1991

SOUTH AMERICAN HANDBOOK

SIXTY SEVENTH EDITION

Editor
Ben Box

"The accidental traveller who has journeyed on
from Stabroek to the rock Saba, and from
thence to the banks of the Essequibo...can
merely mark the outlines of the path he has
trodden, or tell thee the sounds he has heard,
or faintly describe what he has seen in the
environs of his resting-places; but if this be
enough to induce thee to undertake the
journey, and give the world a description of it,
he will be amply satisfied."

Charles Waterton

**TRADE & TRAVEL
PUBLICATIONS**

TRADE & TRAVEL PUBLICATIONS LTD
6 RIVERSIDE COURT
RIVERSIDE ROAD
BATH BA2 3DZ
ENGLAND
TEL 0225 469141
FAX 0225 462921

ISBN 0 900751 30 4

Published in the United States of America and Canada by
Prentice Hall Press
Division of Simon & Schuster Inc.
15 Columbus Circle
New York, NY 10023

In North America, ISBN 0-13-826249-7

COVER—Emperor Penguins

Emperor Penguins live and breed on the inshore icepacks of Antarctica, and around the southern tip of South America. Standing 120 centimetres tall, it is the largest of the penguin family.

After mating, the female lays her single egg at the beginning of winter and returns to sea, leaving the male to incubate the egg on his feet, protected by a fold of skin and feathers, for 64 days. The males fast during the incubation period, drawing on their reserves of fat and gathering in huge colonies to survive the bitter-cold winter.

Just as the ice is breaking, the female returns to take over the newly-born chick and the male swims out to sea to fatten up.

Satellite tracking has recently shown the wandering Albatross, the largest flying seabird, capable of covering up to 600 miles a day. With a wingspan of over 3 metres, the birds can glide motionless for hours and are able to navigate over long distances at speeds up to 50 mph in total darkness.

Cover illustration by Jeremy Pyke
Printed and bound in Great Britain by Clays Ltd., Bungay, Suffolk.

CONTENTS

WILL YOU HELP US?

We do all we can to get our facts right in **The Mexico & Central American Handbook.** Each chapter is thoroughly revised each year, but the territory covered is vast, and our eyes cannot be everywhere. A new highway or airport is built; a hotel, a restaurant, a cabaret dies; another, a good one is born; a building we describe is pulled down, a street renamed. Names and addresses of good hotels and restaurants for "budget-minded" travellers are always very welcome. We would especially like to receive diagrams of walks, national parks and other interesting areas to use as source material for the Handbook and other forthcoming titles.

Your information may be far more up-to-date than ours. If your letter reaches us early enough in the year it will be used in the next edition, but write whenever you want to, for all your letters are used sooner or later.

Thank you very much indeed for you help.

Trade & Travel Publications Limited
6 Riverside Court
Lower Bristol Road
Bath BA2 3DZ. England

PREFACE

Over many years, the *South American Handbook* has expanded with the help of countless travellers who have sent in details of their experiences, corrections to the text and additions of new routes and places to visit. The point has now been reached where it is no longer possible to accommodate all the information in one volume. The type face can get no smaller, nor the pages thinner and many readers have suggested that we split the book. Having already extracted the Caribbean islands into a companion volume, it has been decided to do the same for Mexico and Central America. After making a survey from letters received of the routes people travel, the Darién Gap appeared to be the logical place to make the division. This is therefore the first edition of a *South American Handbook* for the South American continent alone, although it carries the title of 67th in the series. The first *Mexico and Central American Handbook* appears simultaneously with the second edition of the *Caribbean Islands Handbook*.

This year the chapter on Chile has been extensively revised following a trip by the editor as far south as Cochrane on the Carretera Austral. The northern section has been greatly extended with the aid of vulcanologist Dr Lyndsey O'Callaghan. Other major contributions have been received from Sean O'Flynn and Conor O'Sullivan of Tatu Tours, who thoroughly revised the Bahia section and Fernando de Noronha, Brazil; Wayne Berhardson, who rewrote the north of Mendoza section, Argentina; Mark Wilson, who rewrote most of the Guyana chapter; Betsy Wagenhauser and Petra Schepens, of the South American Explorers Club, who kindly shared with us their knowledge and experience of travelling in Ecuador, Peru and Colombia; Hallam Murray for a new cycling section. Thanks are also due to the team of subeditors who helped with the preparation of this edition: Sylvia Brooks, Janet Krengel, Charlie Nurse and Peter Pollard, to Sarah Cameron, who once again edited the economy sections, and to Debbie Wylde for many weeks spent at the keyboard. A number of new maps have been incorporated this year and we are grateful to Katherine Jarvis for her assistance in drawing new maps. The programme of adding new maps to this volume is not as far advanced as had been hoped, but we plan to address this matter for future editions.

We have had considerable difficulty this year in converting local prices into US dollars because of massive swings in inflation and exchange rates in many countries. Relative prices have often become severely unbalanced, an example of which occurred in Brazil where, in the summer season, a small bottle of suntan oil cost the equivalent of several bikinis. Distortions are likely to continue while governments grapple with financial problems in an effort to stabilize their economies. It is possible therefore that our prices are not as accurate as we should like and we advise readers to be flexible when planning their budgets.

After many years of concentration of travellers in the northern Andean countries and Brazil, it is encouraging to see greater interest in the southern cone. Two recent events have helped: the restoration of full diplomatic relations between Argentina and the UK and the election of a civilian government in Chile. Disturbances in Peru and Colombia have undoubtedly influenced this shift in emphasis, but Ecuador and Brazil remain as popular as ever. Finally, we should like to thank the 740 readers of the *Handbook* who took the time to write to us in 1989-90 to share their experiences of travelling in Latin America.

The Editor

HOW TO USE THIS HANDBOOK

The South American Handbook is the most complete and up-to-date package of information for independent travellers on the sub-continent of South America (from the Darién gap to Tierra del Fuego) currently in print. Its text is updated every year for the new edition which is published on 1 September. The text is based on the Editors' travels, contributions from national tourist authorities, notes from correspondents living in the countries we cover, detailed material and maps which Handbook users send us, and the extensive sources of information on Latin America available in London and elsewhere.

Editorial Logic Users of the Handbook will find that we employ a logical system of arrangement, which we believe is the most useful for travellers. The capital city is (with one exception, dictated by geography—Chile) the first place covered in detail. The territory is then divided into subsections which are numbered on the country contents and map as well as in the text. In the subsections, towns appear in sequence along a route, which falls within the natural geography of the region. The routes cover the most interesting places to visit and do not necessarily constitute the shortest possible distance from A to B. Details are also given of any interesting excursions or other sights that are off the route. Travellers can therefore plan their own itineraries according to the time available, and their own special interests.

Cross Referencing and Indexing There is a complete index of place names at the end of the book.
   To make it easier for Readers to find their way around the text, we have a comprehensive system of cross-references. For ease of use, the "see page" entry has been highlighted in heavier type. On the page referred to, you will find the entry again emphasised in some form of heavier type.

Maps The South American Handbook maps within the text are undergoing a programme of updating, improvement and expansion. Three types are used:

A. Country Maps These appear at the start of each country chapter and show main access routes (not necessarily major roads in all cases), main towns, and divisions of the country as described in the text. These divisions are numbered on the map, in the country's contents list and at the text divisions in the chapter. The numbers are not recommendations as to which parts of the country are most interesting to visit, they are only for easy identification.

B. Regional Maps By the 1992 edition, each subsection of the country listed in the country contents will have its own regional map. These give extra information on a more detailed scale and show the main physical features, towns, means of communication and points of interest.

C. City and Town Maps Generally these are detailed maps of town centres, showing means of access to bus and railway stations and airports. The main points of interest are indicated by means of a numbered key.

Introduction and Hints This first section in the book gives information and hints

Roads ———————	Capital Cities ■SANTIAGO
Railways ++++++++++++	Cities/Towns ●córdoba
Trails/Paths/Tracks — — — —	Archaeological sites ▲
Rivers RÍO ARUÑA	Mountains ⌄⌃
Ferries	Streets SAN MARTÍN
Waterfall 〜	Parks
Barrier Reef 〜 〜 〜	Train Station T
Borders	Bus Station B
Country Subdivisions //////	Airport ✈
Metropolitan areas ▨	Key Numbers 6
Major Highway	

that apply generally to all the countries we cover on

- ● travel to and in Latin America
- ● money
- ● law enforcement
- ● security
- ● travelling with children
- ● camping
- ● language

- ● photography
- ● surface transport
- ● hitch-hiking
- ● motoring and motorcycling
- ● hiking and trekking
- ● river boats
- ● cycling

Health Information This major section by Dr David Snashall of St Thomas's Hospital Medical School, London, gives details of the health risks common in South America, and the sensible precautions travellers should take to combat them.

Country Sections Information is set out country by country in a constant sequence as follows:
- ● List of contents
- ● Description of physical geography
  - history
  - people
  - economic report
  - present form of government
- ● Survey of Cities, Towns and places of interest
  - things to do
  - things worth seeing
  - where to stay
  - eating out
  - services for visitors
- ● Information for visitors

what documents are necessary
how to get there
food
health precautions
the best time for visiting
clothing
currency regulations
other essential information

All those readers who have written with valuable updating material are listed with thanks at the end of each chapter.

Hotels and Restaurants In large cities, lists of hotels and restaurants include only those establishments for which positive recommendations have been received. In smaller towns, these lists contain both the favourable recommendations and others. In general, restaurants are grouped by neighbourhood and by type of cuisine.

Prices Our hotel price ranges, for double rooms with taxes and service charges but without meals unless stated, are as follows:

L+—Over US$125	**L**—US$71-US$125	**A**—US$46-70
B—US$31-45	**C**—US$21-30	**D**—US$12-20
E—US$7-11	**F**—US$4-6	**G**—Up to US$3

Other abbreviations used in the book (apart from p.p. = per person; a/c = air conditioned; rec. = recommended; T = telephone) should be self-explanatory.

We are grateful to those travellers, listed below, who have sent us important information for the "Introduction and Hints" section which follows: Tam Agosti-Gisler (Anchorage, Alaska), Vladimir Antonowych (Toronto), Peter Caesar (Bogotá), Bryan Crawford (Beauly, Inverness-shire), Philipp Dyckerhoff (München), Dag K. Ellingsen (Oslo 2), Pauline Fearon (Hornchurch), Margaret Fleming (Karlsfeld, W. Ger.), C. Gammell (London SE 20), Jim Hardy (Waukesha, Wis.), Dr Paul Heaton (London NW6), Bill Hite (Forest, VA), Marcel Kersten (Roosendaal, Neth.), Ole W. Lund (Oslo 3), Sasha Macmiadhachain (Swanage), Herbert P. Minderhond (Amsterdam), S.D. Minks (Thos and Jas Harrison Ltd, Liverpool), Eitan Nir (Beit Ha'emek, Israel) and Orit Sela (Cabri), Barry Oldham (Plymouth, Devon), Sarah Parry (Southampton), Sandrine Pétremand and Gilles Maitre (Bevaix, Switz.), John M. Raspey, Louise Santamera (Liverpool 3), Piero Scaruffi (Redwood City, CA), Karen Schulpzand and Rudy Cruysbergs (Dilbeek, Belgium), von Schubert (Kehl, W. Ger.), R.W. Le Sueur (Jersey), Eileen Synnott and Paul Gurn (Waterbury, CT), Marian Temple (Mérida, Mexico), Ingrid Walter and Norbert Eisinger (Schnelldorf, W. Ger.), Jonathan Weiland (Philadelphia, PA) and Meg Worley (Maryville, TE).

WARNING: Whilst every endeavour is made to ensure that the facts printed in this book are correct at the time of going to press, travellers are cautioned to obtain authoritative advice from consulates, airlines, etc. concerning current travel and visa requirements and conditions before embarkation. The publishers cannot accept legal responsibility for errors, however caused, which are printed in this book.

INTRODUCTION AND HINTS

AIR TRAVEL TO AND WITHIN LATIN AMERICA

Travel to and in South America All the main airlines plying to each country are given in the "Information for Visitors" sections. Airlines will only allow a certain weight of luggage without a surcharge; this is normally 30 kg. for first class and 20 kg. for business and economy classes, but these limits are often not strictly enforced when it is known that the plane is not going to be full. Passengers seeking a larger baggage allowance can route via USA, but with certain exceptions, the fares are slightly higher using this route. On the other hand, weight limits for internal flights are often lower; best to enquire beforehand.

Chris Parrott, of Journey Latin America, has told us:

1. Generally it is cheaper to fly from London rather than a point in Europe to South American destinations.

2. Most airlines offer discounted fares of one sort or another on scheduled flights. These are not offered by the airlines direct to the public, but through agencies who specialize in this type of fare*. The very busy seasons are as follows: South America; 7 Dec.–15 Jan. Peru/Ecuador/Colombia/Venezuela 10 July–10 Sept. If you intend travelling during those times, book as far ahead as possible.

3. Charter flights to Brazil, for 1990, were all cancelled before the service began. At the time of going to press, there are charters scheduled to Margarita, off the Venezuelan coast.

4. Other fares fall into three groups, and are all on scheduled services:
    A. Excursion (return) fares with restricted validity e.g. 5-90 days. These are fixed date tickets where the dates of travel cannot be changed after issue of ticket.
    B. Yearly fares: these may be bought on a one-way or return basis, and usually the returns can be issued with the return date left open. You must, however, fix the route (some of the cheapest flexible fares now have 6 months validity).
    C. Student (or Under 26) fares. (Do not assume that student tickets are the cheapest; though they are often very flexible, they are usually more expensive than A or B above).

---

*In London, these include Journey Latin America, 16 Devonshire Road, Chiswick, London W4 2HD (T 081-747 3108); Trailfinders, 48 Earl's Court Road, London W8 6EJ. (T 071-938 3366); Melia Travel Ltd., 12 Dover Street, London W1X 4NS (T 071-491 3881); Steamond Ltd., 23 Eccleston Street, London SW1W 9LX (T 071-730 8646); and Transatlantic Wings, 70 Pembroke Road, London W.8. (T 071-602 4021). (Ed.)

Some airlines are flexible on the age limit, others strict. One way and returns available, or "Open Jaws" (see below). NB Some student tickets carry standby status only, and should be avoided in the busy seasons (see above).

5. For people intending to travel a linear route and return from a different point from that which they entered, there are "Open Jaws" fares, which are available on student or yearly fares, or occasionally on excursion fares.

6. Many of these fares require a change of plane at an intermediate point, and a stopover may be permitted, or even obligatory, depending on schedules. Simply because a flight stops at a given airport does not mean you can break your journey there—the airline must have traffic rights to pick up or set down passengers between points A and B before it will be permitted. This is where dealing with a specialized agency (like Journey Latin America!) will really pay dividends. There are dozens of agencies that offer the simple returns to Rio or Lima at roughly the same (discounted) fare. On multi-stop itineraries, the specialized agencies can often save clients hundreds of pounds.

7. Although it's a little more complicated, it's possible to sell tickets in London for travel originating in Latin America at substantially cheaper fares than those available locally. This is useful for the traveller who doesn't know where he will end up, or who plans to travel for more than a year. But a one-way ticket from Latin America is more expensive than a one-way in the other direction, so it's always best to buy a return. (I have heard of travellers buying an unused return seat on French charter flights—they're advertised in the small ads in some of the cheap hotels in Lima—and the charter company doesn't seem to mind who sits in the seat; very hit and miss though).

8. Certain Latin American countries impose local tax on flights originating there. Among these are Uruguay, Peru, Ecuador, Colombia and Mexico. This often applies if you happen to have bought a ticket, say, London—Rio—Santiago—Lima—Los Angeles and then on to Australia. Depending on the way it's issued the passenger could get charged tax on all the sectors from Lima onwards.

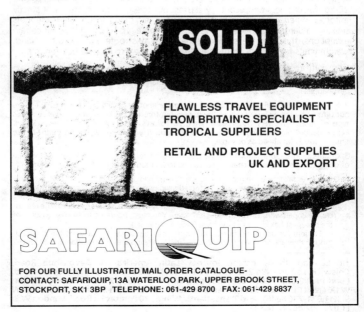

9. There are several cheap French charters to Colombia, Ecuador, Peru, Bolivia and the southern countries, but no-one in the UK sells them. Try: Uniclam-Voyages, 63 rue Monsieur-le Prince, 75006 Paris. A cheap Swiss charter firm is Sindbad, 3 Schoffelgasse, 8025 Zürich. Aeroflot flies cheaply from Shannon to Lima and Buenos Aires, as well as Mexico, Havana and Managua.

10. If you buy discounted air tickets *always* check the reservation with the airline concerned to make sure the flight still exists. Also remember the IATA airlines' schedules change in March and October each year, so if you're going to be away a long time it's best to leave return flight coupons open.

In addition, check whether you are entitled to any refund or re-issued ticket if you lose, or have stolen, a discounted air ticket.

Purchasable only in the USA and still one of the cheapest ways of flying around the continent, AeroPerú's "Around South America Airpass" offers a 45-day return ticket to Miami for US$759. It includes Lima and six other South American cities (all flights originating in Lima), plus discounted flights within Peru. Avianca and LAP offer similar multi-country passes out of Miami, so for European travellers who can take a cheap transatlantic flight to Miami, as well as US travellers, this may be an economic option. Aerolíneas Argentinas offer an airpass that covers Argentina, Brazil, Venezuela, Colombia, Ecuador, Peru, Bolivia and Chile, valid 7-30 days for US$1089 or US$981. These can be bought in London before departure; transatlantic travel must be with Aerolíneas Argentinas.

N.B. At the time of going to press, American Airlines were on the point of taking over Eastern Airlines' routes to the region. American's precise schedules had not been released and we advise readers to check in advance before planning a route.

Beware buying tickets from the general sales agents in Europe of minor Latin American airlines. They are sometimes incorrectly made out and therefore impossible to transfer or cash in. If you buy internal airline tickets in Latin American countries you may find cash refunds difficult to get if you change your plans: better to change your ticket for a different one. On the other hand you can save money by buying tickets in a country with a black exchange market, for local currency, for flights on its national airline. Overbooking by Latin American airlines is very common (largely due to repeated block bookings by travel agents, which everyone knows will not be used), so always reconfirm the next stage of your flight within 72 hours of your intended departure. And it does no harm to reconfirm yet again in the last 24 hours, just to show them you mean it, and turn up for the flight in good time (at least 2 hours before departure).

We advise people who travel the cheap way in Latin America to pay for all transport as they go along, and not in advance. This advice does not apply to people on a tight schedule: paying as you go along may save money, but it is likely to waste your time somewhat. The one exception to this general principle is in transatlantic flights; here money is saved by booking as far as possible in one operation.

The national airlines of Argentina, Bolivia, Brazil, Chile, Colombia, Peru and Venezuela operate schemes for unlimited travel within those countries at a set price. See the respective country sections.

There is also an "Amerailpass", giving unlimited travel on the railways of Argentina, Bolivia, Brazil, Chile, Paraguay and Uruguay, which can be bought for 16 (US$120), 23 (US$140), 30 (US$175) or 60 (US$260) days. Payment must be in US dollars, so the savings may not be that great. Details in the paragraphs on rail travel under the principal cities, but remember that railway services are being progressively withdrawn. *Warning*: Not all railway staff know about the pass.

The Amerbuspass covers the whole of Latin America, from Mexico City to Ushuaia, and entitles the holder to 15-20% discounts on tickets with participating operators; bookable in all Latin American capitals, Europe, Asia, Africa, Oceania, it is valid for 9,999 miles, up to 180 days. Unlimited stopovers, travel with either a confirmed or open itinerary. Contact TISA Internacional, B. Irigoyen 1370, Oficina 25/26, 1138 Buenos Aires, Argentina, T 642-7028, or Av. Larrazabal 493,

1408 Buenos Aires, P.O. Box 40 Suc. 1 (B), 1401 Buenos Aires.

Travel to the USA Until July 1988 all foreigners (except Canadians) needed visas to enter the USA. Despite subsequent relaxations of visa requirements for British air travellers with round-trip tickets to the USA, it is advisable to have a visa to allow entry by land, or on airlines from South and Central America which are not "participating carriers" on the Visa Waiver scheme. If you are thinking of travelling via the USA, or of visiting the USA after Latin America, you are strongly advised to get your visa from a US Consulate in your own country, not while travelling. If you wish to visit a little-known part of the USA (and W Canada), David Stanley's *Alaska-Yukon Handbook* (Chico, CA 96927, Moon Publications), 230 pages, will be of the very greatest use. It costs only US$8 (book postage anywhere).

Shipping Voyages on passenger-carrying cargo vessels between South America and Europe, the USA, or elsewhere, are listed here: the Blue Star line sails from Tilbury to Hamburg, Bremen, Antwerp, thence to Montevideo via the Brazilian ports of Salvador, Santos and Rio de Janeiro, returning via Rio Grande, Santos, Salvador and Recife, and Rotterdam. 12 passengers are carried; fare to Montevideo, £1,610, round trip £2,950 p.p. The Grimaldi Line sails from Tilbury to Brazil (Rio, Santos, Paranaguá), via Hamburg, Rotterdam and West Africa, round trip about 8 weeks, £2,140 p.p. (outside cabin). The Polish Ocean Line serves both the East and West coasts of South America from Hamburg, Antwerp and Bremen: ports of call include La Guaira, Puerto Cabello, Maracaibo (Venezuela), Santa Marta, Barranquilla, Cartagena, Buenaventura (Colombia), Guayaquil (Ecuador), Callao (Peru), and Rio de Janeiro, Santos, Salvador, Ilheus (Brazil), Montevideo and Buenos Aires. The cheapest fare is £755, rising to £2,148 for a 7-week round trip to the East Coast; destinations vary.

From the USA, the Chilean Line sails from Long Beach, California to Esmeraldas, Guayaquil (Ecuador), Callao (Peru), and the Chilean ports of Valparaíso, San Antonio, Antofagasta, Iquique and Arica (round trip US$3,750-4,050); it serves the same ports from the US East Coast (New York, Baltimore, Charleston, Savannah, Miami, Houston, New Orleans and back to Philadelphia) via the Panama Canal (round trip US$4,200-4,500). Ivaran Lines serve East Coast USA, Brazilian ports, Montevideo and Buenos Aires, while Lykes Line sail from Miami/New Orleans to Cartagena, then through the Panama Canal to Guayaquil, Callao and Valparaíso (a round trip costs US$3,300-3,500 p.p.). Egon Oldendorff carries passengers on its USA or Canada/South America routes.

Our thanks are due to John Alton of Weider Travel, Charing Cross Shopping Concourse, The Strand, London WC2N 4HZ, T 071-836 6363, Telex 918791, for the above information. Enquiries regarding passages should be made through agencies in your own country, or through Weider Travel.

Details on shipping cars are given in the relevant country sections.

Warning Many countries in Latin America are reluctant to let travellers enter their territory if they do not already have onward or return tickets. (Look under "Information for Visitors" sections for the countries you intend to visit.) The purchase of a Miscellaneous Charges Order (open ticket) from an IATA airline for (say) US$100 will satisfy this requirement in many but not all countries; it is valid for 12 months, can be exchanged for a ticket, or cashed at the airline offices in the country of issue. (The onward ticket requirement does not apply to travellers with their own vehicles.) If you have no onward ticket, a consular letter verifying a statement from your bank at home, giving details of your account with them, might be helpful.

DOCUMENTATION AND SECURITY

Passports Remember that Latin Americans, especially officials, are very document-minded. You should always carry your passport in a safe place about your person, or if not going far, leave it in the hotel safe. If staying in a country for several weeks, it is worth while registering at your Embassy or Consulate. Then, if your passport is stolen, the process of replacing it is simplified and speeded up. Keeping photocopies of essential documents, and some additional passport-sized photographs, is recommended

Remember that it is your responsibility to ensure that your passport is stamped in and out when you cross frontiers. The absence of entry and exit stamps can cause serious difficulties: seek out the proper migration offices if the stamping process is not carried out as you cross. Also, do not lose your entry card; replacing one causes a lot of trouble, and possibly expense.

If travelling from the West Coast of the USA to Latin America and you require visas, most can be obtained in one building in San Francisco, at 870 Market Street (in 1989, represented here were Mexico, Guatemala, Honduras, Costa Rica, Panama, Colombia, Venezuela, Argentina, Chile, Paraguay, Bolivia, Peru, Ecuador—and Brazil only 300 m. away). You are advised to check in advance that the office you want is still there.

Identity and Membership Cards Membership cards of British, European and US motoring organizations have been found useful for discounts off hotel charges, car rentals, maps, towing charges, etc. Student cards must carry a photograph if they are to be of any use in Latin America for discounts. (If you describe yourself as a student on your tourist card you may be able to get discounts, even if you haven't a student card.). Business people should carry a good supply of visiting cards, which are essential for good business relations in Latin America.

Money is best carried in US dollar travellers' cheques (denominations of US$50 and US$100 are preferable, though one does need a few of US$20) or cash. Sterling and other currencies are not recommended. Travellers' cheques are convenient but they attract thieves (though refunds can of course be arranged) and you will find that they are more difficult than dollar bills to change in small towns. Though the risk of loss is greater, many travellers take part of their funds in US dollar notes; better rates can usually be obtained for them. In some countries you can exchange dollar travellers' cheques into dollars cash, but as the regulations change frequently, you are advised to see the individual country chapters below. Low-value US dollar bills are very useful for shopping: shopkeepers and exchange shops (*casas de cambio*) tend to give better exchange rates than hotels or banks. The better hotels will normally change travellers' cheques for their guests (often at a rather poor rate), but if you're travelling on the cheap it is essential to keep in funds; watch weekends and public holidays carefully and never run out of local currency. Take plenty of local currency, in small denominations, when making trips into the interior. Spread your money around your person: less chance of thieves finding it all. Don't leave cash in your shoe for a long time, it may become too damaged to exchange or use.

American Express (Amex), Carte Blanche and Diners Club credit cards are useful, and so are those of the Visa and Master Charge groups. Conceal them very carefully (*not* under the insole of a shoe, however: that may render them unusable!), and make sure you know the correct procedure if they are lost or stolen. We advise using credit cards only for dollar transactions, or in countries where there is no black market exchange rate. Remember that credit card transactions are always at an officially recognized rate of exchange (sometimes, if there are several, the least favourable one); you may find it much cheaper to pay cash and get the parallel rate. Note that the Eurocard/Eurocheque system is virtually unknown in Latin America. For credit card security, insist that imprints are made in your presence and that any imprints incorrectly completed should be torn into tiny pieces. Also destroy the carbon papers after the form is completed

(signatures can be copied from them).

We recommend in general the use of American Express or Thomas Cook US$ travellers' cheques, but should point out that less commission is often charged on Citibank or Bank of America cheques, if they are cashed at Latin American branches of those banks. These cheques are always accepted by banks, even though they may not be as well known outside banks as those of American Express or Thomas Cook. It is a good idea to take two kinds of cheque: if large numbers of one kind have recently been forged or stolen, making people suspicious, it is unlikely to have happened simultaneously with the other kind. Several banks charge a high fixed commission for changing travellers' cheques—sometimes as much as US$5-10 a cheque—because they don't really want to be bothered. Exchange houses (*casas de cambio*) are usually much better for this service. Some establishments may ask to see the customer's record of purchase before accepting travellers' cheques.

In those countries where there is a black market, find out how much of their currency you are allowed to take in, and *buy before you enter*, preferably in a big city where banks are unlikely to make a charge on the transaction. (In small places the bank may charge up to 50 cents on a 10-dollar travellers' cheque.) There is always an active (but illegal) black market in local currency in all those countries that have no free exchange; it is, however, not illegal to buy currency outside the country you are about to enter, up to any limit that may be imposed. The City of London currency dealers are worth checking with: some find themselves overloaded from time to time with exotic currencies they can't get rid of, and let them go at a large discount. Check in the publication *Banknotes of the World* (the dealers usually have it for consultation) that the notes you are being offered are still current, however.

N.B. If you are having additional sums of money sent out during a tour of Latin America, try to have it sent to one of the countries where you can easily exchange dollar travellers' cheques for dollars cash; at present these are Bolivia, Chile, Ecuador and Uruguay. These countries are also good for getting US$ travellers cheques for a Eurocheque or Amex card, and for buying other Latin American currencies at favourable rates. In many countries, one can get at least US$500 in Amex travellers' cheques on the American Express card (US$1,000 on the gold card): quite the easiest way of adding to one's funds. Remember that a transfer of funds, even by telex, can take several days, and charges can be high; a recommended method is, before leaving, to find out which local bank is correspondent to your bank at home, then when you need funds, telex your own bank and ask them to telex the money to the local bank (confirming by air mail). It is possible to obtain money within hours by this method.

Whenever you leave a country, sell any local currency before leaving, because the further away you get, the less the value of a country's money.

Americans (we are told) should know that if they run out of funds they can expect no help from the US Embassy or Consul other than a referral to some welfare organization. In this regard, find out before you go precisely what services and assistance your embassy or consulate can provide if you find yourself in difficulties.

Law Enforcement Whereas in Europe and North America we are accustomed to law enforcement on a systematic basis, in general, enforcement in Latin America is achieved by periodic campaigns. The most typical is a round-up of criminals in the cities just before Christmas. In December, therefore, you may well be asked for identification at any time, and if you cannot produce it, you will be jailed. At first sight, on arrival, it may seem that you can flout the law with impunity, because everybody else is obviously doing so. If a visitor is jailed his friends should take him food every day. This is especially important for people on a diet, such as diabetics. It must also be borne in mind that in the event of a vehicle accident in which anyone is injured, all drivers involved are automatically detained until blame has been established, and this does not usually take less than two weeks. Sometimes these problems can be avoided by offering a bribe, but this, naturally, is illegal and may be extremely dangerous. Imported cigarettes from airport duty-free shops are very much appreciated by customs officials.

Never offer a bribe unless you are fully conversant with the customs of the country. (In Chile, for instance, it would land you in serious trouble if you tried to bribe a *carabinero*.) Wait until the official makes the suggestion, or offer money in some form which is apparently not bribery, e.g. "In our country we have a system of on-the-spot fines. Is there a similar system here?" Do not assume that an official who accepts a bribe is prepared to do anything else that is illegal. You bribe him to persuade him to do his job, or to persuade him not to do it, or to do it more quickly, or more slowly. You do not bribe him to do something which is against the law. The mere suggestion would make him very upset.

Security Try and look as little like a tourist as possible, especially in poor areas of cities. Most crime is opportunistic so if you are aware of the dangers, act confidently and use your common sense you will lessen many of the risks. The following tips, all endorsed by travellers, are meant to forewarn, but not alarm, you. Keep all documents secure; hide your main cash supply in different places or under your clothes (extra pockets sewn inside shirts and trousers, moneybelts, neck or leg pouches, and elasticated support bandages for keeping money and cheques above the elbow or below the knee have been repeatedly recommended—the last by John Hatt in *The Tropical Traveller*). Keep cameras in bags (preferably with a chain or wire in the strap to defeat the slasher) or briefcases; take spare spectacles (eyeglasses); don't wear wrist-watches (unless they're digital—too cheap and plentiful to attract thieves nowadays) or jewellery. If you wear a shoulder-bag in a market, carry it in front of you. Backpacks are vulnerable to slashers: a good idea is to cover with a sack with maybe a layer of wire netting between. Use a pack which is lockable at its base.

Ignore mustard smearers and paint or shampoo sprayers, and strangers' remarks like "what's that on your shoulder?" or "have you seen that dirt on your shoe?". Furthermore, don't bend over to pick up money or other items in the street. These are all ruses intended to distract your attention and make you easy for an accomplice to steal from. If someone follows you when you're in the street, let him catch up with you and "give him the eye".

Be wary of "plainclothes policemen"; insist on seeing identification and on going to the police station by main roads. Do not hand over your identification (or money—which he should not need to see anyway) until you are at the station. Be even more suspicious if he seeks confirmation of his status from a passer-by. If attacked, remember your assailants may well be armed, and try not to resist.

It is best, if you can trust your hotel, to leave any valuables you don't need in safe-deposit there, when sightseeing locally. If you don't trust the hotel, lock everything in your pack and secure that in your room (some people take eyelet-screws for padlocking cupboards or drawers). If you lose valuables, always report to police and note details of report—for insurance purposes.

When you have all your luggage with you at a bus or railway station, be especially careful: don't get into arguments—or even conversations—with any locals if you can help it, and lock all the items together with a chain or cable if you are waiting for some time. Take a taxi between airport/bus station/railway station and hotel, if you can possibly afford it. Avoid night buses; never arrive at night; and watch your belongings whether they are stowed inside or outside the cabin. Finally, never accept food, drink, sweets or cigarettes from unknown fellow-travellers on buses or trains. They may be drugged, and you would wake up hours later without your belongings. In this connection, never accept a bar drink from an opened bottle (unless you can see that that bottle is in general use): always have it uncapped in front of you.

A last point, from Canadian film-maker Russ Bentley: a courteous, friendly manner of speaking, including to beggars and market vendors, may avoid your being "set up" for robbery or assault. For specific local problems, see under the individual countries in the text.

ACCOMMODATION

Hotels A cheap but not bad hotel might be in the region of US$5 a night in Argentina or Brazil, but is less in the Andean countries. For the indigent, it is a good idea to ask for a boarding house—*casa de huéspedes, hospedaje, pensión, casa familial* or *residencial*, according to country; they are normally to be found in abundance near bus and railway stations and markets. Good value hotels can also be found near truckers' stops/service stations; they are usually secure. There are often great seasonal variations in hotel prices in resorts. Remember, cheaper hotels don't always supply soap, towels and toilet paper. A useful tip: ask the car rental agency employees at the airport for advice when you arrive—as long as they are not busy. And another, always ask for the best room.

Warning The electric showers used in innumerable cheap hotels are extremely dangerous. If you can't avoid using them, check the wiring for obvious flaws and try not to touch the rose while it is producing hot water.

Youth Hostels Organizations affiliated to the Youth Hostels movement exist in Argentina, Brazil, Colombia, Chile, Peru and Uruguay. There is an associate organization in Ecuador. Further information in the country sections and from the IYHA.

Meals In all countries except Brazil and Chile (where cold meats, cheese, eggs, fruit etc. generally figure) breakfast usually means coffee or tea with rolls and butter, and anything more is charged extra. There is a paragraph on each nation's food under "Information for Visitors". For reliable cheap meals, look in and near the markets and eat what the locals are eating, making sure that you can see it being cooked.

Camping There is a growing network of organized campsites, to which reference is made in the text immediately below hotel lists, under each town. If there is no organized site in town, a football pitch or gravel pit might serve. Géraldine des Cressonnières, of Linkebeek, Belgium, gives the following rules for "wild" camping: (1) arrive in daylight; (2) ask permission to camp from the parish priest, or the fire chief, or the police, or a farmer regarding his own property; (3) never ask a group of people— especially young people; (4) never camp on a beach (because of sandflies and thieves). If you can't get information from anyone, camp in a spot where you can't be seen from the nearest inhabited place.

Gas cylinders and bottles are usually exchangeable, but if not can be recharged; specify whether you use butane or propane. (Liquid fuels are readily available.) The Camping C ube do Brasil gives 50% discounts to holders of international campers' cards.

Toilets Many of the cheapest hotels in the poorer areas, also restaurants and bars, have inadequate water supplies. This may mean that used toilet paper should not be flushed down the pan, but placed in the receptacle provided. This is not very sanitary, of course, but a blocked pan or drain is infinitely more of a health risk. It is quite common for people to stand on the toilet seat (facing the wall—easier to balance), as they do in Asia. If you are concerned about the hygiene of the facility, put paper on the seat.

Cockroaches These are ubiquitous and unpleasant, but not dangerous. Take some insecticide powder if staying in cheap hotels; Baygon (Bayer) has been recommended. Stuff toilet paper in any holes in walls that you may suspect of being parts of cockroach runs.

ETIQUETTE AND LANGUAGE

Travellers' Appearance There is a natural prejudice in all countries against travellers who ignore personal hygiene and have a generally dirty and unkempt appearance. Most Latin Americans, if they can afford it, devote great care to their clothes and appearance; it is appreciated if visitors do likewise. The general prejudice previously reported against backpacks has virtually disappeared, unless carried by those whom officials identify as "hippies". One tip we have received; young people of informal dress and life-style may find it advantageous to procure a letter from someone in an official position testifying to their good character, on official-looking notepaper. John Oliver, of Durban, tells us that a photograph of a pretty blonde young woman inside one's passport can have a similar salutary effect on Latin American officials!

Some countries have laws or prejudices against the wearing by civilians of army-surplus clothing. In many places there is also a prejudice against shorts, which are only appropriate on the beach, or for jogging, or for sports and games. A medium weight shawl with some wool content is recommended for women: it can double as pillow, light blanket, bathrobe or sunscreen as required.

Drugs Users of drugs, even of soft ones, without medical prescription should be particularly careful, as some countries impose heavy penalties— up to ten years' imprisonment—for even the simple possession of such substances. In this connection, the planting of drugs on travellers—by traffickers or the police—is not unknown. If offered drugs on the street, make no response at all and keep walking. Note that people who roll their own cigarettes are often suspected of carrying drugs and subjected to intensive searches. Advisable to stick to commercial brands of cigarettes—but better still not to smoke at all.

Courtesy Remember that politeness—even a little ceremoniousness—is much appreciated. In this connection professional or business cards are useful (and have even been known to secure for their owners discount prices in hotels). Michael Davison makes the following suggestions: men should always remove any headgear and say "con permiso" ("com licença" in Brazil) when entering offices, and be prepared to shake hands (this is much commoner in Latin America than in Europe or North America); always say "Buenos días" or "Buenas tardes" ("Bom dia" or "Boa tarde" in Brazil) and wait for a reply before proceeding further; in a word, don't rush them! Always remember that the traveller from abroad has enjoyed greater advantages in life than most Latin American minor officials, and should be friendly and courteous in consequence. N. F. Hawkes adds: never be impatient or criticize situations in public: the officials may know more English than you think and they can certainly interpret gestures and facial expressions. Be judicious about discussing politics with strangers (especially in Guatemala, Honduras and El Salvador). Politeness can be a liability, however, in some situations; most Latin Americans are disorderly queuers. Russ Bentley stresses that politeness and friendliness, with small useful gifts for children such as pencils and scratchpads, not only increase the pleasure of one's trip, but may well improve one's personal security.

Moira Chubb, from New Zealand, suggests that if you are a guest and are offered food that arouses your suspicions, the only courteous way out is to feign an allergy or a stomach ailment.

Language Without some knowledge of Spanish you can become very frustrated and feel helpless in many situations. English is absolutely useless off the beaten track. Some initial study, to get you up to a basic Spanish vocabulary of 500 words or so, and a pocket dictionary and phrase-book, are most strongly recommended: your pleasure will be doubled if you can talk to the locals. Not all the locals speak Spanish, of course; apart from Brazil's Portuguese, you will find that some Indians in the more remote highland parts of Bolivia, Guatemala and Peru, and lowland Indians in Amazonia, speak only their indigenous languages, though there will usually be at least one person in each village who can speak Spanish.

The basic Spanish of Hispanic America is that of south-western Spain, with soft "c's" and "z's" pronounced as "s", and not as "th" as in the other parts of Spain. Castilian Spanish is readily understood, but is not appreciated when spoken by non-Spaniards; try and learn the basic Latin American pronunciation. There are several regional variations in pronunciation, particularly in the River Plate countries, which are noted in the Argentine section "Information for Visitors". Differences in vocabulary also exist, both between peninsular Spanish and Latin American Spanish, and between the usages of the different countries.

If you are going to Brazil, you should learn some Portuguese. Spanish is not adequate: you may be understood but you will probably not be able to understand the answers.

INTERNAL SURFACE TRANSPORT

Surface Transport The continent has a growing road system for motor traffic, with frequent bus services. The buses are often comfortable; Brazil, Chile and Venezuela are the best; Ecuador is quite good; the other Andean countries are a long way behind, because of difficulties of terrain. In mountainous country, however, do not expect buses to get to their destination, after long journeys, anywhere near on time. When the journey takes more than 3 or 4 hours, meal stops at country inns or bars, good and bad, are the rule. See what the locals are eating—and buy likewise, or make sure you're stocked up well on food and drink at the start. For drinks, stick to bottled water or soft drinks or coffee (black). The food sold by vendors at bus stops may be all right: watch if locals are buying, though unpeeled fruit is of course reliable. (See above on **Security** in buses.)

In most countries trains are slower than buses. They do tend, however, to provide finer scenery, and you can normally see much more wildlife than from the road—it is less disturbed by one or two trains a day than by the more frequent road traffic. Moreover, so many buses now show video films that you can't see the countryside because the curtains are drawn. Complaining to the conductor that you cannot see the beautiful landscape may persuade him to give you his seat at the front.

Hitch-hiking This custom is increasing in Latin America, and travellers have reported considerable success in virtually all countries. Neatness of appearance certainly helps. Argentina, Brazil, Chile, Ecuador and Venezuela are reported as good; Peru and Bolivia less so ("paying trucks" recommended here). If trying to hitchhike away from main roads and in sparsely-populated areas, however, allow plenty of time.

Joanna Codrington writes: Hitch-hiking in Latin America is reasonably safe and straightforward for males and couples, provided one speaks some Spanish/Portuguese. In Peru and Bolivia there is little private transport and trucks charge about 2/3 the equivalent fare. But elsewhere cars and trucks will carry you free of charge, and will generally treat you as their guests. It is a most enjoyable mode of transport—a good way to meet the local people, to improve one's languages and to learn about the country. Truck drivers in particular are often well versed in things of interest one is passing, e.g. crops and industries.
    Here are a few general hints: in remoter parts, make enquiries first about the volume of traffic on the road. On long journeys, set out at crack of dawn, which is when trucks usually leave. They tend to go longer distances than cars.

Motoring The car freely crosses international frontiers without payment of customs duties provided it is eventually returned to its country of origin. In parts of South America, it is controlled by a separate document, the *Carnet de Passages en Douanes* or *Libreta de Pasos por Aduana*, which is obtainable at the automobile touring club in the country where the vehicle is registered, and must be stamped at both sides of each frontier. Failure to obtain a stamp will result in your being turned back, perhaps after driving as much as 200 km., so it is important to find the Customs Office (*Aduana—Alfândega* in Brazil) in order to avoid this inconvenience; it may be at the border or in the town nearest the border. In 1989 it was reported that Argentina, Brazil, Chile, Uruguay and Venezuela were not insistent upon a *Carnet de Passages*. In Ecuador, it is obligatory and must be obtained before entry. Difficulties have been experienced in entering Peru and Bolivia: check with the Consulates before setting out. (N.B. Since the AAA stopped issuing *Carnets de Passages*, and since the AA charges two-and-a-half times the maximum estimated duty which may be levied on the vehicle, check if you can purchase the *carnet* in country of entry.) Most countries have special (and cheaper) arrangements for motorists visiting neighbouring countries only.
    A separate insurance policy has to be issued in each country if a claim is to be legally payable in the country where an accident occurs. Very few companies have the necessary international connections, but one which does is American International Underwriters, 700 Pine Street, New York, T (212) 770-7000. Give them at least four months' notice of your requirements. Remember that in many countries third-party insurance for drivers may not be compulsory, or if compulsory, not enforced; you may have no claim on the other driver after an accident, except through the courts—a time-consuming exercise. If you are injured in an accident, people may refuse to take you to hospital; if you are found dead on arrival they could be jailed until it is proved that they were not responsible for the accident. An additional reason for always driving carefully.
    The normal saloon car reaches most destinations of interest to the tourist. High ground clearance is useful for badly surfaced or unsurfaced roads and is of greater value than 4-wheel drive. The latter is recommended for mountainous terrain and unmade roads off the beaten track. In some places, service is not available for sophisticated items like automatic transmission, electronic ignition and fuel injection, so the simpler the car the better. Most mechanics in Latin America are great improvisers, preferring to repair rather than replace. Japanese makes are a good choice (Toyota or Nissan, for example) since they are represented in every country. It's an advantage if you can sleep comfortably in your vehicle; hence the liking for minibuses such as the VW, which can be "Africanized" by the makers, with protective grills and additional cranked exhaust pipe added and a converter for high altitudes; there is also a good VW service network throughout the continent. VW drivers should note that, despite VW's wide network in South America, post-1985 models from Europe are difficult to service and repair, not so the earlier models. VW minibuses should have the normal diesel engine, not a turbo, or 4-wheel drive version, for the same reason.
    Theft of all vehicles is common. Apply at least two anti-theft devices when parked, even in car parks, and remove easily detachable items such as hub-caps, mirrors and windscreen wipers. At least one locking wheel nut per wheel is useful. A policy of insurance may not satisfactorily solve the problem of a car stolen outside its country of origin. There will be a

delay of at least a month in paying the claim, and the sum insured may be inadequate if the theft occurs in a country where cars are more expensive than in the country of origin. Import duty becomes payable on the stolen car, and again on any car bought for the return trip home. If, on the other hand, a cash settlement is made, there may be difficulties with exchange control. The same is largely true if a vehicle becomes a total loss in an accident.

Unleaded petrol (gasoline) is not available. Spare fuel should be in steel, not plastic, cans. You won't have travelled far before the plastic can will spring a leak, and there is danger of a spark from static electricity igniting the petrol when pouring. (In Venezuela, it is illegal to carry petrol from a garage in a can without a permit from the police, and this can only be obtained after paying a fine of Bs 500 for running out of fuel.) In remote areas, gas stations (few and far between, so keep well topped up) are unmarked. Look for a building with empty oil drums outside or ask. In this connection, it is wise to carry a funnel and/or hose to help fill the tank; often in rural areas there are no pumps and fuel must be taken from a drum. An in-line fuel filter is an advantage.

If the engine is not to fail at high altitudes, the spark must be advanced and cold spark plugs changed for hot; alternatively, take sets of smaller carburettor jets for use at altitude, which is a more fuel-economic solution. You can reduce the risk of a broken windscreen on gravel roads by not following closely behind other vehicles, and reducing speed when other vehicles (especially trucks with double rear wheels) are passing. (Wire over-screens are available in some cities, such as Buenos Aires.) A reversing light is needed for driving on narrow mountain roads at night or in narrow unlit tunnels built on curves. Landslides are frequent in the mountains in the rainy season. Keep enough reserve of fuel to be able to turn back, and take warm clothes and food in case you are delayed a day or so. Take plenty of water (for radiator and yourself). The car is liable to be searched for arms and drugs with some frequency in certain areas.

In addition to the normal spares carried, fan belt, spark plugs etc., the more adventurous driver needs a spade, tow cable, planks for placing under the wheels when stuck in dust or sand, filters for fuel, air, water and oil, light bulbs, wiper blades, spare parts for the suspension and steering, jump leads in case of battery failure, extra battery as back-up, and either an extra spare wheel or repair patches, air pump and valve screw. Help to repair a tyre is sometimes only available if you can provide these items yourself. An emergency fan belt which can be fitted without the use of tools is available from Flexicom Ltd, North Wing Mills, Bradford BD1 4EP, England.

Make a check list to ensure you have everything before you start each journey. The list is also useful for establishing what it is essential to replace after the theft of a car's contents. If you carry a cooler for food and drink, any official on the highway who spots it is likely to ask for refreshments, so take plenty or you may end up with none for yourself.

A book containing much practical information on South American motoring conditions and requirements, as well as being a travelogue, is *Driving to Heaven*, by Derek Stansfield (available from Remous Ltd, Wyvern Building, North Street, Milborne Port, Sherborne, Dorset, DT9 5EP, UK, or from the author, 13, The Meads, Milborne Port, Sherborne, DT9 5DS, £8.95 incl. postage and packing).

If driving and camping, the purchase of a 12-volt low-consumption neon light will add greatly to convenience.

If travelling from Europe with a car, do not sail to Panama if you are going south. You will still have the Darién Gap to negotiate. Much better to take the ship to Curaçao, where there is a car ferry to Venezuela. If shipping a car further south, Montevideo has much less bureaucracy and paperwork than any Argentine or Brazilian port. In any event you need a *Carnet de Passages* and an International Certificate of Registration.

Motorcycling Charles and Lucia Newall write: Motorcycling in South America is a great adventure, exhausting sometimes but not beyond the capacity of any experienced rider.

Machine: The bike should be tough and simple and capable of handling dirt roads if you plan on going into the Andes. If riding solo a large 4-stroke trail bike, e.g. Honda or Yamaha 500, would be ideal; if carrying a passenger a larger machine might be needed. We used an 800cc BMW road bike which handled a variety of conditions with ease.

Preparations: Fit a handlebar windscreen rather than a large touring fairing, which will hamper low-speed handling and complicate shipping from Panama. Standard air filters should be replaced by cleanable types e.g. K and N. You may need to carry a set of smaller carburettor jets to adapt the engine for high altitudes; chech with the manufacturer.

The standard rear suspension on motorcycles may give trouble if you are going to travel on unmade roads; again, check with the manufacturer. If so, fit high-quality replacement units (Konis) with springs matched for the weight carried.

The luggage panniers and rack should be very robust; distribute the weight of luggage around the bike rather than just piling it on the back. A fuel range of about 250 (400 km.) miles is useful and also the ability to run on 80-octane fuel.

Spares: A modern well-maintained machine shouldn't need any major repairs on a 25,000-mile trip. Take the usual consumables with you, such as plugs, points, filters, bulbs, chains, tubes and a set of cables; add to this any other parts which might be weak points on your machine. If possible, take spare tyres. Make arrangements to have parts sent out from home if you need anything unusual; a parts book and a good manual are invaluable. Find out how to service your machine and carry the correct tools. (Local mechanics are very good at making do without the proper parts.)

Clothes: Your clothing should keep you comfortable from 20° to 85°F and include a tough waterproof outer layer complete with overboots and overgloves.

Security: Security is not a problem; use a strong chain and lock. Hotel owners are very helpful and good about letting you bring your machine inside, but don't leave a loaded machine unattended. In general much safer than taking night buses or trains; cheaper too.

Documents: Passports, international driving licences, *Carnet de Passages*, or *Libreta de Paso* (if required, see **Motoring** above), motoring association membership card (for discounts etc.), registration certificate, Hoja de Ruta required in Bolivia. A letter from your Embassy, saying that you are a bona-fide tourist and have no intention of selling your bike, is very useful.

Shipping: It is much easier to fly a motorcycle from Panama than a car. SAM and Copa, space permitting, will take bikes in the baggage holds of their 737s. (It cost us US$130 for a 200-kilo machine.) For the adventurous, possibility of taking small boats down to Turbo, but at the high risk of losing the machine. *Warnings*: Do not try to ride the Andean roads in the rainy season as conditions are very dangerous, with muddy roads and deep river fords. Do not attempt to take a bike through the Darién Gap.

Cycling Hallam Murray writes: Over the past decade, bicycle technology has improved in leaps and bounds. With the advent of Kevlar tyres and puncture-resistant inner tubes it is now theoretically possible to cycle from Alaska to Tierra del Fuego without so much as a single puncture. For the traveller with a zest for adventure and a limited budget there is unlikely to be a finer way to explore. At first glance a bicycle may not appear to be the most obvious vehicle for a major journey, but given ample time and reasonable energy it most certainly is the best. It can be ridden, carried by almost every form of transport from an aeroplane to a canoe, and can even be lifted across one's shoulders over short distances. On my most recent journey from Lake Titicaca to Tierra del Fuego—largely on unpaved roads, many of which would have defeated even the most robust car or truck—I was often envied by travellers using more orthodox transport, for I was able to travel at my own pace, to explore more remote regions and to meet people who are not normally in contact with tourists.

Choosing a Bicycle: The choice of bicycle depends on the type and length of expedition being undertaken and on the terrain and road surfaces likely to be encountered. Unless you are planning a journey almost exclusively on paved roads—when a high quality touring bike such as a Dawes Super Galaxy would probably suffice—I would strongly recommend a mountain bike. The good quality ones (and the cast iron rule is **never** to skimp on quality) are incredibly tough and rugged, with low gear ratios for difficult terrain, wide tyres with plenty of tread for good road-holding, cantilever brakes, and a low centre of gravity for improved stability. Expect to pay upwards of US$800 for such a machine. Although touring bikes, and to a lesser extent mountain bikes, and spares are available in the larger Latin American cities, remember that in the developing world most indigenous manufactured goods are shoddy and rarely last. In some countries, such as Mexico, Chile and Uruguay, imported components can be found but they tend to be extremely expensive. Buy everything you possibly can before you leave home.

Bicycle Equipment : A small but comprehensive tool kit (to include chain rivet and crank removers, a spoke key and possibly a block remover), a spare tyre and inner tubes, a puncture repair kit with plenty of extra patches and glue, a set of brake blocks, brake and gear cables and all types of nuts and bolts, at least 12 spokes (best taped to the chain stay), a light oil for the chain, tube of waterproof grease, a pump secured by a pump lock, a Blackburn stopblock (my choice for the most invaluable accessory and they are cheap and virtually weightless), a cyclometer, a loud bell, and a secure lock and chain. *Richard's Bicycle Book* makes useful reading for even the most mechanically minded.

Luggage and equipment: Strong and waterproof front and back panniers are a must. A top bag cum rucksack (e.g. Carradice) makes a good addition for use on and off the bike. I used a Cannondale front bag for my maps, camera, compass, altimeter, notebook and small tape-recorder. My total luggage weighed 27 kg.—on the high side, but I never felt seriously overweight. "Gaffa" tape is excellent for protecting vulnerable parts of panniers and for carrying out all manner of repairs. My most vital equipment included a light and waterproof tent, a 3 season sleeping bag, an Optimus petrol stove (the best I have ever used for it is light and efficient and petrol can be found almost everywhere), a plastic survival bag for storing luggage at night when camping, 4 elastic straps, 4 one-litre water bottles, Swiss Army knife, torch, comprehensive medical kit, money belts, a hat to protect against hours of ferocious tropical sun and small presents such as postcards of home, balloons and plastic badges. A rubber mouse can do wonders for making contact with children in isolated villages.

All equipment and clothes should be packed in plastic bags to give extra protection against dust and rain. Always take the minimum clothing. It's better to buy extra items en route when you find you need them. Naturally the choice will depend on whether you are planning a journey through tropical lowlands, deserts, high mountains or a combination, and whether rain is to be expected. Generally it is best to carry several layers of thin light clothes than fewer heavy, bulky ones. Always keep one set of dry clothes, including long trousers, to put on at the end of the day. I would not have parted with my incredibly light, strong, waterproof and wind resistant goretex jacket and overtrousers. I could have sold them 100 times over and in Bolivia was even offered a young mule in exchange! I took two pairs of training shoes and found these to be ideal for both cycling and walking.

Useful Tips: Wind, not hills is the enemy of the cyclist. Try to make the best use of the times of day when there is little; mornings tend to be best but there is no steadfast rule. In parts of Patagonia there can be gusting winds of 80 kph around the clock at some times of year, whereas in other areas there can be none. Take care to avoid dehydration, by drinking regularly. In hot, dry areas with limited supplies of water, be sure to carry an ample supply. For food I carried the staples (sugar, salt, dried milk, tea, coffee, porridge oats, raisins, dried soups, etc.) and supplemented these with whatever local foods I could find in the markets. Give your bicycle a thorough daily check for loose nuts or bolts or bearings. See that all parts run smoothly. A good chain should last 2,000 miles, 3,200 km. or more but be sure to keep it as clean as possible—an old toothbrush is good for this—and to oil it lightly from time to time. Always camp out of sight of a road. Remember that thieves are attracted to towns and cities, so when sight-seeing, try to leave your bicycle with someone such as a café owner or a priest. Country people tend to be more honest and are usually friendly and very inquisitive. However, don't take unnecessary risks; always see that your bicycle is secure. In more remote regions dogs can be vicious; carry a stick or some small stones to frighten them off. Traffic on main roads can be a nightmare; it is usually far more rewarding to keep to the smaller roads or to paths if they exist. Most towns have a bicycle shop of some description, but it is best to do your own repairs and adjustments whenever possible. In an emergency it is amazing how one can improvise with wire, string, dental floss, nuts and bolts, odd pieces of tin or "Gaffa" tape!

The Expedition Advisory Centre, administered by the Royal Geographical Society, 1, Kensington Gore, London SW7 2AR has published a useful monograph entitled *Bicycle Expeditions*, by Paul Vickers. Published in March 1990, it is available direct from the Centre, price £6.50 (postage extra if outside the UK).

River Transport Geoffrey Dempsey has sent us the following note, with particular reference to Amazonia:

Because expanding air services have captured the lucrative end of the passenger market, passenger services on the rivers are in decline. Worst hit have been the upper reaches; rivers like the Ucayali in Peru, but the trend is apparent throughout the region. The situation has been aggravated for the casual traveller by a new generation of purpose-built tugs (all engine-room and bridge) that can handle up to a dozen freight barges but have no passenger accommodation. In Peru passenger boats must now supplement incomes by carrying cargo, and this lengthens their journey cycle. In the face of long delays, travellers might consider shorter "legs" involving more frequent changes of boat; though the more local the service, the slower and more uncomfortable it will be.

Hammocks, mosquito nets (not always good quality), plastic containers for water storage, kettles and cooking utensils can be purchased in any sizeable riverside town, as well as tinned food such as sardines, meat loaf, frankfurters, ham and fruit. Fresh bread, cake, eggs, fruit—papayas, bananas, pineapples, oranges etc.—are available in most villages. Cabin bunks are provided with thin mattresses but these are often foul. Replacements can be bought locally but rolls of plastic foam that can be cut to size are also available and much cheaper. Eye-screws for securing washing lines and mosquito nets are useful, and tall passengers who are not taking a hammock and who may find insufficient headroom on some boats should consider a camp-chair. The writer yearned for a cushion.

Travelling with Children We are grateful to Tim and Arlene Frost, of New Zealand, for the following notes:

People contemplating overland travel in South America with children should remember that a lot of time can be spent waiting for buses, trains, and especially for aeroplanes. On bus journeys, if the children are good at amusing themselves, or can readily sleep while travelling, the problems can be considerably lessened. Travel on trains, while not as fast or at times as comfortable as buses, allows more scope for moving about. Some trains provide tables between seats, so that games can be played.

Food can be a problem if the children are not adaptable. It is easier to take biscuits, drinks, bread etc. with you on longer trips than to rely on meal stops where the food may not be to taste. A small immersion heater and jug for making hot drinks is invaluable, but remember that electric current varies. Try and get a dual-voltage one (110v and 220v).

Fares: On all long-distance buses you pay for each seat, and there are no half-fares if the children occupy a seat each. For shorter trips it is cheaper, if less comfortable, to seat small children on your knee. Often there are spare seats which children can occupy after tickets have been collected. In city and local excursion buses, small children generally do not pay a fare, but are not entitled to a seat when paying customers are standing. On sightseeing tours you should *always* bargain for a family rate—often children can go free. (In trains, reductions for children are general, but not universal.)

All civil airlines charge half for children under 12, but some military services don't have half-fares, or have younger age limits. Children's fares on Lloyd Aéreo Boliviano are considerably more than half, and there is only a 7kg. baggage allowance. (LAB also checks children's ages on passports.)

Hotels: In all hotels, bargain for rates. If charges are per person, always insist that two children will occupy one bed only, therefore counting as one tariff. If rates are per bed, the same applies. In either case you can almost always get a reduced rate at cheaper hotels. (In restaurants, you can normally buy children's helpings, or divide one full-size helping between two children.)

Generally, travel with children presents no special problems—in fact the path is often smoother for family groups. Officials tend to be more amenable where children are concerned. Moreover, even thieves and pickpockets seem to have some of the traditional respect for families, and may leave you alone because of it!

Hiking and Trekking Hilary Bradt, the well-known trekker, author and publisher, writes: A network of paths and tracks covers much of South America and is in constant use by the local people. In countries with a large Indian population—Ecuador, Peru and Bolivia, for instance—you can walk just about anywhere, but in the more European countries, such as Venezuela, Chile, and Argentina, you must usually limit yourself to the many excellent national parks with hiking trails. Most South American countries have an Instituto Geográfico Militar which sells topographical maps, scale 1:100,000 or 1:50,000. The physical features shown on these are usually accurate; the trails and place names less so. National Parks offices also sell maps.

Hiking and backpacking should not be approached casually. Even if you only plan to be out a couple of hours you should have comfortable, safe footwear and a daypack to carry your sweater and waterproof. At high altitudes the difference in temperature between sun and shade is remarkable. The longer trips mentioned in this book require basic backpacking equipment. Essential items are: backpack with frame, sleeping bag, closed cell foam mat for insulation, stove, tent or tarpaulin, dried food (not tins), water bottle, compass. Some but not all of these things are available locally.

When planning treks in the Andes you should be aware of the effects and dangers of acute mountain sickness, and cerebral and pulmonary oedema (see Health Information, **page 33**). These can be avoided by spending a few days acclimatizing to the altitude before starting your walk, and by climbing slowly. Otherwise there are fewer dangers than in most cities. Hikers have little to fear from the animal kingdom apart from insects (although it's best to avoid actually stepping on a snake), and robbery and assault are very rare. You are much more of a threat to the environment than vice versa. Leave no evidence of your passing; don't litter and don't give gratuitous presents of sweets or money to rural villagers. Respect their system of reciprocity; if they give you hospitality or food, then is the time to reciprocate with presents.

Maps Those from the Instituto Geográficos Militares in the capitals (see above) are often the only good maps available in Latin Amercica. It is therfore wise to get as many as possible in your home country before leaving, especially if travelling by land. A recommended series of general maps is that published by International Travel Map Productions (ITM), PO Box 2290, Vancouver BC, V6B 2WF, Canada, compiled with historical notes, by Kevin Healey. Available are South America South, North East and North West (1:4,000,000), Amazon Basin (1:4,000,000), Central America (1:1,800,000), Costa Rica (1:500,000), the Yucatán (1:1,000,000) and Baja California (1:1,000,000).

Other Travel Books We should mention the "Backpacking Guide Series" published by Bradt Publications, 41 Nortoft Road, Chalfont St. Peter, Bucks, SL9 0LA, UK. They give detailed descriptions of hiking trails (mentioned in our country "Information for Visitors" sections) and much fascinating information, with many illustrations, in the following volumes: *Peru and Bolivia; Chile and Argentina, plus the Falkland Islands; Climbing and Hiking in Ecuador; South American River Trips*. (Bradt Publications also publish and sell other trail guides, and import trekking and topographical maps from South America, including the ITM series.) *South America on a Shoestring*, by Geoff Crowther (Lonely Planet Publications) has been recommended repeatedly for the quality of its maps. Lonely Planet's growing number of individual country guides have also been praised.

Another very useful book, highly recommended, aimed specifically at the budget traveller is *The Tropical Traveller*, by John Hatt (Pan Books, 2nd edition, 1985).

GENERAL ADVICE

Souvenirs Remember that these can almost invariably be bought more cheaply away from the capital, though the choice may be less wide. Bargaining seems to be the general rule in most countries' street markets. Visitors should remember that souvenirs made from endangered species, for example, sea-turtle shells, may not be imported into their home countries, and are advised to ask the responsible government agency at home for a complete list of the endangered species concerned.

If British travellers have no space in their luggage, they might like to remember Tumi, the Latin American Craft Centre, at 23 Chalk Farm Road, London NW1 (T 071-485 4152) and 2 New Bond Street Place, Bath (T 0225 62367), who specialize in Mexican and Andean products. There are similar shops in the USA; one good one is on the ground floor of Citicorp Center, Lexington Avenue and 53rd Street, New York.

Mail Postal services in most countries are not very efficient, and pilfering is frequent. All mail, especially packages, should be registered. Some travellers recommend that mail should be sent to one's Embassy (or, if a cardholder, American Express agent) rather than to the Poste Restante/General Delivery (*Lista de Correos*) department of a country's Post Office. Some Embassies and post offices, however, do not keep mail for more than a month. If there seems to be no mail at the Lista under the initial letter of your surname, ask them to look under the initial of your forename or your middle name. For the smallest risk of misunderstanding, use title, initial and surname only. (If you're a British male, and all else fails, ask them to look under "E" for "Esquire"!—Geoffrey van Dulken.)

Explorers The South American Explorers' Club is at Avenida Portugal 146 (Casilla 3714), Lima, Peru (T 31-44-80), 1254 Toledo, Apartado 21-431, Eloy Alfaro, Quito, Ecuador (T 566-076), and 1510 York Street, Denver, CO 80206, T(303) 320-0388. (For further details see under Lima and Quito.)

Wildlife Wildlife lovers might like to know about Kilverstone Wildlife Park, Thetford, Norfolk, IP24 2RL, England. This is a private zoo, open to the public, which specializes in Latin American fauna and is helping to preserve species threatened with extinction, by breeding and returning them to their native habitat.

Photography Take as much film in from home as you can; it is expensive in most places. Some travellers have advised against mailing exposed films home; better to take them with you. The postal authorities may use less sensitive equipment for X-ray screening than the airports do.

Dan Buck and Anne Meadows write: A note on developing film in South America. Black and white is a problem. Often it is shoddily machine-processed and the negatives are ruined. Ask the store if you can see an example of their laboratory's work and if they hand-develop.

Jeremy Till and Sarah Wigglesworth suggest that exposed film can be protected in humid areas by putting it in a balloon and tying a knot.

Final Hints Everbody has his/her own list. Items most often mentioned include a small portable stove (liquid fuel is more readily available than gas— though the latter is becoming more common—and you need a combination canteen to go with it), air cushions for slatted seats, strong shoes (and remember that footwear over 9½ English size, or 42 European size, is difficult to obtain in Latin America except Argentina and Brazil), money-belt or neck pouch, obtainable from Journey Latin America (address on **page 11**); a small first-aid kit and handbook, rubber window wedges, fully waterproof top clothing, wax earplugs and airline-type eye mask to help you sleep in noisy and poorly curtained hotel rooms, rubber-thong Japanese-type sandals (flip-flops), a polyethylene sheet 2 x 1 metres to cover possibly infested beds and train floors and shelter your luggage, polyethylene bags of varying sizes, a toilet bag you can tie round your waist, a sheet sleeping-bag and pillow-case or separate pillow-case—in some countries they are not changed often in cheap hotels, a mosquito net (or a hammock with a fitted net), a clothes line, a nailbrush (useful for scrubbing dirt off clothes as well as off oneself), a vacuum flask, a water bottle, a small dual-voltage immersion heater, a small dual-voltage (or battery-driven) electric fan, tea bags, a light nylon waterproof shopping bag, a universal bath- and basin-plug of the flanged type that will fit any waste-pipe (or improvise one from a sheet of thick rubber), string, electrical insulating tape, large penknife preferably with tin and bottle openers, scissors and corkscrew—the famous Swiss Army range has been repeatedly recommended, collapsible drinking beaker, electric motor-cycle alarm for luggage protection, a flour sack and roll of wire mesh for ditto, alarm clock or watch, candle, torch (flashlight)—especially one that will clip on to a pocket or belt, small transistor radio or battery cassette-player (Walkman type) with earphones, pocket calculator, an adaptor and flex to enable you to take power from an electric-light socket (the Edison screw type is the most commonly used), a padlock for the doors of the cheapest and most casual hotels, spare chain-lengths and padlock for securing luggage to bed or bus/train seat. Small coins, postage stamps, visiting cards and postcards of views from your own country to give away as souvenirs to friendly locals. Useful medicaments are given at the end of the "Health Information" section (**page 37**); to these might be added some lip salve ("Lypsil" has been recommended), and pre-moistened wipes (such as "Wet Ones"). Always carry toilet paper. Women travelling alone may find it useful to wear a wedding ring. Extra passport photos may be useful, also photocopies of essential documents (passport, credit cards, air tickets). **Never** carry firearms. Their possession could land you in serious trouble.

A note for **contact lens wearers**: most countries have a wide selection of products for the care of lenses, so you don't need to take kilos of lotions.

Be careful when asking directions. Women probably know more about the neighbourhood; men about more distant locations. Policemen are often helpful. However, many Latin Americans will give you the wrong answer rather than admit they do not know; this may be partly because they fear losing face, but is also because they like to please. You are more likely to get reliable information if you carefully refrain from asking leading questions.

Lastly, a good principle is to take half the clothes (trousers with plenty of pockets are very useful), and twice the money, that you think you will need.

HEALTH INFORMATION

The following information has been very kindly compiled for us by Dr. David Snashall, who is presently Senior Lecturer in Occupational Health at St. Thomas's Hospital Medical School in London and Chief Medical Advisor of the British Foreign and Commonwealth Office. He has travelled extensively in Central and South America, worked in Peru and in East Africa and keeps in close touch with developments in preventative and tropical medicine. We incorporate also some welcome observations on the text by Dr. C. J. Schofield, editor of Parasitology Today. The publishers have every confidence that the following information is correct, but cannot assume any direct responsibility in this connection.

THE TRAVELLER to Latin America is inevitably exposed to health risks not encountered in Britain or the USA, especially if he spends time in the tropical regions. Epidemic diseases have been largely brought under control by vaccination programmes and public sanitation but, in rural areas, the latter is rudimentary and the chances of contracting infections of various sorts are much higher than at home.

There are English-speaking doctors in most major cities. If you fall ill the best plan may be to attend the out-patient department of a local hospital or contact your Embassy representative for the name of a reputable doctor. (We give the names of hospitals and some recommended doctors in the main city sections.— Ed.) Medical practices vary from those at home but remember they have particular experience in dealing with locally-occurring diseases.

Self-medication is undesirable except for minor complaints but may be forced on you by circumstances. Whatever the circumstances, be wary of medicines prescribed for you by pharmacists; many are poorly trained and unscrupulous enough to sell you potentially dangerous drugs or old stock they want to get rid of. The large number of pharmacies throughout Latin America is a considerable surprise to most people, as is the range of medicines you can purchase over the counter. There is a tendency towards over-prescription of drug mixtures and in general this should be resisted. Many drugs are manufactured under licence from American or European companies so the trade names may be familiar to you. This means that you do not need to carry a whole chest of medicines, but remember that the shelf-life of some items, especially vaccines and antibiotics, is markedly reduced in tropical conditions. Buy your supplies at the better outlets where they have refrigerators, even though it is more expensive. Check the expiry date of all preparations you buy.

Immigration officials sometimes confiscate scheduled drugs (Lomotil is an example) if they are not accompanied by a doctor's prescription.

With the following precautions and advice, you should keep as healthy as usual. Make local enquiries about health risks if you are apprehensive and take the general advice of European or North American families who have lived or are living in the country.

Before you go take out medical insurance. You should have a dental check-up, obtain a spare glasses prescription and, if you suffer from a chronic illness (such as diabetes, high blood pressure, ear or sinus troubles, cardiopulmonary disease or a nervous disorder) arrange for a check-up with your doctor, who can at the same time provide you with a letter explaining the details of your disability, if possible in English and Spanish (or Portuguese for Brazil). Check current practice in malaria prophylaxis (prevention).

Inoculations Smallpox vaccination is no longer required anywhere in the world. Cholera vaccination is not required for Latin America. The following vaccinations are recommended:

Yellow fever: this is a live vaccine not to be given to children under nine months of age or persons allergic to eggs. Immunity lasts ten years. An international certificate of yellow fever vaccination will be given and should be kept because it is sometimes asked for.

Typhoid (monovalent): one dose followed by a booster in a month's time; Immunity from this course lasts two to three years.

Poliomyelitis: this is a live vaccine generally given orally and a full course consists of three doses with a booster in tropical regions every three to five years.

Tetanus: one dose should be given with a booster (vital) at six weeks and another at six months, and ten-yearly boosters thereafter are recommended.

Children should, in addition, be properly protected against diphtheria, and against pertussis (whooping cough) and measles, both of which tend to be more serious infections than at home. Measles, mumps and rubella vaccine is now widely available but those teenage girls who have not had rubella (German measles) should be tested and vaccinated. Consult your doctor for advice on tuberculosis inoculation: the disease is still widespread.

Infectious Hepatitis (jaundice) is endemic throughout Latin America and seems to be frequently caught by travellers. The main symptoms are pains in the stomach, lack of appetite, lassitude, and the typical yellow colour of the skin. Medically speaking there are two different types, the less serious but more common is hepatitis A, for which the best protection is the careful preparation of food, the avoidance of contaminated drinking water and scrupulous attention to toilet hygiene. Human normal immunoglobulin (gamma globulin) confers considerable protection against the disease and is particularly useful in epidemics; it should be obtained from a reputable source and is certainly useful for travellers who intend to live rough: they should have a shot before leaving and have it repeated every six months. The dose is 250 mg under 10 years of age and 750 mg above. The dose of gamma globulin depends on the concentration of the particular preparation used, so the manufacturer's advice should be taken. A smaller dose than usual can be given if exposure is for one or two months only.

The other, more serious, version is hepatitis B which is acquired usually by injections with unclean needles, blood transfusions, as a sexually transmitted disease and possibly by insect bites. This disease can be effectively prevented by a specific vaccination requiring three shots over six months before travelling but this is quite expensive. If you have had jaundice in the past it would be worthwhile having a blood test to see if you are immune to either of the two types because this might avoid the necessity for vaccination or gamma globulin.

If at a particular occupational risk (e.g. zoologists or veterinarians), or in the case of epidemics, there are vaccines against other diseases such as rabies.

AIDS in South America is increasing in its prevalence, as in most countries, but is not wholly confined to the well known high risk sections of the population, i.e. homosexual men, intravenous drug abusers, prostitutes and children of infected mothers. Heterosexual transmission is now the dominant mode and so the main risk to travellers is from casual sex. The same precautions should be taken as when encountering any sexually transmitted disease. The AIDS virus (HIV) can be passed via unsterilized needles which have been previously used to inject an HIV positive patient, but the risk of this is very small indeed. It would however be sensible to check that needles have been properly sterilised or disposable needles used. Be wary of carrying disposable needles yourself: customs officials find them suspicious. The risk of receiving a blood transfusion with blood infected with the HIV virus is greater than from dirty needles because of the amount of fluid exchanged. Supplies of blood for transfusion should now be screened for HIV in all reputable hospitals so again the risk must be very small indeed. Catching the AIDS virus does not usually produce an illness in itself; the only way to be sure if you feel you have been put at risk is to have a blood test for HIV antibodies on your return to a place where there are reliable laboratory facilities. The test does not become positive for many weeks. Presently the higher risks are probably in Brazil and the West Indies.

Common Problems, some of which will almost certainly be encountered, are:

Heat and Cold Full acclimatization to high temperatures takes about two weeks and during this period it is normal to feel relatively apathetic, especially if the relative humidity is high. Drink plenty of water (up to 15 litres a day are required when working physically hard in the tropics), use salt on your food and avoid extreme exertion. Tepid showers are more cooling than hot or cold ones. Large hats do not cool you down, but do prevent sunburn. Remember that, especially in the highlands, there can be a large and sudden drop in temperature between sun and shade and between night and day, so dress accordingly. Warm jackets and woollens are essential after dark at high altitude.

Altitude Acute mountain sickness or *soroche* can strike from about 3,000 metres upwards. It is more likely to affect those who ascend rapidly (e.g. by plane) and those who over-exert themselves. Teenagers are particularly prone. Past experience is not always a good guide: the author, having spent years in Peru travelling constantly between sea level and very high altitude, never suffered the slightest symptoms, then was severely affected climbing Kilimanjaro in Tanzania.

On reaching heights above 3,000 metres, heart pounding and shortness of breath, especially on exertion, are almost universal and a normal response to the lack of oxygen in the air. *Soroche* takes a few hours or days to come on and presents with headache, lassitude, dizziness, loss of appetite, nausea and vomiting. Insomnia is common and often associated with a suffocating feeling when lying in bed. Keen observers may note their breathing tends to wax and wane at night and their face tends to be puffy in the mornings—this is all part of the syndrome. The treatment is rest, pain killers (preferably not aspirin-based) for the headache and anti-sickness pills for vomiting. Oxygen may help at very high altitudes. Various local panaceas ("Coramina glucosada", "Effortil", "Micoren") have their advocates and *mate* (or *te*) *de coca* (an infusion of coca leaves, widely available) certainly alleviates some of the symptoms. (The drug acetazolamide (Diamox) is said to facilitate acclimatization to altitude; detailed information is available from the Mountain Medicine Centre, c/o Dr. Charles Clarke, Dept. of Neurological Sciences, St. Bartholomew's Hospital, 38 Little Britain, London EC1A 7BE.—Ed.)

On arrival at places over 3,000 metres, a few hours' rest in a chair and avoidance of alcohol, cigarettes and heavy food will go a long way towards preventing *soroche*. Should the symptoms be severe and prolonged it is best to descend to lower altitude and re-ascend slowly or in stages. If this is impossible because of shortage of time or if the likelihood of acute mountain sickness is high then the drug Acetazoleamide (Diamox) can be used as a preventative and continued during the ascent. There is good evidence of the value of this drug in the prevention of *soroche* but some people do experience funny side effects. The usual dose is 500 mg of the slow-release preparation each night, starting the night before ascending above 3,000 metres.

Other problems experienced at high altitude are sunburn, excessively dry air causing skin cracking, sore eyes (it may be wise to leave your contact lenses out) and stuffy noses. It is unwise to ascend to high altitude if you are pregnant, especially in the first 3 months, or if you have any history of heart, lung or blood disease, including sickle-cell.

There is a further, albeit rare, hazard due to rapid ascent to high altitude called acute pulmonary oedema. The condition can affect mountaineers; but also occurs in Andean natives returning from a period at the coast. The condition comes on quite rapidly with breathlessness, noisy breathing, cough, blueness of the lips and frothing at the mouth. Anybody developing this must be brought down as soon as possible, given oxygen and taken to hospital.

Rapid descent from high places will aggravate sinus and middle ear infections, and make bad teeth ache painfully. The same problems are sometimes experienced during descent at the end of a flight.

Despite these various hazards (mostly preventable) of high-altitude travel, many people find the environment healthier and more invigorating than at sea-level.

Intestinal Upsets   Practically nobody escapes this one, so be prepared for it. Most of the time it is due to the insanitary preparation of food. Don't eat uncooked fish or vegetables, fruit with the skin on (always peel your fruit yourself), food that is exposed to flies, or salads. Tap water is rarely safe outside the major cities, especially in the rainy season, and stream water is often contaminated by communities living surprisingly high in the mountains. Filtered or bottled (make sure it is opened in your presence—Ed.) water is usually available and safe. If your hotel has a central hot-water supply, this is safe to drink after cooling. Ice for drinks should be made from boiled water but rarely is, so stand your glass on the ice cubes rather than putting them in the drink. Dirty water should first be strained through a filter bag (available from camping shops) and then boiled or treated. Water in general can be rendered safe in the following ways: boil for 5 minutes at sea level, longer at higher altitudes; or add three drops of household bleach to 1 pint of water and leave for 15 minutes; or add 1 drop of tincture of iodine to 1 pint of water and leave for 3 minutes. Commercial water-sterilizing tablets are available, for instance Sterotabs from Boots, England.

Fresh, unpasteurized milk is a source of food poisoning germs, tuberculosis and brucellosis. This applies equally to ice-cream, yoghurt and cheese made from unpasteurized milk. Fresh milk can be rendered safe by heating it to 62°C for 30 minutes followed by rapid cooling, or by boiling it. Matured or processed cheeses are safer than fresh varieties. Heat-treated (UHT), pasteurized or sterilized milk is becoming more available.

The most effective treatment for simple diarrhoea is rest and plenty to drink. Seek medical advice, however, if there is no improvement after three days. Much of the exhaustion of travellers' diarrhoea derives from the dehydration: water and salts are lost from the body and are not replaced. This can be remedied by proprietary preparations of salts which are dissolved in water, e.g. Electrosol (Macarthys) Dioralyte (Armour) Rehidrat (Searle) or ask for "suero oral" at a pharmacy or health centre. Marsha Stuart, of Save the Children, Westport, Conn. states that adding ½ teaspoon of salt (3.5g) and 4 tablespoons of sugar (40 g) to a litre of pure water makes a perfectly good substitute for the proprietary preparations. If rest is not possible, or the lavatory is full of other people with the same trouble, or if the stomach cramps are particularly bad, then the following drugs may help:

Loperamide (Imodium, Janssen, or Arret) up to eight capsules a day. This is now available in the UK without prescription.
Diaphenoxylate with atropine (Lomotil, Searle) up to 16 tablets in any 24 hours, but do *not* use for simple diarrhoea, only to relieve cramps and never in children.
Codeine phosphate 30 mg. One tablet every 4 hours.
Kaolin and morphine or Paregoric, as directed by the pharmacist.
 Severe vomiting may be calmed by metoclopramide (Maxolon, Beechams; Primperan, Berk) 10 mg. tablet or injection every 8 hours, but not more frequently.

The vast majority of cases of diarrhoea and/or vomiting are due to microbial infections of the bowel plus an effect from strange food and drink. They represent no more than a temporary inconvenience which you learn to live with and need no special treatment. Fortunately, as you get accustomed to Latin American germs, the attacks become less frequent and you can be more daring in your eating habits.

If, in addition to cramps and diarrhoea, you pass blood in the bowel motion, have severe abdominal pain, fever and feel really terrible, you may well have dysentery and a doctor should be consulted at once. If this is not possible, the recommended treatment for bacillary dysentery is Tetracycline or Ampicillin 500 mg. every 6 hours plus replacement of water and salts. If you catch amoebic dysentery, which has rather similar symptoms, do not try to cure yourself but put yourself in proper medical hands; the treatment can be complex and self-medication may just damp down the symptoms with the risk of serious liver involvement later on.

Another common bowel infection is with the parasite Giardia Lamblia, which causes prolonged diarrhoea, bloating, persistent indigestion and sometimes loss of weight. This needs treating with a drug such as Metronidazole, best taken under medical supervision.

There are many travellers' tales about special diets, herbal medicines and the consumption of vast quantities of yoghurt as an aid to rehabilitating one's bowels after such attacks. None of them has proved to be useful, in contrast to the widespread success of oral rehydration (water and salt replenishment by mouth) in thousands of children seriously ill with diarrhoea throughout the third world. There is some evidence that alcohol and milk products can prolong diarrhoea so these are best avoided after an attack.

Enterovioform (Ciba), "Mexaform" in Latin America, can have serious side effects (nerve damage, especially to the eyes) if taken for long periods. The active agent, diodochlor-hydroxy-quinoline, is used in many antidiarrhoeals sold in Peru and Ecuador. If it is impossible to control the source of your food and you are likely to be far from medical attention (such as on Amazonian river trips) it is justifiable to take diloxanide furoate (Furamide) 500 mg. daily *plus* a sulphonamide drug e.g. Phthalylsulphathiazole (Thalazole, May & Baker) 500 mg. twice daily. Many businessmen and, for example, athletes who are on short visits of great importance take Streptotriad (May & Baker) one tablet twice daily to prevent diarrhoea and this has been proved to be effective.

Paradoxically, constipation is also common, probably induced by dietary change, inadequate fluid intake in hot places and long bus journeys. Simple laxatives are useful in the short term (the Editor recommends Senokot) and bulky foods such as maize, beans and plenty of fruit are also useful.

Insects These can be a great nuisance, especially in the tropics, and some, of course, are carriers of serious diseases. The best way of keeping them away at night is to sleep off the ground with a mosquito net and to burn mosquito coils containing pyrethrum. The best way to use insecticide aerosol sprays is to spray the room thoroughly in all areas and then shut the door for a while, re-entering when the smell has dispersed. Tablets of insecticide are also available which, when placed on a heated mat plugged into a wall socket, fill the room with insecticide fumes in the same way. The best repellants contain di-ethyl-meta-toluamide (DET) or di-methyl phthalate—sold as "Deet", "Six-Twelve Plus", "Off", "Boots' Liquid Insect Repellant", "Autan", "Flypel". Liquid is best for arms and face (care around eyes) and aerosol spray for clothes and ankles to deter chiggers, mites and ticks. Liquid DEET suspended in water can be used to impregnate cotton clothes and mosquito nets.

If you are bitten, itching may be relieved by baking-soda baths, anti-histamine tablets (care with alcohol or driving), corticosteroid creams (great care—never use if any hint of sepsis) or by judicious scratching. Calamine lotion and cream have limited effectiveness and antihistamine creams (e.g. Antihisan, May & Baker) have a tendency to cause skin allergies and are, therefore, not generally recommended.

Bites which become infected (commonly in the tropics) should be treated with a local antiseptic or antibiotic cream, such as Cetrimide BP (Savlon, ICI) as should infected scratches.

Skin infestations with body lice (crabs) and scabies are, unfortunately, easy to pick up. Use gamma benzene hexachloride for lice and benzene benzoate solution for scabies. Crotamiton cream (Eurax, Geigy) alleviates itching and also kills a number of skin parasites. Malathion lotion 5% (Prioderm) kills lice effectively, but do not use the toxic agricultural insecticide Malathion.

In remote grassland or jungle areas, insect larvae such as that of the bot-fly, which burrow into the flesh, are best removed by covering the breathing hole in your skin with vaseline, then a circular piece of adhesive tape with more vaseline round the edges. If this is allowed to dry well, with no lymph leaking out round the edges, you will be able to squeeze the maggot out next day. The condition is identifiable by a clear hole in the middle of a growing boil or pimple.

Malaria in South America is theoretically confined to coastal and jungle zones but is now on the increase again. Mosquitoes do not thrive above 2,500 metres so we are safe at altitude. There are different varieties of malaria, some resistant to the normal drugs. Make local enquiries if you intend to visit possibly infected zones and use one of the following prophylactic regimes. Start taking the tablets a few days before exposure and continue to take them for six weeks after leaving the malarial zone. Remember to give the drugs to babies and children also. Opinion varies on the precise drugs and dosage to be used for protection; all the drugs may have some side effects, and it is important to balance the risk of catching the disease against the albeit rare side effects. The increasing complexity of the subject as the malarial parasite becomes immune to the new generation of drugs has made concentration on the physical prevention of being bitten by mosquitoes more important, i.e. the use of long-sleeved shirts/blouses and long trousers, repellants and nets.

Prophylactic regimes:
  Proguanil (Paludrine ICI 100 mg, 2 tablets daily) *or* Chloroquin (Avloclor; ICI, Malarivon; Wallace MFG, Nivaquine, May & Baker; Resochin, Bayer; Aralen 300 mg base (2 tablets) weekly).
  Where there is a high risk of Chloroquin-resistant falciparum malaria, take Chloroquin plus Proguanil in the above-mentioned doses and carry Fansidar (Roche, also spelt Falsidar) for treatment; *or* add Paludrine 2 tablets per day to your routine Chloroquin prophylaxis.

You can catch malaria even when sticking to the above rules, although it is unlikely. If you do develop symptoms (high fever, shivering, headache, sometimes diarrhoea) seek medical advice immediately. If this is not possible, and there is a great likelihood of malaria, the *treatment* is:

Normal types: Chloroquin, a single dose of 4 tablets (600mg) followed by two tablets (300 mg) in 6 hours and 300 mg each day following.
Falciparum type or type in doubt: Fansidar, single dose of 3 tablets. (We have been told that this drug does not combine well with alcohol, so best to avoid drinking during treatment period.)

If Falciparum type malaria is definitely diagnosed, it is wise to get to a good hospital as the treatment can be complex and the illness very serious.

Pregnant women are particularly prone to malaria and should stick to Proguanil as a prophylactic. Chloroquin may cause eye damage if taken over a long period. The safety of Fansidar has been questioned and, at the time of writing, it is not recommended for prophylaxis.

Chagas' Disease (South American Trypanosomiasis) is a chronic disease, very rarely caught by travellers, but very difficult to treat. It is transmitted by the simultaneous biting and excreting of the Reduvid bug (Triatoma or Rhodnius), also known as the *vinchuca*, or *barbeiro*. Somewhat resembling a small cockroach, this nocturnal "kissing bug" lives in poor adobe houses with dirt floors often frequented by oppossums. If you cannot avoid such accommodation, sleep off the floor with a candle lit, use a mosquito net and wash any bites thoroughly with soap and water, or a disinfectant.

Sunburn The burning power of the tropical sun, especially at high altitude, is phenomenal. Always wear a wide-brimmed hat and use some form of suncream lotion on untanned skin. Normal temperate-zone suntan lotions (protection factor up to 7) are not much good; you need to use the types designed specifically for the tropics, or for mountaineers or skiers, with a protection factor between 7 and 15. These are often not available in South America; a reasonable substitute is zinc oxide ointment. Glare from the sun can cause conjunctivitis, so wear sunglasses. especially on tropical beaches, where high protection-factor sunscreen cream should also be used.

Snakebite If you are unlucky enough to be bitten by a venomous snake, spider, scorpion or sea creature, try (within limits) to catch the animal for identification. The reactions to be expected are: fright, swelling, pain and bruising around the bite, soreness of the regional lymph glands, nausea, vomiting and fever. If any of the following symptoms supervene, get the victim to a doctor without delay: numbness and tingling of the face, muscular spasms, convulsion, shortness of breath and haemorrhage. The tiny coral snake, with red, black and white bands, is the most dangerous, but is very timid.

Commercial snakebite and scorpion kits are available, but only useful for the specific type of snake or scorpion for which they are designed. The serum has to be given intravenously so is not much good unless you have had some practice at making injections into veins. If the bite is on a limb, immobilize the limb and apply a tight bandage between the bite and the body, releasing it for 90 seconds every 15 minutes. Reassurance of the bitten person is very important because death from snakebite is very rare. Do not slash the bite area and try to suck out the poison because this sort of heroism does more harm than good. Hospitals usually hold stocks of snake bite serum. Best precaution: don't walk in snake territory with bare feet or sandals—wear proper shoes or boots.

Spiders and Scorpions These may be found in the more basic hotels in the Andean countries. If bitten by *Latrodectus* or *Loxosceles* spiders, or stung by scorpions, rest and take plenty of fluids, and call a doctor. Precaution: keep beds away from the walls, and look inside shoes in morning.

Other Afflictions Remember that **rabies** is endemic throughout Latin America so avoid dogs that are behaving strangely, and cover your toes at night to foil the vampire bats, which also carry the disease. If you are bitten, try to have the animal captured for observation and see a doctor at once. Treatment with human diploid vaccine is now extremely effective and worth seeking out if the likelihood of having contracted rabies is high.

Dengue fever has made its appearance in southern Mexico and the lower-lying parts of Central America; also in Brazil. No treatment: you must just avoid mosquito bites.

Typhus can still occur, carried by ticks. There is usually a reaction at the site of the bite and a fever: seek medical advice.

Intestinal worms are common, and the more serious ones such as **hookworm** can be contracted from walking barefoot on infested earth or beaches. Various other tropical diseases can be caught in jungle areas, usually transmitted by biting insects; they are often related to African diseases and were probably introduced by the slave trade from Africa.

Onchocerciasis (river-blindness), carried by blackflies, is found in parts of Mexico and Venezuela. Cutaneous **leishmaniasis** (Espundia) is carried by sandflies and causes a sore that won't heal; wearing long trousers and long-sleeved shirt in infectious areas helps one to avoid the fly. Epidemics of meningitis occur from time to time. Be careful about swimming in piranha- (or caribe-) infested rivers. It is a good idea not to swim naked: the candiru fish can follow urine currents and become lodged in body orifices; swimwear offers some protection.

Dangerous animals Apart from mosquitoes, the most dangerous animals are men, be they bandits or behind steering wheels. Think carefully about violent confrontations and wear a seatbelt, if you are lucky enough to have one available to you.

Prickly heat, a very common itchy rash, is avoided by frequent washing and by wearing loose clothing. Cured by allowing skin to dry off through use of powder, and spending 2 nights in an air-conditioned hotel! **Athlete's foot** and other fungal infections are best treated with Tinaderm.

When you return home, remember to take your anti-malarial tablets for 6 weeks. Thousands of people develop malaria after tropical holidays because they do not take this precaution and some of them die, because it is not realized at home that they are suffering from malaria. If you have had attacks of diarrhoea, it is worth having a stool specimen tested in case you may have picked up amoebic dysentery. If you have been living in the bush, a blood test may be worthwhile to detect worms and other parasites.

Basic supplies The following items you may find useful to take with you from home:

Sunglasses.
Suntan cream.
Insect repellant, flea powder, mosquito net and coils.
Tampons (they can be bought in the main cities), and contraceptives (not easy to obtain everywhere).
Water-sterilizing tablets, e.g. Sterotabs (Boots), Globaline, Puritabs (Kirby & Co. Ltd.).
Antimalarials.
Anti-infective ointment, e.g. Savlon (ICI).
Dusting powder for feet, e.g. Tinaderm (Glaxo), Desenex.
Travel-sickness pills, e.g. Dramamine (Searle), Gravol (Carter-Wallace).
Antacids, e.g. Maalox.
("Tiger balm", an apparently all-purpose remedy, recommended by two overland travellers from New Zealand).
Antidiarrheals, e.g. Lomotil (Searle), Imodium (Janssen) or Arret. (Charcoal tablets are useful for minor stomach ailments.)
First-aid kit.

The following organizations give information regarding well-trained, English-speaking physicians in Latin America:

International Association for Medical Assistance to Travellers, 745 Fifth Avenue, New York 10022.
Intermedic, 777 Third Avenue, New York 10017 (Tel.: 212-486-8974).

Information regarding country-by-country malaria risk can be obtained from the World Health Organization (WHO), or the Ross Institute, London School of Hygiene and Tropical Medicine, Keppel Street, London WC1E 7HT, which publishes a book strongly recommended, entitled *Preservation of Personal Health in Warm Climates*. Medical Advisory Services for Travellers Abroad (Masta), at the Keppel Street address above, prepares health briefs on every country for a fee.

The new edition of *Travellers' Health: How to Stay Healthy Abroad*, edited by Dr. Richard Dawood (Oxford University Press, 1989, paperback, £5.95), has been fully revised and updated, and will even help you survive travel closer to home. We strongly recommend this book, especially to the intrepid travellers who go to the more out-of-the-way places.

ARGENTINA

INTRODUCTION

ARGENTINA is the second largest country in area and third in population in South America. It covers an area of 2,807,560 square km., or 29% of the area of Europe; it is 3,460 km. long from N to S and is, in places, 1,580 km. wide. The population is about 32 million. Apart from the estuary of the Río de la Plata its coast line is 2,575 km. long. Its western frontier runs along the crest of the high Andes, a formidable barrier between it and Chile. Its neighbours to the N are Bolivia and Paraguay and (in the NE) Brazil. To the E is Uruguay. Its far southern limit is the Beagle Channel. The area figures exclude the sector of Antarctica claimed by Argentina.

Argentina is enormously varied both in its types of land and its climates. Geographers usually recognize four main physical areas: the Andes, the North and Mesopotamia, the Pampas, and Patagonia.

The first division, the Andes, includes the whole length of the Cordilleras, low and deeply glaciated in the Patagonian S, high and dry in the prolongation into NW Argentina of the Bolivian Altiplano, the high plateau. S of this is the very parched desert and mountain region S of Tucumán and W of Córdoba. The oases strung along the eastern foot of the Andes—Jujuy, Salta, Tucumán, Catamarca, La Rioja, San Juan, Mendoza and San Rafael—were the first places to be colonized by the Spaniards.

1. Buenos Aires and the Pampas.
2. The Córdoba Region.
3. Santiago del Estero, Tucumán, Salta & Jujuy.
4. The Cuyo Region: over the Andes to Chile.
5. North of Mendoza.
6. The Chaco.
7. Mesopotamia.
8. The Iguazú Falls.
9. The Lake District.
10. Patagonia.
11. Tierra del Fuego.

ARGENTINA

The second division, the North and Mesopotamia, contains the vast forested plains of the Chaco, and the floodplain and gently rolling land known as the Argentine Mesopotamia lying between the rivers Paraná and Uruguay. The Province of Misiones in the NE is actually on the great Paraná plateau. These plains cover 582,750 square km.

The third division, the flat rich pampa, takes up the heart of the land. These vast plains lie S of the Chaco, E of the Andes, W of the Atlantic and the Río Paraná and N of the Río Colorado. The eastern part, which receives more rain, is usually called the Humid Pampa, and the western part the Dry Pampa. The Pampas stretch for hundreds of km. in almost unrelieved flatness and cover some 650,000 square km.

The final division is Patagonia, the area S of the Río Colorado—a land of arid, wind-swept plateaux cut across by ravines. In the deep S the wind is wilder and more continuous. There is no real summer, but to compensate for this the winters are rarely severe. Patagonia has about 780,000 square km.

Three-quarters of Argentina's territory cannot be cultivated without irrigation but only 400,000 hectares are artificially watered.

Climate ranges from sub-tropical in the N to cold temperate in Tierra del Fuego, but is temperate and quite healthy in the densely populated central zone. From mid-December to the end of February Buenos Aires can be oppressively hot and humid, with temperatures ranging from 27°C (80°F) to 35°C (95°F) and an average humidity of 70%. Beware of the high pollen count in the pollinating season if you have allergy problems. The winter months of June, July and August are best for a business visit, though spring weather in Buenos Aires is often very pleasant indeed. The skiing season in Bariloche ends by August 30. Corrientes and Misiones provinces are wet in August and especially September.

History When, in the early 16th century, the first white men came to Argentina, the native Indians had already halted the Inca drive southwards from Peru through Bolivia into northern Argentina. The Spaniard Juan de Solís landed on the shores of the Plata estuary in 1516, but he was killed and the expedition failed. Magellan touched at the estuary four years later, but turned southwards to make his way into the Pacific. In 1527 both Sebastian Cabot and his rival Diego García sailed into the estuary and up the Paraná and the Paraguay. They formed a small settlement, Sancti Spiritus, at the junction of the Caraña and Coronda rivers near their confluence with the Paraná, but it was wiped out by the Indians about two years later and Cabot and García returned to Spain. Eight years later, in 1535, Pedro de Mendoza, with a large force well supplied with equipment and horses, founded a settlement at Buenos Aires. The natives soon made it too hot for him; the settlement was abandoned and Mendoza returned home, but not before sending Juan de Ayolas with a small force up the Paraná. Ayolas set off for Peru, already conquered by Pizarro, leaving Irala in charge. It is not known for certain what happened to Ayolas, but in 1537 Irala and his men settled at Asunción, in Paraguay, where the natives were friendly. There were no further expeditions from Spain to colonize what is now called Argentina, and it was not until 1573 that the settlement at Asunción sent forces S to establish Santa Fe and not until 11 June, 1580 that Juan de Garay refounded the settlement at Buenos Aires. It was only under his successor, Hernando Arias de Saavedra (1592-1614), that the new colony became secure.

In the meantime there had been successful expeditions into Argentina both from Peru and Chile—the first, from Peru, as early as 1543. These expeditions led, in the latter half of the 16th century, to the foundation at the eastern foot of the Andes of the oldest towns in Argentina: Santiago del Estero, Tucumán, Córdoba, Salta, La Rioja and Jujuy by Spaniards from Peru following the old Inca road, and San Juan, Mendoza, and San Luis by those from Chile, across the Andes. Peru was given the viceroyalty over all the Spanish possessions in South America in 1543.

For 270 years after its foundation Buenos Aires was of little importance. Spanish stress was upon Lima, and Lima did not send its treasures home by way of Buenos Aires but through Panama and the Caribbean. Buenos Aires was not allowed by Spain to take part in any overseas trade until 1778; its population then was only 24,203. It was merely a military outpost for Spain to confront the Portuguese outpost at Colonia, across the estuary, and lived, in the main, by smuggling. Even when in 1776 the Viceroyalty of Río de la Plata was formed, it made little difference to Buenos Aires as a capital, for its control of the *cabildos* (town councils) in distant towns was very tenuous. When the British, following Spain's alliance with Napoleon, attacked Buenos Aires in 1806 and again in 1807 before being repulsed by local levies, there was no inkling of its future potential. But the defeat of these attacks, known as the Reconquista, had one important result: a great increase in the confidence of the *porteños* (the name given to those born in Buenos Aires) to deal with all comers, including the mother-country, whose restrictions were increasingly unpopular. On 25 May, 1810, the *cabildo* of Buenos Aires deposed the viceroy and announced that it was governing henceforth on behalf of King Ferdinand VII, then a captive of Napoleon. Six years later, when Buenos Aires was threatened by invasion from Peru and blockaded by a Spanish fleet in the River Plate, a national congress held at Tucumán declared independence on 9 July, 1816. The declaration was given reality by the genius and devotion of José de San Martín, who boldly marched an Argentine army across the Andes to free Chile, and (with the help of Lord Cochrane, commander of the Chilean Navy), embarked his forces for Peru, where he captured Lima, the first step in the liberation of Peru.

When San Martín returned home, it was to find the country rent by conflict between the central government and the provinces. Disillusioned, he retired to France. The internal conflict was to last a long time. On the one hand stood the Unitarist party, bent on central control; on the other the Federalist party, insisting on local autonomy. The latter had for members the great *caudillos*, the large landowners backed by the *gauchos*, suspicious of the cities. One of their leaders, Juan Manuel de Rosas, took control of the country in 1829. During his second term as Governor of Buenos Aires he asked for and was given extraordinary powers. The result was a 17-year reign of terror. His rule was an international scandal, and when he began a blockade of Asunción in 1845, Britain and France promptly countered with a three-year blockade of Buenos Aires. But in 1851 Justo José de Urquiza, Governor of Entre Ríos, one of his old henchmen, organized a triple *entente* of Brazil, Uruguay, and the Argentine opposition to overthrow him. He was defeated in 1852 at Caseros, a few km. from Buenos Aires, and fled to England, where he farmed quietly for 25 years, dying at Southampton.

Rosas had started his career as a Federalist; once in power he was a Unitarist.

His downfall meant the triumph of federalism. In 1853 a federal system was finally incorporated in the constitution, but the old quarrel had not been solved. In 1859, when the constitution was ratified, the capital was moved to Paraná, the province of Buenos Aires seceded, and Buenos Aires, under Bartolomé Mitre, was defeated by the federal forces under Urquiza. Two years later Buenos Aires again fought the country, and this time it won. Once again it became the seat of the federal government, with Bartolomé Mitre as its first constitutional president. (It was during his term that the Triple Alliance of Argentina, Brazil, and Uruguay defeated Francisco Solano López of Paraguay.) There was another political flare-up of the old quarrel in 1880, ending in the humiliation of Buenos Aires, which then ceased to be the capital of its province; a new provincial capital was founded at La Plata, 56 km. to the SE. At that time a young colonel, Julio A Roca, was finally subduing all the Indian tribes of the pampas and the South. This was an event which was to make possible the final supremacy of Buenos Aires over all rivals.

Politically Argentina was a constitutional republic with a very restricted suffrage up to the passage in 1912 of the Sáenz Peña law, which established universal manhood suffrage. From 1916 to 1930 the Unión Cívica Radical (founded in 1890) held power, under the leadership of Hipólito Yrigoyen and Marcelo T de Alvear, but lost it to the military uprising of 1930. Though seriously affected by the world depression of the 1930s, Argentina's rich soil and educated population had made it one of the ten wealthiest countries in the world, but this wealth was most unevenly distributed, and the political methods followed by the conservatives and their military associates in the 1930s denied the middle and working classes any effective share in their own country's wealth and government. In 1943 came another military coup, which had a distinctly fascist tinge; in 1946 emerged, as President, Gen. Juan Domingo Perón, who based his power on an alliance between the army and labour; his contacts with labour were greatly assisted by his charismatic wife Eva (since commemorated in the rock-opera "Evita") and the living conditions of the workers were greatly improved—but at the expense of the economic state of the country. By the time a military coup unseated Perón in 1955 serious harm had been done; ever since, Argentina has been struggling to recover its lost economic health.

After an uneasy alternation of three military and two constitutional regimes between 1955 and 1973, Gen. Perón again became President in October 1973, but died on 1 July, 1974, leaving the Presidency to his widow, Vice-President María Estela Martínez de Perón. A chaotic political situation, of which a high level of violence (including guerrilla warfare) was a regrettable feature, followed his death; by March 1976 conditions in the country, both of violence and of economic crisis, had deteriorated to the point when the military felt again obliged to intervene. Sra. de Perón was deposed from the Presidency by a military junta, led by Gen. Jorge Videla, and guerrilla warfare and the other features of dissidence were repressed with great brutality: about 9,000 people (according to official statistics; human rights organizations believe the total at least doubles this) disappeared without trace during the so-called "dirty war". General Videla was appointed President in 1978 by the military leaders, for a three-year term. His nominated successor, General Roberto Viola, took over as President for three years in March, 1981 but was replaced by General Leopoldo Galtieri in December 1981. The latter was in turn replaced in June 1982 by General (ret) Reynaldo Bignone.

Confidence in the military began to ebb when their economic policies began to go sour in 1980. In 1982-83 pressure for a democratic restoration grew apace particularly after the South Atlantic conflict with Great Britain in 1982. General elections were held on 30 October, 1983 and the Unión Cívica Radical was victorious, winning the Presidency and an absolute majority in the Chamber of Deputies, with 52% of the vote. Accordingly, Dr. Raúl Alfonsín, its candidate, assumed the Presidency on 10 December, 1983. During 1985 Generals Videla, Viola and Galtieri were sentenced to long terms of imprisonment for their parts in the "dirty war". President Alfonsín's popularity gradually waned as his Government failed to solve economic problems. Presidential elections held on 14 May, 1989, were won by a 10% margin by Sr. Carlos Saúl Menem of the Partido Justicialista (Peronists), who took office ahead of schedule in July 1989 because of economic instability.

The Transformation of the Pampas The pampas, the economic heart of the country, extend fanwise from Buenos Aires for a distance of between 550 and 650 km. Apart from three groups of *sierras* or low hills near Córdoba, Tandil and Bahía Blanca, the surface seems an endless flat monotony, relieved occasionally, in the SW, by sand dunes. There are few rivers. Drinking water is pumped to the surface from a depth of from 30 to 150 metres by the windpumps which are such a prominent feature of the landscape. There are no trees other than those that have been planted, except in the *monte* of the W. But there is, in most years, ample rainfall. It is greatest at Rosario, where it is about 1,020 mm, and evenly distributed throughout the year. The further S from Rosario, the less the rain. At Buenos Aires it is about 940 mm; it drops to 535 at Bahía Blanca, and is only 400 along the boundary of the Humid Pampa. The further from Rosario, too, the more the rainfall is concentrated during the summer. Over the whole of the pampa the summers are hot, the winters mild, but there is a large climatic difference between various regions: at Rosario the growing season between frosts is about 300 days; at Bahía Blanca it falls to 145 days.

When the Spanish arrived in Argentina the pampas were an area of tall coarse grasses. The cattle and horses they brought with them were soon to roam wild and in time transformed the Indian's way of life. The only part of the pampa occupied by the settlers was the so-called Rim, between the Río Salado, S of the capital, and the Paraná-Plata rivers. Here, in large *estancias*, cattle, horses and mules in great herds roamed the open range. There was a line of forts along the Río Salado: a not very effective protection against marauding Indians. The Spaniards had also brought European grasses with them; these soon supplanted the coarse native grasses, and formed a green carpet surface which stopped abruptly at the Río Salado.

The *estancia* owners and their dependent *gauchos* were in no sense an agricultural people, but towards the end of the 18th century, tenants—to the great contempt of both *estanciero* and *gaucho*—began to plant wheat in the valleys along the Paraná-Plata shore. The fall of Rosas in 1852, and the constitution of 1853, made it possible for Argentina to take a leap forward, but it must be remembered that its civilized population at that time was only 1,200,000.

The rapidly rising population of Europe during the latter half of the 19th century and the consequent demand for cheap food was the spur that impelled Argentina (as it did the United States and Canada) to occupy its grasslands and take to agriculture. This was made possible by the new techniques already developed: agricultural machinery, barbed wire, well-drilling machines and windpumps, roads and railways, and ocean-going steamships. Roads were, and are, a difficulty in the Argentine pampa; the soil lacks gravel or stones to surface the roads, and dirt roads become a quagmire in wet weather and a fume of dust in the dry. Railways, on the other hand, were simple and cheap to build. The system grew as need arose and capital (mostly from Britain) became available. The lines in the pampa radiate out fanwise (with intricate inter-communication) from the ports of Buenos Aires, Rosario, Santa Fe and Bahía Blanca. Argentina, unlike most other countries, had extensive railways before a road system was built.

The occupation of the pampa was made finally possible by a war against the Indians in 1878-83 which virtually exterminated them. Many of the officers in that campaign were given gifts of land of more than 40,000 hectares each. The pampa had passed into private hands on the old traditional pattern of large estates.

Cattle products—hides, tallow, and salt beef—had been the mainstay of Argentine overseas trade during the whole of the colonial period. In the early 19th century wool challenged the supremacy of cattle. The occupation of the grasslands did not, at first, alter the complexion of the foreign trade; it merely increased its volume. In 1877, however, the first ship with refrigeration chambers made it possible to send frozen beef to England, but the meat of the scrub cattle was too strong for English taste. As a result, pedigree bulls were imported from England and the upgrading of the herds began. The same process was applied to sheep. But the improved herds could only flourish where there were no ticks—prevalent in the N—and throve best where forage crops were available. Argentina adopted as its main forage crop alfalfa (lucerne), a plant like clover which proved extremely suitable on the pampa. It has since been supplemented with barley, oats, rye and particularly maize and sorghums.

A striking thing about the Pampas is the bird life. Flamingoes rise in a pink and white cloud, heron egrets gleam white against the blue sky, pink spoonbills dig in the mud and rheas stalk in the distance. Most fascinating are the oven birds, the *horneros*, which build oven-shaped nests six times as big as themselves on the top of telegraph and fence posts.

To sum up, the transformation of the pampa has had two profound effects. Because its newly-created riches flowed out and its needs flowed in mainly through Buenos Aires, that port grew from comparative insignificance into one of the great cities in the world. Also, the transformation of the Humid Pampa led, through immigration, to a vast predominance of the European strain. The first immigrants settled NW of Santa Fe in 1856. Between 1857 and 1930 total immigration was over six million, almost all from Europe. The process has continued; Italians have been by far the most numerous, followed by Spaniards, and then, far behind, groups of other Europeans and Latin Americans. British and North Americans normally came as stockbreeders, technicians and business executives.

The Argentine People In the Federal Capital and Province of Buenos Aires, where almost 40% of the population lives, the people are almost exclusively of European origin. In the far northern provinces, colonized from neighbouring countries, at least half the people are *mestizos* though they form less than 2% of the population of the whole country. In the highlands of the NW and in the Chaco, there are still a few pure-blooded Indians.

In 1989 the population was 31,929,000 million. Some 81% are urban and 40% live in cities of 100,000 or more. Population growth: 1.4%; urban growth, 1.1%. Death rate per thousand: 8.6; infantile mortality per thousand live births, 32; birth rate, 23.2. It is estimated that 12.8% are foreign born and generally of European origin. About 94% can read and write.

Not surprisingly, the traditional image of the Argentine is that of the *gaucho*; *gauchismo* has been a powerful influence in literature, sociology and folklore, and is celebrated each year in the week before the "Day of Tradition", 10 November.

Argentina is also celebrated for the tango, a music and dance form that had its origins in the less desirable districts of Buenos Aires in the 1880s. The tango descended primarily from the Cuban habanera and it acquired its own characteristics gradually, with notable changes in the second decade of the 20th century. By then it had fascinated the French, who popularized the tango internationally. To begin with, respectable Argentine society tried to suppress the tango, but its global success led to its acceptance as the national music and dance. The zamba (no relation to Brazil's samba) and milonga are the most prominent of Argentina's other musical forms. (John Rapsey)

The Economy Argentina is one of the more highly developed countries of the region and is potentially one of the richest farming countries in the world. The importance of agriculture and livestock production is shown by the fact that this sector still provides about 70% of export earnings with sales of cereals, oilseeds, meat and processed foodstuffs. Although Argentina has lost its dominant position as an exporter of cereals and beef, it has great resources in relation to its population, which increases at a rate of only 1.6% a year. Per capita income is therefore relatively high, at about US$2,500. Agriculture, livestock, forestry and fishing account for about 15% of gdp. There has been a shift from livestock to crop production since the 1960s in line with changes in relative prices and the introduction of new technology which has sharply increased crop yields. Cereals account for a substantial proportion of crop production, with 11m hectares under cultivation in the late 1980s, of which about 5m were sown to wheat and produced about 9m tonnes a year. The area sown to oilseeds has risen steeply, now exceeding that of wheat, and producing about 11m tonnes of soyabeans and sunflower seed a year. Livestock, faced with stiff competition abroad from other exporting countries, has declined in importance. The cattle stock fell from around 57m head in the late 1970s to 50m in the late 1980s. Exports declined but annual domestic consumption stayed high at about 85-90 kg per person.

The manufacturing sector has developed behind high import protection barriers; it accounts for a quarter of gdp and benefits from increased agricultural activity, so that natural resource-based and labour-intensive industries such as food processing, textiles and clothing are reasonably dynamic. Food processing and beverages account for a quarter of manufacturing output and a fifth of industrial employment, while they are the second largest foreign exchange earners after farming. Metal working, engineering and the steel industry were depressed in the 1980s as inflation surged, dampening domestic demand and creating investment uncertainties. In the construction industry, output halved in the 1980s.

Energy development has been a priority with emphasis on hydro and nuclear power sources to reduce dependence upon thermal power. Liquid fuels supply 44% and natural gas 31% of energy consumption, while hydroelectricity is only 13%. By the end of the century it is planned to reduce liquid fuels' share to 37% and raise natural gas to 35%. Argentina is virtually self-sufficient in oil and there is an exportable surplus of natural gas and petroleum derivatives. The country's hydroelectric potential lies on the rivers Paraná and Uruguay in the north and on the network of rivers in Río Negro and Neuquén provinces. However, severe drought in the late 1980's reduced output from hydroelectricity plants from half to only a third of total electricity generation, while thermal plants increased their share from 40% to 55%, with nuclear power plants supplying the balance.

Extremely high rates of inflation were recorded in the 1980s through a combination of large fiscal deficits, monetary expansion and a high velocity of circulation. These were difficult to contain because of structural imbalances in the economy arising from supply shortages caused by inadequate levels of investment and inefficiencies in both the public and private sectors. As the economy reached hyperinflation at a rate of 1,129% in the twelve months to June 1985, the government introduced a stabilization programme known as the Austral Plan. This included a price and wage freeze, a new currency, the Austral, and attempted to cut the fiscal deficit by raising tax revenues and suspending financing of the deficit by the central bank. The initial positive results were weakened by the failure to cut the fiscal deficit and within 18 months 3-digit inflation had returned.

The economic crisis deepened as management of public finances deteriorated, leading to hyperinflation and a sharp contraction in output and investment as confidence was eroded and the economy became increasingly dollarized. Domestic government debt rose from 1% of gdp in 1988 to 10% in 1989 under the burden of mounting losses from inefficient public enterprises. The new Government which took office in July 1989, attempted to curb hyperinflation by cutting spending and raising revenues, closing or privatising state companies and banks, eliminating price controls and floating the exchange rate. Political opposition to structural economic reform, which would initially bring further recession, unemployment and declining living standards, prevented speedy implementation of the programme, thereby delaying recovery.

The Government also tackled the problem of servicing the external debt, which had risen sharply by an annual average of 35% in 1978-82 to nearly US$60bn in the late 1980s, making Argentina the third largest debtor in the region. Several debt rescheduling agreements were negotiated with commercial bank creditors together with new loans and IMF financing facilities. Several World Bank loans were granted for restructuring a number of economic sectors, such as agriculture and foreign trade, but agreements with all creditors repeatedly collapsed as the Government failed to implement fully its policy commitments. By the end of the 1980s, Argentina was seriously in arrears and the newly elected Government inherited an unsustainable debt burden.

Government The country's official name is La República Argentina (RA), the Argentine Republic. The form of government has traditionally been a representative, republican federal system. Of the two legislative houses, the Senate has 46 seats, and the Chamber of Deputies 254. By the 1853 Constitution (amended in 1880) the country is divided into a Federal Capital (the city of Buenos Aires), 22 Provinces and the National Territory of Tierra del Fuego, Antarctica and South Atlantic Islands. Each Province has its own Senate and Chamber of Deputies. The municipal government of the Federal Capital is exercised by a Mayor appointed by the President with the approval of the Senate.

Communications Argentina has only four good seaports: Buenos Aires, La Plata, Rosario and Bahía Blanca. The two great rivers flowing southward into the Plate, the Paraná and the Uruguay, are not very reliable shipping routes. The Colorado and the Negro rivers in northern Patagonia are navigable by small vessels only. Internal air services are highly developed.

Most of Argentina is served by about 140,000 km. of road, but only 30% are paved and a further 25% improved. Even so, the network carries 80% of freight tonnage and 82% of medium and long-distance passengers. The 43,100 km. of railway line, owned mostly by British companies until they were taken over by the State in 1948, carry less than 10% of passengers and freight, and are very heavily subsidized.

BUENOS AIRES AND THE PAMPAS (1)

The pampa is little more than a fifth of the total area of the country, but 35% of the people live in Greater Buenos Aires and 32% in the Pampas outside Buenos Aires. The Pampa area has 70% of all the railways, 86% of the land used for cereals and linseed, 65% of the cattle, 40% of the sheep, 77% of the pigs, and nearly 90% of the industrial production.

The River Plate, or Río de la Plata, on which Buenos Aires lies, is not a river but an estuary or great basin, 160 km. long and from 37 to 90 km. wide, into which flow the Rivers Paraná and Uruguay and their tributaries. It is muddy and shallow and the passage of ocean vessels is only made possible by continuous dredging. The tides are of little importance, for there is only a 1.2 metre rise and fall at spring tides. The depth of water is determined by the direction of the wind and the flow of the Paraná and Uruguay rivers.

Buenos Aires, the capital, spreads over some 200 square km. The population of the Federal Capital itself is about 3,323,000, but the population of greater Buenos Aires (including the suburbs in the province of Buenos Aires) is already estimated at 12.6 millions.

To Rosario and the North
San Nicolás
To Concordia
U R U G U A Y
N
Firmat
Río Paraná
Zárate
Venado Tuerto
Pergamino
Tigre
Colonia
San Antonio de Areco
To Mendoza and Chile Santiago
Junín
Mercedes
Luján
BUENOS AIRES
Gral. Villegas
Quilmes
Río de la Plata
MONTEVIDEO
La Plata
9 de Julio
Saladillo
Choscomús
Pehuajó
Las Flores
Dolores
San Carlos de Bolívar
Azul
Guaminí
Tandil
Pinamar
Villa Gesell
To Santa Rosa
Comué
Juárez
Balcarce
Camet
Mar Chiquita
Saavedra
Sierra de la Ventana
Tres Picos
Tres Arroyos
Quequén
Mar del Plata
0 50 100 150 200
Bahía Blanca
To Neuquén and the Lakes
VIEDMA and PATAGONIA
Pehuén-Co
Monte Hermoso
Claromecó
Necochea
Miramar

BUENOS AIRES AND THE PAMPAS
2u

To the North
Tigre
BUENOS AIRES
2L
0 10
Km.
San Isidro
Río de la Plata
Martínez
Olivos
Aeroparque
Palermo Parks
T **stations**
1 **Retiro**
2 **Lacroze**
3 **Once**
4 **Constitución**
5 **Buenos Aires**
La Recoleta
Dársena Norte
Area of central map
Plaza de Mayo
Dársena Sud
S.Telmo
La Boca
To Luján and Mendoza
Morón
Avellaneda
Quilmes
To Bahía Blanca and Patagonia
Ezeiza
To Mar del Plata
To La Plata

NB In spite of its name (good air), extreme humidity and unusual pollen conditions can affect asthma sufferers if they stay over an extended period of time (i.e. after a month or so).

Buenos Aires has been virtually rebuilt since the beginning of this century and very few of the old buildings are left. In the centre, which has maintained the original lay-out since its foundation, the streets are often very narrow and are mostly one-way.

The heart of the city, now as in colonial days, is the Plaza de Mayo, with the historic Cabildo, the Town Hall, where the movement for independence from Spain was first planned; the pink Casa Rosada (Presidential Palace); the City Hall; and the Cathedral, where San Martín, the father of Argentine independence, is buried. (For a note on the Mothers of the Plaza de Mayo, **see page** 53). Within a few blocks are the fashionable church of Nuestra Señora de la Merced, the National Library and the main banks and business houses.

Running W from the Plaza, the Avenida de Mayo leads 1½ km. to the Congress building in the Plaza del Congreso. Halfway it crosses the wide Avenida Nueve de Julio. A tall obelisk commemorating the 400th anniversary of the city's founding stands at its centre in the Plaza de la República, surrounded by sloping lawns. The Av Nueve de Julio itself, one of the widest in the world, consists of three carriageways separated by wide grass borders. In the N the Av Nueve de Julio meets the Avenida Libertador, the principal way out of the city to the N and W.

N of the Plaza de Mayo is the shopping, theatre and commercial area. The city's traditional shopping centre, Calle Florida (with excellent newsstands), is in this district. This is the popular down-town meeting place, particularly in the late afternoon; it is reserved for pedestrians only and the buskers in the 500 block are worth visiting. Another shopping street is Avenida Santa Fe, which crosses Florida at the Plaza San Martín; it has become as touristy and as expensive as Florida. Avenida Corrientes is the entertainment centre, a street of theatres, restaurants, cafés and night life. Close by, in Calle Lavalle (part reserved to pedestrians) and in nearby streets, there are numerous cinemas and many good and reasonable restaurants.

A broad avenue, Paseo Colón, runs S to the waterfront and the picturesque old port district known as the Boca (now very touristy), where the Riachuelo flows into the Plata (reached by bus 152 from Av L N Alem, or bus 29 from Plaza de Mayo, in the centre, US$0.10). It was here, near Parque Lezama, that Pedro de Mendoza founded the first Buenos Aires. For a tour of the Boca, start at Plaza Vuelta de Rocha, near Av Pedro de Mendoza and Dr. Del Valle Iberlucea, then walk up Caminito, the little pedestrian street used as a theatre and an art market. Visit the Museo de Bellas Artes de la Boca (**see page** 60). The Boca, mostly Italian, has its own distinctive life, but the area, with the adjacent industrial and meat-packing suburb of Avellaneda across the high Avellaneda bridge, is now dirty and run down, and assaults are frequent. Calle Brasil leads from this area to the far side of the docks and the spacious Avenida Costanera which runs along the river front. Here are bathing places (Balneario Municipal), gardens, many restaurants and public concerts: a pleasant place on a hot summer's day but overcrowded on Sundays and holidays. (The food at the outdoor restaurants is now said to be reliable, particularly barbecues; reached by 33 bus from Retiro Station or Av LN Alem.) Bathing in the River Plate is no longer allowed; the water is heavily polluted.

One of the few places which still have late colonial and Rosista buildings is the *barrio* of San Telmo, S of Plaza de Mayo, centred on Plaza Dorrego along the slope which marks the old beach of the River Plate. It is a recognized artistic centre, with plenty of cafés and a pleasant atmosphere; and there is a regular Saturday and Sunday morning antiques market at the Plaza Dorrego (**see page** 57). The 29 bus connects the Boca with San Telmo, and passes the end of Calle Florida, the shopping street.

BUENOS AIRES CENTRE

The theatre retains its hold on the people of Buenos Aires. About 20 commercial theatres play the year round. Recommended is the Teatro Liceo. There are many amateur theatres. You are advised to book as early as possible for a seat at a concert, ballet, or opera.

NB Street numeration: numbers start from the dock side rising from east to west, but north/south streets are numbered from Av de Mayo rising in both directions. Calle Juan D. Perón used to be called Cangallo; M.T. de Alvear used to be Charcas.

Principal Public Buildings

Casa de Gobierno on the E side of the Plaza de Mayo, and called the Casa Rosada because it is pink, contains the offices of the President of the Republic. (The Foreign Minister's offices are at the Palacio de San Martín, Plaza San Martín). The Casa Rosada is notable for its statuary, the rich furnishing of its halls and for its libraries, but it is not at present possible to visit the interior. The Museo de los Presidentes is on the lower floors (see under **Museums**).

The **Cabildo** on the W side of the same Plaza, the old town hall, was put up in 1711 but has been rebuilt several times. Its original structure, fittings and furniture were replaced in 1940 and it was declared a national monument; it is guarded by soldiers in the red and blue uniform of San Martín's grenadiers. See under **Museums**.

Old Congress Hall on the S of the Square, built 1863, is a National Monument. It has been encircled and built over by a palatial bank building. Open Thursday.

Congress Hall (Palacio del Congreso) to the SW at the far end of Avenida de Mayo, of great size and in Greco-Roman architecture, is the seat of the legislature. It contains the Senate and the Chamber of Deputies. There is limited accommodation for the public at the sittings. It is open from 1700 onwards. Queue in front of desk assigned for minor parties, there they take your passport and give you a ticket for your seat and a pink slip to reclaim your passport. You may stay as long as you wish, but must remain seated. A guided tour (in English) can be taken on Mon., Tues. and Fri. at 1100 and 1700 when Congress is not sitting.

Teatro Colón, one of the world's great opera houses, overlooks Avenida 9 de Julio, with its main entrance on Libertad, between Tucumán and Viamonte. The Colón's interior is resplendent with red plush and gilt; the stage is huge, and salons, dressing rooms and banquet halls are equally sumptuous. Open daily to visitors 1200-1800 (but not always), guided tours hourly, 0900-1100 and 1400-1700 (English/German, six a day on the hour, US$0.25), book in advance (closed Jan.-Feb., so check, T 35-5414/15/16). Male visitors must wear jacket and tie to gala performances, but dress smartly anyway. Tickets, sold three days before performance, on the Calle Tucumán side of the theatre. The season runs from April to early December, and there are concert performances most days. The cheapest seat is about US$25, although there are free performances most days at 1800 in the Sala Dorado—check programme in the visitors' entrance.

The **Bolsa de Comercio**, built in 1916, a handsome building in Calle 25 de Mayo, corner Sarmiento, contains a stock exchange, a grain market and a general produce market.

Churches

All historic churches are open 1630-1900; some at 0900-1100 also.

The **Cathedral**, Rivadavia 437, on the N of Plaza de Mayo is flanked by the former residence of the Archbishop. On this site was built the first church in Buenos Aires, which after reconstruction in 1677 collapsed in 1753 and the rebuilding was not completed until 1823. The eighteenth century towers were never rebuilt, so that the architectural proportions have

---

Buenos Aires: Key to Map

1. Plaza de Mayo; 2. Plaza del Congreso; 3. Plaza de la República, and Obelisk; 4. Plaza San Martín; 5. Plaza de la Fuerza Aérea; 6. Parque Lezama; 7. Plaza Constitución; 8. Plaza Lavalle; 9. Plaza Libertad; 10. Parque Colón; 11. Plaza Dorrego; 12. Cathedral; 13. San Ignacio de Loyola; 14. San Francisco; 15. Cabildo and Museum; 16. Casa Rosada and Museo de los Presidentes; 17. City Hall; 18. Congress; 19. Teatro Colón; 20. Museo Histórico Nacional; 21. Museo de la Ciudad; 22. Teatro Municipal General San Martín and Museo Municipal de Arte Moderno; 23. "Presidente Sarmiento" museum ship; 24. Museo Nacional Ferroviario at Retiro Station; 25. Central Post Office; 26 National Tourist Office (3 locations); 27. Buenos Aires Municipal Tourist Office; 28. Railway booking and information office.

suffered. A frieze upon the Greek façade represents Joseph and his brethren. The tomb (1878) of the Liberator, General José de San Martín, is imposing.

The **Church of San Ignacio de Loyola**, at Calles Alsina and Bolívar 225, founded in 1710, is the oldest Colonial building in Buenos Aires. It has two lofty towers. The **San Francisco**, Calles Alsina and Defensa, controlled by the Franciscan Order, was inaugurated in 1754 and given a new façade in 1808.

La Merced, Calles Juan D. Perón and Reconquista 207, was founded 1604 and rebuilt 1732. One of the altars has a wooden figure of Our Lord, carved during the 18th century by an Indian in Misiones. It has one of the best organs in the country, and one of the few fine carillons of bells in Buenos Aires.

Santo Domingo, on Defensa and Av Belgrano, was founded in 1756. During the British attack on Buenos Aires in 1806 some of Whitelocke's soldiers took refuge in the church. The local forces bombarded it (some of the hits can still be seen on one of the towers); the British capitulated and their regimental colours were preserved in the church. Adjoining is the Salón Belgraniano (with relics of General Belgrano and much colonial furniture). There are summer evening concerts in the church; check times.

El Pilar, Junín 1904, is a jewel of colonial architecture dating from 1717, in a delightful setting of public gardens. An exceptionally fine wooden image of San Pedro de Alcántara, attributed to the famous 17th century Spanish sculptor Alonso Cano, is preserved in a side chapel on the left. It has a huge, unusual graveyard.

Visitors may like to know about the following religious establishments: The **Holy Cross**, Calle Estados Unidos 3150, established by the Passionists. **St John's Cathedral** (Anglican), 25 de Mayo 282 (services, Sun. 0900 in English, 1030 in Spanish), was built half at the expense of the British Government and dedicated in 1831. **St Paul's, St Peter's, St Michael and All Angels** and **St Saviour's** are Anglican places of worship in the suburbs. **St Andrew's**, Calle Belgrano 579, is one of the 8 Scottish Presbyterian churches. The **American Church**, Corrientes 718, is Methodist, built in 1863. Service at 1100. **First Methodist** (American) Church, Av Santa Fe 839, Acassuso.

German Evangelical Church, Esmeralda 162. **Synagogues** Anshe Galitzia at Uriburu 234; Temple at Alvear 1222. **Swedish Church**, Azopardo 1422.

The **Armenian Cathedral** of St Gregory the Illuminator at the Armenian Centre, and the **Russian Orthodox Cathedral** of The Holy Trinity (Parque Lezama) are interesting.

The **Cemetery of Recoleta**, entrance at Junín 1822 near Museo de Bellas Artes (see below), is one of the sights of Buenos Aires (open 0700-1800). Evita Perón is now buried there; her tomb is now marked besides the inscription, Familia Duarte—guards will point out the grave. "A Doric portico gives on to the main, paved, cypress-lined avenue of a little city of the dead. At the end of the avenue there is a great bronze statue of the resurrected Saviour; on either side, hard up against each other, like houses in a street, there are the family vaults of Argentine patricians. Every possible style of architecture is represented." G.S. Fraser, in *News from Latin America*. Bus 17 on Esmeralda, to Recoleta, then 10 mins walk. On Sundays there is a good craft market near the entrance. A new cultural centre has been opened alongside the Recoleta cemetery: exhibitions, concerts, films. Another well known cemetery is that of La Chacarita, reached by Subte to the Federico Lacroze station, which has the much-visited, lovingly-tended tombs of Juan Perón and Carlos Gardel, the tango singer.

Parks and Squares

Parque Lezama, Calles Defensa and Brasil, originally one of the most beautiful in the city, has been somewhat vandalized. Very lively on Sunday. It has an imposing statue of Pedro de Mendoza, the founder of the original city in 1535. The tradition is that the first founding took place on this spot. The Museo Histórico Nacional (**see page 59**) is in the park.

The **Palermo Parks** with their magnificent avenues are the city's Bois de Boulogne. They are famous for their rose garden, Andalusian Patio, Japanese garden with fish to feed (admission US$0.05) and the Hipódromo Argentino, the Palermo race course, with seats for 45,000. Opposite the parks are the Botanical and Zoological Gardens (the Palermo Zoo and Japanese Garden are closed on Mondays). Nearby are the Municipal Golf Club, Buenos Aires Lawn Tennis Club, riding clubs and polo field, and the popular Club de Gimnasia y Esgrima (Athletic and Fencing Club). The **Planetarium** (just off Belisario Roldán, in the Park), is open Sat. and Sun. only (March-Nov., 1630, 1800, 1930, Dec.-Feb., 1800, 1930, 2100), entry US$0.22. The official name of the Palermo parks is the Parque Tres de Febrero. Reached by Subte line D.

The **Show Grounds** of the Argentine Rural Society, on a site next to Palermo Park, stage the Annual Livestock Exhibition in July.

There is another large and modern race course (one of the best of its kind) with grass track at San Isidro, 25 minutes from the city centre by train or road. The meetings alternate with those at Palermo. There are Saturday and Wednesday races throughout the year, and on certain holidays. Betting is by totalizator only.

The **Municipal Botanical Gardens**, Santa Fe 3951, entrance from Plaza Italia (take Subte, line D), contain characteristic specimens of the world's vegetation. The trees proper to the several provinces of Argentina are brought together in one section. The Gardens are full of stray cats, fed regularly by benevolent local residents. The **Zoo** is next to the Botanical Gardens; it is temporarily closed.

The new **Costanera Sur Wildlife Reserve**, S of the city along the River Plate (entrance at Av España y Brasil), has several coypu and many types of birds. It opens at 0800 but much can be seen from the road before then. For details, contact Fundacíon Vida Silvestre, Defensa 251, 6piso, 1075 Bs. as., T 331-4864.

Plazas   The most interesting is the Plaza de Mayo, containing so many public buildings, where the **Mothers of the Plaza de Mayo** still march, Thursdays at 1530, in remembrance of their children who disappeared during the crisis of the 1970s. Others are the Plaza San Martín, with a monument to San Martín in the centre; the former Plaza Británica, now known as the Plaza de la Fuerza Aérea, with the clock tower presented by British and Anglo-Argentine residents, "a florid Victorian sentinel, royal crest upon its bosom" (frequently vandalized); the Plaza Lavalle, which has secondhand bookstalls at the Calle Lavalle end; the Plaza del Congreso, the largest in the city, with a waterfall, floodlit at 2145. There is also the great Plaza de la República, with a 67-metre obelisk at the junction between the Diagonal Norte and the Avenida Corrientes.

Warning   Street crime has risen alarmingly since 1988, especially in the tourist season. Be particularly careful of boarding buses and bagsnatching gangs in parks, markets and in the Subte: they are not violent, but particularly skilful. A common distraction is to spray the victims back with mustard. If your passport is stolen, remember to get a new entrada stamp at the Dirección Nacional de Migraciones. Also changing money on the street is fraught with difficulties: stick to the *cambios*.

Hotels   The Dirección de Turismo fixes maximum and minimum rates for 1, 2 and 3-star hotels, guest houses and inns, but there have been complaints that at 3 stars and below the ratings do not provide very useful guidance. Four and five-star hotels are free to apply any rate they wish. The rates can be taken only as an indication especially since, above 2 stars, hotels charge at the parallel exchange rate, adjusting tariffs daily. All hotels, guest houses, inns and camping sites are graded by the number of beds available, and the services supplied.

5-star hotels in our L+ range are: *Libertador*, Av Córdoba y Maipú, T 322 2095, *Plaza*, Plaza San Martín, T 312 6001/99, *Elevage*, Maipú 960, 145, T 313 2082/2982, *Alvear Palace*, Av Alvear 1891, T 804-4031, an older-style hotel, near Recoleta, with roof garden, shopping gallery, good, *Sheraton*, San Martin 1225, T 311 6311, *Claridge*, Tucumán 535, T 383 7212; and in our L range *Panamericano*, Carlos Pellegrini 525, T 393 6017, *Bauen*, Callao 346, T 804 1600. Also in our L range, but 4-star are *Bizonte Palace*, M.T. de Alvear y Suipacha, very good, welcoming, rec. *El Conquistador*, Suipacha 948, T 313 3012, *Rochester*, Esmeralda 542, T 393 9339, *Las Américas*, Libertad 1020, T 393 3432, pleasant but overpriced, and *Lafayette*, Reconquista 546, T 393 9081.

There are several 4-star hotels in our A price range: recommended in this bracket is the *Gran King*, Lavalle 560, T 392 4012/4052, helpful, English spoken; also *Wilton Palace*, Callao 1162, T 42 6639, *Torre*, Corrientes 6800, T 552 6034, *Sheltown*, M.T. de Alvear 742, T312 5070, *Los Dos Chinos*, Brasil 780, T 23 2021. 2 hotels in this range which have received poor reports, in terms of value and of service, are *Gran*, M.T. de Alvear 767, T 312 3001, and *Continental*, Diagonal Norte 725, T 493251. If any favourites have been omitted from this list we apologize; travellers are welcome to send their recommendations.

Other hotels: C price range, *Ayamitre*, Ayacucho y Bartolomé Mitre, 2 blocks from Congreso Subte station, pleasant; *Orly*, Paraguay 474, good position, helpful, has some rooms for 4; *Bristol*, Cerrito 286; *Savoy*, Av Callao 181, friendly and helpful; *Regis*, Lavalle 813, good value, nice atmosphere; *Camino Real*, Maipú 572, pleasant, clean, central.

D range: *San Antonio*, Paraguay 372, with bath, nice atmosphere, clean, rec.; *Eibar*, Florida 328, breakfast included, quiet, friendly, helpful, rec.; *Tucumán Palace*, Tucumán 384, moderate, front rooms noisy; *Phoenix*, San Martín 780, with bath, "faded gentility", clean, large rooms, use of kitchen, rec.; *Novus*, Sarmiento 631 (near Plaza de Mayo), rec. *Waldorf*, price excludes breakfast, Paraguay 400 block, clean and comfortable, rec. repeatedly; *Orleans*, Callao 465, clean, small rooms (some F), safe and friendly; *Astoria*, Av de Mayo 916, friendly, very clean; *Chile*, Av de Mayo 1297, will mind luggage; *Novel*, Av de Mayo 915, good; *Concorde*, 25 de Mayo 630, TV and fridge, helpful, comfortable, a/c, rec., best above 8th floor to avoid traffic noise; *Majéstic*, Libertad 121, metro Lima, colonial, very clean, good value, breakfast included; *Viamonte*, Viamonte 833, clean and helpful; *Florida House*, Florida 527, comfortable, hot shower, friendly, a little noisy, no fans or a/c so can get uncomfortably hot in summer, safe-deposit, rec.; *Don Juan*, Calle Dr. Finochitto 842, rec. *Super*, Gallo nr. Av Santa Fe (Subte D, Agüero), out of centre, a/c, pleasant.

E range: *Tres Sargentos*, Tres Sargentos 345, clean, secure, dark rooms; *Frossard*, Tucumán 686, inexpensive, hot showers, but not quiet; *Apolo*, Tucumán 951, friendly, central; *O'Rei*, Lavalle 733, with bath (F without), clean, friendly; *Acapulco*, Lavalle 472, hot-shower (cheaper without bathroom), friendly, convenient, good value, rec.; *Odeón*, Esmeralda 368 with Corrientes, clean, friendly; *Parada*, Rivadavia 1291, hot showers, central, friendly; *Gran Vedra*, Av de Mayo 1350, good value, rec.; *Marbella*, Av de Mayo 1261, clean, friendly, quiet, fans, newly decorated; *De Mayo*, Av de Mayo 776, central and friendly; *La Argentina*, Av de Mayo 860, with bath, friendly, central, rec.; *Mundial*, Av de Mayo 1298, with bath, clean, comfortable; *Central Córdoba*, San Martín 1021, safe and friendly, cheaper on 4th floor, rec.; *Sportsman*, Rivadavia 1426, clean, old fashioned, cheaper without bath, rec.; *Suipacha Palace*, Suipacha 18, clean, spacious, charming; *España*, Tacuari 80, with bath, helpful, hot water, lift, rec., T 30-5541/4; *Uruguay*, Tacuari 83, central, clean, friendly, good value, rec.; *Ayacucho Palace*, Ayacucho 1408, 10 mins from centre bus 10, T 825-0943, 2 star, better value than central hotels, rec.; *Hispano Argentino*, Lima Oeste 1483, T 235855/267562, some rooms with bath, clean, quiet, convenient; *Victoria*, Chacabuco 726, clean and cheap, use of kitchens; *Brisas*, Tacuari 1621, bath, etc., clean; *Varela*, Estados Unidos 324 (San Telmo), pleasant; *Ecuador*, Adolfo Alsina 2820, nr. Plaza Once, rec.; *Roxy*, Santiago del Estero 1677 (cheaper per week's stay), hot water, close to cheap restaurants. *Gran Vía* , Sarmiento 1450, T 40-5763, with bath, clean, friendly.

F range: *Aguila*, J.D. Perón 1554, clean; *Bahía*, Corrientes y Libertad, with bath, pleasant, clean, central but very noisy; *Sarmiento*, Sarmiento 1169, clean, central, back rooms quieter; *Mediterráneo*, Rodríguez Peña 149 basic, central, helpful, safe, clean, some rooms are dark, shared showers; *Vila Seca*, Av de Mayo 776, friendly; *Universal*, 25 de Mayo 740, hot water, clean, basic; *Mendoza*, 25 de Mayo 674, dirty, friendly, cheap, hot shower, many similar in same street; *Maipú*, Maipú 735, often crowded, clean, friendly, basic, T 322-5142; *Auzmendi*, Tacuari 242, F, with or without bath, basic, safe, clean; *Central*, Alsina 1693, friendly and clean; *Ostende*, Sarmiento y Talcahuano, very cheap; *De France*, San José 9 near Sáenz Peña Subte, clean, hot water; *Patagones*, B. de Yrigoyen 1692, T 28-6775, friendly, safe to leave luggage, rec.; *Cibelles*, Virrey Cevallos, 2 blocks from Congreso, T 37-3143, with bath, safe (next to police HQ). *Bolívar*, in Bolívar (San Telmo), with bath, clean; *Youth Hostel*, Brasil 675 near Constitucíon station, T 362-9133, G p.p. with YHA card; doors closed 1200-1800 and from midnight. Women should be aware that they could attract unwelcome attention near Constitución station as prostitutes operate there. Otherwise, this area is a short walk to centre and convenient for boats to Uruguay and trains to the N.

One can rent flats on a daily basis in *Edificios Esmeralda*, Marcelo T. de Alvear 842, T 31-3929, US$20-30 for two a day, cleaning included. Facilities for up to 6 persons; also Edificio Suipacha, Suipacha 1235, US$35 a day. Weekly renting at *Edificio Charcas*, MT de Alvear 776, US$128 d for one room per week, rec. (visiting singers at the Colón often stay there). Also *Aspen Apartment Hotel*, Esmeralda 933; *Edificio Lemonde*, San Martín 839, rec., US$750 a month; *Residencial Trianon*, Callao y Alvear, 3-bed apartment US$80 a night. Rooms in private house, E, at Cochabamba 771 (San Telmo) owned by Elizabeth Miles, T 27-5839.

NB All the rates quoted are subject to alteration, particularly in view of exchange rate fluctuations (**see Cost of Living**, page 192). It should be noted that for the most part they are the basic or minimum rates. Room tax is 15% and is not always included in the price. Check when booking into a hotel whether breakfast is included or not. Air conditioning is a must in high summer, but be prepared for frequent power cuts. Many of the cheaper hotels in the central area give large reductions on the daily rate for long stays. International telephone calls from hotels may incur a 40%-50% commission in addition to government tax of about the same amount. Tokens can be obtained and the call made from a public telephone box. International calls can be made from the central office on the corner of Maipú and Corrientes, about US$1 a minute.

Hotels with red-green lights or marked *Albergue Transitorio* are hotels for homeless lovers.

Tips In spite of the high service charge it is customary to tip 10% of the total bill; porters at hotels expect a tip—about US$0.50 per day of stay or service rendered. Hairdressers expect 10% of the bill, cinema ushers about US$0.20.

Camping Closest camp site to the city is about 15 km. out at Lomas de Zamora, US$3 p.p. per night, inc. swimming pool, take bus 141 from Plaza Italia to Puerta La Noria then No. 540 to Villa Albertini which passes the entrance; information on all sites is available from the Automóvil Club Argentino. Those travelling by car might try at the German Sports Club, Sociedad Alemana de Gimnasia, 9 de Julio and Av Márquez, Villa Ballester, 30 km. N of centre, cheap, or free. Easy to reach by Línea Suárez bus 90, get off at Chilavert.
    Sleeping bags and tents direct from the factory at Acoyte 1622, T 855-0619, English, German spoken, reasonable prices, open 0800-1200, 1430-1900, Saturday 0900-1300. Good equipment and fuel from Fugate, Gascón 232 (off Rivadavia 8000 block), also repairs equipment. Camping gas available at América Pesca, Alfredo Pollini Alvear 1461 and El Pescador, Paraguay y Libertad.

Restaurants "The Buenos Aires Herald" publishes a handy *Guide to Good Eating in Buenos Aires* (with a guide to local wines) by Dereck Foster. Eating out in Buenos Aires is very good but is getting more expensive, especially in the posher places which charge in dollars. David Mackintosh tells us that five of the best restaurants are: *Catalinas*, Reconquista 875 (very expensive though); *Francis Malman*, Honduras 4963; *Blabs*, Florida 325; *Au Bec Fin*, Vicente López 1825; and *Montmartre*, Av Libertador 3302, La Lucila.
    Other excellent restaurants include *Clark's*, Sarmiento 645, in old English outfitter's shop (also at Junín 1777), well cooked food, US$10 p.p.; *La Emiliana*, Av Corrientes 1443; *London Grill*, Reconquista 435; *El Imparcial*, H Irigoyen 1201, first-class service (Spanish); *Escorpión*, Av Montes de Oca y Uspallata, good food and service; *Pippo's*, Paraná 356, near corner with Montevideo, and Corrientes near Montevideo (specializes in pasta and meat), cheap, fast service, good simple food. *El Figón de Bonilla*, rustic style, Junín 1721, and Av LN Alem between Tucumán and Viamonte, good. *Le Coq Hardi*, Av Tres Sargentos 496, corner with San Martín, food, service and atmosphere highly rec., first class; *El Ceibal*, food from the NE, at Pueyrredón and Las Heras, distinguished, expensive; *Irish Pub-Downton Matias*, San Martín 979, lunch only. *Portobello*, J.E. Uriburu 1629, romantic atmosphere, fine quality, modest prices. *Claridge Hotel Grill*, excellent for venison and wild boar, haunt of top executives and English community, expensive but worth it; *La Cautiva*, Sucre 1546, typical local game dishes. "Business" restaurants, *ABC*, Lavalle 54-5, traditional (US$8-10); *El Faisán*, Corrientes 260, and *Bolsa de Comercio*, 25 de Mayo 359, downstairs at the Stock Exchange.
    Typical Argentine restaurants: *La Estancia*, Lavalle 941, popular with business people, excellent grills and service, inexpensive; *La Cabaña*, Entre Ríos 436, old tavern style, US$25-30. The typical parrilla (mixed grill) is a speciality of *Tranquera*, in Palermo Park; also in Palermo is *La Placita*, on Plaza Recado (5-6 blocks from Subte D, Plaza Italia station) fine atmosphere and good food; *Viga*, J.D. Perón 1116, excellent value, meal with milanesa for US$3. *Los Troncos*, Suipacha 732, good grills. *Yapeyú*, Maipú 389, rec. as good value and friendly; *El Fogón de Martín Fierro*, Palermo, highly rec., huge barbecue; *Mercado del Puerto*, Av Córdoba 518, warmly rec. for grills. *El Suiza*, Viamonte y Reconquista, typical and reasonable, rec.; *Pichín No 1* or *No 2*, Paraná y Sarmiento, for gigantic asado de tira; *La Rural*, Suipacha 453, rec. for parrillada and bife de lomo, English-speaking head waiter is excellent; *El Repecho de San Telmo*, Carlos Calvo 242, excellent, expensive, reserve in advance. *El Apero*, Av Córdoba 820, very good bife de lomo; *City Grill*, San Martín and Av Córdoba, good steaks with salad and wine; *Florida Grill*, at Florida 122, standing-only steak restaurant, excellent value; *El Comité*, Carlos Calvo 375, very good, not too dear; *Nazarenas*, Reconquista 1132, good for beef, excellent atmosphere, rec.; *El Tronio*, Reconquista 918, is very cheap and good.
    There are good restaurants all along Calles Lavalle and Maipú, serving full meals at US$3-5. *Las Delicias Papas Fritas*, Maipú near Florida, good wines, rec.; *El Palacio de la Papa Frita*, Lavalle 735, also good, smart and courteous service; *Los Inmortales*, Lavalle 746, specializes in pizza, highly rec.; there are other locations; some serve *à la carte* dishes which are plentiful (US$ 5 each, upwards), and are open from 1500-2000 when most other restaurants are closed. There are also several economical restaurants along Florida. Several good restaurants on Defensa, between Alsina and Plaza de Mayo. *El Rocío*, Salta 151, 1 blocks from Av de Mayo, excellent, cheap, everything on menu is good, popular, good value.
    Good restaurants near Teatro Colón include *Posta del Gaucho*, Pellegrini 625, very good, accepts Visa. Several good places near entrance to Recoleta cemetery: *Munich Recoleta*, Junín 1871, good; *Montevideo 352* (address as name), parrillada, good and cheap; *Café Victoria*, Roberto M Ortiz 1865, typical of the Recoleta area; on same street, *Don Juan*, No

1827, and *Lola*, No 1805, good but expensive. The Costanera along the river front is lined with little eating places: *El Rancho Inn* is best, try also *Happening* and *Los Años Locos*.

Seafood: *El Pulpo*, Tucumán y Reconquista, great variety, big portions, moderate prices; *El Pescadito*, P de Mendoza 1483, rec. for pasta and sea-food. *Hispano*, Rivadavia 1200, reasonable, good sea-food. *Ostramar*, Santa Fe 3495 y Lunín Alvarez (Subte station Canning, then walk back towards town), good quality fish.

Italian: *Pizzería Los Idolos*, Suipacha 436, said to be best pizzería in the city; *Broccolino*, Esmeralda 776, excellent, very popular, try pechuguitas; *Le Grand Caruso*, Córdoba y Medrano, rec.; *Mama Liberata*, Cabildo 3800, Palermo, excellent; Italian restaurant at *Sheraton* hotel, good service.

Typical Boca restaurant: *Spadavecchia*, Necochea 1180, set menu with wine US$8, seats some 500 people, dancing. There are several others in the same street. They all serve antipasto, pasta and chicken; no point in looking for beef here. All bands are loud; offputting for those with sensitive ears. Nearby is *Restaurant Napolitano*, which serves excellent set lunches of seafood (US$10 for 2), good atmosphere and young wine. Try a family restaurant at corner of Necochea and Suárez known as *Cantina Los Tres Amigos*; live music from 2130, complete meal with wine under US$6 each, excellent, about 4 blocks from commercial centre. The seafood restaurant *La Barca*, on river bank near Avellaneda bridge, US$16 for 2, rec.; also rec. for seafood and good value, *Viejo Puente*, Almirante Brown 1499.

Swedish food at *Swedish Club*, Tacuari 147, open to non-members. Hungarian, *Budapest*, 25 de Mayo 690, cheap. *Chez Moi*, Av San Juan 1223 (T 270890), French, and Iranian food on Fri. and Sat. lunch, reservations necessary.

Vegetarian: *Granix*, Florida 126 and 461, plenty of cheap food, open lunchtime Mon.-Fri. *Ever Green* is a chain of "tenedor libre" (eat as much as you like for a fixed price) vegetarian restaurants with branches in Paraná 746, Tucumán 666 (T 322-6280, good, Chinese and Argentine, take-away), Sarmiento 1728, Cabildo 2979 and Maipú 338 (Pte Saavedra); *Apio's*, Sucre 2425 at Cabildo, vegetarian buffet, US$4; *Sai Kai*, Suipacha 920 (lunch only, closed weekend); *Za Zen*, Talcahuano 434, T 407844, lunch and dinner; *Sr. Sol*, Billingshurst 1070 (p.m. except Sat., Sun., lunch also, closed Mon.); *Yin Yang*, Paraná 868 (health-food shop too, lunch only, closed Sun.); *Manantial*, Montevideo 560 (closed Sun.). *La Esquina de las Flores*, Montevideo and Córdoba, excellent value, also good health-food shop. *Verde Esmeralda*, Esmeralda (nr. Av Corrientes); *Giardino*, Suipacha 429 and Lavalle 835 (in arcade), 1st floor, rec., US$3 complete meal, take-away also; *La Huerta*, Paraguay 445, T 311-0470, macrobiotic, rec.; *La Huerta II*, Lavalle 895 y Suipacha, 2nd floor, all you can eat for US$3.

Oriental: *Chung Kin*, Calle Paraguay, near Maipú, Chinese, set lunch, US$2; *Oriente*, also Chinese, Maipú 512, good; *Nuevo Kow Loon*, also Maipú, excellent and reasonable; *Los 9 Platos*, B. Mitre 1177, Chinese, good, cheap, 3-course set menu, closed Sun.; *Macau*, Suipacha 477, good Chinese buffet; Chinese restaurant next to *La Rural* on Suipacha is good; *Doll*, Suipacha 544, cheap, Chinese "tenedor libre"; *China Doll*, Paraná 342, self-service, rec.; Tucumán 666, nr. Florida, Chinese/Vegetarian, excellent value, US$3 for all you can eat; *El Balcón*, Carlos Pellegrini 525 (Hotel Panamericano), Japanese, very good.

Pumper-nic is a chain of rather pricey fast food restaurants. *Kentucky Fried Chicken*, Roberto M. Ortiz 1815, Paseo de la Recoleta.

Cheap meals at *Restaurant Bar Salamanca*, at back of Galería de las Américas, Suipacha 927, platos del día for US$1.50. *Los Teatros*, Talcahuano 354, good, cheap (live music 2300-0100, open 24 hrs.). *La Mosca Blanca*, right hand side of Retiro station, very good and busy. Good snacks all day and night at Retiro and Constitución railway termini, also at *La Escalerita*, Lavalle 717. For quick cheap snacks the markets are rec., e.g. El Retiro market on the 900 block of Av Libertador. Stalls of the Cooperadora de Acción Social offer cheap snacks, and can be found in several public areas, e.g. near the Recoleta. The snack bars in underground stations are also cheap; also *Hogar Obrero*, Rivadavia y Esmeraldas, US$0.65 for full meal (but not too good).

For restaurants with shows, see **Night Clubs and Folklore** below.

Tea Rooms, Cafés and Bars *Richmond*, Florida 468 between Lavalle and Corrientes, genteel (chess played between 1200-2400); *La Estrella* and *El Reloj*, Lavalle and Maipú; *Queen Bess*, Santa Fe 868; well-known are the *Confitería Suiza*, Tucumán 753, and the *Florida Garden* at Florida and Paraguay. *Café El Convento de San Telmo*, Bolívar with Humberto 1, good coffee, cakes and atmosphere. *En El Patio*, Paraguay 886, very pleasant. *Exedra* at Carlos Pellegrini and Av Libertador and many on Av Libertador in the Palermo area, such as *Round Point*, *Café Tabac*, are fashionable. *Café Piazza*, Rivadavia 1400 block opp Plaza Lorea, exellent coffee, pretty setting. *Café Merlyn*, Montevideo 1655, great cakes, nice atmosphere. The more bohemian side of the city's intellectual life is centred on Avenida Corrientes, between Cerrito and Callao, where there are many bars and coffee shops, such as *La Paz* (open very late). *Siglo XIX* on Suipacha, rec. for traditional atmosphere; *El Molino*, Rivadavia and Callao, popular with politicians, nr. Congress, Belle Epoque décor, frequent art sales. Excellent ice-cream at *Freddo*, Ayacucho y Quintana. On Lavalle there are *whiskerías* and *cervecerías* where one can have either coffee or exotic drinks, *Bar Suárez*, Lavalle and Maipú, is a good place to watch the world go by. *Café Mozart*, Reconquista 1050, offers variety of music (US$5) along with tea and snacks. *Bar-baro*, cosmopolitan, Tres Sargentos and San Martín. *Bar Rua Nova*, corner of Chacabuco and Av de Mayo, cheap snacks. *Arrayanes*, Córdoba and San Martín, open Sunday. *Young Men's Bar*, Córdoba and Esmeralda. *Barila*, Santa Fe 2375, has excellent confectionery. *Café Tortoni*, Av de Mayo 829-35, a haunt of artists, very elegant, over 100 years old, interesting *peña* evenings of poetry and music. On Saturdays at 2315, it becomes a 'Catedral del Jazz', with Fenix Jazz Band, US$1 entrance. Good local atmosphere in bars along Pasaje Bollini. *Bar Verona* in the Boca. Watch whisky prices in bars: much higher than in restaurants.

Markets Sunday markets for souvenirs, antiques, etc.: **Plaza Dorrego (San Telmo)** with food, dancers, buskers, Sunday 0900-1700, on Humberto 1 and Defensa (only "antiques"). Also Feria de Las Artes (Fri., 1400-1700) on Defensa and Alsina. Saturday craft, jewellery, etc. market, at Plaza Belgrano, nr. Belgrano station. At Parque Rivadavia, Rivadavia 4900, around the *ombú* tree, stamps and coins, Sun. 0900-1300, Plazoleta Primera Junta, Rivadavia and Centenara, books and magazines, Sat. 1200-2000, Sun. 1000-2000. Plazoleta Santa Fe, Santa Fe and Uriarte (Palermo) old books and magazines, same times as Primera Junta, and again, plastic arts in the Caminito (Boca) section. Sat. market in Plaza Centenario, local crafts, good,cheap hand-made clothes. Auction sales: some bargains at weekday p.m. auctions, Edificio de Ventas, Banco de la Ciudad de Buenos Aires, Esmeralda 660. Souvenirs can be found in area around San Martín and Paraguay (not markets). Once market is "cheap and cheerful, with many bargains." Interesting gaucho market at Mataderos, bus 126 from Plaza de Mayo, 50 mins (Sun.).

Shopping Most shops close lunchtime on Sat. Visit the branches of *H Stern*, for fine jewellery at the Sheraton and Plaza Hotels, and at the International Airport. *Kelly's*, Paraguay 431, has a very large selection of Argentine handicrafts in wool, leather, wood, etc. Excellent leatherwork at *LYK*, Paraguay y Maipú. *Artesanías Argentinas*, at Montevideo 1360 and Córdoba 770, a non-profitmaking organization selling handicrafts (clothing, weaving, basketware, wooden goods etc.) all with certificate of origin; also *Matra*, Defensa 372, and the handicrafts centre at Defensa 788, 1st floor. *Señora Luna Arte Popular*, Paraguay 729, wide selection of Argentine, Bolivian, Chilean and Peruvian crafts, new and antique, expensive. *Campanera Dalla Funtana*, Reconquista 735, leather factory which is fast, efficient and reasonably priced for made-to-measure clothes. Good quality leather clothes factory at Boyacá 2030, T 582 6909 to arrange time with English speaking owner. *Aida*, Florida 670, can make a leather jacket to measure in 48 hours. Apart from shops on Florida and Santa Fe (especially between 1000 and 2000), Av Corrientes has many shops for men's clothes between 600 and 1000 blocks, and the shops on Arenales N of Av Santa Fe, and on Av Alvear on the way to Recoleta, have been recommended. Av Cabildo in Belgrano district can be reached by 152 bus from Retiro for good shopping between 1600 and 2800 blocks. Many boutiques and places for casual clothes in Martínez suburb. The Mercado de Abasto, originally built in 1893, at Avs Corrientes, Anchorena, Lavalle and Agüero, has been reopened as a commercial, cultural and entertainment centre. There is a new shopping mall, Patio Bullrich, Av Libertador y Posadas, between Montevideo and Libertador, entrances on Posadas and Av Libertador (No 750); boutiques are very expensive, but leather goods are of high quality. In the Munro district on Av. Mitre (buses, 130, 314, 41 from Av. Libertador, 50 mins.) are cheap and varied fashion clothes, fake designer labels, some secondhand.

Bookshops *ABC*, Av Córdoba 685 (good selection of second-hand and new English books, sells *South American Handbook*) and Av Libertador 13777 in Martínez suburb. *Librería Rodríguez*, Sarmiento 835, good selection of English books and magazines; French bookshop at Calle Rivadavia 743; *Librería Goethe*, San Martín 577 and *Librería Henschel*, Reconquista 533, both have good selection of secondhand German books. Italian books at *Librería Leonardo*, Av Córdoba 335, also (with newspapers and magazines) *La Viscontea*, Libertad 1067. Secondhand/exchange inside shopping arcade under Av 9 de Julio at the Obelisco—good stock and prices. Good bookshop at Florida 340, *El Ateneo* (basement, good selection of English books), and *Atlántida*, *Kel Ediciones*, Talcahuano 1063, and Laprida 2488 in Florida suburb, also maintain a good stock of English books. Prices at *Harrods* on Florida are lower than most. For used and rare books: *Fernández Blanco*, Tucumán 712; *Casa Figueroa*, Esmeralda 970; and *L'Amateur*, Esmeralda 882. Second-hand English language books from British and *American Benevolent Society* (BABS); look in *Buenos Aires Herald* for address, which changes often.

Foreign newspapers at newsstands on Florida.

Camera Repairs and Film Developing　Film developing to international standards. Recommended for best quality is Expofoto, Lavalle 1250. Kodak, Paraná 515, good and cheap developing. Fotospeed, Av Santa Fe 4838 (20% discount to SAHB owners!) for quality 2-hour service. Park Color, Av. Corrientes 614, 1-hr. developing, good prices for Kodak products. Camera repairs: Casa Schwarz, Perú 989, international brands; Golden Lab, Lavalle 630, good prices for film; Horacio Calvo, Río bamba 183, all brands and variety of rare accessories; for Olympus cameras, Rodolfo Jablanca, Corrientes 2589. German spoken at Gerardo Föhse, Florida 890, fast, friendly.

Taxis　are painted yellow and black, and carry *Taxi* flags.　About US$1 per km.; meters show the number of "points" (zones) crossed, *not* the fare in australes, which is shown on a chart held by the driver. A charge is made for each piece of hand baggage. Tips not necessary. Beware of overcharging especially with remise (private clubs) and late at night. Check the notes you offer the driver; they have been known to switch a low-value note for your high one and demand the balance. Fares double for journey outside city limit (Av General Paz). Alberto Pommerenck, T 654 5988, offers reasonable ½ day hire, knows suburban leather factories well, good driver.

Car Hire　Cars for hire, expensive, can be got through hotel reception clerks. Use of Avis Car Credit card with central billing in one's home country is possible. Traffic drives on the right. Driving in Buenos Aires is no problem, provided you have eyes in the back of your head and good nerves. Avis agency in the *Sheraton Hotel* (vehicles reported not well serviced); A1 International, MT de Alvear 680, T 32-9475/76, 31-0247, both have branches in all main cities. Hertz in Buenos Aires and Bariloche. Average rental for a small car is US$50 per day including mileage, fuel and insurance. If you want to travel to another country you need a special authorization from the car hire company.

Local Bus　services (*colectivos*) cover a very wide radius, and are clean, frequent, efficient and very fast. The basic fare is about US$0.20. **NB**. The number of the bus is not sufficient indication of destination, as each number has a variety of routes. Look for the little plaques displayed in the driver's window. Lumi guide to all routes is available at newsstands, US$3.

Tram　A green and white old-fashioned street car operates on Sat. 1500-2000 and Sun. 1000-1200, 1500-2000 (not Easter Sun.), free, from Emilio Mitre and Directorio (Emilio Mitre Subte), and from near Primera Junta Subte. Operated by Asociación de los Amigos del Tranvía.

Underground Railways ("Subte")　Five lines link the outer parts of the City to the centre. "A" line runs under Calle Rivadavia, from Plaza de Mayo up to Primera Junta. "B" line from central Post Office, Avenida L. N. Alem, under Av Corrientes to Federico Lacroze railway station. "C" line links Plaza Constitución with the Retiro railway station, and provides connections with all the other lines. "D" line runs from Plaza de Mayo, under the Diagonal Norte, Córdoba and Santa Fe to Palermo. "E" line runs from Plaza de Mayo through San Juan to Avs Directorio and José María Moreno. The fare is about US$0.10, the same for any direct trip or combination between lines; tokens must be bought at booking offices (*boleterías*); buy a few in advance to save time. System operates 0530-01300. Some stations on lines C and D have some very fine tile-work. Backpacks and luggage allowed. Beware bag- and jewellery-snatchers and pickpockets. The tourist office gives out a map, which can also be bought on station platforms with a booklet giving bus schedules.

Night Clubs and Folklore　*Michelangelo*, impressive setting, restaurant and nightclub in an old converted monastery, US$10 each, including cover charges and first drink, good show, Balcarce 433, go at about 2300 on Fri.; *Hippopotamus*, Junín 1787, also good restaurant (nouvelle cuisine) and night club; *Mesón Español*, Av Caseros 1750, good folk music show and good food; *Karim*, Carlos Pellegrini y Av Santa Fe, good; *Caño 14*, Talcahuano 975, *El Viejo Almacén*, Independencia and Balcarce, tango shows at 2230 and 0115, rec. but touristy, (entrance US$10, including transport from hotel—no dancing for guests); nearby are *Casablanca*, Balcarce 668, and *Taconeando*, San Lorenzo and Balcarce 725, tango shows, entrance US$17, more authentic, rec. *La Casa del Cantor*, P.Gollena 603. *El Rancho Ochoa*, Catamarca 999, has a good show and a reasonable meal. Good show also at *La Veda*, Florida 1, US$30 for reasonable meal with wine and other drinks. The best affordable tango bars are in the Boca, but it is apparently becoming increasingly difficult to find authentic tango for locals; most are tourist-oriented. One recommended place is *Italia Unita* in the 2300 block of JD Perón. Recommended night club/discos include *Le Club*, small and exclusive, Quintana

111; *Dimensión*, new and large but pleasant, Av Córdoba 3653; *Paladium*, "extravagant", on Reconquista next to *Pumper-nic* restaurant. Three gay discos: *Contramano* (the best), Rodrgúez Peña 1082; *Bunker*, Anchorena 1170; *Area*, Junín y Santa Fe. Andean music at *Ollantaytambo*, Estados Unidos 541.

Bars and restaurants in San Telmo district, with live music (usually beginning 2330-2400, Fri., Sat., Sun., cover charge US$2): *San Telmo Tango*, Cochabamba 435, US$25 for large meal, show and unlimited drinks, popular with locals, not touristy; *Jazz y Pop*, Venezuela y Chacabuco; *Jazz Café*, Chile 400; *Players*, Humberto I 528 (piano bar); *La Peluquería*, Bolívar, nr. Carlos Calvo (Samba).

Cultural Events The Luna Park stadium holds pop/jazz concerts. Teatro Alvear has free concerts Thursday at 1300, usually Orquesta de Tango de Bs. As. Teatro Municipal General San Martín, Av Corrientes 1530, organizes many cultural activities of which quite a few are free of charge, including concerts Sat. evenings; the theatre's Sala Leopoldo Lugones shows international classic films, US$0.75 Sat.-Sun. Free concerts at ProMusica music shop, Florida 638; schedule in window. Centro Cultural General San Martín, Sarmiento 1551, and the Centro Cultural de Buenos Aires, Junín 1930, next to the Recoleta cemetery, have many free activities. The Teatro Liceo, Plaza de Congreso has been giving performances of a hugely popular revue, "Salsa Criolla", nightly for the last six years, dealing with Argentine history, people and customs. Tickets from US$2.50. Theatre ticket agency, La Cartelera, Lavalle 828. Look for details in main newspapers.

Cinemas Many, centred on Lavalle and nearby blocks. The selection of films is as good as anywhere else in the world. Films are now shown uncensored. Average ticket price US$1, best booked early afternoon to ensure good seats. Tickets obtainable, sometimes cheaper, from ticket agencies (*carteleras*), such as the one in the gallery at Maipú y Lavalle. Most foreign films are shown with subtitles, but dubbing increasingly used for major box-office successes. Free films at Asociación Bancaria, Sarmiento 337/341, T 313-9306/312-5011/17; old films at Ciné en el Teatro Hebraíco, Sarmiento 2255, and at Sarmiento 2150, T 48-2170, US$1. On Sat. nights many central cinemas have *transnoches*, late shows starting at 0100.

Sports Association and rugby football are both played to a very high standard. Entry to the River Plate Stadium (bus 130) for match, US$3 (enclosure); matches Sun. 1600, Wed. evenings. Next to the stadium is a sports centre, good climbing wall. Ice-hockey is becoming popular. Cricket is not unknown. Polo is played from Oct. to Dec.; a visit to the national finals at Palermo in Nov. is recommended, entrance free. The Tigre Boat Club, founded in 1888, is open to British or American visitors for a small fee and a limited period. The leading golf clubs are the Hurlingham, Ranelagh, Ituzaingó, Lomas, San Andrés, San Isidro, Sáenz Peña, Olivos, Jockey, Campos Argentinos and Hindú Country Club; visitors wishing to play should bring handicap certificate and make telephone booking. Weekend play possible only with a member. Good hotels may be able to make special arrangements. Tennis and squash are popular: there are 5 squash clubs.

Gambling Weekly lotteries. Football pools, known as *Prode*.

Chess Club Argentino de Ajedrez, Paraguay 1858, open daily, arrive after 2000; special tournament every Sat., 1800. High standards.

Museums, Libraries, Art Exhibitions Note: Most museums close on Monday, and some in January and most of February for summer holidays. State museums and parks are free on Wednesdays. Check opening hours with Tourist Office.
Museo de los Presidentes (basement of Casa Rosada), Hipólito Irigoyen 218. Historical memorabilia, particularly of former Presidents.
Museo de Bellas Artes (National Gallery), Avenida Libertador 1473. In addition to a fine collection of European works, particularly strong in the 19th century French school, there are paintings representing the conquest of Mexico, executed 300 or 400 years ago, many good Argentine works, and wooden carvings from the Argentine hinterland. Open Tues.-Sun. (free Thurs.), 0900-1245, 1500-1845. Entrance US$2. Warmly rec.
The National Museum of the Decorative Arts is at Av Libertador 1902. The building is shared with the **Museo Nacional de Arte Oriental**; both are open Wed.-Mon., 1500-1900.
Biblioteca Nacional (The National Library). Calle México 566, founded in 1810, moved here in 1902. About 500,000 volumes and 10,000 manuscripts.
Museo Histórico Nacional, Defensa 1600. Trophies and mementoes of historical events. Here are San Martín's uniforms, a replica of his famous sabre, and the original furniture and door of the house in which he died at Boulogne. Open Tues.-Fri. and Sunday, 1500-1900. Entrance US$0.10.
Museo de la Ciudad, Alsina 412, open Mon.-Fri., 1100-1900, Sat., 1600-2000. Permanent

exhibition covering social history and popular culture, special exhibitions on daily life in Buenos Aires changed every two months, and a reference library open to the public.

Museo y Biblioteca Mitre, San Martín 336, preserves intact the household of President Bartolomé Mitre. Open 1500-1700.

Museo de Ciencias Naturales at Avenida Angel Gallardo 490, facing Parque Centenario. It houses palaeontological, zoological, mineralogical, botanical, archaeological and marine sections. Open Tues., Thurs., Sun. 1400-1800, US$0.20. Library, Mon.-Fri., 1100-1700.

Museo Municipal de Arte Moderno (Tues.-Sun. 1600-2000) at Avenida Corrientes 1530, and **Museo Municipal de Artes Plásticas Eduardo Sivori** (Tues.-Sun. 1600-2000) at Centro Cultural de Recoleta, Junín 1930, where there are also a cinema, a theatre, and the **Museo de Artes Visuales**, Tues.-Fri. 1600-2000. Free entry on Wed. 19th century and contemporary Argentine painting.

Museo de Bellas Artes de Boca, Pedro de Mendoza 1835, Boca, has many works on local life, entrance free.

Centro Cultural Las Malvinas, Florida 853, stages many art exhibitions by Argentine and foreign artists.

Museo de Motivos Populares Argentinos José Hernández, Av Libertador 2373, Gaucho collection, open Tues.-Sun., 1400-1800.

Museo del Instituto Nacional Sanmartino, Sánchez de Bustamante and Av A M de Aguado; Mon.-Fri. 0900-1200 and 1400-1700; Sat., Sun. 1400-1700.

Museo de Arte Español Enrique Larreta, Juramento 2291, in Belgrano. 1500-1945. Closed Thurs. The home of the writer Larreta. Also **Biblioteca Alfonso El Sabio**, Mon.-Fri., 1300-1930.

Museo de Cabildo y Revolución de Mayo, Bolívar 65, is the old Cabildo building, converted into a museum in 1940. It contains paintings, documents, furniture, etc., recording the May 1810 revolution, and memorabilia of the 1806 British attack. Entry US$0.33. Open Wed.-Sun., 1500-1900. Library, Mon.-Fri., 1100-1900.

Museo de Arte Hispanoamericano Isaac Fernández Blanco, Suipacha 1422. Contains a most interesting and valuable collection of colonial art, especially silver, in a beautiful colonial mansion. Open Tues.-Sun., 1400-1900, admission US$0.35. Thursdays free. Latin American art and history library at Suipacha 1444 nearby, 0900-1900, Mon.-Fri.

Museo y Biblioteca Ricardo Rojas, Charcas 2837, open Wednesdays and Fridays 1500-1800, US$0.10. The famous writer Rojas lived in this beautiful colonial house for several decades. It contains his library, souvenirs of his travels, and many intriguing literary and historical curios.

Numismatic Museum; fascinating, well kept, little known, at the Banco Central in San Martín, overlooks central foyer, ask guard for directions.

"**Presidente Sarmiento**", Dársena Norte, a sailing ship used as a naval training ship until 1987; now a museum. Open daily 1000-1800, US$0.40. The corvette "**Uruguay**", tied up by the Boca bridge, is a museum of Antarctica, open Sat. and Sun. 1300-1800, US$0.40.

Bank of London and South America (now Lloyds Bank (BLSA)), Bartolomé Mitre and Reconquista, has a miniature museum on its fifth floor. Open during banking hours; the building, designed by SEPRA (Santiago Sánchez Elia, Federico Peralta Ramos, and Alfredo Agostini) and completed in 1963 is worth seeing for itself. Next door is the **Banco de Córdoba**, designed by the brilliant Córdoba architect Miguel Angel Roca, completed in the early 1970s.

Museo Nacional de Aeronáutica, Av. Costanera Rafael Obligado, next to Jorge Newbery airport, Thurs., Sat. and Sun., 1600-1900. Many civil and military aircraft.

Museo Nacional Ferroviario, Av Libertador 405, in Retiro station. Mon.-Fri., 0900-1800, free. Archives 1100-1800. For railway fans; no photographing.

Museo Botánico, Las Heras 4102 and Malabia 2690. Open 0800-1200 and 1400-1800, Mon.-Fri. Herbarium pleasant. Some 1,000 cats in residence.

Museo de la Dirección Nacional del Antártico, Angel Gallardo 470, Tues., Thurs. and Sun., 1400-1800. Dioramas.

Museo del Teatro Colón, Tucumán 1161. Mon.-Fri. 1200-1800. Documents and objects related to the theatre.

Museo Histórico Saavedra, Crisólogo Larralde (Republiquetas) 6309. Wed.-Fri., 1400-1800; Sat., 1800-2200; Sun., 1500-1900. City history from the eighteenth century. Free on Wed.

Yuchán Centro de Artesanía Aborigen, Defensa 788, has many interesting native artefacts on view, for sale.

Federal Police Museum San Martín 353, 7th floor, worth visiting, small entrance fee. The interesting forensic part can only be seen if you offer a police, medical or journalist's identification.

Museo Internacional de Caricatura y Humorismo, Lima 1037, open Fri., 1700-2100 only, originals of cartoons and caricatures of 20th century, but small international section, admission US$0.05.

Museo de Armas, Maipú y Santa Fe. Open 1500-1900 daily, US$0.15. All kinds of weaponry.

Retiro Art Gallery, an excellent, small art gallery in two train carriages on Platform 9 at Retiro station; sometimes tours the country. Access is from platform 8; small entrance fee. Also shows documentary films.

Exchange Most banks charge very high commission. Lloyds Bank (BLSA) Ltd, corner of Reconquista and Bartolomé Mitre. It has 13 other branches in the city, and others in Greater Buenos Aires. Royal Bank of Canada, corner of Florida and J. D. Perón; branch at Av. Callao 291. Citibank, B Mitre 502; branch at Florida 746. First National Bank of Boston, Florida 99. Bank of America, J. D. Perón and San Martín changes Bank of America travellers' cheques am. only, into US$ at very high commission; branch at Paraguay 901 doesn't take American Express or Thomas Cook cheques. Banco Holandés Unido, Florida 361. Deutsche Bank, B. Mitre and Reconquista. Banking hours 0800-1200, Mon.-Fri., although exchange may be possible in some casas de cambio to 1400 or 1600. Banco de la Provincia de Buenos Aires, San Martín, close to Plaza de Mayo, and Banco Río de la Plata, San Martín 77-97 both advance cash on Visa Card. American Express offices are in a new building at the corner of Arenales 707 and Maipú, by Plaza San Martín, where one apply for a card, get financial services, etc., changes Amex travellers' cheques into US$ with commission of US$5 up to US$500. For client mail, go to the office at *Hotel Plaza*, Florida 1005, 2nd floor, Mon.-Fri. 0800-2000, Sat.

There are many exchange shops, and increasing numbers deal in travellers' cheques; most are concentrated around San Martín and Corrientes, those on Lavalle and Maipú are reported to give better rates than those on Florida (although Onda has been rec.); open from 0900 to 1630, Mon.-Fri. Many *cambios* will exchange US$ travellers' cheques for US$ cash at commissions varying from 1.25 to 3%. If all *cambios* closed, try Mercadería de Renate de Aduana, Florida 8, or Olympia leather shop on Tucumán between Florida and San Martín. There is no service charge on notes, only on cheques. Many exchange shops ask for receipt of purchase of cheques, and practices vary all the time. Major credit cards widely accepted; general Master Card office at Hipolito Yrigoyen 878, open 1000-1700, T 331-1022/2502/2549.

Language Schools Spanish classes at Academia Toil And Chat, Suipacha 443, T 322-9739 and at Interact, Ramón Freire 1047, T 562-8776. For other schools teaching Spanish, look in *Buenos Aires Herald* in the classified ads. Enquire also at the Goethe Institut. Schools which teach English to Argentines are: International House, Larrea 1333, and the Victoria School of English, Uruguay 782, both British-owned and -run. Masters, Av de Mayo 791; Berlitz, Av de Mayo 847 (low rates of pay); Central Consultaret de Personal, Lavalle 1290 (office at 1103); Pullmen, Santiago del Estero 324. Before being allowed to teach, you must have a work permit; if unsure of your papers, ask at Migraciones (address below).

Libraries, Cultural and Trade Associations Harrods (2nd floor), on Florida, US$6 a month. Argentine Association of English Culture, Suipacha 1333 (library for members only); British Chamber of Commerce, Av Corrientes 457; British Community Council, 25 de Mayo 444. Goethe Institut, Av Corrientes 311, German library (open 1300-1800 exc Wed.) and newspapers, free German films shown; in the same building, upstairs, is the German Club, Corrientes 327. USA Chamber of Commerce, Diagonal Norte 567; US Information Library (Biblioteca Lincoln), Florida 935, reference and lending library, free, take passport (closed Wed., Sat., Sun.). St Andrew's Society, Perú 352.

Clubs American Club, Viamonte 1133, facing Colón Theatre, temporary membership available; American Women's Club, Av Córdoba 632, 11 piso. English Club, 25 de Mayo 581, T 311-9121; temporary membership available to British business visitors. The American and English Clubs have reciprocal arrangements with many clubs in USA and UK. Swedish Club, Tacuari 147.

Embassies and Consulates Bolivian Consulate, Belgrano 1670, 2nd floor, open 0900-1400. **Brazilian Consulate**, Pellegrini 1363, 5th floor, open Mon.-Fri., 1000-1800 (easier to get a Brazilian visa, in 2 hrs., US$12 for Australians, free for US, from this consulate than in Montevideo; 2-day wait at latter), T 394-5620. **Paraguayan Consulate**, Maipú 464, 3rd floor, 0900-1300. T 392-6535. **Peruvian Consulate**, Tucumán 637, 9th floor, 0900-1400, visa US$5, takes 1 day. **Uruguayan Consulate**, Ayacucho 1616, open 1000-1800, T 821-6031.

US Embassy and Consulate General, Colombia 4300, Palermo, T 774-7611 (US Embassy Residence, Av Libertador 3502). **Australian Embassy**, Av Santa Fe 846 (Swissair

Building), T 312-6841. **Canadian Embassy**, Suipacha 111 y Santa Fe, T 312 9081. **South African Embassy**, Marcelo T. de Alvear 590,8 piso, T 311-8991. **Israeli Embassy**, Arroyo 910, T 392 2903/4987/4885/4481/4611/4781.

Austrian Embassy, French 3671, T 802-7095/6. **British Consulate General**, Luis Agote 2412/52 (near corner Pueyrredón & Guido), Casilla de Correos 2050, T 803-7071, open 0915-1215, 1415-1615 (as of June 1990 an Embassy had not reopened). **Finnish Embassy**, Av Santa Fe 846, 5 piso. **French Embassy**, Av Santa Fe 846, 5 piso. **West German Embassy**, Villanueva 1055, Belgrano, T 771-5054/9. **Irish Embassy**, Av Santa Fe 1391, 4 piso, T 41 6672. **Italian Embassy**, Billinghurst 2577, consulate at M.T. de Alvear 1149. **Netherlands Embassy**, Maipú 66, 1084 Buenos Aires, T 33-6066. **Spanish Embassy**, Mariscal Ramón Castilla 2720, esq Av del Libertador 2075. **Swedish Embassy**, Corrientes 310, 3 piso, T 311-3088. **Swiss Embassy**, Av Santa Fe 846, 12 piso, T 311-6491, open 0900-1200 (see also British Interests Section above).

Useful Addresses Youth Hostel Association—information for all South America; Talcahuano 214, 6 piso T 45-1001 (post code: 1013 Buenos Aires). Buenos Aires hostel at Brasil 675. **N.B.** A YHA card in Argentina costs US$12. Secretariat open Mon.-Fri. 1300-2000. (There are very few hostels near road S from Buenos Aires on Route 3.)
YMCA (Central), Reconquista 439.
YWCA, Tucumán 844.
Salvation Army, Rivadavia 3255.
Municipality, Av de Mayo 525, facing Plaza de Mayo.
Central Police Station, Moreno 1550, T 38-8041 (emergency, T 101).
Migraciones (Immigration), Antártida Argentina 1365.
Comisión Nacional de Museos y Monumentos y Lugares Históricos, Av de Mayo 556; professional archaeology institute.

Urgent Medical Service (day and night) (Casualty ward: *Sala de guardia*). T 34-4001/4. British Hospital, Perdriel 74, T 23-1081, US$6 a visit; cheap dental treatment at Av Caseros y Perdriel 76. German Hospital, Pueyrredón 1658, between C Berruti and C Juncal, T 821-4083. Both maintain first-aid centres (*centros asistenciales*) as do the other main hospitals. Hospital Juan A Fernández, Ceviño y Bulnes, good, free medical attention. If affected by pollen, asthma sufferers can receive excellent free treatment at the University Hospital de Clínicas José San Martín, Córdoba 2351.

Inoculations Centro Médico Rivadavia, S de Bustamante 2531, Mon.-Fri., 0730-1900, or Sanidad de Puerto, Mon. and Thurs., 0800-1200, at Av Ing. Huergo 690, free, bus 20 from Retiro, no appointment required (typhus, cholera, Mon./Thurs. 0800-1200; yellow fever, Thurs. 1400-1600). Hospital Rivadavia, Calles Las Heras y Tagle, for polio inoculation. Free. Centro de Inmunización reported not to give vaccinations any more.

Laundries Tintorería Constitución, Av Santiago del Estero 1572 (suits only). Laundry at Esmeralda 1077 takes 2 hrs. Many dry cleaners, efficient and friendly. Several launderettes, e.g. Marcelo T. de Alvear 2018, in centre, US$1.50 wash and dry; Junín 15 with Rivadavia, Mon.-Sat. 0800-2100; Junín 529 with Lavalle; Lavarap, US$0.50 wash, same for drying, Paraguay 888 with Suipacha San Martín with Córdoba, Arenales 894, and many other sites; Marva, Juan D. Perón 2000 with Ayacucho. Typical charge: US$2 for 6 kg. wash.

General Post Office (Correo Central), corner of Sarmiento and L.N. Alem. Poste Restante (US$0.30 per letter); very limited service on Saturday (closes 1400). Centro Postal Internacional, for parcels over 1 kg, at Av Antártida Argentina, near Retiro station, open 1100 to 1700.

Cables and Telephones Entel on Av Corrientes, near corner of Calle Maipú (open 24 hrs.), public telex in basement; alternatively in Central Post Office, Leandro N Alem 300, also telex. Another office at San Martín 322. There are Entel offices for international calls and cables in Once station, open 7 days, 0700-2400. Entel also on Agüero/Las Heras. Calls are cheaper after 1800 on Sat. and all day Sun. *Fichas* (tokens) for calls in the city cost US$0.10, obtained at newspaper stalls and Entel offices.

Tourist Information National office at Santa Fe 883 with masses of maps and literature, and said to change money. Open 1000-1700, Mon.-Fri.; T 312-2232, 312-6560. Has addresses of some campsites throughout Argentina, and laundromats in Buenos Aires. There is also a branch on 1st floor of Retiro bus station, with free city maps.

There are also helpful *Casas de Turismo* for most provinces (open Mon.-Fri. usually, 1200-1900, depending on office, check): on Callao are Buenos Aires (no 237), Córdoba (332), Chaco (322), La Rioja (745), Mendoza (445). Río Negro, Tucumán 1920; Chubut, Paraguay

876; Entre Ríos, Suipacha 848; Formosa, B. Mitre 1797; Jujuy, Santa Fe 967; Misiones, Santa Fe 989; Neuquén, J. D. Perón 687; Salta, Diagonal Norte (Roque Sáenz Peña) 933; Santa Cruz, Córdoba 1345, 14th floor, Catamarca, Córdoba 2080; Corrientes, San Martín 333; La Pampa, Suipacha 346; San Juan, Sarmiento 1251; Santa Fe, Maipú 356; Santiago del Estero, Florida 274; Tucumán, Mitre 836; Tierra del Fuego, Sarmiento 745; Ushuaia and Lago Argentino, Av Santa Fe 790. Bariloche hotel, flat and bungalow service at Florida 520, enter *Galería* and walk up to room 116. Calafate bookings for *Motel La Loma* and *Refugio and Autocamping Lago Viedma*, excursions with Transporte Ruta 3 and lake excursions with Empresa Paraíso de Navegación booked from Turismo Argos, Maipú 812, 13th floor C, T 392-5460.

Municipalidad de Buenos Aires, Sarmiento 1551, 4th floor, has an excellent free booklet about the city centre and maps. Further offices at Aeroparque (Aerolíneas Argentinas), Mon.-Fri., 0830-2000 and Sat. 0900-1900, and Ezeiza Airport, Mon.-Fri. 0830-2200; also Florida with Diagonal Norte and Florida with Córdoba, open at 0830-1930 Mon.-Fri. and 0900-1900 Sat.

On Fri., the youth section of *Clarín—Sí*—lists free entertainments. *Where*, a tourist guide in English, published monthly, is available free in hotels, travel agencies, tourist kiosks on Florida, and in some newsstands at US$2.50. The *Buenos Aires Times* is a bilingual monthly newspaper covering tourist topics. A good guide to bus and subway routes is *Guía Peuser*, US$3, available from newsstands; there is one for the city and one covering Greater Buenos Aires. Country-wide maps at Instituto Geográfico Militar, Cabildo 381, reached by 152 bus from Retiro station, open 0800-1300 Mon.-Fri. Federico B. Kirbus has written the highly informative *Las mil maravillas de la Argentina* (with comprehensive English index—1989), obtainable at El Ateneo, or from the author at Casilla de Correo 5210, RA-1000, Buenos Aires. The Fundación Vida Silvestre (conservation organization and bookshop), Defensa 245/251, has information and books on Argentine flora and fauna. Field guide to Argentine birds: *Las aves argentinas*, by Claes Chr. Olrog, US$35, poor drawings but good range maps.

Tourist Agents *Exprinter*, Santa Fe, and San Martín 176, Galería Güemes (their 5-day, 3-night tour to Iguazú and San Ignacio Miní for US$60 has been recommended); *American Express*, Arenales y Maipú; *Thos. Cook & Son*, Av Córdoba 746; *Fairways*, Viamonte 640, 3° piso (392-1716). *City Service Travel Agency*, Florida 890, 4th floor (32-8416), with British staff to advise people travelling to the UK; *Sol-Jet*, Cerrito 1328, warmly rec.; *ATI*, Esmeralda 516, very efficient and helpful, with branches in Brazil; *Astra Travel*, Tucumán 358, 5th floor, English spoken by director, efficient; *Agencia Maritima Mundial*, Av Córdoba 653, helpful and efficient. *Turismo Flyer*, Reconquista 621, 8° piso, T 312-9164/313-8165, English, Dutch and German spoken, accepts credit cards, rec. *Schenker Argentina*, Lavalle 530, German (T 394-2074). *Diners Travel*, Avenida Sarmiento, takes Diners card, unlike most other travel agents. *Germania*, Lavalle 414, excellent service (English not spoken), especially for tours to the N, branch in Salta (T 393-1265/0035). *Patagonia Turística*, specialists on that region, Florida 755 (T 311-9216). English is widely spoken.

ASATEJ, a non-profit making youth and student travel association, Florida 833, piso 1, oficina 104, T 312-8476, Fax 334-2793, gives general information, organizes trips, books youth hostels in Patagonia, Iguazú, Mendoza, Bariloche and elsewhere in the country, transport, Spanish courses, etc., discounts for YHA and student holders.

Tours A good way of seeing Buenos Aires and its surroundings is by Autobuses Sudamericanos (TISA), information and booking office at Bernardo Irigoyen 1370, 1st floor, Offices 25 and 26, T 27-6591 or 631-1108, or Av Larrazabal 493, T 642 7028 (Liniers). For reservations in advance for sightseeing or other tours, with a 20%courtesy discount to *South American Handbook* readers, write to Casilla de Correo No 40, Sucursal 1(B), 1401 Buenos Aires. A 3-hour tour of Buenos Aires in English and Spanish is run by City Tours, book through *Florida House* hotel, US$9, rec., as is Eurotur (T 312-6170), US$6.50, in English. Some tours (e.g. Buenos Aires Tur, Carlos Pellegrini 509, cheaper than TISA) include dinner and a tango show, or a gaucho *fiesta* at a ranch.

Motoring Associations See page 188 for details of service. Parking, safely, at El Balneario within the old port, but ask the military post for permission first.

Passenger Boats The *Buenos Aires Herald* (English-language daily) notes all shipping movements. Flota Fluvial del Estado (Corrientes 489, T 311-0728) organizes cruises from Buenos Aires, Dársena Sud; up the Paraná river. South Coast, down to Punta Arenas and intermediate Patagonian ports, served by the Imp & Exp de la Patagonia and Elma (state shipping line). Very irregular sailings. For connections with Uruguay, **see page** 66.

Airports Ezeiza (sometimes referred to as Ministro Pistarino), 35 km. from the centre by a good divided lane highway, which links with the General Paz circular highway round the city. The airport is up-to-date, has a duty free shop, exchange facilities (beware short-changing, no commission on bills, 6% on travellers' cheques), but its hotel, the *Internacional*, is closed for renovation. Airport information, T 620-0217. Ezeiza is used by international services but Jorge Newbery airport (normally known as Aeroparque), on the N side river front at the end of the New Port, 4 km. from the centre, is used for internal services and also flights to Punta del Este, Montevideo and Aerolíneas flights to Asunción, Santiago and Santa Cruz (Bolivia). If stuck for cash because banks are closed you can try the Newbery airport exchange facilities (bills only), run by Banco de la Nación (close at 2100).

There is a reliable standard taxi service operating from Ezeiza, US$15. Do not take an unmarked car, however attractive the fare may sound; the drivers are adept at separating you from far more money than you can possibly owe them for the journey. Buses from the Manuel Tienda León counter in the airport, T 89-0661/6, operate at a fixed price (US$7), from the centre they leave from near *Hotel Colón*, at Carlos Pellegrini 509, more-or-less hourly, every day from 0530 (0630 Sat.) to 2030 (1930 Mon.). When landing at Ezeiza, buy tickets for city centre at the kiosk in the terminal building, before boarding the bus. No 86 bus (blue, marked "Fournier") can be caught outside the airport terminal to city centre; coming to the airport from town, catch the bus in Plaza de Mayo, or at corner of Perú and Av de Mayo (500—starts at Irala 800 block in the Boca, service from 0500 to 2400), US$1 but no good if you have much luggage (conductor may be persuaded with a dollar extra), and takes 1 hr. for the journey. Make sure bus has sign "Aeropuerto" in the front window; many 86's stop short of the airport. Two or three stops in the Ezeiza airport area, *servicio diferencial* akin to shuttle bus comfort, every 20-30 mins from Av Colón y Estados Unidos, US$1. Other routes to the airport: train to Liniers, then bus 86, or train from Constitución to Ezeiza, then bus 138.

Journeys to and from Jorge Newbery (Aeroparque) by *remise* taxi, e.g. US$8 to Retiro, US$25 to Ezeiza. Taxis are charged according to meter (about US$3 from the centre, but up to US$5 to the centre), or you can catch the local No 33 or 56 bus (US$0.25) from outside the airport to the Retiro railway station. You can also use your Pase Americano from De la Torre station (just past the race track) after having walked across the Palermo park or having taken a US$0.35 bus-ride to the station. Take train from there to Retiro. Manuel Tienda León operates buses between Ezeiza and Jorge Newbery airports, stopping in city centre, US$5.

Aerolíneas Argentinas and Austral offer daily flights to the main cities, for details see text under intended destination; **see also page** 187 for the Visit Argentina fare. If travelling in the south, book ahead if possible with LADE, whose flights are cheaper than buses in most cases.

Local Airline Offices Aerolíneas Argentinas, Calle Perú 2, with a branch office at Santa Fe and Esmeralda; reservations and enquiries, T 393-5122. Austral Líneas Aéreas, Flórida 429, T 774-1076. Líneas Aéreas del Estado (LADE), Calle Perú 710, T 361-7071.

Railways There are 4 main terminals:

Retiro: Ferrocarril Nacional Mitre (Central)—312-6596; Ferrocarril Nacional San Martín (Pacific)—311-8054; Ferrocarril Nacional Belgrano (North-Western)—311-5287/8/9. Services to Córdoba*, Mendoza*, Rosario, Sante Fe and Tucumán. The station has a good left-luggage facility, but it is said to be a haven for pickpockets and bagsnatchers.
Constitución: Ferrocarril Nacional Roca (Southern)—23-0021. Services to Bahía Blanca, Bariloche, San Antonio Oeste and Zapala.
F. Lacroze: Ferrocarril Nacional Urquiza (North-Eastern)—55-5214. Services to Concordia*, Paraná*, Paso de los Libres*, and Posadas*.

Once: Ferrocarril Nacional Sarmiento (Western)—87-0041/2/3.

Fuller details will be found under destinations in the text below; prices given there are only approximate, but as a rough indication US$1.70 per 100 km. for first class and US$1.25/100 km. tourist class in late 1989.

* Some trains have car-transporters

NB The railways maintain an information centre and booking office beside the Galerías Pacífico, Florida 729 (311-6411/14), open 0700-2100 Mon.-Fri., 0700-1300 Sat. Book tickets well in advance wherever possible (especially in July and December), also for connecting services, especially those going south of Buenos Aires. Outward journeys may be booked 45 days in advance, return journeys 60 days, but not later than 7 days in advance. Telephone reservations for named trains (details in text under destinations): 312-5680, 312-5686/9, 312-3686/9, 311-6325/9, 312-8610 and 312-8616/9. Pullman services are usually air conditioned but a/c often does not work, resulting sometimes in very hot journeys as carriage windows do not open. Tourist fares are about 40% cheaper than buses (prices even less for those under 20 years or over 65, for the just married, teachers, students, groups and public sector workers), but much slower and less reliable, and there is no guarantee of being able to stretch out to sleep. Buffet cars usually offer coffee and drinks; sandwiches and refreshments are usually touted down the train during journeys.

Buses The long-distance bus station, Estación Terminal de Omnibus, is behind Retiro, on Av Ramos Mejía and Antártida Argentina (Subte C) T for information 311-6073/6088. All long distance buses leave from here. There are two left-luggage offices, open 0600-2300. Some bus companies charge extra for luggage. Fares charged by the country-wide **Chevallier** company are: Bariloche, US$62; Córdoba, US$17; Mar. del Plata, US$9.50; Mendoza, US$39; Rosario, US$8.10; San Martín de los Andes, US$30; and Tucumán, US$20. Fares may vary according to time of year and advance booking is advisable Dec.-March. Be sure to ask for price in australes; we have received reports that companies quoting US$prices overcharge the hapless tourist. See **Cost of Living, page 192**. Some companies may give discounts, such as 20% to YHA or student-card holders and foreign, as well as Argentine, teachers and university lecturers. Travellers have reported getting discounts without showing evidence of status, so it's always worth asking. For further details of bus services, look under proposed destinations. No exchange shop at bus station: only bank, giving official rate. Tourist office open from 1000, makes hotel reservations. TISA, see above under **Tours**, is the agent for Amerbuspass, for Argentina and Bolivia.

Hitch-hiking Heading S, take bus 96 to Ruta 3 for Comodoro Rivadavia, etc., US$0.35. Best to hitch from a service station The police control point at Km. 43 (southwards) is reported to be friendly and will help to find a lift for you.

Travel into Neighbouring Countries

By Road

Four branches of the Inter-American Highway run from Buenos Aires to the borders of Chile, Bolivia, Paraguay and Brazil. The roads are paved except when otherwise stated.

To Chile via Río Cuarto, Mercedes, San Luis, and Mendoza, Total: 1,310 km. paved throughout. (Three direct buses a week to Santiago, US$40, 23 hrs. e.g. TAC or Chevallier, 1,459 km.; same price to Valparaíso or Viña del Mar.) Car-transporter train to Mendoza on Fridays. There are also road connections between Bariloche and Osorno and Puerto Montt, and between Salta and Antofagasta.

To Bolivia via Rosario, Villa María, Córdoba, Santiago del Estero, Tucumán, and Jujuy. Total: 1,994 km. There is no direct bus service from Buenos Aires to La Paz but through connections can be booked, about US$80. Also a train/ bus combination, train to Tucumán and then bus to Jujuy, but no sleepers. Try travel agent in Bernardo de Yrigoyen 957 shopping arcade. Car-transporter train to Tucumán, Mon., Tue, Wed. and Fri.

To Paraguay via Rosario (as for Bolivia), Santa Fe, Resistencia, Clorinda and Asunción (via toll bridge). Total: 1,370 km. (all paved). Buses take 20-22 hours, with NS de la Asunción, Juan D. Perón 2760; or Chevallier, Empresa Godoy, La Internacional or Expreso Brújula (all next to each other at the Retiro bus terminal). You have choice between *diferencial* (with food, drinks, about US$42) and *común* (without food, about US$32.50) services. Tickets can be bought up to 30 days in advance.

Those who wish to drive to Misiones to visit San Ignacio Miní or the Iguazú Falls can cross the river by the bridge between Santa Fe and Paraná, or the one between Resistencia and Corrientes. From there Route 12 leads NE through Posadas to the Iguazú Falls. The direct road from Buenos Aires to Posadas via the Zárate-Brazo Largo bridges is fully paved. From Corrientes to Esperanza is paved, and from Posadas to Iguazú. (Singer and Tigre-Iguazú buses to Puerto Iguazú leave daily at 1130 and 1500 respectively, US$28.75, 22 hrs.) From Posadas you can cross the river to Encarnación by the ferry (check if new bridge is open) and take a good 370-km. road to Asunción (see Paraguayan chapter). Car-transporter train to Posadas, Tues. and Fri.

To Brazil To the Iguazú Falls, go by the bridge from Puerto Iguazú, reached via Posadas. Another road to the border with Brazil, at Paso de los Libres, goes to Rosario, Santa Fe, cross by bridge and tunnel to Paraná; Villa Federal, Curuzú Cuatiá, Paso de los Libres, opposite Uruguaiana (Brazil), across the Río Uruguay. Total: 960 km. Direct buses to Brazil via Paso de los Libres by Pluma: São Paulo, 40 hrs. US$63.25, Curitiba, US$51.75, 38 hrs.; Florianópolis, US$46, 32 hrs.; daily at 1000 to Porto Alegre, US$40.25, 26 hrs. (The route across the River Plate and through Uruguay is a bit cheaper, not as long and offers a variety of transport and journey breaks; see also Uruguay under next section). Tickets from Onda, Florida 502 y Lavalle (392-5011), for any information also to combine travel via Uruguay. Buen Viaje, Av Córdoba 415 (31-2953) or Pluma, Av Córdoba 461 (311-4871 or 311-5986) or office branches in Rosario, Santa Fe and Paraná. Journey direct to Rio takes about 44 hrs., US$75; at least one bus per day; to Rio, changing buses at Posadas and Foz do Iguaçu is almost half price, 50 hrs. Car-transporter train to Paso de los Libres, Tues. and Fri.

To Uruguay Direct road connections by means of two bridges over the River Uruguay between Puerto Colón and Paysandú and between Puerto Unzué and Fray Bentos. "*Bus de la carrera*" links Montevideo and Buenos Aires (8½ hrs.). Departure from each city at 1000, 2200 and 2300 via Zárate-Gualeguaychú-Puerto Unzué-Fray Bentos-Mercedes, US$11.80. Book at Onda.

To Peru Ormeño has a direct service Buenos Aires-Lima, from Retiro bus station, Tues. 1800, 3½ days, all meals included, one night spent in Coquimbo, Chile (if you need a visa for Chile, get one before travelling), US$120. the route is: Mendoza, Coquimbo, Arica, Tacna, Nazca, Ica, Lima.

Air, River and Railway Services

Brazil Daily air services to São Paulo, Rio de Janeiro and other Brazilian cities. To Porto Alegre by train, a service runs between Bs. As. and Uruguaiana, from where an onwards connection can be made. Shipping service between Buenos Aires and Brazilian ports by various transatlantic lines. See *Buenos Aires Herald*, English-language daily.

Chile Information about travel to Chile is available from Av Córdoba 879. The passenger-train service across the Andes between Mendoza and Santiago has been discontinued, but bus services are available. The train service to Antofagasta via Salta and Socompa has also been suspended, but there are buses between Salta and Antofagasta.
    Foreign and national lines fly daily between Buenos Aires and Santiago. Time taken: 1½ to 2 hours. Aerolíneas Argentinas also flies to Antofagasta via Salta.

Bolivia The connecting service from Tucumán and Jujuy to La Quiaca has been restored: the *Panamericano* leaves Tucumán on Tues. and Fri. 1500, arriving La Quiaca next day at 0920. On arriving in La Quiaca one must cross on foot to the Bolivian side and purchase a train ticket for the remainder of the journey, Villazón-La Paz. The Friday train from Tucumán has one Pullman coach (leaving Buenos Aires on Thurs.) which passes over the border to Villazón. There it is coupled to a Bolivian train which departs Villazón Sat. at 1530 for La Paz, arriving Sun. 0930. *El Norteño* train has no sleepers, leaves Retiro Tues. and Fri. at 1000, via Tucumán to Jujuy. Bus Panamericano Jujuy to La Quiaca. Villalonga Furlong, Balcarce 473, 2nd floor, open Mon.-Fri. 0900-1700, has information about trains (not Retiro); it is also a freighting company and sells the tickets. See under Tucumán (**page 89**) for other train services. There are no sleepers beyond Tucumán. Sleeper tickets to Tucumán carry no seat entitlement elsewhere in the train. Sanitary facilities poor. Hot soup and local dishes brought round carriages. Bar and restaurant car with same food, adequate. Travel rug recommended on this part of the journey. Train Villazón-La Paz has sleepers, worthwhile but may need paying over the odds to secure. Carriages, old, noisy and crowded; bad sanitary facilities. Local food available on train. Cold night. Free baggage allowance 30 kg, and excess is charged. A weekly train (no sleepers) to Santa Cruz de la Sierra from Retiro Station (details and ticket from office at Florida 729) via Salta, Güemes, Pocitos and Yacuiba takes 3 days, US$67; leaves Buenos Aires Sun. at 1000, arrives Santa Cruz 1015 (but more often 1400) Wed. From Santa Cruz, dep 1000 Thurs., arrival 2100 Sat. at Retiro. See page 97.

There are also regular air services 5 or 6 times a week to La Paz by Eastern, Aerolíneas and Lloyd Aéreo Boliviano.

Paraguay The direct train to Asunción was withdrawn in 1984, but trains run daily to Posadas, and once a week from Encarnación to Asunción. From Encarnación you can get a connecting train (if it waits) or bus (saving up to 16 hrs.) to Asunción. There is a daily air service to Asunción by various companies. Time taken: 2 to 6 hours. See also Posadas, **page** 133. Occasional river boats to Asunción in winter and spring, 6 days, cabins cost US$300-560 p.p., food and nightly entertainment reported good.

Uruguay Tickets heavily booked Dec.-March. **NB:** No money changing facilities in Tigre, and poor elsewhere. For boat services, take the train to Tigre (Mitre suburban line), 50 mins (US$0.25), leaves at 5 min intervals from Retiro. (No good hotels in Tigre, but try Astor, reasonable-looking.) Two daily boats to **Carmelo**: Cacciola at 0800 and 1330, 3 hrs., and Delta Nav, Mon.-Sat. 0830 and 1700, Sun. 0830,1700 and 2400, 2½ hrs., both services US$3; tickets at Movilan, Lavalle y Florida, Bs. as. (T 392-5011) or Estación Fluvial, local 13 (T 749-4119), Tigre. It is advisable to book in advance; connecting bus to Montevideo (Onda, Florida y Lavalle, book in advance), arriving at 1530 and 1600.

From Dársena Sud, night boat (vapor carrera) goes to Montevideo, Ferrytur (bus from their office at Florida 780 at 0615 and 1500) leaves at 0745 and 1630, boarding finishes ½ hr. before departure; single fare, shared cabin and breakfast, US$11 for seat, 20 for sleeper; cars charged by weight. Ferry services to Colonia 0730 and 0900, 3 hours, US$16, including bus connection to Montevideo (2½ hrs.), with Ferrytur, Florida 780, 2nd floor, bus leaves from Florida and Córdoba to ferry. Also Buquebus, Suipacha 776, T 392-0365, 3-5 sailings a day, depending on season, 3½ hrs. to Colonia, total of 6½ to Montevideo. It is cheaper to buy a through ticket to Buenos Aires-Montevideo than to buy tickets for each stage separately. Uruguayan immigration officer on ferry.

Atlantic car ferry, daily, at 0800 arr Colonia 1100, Montevideo 1430, US$32.65-53.35 p.p. w/o car, US$90 upwards per car; food on the ferry is not good, so take your own. Tickets from Flota Fluvial, Corrientes 375 or Onda.

Puente Fluvial runs hydrofoils (aliscafos) to Colonia six times a day (winter) or five times a day (summer), 4½ hrs. to Montevideo including Onda bus journey, US$24. All tickets from Onda, Florida 502, T 392-5011; reconfirm seat at Onda in Montevideo, Plaza Cagancha. Beware of overcharging by taxis from the harbour to the centre of Buenos Aires. Buquebus offers services similar to those of Onda, has built a new ferry station at Dársena Sud; taxi from Dársena Sud to Ezeiza airport, US$15.40

Several airlines fly from Jorge Newbery Airport (Aeroparque) to Colonia 15 mins; US$22 one way. Tickets at Onda, or Aero Uruguay, Reconquista 885. Continue by bus to Montevideo, or from Jorge Newbery, air service to Montevideo: shuttle 10 daily, 0730 to 2200, known as Puente Aéreo and run by AA and Pluna. Book at Jorge Newbery Airport or T 361-5008. Fare US$41; flight takes 35 mins. Punta del Este, daily with AA and Pluna US$66, 40 mins.

Suburbs of Buenos Aires

Avellaneda, a separate municipality of over 650,000 people, is one of the most important industrial centres in the country; the handling of hides, wool and animal produce is concentrated here. It is 5 km. from Plaza Constitución station, on the other side of the Riachuelo river from Boca.

Olivos, on the River Plate coast, 20 minutes by the Bartolomé Mitre Railway, is a favourite residential district. The presidential residence is there, many foreign residents. Population, about 160,000. (A rec. restaurant here is Grinzing, Córdoba 2864, European specialities, about US$20 p.p. inc. wines, historical objects in house, garden with swimming pool.) Nearby, at La Lucila, there are many American families.

San Isidro, just beyond Olivos, a resort for golf, yachting, swimming, and athletics, is one of the most attractive suburbs on the coast. There is a magnificent turf racecourse, an attractive central plaza and fine colonial buildings. Pop: 80,000.

Martínez, nearby is an attractive residential area overlooking the River Plate, with an interesting shopping area. Sailing and windsurfing are well represented and river launches and other craft may be hired.

Quilmes (Bs.As.), with one of the world's largest breweries, an important industrial centre, was given that name because the Quilmes Indians were forcibly moved there in 1665 from the famous Inca site in Tucumán Province (see page 91). Population about 150,000. St

George's College, an English boarding school, is here. Bathing is now both dangerous and prohibited; in one day 19 lives were lost. It is served by the Roca Railway and buses.

The naturalist and writer W H Hudson (1841-1922) was born at Florencio Varela, near Quilmes, about 32 km. from Buenos Aires. His birthplace is now a national monument.

Tigre, on the delta of the Paraná, is about 29 km. (50 minutes) by train from Buenos Aires. Take the train from platform 1 or 2 at Retiro station (FC Mitre) to the end of the line, US$0.70. It can also be reached by bus 60 bajo, which takes a little longer; the 60 alto bus takes a faster road but is less interesting for sightseeing. Regattas are held in November and March on the River Luján. There are numerous "recreos" and restaurants on the river front, but sleeping accommodation is not good. There is an excellent fruit market on Sundays; craft market is tacky. Inland from Tigre are innumerable canals and rivulets, holiday homes, clubs, a profitable fruit growing centre and an attraction for holiday makers. The fishing is excellent and there is peace on the waterways, apart from motor-boats at week-ends. Regular launch services, each company with its own routes, for all parts of the Delta, including taxi launches—watch prices for these!—leave from wharf opposite railway station. The wharf where these are moored can be quite smelly. Be warned that if you leave just before lunch the launch crew may stop along the way for a 1-1½ hr. lunch break! A journey through the Delta, with its lush tropical vegetation (even in winter) is fascinating. The best option is a 2-hr. ride by catamaran; they dock on the other side of the bridge from the railway station and leave at 1330 and 1600 Mon.-Fri., and hourly from 1300 on Sat. and Sun. the excursion lasts 1½ hrs.; longer trips (4½ hrs.) to the open River Plate estuary are available. Snacks and refreshments on board. Do not confuse the tourist catamarans with the *lanchas* which run regular passenger services between islands. Population: 40,000. In delta is *El Tropezón*, an old inn on Paraná de las Palmas island (the boat crews know it; Lucy Krause writes that the inn is a "decaying old world hotel of great charm, run by 3 old ladies. Tranquil garden, haunt of Hemingway and a suicidal Argentine writer, good food and extremely cheap (F p.p.). A wonderful experience". Delta **Youth Hostel** at Río Luján y Abra Vieja, Canal de San Fernando (take bus 60 from train station, US$0.15) US$0.90 clean, hot showers; ask at Talcahuano 214, Buenos Aires. Good restaurant near Youth Hostel, around the corner. Direct ferry to Carmelo, Uruguay (**see page 67**) from opposite railway station. (If you miss the boat, Antonio J Pissini has guest rooms for US$5 a night at Montes de Oca 142, Tigre, or try *Hotel Astor*.)

The Naval Museum is worth a visit. It contains models old and new, navigation instruments, flags and banners, and paintings of naval battles. There are also relics of the 1982 South Atlantic war on display outside. The Reconquista Museum celebrates the reconquest of Buenos Aires from the British in 1806-07.

Excursion to **Martín García** island (Juan Díaz de Solís' landfall in 1516) in the River Plate, 45 km. from Buenos Aires, with La Valette Turismo, through channels in The Delta (approx 12 hours there and back with day on the island; T 921-2050/2055).

Other Towns in the Pampas

There is one town which belongs to Argentina as a whole rather than to any province or area, though it is actually in the Province of Buenos Aires and only 71 km. W of the capital by Sarmiento railway from Once station (change at Moreno, 2 hours, US$2.30) or by bus from Once station, 1 hr. This is

Luján, a place of pilgrimage for all devout Catholics in Argentina. An image of the Virgin was being taken from church to church in the area in 1630 by ox cart. At a certain spot the cart got stuck, in spite of strenuous efforts by men and oxen to move it. This was taken as a sign that the Virgin willed she should stay there. A chapel was built for the image, and around it grew Luján. The chapel has long since been superseded by an impressive neo-Gothic basilica and the Virgin now stands on the High Altar. May 8 is her day. Each arch of the church is dedicated to an Argentine province, and two of the transepts to Uruguay and Paraguay. Population: 30,000. Very heavy traffic at weekends.

Museo Colonial e Histórico (The Colonial and Historical Museum) is in the old Cabildo building. Exhibits illustrate the historical and political development of the country. One of the most interesting museums. Open daily, except Monday and Tuesday, 1200-1800. No cameras allowed, and nowhere to store them, stroppy caretaker. General Beresford, the leader of an attempt to capture Buenos Aires, was a prisoner here, and so, in later days, were Generals Mitre, Paz, and Belgrano. There are also museums devoted to transport and to religious ex-votos. The River Luján is picturesque at this point, a favourite spot for picnic parties.

Hotels *España, La Paz*. There are numerous **restaurants**: an excellent one is *L'Eau Vive* on the road to Buenos Aires at Constitución 2112; it is run by nuns, pleasant surroundings.

There are dozens of small, prosperous towns scattered throughout the vast area of the pampas. They serve as clearing centres for the cattle and grain and supply the rural population, which is much denser in the Humid Pampa than elsewhere in Argentina. Only the larger towns and resorts are dealt with here.

La Plata, capital of Buenos Aires Province, on the River Plate and only 56 km. SE of Buenos Aires, is reached by Roca railway and by many buses. This modern city, founded in 1882, has a population of about 454,000. Its port is accessible to ships of the largest tonnage. Its major industrial interest is the YPF petroleum refinery; a 72-km. pipeline runs to the South Dock at Buenos Aires. Its Museum of Natural History is one of the best in Argentina and has several unique exhibits (open 1300-1800). A motorway is being built to link La Plata with Buenos Aires, via Riachuelo, Avellaneda, Berazátegui, Gonnet and Tolosa (expected to be finished in 1990).

Points of Interest The Museum at La Plata, famous for its collection of extinct animals, is open daily except in January and on public holidays (admission US$0.30, but free on Mon., highly rec.). Its treasures are largely ethnological and include human skulls, mummies, and prehistoric implements. There are zoological, botanical, geological, mineralogical, palaeontological and archaeological sections, guided tours in Spanish. Well laid-out Zoological Gardens; fine racecourse and Observatory. The Museum, Zoological Gardens, and Observatory are all in the public park; park entrance at Calle 1 y 53. The city has a Garden of Peace behind the Museum, each country in the world represented by one flower, with a plaque in front of it; on October 12 flags are put up there. The Town Hall and Cathedral (an unfinished but magnificent copy of Cologne's Gothic cathedral) are in the Plaza Moreno. Ten minutes in the train takes one to the Islas de Río Santiago and to the Yacht Club, Arsenal, and Naval Academy. Nearby is an interesting children's village with scaled-down public buildings, built under the first Perón administration; take a green microbus 273 or a red and black 518 to República de los Niños, going N along Av 7 from Plaza San Martín. There is a small, interesting nature reserve at Punta Lora, a short bus ride from town, slide show and tour, open to public Sat.-Sun., 1000-1300 and 1400-1800.

Local Holiday Foundation of the City, 19 November.

Hotels *Corregidor*, new, expensive; *Roga*, Calle 54 No 334, E, close to museum, visiting scientists stay here. *Plaza*, Calle 44 y 2, E with bath; *Roca*, Calle 1 y 42, F with bath.

Restaurant *El Fogón*, Av 1, Calle 49; *Ianno*, rec., Calle 46 y 10. Restaurants rarely open before 2100. *Don Quixote*, Plaza Passo, good value, best in town, can get very crowded; Chinese "tenedor libre" at *Guinga*, also on Plaza Passo; *La Linterne*, Calle 60 Av 1, upmarket but good value; *El Chaparral*, good parrillada, Calle 60 in the Bosque. Several reasonable restaurants around the bus station (which is in the red light area, though quite safe even at night). Recommended bar, with steak sandwiches, *El Modelo*, Calle 52 and 4. Best empanadas at *La Madrileña*, a hole-in-the-wall on Calle 60 between 5 and 6. Best bakery is *El Globo*, Calle 43 y 5.

Entertainments Tango and tropical music at *El Viejo Almacén*, on Diagonal 74, Calle 2. there are free concerts during the summer in the Bosque amphitheatre.

Tourist Office In the old white theatre on the main plaza, also at bus terminal. Turismo San Martín, Calle 51 between 7 and 8, rec.

Buses To Buenos Aires, 1½ hrs. Fare US$0.85, about every quarter hour, Río de la Plata company (from Retiro in Buenos Aires day and night; also from Plaza Constitución, daytime, more convenient).

On the coast 400 km. S of Buenos Aires, lies Mar. del Plata, the most celebrated Argentine seaside resort. The road and rail routes S to it are through Chascomús and Dolores.

Chascomús, 126 km. from Buenos Aires, is on a wide plain on the shores of Lake Chascomús, which covers 3,000 hectares and swells greatly in size during the rains. Its slightly brackish water is an important breeding place for *pejerrey* fish; up to 1,000 kg have been caught in one day during the winter season, when amateur fishing competitions are held. There is a *gaucho* museum, and also a Regatta Club and bathing beaches and camping grounds at Monte Brown, on the far side of the lake. Chascomús is the birthplace of President Alfonsín.

Hotels *Del Lago; Riviera; Americano; Santa María.*

Camping Sites *Estancia El Carmen* (US$2.10 p.p.) and *Casa Amarilla.*

Dolores, 204 km. (3½ hrs. by bus) from Buenos Aires, has a district population of 30,000; it was founded in 1818, destroyed by Indians three years later, and rebuilt. It is a grain and cattle farming centre which is said hardly to have changed in 50 years. The Museo y Parque Libres del Sur, commemorating the revolt of the district against Rosas in the early 19C., is interesting and well displayed.

Hotel *Plaza*, very pleasant.

About 130 km. N of Mar. del Plata a charming new seaside resort, **Villa Gesell**, (population 9,700) has sprung up, very popular with young people and families. The town offers dunes, pine forests and sandy beaches (less crowded than Mar. del Plata). The only paved road in town is Avenida3 (third street parallel to seafront); all the cross streets are sand-covered, leading to the sea, so you can walk barefoot almost everywhere. Direct bus service to Buenos Aires by Empresas Antón and Río de la Plata.

Hotels *Terrazas Club*, 4 star, suite accommodation, Av 2 between Calles 104 and 105, T 6 2181; *Colón*, 2 star, 3 blocks from beach at Av 4, Calle 104, T 62310, private bath, restaurant; *Hostería Gran Chalet*, Paseo 105 No 447 y Av 4-5, D, clean, rec. Many others of all classes within 800 metres of sea.

Youth Hostel *Albergue Camping El Coyote*, Calle 212 y 306, Barrio Norte.

Camping Sites *Del Sol, El Faro, California.* The first is open all year round.

Air Aerolíneas Argentinas flies to Villa Gesell several times daily in summer.

Pinamar, 22 km. N of Villa Gesell, is a rapidly growing resort, with a casino (population 2,850). It is now very much the "in" place, with good water-skiing. Fish, including conger eel (*congrio*) may be bought on the beach from local fishermen. Tourist office, friendly and honest, is in the main square.

Hotels Many, from **Arenas**, Av Bunge 700, T 322 7877, 4 star, to **Berlín**, Rivadavia 326, T 82320, 1 star. All hotels fully booked throughout Jan.- March (as much as two years in advance!). **Youth Hostel**, Nuestras Malvinas y Sarmiento, and **Moby Dick** campsite at Ostende. Many other campsites close to town.

Mar. del Plata is 400 km. from the capital. The normal population is 407,000, but during the summer about two million visitors stay there; there are all classes of apartment blocks, boarding houses and lodgings. It is necessary to book in advance between late December and mid- March (when the night-life continues all night). For the rest of the year the town is fairly quiet. The city is famous for its casino: the upper floor is open to the public, for a small admission charge. Small but pleasant natural history museum in Plaza España off Playa la Perla. Interesting municipal art museum at Villa Ortiz Basualdo, Av Colón 1189.

There are fine squares, especially Plaza San Martín, and eight km. of beaches, including fashionable Playa Grande, with its private clubs and the summer estates of wealthy *porteños*; Bristol Beach, where the casino is; and Playa la Perla, with moderately priced hotels. At Punta Iglesia there is a large rock carving of Florentino Ameghino, the palaeontologist who collected most of the fossils in the museum at La Plata. The wooded municipally owned Parque Camet is 8 km. to the N. It has polo grounds and playing fields. For those who do not care for surf bathing, there are salt-water pools. Fishing is good all along the coast and *pejerrey, corvina* and *merluza* (hake) abound; it is possible to charter a private launch for shark fishing. Football fans might enjoy seeing San Lorenzo play at their stadium—a very good atmosphere.

The port can be reached by bus, 15 mins from bus terminal. There are a large fishing fleet, excursion boats, seafood restaurants.

Visits can be paid to the rocky promontory of Cabo Corrientes to watch the breakers; to Punta Mogotes lighthouse (open Thursdays 1330-1700); to the Gruta de Lourdes, and the Bosque Peralta Ramos.

Local Holidays 10 Feb. (Foundation of City); 10 Nov. (Day of Tradition); 22 Nov. (St Cecilia). Mar. del Plata is known for its hand-finished sweaters.

Hotels Four-star (category A) are the *Provincial*, 500 rooms, Boulevard Marítimo 2300, T 24081/9; the *Dos Reyes*, Av Colón 2129; the *Hermitage*, Blvd Peralta Ramos 2657, 150 rooms; and the *Sasso*, M de Hoz 3545. Among the 3-star hotels (category B) are the *Astor*, Entre Ríos 1649; *Benedetti*, Av Colón 2198, rec., T 30031/2; *Gran Continental*, Córdoba 1929; *Presidente*, Corrientes 1516; and *Gran Dora*, Buenos Aires 1841. 2-star hotels (category C) include the *Flamingo*, Moreno 2155, has seen better days, but comfortable; *Finisterre*, Garay 1786, without breakfast, clean, comfortable (near the bus station). There are scores of good hotels at reasonable rates e.g. *Boedo*, Almirante Brown 1771 (T 24695), D, with bath, hot water, clean, good value, near beaches (open Jan.-Feb. only); *Europa*, Arenales 2735, 2 blocks from bus station, E p.p. (low season), clean, quiet, hot water; *Residencial San Mateo*, Arenales nr. Alberdi, E with bath, friendly; *Peley*, on Alberdi near bus station, E, clean, comfortable, open all year, rec.; *Hospedaje Paraná*, Lamadrid 2749, near bus terminal, E, with bath; *Niza*, Santiago del Estero 1843, E (F out of season), bath, clean, safe, friendly, restaurant; *Little Hotel*, Lamadrid 2461, near bus station, nice and cheap; *Monterrey*, Lamadrid 2627, F, clean, good; *Don Quijote*, Sarmiento 2478 near bus station, F, quite clean; *Hospedaje Alfa*, Garay 1731, close to bus station, cramped but very friendly. During summer months it is essential to book in advance. In the off-season, bargain everywhere. *Youth Hostel*, Tucumán 2728. Many hotels and restaurants close when the summer is over; worth looking round the bus-station area out of season.

There are many houses and apartments for rent, built for, but not yet filled by, retirees.

Camping *Pinar de la Serena* and other sites, reasonable prices. Several on the road S out of town; *Los Horneros* has been rec.

Restaurants *Taverna Vaska*, 12 de Octubre 3301, very popular seafood. *Sorrento*, Av H Yrigoyen 1549, Italian family style, excellent and reasonable. *Hostería del Caballito Blanco*, Av Rivadavia, excellent, German decor. *Cantina Capri*, Belgrano 2161 (near Casino), not cheap but excellent value; *Los Cercos*, Belgrano, between Entre Ríos and Corrientes, for meat; *La Paella*, Entre Ríos, between Bolívar and Moreno, good; *La Caracola*, Nuevo Complejo Comercial Puerto, seafood, good but dear; *Don Pepito*, opposite casino, big portions, reasonable prices, very popular, rec.; *Raviolandia*, Colón y Heras, good, cheap, try the seafood with rice; *La Tablita*, Av Rivadavia, excellent asado. *Montecatini*, Av Colón, good and cheap; *Comedor Naturista*, vegetarian, Av Salta 1571, cheap, highly rec. Also vegetarian: *El Jardín*, Plaza de San Martín, all you can eat for US$1.25 ("tenedor libre"), and *La Huerta*, close to pedestrian shopping street in centre. Many "tenedor libre" restaurants of all kinds along San Martín. *Los Inmortales*, Corrientes 1662, good, moderately priced. Tea, coffee and spirits in port area at Cristóbal Colón.

Casino Open December to end-April, 1600-0330; 1600-0400 on Sats Winter opening, May-December, Mon.-Fri. 1500-0230; weekends 1500-0300. Entrance US$2.

Exchange Lloyds Bank (BLSA) Ltd, Av Luro 3201. Open 1000-1600. American Express, Av Colón 2605. Exchange houses on San Martín and surroundings. Jonestur, San Martín 2574, will collect on personal US bank cheques in 15 working days, at 2½% fee.

Sociedad de Cultura Inglesa, San Luís 2498.

Post Office on Santiago del Estero, Pedro Luro.

Tourist Office opp. Casino, near beach, free maps; also at bus terminal.

Trains (ten each day) leave Buenos Aires from Constitución, 10 minutes from the centre by any bus marked "Constitución". The best trains (a/c) take 5 hours (US$5 tourist, US$7 first, US$9 Pullman), 3 times a day each way; from Buenos Aires at 0800, 1530 and 2330, returning at 0825,1545 amd 2350. Book very early for Dec.-March trips. 25% reduction for persons under 20 years of age. In Buenos Aires tickets from Galerías Pacífico, Florida 753. Mar. del Plata station is at Av Luro 4700, about 13 blocks from centre.

Buses Bus station at corner of Alberti y Las Heras, convenient. Companies from Retiro terminal in Buenos Aires: El Cóndor (very luxurious, 3 seats a row, self service bar, US$14.20), Micromar, Costera Criolla. Chevallier US$9.50, 5½ hrs. Bus to Miramar from Mar. del Plata, US$2.80. El Cóndor and Rápido Argentino to La Plata, day and night, US$9. La Estrella goes to San Martín de los Andes, US$26, and Bariloche US$32.50 (none direct; change at Bahía Blanca or Tres Arroyos). To Bahía Blanca, only Pampa, 6 daily, US$17, 7½ hrs. To Puerto Madryn and Trelew, Wed. and Sat. night. For hitch-hiking S, take a colectivo to the monument to El Gaucho.

Air Services Camet airport, 10 km. from town. Many flights daily to and from Buenos Aires with Austral and Aerolíneas Argentinas. *Remise* taxi from airport to town, US$6.

Outside the city the country is undulating. To the N (34 km.) is a lagoon—the Mar. Chiquita—joined to the sea by a narrow channel. There is good fishing, yachting, boating and bathing here. Picturesque spots reached from the road to Balcarce are (19 km.) Laguna de los Padres (a **reserva provincial**), and Sierra de los Padres and (32 km. beyond) the Laguna La Brava, at the foot of the Balcarce hills.

In these hills, 68 km. by paved road from Mar. del Plata, is the town of **Balcarce**, a centre for hill visits to La Brava, above Ruca-Lauquén, and the Cinco Cerros, five hills most strangely shaped. Balcarce is the birthplace of the great racing driver Juan Fangio; it has a racing circuit.

Hotel *Balcarce*, Mitre y Balcare, T 22055, good, D.

Beyond Balcarce a paved road runs 103 km. to Tandil. Tandil is reached by road from Buenos Aires (6 buses a day, US$8, 6hrs) via Azul.

Tandil, at the northern end of the Sierra del Tandil, a ridge of hills which run W from the sea into the pampa for 250 km., is 390 km. by road from Buenos Aires. It is a resort with fine views of *sierra* scenery. The air is splendidly clear and refreshing, and the Holy Week festivities are outstanding. Excursions to the Sierra La Aurora. Population: 125,000.

Hotels *Plaza*, General Pinto 438 T 27160, 3 star, E, very friendly, clean, comfortable and quiet. *Kaiku*, Mitre 902, F, basic; *Turista*, 14 de Julio 60, T22626, 1 star, F. Others near railway station.

By Air Lapa flight Buenos Aires-Tandil.

From Mar. del Plata, along the rocky sea-front to the SW, there are a road (53 km.) and railway line to Miramar.

Miramar (population 17,500), like Mar. del Plata, is a summer bathing resort, but the cliffs backing the beach are higher, the surrounding hills more picturesque, and it is a good deal cheaper to stay at. There is a fine golf course at *Hotel Golf Roca* and a casino. Fourteen km. by road or railway to the S, among dunes and black rocks, is Mar. del Sur (*Atlantic Hotel*) with good fishing in a lagoon and bathing on the beach.

Hotels Dozens of hotels and apartments. *Santa Eulalia*, Calle 26 No 851, D, friendly but run down. *Grand*, Calle 29 No 586 esq 12, T 20358, 3 star; *Palace*, Calle 23 No 774, T 20258, 3 star; *Villa Cruz,* friendly, clean, near the beach, D.

Camping *Escargot, El Fortín, Miramar*. Many sites, reasonably priced.

Restaurant *El Aguila*, good value; *El Pescador Romano*, good seafood take-away.

Exchange None for travellers' cheques; must go to Mar. del Plata. Money changers (cash) in front of Banco de la Provincia.

Railway *Cruz del Sur* daily train, via Mar. del Plata, leaves Buenos Aires (Constitución) daily at 2345, arrives Miramar 0550; leaves Miramar 2205, arrives Buenos Aires 0500. Fares are US$13.25 Pullman, US$7.60 first and US$6 tourist class. *El Atlántico* train, daily at 1520 from Buenos Aires to Mar. del Plata arriving at 2000, connects with a railcar service (*automotor*) to Miramar (US$5 extra), arriving 2140.

Bus Buenos Aires-Miramar with Cóndor, five daily, and Costera Criolla, four a day.

About 110 km. further by road along the coast to the SW is another famous seaside resort:

Necochea, 500 km. from Buenos Aires, is reached by Roca Railway in 10½ hours. It stands next to Mar. del Plata in repute. The surroundings are picturesque. Visits can be paid to the Paseo del Puente, Punta Negra, the Cascada (or waterfalls) 16 km. up the Río Quequén Grande, Los Manantiales, and the Laguna de los Padres. Grain is exported from the port. Urban population: 52,000 including large Danish colony: there are a Danish club and consulate. About 100,000 tourists visit during the season, for the 24-km. long beach is one of the best in the country. There is a municipal recreation complex, boasting a large modern casino, various sports facilities, including skating rink, swimming pool, bowling, a cinema and children's play area. The Parque Miguel Lillo (named after the Argentine botanist) faces the beach, comprising 400 hectares of conifers, nature park, swan lake with paddle boats, an amphitheatre, museum and go-cart track. The casino is open in summer. Airport.

Hotels The Hotel Association is at Av 79 with Calle 4. Most hotels are in the downtown area from Calle 2 (parallel with beach) northwards between Av 71-91; there are at least a hundred within 700 metres of the beach. **Camping** Beach sites reported expensive in summer.

Restaurants *Parrilla La Rueda*, excellent beef, cheap, rec.; *La Vieja Taberna*, Calle 85, reasonable, good chicken and beef dishes; *Caviar*, by fishing wharf, good steak, chicken, seafood. *Mi Cantina*, excellent family restaurant. *Parrilla El Palenque*, Av 79 y 6; *Pizzería Kapotte*, Av 79 next beach, both rec.

Tourist Office At the bus terminal by the river at corner of Av 47 and Calle 582; also on beach front at Av 79.

Railway Train No 117 (Mon.-Wed.-Fri.) leaves Buenos Aires (Constitución) at 1930, arrives Necochea 0645; leaves Necochea at 0025 Sun.-Wed.-Fri. arriving at 1150 at Buenos Aires. Fares are US$10 Pullman, US$6 first, US$4.80 tourist class.

Bus El Cóndor from Buenos Aires six times a day, Costera Criolla 5 times a day.

About 3½ km. across the mouth of the river from Necochea is **Quequén**, with an excellent beach, good bathing, and pleasant scenery. The channel to the port has to be dredged daily.

Hotels *Quequén; Faro; Costa Azul.*

Camping *Monte Pasuvio* and *Doble J* (rec.) sites.

Over 320 km. westwards from Necochea by paved road through the coastal area is the port of Bahía Blanca, which can be reached by rail (900 km.), by air, or by a 688-km. paved road (Route 3) through Las Flores (pop 20,200), Azul, Juárez and Tres Arroyos.

Azul, 264 km. from Buenos Aires, is a cattle centre with an attractive plaza. Population: about 45,000. A good stopping place if driving S from Buenos Aires. The river has been dammed to provide a water-sports centre.

Hotels *Gran Hotel Azul*, C, excellent cafeteria; *Argentino; Roma; Torino.*

Restaurant *Mitre*, Av Mitre, *Londres*.

Tres Arroyos, about 195 km. from Bahía Blanca, is a cattle and wheat growing centre of 70,000 people. Many inhabitants are of Dutch origin; there are a Dutch consulate and a primary school named Holanda, supported by funds of the Argentine Dutch. There is also an important Danish colony, with school, club and consulate. A 68-km. paved road runs S to the sea at the pleasant little resort of **Claromecó**, with a beautiful beach of dark sand backed by high dunes.

Hotels at Tres Arroyos *Alfil, Parque*, rec. (restaurant) and *Andrea* are best. *City, París, Plaza* and *Tres Arroyos* (friendly), all modest. **Restaurant** *Di Troppo*, near *Hotel Parque*, good.

Hotels at Claromecó *Claromecó* (only open in summer; restaurant); *Residencial La Perla*;

Comercio, D, good restaurant, pleasant atmosphere; *Pablo Satini's Bar*, on main street, 5 mins from beach, F off season, OK, safe deposit.

Camping at Claromecó Good campsite *Dunamar*, hot showers, fire pits and laundering basins, US$1 a day; also ACA campsite.

Bus Buenos Aires-Claromecó with El Cóndor, US$20. Tres Arroyos-Claromecó twice daily off season, extra buses from mid-December in season. Pampa bus to Mar. del Plata 0650, 4½ hrs., US$5.50. Modern, efficient bus terminal a few blocks from centre of Tres Arroyos.

Bahía Blanca, population 300,000, the most important centre S of Mar. del Plata, stands at the head of a large bay where the river Naposta runs into it. The region has over a million people. Bahía Blanca consists of the city itself, built back from the river front, and five ports at various distances from the city strung along the N bank of the Naposta: Arroya Pareja and the naval base of Puerto Belgrano at the mouth of the estuary; Puerto Ingeniero White, 23 km. inland, Puerto Galván, 3½ km. beyond, and Cuatreros, 8 km. upstream. Bahía Blanca is also a rail, air and pipeline transport terminal for the rich Río Negro valley.

The city has some fine modern buildings and two parks. In the Parque de Mayo are lakes fed by the River Naposta and interesting statuary. There is a very poor Zoological Garden in Parque Independencia, on the outskirts.

To the E of Bahía Blanca is an enormous stretch of sandy beaches, scarcely developed for visitors (in the afternoon, however, it is usually windy). Pehuén-Có, 70 km. away, is an example of the beaches with camping places, well shaded by pine trees. Signs to it on the main road 24 km. from Bahía Blanca. Another fine beach, with hotels and camping places (*El Americano* and *Monte Mar.*), is **Monte Hermoso**, 2 hours by bus at 0830 and 1830, US$2.50 (106 km.) from Bahía Blanca. Return daily at 0900 and 2100. Good cheap meals, several restaurants. (Its hotels are open only Jan.-March: *Isabel, Americano, Ameghino*, E, *América*).

Local Holidays Sept. 24 (Our Lady of Mercy); Nov. 10 (Day of Tradition).

Hotels *Austral*, C, and **Del Sur**, C, with restaurants (not good in the former), noisy with traffic; *City Hotel*, Chiclana 132, D. *Atlántico*, Chiclana 251, E; *Argentino* (restaurant), Chiclana 466, E. Opposite railway station: *Residencial Roma*, D with private bath, cheaper without. Cheap: *Hogar*, Rodríguez 64, F, clean, good, near Plaza; *Tizón*, Chiclana 422, E. *Victoria*, Gral. Paz 82, F, nice rooms, hot water; *Hospedaje Brandsen*, Brandsen 276, F with private bath, friendly, near railway station.

Camping Balneario Maldonado, 2 km. from centre, next to petrochemical plant, bus 514 along Av. Colón every ½ hr. but only when beach is open, i.e. when sunny and not in evening, US$0.30 p.p.; salt water swimming pool, US$0.80. Many others.

Restaurants *La Cigala*, opp railway station, very good; *Il Vesuvio*, Chiclana 231, cheap and good. *Gambrines*, Arribeños 174, central. Very good seafood and fish at Ingeniero White, e.g. *Michos* and *El Greco*; buses go there.

Shopping Good gaucho shop on Soler, nr. Fortur, genuine articles.

Motoring 2 VW franchises in centre, good.

Exchange Lloyds Bank (BLSA), Calle Chiclana 102. Citibank. Open 0800-1400 on Nov. 15-March 31, 1000-1600 on April 1-Nov. 14. AmEx, Fortur, Soler 38, *poste restante*, English spoken. **Casa de Cambio** Pullman, Av San Martín close to main plaza, will change US$ cheques into US$ notes; good rates (closes 1600).

Tourist Office In town hall, friendly and helpful, good map.

Airport Comandante Espora, 15 km. from centre. Austral and Aerolíneas Argentinas flights to Buenos Aires daily. To Comodoro Rivadavia, Sun. at 0800 arrive 1005. To Neuquén daily at 1900, arrive at 1955. Flights to Río Gallegos and Trelew on Sun., at 0800 arrive at 1135 and 0905, respectively.

Trains Two trains daily from Buenos Aires, fairly comfortable, go via Olavarría from Constitución; *Estrella del Valle* daily at 1000, arrive at 2115, with dining car, return 0910 daily, arrive 2050; and at 0910 daily, arriving 0840, returning at same time, arriving Buenos Aires 0825. Five other trains on different days of the week. Sleeper US$27; Pullman US$20; 1st class US$12.40, tourist US$9. Daily train to Bariloche, 19 hrs., sleeper US$24, pullman

US$19.25, first class US$13.60, tourist, US$9.60. To Zapala at 2150 (arrive 1000), same classes as Bariloche. Can be cold. There is no other link between the Bahía Blanca-Bariloche line and the more northerly Bahía Blanca-Zapala line.

Roads Well built paved highway (Route 3) S to Comodoro Rivadavia; major paved route W to Neuquén and the Lake District. Several routes go North.

Buses Terminal is 2½ km. from centre in old railway station; no hotels nearby. To Trelew, 3 per week, US$20, 734 km. Río Gallegos with Don Otto US$60; Mar. del Plata bus, US$17 with Pampa, 7-8 hrs., 469 km. Bus Río Colorado US$5.20. Bus to Buenos Aires frequent US$17. To Neuquén, 6 a day, 9hrs, US$15.50, 580 km., one company only. To Zapala daily at 0630 and 1030. To Viedma daily at 0740, 1230, 1800, 4 hrs.

Hitch-hiking S or W from Bahía Blanca is possible but not too easy. N to Buenos Aires, take bus 10 to outskirts, or bus 510 from centre to Ruta 51 (10 km.).

Some 100 km. to the N is the Sierra de la Ventana, a favourite and recommended area for excursions from Bahía Blanca, and a **reserva provincial**, protecting the range's flora and fauna. The small town of Tornquist, with an attractive church on the central plaza (post and phone office open 0800-1800), is a good starting point. Leave Route 33 on Route 76 to the town of Sierra de la Ventura. After 32 km. is the entrance to the Parque Provincial, with massive ornate gates from the Tornquist family home. From here it's a 3-hr. walk to the summit of Cerro La Ventana, which has fantastic views from the "window" in the summit ridge (camping at the base, free, basic facilities, canteen). 5 km. further is the forestry station, with audio-visual display, trips to see wild deer, wild horses, guanacos, and on Fri. and Sun. trips at 0900 to 2 caves, one an Indian cemetery, the other with petroglyphs (US$0.70). Villa Ventana, 10 km. further, is a wooden settlement with excellent teashop, Casa de Heidi, and wholefood available from Jardín de Aylem. Municipal campsite by river with all facilities, US$1.50 p.p. **Sierra de la Ventana**, further east, is a good centre for exploring the hills, with hotels (Golf, near station, is OK) and the excellent Don Diego campsite (hot water, open all year round); also 2 more campsites. Excellent tourist information in town. Tres Picos, rising bare and barren from the rich farmlands to 1,070 metres, is only 6¼ km. away. There is a 9-hole golf course, and good trout fishing in the Río Sauce Grande. Train Bahía Blanca-Sierra de la Ventana 3 hrs., US$0.80; all points can be easily rached by bus from Bahía Blanca or Tornquist.

193 km. N of Bahía Blanca by road/rail through Saavedra is **Carhué**, served by three railways, one of which, via Bolívar, runs to Buenos Aires (603 km.). Five km. away is a sheet of water, Lake Epecuén, which covers over 40,000 hectares and is over twenty times saltier than the sea. No fish can live in it. These waters are recommended for chronic rheumatism and skin diseases. There are many hotels and residenciales at the lake side and the area is fast being developed as a tourist resort. A health spa is planned. There is a museum of the wars against the Indians behind the town hall. Visit the ruins of Villa Epequén, drowned by the lake in 1985. Carhué suffered severe flood damage in late 1989. Pop.: 18,000. Tourist information at bus station.

Hotels at Lake Epecuén With restaurant: Gran Parque Patera, Plage, Elkie, Victoria, Rambla, Cuatro Hermanos, Villa Marta, Italia, Española, Las Familias, Gran Rose. Also: El Lago, Castello.

Hotels at Carhué With restaurant: Buenos Aires, Marconi. Without: Volpe, Bristol.

Camping Free camping in the beach area, no facilities. Rotary Club campsite, 2 km. from Carhué, US$1 p.p.

About 38 km. by road NE of Carhué, on the Roca Railway, is **Guaminí**, a pleasant summer hill resort of 3,500 inhabitants on the shore of Laguna del Monte, not as salty as Lake Epecuén; pejerrey fishing is one of the attractions. (Hotels: La Aragonesa, Roma; Camping Municipal on lake.) From Guarminí take routes 65 and 205 back to Buenos Aires, via Lobos (excellent ACA campsite at lake 10 km.

S of Lobos).

Santa Rosa (Population 55,000, hotel: *Calfacura*, Av San Martín 695, T 23612, 4-star, no restaurant, C without breakfast, but excellent steak restaurant around the corner; *Motel Calden*, Route 35, km. 330, D, good restaurant attached, large rooms, a bit run down), capital of the Province of La Pampa, is 332 km. NW of Bahía Blanca by road, and can be reached (619 km.) by Route 5, via Chivilcoy (pop 47,500) and Pehuajó (pop 26,800), from Buenos Aires.

THE CORDOBA REGION (2)

The pattern of the land in Northern Argentina, from the crest of the Andes in the W to the river Paraguay in the E, consists of a high, dry Altiplano rising to a Puna cut into on its eastern face by rivers which flow into the Lowlands. This configuration of the land, similar to Bolivia, is carried southwards into all the north-western provinces of Argentina as far S as Tucumán, but the altitudes in Argentina are not so great as in Bolivia, and the whole area not so large. The E-running rivers born on the Puna flow into the Chaco; their broad valleys, or *quebradas*, make access to the heights comparatively easy. Between the base of the Puna and the Chaco lie a series of front range hogback hills running roughly from N to S; the lowlands between them are known in Argentina as the *valles*. Tucumán is the southern boundary of this kind of land. N of Tucumán crops can be grown without irrigation (though there is irrigation where the soil is absorbent) but S of Tucumán is droughty land, with long N-S ranges of low hills such as the Sierras de Córdoba, set in plains which have salt flats and swamps in the depressions.

Settlement and Economy The Puna is windswept, stony and treeless: the only growth is a low, blackish shrub (*tola*), and an occasional cactus. The first Spanish expedition from Bolivia came down the main Inca road (long since disappeared in Argentina) in 1542. A little later a better and lower route was discovered—the main route used today—descending from La Quiaca to Jujuy through the Quebrada de Humahuaca, with rugged and colourful mountain ranges closing in on both sides. Along this new route the Spaniards pressed S and founded a group of towns in the north-west: Santiago del Estero (the first) in 1551, Tucumán in 1565, Córdoba in 1573, Salta in 1582, La Rioja in 1591, and Jujuy in 1592. Mendoza (1561), San Juan (1562), and San Luis (1598) were all colonized by people who crossed the passes from Chile. All these colonies were hemmed in by the warlike tribes of the Pampas, and until the war of extermination in 1880 the route from Buenos Aires to Córdoba was often unsafe. The Indians raided frequently for cattle, which they drove S and over the Andes for sale in Chile.

During the whole of the colonial era the trade of the area, mostly in mules, was with Bolivia and Peru rather than with Buenos Aires, which was little more than a garrison and smuggling port. The mules were bred mainly in the plains between Rosario, Santa Fe, and Córdoba, and driven finally into Salta for the great fair in February and March.

Historically, Tucumán was always important, for the two river routes of the Salado and the Dulce across the dry belt forced the mule traffic to pass through Tucumán on the way to Salta. Tucumán still produces most of Argentina's sugar. Tobacco is becoming important in the area, and an important factor in the North West is the growth of tourism.

In nearly all the provincial towns everything shuts between 1200 and 1600 except restaurants, hotels and post offices. There is nothing to do or see, and we suggest that this is a good time for travelling; buses are generally preferable to trains, being faster (except to Córdoba). (Panamericano buses have been recommended in the NW as new, clean and with a good service.)

NORTH-WEST ARGENTINA

From Buenos Aires to Córdoba

If hitch-hiking, take the train from Retiro (San Martín line) to Pilar to reach the main Córdoba highway via Rosario. There are two main road routes: the shorter (713 km.) via Rosario and the longer (835 km.) via Río Cuarto. The latter goes through **San Antonio de Areco**—also on the Mitre Railway—113 km. NW of Buenos Aires (also Chevallier bus, 2hrs, US$3, every hour). Here is the Museo Gauchesco Ricardo Güiraldes, on Camino Güiraldes and Aureliano, a typical *estancia* of the late 19th century with manor house, mill, tavern, open Wed.-Sun., 1000-1200, 1500-1800 in summer; in winter 1000-1200 and 1400-1700. Check if it is open in Jan.-Feb. Souvenir shop opposite. Güiraldes was a writer who described *gaucho* life; his best-known book is *Don Segundo Sombra*. Visitors can also see over Cina-Cina, a working *estancia*, tour for US$20 includes visit, typical lunch and riding display. Día de la Tradición is a *gaucho* festival with traditional parades, games, events on horseback, music and dance, celebrated on Nov. 10, 11 and 12 each year.

Camping near the centre of town; 12 km. from centre, Auto-camping *La Porteña* on the Güiraldes *estancia*, good access roads. Six hotels. Many handicrafts, mainly *gaucho* objects, ceramics, silver, leather, colonial furniture. The Argentine artist Gasparini has a museum-school where he sells his drawings of *gauchos* to tourists; Calle de los Martínez, between Bolívar and Rivadavia. There is also a local natural history museum, Parque Metri, on Matheu and Hernández. For tourist information go to the Sub-Dirección de Turismo at Alsina and Lavalle. T 2101. *Hotel San Carlos*, opp tourist office, E, clean and friendly, ask in advance for meals; *Residencial Areco*, Segundo Sombra y Rivadavia, T 2166, good, E, comfortable, clean. Opposite Museo Gauchesco is *Hostería del Palomar*, typical barbecue; *Restaurant La Porteña* on the riverside, typical, very good.

Beyond Pergamino, 146 km., is **Venado Tuerto**, a pleasant town of 58,000 people with a fine Country Club at which race meetings and tournaments are held twice a year (*Hotel Touring*, cool, quiet, rec., D). At **Río Cuarto**, 110,000 people, there is a golf club and a fine old municipal building with an outlook tower worth seeing.

Hotels *Gran*, on Plaza, D, 1st class; *City Hotel*, good, D. *Opera*, 25 de Mayo, C; *Victoria*, Buenos Aires 183, E, small beds; *Gran Hotel Mendoza*, Constitución 483; *Alihué*, Sarsfield 69, E, good value, very friendly, big rooms. Near bus station on Calle Sobremonte 100-200 block are 3 cheap *residenciales*, *El Ciervo*, *Hospedaje El Bambi*, *Residencial Monge*, all F.

Restaurants *Cantina Italiana Sorrento*, fair. Best exchange rate at Banco de la Nación; post office on plaza. *Pizzería Costa Azul*, Belgrano 67, sit in or out, pleasant.

Buses　Buenos Aires, US$12. Bus to Mendoza, US$24; to Córdoba US$7.75; frequent departures to Santiago US$35, daily.

Córdoba is 225 km. N of Río Cuarto across flatlands and rolling hills. About half-way along the road runs on the retaining wall of the great Río Tercero dam; the artificial lake here is used for recreation. Río Tercero has gained in importance with the development of groundnut plantations and a local military factory. *Hotel Argentino*, adequate, D, with a/c.

Villa María, on the Mitre Railway and at a vital crossroads on the main Buenos Aires-Córdoba road, where it meets the most convenient highway route linking central Chile with Paraguay, Uruguay and Brazil, is a prosperous agricultural town (population 68,000). Hotel: *City*, D. Restaurant: *La Churrasquita*.

Córdoba, capital of Córdoba Province and Argentina's second city, has about a million inhabitants; it stands at an altitude of 440 metres. The district is well known for its countryside and the city for its buildings; it was founded as early as 1573. Its university, founded in 1613, was the first in the country. The heart of the city is Plaza San Martín (the Liberator's statue is there). On the western side is the old Cabildo, now the police headquarters. Next to it stands the Cathedral, started in

1. Plaza San Martin
2. Plaza España
3. Plaza General Paz
4. Parque Sarmiento and Zoo
5. Cathedral
6. Santa Teresa
7. La Merced
8. La Compañia
9. Old Cabildo
10. Casa del Virrey/Historical and Colonial Museum
11. Natural History Museum
12. Museum of Minerology
13. Museum of Fine Arts
14. Theatre
15. Post Office
16. Tourist Office

NOT TO SCALE

CÓRDOBA

1697 and finished 1787. The neo-gothic church of the Sacred Heart (Sagrado Corazón), built in 1933, at Buenos Aires e Yrigoyen, is worth a visit. Córdoba was once a very picturesque place, but modernization is catching up fast. Pedestrianization schemes have recently improved the centre.

On Calle Independencia, leading S from the Plaza San Martín, is the church and convent of Santa Teresa, open Wed. and Thurs., 1000-1200 (beautiful doorway, 1770). An old colonial building, the Viceroy's House (Casa del Virrey), is on Calle Rosario, E of the central plaza; it houses the Historical and Colonial Museum, open Tues.-Fri. 0830-1300, 1530-1930, Sat.-Sun. 0900-1200. N of Plaza San Martín, on Calle Rivadavia, is the church of La Merced, whose old colonial pulpit is well worth seeing. The church of La Compañía, on Calles Trejo y Caseros, with a simple façade, dates from about 1650 and is a far better building than the Cathedral; its façade was rebuilt in the 20th century. The barrel vault and cupola of the Capilla Doméstica of this church, built entirely of Paraguayan cedar, are unique. There are some pleasant small 18th century churches with striking bell gables and undulating pediments. The C16 Carmelite convent at Independencia 122 has a religious art museum, some very interesting items, Spanish-speaking guide, open Wed., Sat., 1000-1200. La Merced, on Rivas, has fine modern tile murals, showing angels wearing blue jeans. Natural History Museum, Av Yrigoyen 115 (open Mon.-Fri. 0830-1230 and 1430-1830, Sat.-Sun. 0900-1200). There is a very interesting and well laid out Museum of Mineralogy, Av Vélez Sarsfield 299; ask permission to visit from Dra Hebe Gay at Universidad de Ciencias Exactas.

The Academy of Fine Arts, the theatre and the Olmos School are near the Plaza Vélez Sarsfield (there is a statue to this jurist, who gave Argentina its civil code). A diagonal, Avenida Yrigoyen, runs to the round Plaza España, where the Museum of Fine Arts (open Mon.-Fri., 0900-1300) is housed in a pillared building. E from this plaza is Parque Sarmiento, where there is a Zoological Garden with a serpentarium and a small waterfall. Argentina's main observatory is at Calle Laprida (open to public on Wed. 2000-2200). Around the corner at Calle San Luis 801 is the Museum of Meteorology. Córdoba is a good shopping city; leather goods are cheaper than in Buenos Aires. **NB:** Churches are open mornings and after 1600.

Local Holidays 6 July (Reconfoundation of the City); 30 September (St Jerome), 7-10 October.

Industries Córdoba is the centre of Argentina's motor industry.

Hotels Best are: *Crillón*, Rivadavia 85, A, very friendly, good restaurant, comfortable; *Ritz*, San Jerónimo 495, B, "clean but dilipidated"; *Mediterráneo*, Av M.T. de Alvear 10, B; *Cañada*, Av M.T. de Alvear 580, B, good, recently modernized to include conference facilities with full technical back-up, a/c, private bath, TV and video, restaurant, laundry, transport; *Sussex*, Buenos Aires 59, B, comfortable, roomy, discounts for ACA members; *Palace*, Buenos Aires 101, C; *Royal*, Blvd Reconquista 180, C; all these have garages. *Del Sol*, Balcarce 144, C with bath, clean, fan, a/c extra, piped music, close to stations, rec. More economical: *Rivera*, Balcarce 74, near bus station, D, friendly, clean. *Damar*, Illia, 2 blocks from bus station, D, pleasant, a/c.

In the cheaper brackets: On Corrientes, *Grand Hotel Bristol*, No 64, F, bathroom, a/c, telephone; *Hospedaje Suiza*, (No 569), near bus terminal, very friendly but not too clean, F; *Hospedaje My House*, near *Suiza* on Corrientes, clean, quiet, very friendly, rec.; *Residencial Mi Valle* (No. 586), small, clean and nice, family-run, washing facilities, F, rec.; *Pasajeros* (No. 564), F, pleasant; *Res Corrientes* (No. 540), F, good rooms. Plenty of hotels of all classes on San Jerónimo: *Sportsman* (No. 590), F, very good, near bus and railway station; *Corona* (500 block), E not inc. breakfast, clean, comfortable, friendly; *Dallas* (No. 339), E, rec.; *Soledad* (not very clean), San Jerónimo, friendly, cheap. On Balcarce: *Residencial Plaza* (No. 336), 150 metres from bus station, clean, friendly and quiet, E; *Mallorca*, on Balcarce, E, quite clean and near bus and railway station; *Hospedaje El Progreso*, also on Balcarce, F, not too clean but pleasant. Plenty of hotels of all classes on San Jerónimo, *Roma Termini* (ex-*Entre-Ríos*, close to bus terminal on Entre Ríos, E, recently renovated by Italian family, spotless, welcoming. *Florida*, E, clean, Rosario de Santa Fe 459, friendly, rec., some rooms with a/c, D. Across the pedestrian bridge from the top of the bus station into a residential precinct are many low cost hotels and restaurants, around the precinct park or 1/2 block into bordering streets. No cheap hotels near Alta Córdoba railway station.

Camping Nearest site in Alta Gracia. Local bus takes 40 mins.

Restaurants *Florida Grill*, opp *Hotel Crillón*, informal meals, good, moderate prices. Next to *Crillón* is *Jerónimo*, simple, pleasant; nearby is **Casino Español**, good. *El Recodo*, Rivadavia 0-100 block, very good and reasonable. There are also numerous grills of all categories on the outskirts of the city, especially in the Cerro de las Rosas district, for meals out-of-doors when the weather is suitable. Many cheap restaurants along San Jerónimo. Restaurant in **Hotel Familiar**, S. Jerónimo, near railway station, cheap and good, rec. **Restaurant Alborada**, nr. bus station, good meals; *Romagnolo*, opposite the Mitre railway station, rec., and *Comedor Albéniz*, opposite Alto Córdoba station, a bit noisy. *Rigoletto*, Entre Ríos 73, cheap meals, *La Cabaña*, Maipú 230, cheap and good. *Don Pipo*, Santa Rosa 212, good, cheap *parrilladas*; similar is *Don Siriacoo*, opposite the *Damar* hotel on Illia. Excellent fruit juices (*licuados*) at *Kiosco* Americano, Tucumán 185. Recommended for vegetarian food is *La Pepperoni*, San Martín 114; also *Granix*, 9 de Julio 479.

Rent-a-Car Avis and AI International at airport and in the centre. Entre Ríos 70. T 42-036/38 central depôt.

Casino Nearby, at Alta Gracia.

Exchange Lloyds Bank (BLSA), Buenos Aires 23. Citibank. Oct.-March, 0730- 1330; April-Sept., 0800-1400. American Express, 25 de Mayo 125. Exchange at banks and following travel agencies: Exprinter (changes travellers' cheques), Rivadavia 39, opposite is Maguitur, Rivadavia 30, good rates, Viacor, Avincor, Epoca and Barujel, San Martín 37. Also Cambio Coín, Rivadavia y 25 de Mayo, best rate for US$ cash. Many *cambios* on Rivadavia just off Plaza.

Post Office Parcel Service on the ground floor of the Correo Central, Av Colón 201, beside the customs office, up to 20 kg; wrapping service for small fee.

British Council Blvd San Juan 137, has a good library.

Goethe Institut, Chacabuco 476, open Mon.-Fri., 1700-2100.

Laundry Laundromat (self-service) at Tucumán 135; also Chacabuco 32, and Av Colón 300.

Tourist Office Dirección Provincial de Turismo, Tucumán 25. Information centres: Plaza San Martín on Obispo Mercadillo, Rosario de Santa Fe 39. Also at bus station, has free maps; will make hotel reservations for you on arrival. Tourist Office desk at airport often unmanned, but car-hire desks next to it are most helpful.

Club Andino, Duarte Quirós 1591.

Air Pajas Blancas airport, 15 km. from the city, is modern and has a good restaurant. Taxi to airport, US$10. Airport bus leaves terminal opposite railway station; irregular schedule, 30 mins, US$0.50. Several flights to Buenos Aires daily, about 1 hr.; to Mendoza daily at 1400 (55 mins); to Tucumán at 1235 daily exc Sun. arr 1335. To Iguazú, AA. Night flights: Buenos Aires to Córdoba Thurs. at 2230. Córdoba-Mar. del Plata Thurs. and Sat. at 2350, returns Tues. and Fri. at 2330. Aerolíneas Argentinas, Av Colón 520. Austral, Av Colón 678.

Buses Excellent new bus station with Tourist Office, many public telephones, shops, bank, post office, restaurants, and showers in bathrooms (about 6 blocks from centre), crowded at weekends. Buenos Aires-Córdoba (US$17.50 with Costera Criolla or with Cacorba) by bus takes about 10 hours, and on from Córdoba to Salta (US$15) and Jujuy (US$20) with Panamericano, about 12 and 15 hours. Chevallier, Buenos Aires to Córdoba via Route 8, four services, at 0600, 1600, 2015 and 2345; via Route 9 at 0745, 2100, 2200, and 2340. Many buses on both routes, 101/2 hrs., US$17. Bus to Mendoza (10 hours), 4 a day with TAC, frequent delays and breakdowns, 1 daily with Upsalla, US$13. Bus to Tucumán, US$13, about 8 a day, Panamericano has more than other companies (T 223569). To Posadas (Expreso Singer) Tues., Thurs., Sat., 1730 arrive at Posadas at 1335; Thurs. and Sat. bus continues to Iguazú arriving 1930 next day, no air-conditioning. Onda operates a service from Paraná via Santa Fe and Rosario to and from Córdoba. Bus Córdoba-Asunción (Paraguay) direct with Brújula, four times a week, also with Cacorba 19 hrs., US$25. Regular bus between Córdoba and Montevideo (Uruguay). In general, it is best to travel from Córdoba if you are going N, as at stations in between it may be hard to get a seat; a seat is only guaranteed if one pays US$1 extra. To Santiago del Estero, US$8. To La Rioja 3-4 a day with Cotil and El Cóndor; some go on to Catamarca. Córdoba-La Rioja-Aimogasta-Tinogasta-Fiambalá with El Cóndor,

Tues., Thurs., Fri.; leaves Tinogasta 1140 arr Fiambalá 1240, returns from Fiambalá same day 1445, from Tinogasta at 1600 (**see also page** 119). La Calera bus leaves for Belén (Catamarca) on Mon., Wed., Fri., at 2100, arr Belén 1030; return journey, also via Andalgalá, Wed., Fri., Sun., dep 1600 arr Andalgalá 1735, dep 1750, arr Córdoba 0055. Cacorba, efficient a/c buses, serve Villa Carlos Paz, Cosquín and La Falda in the Sierras de Córdoba.

Railways The Mitre Railway (next to bus station) *Rayo de Sol* night train takes 11 hours to and from Buenos Aires. Tourist class US$12.55, 1st class US$21, Pullman US$28.25, Sleeper US$36.65, car transporter daily. *Rayo de Sol* leaves Buenos Aires (Retiro) 2100 daily and Córdoba 2030 daily. The Belgrano Railway runs *El Norteño* train on Tues., and Fri., from Buenos Aires (Retiro) at 1000; from Córdoba, 0750, Wed., Sat. (12 hours), no sleepers. The Alta Córdoba railway station for long-distance journeys is a good 2 km. from the city centre. The No 71 and 73 buses will transport you from the Mitre railway station to the Belgrano station. Three trains per week to Tucumán, Wed., Fri. and Sun., 2200 (15 hours). It is advisable to check all trains as services are sometimes suspended without notice. The *Rayo de Sol* trains connect with bus services to various resorts in the Sierras de Córdoba, and the *Norteño* to La Rioja and Catamarca.

The *Sierras of Córdoba*, rising in undulating hills from the pampas, their lower slopes often wooded, particularly in the S, attract each year a large number of visitors. The highest peak, Champaquí (2,975 metres) has a small lake about 2,550 metres up. The hills run, roughly, for 500 km. from N to S; west of Córdoba they are 150 km. wide. There are three ranges of them: the Sierra Grande, the longest, in the middle, with Sierra Chica to the E and Sierra de Guisapampa and its continuation, the Sierra de Pocho, to the W A network of good roads gives pleasant contrasts of scenery, but there are few footpaths and trails for the walker. The region's climate is dry, sunny and exhilarating, especially in winter.

At the foot of the Sierra Chica are large dams to contain the waters of the Río Primero at Río Molinos (29 km. from Córdoba, Route 5, good *pejerrey* and trout-fishing; bus to Villa Carlos Paz, US$2), San Roque, and Río Tercero. There are two other large dams in the hills, at Cruz del Eje and La Viña. They provide power and irrigation, and the lakes are in themselves attractive. The Government keeps them stocked with fish. Sailing is popular.

Information can be obtained at travel agencies, at the Dirección Provincial de Turismo or at Casa de Córdoba at Callao 332, Buenos Aires.

Note There are innumerable good hotels and *pensiones* in the Córdoba mountain region; names are therefore not always given.

A road running NW from Córdoba through the Punilla valley leads to the following string of popular resorts shadowed by the Sierra Chica (note that many services are closed out of season). Many of them have daily bus connection with trains between Buenos Aires and Córdoba.

Villa Carlos Paz (buses from Córdoba bus terminal every 15 mins, 36 km., US$ 1; taxi from Córdoba airport, US$8; Buenos Aires-Villa Carlos Paz with Costera Criolla,US$18—bus terminal on Calle Alvear), on man-made Lake San Roque, in the Punilla valley. It is the nearest resort to Córdoba and is therefore often crowded. Tours possible on amphibian buses which go as far as the two dams on the lake. Launch trips, US$2.40 for 2½ hours. There is a pleasant 5 km. walk to the dam from the outskirts of Villa Carlos Paz. Much frequented by the British community in Argentina. At the Casa de Gaspar, Miguel Cané and El Redentor, roller-skating and optical illusions, Fri.-Sun. 1400-1900 out of season. A chair-lift (US$2.10) runs up the slopes to a tearoom and night club overlooking the valley, between 0900 and 1900. Bus tours to areas such as Sierra Chica, for those who like snack bars, fun slides and gravity-defying houses.

Accommodation, Restaurants and Services Plenty of hotels, big and small, e.g. *El Ciervo de Oro*, Hipólito Yrigoyen 995, on the lake, B-C, rec. *Las Junturas*, Florida 181, excellent, clean and friendly, hot shower, use of barbecue and fridge. *Mar. del Plata*, E, friendly, rec.; *Riviera*, E with bath, clean, rec. Cheap *Recreo El Ancla* across the road. Camping at ACA campground, and associated sites at *Las Tolderías* and *El Mirador Lago San Roque*; there is a municipal campground with swimming at Bialet Massé, N of Carlos Paz. Best buys: leather mats, bags, pottery. *Restaurant Carlos Paz* highly rec. for food and setting. *Restaurant Pamilla*

Mingo, Av Uruguay opp *Hotel Uruguay*, not cheap but good. Banco de Córdoba, Av San Martín, will change US$ cash only. Post Office and telephone on Av Gral. San Martín. **Tourist office** at bus station, very friendly.

Cosquín, Bus Córdoba-Cosquín US$2. with Cacorba; 1½ hrs., via Carlos Paz or with La Calera via the San Roque dam. 63 km. by Route 38 from Córdoba, on the banks of a river. Altitude, 720 metres. Camping on south bank of river. Tourist office at San Martía 560, *Hotel La Serrana*, P Ortiz 740, near bus station, F, friendly, good; likewise *Hotel Italia*, across from bus station, F, rec. and *Hotel Petit*, Calle Sabattini, F, 2 blocks from bus station. Take a bus to the Pan de Azúcar hill from where there is a good view over the Punilla valley, at 0930, return 1630 or 2 hrs. walk. Chairlift to top (all year round). 19 km. on is **Valle Hermoso**, near La Falda (buses from Villa Carlos Paz). Altitude, 850 metres. Old restored chapel of San Antonio, a little gem. Riding, motoring. Youth hostel, address "Steinhaus", dirty, no heating, very cold, US$2 p.p., pay extra for gas. Camping near river, US$0.60 p.p., all facilities, but not too clean. A folklore festival is held in the last half of January at Cosquín, from 2200-0500, tickets from US$6 per night. (Recent reports suggest that the festival is becoming commercialized.)

La Falda, 82 km. from Córdoba, a good touring centre. Bus 2 hrs., US$2.20. Altitude, 933 metres. Helpful tourist offices at bus station and in old railway station building. Model railway museum at Las Murallas zoo at the end of Av 25 de Mayo. Nearby is the privately run Ambato Archaeological Museum; articles are well displayed, worth a visit, open Sat., Sun. and public holidays, 0930-1230 and 1530-1830, US$0.50 entrance. *Hotel Fénix*, 25 de Mayo 218, good, F. *Restaurant El Bochín*, Av España 117, good, cheap. Students of all nations welcome at Córdoba University holiday centre at Vaquerías, 2 km. from La Falda. Camping near small river. (Bus from Buenos Aires, US$19.50) Excursions to Quebrada Chica, Cascada del Molino. 3½ km. on by Route 38 is **Huerta Grande**, at 971 metres, a bathing resort with good fishing and medicinal waters.

Round trip excursion to **Cascadas de Olaén**. Take the road to Valle Hermoso back 10 km. towards Cosquín, then follow dirt road about 12½ km. to the crossing marked "Cascadas de Olaén"; from here walk 4½ km. to the falls: quite spectacular canyon—the water splashes into a small lake full of little fish. Return to the dirt road and 2½ km. to a monolith and another dirt road, which leads to La Falda. See the Pampa de Olaén, where there are many quartz mines.

Bus connections with Uruguay from La Falda on Mon., Fri., Sat. and Sun. at 1730, arriving at 1200 next day with CORA (of Uruguay). Connections to Rosario, Mendoza, Catamarca, Santiago del Estero, Tucumán, Salta and Jujuy. Route: La Falda-Córdoba-Santa Fe-Paraná-Colón-Paysandú-Montevideo. Expreso Encón operates a similar service with similar connections.

Candonga, altitude 810 metres, 11 km. from Huerta Grande, is in the Sierra Chica. The road from Córdoba (55 km.) goes through Argüello, Villa Allende, Río Ceballos (*Albergue La Gloria*, affiliated to IYHA, E, warmly rec., and campsites *Río Camping* and *La Quebrada*), and Salsipuedes (*AT Camping*) to El Manzano, where it branches off to the left leading to La Cumbre. The historic colonial church at Candonga, now a National Monument, was built in 1730 as an oratory of the Jesuit Estancia of Santa Gertrudis. The arch protrudes to form a porch which covers the entrance.

La Cumbre, 97 km. from Córdoba. Bus, US$3, 2½ hrs. Altitude, 1,141 metres. Trout streams with good fishing from November to April. Swimming, golf, tennis. Has an airport. *Hotel Lima*, swimming pool, D, quiet, clean. Charming small inn, *Victoria*; *La Cumbre Inn*, large and commercial, good views; *Residencial Peti*, good, friendly, D/E. Good restaurants. *El Toboso*.

Los Cocos, just N of Cruz Chica and 8 km. from La Cumbre, is a delightful, extremely popular mountain resort with 3 first rate hotels and many holiday houses. *Hostería Zanier*, E, full board C, rec. Hang-gliding nearby at Cuchi Corral.

Cruz Chica, altitude, 1,067 metres, has very English houses and gardens in pine woods. Most attractive. Good English boys' school.

Capilla del Monte, 106 km. from Córdoba (bus US$4, *Hospedaje Italiano*, F, clean, showers, opposite bus station; municipal campsite on the way to Cerro Uritorco and also some 9½ km. from Capilla del Monte) in the heart of the Sierras. Altitude, 914 metres. Medicinal waters (good baths at La Toma), rocks and waterfalls and wide views; see particularly El Zapato rock, despite its graffiti. Excursions in the hills, particularly to Cerro Uritorco (1,950 metres). Good trout fishing at Los Alazanes dam; and good path on to Uritorco, walk takes 2½ hrs. Permission to walk obtainable from a house beyond the river crossing (US$0.60). You can walk on to the direct dirt road to San Marcos Sierra (22 km.); many parakeets and small farmhouses. Along the way you will also get views down to the **Cruz del Eje** dam (camping possible at foot of dam, or stay at friendly, family-run *Hotel España* in village, F, some private baths; rowboats for rent on dam's lake, where there is good fishing). Cruz del Eje (pop 23,100) is one of two towns with its own "micro-climate" (the other is Merlo in San Luis Province) and own honey production—try that made from carob (*algarrobo*) blossom (1 kg about US$2). Excellent trout fishing at Tío Mayo, an hour from Capilla del Monte by car.

A road runs N from Córdoba to Ascochinga and Jesús María via pleasant little townships such as Villa Allende, Unquillo, and La Granja. Near **Ascochinga** (63 km. N of Córdoba by road; altitude, 700 metres), is Santa Catalina, originally a Jesuit mission founded in 1622 and the most elaborate Jesuit establishment in the hills around Córdoba (no bus from Ascochinga, but 2 a day from Jesús María). (See the church begun in 1754, workshops and stone conduits; the families who now occupy the place as a summer home will show you round.)

Hotels in Ascochinga *Hostería El Cortijo*, D, full board only, good value, with bath, small swimming pool and river outside, horses for rent, US$1/hr.; 5 km. walk to Tres Cascadas falls and *balneario*. During winter, open weekends only.

Jesús María, 51 km. N of Córdoba. Altitude, 533 metres. Good 18th century Jesuit church and the remains of its once famous winery; in the cloister is an excellent Museo Jesuítico, said to be one of the best on the continent (open Mon.-Fri. 0900-1200 and 1400-1900, Sat. and Sun. 1600-2000). Each January there is a gaucho and folklore festival, lasting 10 nights; very popular, entrance fee US$1-2. Good trout, *dorado*, and carp fishing in winter. Road to Córdoba paved but rough, direct bus from Córdoba, US$1.50, 1½hrs. Some 4 km. N of Jesús María is Sinsacate, with an interesting church. There is also a fine colonial posting inn, with long, deep verandah and chapel attached. Beyond Jesús María the paved road runs another 132 km. to **Villa de María**, the birthplace of Leopoldo Lugones, a poet of country life. His house is a museum. *Hotel City*, good, at Villa de María, D.

From Córdoba (1 bus a day at 1530, 4½ hrs, US$4), or Jesús María (daily, 1610) you can take a bus to **Cerro Colorado**, 160 km. N of Córdoba and 14 km. W of Route 9 at Argañadas, near Santa Elena. There are more than 30,000 rock paintings by the Comechingones Indians in the Cerro Colorado archaeological park, where there is cheap accommodation (e.g. with Sosa family) and camping. You can stay with Don Elvio, who runs the *pulpería* near the archaeological station, but watch prices. The bus back to Córdoba leaves Cerro Colorado 0600 Mon.-Sat., 1800 Sun.

South-west of Córdoba a scenic road climbs through the Sierra Grande to another chain of resorts, Mina Clavero, Villa Dolores and Yacanto.

Mina Clavero is 140 km. from Córdoba by bus (0845, 6 hours, US$9), beautiful ride through grand lake and hill scenery, and curious palm trees. A good centre for exploring the high *sierra*. No money exchange available. There is a nice church and a most interesting museum, dedicated by a French archaeologist, 13 km. south from Mina Clavero and about 5 km. from the village of Nono, entrance US$0.60, called "Rocsen" open 0900 till sunset, with furniture, minerals, instruments, animals, etc. Altitude, 915 metres. (Restaurant: *Rincón Suizo*, Calle Champaquí, good pastries.) Road from Mina Clavero over the Sierra Grande to *Hotel El Cóndor*, goes to Carlos Paz (bus leaves Mina Clavero at 0800)—not yet paved. Views from El Cóndor over Lake San Roque. If hitching from Córdoba down this route to Mendoza, best starting point is Ycho Cruz, beyond Carlos Paz.

Villa Dolores, 187 km. from Córdoba (bus takes 5 hrs.), 48 km. from Mina Clavero. Altitude, 529 metres. Population: 10,000. The road from Córdoba crosses the two mountain ranges to reach finally the Pampa de Achala, a huge desert plateau of grey granite. (Camping: nearest site is Piedra Pintada, 15 min-bus-ride away, pleasant little village well situated for walks into mountains.) Bus to San Luis 5¼ hrs.

Rail Buenos Aires (Retiro)-Villa Dolores: *Sierras Grandes* train via Villa Mercedes, Mon., Wed., Fri. at 1615, arriving 0800; leaving V Dolores 2240 Tues., Thurs., Sun., arriving Retiro 1350. Fares: Pullman US$20, first US$14, tourist US$10.85. Car transporter from Buenos Aires on Fri., from Villa Dolores on Sun.

From San Javier you can explore **Champaquí** (altitude, 2,975 metres). For top, follow path to Capilla La Constancia, set in river valley with pine and nut trees, 2-3 hrs. Take water from here, then cross the river (path), keep left through a pinewood up to a mountain range and follow it up to the top of a huge plateau. Good path, about 4-5 hrs., and then you reach a square enclosure, whence you keep left. Follow stone mounds about 2 hrs. until you see the higher of two peaks, which is Champaquí. Lovely views, descent 4 hrs. to La Constancia. Not to be attempted in misty weather.

Yacanto, near Villa Dolores, at the foot of Champaquí, in a region of woods and waterfalls. Reached by road from Villa Dolores railway station. Curative waters.

A road S from Córdoba runs to Alta Gracia and to the Río Tercero dam.

    Alta Gracia, altitude 580 metres, population 33,800, 48 km. SW of Córdoba. (Bus 1 hr., every 15 mins, US$0.75.) Interesting colonial church, finished c1762, open am. and after 1700, and buildings housing Museo del Virrey Liniers, about the Estancia de Alta Gracia, founded in 1588 and taken over by the Jesuits in 1643, beside Lake Trajamar, open Tues.-Sun. 0900-1200 and 1500-1800 (all day in summer). There is also the Museo Manuel de Falla on Pellegrini Final, open Tues.-Fri. 0900-1900, entry US$0.30, where the Spanish composer spent his last years. Take the local bus to La Paysanita or La Serranita for a quiet environment (but no cheap accommodation). *Hostería Reina*, Urquiza 129, good. Two camping sites, one scruffy, the other better and free in winter, which is by golf course. A few reasonably priced restaurants in town centre. Tourist office inside clock tower by Lake Trajamar. New casino. To the Bosque Alegre and Observatory it is 24 km., open Thurs. 1600-1800 Sun. 1000-1200 and 1600- 1800. Good views over Córdoba, Alta Gracia and the Sierra Grande. To the Río Tercero dam is 79 km.; on the lake is a workers' holiday colony and an ACA *Unidad Turística*. Gruta de la Virgen de Lourdes, 3 km. out of town, beautiful views from cross on top of hill.

Villa General Belgrano, 85 km. S of Córdoba on Route 36, is a completely German town founded by the surviving interned seamen from the *Graf Spee*, some of whom still live in the town. It is a pleasant resort and a good centre for excursions in the surrounding mountains. If walking between here and La Cumbrecita, lodge with Siegfried at *Alta Vista*, F, friendly. There are two Youth Hostels, one at Estancia Alta Vista, 14 km. from the town, and one, El Rincón, in the town.

La Cumbrecita, a German village reached from General Belgrano by daily bus at 1500 or by taxi (US$25-30, 1-1½ hrs.) along a dirt road, is another Sierra resort. Good walking and riding. Hotels: *Cascadas*, B, with pool, tennis etc.; *Panorama*, C, higher up hill (T 98406); three others (C) and *Residencial Casa Rosita*, E. Youth Hostel at Villa Alpina, 17 km. from the town.

Some 200 km. NE of Córdoba the Río Dulce, flowing in places through salt flats, runs into the shallow Mar. Chiquita on the southern margin of the Chaco. People who live in the valley of the Río Dulce are so used to the taste of its water that they often add a pinch of salt to the water they drink when away from home. Mar. Chiquita, which is now growing rapidly, is naturally salty, and the water is warm. No river drains it, though two other rivers flow into it from the Sierras of Córdoba in the flood season. There are several islands in the lake. On its southern shore is the small town of **Miramar**, which is being gradually overwhelmed by the expanding Mar. Chiquita. The area is a very popular resort during the summer months; its salt waters are used in the treatment of rheumatic ailments and skin diseases. It is best reached by a railway W from Santa Fe to Deán Funes, which runs within a few km. of the southern shore. The lake is about 320 km. SE of Santiago del Estero.

Hotels *Savoy*, cheap, very friendly

Camping Autocamping Lilly. Bahía de los Sanavirones.

(**Note** This Mar. Chiquita and its town, Miramar, must not be confused with the other Mar. Chiquita to the N of Mar. del Plata and the seaside resort of Miramar, S of Mar. del Plata.)

SANTIAGO DEL ESTERO, TUCUMAN, SALTA AND JUJUY (3)

The broad-gauge Mitre Railway and the metre-gauge Belgrano Railway (slower) both run N past Santiago del Estero to Tucumán, 522 km. away. From Recreo on the Belgrano a branch runs W to Chumbicha, where it connects with a line N to Catamarca and S to La Rioja; they will be described later.

Santiago del Estero, the oldest Argentine town, was founded in 1553 by settlers pushing S from Peru. It is about 360 km. N of Córdoba and 167 km. SE of Tucumán. A 1½-km. steel bridge across the Río Dulce carries the Mitre railway from La Banda (6½ km., pop 47,900.) on the Buenos Aires-Rosario-Tucumán route. There is a branch line via Forres to Córdoba. Population, 148,000. The main square, Plaza Libertad, contains the Casa de Gobierno, and the Cathedral (the 5th on the site) stands next to it. Also on the plaza is the tourist office, open 0800 to 2000 daily, and very helpful. On Plaza Lugones is the pleasant old church of San Francisco, the city's first, which was founded in 1590 by San Francisco Solano, patron saint of Tucumán. His cell is in the near-by convent; his festival, celebrated with folk-music (he himself played the viol), is on July 24. Beyond the church is the pleasant Parque Aguirre, with a good zoo. Airport (Aerolíneas Argentinas flights daily, except Thurs.).

In the convent of Santo Domingo is a "Holy Sheet", one of the three copies of the sheet that covered the body of Christ, given by Philip II to his "beloved colonies of America". The Provincial Museum of Archaeology (Calle Avellaneda) founded by Emil and Duncan Wagner, has over 10,000 samples of Indian pottery. There is also a provincial history museum, previously known as the Museo Gancedo.

Festival Carnival in February is to be avoided: virtually everything throwable gets thrown by everyone at everyone else.

Hotels *Gran Hotel*, Avellaneda and Independencia; *Residencial San Antonio*, Belgrano 485, E, very basic rooms but clean bathrooms. *Residencial Rodas*, Pedro L. Gallo 432, E, next to bus station, café attached, very friendly. *Hotel-Residencia Iovino I*, on Moreno y San Martín, D; *Residencial Iovino II*, Santa Fe 259, 2 blocks from bus station, E with bath, clean, fan, but doors and windows don't close properly; *Residencial Santa Fe*, F, next to *Iovino II. Embajador*, Buenos Aires 60, E, reductions for longer stays; unmarked *pensión*, Moreno 665, F, adequate.

Restaurant *La Rotonda*, at edge of town on road to Tucumán, reasonable *asado*. Easy to hitchhike N from here. *Mía Mamma*, on Plaza is good restaurant/salad bar.

Exchange Noroeste Cambio, 200 block of 24 de Septembre, good rates.

Buses to Resistencia, 3 a day, US$12, 11 hrs., run by El Rayo company, via Quimili and Roque Sáenz Peña (US$9, 8 hrs.); also to Córdoba, 12 a day, US$8; to Tucumán (via Río Hondo) US$3. To Buenos Aires, 3 a day, 12 hrs., US$20. Three a day to Salta, 5½ hrs., and to Jujuy, 6¼ hrs. Tourist Office extremely helpful.

The **Termas de Río Hondo** are 65 km. from Santiago del Estero along the road to Tucumán, at 264 metres. Their water is recommended for blood pressure and rheumatism; good to drink, too, and used for the local soda water. Swimming in public baths. Bus US$1.50 from Santiago del Estero, 1 hr. Aerolíneas Argentinas have combined flight and bus excursion from Buenos Aires, via Santiago del Estero, to the Termas, daily 1030, return 1245 from Santiago. The huge Río Hondo dam on the Río Dulce is close by; it forms a lake of 33,000 hectares, used for sailing and fishing. Very popular in August, so book accommodation well in advance.

Hotels *Grand Hotel Río Hondo*; *Los Pinos*, the most pleasant; *Panamericano; Palace; Ambassador; Aranjuez*, C, newest. Three campsites by river.

Food In the main street is a corner shop where you can watch *alfajores*, the local sweet (**see page** 190) being made. Around the corner from there is a small restaurant with excellent home-made pasta. There are two restaurants on the plaza: *Sabot* is quite good.

NB In Tucumán, Salta and Jujuy the only fuel one can get at the service station is *alconafta* (85% gasoline, 15% ethanol) which is a harmless substitute for gasoline.

Tucumán (properly San Miguel de Tucumán), capital of its province and with a population of almost a million, is the busiest and the most populous city in the N. Its natural beauties are great: it stands on a plain, at 450 metres, but to the W towers the Sierra de Aconquija. The city was founded by Spaniards coming S from Peru in 1565. There are still many colonial buildings left, and among rows of elaborately stuccoed, spacious, one-storey houses (many of them sadly dilapidated) rise three or four handsome churches with blue, yellow and white tiled domes. Summer weather can be very hot and sticky.

Tucumán's main square is Plaza Independencia. On its W side is the ornate Government Palace, next is the church of San Francisco, with a picturesque façade. On the S side is the Cathedral, with an old rustic cross, kept near the baptismal font, used when founding the city.

To the S, on Calle Congreso, is the Casa Histórica where, in 1816, the Congress of the United Provinces of Río de la Plata met to draft and proclaim Argentina's Declaration of Independence. The simple room in which it was proclaimed survived the destruction of the original house in 1908 and has now been enclosed in a modern museum. A bas-relief on the museum walls shows the delegates proclaiming independence. Some distance to the W is Plaza Belgrano, with a statue to General Belgrano, who won a decisive battle against the royalists here in 1812. Two blocks E is the University, with a grand view from the *vivero*. Nightly, at 2030, *son et lumière* programme at **Casa Histórica**, in garden, in Spanish only, US$0.70, tickets from tourist office on Plaza Independencia, no seats.

In the large Nueve de Julio park (avoid at night) is the house of Bishop Colombres, who introduced sugar cane to Tucumán in the early 19th century. In the house is his first milling machine.

Local Holiday 24 Sept. (Battle of Tucumán). Independence celebrations include music and speeches at the Casa de Independencia on 8 July, followed by *gauchos* bringing in the National Flag at midnight. Next day there are many folklore markets and music. Also Día de la Tradición, 10 Nov.

Hotels *Grand Hotel del Tucumán*, Av. de los Próceres 380, B, large, new five-star hotel opposite the Parque Centenario 9 de Julio, efficient, outstanding food and service, swimming pool, tennis courts, discotheque; *Carlos V*, 25 de Mayo 330, T 215042/221972, central, good service, a/c, bar, restaurant, excellent pasta, rec.; *Metropol*, 24 de Septiembre 524, T 311180, expensive, C, but good service, worth it; *Premier*, with a/c, good, friendly, accepts Visa credit card, C. Alvarez 510, D. In summer, best to stay at *Hotel St James*, on top of Sierra de Aconquija, expensive, comfortable, good food, swimming pool, good views, and fine walking. Also good: *Viena*, Santiago del Estero 1054, E; *Corona*, on main square next to Tourist Office; *Plaza*, E, San Martín 435, built round a pretty central courtyard, basic but clean. *Congreso*, Congreso 74, clean but old, rec., friendly, E, with bath, extra charge for fan. There are other cheap hotels near the bus station, e.g. *Boston*, F, on Sáenz Peña, nice courtyards, restaurant, but some are very dirty. *Palace*, 24 de Septiembre 233, E, friendly, clean, rec.; *Colonial*, San Martín 35, E, 5 mins from bus station, very clean, private bath, fan, laundry service, rec.; *Estrella*, just outside bus station, 24 de Septiembre, clean, cheap and basic, a bit noisy, open 24 hrs. Nameless hotel opp bus terminal, F with bath, radio and heating; *Florida*, 24 de Septiembre and 9 de Julio, E, very good value; *Italia*, Catamarca and Corrientes, F, by Mitre station, friendly, hot water, reasonably clean, hot-pillow place; also by the station is *Tucumán*, Catamarca 573, G, clean, OK; *Petit*, C Alvarez 765, a bit noisy, spacious, friendly, clean, E with bath, highly rec. *El Parque* or *El Bosque* (both names used), across from bus station, E, fan, clean (though used as a brothel), friendly, safe. Many cheap hotels in streets around General Belgrano station. Marta Ruiz offers accommodation in her house at Rondeau 1824, F, not including food, very comfortable. If they arrange beforehand, students can stay in the University residence of Horco Molle.

Camping Parque Nueve de Julio, one site for locals, one for tourists (US$0.25 per tent, US$0.25 p.p.): reported to be dirty. Two roadside camp sites 3 km. E and NE of city centre.

Restaurants *El Duque*, San Lorenzo 440, very large, popular, excellent, and *La Chacha*, Córdoba 476, good value. Good meat in open air at *La Rural*, Parque 9 de Julio, reasonable prices; *Isoscelles*, Junín 583, original dishes, good service, US$6 for 2 with wine; both warmly

TUCUMÁN
CENTRE
NOT TO SCALE

1. Plaza Independencia
2. Parque Avellaneda
3. Plaza San Martín
4. Plaza Urquiza
5. Plaza Belgrano
6. Cathedral
7. San Francisco
8. Government Palace
9. Casa Histórica
10. University of Tucumán
11. Casa del Obispo Colombres
12. Folklore Museum
13. Instituto Miguel Lillo
14. Casa de Padilla
15. Museo Iremain
16. Telephone Office
17. Post Office
18. Tourist Office
19. Campsites

rec. *El Rincón de Cholo*, Chacabuco 31, Arab and other food, esp lunches, very friendly, good, cheap. *La Leñita*, 25 de Mayo, inexpensive, good meat. *El Ruincho*, in patio behind tourist office, cheap regional dishes, popular with locals, open air; *La Parrilla del Centro*, San Martín 381, excellent, reasonable prices; *Panchería Las Piñas Doradas*, 25 de Mayo 119, self-service hot dogs with choice of 20 toppings, good and cheap; *Bar Risco*, B. Araoz and Avellaneda, nr. bus station, good cheap sandwiches. *Rocca Bianca*, Congreso 32, good all round, very popular; *La Cantina*, San Martín 750, good; also good, cheap meals at *Champaquí*, Av Sarmiento, corner with Catamarca, opp Mitre station, and at *Las Brasas*, Maipú 700 block. Good fast food at *Palacio de las Empanadas*, Maipú 900 block; and at *Pic Nic*, San Juan 600 block and Ayacucho 500 block, meal US$1.50. *Comilandia*, cheap set meals, San Martín 181. *Bar Sandwichería*, Junín y Corrientes, nice atmosphere; *Café and Sandwichería*, corner of 24 de Septiembre and Buenos Aires, good. Set lunches near bus station good value. The local beer is very good (Cervecería del Norte), and in this part of Argentina "black beer" (e.g. Salta Negra) is available; also in Salta and Cafayate.

Shopping An active centre, cheaper than Buenos Aires. *Valles Colchaquíes*, Congreso 178; Mercado Artesanal, at the tourist office in Plaza Independencia, small, but nice selection of lace and leather work. *Discoteque*, Galería at San Martín 675, good selection of records, English-speaking owner. *Librería Sarmiento*, San Martín 600 block, for maps. All shops close 1200-1630. Good 2nd-hand book shop in centre, *Los Primos*, with English, French, German books.

Taxis Many unscrupulous drivers, who "rig" their meters. Better to arrange price in advance if possible.

Car Hire Al International and Avis; airport and in centre.

Car Repairs Rubén Boss, Av Aconquija 947, rec. esp for Volkswagen.

Casinos The Winter Casino is in an elegant 19th century building on the outskirts. It is open all year except January. The Summer Casino at the top of Aconquija is now closed.

Museums Casa Histórica, Calle Congreso, open Tue-Sun. 0830-1200 and 1730-2000, US$0.20, but you're encouraged to buy a guide, see previous page; Anthropological Museum, 25 de Mayo y Mendoza in University building, not well staffed, good exhibits; Folklore Museum, 24 de Septiembre 565, open every day 0800-1230 and 1730- 2030; the Instituto Miguel Lillo, associated with the natural history department of the University, has a large collection of animals, insects, and a herbarium, with the display greatly improved. One of the library's treasures is one of eight copies of the original edition of von Humboldt's travels in Spanish America; another is a sixteenth-century Pliny. Open Mon.-Fri. 0900-1300. All these four museums have been described as "quite exceptional". Casa de Padilla, next to government palace, houses a collection of international art and antiques in the home of a prominent Tucumán family. Next to *Hotel Colonia* on Av Entre Ríos is Museo Iremaín, a very interesting memorial to the sculptor, open 0830-1200 and 1500-1800, Mon.-Fri. All museums now make a small charge.

Exchange Lloyds Bank (BLSA), San Martín 622. Open 0700-1300; charges high commission on traveller's cheques. American Express, San Martín 845. Noroeste Cambios, 24 de Septiembre 549 (3% commission on cheques, open Sat. a.m., does not give dollars for travellers' cheques) Dinartur, San Martín 678, cheques and cash, and Maguitur, San Martín 765, near main square, good rates for cash; also Imperio de Oro, *local* 3, Galería Pezza, San Martín 650, good rates for cash. (See note on provincial bonds used as currency, **page 192**.)

Immigration Office Buenos Aires 2719, take bus No 6.

Library North American Centre, Alliance Française, Mendoza 255, free events in French.

Laundry Lavarap (self-service), Las Piedras y 9 de Julio; also at San Martín 927, and Santiago and Laprida.

International Calls Entel, Maipú 481.

Tourist Office In Plaza Independencia, 24 de Septiembre 484, 1st floor, open 0800-1300 and in summer 1600-2000; helpful in finding accommodation in private houses (about US$3 with cooking facilities), English spoken. Has details on Tafí (**see page** 90).
    Delfín Turismo, on 24 de Septiembre, very helpful, good excursions, operates in conjunction with Saltur of Salta. Excursions around the city are run by Disney Tour, San Lorenzo 435.

Rail 1st class and Pullman often booked up 2 weeks in advance. The daily *Estrella del Norte* train leaves Retiro station, Buenos Aires, at 1800, returns daily from the Mitre station in Tucumán at 1845, costs US$51 sleeper, US$38.75 Pullman, US$25.50 first, US$17.85 tourist class; takes 18½ hours. The Belgrano train, the *Norteño*, leaves Buenos Aires 1000, Tues. and Fri.; and Tucumán (Belgrano station opp bus station) 1845, Tues., Fri., taking 25 hours, no sleeper. *Independencia* train leaves Buenos Aires Tues. and Fri. at 1600, returns Sun. and Wed. at 1715 (Mitre station) sleeper, car transporter, can combine with bus La Veloz del Norte (5½ hrs.) to Salta, for about US$7 more, also to Jujuy (US$10, 5 hours) as can *Estrella del Norte* (to Salta only, daily at 1300). *Panamericano* train leaves Mitre station, Tucumán, Tues., Fri. 1500, arrives La Quiaca 0920 next day, fare US$11.50 1st class, the Friday train has a Pullman coach which passes the border to Villazón, where it is coupled to a Bolivian train leaving for La Paz at 1530 (Sat.), arriving La Paz Sun. 0930. Three trains a week to Córdoba, 1745, 14 hrs., 1st US$20, 2nd US$15.

Beyond Tucumán the Belgrano line runs N via Rosario de la Frontera to Jujuy, and La Quiaca, on the Bolivian border, 644 km. from Tucumán. There are also buses to all these places and their use seems preferable; the trains N of Tucumán, though comfortable (with a dining car and crowded only when there are *fiestas*), are slow.

Road For travellers to Salta from Tucumán the road via Santa María and Cafayate (a very interesting journey through many microclimates, **see page** 91) is longer but more interesting than the direct road. Aconquija bus Tucumán to Cafayate (7 hrs., US$8) via Tafí and Santa María (6 hrs.) leaves daily at 0600. Direct bus in summer from Tucumán to Cafayate Tues., Thurs., Sat., 6½ hrs., at 1000 (0600/0700 in winter). Direct Tucumán bus to Salta (but not via Cafayate), 4 hours, several daily, US$8. (slow bus 5½ hrs.). Hitch-hiking from Tucumán to Salta is difficult beyond Tafí del Valle. Plenty of buses to Jujuy, e.g. Veloz del Norte, leaves at 0900, 6 hrs. (US$7).

Bus to La Rioja, 7 hours, US$10. To Catamarca, 7 a day with Bosio, about US$5.50. Buses also to Santiago del Estero (US$3), Paraná, Termas de Río Hondo, Orán (US$12), Resistencia and Tinogasta. Bus to Buenos Aires, Chevallier at 1250 and 2100, 19 hours, US$20; El Trébol at 1600, 16 hrs., US$20.

For those who wish to travel direct from N Argentina to Central Chile, there are daily La Estrella buses (US$20) from Tucumán to Mendoza, leaving 1300, 1400 and 2000 (19 hours), via Catamarca, La Rioja, and San Juan. Bus to Córdoba 480 km., US$14, 8 hours, many companies (incl. El Tucumano Panamericano). *La Veloz de Norte* serves free coffee, cake and soda. To La Paz, take train or bus to the frontier, then at Villazón, connect with train to Oruro and La Paz.

Air Airport: Benjamín Matienzo, 9 km. from town. Bus for each flight, US$0.60, starts from *Hotel Mayoral*, 24 de Septiembre 364. Day flights to Buenos Aires with Aerolíneas Argentinas and Austral; discounts on night flights. Austral Tucumán-Mar. del Plata at 0240 on Mon., Mar. del Plata-Tucumán Tue and Sat. at 0150; Tucumán-Córdoba with Austral daily exc Sun. at 1355. Alfa to Iguazú, Thurs. 1710.

Excursions Simoca, 50 km. S of Tucumán on Route 157, has an authentic Saturday morning market, handicrafts and produce; essential to get there early. 36 km. to Villa Nougués, an hour up the mountain side (one of the most interesting tours), the summer residence of the well-to-do Tucumanos; it has an excellent private hotel; Aconquija park, with glorious trees, is at the foot of the mountains. Bus at 1130 (the only one; returns immediately); tours from Terra, 9 de Julio 80, US$5.25. El Cadillal dam, in the gorge of the Río Sali, 26 km. N of Tucumán, supplies electricity and water for the city and permanent irrigation for 80,000 hectares of parched land. There are restaurants, a good ACA campsite, good swimming, and a small museum at the dam. Reached by frequent bus from the depot near the railway station, US$1. Another possible excursion is to San Javier (hotel), plenty of buses to foot of hill, 20 km., beautiful views. To Salta via Cafayate, take the Ruta Nacional 38 SW, passing the Quebrada de Lules (20 km.), which is worth visiting.

At Km. 46, Route 307 branches NW to **Tafí del Valle** (population 27,000, 97 km. from Tucumán, not to be confused with Tafí Viejo which is 10 km. N of the city) known to archaeologists as a holy valley of the precolumbian Indian tribes. Just before Tafí del Valle are Dique El Mollar, formerly La Angostura dam, and nearby the menhir park of **El Mollar**, with 129 standing stones (collected from various sites apparently) and good views (closed in winter). Paved road between

Tafí and El Mollar. Tours to El Mollar and Tafí from the agency next door to the tourist office, US$11.50 each for 4 people minimum. Local buses from Tafí, several a day, US$0.05, and the Tucumán-Tafí bus stops nearby. Entrance to the park is 10 km. S of Tafí del Valle; you can drive around it (but not within it) by car, or walk.

Tafí del Valle, which is becoming touristy, and El Mollar are often shrouded in fog because of the dam. Ten mins from Tafí is Museo La Banda in the old chapel of San Lorenzo.

Hotels *Hostería ACA*, C; *Hotel Nuñorco*, D; *Colonial*, nr. bus station, no singles, friendly, clean, F. *Pensión La Cumbre*, F, hot water, basic, no locks on doors; better one opposite *Colonial*, in billiard hall. Hotels and bungalows (D) at El Pinar del Ciervo. Camping, *Los Sauzales*, very clean, hot showers, rec. Try local cheese.

Bus, Tucumán-Tafí, with Aconquija, sit on left-hand side, travels through luxuriant gorge with sub-tropical vegetation, 0700 and 1600, 3½ hrs., US$3.25, returning at 0600, 1630 and 1930.

NW of Tafí is **Amaicha del Valle** (bus from Tucumán, US$5, 0600) with 360 sunny days a year, free municipal campsite, *Juan Bautista Alberdi*, 10 min out of town (blue gate) (*Hostería Provincial*, D full board, showers not always hot, clean and friendly, rec., *Pensión Albarracín*, F; *Hostería Colonial*, F with bath, friendly). La Pachamama festival at end of pre-Lent Carnival; also see Sr. Cruz' craft workshop.

Over the 3,040 metre Infiernillo pass 21 km. from Tafí and 15 km. from Amaicha the road is paved and again after Amaicha to the junction with the Ruta Nacional 40 (15 km.) which leads N to Cafayate (55 km.- **see page** 97) and S, 24 km. to **Santa María**, population 18,000.

Hotels *Plaza*, on plaza, clean, modern, rec., D; *Provincial de Turismo*, San Martín, friendly, rec., dining room, D, with bath; *Residencial Palacios*, Mitre 592, F, basic, hot water, clean, reasonable and friendly; *Residencial Reinoso*, Av 1° de Mayo 649, G, good, 2 blocks from plaza, hot showers, clean, friendly. Municipal **campsite** at end of Sarmiento.

Restaurants *El Cardón*, Abel Acosta 158, cheap and good, regional dishes.

Buses To Tucumán 6 hrs., 0220, 0800 (US$6). To Cafayate daily at 0700 exc Thurs. at 1030. Empresa Bosio goes to Catamarca, Sat.; via Tucumán Sun. at 1230, 9 hrs. Most start from Belgrano 271 on main Plaza; Empresa San Cayetano (600 block of Esquiú) goes to Belén (**see page** 120) 4 hrs., Mon., Wed., Fri. at 0500.

Excursions to Fuerte Quemado (Indian ruins) 15 km. away, not as impressive as Quilmes (see below); Cerro Pintado, 8 km., coloured sandstone mountains; important ruins of Loma Rica, 18 km. away; Ampajango, 20 km. away, important indigenous finds.
  Quilmes (Tucumán), 37 km. away, with splendid views from the fortifications and interesting cacti, has the most southerly Inca ruins (dam, village and posting house—*tambo*), an *hostería* (summer only), camping facilities and a guide at the site from 0700 to 1730. It is 5 km. along a dirt road off the main Santa María-Cafayate road, and 16 km. from Amaicha del Valle. There is also a provincial archaeological museum. Bus from Santa María at 0655, 1½ hrs., US$1.50, returns about 1030.

A railway and road run N from Tucumán to (145 km.) **Rosario de la Frontera**, a popular resort from June to September. Altitude: 769 metres. Eight km. away there are sulphur springs. Casino. From Buenos Aires, by Belgrano Railway: 1,296 km.

Hotels *Termas*, rambling place, being remodelled, but beware of loose accounting, good food but many rooms without private bath (6 km. from bus station, taxi US$5), room with bath and 3 meals, C (T 81004). Baths US$1.50. About 1 km. from *Hotel Termas* is ACA motel. Across the road is man-made lake owned by Caza y Pesca Club—ask in your hotel for permission to fish. *Real*, E, basic, clean, not all doors close.

Bus Rosario de la Frontera-Tucumán, Veloz del Norte, with stewardess, coffee and biscuits.

Excursions To **El Naranjo** (19 km.) a Jesuit colonial town; a church contains images and carvings made by Indians.
  About 80 km. N of Rosario de la Frontera, at Lumbreras, a road branches off the Inter-

American Highway and runs 80 km. NE to the Parque Nacional *Finca El Rey*, a 44,160-hectare tropical forest and wildlife preserve set among 900-1,500 metre hills with clear streams (good fishing). It can also be reached from Salta, 196 km., US$20 p.p. round-trip excursions of at least 6 with agencies. There is a Park office in Salta, Leguizamon 925. Check here on timetable for Park truck. From Salta, take bus to Sarana, daily at 1630, 3 hours, US$3. Bus drops you at a dirt track 40 km. from park entrance and 50 km. from the park headquarters. No public and little other traffic after this, but you may get a lift with local farm or roadbuilding vehicles. A truck leaves the Park HQ for the main road on Sun., Tues. and Fri. at 1600 to meet the bus going to Salta at 1825, but it rarely connects with the 1630 coming from Salta. *National Tourist Hotel*, E, is usually but not always closed at the height of the rainy season, Jan.-March (check at Terra Tours, Tucumán, T 214333, ask for Eduardo Cendoyo). It is clean and comfortable, has a large enclosed veranda overlooking the park. Also bungalows, and basic student accommodation. Mosquitoes, ticks and chiggers thrive; bring lotion. Camping is free, there are several tent sites, but few facilities. Horseback riding. Landing strip for small planes. The access road is still poor and fords the river 9 times; passable for ordinary cars only in the driest of times.

From Güemes, 148 km. N of Rosario de la Frontera, a branch line and road run W through the mountains for 43 km. to

Salta, at 1,190 metres, 294,000 people, on the Río Arias, in the Lerma valley, in a mountainous and strikingly beautiful district. Salta, capital of its province, is a handsome city founded in 1582, with fine colonial buildings. Follow the ceramic pavement plaques, or get map from Tourist Office, for an interesting pedestrian tour. The Cathedral (open mornings and evenings), on the N side of the central Plaza 9 de Julio, was built 1858-1878; it contains the much venerated images of the Cristo del Milagro and of the Virgin Mary, the first sent from Spain in 1592, and has a rich interior mainly in red and gold, as well as a huge late baroque altar. The miracle was the sudden cessation of a terrifying earthquake when the images were paraded through the streets on September 13, 1692. They still are, each September, when 80,000 people visit the town. The Cabildo, on Calle Caseros, was built 1783. The Convent of San Bernardo, at Caseros and Santa Fe, was built in colonial style in the mid-19th century; it has a famous wooden portal of 1762. San Francisco church, at Caseros and Córdoba, built around 1880, is said to have the tallest church tower in South America. The Museo Arqueológico (US$1) on Paseo Güemes has many objects from Tastil (**see page** 100). Salta, 1,600 km. from Buenos Aires by rail or paved road, is now a great tourist and handicraft centre (visit the craft market at La Casa el Alto Molino and shops—open 0800-2000 weekdays, 0800-1300 Sat. and the onyx factory; prices are lower than in Tucumán or Buenos Aires) and the best starting place for tours of the NW.

In Salta, visit the Cerro San Bernardo (1,458 metres), accessible in the afternoon by cable car (teleférico, closed for maintenance Tues.), US$2.50 return, from Parque San Martín. Very beautifully set at the foot of the hill is an impressive statue by Víctor Cariño, 1931, to General Güemes, whose *gaucho* troops repelled seven powerful attacks by the Spaniards between 1814 and 1821. A steep path behind the Archaeological Museum with Stations of the Cross leads to the top of the hill, where there is an old wooden cross, together with restaurant and artificial waterfalls. The guards at the provincial government palace on the Plaza 9 de Julio wear red ponchos with black stripes to commemorate the death of General Güemes; extended ceremony on Sats,—but not always.

NB All east/west streets in the centre are pedestrian only.

Festivals 24 Sept, commemorating the battles of Tucumán and Salta. On 16-17 June, folk music by youngsters in the evening and *gaucho* parade in the morning around the Güemes statue at the foot of the San Bernardo hill. Salta celebrates Carnival with processions on the four weekends before Ash Wednesday at 2200 in Av Belgrano (seats optional at US$2-4); lots of shaving foam (*nieve*) in the early morning; also Mardi Gras (Shrove Tuesday) with a procession of decorated floats and dancers with intricate masks of feathers and mirrors. It is the custom to squirt water at passers-by and *bombas de agua* (small balloons to be filled with water) are on sale for dropping from balconies on to unwary pedestrians below. Wear a light waterproof!

Hotels Salta is a favourite convention town. Some hotels close for a vacation during the

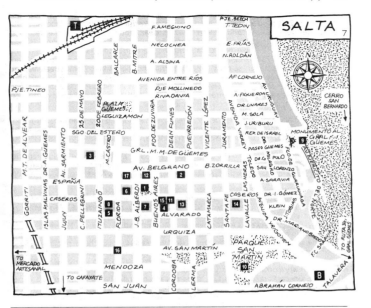

Salta: Key to Map

1. Plaza 9 de Julio, 2. Post Office, 3. Telphone Office, 4. Tourist Office, 5. Municipality, 6. Casa de Gobierno, 7. Cabildo Museum, 8. Museo de Bellas Artes, 9. Museo Arqueológico, 10. Museo de Ciencias Naturales, 11. Casa Uriburu, 12. Cathedral, 13. San Francisco, 14. Convento de San Bernardo, 15. Aerolíneas Argentinas, 16. Market and local buses, 17. Banco de la Nación.

Christmas season until January 10, so check. The last two weeks in July are often fully booked because of holidays. *Victoria Plaza*, B, Zuviría 16, excellent restaurant, the foyer overlooking the plaza is one of the centres of *salteño* life; *Salta*, Buenos Aires 1 (B), in main plaza, first class, refurbished, swimming pool, restaurant from 2100 only, and *California*, Alvarado 646 (C), 1st class, one block from main plaza, singles are small, rec. Also on main plaza is *Cabildo*, Caseros 527, D, pleasant, above 24-hour café, so noisy, a bit run down. *Regidor*, Buenos Aires 9, opp the *Salta*, English-speaking owner, avoid 1st floor, D, lunch US$5. *Colonial*, D, with bath, Zuviría 6, a/c 24-hr. cafeteria; *Crystal*, Urquiza and Alberdi, D, clean, rec.; *Colón*, J. B. Alberdi 165, old fashioned, central, opposite railway station, no hot shower, F; *Plaza*, España 508, E, old, fair; *Motel Portezuelo*, very good hotel at foot of Cerro San Bernardo, T 216027, C with breakfast, some rooms a/c, swimming pool, clean, helpful, better and cheaper than the ACA's *Motel Huaico*, Av Bolivia, Campo Castanares; *Crillón* (near main plaza, Ituzaingó 30), good;*Continental*, H. Yrigoyen 295, D, pleasant, 15% reduction for cash payments; *Petit*, H Yrigoyen 225, D, some rooms shared, swimming pool, nice; *Italia*, Alberdi 210, E, next to jazz club/casino, very clean and friendly, rec.; *Residencial Güemes*, on Necochea (600 block) near railway station F, basic, clean, private bath, laundry service; *Savoy* (near railway station), E, or F without bath, basic, clean, with cheap restaurant; *Residencial Elena*, E, clean, friendly and quiet, "charming", Buenos Aires 254; *Residencial San Jorge*, Esteco 244 y Ruiz de los Llanos 1164, highly rec., F with bath, parking, safe deposit, garden, washing and cooking facilities, horse-trekking advice by friendly proprietor, Sr. Dejean; *Hospedaje Doll*, Pasaje Ruiz de los Llanos 1360 (7 blocks from centre), F with bath, friendly, safe; *Residencial Viena*, Florida 184, F without bath, clean, a/c; *Florida*, F with bath, very friendly, clean, will store luggage, Calle Florida y Urquiza 722, rec. *Residencial Italia*, Alberdi 210, modern, good value, E, with bath; *Residencial Cepmer*, Yrigoyen 1195, E, good. *Residencial Cayetano*, Balcarce 747, E, clean, hot water; *Residencial Balcarce*, Balcarce 460, friendly, clean. *Residencial Centro*, Belgrano 657, friendly, F. *España*, F, España 319, central but quiet, simple, rec.; *Casa Familiar*, San Martín 540, 1st floor, Apt 2, run by Sra. María Florencia Zavalia de Márquez Valladares, E, hot showers, cooking facilities, very friendly but near bus station, so noisy. Very cheap fruit and veg market in same street. *Nápoli*, Mitre 1021, F, fairly near railway, laundry, friendly, quiet; *Candilejas*, Balcarce 980, F, without bath, erratic water supply, clean, comfortable, close to railway station. Many other cheap hotels near railway station (e.g. *Internacional*, F, opp station, hot water, basic, with good cheap restaurant), but few near new bus station.

Camping Casino Provincial municipal grounds, by river, swimming pool available, 3 km. from centre. Bus 13 to grounds. There is no signposting. In front of the Casino turn left, go to the *balneario* administration office, US$2.15 each, car US$3. Free hot showers available if there is gas, safe and excellent facilities. At *Motel Huaico*, Campo Castanares, and *Residencial Hispano*, San Juan 619. Campo Quijano, 30 km. W of Salta, at the entrance to Quebrada del Toro gorge, hot showers, bungalows, plenty of room for pitching tents, rec., bus from Salta bus terminal. Camping shops: H.R. Maluf, San Martín y Buenos Aires, and one at La Rioja 995.

Restaurants *La Quincha*, rec., near bus station, with excellent cold buffet and bife; *Balcarce*, near railway on Balcarce 934, delicious and reasonable. *El Monumento*, Gurrachaga 300 (opp Güemes monument), good food, slow service, good atmosphere, reasonably priced; *Jockey Club*, Güemes 452; *La Castiza*, Alberdi 134, huge, little atmosphere, reasonable; *Italiano*, Buenos Aires y Urquiza, 1st floor, highly rec. and reasonable, good *pizzería* opposite. *Don José*, Urquiza 484, good, cheap, popular on Sun., asado de tira and grilled kid warmly rec. *La Madrileña*, España 421, good; *La Posta*, España 476, food and atmosphere both excellent, highly rec.; *La Casona*, Caseros 511, good, reasonable; *Capricornio*, Caseros y Catamarca, good food and value; *9 de Julio*, Urquiza 1020, rec.; *Green Park*, Caseros 529, good pizzas, and milk shakes; *El Mesón de Pepe*, Rivadavia 714, fish specialities. Pleasant outdoor restaurants in Parque San Martín, at foot of Cerro San Bernardo. Good pizza at *La Selecta*, Belgrano 511. *El Quebracho*, near bus station, has peña show, at 2030. *El Antigal*, Balcarce, ½ block from railway station, cheap and good. Good set menu at *El Sorpaso* on Balcarce, cheap; *Miguel's Rotisería y Pizzería*, Balcarce nr. Belgrano, cheap, popular. Many good cheap restaurants on and near San Martín, by market. *Rotisería Pizzería Roque*, Alberdi y San Martín, cheap; *JA*, HYrigoyen y San Martín, excellent kid; *Boliche Balderrama*, San Martín 1126, has folk music, US$5 entrance for the show, also US$1 for good 4-course lunch. *Gauchos de Güemes*, for hearty late dinner and music, US$10, Uruguay 750. Opposite the church of San Francisco is a more humble but equally entertaining peña, where in addition to the modest cover charge one can order a drink and empañados. Good, cheap pasta at *Sitoco*, Alberdi y San Martín. *El Rincón del Artista*, in 1200 block of San Martín, also rec. *Tobi*, Urquiza y Buenos Aires, popular, cheap, good hamburgers; *Alvarez*, Buenos Aires y San Martín, cafetería style, cheap and good. *Rubero 88*, Buenos Aires 88, good pizza/pasta. Vegetarian food at *El Jardín*, Alberdi 420, small, good. *Casa de Té*, Paseo Alberdi 422, chocolate and cakes; *Café del Paseo* at Hotel Colonial, Zuviría 6, open 24 hrs. *Confitería Milk 1000*, 20 de Febrero y España, good ice cream. *Heladería Gianni*, España 486, ask for copa del amor; excellent coffee served. *Heladería Cercena*, Pasaje Continental 7, Mitre 55 by Plaza 9 Julio, excellent natural ice-cream. Cheap restaurants near the railway and bus stations, many lunch-only restaurants (closed Suns) with meals at US$1-2. *Unión Sirio Libanesa*, San Martín 677, has a good restaurant open to the public. Cheapest food is from the numerous superpanchito stands (huge cheesedogs, US$0.50).

Try local Cafayate wines, such as Michel Torino and Echart Privado, and typical Torrontés-grape wine. Also, the good local water makes excellent beer.

Shopping Mercado Municipal, corner of San Martín and Florida, for meat, fish, vegetables and other produce and handicrafts, closed 1200-1700 and Sun. Mercado Artesanal, San Martín 2555, T 219195, 0800-1930, take bus 2 or 3 from the centre, has become very touristy and expensive; the smaller shops further up the street are better. Woodcarvings of birds etc. from *RUD*, Santiago del Estero 202. *Tiwanaku* handicrafts store, museum upstairs, Caseros 424, will safely pack and send purchases to any Argentine destination. *Centro de Comercialización de Artesanías*, Catamarca 84, cheaper handicrafts than in tourist shops. High quality, hand-made *salteño* boots from Calle Vicente López 1046. Shoemakers on Calle Urquiza make boots to order in 48 hours. Fair selection of books in English at *Feria del Libro*,

Buenos Aires 69.

Rent-a-Car   Avis, airport and Alvarado 537; Al International in centre; several local companies, e.g. at Jujuy 997, very cheap.

Bathing   Balneario Municipal on outskirts, reached by bus No 13 from Calle Ituzaingó, entry US$1.00. Bus fare US$1.20.

Museums   Cabildo Histórico, Caseros 549, colonial and historical museum, free guided tour, ½, open Mon.-Fri., 0900-1400, US$0.20. Museo de Bellas Artes, Florida 51, open every day 1600-1900 and Wed.-Sun. 0900-1200. Casa Uriburu, Caseros 421, has relics of a distinguished *salteño* family. Museo Folclórico Pajarito Velarde, Pueyrredón 106. Museo Arqueológico, interesting, on Paseo Güemes, behind the Güemes statue. Museo de Ciencias Naturales, Mendoza 2, has a full display of stuffed birds. Museo de Arte Popular y Artesanías Iberoamericanas, Caseros 476, T 215289, Mon.-Sat. 0900-1300, 1700-2100, Sun. 0900-1300, good display of Latin American handicrafts. In the Casa el Alto Molino (Av San Martín 2555), much rawhide work is on display. Centro Cultural, on Calle Caseros, has slide shows on Fridays about the local countryside, free.

Exchange   Banco de la Nación on Mitre and Belgrano, open 0730 until 1330 (pays 5% more on cheques than on notes, but doesn't change money after 1000); Banco Provincial de Salta, España 526 on main square, closes at 1200 but changes travellers' cheques. Amex representative, Chicoana Turismo, Caseros 665, Galeria Margolet, *local 20*. Many *cambios* on España: Cambio Dinar at 609 changes cheques (3% commission) and cash (poor rates); Saltur on the main square. Maguitur, España 666, only cash. (See note on provincial bonds used as currency, **page 192**.)

Laundry   Lavarap, self-service, Alvarado at Yrigoyen. Also Santiago del Estero 221 (open Sun. a.m.), Speed Queen (cheap) Juramento 315.

Post Office   Deán Funes 140, corner of España; also in shopping arcade at corner of Florida and Gral. San Martín. **Telephone** office at Av Belgrano 824, 24 hrs., international calls at Av Vicente López 124, 0800-1930.

Immigration Office   Maipú 35.

Consulates   **Bolivia**, Santiago del Estero 179; open Mon.-Fri., 0900-1300. **Chile**, Ejército del Norte 312; **Peru**, 25 de Mayo y Santiago del Estero; **Paraguay**, Los Almendros 161; **Spain**, Las Heras 1229; **Italy**, Zuviría 380; **France**, Santa Fe 20; **West Germany**, España 671.

Tourist Office   Buenos Aires 93 (one block from main square). Open every day, inc. Sun., till 2100. Very helpful, gives free maps and offers slide shows some evenings, also a self-guiding tour, Circuito Peatonal, to see important landmarks on foot. This office will also arrange accommodation in private houses. Ask for the Tourist Market here, excellent leather goods.

Travel Agencies   *Saltur*, Caseros 525, T 212012, very efficient. Next door at Caseros 527 is *Mallorca Naturaleza y Aventuras*, specializes in horse trekking, very good value. *Continente Viajes*, Zuviría 60 (on main plaza), has a wide variety of tours, rec. *Chicoana Turismo*, Caseros 565 (Local 20), T 218134, very helpful, rec. *Puna Expediciones*, Braquiquitos 399, T 212-797 (well qualified and experienced guide Luis H. Aguilar can also be contacted through the *Residencial San Jorge*), organizes treks in remote areas, US$25 a day including transport to trekking region, food, porters, highly rec. *Juan Kühl*, Córdoba 202, at Urquiza, tours by light aeroplane, horseback, caravan, boat, German and English spoken, also runs photographic company.

Bus Services   There is no direct bus from Salta to Asunción, but Salta provides the most reliable cheap land connection between Bolivia and Paraguay. Buses daily 1700, US$18 (with La Veloz del Norte, 20% reduction for students), 14-16 hrs. to Resistencia, 1700 and 2200 for crossing into Paraguay (an arduous journey, but a/c, many stops in the night); for description of road, **see page** 130. Salta-Formosa with Atahualpa, which would provide the shortest route to Asunción, operates only twice weekly because of the state of the road. Bus to Córdoba, 8 a day, 14 hrs., US$15, US$27 with Expreso Panamericano (T 212460), no faster but luxury service with hostess. Bus to Cafayate, US$4, 3½ hrs., three a day, with El Indio at 0700, 1130 and 1800. To Cachi (5 hrs.) and Molinos (7 hrs.) Marcos Rueda daily at 0700 (or 0630 from bridge near Islas Malvinas 339). Marcos Rueda also has a service from Salta (Sat., 1300) to **La Poma**, arriving 1945 (via Cachi at 1750). The bus returns from La Poma next day at 1320. La Poma is reportedly a beautiful hamlet, and there is a *hostería*. Trout fishing is currently forbidden while stocks recover.

The road (no buses) between La Poma and San Antonio de los Cobres (**see page** 100) crosses the highest pass in South America negotiable by car, the Paso Abra del Acay (4,900 metres).

To Santa María, El Indio, 6½ hrs., 0700, US$10. To Mendoza via Tucumán, US$20, Mon., Wed., Fri., Sat., 20 hrs. with Andesmar; the Monday bus continues all the way to Río Gallegos, arriving Thurs. 1430, the other three services continue as far as Comodoro Rivadavia. Bus to Tucumán, 4½ hrs., several firms (La Veloz del Norte rec.), US$8. Bus to Embarcación daily at 0700. Bus to Jujuy, Atahualpa 16 a day between 0600 and 2300, "directo", US$2.40, 2¾ hours; to La Rioja, US$13.30; to La Quiaca, 11 hours, US$7 (see below).

Bus to Calama and Antofagasta (Chile) leaves Wed. at 0830, US$33 to Calama, US$34 to Antofagasta (20-hour journey at least, very cold), run by Atahualpa, tickets from Balturis, Urquiza 272. Take own food and a sheet to protect luggage against dust. Gemini (Caseros 665, T 212758) bus to Antofagasta on Sat. at 1600 (said to be better than Atahualpa); reservations are hard to get on either service, have your name added to the list of reservations and try again on the evening before departure. The route only open in Oct.-Dec., and even then may be suspended if there is heavy rain. Bus to Rosario de la Frontera, US$3.50, 2½ hrs., stewardess service, very pleasant trip. The new bus station is eight blocks from the main square. Taxi from bus station into Salta US$2.

Airport Bus connection from town on corner of the main Plaza to El Aybal airport (35 mins, US$1.20). From London, cheapest to fly standby to Miami, connect with LAB flight via Santa Cruz once a week to Salta. Two AA flights a week to Santa Cruz (Bolivia), Mon. and Sat. at 1145, arr 1215 Bolivian time, and also Lloyd Aéreo Boliviano (LAB office on Caseros 376). To Orán and Tartagal (Bolivia) with SEAL. AA flies Antofagasta (Chile) on Sat., 1700. AA flies to Bs. Aires (2 hrs., US$103) Tucumán, Córdoba (US$70) and Rosario. There are flights across the N of Argentina, e.g. Salta to Resistencia by Aerolínea Federal Argentina Alfa (office in España building between main square and Dean Funes), US$37 via Tucumán, Sat. and Salta-Formosa on Wed. (tickets and reservations only in these towns, prop-jets). There is a flight to Iguazú on Tues., return Sun. Special, regular, bus service between airport and Plaza 9 de Julio, US$1.50; don't be fooled by taxi touts who tell you there is no bus for 3 hours! Taxi from airport to bus station US$9.

Railways Ticket office open weekdays 0900-1100, 1700-1900. (Salta is not on a direct line, it is connected with Güemes by local trains and by bus. In Güemes, the bus terminal is 1 km. from the railway station; bus Salta-Güemes every 15 mins, US$1.30). Services to Buenos Aires also serve Tucumán (6 hrs.). Also bus/train combination with La Veloz del Norte Wed., Fri., Sun. leaving at 0820; see Tucumán section for details to Buenos Aires. **NB** If buying ticket from Buenos Aires to Salta via Tucumán, purchase train ticket to Tucumán and bus ticket to Salta at the same time so that you can transfer directly to the bus which meets the train, otherwise you must take local bus to bus terminal and wait (fare Buenos Aires-Salta US$38.40 and US$26.75). Ordinary train to Tucumán (continues to Córdoba), Tues., and Fri., 0835, 11½ hours (very slow). Train to Córdoba, leaves Tues. and Fri. at 1430, 20 hrs., no sleepers. From Salta to Mendoza, one takes a train to Villa María, near Córdoba, and after a 3-hr. wait gets another to Mendoza, takes about 40 hours. Slow but pleasant. Avoid during rainy periods as the track can get washed out; in summer can be hot and dusty. The Salta-Resistencia passenger service has been abolished, but for the hardy there is a regular freight service that leaves Metán (150 km. SE of Salta and a steam locomotive graveyard) after 1000 daily. The journey takes about 3 days, is very uncomfortable and involves frequent changes. It is best to buy all food before starting and to take plenty of drinking water with you. No direct train to Formosa. No direct trains between Salta and Jujuy, but connections are possible; buses much quicker.

In October 1980 Chile suspended its rail service from Socompa to Antofagasta, so it is not now possible to travel from Salta to Antofagasta direct except by air (see above) or by Atahualpa or Gemini bus. Argentine railways still maintain a train service from Salta to Socompa, where tourist cards are available (**see page** 100 for description of line, tourist train to San Antonio de los Cobres, and goods train, and also for road taking similar route.)

Routes to Bolivia To La Quiaca, on Bolivian frontier, 4 buses daily, Atahualpa (US$13), 9 hrs., at 0630 (direct), 1000 and 2130 (via Jujuy, prolonged stop), can be very cold, dusty. Buses also NE to Orán, six hours, for connection with Tarija, Bolivia, which can involve taking overnight bus (Atahualpa, 7-10 hrs.) to Aguas Blancas at 2200 (road now paved), arriving before dawn—cold—then crossing river in motor boats to Bermejo, Bolivia and the next bus out is often full. Spectacular 8 hr. mountain ride alternative to the latter in open-air pick-up: hair-raising! Also to Yacuiba, via Pocitos (Bolivian frontier), for Santa Cruz, Bolivia. US$10 with Atahualpa to Pocitos, 7-10 hrs., very full, with passengers standing, can be uncomfortable, but road now paved. Customs at Pocitos not to be trusted—beware of theft;

and overcharging for "excess baggage" (on bus), for which there is no official limit written up anywhere. (Hotel at Pocitos, *Buen Gusto*, F, just tolerable.)

Trains to La Quiaca run via Jujuy, but not direct from Salta. The other route is served by train: Salta to Pocitos, Mon. 2015, arrive 1440 Tues.; go through Argentine exit formalities, **cross the bridge into Bolivia** then take a taxi to Yacuiba (US$0.25), whence the train leaves at 1820 to Santa Cruz, arrive 1015 Wed. (if you miss it, other trains to Santa Cruz on Wed. and Sat. at 1230—*rápido*, or Mon. and Fri. at 1900—*mixto*). See also page 107 on the route via Orán.

Excursions Just S of Salta you pass Coronel Moldes: 26 km. from there is the dam of Cabra Corral, one of the largest artificial lakes in Argentina; water skiing, fishing, no hotels, just a camping site, restaurant and sailing club; the *Hostería Cabra Corral* is 10 km. from the lake, Route 68, D full board p.p., swimming pool, good. Paved road ends at the Presa General M. Belgrano, impressive views of the bridge across the lake. 11 km. NW of Salta, along a steep wooded valley (*quebrada*), is the wealthy neighbourhood of San Lorenzo (new restaurant in high tower, *El Castillo*, owned by John Johnston (US), good food and music, T 921052 for free taxi, 4-6 people; 2 *hosterías* opened recently; otherwise camping and picnicking beside rocky stream—meals also at hillside lodge). 2 km. further are the Lomas de San Lorenzo with a little river and subtropical vegetation (a popular Sunday picnic spot). Can be reached by hourly bus from Salta, ½ hr. journey. To Jujuy and Humahuaca, day trip through many agencies, about US$15 p.p. To Cuesta del Obispo and the Forgotten Valley, on return, with Saltur day trip, superb. In summer, guided tours are few and far between because of a lack of tourists. Saltur also does US$8 guided trip to Cafayate, with stops at major rock formations along road. The El Rey National Park (**see page** 92) Finca is about 200 km. E of Salta, at junction of Chaco and pre-Andean regions. Much wildlife and varied scenery. *Hostería*, D p.p. full board, and campsite next to it. Horses can be hired. Best time to visit is winter (drier). Tours arranged from Salta, e.g. by Mallorca, Caseros 527.

A magnificent round trip of about 520 km. can be taken going SW from Salta to Cafayate (well paved, through a splendid canyon), then N through the Valles Calchaquíes and Cachi, and back E to Salta. (Most travel agencies in Salta offer the round trip, US$11, no student discounts, 12 hours.) The first part of this trip, S from Salta, goes through El Carril (30 km.) where a road from Cachi intersects; continuing S for 25 km. Coronel Moldes is reached. Here, a side road to the left goes to Embalse Cabra Corral (see above). After Coronel Moldes, Route 68 goes through the Quebrada del Río de las Conchas with fascinating rock formations, all signposted: Anfiteatro (a gorge), El Sapo, El Fraile, El Obelisco, Los Castillos. The road goes through wild and semi-arid landscapes with many wild birds, including *ñandúes* (rheas).

Cafayate (altitude 1,660 metres, population 4,800) is a quiet, clean, little town, with low rainfall, lying between two ranges of Andean foothills and surrounded by vineyards. Its church is narrow but has 5 arches. About 18 km. S. is Tolombón, where there are reported Indian ruins among giant cacti and other scrub plants. (The ruins are vestigial; the cacti are far more interesting.) Cafayate is much frequented by Argentine tourists and accommodation is hard to find (virtually impossible for a single person) in Jan.-Feb. A walk to La Cruz (3 hrs.) takes you to a view of the Aconquija chain in the S to Nevado de Cachi in the N.

See Sr. Rodolfo Bravo's private museum of Calchaquí archaeology on Calle Colón, full of Indian artefacts dug up nearby, interesting slide show, advance group bookings only (US$0.50 p.p.). Excursions to *bodegas* and vineyards possible, e.g. La Rosa owned by Michel Torino, open Mon.-Fri., 0800-1200 and 1600-1900, weekends a.m. only, no need to book, 30 min. tours and tasting; also Etchart, 2 km. on road to Tucumán, now has tours: the Etchart Cabernet Privado, red, has been recommended. La Banda, a small vineyard near La Rosa, is interesting because it is more primitive. Near Bodega La Rosa a local kiln makes enormous pots. The Museo de Vitivinicultura is in an old cellar on Av. Güemes, 2 blocks from main square, US$0.40, very well laid out. Locally woven tapestries are interesting, and very expensive; see them at workshops of Ricardo Miranda, Av. Güemes 330. Also Platería of Jorge Barraco, Colón 147, for silver craft work. Handicrafts in wood and silver by Oscar Hipaucha on main plaza. Pancho Silva and his family have a workshop at 25 de Mayo selling and displaying their own and locals' handicrafts.

Hotels *Hostería Cafayate* (ACA), modern, quiet (but cold), colonial-style, D, good food;

Gran Real, Güemes 128, *Asturias*, Güemes 158, *Melchor*, Güemes y Almagro, all C; *Pensión Arroyo*, Camila Q. de Niño 160, rec., friendly, clean, F; *Colonial*, Almagro 134, E, charming patio; *Parador*, colonial style; *Güemes*, Salta 13, one block off main square, E; *Briones*, on main square, clean and comfortable, D with bath and hot water, accepts Amex card; *La Posta del Rey*, Güemes, E, clean; *Aserbal*, Güemes, 1 block from main square, E, new, nice rooms with bath, good; *Savoy*, off main square, with nice restaurant, D; *Confort*, on main street, E with bath, clean, comfortable. Accommodation in private houses is available. Municipal **campsite** Lorohuasi at S access to town, hot water, swimming pool, well maintained, bungalows for rent.

Restaurants *Cafayate*, simple, on plaza, good regional dishes and nice atmosphere; *Bárbara*, also on plaza, good food, expensive; *Café La Barra*, also on plaza, rec. *La Carreta de Don Olegario*, also on plaza, good, pleasant, and spotless but rather expensive; *Recova*, next to *Hotel Briones* on Güemes, very good; *La López Pereyra*, Av. Güemes between La Banda and Lamadrid, well rec. *El Criollo*, Güemes 254, tourist menu US$1.25, clean, fan, rec. *El Rancho*, for parrilla. Another *parrillada* is *La Tinaja* on the corner of the main square. Good cheap wine at café opposite El Indio bus station in street off plaza, provide own container. Try excellent pan casero (local bread).

Exchange The intendente at a white house opposite *Hotel Gran Real* changes dollar bills. Try also at El Indio bus station or in artesanía shops.

Tourist Office at the municipal building next to the cathedral.

Bus Service (Aconquija) to Tucumán (US$8) daily at 0630 and 1500, 7 hours. Alternatively go to Santa María with 1100 El Indio bus (2 hrs.) over good dirt road and take bus to Tucumán, Empresa Aconquija, leaving at 0200 and 0600, daily, taking 5-6 hrs. Colectivo leaves at 0400, taking 3½-4 hrs. (minimum 4 or 5 passengers). Bus to and from Salta 3 times a day, 3½ hrs., US$4. To Angastaco (El Indio) 1100 daily, leaves Angastaco for the return journey at 0630. Taxi owner, Millán, can usually be found in *La Tinaja*, Cafayate, but he is expensive.

Reinhard Böhm-Raffay writes: "On entering Cafayate from Tucumán there is a municipal campsite (US$2). If you follow the Río Colorado on foot just before this campsite, you can cross and follow the road towards the mountains. (An alternative is to take Calle 25 de Mayo, a dirt road, 4 blocks from the main plaza; carry on along this road, including a sharp left turn, and you reach the start of the road to the ridge.) Adobe houses with orange trees and chickens, dogs and horses along the riverbank. The road becomes a path, leading past Indian village up 3,500 metres to a mountain ridge. Spectacular view down the river valley and towards Cafayate and its vast, flat valley. From the last hut in the valley is where the path leads up for about 3-5 hrs." Alternatively, hitch-hike, or take the El Indio bus to Salta as far as Km. 30, then walk the Quebrada de Cafayate; best done in the afternoon, take fruit and/or water.

Horses can be hired for US$1 for 1½ hrs. from La Florida, Bodega Etchart Privado (2 km. from Cafayate on road to Tucumán).

Continuing S from Cafayate, the road goes to Santa María (**see page** 91), and SE to Tafí del Valle and Tucumán.

About a day is needed for the 160 km. trip from Cafayate to Cachi (Route 40). The road is mainly gravel and can be very difficult after rain, but the views of the Andean-foothill desert country are fascinating for those to whom strange rock formations and unexpected colours have an appeal. The population is largely Indian, and regional costumes abound. Salta and the Valles Calchaquíes are the centre for US archaeologist John Hyslo's study of Inca roads in the Andes. Between Cafayate and San Carlos is Aninominá, with municipal campsite.

About 24 km. N of Cafayate is **San Carlos** (altitude 1,660 m), a small settlement destroyed four times by Indians. It has a pleasant white church completed 1854, and another ACA *hostería*, as well as a municipal campsite. The Quebrada de Flechas, N of Cafayate on the road to Angastaco, is beautiful and desolate.

Bus The El Indio bus on the Salta-Cafayate-Angastaco run arrives in San Carlos by noon and on the return journey at 0745. Cafayate to San Carlos daily at 1535 and 2205, 45 mins., US$0.60; returns at 0500 and 1655.

Entering the Calchaquí valley, one comes N into a hillier region centred on

Angastaco, 2 km. off the main road, another small town, expanding rapidly, surrounded again by vineyards. You can sample the local Vino Patero, red or sweet white, in a house close to the river bridge; apparently *bodegas* can be visited, *vino patero* is supposed to be made by treading the grapes in the traditional manner. The Fiesta Patronal Virgen del Valle is held on the second weekend of December, with processions, folk music, dancing, many gauchos and rodeos. *Hostería* with pool, run by municipality, D, good, cheap and delicious meals on request, has its own small but informative archaeological museum; also a small *residencial* off the main plaza, G, clean, comfortable. Weekly bus Angastaco-Molinos, leaves Molinos Thurs. 2025, returns from Angastaco Fri. 1200. Ask in the main square for alternative transport to Molinos, Cachi or Cafayate. Also ask for Sr. Gutiérrez in the shop by the bus stop, or for Yapura in the shop on the side of the same block; it's 1-1½ hrs. to Molinos, locals charge US$10-15. From the Angastaco turn-off it is 40 km. on a winding road through beautiful and desolate rock formations to **Molinos** (*Hostería Provincial*, very highly recommended, C with breakfast, meals, in Isasmendi house with small museum, manager, Jorge Staude, speaks English, French and some German, and sells good local *artesanía*). Its church (a national monument, built c. 1720, now covered in a yellowish paste to preserve it), contains the mummified body of the last governor appointed by Spain, Colonel Severo Siqueira de Isasmendi y Echalar, who died in 1837. To protect it from visitors plucking its hair, this relic can no longer be viewed by the public. The priest is very knowledgable about local history. A pleasant walk is down from the church, crossing a creek and then climbing a gentle hill, from which there are good views of Molinos and surrounding country. Sra. de Guaymas runs a restaurant and rents beds (3 to a room); there are other rooms to rent around the main square. On the left bank of the river, ask at the village of Seclantás for the authentic *ponchos de Güemes* (red with the black mourning stripe for General Güemes). Daily bus to Salta via Cachi (with Marcos Rueda company), leaves Molinos daily at 0630 except Fri. (1315) and Sun. (1130); 2 hours to Cachi, 8 hours to Salta.

We are informed that *ponchos de Güemes* are made in most of the villages in the Valles Calchaquíes.

From Molinos it is 46 km. to **Cachi** (Quechua for "salt"), a beautiful little town renowned for its weaving and other crafts; the natives claim people die only of old age, because the climate is very invigorating; height above sea level, 2,280 metres. The church's floor, roof and confessional are made from the wood of the *cardón* cactus. The local archaeological museum is interesting. It is in the "Land of the Pimentón", the pepper-growing area. *Hotel Nevado de Cachi*, G, near bus station, basic but good restaurant, owned by Marcos Rueda bus company also a good one opposite; good *ACA Hostería Cachi*, E; *Albergue Municipal*, F, good restaurant, also has good municipal campsite with swimming pool, on hill at S end of town. From Cachi, you follow Route 40 for 11 km. N, then turn right to Route 33. This road climbs continuously to the Cuesta del Obispo passing a dead-straight stretch of 14 km. known as Recta Tin-Tin with magnificent views of the **Los Cardones National Park** with the huge candelabra cacti, which grow up to 6 metres in height, reaching the summit (3,620 metres) after 43 km. Then it plunges down through a luxuriously-wooded steep valley populated by Indians in local costumes. The road rejoins Route 68 at El Carril, from where it is 37 km. back to Salta.

If you wish to make a round trip just to Cachi, take a bus at 0630 from Salta (6 hrs.) stay the night and return the next morning at 0830. Take the bus from the bridge near Islas Malvinas 339, *not* at bus station, where it arrives full (buy bus ticket the day before, from the Terminal Terrestre); sit on left-hand side to see remarkable Quebrada de Escoipe. The bus goes on to Molinos. One-day excursions to Cachi from Salta (US$10) give insufficient time.

Ask also at tour agencies about excursions to Quebrada del Toro, rugged and striking countryside (see below).

A trip to the Indian ruins at Las Pailas, 10 km. from Cachi, provides a fine afternoon's walk in splendid surroundings. Take the 1230 bus from Cachi to the schoolhouse at Las Pailas, walking from there on a track towards the mountains. After about 1 hour, you cross a river by a small wooden hanging bridge. Ask at the house there for a guide to take you to the ruins. The ruins themselves are not especially impressive but the view is breathtaking, with huge cacti set against snow-topped Andean peaks. The walk back to Cachi is an easy going 3 hours downhill; alternatively there is a bus which arrives at Cachi at 1800.

There is a metre-gauge railway from Salta through the little town of **San Antonio de los Cobres** to Antofagasta, in north Chile (trains only as far as Socompa, on the Chilean frontier). It is 900 km. long and reaches an altitude of 4,453 metres as it passes over the Chorrillos pass. Do not eat, drink, smoke in excess on the way up; resident doctor on board for altitude problems. Take plenty of film, but do not take pictures in San Antonio: it is a military zone. From Salta to San Antonio de los Cobres it passes through the Quebrada del Toro, even more picturesque and impressive than the Humahuaca valley. Muñano, on a desert plateau after one goes over the mountains at Abra Muñano (4,165 metres), is the highest railway station in Argentina, 3,936 metres. The gorge is peculiar in that there is no pass over the mountains. The line is hewn out of the wall closing the end of the valley, zig-zags up and then across the top of the ridge at both El Alisal and Chorrillos. The Argentine side is a barren, rocky plateau 2,150-3,350 metres above sea level and inhabited by Coya Indians who bear a far closer resemblance to their cousins in Bolivia than to the Salteño lowlander. The train turns E at Puerto Tastil to climb to Muñano and misses the archaeological areas, which can however be reached by bus or car. The vertiginous, many-forded road from Salta to San Antonio de los Cobres follows much the same route as the railway but is at a much lower level, which makes it prone to flooding, and the view from the train is much more impressive. The vegetation is low scrub and cactus.

San Antonio is a squat, ugly mining town on a bleak, high desert at 3,750 metres, pop.: 2,200 only of interest if you want to visit the copper, zinc, lead and silver mines with shuttle bus from La Concordia company office, about 20 km., from the mine you can walk to La Polvorilla viaduct, 20 mins., vicuñas and condors en route; *Hospedaje Belgrano*, painted blue, F, no heat, basic, expensive restaurant; *Pensión Los Andes*, G, breakfast extra, very basic, both on main street.
    Bus from Salta to San Antonio de los Cobres, 6 hrs., daily except Sat., US$2.30. Empresa Quebradeña also runs, and serves Muñano 3 times a week, unreliable timetable. On a day trip from Salta by minibus US$6, stop at Santa Rosa de **Tastil** to see Indian ruins (the roofs of the houses are said to have been made of cactus). Alternatively, take the Empresa Quebradeño bus, Fri. 1010 only, arriving 1600 at Tastil, which leaves you 4 hours at ruins (plenty of time) before catching the bus (1955) on its way back from San Antonio de los Cobres. Try the quesillo de cabra (goat's cheese) from Estancia Las Cuevas. If hiking, take your own water, there is none in the mountains.

From Salta the main connection with San Antonio is now the train to **Socompa on the Chilean frontier** (570 km.). Train to Socompa leaves Salta 1615, arr 1245 Sun., first class US$8, tourist class US$6, returns Sun. at 1455 arriving in Salta 1145 Mon. Wait in Socompa for the freight train which runs to and from Calama and ask officials if you can take this, a long, hard, cold ride, but cheap (total cost Salta-Baquedano, Chile, US$18). No through trains to Chile.
    The *Tren a las Nubes* (Train to the Clouds) runs the 218 km. between Salta and La Polvorilla viaduct. The service (1st class) operates on Sat. from April to November (July and August Thur., Fri. and Sun. as well), leaving at 0645 and arriving back at 2205, US$11, US$2 for lunch. Book up to 45 days in advance at station; or in railway office, Florida 753 Buenos Aires. Be warned, though, that its departure and arrival points are at 1,200 metres while it climbs to and descends from 3,960 metres in 15 hours—you will need a remedy for *soroche*. Furthermore, if the service is cancelled because of inclement waether, it can be difficult to obtain a refund.
    A goods train goes on Weds. from Salta at 1910 (arrive 0820) to Pocitos, beyond San Antonio. It serves the British-built borate plant at Campo Quijano. It is a single track line so you can change to come down at e.g. Diego de Almagro at dusk. Obtain authorization for

travel by this train at the "Movimientos" bureau, 1st floor Office No. 110, change voucher for ticket at the downstairs counter. The train leaves from the goods depôt, a few metres from the Belgrano Railway station. Show up ½ hour early, on the platform where the big bell hangs and where the conductors (guards) meet; there is now one passenger coach (first class US$7.90, tourist US$5.90).

The road from San Antonio de los Cobres over the pass of Huaytiquina (4,200 metres) to San Pedro de Atacama is no longer in use. At its highest, this road is 4,560 metres but it has been replaced by the less steep Sico Pass, which runs parallel to Huaytiquina. Fork left just before Catúa, cross the border at Sico (4,079 metres) and continue via Mina Laco and Socaire to Taconao (road very bad between these two points) where the road joins the Huaytiquina route. It is a very beautiful trip: you cross salt lakes with flamingoes and impressive desert around. The road on the Argentine side is very good. Gasoline is available in San Pedro and Calama. Because of snow, this route is available only part of the year. A car must be in very good condition to cope with the heights. Ask the carabineros in San Antonio de los Cobres about road conditions, and complete exit formalities here.

The direct road from Salta to Jujuy is picturesque with its winding 92-km. stretch through the mountains, now paved, known as *la cornisa*. The longer road, via Güemes, is the better road for hitch-hiking.

Jujuy (pronounced Hoo-hooey) properly San Salvador de Jujuy, the capital of Jujuy province, 66 km. by rail N of the Güemes junction on the Belgrano railway, was founded first in 1565 and then in 1575, when it was destroyed by the Indians, and finally established in 1593. The Government House is in a fine square lined with orange trees, Plaza Belgrano, in the eastern part of the city. On the western side of this plaza is a colonial Cathedral (shuts 1230-1500 daily) with very fine 18th century images, pulpits, walls and paintings finished about 1746. It has been heavily restored, but in the nave is a superb wooden pulpit, carved by Indians and gilded, a colonial treasure without its equal in Argentina. You can see the doorway on Calle Lavalle through which General Lavalle, the enemy of Rosas, was killed by a bullet in 1848, but the door is a copy; the original was taken to Buenos Aires. On Alvear, between Senador Pérez and Lamadrid, are the Teatro Mitre (worth a visit) and the Mercado Artesanal. In the western part of the city are the Parque San Martín and an open space, La Tablada, where horses, mules and donkeys used to be assembled in caravans to be driven to the mines in Bolivia and Peru. See the Palacio de Tribunales near the river, one of the best modern buildings in Argentina. Jujuy stands at 1,260 metres, completely surrounded by wooded mountains. Streets are lined with bitter-orange trees. Pop.: 124,500. The scenery is varied and splendid, although the city itself has become a little shabby.

Public Holidays 6 and 23-24 August. Festival on 6 Nov.

Hotels Best is *Augustus*, Belgrano 715, 4 star, A, modern, comfortable but noisy. *Fenicia*, B, on riverside at 19 de Abril 427. *Internacional*, Belgrano 501 (main square), B. *Alto la Viña*, attractive, on hill 5 km. away, C, swimming pool. *Sumay*, Otero 232, C, central, clean; *Avenida*, 19 de Abril 469, on riverside, with fair restaurant, D (F off season, cafeteria only); *Residencial Belgrano*, Belgrano, E, some rooms with bath, not too clean, very central; *Residencial Los Andes*, Rep. de Siria 460, clean, hot water, F. Across the street is *Residencial San Carlos*, Siria 459, E, friendly, clean, some rooms a/c; *Motel Huaico* (good), just outside on road to Humahuaca. *Residencial Lavalle*, Lavalle 372, near station, rec., E (dog bites if touched). *Del Norte*, Alvear 444, F, clean and friendly, near railway station, with good cheap restaurant; next door is *Carlitos*, also F, very friendly. *Chung King*, Alvear 627, friendly, very noisy, many mosquitoes, E, good restaurant. *Savoy*, F, basic and very clean, but damp.

Camping *Autocamping Municipal*, US$2.40 per tent, ask for a cheaper rate for one person. 14 km. N of Jujuy on Humahuaca road, also *Autocamping*, 3 km. N outside city at Huaico Chico, US$1.50 per tent, motel opposite. Buses frequent. Hot showers, clothes washing facilities, very friendly.

Restaurants *Casa del Médico*, Alto La Viña, French cooking, expensive and excellent; *Chung-King*, very good, Alvear 627; *Conrad*, Belgrano 952, good; *La Royal*, on Belgrano, good food and atmosphere. *Bar-Restaurant Sociedad Obrera* for cheap food, General Balcarce 357, but not attractive, cheap bar opposite. *Restaurant Sirio Libanesa*, Lamadrid 568 (don't be put off by the uninviting entrance). *La Ventana Salón Club Social*, Belgrano

751, good cheap menu. *La Rueda-Parrillada*, Lavalle 320, excellent meat, very popular; *Ruta 9*, Costa Rica 968, good local food, Bolivian owners in Barrio Mariano Moreno, take taxi. Very good ice cream around the corner of the Cathedral, made by Greek owner.

Shopping Camera Repairs Sr. Calve, Siria 345. Backpack repairs, San Martín y Gorriti. Good cheap ponchos at cooperative on Necochea, near Belgrano.

Museums Histórico Provincial, Lavalle 266; Museo de Paleontología y Mineralogía, Independencia and Lavalle. Museo de Bellas Artes, Güemes 956, open Mon.-Fri., 0800-1300, 1600-2100, Sat. 0900-1200.

Exchange at travel agencies on Calle Belgrano change cash and dollar travellers' cheques (e.g. Noroeste Cambio, No. 592). Cheques can also be changed at Horus, about 50 metres from the Tourist Office, on Belgrano. If desperate, ask the dueña of the *confitería* at bus station, rates not too unreasonable. (See note on provincial bonds used as currency, **page** 192).

Consulates Bolivia, Av. Mitre 32, Barrio V. San Martín, price of visa should be US$5, pay no more; Spain, R. de Velasco 362; Italy, Av. Fascio 660. **Migración** is on Belgrano 499.

Post Office Otero 262; Independencia y Lamadrid; bus terminal. Entel, Senador Pérez 141.

Tourist Office on corner of Belgrano 690 and Lavalle, very helpful, open till 2100.

For information on bird watching, contact Mario Daniel Cheronaza, Pratonal 38, No. 848-830, Viviendos "El Arenal", Jujuy. The Estación Biológica de Fauna Silvestre, Av. Bolivia 2335, Jujuy, is open to the public on Sundays (for private tours on other days, contact Dr. Arturo A.Canedi, T 25617-25845), very interesting.

Travel Agencies Many along Belgrano. Turismo Lavalle, Belgrano 636, does car tours through the Quebrada de Humahuaca, US$10 to see the villages.

Train No direct services to Salta. Train to Buenos Aires only Tues. and Fri. at 1240, very crowded and can be endlessly delayed. There is also a bus/train combination via Tucumán with La Veloz del Norte (US$10) Sun. and Wed. at 1100 arr. Tucumán 1600; Independencia train leaves at 1715, Bs. As. to Jujuy, Tues. and Fri. with *El Norteño* at 1000; Sun. and Thurs. at 1800. No sleepers. There are two trains a week to La Quiaca for Bolivia, leaving 2319 Tues. and Fri., arriving 0930 Wed. and Sat. respectively.

Airport 40 km. out of town or 45 mins. by bus. Service to Buenos Aires by Aerolíneas Argentinas, two flights a day via Salta, Tucumán, Córdoba; cheap flight on Sun. 0315. Check for weather conditions in connecting airports before you fly or you may find yourself stranded elsewhere.

Buses To and from Buenos Aires Mon., Wed., Fri., Sun. at 1200 arriving 0930 following day; Mon., Tues., Thurs., Sat. leaves 2200, arrives 1945. Via Tucumán to Córdoba, at 0800, 1400, 1845, 2130 (Panamericano T 27281/27143), at 0800, 1100, with La Veloz, daily, Tucumán 5 hrs., US$7, and Córdoba, 14 hrs. US$20 with Atahualpa. To Salta, from 0700 to 0930, 2¾ hours, US$2.40. To La Quiaca, leaves 0745, 1100, 1800, 2315, 6½ hrs., Panamericano, US$6.50. Road paved only as far as Humahuaca, reasonably comfortable, but cold. To Orán daily at 1700; to Humahuaca, US$3, 3 hrs., sit on left side. To Embarcación, US$5.25 with Agencia Balut, via San Pedro and Libertador San Martín. Jujuy-Purmamarca-Susques, leaves Purmamarca at 1330 on Wed. and Sat., returning Thurs. and Sun., crossing the Abra Potrerillos (4,164 m.) and the Salinas Grandes of Jujuy. Jujuy-Tilcara 1½ hrs., US$2.50.

Some 19 km. from Jujuy is ***Termas de Reyes***, where there are hot springs. This resort, with the *Gran Hotel Termas de Reyes*, (C, run down but friendly, good meals), is set among magnificent mountains 45 mins. by bus from Jujuy (No. 14 from corner of plaza, 6 times a day). US$2 to swim in the thermal pool at the hotel; municipal baths free but closed Weds. It is possible to camp below the hotel free of charge.

East from Jujuy The Loving Team of London write: ***San Pedro de Jujuy*** is a sugar town of 60,000; interesting factory area with houses, hospital, Anglican church, recreation centre built by the English Leach family who owned the sugar mill; now all falling to rack and ruin. *Hotel Alex*, opp. bus station, E, clean; *Residencial Gorritti*, on Gorritti, F. Bus to Jujuy, US$2, 1½ hrs.; Atahualpa to Embarcación, US$3.50, 2½ hrs.

North from Jujuy
Lovers of old churches will find Salta and Jujuy excellent centres. Franciscan and Dominican friars arrived in the area from Bolivia as early as 1550. The Jesuits followed about 1585. Along both the old Camino de los Incas and the new route through the Quebrada de Humahuaca the padres, in the

ANDEAN CHURCHES
IN ARGENTINA
CROQUIS.

course of two centuries, built simple but beautiful churches, of which about 20 still exist. They are marked by crosses on the map. All of them can be visited by car from Salta or Jujuy, though some of the roads are very rough. A spare fuel can should be carried because service stations are far apart. (There are ACA stations at Jujuy, Humahuaca and La Quiaca, and YPF stations at Tilcara and Abra Pampa.)

One group, in the Puna de Atacama, on the old Camino de los Incas (which has completely disappeared), can be reached by the road which runs W from Salta through the picturesque Quebrada del Toro to San Antonio de los Cobres (**see page** 100). The road S from San Antonio to Antofagasta de la Sierra is pretty severe going. The road N to Susques (105 km.), is comparatively comfortable, but runs through utter desert. There is lodging at Susques and an interesting 16th century chapel. Close to the Bolivian and Chilean frontier is El Toro, lovely ride through *altiplano*, past Laguna Turilari, mining territory, bizarre rock formations. Lodgings may be available in first-aid room, ask male nurse, Don Juan Puca. From El Toro on to Coranzulí is very rough.

The second group can be reached from the road N from Jujuy to La Quiaca through the Quebrada de Humahuaca, which is itself extremely beautiful, with spectacular and dramatic rock colours and giant cacti in the higher, drier parts; the Inter-American Highway through it has been paved as far as Humahuaca.

Beyond Tumbaya, where there is a church originally built in 1796 and rebuilt in 1873, a road runs 5 km. to **Purmamarca**, a very poor but picturesque village; there is a *hospedaje*, or lodging can be obtained by asking at the ceramic shop opposite the church (mid-17th century) or at the police station, and there is a campsite (no facilities). At the entrance to Purmamarca a right turn leads to a new gravel road, which leads through another *quebrada* over a 4,170-metre pass to the Salinas Grandes salt flats at about 3,500 metres on the Altiplano. The road continues on to Susques (see above).

Not far N of the turn, on the main road, is Maimará (*Albergue Maimará*, also camping, 5 km. from Maimará, US$1.20 a day). Between the turning to Purmamarca and Maimará is a new folk museum called Posta de Hornillos, a recently restored old colonial posting house, of which there used to be a chain from Buenos Aires to the Bolivian border. Highly recommended. **Tilcara**, a short distance N in the *quebrada*, has a folk museum run by Buenos Aires University (closed in June), the Ernesto Soto Avendaño museum where a scaled-down model of the independence monument at Humahuaca can be seen, the regional museum José A. Terry with paintings, and the *Hotel Tilcara* (D, closed in winter, swimming pool—usually dry); *Hotel Edén*, Av. Rivadavia, one block from plaza, clean, friendly, F; *El Antigal*, on same street, E, warmly rec., popular meeting place for travellers, good restaurant. *Restaurante Pucará*, on main square, rec. Within walking distance is a *pucará*, or Inca fort, entry US$0.40, incorrectly reconstructed but with good views of the valley, closed in June. Botanic garden at the foot of the *pucará* and museum at the main square with excellent display of Andean items.

The churches of Huacalera, Uquía, and Humahuaca are on the main road. At Huacalera is the entirely new *Hotel Monterrey*, D, friendly but run down. Two km. S of Huacalera, a small obelisk 20 metres W of the road gives the exact latitude of the Tropic of Capricorn. At Uquía (church built 1691, with *cuzqueño* paintings) and Casabindo, the walls of the naves are hung with 17th century paintings of winged angels in military dress: the so-called *ángeles caballeros*. Cactus-wood decoration is found in many local churches.

Both in Tilcara and Humahuaca there are displays of pictures of the Passion made Hotel entirely of flowers, leaves, grasses and seeds at Easter and a traditional procession on Holy Thursday at night joined by thousands. No beef is sold during Holy Week in shops or restaurants. All along the Quebrada de Humahuaca the pre-Lent carnival celebrations are picturesque and colourful.

Humahuaca (alt. 2,940 metres), 126 km. from Jujuy (3 hrs., US$3, by bus), is a small traditional town with an attractive church (originally begun 1631, but totally reconstructed in 1873-80), a mechanical figure of San Francisco Solano which blesses the town from the town hall at 1200, and a large independence monument flanked by huge cacti. See the Estudio Museo Ramoneda, combined studio and museum, entrance US$0.50. Museo Folklórico Regional, Buenos Aires 435, open daily 0800-2000, US$0.80, privately owned (run by Sr. Sixto Vázquez Zuleta, an authority on the area's folklore), well worth seeing. Market near Humahuaca railway station, where *colla* women sell everything from homeopathic herbs to fresh bread. Folklore festival at Rodero, close to Humahuaca, around January 13-15, with local groups and dancing. Humahuaca's main festival is Candelaria, February 2, with a procession after 1400 with traditional dress and music. Near Humahuaca, 9 km. NE, is Cotaca, a large unexplained archaeological site with an Indian village nearby, a nice walk; you can also see Indian artistic remains nearby at Hornaditas (18 km. on La Quiaca road) and Incacueva, and an Indian mine at Rinconada.

Humahuaca, to its detriment, is becoming increasingly geared towards tourism; an influx of tourist coaches arrives from Salta and Jujuy in the early afternoon, when prices for handicrafts rise steeply; if buying wait till the late afternoon when the coaches have gone.

The Instituto de Cultura Indígena offers guided tours of Indian communities, information, Quechua classes, exhibitions, concerts, lectures and a public library specializing in anthropology, folklore, history and archaeology, on Buenos Aires 740.

Hotels *Provincial de Turismo*, Buenos Aires 650, D, swimming pool dry even in summer, poor service, modern building is sadly out of keeping with surroundings; *Hotel Humahuaca*, Córdoba y Corrientes, E, basic, run down, with hot water, food is not rec.; **Residencial Humahuaca**, E, some a/c, traditional, clean, friendly. **Residencial Colonial**, E, gloomy, windowless rooms, but clean, on Entre Ríos, one block from bus station. Several **residenciales** (F). Youth Hostel, *Albergue Humahuaca*, Buenos Aires 447, F.

Camping Across bridge by railway station, small charge includes use of facilities.

Restaurants *Del Norte*, Belgrano 346 nr. market, good and cheap, opens Sun. night when most other restaurants are shut; *La Cacharpaya*, near church, good food and music, but avoid middle of the day when bus tours invade. Good place at bus station, which is open in the evening; *Hotel Provincial de Turismo* is also open p.m. Most restaurants only open during the day.

North of Humahuaca, at Iturbe (also called Irigoyen, one bus a day), a road leads right to La Cueva (6 km.) and on 70 km., a spectacular ride over the 4,000-metre Abra del Cóndor to **Iruya**, a beautiful village with a fine 17th-century church and Rosario festival on first Sunday in October; two buses a week from Humahuaca, on other days take the bus to Iturbe and ask in one of the village's few shops for a lift. The trips to Iruya offered by *pensiones* in Humahuaca, or even by people in the street, are overpriced; check at the ACA petrol station for correct information on public transport. It is worthwhile staying in Iruya for a few days; it makes an extremely pleasant and friendly centre for walking trips. Puna Expediciones (**see Salta page** 95) runs a 7-day trek, Salta-Iruya-Nazareno-La Quiaca, walking between Iruya and Nazareno on small, remote paths where there are no tourists or motorvehicles, sleeping in local schoolhouses; rest of route is by truck.

Roads to Cochinoca (25 km.) and Casabindo (62 km.) branch off left at a point 4 km. N of Abra Pampa, where mining is important. (*Residencial* nr. plaza in Abra Pampa on Senador Pérez, clean, hot water; meals in the bus station.) About 60 km. away is Laguna Pozuelos, a natural monument and flamingo reserve. Truck transport daily exc. Sun. If driving, the Laguna is 5 kms from the road, the turning is marked by a post with a wheel hanging on it, the road is private and permission to use it is necessary; walk last 800 metres to reach the edge of the lagoon. 15 km. from Abra Pampa is the vicuña farm at Miraflores, the largest in Argentina. Information offered, photography permitted; colectivos go a.m. Mon.-Sat. from Abra Pampa to the vicuña farm.

Yavi, with the fine church of San Francisco, which has magnificent gold decoration and windows of onyx, is reached by a good, paved road (16 km.) from La Quiaca; taxi available. (Find the caretaker at her house and she will show you round the church, open Tues.-Sun. 0900-1200 and Tues.-Fri. 1500-1800.) Opposite this church is the house of the Marqués Campero y Tojo. Three-room *hostería* at Yavi. Only a mule track leads on to the two churches of Santa Victoria (a forlorn Indian village in a rain forest valley) and Acoyte.

Beyond Humahuaca the *puna* is bleak and barren all the way, and the road unpaved, for the 167 km. to **La Quiaca**, on the Bolivian border and 292 km. from Jujuy. There is a market across the footbridge over the railway tracks, then one block on. La Quiaca is joined to its Bolivian neighbour, Villazón, by a concrete bridge. Altitude, 3,442 metres. On the third Sunday in October the Manca Fiesta, or the festival of the pots, is held here, and the Colla Indians from Jujuy and the Bolivian *altiplano* come, carrying all sorts of pots; local food is eaten. The climate calls for warm clothing the year round. If going on into Bolivia, buy your basic rations, medicaments etc. in La Quiaca. If it rains heavily when you are travelling by car between Jujuy and La Quiaca, wait, or you may find yourself on flooded roads.

Hotels *Turismo*, D, rec., clean, modern, comfortable, two blocks S and one W of bus station; *Cristal*, best, four blocks from railway station, E, clean and comfortable, with café and bus office adjacent. *Residencia Argentina*, clean; *Grand*, opp. railway station, clean, good hot showers, F; *Residencial El Turista*, very good, but expensive, has garages and swimming pool; *Alojamiento Cruz del Sur*, cheap; cheap alojamiento, *Pequeño*, Av. Bolívar 236, friendly and clean. *Residencial Independencia*, rec., near railway station and church, F, hot water but no room heating even in winter when temperatures can drop to -15˚C. *La Frontera* hotel and restaurant, uphill from Atahualpa bus stop, good and cheap.

Camping is possible near the control post on the outskirts of town.

Restaurant *Cristal*, opposite the Atahualpa bus office in small shopping arcade on the main shopping street, good, cheap; *Café Victoria* and *Panamericano* in same building as *Grand Hotel*.

Exchange Travel agency around corner from *Hotel Cristal* gives good rates for cheques; there are few other exchange facilities in town.

Transport Difficult to obtain information in La Quiaca about buses leaving Villazón for points in Bolivia (see page 243 for Villazón), though Bolivian buses tend to be more reliable than Bolivian trains. New bus station in La Quiaca, 4 blocks from railway station, accepts payment in US$. 4 Atahualpa buses (next to *Hotel Cristal*) a day to Salta (US$13) via Jujuy, 1100, 1600, 1800, 2130 (5-8 hrs. to Jujuy, 9-11 hrs. to Salta), also several to Jujuy. Panamericano (T 396, next to *Hotel Grand*) has 5 buses a day to Jujuy, US$6.50, 6½ hrs. Some meal breaks, but take own food, as sometimes long delays. Buses may be stopped and searched for coca leaves. *Común* bus at 2130, 12 hours. The railway line between Jujuy and La Quiaca has been restored following storm damage in February 1984; train leaves for Jujuy and Tucumán Thurs. and Sat. at 1015, arriving Jujuy at 2030, Tucumán at 0630 Fri. and Sun. On the days when trains from La Paz to Villazón arrive (Wed., Fri., and Sat., but check), there is reported to be a connection from La Quiaca to Buenos Aires at 2100, good meals in 1st class, crowded. Fare to Güemes (for Salta), US$4. The railway goes up to 3,692 metres at Tres Cruces. Take warm sweaters, as temperature drops sharply after sunset.

To Bolivia Take a taxi or hire a porter with a luggage barrow to take you through the immigration office opposite the Automóvil Club, and customs and final control on the frontier. There are few exchange facilities on the Argentine side (only until 1300 at Banco de la Nación in La Quiaca). Travellers' cheques can no longer be cashed at the Turismo building; only dollar notes are accepted there (good rates) and at the exchange shops. In La Quiaca some of the large supermarkets give good rates for the Argentine austral. You can also buy australes in Villazón for US notes, but not for travellers' cheques. *Cambios* are open on Sundays at Villazón but give a very poor rate. Food is good and cheap. Tip conductor at start and end of trip for service. Motorists should visit the Argentine Automóvil Club just off the international bridge for maps, gasoline, etc., and information; and in Villazón, the Servicio Nacional de Turismo to obtain the Hoja de Ruta, which all motorists must have. It is not restrictive in any practical sense; just a nuisance! If the Bolivian Immigration Officer at Villazón is not in his office, you can ask for him at *Hotel Panamericano*, just up from the Post Office. Taxis are available from the Argentine station, or the frontier, to the Bolivian station.

Warning Those travellers who need a visa to enter Bolivia are advised to get it before arriving in La Quiaca because the consular staff there try to charge US$15 per visa; pleading may reduce the charge.

Medical There are a good hospital in La Quiaca and a doctor in Villazón. Farmacia Nueva, 1/2 block from Church, has remedies for *soroche* (mountain sickness).

Entering Argentina from Bolivia, Argentine immigration and customs are open 0730- 1200, 1500-1800; Sats., Suns., and holidays pay special fee of US$3 after 1100. Buses arriving outside these hours will have to wait, so check before travelling. Porters US$1 from Villazón bus station to border; another US$1 from border to Argentine station. You can cross the border at night, without luggage, and your passport will not be stamped. Very thorough customs searches are made some 20 km. after the border in Argentina; be prepared for camera search. Border crossing into Argentina may take up to 1 1/2 hours: formalities are very thorough.

N.B. Bolivian time is one hour earlier than Argentine (2 hours in summer). Lunch Bolivian side is 1200-1400 (Bolivian time) and Argentine side 1200-1500 (Argentine time) so customs reopen at same time.

Make sure you book a seat when buying a railway ticket; it is also essential to arrive well in advance of advertised time of departure to get your seat.

Bolivia can also be reached by road from **Orán**, an uninteresting place, pop. 34,000 (*Hotel Centro*, E; dirty room at *Hotel Crillón*, E; *Residencial Crisol*, General San Martín, near bus stations, F, without bath, hot water, friendly, rec.; several hotels near bus station) where there are bus services to Agua Blanca (45mins., US$1.30, luggage checks on bus), on the frontier. There is nowhere to stay at Agua Blanca nor anywhere to change money, but there are restaurants (*El Rinconcito de los Amigos*) and shops; spend your remaining Bolivian money here, not accepted in Orán; buses to Orán every 45 mins. The passport office at Agua Blanca is open from 0700 to 1200 and 1500 to 1900 hrs. There is no exit tax. There is a through bus service from Agua Blanca to Salta at 1100 daily. Buses run twice daily from Bermejo, across the river (ferry US$0.10), to Tarija (10 hours, US$6). There is no direct bus from Orán to Asunción, Paraguay; take bus to Embarcación, from there train to Formosa, then bus to Asunción.

Buses, five daily from Orán to Salta, last at 2100, 8 1/2 hrs.; direct bus to Tucumán at 2130, connecting for Mendoza bus which leaves at 1300. Bus to Tartagal daily at 0630 and 1800; to Jujuy at 1200 daily; to Formosa, US$22, 14 hrs., leaving Tues., Thurs., Sat. at 0930; Orán to Embarcación, US$1.30.

Embarcación (pop. 24,000) has several hotels (*Punta Norte*, on España, D, new, clean, a/c, friendly; Sr. Sarmiento's Hotel; *Universal*, hot water), of which the cheaper are near the railway station. Restaurant of *Sociedad Sirio Libanesa*, H. Irigoyen and 9 de Julio, cheap and good. 2 km. from Embarcación you can walk to the Loma Protestant mission for Mataes and Toba Indians, who sell unpainted pottery there. These Indians lead a fairly miserable existence. Buses go to Orán, 1 hour, US$1.30 on a paved road, from whence there are frequent buses to Agua Blanca (1 hour, US$1). Buses Embarcación-Pocitos. Bus Embarcación-Salta US$10. Embarcación-Formosa railway (dusty in summer) has *coche-motor* link leaving Embarcación 1325 Mon. and Fri., 20 hours, US$10 1st class, US$6 tourist, plenty of wildlife to see, but check details as this service is sometimes replaced by a bus when there is weather damage to the line. (Regular bus runs Tues. 1445.)

THE CUYO REGION: OVER THE ANDES TO CHILE (4)

In the Cuyo region, in the W, there is little rain and nothing can be grown except under irrigation. On the irrigated lands grapes and fruit are possible, and alfalfa takes the place of the maize grown in the N. Three of the more important oases in this area of slight rainfall are Mendoza itself, San Rafael, 160 km. to the S, and San Juan 177 km. to the N.

Of the 15 million hectares in Mendoza Province, only 2% are cultivated. Of the cultivated area 40% is given over to vines, 25% is under alfalfa grown for cattle, and the rest under olive groves and fruit trees. Petroleum is produced in the Province, and there are important uranium deposits.

The Transandine Route Travelling by rail or road from Buenos Aires westward across the pampa, one comes first to:

Mercedes, in Buenos Aires Province, a pleasant city with a population of 40,000. It has many fine buildings, and is a railway junction of some importance. Travellers have been told here that it is against the law to take one's shoes off in the station! (Not to be confused with Villa Mercedes in San Luis Province—see below.) Tourist Office on plaza, very friendly.

Hotels *Aragón*, ½ block from Plaza, friendly, F, hot water. *Libertador*, E, opp. bus station, good.

The workshops of the San Martín railway are at *Junín*, 256 km. from Buenos Aires. (Eva Perón was born near here.) Also served by Mitre railway, the town is close to lagoons from which fish are taken to the capital. Population, 63,700.

Hotels *Junín; Central. La Piemontesa*, E, reasonable.

Camping Chimihuin municipal campsite, US$1.50.

At Rufino, on Route 7, 452 km. from Buenos Aires, is the very reasonable, rec. *Hotel Astur* (Córdoba 81), D with ACA discount; also at La Boulaye, on Route 7, 517 km. from Buenos Aires, there are several good and cheap hotels, e.g. *Victoria*.

At *Villa Mercedes* (San Luis Province, pop. 77,000), 693 km. from Buenos Aires (where the old municipal market is now an arts and community centre), a line runs NE to (122 km.) Río Cuarto. About 65 km. beyond Villa Mercedes we begin to run into the rolling hills of San Luis; beyond there are stretches of woodland.

Hotels ACA hotel *San Martín*, Lavalle 435, D, restaurant, garages, clean, friendly; the ACA restaurant at the service station on Route 7, outside town, is very good value; *Hostal del Sol*, on main highway; *Avenida*, in centre, E.

Bus Villa Mercedes - Buenos Aires US$20.

Train Buenos Aires-Villa Mercedes, *El Aconcagua* daily at 2115, arrives 0730; returns 2206, arrives 0830; sleeper US$28.50, Pullman US$20.60; 1st Class US$13.50, tourist US$9.40.

Air Airport: Villa Reynolds, 10 km. from Villa Mercedes. Austral to Buenos Aires and to San Juan on Mon., Tues., Wed. at 1225, Fri., at 2000.

San Luis, 98 km. from Villa Mercedes, is the capital of the Province of San Luis. It stands at 765 metres at the southern end of the Punta de los Venados   hills. It was founded by Martín de Loyola, the governor of Chile, in 1596, and is still faintly colonial. The area is rich in minerals and an onyx quarry is worked. Visit the Centro Artesanal San Martín de Porras, run by the Dominican fathers, on 25 de Mayo, opp. Govt. Palace, where rugs are made. Open 0700-1300 exc. Sat. and Sun. Population: 150,000. San Luis to Mendoza is 264 km.

A "Via Crucis" sculptured in white marble skirts the mountainside. Beyond Salto Grande, Salto Colorado and the Gruta de la Virgen de las Flores is El Volcán, in whose neighbourhood is Cruz de Piedra dam (drives, fishing), and Cañada Honda (placer gold mining, riding and fishing). Hotels and inns along the road.

Hotels *Dos Venados*, Junín and Sucre; *Gran Palace*, Rivadavia 657; *Aiello*, Av. Pres. Illia 431 T 25644, a/c, private bath, garages. *Gran San Luis*, Av. Pres. Illia 470, pool, 50 metres from ACA; *Regidor*, San Martín 804; *Gran Hotel España*, Av.Pres. Illia 300,T 25051, 3 star; and *Novel*, Junín 748, all category C. *Castelmonte*, Chacabuco 769; *Grisel*, Bolívar 321; and *Miramar*, Maipú 874, all category D. *Mitre*, Mitre 1043; *Rivadavia*, Rivadavia 1470; *Casino*, Uruguay 804; *Los Andes*, Los Andes 1582; *Royal*, Colón 878; and *Buenos Aires*, Buenos Aires 834; all category E. *Hotel Residencial 17*, hot water, friendly, opp. bus station, basic, F. *Hotel San Antonio*, with restaurant; many others opposite bus and railway station; these are category F.

Camping No site but plenty of waste ground between bus and railway stations.

Restaurants *Suany*, Bolívar 991, rec.; *Los Venados*, Colón and Bolívar. *Michel*, rec.

Exchange House *Alituris*, Pringles 983, opp. Plaza, no commission.

Tourist Office San Martín 741, excellent.

Train Buenos Aires-San Luis leaves at 2115, *El Aconcagua*, costs US$10.75 tourist, US$15.25 first, US$23.30 Pullman, and Sleeper US$30.80. Can continue on train to Mendoza, 4 hrs. Return daily at 2006, arrives 0830 next day.

29 km. NE of San Luis is **La Toma** (*Hotel Gran Italia*, F, hot showers; *Residencial Days*, P. Graciarena 158, private bath) the cheapest place to buy green onyx - about 20 shops. From here you can make an excursion to Cerros Rosario, interesting hills and rock scenery, 10 km. NW; and San José del Morro, a group of mountains which were originally volcanoes (there is a model in the Museo de Ciencias in Buenos Aires). You will find a lot of rose-quartz.

Beyond San Luis (27 km.) the line climbs to a height of 460 metres and descends again along the valley of the Río Desaguadero. From the small junction of Las Catitas, 92 km. from Mendoza, a branch line runs S to (183 km.) San Rafael, through country typical of this region: sometimes arid, sometimes marshy, and sometimes cultivated. At **San Rafael** itself, at the foot of the Andes, irrigation makes it possible to grow fruit in large quantities. The town - there are some oil wells near - has a population of 72,200. There is a small but interesting natural history museum. A road runs W over El Pehuenche pass to Talca (Chile). Bus to Mendoza, frequent, US$4. Bus to Neuquén, US$15.

Hotels *Rex; España*, corner of San Martín and España, D with bath, clean but shabby, no restaurant. *Luis 1*, España 23, E with bath, a/c, clean; *Hospedaje Residencial Comercio*, F, opp. station on Rivadavia.

Campsite at Tunuyán, 77 km. S of Mendoza on road to San Rafael; there are three more campsites on the road from Luján outside Mendoza to Potrerillos (52 km.).

Above the town, up the Río Atuel valley, there is beautiful scenery in the Valle Hermoso up to the dams of El Nihuil which provide irrigation water and hydroelectric power to Mendoza. There is fishing in the reservoir above the highest dam. Good skiing at **Las Leñas**, 2,250 metres up in Valle Hermoso, a new resort with 15 ski-courses, three T-bars, three ski-lifts. It claims to be the foremost ski resort in the southern hemisphere and hopes to host the World Ski Championships in 1991 or 1993. Three stonebuilt hotels: *Escorpio, Acuario* and *Gemini* and a disco, shop renting equipment and expensive restaurant. All the hotels are L; for cheaper accommodation you have to stay in Los Molles (bus from San Rafael US$3.80; from Las Leñas US$0.50) where is *Hotel La Huenca*, B, a/c, clean. There is an airport in **Malargüe**, pop. 8,600 (*Hotel del Turismo, Restaurant El Cisne*, both rec.), 70 km. from Las Leñas, with flights to Buenos Aires.

Mendoza, at the foot of the Andes, 1,060 km. from Buenos Aires, is linked to it by air, the San Martín railway and a paved road, which continues across the Andes to Chile. (No rail service now between Mendoza and Chile.)

Mendoza (756 metres) is an expanding and very pleasant city. Rainfall is slight, but irrigation has turned the area into a green oasis of fruit trees and vineyards. The city was colonized from Chile in 1561 and named in honour of the then governor of Chile. It was from here that the Liberator José de San Martín set out to cross the Andes, to help in the liberation of Chile. Mendoza was completely destroyed by fire and earthquake in 1861, so today it is essentially a modern city of low dwellings (as a precaution against earthquakes), thickly planted with trees and gardens. There was a serious earthquake, which made 40,000 homeless, in January 1985. The main street is Calle San Martín, which runs S to N parallel to the San Martín railway line. Population of city 148,000, but with suburbs included, it is about 600,000.

See the Cerro de la Gloria, a hill above the great Parque San Martín on the W side of the city, crowned by an astonishing monument to San Martín. There is a great rectangular stone block with bas-reliefs depicting various episodes in the equipping of the Army of the Andes and the actual crossing. In front of the block, San Martín bestrides his charger. In the park at the foot of Cerro de la Gloria steep and twisting paths run to the Zoological Gardens. There are watercourses and an artificial 1 km.-long lake in the park too, where regattas are held, and views of the Andes (when the amount of floating dust will allow) rising in a blue-black perpendicular wall, topped off in winter with dazzling snow, into a china-blue sky. The entrance to the Parque San Martín is ten blocks W of the Plaza Independencia. Bus 11 from the centre will take you half-way up the hill, at the entrance to the zoo (the zoo itself is rather run down). There is an hourly open-topped bus ("Oro Negro") that will take you to the top of the Cerro de la Gloria, which runs from the eastern end of the park, on Av. Libertad, to the monument - it's a long walk (45 mins.).

The best shopping centre is Avenida Las Heras, where there are good souvenir and handicraft shops; leather goods are cheaper here than in Buenos Aires. The municipal market is clean and well-stocked; worth a visit. The vintage festival, Fiesta de la Vendimia, is held in the amphitheatre of the Parque San Martín in the first week of March. There is a wine museum (at the Giol *bodega*), with good guides and wine tasting, just behind the Palacio de Gobierno, opening hours from the tourist office. Outside Mendoza, about 40 km. due E, there is a satellite town, very modern, called San Martín. N.B. Official tours of the city are a waste of time and money.

Wine Wine *bodegas* (wine-making season March/April) and fruit preserving; visiting times available from Tourist Office. Giol winery, one of the world's biggest, was closed and up for sale in early 1990, after economic difficulties in 1989. Take 15 bus marked "Maipú" (every hour), but check if winery is open before going. Also in Maipú district is Peñaflor, 1/2 hr. by taxi SW of city, good visit and generous tasting. Bodega de Arizú is open to inspection any time, bus No 7 from city centre; so are many of the others, and they offer you a glass after the visit. Try Bodega Escorihuela (bus 15 from centre) if you are more interested in the information than the wine-tasting. The Toso bodega is close to the city centre and has excellent wines. San Felipe winery visit rec., with museum, bus 17, tours 0900-1400, 1600-1800, tasting. Prices at the bodegas have roughly a 100% mark-up from supermarket prices. Recommended: Cruz del Sur from Bodega Arizú, Cuesta del Parsal, Valroy-Borgoña, Valroy-Cabernet Sauvignon, Viejo Toro, Trapiche from Bodega Peñaflor, and Vino de Mesa Arizú Tinto Seco. Many tourist agencies include the bodegas in their half-day or day-long tours (US$4-8 but these visits are too short, with too few guides and little tasting - only of the cheaper wines).

Local Holidays 18 January (Crossing of the Andes); 25 July (St. James); 8 September (Virgin of Carmen de Cuyo). Annual wine festival at the beginning of March, when hotels fill up fast; book ahead! Prices rise at this time, and in July (the ski season) and September (the spring festival).

Hotels *Aconcagua*, 4 star, C, comfortable, San Lorenzo 545, good restaurant, pool, tourist advice and bookings available; *Plaza*, Chile 1124 on main plaza, B, not too clean, but obliging; *Blabi*, Las Heras 340, C, small swimming pool, a/c but you must phone to have it turned on each time you return to your room, nice rooms; *Nutibara*, Bartolomé Mitre 867, C, central, modern swimming pool, rec.; *Vecchia Roma*, España 1617 (next door to restaurant of same name), C, comfortable, safe.

In our price range D: *Crillón*, Perú 1065, small, clean. *Petit*, Perú 1459, without breakfast, 11/2 blocks from railway station, clean, friendly, rec.; *City*, Gen. Paz 95, T 253143, clean, helpful; *Royal*, old part, Las Heras 145, adequate value, ask for fan in summer; *Palace*, Las Heras 70, a/c, bath, no breakfast, central; *Vigo*, Necochea 749 (T 250208), good value, good *comedor*; *Santa Clara*, 9 de Julio, central, clean, hot water, own bath. Lower ratings: *Pacífico*, San Juan 1407, modern, comfortable, clean; *Milena*, Pasaje Babilonia 17 (off San Juan nr. Don Bosco), T 240248, 2 star, clean, nice atmosphere; *1 de Mayo*, on first block of Garibaldi, highly rec., 0800 checkout time; *Messidor*, Alberdi 690, reasonable, friendly, clean, comfortable, arranges tours; *El Piño Azul* apartments, San Martín 2872 (T 304593), D per day.

In the cheaper categories: On Calle Juan B. Justo, *Penitentes*, (No 67), T 230208, E with bath, a/c and heating, good, snack bar; *Margal* (No 75), cean, F, mixed reports; *Ideal* (No 270), E, transport to bus station; *Premier* (700 block), E, private parking, clean, good value. On Perú: *Zamora* (No 1156), reasonable and friendly, converted house, E; *Residencial D'Amore* (No 1346), E, clean, use of kitchen, used as brothel. *Dardex* (Perú No.1735), 2 blocks from railway station, G, friendly. On General Paz: *Alcor* (No. 86), central, good, accepts Amex; *Líbano* (No. 227), excellent, clean, from E; *Gran Marta* (No. 460), clean, but only cold showers, rec. (*El Descanso* next door is not rec.); *Imperial*, Las Heras 88, E, washing facilities, friendly, rec.; *República*, Necochea 541, E, pleasant, cheerful, English spoken;

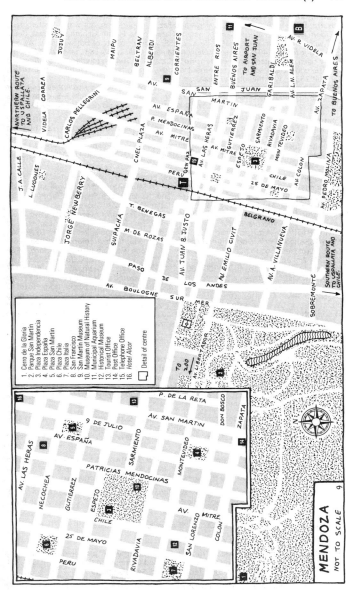

MENDOZA
NOT TO SCALE

1. Cerro de la Gloria
2. Parque San Martín
3. Plaza Independencia
4. Plaza España
5. Plaza San Martín
6. Plaza Chile
7. Plaza Italia
8. San Francisco
9. San Martín Museum
10. Museum of Natural History
11. Municipal Aquarium
12. Historical Museum
13. Tourist Office
14. Post Office
15. Telephone Office
16. Hotel Alcor

☐ Detail of centre

Residencial Miami, Necochea 278, E, very clean; *San Martín*, on Espejo at Plaza, E, rec.; *El Rosario*, Chile 1579, between Las Heras and Paz, E, good, clean, hot water, heating, rec.; *Residencial Unión*, Patricias Mendocinas, nr. Plaza España, E, without bath, breakfast, clean, hot water; *Residencial Central*, 9 de Julio 658, F, clean, plenty of hot water. On Av. San Juan, *Quijote* (No. 1407), E, clean, friendly, restaurant; *Galicia* (No. 881, near Av. L. M. Alem), F, very clean, hot water; unnamed *pensión* at Catamarca 264, F, crowded. *Savoy*, Belgrano 1377, E, good, clean, some rooms without window, tours offered at 20% discount; *Escorial*, San Luis 263, E, very friendly and clean, rec.

Lodgings (F) in private houses: ask at Escuela de Hotelería, Paso de los Andes 1249, near entrance to Parque San Martín. Sra. Ada Zárate, San Juan 564, 1, Dept. 5-6, close to bus station, E in dormitory, has been rec. Small *Youth Hostel* at Paso de los Andes 1249.

Camping In Parque General San Martín permitted, free, in cars, but not in tents. Three campsites at Challao, about 14 km. from the city centre, reached by colectivo No. 11 leaving every hour. *Camping Suizo* best value, has shop, US$1.50 p.p. and US$1.50 for tent, safest of all sites, friendly but loud music at night from nearby amusement arcade. About 13 km. from Mendoza, two sites near the turn-off for Barballón. *El Salto*, 50 km. W of Mendoza, near mountains, well situated.

Restaurants *Trevi*, Las Heras 68, good. Good ones are the *Automobile Club*, Italian restaurants *Montecatini*, Gral. Paz 370, *Mi Piace*, on Sarmiento, and *Marchigiana*, Patricias Mendocinas 1550; *San Marco*, on Las Heras, and the *Mendoza Regatta Club*, Av. de las Palmeras, Parque San Martín. *Bárbaro*, San Martín 914, English spoken, speciality is roast kid. *Tristán Barraza*, 658 Av. Sarmiento (parrilla), good. *Trattoria Aveni*, 25 de Mayo 1162, crowded, good. *Vecchia Roma*, Av. España 1619, rec. for good food, atmosphere and service. *Parrillada Arturito*, Chile 1575, good cheap steak, popular with locals; *La Rueda*, Mitre 1468, good grill. *Don Angelo*, Lavalle 148, cheap; *Club Alemán*, Necochea 2261, Godoy Cruz, rec. Good value is *Petit Progreso*, Córdoba with San Juan; *Boccaccio*, Mitre 1976; *La Nevada*, Chile 1495, 3-course meal for US$2, excellent value; *Govinda*, San Juan 840, excellent and cheap, open 1200-1600, 1900-2200; *San Agustín*, Av. L. M. Alem 477 opposite hospital, big meals at reasonable prices. *El Dragón del Oro*, Chinese, 25 de Mayo 1553 (near Las Heras), very good; *La Tapita*, 25 de Mayo, 11/2 blocks from *Hotel El Descanso*, serves 4 course set meal at low price. *Pizzería Pic-Nic*, Las Heras 475, good, cheap pizzas. Also on Las Heras is *Cervecería Zurich*, good food and service, cheap, rec. Ice cream at *Soppelso*, Las Heras 409, rec. *Sr. Cheff*, good restaurant/confitería at *Hotel 1 de Mayo* on Garibaldi. *São Paulo*, San Martín 1214, very popular standup coffee bar. *El Gran Lomo*, Rivadavia and San Martín, cheap filling sandwiches, open 24 hrs. *IL Tucco*, Emilio Civit 556 (nr. park gates), also same name and owner in centre on Montevideo, excellent new Italian restaurants, reasonable prices; also on Emilio Civit, No. 275, *Dis Cepolin*, meals at 2200, good tango show at 2300. Good snacks at *Cerrito Bar*, L.M. Alem 41. Vegetarian: Mitre 523, US$2 for all you can eat. Cheap and good eating places near San Martín railway station. In bars 20% extra is charged if you sit at a table rather than at the counter; bar on Belgrano opp. *Hotel Belgrano* is recommended. Out of town, *Lomo Loco*, a few km. S on Luján road, locals' favourite *parrilla* but not cheap. *Chopería Bull and Bush*, José Zapata, large sandwiches and good draught lager.

Shopping Leather goods good and cheap; try *Jorge Ruben Pacheco*, 9 de Julio 1455, subsuelo Loc. 1. Books (English and German selection) from *Historias* on Av. San Martín. English language magazines and *Buenos Aires Herald* usually available at kiosk at corner of San Martín and Alem.

Car Hire Avis, Espejo 228; Lis Car, San Lorenzo 110, T 291416; A.S. Rent-a-Car, Garibaldi 186, T 248317. **Motorcycle repairs** César Armitrano, Rubén Zarate 138, 1600-2100, highly recommended for assistance or a chat; he will let you work in his workshop.

Nightclubs in the suburb of Chacras de Coria. Discothèques: *Blow Up*, Mitre 1520; *Kangaroo*, Rivadavia 430; *La Cueva*, Chile 1285; *El Grillo*, Chile 1243; *Casino*, 25 de Mayo 1123; *Al Diablo*, Ruta Internacional Vistalba Luján.

Cinema Free film shows at Salón Cultural Rivadavia, José V. Zapata 349.

Casino 25 de Mayo 1123, daily 2100-0300.

Mountain Climbing Information from Tourist Office. There is a three-day (Thurs.-Sat.) climbing and trekking expedition via Godoy Cruz and Cacheuta to Cerro Penitentes (4,351 metres), sleeping in mountain refuge, food included. See also page 116.

Museums The **San Martín Museum** (US$0.15) is at Av. General San Martín 1851, some 8 blocks N of the city centre (closed weekends). The **Historical Museum**, on Calle Montevideo near Calle Chile, beautifully furnished, has a collection on San Martín and history of Mendoza. The **Museum of Natural History** is on Plaza Independencia, lodged underground; this, too, has some colonial exhibits but is best known for its collection of Argentine plants and animals (open Tues.-Fri. 0900-1300, Sat.-Sun. 1500-1900). **Museum of Modern Art**, San Martín 1143. The **Palacio Municipal** has a rooftop observation platform, no charge. The **Municipal Aquarium** is underground at Calle Buenos Aires and Ituzaingó, very interesting, admission US$0.50, open Mon.-Fri. 1000-1200 and 1530-2100, Sat. and Sun. same times a.m. but open an hour longer in the evening, until 2200. Worth seeing, also, are the ruins of the **San Francisco church** near Plaza Pedro de Castillo.

Language Classes Sra. Inés Perea de Bujaldon. Rioja 620, teaches Spanish to German speakers, rec.

Exchange Lloyds Bank (BLSA), Av. San Martín 1498. Banco de Credito Argentino, España 1168, gives cash advance on Visa card. Good rates at Bank of America (not travellers' cheques though). American Express, Rivadavia at 9 de Julio, and Citibank Av. San Martín 1099, do not give dollars for US travellers' cheques. Citibank open 0715-1315. Currency changed between 0715 and 1030 only. **N.B.** No travellers' cheques changed at weekends, except at the *cambio* at Galería Tonsa, Av. San Martín 1177, open till 2000 on Sat. Best rate for Chilean currency at the bus terminal (open from 0715). Many *cambios* at Espejo y Catamarca and along San Martín. Good exchange house opposite LAN-Chile office in San Martín. Exprinter, San Martín 1198, and Santiago *cambio* opposite, well rec. Also rec.: Maguitur, Av. San Martín 1203. Another at 9 de Julio, by Av. Las Heras.

Consulates **Bolivia**, Sarmiento 163; **Ecuador**, Boulogne Sur Mer 1397; **Peru**, Perú 8185 Carrodilla; **Chile**, Av. Emilio Civit, esq. Rodríguez; **Uruguay**, 9 de Julio 200.

Goethe Institut Morón 265, Mon.-Fri. 0800-1200, 1600-2230. German films.

Coin-operated **laundromat**, Colón 543, also on Garibaldi near La Rioja, on Salta near San Luis, and at corner of San Juan and Rondeau.

There is a **gynaecological clinic** about three doors away from *El Descanso* hotel; helpful and relatively inexpensive.

Post Office Av. San Martín and Av. Colón. **Telefónico Central**, Chile 1574.

Tourist Offices at airport, T 306484, helpful (frequently closed), and at the bus terminal, T 259709, at Av. San Martín 1143, T 242800, which is also the Museum of Modern Art. They have a list of reasonable private lodgings, but not much other literature apart from lists of *bodegas* and a free town map; the latter is also available at most kiosks.

Travel Agencies Lots in Las Heras, between Perú and San Martín. *Turismo Cóndor*, Las Heras 702 (also at bus station), rec. for tours in and around the city, and to El Cristo Redentor statue, US$12 for whole day, good guides, Spanish only. *Turismo Sepeán*, San Juan 1070, friendly and helpful, have branch in Santiago. *Ibiza*, Espejo 217, T 258141, helpful and efficient. *Hunuc Huar Expediciones*, Av. España 1340, 8 piso, oficina 7, specializes in assistance to climbers, especially on Aconcagua.

Airport Plumerillo, 8 km. from centre; *remise* taxis (US$2-3) and buses (infrequent) run. Bus No. 6 stops at corner of San Juan and Alem and takes you close to the terminal; make sure there is an "Aeropuerto" sign on the driver's window. Flying time from Buenos Aires: 1¾ hours. Aerolíneas flies three times a day (US$70), and has Tuesday night flight (US$42); Austral twice a day. 40% discount on night flight from Buenos Aires (night flight to Buenos Aires, Sat. 2315). AA to Santiago, 5 times a week, fare must be paid in US$. AA to and from Bariloche, 3 times a week. Several flights to Córdoba with AA and Austral (1515). Neuquén 3 weekly with TAN.

Trains to Buenos Aires: *El Libertador*, leaves Mendoza Mon. and Fri. at 2015, arrives at 0930; car transporters, luxurious bar, film show and airconditioning, steward service, good dining cars, meal US$4, good value; take drinks with you. *El Aconcagua* leaves Mendoza daily at 1600, arriving the next day at 0830; *El Cóndor* leaves at 1845, arrives Bs. As. at 0930 (Sun.). Trains from Buenos Aires to Mendoza: *Libertador*, leaves at 2015, Sun. and Thurs., arrives 1000. *El Aconcagua* leaves daily at 2115, arrives at 1400; *El Cóndor* leaves Fri. at 2015, arrives 1130: sleeper US$37.65, pullman US$30, first, US$19, tourist US$17.50. There are no trains to Chile but local buses meet train to take you to bus station, to catch buses for Chile. Train from Mendoza to San Luis 4 hrs.; to San Juan, 1420 daily, 1020 four a week, 2½ hrs. daily. Book pullmans well ahead in winter; they're heated. No direct trains to Salta, Tucumán or

Córdoba, but connections are possible. A tourist train runs to Puente del Inca: ask for details at the tourist office or Belgrano station. The train runs on the one-metre gauge Transandino line (built at the end of the 19th century), which has been neglected and partly disused on the Chilean side. Bus from railway to bus terminal, No. 5, US$0.15.

Buses (all from smart new bus station) to Santiago, **see page** 116. Buses run to Bariloche, TAC, leave 1300 Sun., Thurs., US$25, on a mostly paved road, about 22 hours, book well ahead; to Córdoba, TAC 4 daily, 9 hrs., US$13; to San Rafael, US$4; to San Juan every 2 hours, US$3.75, 2 hrs. (2 companies, TAC and Villa del Sur y Media Agua). To La Rioja US$11 (US$15 luxury), 10 hrs., leaves 1430, 1930 or 2130. Catamarca overnight only, 12 hrs., daily, US$15. Daily at 1730 to Tucumán, US$17.25. to Salta, Andesmar on Tues., Thurs., Fri., Sun. (via Tucumán) at 1300, 20 hrs. Bus to Mar. del Plata US$32; to Puerto Iguazú at 0700, Tues. and Thur. US$50, 38 hrs., Argentina Central company; alternatively take daily Vila Marta bus to Santa Fe and change for Iguazú bus, about 40 hrs. inc. waiting time, US$50. To Comodoro Rivadavia, daily with Andesmar, at 2000, US$80, 32 hrs. including 4 meal stops; the Tues. departure continues to Río Gallegos, arriving 1450 Thurs. To Buenos Aires via Route 8, 2nd class daily at 1315, arrives 0550, US$26, 1st class daily at 1630, arrives 0700, US$32; luxury service daily at 2100 (Chevallier), US$39 including meals; via Route 7 (Junín-Mercedes) at 2020, arrive 1205, US$26. Dull scenery, and very cold across the Pampas at night.

Hitch-hiking between Mendoza and Buenos Aires is quite easy. If hitching to San Juan, take bus No. 6 to the airport near the highway. Hitching from Mendoza to Los Andes (Chile) is easy; go to the service station in Godoy Cruz suburb, from where all trucks to Chile, Peru and elsewhere leave.

Excursions If driving in mountains remember to advance the spark by adjusting the distributor, or weaken the mixture in the carburettor, to avoid the car seizing up in the rarified air. Buses run to the hot springs at *Cacheuta*, US$2.40 round trip, US$5 entry (thermal baths for a variety of ailments, can be arranged at travel agents for US$4), 45 km. to the SW (hotels not rec.). The charming resort of *Potrerillos* is 13 km. from Cacheuta, with ski slopes not far away and excellent birdwatching in summer. *Gran Hotel; Hotel de Turismo*, B, with meals; ACA campsite (US$2 for members) *Restaurant Armando* rec. In summer, you can hike 20 km. from the resort of Potrerillos to Vallecito, a closed ski resort, taking two days. On the first you will see desert scenery, blooming cactus flowers, birds and an occasional goat or cow. The second you walk surrounded by peaks, a steep but not difficult climb to the San Antonio refuge, usually open with beds and meals. Two other popular resorts within a few km. of the city are Barballón, to the NE, and Challao, to the NW. An excursion is also available from the Mendoza bus station to the small ski resort of Los Penitentes, 170 km. away; equipment hire US$5 a day, lift ticket for a day US$9. The best skiing is at (2,250 metres) Valle de las Leñas, S of Mendoza in the Valle Hermoso (**see page** 109). Excursions also to the dam at El Nihuil, with artificial lake, and to the Río Atuel canyon (although the 16 hour round trip from Mendoza can be uncomfortable in hot weather, better to visit the canyon from San Rafael). On the road to Luján de Cuyo (buses go every 15 mins. from near bus terminal) is a fine arts museum dedicated to Argentine artists, surrounded by sculpture in gardens, admission free (Museo Provincial de Bellas Artes Emiliano Guiñazu, Casa de Fader). Day-trips can also be made to Puente del Inca with Turismo Vitar for about US$10 (see page 115). Turismo La Cumbre, Necochea 541, also includes it on its 19-hour circular tour, as does Cata Turismo, Las Heras 426, 13 hours.

Hotel Termas at Villavicencio is closed. Many tourists come to visit the springs, which are all set in concrete. Pleasant walks round the area.

N.B. It is no longer possible to go from Mendoza to Santiago via the statue of Christ the Redeemer at 4,200 metres. To see the statue you must go on a 12 hr. excursion from Mendoza (US$15 return, weekends early a.m., all travel agencies) since the Chilean side of the frontier at the statue is closed. The excursion also includes Puente del Inca (see below). All buses and cars go through the tunnel to Chile, leaving the statue unseen above.

Over the Andes to Chile

N.B. No visas into Chile are available at the border, so if you need one and haven't got it, you will be turned back. There is a time change: travelling from Argentina into Chile remember to move your watch back 1 hr. between mid-March and mid-October.

There are 2 alternates of Route 7, which meet at *Uspallata*, the only settlement of any size between Mendoza and the Chilean frontier. Near Uspallata are the ruins of Las Bóvedas, built by the Huarpe Indians under the Jesuits, and an Inca *tambería*. They are just off the road which leads to Barreal and Calingasta (**see page** 118), unpaved for its first part and tricky when the snow melts and floods it in summer. (Prices are usually much higher at frontier, temperatures much lower. Frontier closes early.) The fully-paved southern branch, via Cacheuta and Potrerillos, is wider and better than the northern branch, which goes via Villavicencio with a stretch of one-way traffic just beyond the resort, where the road leads up spectacularly to the 3,050 metres high Cruz del Paramillo. (The return loop, a little longer and less steep, is through the picturesque Quebrada del Toro.) This northern branch is still unpaved.

Hotels *Hotel Uspallata*, C, dinner at 2100; payment for meals and drinks in cash, bowling alley, nice location, but hotel run down, service friendly, but vast herds of people get driven through it. *Hostería Los Cóndores*, clean, friendly, cheap.

Camping There is a pleasant ACA site at Uspallata, US$3 per head, full washing facilities, hot water.

People travelling by car over the Andes in winter are advised to enquire about road conditions from ACA in Mendoza (San Martín y Amigorena).

The crossing of the Andes, taken by San Martín, is the old mountain trail the Spaniards named the Camino de los Andes. Beyond Uspallata is a vast, open, undulating plain, wild and bare. On all sides stand the grey, gaunt mountains. On the far side of this plain the valley narrows till Río Blanco is reached, and there the mountain torrents rush and froth into the river. At Punta de Vacas we look left up the Tupungato Valley at the majestic cone of Tupungato, one of the giants of the Andes, rising 6,550 metres. An equally majestic mass of pinnacled rocks, Los Penitentes, is passed on the left; they are about 7 km. away. The climber to their base (an easy task from Puente del Inca with a guide) sees a remarkable sight. The higher rocks look like a church and the smaller, sharper rocks below give the impression of a number of cowled monks climbing upwards.

In a short time we are at **Puente del Inca**, 2,718 metres above sea level, 160 km. from Mendoza, a sports resort set among mountains of great grandeur. (*Hostería Puente del Inca*, E for room, less off-season, very pleasant, about US$50 extra for full board, also bookable from *Plaza Hotel* in Mendoza; opposite is an army base which obscures the view of Aconcagua and prohibits photography.) Camping possible next to the church, if your equipment can withstand the winds. 5 km. from Puente del Inca on the road to Mendoza is a ski club, *Cruz de Caña*, with comfortable dormitories, E, and a good restaurant. The owner organizes trekking expeditions; prices: US$50 a day full board during expedition, and US$20 per mule.

The natural bridge after which Puente del Inca is named is one of the wonders of South America; it crosses the river Mendoza at a height of 19 metres, has a span of 21 metres, and is 27 metres wide, and seems to have been formed by sulphur-bearing hot springs. Puente del Inca is the best point for excursions into the higher Andean valleys or for a visit to the base of Aconcagua, which was first climbed by Zurbriggen of the Fitzgerald Expedition in 1897. Visits can be paid on horseback from Puente del Inca to Los Penitentes (*La Taberna del Gringo*, Km. 151, Villa Los Penitentes, E, rec.); or on foot to the green lake of Laguna de los Horcones; or by car (only with a well regulated engine) or bus or on horseback to the statue of Christ the Redeemer set above La Cumbre (or Uspallata) pass on the frontier at an altitude of 4,200 metres. It was erected jointly by Chile and Argentina in 1904 to celebrate King Edward VII's decision in the boundary dispute of 1902. It is, unfortunately, somewhat disappointing from the road, for it is completely dwarfed by the landscape. (The road from the tunnel to the statue is closed for the season after the first snowfall in April.)

Local bus (Expreso Uspallata) for Uspallata and Puente del Inca 4 hrs., 0600 and 1000, returning from Puente del Inca 1300 and 1615; local buses also go on from Puente del Inca to Las Cuevas, Expreso Uspallata, US$4. (See above under Mendoza **Trains** for tourist rail service.)

After Puente del Inca, on the right, we get a good view of Aconcagua (6,960 metres), sharply silhouetted against the blue sky. In 1985, a complete Inca mummy was discovered at 5,300 metres on the mountain.

Best time for climbing **Aconcagua** (the highest peak in the Americas and a **national park**) is from mid-January to mid-February. Rob Rachowiecki writes: it is first necessary to obtain a permit from the Dirección de Deportes, Recreación y Turismo Social (offices at the Mendoza football stadium). The Club Andinista Mendoza (at end of Lemus, between Rioja and Salta, open 2000-2200) will help you with the paperwork; Sr. Luis Alberto Parra is particularly helpful, Güiraldes 246, 5519 San José, Mendoza. T 242003. Allow a couple of days for this. From Mendoza take a bus or colectivo to Puente del Inca. From here mules are available but cost US$20 per mule per day; you have to pay for 3 days there and back (1 day rest) and for the muleteer and his wages. This only takes you to the base camp at Plaza de Mulas (4,200 m). Of the huts above this point only La Libertad (Berlín) hut at about 6,000 m is in serviceable condition. Both huts are small with no facilities. Bring a tent able to withstand 100 mph + winds, and clothing and sleeping gear for temperatures below -20C. Allow at least one week for acclimatization at lower altitudes before attempting summit (4 days from Plaza de Mulas). Treks and climbs organized by Sr. Fernando Grajales, the famous climber, in *Hostería Puente del Inca*, or at J.F.Moreno 898, 5500 Mendoza, Telex 55-154. Other guides can be found at the airport in Mendoza.

The frontier railway tunnel is no longer used by road traffic, which now takes the new 4-km. El Libertador-Las Cuevas toll road tunnel (US$2 toll). The Chilean frontier is beyond **Las Cuevas**, a neat, modern settlement being developed as a ski-ing. resort (though there is no ski-lift as yet), but recently damaged by landslides and a fire. It is wise to take snow chains from June to October. Officially, driving without chains and a shovel is prohibited between Uspallata and the border, but this can be resolved in a friendly way with border policemen. Both ACA and Chilean Automobile Club sell, but do not rent, chains.

Hotel *Hostería Las Cuevas*, only one, poor food, no heating in annex. Food available at kiosk at Expreso Uspallata bus terminal point.

Beyond Las Cuevas, the road, now completely paved, goes through the new road tunnel (charge for car, US$2, for a VW bus, US$3). The old road over La Cumbre pass is now closed to through traffic; the famous statue of Christ can be visited only by excursion from Mendoza (see above).

Transport to Chile Turismo cars (Chi-Ar - some adverse reports - and Nevada) carrying 4 to 5 passengers (US$19, 5 hrs.) and minibuses (51/2-6 hrs.) do the trip to Santiago daily. If travelling by bus from Mendoza to Santiago take a direct bus as it is not possible to walk across the border. Buses Mendoza to Santiago daily at 0600-1200; several companies, TAC-Choapa at 0830 (meals included, films shown) recommended for cheapness and service; also Félix Pullman Norte; adverse reports on Chile Bus. Most buses are comfortable and fast (6½-8 hrs.) and charge about US$10 (US$12 to Viña del Mar. and Valparaíso), those with air-conditioning and hostess service (including breakfast) charge more, worth it when crossing the border as waiting time can be a matter of several hours. All companies in same part of Mendoza bus station: you can easily shop around. Children under 8 pay 60% of adult fare, but no seat; book two days ahead, if all seats booked try CATA, its service is reportedly less good than others thus it usually has some empty seats. Passport required. The ride is spectacular. Information at main bus station. If you want to return, buy an undated return ticket Santiago-Mendoza; it is cheaper. A taxi Mendoza-Santiago costs about US$70 for 4-5 people. Covalle runs direct service to La Serena, Chile, twice a week.

All Argentine entry and exit formalities are now dealt with at Punta de Vacas, 30 km. from Las Cuevas. A new customs post, Ingeniero Roque Carranza has been built near Laguna Los Horcones, nearer Las Cuevas. One can hitch-hike, or possibly bargain with bus drivers for a seat, from Punta de Vacas to Santiago, but if one is dropped at the entrance to the tunnel in winter, one cannot walk through. Travellers however report that customs men often help by asking passing motorists to take hitch-hikers through the tunnel to Chile. Chilean migration and customs check is after the tunnel - searches for fruit, meat, vegetables, which may not be imported into Chile, in a new building with the bus parked inside. Customs at the frontier are closed 1200-1400. Members of ACA need only the *Libreta de Pasos por Aduana*, otherwise you need the *Documento de Exportación* to enter Chile. Good food at frontier hotel, and there is an excellent motel on the Chilean side about an hour down.

NORTH OF MENDOZA (5)

In the large more arid zone N of Mendoza, there are three other oases between the plains and the Andes. San Juan is the most prosperous, wine and olives support La Rioja, but Catamarca is economically depressed. The first, 177 km. from Mendoza by paved road, is

San Juan, population 122,000 at 650 metres, founded 1562 by Don Juan Jufré de Loaysa y Montese and capital of its namesake province. The city is proud of its sunny climate and clean, tree-lined streets. Nearly destroyed by a 1944 earthquake, the centre has been completely rebuilt, with a modern cathedral. The birthplace of Domingo Sarmiento (President of the Republic, 1868-1874, also an important historian/educator) is a museum; nominal entrance fee, closed Mondays. Museum of Natural Sciences, open daily, features geological exhibits anjd fossils from Ischigualasto Provincial Park (see below). Archaeological museum at La Laja, 25 Km. N, has mummies, basketry, and textiles; inexpensive thermal baths nearby. Only one direct bus station, but take No. 20 bus to Piedritas for easy hitch. At vallecito, some 60 Km. E, is the famous shrine to the **Difunta Correa**, an unofficial saint whose infant (according to legend) survived at her breast even after the mother's death from thirst in the desert. During Holy Week, up to 100,000 pilgrims visit the site, some crawling the final kilometer on their backs. See the remarkable collection of personal items left in tribute, including number plates from all over the world and even one policeman's detective school diploma!

Hotels The Cámara Hotelera, a central clearing office, is opposite **Hotel Nogaró**, Ignacio de la Roza 132, T 227501/5, best, pool, B (ACA discount); **Jardin Petit**, 25 de Mayo 345, B (ACA discount), T 211825; **Selby**, Rioja 183, C, T 224777; **Bristol**, Entre Rios 368, T 222629, C, a/c, hot water, clean, rec.; **Plaza** Sarmiento 344, T 225179, E, friendly, noisy disco behind, **Brescia**, España 336 near train station, T 225708, D; **Austria**, Sarmiento 234, T 210274, E, warmly recommended. Better cheap hotels include **Central**, Mitre 131, T 223174, very clean and quiet, good beds, friendly owner, F; **Lara**, Rivadavia 213, T 227973, clean and friendly but a bit noisy, with resident families, F; **Rawson** 561, F, near bus station, hot water, basic.

Camping Possible along San Juan-Mendoza road. Organized sites at Cerro Blanco, Zonda, Rivadavia and near Ullum Dan, W of San Juan. Other sites at an olive grove 7 km. S of Jachal and 23 km. beyond Jachal, on Villa Unión road.

Restaurants **Hostal de Palito**, Circunvalación Sur 271 (between San Martin and Ignacio de la Roza, some way out), excellent; **Wiesbaden**, Circunvalación y San Martin, German-style, pleasant setting; **La Cabaña**, edge of town at Salta y Circunvalación, *parillada*; **Comedor Sirio Libanés**, Entre Rios 33 S, pleasant decor, good food. **Comedor Central**, Ignacio de la Roza 171 E, not luxurious but good locro (stew) and chivito (goat). **Parilla Bigotes**, Las Heras y Ignacio de la Roza, inexpensive "all you can eat" meat, chicken, salads. **Club Español**, more expensive, large portions of mediocre food, indifferent service. Many *pizzerias, confiterias*, and sidewalk cafes, including **Café Amadeus** and **Café del Aguila** (where one waiter resembles John Cleese). **Un Rincón de Napoli**, Rivadavia 175 Oeste, good; large glasses of fresh orange juice, good delicatessen next door. Eat under thatched shelters (*quinchos*) at **Las Leñas**, a *parillada* on San Martin, some distance from centre.

Car Hire Parque Automotor, España y San Martin, Tel: 226018. Cash discount on request.

Exchange Good rates at Cambio Santiago, Gral. Acha 52, weekdays until 20000, Sat. a.m.

Tourist Office, opposite Sarmiento Museum, helpful, good brochures, closed weekends. Arranges tours in summer only. Large-scale provinical maps available at bookshops. For information on Difunta Correa, consult Fundación Vallecito at Caucete.

Travel Agent Yafar Turismo, Laprida and Aberastain, rec.

By Air Chacritas Airport, 14 Km. SE. From Buenos Aires with Austral and Aerolíneas Argentinas. Aerolínea Federal Argentina to Tucumán, Santa Fé, Mendoza, and the Chaco.

Buses Terminal at Estados Unidos 492 S. Long distance services to La Rioja (550 km., 6½ hours, US$10), Catamarca (660 km. over secondary roads, US$13, with connection to Salta), Tucumán (3 a day, 13 hrs., Libertador is cheapest, US$9.50), Córdoba, Santa Fé, Mar. del

Plata, Bahía Blanca and Bs.As. Fifteen departures daily from Mendoza with TAC. Also service to provincial tourist destinations.

To Chile: only connection with Santiago (Chile) is via Mendoza; catch the TAC bus at 0600, arrives in Mendoza 0830 in time for bus to Santiago which connects with train to Puerto Montt. To La Serena, Covalle Bus Thurs. at midnight, 17 hrs. (no longer goes over the Agua Negra pass as it was blown up some years ago).

Rail The San Martin line's *Aconcagua* train, between Retiro and Mendoza (**see page** 113) also serves San Juan daily, arriving 2½ hours later than in Mendoza westbound, departing 2½ hours earlier eastbound. Sleeper service (from Mendoza only), Pullman, first and tourist classes.

From San Juan Hitchhiking to La Rioja, take route 141 to Chepes (ACA *Hostería*), then N to Patquía; more traffic on provinical route 29, a good paved, but less interesting road than that via San Agustin or Jachal (see below).

Along scenic provincial route 12 (open westbound mornings, eastbound afternoons), 135 km. W of San Juan, lies **Calingasta**, in the valley of same name (annual cider festival in April). 40 km. S on the road to Uspallata is **Barreal** (*Hotel Barreal*, recently improved, good value in restaurant; also *Hotel Jorge*, F, clean, very simple. *Hosteria San Eduardo*, small, quaint, few rooms with bath, open summer only; *Restaurant Isidoro*, owned by local baker and sandyacht champion, reasonable). Free tours of observatory at El Leoncito, 26 km. from Barreal (no public transport) can be arranged from San Juan.

Sr. Ramón Luis Ossa, physical education teacher at Barreal's high school, runs mule treks into the Andes, crossing the foothills in summer, from 10 to 21 days between November and April; he can be reached at 5405 Barreal, Pcia. San Juan, T (0648) 4 1024. We are grateful to Herbert Levi for a detailed account of Sr. Ossa's treks. In addition to the organizer's list of essentials, Sr. Levi recommends the following on any Andean trip: metal drinking mugs, metal containers to prevent tubes of toothpaste etc. emptying themselves in mule packs, long underpants to protect against chafing, woollen cap, insect repellent, sunburn cream, laxatives, soap, nylon groundsheet for sleeping bag (depending on weather), portable tent for privacy, and fishing gear for those who prefer catching their own meals (No. 3 spoons best for Andean streams--permit required).

Route 40, the principal tourist route on the eastern Andean slope, heads N toward Cafayate and Salta, via San José de Jachal. At Talacasto, 55 km. from San Juan, route 436 branches toward Las Flores and the Chilean border at Agua Negra pass (4,765 metres). Since this road was dynamited during the 1979 dispute over the Beagle Channel, it is impossible to cross to La Serena via the Elqui valley.

At Pismanta, 5 km. N of Las Flores, the moderately priced *Hotel Termas de Pismanta* (D p.p., B with full board) features rooms for 120 guests, thermal baths between 38° and 44°C, a large swimming pool, medical attention, library, cinema, casino, and hairdressers. Reservations in Buenos Aires (Maipú 331) and San Juan (San Martin y Sarmiento). From San Juan, two buses daily with TAC, four weekly with Empresa Iglesia, also from Mendoza. Nearby, in Rodeo, Ing. Meglioli raises guanaco and vicuña, and sells local produce and crafts. A scenic road, with several tunnels, follows the Rio Jachal 61 km. to **San José de Jachal**, a wine and olive-growing center (pop 9,300), with many adobe buildings (hotel, C; *Plaza*, E, basic but clean; good *El Chato Flores* restaurant; several camping sites). Expreso Argentino bus from San Juan at 0730 arrives at 0940.

From Jachal, route 491 offers a scenic alternative to Villa Unión (see below), but buses now take new route 40 via Huaco. The undulating road, paved to the La Rioja border, crosses dozens of dry watercourses.

E of San Juan, one can make a loop via San Agustin del Valle Fértil and Villa Unión (La Rioja province). Turn off route 141 at Marayes (133 km.), from which paved route 510 (poor) goes N 114 km. to **San Agustín del Valle Fértil** (ACA hillside *hosteria*, good desert views, campsite). Pensiones (*Andacollo*, *Los Olivos*, both E) and private houses also provide lodging. There is a municipal swimming pool, and a lake with fishing. Local weavers offer ponchos and blankets. Bus from San Juan at 2000, arr. 2300; San Juan-La Rioja bus stops in San Agustín about midnight.

N of San Agustín, at a police checkpoint, 56 km. by paved road, a side road goes 17 km. to the 62,000-ha *Ischigualasto* Provincial Park, also known as *Valle de la Luna* for its exotic desert landforms. All private behicle must be accompanied by rangers whose knowledge and interest vary greatly; fee US$1.25 p.p. The circular tour, on an unpaved road, last 2-3 hours. the Dirección de Turismo in San Juan can arrange group visits. Local bus from San Juan Sat. afternoon, if demand is sufficient.

Just beyond the police checkpoint, over the provincial border, paved route 150 heads E to Patquia and then to La Rioja or Chilecito, while provincial route 26 heads N. 58 km. N of the junction a paved road goes to *Puerta de Talampaya* Provincial Park, another collection of spectacular desert landforms. Tours follows the dry bed of the Río Talampaya in four-wheel drive vehicles operated by park rangers (entrance fee US$3 p.p. for up to 8 people). Herbert Levi writes "There are 6,000 year old petroglyphs with pictures depicting animals. The whole area is said to have been covered with water long ago; now there are two visible strata, the *tarjado* and the *talampaya*. After that one enters a canyon with "balconies", sheer overhanging walls. Across these is a wood with many wild plants which are used for curative purposes. Coming out of the canyon there are rocks shaped like a cathedral, a bird, a castle, a chessboard, a monk, and three kings on a camel". Before returning, one can climb a small hill with a good view. Tours, arranged through Dirección Provincial de Turismo in La Rioja, last about two hours. Chilecito-San Juan buses pass Talampaya.

From the park junction route 26 coninues to *Villa Unión* (*Hostería Provincial*, simple, E, highly recommended; under new ownership. *Hospedaje Paola*, main street opp. police station, G, basic; next door is *Hospedaje Chaguito*, G, restaurant). Jeep excursions can be made to Ischigualasto and Talampaya, Laguna Verde and Laguna Veladero. Bus station behind plaza.

From Villa Unión, partly paved route 40 crosses the Cuesta de Miranda, dropping through a deep narrow canyon in a series of hairpins. After 92 km., it intersects the paved Patquía-Chilecito road. 18 km. N of the junction is

Chilecito , La Rioja province's second town, pop. 15,000, has good views of Sierra de Famatina. Sra. Inocente de Pizetti's souvenir shop features her own unique ceramic statuettes, with religious motifs.

Hotels *ACA*, T. Gordillo y 9 de Julio, good, E; *Belsavac*, 9 de Julio y Dávila, good but paperthin walls; *Ferrito*, Pelagio Luna 661; *El Cordobés*, Dávila y Libertad; *Los Cerros*, Caminito 270; *Riviera*, Castro Barros 133, F, rec., clean, hot showers; *Americano*, Libertad 68; *Bellia*, El Maestro y A. Marasso; *Mis Montañas*, J.V. González 27.

Camping Club Atlético Chilecito has site near ACA hotel. Unofficial sites at Guanchín, 15 km. from Chilecito, near 17th-century Jesuit *estancia*, also at Santa Florentina, 6 km. from Chilecito and Los Tabas, 2 km. beyond.

Restaurants *Yayo y Silvia*, Independencia y 9 de Julio, good chivito, *Capri*, on main square; *Comedor Club Atlético Newells Old Boys*, La Plata, near bus station.

Tourist Office 19 de Febrero y La Plata, very helpful.

Transport Líneas Aéreas Riojanas fly La Rioja-Chilecito, 20 min., US$10. Buses: to San Juan, Tues., Thur., Sat. at 2200, arr. 0705; to Tinogasta (Catamarca), Mon.-Fri., direct at 0700 via route 11, returning same day at 1600; to Tinogasta via Pituil, Tues. 0700 and Sat. 1330, returning Wed. 0600 and Sun. 1400. Connections with Catamarca and Córdoba (see relevant sections).

Excursions La Mejicana mine via Santa Florentina road: a cable car system which brought ore 39 km. to the railhead at Chilecito is now out of use. **Samay Huasi**, the house of Joaquín V. González, founder of La Plata University, open 0800-1200 and 1500-1800, pleasant gardens, good views of Chilecito, the Famatina ridge and connecting valley. Molino San Francisco Museum, at J. de Ocampo 363, has archaeological, historical and artistic exhibits. Art gallery "Osman Páez" at González 161. For treks, and trips to see gold washers at Famatina or to Talampaya, see Carlos de Caro, at tourist office near bus terminal.

With construction of an excellent new road, route 40 now goes via Salicas, since the Cuesta de Zapata, N of Tinogasta, was closed after 1981 floods. 21 km. N of Chilecito, the old road (now route 11) goes via Famatina (ACA *Hostería*) to **Tinogasta**, a half-Indian copper mining town in an oasis of vineyards, olive groves, and poplars (population 9,000).

Hotels *Provincial de Turismo*; *Hostería Novel*, near airport.

Restaurants *Persegoni*, Tristán Villafane 373; *Rancho Huairipaca*, on Moreno.

Transport Buses: to Tucumán, Empresa Gutiérrez, Tues., Fri., Sun. 1700, Mon., Tues., Fri., Sun. 0615, Fri. 0845; return Tues., Fri., Sun. Services to Chubut, Comodoro Rivadavia, and Caleta Olivia, with Empresa Ortiz, reflect that this is the source region for labour in the Patagonian oilfields. For air services, see under Catamarca.

Fiambalá is reached from Tinogasta with El Cóndor on the mountainous Córdoba-Fiambalá route. *Hospedaje* at the end of route (excellent *locro*). Drive from here to *aguaditas*, hot springs; the entire province is rich in thermal mineral waters. Empressa Gutiérrez daily at 1345 to Catamarca via Tinogasta (1500) and Cerro Negro junction (1610), connect with Coop. Catamarca bus to Belén (from Catamarca), about 2 hrs. by bad road. Also 0530 departure from Fiambalá. 36 km. beyond Fiambala is Palo Blanco, in the *pre-puna* foothills.

At the junction, new route 40 goes to Pituil, where pavement ends, and on to Salicas (ACA *Hostería*) and Cerro Negro junction (59 km.) with route 60, the Tinogasta-Aimogasta road. Turning left at Cerro Negro for 2 km., paved route 40 heads N to **Londres**, founded in 1558 and the second-oldest town in Argentina, named in honour of the marriage of Mary Tudor and Philip II. The town hall displays a glass coat-of-arms of the City of London and a copy of the marriage proposal. 15 km. further (paved) is **Belén**, population 8,800 (*Hotel Samai*, Urquiza 349, E, new; *Hotel Provincial*, dilapidated. Good breakfast at bus terminal; *Restaurant Dalesio*, near YPF gas station, excellent and cheap). The Huaco district is famous for weavings, ponchos, saddlebags and rugs. There are good views from the new statue of Virgin of Belén at the summit of the path beginning at Calle General Roca, and an interesting archaeological museum, Condor Huasi. Folklore festivals October and Christmas. Belén is encircled by mountains, except to the SE; lush vegetation along Río Belén. Then 176 km., largely unpaved, to Santa María at Tucumán provincial border (**see page** 91), and on to Cafayate (page 97.

Transport Belén-Villavil (springs), including side trip to Corral Quemado and end of line at Barranca Larga, 19 km. N of Villavil, Tues., Thur., Sun. at 0800, returns from Villavil at 1830. Sit on right-hand side for best views of impressive canyon and Rio Bolsón reservoir. Belén-Santa María Tues. 1330, Fri. and Sun. 2020; return Tues. and Thur. 0930, Sun. 1945. Belén-Salta via Haulfín (mineral hot springs), Santa María, Cafayate Thur. 0600.

From Cerro Negro it is 38 km. SE to Aimogasta (national olive festival in May) and another 30 km. to turnoff to Termas Santa Teresita (ACA *Hostería*, thermal baths each room, heated pool, excellent, reasonably priced food). 15 km. E on route 60 a good new road branches N to Saujil (60 km.) and **Andalgalá** (130 km., pop. 7,800), renowned for strong alcoholic drinks; *Hostería Provincial*. The road parallels the Salar de Pipanaco on the W and Sierra de Ambato on the E. Beyond Andalgalá, there is no public transport on the difficult but beautiful road to Santa María over the Cuesta de Capillitas, although trucks go weekdays to the mines just beyond the pass.

An alternative route to Salta turns W 52 km. past Belén on route 53, via Antofagasta de la Sierra and San Antonio de los Cobres (petrol available—**see page** 100). This route is possible in passenger cars, but requires enough fuel for 600 km. at high altitudes on unmaintained rods (fill up at Haulfín, 10 km. past turnoff to Route 53). Also, the stretch beyond the right turn at Puerto de Corral Quemado is very difficult (37 km. of fords), to be avoided in summer rainy season. At Km. 87 is Cerro Compo (3,125 metres), magnificent descent; at Km. 99 the road turns left to Laguna Blanca (**don't go straight at the junction).** **Antofagasta de la Sierra** (260 km.) can be reached only by hiring a pickup or hitching, or by plane, inquire at Dirección de Aeronaútica, Aerodromo de Choya, T 24750, bus L22 from airfield to centre (*Pensión Darín*). No petrol station, but fuel obtainable from *intendencia*. Together with El Peñón and Laguna Blanca in the *puna*, and Villavil and La Hoyada in the *pre-puna*, this is the main township of NW Catamarca. La Hoyada can be reached from Santa María in the NE via provincial route 118. There are lunar landscapes, with salt lakes, around Antofagasta and many peaks over 5,000 metres. Deposits of marble, onyx, sulphur, mica, salts, borates, and gold are present. Wildlife in the sparsely populated region includes vicuña, guanaco, vizcacha, flamingoes, and foxes.

La Rioja, founded 1592, 66,000 people, is capital of its province and home of new Argentine president Carlos Menem. Some colonial buildings survive, despite a major earthquake in 1894. Some colonial buildings survive, despite a major earthquake in 1894. There are many museums: Instituto del Folklore Riojano in a traditional house at Pelagio B. Luna 811 (Tues.-Sat. 0900-1300, 1600-2300, Sun. 0900-1300); Museo Arqueológico Inca Huasi, Alberdi 650 (Mon.-Fri. 0900-1300, 1600-1900, Sun. 0900-1300, Diaguita Indian relics, including skulls, textiles, funerary urns and ceramics); Museo Histórico de la Provincia, Alfredo E. Dávila 87 (Sat. 1430-2000, Sun. 0900-1230), with military exhibits; Museo Municipal de Bellas Artes (Mon.-Fri. 0700-1400, 1430-2130, Sat.-Sun. 0900-1200), Copiapó 245, works by local, national, and foreign artists; Museo de Arte Sacro, Catamarca 218. The adobe ruin of the Jesuit church in which San Francisco Solano baptized local Indians also merits a visit. The convent of Santo Domingo (built with Indian labour in 17th century), Lamadrid y Pelagio B. Luna, is a national historical monument. The *Niño Alcalde*, a remarkable image of the Baby Jesus at the church of San Francisco (25 de Mayo 218) is an object of local devotion. The castle-like Casa de Joaquín V. González at Rivadavia 952 is open to the public, free. There is also a famous casino at Sarmiento (renamed Juan D. Perón) and Quiroga.

La Rioja is known as "City of the Orange Trees," but there are also many specimens of the contorted, thorn-studded *palo borracho* tree, whose ripened avocado-like pods release large brown seeds in a kapok-like substance. It is also a common ornamental in Buenos Aires.

NB Avoid arriving on Saturday night as most things are shut on Sunday.

Hotels *International Sussex*, Ortiz de Campo 1551, adverse report; *King's*, Quiroga 1070; *Luxor*, Quiroga 25; *Provincial Casino*, Perón 1235; *Libertador*, Buenos Aires 223; *Talampaya*, Perón 951; *Provincial de Turismo*, Santa Fé 950, well set up but poorly run; *Emperador*, San Martín 258; *Centro*, Rivadavia 499; *Plaza*, Mitre y 9 de Julio, recommended but street noisy; all D. *Parlamento*, Rivadavia 549; *Ritz* 25 de Mayo 195; *El Gringo*, Coronel Lagos 427; *Aparicio*, Copiapó 119, all E, recommended. *Savoy*, Roque A. Luna y Mitre, excellent value, F, hot shower. Good value from *La Rioja*, *Libertador*, and *Central*. Best of the *residenciales* is *Sumaj Kanki*, Castro Barros y Lagos, but can't leave before 0730. At Aniliaco, on Highway 75 between La Rioja and Aimogasta, there is an *ACA Hostería*. The Tourist Office keeps a list of private lodgings, such as Familia Lazzarotto, San Martin 156, friendly, hot showers, cooking facilities.

Restaurants *Café Corredor*, San Martín y Pelagio Luna, good, cheap; *La Cantina de Juan*, Yrigoyen 190, excellent empanadas, local white wine, local cheese with nuts; *La Posta* and *Don Facundo*, both on Perón. Good takeaway food at *Tres Bien* on 9 de Julio near cathedral.

Exchange Banco de la Provincia, behind main office on Plaza (see note on provincial bonds used as currency, page 192).

Tourist Office at Perón y Urquiza and near plaza, one of most helpful in Argentina. Maps, information, bus schedules for routes off main road.

Transport No direct passenger service by rail; Belgrano railway from Retiro to Córdoba, Tues., Fri. at 1000, connects with bus to La Rioja and Catamarca. Return journeys (*automotor* from Córdoba Wed., Sat. at 0751) can be booked at La Rioja and Catamarca bus offices.

By Air: Aerolíneas daily from Bs.As; Aerolínea Federal Argentina to Resistencia, Tucumán, San Juan and Mendoza; Líneas Aéreas Riojanas to Catamarca (0800 and 1330 weekdays), Chilecito.

Buses: Buenos Aires with Empresa Cotil, combination Ablo and General Urquiza, via Córdoba and Rosario. To Mendoza and San Juan, night service only, with La Estrella or Libertador. To travel to San Juan by day (good scenery), take 0715 Cotil bus to Chepes (new bus station and ACA motel), then Cotil again next day to San Jauan at 0900 or 20 de Junio bus at 1000 for San Juan or 1230 to San Luis. To Tucumán (US$10), with Bosio and La Estrella. Also provincial services. Terminal about 5 blocks from centre.

Excursions To Ischigualasto and Talampaya (via Nonogasta, Cuesta de Miranda and Villa Unión, including transport and guide), and to Samay Huasi (**see page**

119). Fishing at El Portezuelo dam (see below). Swimming and fishing at Los Sauces dam, 15 km. away; beyond Los Sauces is Villa Sanogasta, nicely run, El Cóndor buses daily at 1200 and 1500, cheap, returning 1400 and 1700, 45 mins. Good views of La Rioja from Cerro de la Cruz (1,680 m). There is a bad road from the dam to the summit, now a centre for hang-gliding, where condors and falcons may be sighted. Two hours to thermal springs at Santa Teresita.

A paved road runs to the third oasis.

Catamarca (San Fernando del Valle de Catamarca), population 88,000, capital of its province, at 490 metres on the Río del Valle, between two southern slopes of the Sierra de Aconquija, about 240 km. S of Tucumán. Cattle, fruit, grapes and cotton are the main agricultural products, but it is also renowned for hand-woven ponchos and fruit preserves (try Casa Valdés, Sarmiento 586). Pilgrimages to church of the Virgen del Valle. There are therapeutic mineral springs. The *Zonda*, a strong dry mountain wind equivalent to the European *Föhn* or North American chinook or Santa Ana, can cause dramatic temperature increases. In July, regional handicrafts are sold at Festival del Poncho, a *feria* with four nights of music, mostly folklore of the NW.

Hotels *Provincial del Turismo*, at República y Caseros, resembles its La Rioja counterpart; *Ancasti*, Sarmiento 520, D, costly rooftop restaurant; *Inti Huasi*, República 297, E; *Pucará*, Avenida Esquiú, near ACA station, E, clean, a/c friendly; *Colonial*, República 802, E, no food but rec. as clean, welcoming, good value; *Suma Huasi*, Sarmiento 547, F, avoid TV lounge and rooms above it; *Centro*, Rosas y 9 de Julio, basic. Many *residenciales* clustered around Avenida Güemes. Discounts to ACA members at *Ancasti*, *Inti Huasi*, and *Suma Huasi*. Cheap, basic, nameless *pensión* at Tucumán 1294, friendly, shared rooms, no showers or hot water.

Restaurants *Club Español, El Encuentro, La Cabaña*, on Esquiú and *Carlos I* (at weekends) have folkloric dancing. *La Tinaja*, excellent, cheap, with live music, warmly rec.; *Pizzería Maryeli*, Esquiú 473, basic (but good empanadas). Local custom of soup after meal is said to be of Chinese origin. Many cheap restaurants along Av. Guemes, bars and cafés along Rivadavia (pedestrian street).

Shopping *Regionales Sevita*, next to Aerolíneas Argentinas, has Catamarca specialities. *Casa del Poncho*, artisanal exhibition hall, Urquiza at Mota Botello, has handwoven articles, open 0700-1330. The value of these depends on the number of knots used. Reached by infrequent colectivo 23 from centre.

Museums Instituto Cultural Esquiú, Sarmiento 450, archaeology, colonial history, iconography, mineralogy; Museo Arqueológico Adán Quiroga open Mon.-Fri. 0800-1300, 1530-2130, Sat.-Sun. 0830-1230. There are traces of Indian civilizations, including extensive agricultural terraces (now mostly abandoned), throughout the province.

Post Office San Martín 753, slow, closes noon. Telephones at Rivadavia 758.

Exchange No *casa de cambio*, try Yuri Tat travel agency in 800 block of República, or tourist shops.

Tourist Office At Plaza, 500 block of San Martin, very helpful but not too reliable. Also at Manzana del Turismo, Urquiza 951. Try Yokavil agency, Salta 1179, T 25403.

Buses To Tucumán, 7 daily with Bosio, 5½ hrs., US$5.50; road paved, in good condition except for rough stretch at provincial border (Cuesta del Totoral has steep gradients, hairpins, potholes). To Bs.As, 2nd class at 2200 US$30, 1st class at 1900, US$37 daily. To Belén via Cerro Negro with Coop Catamarca, returns from Belén daily 1300 (see page 120). Also Belén-Catamarca via Andalgalá; Coop Catamarca via Saujil, Poman, Chumbicha, Tues., Thur. 1000, Fri., Sun. 1300, about 8 hrs. Catamarca-El Rodeo-Las Juntas daily at 1300, returns from Las Juntas 1700. Twice weekly, buses to Córdoba connect with train to Bs.As.; in total, five buses daily to Córdoba. To Santiago del Estero, 1630, US$6.

Air Cooperativa de Transportes Catamarca, less dependable than Aerolíneas Riojanas, twice weekly Tinogasta to Belén. Officially departs Tinogasta 0810, but one is told to appear at municipal building at 0815 to be at plane at 0830. Route is circular: Catamarca-Tinogasta-Belén-Andalgala-Catamarca, in small Piper or Cessna. AA offices on Sarmiento, next to *Hotel Suma Huasi*.

Excursion To Dique Las Pirquitas, 3 hrs. with local bus 1A from bus station, or with Yokavil agency, terminus at Isla Larga (pleasant hills and woods). Bus stops at *Hostería de Turismo* at Villa Pirquitas, about 45 min. walk. Five morning buses from 0700, last returns at 2200. Opening hours Mon.-Fri. 1000-1900. Sat., Sun. and holidays 0830-1900.

A road runs NE to Lavalle (toward Santiago del Estero). This 116 km. run over the *Cuesta El Portezuelo* (1,980 m), is scenic, but steep and difficult. No bus service over Portezuelo to Lavalle, but a service to Frías, E, and also in Santiago del Estero province—No. 9 and not No. 18 (which crosses the Totoral), run by Coop. de Transportes de Catamarca. Leaves 0500 Tues., Thur., Fri. and Sat., arrives at Frías 1000, returns 1400, arrives in Catamarca 1900. From Frías travel to Lavalle.

Catamarca-Frías via Totoral, No. 18 Mon., Wed., Fri., Sat. 0500, arrives 1030, return 1330, arrives Catamarca 1900. No. 14 via El Alto, longer trip, arrives Frías 1045. Catamarca-Lavalle via Totoral, same No. 18, leaves Tues., Thur., and Sun. 1100, arrives Lavalle 1510.

THE CHACO (6)

Between the north-western highlands already described and the Río Paraná to the E lies the Argentine Chaco, containing the provinces of Formosa and Chaco, part of Santiago del Estero, and northern Santa Fe. Its southern limit is the Río Dulce valley. This great lowland is covered with thorn scrub and grassy savanna, the thorn bushes sometimes impenetrable and sometimes set widely apart on grassland. The highest summer temperatures in all South America have been recorded in the Argentine Chaco; the winters are mild with an occasional touch of frost in the S. Rain falls in the winter according to location: the further W, the less the rain.

Communications Before the recent building of highways, the only all-weather routes were provided by the Belgrano Railway. There are two main north/south lines from Buenos Aires: the international route to La Paz and the line through Rosario and Santa Fe to Resistencia. There are two east/west rail connections, Resistencia-Metán and Formosa-Embarcación; only the latter carries passengers regularly (**see page 132**). A third line runs SW from Roque Sáenz Peña to Anatuya in the province of Santiago del Estero. (It is advisable to check all rail services, since many were suspended years ago without being formally abolished.) Roads are given in the text and air services link the major towns.

Tannin and cotton are the two great industries of the Chaco. The iron-hard *quebracho* (axe-breaker) tree grows only in the Chaco of northern Argentina and Paraguay; it is the purest known source of tannin. The industry is struggling against competition from synthetic tannin and the huge mimosa plantations in South Africa. The most accessible forest is worked out; most of the cutting is now in the N and W of the province.

Cotton growers, around Roque Sáenz Peña in Chaco Province, have had difficulty in maintaining production in the face of soil exhaustion. Sunflower is the chief crop replacing cotton, and there is also some maize and sorghum.

Roque Sáenz Peña (population 50,000) can be reached by an excellent road from Puerto Pilcomayo. Hot springs have been found here and a modern hotel has been built to develop the city as a spa. Other hotels are: *Residencial Sáenz Peña*, near bus station, cheap, clean and friendly; *Residencia Asturias*, D, fair. Daily bus, La Internacional, to Buenos Aires, 2000, 19 hrs. From Buenos Aires, also 2000. Bus from Salta at 1700, 10 hrs., US$12.50; bus to Resistencia, US$3. North of Roque Sáenz Peña is the village of Castelli, which has a large Tobas Indian community and an *artesanía* shop. *Hotel Guc*, F, basic. 23 km. SE of R.S.Peña, on Route 16, is Quitilipi, with municipal campsite.

The rest of the Chaco is cattle country but there are few animals to the square km. Large *estancias* are the rule, some growing cotton, linseed and other crops by irrigation. The bird life of the area—flamingoes, black-necked swans, heron egrets, storks and various birds of prey—is most interesting.

Towns of the Chaco The most important ones—Resistencia and Formosa—are on the W bank of the Paraná and Paraguay and will be described, for convenience's sake, under Argentine Mesopotamia. Apart from Roque Sáenz Peña, the only other town of any importance is Santiago del Estero, on the western boundary of the Chaco (**see page** 86).

Federico Kirbus tells us that on the border of Chaco and Santiago del Estero provinces is Campo de Cielo, a meteorite impact field about 15 km. by 4 km. where about 5,000 years ago a planetoid landed and broke into 30 main pieces. Some of the meteorites are on display in Buenos Aires (the Rivadavia museum and the Planetarium), but the largest, "El Chaco", (33.4 tonnes), is on display at the Campo. Access from Route 89 (between Resistencia and Santiago del Estero) at Gancedo, where you travel 15 km. S to Las Víboras (many buses).

MESOPOTAMIA (7)

Between the rivers Paraná and Uruguay lies Argentine Mesopotamia: the provinces of Entre Ríos, Corrientes, and Misiones. The distance between the rivers is 390 km. in northern Corrientes, but narrows to about 210 km. in the latitude of Santa Fe. Mesopotamia was first colonized by Spaniards pushing S from Asunción to reoccupy Buenos Aires; both Corrientes and Paraná were founded as early as 1588. Alison Brysk and Mark Freeman (San Francisco) tell us that there was Jewish agricultural settlement in Entre Ríos at the beginning of C.20 ("Los gauchos judíos"). Vestiges of these settlements remain at Domínguez (museum) and Basavilbaso, and across the river in Moisesville (Santa Fe).

Much of Entre Ríos and Corrientes is still pastoral, a land of large *estancias* raising cattle and sheep. Maize (a gamble in the N) is largely grown in southern Entre Ríos, which is also the most important producer of linseed, citrus fruit and poultry in Argentina. In Corrientes, along the banks of the Paraná between the cities of Corrientes and Posadas, rice and oranges are grown.

The province of Corrientes, in the N, is marshy and deeply-wooded, with low grass-covered hills rising from the marshes. The normal rainfall is about 2,000 mm, but the rains are not spread uniformly and drain off quickly through the sandy soil. Entre Ríos, to the S, has plains of rich pasture land not unlike those of Uruguay. Winters in Mesopotamia are mild; the summers are hot and much rain falls in short, sharp storms, though both Entre Ríos and Corrientes often suffer from summer drought.

Misiones Province, in the far NE, was first occupied by the Jesuit Fathers fleeing from the Brazilian Alto-Paraná region with their devoted Indian followers before the slave-hunting Bandeirantes. These missions and their history are described under Posadas (**see page** 133). Misiones is a hilly strip of land between the Alto Paraná and the Uruguay rivers, 80-100 km. wide and about 400 km. long; its capital is the river port of Posadas. Its boundary to the N is the river Iguazú, which here tumbles over the great Iguazú Falls. Misiones is on the Paraná Plateau; much of it is covered with forests of pine and cedar and broad-leaved trees, and the look of the land, with its red soil, reminds one strongly of Brazil. Here too the rainfall is heavy: twice as heavy as in Entre Ríos. The days are hot, and the nights cool.

It was the Jesuits who first grew *yerba mate* in plantations; Misiones has always been a large producer of this leaf, and also of citrus, tobacco, timber and tung oil. The province has of late years attracted immigrants from Eastern Europe, from Paraguay and from the rest of Mesopotamia. There is good fishing in many of the small river-towns. In NE Corrientes and in Misiones more Indian tea is now

NORTH-EAST ARGENTINA

grown than can be absorbed by the internal market.

The Indian-tea industry was started by Sir Herbert Gibson, who sent for seed from Assam in 1929; it was sown in Playadito, Corrientes province. Six seeds developed into sturdy bushes. Year after year their seed was given to anyone interested. All Argentina's tea plantations today have their origin in Sir Herbert Gibson's enterprise.

Communications in the area are by road (now greatly improved), by railway, and by the two rivers the Paraná and the Uruguay, which bound it to E and W. Neither river is very good for navigation. Bridges between Fray Bentos (Uruguay) and Puerto Unzué, near Gualeguaychú, and between Paysandú (Uruguay) and Colón were opened in 1976, and there are a road and railway over the Salto Grande dam, near Concordia.

The area is served by the Urquiza railway, the only standard-gauge line in the country; the most important line runs from Buenos Aires to Posadas with connection over the river to Asunción, the capital of Paraguay, and a branch at Monte Caseros for Corrientes.

Most of the important towns of Mesopotamia lie on the E bank of the Paraná or the S bank of the Alto Paraná. A journey up these rivers is given here; the towns on both banks are described.

Up the Paraná River

Navigation River boats carry passengers along various stretches of the river, but there are no long-distance passenger services up the river from Buenos Aires, except those to Asunción, Paraguay. According to the tide, boats enter the Paraná river by either the Las Palmas reach of the delta, on which is Zárate, or the Paraná-Guazú reach, on which is Ibicuy.

Zárate, with 65,000 inhabitants, is industrially important, with large *frigoríficos* and paper works (*Hotel San Martín*, Ameghino 773, D, clean; *Restaurant La Posta de Correa*, cheap, good service). It is served from Buenos Aires (90 km.) by bus (US$2) and two railways: the Mitre and the Urquiza. Urquiza trains used to be ferried 84 km. across the river, but a link including two large and beautiful bridges has been built between Zárate and Brazo Largo, accelerating rail and road journeys alike (the bridge toll is US$6). The picturesque Ibicuy Islands can be visited by boat. Near Zárate is San Pedro (28,000 people) where fine riverfront camping can be had at either the *Centro Turístico, Club Pescadores* or *Camping Municipal*.

On the way upstream to Rosario, on the western bank, are two ports which export grain: San Nicolás (97,000 people), 80 km. below Rosario, and Villa Constitución (34,000 people), 37 km. below Rosario. Both are served by a railway from the capital. At San Nicolás is the General Savio steel plant. Pergamino, an important road/rail junction in the pampas, is 72 km. S by road or rail.

About 108 km. N of Ibicuy is **Gualeguay**, with a population of 26,000. It is the centre of one of the richest cattle and sheep ranching regions in Entre Ríos. The house in which Garibaldi was tortured by the local chief of police in 1837, in the time of Rosas, still exists. Eight km. S is its river port, Puerto Ruiz. The road from Gualeguay northwards along the E bank of the Paraná is paved most of the way to Posadas.

Hotels *Gran Hotel Gualeguay*, Monte Caseros 217, C; *Italia*, F with bath, friendly. There is a municipal **campsite**. In the centre there are practically no **restaurants**, but the *Jockey Club* and the *Club Social*, both on the main square close to the *Gran Hotel Gualeguay*, cater also for non-members. The *Club Social* has a very nice atmosphere, good food, and you might be invited to see films on certain nights.

Rosario, chief city of the province of Santa Fe, 320 km. N of Buenos Aires, is the third city of the republic, with a population of well over a million. It is a great industrial and export centre. The streets are wider than those of Buenos Aires, and there are fine boulevards and handsome open spaces. From October to early March it is warm, and from December to the end of February uncomfortably hot.

Changes of temperature are sudden.

Points of Interest Monument of the Flag, a memorial on the river bank in honour of General Belgrano, designer of the Argentine flag, who raised it on this spot for the first time; Parque Independencia (Rose Garden): Boulevard Oroño; Cathedral in Calle 25 de Mayo; St. Bartholomew's Church (Anglican), Calle Paraguay; racecourse, the Alberdi and Arroyito boat clubs, and Saladillo Golf Club, with its own Links station on the Mitre line. The Aero Club is at the fashionable suburb of Fisherton, headquarters of the British community. The Juan B. Castagnino Municipal Museum and the provincial Historical Museum (open Thurs. and Sat. 1500-1800, and Sun. 1000-1200, 1500-1800) are in Parque Independencia. Swimming at sandy Florida beach, about 8 km. N of Rosario. The boat *Ciudad de Rosario* does a short trip round the nearby river islands Sat. 1730, Sun. 1600 and 1830, US$1, leaving from the Estación Fluvial near the Monument of the Flag.

Local Holiday 7 October (Foundation of the City).

Hotels *Riviera*, San Lorenzo 1460, air conditioned, B; *Plaza*, Barón de Mauá, C; *La Paz*, Barón de Mauá 36, T 210905, E, clean, quiet, friendly, rec.; *Presidente*, Av. Corrientes 919, C, good; *Micro*, Santa Fe 3650, D; *Onix*, Vera Mujica 757, D; *Río*, opp. railway station, E, clean, friendly; *Moderno*, by Norte railway station, F with bath, OK; *Oviedo*, near railway station, F, with bath.

Restaurants *Don Rodrigo*, Sante Fe 968, and *Fenix*, Santa Fe next to Citibank, are both very good. *Doña María*, also on Santa Fe, does good Italian food; *Catay*, off Plaza Murillo, rec. for Chinese food; *Scaramouche*, just off Prado, on Loaysa, excellent US$4 menú del oficinista; *Casa Uruguaya*, Alvear 1125 (T 69320), away from centre, good.

Markets Mercado Central, Calle San Martín; also Mercados Norte, Sud, and Abasto. Best time, 0600-0800.

Exchange Lloyds Bank (BLSA), Calle La Rioja 1205; Citibank, Santa Fe 1101; First National Bank of Boston, Córdoba esq. Mitre. Open 1000-1600.

Tourist Office At Monument of the Flag, helpful but information inadequate.

Airport at Fisherton, 8 km. from centre. Taxi charges vary. Several flights daily to Buenos Aires. Austral to Corrientes once a week, to Posadas, three times and to Resistencia twice a week.

Rail Rosario is 4 hours from Buenos Aires (320 km.) on the Mitre Railway by express train, Pullman US$10.60, 1st class US$7.90, tourist US$5. It is served also by the Belgrano (metre gauge—5 hours). All trains heading N stop at Rosario.

Road Transport There are regular bus services to Arroyo Seco, Casilda, Cañada de Gómez, San Lorenzo and other important centres up to 80 km. from the city. Also from Buenos Aires, by paved roads via San Nicolás and General Pacheco on Route 9 (3¾-4 hrs.) or via Pergamino, 309 km. less frequent on Route 8 (Chevallier bus, US$8.10), and from Rosario via Bell Ville NW to Córdoba (bus, US$8) and Tucumán. To Santa Fe, US$3.25. Local bus fare, US$0.50.
    Rosario can be reached from Buenos Aires by Route 8 (marked Córdoba) to Pergamino, and then, following signs, by Route 188, and then 178 to Rosario. This is a better way than lorry-packed Route 9. Hitching to Salta along Route 34 is possible.

Ferries to Victoria, in Entre Ríos, which has a municipal **campsite**.

Above Rosario the river is very braided and islanded. Boat trips to river islands can be made at weekends. Canoes can be hired. Some 23 km. N of Rosario is **San Lorenzo** (pop 28,700), where an associate company of ICI has one of the largest chemical works in Argentina. See the restored San Carlos monastery on the river bank, where in 1813 San Martín won his first battle in the War of Independence. Visitors are shown a pine tree grown from a cutting of the tree under which the Liberator rested after the battle. Some 180 km. above Rosario, on the E bank, is

Paraná, capital of Entre Ríos (pop., 200,000), founded in 1588. From 1853 to 1862 the city was the capital of the Republic; it is a handsome place, with a fine centre, the Plaza San Martín, where there are fountains and a statue of the Liberator. The Cathedral, E of the plaza, is notable for its portico and its interior; opposite it is the tourist information office. A modern building on Plaza Alvear houses the Bazán Museum of Fine Arts (good) and the local history museum, open 0900-1200 and 1500-1800 except Mon. The Government Palace (Casa de Gobierno), in another plaza, has a grand façade. But the city's glory is the Parque Urquiza, to the NW. It has an enormous statue to General Urquiza, and a bas-relief showing the battle of Caseros, at which he finally defeated Rosas; also an open-air theatre. There are excellent views of the country and of Santa Fe on the other side of the river (launch trips). There is a paved road to Paso de los Libres, 483 km., on the Brazilian frontier (see page 142).

Hotels *Mayorazgo*, Etchevehere y Córdoba, on Costanera Alta, T 216111, with fine view of park and river, has casino and swimming pool, B; *Super Luxe*, Villaguay 162, T 212373, C; *Gran Hotel Paraná*, Urquiza 976, T 223900 D; *Almafuerte*, Av. Almafuerte 1295, T 240644 D. Cheap hotels near railway station, and *Plaza*, San Martín 915, T 211220, and *Bristol*, Alsina 221, T 213961, close to the bus terminal. The *Centro Autoturismo* motel on the road to the Hernandarias tunnel, C.

Santa Fe and Paraná do not face one another. It takes 20 mins. to get from one to the other by car, and 1 hour by bus, US$1, every half-hour. You cross a bridge close to Santa Fe, an uninhabited island, another bridge, and another uninhabited island to dive into the 2-km. Hernandarias tunnel, which leads up to Paraná city (toll US$1.90).

Air Service Airport: General Urquiza, 12 km. from town; two flights to Buenos Aires daily with Austral. To Goya and Reconquista at 0820 thrice weekly.

Train *Río Paraná* train to Buenos Aires daily except Sat. at 2020, arrives 0710. From Buenos Aires (F. Lacroze) 2215, arrives 0857.

Bus E across Entre Ríos to Concordia on Río Uruguay, 5 a day, 5 hours.

Santa Fe, a larger city of some 300,000 inhabitants, is the capital of its province and the centre of a very fertile region. It was founded by settlers from Asunción in 1573, though its present site was not occupied until 1651. It was in its Cabildo (town hall) that the Constitution of 1853 was adopted. The oath of allegiance was taken before the crucifix in the sacristy of the church of San Francisco, built in 1680 from materials floated down the river from Paraguay; this old colonial church has been tampered with but is still fine, especially the carved wooden ceilings, which were fitted without nails.

Most of the best buildings are grouped round Plaza Mayo and Plaza San Martín in the eastern part of the city. Plaza Mayo, on Calle General López, has the small Jesuit church of La Merced (1660-1754), next to the majestic Casa de Gobierno, and (on the N side) a church begun in 1741 (see an old painting from Cuzco and the interesting archives). A block SE of the Plaza has the famous church of San Francisco (see above). Opposite it is the Museo Histórico Provincial. In Calle General López is the Rosa Galisteo de Rodríguez Museum of Fine Arts, where local painters hold their exhibitions. The church of Nuestra Señora de Guadalupe has beautifully painted glass windows and may be reached by bus 8 or 14 from the centre. Twice weekly boats from Buenos Aires, 483 km. to the south; regular only in winter.

Local holidays 30 Sept. (St. Jerome); 15 Nov. (Foundation of City).

Hotels *Hostal de Santa Fe de la Vera Cruz*, best, genial management, well-kept and run, San Martín 2954, T 21115/8, C; *Río Grande*, San Gerónimo 2586, B, modern, rec.; *El Conquistador*, 25 de Mayo 2676, C; *Corrientes*, Corrientes 2520, C; *Colón*, San Luis 2862, D; *Pacífico*, Obispo Gelabert 2950, D; *Hospedaje Nueva Tripolitania*, Vera 2230, F, friendly, good restaurant; *Royal*, clean, modern, private bath, opposite bus station, D; *Niza*, Rivadavia 2755, T 22047, D, very clean, friendly; *Brigadier*, San Luis 3148, E, two blocks from bus station, good, clean, friendly, 50 rooms, a/c extra, but rec. if the river is in flood and there are lots of mosquitoes, some English spoken, private parking; *Bristol*, Belgrano 2859 by bus terminal, E; next door to it is *Gran Hotel Terminal*, Belgrano 2839, opposite bus terminal, E/F, basic, clean, water shortage; *Astur*, near the bus station, F (cheaper than most).

Camping Possible in free municipal site near town centre, Parque Sul, bus No. 5; beware ferocious mosquitoes. Site at Guadalupe beach by the lake.

Restaurants Many good ones, offering excellent meals with good wine for US$5. *El Quincho de Chiquito*, Obispo Príncipe y Almte. Brown, excellent and cheap, huge helpings. Excellent grills including *surubí* (local fish) at *Gran Parrillada Rivadavia*, Rivadavia 3299. Surubí also at *Aston*, San Jerónimo 2619, said to be best in town, and *España*, cheaper, San Martín 2644. *Apolo*, opposite bus terminal, good, cheap. Also good and cheap, *Comedor Tío Carlos*, Rivadavia y Suipacha, US$2 for unlimited antipasto and pasta or meat; and *Nochera Española*, next to railway station.

Exchange Lloyds Bank (BLSA), Calle 25 de Mayo 2501, open 0715-1315. Amex representative, Vacaciones Felices, San Martín 2347. Tourfé, San Martín 2901, changes travellers' cheques.

Laundromat San Martín 1750.

Swimming On river at Guadalupe beach; local bus.

Tourist Office at the conveniently situated bus terminal: maps, friendly.

Railways The quickest link from Buenos Aires is by Mitre railway to Rosario, and connecting bus (7 hours). Belgrano railway to Buenos Aires, 483 km., 8-10 hours (US$8 tourist, US$10.25 first class), also N to Resistencia.

Roads Fully paved to Rosario, 160 km. (3 hours by bus); to Formosa, 894 km.; to Roque Sáenz Peña, with spurs S to Villa Angela and General Pinedo and N to San Martín. Large and modern bus terminal. Bus for Asunción (Paraguay) leaves daily at 2125, US$28, 17 hrs. Bus to Córdoba, US$7, 5 hrs. Many buses to Buenos Aires, Paraná and Rosario; daily to Mendoza (2100) and Santiago del Estero/Tucumán (2010).

Airport At Sauce Viejo, 17 km. from the city. Three daily flights (2 on Sun.) to and from Buenos Aires.

Upstream from Santa Fe the Paraná rapidly loses depth and is navigable only by river boats and small coastal vessels.

Between Paraná and Goya, on the left bank, is **La Paz (Entre Ríos)**, a small port (pop. 15,200) with regional museum, riverside park and golf club. Buses to Buenos Aires, Rosario and Concordia. Small restaurants in port and near bus station.

Hotels *Milton*, San Martín e Italia, modern; *Plaza*, main square; *Rivera*, San Martín 376; *San Martín*, San Martín 551, E, clean.

Between Santa Fe and Corrientes the boat calls at several river ports, including La Paz, Goya and Empedrado. **Goya** (airport 7 km. from centre), on the E bank, the second town of the Province of Corrientes, is near the junction of the Paraná with the Santa Lucía river. It is a large tobacco centre on the Urquiza railway, with a population of 47,000. There is a vehicle-ferry service across the river to **Reconquista** (34,800 people). Both towns are served by Austral (which flies from the military base at Reconquista, between the airport and town, 10 km. from town). Austral, Bs. As.—Reconquista, stopping at Paraná on Tues., Thurs. and Sat. at 0955. The road N from Goya to Empedrado and Corrientes is paved; many buses.

Hotels at Goya *Hotel de Turismo*, modern, rec. *Cervantes*, J. E. Gómez 723; *Goya*, Colón 929; *España*, España 345, F, clean, hot water, friendly, near bus station. *Hoguimarsa*, B. Mitre 880/90 (the last-named also has establishments at Curuzú Cuatiá, Esquina, Empedrado and Mercedes in Corrientes province). *Restaurant El Colonial* said to be the best, US$4 for full meal, near bus station at Loza 415.

Hotels at Reconquista *Magni*, D, on main street, adequate, excellent restaurant. *Olessio*, opposite bus terminal, F. *Residencial San Martín*, F, with bath, on B. Mitre and Bolívar. *Motel Hostal del Rey*, located on the edge of town, clean, new, D, with bath. Many around bus station, e.g. *Ideal*, E, good.

Empedrado, further up the river on the E bank, has a population of 46,000. It is on the railway line between Buenos Aires (1,014 km.) and Corrientes. Oranges and rice are grown in the neighbourhood.

Hotel *Turismo*, with swimming pool and fine views. **Campsite**.

About 600 km. upstream from Santa Fe, on the W bank, is the little port of Barranqueras, served also from Santa Fe by railway (17 hours). It is on a steep bluff overlooking the Paraná. A paved road connects it with

Resistencia, the bustling, hot and energetic capital of the Province of Chaco, a galaxy of neon after dark, 6½ km. up the Barranqueras stream. Pop.: 218,000. The road N from Resistencia to Formosa (200 km.) and on to Puerto Pilcomayo (137 km.) is paved. There are many modern statues, mostly female nudes, promoted by the *Fogón de los Arrieros* (see below), along the streets and a museum, the Museo Histórico Ichoalay, at Donovan 425, in the Catholic girls' school, which traces the development of the city. International airport.

Area Products Cotton, *quebracho*, cattle. Sculptured Chaco woods from Domingo Arenas, cubist-type wood-statues. Tradicional Pampeya, on Güemes 154, sells local handicrafts and has an Indian handicraft display. Handicrafts also sold by Toba Indians in the Toba district.

Hotels Many accept Visa cards. *Covadonga*, Güemes 182, T 22875, D, small rooms, clean, a/c, *Tabaré* snack bar; *Lemirson*, Rawson 167, C; *Colón*, Sta. María de Oro 139, C, friendly, clean, rec.; *Sahara*, Güemes 169, D, Telex 71104. *Esmirna*, H. Irigoyen 83 on corner of Plaza, D with bath, good. *Residencial*, Av. Alberdi 317, F; *Las Torres*, Güemes 757, D; *Residencia Monaco*, Tucumán 350, E, OK. Several cheap ones near bus station, e.g. *Alfi*, E; *Aragón*, Santiago del Estero, F; *Comedor El Oriente*, Av. 25 de Mayo 554, E, with bath; *Residencia Alberdi*, Av. Alberdi 317, one block from bus station, F, clean, friendly new owner, rec.

Camping *Parque Dos de Febrero*, very pretty, near artificial lake, tent US$2; adequate free site nearby. *Parque Mitre*, showers and toilets. There is another site, shady but no facilities, NW of Resistencia on Route 16.

Restaurants *Círculo Residentes Santafecinos*, tasty meals at family style restaurant, US$6 for large meal, on Vedia 152. Try chupín de surubí, a sort of bouillabaisse, delightful. Nearby is *Cirilo*, Vedia 164, lunch for US$1.35, good. *Parrillada Clemente*, Santa María de Oro 399 near bus station, *Parrillada Las Brasas*, Brown 71, less good. Meat also at *Kebon*, on 200 block of Brown. Good pizzas at *San José* in main square. *Antiguo Farol* and *La Recova* both on Güemes and Don Bosco. Several cheap restaurants near bus station.

Fogón de los Arrieros, Brown 350, between López and French, a famous house-and-club full of local art and "objets" from abroad. No fee. Anyone can drink at the bar, open to the public from 2100 to 2300, Tues.-Thurs. Good place to meet local people.

Car Hire Avis, French 701 and at airport.

Exchange Banco del Chaco, Güemes on main plaza, high commission on travellers' cheques, good for buying guaraníes. Cambio Espinoza (also travel agency), Güemes 160 good rates.

Tourist Office Marcelo T. de Alvear with Escalada, maps, very helpful; open 0800-2000.

Air Airport 8 km. from town (no bus). Austral weekend night flights to and from Buenos Aires with 40% discount. Two flights a day to Buenos Aires, some stopping at Rosario. Alfa flies to Salta Sat. 0800.

Rail S to Santa Fe, leaves on Tues. and Sat. at 1830 (0600 in winter), 15½ hrs., nothing to eat or drink on train (Belgrano Railway). No regular passenger service to Formosa, Metán or Salta.

Buses Buses leave every 15 mins. to Corrientes over the Paraná River bridge, 40 mins., US$0.40, the Resistencia terminal is on Sta. Maria del Oro, 3 blocks from main plaza. 3 *especiales* a day to Buenos Aires (US$23) 14 hrs., 3 *comunes* a day (US$19), 17 hrs.; bus to Santa Fe (US$11.50). 8 a day to Formosa (2½ hrs.) and Puerto Pilcomayo, 6-7 hours, US$6.50. To Posadas, 6-7 hours, 4 a day, US$9, dull, hot journey. Two Veloz del Norte buses direct to Salta (US$18) at 1700 and 2300, 14-16 hours, bus may get bogged down on dirt roads; can be crowded; few stops and no toilet on bus. To Bolivian border at Agua Blanca/Bermejo, take 1700 bus, change at Joaquín V. González, US$11, 10 hrs., for direct connection to Orán, from where it is a 45 min. ride to border. El Rayo to Tucumán at 1930 and 2200, 15 hrs., US$14.50. Bus to Rosario, daily, 2015, US$17.25. Bus to Clorinda and Paraguayan border US$6, 5 hours. Many searches, watch your belongings and make sure everything is there afterwards. Also to Asunción daily, via Formosa, with Godoy (at 0300, 0600, 1400) and Brújula, US$7.50, 6½ hrs.

Roads between Resistencia and Salta: Most of Route 16, through Roque Sáenz Peña (**see page 123**), Avia Teray, Pampa del Infierno (good ACA *Hostería*), Río Muerto, Monte Quemado, El Quebrachal, Joaquín V. González (good municipal campsite at YPF service station and *Hotel Mallorca*, Av. Güemes 110, E with bath, café; impressive railway station, good restaurant opposite), then on Route 30 to Las Lajitas and Lumbrera, is paved, but there is a very bad stretch of 60 km. between Avia Teray and Río Muerto. No service stations along most of the route. It is 830 km. and can be done in one day by car, but it may be hot and there are several police check points; beware of cattle crossing the road. A south-western route (No. 94), from Avia Teray to Quimili, thence to Santiago del Estero, is very bad. Fill up in Resistencia if driving to Formosa, there are no service stations on the road, camping possible but no facilities, frequent police checks looking for stolen cars and contraband (especially electrical goods).

On the other side of the river from Resistencia (25 km.) is Corrientes. The 2¾-km. General Belgrano bridge crosses the river (toll free); the best view of it is from the Corrientes side.

Corrientes, the site of Graham Greene's *The Honorary Consul*, is the capital of Corrientes Province. The river can make the air heavy, moist and oppressive, but in winter the climate is pleasant. Population, 200,000. The city was founded in 1588. The church of La Cruz (1808) houses a miraculous cross placed there by the founder of the city, Alonzo de Vera—Indians who tried to burn it were killed by lightning from a cloudless sky. The Cathedral is in the renaissance style. Plaza Sargento Cabral has a statue to the sergeant who saved San Martín's life at the battle of San Lorenzo. A beautiful walk along the Paraná river leads to Parque Mitre, from where there are good views of sunsets over the river. On the Costanera, above the bridge to Resistencia, is a zoo with animals of the region. There is a Colonial, Historical and Fine Arts Museum. The pre-Lenten carnival is said to be interesting; reserve hotel in advance; otherwise stay in Resistencia, which is cheaper. Calle Junín is pedestrianized, with restaurants and shops, crowded at night. Road to Posadas, 320 km., now paved.

Hotels *Corrientes*, Junín 1549, T 65025, C; and *Gran Hotel Guaraní*, Mendoza 970, B; *Turismo Provincial*, Entre Ríos 650; *Cadena de Oro*, Ruta Nacional 12; *Orly*, San Juan 861, C; *Waikiki*, Gobernador A. Ruiz 2260, D; *Sosa*, España 1050, D, a little overpriced; *Pavón*, Av. Maipú, km. 3. Residenciales *Aialay*, Córdoba 314; *Avenida*, Av. 3 de Abril.

Camping Near bus terminal and railway station is *Camping-club Teléfono*, US$1 p.p., hot showers or bath, friendly.

Restaurants *Maximiliano*, H. Irigoyen 1331, open until 0300; *Yapeyú*, Av. Vera 1352; *Michelangelo*, C. Pellegrini y Catamarca; *Raviolandia*, Nueve de Julio 652; *Che Camba*, Av. Independencia 4175; *El Mangrullo*, Junín y Don Bosco. *La Rueda*, Av. 3 de Abril. *La Reforma*, Rioja and Julio. Ice creams at *Italia*, Nueve de Julio 1301 and *Verona*, Av. Ferré 1750. Tea rooms: *Confitería Viki*, San Juan 721 y Maipú 1198. *Café Mecca*, Junín 1264/66; *Gualeyán*, Junín 1426. Several on San Juan. *Pizzerías: Gaselli*, Av. Tres de Abril 686, *San Jorge*, Irigoyen 2265; *Los Pinos*, Catamarca and Bolívar; *Gandolfo*, Av. Tres de Abril 563.

Nightclubs Several on or near Mendoza, and on or near Pellegrini.

Car Hire Avis at *Gran Hotel Guaraní* and airport; only credit cards accepted from foreigners.

Exchange Virtually unobtainable. Aerolíneas or travel agents may help.

Tourist Office La Rioja 149.

Travel Agencies Quo Vadis, Pellegrini 1140; El Cabure, San Juan 671; Viamir, Junín 1459; Viajes Atlas, Mendoza 1073.

Airport Camba Punta, 10 km. from city. Aerolíneas Argentinas office Junín 1301, T 23850; Austral, Córdoba 935, T 25278. Daily AA and Austral flights to and from Buenos Aires. Austral to Rosario twice a week.

Rail Office on Córdoba 990, T 22009. Daily train leaves Lacroze station, Buenos Aires at 1230 or 1500 daily, arriving at Corrientes (1,046 km.) at 0900 or 1230 next day; it leaves Corrientes at 1825 daily, reaching Buenos Aires at 1545 next day. Fares: sleeper US$38.85, first US$23, tourist US$14.30.

Bus New terminal 5 km. from centre; bus No. 6 from terminal to town centre (US$0.15). Corrientes-Posadas US$7.50, 4½ hrs. Buses to Resistencia US$0.40, Cota, every 15 mins., 40 mins. journey, labelled "Chaco", leave from harbour; Buenos Aires-Corrientes, US$21.50; there are many more buses to Buenos Aires, Rosario and Santa Fe from Resistencia than from

Corrientes.

At 20 km. along Route 12 from Corrientes is Santa Ana de los Guacaras, a 17th-century settlement with attractive colonial architecture. To the N of Corrientes is the small town of **Paso de la Patria** (38 km., Route 12), a paradise for *dorado* fishing, with plenty of bungalows to stay. (Hotels: *Hostería Oficial*, C; *Cabaña Don Julián*, C, full board.)

A tiny port on the Alto Paraná—**Itatí** (pop. 5,700)—is reached by bus (73 km. on Route 12). Here, on July 16, is held a gala festival which celebrates jointly the crowning of the Virgin of Itatí (housed in a sanctuary built 1638), and St. Louis of France. Thousands of pilgrims arrive on the 16th (when the religious ceremonies begin) from San Luis del Palmar (pop. 15,000) in picturesque procession. Also on Route 12 (250 km. from Corrientes) are the Saltos de Apipé, where one can fish or swim.

210 km. SE of Corrientes, on the edge of the Iberá marshes, is the Estancia of San Juan Poriahú (16,500 hectares), a wildlife reserve with a superb array of animals and birds. Among the species are the endangered aguará-guazá (a large, red fox), deer, otters, the Juan Grande stork, kingfishers, snakes, etc. Visitors can explore the estancia on horseback, or in pick-ups or tractors. Iberá itself is a nature reserve containing more species, it is claimed, than the Pantanal in Mato Grosso, Brazil.

Corrientes is 40 km. below the confluence of the Paraguay and Alto Paraná rivers. Up the former are Formosa and Asunción; up the latter are Posadas and Iguazú.

The only Argentine port of any note on the Paraguay river is **Formosa**, 240 km. above Corrientes. It is the capital of Formosa Province, and has a population of 95,000. There is an interesting colonial museum in the town centre. There are many Indians in the area (bus from Rivadavia y San Martín, No. 1 ("Lote 68"), 15 mins., to the Barrio de los Indios.) At the Casa de Artesanía ask about the ACA in Ingeniero Juárez, from where excursions to see Chaco Indian settlements may be made. The surroundings are flat and swampy, the climate and vegetation tropical. From the port a trip can be made to Isla Alberdi, a Paraguayan duty-free spot; no possibility of continuing into Paraguay, and can only be done if you have a multiple entry visa. By road from Buenos Aires; 1,365 km. Airport (at least one Aerolíneas Argentinas flight per day).

Hotels *Turismo*, best, San Martín 759, T 26004, B; *Residencial City*, near railway station, D; *Colón*, Belgrano 1068, a/c, colour TV, spacious, D 1st floor, C 2nd floor, good; *Plaza*, J.M. Uriburu 905, D; *San Martín*, 25 de Mayo 380, D, overpriced, rundown. Several others on San Martín, E, e.g. *Residencial Italia*, nr. station, E, clean, hot showers; *Colonial*, F with private bath, clean, a/c, basic but good value, private parking available. *Residencial Rivas*, ½ block from bus station, F with bath, clean, friendly. Many along Belgrano.

Camping Possible on the river about 2 km. from the centre along a dirt road, upstream and over the railway lines.

Restaurant *Ser Bran*, near bus terminal, cheap and good. *El Ciervo*, Av. 25 de Mayo 65, excellent fish (surubí) and empanadas; *Latino American Bar*, 25 de Mayo 55, good Italian food, nice atmosphere, expensive.

Exchange Banks close at about noon and there are no exchange shops; buy australes in Asunción or Clorinda if en route when they're closed. Banco de la Provincia de Formosa changes travellers' cheques.

Tourist Office San Martín y 25 de Mayo, open 0800-1200 and 1600-2000, near the port, helpful.

Shipping Bolivian vessels (cargo and passenger) to Puerto Suárez (Bolivia), with call at Asunción. Irregular.

Roads S to Resistencia (200 km.); N to Clorinda and Asunción, paved, 150 km., via new toll bridge. Direct road to Salta very bad: the bus service appears to run only rarely.

Bus Formosa-Puente Loyola US$4.25. Formosa-Asunción US$4, 0800 and 1630, Expreso Brújula and other companies on main street. Empresa Godoy to border. Six a day to Resistencia.

Railway across the Chaco to Embarcación, N of Jujuy and Salta. *Cochemotor* passenger service, dusty in summer, Sun. and Thurs. 1200, 1st class US$15, tourist class US$10, buy ticket at 1000 and get on train as soon as you can; 20 hrs., noisy, uncomfortable but worth it for the birdlife.

Excursion Nature reserve (flora and fauna) at Guaycotea, 6 buses a day from Formosa, ½ hr.

About 137 km. N of Formosa, almost opposite Asunción (Paraguay), is **Clorinda**, whence the new Loyola bridge crosses to Puerto Falcón, Paraguay. Border crossing is easy. Many buses from Argentine end of bridge: to Formosa (10 a day), Resistencia (4) and Santa Fe/Rosario/Buenos Aires (3). Clorinda has a well-known banana festival in early October. Street money changer at Clorinda bus station, gives good rates austral/guaraní. From Puerto Pilcomayo, close to Clorinda (bus US$0.30) one can catch a ferry to Itá Enramada (Paraguay), a US$0.50 five-minute journey every 20 minutes. Argentine migration office at Puerto Pilcomayo is open 7 days a week.

At the confluence of the two rivers above Corrientes the Paraguay river comes in from the N, the Alto Paraná from the E. The Alto Paraná is difficult to navigate; it is, in parts, shallow; there are several rapids, and sometimes the stream is braided, its various channels embracing mid-stream islands. Much rice is grown on its banks.

The main Argentine port, on the S bank, is **Posadas**, capital of the province of Misiones, 377 km. above Corrientes, and very hot in summer. Many street numberings have been changed: beware! A bridge has been built across the 2½ km. of river between Posadas and the Paraguayan town of Encarnación opposite, to link the road systems of the two countries. A motor launch and car ferry link Posadas and Encarnación (buses to Asunción leave from here); the former runs 6 times a day Sat. and Sun., 7 daily in the week (US$1 plus US$0.10 for baggage). The car ferry runs 4 times a day. Mon.-Fri. at 0800, 1100, 1500, 1800, Sat. at 0700, 1100, 1400, 1900, and Sun. at 1000, 1130, 1800, 1900. Thorough baggage and body searches when entering Argentina. Population, 141,000. *Yerba mate*, tea and tobacco are grown in the area. There is a Museo Regional near the amphitheatre on J. B. Alberdi, open daily 0800-1000, US$0.15. (not rec., dilapidated). Better is the Museo Arqueológico e Histórico Andrés Guacurarí (on Gen. Paz, near municipal market), which has Jesuit remains and archaeological pieces from the areas to be flooded by the Yacyretá hydroelectric project. The Montoya Natural History Museum in the centre of Posadas, with live birds and snakes, well-kept, extensive range. The Palacio del Mate houses a good collection of Argentine painting and sculpture. There is a relatively expensive Mercado Artesanal (craft market). The roads to Corrientes and Iguazú are paved.

Route 12 along the Río Uruguay from Zárate north (now fully paved) is the shortest and least crowded route from Buenos Aires to Posadas and Iguazú and avoids the major population centres. On this route, S of Posadas, is San Miguel Apóstoles, where a *mate* festival is held at the beginning of November.

Hotels Prices in the Province of Misiones are on the whole significantly higher than elsewhere, and double if you want a private bathroom. Best is *Libertador*, San Lorenzo 2208, C; *Continental*, Bolívar 314, D, comfortable, but noisy, reasonable breakfast; *City*, Colón 280, D, shower, a/c, clean and reasonable, good restaurant (colectivo bus service from airport to this hotel); *Residencial Colón*, also on Colón, E, good and clean; *Posadas*, Bolívar 272, T 30801/31221, D with bath and breakfast, good service, snack bar, laundry, highly rec.; *Grand Hotel*, Ayacucho 172, swimming pool, central, threadbare, but clean and friendly, E; *Turismo*, Bolívar 171, D, modern but poor maintenance; *Savoy*, Sarmiento 296, clean and pleasant, D/E; *Residencial Nagel*, Pedro de Mendoza 211, near bus station, noisy, basic, F; *Argentina*, corner of Colón and Sarmiento, basic, with fan; *Gran Hotel Misiones*, E, on Líbano, a/c, restaurant, dirty, rundown, one block from bus terminal; next door to it at Líbano 2655 is *Horianski*, E with bath, garage for cars, family atmosphere but many mosquitoes in season, Familiar Mitre 58 near railway station, F, good restaurant, rec. Many adequate *residenciales* in the centre, F: *Residencial Marlis*, F with bath, clean, German-run, rec.

Camping Municipal camping ground on the river, off the road to San Ignacio Miní, hot showers and shop, good.

Restaurants *El Tropezón*, San Martín 185, good, inexpensive; *Jockey Club*, San Martín 159; *El Encuentro*, also on San Martín, one block from plaza; *Los Troncos*, Colón y San Martín, excellent food and service; *Pescadería Bárbara*, corner of Junín and Entre Ríos, good, wide selection; excellent US$3 buffet on ground floor of *Hotel Savoy* . There is an excellent restaurant *La Querencia*, on Plaza 9 Julio *Pizzería Los Pinos*, San Lorenzo 286, excellent and cheap; *Pizzería La Grata Alegría*, Bolívar y Junín, good. Breakfast at ACA.

Discos on Bolívar between 3 de Febrero y 25 de Mayo (*Power*) and at San Martín y Jujuy, open 0100-0500 Thur.-Sun.

Exchange Banco de La Nación changes travellers' cheques. Opens very early, 0615-1215. *Caneva*, Bolívar 609, changes Amex cheques; *Cambio Mazza*, Bolívar 1995, near main square, changes travellers' cheques and other currencies. If stuck when banks and *cambios* are closed, cross the river to Encarnación and use the street changers.

Paraguayan Consulate San Lorenzo 179. **Brazilian Consulate** Mitre 631, T 24830, 0800-1200, visas issued free, photo required, 90 days given.

Tourist Office Colón 1985, corner Rioja, on central plaza, T 24360, helpful, open late at weekends, maps and brochures in English of Posadas, Formosa and Iguazú Falls. Hotel listings for Misiones province.

Travel Agent Viajes Turismo, Colón 1901, ask for Kenneth Nairn, speaks English, most helpful, good tours to Iguazú and local sights.

Buses from Buenos Aires, US$20 (US$2 extra for *servico diferencial*, i.e. supper and breakfast) 16½ hrs.; Expreso Singer, 1130, 1600, 2200, plus *diferencial* at 2000, *rápido* at 2200 and an extra service in summer (to Bs.As., 1340, 1750, 2055, *diferencial* 2000 and *rápido* 2030 Tigre-Iguazú at 1500; some go via Resistencia, some via Concordia. Expreso Singer (Av. Mitre 2447, T 24771/2) and Tigre bus terminal is 5 mins. walk from the main bus terminal. Express bus to Puerto Iguazú leaves at 0900 and 0500, 4½ hrs., US$9, daily; stops at San Ignacio Miní. Another service to San Ignacio and Puerto Iguazú is by A. Martignoni. Bus to Córdoba with Singer and Litoral on alternate days at 1200, arrive at 0735 next day. Bus to Corrientes US$7.50; to Formosa US$6.50; to Santa Fe US$11.50. La Estrella bus to Tucumán, Tues., Thurs., Sun. at 1720, 16 hrs., US$20. Bus to Rosario US$14; to Paso de los Libres (7 hrs.) US$7.75, interesting, 60 km. not paved. To Resistencia, 6-7 hrs., dull trip, US$9. To Concordia (Expreso Singer) US$11.50, 2100 daily, 8¾ hrs. Singertur, Av. Mitre 54 (T 4771, 4772) in Posadas. **N.B.** The main bus station, at junction of Av. Uruguay and Av. Bartolomé Mitre, is on the upper level of the town, some distance from the ferry terminal taxi between the two, US$2.

International To Asunción (Expreso Singer, daily 1400, 7 hrs., and Empresa Godoy), US$10. To Montevideo, a roundabout journey because the main Asunción-Montevideo route passes through Corrientes. One can take Expreso Singer bus to the junction for Colón, at Villa San José (ACA hostel), D, (US$15), local bus to Colón; two local buses over the bridge to Paysandú (US$1.50), then plenty of buses to Montevideo (US$8). For those continuing to Brazil (Uruguaiana) have the bus drop you off about 3 km. before Paso de los Libres at Puente Internacional—Argentine customs—the bus from here to the Brazilian border on the other side of the Río Uruguay costs US$0.25. Expreso Singer bus to Porto Alegre (via Oberá, Panambí, Santo Angelo and Carazinho, Tues., Thur., Sun. at 1400, arriving 0345 next day, US$18. If the bus is full it is possible to buy a ticket (without a seat) in Oberá. The bus usually empties before long and you can get a seat.

Train from Buenos Aires (Lacroze Station). Information available in Galerías Pacífico, Florida 729, T 31-6411/5. *El Gran Capitán*, which leaves at 1130 daily, arrives at 0530. Transfer (free) to the bus station where there is a connecting bus to San Ignacio Miní (1 hr.). From Posadas *El Gran Capitán* leaves at 1745 daily, arrives in Buenos Aires about 1545 next day, sleeper US$37.25; pullman US$32; 1st class US$19; tourist US$15, not crowded. There is a car transporter on the Mon. and Fri. trains, returning to Buenos Aires on Thurs. and Sun. *Cataratas*, leaves Lacroze 1800 Fri., arrives 1123 Sat., returns 2300 Sat., arriving Buenos Aires 1617 Sun., cinema, a/c sleepers, pullman, car transporter. One advantage over the buses is that the wild life in woods and swamps may be seen more easily (because it is less often disturbed) from the railway than from the road. Meals on board, US$4.45. Train to Asunción leaves Encarnación 1100 Wed., arrives 0600 next day. Returns Tues. at 2000. There is a 4 hr. layover between Bs.As. and Asunción at Posadas (where one must leave the train and cross to Encarnación by ferry).

Airport General San Martín (12 km.), reached from Posadas by Bus No. 8 from opp. bus terminal in 20 mins., US$0.30. Daily flights to Buenos Aires with Austral (with one connection a week to Rosario), and Aerolíneas Argentinas; one night flight a week to Buenos Aires with each company: 40% discount.

From Posadas a visit should be paid to the impressive ruins of Jesuit settlements and to the magnificent Falls of Iguazú. The express bus takes 4½ hours (US$6.50), 4 a day from Posadas to Puerto Iguazú, but may not stop at San Ignacio Miní (**see below**); the ordinary buses, which will, take 8 hours for the journey and there are hourly departures from Posadas; these buses make 35 stops in all.

Not far from Posadas are the ruins of thirty old Jesuit missions among the Guaraní Indians, from which the province of Misiones derives its name. Tourists should see those at San Ignacio Miní (very well maintained), reached by paved road in 1¼ hours (bus, US$1.45, every 1-1½ hours, from terminal, Nuestra Señora, check return time with office). You need about 1½ hrs. for a leisurely look; the ruins begin 3 blocks from the road where the bus stops. There are heavy rains at San Ignacio in February. 16 km. before San Ignacio are the ruins of Santa Ana, only partially cleared but very impressive.

At **San Ignacio Miní**, founded on its present site in 1696, the grass-covered plaza, a hundred metres square, is flanked north, east and west by 30 parallel blocks of stone buildings with ten small, one-room dwellings to the block. The roofs have gone, but the massive metre-thick walls are still standing except where they have been torn down by the *ibapoi* trees; it looks as if there was an arcade in front of each block. The public buildings, some of them still 10 metres high, are on the south side. In the centre are the ruins of a large church finished about 1724. To the right is the cemetery, to the left the school and the cloisters of the priests. Beyond are other buildings which were no doubt the workshops, refectory and storerooms. The masonry, a red or yellow sandstone from the Paraná River, was held together by a sandy mud. There is much bas-relief sculpture, mostly of floral designs. Now maintained as a National Monument (open 0700-1900, entry free, but tip appreciated if the guards look after your luggage; you have to pay to park by the ruins' fence; park on the other side of the street, it's free!). Mosquitoes can be a problem.

The Jesuits set up their first missions among the Guaraní Indians about 1609, in the region of Guaíra, now in Brazil. The missions flourished: cotton was introduced, the Indians wove their own clothes, dressed like Europeans, raised cattle, and built and sculpted and painted their own churches. But in 1627 they were violently attacked by the slave-hunting Bandeirantes from São Paulo, and by 1632 the position of the mission had become impossible: 12,000 converts, led by the priests, floated on 700 rafts down the Paranapanema into the Paraná, only to find their route made impassable by the Guaíra Falls. They pushed for eight days through dense virgin forests on both sides of the river, then built new boats and continued their journey; 725 km. from their old homes they founded new missions in what is now Paraguay, Argentine Misiones, and Brazilian Rio Grande do Sul. By the early 18th century there were, on both sides of the river, 30 mission villages with a combined population of over 100,000 souls. Only four of these show any signs of their former splendour: San Ignacio Miní, São Miguel (Brazil), and Jesús and Trinidad (Paraguay). At the height of its prosperity in 1731 San Ignacio contained 4,356 people. In 1767, Charles III of Spain expelled the Jesuits from Spanish territory; the Franciscans and Dominicans then took over. After the Jesuits had gone, there was a rapid decline in prosperity. By 1784 there were only 176 Indians at San Ignacio Miní; by 1810, there was none. By order of the Paraguayan dictator Francia, all the settlements were evacuated in 1817, and San Ignacio was set on fire. The village was lost in the jungle until it was discovered again in 1897. In 1943 an agency of the Argentine Government took control. Some of the craft work produced at the settlement can be seen at two museums in Buenos Aires: the Museo Colonial Isaac Fernández Blanco and the municipal Museo de Arte Colonial. The Museo Jesuítico at the site is close to ruins on the main avenue. The caretaker, Sr. Miguel Nadasdy, will show you a 350-mm. statue of Moses, said to be by Michelangelo, kept in the museum, and tell you of other worthwhile sites. Also Museo Provincial in main street. Interesting local crafts sold opposite ruins. Wooden carvings are especially worthwhile. Son-et-lumière show after dark (1930) at the ruins, Spanish only, tickets from museum. Dr. Hector Alvarez has been recommended as an informative and friendly guide; he gives tours of the ruins for a nominal fee, and will also take visitors to the quarry used for the original stone buildings, speaks English, French, Portuguese, Italian and some German.

Accommodation ACA hostel (E; lunches at US$5 each); *Hotel San Ignacio*, friendly, good, clean, restaurant with light meals (closed in August), E; 3 blocks away is *Hospedaje El Descanso*, Pellegrini 270, F, friendly German owners, modern, quiet, rec.; sign posted from the main road. *San Martín* church in main street close to Museo Provincial has hostel, E; ask the padre. *Hospedaje Alemán*, Quiroga 870 near bus station, Clemens speaks German and English. There are *Restaurant Artemio I*, good and cheap, open till midnight, and two *comedores* (lunch only) opposite the entrance to the ruins. Festival July 30-31.

Camping outside the ruins in municipal site; cold showers and toilets. Two pleasant sites by small lake about 5 km. S of San Ignacio, on Route 12.

At Jardín América, 48 km. N of San Ignacio, there is an excellent municipal campsite 2 km. off Route 12. Flights can be taken over Misiones province for US$30. At Puerto Rico, 21 km. N of Jardín América, there is a good hotel, *Suizo*, D; campsite at Club de Pesca; rec. restaurants are *Don Luis* and *Churrascaría Flach*, both on main street. The ACA *hosteria* at Montecarlo, half way between San Ignacio and Iguazú, is warmly rec.; take town bus from centre. In Montecarlo is the Museo de Ciencias Naturales Juan Foerster, dedicated to flora, fauna and history, open Tues.-Sun., 0800-1200, 1400-1800, worth a visit; it is run by Sr. Foerster's widow.

The most successful colonization in Argentina of late years has been at **Eldorado**, on this route. This prosperous small town is surrounded by flourishing *mate*, tung, citrus, eucalyptus and tobacco plantations. There are tung oil factories, sawmills, plywood factories, *mate* drying installations and a citrus packing plant. The ACA office is very helpful and has a large illuminated map of Eldorado and its surroundings.

Hotels at Eldorado *Alpa*, D; *Hostería ACA* and *Atlántida*, both E; *Castellar*, D with bath. *Ideal*, F, clean, opp. bus station; *Gran Riojano*, Av San Martín 314, T 22217, very friendly, 5 min walk from main road crossing. **Restaurant** : *Copetín al Paso*, excellent, reasonable for price, but doesn't cook every day. Also try restaurant at *Gran Riojano* .

Camping Camping site with showers and toilets; take the road toward the river from the main highway, for 2 km.

To see something of the Province of Misiones, the following way to return from Puerto Iguazú to Posadas is suggested by Reinhard Böhm-Raffay. If you are interested in flora and fauna, travel from Puerto Iguazú on Route 12 to Wanda (*Hotel Prisa*, Swiss-owned, 20% discount for Swiss nationals); nearby are two open-cast amethyst and quartz mines which sell gems, but they are much more expensive than in Brazil, there are free guided tours. Carry on to Eldorado, then follow Route 17 (buses 0800 and 1530), paved to Bernardo Yrigoyen, a nice village, lovely vegetation en route. The direct (dirt) road from Puerto Iguazú to Bernardo Yrigoyen crosses the National Park of Iguazú, passing Andrecito, Cabuneí and San Antonio. Local buses ply the route if the weather is dry. From B. Yrigoyen follow Route 14 to Tobuna, where you will see the Alegría falls. On to the small village of Paraíso, see Moconá falls 82 km. from there, then Dos de Mayo (*Hotel Alex*). Pass through **Oberá** (*Hotel Quatro Pinos*, Av. Sarmiento 853, good value; campsite just outside town, with swimming pool and waterfall nearby; *Enqüete* restaurant, Alvar Núñez Cabeza de Vaca 340, good),and follow Route 103 W to Santa Ana, with Jesuit ruins of Loreto, not fully restored; best at sunrise, museum opens 0700-1900, US$0.75. From here you can return via San Ignacio to Puerto Iguazú or turn 16 km. in opposite direction to Posadas. In Oberá, a Parque de Naciones is being built, with houses to commemorate the nationalities of all the immigrants who founded the town. Many maté-leaf drying factories can be visited. Tourist information centre in a pavilion on Av Libertad, T 21808

THE IGUAZU FALLS (8)

For specific references to the Brazilian side of the Falls, with accommodation and transport links, see Brazilian section page 379. For a general description, local transport arrangements, and specific Argentine references, see below.

The **Iguazú Falls** are the most overwhelming falls in South America. They lie about 350 km. upstream from Posadas where, 19 km. above the confluence of the Iguazú with the Alto Paraná, the waters fall thunderously in virgin forest bright with orchids and serpentine creepers festooning the branches. Above the impact of water on basalt rock hovers a perpetual 30-metre high cloud of mist in which the sun. creates blazing rainbows. The Iguazú (Guaraní for great waters) rises in the Brazilian hills near Curitiba and receives some 30 streams on its course across the plateau. Above the main falls the river, sown with wooded islets, opens out to a width of 4 km. There are rapids for 3½ km. above the 60-metre precipice over which the water plunges in 275 falls over a frontage of 2,470 metres, at a rate of 1,750 cubic metres a second. Their height is greater than Niagara's by 20 metres or so and their width by one half, but most of the falls are broken midway by ledges of rock. The tumbling water in its setting of begonias, orchids, fern and palms with toucans, flocks of parrots and cacique birds, swifts (*vencejos*) dodging in and out of the very falls, and myriads of butterflies (at least 500 different species), is majestically beautiful, especially outside the cool season (when the water is much diminished, as are the birds and insects). One cannot cross the river at the Falls themselves; this can only be done by bridge between Porto Meira and Puerto Iguazú.

Visitors to the Falls should note that the Brazilian side (best visited in the morning because the light then is better for photography) shows the best panorama of the whole falls and should therefore be preferred if your visit is limited to, say, half a day, but the Argentine side (which needs most of a day to explore properly: the area is much greater) shows more close detail of the individual falls and is much more interesting from the point of view of seeing the forest with its wildlife and butterflies. There are a bird hide overlooking a marsh (Bañado), an interpreted (Spanish) nature trail (Macuco) in the jungle, a self-guided trail around the *Circuito Inferior*, all of which are very lovely. (An advantage in visiting the Argentine side first is that the information provided at the Visitors' Centre is far superior to anything offered in Brazil.)

The Devil's Throat, the most spectacular fall (for which you need waterproof clothing or swimming gear), is best seen from Puerto Canoas, to which buses run (see below), or you can drive (parking US$1). On the Argentine side the upper series of catwalks on the river, *Circuito Superior*, were largely destroyed by floods in 1983. The 1 km. catwalk from the river bank to the Devil's Throat has been replaced. There is also a short boat trip from Puerto Canoas to join the catwalk. Recommended in the evening when the light is best and the swifts are returning to roost on the walls, some behind the water. Below the falls the Iguazú runs swiftly for 19 km. through a deep canyon before it joins the Alto Paraná.

To walk along the lower series of catwalks, at the level of the midway ledge, waterproof coats or swimming costumes are advisable but not absolutely necessary. Wear shoes with good soles when walking around, as the rocks are very slippery in places. Put your camera in a plastic bag. At the base of Dos Hermanas fall is a natural, idyllic swimming pool, so take bathing gear in summer to cool off.

The Argentine Iguazú National Park embraces a large area. The fauna includes the black howler monkey, capybara, jaguar and puma, along with a huge variety of birds; neither hunting nor fishing are allowed. The months to avoid are July (holidays) and December-March (hot). Information and permits can be got from the Visitors Centre information desk, open daily 0800-1800 in the old, Argentine Cataratas Hotel, now converted. The Visitors' Centre organizes a 4-hour walk (8 km.) through the jungle, beginning at 0900 daily; fixed price US$25 to share among the party. Catch 0825 bus from Puerto Iguazú. It also runs night-time walks between *Hotel Internacional Iguazú* and the falls when the moon is full; on clear nights the moon casts a blue halo over the falls. Helicopter rides over the Falls, about 15 mins. for US$30, start from the Brazilian airport. The Argentine National Park keepers regard the helicopter rides as a serious noise pollutant; they are collecting visitors' complaints about the problem in a book to which they welcome additions. It is also reported that the helicopter noise is a threat to some bird species which are laying thinner-shelled eggs.There is a museum of local fauna and an auditorium for periodic slide shows (on request for 8 or more people), no commentary, just music. A good guide book on Argentine birds is for sale. Administration for the park's headquarters is in a colonial-style building at Puerto Iguazú.

There is a US$0.60 charge which allows one-day entry to the Argentine Park, free information leaflet provided with ticket (guests at *Hotel Internacional* do not have to pay).

Getting to the Falls Transportes Cataratas buses run hourly from the Puerto Iguazú bus station to the Falls, stopping in town outside the Aerolíneas Argentinas office, taking about 30 minutes for the 22½ km. These buses are sometimes erratic, even though the times are clearly indicated, especially when it is wet. They stop at the National Park entrance for the purchase of entrance tickets. Fare to the Falls, US$1; first bus at 0700, last at 1700; first back at 0815, last at 1900. Inclusive fare, including ride to Puerto Canoas and boat to San Martín island (US$2 return), is US$3.50. The bus continues from the Park Adminstration to Puerto Canoas (for Devil's Throat), hourly on the half-hour, US$0.20; returning hourly at quarter-to-the-hour. There are fixed rates for taxis, US$10, up to 5 people. A tour from the bus terminal, taking in both sides of the Falls, costs US$11. Hitch-hiking to the Falls is difficult, but you can hitch up to the Posadas intersection at Km. 11, then it is only 7 km. walk. A trail starting behind the *Hotel Internacional* leads down to the Río Iguazú ferry to Isla San Martín; ferry takes 2-3 mins., leaves on demand.

Frontier crossing to see both sides is easy. If you are coming from one side and you just want to see the other, returning on the same day to the side you came from, tell the officials, and they won't stamp your passport. Holders of British passports may on occasion be subjected to a certain amount of verbal abuse in local bars, but there is now no problem entering without a visa. Check relevant **Information for Visitors** sections for those who need visas. Some say that, for fear of being stranded in no-man's-land, it is best to insist on having one's papers stamped at all posts. International buses won't wait if you alight to be stamped out of a country, but if you keep your bus ticket you can get on the next one.

Travel between Argentina and Brazil has been greatly improved by the opening of the 480 metre Puente de Fraternidad/Ponte Presidente Tancredo Neves, which joins Puerto Iguazú (Route 12) and Porto Meira (BR-469). Six buses run each hour (US$0.70) from the Puerto Iguazú bus terminal on Av. Córdoba to the Terminal Urbana in Foz do Iguaçu, pausing at the border but not stopping long enough for passport controls (US$0.60); you have to wait for the next one if you need a stamp (keep the ticket so as not to pay twice); on the other hand if you are simply crossing to see the other side of the Falls, you can stay on the same bus. The passenger and car ferries between Puerto Iguazú and Porto Meira no longer run a regular schedule, and there are no immigration offices on either side; motorists visiting the Argentine side from Brazil can park overnight in the National Park, free.

Change some money into new cruzeiro before going into Brazil: they try to charge you triple the true cost if you use Argentine money. The new cruzeiro exchange rate is better in the town of Puerto Iguazú than in Brazil itself. Foz do Iguaçu being much the larger town, tends to be cheaper, with more choice than Puerto Iguazú for hotels and food.

There is a Brazilian immigration office on the road between Foz do Iguaçu and the bridge. Customs on Brazil-Argentina border do not now close until 0200; they can be very thorough with their luggage checks.

It is not possible to go direct by road to Puerto Franco (Paraguay) from Puerto Iguazú; one must go through Brazil. If passing through Foz do Iguaçu en route from Puerto Iguazú to Paraguay, make sure that Brazilian officials stamp your passport. "Ponte-Ponte" buses ply (US$0.20) between the Brazilian ends of the bridges into Argentina and into Paraguay, via Foz do Iguaçu. However, there are launches plying on the rivers Paraná and Iguazú between Puerto Franco and Puerto Iguazú: every 2 hours or so, US$0.50.

On the Argentine side is **Puerto Iguazú**, a small modern town above the river. There is a helpful tourist office (English spoken) at Av. Victoria Aguirre and Brasil, open 0800-1200, 1500-2000 Mon.-Fri., 0800-1200, 1630-2000 Sat. and Sun.

Museum Imágenes de la Selva, housed in a shop on Av. Victoria Aguirre, open daily, free, has wood sculptures by Rodolfo Allou who uses natural shapes of roots and branches.

Hotels Crowded during summer (Jan.-Feb.), Easter and July holiday periods. *Internacional Iguazú*, L, five-star, pool, casino, good restaurant, business facilities, overlooking the falls. Reservations at Av. Eduardo Madero 1020 (T 3114259, or 3136292), Buenos Aires. *Iguazú*, on Paraguay, in the town (no swimming pool), is being used to offer rest accommodation to the elderly, but transients are still welcome, D. The *Paraná*, E, is clean and friendly, Brasil 367. *La Cabaña*, Av. Tres Fronteras 434 D, with shower and breakfast, a/c, good, clean and friendly) with an older part and a new annexe, and has communal washing facilities and swimming pool, rec.; opp. is *Residencial Tres Fronteras*; in same street (No. 341) is *Residencial Tucán*. *Tierra Colorada*, Av. Córdoba and El Urú 265, very good, E with fan and bath, nice restaurant, trips arranged. *Esturión*, L, Av. Tres Fronteras 650, clean, arbitrary pricing, comfortable, swimming pool, good restaurant, reservations at Belgrano 265, 10th floor, Buenos Aires. *Libertador*, San Martín 441, central, helpful, large bedrooms and public rooms, rooms at back have balconies overlooking garden and swimming pool, C. *Las Orquídeas*, Ruta 12, Km. 5 (T 2472), very comfortable, clean, set right in the jungle outside Puerto Iguazú, restaurant, C. *Alexander*, Córdoba 685, opp. bus station, C incl. meagre breakfast, swimming pool; *El Yaguareté*, Av. Victoria Aguirre (entrance to town), bungalows, D, with kitchen, excellent value; *Residencial San Fernando*, Av. Córdoba 693, close to bus station, E, with bath, clean, quiet, restaurant, highly rec. *Residencial Paquita*, Av. Córdoba 731, F, noisy but friendly, nice setting, small, some rooms with terrace opposite bus station, rec. Two blocks from bus station is *Residencial San Diego*, E, clean, friendly. *Turismo de Iguazú*, D with bath, hot water, charmingly old fashioned, spectacularly set above river. *Saint George*, Av. Córdoba 745, opp. bus station, C, with breakfast, comfortable, has good, expensive restaurant. Behind this hotel is *Residencial Los Helechos*, E, with bath, owner speaks German, clean, new, motel-style accommodation. *Residencial Gloria*, Av. Uruguay, E with bath (electric showers) and fridge, clean, quiet, friendly. *Residencial Los Naranjos*, E, clean, mosquito-free, private bath. *Residencial Arco Iris* (with private shower), basic, cooking facilities available, E. Cheapest hotel is *Misiones*, E, Av. Victoria Aquirre opp. Tourist

Office, clean, friendly and less busy than many other hotels; there are some *hosterías* in the F range of which *Lilian*, behind the *Paquita* hotel, is recommended, F with bath, clean, safe; also *Residencial Río Selva*, San Martín 147, G. There is a hostel affiliated to the IYHA (G) between immigration and international bridge, pleasant, 90 beds.

Camping Free site 600 metres past parking area at Puerto Canoas. Tables, but no other facilities. Camping sometimes permitted at the school just inside the Park entrance. Municipal campsite in Puerto Iguazú reported "grim". Camping Pindó at the edge of town, charges US$0.60 p.p, US$6 per tent and US$1.00 for use of pool, friendly, but very run down. There are better facilities at Camping América (T 2820/2788), incl. swimming pool.

Restaurants Restaurant (nameless), ½ block from *Hotel Sol de Iguazú*, Brazilian food, all you can eat for US$5. *La Rueda*, Av. Córdoba, good food at reasonable prices, but service less than good. *Don Nicola*, Av. Bompland, good. *El Tío Querido*, Perito Moreno 345, friendly service, excellent cooking, guitarist at night; *Casa de Comercio*, Aguirre 327 through arch, on square opp. church, good food, moderate prices; *Ser Barbas* and *Trébol*, rec. Good meals in the bus terminal.

Money Exchange three *casas de cambio* opposite the tourist office, change cash at good rates (though rates may vary between the *casas*; shop around!) only one, Dick, changes travellers' cheques, at 4% commission.

Car Hire Al International at airport and in town; *Hotel Internacional*; Avis plan to open an agency. Cars may be taken to the Brazilian side for an extra US$5.

Brazilian Consulate Victoria Aquirre 773, 0800-1200, arrive early with 1 photo for a free, 90-day, multiple early visa (applicable to US citizens, Australians, New Zealanders, French citizens—check Brazil chapter).

Travel Agent Turismo Dick, Av. Victoria Aguirre 425, also in Foz do Iguaçu, good rates of exchange; does not close at lunchtime. Reports vary. Reinhard Foerster, Privat Servis, Av. Tres Fronteras 335, T 2774, offers naturalists' and birdwatchers' programmes. Turismo Caracol, Moreno 357, T 2124, does good all-day tour of both sides of falls, US$10 including meal in Brazil. Agency at bus terminal does tour of Argentine side of falls for US$2.50.

Airports There is an Argentine domestic airport near the Falls, and a Brazilian international airport about half-way between Foz do Iguaçu and the Falls. Taxi between the two airports over the new bridge costs US$20. Aerolíneas Argentinas office in centre of Puerto Iguazú (bus from here to airport about 2 hours before plane's departure, 1445 and 2145).

Air Transport By Boeing 737 (Aerolíneas Argentinas and Austral) from Buenos Aires, via Rosario, Corrientes or Posadas, or direct to improved Iguazú airport (1 hr. 40 mins.) several daily. Direct flights (AA) from Córdoba. For best view on landing, sit on left side of aircraft. Flights back to Buenos Aires are very crowded. The Argentine side can be seen in one day from Buenos Aires: there is a flight between 0730 and 0830 with either Aerolíneas Argentinas or Austral on most days of the week from BSA. domestic airport, flight time 1 hr. 40 mins; bus to falls takes ½ hr., leaving according to plane arrivals. There is only one smallish bus meeting each flight; it is advisable to buy tickets (US$1.50) even before collecting luggage because when the bus is full the only alternative is a taxi, US$8 to *Hotel Internacional* and considerably more to Puerto Iguazú. Bus from *Hotel Internacional* to airport leaves according to flight departure times. Aerolínea Federal Argentina (ex Alfa); flies to Resistencia on Tues., Wed. and Sun., with connecting flights to Tucumán, Mendoza and Salta.

Rail Transport from Buenos Aires is comfortable and cheap. There are sleeping and restaurant cars, good meals and wines. Passengers take a train from **Lacroze Station** in Buenos Aires to Posadas (for details, see under Posadas, page 133). There is a road, now paved, from Posadas to Puerto Iguazú; express bus to Iguazú meets train, 4½ hrs.

Road Transport From Buenos Aires N to Clorinda, then by new toll bridge to Asunción. Or crossing the Paraná at Santa Fe or Resistencia, taking the paved road to Posadas, and on to the falls. The more direct run via Zárate and Concordia is now completely paved. Direct buses take some 21 hours, leaving at 1130 (returns at 1200), with Singer (Av. Perito Moreno 366, T 2581) no a/c, and Buenos Aires-Posadas-Iguazú (returns at 1600 to Buenos Aires) Expreso Tigre-Iguazú, daily at 1500, offices at Plaza Once, Buenos Aires leaving from Retiro terminal (US$28.75). Expreso Iguazú offers discounts to students. To Santiago del Estero, Wed. and Sat. at 0130 (20 hours) with Cotal, gives student discount. To Córdoba, daily at 1130, via Posadas 26 hrs., US$34.50, with Singer or El Litoral. To Rosario daily except Thurs., 24 hrs. Expreso Iguazú to Posadas, 5 hrs., US$6.50 (310 km.) e.g. with Transportes Iguazú at 0930 and 1530; ordinary bus takes 8 hrs., every 1½ hrs. All go by the Falls and stop at San Ignacio

Miní (US$8). To Resistencia daily 0900 and 2000, 11 hrs., US$16; change there for Bolivian border at Agua Blanca/Bermejo, via Joaquín V. González and Orán. Alternative to direct bus to Buenos Aires (**see above**), take bus to Posadas and take train from there; slower, but more comfortable. Puerto Iguazú to Eldorado, 2 hrs., US$3.50 with Cotal.

Up the River Uruguay

The Río Uruguay is the eastern boundary of Mesopotamia and forms the western border of the Republic of Uruguay. There are no regular passenger shipping services.

Boats leaving Buenos Aires go past Martín García island, and enter the wide estuary. At 193 km. from Buenos Aires, the Uruguayan town of Fray Bentos is to the right; there is a bridge between Fray Bentos and the Argentine town of Puerto Unzué, near Gualeguaychú, but pedestrians and cyclists cannot cross it other than on motor vehicles; officials will give lifts on either side. The river now becomes braided into channels and islands. Opposite Fray Bentos, on the left, is the mouth of the Río Gualeguay; 19 km. up is **Gualeguaychú**, which can be reached by good road from Buenos Aires (370 km.) and Concordia. It is a very pleasant town with a river promenade, a country club (free for tourists), street entertainment and a camping site (La Delfina, US$3.50 p.p. good; also possible in Parque Saturnino Unzué). Lively Carnival at beginning of March. Population, 61,000, with quite a large German contingent. Airport. Customs formalities at Puerto Unzué take 10 minutes.

Hotels *Embajador*, San Martín y 3 de Febrero, T 4414, C, casino; *Posada del Charrúa*, D; *El Faro*, E; *París*, E; *Yapo*, E; *Entre Ríos*, F; *Mayo*, F; *Alemán*, F, friendly, German-speaking, rec.

Exchange There are banks on either side of the bridge, but in Uruguay you can obtain only Uruguayan pesos and the Argentine-side bank is almost always closed. Next bank at Gualeguaychú has very good rates. There is also a service station a few km. beyond the border in Argentina, where you can sell Uruguayan pesos.

Transport Buses to Fray Bentos, Uruguay, 0845, 1230, 1800.

Concepción del Uruguay, the first Argentine port of any size on the river, was founded in 1778. There are train services to all parts of Mesopotamia. Population, 47,200. Paved roads to Paraná and Colón.

Hotels *Virrey*, Aceso Ruta 131, D; *Gran Hotel*, Colón 134, D; *General Ramírez*, Galarza y Blvd. Ramírez, E; *Residencial 3 de Febrero*, E; *Residencial La Posada*, E; *Centro Hotel*, E. Many hotels of all classes by the bus station, none near the railway station.

Local Boats Daily to Paysandú (Uruguay).

Colón (17,000 people), 350 km. from Buenos Aires, is 37 km. above Concepción del Uruguay. The river is more picturesque here with sandy beaches, and cliffs visible from a considerable distance; a road bridge now links Colón and Paysandú. (Toll for cars US$1.40. All border formalities, including stamping of vehicle carnets, are conducted at both ends of the bridge, easy crossing.) The town is known for *artesanía* shops down San Martín, the main street, and there is a large handicrafts fair at Carnival time (Feb.). Tourist office by river not very helpful. It is possible to get a bus from Colón to Paysandú, US$1.50, but there are none between 1145 and 1645, and none on Sundays. There are 2 buses a day to Buenos Aires, US$8, 5 hrs., daily buses to Concordia (2½ hrs., US$2.65), Paraná and four a week to Córdoba.

Hotels *Quirinale*, Av. Quirós s/n, 5-star, A (with casino), *Nuevo Hotel Plaza*, D, 12 de Abril y Belgrano; *Palmar*, D, Blvd. Ferrari 285, T 21952, good; *Vieja Calera*, E, Bolívar y Maipú; *Holimazu*, E, Belgrano 28; *Ver-Wei*, F, 25 de Mayo 10; *Residencial JR*, Chacabuco 185. Several **campsites** along river bank.

Restaurant *Marito*, good and cheap.

Parque Nacional El Palmar lies between Colón and Concordia, has both free and paying camping facilities, a small hotel 8 km. N of the Park, with restaurant opposite, and a small shop. The Park contains varied scenery with a mature palm forest, Indian tombs and other remains, and many rheas and other birds. Buses from Colón, 40 mins, US$1.75.

Concordia, about 105 km. above Colón, a little downriver from Salto, Uruguay, is a prosperous city, with a population of 92,000, which has some fine public buildings, a racecourse, rowing clubs, and a 9-hole golf club. Five km. out is Parque Rivadavia, with a circular road used occasionally as a motor-racing track; there are pleasant views here of the river and a ruined French-style palace. Paved roads to Buenos Aires, Paraná and Posadas.

The river is impassable for large vessels beyond the rapids of Salto Chico near the town, and Salto Grande 32 km. up-river, where there is a large international hydro-electric dam, providing a route for an international road and railway. Take No. 2 bus from bus terminal marked "Puerto", for ferry crossing to Salto from Concordia US$1 (tickets obtainable at a small kiosk, which shuts 15 mins. before departure, outside customs) departures 0730, 0900, 1130, 1500, 1815, weekdays, twice a day Sat. but none Sun.; takes 15 mins. Few cars, but people willing to give rides. Above Salto Grande the river is generally known as the Alto Uruguay.

Hotels *San Carlos*, Parque Rivadavia, T 216725, C; *Salto Grande*, Urquiza 581, T 210034, C; *Palmar*, Urquiza 517, T 216050, D; *Imperial* Argentino, E, very friendly; *Central*, 1° de Mayo 185, E; *Gran Hotel Colón*, E, Pelligrini 611, highly rec., simple, clean and charming, highly rec.; *Embajador*, San Lorenzo 75, F, nr. bus station, good value, neat and clean. *Terminal* above bus station, surprisingly quiet, good value, F.

Camping La Tortuga Alegre. La Posada de Suárez—Club Viajantes on Av. Costanera near the park, warmly rec., with good *parrillada* alongside.

Restaurants *Lion d'Or; Don Juan*, H. Yrigoyen 602, near main plaza, excellent and cheap. *El Abrojito*, Pellegrini 1203, rec.

Tourist Office Plaza 25 de Mayo, helpful.

Rail *El Correntino* train has sleepers, pullman, 1st class (heating ineffective) and tourist class (US$24, US$15.50, US$10, US$7) and leaves Lacroze station at 1500, daily, arriving at 2314, returns daily at 0729, arr. 1545. *El Gran Capitán*, same prices, leaves at 1500 daily, arrives at 2314 daily. Returns daily at 0729, arrives 1545. This train also goes on at 2017 to Paso de los Libres and Posadas (sleeper US$28.50, pullman US$19, 1st US$13.20, tourist US$9.30 from Buenos Aires), arrives at 0230 and 0800, respectively.

Buses To Buenos Aires, 6 daily; to Paraná 5, to Posadas 3 (8½ hrs., US$11.50), to Iguazú one (1810, 13½ hrs.). Bus to La Paz (Entre Ríos)—see page 129, 1100, US$7.70, 8 hrs. Possible to sleep overnight on benches in bus terminal.

About 153 km. upstream from Concordia lies the small port of **Monte Caseros**, with the Uruguayan town of Bella Unión, on the Brazilian border, almost opposite. Above Bella Unión, the **Alto Uruguay** is the boundary between Argentina and Brazil. Ninety-six km. above MonteCaseros is **Paso de los Libres**, with the Brazilian cattle town of **Uruguaiana** opposite: a bridge joins the two. From Uruguaiana into Brazil the buses are much quicker than trains, though there is a comfortable railway service to Porto Alegre. Paso de los Libres was founded in 1843 by General Madariaga; it was here that he crossed the river from Brazil with his hundred men and annexed Corrientes province for Argentina. Road (paved) to Paraná.

Hotel in Paso de los Libres, *Alejandro* I, Coronel López y Pago Largo, best in town.

Rail See above under Concordia. Fares a/c sleeper US$22, Pullman US$22.20 first US$14.50, tourist US$10.25 Buenos Aires-Paso de los Libres.

N of Paso de los Libres, on the road to Alvear, is *Yapeyú*, famous as the birthplace of the liberator, José de San Martín. There is a pleasant little museum and part of the house where he was born is well preserved, inside another building.

THE LAKE DISTRICT (9)

Northern Patagonia has two railway lines. The more northerly runs westwards from Bahía Blanca to Neuquén and Zapala; the southern line runs from Bahía Blanca southwards across the Colorado to Viedma and then westwards through San Antonio Oeste to Bariloche and the Lake District. The roads along which buses ply, and airlines are mentioned in the text. (For map, see the Chilean section, **page 558**.)

The **Lake District** contains a series of great lakes strung along the foot of the Andes from above 40° South to below 50° in the Los Glaciares National Park area. In the N the western ends of these lakes cut deeply into the mountains, their water lapping the forested skirts of some of the most spectacular snow-capped peaks in the world; their eastern ends are contained by the frontal moraines deposited there by the ancient glaciers which melted to form these huge fjord-like lakes. The water is a deep blue, sometimes lashed into white froth by the region's high winds.

On the far side of the Andes, in Chile, lies another system of lakes: these can be visited (unpaved roads) through various passes. The Puyehue route is given on page 150, with an alternative in the Chilean section.

National Park Lake Nahuel Huapí with its surroundings, an area of 7,850 square km., was set aside in 1903 as a National Park. It contains the most diverse and spectacular natural phenomena: lakes, rivers, glaciers, waterfalls, torrents, rapids, valleys, forest, bare mountains and snow-clad peaks. Most of the area is covered with abundant vegetation, though it is notably more abundant on the Chilean side, which gets more rain. Many kinds of wild animals live in the region, but they are extremely shy and seldom glimpsed by the explorer. Bird life, on the other hand—particularly swans, geese and ducks—is seen at any time and everywhere in large flocks. In the far N of this region, near Zapala, these species and many others can be seen in their hundreds in the nature reserve of Laguna Blanca.

The outstanding feature of this National Park is the splendour of the lakes. The largest is **Lake Nahuel Huapí**, 531 square km. and 460 metres deep in places. It is 767 metres above sea level, in full view of the snow-covered peaks of the Cordillera and of the forests covering the lower slopes. Towering over the scene is Cerro Tronador. Some 96 km. long, and not more than 12 km. wide, the lake is very irregular in shape; long arms of water, or *brazos*, which look like fjords, stretch far into the land. There are many islands: the largest is **Isla Victoria**, on which stands the forest research station where new species of vegetation are acclimatized. The Zoological Board is adding to the indigenous fauna; the trout and salmon of the lakes, for instance, have been introduced from abroad. Lake Nahuel Huapí is drained eastwards by the Río Limay; below its junction with the Río Neuquén it becomes the Río Negro. The Limay has good trout fishing but the rivers farther N—the Quilquihue, Malleu, Chimehuín, Collón-Curá, Hermoso, Meliquina and Caleufú—are much less fished. They are all in the neighbourhood of San Martín de los Andes (**see page** 157). The season is from early November to the end of March. Do not take fishing equipment out-of-season; it will only cause suspicion.

A mere sand bar in one of the northern *brazos* separates Lake Nahuel Huapí from Lake Correntoso, which is quite close to Lake Espejo. Lake Traful, a short distance to the NE, can be reached by a road which follows the River Limay through the Valle Encantado, with its fantastic rock formations. S of Nahuel Huapí there are other lakes: the three main ones are Mascardi, Guillermo, and Gutiérrez. On the shore of Lake Gutiérrez, in a grotto, is the Virgen de las Nieves (Virgin of the Snows). There is a road to these lakes from Bariloche.

Fishing   The lakes are full of fish, and the best time for fishing is at the beginning of the season, that is, in November and December. Among the best are: Lakes Traful, Gutiérrez, Mascardi, Futalaufquen (in Los Alerces National Park), Meliquina, Falkner, Villarino, Nuevo, Lacar, Lolog, Curruhué, Chico, Huechulafquen, Paimún, Epulafquen, Tromen (all in Lanín National Park), and, in the far N, Quillén. In the far S, the fishing in Lake Argentino is also good. **NB** fishing anywhere in Argentina requires a permit.

Bariloche (San Carlos de), on the southern shore of Lake Nahuel Huapí, founded 1898, is the best centre for exploring the National Park. It is a Swiss-looking town of steep streets, its wooden chalets perched upon a glacial moraine at the foot of Cerro Otto. To the S lie the heights of the Ventana and the Cerro Colorado (2,135 metres). The place is full of hotels and cheap *hosterías*. The cathedral, built in 1946, dominates the town; interior unfinished. There is a belvedere at the top of Cerro Otto with wide views of lake and mountain. The main road into Bariloche from the E is paved and in good condition. Unhappily, because of its phenomenal growth, the town has become noisy and overcrowded, and the best time to visit it is out of season either in the spring or autumn (the forest is particularly beautiful around May). The 24 km. road to Llao-Llao (bus No. 20, ¾ hr., US$1) is ribbon-developed, except near Cerro Catedral. Population, over 70,000. Lido swimming pool on the lake shore is beautifully sited but somewhat run down.

Hotels   The most complete listing with map is published by the Oficina Municipal de Turismo, which you are advised to consult if you arrive in the high season without a reservation. It also has booking service at Florida 520 (Galería), room 116, Buenos Aires. Out of season, prices are quite reasonable, in all ranges, but in season everything is very expensive. Most hotels outside the town include half-board, and those in the town include breakfast. Hotels with high-season lake views normally charge US$3-4 extra, per room per day, for the view; we give lake-view high-season prices where applicable. The best outside town are: *Huemul* (road to Llao-Llao, 1.5 km.); *El Casco* (Av. Bustillo, road to Llao-Llao 11 km.), German-run, excellent, luxurious, warmly rec.; *Apart-hotel Casablanca* (same road, 23.5 km.), good, on a peninsula between Lakes Nahuel Huapí and Moreno, all L, some offering half-board. Also at Llao-Llao, 24 km. from Bariloche, are *Tunquelén*, L, and *Hostería Aunancay*, L, including 2 meals, friendly and delightful setting. *Hostería Katy*, on Llao-Llao road Km. 24, warmly rec., reasonable, B. *La Caleta*, Km. 1.9 on Llao-Llao road, bungalows run by Neil Callwood, E for an apartment sleeping 4, shower, open fire, excellent value, self-catering, rec., T 25650. *Residencial Matterhorn*, Swiss-run, Pasaje Gutiérrez 1122, D, rec., good breakfast; *Hotel Los Andes*, Moreno 594, affliated to youth hostel organization, good and cheap. Out of town (many birds to see) is *Hostería del Viejo Molino*, Av. Bustillo km. 6.4, D, buses to town, T 22411, friendly, rec.

In the town are the following: *Edelweiss*, Av. San Martín 232, L, 5-star, modern, spotless, excellent food; enclosed pool, highly rec.; *Panamericano*, San Martín 536, L, 5-star, heated swimming pool; *Bariloche Sky*, San Martín 352, L, 4-star, T 311-3235, Telex 18273, good; *Interlaken*, V.A. O'Connor 383, L, lake view, 4-star; *Tres Reyes*, 12 de Octubre 135 T 26121, L, lake view, 4-star. First class: *Residencial Tirol*, Libertad 175, C, clean, friendly, good; *Casita Suiza*, Quaglia 342, very nice, 4-star. At Rolando 197 is *Val Gardena*, B with breakfast, excellent service, clean, no restaurant, 2-star; opp. is *Sunset*, B, 4-star. *Residencial El Ciervo*

BARILOCHE

LAKE NAHUEL HUAPI

1. Civic Centre, Tourist Office, Post Office and Museum,
2. Municipality, 3. National Park Office, 4. Banco de la
Nación, 5. Banco de Río Negro, 6. Hospital,
7. Cathedral, 8. Market, 9. Catedral Turismo,
10. Transporte Mercedes.

To RAILWAY, AIRPORT; NEUQUEN, BUENOS AIRES

LARIDA

A. SAENZ PEÑA

RIVADAVIA

SARMIENTO

RUIZ MORENO

G. ELORDI

C. ONELLI

T. SCORNIA

ALBARRACIN

N. FAGNANO

25 DE MAYO

O. GOEDEKE

J. O'CONNOR

E. FREY

F. BESCHTEDT

PALACIOS

ROLANDO

VILLEGAS

QUAGLIA

MORALES

TACUARI

AVDA 12 DE OCTUBRE

VTE O'CONNOR

BME MITRE

FP MORENO

A M ELFLEIN

A GALLARDO

N ANASAGASTI

CONSTITUCION

DIAGONAL CAPRARO

NUEVA ANTARTIDA ARGENTINA

TO EL BOLSÓN

JUAN MANUEL DE ROSAS

ESPAÑA

AVDA SAN MARTIN

SALTA

TUCUMÁN

GRAL BELGRANO

24 DE SEPTIEMBRE

LIBERTAD

FRANCIA

PANOZZI

RECONQUISTA

URQUIZA

INDEPENDENCIA

JURAMENTO

J NEUMEYER

JJ PASOS

20 DE FEBRERO

GÜEMES

CAMPICHUELO

PRIMERA JUNTA

30 DE JUNIO

20 DE FEBRERO

BAJADA DE

PARANA

GUTIERREZ

CASTAÑARES

CERRO OTTO

PARQUE CERRO OTTO

TO LLAO LLAO

TO CERRO OTTO

Rojo, Elflein 115, B, 2-star, very pleasant; *Austral*, San Martín 425, B, 2-star, restaurant, small rooms; *Hostería Madinette*, Morales 534, very well run, half-board; *Los Pinos*, 20 de Febrero 640, C, clean, spacious rooms, private bath, central heating, rec.; *King's Hotel*, Moreno 136, very nice, clean, warm, C, with bath (E off-season); *La Pastorella*, Belgrano 127, C, with bath and breakfast, German-run, English and German spoken, central, rec.; *Residencial Portofino*, Morales 439, two blocks from plaza, C, small but spotless. *Venezia*, also on Morales, D, rec.; *Nevada*, Rolando 250, C with shower, and heating, breakfast included, nice rooms; *Residencial Elisabeth*, J. J. Paso 117, D, cheaper rates for longer stays, German-run, clean, central, private bath, hot water, towels, clean, good value; *La Negra*, Apartado Postal 21, T 25720, D, original wooden house with view of lake, good food and service, rec., especially for motorcyclists; *Residencial Piuké*, Beschtedt 136, E inc. breakfast (A in skiing season), clean, friendly, rec.; opposite is *Residencial Sur*, Beschtedt 101, excellent value, D with bath and breakfast. *Residencial La Fontana*, Saavedra 689, Plaza Belgrano, clean, friendly, A; *Ideal*, Libertad 121, behind police station, pleasant, clean, quiet, away from the commercial centre, C with private bath, cheaper without, restaurant, some doubles have lake view; *Hospedaje Nahuel*, Gallardo 454, C, warm and clean, hot showers; *Residencial Panorámico*, Moreno 646, A, private shower, rec.; *Hostal de Los Alpes*, Diagonal Capraro 1034, C, very modern, clean, friendly; *Monte Grande*, 25 de Mayo 1544, T 22159, with bath, heating, breakfast room, camping, parking, economical prices, Ruca Malen travel agency here; *Victoria*, F, shared rooms Mitre 815, friendly but grubby, information service helpful. *Internacional*, also on Mitre, C, rec.

Others: *Hostal Las Moiras*, Reconquista, E, central but quiet, hot shower, comfortable; *El Mirador*, Moreno 652-76, E, hot water, eccentric owner speaks German, very pleasant, with lake views; *Residencial Premier*, Rolando 263, ½ block from main street, E, clean, hot showers, English and German spoken, rec.; *Kent*, E, near Club Andino on 20 de Febrero, new, modern. Also new is *Residencial Wikter*, E, Güemes 506; *Hostería El Radal*, 24 de Septiembre 46, E, clean, friendly; *Residencial Adquintue*, V.A. O'Connor 776, E, clean and comfortable; *Residencial El Ñire* (T 2-3041), V.A. O'Connor 710, corner J. O'Connor, hot showers, clean, very pleasant, E, prefers longer-stay visitors, highly rec. *Huecho Ruca*, Moreno 816, D with bath, hot shower, rec. *Residencial Rosán* (Sra. Milena de Arko), E, strongly rec., Güemes 691, T 23109, English and German spoken, cooking facilities, four rooms, two showers. Also rec., *Residencial Güemes* on street of same name (No. 715), T 24785, E with breakfast, helpful; *Hostería Maribor*, Angel Gallardo 950, Sra Adriana, bath, breakfast extra, laundry, excursions, rec.; and *pensión* of Sra. Carlota Baumann, Av. de los Pioneros 860 (T 24502), follow 20 de Febrero for 10-15 minutes, F p.p., kitchen, bath, hot water, laundry service, friendly, Sra. Baumann speaks English and German. *Residencial Alpina*, Discornia 90, D, clean, friendly, good value. *Residencial Millaray*, Libertad 125, D, good and cheap, shower, closed in off-season; *Los Andes*, F.P. Moreno y J. O'Connor, F, youth hostel style, clean friendly; *Belgrano*, Güemes 648, E, friendly. Rec. family *pensión* at Salta 571, heated; similar at Salta 188, F, excellent food, warm and friendly reception, rec. Ask at tourist office, which has private homes listed. For longer stays try private house at Elflein 507 (Sra. Heidi Landolf), F, or Anasagasti 345, US$3; also at 12 de Octubre 2008 (road to airport), US$3. *Alojamiento Familiar Pire-Cuyen*, Anasagasti 840, E, clean, good, no single rooms. *Alojamiento Familial*, Frey 635, F, 6 rooms, clean, hot shower, reasonable, friendly, rec., has space for motorcycles. Youth hostel: *Alaska*, Marcelo Ferrante, Estafeta Postal No. 4, about 7 km. from centre, 6 blocks from beach, G p.p., warm water, good atmosphere and neighbourhood.

Camping Several sites (Km. 2.7, 5.8, 13.2) on road to Llao-Llao: *Petunia* rec.; list from Tourist Office. Selva Negra at Km. 2.8 is US$1 p.p. but not rec., very unfriendly. Note that in Bariloche the only type of camping gas on sale fits only Argentine-made stoves (which can be bought for US$10) and not the small, international stoves.

Restaurants *Casita Suiza*, Quaglia 342, excellent and rec. (fondue US$11 for 2); *Viejo Munich*, good, Mitre 102; *Sobremonte*, Mitre 420, good meat and wine; *La Marmita*, Mitre, small, cosy, excellent, mixed fondues particularly rec.; *La Costa*, Rosas 485, excellent fillet steak; *La Andina* on Elflein and Quaglia specializes in inexpensive but good "fast food", rec.; *Caza Mayor*, Quaglia and Elflein, game and fish, good but expensive; *Nikola*, Elflein 49, very good value; *Kandahar*, 20 de Febrero 698, T 24702, excellent, run by Argentine ski champion Marta Peirono de Barber; *Parrilla 1810*, Elflein 167, T 23922, good meat and reasonable, highly rec.; *Parilla La Vizcacha*, Rolando, rec.; *El Barrilito*, Moreno 180, good and reasonable; *Asociación Española*, Rolando 142, fine paellas; *Mangiare*, pizzas and other Italian, Palacios 86. Good pastries and hot chocolate at *Hola Nicolás*, Moreno 66 and Urquiza. *El Jabalí*, Av. San Martín, specialises in wild boar, interesting fish buffet. *Jauja*, Moreno (near Villegas), good typical dishes; *Canguros*, Palacios 153, excellent steaks, try the hot wine (ask, not on menu) very friendly, rec. *La Andinita*, Mitre 56, rec., reasonable, trout a speciality, friendly; *La Sandina*, Elflein 95, rec. for pizzas; *Pizza Vía Roma*, Mitre 5, big choice of good pizzas; *Villegas*, Villegas 363, rec. for trout and friendly service. Vegetarian: *La Huerta*, Morales 362, good, cheap, pleasant. On Av. Bustillo (the road to Llao-Llao), Km. 10, is *La Posta del Río*, reasonable, *Dirty Dick's Pub*, Km. 5 and *La Glorieta*, Av. Bustillo, km. 3.8, good. Superb coffee and cakes at *Chocolate Casero del Turista* at Mitre 239, but nowhere to sit. *T-Bar Café*, Mitre 201, good hot chocolate. *Ermitage*, new tea rooms, on road to Llao-Llao at Km. 18, owner speaks Slovenian. *La Mamadera*, Mitre 358, rec. *Saloom*, Mitre 208, restaurant with video films, open 24 hours, as are others on Mitre; *Oso Panda*, Rolandio 257, good, reasonably priced Chinese. *Friends*, San Martín, good sandwiches, gateaux, quick meals. Good breakfasts at *Bar y Leche*, on Quaglia. *Crêperie Bretonne*, nr. Civic Centre, cheap and very good. Many good delicatessens in the area with take-away food, including chicken pizzas and cheeses, for picnics.

Best Buys Woollen goods, e.g. at *Arbol* on Mitre, or *Manos del Uruguay*, Mitre 216. The products of the local chocolate industry are excellent: *Fábrica de Chocolate Cerro León* on Av. 12 de Octubre, near railway station. You can watch chocolates being made at *Turista*, San Martín 220. Very good chocolate at *Gallardo* (be sure to get the 10% discount). Try "Papas de Bariloche", the local chocolate speciality. Also chocolates at *Benroth*, Beschtedt 569, above Gallardo. Handicraft shops all along San Martín; some will change money. Artesanía cooperative on Moreno y Rolando, rec.

Car Hire Hertz, Avis, and A1 International, at airport and in town (latter at Bartolomé Mitre 26, T 24869, 22038); no flat rates. Permission to enter Chile may be obtained.

Car mechanic Auguen SA, V.A. O'Connor 1068, fast, reasonable, highly rec.

Bicycles may be hired beside the lake in high season. Mopeds from Vertigo Rental, San Martin 594, US$3.50 per hour.

Cinemas Arrayanes, Moreno 39; Coliseo, Mitre 281; Ciné Club, Tues. 2115 only, Biblioteca Sarmiento in the Centro Cívico.

Museums The Museo de La Patagonia in the Civic Centre, has a nice collection of stuffed animals, also well worth seeing for collection of Indian artefacts, houses, open 1000-1200, 1400-1900 Tues.-Fri., 1000-1300 Sat. US$0.50. The clock in the Civic Centre has four figures which rotate at noon; photos with St. Bernard dogs may be taken in the Civic Centre square.

Exchange There are several banks and exchange shops, which buy and sell virtually all European and South American currencies, besides US dollars; Sat. is a bad day. Exchange houses cash cheques for 5-10%. Casa Piano, B. Mitre 131, T 23733, rec., open 0900-1300 and 1600-2000 and Sat. a.m. (charges US$2 on all cheques below US$100, 2% over US$100, changes travellers' cheques into US$ cash 2% commission). Kiosko Suyoi, Elflein 87, cash only. Austral, Quaglia 230, good both for cash and cheques. Kiosko Anri, Mitre 339 (rear of Galería Arrayanes), US$ cheques and Chilean pesos accepted, good rates, highly rec. Good exchange rates at *Kiwanis* (boot rental), Mitre 210. The American Express Co., B. Mitre 139, sends you across the street to the Banco Provincia to buy travellers' cheques. Beware forged Argentine banknotes.

Laundry Prices are generally 60% higher than elsewhere in Argentina. Lavamatic, Villegas 258, English manager, friendly, opp. cathedral, open till 2230 Mon.-Sat., 2100 Sun. Laundromats at Quaglia 427 (US$2 for 2 kg.), on Palacios, on San Martín, and on Villegas nr. Mitre.

Chilean Consulate Villegas, near Mitre, friendly, helpful.

Post Office Centro Cívico (same building as tourist office).

Immigration Office Next to *Hostería Tirol*, Libertad 175.

Clinic Cruz Azul, Capraro 1216.

Tourist Office Oficina Municipal de Turismo in Centro Cívico, open Mon.-Sat., (ski season) 0800-2000, daily at those times in summer but check times out of season (March-April, October-November) when closed at weekends; very helpful. Has details of hikes and campsites in the area. Also has the address of a motorcycle hire company—a good way of getting around the National Park. National Park information (scanty) at San Martín 24, open 0800-2000. Information also from Sociedad Profesional de Guías de Turismo, Casilla de Correo 51, 8400 S.C. de Bariloche (President: Ama Petroff).

Tourist Agencies Tour buses pick you up from your hotel. *Patagonia Travel*, Mitre 150 (Telex

80746 Patra), efficient, rec., English spoken; their guide Daniel is a good naturalist. *Catedral Turismo*, Mitre 399, T 25443/5, runs boats to Chile for Peulla-Puerto Montt trip; *Alunco Turismo*, groups first, friendly. *Transport Mercedes*; *Turisur*, Quaglia 227, T 26109, organizes US$10 trips on lake. *Lake Travel Service*, Moreno 126, 3rd floor, efficient, English spoken. *Polvani Tours*, Quaglia 268 (T 23286), see Hans Schulz (speaks Spanish, German and English) to arrange horse trekking at the Estancia Nahuel Huapí, run by Carol Jones (from US$24 for 1/2 day to US$75 overnight incl. meals and gear); both the agency and the treks rec. Arrange trekking with Sr. Daniel José Gorgone, San Martín 127, DT 0706, T 26181. *Tur Acción*, Quaglia 219, has been recommended for "adventure" tours.

Air Services Airport, 11 km. from town. Many flights to Buenos Aires. Aerolíneas Argentinas, 2 a day, US$150; no night flight. Also Austral, 25% cheaper with an extra US$35 reduction for cash, and CATA, US$70. AA has a Mendoza-Bariloche flight via Neuquén and there is an Austral Neuquén flight daily, exc. Sun., from Bariloche at 1320, arrival 1405. LADE to Trelew, Mon. 1255, Fri. 1304 and to Comodoro Rivadavia Tues., Fri. and Sun. LADE to Río Gallegos, 3 a week, US$36, usually booked 2 weeks in advance in season; continues to Calafate. AA also to Comodoro Rivadavia and Rio Gállegos. Flights, 3-4 times a week, with Aerolíneas and LADE to Esquel. (It is reported that it is difficult to obtain LADE flights from Bariloche now, especially the cheaper night flights to Buenos Aires.) LAN flies to Santiago (Chile), US$110. Small tax at airport on leaving. Taxi to or from airport, US$8-10; bus US$2 from Austral or Aerolíneas office. Turismo Catedral, Mitre 399, has US$1 airport bus service into town.

Rail Services The railway station is 5 km. E of centre (booking office closed 1200-1500 weekdays, Sat. p.m. and all Sun.), reached by local buses 70 and 71 (US$0.20). Information from San Martín 127 in centre; tickets also available from *Hotel Pagano y Pamozzi*, 3 blocks from Centro Cívico. *Expreso Lagos del Sur*, leaves Buenos Aires, Constitución, Sun. (with car transporter), 0730, 34 hrs. (not much heat); *Lagos del Sur* Tues., Thurs. 40 hrs.; both at 2300; good buffet car, cinema car (3 films), children half price. *Expreso* leaves Bariloche, Tues. 2230, *Lagos del Sur* 1955 Thurs. and Sun., all arrive at 0550 two days after, fares US$56 sleeper, US$51 Pullman, US$32 first, US$20 tourist class. Trip can be extremely dusty, take a wet towel in a plastic bag for face and hands. Scenery only interesting between Bariloche and Jacobacci (41/2 hrs.), where you catch the train to Esquel; food on board reasonable (US$4 for 3 courses), but not always available and water sometimes runs out.

Road Services Paved road from Buenos Aires via Neuquén, 1,600 km. Chevallier, Buenos Aires to Bariloche, daily at 1215, 221/2 hrs., US$62. Also La Estrella daily at 1315 (US$56.50) and El Valle via Neuquén at 1300 (US$55). These three return daily between 1500 and 1600, respectively. For Mar. del Plata, take Buenos Aires bus and change at Bahía Blanca or Tres Arroyos (e.g. La Estrella, 1500, arrive Tres Arroyos 0555, US$26). Bus to Mendoza, TAC, Tues., Thurs. and Sat., US$25, 22 hrs., on a paved road via Zapala, Buta Ranquil and San Rafael. Bus Córdoba-Bariloche, TUS, 25 hrs., US$46, Mon., Wed., Fri., and Sun. at 1000. Buses to El Bolsón (US$4.50 31/2 hrs.) and Esquel (US$9.50 with Don Otto or Mercedes) exc. Sun., with a 4 times weekly extension on paved road to Comodoro Rivadavia, US$40 (Don Otto). To Puerto Madryn, 24 hrs. via Esquel and Trelew. To Jacobacci (for Esquel train) only one bus a day, arrives after train has left. To San Martín de los Andes, 0800, US$10, 41/2 hrs. Buses also to Neuquén (550 km.) US$11.50 by Transportes Mercedes on Bartolomé Mitre or daily with La Estrella, Palacios 246 at 1415, 61/2 hrs. (a dull journey). (No direct bus to Río Gallegos; you have to spend a night in Comodoro Rivadavia en route.) To Santiago (Chile), Tues., Fri. and Sun., 24 hours with tea and breakfast served en route. To Puerto Montt, see the route to Chile from Bariloche, **page 150.**

Activities Apart from sailing and boating, there are golf, mountaineering, walking, birdwatching, skiing, and fishing (for which you need a permit). Racquet Club, Ruta Llao-Llao, Km. 13.5, tennis and squash, snack bar. Before going hiking you are recommended to buy moisturizing creams for exposed skin areas and lips. Excellent trout fishing Nov.-March; boat hire arranged with tackle shops. Horseflies (*tábanos*) frequent the lake shores and lower areas in summer; lemon juice is good for keeping them away. For horse riding, see above under Tourist Agencies.

Mountain Climbing In the area there is something for every kind of mountaineer. National Park mountain guides are available but can be expensive. Book: *Excursiones, Andinismo y Refugios de Montaña en Bariloche*, by Tonek Arko, available in local shops, US$2, or from the author at Güemes 691. In treks to *refugios* remember to add costs of ski lifts, buses, food at *refugio* and lodging (in Club Andino *refugios*: US$3 per night, plus US$1 for cooking, or US$1 for breakfast, US$2 for lunch, US$3 for dinner). Information from Club Andino Bariloche, 20 de Febrero 30, open 0900-1200 and 1500-2000 Mon.-Fri. and Sat. 0900-1200.

The climbing may mean a ride on horseback or a skilled ascent of the slopes of Cerro Tronador (excursion by bus US$15, full day, including 1 hr. walk to black glacier, leaves at 0800, but too much time spent on the bus) which looms over the area. The Club Andino Bariloche arranges for guides; ask for Sr. Ricardo, the secretary, who organizes easy weekend climbs and walks with friendly visitors. It also provides maps and details of all campsites, hotels and mountain lodges. The Government has convenient rest lodges at from 1,000 to 2,000 metres on the mountains. Firing, light and food are provided at these points. Note that at higher levels, winter snow storms can begin as early as April, making climbing dangerous.

Swimming in the larger lakes such as Nahuel Huapí and Huechulafquen is not recommended, for the water is cold. But swimming in smaller lakes such as Lolog, Lacar, Curruhué Chico, Hermoso, Meliquina, Espejo, Hess and Fonck is very pleasant and the water—especially where the bottom shelves to a shingly beach—can be positively warm.

Skiing There is good skiing during the winter season (July to early October), supervised by the Club Andino at Bariloche. It is best organized with a tour company, through whom you can secure discounts as part of an inclusive deal. (Skiing is cheaper, however, at smaller resorts, such as Esquel, though more expensive at San Martín de los Andes.) The favourite skiing slopes are on Cerro Catedral, and a new ski-lift is to be built higher up, to permit a longer skiing season. (Regular bus service with seasonal timetable from Mercedes bus company on Mitre 161, US$2 return.) There are a cable car (US$6 single, 7.50 return) and a chair lift (US$22.50 full day, 17.50 afternoon only) from the foot of Cerro Catedral to points high on the ridge. Red and yellow markers painted on the rock mark a trail from the top, which leads to Refugio Frey (well equipped, blankets, meals, accommodation E) on the edge of a small mountain lake (allow 6 hours; one can return through the forest to the ski complex the next day and take a bus back to Bariloche). The seasonal cable car, with a chair lift from its upper terminus, takes one higher than the main (2-stage) chair lift. Bus tours from Bariloche to the foot of Cerro Catedral give time for less than 2 hours on top of the mountain. Entrance to the Cerro Catedral ski slopes, below the snowline, is US$ 0.40. The only disadvantage at Bariloche is that the snow is unreliable except at the top. There are other skiing slopes 5 km. out of Bariloche, on Cerro Otto (cable car, US$7 p.p.; open 0900-1900 Jan., Feb., July, August, and 1400-1800 rest of year; station at foot reached by bus No. 50 "Teleférico", 15 mins., US$0.30, entry to revolving restaurant at top, US$3.50), which can be reached in 2-3 hours' walk from the town; take the paved Av. de los Pioneros, then switch to the signed dirt track 1 km. out of Bariloche (splendid views), or in a minibus which goes every ½ hour from a car park near the National Park headquarters (closed public holidays), between 1400 and 1600, US$5 round trip (local bus US$1.50 return); at Piedras Blancas (bus US$5 return); also on López (try a car trip, rough road, US$10 for a tour, 1400-1830), Dormilón and La Ventana. Ski hire US$5-9 a day, depending on quality, dearer at Cerro Catedral than in town. Ski clothes can also be rented by the day, at US$1-2 per item, from Kiwanis sport stores in Bariloche or El Iglú, Galería Arrayanes II, Rolando 244. **N.B.** Summer skiing on grass has been organized 20 km. S of Bariloche, on Route 258 to El Bolsón.

Excursions Whole-day trip to Lakes Gutiérrez, Mascardi, Hess, the Cascada Los Alerces and Cerro Tronador (3,554 metres) leaves at 0800, US$20. Turismo Llao-Llao organizes the following: 8-hour excursion to Río Limay, Valle Encantado, Lake Traful, Lake Correntoso, Villa La Angostura, returning via Paso Coihue. Catedral and Turisur have a 9-hour excursion, leaving at 0900 (afternoon dep. also Dec.-March), to Puerto Pañuelo, sailing down to Puerto Blest and continuing by bus to Puerto Alegre and again by launch to Puerto Frías (US$14). A visit to the Cascada de los Cántaros is made. Several 12-hour excursions to San Martín de los Andes, US$25, through 2 national parks, passing 7 lakes, returning via Paso de Córdoba and the Valle Encantado. Beautiful scenery at Llao-Llao for walking; one can walk the 15 km. Circuito Chico, or the 17 km. "motor tour" route back to Bariloche (take the 3 de Mayo bus there from Moreno and Rolando, and the ferry for Isla Victoria; there is a chairlift at km. 17.7 on Llao-Llao road (Campanario) one can walk to km. 18.3 and take the road to the left to Colonia Suiza and Punto Panorámico, which winds around Lago Moreno, unspoiled surroundings, all in 16 km. to Puerto Pañuelo. The chairlift at Campanario offers fine views of Isla Victoria and Puerto Pañuelo, 0900-1200, 1400-1800 daily, US$4. Another excursion involves going to Pampa Linda, which is 8 km. from the road ending at Tronador and has the *guardaparque* station. From there you can ask the ranger to show you a path for a two-day walk over Paso de las Nubes to Laguna Fría, which is not always well marked, especially one place early on where the track branches after crossing a river by a series of temporary footbridges. The right hand track should *not* be attempted by inexperienced walkers. The left hand track, once a road, leads one west up a spur to the edge of the glacier with a well appointed hut (3-4 hours journey). **NB** If driving or hitching to Pampa Linda, the road has a one-way system: up only in the morning, down only in the afternoon.

From Pampa Linda ranger post you can also walk past the glacier on Tronador to Peulla in Chile (accommodation at one expensive hotel, A in high season, one *residencial* and a private house) 2½ days; details in *Backpacking in Chile and Argentina* (Bradt Publications) Turismo Catedral has 11-12 hr. excursion, US$36, crossing Lake Todos los Santos into Chile taking in Peulla (lunch at hotel, US$6.50) and the Petrohué falls. Alun-Co Turismo, Mitre 22, 2nd floor, operates a rubber raft excursion mid-Nov. until mid-April to Confluencia, leaves Bariloche at 1000 up River Limay, stopping for lunch at Valle Encantado, returns to Bariloche at 1900, US$16. A half-day excursion is possible taking a bus to Virgen de las Nieves, walking 2 km. to arrive at beautiful Lake Gutiérrez; walk along lake shore to the road from El Bolsón and walk back to Bariloche (about 4 hrs.).

A recommended one-day trip by car is Bariloche-Llao Llao-Bahía-Colonia Suiza-Cerro Catedral-Bariloche; the reverse direction misses the sunsets and afternoon views from the higher roads, which are negotiable in winter (even snow-covered). If one is staying only 1-2 days in the area the best excursions are to Cerro Tronador the 1st day, and on the 2nd to Cerro Catedral in the morning and Isla Victoria in the afternoon (possible only Dec.-March when there are afternoon departures for the island). Camping facilities for firing, food and water are good. Good walks to Lake Correntoso (4 km.) and Quetrihué Peninsula (15 km. to forest of Arrayanes). Also to the *refugio* at Laguna Negra (16 km. trail) and to Cerro López (3 hrs., with a *refugio* after 2); in both cases take Colonia Suiza bus and for the former alight at SAC, for the latter at Picada. Hitching to local sights is difficult.

A half-day excursion (1300-1830) may be taken from Bariloche to Puerto Pañuelo, then by boat to Isla Victoria. The full-day excursion (0900-1830, or 1300 till 2000 in season) at US$18-20 includes the Arrayanes forest on the Quetrihue peninsula and 3 hours on Isla Victoria, picnic lunch advised. Half-day excursions to Isla Victoria are available. Some boats going to Arrayanes call first at Isla Victoria, early enough to avoid boat-loads of tourists. These boats carry the names of Paraná river provinces—Corrientes, Misiones, Santa Fe—and they have no open deck. For open decks try the *Modesta Victoria* or the *Don Luis*. (Turisur have 4 catamarans with a bar and cafeteria.) For a cheaper excursion take Transporte 3 de Mayo bus marked Estación Llao-Llao from Moreno and Rolando at 0900 or 0930 (Rte 6091) for 1030 dep. from Puerto Pañuelo (1130 or 1200 for 1300 dep.) to go to Isla Victoria and Arrayanes by boat (US$7). From Puerto Pañuelo, opposite the *Hotel Llao-Llao*, boats also leave for Puerto Blest. All boats are very crowded in season, but operators have to provide seating for all passengers. The Arrayanes forest can also be visited by walking 12 km. from Villa la Angostura (**see next page**).

Roads There are 500 km. of highways (mostly unpaved) running through the park. There are numerous excursions; prices vary very widely, and it is best to buy tours on the spot rather than in advance, although they get very booked up in season. The old road to El Bolsón and Esquel (a new, faster, but less interesting road is being built between Bariloche and Esquel) is paved for the first 30 km. (very poor condition thereafter, take care), and goes past the beautiful lakes of Gutiérrez, Mascardi and Guillelmo and over fine mountain passes.

The Route to Chile from Bariloche The preferred route is over Puyehue pass, being 50% times cheaper than via the lakes, on a good broad highway which is paved on the Chilean side up to Termas de Puyehue, while on the Argentine side work is progressing with only a few sections remaining unpaved. Road from Bariloche goes around east end of Lake Nahuel Huapí, then follows north side of lake through resort town of Villa La Angostura to junction with "Ruta de Siete Lagos" for San Martín at Km. 94, Argentine customs at Km. 109 and pass at Km. 125 at elevation of about 1,280 metres. (About 22 km. from the Argentine customs is Camping Correntoso; 4 km. further is Camping El Cruce, ACA, and another 2 km. brings you to Camping Osa Mayor, ACA.) Chilean customs at Km. 146 in middle of a forest. The frontier is closed at night. *Hotel Termas de Puyehue* is at Km. 168. Possible to camp nearby, but bring own food as restaurant is expensive. Very pleasant *Motel Ñilque* on Lake Puyehue (Chile) is at Km. 174. A six-hour drive.

The alternative is to go via the lakes. The route is Bariloche to Llao-Llao by road, Llao-Llao to Puerto Blest by boat (2½ hrs.), Puerto Blest to Puerto Frías (20 mins. by boat), then 1½ hrs. by road to Peulla. (A Bariloche-Peulla day excursion costs about US$25 p.p.) Leave for Petrohué in the afternoon by boat (2½ hrs.), cross Lake Todos Los Santos, passing the Osorno volcano, then by bus to Puerto Montt.

Several bus companies run services from Bariloche to Puerto Montt, Osorno and Valdivia, there is at least one bus every day from Argentine side. The majority go via Osorno and fares range from US$15-20; it is no cheaper to go to Osorno and buy a separate ticket from there to Puerto Montt. Companies include Bus Norte, Mitre 10, T. Lanin (not rec.), Moreno 138, Mercedes, Tas Choapa, and Cruz del Sur. Sit on left side for best views. You can buy a ticket to the Chilean border, then another to Puerto Montt, or pay in stages in Chile, but there is little advantage in doing this. Turismo Catedral operates a 12-hour crossing to Puerto Montt, via the lake with lunch at Peulla, about US$36. All other agencies sell excursions to Puerto Frías using a Mercedes bus to Puerto Pañuelo, a Turisur boat to Puerto Blest and share a bus and boat to Puerto Frías with excursion groups going on to Chile. Request information at Turismo Catedral which owns the exclusive rights to the excursion via the lakes, using their own boats and bus from Puerto Pañuelo to Puerto Frías (Andina del Sud operates with them on the Chilean side). The most satisfactory way of doing the trip full-circle is by car from Bariloche, going first via Puyehue to Puerto Montt, returning via Tromen Pass (see the Villarrica volcano, good road), then Junín and San Martín de los Andes. No cars taken on ferry on Lake Todos Los Santos. There are daily boats from Puerto Pañuelo to Puerto Blest, with daily through connections by boat and bus to Puerto Montt.

N.B. You are strongly advised to get rid of all your australes before leaving Argentina; it may be useful to have some Chilean pesos before you cross into Chile from Bariloche. The Argentine and Chilean border posts are open every day; the launches (and hence the connecting buses) on the lakes servicing the direct route via Puerto Blest to Puerto Montt generally do not operate at weekends; check. There is an absolute ban in Chile on importing any fresh food—meat, cheese, fruit—from Argentina. Bariloche Tourist Office may not be up to date on lake crossings to Puerto Montt, check details at travel agencies, particularly if travelling to meet connections.

Further information on border crossings in the Lake District, and details of accommodation in Peulla will be found in the Chilean section, **page 578.** Older travellers are advised not to attempt the Bariloche-Puerto Montt trip all in one day; parts of road on the Argentine side of the Puyehue route are being reconstructed, and the lake route is long and tiring.

N.B. Obtain maps and information about the district in Buenos Aires at the National Park Tourist Office at Santa Fe 690, or at the provincial offices (addresses given on **page 62**); it is hard to obtain these in the provinces themselves. Park wardens are also useful sources of information.

Río Villegas, about 80 km. S of Bariloche on the road to El Bolsón, is very beautiful. Cheap but pleasant *hostería* just outside the gates of the National Park, by the river.

Villa La Angostura on Lake Correntoso is picturesque, 90 km. W of Bariloche on the way to Chile, by excursion bus (day trip; try Turismo Llao-Llao, 8 hrs.) or local bus (at 1900 daily, returning 0730, Transporte Mercedes, US$5) which requires staying overnight; hotels a little dearer than Bariloche. The port, 3 km. from town, is spectacular in summer. It is best to return to Bariloche if going on to Osorno (Chile): otherwise you have to pay twice the fare to Osorno from Bariloche and arrange for the bus company to pick you up at La Angostura. Daily bus at 1700 to San Martín de los Andes.

Hotels *Correntoso*, A; has a chalet next door, C for 2 bedrooms, shared use of kitchen and sitting room, luxurious. Cheaper are *La Cabañita* (Belvedere s/n)and *Don Pedro* (El Cruce), both E. Ask in the tourist office, opposite ACA, for lodgings in private houses, cheaper than hotels. *Hotel Ruca Malen*, 24 km. away on lake shore, under new management.

Camping *El Cruce, ACA Osa Mayor* (2 km. along Bariloche road, pleasant, US$1.35 p.p., open late Dec. to mid-May), *Autocamping San Martín, Municipal Lago Correntoso.*

Restaurants *Guatraché*, grills; *Cuernavaca*; *Parrilla Gallegos, Confitería de los Amigos* (also lets rooms, E, no bath).

Excellent *Hostería Los Peraltoches* on Lake Gutiérrez, 116 km. from Bariloche, A with meals; magnificent views, English spoken, very homelike, open Nov.-March and June-Aug.

El Bolsón is 130 km. to the S, on the old road to Esquel (very rough from Bariloche, fully paved to Esquel). It is a most attractive small town (pop. 8,000) in beautiful country, with many mountain walks and waterfalls nearby, though as it lies in a hollow at about 200 metres, it can be very hot in summer. It has good fishing and is fully developed as a tourist resort. Within half an hour's drive are Lakes Puelo (see below) and Epuyén (shops and petrol available). The farms and the orchards sell their produce at Bariloche. Famous local fruit preserves can be bought at the factories in town. Handicraft market every Saturday. The Balneario Municipal is 300 metres from the town centre, pleasant river swimming. There is a full-day tour from Bariloche, about US$9, at 0800 (stops at Lake Puelo) Empresa Don Otto (very crowded and difficult to get on in high season), Mercedes or Turismo Llao-Llao, 11 hrs. Mercedes bus from Bariloche US$4.50, 3¼ hrs.

Accommodation *Hostería Steiner*, clean and pleasant,wood fire, lovely garden, on the Lake Puelo route, F; *Motel La Posta*, smart and new (Route 258). *Residencial* at Playa Onelli 3076, clean, friendly, E. *Piltriquitrón*, E, large, clean rooms. *Rhona-Hué*, Villa Turismo, E, T 0944-92416, run by John and Rhona Gough, who speak English and Welsh, friendly and hospitable, rec. Up to 2 days' stay possible at the Franciscan school, but get recommendation from tourist agent. *Hotel Salinas*, Rocas 641 in private house, E, friendly, clean, rec. Very difficult to find accommodation in the high season.

20 km. N of El Bolsón, at Rinconada del Mallín Ahogado (daily bus from El Bolsón) is *Hostería María y Pancho Kramer*, D, warmly rec., wholefood meals, hot shower, sauna, swimming pool, chess, volleyball, horseback and trekking excursions to lakes and mountains. E of El Bolsón, at El Maitén, is *Hostería La Vasconia*, no other accommodation around here on Route 40.

Camping Municipal site at Balneario, US$0.50, basic; many other sites in surrounding area. Several *residencias* and camping sites nearby; the *Aldea Suiza* camping site has been especially recommended, tennis courts, hot showers, good restaurant. The paying campsite (US$1) at Lake Puelo has beautiful views across the lake to Tres Picos, but the walking is limited, shop and café; free campsite also at Lake Puelo. Frequent public transport from El Bolsón.

Restaurants *Don Diego*, good; *Ricardo*, on Rocas, good coffee. Welsh tea room, *Casa del Té Galés*. *El Viejo Maitén*, good.

Exchange *Hotel Cordillera*, tourist agency ½ block from plaza, or Inmobilaria Turneo shop, all cash only.

Tourist Office. Office on main plaza, open 0900-200. Ask for sketch maps of the beautiful walks in the neighbourhood including up Cerro Piltriquitrón.

Lake Puelo Regular buses from El Bolsón go to the lake and continue into the Parque Nacional Lago Puelo. Villa Lago Puelo has a bank, shops, fuel and *hosterías*. Good information on the park is available from the wardens at the entrance. Trans Lagos excursions from the paying campsite, or from office in town: ½-day trip across the lake to Valle Río Turbio below Cerro Tres Picos, US$10; also to the Chilean border and Lago Inferior. Canoes can be rented for US$3/hr. to appreciate the beauty of the lake. There is a path to Chile from Villa Lago Puelo, 12 km.

On the way from Epuyén to Esquel is **Cholila**, with superb views of Lake Cholila, crowned by the Matterhorn-like mountains of Cerros Dos and Tres Picos. There are bus services between Bariloche, El Bolsón, and Esquel, and between Comodoro Rivadavia and Esquel. A recommended journey for motorists is to spend the night at El Bolsón, enter the Los Alerces park via Cholila and drive right through it to Esquel, travelling the whole length of Lakes Rivadavia and Futalaufquen.

Hotel *El Trébol*, E with bath, US$1.50 farm breakfast. **Restaurant** *Hue Telén*, open 24 hrs., near ACA.

Esquel, about 260 km. S of Bariloche, was originally an offshoot of the Welsh colony at Chubut, nearly 650 km. to the E. It is now a modern town with reasonable amenities (population 17,000). Major skiing location at La Hoya, 7 ski-lifts, 15 km. north of Esquel (skiing much cheaper than at Bariloche). Restaurant. For skiing information ask at Club Andino Esquel; bus to La Hoya from Esquel, 3 a day, US$3, lift tickets US$7 a day, gear hire US$6 a day. Esquel is known for its tulips, chocolate, jellies and jams (also for the mazard berry liquor made by the Braese family, interesting, but expensive). There is a museum on Belgrano and Ameghino, very varied exhibits, including stuffed local animals. Free, open Mon.-Fri., 0900-1200 and 1800-2100. Sat. at 1900-2100; 15 min. tour.

Hotels *Tehuelche*, 9 de Julio 961 y Belgrano, C with shower, heating and breakfast, excellent restaurant, some staff speak English; *Residencial Gingin*, Rivadavia 1243, E, friendly, grubby; *Hostería los Tulipanes*, Fontana 365, D, good rooms and service;

Residencial Angelina, Av. Alvear 18 (Luis Scaglioni), D, very friendly and clean; *Residencial Huemul*, Alvear 1015, D; *Hostería*, at Italian consulate, Ameghino 505, F, nice, friendly, clean, quiet, meals; *Hotel-Restaurant Vascongada*, Mitre y 9 de Julio, E with shower, friendly, good cheap food. *Motel La Hoya*, Ameghino 2296, D, on road to airport, 1 km. Also *Hostería La Hoya* at the Centro Deportivo de Ski at La Hoya itself, E. *Hosksia Huentru Niyeu*, Chacabuco 606, F, clean, quiet, friendly. Mrs Megan Rowlands' guesthouse at Rivadavia 330, F, meals available, Welsh and English spoken, rec. *Hospedaje Beirut*, 25 de Mayo 200, Ameghino, F, shared room, not very clean but friendly. Many others. Ask at tourist office for lodgings in private houses.

Camping Municipal site 5 km. from centre on Trevelin road, near gravel-crushing plant, hot showers, US$1.50 p.p., rec. In the Parque Nacional there are numerous paying and free campsites beside the lakes; the nearest is at Villa Futalaufquen, about 1 km. from the Intendencia (private, not Parque Nacional property, easily reached by bus from Esquel, 60 km.). Permit needed from Intendencia, who also provide fishing permits (US$51.35 for a whole season, with reductions for shorter periods). Camping facilities closed in winter; also on the way to El Bolsón. Free campsite at Laguna Z, 5 km. along Calle Fontana. Camping at *Cabañas Tejas Negras* (C), good facilities for US$3.50, by *Pucón Pai Motel*, which has its own campsite. Those with sleeping bags can go to the Salesian school and sleep in the school classrooms, Dec. to March; get recommendation from tourist office.

Restaurants *Jockey Club*, Alvear 947, excellent, reasonably priced; *El Cóndor*, rotisería, near bus station, Alvear 1250, good for packed lunches; also for snacks. *Rotisería Las Brasas*, clean, friendly, cheap. *Ahla Wasahla*, San Martín 1100, opposite Tour d'Argent, good cheap, friendly, TV, closed Sun.; *Red Fox*, Sarmiento 795 and Alvear, a British-style pub with light, but expensive meals, open from 2200, closed Tues. *Parrilla La Estancia*, 25 de Mayo 541, quite good; *El Mesón*, 25 de Mayo 462, reasonable, but slow service *Pizzería Don Pipo*, Rivadavia 820, good pizzas and empanadas. Excellent pasta at reasonable prices at *Trattoria de Julio*, Rivadavia 1080. *Casa Suiza*, good confitería. Rugby fans will enjoy the *Confitería Las Tejas*, which shows videos of the game.

Bank and Post Office Banco de la Nación on Güemes and San Martín cash; open Mon.-Fri., 1000-1300; no where to change cheques. Post and telecommunications office opposite the bus terminal on Fontana and Alvear (open 0800-2000).

Tourist Office Operates from the bus terminal, very friendly, can arrange lodgings in private homes. Closed Sat. p.m. and Sun. off-season.

Tourist Agencies Esquel Tours, Fontana 754, T 2704, run a service to and from the airport (US$0.70) where they also have an office, good for local tours, to Lakes Menéndez and Cisnes.

Airport 20 km. E of Esquel, by paved road, US$10 by taxi. US$1.60 by bus; US$2 by Esquel Tours bus 1 hr. before each LADE flight. One flight daily to Buenos Aires: 3 a week via Bariloche; 4 a week via Trelew. LADE flight to Ushuaia; also to Trelew, to Bariloche, and to Río Gallegos, US$50.

Rail From Buenos Aires, Constitución, *Lagos del Sur* train leaves Sun. 0730 and Thurs. 2300 arrives in Ingeniero Jacobacci (E of Bariloche) after 27½ hrs., returning Mon. 0045 and Wed. 0305, arriving Bs.As. Tues. 0600 and Thurs. 0600. A steam-operated, narrow-gauge train (known locally as El Trencito, described by Paul Theroux in *The Old Patagonian Express*) waits for the train from Buenos Aires, and normally leaves Jacobacci Sat. 0600, for Esquel, arrives 1945 Sat., which is the most southerly point in the connected South American railway system. It returns Sun. (0800), arriving at Jacobacci at 2200 (hotel in Jacobacci: *Gran Hotel Argentino*, nearly opp. station, D with shower and heating, very good, restaurant nearby). Fares from Bs.As. to Esquel: tourist US$23.50, 1st class US$35, pullman and sleeper, available only as far as Jacobacci, US$42 and US$56. Enquire at station for bookings. Sleepers from Jacobacci to Bs.As. are usually fully booked from Bariloche; only a small quota of first class tickets are available in Esquel for connections to Bs.As. The Jacobacci-Esquel branch line was under threat of closure in 1990, check in Buenos Aires at the railway office on Florida in advance. Tourist train to Nahuel Pan leaves Mon. at 1500, returns same day, US$7.75. Tickets from Tehuelche Viajes, Fontana 574, or Esquel Tours, Fontana 754. There are only two engines at Esquel, so go to El Maitén (train from Esquel, Sun. and Thurs. 2200, arrives 0300, cold), where there are about 12, arriving at 0830. From El Maitén it is possible to hitch to Bariloche or take the Esquel-Bariloche bus.

Buses None direct from Buenos Aires to Esquel so travel via Bariloche. To Comodoro Rivadavia (paved), Tues. and Fri. via Río Mayo, 0100, and Thur. direct at 2100, US$10, Transportes Patagónicos (Don Otto) leaves Comodoro Rivadavia on Tues., Thurs., Fri., and

Sun., passing through Esquel at midnight. This bus runs slowly to El Bolsón, where it stays over one hour before leaving for Bariloche. Empresa Mercedes goes daily (9 hrs.) to Bariloche at 0800 (also at 2200), US$9.50. To El Bolsón, 5 hrs., US$8, rough road, goes alternate days via El Maitén (for train buffs) and via Cholila (for views). To Trelew, US$12, 10½ hrs., leaves 0900 Tues., Thurs., Sat., and 1900 Mon., Wed., Fri.; other bus companies on Av. Fontana and Alvear (bus terminal) are Empresa Don Otto, Chubut, Denis. Bus terminal T 2233, also for taxis.

Los Alerces National Park Sixty km. W of Esquel, which can also be reached by road from Rawson, is the Los Alerces National Park, with centuries-old larch trees. An interesting part of the park can be reached from a separate entrance through Trevelin (see below) following the Río Futaleufú, but one can go only 22 km. W because of the new Futaleufú hydroelectric dam. Behind it is Lake Amutui Quimei, which has swallowed Lake Situación and 3 others stretching almost to the frontier. (Futaleufú supplies power to the alumina plant at Puerto Madryn, 500 Km. to the E.) Entrance by car to see Futaleufú dam is only allowed at 1500, under police supervision; photography not permitted, except on top of the dam itself. There is no public transport to the dam, but buses pass the eastern side of the lake. (Hotels on Route 258, on S side of Lake Futalaufquen are, *Quime Quipán* and *Cume-Hué*, both closed in winter). The eastern side of Los Alerces has much the same natural attractions as the Nahuel Huapi and Lanín parks, but is much less developed for tourism. Esquel to Los Alerces, Mon. and Sat. at 0630, returns at 1800, US$4 round trip—check schedule as it varies. Its great Lake Futalaufquen has some of the best fishing in this huge area, begins Nov. 15. Bus to Lake Futalaufquen, on Thurs., Sat. and Sun. at 0830 and 1730 (it passes 3 hotels and drives into 2 camp sites). The 0830 bus connects with the Trelew bus. Off-season, the bus only goes to the southern tip of the lake (Villa Futalaufquen and the administration building, or Intendencia). On Mon. at 0630 and 1830, returning 0800 and 2000, US$1 one way, buy ticket from kiosk at terminal in Esquel. Taxi, US$72. The Intendencia has a small museum about the park and a slide show of Argentina's National Parks. Petrol station, 2 supermarkets in Villa Futalaufquen and a lady sells bread and vegetables from her house (buy bread early, or order the day before; meat can be hard to get). Camping at Villa Futalaufquen and at Los Maitenes, on road to Cholila (closed May-Sept.), US$1.20 per tent and US$1.20 p.p., hot water, store. The *Hostería Los Tepúes*, on the E side, is simple, rustic, and frequented by teenagers, A, open all year round, also has a family bungalow for rent. Recommended for fishermen are the *Quime Quipán* and *Pucón Pai* motels. (The *Pucón Pai* holds a fishing festival to open the season, A, friendly, opens out of season for large groups only; reservations: Casilla 150, Esquel. It has a good restaurant.) On the W side, which is untouched by tourism (by law), is *Hotel Futalaufquen* just N of Puerto Limonao, rec., especially rooms 2/3 and 4/5 which have balconies overlooking the lake, L, open all year (no heating in rooms); good walking around the hotel, e.g. to Cinco Saltos, and El Dedal. Regular full day launch trip from Puerto Limonao (reached by early morning minibus) on Lake Futalaufquen (a sheer delight) through Arrayanes river to windless Lake Verde (2 campsites, one US$1 p.p., one free). From there one can walk out to Lakes Rivadavia and Cholila - 2 days minimum (*Hostería El Trébol* on Lake Mosquito), and to the end of Lake Menéndez, famous for its giant larch trees (US$15 incl. launch trip on Lake Menéndez, with Tehuelche Viajes y Turismo, Av. Fontana 574, from Esquel); the boat leaves at 1330 but book the day before in Esquel, preferably, as it will not leave if there are not enough passengers. The dock can be reached by a 30-minute walk across the bridge between lakes Futalaufquen and Verde. There are local guides with outboard motor boats for fishermen. Lovely view of Lago Cisne (Swan Lake) to the NW end of Lake Menéndez. One then walks a 3 km. nature trail looking across the Andes to Chile before returning. Tours arranged at Esquel (e.g. Elentur's Lacustre excursion visiting lakes Futalaufquen, Verde, Menendez and a guided tour around the 2 km. walk to Lake Cisne, on which you will see a 2,600-year old alerce, US$11 p.p. from Puerto Limonao, take food and drink). Other excursion tours offered are less interesting because they only involve short stops in front of points of interest. A road connects all the lakes. The tourist office in Esquel has a pamphlet on all the walks in the Park.

From Esquel one can also drive to Perito Moreno (**see page** 170) via Teckia (95 km. paved), Gobernador Costa (84 km. unpaved), La Laurita (last 61 km. paved, ACA service station, breakdown truck and snack bar), 65 paved km. to join route 22 (60 km.) which is being paved, and on to Río Mayo, with 121 km. unpaved road to Perito Moreno.

Crossing into Chile Colectivos leave Esquel for the frontier at La Balsa, 70 km., 2 hrs., US$3. Campsite (Camping Río Grande) on Argentine side of river. Cross the frontier river by barge (*balsa*) after passing Argentine customs; Chilean customs is 1 km. on the other side of river (1 hr. for all formalities). Colectivo from Chilean customs to Futaleufú (8 km.) is US$1.25.

Very little traffic for hitching. The colectivos from Esquel pass through Trevelin on the way.

N.B. At the Futaleufú and Palena border crossings, Argentine border officials only give transit visas: legalize your stay within 10 days either by leaving the country or by renewing entry stamp at an immigration office.

Trevelin (pop. 5,000), 23 km. SW of Esquel (local bus, US$0.60, every ½ hour, 0700-1900; *Hostería Estefania*), is also an offshoot of the Welsh Chubut colony (**see page 161**). There is a modern Anglican church beside the Catholic church. It has a historical museum (entrance US$0.30) in the old mill.

Food and Lodging Grills at *Che Ferrada*, good mixed *parrillada* at *El Quincho*, and tea rooms offering *té galés* and *torta negra* (e.g. *El Adobe* on Av. Patagonia). *La Cabaña*, 7 km. out on the road from Trevelin to Lake Futalaufquen, serves Welsh teas. There is a custom of giving a newly-married couple a "black cake" on their wedding day, to be eaten on their first anniversary. Municipal campsite near centre. On the road to Esquel 3 km. from Trevelin, signposted on the righthand side, is *La Granja Trevelin*, owned by Domingo Giacci, macrobiotic meals and good Italian cooking, sells milk, cheese and onions; camping US$0.90, hot water and w.c., bungalows US$15 a day; excellent horses for hire.

Tourist Office Good office in central plaza.

Excursion 17 km. on road to frontier are Nant-y-fall Falls, entrance US$0.50 p.p. includes guide to all 7 falls (1½ hr. walk).

Neuquén, capital of Neuquén Province, was founded 1904 on the W side of the confluence of the Limay and Neuquén rivers. It is a pleasant, clean industrial city of 90,000 people. A major stop on paved Highway 22, 540 km. from Bahía Blanca and 474 km. from Bariloche, it serves the rich oilfields to the W with heavy equipment and construction materials, and the irrigated fruit-producing valley to the E. There are also many wine *bodegas* nearby. Much farm machinery is sold to the orchards where apples, pears, grapes, hops and plums are grown. At the Parque Centenario is a *mirador* with good views of the city and the confluence of the rivers, where they become the Negro (be sure *not* to take the bus to Centenario industrial suburb). Facing Neuquén and connected by bridge is Cipolletti (pop. 43,600) a prosperous centre of the fruit-growing region. The Museo Provincial Carlos Ameghino, Yrigoyen 1047, is modest but interesting.

Hotels *Apollo*, D-C, Av. Olascoaga 361, very good; *Cristal*, D-C, Av. Olascoaga 268, adequate; *del Comahue*, Av. Argentina 4-star, new, very good; *ACA Cipolletti*, just outside Neuquén; other *Hospedajes* on San Martín, all E; 13 km. S on Zapala road is *Hostal del Caminante*, T 33118, with pool and garden, popular. *Residencial Libeam*, M.Alcorta 41, E with bath, fairly clean, near bus station. Some 50 km. W of Neuquén there is a motel at Arroyitos. Municipal camping site at Neuquén and various camping sites, mostly by the river.

Restaurants *Las Tres Marías*, Alberdi 126, excellent; *Bariloche*, good food but poor service. Pleasant bars on Av. Argentina.

Exchange *Casa de cambio* at Ministro Alcorta 144; also *Pullman*, Alcorta 163, T 22438.

Museums Museo Histórico Provincial, Santa Fe 163; Museo de Ciencias Naturales, at entrance to airport (as is the Casino).

Tourist Office Félix San Martín y Río Negro.

Transport El Cóndor (La Estrella), El Valle and Chevallier bus Buenos Aires-Neuquén, daily US$24, 18½ hours; paved road throughout. Connections with Copahué and Córdoba; also with San Rafael (US$15) and San Martín de los Andes (US$12.25). Bus to Zapala daily, 7 hours. To Bariloche, take La Estrella or Chevallier (not El Valle as it stops too often), and sit on left. Bus La Unión del Sud to Temuco (Chile) via Zapala all year three times a week each way, and Ruta Sur twice a week, US$16, 16 hrs.

   Daily train, *Estrella del Valle*, leaves Constitución station, Buenos Aires, at 1000, arriving Neuquén 0745; sleeper US$32, pullman US$23, first class US$23, tourist US$15.75; goes on to Zapala, 4 hours. Leaves Neuquén 2330, arrives Buenos Aires 2050. Takes car transporter Buenos Aires-Neuquén Thurs.; returns Fri.

If driving from Neuquén to Buenos Aires on Routes 151 and 21, via Catriel, fill up with fuel here because there is no other fuel for 323 km. of desert before General Achá. Driving from

Neuquén to Bariloche, go via El Chocón hydroelectric lake, Junín and San Martín (both "de los Andes"), taking Routes 237, 40 and 234; route more attractive than that via Zapala.

Air There is a jet airport 7 km. from centre. Daily flights to and from Buenos Aires with AA and Austral (one night flight each). Connecting flights to San Martín de los Andes with TAN, Av. Argentina 383, T 23076/24834 (30096 at airport), who also fly to Mendoza five times a week, also Bariloche and Puerto Montt and Temuco in Chile.

Excursions Paved roads lead 33 km. N to the artificial and natural swimming pools at the Ballester dam; nearby is artificial Lake Pellegrini, where various watersports are held. A narrow-gauge railway runs with sporadic services via Cipolletti to Contralmirante Cordero, 7 km. from the dam. Extensive irrigation has turned the Río Negro valley into a major fruit-producing region, with apples the principal crop. All the towns in the valley celebrate the Fiesta Nacional de la Manzana in the second half of March.

A road and railway go W from Neuquén to **Zapala** (179 km., pop. 20,000) through the oil zone at Challacó, Cutral-Có and Plaza Huincul. There is an excellent geology museum in Zapala, visited by specialist groups from all over the world (closed weekends). Among the collections of minerals, fossils, shells and rocks, is a complete crocodile jaw, believed to be 80 million years old. There is an airport and an ACA service station.

Hotels *Huincul*, Roca 313, F; *Coliqueo*, Etcheluz 159, E; *Petuién*, Vidal y Etcheluz, E, rec. *Odetto's Grill*, Ejército Argentino 455, moderate prices, 2 mins. from bus terminal. There is a municipal camping site.

Transport A Pullman bus, with hostess service, plies twice daily between Bahía Blanca and Zapala (15 hrs.). El Petróleo bus leaves Zapala 0230 and 1630 for San Martín de los Andes (5½ hrs.) via Junín de los Andes. In winter the direct route from San Martín de los Andes via the lakes may be impassable, so a bus must be taken back from San Martín to La Rinconada and then round to Bariloche (4 hrs.). There is also an overnight (at 2200) Neuquén-Zapala-San Martín bus that comes through Zapala at 0230; same service at 0915 (US$23). From Zapala to Bariloche by bus, one must change at La Rinconada. Zapala-Temuco (Chile) all year with La Unión del Sud and Ruta Sur, at 0500, US$10-15, 10-12 hrs., as under Neuquén (see above). Also with Igi-Llaimi Wed. and Fri. at 0530, return 0330, twice weekly. Buy Chilean currency before leaving.

Train from Buenos Aires to Zapala, *Estrella del Valle*, 1,367 km., 26 hrs.; daily via Bahía Blanca at 1000 from Constitución station, arr. 1140. Zapala-Buenos Aires at 1925, arrives 2050 next day. On Sundays tickets go on sale at 1500, buffet car on train, scenery largely uninteresting. The line follows the Río Colorado for some distance, then crosses it into the valley of the Río Negro where large fruit growing areas at (343 km.)

Choele-Choel (ACA motel on edge of town, D, with bath, good restaurant at bus station and fine modern *Hotel Choele-Choel*) and at (472 km.) Villa Regina are irrigated from the Río Negro dam. Two low-priced clean places: motel and *residencial* at edge of town near the main road. Cheap food at one of the service stations. There is an excellent free municipal campsite at Choele-Choel; shady, beside the Río Negro; no showers. Many local buses ply from Choele-Choel to El Chocón (large hydroelectric plant) and Zapala.

North of Zapala on the Chilean border is the Copahué National Reservation, best-known for its thermal baths and volcano of the same name. At 1,980 metres above sea-level in a volcanic region, **Copahué Termas** is enclosed in a gigantic amphitheatre formed by mountain walls, with an opening to the E. Near Copahué, Caviahue is being developed; accommodation is available in prettier surroundings (there are trees), and a bus service connect the two. There are bus services from Neuquén and Zapala to Copahué, which may also be reached by road from Mendoza. The **Laguna Blanca National Park** 35 km. SW of Zapala on a good, consolidated road is famous for its animal and bird life (notably black-necked swans), but has not yet become a tourist centre.

Hotels N of Zapala include those at Churriaca (131 km.), Chos Malal (202 km.) and Río Barrancas (at 340 km.). The road via Las Lajas is paved as far as Chos Malal, founded as a military fort in 1889 (restored as a historic monument, with Museo Histórico Olascoaga). ACA service station and hotel (San Martín y Sarmiento). Routes 143 and 151 from Neuquén to Mendoza via San Rafael are almost fully paved (apart from 40 km. around Santa Isabel) and provide faster, though less scenic alternatives to Route 40 via Zapala, Chos Malal and

Malargüe.

Bariloche is 418 km. S of Zapala by a road through Junín de los Andes and San Martín de los Andes. A short detour from Junín leads to the very beautiful lake of Huechulafquen; from Junín, too, a road runs W over the Tromen Pass through glorious scenery to Pucón (135 km.) on Lake Villarrica, in Chile (easy to hitchhike to Villarrica from the Argentine border post); on the way there are splendid views of Lanín volcano, extinct and 3,747 metres high, one of the world's most beautiful mountains. At **Junín de los Andes**—a famous spot for salmon and rainbow trout, known as the trout capital of Argentina—is the *Chimehuín*, a very small fishing hostelry (C); *Restaurant Ruca Hueney* is the town's social centre. Some 30 km. N of Junín are the *ACA Las Rinconadas* facilities; paved road. There is an airport between Junín and San Martín, but it is mainly used by the military.

The Tromen (Chileans call it Mamuil Malal) pass route between Argentina and Chile is much less developed than the Puyehue route, and definitely not usable during heavy rain or snow. Parts are narrow and steep. Argentine customs are at the pass. The Chilean *aduana* is at Puesco, 58 km. SE of Pucón and 16 km. from Tromen. Ferry at Lake Quilleihue, which is halfway between the posts, has been eliminated by road blasted across cliffs. It is possible to camp in the area (though very windy), but take food as there are no shops at the pass. From the border, it is 24 km. to Curarrehue, from where several buses a day go (either at 0600 or at the latest at 1400) to Pucón. The international bus will officially only pick up people at Tromen but at the discretion of the driver can pick up passengers at Puesco (customs, but no hotel) at 0900 and Currarehue stops. Hitch-hiking over to the Tromen Pass is difficult.

San Martín de los Andes, 40 km. S. of Junín (paved road), and 196 km. from Zapala, is a lovely but expensive little town, population 14,000, at the eastern end of Lake Lacar; it is the best centre for exploring **Lanín National Park**, with its sparkling lakes, wooded mountain valleys and the snow-capped Lanín Volcano. The numerous deer in the park are the red deer of temperate Europe and Asia. There is excellent ski-ing. on Cerro Chapelco, to which there is a road, and facilities for water ski-ing., windsurfing and sailing on Lake Lacar.

Lanín Volcano A 4-hour hike from the Argentine customs post at Tromen pass (speak to the *guardaparque* at the border) to *refugio* at 2,400 metres. Climb from *refugio* to summit is easy but crampons and ice-axe are needed. Permission for the climb must be obtained from the army post in Junín de los Andes.

Hotels Motel, *El Sol de los Andes*, very expensive and nice, set above the town (Cerro Cnl. Díaz), 5-star, A-L, shopping gallery, swimming pool, sauna, night club, casino, regular bus service to centre of town. *La Cheminée*, Roca y Moreno, B, very good, breakfast included, but no restaurant; *Hostería Villa Lagos*, Av. Villa Lagos, E, good, ski hire. *Posta del Cazador*, very highly rec. *Hostería Arrayán*, 5 km. from San Martín, is an English tea room with 2 self contained log cabins for rent with full cooking facilities, dining and sitting rooms etc., superb view over Lake Lacar, very peaceful, US$25 a day, all in. At San Martín is *Los Pinos*, D with breakfast, Almte. Brown 420, German-run, with a/c and heating, clean, friendly; *Hostería Cumelén*, Elordi 931, F p.p. (low season), E high season, with bath, hot water, breakfast, nice lobby with fireplace, rec.; also *Residencial Pinos*, E, pleasant, nice garden. *Turismo* is rec., Mascardi and R. Roca, D-C, shared bathroom; *Hostería Anay*, Cap. Drury 841, E, central, good value, rec. Also good, *Casa Alta*, Gabriel Obeid 659 E; *Residencial Peumayen*, Av. San Martín 851, very clean, C-D, with bath and breakfast. Cheapest is *Posta del Caminante*, Caballería 1164, basic, friendly, good atmosphere, noisy; *Cabañas del Sur*, on main road out of town towards Junín, sleeps up to 6 in comfortable cabin, D per cabin, rec. *Casa del Amigo*, Obeid y Cnel. Pérez, E, very friendly. Consult very good tourist office for other private addresses, but these are not available in winter. *Residencial Villa Bibi*, E, with private bath, breakfast extra, clean, family-run, near lake, Cnl. Díaz 1186, rec. At 24 km. from Villa La Angostura (**see page** 151) is *Hotel Ruca Malen* on Lake Correntoso, warmly rec.; at 53 km. *Hotel Pichi Traful*, and at 75 km. *Hostería Lago Hermoso*.

Camping ACA Camping and Autocamping San Martín de los Andes, both with hot water and laundering facilities US$2.20 p.p. Municipal, with shop and showers, US$2.50 p.p. Cabins on the camp site are US$5 p.p. Not open all year round. *Camping Los Andes*, El Valle 611, other side of bridge, US$2, clean, bunk beds, shared bath. Pleasant site by the lake at Quilaquina, 27 km. from San Martín, with beaches, and another on the lake at Catritre, just

6 km. from town. Hitchhiking to Bariloche and San Juan is slow.

Restaurants Try smoked venison, wild boar or trout, at *El Ciervo* restaurant; *Don Eugenio, Piscis, Betty, La Raclette* and *El Peñon*, all good. *Parrilla La Tranquera*, good value; and *Parrilla del Esquiador* on Belgrano 885, reasonable home-cooked food. *El Jockey*, also good. It is difficult to get dinner before 2200, but there are various good restaurants in the area. *Pizzería La Strada*, San Martín 721, excellent; *Fanfani*, on Rodhel, has good pasta.

Exchange Banco de la Nación on San Martín exchanges cash and Amex cheques only; American Express office on San Martín, 1 block from tourist office, 10% commission on cheques; also at San Martín 886, 2nd floor and at Avis office, San Martín 998 (rates not as good).

Laundry Lavarap, Drury 980, 0800-220 daily; Villegas 968, cheaper, 0900-1300, 1600-2130 Mon.-Fri., 0900-1300 Sat.

Tourist Office at Rosas 790, on main square, corner of San Martín, open 0800-2200, very helpful. Police station at Belgrano 611.

Buses Station at Gral. Villegas 251, good toilet facilities. Bus Buenos Aires-San Martín, US$30, three a week, Chevallier goes Mon. and Fri. at 1430, arrives 1520 next day.

Air There are 6 flights a week from Buenos Aires with AA to Chapelco Airport, 20 km. from San Martín, and daily flights with TAN from Neuquén.

Excursions The most popular trips by car are to Lakes Lolog, Alumine, Huechulafquen and Paimún, to a campsite in the shadow of Lanín Volcano. Shorter excursions can be made on horseback or by launch; recommended day excursion by El Valle at 0930, return 1700 on Lake Lacar for US$10. The road goes on via Lake Hermoso and Villa La Angostura to Bariloche, a beautiful drive of 220 km., 10 hours (US$7) by bus, which stops for views and an hour for lunch at La Angostura—an excellent, well organized bus route, but not in winter. (Beware bad connections at La Angostura if you change buses there.) Many buses, however, use a rather less scenic route following Río Traful, then Lake Lanín and joining the paved Bariloche highway at Confluencia (ACA station and a hotel, also motel *El Rancho* just before Confluencia). A small road runs W from San Martín along the southern edge of Lake Lacar for 10 km. to Quila Quina, where there are Indian engravings and a lovely waterfall.

   Villa Traful, beside Lake Traful about half-way between San Martín and Bariloche on a side road, is described as a "camper's paradise". Marvellous views, fishing (licence needed) excellent. All roads are dirt; drive carefully, avoiding wild cattle! Hotel *Pichi Traful* and *Hostería Traful* provide accommodation.

   Camping along this "Seven Lake Drive" route is freely allowed to National Park permit-holders. No buses from Seven Lakes to San Martín de los Andes. If however you want to travel from **Bariloche to San Martín via Junín and the Seven Lakes**, you must buy a round trip excursion from one of the tour companies (e.g. Velox in Bariloche) for US$17.75, leaving at 0800, and not return with them. This is actually cheaper than a one-way ticket with the El Valle company who go there direct, via the less scenic route (US$20, at 1430). It is difficult to hitch-hike along this route as there is little traffic. When there is sufficient demand, there are two buses a day San Martín-Bariloche, 5 hours, making tourist day trips via the Seven Lakes, US$10.35. There are also daily buses San Martín-Bariloche via a paved road (least scenic) leaving San Martín at different times through four days in the morning and three days in early afternoon.

Skiing There are several chair-lifts of varying capacity on Cerro Chapelco and a ski-tow higher up. Bus from San Martín to slopes, US$5 return. Very good slopes and snow conditions. As yet uncrowded. Lift pass US$23, ski hire US$5 a day from *Hostería Villa Lagos*. At the foot of the mountain are a restaurant and base lodge. There are three more restaurants on the top, and a small café at the top. For information on trout fishing or duck and geese shooting, contact Logaine and David Denies at Trails, Pérez 662, San Martín.

To Chile Excursion San Martín de los Andes-Panguipulli (Chile): boat leaves San Martín Tues., Thurs., Sat. to Hua-Hum at the end of Lake Lacar, at 0900, US$4.25. Camping with shop at Hua-Hum. Excursion buses run to Hua-Hum when the launch arrives across the border to Pirehueico, US$2.35. There is now a road between San Martín and Puerto Pirehueico (Chile). Buses daily at 1000 (US$3), 2 hr. journey through Lanín National Park. The ferry across Lake Pirehueico (Tues., Thurs., Sat. 1730; at 0830 in other direction) takes 2 hours (US$2) to Puerto Fuy; beautiful scenery. Daily bus 0600, US$1.50, 3 hrs., Puerto Fuy-Panguipulli; or ask for lift among vehicles on ferry (friendly boat crew may help). Boats also leave Puerto Fuy Mon., Tues. and Thurs. to Pirehueico for a day trip, US$3.45, and there is a daily ferry at 0600. From

Puerto Fuy to Panguipulli transport goes on the new road via Choshuenco around the N shore of Lake Panguipulli. This route is open all year round and is an alternative service from Temuco to San Martín when the Tromen Pass is blocked by snow (usually June-mid-Nov.). When the pass is closed, the buses drive right on to the boat to cross between Puerto Fuy and Puerto Pirehueico. Check with customs at Hua-Hum about arrangements.

Bus San Martín de los Andes to Pucón and to Temuco, US$12 to all destinations, rough ride; mid-Nov.-May Empresa San Martín Mon., Wed. and Fri., at 0700, returns from Temuco the following day at 0500, Igi-Llaimi Tues., Thurs. and Sat. at 0700, ret. next day at 0630, US$12 for Pucón, Villarrica and Temuco. When the pass is closed Empresa San Martín switches its return and forward journey days but not the times. Igi-Llaimi goes Wed. and Fri. only at 0500, returning from Temuco Tues. and Thurs. at 0330. This route passes through Panguipulli, Villarica and Temuco only. For Pucón change to JAC bus in Villarrica. JAC also runs a service between Temuco and San Martín, via Junín de los Andes and continuing to Neuquén. The companies will not give information about each other, and do not run buses in winter when the pass is blocked.

PATAGONIA (10)

South of the Río Colorado is the vast plateau known generally as Patagonia. The area is sub-divided into the provinces of Neuquén, Río Negro, Chubut, Santa Cruz and the Territory of Tierra del Fuego. The area covers 780,000 square km.: 28% of the national territory, but has a population of only 600,000, little over 2.7% of the total population; and 57% of it is urban. Wide areas have less than one person to the square km., and there are virtually no trees except in the north and the Andean foothills.

Over the whole land there blows a boisterous, cloud-laden strong wind which raises a haze of dust in summer, but in winter the dust can turn into thick mud. Temperatures are moderated by the proximity of the sea and are singularly mild, neither rising high during the summer nor falling low during the winter. Even in Tierra del Fuego, where the warmest summer months average 10½°C, the winter days' average can reach a high of about 2°C. Make sure you have plenty of warm clothing, and anti-freeze in your car, available locally. Rain falls mostly in the winter, but not more than 200-250 mm. a year. The whole eastern part of the area suffers from a lack of rainfall and the land is more or less desert. Deep crevices or canyons intersect the land from E to W. Few of them contain permanent water, but ground water is easily pumped to the surface. The great sheep *estancias* are along these canyons, sheltered from the wind, and in the depression running N from the Strait of Magellan to Lakes Argentino and Buenos Aires and beyond. During a brief period in spring, after the melting of the snows, there is grass on the plateau. Most of the land is devoted to sheep raising. The wool, which is shipped N to Buenos Aires, is mostly the fine and finecrossbred wool used by the Argentine mills, and is often heavy with sand. Over-grazing leads to much erosion. Wild dogs and the red fox are the sole enemies of the sheep.

Because of the high winds and insufficient rainfall there is little agriculture except in the N, in the valleys of the Colorado and Negro rivers. Some cattle are raised in both valleys where irrigation permits the growing of alfalfa. A large area has been irrigated from the Río Negro dam near Neuquén and here, as a supplement to cattle raising, fruit growing has been highly successful: apples and pears are the chief crops, and many are exported.

Patagonia is rich in extractive resources: the oil of Comodoro Rivadavia and Tierra del Fuego, the little exploited iron ore of Sierra Grande, the coal of Río Turbio, the hydro-electric capacity of El Chocón, plentiful deposits of minerals (particularly bauxite) and marine resources, but their exploitation has been slow. Tourism is opening up too. The wildlife is attractive. *Guanacos* and rheas are a common sight: there are also *maras*, Patagonian hares. On and off parts of the coast, particularly the Valdés peninsula, seals, sea-elephants, right whales and

PATAGONIA

other aquatic mammals may be seen, as well as penguins, especially between October and April. Further S, particularly in Tierra del Fuego, the antarctic wild goose (*quequén*) is the most commonly seen of the 152 species of birds. Patagonia Turística, Florida 755, Buenos Aires (T 311-9216) are very helpful on travel to the region.

N.B. We are informed that in summer hotel prices are grossly inflated (by as much as 100% in Ushuaia, 75% in Calafate); also that in some places there may not be enough hotel beds to meet the demand. Camping is increasingly popular, and *estancias* seem hospitable to travellers who are stuck for a bed. During Argentine summer holidays (Jan., Feb., March) getting a hotel room in Ushuaia, Río Grande, Río Gallegos and Calafate is practically impossible. In this connection, remember that ACA establishments, which charge the same prices all over Argentina, are a bargain in Patagonia and Tierra del Fuego, where all other accommodation is expensive. Very few hotels and restaurants have a/c or even fans, it can get uncomfortably hot in January.

Discovery and Colonization   The coast of Patagonia was first visited by a European late in 1519, when the Portuguese Fernão Magalhães (Magellan), then in the service of Spain, was on his voyage round the world. Early in 1520 he turned W into the strait which now bears his name and there struggled with fierce headwinds until he reached that Sea of Peace he named the Pacific. Later European expeditions that attempted to land on the coast were repulsed by the dour and obdurate local Indians, but these were almost entirely wiped out in the wars of 1879-1883, generally known as the "Campaign of the Desert". Before this there had been a long established colony at Carmen de Patagones; it shipped salt to Buenos Aires during the colonial period. There had also been a settlement of Welsh people in the Chubut Valley since 1865 (see below). After the Indian wars colonization was rapid, the Welsh, Scots and English taking a great part. Chilean sheep farmers from Punta Arenas moved northwards along the depression at the foot of the Andes, eastwards into Tierra del Fuego, and northwards to Santa Cruz.

The Welsh settlement   On July 28, 1865, 150 Welsh immigrants landed at Puerto Madryn, then a deserted beach deep in Indian country. After three weeks they pushed, on foot, across the parched pampa and into the Chubut river valley, where there is flat cultivable land along the riverside for a distance of 80 km. upstream. Here, maintained in part by the Argentine Government, they settled, but it was three years before they realized the land was barren unless watered. They drew water from the river, which is higher than the surrounding flats, and later built a fine system of irrigation canals. The colony, reinforced later by immigrants from Wales and from the United States, prospered, but in 1899 a great flood drowned the valley and some of the immigrants left for Canada. The last Welsh contingent arrived in 1911. The object of the colony had been to create a "Little Wales beyond Wales", and for four generations they kept the Welsh language alive. The language is, however, dying out in the fifth generation. There is an offshoot of the colony of Chubut at Trevelin, at the foot of the Andes nearly 650 km. to the west, settled in 1888 (**see page 155**). It is interesting that this distant land gave to the Welsh language one of its most endearing classics: *Dringo'r Andes* (Climbing the Andes), written by one of the early women settlers.

Gary Luton, of the Welsh Patagonia Expedition 1980, writes: "To me Chubut will always foster memories of horses on an open wind-swept plain, or tethered, with brown sheepskin saddles, outside a *pueblo* inn. It is shuttered houses with poplar windbreaks. Chubut is relative prosperity surrounded by shanties of mud brick and tin; it is Coca-Cola and tea houses, sea lions and right whales sounding a short distance from shore; and *asados* washed down with red wine and *mate*. Chubut is a moonscape of neutral colours where sheep lose themselves in the grey-green saltpans of thornscrub, and dust and wind blow across scattered pockets of civilization. And it is the Eisteddfod at Gaiman, a Welsh festival of the arts in a chapel nestled among the poplars, on a cloudless night, where boys in white shirts recite poetry and choirs sing as a culture fights a subsiding battle to maintain itself."

Recommended Reading   *In Patagonia* by Bruce Chatwin, a good introduction to the area and its people.

In all Patagonia there is only one town—Comodoro Rivadavia—with a population over 100,000. Most of the towns are small ports, which used only to work during the wool-shipping season but have livened up since the local economy began to diversify. The high tidal range makes it impossible in most of them for ships to tie up at the docks (except at Madryn and Punta Arenas, Chile). The short railways inland from the ports have little traffic except during the sheep-shearing season.

Communications Calls at the chief ports by passenger/cargo ships of the Flota Carbonera del Estado. Navy transport ships go as far as Ushuaia (Tierra del Fuego) once a month and carry 60 passengers for a nine-day trip.

Air Services Aerolíneas Argentinas from Buenos Aires either direct to Río Gallegos or calling at Bahía Blanca, Trelew and Comodoro Rivadavia on the way. Austral from Buenos Aires to Río Gallegos via Bahía Blanca, Trelew and Comodoro Rivadavia daily. Cía. Argentina de Transportes Aéreos (CATA) from Buenos Aires to Bahía Blanca, Trelew, Comodoro Rivadavia and Río Gallegos. Beware delays for bad weather.

Many air force LADE flights in the region S of Bariloche—Río Gallegos to Bariloche, to Ushuaia, to Calafate—must be booked in advance from departure point of flight. The planes are small and fly low; passengers miss little of what there is to be seen, highly recommended for those who enjoy flying. The baggage allowance is 15 kg. Travellers are warned that the flights are often heavily booked ahead, but always check again on the day of the flight if you are told beforehand that it is sold out. Sometimes, individual passengers are allowed to fly on air force carriers if planes are full or inopportune, through LADE. Also, LADE tickets are much cheaper for a long flight with stops than buying separate segments. LADE's computer reservation system is linked to Aerolíneas Argentinas, so flight connections are possible between these airlines. Also LADE's flights synchronize with both AA and Austral flights.

Roads The main road, Route 3, which runs near the coast, is now paved from Buenos Aires via Fitz Roy and down to Río Gallegos. S of this town to Ushuaia is all-weather in a bad state of repair as it is awaiting asphalt. Sometimes passengers going South have to pay for baggage by weight.

The principal roads in Patagonia roughly form an inverted triangle. Route 3 has regular traffic (hitch-hiking good in spring and summer) and adequate services. At the southern end, this route enters Chile and crosses the Magellan Straits to Tierra del Fuego by the car ferry at Primera Angostura. The western route (Route 40) zigzags across the moors, is lonely and is good in parts, poor in others (more details given below); there is hardly any traffic except in December, January and February, the tourist season. However, it is by far the more interesting road, with fine views of the Andes and plenty of wild life as well as the Alerces and Glaciares National Parks. Camping is no problem, and there are good hotels at Esquel, Perito Moreno, Calafate and (in Chile) Puerto Natales. Third class accommodation also at Gobernador Gregores, Río Mayo and Esperanza. There is also in Coyhaique, Chile. The northern part of the triangle is formed by the paved highway running from Bariloche through Neuquén to San Antonio Oeste.

Many of the roads in Southern Argentina are gravelled. The price of a good windscreen protector varies according to make of car, but can be US$50 in Buenos Aires. For a VW Kombi they are hard to find at a reasonable price. More primitive versions can be bought for much less—e.g. US$5 in San Julián, and probably elsewhere - or made from wire mesh, wood and string. The best types to buy are the grid-type, or inflatable plastic ones which are made for some standard-type vehicles, the only disadvantage being some loss of visibility.

N.B. Keep passport handy as examination is required when passing from one province to another. Also, be prepared for roadblocks at which one has to declare one's destination, nationality, vehicle particulars, etc.

The upper course of the Río Colorado is the northern limit of Patagonia. 160 km. S of where it reaches the sea (250 km. S of Bahía Blanca), about 27 km. from the mouth of the Río Negro, is

Carmen de Patagones (16,000 people), standing on high ground on the northern bank, with **Viedma** (26,000 people) the capital of Río Negro Province, across the river, which is spanned by a connecting rail and road bridge. There is also a frequent ferry service for pedestrians. On a hill behind Patagones a monument commemorates an attack on the twin towns by a Brazilian squadron in 1827. (Beware of pleasant-looking campsites near this monument; there is an artillery range nearby.) There are three museums, open 1000-1200 only. There are air services to Viedma, 966 km. from Buenos Aires daily except Thursday (continuing either to Bariloche or General Roca). The swimming is recommended on the Viedma side of the river, where there is a nice shady shore. A law has been passed nominating Viedma as the site of the new federal capital, but building has not yet begun.

Hotels at Carmen de Patagones: *Percaz; Gran Argentino*. At Viedma: *Peumayen*, Buenos

Aires 334, D; *Viedma; Austral*, rec., modern. *Hotel Roma*, basic, has good restaurant. *Restaurant Munich*, Buenos Aires 161, open late.

Camping   Good municipal site 500 metres after crossing the river on the new road bridge on the right, all facilities.

Exchange   Travel agency at Namuncurra 78, Viedma, exchanges Am Ex cheques.

Tourist Office   Belgrano 544, 9th floor, Viedma.

Buses   Bus terminal at Calle A Zatti y Lavalle about 6 blocks from main plaza.

Excursion   Beautiful beach, El Cóndor, 30 km. S of Viedma, 3 buses a day, hotel open Jan.-Feb., restaurants and shops, free camping on beach 2 km. S. 30 km. from El Cóndor is a sealion colony (*lobería*); no public transport, but hitching easy in summer.

Camping   Further camping sites on the Río Negro where the main route into Patagonia meets the river (some 170 km. from Viedma due NW) with all facilities including a small shop. Additional shops at General Conesa, 2 km. away. Mosquito repellant needed. There is another campsite N of General Conesa (about 140 km.) at Río Colorado again alongside the Patagonian road. All facilities.

Almost due W and 180 km. along the coast, on the Gulf of San Matías, is **San Antonio Oeste** (10,000 people). 17 km. S is a seaside resort, **Las Grutas**, developed in the 1960s with good safe beach; the caves are not really worth visiting, but there is a good seafood restaurant, *Parrilla Bariloche*. ACA has a *Unidad Turística*, with 6-bed rooms, no restaurant. *Tour du Golfe*, friendly, 3-bed rooms, E, provide cooking facilities. There is also a camping ground. *Restaurant Rambla* recommended. The whole of Las Grutas closes down in mid-March and retires to Buenos Aires. Between San Antonio and Puerto Madryn is Sierra Grande, where iron-ore deposits are being rapidly developed. The ore is piped in solution to an ocean terminal 32 km. E.

Hotels at San Antonio   *Iberia*, Sarmiento 241, E with bath, but without breakfast, small rooms; *Kandava*, 2 blocks from bus and railway station, E with bath, hot water, clean, good; *Vasquito*, just acceptable, F; *Americana*, F, cheap and pleasant. Good beach 7 km. away.

Railway   via Viedma to Bahía Blanca and Buenos Aires and westwards to Bariloche. Trains from Buenos Aires (Constitución) (19 hours) 0820 Wed. and Sat. (*Lagos del Sur*). Leaves San Antonio Oeste 2225 Tues., Wed., Fri. and Sat. Fares: sleeper US\$39.20, pullman US\$32, first US\$21.75, Tourist US\$14.75.

Buses   From San Antonio N to Bahía Blanca and S to Río Gallegos and Punta Arenas by Transportes Patagónicos. To Viedma 0700 daily. To Puerto Madryn and Trelew, Don Otto, 0430 and 1400, 4 hrs., US\$6.50, leaving 45 mins. after arrival of trains from Buenos Aires. To Buenos Aires, US\$23 via Bahía Blanca, frequent.

Route to Bariloche: paved. Continue 201 km. through bush country providing fodder for a few cattle, with a view to the S of the salt flats called Salina del Gualicho. The road then meets the Zapala-Buenos Aires highway at Choele Choel. Then 223 km. to Neuquén through an unbroken series of groves of tall trees sheltering vineyards and orchards. On (424 km.) to Bariloche along fast road, skirting the entire length of the reservoir formed by the Ezequiel Ramos Mejía dam. Then it drops over an escarpment to cross the Collón Curá river. Continue through the valley of the river Limay to Confluencia and the Valle Encantado. The journey can be completed in 11 hours.

About 250 km. to the S, in Chubut, is

Puerto Madryn, a port on the Golfo Nuevo. It was founded by the Welsh colonist, Parry Madryn, in 1865. Population, 40,000. A large aluminium plant is now operating (ask at tourist office for details of visits), and the town is becoming a popular tourist centre, with a casino, skin-diving and nature reserves, both near the town and on the nearby Valdés peninsula. Museo de Ciencias Naturales y Oceanográfico on Domecq García and J. Menéndez, informative and worth a visit, US\$0.60, open Mon.-Fri. 0900-1130, 1800-2100, 1500-1830 Suns. Airport. No Youth Hostel.

Hotels   (Very full in summer, make bookings early.) *Península Valdés*, J.A.Roca 163, T 71292

B, 4-star, sea view, suites available, comfortable, rec.; *Tolosa*, R. Sáenz Peña 250, T 71850 B, 3-star, friendly; *Gran Madryn I*, L. Lugones 40, T 72205, C, 2-star, friendly but rooms just acceptable; *Hostal del Rey*, Blvd. Brown 681, T 71156, on beach, rec., C, 2-star, with radio, breakfast included, loud disco at night; *Motel ACA*, Ribera Marítima Norte, D; *Yanco*, Av. Roca 627, T 71581, on beach, nightly entertainment programme, free, C, has rooms for up to 6; *Argentino*, 25 de Mayo 275, E p.p., clean, popular, friendly, hot water, with shared bath; *Atalaya*, Domecq García 149, T 73006 D, with bath, clean; *Muelle Viejo*, Yrigoyen 410, opposite pier, E with breakfast, good; *París*, Roque Sáenz Peña and 25 de Mayo, E without bath, very friendly, good restaurant, rec.; *Vaskonia*, 25 de Mayo 43, T 74427, E, hot water sometimes, noisy, unfriendly; *Apart-Motel Palma*, Av. Roca 7, new, E, heated, showers, no food but clean; *Español*, San Martín 233, 2 blocks from bus station, E, restaurant; *El Dorado*, San Martín 545, T 71026, E, clean, shower, patio, but landlady not keen on backpackers; *Residencial La Posta*, J.A.Roca 33, T 72422, E with bath (cheaper without), cooking facilities, clean, good, British not welcome; *Residencial Paula*, Albarracín 249, T 74384, E, good; *Residencial Petit*, Alvear 845, T 71460, E with bath.

Camping All closed out of season. At far end of bay, 6 km. S of town, is ACA site with hot showers and shady trees (Punta Cuevas) but many people camp on beach. There is a swimming pool in the rocks near the ACA camp site, which gets its water at high tide, very pleasant, and free. Also municipal, US$0.75 p.p. and per tent (gives student discount) at Ribera Sur, 4-5 km. S of town on same road along beach. All facilities, very crowded. Bus from centre goes to within 1 km. of municipal site. Camping out can be interesting as one can watch foxes, armadillos, skunks and rheas roaming around in the evening. Charges about US$2.50 a night p.p. and per car; discounts at ACA sites for automobile club members and holders of International Driving Licence.

Restaurants *Aguila*, M.A.Zar and R.S.Peña, highly rec., good for seafood; *La Caleta*, San Martín 156, excellent, seafood, reasonable prices; *Cantina El Náutico*, Julio Roca and Lugones, good food, especially fish; *Comedor ACA*, Costanera Norte; *París*, R.S.Peña 112, excellent and reasonable; *Parrilla Mayoral*, R.S. Peña 12; *Pizzería Quine*, Roca y R.S.Peña, good and not only for pizzas; *Pizzería Roselli*, Peña y J.A. Roca, cheap, good, with vegetarian selections; *Parrilla El Soledad*, R.S.Peña 214, good salads; *Pleno Centro Confitería*, 28 de Julio y 25 de Mayo, good.

Tea Rooms *Panadería La Proveedura*, good pastries; *Centenario*, on Belgrano and Paraguay. For excellent Welsh afternoon teas, *La Goleta*, Roca 87, 1700-1900 (poor sign).

Exchange Banco de la Nación, 25 de Mayo y 9 de Julio, best rates, go early to avoid long queues. There are no *cambios* as such, apart from Turismo Pu-Ma, 28 de Julio 46, but fair rates from travel agents (e.g. Golfo Nuero viajes, Safari Submarino, addresses below; go in the morning). Gold dealer La Moneda, next to Golfo Nuero Viajes on 28 de Julio, will exchange large sums, not very good rates. Some shops will change US$ cash.

Car Hire On Roca next to *Hotel Península Valdés*. **Bicycles** rented at Roca and Yrigoyen on harbour, US$1.75 for 2 hrs.

Laundromat Lavarap, 25 de Mayo near Sarmiento.

Sport Puerto Madryn is being promoted as a diving centre. Tours for those who have never dived before are organized by Safari Submarino, Mitre 80; Turismo Submarino, Av. Roca 743; Pimino in the harbour, all about US$16 per excursion. A few others along the harbour; all show nature videos at about 1930. Swim in the so-called *parque submarino* amid sunken cars and a few fish! Trained divers seriously interested in marine life who have at least a week's stay should contact the Centro Nacional Patagónico at Av. Roca. Windsurfing lessons and equipment hire at Brown 871.

Tourist Agencies Several agencies do tours to the Valdés Peninsula, all are for 12 hours, US$10, take lunch, swimsuit and towel. Prices are fixed by law, but itineraries may differ. Tour rates increase by 75% on 15 November and again on 15 December by the same amount. *Tur-Mar.*, T 74104, 25 de Mayo 167; *Pu-Ma*, 28 de Julio 48, T 71482; *Mar. y Valle*, Roca 37, T 72872, rec. *Receptivo*, Roca 303 y Belgrano, T 71048, An Ex agent, weekend and off-season tours, mixed reports; *Sur Turismo*, J.A. Roca 612, T 73585; *Golfo Nuevo Viajes*, 28 de Julio 21, T 72117, Nelson speaks English. Recommended guide: Dr. Pedro Fuentes Galliardo.

Tourist Office, at Julio Roca 444, open until 2200 in the tourist season, but only 0700-1300 Mon.-Fri. in winter; helpful, has notice board for messages.

Transport Buses from Buenos Aires, 2 a day with La Puntual, 21 hrs., comfortable, US$34; Sun., Mon., Thurs. and Fri., at 2030, with El Cóndor, daily with Costa Criolla at 2130, via San

Antonio Oeste, change at Bahía Blanca (US$29), 22-24 hrs. To Río Gallegos, also 24 hrs., four times a week. Bus to Bahía Blanca 0800 and 1000 daily, 12 hrs. (US$8 with Don Otto); 10½ hrs., US$18, with La Puntual to Mar. del Plata, changing at Bahía Blanca. Patagónicos to San Antonio Oeste at 0800 and 2230, US$6.50. Same times to Buenos Aires, US$29 (cheaper to go to San Antonio Oeste and change to the train, but 9 hr. wait). Bus to Trelew with 28 de Julio company. (April to November, every 75 mins. between 0615 and 2230, Mon.-Sat., Sun. and holidays 11 a day, every 90 minutes between 0800 and 2230—more frequent in summer, 65 mins., US$1.60); driver will stop at entrance to Trelew airport if asked. Don Otto to Comodoro Rivadavia, Wed., Thurs., Fri., Sun. 0915 and daily at 1600, US$15.50. No direct bus to Bariloche, change at Trelew and Esquel (Aerolíneas Argentinas flight to Esquel Mon. and Tues. 1215). Taxi rank on the plaza.

Excursions There are nature reserves nearby at Punta Loma on Golfo Nuevo (sea-lions), only 15 km. from Puerto Madryn (sea-lions, whales, penguins and flamingoes also frequent the Puerto Madryn area itself, sea-lions even invading the harbour); Punta Pirámides (sea-lions) and Isla de los Pájaros (sea birds) Golfo San José and Punta Norte (right whales), on the Valdés Peninsula (see below). (Check opening times of reserves in Puerto Madryn; they vary.) The natural history of the region is most interesting, with other seal and penguin colonies, breeding ground at Golfo Nuevo for right whales, fossils in the cliffs, and *guanacos*, rheas and armadillos in the countryside. Most animals (except the whale) can be seen in the warm seasons, from October to April. See whales at Puerto Madryn from perhaps as early as June to, at the very latest, end- November. Past the lighthouse and Naval Zone at Punta Delgada on the other side of the Valdés peninsula is Salina Grande, Argentina's lowest point, 35 metres below sea level.

Take bus or hitch-hike (28 de Julio bus 0825 Tues., Thurs., Sat. US$3, return 1855) to **Puerto Pirámides**, with a population of 70 (ACA motel, C, restaurant poor for food and value; also municipal campsite, US$1 p.p., hot showers in evening only; *hostería* on seaward side of main street with café attached, excellent value, clean; and small friendly *hostería*, open Sept.-March, the *Posada del Mar.*, 10 minutes from the sea, D. Also *Cantina El Salmón*, on the beach, poor food and service. There is a shop that sells original Patagonian Indian work). Hydro Sports rents scuba equipment and boats, has a small restaurant, and organizes land and sea wildlife tours (ask for Mariano), boat trips US$10 for 1 hour. About 79 km. from Puerto Madryn is Isla de los Pájaros, on a good road. No one is now allowed to visit the island without special permission (only granted to recognized ornithologists). At Punta Norte (176 km.) on the Valdés Peninsula, there are sea-elephants (breeding time in first fortnight in August, best seen at low tide), late spring and summer (Nov.-March), reasonably priced restaurant for meals and snacks. At Caleta Valdés, you can see penguins and sea elephants at close quarters, but not at any specific point. Camping at hangar nearby, but bring fresh water with you as supplies are unreliable. At Punta Delgada (at the S of the peninsula) most wildlife can be seen except the penguins, which have moved away. The peninsula is private property. One third belongs to one man, who grazes 40,000 sheep. In theory, US$1 is charged to visit each nature reserve on the peninsula; moreover, the beach on the entire coast is out of bounds, although this is not strictly enforced.

Tourist excursions are organized by Tur-Mar., Receptivo (guide, Luis, has been recommended and Coyun-Co Turismo, Av. Roca 37, Puerto Madryn. The usual tour takes in Puerto Pirámides, Caleta Valdés (or Punta Norte) and Isla de los Pájaros: the costs are US$10 p.p. on a 1 hr. bus tour, US$15 on a 11-hour minibus (minimum 6 persons, e.g. Tur-Mar.), US$90 for a car with guide, for 4-5 people, US$55 in a taxi for 4 (will stay as long as you like and may also go to Riacho San José to see flamingoes); tours including a boat trip to see whales charge up to US$10 extra; there are two companies running boat trips from Puerto Pirámides into Golfo Nuero to see whales, the one on the right as you face the water is better. Trips last about 3 hours, starting at 0800. On all excursions take drink with you (binoculars are also a good idea). Most tour companies stay 50-60 minutes on location, not considered sufficient by some. The excursion buses run in Jan.-March, but the peninsula is easily reached if one has one's own car, in fact the best way to see the wildlife is by car and hiring a vehicle is worth considering if you can get a group together. Hitching is very difficult. Peninsular roads are variable: from Puerto Pirámides to Punta Norte is degenerating and that parallel to Caleta Valdés consists of large pebbles which may cause problems for low-clearance vehicles (tours will not run after heavy rain in the low season). There is a permanently-stationed Conservation Officer at the entrance to the Peninsula (he is very helpful). Tour to Punta Tombo (**see page** 168) including a little sight-seeing tour of Rawson, Trelew and Gaiman, US$16.50. Turismo Receptivo runs full-day excursions to Punta Tombo, Gaiman, Rawson and Trelew (US$20); this trip involves more time travellings than sight-seeing. Taxis to Punta Loma for sealions charge official price, US$12; Tur-Mar. does 12-hour US$20 p.p. trip to Punta Loma and the

Ameghino dam (see below). The Punta Loma sealion reserve is open 0900-1200, 1430-1730 (easy hitch-hike from Madryn), Sept. and Oct. are best months. Sur Turismo is the only agency that will arrange a minibus out of season, if you can gather eight people, to go to Punta Norte, Punta Pirámides and the shore opposite Isla de los Pájaros. You will not see whales between Dec. and June and there will only be young sealions as the older ones will have gone south.

N.B. If possible check all excursion dates in advance; it is very disappointing to arrive in Puerto Madryn only to find that one cannot reach the wildlife reserves. From March to September (when there is less wildlife to be seen) it has been necessary to take a taxi but we are now informed that the tours run all year, depending on numbers. Tours seem cheaper from Madryn than from Trelew, probably because Trelew has the airport.

The roads between Puerto Madryn and Puerto Pirámides (94 km.) and between **Puerto Pirámides** and San Antonio Oeste (328 km.) are now paved.

The Florentino Ameghino dam, 110 km. inland on the River Chubut, covers 7,000 hectares with water and irrigates 28,000 hectares in the lower Chubut valley, as well as producing electric power.

The Florentino Ameghino dam, 110 km. inland on the River Chubut, covers 7,000 hectares with water and irrigates 28,000 hectares in the lower Chubut valley, as well as producing electric power.

Along the Río Chubut are several towns. **Rawson** (pop 9,000), the capital of Chubut Province, 7 km. from the sea (Hotel Provincial, Mitre, C, good restaurant, hotel clean, but seems to be falling down), has law courts, a museum in the Colegio Don Bosco, a fishing port, and a riverside Tourist Office, 9 de Julio 64, T 213. Puerto Rawson is about 5 km. down river; you can camp on the beach, and Cantina El Marinero serves good seafood.

Some 20 km. up the Río Chubut is **Trelew** (90,000 people), a prosperous town which has lost its Welsh look. There is a pretty red-brick chapel in the centre, and a small, interesting museum in the old railway station, open 0900-1300, 1500-2045. On the road to Rawson, 500 metres before the bridge is Chapel Moriah, a beautiful 1880 Welsh chapel, with the graves of many original settlers. A paved road runs from Rawson through Trelew, Gaiman (**see page 167**) and Dolavon, all on the river, to Las Plumas (mind the bridge if driving) and the upper Chubut Valley, all the way to Esquel (**see page 152**) and Trevelin.

Local Holidays 28 July (Founding of Chubut); 13 Dec. (Petroleum Day).

Hotels Centenario, San Martín 150, T 30041, C, good and cheap restaurant, best to stick to simpler dishes; **Libertador**, Rivadavia 73, T 35316, D, without breakfast 4 blocks from Plaza, service good, quiet, **Plaza**, F, on main square, clean, friendly, helpful; **Parque**, Irigoyen and Cangallo, T 30098 D, good; **Rivadavia**, Rivadavia 55, T 34472, E with bath, clean, rec.; **Touring Club**, Av. Fontana 240, T 33998, excellent, D (with bath), the social hub of Trelew, chess is played here, colour TV, breakfast rec., coffee the best in town; **Galicia**, 9 de Julio and Rivadavia, T 33803 very warm, E, without bath, clean. **Residencial San Carlos**, F, with private bath, Sarmiento 758, rec., and **Provinciano**, Yrigoyen 525, F, poor and noisy. **Argentino**, Abraham Matthews and Moreno, E, clean, quiet, near bus station. **Hostal Residencial Plaza**, F in triple, clean, friendly, rec. **Hostal Avenida**, Lewis Jones 49, F, close to bus station, friendly, quiet, "rec., cheapest in town, nice rooms".

Camping possible south of the town on the road to Rawson and Comodoro Rivadavia, on right about 200 metres beyond the bridge over River Chubut, one can camp by the river, but beware of mosquitoes (US$3 for 2 people + van). The site belongs to the Sports Club and has a public swimming pool.

Restaurants Martín Fierro; **Luque**, H. Yrigoyen and Chile; **Parrilla Don Pedro**, intersection of Routes 3 and 25; **El Quijote**, 25 de Mayo 86, good food, better than service; **El Mesón**, Rivadavia 588; **El Progreso**, San Martín 140; **Galicia**, Rivadavia and 9 de Julio; **Cantina Acapulco**, Belgrano and San Martín. **Pizzería Rosselli**, 25 de Mayo on Plaza, good and cheap.

Shopping Mr Sturdee Rogers, Rogers Shop, Moreno 463, T 20696, serves Welsh afternoon teas between 1700 and 1900, US$4, and sells traditional cakes; also gives information on the Welsh of Patagonia. Welsh and English spoken; rec.

Car Hire Information at the airport; fixed rate plus charge per km. Also Alquilauto Fiorasi, España 344, T 30589, very reasonable.

Exchange Lloyds Bank (BLSA), Av. 9 de Julio esq. Belgrano; Banco Provincia del Chubut. Local banks. Open 0800-1200. (1% commission). Sur Turismo, Belgrano 326, accepts travellers' cheques at poor rate. Banco del Sud, España 197, only accepts dollar bills in mint condition!

Post Office and Entel 25 de Mayo and Mitre.

Tourist Office, room 20 on 1st floor of Terminal Terrestre, additionally opens briefly at 0515 for travellers arriving from Esquel, also at airport and at Italia y Rioja, friendly but not always accurate. Free maps.

Tourist Agencies *Sur Turismo* (exchanges cash and travellers' cheques), Belgrano 326-330, organize a few excursions to Punta Tombo US$15, to Punta Norte US$25, T 34550; *Estrella del Sur Turismo*, San Martin 129, T 31282, tours to Valdés Peninsula and Punta Tombo, rec.; *Punta Tombo Turismo*, in *Hotel Centenario* T 30658; and others. Tours to Valdés Peninsula take about 12-13 hours, best to go in a small tour bus which can get closer to main wildlife viewing sites. Recommended tours by taxi to the Valdés Peninsula (see above) cost US$75 for 4 for a whole day.

By Air Airport 5 km. from centre; taxis cost about US$4. Buses from Puerto Madryn do stop at the airport, however. LADE (Av. Fontana 227, T 35244) flies, Trelew-Río Gallegos, 1-3 flights daily; also with Aerolíneas (25 de Mayo 33, T 35297). Daily to Buenos Aires, AA and Austral (25 de Mayo 259, T 34799). To Ushuaia, with Aerolíneas. Buenos Aires-Trelew night flights once a week in each direction with AA and Austral. LADE also Buenos Aires-Trelew. Río Grande (via Río Gallegos), 2 flights a week, with Aerolíneas or Austral, stopping at Comodoro Rivadavia, and Río Gallegos; to Comodoro Rivadavia- Esquel-Bariloche with LADE; crowded, book preferably in Buenos Aires in advance; 4 times a week, to Esquel with Aerolíneas.

Buses from Buenos Aires to Trelew daily at 2100, 21½ hrs., US$25 (return 0700 and 2130 daily, 1705 Tues., Thurs., Fri. and Sat.). Bus to Bahía Blanca, 734 km., US$20 daily with Don Otto, 0600, few a week with La Puntual, 0600; to Mar. del Plata, changing at Bahía Blanca, US$17.25 with La Puntual; to Esquel, US$12, 2130, 9¾ hrs. with Empresa Chubut; bus to Bariloche daily. Buses to Rawson every 15 min.; every 1½ hours to Gaiman, US$0.60; hourly on the hour to Puerto Madryn (every 1½ hrs. in low season, 0600 to 2215, every 90 minutes approx., Sundays and holidays between 0800 and 2230), US$1.60 with 28 de Julio; to Comodoro Rivadavia daily at 2000, and Sun., Wed., Thurs. and Fri. at 1035, US$9.20, 6 hrs.; to Río Gallegos, Sun., Tues., Thurs. 2005, via Puerto Deseado. If **hitching** from Trelew, take the Rawson bus to the flyover 5 km. out of town.

Gaiman, 18 km. from Trelew, a pretty place with well-built brick houses, is now the most Welsh of the Chubut valley towns, and has a museum of the colony, US$0.30, in the old railway station (open in summer, Tues.-Sat. 1600-2000). The only restaurant seems often to be closed, but tea rooms such as *Casa de Té Gaiman*, Yrigoyen 738 (US$3 with lots of cakes) and those opposite the square, *Plas y Coed* (oldest, good value, Marta Rees speaks English) and *Ti Gwyn, Ty Nain* (frequented by tour buses), and *Elma*, Tello 571, are open from 1500. Small municipal campground by river (poor, no facilities). Interesting local agriculture. Welsh-speakers will be interested in the cemetery above town. The Eisteddfodd, Welsh festival of arts, is held in early October each year. Interesting walking tours led by volunteer guides (Spanish-speaking—meet in main plaza) include a private, hand-made (out of beer bottles and string!) theme park, a seaweed factory and the *Ty Nain* tearoom which has a nice display of historical items. All facilities are closed out of season.

Dolavon, 20 km. past Gaiman, is easily reached by bus from Trelew. It still retains much Welsh character and provides an interesting view of the irrigation system built by the settlers. The old flour mill/museum is superb; it is completely intact and demonstrations will be given. There is a campsite: turn right by the service station on the way into town, excellent facilities, free (Wendy Chilcott and Steve Newman).

Wildlife may be seen at **Punta Tombo** and Camarones. Punta Tombo is 120 km. S of Trelew, on a dirt road branching off 5 km. SE of Trelew on the road to Rawson, driving time 1¾ hours (this is incorrectly shown on ACA maps). There the wildlife is very varied: penguin, *guanacos*, etc. Season for penguins, Sept.- March (Dec.- Jan. is the time when the young are taking to the water). Check with the Tourist Office that it is all right to visit the penguins as from late March they are "off limits" as they prepare to migrate. When visits are permitted it is a fantastic experience. You can share a taxi from Trelew; US$70 for one, US$90 for up to 4 passengers. Taxis available from San Martín y Belgrano, 25 de Mayo corners of Rivadavia and Belgrano, España y Moreno. Sur Turismo takes you there and back in a morning (0800-1300) for US$10. About mid-way between Rawson and Punta Tombo, a road leads off Ruta 1 to Isla Escondida (9 km. signed), no facilities, but lovely rock and sand beach with bird and wildlife (badly littered unfortunately); secluded camping. Good place to camp if you are visiting the wildlife at Punta Tombo early a.m. (the best times).

Camarones, 275 km. from both Trelew and Comodoro Rivadavia, is less crowded. There is a large **penguin colony** 35 km. away at Cabo Dos Bahías along a dirt road (open in season only); free camping is possible there and in the town itself (three *hosterías*, all F, the one by the power station is not recommended). Local buses very scarce; two a week, US$10, on Mon. and Fri. from Trelew (Don Otto), book at Uruguay 590, Trelew; bus leaves 0800 from San Martín and Belgrano, arrives 1130, returns to Trelew same day 1600 (reports disagree on whether Don Otto bus continues from Camarones to Comodoro Rivadavia). In Camarones take a taxi (if you can find one) to the penguin colony (US$15 return), or ask the Guardia Fauna for a lift, hitchhiking possible at weekends and return to Trelew Tues. Hotel and restaurant at Camarones, *Kau-i-Keuken*, E, clean, friendly, good food, highly rec.

Comodoro Rivadavia, the largest city in the province of Chubut, is 396 km. S of Trelew. Petroleum was discovered here in 1907 and about 30% of all Argentina's oil production comes from wells to the S and W. A 1,770-km. pipeline carries the natural gas to Buenos Aires, and a petrochemical plant has been built. Renewed interest in the local oil industry is making the town boom. Population: 150,000. From here southward, prices begin to rise very rapidly, so stock up before reaching Río Gallegos. Good beach at Rada Tilly, 5 km. south; walk along beach at low tide to see sealions

Local Holidays 28 July (Founding of Chubut); 13 Dec. (Petroleum Day).

Hotels *Austral*, Rivadavia 190, D, noise from street traffic but otherwise comfortable, being modernized in 1990, reasonable restaurant; *Colón*, on San Martín, E, run down, but quiet, safe and cheap; *Hospedaje Praga*, España y Sarmiento, E, shower, clean; *Residencial Azul*, C, good service, Sarmiento 724; *Comercio*, Rivadavia 341, friendly, near bus station, hot showers, E (may be bargained lower), good meals, US$3.80; *Pensión Boedo*, Rivadavia 453, cheap restaurant, mediocre food; *Hospedaje Belgrano*, Belgrano 546, D, with bath, clean, hot water; *Cari-Hué*, Belgrano 363, clean, quiet, cheap, F; *Rada Tilly*, E, modern, clean, 5 km. S. *España*, 9 de Julio 935, F, basic. *Hosp. Nanet*, España 1095, T 28867, F, clean, friendly. *El Patagón Motel*, access (S) of Route 3.

Camping Municipal and ACA, 10 km. S at Rada Tilly, may be reached by hourly Expreso Rada Tilly bus from town. Excellent facilities, hot and cold water. There is another, free, campsite at N end of beach, cold water only (watch out for clayslides when it rains).

Restaurants No one eats at night until 2200. *Austral*, fair; *La Rastra*, Rivadavia 384, very good for churrasco, but not much else; *El Ancla de Oro*, Caleta Córdoba (18 km. from Comodoro); *Los Troncos*, Av. Costanera and Rada Tilly; *Cocorico* (better) and *El Náutico*, Playa Costanera. *Café Bierhaus*, San Martín, highly rec. Several *rotiserías*, much cheaper, on 400 block of Rivadavia, in municipal market.

VW dealer, Comercial Automotor, Rivadavia 380, rec. VW concession in Barrio Industrial, Av. Irigoyen, also rec.

Exchange Lloyds Bank (BLSA), Av. Rivadavia 264. Oct.-March 0700-1300; April-Sept. 1200-1800; no exchange transactions after 1000 in summer, 6% commission on travellers' cheques; the Banco de la Nación, San Martín 108, has the best rates on US$ but does not change travellers' cheques. *Hotel Comodoro* changes US$ at poor rate. Roqueta Travel, Rivadavia y Pellegrini, Ceferino, 9 de Julio 852, San Julián travel agency, and CRD Travel, Moreno 844 (travellers' cheques) will change money. Bill Fitzpatrick in the insurance company at Moreno y Rivadavia. Video shop Ostoich, 25 de Mayo 957, will change at back counter.

Post Office San Martín y Moreno. Branch in central bus station (beware of overcharging) closed Jan.-Feb.

Consulates Belgian Vice-Consul, Rivadavia 283; Chilean Consul, Sarmiento 936; Italian Vice-Consul, Belgrano 1053.

Travel agencies: *Puelche EVT*, Rivadavia 527; *Richard Pentreath*, Mitre 952; *San Gabriel*, *Atlas*, *Monitur* and *Ceferino*, at San Martín 488, 263, 811 and 372, respectively.

Tourist Office On Rivadavia.

Buses Bus service to Buenos Aires daily at 1530 (Don Otto), 32 hrs., US$39 (also daily with La Puntual/Cóndor at 1300 and Sat. 2400). Angel Giobbi buses to Coyhaique (Chile), US$20, 12 hrs., twice a week (Tues. and Fri.), 0100, June-Sept. and 3 a week (Mon., Wed., Fri.), 0100, Oct.-May (weather permitting). Three buses a week to Bariloche, US$40 (Don Otto leaves 1400, Sun., Tues., Thurs., stops at Esquel midnight (US$30), arrives 0600 at Bariloche). To Esquel (paved road) direct, Fri. 1230, 10 hrs., via Río Mayo, Mon., Thurs., 0100, 15½ hrs., to Río Mayo Tues., Thurs., Sun., 1700 and 1900, 5½ hrs. Three a week to Río Gallegos (Patagónica, US$35 and Andesmar, Thurs. at 0320). To Puerto Madryn US$15.50 (Don Otto at 1600). La Unión colectivo to Caleta Olivia, hourly, US$2.50. To Sarmiento, US$5, 2½ hrs. at 0700, 1300, 1900. To Mendoza, daily at 0130, 20 hrs.; to Córdoba, Tues., Fri., Sun., 1200, 33 hrs.

Air Services Airport, 9 km. Bus to airport from downtown terminal or opp. Aerolíneas Argentinas in main street hourly (45 mins), US$0.30; take bus No.6. 4-7 flights to Buenos Aires a day with Aerolíneas or Austral, stopping at Trelew, Bahía Blanca or both; offices on San Martín 421 and 291; Aerolíneas and Austral flight daily to Río Gallegos. Aerolíneas fly to Ushuaia; LADE flies twice a week Comodoro Rivadavia-Perito Moreno-Gobernador Gregores-Calafate-Río Gallegos-Río Grande-Ushuaia, with detour over Calafate glacier, weather permitting. Also to Río Gallegos via Puerto Deseado, San Julián, Santa Cruz. Taxi to airport, US$6.

Hitch-Hiking There is a truck stop outside Comodoro Rivadavia on the road to Bahía Blanca, where you can contact drivers if hitching. Take the bus leaving at 1200 from the bus station marked "Astra Km. 20'. Expensive truckdrivers' restaurants along the road; buy food in supermarkets.

The road to Chile runs inland from Comodoro Rivadavia, amid oil wells, to (156 km.) Colonia Sarmiento (commonly known just as **Sarmiento**), population: 12,000 (archaeological museum with tourist office next to cathedral, check opening times, may be closed at weekends), on Lake Musters, near the large Lake Colhué Huapí. 30 km. by dirt road S of Sarmiento there is a large petrified forest (Ormachea), well worth a visit (see below). Taxis, US$12, leave from opposite *Hotel Lago Musters*, there are not many so book early. Sr. Gómez is reputed to do the cheapest tour, ask at bus station. The taxi allows only one hour to see the forest; bargain for longer, or hitch; in summer it's not too difficult. However, the friendly warden, Juan José Valera, lives at Uruguay 43, Sarmiento, and is willing to give lifts to those in need when he makes his frequent journeys to the park. No bus station; all buses stop and start at a little office beside *Hotel Lago Musters*.

Hotels *Lago Musters*, P. Moreno and Ing. Coronel, run down; *Hostería Los Lagos*, Roca and Alberdi, D, good, friendly, heating, has restaurant. Food at *Colón*, P. Moreno 645, F, clean and friendly, and *El Gaucho*, Route 20, access Sarmiento. *Ismar*, 200 block of Patagonia; *Oroz*, 200 block of Uruguay. In Dec.-March you may be permitted to sleep in the Agricultural School (bring sleeping bag) on the road to petrified forest, opp. the ACA petrol station.

Camping Municipal site 2 km. N of centre on Route 24, basic but free, beside river.

Travel Agency Julio Lew, Roca and Alberdi.

Bus Overnight buses to Esquel on Sun. Tues. and Thurs., stop at Rio Mayo, 0630, take food for journey as cafés on route tend to overcharge. 3 buses a day to Comodoro Rivadavia, 0700, 1300, 1900 and Giobbi buses to Chile leave at 0200.

The road runs West from Sarmiento via **Río Mayo** (which has three hotels, the *Covadonga*, E, very good, *La Ruta* and *San Martín*), to Puerto Aysén in Chile. The Giobbi buses from Comodoro Rivadavia to Coyhaique, Chile, leave Río Mayo at 0600. A branch from this road goes 134 km. S to Perito Moreno, by Lake Buenos Aires. Another branch on the Río Mayo-Perito Moreno road turns W at 31 km. to Lago Blanco, where there is a small *estancia* community, 30 km. from the border with Chile (about 150 km. from Río Mayo). No hotel, but police are friendly and may permit camping at the police post. No public transport to Chile; wild but beautiful place. From Sarmiento you can reach Esquel (448 km.), at the southern edge of the Lake District (**see page** 152). The first 210 km. from Sarmiento are paved, then it is mostly a dirt or all-weather road, though short stretches have been paved.

Perito Moreno (population 1,700), at 400 metres, is close to Lake Buenos Aires, which extends into Chile as Lake General Carrera (do not confuse the town with Ventisquero Perito Moreno, the glacier on Lake Argentino; see under Calafate, below). Also nearby are Lakes Belgrano and Burmeister, and the source of the River Deseado. Daily buses (US$2, 1½ hrs.) to Los Antiguos (*Hotel Argentino*, E, comfortable restaurant; municipal campsite; service station) on the Chilean border at Lake Buenos Aires (67 km. along Route 520), surrounded by orchards, where *pejerrey* can be caught. Halfway is Las Chilcas where Indian remains are found.

The famous Cuevas de las Manos, a series of galleries with 10,000-years-old paintings of human hands and of animals in red, orange, black, white and green, are interesting even for those not interested in rock art; the canyon in which the caves are situated is very beautiful. 118 km. S of Perito Moreno on Route 40, a marked road goes directly to the caves (68 km.) No buses, but the tourist office at Perito Moreno can supply names of drivers who can take you there, prices between US$40-60, to be split among a party of visitors. On leaving Perito Moreno on the way to the caves you will pass Cerro de El Volcán, its crater is accessible; after pasing the Gendarmería on your right, take the first left (dirt road) at the 3-road junction with Route 40. It is 12 km. to the path to the crater—ask permission at the Estancia to continue.

Hotels *Belgrano*, D with shower, clean, no heating, with good restaurant; *Austral*, D, modern, clean, open Dec. to Feb., both on San Martín; *Fénix*, F, no heating or hot water, confirm price in advance, not rec; *Argentino*, E, dirty, no showers; *Santa Cruz*, on Belgrano, E, heating, shared bath and hot water. Food is very expensive in Perito Moreno. **Restaurant** *Americano*, opp. *Hotel Fénix*, good and cheap.

Camping Parque Laguna in town, opposite Laguna Cisnes, good hot showers, well shielded, US$0.50 p.p. (slide shows at the tourist office there, information given).

Exchange US dollars can be exchanged at Banco de la Nación and Banco de la Provincia de Santa Cruz (both change cash), *Hotel Austral* and *Hotel Belgrano*, latter gives better rates. Difficult to exchange travellers cheques.

Transport Airport is a long way from town, try to hitch as there is only one taxi; LADE flies from Perito Moreno to Calafate (Tues.) and Río Gallegos and Ushuaia (Thurs.). Hitch-hikers to the S are warned that, outside the tourist season (Jan.-mid-Feb.), it is usually quicker to head for the coast at Caleta Olivia and go S from there than to take the road via Gobernador Gregores and Piedra Buena.

There are various routes from Perito Moreno to Coyhaique in Chile: Perito Moreno to Chile Chico, then by twice-weekly *El Pilchero* ferry boat across Lake General Carrera to Puerto Ibáñez, and then on by road to Coyhaique (public transport on the days the ferry sails). On this route there is a bus connection from Caleta Olivia (see below) through to Los Antiguos (2 km. from border with Chile) every Mon. and Thurs., at 1500 (from Perito Moreno, leaves from *Hotel Argentino*) and back to Caleta Olivia every Tues. and Fri. at 0730 (0930 from Perito Moreno), 1030 other days except Sun., US$10, with Empresa Comi; returns daily at 1030. Chile Chico is 8 km. from Los Antiguos; several jeeps a day cross border (not suitable for ordinary cars—the water is waist-deep if you want to walk); ask in *Hotel Argentino*. A second route is to go N to Río Mayo, then W to Coyhaique Alto on the border, and on to Coyhaique. The third alternative is on this same route, but head W at Río Guenguel to the border at Paso Huemules and on to Coyhaique via Balmaceda. Fourthly, there are the roads which go around the northern side of Lake Buenos Aires to Puerto Ibáñez, but there are no sign posts and it is easy to get lost among the *estancias*; it is not worth attempting this route.

The road to Fitz Roy, 110 km. S of Comodoro Rivadavia, is paved, and a major short-cut now bypasses Puerto Deseado. Fitz Roy to Río Gallegos is now also paved (goes via Piedra Buena, see page 172). Fitz Roy (named for the captain of Darwin's *Beagle*) is a tiny town, only two small *hosterías*, very primitive, not rec. Better stay 22 km. N at **Caleta Olivia** on Route 3 (13,400 inhabitants); hotels *Residencial Robert*, *Grand* and one other, all D; and camping at Yacht Club. Caleta Olivia, a good start-point for hitching S, is the urban centre for important oilfields, and is near Pico Truncado, the gas field which feeds the pipeline to Buenos Aires. El Pingüino bus runs daily from Caleta Olivia to Rio Gallegos at 2200, 11 hrs.

This is the area of the **petrified forests,** 70,000 years old, of fallen araucaria trees, nearly 3 metres round and 15-20 metres long: a remarkable sight. Taxi, Sarmiento to forests, US$12. There are two sites you can visit: the Bosque Petrificado José Ormachea, due W of Comodoro Rivadavia, about 140 km. by road (116 km. paved—the unpaved part is practically impassable in the wet season), 32 km. S of Sarmiento, in Chubut entry US$1, jeep trip to larger trees US$5 but can be walked in 20 mins.; the Víctor Szlapelis, some 40 km. further SW along the same road (follow signposts, road from Sarmiento in good condition). The **Monumento Natural Bosques Petrificados,** W of Puerto Deseado in Santa Cruz, surrounding the Laguna Grande on a road SW from Fitz Roy, 113 km. away was closed indefinitely in 1989. A new road has been built from Route 3 about 65 km. S of Fitz Roy to the Bosques Petrificados, which reduces the journey by several km.

At Piedra Negra, the previous turn-off for Puerto Deseado, there is a cheap hotel, *Florida Negra.* The only other building is a police post.

About 300 km. S of Comodoro Rivadavia is **Puerto Deseado**, with a population of 3,750 (airport), at the mouth of the river Deseado which drains Lake Buenos Aires, far to the W. (Hotels: *Los Acantilados,* C, and *Colón,* D.) The town was founded on July 15, 1884; its harbour takes large ships. A local tourist attraction is the Cañadón de las Bandurrias, sometimes known as the Grotto of Lourdes, 40 metres high. Nearby are islands with penguins and other birds, including the unique grey cormorant; local launches available. Lake Buenos Aires is reached by road in 7 hours; 280 km. to Las Heras, on to Perito Moreno, near the lake, 177 km., and a further 67 km. to the Chilean border at Los Antiguous (see above).

It was at Puerto Deseado that a Welshman in Cavendish's expedition of 1586 gave the name of *pengwyn* (white head) to a certain strange-looking bird. It is only fair to mention the opposing theory that the name is derived from a Spanish word, *pingüe,* meaning fat.

Local holidays Jan. 31 (St. John Bosco); Oct. 9 (Coat of Arms day).

From Puerto Deseado to Santa Cruz by the old road is about 470 km. Some 156 km. short of Santa Cruz and 4 km. off Route 3, it reaches **San Julián** (founded 1901, population of 4,480), the best place for breaking the 925 km. run from Comodoro Rivadavia to Río Gallegos. There is much wildlife in the area: red and grey foxes, *guanacos,* wildcats in the mountains, rheas, etc. The main activities are sheep raising for export, fish canning, and production of kaolin and clay. Clay grinding can be seen at Molienda Santa Cruz and ceramics made at the Escuela de Cerámica; good handicraft centre next door, on Moreno. There is a regional museum at the end of San Martín on the waterfront. The ruins of Florida Blanca, a colony founded in 1870 by Antonio Viedma, can be visited. The cascade of San Julián is formed by two different tides. Punta Caldera is a popular summer beach. The first mass in Argentina was held here after Magellan had executed a member of his crew. Francis Drake also put in here to hang Thomas Doughty, after amiably taking breakfast with him. Near San Julián (15 km.) is Cabo Curioso beach, with an attractive natural cave.

Hotels *Municipal,* Av. Costanera and 25 de Mayo, very nice, well-run, good value, D, but no restaurant. *Residencial Sada,* on San Martín, D, nice, clean, hot water, own bathroom, but sited on busy main road. Also older *Colón,* D, Av. San Martín 301 and Águila, F, friendly, clean. Good municipal campsite on the waterfront, all facilities, Av. Costanera betweeen Rivadavia and Roca.

Restaurants *Sportsman,* Mitre and 25 de Mayo; *Dos Anclas,* Berutti 1080; *Mi Refugio,* Mitre and Vélez Sársfield, *Soc. Chilena de Socorros Mutuos,* Ameghino 961; *Astra* on Route 3. Restaurant at San Martín 1375. Bars and tearooms: *Nos Amis,* Ameghino 1091; *Sweet Helen,* San Martín 485, *Aero Bar,* J. B. Alberdi and Pellegrini. Dancing at *Franoi,* 25 de Mayo 1198.

Post Office At Belgrano and Av. San Martín; telephone exchange also.

Banks Banco de la Nación on Mitre and Belgrano, and Banco de la Provincia de Santa Cruz on San Martín and Moreno.

Pharmacy *Del Pueblo* on San Martín 570. **Hospital** on Av. Costanera between Roca and Magallanes.

Tourist Office In centre of San Martín.

Air Weekly services to Río Gallegos, other routes end in Buenos Aires; many connect with flights from Comodoro Rivadavia by Austral and Aerolíneas.

Bus Transportadora Patagónica comes from Río Gallegos en route to Buenos Aires; Transportes Staller goes weekly to Lago Posadas stopping in Gobernador Gregores, Hotel Riera, Las Horquetas, Caracoles and Río Blanco. Transportes El Cordillerano cover the previous route but also stop at Olivia.

Santa Cruz, one of the best of the coastal harbours (airport) is near the mouth of the Santa Cruz river which drains Lake Argentino. Founded on December 1, 1878 and capital of Santa Cruz province until 1904. A deep-water port is being built 22 km. outside Santa Cruz at Punta Quilla. Population 3,000 (ACA *Hostería*, D; *Hotel Anel Aike*, D). Isla Monte León, 66 km. away (Route 1601, then Route 3 and dirt track) has walruses, penguins, beaches, fishing and camping facilities.

An unpaved road (Route 521) runs NW from San Julián to Route 40 along the foothills of the Andes. About halfway is **Gobernador Gregores** (*Hotel San Francisco*, acceptable, similarly *Adelino*, C; municipal campsite; good mechanic in town and all grades of fuel available).
    At **Piedra Buena** (population 2,600), 35 km. W of Santa Cruz (paved road) is ACA motel, simple, functional but good, warm and nice food (E), also campsites N of town on Route 3. ACA breakdown station at Km. 247 on Route 3. The *Select* restaurant is very dear for what it offers. Provincial Route 9 (1603 on some maps, unpaved, no petrol) from 43 km. S of Piedra Buena to Calafate runs along the edge of a plateau with occasional panoramic views across the valley of the River Santa Cruz below. Then at about 170 km. it drops down into the valley itself to follow the river into the hills and to Lake Argentino. A pleasant run, without being spectacular. Route 288 runs direct to Calafate from Piedra Buena via Tres Lagos. Most traffic to Calafate goes via Río Gallegos.

Río Gallegos, at the mouth of the Río Gallegos, the capital of Santa Cruz Province, is 265 km. S of Santa Cruz; it has a deep-water port with a dry-dock. The tidal range here during spring tides may be as high as 16 metres. There is a large trade in wool and sheepskins. The town has recently improved greatly and has a good shopping centre, although it is still somewhat drab. (The cave paintings at Laguna Azul, 60 km. from Río Gallegos, are now reported not available for visiting.) Population: 43,400. Foundation Day: 9 Dec., 1885. Museum at Perito Moreno 35. The Regional Provincial Museum, Mendoza y Roca, has collections of local flora, fauna, rock samples. Colonial museum at Alberdi y Córdoba. ACA service centre with excellent restaurant. Cheap sheepskins (tanned) and very warm leather coats (*gamulanes*) at Puerto Aymond factory of Mr. Szasack (half the Buenos Aires price). Handicraft market at Roca 658, open 0800-2000.

Hotels Strongly recommended: *Alonso*, Corrientes 33, C, simple, very clean and comfortable. *Aparthotel Niza*, Alcorta 190, T 20958, C quiet, good breakfast included, clean, rec.; *Santa Cruz*, Roca 701, C with shower and heating, discount for cash, receptionist speaks English, good coffee bar, breakfast, Avis office here; *Covadonga*, Roca 1214, D, clean, comfortable, warm; *Comercio*, Roca 1302, C, reported not too clean, overpriced, very busy; *Residencial Sachas*, Rivadavia 122, E, clean; *Caabo Vírgenes*, Rivadavia 150, E with bath, rec.; *Río Turbio*, Zapiola 486 (opp. bus station for Punta Arenas), D, with bath, English spoken, good. *Central*, Av. Roca 1127, E, central, quiet, cold shower, no heating; *Pensión Belgrano*, Calle Belgrano 119, very cheap, has good restaurant; *Hotel y Confitería Florida*, Roca 1202 y Vélez Sarsfield, E (F without bath), clean, hot water; private house at Vélez Sársfield 505; *Residencial Internacional*, at Roca and Sphur 78, E, with heating, friendly, but insecure; *Colonial*, Urquiza y Rivadavia, T 22329, E, shower, cheaper without, hot water, friendly, clean, can be noisy; close by is *Laguna Azul*, E, a little rundown but clean and good value; *Entre Ríos*, Entre Ríos, E, fairly good; *Viejo La Fuente*, Vélez Sarsfield 64-70, T 20304, F, basic, hot water, dinner for US$3 incl. wine; *Puerto Santa Cruz*, round corner from LADE office, F, hot shower.

N.B. Accommodation is hard to find in Río Gallegos because of the number of transient workers in town. Apparently no camping is allowed around Río Gallegos because it is a military zone apart from authorized municipal site on Italia y Costa Rica, turn off Route 3 at edge of town heading south (US$0.20 p.p., small, basic). Ask at tourist office for new site, being developed alongside a children's playground, cheap, free, hot showers. One is not allowed to take photographs either, for the same reason.

Restaurants Plenty and good, some specializing in sea food. *La Casa de Miguel*, Roca 1284, good. *Restaurant Díaz*, Roca 1143, good, mixed reports about the mixed grill; *Montecarlo*, Zapiola 558, good seafood, not the cheapest; opp. is good *heladería*. *El Palenque*, Corrientes 73, rec. *Café Carrera* has good but expensive breakfast, on Fagnano and Pres. Roca. *Pizzería Don Pizza*, excellent.

Car Hire Andrés Etura, Sarmiento 204.

Car parts and repairs at Repuestos Sarmiento, on Sarmiento, owner very friendly and helpful.

Motorcycle Mechanic Juan Carlos Topcic, Costa Rica 25, friendly and helpful.

Exchange Lloyds Bank (BLSA), Sarmiento 47. Open 1000-1600. Banco de Santa Cruz, 900 block of Roca, good rates; Sur Cambio, San Martín y Roca (no travellers' cheques); *casas de cambio*, best rates. Change travellers' cheques in Río Gallegos if going to Calafate, where it is more difficult; good rates at Cambio El Pingüino (Zapiola 469); may also change European and South American currencies.

Chilean Consulate Mariano Moreno 144, Mon.-Fri., 0900-1400.

Post Office Roca 893. **Telephones**, Entel, Roca 613.

Tourist Office Roca y Córdoba friendly, helpful. (Also Alberdi 154.) They will phone round hotels for you.

Road Travel New bus terminal at corner of Route 3 and Eva Perón, 3 km. from centre, taxi to centre US$0.75, occasional bus US$0.25. Calafate (Interlagos and Pingüino in summer, in winter pooled service, 1130, 6 hrs., US$14, very crowded; turn up with ticket 30 mins. before departure) Bus (Interlagos), Río Gallegos-Calafate, daily (Tues., Thurs., Sat. in winter) 1600, 5 hrs.; Pingüino in summer daily 1600. Route 40, which goes to Calafate (312 km.) is paved with a service station and motel at La Esperanza (146 km.).

Daily to Río Turbio: Expreso Pingüino goes at 1200 plus 1530 Mon., Wed., Fri., 5½—6½ hrs., US$15; San Caferino (Entre Ríos 371) Mon., Thurs. at 1130, US$12.30; same company to Puerto Natales Tues., Thurs., Sat. 1300. Make sure your car papers are in order if driving to Puerto Natales, Chile (go first to Tourist Office for necessary documents, then to the customs office at the port, at the end of San Martín, very uncomplicated). Poor road to turn-off to Puerto Natales, then good road to Punta Arenas, 303 km. (one lane only); taxi US$50-70; buses US$13 daily at 1300 (1000 Mon., 1230 Sat.), by Expreso Pingüino (booking office Zapiola 455, T 22338, 0800-1300 and 1500-2100 Mon.-Sat. 0900-1300 and 1700-2100 on Sun.), take 6 hours including border-crossing process, now greatly simplified following the settlement of the Beagle Channel dispute.

Pingüino daily at 2100 to Caleta Olivia, US$20, 11-14 hrs. Bus to Puerto Madryn 28 hrs. To Comodoro Rivadavia, 808 km., stops at Fitz Roy daily at 2200, arr. 1000 next day, US$28; a bus (Andesmar) now goes all the way to Mendoza, leaves Fri. 1300, arrives 0900 Sun., via Comodoro Rivadavia, Puerto Madryn and Neuquén. No direct bus to Bariloche; you have to spend a night in Comodoro Rivadavia.

Occasional ships and buses (Don Otto, US$81, 48 hrs.), to Buenos Aires, 2,575 km. Buses (Transportadora Patagónica, Gobernador Lista 330, T 2330) Tues., Thurs., Sat. at 2330, 14 hrs., **Hitchhiking** to Buenos Aires is possible in about 3½ days; appearance important.

Air Travel In summer, it is best to make your bookings in advance. AA and Austral fly daily to Buenos Aires, fare US$100 (daytime). To get on cheaper night flight from Buenos Aires (Austral—may be seasonal) go to Aeroparque at midnight on Sun., purchase ticket at Austral desk to get on waiting list, go to airport again at 2135 on Mon. for 2235 flight and hope there's a seat, 4-hr. flight. LADE flies to Buenos Aires (making 12 stops on the way; wonderful topographical views) and Mar. del Plata. AA's Buenos Aires-Auckland-Sydney flight (twice a week) stops at Río Gallegos, but the return journey does not. Numerous flights to Ushuaia (Tierra del Fuego), direct or via Río Grande (AA and LADE, cheaper than by bus, always booked, try waiting list). To Río Grande, 40 mins, LADE, or Aerolíneas Argentinas. LADE flights to Calafate US$14, 2 a day in summer (about 3 a week out of season—also local airline Aeroposta, daily); to Río Turbio (2 per week). LADE flights also to Bariloche via Santa Cruz, San Julián, Puerto Deseado, Comodoro Rivadavia (3 a week), Trelew (twice a week) and Esquel, twice a week. To Comodoro Rivadavia with Aerolíneas Argentinas, daily, 1 hr.; LADE to Perito Moreno, Tues. 1130 and Thurs. 1545, US$26, 3 hrs. Book seats in Buenos Aires to avoid difficulties with departures. Airport bus, No 6, from Av. Roca, US$0.50, once or twice an hour. Taxi (*remise*) to/from town, e.g. opp. *Hotel Colonial* US$1.20; Interlagos and Pingüino buses stop at airport; hitching from car park is easy. **N.B.** Flights may leave early, sometimes up to 40 mins. LADE flights should be booked as far in advance as possible.

Excursion   134 km. S, there is a penguin colony at Cabo Vírgenes (totally undeveloped); follow Route 3 then branch off on Route 1 for 3½ hrs. (unpaved). (On the way is El Cóndor ranch, where the manager, Mr Blake, is reported to welcome visitors.) The Navy allows visitors to climb up Cabo Vírgenes lighthouse for a superb view. Likewise, undeveloped, is Isla de Monte León, N of Río Gallegos, take Route 3 (paved), then a dirt track in good condition.

From Río Gallegos a railway runs 260 km. to **Río Turbío** (6,000 people) where is found Argentina's largest coalfield; reserves are estimated at 450m tons and the state coal company YCF is building a deep-water port at Punta Loyola to service it. There is a director of tourism, Prof. César Cetta, in the municipality on San Martín. Hotels, always almost full: *Hostería Capipe*, Dufour (9 km. from town), C; *Gato Negro*, E, recently renovated; *Azteca*, E; *Hostería Municipal*, by ski-run in hills, 6 km. from town. Visitors can see Mina 1, where the first mine was opened in the hills; area good for trekking and horseback riding. The present mining and industrial area, with the school museum, can also be visited. Unfortunately, it is no longer possible for tourists to ride the coal train (steam locomotives) to Río Turbio, although advance warning to the management *may* provide a truck on the train. Río Turbio is reported to have better travel connections than Puerto Natales and once in Río Turbio it is easy to catch a local bus into Chile. (Río Turbio to Argentine border post: 3 km.,—bus, US$0.30, last at 2230, some reports suggest that there are no buses either side of the border, though—a further 4 km. to Chilean post and then 14 km. to paved section of road connecting Puerto Natales with Punta Arenas.) The bus from Río Turbio to Puerto Natales (31 km.) connects with the bus arriving from Río Gallegos. No direct bus to Calafate. There is a LADE office and Expreso Pingüino runs daily at 0600 (plus 1300 Tues., Thurs., Sat., 6 hrs.) in summer or 1300 Wed., Thurs., Sat. in winter to Río Gallegos, but flights are cheaper and avoid the numerous passport checks as well as the essentially uninteresting ride. *Restaurant El Ringo*, near bus station, will shelter you from the wind.

Calafate (properly El Calafate), on Lake Argentino, 320 km. NW of Río Gallegos, pop. 3,000, is an expensive and developing tourist centre (more expensive than Ushuaia). There is a chapel dedicated to Santa Teresa in the centre; behind it Calle Perito Moreno gently climbs the large hill S of the town, from which one can see the silhouette of the S end of the Andes, the Laguna Redonda and Isla de la Soledad on Lake Argentino. It is the southern gateway to the **Parque Nacional de los Glaciares**, which is 50 km. away (the northern end is at Lake Viedma). On the alluvial plain by the lake there are many interesting birds, and in the other direction there is scope for good hill-walking. Colourful cave paintings (now closed except with special permission at Punta Gualichú) some 8 km. from Calafate, walking through the fields bordering the lake, or 12 km. by road. The Lake Argentino area is very popular, booking all transport in advance is a *must*; accommodation is very difficult to find in Jan.-Feb. The store *Las Plantas* in Calafate is helpful with travel arrangements and exchange. The tourist office has a list of taxis but undertakes no arrangements; it is helpful but some information may be incorrect, so check. Small museum at airport. Note that credit cards are not popular, apart from hotels, while most places quote in US dollars.

Camping and fishing permits, limited to official sites, from the Parque Nacional rangers in Calafate. Although the mountains are snow capped, you can camp out in the pleasant woods around the lake in summer and even swim in it on warm days. (Campsite details below.) There is utter stillness apart from squawking flocks of parakeets and an occasional roar as ice falls off the glacier and thunders into the lake. In November, 1989, all accommodation and restaurant facilities at the glacier's edge were closed. Visitors must take their own food and drink.

Festivals   People flock to the rural show on 15 February (Lago Argentino Day) and camp out with much revelry; dances and *asados* (barbecued sides of sheep). There are also barbecues and rodeo etc. on Día de la Tradición, 10 November.

Hotels   *Los Alamos*, A, comfortable, good food and service, has a mixed-media show, with dinner afterwards, rec.; *Amado*, A, Av Libertador, good; *La Loma*, B. Roca and 15 de Febrero (can be booked in Buenos Aires at Av. Callao 433, 4° H, T 40-7476/40-9123), with bath, breakfast not included, excellent view, modern, rec., multilingual, restaurant, tea room: the hotel itself is B (high season Oct.-May, cheaper in low season, behind it there are 14 cheaper rooms, E, with special rate for International Youth Hostel members (F p.p. with bath between Oct.-Dec., E from 20 Dec.-31 March), special rates for owners of *South American Handbook*, between Oct. and Dec., also has two kombis for excursions for guests (run on most days, closed in winter); ACA *Hostería El Calafate*, on Manzana 36, D, modern, good view, 26 rooms; *El Quijote*, D, friendly, comfortable, good restaurant; *Carlitos*, Comandante Espora, D, modern, clean and very friendly; *Michelangelo*, Espora, D, modern, clean, excellent, reasonable, good restaurant, will accept travellers' cheques in payment (at a poor rate, though); *Cabañas Nevis*, Av. Libertador 1956, friendly, clean, D, good meals, rec.; *Hostería Kau-Yatún*, A, with bath, many facilities, 25 de Mayo (10 blocks from town centre), old *estancia* house, comfortable, restaurant and barbecues, horses for hire; *Upsala*, Comandante Espora 139, C, with bath, good and clean; *Hospedaje Belén*, E, clean, warm, hot water, cooking facilities. Several slightly cheaper hotels but none less than E, e.g. *Hospedaje Jorgito*, Gob. Moyano 934, D, clean, hot water, heating, breakfast extra, always full; *Hospedaje del* Norte, Los Gauchos 813, E open all year, comfortable, a similar place across the street; *Hospedaje Echevarría*, Libertador 989, E, quiet, very clean, highly rec.; Libertador 1311, Jorge Hazembuller, T (0902) 91435, far end of town from airport, E with breakfast, 2 shared rooms, will store luggage, very helpful, trips to glacier, rec.; *Residencia Los Lagos*, Moyona and 25 de Mayo, bakery pizzeria on ground floor (so ground floor rooms noisy from singing baker in a.m.), E with bath, very comfortable and clean, good value; *Residencia Bórquez*, also on 25 de Mayo, E, friendly. Rec. bed and breakfast at Espora 60, E p.p.; *Casa de Familia Del Norte* 25 de Mayo 345, E with and without bath, clean, use of kitchen. *Cabañas Nevis*, about 1 km. from town towards glacier, for 4 or 8, new, lake view, full board good value; *Youth Hostel, Albergue del Glaciar*, Calle los Pioneros, 200 metres off Av. Libertador (reservations in Buenos Aires T 71-9344, 312-8486/9, Fax 054-1-3124700), open October-April, IYHF member, rec., F-E, hot water, information on bikes, horses, etc., runs good tours to Moreno glacier, US$5 with plenty of time to see the glacier and its surroundings. Calafate has a tourist office from which caravans, tents (US$2 each, sleep 4) and 4-berth *cabañas* (US$3 p.p.) may be hired, showers extra. Note that all hotels except ACA are open only from October to April/May. Some private houses offer accommodation such as Enrique Barragán, Barrio Bahía Redonda, Casa 10, E, rec. Ask at tourist office if in difficulty.

Camping In Calafate is a municipal camp site (cheaper than Lago Roca site, see below), new facilities, behind YPF service station, US$0.50, and US$2.50 for warm showers, no tents for rent at site, but beds in trailers, US$3.75, near airport. 3 campsites in the Park en route to the glacier: the first is 10 km. past the park entrance, US$1 p.p., prone to flooding; the second is 10 km. before the glacier, free, no facilities, but nice riverside location and lots of firewood, warden visits site to issue permits; the third is 8 km. before the glacier, with all facilities, US$1 p.p. Take food to all three.

Restaurants Prices rise during November and high season lasts until May. *ACA* Grill; *Pizzería Onelli*, Libertador 1197, reasonable, stays open out of season; *Michelangelo*, Tomás Espora, good food and atmosphere, rec.; *La Tablita*, used by locals, barbecues; *El Mirador del Lago*, excellent food, beautiful views; *Kauyatun*, for barbecues; *Tehuel Aike*, Av. Libertador 992, central, good food, slow service; *La Loma*, friendly, home food, picnic lunches supplied, good cakes and chocolates, beautiful view. Tea rooms: *Maktub*, Libertador 905, excellent pastries, expensive; *Mirador del Lago*, Kasbah. *Bar Don Diego de la Noche*, at end of main road in direction of the glacier, good atmosphere.

Exchange Banco de la Provincia de Santa Cruz (Av. del Libertador) changes cash but not travellers' cheques. Advances (costly) on some credit cards given. Tourist office reported to change money. Travel agencies such as Interlagos and Lake Travel may be able to help. YPF garage and Chocolate El Calafate and some other shops give good rates for cash; also El Pingüino bus company for good rates; the *Scorpio* snack bar in the main street is reported to give best rates; try also the supermarket in the main street and reception of *Hotel La Loma* for travellers' cheques and cash.

Tourist Information In new building by bridge over Río Calafate. Tourist office friendly. Tour to Moreno glacier information available here, US$10. Hotel prices detailed on poster at the airport and on large chart at tourist office. Sr. Jorge Antolín Solache owner of *Hotel La Loma*, Casilla de Correo 36, 9405 Calafate (T 0902-91016, Dec.-May), rest of the year Callao 433-4°H, 1022 Buenos Aires (T 40-7476), to whom we are very grateful for updating the Calafate section, has kindly offered to provide any information to travellers in the region. He speaks English, French, Italian and Portuguese.

Travel Agents Interlagos, Libertador 1175; Lake Travel Tours, Libertador 932; and Gador Viajes, on Libertador. All agencies charge the same rates for excursions to the glazier: US$6 for a trip leaving 0830, returning 1200, without lunch, 3 hrs. at glacier; to Lake Roca, at 0930 return 1700, US$14; Fitz Roy, at 0700 return 1900, US$25, Gualichu caves, 2 hrs., US$4; Upsala and Onelli glaciers (boat trip and bus to Punta Bandera), US$18. Also try at *Hotel La Loma*, with *kombis*, where prices are usually lower. Aeroposta at Calafate airport flies over Moreno glacier in Aero Commander twin-engined planes, 5 passengers, US$35 p.p. Jorge Lemos, Aventrek, AP Postal Esp. No. 7 (9405) El Calafate, Telex Cab. pública 86905, runs recommended treks in Glaciares National Park and Fitzroy.

Film and slide show about Calafate, the Moreno glacier and climbing the Cerro Torres at *Tío Cacho* discothèque, every night, 2000, US$2 (prefers large groups with reservations), better for non-groups is the audiovisual at *La Posta* restaurant every day in summer at 1845, US$2.

Transport By air from Río Gallegos (US$14, LADE, 2 a day in summer, out of season 3 per week) and Comodoro Rivadavia (often fully booked), US$38, Tues. only, also Río Grande Ushuaia (AA, US$35, LADE US$25), daily in summer and Perito Moreno, US$20 with LADE. Aeroposta also flies daily to Río Gallegos and back. To Esquel weekly on Tues., US$45. In winter there are often no flights for weeks if the weather is bad. The airport is about a ten-minute walk from the centre of town; it may close in autumn after rain.

Bus Calafate to Ushuaia requires four changes, and ferry; total cost of journey US$43. Interlagos Turismo bus runs daily at 0700 (summer) or 0915 (winter) to Río Gallegos; in addition El Pingüino runs daily at 0700 5 hrs. US$14, passengers on this bus wishing to go to Chile get off at Güer Aike to catch Pingüino's Gallegos-Río Turbio bus 50 mins later, arriving at 1700. Taxi to Río Gallegos, 4 hours, US$165 irrespective of number of passengers, up to 5 people. The Río Gallegos-Calafate road (323 km., of which about 220 km. paved) trip is worth while for the number of animals and birds one sees. No direct bus Calafate-Río Turbio.

Direct services to Chile: Pingüino, Av. Libertador, to Puerto Natales from 4 Dec. to Feb., US$42; Lake Travel Tours' (Mon., Wed. and Fri., 0600) to Puerto Natales (US$36) via La Esperanza and El Turbio. Other reported services: a semi-scheduled service in season on Tues., Thur., Sun., US$18, ask travel agents; Chilean minibuses to Puerto Natales 3 times a week, US$18-20 in dollars, ask at Youth Hostel; lorry service, ask Gador Viajes, Libertador 1046. The road trip from Calafate to Punta Arenas is very interesting for animal and bird watchers: from Calafate take Route 40 (a new road is almost complete) and "Complementaria O" to La Esperanza (150 km., after 1½ hrs. there is a 45 km. short cut avoiding La Esperanza, in terrible condition), where there is a petrol pump and hotel; thence to Cancha Carrera (border post Dec.-April), 63 km. to La Laurita, pay US$0.50 at control, then 4 km. to border, then paved road (14 km.) to Puerto Natales and 245 km. to Punta Arenas, 42 km. paved. To Torres del Paine National Park, the quickest, but not the cheapest, way to take a Kombi from either Gador Viajes or Lake Travel Tours, leaving Calafate at 0600, which travels to Puerto Natales (US$36) on a private road through an estancia; get off at Cerro Castillo (Chilean border post, closed Dec.-April) from where it is possible, with some patience, to hitch a lift to the park, or to take the bus coming from Puerto Natales to the Park. It is not possible to change Australes once inside the Park.

The easiest way to Río Turbio for Puerto Natales is to fly to Río Gallegos then take the daily bus; this avoids a long wait to change buses at La Esperanza.

Road routes to Calafate By a rough but interesting road from Santa Cruz, Provincial Route 9 (Route 288) is 100 km. longer with two bridges replacing old ferry crossings, 5 or 6 hrs. by car, but not always possible after rain. Route 40 from Esquel is a mixture of asphalt and gravel to Perito Moreno, then to Bajo Caracoles (small but friendly hotel/bar, petrol pump—"normal" grade fuel only) it is very bad for the first 10 km. before improving a little. This route has little traffic and extreme winds can double your fuel consumption, carry some spare. Route 40 continues to Tres Lagos, but it may be wise to make an extra 50 km. detour on good roads to Gobernador Gregores (see page 168) for fuel or accommodation. At Tres Lagos there is only "normal" grade fuel. From Tres Lagos to Calafate is very bad, slow going. South of Calafate, Route 40 to Río Gallegos is paved and in excellent condition.

N.B. It is nearly impossible to hitchhike from Calafate to Perito Moreno.

Excursions At the far end of Lake Argentino (80 km.) the Ventisquero Moreno, one of the few glaciers in the world that is growing descend, descends to the surface of the water over a five-km. frontage and a height of about 60 metres. In a cycle of roughly three years it advances across the lake, cutting the Brazo Rico off from the Canal de los Témpanos; then the pressure of water in the Brazo Rico breaks up the ice and reopens the channel. Pieces break off and float away as icebergs. When visiting the glacier, do not go down too close to the lake as these icebergs can cause great waves when breaking off, and wash people off rocks; in fact, new wooden catwalks prevent you from going to the water's edge. From Calafate there are daily Pingüino and Interlagos (rec.) bus trips Sept.-May only, to the glacier's edge (return, US$14 from Av. Libertador at 0930 returning 1700, giving 3 hrs. at glacier); you can use the return fare at no extra cost if you come back next day. Taxis, US$40 for 4 passengers round trip. The Parque Nacional truck leaves Calafate most weekday mornings at 0800 and may give lifts (but arrive at 0500!); It may be possible to camp in the guardaparque's backyard, but you must ask first. Out of season, trips to the glacier are difficult to arrange, but one can gather a party and hire a taxi, about US$43 for 1 hr. 20 mins. one way; take warm clothes, and food and drink; try asking at *Hotel La Loma* (where they have 2 station wagons/kombis) or taxis at cooperative, T 91044 (for 4 people).

Travel by road to the most interesting spots is limited and may require expensive taxis; the best connections are to Perito Moreno. Tours can be arranged at travel agencies, *Hotel La Loma* or with taxi drivers at the airport who await arrivals. Two recommended walks: (1) From the Centro Cívico in Calafate, visit Capilla Santa Teresita in Plaza San Martín; behind it is Calle Perito Moreno; walk to the top of the hill for a view of Calafate. Then go S to the Río Calafate, then to the new section of the town, where the ACA grill is. (2) From the Intendencia del Parque, follow the new road among cultivated fields and orchards to Laguna de Los Cisnes, a bird reserve, with flamingos, ducks, etc. Walk down to Lake Argentino; 15 km. along the lakeside are the painted caves at Punta Gualichú. Unfortunately the paintings have greatly deteriorated and only tour groups are allowed to visit them, but there are fascinating geological formations caused by erosion, on the edge of Lake Argentino, 12 km. from Calafate on the road to Río Gallegos. Excursion to Lake Roca, 50 km. S from Calafate. Trout and salmon fishing, climbing, walking, camping and branding of cattle in summer.

Lake Travel arrange trekking tours over the glacier, from 0900 to 1700: minibuses go to Lago Rico where a rubber boat crosses to the other side, specialized guides then take you over the glacier, a 2½ -hr. trek. Lake Travel also organize treks with specialized guides in the Fitzroy area.

Horse riding can be arranged at Estancia Huiliches, who pick you up by car at your hotel, take you to the estancia, 4 km. from Calafate, for 2 hrs. riding with beautiful views of Calafate and its surroundings, US$15 p.p.

A worthwhile trip is by motor-boat (120-150 passengers, take your own food) from Punta Bandera, 50 km. from Calafate, to the Upsala glacier at the end of Lake Argentino, Lake Onelli and glacier (restaurant) and Spegazzini glacier, leaves 0800 daily in summer from Punta Bandera, returns 1600. Cia. Paraíso de Navegación (9 de Julio y Gregores) runs the lake excursions, tickets US$38 (in dollars) including transport to the port. Nova Terra does similar trip, same price lunch US$6.50 extra, leaves 0645, (tours end 30 April). The boat passes by the 30-metre high glacier; it is reported however that the master sometimes decides the weather is too rough and does not go to Upsala. Put inshore and cross a little forest to reach the small Lake Onelli, quiet and very beautiful, beech trees on one side, and ice-covered mountains on the other. Small icebergs in the lake. Out of season it is extremely difficult to get to the glacier. Smaller boats (39 passengers) may run in winter; sometimes they don't run because of the danger of the glaciers "calving". Book tickets at Empresa Nova Terra, and at least two days in advance; take a taxi (US$35 round trip for up to 5 people); bus Calafate-Punta Bandera US$6, at 0700. On the road from Calafate to Punta Bandera, at the foot of Cerro Comisión, is a rock formation that looks like a herd of elephants facing down.

Another worthwhile excursion is to the N end of the Glaciares National Park to **Cerro Fitzroy** and Cerro Torres, 230 km. from Calafate; organized trip US$25 p.p. return. Interlagos and Chaltén now run a daily bus in summer at 0645 and 0800 respectively from Calafate to Cerro Fitzroy, about US$15, 4½ hrs., returns 1500, allowing 2-3 hrs. at site. A new road has been built from Route 40 to Fitzroy. The village at the base of Cerro Fitzroy is El Chaltén. There is a very friendly hostel there, *Lago Viedma* (expensive, D p.p. in dormitory with communal bathroom, inc. breakfast and dinner) providing also a restaurant, shop, horse-hire and guide service. They have a free campsite nearby, use of the hostel's facilities may be possible; second, free campsite at end of village near the paths to Cerros Fitzroy and Torres (the bus from Calafate goes to and from this site), no facilities. An *estancia* offers *hospedaje* at the same price as *Lago Viedma*. The Fitzroy massif can be seen from the hostel, and one can walk for 2½ hours (stupendous views: "anyone within 500 miles would be a fool to miss them"—Julian and Cordelia Thomas) to see Cerro Torres, where there is a *refugio*. There is also a *refugio* at Fraile Muerto, beyond the base of Cerro Fitzroy, good day's hike from Chaltén; Chaltén Patagonia Tours offers day trips Mon., Wed., Fri. To reach either refugio, one must cross the Río Fitzroy; by the new bridge; Cerro Fitzroy base camp is 2-2½ hrs. easy walk from the campsite at the edge of the village. Ask at the *gendarmería* (border-police) in Calafate if you can join their truck which goes once or twice a week. On the way to Cerro Fitzroy (often bad weather) on Route 40, is the Southern Astronomical Observatory, managed by the Observatory of La Plata.

A certificate is required from the National Park Office in Calafate to camp in the Park.

Organized trips to the Glaciares National Park are too short to appreciate it fully; either go on a tour bus, then camp (good gear essential) or hire a taxi/minibus. The travel agencies charge US$200 for up to 8 people, US$300 to take you and return later to collect you; private drivers (e.g. Martín Drake, Bo. Plan Alborada 390—speaks English) charge US$300 for up to 8 to take you and collect later (also does similar arrangements for the Moreno glacier).

TIERRA DEL FUEGO (11)

Tierra del Fuego is the island at the extreme south of South America. It is bounded by the Magellan Strait to the north, the Atlantic Ocean to the east, the Beagle Channel to the south—which separates it from the southern islands—and by the Whiteside, Gabriel, Magdalena and Cockburn Channels etc., which divide it from the islands to the west. The western side belongs to Chile and the eastern to Argentina. The local Ona Indians are now extinct. Throughout Tierra del Fuego the main roads are narrow and gravelled. The exceptions are the road for about 50 km. out of Porvenir (Chile), which is being widened, and Río Grande-Ushuaia, which is being improved. The south has beautiful lakes, woods and mountain scenery. Part of this country is a National Parks Reserve: trout and salmon in nearly all the lakes and rivers, and in summer wild geese, ducks, 152 other species of birds, and imported musk rats and beaver. Local tax exemptions apply throughout Tierra del Fuego. **Note** that accommodation is sparse and the island is becoming popular among Argentines in summer. Hotel beds and seats on aircraft may begin to run short as early as November.

N.B. Argentine time is normally one hour ahead of Chilean time.

Books *Tierra del Fuego* (3rd edition), in English, by Rae Natalie Prosser de Goodall, US$7.50 (obtainable in Ushuaia and Buenos Aires), colourful maps by the same author. Also *Tierra del Fuego: The Fatal Lodestone*, by Eric Shipton, and *Uttermost Part of the Earth*, by E. Lucas Bridges. Available in U.S.A.: *Birds of Isla Grande* (Tierra del Fuego) by Philip S.Humphrey, and *A Guide to the Birds of South America*, by Rodolphe Meyer de Schauensee.

March-April is a good time to visit because of the beautiful autumn colours.

Camping is very easy in Tierra del Fuego. You can, if so inclined, camp at most service stations. Many towns have municipal campsites which are either free or cost up to US$1. Private campsites can be very expensive.

There are two ways of crossing the Straits of Magellan to Tierra del Fuego. Coming S from Río Gallegos, an unpaved road turns left for Punta Delgada (1 hotel, 2 *hosterías*). (On the road Río Gallegos-Punta Delgada is Laguna Azul—3 km. off main road in an old crater; an ibis breeding ground, beautiful colours). A 30-minute crossing can be made by fast modern ferry from Punta Delgada to Punta Espora (no hotel—if desperate, ask the lighthouse keeper). The boats, which take 4 lorries and 2 cars, run every hour, with schedule determined by tides and a 1200-1400 lunch hour rest. Under normal conditions they run from 0800 to 2100 daily, with tidal breaks lasting 4 hours (autumn and winter timetable). Ferry-operators accept US dollars or Argentine or Chilean currencies. If going by car, do not go before 1000, as first crossings are taken by buses, etc. However, there is no bus service from Punta Espora (or Punta Delgada); buses to and from the island only through Porvenir. From Punta Espora (Bahía Aril is ferry terminal) a road runs through Chilean territory to San Sebastián (Chile) and 14 km. further to San Sebastián (Argentina) (usually 15 min. delay in crossing borders), Río Grande (road San Sebastián-Río Grande is appalling) and Ushuaia. There is an Esso service station 38 km. from Punta Espora. Accommodation is scarce in the Chilean part (except for Porvenir—**see page 607**), and it is not always possible to cross it in one day because of the irregularity of the ferry. It is sometimes possible, coming and going, to spend the night at the guest house of ENAP at Cerro Sombrero (petrol there for employees only, but if you are running out, they may help), but do not count on it. Try *Hostería Karu-Kinka*.

The road from Río Gallegos goes on to Punta Arenas, from where (dock at Tres Puentes

5 km. E of town) there is a daily crossing to Porvenir (passenger US$2, motor car US$33, 2½-3 hours; there is a passenger saloon with small cafeteria; get on first and you are invited on the bridge, get on last and you stand outside in the cold), from Porvenir at 1400 (Sun. 1700). If crossing with car, don't allow it to be parked too close to other vehicles; the ferry company will not accept responsibility for damage caused by onboard "crashes". If you want to continue, Senkovic buses to Río Grande leave at 1400 on Sat. and Wed. A 225-km. road runs from Porvenir E to Río Grande (6 hours) via San Sebastián; or by alternative route through Cerro Sombrero (see previous paragraph). On Chilean side of Tierra del Fuego, petrol available only at Porvenir. Reservations must be made at the hi-fi shop at Bulnes 637, Punta Arenas. The Argentine Consul in Punta Arenas is at Calle Valdivia 961 (T 22887). Border police at San Sebastián (ACA motel) will sometimes arrange lifts to Ushuaia or Río Grande. Hitching after San Sebastián is easy. Distances are roughly as follows in this area: Border with Chile at Monte Aymont; to Río Gallegos 73 km.; road to Río Grande via Kimiri-Aike (114 km. from Río Gallegos)—no buses; from here to Punta Delgada 30 km.; Punta Delgada-Punta Espora (ferry, free for pedestrians) 20 km.; on to Punta Sombrero (60 km.) and San Sebastián (60 km.) reaching Río Grande 80 km. on. The best way to hitch from Río Gallegos to Punta Arenas is to take any lorry as far as the turn-off for Punta Delgada ferry. Then there is plenty of Chilean traffic from Punta Delgada to Punta Arenas. *Hotel San Gregorio* will put you up if you get stuck near the turn-off.

Entering Argentina from Chile, be firm about getting an entry stamp for as long as you require. Going in the other direction, don't stock up with food in Argentina, as Chilean border guards will confiscate all fruit, vegetable, dairy and meat products coming into Chile.

N.B. If wishing to visit both sides of Tierra del Fuego, Punta Arenas, Torres del Paine, Calafate, Fitzroy, etc., the transport arrangements work much better if you start in Ushuaia and work north, via Chile, rather than starting in Calafate and working south.

The largest town in the Argentine part, with a population of 35,000 and growing, as industrialization spreads, is **Ushuaia**, the most southerly town in Argentina, and among the most expensive. Its steep streets (there are mountains, the Cerro Martial, at the back of the town) overlook the green waters of the Beagle Channel, named after the ship in which Darwin sailed the Channel in 1832, on Captain Fitroy's second expedition. It is reached from Buenos Aires by plane (5 hours). There are impressive views of the snow-clad peaks, rivers, waterfalls and dense woods. There is a naval station at Isla Redonda. The people are engaged in timber cutting, fishing and, nowadays, increasingly in factories. The tourist industry is also expanding rapidly and Ushuaia's main street is lined with tax-free shops. A new road has been built between Ushuaia and Río Grande via Paso Garibaldi. Ushuaia and its environs are worth a 2-3 day visit. See Documents, **page 185**.
Warning There have been complaints about the tap water in Ushuaia.

Note: Prices double on December 12.

Hotels *Monte Cervantes*, San Martín y Sarmiento, T 22153, A, run by owners of the Barracuda ship (see **Excursions**, page 184), rec.; *Cabo de Hornos*, San Martín and Triunvirato, T 22187, B, comfortable, TV, spotless, good value (but surcharge on credit cards), restaurant not open to non-residents; *Las Lengas*, Goleta Florencia s/n, T 22668, C, cold, no English spoken, breakfast only meal; *Maitén*, 12 de Octubre 138, T 22745, D-C, good value, clean, but a long walk from town centre. *Canal Beagle*, Maipú 599, T 21117, B (reductions for members of the ACA), good restaurant (catering usually for tour groups); *Albatros*, Maipú 505 and Lasserre, T 22504, clean, modern, good service, B including large breakfast, but lighting poor; *Malvinas*, Deloqui 609, T 22626, C, with bath, breakfast included, pleasant, helpful, central heating; *Antártida*, San Martín 1600, T 21896, C, friendly, restaurant with fine views, rec.; *Capri*, San Martín 720, T 21833, D, clean, friendly; *César*, San Martín 752, T 21460, D, with bath, comfortable, friendly, clean, no breakfast, rec.; *Mustapic*, Piedrabuena and Deloqui, T 21718, friendly multi-lingual owner (Sr. Miro, from Yugoslavia), C/D (may bargain lower), no singles, highly rec., exceptionally clean, can leave luggage, rooftop restaurant for breakfast; *Hospedaje Ona*, 9 de Julio 27, on waterfront, noisy, E (without breakfast, price drops to F after 5 nights stay), heater in room, used by lorry drivers, difficult to get into, but rec. *Las Goletas* (no sign) Maipú 857 on waterfront, D, some rooms shared (3-6), in bunk beds, TV room (where they will allow sleepers if there is scarce accommodation), hot showers, heating. *Fernández*, Onachaga 68, T 21453 very friendly, hot water, good but expensive meals, D, but cheaper in bunk-bed accommodation. *Bungalows Río Olivia*, 6 km. from town, Salón La Tía Tata, T 23714, owned by taxi driver Victor H. Ibiris (T 21282, 23241),

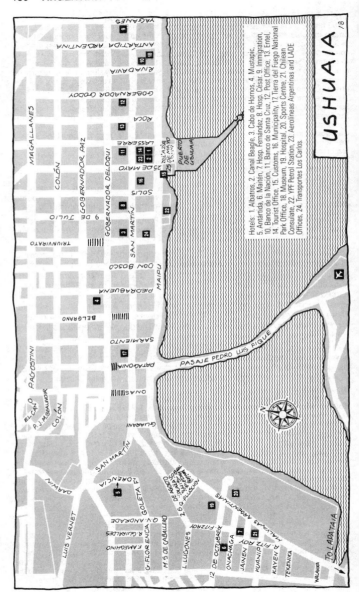

USHUAIA

Hotels: 1, Albatros, 2, Canal Beagle, 3, Cabo de Hornos, 4, Mustapic, 5, Antártida, 6, Maitén, 7, Hosp. Fernández, 8, Hosp. César, 9, Immigration, 10, Banco de la Nación, 11, Banco de Santa Cruz, 12, Post Office, 13, Entel, 14, Tourist Office, 15, Customs, 16, Municipality, 17, Tierra del Fuego National Park Office, 18, Museum, 19, Hospital, 20, Sports Centre, 21, Chilean Consulate, 22, YPF Petrol Station, 23, Aerolíneas Argentinas and LADE Offices, 24, Transportes Los Carlos.

D, good views. *Ushuaia Apartment Hotel* for self-catering visitors, very friendly. *Club Naval*, on hill 3 km. out of town, has begun taking visitors, D, restaurant. *Casa de Sra. Hilda Sánchez*, Deloqui 395, G p.p., triples only unless "matrimonial" requested, crowded but rec., clean, students and backpackers catered for; camping at the back, with use of facilities; cheap meals available, Sra. Marta Alanis, Magallanes 229, T 24150, E-D, good d and comfort; restaurant *Kayu* downstairs. Rooms, D, at home of Ismael Vargas (some way from centre), Kayen 394 (T 21125) Sra. Vargas speaks English; 25 de Mayo 345, near top of hill, E, rec.; *Albergue Ushuaia*, cheap and clean, ask at the bookshop at Piedrabuena y San Martín; *Kau Pen*, Piedrabuena 118 y San Martín, F, sheets extra, a travellers' meeting place, clean, warm, hot water, kitchen, but little privacy. *Hospedaje Turístico*. Deloqui 271, E with private bath, very clean, friendly, rec. *Cabaña* at Colón 631, sleeps up to 4, E p.p., modern, comfortable. There is no YHA in Ushuaia. Hostel for sporting groups only at Sports Complex. Lodging in Ushuaia has recently become rather a problem esp. Jan.-March., but even in winter hotels are very expensive. Enquire at Tourist Office for accommodation in private homes (they are said to have a list of 200), and for campsites, some of which are free. Many people go to the airport to offer rooms in private houses, in our E range.

36 km. from Ushuaia on the road to Río Grande is *Haruwen*, cabin accommodation, saunas, good restaurant, centre for cross country skiing in winter.

Camping None in town. After paying US$1 entrance fee to park, there are 4 camping sites to choose from, of which 3 are free, but have few or no facilities. The fourth is Camping Lago Roca, at Lapataia, by forested shore of Lake Roca in Parque Nacional, with facilities for car and tent, US$5, caters for travellers without car, hires horses, Dec.-March, including gas (18 km. from Ushuaia; weather can be bad). Can be reached by bus Jan.-Feb. Hot showers evenings, small shop, cafeteria. One free site is by restaurant, with no facilities, on road to Parque Nacional about 4 km. from Ushuaia at Cascadas de Río Pipo, and another, 2 km. from the Lake Roca campsite close to a beaver dam. The third free site is at Monte Susana, 10 km. W, Ensenada, 14 km. W, and Río Olivia, 12 km. E of Ushuaia. Tents for hire at Parque Nacional Tierra del Fuego, US$3 per night. Hot showers at Sports Centre on Malvinas Argentinas.

Restaurants *Los Canelos*, Maipú y 9 de Julio, excellent seafood, friendly, good value, rec., *Tante Elvira*, Av. San Martín 238 near Rumbo Sur, very poopular, make advance booking, good seafood; *Moustacchio*, San Martín y Godoy, sea food, expensive, warmly rec.; unnamed green, wooden restaurant at Maipú y Triunvirato, good centolla, rec.; *Asturias*, Triunvirato between San Martín and Maipú, pleasant, reasonable, open 1200-1500, 2030-2300. *Parillada* at San Martín 371 has good steaks but poor parillada; *ACA Grill*, good value and food. *Barcleit 1912*, Solis 148, cordon bleu cooking at reasonable prices. Best place to eat lamb is at *Tolkeyen*, Estancia Río Pipo, 5 km. from town, meal US$4-5, taxi US$2. Cheap and good food at restaurant above the sports gymnasium at Maipú and 12 de Octubre. *Blanco y Negro Importaciones*, delicatessen; *Tío Carlos*, Colón 756, good *Parrillada*; *Cafetería, pizzería Ideal*, San Martín 393 y Roca, popular with travellers. Also well rec. is *La Pasiva*, San Martín 1275, very good for pasta and milanesa. *Quick*, San Martín 130, clean, good service, inexpensive, rec.; *Der Garten*, Swiss *confitería*, San Martín 620, in Galería shopping arcade, rec. Excellent homemade chocolate sold at a shop at San Martín 785. *Panadería Primavera*, San Martín, good. The coffee bar at the airport is very expensive. Ask around for currently available centolla (king crab) and cholga (giant mussels). Food and drink (apart from the duty-free items) in Ushuaia are very expensive. Supermarkets: Surty Sur (with clean toilets, San Martín y Onas) and Sucoop, Paz 1600. Popular spots at night include *Yoppen* at Rivadavia 200 and the disco *Alexander* at 9 de Julio y Maipú.

N.B. Restaurants here and elsewhere on Tierra del Fuego do not begin to serve until 2100-2130 in summer; it is advisable to book in advance in the high season.

Shopping Many duty-free shops along main shopping street. Cheap cigarettes, perfume, clothing, drink and chocolates available. Prices said to be lower, and stocks better, than in Punta Arenas or Ciudad del Este (Paraguay). Good boots at Stella Maris, San Martín 443. Bookshop at San Martín y Sarmiento. Film is cheaper in Chile.

Car Hire Rent Austral, 25 de Mayo 130, T 22363; Rentacar, Antártida Argentina 75, T 22620, Avis, Maipú 329, T 23350 code 347; Autograd, Deloqui 368, T 23350 code 223; Aukiler, T 23424; Tagle, San Martín y Belgrano, good, also at airport, US$24/day plus US$0.18 per km., or US$60 inclusive (inc. insurance) for Fiat 147, 1300 cc.

Museum Museo Territorial, Maipú y Rivadavia, open Mon.-Sat. 1500-2030, US$0.60, small but interesting display of early photos and artefacts of the local Indian tribes; relics from the missionaries and first settlers, etc. Also known as the "museum at the end of the world". Highly recommended. Good bookshop in building. Also Post office in building, open afternoons when the main one is closed.

Exchange Banks are open mornings only in Ushuaia. Travellers' cheques can be changed at Banco del Sud (Roca 30), good rates. No cash advance on Visa card available. Tourist agencies give poor rates. Try also *El Globo Naranjo*, Av. San Martín, the desk by the tourist information office in *Hotel Albatros*, or *La Ponderosa* shop at Antártida Argentina 209, or other duty-free shops, or Caminante, Deloqui 368.

Laundromat Triunvirato 139, between San Martín and Deloqui, open weekdays 0900-2100.

Chilean Consulate Malvinas Argentinas 236, at corner of Jainen, Casilla 21, T 21279.

Tourist Office Av. San Martín 512 office 2 (T21423), friendly and helpful (will look after luggage while you trek). Large chart of hotels and prices and information on staying at Estancia Harberton, off road to Río Grande. Tourist Office at airport has information on hotels. National Park Office, on San Martín between Patagonia y Sarmiento, has small map but not much information.

Travel Agents All agencies charge the same fees for excursions. *Rumbo Sur*, San Martín 342, does 5 tours: 2 on land, 2 on water, 1 mixed (1000-1600, US$18, rec.), and organizes bus to ski slope, very helpful; *Antartur*, in *Hotel Cabo de Hornos*. Onas Tours, 25 de Mayo 50, just off main street, very friendly. *Tiempo Libre*, San Martín 154, T21296, recommended, English spoken. *Caminante*, Deloqui 368, organizes walking and climbing tours to suit all levels of experience, provides food, tents, equipment, outdoor clothing, detailed map, very friendly and helpful, English and German spoken, highly rec, T 22723. Recommended guides: Domingo Galussio, Intervú 15, Casa 211, 9410 Ushuaia, bilingual, not cheap (US$120); and Karl Renoth, Don Bosco 321, 2410 Ushuaia, T 22723, speaks English and German.

Buses run daily between Ushuaia and Río Grande (4 hrs.) at 0800 and 1200, also at 2400 on Sat. and Sun., US$13, Transporte Los Carlos, Triunvirato 57. Taxi to Río Grande about US$75. There are bus services between Río Grande (**see page** 184) and Porvenir in the Chilean part of the island (242 km., 6-8 hrs.) but no air connection.

Airport Aerolíneas Argentinas flights daily (twice, except Tues., and Sat.) from Buenos Aires all year round (change at Río Gallegos); flights also with Austral. (LADE office on Av. San Martín, Aerolíneas at Maipú y Lasserre, open Mon.-Fri. 0900-1200, 1500-1800). To Río Grande US$10 (LADE and AA), daily at 0900, and several afternoons at 1300-1400; to Calafate via Río Grande and Río Gallegos (book early) US$35, 4 a week at 0900, or US$25 with LADE to Trelew; to Comodoro Rivadavia, via Río Gallegos; to Río Gallegos, heavily booked (US$25, daily). To Bariloche, Tues. and Sun. at 0800, stops at Río Grande, Río Gallegos, Santa Cruz, San Julián, Puerto Deseado, Comodoro Rivadavia, Trelew and Esquel. To Buenos Aires, day flight US$90, night flight (Austral only) US$50 (booked up at least 5 days ahead). LADE flies every day: Ushuaia, Río Grande, Río Gallegos, Calafate (US$35), Gobernador Gregores, Perito Moreno (US$41), Comodoro Rivadavia; with small detour over complete glacier, weather permitting. Get window seat on left side.

Weather often impedes flights in winter, and in the summer tourist season it is sometimes difficult to get a flight out. Since Río Grande airport can take larger planes than Ushuaia (until the new airfield is built), it may be easier to get a flight to Río Grande and travel on from there. At the airport ask around for a pilot willing to take you on a 1/2 hr. flight around Ushuaia; US$20 for 2 people (best to go in p.m. when wind has dropped). Alternatively ask about flights at the tourist office. Taxi to airport, US$1, or 15 mins. walk (no bus).

New airport being built, but some say it won't be ready until 2000.

Sport Sports Centre on Malvinas Argentinas on W side of town (close to seafront). Ice skating rink at Ushuaia gymnasium in winter (when lagoon is frozen). Diving: write to Club de Actividades Subacuáticas for information about scuba diving in the Beagle Channel. Beachcombing can produce whale bones. Fishing: trout, contact Asociación de Caza y Pesca at Maipú and 9 de Julio, with small museum. Fishermen may be interested in visiting the fish hatchery 7 km. E of Ushuaia, visiting hours daily 1400-1700. There are brook, rainbow and brown trout and land-locked salmon. Take No. 1 bus E-bound on Maipú to the end of the line and continue 2 1/2 km. on foot to the hatchery. Birdwatchers will also find this ride rewarding. Skiing, hiking, climbing: contact Club Andino, Solís 50, or Caminante. Skiing: A downhill ski run (beginner standard) with chairlift (US$3), equipment rental (US$5.70), lessons and cafeteria is found on Cerro Martial. There is another ski run 3 km. from Ushuaia, open June-August, has lights for night-skiing and is run by Club Andino; bus leaves Rumbo Sur, San Martín 342, each hour for ski slope, US$1.50 return. The area is excellent for cross country skiing; Caminante organizes excursions "off road". 20 km. E of Ushuaia is Valle Tierra Mayoria, a large flat valley with high standard facilities for cross country skiing, snow shoeing and snowmobiling; rentals (US$7 the day) and a cafeteria; bus a.m. and 1400 from *Hotel Las Lengas*, US$3 return.

Excursions For **Lapataia** bay, take van from Solís 50, 4-6 times a day, about US$4 p.p. plus US$1 National Park fee; also good catamaran trips. Lake Escondido US$8, 50 km., 3-4 hrs., to *Petrel Inn*. There is a minibus (US$7 return) into the National Park, from Deloqui 368 at 1000 and 1500, returning 1100 and 1600 from restaurant car park at Lago Roca. There are excursions to the Martial glacier (itself unspectacular but fine scenery) about 7 km. behind the town; take road behind *Hotel Antártida*, 2 km. to small dam, then 3-4 hour walk along trail. There is a chairlift to the glacier (operating schedule unclear), US$3 round trip, but it follows a narrow valley which does not offer good views. (In winter the glacier is inaccessible, even on foot; a bus leaves every hour in summer from in front of Rumba Sur office to the chairlift, US$1.) Also to Lendegaia and Lapataia bays, the falls of the Olivia river. In winter the temperature drops to as low as -12°C, in summer it goes up to 25°C. Beaver inhabit the Parque Nacional near the Chilean border; one may see beaver dams and with much luck and patience the beavers themselves after dark, stand still and down-wind of them: their sense of smell and hearing are good, but not their eyesight. No maps of the Park are available and hiking can be interrupted by the Chilean border (you cannot, for instance, cross to climb Cerro Cóndor.)

At Lake Fagnano: *Hostería El Kaiken* (ACA) also bungalows, nice site, well-run facilities, cheap drinks, on a promontory 93 km. from Ushuaia, C including real bath. At Lake Escondido *El Petrel Inn*, 54 km. from Ushuaia, D (after a spectacular climb through Garibaldi Pass, on the road to Río Grande). Facilities at *Kaiken* and *Petrel* are open all year round. These inns are rec. for peace and quiet.

The old Route 3 circles close to the lake, but comes to a dead end at the hotel; it does not go over the pass. The newer Route 3 bypasses most of the lake. Even in the summer the climate can often be cold, damp and unpredictable. It is possible to hitch-hike, though with difficulty, as far as Lapataia; only tour buses go there. Rangers in the park are friendly and will sometimes put people up for a couple of days (as will police) and help with places to visit. A ranger truck leaves Ushuaia every weekday at 1300 and picks up hitch-hikers along the road. Park entrance US$1.

At the very end of the Park road are several posts covered with momentos left by travellers from all over the world.

Taxi to Park US$15. Los Carlos bus to Lake Fagnano, 2½ hrs., US$4.70, then from Lake to Río Grande 2 hrs., US$5. Tours also arranged to Lake Fagnano and aerial excursions over the Beagle Channel (with local flying club, hangar at airport, 3-5 seater planes, 30 mins. US$19), Lake Fagnano, Lapataia and Ushuaia Bay. To Lake Escondido/Fagnano US$24; bus to Puerto Almanza (on Beagle Channel), 75 km., 4-5 hrs., US$9. Rumbo Sur does a whole-day, trip by catamaran down the Beagle Channel to see wildlife, with return by bus, highly rec. (see above under **Travel Agents**). Caminante runs a one day excursion to the Parque Nacional, including trek, canoeing, *asado* lunch, US$30 inclusive. It also runs a bus to the national park at 1000, 1500 and 1900, returning 1100, 1600, 2000, US$6.

Off the road to Río Grande from Ushuaia is the Estancia Harberton, the oldest on the island, which now offers tours and tea, and where you can camp. It can only be reached by rented car from Ushuaia (not by boat as some brochures imply - they only go to the boat). Leave Ushuaia on Route 3, after 40 km. fork right on Route J, passing Lake Victoria, then 25 km. through forest before the open country around Haberton (85 km. in all). Some parts of the road are bad; tiring driving, 5 hrs. there and back.

Sea Trips Boat and bus 7 hr. tour to the Isla de Los Lobos y Pájaros along the Beagle Channel, US$36. Take food, on board it is overpriced. In summer, 3 hr. trips may be taken to see the sealions on Isla de Los Lobos, also to Les Eclaireurs lighthouse, the Bridges islands and Isla Redonda, where the Government is breeding guanacos. Ask at Rumbo Sur; the *Ana B* leaves 0930 daily, the *Angel B*, at 1500 daily. Interesting boat trips of 3 weeks' duration on the 2,346 ton *Lindblad Explorer* cost from US$4,600. The ship *Ethel B* (owner Vincente Padin, enquire at Don Bosco 56, T 22253) does trips up the Beagle Channel to the Chilean border.

To Puerto Williams, Chile, Onas Tours, 25 de Mayo, organizes trips on the *Barracuda*, US$35 p.p., take own lunch, post office and postcards available in Puerto Williams, immigration formalities dealt with on board. El Caminante, Deloqui 368, has also been recommended for trips to Puerto Williams.

Ultragas (Chile) runs a boat between Puerto Williams and Punta Arenas (departing midnight both ends 17 hours), making it possible to do a round trip Porvenir—Río Grande—Ushuaia—Puerto Williams—Punta Arenas. Buy ticket in Porvenir Tues. for early Wed. a.m. bus to Río Grande, arrives 1400; bus from there to Ushuaia arrives Thurs. allowing time to book ticket on Puerto Williams boat, leaves Sat. 0800 weather permitting. it has been reported that boat (*Barracuda*) to Puerto Williams from Ushuaia is unreliable, both because of weather and because it will not leave unless full; however, with more companies organizing trips this may improve. One alternative is to ask at the Club Náutico for trip in private launch (about US$90 p.p.).

Río Grande (40,000 people) 236 km. from Ushuaia, is a port in windy, dust-laden sheep-grazing and oil-bearing plains; the oil is refined at San Sebastián (with ACA motel, D) in the smallest and most southerly refinery in the world (service station open 0700-2300). The *frigorífico* plant in Río Grande is one of the largest in South America; so is the sheep-shearing shed. Accommodation is very difficult (especially if arriving at night); we hear that one can sleep in the hospital's emergency room, if it's not in use. ACA garage on sea-front has free hot showers for men, as has the gymnasium. Fill up with gasoline here.

Local Festivals   *Trout Festival*, 3rd Sunday in February; *Snow Festival*, 3rd Sunday in July; *Woodsman Festival*, 1st week of December.

Hotels   *Hospedaje Irmary*, Estrada 743, clean and pleasant, A, rec.; *Federico Ibarra*, Rosales and Fagnano, rec., good restaurant, B; *Villa*, San Martín 277, C, very warm; *Hospedaje Noal*, Rafael Obligado 557, D, clean, cosy, friendly, rec.; *Atlántida*, Av. Belgrano and Rosales, said to be best, always full; *Yaganes ACA*, Av. Belgrano 319, A, clean, comfortable, has a restaurant; *ACA Albergue*, on Luis Piedrabuena near Gymnasium, B, 4-bed rooms, very comfortable, central heating, hot showers, restaurant, US$10 a meal; *Miramar*, Belgrano and Mackinlay, E-D without bath, no breakfast, heated, hot water ("a plywood palace"); *Hospedaje Dany*, Moreno 781, E, heated, hot shower, clean; *Residencial Arboles*, Rivadavia 637, E, clean, heated, hot showers; *Motel Sur*, on beach, truckers' place, clean and cheap, being enlarged. *Residencial Las Lenguitas*, Piedrabuena 436, E, bathroom shared between 2 rooms, good value; ; *Residencial Rawson*, Estrada 750, E with bath, no singles, clean, rec.; *Pensión La Cabaña*, 9 de Julio 1025, E; *Tierra del Fuego*, Perito Moreno 98, F, basic, clean. *Pensión Río Bueno*, J. B. Alberdi 616, E, simple, clean and friendly, men only.

Youth Hostel, for males only, but apparently always filled by local workers.

Restaurants   *Las Malvinas*, reasonable; *Yaganes* (good for centolla) expensive; *Rotisería El Trébol*, Calle Belgrano, counter snacks; *Don Rico*, in ultra-modern building in centre, interesting; *Confitería Roca*, Roca 629, open all hours, reasonably priced food and bar; likewise *A Todas Horas* in same street. Good workmen's café, *Mary's*, Moyano 373. *Supermarket Sados* on San Martín, near 25 de Mayo. Smart place for a drink, *Paris*, Rosales 448.

Exchange   Import shops, e.g. Yehuín, San Martín y Rivadavia, Avepí on Belgrano. Try *Confitería Roca*, Roca 629. Tends to be difficult: if coming from Chile, buy australes there.

Car Hire   Rent-a-Car, Belgrano y Ameghino, T 22657.

Car mechanic   and VW dealer Viaval SRL, P. Moreno 927.

Tourist Information   at the Municipalidad, Mon.-Fri., on Calle Sebastián El Cano.

Airport   4 km. W of town. Río Grande-Buenos Aires flight (Aerolíneas Argentinas, several daily, 3 night flights weekly), 5 hours, stops at Río Gallegos and Comodoro Rivadavia (some also at Bahía Blanca). LADE to Buenos Aires, Wed. and Fri., many stops, always full; to Bariloche, 8 hrs. LADE flight Río Grande to Ushuaia, US$15.50 return, heavily booked (also Aerolíneas, US$10 one way). A bus Río Grande-Ushuaia also connects with the Aerolíneas night flight from Buenos Aires. To Río Gallegos, 40 mins. (book early in summer) and to Comodoro Rivadavia. To Calafate, stopping at Río Gallegos, US$38. Telephone LADE office (behind *Hotel Yaganes*) open Mon.-Fri., 0900-1200 and 1530-1900, 0700-1200 on Sat., T 308. Conversely, travel with Aeronaval (if you're lucky), mostly Hercules transports, for half the price—enquire at airport. "Rent-a-plane" at airport, US$25 an hour. No flights to Chile.

Buses   leave at 0600 Wed. and Sat. US$10 (Senkovic, San Martín 959, T 22345), for Porvenir, Chile (about 230 km.), no food or drink provided, no toilets, nor stops, for 6 hrs., always heavily booked but especially over Christmas/New Year period, meticulous passport and luggage control at San Sebastián (ACA motel, 144 km. before Porvenir). Ferry journey from Porvenir to Punta Arenas (2 hrs.) can be very rough and cold, US$2 p.p., US$33 per car. Bus from landing stage, Tres Puentes, into Punta Arenas (5 km.) necessary (US$0.85). Flight across Strait, US$20 each. Transportes Turicisne go to Porvenir, very crowded and filthy, avoid at all costs. Daily bus service at 1230 and 1930 except Thurs., 1230 only with Los Carlos, Estrada 568 to Ushuaia, 234 km., on an unpaved road, US$13, 4 hours, stopping at *Hosteria El Kaikén*, Lake Fagnano, for a drink. Don Carlos office is round corner from Senkovic bus terminal. Bus departs from Los Carlos office; arrive 15 mins early. In winter the bus leaves on Mon., Wed. and Fri. only (1830).

Excursion 11 km. N lies the Salesian mission and the regional museum housed in the original chapel and first parish church of Río Grande. Although the exhibits are not at all organized or classified, there is a great deal to see. There are Ona Indian materials, Salesian mission works, fossils, handicrafts and flora, fauna and mineral exhibits of the area. Just past the mission, on the right side of the road, is the old cemetery.

Isla de los Estados Robert T. Cook writes: "This long (75 km.) and guarded island lies east of Tierra del Fuego. Except for the caretakers of the lighthouse and an occasional scientist few people ever set foot on this cloud-shrouded reserve of Fuegian flora and fauna that no longer exist on the main island. During the 18th and 19th centuries hundreds of ships were wrecked or lost in the treacherous waters surrounding this island. Much gold, silver and relics await salvage." Information and tours from Rumbo Sur, San Martín 342, Ushuaia.

Argentina apparently has plans for tourist developments in ***Antarctica*** (accommodation at Marambio and Esperanza stations) and Argentina and Chile are planning a mountaineering camp about 600 km. from the South Pole.

INFORMATION FOR VISITORS

Documents Check visa requirements as they change frequently. In 1990, following the renewal of diplomatic relations between Argentina and the UK, British tourists were permitted once more to visit Argentina without a visa. Passports are not required by citizens of neighbouring countries who hold identity cards issued by their own Governments. No visa is necessary for US citizens and nationals of other Western Hemisphere countries (excluding Cuba), Western European countries (excluding Portugal), and Japan, who may stay for 3 months, a period which can be renewed for another 3 months at the National Directorate of Migration. For all others there are three forms of visa: a business "temporary" visa, a tourist visa, and a transit visa. Australians, New Zealanders and South Africans need visas. Tourist visas are usually valid for three months in Argentina and for any number of exits and entrances during that period. Visitors should carry passports at all times; backpackers are particular targets for thorough searches - just stay calm; it is illegal not to have identification handy. When crossing land frontiers, remember that though the migration and customs officials are generally friendly, helpful and efficient, the police at the control posts a little further into Argentina tend to be extremely bureaucratic in their approach.

Airport Tax US$10 for international flights, including to Uruguay, Chile, Brazil and Bolivia, but flights from Aeroparque to Montevideo are subject to US$3 tax (Punta del Este, US$10); US$1 for internal flights. When in transit from one international flight to another, you may be obliged to pass through immigration and customs, have your passport stamped and be made to pay an airport tax on departure. A 3% tax on the purchase of air tickets has been reported.

N.B. Do not send unaccompanied luggage to Argentina; it can take up to 3 days of form-filling to retrieve it from the airport. Paying overweight, though expensive, saves time.

How to reach Argentina
By Air from Europe Flights between London and Buenos Aires were resumed in January 1990, with British Airways and Aerolíneas Argentinas each flying the route twice a week (BA via Rio de Janeiro and São Paulo on Tues. and Sat.; AA on Wed. and Sun.). AA also fly to the following European destinations (with other carriers in parentheses): Amsterdam (once a week; KLM twice); Frankfurt (three a week, similarly Lufthansa); Madrid (5 a week, Iberia three times); Paris (and Air France, three a week each); Rome (three a week, also Alitalia, who also fly to

Milan); Zurich (twice, Swiss Air, three times and to Geneva once). Aeroflot flies Moscow, via Dakar, on Sunday.

From North America   Aerolíneas Argentinas fly from the following US destinations (with other carriers in brackets): Los Angeles (three times weekly, Ecuatoriana, Avianca); Miami (daily, Pan Am, Lan-Chile, American); New York (6 a week, Lan-Chile, Pan Am). AA and Canadian Air International fly from Toronto (the latter twice a week); AA and Lan-Chile fly once a week from Montreal.

Aerolíneas Argentinas fly from Sydney, Australia, via Auckland, New Zealand, on Wed. and Fri.; Qantas also fly from Sydney on the same days. On the outward flight from Argentina, AA stops at Río Gallegos, but it is difficult to board there in high season.

From Latin America   AA (5 times a week) and Líneas Aéreas Paraguayas (3) from Asunción; AA (2) and Avianca (3) from Bogotá; AA and Viasa from Caracas (twice each); Eucatoriana from Quito and Guayaquil, AA from the latter only; AA (twice) and LAB (once a week via Santa Cruz) from La Paz, but LAB has two other flights from Santa Cruz (one via Tarija), AA one other; from Lima, AA (3), AeroPerú (4) and Lan-Chile once; AA (3), Avianca (2) and Eucatoriana (1) from Mexico City; from Montevideo (apart from those given in the Buenos Aires section), AA, Pluna, Avianca, Varig, Cruzeiro do Sul and Iberia (frequent flights also to Punta del Este, with many more in holiday season); from Santiago, Chile, daily with AA and Lan-Chile and other Latin American, European and North American carriers on various days; from Panama City, AA once a week.

From Brazil, AA, Varig and Cruzeiro do Sul fly daily from Rio de Janeiro, AA and Cruzeiro do Sul daily from São Paulo; Cruzeiro stop over in Porto Alegre, AA also fly from Porto Alegre, via Montevideo.

NB   The abbreviation "AA" in this chapter refers to Aerolíneas Argentinas, not to the international code for American Airlines.

Customs   No duties are charged on clothing, personal effects, toilet necessities, etc. Cameras, typewriters, binoculars, radios and other things which a tourist normally carries are duty-free if they have been used and only one of each article is carried. This is also true of scientific and professional instruments for the personal use of the traveller. Travellers may only bring in new personal goods up to a value of US$150 (up to US$50 for tourists entering from neighbouring countries); the amount of duty varies per item and according to exchange rates. However, the Argentine authorities allow goods to the value of US$500 to be introduced duty-free by travellers arriving in Tierra del Fuego. There are red and green divisions at airport customs, but officials make no difference between them. All incoming baggage is normally inspected.

Two litres of alcoholic drinks, 400 cigarettes, 50 cigars and 5 kg. of foodstuffs are also allowed in duty-free; for tourists originating from neighbouring countries the respective quantities allowed are 1 litre, 200, 20 and 2 kg. You can buy duty-free goods *on arrival* at Ezeiza airport.

If having packages sent to Argentina, do not use the green customs label unless the contents are of real value and you expect to pay duty. For such things as books or samples use the white label if available.

Internal Air Services   are run by Aerolíneas Argentinas, Austral, Lapa (reliable turbo-prop services from Buenos Aires to Córdoba, Rosario, seaside resorts in Buenos Aires province and to Colonia, Uruguay, with bus connection to Montevideo), Cata (tubo-prop service from Buenos Aires to Bariloche and Iguazú), Aerolínea Federal Argentina and the army airline LADE (in Patagonia, highly rec.). (services in the north, from Tucumán to San Juan, Mendoza, Resistencia, Cordoba, Santa Fe, Posadas and Iguazú, Salta, Jujuy, Famosa and Tartagal). LADE flights are cheaper than the others, and there is a good extended schedule with new Fokker F-28 jets. **N.B.** LADE will not accept IATA MCOs. (Even though sometimes offices in various towns may tell you the flights are full, it is usually worth a try out at the airport.) The naval air passenger service, Aeronaval, carries paying civilian passengers, ⅓ cheaper than LADE. No firm schedule though; 2 flights a week between Ushuaia, Río Grande and Río Gallegos; once a week between Ushuaia and Buenos Aires. Aerolíneas and Austral have introduced a service of night flights, at fares 40-50% lower than the normal day tariff. Plan familiar tickets allow couples to travel with a 25% discount for the spouse. Children under 3 travel free. LADE also operates discount spouse (65%) and children (35%) tickets. If travelling by AA or Austral a long linear distance, e.g. Río Gallegos-Buenos Aires, but wishing to stop en route, cheaper to buy the long flight and pay extra (about US$2) for stopovers. **N.B.** All local flights are fully booked way in advance for travel in December. Don't lose your baggage ticket; you won't be able to collect your bags without it.

Visit Argentina Fare   Aerolíneas Argentinas sells four Visit Argentina tickets: four flight coupons costing US$199, six coupons costing US$249, eight coupons US$299 and ten coups costing US$349. All are valid for 30 days and must be purchased outside Argentina and in conjunction with an international flight ticket. Routing and dates must be booked when the coupons are issued, and any changes incur US$25 per alteration. One stop only is permitted per town, except for making a connection (maximum time allowed for awaiting connecting flight is 24 hrs.). If you wish to visit Tierra del Fuego and Lago Argentino it is better fly on the Visit Argentina pass to Río Grande or Ushuaia and travel around by bus or LADE from there than to stop off in Río Gallegos, fly to Ushuaia and thence back to Buenos Aires, which will use 3 coupons. If possible, plan radial routes from Buenos Aires. Children travel at a 50% discount, infants 10%. Domestic timetables are given in *Guía Argentina de Tráfico Aéreo* and *Guía Internacional de Tráfico*. It is unwise to set up too tight a schedule because of delays which may be caused by bad weather. Flights between Buenos Aires and Río Gallegos are often fully booked 2 to 3 weeks ahead, and there may be similar difficulties on the routes to Bariloche and Iguazú. It is advisable to have an "OK" status put on your flight coupons even if you are "wait- listed", to be sure of your seat. Reconfirmation at least 24 hours ahead of a flight is important and it is essential to make it at the point of departure. Extra charges are made for reconfirming LADE flights (useful in Santa Cruz and Tierra del Fuego) but they are not high.

Railways   A permit (Argenpass) to travel anywhere by the Argentine railways costs US$95 a month, and US$150 for two months. There is no connected railway system south of Bariloche and Esquel. A "Pase Americano" (Amerailpass—check if still available) which enables you to travel on Pullman coaches through Uruguay, Argentina, Brazil, Chile, Bolivia, Paraguay, without mileage limit is US$120 for 16 days, US$140 for 23 days, US$175 for 30 days, US$260 for 60 days, also available for 90 days (payable in US$ only) free carriage, 30 kg. (children ½ price) and obtainable at the Centro de Información de Ferrocarriles Argentinos (CIFA) in Galerías Pacífico, Florida 729, Buenos Aires, open Mon.-Fri. 0700-2100 Sat. 0700-1300, closed Sun.; also available in Mar. del Plata, Bariloche, Mendoza, Córdoba, Tucumán and Posadas. There is no great difference between 1st and tourist class in trains, but if uncrowded, you can sleep across 5 seats in the latter (3 + 2), and only 4 in 1st class. As a rule, tourist class is 40% cheaper than 1st class, Pullman 50% more than 1st. 25% discount for rail tickets for "jóvenes", aged 13-30, for senior citizens, newly-weds. and others. Note, when travelling in winter, that heating may be available only in sleepers and pullmans, not 1st or 2nd.

In 1990 it was proposed; for budgetary purposes, to terminate about 34 long distance rail services. Exact details were not known at the time of going to press, so rail travellers are advised to check in advance before planning a route.

N.B. Once out of Buenos Aires, train information is hard to come by, although we are informed that the CIFA has 328 agencies to book facilities for the named-train principal services from Buenos Aires. Stations have wall time-tables of complete schedules for their own line but no information for other systems. To avoid disappointments, make long-distance call to nearest station on the line you require—although this requires fluency in Spanish. The only general time-tables in circulation at present are those for named trains on the main lines to Mendoza, San Juan, Tucumán, Posadas, Córdoba, Mar. del Plata, Bariloche, Zapala and Corrientes, which are available from the information centre at Galerías Pacífico. The main services have been accelerated in recent years, but others remain slow and infrequent.

Motoring   For entering Argentina by automobile the *Carnet de passages en douanes* (*Libreta de aduana*, is not required. Tourists can bring their cars into Argentina temporarily under international documentation. No specific papers are usually required to bring a Brazilian registered car into Argentina. A British international driving licence is valid only if it is endorsed by the Automóvil Club Argentino (ACA), and if the holder has a visa. Most main roads are paved, if rather narrow (road maps are a good indication of quality), and roadside services are good. Road surface conditions vary once one leaves main towns: high speeds are quite possible on the dirt and gravel roads, as long as you have the essential guard for the windscreen. All motorists are required to carry 2 warning triangles, a fire-extinguisher, a rigid tow bar, a first aid kit, full car documentation together with international driving licence (for non-residents), and the handbrake must be fully operative. However, few checks are made in most of country, with the notable exceptions of roads into Rosario and Buenos Aires. You may not export fuel from Argentina, so use up fuel in spare jerry cans while you are in the country. Always fill up when you can in less developed areas like Chaco and Formosa as filling stations are infrequent. Diesel fuel "gas-oil" prices are about 60% of those for gasoline ("*nafta*"). Octane rating is as follows: regular gasoline 83 (US$0.35 per litre); super 93 (US$0.50).

To obtain documents for a resident (holder of resident visa, staying at least 6 months in the country) to take a car out of Argentina, you can go to ACA in Buenos Aires, which may take up to 4 working days, or you can ask for a list of other ACA offices that can undertake the work; take forms with you from Buenos Aires, and papers may be ready in 24 hours. You will need at least 1 passport-size photo, which you can have taken at ACA at a fair cost. If the car is not your own, you require a special form signed by the owner and witnessed by a notary public. **NB** Non-residents may buy a car in Argentina but are in no circumstances allowed to take it out of the country; it must be resold in Argentina, preferably in the province where it was purchased.

Sometimes one may not be allowed to reach a border if one does not intend to cross it, stopping e.g. 20 km. from the border.

Automóvil Club Argentino (ACA), Av. Libertador General San Martín 1850, 1st floor, 1425 Buenos Aires, T 802-6061, office on Florida above Harrod's, 2nd floor, has a travel document service, complete car service facilities, insurance facilities, road information, road charts (*hojas de ruta*-about US$1 each to members, if available) and maps (dated with the code letters in the bottom corner—road map of whole country, with service stations and *hosterías* shown, US$3.20 to non-members, and of each province), a hotel list, camping information, and a tourist guide book sold at a discount to its members and members of other recognized automobile clubs upon presentation of a membership card. (YPF, the state oil agency, also produces good maps for sale.) Members of other recognized automobile clubs can also, on presentation of membership cards, benefit from lower prices for their rooms and meals at ACA *hosterías*. The Club has service stations, some with parking garages, all over the country. The organization is efficient. Travellers do report, however, that if you are not a member of ACA you will not get any help when in trouble. ACA membership for 3 months costs US$40, which permits you to pay with Eurocard

(Argencard) for fuel at their Service stations, gives 20% discount on hotel rooms and maps, and discounts at associated hotels, and 10% discount on meals.

ACA accommodation comes in 4 basic types: *Motel*, *Hostería*, *Hotel*, and *Unidades Turísticas*, and they also organize campsites (see below). A *motel* may have as few as 3 rooms, and only one night's stay is permitted. *Hosterías* have very attractive buildings and are very friendly. *Hotels* are smarter and more impersonal. All have meal facilities of some kind. Anyone can get in touch with the organization to find out about accommodation or road conditions.

Hitch-hikers, as well as motorists, are recommended to contact the ACA for its wealth of information.

Touring Club Argentino, Esmeralda 605 and Tucumán 781 3rd floor, T 392-6742 has similar travel services but no service stations.

Maps The best road maps are those of the ACA (see above). Topographical maps are issued by the Instituto Geográfico Militar, Cabildo 381, Casilla 1426, Buenos Aires (reached by *Subte* D to Palermo, then train to Carranza, where IGM is one block from station).

Car Hire To rent a small car (for four plus luggage) costs about US$50 a day, including mileage, fuel and insurance. You must ensure that the renting agency gives you ownership papers of the vehicle, which have to be shown at police and military checks. At tourist centres such as Salta, Posadas, Bariloche or Mendoza it may be more economical to hire a taxi with driver, which includes the guide, the fuel, the insurance and the mechanic. Avis offers a good and efficient service with the possibility of complete insurance and unlimited mileage for rentals of 7 days or more, but you should prebook from abroad. No one-way fee if returned to another Avis office, but the car may not be taken out of the country. Other companies are given in the text.

Motorhomes US Motorhomes "Winnebago" is represented at Todotur, Av. de Mayo 1370-5th Floor, Room 92 (T 371552 or 380406) Buenos Aires. "Coachmen" Motorhome and "Pick-up" camper dealer at Av. Debenedetti 1285, (1871) Dock Sud, Avellaneda, Buenos Aires also represents Jensen, Wemac, Monogram, Peterson, Winegard, Monarch and Coleman (T 201-5289/6379). The best dealer for Motorhome equipment and repairs is Merello Hermanos S.R.L., Maipú 742, Vicente López, Prov. of Bs. As (T 795-3503/4335). Porta-Potti toilets are widely sold in Argentina, sometimes under a different name.

Buses The price of bus journeys is approximately US$2.50 per 100 km. Most bus companies give a 20% student discount, but persistence is required to prevail with an international student card; a YHA card is useful. The same discount may also be given to foreign, as well as Argentine, teachers and university professors but you must carry documentary proof of your employment. Express buses between cities are dearer than the *comunes*, but well worth the extra money for the fewer stops. When buying tickets at a bus office, don't assume you've been automatically alloted a seat: make sure you have one.

Hitch-hiking Argentina is on the whole a good country for this (especially in Dec.-March), though recent problems with robberies have made drivers cautious. Carry little foreign cash on you, because of frequent stoppages along the road. Don't rely on hitching absolutely, though; traffic can be sparse, especially at distances from the main towns, and in Patagonia out of season. It may be useful to carry a letter from your Consulate. Though they tend to be more reserved in manner than most Latin Americans, Argentines are generally friendly and helpful. Sirikit Bhagwanani, of Walchuil, Switzerland, says there are no problems at all for a reasonably careful woman on her own in Argentina.

Walking Information on trails in NW Argentina, the Lake District, Patagonia and Tierra del Fuego is given in *Backpacking in Chile and Argentina*, edited by Claire Hargreaves (Bradt Publications).

Camping is very popular in Argentina (except in Buenos Aires) and sites with services are being installed, as well as good free municipal and paying private campsites in most tourist centres. Many are closed off-season. Camping is now allowed at the side of major highways and in all national parks (except at Iguazú Falls), at no cost. Many ACA service stations have a site where one can camp, and in general service station owners are very friendly to campers. A list of camping sites is available from ACA (labelled for members, but should be easily available and from the main tourist office in Av. Santa Fe, Bs. As.); see Autoclub magazine. References to sites will be found in the text. ACA campsites offer discounts to members, and to holders of the International Driving Licence. There are few **Youth Hostels** (many open only February to March), but some towns offer free accommodation to young travellers in the holiday season, on floors of schools or church halls; some fire stations will let you sleep on the floor for free (sometimes men only). Many garages have showers that you can use. Good lightweight tents now available, e.g. Cacique. Regular (blue bottle) Camping Gaz International is available in Buenos Aires, at an electrical goods store on Av. 9 de Julio, near Teatro Colón, and Suntime, Lima 225, Guatemala 5908 (Palermo), Juramento 2452 (Belgrano) at América Pesca, Alfredo Pollini Alvear 1461.

Food National dishes are based in the main upon plentiful supplies of beef. Many dishes are distinctive and excellent; the *asado*, a roast cooked on an open fire or grill; *puchero*, a stew, very good indeed; *bife a caballo*, steak topped with a fried egg; the *carbonada* (onions, tomatoes, minced beef), particularly good in Buenos Aires; *churrasco*, a thick grilled steak; *parrillada*, a mixed grill, mainly roast meat, sausages (including *morcilla*, black pudding to the British, or blood sausage) and offal; and *humitas*, made with sweet corn, tasty but not strictly national. *Arroz con pollo* is a delicious combination of rice, chicken, eggs, vegetables and strong sauce. *Puchero de gallina* is chicken, sausage, maize, potatoes and squash cooked together. *Empanada* is a tasty meat pie, and *chorizo* a highly spiced sausage, though do not confuse this with *bife de chorizo*, which is a rump steak (*bife de lomo* is fillet steak). *Ñoquis* (gnocchi), potato dumplings normally served with meat and tomato sauce, are tasty and often the cheapest item on the menu. *Locro* is a thick stew made of maize, white beans, beef, sausages, pumpkin and herbs. Pizzas come in all sorts of exotic flavours, both savoury and sweet. Almost uniquely in Latin America, salads are quite safe. A popular sweet is *dulce de leche* (especially from Chascomús), milk and sugar evaporated to a pale, soft fudge. Other popular desserts are *almendrado* (ice-cream rolled in crushed almonds), *dulce de batata* (sweet potato preserve), *dulce de membrillo* (quince preserve), *dulce de zapallo* (pumpkin in syrup); these *dulces* are often eaten with cheese. *Postre Balcarce*, a cream and meringue cake and *alfajores*, maize-flour biscuits filled with *dulce de leche* or apricot jam, are also very popular. Sweets: the Havana brands have been particularly recommended. Excellent Italian-style ice-cream with exotic flavours. For local recipes (in Spanish) *Las Comidas de Mi Pueblo*, by Margarita Palacios, recommended.

Offices close for 2 to 2½ hours for lunch between 1200 and 1500. Around 1700, many people go to a *confitería* for tea, sandwiches and cakes. Dinner often begins at 2200 or 2230; it is, in the main, a repetition of lunch.

Drink Argentine wines (including champagnes, both charmat and champenoise) are sound throughout the price range. The ordinary *vinos corrientes* are wholesome and extremely cheap cost about US$3.50 a bottle in shops (US$8 in a restaurant—US$15-20 for a good wine); reds better than the whites. The local beers, mainly lager-type, are quite acceptable and cost about US$0.50 a litre in supermarkets. Hard liquor is relatively cheap, except for imported whisky, at about US$3 in shops for gin and vodka. Local liqueurs may be as cheap as US$0.70 a litre. *Clérico* is a white-wine *sangría* drunk in summer. Tap water in the main cities is safe, but often heavily chlorinated. It is usual to drink soda or mineral water at restaurants, and many Argentines mix it with their cheaper wine, with ice, as a refreshing drink in summer. *Yerba mate*, a very popular home-grown tea, is widely drunk, especially in the interior, continuing the old *gaucho* custom.

Best Buys Local leather goods in Buenos Aires, men's leather coats, US$200; suede, US$200-250 three-quarter-length coats are about US$130 and suede blousons about US$80; handbags and shoes (leather is much cheaper in Uruguay). *Ciudad del Cuero*, Florida 940, has clothing, footwear and luggage from 40 manufacturers. A gourd for drinking *yerba mate* and the silver *bombilla* which goes with it, perhaps a pair of *gaucho* trousers, the *bombachas*. Ponchos (red and black for men, all colours for women). *El Guasquero* in Calle Anasagasti specializes in old *gaucho* objects, saddlery, *bolas*, horn items, all genuine and reconditioned by Sr. Flores, the owner. The shop is N of Av. Santa Fe, near Calle Bulnes, Buenos Aires (postcode 2028). Articles of onyx, specially in Salta. Silver handicrafts. In Buenos Aires, there is a good, reasonable and helpful souvenir shop on Av. de Mayo near Chacabuco. Knitted woollens, especially in Bariloche and Mar. del Plata. If you like honey, the Casa de Miel has different honeys from every province. Try Mendoza or Tucumán varieties.

N.B. Never carry weapons, or drugs without prescriptions. The open season for fishing is between November and February or March. Enquire as to dates, so as to avoid carrying equipment unnecessarily, and remember that fishing anywhere requires a permit.

Health Argentina is in general a healthy country to visit, with good sanitary services. In some provinces, like Neuquén and Salta, medical assistance, including operations, X-ray and medication, is free in provincial hospitals, even for foreigners. All private clinics, on the other hand, charge. Smallpox vaccination no longer required to enter Argentina. If intending to visit the low-lying tropical areas, it is advisable to take precautions against malaria. **See page** 62. Chagas' disease (**see page** 35) is found in NW Argentina.

British Business Travellers are strongly advised to read "Hints to Exporters: Argentina", obtainable from Department of Trade, Export Services Division, Sanctuary Bldgs, 16-20 Great Smith Street, London SW1P 3DB. Similar information is provided for US citizens by the US Department of Commerce.

Clothing Shorts are not worn in city centres, though their use has become more common in residential suburbs in spring, summer and autumn, and in Buenos Aires in the hottest months. In general, dress tends to be formal (unless casual wear is specified on an invitation) in Buenos Aires and for evening outings to shows, etc. The general standard of dress among Argentines is very high: collar and tie, with jacket, are very much the standard for men, and women "should always err on the side of elegance"—David Mackintosh.

Hours of Business Banks, government offices, insurance offices and business houses are not open on Saturdays. *Government Offices*: 1230-1930 in the winter and 0730-1300 in summer. *Banks*: generally 1000-1600 but time varies according to the city, and sometimes according to the season. (See under names of cities in text.) *Post Offices*: 0800 to midnight for telegrams. Stamps on sale during working days 0800-2000 but 0800-1400 on Saturdays. *Shops* are open from about 0900 to 1900, though many close at midday on Saturdays. Outside the main cities many close for the daily afternoon siesta, reopening at about 1700. 24-hour opening is allowed except on Mondays; this applies mainly to restaurants, foodshops, barbers, newspaper shops, art, book and record stores.

Dance halls open at 2300 but don't fill up till after midnight; night clubs open after midnight. In city centre, cafés and restaurants are busy till after midnight and many evening events, such as lectures, may not start before 2200.

Holidays The main holiday period, generally to be avoided by business visitors, is January-March, though some areas, such as Tierra del Fuego, begin to fill up in November/December. Winter school holidays, in which travelling and hotels may be difficult, are the middle two weeks of July. No work may be done on the national holidays (1 May, 25 May, 20 June, 9 July, 17 August, 12 October and 25 December) with the exceptions specifically established by the legislation in force. There are no bus services on 1 May. On the non-working days (1 January, Holy Thursday and Good Friday, and 8 December) employers are left free to decide whether their employees should work, but banks and public offices are closed. Banks are also closed on 31 December. There are gaucho parades throughout Argentina, with traditional music, on the days leading up to the Día de la Tradición, 10 November. On 30

December (not 31 because so many offices in centre are closed) there is a ticker-tape tradition in downtown Buenos Aires: it snows paper and the crowds stuff passing cars and buses with long streamers.

Standard Time is 3 hours behind GMT; 2 hours behind October to March (check precise date of change)

Currency In mid-1985, a new currency was introduced, the *austral*, divided into 100 centavos, worth 1,000 of the existing pesos argentinos (themselves introduced as recently as mid-1983). Austral notes are being issued, but peso argentino notes not overprinted with austral denominations went out of circulation at end-March 1988. Notes in circulation: A50,000, A10,000, A5,000, A1,000, A500, A100, A50 (beware forgeries of these two from street money-changers), A 10, A 5, 5 and 1 centavo coins have been introduced to co-exist with 50, 10 and 5-peso argentino coins, and coins for up to 50 centavos bearing the austral sign (A with an extra crossbar) are being struck. There is an acute shortage of small change, and the different series of coins in circulation are very confusing. It is often difficult to change travellers' cheques, particularly in the smaller towns. Commissions can be as high as 6% and in general it takes a long time and many forms to transact these cheques. Other travellers have warned not to engage in unsolicited currency transactions in the streets, etc. as you may be tricked or land in prison. Some of the major towns have exchange shops (*casas de cambio*) and these are given in the text. There is a 3% tax on cheques and an extra commission which can be avoided if you go to a branch of the issuing bank, especially if changing small amounts. In December 1989, the exchange rate was freed and exchange controls were lifted, so there was no market rate from which travellers could benefit as opposed to the official exchange rate. This regime was in force at the time of going to press, but you are advised to check for changes at the time of your visit. Exchange rates are quoted in major newspaper daily. Money remitted to Argentina from abroad is normally paid out in australes. It is possible to obtain money from Europe through an express transfer, which takes 2-3 days, and the currency will be subject to tax.

Various Argentine provinces (Tucumán, Salta, Jujuy, La Rioja are examples) have issued *bonos* (bonds) which circulate at face value alongside the national currency. Two warnings: they are not accepted outside the province of issue; and they bear redemption dates, after which they are valueless. Beware!

When crossing a land frontier into Argentina, make sure you have some Argentine currency as there are normally no facilities at the border.

Credit Cards It is reported that American Express, Diners Club, Visa and Mastercard cards are all useful. All shops, hotels and places showing Argencard (head office, H.Yrigoyen, Buenos Aires) signs will accept Eurocard and Access, but you must state that these cards are affiliated to Mastercard. Argencard will not permit cash advances on these cards in outlying regions, and is itself very slow in advancing cash. The use of Mastercard/Access and Eurocard is very limited in the south.

Note that, in 1990, the use of both credit cards (for purchases) and travellers' cheques (for exchange) was increasingly restricted, so travellers had to rely heavily on hard currency.

Cost of living The cost of living for the foreigner travelling with dollars varies according to the currency exchange regime in force. If the currency is fixed against the dollar, Argentina becomes expensive; if the currency is free, the country should become cheaper. Travellers should therefore be prepared for unpredictable swings in prices and, for this reason, should only regard the prices given in this chapter as representative.

Value-Added Tax VAT is not levied on most medicines and some foodstuffs but on all other products and services 13%.

Weights and Measures The metric system is used.

Electric Current 220 volts, 50 cycles, A.C., European Continental-type plugs in old buildings, Australian 3-pin flat-type in the new. Adaptors can be purchased locally for either type (i.e. from new 3-pin to old 2-pin and vice-versa).

Postage and Telephone Rates The minimum rate for airmail is about US$0.30. Letters from Argentina take up to a month to get to the UK and x 3 the USA.

Small parcels only of 1 kg. at post offices; larger parcels from Encomiendes Internacionales, Centro Postal Internacional, Av. Antártida Argentina, near Retiro Station, Buenos Aires, and in main provincial cities, about US$40 or 5 kg. Larger parcels must first be examined, before final packing, by Customs, then wrapped (up to 2 kg., brown paper; over 2 kg. must be sewn in linen cloth), then sealed by Customs, then taken to Encomiendas Internacionales for posting. Cheap packing service available (US$3.50). Open between 1100 and 1700 on weekdays. Used clothes have to be fumigated before they will be accepted. Having parcels sent to Argentina incurs a customs tax of about US$3 per package.

The local telephone system is hopelessly overloaded. On weekdays, 2200-0800, there is a 20% reduction, and from Sat. midnight to 1200 Sun. and Christmas to New Year and Easter Week, international calls are 40% less. The normal rate for international calls is from US$2 to US$7.50 a minute, and for telex about US$1.00-1.75. Direct international telephone dialling is almost unknown in hotels and private homes. No reverse-charge calls to Australia or South Africa.

Press Buenos Aires dailies: *La Nación, La Prensa*. Tabloids: *Clarín, La Razón, Tiempo Argentino* Evening papers: *Crónica*. English language daily: *Buenos Aires Herald*. Magazines: *Siete Días, Gente, La Semana, Redacción, Mercado, El Gráfico* (sports). New daily, *Página Doce*, very popular among students and intellectuals. English language magazines: *The Review of the River Plate* (commercial, agricultural, political and economic comment), and *The Southern Cross* (Irish community).

Radio English language radio broadcasts can be heard daily on short wave: 0100-0130 on 6060 KHz 49m, 0230-0300 on 11710 KHz 25m, 0430-0500 and 2230-2300 on 15345 KHz 19m; Radiodifusión Argentina al Exterior, Casilla de Correo 555, Arg 1000, Buenos Aires. This is a government station and broadcasts also in Japanese, Arabic, German, French, Italian and Portuguese. Broadcasts by foreign radio stations (including the BBC) are receivable on short wave.

Language Spanish, with variant words and pronunciation. English comes second; French and Italian (especially in Patagonia) may be useful.

The chief variant pronunciations are the replacement of the "ll" and "Y" sounds by a soft "j" sound, as in "azure" (though note that this is not done in Mendoza), the omission of the "d" sound in words ending in "-ado", the omission of final "s" sounds, the pronunciation of "s" before a consonant as a Scottish or German "ch", and the substitution in the north and west of the normal rolled "r" sound by a hybrid "rj". In grammar the Spanish "tú" is replaced by "vos" and the second person singular conjugation of verbs has the accent on the last syllable e.g. *vos tenés, podés*, etc.

We wish to offer our profound thanks to Janet Krengel of Lloyds Bank Group Economics Department for doing the updating. We also wish to thank the following residents and travellers : Rop Bomer and Wilhelmien Tar Haar (Mexico DF), Tom Brandt (Buenos Aires), Wendy Chilcott and Steve Newman (Watford) for a very useful contribution, Jorge Antolín Solache (El Calafate), Tam Agosti-Gisler (Anchorage, Alaska), Martin Anderle, Susanne Riller and Tilo Timmermann (Fürth, W. Ger.), Rick Ansell and Paulette Milego (Porto Alegre) for a very useful contribution, Vladimir Antonowych (Toronto), Haz Arad, Lucie Armstrong (Ithaca, NY), Hans and Verónica Liechti-Avaneda (Santiago de Chile), Eberhard Baer (Koeningsbrunn, W. Ger.), Maarten Beeris (San Pedro de Atacama), Hans and Lena Bengtsson (Gothenburg, Swe.), Lisbet Bengtsson (Gothenburg, Swe.), Momik Bernaerts (Amsterdam) and Thomas Hartmann (Copenhagen), R. Billman (Stockholm), Fearon and Richard Blair (Kamloops BC, Canada), O. Blane, Astrid Bombosch (Heidelberg), Aad Bol (Poelijk, Neth.) and Trish Clements (Faullconbridge, Australia), Marcela M. Bonilla (Bogotá), Jens Borchers (Herzberg/Harz, W. Ger.) and Michael Frantz (Sieber, W. Ger.), Dorothea Bornholdt (Lutzhorn, W. Ger.), Alex Brand (Heidelberg 1), Kirsten Bruun and Jesper Juel Rasmussen (Copenhagen), Felicity and Charles Buchan (Fraserburgh), Daniel Buck and Anne Meadows (Washington DC), David M. Butler (Belmont, Victoria), Jan Camps and Silvia Bogdanski (Leiden, Neth. and Mönchengladbach, W. Ger.), Ken Chitty (Rochester, Kent) for a very useful contribution, Tage Christensen and Palle Kangstad (Århus, DMK.), Jim Cilek (Twin Falls, ID), Lucinda Coates (North Ryde, NSW), Andrew Cresswe.ll (Worcester), Jörg Cusker (Ushuaia), Daniel Darwish (Oxford),

Louis-François Debêtaz (Concise, Switz.), Patrick Debergh (Cressier, Switz.), Jorge Carlos Dejean (Salta), Janet Dickinson (San Martín de los Andes), Albert Dietschi (Sunnyside, NY), Rolf Ditsch (Steinbach, W. Ger.), Bill Dixon (Flitwick, Beds.), Larry Dolan (Helena, MT), Hermien Don (Amsterdam), C. Dragonat (Stuttgart 75), Rosetta Drioli, Joy Jarvis, Dorothy Mitchell and Anneli Soininen (Waverton, NSW), Frank Dux (Detmold 18, W. Ger.), Jennifer Eberle (Westwood, NJ), John Edmonds (Harpenden, Herts), Paula Egli (Wallenwil, Switz.), Dag K. Ellingsen (Oslo 2), Fred and Marianne Emery (London SE26), David K. Erdin (Gansingen, Switz.), Sheila and Dennis Fabricant and Matt Linn, Men Färber (Dübendorf, Switz.), Alexandra Fisher (London W8), Bruce Fitzwater (Portland, OR), Margaret Fleming (Karlsfeld, W. Ger.), Harry Floyd (London W8), Olivier and Paloma Foro (St-Moritz), Paul Forte (London NW1), D. Friend (Melbourne), John N. Fugelso (Durham N. C.), Roman Füglister (Alpnach Dorf, Switz.), Anita Gee and Ian Boonin (Ilford), Theodor A. Gevert (Barueri, SP, Brazil), Gustavo Giorgis (Ushuaia), Rod Glaubitz (Köln 91), Martin Gorst (London W13), Tony Gowers (Bristol), M. De Graaf (Hilvarenbeek), Tamar Grossman (Montreal), Jon and Julia Gruffydd (Lima) Christian Gurney (Thornhill, Ont.), Simon Gustafson (Taby, Swe.), Monika Gwerder (Muotathal, Switz.), Jim Hardy (Waukesha, Wis.), Roy and Joan Harris (Nanaimo, BC), Wayne Harvey (South Australia), Kevin Healey (Melbourne, Vic.), Dr Paul Heaton (London NW6), Judith and Stephen Adler Hellman (Toronto), David W. Heumann (Los Angeles, CA), Ursula Hochuli (Switz.) and Vincent Choblet (Paris), Thomas Hodel and Elsbeth Flükiger (Kaufdorf, Switz.), Mary Hodgson (Sydney, NSW), Jorge Hopff (Rio de Janeiro), Rosemary J. Hughes (Ormskirk), María Iglesias (Dirrección de Turismo Territorial, Ushuaia), Jeff Inglis (Seattle), Volkmar E. Janicke (München 40), Simon Jeffreys (Peterborough), Ursula Jenny (Bottmingen, Switz.), Allan Jensen and Vibeke Nageh (Munke-Bjergby, Dnmk.), Tobias Kämpf (Rupperswil, Switz.), Bill Kauffman (Sydney, NSW), Rosi Kerler (München 40), Marcel Kersten (Roosendaal, Neth.), Federico Kirbus (Buenos Aires), Peter Kocan (Summit, NJ), Carsten Kolbe (Marburg, W. Ger.), Justin Koprowski (High Wycombe), Lucy, Ian and Laura Krause (Newcastle-upon-Tyne), Philip Krippendorff and Matthias Bertsch (Marburg), Juan C. Kühl (Salta), Antony and Elisabeth Lancaster (Lima 18), Marie-Anne Lejen (Switz.), Jo Lerner (Grimbergen, Belg.), Herbert S. Levi (Buenos Aires), John Lewis (London NW2), Udo Lichtenthäler (Berlin 21), Mika Määttänen (Tampere, Fin.), Susan MacCallum and Peter Hedvlin (Sydney, Aust.), Raphael Marti, René Luthi and Raymond Burri (Bern), Nelly Matthey (Lausanne), Brigit McCarthy (Rome), Dean McCauley (San Francisco, CA), David McDonnell (London N13), A. Mckenzie Brockman (Deux-Montagnes, Quebec), Sarita McLuskie (Great Missenden), Barbara Meier and Thomas Ester (Essen 15, W. Ger.), Karssen Mengel and Birgit Borkholm Nielsen (Langeskov, Dmk.), Valerie and Bob Mitchell (Cottesloe, Western Australia), Daniel Morgan (Wellington, NZ), Regina Moser and Jürg Bächli (Mutschellen, Switz.), Dimitri Moursellas (Manhattan Beach, Ca), Richard Müller (Gümligen, Switz.), Hallam Murray (London SW11), David, Christine, Philip and Catherine Mylan (Worksop) for a very useful contribution, Ruth Nebiker (Diegten) and Martin Bachmann (Riehen, Switz.), Dr Hannes Neuhauser (München 70), Stephen Newcomer (Centrevill, Iowa), Jonas Noreús (Varberg, Swe.), Claus Nøgaard and Bitten Pedersen (Silkeborg, Dmk.), Bryan F. O'Leary (Redondo Beach, CA), Justine O'Keefe and David Couper (N Z), Shawn and Jeff Olsen (St Paul, Minnesota), Ingrid Østergaard (Vestervig, Dnmk.), Karin Ottiger (Ottikon, Switz.), Ruth Owen (Lima 4), Lucy Paine and William Petrie (Watlington, Oxon.), Mark Pangbourne (Hastings), Dave and Laurie Parker (Pedro Juan Caballero), Dirk Partridge (Fredericton, NB, Canada), Angus Pelham Burn (Banchory, Kincardineshire), Barry M. Pell and Judith L. Katz (Brookline, MA), Jeff Perk (Carbondale, IL), Jérôme De Perlinghi and Rosa Gobien (Brussels), Wulf Peters (Querenhurst, W. Ger.), Sandrine Pétremand and Gilles Maitre (Bevaix, Switz.), Ortrun Poettering (Rio de Janeiro), Louis Prefontaine (St Malo, Manitoba), Antonio Righetti and Daniela Wenger (Bern), Marvin and Pat Rosen (New York), Richard Rosenberg (New York), Yves Rougeaux (Montreuil, France), Richard and Yvonne Ruming (Bathurst, NSW), Silvia Salzmann (Mettmenhasli), R.O. Sanchez, Louise Santamera (Liverpool 3), Rick and Su Sareen (Thailand), Piero Scaruffi (Redwood City, CA), Thomas Schemmel (Bonn 1), Kathrin Schildknecht and Jürg Schmutz (Bern, Switz.), Ueli Schlatter (Hemmental, Switz.), Andrea Schneiber (Herborn, W. Ger.), Jolanda Schneider (Malans, Switz.), Rolf Schneider (Effretikon, Switz.), Karen Schulpzand and Rudy Cruysbergs (Dilbeek, Belgium), von Schubert (Kehl, W. Ger.), Daniel Schweimler and Claudia Ricca (London E7), Vivienne Shave (Truro), Bette Smith and James Amidon (Winter Park, CO), David Sosa and Alison Boegehold, John Spraos (London NW11), Hans, Helen, Florian and Simon Sprecher (Chavos, Switz.), Nikita Stampa and Christian Rousseau (Brussels), Jochen Steuer (Brüttisellen, Switz.), Hans and Ina Stoffregen (Celle, W. Ger.), Hal Stufft and Dorothy Young (Imler, PA/Evesham), Joseph Syfrig (Riehen, Switz.), Thomas Thanner (München 40), Dominik Thumfart (Vienna), Nicholas Tongue and Uta Rössler (Brussels), Trevor Toone (Burnaby, BC, Canada), Scott Tremaine (Toronto), Douglas B. Trent (Focus Tours, Belo Horizonte), Karen Uemura (Hollister, CA), T.C. Walker (Chobham,

Sy.), William Walker (Washington DC), Patrick Wallerand (Liège, Belg.), Anne H. Walton (US Embassy, Buenos Aires), Ingrid Walter and Norbert Eisinger (Schnelldorf, W. Ger.), Ignaz Wanders (Haarlem), Roland Weitkamp (Braunschweig, W. Ger.), Regina Wetzer and Richard C. Brusca (San Diego, Ca), Urs Wigger (Menznau, Switz.) and Helmut Zettl (Ebergassing, Austria).

BOLIVIA

INTRODUCTION

BOLIVIA, straddling the Andes, is a land of gaunt mountains, cold desolate plateaux and developing semi-tropical and fertile lowlands. Its area of about 1,098,580 square kilometres makes it twice the size of Spain. It is land-locked, with Chile and Peru to the W, Brazil to N and E, and Argentina and Paraguay to the S.

The Andean range is at its widest—some 650 km.—in Bolivia. The Western Cordillera, which separates Bolivia from Chile, has high peaks of between 5,800 and 6,500 metres and a number of active volcanoes along its crest. The passes across it are above 4,000 metres. To the E of this range lies the bleak, treeless, windswept Altiplano, much of it 4,000 metres above sea-level. It has an average width of 140 km., is 840 km. long, and covers an area (in Bolivia) of 102,300 square km., or nearly 10% of the country. Its surface is by no means flat, for the Western Cordillera sends spurs into it which tend to divide it into basins. The more fertile northern part is the more inhabited; the southern part is parched desert and almost unoccupied, save for a mining town here and there. Nearly 70% of the population lives on it, for it contains most of the major cities; almost half of the people are urban dwellers.

Lake Titicaca, at the northern end of the Altiplano, is an inland sea of 8,965 square km. at 3,810 metres: the highest navigable water in the world. Its maximum length and breadth are 171 and 64 km., and the greatest known depth is 280 metres. There are large annual variations between high and low water levels; 95% of the water flowing into it is lost by evaporation, making it more salty than most freshwater lakes. The immense depth of the water keeps the lake at an even all-the-year-around temperature of 10°C, and modifies the extremes of winter and night temperatures on the surrounding land. There is therefore a large farming population of Indians in this basin, tilling the fields and the hill terraces and tending their sheep and llamas.

The Altiplano is a harsh, strange land, a dreary grey solitude except for the bursts of green after rain. The air is unbelievably clear—the whole plateau is a bowl of luminous light. A cold wind blows frequently in the afternoons, causing dust storms. During the winter temperatures fall below freezing point; there is frost every night in July and August, but during the day the tropical sun raises temperatures over 20°C.

The animals of the Altiplano are fascinating. Llamas serve as pack animals—they carry up to 22 kg. loads up to 20 km. a day and yield about 2½kg. of wool when sheared at intervals of from two to five years. The alpaca, bred not for work but for wool, belongs to the same group; the two may be distinguished by differences in the texture of their coats and shape of their tails. The vicuña, chinchilla and red fox are the main wild animals. The vicuña, an untamed smaller member of the family to which the llama and the alpaca belong, is found, though in diminishing numbers, on the bleak pampas. It may not be hunted, but its fine silky, tawny coloured wool may be sold.

Agriculture in the Altiplano is also interesting: the potato and the oca (another tuber), eaten in the dehydrated form of *chuño* and *tunta*, are the main crops. *Quinoa*, a kind of millet, and *cañava*, a smaller and darker grain, are the main cereals; both are extremely nutritious. *Chicha*, the national intoxicant, is brewed from maize (corn). Edible fish (small *boga*, large white-fleshed *pejerrey* and rainbow and salmon trout—Lake Titicaca has been stocked with the last two) are widely sold in the towns of the Altiplano.

Far more important to the economy of the Altiplano than agriculture is mining. 210 km. S of La Paz along the passageway at the base of the Eastern Cordillera is Oruro, where a low belt of hills supplies tin, copper, silver and tungsten. The Spaniards of Peru discovered the Cerro Rico in 1545. It is a mountain rising out of the Puna to a height of 4,780 metres, and was almost a solid mass of ore containing tin, silver, bismuth and tungsten. The Spaniards, interested only in silver, built Potosí at its base, 4,065 metres above sea level. The city grew till it had a population of 150,000, but rapidly dwindled after the richest deposits had been worked out. It remained a dead town till demand for tin rose early this century.

The presence of tin also accounts for the mining communities in the Cordillera to the SE of Oruro: the ex-Patiño mines at Catavi, to which there is a branch railway from Oruro, produce nearly half the tin of Bolivia. The high cost of producing Bolivian tin was a major contributor to the industry's decline in 1986, when the world tin market collapsed. Silver is still mined or extracted from the tailings left by past generations, and variable amounts of lead, bismuth, antimony, tungsten and zinc from pockets in the Cordillera are exported. Large deposits of silver have been found south of the Altiplano, near Lípez, and mines are being reopened, and their tailings reprocessed, two centuries after the Spaniards abandoned them.

Recommended reading: *We Eat the Mines and the Mines Eat* Us by June Nash, New York, 1979, and *The Potosí Mita* 1573-1700 by Jeffery Cole, Stanford University Press, 1985.

From the Altiplano rises, to the E, the sharp façade of the Eastern Cordillera. As luck would have it there is a gently graded passageway along the plateau at the foot of the Eastern Cordillera from Lake Titicaca in the N, to the Argentine frontier, in the S. From Viacha, near La Paz, the main line of the Bolivian railways runs along this passageway to Villazón, with connections to Chile (from Uyuni) and Buenos Aires. The giant masses of the northern parts of the Eastern Cordillera rise to very great heights in the Cordillera Real to the east of Lake Titicaca: four peaks soar to above 6,000 metres. This magnificent sight can be seen on a clear day from the top of a ridge on the more southerly Titicaca-La Paz road, which goes past Tiahuanaco. Their far sides fall away to the NE, very sharply, towards the Amazon basin.

These heavily forested north-eastern slopes are deeply indented by the fertile valleys of the Nor Yungas and Sud Yungas, drained by the Río Beni and its tributaries, where cacao, coffee, sugar, coca and tropical fruits are grown. The problem of transport to the consuming centre of La Paz is formidable: the connecting all-weather road, hair-raising in places, climbs 3,430 metres in 80 km. to surmount La Cumbre pass, at 4,725 metres within 24 km. of La Paz.

From a point just N of Cochabamba to the S the Eastern Cordillera is tilted, not to the NE, but to the E. This part of the Eastern Cordillera rises abruptly in sharp escarpments from the Altiplano, and then flattens out to an easy slope eastwards to the plains: an area known as the Puna. The streams which flow across the Puna are tributaries of the Río Grande flowing NE to the basin of the Amazon, and of the Pilcomayo flowing SE through the Chaco to the River Plate system. They cut increasingly deep incisions as they gather volume until, to the E, the Puna is eroded to little more than a high remnant between the river valleys. These valleys deeply incising the surface of the eastern-sloping Puna are densely inhabited; a variety of grain crops and fruits is grown. All these semi-tropical mountain valleys are known as Yungas: the generic name is not confined to the valleys of the Provinces of Nor and Sud Yungas to the E of La Paz. Rainfall in the Yungas is from 700 to 800 mm. a year, as opposed to the 400 to 700 mm. of the northern Altiplano and much less further S. The heaviest rain is during December, January and February. The mean average temperature is between 16° and 18°C, but in spite of a high humidity the Yungas are not unhealthy. Chulumani in the Sud Yungas and Coroico in the Nor Yungas are popular resorts.

Typical valleys are the very fertile basins in which Cochabamba, Sucre, and Tarija lie. These send food and cattle to the towns of the Altiplano, but other valleys have no way of doing so. The basins and long ribbons of valley farmland are isolated, and transport to the areas where they might sell their produce is only now being developed.

The lowland tropics, stretching from the foothills of the Eastern Cordillera to the frontiers with Brazil to the NE and E and with Paraguay and Argentina to the SE and S, take up 70% of the total area of Bolivia, but contain only about 20% of its population. Rainfall is high but seasonal, and large stretches suffer from alternate flooding and drought. The climate is hot, ranging from 23° to 25°C in the S and to 27°C in the N. Occasional cold dust-laden winds from the S—the *surazos*—lower the temperature considerably. In the N and E the Oriente has dense tropical forest. Open plains covered with rough pasture, swamp and scrub occupy the centre. Towards the end of the 18th century this was a populous land of plenty; for 150 years Jesuit missionaries had controlled the area and guided it into a prosperous security. A symbol of their great effort is the cathedral at San José de Chiquitos: a gem of elegance and dignity. But the Jesuits were expelled in 1767; years of maladministration, spoliation and corruption reduced the area to lethargy.

This once rich land, drained by the Madre de Dios, Beni and Mamoré rivers into the Madeira, a tributary of the Amazon, has been isolated from the rest of the country. It is as difficult to get at from the E as from the W, for there are rapids and falls in the Madeira which limit navigation. In its heart lie the seasonally inundated tropical Llanos de Mojos, ringed in by rain forest or semi-deciduous tropical forest—230,000 square km. with only 120,000 people. Roads and river connections are still being improved; there are roads between La Paz and Trinidad, Santa Cruz and Trinidad, and Cochabamba and Todos Santos and Puerto Villarroel. Meat is already brought in from Trinidad, capital of Beni Department, and from airstrips in the area, to the urban centres of La Paz, Oruro, and Cochabamba.

The forests and plains beyond the Eastern Cordillera sweep S towards the Pilcomayo River, getting progressively less rain and merging into a comparatively dry southern land of scrub forest and arid savanna. The main city of this area is Santa Cruz de la Sierra, founded in the 16th century, now the second city of Bolivia and a large agricultural centre. Here conditions favour the growing of sugar-cane, rice, oil plants and citrus fruit. The plains to the E are mainly used as grazing lands with small areas under cultivation, but in this area are extensive oil, gas, and iron-ore deposits, possibly Bolivia's greatest asset when developed.

Climate There are four distinct climatic zones: (1) The tropical departments of Santa Cruz and Beni, drained by the Amazon; altitude between 150 and 750 metres; average temperature, 29°C. (2) The Yungas, or low valleys, north of La Paz and Cochabamba, among the spurs of the Cordillera; altitude, 750-1,500 metres; average temperature, 24°C. (3) The Valles, or high valleys and basins gouged out by the rivers of the Puna; average temperature, 19°C. (4) The Puna and Altiplano; average temperature, 10°C, but above 4,000 metres may get down to -25°C at night in June-August (don't forget antifreeze). Little rain falls upon the western plateaux between May and November, but the rest of the year is wet. There is rain at all seasons in the eastern part of the country, and heavy rain from November to March.

History At Tiahuanaco (Tiwanaku), near Lake Titicaca, stand the impressive remains of a pre-Inca civilization. The Aymará-speaking Indians in this area emerged around 1000 BC into a civilization characterized by massive stone buildings and monuments, exquisite textiles, pottery and metalwork. This phase seems to have been ended abruptly by some unexplained calamity, which greatly reduced the size of Lake Titicaca, around AD 900. When the Quechua-speaking Incas of Cuzco conquered the area around AD 1200, they found the Aymarás at Tiahuanaco living among ruins they could no longer explain. The Aymarás resisted obstinately and were not finally conquered until the latter part of the 15th century under the reign of Inca Túpac Yupangi (1471-93). Even so, they kept their traditional social structures and language, and fought for the Incas under their own leaders. Only religion was formally imposed by the Incas.

Francisco Pizarro landed in Peru in 1532. Six years later Spain conquered Bolivia, and the next year Sucre (then Charcas), still the official capital, was founded. By 1559 Bolivia had become the *audiencia* of Charcas, in the Viceroyalty of Peru, for it had become extremely important for the Spaniards after the discovery of the silver mountain at Potosí in 1545.

The excellent Inca communications and economic organization fell into ruin. Revolutionary movements against the colonial rule of the Spaniards began early; there were revolts at La Paz in 1661, at Cochabamba in 1730 and at Sucre, Cochabamba, Oruro and La Paz from 1776 to 1780. In 1809 the University of San Francisco Xavier, at Sucre, called for the independence of all Spain's American colonies. Finally, on December 9, 1824, Bolívar's general, Sucre, won the decisive battle of Ayacucho in Peru and invaded what is now Bolivia, defeating the Spaniards finally at the battle of Tumusla on April 2, 1825.

On February 9, 1825, when he first entered La Paz, Sucre had already promulgated the decree of independence, but his second in command, Santa Cruz, was for retaining links with Peru; Bolívar was in two minds. Sucre had his way and Bolivia was declared independent. On August 25, 1825, Bolívar named the new country after himself. In 1828, when Sucre left the country, Santa Cruz became President; pursuing his dream of amalgamation he proclaimed a Peruvian-Bolivian confederation in 1836, but Chile and Argentina intervened, and in 1839 Santa Cruz was overthrown and the confederation dissolved.

Since its independence, Bolivia has suffered a grievous contraction of its territory. In the War of the Pacific (1879-1883) Bolivia in alliance with Peru fought the Chileans for the right to retain the nitrate-rich Atacama desert. After a year the Bolivians withdrew and Chile took over the desert and the port of Antofagasta, though it later compensated by building Bolivia the railway between Arica and La Paz. Railways traded for valuable territory has been Bolivia's fate. A railway to Yacuiba was Argentina's return for annexing some of the Chaco. When

Brazil annexed the rich Acre Territory in 1903, Bolivia was compensated by yet another railway, but this Madeira-Mamoré line never reached its destination, Riberalta, and proved of little use; it was closed in 1972. A fourth railway, completed in the 1950s, connects Santa Cruz in East-Central Bolivia with Corumbá in Brazil.

There was not even an unbuilt railway to compensate Bolivia for its next loss. Constant disputes between Bolivia and Paraguay over the Chaco led to open warfare between 1928 and 1930, and again between 1933 and 1935. In 1938, by arbitration, Bolivia ceded to Paraguay three-quarters of the Chaco, but obtained a doubtfully valuable outlet to the Río Paraguay. Bolivia's failure to occupy its empty spaces is partly the explanation for these losses.

The moral results of this last defeat had revolutionary consequences. After over fifteen years of disorder, Víctor Paz Estenssoro was elected to the presidency in 1951 on a left-nationalist ticket. A military junta intervened, but in April 1952 a popular revolution overthrew it: Paz Estenssoro returned as president. His government committed itself to a profound social revolution, introducing the expropriation and the nationalization of the tin mines; universal suffrage without literacy or income qualifications; and a policy of land reform and redistribution of the large estates. Hernán Siles Zuazo, a revolutionary leader and vice president under Paz from 1952-56, was president from 1956-60. During his term the economy was stabilized. Paz Estenssoro was again elected president from 1960-64, but shortly after beginning a third term was overthrown in 1964 by General Barrientos, killed in an air crash in 1969. After three ephemeral governments, power was taken in August 1971 by a right-wing general, Hugo Banzer Suárez, who after seven years' rule called for elections in July 1978. Then came another sequence of short-lived military governments, despite disallowed elections which gave victories to ex-President Hernán Siles Zuazo. In August 1982 the military returned to barracks and Dr. Siles Zuazo assumed the Presidency in a leftist coalition government with support from the communists and trade unions. Under this regime inflation spiralled out of control. The elections of July 14, 1985 were won again by Víctor Paz Estenssoro, who imposed a most rigorous programme to stabilize the economy. In the elections of May 7, 1989, Gonzalo Sánchez de Losada of the Movimiento Nacionalista Revolucionario (chief architect of the stabilization programme) won most votes but the result was so close that Congress had to choose a president from the three leading contenders. Jaime Paz Zamora of the Movimiento de la Izquierda Revolucionaria (MIR) who came third in the elections, was inaugurated as President on 6 August 1989 after having made an unlikely alliance with the right wing former military dictator, Gen. (retired) Hugo Banzer (Acción Democrática Nacionalista), in return for certain cabinet posts.

The People Of the population of some 7.11m people some 70% are Indians, 25% *mestizo* and 5% European. The racial composition varies from place to place: pure Indian around Lake Titicaca; more than half Indian in La Paz; three-quarters *mestizo* or European in the Yungas, Cochabamba, Santa Cruz and Tarija, the most European of all. During the 1980s, regional tensions between the "collas" (*altiplano* dwellers) and the "cambas" (lowlanders) have become more marked. Under 40% of children of school age are attending school even though it is theoretically compulsory between 7 and 14.

About two-thirds of the population lives in adobe huts, and medical services are sketchy outside the towns and mining camps; birth rate, 44.0, general death rate, 15.8 per 1,000, but infantile mortality is 124 per 1,000 during the first year (local estimates put this rate at 300 per 1,000). Epidemics are comparatively rare on the Altiplano, but malaria and yellow fever are still problems in the Oriente and Santa Cruz, and hepatitis and Chagas disease (**see page 35**) are endemic in the warmer parts of the country. About 50.4% is urban. Annual population growth: 2.8%; urban growth: 4.3%. Life expectancy at birth: 51 years; unemployment in 1986 was estimated at 22% of the work-force.

The Indians are mainly composed of two groups: those in the north of the Altiplano who speak the guttural Aymará, and those elsewhere, who speak Quechua, the Inca tongue. Outside the big cities many of them speak no Spanish, but knowledge of Spanish is increasing.

The most obdurate of Bolivian problems has always been that the main mass of population is, from a strictly economic viewpoint, in the wrong place, the poor Altiplano and not the potentially rich Oriente; and that the Indians lived largely outside the monetary system on a self-sufficient basis. Since the land reform of 1952 isolated communities continue the old life but in the agricultural area around Lake Titicaca, the valleys of Cochabamba, the Yungas and the irrigated areas of the south, most peasants now own their own land, however small the plot may be. There has also been appreciable migration to the warmer and more fertile lands of the eastern region, encouraged by the Government.

The Indian women retain their traditional costume, with bright petticoats, and in the highlands wear, apparently from birth, a flattish brown or grey bowler. In Cochabamba they wear a white top hat of ripolined straw. However, traditional headgear is being replaced by the baseball cap which sells for US$2.50 against US$7 for a bowler. Indians traditionally chew the coca leaf, which deadens hunger pains and gives a measure of oblivion. On feast days they drink with considerable application, wear the most sensational masks and dance till they drop.

N.B. Remember to refer to rural Indians not as "indios" (an insult) but as "campesinos" (peasants).

The Economy Bolivia is the poorest country on the South American mainland, with annual income per head estimated at about US$650. Its backwardness is partly attributable to its rugged terrain, which makes communications between the various parts of the country extremely difficult, and to its landlocked position.

The agricultural sector employs over 56% of the working population and contributes about 20% to gdp, but less than 2% of export earnings. Employment in agriculture has fallen since the mid-1960s because of increasing urbanization. Production of crops for food takes place primarily in the Altiplano, mainly by subsistence farmers, while crops for industrial use (cotton, sugar and soya) are concentrated around Santa Cruz. Croplands cover about 5% of total land area. Most commercial agriculture is in the east, where there are a number of food-processing plants: vegetable oils, a maize mill and sugar refineries. One of the major growth areas in agriculture is the cultivation of the coca leaf, used for chewing by the Indians and to make the drug cocaine. The extreme economic depression and rising unemployment have driven increasing numbers in search of the lucrative cocaine trade. Coca is easy to grow, up to four crops a year can be harvested, and Bolivia's production is believed to be worth about US$2bn a year, although less than a quarter of that actually returns to the country.

In contrast to agriculture, mining, including oil, employs only 2-5% of the labour force and contributes less than 10% of gdp, yet 95% of export earnings. Bolivia is a major producer of tin, antimony, wolfram and bismuth. Silver, lead and zinc are also produced and there are large unexploited reserves of lithium and potassium. Tin is the major mineral export, but because of the collapse of the world tin market, it has lost its first position in overall exports to natural gas. The mining sector is in decline and many mines are being closed.

Estimated reserves of natural gas are sufficient to meet domestic demand and export commitments for 30 years, but oil reserves, at 155m barrels in the mid-1980s, were being exploited faster than the rate of discovery. Production of around 20,000 b/d was just sufficient to meet domestic demand, but would be insufficient were there to be a general economic recovery.

The recession which afflicted most Latin American countries from 1980 hit

Bolivia with six consecutive years of contraction of gdp, accompanied by accelerating inflation, massive and frequent devaluations of the currency and social unrest. Government spending to support key export sectors was hampered by widespread inefficiency, corruption and strikes in state enterprises, which led to massive public sector deficits and external indebtedness. Economic problems were compounded in 1983 by a severe drought in the Altiplano and floods in the eastern lowlands, which devasted farming. The resulting food shortages exacerbated existing inflationary pressures and led to hyperinflation with annual rates reaching over 20,000%.

In the mid-1980s the government of President Paz Estenssoro introduced severe austerity measures to stabilize the economy, in which price controls were lifted, subsidies removed, public sector wages frozen and the currency linked to the US dollar in a controlled float. Tax reform was passed, a new currency, the boliviano, was created, worth 1 million pesos, the IMF agreed to disburse a standby credit, bilateral and multilateral lending began to flow again and steps were taken to reschedule or buy back the external commercial bank debt. Inflation came down to 10% a year, although unemployment continued to rise and living standards to fall. Nevertheless, by the end of the decade there were encouraging signs that growth was recovering and structural adjustment would put Bolivia on a firmer footing for the 1990s.

Government The Constitution of 1967 vests executive power in the President, elected by popular vote for a term of 4 years; he cannot be immediately re-elected. Government is by two legislative houses, the Chamber of Senators, with 27 seats, and the Chamber of Deputies, with 130 seats. There are nine departments; each is controlled by a Delegate appointed by the President.

Bolivia has, in effect, two capitals. Although Sucre is the legal capital, La Paz is in almost all respects the actual capital, being the seat of the Government and of Congress. On the other hand, the Supreme Court still holds its sessions in Sucre.

Communications After centuries of isolation new roads are now integrating the food-producing eastern zones with the bulk of the population living in the towns of the Altiplano or the westward-facing slopes of the Eastern Cordillera. Under Spanish rule there were four great trails in use within the country: three of them led through passes in the Western Cordillera to the Pacific; the fourth led from La Paz southwards into Argentina. At the turn of the century, railways replaced the llamas and mules. By far the shortest line is the one from La Paz to Arica (Chile), completed in 1913. Arica ships a large part of the exports together with Antofagasta (Chile) and Matarani (Peru).

Bolivia has 3,774 km. of railway. There are two private railways: Machacamarca-Uncia, owned by the Corporación Minera de Bolivia (108 km.) and Uyuni-Pulacayo (52 km.) owned by the Empresa Minera Pulacayo. Plans to construct a railway to link Cochabamba and Santa Cruz, as part of a Pacific-Atlantic rail network, were under study with Inter-American Development Bank assistance in 1989. Bolivia has over 14,000 km. of navigable rivers, which connect most of the country with the Amazon basin. The national highway system at the end of 1985 totalled 40,987 km., of which only 3.75% were paved and 22.6% gravel-surfaced.

Recommended reading: Herbert S.Klein, *Bolivia: The Evolution of a Multi-Ethnic Society* (Oxford University Press).

LA PAZ (1)

La Paz, the highest capital in the world, lies at 3,636 metres in a natural basin or canyon; it is sunk about 370 metres below the level of the Altiplano in its north-eastern corner. Mount Illimani, with its snow-capped peaks (6,402 metres),

towers over the city. The Spaniards chose this odd place for a city on October 20, 1548, to avoid the chill winds of the plateau, and because they had found gold in the River Choqueyapu, which runs through the canyon. The mean average temperature is 10°C, but it varies greatly during each day, and the nights are cold. It rains almost every day from December to February, but the sun usually shines for several hours. The rest of the year the weather is mostly clear and sunny. Snow is rare. At first the visitor will probably feel some discomfort, known as *soroche* (altitude sickness), from the rarified air; a few hours resting when you arrive will put that right, though visitors with heart problems should consult a physician. Oxygen is available at the better hotels.

In 1986, the population of La Paz was 1.1 million, over half of it Indian. Most of the Indians live in the higher terraces. Below are the business quarter, the government offices, the main hotels and restaurants and the university. The wealthier residential district is lower still: strung from Sopocachi to the bed of the valley at Obrajes, 5 km. from the centre and 500 metres lower than Plaza Murillo. Beyond Obrajes are the upper-class districts of Calacoto and La Florida. The main sports and social clubs have moved to these districts.

The neighbourhood of El Alto has now become a city in its own right, with a population of between 400,000 and 500,000. Apart from the district known as Ciudad Satelite, it is almost 100 per cent indigenous; almost everyone is an emigrant from the countryside. There is a fair every Sunday in Plaza 16 de Julio, more interesting for its size than the items for sale. Buses from Plaza Aguino and Pérez Velasco leave regularly for Plaza 16 de Julio.

There is some colonial building left; probably the best examples are in the Calle Jaén, but much of La Paz is modern. Plaza Murillo, on the north-eastern side of the river, is the traditional centre. Facing its formal gardens are the huge Cathedral (modern but very graceful); the Presidential Palace in Italian renaissance style, usually known as the Palacio Quemado (burnt palace) twice gutted by fire in its stormy 130-year history; and on the E side the National Congress. Across from the Cathedral on Calle Socabaya is the Palace of the Condes de Arana, now the Museo Nacional del Arte. Calle Comercio, running cross-wise past the Plaza, has most of the stores and shops. On Av. Bolívar (to which Mount Illimani provides a backdrop), continuing the Av. Camacho, is the Central Market (called "Mercado Camacho"), a picturesque medley of Indian victuals and vendors presiding raucously over stalls, their black braids topped by hard-brimmed bowler hats. Av. Camacho leads to the residential district of Miraflores.

From the Plaza Venezuela, Avenida Mariscal Santa Cruz leads to the Plaza San Francisco and to the church and monastery of San Francisco, well worth seeing; the church is colonial, richly decorated on native religious themes, and Indian weddings can be seen on Sats. 1000-1200. SW from Plaza San Francisco runs Calle Sagárnaga, with rows of handicraft shops. Going higher still up Sagárnaga is a local market, and turning right on Max Paredes, heading west, one reaches Avenida Buenos Aires, one of the liveliest streets in the Indian quarter. A worthwhile walk is to Mirador Laicacota on Avenida del Ejército.

Other churches of more than passing interest are Santo Domingo (originally

---

La Paz: Key to map

1. Plaza Murillo; 2. Congreso Nacional; 3. Museo Nacional de Arte; 4. Cathedral; 5. Government Palace (Palacio Quemado); 6. General Post Office; 7. Iglesia La Merced; 8. Museo de Costumbres; 9. Museo y Casa de Murillo; 10. Iglesia Santo Domingo; 11. Museo Nacional de Etnografía y Folklore; 12. Villaverde Palace; 13. Casa de la Cultura; 14. Basílica de San Francisco; 15. Witchcraft Market (Mercado de Hechicería); 16. Parque Prehistórico Tiahuanaco (Museo Semisubterráneo); 17. Alcaldía; 18. U.S. Embassy and Citibank; 19. Banco Central; 20. Tourist Office; 21. TAM; 22. Museo Arqueológico de Tiahuanaco; 23. Lloyd Aéreo Boliviano; 24. Mercado Camacho; 25. Biblioteca Municipal. Hotels: 26. *La Paz*; 27. *Sucre Palace*; 28. *Gloria*; 29. *Libertador*; 30. *Plaza*; 31. *El Dorado*; 32. *Panamericano*; 33. *Res. Rosario*; 34. *Milton*; 35. *La Paz*.

the cathedral) on the corner of Calles Ingavi and Yanacocha; La Merced, with its decorative 18th-century façade, on Calles Colón and Comercio; and San Sebastián, the first church to be built in La Paz, in Plaza Alonso de Mendoza (named after the church's builder).

Festivals Particularly impressive is the Alacitas Fair held from 24 Jan. to 15 Feb., on the upper part of Plaza Villarroel, mostly on Calle Tejada Zorzano (take *micro* B, K, H, 131 or X). "It is dedicated to Ekeko, an Indian household god. You can buy plaster images of him at many of the booths. He is a red-nosed cheerfully-grinning little personage laden with an assortment of miniature cooking utensils, coins, balls of wool, tiny sacks of sugar, coffee, salt, rice and flour; a kind of Bolivian Santa Claus. Ekeko is said to bring prosperity and to grant wishes. If you buy a toy house, or a cow, or a sheep at the Alacitas, you will get a real one before the year is out. There are also model motor-cars and planes, for the extreme optimists." (Christopher Isherwood, "The Condor and the Cows.") Beginning of May, Corpus Christi, End May, early June, Festividad del Señor de Gran Poder, huge procession of costumed and masked dancers. Fiestas de Julio, a month of concerts and performances at the Teatro Municipal, offers a wide variety of music. 8 December, festival around Plaza España, not very large, but colourful and noisy. On New Year's Eve fireworks are let off and make a spectacular sight, and a din, view from higher up. **See also page 262** for festivals outside La Paz.

Hotels Try to arrive in La Paz as early in the day as possible, as accommodation, especially at the cheaper end of the market, can be hard to find. Prices are inclusive of tax and service charge (20% in all).
    Expensive Hotels: *Plaza*, Av. 16 de Julio, T 378311, L, excellent, and its restaurant is open to the public; peña show on Fridays. *Sucre Palace*, Av. 16 de Julio 1636, T 355080, A, good value, but hot water a problem, 2 restaurants in the building, *Karin* snack bar on 1st floor, excellent, and an expensive restaurant on 2nd floor; *Hotel La Paz*, Av. Arce, T 356950, A, good views from upper floors; *Libertador*, Obispo Cárdenas 1421, T 343360, B, very good value (although continental breakfast is reported to be poor) and nearest the business section, helpful (baggage stored); *Eldorado*, Av. Villazón, T 363355, B, may be able to bargain for longer stays, highly rec., secure parking nearby. *Gloria*, Potosí esq. Sanjinés, T 370010, B;

Hotel Copacabana, Av. 16 de Julio 1802, T 351240/342241-4, C, with bath, central, restaurant and grill room (lunch only at latter), good service, safe deposit, rec. *Crillón*, Plaza Isabel La Católica, T 352121, C, not central, old fashioned, good restaurant on 10th floor, good views; *Emperador*, Plaza del Stadium 90, T 367327, C.

For people staying several weeks, often looking for permanent residences, boarding houses (*pensiones*) are popular, eg Illmeier, Sopocachi, Calle Resequin 1978, D with breakfast, English and German spoken. For those wanting to stay in the suburbs at a lower altitude there is the *Calacoto*, Calle 13 No. 8009 on the corner of Bustamente, in Calacoto, D, with bath.

The following medium-priced hotels have been recommended: *Residencial Rosario*, Illampu 704, travel agency downstairs, organizes trips to Puno and Tiahuanaco (Turisbus, 10% discount on some tours), D with bath (electric shower—safe design), E without, popular with foreigners, laundry and restaurant expensive, recently modernized and extended, stores luggage, (T 326531); *Residencial Copacabana*, Illampu 734, T 367896, 3-star, E, hot water, but few showers safe; *Continental*, Illampu 626, T 378226, D with bath, hot water, clean, friendly; *Milton*, Illampu and Calderón No. 1124, T 368003/353511 (P.O. Box 5118), D with bath, hot water, friendly, popular with travellers, helpful, will store luggage, rec., local market outside, so no taxis to the hotel at weekends; *Sagárnaga*, Sagárnaga 326, D with bath, (try bargaining), E without, basic breakfast included, friendly, helpful, good location, laundry; next door and slightly cheaper, is *Alem*, No. 334, hot water but inadequate plumbing; *Panamericano*, Manco Kapac 454, clean, E with hot electric showers; *Hostería Florida*, on Viacha off Av. Muñecas, E with bath, clean, good views, cheap breakfast; *Avenida*, Av. Montes 690 y Bozo (Casilla No. 48), D with bath, clean, central, near market; *Neuman*, Loayza 442, D with bath; *Viena*, Loayza 420, C with bath, E without, beautiful renovated old building, friendly staff, arrive early often full; *Residencial La Estancia*, Mexico 1559, D with breakfast, helpful; *Hostal Residencial*, Sucre 949, F, clean, hot showers, friendly.

Cheaper (bargaining possible for students): *Florida* (also *Hostería Florida* above), Ingavi 727, E with bath, good, warm water for shower; *Yanacocha*, Yanacocha 540, E, expensive for what is offered (no breakfast) with bath, clean, but has seen better days (check bill carefully); *Austria*, Yanacocha 531, E with bath, F without, rec.; *Torino*, Socabaya 457, safe, clean, central, noisy, hot water on request, (electric showers) E with bath (F without), washing facilities, stores luggage, book exchange, bar, generally popular with young travellers, beware of drug-raids by police; *Residencial Illimani*, Av. Illimani 1817, F, very friendly, washing facilities, often full; *Claudia*, Av. Villazón, op.. *Eldorado*, nr. Plaza Estudiante, E with bath (cheaper without), clean, secure, friendly. Cheap hotels located in the Indian quarter include: *Andes*, Av. Manco Kapac 364, E with shared bath, clean, hot water, good value (one of the few that offers single rooms at F), radio played loud all day, cafeteria on 1st floor (poor service and food); *Pullman*, Av. Montes 665, F, likely to be "full", spartan, good cheap restaurant. *Bolivia*, opp. railway station, F, clean, shared hot showers. *Max Paredes*, on street of same name No. 660, modern, clean, F; *Urkupiña*, Max Paredes 527, hot shower, good, clean, F; *Residencial Don Guillermo*, Colombia 222, E, good value, clean, hot water, rec.; *Alojamiento Universo*, Inca 175, T 340431, F, good value, hot water, a/c, clean, friendly, safe to leave luggage; *Alojamiento Illampu*, Illampu 635, F, hot water, washing facilities, mixed reports; *Conquistador*, upper end of Tumusla, F without bath, clean; *Hostal República*, Comercio 1455 (T 357966), remodelled, clean, hot water, D with bath, cheaper without, discounts for longer stay, hot water, luggage stored, helpful, laundry service. *Alojamiento Metropoli*, Tumusla, F p.p., under renovation, poor water supply, safe to leave luggage; *Plaza* on Plaza Pérez Velasco 785, clean and hot water, F, without bath, E with. Cheapest possibly is *El Carretero*, Catacora 1056, G p.p., 5 beds to a room, helpful, pleasant, hot shower extra.

Motels *Kori-Tambo*, Achocalla, outside the city, Tel.:327078. *San Bartolomé* rec., own bus service to and from La Paz.

Youth Hostel and camping club (with equipment for hire), Ciudad Satelite Plan 561, Calle 3 N 1073, Sr. Gonzalo O. Rodríquez, T 812341, US$3/night with cooking and washing facilities (tours and treks also arranged, and Spanish and Portuguese classes given—Fastalk, Casilla 11106). Take *trufi* "Satelite" from Calle Mercado, 1/2 hr., US$0.30.

Camping No organized site, but Mallasa (Municipal Park, unmarked, turn left at Alders Infantiles S.O.S.), Valencia and Palca below the suburb of La Florida have been recommended Club Andino Boliviano (T 794016) rents equipment. Camping gas is available at Camino Real, Calle Sanginés, US$2.50. Kerosene for pressure stoves is available from a pump in Plaza Alexander. Public showers at Duchas La Paz, 20 de Octubre 1677.

Restaurants in La Paz can be roughly divided into two categories: either they serve international cuisine and are expensive or they serve local dishes and are fairly cheap. The restaurants with international cuisine are to be found mainly on three streets, Av. 16 de Julio (the Prado), Av. 6 de Agosto and Av. 20 de Octubre. Service charges and tax of up to 23% are usually included on the bill but it is customary to leave a tip anyway of a few bolivianos. Always check prices before ordering, and then your bill and change.

Av. 16 de Julio: (street numbers given in brackets.)As well as the hotel restaurants, there is, in the expensive range: *New China* (1577), good international cooking. Slightly cheaper restaurants include the *China* (1549), good Chinese food; *Picol*, corner of Prado and Bueno, good value. *Bistro Paragayo*, nr. *Hotel Plaza*, German food, cheap. There are many snack bars, including *Confitería Elis* (1497), with good plate lunches, excellent soups, breakfasts and pastries, English and German spoken. *Capri* (1605) English spoken, rec. *California Donuts* II (1695), food, American-style, expensive, US$2-10, (No I is at Av Camacho 1248); *Tokio* (No. 1832), good, also has tea room and patisserie.

Off the Prado, on Calle Campero, one can recommend the *Club de la Prensa*, set in a pleasant garden, the limited menu is typical Bolivian and the company is lively. *Club de La Paz*, Camacho 203, is a good tea room. The *Club Alemán*, off Calle Reyes Ortiz, with reasonable prices.. The *Carreta*, an Argentine-type restaurant at Batallón Colorados 32, serves a recommended mixed grill and very good steaks, a favourite of businessmen for lunch; *Panchos*, Landaeta 402, T 342518, steakhouse, Chilean wine, English spoken, rec;

At the eastern end of the Prado, at Edificio Villazón, Av. Villazón, is *Monaco* (T 365014), good, reasonably-priced international and Bolivian dishes. *Pizzeria Morello*, Av. Arce, very good, opp the *La Paz*, also *Maison Suisse*, Av. Arce, good steaks and raclette, closed Sat. and Sun., gourmet restaurant on first floor. *Viva La Pizza*, J. José Pérez 322, rec., expensive.

Among those on Av. 6 de Agosto: *El Arriero* (No 2535, Casa Argentina), best barbecue with large portions, but quite expensive; *Hoyo 19* (T 322320), international and local dishes, and *Casa del Corregidor*, Calle Murillo 1040, a colonial mansion, attractive, rec. (see **Entertainments** below).

Av. 20 de Octubre: there is *Max Bieber's Restaurant and Tea-Room*, ice-cream, cakes and other dishes, owner speaks German (2080); next door is *Stefano's*, art gallery by day, good Italian restaurant at night; *Churrasquería La Maison* (2344), good steaks. *Patito Pekin* (2463), very good Chinese, about US$5 p.p. *Le Grand Chevalier*, Belisario Salinas 530, charming bar serving crêpes. *Arte y Cocina*, Aspiazu 637, restaurant and bar at night, good, small selection.

On the continuation of the Prado going west, in Av. Mariscal Santa Cruz, is *Los Escudos* (Edif. Club de La Paz, T 322028/350586), Munich-type bierkeller with fixed 4-course lunch for US$6, food and shows. Friday and Saturday nights (2000-2400, US$10-12 p.p.). *Lido Grill* (restaurant and confectionery), at No.815, popular meeting place, good food, reasonably-priced. *Parrillada Las Tablitas*, at Mariscal Santa Cruz 1283, excellent steaks, US$12; on the corner of Colón with Santa Cruz is *Restaurant Verona* for good economical plato del día. At Av. Ayacucho 206 is the *Internacional*, a lunch-time favourite of local businessmen and has good shows Friday and Saturday nights.

In the shopping and business district: there are numerous snack bars and cheap restaurants. One can recommend: *Marilyn*, corner of Potosí and Socabaya, salteñas, 3-course lunches for US$1.50; *Paulo*, on Potosí between Colón and Ayacucho for confectionery and coffee, offers excellent, cheap family lunches; also on Potosí, *Colorado* (No 1240), cheap and good, and *Hogar Austriaco*, good lunches, pleasant; *Lasky*, on Plaza Venezuela, offers huge helpings and varied meals for less than US$4. *El Lobo*, Illampu y Santa Cruz, good, clean, rec; good cheap meals at Illampú 773, closed Sun evening. On Yanacocha, *La Fregata* (No 525), 2 courses for US$5.50, good value, and *La Tertulia*, near Ingavi, small, simple, charming, hot drinks and pastries. *Casa Chan*, Juan de la Riva y Bueno, good set course Chinese meals, US$1.50, *Arabesque*, corner Loayza and Juan de la Riva. Rec. Mexican place: *Tacos Teru K*, Ignacio Cordero 1294, San Miguel (behind Loreto College) T 794513. There are many other snack bars and Chinese restaurants on Calles Comercio (eg *Café Comercio*, next to *Hostal República*, and *Salteñería Comercio*, Comercio 1439, excellent salteñas and Bolivian food, outdoor seating, inexpensive. Colón. *Helados Kivon*, Plaza Murillo 542, snack bar open Sunday morning.

On Sagárnaga: there is a good restaurant next to *Pería Naira* (No 161), which serves good food (see **Entertainments** below); *El Montañés*, opposite *Hotel Sagárnaga*, good, clean, family-run, homemade dishes; good café, *Snack Carabelas* (No 315), recommended for coffee and cakes. In same area, *Snack América*. Av América 192, good hamburgers from US$2.50. *El Refugio*, Plaza Avaroa, not cheap, but best meal in La Paz.

Cheap vegetarian restaurants to recommend are the *Hotel Gloria Naranjos*, Potosí 909, buffet lunch; *Aquarius* México 1844 (Tues.-Fri. lunch only); *Man Jari*, Potosí 1315, Mon.-Sat. 0900-2100, good value vegetarian meals (US$2), bread, muesli; *Nutricentro*, Comercio 1013, 2nd floor, rec., and Av. 16 de Julio 1655, local 11, open Sun.

Burgers: Stalls in the Indian quarter sell hamburgers for US$0.75 each including chips, egg and tomato, have 2 for a filling meal, but don't have aji, mayonnaise or mustard if worried about hygiene and watch your burger being cooked; also *Chingo's Hamburgers*, Av. Saavedra, clean. There is a *MacDonalds* on Plaza del Estudiante (a poor imitation of the real thing).

Comedor Popular, often referred to as *Comedor Familiar*, for the strictly limited budgets, cheap but filling local meals around US$1.50, available at Camacho and Loayza markets. The foodstalls at the top of Jiménez sell good T-bone steak cheaply. Bread from street vendors. Fresh dairy produce at *Pil* on Bueno y Cárdenas.

Bookshops Foreign language books at *Los Amigos del Libro*, Mercado 1315, and El Alto airport; they also sell tourist maps of the region from Puno to the Yungas, and walking-tour guides. Treat the details with caution. *Gisbert* on Calle Comercio 1270 (corner Plaza Murillo), and *Juventud* on Mercado and Yanacocha have good stocks (Gisbert also stocks maps). Amigos del Libro and Gisbert will ship books. There are 2nd-hand stalls on Av. Ismael Montes.

Films For Kodak, Casa Kavlin, Calle Potosí 1130; Laboratorio Fuji Color, Potosí 1316; Foto Linares, Mercado y Loayza, will develop both Ansco and Agfa colour film 1-day service on black-and-white, but only repairs Minolta cameras. Repairs also at Av. Sánchez Lima 2178 by Rolando Calla C, just ring bell (1000-1200), there is no sign; also at Potosí 1316, between 1400—1900, T 373621, very helpful, professional, fair prices. Film is available at black market prices around Av. Buenos Aires and Pasaje Ortega, Calle Granerdo, but otherwise it is expensive, as is developing. Fuji transparency film available at half shop price in market. In all cases check dates on film.

Shopping Look around and bargain first. There is inexpensive silver and jewellery in the little cabinets outside Lanza market on Av. Santa Cruz. Up Sagárnaga, by the side of San Francisco church (Mercado Artesanal), are booths and small stores with interesting local items of all sorts, best value on Sunday am when prices are reduced. There are good jewellery stores throughout the city but visit the gold factories for lower prices and special orders. *Schohaus* at Calle Colón 260 has good pewter. At Sagárnaga 177 is *Artesanía Nacional Tiwanaku*, for paintings, silver jewellery and woven goods, although there have been complaints about quality and price, a visit is a must. *Pacha-Marka*, Sagárnaga 272, good selection of antiques, knowledgeable owner. Many Indian objects are sold near Av. Buenos Aires, and Indian musical instruments on Calle Granier, near the General Cemetery. *Puma Punku*, Av. 16 de Julio, for weaving. *Artesanías Titicaca*, Av. Sánchez Lima 2320, and *Marka Tambo*, Jaén 710, retail and wholesale weaving. *Millma*, Sagárnaga 225, and in *Hotel Plaza*, for alpaca sweaters (made in their own factory) and antique and rare textiles. *Wari* on Sagárnaga will make to measure very quickly, prices reasonable. *Suri*, Av. Jua de la Riva 1431. *El Cuerito*, Av Montes 446, T 326982 (Casilla 2177-100), for all leather goods and for camping equipment, including tents, sleeping bags, hammocks, mosquito nets, etc. *Curerex* has four shops in La Paz, rec. for leather goods. Good value is to be had at the *Hotel La Paz* shops. Try *Inti Art* on the Prado (expensive modern designs), which is next to an antique store, in turn next to the *Restaurant China* and another on Calle Goitia. *Algo Más* on the Prado has an unusual selection of handicrafts. *Artículos Regionales* in Plaza de los Estudiantes is rec. *Suma Ampara*, Av. Villazón 1958, wide variety of woven goods, but prices not as low as in street markets. *Punchay Artesanías y Folklore*, Calle Santa Cruz 156 (T 362253), has been highly rec.—worth a visit;

also *Rumillajta*, one of the Galería shops adjacent to the San Francisco church entrance. *Artesanía Sorata*, Linares 862, specializes in dolls made by a women's cooperative and handmade textiles. Along Murillo and between Sagárnaga and Santa Cruz are various little shops selling old ponchos and rugs. Generally, the higher up one goes along Calle Santa Cruz, the cheaper woollen goods seem to become. Also weavers' co-operative in central plaza. Alpaca goods are about 50% dearer than in Puno. The maximum you can bargain prices down is 20%. Handmade clothing for children is good value. Many shops closed Saturday afternoon and Sunday.

The Indian market is a good place for ponchos and local handicrafts. See also the "witchcraft market" on Melchor Jiménez, 3rd street on left walking up Calle Santa Cruz from Av. Mariscal Santa Cruz, fascinating items for sale. Food market is the Mercado Camacho (Camacho y Bolívar). The Tourist Office has a full list of all markets.

Local Buses There are three types of city bus: large Fiat buses run by the city corporation, on fairly limited routes; *micros* (Bluebird-type buses), which charge US$0.15-0.20 depending on length of route; and *trufis*, minivans flying variously coloured flags and following fixed routes, which charge about US$0.35 pp.

Taxis US$0.35 p.p., for short trips within city limits. Sharing of taxis is common. Fares out of town are given under **Excursions** below. Taxi drivers are not tipped. Radio taxis, T 371111 or 322424.

Car Hire Cars may be hired direct from Imbex, Av. Arce 2303, T 379884, inc. Suzuki jeeps; Rent-a-Car International, F. Suazo 1942, T 357061; Kolla Motors, Rosendo Gutiérrez 502, T 341660/351701 who have well-maintained four-wheel drive Toyota jeeps (which seat 6), insurance and gasoline extra; Bolivia Rent-a-Car, Cap. Ravelo 2445, US$25, or through a travel agent. Oscar Crespo, Av. Bolívar, rents Brazilian-made VWs; Ruben Hidalgo Nogales of Domicilio Graneros 304, Zona Rosario, hires out Dodge Darts. One can also hire experienced drivers for US$25 a day plus accommodation and meals. You must have an international driving permit to drive in Bolivia, and outside the city you need an Hoja de Ruta (**see page 260**). Long queues for fuel, few stations.

Garage for VW and other makes: Ernesto Hug, Av. Jaime Freyre 2326, T 342279.

Entertainment Best entertainment for visitors are the folk shows (*peñas*), though they are reported as packed with tourists and increasingly commercialized. Outstanding (up to 7-group) folk show at *Peña Naira* (US$5, includes first drink), Sagárnaga 161, every night about 2215. Various restaurants have shows worth seeing. At these folk shows, visitors will be able to listen to the wide variety of local musical instruments, the different types of flutes, including the *queña*, and the *charango*, a small guitar with five strings, the back often made from the hide of an armadillo. Enquire at the *Rumillajta* shop (in the *galería* close to San Francisco church) about future performances by the famous folk group of that name. Good *peña* at *Casa del Corregidor*, Calle Murillo 1040, US$5 good food, rec., Fri. and Sat. p.m. only; similarly *Marko Tambo* on Calle Jaén, US$7 (all incl.) repeatedly rec. Indian dance halls, for example on Max Paredes, should only be visited in the company of Bolivians.

There are a few **discotheques** of which the best are *Alambra, Onix, Michelangelo's*, Av. 20 de Octubre 1832, and the *Viejoteca*, in Obrajes, which also has shows at week-ends, or the *Baccara* in Calle 25 de Agosto. For **drinks**, there is *Giorgissimo* on Loayza, which is very popular (but not cheap by Bolivian standards) and also serves good meals, *Charlie's Bar* on Plaza Isabel La Católica, *St. George's Pub* at Av. 20 de Octubre 2019 (both expensive lounge bars) and *Whiskería Brigitte*, downtown The *Sky Room* in the *Hotel Gloria* has been rec.

La Paz has a resident ballet and symphony orchestra (*Teatro Municipal* on Sanjinés and Indabura) but no theatre company. There are some good **cinemas**, films being mainly in English. For film buffs there is the excellent Cinemateca Boliviana, corner of Pichincha and Indabura, La Paz's art film centre with festivals, courses, etc. (entry US$0.75 for students). The Casa de Cultura (almost opposite Plaza San Francisco) sometimes has exhibitions, concerts or film festivals, most of which are free.

There are clown and mime shows in Parque del Ejército on Sunday, colourful and popular; the Parque Central has a children's amusement park, US$0.20.

Sport There are two golf clubs (Malasilla, the world's highest, and Pinos.—non-members can play at Malasilla on weekdays subject to the usual payments, but it may be difficult to hire clubs); two tennis clubs (La Paz Tennis and Sucre Tennis); and two riding clubs. Football is popular and played on Thursday and Sunday at the Siles Stadium in Miraflores, two clubs (Micro A); there are reserved seats. Basketball is played in Plaza del Estudiante on Mon., Wed. and Fri. in season. Fishing and duck-shooting on Lake Titicaca and other lakes and rivers. There is a yacht club at Huatajata on Lake Titicaca (**see page 224**); sail and motor boats can be hired there and at Chúa. YMCA sportsground and gymnasium, opposite the side of the University of San Andrés, Av. Villazón, and clubhouse open to the public, Av. 20 de Octubre 1839 (table tennis, billiards, etc.), regular meetings Tues. and Thurs. 1930 of a mountaineering group which runs weekend excursions.

Mountaineering See page 219.

Museums
Museo Nacional de Arte, across from the Cathedral at Calle Socabaya 432, housed in the 18th century baroque palace of the Condes de Arana, with beautiful exterior and patio. It has a fine collection of colonial paintings and also exhibits the works of contemporary local artists. Open Tues-Fri, 0900-1230, 1500-1900, US$0.70, Sat, 0930-1330 free. There are other exhibits at the Galería Municipal, on Colón, and at Galería Naira, on Sagárnaga.
Museo Tiahuanaco (Tiwanaku), or National Museum of Archaeology, easily reached by the flight of stairs by María Auxili church on the Prado. This modern building, simulating the Tiahuanaco style, contains good collections of the arts and crafts of ancient Tiahuanaco and items from the eastern jungles. Admission US$0.50; Tues.-Fri. 0900-1200, 1500-1900 (summer 1530-1700, Sat 0930-1230, 1430-1830).
Museo Semisubterráneo, in front of National Stadium, with restored statues and other artefacts from Tiahuanaco. It's in a sunken garden out of doors, and much can be seen from street level.
Museo Nacional de Etnografía y Folklore, on Calle Ingavi 916, is housed in the palace of the Marqueses de Villaverde, worth seeing (especially the exhibit on the Chipaya Indians), small contribution requested. Mon.-Fri. 0830-1130, 1430-1700.

The following four museums, all on Calle Jaén, are included on a single ticket, which costs US$2, from Museo Costumbrista. All are open Tues.-Fri. 1000-1200, 1430-1830, Sat. and Sun. 1000-1230. Calle Jaén, a picturesque colonial street with many craft shops, is well worth seeing for itself.

    Museo Costumbrista, Plaza Riosinio, at top of Jaén. Miniature displays depict incidents in the history of La Paz and well-known Paceños. T 378478.

    Museo Murillo, on Jaén, T 375273 (closed in 1987 for renovating) was originally the home of Pedro Domingo Murillo, one of the martyrs of the abortive La Paz independence movement of July 16, 1809. This colonial house has been carefully restored and has a good collection of paintings, furniture and national costumes of the period; there is also a special room dedicated to herbal medicine and magic. Warmly rec.

    Museo de Metales Preciosos, Jaén 777, well set out and warmly rec., T:371470.

    Museo de Litoral, Jaén 789, with artefacts of the War of the Pacific.
Mineral Museum, Banco Minero, 6 de Agosto 2382, esq Belisario Salinas. Open Mon.-Fri. 0900-1300, 1430-1630. Good gold and silver exhibits; free.
Núñez del Prado, Ecuador 2034, Mon.-Fri., 0900-1200, 1400-1800, excellent sculpture.
Museo Tambo Quirquincho, Calle Evavistovalle, nr. Plaza Mendoza (Tues.-Fri., 0930-1300, 1600-2000, Sat.-Sun., 1000-1300, US$0.50, Sat. free), in a restored colonial building, displaying modern painting and sculpture, carnival masks, silver, early 20th century photography and city plans, highly recommended.

Zoo at the upper end of Av. Bolivia, small, US$0.20.

Banks Citibank, on the Prado (cashes its own travellers' cheques, 1% commission and will receive money sent from any US bank), but will not advance cash to holders of Citibank Mastercard; other banks; American Express agent: Magri Turismo, Av. 16 de Julio 1490, 5th Floor (doesn't change Amex travellers' cheques). Open 0900-1200, 1400-1630. Closed Saturday. Cash advance on Visa and Mastercard at Banco de La Paz on Prado (limit US$300), Banco Santa Cruz de la Sierra, and Banco Boliviano Americano, among others. Money is changed in hotels or *casas de cambio* rather than in banks.

Exchange Houses Sudamer, Colón 256, good rates also for currencies other than US$ (2% commission on travellers' cheques into dollars); Titikaka Tours, Loayza 203; Tony Tours, Yanacocha y Asbún. Shampoo shop *perfumeria* at Yanacocha 319, where you ask for Sr. Koli will cash US$ from travellers' cheques, 1% commission, (will take back bolivianos at same rates); Casa de Cambio Silver, Mercado 979, charges 1% commission to change travellers cheques into dollars cash; similarly *D'Argent*, Mercado 1328. Airport exchange booth will only change up to US$50 (commission) in travellers' cheques. *Casas de cambio* and street changers can be found on Camacho, Colón and Prado. It is not worth dealing on the black market since there is virtually no difference between black and official rates. N.B. if arriving on Friday night, bring bolivianos or US dollars cash as it is difficult to change travellers' cheques at the weekend. If you leave Bolivia with bolivianos you may not be able to change them in neighbouring countries. Watch out for forged currency, especially dollars and Chilean pesos.

Spanish Courses Centro Boliviano Americano (address under **Libraries** below) US$140 for 2 months, 1½ hrs. tuition each afternoon; Centro de Estudios Brasileños, Av. Sánchez Lima 2226, T 3-22110, 2 hrs. tuition each morning, US$125 for 6 weeks. Christiane Hasselmann, Casilla 7903, La Paz, offers Spanish classes, with emphasis on local pronunciation and customs.

Libraries Centro Boliviano Americano (CBA), Parque Zenón Iturralde (near Av. Arce), has public library and recent US papers (Mon.-Fri. 0900-1200, 1430-1920). USIS has lending library and 2nd-hand paperbacks. Alliance Française, Calle Ingavi (open Mon.-Fri. 1600-2000), has an old library. Goethe-Institut, Av. 6 de Agosto 2118 (Mon.-Thurs., 1600-1900), good library, recent papers in German, videos in German and Spanish.

Embassies and Consulates **Argentine Consulate**, Av. 16 de Julio 1480, over Aerolíneas Argentinas T 353233/353234; **Brazilian Consulate**, Fernando Guachalla 494, T 350718; visa office is round corner at Sánchez Lima 2199, 0900-1300, Mon.-Fri. **Paraguayan Consulate**, 7th floor Edificio Montevideo, Av. Arce, just below Calle Montevideo; **Peruvian Consulate and Embassy**, 6 de Agosto 2190 y Calle F.Guachalla, 0930-1300 (a visa costs US$5 in US$ bills, issued same day if you go early); **Venezuelan Embassy and Consulate**, Av. Arce 2678, Ed. Illimani, 4th floor (consulate open Mon., Wed., Fri. 0900-1200).
    United States Embassy, Calle Colón and Mercado (has a good reading room, closed 1200-1400), Consulate on Av. Potosí—(T 350120/350251); **Canadian Consulate**, Av. Arce 2342 (1000-1400), T 375224.
    Austrian Consulate, Edif. Petrolero, 7th floor, Oficina 1, Av. 16 de Julio 1616, T 326601, 1600-1800; **British Embassy and Consulate**, Av. Arce 2732-2754, T 351400/329401-4, Casilla 694,, closed 1200-1300 and Wed. p.m.; **Danish Consulate**, Calle Layanza 250, Edif. Casilla, 5th floor, No. 509, T 322601/325589; **French Consulate**, Av. Hernando Siles 5390, esq. Calle 08, Obrajes, T 782849 (take bus No 11 down Av. 16 de Julio); **Belgian Embassy** is 1 block from French; **West German Embassy**, Av. Arce 2395. T 352072 or 352389; **Netherlands Consulate**, Av. Arce 8031, Edif. Victorio, 2nd floor; **Norwegian Consulate**, Av. Mcal. Santa Cruz, Edif. Esperanza, 11th floor, T 322528; **Spanish Consulate**, Calle Cordero T 343518; **Swedish Consulate**, Av. Arce 2856, Casilla de Correo 852, T 327535; **Swiss Embassy**, Av. 16 de Julio 1616, 6th floor, T 353091, open 0900-1200, 1300-1400; **Israeli Embassy**, Av Mcal Santa Cruz, Edificio Esperanza, 10th floor, T 358676/325463, Casilla 1309/1320.

Addresses Instituto Nacional de Arqueología de Bolivia, Calle Tiwanaku 93.
Immigration, Ministerio del Interior, Avenida Arce.
YMCA, 20 de Octubre 1839, Casilla 963.
Asociación Boliviana de Agencias de Viajes y Turismo, Edif. Litoral, Mariscal Santa Cruz 1351, Casilla 3967.

Doctor Dr René Coloma Rector, Edificio Cosmos, 11th floor, Office 1, Av. 16 de Julio (El Prado) T 377914 (private surgery, Mon.-Fri. from 1500), or 355456 (home—any time). Rec., speaks good English. Dr Jorge Muñoz A. Ed Alianza, Av. 6 de Agosto y F. Guachalla, speaks German, rec; also Dr Villarreal whose office is on 9th floor of *Café Verona* building, Colón y Santa Cruz, works at German hospital, speaks fluent German. **Dentists** Dr and Dra Osorio at *Hostal Austria*, Yanacocha 531. Tourist Office has a list of doctors and dentists who speak foreign languages.

Hospital Clínica del Accidentado, Plaza Uyuni 1351, T 328632/321888 offers first aid. Efficient and well run nursing homes such as Clínica Americana, Clínica Alemana, Clínica Rengel (T 390792/8), Clínica Santa María, Av. 6 de Agosto 2487, efficient and not too expensive. Red Cross opposite Mercado Camacho will give inoculations if required. The Methodist Hospital (12th block of Obrajes, take "A" *micro* from the Prado) runs clinic at US$5, telephone for appointment.

Health and Hygiene If suffering from *soroche*, ask in chemists/pharmacies for suitable medication. Tampons may be bought at most *farmacias* and supermarkets.

Laundromats Wash and dry, US$2 per 4-kilo load, 6-hour service, at Gelmi-Lava-Sec, 20 de Octubre 2019, suite 9, T 352930, helpful service, US$1.40 for 1 kg.; Lavandería Cinco Estrellas, 20 de Octubre 1714. Lavandería Select, Av. Arce, down from *Hotel La Paz*; 3-hour service, rec. Finesse Limpieza, Illampu 863; Av. Mcal. Santa Cruz 1154, central; laundry service at Oficina Gregoria Apazá, Colombia y Almirante Grau, T 369607, phone first. Dry cleaning, Calle Murillo 1366, US$.15 per kg., La Esmeralda, Colon 558.

Church   Protestant Community Church (inter-denominational), in English, American Co-operative School, Calle 10 Calacoto (T 795639 or 792052). The former pastor and his wife (The Rev. & Mrs. Charles F. King) have written an excellent duplicated guide to "Life in La Paz" which can be got on Sunday at the Community Church. Sunday service at 1045, but there are "lots of activities during the week". Anglican-Episcopalian services are held at the Community Church on the third Sunday of each month.

Synagogues   Calle Landaeta 330 (Sat. a.m. services only); Colegio Boliviano Israëlito, Canada 1846 for Friday service—it looks like a private house.

Telecommunications   Entel office for telephone calls is in Edif. Libertad, Calle Potosí, English spoken, and at Ayacucho 267 y Mercado and in *La Paz Hotel*, lower ground floor, in both these locations there are also public telex booths.

Post Office   Av. Mariscal Santa Cruz y Oruro (open Mon.-Sat. 0800-2000, and until 1200 on Sun. and holidays). Stamps are sold only at the post office. Poste Restante keeps letters for 3 months. Procedure for sending parcels: customs (upstairs) must check contents first; then go to stamp counter to fill in customs declaration and purchase stamps; next have value of stamps checked and stamps franked, at a separate counter; finally, go to opposite window for *certificado* ticket. (Don't forget sack, needle and string for sewing up, and moth balls for textile items). To collect parcels costs at least US$0.50.

Tourist Office   Instituto Boliviano de Turismo (IBT) Plaza Estudiante 176, 2nd floor, corner of México y 16 de Julio; 0830-1200, 1430-1830. Very helpful. English spoken. Maps and leaflets are available and there is a tourist information guide listing hotels, restaurants and other practical details.

Maps   Instituto Geográfico Militar, Av. 16 de Julio 1471 (take Micro C or N), head office open 1500-1700 only, collect maps next day, delivery to your hotel not reliable. Passport is needed to get in, but worth it as they have the only railway map available in La Paz and a wide selection of others invaluable for the traveller. Topographic maps cost US$10 per sheet (scale 1:50,000) and about US$8 for standard tourist maps. Departmental road maps are meant to be available in the tourist offices in the capitals of each department but often they are out of stock. Senac (the national road service) publishes a Red Vial 1989 map, which is probably the best, but is still inaccurate, about US$6.50. Also reported as inaccurate are the maps of the Automóvil Club Boliviano. Maps are generally hard to find. Maps are sold at Ichthus bookshop on the Prado; also at Librería La Paz, Amigos del Libro and Gisbert (**See page** 209).

Guides   *La Paz Insólita* (7 maps) US$3 and *Guía de La Paz* by Jorge Siles Salinas (historical) US$5. *Guía Central de Bolivia*, US$2, information on transport, statistical and geographical data. In particular it contains the La Paz minibus schedules, which are unobtainable elsewhere. *An Insider's Guide to Bolivia*, by Peter McFarren (Fundación Cultural Quipus, Casilla 1696, La Paz, 1988, US$12) has been recommended, especially for its section on culture. *Descubriendo Bolivia*, Hugo Boero Rojo, 1989.

Travel Agents   *Crillon Tours*, Av. Camacho 1223, Casilla 4785 (T 374566), expensive; they run a hydrofoil-bus service to Puno, US$160, via Copacabana and Isla del Sol, incl. lunch and breakfast; they also have a sunset to sunrise programme, based at the *Inca Utama Hotel* at Huatajata, involving trips on the lake, meals and lodging. *Transturin*, Camacho 1321 (T 328560/363654, Telex 2301 TRTURIN BV), also very expensive, La Paz-Puno, inc. boat crossing on Lake Titicaca, US$80. *Diana Tours*, Sagárnaga 328, T 358757, very good value. *Turismo Balsa*, Av. 16 de Julio 1650 (T 356566 and 355817), has reservation service for air tickets; *Turisbus* (Illampu 704, Casilla 442, T 325348/326531), helpful, again mixed reports on its services (to Puno and Cuzco—US$29), and *Marka Tambo*, Calle Mercado 1328 (Ed. Mscal. Ballivián, Local 24) for local tours. *Tourismo Tours*, Bueno, rec.; *Vicuna Tours, Hotel Copacabana*, rec. *Exprinter*, Loayza 107, has tickets to Tumbes and Guayaquil (also operates exchange facilities) to Cuzco via Copacabana, US$30. *Tawa Tours*, Sagárnaga 161, run jungle tours to their own camp as well as the Salt Lake areas, and the Amazon, friendly, good guides (also charter flights to Europe and USA); *Profian Tours*, Sra. Perales, Fernando Guachalla 319, rec. for local bus tours. *Magriturismo*, Av. 16 de Julio 1490, very helpful. *Diplomatic Tours*, managed by Rosario Zambrana, located at 2nd floor of Plaza Venezuela 1920, has been rec. (T 372611); will provide airport transfer (US$8). *Shima Tours*, Potosí 1310, very helpful, good for flight tickets; *Cóndor Tours*, Sagárnaga, good and cheap; *Seul Travel*, Plaza San Francisco, arranges tours to the Yungas for more than one day, helpful. *Leslie Iruzoque* organizes "alternative" trips while her mother can provide accommodation near Moon Valley (T 360777 or 791767). *Paititi S.R.L.*, Av. Arce 2630, and Calle Juan de la Riva, Ed. Alborada (oficinas 106-107, Casilla 106, T 329625), organizes adventure tours, rec., Javier Prudencio is helpful

TITIKAKA LAKE ON A CATAMARAN CRUISE SHIP

LA PAZ • SUN ISLAND • PUNO • CUZCO

INTERNATIONAL SERVICE REGULAR SCHEDULE

LV. 06:00		LA PAZ	AR.		18:30
AR. 07:30		HUATAJATA	LV.		17:00
LV. 08:00			AR.		16:30
AR. 10:30		SUN ISLAND	LV.		14:00
LV. 11:00			AR.		13:30
AR. 12:00		COPACABANA	LV.		12:30
LV. 13:30			AR.		11:00
AR. 16:00*		PUNO	LV.		06:30*
LV. -	06:55*			AR 19:00*	
AR. -	18:50*	CUZCO	LV. 07:00*		

DAILY SERVICE

* PERUVIAN TIME

TRANSTURIN LTDA.
TRAVEL AGENTS & TOUR OPERATORS

MAIN OFFICE: Av. MARISCAL STA. CRUZ 1295
(3rd FLOOR) P.O. BOX 5311
TELEX: 2301 TRTURIN BV
PHONE 320445-341787   FAX: 391162

SALES OFFICE: AV. CAMACHO 1321
PHONE 328560-363654

OFFICE IN PUNO: AV. GIRON TACNA, 149-147
PHONE 352771

OFFICE IN CUZCO: AV. PORTAL DE PANES 109 OF. 1
(PLAZA DE ARMAS) PHONE 222332

and speaks several languages. *Bolivian Adventure Tours* in hall of *Hotel Sucre* has tents for hire. Also *Carmoar Tours*, Calle Bueno 159, which is headed by Günther Ruttger, (T 340633), rec. as among the best, has information and maps for the Inca Trail to Coroico. *Reinaldo Pou Munt*, Capitán Ravelo 2401, T 327226, expensive; Casilla 13632, offers excellent, tours of the city and environs, speaks English and German. Many agencies arrange excursions or travel to Peru (Puno, Cuzco, Arequipa), as well as local tours. See also names and addresses under "Exchange Houses", **page** 211.

N.B. Unless indicated in the list above, services offered by travel agents are expensive, some being criticised as overpriced. We have also been told that many services to Peru and beyond deteriorate markedly once Bolivia has been left (commitments unfulfilled, buses changed, extra passengers taken on—but **see also page** 947).

Airport El Alto, above La Paz, the highest commercial airport in the world (4,018 metres) connected to the city by motorway. A taxi between the centre and airport takes at least 15 minutes, US$8-9 but may be negotiated down to US$6; current prices, including luggage, should be on display at the airport exit (enquire at the tourist office in town, or at the airport—not too reliable). *Trufi*/bus leaves from Plaza Isabel La Católica, from 0700, frequent; US$0.85, best to have little luggage; colectivos from opposite *Hotel Crillón* (same square) charge US$2, carrying 4 passengers. There is a duty-free shop but it can sometimes forget to open. No bank. The small tourist office at the Airport should know the price of a taxi to town, some maps available, English spoken, helpful (when manned). The coffee shop is slow but inexpensive.

Air Taxis US$250 per hour, contact Major Pericón of Taxi Aéreo Urkupiña, T 350580, 812099. Aero Inca, T 361018. Alas Doradas T 354070.

Air Services Lloyd Aéreo Boliviano (LAB), Camacho y Loayza, T 367701/7, and TAM, Av. Montes near Plaza Velasco (the air force and not recommended) fly to the main cities and towns, and also to Lima and Arica daily. Fares are comparatively low for internal flights. (For details of internal flights, see under proposed destinations.) The Faucett office in La Paz provides unreliable information.

Bus Services (for information, T 367276); Micros to the main bus terminal at Plaza Antofagasta are 2,M,CH or 130, for buses to: Oruro (3 hours, US$3-5), Potosí (12 hours, US$9.50, very cold, all at night—1730-1830), Sucre (18 hours, US$11.50), Cochabamba (several companies, e.g. Trans Nacional, 11 hrs., US$4.90, San Francisco, US$5, El Dorado, 8 hrs., Nóbleza, 5 hrs. at 0900 and 1600), Santa Cruz (23 hours, US$14), Tarija (26 hours, 1450, US$16), For Coroico and the Yungas, **see page** 245. Villazón, 26 hrs. with a change of bus in Potosí, may have to wait 11 hrs (US$15),

Buses to Sorata, Copacabana and Tiahuanaco do not leave from the bus station but from the Cementerio district (Micros C,I,K,S,M,P,X,132 and 134 go there). See under each destination for details. Companies located in the Cementerio district include Flota Copacabana, Manco Kapac, 2 de Febrero, Ingavi, Morales. As so few roads are well paved, train is usually preferable to bus when there is a *ferrobus* service (see below). The services of Cóndor are best avoided.

International Buses To Buenos Aires, daily at 1800, Expresos Panamericanos. Bus to Arica at 0530 Tues. and Fri, in each direction, check schedule in advance, US$20, Litoral (office at back of bus terminal), 20-22 hrs. (It is reported that Litoral buses are in poor condition and are liable to break down). Senobus (Calle Hujutri, 400 m. from train station in direction of Cementerio), Mon. and Fri. (US$8.50) or (cheaper) El Cariñoso to Charãna on the frontier then Sanga from Visviri (Chile) to Arica, US$5, or take a taxi, a very hard trip on a dirt road in the Bolivian section to Tambo Quemado, subject to cancellation in the wet, no food but beautiful. Colectivos to Puno daily with different companies (eg Colectur) most easily booked through travel agencies, US$9-12, 10 hrs. **N.B.** Of the various La Paz-Puno services, only Turisbus (Illampu 704) does not make you change to a Peruvian bus once over the border. For luxury and other services to Peru see **Travel Agents** above.

Trains It is imperative to check times before travelling as changes are frequent. For this reason, we do not give exact schedules in the text. Micros which go to the station are A,M,N,P,130,131,C. There is an acceptable *ferrobus* (railcar) service (with food and drink served) between La Paz and Cochabamba (8 hours, 3 times a week US$7 Pullman, US$6 special); to Potosí (11½ hours), *ferrobus* once/twice a week, US$8 Pullman, US$5.50 special, and train once a week US$5.75 Pullman, US$4 special; train goes to Sucre, US$7.50 Pullman, US$5 special, also *ferrobus* to Sucre, booked up 1 week in advance in January. In theory, however, you may only buy tickets the day before you travel; office opens 0700, but get there beforehand.

To Villazón (24 hrs.) for Argentina, Tuesday, Thursday at 1630 and Friday at 1900; no food or drink is served (very dusty journey, arr. 1230 next day), no sleepers; *tren mixto* leaves Wed. and Sun. at 1915, fares for both, US$19 Pullman, US$13 special. Book ahead at central station; queue for booking at 0600 on previous day (queuing numbers are given out), take passport. All trains South (to Oruro and Villazón) are sold out by 0700 on Monday, so 1) go to station 2 hrs. before departure for returned tickets, 2) bus to Oruro then catch train, 3) try Exprinter travel agency, 4) try and board train anyway and pay the guard, 5) fly to Tarija and then go by road to Villazón. Phone to check times etc.: 352510.

Railways to/from the Coast (1) By the Southern Railway of Peru from Arequipa to Puno, on Lake Titicaca. Getting to La Paz from Puno: by road (several lines, 10-hour journey); Crillon Tours run a daily hydrofoil service (0600 from La Paz; 0830 bus departure from La Paz).

From Guaqui to El Alto. above La Paz, a railway follows the broad plateau on an almost level gradient, rising only about 300 metres to El Alto. This line carries only freight.

(2) **La Paz-Arica International Railway**, 447 km.: there is a Bolivian *ferrobus* service straight through to Arica, twice a week in summer (Tues and Fri, 0700, about 11 hrs), US$35 incl. meals, but not drinks, worth it for the views, book ticket one-two weeks in advance, or a Chilean *coche motor* once a week, 10 hrs., US$48, reserve at *Hotel Bolivia* opp. station, T 375030, Tues.-Fri. of preceding week (many are taken up by travel agencies: ask around, e.g. Exprinter, if none on sale at station). The service is less frequent in winter. Alternatively take a train to Charaña, then change to a bus to Arica, or, on 2nd and 4th Wed. of each month a train leaves Charána at 0930, arriving Arica at 1800. Fares: La Paz-Charaña: Pullman slow train US$23; special US$15; train leaves La Paz every Tues. at 2300, arriving Charaña at 0530 (ie no chance of seeing the spectacular scenery).

In the Bolivian section the line runs to Viacha, the junction of the several railways running to Antofagasta, Guaqui, and Buenos Aires. It coninues to Corocoro, the copper mining town, thence to the border. The mountain peaks visible include Illimani, Sorata, Huayna-Potosí, Muruata, and many others. For description of the Chilean section, **see page 495**.

(3) La Paz-Antofagasta, by Antofagasta and Bolivia Railway, 1,173 km., now definitely a trip for the adventurous who are impervious to cold, is by bus to Oruro, then train as far as Calama in Chile, then by bus (240 km.) to Antofagasta; the bus ticket (US$3) is given when entering Chile. This, the most southerly of the three railway routes connecting La Paz with the Pacific coast, passes through magnificent scenery but the timetable has been described as "pure fantasy". Having taken a bus from La Paz to Oruro (US$3), you take the train from Oruro at 2000 on Friday, US$15 to Calama: it is 8 hrs. to Uyuni, where there is a 4½ hr. wait, then another 4 hrs. to the border; 1 hr. to change trains, then 40 minutes to Ollagüe, where Chilean customs take 4-12 hrs. (gringos usually dealt with last). After that it is 6 uncomfortable hours to Calama. In Bolivia, seats can be reserved as far as the border, food is served (waiter service), but no water; in Chile, only sandwiches, no other food, or lights. At the change-over before Ollagüe it is possible to walk through customs and take a colectivo to Calama, 5 hrs., US$8, the road Ollagüe—Calama is in good condition. Money changers not allowed on the train, but still manage to operate. Watch out for forged Chilean notes especially if the light is bad. It is advisable to buy Chilean currency and sell bolivianos before journey. All passports are collected and stamped in the rear carriage, they should be ready for collection after 1-2 hours (beware, as the train goes down to Chile, carriages are added; the reverse happens in the other direction).

(4) La Paz-Buenos Aires: This railway journey of about 2,400 km. takes 71 hours. Either take Tuesday or Thursday (1630) train to Villazón (arrives 1230—tickets sold day before 0800-1100), then cross frontier to La Quiaca (1-1½ km. walk) to catch train or bus to Jujuy or train to Tucumán for another train to Buenos Aires (Retiro). On Friday the 1900 La Paz-Villazon train takes an expensive Pullman coach which crosses the border and is connected to an Argentine train for Buenos Aires.

Note that many travellers from La Paz on the Buenos Aires line take a bus to Oruro (more comfortable and quicker than the train) and board the train there. Again, you may have trouble getting a sleeper if you do this. Remember that in northern Argentina buses tend to be much quicker than trains.

Excursions from La Paz There is trout fishing in the many glacier lakes and streams near La Paz.

The best near-by excursion is to Río Abajo and Malasilla golf course: through suburbs of Calacoto and La Florida follow the river road past lovely picnic spots and through some weird rock formations, known as the "Moon Valley". About

3 km. from bridge at Calacoto the road forks; sharp right leads to the Caza y Pesca Club and Malasilla golf course. Moon Valley can also be reached by Micro 11 ("Aranjuez") from Plaza San Francisco, which runs along the Prado and goes as far as Aranjuez Forest (US$1); cross the bridge on your right then walk 2 km. uphill past the cactus garden to Moon Valley. Most of the local travel agents organize tours to Moon Valley, (which are very brief, 5 minutes stop for photos in a US$9 tour of La Paz and surroundings); taxis are not dear (US$12), especially if shared; make sure the price is per car and not per person. Near the Arcillo Arce cactus gardens (dilapidated) is the *Balneario Los Lobos*, popular for lunch at weekends.

To the ice cave in the Zongo Valley: a steep but scenic ride down past several of La Paz's electric power plants. In 32 km. the altitude drops from 4,265 to 1,830 metres. The beautiful ice cave under the Chacaltaya glacier may be visited. Either take taxi for a day US$35-40, or take Micro 52, EMTA or 101 to Plaza 16 de Julio, El Alto (US$0.50) from where you can hire a taxi for US$2.25-4.50 p.p. or take Trans 16 de Julio (Plaza Ballivián) on Tues., Thurs. and Sat., 0600. The road follows an aqueduct (on left); at each junction en route turn left, 20 minutes past a cemetery (also on left), you come to the last hydroelectric dam and on the right, a white guard house. Alight here. Walk up and over the small hill on the righthand side of the road until you meet the aqueduct again. Follow the water course for 35-45 minutes (take care and don't look down) until you come to a bridge. You can either cross this, straddling the water, or walk beneath to the other side. At the end of the bridge, turn right up hill to a marker of rocks piled one on top of the other. Continue over the hill, cross a stream and go straight up the next hill at a similar rock marker. From the top of the hill, you should see the cave ahead of you (about 1 hour's walk in all).

To Ashumani (past Valley of the Moon) for good views of the valley and houses of the wealthy (no buses). Walk back along the valley and catch frequent buses into town.

To El Organo del Diablo—a gigantic, tooth-shaped rock, take Micro "Ñ" (last stop Cota Cota) or Trans EMTA from Calles Murillo and México to the end of the route, then continue for 1 km. more and you will see the rock on the left—"more impressive especially if the wind is blowing than Moon Valley". A further 4 km. on is the top of the mountain with a superb view of Illimani. The road continues to Ventilla, the start of the Inca trail.

For the acclimatized only: A climb to Corazón de Jesús, the statue at the top of the hill reached via the steps at the north end of Calle Washington, then left and right and follow the stations of the cross. Worth the climb for the views over the city and the Altiplano, but watch out where you put your feet.

To see Puya Raimondii flowers, go to the village of Comanche, 2½ hrs. from La Paz (micros from railway station to Viacha—1 hr.—then truck to Comanche—rough, dusty and cold); some travel agencies arrange tours.

Hikes near La Paz For the *Takesi* (Inca) road hike, take a Sector Bolsa Negra bus at 0900, US$1.25, daily from Calle González y Grau, Plaza Belsu (which is below the Mercado Rodríguez) to Ventilla on Palca road, arrive 1 hr. early for seat, 3 hrs., return 0930 (alternatively take a Cota Cota bus to the end of the line or a taxi to Ovejura vehicle checkpoint above Cota Cota, US$6.35, then truck to Ventilla). Take the track to the left, parallel to the Río Palca for 10 km. track to San Francisco mine. At Choquecota, before San Francisco, there are shops, and you can stay at the mine if necessary. If you leave Ventilla before 1300, you should reach Takesi village before nightfall (it's worth seeing the village). The "camino de Takesi" goes over the pass (4,650 metres), passes the Laguito Loro Keri and then follows the valley which ends at Chojlla and on 5 km. to Yanacachi, some meals available in private homes also some accommodation— only colectivo to La Paz at 0700 US$2.85, daily except Sat. (or Sun., check, buy ticket day before), 4 hrs. (If you miss that, it's a 45-min. walk down to Santa Rosa, which is on the main La Paz-Chulumani road). One powerful river can be crossed by applying to houses on the bank, where they will rig up a pulley for you US$1-2. *Backpacking in Peru and Bolivia* (Bradt Publications), and the La Paz tourist office leaflet with sketch map both describe this 3-5 day walk, which shows exceptionally fine Inca paving in the first part. Please take care not to add to the litter already on the route. The highest point is 4,650 metres and the lowest 2,100. The trail can also be used as a starting point for reaching Chulumani or Coroico. The scenery changes dramatically from the bitterly cold pass down to the humid Yungas. Take sweets and fruit for children and, if you feel confident in this respect, disinfectant, bandages, etc to treat their wounds and ailments. At Chojlla one can sleep at the school house for US$0.80, or the *Sheraton Inn*, basic, US$1 or less.

Another trail is the **Choro** hike from La Cumbre pass to Coroico, descending from the snow-covered heights to tropical vegetation. Take a bus to Villa Fátima, from Av. Mariscal Santa Cruz, then a Flota Yunguena bus or a truck (see page 246 for transport details) to the statue of Christ at La Cumbre where the trail starts (a pick-up is unlikely to take you). If asked to pay at the checkpoint out of La Cumbre, there is no need to, the fee is not legal. Look out for condors at the start of the trail. The speedy can do the hike in under 3 days, lesser mortals will need about 4 days. It is 4-5 hours from La Cumbre to Chucura (campsite); 8-9 hours to the village of Choro (campsite en route at Challapampa); 5-6 hrs. to Sandillani (camping possible all along this stretch); in Sandillani a Japanese man welcomes visitors and will let you camp in his orchard, he likes postcards, stamps, money from your home country; thereafter it is 3 hours/7 km. to Chairo. Water is available all the way, but take water purification pills. A tent is essential. (The tourist office has a map of the trail.) From Chairo (accommodation—US$2.50—,or sleep under eaves of the school, and food with Família Paredes de la Tienda, very friendly, swimming pool), there is a stiff climb remaining up to Coroico. Usually, jeeps run from Chairo to Coroico for US$0.60 and colectivos to La Paz, but in 1989 2 bridges were washed away, so walk to the junction with the main road and hitch to Yolosa for a truck to Corocoi.

There is a real possibility of theft between Chucura and Choro; try to camp away from villages and banana plantations, team up with other walkers and set a guard if possible. There is also constant pestering for sweets and money. You are advised to check the safety of this, and the Takesi hike before setting out.

For both the above hikes, Carmoar Tours in La Plaz (address above) has been recommended for equipment rental (tents US$4.10/night) and maps.

A third hike is **Yunga Cruz**, from Chuñaví to Chulumani in the Sud Yungas (sketch map available from La Paz tourist office).

Mountaineering Increasing numbers are visiting the Cordillera Real, to the east of La Paz. The range has the marked advantages over many high massifs of settled weather from May-Sept., easy access via numerous mine tracks, and favourable starting altitudes (4,200-4,700 m.). The Cordillera Real is 150 km. long with six peaks over 6,000 m. (20,000 ft.)—Illampu 6,380 m. (see under Sorata, below) Ancohuma 6,420 m., Chearoco 6,100 m., Chachacomani 6,100 m., Huayna Potosí 6,090 m., Illimani 6,460 m. All can be reached relatively easily from La Paz, the latter two within a few hours' driving. There are also a large number of impressive 5,000 m.-plus peaks.

The route to Illimani is 4-5 hours via Colacoto and Huancapampa.The route to **Huayna Potosí**, an attractive peak (2 days) starts from Zongo Lake. The only access is by taxi to Zongo Lake (US$35 one way), or by truck on Sunday. Huayna Potosí (about 6,000 metres) requires mountaineering experience with ice and crevasses on the way to the top; however bad weather, apart from mist, is rare. Alternatively Condoriri or Pequeño Alpamayo are reached in one or two days from Tuni at Km. 21 on the La Paz-Tiquina road.

Normal alpine experience and equipment will enable most peaks to be ascended, and many new routes remain to be explored. Several peaks can be climbed in a day, but the 6,000

LAKE TITICACA
La Paz, Lake Titicaca and
the Peruvian Frontier. 2.1

m. mountains usually require 2-4 days. There are no huts (except Chacaltaya ski-lodge). Do not underestimate altitude problems: at least 1-2 weeks' acclimatization is usually necessary before exceeding 5,500 m. (A visit to Chacaltaya and its ski-slopes is an easy way of judging one's reaction to altitude). Also rescue services are virtually non-existent; prudence and proper gear (incl. crevasse rescue abilities) are indispensable. Note that mountaineering gear and high altitude camping equipment cannot be bought in Bolivia.

Other ranges: Western Cordillera including Sajama (6,530 m.)—mainly extinct volcano ice cones. Also Cordillera Apolobamba, northern extension of Cordillera Real extending into Peru with many 5,000 m.-plus peaks.

A good guidebook is *The Southern Cordillera Real*, R.Pecher & W.Schmiemann, Plata Publishing Ltd (1977), possibly obtainable in La Paz; distributor: Los Amigos del Libro (W.Guttentag), Casilla 450, Cochabamba. Also numerous expedition reports. The Club Andino Boliviano, Calle México 1638, PO Box 1346, will help with advice on routes and has maps on access, etc. Maps covering most of the range are the photo-surveyed 1:50,000 IGM Series, US$5 each (the only ones available). Club Andino Boliviano will be very pleased to accept "surplus" gear after climbing is finished.

Alfredo Martínez at the Club Andino is the country's foremost guide, or contact the well-regarded and friendly Bernardo Guarachi, Plaza Alonso de Mendoza, Edif. Santa Anita, oficina 314, T 320901, Casilla 20886, La Paz (he has equipment for hire) or Norbert Kloiber, Herrenstrasse 16, 8940 Memmingen, West Germany (T 08331-5258). Iván Blanco Alba, Asociación de Guías de Montaña y Trekking, Calle Chaco 1063, Casilla 1579, La Paz, T 350334, has been recommended (the association has about 10 guides in all and arranges climbing and hiking expeditions). Also recommended, José Camarlinghi (licensed by the German Alpine Club), Casilla 3772, Pedro Kramer 924, La Paz (T 352266).

Skiing Ninety minutes by car from La Paz (36 km.) is Chacaltaya, the highest ski run in the world. Season: November to March, sometimes longer. Skiing equipment may be hired, and a rope-tow reaches 5,221 metres. The facilities are basic, emergency services practically non-existent and the rope tow should be used with caution (it is of a design no longer permitted in Europe). Taxi US$30 (whole car) for a half-day trip, or similar to the top by rented car costs about US$60, and really only at weekends; no visitor should miss the experience and the views. However the trip can be hair raising, buses carry no chains and the drivers have little experience on snow. Occasionally the buses only go half way. The Club Andino, México 1638 y Otero de la Vega, runs its own Saturday and Sunday buses; the day trip, beginning at 0830 and returning at 1730, comes to about US$24 for bus ticket and ski pass for the day; your bus ticket (US$10) gives free access to the ski station restaurant, otherwise US$2 entrance, hot drinks only. Equipment for hire is available (US$10 skis and boots from the Ski School—in the same building as the Ski Club, limited equipment for hire, queue at once) or Ricardo Ramos, 6 de Agosto 2730, about US$10 per day (T 343441 or 372920). A good tip is to share equipment since, at that altitude, you will need a long break between activities. The lift pass costs US$4—out of season the lift only goes if there are 5 or more people (N.B. Club Andino's oxygen bottle at the Chacaltaya station is reported to be empty). Crillon also does a day trip, US$15. Club Andino also occasionally arranges trips to Mount Illimani. One can walk to the summit of Chacaltaya for views of Titicaca on one side, La Paz on the other, and Huayna Potosi. Tiring, as it is over 5,000 metres, but one has most of the day to do the climb. Take plenty of mineral water when going to the mountains as it's thirsty work in the rarefied air. Laguna de Milluni, near Chacaltaya, is a beautiful lake to visit, but do not drink its water; it is dangerously contaminated by acid residues from mining.

Urmiri Take road S towards Oruro, turn left at Urmiri sign at Km. 75. To get this far take Flota Bolívar or Flota Copacabana bus; lifts from the crossroads are few and far between. A steep scenic descent leads to pool filled by mineral springs and a pleasant primitive inn. Worth visiting, it's a 2½ hour trip one way. The La Paz Prefectura runs buses to Urmiri, where they have a hotel (D), price includes food.

Sorata is 105 km. from La Paz at 2,695 metres, giving appreciable relief, and is very beautiful. A 4-6 hour trip each way, bus every day with Transportes Larecaja, Calles Angel Bavia y Bustillos (Av. Kollasuyo), daily 0700, 0715, 0730, returning at 1230 and 1300. Plenty of trucks to Sorata from by cemetery, US$2. It is in a valley at the foot of Illampu. Area has lovely views, mountain climbing, cave exploring. Climbers of **Illampu** (experience and full equipment necessary) start here: hire horses at Candelaria mine and on to Coóco where llamas are hired to reach the base camp at 4,500 metres. Swimming pool 2 km. along road to river. Sunday market. Also Sunday market festival, including bull market, at village of

Achacachi (*Pensión*, F, tiny) on the road. Not far from Sorata, along E shore of Lake Titicaca, is a tremendous marsh. Typical *fiestas*, both at Sorata and Achacachi, on 14 Sept. Pleasant walks: splendid one to San Pedro village and cave with ice-cold swimming in underground lake, 75 metres below surface (take torch). Ulla Ulla vicuña reserve off the Achacachi-Puerto Acosta road around the northeast corner of Lake Titicaca, about 200 km. from La Paz.

Sorata Hotels *Prefectural*, rec., good value, C, with meals, hot water. **Residencia Sorata** above Casa Gunther, C (rec.) with good meals. **Alojamiento Central**, main plaza, No. 127, F, basic, no showers, but nice rooms. **San Cristóbal**, near market, F, bargain. **Copacabana**, F, basic, clean and cheap, German-run, vegetarian meals.

Sorata is the starting place for the "Camino del Oro" or "Gold-digger's Trail", a strenuous 7-8 day hike to Guanay (**see page** 247), via La Cumbre, 4,800 metres (8-11 hrs. straight up from Sorata, best done in 2 stages). Ancoma, (3-4 hrs. from the pass, very cold), Wainapata, Chusi, Llipi, and Unutulumi (2-3 hrs. from Llipi; from here a camioneta runs daily at 0930 to Guanay, for US$5, winding through the many gold-mining towns along the Tipuani valley). After Ancoma it is very hot; in the dry season take water. There is a shop in Chusi. The Ancoma-Llipi section is the most interesting, following the Tipuani river, climbing Inca staircases, crossing rivers on precarious plank bridges and going throuh an Inca tunnel (fully repaird in 1989 after having caved in). (Details in *Backpacking in Peru and Bolivia*—see above).

Tiahuanaco (Tiwanaku) The ruins of Tiahuanaco are near the southern end of Lake Titicaca, by partly paved, but bad road through the village of Laja (solid silver altar in church, but church closed to visitors), the first site of La Paz. Simple meals at US$0.80 available in village. There is a good restaurant near the ruins. The village church is in striking contrast with the pre-Incaic statuary in front of it. The ruins, which are being reconstructed, comprise four main structures: the Kalasasaya compound, the Acapana pyramid (the 6 pillars on top are magnetic, probably by accident rather than design), the underground temple, and the Gate of the Sun, with carved stone blocks weighing many tons; this is reported in a bad state as the locals used it for shooting practice. Many archaeologists believe that Tiahuanaco existed as early as 1600 BC. Recent research suggests that the site was a ceremonial complex at the centre of an empire which covered almost half Bolivia, southern Peru, northern Chile and northwest Argentina. It was also a hub of trans-Andean trade. The reason for the demise of the Tiahuanaco civilization is not entirely clear, although studies by Alan Kolata of the University of Illinois indicate that the area had an extensive system of raised fields, capable of sustaining a population of 20,000, which may have been flooded by rising water levels in Lake Titicaca. This could have precipitated the empire's fall. The raised field system is being reutilized in the Titicaca area. The entrance ticket to Tiahuanaco (US$2.20) also gives entrance to Puma Punku (down the road 1 km.), which contains a pair of andesite gates (among the finest examples of stone cutting in South America) while its sandstone platforms are made up of cut slabs weighing 13 tonnes each. There is a museum near the ruins: entrance free to those with admission tickets for the site (open 0900-1700). There is also a small museum at the ticket window. However most of the best statues are in the Museo Tiahuanaco or the Museo Semisubterráneo in La Paz. Indians trade arrowheads and bronze figures (almost all fakes). Allow 4 hours to see the ruins and village. There is a very basic *alojamiento* on Calle Bolívar, cheap but good views.

Guidebook in English *Tiwanaku*, by Mariano Baptista, Plata Publishing Ltd., Chur, Switzerland, or *Discovering Tiwanaku* by Hugo Boero Rojo. They are obtainable from Los Amigos del Libro (or 2nd-hand from stalls in Av. Ismael Montes). *Guía Especial de Arqueología Tiwanaku*, by Edgar Hernández Leonardini, a guide on the site, recommended. Written guide material is very difficult to come by, so if you can hire a good guide take him with good grace (US$10).

Buses for Tiahuanaco (72 km.) can be caught opposite the Cemetery off Plaza Garita de Lima but may be full already! Taxi for 2 costs about US$20 (can be shared), return, with unlimited time at site. Transportes Ingavi, José María Azú y Eyzaguirre (take any Micro marked

'Cementerio') US$1 (2½-3 hrs.), Mon-Sat. 0700, 0900, 1030, 1300, 1500, Sun. 0700, 0900, 1100 and 1230 (frequency may change according to demand—the earlier you go the better). (Tourist buses cost US$15 return; some tours include Moon Valley.) Some buses go on from Tiahuanaco to Desaguadero; virtually all Desaguadero buses stop at Tiahuanaco, US$0.50. Return buses (last one back at about 1700) can be caught at the crossroads in the village at the "Tránsito" sign; cannot be booked in advance (return is often difficult).

LAKE TITICACA

The road and railway go to **Guaqui**, the port for the Titicaca passenger boats (service suspended in 1985/86; in 1989 the ferry and railway were carrying only freight. *Hotel Guaqui*, G, good value; tiny restaurant on the Plaza de Armas has been rec.). The road crosses the border at Desaguadero into Peru and runs along the western shore to the Peruvian port of Puno, at the northern end. Desaguadero is noted for its lack of accommodation. At Yunguyo a side road to the right re-enters Bolivian territory and leads to Copacabana. (Hourly buses, taking 45 minutes, US$0.40.)

Copacabana, 158 km. from La Paz, is an attractive little town on Lake Titicaca. It has a heavily restored cathedral containing a famous 16th century miracle-working Dark Virgin of the Lake, also known as the Virgin of Candelaria, the patron saint of Bolivia. Candlelight procession on Good Friday. The cathedral itself is notable for its spacious atrium with four small chapels; the main chapel has one of the finest altars in Bolivia. An *hospicio* (serving now as an almshouse) with its two arcaded patios is worth a visit; ask permission before entering. There are 17th and 18th century paintings and statues in the sanctuary and monastery. Good food and drink at the hotels and in the market. Bank only opens Wednesday-Sunday (does not change travellers' cheques); a few restaurants and shops give poor rates, so buy Bolivian money in Yunguyo (beware, much counterfeit money here) before crossing frontier, if coming from Peru. Major festival on August 5-8 makes town full, and dangerous. Vehicles are blessed in front of the church daily, especially on Sunday. There are good walks beside the lake for those unwilling to do penance on the hill, or to an Inca site, Horca del Inca, on the hill behind the town overlooking the lake (rec. sunset walk). On the other side of the lake is El Baño del Inca, about 2 km. (an hotel and museum are under construction here). Ask for directions on reaching the woods. Copacabana's water supply can be intermittent. **NB** The local police need watching: they have been known to accuse travellers of "photographing secret buildings" and "fine" them US$10.

Hotels *Playa Azul*, C, full board (rooms fair, half-board a possibility), hot showers, water supply poor, good food, T 320068. *Ambassador*, E; *Patria*, in main square, E, dirty, cold water, good food; *Prefectural*, E with good meals, clean, helpful, some rooms have lake view; *Alojamiento Imperio*, Calle Visconde de Lemos, F, clean, new, some hot water (shower US$0.50 extra), repeatedly rec., will change money; *Kota Kahuaña*, Av. Busch 15, pink house, F, hot showers, cheap, clean, some rooms with lake view, rec. *Emperador*, behind the Cathedral, F, clean, rec., popular with travellers, washing done and washing facilities, communal baths, hot showers 0600-1300; *Las Playas*, overlooking beach, F, clean, hot showers, laundry facilities; *El Turista*, 13 de Mayo and Jaure, F, rec., cheap and clean; *Residencial Porteñila*, F, clean, safe, rec. Many basic, but cheap and clean *pensiones*, F.

Restaurants *Napolés*, on main plaza, clean, reasonable prices, will change money; *Aransay*, Av. 6 de Agosto 130 friendly, good food; *6 de Agosto* on street of same name, good trout, salad and chips, US$2; *Puerto del Sol*, on road to lake just off main square, cheap, filling set menu; *Tito Yupanqui* Av. Gonzalo Jauregui 123, rec., good value cena or almuerzo. Watch out for gringo pricing of food and in restaurants. *Peña Clima* has music on Saturdays, behind the market; *Turistas* is not rec., but *La Patria* is on Plaza Principal, left-hand corner of the Cathedral. Many other restaurants offer acceptable US$2 meals; trout rec.

Transport By car from La Paz to Copacabana (direct), 4 hours. Bus: either take an agency bus for US$5 and up (pick up at your hotel; US$0.65 ferry fare at Tiquina not normally included, e.g. Turibus, US$13 return); or public bus: 2 de Febrero, José María Aliaga 687, T 377181, US$2.50, 5 hrs., 0800, 1500 each direction; Manko Kapac, José María Aliaga, T 350033, US$2, 0700 and 1315 each way; book one day in advance. Bus, Copacabana-Yunguyo (for Peruvian frontier), hourly, US$0.40, from plaza below *Hotel Playa Azul* . Minibuses to Puno leave 1200-1400, US$4 from *Hotel Litoral* on Plaza, *Hotel Patria*, Cóndor bus (office near cathedral, will store luggage), or *Playa Azul* (Colectur); they leave same time same place for La Paz. To reach Copacabana (or Tiquina) you cross the lovely straits of Tiquina (coming from Peru, the ferry fare has to be paid in Peruvian currency). On the La Paz side of the Strait, there is a clean blue restaurant with excellent toilets. Vehicles are loaded on to a barge equipped with outboard motors. The official charge for a car is US$2, though they ask for more and there is a US$0.50 municipal car toll to enter Copacabana. Delays on the lake crossing during rough weather, when it can get very cold. Even when one has a bus ticket passengers pay US$0.65 each to cross and passports are checked (checks are also made in Copacabana, even if you aren't going to Peru. **N.B.** It is impossible to travel from Copacabana to Guaqui direct, because of border crossings.

Visiting the Lake Sailing boats and motor-boats can be hired in Copacabana to visit the **Island of the Sun**. It contains a sacred rock at its NW end, worshipped as the site of the Inca's creation legend. In the middle of the E shore are Inca steps down to the water. A 2-km. walk from the landing stage to the SE takes one to the main ruins of Pilko Caima—a Sun Gate (not as impressive as at Tiahuanaco), a two-storey building with false domes and superb views. The Island of the Moon (or Coati) may be visited—the best ruins are an Inca temple and nunnery. A cheap way to visit the Island of the Sun is to catch the public ferry from the Bolivian naval station (passport required); it leaves 1300 on Wed., Sat. and Sun. Worth taking camping equipment and food as there is no boat back on the same day nor any accommodation. Ask permission at the *hacienda*, good spring water available opposite hydrofoil landing. Beware of constant harassment for photographs and of thieves. Boats (not tackle) are hired at reasonable rates for fishing. Dawns and sunsets are spectacular. At **Chúa**, on the lake, there is duck shooting, fishing, sailing and at **Huatajata** a yacht club—restaurant open to public, serves reasonable trout, and Crillon Tours International Hydroharbour and *Inca Utama Hotel* (*Hotel Chúa*, situated on lake between Huatajata and Tiquina, good). Bus La Paz—Huatajata/Tiquina, Transportes Titikaka, Av. Kollasuyo 16, daily from 0400, returning between 0700 and 1800.

In Huatajata there are several *alojamientos*, which only seem to come to life at weekends and in the high season. In the village contact Máximo Catari who has rooms for G p.p. and serves meals at *Inti Karka*, a 3-storey building on the waterfront (contact him also at Turismo de Aventura, Av 16 de Julio 1639, P O Box 8412, La Paz). He can also arrange boats to the islands of Pariti, Kalahuta and Suriqui for about US$30. On Suriqui you can visit the museum/craft shops of the Limachi brothers and Paulineo Esteban, who helped in the construction, out of totora reeds, of Thor Heyerdahl's *Ra II*, which sailed from Morocco to Barbados in 1970. Heyerdahl's *Tigris* reed boat, and the balloon gondola for the Nazca (Peru) flight experiment (**see page** 930), were also constructed by the craftsmen of Suriqui. Reed boats are still made on Suriqui, probably the last place where the art survives.

Boats on Lake 6 hours to Island of Sun and back, about US$35 for boat taking 8 (you can bargain), best ruins on S, good scenery on N side, but difficult to persuade boatmen to go there. As it is a 4-hour round trip to see all the temples, it may not be possible to do it all in a day. There is accommodation, bed and blankets, near the Inca steps and at Challa on the other side of the island, and some basic supplies from villagers. Ask for Juan Mamani Ramos in Challa. Similar rates for Island of the Moon. Motor boat trips from Copacabana to Suriqui may be arranged. (Sailing boats, which take five and cost less, often suffer from lack of wind in the morning.) Rowing boat, US$6.50 an hour. Cheaper boats can be found by walking 15 km. along the lakeside outside Copacabana to Yampupata where fishermen cross in ½ hour, US$1-2. Danger of sunburn on lake even if it does not feel hot.

Crillon Tours, Avenida Camacho 1223, run a hydrofoil service on Lake Titicaca with a bilingual guide. Leaving La Paz at 0600 (except Saturday), you get to Huatajata on Lake Titicaca for breakfast by 0800. The hydrofoil sets off at 0830, moves past groups of reed fishing boats, and stops in the Straits of Tiquina for a few minutes to watch the wooden ferry boats crossing. Only the Island of the Sun is visited to see the ruins. You arrive at Copacabana for sightseeing and a trout lunch, with local folk music. The short tour returns to La Paz from Copacabana; the longer one continues to Puno (Peru). Charge: US$160 from La Paz to Puno. Expensive but fascinating, not least for the magnificent views of the Cordillera on a clear day. Turismo Balsa's tour of the Lake, including Isla de Suriqui, has been recommended, except for the fact that the motor boat has no liferafts.

Tristan Jones, who crossed South America in his sailing cutter *Sea Dart* (see his book *The Incredible Voyage*, Futura Publications), spent over eight months cruising Lake Titicaca. He recommends visiting the islands of **Pariti**, where the weaving is very good indeed and, only a mile or so away, **Quebraya**, where there are pre-Inca *chulpas*, or tombs, stretching along the shore. "This was the ancient port for Tiahuanaco, when the lake fell back from that city. No-one lives there, and it is best always to go with an Aymará guide, for the locals are very jealous of the place.

"The only hotel on Lake Huanamarca, at Chúa, is now expensive, but the trout is good. "**Note** The Titicaca Indians' most interesting music, and quite rare, is at masses held for the dead."

CROSSING THE PERUVIAN FRONTIER

We give below the journey by road (see Peruvian section **page 947 for other routes**). A visa to Peru will cost US$5 in US currency (if you need one). Also, the Bolivian navy (assorted hovercraft and motor boats) may be seen at Tiquina. The road between La Paz and Tiquina is now motorway to El Alto, then surfaced.

No hotel at Tiquina, but ask for the Casa Verde, where you can stay for US$0.50 p.p. Two cheap eating places at Yunguyo.

Just as interesting as the water route is the bus journey to Puno along the western side of the lake via Desaguadero at the border, the junction to Yunguyo (13 km. from Copacabana), Pomata, Juli and Ilave. Desaguadero-Puno takes 5 hours by taxi and 6 hours by bus. This is a colourful trip, with wonderful views of the lake against the snow-capped Cordillera. The La Paz-Desaguardero road is mostly good gravel with some fords (treacherous in the dark) and railway level crossings. The road on the Peruvian side is nearly all paved, and you really see the Indian life of the Altiplano. There are many checkpoints for motorists.

A colectivo from La Paz to Puno costs US$9-12 p.p. (8 hours). Colectivos can be caught at Desaguadero for Puno. One problem with the Desaguadero route is that on Tuesday and Friday it is reported that cars are not allowed to cross because these days are set aside for "interchange of national produce". At the risk of another change it may be better (and certainly more scenic) to catch buses La Paz—Copcabana via Tiquina, Copacabana—Yunguyo (for Peruvian entry formalities) and Yunguyo-Puno, (**see page 224**). This is possible in one day.

If you are leaving Copacabana for Peru, get exit stamp at Bolivian immigration office (open 0800-1900) on Yunguyo road. Be careful that dates stamped are correct on all documents. Generally, though, this is now a very straightforward border crossing, with customs and immigration posts at either side of the border; the buses/colectivos stop at each one, 4 in all (or you can walk, but it is over 1 km.). Make sure, however, if arranging a through ticket La Paz-Puno, that you get all the necessary stamps en route, and ascertain whether your journey involves a change of bus. Note the common complaint that through services La Paz-Puno (or vice versa) deteriorate once the border has been crossed, eg smaller buses are used, extra passengers taken on, drivers won't drop you where the company says they will.

It is also possible to enter/leave Bolivia via the east side of the lake. However, the Peruvians do not officially recognize the road as being a border crossing. (Officially, you must get your entry stamp in the Department of Puno, but as this is next to impossible on this route, you will run into difficulties later on.) The Bolivian frontier is at **Puerto Acosta** (there is an immigration office, but it is advisable to get an exit stamp in La Paz first, especially if you have not been staying at a recognized hotel (**see page 258**). One *alojamiento* (G) and one restaurant (*pensión*) on the main plaza (2 smaller *pensiones*/kitchens on the smaller plaza).The road to La Paz (fine during the dry season only) passes through splendid scenery while the area around Puerto Acosta is good walking country and the locals are friendly. Ask for directions to the thermal water swimming pool. The Acosta road northwards to Peru rapidly deteriorates and is only recommended in the dry season (approximately May to October). The only transport beyond Acosta is early on Saturday mornings when a couple of trucks go to the markets, some 25 km. from Puerto Acosta on the border (no formalities); the Peruvian and Bolivian markets are completely different.

N.B. Remember that if you wish to enter Peru from Bolivia you must have an onward ticket (or return ticket) out of Peru. A ticket outward from Peru can be purchased at Exprinter in La Paz, but you will have to pay in foreign currency rather than bolivianos.

SOUTH FROM LA PAZ (2)

Oruro is built on the slopes of a hill at an altitude of 3,704 metres. The population, mostly Indian, is 178,393. It is about 190 km. from La Paz, and is important as a railway centre and for its tin, silver, and tungsten. A 20,000 tons-a-year tin smelter has been built nearby at Vinto; reported no longer open to visitors, following an accident. There is good *pejerrey* fishing on a large nearby lake. Excellent daily market, near railway station. The zoo is not really worth a special visit. Rail travellers from Buenos Aires can, and from Antofagasta have to, alight at Oruro and continue to La Paz by bus. A severe water shortage puts showers at a premium. We are informed that in hotels water is only available in the mornings, owing to city ordinances.

La Diablada At carnival on the Saturday before Ash Wednesday, Oruro stages the Diablada ceremony in gratitude to Pachamama, the Earth Mother. Two figures, a bear and a condor, clear the way for a procession of masked dancers, led by two luxuriously costumed masqueraders representing Satan and Lucifer. Alternating with them in the lead are St. Michael the Archangel and China Supay, the Devil's wife, who plays the role of carnal temptress. Behind them come hundreds of dancers in ferocious diabolical costumes, leaping, shouting, and pirouetting. The parade ends in the crowded football stadium, where the masqueraders perform various mass and solo dances. These are followed by two masques: the first is a tragic re-enactment of the Conquest, in the second the golden-haired Archangel conquers the forces of evil in battle.

In the contest between good and evil, the result in favour of the good is pronounced by the Virgen del Socavón, the patroness of miners, and after the performance the dancers all enter her chapel, chant a hymn in Quechua and pray for pardon. The Diablada was traditionally performed by Indian miners, but three other guilds have taken up the custom.

The costume always features the heavy, gruesome mask modelled in plaster, with a toad or snake on top; huge glass eyes; triangular glass teeth; a horsehair wig; and pointed, vibrating ears. Tied around the neck is a large silk shawl embroidered with dragons or other figures, and the dancer also has a jewelled, fringed breastplate. Over his white shirt and tights he wears a sash trimmed with coins, and from it hang the four flaps of the native skirt, embroidered in gold and silver thread and loaded with precious stones. Special boots equipped with spurs complete the elaborate outfit. Satan and Lucifer wear scarlet cloaks, and carry a serpent twisted around one arm and a trident. The working-class Oruro district known as La Ranchería is particularly famous for the excellence of the costumes and masks made there. One of the most famous folklore groups is the stately Morenada. Carnival lasts 8 days with displays of dancing by day and night often superior to those given on the opening Saturday. There are two options for seating: municipal seats around the main plaza and on Av. Cívica, which cost US$9 for 3 days; Av. Cívica is a good spot because the street is wide and the dancers are unrestricted. The alternative is seating outside shops, also US$9, the streets are narrower so you are closer to the dancers, and to the water-bombers. To wander among the dancers you are officially supposed to purchase a photography ticket for US$15, but little checking seems to be done. Seats can be booked at the town hall. Take raincoats as protection against water pistols and *bombas de agua* (water-filled balloons). Latest reports suggest that the processions on Saturday before Ash Wednesday are fine, but degenerate thereafter as all the participants are drunk; also participants now have to be wealthy to afford to take part, so *campesinos* have been forced to the periphery (selling food, etc.). Beware of sharp practices and doubling of hotel prices during the period of carnival.

Guide *Carnival de Oruro*. Dance costumes and masks, Calle La Paz, 400 block.

Hotels *Repostero*, Sucre 370, good by local standards but unfriendly, C with bath, hot water unreliable on upper floors; *Prefectural-Oruro*, Pagador y Galvarro, D, near station, bleak but quite comfortable, good restaurant; *Terminal*, above bus depot, D, modern, but with technical defects, hot water, night club, expensive restaurant. *Lipton*, Av. 6 de Agosto 225, E, with bath, TV and hot water (cheaper without bath and TV), breakfast; *Residencial Ideal*, Bolívar 386, F, clean but no hot water. *Alojamiento Bolívar*, Bolívar y Sargento Tejerina, F, poor, but restaurant is good and cheap. *Osber*, Murguía y Washington, basic; *Residencial Familiar* annex, F, 25 de Mayo, is clean. *Hispanoamericano*, Galvarro y Aldana, opposite station, F, no hot water and no running water after 2200. *Alojamiento Central Oruro*, Potosí 5917, F, clean, warm showers; *Alojamiento Ferrocarril*, Galvarro 6278, F, basic, no hot water, opp. railway station, nearby is *Alojamiento San Juan de Dios*, Galvarro 6338.

Restaurants   *La Prensa*, Murguía (500 block, Press Club restaurant), quite good; *Pigalle*, Plaza 1° de Febrero, fair, not cheap; *El Chef*, 6 de Octubre 6056, T 50712, good, not cheap; *Quick Lunch*, 6 de Octubre, good, big meals, cheap; *Don Pepe*, Pagador y 1° de Noviembre, above Ciné Elisa, good; *pizzería* at S Galvarro 5865 has good salteñas; good *pizzería* opp. Post Office on Pres. Montes; *Prague*, 6 de Octubre, near centre, good bakery; *Le Grill*, Bolívar, near plaza, good, cheap; cheap food at *Pensión 10 de Febrero*, at bottom end of Bolívar. Vegetarian: *El Huerto*, Bolívar 359. *Pastelería La Polar*, C. Presidente Montes 5985, is good place to get warm; *Pastelería Suiza*, Bolívar, near 6 de Octubre, clean and excellent tea and pastries. *Donut Shop*, 6 de Octubre y Mier, for the obvious, and good hamburgers and beer; rec. nameless restaurant at 6 de Agosto 1166, huge portions.

Shopping   *Infol*, Ayacucho 426 for alpaca, high quality but not cheap nor a large selection and *Reguerín* on the junction with Mier; also sell devil masks. Handicraft market at bus station, cheap souvenirs. Items are generally cheaper in Cochabamba.

Museums   Worth a visit are Patiño legacies, e.g. the Sala de Conciertos (now a cinema). Museo Arqueológico Vivero Municipal, near the zoo on Calle Lizarraga (reached on foot, or Micro 'A Sud') has unique collections of stone llama heads and carnival masks. Guide available, US$0.75. Geology Museum at the university. Ask the tourist office whether they are open.

Exchange   Banks not helpful. It is quite easy to change dollars (cash) on the street, specifically 1 block E of main plaza, or at Ferretería Finkel, Calle Pagador 1491, near the market (large hardware store; owner, Don Ernesto, speaks English and is helpful and friendly). Cheques can be changed at pharmacy close to Ferretería Finkel. Many dealers on the corner opp. railway station offer good rates.

German Consulate   at Adolfo Mier.

Sauna   Ayacucho y Galvarro, wet or dry, showers US$0.75. Duchas Oruro, 500 block of Av. 6 de Agosto (near bus terminal); Santa Bárbara, Pagador 6801.

Laundry   Alemania, Aldana 280.

Post Office   Presidente Montes 1456.

Cables   Cables can be filed at the Empresa Nacional Office (Entel) with the routing via: Cable West Coast.

Tourist Office, Edificio Prefectural, Plaza 10 de Febrero (T 51764), open Mon.-Fri., 0900-1200, 1400-1800, has map of city, helpful. Also on Bolívar and Galvarro, Mon.-Fri., 0900-1200, 1400-1800, Sat. 0900-1200.

Trains   About 5 hours to La Paz (if running, US$4 Pullman, US$3 special) and 7 to Cochabamba (daily) ferrobus US$3, Pullman US$1.60 special; to Potosí, ferrobus three a week, express (2 a week), US$3.75 Pullman, US$2.25 special; to Sucre, same timetable, US$7 Pullman, US$5.50 special. To Villazón, *mixto*, coming from La Paz, Mon. and Thurs., 0100, 18 hours, exhausting but exhilarating to hardy traveller, Express, Tues, Thurs, Fri, US$13 Pullman, US$9 special. Ticket office opens at 0700, best to be there early. Calama, for Antofagasta (Chile), 29½ hours, Fri., 2000, very crowded and dusty for first few stops. There is no train connection to La Paz on this route; for details see above under La Paz, **Railways to/from the Coast**.

Buses   To La Paz, 3 hours, seven bus lines work the route, US$3-5; to Potosí, 10 cold and rough hours, US$6.85, two companies, both at 1900 daily; to Llallagua, Bustillo, 7 a day, US$1.65, Enta 0900 and 1700 daily US$1.45; to Cochabamba, 4½ hours, US$5, six lines, most leave 0800-1000 (one night bus 2000). To Sucre, best to go via Cochabamba if wet as the road to Potosí is so bad. Roads to Río Mulato and Uyuni are very bad, but some trucks work the route; train (8 hours) recommended. Bus agencies are all at the new terminal 6-8 blocks from the railway station in the centre. Trucks to Potosí and Sucre leave from Av. Cochabamba near the Mercado Bolívar.

Excursions From Machacamarca, 24 km. S of Oruro, a branch line runs to Uncia (108 km.) and the ex-Patiño tin mines.

A taxi to Lake Uru Uru costs US$5-7.50 (agree price and waiting time in advance); or take Micro A to its terminus and then walk 1 hour along road, take Micro B for return trip, US$0.15 each way: flamingoes and other water-birds, highly recommended, but not at the height of the dry season (October) when wild life moves elsewhere. Boats may be hired only out of the rainy season.

There are hot springs at Obrajes, where there is the choice of private baths or swimming pool, both hot. Wait at the bus stop at 6 de Octubre 1420 for the (intermittent) bus. Taxis sometimes make the run. Take picnic lunch.

Visitors with a Land Rover might explore the country W of Oruro towards the Chilean frontier. It's a day's drive to the western mountains following tracks rather than roads. There are no hotels in any of the towns, such as Escara or Sabaya, but lodging could be found by asking a school-teacher or local mayor. From Escara it is only 25 km. S to **Chipaya**, the main settlement of the most interesting Indians of the Altiplano. They speak a language closely related to the almost extinct Uru, their dress is distinctive and their conical houses unique. This is a very difficult trip without your own transport. Sometimes trucks leave from Plaza Walter Khon in Oruro for Chipaya; or the village may be reached by taking a bus to Sabaya or Turco, then a truck. Bring your own food; shelter for US$0.25 per head in adobe *alojamiento* . Bicycles may be hired in Chipaya to visit lake 2 hours away with great variety of bird life.

A one-day drive to the west is the **Parque Nacional Sajama**, the world's highest forest. The road is reported to be very bad. To climb **Sajama**, Bolivia's highest mountain (6,530 metres) take the Litoral La Paz-Arica bus and pay the full fare. Ask for the Sajama stop, 20 minutes past the village of that name, before Lagunas, and about 11 hrs. from La Paz. A cheaper way is to take a La Paz-Oruro bus as far as Patacamayo (1½ hrs. from La Paz), then take a truck to Estación Tomarapi (dusty, but very interesting, US$2). Tomarapi is in the Parque Nacional Sajama; no fresh food is available in the Park, so take plenty from La Paz. If continuing into Chile (by truck—possible but hard) remember that no meat, dairy products, fruit or vegetables may be taken across the border. To return to La Paz, walk to Lagunas and take a truck or the Litoral bus (twice weekly). Crampons, ice axe and rope are needed for the climb, which is not technically difficult; the routes to base camp and beyond are fairly obvious. In Sajama village, Peter Brunnhart (El Gringo, in the first house you come to in town) has a book with descriptions of the various routes to the summit. Water is available, but beware of sulphurous streams. It can be very windy.

About 100 km. S of Oruro is **Llallagua** (*Hotel Bustillo*, F; *Santa María, Hotel Llallagua*, F, the best). Nearby is the famous Siglo Veinte, the largest tin mine (ex-Patiño) in the country (trucks up from town). Tourist visits start at 0700. Prior permission to visit must be obtained from Comibol in La Paz. There is an acute water shortage. Llallagua can be reached by bus from Oruro, but only trucks make the journey to Sucre (without going via Potosí), beautiful but uncomfortable. Also buses 1900 from La Paz.

On the road to La Paz is Patacamaya which has a Sunday market (no tourist items); *Alojamiento 18 de Julio*, F (no w/c). A recommended driver is Freddy Barron M., Casilla 23, Oruro, T 55270, for excursions.

From Oruro a railway runs eastwards to Cochabamba (204 km.). It reaches a height of 4,140 metres at Cuesta Colorada before it begins to descend to the fertile basin in which Cochabamba lies. It is 394 km. from La Paz to Cochabamba by road, now paved to Oruro and from there paved except for 50 km. midway, where the going is very rough; about 8 hours by private car. A new highway is being built to Cochabamba, via Quillacollo. On the present road, a short cut from Caracollo to Colhuasi avoids Oruro and saves 65 km.

Cochabamba, Bolivia's third-largest city, founded in 1542, is set in a bowl of rolling hills and is an important agricultural centre. Population: 954,790; altitude 2,570 metres; excellent climate with average temperature of 18° C. It has fine buildings (though much of the modern building looks seedy), a University, an excellent archaeological museum, 25 de Mayo Norte 145, with a small but interesting collection of prehistoric pieces and Indian hieroglyphic scripts, and little-known collection of pre-Inca textiles (Mon.-Fri. only, 0830-1200, 1400-1800, US$1.50 with guide). Many Spanish houses with overhanging eaves, and much for the tourist: a grand view from San Sebastián, a hill on the edge of the city (robberies reported, beware even of police); the Golf Club on Lake Alalay (you need a member to introduce you), and Los Portales, the Patiño mansion in the northern part of the city (take Micro G), set in beautiful grounds, completed after 10 years' effort in 1927 but never occupied (check times with tourist office). The Cathedral in the main plaza is pleasantly decorated; panels painted to look like marble. Just off the plaza is La Compañía, whose whitewashed interior is completely innocent of the usual riot of late Baroque decoration. The municipal market and the Cancha, a retail market (Wednesday and Saturday), are also full of local colour. Beware: street numbering can be chaotic.

An imposing monument overlooks the town from La Coronilla, part of the same hill as San Sebastián. It commemorates the heroic defence of Cochabamba by its womenfolk during the War of Independence. It has fine views and just below it is a charming little old bull ring, little used. There are thermal baths near the city. The Palacio de Cultura, Av. Heroínas y 25 de Mayo, has a group of local museums under one roof (entrance free, but exhibits usually locked). Churches worth a visit include Santo Domingo (Santiváñez and Ayacucho) and Santa Teresa (Baptista and Ecuador). The water is notoriously bad, especially in the rainy season.

Festivals *Fiestas* are frequent and fascinating. Carnival is celebrated 15 days before Lent. Rival groups (*cumparsas*) compete in music, dancing, and fancy dress, culminating in El Corso on the last Saturday of the Carnival. Beware the rains around and after Carnival, and water-throwing the day after, when you are likely to get drenched. *Mascaritas* balls also take place in the carnival season, when the young women wear long hooded satin masks.

Fiesta de la Virgen de Urkupiña, Quillacollo, mid-August, see below; and 14 September, dancing.

Hotels *Gran Hotel Cochabamba*, Plaza Ubaldo Arze, T 43524, beautifully set in the northern part of the city (2 blocks from Los Portales at La Recoleta), with garden, swimming pool (guests only) and tennis courts, good food, the most expensive. *Portales*, Av. Pando 1271, T 48507, 5-star, swimming pool, a long way from centre, new. In the city: motel-type *Berkeley* (French run, solarium with each room, swimming pool); *Ambassador*, Calle España 349 (T 48777), private bath, hot water, telephone, modern, central and reasonable, A, good restaurant. *Capitol*, Colombia 418 y Mayo, T 24510, C, private bath, TV, clean and friendly. *Residencial Escobar*, Uruguay y Nataniel Aguirre, T 29275, D with bath, but no toilet paper (hotel sells it at a price), hot shower, modern mediocre; *Hostal Doria*, Junín 765, D with bath, good, clean; *La Coruña*, Junín 5961 (garden), rec., D; *Las Palmas*, Av. Salamanca 0617, D, spotless. *Residencial*, Calle Uruguay 213, F, good; *Gran Hotel Las Vegas*, D, bath, rec., Esteban Arce 352, behind Cathedral. *El Dorado*, D, rec., clean, hot water, is in 25 de Mayo; *Colón*, in Plaza Colón T 48101, E, hot water, breakfast included. *City Hotel*, Jordán 341, T 22903, near centre, F with shower but without breakfast, cheaper rooms on upper floors, clean, noisy but modern. Both *Alojamiento Oruro*, Junín S-0680, T 24107, F, and *Residencial Agustín López*, Agustín López 0859, T 27250, near bus station, F, clean, comfortable, hot water. *Residencial Pullman*, Av. Aroma L-0870, T 24073, F, hot showers. *Alojamiento Cochabamba*, F, clean, rec., Calle Nataniel Aguirre S-0385, T 25067; *Florida*, 25 de Mayo 583, T 27787, clean and friendly, E (hot showers); *Res El Salvador*, 25 de Mayo 0420, T 27307, E with electric shower, clean, beware theft close to market but inconvenient for restaurants; *Residencial San Severino*, 25 de Mayo 621, hot showers and clothes washing facilities; *Residencial Lanza*, Lanza 929, T 2-4494, E with bath (F without), friendly, by market, rec.; *Residencial Urkupiña*, Esteban Arce 750, F, clean, hot water, near bus station, peepholes in the bedroom walls and ladies' bathrooms. *Residencial Elisa*, C. Agustín López, 0834, T 27846, E with bath, F without, breakfast and water for clothes washing extra, modern, clean, garden, 2 blocks from bus station, friendly, rec. *Residencial Palace*, Av. San Martín 1023, E, hot shower. *Casa de Huéspedes San Martín*, Antezana, between Jordán y Calama, pleasant.

Restaurants *Pasatiempo* on Plaza Colón serves very large steaks. Behind *Doña Lucha's* store, Av. Simón López, *Cala Cala* (1st corner past 1st bridge), is a good bar and restaurant, inexpensive. *La Taquiña*, 500 metres down from brewery 12 km. from city, roast duck lunches Friday, Saturday and Sunday (US$5), superb views, take bus No.3 to Cruce La Taquiña, then walk 30 mins. uphill, or take taxi from Cala Cala, reached by Micro A from plaza. *Suiza*, Av.

Ballivián 820, T 45485, highly rec; *Langostinos*, nearby on same street, good seafood. *El Grill*, next to Los Portales, good, not expensive, you can eat in the garden. Oriental: medium-price *Shangai*, good food although like the *China* nearby, on Av. San Martín, good but dear. *Ming Ming*, on España, opp *Hotel Ideal*, good; *La Puerta del Dragón* on corner of Avenida Arce and Ravelo, 2nd floor. International menu available at *Don Quixote*, Plaza Colón, and *La Costilla de Adán*, Aniceto Padilla 120, good value. *Karpels* on Calle Achá serves Black Forest cake. Rec. is *La Estancia*, in a side street off Plaza Recoleta; just beyond are *Casa del Campo*, Av. Aniceto Padilla, good (Bolivian dishes), *Black Angus* (Argentine style) and *Lai Lai* (good, but slow service). Good Bolivian food at *El Paraje*, Av. Salamanca, half way between Plaza Colón and the bridge to Plaza Recoleta; *El Sauce* on Quijarro 70 serves local specialities, not too cheap but worth it; *Gallo de Oro*, Calle Lanza Sur 0567, rec. Also worth trying is *El Mesón*, Colombia Este 379 and 25 de Mayo—Argentine style. Vegetarian restaurant opposite Jasmín on M. Rocha and Ayacucho, lunch US$1, rec; *Govinda*, between Plaza Colón and España, vegetarian, good value. On Av. España are *Don Corleone* (pizzas, opp. *Hotel Ambassador*), *España* (No. 272), *Heladería España* and many *confiterías*; many cheap places on 25 de Mayo (incl. *California Donuts, Dallas*) and Bolívar. *Don Pollo*, top of the Prado next to the roundabout, good ceviche, US$1.50, friendly management. *Burger House* and *Kentucky Chicken* on main square. *Heladería Imperial* (off Plaza de Armas) for good ice cream; also *H. Sabor* at Esq. Colón and Prado, nice surroundings. Excellent pastries and ice cream at the *Zurich Tea Room*, Av. San Martín Norte 143, closes 2000, and *Café Berneck* on Colombia and San Martín, both expensive; *Salón Berna*, Av. San Martín Norte 209 y Colombia, Swiss pastry, ice creams inexpensive. Rec. salteñas at *Confitería Caravelle* on Calle Sucre. The local place for cakes is *Dulce Ilusión* on Calle España.

Shopping Main market is called San Antonio. Large market (La Cancha) near railway station (tourist items). *Fotrama* Cooperative for alpaca sweaters, stoles, rugs, etc. (expensive); there is also a branch at Av. de Heroínas, or Madame Eleska's *Adam* shop, (Jordán 0148, T 25791) now run by her son (expensive), or *Amerindia* for good rugs and lengths of alpaca material, as well as ponchos and jumpers, T 49994 to visit offices and purchase items; or picturesque Indian market and nearby shops. *Artesaniás Casa Fisher*, Plazuela de la Recoleta, T 45625, good woollen goods. For leather try *Confecciones Gamucuer*, Destacamento 317. Market fruit and vegetables excellent and very cheap, but on more expensive articles do not expect prices to drop very much when bargaining. Try local hot drink, *api*, made from maize. Main markets Wed. and Sat.; beware pickpockets and thieves. **Cycle repairs** : parts in market at Lanza 700 Sur. **Camera repairs** recommended at shop on General Achá, next door to *Cromos* . Foto Broadway, España y Colombia, for developing at reasonable prices. A very good bookshop is *Los Amigos del Libro*, Av. de Heroínas 311 y España, and Gral. Achá 110. Books cheaper than in La Paz.

Local Transport Micros and colectivos, US$0.10; *trufis* (vans), US$0.12; anything marked "San Antonio" goes to the market. Taxis: agree fare before getting in; about US$0.50 from anywhere to the Plaza; double after dark.

Entertainment *Camel* (discotheque), *Colonial* (discotheque), *El Trocador* (peña), *Alexander* (restaurant/ peña), all near intersection of Heroínas and Oquendo (all start around 2300); *Pier Seven* (disco) Heroínas 464.

Swimming *El Paraíso*, halfway to Quillacollo (Km. 10), sauna and pool, US$0.50 entrance, accessible by bus or train. Pool at Club Social, Calle Méjico (US$1.60), is open to the public as well as La Rivera on Simón López (Micro A) or Los Chorrillos, both US$1, crowded on Sunday (Micro G), or outside town then *Posada de los Cisnes* at Quillacollo, at Km. 13 on Cochabamba road (entrance US$1.60). Also at *Don Gerardo* at Km. 7, with restaurant. Pool, sauna, restaurant at Estancia El Rosedal at Tiquipaya, take bus number 12 from Antezana y Cabrera to end of line. Most are open only at weekends.

Tennis Club de Ténis de Cochabamba admits non-members for US$5 per day.

Fishing Excellent trout fishing in lake formed by the Corani dam, 48 km. N of Cochabamba.

Exchange Houses Exprint-Bol, Plaza 14 de Septiembre 252 (will change travellers' cheques into dollars at 2% commission); American Ltda., Plaza 14 de Septiembre. Universo, on España, 1 block from plaza. Money changers congregate in Plaza Colón. Try also Los Amigos del Libro and Librería Juventud in main plaza.

Language Classes Sra. Blanca de La Rosa Villareal, Av. Villazón 5218 (T 44298) charges US$3 for a 45 minute lesson. Instituto de Lenguaje (Idelco), Plaza Busch, Bolívar 826, T 44868.

Consulates W. Germany, España 149; US, Av. de Heroínas 464, office 115, T 25896; Brazil, Potosí 1455 (opp. Patiño Museum), open 1400-1800; Argentina, Av. Pando 1329, visa applications 0900-1300; Perú, Av. Pando 1143.

Addresses At 25 de Mayo 25698, Telephone 21288, is the Centro Boliviano Norteamericano with a library of English-language books, open 0900-1200 and 1500-1900. Alliance Française, Santiváñez 187.

Post Office Av. Heroínas, next to TAM office; Mon.-Sat. 0800-1900, Sun. 0800-1200.

Cables can be filed at Empresa Nacional Office.

Tourist Office Calle General Achá, and Plaza 14 de Septiembre (helpful). Kiosks at Jorge Wilstermann airport and near Entel building. A useful photocopy map of the city can be obtained from Los Amigos del Libro, who also publish a guide book. Recommended travel agency, Gitano Tours.

Railway Tickets available on day before travel (office opens 0600-1000, be there early). There are ferrobuses leaving for La Paz 3 times a week, 8 hours; fares US$7 Pullman, US$6 special. Express train to Oruro 0830, 3 a week; ferrobus daily at (rec), US$3 1st, US$1.60 2nd. Sit on left side for the best views.

Air Service Jorge Wilstermann airport. Airport bus is Micro B from Plaza 14 de Septiembre, taxis about US$2 (no set rates, so bargain). Daily by LAB to and from La Paz (½ hour), US$23 one way (15 kg. baggage allowance), book early for morning flights, and to Santa Cruz (½ hour, US$30). Three flights a week to Sucre and Tarija (US$32), also to Trinidad (connects with Riberalta flight). LAB in town at Ayacucho and Heroínas, open 0800; at airport LAB office opens 0500. TAM (Hamiraya 122, nr. Av. Heroínas) to La Paz, US$16; flights to Riberalta US$100, but infrequent; best to fly from La Paz or Santa Cruz, via Trinidad.

Bus Services Buses (overnight) and colectivos (day and night) to Santa Cruz, taking 12 to 16 hours (US$11); the road goes via Villa Tunari, Puerto Villarroel, Buena Vista and Montero, a more northerly and lowland alternative to the mountain road via Epizana. The new route is through cocaine country so there are many checkpoints. To La Paz via Oruro (0800, 1000 and 1300 with Nobleza, 2000 with Trans Nacional, and others) US$4.90, 8 hrs., over a terrifying road (but good surface for all but 1½ hours), you have to change buses in Oruro and get a new ticket at the same time on a different floor, luggage is automatically transferred to the new bus; or via Caracollo, by night or by day, 10-12 hours. Bus to Oruro, US$5, 6½ hrs. Epizana (US$3.35). To Potosí, via Oruro. Daily to Sucre, by Flota Minera, Aroma 120, or Flota Unificada, between 1800 and 1830, 12 hours, US$7, all but the first 2 hours are very bad. To Sucre by day; take a bus or truck to Aiquile (bus every other day 1300), spend the night there, then take a truck to Sucre. There are 3 bus stations: along Av. Aroma, near Plaza San Sebastián, for long-distance bus offices; the Avenida at the foot of La Coronilla for local buses to Tarata, Punata and Clisa; Av. Oquendo (at the edge of Lake Alalay) to Villa Tunari, US$3.50; Chimoré, US$4.50; Eterazama, US$4.50; Puerto Villarroel, US$6; Puerto San Francisco, US$5; and other destinations—all leave 0800-1000 if sufficient passengers. Trucks to Oruro leave from Plaza San Sebastián. Trucks to Sucre leave from end of Av. San Martín (US$3.30). Trucks to Puerto Villarroel from Av. República, US$3.30.

Excursions To the N, in a high fault-block range of mountains, is Cerro Tunari, 5,180 metres. A road runs to within 300 metres of the top, usually sprinkled with a little snow. There are beautiful views of the Cochabamba valley from the mountain road which goes into the Parque Tunari from Cala Cala, ending at the lake which supplies drinking water; best in the afternoon, but no public transport. Another somewhat difficult mountain road to the north, with little local traffic, climbs from Tiquipaya (take bus No. 12 from Cochabamba, US$0.15) to Chapisicca. Trucks leave Mon., and Thur., returning Tues. and Fri. with potatoes and wool for the Cochabamba market. Beautiful views on the ascent: good walks on the plateau to mountain lakes in lovely scenery.

The Cochabamba basin, dotted with several small townships, is the largest grain and fruit producing area in Bolivia. **Quillacollo** (20,000 people), a 20 minute bus ride from Av. Ayacucho y Av. Aroma, just beyond the markets in Cochabamba (good Sunday market but no tourist items; the campesinos do not like being photographed). Fiesta de la Virgen de Urkupiña in mid-August lasts 4 days with much dancing and religious ceremony (designed to make you rich); very interesting, plenty of transport from Cochabamba. 2-3 km. beyond Quillacollo is a road to the beautiful Pairumani *hacienda*, centre of the Patiño agricultural foundation. The house may be visited (T 60082 to arrange visit, or check times at Los Portales in Cochabamba); the Patiño mausoleum may be visited if one is accompanied by a member of the family. Don't miss Tarata, a sleepy old village with beautiful Plaza, nearby, market day Thursday (bus also from Av. Ayacucho, US$0.50). Punata, an hour's bus ride from Cochabamba, has an interesting, lively market on Tuesday. Behind the main church, new vehicles are lined up to be blessed by the priest. The local speciality is *garapiña*, a mixture of *chicha* and icecream. Beyond Punata, at Villa Rivera, woven wall hangings are produced. Another 6 km. from Torata is Huayculi, the population of which consists almost entirely of potters, who produce good ceramics for the Cochabamba market. Several houses may be visited to see the kilns and painting areas. No public transport from Torata, but you may get a ride. A railway line runs from Cochabamba through the Punata valley as far as Arani. Another runs to Vila-Vila (132 km.). There is a large Sunday market at **Clisa**, accessible by bus from Av. Ayacucho. For those interested in *charangos* (of wood) a visit to Aiquile (6 hrs.) is recommended (by bus US$3.50; *Hotel Escudo*, F, basic). To the north is the Parque Tunari, which is partly forested, and Laguna Wara Wara at 4,000 metres surrounded by 4,500 metre mountains.

Three seldom visited Inca ruins might be of interest: Inka-Rakay, a small outpost about 45 minutes' drive from Cochabamba and a 2-hour hike up a mountain; and Inkallajta and Samaipata (see below).

The Inka-Rakay ruins are near the village of Sipe-Sipe; the main attraction is the view from the site over the Cochabamba valley, as well as the mountains ringing the ruins. Take a bus to Quillacollo where the bus for Sipe-Sipe waits until there are enough passengers. From Sipe-Sipe to the ruins there is either a 4 km. footpath, or a 12 km. road with almost no traffic, which, to walk, takes three hours. Either hitch or hire guides and Land Rover in Cochabamba. Several letters indicate that it might be less terrifying to walk but all admit that this is a beautiful trip. Start early for it is a full day. Leave the Square at Sipe Sipe going up the street past the church, then left at the top and then right when you come to the wider road. Follow this road to the ridge ahead. Just below the ridge, the road loses a little height to take a bend. There is an outcrop of rock and here look for a track leading away downhill. The Inka-Rakay ruins are about 200 metres below. **N.B.** Carry plenty of water as there is none available and beware of theft on the footpath.

The 500-km. road via the mountains and Epizana to Santa Cruz (**page 251**) is paved, but the surface has greatly deteriorated. Before the Siberia pass, 5 km. beyond Montepunco at Pocona (Km. 119), the 23-km. road to Inkallajta (unpaved and very bad) turns off. The ruins, on a flat spur of land at the mouth of a steep valley, are extensive and the temple is said to have been the largest roofed Inca building. To get there without your own transport a reader advises: "Take a micro to the checkpoint 10 km. from Cochabamba, take a truck to Km. 122, walk on towards Pocona or take a truck for 12 km. A large yellow sign indicates the trail. After approx. 10 km. the trail divides, take the downhill path and the ruins are a further 2 km. Take food and camping gear". At Km. 386 are the ruins of Samaipata, worth a stop. At **Epizana**, a lovely dilapidated colonial village, 13 km. beyond Montepunco (Km. 128), with poor hotels and service stations, a branch road, right—dusty, stony, and narrow in parts, but very scenic—goes 233 km. to Sucre, 7-8 hours drive. Totora, described as one of the loveliest sleepy, friendly colonial villages, is said to be better to stay in than Epizana.

S of Oruro the railway from La Paz skirts Lake Poopó, over 90 km. long and 32 km. wide. From Río Mulato a branch line runs eastwards to Potosí (174 km.) and Sucre. The track reaches the height of 4,786 metres at Cóndor: one of the highest points on the world's railway lines.

Potosí, with a population of 103,183, stands at 4,070 metres, the highest city of its size in the world. The climate is often bitterly cold and fireplaces are few; warm clothes essential. It was founded by the Spaniards on April 10, 1545, after they had discovered Indian mine workings at Cerro Rico, the hill at whose foot it stands.

Immense amounts of silver were once extracted from this hill. In Spain "éste es un Potosí" (it's a Potosí) is still used for anything superlatively rich. Early in the 17th century Potosí had a population of 113,380, but two centuries later, as its lodes began to deteriorate and silver had been found in Peru and Mexico, Potosí became little more than a ghost town. It was the demand for tin—a metal the Spaniards ignored—that lifted the city to comparative prosperity again. Silver, copper and lead are also mined. A new seam of silver has been discovered recently.

Large parts of Potosí are colonial, with twisting, narrow streets and an occasional great mansion with its coat of arms over the doorway. UNESCO has declared the city to be "Patrimonio de la Humanidad." Some of the best buildings are grouped round the Plaza 10 de Noviembre, the main square. The Convent of Santa Teresa (entry US$1.50, opening times vary, check at Tourist Office) has an interesting collection of colonial and religious art. The old Cabildo and the Royal Treasury—Las Cajas Reales—are both here, converted to other uses. The Cathedral (open only between 0900 and 1000 on Sundays) faces the square, and near-by is the Mint—the Casa Real de Moneda (founded 1572, rebuilt 1759)—one of the chief monuments of civil building in Hispanic America. The Moneda (entrance US$1, tours at 1000 and 1430) has a museum in many sections. The main art gallery is in a splendid salon on the first floor: the salon better than the paintings. Elsewhere are coin dies and huge wooden presses which made the silver strip from which coins were cut. You are advised to wear warm clothes, as it is cold inside; a guided tour (essential) starts at 0900 and 1400. The smelting houses have carved altar pieces from Potosí's ruined churches. Open Mon.-Sat. 0900-1200 and 1400-1700. Among Potosí's baroque churches, typical of the Andean or "mestizo" architecture of the 18th century, are the Compañía (Jesuit) church, with an impressive bell-gable (1700), San Francisco with a fine organ (monastery closed to visitors, church can be visited in morning and evening, museum of ecclesiastical art, open 1400-1600, Mon.-Fri.), and San Lorenzo, with a rich portal (1728-1744); fine views from the tower. San Martín, with an uninviting exterior, is beautiful inside, but normally closed for fear of theft. Ask the German Redemptorist Fathers to show you around; their office is just to the left of their church. Other churches to visit include Jerusalén, close to the Hotel Centenario, and San Agustín (only by prior arrangement with tourist office) on Bolívar, with crypts and catacombs. Tour starts at 1700, US$0.10 admission. From San Cristóbal, at Pacheco with Cañete, one gets a fine view over the whole city. The University has a museum (Mon.-Fri., 1000-1200, 1500-1700, entrance US$1).

Festival San Barolomé, 24 August, costumes for hire in artesanía market on Calle Sucre.

Hotels Best hotel is **Hostal Colonial**, Hoyos 8, C, a pretty colonial house (T 24265) near the main plaza rec, has names and T numbers of guides, even if you're not staying there. **Turista**, Lanza 19 (T 22492), D, helpful, now remodelled, but no heating or hot water, breakfast (US$1 only) highly rec. **Casa de Huéspedes Hispano**, Matos 62, clean rooms with or without bath, F; **Res. San Antonio**, Oruro 140, E, hot shower, basic and run down; **Residencial Sumaj**, Gumiel 10, F, friendly, small but warm rooms, good breakfast. **Hotel IV Centenario**, D, hot water, but no heating, has seen better days but friendly, central; **Santa María**, Av. Serrudo 166, E, clean, hot water; **Casa de Huéspedes**, San Agustín, 1st floor, opp Hidalgo Tours, E with bath, clean, **Alojamiento Ferrocarril**, Av. E. Villazón 159, F, basic, uncomfortable beds but clean (no hot water but hot showers available for US$0.55), friendly, close to the railway station. The best cheap lodgings (for which Potosí has a bad reputation) between Av. Oruro and Av. Serrudo, clean, but rarely with hot water; **Alojamiento Tumusla** (avoid ground floor—cold), near the bus station, F, grubby; **Hostal Oruro**, Oruro 292, F, shared shower, clean and basic; **Alojamiento La Paz**, Oruro 242, F pp, hot shower US$0.50, clean, pleasant, washing facilities; **Residencial Copacabana**, Av. Serrudo, F, shared room, restaurant, safe car park; **Villa Imperial**, dirty, noisy, same prices, good motorcycle parking, US$0.20 for hot

Potosí: Key to Map

1. Plaza 10 de Noviembre, 2. Plaza 6 de Agosto, 3. Plazuela Daniel Campos, 4. Cathedral, 5. Jerusalén, 6. San Lorenzo, 7. San Agustín, 8. La Compañía, 9. San Martín, 10. Convent of Santa Teresa, 11. Convent of San Francisco, 12. Casa Real de Móneda, 13. University Museum, 14. Alcaldía, 15. Central Market, 16. Handicrafts Market, 17. Tourist Office, 18. Post Office

shower. *Alojamiento San Lorenzo*, Bustillos 967, G, close to market, very basic, no shower or hot water. In times of drought there may be rationing of water for showers etc.

Restaurants *Sumac Orko*, 25 de Mayo, near Bolívar, reasonable, friendly; *Confitería Royal*, just off main plaza, small selection of good cakes and coffee; *El Aldabón*, Plaza 10 de Noviembre 35, good set meal, US$1; *El Mesón*, corner of Plaza 10 de Noviembre near Tarija, irregular opening, European-style, variously reported as excellent, and pretentious; *Scaramuch*, Bolívar 843 and *La Tranquita* at Bolívar 957, good and cheap. *La Salteña*, Linares 20, rec, cheap, tasty salteñas, good service, also pizzas. *Siete Vueltas*, Bolívar 816, serves a decent almuerzo. *Bolívar*, Sucre y Bolívar, 4 course lunch US$1.25, rec.; *Colonial*, US$1 for 4 courses, food clean and fresh. Cakes and ice creams along Linares and in Plaza 25 de Mayo. *Don Lucho*, Bolívar 765, meat good (but not rec. for chicken), *peñas* at weekends, check entrance fee for show before eating. *The Sky Room* at Bolívar 701 has interesting views of the town and the Cerro, mediocre food. *Snack bar Bamby*, just off top of main square, good cheap lunches. Breakfast can be a difficult meal to find, but it is available in the Mercado Central, Calle Bolívar: worthwhile to see if the hotel serves it as most restaurants seem to be closed at this time. *Alemania Confitería*, Hoyo y Sucre (opp. tourism kiosk), very good (but check bill); *Coffee Shop*, Boulevard 20, good coffee and cakes. To get fresh bread you have to be up at 0630-0700 and go to Bustillos between Ingavi and Oniste and up a passage on the upper side of the street.

Shopping Silver (sometimes containing nickel) and native cloth; there are stalls in Calle Bustillos. Silver coins, jewellery and coca leaves in market between Av. Camacho and H. del Chaco. There is an interesting gift shop in the post office. Silver is sold in the main market near the Calle Oruro entrance. There is an informal swap market every Friday night at the Plaza, at Bolívar and Quijarro. There is a handicraft market at the junction of Calle Sucre and Plaza Saavedra (rec). Some Fridays the merchants organize music, food and drink (*ponche*), not to be missed. The best bookshop is at the University, open Mon.-Fri., 1000-1200, 1500-1700.

Local Transport   Taxi within city limits US$0.30; approx US$0.50/km. for longer journeys. Buses US$0.10.

Car Spares   VW spares are obtainable at Hauwa Ltd, but it takes several days to get parts from La Paz.

Exchange   Ask at Tourist Office. Street changers around Oruro 430; also shops and restaurants around main plaza. Amex cheques may be changed at Hidalgo Tours, Junín y Bolívar (2% commission). Morales, Bertram y Schuett, Matos 19, and Distribuidora Cultural Sud, Bolivar 876, both change travellers cheques.

Clinic   Clínica Británica, on Oruro near *Alojamiento La Paz*, clinics a.m. and p.m. English spoken, US$6.

Sauna   Bath and showers in Calle Nogales. Sauna Florida, Plaza Chuquimina, near bus station, open Thurs. and Fri., US$1.50.

Post Office   Lanza and Chuquisaca; unreliable for overseas mail.

Police station   On Plaza 10 de Noviembre. Beware so-called "plain-clothes police"; they are not authentic.

Tourist Agents   Potosí Tours, on the Plaza, good city tours; Candería Tours, Bolívar 634, T 22458 and Tursul Ltda, Calle San Alberto, 24, T 21360.

Tourist Office   On 2nd Floor, Cámara de Minería, Calle Quijarro (T 25288). ½ block from main plaza, and booth on main plaza (both closed Sat. and Sun.); sells town maps (US$0.25), information booklet (US$2.50), helpful.

Trains   To La Paz, *ferrobus*: book previous day only: once/twice a week, 10½ hrs., US$8 Pullman, US$5.50 special; express train once a week: Thurs., US$5.75 Pullman, US$4 special. To Sucre, *ferrobus* twice a week, US$4.50 Pullman, US$3 special. To Oruro, 8 hrs., *ferrobus* and express US$3.75 Pullman, US$2.25 special, with connection to Cochabamba.

To Calama for Antofagasta, take the bus to Uyuni daily between 1000 and 1400 from Villa Imperial, Toledo 216, off Av. Antofagasta where it crosses the railway, US$5, or there's a microbus on Wed. from about 50 metres from the station, US$6 (buy ticket night before or early same day and arrive in good time for the bus) and connect with the La Paz-Antofagasta train/bus route on Fri. night. Alternatively, take the Tues. *ferrobus* to Oruro and then book Pullman on Fri. train to Calama; fares can be paid in bolivianos. To Villazón, go to Uyuni and connect with La Paz-Villazón train there. Apparently there is a Sunday train as far as Tupiza, but little information at the station; it should take 18 hrs. but may be 24 hrs. late.

Buses   Bus station out of town, below railway station and 20 minute walk (or *micros* C, I or L) from main Plaza; through buses from La Paz call here at the toll gate, as they are not allowed to enter city limits. To Tarija, 10 de Noviembre, Fri. and Sun. 0830, very poor buses; Tarija is reached by car or lorry leaving Plaza Minero (Bus "A"), full range of scenery. To Villazón, daily at 1800, 12 hrs., or 0800, shop around for best price. To Sucre, Soltrans, Quijarro 34, just off Plaza 10 de Noviembre, US$5, several daily, 5½ hrs., first at 0700; also Hidalgo (minibus), Bolívar y Junín, 0700, 1830, 4 hrs., US$5 incl. snack. La Paz (12 hrs., overnight only, US$9.50) leaves 1800 daily. Oruro, US$6.85. Trucks for Tarabuco leave from Plaza San Francisco. Heavy overbooking reported on buses, also, timetables change frequently; the trucks from the plaza are an alternative if you are in a hurry.

Warning   It has been reported that men with false police I.D. cards meet trains and buses. They demand to see passports and currency and confiscate dollars. Insist on going to the police station, if possible with a witness.

Airport   under construction.

A suggested tour round the town is to walk down Quijarro from San Agustín on Bolívar as far as Oniste then return by Junín, looking at "the passage of the seven turns" on the way. There is a fine stone doorway (house of the Marqués de Otavi) in Junín between Matos and Bolívar. Calle Lanza 8 (now a school) was the house of José de Quiroz and of Antonio López de Quiroga. Along Millares between Chuquisaca and Nogales one sees on the right a sculpted stone doorway and on the left a doorway with two rampant lions in low relief on the lintel. Turning left up Nogales one comes to an old mansion in a little square. Turn left along La Paz and three blocks along there is another stone doorway with suns in relief. At the corner with Bolívar is the Casa del Balcón de la Horca. Turn left and one comes to the Casa de las Tres Portadas.

Excursions A recommended guide to the cooperative mines and ore-processing plant is Eduardo Garnica Fajardo, Hernández 1035, Casilla 33, T 24708 (or via *Hotel Ferrocarril*, or in main plaza 0800-0830); he speaks English, French and some Hebrew. He charges about US$3 for a 4½ hr. morning tour, which involves meeting miners and seeing them at work in conditions described as "like stepping back into the nineteenth century"; a contribution to the miners' cooperative is appreciated, take cigarettes and coca leaves as presents. If visiting the mines, wear old clothes and take a good torch and a handkerchief to filter the dusty air, visitors need to be reasonably fit. Eduardo Garnica has written to assure us that he works independently and is not connected with either Potosí Tours or Hidalgo Tours, both of whom claim that he is in their employ. Another guide is Salustio Gallardo, Calle Betanzos 231, near Plaza Minero, price negotiable; also Braulio Mamani (T 23396, he operates from Plaza 10 de Noviembre, 0800-0830), about US$2 p.p., to Mina Rosario. Spanish only. Juan Carlos González, Av. Japón 10, T 24074 or 26740/25591 (Agencia Hidalgo), takes small groups to private mines, Spanish spoken only. Visitors can approach Padre Gustavo, a Belgian priest at the Concepción church who occasionally organizes visits to the cooperative mines. More interesting than a visit to the State mine, which is now automated (visits daily at 0900, take microbus 100 from main square; US$2 pp, including rubber boots, lamp, helmet and jacket).

A recommended Sunday trip is to Manquiri, a sanctuary in the mountains. Wait from 0730 at Garita de San Roque for a truck. Another trip is to Caiza on the fork off the Tarija road at Ingeniero Cucho; for this you will need a tent, etc., as there is no hotel. Only one bus a day from Potosí: it should leave from Plaza del Minero at 1330 but is often late. Caiza is where cooperatives produce handicrafts in tin. Their Caiza outlet is the Belgian Catholic Agricultural School in the main square. Cheap *mantas* and other hand woven goods can be purchased at villages betweeen Challatapa and Potosí, on the road from Oruro along Lake Poopó. At Betanzos (1 hour on the Sucre road), the Feria de Papas is held on 14-15 May: folk dances, music and costumes, especially on the 15th (buses from Plaza Uyuni, Potosí).

Thermal Baths at lake below city. Laguna de Tarapaya, Miraflores truck or van from Plaza Chuquimina to 25 Km. post, just before crossing the bridge. Above Tarapaya is the crater, which is reached by a track from 23 Km. point. When bathing take great care as the current is very strong; whirlpools can develop, which have claimed many lives. There are buses back from Tarapaya at 1400 and 1600. A good place to spend a lazy day resting. Also Chaqui (by truck or bus from Plaza Uyuni, tiring journey, but clean, pleasant baths), Tora and San Diego (on the main road to Sucre, it also has a restaurant). Alternatively there is a thermal pool 1 km. before the village on the other side of the river. It is best to get off bus at the bridge 400 metres on the Potosí side of the river and pool.

Hallam Murray writes: One of the most interesting and varied mountain walks I have experienced in Bolivia can be made from Potosí. It takes 8 hours at a gentle pace and covers about 24 km. (map Hoja 6435, serie H631, from Instituto Geográfico Militar is helpful but not essential). Take Av. Hoyos east out of Plaza Alonso Ibáñez and continue beyond the Iglesia San Martín. Follow the road or path south east and climb the hill above the city, aiming for Laguna San Ildefonso. Ask directions if in doubt. This lake was built in 1767 to provide water for the city and is in a wonderful position. It has duck, and fish deep down in the clear water. Beyond, to the east, are some very inviting-looking, lumpy hills and mountains. Follow up the valley, passing herds of llama and old mine openings. It is probably best to start on the path to the south east of the lake (to right). This valley is full of fascinating plants, animals, and rock formations.

Continue beyond a second unnamed, and possibly dried-up lake and turn south to climb steeply to the adjoining valley, just beyond the peak of Cerro Masoni. The time from Plaza Alonso Ibáñez to the highest point between the two valleys is 4 hours. The views from this point are spectacular, with mountain peaks to the south towards Argentina. Closer at hand is moon-like scenery. This is an excellent spot for a picnic. Continue down and back to Potosí via the small lake which can be seen from the high point. Probably best to keep high to the left (south) of Lagunas San Sebastián and to approach Cerro Rico on its eastern flank. The walk back into Potosí is depressing and bleak, passing miners' houses, close to a heavily polluted stream and with the most extensively worked face of Cerro Rico to your left, but this is a side of Bolivia which should also be seen.

Sucre, (pop. 86,609) the official capital of Bolivia, is reached from Potosí (175 km.) by daily train (a grand trip) or by road (the best *dirt* road in Bolivia). A branch road runs to it from the Cochabamba-Santa Cruz highway. The altitude is 2,790 metres, and the climate is mild (mean temperature 12°C, but sometimes 24°C in November-December and 7°C in June).

Sucre (originally Charcas) was founded in 1538. Long isolation has helped it to preserve its courtly charm; local law now requires all buildings to be painted original colonial white. Public buildings are impressive. Opening times are as reported but seem to be variable. Be prepared to get frustrated. Among these are the Casa de la Libertad (open 0900-1200 and 1400-1700, Sats., 0900-1200, US$0.50, US$1 to take photographs), where the country's Declaration of Independence was signed; the modern Santo Domingo (Palace of Justice), the seat of Bolivia's judiciary, R. Moreno y Ravelo (entry free but must leave passport with guard, no photographs allowed); the modern Government Palace; the beautiful 17th century Cathedral, open 0730-0915, and museum (US$0.25), open 1000-1200 and 1500-1700 (1000-1200, Sat.) (worth seeing are the Chapel of the famous jewel-encrusted Virgin of Guadalupe, 1601—closed in 1989, and the monstrance and other church jewels by appointment with the Padre Tesorero); the Consistorial building; the Teatro Gran Mariscal Sucre, and Junín College. Sucre University was founded in 1624. Early 17th century wooden ceilings (*alfarjes*) with intricate patterns of Moorish origin are found in San Miguel (see below) and San Francisco (0700-0930 and 1600-1930).

Behind the town a road flanked by Stations of the Cross ascends an attractive hill, Cerro Churuquella, with large eucalyptus trees on its flank, to a statue of Christ at the top. There is also a *mirador* in the square opposite La Recoleta, at the end of Calle Dalence. The cemetery is worth a visit, to see mausoleums of presidents and other famous people; take Calle Junín south to its end, 7-8 blocks from main plaza.

Churches San Miguel is being restored (closed in 1989) and is very beautiful with carved and painted ceilings, pure-white walls and gold and silver altar. In the Baptistery there is a painting by Viti, the first great painter of the New World, who studied under Raphael. In the Sacristy are another of his paintings and some early sculpture. It was from San Miguel that Jesuit missionaries went south to convert Argentina, Uruguay and Paraguay. San Felipe Neri, church and monastery, attractive courtyard with cloisters. Roof gives view of city; open 1630-1700, US$0.50 entrance. Entrance requires a guide from Universidad de Turismo office, opposite the convent, at N. Ortiz 182. Santa Mónica (Arenales with Junín) is perhaps one of the finest gems of Spanish architecture in the Americas, note the main altar and pulpit in filigree (closed in 1987, but the ex-convent—now a school—can be visited). San Francisco in Calle Ravelo has altars coated in gold leaf; the bell is the one that summoned the people of Sucre to struggle for independence. Capilla de la Rotonda (Av. L. Cabrera, near the station), Santa Rita, San Sebastián and Sta. Bárbara (Plaza Pizarro). Santo Domingo, corner of Calvo and Bolívar (1545), open only Fridays and Sunday night. Next door at Calvo 212 is the Santa Clara museum with art gallery and silver collection (see below), and Church of San Lázaro, built in 1538 and regarded as the first cathedral of La Plata (Sucre). On the nave walls are six paintings attributed to Zurbarán; it has fine silverwork and alabaster in the Baptistery, open 0700-0745 Sat., and Sun. after church service at 1900. La Merced (Azurduy and Pérez) has gilded altar pieces.

Warning Police all wear uniform and carry I.D. cards with photographs. Insist on going to the police station, if possible with a witness, before showing passport or money to anyone without these credentials.

Festival Independence celebrations, 24-26 May, most services, museums and restaurants closed.

Hotels Best hotel is *Hostal Cruz de Popayán*, Calle Loa, C, rec., a beautiful colonial house with interior courtyard, no heating, good breakfast served in rooms; *Hostal Sucre*, 3 stars, Bustillos 113, D, good, clean, rec.; *Hostal los Pinos*, Colón 502, clean, comfortable, hot showers, D. *Londres*, Av. Hernando Siles, 3 blocks uphill from station, D with shower, restaurant, good ; *Residencial Bolivia*, near plaza in Calle San Alberto, E, with dangerous electric showers, hot water, noisy, unfriendly, breakfast included (clothes washing, cooking not allowed); *Residencial Oriental*, Calle San Alberto 9, E, clean, friendly but basic, hot

Sucre: Key to map

Public Buildings: 1. Casa de la Livertad, 2. Palace of Justice/Santo Domingo. *Churches:* 3. Cathedral, 4. San Miguel, 5. San Lázaro, 6. Santa Mónica, 7. San Francisco, 8. San Felipe Neri, 9. Santa Rita, 10. San Sebastián, 11. Santa Bárbara, 12. Santo Domingo, 13. Santa Clara. *Museums:* 14. Charcas, Anthropology & Modern Art, 15. Teatro Mariscal. *Services:* 16. Post Office, 17. Entel —communications, 18. Tourist Office, 19. LAB, 20. Hostal Sucre.

water; *Residencial Charcas*, Ravelo 62, T 23972, E with or without bath, clean, helpful, opp. market, laundry, rec.; *Alojamiento El Turista*, Ravelo 118, F, clean, showers, friendly, good; *Alojamiento La Plata*, Ravelo 32, F, clean, central, hot showers; *La Plata*, Ravelo, F, rec. *Alojamiento San Francisco*, esq. Av. Acre and Camargo, bath or shower, E with breakfast and bath, has seen better days, but pleasant, meals available; also near station, *Municipal*, Av. Venezuela, E (T 21074), rec., restaurant; *Residencial Bustillo*, Calle Ravelo 158, F, clean and modern, hot water, shared showers, will store luggage at a price; *Alojamiento Austria*, Av. Ostria Gutiérrez 33, E, hot showers, good value, near bus station as well as *Alojamiento Central*, E, rec. (beware the buses which stop at 2000).

Restaurants Best restaurant is *Aranjuez*, Calvo 16 (closed Tues.), expensive. *Piso Cero*, Venezuela 241, good but expensive; *Las Vegas* on east side of Plaza (icecream, no breakfast, at lunchtime no drink without food, good evening meals); *Pizzería Napoletana*, on Plaza, excellent pizzas and good home-made ice cream; *Pecos Bill Pizza*, Bustillos, between plaza and *Hostal Sucre*, rec; *China*, Ravelo y Arce, 1st floor, not cheap but good. The *Alliance Française*, Aniceto Arce 35, 1/2 block from main square, serves crêpes, ratatouille (rec) Mon. and Fri. 1100-1300, 1600-2000, soft music etc—also occasional films and cultural events; good breakfast at *Leblon*, Aniceto Arce 99, opp. San Francisco church. *Medeval*, Plaza San Francisco 105, international food (reports vary). *Las Tablitas*, Bustillo 198 esq Colón, good lunches; good almuerzo at Hernando Siles 953. *Mesón de don Enrique*, N. Ortiz, good; other places along Ortiz, near Plaza 25 de Mayo, are *Snack Paulista* (no. 14) and *Bibliocafé Sureña* (No. 30), good coffee and crêpes, "bohemian", with English and German magazines, closed Monday, and 2230-2300, nightly; *Kultor-Café Berlin*, Avaroa 326, good food, German newspapers, *peña* every other Friday, closed Sunday (in same building as Instituto Cultural Boliviano Alemán—ICBA); *Palace*, Plaza 25 de Mayo 38, good, reasonably priced.

Los Bajos, Loa 761, serves special sausages. *Doña Máxima*, Junín 411; *Austria*, good, attached to hotel, near bus station. Good value is given at *El Solar*, Bolívar 800 (Sun. closed); *Snack Anni*, Avaroa y Bolivia, for the best empanadas; *La Casona*, Av. Ostria Gutiérrez 401, local food. Foodstores in the new market, highly rec., serve clean cheap meals for US$1 until 1400. *Snack Miriam*, España 67, good *salteñas*; *Bar El Tío*, Calle España, is pleasant as is *Pip* (breakfast especially), esq. Ravelo and Lourdes, Loa 581. *Ghandi*, Arenales 15, excellent curry, US$1.50. *Sagitario*, Arenales 17, good cakes and pastries. The local brewery produces an interesting sweetish porter or stout. *Café Hacheh*, Pastor Sainz 241, coffee bar and art gallery near university, interesting to visit. The local chocolate is recommended.

Shopping Antique woven items must be sought. Permanent market along Av. Jaime Mendoza, for food and household goods. There is a wide selection in Calle Argentina, opposite Post Office, and *Coinca*, Loa 616, and *Candelaria* at Bolívar 634 (expensive). *Artesanías Calcha*, Calle Hernando Siles 713, rec., very knowledgeable proprietor. *ASUR* project shop, San Alberto 413, T 32194, weavings from North Potosí and Tarabuco at very good prices, rec. Good selection in arcade at Junín 403. Doña Máxima sells woven goods from the basement of *Alojamiento Guadalupe*, Junín 411, opp. Central Market; best to know what you're looking for, not especially cheap. *Charangos* from Tarabuco are obtainable in the main plaza. Prices for souvenir items tend to be much higher than in La Paz.

Taxis US$0.30 p.p. within city limits.

Motor-cycle Mechanic Sr Jaime Medina, Motorservi Honda, Calle René Calvo Arana, T 5484. Will service all makes of machine.

Night Clubs *Night Club Municipal*, Av. Venezuela; *El Sótano* at the Parque Bolívar, acceptable; *El Cuerno Colonial*, España 162. Disco-Viva María, US$2.80, entrance includes a beer, San Alberto 6. *Charleston Piano Bar*, cover charge US$1.50. *peña* Fri. and Sat.

Folklore Centro Cultural Masis aims to promote traditional culture. It offers instruction in Quechua, traditional Bolivian music making and handicrafts; once or twice a week there are musical events and the snack bar holds exhibitions of textiles and photographs. Open 1530-2130. The director, Roberto Sahonero, who will give further details, is to be found at Bolívar 561 DS (T 23403, Casilla 463); he is usually at the centre Mon., Wed. and Fri., 1900.

Museums These include the University's anthropological, floric, and colonial collections at the Charcas Museum (Bolívar 700), and its presidential and modern-art galleries. There are also the Museo de Santa Clara (Calle Calvo 212), paintings, and the Museo de la Recoleta (Calle Pedro de Anzúrez), open 0930-1130 and 1500-1730 US$0.50 for entrance to all collections. The Recoleta monastery on a hill above the town is notable for the beauty of its cloisters and gardens; the carved wooden choirstalls in the chapel (upstairs) are especially fine (0930-1130 and 1400-1730). The Glorieta mansion (now very neglected), with the Princesa collection (leaflet available from tourist office), 5 km. outside the city bus E on the road to Potosí, has beautiful painted ceilings and Arabian gardens; worth a visit: "a delightful mixture of many styles", open Mon.-Fri. 0900-1200 and 1400-1800. It is in the military compound, passports must be surrendered at the gate, do not cross the river. At the back of the Grand Marshal's theatre, the faculty of medical sciences recently opened a museum of human anatomy and pathology—open 0830-1200 and 1400-1800 Mon.-Fri.

Exchange Banco del Estado, no exchange facilities; Banco Nacional, cash only at a poor rate. Banco Santa Cruz, Calle España will change cash and travellers' cheques. Travel agencies' rates are good. Ambar, *casa de cambio*, San Alberto 7, T 31339, good rates. Turismo Sucre, Bustillos 107, good rates. Most shops and hotels will change money. Street changers on Hernando Siles/Camargo between España and Junín.

Cultural Institutes The Goethe Institute shows films, has German newspapers and books to lend (1030-1230 and 1700-2000), and its bar is a good meeting place. Instituto Cultural Boliviano Alemán (ICBA), Avaroa 326, offers courses in Spanish and Quechua and in various dance forms at reasonable prices (US$10 for 12 lessons, twice a week for 6 weeks), term dates variable.

Consulates West German, Arenales 215 (T 21862). Spain, Pasaje Argandoña (T 21435); Italy, Defensa 33 (T 22650).

Laundry Lavarap, Bolívar 609; Lavandería Cristal, Bolívar y Camargo, under 24 hrs.

Hospital Recommended, staffed by Japanese and locals. Doctor Roger Mortojo Panoso, Av. Hernando Siles 911.

Saunas San Roque and Acuario, Sat and Sun only, 1430-2000; Copacabana, just out of town (take taxi), Wed to Sun, 1400-2000.

Post Office Argentina 50, between Estudiantes and Olañeta. **Telephone** Entel, España 271.

Tourist Office Calle Potosí 102 esq. San Alberto, T 25983, helpful, map US$0.25. Check church and museum opening hours. Sub-office at airport, helpful. Tourist information office opp. San Felipe Neri, at Nicolás Ortiz 182, is run by students studying tourism, who will show you around tourist sites for free (see above under **Churches**). All offices closed Sat. and Sun.

Travel Agencies Candelaria Tours, Bolívar 634; Teresita's Tours, Bustillos 146; Solarsa Tours, Arenales 212; Hidalgo Tours, Bustillos 105; Sucre Tours, Bustillos 107. Soltours, N.Ortiz 6, next to Cathedral, T 30500.

Train Service to Potosí, Oruro and La Paz usually twice a week (book seats as far in advance as possible: to Potosí, US$4.50 Pullman, US$3 special—often no connection in the rainy season; to Oruro, US$7 first, US$5.50 second class, *ferrobus* 3 times weekly (if trying to make connection with train to Calama on Fri. and it looks like you will be late, get out at Río Mulato); to La Paz 20 hours (take food), US$7.50 Pullman, US$5 special. Station, behind Parque Bolívar, T 21114-21115, only open after 1500.

Air Service By LAB there is a Mon., Wed., Fri. La Paz-Sucre direct (US$35) air service, to La Paz via Cochabamba (US$20) on Tuesdays, Thursdays and Saturdays (US$40) and Santa Cruz (US$25) daily. Puerto Suárez, 0900 Mondays, TAM. There are also LAB flights to Tarija (Mon., Wed. and Fri., US$24) and Yacuiba, and F27 flights to Camiri (Tues., Thurs., Sat.). TAM fly on Wed. to La Paz, Santa Cruz and Puerto Suárez, and on Sundays to Santa Cruz. All flights heavily booked but some "stand by" available. Your best chance is to lie in wait at the airport; they know nothing in town. Airport 5 km. from town (T 24445). LAB office is at Bustillos 121-127 (T 21140), from where free bus for passengers leaves 1½ hrs. before flight. Taxi US$2; buses from main road (difficult to get on with luggage). Beware of pickpockets at airport. Local airport taxes total US$2 (3 in all), pay before checking in.

Bus daily to La Paz via Cochabamba (18 hrs., US$11.50), very rough and roads liable to flooding during the rainy season, but worthwhile; via Potosí, US$17 (18 hrs.); to Cochabamba daily, 1800, 12½ hrs., US$7 (also by truck for about US$4, night trip caught at cement works 1½ km. off Cochabamba road—Micro A goes as far as turning); daily buses and *micros* to Potosí (0700, 1700 with Hidalgo, US$5), 4½ hrs., US$5 with Soltrans, N Ortiz 6, 0700, US$4.50, with Transtin, Estudiantes 17). Bus to Santa Cruz, via Cochabamba, Flota Unificada, Mon. and Thurs., 1700, 18 hrs., US$16, also Mopar (rec). Once a week to Tarija at 1030, Saturday, US$16, 18 hrs. To Monteagudo, Thurs. and Sun., 1500, US$5.30. Oruro, via Potosí or Cochabamba, none direct. To Llallagua, Wed. and Sat., 0700, US$8.20, 10 hours. (Take Micro A to bus station 3 km. from centre, taxi US$0.80, T 22029.)

Excursion   *Tarabuco*, 3,295 metres, 64 km. by road and 78 km. by rail from Sucre, has a most colourful Indian market on Sundays, starting about 0930. Buses and trucks leave 0500-0900 from top of Calle Calvo, Sucre, 2 ½ hr. journey, US$1.50 (or taxi, US$40). Train (*ferrobus*) from Sucre, Sun. 0700, 2½ hrs., US$1.50, returning 1400, buy ticket at 0600 on day of departure (check in advance, track is liable to mudslides in rainy weather).
There is a direct bus to Cochabamba, US$9.50, 11 hrs. There are at least 2 budget hotels, including *Residencial Florida*, basic, dirty but friendly, lovely garden, G, restaurant not rec; try *Bar California*, basic, or other restaurants. Festival with fair: Virgen de Rosario, 1st Sunday in October and 12 March. If you are hardy take a sleeping-bag and sleep in the only restaurant.
   "Surely this is one of the most colourful Indian markets in S America. The costume of these Indians is unique and fantastic. Women do most of the work. The woven skirts and belts of the women are some of the finest to be found in Bolivia, and good weaving may be bought."—Hilary Bradt. Although the market is popular with tourists, it is still worth a visit. Best bargains are to be had on weekdays, or before the bulk of tourists arrive, or late in the day. Our latest reports indicate that prices at the market are high, but that the real appeal is the Indians in their authentic dress. To see the weaving in progress, visits to Candelaria (two hours truck from Tarabuco) or Macha (8 hours from Sucre), Pocata (one hour from Macha), or Ravelo will save you from hordes of other tourists (travel to Ravelo: by lorry or *micro*, mostly in the morning from departure point near airport, 3 hrs. one way; *micro*, US$1.30, check at shop at Hernando Siles 843 if it's running, it's supposed to leave at 0900, return 1600—lorries back to Sucre invariably full). Specially recommended is a trip to Potolo, where they weave red animals on a black or brown background. Trucks (Thurs. and Fri. in the dry season) go direct from near Sucre airport; in the wet, you can only get to Challanaca and you walk for 3 hours to get there—the prices will probably be lower in the wet season. It has even been suggested that it is cheaper to buy in Peru or from street vendors in Sucre—so check and

compare. Swimming in the rainy season only at Cachimayo, Yotala and Ñujchu on the road to Potosí.

A main road runs SE from Sucre through Tarabuco and **Monteagudo** (*Hotel Salamanca*, F) for 216 km. to **Villa Serrano**, where the musician Mauro Núñez lived. A music festival is held on 28-29 December. (The journey is beautiful through wild mountains.) 460 km. from Sucre is **Camiri** (20,000 people), growing rapidly because of nearby oilfields—the oil refinery may be visited. Flota El Chaqueño runs from Sucre to Camiri on Fri., theoretically at 0700, at least 20 hrs., US$16, returns, again in theory, on Tues. From Camiri there is a bus to Santa Cruz which should be booked up well in advance as it is always crowded (terrifying road), office on Av. Busch next to *Gran Hotel Londres*, goes 4 times a week if enough passengers, 8 hrs., US$11; *camioneta* leaves from in front of the market when there are enough passengers, US$7.80, 7 hrs. (boring journey, dusty). As a garrison town it has some hotels (*Hotel Ortuño*, Calle Comercio, E; *Residencial Marieta*, Av. Petrolera 15, E; *Residencial Premier*, Av. Busch 60, E; *Residencial Familiar*, Calle Comercio, F; *Gran Hotel Londres*, Av. Busch 36, F), restaurants, bars (nothing is cheap) and also flights to La Paz and Santa Cruz, 180 km. If you arrive by car: at Tránsito checkpoint pick up a slip of paper with instructions on how to reach Guardia where you collect permits to stay overnight. Next visit army post on Plaza de Armas to be checked there. Before leaving town visit Guardia again to collect a permit to proceed—all permits cost about US$0.50 each. Hotels will *not* accept car passengers without permit. S along a very bad road is **Villa Montes**, more easily reached from Tarija (260 km., bus leaves Tues., Fri. and Sat. at 0700, US$11), famous for the highest temperatures in Bolivia; take mosquito repellant. Opposite the railway station 2 km. out of town is *Hotel El Rancho*, F, with bungalow-type accommodation; the food is expensive so eat in town. It is on the edge of the Gran Chaco and has a road and railway S to Yacuiba and Argentina and another dry-season road E to Paraguay which is O.K. for high clearance vehicles. *Hotel Pilcomayo*, F, dirty, communal bath, and *Hotel Demia*, F, clean and friendly. The bus trip via Tarabuco and Camiri to Argentina is very rough; poor road and little comfort. Two buses a week (Wed. and Sat. 0730) to Llallagua (**see page 228**).

It is possible to drive from Camiri into Paraguay direct in a truck or 4-wheel-drive vehicle, carrying food and water for a week. No help can be relied on in case of a breakdown. At Camiri, obtain a US$3 permit from the Guardia to go 64 km. (1½ hours) over a rough road to **Boyuibe**, the last town in Bolivia (*Hotel Guadalquivir*, or *Hotel Chaqueño* next door, both F, both serve meals); once there pay US$2 at Customs for an exit stamp. Passports must be stamped by commander of the army post south of the town. There are some rivers to ford and although they are dry in the dry season they can be impassable if there is rain in the area. Some road junctions are unmarked; get accurate directions from the army before leaving Boyuibe. At Boyuibe gas and water are available, and it is on the Yacuiba railway. A new line is being built West out of Boyuibe, then North, to Tarabuco, to link up with Cochabamba (it has reached Monteagudo).

Tom Courtenay-Clack tells us: "¾ km. after the military checkpoint turn left past a large water tower. From then on just follow the most used road. The road is much better now than it used to be, owing to black market fuel truck traffic. It's still quite difficult though and four wheel drive and high clearance is essential. A winch is also advisable especially if there's been rain. The insects are appalling.

"The road turns disconcertingly South for several km. at one point but it's O.K. We saw a tapir and a puma on this road. It is 134 km. from Boyuibe to the Bolivian border post at Villazón (not to be confused with the other Villazón on the frontier with Argentina—Ed.). It took us 6 hours. (It is reported that this trip can take up to 3 days if there are unseasonable storms—Ed.) The officer at Villazón will give you your exit stamp. The nine soldiers at each of the fly-infested lonely posts on either side of the border will vie for your company if you arrive at nightfall. Enormously appreciated by these poor fellows are small gifts of soft drinks, beer, cigarettes or canned fruit. They do six month stints here.

"The Paraguayan post is 3 km. from the Bolivian post. Just a passport check here. Camping is better here than at the Bolivian post because they have a shower and will let you use their kitchen. 13 km. from the Paraguayan border post is Fortín Garay. Here the commanding officer will give you entry stamps. The road is somewhat better from here on, sandy and bumpy but straight.

"There is a police check point later at Mister Long, and still one more at an airforce base. All these take time. It took us nearly nine hours to get to Mariscal Estigarribia. Here there's a large military base and passports are cleared by the commandant. He is unavailable from 1300 to 1600, so be prepared for a wait. If you have to wait, there's a nice German-run pension 100 yards away where you can get excellent ice-cream, a meal and a room. They have a pet rhea (ostrich) if you want to see one close up.

"One and a half hours from Mariscal is Filadelfia (340 km. from Fortín Garay). About 20 km. South of Filadelfia the road is newly and beautifully asphalted all the way to Asunción. The birds along this road are incredible."

There are no buses beyond Camiri on this road. Fuel tankers and other trucks go through to Paraguay (about one a week on average); they will sometimes take one passenger, as regulations forbid more, from Camiri to Filadelfia for US$5—possibly less. The army goes to Villazón once or twice a month; you can camp at Villazón, but no food is available, nor is there much water. Not much food on the Paraguayan side until Mariscal Estigarribia.

The railway line S from Río Mulato goes through **Uyuni** (3,660 metres), the junction for the line to Chile. Warning: do not take photos between Uyuni and the border. Trains to La Paz (US$5.60 Pullman, US$3.75 special) and Oruro (5 a week: 3 express, 2 *trenes mixtos*). Tickets for the train to Calama (coming from Oruro) can be bought on Fri. between 1700 and 1800. The road down from Oruro is sandy, and after rain very bad. Buses to Potosí, 1300, 12-18 hrs., microbus Thurs and Fri, 1300, US$6, 7 hrs., truck on Sunday from near Banco del Estado. Uyuni lies bitterly cold and unprotected on the plain at the edge of a vast salt lake, the Salar of Uyuni. Julián Quispe charges US$25 for 3 hour trip to the Salar. His green jeep holds 8 and is in front of the cathedral around 1000-1100.

"When it still has water in it (up to 4 or possibly 6 inches), being in the middle of the Salar de Uyuni is like being an ant on a gigantic mirror. The blue sky merges into the blue water, the islands are perfectly reflected and since there is no horizon they appear suspended in space. Some areas may be dry, in which case the salt crust is as blinding-white and featureless as the most perfect snowfield (sunglasses essential)."—Stephen Saker, who endorses our warning on the **Ollagüe-Uyuni track (see below).**

Uyuni's 20,000 inhabitants are mostly Indian. Its market is the only point of interest, best on Thurs. and Fri. (public showers). There is also supposed to be gasoline available at YPFB near cemetery.

Hotels and Services *Avenida*, F, renovated, clean, hot showers, bar. The *patrón*, Don Jesús Rosas, runs jeep excursions to the Salar (US$35). *Residencial Uyuni*, F, *Residencial Copacabana*, F, *Residencial Urkipiña*, F, all three on Av. Acre, basic and quite clean. *Restaurant Ferrocaril* cooks very good llama meat in the traditional manner, order several hours before. Banco del Estado will not change money. The pharmacy on the main street will change money, but it is very difficult to find out the current rate of exchange.

Motorists must be warned against a road from Río Mulato to Chile by way of Ollagüe. "Between Río Mulato and Uyuni it is deep soft sand and possible only for 4-wheel drive vehicles and trucks. Beyond there is the danger of getting lost on the many tracks leading over the deserted salt lakes, no gasoline between Uyuni and Calama (Chile), and little hope of help with a breakdown on the Bolivian side unless you don't mind waiting for perhaps a week. After rain the route is impassable. Where the road has been built up, *never* forsake it for the appealing soft salt beside it. The salt takes a man's weight but a vehicle breaks through the crust into unfathomable depths of plasticine mud below."—Andrew Parkin.

Excursions Dan Buck and Anne Meadows write: "**Laguna Colorada**, about 350-400 km. SW of Uyuni, 12 hours' straight driving over unmarked, rugged truck tracks, is featured in Tony Morrison's two books, *Land Above the Clouds* and *The Andes*. It is one of Bolivia's most spectacular and most isolated marvels. The rare James flamingoes, along with the more common Chilean and Andean flamingoes, breed and live in its red algae-coloured waters. The shores and shallows of the lake are crusted with gypsum and salt, a bizarre arctic-white counterpoint to the flaming red waters.

"The standard rate for hiring a truck or jeep, Uyuni-Laguna Colorada 3 day round trip, is US$300-400, negotiate. The Uyuni *Hotel Avenida* is a good contact for making arrangements. There is a welter of tracks, and even locals easily get lost. Truck rides can be arranged at the Sindicato de Chóferes in town, behind the church. A map, compass, and a guide are all useful, plus asking directions of every person one meets along the way— which won't be many. In our round trip we met no vehicles, only 4 *campesinos* on bicycles and a handful on foot. Going out we went Uyuni-Corpina-Quetena Chica-east side Laguna Colorada; on the return we travelled west side Laguna Colorada-Alota-Uyuni. Beware: if approaching the lake from the east side, take the south shore of the lake to the *campamento*, it is longer but better than the north shore which is deep, treacherous volcanic ash and sand.

A map of Laguna Colorada may be obtained from Instituto Geográfico Militar in Uyuni. Sr. Erasmo Ansa, Calle Loa between Uruguay and Mexico, drives a truck to Laguna Colorada twice a week. He will leave you there and pick up after 2 or 3 days on his way back, US$25-50 depending on his load.

"There is no dependable transport linking any of the towns and mining camps in the Uyuni-Laguna Colorada area. No one should travel in the area without cold-weather camping gear, sufficient food, etc." At Laguna Colorada, you must camp out of doors, no alternative. A map of Laguna Colorada may be obtained from the Instituto Geográfico Militar in Uyuni. Sr. Erasmo Ansa, Calle Loa between Uruguay and México, drives a truck to Laguna Colorada twice a week. He will leave you there and pick up after 2 or 3 days on his way back, US$25-50 depending on his load.

There is a truck on Saturdays which leaves Chiguana, a town on the Uyuni-Antofagasta railway, once the La Paz train arrives, going to Laguna Verde, 3 hrs., south of Laguna Colorada. There are also trucks which go to the Laguna Colorada and the Susana sulphur mine. A lorry back sometimes leaves on Friday afternoon, but this is by no means certain. There is transport from Uyuni with people taking petrol to the *campamento* at Laguna Colorada—ask at the mining offices at Uyuni. At Chiguana and Laguna Verde the army will normally provide a place to sleep (no bedding). You may also be able to sleep on a floor at the sulphur mine at Laguna Verde, or at the workers' quarters for the Sol de Mañana geothermal project, 45 km. from Laguna Colorada. Hot food can also be purchased although there is none at Laguna Colorada. Travel in this region is possible anytime between May and October, but there is no petrol, mechanical assistance or supplies S of Salinas de Garci Mendoza (270 km. from Oruro) or Uyuni (petrol in Salinas de Garci Mendoza is twice as expensive as in Uyuni). The army can be helpful for transport in the area if you persist.

The scenery between Laguna Colorada and Laguna Verde is spectacular (geysers, boiling mud pools, steaming streams, lakes with flamingoes, wind-eroded rocks). Just past Laguna Verde is a deserted Bolivian border sign, from where it is possible to walk 40 km. to a small Chilean border town, with regular transport to Calama.

One can visit **Llica**, the capital of Daniel Campos Province, in 5 hours over the Salar by truck, or about 12 hours by boat, if there is enough water in the lake. There is a new, basic *Alojamiento Municipal* in town, F. Also Angel Quispe in the plaza has 3 beds. Food is "difficult". There is a teachers' training college but not much special to see. Two fiestas: July 26 and August 15. Good for llama and other wool handicrafts.

SW of Atocha, 2 hours by irregular bus or truck is San Vicente where Butch Cassidy and the Sundance Kid are said to be buried in an unmarked grave, following a gun battle with the police in 1908.

S of Uyuni, 200 km., is **Tupiza** (2,990 metres, 11,000 people), a centre of the silver, tin, lead, and bismuth mining industries (*Hotel Mitru*, F, private shower and bath; next to it is *Residencial Crillón*, F, very run down, with good motorcycle parking; much better for motorcyclists is *Res. Valle Hermoso*, Av. Pedro Arraya, T 589, F, hot showers, good, will let you park bikes in restaurant; also *Hotel Americano*, G, opposite railway station). Chajra Huasi, a palazzo-style, abandoned home of the Aramayo family, may be visited, across Río Tupiza. The statue in the main square of Tupiza is to the founding member of the Aramayo mining dynasty, pre-eminent in the late 19th, early 20th centuries, together with the Patiños and the Hoschilds. Chajra Huasi was expropriated by the government after the 1952 revolution. IGM office, for maps, is in the Municipal building. Three trains to border every week. Fri train to Potosí at 1400, late, uncomfortable, not recommended. Bad road from Potosí which goes on S to Villazón; often closed in rainy season because there is no bridge over the Río Suipacha. Bus to Villazón 3 hrs., US$2 (many daily).

From **Villazón** (13,000 people, good local market), on the border with Argentina, there is an improved road to Tarija, 965 km. by road from La Paz. The road linking Potosí with Villazón via Camargo is in poor condition and about 100 km. longer than the better road via Tupiza. For information on border crossing with Argentina **see page** 106; US$1 usually charged for crossing; remember Argentina is 1 hour ahead (2 hours in summer) if making a connection. Little to see in Villazón (has two cinemas) and not at all welcoming; border area must not be photographed.

Hotels at Villazón *Panamericano*, F, breakfast and lunch (showers extra); *Residencia*

Martínez, ½ block from bus station, well signed, F, hot water when town's supply is on; *Residencial El Cortijo*, clean, E, good value, hot water, restaurant; *Residencial Avenida*, F, but try bargaining. *Grand Palace*, clean, E. Restaurants opposite bus station and on first floor of covered market.

Argentine Consulate in main plaza, open 1400-1700, Mon.-Fri.; not very helpful.

Exchange Money-changing at Cambio Porvenir or other *cambios* on main street, rates said to be good (cash only); Banco del Estado does not change travellers' cheques. Out of hours try the Ciné Rex. Warning: do not show passport or money to men claiming to be plainclothes police.

Buses from Villazón To Potosí at 1600 and 1700, 13-15 hrs., US$7 (terrible in the wet); to Tupiza, 0700 and 1500; to Tarija, Mon., Tues., Thur., Sun. at 1100, Wed. and Sat. at 0900 (US$6.50-7), 7 hours; trucks for Tarija from beside bus station. Bus passengers for La Paz must cross from Argentina the previous day. Watch out for overcharging by Panamericano bus company— the "direct" La Paz bus usually goes only as far as Potosí, and is very slow. Bus station is near the main square, behind Ciné Teatro Libertador Bolívar; it is about 6 blocks from the border. Taxi to border, US$0.20 or hire partir, US$1, and walk across.

Trains from Villazón To La Paz (very dusty and cold journey), Tues., Fri., at 1450, arr. La Paz 1110 next day (US$9 Pullman, US$6.50 special). On Sat. at 1530 a train leaves for La Paz with an expensive Pullman coach which has come right through from Buenos Aires (dep. Thurs) and Tucumán (dep. Fri. 1500); arrival in La Paz scheduled for 0930 Sunday. Journey very crowded, especially 2nd class. Train stops at Tupiza for evening meal at 1900 (no cutlery or napkins provided), Atocha, Uyuni and Oruro, *tren mixto* twice a week to Oruro, Mon. and Thur. at 1340 (cold journey). The express from La Paz/Oruro connects with a bus to Tarija (in theory), tickets from railway station, about 1 km. out of town on main road.

At **Camargo**, on road from Potosí to Tarija, is an excellent restaurant, *Media Luz*. Guest rooms have been built for overnight stop.

Tarija, at 1,956 metres (population, 60,621) was founded July 4, 1574, in the rich valley of the Guadalquivir river. The road from Villazón, 183 km., is the shortest route from Argentina; there is also a road to Potosí via Camargo. The alternative route from Argentina via Bermejo (13,000 people, *casas de cambio* on main street, thorough customs searches), 216 km., is at a fairly low altitude and in a mild climate, but the views are rewarding; not recommended in the rainy season or a month or so after. The road is in an appalling condition apart from 50 km. which are paved. Daily buses take 5 or 6 hours. Do not try to cycle. There is no railway. Tarija had a tumultuous struggle against Spain, declaring itself independent in 1807, and has a strong cultural heritage. Its own university was founded in 1946. There is a large archaeological collection; the entrance is at the corner of the building. Maize, vegetables, wheat, potatoes and splendid grapes thrive in the basin. Bolivia's best wines are produced here (no organized tours to *bodegas*, phone for appointment). Its people are markedly religious and strongly individualistic, and the Indian strain is less marked here than elsewhere in Bolivia. The modern Avenida Costanera gracefully flanks the curves of the river. The Casa Dorada is being reconstructed with a view to becoming the Casa de Cultura (interested visitors may be shown round by the restorer), note the figures in the roof. A good view can be had from Cerro San Juan; follow Calle D.Paz to the top of the rise where the buses gather, turn right on the cobbled street, then right through the gate and follow the Stations of the Cross to the top (it's about 4 blocks up from zoo).

The city is famous for its *niño* (child) processions: colourful and charming. During processions of San Roque in a 3-day festival from the first Sunday in September the richly dressed saint's statue is paraded through the streets; wearing lively colours, cloth turbans and cloth veils, the people dance before it as it goes, and women throw flowers from the balconies. Dogs are decorated with ribbons for the day. On the second Sunday in October the flower festival commemorates the Virgen del Rosario, and another in Easter week.

Hotels *Prefectural*, D with bath and pool, shabby, poor service (2 km. from city centre, upstream on road); *Hostal Carmen*, Ingavi 0-0784, T 3372/4342, E, shower, clean, good value; *Hostal Costanera*, Av. Las Américas, rec., reasonably-priced, modern facilities; *América*, Bolívar 257, hot showers, good, F, restaurant attached (good); opp. is *Residencial Bolívar*, E with bath, rec., clean, comfortable, hot water, breakfast US$1; *Residencial Miraflores*, Calle Sucre, F, clean and rec. *Terminal*, behind bus station, family-run, good lunches, suitable for a night's stop-over; *Residencial Familiar*, F, hot shower, friendly, good food; *Residencial Ocho Hermanos*, near main plaza, F, clean, collective rooms only.

Restaurants *Chapaco*, on main plaza, expensive. *Guacho*, Av. Costanera, is rec. *Arlequín*, Gral. B.Trigo, just off plaza, nice but expensive bar; *La Cabaña de Don Pepe*, Campos 138, has excellent steaks at reasonable prices; *El Rinconcito Andaluz* on the Plaza is cheap and the food reasonable. On La Madrid, *La Princesa* (excellent keperi—meat that is first boiled, then fried); for pizza and icecream on same street, unnamed parlour at the Agencia Kohlberg sign near Suipacha (opp. No. 268); ice cream also at *Gloria*, Ingavi y Gral. B. Trigo; *Café Puschkin*, Ingavi 0277, *Café Show*, Ingavi y Mariscal Sucre; *Snack Te Ve*, Sucre 622, just off plaza, popular. *Al Solar*, vegetarian, US$1.50 set menu. Excellent food, cheap breakfast, in market, but get there before 1300. After, go to Calle Carrero. Try the local wines, e.g. the white Aranjuez, Arce, Colonial or Kohlberg, also local beer.

N.B. Restaurants (and everything else in town) close in the middle of the day.

Shopping Craft goods in market and in co-operative shop in plaza; some cheap stuff, shoddy. Ceramics at Frial Susy, Sucre 776. Felt for hats at La Nueva Italia, Ingavi y Sucre; they will show you where to have your hat made up for US$3.50.

Zoo Out on Av. Costanera ("a tatty children's park, but worth the US$0.15 to see the condors", Michael J.Finnerty).

Exchange Banco del Estado will change money. Try Comercial Salinas at Mcal. Sucre 758. Money changers on Bolívar at Daniel Campos, also at shops in the vicinity, between Colón and Suipacha. Better rates for australes than in Villazón.

West German Consulate Sucre 665, helpful.

Argentine Consulate Corner of Ballivián and Bolívar, Mon.-Fri., 0800-1300.

Travel Agents Internacional Tarija, Sucre 721, Tel.:4446/7, helpful.

Tourist Office J.M.Saracho 685, just off Calle Bolívar, very helpful, free map.

Air Service TAM and LAB to Cochabamba, La Paz (Mon., Wed., Fri., US$39), Santa Cruz, Trinidad, Yacuiba, and Sucre (Tues). Flights are frequently cancelled and/or strike-bound. LAB office, Ingavi 244; TAM office between Sucre and Bolívar. Free LAB bus to airport. Taxi to airport, US$1 p.p., or *micro* drops you 2 blocks away.

Buses Mon., Wed., Thurs. and Sat. on 935-km. route Potosí-Oruro-La Paz, leaving 1700 (26 hrs., US$16; check which company operates the best buses). To Potosí (386 km.), with 10 de Noviembre, takes 13 hrs. (US$12.50), cold. For Sucre, you must change buses in Potosí. To Villazón: EMTV, Tues., Thur., Sat. 0830, US$6.50, Veloz del Sud, Mon., Wed., Sat. 0900, US$7, taking 6½ hrs.; otherwise you need to take a local truck (US$5). On Tues. and Fri. there is a combined bus/train service to Villazón and La Paz, US$22.75, leaves Tarija 0630, seat guaranteed on both services. Daily buses to Bermejo (1900-1930, 10 hrs., US$6, truck US$3.50) not recommended in rainy season; at Bermejo cross river by ferry to Agua Blanca, Argentina. To Villa Montes (**see page** 241), 12 hrs., Wed., 0730, US$11. Also to Yacuiba, daily by Flota Tarija. The new bus station is in the outskirts on Avenida de Las Américas (30 mins. walk from centre, 7-8 mins. from airport). Cía. El Chapaco uses poor quality vehicles. Trucks to all destinations leave from Loma, near the market.

Swimming Municipal swimming bath down the hill from the Mercado Negro. Tomatito, bus from San Juan at 0800, a trip of 5 km., popular picnic area. For those with their own transport El Rincón de la Victoria, 18 km., or Tolomosita, 7 km., sandy beach on river bank, and Los Churros de Jurina with natural rock pools, 22 km., or the Ancón gorge. Sauna at Acuario, 15 de Abril 679. Also interesting walking tours.

THE YUNGAS (3)

NE of La Paz a road runs to the Yungas. It circles cloudwards over La Cumbre pass at 4,725 metres; the highest point is reached in an hour; all around stand titanic snowcapped peaks and snowfields glinting in the sun. Then at Unduavi the paving ends; the road becomes "all-weather" (dangerous, especially in the rainy season, but it has been widened) and drops over 3,400 metres to the luxuriant green rain forest in 80 km. The little town of **Coroico** is perched on a hill at 1,525 metres; the scenery is beautiful (a walk to the river for a swim is a must). A visit to the old cemetery is recommended especially for camera buffs.

The roads to Coroico and to Coripata and Chulumani divide at Unduavi at a height of about 3,000 metres on the E side of La Cumbre. Here the well-surfaced road ends; the only petrol station is at Unduavi. There is no good place to eat at Unduavi, nor at Santa Rosa on the road to Coripata. From Coroico one can go by road into the Alto Beni beyond Caranavi; both Rurrenabaque and Trinidad can be reached by road. Note, if travelling by truck from La Paz to the Yungas via La Cumbre, the best views can be seen in May and June, when there is least chance of fog and rain on the heights. If you want to alight at La Cumbre, ensure you tell the driver beforehand for it is easy to miss in fog or cloud. It is very cold at La Cumbre and, further down, there are waterfalls at San Juan that baptise open vehicles—be prepared.

Festivals There is a colourful four-day festival on 19-22 October. On 2 November, All Souls' Day, the local cemetery is festooned with black ribbons.

Hotels *Prefectural*, C, up the hill, biggest in town with full board (F without food) but very run down, water 0700-1030 and 1400-1700, and food poor. *Sol y Luna* (formerly *Bel Jardín en los Pinos*), uphill past cemetery, and Umopar (narcotics police) station, ½-hr. walk from town (ask for La Alemana, La Gringa, Victoria or Sigrid Fronius—all the same person!), F p.p. bed and breakfast, E full board, separate meals available, cooking facilities, also 2 small houses for rent, swimming pool, garden, rec. (also, Sigrid offers Shiatsu massage for US$7). *Lluvia de Oro* (good value, food rec.), billiards downstairs, cheap), swimming pool, F, top floor rooms are best. *Alojamiento Pijoán* is very basic, F, cold water. *Hostal Kori*, swimming pool (open to all), good value, F, top floors rec., clean, good restaurant. The hotel near the junction of the La Paz-Chulumani and Coripata-Chulumani roads has been rec.; C. A camping site will be found by the small church on the hill overlooking the town—a stiff climb though; at the church take the left-hand path for another stiff climb to a waterfall (only worth it in the wet season). Coroico is an attractive place to wander around, especially towards evening. Hotels can be difficult at holiday weekends.

Restaurants *La Tasca*, only one menu and under new ownership, not as good as before; *La Casa* is German-run, good food and setting, excellent fondue for dinner, wonderful views, rec.; *Don Pepe*, good food. *Kory*, good breakfast; *El Rodeo*, Caranavi road, brilliant view, good food. The convent has been rec. for its chocolate biscuits, peanut butter and coffee liqueurs, and interesting cheap wine.

Horse Riding Patricio and Danny (French), who live by the new hospital in Comunidad de Aparto, have 6 horses for hire, US$3.80/hr., for trekking in the mountains or just a few hours' riding; very friendly. Reservations in La Paz: Shuriya, Plaza Abaroa, Av. 20 de Octubre 2463, T 322041, 1100-1300, 1530-1930.

Buses from La Paz to Coroico (US$3.25) leave from the main bus terminal at 0830, on Tues., Thur., Fri. and Sat., returning from Coroico on Wed., Fri. and Sat. at 0700 and Sun. at 1300 and take 5 hours each way; sit on left hand side (book return to La Paz well in advance). Flota Yungueña (Av. de las Américas 354, Villa Fátima, La Paz) runs between La Paz, Coroico and other towns in the Yungas. Take Micros B,V,X,K, 131 or 136, or *trufis* 2 or 9, which pass Pérez Velasco coming down from Plaza Mendoza, and get off at the service station, 20 metres before the booking office (it's 25 minutes from or to the suburb of Villa Fátima). Trucks to and from La Paz are more frequent (daily) and cheaper, US$2.20; they leave two blocks above the bus company. Pick-ups also take passengers, usually from outside the bus office, ask around. Trucks and pick-ups may drop you at Yolosa, the road junction 7 km. from Coroico; there is usually transport Yolosa-Coroico, US$0.50, or you can walk, uphill all the way. Transport can be a problem at holidays. Reconfirm onward bookings to and from Coroico as it is possible to get stuck for days at a time. In Coroico trucks leave from the market.

Chulumani, the capital of Sud Yungas, is the main regional centre. Citrus fruits are the main products from this area as well as some coffee. Along the road from Puente Villa to Coripata you enter the main coca growing area of northern Bolivia and the countryside is quite different from that near Coroico, where coffee, as well as coca and fruits, is the main crop.

Hotels *Hotel Prefectural*, D; *Motel San Bartolomé* (T 358386), B, pleasant and *Motel San Antonio*, C, with pleasant cabins and swimming pools. *Hotel Bolívar*, cheap, clean and friendly.

Hotel Tamapaya, 95 Km. from La Paz, just outside Puente Villa, is in a beautiful setting, C with shower, good rooms, swimming pool, rec except for variable, espensive restaurant.

Bus La Paz-Chulumani, Flota Yungueña, 120 km., 6 hours, US$3.30.

From below Coroico the road forks, the lower fork following the river NE to **Caranavi**, a very ugly town 164 km. from La Paz, at times along a picturesque gorge, towards the settled area of the Alto Beni . Market day is Saturday; lots of transport in late afternoon.

Hotels *Esplendido, Universo* and *Alojamiento Buen Amigo*, E; *Caranavi*, F, clean and friendly. *Prefectural*, F, not rec., but has a swimming pool. *Avenida*, F, very basic; *Residencial Rosedal*, clean, friendly, cheap.

Bus Yungueña buses leave La Paz for Caranavi at 0900 each day, US$5.20; the 164-km. journey has 6-7 hours and trucks 12½ hours. Direct bus Coroico-Caranavi on Sundays, or you can take a truck, US$1.65. At Yolosa you may also be able to get transport to Caranavi. If you want to continue into the Beni Lowlands without going into Caranavi, wait at the checkpoint before the town where all transport has to stop and ask for a ride there.

Some 70 km. from Caranavi lies the gold mining town of **Guanay**, an interesting, friendly place at the junction of the Tipuani and Mapiri rivers. To stay, *Alojamiento Los Pinos*, opp. football pitch, G p.p., cold water, basic, clean, may arrange exchange of travellers' cheques (with commission—cash can be changed with shopkeepers or gold dealers). Camping is possible next to the football field. *Restaurant La Bamba*, opp old *Panamericana Hotel* (apparently closed) good value, English spoken. Many other eating places on main street have fixed-price meals; one, with courtyard, monkey and parrot, serves excellent value breakfast of steak, eggs and tomato for US$0.75. Electricity is rationed—every 10 mins. or so. Other gold mining sites are Tipuani and Mapiri (canoe trips to Mapiri can be arranged, with overnight stay, or you can go up the Rio Mapiri for US$2 to see *La Draga*, a dredger which is sifting the river for gold and turning it into a "mud bath"—Richard and Yvonne Ruming, Bathurst, NSW). Buses direct from La Paz, Yungueña and Estrella Azul, about US$8, also trucks, which make frequent stops and diversions.

Canoes go down the Río Beni from Guanay to Rurrenabaque (**see page** 248), 8-12 hrs., US$11-18 depending on how successfully you negotiate and availability of canoes. The journey goes through gold mining settlements, then narrow, fertile river banks sown with peanuts.

N.B. The Yungas are a coca-growing region, so it is advisable not to wander too far off the beaten track.

THE NORTHERN LOWLANDS (4)

From Caranavi to the Beni Lowlands From Caranavi, you can take a bus (once a week) to Sapecho (with a cocoa cooperative), where a bridge over the Rio Beni has effectively cut off the old port for river access to the Lowlands, Puerto Linares. Beyond Sapecho, the road passes through Palos Blancos 20 km. from the bridge (market day, Saturday; *Hotel Magdalena*, G p.p., no running water; *Doña Luisa's* restaurant, good non-alcoholic *chicha*), from where a road has been opened to Yucumo, the centre of a large area of colonization. The road is passable only with 4 wheel drive, but there are occasional buses from Caranavi (13-15 hrs.). There are *hospedajes* (F) and restaurants in Yucumo. 550,000 ha. of jungle are under cultivation, rice, sugar, corn and fruit being planted. The Chimanes indians are trying to survive the influx of settlers from the altiplano. From Yucumo it is 50 km. to San Borja, a cattle-raising centre with hotels (F) and restaurants. It is also a cocaine district and in the centre are three identical, ugly cocaine mansions. From San Borja it is 7 hrs. by pick-up, US$12.50, to Trinidad (bus service expected to start in 1990); there are 5-6 river crossings and, in the wetlands, flamingoes, blue heron and a multitude of waterfowl.

At Yucumo, a second road branches NW to Rurrenabaque.

In the wet season, when the road is impassable, small boats take a day (at least) from Puerto Linares to Rurrenabaque. In Puerto Linares there is *Alojamiento Don Pancho*, best beds, shared showers, no doors, friendly, *alojamiento*, opposite is dirty, sleep on mats, no locks on doors. Across the river is Santa Ana, originally an Indian village, more interesting than Puerto Linares.

Rurrenabaque is a small, picturesque jungle town, with San Buenaventura on its opposite bank. Plans to build a brewery are enforcing change. The main square was remodelled in 1989. You must register with the police on arrival.

Hotels and Restaurants *Santa Ana*, E with bath, less without, near main square, G p.p., clean, basic, cold water, good cake in kiosk; *Berlin*, near wharf, from G to F but all rooms dirty, insanitary, cold water, to be avoided.; *Porteño*, E with bath, less without, quite good; *Safari*, on outskirts, for tours, all rooms with bath, not open all year round; an unnamed place by the river, cheapest, dirty, rooms with or without bath. Best meals at *Club Social Rurrenabaque*, US$1.25; *Snack Horeb*, no sign, run by Jorge Pacheco, friendly, helpful, a good meeting place. Several restaurants offer fixed-price meals which are good value; several "shanty" type restaurants, 1½ blocks up from canoe dock, offer beef or chicken kebabs with rice, empanadas and chicha, all under US$1 an item. Try banana or papaya milk shakes from stop opp. *Hotel Berlin*.

Transport Bus to/from La Paz twice a week, 20 hrs., US$18. TAM flies to Los Reyes from La Paz (50 mins, US$32), jeep Los Reyes—Rurrenabaque 1 hr., US$3.50. Trucks go Riberalta, but boats are infrequent; the fastest and largest is the *Don Carlos* (Captain Fong), US$30 incl. meals, 5 days to Riberalta (take a hammock). In the rubber season, the *Don Carlos* stops at the *estancia* of the Fong Rocas family, where you can see the rubber process and the conditions of the indebted workers. There may also be boats to Santa Cruz (try radioing in advance to the Capitanía del Puerto at Rurrenabaque to find out about boats).

Excursion Agencia Fluvial, to left of canoe dock runs a 4-day jungle tour on the Río Tuichi, US$50 (payable in dollars, travellers' cheques accepted at 2% commission). 3 nights are spent in the jungle, learning about plants, survival and the culinary specialities of the region (turtle eggs, wild pheasant, alligator tail, stingray, wild pig, duck, fish, fried bananas and "the sweetest grapefruit you'll ever taste"—Richard and Yvonne Ruming). You must take swimming costume, insect repellant to ward off sandflies and mosquitoes, and a camera.

Another route into Beni Department runs from Cochabamba NE for 200 km. to Todos Santos, on the Chaparé river, a tributary of the Mamoré (the previous narrow road has now been much improved and paved). To **Villa Tunari** by bus between 0800 and 1000 (no standing allowed, won't go if not enough passengers) from Av. Oquendo 985, Cochabamba, US$3.50, 3-6 hrs. Ask for the Piscinas Naturales for beautiful swimming. *Hotel Las Pozas*, 1 km. out of town, wonderful setting near Piscinas Naturales, own small pool, D with shared shower, excellent restaurant; *Hotel San Antonio*, E, water intermittent, *Hotel Las Vegas*, basic but clean; *Pilundui*, F; *Las Rosas*, not clean but friendly, full board available; *La Querencia*; probably best in town, E, basic, insect repellent provided, and toads. Sr. Carlos at the *Hotel Rosas* does jungle trips to see birds and crocodiles (his tours have to be booked in advance in Cochabamba).

The Cochambamba—Santa Cruz lowland road goes through from Villa Tunari to **Puerto Villarroel** (Hotels Rivera, Hannover, best, E, and some cheap *alojamientos*) from where cargo boats ply irregularly to Trinidad in about 4-10 days (see below). You can get information from the Capitanía del Puerto notice board. (There are very few stores in Villarroel. Sr. Arturo Linares at the Cede office organizes boat trips to the jungle—not cheap.) The Cochabamba-Villa Tunari run is highly recommended for scenery, and fishing at San Fernando.

From Cochabamba you can get a bus to Puerto San Francisco (US$5), Todos Santos or Puerto

Villarroel. Bus Cochabamba—Puerto Villarroel US$5.30, from 0800 when full, 6 hrs., occasional searches and 5 checkpoints. As this is coca-growing territory the police advise: don't stray from the main road, don't talk to strangers and don't take other people's luggage. From Puerto Villarroel you can continue by road to Santa Cruz, or by boat down the Securé, Chaparé or Mamoré rivers to Guayaramerín, then by road to Riberalta and back up river to Santa Ana on the River Santa Elena, or Rurrenabaque, thence by road to Coroico and back to La Paz.

Boat trip from Puerto Villarroel to Trinidad Puerto Villarroel is the main port for the river transport to the north of Bolivia. The road network is being extended, but many roads can only be used in the dry season, so river transport is still an important means of communication. There are boats running between Puerto Villarroel, Trinidad and Guayaramerín on the Brazilian border, taking passengers. This trip is only for the hardy traveller. In the rainy season when the river is high it takes about 3 to 5 days to go from Puerto Villarroel to Trinidad, but in the dry season, i.e. between May or June and August-November, it may last 8 to 10 days (the river is lower, cleaner and there may be more animals to see on the shore). It is another 5 days to Guayaramerín. The launches do not provide berths; you just have to sleep on the cargo which, if you are lucky, may be sugar bags and the like. The fare to Trinidad is US$22 for 3 days and nights, including meals. The food is native, that is to say all kinds of fish, dishes like *massaca* (stewed yuca with cooking bananas, *charque* or dried meat, oil and salt) and turtle eggs (delicious!). If you are fussy about food, don't make the trip because the kitchen is beyond description and the toilet facilities, too. Take your own drinking water, or water sterilizing tablets as the water served is taken from the river. The food served is very starchy and heavy because it is nearly always fried in oil, so supplement the diet with fruit and any other interesting food you can find beforehand (you can also take cigarettes and drink for the crew if you want). The trip is not as exciting as those in the real jungle; the countryside between Puerto Villarroel and Trinidad is more or less cultivated, with plantations of bananas and cattle ranches, some with 20-30,000 head. There is no jungle with orchids, crocodiles, etc., but one can see *petas*—small turtles basking in the sun, capibara, river dolphins, jumping fish, now and then monkeys playing on the beach, and many types of birds. At night, there are never-ending frog concerts. This trip could be described as quite relaxing if it was not for the poor food and the spartan accommodation.

Bathing in the river can be done without any harm.

If one does not know how to enjoy the "green symphony" as it is passing by, one should take a good book, as the trip might otherwise get very long!

A mosquito net is a "must", a hammock a good idea, and binoculars for watching the wildlife a useful extra.

Trinidad, the capital of the lowland Beni Department (237 metres), founded 1686, population 40,288, is reached by air from La Paz, Cochabamba, Riberalta or Santa Cruz, by road from Santa Cruz or by river from Puerto Villarroel. Sleeping-bag and mosquito-net essential on boats; passengers sleep on the deck. There are two ports, Almacén and Parador, check which one your boat is docking at. Parador is 3 km./1 hr. walk from town; cross the river by the main bridge by the market, walk down to the service station by the police checkpoint and take a truck, US$1.30. In the dry season, Oct.-Dec., boats do not reach Villarroel from the north. Food quite varied. The main mode of transport (even for taxis) is the motorbike.

Hotels *Ganadero*, B, rec., friendly, roof top pool. *El Bajío*, Av. Nicolás Suárez 622, T 21344/20203, C with bath and fan, breakfast extra, modern, swimming pool; *Mi Residencia*, near plaza, D, friendly, clean; *Residencial Loreto*, Calle La Paz, E, clean. *Yacuma*, La Paz y Santa Cruz, upstairs rooms rec., clean, bargaining possible, E, restaurant, washing facilities, fan, unfriendly. Some cheaper alternatives on Calle 18 de Octubre. *Residencial Palermo*, E, Av. 6 de Agosto, clean with hot water. Slightly out of town (no transport) is *Hostelería*, D, swimming pool, air-conditioned, friendly.

Restaurants *Loreto*, rec., between Plaza and Calle La Paz; *Moron*, Bolívar, almost opp. hospital, family run, excellent value fish dishes. Also *Churrasquería El Cachón de Mamita*, Av. Sucre 737, expensive; *Dragón China*, Calama 700, good Chinese food; and *Chifa Hong Kong* on the Plaza. *Pacumutu*, Nicolás Suárez, for plato común; *El Dorado*, Santa Cruz 522, cheap; *Snack Brasilia*, La Paz 662, serves a good dinner. *Carlitos*, on main square, rec. Sugar cane juice with lemon sold near the market—delicious.

Exchange cash dollars at Farmacia de Tarno, Santa Cruz 470.

Transport A road has been built to link La Paz with Trinidad (via San Ignacio, San Borja and Sapecho), and occasional colectivos and trucks use it (the latter attempt it all year, 24 hrs. if you're lucky); the road is of typical "penetration" standard, not for use during the rainy season, and gasoline is very difficult to come by. Take water, and a compass. Bus service to Cochabamba leaves 0700. Trinidad to Santa Cruz by road: 2 companies, Flota Puñata, US$13.50, and Trans Beni, US$12.50, each runs twice a week in the dry season, March-October; the route (Federal No 9) is 612 km., via Casarabe (56 km.), Villa Banzer (68 km.), Santa Maria (208 km.), Ascención (250 km.), El Puerte (312 km.), San Ramón (372 km.), San Julián (382 km.) and Montero (564 km.—all distances from Trinidad). From Casarabe to Villa Banzer is poor gravel, then it's dirt, tough going and impassable in the wet to San Julián, from where a good gravel surface goes to the Río Guapay and thereafter it is paved. A railway from Santa Cruz to Trinidad, via Montero and Colonia San Juan, has reached the confluence of the Ichilo and Grande rivers, 105 km. from Trinidad. The flight to La Paz is cheaper by TAM than by LAB (book early in either case). TAM to Cochabamba, US$22, plus US$1.20 tax, plus US$0.40 for each kg. of baggage over 15 kg. A fleet of over 20 air taxis also provides local transport. LAB tend to cancel flights, especially during rainy season. Ask around at airport for private-hire air fare prices.

Excursions Interesting for wildlife, as is the river trip (hire a motorbike or jeep to go to the river; good swimming on the opposite bank; boat hire US$5). 4 km. from town is the Laguna, with plenty of wildlife; the water is very warm, the bathing safe where the locals swim, near the café with the jetty (elsewhere there are stingrays and crocodiles). Motorbike taxi from Trinidad, US$1.

Guayaramerín A primitive small town (12,500 people) and centre for gold prospectors, is on the bank of the Mamoré river, N of Trinidad, opposite the Brazilian town of Guajará-Mirim. Passage between the two towns is unrestricted, but if going from Brazil into Bolivia you need your passport stamped by the Bolivian consul in Guajará-Mirim before leaving Brazil, and by the Bolivian immigration office. Similarly, if you are travelling on into Brazil and not just visiting Guajará-Mirim, get your passport stamped when leaving Bolivia and entering Brazil (US citizens need visas to enter Brazil). Exchange money (cash and travellers' cheques) in Bolivia, as this is very difficult in the State of Rondônia in Brazil. Boat trip, US$0.75, speed boat US$5 during day, more at night. If you don't want to stay, check the notice of boats leaving port on the Port Captain's board, prominently displayed near the immigration post on the river's bank. Boats up the Mamoré are fairly frequent—a three-day wait at the most.

Hotels *Santa Carlos*, 6 de Agosto, a few blocks from launch dock, C for a suite, D for other rooms, some a/c, hot showers, clean, money exchange (dollars and cruzados), swimming pool, reasonable restaurant; *Santa Ana*, E, rec. *Playa*, F. *Litoral*, F, cold water only, friendly. *Central*, F, just off the Plaza, and *Mexo Plaza*, E, on the main Plaza.

Restaurants *La Querencia*. Best is *La Puerta del Sol* for US$4-6 evening meals, or the old municipal market, two blocks west of the main square. *Snack Gino* at Av. 25 de Mayo 511 is also a possibility. At mid-day try the port area, where rapid short-order meals can be had for US$1-1.50.

Buses to Riberalta 3 hrs., US$4.75, 0930 and 1600 daily (first return bus at 0700). Also trucks available from the 1100 block of Gral. Federico Román.

Air Transport Daily flights to Trinidad and to La Paz (0930), and others to San Joaquín and Santa Ana. LAB and TAM offices at airport, 10 minute walk from town.

Riberalta Only 175 metres above sea level, another expanding town (40,000 people) which, with the whole region, attained temporary importance during the natural-rubber boom of the late 19th century; the cattle industry is providing a new boost for the town. It is at the confluence of the Madre de Dios and Beni rivers, which together flow into the Mamoré a few km. N of Guayaramerín.

Hotels *Noreste*, clean, friendly, *Cochabamba, Residencia, Santa Rita*, all F (without breakfast). *Residencias Julita*, F, good, clean; *Comercial Lazo*, Calle N.G. Salvatierra (F, p.p., D with a/c, clean, basic; comfortable; washing facilities), *Colonial*, Plácido Méndez 1, F, dirty, cold showers, poor; *Residencial Los Reyes*, near airport, D, with fan, clean.

Restaurants *Club Social Progresso*; *Club Social Riberalta*, better, on Maldonado; *Club*

Social Japonés, Sucre opp. market, reasonable, about US$2.50 p.p.; *Restaurant Popular Cochabamba*, US$0.50. Restaurants on main square are mediocre; good meals in market, about US$1 for 2 courses; food stalls outside *Comercial Lazo*, tasty meals.

Exchange Bazar La Paz on main Plaza buys dollars cash and travellers' cheques.

Transport Flight, Riberalta-Cochabamba (US$100 TAM, US$105 LAB). LAB to La Paz, via Santa Cruz and Tarija (TAM to La Paz, US$65). Expect delays in the wet season. LAB office Linares 31, TAM office is opposite LAB. Air taxi Riberalta-Cobija, US$400 in dollars. A bus runs to La Paz only after the wet season (ie after September). A motorcycle can be hired for US$2 an hour (no licence or deposit required) for visits to jungle; taxi drivers can give you the address.

Boat trip from Riberalta to Puerto Rico via River Aruña, from there to Conquista by road (US$4.10) and thence by River Madre de Dios to Riberalta (US$5.25). There are long gaps between boats from Riberalta.

N.B. Food in the Beni tends to be expensive, but the steaks are good.

Cobija, capital of the lowland Department of Pando, N of La Paz, population, 4,989 (252 metres), only connections by air (e.g. TAM to Puerto Rico, Trinidad, La Paz, US$70, and LAB to Guayaramerín and Riberalta) and river transport. It is close to the Brazilian and Peruvian frontiers and the area has many Brazilian residents. Taxis charge US$12-15 for a day trip to Brasileia across the International Bridge. It is difficult to get more than a month-long entry stamp in your passport here; if needing longer, press for it.

Hotel *Prefectural*, Av. 9 de Febrero, central, F, cold showers, others more expensive.

EASTERN BOLIVIA (5)

Santa Cruz de la Sierra (437 metres) is the only other city of note, capital of the Department of Santa Cruz, Bolivia's largest and richest in natural resources, lying in the vast and now rapidly developing plains to the E of the Eastern Cordillera, 552 km. by air from La Paz. This hot, windswept (May-August) boom town, whose population is now 600,000, making it Bolivia's second city, was founded in 1561 by Spaniards who had come from Paraguay.

Santa Cruz is usually hot and dusty, although when the cold *surazo* blows from the Argentine pampas the temperature drops sharply (May-August); the rainy season is December-February. The Plaza 24 de Septiembre is the city's main square with the Cathedral (interesting hand-wrought colonial silver), the University and prefecture set around it. The Cathedral museum is open on Tuesdays and Thursdays (1000-1200, 1600-1800), and Sunday (1000-1200, 1800-2000). Worth seeing if only to wonder how such an isolated community maintained such high artistic standards (but entry is expensive). Pleasant residential areas are being developed on the outskirts of town. The water supply is quite good, though typhoid and hepatitis are endemic in the area.

Cruceños are famous for their gaiety—their music, the *carnavalitos*, can be heard all over South America. Of the various festivals, the brightest is Carnival, celebrated for the 15 days before Lent: music in the streets, dancing, fancy dress and the coronation of a queen. Beware the following day when youths run wild with buckets and balloons filled with water—no one is exempt. The *mascaritas* balls also take place during the pre-Lent season at *Caballito Blanco*: girls wear satin masks covering their heads completely, thus ensuring anonymity!

Until recently Santa Cruz was fairly isolated, but new rail and road links in the 1950s ended this isolation and now there is an ever-increasing flow of immigrants from the highlands as well as Mennonites mostly from USA and Canada and Japanese settlers, such as the Okinawan colony 50 km. from Montero, to grow cotton, sugar, rice, coffee and other crops, which yield profusely. Cattle breeding and timber projects are also becoming important. A trip out of Santa Cruz to see these newly-settled areas is interesting, especially towards the Río Grande or

SANTACRUZ
26

To VIRU
VIRU AIRPORT
AND THE NORTH

SEGUNDO ANILLO

Av. CRISTÓBAL
DE MENDOZA

SANTA FE

PATANILLOS

CAÑADA STRONGEST

J.R. COIMBRA

MJ. JUSTINIANO

QUIJARRO

CAMPERO

C.C. LLANOS

ACRE

ITENEZ

FORTÍN TOLEDO

P. RICO

FORTÍN CORRALES

ASUNCIÓN

D'ORBIGNY

CENTRO CÍVICO

BAURES

MOXAS

MAMORE

ABUNA

Av. BUSCH

PERU

Av. CAÑOTO

MONS. RIVERO

CELSO CASTEDO

Av. URUGUAY

RIBERALTA

PRIMER ANILLO

HOSPITAL SANTA CRUZ

HOSPITAL S. DE DIOS

SANTA BÁRBARA

ANDRES IBÁÑEZ

RAFAEL PEÑA

VACA DIEZ

3

PARQUE EL ARENAL

6 DE AGOSTO

6 DE AGOSTO

OBISPO AGUIRRE

10

CUELLAR

CABALLERO

SUÁREZ ARANA

SEOANE

CHARCAS

CORDILLERA SARAH

VALLE GRANDE

BUENOS AIRES

CHARCAS

JOSE CALLAU

FLORIDA

8 24 DE SEPTIEMBRE

ARENALES

ARENALES

2

INGAVI

COLÓN ESPAÑA

JUNÍN

VELASCO 21 DE MAYO

INDEPENDENCIA LIBERTAD

8

1

BOLÍVAR

LA PAZ MURILLO

COCHABAMBA AROMA

POTOSÍ QUIJARRO

TARIJA CAMPERO

BOLÍVAR

AYACUCHO

PLAZA 24 DE SPTBRE

B. RENEMORENO

BENI

SUCRE

SUCRE

5

INGAVI

CHUQUISACA

BALLIVIÁN

BALLIVIÁN

CAMIRI

SUÁREZ DE FIGUEROA

ÑUELO DE CHÁVEZ

9

WARNES

Av. ISABELLA CATÓLICA

Av. CAÑOTO

PARI

WARNES

REPUBLIQUETAS

MERCADO

MONS. SALVATIERRA

ASILO DE HUERFANOS

MOLDES

LEMOINE

SAAVEDRA

PARAPETI

LA RIVA

PRIMER ANILLO

Av. IRALA

B 6

To COCHABAMBA

Av. IRALA

PICADA

DIEGO DE MENDOZA

POTOSÍ

Av. IRALA

CAÑADA

H. DE ZALAZAR

PLAZA HEROES DEL CHACO

1

SENDA

4

7

SOLÍS DE OLGUIN

To EL TROMPILLO
AIRPORT

Av. ARGENTINA

TTE. A. PEÑA

Yapacaní (beautiful birds and butterflies; the fish are highly recommended). About 7 km. E of town new Botanical Gardens are being developed. At the N edge of town (Barrio Equipetrol, towards airport) is a good, small zoo, take bus 8 or 16.

The exploitation of oil and gas in the Department of Santa Cruz has greatly contributed to the city's rapid development. There are several oil fields: at Caranda, 50 km. to the NW, at Colpa, 32 km. to the N and a large gas field at Río Grande, 40 km. to the SE. YPFB has an oil refinery at Santa Cruz.

Warning The influence of drug-trafficking has made Santa Cruz into an expensive and, according to most travellers, unpleasant place. Always carry your passport with you as there are constant checks by Immigration. Failure to do so will result in extra hours at the police station. There seems to be no escape from plainclothes policemen "fining" foreigners for some misdemeanor or other: "having an invalid visa"; at the airport "failing to pay the airport tax"; needing "safe conduct" to travel to Brazil. Bribes are charged arbitrarily at the bus station and, especially, at the railway station en route to Brazil. Watch out also for the "planting" of drugs. If possible never be without a witness, always ask for the policeman's identity card (green, embossed with a coat of arms), take his name and number, and say you will take the matter to his superior. Try also to enlist the help of the military police. There may be no alternative but to pay up: complaints, or even requests for a receipt, have often led to jail. If troubled by the police, you may be able to get help from Radio Santa Cruz, Calle Marioflorés y Güenda.

Hotels *Los Tajibos*, the biggest and most expensive, A, Av. San Martín in Barrio Equipetrol out of town, restaurant good but overpriced, swimming pool for residents only; *Cortez*, Av. Cristóbal de Mendoza 280, also out of town, on 2nd Anillo near the Cristo, also has pool and good reputation, C, rec. for medium or long stays; *Las Palmas*, Av. Trompillo, near airport, new, friendly, rec.; in the centre of town is the *Gran Hotel Santa Cruz*, Pari 59, T 48811/48997, good with pool, B, much used by British visitors (with English managers), not really rec. for families; *Asturias*, Moldes 154 with 2 pools, rec. for families C; all those mentioned above are air-conditioned. *Colonial*, Buenos Aires 57, comfortable, rec., C; *Brasil*, Santa Bárbara 242, T 23530, D, breakfast, bath and friendly; *Roma*, 24 de Septiembre 530, D, pleasant, good value, helpful, no restaurant; *Cataluña*, 10 km. N on Montero road, pool, basketball, grounds, D, very popular at weekends with cruceños; *Residencial Bolívar*, Sucre 131, F with breakfast, hot showers, some rooms with bath, nice courtyard with hammocks; *Hotel Copacabana*, Junín 217 D, with bath (E without), laundry facilities, rec.; *Bibosi*, Junín 218 (T 48887/51791), D-E, hot showers, breakfast extra, good; *Alojamiento Santa Bárbara*, Junín y Santa Bárbara 151, E, cold showers, helpful, clean, will store luggage, rec; *Los Pozos*, opp. Mercado Los Pozos, F, hot shower, clean, safe; *Res Ballivián*, Ballivián 71, F, clean, nice patio. The better hotels have some air-conditioned rooms but there is usually an extra charge. For those taking buses, *Residencial Arze* at the back of the terminal, F, or *Querencia*, F, is about half a block north of the bus terminal and *Alojamiento San José*, Canadá 136, hot showers, clean, F, about 1½ blocks. *La Quinta*, 4-star, Barrio Urbari, has individual chalets, good for families but out of town. For all hotels there is 3-tier pricing: locals, South Americans and others. All prices include taxes.

Restaurants The best restaurants are the *Floresca*, Av. Velarde 136, which has a good discotheque upstairs; the *"85"* at Bolívar 85 is good with reasonable prices; *La Fonda de Ariel* (chicharrón on Sundays and pork), Av. Irala, and the *Ambassador*, Av. San Martín (all air-conditioned). *La Empalizada*, Barrio Cooper 3, has very good parrilladas (grills) in a very pleasant outdoor setting with discotheque. *Amadeo*, 21 de Mayo, just off Junín, Spanish, good value, rec. *Candilejas*, next to *Hotel Cortez*. *El Fogón*, Av. Viedma 436 and *La Buena Mesa*, 2nd Anillo near Cristo, both excellent for parrillada and churrasquería; *Churrasquería El Palenque*, Av. El Trompillo y Santos Dumon, good; *Amadeus Pizzería*, Tercer Anillo 761, Barrio Equipetrol, T 45319, good; *El Mauricio Rancho*, Av. Ejército Nacional 505 for excellent steaks. Two quite good duck restaurants are located on Km. 2 (*Los Patos*) and Km. 8 on the road to Cochabamba. *London Grill* in Bolívar is run by British ex-airman and his Bolivian wife. *El Surubí*, Av. Irala, serves only surubí (fish); *El Boliche*, Bení 222, serves good crêpes. Chinese restaurants include *China*, Sucre 209; *China Law*, Castedo Barba 127; *China Town*, Velasco 58; *Patito*, 24 de Septiembre 301; *El Pato Pekín*, 24 de Septiembre, excellent,

SANTA CRUZ: Key to map

1.Plaza 24 de Septiembre; 2. Plaza Ñuflo de Chávez; 3. Parque Arenal; 4. Plaza Héroes del Chaco; 5. Cathedral; 6. Bus Terminal; 7. Railway Station; 8. Post Office; 9. Tourist Office; 10. Mercado Los Pozos.

authentic Chinese; *Shanghai*, Av. 27 de Febrero 33, *Nueva China* on 24 de Septiembre or the expensive *New Hong Kong* on Ballivián 137. *El Mandarín*, Av. Irala 673, excellent. Japanese *Kiku*, near Los Pozos market. Also good value is the *Bonanza*, Junín 177, across from the Post Office, clean; next door is *Gandhis*, opinions divided on the curries (ask if you want a hot one), English-speaking, helpful Indian owner. *El Dorado*, Libertad y Junín (main square), good; *Café España*, Junin y Colón España, good coffee, salteñas (a.m. only), snacks all day; *Cochero's Bar*, Bolívar 165, good lunches; *Monterrey*, René Moreno, good value with cheap meals and snacks. *Hannes*, Calle Campero, serves continental food, both English and German spoken. Outside the centre, *Chopp Rudi*, Av. Paraguay 739, before that on same road, *La Corona Krone*, German and English is spoken in both and they serve good continental food. Many cheap restaurants near the bus terminal on the main avenida. Also on the extension of Calle 6 de Agosto behind Los Pozos market (daytime). Excellent empanadas are sold in the food section of Los Pozos market. The bakeries on Junín, Los Manzanos and España look scruffy but sell the local specialities: empanadas de queso (cheese pies), cuñapés (yuca buns), rice bread and humitas (maize pies); try the *Panadería Trieste*, 21 de Mayo 369, not the cheapest, but good breakfasts as well. *El Patio* and the *Palace* on the main square sell good cakes. *La Pascana* on the Plaza is a favourite of tourists and locals alike for ice-cream and snacks, though service is slow. Ice-cream specialities at *Ca-Ri-Na*, Ingavi 213, *Helados Alpine*, Junin 269, 2 blocks from main plaza, wide range of flavours, and at *Kivón*, Ayacucho 267, highly rec.

Books Los Amigos del Libro, René Moreno 26, sells foreign language books (expensive) and *Newsweek*, and a useful guide *Con Usted La Señorial Santa Cruz de la Sierra* for US$0.25 (list of cheap boarding houses); Cruz del Sur, 21 de Mayo 62, sells *Time*.

Shopping Leather goods (Dorian, Florida 39, esq. Libertad, honest), baskets, hammocks. Carvings and other objects made from beautiful *guayacán* and *jacarandá* wood (though reported these crack in drier climates). The Los Pozos market is new, clean, good for mid-day meals and worth going to in summer for its exotic fruits: *ambaiba* (looks like a glove and the fruit is sucked out of the "fingers"), *guaypurú* (like a cherry), *ocoro* (like a prickly mandarin), *achachayrú* (mandarin-like with hard skin), *pitón* (like sour grapes) as well as better-known tropical fruits. There are plenty of smuggled Brazilian goods on sale, exchanged for Bolivian coca (made into cocaine). Beware of bag-snatching in the market. Another market (nothing for tourists, but also has a wide variety of fruit) is *Bazar Siete Calles*: walk down Vallegrande, past Ingavi.

Taxis about US$0.40, fix fare in advance. Luggage extra.

Entertainment Discotheques: *El Mau-Mau*, open only during Carnival (a vast auditorium), The *Viva María* is the largest night club. Another recommended night club is *El Cuerno Colonial* at España 162; on El Paso, *Tramps Bar* and *The New Orleans Bar* (both expensive). Also *Caaly* and *Mermelade* (Av. Uruguay 30). *Tijuana Piano Bar Saloon* has offered a courtesy drink to bearers of the *South American Handbook* at Av. Velarde 230. They also co-own *Number One Disco*, Calle Boquerón 83. The bar at Hotel Los Tajibos usually has live music. There are numerous cinemas in town; see local press for details.

Sports/Clubs Tennis Club; Club Las Palmas, 2½ km. on road to Cochabamba, has 9-hole golf course and pool; Club Hípico, riding club, nearby.

Museums Casa de la Cultura, on the plaza, with occasional exhibitions and also an archaeological display; has plays, recitals, concerts and folk dancing. Museo de Historia Natural in the university campus.

Exchange Bank of America, Velasco 19; Banco do Brasil, Ayacucho 168; Banco Popular del Perú, 24 de Septiembre 156; Banco de la Nación Argentina, Sucre 31; also local banks. Open 0730 to 1300. US$ can be telexed from anywhere in the world to Banco Nacional de Bolivia, who issues a cheque drawn on its own Brown Brothers, Harriman account in New York. This can be exchanged at one of two nearby *Cambios*, paying 2% to the bank and 2% to the *cambio*. Use *Casas de Cambio* for money exchange, on 24 de Septiembre for example; in NW corner of Plaza 24 de Septiembre in entrance to a restaurant; Ambar, Arcey San Alberto; Mendicambio on main plaza will change travellers' cheques into dollars at 3% commission. Magri Turismo, Edificio Oriente, Of. 215, T 45663, 2 blocks from main plaza, the American Express agent doesn't change American Express travellers' cheques, but you may have to go there to have cheques certified before a *casa de cambio* will accept them. Money changers on Av. Libertad, and Plaza de Armas.

Consulates Brazil, Av. Busch 330; **Argentina**, Banco de la Nación Argentina building, Sucre 31. Uruguay, Colón 58, Mon.-Fri. 0900-1100; **Paraguay**, Bolivia 568; **Peru**, La Paz 726; **British**, P.O. Box 3181, Centro Comercial Urbari, oficina 22 y 23, T 43874/43931.

Health Clínica Lourdes, René Moreno 362, T 25518. Dr. Pepe Arzabe, Quiroga Felix Romero 65, is reported to have specialised knowledge of regional illnesses.

Post Office Calle Junín 146.

Cables can be sent from Entel just off the Plaza at Warnes 83.

Tourist Agents Santa Cruz Tur and Orientur are on the Plaza; Exprinter is at Libertad 149; Magri Turismo, address under **Exchange**, helpful, rec.; Chovy Tours, 21 de Mayo 309/317, T 24445, recommended; Camba Tur, Sucre 8; and Turismo Balas, Bolívar 16, recommended. Many agencies (there are over 100) are to be treated with caution since travel is not their primary business.

Tourist Office Chuquisaca and Ñuflo de Chávez (T 48644). Open Monday-Friday, business hours only, no city maps (reported closed in mid-1989). Also kiosk at bus station.

Air Service LAB flies daily to La Paz and Cochabamba (US$39). LAB (once a week) and Líneas Aéreas Paraguayas (LAP—rec., once a week) fly Asunción-Santa Cruz. It is reported that up to US$40 can be saved by breaking your flight at Santa Cruz from Asunción and buying a La Paz ticket, rather than flying direct. Cruzeiro do Sul and LAB have 4 a week each to São Paulo and Rio de Janeiro (LAB, 2 to Rio). LAB and Aerolíneas Argentinas also fly to Salta (2 flights in all, US$79) and Buenos Aires (5 in all, US$214). There are also flights by LAB to Manaus, Caracas and Miami. LAB flies to some of the outlying towns in the Dept. of Santa Cruz and to Trinidad, Camiri, Sucre (US$25), Puerto Suárez, 3 a week, US$50, book well in advance, San Ignacio de Velasco (Mon., Wed., Fri. but check with LAB), Tarija and Yacuiba (US$35.90). There is a weekly flight to Roboré and San Matías every Tues.—one can then enter Brazil via Cáceres, taxi US$2.40.

   The international airport is at Viru-Viru, about 16 km. from the town. T 44411 or 33473 (has Emigration/Immigration office, luggage lockers, duty free shop, and restaurant; no exchange facilities). The bus every 20 minutes to Viru-Viru leaves from the old Trompillo airport, or the bus terminal (US$1). Viru-Viru taxi, US$9 (beware of overcharging). TAM, office at Aeropuerto Trompillo, flies to Puerto Suárez (US$16.50 Tues., Fri., Sun.) fills up quickly, book well in advance. Sucre (US$17, excess baggage over 15 Kg., US$1/Kg), and Yacuiba (US$12, daily). LAB office is at Chuquisaca y Suárez de Figueroa. On LAB internal services baggage allowance is 15 kg. (excess US$0.35 per kg.). Tax: internal US$2.75, international US$10. Often it is worth going out to the airport as neither LAB or TAM seems to be very aware of empty seats.

Buses Bus terminal on corner of Av. Cañuto and Av. Irala. Most buses seem to run at night. Daily buses to Cochabamba (US$11, 15 hrs.) 0700 by Bolívar (sit on left for best views), 1000, or 1700 with connections to Sucre (US$16). Buses to Cochabamba now take the new, lowland route, via Montero, Buena Vista and Puerto Villarroel, which is no quicker than the old mountain route via Epizana. Some afternoon buses direct to Sucre US$12. Oruro and La Paz (US$14, 23 hrs.). For Sucre it is sometimes quicker and cheaper to fly, avoiding changing buses at Cochabamba, i.e. an extra 300 km. The only day time possibility for travel is by colectivo or truck to Cochabamba: either take Micro 17 to Km. 12 where there is a police checkpoint at which all the trucks stop, or go to the office of Transportes Peco in Av. Landívar, half a block west from the Cañuto statue, on Calle Ayacucho. The fare after negotiation will only be marginally less than that for the bus, but at least you will get good views. Note that trucks to Cochabamba (if taking the old road) and Sucre traverse 3,000-metre plus mountains at night, so it's very cold: to Cochabamba 22 hrs., Sucre 32 hrs. Flota Chiquitana leaves for San Ignacio Mon., Wed. and Fri. (US$12), 18 hrs., more if raining. To Camiri, bus US$11, 8 hrs., *camioneta*, 7 hrs., US$7.80. 2 companies to Trinidad, Flota Puñata on Wed. and Sat. at 0600, US$13.50, and Trans Beni, same days at 1630, US$12.50; in the wet season, Nov.-Feb., the service may be cancelled. Lorries also leave for Trinidad from the Plaza behind the statue.

Excursions The new road route to Cochabamba passes through fertile lowland to the NW of Santa Cruz. It goes 37 km. N to **Montero** (30,000 people), where sugar and cotton are grown and processed, and on to Puerto Grether, high on the River Ichilo, a tributary of the Mamoré. It then connects at Todos Santos with the 200-km. road to Cochabamba. A non-stop shuttle minibus service leaves from Santa Cruz bus station for Montero when full. From Santa Cruz buses and from Montero minibuses run to Buena Vista (*Pensión*); from there trucks run to El Terminal after which one can walk to the Surutú river, the eastern boundary of **Amboró National Park** (180,000 hectares)—walk to Cerro Amboró (guide required) recommended. There is a national park office in Buena Vista. The park is home to butterflies, humming birds, macaws, hoatzin and other native fauna (many of them endangered species). Beware of the insects—do not wear shorts or short-sleeved shirts; much wading is required to get around the park.

The country surrounding the city is flat and scenically uninteresting—except to the agriculturist. The sand-dunes (Las Lomas de Arena) 20 km. to the south are worth a visit; the scenery has been described as similar to deserts in a Walt Disney cartoon. You may be able to get there by taxi, but private transport is best. It may be possible to hitch at weekends. There are two fresh-water lakes in the dunes, but a 4-wheel drive vehicle is normally required. Los Espejillos, where a mountain stream plunges over a waterfall and carves its way through limestone rocks down a beautiful green and forested valley is well worth the effort to get to—4-wheel drive, only in the dry season. Turn right at Km. 26 on the old Cochabamba road, cross the Piray river and drive some 12 km. up a forested valley. At a green field on the left (football goal posts) stop and walk a few hundred metres up to the stream. A favourite day trip is to the Yapacaní bridge where *surubí* from the river or *jochi* and *tatú* (armadillo) from the forest may be eaten in one of the riverside eating houses. The drive up to Samaipata, 120 km. along the old Cochabamba road, takes a full day—visit the Inca site, El Fuerte, near the town, an exhausting walk, but the drive up the Piray gorge and "over the top" makes a splendid trip. The ruins are some kilometres before Samaipata, coming from Santa Cruz; the side road to the left is signed to El Fuerte. In Samaipata is a hotel (try the local wine); a taxi from the town will go part of the way to the ruins. Take daily bus to Vallegrande which passes the site (2½-3 hrs.)

South of Vallegrande is Pukara, from where a day's horse or donkey ride will take you to the village of Higuera, where Che Guevara was killed. On 8 October each year, many people gather there to celebrate his memory; ask at the Universidad Gabriel René Moreno or Radio Santa Cruz about collective transport.

A recommended round trip taking about a week starts by arriving by train at San José de Chiquitos (with beautiful church that looks like a candle—see below. From there by truck to San Rafael (134 km.), San Miguel (169 km.) and then San Ignacio, and Concepción, all with interesting old churches. From **Concepción** there are daily tours to San Javier or Santa Cruz. Accommodation is limited, but best at **San Ignacio** (*Hotel Santa Cruz*; also luxury bungalows, US$55d, or US$150 weekly for groups of over 6, contact Lucy Hartmann, Cochabamba, T 24258). Concepción is roughly 300 km. NE of Santa Cruz. Still reasonably wild though being opened up. Accommodation at *Grand Hotel Guarayas*, F; *Residencial 6 de Agosto*, shower, clean.

Travel to Brazil The Santa Cruz-Corumbá railway (take bus 4 from the centre to the station) is still rather primitive (and the time-table has been described as flexible, or pure fantasy) but has recently been improved; toilets are still dirty but there is an adequate dining car. Trains stop at Quijarro near the frontier. From there travellers must go by taxi to Corumbá in Brazil; these meet the trains as they arrive and try to overcharge (fare should be about US$0.50 per seat); it's a further US$0.50 by bus from the border to Corumbá. The *ferrobus* train service is much faster and better, but also ends at Quijarro; it leaves Santa Cruz at 0800 Mon., Wed., Fri. 12-hr. trip, returning from Quijarro the following day at 1800 (meals served at seats). *Ferrobus* tickets are only available at the station (T 48488), and are sold out 1 week in advance; ticket office opens 0800-0830, but queuing starts at 0500; don't buy tickets for seats 2c and 2d, they don't exist. There is also a "fast" train (*rápido*) that leaves Santa Cruz Sun., Tues. and Thurs., but maybe daily, at 1100; returns following day at 1800, about 20 hrs. Stopping trains leave Thurs. and Sun. at 1404 and goods trains (mixed) Mon. and Fri. at 2115. Slow trains from Quijarro leave Mon. and Fri. at 1150 or goods (mixed) train at 1500 on Wed. or Sun. Fares: for ordinary trains Pullman, US$12 (comfortable, but sways a lot) first class US$10, second class US$6; *ferrobus*, Pullman, US$20, special, US$15. Check *all* times before setting out. Take a torch, whichever class you are travelling. It is a monotonous journey through jungle except for the frequent stops at trackside towns, where the train's arrival is the chief event in life. A rail flat-car can be hired to transport cars, US$185; you may have to wait several days for a flat-car, however. Only men are allowed to ride on the roof of the train. Food is available on the train or at frequent stops.

The ticket office at the station is not open before 0800 to Corumbá and Yacuiba (start queing at 0400-0500); purchase only the day before. The customs and emigration post at Quijarro closes very soon after the arrival of the *ferrobus*. You are advised to book as early as possible on all services to Corumbá, which are reported to be getting very crowded. Failing that you can try to buy a ticket on the platform 1/2 hr. before train departure. Foreign exchange generally little problem, but you are likely to be sold cruzeiros in largish denominations; also you will probably only be able to sell bolivianos in Bolivia, while a few dollars in cash have been known to make irritating border formalities less troublesome. However do beware of showing large quantities of money around. If there are heavy rains check that the line has not been washed out.

It is possible to go by road between Santa Cruz and the Brazilian border, but this is not recommended, especially in the rainy season. Take water, map, food and compass. The stretch between Santa Cruz and San José de Chiquitos has been washed away, so road traffic must go via Concepción and San Ignacio de Velasco (see above). After San José the road heads S from the railway at 7 de Mayo in a 128 km. detour until the railway is rejoined at Roboré (check compass because many tracks go to Paraguay). At Roboré the road narrows and deteriorates, being the worst stretch, to Corumbá. It is a 1,050 km. journey in all, without paving; in the wet allow 2 weeks.

Travellers who need a visa for Brazil are advised to obtain a visa before arriving in Santa Cruz. The Brazilian consulate in Santa Cruz normally takes 24 hrs. to process applications (if you apply at 0900, may be ready by 1200). Such travellers will be refused entry to Brazil unless they have a visa. Yellow-fever certificates are often asked for (failure to produce one is another "fineable" offence—**see warning on page** 253). All travellers, except Brazilian citizens, have to pay US$3 to the Bolivian Ministry of the Interior at the border; an official receipt is given.

On the railway, half way between Santa Cruz and Corumbá, is **San José de Chiquitos**, with huge Jesuit church. (*Hotel San Sebastián Silvestre*, F, basic, clean, good food, near railway station.)

Puerto Suárez Beware thieves. *Hotel Sucre* on main plaza, F, barely adequate; *Hotel Banidi* (more comfortable and the most obvious), and *Residencial Puerto Suárez*, E, clean, fans and showers. *Hotel Bolivia*, D; *Hotel Beby*, Av. Bolívar 111, E, clean, welcoming. Beware the water, it is straight from the river. Most people prefer to go on to Corumbá where hotels are better.

The simplest way to Brazil is to fly La Paz-Puerto Suárez, US$100, then share a taxi to the border, US$4 (per car). Flights to Santa Cruz: LAB Mon., Wed., Sat., US$50, TAM Tues., Sat., US$45.

A tip if travelling from Brazil to Bolivia is to arrive a week in advance, take a day trip from Corumbá to Puerto Suárez to purchase a train ticket at a travel agency (or book a flight), return to Brazil (to the Pantanal, say) and prepare yourself for the journey.

Travel to Argentina To Buenos Aires by train via **Yacuiba** (11,000 people; many cheap hotels in town centre) takes 3 days and is a long and tiring trip. First class and second class passengers must disembark at Yacuiba, taking taxi (US$0.25) to Pocitos on the border and walking across to Argentine side before boarding train for Buenos Aires. Tickets should be purchased from Incatur travel agents in Santa Cruz. A more comfortable alternative is to take the *ferrobus* from Santa Cruz to Yacuiba (9-10 hour journey) and then to take a bus from Pocitos on the Argentine side of the border to Güemes (2 buses daily with connections to Salta and Buenos Aires). Trains Yacuiba-Santa Cruz: Mon. and Fri., *mixto*, at 1900, 24 hrs., US$3.10; Wed. and Sat., *rápido*, at 1230, Pullman, US$12, 1st class US$6.20, 2nd US$3.80, 10 hrs.; or Tuesday at 1820. Trucks for Santa Cruz leave from Lourdes market, not advisable after rain. Be warned that the immigration police have been shaking tourists down for "smuggling dollars" and will offer you the option of jail or a fine. Contact a superior officer and/or Consulate to help stop this banditry. LAB flies to Santa Cruz and La Paz (US$60) on Tues. and Sun., 1500 (supposedly); TAM also flies from here but has a much more flexible timetable.

INFORMATION FOR VISITORS

Documents A passport only is needed for citizens of the Western European and Scandinavian countries, USA and Israel; all others need visas unless they have tourist cards, which can be obtained free from Consuls and travel agencies; they are good for 30 days and can be renewed, free, up to 90 days at the Ministerio del Interior in La Paz, Avenida Arce, Mon.-Fri. 0900-1830, Sat. 0900-1200. Extending tourist visas is time-consuming, and costs US$25; ensure that visas and passports are stamped with the same, correct date of entry or this can lead to "fines" later. Beware also of illegal charging on entry into Bolivia. Business visitors (unless passing through as tourists) are required to obtain a Determined Object Visa quoting reference Tasa-03.03. D from a Bolivian consulate. This costs US$60. Hotels automatically register their guests with the immigration authorities but visitors staying as private guests should present their passports at the nearest immigration office.

We have repeatedly been asked to warn against people impersonating Interpol men who want to see all your money—ask (politely) to see identification first and then only in front of friendly witnesses. This warning applies especially to Santa Cruz and the rail link to Brazil, also the La Paz-Arica railway (point to the "Gratis" on the stamp, and stand your ground). Now reports state that this happens in La Paz, Sucre and Potosí also. Do not show money or passport to anyone not in police uniform. Genuine police and immigration staff are not above pretending that your documents are not in order, and demanding US$10 or so p.p. to "rectify" them. In such cases it is probably best to pay up with good grace.

Airport tax of US$12 (only US$0.75-3 on internal flights, payable in bolivianos) is levied on leaving. Tax on airline tickets 12.3%. No tax if leaving overland, or if you stay in Bolivia less than 24 hours, although there have been reports of US$10 being charged overland.

To Bolivia by Air

(1) *From Europe*: Either fly to Lima by Air France, etc., whence 11 flights a week to La Paz, or fly with Lufthansa from Frankfurt, with a change of aircraft in Lima; or via Rio de Janeiro, São Paulo or Buenos Aires. Tawa Tours, Sagárnaga 161, La Paz, T 329814, sells and confirms Aeroflot flights to Europe (probably the cheapest, but you need to reserve seat 3 weeks in advance in Bolivia). Another route is with Líneas Aéreas Paraguayas: Frankfurt-Brussels-(Madrid)-Asunción-Santa Cruz; on the outward journey you will have to stay for 1,2 or 6 nights in Asunción (first night may be paid for by LAP), but the return connection is immediate.

(2) *From North America*: American from Miami to La Paz. Lloyd Aéreo Boliviano (LAB, no 1st class on international flights, but good service), daily from Miami via Caracas, Manaus and Santa Cruz, or Panama to La Paz. Otherwise, connections via Lima.

(3) *Within South America*: From Caracas twice weekly by LAB. From Lima, 11 a week by Aero Perú, LAB or Lufthansa. From Arica, three times weekly by LAB and LAN-Chile; this is a good route to Ecuador because from Arica AeroPerú flies to Guayaquil for US$140, Fri. and Sun., but this ticket is only available in Chile. From Santiago, 4/5 a week, 2/3 by LAN-Chile (via Arica and Iquique), and 2 by LAB. From Buenos Aires, 4 flights by LAB and Aerolíneas Argentinas; to Salta, via Santa Cruz and Tarija with LAB (US$137, little food served). LAB to Montevideo once a week, with a change of flight in Santa Cruz. From Asunción, one a week by LAB, 3 by Eastern (US$50 more). From Rio and São Paulo (US$277), 4 a week by Cruzeiro do Sul and 1 a week by LAB (to São Paulo only). *Note*: LAB international flights to and from points E of La Paz tend also to call at Santa Cruz or Cochabamba, or both. TAM services are one third cheaper than LAB.

By Rail From Argentina and Chile (**see page** 217).

By Road From Cuzco or Puno, several services. Peruvian and Bolivian roads partly paved. Also links with Argentina and Chile (see below).

Motoring (1) From Puno (Peru) via border stations at Desaguadero (for Guaqui and La Paz) or Yunguyo (for Copacabana, the straits of Tiquina, and La Paz). Peruvian customs at Desaguadero do not work after 1730 unless you are prepared to seek out the officials and pay them "overtime" (US$3 at weekends). Bolivian customs now operate to 1900 but immigration formalities can be completed at Copacabana if the border post is closed. Peruvian time is an hour behind Bolivian time.

(2) From Salta-Jujuy-La Quiaca (Argentina) to Potosí or Tarija. Roads ford many rivers in Bolivia and are impassable in wet weather (Argentine section, despite much work, is reported still to be bad). Bolivian border controls work mornings and 1400-1800 only. Argentina is one hour ahead of Bolivia, 2 in summer.

(3) Alternative routes lead from the Argentine province of Salta via Bermejo or Yacuiba into Tarija. Dry weather only.

(4) From Ollagüe (Chile) to Uyuni, very bad. A new dirt road has been built from Arica (Chile) via Tambo Quemado.

Travel to Paraguay Apart from the adventurous journey described on **page** 241, a cheap way of getting to Paraguay is to travel by bus to Salta or Orán (Argentina), then on to Asunción via Resistencia (Argentina).

Duty-free Imports 200 cigarettes, 50 cigars and 1 lb. tobacco; one opened bottle of alcoholic drink.

Internal Air Services are run by Lloyd Aéreo Boliviano (LAB) and TAM, the army airline, between the main towns. LAB offers a 28-day unlimited domestic flight ticket for US$119 for international travellers using LAB, which must be bought outside Bolivia (only one stopover per city is allowed, except for connecting flights; note that many flights radiate from La Paz or Cochabamba). To avoid paying the 12.3% tax on the air-pass, purchase it as an MCO outside the country, then exchange this for flight tickets later. You must enter Bolivia using LAB or on a foreign carrier with whom LAB may have a pooling arrangement. Also LAB is promoting limited stay tickets as well as the normal Apex type fares. Spouse fares (i.e. one goes free with one paying full fare) available on certain international flights. There are also reductions for special excursion flights. LAB will be glad to supply current information on request. Although LAB's services have been recommended, in out-of-the-way places TAM is more reliable than LAB, which will not go if there are insufficient passengers. Your seat priority on TAM is low, though. Insure your bags heavily as they tend to get left around.

NB If your internal flight is delayed keep your baggage with you and do not check it in until the flight is definitely announced. There have been robberies of prematurely checked-in baggage.

Internal Roads La Paz-Oruro, completely paved; Oruro-Challapata, paved first 30 km., then dirt (or mud in the wet season); La Paz-Tiquina: *autopista* to El Alto (toll US$0.25), then surfaced to Tiquina; La Paz-Cochabamba paved; Oruro-Cochabamba, all-weather; Cochabamba-Santa Cruz, mountain route paved, but in a very bad state, lowland route paved Cochabamba—Puerto Villarroel, Villa Yapacaní—Santa Cruz, with good gravel between; Cochabamba-Sucre and on to Potosí, S of paved road, paved for 127 km. to Totora, then dirt (bad in rainy season). Oruro-Potosí, dirt, very bad in rainy season. La Paz-Yungas, well-engineered and surfaced to Unduavi, but most roads in the Yungas offer "hair-raising driving". La Paz-Beni-Trinidad, mixed reports. Santa Cruz—Trinidad: paved from Santa Cruz to Puerto Banegas on Río Guapey, then gravel to San Julián, thereafter dirt (impassable in the wet) to Casarabe, whence poor gravel to Trinidad. Puerto Suárez-Arroyo Concepción open. Nearly all Bolivian road surfaces, even the paved sections, are bad, and after flooding or rough weather they are even worse. Even main roads may be closed in the rainy season.

Buses (interurban ones are called *flotas*, urban ones *micros*) ply on most of the roads. Reporting time is half an hour before the bus leaves, but you should always try to reserve a seat as far as possible in advance. In the wet season, bus travel is subject to long delays and detours at extra cost. On all journeys, take food and toilet wipes.

Trucks congregate at all town markets, with destinations chalked on the sides, they are not much less comfortable than buses or ordinary trains and are normally about half the cost when there is competition. Otherwise they charge what they judge the market will bear and can therefore seem expensive.

Motorists (including motor-cyclists) must buy an **Hoja de Ruta (driving permit)** from local offices of the Servicio Nacional de Tránsito for every road journey, specifying final destination and date. A *carnet de passages* is essential for those bringing a car into Bolivia. If hiring a car, the company can arrange a "blanket" driving permit for tourist purposes which is valid for several days and destinations. Tolls vary from US$0.50 to US$2.50 for journeys up to 100 km. You also need an International Driving Permit (and, since a driving licence number is requested, also your national driving licence, or some ingenuity). For hints on high-altitude motoring, see **Introduction and Hints** at front of book.

Petrol (gasoline) 2 grades: 85 and 92 octane. Gas oil is slightly cheaper. Costs are higher in Guayaramerín, Riberalta and Puerto Suárez.

Travel by Train The "Pullman" services are reported to be improving the general slow train service. The railways have recently renewed their rolling stock with Fiat railway coaches from Argentina. "Slow" trains have speeded up but they cannot take the curves and gradients at the same rate as the *ferrobuses*. Always check departure times in advance; timetables change too frequently for us to quote precise schedules.

Walking *Backpacking and Trekking in Peru and Bolivia*, 5th edition, published by Bradt Publications, describes 3-9 day hikes in the Cordillera Real within easy reach of La Paz. The local tourist office also produces a leaflet with sketch maps on walks available from La Paz. There are also some excellent guides available through local clubs.

Camping Chet and Jeri Wade, of Sacramento, California, tell us that one can camp almost anywhere in safety. Warm sleeping gear essential, even in the lowlands in the winter. Sleeping bags are also useful for getting some sleep on the buses or long distance trains, especially those crossing the Andes. Mosquito nets can be purchased in La Paz, but they are not cheap. Beware sandstorms S of Oruro. Camping gas is available in La Paz.

Hotels Throughout Bolivia the cheaper hotels impose their own curfews. In La Paz it tends to be midnight (check) but it can be as early as 2130 in Copacabana. These locking up times are strictly adhered to by hotel keepers. Accommodation at the cheaper end of the market costs about US$1.50 p.p. in a *posada*, US$2-3 in an *alojamiento* and US$3 upwards in a *residencial* (1990).

Food and Drink The normal international cuisine is found at most good hotels and restaurants. Some local dishes are interesting (see below). The 3 makes of local beer (Pilsener), lager-type, are recommendable; the local hot maize drink, *api* (with cloves, cinnamon, lemon and sugar), should be tried (usually US$0.12), as well as *singani*, distilled from grapes, good, cheap and bracing. *Chicha* is a fermented maize drink, popular around Cochabamba. Bottled water cannot always be found (rain water is sometimes offered as alternative); the local tap water should not be drunk without first being sterilized. We do not recommend Bolivian market food except to the desperate and, of course, to those accustomed to South American food, but buy it only if it is cooked in front of you. Be very careful of salads; they may carry a multitude of amoebic life as well as vile green bacteria.

In the *pensiones* and cheaper restaurants a basic lunch (*almuerzo*—usually finished by 1300) and dinner (*cena*) are normally available. Lunch can also be obtained in many of the modern market buildings in the main towns.

Salteñas are meat stew pies, eaten regularly by Bolivians, mostly in the morning. Some are *muy picante* (very hot) with red chili peppers, but *medio picante* and *poco picante* ones can normally be obtained. For milk, try sachets of Leche Pil (plain, chocolate or strawberry-flavoured), at US$0.25 each.

N.B. Bolivian highland cooking is usually very tasty and often *picante*, which means highly spiced with chili peppers. Local specialities, which visitors should try, include *empanadas* (cheese pies) and *humitas* (maize pies); *pukacapas* are *picante* cheese pies. Recommended main dishes include *sajta de pollo*, hot spicy chicken with onion, fresh potatoes and *chuño* (dehydrated potatoes), *parrillada* (a Bolivian kind of mixed grill), *fricase* (juicy pork dish served with *chuño*), *silpancho* (fried breaded meat with eggs, rice and bananas), and *ají de lengua*, ox-tongue with chilis, potatoes and *chuño* or *tunta* (another kind of dehydrated potato). The soups are also good, especially a *chairo* soup made of meat, vegetables, *chuño* and *ají* (hot pepper) to which the locals like to add *llajua* or *halpahuayca* (hot sauces always set on restaurant tables) to make it even more *picante*.

Best Buys Llama-and alpaca-wool knitted and woven items are at least as good as those from Peru. La Cancha market in Cochabamba is highly recommended but you *must* bargain. Ponchos, *mantas*, bags, *chullos* (bonnets). Gold and silverware. Musical instruments such as the *charango* (mandolin with armadillo-shell sound-box) and the *queña* (Inca flute), and other assorted wooden items.

Security Apart from the warnings given in the text, note that in some cities there is hostility to foreigners, mainly out of resentment to foreign involvement in anti-narcotics policies.

Health Whatever their ages, travellers arriving in La Paz by air (too quickly, that is, for a progressive adaptation to the altitude) should rest for half a day, taking very little food and drink. They will be up and doing the next morning. In Bolivia, do as the Bolivians do: above 3,000 metres, walk slowly, very slowly uphill. Never go out for the whole day without taking an outer garment: the temperature drops sharply at sunset. Inoculate against typhoid and paratyphoid (also have yellow fever inoculation and anti-malaria tablets if visiting the lowlands) and stock up on necessary medicines; they are dear in Bolivia. Visitors are being asked for yellow-fever vaccination certificates when visiting Santa Cruz or the Oriente. A yellow fever vaccination certificate, at least 10 days old, is required for leaving the country; LAB is very strict about this. We have also been asked to mention that hepatitis is very common. Chagas disease is endemic in the Yungas and other warmer parts of Bolivia. There is no known cure, so that adobe huts with thatched, or leaf-protected, roofs should be avoided as sleeping places because they play host to the *vinchuca* beetle which is the vector; half Bolivia's population has the disease, which leads to heart failure but shows few other immediate symptoms (see **Health Hints**, page 35).

Clothing suitable for Great Britain, with a raincoat or light overcoat, should be worn by visitors to the Altiplano and the Puna, where it is particularly cold at night. The climate in the Eastern Lowlands is tropical. Oruro and Potosí are colder than La Paz; Cochabamba can be very warm. There is a prejudice against the wearing of shorts in town centres.

The best time for a visit is May to November, the dry season. May, June, and July are the coldest months.

British Business Visitors are strongly advised to consult "Hints to Exporters: Bolivia", which can be obtained from Dept. of Trade, Export Services Division, Sanctuary Blgs, 16-20 Great Smith Street, London SW1P 3DB. Similar publications for U.S. business visitors may be obtained from the Department of Commerce.

Hours of Business are normally 0900-1200 (sometimes 1130 in La Paz), and 1400-1800. Saturday is a half day. Opening and closing in the afternoon are several hours later in the provinces. Government offices are closed on Saturday. Banks 0900-1200, 1400-1630, but closed on Saturday.

Public Holidays 1 January, New Year's Day; Carnival Week, Monday, Shrove Tuesday, Ash Wednesday; Holy Week, Thursday, Friday and Saturday; 1 May, Labour Day; Corpus Christi (moveable); 16 July, La Paz Municipal Holiday; 5-7 August, Independence; 12 Oct., Columbus Day; 2 November, Day of the Dead; Christmas Day.

There are local holidays at Tarija, on 15 April; at Sucre on 25 May; at Cochabamba, 14 Sept.; at Santa Cruz and Cobija 24 Sept.; at Potosí, 10 Nov.; at Beni, 18 Nov., and at Oruro, 22 Feb.

Festivals January (last week), La Paz, "Alacitas". 2 Feb., 25 Aug.: Virgin Copacabana. 3 May: Fiesta de la Invención de la Santa Cruz, various parts. In La Paz El Gran Poder, end May/early June, at the "Calvario". 23 June: San Juan, all Bolivia. 29 June: San Pedro y San Pablo, at Tiquina. 28 July: Fiesta de Santiago (St. James), Altiplano and lake region; Achocalla a convenient place to go to. 1 and 2 Nov.: All Saints and All Souls, any local cemetery. For other festivals on the Altiplano enquire at hotels or tourist office in La Paz. Remember that the cities are very quiet on national holidays, but colourful celebrations will be going on in the villages.

Local time 4 hours behind GMT.

Currency The unit of currency is the boliviano (Bs.), divided into 100 centavos. There are notes for 200, 100, 50, 20, 10, 5 and 2 bolivianos, and coins of 1 boliviano and 50, 20, 10, 5 and 2 centavos. The boliviano replaced the peso boliviano in 1986 at the rate of 1:1,000,000; bank notes and other paper denominated in pesos are legal tender until 31 December, 1989. Change is often given in forms other than money: e.g. cigarette, sweet, or razor blade. It is almost impossible to buy dollars at points of exit when leaving or to change bolivianos in other countries. Inflation is low; there is no need to buy bolivianos in small amounts to avoid depreciation. The black market is more-or-less dead, since rates are no different on the street and in *casas de cambio*. *Cambios* in all the major cities will change travellers' cheques, and changing US$ cash presents no problems anywhere.

Credit cards are accepted hardly anywhere; it is possible to get cash against Visa and Mastercard in La Paz in some major banks (**see page** 211). Many shops displaying credit card signs do not, in fact, accept them.

Cost of Living Rents, appliances, and some clothing, and especially toilet goods and medicines, are high priced. With inflation now under control, Bolivia has become much more expensive for the traveller. La Paz, Cochamba and Santa Cruz, and indeed anywhere else touched by the drugs or gold trades are expensive. For basic hotel rates, see above; *almuerzos* cost from US$1-2; all other meals are dear.

Electric Current Varies considerably. Generally 110 volts, 50 cycles A.C. in La Paz, 220 volts 50 cycles A.C. elsewhere, but check before using any appliance. (You may even find 110 and 220 in the same room). US-type plugs can be used in most hotels.

Post, Telegraph, and Telephone Post offices use the post box (*casilla*) system. Items sent by post should therefore bear, not the street address, but the *casilla* number and town. Hours are Mon.-Sat. 0800-2000, Sun. 0800-1200. There is a national and international express post system; special counters and envelopes provided. Air-mail letters to and from Britain take between 5 and 10 days.

Radio telephone services run by the Serval Company serve Cochabamba and other parts of the interior. There is now direct satellite communication with Bolivia. Direct calls possible from major cities to Europe, clear lines, delays minimal (station to station, US$7.20/3 mins.). No collect calls can be made. When making overseas calls, your passport is kept to ensure prompt payment. Reduced rates on Sunday. Phone calls within city limits are free for private calls; for public phones, coins/fichas are necessary.

Media In La Paz: morning papers—*Presencia*, daily (available in other main cities), about

75,000, the largest circulation, largely Catholic, with good coverage of world events; *Hoy* and *El Diario*. *Meridiano* (midday): *Ultima Hora*, and *Jornada* (evenings). In Cochabamba—*Los Tiempos*, *Extra*. In Oruro—*La Patria*, mornings (except Mondays). *El Mundo* and *Crónica Deber* are the Santa Cruz daily papers; *Deber* also appears in Trinidad. La Paz papers are on sale in other cities. The *Miami Herald* is sometimes available in La Paz. Also, there are about 85 radio stations, a commercial government T.V. station as well as a university T.V. service.

We are deeply grateful to the following residents and travellers for new information on Bolivia: Phineas Gosselink (La Paz), Richard and Yvonne Ruming (Bathurst, NSW), Franck Abadie (Megève, France) and Marianne Joelius (Stockholm), Dean A. Alper (Mill Valley, CA), Martin Anderle, Susanne Riller and Tilo Timmermann (Fürth, W. Ger.), Stan Anderton (Preston, Lancs), Haz Arad, Lucie Armstrong (Ithaca, NY), Eberhard Baer (Koeningsbrunn, W. Ger.), Robin E. Baronas (Pittsburgh, PE), Maarten Beeris (San Pedro de Atacama), Hans and Lena Bengtsson (Gothenburg, Swe.), Lisbet Bengtsson (Gothenburg, Swe.), Momik Bernaerts (Amsterdam) and Thomas Hartmann (Copenhagen), O. Blane, Dorothea Bornholdt (Lutzhorn, W. Ger.), Lucy Broadbent and Rick Palmer (Palmerston North, NZ), Daniel Buck and Anne Meadows (Washington DC), Lucinda Coates (North Ryde, NSW), Jane Coburn (Thirroul, NSW), David S. Cousens and Antonia E. Melvin (London E18), G.G.A. Cumming (Viña del Mar), Karen Dahl (Hamden, Conn.), Jan Van Dalfsen and Tineke Puister (Neths.), Louis-François Debétaz (Concise, Switz.), Christian Delbrouck (Freiburg, W. Ger.), Peter Driesch (Essen 1), Scott Duffton (Aberdeen) and Alison Barrit (Inverness), Sonia and Tzvi Dugan (D.N. Eilot, Israel), Frank Dux (Detmold 18, W. Ger.), Kate Edwards (Freeport, Grand Bahama), Dag K. Ellingsen (Oslo 2), Fred and Marianne Emery (London SE26), Dr Dietz Evers (Krumesse), Volker Filss (Oberhausen, W. Ger.), Elisabeth Fischer and Thomas Winter (München 40), Alexandra Fisher (London W8), Margaret Fleming (Karlsfeld, W. Ger.), Olivier and Paloma Foro (St-Moritz), John N. Fugelso (Durham NC), Katy Gardner (Liverpool 8), Eduardo Garnica (Potosí), Theodor A. Gevert (Barueri, SP, Brazil), Jens Gjerlev (Bodøn, Norway), Rudolf Graf (Genthod, Switz.), Jacqueline Greig (Cuckfield, E. Sussex), Tamar Grossman (Montreal), Jon and Julia Gruffydd (Lima), Christian Gurney (Thornhill, Ont.), Rupert Hafner (Vienna), Anita Hammel (São Paulo), Mrs R.M. Hampson (Nassau), Astrid Hansen (Aars) and Jane Harfeld (Hornsyld, Dnmk.), Ellen Hansen and Morten Volden (Saupstad, Norway), Roy and Joan Harris (Nanaimo, BC), Kevin Healey (Melbourne, Vic.), Dr Paul Heaton (London NW6), Judith and Stephen Adler Hellman (Toronto), Olav Holger Helø (Copenhagen), Ursula Hochuli (Switz.) and Vincent Choblet (Paris), Edward Hutt (Stowmarket), Jeff Inglis (Seattle), Simon Jeffreys (Peterborough), Allan Jensen and Vibeke Nageh (Munke-Bjergby, Dnmk.), Martina Jost and Heinz Eisenhauer (Darmstadt), Tobias Kämpf (Rupperswil, Switz.), Rosi Kerler (München 40), Marcel Kersten (Roosendaal, Neth.), Carsten Kolbe (Marburg, W. Ger.), Lucy, Ian and Laura Krause (Newcastle-upon-Tyne), Thomas Krauss and Petra Fadi (Glasgow 12), Philip Krippendorff and Matthias Bertsch (Marburg), Daniel Küng (Wohlen, Switz.), Loren Lacelle (Willits, CA), Toby Lanzer (Santiago de Chile), Udo Lichtenthäler (Berlin 21), Carl Loeber (San José, CR), Kirsten Lührs (Stuttgart, 1), Mika Määttänen (Tampere, Fin.), Jan Madsen (Agedrup, Dmk.), S. D Manley (London E12), Nelly Matthey (Lausanne), A. Mckenzie Brockman (Deux-Montagnes, Quebec), Sylvia Meichsner (La Paz), Karssen Mengel and Birgit Borkholm Nielsen (Langeskov, Dmk.), Cindy Miller (Vancouver, BC), Valerie and Bob Mitchell (Cottesloe, Western Australia), Helene Monsme (Leiden, Neth.), Daniel Morgan (Wellington, NZ), David, Christine, Philip and Catherine Mylan (Worksop), Stephen Newcomer (Centrevill, Iowa), Mette Nordaw and Claus Jørgensen (Lyngby, Dnmk.), Jonas Noreús (Varberg, Swe.), Dave Nutting (Melbourne), Justine O'Keefe and David Couper (N Z), Lucy Paine and William Petrie (Watlington, Oxon.), Sandrine Pétremand and Gilles Maitre (Bevaix, Switz.), Ian Powell (Stafford) and Judy Proctor (London), Louis Prefontaine (St Malo, Manitoba), Robert Jan Prenger and André Kuipers (Amsterdam), Bernd Proissl (Wernau, W. Ger.), Johan Reinhard (La Paz), Jörg Retzluff (Aurich, W. Ger.), David Reynolds (Westerham, Kent), Antonio Righetti and Daniela Wenger (Bern), Gonzalo O. Rodríguez (La Paz), Jan and Ernest Rolland (Papendtecht, Neths.), Dafna and Yoram Rozy (Tel-Aviv), Silvia Salzmann (Mettmenhasli), J.J. Schat (Zoetermeer, Neths.), Kathrin Schildknecht and Jürg Schmutz (Bern, Switz.), Ueli Schlatter (Hemmental, Switz.), Andrea Schneiber (Herborn, W. Ger.), Isabelle and Heinz Scholl-Kalt (Zürich), Horst H. Schulz (Hamburg), Eleanor Sepora (New Zealand), John Spraos (London NW11), Mr and Mrs Ernest Stead (Pudsey, W. Yorks), Hans and Ina Stoffregen (Celle, W. Ger.), Christian Stückle (Ingolstadt, W. Ger.), Martin and Susanna Theander (Malmö), Shawn Toscano Olsen (Minnesota USA), Richard D. Tucker (Amsterdam), Maarten van Vlerken (Amsterdam), Thomas Walbaum (Steinheim, W. Ger.), Rob Ward (Sutton, Sy.), Roland Weitkamp (Braunschweig, W. Ger.), Lorraine Westerink (Old Toongabbie, NSW), Regina Wetzer and Richard C. Brusca (San Diego, Ca), Urs Wigger (Menznau, Switz.), Jacqueline P. M. Williams (London SW1) and Tim Woodward (Tottenham, N15).

VARIG ARE NEVER FAR FROM BRAZIL.

Brazil is a country at the forefront of technological achievement. But it is also much more. There's a spirit about Brazil. A spirit of warmth and vitality. A spirit that's perfectly reflected in the friendly efficiency of its national airline.

VARIG is Brazil.

VARIG

Brazilian Airlines

BRAZIL

Maps Country, 267; Brasília, 276; Rio de Janeiro environs, 283; Rio de Janeiro detail, 286; Copacabana, 305; Roads from Rio de Janeiro, 314; Minas Gerais and Espírito Santo, 320; São Paulo Orientation, 336; São Paulo Centre, 339; São Paulo Centre detail, 341; Southern Brazil, 357; Porto Alegre, 359; Curitiba, 374; Salvador, 386; Recife, 410; Manaus, 443.

INTRODUCTION

BRAZIL, the fifth largest country in the world, has the eighth largest population. It is almost as large as the United States of America. Its 8,511,965 square km. is nearly half that of South America. For neighbours it has all the South American countries save Chile and Ecuador. Distances are enormous: 4,320 km. from north to south, 4,328 km. from east to west, a land frontier of 15,719 km. and an Atlantic coast line of 7,408 km. Its population of 147 million (1989) is half that of all South America, and one in every two is under 25 years of age.

Brazil's topography may be divided roughly into five main zones: the Amazon Basin; the River Plate Basin; the Guiana Highlands north of the Amazon; the Brazilian Highlands south of the Amazon; and the coastal strip. The two great river basins account for about three-fifths of Brazil's area.

The Amazon Basin, in northern and western Brazil, takes up more than a third of the whole country. This basin is plain, broadly based on the Andes and funnelling narrowly to the sea; most of the drained area has an elevation of less than 250 metres. The rainfall is heavy, for the winds from the north-east and south-east lose their moisture as they approach the Andes. Some few places receive from 3,750 to 5,000 mm. a year, though over most of the area it is no more than from 1,500 to 2,500 mm. Much of the basin suffers from annual floods. The region was covered by tropical forest, with little undergrowth except along the watercourses; it is now being rapidly cut down. The climate is hot and the humidity high throughout the year.

The River Plate Basin, in the southern part of Brazil, has a more varied surface and is less heavily forested than the Amazon Basin. The land is higher and the climate cooler.

Most of the remainder of Brazil's territory is highland. The Guiana Highlands, north of the Amazon, are partly forested, partly hot stony desert. Those that face the north-west winds get heavy rainfall, but the southern slopes are arid. The rainfall, which comes during the hot season, is about 1,250 mm. a year. The summers are hot and the winters cool.

The Brazilian Highlands lying SE of the Amazon and NE of the River Plate Basin form a tableland of from 300 to 900 metres high, but here and there, mostly in South-Eastern Brazil, mountain ranges rise from it. The highest peak in southern Brazil, the Pico da Bandeira, north-east of Rio de Janeiro, is 2,898 metres; the highest peak in all Brazil, the Pico da Neblina on the Venezuelan border, is 3,014 metres.

For the most part the Highlands cascade sharply to the sea. South of Salvador as far as Porto Alegre the coast rises steeply to a protective barrier, the Great Escarpment. In only two places is this Escarpment breached by deeply cut river beds—those of the Rio Doce and the Rio Paraíba; and only in a few places does the land rise in a single slope making for comparatively easy communication with the interior. Along most of its course, the Great Escarpment falls to the sea in parallel steps, each step separated by the trough of a valley.

The few rivers rising on the Escarpment which flow direct into the Atlantic do so precipitously and are not navigable. Most of the rivers flow deep into the interior. Those in southern Brazil rise almost within sight of the sea, but run westward through the vast interior to join the Paraná. In the central area the Escarpment rivers run away from the sea to join the São Francisco river, which flows northwards parallel to the coast for 2,900 km., to tumble over the Paulo Afonso Falls on its eastward course to the Atlantic.

The Great Escarpment denies to most of Brazil the natural valley outflows and lines of travel from the interior to the sea. Of its rivers the Amazon alone is directly navigable for a great distance inland.

Climate The average annual temperature increases steadily from south to north, but even on the Equator, in the Amazon Basin, the average temperature is not more than 27°C, and the highest recorded has been only 36°C. Six degrees more have been recorded in the dry north-eastern states. From the latitude of Recife south to Rio de Janeiro, the mean temperature is from 23° to 27°C along the coast, and from 18° to 21°C in the Highlands. From a few degrees south of Rio de Janeiro to the boundary with Uruguay the mean temperature is from 17° to 19°C. Humidity is relatively high in Brazil, particularly along the coast.

It is only in rare cases that the rainfall can be described as either excessive or deficient: few places get more than 2,000 mm.—the coast north of Belém, some of the Amazon Basin, and a small area of the Serra do Mar between Santos and São Paulo, where the downpour has been harnessed to generate electricity. The north-eastern droughts are caused not by lack of rainfall, but by irregular rainfall; the area is also subject to floods.

The rainy season in the South is from December to March; as this is also the holiday season in Brazil when hotels and flights tend to be booked solid, it seems a good time for tourists to stay away—unless, of course, they want to see the famous Carnival seven weeks before Easter.

Political and Social History Brazil was discovered by the Portuguese, Pedro Alvares Cabral, in 1500. The first system of government adopted by the Portuguese was a Capitânia, a kind of feudal principality—there were thirteen of them, but these were replaced in 1572 by a Viceroyalty. In the same year it was decided to divide the colony into two, north and south, with capitals at Salvador and Rio de Janeiro; it was not until 1763 that Rio became the sole capital. The Portuguese crown expected both a personal and a state revenue from its colony. This was raised partly by payment of a tenth of the produce from grants of land

N.W. BRAZIL 0 Km 500
Not to same scale

1 Brasília.
2 The state of Rio de Janeiro.
3 Espírito Santo.
4 Minas Gerais.
5 The state of São Paulo.
6 Southern Brazil.
7 The North East.
8 Northern Brazil.
9 Southern Amazonia.
10 The centre West.

BRAZIL

27

made to colonists, a fifth from mining production, and about forty other taxes.

Three hundred years under the paternal eye of Portugal had ill-prepared the colonists for independent existence, except for the experience of Dutch invasion (1624 in Salvador, and 1630-1654 in Recife). The colonists ejected the Dutch from Brazil with little help from Portugal, and Brazilians date the birth of their national sentiment from these events. In 1789 infiltration of European thought led to the first unsuccessful revolution against Portuguese rule, the Inconfidência in Minas Gerais, led by Tiradentes. When the troops of Napoleon caused the Portuguese Royal Family to sail in British ships to Brazil in 1808, the fate of the colony was decided: Brazil became the senior partner, as it were, in the Portuguese empire. King João VI returned to the mother country in 1821, leaving his son, the handsome young Pedro, as Regent. The Portuguese Parliament (the Cortes) mistrusted this arrangement, and called on Pedro to return, but the Brazilians asked him to stay. On 13 May, 1822, he agreed to stay, and assumed the title of "Perpetual Defender and Protector of Brazil". On 7 September he declared Brazil's independence with the cry "Independence or Death" by the Ipiranga River; on 12 October he was proclaimed constitutional emperor of Brazil, and on 1 December he was crowned in Rio de Janeiro.

Dom Pedro the First had the misfortune to be faced by a secession movement in the north, to lose the Banda Oriental (today Uruguay) and to get somewhat involved in his marital relations. Finally, he abdicated as the result of a military revolt in 1831, leaving his five-year-old son, Dom Pedro the Second, in the hands of a regent, as ruler. On 23 July, 1840, the lad, though only 15, was proclaimed of age and the regency discontinued. Dom Pedro the Second, a strong liberal at heart, promoted education, increased communications, developed agriculture, stamped on corruption and encouraged immigration from Europe. Under his rule the war with the dictator López of Paraguay ended in Brazilian victory. Finally, he declared that he would rather lose his crown than allow slavery to continue, and on 13 May, 1888, it was finally abolished by his daughter, Princess Isabel, who was acting as Regent during his temporary absence.

There is little doubt that it was this measure that cost him his throne. Many plantation owners, who had been given no compensation, turned against the Emperor; they were supported by elements in the army and navy, who felt that the Emperor had not given due heed to their interests since the Paraguay War. On 15 November, 1889, the Republic was proclaimed and the Emperor sailed for Europe. Two years later he died in a second-rate hotel in Paris, after steadfastly refusing a pension from the conscience-stricken revolutionaries. At the time of the first centenary of independence in 1922 the imperial family was allowed to return to Brazil, and the body of Dom Pedro was brought back and buried in the cathedral at Petrópolis.

The history of the "Old Republic" (1889-1930), apart from the first ten years

which saw several monarchist rebellions, was comparatively eventless, a time of expansion and increasing prosperity. Brazil declared war on Germany during both wars and Brazilian troops fought in the Italian campaign in 1944-45. In 1930 a revolution headed by Getúlio Vargas, Governor of Rio Grande do Sul, who was to become known as "the Father of the Poor" for the social measures he introduced, deposed President Wáshington Luís and Vargas assumed executive power first as provisional president and then as dictator. He was forced to resign in October 1945. In 1946 a liberal republic was restored and the following 18 years saw considerable economic development and social advance. There was, however, increasing government instability and corruption leading to growing military intervention in civil affairs; this culminated in the military movement of March 1964, which ruled until March 1985 with increasing liberalization and great economic success (up to 1980). In January 1985 a civilian, Tancredo Neves, representing a broad opposition to the military regime, was elected President by the electoral college introduced under the military's 1967 constitution. He was unable, because of illness, to take office: the vice-president elect, Sr. José Sarney, was sworn in as acting President in March 1985, and became President on Sr. Neves' death in April. A Constituent Assembly completely revised Brazil's constitution in 1987-88. A new constitution was approved in 1988 which opened the way for direct presidential elections to be held in November 1989. The elections were held in two rounds, the final result giving Sr. Fernanado Collar de Melo, of the small Partido da Recontrução Nacional, 53% of the vote, narrowly defeating his left-wing rival, Luis Inácio da Silva (Lula). President Collar took office on 15 March for a five-year term, pledging to fight corruption, injustice and inflation, and immediately announced an economic programme which combined free market principles with authoritarian state intervention.

Settlement and Economic History   The first European settlement was at Salvador da Bahia, and the settlers came mainly from southern Portugal, with its feudal tradition of great estates. For the first few years Portugal, then much concerned with the Orient, paid little attention to Brazil. But about 1507 a second colony was settled at São Vicente, near Santos, and in 1537 a third at Olinda, near Recife. The settlers at São Vicente, who founded the first settlement in the highlands at São Paulo in 1534, were unlike those at Salvador and Recife: they came from the poorer and more energetic north of Portugal. All of them were attracted less by the prospect of earning their living by self-supporting labour than by opportunities of speculative profit. To do the work they impressed the primitive Tupi-Guarani Indians, many of whom died from European diseases (see *Red Gold*, by John Hemming). They cohabited freely with the Indians and, later, with slaves imported from Africa to run the huge estates.

Sugar cane had been introduced at São Vicente in 1532, but it was the wealthy settlers of the north-east who had the necessary capital to establish the crop and to buy African slaves to work it; the Indian, with his hunting-and-gathering culture, was a disappointment as a labourer. In the matter of sugar, Salvador and Recife had the advantages over São Vicente of being very much nearer home, and of having better ports and easier access to the interior. During the latter half of the 16th and the whole of the 17th centuries, the provinces of Bahia, Pernambuco, and Paraíba were the world's prime source of sugar.

The settlers at São Paulo, envious of the more fortunate north-east, sent out expeditions to explore the interior for gold, which had already been found in small quantities in their own streams. These hardy Bandeirantes pushed as far south as Colonia, opposite Buenos Aires, as far west as the River Paraguay, and north into the area west of the sugar plantations of the north-east. In 1698 they struck gold in central Minas Gerais. More was found soon after in central Mato Grosso, and in 1725 in Goiás. Diamonds were discovered in 1729 north of the goldfields of Minas Gerais.

There was a great gold and diamond rush in which the sugar planters took part. Sugar by that time was on the decline: there was competition from the Caribbean; profits had fallen, and the Brazilians had made no attempt to lower costs by ploughing back profits: that was not in their tradition. The gold boom started early in the 18th century, lasted a hundred years, and then petered out. Minas Gerais was transformed from a wilderness into a well populated agricultural, pastoral, and mining region. It was as an outlet for this area that Rio de Janeiro was developed. Some of the wealth went to create the extraordinarily beautiful city of Ouro Preto, to-day a national monument of superb building, painting and sculpture, and the similarly attractive cities of São João del Rei, Mariana, Congonhas do Campo, Diamantina and others.

Brazil was ready for the next speculation, coffee, introduced about 1720 from French Guyane. Coffee planting began near Rio de Janeiro and at many places round the coast as far as the Amazon, but by 1825 it had mainly been concentrated in the Paraíba valley, west of the capital. From there it spread into São Paulo, where its cultivation attracted a large number of immigrants after 1850. About a third of the total production normally still comes from São Paulo state.

There have been many other typical Brazilian booms and recessions. The best known is the rubber boom in the Amazon valley; competition from SE Asia wiped it out after 1912. Sugar, coffee, and cocoa were alike the subject of booms. In each case Brazil was challenged by other sources of supply, where more intensive methods of production were applied.

This boom tradition still holds, but it is shifting from agriculture to industry: Brazilians today prefer to think of themselves as a rising industrial nation. Nevertheless, a great increase in production and export of manufactured goods has not prevented oases of prosperity being edged by deserts of poverty and wilderness.

The People   At first the new colony grew slowly. From 1580 to 1640 the population was only about 50,000 apart from the million or so indigenous Indians. In 1700 there were some 750,000 civilized people in Brazil. Early in the 19th century Humboldt computed there were about 920,000 whites, 1,960,000 Africans, and 1,120,000 Indians and mestiços: after three centuries of occupation a total of only four millions, and over twice as many blacks as there were whites.

Modern immigration did not begin effectively until after 1850. Of the 4.6 million immigrants from Europe between 1884 and 1954, 32% were Italians, 30% Portuguese, 14% Spanish, 4% German, and the rest of various nationalities. Since 1954 immigrants have averaged 50,000 a year. There are some 1 million Japanese-descended Brazilians; they grow a fifth of the coffee, 30% of the cotton, all the tea, and are very active in market gardening.

Today the whites and near-whites are about 53% of the population, people of mixed race about 34%, and blacks 11%; the rest are either aboriginal Indians or Asians. There are large regional variations in the distribution of the races: the whites predominate greatly in the south, which received the largest flood of European immigrants, and decrease more or less progressively towards the north.

Most of the German immigrants settled in the three southern states: Santa Catarina, Rio Grande do Sul, and Paraná. The Germans (and the Italians and Poles and other Slavs who followed them) did not in the main go as wage earners on the big estates, but as cultivators of their own small farms. Here there is a settled agricultural population cultivating the soil intensively. It is only by such methods and by such an expansion that the wastes of the Sertão, given sufficient water, can be put to effective use. However, the Sertão has been relatively unaffected by European and Far Eastern immigration. Its inhabitants are people of mixed Portuguese and Indian origin (mestiço); most live off a primitive but ecologically effective method of cultivation known as "slash and burn", which involves cutting down and burning the forest for a small patch of ground which is cultivated for a few years and then allowed to return to forest.

The decision to found a new federal capital, Brasília, deep in the interior, was a symbolic act of faith in the future of the Sertão: a bold attempt to deflect population from the coastal regions to the under-developed central and western plateaux of the country.

Though there is no legal discrimination against black people, the economic and educational disparity—by default rather than intent of the Government—is such that successful Afro Brazilians are active almost exclusively in the worlds of sport, entertainment and the arts. By the way, don't refer to black people as "pretos" or "negros": describe them as "oscuros" or "gente de cor "—more acceptable terms.

The seven censuses of the present century show the growth of the population, from 17.3 million in 1900 to 119.0 million in 1980. Official estimates give the total popoulation at 148.9 million in 1985, compared with a total in 1989 of 147.4 million, estimated by external sources. In 1970, 56% of the population was urban; by 1980 this proportion had risen to 71%. Of the total labour force in 1980, 30% was occupied in agriculture and fishing, compared with 44% in 1970, 24% worked in industry (18% in 1970), 9% in commerce (8% in 1970) and 36% in government and services, compared with only 19% in 1970. The average life span has increased from 39 years in 1939 to 58 years today. The population grew 2.5% between 1970 and 1980. By region, population growth 1970-80 was: N, 5.0%; NE, 2.2%; S, 1.4%; and SE, 2.7%.

The population has historically been heavily concentrated in a comparatively small area—chiefly along the coastal strip where the original Portuguese settlers exploited the agricultural wealth, and further inland in the states of Minas Gerais and São Paulo where more recent development has followed the original search for gold, precious stones and slaves. Much of the interior of Pará, Amazonas, Goiás and the Mato Grossos has densities of one person per sq. km. or less. Brazil's attention is officially focused on these relatively underpopulated regions as a means of syphoning off some of the population excess in the urban centres—the industrialized South-East contains more than 50% of the total urban population and its two largest cities, São Paulo and Rio de Janeiro, both have over ten million people in their metropolitan and surrounding areas.

The urban population of Brazil increased at rates more than double the overall average rate, until the 1980s, and much of this growth has been concentrated in the larger cities—those over 100,000 (which numbered 95 in 1980). Internal migration is the major cause of these phenomenal growth rates, bringing to the cities problems of unemployment, housing shortage, and pressure on services which are already stretched to breaking point; shanty towns—or *favelas*, *mocambos*, *alagados*, according to the region—are an integral part of the urban landscape and a constant reminder of the poverty of some of the rural areas from which these people come. But while the North-East, because of its poverty, has lost many workers to the industries of the South-East, many rural workers from southern Brazil have moved north, drawn by the rapid development of Amazonia, creating unprecedented pressures on the environment.

The most recent official surveys indicate that 31% of the population is illiterate. Of the 13 million children between 7 and 14, 2 million have no school to go to. Of those who go to school, not all stay long enough to learn how to read and write. Adult literacy campaigns have, however, recently improved the picture.

The Economy Brazil is the world's tenth largest economy and eighth largest market economy. It has abundant and varied natural resources and a long-standing development record, obtaining a positive growth rate every year since 1931 apart from 1963 and 1981-83 and 1988. The most striking features of economic development since 1945 have been state intervention and control, and industrialization, -particularly in the areas of energy, heavy industry, transport equipment and capital goods. The vast majority of consumer goods are now manufactured locally, as well as a wide range of capital goods. Since the 1970s there has been a rapid expansion of technology-based industries. Manufactures now account for 70% of total exports. Industry accounts for 38% of gdp and 25% of total employment.

Brazil remains a large farming country and is generally self-sufficient in food production. It is the world's largest producer and exporter of coffee and sugar cane. Since the mid-1970s soya and orange juice production have been developed, so that dominant positions in international markets in these products have been secured. Agriculture customarily produces about two-fifths of exports, 10% of gdp and 30% of total employment. However, the sector is backward in its use of techniques and yields are comparatively low. Mechanization is largely limited to southern areas. A concentrated land holding structure and a preference for export cash crops have generated structural problems which have prevented satisfaction of domestic demand for food.

The country is richly endowed with metals and other minerals. Their exploitation has only recently begun, since low demand and high transport costs have previously rendered them uneconomic. Brazil has up to a third of the world's total iron ore reserves, found mainly in Minas Gerais and certain parts of the Amazon basin, especially the Serra dos Carajás region (Pará). Brazil is also a significant exporter of manganese and gold and produces increasing amounts of tin and copper.

Energy sector development has aimed at substituting local for imported energy. Oil reserves are estimated at 2.1 bn barrels with substantial additions in recent years from the Campos basin off the coast of Rio de Janeiro state. Oil production has steadily risen to 0.6 m barrels a day, and this satisfies two-thirds of local requirements. Large investments have been made in hydroelectricity, alcohol and nuclear power. Hydroelectric plants produce 90% of electricity and several major schemes are in preparation, including Itaipú on the River Paraná, a joint project with Paraguay and reportedly the world's largest. The Proálcool programme begun in 1974 aimed to substitute alcohol derived mainly from sugar cane for oil products, and 90% of the country's vehicles are powered by alcohol. However, the fall in oil prices in the 1980s rendered this programme uneconomic because of the massive subsidies to cane growers. A 620-Mw nuclear reactor at Angra dos Reis (Rio de Janeiro) came on stream in 1985, but financial restrictions have slowed nuclear power development.

High rates of inflation have been recorded particularly in the 1980s because of domestic and external factors. These included urbanization and food supply bottlenecks, energy consumption patterns heavily dependent on oil imports, public accounts disequilibrium, and generalized indexation covering wages, prices and financial instruments. A stabilization programme, known as the Cruzado plan, was introduced in February 1986, including a price freeze, introduction of a new currency, the new cruzados, and partial dismantling of indexation. Inflation was sharply cut, but the generation of excess demand caused the plan to collapse by the end of the year and inflation soon rose again. In 1989 a new stabilization plan, dubbed the summer plan, was introduced when inflation rose to 1,000%. The new cruzados was created, worth 1,000 cruzados, but failure was inevitable considering the lack of political will to tackle the structural causes of inflation. It was left to the newly-elected Government in 1990 to introduce sweeping economic reforms which effectively froze all savings and bank accounts, removed all subsidies and tax incentives and raised tax revenues. By keeping a very tight fiscal and monetary policy coupled with liberalization of foreign trade and the exchange rate, the Government hoped to eradicate inflation prior to easing liquidity and generating economic recovery.

During the 1970s large-scale, high cost projects and current account deficits were financed by foreign borrowing, and Brazil accumulated the region's largest external debt, estimated at US$113 bn at end-1988. From 1982 annual rescheduling agreements were concluded with creditors, with new money and, in 1983-85, IMF standby facilities. The World Bank and Inter-American Development Bank granted large loans for sectoral development. These arrangements did not, however, help to reduce the burden of interest payments and in February 1987 Brazil declared a moratorium on interest in order to preserve foreign exchange reserves and halt the net transfer of resources to creditors. The plan did not prosper and a year later reserves were even lower as lenders declined to extend credit and favourable terms were being awarded to other borrowers. In 1988 Brazil returned to the international financial community and negotiated a financing package from all creditors aimed at restoring its creditworthiness, but by 1989 it had moved back into arrears to preserve foreign reserves. The new administration was expected to negotiate a new debt package with all creditors in 1990.

Government The 1988 constitution provides for an executive president elected by direct popular vote, balanced by a bicameral legislature (72 seats in the Federal Senate, 487 seats in the Chamber of Deputies) and an independent judiciary. The vote has been extended to 16-year olds and illiterates. Presidential elections are held every 5 years, with a second round one month after the first if no candidate wins an outright majority. Congressional elections are held every four years, the deputies being chosen by proportional representation. Congressional elections were due in November 1990.

Local Administration Each State has a popularly-elected Governor who exercises the executive power, and a Legislative Assembly which legislates on all matters affecting provincial administration and provides for State expenses and needs by levying taxes. Each municipality has a similar structure, with a mayor (*prefeito*), also popularly elected, and a local council (*câmara de vereadores*). Municipal elections were held in November 1988.

Railways, of which there are about 30,500 km., were originally built to supply export markets and did not combine into a unified system. To join them effectively, however, would mean—besides 3,200 km. of new construction—the unifying of Brazil's two existing gauges. Three more gauges exist for the isolated Amapa Railway and a number of abandoned lines. the About 2,450 km. have now been electrified. Many lines have been closed in recent years.

Roads Though the best paved highways are still heavily concentrated in the South-East, those serving the interior are now being improved to all-weather status and many are paved. Brazil has over 1.4 million kilometres of highways, of which in 1986 about 127,000 km. were paved, and the recent road-building programmes have emphasized inter-regional connections and the opening up of the Centre, North and West of the country. Interurban bus services are frequent and good.

Air Services The first commercial flight in Brazil was in 1927. Because of the great distances and the comparative paucity of good highways and railways, aircraft have eased the traveller's lot more spectacularly in Brazil than in any other country. The larger cities are now linked with each other several times a day by air, and even the more remote points in the country can now be reached by light aircraft.

BRASILIA (1)

Brasília On April 21, 1960, Rio de Janeiro ceased to be the Federal Capital of Brazil; as required by the Constitution, it was replaced by Brasília, 960 km. away in the unpopulated uplands of Goiás, in the heart of the undeveloped Sertão. The population of the Plano Piloto (the official name for central Brasília) was 411,000 (1980 census—the Federal District as a whole, with an area of 5,814 square km., now has nearly 1.9 million inhabitants).

The new capital lies 1,150 metres above sea-level on undulating ground. The climate, unlike that of the old capital, is mild and the humidity refreshingly low, but trying in dry weather. The noonday sun beats hard, but summer brings heavy rains and the air is usually cool by night.

The creation of an inland capital had been urged since the beginning of the last century, but it was finally brought into being after President Kubitschek came to power in 1956, when a competition for the best general plan was won by Professor Lúcio Costa, who laid out the city in the shape of a bent bow and arrow.

Along the curve of the bow are the residential areas made up of large six-storey apartment blocks, the "Super-Quadras". They lie on either side (E and W) of the "bow" (the Eixo Rodoviário) and are numbered according to their relation to the Eixo and their distance from the centre. Thus the 100s and 300s lie west of the Eixo and the 200s and 400s to the east; Quadras 302, 102, 202 and 402 are nearest the centre and 316, 116, 216 and 416 mark the end of the Plano Piloto. The numbering applies equally on either side of the centre, the two halves of the city being referred to as Asa Sul and Asa Norte (the north and south wings). Thus, for example, 116 Sul and 116 Norte are at the extreme opposite ends of the city. All Quadras are separated by feeder roads, along which are the local shops. There are also a number of schools, parks and cinemas in the spaces between the Quadras (especially in Asa Sul), though not as systematically as was originally envisaged. On the outer side of the 300s and extending the length of the city is the Avenida W3 and on the outer side of the 400s is the Avenida L2, both of these being similarly divided into north and south according to the part of the city they are in.

Asa Sul is almost complete and Asa Norte (which for years was looked down on) is growing very fast, with standards of architecture and urbanization that promise to make it more attractive than Asa Sul in the near future. The main shopping areas—with more cinemas, restaurants and so on, are situated on either side of the old bus station. Several parks—or at least green areas—are now in being. The private residential areas are W of the Super-Quadras, and on the other side of the lake.

At right angles to these residential areas is the "arrow", the 8-km. long, 250-metre wide Eixo Monumental. At the tip of the arrow, as it were, is the Praça dos Tres Poderes, with the Congress buildings, the Palácio do Planalto (the President's office), the Palácio da Justiça (Supreme Court) and the Panteão Tancredo Neves (a memorial to the president-elect who died in 1985 before taking office). The Cathedral and the Ministry buildings line the Esplanada dos Ministérios, W of the Praça. Where the bow and arrow intersect is the city bus terminal (Rodoviária), with the cultural and recreational centres and commercial and financial areas on either side. There is a sequence of zones westward along the shaft of the arrow; a hotel centre, a radio city, an area for fairs and circuses, a centre for sports, the Praça Municipal (with the municipal offices in the Palácio do Buriti and a great cross marking the spot on which the first mass was said in Brasília, on May 3, 1957), and, lastly (where the nock of the arrow would be) the combined new bus and railway station (Rodoferroviária) with the industrial area nearby. The most impressive buildings are all by Oscar Niemeyer, Brazil's leading architect.

The main north-south road (Eixo Rodoviário), in which fast-moving traffic is segregated, follows the curve of the bow; the radial road is along the line of the arrow—intersections are avoided by means of underpasses and cloverleaves. Motor and pedestrian traffic is segregated in the residential areas.

The Palácio da Alvorada, the President's residence, which is not open to visitors, is close to the lake. The 80-km. drive along the road round the lake to the dam is attractive. There are spectacular falls below the dam in the rainy season. Between the Praça dos Tres Poderes and the lake are sites for various recreations, including golf, fishing and yacht clubs, and an acoustic shell for shows in the open air. The airport is on the far side of the lake. Some 250 hectares between the lake and the northern residential area (Asa Norte) are reserved for the University of Brasília, founded in 1962. South of the university area, the Avenida das Nações runs from the Palácio da Alvorada along the lake to join the road from the airport to the centre. Along it are found all the principal embassies. Also in this area is the attractive vice-presidential residence, the Palácio do Jaburu, again not open to visitors. This area is almost completed and very scenic.

Sightseeing A fine initial view of the city may be had from the television tower, which has a free observation platform at 75 metres up (lift will not ascend with fewer than 5 people; also bar and souvenir shop; open 0800-2000, long queues

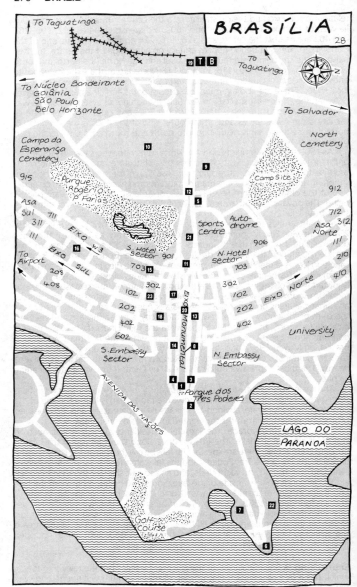

BRASÍLIA

28

To Taguatinga

To Taguatinga

Z

To Núcleo Bandeirante
Goiânia
São Paulo
Belo Horizonte

To Salvador

Campo da
Esperança
Cemetery

North
Cemetery

915

Parque
Rogério
P. Farias

Camp Site

912

Asa
Sul   711

311

111

EIXO   W 3

S. Hotel
Sector   901

Sports
Centre

Auto-
drome

712 312
Asa
Norte

111

To
Airport

208

408

EIXO
SUL

703 15

302

102

202

402

602

S. Embassy
Sector

N. Hotel
Sector

906

703

302

102

202

402

210

Eixo Norte   410

University

Eixo Monumental

N. Embassy
Sector

AVENIDA DAS NAÇÕES

Parque dos
Tres Poderes

LAGO DO
PARANOA

Golf
Course

Sat. and Sun.; the TV tower sways quite a bit), or from the old Rodoviária tower. A general impression can be gained in a day by bus or taxi tour—don't try walking much unless fit and fairly impervious to heat (and even so not recommended for single females). This impression is best gained at weekends when the city is quieter, though then there are fewer buses to move you around (some say the city is "totally dead" at weekends). The city can also be seen at night by taking the Alvorada circular bus from the old Rodoviária. Congress is open to visitors Mon.-Fri. 0800-1200 and 1400-1700, guides free of charge (in English 1400-1600), and visitors may attend debates when Congress is in session. The Planalto may be visited; admission restricted to men in long-sleeved shirts and trousers and women in skirts, Fri., 0900-1100 and 1500-1700. The marvellous building of the Ministry of Foreign Affairs, the Itamarati, has modern paintings and furniture, beautiful water gardens and offers one of the most rewarding visits (guided visits at 1000 and 1600, free). Opposite the Itamarati is the Palácio de Justiça, the Supreme Court building, with artificial cascades between its concrete columns. Visiting (dress as for the Planalto, Mon., Wed., Fri) 1400-1900; Tues. and Thurs. 0800-1030. The Cathedral, on the Esplanada dos Ministérios, a most spectacular circular building in the shape of the crown of thorns (still under construction), is open 0900-1100, 1400-1700; see also the Ceschiatti statues of the evangelists and the baptistery in the shape of a large pebble. The outdoor carrillon was a gift from the King of Spain. W of the TV tower on Avenida W3 Sul, at Quadra 702, is the Sanctuary of Dom Bosco, a square building constructed largely of blue glass. Other religious buildings worth seeing are the Fátima church (the Igrejinha) in the Asa Sul at Quadras 307-308, the Sanctuary of Our Lady of Fátima, the "orange caterpillar" on Av. W5 a little S of the Dom Bosco sanctuary, and the chapel (Ermida) of Dom Bosco, on the other side of the lake opposite the Alvorada, though the site is not well maintained. Some 15 km. out along the Belo Horizonte road is the small wooden house, known as "O Catetinho", in which President Kubitschek stayed in the late 1950s during his visits to the city when it was under construction; it is open to visitors and most interesting. A permanent memorial to Juscelino Kubitschek, the "Memorial JK", containing his tomb together with a lecture hall and exhibits, is worth visiting (open Mon.-Fri. 0900-1200, 1300-1800, Sat.-Sun. 0900-1900, entry US$0.50). The Brazilian Army headquarters, designed by Oscar Niemeyer, is interesting; The Monumental Parade Stand has unique and mysterious acoustic characteristics (the complex is north of the Eixo Monumental, between the "Memorial JK" and the Rodoferroviária).

Light industry alone is allowed in the city and its population was limited to 500,000; this has been exceeded and more people live in a number of shanty towns, with minimal services, located well away from the main city.

Sculptures Brasília is famous for its wealth of modern sculpture, Examples are: "Culture" (on the University campus), "The Meteorite" (above the Itamarati water-mirror), and "The Warriors" (in front of the Planalto)—all by Bruno Giorgi; "Justice" (in front of Supreme Court building), the four evangelists in front of the Cathedral and "The Water-Nymphs" (above the Alvorada water-mirror)—all by Alfredo Ceschiatti; "The Rite of Rhythms" (Alvorada gardens), by Maria Martins; and the beautiful "Mermaid" in front of the Navy Ministry on the Esplanada dos Ministérios. A statue of Juscelino Kubitschek is adjacent to the "Memorial JK".

Ceremonies The guard is changed ceremonially at the Palácio do Planalto on Tues., 0830

Brasília: Key to map

1. Congress; 2. Palácio de Planalto; 3. Palácio da Justiça; 4. Itamarati; 5. Buriti; 6. Palácio da Alvorada; 7. Palácio do Jaburu; 8. Ministries; 9. Army Ministry; 10. Observatory; 11. TV Tower; 12. J.K. Monument; 13. National Theatre; 14. Cathedral; 15. Dom Bosco; 16. Igrejinha/Fátima; 17. Post Office, Telegraph and Postal Museum; 18. S. Banking Sector and Gold Museum; 19 Rodoferroviária; 20. Municipal Rodoviária; 21. Convention Centre and Tourist Office; 22. *Hotel Brasília Palace*; 23. Hospital.

and 1730. The President attends if he is present.

Local Holidays Ash Wednesday; Maundy Thursday, half-day; 8 Dec. (Immaculate Conception); Christmas Eve.

Hotels Prices include breakfast, but 10% must be added. In the Southern Hotel Sector: *Nacional*, Lote 1, T 226-8180, A, 4-star, pool; *Carlton*, Quadra 5 bloco G, T 224-8819, A, 4-star, pool; *Bristol*, Quadra 4, bloco F, T 225-6170, A, 3-star, pool; *Riviera*, Quadra 3, bloco I, T 225-1880, B, 3-star; *Brasília Imperial*, Quadra 3, bloco E, T 225-7050, B, 2-star, deposit for room requested, good breakfast, motel-style; *Planalto*, Quadra 3, bloco A, T 225-6860, comfortable, reasonably-priced, city tours.

In the Northern Hotel Sector: *Eron Brasília*, Quadra 5, Lote A, T 226-2125, 4-star, A; *Aracoara*, Quadra 5, bloco C, T 225-1650, 4 star, A; *Casablanca*, Quadra 3, Lote A, T 226-0255, A, good; *Diplomat*, Quadra 2, bloco L, T 225-2010, B, good; *El Pilar*, Quadra 3, bloco F, T 224-5915, B, friendly; *Byblos*, Quadra 3, bloco E, T 223-1570, C; *Aristus*, Quadra 2, bloco O, T 223-8675, good; and *Mirage* D, Q2N, T 225-7150, fan, good, clean. Moderately-priced hotels can be found in the Northern Hotel Sector only.

The *Petrobrás Motel* at the Saída Sul is far from the centre but clean and cheaper (D) for motorists. Also at Saída Sul: Shell's *Motel Sabataia*, D, no breakfast; *Paranoá*, E, basic. Cheaper pensions available; enquire at airport information desk, which also has the phone number of the Youth hostel, Albergue Projeto Rondon, Av. W Sul, Superquadra 712, Bloco O, Casa 44. At weekends discounts can be obtained, worth bargaining.

However, the hotels outside the city in Taguatinga (take 102 or 106 bus, E1XO) and Núcleo Bandeirante, though fairly basic, tend to be recommended for cheapness, but reported very difficult to get single rooms. Núcleo Bandeirante: *Jurema*, at Av. Central 1390, D; *São Judas Tadeu*, E, noisy, clean but cockroaches, poor breakfast; *Ypacaraí*, round corner from *Hotel Rio de Janeiro*, E, O.K. for "young and hearty" but many mosquitoes; *Buriti*, 2° Avenida 1415, E, with bath; has cheaper single rooms. Taguatinga is pleasanter than the Núcleo, which is full of shanties; there are many cheap hotels and restaurants of a reasonable standard, for example, *Solar*, near Jumbo Supermarket, F, basic and clean. *Colorado*, Setor Hoteleira, Projeção B, T 561-3500, D, with bath, fridge, TV, good, in the centre; *Pousada Brasília*, next door, T 562-5055, E with bath and breakfast; *Globo*, CNB4, Lote 1, T 561-1716, E, without breakfast, friendly, basic. *Rodoviária*, E, without bath, more with, including breakfast, clean and friendly. Bus "Estrutural" from Brasília Rodoferroviária to Taguatinga Rodoviária where you change, without extra charge to 700 bus which passes, in order: *Rio Verde*, Bloco Norte QNE 26, E; *Camará*, QNE 16, F (hourly rentals also); *Palace*, CNB 11, E, clean, basic, hot water, communal shower; *Taguatinga*, by roundabout near clocktower, about 10 mins. from Rodoviária, F, hot showers, TV, back rooms are quieter, clothes-washing facilities, used by prostitutes. Bus 700 or 800 (marked "Eixo") goes from opp. Jumbo Supermarket in Taguatinga to old Rodoviária in Brasília.

Camping The city's main site is 2 km. out, by the Centro Esportivo, near the motor-racing track, with room for 3,100 campers. US$1.50 p.p., average charge, though apparently some travellers have stayed free. Take bus 109 (infrequent) from municipal Rodoviária. Agua Mineral Parque, 6 km. NW of city, direct buses only at weekend; US$1 p.p., mineral pool, showers. One site a few km. S on Belo Horizonte road, another out in the country about 70 km. E. Associação Brasileira de Camping (Edif. Márcia, 12th floor, Setor Comercial Sul, T 225-8768) has two sites: one at Km. 19 on the Belo Horizonte road and one 25 km. NE of Brasília at Sobradinho. Camping Clube do Brasil has site at Itiquira waterfall, 100 km. NE of the city, near Formosa; information from Edif. Maristela, room 1214, Setor Comercial Sul, T 223-6561. There is a Forestry Commission site 10 km. out of Brasília on the BR-041. There are signs to the sites. "Wild" camping is possible.

Restaurants There are new restaurants opening in Brasília every week. (The Southern Hotel Sector tends to have more; there are many cheap places on Av. W3 Sul. e.g. at Blocos 502 and 506.) At weekends few restaurants in central Brasília are open. The following are classified by their speciality:

International Cuisine: *Aeroporto*, terrace of international airport, very pleasant, food reported very good. Most of the big hotels' restaurants. *Restaurant Gaff*, Centro Gilberto Salomão, South Lake (very good, especially meat, but expensive).

Churrascarias (barbecues): *Brasas*, first floor of Conjunto Nacional; *Boi na Brasa*, Km. 15 on Brasília-Belo Horizonte road; *Galetão*, Galeria dos Estados; *Júlio*, on road to Taguatinga; *Churrascaria do Lago*, beside *Brasília Palace Hotel*; *Pampa*, beside Carrefour hypermarket, *Tordilho*, on edge of lake near *Brasília Palace Hotel*; *Muken*, in Taguatinga; *Toys*, a rancho among the trees below the Avenida das Nações; *Churrascaria do Paranoá*, beside the dam.

Brazilian food: *Cantina Caipira*, 104 Sul; *Fogão de Lenha*, 402 Sul; *Maloca Querida*, 107 Sul.

Northern Brazilian/Amazonian: *Pororoca*, 411 Sul; *Marajoara*, 113 Sul.

Seafood/Fish: *Panela de Barro*, Galeria Nova Ouvidor, Setor Comercial Sul; *Chorão*, 302 Norte; *Jangadeiro*, 213 Sul; *Sereia*, 212 Sul (open until the early hours); *Kastelinho*, 411 Sul.

Portuguese: *Cachopa*, Galeria Nova Ouvidor; *Ginga*, 104 Sul.

Spanish: *O Espanhol*, Avenida W3 Sul, quadra 506; *Salamanca*, 113 Sul.

French: *Français*, 404 Sul; *Forty Five*, 203 Sul (overpriced); *Le Coq*, Galeria Karim, 110/111 Sul; *La Chaumière*, 408 Sul.

Chinese: *China*, 203 Sul; *New China*, 209 Sul (the best according to Chinese diplomats); *Fon Min*, 405 Sul; *Fon Pin*, 403 Sul; *Fon Shian*, 201 Sul; *Pequim*, 212 Sul; *Ran Gon*, Praça dos Tres Poderes.

Japanese: *Nipon*, 314 Sul and 112 Sul.

Lebanese/Middle Eastern: *Alef*, 302 Sul; *Arabeske*, 109 Sul; *Beirute*, 109 Sul; *Beduino*, 102 Sul; *Almenara*, 204 Sul. *Chez Karam*, Centro Gilberto Salomão; *El Hadji*; *Hotel Torre*, N. Hotel Sector (self-service, very good).

German: *Tirol* and *Bierfass*, both in Centro Gilberto Salomão, South Lake.

Italian/Pizzerias: *Kazebre 13*, Avenida W3 Sul, quadra 504; *La Grotta Azzurra*, 208 Sul; *Roma*, Avenida W3 Sul, quadras 501 and 511, good, quite cheap; *La Romanina*, 303 Sul; *Tarantela*, 202 Sul; *Pizzaiola*, 310 Sul; *Prima*, 106 Sul; *Roma*, 311 Sul; *Romassas*, Avenida W3 Sul, quadra 505.

Macrobiotic/Vegetarian: *Coisas da Terra*, Avenida W3 Norte, quadra 704; *Boa Terra*, Quadra 702, open for dinner, rec; *Portal*, 209 Sul, one at front of Setor Comercial Sul, close to Rodoviária, lunch only, set-price meal; *Ken's Kitchen*, Quadra 302 Norte (English spoken).

Local: *Bom Demais*, Av. W3 Norte, Quadra 706, comfortable, inexpensive, serving fish, beef and rice, etc., live music at weekends (cover charge US$0.50). "For a good, cheap meal, eat at the crew's canteen at the airport, in a building to the right as you leave the main exit."

Pubs   There are two "English style" bars: *Gates Pub*, 403 Sul and *London Tavern*, 409 Sul. The *Grenada* bar near the *Hotel Nacional* (pedestrian area across road, 250 metres away) has good pavement atmosphere in early evening.

Snack Bars   (i.e. those serving *prato feito* or *comercial*, cheap set meals) can be found all over the city, especially on Avenida W3 and in the Setor Comercial Sul (e.g. *Max Burger*). Other good bets are the Conjunto Nacional and the Conjunto Venâncio, two shopping/office complexes on either side of the municipal bus station (Rodoviária), which itself provides the best coffee and *pastéis* in town (bottom departure level). For ice creams (especially tropical fruit flavours) try the two ice-cream parlours in 302 Norte or the *Marajoara* restaurant. Freshly made fruit juices in all bars; for Amazonian fruits try the bar at the eastern (i.e. Setor Bancário) end of the Galeria dos Estados.

Shopping   There are eight big shopping complexes, including the vast *Conjunto Nacional* on the north side of the Rodoviária, the *Conjunto Venâncio* on the south side, the *Centro Venâncio 2000* at the beginning of Avenida W3 Sul and *Park Shopping* and the *Carrefour* hypermarket just off the exit to Guará, 12 km. from centre. For fine jewellery, *H. Stern* has branches in the *Nacional* and *Carlton* Hotels and at the Conjunto Nacional and Park Shopping (with *McDonald's* and other restaurants). The embassy sector is good for low-priced, high quality men's wear. For handicrafts try *Galeria dos Estados* (which runs underneath the *eixo* from Setor Comercial Sul to Setor Bancário Sul, 10 mins. walk from municipal Rodoviária, south along Eixo Rodoviário Sul) with shops selling handicrafts from all the Brazilian states; *Lampião*, 208 Sul; *Di Barro*, 302 Norte; *Zé Artesanato*, 215 Sul. For Amerindian handicrafts, *Artindia* in the bus station and at the airport. Also at the bus station is a *Funai* shop. Dried flowers (typical of the region) outside the Cathedral. There is a *feira hippy* at the base of the TV tower every Saturday, Sunday and holiday: leather goods, wood carvings, jewellery, bronzes. English books (good selection) at *Livraria Sodler* in Conjunto Nacional and at the airport.

Car Hire   Critical reports on Hertz cars hired at airport.

Entertainment   There are three auditoria of the Teatro Nacional, the Sala Villa-Lobos (1,300 seats), the Sala Martins Pena (450), and the Sala Padre José Maurício (120); the building is in the shape of an Aztec pyramid.

The Federal District authorities have two theatres, the Galpão and Galpãozinho, between Quadra 308 Sul and Av. W3 Sul. Concerts are given at the Escola Parque (Quadras 507-508 Sul), the Ginásio Presidente Médici (Eixo Monumental, near TV tower), the Escola de Música

(Av. L2 Sul, Quadra 602) and the outdoor Concha Acústica (edge of lake near Brasília Palace Hotel). The Planetarium, on the Eixo next to the TV tower, gives shows Sat. and Sun. at 1600 and 1700.

There are 15 cinemas in the Plano Piloto; programmes are available daily by dialling 139 on the telephone.

Information about entertainment etc. is available in two daily papers *Jornal de Brasília* and *Correio Brasiliense*. Any student card (provided it has a photograph) will get you into the cinema/theatre/concert hall for half price. Ask for "uma meia" at the box office.

Nightclubs *Aquarius* (gay), *Bataklan*, *Le Bateau*, all in Conjunto Venâncio; *Kako*, *Senzala*, in Centro Gilberto Salomão; *Tendinha*, *Odara*, 405 Sul; *Xadrezinha*, Avenida das Nações. Also in the main hotels.

Historical Museum Praça dos Tres Poderes, really a hollow monument, with tablets inside; open Tues.-Fri. 0800-1200, 1300-1800.

Museum of Gold at the Banco Central exhibits old and new notes and coins and gold prospecting in Brazil; open Mon.-Fri. 1000-1600, Sat. 1400-1800.

Museo Postal e Telegráfico da ECT, Setor Comercial Sul, Ed. Apolo, Quadra 13, Block A. Very interesting, stamps, telegraphic equipment, etc. Entry, US$0.30. Closed Sun.-Mon.

Museo da Imprensa Nacional, Setor de Indústrias Gráficas, Quadra 6; bus 152 from municipal Rodoviária: admission free. Old printing and embossing equipment, etc.

Exchange Lloyds Bank, Avenida W3 Sul, quadra 506; First National Bank of Boston, Avenida W3 Sul, quadra 501; Citibank, Edifício Citibank, Setor Comercial Sul; Banco Francês e Brasileiro, Avenida W3 Sul, quadra 506; local banks. Open 0930-1630. Foreign currency (but not always Amex cheques) can be exchanged at these banks and at the branches of: Caixa Econômica Federal at the airport; Banco Regional de Brasília and Banco do Brasil, Setor Bancário Sul. American Express, Kontik-Franstur, Setor Comercial Sul, Edifício Central, S/1007. Diners Club office, Av. W3 Norte 502. Use of international credit cards in Brasília tends to be difficult, though it should not be. Good exchange rates from hotels with "exchange-turismo" sign (e.g. *Nacional*).

British Commonwealth Chamber of Commerce, at the British Embassy.

Cultural Institutes British Council: CRN 708/709 Bloco 3 Lotes 1 e 3, T 272-3060. Cultura Inglesa, SEPS 709/908 Conj. B. American Library: Casa Thomas Jefferson, Avenida W4 Sul, quadra 706, T 243-6588 and 243-6625. Institut-Cultural Goethe, Edifício Dom Bosco, Setor Comercial Sul, Bloco A, 114-118, Mon.-Fri., 0800-1700, 1600-2000.

Embassies British: SES, Quadra 801, Conjunto K, 70.408 Brasília, D.F., or Avenida das Nações, Caixa Postal 070586, T 225-2710. **USA**: SES, Avenida das Nações 3, T 223-0120. **Australian**: Caixa Postal 11-1256, SHIS QL-09, Conj 16, Casa 1, T 248-5569 (in residential district, S of the lake). **Canadian**: SES, Avenida das Nações 16, T 223-7615. **West German**: SES, Avenida das Nações 25, T 243-7466. **Netherlands**: SES, Av. das Nações 5, T 223-2025. **Swiss**: SES, Av. das Nações 41, T 244-5500; **Austrian**: SES, Av. das Nações 40, T 243-3111; **Swedish**: Av. des Nações 29, T 243-1444 (postal address: Caixa Postal 07-0419, 70.000 Brasília, D.F.).

Immigration Office, at end of W3 Norte.

Poste Restante Central Correio, 70001; SBN-Cj 03, BL-A, ED. SEDE DA ECT.

Electric Current 220 volts, 60 cycles.

Tourist Offices at the Centro de Convenções (Detur); small stand at Rodoferroviária, not very helpful (open 24 hours, every day). Tourist office at the Air Terminal is on the international arrival side only, will book hotels, generally helpful; French and English spoken. Tours by bus (US$12-20), may be booked at the airport or *Hotel Nacional*: check that you will be taken back to the airport if you have a flight to catch. Touring Club do Brasil, on Eixo, has maps (members only).

Tours A good and cheap way of seeing Brasília is by taking bus rides from the municipal Rodoviária at the centre: the destinations are clearly marked. The circular bus route 106 goes right round the city's perimeter (you can also take buses 108 or 131). If you go around the lake by bus, you must change at the Paranoá dam (to visit the dam take bus 104); from Paranoá Norte take bus 100, "Rodoviária", back to centre, bypassing the airport. A one-day visit by air from Rio gives 4 hours in Brasília for a minibus tour, starting and ending at airport (but the city is worth much more of anyone's time than this). Cheaper tours, from 1300-1700, from US$7 up, start from the downtown hotel area and municipal Rodoviária. All tour operators have their offices in the shopping arcade of the *Hotel Nacional*; Toscana has been recommended as cheap and good. Presmic Turismo, Galeria do Hotel Nacional, lojas 33/34, T 225-5515, offers full-, half-day and nighttime tours (0845, 1400 and 1930 respectively), from US$11.45 p.p. Kubitschek Turismo (Lucas Milhomens—speaks English), T 347-1494, rec. for city tour and information. Some tours have been criticised as too short, others that the guides speak poor English. Tour guides meet arriving air passengers at the airport, offering city tours, ending at a destination of your choice (3-4 hrs., English commentary, inexpensive but bargain)—a convenient way of getting to your hotel if you have heavy baggage.

Roads From Saída Sul (the southern end of the Eixo) the BR-040/050 goes to Cristalina where it divides; the BR-040 continues to Belo Horizonte and Rio de Janeiro, the BR-050 to Uberlândia and São Paulo (both paved).

Also from Saída Sul, the BR-060 to Anápolis, Goiânia and Cuiabá; from Anápolis the BR-153 (Belém-Brasília) heads north to Belém (paved—for a description of this road, **see page** 461) and from Goiânia the BR-153 goes south through the interior of the states of São Paulo and Paraná (also paved).

From Saída Norte (the northern end of the Eixo) the BR-020 goes north to Formosa, Barreiras, and after Barreiras on the BR-242 (all paved) to Salvador and Fortaleza.

Road distances, in km.: Belém, 2,110; Campo Grande, 1,405; Corumbá, 1,834; Cuiabá, 1,127; Foz do Iguaçu, 1,415; Goiânia, 202; Manaus, 3,421; Porto Alegre, 2,021; Recife, 2,303; Rio, 1,204; Salvador, 1,529; São Paulo, 1,015.

Buses To Rio: 20 hours, 6 *comuns* (US$20) and 3 *leitos* (about US$40) daily. To São Paulo: 16 hours, 7 *comuns* (about US$14) and 2 *leitos* (about US$28) daily (Rápido Federal rec.). To Belo Horizonte: 12 hours, 9 *comuns* (US$12) and 2 *leitos* (US$24) daily (alight at Curvelo, 8½ hrs., US$7 for Diamantina). To Belém: 36 hours, at 0715, 1200, 1915, 2400 (US$36, Trans Brasília, buses poorly-maintained, but no alternative), *leito* (US$68) Tues., Wed. and Sat. To Goiânia: 2½ hours, every hour from 0600 to 2000 and at 2200 and 2400 (US$3). To Cuiabá, twice daily 1200 and 1945 (São Luiz), US$22, 20-24 hours, book journey in advance. To Curitiba, US$25, Tues., Thurs. and Sat. To Porto Alegre: 35 hours, every evening at 2100 (US$35). To Natal: every evening at 2000. To Campo Grande, US$23, 23 hours. To Fortaleza: 40 hours, every day at 0800 (US$40). To Recife: 40 hours, daily at 1100 and Mon., Wed. and Fri. at 1830. To Salvador: 23 hours, daily at 1200 and 2000 (US$28). To Barreiras, 9 hrs. To Teresina: daily at 0900 and 2130. To São Luís: daily at 1400. To Anápolis, 2½ hours, US$2.50. Manaus via Porto Velho and Cuiabá involves several changes, taking up to 6 days (road is good as far as Porto Velho). Bus tickets for major companies are sold in a subsidiary office in Taguatinga, Centro Oeste, C8, Lotes 1 and 2, Loja 1; and at the city bus terminal. Left luggage, post office, telephone and telegram facilities available at new bus terminal (Rodoferroviária) beside the railway station, from which long-distance buses leave; bus 131 between Rodoviária, the terminal for city buses, and Rodoferroviária, US$0.25. The waiting room at the Rodoferroviária is very comfortable, but one is not permitted to sleep stretched out. There are showers (US$0.50). Both bus stations have large luggage lockers.

Rail In 1981 a metre-gauge rail link from Brasília to Campinas was opened; at Campinas one changes train for São Paulo. The train "O Bandeirante" leaves Brasília on Friday only at 2050, arriving at São Paulo at 1920 next day; US$13.50 sleeper, US$8.50 first class. A cheap and interesting way to the South; very slow, but it passes through some interesting country. Cheap meals are served. The station is at the far end of the Eixo Monumental, past the TV tower.

Air Services Varig to Rio and São Paulo regular shuttle service (2½ hours in both cases); daily flights to other main cities; regional services to the interior of Goiás, São Paulo, Pará, etc. Vasp to Corumbá via Goiânia and Cuiabá, daily. Transbrasil offers reduced-fare night flights to Manaus at 0145 twice weekly. Bus 102 or 118 to airport, regular, US$0.35, ½ hour. Taxi is US$4.50, worth it. Left luggage facilities at airport (tokens for lockers, US$0.50). Airport tax US$1.25.

Of the seven *cidades satélites* that contain between them over half the Federal District's population, five are new and two (Brazlândia and Planaltina) are based on pre-existing settlements.

Planaltina, 40 km. N of the Plano Piloto via Saída Norte, was originally a settlement on the colonial pack route from the mines of Goiás and Cuiabá to the coast. The old part of the town (50,000 inhabitants) still contains many colonial buildings. There are two good *churrascarias* on the main street and it is a good place for a rural Sunday lunch. 5 km. outside Planaltina is the Pedra Fundamental, the foundation stone laid by President Epitácio Pessoa in 1922 to mark the site originally chosen for the new capital.

Just before Planaltina, at Km. 30 on the road from Brasília, lies the point known as Aguas Emendadas: from the same point spring two streams that flow in opposite directions to form part of the two great river systems—the Amazon and the Plate. Permission from the biological institute in Brasília is now required to visit the site. Continuing along the same road (BR-020), at Km. 70 is the town of Formosa (*Hotel Mineiro*, E). Some 20 km. north of the town is the Itiquira waterfall (158 metres high). From the top are spectacular views and the pools at the bottom offer good bathing. It is crowded at weekends. There are four smaller falls in the area. Camping is possible. To get there take the road into the centre of Formosa and follow the signs or ask. It is not possible to get by bus to the Itiquira falls from Brasília in one day; the only bus from Formosa to Itiquira leaves at 1500 and returns the next morning.

In the other direction (S) is the Cristalina waterfall; take the BR-040 (Belo Horizonte road) and at Km. 104 take a left turn along a dirt road just after the highway police post. The waterfall is 11 km. along this road. The town of **Cristalina** is famous for its semi-precious stones, which can be bought cheaply in local shops.

Nearer Brasília, good bathing can be had at Água Mineral, two mineral pools 10 km. from the centre of the city. The newer pool is the better; turn right immediately after entering the main gate.

North West of Brasília, but only 15 minutes by car from the centre is the **Parque Nacional de Brasília** (about 28,000 hectares), founded in 1961 to conserve the flora and fauna of the Federal Capital. For information, contact Delegacia Estadual do IBDF, Av. W-3 N, Q513, Edif. Imperador, rooms 301-320.

For information on the State of Goiás, which surrounds the Federal District, **see page 459.**

STATE OF RIO DE JANEIRO (2)

The State of Rio de Janeiro covers 43,305 sq. km. (the size of Denmark) and in 1985 had a population of 13.5 m., 88% of whom lived in metropolitan areas. The State is Brazil's second-largest industrial producer.

Rio de Janeiro, for 125 years the national capital, is on the south-western shore of Guanabara Bay, 24 km. long and from 3 to 16 km. wide. The setting is magnificent. The city sweeps twenty kilometres along a narrow alluvial strip between the mountains and the sea. The combination of a dark blue sea, studded with rocky islands, with the tumbling wooded mountains and expanses of bare grey rock which surround the city is very impressive. Brazilians say: God made the world in six days; the seventh he devoted to Rio. God's work is now under threat from too many high-rise buildings and failure to maintain or clean the city adequately.

The best known of these rocky masses are the Pão de Açúcar (Sugar Loaf, 396 metres), the highest peak of a low chain of mountains on the fringe of the harbour, and the Corcovado (Hunchback), a jagged peak rising 710 metres behind the city. There are other peaks, including Tijuca (1,012 metres), the tallest point in the foreground, and 50 km. away rise the strangely shaped Organ Mountains with the "Finger of God".

Rio has one of the healthiest climates in the tropics. Trade winds cool the air. June, July and August are the coolest months with temperatures ranging from 22°C (18° in a cold spell) to 32°C on a sunny day at noon. From December to March temperatures are high, from 32°C to 42°C. Sunstroke is uncommon, but humidity is high. It is important, especially for children, to guard against dehydration in summer by drinking as much liquid as possible. October to March is the rainy season, and the annual rainfall is about 1,120 mm. The population in 1985 was 5,650,000.

History The Portuguese navigator, Gonçalo Coelho, discovered Rio de Janeiro on January 1, 1502, but it was first settled by the French, who, under the

RIO DE JANEIRO
ORIENTATION MAP   29

1 Pico da Tijuca.
2 Corcovado and Statue of Christ.
3 Station for Corcovado.
4 Vista Chinesa.
5 Parque da Cidade.
6 Jardim Botânico.
7 Jockey Club.
8 Lagoa Rodrigo de Freitas.
9 Largo do Boticário.
10 Pão de Açúcar (Sugar Loaf).
11 Station for Pão de Açúcar.
12 Botafogo (end of Metro Line 1).
13 Largo do Machado.
14 Catete (cheap hotel area).
15 Glória.
16 Parque do Flamengo.
17 Santa Teresa.
18 New cathedral.
19 Business centre.
20 Sambódromo.
21 Maracanã Stadium.
22 Quinta de Boa Vista.
23 Santos Dumont Airport.
24 Galeão International Airport.
25 Rodoviária Novo Rio.
26 Pedro II Railway Station.
27 Ferries to Paquetá and Niterói.

Huguenot Admiral Villegaignon, occupied Lage Island on November 10, 1555, but later transferred to Sergipe Island (now Villegaignon), where they built the fort of Colligny. The fort has been demolished to make way for the Naval College (Escola Naval), and the island itself, since the narrow channel was filled up, has become a part of the mainland. In January 1567, Mem de Sá, third governor of Brazil, defeated the French in a sea battle and transferred the Portuguese settlement to the São Januário hill—the Esplanada do Castelo covers the site today. Though constantly attacked by Indians, the new city grew rapidly, and when King Sebastião divided Brazil into two provinces, Rio was chosen capital of the southern captaincies. Salvador became sole capital again in 1576, but Rio again became the southern capital in 1608 and the seat of a bishopric. There was a further French incursion in 1710-11.

Rio de Janeiro was by now becoming the leading city in Brazil. On 27 January, 1763, it became the seat of the Viceroy. After independence, in 1834, it was declared capital of the Empire, and remained the capital for 125 years.

Points of Interest   Two of the main streets are particularly impressive. The Avenida Rio Branco, nearly 2 km. long and 33 metres wide, is intersected by the city's main artery, the Avenida Presidente Vargas, 4½ km. long and over 90 metres wide, which starts at the waterfront, divides to embrace the famous Candelária church, then crosses the Avenida Rio Branco in a magnificent straight stretch past the Central do Brasil railway station, with its imposing clock tower, until finally it incorporates the palm-lined, canal-divided avenue formerly known as the Avenida Mangue. The Avenida Rio Branco is lined with ornate buildings, including the Brazilian Academy, National Art Museum, National Library, Municipal Council Chamber, and Municipal Theatre. The Rua Ouvidor, crossing the Avenida Rio Branco half way along its length, contains the centre's principal shops. Other shopping streets are the Ruas Gonçalves Dias, Sete de Setembro, Uruguaiana, Assembléia, and also the arcade running from Av. Rio Branco to the Rua Gonçalves Dias. The most stylish shops, however, are to be found in Copacabana and in the various large shopping centres in the city (see under **Shopping** below). (The quality of souvenirs is higher in Copacabana than in the centre, and higher still in São Paulo.) The Av. Beira Mar, with its royal palms, bougainvilleas and handsome buildings, coasting the Botafogo and Flamengo beaches (too polluted for bathing), makes a splendid drive; its scenery is shared by the urban motorway along the beach over reclaimed land (the Aterro), which leads to Botafogo and through two tunnels to Copacabana, described on **page** 303. Some of the finest modern architecture is to be found along the Avenida Chile, such as the Petrobrás and National Housing Bank buildings, and the new Cathedral, dedicated in November 1976.

Sightseeing   See, within the city, Candelária church, the monastery of São Bento, the convent of Santo Antônio, the Glória church (see under Churches), the Museum of National History, the National Museum of Fine Arts, the Municipal Theatre, the National Library, the Ruy Barbosa Museum (see under Public Buildings). Outside the centre you should see Copacabana, Ipanema, Leblon and Barra da Tijuca beaches, the Sugar Loaf, Corcovado, Tijuca Forest, Botanical Gardens, Quinta da Boa Vista and Zoological Gardens, the Maracanã Stadium, Santa Teresa and, if there is time, Niterói and Icaraí, Paquetá Island and Petrópolis, where you can visit the Imperial Palace.

Carnival   Carnival in Rio is spectacular. On Shrove Tuesday and the three preceding days, the main avenues are colourfully lit, and many young people and children wear fancy dress. Special bandstands throughout the city are manned for public street-dancing (see *Daily Post/Brazil Herald* for where and when) and organized carnival groups, the *blocos carnavalescos*, are everywhere, dancing, drumming and singing. There are numerous samba schools in Rio. They are divided into four leagues, the first and second of which are allowed to parade in the Sambódromo. The second league (10 schools) parades on Saturday, the first league (16 schools) on Sunday and Monday. The order of appearance of the first league is determined by lottery, so there is no better day. Each school parades with 3,000-5,000 participants, divided into 40 groups and as many as 30 floats. Each school has 90 minutes to parade, and will lose points if it takes longer. The third and fourth leagues parade on Av. Rio Branco (less spectacular -has been described as a "mass of people walking up and down with three or four music groups"- but free).

Each school chooses a theme, then composes a samba, and designs costumes and floats to fit it. All the schools are judged on each element, the best ones being promoted to a higher league, those with fewest points being relegated, as in a football league. Competition is intense. For the winners there is a monetary prize, funded by the entrance fees.

To understand the traditions of the schools, the meanings of the different parts of the parade, and carnival as a whole, visit the carnival museum in the Sambódromo; although small, it has lots of photographs and the English-speaking staff are very informative (entrance free).

The Sambódromo parades start at 2030 and last about 12 hours. Gates (which are not clearly marked) open at 1800. The best places are those reserved for tourists, and sectors 4 and 11 (sectors 6 and 13 are not recommended). Seats are closer to the parade, but because they are not elevated you see mostly the people in front of you. Tickets are sold through Banco do Brasil, and start at about US$30; tickets are also sold at the Maracanã Stadium box office, but touts outside will try to sell you places at double the price. Check availability, even if they say all tickets are sold. Tourist tickets range from US$138-240 to US$1,000 for the most expensive cabin and are available through Riotur or travel agencies. On Tuesday there is an amalgam of events including a huge float parade by the *grandes clubes carnavalescos*, and exhibitions by the previous year's champion samba groups, *blocos carnavalescos* and *frevo* and *rancho* groups. On the Saturday after carnival, the samba schools voted best on Sun. and Mon. parade in the Sambódromo (admission from US$20).

The **Sambódromo**, a permanent site at Rua Marquês de Sapucaí, Cidade Nova, not far from the centre, has a length of 600 metres, with seats for 60,000 people.

There are also innumerable fancy-dress balls (highly recommended); the main public one is at the Canecão (Sat. night) but there are scores more in hotels and clubs. Two that have been recommended are those at Clube Monte Líbano in Ipanema which have a different theme each night (you don't have to go in fancy dress), very crowded after midnight, and the Grande Gala Gay on Tues. (entry US$10). The Tourist Office has a list of all balls.

Carnival takes place at a time when Rio is packed with summer visitors enjoying the beaches. So visitors wishing to attend the Carnival are earnestly advised to make sure of their accommodation well in advance. Virtually all hotels raise their prices during Carnival.

Pickpockets and thieves are very active during Carnival (but the Sambódromo itself is quite safe—it's getting in that's the problem). Don't wander into dark corners on your own, don't brandish your camera, and take with you only as much money as you need for fares and refreshments (food and drink is expensive in the Sambódromo). It gets hot! Wear as little as possible (shorts or Bermudas and a T-shirt).

If you can't be there at Carnival time, rehearsals are held at various places from November onwards; e.g. the Portela *escola* at Rua Arruda Câmara 81, Madureira, late Sat. nights. Samba shows are given at the Teatro Tereza Rachel, Rua Siqueira Campos 143, Copacabana, on Mon. nights (not December), T 235-2119 (**see also page** 298); rec. Also, Beija Flor, one of the best samba schools, performs on Mon. nights at Urca (half-way up to Sugar Loaf Mountain), dinner

available at 2000, show, US$10, starts 2200. Reservations required (on Fri. and Sat. at this venue is the "Noite Carioca" show, or a disco).

Other Festivals Less hectic than Carnival, but very atmospheric, is the festival of Iemanjá on the night of 31 December, when devotees of the spirit cults brought from Africa gather on **Copacabana, Ipanema and Leblon beaches**, singing and dancing around open fires and making offerings, and the elected Queen of the Sea is rowed along the seashore. There is a firework display on Copacabana beach at midnight, so the crowds tend to concentrate there, in front of the Copacabana Palace and Meridien hotels. At midnight small boats are launched as sacrifices to Iemanjá. Again, if you go, beware thieves.

The festival of São Sebastião, patron saint of Rio, is celebrated by an evening procession on 20 Jan., leaving Capuchinhos Church, Tijuca, and arriving at the cathedral of São Sebastião. The same evening an *umbanda* festival is celebrated at the Caboclo Monument in Santa Teresa.

Museums and other Public Buildings

All museums and the Jardim Botânico are closed over Carnival.

The **National Museum** in the Quinta da Boa Vista is said to be one of the most important museums in South America but is disappointing, and the park surrounding it is dangerous. The building was the principal palace of the Emperors of Brazil, but only the unfurnished Throne Room and ambassadorial reception room on the 2nd floor reflect past glories. In the entrance hall is the famous Bêndego meteorite, found in the State of Bahia in 1888; its original weight, before some of it was chipped, was 5,360 kg. Besides several foreign collections of note, the Museum contains collections of Brazilian Indian weapons, dresses, utensils, etc., and of minerals and of historical documents. There are also collections of birds, beasts, fishes, and butterflies. Open 1000-1645, closed Mon.; entrance US$0.50 (free Thursday). Buses: 472, 474, 475 from centre, Flamengo and Copacabana, 583 from Largo do Machado. Nearest metro São Cristóvão, but thieves operate by park entrance and in the park, taxi to the main door is safer. Some of the collections are open to qualified research students, but not to the general public.

Museu de Fauna also at Quinta da Boa Vista, contains a most interesting collection of Brazilian fauna. Open Tues.-Sun. 1200-1700.

The **National Library** (Biblioteca Nacional), at Avenida Rio Branco 219, was founded in 1810. Its first collection came from the Ajuda Palace in Lisbon, and today it houses over 2 million volumes and many rare manuscripts. The library is open Mon.-Fri. 1030-1830, and Sat. 1200-1800.

National Museum of Fine Art (Museu Nacional de Belas Artes), at Avenida Rio Branco 199. There are about 800 original paintings and sculptures and some thousand direct reproductions. Exhibitions of works by contemporary Brazilian artists are often held here. Open Tues.-Fri. 1230-1800; Sat., Sun. and holidays 1500-1800; free.

Those interested in contemporary art will also visit the former Ministry of Education, designed by Le Corbusier, to see the great murals of Cândido Portinári, whose canvas, "Café", is in the Museum of Fine Art.

Opposite the Art Museum is the **Municipal Theatre**. Opera and orchestral performances

Rio de Janeiro: Key to map

1. Praça Mauá; 2. Praça da República and Campo de Santana; 3. Praça Duque de Caxias; 4. Praça Tiradentes; 5. Largo da Carioca; 6. Praça 15 de Novembro; 7. Passeio Público; 8. Parque do Flamengo; 9. Praça Mahatma Gandhi; 10. Praça do Expedicionário; 11. Aqueduto da Carioca (Arches, or *arcos*); 12. New Cathedral; 13. Monastery and church of São Bento; 14. Church of Candelária; 15. Church of Santa Cruz dos Militares; 16. Old Cathedral and Church of Carmo; 17. Monastery of Santo Antônio and Church of São Francisco da Penitência; 18. Church of Santa Luzia; 19. Church of São Francisco de Paula; 20. Itamarati Palace; 21. Viceroys' Palace (Paço Imperial); 22. National Archive; 23. Museu de Belas Artes; 24. Museu da Imagem e do Som; 25. Museu Histórico Nacional; 26. Instituto Histórico e Geográfico; 27 Museu de Arte Moderno; 28. Second World War Memorial; 29. National Library; 30. Tram terminus; 31. Ferry dock; 32. Riotur and Flumitur offices; 33. Central Post Office; 34. Teatro João Caetano; 35. Teatro Municipal; 36. Flower Market; 37. Mariano Procópio bus terminal (for greater Rio de Janeiro); 38. Menezes Cortes bus terminal (Castelo–a/c buses to Zona sul).

are given here; the small museum that used to be below the theatre is now at Rua São João Batista 103/105, Botafogo, normally open 1100-1700 Tues.-Sun, but reported closed since 1987.

The **Paço Imperial** (former Royal Palace on Praça Quinze de Novembro), a beautiful colonial building begun in 1743, has been restored. It has a gallery for tempory exhibitions and the occasional free concert.

The **Museum of Modern Art** (Museu de Arte Moderna), is a spectacular building at Avenida Infante D. Henrique 85, near the National War Memorial (**see page 290**). It suffered a disastrous fire in 1978; the collection is now being rebuilt, and several countries have donated works of art. There is also a non-commercial cinema. Entrance US$0.85, Tues.-Sat. 1200-1900 (open till 2200 on Thurs.), Sun., 1400-1900. Closed for repairs 1989, except for special exhibits.

The **National Historical Museum** on Praça Rui Barbosa (formerly Praça Marechal Âncora) contains a most interesting collection of historical treasures, colonial sculpture and furniture, maps, paintings, arms and armour, silver, and porcelain. The building was once the old War Arsenal of the Empire, part of which was built in 1762. Open Tues. to Fri., 1100-1700; Sat., Sun. and holidays 1400-1700; admission US$0.40. The building also houses the **Military Museum**.

Naval and Oceanographic Museum, Rua D. Manoel 15, daily 1200-1645. There is a particularly large collection of paintings and prints, besides the more usual display of weapons and figureheads.

The warship *Bauru* (ex-USS *McCann*) has been made into a floating museum, in the Glória Marina, opposite the war memorial on the Praia do Flamengo.

Museum of Image and Sound, also on Praça Rui Barbosa, has many photographs of Brazil and modern Brazilian paintings; also collections and recordings of Brazilian classical and popular music and a non-commercial cinema open Fri.-Sun. Closed for repairs.

The **Museum of the Indian** (Museu do Índio) is at Rua das Palmeiras 55, Botafogo, T 286 0845, open Tues.-Sun., 1000-1800. Highly rec.; has handicrafts shop, which closes for lunch 1200-1400. It contains 12,000 objects from many Brazilian Indian groups.

The **Museum of the City** (Museu da Cidade) at Estrada Santa Marinha, Gávea, in the delightful Parque da Cidade (**see page 291**), contains a collection of Rio's historical objects. Open Mon.-Fri., 1300-1700; Sat.-Sun., 1100-1700. Buses from centre, 176, 178; from Copacabana, 591, 593 and 594.

The Fundação Raymundo Ottoni de Castro Maia, generally known as Chácara do Céu, Rua Murtinho Nobre 93, has a wide range of art objects and particularly works of modern Brazilian painters. Take Santa Teresa tram to Rua Dias de Barros, then follow signposts. Open Tues.-Sat. 1400-1700, Sun. 1300-1700, US$0.30. Castro Maia's former residence on the Estrada do Açude in the Tijuca Forest bears the same name and is also a museum, currently under restoration.

Museo do Instituto Histórico e Geográfico, Av. Augusto Severo 8 (10th floor), just off Av. Beira Mar, has a very interesting collection of Brazil's products and the artefacts of its peoples. Open Mon.-Fri. 1300-1700.

The **São Cristóvão Pavilion**, designed by Sérgio Bernardes, has the world's largest open floor space without columns or transverse walls, but is now closed to the public. It is in very poor condition. Sunday market is worth visiting for North Eastern food and hammocks. Bus 472 or 474 from Copacabana or centre.

The **National Observatory** (founded 1827) is on São Januário hill, Rua Gen. Bruce 586, São Cristóvão. Visitors advised to call 248-1182 after 1700 to arrange a night viewing.

The **House of Rui Barbosa**, Rua São Clemente 134, Botafogo, former home of the Brazilian jurist and statesman, containing his library and other possessions, is open Tue.-Fri. 1000-1615, Sats., Suns. and holidays 1400-1700. The large garden is also open to the public. Buses 106, 176, 178 from centre; 571 from Flamengo; 591 from Copacabana.

Itamarati Palace, the former Foreign Ministry, at Avenida Marechal Floriano 196, contains much interesting old furniture, tapestry and other objects of art. Now called Museu Histórico e Diplomático, open Tues.-Fri., 1200-1615 (doors close at 1700); admission free on Thurs.

Museum of the Republic, in Catete Palace (Rua do Catete 179), entrance in Rua Silveira Martins, was the official residence of the President for 63 years when Rio was the Federal

Capital. Under renovation in 1988, but good Folklore Museum in same building was open. Bus 571 from Copacabana, and close to Catete metro station.

Guanabara Palace, once the residence of the Princess Isabel, daughter of Dom Pedro II, is now the office of the Governor of the State of Rio de Janeiro.

Carmen Miranda Museum, Tues.-Sun. 1100-1700, Flamengo park area in front of Rui Barbosa 560 (small display of the famous singer's gowns etc). **Museum of Fringes of the Unconscious**, Ramiro Magalhães 521, Engenho de Dentro, Mon.-Fri. 0800-1600. Closed for repairs 1987. **Villa-Lobos Museum**, Rua da Imprensa 16, Tues.-Sat. 1000-1600, with instruments, scores, books, recordings. **Capão do Bispo Estate**, Av. Suburbana 4616, Del Castilho, Mon.-Fri. 1400-1700 with archaeological exhibition.

Planetarium, Padre Leonel Franco 240, Gávea, Sat. and Sun. at 1600, 1700, 1830: inaugurated in 1970, sculpture of Earth and Moon by Mario Agostinelli. Free *choro* concert Fri. at 2100. Buses 176 and 178 from centre and Flamengo; 591 and 592 from Copacabana.

Aerospace Museum, Av. Marechal Fontenelle 2000, Campo dos Afonsos, Tues.-Fri. 0900-1600, early Brazilian civil and military aircraft.

Carnival Museum, Av. dos Desfiles, entrance by Rua Frei Caneca, Tues.-Sun. 1000-1600.

Antônio Lago Museum, R. Andradas 96, centre, Mon.-Fri. 1400-1700. Reproduction of historical apothecary's shop.

Amsterdam Sauer Museum, Garcia d'Avila e Visconde de Pirajá, reproduction of a Brazilian mine and exhibition of gemstones. Open Mon.-Fri. 1000-1700.

Churches and Religious Foundations

Check opening hours before attempting to visit.

The oldest foundation is the **Convent of Carmo**, built early in the 17th century on Rua Primeiro de Março close to Praça 15 de Novembro, now used as a school. Its present church, the Carmo Church in Rua Primeiro de Março, next to the old cathedral, was built in the 1770s and rebuilt between 1797 and 1826. It has strikingly beautiful portals by Mestre Valentim, the son of a Portuguese nobleman and a slave girl. He also created the main altar of fine moulded silver, the throne and its chair, and much else.

The second oldest convent is the seventeenth-century **Convent of Santo Antônio**, on a hill off the Largo da Carioca, built between 1608 and 1615. Its church has a marvellous sacristy adorned with blue tiles. St. Anthony is a particular object of devotion for women who want to find husbands, and many will be seen in the precincts.

The crypt contains the tomb of a Scottish soldier of fortune known as "Wild Jock of Skelater". He was in the service of the Portuguese Government during the Napoleonic War, and had the distinction of being appointed the first Commander-in-Chief of the Army in Brazil. The statue of St. Anthony was made a captain in the Portuguese army after his help had been sought to drive out the French in 1710, and his salary paid to the monastery. In 1810 he became a major, in 1814 a lieutenant-colonel, and he was granted the Grand Cross of the Order of Christ. He was retired without pay in 1914.

Separated from this church only by some iron railings is the charming church of **São Francisco da Penitência**, built in 1773. The carving and gilding of walls and altar are superb. In the ceiling over the nave is a fine panel painted by José de Oliveira. There is a museum attached to the church, open first and third Sun. of the month, 0700-1000.

The **Monastery of São Bento** (1641); entrance at Rua Dom Gerardo 68, contains much of what is best in the 17th and 18th century art of Brazil. "O Salvador", the masterpiece of Brazil's first painter, Frei Ricardo do Pilar, hangs in the sacristy. The carving in the church is particularly good. The Chapels of the Immaculate Conception and of the Most Holy Sacrament are masterpieces of colonial art. The organ is very interesting. The monastery is a few minutes' walk from Praça Mauá, turning left off Av. Rio Branco just before the Rua São Bento. The intimate view of the harbour and its shipping from the grounds of the monastery (behind the church) is in itself worth climbing the hill on which it stands. (Male visitors must wear long trousers.)

The **Old Cathedral** of São Sebastião, in the Rua Primeiro de Março, was built between 1749 and 1770. In the crypt are the alleged remains of Pedro Alvares Cabral, the discoverer of Brazil (though it is only fair to note that Santarém, Portugal, also claims to be his last resting-place).

The **New Cathedral**, on Avenida República de Chile not far from the Largo da Carioca, dedicated in 1976, is a very exciting cone-shaped building. Its internal height is 68 metres, diameter 104 metres, external height 83 metres; capacity 5,000 seated, 20,000 standing. The most striking feature is four enormous stained-glass windows (60 metres high). It is still incomplete.

The Church of **São Francisco de Paula**, at the upper end of the Rua do Ouvidor, was built in 1759. It contains some of Mestre Valentim's work—the carvings in the main chapel and the lovely Chapel of Our Lady of Victory. Some of the paintings, and probably the ceiling, are by Manuel da Cunha. The beautiful fountain at the back plays only at night.

The Church of **Nossa Senhora da Candelária** (1775-1810), on Praça Pio Dez, at the city end of Avenida Presidente Vargas, is well worth a visit to see its beautiful interior decorations and paintings. It is on the site of a chapel founded in 1610 by Antônio da Palma after he had survived a shipwreck, an event depicted by paintings inside the present dome.

In the Rua de Santa Luzia, overwhelmed by tall office buildings, is the attractive little church of **Santa Luzia**. When built in 1752 it had only one tower; the other was added late in the 19th century. Feast day: 13 December, when devotees bathe their eyes with holy water, considered miraculous.

In the Rua Primeiro de Março, at the corner of Ouvidor (near the Old Cathedral), is the church of **Santa Cruz dos Militares**, built 1780-1811. It is large, stately and beautiful.

The beautiful little church on the Glória hill, overlooking the Parque do Flamengo, is **Nossa Senhora da Glória**. It was the favourite church of the imperial family; Dom Pedro II was baptized here. Built in 1791, it contains some excellent examples of blue-faced Brazilian tiling. Its main altar, of wood, was carved by Mestre Valentim. The church, open 0900-1200 (only Sat.-Sun.) and 1300-1700 weekdays, is reached by bus 119 from the centre and 571 from Copacabana. The adjacent museum of religious art is open on application to the priest.

The church of **Nossa Senhora da Penha**, in the N suburb of Penha (early 20th century), is on a bare rock in which 365 steps are cut. This staircase is ascended by pilgrims on their knees during the festival month of October; there is a funicular for those unable to do this. Bus 497 from Copacabana, 340 and 346 from centre.

When the Morro do Castelo was levelled to build the Esplanada do Castelo, the old church of São Sebastião had to be demolished. Its successor, the Capuchin church of São Sebastião in the Rua Haddock Lobo, Tijuca, built in 1936, contains the tomb of Estácio de Sá, founder and first Governor of Rio de Janeiro.

Churches where worship is conducted in English:

Christ Church, Rua Real Grandeza 99, Botafogo (Church of England/American Episcopalian). The British School, for children of 5-16, is nearby.

Chapel of Our Lady of Mercy, Rua Visconde de Caravelas 48, Botafogo (Roman Catholic, with primary school).

Union Church (Protestant undenominational) Services held at Rua Parque da Lagoa de Marapendi, C.P.37154-CEP 22609 Barra da Tijuca.

International Baptist Church, Rua Desembargador Alfredo Russel 146, Leblon.

First Church of Christ Scientist, Av. Marechal Câmara 271, room 301.

Masonic Temple, in the British School at Rua da Matriz 76, Botafogo.

Synagogues, General Severiano 170, Botafogo; Rua Barata Ribeiro, Copacabana.

Swedish Church, Igreja Escandinava, Av. Rui Barbosa 170, Bloco B 1, 5 And.

British Cemetery, Rua da Gamboa 181, granted to the British community by Dom João, Regent of Portugal, in 1810. It is the oldest cemetery in Rio.

Parks, Squares and Monuments

The city abounds in open spaces and squares, many of which have ornamental gardens and statuary.

On the Glória and Flamengo waterfront, with a view of the Sugar Loaf and Corcovado, is the **Parque do Flamengo**, designed by Burle Marx, opened in 1965 during the 400th anniversary of the city's founding, and landscaped on 100 hectares reclaimed from the Bay. Behind the War Memorial (see below) is the public yacht marina.

In the park are many sports fields and a botanical garden; for children, there are a sailboat basin, a marionette theatre, a miniature village and a staffed nursery. There are night amusements, such as bandstands and areas set apart for dancing.

The National War Memorial to Brazil's dead in World War II and the Modern Art Museum (see page 287) are at the city end of the park, opposite Praça Paris. The Memorial takes the form of two slender columns supporting a slightly curved slab, representing two palms uplifted to heaven. In the crypt are the remains of the Brazilian soldiers killed in Italy in

1944-45. It is well worth a visit, but beach clothes and rubber-thonged sandals will get you ejected—and don't sit on the wall. The crypt and museum are open Tues.-Sun. 1000-1700.

Those who want to see what Rio was like early in the 19th century should go by bus to the **Largo do Boticário**, Rua Cosme Velho 822, a charming small square in pure colonial style. Buses to Cosme Velho from all parts of the city. The square is close to the terminus for the Corcovado rack railway (see page 306).

Botanical Gardens (Jardim Botânico) founded 1808, closed Mon, open 0800-1800 in summer and 0830-1730 in winter (US$0.30); well worth a visit. The most striking features are the transverse avenues of 30-metre royal palms. There are over 7,000 varieties of plants, herbarium, aquarium, and library (some labels are unclear), some parts reported closed in 1989. The Gardens are 8 km. from the centre, 140 hectares in area; take any bus from the centre, e.g. 104, to Leblon, Gávea or São Conrado marked "via Jóquei". From Copacabana any bus whose number begins with 5 and ends with an even number, except 592.

Bird-watchers should visit the Botanical Gardens, preferably early in the morning. 140 species of birds have been recorded there. Flycatchers are very prominent (the social flycatcher, great and boat-billed kiskadees, cattle tyrant); also tanagers (the sayaca and palm tanagers, and the colourful green-headed tanager), and over 20 different kinds of hummingbird. Birds of prey include the roadside hawk, the laughing falcon and the American kestrel, and there are doves, cuckoos, parakeets, thrushes and woodpeckers, and occasional flocks of toucans. (John and George Newmark, Eastbourne.)

Parque Laje, near the Jardim Botânico at Rua Jardim Botânico 414, almost jungle-like, has small grottoes, an old tower and lakes. (The Institute of Fine Arts is housed in the mansion.) Open daily, 0730-1730, admittance free.

Quinta da Boa Vista, formerly the Emperor's private park, contains the zoo (see below) and many specimen trees. The Palace now houses the National Museum (see page 287).

Zoological Gardens, which contain Brazilian and imported wild animals, and a fine collection of birds (as well as many "visitors"—also good for bird-watchers), are in the Quinta de Boa Vista (admission US$1). Open 0800-1800 daily, except Mon. The gateway is a replica of Robert Adam's famous gateway to Syon House, near London. Near the Zoological Gardens is the Museum of Natural History which is small but excellent. Take bus 474 or 472 from Copacabana or Flamengo; bus 262 from Praça Mauá.

Parque da Cidade A pleasant park a short walk beyond the Gávea bus terminus. It was previously the grounds of the home of the Guinle family, by whom it was presented to the City; the house itself is now the Museu da Cidade (see page 288). Admission to the park is free; open Tues.-Fri. 0730-1730, Sat., Sun. and holidays 1100-1700. The proximity of the Rocinha favela means that the park is not very safe. It is advisable to carry your passport (or copy) here because of frequent police checks.

Jockey Club Racecourse, at Praça Santos Dumont, Gávea, meetings on Mon. and Thurs. evenings and Sat. and Sun. 1400, entrance US$0.30. Take any bus marked "via Jóquei". Betting is by totalizator only.

Praça da República and **Campo de Santana** is an extensive and picturesque public garden close to the Central Railway station. At Praça da República 197 lived Marshal Deodoro da Fonseca, who proclaimed Brazil a republic in 1889 (plaque). The Parque Júlio Furtado in the middle of the square is populated by playful agoutis (or gophers), best seen at dusk; there is also a little artificial grotto, with swans.

Passeio Público (turn right at S end of Avenida Rio Branco) is a garden planted by the artist Mestre Valentim, whose bust is near the old former gateway. Coin and stamp market on Sun., a.m.

Praça Quinze de Novembro contains the original royal palace (see page 288). Every Sat. 0900-1900, handicraft fair and flea market; nearby on waterfront is Sun. antiques market, 1000-1800.

Praça Tiradentes, old and shady, has a statue to D. Pedro I, first Emperor of Brazil. Shops in nearby streets specialize in selling goods for *umbanda* and *macumba*—African-type religion and magic respectively. Several theatres nearby.

Praça Mahatma Gandhi, at the end of Avenida Rio Branco, is flanked on one side by the cinema and amusement centre of the city, known as Cinelândia. The fountain (1789) by Mestre Valentim in the ornamental garden was moved here from Praça Quinze de Novembro in 1979.

Parque do Catete is a charming small park between the Catete Palace (Museum of the Republic) and Praia do Flamengo; it has many birds and playful monkeys.

Praça Paris, built on reclaimed ground near the Largo da Glória, is much admired for the beauty of its formal gardens and illuminated fountains.

Fountains   The oldest, the Fonte da Glória (1789), has eight bronze spouts. Possibly the finest, although now sadly neglected, is at the back of the church of S. Francisco de Paula, at the inland end of the Rua do Ouvidor. These, and nine other old fountains, are illuminated by night.

Crime   Rio has been getting worse, both for assaults and for pickpocketing, but the number of patrolling police has been steadily expanded in recent years. Precautions are advisable, especially on the famous beaches, where small boys work in gangs, some distracting your attention while others go through pockets and bags. It is best not to take any belongings to the beach. It is suggested to women that they do not visit the cinema alone. Venturing out alone at night is not advisable for anyone. Always carry some money (but never large amounts): robbers may be incensed and very aggressive if their victims have nothing at all. Do not wear jewellery or carry openly tourist goods such as a camera, maps or guide books to make yourself an obvious target. Carry your belongings in a "day-pack", as the locals do (can be bought at any street corner—joggers' arm-bands have also been suggested; leg money belts have been recommended if larger sums of money have to be carried). Pickpockets and purse-snatchers operate at bus stops, bus turnstiles and among passengers while the bus is passing through a tunnel; also at street-corner newsagent stands. The centre of Rio can be dangerous at weekends, when most of the police force is patrolling the beaches. Among the more problematic areas at any time are Dois Irmãos, Santa Teresa, on Copacabana's Av. Atlântica and Rua Belfort Roxo, on the train between the zoo and Maracaña stadium, Pão de Açúcar, Corcovado, Quinta da Boa Vista, Jardim Botânico/Jóquei Clube racecourse area, and beyond Leblon out to Barra da Tijuca. To avoid swindling in bars, especially if sitting outside, pay as soon as you receive your order (although contrary to custom) and always ask for an itemized bill and check your change; alternatively, pay at the cash desk. Be especially careful after changing money in a public place; thieves often wait outside *câmbios*. Drivers, watch out for live snakes being thrown through open car windows: you jump out, the thief jumps in. The Tourist Police (Poltur) office is at Rua Humberto de Campos 319, Leblon, but, if robbed, you must report the incident at the station in the district where the incident occured.

   It should be added that Rio remains a beautiful and fascinating city. Whilst warnings should not be ignored, using your common sense should help towards a trouble-free visit.

Hotels   All hotels in the following list are air-conditioned. A 10% service charge is usually added to the bill. Note that not all higher-class hotels include breakfast in their room rates.

	Single US$	Double US$	Stars	Phone
Centre (Well placed for transport, 30 min. from the beaches. Most offices and commerce are located here, but no night life);				
Ambassador, Senador Dantas, 25	45	50	3	297-7181
Ambassador Santos Dumont, Sta. Luzia 651	52	58	3	210-2119
Granada, Gomes Freire, 530	45	49	3	224-6652

Grande Hotel OK, Senador Dantas, 24	46	51	3	292-4114
Othon Aeroporto, Av. Beira Mar, 280	50	56	3	262-8922
Presidente, Pedro I, 19	44	48	3	297-0110
São Francisco, Visc. de Inhaúma, 95,	44	47	3	233-8122

Flamengo (Residential area midway between centre and Copacabana.);

Flamengo Palace, Praia Flamengo, 6	47	49	3	205-1552
Glória, Rua do Russel, 632	76	84	4	205-7272
Novo Mundo, Praia Flamengo, 20 (well rec.)	52	55	3	225-7366

Copacabana (Seaside residential and commercial area.);

Apa, República do Peru, 305	54	56	3	255-8112
Bandeirante Othon, Barata Ribeiro, 548	52	55	3	255-6252
Castro Alves, Av. Copacabana, 552	52	55	3	257-1800
†*Copacabana Palace*, Av. Atlântica, 1702	95-145	110-160	4	255-7070
Califórnia Othon, Av. Atlântica, 2616	73	79	4	257-1900
Debret, Av. Atlântica, 3564	50	54	3	521-3332
International Rio, Av. Atlântica 1500	140-180	150-195	5	
Lancaster Othon, Av. Atlântica, 1470	60	70	4	541-1887
Leme Palace, Av. Atlântica, 656	67	73	4	275-8080
Luxor Continental, Gustavo Sampaio, 320		100	4	275-5252
Luxor Copacabana, Av. Atlântica, 2554		50-60	4	257-1940
Luxor Regente, Av. Atlântica, 3716		50-60	4	287-4212
†*Meridien*, Av. Atlântica, 1020	160	170	5	275-9922
Miramar Palace, Sá Ferreira, 9	72	77	4	247-6070
Olinda Othon, Av. Atlântica, 2230	72	78	4	257-1890
Ouro Verde, Av. Atlântica, 1456	90	100	4	542-1887
Rio Copa, Av. Princesa Isabel, 370	45	48	3	275-6644
†*Rio Othon Palace*, Av. Atlântica, 3264	104	114	5	255-8812
†*Rio Palace*, Av. Atlântica, 4240	145-185	170-210	5	521-3232
Savoy Othon, Av. Copacabana, 995	75	80	4	257-8052
Trocadero, Av. Atlântica, 2064	55	60	3	257-1834

Ipanema/Leblon (Outer seaside residential and commercial area.);

Arpoador Inn, Francisco Otaviano, 177	43	48	3	247-6090
†*Caesar Park*, Av. Vieira Souto 640	140	160	5	285-6622
†*Everest*, Prudente de Morais, 1117	102	110	5	287-8282
Marina Rio, Av. Delfim Moreira, 696	150	150	4	239-8844
Marina Palace, Av. Delfim Moreira 630	200	200	5	259-5212
†*Praia Ipanema*, Av. Vieira Souto, 706	75	80	4	239-9932
Sol Ipanema, Av. Vieira Souto, 320	72	77	4	227-0060

São Conrado and further out (Spectacular settings, but isolated and far from centre.);

†*Sheraton*, Av. Niemeyer, 121	145-205	165-225	5	274-1122
†*Nacional*, Av. Niemeyer, 769	110	118	5	322-1000
†*Intercontinental*, Av. Litorânea, 222	170-180	180-190	5	322-2200
Atlântico Sul, Av. Sernambetiba 18000 (Recreio)	39	45	3	327-8411

Airport, Galeão

Luxor Hotel do Aeroporto	104	114	3	398-5960

†Swimming pool.

Other Hotels in Copacabana (all air-conditioned; number of stars in brackets) Our categories A-B: *Royalty Copacabana*, Toneleros 154, T 235-5699 4 blocks from beach (4), a/c, swimming pool on 13th floor with view; *Praia Leme*, Av. Atlântica 866, pleasant, Austrian run, overlooking beach, English and German spoken (2); *Riviera*, Av. Atlântica 4122, T 247-6060, very good, excellent breakfast but other meals disapping, well placed, (3). *Atlantis Copacabana*, Av. Bulhões de Carvalho 61, T 521-1142, a/c, TV, very good, close to Ipanema and Copacabana beaches (2). *Ipanema Inn*, Maria Quitéria 27 (Ipanema) T 287-6092, good, swimming pool.

Our category C, unless stated E: *Biarritz*, Rua Aires Saldanha 54 (2) T 255-6552, good, accepts American Express; *Angarense* (2), Trav. Angarense 25, clean, friendly, C-D with shower, a/c, breakfast in room; *Toledo* (2), Rua Domingos Ferreira 71, T 521-4443 or 257-1990, friendly, good breakfast, safe, luggage stored, warmly rec. (except for single rooms which are gloomy); *Santa Clara* (2), Rua Décio Vilares 316, T 256-2650, rec., quiet; *Copa Linda*, Av. Atlântica 956, T 255-0938, incl. breakfast, friendly and clean, D (2); *Plaza*

Copacabana, Av. Princesa Isabel 263 (3), T 275-7722, highly rec. as most hospitable.

Economy Hotels are found mainly in three districts of Rio: Flamengo/Botafogo (best), Lapa/ Fátima and Saúde/Mauá. Rates are for doubles, and include continental breakfast.

Flamengo/Botafogo (Residential area between centre and Copacabana, with good bus and metro connexions.) Walking from the centre, you will come across the hotels in this order: Rua Cândido Mendes, off Rua da Glória: *Alameda*, No. 112/118, D with bath, TV, radio, phone, good value, near Glória metro and Copacabana buses; *Monte Castelo*, No. 201 (T 222-1733), E (with bathroom), clean, central, safe deposit (but get a receipt for your valuables), rec. *Benjamin Constant*, Rua Benjamin Constant 10, nr. Glória metro, F, men only; *Bahia*, Santo Amaro 42, F (without bath), clean; on same street, No. 75, *Opera*, E (a/c extra, cheaper without bath), also good, safe, near Glória metro (T 221-8759/242-3583). Across from here, on the hillside is Ladeira da Glória: *Turístico*, Ladeira da Glória 30, sold out Dec.-March, E, with bath, including breakfast, a/c, money and valuables can be left safely, tourist information provided, rec., under new management in 1990. *Victória*, Rua do Catete 172, E, with breakfast, bath and hot water, a/c, clean and friendly, also on Rua do Catete: No. 233, *Rio Claro*, E, recently renovated, breakfast, shower, a/c, safe, rec.; No. 160, *Monte Blanco*, E, breakfast, bath, a/c, radio, refurbished, clean, friendly, safe, very popular (try for a room about 1200), rec. To the left is Rua Silveira Martins: No. 20, *Inglês*, D, reasonable breakfast; at No. 135, *Hispano Brasileiro*, E, a/c, with bath, friendly owner speaks Spanish, but little else to recommend it. Walking down Praia de Flamengo you will come across the next streets: Ferreira Viana: No. 20, *Mayflower*, E with bath, no breakfast, simple; *Regina*, No. 29, 2-star, C-D, a/c, bath, fridge, TV, poor service; No. 58, *Ferreira Viana* (E, with bath and breakfast, always heavily booked, valuables may be left safely); No. 69-81, *Florida*, private shower and breakfast, good souvenir shop, highly rec., safe-deposit, D and up. Correia Dutra: *Mengo*, E (not very clean, friendly), No. 31 (T 225-5911); No. 141, *Leão*, E, clean, bath, a/c, unfriendly staff; *Caxambu*, E with breakfast and radio, good. *Unico*, Buarque de Machado 54, T 205-9932, E, a/c, clean, friendly, rec. (nr. Largo do Machado metro). *Monterrey*, Rua Artur Bernardes 39, E with bath, very good; at No. 29, *Rio Lisboa*, E with bath, a/c, cheaper rooms without bath, clean, safe, rec.—both hotels in this quiet street are family hotels. Rua Paissandu: No. 34, *Venezuela*, E, with bathroom, very clean, but rooms small and breakfast poor; *Paysandu*, opposite *Venezuela*, E, very clean, comfortable and good value. Beyond Largo de Machado: Rua Gago Coutinho: No. 22, *Serrano*, D, pleasant; and *Argentina*, Cruz Lima 30, C, rec.

Lapa/Fátima (Area between Lapa and Praça Tiradentes, inner residential area, less desirable than Flamengo.) *Hospedaria Sul América*, Rua da Lapa, E, without breakfast, rec. *Universo*, Visconde do Rio Branco 61, E, good, but area deserted from 2200 on. Near Cinelândia metro station are *Itajubá*, Rua Alvaro Alvim 15, E, good, and *Nelba*, Senador Dantas 46, E, with shower, friendly, also good. There are a lot of cheap hotels in this area, but many are hot-pillow establishments. In Lapa itself, near the Arches just beyond Passeio Público, is Rua Joaquim Silva: No. 87, *Ipiranga*, E, old but clean; and No. 99, *Marajó*, D, with breakfast, varied rooms, clean; also *Love's House*, Rua Joaquim Silva, E, ask for room with window, safe, respectable, good value. Passing under the Arches you come to Av. Mem de Sá (bus 127 from bus terminal): No. 85, *Mundo Novo*, E, clean, a/c. Turning towards Praça Tiradentes is Rua Resende, No. 31, *Estadual*, D, good; No. 35, *Pouso Real*, D, good, but the area is dubious. *Marialva*, Gomes Freire 430 (nr. New Cathedral, convenient for Av. Rio Branco, buses etc.), 2 star, D with bath, a/c, breakfast in room, rec. Praça Tiradentes, *Rio Hotel*, clean, noisy rooms on Praça, quieter overlooking São Sebastião cathedral, D with breakfast (only served in rooms). Beyond Praça Tiradentes is Rua dos Andradas (towards centre): No. 19, *Globo*, D a/c, shower, TV, very good (beware the sharp lift doors).

Saúde/Mauá (Area between the railway station and the docks, a dubious part of town.) *Rio Grande*, Rua Senador Pompeu 220, E, rec.; *Internacional*, Rua Senador Pompeu 82, E, clean and friendly. The very cheapest hotels in town are in this area, but it is not too safe at night.

Near the Rodoviária *Conceição*, Rua Garibáldi 165, good and cheap; *Rodoviária*, adequate, cheap, E without breakfast, fan, clean, hot water.

In the traditional **Santa Teresa** district, Rua Almirante Alexandrino 660, is the *Santa Teresa Hotel*, C, with swimming pool and full board. Also Dona Ana's hostel on the same street at No. 501, C, T 232-9603. Take the "Dois Irmãos" tram from Largo da Carioca.

The Federal University puts up men during vacations. *Pousada Estácio*, Rua do Bispo 83, F in 4-bedded apartments with breakfast, rec. (in campus of Faculdades Integradas Estácio de Sá). There is a **Youth Hostel** on the tenth and eleventh floors of the *Casa do Estudante*, at Praça Ana Amélia 9 (Rua Sta. Luzia), near Santa Luzia church, T 220-7123/7223, open all year, F—student card required—international youth hostel card is best, you can check in at any time of day, and can come in at any time of night, but after 0100 you must pay the lift man US$0.10. (Adverse opinion from some travellers—uncomfortable, showers not working.) Adverse reports of *Casa do Estudante Universitário*, Av. Rui Barbosa 762; said to be unsafe for property. Cheap food at canteens for those with international student cards. Other Youth Hostels at Rua Almte. Alexandrino 2840, Santa Teresa (*Pousada do Garuda*, T 225-0393/326-1419), Santa Amaro 162, Glória, T 222-8576; and Rua Emílio Burla 41, Copacabana (T 236-6472), good, YHA card not necessary, but you pay a bit more without it, cleaner than the one at Sta. Luzia. Youth hostels are fully booked between Christmas and Carnival; if intending to stay at this time reserve well in advance. Remember that the "motels" in the suburbs and along the main highways are mainly for the use of very-short-stay couples.

The city is extremely noisy. An inside room is cheaper and much quieter. (If you are desperate and it is late, some smaller hotels and hostelries may let you sleep on the floor.)

Apartments   If they prefer, tourists can look after themselves in flatlets (small apartments) in Copacabana, Ipanema, Leblon, or, more cheaply, in the centre or more northerly areas (for example, furnished apartments, accommodating up to 6, cost US$200 per month in Maracanã, about US$300 per month in Saúde, Cinelândia, Flamengo). Bookings for Copacabana at Rua Barata Ribeiro 90, room 205, Copacabana, Av. N.S. da Copacabana 583, room 1007, T 235-3748, and at Rua Barata Ribeiro 87/ 202, T 255-2016 or 237-1133. Also Rent Fiat Imobiliária Ltda, Rua Barata Ribeiro 207 s/101—CEP: 22011, T 256-9986. The *Praia Leme Hotel*, Av. Atlântica 866, has apartments, with maid and laundry service at Av. Princesa Isabel 7, close to the beach; US$27d in low season, US$30 in high season (when reservation is necessary). José Silva da Ferreira, Rua Pompeu Loureiro 56A, Apto. 401, Copacabana (T 256-9957) lets good apartments (US$30/day); Hans Peter Corr, Rua Belfort Roxo 158, Apto. 701, Copacabana (T 541-0615), several apartments from US$50 upwards, 30% reduction for people staying 4 weeks or more (U.K. representative Mrs M.A.Barker, 20 Farrer Rd, London N8 8LB, T 01-340 4163). Yvonne Reimann, Av. Atlântica 4.066, apto. 605, T 227-0281, rents very safe apartments, well furnished and clean, a/c, maid service, starting from US$30; also Ruth Haeberlin, Rua Hilario Gouveia 88, Apt. 702, T 236-4496, from US$30 per day (1-3 people). *Rio Hotel Residencia*, Av. Sernambetiba 6250, Barra da Tijuca, offers one-bedroom suites (for 2) with sitting-room and kitchen for US$50 a day, two -bedroom suites (for 4) for US$70. *Rio Flat Service*, Almirante Guilhém 322, Leblon, reservations through SASS Ltda, Ataulfo de Paiva 566/305, T 274-9546, Telex: 30245. *New Rio Home Service*, Visconde de Pirajá 414, sala 522, Ipanema, T 521-2332, Fax 267-6090, Swedish-run, rec. Estate agents dealing in more expensive apartments include Tower Real Estate, Rua Aníbal de Mendonça 157, Ipanema; Coroa Real, Rua Buenos Aires 4 and Av. Copacabana 647, Loja 205/206; Lowndes and Sons S.A., Av. Presidente Vargas 290, 2° andar, T 253-5622. Appartur Imovéis Ltda, R Visconde de Pirajá 371, S/L 204, Ipanema RJ, T 287-5757/5797, TV, a/c, clean quiet US$11-40. For cheaper apartments, and rooms in private homes, try classified ads, e.g. *Balcão* (like *Exchange and Mart*), twice weekly, look for word "proprietário", or *Jornal do Brasil*, under section 100, subsection 101—Temporada. The word "conjugado" abbreviated to "conj" means bedsitter, "vaga" a bed in a private home or a shared apartment and "quarto" a room in a private house. Do check security arrangements in apartment buildings since robbery is common.

Camping   Camping Clube do Brasil has beach site at Av. Sernambetiba 3200 (bus 233 from centre or 554 from Leblon, US$1.20—a long way from the centre), Barra da Tijuca, costing US$6 p.p. per night (half price for members). During January and February this site is often full and sometimes restricted to members of the Camping Clube do Brasil. Also at Recreio dos Bandeirantes, Estrada do Pontal 5900, and *Ostral*, Av. Sernambetiba 18790, US$2 p.p. and *Novo Rio*, at 17.5 km. on Rio-Santos road, US$2.50 p.p. "Wild" camping possible on beaches further out; if trying it nearer centre, risk of thieves. If travelling by trailer, you can park at the Marina Glória car park, where there are showers and toilets, a small shop and snack bar. Pay the guards to look after your vehicle. Camping gear for sale at Montcamp, Teixeira de Melo 21, Ipanema, T 287-1143.

Restaurants: In Rio, avoid mussels! **Centre:** *La Tour*, revolving restaurant, Clube Aeronáutica building, Rua Santa Luzia 651, 45th floor. Marvellous views, but food said to be poor and expensive. (Reservations, T 224-2221 for French meals, 242-3221 for international and 252-8234 for fish). *Alba Mar* (fish, very good and reasonable, Praça 15 de Novembro overlooking ferry station): *A Cabaça Grande*, Casa das Peixadas, Rua do Ouvidor 12, best for fish, closed Sun./holidays) *Spaghetti*, Av. Rio Branco 25, Italian, self-service, good salads, cheap; *Miura*, Av. Rio Branco 156, 2nd mezzanine, No. 324/325 (Japanese); *Rio Minho*, Rua do Ouvidor 10, for seafood, expensive, old-fashioned, very good. Vegetarian: *Naranda*, Rua da Alfândega 112—1st floor, good value; *Health's*, Rua Benedito 18, Mon.-Fri. lunch only

Superbom Rio Branco 130, rec., lunch only; *Zan*, Travessa do Ouvidor 25, *Lida* and *Saúde*, Rua Rosário 142, 2nd floor. There are several Arab restaurants on Av. Senhor dos Passos, also open Sat. and Sun. *Buksky (Paulista)*, Rua do Rosário 133 (German), rec. for wholesome food and speedy service: on same street, *N.S. de Guia*, good, lunch only; and *La Table*, pancakes, good and cheap; *Oxalá*, Rua Álvaro Alvim 36, good Bahian food, quick service, reasonable; *Pensão Guanabara*, Rua Buenos Aires by flower market, meal for US$1. *Kit-Kat*, Primeiro de Março, near Post Office, Chinese, self-service, good selection. *Café Nice*, Av. Rio Branco 277, beside main Varig-Cruzeiro do Sul office, interesting, old-fashioned, not cheap. *Taverna do Galeto*, near Cinelândia metro station, good. *Navona*, Rua da Carioca, very good Italian food; *Lanchonete Brasilândia*, Rua das Marrecas, and in same street, No. 44, *Luciano*, all you can eat at buffet, and *Portuense*, rec. Many lanchonetes for good, cheap meals in the business sector. Cheap eating places on Praça Tiradentes. *Bar dos Estudantes*, opp. Casa dos Estudantes, prato comercial is cheap, filling and balanced, friendly staff.

Santa Teresa: *Maçã d'Ouro*, Largo da Neves opposite church at end of Paula Mattos tram line, excellent, American-run, will change money; *Bar do Arnaudo*, Alm. Alexandrino, rec.; **Lapa**: *Mario*, Rua Joaquim Silva 130, and *Semente*, same street No. 138, both vegetarian. **Glória**: *Braseiro Galeto*, R. Cândido Mendes 116-C, good, cheap barbecued chicken, meats; *Vila Rica*, Rua Cândido Mendes, corner with Rua da Glória, good selection, inexpensive; *St. Moritz*, in same building as Swiss Consulate, Rua Cândido Mendes 157, bar/restaurant, good atmosphere; *Hobby Lanches*, R. da Glória, near Metro, good, cheap.

Flamengo and Catete: *Planalto do Flamengo*, churrascaria, Rua Barão do Flamengo 35-S (Praça José de Alencar), rec. *Bar KTT*, Rua do Catete, US$2 for 2-course meal, excellent; same road, No. 212, *Catetelândia*, reasonable meals at the bar; No. 239, *Pastelaria* Wong, very cheap, good and, No. 234B, *Amazônia*, downstairs, one-price counter service, upstairs for good, reasonably-priced evening meals, over-zealous service, rec. *Restaurante e Pizzaria Guanabara*, Rua do Catete 150, excellent value and selection; *Rio Galícia*, Rua do Catete 265, near *Hotel Vitória*, very good pizza, good service; *Machado*, Rua do Catete 286, good Italian food at reasonable prices; *Rio's*, Parque de Flamengo, opp. Morro da Viúva, T 551-1131, French, expensive, good service, piano bar; *Restaurante Praia Bar*, Praia do Flamengo 144, elegant Italian, reasonable; *Galeto, Restaurante e Bar Cabanas*, Praia do Flamengo 122A, bar meals, reasonable; *Lamas*, Marquês de Abrantes 18-A, excellent value, good food, go early; *Churrascaria Majórica*, many steak specialities, rec.; *Gaúcha*, Rua Senador Vergueiro 114, good and cheap. *Cozinha Arabe Brasileira*, Severo 176, cheap, small Arab dishes; *Pensão*, Rua Arturo Bernardes 9, cheap meals, good. **Largo do Machado**: *Adega Real*, Rua Gago Coutinho, very good. Plenty of pizza places.

Botafogo: *Aurora*, Capitão Salomão 43 (Mon.-Sat. till 2330) good food, excellent value; *La Mole*, Praia de Botafogo 228, good, cheap Italian food (other locations in Rio); *Churrascaría Estrela do Sul*, Av. Repórter Néstor Moreira, s/n, excellent rodízio. *Neal's*, Rua Sorocaba, US-style, burgers, chili, steaks, good value; *Café Pacífico*, Rua Visconde Silva 14, good, cheap, Mexican; *Manolo*, Bambina e M. de Olinda, very good value; *Restaurante Natural*, Rua 19 de Fevereiro 118.

Copacabana and Leme: The main hotels, including particularly *Rio Palace* and *Ouro Verde* (international food, highly rec.); *Churrascaria Marius*, at Leme end of Av. Atlántica, excellent but not cheap; *Príncipe Legítimo das Peixadas*, Av. Atlántica 974B, good but expensive; *Churrascaria Palace*, Rua Rodolfo Dantas 16-B, 22 different kinds of meat, very good value; *Baalbeck*, Rodolfo Dantas 225, Arab food and pastries, reasonable; also Arabic is *Novo Stambul*, Rua Domingos Ferreira 221-B, good; same street, No. 242-A, *Nino*, good but not cheap; *El Pote Galetos*, Rua República do Peru 143B, good chicken; *Moenda*, Av. Atlántica 2064, live music but formal, good food; *La Mole*, Av. N.S. de Copacabana, good service; *Beliscão*, Rua Siqueira Campos 23A e B, good beef stroganoff; nearby is *Cantina Veneziana*, good and cheap. *Akasaka* (Japanese) Av. Copacabana and Rua Joaquim Nabuco, rec.; *Zingaro's* (Italian) Rua Figueiredo Magalhães, reasonable. *Arataca*, Figueiredo de Magalhães 28, try carne-de-sol and lagosta ao molho; *A Marisquera*, Barata Ribeiro 232, good seafood; *Ponto d'Encontro* at 750, Portuguese, try baked bacolhão; *Ariston*, Santa Clara 18A and B, good; *Rian*, Santa Clara 8 (international), excellent and reasonable, especially seafood. *Le Streghe*, Rua Prudente Morais 129, *Barone Fasoli*, Rua Jangadeiros 14-D, and *Enotria*, R. Constante Ramos 115, all Italian and 4 star. Cheap and good inclusive meal at *Frango na Brasa*, Rua Constante Ramos 35; *Cabral 1500*, Rua Bolívar 8, good; *Maxim*, Av. Atlántica 1850, good and reasonable, pleasant place and atmosphere; *La Tratoria*, Av. Atlántica (opp. *Hotel Excelsior*), Italian, good food and service.

Ipanema: *Hotel Caesar Park*, rec. for Saturday feijoada, all you can eat; *Bardo Beto*, Rua Farme de Amoedo 51 (T 267-4443) excellent food, big servings, good value; *Il Capo*, Visconde de Pirajá 276, T 267-8747, rec; *Satiricon*, Barão da Torre 192, Italian food and fish excellent. Ipanema is quieter than Copacabana, many nice places round main square, Praça

General Osório, such as *Romanos*. At corner of Prudente de Morais and Vicícius de Morais there are 4 restaurants: *Del Mare* particularly rec. Health food at *Restaurante Natural*, Rua Barão de Torre 171. *Delicats*, Av. Henrique Dumont 68, good Jewish deli.

Jardim Botânico *O Philippe*, R.Jardim Botânico 617, very good and reasonable, close to the Garden. **Lagoa**: *Castelo da Lagoa*, on Av Epitácio Pessoa: on same road. *Rive Gauche*, No. 1484 (T 247-9993), French, excellent. **Gávea**: *Schwarze Katz*, Estrada do Vidigal 471, German and international. **Leblon**: *Un, Deux, Trois*, Rua Bartolomeu Mitre 123, very fashionable; restaurant and night club; *Antiquarius*, Rua Aristides Espínola 19, restaurant-cum-antique shop, seafood and international cuisine. *Sabor Saúde*, Av. Ataulfo de Paiva 624, very nice. *Mediterráneo*, Rua Prudente de Morais 1810, excellent fish, reasonable prices; *Celeiro*, vegetarian and health food, on Dias Ferreira between Aristides Espínola and Rainha Guilhermina, rec. (good bookshop 3 doors away). *Bar Degrau*, Av. Ataulfo de Paiva 517b, good atmosphere. In **São Conrado**, *El Pescador*, Praça São Conrado 20, Spanish-style fish restaurant, excellent value and variety of paellas. The *Sheraton* coffee shop has good feijoada on Sat. p.m.

Grill or barbecue houses (churrascarias) are relatively cheap, especially by European standards. There are many at São Conrado and Joá, on the road out to Barra da Tijuca (**see page 307**). Look for the "Churrascaria Rodízio", where you are served as much as you can eat. There are plentiful hamburger stands (literally "stands" as you stand and eat the hamburger) and lunch counters all over the city. *McDonalds* and *Big Bob's* (similar) can be found at about 20 locations each. *Galetos* are lunch counters specializing in chicken and grilled meat, very reasonable. In the "shopping centres" there is usually a variety of restaurants and snack bars grouped around a central plaza where you can shop around for a good meal. Most less-expensive restaurants in Rio have basically the same type of food (based on steak, fried potatoes and rice) and serve large portions; those with small appetites, and especially families with children, can ask for a spare plate, and split helpings. There are many juice bars in Rio with a wide selection. Most restaurants are closed on 24 and 25 December.

Tea Rooms For those who like their teas served English style, the sedate Belle Epoque 80-year-old *Confeitaria Colombo*, Rua Gonçalves Dias 32, is highly rec. for atmosphere, being the only one of its kind in Rio, with the original décor, open 0900-1800. It has also a most attractive branch at Av. Copacabana 890. More modern but similar establishments in some of the main hotels, and at *Casarão*, Souza Lima 37A, Copacabana; *Traiteurs de France*, Av. Copacabana 386, delicious tarts and pastries, not expensive; *La Bonne Table*, Visc. de Pirajá 580 sala 407, Ipanema; and *Ponto de Encontro*, Barata Ribeiro 750B, Copacabana. *Café de la Paix*, Av. Atlântica, 1020; *Chá e Simpatia*, Av. Atlântica 4240; *Um Chorinho chamado Odeon*, Gávea Shopping Centre; *Bolo Inglês*, Cassino Atlântico Shopping Centre; *Concorde*, Av. Prudente de Morais 129. These establishments have become very fashionable.

Shopping A good jewellery shop is *Badofsky Brothers*, Av. Copacabana 680, Room 315, 3rd floor; English, German, French spoken. *Maximino Jeweler*, Av. Rio Branco 25, 11th floor, and other branches. *H. Stern*, jewellers, Rua Garcia D'Avila 113, Ipanema; they also offer a tour, with head-phone commentary, of their lapidary and designing workshops, arranged through representatives at better hotels. *Gregory & Sheehan*, jewellers, Rua da Alfândega 65, 1st & 2nd floors; *Corcovado Jóias*, Av. N.S. de Copacabana 209, Loja F; *Roditi* and *Amsterdam Sauer* offer free taxi rides to their workshops. For mineral specimens as against cut stones, try *Mineraux*, Av. Copacabana 195, Belgian owner. *Saara* is a multitude of little shops along Rua Alfândega and Rua Sen. dos Passos (between city centre and Campo Sant'ana) where clothes bargains can be found (especially jeans and bikinis). Good "hippy fair" at Ipanema (Praça General Osório on Suns.). Sunday market in Glória district (Rua da Glória), colourful, cheap fruit, vegetable and flowers. "Shopping centres:" Rio Sul, at Botafogo end of Túnel Novo, Cassino (Copacabana), Norte Shopping (Meier), Plaza Shopping (Niteroi), Barra on Barra de Tijuca (**see page 307**). At São Conrado The Fashion Mall is smaller and more stylish. The *Funai* shop (Government Indian Agency) is very disappointing.

Cameras and Film Processing *Dino's*, Rua Buenos Aires 241; others in same street. Camera repair, Av. Rio Branco 151, 2nd floor, room 204. Kodachrome slide film difficult to get in Rio. For processing, *One Hour Foto*, in the Rio Sul and Barra shopping centres, is rec.; also a laboratory at Rua do Russel 344, Glória (1 hour for transparencies). Nikon camera repairs, T Tanaka cia Ltd, Av Franklin Roosevelt 39, of 505, T 220-1127

Electronics repair (radio, walkman, etc.), *Eletrônika Tekron*, Rua Figueiredo Magalhes 870, Copacabana, T 235-4096, efficient, friendly.

Bookshops For international stock, *Livraria Kosmos*, Rua do Rosário 155, good shop (in the centre and Av. Atlântica 1702, loja 5) and there are many others, e.g. *Livros Técnicos*, Rua

Miguel Couto 35, wide selection; *Nova Livraria Da Vinci*, Av. Rio Branco 185 loja 2/3, all types of foreign books; *Livrarias Siciliano*, Av. Rio Branco 156, loja 26, English, French and German books, also at N.S. de Copacabana 830 and other branches. *Unilivros*, Largo do Machado 29C, French and English bestsellers; *Livraria Nova Galeria de Arte*, Av. Copacabana 291D, international stock. *El Dorado*, Av. das Américas 4666, loja 207. Second-hand books also at *Livraria São José*, Rua Carmo 61 (only a few in English); *Livraria Brasileira*, Av. Rio Branco 156, S/Loja 229 (some in English); under *Rio Hotel*, corner of Rua da Carioca and Praça Tiradentes; *Livraria Antiquário*, Sete de Setembro 207 and in Rua Pedro I, all in centre. Also on Av. Marechal Floriano, near Av. Rio Branco, especially at No. 63. On S side of Praça Tiradentes, *Casa dos Artistas* trades in second-hand paperbacks. Second-hand English books at the Anglican church, Rua Real Grandeza 99, Botafogo.

Markets North-eastern market at Campo de São Cristóvão, with music and magic, on Sun. mornings. Saturday antiques market on waterfront, near Praça 15 de Novembro (1000-1800) and handicraft and flea market Sat. (0900-1900) in Praça 15. Sunday stamp and coin market in Passeio Público, a.m. Sunday open-air handicrafts market at Praça General Osório, Ipanema. Excellent food and household-goods markets at various places in the city and suburbs (see newspapers for times and places).

Buses Good services to all parts, very crowded, not for the aged and infirm during rush hours. Hang on tight, drivers try to emulate Nelson Picquet and Ayrton Senna. Fare normally about US$0.10, watch your change. Bus stops are often not marked. Four private companies operate air-conditioned buses which can be flagged down practically anywhere: Real, Pegaso, Anatur and Carioca. They run from all points in Rio Sul (Barra, São Conrado, Leblon/Ipanema, Copacabana) to the city centre, Rodoviária and the airports. Fares about US$1 (US$2 to international airport).

Trams Try the remaining tram from Largo da Carioca (where there is a museum, open only Fri. 0830-1700) across the old aqueduct (Arcos) to Dois Irmãos or Santa Teresa— historical and most interesting, and now refurbished, US$0.05.

Taxis start at US$0.60 and are quite reasonable. There is a 40% surcharge between 2300 and 0600 and on Suns. and holidays. Taxis have red number plates with white digits (yellow for private cars, with black digits) and have meters. Smaller ones (mostly Volkswagen) are marked TAXI on windscreen or roof. Meters are often out-of-date because of inflation and drivers will consult updating sheets (make sure the updating sheet is an original in black and red, and not a photocopy—this is a well-known fiddle!); all the same, beware of overcharging, which is rife (**See also page** 303 in Rodoviária section). Make sure meters are cleared and on tariff 1, except 2300-0600 and in Dec. when 2 is permitted. If there is no meter, you *must* fix the fare before entering. Don't hesitate to argue if the route is too long or the fare too much. Radio Taxis (white with red and yellow stripe) are safer and not much more expensive, e.g. Cootramo, 270-1442, Coopertramo, 260-2022. Luxury cabs are allowed to charge higher rates.

Underground Railway Line 1 operates between Tijuca and Botafogo, via the railway station and Glória, with 19 km. in operation; it is being extended 1 km. at the Tijuca end and 7 km. at the other. It will go from Botafogo via Copacabana and on to Ipanema and Leblon (Jardim de Allah). Line 2, running past the Maracanã stadium northward to Irajá, will eventually run from Praça 15 de Novembro (Estação das barcas Rio-Niteroi), through the city centre, to Estácio. Line 1 operates 0600-2300, Line 2 0600-2000, but closed Sun and holidays. Fare US$0.15; integrated bus/metro tickets available (cheaper if bought in block). Substantial changes in bus operations are taking place because of the extended metro system; buses connecting with the metro have a blue-and-white symbol in the windscreen. The metro system is due for completion in 1993. If you speak Portuguese, apply to the Municipality and allow 10 days for arranging a sightseeing tour.

Car Hire For self-drive, try Avis, Rio International airport, less helpful than office at Praia do Flamengo 224 (205-5796); Nobre, Gustavo Sampaio 826 (275-5297) and Av. Princesa Isabel 350 (T 541-4646) Copacabana, has special deal for 7 hrs. Telecar, Rua Figueiredo Magalhães 701 (257-2620). Many agencies on Av. Princesa Isabel, Copacabana. Credit card virtually essential. Recent reports suggest it is cheaper to hire outside Brasil, Budget rec. Remember service stations are closed in many places on Saturdays and Sundays; some agencies will supply gas to customers at the weekend.

Night Clubs Note that respectable night clubs permit entrance only to couples. Of most interest to the visitor will be shows featuring samba dancing. *Hotel Nacional* at São Conrado has the most lavish show in town, price for entrance and one drink is US$20. Other good samba shows at: *Solaris*, Rua Humaitá 110; *Oba-Oba*, Visconde de Pirajá 499 e.g. US$32 for two dinners and show considered one of the best in Rio. For the best Brazilian shows try *Canecão*, Rua Venceslau Bras 215, where the best-known Carnival ball is now held. *Plataforma I*, Rua Adalberto Ferreira 32, Leblon, getting better and better but beware of overcharging on drinks. Rio has its share of lively discotheques; among the best are; *New Jirau*, Rua Siqueira Campos 12-A, Copacabana; *Ye Bateau*, Praça Serzedelo Correia 15-A, Copacabana; *Crocodilus*, Rua Xavier da Silveira 7, Copacabana; *Privé*, Praça General Osório, Rua Jangadeiros 28-A; *Papagaio Disco Club*, Av. Borges de Medeiros 1426, Lagoa (Fri. and Sat. only); *Zoom* at São Conrado is very good. For something quieter and more intimate, look in at any of the following piano bars: *Balaio* (Hotel Leme Palace), Av. Atlântica 656. *Crazy Rabbit* on Av. Princesa Isabel. 3 rec. bars in Flamengo area: *Tronbada*, Rua M. de Abrantes 64, Spanish-style tapas, very popular; *Planalto Flamengo*, Largo de Machado end of Rua do Catete, very friendly and crowded and, nearby, a bar at the corner of Paiçandu and Senador Vergueiro. Two good (and expensive) restaurants with live shows are *Fossa*, Rua Ronaldo de Carvalho 55, Copacabana, and *Carinhoso*, Rua Visconde de Pirajá 22, Ipanema. On the beach, not far away, is *Albericos*, Av. Vieira Souto 240. *Scala*, Av. Afranio de Mello Franco, Leblon, large, 1¾ hr. show at 2300, lavish and loud, reasonably-priced drinks, entry US$11. Also in Ipanema on Rua Vinicius de Morais 49-A, *Garota de Ipanema*, where the song "Girl from Ipanema" was written, excellent atmosphere, food reasonable. *Help*, Av. Atlântica 3432, is also very popular with young people, but many prostitutes, dangerous for drinkers. *Forró de Copacabana*, Av. N.S. de Copacabana 435, forró music upstairs on first floor, disco on second floor, very popular, cheap, safe for single women. On Fri., Sat. and Sun. nights, 2100-0200, there is dancing to live bands at *Circo Voador* beneath Arcos da Lapa, in a circus tent, popular (other events during the week).

One of the centres of gay life is Cinelândia, in the centre (another is Galeria Alaska); in this area extending up to the Viaduto is found the whole gamut of human life. The essentially local character of night life in this area seems to make it relatively safe. Other gay places are *Papagaio* (see above); *Cochrane*, Rua das Palmeiras 66, Botafogo, done out like a traditional English pub; *Tamino*, Rua Arnaldo Quintela 30, near Rua da Passagem, Botafogo.

Another good place to see Brazilians at play, and at the same time for the English to feel some saudades (homesickness), is *Lord Jim Pub*, Paul Redfern 63 (Ipanema). Authentic pub atmosphere, afternoon tea, English food upstairs—steak-and-kidney pie, fish and chips. Phone in advance to check opening hours (usually closed Mon).

There are also gafieras, restaurants or night clubs with live Brazilian music for dancing. The best (and most expensive) is *Carinhoso*, Rua Visconde de Pirajá 22, Ipanema. Others, *Elite Club*, Rua Frei Caneca 4, 1st floor, in the centre. *Asa Branca*, Av. Mem de Sá 17, Lapa, high class, expensive, live music daily. *Roda Viva*, beside the Sugar Loaf cable car station, and *Cordão da Bola Preta* (pretty rough, but typical, only on Friday evening), Av. Treze de Maio 13, 3rd. floor, beside the Municipal Theatre, centre; *Gafiera Estudiantina*, Praça Tiradentes and one, enthusiastically rec., at Botafogo under the beach highway. Other bars which have music shows include: *Chucrute*, Largo de São Conrado; *Barbas*, Álvaro Ramos 408, Botafogo; *Equinox*, restaurant/bar, Rua Prudente de Morais 729 (piano music); *Jazzmania*, Av. Rainha Elisabeth 769, T 227-2447, show at 2200; *Western Club*, Rua Humaitá 380; *Gente da Noite*, Rua Voluntários da Pátria 466, both in Botafogo; *Klaus Bar*, Rua Dias Ferreira 410, Leblon (live music irregularly on Fri. and Sat.); *Existe um Lugar*, Estrada das Furnas 3001; *Four Seasons*, Paul Redfern 44, Ipanema, for jazz; *Vogue*, Rua Cupertino Durão 173, Leblon; *People*, Av. Bartolomeu Mitre 370, Leblon. In Barra de Tijuca there are a multitude of small night clubs, discotheques and gafieras, as well as some very luxurious motels for very-short-stay couples.

Many people look for Macumba religious ceremonies. Those offered on the night tours sold at hotels are not genuine, and a disappointment. You need a local contact to see the real ones, which are usually held in *favelas* and are none too safe for unaccompanied tourists.

Theatres   There are about 20 theatres in Rio. The best known are: *Teatro Municipal*, Av. Rio Branco, for concerts, opera and ballet; *Tereza Rachel*, R. Siqueira Campos 143, Copacabana (has samba shows, much cheaper than night clubs); *Sala Cecília Meireles*, Largo da Lapa (often free classical concerts); *Teatro Villa-Lobos*, Av. Princesa Isabel, Copacabana; *Senac*, Rua Pompeu Loureiro 45, Copacabana. Good value entertainment at "Seis e Meia" (1830) shows at various downtown theatres (e.g. *João Caetano* on Praça Tiradentes): 1½ hr. musical shows with top-name Brazilian artists—check local papers.

Cinemas   A very few give cheaper tickets to students, but not at weekends. Listings in *Jornal do Brasil* newspaper (best) and *O Globo*.

Sports   Paissandu Athletic Club, Av. Afrânio de Melo Franco 330, Leblon—Tennis, bowls, swimming. Leme Tennis Club, Rua Gustavo Sampaio 74—Tennis. Rio de Janeiro Country Club,

Rua Prudente de Morais 1597, Ipanema—Tennis and swimming. Gávea Golf and Country Club, Estrada da Barra da Tijuca 2005—Golf and polo. Itanhangá Golf Club, Jacarepaguá, visiting cards from Avenida Rio Branco 26, 16th floor. Clube Hípico Brasileiro, Av. Borges de Medeiros 2448, Jardim Botânico—Riding. late Clube do Rio de Janeiro, Av. Pasteur, Botafogo—Yachting. Squash at Rua Cândido Mendes 581, Glória, T 242-0642. Ice skating at Barra Shopping, Av. das Américas 466, Barra da Tijuca. Roller-skating at Roxy-Roller, opp. Clube de Regatas Flamengo on Av. Borges de Medeiros, Lagoa.

Banks Lloyds Bank (ex-BOLSA), Rua da Alfândega 33; Banco Internacional (Bank of America and Royal Bank of Canada), Rua do Ouvidor 90; Banco Holandês Unido, Rua do Ouvidor 101; Citibank, Rua Assembléia 100; The First National Bank of Boston, Av. Rio Branco 110; Banco de Crédito Real de Minas Gerais, S.A., Av. Rio Branco 116; Banco Lar Brasileiro, Rua do Ouvidor 98; and many others. Banks are open 1000 to 1630. Closed on Sat. Banco do Brasil at the International Airport is open 0800-2000 every day, Bolzano-Simonsen in Sector B is open to 2300. Banks use the legal tourist exchange rate.

Exchange Houses American Express, Av. Atlântica 2316, CEP 22-041, Copacabana; at Exprinter, Av. Rio Branco 57A, cash and cheques (good rates also at their Av. N.S. de Copacabana branch), Casa Piano, Rua Visconde de Pirajá 365, Ipanema, also Praça da Paz, Ipanema, and Av. Rio Branco 88; Turismo Portuguesa, Av. Rio Branco 45; Cualitour, Av. Rio Branco 25B; Behar Turismo, Av. Rio Branco esq. Teófilo Ottoni-Visc. de Inhaúma, rec. for cheques; nearby Casa São Jorge changes Amex cheques at parallel rate; Kontik, Av. Presidente Vargas 309, Irmãos Capello, Av. Rio Branco 31A; Sultur, Av. Rio Branco 151C, Xanadu, Rua do Rosário 171. In Copacabana (where parallel market rates are generally worse than in centre): P. M. (no travellers' cheques), Av. Copacabana 391-B and Av. Rio Branco 124-A; Sala 309 (3rd floor), Ed. Monte Carmel, Av. N.S. de Copacabana 680, good rates; Paladium Travel, 3rd floor of Shopping Cassino Atlântico, Ipanema end of Av. Atlântica, Copacabana, Kraus, Praça Pio X 55, 2nd floor (German spoken), and Passamar, Rua Siqueira Campos 7. (Try Atlântica Joias, Rua Fernando Mendes 5). **N.B**. Many câmbios will give you the parallel rate for cash, but a worse rate for cheques; some will also change US$ cheques for US$ cash with a 4% commission. These transactions are not strictly legal, so you will have to look around for the câmbios that do them.

Portuguese Instituto Brasil-Estados Unidos, Av. Copacabana 690, 5° andar, only for those with student visas; tourists will be referred to private teachers. Good English library at same address. Curso Feedback, branches in Botafogo, Centre, Copacabana and Ipanema (addresses in yellow pages): individual tuition from girl students about US$10/hr., rec.

Cultural and Trade Institutions The British Council, Rua Elmano Cardim 10 (formerly Rua Iguatu), Urca. T 295-7782. The British School of Rio de Janeiro, Rua da Matriz 76. Sociedade Brasileira de Cultura Inglesa, Av. Graça Aranha 327, and in Copacabana, T 227-0147. American Chamber of Commerce for Brazil, Praça Pio Dez 15, 5th floor. American Society and American Club, Avenida Rio Branco 123, 21st floor. USICA Reference Library, U.S. Consulate General, Av. Presidente Wilson 147. The American School of Rio de Janeiro, Estrada da Gávea 132. German Cultur-Institut (Goethe), Av. Graça Aranha 416, 9th floor; open Mon., Wed., Thurs., 1000-1400, 1500-1930, Fri., 1000-1300. Australian Trade Commission, Rua Voluntário da Pátria 45, 5°, Botafogo, T 286-7922; for visas etc. you must go to Brasília.

Embassies and Consulates Argentine Embassy, Praia de Botafogo 242; **Consul**, Praia de Botafogo 228, T 551-5198, very helpful over visas, 1130-1600; **Uruguayan Embassy**, Rua Artur Bernardes 30; **Paraguayan Embassy**, Av. N.S. de Copacabana 427, room 303, 0900-1300, visas US$5; **Venezuelan Consulate**, Praia de Botafogo 242, 5th floor, open 0830-1300.

U.S. Consulate General, Avenida Presidente Wilson, 147, T 292-7117.

British Consulate, Praia do Flamengo 284, T 552-1422; **Irish Consulate**, Rua Fonseca Teles 18, CEP 20940, T 254-0960; **Swiss Consulate**, Rua Cândido Mendes 157, 11° andar, Cx. Postal 744-7c-00, T 242-8035 (open 0900-1200, Mon.-Fri.); **West German Consulate-General**, Rua Presidente Carlos de Campos 417, T 285-2333; **French Consulate**, Av. Pres. Antônio Carlos, 58, T 220-6022; **Austrian Consulate**, Av. Atlântica 3804, CEP 22070, T 227-0040/048/049; **Netherlands Consulate**, Rua Sorocaba 570. T 246-4050. (Dutch newspapers here; also at KLM office on Av. Rio Branco.); **Swedish Consulate-General**, Praia do Flamengo 344, 9° andar, 22210, Rio de Janeiro, T 552-2422; **Danish Consulate**, Praia do Flamengo 284, Apt. 101, T 552-6149.

Israeli Embassy, Av N.S. Copacabana 608-C, Copacabana, T 255 5432, Caixa Postal 12353; **S. Africa Consulate**, Rua Voluntários da Pátria 45, 9th floor, Botafogo, T 266-6246.

Policia Federal, Av. Venezuela 2 (near Praça Mauá), for renewal of 90-day visa, US$4.

Y.M.C.A., Rua da Lapa, 40.

Doctor Vaccinations at Saude de Portos, Praça 15 de Novembro. Policlínica, Av. Nilo Peçanha 38, rec. for diagnosis and investigation. Hospital Miguel Couto, Mário Ribeiro 117, Gávea, has a casualty ward (free), but no eye doctors T 274-2121; these can be found at Hospital Souza Aguiar, Praça da República III (casuality ward also free), T 296-4114.

Dentist English-speaking, Amílcar Werneck de Carvalho Vianna, Av. Pres. Wilson 165, suite 811. Dr Djorup, Av Beira Mar.

Hairdresser Cabral's, Rua do Catete 228, 2nd floor, T205-4398.

Laundromats Lavandaria Automática, Rua Barão do Flamengo 42, and Rua Bambina 164 (Botafogo); Automática do Catete, Rua Andrade Pertence 42, Loja 6; Fénix, Rua do Catete 214, Loja 20; Rua Marques de Abrantes, about No. 80 (Flamengo); Laundromat at 1216 Av. N.S. de Copacabana. In Rio Sul are self-service laundrettes such as Lavlev, about US$3-4 for a machine, including detergent and drying, 1 hr, also at Rua Voluntário da Patria 248, Botafogo, Av. Prado Jnr 6313, Copacabana.

Public Conveniences There are very few in Rio de Janeiro, but many bars and restaurants (e.g. Macdonalds) offer facilities; just ask for the "banheiro" (banyairoo). Try the Castelo bus terminal in city centre. Also Praça Tiradentes, and 5th floor of Rua da Assembleia 10 (same building as Riotur). Best conveniences are to be found in the Shopping Centres.

Electric Current 110-220 volts, 60 cycles, A.C.

Post Office Central Post Office, Rua Primeiro de Março, at corner of Rua do Rosário. Overseas parcels may be sent from here. **Poste Restante** American Express, Av. Atlântica 2316, Copacabana (for customers), and all large post offices (letters held for a month, rec., US$0.10 per letter).

Telephones Buy *fichas* for calls from public phones (in acoustic shells) at chemists and news stands; they are hard to come by late at night. International calls at Av. Copacabana 462, 2nd floor, international airport, Praça Tiradentes (centre), Rodoviária, or Rua Dias da Cruz 182-4, 24 hrs, 7 days a week, or at Santos Dumont airport, 1st floor (0530-2300). Collect calls, national and international, dial 107 (no charge).

Cables Embratel, Av. President Vargas 1012. Telegrams may be sent through any post office. Larger offices have telex.

Travel Agents *American Express Kontik Franstur*, Av. Atlântica 2316A; *Roxy*, Av. Winston Churchill 60, helpful, rec. (ask for Michael Oeary who speaks English); *Exprinter*, Av. Rio Branco, 128 (said to be particularly good for money-changing); *Itatiaia Turismo*, Av. Rio Branco 120, helpful, will sometimes change money; *Manhattan Turismo Ltda*, Rua da Assembléia 10, GR 3503, Centro, CEP 20-031, T 242-3779/3064, very helpful, cheap flights, English spoken; *Creditur*, Av. Almirante Barroso 63, suite 2508, for non IATA flights to N. America and Europe; for cheap flights to Europe, Líneas Aéreas Paraguayas, Rua Santa Luzia 827 and *A.G.S. Viagem e Turismo Ltda*, same street No. 799, T 262-5867 (N.B. LAP will not accept American Express cards); *Brazilian Holidays*, Rua Visconde de Pirajá 414, Suite 819/820, T 267-5749, Ipanema, English and German spoken, helpful regarding tickets and information; *Soletur*, Visconde de Pirajá 550, sala 1708, rec; *Tour Brazil*, R. Farme de Amoeda 75/605, nr. Ipanema, T 521-4461, Fax 021-521-1056, very good English spoken; *Victor Hummel*, Av. Presidente Vargas 290/4, T 223-1262, Swiss-run, rec. T 231-1800. Also Swiss-run and highly rec., *South American Turismo Ltda*, Av. N. S. de Copacabana 788, 6th and 7th floors, T 255-2345. *Americatur*, Av. Rio Branco 156 (T 262-4293, 262-2659) runs tours on the Rio São Francisco, flying from Rio to Belo Horizonte (**see page** 331). Regular sightseeing tours operated by *Gray Line* (294-0393), *American Sightseeing* (236-3551), *Sul América* (257-4235), *Canbitur* (of Copacabana), *Passamar Turismo*, Av. Rio Branco 25 (233-8883, 233-4833, 253-1125; also at *Hotel Nacional*). *Adrianotour*, T 208-5103, for guided tours, reservations and commercial services (English, French, German and Spanish spoken). *Enasa*, for Amazon river travel, Rua Uruguaiana 39 (Sala 1402); they try to sell tickets on first-class boats only.

For a good, private walking tour of Rio's cultural sights, contact Prof. Carlos Roquette, a professor of history, who charges US$20 p.p., T 322-4872, 24 hrs, write to Rua Santa Clara 110/904, Copacabana, Rio de Janeiro, RJ 22041, English and French spoken.

Tourist Information There are several excellent information centres. Embratur, Rua Mariz e Barros 13, near Praça da Bandeira, T 273-2212, gives information on the whole country. Riotur (for the city of Rio), Rua da Assembléia 10, 8th floor (T 297-7117), sells a huge map of the city. Official Riotur information stands at Pão de Açúcar cablecar station (0800-2000); Marina da Glória, Flamengo; Rodoviária Novo Rio (the bus station—0600-2400; very friendly and helpful in finding accommodation). Riotur also has a multilingual telephone service operating 24 hours, T 580-8000. Flumitur (for the state of Rio de Janeiro) at Rio International Airport, helpful with hotel information and booking, can sometimes arrange discounts, and Rua da Assembléia 10, 8th floor, very helpful. Touring Club do Brasil, Pres. Antônio Carlos 130 and Av. Brasil 4294 (out of town) no English spoken.

N.B. Tourist packs are sold for US$15 at the International Airport—these contain a map, restaurant list and a blank passport facsimile, which has no legal standing even though they may try to persuade you otherwise. Best guide to Rio, with excellent map, *Guia Quatro Rodas do Rio* in Portuguese and English, US$3.(the *Guia Quatro Rodas do Brasil*, published annually in Nov, also has a good Rio section) *Guia Rex* street guide, US$8. *Guia Schaeffer Rio de Janeiro* (US$3) is an excellent sheet. Also, *The Insider's Guide to Rio de Janeiro*, an annual guide book by Christopher Pickard, published by Streamline Ltda, Av. N.S. de Copacabana 605/1210 (distributed in UK and Europe by Roger Lascelles, 47 York Rd., Brentford, Middlesex, TW8 0OP, and in USA by Luso-Brazilian Books, 33 Nevins St., Brooklyn, New York 11217). Many hotels provide guests with the weekly *Itinerário* (*Rio This Month*).

Maps are available from Riotur information desks (US$1), Touring Clube do Brasil (US$0.40), newsstands (US$0.65), touring agencies and hotels; Geomapas tourist map is clear, US$1.20. Also maps free from H. Stern, the jeweller, at Rua Visconde do Pirajá 490, Ipanema. Also from Paulini, Rua Lélio Gama 75 (outside the entrance of the downtown tram station): topographical and other maps of Brazil and of South America. **Note** Tourist agencies do not normally provide lists of cheap accommodation for travellers; some initiative is required.

Airports Rio has two airports. The Santos Dumont airport on Guanabara Bay, right in the city, is used exclusively for Rio-São Paulo shuttle flights (US$55), air taxis and private planes. The shuttle services operate every half hour throughout the day from 0630 to 2230. Sit on right-hand side for views to São Paulo, other side coming back. The main airport (Galeão), on Governador Island, some 16 km. from the centre of Rio, is in two sections, international and domestic (including Vasp and Transbrasil's jet shuttle from Rio to São Paulo). Duty-free shops are well-stocked, but not especially cheap. The Real company runs an air-conditioned bus (*frescão*) from Galeão to Santos Dumont Airport, via the city centre, every half-hour (for Flamengo/Catete hotel area, take this bus, then a taxi from Santos Dumont) and another goes to Copacabana at approx. half-past every hour, with space for baggage, US$2 (also stops at Rodoviária). Difficulties reported in locating this bus in Copacabana for return to the airport. Air-conditioned taxis (Cootramo and Transcopass) have fixed rates (US$6 downtown, US$8 Copacabana) and you buy a ticket at the counter near the arrivals gate before getting into the car. The hire is for taxi, irrespective of number of passengers, and therefore the possibility of sharing with other passengers arises. Ordinary taxis also operate with the normal meter reading—make sure you are given the card which gives the number to phone if you are overcharged (about US$8 downtown, US$10 Copacabana). A good policy is to check at the Riotur counter before leaving, for folders, maps and advice; watch out for pirate taxis, whose drivers will want to charge up to US$50! Town bus No. 322 goes to Rio International airport, first one with direction Bananal. No bank or *câmbio* in departure hall of airport, and the 24-hour banks before passport control give worse rates than the lift attendants, etc. (if you can wait, on arrival, till you get into town, so much the better). There is a wider choice of restaurants before passport control, but seats for flights are not allocated until after passport control. We have been told that X-ray machines at Galeão are not safe for film.

Rail Central do Brasil Railway to São Paulo and Belo Horizonte. To São Paulo there are only the "Santa Cruz" night trains with sleepers and lounge cars, no seats, US$15 for a double cabin, 9 hrs., leaving 2300— rec., book cabins 2 weeks ahead for weekend journeys, 3-5 days for weekdays in holiday times), provision of service is erratic, check! Fri and Sun. night service to Belo Horizonte (US$10 pullman, US$27 cabin for two, 12½hrs., leaves 2015). No service to Brasília. There are suburban trains to Nova Iguaçu, Nilópolis, Campo Grande and elsewhere. Buses marked "E. Ferro" go to the railway station. For guided excursions by rail, contact Platur.

Buses Bus fares to the following cities, with approximate journey times (book ahead if you can), are as follows:

	distance km.	ordinary US$	executive US$	leito US$	hours
São Paulo	434	6.00	9.00	12.00	6
Brasília	1,134	20.00	31.00	40.00	20
Belo Horizonte	429	8.00	12.00	16.00	7

Curitiba	839	13.00	—	26.00	11
Florianópolis	1,154	16.00	—	32.00	20
Foz do Iguaçu	1,500	18.00	—	36.00	23
Porto Alegre	1,603	24.00	—	48.00	26
Juiz de Fora	177	3.00	4.50	—	4
Vitória	519	8.00	—	16.00	8
Salvador	1,690	25.00	—	50.00	28
Recife	2,309	34.00	—	68.00	38
Fortaleza	2,861	45.00	—	90.00	48
São Luís	3,093	49.00	—	—	50
Belém	3,187	52.00	—	—	52

To Campo Grande, 21 hrs. with Andorinha, US$11. To Santos, 6 a day with Normandy, US$6, 7½ hrs., but not along coast road—which can only be done by taking local buses (Atlântico to São Sebastião, US$6, 7 hrs., 1030 and 1800) and changing at Ubatuba, Caraguatatuba or São Sebastião. The trip to Santos along the coast road can be done in one day, in either direction, but it needs at least a 0600 start. To Ouro Preto, direct bus (Util) at 0830 and 2330 daily US$5, 8 hrs.

International: Asunción, 1,511 km. via Foz do Iguaçu, 30 hrs., (Pluma) US$35, *leito* US$70; Buenos Aires (Pluma), via Porto Alegre and Santa Fe, 44 hrs., 1230, US$75, *leito* US$150 (book 2 days in advance); Montevideo, only from São Paulo; Santiago de Chile, US$100 with Pluma or Gral. Urquiza, about 70 hours. The Buenos Aires and Montevideo services are fully booked a week in advance.

You are allowed to sleep at the bus station, if you don't lie down. The main bus station (the Rodoviária, at Av. Rodrigues Alves, corner with Av. Francisco Bicalho, just past the docks, reached by buses 104 from the centre, 127 and 128 from Copacabana and 136, 456, 172 from Flamengo, and 170 from Largo do Machado and Flamengo, or taxi about US$8), has a Riotur information centre, very helpful. From Rodoviária, take bus 104 to Largo do Machado or to Catete for central location with buses and cheap hotels. The local bus terminal is just outside the Rodoviária: turn right as you leave and run the gauntlet of taxi drivers. The Real bus goes along the beach to São Conrado and will take luggage. **If you do need a taxi collect a ticket**, which ensures against overcharging, from the official at the head of the taxi queue. On no account give the ticket to the taxi driver.

Hitch Hiking To hitch to Belo Horizonte or Brasília, take a C-3 bus from Av. Presidente Antônio Carlos to the railway station, cross through the station to a bus station, and catch the Nova Iguaçu bus. Ask to be let off at the Belo Horizonte turn off. For the motorway entrance north and south take bus 392 or 393 from Praça São Francisco.

Ferry Service From the "barcas" at Praça 15 de Novembro, ferry boats and launches cross every 10 mins. to Niterói (20-30 mins., US$0.05); to Paquetá Island (70-90 mins., **see page 307** for fares). There are also hydrofoils ("aerobarcas") to Niterói every 10 mins. (about 10 mins., US$0.70). The Niterói ferry service is still being maintained, despite the competition from the 14 km. bridge linking the two sides of Guanabara Bay. (The approach to the bridge is on the elevated motorway from the centre, or via Av. Rio de Janeiro, in the Caju district; take the Av. Rodrigues Alves past the docks.) Bus 999 from the Passeio Público crosses the bridge.

The Suburbs of Rio de Janeiro

Copacabana, built on a narrow strip of land—only a little over 4 square kilometres—between mountain and sea, has one of the highest population densities in the world: 62,000 per square kilometre, or 250,000 in all. Its celebrated curved beach backed by skyscraper apartments is an unforgettable "must" for visitors. On all Rio's beaches you should take a towel or mat to protect you against sandflies; in the water stay near groups of other swimmers; bathing is generally dangerous.

Copacabana began to develop when the Old Tunnel was built in 1891 and an electric tram service reached it. Week-end villas and bungalows sprang up; all have now gone. In the 1930s the Copacabana Palace Hotel was the only tall building; it is now one of the lowest on the beach. The opening of the New Tunnel in the 1940s led to an explosion of population which shows no sign of having spent its force. Buildings of less than 12 storeys are still being replaced by high flats and luxury hotels.

There is almost everything in this fabulous "city within a city". The shops, mostly in Avenida Copacabana and the Rua Barata Ribeiro, are excellent; this is the area in which to watch, or participate in, the city's glamorous night life. A fort at the far end of the beach commands the entrance to Rio Bay and prevents a seashore connection with the Ipanema and Leblon beaches. However, parts of the military area are now being handed over to civilian use, the first being the Parque Garota de Ipanema at Arpoador, the fashionable Copacabana end of the Ipanema beach. Buses to and from the city centre are plentiful and cheap, about US$0.10. If you are going to the centre from Copacabana, look for "Castelo", "Praça 15", "E. Ferro" or "Praça Mauá" on the sign by the front door. "Aterro" means the expressway between Botafogo and downtown Rio (not open Sundays). From the centre to Copacabana is easier as all buses in that direction are clearly marked. Aterro bus does the journey in 15 minutes.

Beyond Copacabana are the beautiful seaside suburbs of Ipanema and Leblon; they are a little less built-up than Copacabana, and their beaches tend to be cleaner, though no less dangerous, than Copacabana's. (Posto 9 beach in Ipanema is a gay beach.) Backing Ipanema and Leblon is the Lagoa Rodrigo de Freitas, a salt-water lagoon on which Rio's rowing and small-boat sailing clubs are active; too polluted for bathing. Beyond Leblon the coast is rocky; the Avenida Niemeyer skirts the cliffs on the journey past Vidigal, a small beach where the *Sheraton* is situated, to the outer seaside suburbs of São Conrado (beach polluted) and Barra da Tijuca (see next page). The flat topped Gávea rock can be climbed or scrambled up for magnificent views, but beware snakes. Buses from Botafogo Metro terminal to Ipanema: some take integrated Metro-Bus tickets, saving 25%; look for the blue signs on the windscreen. Many buses from Copacabana to Ipanema (buses 154 and 158 from Flamengo) and Leblon (buses 158, 434 and 488 from Flamengo, continuing to Barra da Tijuca).

On New Year's Eve the festival of Iemanjá is held by the *umbandistas* on the beaches of Copacabana, Ipanema and Leblon (see page 287).

Santa Teresa, a hilly inner suburb SW of the centre, well known as the coolest part of Rio, still has many colonial and 19th-century buildings, set in narrow, curving, tree-lined streets. See particularly the Convent (only the outside; the Carmelite nuns do not admit visitors), the Chácara do Céu Museum (see page 288), the Hotel Santa Teresa (the oldest house in the area), Vista Alegre, the Rua Aprazível, and Largo de Guimarães. Santa Teresa is best visited on the traditional open-sided tram, the only one left in Rio, which leaves from the Largo da Carioca in the centre of the city, for Dois Irmãos, crossing to Santa Teresa on top of the old 18th-century aqueduct known as the Arcos.

Maracanã Stadium is one of the largest sports centres in the world. The football ground has seating capacity for 200,000 spectators and most matches are played on Sun. about 1700 (entrance from US$0.50-*geral*-, to US$2 for a seat, good, safe, to US$8; matches are worth going to for the fireworks and samba bands of the spectators, even if you're not a football fan. N.B. agencies charge about US$20). Buses 433, 434 and 455 from Copacabana; 433 and 434 from Flamengo; from Leblon, 464 via Ipanema and Copacabana; 221 and 231 from Castelo; 249 and 269 from Praça Tiradentes; and 238 and 239 from Praça 15 de Novembro; from Praça Mauá, 241 or 262; also Metro from Botafogo and centre. Hotels can arrange visits to football matches: good idea Sundays when the metro is closed and buses very full. If you want the real football experience, take a bus three hours before the game, buy a ticket in the upper ring, people very friendly.

Corcovado (710 metres) is the hunch-backed peak surmounted by a 40-metre high statue of Christ the Redeemer completed in 1931, weighing, with its base, 1,200 tons. There is a superb view from the top (sometimes obscured by mist), to which there are a cog railway and a road; both car and train (30 mins. each way) put down their passengers behind the statue—there is a climb of 220 steps to the top, near which there is a café for light refreshments. To see the city by day

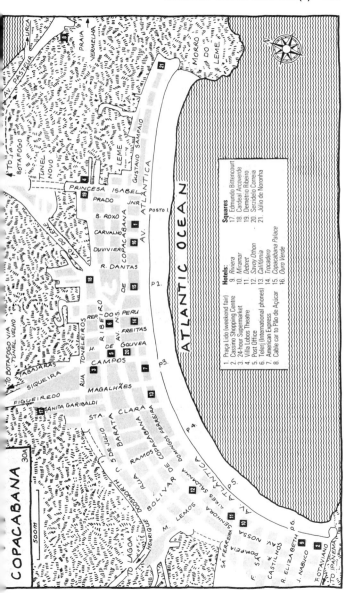

COPACABANA

ATLANTIC OCEAN

Hotels:
9. Riviera
10. Miramar
11. Debret
12. Savoy Othon
13. California
14. Trocadero
15. Copacabana Palace
16. Ouro Verde

1. Praça Lido (weekend fair)
2. Cassino Shopping Centre
3. 24-hour Supermarket
4. Villa Lobos Theatre
5. Post Office
6. Telerj (international phones)
7. American Express
8. Cable car to Pão de Açúcar

Squares
17. Edmundo Bittencourt
18. Cardeal Arcoverde
19. Demetrio Ribeiro
20. Serridelo Correia
21. Júlio de Noronha

and night ascend at 1500 or 1600 and descend on the last train. Mass is held on Sun. in a small chapel in the statue pedestal. The floodlighting was designed in 1931 by Marconi himself.

Take a Cosme Velho bus (422, 497, 498) to the **cog railway station at Rua Cosme Velho 513**. Service every 10-20 minutes according to demand, journey time 10 minutes (cost: US$3 return; single tickets available). Minibuses also operate from the station, return trip (1 hour stop) US$1.50, tickets obtained from office. Also, a 206 bus does the very attractive run from Praça Tiradentes (or a 407 from Largo do Machado) to Silvestre (the railway has no stop here now). An active walk of one hour will bring one to the top, and the road is shady. (Best done in company; robberies are very common in this neighbourhood.) Coach trips tend to be rather brief. N.B. There is too much interference around the statue for taking video pictures.

Pão de Açúcar (Sugar Loaf, 396 metres) is a massive granite cone at the entrance to Guanabara Bay. The bird's eye view of the city and beaches is very beautiful. There is a restaurant (excellent location, mixed reports on food, closes 1900) and a playground for children on the Morro da Urca, half way up, where there are also shows at night (weekends and Mon., 2200). You can get refreshments at the top. On the small path that leads down in the direction of Morro Cara de Cão there are toucans and macaws in cages. Buses 107 or 442 (from the centre or Flamengo) and 511 or 500 "jardinière" (from Copacabana) take you to the cable-car station, Av. Pasteur 520, at the foot.

The cable car timetable: Praia Vermelha to Urca: first car goes up at 0800, and the last comes down at 2215. From Urca to Sugar Loaf the first connecting cable car goes up at 0815 and the last leaves the summit at 2200; the return trip costs US$2.50 (US$1.25 to Morro da Urca, half-way up). The old cableway has been completely rebuilt. Termini are now ample and efficient and the present Italian cable cars carry 75 passengers. Even on the most crowded days there is little queuing. Beware of thieves at the cable car starting point. If you want to climb the Pão de Açúcar, contact the Clube Excursionista de Rio de Janeiro, or the rock-climbing club, Andre Illa and Xavier de Silvera, Copacabana, T 237-5229. There are 35 routes up the mountain, with various degrees of difficulty (best months for climbing: April to August).

Tijuca National Park, open 0600-2100, is for those interested in taking a forest walk through mountain scenery. An approximately 2-3 hr. walk will bring you to the summit of the Pico da Tijuca (1,012 metres), which gives a good idea of the tropical vegetation of the interior and a fine view of the bay and its shipping. On entering the park at Alto de Boa Vista, follow the signposts (maps are displayed) to Bom Retiro, a good picnic place (1½ hrs walk), passing by the Cascatinha Taunay, Mayrink Chapel (built 1860) and the restaurant *A Floresta*. At Bom Retiro the road ends and there is another hour's walk up a fair footpath to the summit; take the path from the right of the Bom Retiro drinking fountain, not the more obvious steps from the left. The last part consists of steps carved out of the solid rock; take care of children at the summit as there are several sheer drops, invisible because of bushes. The route is shady for almost its entire length. The panels painted in the Mayrink Chapel by Cândido Portinari have been replaced by copies and the originals will probably be installed in the Museu de Arte Moderna. Maps of the Park are available.

Take a 221 from Praça 15 de Novembro, 233 or 234 bus from the Rodoviária (it is reported that the 233 bus becomes the 234 on the return journey) or 454 from Copacabana or from Praça Sáenz Pena, Tijuca (reached by metro) to Alto da Boa Vista, for the park entrance. Other places of interest not passed on the walk to the peak are the Paul and Virginia Grotto, the Vista do Almirante and the Mesa do Imperador (viewpoints). A good restaurant in Parque Floresta is *Os Esquilos*. Allow at least 5 to 6 hrs. for the excursion. Also, one of the Raymundo

Castro Maia museums is nearby (**see page** 288).

Barra da Tijuca This new and very rapidly developing residential area can be reached from the Tijuca Forest by continuing on the 233 or 234 bus (from Praça Sáenz Pena, very good views of São Conrado and Barra), or from the city bus station at Rua São José, from Santos Dumont airport, and from Copacabana via Leblon beach (bus 553). From Botafogo metro terminus, take bus 524. A comfortable bus, Pegasus, goes along the coast from the Castelo bus terminal to Barra da Tijuca and continues to Campo Grande or Santa Cruz. Robberies on the buses have been reported.

Barra da Tijuca is also one of the principal recreation areas of Rio, the prime attraction being its 20-km. sandy beach, with good waves for surfing; somewhat cleaner than Copacabana but fast becoming another "Costa del Sol". Bus 700 from Praça São Conrado (terminal of bus 553 from Copacabana) goes the full length of the beach to Recreio dos Bandeirantes. Apart from this, there are innumerable bars and restaurants, campsites (**see page** 295), motels and hotels. The facilities include Riocenter, a 600,000 sq.m. convention complex and the huge Barra Shopping and Carrefour shopping centres. The stylish Fashion Mall is opposite the golf club. Watch the hang-gliders jumping from the hilltops at weekends. View the beaches and hills from the air, Ultra Força Ltda, Av. Sernambetiba 8100, T 399-3114, 15 mins, US$10. Live concerts on São Conrado beach during summer (Nov.-Feb.).

The Autódromo (motor racing track) is beyond Barra in the Jacarepaguá district. The Brazilian Grand Prix is held here or at Interlagos, São Paulo, alternately in January.

Viewpoints Apart from the Pico da Tijuca, Corcovado and Pão de Açúcar, splendid views of different parts of Rio can be seen from the Vista Chinesa (420 metres), where from a Chinese-style pavilion one can see the inland lake (the Lagoa), Ipanema and Leblon; the Mesa do Imperador (Emperor's Table) and Vista do Almirante (Admiral's View) in the Tijuca Forest; and the Mirante de Dona Marta (340 metres) off the Corcovado road, with the same direction of view as the Corcovado, but as it is lower the details can be seen more clearly. There is as yet no public transport to any of these places.

Paquetá Island in Guanabara Bay can be visited by more or less two-hourly ferry services from Praça Quinze de Novembro (fare US$0.15 by boat, 1 hr., US$1 by hydrofoil, every ½ hr., 20 mins. journey, which more than doubles its price Sats., Suns. and holidays). Horse-drawn carriages hire for US$6 per hr. (many have harnesses which cut into the horse's flesh); they do not stop at the interesting Parque Darke de Mattos. Tour by "trenzinho", a tractor pulling trailers, US$0.80. Bicycles for hire from US$1 per hr. (deposit US$2). The island is noted for its gigantic pebble shaped rocks, butterflies and orchids. Very crowded at weekends and public holidays, but usually very quiet during the week, though there can be aircraft noise. Reasonable food and drink prices.

Hotel Paquetá, E, Flamboyant and Lido. Porto Fino Restaurant, expensive and poor food.

Other boat trips, Aquatur (T 230-9273), Brazilian Marina Turismo, Camargo (T 275-0643), Passamar, Siqueira Campos 7 (T 236-4136), Greyline (T 274-7146), Soletur (Bay trips Sat. and Sun. only) and American Sightseeing, Av. N.S. Copacabana 605, Sala 1204 (T 236-3551). The last three offer a day cruise, including lunch, to Jaguanum Island (**see page** 313, under Itacuruçá) and a sundown cruise around Guanabara Bay, also deep-sea fishing expeditions and private charters.

Entering Rio from the W, an alternative to the BR-101 and Avenida Brasil, is to leave BR-101 on the road to Santa Cruz, continuing 6 km. to the fishing village of Sepetiba, quiet other than at weekends. Along the coast is Pedra de Guaratiba, from where you join Avenida das Américas, turning off right soon afterwards to Ponta do Picão and Guaratiba, a pretty seaside resort on a rocky, narrow, steep ledge between mountain and sea (good beaches and a playground for the rich). Another 2 km. along the main road is another (unmarked) right turn leading to a restaurant at the summit, with fantastic views, then down to Praia de Grumari, which is unspoilt except for 2 restaurants and a campsite (US$1 p.p.). It is then 30 km. to Copacabana, via Recreio dos Bandeirantes (Dieter Reinmuth).

The State of Rio de Janeiro: East from Rio

Niterói, (pop. 441,000) founded in 1573, the ex-capital of the State of Rio de Janeiro, is reached across the bay by bridge or ferries,

Of the frequent ferry boat and hydrofoil services (**see page** 303) from Praça 15 de Novembro, Rio, the slow, cheaper ferry gives the best views. There is a Flumitur tourist information booth to the right of the ferry-boat station. Nearby you can take the 33 bus (marked "via Froes") to the beaches of Icaraí, São Francisco and Jurujuba on the bay, a beautiful ride. Sit on the right-hand side. A few minutes' walk from where the bus route ends at Jurujuba are the attractive twin beaches of Adão and Eva, with lovely views of Rio across the bay. From Praça General Gomes Carneiro, near the ferry boats, take a 38 bus to Piratininga, Itaipu and Itacoatiara, fabulous ocean beaches and the best in the area, about 40 minutes' ride through picturesque countryside. The beaches inside the bay, though calm, are often overcrowded and polluted, but no more so than those opposite in Rio. The forts on this side of the bay include Santa Cruz (16th century, still a military establishment), Barão do Rio Branco (1633), Gragoatá and Nossa Senhora da Boa Viagem.

You should also visit the church of Boa Viagem (1633), built on an island connected to the mainland by a short causeway, a few minutes' walk from Icaraí beach. Nearby, on Rua Tiradentes, is the Antônio Parreira Museum, opens 1300, dedicated to the eponymous artist. The Museu de Arqueologia de Itaipu is in the ruins of the 18th century Santa Teresa Convent, and also covers the archaeological site of Duna Grande on Itaipu beach.

The Rio-Niterói bridge (Ponte Costa e Silva) has a length of 14 km. Toll for cars, US$0.30. Motorway connection to centre of Rio. Bus 999 from the corner of Senador Dantas and Av. Beira Mar, Rio, crosses the bridge to Niterói and Icaraí (US$0.30); also 996 and 998 from the Jardim Botânico (all three go to the Rodoviária in Rio).

Hotels *Novotel Rio-Niterói*, Praia de Gragoatá, Telex 021-7252, A; *Samanguaia*, D; *Niterói Palace*, Rua Andrade Neves 134, D-C; *Imperial*, D.

Clubs Rio Cricket, bus 57 from ferry. Rio Sailing, bus 33 marked "via Froes".

Electric Current 110 volts, A.C., 60 cycles.

Laundromats, Lavlev, Rua Presidente Backer 138.

To the east of Niterói lie a series of salt-water lagoons, the Lagos Fluminenses. Two small lakes lie behind the beaches of Piratininga and Itaipu near Niterói, but they are polluted and ringed by mud. The next lakes are much larger, those of Maricá and Saquarema; though they are still muddy, the waters are relatively unpolluted, and wild life abounds in the scrub and bush around the lagoons. At the outlet to the lake of Saquarema (turn right off the main road at Bacaxá) is the holiday village of **Saquarema**. Of particular interest is the little white church of Nossa Senhora de Nazaré (1675) built atop a green promontory jutting into the ocean. Saquarema is the centre for surfing in Brazil, and the national championships are held here each year in May. Beware of strong currents, though.
    The largest lake is that of **Araruama**, famous for its medicinal mud. It is so large that it seems more like a bay than a lagoon. The salinity is extremely high, the waters calm, and almost the entire lake is surrounded by sandy beaches, making it very popular with families looking for safe, unpolluted bathing. The major industry of the area is salt, and all around one can see the saltpans and the wind pumps used to carry the water into the pans. At the eastern end of the lake lies the village of **São Pedro de Aldeia**, which, in spite of intensive development, still retains much of its colonial charm, and has a lovely Jesuit church built in 1723.

Hotels in the lake district: Saquarema: *Sol e Mar*, B; *Katy Motel*, B; *Pousada do Holandés*, Av. Vilamar 377, at Itaúna beach, D, highly rec., many languages spoken by Dutch owner and his Brazilian wife (who runs the local day-care centre), good meals—follow the signs, or take a taxi (US$0.50), from Saquarema. Restaurant in Saquarema, *Tem Uma Né Chama Teré*, very good, in main square. Araruama: *Senzala*, on Iguabinha beach, 10 km. from Araruama, A with meals; *La Gondola*, on the lake beach, C, overpriced; *Parque Hotel*, A; *Lakes Hotel*, over the bus station, A; *Chalés do Coqueiral*, chalets on lake beach, A. São Pedro de Aldeia: *Solar de Iguaba*, C; *Vilabranca Village*, over 100 chalets, A with meals, and *Costa do Sol*, A, on Iguaba Grande beach, 14 km. from São Pedro. At Ponta Negra is *Pousada Colonial*, suites and bungalows in B. range, breakfast included, T Rio, 451-6254 for reservations.

The ocean beaches beside these lagoons, except for the sheltered coves of Ponta Negra and Saquarema, are rough and lonely. The whole area is perfect for camping; there are campsites (including Camping Clube do Brasil) at Araruama (close to the *Parque Hotel*) and São Pedro de Aldeia. A very steep road connects the beaches of Itaipu and Itacoatiara with BR-106 (and on to Araruama) via the village of Itaipu-Açu, with beach and good camping. Most maps do not show a road beyond Itaipu-Açu; it is certainly too steep for buses.

An alternative to the route from Niterói to Araruama through the lagoons is via Manilla, Itaboraí and Rio Bonito, on the BR-101 and RJ-124; this is a fruit-growing region.

Cabo Frio, 156 km. from Rio, is a popular holiday and week-end haunt of Cariocas because of its cool weather, beaches, scenery, sailing and good under-water swimming (but mosquitoes are a problem). The ocean beach is much less frequented than the bay beach. The São Mateus fort nearby was built by the French; it is in a state of disrepair. If in the area, take a look at the huge church under construction at Arraial do Cabo nearby; it totally dominates the town (bus every 20 mins. from Cabo Frio).

Hotels *Marliru Acapulco*, A; *Cabo Frio Sol* (motel), C. 20 other hotels with descending prices down to *Caravela* and *Colonial*, both D. *Jangada*, Granaola 220, near canal, D, very friendly, good breakfast, rec. *Nanaque*, 2 blocks from bus station, follow signs, 3 blocks from sea, E with bath and breakfast, clean, highly rec.; two similar nearby. Youth Hostel, both sexes, open all year to IYHF members (F p.p., more for non-members), on Rua Kubitschek, 1 block from bus station, very friendly. 2 youth hostels in Arraial do Cabo, one at Escola Municipal Ione Nogueira (T 43-0369) and the other at Rua Gen. Bruno Martins 9881 (T 262-6360).

Camping Camping Clube do Brasil sites at Estrada dos Passageiros, near town; at Km. 135 on the Rio road, 4 km. outside town, in Palmeiras; and at Arraial do Cabo on Praia dos Anjos, crowded beach. 10 km. to S. Cambrás has a site at Estrada dos Passageiros. Also site at Cabo Yacht club.

Buses Rodoviária is 2 km. from centre. Bus from Rio every ½ hr., 2½ hrs., US$4. To Búzios, from local bus terminus in town centre, every hour, US$0.50.

Búzios, NE of Cabo Frio, is a resort built up in Portuguese colonial styles, with unmade roads so as to discourage fast drivers. It has 27 sandy coves, calm unpolluted waters (superb for windsurfing), beautiful scenery, plenty of good hotels and *pousadas* (mostly C upwards, e.g. *Casa D'elas Pousada*, and *Pousada do Sol*, Praia da Armação; *Pousada Casa de Pedra*, Trav. Lúcio A. Quintanilha 57, T (0246) 231499, D, TV, fridge, safe, in centre of town, rec.), but very expensive, as is everything else (except the vicious mosquitoes). Best route from Rio (2 hrs. by car) is the paved road towards Macaé, with a paved turnoff to Búzios. Direct road from Cabo Frio (bus 45 mins.) is unpaved. Camping is allowed but dangerous. Tourist information office near bus station. Very crowded during Brazilian holiday season and extremely difficult to get hotel booking. Good restaurants: *Frank's* in Ossos and *Natural* in Armação (try the camarão tropical). Popular bars are *Delikatessen* and *Tempero's*. Tartaruga beach is not marked and not developed (take dirt road up small hill opp. *Pousada Baer Búzios*); there is a restaurant and snack bar in season.

Continuing to the north, one comes to the seaside resorts of Barra de São João, **Rio das Ostras** (*Hotel Saint Tropez*, C; *Hotel Mirante do Poeta*, C) and **Macaé** (Hotels: *Colonial*, C, friendly, helpful, comfortable; *Turismo* and *Panorama*, C; *Central*, Rua Rui Barbosa, E, clean, nice, friendly, good breakfast, secure parking), all containing sheltered coves with good swimming and scuba diving. Macaé is also the supply centre for the offshore oil industry so there are usually several foreigners in town enjoying a beer.

From Rio and Niterói a first class highway, the BR-101, runs NE past Macaé to Campos (bus Rio-Macaé 2½-3 hrs., every ½ hr., Mil e Um or Rápido Macaense; bus Macaé-Campos, 1¾ hrs., US$1.50). At Km. 222 is the **Biological Reserve of Poço das Antas** (2 hrs. drive from Rio; it is not open to the general public, for details, Delegacia Estadual do IBDF, Av. Pres. Antônio Carlos 607-12°, CEP 20.000, Rio de Janeiro). Many animals (including the *mico-leão* marmoset—this is its only natural habitat) roam in the forest.

Campos (pop. 367,000) is a busy industrial city, some 276 km. (4½ hrs. by Mil e Um bus, hourly) from Rio de Janeiro (70 km. from Macaé). It stands 56 km. from the mouth of the Rio Paraíba, up which coffee planting originally spread to São Paulo state. Coffee is still grown near Campos, though the region is now one of the largest sugar-producing zones in Brazil. Important offshore oil discoveries have been made nearby. Town is quite interesting.

Hotels *Terraza Tourist*, D, 2-star; *Planície*, Rua 13 de Maio 56, D; *Palace*, Av. 15 de Novembro 143, D. *Silva*, some way behind church on municipal square, E, breakfast, clean, safe parking.

Travelling N, as an alternative to BR-101 to Vitória, one can take a detour inland, going through São Fidélis, Cambiasca, Itoacara and on to **Santo Antônio de Pádua**, 130 km. from Campos, a pleasant town on the Rio Pomba. (*Hotel das Aguas*, a short walk from the centre, D, a resort hotel in a park with pool; health centre and bottling plant for the local mineral water which is used for treating cardiovascular illness; *Braga*, in town, E, clean, friendly, good food.) Take road No. 393 to Itaperuna, Bom Jesus do Itabapoana and into Espírito Santo, then road No. 484 to Guaçuí (*Grande Hotel Minas*, F, friendly, clean; *Restaurant Kontiki*, very good), one of the starting points for the Parque Nacional do Caparaó (**see page 333**). Then take the road 482 to Cachoeira do Itapemirim and the BR-101 (**see page 316**).

Petrópolis (population: 275,000) is a summer hill resort and industrial city at 840 metres, 68 km. N of Rio. It is reached by bus along a steep, scenic mountain toll road (US$1 weekdays, US$1.50 weekends). Until 1962 Petrópolis was the "summer capital" of Brazil; it was founded in 1843 as a summer refuge by Dom Pedro II. Now it combines manufacturing industry (particularly textiles, which may be bought cheaply) with floral beauty and hill scenery. The Imperial Palace (Museu Imperial), which seems to express very faithfully what we know of Dom Pedro II's character, is a modest but elegant building, fully furnished and equipped, containing the Crown Jewels and other imperial possessions. It is assiduously well-kept: one might think the imperial family had left the day before one's visit, rather than in 1889. Open Tues.-Sun., 1200-1730. Entry US$0.30. Well worth a visit is the Gothic-style Cathedral, completed in 1925, which contains the tombs of the Emperor and Empress (guide in English, US$0.20).

Hotels *Casa do Sol*, 4-star hotel out on road to Rio, B; *Margaridas*, Monsenhor Bacelar 126, chalet-type hotel set in lovely gardens with swimming pool, charming proprietors, C; *Auto-Tour (Fazenda Inglesa)* at km. 51 on the Petrópolis by-pass, very chic, A, with meals; *Riverside Parque*, Rua Hermogéneo Silva 522, C; *Casablanca Center*, General Osório 28, B; *Casablanca*, Sete de Setembro beside Imperial Palace, C, good atmosphere in older part, pool, very clean; *Casablanca Palace*, Primeiro de Março 123, C; *Gran Solar (Pousado do Carmo)*, Benjamin Constant 288, C; *Dom Pedro*, D, on main square, pleasant; *Comércio*, opp. bus station, E, with breakfast; *Pensão Esther*, Rua do Imperador, E, incl. breakfast.

Camping Associação Brasileira de Camping and YMCA, Araras district. Can reserve space through Rio YMCA, T 231-9860.

Restaurants *Churrascaria Majórica*, Av. do Imperador (ex 15 de Novembro) 754; *Mirthes Paranhos*, Irmãos d'Angelo 99; *Cantina Italiana*, Paulo Barbosa 48, clean, pleasant; *Maloca*, Wáshington Luís 466; *Bauernstube*, João Pessoa 297. *Vegetariano*, Rua do Imperador 288, sobreloja 1, good and cheap.

Attractions and Excursions Museu Ferreira da Cunha, Fernandes Vieira 390 (old road to Rio) shows large collection of arms, open Sat. and Sun. (only to groups; need to arrange in advance) 0900-1700. Summer home of air pioneer Santos Dumont, showing early inventions. Crystal Palace in Praça da Confluência, former imperial ballroom and now exhibition centre. Orquidário Binot, Rua Fernandes Vieira 390 (take bus to Vila Isabel; open Mon.-Sat., 0800-1100, 1300-1700), a huge collection of orchids from all over Brazil (plants may be purchased).

Buses leave from Rio every 10 mins. throughout the day (US$1), sit on the left hand side for best views. Return tickets are not available, so passengers must buy tickets for the return bus as soon as they arrive in Petrópolis. Journey 75 mins. each way. The ordinary buses leave from the Rodoviária in Rio; there is a new service of air-conditioned buses, hourly from 1100, from Av. Nilo Peçanha, US$1.50. There is a direct overnight bus from São Paulo.

Teresópolis (pop. 115,000; 910 metres), near the Serra dos Órgãos, is 124 km. NE of Rio. It was the favourite summer residence of the Empress Teresa Cristina. See the Colina dos Mirantes hill, the Sloper and Iaci lakes, the Imbui and Amores waterfalls, and the Fonte Judith. Tourist information office some way from bus station (not very helpful). São Pedro festival on June 29 is celebrated with fireworks.

Martin Crossland writes: Leave the Rodoviária bus station in Rio on the 0800 bus or before (Viação Teresópolis) for the 1¾-hour ride and up into the mountains to Teresópolis (sit on right side of bus). Upon arrival at the bus station, buy another ticket right away for Petrópolis (Viação Teresópolis) for the 1200 bus in order to get a good seat, as the bus fills rapidly. This gives you 2¾ hours to wander around. If you feel up to a steep ½-hr. climb, try the Colina dos Mirantes for a sweeping view of the city and surroundings. For the less energetic, a taxi is not dear.

The 90-minute drive from Teresópolis to Petrópolis is beautiful. (Sit on left side.) The views on either side are spectacular. Again, upon arrival in Petrópolis at 1330, buy your ticket to Rio (Facil or Unica). Take the 1715 bus "via Quitandinha", and you might catch the sunset over the mountains (in May, June, July, take the 1615 bus). This gives you time to visit most of the attractions listed in the city description.

Hotels *São Moritz*, Swiss-style, outside on the Nova Friburgo road, Km. 36, lowest rates, B, with meals; *Clube Caxangá*, resort-type, not well kept, B; *Philips*, Rua Duval Fonseca, B; *Alpina*, Parque Imbui, on Petrópolis road, B; *Higíno Palace*, Av. Oliveira Botelho 328, C; *Vila Nova do Paquequer*, Av. Alberto Torres 1149 (by the Guarani waterfall), D; *Várzea Palace*, Rua Sebastião Teixeira 41, E. *Florida*, Av. Lúcio Meira 467, E, with bargaining. Youth hostel: Retiro da Inglesa, 20 km. on road to Friburgo, Fazenda Boa Esperança (reservations, Rua Papa Pio XII 50, Jardim Cascata 25963 Teresópolis).

Camping National Park, entrance to Teresópolis from Rio, full facilities; Quinta de Barra, km. 3 on Petrópolis road; Vale das Choupanas, km. 30 on Rio road.

Restaurants *Taberna Alpina*, Duque de Caxias 131; *Cantina Riviera*, Praça Baltazar de Silveira 112; *La Cremaille*, Av. Feliciano Sodré 1012; *De Stéfano*, Av. Lúcio Meira 695. *Bar Gota d'Água*, Praça Baltasar da Silveira 16 for trout or feijoada (small but rec.).

Bus, Rio-Teresópolis Buses leave every half-hour from Rodoviária. As return tickets are not issued, passengers should book for the return journey as soon as they arrive at Teresópolis. Time, 1¾ hrs. each way; fare US$1.50. From Teresópolis to Petrópolis, every 2 hrs. from 0900-2100, US$1.75.

About 30,000 hectares of the Serra dos Órgãos, so called because their strange shapes are said to recall organ-pipes, are now a **National Park**. The main attraction is the precipitous Dedo de Deus (God's Finger) Peak. There is also the rock formation Mulher de Pedra 12 km. out on the Nova Friburgo road, and the Von Martinó natural-history museum. The highest point is the Pedra Açu, 2,400 metres. A path leads up the 2,260-metre Pedra do Silo, 3-4 hours' climb. Entrance to park, US$0.25. IBDF (The National Forestry Institute, office in Teresópolis, Serra dos Órgãos, Casa 8, CEP 25.950) has some hostels, US$4.60 full board, or US$3.10 first night, US$1.50 thereafter, a bit rough. Camping, US$0.50. A good way to see the Park is to do the Rio-Teresópolis-Petrópolis-Rio circuit; a scenic day trip. The Rio-Teresópolis road, which passes right next to the Serra dos Órgãos, is a toll road (cars US$1, US$1.50 at weekendsa) from Km. 10.6.

Nova Friburgo (pop. 143,000, 850 metres above sea-level), is a popular resort during summer months (around 30 hotels), in a beautiful valley with excellent walking and riding possibilities. Founded by Swiss settlers from Fribourg, it can be reached by bus (US$3) from Rio (every hour) in 2 hrs. or by car in 1 hr. 45 min. Cable car from Praça dos Suspiros 650 metres up the Morro da Cruz, for view of rugged country. Road to Teresópolis paved.

Hotels *Bucsky*, T 22-5052, 5 km. out on Niterói road, B, with meals; *Everest*, T 22-7350, behind Chess Club, E, comfortable, good breakfasts; *Sans-Souci*, T 22-7752, 1 km. out, B, with meals, D without; *Garlipp*, German-run, in chalets, B, with meals, at Muri, km. 70.5 from Rio, 10 km. from Nova Friburgo, T 42-1330. Under same ownership is *Fazenda São João*, C, T 42-1304, 11 km. from *Garlipp* up a side road (impassable in the wet), riding, swimming, sauna, tennis, hummingbirds and orchids; owner will meet guests in Nova Friburgo or even in Rio. Also *Mury Garden*, T 42-1120, with swimming pool, B, with meals, reasonable, 10 km. away at Muri (Km. 70 on Niterói road). 12 km. from Nova Friburgo at Amparo is *Jequitibá*, C, T 22-1831, sports facilities, restaurant.

Camping Camping Clube do Brasil has sites on Niterói road, at Cônego (7 km. out) and Muri (10 km. out). Cambrás site also at Cônego, and private site at Fazenda Sanandu, 20 km. out on same road.

Restaurants *Majórica*, traditional churrascaria. *Natural*, Rua Farinha Filho 2515, in centre, vegetarian, good and cheap.

The State of Rio de Janeiro: West from Rio

Volta Redonda (pop. 219,000) stands on a broad bend of the Rio Paraíba at an altitude of 565 metres, 113 km. W of Rio along the railway to São Paulo. In 1942 it was a little village; today it has one of the largest steel works in Latin American. The mills are on the river bank and the town spreads up the surrounding wooded and gardened slopes.

Hotels *Sider Palace*, Rua 33 No. 10, C; *Embaixador*, 1-star, E; *Bela Vista*, Alto de Boa Vista, on a hill overlooking town, B.

Visitors who have a permit from the Companhia Siderúrgica Nacional, Av. Treze de Maio 13, Rio de Janeiro (apply ten days in advance), or locally from the *Bela Vista* hotel, are allowed to inspect the mills. Visits start at 0900, and last 2½-3 hrs. The town can be reached from Rio by buses or minibuses in 2½ hrs., US$1.50.

North of Volta Redonda is Miguel Pereira, set in the mountain region with an excellent climate; nearby is the Javari lake, a popular recreational spot. Two *Hotel-Fazendas* (both C) near Miguel Pereira are *Quindins* and *Javari*, both with restaurant, swimming pool, sports grounds, etc. In town is the *Rei dos Montanhas*, F, Swiss-chalet style, clean, chilly at night. A tourist steam train runs from Miguel Pereira to Conrado, very scenic. Further north, and still in the mountains are the university centres of Vassouras and Valença; both are historical monuments. 35 km. from Valença is Conservatória, another colonial town. This region can also be reached via the Japeri turn-off on the BR-116 (a beautiful mountain drive). Some 30 km. W of Volta Redonda, in the town of Resende, is the Military Academy of Agulhas Negras. Grounds, with captured German guns of World War II, are open to the public. **Resende** can be reached by bus from Aparecida do Norte (see page 355), several daily, US$1.25, or from Rio, frequent, 1¾ hrs., US$1.75, also from São Paulo and Volta Redonda.

Hotels *Leme*, Rua Dr. Cunha Ferreira, 100 m. from Rodoviária, clean, basic, F p.p.; *Dormitórios Amazônica*, Dr. Cunha Ferreira esq. Praça Oliveira Botelho. Shops across river before railway station.

In the same region, 175 km. from Rio, is the small town of **Penedo** (5 buses a day from Resende) which in the 1930s attracted Finnish settlers who brought the first saunas to Brazil. This weekend resort, popular with the prosperous of São Paulo and Rio, hippies and naturalists, also provides horseback riding, and swimming in the Portinho river. Some 33 km. beyond Penedo (part of road unpaved) is the small village of **Visconde de Mauá**, which has cheap lodgings: enquire at **Vendinha da Serra** (run by John from Leeds), excellent natural food restaurant and store. Fine scenery and walks, lots of holidaymakers, pleasant atmosphere; roads to 3 other small hill towns, Maringá (several E hotels), Marumbá and Mirantão, at about 1,700 metres. 6 km. up river from Maringá are the well-known Santa Clara falls. Buses to Visconde de Mauá from Resende, 1500 and 1630, 1½ hrs., US$1.50 (you reach Maringá before Visconde de Mauá). Further along the Dutra Highway (186 km. from Rio) is the small town of **Engenheiro Passos**, from which a road (BR-354) leads to São Lourenço and Caxambu in Minas Gerais **(see page** 333), passing Agulhas Negras. One can climb Agulhas Negras from this side by taking the road from Registro pass (1,670 metres) to the Abrigo Rebouças refuge, which is manned all year round (take your own food, US$0.80 to stay), at 2,350 metres.

Hotels Penedo: *Bertell*, B, with meals; also *da Cachoeira*, *Moradas do Penedo*; *Pousada Penedo*, D, safe, clean, pool, rec. 2 campsites. Restaurants *Viking*, *Mariska* (Hungarian), and *Baianinha*. Engenheiro Passos: *Villa Forte*, B, with meals; *Pensão das Flores*, Visconde de Mauá, D, with meals. Nine campsites in the area.

The **Itatiaia National Park** (founded 1937), on the Serra de Itatiaia in the Mantiqueira chain of mountains, is a few km. N of the Via Dutra (Rio-São Paulo highway). The road to it is paved. The town of Itatiaia is surrounded by picturesque mountain peaks and lovely waterfalls. It has good hotels, and plenty of camping sites: the Camping Clube do Brasil site is entered at Km. 148 on the Via Dutra. This is a good area for climbing (Pico das Agulhas Negras 2,787 metres, Pico da Prateleira 2,540 metres), trekking and birdwatching; information and maps can be obtained at the park office. Worth seeing are the curious rock formations of Pedra de Taruga and Pedra de Maçã, and the waterfall Véu de Noiva (many birds). Basic accommodation in cabins and dormitories is available in the park; you will need to book in season, say 30 days in advance, by writing to Administração do Parque Nacional de Itatiaia, Itatiaia 27540, RJ. A Administração operates a refuge in the park which acts as a starting point for climbs and treks: information on these from Club Excursionista Brasileira, Av. Almirante Barroso 2, 8th floor, T 220-3695, Rio. Tres Picos wildlife trail near *Hotel Simon*; ask at hotel desk for info. There is a Museum of Flora and Fauna, closed Mondays. Entrance to Park, US$0.35. A bus from Itatiaia, marked *Hotel Simon*, goes to the Park, 1200, returns 1700; coming from Resende this may be caught at the crossroads before Itatiaia.

Hotels *Simon*, Km. 13 park road, A, with meals, lovely views; *Repouso Itatiaia*, Km. 10 park road, A, with meals; *Hotel do Ypé*, Km. 13 park road, B, with meals; *Fazenda da Serra*, Via Dutra Km. 151, B, with meals; *Tyll*, Via Dutra Km. 155, B, with meals. *Jahu*, Via Dutra Km. 156, D, very friendly, clean, comfortable.

The new **Rio-Santos highway**, and even more the parallel road along the coast, are making the forested and hilly coastal region SW of Rio more accessible. It is now complete right through to Bertioga **(see page** 350), which has good links both with Santos and (avoiding Santos) to São Paulo. There are direct Rio-Santos buses, and direct services from Rio to Angra dos Reis, Parati, Ubatuba, Caraguatatuba, and São Sebastião. Hotels and *pousadas* have sprung up all along the road.

Itacuruçá, 91 km. from Rio, is a delightful place to visit if you like fine scenery and peace and quiet, with islands off the coast.

Hotels On Ilha de Itacuruçá, is *Hotel Pierre*, reached by boat from Coroa Grande, north of Itacuruçá on the mainland, 5 mins. (boats also go from Itacuruçá); hotel has 27 rooms in price range L, restaurant, bars, sporting facilities. For bookings T Rio 521-1546 or 289-7546, or Saveiros Tours, 267-2792. At S end of the island is *Pousada do Artur*, A; T Rio 256-6227. The *Hotel Jaguanum*, Ilha de Jaguanum, Itacuruçá, has apartments and chalets with private bathrooms. There are beautiful walks around the island. Reservations for the hotel, which include the boat trip to and from the island (at 1000 and 1700), cost US$120-130 per day

RIO DE JANEIRO,
EASTERN SÃO PAULO&
SOUTHERN MINAS GERAIS
NOT TO SCALE   31

for two with all meals. The only extra is the bus, US$3 return, which picks you up at your hotel. Book by calling 235-2893 or 237-5119, in Rio, or enquire at Sepetiba Turismo, Av. N.S. de Copacabana 605, s. 202.

The sea is now reported to be too polluted for bathing, but you can walk along the railway to Castelo where the beach is cleaner. Ilha de Itacuruçá can also be reached from Muriqui, a popular beach resort 9 km from Itacuruça ; bathing also in the Véu de Noiva waterfall. The next beach along the coast is Praia Grande.

Mangaratiba, half-way from Rio to Angra dos Reis, has muddy beaches, but pleasant surroundings and better beaches outside the town, for example Ibicuí, São Brás, Praia Brava, Saco, Guiti and Cação.

Hotels *Moreira,* and *Mendoza* (both have same owner), E without breakfast (US$1.90 extra), without bath, good, clean; 2 others, more expensive. None is crowded because the town is not a tourist resort.

Daily ferry (Conerj) to Ilha Grande island (see below), at 0830 daily, 1½ hrs., highly rec.; return ferry Mon., Wed., Fri. at 1700, Wed. at 1600, other days at 1100. Fare US$0.45, US$0.90 weekends. Tues. and Thur. departures continue on to Angra dos Reis. Ferry departures and destinations can be checked at ferry station at Praça Quinze de Novembro, Rio. Buses from Rio Rodoviária 7 a day, US$1.50.

Angra dos Reis (pop 70,000), said to have been founded in 1502, is 197 km. SW of Rio by road. A small port with an important fishing and shipbuilding industry, it has several small bays with good bathing within easy reach and is situated on an enormous bay full of islands. Boat trips around the bay are available, some with a stop for lunch on the island of Jipóia (5 hrs., US$7.50 p.p.; boats for hire US$10/hour). Of particular interest are the convent of Nossa Senhora do Carmo, built in 1593, the parish church (1626), the ruins of the Jacuecanga seminary (1797), and the Senhor do Bonfim church (1780).

Hotels *Frade* (A, the most expensive), *Da Praia* and *Pousada do Retiro*, small resort hotels, bookings 267-7375, all B; *Palace,* C, and *Londres,* C; *Caribe,* D, central, and *Acrópolis,* Rua de Conceição 255, T 65-1022, D, clothes washing facilities, rec. *Porto Rico,* E without breakfast, clean, quiet. At Km. 115 on BR-101 is *Hotel Porto Bracuhy,* B, with lots of facilities for watersports, nightly shows and dancing, restaurant, etc. (23 km. from Angra dos Reis). *Porto Atlântico,* A, also beyond Angra.

Restaurants *Costa Verde, Verde Mar,* both specializing in sea food. For meat, *Adega dos Dragos,* good. *Taberna,* Raul Pompeia 33, good, popular, moderate prices; *Jacques,* Rua de Comércio, good for seafood, also *Tropicalitá,* Largo do Convento do Carmo.

Bus Hourly from Rio's Rodoviária, Viação Eval, take the "via litoral" bus and sit on the left, US$3, 2½ hrs. Tourist information opposite the bus station.

The Hotéis do Frade group (*Frade do Retiro, Pousada Dom João* in Parati and *Hotel Portogalo,* 1½ hrs. from Rio on a cliff top) in conjunction with Aquatur owns a schooner, the *Frade-Mar,* which runs cruises off Angra dos Reis, exploring islands, snorkelling, diving, etc. Trips are Mon.-Wed., or Fri.-Sun.; bookings for cruises,and for Frade hotels: Rua Joaquim Nabuco 161, Copacabana, 22080 Rio de Janeiro, T 267-7375, Telex: 31034, or Portuguese Tours Inc., 321 Rahway Av., Elizabeth, N.J. 07202, T 352-6112, Telex 138-203 or 178-051.

A road runs inland (about 18 km. beyond Angra), through Getulândia, to join the BR-116 either just S of Pirai or near Volta Redonda, through nice mountain scenery.

Two hours by ferry boat (Mon., Wed., Fri. at 1530, return 1015—so you have to stay 2 nights; for day trips, go from Mangaratiba) takes you on a most attractive trip through the bay to **Ilha Grande**, once an infamous pirate lair, and now occupied principally by fishermen and one of Brazil's larger prisons, with two good hotels, *Paraiso do Sol* (A, inclusive of meals, reservations, Rio, T 252-9158) and *Mar da Tranqüilidade* (B, reservations Rio, T 392-8475). Hotel reservations are necessary; alternatively you can camp on beaches; ask in the port at Angra dos Reis for a fishing boat going to Proveta, where you can stay in boat sheds or, if lucky, with a fisherman. It is a beautiful village, from which you can walk through tropical forest on a mountain to Praia do Aventureiro (a day's leisurely walk each way). Take mosquito precautions and register with police post in village of Abraão.

Beyond Angra dos Reis, the road continues 100 km. along the coast (on the way is *Pousada do Bosque*, Mambucaba, B, rec.), past the nuclear-power plant at Itaorna, to **Parati**, (pop. 23,300) a charming colonial town only recently accessible with the opening of the road. The centre has been declared a national historic monument in its entirety. It used to be a very important place, being the chief port for the export of gold in the 17th century. The churches were built separately for each race, Indian, black and white. There is a great deal of distinguished Portuguese colonial architecture in delightful settings. On the northern headland is a small fort, 15 mins.' walk, pleasant views. There is a festival of sacred music in September. The town centre is out of bounds for motor vehicles. It is now very popular with tourists, and an expensive place to visit. Local patchwork is for sale in the community centre on the waterfront, quilts for sale in gift shop in Santa Rita de Cassia church. Boat trips round the bay daily at 1200, returning 1700, US$10.50 p.p., beautiful trip; alternatively you can hire small boats by the hour. Take mosquito repellent.

Hotels *Pousada Pardieiro*, A, attractively housed in colonial building with lovely gardens, but always full at week-ends, does not take children. Also *Pousada Dom João*, A, bookings Rio 267-7375; *Pousada Parati*, A, reasonable value; *Santa Rita*, Rua Santa Rita 2, D, good, with bath and breakfast; other central *pousadas*: *do Ouro*, A, *das Canoas* (rec., clean, swimming pool, a/c) and *Aconchego*, both C; *Hotels Pescador* and *Sila Coupê*, central, C; *Pouso Familiar*, Rua J.V.Ramos 262, E, run by Belgian (Joseph Yserbyt) and his Brazilian wife (Lucia), near bus station, laundry facilities, English spoken, T 0243-711475, rec.; *Hotel Solar dos Gerânios*, Praça da Matriz, D, clean, friendly, good breakfast; *Estalagem Colonial*, Rua de Matriz 9, T 71-1626, D, clean, rec; *Posada Patitiba*, E, without bath or breakfast, basic, hot; *Tia Palminas*, opposite Entel caravan, G, basic.

Good **restaurants**, *Vagalume*; *Paulinho*, a "sort of shed" on the waterside, good, cheap churrascaria; cheaper places away from older centre. e.g. *Ceu de Boca*, good; *Couto Marquese*, good, cheap, but small portions. Snack bars, *Maré Alta*, *Sem Nome* (expensive).

There is a small Camping Club site on the fine Pontal beach, very crowded in January and February, and also a private camping site and a site next to the police station after the bridge, US$2 p.p. Apart from camping, very little cheap accommodation.

Tourist Information, Praça Chafariz.

Bus 7 a day to Rio (4 hrs., US$4.25) and to Angra dos Reis (1½ hrs., every 2 hrs., US$1.75); three a day to Ubatuba (70 km.), Taubaté (170 km.) and Guaratinguetá (210 km.); four a day to São Paulo (0930, 2230, 5½ hrs., US$5, booked up quickly) and São Sebastião.

The coast road continues from Parati into the State of São Paulo. Another road, rough but scenic, climbs the Serra do Mar to Cunha and Guaratinguetá, also in São Paulo.

ESPIRITO SANTO (3)

N of Campos (**see page** 310) is the State of Espírito Santo (pop. 2,429,000) with its capital at Vitória. The State has a mountainous interior and a hot, damp seaboard. It is an important grower of coffee. In the north there are large forests containing hardwoods. The people are known as Capixabas, after a former Indian tribe. Just across the frontier between the states is the resort town of **Marataizes**, with fair hotels and good beaches.

Hotels *Praia*, Av. Atlântica 99, on beach, D; *Saveiros Palace*, Av. Miramar 119, on beach, D; *Dona Judith*, Av. Lacerda de Aguiar 353, D; *Jona Balbina*, same street, No. 397, similar prices.

Camping Municipal site on Praia do Siri, 10 km. from centre; Xodó private site, Av. Atlântica, 2 km. from centre.

The main road N passes **Cachoeira do Itapemirim**, a busy city on both banks of the fast-flowing Rio Itapemirim; many hotels of all classes, a cheap one being *Planalto*, facing the river, E.

Further north, 58 km. south of Vitória, is **Guarapari**, whose beaches attract many people seeking cures for rheumatism, neuritis and other complaints, from the radioactive monazitic sands. Bus from Vitória, 1 hr., US$0.80. (Both Marataizes and Guarapari are very crowded mid-Dec. to end Feb.)

Hotels *Porto do Sol*, Mediterranean style village on rocky point overlooking a calm beach, pool, sauna, etc., A, rec., T 261-0011, Telex: (27) 3178; *Coronado*, Av. Lourival de Almeida 312, B, T 261-1709; *Hostess*, Rua Joaquim Silva Lima 701, B; *Atlántico*, Av. Edísio Cirne 332, T 261-1237 on beach, rec., D;

Camping Camping Clube do Brasil, Setiba beach, 9 km. from centre. Cambrás site off Vitória highway close to beach, 4 km. from centre. Private site near Cambrás site. Less crowded than Guarapari is Praia Iriri, 30 km. to the South, served by a regular bus; 2 beaches, beautiful setting, lodging in private houses is possible.

1 hour S of Guarapari, is Praia dos Castelhanos, near Anchieta (*Hotel Thanharu Praia*, good; *Restaurant Moacyr*, main courses US$2.75-4). Fishing/diving boat hire from Sr. Romildo, Peixaria do Onça (2 km. N of Anchieta) US$12 for 3 hrs., US$25 to Ilha dos Franceses.

There are coastal and inland road routes to **Vitória** (pop. 253,000) 509 km. from Rio de Janeiro, reached several times a day by plane (80 min.), and by bus (9 hrs.). Two bridges connect the island on which it stands with the mainland. The town is beautifully set, its entrance second only to Rio's, its beaches quite as attractive, but smaller, and the climate is less humid. On Avenida República is the huge Parque Moscoso, an oasis of quiet, with a lake, playground and tiny zoo. The Teatro Carlos Gomes, on Praça Costa Pereira, often presents plays, also jazz and folk festivals. The upper, older part of town, reached by steep streets and steps, is much less hectic than the lower harbour area which is beset by dreadful traffic problems. Vitória is a growing centre for the sport of sea fishing.

Its importance is due to its connection westwards with Minas Gerais by the Vitória-Minas railway, which transports for export millions of tons of iron ore and a large tonnage of coffee and timber. Ships drawing 11 metres and 240 metres in length can enter the port. A supplementary iron-ore port has been built at Ponta do Tubarão, near Vitória, to load ships up to 250,000 tons. These installations have led to some beach and air pollution at places near Vitória, such as Camburi (quite a pleasant beach, though, partly built up, palms, drink stands, fair surf).

See the fortified monastery of Nossa Senhora da Penha, on a high hill above the small settlement of Vila Velha. Most of the (unremarkable) structure, now in ruins, is of the 17th and 18th centuries; the views are superb. The Dutch attacked it in 1625 and 1640. Vila Velha has an excellent beach, but it is built up and noisy: take bus from Vitória marked Vilha Velha. A fine bridge has been built across the bay to Vila Velha; for bigger waves go to Barra do Jucu. Pleasant excursions in ferry-boats to Vila Velha.

Warning Robberies on the street are common. If you are robbed, yell "thief" or "*ladrão*" and give chase (if you think it safe to do so); most likely most of the street will join you and if the thief is caught he will receive a severe beating.

Hotels *Senac Hotel* (Government-run hotel school), luxurious, swimming pool, restaurant, guests attended by student staff, on the ocean at Rua Sete, 417 Ilha do Boi, B, T 227-3222; *Novotel*, Av. Adalberto Simão Nader 133, A, T 227-9422. *Helal*, Jerônimo Monteiro 935, B, T 222-2955; *São José*, Av. Princesa Isabel 300, C, T 223-7222; *Estoril*, Praça Pres. Roosevelt 532, D, a/c, some rooms overlook the port; *Vitória*, Cais de São Francisco 85, near Parque Moscoso, E with bath, excellent restaurant, changes money, good, clean; *Minister*, Av. Cleto Nunes, off Parque Moscoso, F; *Europa*, Sete de Setembro, corner of Praça Costa Pereira, F, clean, noisy but cheap, good value restaurant (nearby is a good value vegetarian restaurant and a money changer, ask at the hotel); *Catedral*, opp. Cathedral in upper part of city, E, clean; *Avenida*, Av. Florentino Avidos 350(ish) (T 223-4317/ 0770), E with breakfast, friendly, clean. Hotels located in beach areas, Camburi to the N, Vila Velha to the S, both about 15 mins. from city centre. *Walter*, across from Rodoviária, adequate, but *Lisboa*, opp. Rodoviária, is not rec.

Camping Serra Verde and Dalla's, private sites with some facilities, about 30 km. N of the city on Manguinhos beach.

Restaurants *São Pedro* (fish a speciality). *Trattoria Toscana*, Av. República and Cleto Nunes, by Parque Moscoso, on first floor, good food and service. *Acácia*, Cleto Nunes 273, good; *Mar e Terra* opp. Rodoviária, good food, live music at night; *Lavacar* and many others at Praia Camburi offer food and live music; *Lambahias* is a lively dancing place for the young, 1/2 km west of Bambini, buses each hour on the hour.

Banks Local banks. *Casa de Câmbio* at Vitur, Av. Getúlio Vargas, big ESCAL sign, next to *Bar Scandinave* (where moneychangers of a less trustworthy type can be found); Plumatur, Av. Governador Bley 465, Edif. Glória, Conj. 101, T 222-5955.

Cables Embratel, Palácio do Café, Praça Costa Pereira 52. Tel.:30914.

Tourist Information Emcatur, Av. Getúlio Vargas (corner of Av. Jerônimo Monteiro), and at Rodoviária (bus. station, friendly, good free map). Plumatur, Av. Governador Bley (first floor), tourist information, coffee and parallel exchange rate.

Roads (distances in km.): Belém, 3,075; Brasília, 1,238; Belo Horizonte, 541; Foz do Iguaçu, 2,002; Manaus, 4,489; Porto Alegre, 2,038; Recife, 1,948; Rio, 509; Salvador, 1,175; São Paulo, 932.

Buses Rodoviária is 15 mins.' walk from centre. Rio, 8 hrs., US$8. To hitch to Rio, take Itapemirim bus to Aracatiba (26 km). 5 buses a day to Campos, US$2.40 (Itapemirim), one to Macaé, 2330. Salvador, 18 hrs., US$16; Porto Seguro direct 11 hrs. with lots of stops (Agua Blanca, dep. 0900), US$8, *Leito* direct leaves 2100, alternatively, take bus to Eunápolis, then change buses which run every hour, US$1. To hitch to Salvador, take a bus to Sara, which is beyond Carapina; alight where the bus turns off to Sara. Diamantina, 51/2 hrs., US$5. To Ouro Preto, 2215 only, Thurs., US$5.50; to Belo Horizonte, by bus, 8 hrs., US$6. Daily to Porto Velho, 61 hrs.

Excursions Visit **Santa Leopoldina** or **Domingos Martins**, both around 45 km. from Vitória, less than an hour by bus (2 companies run to the former, approx. every 3 hrs.). Both villages preserve the architecture and customs of the first German and Swiss settlers who arrived in the 1840s. Domingos Martins (also known as Campinho) has a Casa de Cultura with some items of German settlement (Hotels *Campinho*, E, clean, breakfast, *Imperador*, 2 star, D). Santa Leopoldina has a most interesting museum (open Tues.-Sun., 0900-1100 and 1300-1800) covering the settlers' first years in the area, and a large number of fascinating constructions dating from the end of the last century showing Swiss and German influence.

To **Santa Teresa**, a charming hill town 21/2 hours by bus from Vitória, US$1.75 (beautiful journey). 2 hotels, *Pierazzo*, E, *Glebo*, G, clean, and many restaurants. There is a unique hummingbird sanctuary—difficult to visit. Also the **Nova Lombardia National Biological Reserve**. Previous permission must be obtained to visit from Instituto Brasileiro de Desenvolvimento Florestal, Av. Mal. Mascarenhas de Moraes 2487, CP 762, CEP 29.000, Bento Ferreira.

75 km. N of Vitória is the town of Aracruz. A whole new town is being built beside the impressive Scandinavian/Brazilian cellulose plant, surrounded by vast new eucalyptus forests.

136 km. N of Vitória is **Linhares**, on Rio Doce, with good hotels, for example *Linhares*, C, best in town; *Grande*, E, pleasant, and others; *Restaurant Mocambo*, good and cheap. Mid-way between Linhares and Vitória, 5 km. off BR-101 between Fundão and Ibiraçu, is a Zen Buddhist monastery. 84 km. N of Linhares is São Mateus, a pleasant town with no decent hotels (*Grande*, E, tiny, bad rooms), 13 km. from good beaches (buses). The **Comboios Biological Reserve**, just S of Linhares, is designed to protect the species of marine turtles which frequent this coast (for information, contact IBDF at address above). Similarly the **Sooretama Biological Reserve**, also in the vicinity of Linhares; this protects tropical Atlantic rain forest and its fauna and birds.

The most attractive beaches in the State are around **Conceição da Barra**, 242 km. N of Vitória. Basic hotels *Cricaré*; *Nanuque*; and *Rio Mar*, E. Camping Clube do Brasil site with full facilities. An interesting excursion is to Itaúnas, 21 km. up the coast; the small town has been swamped by sand dunes, so it has been moved to the opposite river bank. There is now a fantastic landscape of huge dunes and deserted beaches. A few pousadas and a small campsite can be found. Bus from the *padaria* in Conceição da Barra at 0700, returns 1700.

MINAS GERAIS (4)

The inland State of Minas Gerais (pop. 15,239,000) somewhat larger than France, is mountainous in the S, rising to the 2,787-metre peak of Agulhas Negras in the Mantiqueira range, and in the E, where there is the Caparaó National Park containing the Pico da Bandeira (2,890 metres). From Belo Horizonte north are undulating grazing lands, the richest of which are in the extreme W: a broad wedge of country between Goiás in the N and São Paulo in the S, known as the Triângulo Mineiro. Most of the upland is also good grazing country. Being frost-free, Minas Gerais is again becoming one of the main producers of coffee.

Minas Gerais was once described as having a heart of gold and a breast of iron. Half the mineral production of Brazil comes from the State, including most of the iron ore. Diamonds and gold are still found. Its exports move through Rio de Janeiro, Santos, Vitória and Angra dos Reis. The easy availability of power and the local agricultural and mineral production has created a large number of metal-working, textile, mineral water, food processing and timber industries.

There is much to interest the tourist: the old colonial cities built during the gold rush in the 18th century, some splendid caves, the Rio São Francisco in the N, and a number of fine spas and hill resorts. You can easily visit the colonial cities from Rio or Belo Horizonte; many companies provide tours. The chief glory of the colonial cities is the architecture and, even more, the sculpture of one of the world's great creative artists, Antônio Francisco Lisboa (1738-1814), the son of a Portuguese architect and a black slave woman. He is known as "O Aleijadinho" (the little cripple) because in later life he developed a maiming disease (possibly leprosy) which compelled him to work in a kneeling (and ultimately a recumbent) position with his hammer and chisel strapped to his wrists. His finest work, which shows a strength not usually associated with the plastic arts in the 18th century, is probably the set of statues in the gardens and sanctuary of the great Bom Jesus church in Congonhas do Campo, but the main body of his work is in Ouro Preto, with some important pieces in Sabará, São João del Rei and Mariana (see following pages).

We survey first the places on, or easily reached from, the Rio de Janeiro-Belo Horizonte highway, then the colonial cities of central Minas, then the outlying parts of the State. 129 km. north of Rio by air and 155 km. by road is the pleasant city of **Juiz de Fora** (pop. 350,000). It lies on the Paraibuna river, in a deep valley between the Mar and Mantiqueira mountain chains, at 640 metres. The Museum of Mariano Procópio is well worth a visit.

Industries Steel-making, textiles, brewing, timber sawing, sugar refining.

Hotels *Ritz* (best), *Barão do Rio Barras* 2000, T 212-7300, C; *Imperial*, Batista de Oliveira 605, T 212-7400, D, simple, but well run. Many hotels on Rua Getúlio Vargas of (our) category E: declining street numbers for Hotels *Glória* (good), *Transmontana*, *Hilton* (no relation), *Brasília*, *Mauá* and *Big. Picache*, opp. Rodoviária. Boarding houses (F) in side streets, e.g. Rua Marechal Deodoro, *Pensão Sulamericana* at No. 86, *Belo Horizonte* at No. 120..

Camping Camping Clube do Brasil site at Represa Dr. João Penido.

Bus Hourly from Rio 0600-2200, US$3, 3½ hrs. (spectacular trip), Belo Horizonte (many, US$5.50) and Petrópolis. Bus station outside town, Av. Brasil 3405.

From **Barbacena**, 103 km. on (with an important horse and cattle fair, and a rose festival in October), a paved road runs W to the colonial city of **São João del Rei** (pop. 75000), at the foot of the Serra do Lenheiro, with a fine bridge and three splendid 18th century churches: Pilar, the earliest, with rich altars and bright ceiling, and good *azulejos* in choir, and a sacristy with portraits of the Evangelists, new sacred art museum next door, entry US$0.10; São Francisco de Assis (1764), with exterior and interior sculptures by Aleijadinho (recent restoration has removed the plaster from the altars, revealing fine carving in

sucupira wood) and the Carmo, on the other side of the river, designed by him and with interior sculptures by him, recently very well restored, all in white. Near São Francisco is the tourist office in the house of Bárbara Heliodora (1759-1819), one of the Inconfidentes (**see page** 327), which also contains the municipal museum, whose chief treasure is a reputed portrait of Aleijadinho. The railway museum (see below) is well worth seeing. Museu da Arte Sacra, small but well recommended. There are also the Museu de Arte Regional do Patrimônio Histórico, in Praça Severiano (open Tues.-Sun., 1300-1600, US$0.25), and a pewter factory (with exhibition and shop) run by an Englishman, John Somers. Tourist office also in old bus station. A good view of the town and surroundings is from Alto da Boa Vista, where there is a Statue of Christ (Senhor dos Montes).

Festivals The morning masses on Sundays and religious festivals at São Francisco (0915) and Mercês (1030)—behind and above Pilar— are accompanied by choir and orchestra who maintain a tradition of over 200 years of local composition.

John Parsons writes: ***Tiradentes*** (originally São José del Rei; pop. 8,500). The centre of this charming little town, 15 km. from São João, with its nine streets and eight churches, at the foot of the green Serra São José, hardly belongs to this century. The Santo Antônio church, first built in 1710, contains some of the finest gilded wood carvings in the country and a small but fine organ brought from Oporto in the 1790s. The reconstructed façade is said to follow a design by Aleijadinho. There is also a sun-dial by him. Also of unusual interest and charm are the Rosário church, with fine statuary and ornate gilded altars; this and Nossa Senhora das Mercês have interesting painted ceilings and the latter a notable statue of the Virgin.

At the bottom of the stone paved road which descends from Santo Antônio is the fine fountain (*chafariz*), installed in 1749. The water is brought by a stone aqueduct from springs in the forest at the foot of Serra São José, which offers fine walks including the lane beside the aqueduct. The museum, housed where Padre Toledo (another Inconfidente) once lived, is of particular interest and there are some good pieces of furniture exhibited. The simple pilgrimage church of Santíssima Trindade is also well worth seeing. Tourist Office in the Prefeitura, Rua Resende Costa 71. See the artists' lithographic printing shop of Largo do Ó. There are attractive walks in the neighbourhood, and a 1½-hr. walk to the natural pools of Águas Santas.

Barbacena Hotel *Grogotó*, excellent, C; operated by Senac.

São João del Rei Hotels *Solar da Ponte*, A; *Novotel Porto Real*, Av. Eduardo Magalhães 254, T 371-1201, comfortable, B; *Lenheiro Palace*, Av. Pres. Tancredo Neves 257, T 371-3914, B/C, good; *Pousada do Sol*, C, 6km out on road to Tiradentes, T 371-1004; *do Espanhol*, R. Marechal Deodoro 131, C; cheap *pousadas* in same street; *Pousada Casarão*, opp. São Francisco church, C, converted mansion, Ribeíro Bastos 94, T 371-1224, swimming pool, delightful; *Colonial*, Manoel Anselmo 22, T 371-1792, D, clean and comfortable. *Pensão N.S. de Lourdes*, near bus station, F, meals US$1.10, good; *Pousada Ramón*, opp. bus station, F, good; *Brasil*, opposite railway station so back rooms much quieter, clean, friendly, cheap, E, rec., no breakfast (*Cafeteria Globo* in the same street, 2 blocks away, is good, though). *Hotel Porto Real* restaurant and *Restaurant Quinta do Ouro*, also good vegetarian restaurant, all rec. Good *Churrascaria* next to railway station.

Buses Rodoviária is 2 km. W of centre of São João. Direct buses to Rio leave 0800, 1600, 2330 Mon-Sat, 1600, 2215, 2350 Sun and hols, 5 hrs., US$4, São Paulo 8 hrs, and Belo Horizonte 3½ hrs.

Tiradentes Hotels *Solar da Ponte*, Praça das Mercês (prop. John and Anna Maria Parsons) T 032-355-1255, atmosphere of country house, A, including breakfast and tea, only 12 rooms. Fresh flowers in rooms, bar, sauna, garden, swimming pool, light meals for residents only, for larger meals, the hotel recommends five local restaurants listed below; also *Pousada Maria Barbosa*, Antônio Teixeira, Carvallio 134, T 355-1227, D, pool, very pleasant, *Hotel Wellerson*, T 355-1226, *Pousada Tiradentes*, E, *Hotel Ponto do Morro*, *Pousada de Laurit*, Direita 187, T 355-1268.

Restaurants Local food: *Quinta de Ouro*, rec.; *Estalagem*; *Padre Toledo*. Meat: *Thé*. Italian: *Donatelli*.

Recommended is the train trip between São João del Rei and Tiradentes (13 km.). The train has been in continuous operation since 1881, using the same locomotives and rolling stock, running on 76 cm. gauge track, all now lovingly restored and cared for. Maximum speed is 20 km. per hour. Price: US$1.20, one class only. Fri., Sat., Sun. and holiday steam train service to Tiradentes, 1000 and 1400, returning 1300 and 1700. Railway museum at the railway station in São João del Rei; open daily 0900-1200, 1330-1730; there are also a round house which has 16 vintage locomotives in supberb condition, an engine shed and a steam-operated machine shop, still working.

From Belo Horizonte, the shortest road to São João del Rei is via Lagoa Dourada. Just past Lagoa Dourada is the turning (12 km. on dirt road) for **Prados**, a small town 15 km. from Tiradentes known for its musical and handicrafts traditions. Near the turn is Entre Rios de Minas (*Hotel Camapuã*).

Belo Horizonte, the capital of Minas Gerais, is the third largest city in Brazil (pop. 2,120,000). It is situated over 800 metres above sea-level, surrounded by mountains, and enjoys an excellent climate (16°-30°C) except for the rainy season. It was Brazil's first modern planned city, founded 12 December 1897. Sights to be seen are the Praça da Assembléia, with three fine modern buildings: Legislative Assembly, church and Banco do Brasil; the Palácio da Liberdade, in Praça da Liberdade amid other fine *fin-de-siècle*-style public buildings (every Sun. morning and Thurs. evening an open-air craft market operates here—very good, also a flower market each Fri. from 1800 and an antique and occultism market each Sun.); the Palácio das Artes, Afonso Pena 1567, which is in the Parque Municipal and contains the Centro de Artesanato Mineiro (craft shop open 0900-1700, Tues.-Sun.); the Museu Mineiro, Av. João Pinheiro, 342 in old Senate building near centre (open Tues., Wed., Fri. 1230-1830, Thur. 1500-2100, Sat., Sun. 1000-1600); the City Museum; the Museum of Mineralogy, Rua da Bahia 1149, a Gothic building near the park, with interesting exhibits (open Mon.-Sat., 0830-1730, entrance free); the Museu Histórico Abílio Barreto, R. Bernado Mascarenhas, in an old *fazenda* house which is the last reminder of Belo Horizonte's predecessor, the village of Arraial do Curral d'el Rey, built by João Leite da Silva Ortiz in the 18th century, with most interesting historical exhibits (open 1000-1700 Wed.-Mon, take bus 2902 from Av. Pena); the Museu do Telefone, Av. Afonso Pena 1180 (open Mon.-Fri., 0900-1800, Sun., 0900-1300); the railway station, with museum on 2nd floor showing a model railway and the railway headquarters in a mansion on the hill above the station, with locomotive and railway coach used by Dom Pedro II; the Municipal Park (an oasis of green, right in the centre of the city, small amusement park and playground, not too safe at night). Museo Histórico Natural, in the Instituto Agronómico, Rua Gustavo da Silveira 1035, T 461-7666, has a local geological and palaeontological display and good archaeological exhibits (take bus 3803A from Praça Rio Branco). An obelisk in Praca Sete de Setembro commemorates Independence, it is the centre for political protest.

Eight km. from the centre is the picturesque suburb of Pampulha, famous for its modern buildings and the artificial lake (many infestations, do not swim in it), many buildings designed by the renowned Brazilian architect Oscar Niemeyer (who later designed much of Brasília); in Pampulha the glass and marble Museum of Modern Art may be visited (Av. Octacílio Negrão de Lima, open 0800-1800 daily, reported disappointing), as well as the Chapel of São Francisco (the interior of which was decorated by the Brazilian painter Cândido Portinári). There is a bus (not the 4403) from the city centre to the Jardim Zoológico (at the far end of the lake from the dam—small selection of birds with some rarities, animals well kept for the most part) that passes the chapel and also the Mineirão stadium about ¾ km. away (see below); bus 2004 goes from Av. Afonso Pena to the chapel.

In the southern zone of the city, on the Serra do Curral, the Parque de Mangabeiras has a good view of the city, forest trails, sports facilities and snack bars. The natural amphitheatre where the Pope spoke in 1982 is nearby; there is an iron monument marking the occasion (take bus 2001 from Afonso Pena between Av. Amazonas and Rua Tamóios). In 1984, the Minascentro, a convention centre for exhibitions and congresses, was opened in the city centre. The huge Mineirão stadium is the second largest in Brazil after the Maracanã stadium in Rio. Belo Horizonte is one of the fastest growing of Brazil's main cities; atmospheric pollution has recently been reported.

The industrial area, about 10 km. from the centre, has now become the third largest industrial centre of Brazil, and apart from being the traditional centre of mining and agricultural industries (as well as diamond cutting and precious stones), it has steelworks and an automobile industry. The city has a good public transport system (red buses serve central and express routes, yellow circular routes, and blue diagonal routes), and taxis are plentiful, although hard to find at peak hours.

Local Holidays Maundy Thursday; Corpus Christi; 15 August (Assumption); 8 December (Immaculate Conception).

Electric Current 120-220 A.C. 60 cycles.

Hotels (number of stars in brackets) *Othon Palace* (5), Av. Afonso Pena 1050, T 226-7844, L, deluxe, best, rec.; *Brasilton* (4), out of town at km. 3.65 on Rodovia Fernão Dias, Contagem, L, very good restaurant; *Real Palace* (4), R. Espírito Santo 904, T 224-2111, A; *Internacional Plaza Palace* (3), R. Rio de Janeiro 109, T 201-2300, A, good but seedy part of town; *Boulevard Plaza* (3), Av. Getúlio Vargas 1640, Savassi district (chic), A, T 223-9000, very nice; *Wembley Palace* (3), Rua Espírito Santo 201, T 201-6966, A, excellent, central, clean, but poor rate for travellers' cheques; *Del Rey* (4), Praça Afonso Arinos 60, A; *Normandie* (3), Rua Tamóios 212, B, excellent grill; *Serrana Palace* (3), Rua Goitacases 450, B, pleasant restaurant but hotel rather run down, seedy area; *Estoril*, Rua Carijós 454, C with bath, comfortable, pleasant; *Ambassy* (3), Rua Caetés 633, near bus station, D, helpful, English spoken, clean, a/c, noisy, good restaurant; *Itatiaia* (2), Praça Rui Barbosa 187, D, near railway station, central, clean, a/c with bath and good breakfast; *Esplanada* (2), Av. Santos Dumont 304, D (E without bath), clean, good restaurant, own garage; *Sul América Palace* (2), Av. Amazonas 50, D, clean, friendly, TV and fridge in rooms, warmly rec.; *Paraná*, Av. Paraná 437 (T 222-3472), D, with shower, clean, noisy at weekends from discothèque; *Casa dos Municípios*, Rua Rio Grande do Norte 1017, Funcionários (in Savassi, chic shopping area), T 226-5177, clean, inexpensive; *Continental* (2), Av. Paraná 241, D, central, clean, friendly; *Minas*, Rua São Paulo 331, D, friendly, rec.; *Dom Pedro II*, R. Curitiba 248, E, clean, rather faded; same street, No. 224, E without bath, good. Cheaper places are: *Magnata*, Rua Guarani 124, F, with breakfast, near bus station, cheap and clean, bath, good hot shower, safe dposit, rec.; near bus station and in Rua Curitiba many hotels are for very-short-stay couples; *Pensão Rodoviária* and away from traffic, *Pensão Nova Rodoviária*, Rua 21 de Abril 89, E, a bit dubious, basic, and many others; *Pensão N.S. Aparecida*, Av. de Fátima 1320 (near Rodoviária), E, basic, friendly but noisy. Within 10 mins. walk of Rodoviária: Rua Espírito Santo, No. 284, *Majestic*, E; No. 227, *São Salvador*, E; No. 237, *Magalhães*, F, basic, clean, friendly, cheap laundry service, good restaurant over the road; *Lux*, No. 220; Rua dos Caetés, *Solar*, No. 265. You may spend the night in the bus station only if you have an onward ticket (police check at midnight); area round bus station said to be dangerous. *Dona Carolina*, Rua dos Timbiras 1969, unsigned, in centre, 20 mins.' walk from Rodoviária F p.p. per day with full board, most residents are students, good atmosphere and food. Youth hostel, *Pousadinha Mineira*, Rua Araxá 514, Bairro Colégio Batista, 31.110 Belo Horizonte, T 442-2049/444-8205.

Camping Wild camping near Alto do Palácio, near river and waterfalls.

Restaurants *Tavares*, Rua Santa Catarina 64 (local dishes), excellent value. Chinese: *Yun Ton*, R. Santa Catarina 946, rec.; Churrascarias: *Carretão Guaiba*, Av. do Contorno 8412; *Rodeio*, Av. do Contorno 8222; *Farrounilha*, Afonso Pena 3300; *Picanha na Tábua*, Rua Curitiba, unprepossessing but highly rec.; *Chico Mineiro*, Rua Alagoas, corner of Av. Brasil, local chicken specialities, good, closed Sun.; *Santa Felicidade*, Rua Dr. Morais, good; *Arroz com Feijão*, typical food, Av. Contorno 6510, Av. Contorno 7438 and R. Antônio de Albuquerque 440, all friendly, reasonably-priced; *Martini*, Rua Curitiba, and *Pizzaiolo*, Av. Contorno 8495, good for pizzas. *Tokyo* (Japanese), R. Guajajaras 909; *Ninho*, (Chinese), Rua São Paulo 1271, Centro, cheap, good; *Via Natural, No. 1*, Av. Afonso Pena 941, vegetarian, open till 2200 (except 2000 on Sun.), *No. 2*, Av. Andradas 367; *O Armazem*, Rua Alagoas 1468, also vegetarian, as is *Alquima Mercearia*, Rua Tomé de Souza 855, and *Folhas*, same street, No. 503; *Superbom* (vegetarian), R. São Paulo, 971, 1100-1500, Mon. to Fri. *Casa do Ouvidor*, near central square highly rec. but expensive. *Degrau*, Av. Afonso Pena 4221, excellent restaurant and bar, very pleasant; *Giovanni*, Av. Afonso Pena opposite park, good Italian; *Pinho's*, Rua Pouso Alto 740, set high above the city, tremendous views by day or night, can be very busy on Fri. and Sat.; *Mangueiras*, at Pampulha, next to Niemeyer chapel of São Francisco, very popular; *Dona Derna*, behind the Palácio de Liberdade, highly rec.; *Buona Távola*, R. Alagoas 777, Savassi, excellent Italian; *Cantina do Ângelo* (Italian), Rua Tupinambás 267, rec., and in same street, No.253, *Torino* (Italian excellent, huge and varied menu, also at Guajajaras 460), and *Alpino* (German), same street, No. 173, both good value and popular, corned beef and fresh boiled vegetables available, open-air; *Flor de Líbano*, opposite *Hotel Magalhães* at Espírito Santo 234, cheap and good; *Quibelândia*, Rua dos Caetés 188, good. *Mister Beef*, Rua Gonçalves Dias, American-style, rec. Good snack bar at corner of Av. Afonso Pena and Rua Bahia, *Doce D'Ocê*, Av. Afonso Pena 2712, also *Formula 1*, Galeria Praça 7, Rua Rio de Janeiro. We are told that the splendid Minas typical dishes are more authentic— and more toothsome—outside Belo Horizonte.

Tea rooms   *Era Una Vez Un Chalezinho*, Rua Paraíba 1455; *Tia Clara*, Rua Antônio de Albuquerque 617.

Shopping   Mercado Central, Av. Aug. de Lima 744, large and clean, open every day, Saturday social centre. Market for fruit, vegetables, meat and other items at corner of Rua Santa Catarina and Av. Amazonas (near Praça Raúl Soares). There are huge hypermarkets just outside the city on the highways to Rio and to São Paulo. Splendid delicatessen with foreign food and wines—and liquors—*Au Bon Gourmet*, Rua Tupinambás 187. For gemstones, try *Manoel Bernardes*, Rua Espírito Santo 835, very reasonable, ask for US saleswoman Manuela, who can arrange tours of workshops; *Gem Centre*, Av Alvares Cabral 45, good prices and selection, rec; "Hippie fair" Thurs. evenings and Sundays in Praça da Liberdade; Food and Antique fair, Praça da Independência, Sats, good home-made food; other fairs on Fri. and Sat. Belo is said to be very good for slide film, cheese and chocolate.

Bookshop   *Daniel Vaitsman*, Rua Espírito Santo 466, 17th floor, for English language books. Foreign language books at *Livraria Van Damme*, Rua das Guajajaras 505, also good local and Portuguese selection (and said to change travellers' cheques). Used foreign-language books at *Livraria Alfarrábio*, Rua Tamóios 320.

Nightlife   *Drosophila*, R. Ouro Preto, Bairro Preto, bar, dancing; *The Great Brasilien Disaster*, R. Tomé, Bairro Savass; funk, dancing; *Angelas Buffet*, R. Tomé, street café; *A Vida*, Av. Getúlio Vargas, bar, dancing.

Exchange   Lloyds Bank Av. João Pinheiro 580; Citibank, Rua Espírito Santo 871; Banco do Brasil, Rua Rio de Janeiro 750; Banco Econômico, Rua Bahia 360, 9th floor, and other local banks, 1000-1630. American Express, Kontik-Franstur, Rua Espírito Santo 1204, T 273-1288. Exchange: H. Pichiommi, Rua Espirito Santo and Rua Guajajanas. Nascente Turismo, Rio de Janeiro 1101, T 224-3334, ask for Luiz Carlos de Oliveira, changes money at a good rate.

Consulates   **British Vice-Consulate**: Av. Afonso Pena 952, s. 500, Caixa Postal 576, T 222-6318; **W. German**, R. Carijós 244; **Austrian**; Rua José Américo Cancado Bahia 199, T 33 33 622. **US**, Av. Cristovão Colombo 400, 1st floor, T 224-9339; **French**, R. Prof Antônio Aleixo 843, 5th Floor, T335-5563; **Italian**, Praça Carlos Chagas 49, 2nd floor, T 335-5394; **Netherlands**, R. Paraíba 1122, 20th floor, T 273-4477; **Denmark**, R. Prof. Jerson Martins 166, T 441-4755.

Churches   Synagoga Beth Yacou, R. Pernambuco 326, T 2246013; Catholic Church, Av. Antônio Carlos 2747, T 442-7743, Rua Bahia 1596, T 222-6059; Presbyterian Church, R. Ceará 1434, T 226-1844; Baptist Church, R. Joaquim de Fiqueredo 332, T 384-1322; Mormon Church, R. Levindo Lopes 214, T 233-7883; Adventist Church, R. Timbras 683, T 226-6144.

Hospital   Mater Dei, Rua Gonçalves Dias 2700, T 335-2200, has been rec.

Post Office   with poste restante, Av. Afonso Pena 1270.

Tourist Information   Turminas, Av. do Contorno 8471; Praça Sete de Setembro; at Rodoviária (particularly polyglot, reasonable free map of centre) ask for the Guia Turistico for events, opening times etc, railway station, airport (very helpful). Touring Club do Brasil.

Travel Agent   *Focus Tours*, R.Grão Mogol 502, in Sion district, T (031) 223-0358, telex (031) 3823 RAPT, run by Douglas and Nancy Trent, offer specialized tours all over Brazil and have a special interest in ecology and tours to the Pantanal. Tours in Minas to see a great variety of wildlife. Reliable information and a portion of their profits is used for conservation project in Brazil. *Mangabeira Turismo*, R. Goitcazes 71-8° andar, and *Unitour*, Av. Tupis 141, organize river trips on the São Francisco (**see page** 332).

Roads (distances in km.): Belém, 2,827; Brasília, 747; Foz do Iguaçu, 1,663; Manaus, 3,948; Porto Alegre, 1,709; Recife, 2,137; Rio, 426; Salvador, 1,355; São Paulo, 588; Vitória, 541.

Buses Rodoviária is by Praça Rio Branco at end of Av. Afonso Pena (left-luggage lockers, attended service 0700-2200). To Rio, 7 hrs., US$8 (ordinary), *leito*, US$16; to Brasília, 12 hrs., 9 a day incl. 2 *leitos*, only one leaves in daylight (0800), US$12, *leito* US$24; to Ouro Preto, 2 hrs., US$0.80, several daily (buy ticket well in advance); to Mariana (via Ouro Preto), 2¼ hrs., US$1; to Congonhas do Campo, 1½ hrs., US$0.75. To Sabará, US$0.30, ½ hr., from separate part of Rodoviária from main departure hall. To São Paulo, 10 hrs., US$10; route passes the great Furnas reservoir. To Salvador US$29, 22 hrs., at 1800 and 1900 daily. **For Porto Seguro** take Gontijo bus to Nanuque, then Rio Doce bus to Eunápolis, then Espresso São Jorge to Porto Seguro, tickets may be booked through Belo, road poor in places, total time 22 hrs., US$18. To Aracaju, US$12, 29 hrs; to Recife, US$32; to Belém, US$48. To Cuiabá, Expresso São Luiz, 0800 and 2000 daily, 26 hrs., US$25; to Vitória, 8 hrs., US$6. To Campo Grande 2000, with Gontigo, a good route to Bolivia, avoiding São Paulo.

Train Railway station is at Praça Rui Barbosa. Trains leave Friday and Sunday at 1230 (the Vera Cruz) for Rio de Janeiro: cabin for two costs US$27 single fare. There are no trains to São Paulo or Brasília. No passenger train to Vitória.

Airport A new international airport near Lagoa Santa, at Confins, 39 km. from Belo Horizonte, has been opened. Taxi to centre, US$12; airport bus, either *executivo* from the exit, or comfortable normal bus from far end of car park every hour on the half-hour, US$1. From centre, catch bus at Terminal Turístico JK, R. Olegário Maciel and R. Guajajaras.

Hitch-hiking to Rio or Ouro Preto, take a bus marked "Shopping", to the shopping centre above Belo Horizonte on the Rio road.

Excursions Within easy motoring distance from Belo Horizonte are several of the 400 caves and grottoes for which Minas Gerais is famous. The best and most famous is the Gruta de Maquiné with 7 chambers, well lit, with guides, but hot—26°C, 126 km. NW of Belo (well signposted and with restaurants nearby, bus at 0915, return at 1500, 2¼ hrs., US$2. In the nearby town of Cordisburgo is a museum to the writer Guimarães Rosa. The Gruta de Lapinha, almost as good, is only 51 km. N of the city (entrance to caves and small museum, US$0.30; bus at 0930, 1130 and others, via Pampulha, return 1230, 1600, 1¼hr., US$0.75 one way—don't alight at Lapinha bus station, it's 6 km. before the cave). Lapinha cave is closed Mon.

10 km. before Lapinha is the town of **Lagoa Santa**, a weekend resort for Belo Horizonte. The sandy beach on the lake (close to the town centre and bus station) is used for fishing, sun-bathing and boating (do not swim, the water is infected with schistosomiasis). Along the beach are bars and restaurants, with more in the nearby main square which also has two small hotels and an interesting modernistic church. The road to Belo Horizonte (half-hourly bus service, US$0.75) passes Belo Horizonte's new international airport. Bus Lagoa Santa-Lapinha every half hour.

To the NE of the city, a few km. off the BR-262, is the Serra de Piedade, a high peak giving spectacular views over the surrounding countryside. A popular excursion point but only accessible by car or special bus service. There are a small chapel and a *churrascaria*. From the peak can be seen the small town of **Caeté**, which has one or two interesting churches and the remains of an old ironworks near the railway station. Take the Conceição do Mato Dentro bus to Alto do Palácio; near there are waterfalls and campsites. Further from Belo, turn off the BR-262 (towards Vitória) at km. 73 and go via Barão de Cocais and Brumal to Caraçá (120 km.), where the monastery has been converted into a hotel (C), the site and region highly recommended. Reservations through Instituto São Vicente in Belo, T 031-441-5399. It is possible to stay in Santa Barbara, *Hotel Karaibe*, E; *Sta Inés*, F, 25 km. away on the road to Mariana and hitch-hike to Caraçá.

From Belo Horizonte, excursions can be made to Nova Lima and the picturesque colonial cities described in the following pages. If short of time, Ouro Preto and Congonhas are the most outstanding. The road follows the Rio das Velhas in which, at points, one can see the *garimpeiros* waist-deep washing for gold.

Nova Lima, (pop 47,000) about 27 km. SE of Belo by a good road, is set in eucalyptus forests. Its houses are grouped round the gold mine of Morro Velho, opened by a British firm in 1834 but sold to Brazilians in 1959, the deepest mine in the Americas. The shaft has followed a rich vein of gold down to 2,591 metres. There are interesting carvings by Aleijadinho, recovered from elsewhere, in the (modern) parish church.

A paved road branching off the Belo Horizonte-Brasília highway leads (30 km., ½-hr.) to the colonial gold-mining (and steel-making) town of Sabará. Return by the old road over the mountain range of Serra do Curral for fine views. There is also a railway: 3 trains a day between Belo and Sabará, taking one hour.

Sabará (pop. 74,000) is strung along the narrow steep valleys of the Rio das Velhas and Rio Sabará. Its old churches and fountains, its rambling cobbled streets, its simple houses with their carved doors, and its museum of 18th century gold mining in the Intendência de Ouro (built 1732, open 1200-1700 Tues.-Fri.) are of great interest. The churches are so spread out that a taxi is advisable if you wish to see them all. Very few places to stay.

Passeio a Sabará, by Lúcia Machado de Almeida, with splendid illustrations by Guignard, is an excellent guide to the place. The main sights are the Prefeitura, in Rua Pedro II, an old mansion, with oratory and main reception room (*salão nobre*) to be seen; the Imperial Theatre (1770, restored 1960) in the same street, for its fine interior; the Casa Azul, in the same street, for its portal; the Churches of Nossa Senhora do Carmo (1774), with doorway, pulpits and choirloft by Aleijadinho and paintings by Athayde; Nossa Senhora do Rosário dos Pretos (left unfinished at the time of the slaves' emancipation); São Francisco; Nossa Senhora da Conceição (1720) with much gilding, and paintings by 23 Chinese artists brought from Macau; and, last of all, Nossa Senhora do O, built in 1698 and showing unmistakable Chinese influence (paintings much in need of restoration), 2 km. from the centre of the town (take local bus marked "Esplanada"). Also the fountains of Kaquende (1757), and Rosário.

Hotel: *Pensão Bobagato*, above an art gallery, E, or ask for Senhor Sérgio at the Sports Centre, he may have accommodation. **Restaurants**: *O Quinto do Ouro*, close to the bus station; *314*, Comendador Viana 314, near main praça; *Imperial Restaurant/Pizzaria*, in Rua Pedro II.

At 27 km. S along the Belo Horizonte-Rio de Janeiro highway a 68 km. road, the Rodovia dos Inconfidentes, branches off to Ouro Preto. On the way (48 km.) it passes Cachoeira do Campo, which was the centre of the regional mining administration in colonial times: now a sleepy, unspoilt village.

Ouro Preto (pop 61,400), the famous former capital of the State, was founded in 1711. There is a famous School of Mining (Escola Minas), founded in 1876, in the fortress-like Governor's Palace (1742), facing the main square (Praça Tiradentes); it has the interesting Museo de Mineralogia e das Pedras, a must, US$0.35, the only one open on Mondays (1200-1700), but closed Sundays. Opposite the Palace, next to Carmo Church, is the Museu da Inconfidência, a fine historical and art museum which has some drawings by Aleijadinho and the Sala Manoel da Costa Athaíde, in an annex; the building, begun in the eighteenth century, has been a prison and also the local chamber of commerce (open 1200-1730, entry, US$0.45). See the Casa das Contas, now also a museum (open 1230-1700), Sun 0800-1300. Another museum, the Casa Guignard, on Rua Conde de Bobadela, displays the paintings of Alberto da Veiga Guignard, open Tues-Sat 0900-1700, Sun 1200-1700, free. Buy soapstone carvings at roadside stalls and bus stops rather than in the cities; they are much cheaper. (However, gems are not much cheaper from freelance sellers in the square than from the shops around the square, and in the shops themselves, the same quality of stone is offered at the same price—Brasil Gemas and De Bernard are recommended.)

The city, built on rocky ground 1,000 metres above sea-level (cold and wet Oct.-Feb.) was declared a national monument in 1933. Its cobbled streets wind up and down steep hills crowned with 13 churches. Mansions, fountains, churches, vistas of terraced gardens, ruins, towers shining with coloured tiles, all blend together to maintain a delightful 18th century atmosphere.

Ouro Preto displays many superb baroque carvings, in wood and in soapstone, of the sculptor Aleijadinho. The church of São Francisco de Assis and the façade of the Carmo church are his work, and so are the two pulpits in the church of São Francisco, and much else.

In the **Praça de Independência** there is a statue of José Joaquim da Silva Xavier, known as Tiradentes, leader of the **Inconfidentes** (unsuccessful revolutionaries of 1789), and regarded in Brazil as the precursor of independence. Another Inconfidente, the poet Tomás Antônio Gonzaga (whose house is close to São Francisco de Assis), was exiled to Africa. (Most Brazilians know his poem based on his forbidden love affair; visitors are shown the bridge and decorative fountain where the lovers held their trysts.) On 24 June of each year Ouro Preto again becomes, for that day only, the capital of the state of Minas Gerais.

Churches The following churches are all closed Mon., but are open at following times on other days: Santa Efigênia (1720, decorated with gold dust washed out of slaves' hair), Padre Faria, 0800-1200; Francisco de Assis, N.S. Conceição, 0800-1130, 1300-1700 (under restoration 1988/89); Senhor Bom Jesus, N.S. Carmo, 0800-1130, 1300-1700 (being restored 1989); N.S. Pilar (1733, heavily gilded work of Aleijadinho's father, Manuel Lisboa), Rosário, 1200-1700; das Mercês e Perdões, are open in afternoons only. The Antônio Dias parish church, Nossa Senhora da Conceição (1722), heavily gilded, contains Aleijadinho's tomb, and a museum devoted to him, Aleijadinho Paróquia, 0800-1130, 1300-1700. At least two days are needed to see them all; the tourist office on Praça Tiradentes (opens 0800, Portuguese only spoken) and the hotels offer a leaflet showing the opening times; also sells good map for US$0.80. Most of the churches now charge for admission, usually about US$0.45. Shorts may not be worn in churches.

The mid-18th century paintings by Mestre Athayde (1732-1827), to be seen in S. F. de Assis, Sta. Ifigênia and elsewhere, are of particular interest: the pigments were obtained from local iron ore and from forest fruits. They are also very fine artistically; he was a worthy colleague of Aleijadinho.

N.B. In most churches and museums, tourists' handbags and cameras are taken at the entrance and guarded in lockers.

Ouro Preto is famous for its Holy Week processions, which in fact begin on the Thursday before Palm Sunday and continue (but not every day) until Easter Sunday. The most famous is that commemorating Christ's removal from the Cross, late on Good Friday. This is very much a holiday period and many shops are shut—as indeed they are on winter weekends. Carnival is also memorable, with samba and happenings in the streets.

Hotels Grande, Rua Sen. Rocha 164, T 551-1488, largest hotel in town and the only modern structure, designed by Oscar Niemeyer, B, not well kept; **Pouso Chico Rei**, a fascinating old house with Portuguese colonial furnishings, very small and utterly delightful, book in advance, Rua Brig. Mosqueira 90, C, T 551-1274 (room No. 6 has been described as a "dream"); **Pousada do Mondego**, A, Largo de Coimbra 38, T 551-2040, beautifully kept colonial house, rec.; **Luxor Pousada**, Praça Antônio Dias 10, converted colonial mansion, no twin beds, friendly, clean, comfortable, T 551-2244, reservations in Rio, T 256-2680, B, restaurant good; **Hospedária Antiga**, Rua Xavier da Veiga 3, T 551-2203, a restored colonial house, reasonable rates, friendly, rec.; **Estrada Real**, 8 km. outside city, good but often fully-booked, T 551-2122; **Pousada e Galeria Panorama Barroco**, Rua Conselheiro Quintiliano 722, fine views, T (031)551-3366, E (F p.p. without bath), with good breakfast, restored house with antique furniture, art gallery, music, videos, bulletin board for local events, reservations made, excursions organized, run by David and Lucia Peterkin (US/Brazilian), exceptionally friendly and helpful, rec.; **Solar das Lajes**, Rua Conselheiro Quintiliano 604 (T 551-3388), C with bath, a little way from centre, excellent view, being extended, friendly and well run; **Pilão**, Praça Tiradentes 51, on main square, T 551-3066, D, noisy; **Pousada dos Bandierantes**, Rua das Mercês 167, D, clean, beautiful views, rec.; **Colonial**, Rua Camilo Veloso 26, D; T 551-3133; **Tófolo**, São José 76, near Contas fountain, D, cheaper rooms available, reasonable, sometimes overcharges, so pay in advance; **Pousada Ouro Preto**, Largo Musicista José dos Anjos Costa 72, T 551-3081, 4/5 rooms, E, clean, laundry facilities, hot showers, English spoken by owner, **Gérson Luís Cotta** (most helpful), rec.; at No. 26, same sheet, Rosana lets rooms, basic, clean, friendly, clothes washing, G; **Pensão** at Rua Coronel Alves 2, T 551-2393, clean reasonable, friendly; **Conde**, Rua Direita, D, old furniture, clean, rec.; **Miranda**, same street, E, shared bath. clean; **N. S. Aparecida**, Praça Cesário Alvim 21, T 551-1091, E, better rooms good, cheaper rooms without bath, restaurant cheap. **Pousada dos Inconfidentes**, Felipe dos Santos 31, E; same street, No. 241, **Pousada Ciclo do Ouro** (T 581-3201/2210), F, clean, laundry facilities, rec. Try **pensões** in Ruas Randolpho Bretas,

Getúlio Vargas, Paraná *(Pensão da Conceição*, E, Paraná 137, has been rec.), also *Vermelha Dormitório*, Praça São Francisco de Assis 30, T 551-1138, quiet, shared shower), E. *Residencia de Doña Iva*, simple and friendly but noisy, D. Also try *casas de família*, reasonably-priced, but more expensive if booked through tourist office. Difficult to get hotel rooms at weekends and holiday periods; a good idea to telephone ahead. A number of travellers have rec. staying in Mariana where hotels are cheaper; two buses an hour to Ouro Preto.

Students may be able to stay, during holidays and weekends, at the self-governing student hostels, known as *repúblicas*, for about US$2 a night (e.g. *República Vaticana*, Rua das Mercês 198, or *Pif-Paf*, in front of the Pilar church, *Tabu*, on road with main Post Office, or *Serigy*). Many are closed between Christmas and Carnival. Enquire at the city's tourist office.

Camping Camping Clube do Brasil, 2 km. N of city, is quite expensive but very nice. Do not camp beside the waterfall, Cachoeira dos Andorinhas, 1½ hrs. walk from city; there have been robberies there. Also a site reached by car up a very steep hill at the top end of town: about 5 km. Also at picnic site 4 km. west of Ouro Preto, and at Rio Acima nearby.

Restaurants *Calabouço*, good, Conde de Bobadela 132, with an antique shop; *Sobrenatural* on the same road, rec.; *Pilão*, in main square (local painters), and good rooms above; *Quinta do Ouro*, Rua Camilo de Brito 21, good, a bit pricey, avoid window seats, rec.; also *Pelique*, US$2 prato do dia rec., another branch at Rua São José 131, no sign; opposite *Pelique* is *Chalet*, warmly rec. *Chafariz*, Rua São José 167, good local food; *Casa Grande* (watch your belongings) and *Forno de Barro*, both on Praça Tiradentes, good local dishes; *Casa do Ouvidor*, Conde de Bobadela 42, above De Bernardis jewellery shop (good), near main square, good. On same street, *Chicken Inn*, No. 40, *Taberna La Luna* (very friendly), No. 138, good and cheap. *Chelvo Verde*, Rua Getúlio Vargas 250 (nr. Rosário church), good vegetarian and other dishes, pleasant, quite cheap. *Bar Tropical*, near *Hotel N.S. Aparecida*, cheap. Cheap *lanchonetes* on opposite side of square to *Hotel Pilão*. Excellent sandwich bar, good breakfast at *lanchonete* on corner of São José and Getúlio Vargas. Tea shop. Students may be able to eat at the School of Mining on Praça Tiradentes. Try the local licor de jaboticaba.

Electric Current 110 volts A.C.

Exchange arranged through Amsterdam Sauer jewellers on main square.

Post Office on Rua Direita, opp. *Hotel Miranda*.

Tourist Office Praça Tiradentes 41, helpful. Enquire here for details of accommodation in *casas de família*, *repúblicas* and other forms. Note, though, that foreigners are expected to want expensive hotels. It shows filmstrips at 0900, 1200 and 1600 on weekdays, 0930, 1030, 1300, 1500, 1600 at weekends and holidays. The tourist office at the bus station is helpful, Portuguese only, map US$0.50.

Guides Bandeira's *Guia de Ouro Preto* in Portuguese and English (US$3.50 with coloured map, US$1 with black and white one), normally available at Tourist Office. Also available is Lucia Machado de Almeida's *Passeio a Ouro Preto*, US$6 (in Portuguese, English and French). A local guide for a day costs about US$3, Associação de Guias de Turismo, T 551-2655. (US$10 if obtained through Tourist Office). Ourotur runs a tour of Ouro Preto in a vintage-style bus for US$5, 0900 and 1430, from the bus station (T 551-2764).

Transport An early plane from Rio to Belo Horizonte and a bus (11 a day) gets to Ouro Preto by lunch (2 hrs.); bus fare, each way, US$0.80. Day trips are run; alternatively take bus from Rio, for example Util at 0830 and 2330 (US$5, 9 hrs), return bus to Rio leaves at same times. There is a new bus station (Rodoviária) at Ouro Preto, above the town near the São Francisco de Paula church. Book your return journey to Belo Horizonte early if returning in the evening; buses get crowded. There are also buses to Conselheiro Lafaiete for connections to Belo Horizonte and Congonhas, and direct to Congonhas at 1400 and 1530, or to Rio via Barbacena and Juiz de Fora (direct bus to Rio is often fully booked 2-3 days in advance). Direct bus Ouro Preto to Vitória at 2100, US$5.50, 5½ hrs., not daily. Direct bus to São Paulo, 1900, 11 hrs., US$10.50. Check that your bus ticket from Ouro Preto is in fact from Ouro Preto and not from Belo Horizonte. Two buses an hour to Mariana (20 mins.). A vintage tourist train, the Trem dos Inconfidentes, leaves Ouro Preto for Mariana 0900 Sat. and Sun., returning at 1600, US$2.50. Hitch-hiking to Mariana is said to be easy, start in Praça Tiradentes.

Mariana (pop. 34,000, 697 metres above sea level), another old mining city, founded 1696, much less hilly than Ouro Preto, is 12 km. E of Ouro Preto on a road which goes on to join the Rio-Salvador highway. See the beautiful old prison (Cadeia, 1768, now the Prefeitura Municipal, closed for restoration in 1988); the Carmo church (1784, steatite carvings, Athayde paintings, chinoiserie panelling), next to it is the fine São Francisco church (1762, granite painted to look like marble, pulpits designed by Aleijadinho, Athayde paintings and tomb, fine sacristy, one side-altar by Aleijadinho, entry, US$0.15) and the old Palace of the Governors connected with it; the Museum (formerly the Bishop's Palace) for its church furniture, gold and silver collection, Aleijadinho statues and ivory cross (open 0900-1100 except Tues. and 1200-1700; entrance US$0.80, good guide book), Capela de Santo Antônio, wonderfully simple and the oldest; the city hall and the former post office, once a mansion. The Cathedral, Basílica de NS da Assunção, built 1711-1760, has been reopened, after repairs (entry US$0.15). Between the old prison and São Francisco is a stone monument to Justice, at which slaves used to be beaten. The house of the poet Afonso de Guimarães (buried behind the Igreja Santuaria), Rua Direita 35, is open to visitors: photographs and letters (free). There are viewpoints at the churches of N.S. do Rosário (1752, with work by Athayde and showing Moorish influence) and São Pedro dos Clérigos (built in 1753). Some people still pan for gold in the river running through the town. Between Ouro Preto and Mariana is the Minas de Passagem gold mine, dating from 1719.

Minas de Passagem A guided tour visits the old mine workings and the processing plant, entrance US$4 each, visiting hours 0900-1800, T Ouro Preto 551-1068, Mariana 557-1340/1255. Bus between Ouro Preto and Mariana, every 20 mins., all stop, US$0.15 to Ouro Preto, US$0.20 to Mariana. Taxi from Ouro Preto, US$4. There is a waterfall, Cachoeira Serrinha, where swimming is possible, ¾ hr walk from the bus stop to the mine. Monik Bernaerts, to whom we are indebted, gives the following directions: walk 100m in direction of Mariana, turn left, the road crosses a paved road, take the left fork, twice, after the second there is a yellow house on the left, where a trail starts, follow this across a paved road, turn left, a little further on there is a path to the right, which leads to the stream, walk up stream.

Hotels *Itacolomi*, 6 km. out on Ponte Nova road, C; *Faisca*, Rua Antônio Olinto 48, T 557-1206, F includes breakfast, spotless, excellent, friendly; *Müller*, Av. G. Vargas 34, T 557-1188, D-E, *Central*, Rua Frei Durão 8, E, on attractive square, pleasant, quiet, clean but poor breakfast; *Dormitório Bandeirante*, Direita 185, F, basic. *Providência*, Rua Dom Silverio 233, T 557-1444, run by nuns, small rooms, D (electric shower), clean, quiet. The modern service station (posto) on the highway above the town offers good clean rooms at F, with hot showers.

Restaurants *Alvorada*, Praça Claudio Mansel 42, US$1-3; *Panetão*, Rua Dom Viçoso; *Taubaú*, Praça da Sé; *Papinha della Nonna*, Praça Gomes Freire 246, Italian, rec. *Fundão 17*, Rua Direita 17, good and cheap.

Tourist Office Praça Bandeirantes, helpful for a guide or pamphlet and good map. Get off bus at first stop in Mariana rather than continuing to Rodoviária. Tourist agency, Transcolta, Praça JK, T 557-2056; enquire also at Embratur, Praça Neves, T 557-1533.

Congonhas do Campo (pop. 35,000, altitude 866 metres) is a hill town with a good road through pleasant farming country connecting with Ouro Preto, and a paved 3½-km. road link with the Rio-Belo Horizonte highway. It is also on the Central do Brasil railway between Rio and Belo Horizonte (but no through train to Rio). The town is dominated by the great pilgrimage church of Bom Jesus do Matozinho (1773), which opens at 0815; indeed there is little else of architectural interest. There is a wide view of the country from the church terrace, below which are six small chapels set in attractive sloping gardens, showing scenes with life-size Passion figures carved by Aleijadinho and his pupils in cedar wood. The church is mainly famous for its group of prophets sculpted by Aleijadinho, standing on the parapets of the terrace. These twelve great dramatic statues (thought of as Aleijadinho's masterpieces), carved in soapstone with dramatic sense of movement, constitute one of the finest works of art of their period in the world—not just in Latin America. Inside the church, as well as the Room of

Miracles, there are paintings by Athayde and the heads of four sainted popes (Gregory, Jerome, Ambrose and Augustine) sculpted by Aleijadinho for the reliquaries on the high altar. (Buses run from opposite the Rodoviária to Bom Jesus, US$0.10.) Pleasant excursion to waterfall with park and swimming, at Cachoeira Santo Antônio.

Congonhas is also celebrated for its Holy Week processions, which have as their focus the Bom Jesus church. The most celebrated ceremonies are the meeting of Christ and the Virgin Mary on the Tuesday, and the dramatized Deposition from the Cross late on Good Friday. Pilgrimage season, first half of September, draws many thousands.

Hotels *Colonial*, opp. Bom Jesus, good and comfortable, breakfast extra, no showers/toilets in room, blankets only, E-D; *Santuário*, Praça da Basílica 76, with fascinating restaurant downstairs full of colonial handicrafts and good local food, right next to Bom Jesus, "a bit run down, but charming", friendly, E; *Freitas*, Rua Marechal Floriano 69, F, basic. There are handicraft shops selling soapstone artefacts.

Bus From Belo Horizonte, US$0.75, 6 times a day, best to buy a return ticket. None direct from Rio; you have to change buses at Conselheiro Lafaiete (*Rhud's Hotel and Restaurant*, D; *Hotel Cupim*, on main Rio road, also D). To Congonhas from São João del Rei, take a São João-Belo Horizonte bus (5 a day) and alight at Murtinho, the crossing with the main Rio-Belo Horizonte highway (US$2); from there (it's an official bus stop) take a local bus (every ½ hr., US$0.50). Bus to Ouro Preto: either go via Belo Horizonte, or bus (every ½ hr.) to Murtinho or Conselheiro Lafaiete, US$0.30 (30 mins.), then 0745, 1200, 1500 or 1845 bus to Ouro Preto, US$1, via Itabirito. Rodoviária is 1½ km. outside town.

Diamantina, the most remote of these cities, is reached from Belo Horizonte by paved road (289 km., 6 daily buses via Pássaro Verde, US$4, 5½ hrs.) but there is no scheduled air service. Take the road to Brasília almost as far as the turnoff for Curvelo (a lively town, *Hotel Sagarana*—5-star, very good; *Restaurant Denise* with sleeping accommodation, on main highway, very clean), then through the impressive rocky country of the Serra do Espinhaço. The old railway service has been discontinued. 30 km. N of Belo Horizonte on this road, is the *Hotel Fazenda* at Ipê Amarelo—horses to ride, etc. Further on, between Paraopeba and Caetanópolis, is the *Flora Eunice* (*Leite ao Pé de Vaca*) snackbar (good toilets) with small private botanic garden and zoo with contented animals, recommended. About 120 km. N of Belo Horizonte, 33,400 square km. of the Serra do Espinaço has been named as the **National Park of Serra do Cipó**, in view of its scenic beauty and rich variety of plant and animal life (IBDF office: Av. do Contorno 8121, CP 1304, CEP 30.000, Belo Horizonte).

Diamantina (pop. 37,000) centre of a once active diamond industry founded in 1729, has excellent colonial buildings. Its churches (difficult to get into, except for the modern Cathedral) are not so grand as those of Ouro Preto, but it is possibly the least spoilt of all the colonial mining cities, with carved overhanging roofs and brackets; try walking through the lower part of the town. This very friendly town is in the deep interior, 1,120 metres up amid barren mountains; it is the birthplace of the late President Juscelino Kubitschek, the founder of Brasília. His house has been converted into a museum.

After repeated thefts, the diamonds of the Diamond Museum, in the house of Padre Rolim, one of the Inconfidentes (see under Ouro Preto) have been removed to the Banco do Brasil. Diamonds are still sought; see traditional methods at Guinda, 7 km. away. *Passeio a Diamantina*, an excellent guide, is written by the author of *Passeio a Sabará*. The town's latest industry is the making of Portuguese Arraiolos-style tapestry carpets by hand, at a cooperative in the centre; it was started by a diplomat, Sr Flecha da Silva, who was perturbed by the amount of local unemployment, and it has become very successful. Also etchings on leather are made locally.

The house of Chica da Silva, an 18th-century slave who married a rich diamond contractor, is at Praça Lobo Mesquita 266 (not worth a visit, entry US$0.30); Chica has become a folk-heroine among Brazilian blacks.

Hotels *Tijuco*, Macau do Melo 211, T 931-1022, C, best, good food; *Grande*, Rua da

Quitanda 70, D, T 931-1520; *Carvalho*, same street No. 12, and *Dália*, Praça JK (Jota-Ka) 25, T 931-1477, fairly good, E. *Pensão Avenida*, Av. Francisco Sá 243. Unnamed *pensão* at Rua Direita 131 (Dona Tazinha), F; *Esplanada*, F; *Nosso*, opp. bus station, F without breakfast, good value; also opp. bus station, *J.K.* Other cheap hotels around the bus station. Wild camping near waterfall just outside town.

Restaurants *Bar-Restaurant Confiança*, Rua da Quitanda 39, good. *Capistrana*, R. Campos Carvalho 36, near Cathedral square, rec. *Serestas* (serenades) Fri. and Sat. nights.

Voltage 110 A.C.

Tourist Information Dept. de Turismo in Casa de Cultura in Praça Antônio Eulálio 53 (no sign), 3rd floor, pamphlets and a reliable map.

Buses 6 a day to Belo Horizonte, via Curvelo, for connections to Brasília, with Pássaro Verde: 2½ hrs. to Curvelo, US$1.70, to Belo Horizonte, US$2.

Excursion Walk along the Caminho dos Escravos, the old paved road built by slaves between the mining area on Rio Jequitinhonha and Diamantina. A guide is essential (ask at the Casa de Cultura—cheap), and beware of snakes. Along the river bank to (12 km.) Biribiri, a pretty village with an abandoned textile factory (its inhabitants are reported to be leaving the village in great numbers). About half-way, swimming pools in the river; opposite them, on cliff face, animal paintings in red, age and origin unknown. Interesting plant life along river, and beautiful mountain views.

Serro, (pop. 17,000) 92 km. by paved road from Diamantina and reached by bus from there or from Belo Horizonte, is an unspoilt colonial town on the River Jequitinhonha with six fine baroque churches, a museum and many beautiful squares. It makes queijo serrano, one of Brazil's best cheeses, being in the centre of a prosperous cattle region. The most conspicuous church is Santa Rita, on a hill in the centre of town, reached by steps. On the main square, by the bottom of the steps, is the Carmo, arcaded, with original paintings on ceiling and in choir. The town has two large mansions: those of the Barão de Diamantina, now in ruins, and of the Barão do Serro across the river, beautifully restored and used as the town hall and Casa de Cultura; there are old mine entrances in the hillside behind the courtyard.

Hotels *Pousada Vila do Príncipe*, T 641-1485, D, very clean, in old mansion on main street, contains own museum, the artist Mestre Valentim said to have been born in slave quarters; other cheap hotels (e.g. *Dormitório*, Rua Rio Branco, opp. Banco do Brasil, F). **Restaurants**: *Itacolomi*, Praça João Pinheiro 20, fair; good one on main square, also *Churrascaria Vila do Príncipe* nearby on main street.

Just by the Serro turnoff is the town of Datas, whose spacious church (1832) decorated in red and blue, contains striking wooden image of Christ with the crown of thorns.

Tres Marias Some 240 km. NW of Belo Horizonte is a lake five times as large as Rio de Janeiro bay, formed by the Tres Marias dam on the upper reaches of the São Francisco river. There is a motel, and **the power company, Cemig, runs a guest house** (book in advance through its head office at Belo Horizonte). At Barreiro Grande is the Clube Náutico Tres Marias, E, simple. There are plans to develop the Tres Marias area for tourism.

Almost the same distance SW of Belo is the even larger lake formed by the Furnas dam. It can be seen from the BR-381 road to São Paulo.

Also north of Belo Horizonte is **Pirapora**, terminus for boat journeys on the River São Francisco (see also page 407). The cutting down of trees, in part as fuel for the boats, and the low rainfall in recent years, has greatly reduced the flow. The Sobradinho lake, which was meant to save the river, is only one third full and it is feared that, in the long term, the production of energy will be reduced. The town itself is a tourist attraction because of the falls in the river which make for excellent fishing: catches weighing 73 kg. (160lb) have been reported. The sandy river beaches are used for swimming. The grotesque figureheads of the riverboats, carrancas, are made in the workshops of Lourdes Barroso, Rua Abaeté 390. There are several hotels: *Canoeiras*, used by river-tour parties, *Pirapora*

Palace, on Praça Melo Viana (7 blocks west and 1 block south of Rodoviária), E, ask for room on garden, clean, friendly, safe, and *Hotel Rex*, Rua Antônio Nascimento 357, F, small breakfast, not very good. Camping near the Praça on riverside. Restaurants: *Borretos* on the riverfront, and *Barrenko*, next door, better value. Watch the fishermen at work in their punt-like canoes.

The old river passenger service of the Companhia de Navegação do São Francisco (Franave) to Juazeiro has been discontinued, but it is still sometimes possible to arrange journeys down the river on cargo boats if you talk to the masters, in the port. The Taina has been rec.: a trip to Ibotirama costs about US$70. If you can get on a cargo boat, the regular stops are at Januária (famous for Brazil's reputed best cachaça) and Bom Jesus da Lapa (a pilgrimage centre with a church built in a grotto inside a mountain, but a very poor town). Between Pirapora and Januária is the colonial town of São Francisco, with many attractive houses and a good handicraft market in the town hall; the boats do not always stop there. If you want to see the real Sertão, get off at Xique-Xique and take a bus to Utinga, Rui Barbosa and Itaberaba, then on to Salvador. Of the two remaining wood-burning stern-wheel boats, allegedly built for Mississippi services in the 1860s and imported from the USA in 1922 to work on the Amazon, one, the *Gaiola*, has been restored for tourist-agency use. A weekly trip (starting Sunday) is made downriver visiting various ports as far as São Francisco, organised by **Unitour or Mangebeira Turismo**, of Belo Horizonte, for about US$200 including return bus journey Belo-Pirapora (reportedly a jaunt for the wealthy).

If you can't get a boat, an adventurous journey to the Bahia coast is as follows: bus 0730 Pirpora-Montes Claros (also reached by train once a week from Belo Horizonte), next morning bus Montes Claros— Almenara (12 hrs.) then bus Almenara-Salto da Divisa (2½ hrs.), then after night in Salto at hotel facing bus station, take 0600 bus to Porto Seguro.

Eastern Minas

Eastern Minas Gerais is not of great cultural or historical interest, but is a centre of semi-precious stone processing and crystal carving, and also contains the Serra do Caparaó, where are found several of Brazil's highest mountains. The two principal towns, Governador Valadares and Teôfilo Otôni, are both on the BR-116 inland Rio-Salvador road, and both have good connections with Belo Horizonte. **Focus Tours (see Belo Horizonte, see page 324)** offers naturetours in this area to see four rare monkey species, including the muriqui, and a number of other animals including tree sloths, maned wolves, and an incredible array of birds.

Douglas Trent writes:

Governador Valadares, (pop. 250,000) 324 km. from Belo Horizonte, 5½ hours by bus (US$5 normal, US$10 leito) and also by regional air service, is a modern planned city. The altitude is 170 metres. It is a centre of semi-precious stone mines and lapidation, as well as for the cut-crystal animals one finds in tourist shops all around Brazil.

Hotels *Governador Palace*, Av. Minas Gerais 550, B; *Real Minas*, Praça Serra Lima 607, C; *Panorama*, C; *São Salvador*, Rua Prudente de Morais 915, D, new, clean.

Restaurants Main hotels; *JB*, Rua Bárbara Heliodora 384, rec., huge servings; *Joazeiro*, Rua Pessanha 639; *Tabu*, good fish dishes.

Hospital São Lucas, Rua Barão do Rio Branco 662, T 70-0121.

Airport is on the BR-381, 6 km. from the city centre with flights to Belo Horizonte and Ipatinga.

Excursion to the top of the Pico de Ibituruna, 960 metres.

Teôfilo Otôni, (335 metres, pop. 129,000), 138 km. from Governador Valadares, is a popular buying spot for dealers of crystals and semi-precious stones. The best prices in the state are found here (try K. Eluwar Ltda, Rua Epamin 458—change money also).

Hotels *Nobre Palace*, Av. Francisco Sá 43; *Teôfilo Otôni*, BR-116 Norte km. 275, 5 km. from centre; *Lancaster*, Rua Frei Gonzaga 142, D; *Metropole*, Av. Francisco Sá 14, D; *Beira-Rio*, Av. Israel Pinheiro 671, E; *São Francisco*, Rua Dr. João Antônio 287; *Presidente*,

Av. Getúlio Vargas 183, F, clean, good breakfast, laundry facilities.

Restaurants *Amigo do Rei*, Rua Benedito Valadares 161, T 521-4927; *Rio Grande*, next to *Teófilo Otôni Hotel*; *Intermezzo*, next to *Lancaster Hotel*.

Bus to Porto Seguro via Nanuque (Hotel Minas, at Rodoviária, F, adequate).

Caparaó National Park, 49 km. by paved road from Manhuaçu on the Belo Horizonte-Vitória road (BR-262), has the Pico da Bandeira (2,890m), Pico do Cruzeiro (2,861m) and the Pico do Cristal (2,798m). The park features rare Atlantic rainforest in its lower altitudes and Brazilian alpine on top. It is best to visit during the dry season (April-October). Camping is permitted within the park at two spots and it can be quite crowded in July and during Carnaval. (IBDF address under Serra do Cipó, **page** 330 **above**).

Hotel *Caparaó Parque*, near park entrance 15 mins. walk from the town of Caparaó, nice, C, T (032) 741-2559.

How to get there There are buses from Belo Horizonte, Ouro Preto or Vitória to **Manhumirim** (Hotel São Luiz, E, meal $1.10, good value, but Cids Bar, next door, Travessa 16 do Março, has better food). From Manhumirim, take a bus direct to Caparaó, 0930, 1630 US$0.50, or to Presidente Soares (several, 7 km.), then hitch 11 km. to Caparaó. By car from the BR-262, go through the Manhumirim, Pres. Soares and Caparaó village, then 1 km. further to the hotel, which is 2 km. from the park entrance (small entry fee). Coming from Rio, leave BR-116 at Fervedouro and take BR-482 to Carangola. Just before this town branch N to Espera Feliz. About half way turn left again to Pres. Soares. From the park entrance it is 6 km. on a poorly-marked road to the car park at the base of the waterfall. From the hotel jeeps (US$12 per jeep) run to the car park at 1,970 metres (2½ hrs.' walk), then it's a 3-4 hour walk to the summit of the Pico da Bandeira, marked by yellow arrows; plenty of camping possibilities all the way up, the highest being at Terreirão (2,370 m). It is very difficult to get to the Pico da Bandeira from Manhumirim and back in a day. This is good walking country. It may also be possible to visit local fazendas, for example Fazenda Modelo, 8 km. from Manhumirim.

Southern and Western Minas

The spas of southern Minas Gerais are easily reached by road and in some cases by air from Rio de Janeiro and São Paulo. They are also popular holiday places; the high season is from December through March.

São Lourenço (pop. 28,000) easily accessible from Rio de Janeiro or São Paulo, stands at 850 metres above sea-level. There is a splendid park, tennis, boating, swimming, a flying field, and fishing from the Ilha dos Amores in a lake ringed by gardens and forests. There is a grand ride through fine scenery to the Pico de Buqueré (1,500 metres).

Its rich mineral waters are used in the treatment of stomach, liver, kidney and intestinal complaints. There is an up-to-date hydro establishment for douches and for the famous carbo-gaseous baths, unique in South America.

Hotels *Brasil*, nice; *Sul Americano Grande; Ponto Chic*, etc.

Bus service from Rio de Janeiro, 277 km., 5-6 hrs.; from São Paulo, 338 km., 6-7 hrs.

Caxambu, (pop. 20,000) N of São Lourenço, at 900 metres, is one of the more sophisticated of these resorts. Its waters are used for treating stomach, kidney and bladder diseases, and are said to restore fertility. They seemed to work for Princess Isabel, daughter of Dom Pedro II, who produced three sons after a visit. The little church of Santa Isabel da Hungária stands on a hill as a thank-offering. The mountains and forests around are very beautiful. View over the city from Morro Caxambu, 1,010 metres. Excellent hotels.

Hotels *Glória; Palace; Avenida; Caxambu; Bragança*, and 20 others.

Lambari, (pop. 14,400) a lesser-known resort, is 56 km. W of Caxambu by road at 900 metres. Efforts are under way to reopen the casino, closed in 1945. Hotels are not luxurious but fairly comfortable. The Parque das Águas has seven springs and a swimming pool. There are boat trips on the Lago Guanabara.

Hotels *Itaicy*, largest, on lake near Casino. Many others.

Cambuquirá, (pop. 11,000) a little N of Lambari by road at 946 metres, very popular, with friendly atmosphere and picnic sites close by.

Hotels *Grande Hotel Empresa*; also *Santos Dumont*, and many others.

Poços de Caldas, (1,180 metres; pop. 110,000) in western Minas, is reached by road or plane from São Paulo (272 km.), Rio (507 km.) or Belo Horizonte (510 km.). The city is sited on the crater of an extinct volcano in a mountainous area. Venetians from Murano settled here and established a crystal-glass industry. It is the best-known of the resorts, and is a traditional honeymoon centre. It has complete and up-to-date thermal establishments for the treatment of rheumatic, skin and intestinal diseases; you need a local doctor's certificate to use these facilities. Excursions include several lakes within a few km. of the city with boating and restaurants; the Véu das Noivas with its three waterfalls illuminated at night; the tall statue of Cristo Redentor at an altitude of 1,678 metres, which can be reached by cable car; nearby is an 80-metre granite rock, Pedra Batão. There are also the lovers' well, Fonte dos Amores, and the Japanese teahouse at the Recanto Japonês. Hippie fair every Sunday in Praça Pedro Sanches. Festivals include Carnival, São Benedito ending on 13 May, and recently established Festival de Música Popular Brasileira. Excellent climate. There is now a small industrial estate.

Hotels Some 80 hotels and pensions. *Palace*, old fashioned but well run, with sulphur baths; *Continental*, Av. Francisco Salles 235; *Pousada Vale das Rosas*, Rodovia a Belo Horizonte Km. 5; *Minas Gerais*, Rua Pernambuco 615.

Restaurants *Castelões*, Praça Pedro Sanches 207; *Lareira*; *Sem-Sem*, Rua Assis Figueiredo 1080; *Cantina do Araújo*, Rua Assis Figueiredo 1705.

Buses Rio, 8 hrs., US$6; São Paulo, 4½ hrs., US$3.50; both by Viação Cometa.

Tres Corações, also in southern Minas but not a spa, is the birthplace of Pelé, the legendary football star (statue). Hotels: *Italian Palace*, E; *Capri*, F; good food at *Cantina Calabresa*. Reached by daily buses from Rio, São Paulo and Belo Horizonte. Daily bus to (32 km.) **São Tomé das Letras**, beautiful hilltop village with frescoed 17th-century church and many caves in surrounding hills. Poçinhos do Rio Verde, a friendly hill resort, bus 1 hr; *Hotel Bosque das Fontes*, rec., at entrance to town, chalets, camp sites, restaurant, low cost steam and mineral baths; lake, horses and many trails.

Note that there are also mountain spa resorts (Serra Negra, Lindóia, Campos do Jordão) in São Paulo State (see page 354).

Araxá, (pop. 62,000) in the Minas Triangle, about 193 km. before Uberaba at 970 metres, is a quiet little place with thorium and radio-active waters and sulphur and mud baths. It can be reached from Rio (848 km.) or São Paulo (549 km.) Belo Horizonte (374 km.), by bus. Airport.

Hotels *Grande de Araxá*, luxury, 8 km. away; *Grande Hotel Pinto; Colombo*.

South of Araxá is the **Serra da Canastra National Park**, in which the Rio São Francisco rises. It is a cool region (temperatures in May and June average 18°C), best reached from Piumhi, on state road 050, 267 km. W of Belo Horizonte.

Uberaba, (pop. 245,000) also in the Minas Triangle, is on the Rio da Prata, 718 km. from São Paulo. It is an important rail and road junction, being on the direct highway between São Paulo and Brasília, and serves a large cattle raising district. At the beginning of May each year the Rural Society of the Minas Triangle holds a famous cattle and agricultural exhibition at Uberaba. Altitude, 700 metres. Hotels: *Palácio*; *Grande*. Bus from Belo Horizonte, US$6 (leito US$12), 7 hrs.

To the N of Uberaba is **Uberlândia** (pop. 312,000), founded in 1888; good communications by air and road (buses to Brasília, 6 hrs., US$5; to Belo Horizonte, 9 hrs., US$7.50, to São Paulo, US$8). *Hotel Nacional*, opposite Rodoviária, F, with view (cheaper without), shower and breakfast, clean.

THE STATE OF SÃO PAULO (5)

The State of São Paulo (pop. 32,090,000), with an area of 247,898 square km., is larger than the states of New York and Pennsylvania together and about the same size as Great Britain and Northern Ireland. A narrow zone of wet tropical lowland along the coast rises in an unbroken slope to the ridge of the Great Escarpment—the Serra do Mar—at from 800 to 900 metres above sea level. The upland beyond the Great Escarpment is drained westwards by the tributaries of the Rio Paraná. The broad valleys of the uplands are surmounted by ranges of low mountains; one such range lies between the São Paulo basin and the hinterland of the state. West of the low mountains between the basin and the rest of the state lie the uplands of the Paraná Plateau, at about 600 metres above the sea. One of the soils in this area is the terra roxa, the red earth in which coffee flourishes. When dry it gives off a red dust which colours everything; when wet it is sticky and slippery. There is ample rainfall in São Paulo State; indeed, the highest rainfall in Brazil (3,810 mm.) is over a small area between Santos and São Paulo; at São Paulo itself it is no more than 1,194 mm. Temperatures on the plateau are about 5°C lower than on the coast, but it is only south of the latitude of Sorocaba that frosts occur and then not frequently. Temperatures are too low for coffee in the São Paulo basin itself, but the State produces, on average, about 7 million bags a year.

Between 1885 and the end of the century a boom in coffee and the arrival of large numbers of Europeans transformed the State out of all recognition. By the end of the 1930s there had arrived in São Paulo State a million Italians, half a million each of Portuguese and immigrants from the rest of Brazil, nearly 400,000 Spaniards and nearly 200,000 Japanese. The population is now equal to that of Argentina or Colombia. Today the State produces 50% of the country's cotton, 62% of its sugar, a third of its coffee and over 50% of its fruit exports. It turns out 90% of Brazil's motor vehicles, 65% of its paper and cellulose, and 60% of its machinery and tools, being also responsible for 60% of the country's industrial consumption of electric energy. All this comes, in sum, to some 20% of Brazil's agricultural output and 65% (40% in São Paulo city alone) of its industrial production. São Paulo provides 33% of the total exports of Brazil and takes 40% of the total imports: nearly all pass through the port of Santos.

São Paulo (pop. 10,100,000) is 429 km. from Rio de Janeiro, and is connected with it by air, the Via Dutra highway, and the Central do Brasil railway. It was founded in 1554 by two Jesuit priests from São Vicente, Blessed José Anchieta and Padre Manuel Nóbrega, as a mission station. The original settlement, not yet effectively preserved, was at the Pátio do Colégio in the centre of the city, where a copy of Anchieta's original church has been built (it is open Tues. to Sun., 1300-1700).

São Paulo (altitude 730 metres) is one of the fastest growing cities in the world. It is already the most populous city in South America, and the continent's leading industrial centre. Until the 1870s it was a sleepy, shabby little town, but it now covers more than 1,500 square km.—three times the size of Paris. The citizens are intensely proud of its skyscrapers, of its well-lit streets, of its efficient water supply, and especially of its Metro system, the first in Brazil, which began operating in September 1975, linking Jabaquara in the south with Santana in the north. (A second line is now open.) The traffic pattern is extremely exasperating: you may have to drive around 10 blocks to reach a point half a block away. Also exasperating is the amount of air pollution: in dry weather eyes and nose are continually troubled.

The two main reasons for the city's development lie in its position at the focus of so much agricultural wealth, and in its climate, which makes the Paulistanos

SÃO PAULO

ORIENTATION MAP

33A

NOT TO SCALE

1. Cathedral
2. São Paulo Museum of Art (MASP)
3. Butantã Snake Farm and Museum
4. University City
5. Ibirapuera Park
6. Parque da Independência and Museu Paulista
7. Parque do Estado, Botanical and Zoological Gardens
8. Pacaembu Stadium
9. Anhembi
10. Morumbi Stadium
11. Parque Água Branca
12. Casa do Bandeirante
13. Museum of Lasar Segall
14. Casa do Sertanista
15. Casa Brasileira
16. Museum of Brasilian Art

the most hard working and energetic people in Brazil. Visitors, however, find the characteristic sharp changes of temperature troublesome and even Paulistanos seem to catch cold often. (Incidentally, one differentiates between Paulistas—inhabitants of the State—and Paulistanos— inhabitants of the city.) There is another and a most potent factor which explains its industrial growth: the availability of plentiful hydro-electric power.

The shopping, hotel and restaurant centre embraces the districts of Av. São Luís, the Praça da República, and Rua Barão de Itapetininga. The commercial quarter, containing banks, offices and shops, is contained within a central district known as the Triângulo, bounded by Rua Direita, Quinze de Novembro, São Bento and Praça Antônio Prado, but it is already rapidly spreading towards the apartment and shopping district of Praça da República. Rua Augusta, near Avenida Paulista, once the home of the wealthier citizens, is now full of boutiques and fashion shops. Avenida Paulista houses most consulates in skyscrapers, many banking head offices, and the Assis Chateaubriand Art Museum of São Paulo (MASP—opened by Queen Elizabeth in 1968). It is becoming a new downtown area, more dynamic than the old centre, and so is Av. Faria Lima, 8 km. from Praça da República. (Good view of the city from Conjunto Nacional, Horsa II, Av. Paulista, free on presentation of passport).

The park in Praça da República is worth going into between 0800 and 1400 on Sun.: birds, trees and Brazilians in all their variety, and a famous handicrafts fair; on Saturday p.m. there is live music, and stalls sell sweets and salgados. Near the Praça is the city's tallest building, the Edifício Itália on the corner of Av. Ipiranga and Av. São Luís. There is a restaurant on top (very reasonable), and a sightseeing balcony.

The Viaduto do Chá, which bridges the central avenue, Anhangabaú, leads to the opera house, one of the few distinguished 19th-century survivals that São Paulo can boast. The Av. Paulista and the "jardins" América, Paulista and Paulistano still contain some mansions of beauty and interest and are on one of the routes to the Butantã Institute or "snake farm". About 10 minutes' walk from the centre of the city is the old Municipal Market, covering an area of 27,000 square metres; a new Municipal Market has been built in the outskirts. The Municipal Library, surrounded by a pleasant shady garden, is well worth visiting.

The Cathedral's foundations were laid over 40 years before its inauguration during the 1954 festivities commemorating the 4th centenary of the city. This massive building in neo-Gothic style, with a capacity for 8,000 worshippers, is in the heart of the city.

The large Municipal Stadium in the Pacaembu valley, a flourishing residential district, is well worth seeing. Built on Olympic lines in an area of 75,500 square metres, it holds nearly 70,000 spectators. Besides the flood-lit football ground and athletics field and basketball court, there are also a covered gymnasium, open-air and covered tennis courts, an illuminated 50-metre long swimming pool, a youth hostel, and a great hall for receptions and rallies. There is a larger stadium holding 100,000 people in Morumbi, one of the more elegant residential districts.

Typical of modern development are the huge Iguatemi, Ibirapuera and Morumbi shopping centres. They include luxurious cinemas, snack bars and most of the best shops in São Paulo. Parking in each for over 1,000 vehicles. On a rather humbler level are the big supermarkets of El Dorado (Av. Pamplona 1704) and Pão de Açúcar (Praça Roosevelt, near the Hilton); the latter is open 24 hrs. a day (except Sun.).

The palatial Jockey Club racecourse is in the Cidade Jardim district with easy access by bus. Race meetings are held on Sat., Sun., Mon. and Thurs. nights. The new town premises of the Jockey Club (Rua Boa Vista) are well worth a visit.

Ibirapuera Take a Monções bus (675-C) from Ana Rosa metro station to Ibirapuera Park for the architecturally impressive new Legislative Assembly. There is also a planetarium equipped with the most up-to-date machinery (shows at 2000 Tues. and Thurs.; 1600, 1800 and 2000 weekends and holidays); a velodrome for cycle and motor-cycle racing; an all-aluminium covered stadium for indoor sports which seats 20,000 people. The Museum of Contemporary Art (of the Universidade de São Paulo), founded in 1963, has an important collection of

Western and South American modern art. The collection is divided between the Bienal building in Parque Ibirapuera (entrance at back of building, open Tues.-Sun., 1300-1800, closed holidays, free) and a building at Rua da Reitoria, 109, Cidade Universitária, open Weds.-Sun. 1000-1700, closed holidays, students free (it is hoped to unite the collection at the Cidade Universitária). Buses to Ibirapuera, 6414 (Gatusa) from Praça da Bandeira; to Cidade Universitária 702U or 7181 from Praça da República.

In this park, too, are the Museums of Modern Art, Aviation (showing the Santos Dumont plane; US$0.40 entrance, open to 1600 only), Folklore (interesting) and Sciences. There is also a unique display of nativity scenes and scenes of the life of Christ. (Concerts held at Christmas-time). At the entrance is a majestic monument to the Bandeirantes, or pioneers. All the Ibirapuera museums (except Aviation) are open Tues.-Sun., 1400-1700. (For other museums **see page 344**.)

Anhembi (Av. Assis Chateaubriand, Santana) is the largest exhibition hall in the world. It was inaugurated in 1970 and all São Paulo's industrial fairs are held there. It has a meeting hall seating 3,500 people, three auditórios, 24 conference rooms (salas de reunião) and two restaurants. Parking space is provided for 3,500 cars. It may be reached by underground (short walk from Tietê station).

Local Holidays 25 Jan. (Foundation of City).

Warning Beware of assaults and pickpocketing in São Paulo.

Hotels Among the most luxurious are the **Maksoud Plaza**, Alameda Campinas 150, T 251-2233; **Caesar Park**, Rua Augusta 1508, T 285-6622; **Mofarrej Sheraton**, Alameda Santos 1437, T 284-5544 (rec); **Eldorado Boulevard**, Av. São Luís 234, T 256-8833 (excellent); **Hilton**, Av. Ipiranga 165, T 256-0033; **Holiday Inn Crowne Plaza**, Rua Frei Caneca 1360, T 284-1144, Fax 251-3121, 5-star, central, small swimming pool, very comfortable; **Grand Hotel Cà d'Oro**, Rua Augusta 129, T 256-8011 (superb restaurant) and the **Brasilton**, Rua Martins Fontes 330, T 258-5811, all in our price category L+ and with swimming pools, nightclubs and convention halls. The **Grand Corona**, Basílio da Gama 101, T 259-8177, A-very fairly priced, and **Cambridge**, Av. Nove de Julho 216, T 239-0399, B (local standard class), have been rec. (although the last named's location is uninspiring).

There are many other good hotels, including in our L category, **Bristol**, Rua Martins Fontes 277, T 258-0011; in our A category, **Othon Palace**, Rua Líbero Badaró 190, T 239-3277; **Samambaia**, Rua Sete de Abril 422, T 231-1333; **Excelsior**, Av. Ipiranga 770, T 222-7377; **Jaraguá**, Rua Major Quedinho 44, T 256-6633 and **Planalto**, Cásper Líbero 117 (Varig-Tropical chain), T 227-7311; and in our B category **Terminus**, Av. Ipiranga 741, T 222-2266, and **Solar Paulista**, Rua Francisca Miquelina 343, T 257-2800.

There are scores of cheaper hotels, of which we append a selection: **Hores Belgrano**, Rua Marquês de Paranaguá, 88, T 258-0255, D, central, English spoken, special rates for long stays, rooms with kitchenette. Another residential hotel, rec. for longer stays, is **Metropolitan Plaza**, Alameda Campinas 474, T 287-4855, A. A rec. "Apart-hotel" for longer stays is **Residencial Alameda Nothman** (Santa Cecília), Al. Nothman 682. **Residence Saint Thomas**, Av. Joaquim Eugênio de Lima 1360, good value service apartments (B); in same chain **Residence Saint James** and 2 others. **Service-Flat Monterey**, Alameda Itu 265, Jardim Paulista, has been rec. for longer stays, at US$600/month; safe parking, comfortable accommodation.

Las Vegas, Rua Vitória 390 (corner Av. Rio Branco), E, excellent; **Continental**, same street, No. 223, F, clean, safe, highly rec.; **Rio Branco**, Av. Rio Branco 234, near corner with Ipiranga, D, central, with bath, rec.; **Itauna**, E, No. 280, well furnished, rec; **Lincoln** No. 47, E, excellent breakfast; **Paris**, 7 de Abril (close to Anhangabaú metro station), D with shower, TV, clean, honest, highly rec.; **Marechal**, Av. Barão de Limeira 339, 67 rooms, D with bath and telephone, safe, excellent; **Kolins**, Alameda Gilete 1017 (off São João, nearest subway Praça República), D, clean, hot water, private toilet; **Metro**, Av. Paulista at Paraíso Metro station, E without breakfast, quiet, convenient; **Banri**, Rua Galvão Bueno 209, C, good; **Isei**, Rua da Glória 288, D, good value, simple, nice, both near metro station Liberdade (Japanese quarter). **Center Bela Vista**, 13 de Maio 198 (T 257-2658), near plenty of restaurants in an old Italian suburb (Rua Santo Antônio/Rua 13 de Maio, nr. Praça da Bandeira).

Also suggested: **S. Sebastião**, 7 de Abril 364 (T 257-4988/255-1594), E, rec., cheap and clean, and now has rooms with bath; **Cineasta**, Av. São João 613, 80 rooms, D, a/c; **Plaza**, Av. São João 407, 42 rooms, D; **Central**, Av. São João 288, E with shower, F without, clean, good if a little run down, central; many others in and around Av. São João. On Rua do Triúnfo: **Condeixa**, No. 145, F, showers; **Maringá**, F, friendly, basic; **Noroeste**, No. 285, F, basic, clean, hot showers; **Saturno**, F, hot water, soap and towel. Very many of the cheap hotels are hot-pillow establishments.

1. Cathedral
2. Praça da República
3. Praça Roosevelt
4. Praça Princesa Isabel
5. Praça Alfredo Issa
6. Praça Júlio Prestes
7. Museum of Sacred Art
8. Luz Station
9. Sorocabana Station
10. Bus Station for Santos
11. Tiete Metro Station
12. Old Municipal Market
13. Anhembi Exhibition Centre
14. Military Hospital
15. Cheap Hotel Area

← SEE MAP 33B
FOR DETAIL

SÃO PAULO
CENTRE
MAIN STREETS ONLY 33

Take the metro to Luz station and in the block behind the old Rodoviária, off Av. Rio Branco, there are scores of cheap hotels with prices ranging from category F to category C; try: Rua Santa Ifigénia: *Trinidade*, No. 737, E, clean, friendly, good value; *Lima*, E, friendly, rec.; *Luanda*, No. 348, F with breakfast, English-speaking owner, helpful, rec.; *Aliança*, No. 235 (corner Santa Ifigénia), E, nice; *Ouro Fino Hotel Familiar*, No. 388, E, friendly; *Uai*, No. 66, E, clean and pleasant, rooms on street are good, rec. Rua dos Gusmões: *Galeão*, No. 394, E, clean, safe, helpful, hot showers; *Hospedaria Apuliense Familiar*, No. 218, F, with shower; *Santa Ifigénia*, E, lunch available for US$1.70. Rua dos Andradas; *Itaipu*, No. 467, E, good, clean. Rua Barão de Piracicaba; *São José*, F without breakfast, basic, good value; *Osiris*, Cásper Líbero 591, E with bath and breakfast, clean, quite good, hot water, near Luz railway station; *Lisboa*, same street, E, basic, shared shower, safe; and *Lepanto*, No. 359, E, shower, TV, clean; *Tatuí*, Praça Princeza Isabel 171 (on corner of Av. Duque de Caxias, 2 blocks from old bus station), F, clean with bath. N.B. the redlight district is in the blocks bounded by Ruas Santa Ifigénia, dos Andradas, dos Gusmões and Av. Ipiranga, and is definitely not rec. for women travelling alone. *Casa do Politécnico*, Rua Afonso Pena 272, cheap accommodation. *Comendadore*, Largo Santa Cecília, E, safe, quiet. Accommodation of the youth-hostel type is available at the Pacaembu Stadium at a fee in (our) category E. A letter addressed to the Secretário de Esportes is present. The Youth Hostel (*Albergue da Juventude*) is in the Ibirapuera gymnasium, Nóbrega e Estados Unidos, very cheap but you must first join the Brazilian YHA (15 de Novembro e Av. São João—office in centre) for about US$5 a year. Also Magdalena Tagkiaferro, Estrada Turística do Jaguarã 651, km. 18, via Anhanguera, 05173 São Paulo (T 229-3787/3011).

Electric Current   110-220 volts A.C., 60 cycles.

Camping   Cemucam, at Cobia (Rodovia Raposo Tavares, Km. 27). List of sites can be obtained from Camping Clube do Brasil, R. Minerva, 156—Perdizes (T 263-024).

Restaurants   Apart from the international cuisine in the first-class hotels listed above, here are only a few out of many:
Portuguese *Abril em Portugal*, Rua Caio Prado 47; and others.
Italian *Tibério*, Av. Paulista 392; *Famiglia Marcini*, Rua Avanhandava 81; *Trattoria do Piero*, Rua Caconde 323, popular and good; *Gigeto*, Avanhandava 63; *A Camorra*, R. de Consolação 3589; *Trattoria del Sargento*, Al. Campinas 3 (establishments), popular; *Leonardo*, Al. Santos 1508 (opp. *Sheraton*), good; *Pastasciutta*, Rua Barão do Triúnfo 427 (Brooklin Paulista); *Cantina Roma*, Rua Maranhão 512 (Higienópolis); *Trastevere*, Al. Santos 1518; *Bongiovanni*, Av. 9 de Julho 5511; *Da Fierella*, R. Bernardino de Campos 294; *Don Ciccillo*, Praça Souza Aranha 185; *L'Osteria do Piero*, Alameda França 1509; *Via Veneto*, Al. Barros 909; *Giovanni Bruno*, Rua Martinho Prado 165; *Il Sogno di Anarello*, Rua José Maria Lisboa 661, Jardim Paulista; *Grupo Sérgio*, Post Office building in Av. São João near Rua Marconi (rec.); *Piemontese*, Al. França 1509, Jardim Paulista, popular, huge meals; and many others in Rua 13 de Maio (Bela Vista)— *Lazzarella, Roperto, La Fontana di Trevi, La Tavola*—and neighbourhood. *Casa de Pizza Rodízio*, Rua Augusta 1585, all you can eat for US$4. *La Farina*, Av. Ipiranga 924, for good cheap pasta, popular.
French *David's*, R. Oscar Freire 913; *La Cocagne*, Rua Amaral Gurgel 378; *La Casserole*, Largo do Arouche 346, US$25; *La Gratinée*, Rua Bento Freitas, 42; *La Maison Basque*, Av. João Dias 239; *Le Bistrot*, Av. Adolfo Pinheiro 510; *Freddy*, Praça Dom Gastão Liberal Pinto 11; *Marcel*, Rua Epitácio Pessoa 98.
German *Juca Alemão*, Av. Santo Amaro and Al. Lorena; *Bierhalle*, Av. Lavandisca 263; *Biergarten*, Av. Ibirapuera 3174; *Kobes*, Av. Santo Amaro 5394; *Zillertal*, Av. Brig. Luís Antônio 909.
Swiss *Chamonix*, Rua Pamplona 1446, very expensive; *Maison Suisse*, Rua Caio Prado 183.
Austrian *Kitzbühel*, R. Frei Gaspar.
Greek *Mikonos*, R. Henrique Monteiro 218.
Middle East *Almanara* (Arab), good and reasonable, Av. São João 1155, Oscar Freire 523,

---

São Paulo (Centre Detail): Key to map

1. Praça da Sé; 2. Praça da República; 3. Parque Dom Pedro II; 4. Pátio do Colégio and Museu Padre Anchieta; 5. Praça Dr. João Mendes; 6. Praça da Bandeira; 7. Praça Roosevelt and Church of Consolação; 8. Praça Dom José Gaspar   and Municipal Library; 9. Praça Ramos Azevedo; 10. Largo do Arouche; 11. Largo Paiçandu; 12. Largo São Bento; 13. Praça Clovis Bevilagua; 14. Praça Antônio Prado; 15. Cathedral; 16 São Bento; 17. São Francisco do Assis; 18. São Gonçalo; 19. Old Municipal Market; 20. Teatro Municipal; 21. Edifício Itália; 22. Central Post Office; 23 Embratel; 24. State Tourist Offices (2 locations). **Hotels:** 25. *Hilton*; 26. *Grand Cà d'Oro*; 27. *Cambridge*; 28. *Othon Palace*; 29. *Excelsior*; 30. *Samambaia*.

SÃO PAULO

CENTRE DETAIL

33B

Av. Vieira de Carvalho 109 and 124; *Rubayat*, Av. Vieira de Carvalho 134, Al. Santos 86 and Av. Faria Lima 5332, excellent meat.

Oriental *Sino-Brasileiro*, Rua Alberto Torres 39 (Perdizes); *Gengis Khan*, Av. Rebouças 3241 (Chinese); *Golden Dragon*, Av. Rebouças 2371; *Yamanga*, R. Tomás Gonzaga 66; *Heike* and *Notre Dame*, both Av. Paulista 2064 (Center 3); *Akasaka*, Rua 13 de Maio 1639; *Shushi-Kiyo*, also 13 de Maio, rec. Many other Chinese and Japanese restaurants in Liberdade, the Japanese quarter, where there is a Japanese food market in the square by the metro station. *Kokeche*, Rua dos Estudantes 41 (Liberdade), good, reasonably-priced *sushi* bar; *Hare Krishna*, Rua Pandiá Calógeras 54, Liberdade, near São Joaquim metro station; *Korea House*, Galvão Bueno 43 (Liberdade).

Vegetarian *Superbom*, Viaduto 9 de Julho 180, Praça da Sé 62, Praça da República 128 (lunch only); *Salade e Chi*, Rua Aurora, US$2.50 for all you can eat; *Sattua*, Rua da Consolação 3140; same street, No. 2961, *Mãe Terra* (shop also); *O Arroz de Ouro*, Largo do Arouche 46 (shop as well); *Cheiro Verde*, Peixoto Gomide 1413; several off Av. Paulista, including *Boy Papi*, on Rua Augusta; *Nectar*, Alameda Gabriel Monteiro da Silva 1931 (open to midnight except Mon.); *Jasmin Casa de Chá*, vegetarian food and tea house, Rua Haddock Lobo 932; *Intergrão*, Av. Rebouças 2036; *Delícia Natural*, Av. Rio Branco 211 (4th floor), corner Av. Ipiranga, lunch only, good; *Sabor Natural* Rio Branco 91, lunch only, good choice, all you can eat for US$1.50; *Herva*, Rua Pinheiros 541; good one next to Geomapas, 300 block of Libero Badaró, buffet lunch US$1.50. "Vida Integral" newspaper (US$0.35) gives details of all health food restaurants and stores in São Paulo.

General *Terraço Itália*, on top of Edifício Itália, 41 floors up, good fixed price lunch, dancing with excellent band and superb view (must consume to be allowed to see the view), shorts and flip flops not allowed; *Mexilhão*, Rua 13 de Maio 62, Bela Vista, very good. *Buffalo Grill*, Rua Bela Cintra 2231, US$20, very good; *O Beco*, Rua Bela Cintra 306, dinner only; *Dinho's Place*, Largo do Arouche 246, Al. Santos 45 and Av. Morumbi 7976, US$25; *Rodeio*, Rua Haddock Lobo 1468, excellent meat dishes, US$25; *Paddock*, Av. São Luís 228 and Av. Faria Lima 1541 (genuine Brazilian, serves feijoada completa, very expensive); *Um, Dois, Feijão e Arroz*, Rua Ipiranga, modest (US$3 or 4) but excellent (4 other branches); *Cantina Amigo Piolin*, Rua Augusta 89, excellent and cheap; *Dewar's*, R Timbiras 607, clean, good service, good and cheap; *Alvear*, Rua Seminario, near Central Post Office, cheap surtido; *Bolinha*, Av. Cidade Jardim 53 for feijoadas (on Wed. and Sat.); *Maria Fulô*, Av. 9 de Julho for Bahia and other regional dishes—fixed menu, fixed price, very expensive; *Oxalá*, Maria Antônia, just off Consolaçáo, Bahian specialities at modest prices; *O Veleiro*, Santo Amaro 15 (Praça da Bandeira), Amazonian specialities; Airport Restaurant (very good); *Jack in the Box*, fast food, several locations. *Pizza d'Oro*, in Vila Mariana (local painters and sculptors); many snack-bars and pizzerias throughout the city. For fast food, there are now several *McDonalds* in São Paulo. There are plenty of atmospheric restaurants in the "artists' quarter" of Bexiga (Bela Vista), best Fri. and Sat. nights. Another atmospheric place is *Recanto Goiano*, just off Praça 14 bis (Av. 9 de Julho), typical dishes, caipira music.

Bars *Bar Brasil*, Bela Ciutra 1209, Jardins; *Spazio Pirandello*, Augusta 371, Zona Central (not expensive, a meeting place for intellectuals); *Scotch Bar*, Rua 24 de Maio 35, conjunto 411; *Pepe's Bar*, Edifício Metrópole; *Finnegan's*, Alameda Itú 1529 (esq. Consolação) and Cristiano Viana 358 (esq. Artur de Azevedo), rec., international clientéle; several outdoor bars in Largo do Arouche and in Moema; all major hotels. Many gay and lesbian bars.

Tea Rooms *Chá Mon* (Edifício Metropole); *Chelsea Art Gallery*, Hotel Eldorado. *Jasmin*, Rua Haddock Lobo 932.

Shopping Rua Augusta for boutiques. All types of stores at Shopping Center Iguatemi, Av. Brig. Faria Lima, Shopping Centre Ibirapuera, Av. Ibirapuera (**see page 337**), and Shopping Centre Morumbi, also El Dorado Shopping Centre (corner of Av. Rebouças and Marginal Pinheiros). Souvenirs from *Mimosa*, Joaquim Nabuco 275, Brooklin Paulista; Indian handicraft, *Artindia*, Rua Augusta 1371 (Galeria Ouro Velho), T 283-2102; *Coisarada*, Rua Tabapuã 390, Itaim Bibi (T 881-4810). Also good for souvenirs is the area between Rua 24 de Maio and bars and pizzerias Rua 7 de Abril (just off Praça da República); bargaining is rec.; plenty of jewellers here. *H. Stern*, jewellers, at Praça da República 242, Rua Augusta 2340 and at Iguatemi, Ibirapuera and Morumbi shopping centres and at main hotels. Open air markets: "Hippy" fair, Praça da República, Sun. 0800-1400, very varied, many tourists, good selection of inexpensive fossils, Bahian food, lots of artists; "Oriental" fair, Praça de Liberdade Metro, Sun. p.m., good for Japanese snacks but not much else; at Praça da Sé, Liberdade, Sun., very picturesque, with remedies on sale, tightrope walking, gypsy fortune tellers, etc. Below the Museu de Arte de São Paulo, a flea market takes place on Sun., 0800-1700; there is another flea market Suns. in the main square of the Bexiga district. São Paulo is cheap for film and clothes. The Ceasa flower market, Tues. and Fri. a.m., is supposedly one of the largest in the world; ask taxi drivers how to get there.

Bookshops *Livraria Cultura*, Eva Herz e Cia., Av. Paulista 2073, loja 153. *Livraria Triângulo*, Alameda Tietê 46. Ilco, Barão do Triúnfo 371, Brooklin Paulista, books in English. *Livraria Kosmos*, Praça Dom José Caspar 134, loja 30, international stock. *Livraria Alemã*, Rua Laplace 159, Brooklin; *Librairie Française*, R. Barão de Itapetininga 275, wide selection. *Book Centre*, R. Gabus Mendes 29 (near Praça de República), books in English and German.

Camera Repairs T. Tanaka Cia Ltd repair Nikon cameras, very helpful. Will give advice and addresses for other makes.

Local Transport The metro is clean, cheap and efficient; it operates from 0500-2400. Book of ten tickets US$1.25; backpacks are allowed. Combined bus and metro ticket are available, e.g. to Congonhas airport. The East-West line (2) is being extended 14 km. from Barra Funda (the interchange with Fepasa and RFFSA railways and site of a future, third Rodoviária) to Itaquera. Local buses are normally crowded and rather slow, but clean. Maps of the bus and metro system are available at depots, e.g. Anhangabaú. Taxis display cards of actual tariffs in the window, for "especial taxis", dearer but fewer hassles, T 251-1733. The municipal transport agency CMTC organizes tours of the city by metro and bus (US$1) or by metro only (US$0.50). Information and tickets at the Sé metro station. Sightseeing tours also leave on Sundays from Praça da República.

Night Clubs There are several first-class night-clubs serving excellent meals; they prefer couples to single people. Besides very good dance-bands, the majority have floor-shows in which internationally-famed artists perform. *A Baiúca*, Praça Roosevelt 256; *Silvio's* and *Plano's*, Oscar Freire 913 and 811 respectively; *Stardust*, Largo do Arouche 336. *Catedral da Samba* (Rua Rui Barbosa 333); *Igrejinha* (Rua Santo Antônio 973) and *O Beco* (Rua Bela Cintra 306), rec. for samba. Also rec.: *O Jogral*, Rua Maceió 66, Higienópolis (reasonable). Several small clubs with live music in the Bela Vista area of Av. Santo Antônio and Rua 13 de Maio.

Discotheques *London Tavern* (Hilton Hotel, subsolo); *Ton Ton* (Rua Néstor Pestana 115); Moustache (Rua Sergipe 160—gay), *Madame Satã*, Conselheiro Ramalho 873, Bela Vista, zona central (new-wave type), among others. Jazz at *Opus 2004*, Rua Consolação 2004.

Entertainment The Teatro Municipal is used by visiting theatrical and operatic groups but has no resident company. There are several first-class theatres: Aliança Francesa, Teatro Arena, Itália, Maria Della Costa, Paiol, Ruth Escobar among others. There are also ballet companies and the usual multitude of luxurious cinemas.

Golf Courses About half an hour's drive from the centre there are two 18-hole golf courses, one at Santo Amaro, and another, the São Fernando Golf Club, in beautiful surroundings. There is a sporting 9-hole course at São Francisco club, beyond the Butantã Institute.

Sport The most popular is association football. The most important matches are played at Morumbi and Pacaembu grounds. At Interlagos there is a first-class racing track (**see page 347**). There is yachting, sailing and rowing on the Santo Amaro reservoir. For nature trails, etc., Free Way, Rua Leôncio de Carvalho 267, Paraíso, CEP 04.003 São Paulo, T 285-4767/283-5983.

Culture and Education There are three universities: the official university of São Paulo, the

Pontifical Catholic University, and the Mackenzie University. The official University of São Paulo is now situated in the Cidade Universitária (buses from main bus station), outside the city beyond Pinheiros. There are a number of architecturally interesting buildings housing different faculties and the four museums of archaeology, ethnology, anthropology and mineralogy. (All keep different hours, but all are open Mon.-Thurs. 1400-1700.)

Galleries and Museums The **Museu de Arte de São Paulo** (founded by Assis Chateaubriand, Av. Paulista 1578, immediately above the 9 de Julho tunnel, nearest metro is Paraíso, or circular bus 805A from Praça da República) has a large group of French Impressionists, Florentine and Umbrian painters (including Botticelli and Raphael), several Hieronymus Bosch and Frans Post, sculptures by Rodin, some interesting work by Brazilian artists, including Portinári. Particularly interesting are the pictures of the North-East done by Dutch artists during the Dutch occupation (1630-54): the exotic tropical landscapes— even the Paulo Afonso falls!—have been made to look incredibly temperate. (Exhibitions vary, not all the arts above may be on view.) Temporary exhibitions are held in the basement. Entrance US$0.25, Tues.-Fri. 1300-1700, Sat.-Sun. 1400-1800. The **Museum of Brazilian Art** is at Rua Alagoas 903, Higienópolis, entrance free, Tues.-Fri. 1000-2200, Sat.-Sun. 1400-1800. Here there are copies of Brazilian sculptures, including those of Aleijadinho. The **Museum of Anthropology and Ethnology** is on the fourth and fifth floors of Bloco D in the main Arts Complex just opposite the entrance to the Butantã Institute (see page 347). Every odd-numbered year the São Paulo Bienal at Ibirapuera has the most important show of modern art in Latin America, open from beginning of Sept. till Nov. For the other museums at Ibirapuera (including the Museum of Contemporary Art), see page 337, and for the Museu Paulista and Casa do Grito at Ipiranga, see page 347.

There are two museums on Av. Tiradentes, near the Luz Park; the **Museum of Sacred Art** in the Convento da Luz, No 676 (open Tues.-Sun. 1300-1700, US$0.20) and the State Art Collection (**Pinacoteca do Estado**) at No. 141 (open Tues.-Sun. 1400-1800, free).

Not far from the Butantã Institute (see page 347) are the **Casa do Bandeirante** (being renovated) at Praça Monteiro Lobato, the reconstructed home of a pioneer of 400 years ago (Tues.-Sun. 1000-1700, free); and the **Casa do Sertanista**, a museum of Indian folklore and handicrafts mounted by the famous expert on the Indians, Orlando Villas Boas, at Av. Francisco Morato 2200, open Tues.-Sun., 1230-1730, entrance free.

The **Casa Brasileira**, Av. Faria Lima 774, has been established as a museum of Brazilian furniture. Open weekdays 0900-1200 and 1400-1700. **Museo Padre Anchieta**, Pátio do Colégio, is a restored mission house; inside are examples and relics of the Jesuit era, entrance US$0.05. The **Sound and Image Museum** is at Av. Europa 158. The **Museum of Lasar Segall**, at Rua Alfonso Celso 362, Vila Mariana (near Santa Cruz metro station), shows the works of a German expressionist painter who emigrated to Brazil. **Museum of Japanese Immigration**, Rua São Joaquim 381, Liberdade, excellent, nice roof garden, ask at desk for English translation of the exhibits. **Museo da Fundação Maria Luisa e Oscar Americano**, Av. Morumbi 3700, Morumbi, a private collection of Brazilian and Portuguese art and furniture, well-displayed; hours Tues.-Sun., 1330-1700. There is a **Museo da Discoteca e Biblioteca da Música** at Rua Catão 611, 5th and 6th floors, open Mon.-Fri., 0900-1300 (take bus 819 P from Praça Princesa Isabel to Lapa district). **Museu do Telefone**, Martiniano de Carvalho 851, Paraíso, Tues.-Fri., 0900-1730, Sat.-Sun., 1400-1800, quite good, but you're not allowed to operate anything. **Transport Museum**, Av Cruzeiro do Sul 780, Tues.-Sun., 0900-1700.

The **Centro Cultural São Paulo**, Rua Vergueiro 1000 (metro Vergueiro) has art and photographic exhibitions, a library, music and dance shows (often regional) and films; open daily until 2200. **Memorial to Latin American Unification**, alongside Barra Funda metro station, relief map of Central and South America under a glass floor, library of photographs and films shown on video, entrance free.

Banks Times when open vary from bank to bank. Lloyds Bank, Rua Quinze de Novembro 143-165. (Open 1000-1630.) Banco Internacional, Rua Quinze de Novembro 240. Banco Holandês Unido, Rua Quinze de Novembro 150. Citibank, Av. Ipiranga 855, or Av. Paulista IIII (T 576-2211) will receive money from abroad (US$20 charge, takes 5 days). First National Bank of Boston, Rua Líbero Badaró 487. Banco Lar Brasileiro (Chase Manhattan owned), 131 Rua Alvares Penteado, and other national banks. Banco Mercantil de São Paulo, Av. Paulista 1450, for cash advances on Access/Master Charge, but slow.

Exchange Many câmbios near Praça da República. American Express (Kontik Franstur—address below) very helpful; Exprinter, Barão de Itapetininga 243, also deals in foreign currencies (cash only). Boreal Turismo, Rua Dom José de Barros 326. Tourist Cambio, Rua Badaró (turn left off Viaduto do Chá); Agency Faro, Av. São Luis 157, for travellers' cheques; Interpax, Praça da República 177, loja 13, changes cheques at good rates. For parallel rates ask at tourist kiosks for details.

Trade and Cultural Institutions British Chamber of Commerce of São Paulo, Rua Barão de Itapetininga 275, 7th floor; Caixa Postal 1621. T 255-0519. Sociedade Brasileira de Cultura Inglesa, Avenida Higienópolis 449. American Chamber of Commerce for Brazil, Rua Formosa 367, 29th floor, T 222-6377. American Library, União Cultural Brasil-Estados Unidos, Rua Coronel Oscar Porto 208, T 287-1022. Goethe-Instituto, Rua Frei Caneca 1246 (open Mon.-Thurs. 1400-2030). Instituto Hans Staden, Rua Cons. Crispiniano 53, 12th floor.

Consulates Argentine, Rua Araújo 216, 8th floor (open 0830-1300, very easy to get visa here); **Bolivian**, Rua Quirino de Andrade 219, 3rd floor, (open 0900-1300), T 255-3555; **Paraguayan**, Av. São Luiz 112, 10th floor, T 259-3579; **Uruguayan**, Al. Campinas 433, 7th floor, T 284-5777; **Venezuelan**, Rua Jerônimo da Viega 164, 16th floor, T 883-3000.

    American Consulate General, Rua Padre João Manuel 933, T 881-6511; **Canadian Consulate General**, Av. Paulista 854-5th floor, T 287-2122; **British Consulate General**, Av. Paulista 1938, 17th floor, Caixa Postal 846, T 287-7722; **Irish**, Av. Paulista 2006, 5th floor, 01310 São Paulo, T 287-6362; **West German**, Av. Brig Faria Lima 1383, 12th floor, T 814-6644; **Swiss Consulate-General**, Av. Paulista 1754, 4th floor, Caixa Postal 30588. T 289-1033; **Austrian Consulate-General**, Al Lorena 1271, 01424 São Paulo, T 282-6223; **Swedish Consulate-General**, Rua Oscar Freire 379, 3rd floor, T 883-3322 (postal address: Caixa Postal 51626, 01499 São Paulo); **Dutch**, Av. Brigadeiro Faria Lima 1698.

Churches St. Paul's Anglican (Episcopal) Church, Rua Comendador Elias Zarzua 1231, Santo Amaro. T 246-0383. Igreja Metodista, Av Liberdade 695, T 278-5895. Mormon Church, Av. Prof. Francisco Morato 2430, T 570-2483. Synagogue Centro Israelista, Rua Newton Prado 76, T 220-0185. Templo Budista, Av. do Cursino 753, T 63-4015. Lutheran church, Av. Rio Branco 34. Swedish Church, Igreja Evangelica Luterana Escandinava, Rua Job Lane 1030, CEP 04639, T 011-247 88 29.

Police T 228-2276; Radio Patrol, T 190. Federal Police, Av. Prestes Maio 700, open 1000-1600 for visa extensions.

Emergency First Aid, T 71-8673, 71-0757 or 852-3649.

Physicians (English-speaking) Edwin Castello, José Maria Lisboa 861, s/104, T 287-9071; Ruy Silva, Conselheiro Brotero 1505, No. 64, T 67-2470; Wilson Frey, Barão de Jacegua 1102, T 241-4474. Christel Schlúnder, Rua Alvares de Azevedo 127, Sto. Amaro, T 247-5963, German speaking, and for children. Also Samaritans' Hospital, Rua Conselheiro Brotero 1486. T 51-2154.

Post Office Praça do Correio, corner Av. São João.

International Telephone Rua 7 de Abril 295, near Praça da República.

Cables Embratel, Av. São Luís 50, and Av. Ipiranga 344.

Tourist Offices Praça da República (very helpful), and Praça da Sé, Praça Dom José Gaspar and Liberdade metro stations (small red kiosks). Office at Guarulhos airport is helpful. For information on São Paulo State, Praça Antônio Prado 9, 6th floor, Av. São Luís 115. On Sundays a free cultural tour of the city starts at the tourist office (buses every 20 mins. from 0900 to 1600), to see Casa do Bandeirante, Casa do Sertanista, Capella do Morumbi, the old market, and Casa do Grito, T 267-2102/2122 for information, for children's entertainment ext 627/640. For weekly information on cultural activities, addresses and recommended bars, see the supplement "Veja em São Paulo", of the magazine *Veja*. Tourist offices have free magazine, *Visão. Guia Turística Carto Plum* available from banks etc. around Praça da República. Also recommended is Quatro Rodas guide to the City.

Maps of São Paulo in train timetables at news-stands (US$2.50), and in the monthly tourist guide published by the Prefeitura. Also obtainable from the tourist offices, the Rodoviária (upstairs), the better hotels, American Express and H. Stern, the jeweller. 2 private map producers: Geo Mapas, Rua Libero Badaró 336, C.E.P. 01008, T 259-2166 (40% discount for volume purchases, excellent 1988 1:5,000,000 map of Brazil, town maps), and Editorial Abril, Rua Geraldo Flaufino Gomez 61, Barrio Brooklin, C.E.P. 04575, T 545-8122.

Travel Agents *Wilson, Sons S.A.*, Av. São Luís 715; *Exprinter*, Rua Barão de Itapetininga 243; *Receptur*, same street, 221; *Wagon-Lits Cook*, Av. São Luís 285; *Woehrle Turismo*, Rua do Tesouro 47, cep 01013, T (011) 37-7594, USA T (011) 532-1105, helpful, German spoken; *Tunibra*, Praça da Liberdade 63, T 36-0101, helpful; *Itatiaia Publicidade e Turismo*, Cons. Crispiniano 69 (for hotel reservations especially); *Transatlântica Turismo*, Rua Coronel Xavier de Toledo 98 (for local excursions); *Kontik-Franstur* (American Express representative), Rua Marconi 71. *Royal Turismo*, Manoel da Nóbrega off Av. Paulista, helpful to budget travellers. Visits to coffee fazendas (May-June) and round trips into the surrounding country are organized by the travel agencies.

Railways The Estrada de Ferro Santos a Jundiaí (ex São Paulo Railway) to Santos "down the hill" (passenger service suspended in 1985), also to Jundiaí and the interior; Fepasa into the coffee, fruit and cattle districts; Central do Brasil Railway to Rio de Janeiro, 9 hrs. journey, night sleeper train (the Santa Cruz) leaving at 2300; warmly rec., US$15 for a double cabin; Cia Mogiana to NE of state, from Campinas through Ribeirão Preto; Fepasa through Sorocaba to Bauru. No through tickets from São Paulo to Campo Grande or Corumbá are sold; you must go by bus or train (0830, 1925, 2225) from Luz station to Bauru (risking a day's wait there for train connections) from where Estrada de Ferro Noroeste do Brasil goes daily across Mato Grosso do Sul to Corumbá (34 hrs. from São Paulo), and on, after crossing frontier by road, from Quijarro (Bolivia) to Santa Cruz de la Sierra by the Estrada de Ferro Brasil-Bolívia (**see page** 354). There is a railway from São Paulo to Brasília, changing at Campinas; US$24.50 sleeper, US$14.50 1st class, leaves on Sun. at 1000, reaching Campinas at 1125, and Brasília 0830 on Mon. (through tickets available). The track is bad, but the journey interesting. The "Expresses" train leaves for Araraquara (**see page** 352) 0715 and 1925, first class only, returns 1129 and 2304, diner, reported to be the best trains in Brasil. There are several railway stations in São Paulo; Júlio Prestes for Suburban trains. A new terminal, Barra Funda handles Fepasa long distance, metro and commuter trains and transfers from CBTU commuter trains. A new terminal will handle RFFSA long distance trains.

RFFSA is planning to restore the uppermost stage of the São Paulo—Paranapiaçaba cog railway and the railway buildings; the line was the first to link São Paulo with the coast and Santos.

Roads Distances in km.: Belém, 2,917; Brasília, 1,100; Belo Horizonte, 586; Curitiba, 397; Florianópolis, 700; Fortaleza, 3,065; Foz do Iguaçu, 1,071; Manaus, 4,052 (last stretch not paved); Natal, 2,992; Porto Alegre, 1,143; Recife, 2,671; Rio, 429; Salvador, 1,944; Vitória, 932. To take the picturesque new coast road to Rio, take the Via Anchieta to the Guarujá turn, before Guarujá take Bertioga turn and you're on the Santos-Rio highway. Motorists leaving the ring road for Curitiba and Iguaçu should follow Regis de Bittencourt signs. To hitch to Rio, take the metro to Ponte Pequeno, then a bus to Guarulhos, alighting where the bus turns off the Rio road for Guarulhos.

Buses To get to the new Rodoviária, take the metro to Tietê, very convenient. Bus to centre, US$0.20. Bus to Rio, 6 hrs., frequent service, US$6 (leito, 12), special section for this route in the Rodoviária; to Curitiba, 6 hrs., US$6 (leito, 12); to Blumenau, 9½ hrs., US$10; to Porto Alegre, 18 hrs., US$16.75 (leito, 33.50); Rio Grande 25 hrs., US$25; to Belo Horizonte, 10 hrs., US$10 (leito, 20); buy ticket and get on bus at Terminal Bresser, T 61.084-018. Salvador, 30 hrs., US$30 (leito, 60); to Recife, 40 hrs., US$42 (leito, 84); to Fortaleza, 48 hrs. US$46 (leito 92); to Natal, US$41, 55 hrs.; to Cuiabá, 24 hrs., US$18 (Andorinha at 1700, connects with Cuiabá-Porto Velho bus); to Campo Grande (Mato Grosso do Sul), 16 hrs., US$14.50; to Porto Velho, 60 hrs. (or more), US$50; to Brasília, 15 hrs., US$14 (leito, 28); to Foz do Iguaçu, 16 hrs., US$15 (leito, 30). To Santos, US$1.50 (there is a bus station for Santos and São Vicente at the southern end of the Metro line, at Jabaquara, buses from here leave every 5 minutes, taking about 50 minutes); São Sebastião, 4 hrs. US$4 (say "via Bertioga" if you want to go by the coast road); to Parati, Angra dos Reis and also to Ilhabela, 2 daily, 8 hrs., US$7.50.

To Montevideo, via Porto Alegre, with TTL, departs 2200, 31 hrs. US$40; to Buenos Aires 36 hrs., US$60 (leito, 120); to Santiago, Pluma or Gral. Urquiza (both start from Rio), 56 hrs., US$110; to Asunción (1,044 km.), 18 hours with Pluma or RYSA, US$24 (leito US$48).

Air Services There are air services to all parts of Brazil, Europe, North and South America from the new international airport at Guarulhos (30 km. from the city); the local airport of Congonhas, 14 km. from the city centre, is used for the Rio-São Paulo shuttle and private flights only. From Guarulhos there are airport taxis which charge US$17 on a fixed rate system. Metro bus service every 25 mins. to Guarulhos from Praça da República, US$3; metro bus trip (US$2.50) to the Rodoviária do Tietê and Congonhas airport, every 20-40 mins., approx. 1 hr. There are about four hundred flights per week to Rio de Janeiro (about US$55). All airline offices in triangle formed by Av. São Luís, Av. Ipiranga and Rua da Consolação. Amex provides free transport for cardholders from airports to city centre.

Air freight Pan Am, at Carga Aérea Terminal, T531-4366/4052/9602, has a small package "sprint" service to the USA, max 30 kg., US$4.46/kg., but not for business purchases (for these you need an export broker)—open Mon.-Fri. 0900-1800. Varig will send anything, anywhere, for US$6.65/kg. (cheaper if paid in new cruzeiros), but involves more red tape, office next to Pan Am.

The Butantã Snake Farm and Museum (Instituto Seroterápico at the University), Av. Dr. Vital Brasil 1500, Pinheiros, is the most popular tourist attraction. The snakes are milked for their poison six times a day but you may not witness this; the antidotes made from the venom have greatly reduced deaths from snakebite in Brazil. Open daily from 0800-1700 (except Mon.), entrance US$1.50. Informative museum; details in English and Portuguese. From Praça da República take bus marked "Butantã" along Av. Paulista, and ask to be let out at the right place.

Parque da Independência, in the suburb of Ipiranga, contains the famous Ipiranga Monument to commemorate the declaration of Brazilian independence; beneath the monument is the Imperial Chapel, with the tomb of the first emperor, Dom Pedro I, and Empress Leopoldina (open Tues.-Sun., 1300-1700). Take bus 4612 from Praça da República. The **Casa do Grito**, the little house in which Dom Pedro I spent the night before his famous cry of **Ipiranga— "Independence or Death"**—is preserved in the park (open Tues.-Sun. 1300-1730). The **Museu Paulista**, housed in a huge palace at the top of the park, has old maps, traditional furniture, collections of old coins and of religious art and rare documents, and a department of Indian ethnology. Behind the Museum is the Ipiranga Botanical Garden. Open Tues.-Sun. and holidays, 1300-1730. Take bus 478-P (Ipiranga-Pompéia for return) from Ana Rosa. There is a *son et lumière* show on Brazilian history in the park on Wed., Fri. and Sat. evenings at 2030.

Parque do Estado (Jardim Botânico), out at Água Funda (Av. Jabaquara), has a vast garden esplanade surrounded by magnificent stone porches, with lakes and trees and places for picnics, and a very fine orchid farm worth seeing during the flowering season, November-December. Over 32,000 different kinds of orchids are cultivated. Open Tue.-Sat., 0900-1700. The astronomical observatory nearby is open to the public Thurs. afternoons. Bus 475 from Brig. Luís Antônio or metro to Jaguaribe (2nd last stop), then a bus marked "Zoológico".

Zoological Gardens Near the Jardim Botânico, not more than half an hour's drive from the city centre. A very large variety of specimens can be seen in an almost natural setting of about 35 hectares of forest: a most interesting site. Open 0900-1800, admission US$0.45 (bus 4742, "Jardim Celeste", from São Judas Tadeu). There is a wild-life park, Simba Safari, nearby, admission US$0.80 per pedestrian, US$2 p.p. with a car, open Tues.-Sun. 0900-1800.

Aquarium The one formerly on Av. Pacaembu has closed, but the "Exotiquarium" on the bottom level of the Morumbi Shopping Centre claims to be the largest in South America, US$2; it has a pink river dolphin.

Parque Água Branca (Avenida Água Branca, 455) has beautiful gardens with specimens of tropical plants, Brazilian birds and wild life. Pavilions house a well stocked aquarium, a zoo, and exhibitions of food produce.

In Tremembé, a little beyond Cantareira, half an hour from the down-town area, is the **Horto Florestal**, containing examples of nearly every species of Brazilian woodland flora (admission daily, 0800-1800).

Santo Amaro Dam (Old Lake), is 3 km. from the centre of Santo Amaro suburb. This is a popular boating resort with several sailing clubs and many attractive cottages along the shore. There is a bus (30 min.) from São Paulo to Santo Amaro.

Interlagos, which has a motor-racing circuit with 18 km. of track, is São Paulo's lake resort on the Santo Amaro dam. It can be reached from Santo Amaro by bus. Close to the track, where the Brazilian Grand Prix takes place every second year, usually in February, is the 32-km. long Guarapiranga artificial lake with good restaurants and several luxurious sailing and sports clubs. Camping Clube do Brasil site. Guarapiranga is less polluted than the other artificial lake, Billings, which also has restaurants.

Pico de Jaraguá (1,135 metres) the highest peak in the neighbourhood, gives good views of Greater São Paulo on a fine day. This peak is reached from Km. 18 on the Campinas highway (Via Anhanguera) by a good road through Taipas and Pirituba.

Embu, 28 km. from São Paulo, is a colonial town which has become a centre for artists and craftsmen. On Sunday afternoons there is a large and popular arts and crafts fair; not to be missed. Buses from close to the Largo de Pinheiros, São Paulo, or Santo Amaro bus.

The Coast of the State of São Paulo

Santos, 63 km. SE of São Paulo and 5 km. from the open sea, is the most important Brazilian port. (Over 40% by value of all Brazilian imports and about half the total exports pass through it.) It is reached from Rio by ship (320 km.) in 12-15 hrs., and a direct highway between the two cities has been completed (**see pages** 313 and 350). A railway (no passenger service) and the Anchieta and Imigrantes highways run to São Paulo. A free-port zone for Paraguay, 1,930 km. by rail or road, has been established. A few km. outside the city there is an important industrial area round the steelworks, oil refinery and hydroelectric plant at Cubatão (known locally as the Valley of Death because of the pollution from chemical factories, among the worst in the world).

The plain upon which Santos, a city of 411,000 people, stands is an island which can be circumnavigated by small boats. The city has impressive modern buildings, wide, tree-lined avenues, and wealthy suburbs. The streets around Praça Mauá are very busy in the daytime, with plenty of cheap shops. In the centre, an interesting building is the Bolsa Oficial de Café, in Rua 15 de Novembro. The night-life can best be seen in the Gonzaga area which has the large hotels. Although best known for its commerce, Santos is also a holiday resort, with magnificent beaches and views. The port is approached by the winding Santos Channel; at its mouth is an old fort (1709).

There are many monuments: one in Avenida Ana Costa to commemorate the brothers Andradas, who took a leading part in the movement for independence; one in the Praça Rui Barbosa to Bartolomeu de Gusmão, who has a claim to the world's first historically recorded airborne ascent in 1709; one in the Praça da República to Bras Cubas, who founded the city in 1534; and one in the Praça José Bonifácio to the soldiers of Santos who died in the Revolution of 1932. There are a disappointing municipal aquarium on Av. Bartolomeu de Gusmão (Ponta da Praia) and a Museu do Mar, Rua República do Equador 81.

Local Holidays (in addition to national): 26 Jan. (Foundation of Santos); Good Friday; Corpus Christi.

Hotels *Parque Balneario*, complex at the centre of Gonzaga, Ana Costa 555, T (0132) 34-7211, Telex (13) 1241PBHS BR, A, with shopping centre; *Mendes Plaza*, Av. Floriano Peixoto 42, T (0132) 37-4243, Telex MHTX 13-3002, A; *Mendes Panorama*, Rua Euclides da Cunha 15, T (0132) 37.2627, Telex MHTX 133003, B-C; *Atlântico*, Av. Pres. Wilson 1, T 37-8823, C, good value; *Gonzaga*, Av. Pres. Wilson 36, T 4-1411, D with bath; *Indaiá*, Av. Ana Costa 431, T 4-1134, C; *Transmontana*, Rua Marechal Floriano Peixoto 202, rec.; *Maracanã Santos*, Pres. Wilson, 172, T 37-4030, beach front, C; *Avenida Palace*, Pres. Wilson 10, T 4-1166, beach front, C; *Santos*, Bartolomeu de Gusmão 16, C with bath; *Estoril*, Rua Bitencourt 55, E, with bath, cheap (has round beds, red lights and mirrored ceilings); small, family-style hotels can be found in this area; many cheap hotels near the Orquidário Municipal, 1-2 blocks from the beach. *Vilazul*, Av. Sen Feijo, nr. Rodoviária, F, clean, a/c, breakfast.

Restaurants *Cibus*, Av Conselleiro Nébias, beach end, considered the best; *Cantina Dom Fabrízio*, Av. Ana Costa 482; *Jangadeiro*, Ponta da Praia; *Hong Kong Palace*, Av. Conselheiro Nébias 288 (Chinese food); *Rincón Argentino*, Av. Manuel da Nóbrega 666, at São Vicente (Gaucho food); *Ilha Porchat Grill*, on Ilha Porchat, off São Vicente, at edge of island, overlooking bays of São Vicente and Santos; *Penhasco*, Ilha Porchat; first class *Pizzaria Zi Tereza*, Av. Ana Costa 451; also *Pizzaria Santa Izabel*, Av. Bartolomeu de Gusmão 165 (also serves seafood); *Churrascaria Tertúlia*, N0190, T (0132) 36-1461; *Chico's Bar*, Av. Floriano Peixoto (Boqueirão), good. *Fonte das Vitaminas*, Ana Costa 534, good for juices, lunches.

Electric Current 220 A.C. 60 cycles.

Taxis All taxis are supplied with meters. The fare is a fixed charge of US$0.25 plus US$0.10 per km. Taxi, Gonzaga to bus station, US$2.

Banks Banco Internacional, Rua General Câmara 24; Banco Holandês Unido, Citibank, Banco do Brasil, all in the Rua 15 de Novembro. The First National Bank of Boston, Praça Visc. de

Mauá 14. Banks open: 1000-1630.

Exchange Houses Casa Faro, Rua 15 de Novembro, 80 & 260; Casa Bancaria Branco, Praça de República 29 and Gonzaga, R Galeão Carvalhal 52/4.

Consulate (British) Rua Tuiuti 58, 2nd floor, Caixa Postal 204, 11010 Santos-SP, T 33-6111/34-6656.

All Saints Church Praça Washington 92, José Menino. Services in English held every Sun.

Cables Embratel, Largo Senador Vergueiro 1 and 2.

Tourist Information Praça dos Expedicionários 10, 10th floor; booths at Aquarium, Rodoviária, Casa do Café, Orquidário Municipal.

Coastal Shipping Irregular services to Brazilian ports by Companhia de Navegação Lóide Brasileiro. Consult their agents, Rua General Câmara 22, 2nd floor, conjunto 34.

Rail The British-built Santos a Jundiaí up the hill to São Paulo is one of the railway wonders of the world; it passes through Cubatão and then, running on toothed tracks up the escarpment, interesting hill scenery. Passenger services were suspended in 1985. From Ana Costa station, a Fepasa (mixed) train may be taken to Embu Guaçu from where there is a bus to São Paulo.

Air Services From São Paulo; Santos has no airport.

Bus Services Buses start for most suburbs from Praça Mauá, in the centre of the city. There are buses to São Paulo (50 mins., US$1.50) at intervals of approximately 15 mins., from the Rodoviária near city centre. Enquire about being picked up or put down outside usual terminal points. Express cars also run to São Paulo at regular intervals. Fare, US$2.75 each way, per passenger. (The two highways between São Paulo and Santos are sometimes seriously crowded, especially at rush hours and weekends.) Buses for Santos are caught in São Paulo in the Jabaquara bus station, not the new Rodoviária. There are direct buses to Rio but not along the coast road (Normandy company, 6 a day, 7½ hrs., US$7, leito at 2230, US$14); to get to Rio along the coast road, you must take an Atlántico bus to Ubatuba or Caraguatatuba, change there for Rio.

Excursions To the coasts E of Santos (Guarujá, Bertioga, Ilhabela) and SW (Praia Grande, Itanhaém). Short excursion along the Guarujá road to José Menino for the orchid gardens in the Praça Washington (flowering Oct.-Feb.). There is an open-air cage containing humming-birds of 20 different species and the park is also a sanctuary for other birds.

The **Ilha Porchat**, a small island reached by a bridge at the far end of Santos/São Vicente bay, has beautiful views over rocky precipices, of the high seas on one side and the city and bay on the other. At the summit is a splendid night club, the Top House Restaurante e Discoteca. No entrance fee but there is a minimum charge of US$8.

To **Alto da Serra**, the summit of the forest-clad mountain range; magnificent views. The return journey can be done in under 2 hrs. by road.

Monte Serrat A funicular railway to the summit (every ½ hr., US$1 return), where there is a semaphore station and look-out post which reports the arrival of all ships in Santos harbour. There is also a quaint old church, dedicated to Nossa Senhora da Monte Serrat, said to have performed many miracles. The top can be reached on foot. Seven shrines have been built on the way up; annual pilgrimages are made by the local people. Fine views.

Guarujá (pop. 186,000).The route from Santos to the resort of Guarujá is along Av. Conselheiro Nébias to the seafront, continuing along the beach to the Guarujá ferry (every 10 min., free for pedestrians) at Ponta da Praia. On the other side proceed as far as Turtle Bay. During the season and weekends there is a long delay at the Ponta da Praia vehicle ferry; to avoid this take the ferry on foot and get the bus on the Guarujá side; motor boats also cross for US$0.06. There is a strong undertow on nearly all the Guarujá beaches; the Jequiti-Mar beach (officially called Praia de Pernambuco) is the safest. Golf club at Guarujá. (Trolleybus from Praça Mauá in Santos to the ferry, then buses.)

Turn left in centre of Guarujá and drive less than 1 km. to reach Delfim Hotel (A) and its restaurant La Popote at the beginning of the long beach of Praia da Enseada. Close by, at Av.

Miguel Stefano 999, is *Casa Grande Hotel*, luxury, A, in colonial style, with clean beach. Facing sea is the luxurious *Ferraretto Hotel*, B (night club, swimming pool). Camping Clube do Brasil site at Praia do Perequé (where the best fish restaurants are), near municipal nursery. Good *churrascaria* opposite Rodoviária.

The Jequiti-Mar holiday complex, 8 km. beyond Guarujá on the road to Bertioga, is extremely attractive. There are private beaches (excellent swimming and boating) and very fine fishing grounds, and chalet accommodation, A or B, according to size and situation. There is an excellent restaurant and two night clubs; they are open each weekend and every night from December to March, in the holiday season. 2 km. further north is a beach where fishing boats land their catch—a number of good seafood restaurants line the seafront.

There are good sea-food restaurants on the road to **Bertioga**, an attractive place, where the fort of São João houses the João Ramalho museum (bus Guarujá-Bertioga, 1 hr., US$0.30). (Hotels: *Marazul*, Av. Tomé de Souza 825; *Indaiá Praia*, same street, No. 1079, both C; restaurants *Zezé e Duarte (2)*, *O Camarão de Bertioga*.) The coastal road beyond Bertioga is paved, and the new Rio-Santos highway, 1-2 km. inland, is completed, and provides a good link to São Sebastião. Going NE, the beaches are Praia de Bertioga. Praia São Lourenço, Praia Guaratuba, Praia Boracéia (campsite, US$0.70 with meals), are all empty except for the light traffic. 30 km. beyond Boracéia is the beach resort of Maresia (hotels, campsite), from where it is 21 km. to **São Sebastião** (two buses a day from Rio, 1030 and 1830, to Rio 0600 and 2330 not along the coast, heavily booked in advance; 4 a day from Santos, 3½ hrs.; buses from São Paulo (US$4) run inland via São José dos Campos, unless you ask for the service via Bertioga, only 2 a day), and **(free ferry) to Ilhabela** (4 hrs. by bus from Santos, 3 a day, US$3). There is a Museu de Arte Sacra in the chapel of São Gonçalo in the town centre. Tourist Office; Av. Dr Altino Arantes 174, friendly and helpful except regarding Ilhabela. The São Sebastião beaches are polluted; foreigners can stay in the Camping Clube do Brasil grounds for US$3 a night. 6 km. S of São Sebastião is Camping do Barraquecaba Bar de Mar de Lucas, US$2 per night, rec. (*Hotel Roma*, on the main square, excellent, E and upwards, very well rec.; *Recanto dos Pássaros*, Porto Grande, both C; *Arrastão*, B with most facilities; *São Paulo*, E with breakfast, clean, friendly.) Ilhabela tends to be expensive in season, when it is cheaper to stay in São Sebastião.

Half-way between Bertioga and São Sebastião, on the Praia de Juqueí beach, is Hotel Timão, C, German-owned, with excellent fish meals.

Ilha de São Sebastião (Ilhabela). The island of São Sebastião, known popularly as Ilhabela, is now easily accessible by car or bus from Santos. A bus runs along the coastal strip facing the mainland. Cavendish, the English pirate, had his secret anchorage in one of the sheltered caves there. Last century it was used as a landing place for illegal slave-traffic.

The island is of volcanic origin, roughly about 390 sq. km. in area. Its highest peak, Morro do Papagaio, rises 1,300 metres above sea-level, with its bare peak often obscured by mist; the slopes are densely wooded. There are many beautiful waterfalls, easily accessible to the enterprising walker. Most of the flatter ground is given over to sugar-cane.

The only settled district lies on the coastal strip facing the mainland, the Atlantic side being practically uninhabited except by a few fisherfolk. The place abounds in tropical plants and flowers of the most extraordinary variety, and many fruits grow wild, whose juice mixed with cachaça and sugar makes as delicious a cocktail as can be imagined.

No alterations are allowed to the frontage of the main township, **Ilhabela**. Visitors abound during summer week-ends; motorists are warned to avoid those days as the car-carrying capacity of the ferry is very limited.

The energetic can climb over the hump of the island down towards the Atlantic, sometimes through dense tropical forest following the old slave trail, but for this 50-km. return journey a local guide is required. There is a rough road to the Atlantic side, but it is very difficult to drive. A visit to the terraced Toca waterfalls amid dense jungle close to the foot of the 970-metre Baepi peak will give you cool freshwater bathing (entry, US$0.50). In all shady places, especially away from the sea, there abounds a species of midge known locally as *borrachudos*. A locally sold repellant (Autum) keeps them off for some time, however. Those allergic to insect bites should remain on the inhabited coastal strip.

Hotels in Ilhabela: *Mercedes*, B, T 72-1071; *Ilhabela*, C, T 72-1083, Av Pedro Paulo de Morais 151, rec., good breakfast. Next door is *Itapemar*, T 72-1329, windsurfing equipment rented at US$3 an hour, A. Also in the C price range are *Bella Vista* (nice position), *Petit Village*, *Solar dos Bandeirantes*, and *Colonial*. *Pousada dos Hibiscos*, Av. P.P. de Morais 714, T 72-1375, C, good atmosphere, swimming pool, rec. There are several other less expensive pensions in D/E range, such as *Sul America*. *Camping Porto Seguro*, accessible by two-hourly bus from Ilhabela, US$8 p.p.

Restaurant *Les Boucaniers*, French-run, rec., US$3.50 per head. *Perequê*, reasonable. *Farol*, Av. Princesa Isabel 1634, Perequê, good, especially seafood, rec.

Sightseeing Visit the old Feiticeira plantation, with underground dungeons. The road is along the coast, sometimes high above the sea, towards the south of the island. You can go by bus, taxi, or horse and buggy.

Pedras do Sino (Bell Rocks) These curious seashore boulders, when struck with a piece of iron or stone, emit a loud bell-like note. Another campsite nearby.

Bathing Bathing on the mainland side is not recommended because of oil, sandflies and jelly fish on the beaches and in the water. Praia dos Castelhanos, reached by a rough road over the island (no buses), is recommended.

Transport Passenger ferry every 2 hours; stops at Perequê and Ilhabela; separate car ferry runs through the night and serves Perequê only.

North of São Sebastião, on the Santos-Rio road, is São Francisco, a village with *Pontal Hotel* (not rec., expensive, noisy), and *Restaurant Flipper* (excellent); good beaches. Further on is **Caraguatatuba**, with 17 good beaches to the NE and SW (several hotels, popular at weekends, good restaurants: *Brisa*, Av. Artur Costa Filho 1821, *Xamagu*, near main square). Good camping site US$1.60 per night on beach and other sites. Direct buses to Caraguatatuba from Rio de Janeiro, São Paulo and Santos; direct buses from São Paulo do not use the coast road. Further E is **Lagoinha**, 34 km. W of Ubatuba, with chalets and sailing boats for hire. Exotic birdlife and virgin forest. *Maier's Mar Virado* is owned by Hans Maier, who speaks English and arranges hirings. Next is **Ubatuba**, with two Camping Clube do Brasil sites at Maranduba and Perequê-Açu beaches. In all, there are 72 beautiful beaches, quite spread out, most with campsites (Grande, just S, and one 6 km. N of Ubatuba, US$1 p.p., are rec.). There is also a yacht haven. The area gets very crowded at Carnival time as people from Rio come to escape the crowds in their city. Jewellery market on beach, Sats. Ubatuba has numerous hotels; rec. are *Tropicana*, Praia da Enseada, C; *Restaurante Beija Flor* with apartments, D; *Solar das Aguas Cantantes*, Praia do Lázaro (11680 S.P., T 0124-42-0178), reached by local bus, swimming pool, restaurant, B; *Saveiros*, Praia do Lázaro (T 0124-42-0172), pool, restaurant, C, run by a Rumanian, Lucian Strass, English spoken, who welcomes users of *South American Handbook*; *Mauricio*, Av. Abreu Sodre 607, nr. Praia do Perequê-Açu, has cheap rooms, friendly, clothes washing possible. Youth Hostel Cora Coralina, Rodovia Oswaldo Cruz, Km. 89, T 229-3787/229-3011, extension (ramal) 286 for details. Furnished flats and cottages may be rented from Lúcio Martins Rodrigues, Rua Amaral Gurgel 158, Apto. 121—CEP.01221, Vila Buarque, São Paulo; T 853-8101, 532-0496, 577-6482, 221-1357. The flats are in the town centre, 400 m from beach, the cottages 7½ km. from the centre with a natural swimming pool, each can sleep a maximum of 5 (bedroom for 2-3, 2 extra in living room), and has kitchen with cooker and fridge, bathroom and laundry facilities. Cost is US$5 a day, payable in US or Canadian dollars, or any Western European currency.

The road from São Sebastião is paved, so a journey from São Paulo along the coast is possible, 5 buses daily. Ubatuba is 70 km. from Parati (**see page 316**), several buses daily, on the hour, from *Lanchonete Nice*, near Rodoviária. If driving from Ubatuba along the coast to Rio, one can stop for lunch at Porto Aquarius, where there is a cave and hotel in a beautiful setting (not cheap). Direct buses from Rio, São Paulo and Santos.

Straddling the border of São Paulo and Rio de Janeiro states is the **Parque Nacional Serra da Bocaina**, which rises from the coast to heights of over 1,900 metres, encompassing three strata of vegetation (IBDF office, Al. Tietê 637, Caixa Postal 7134, CEP 01.312, São Paulo).

In the opposite direction (SW) from Santos, it is 50 km. beside the Praia Grande to the town of **Itanhaém**, with its pretty colonial church and semi-ruined Convento da Conceição on a small hill. There are several good sea-food restaurants along the beach, and a Camping Clube do Brasil site nearby at Peruíbe beach, and many others which are cheaper. There are many attractive beaches here, and hot springs with medicinal mud (hotels *Maison Suisse, Príncipe, Glória*). The whole stretch of coast is completely built up with holiday developments. Frequent buses from Santos US$0.85, 1 hr.

Further south is the town of **Iguape**, founded in 1538. Typical Portuguese architecture, the small municipal museum is housed in a 16th century building. Buses from São Paulo, Santos, or Curitiba, changing at Registro (see below). It has a market, hotels and restaurants. (*Hotel Pousada Aguape*, Rua Padre Homer, F, good; *Hotel Rio Verde*, F, rec.). Camping Clube do Brasil site on beach. Opposite Iguape is the northern end of the Ilha Comprida with beautiful beaches stretching SW for 86 km. A continuous ferry service runs from Iguape (passengers free; cars at a small charge); buses run until 1900 from the ferry stop to the beaches and campsite Britânia (clean, friendly, US$0.70 p.p., drinkable tap water, tastes bad). The island is being developed as a resort; good restaurants, hotels, supermarket—fresh fish is excellent. At the southern end **Cananéia** is more commercialized than Iguape; it has 3 or 4 hotels (mostly E).

From Iguape it is possible to take a boat trip down the coast to Cananéia and Ariri. Tickets and information from Dept. Hidroviário do Estado, Rua Major Moutinho 198, Iguape, T 41 1122. Boats leave Iguape on Mon., Thurs. (but check in advance), returning next day. It is a beautiful trip, passing between the island and the mainland. The boat has a toilet, fresh water, and meals. In wet weather, the cabin gets crowded and uncomfortable. Ariri has no road connections; there is a hostel, F, run by the shipping line.

Caves Inland, W of the BR-116 are the caverns of the Vale do Ribeira; among the best known is the 8-km. Gruta da Tapagem, known as Caverna do Diabo (Devil's Cave—as huge "as a cathedral" with well-lit formations), 45 km. from Eldorado Paulista. The caves are open 0800-1100 and 1200-1700; bar and toilets. *Hotel Eldorado*, friendly, clean, with breakfast, F. Bus to Eldorado Paulista from Santos or São Paulo, US$2.60, 4-5 hrs., then hitch-hike on banana trucks or tourist buses (which run from both cities); most traffic on Sats. and Suns. From Curitiba, change buses at Jacupiranga for Eldorado Paulista. A suitable stopping place for visiting the caves area is **Registro** on BR-116, in the heart of the tea-growing region, populated mainly by Japanese Brazilians. (*Lito Palace Hotel*, D; *Hotel Continental*, F; *Hotel Brasília*, Rua Brasília, round corner from Rodoviária, F, no breakfast, shower, clean, quiet; good *Churrascaria* next to bus station, US$3 p.p.). 43 km. from Caverna do Diabo is Caverna de Santana, 10 km. from the town of Iporanga; it has 5.6 km. of subterranean passages and three levels of galleries. (Iporanga is the most convenient town for visiting both sets of caves; it is 42 km. from Apiaí, which is 257 km. SW of São Paulo.)

Towns in the State of São Paulo

About 13% of Brazil's population lives within 200 km. of São Paulo city, a circle which includes 88 municipalities. Four of them—the big ABCD towns— sharing a population of over a million, are Santo André, São Bernardo, São Caetano and Diadema; they have many of the largest industrial plants. There are some 70 cities in the State with populations of over 50,000 and São Paulo is linked with all of them by road, and several of them by railway. One important line, the broad-gauge Santos a Jundiaí, runs from Santos to São Paulo (passenger services suspended on this stretch), and across the low mountains which separate São Paulo city from the interior to its terminus at

Jundiaí (pop. 315,000), 58 km. from São Paulo, which has textile factories and other industries. The district grows coffee and grain and there is an annual Grape Festival.

Hotel *Grande Hotel*, Rua do Rosário 605, with good restaurant.

The Fepasa Railway, with the same broad gauge, continues from Jundiaí through Campinas, Limeira, and São Carlos do Pinhal—the richest part of the state—to **Araraquara**. A metre-gauge line now links Campinas and Brasília.

Campinas (pop. 850,000), 88 km. from São Paulo by the fine Via Anhanguera highway (many buses, US$1.60), is important as a clearing point for coffee, for its Agricultural Institute, and its rapidly growing industries. The Viracopos international airport is 11 km. from Campinas, which also has its own airport.

See fine cathedral, old market, colonial buildings, 8 museums, arts centre (noted symphony orchestra; the city is the birthplace of the noted 19th century Brazilian composer Carlos Gomes), and the modern university outside the city. Visits can be made to the Agricultural Institute to see all the aspects of coffee growing. Trains to and from São Paulo; trains and buses also to Ribeirão Preto, Araguari, Brasília and Rio de Janeiro, 7 hrs., US$6.

Hotels *Royal Palm Plaza* Praça Rotatória 88, T 2-9085, A; *Vila Rica*, Rua Donato Paschoal 100, T 31-5242, B; *Savoy*, Rua Regente Feijó 1064, T 32-9444, B; *Opala Avenida*, Av. Campos Sales 161, T 8-4115, central, C. *Solar das Andorinhas*, a health farm with pool, sauna, horses, sports, etc. 18 km. outside city on the Mogi-Mirim road, B, with meals, T 39-4411. Many cheap hotels near Rodoviária.

Restaurants *Bar Restaurante Barão*, Barão de Jaguará 1381 and *Churrascaria Gaúcha*, Av. Dr Campos Sales 515, excellent for Brazilian food. *Kirinu's Place*, Av. Moraes Salles 1102, all you can eat for US$4.50. *Papai Salim*, Benjamin Constant 1293, Arab food, good. *Natureza* (vegetarian) at Rua José Paulino 1248, 2nd floor and Av. Francisco Glicério 984; lunch only, closed Sat. *Vegetariano*, Rua Barão de Jaguara 1260, 2nd floor, closed Sat. (and Fri. for dinner).

Shopping H. Stern jewellers at Shopping Centre Iguatemi.

Banks Lloyds Bank, Rua General Osório 859. The First National Bank of Boston, Av. Francisco Glicério 1275, and local banks. Open 1000-1630. Good rates at Valortec (Dona Daiuza), Av. Dr. Moraes Salles 1212, 6th floor.

Community Church Services in English at School of Language and Orientation, Rua Eduardo Lane 270.

Americana (pop. 56,000), an interesting town, is 42 km. from Campinas. This area was settled by Confederate refugees from the south of the USA after the Civil War. Most of the original settlers soon returned to the States, but some stayed, and there still exist reminders of their occupation here. A visit to the cemetery reveals an unusual number of English surnames. (*Hotel Bradesco*, 12 km. away at Km. 118 on the Anhanguera Highway, C; *Cacique*, Rua Wáshington Luís 143, E.)

The metre-gauge Mogiana line, connecting with the broad-gauge Paulista at Campinas, serves the north-eastern part of the state. It goes through Ribeirão Preto and into the Triângulo of Minas Gerais, a great area for fattening beasts which are trucked to the frigoríficos of São Paulo. No São Paulo-Ribeirão Preto tickets are sold, so you may have to wait a day at Campinas for a connection (or go by bus). From Araguari there is a line into the state of Goiás and to Brasília (train from Campinas daily except Sunday). 25 km. from Campinas, at Jaguariúna, is a railway preservation group with steam engines and wagons; hourly bus from Campinas US$0.50. The group meets at weekends, just outside the town centre.

Ribeirão Preto (pop. 385,000), the centre of a rich coffee-growing district, also has a steel industry. The town is 422 km. from São Paulo city by rail via Campinas or paved road (5 hrs. by bus); airport has TAM flights to São Paulo, Rio, Poços de Caldas. Altitude, 420 metres. It is a distribution centre for the interior of São Paulo State and certain districts in Minas Gerais and Goiás. Products: coffee, cotton, sugar, grain and rice.

Hotels *Black Stream*, Rua General Osório 830, T 634-0606, B, with TV; *Umuarama Recreio*, Praça dos Cafeeiros 140, T 625-5790, 6 km. from centre, very pleasant, pool, gardens, C; *Brasil*, Rua General Osório 20, E; *Holiday Inn*, Rua Alvares Cabral 1200, T 625-0186, L-L+.

All the southern part of the state and most of its western part are served by the metre-gauge Sorocabana railway. The main line runs from São Paulo through Sorocaba to Bauru, where it connects with the Noroeste, to Corumbá, 1,223 km. The line from a junction near Sorocaba extending (through connections with other lines) across the southern states to the border with Uruguay is for freight only.

Sorocaba (pop. 327,000), 110 km. west of São Paulo, is an important industrial centre. The altitude is 540 metres, and the climate temperate. It has textile mills; produces cement, fertilizers, footwear, hats, alcohol, wines; there are railway workshops, extensive orange groves and packing house installations. It is an important cotton centre. Other products are timber, sugar, cereals, coffee, and minerals. Communications with São Paulo are better by road than by rail; the Castello Branco highway passes nearby.

Hotels *Terminus,* Av. General Carneiro 474, T 32-6970, C; *Nova Sorocaba,* Rua Mons. João Soares 158, D. *Manchester,* Rua 15 de Novembro 21, E, basic, friendly, excellent breakfast.

There is a picturesque paved road along the Tietê valley from São Paulo to Bauru, via the colonial towns of Pirapora and Itu.

Pirapora de Bom Jesus is a popular place of pilgrimage, in a most attractive setting on both sides of the river. *Itu* was founded by the Bandeirantes in the 17th century. The beautiful falls of Salto de Itu, 8 km. N, are flanked by a park and a textile mill.

Itu Hotels *International,* Rua Barão do Itaím 93, D; *Sabará,* Praça Padre Miguel 90, E.

Camping *Casarão de Itu,* km. 95 on the Jundiaí road; Itu, at km. 89 on the Cabreúva road.

Bauru (pop. 220,000) was founded at the end of the last century. Its points of interest include the Horto Florestal, an experimental forestry station opened in 1928, the Vitória Regia amphitheatre in the Parque das Nações and the Tenrikyo temple, Rua Newton Prado. It is used by Paulistanos as a weekend resort. Currency exchange is difficult.

Hotels *Bekassin,* Av. Duque de Caxias 1717, T 24-3700, swimming pool, C; *Colonial,* Praça Rui Barbosa 248, T 22-3191, D; *Alvorada Palace,* Rua Primeiro de Agosto 619, T 22-5900, D. Cheaper ones too, such as *Hotel Português* near bus station. Opp. railway station, *Lisboa,* E, clean, hot shower, restaurant, rec., very friendly; to right of railway station exit is *Cariani,* E, clean, good breakfast, rec. *Phenix,* near railway station, E.

Restaurant *H 2 Churrascaria* Piauí 8-55; *Cantina Bello Nápoli,* 1° de Agosto 6-52, cheap. Homemade ice-cream at sorveteria near *Hotel Lisboa.*

Rail to São Paulo, US$2.50 1st class, US$2 2nd class, three a day (6½ to 7½ hrs., compared to 4½ hrs., US$4, by bus); three trains a week from Corumbá arrive 1600, many timetable changes on this route, so check in advance (take bus—Expresso da Prata—to São Paulo). Trains to Corumbá via Campo Grande. There are no reliable connections between São Paulo-Bauru and Bauru-Corumbá or Campo Grande trains in either direction.

Marília, W of Bauru, is a pleasant clean town with a good hotel, *Sun Valley Park Hotel,* B, friendly. Texaco garage rec. for car repairs, top of hill, Japanese owner.

Presidente Prudente, in the West, is on the railway which runs to Presidente Epitácio (**see page 382**) on the Paraná river, and is a useful place to make bus connections for Campo Grande (US$9), Porto Alegre and São Paulo; also to Ribeirão Preto, US$8, 9 hrs. *Hotel Aruã,* B, single rooms poor but doubles said to be nice. *Hotel Alves* opp. bus station, E, clean, nice but noisy. Beware of assaults and pickpockets.

Serra Negra (pop. 19,000) is a very pleasant spa town and summer holiday resort up in the mountains at 1,080 metres, 145 km. from São Paulo. Visitors tour the countryside in horse-drawn buggies. There are many first class hotels, a balneário and a small zoo.

Hotels *Rádio Hotel,* T 92-3311, B, very nice indeed, and several others.

Near Serra Negra is the even better-known spa town of Lindóia, whose still waters are bottled and sent all over Brazil.

Another weekend resort, 70 km. north of São Paulo on the Dom Pedro I highway, is **Atibaia**; nearby is the strangely-shaped Pedra Grande mountain summit. There are two campsites, Pedra Grande, and Taba, which is near the

Hotel Village Eldorado (with sports facilities, American-plan accommodation).

Campos do Jordão (pop. 33,000), between Rio de Janeiro and São Paulo, is a mountain resort at 1,710 metres, in the Serra da Mantiqueira. It is prettily set in a long valley. The climate is cold and dry in winter and cool in summer, a great relief from the coastal heat and humidity. There are many hotels; but no airport, as yet.

The resort, about 190 km. from São Paulo, is reached by an 87 km. paved road from São José dos Campos, 100 km. from São Paulo, on the Presidente Dutra (BR-116) highway. By car it takes about 3 hrs. from São Paulo, 6 to 7 from Rio de Janeiro.

Places of Interest Palace of Boa Vista, 4 km. from Abernessia Centre, Governor's residence and museum, open Wed., Sat., Sun., 1000-1200, 1400-1700; Pedra do Baú (1,950 metres), to get there take a bus to São Bento do Sapucaí at 0800 or 1500, then walk to Paiol Grande and then on an unmarked path to the Pedra. Return buses from São Bento at 0915 and 1615. Near Paiol Grande is the small waterfall of Cachoeira dos Amores. Pico do Itapeva (2,030 metres) and Imbiri (1,950 metres) command a beautiful view of the Paraíba valley; see also Morro do Elefante (chairlift available); Gruta dos Crioulos; nature reserve at Horto Florestal (20 km.), signposted from chairlift station, very pretty —go in the morning to avoid crowds; lots of streams with bridges, waterfalls nearby. Campos do Jordão is a popular place for hikers; most of the roads leading off the main avenue lead to quiet areas with nice views, e.g. up Av. Dr. Antônio Nicola Padula, turn left 500 metres past Refugio na Serra for waterfalls and Pico do Itapeva. The villages of Emílio Ribas and São Cristóvão are connected by a railcar which runs frequently, US$0.10.

Hotels *Toriba*, Av. E Diederichsen, T 62-1566; *Vila Inglesa*, Sen. R. Simonsen, T 63-1955; *Refúgio Alpino*, T 63-1660, and others at Capivari. **Refugio na Serra**, Av. Dr. Antônio Nicola Padula 275, T 63-1330, C, comfortable, good breakfast, very helpful owners (some English spoken), rec.; Youth Hostel, Rua Diogo de Carvalho 86, T 229-3787/3011, ramal 286; membership card and permission from Dr. Fernando at Tourist Office in the bus terminal required. Camping Clube do Brasil site in the Descansópolis district. Book accommodation in advance if going June/July.

Restaurants *Sole Mio* (on road to Horto Florestal), Italian, big portions; **Baden Baden**, German, good. Good cheese on sale at a shop just past sports centre on way out of town, also jams and chocolates; plenty of other chocolate shops. "Milbaho" mineral water is produced here.

Stalls on main square Thurs.-Sun. sell local produce. Exchange at Geneve Sweater shop, or Cadij Imóveis, "if they want to", check rates.

Transport Bus from São Paulo, US$3, 3 hrs.; from Rio, changing at São José dos Campos, US$5. No through rail service: railcars make round trips between Campos do Jordão and Santo Antônio do Pinhal, in season between 0800 and 0900 and at 1310, out of season (Oct.-Nov., March-April) at 1310 only, a bit bumpy, but beautiful views (sit on the right on the way there, left coming back): hills, valleys, tight corners. The train is very crowded even though you are assigned a seat; fare US$0.75 (buy ticket in advance, and get return immediately on arrival in San Antônio; watch your belongings on board). Whole trip takes about 3 hrs.: 1 hr. each way on train, 40 mins.-1 hr. in Santo Antônio (not much on offer there: a few snack bars, nice views, statue of Madonna and Child). There is a local railcar service within São Paulo (very crowded but cheap). From Pindamonhangaba buses run to São Paulo and Taubaté; also to Aparecida do Norte, 1030, US$1.00. The short drive down to "Pinda", starting from the paved road 24 km. SW of Campos do Jordão, is now unpaved. Train to Pinda leaves 1705 Mon.-Thurs. and weekends, from Pinda 0600 Tues.-Fri., 0930 weekends. A new road branching off the BR-116 near Caçapava provides a quicker drive from Rio, or São Paulo, than the route via São José dos Campos.

Nearer to Rio than the Pindamonhangaba turn, just off the BR-116, is **Aparecida do Norte**, Brazil's chief place of pilgrimage and the seat of its patron saint, Nossa Senhora Aparecida. This small black image of the Virgin is said to have been taken by a fisherman from the nearby River Paraíba, and quickly acquired a miraculous reputation. It is now housed in a huge modern basilica in Romanesque style on top of a hill, with the clean white-walled, red-roofed town below.

For the route to the Paraná River, from São Paulo to Presidente Epitácio, **see page 382**

SOUTHERN BRAZIL (6)

This consists, from S to N, of the three states of Rio Grande do Sul, Santa Catarina and Paraná. The conformation of the land is not unlike what it is further north; the Great Escarpment runs down the coastal area as far as Porto Alegre, receding from the coast in a wide curve between Paranaguá and Florianópolis. South of Tubarão to the borders of Uruguay the hills of southern Rio Grande do Sul, which never rise higher than 900 to 1,000 metres, are fringed along the coast by sand bars and lagoons.

Rio Grande do Sul

North of the Rio Uruguai the land is deeply forested, but the area of prairie, small in São Paulo, Paraná and Santa Catarina, grows more extensive than the forest in Rio Grande do Sul, south of the Uruguai valley. In southern Rio Grande do Sul, south and west of the Rio Jacuí (draining into the Lagoa dos Patos) there are great grasslands stretching as far as Uruguay to the south and Argentina to the west. This is the distinctive land of the *gaúcho*, or cowboy (pronounced ga-oo-shoo in Brazil), of *bombachas* (the baggy trousers worn by the *gaúcho*), of the poncho and *ximarão* (or *mate* without sugar), the indispensable drink of southern cattlemen. There are many millions of cattle, sheep and pigs, and some 75% of all Brazilian wine comes from the state. Its population (who all call themselves *gaúchos*) now number nearly 9 million. Rio Grande do Sul has the highest proportion of literate people in Brazil.

There are three sharply contrasted types of colonization and land owning in Rio Grande do Sul. During the colonial period, wars with the Spaniards of Uruguay were frequent, and the Portuguese government brought into the grasslands of the south a number of military settlers from the Azores; these soldiers inter-married with the Brazilian herdfolk in the area. In the colonial period, also, the Jesuits built several settlements to acculturate the local Indians; relics of this process include the impressive ruins of the **Sete Povos das Missões Orientais** (São Borja, São Nicolau, São Luiz, São Lourenço, São Miguel, São João, Santo Ángelo). West from Porto Alegre, in the floodlands of the Rio Jacuí and its tributary, the Rio Taquari, rice is cultivated in typical Brazilian fashion: large estates with tenant workers.

At São Leopoldo, north of Porto Alegre, a group of Germans were settled in 1824 on their own small farms, and during the next 25 years over 20,000 more were brought into the area by the Brazilian Government. The Germans concentrated on rye, maize, and pigs. Between 1870 and 1890, settlers from northern Italy arrived, bringing viticulture with them, and settled north of the Germans at Alfredo Chaves and Caxias do Sul.

Porto Alegre, (pop. 1,275,000), capital of Rio Grande do Sul, lies at the confluence of five rivers which flow into the Rio Guaíba and thence into the great fresh-water lagoon, the Lagoa dos Patos, which runs into the sea. It is the most important commercial centre south of São Paulo.

Standing on a series of hills and valleys on the banks of the Guaíba, with its business centre jutting out into the water on a promontory, Porto Alegre is one of the most up-to-date cities in Brazil. The older residential part of the town is on a promontory dominated previously by the Governor's Palace, the imposing modern cathedral, and the two high white towers of the old church of Nossa Senhora das Dores, but Governor and God have now been utterly dwarfed by the skyscraper of the Legislative Assembly. The streets in the centre are famous for their steep gradients. The climate is temperate through most of the year, though the temperature at the height of summer can often exceed 40°C. The surrounding suburbs are very pleasant. For instance, Ipanema, on the banks of

SOUTHERN BRAZIL

the Guaíba, has a selection of bars and small restaurants; a popular rendezvous, with spectacular sunsets over the river.

Do not miss that section of the Rua dos Andradas (Rua da Praia) that is now permanently closed to traffic. It is the city's principal outdoor meeting place, the main shopping area, and by around 1600 it is full of people; at the peak hour of 1900 the street is jammed for about 6 blocks.

Points of Interest The Parque Farroupilha, a fine park near the city centre; the interesting cathedral of the Anglican-Episcopal church of Brazil; the Zoological Gardens near São Leopoldo (bus US$0.50; Hotel: *Rima*, D, standard), the Botanic Gardens (Bairro Jardim Botânico, bus 40 from Praça 15 de Novembro) and the Cidade Universitária are well worth a visit. The Mercado Público (said to be a replica of Lisbon's Mercado da Figueira) is next to the Prefeitura, in the centre of town. In the Cidade Baixa quarter are the colonial Travessa dos Venezianos (between Ruas Lopo Gonçalves and Joaquim Nabuco) and the house of Lopo Gonçalves, Rua João Alfredo 582, which houses the Museu do Porto Alegre, free, 0900-1700 Tues.-Sun. The 5-km. wide River Guaíba lends itself to every form of boating and there are several sailing clubs. A good view of the city may be had from the Morro de Santa Teresa, approached from Av. Padre Cacique (take bus 95 from Rua Salgado Filho).

Porto Alegre is a fresh-water port for ocean-going vessels of up to 7,000 tons and 4.87 metres draught. Vessels must come up through Rio Grande and the Lagoa dos Patos, some 275 km. from the open sea. Large areas of reclaimed land have been used for residential building and to extend the port facilities and quays, now among the most up-to-date in Brazil. Mosquitoes are plentiful.

Porto Alegre's most important industries are food and farm products, textiles, metal-processing, chemicals and leather products. Chief exports are pinewood, rice, wheat, soya, meat, hides, wool, animal hair, semi-precious stones, wine and tobacco. A visit to Varig's installations and workshops is well worth while.

Festivals 2 February (local holiday) is the festival of Nossa Senhora dos Navegantes, whose image is taken by boat from the central quay in the port to the industrial district of Navegantes. Semana Farroupilha, celebrating gaúcho traditions, main day 20 September.

Warning The market area in Praça 15 de Novembro and the bus terminal are dangerous at night; thefts have been reported in Voluntários da Pátia and Praça Parcão.

Hotels *Plaza São Rafael*, Av. Alberto Bins 514, T 21-6100, A; *Conceição-Center*, Av. Senador Salgado Filho 201 (T 26-0610), good; *Alfred Executivo*, Av. Otávio Rocha 270, T 21-8966, B; *Embaixador*, Jerônimo Coelho 354, T 28-2211, B, 4-star, comfortable, unexciting restaurant; *Everest Palace*, Rua Duque de Caxias 1357, T 24-7355 B; *Ritter*, Igo V. J. Veppo 55, T 21-8155, A, opp. Rodoviária, good service, English spoken, conveniently located.
São Luiz, Av. Farrapos 45, T 24-9522, D, spotless, good service, but near Rodoviária and the freeway and so a bit noisy; *Conceição II*, Garibáldi 165, T 24 3987, near Rodoviária, a/c, TV, fridge, OK, D; *Terminaltur*, opp. Rodoviária, T 27-1656, D with bath, a/c, TV, breakfast, heating, but small rooms and tiny bathrooms. *Coliseu*, Voluntários da Pátria, E with shower, clean; *Porto Alegre*, Pinto Bandeirantes 339, good, clean, quiet, rec, F; other hotels (in particular Rua Garibáldi) in this area are used for very short stays. *Minuano*, Farrapos 31, F without breakfast or bath (E with bath), noisy but otherwise good, and *Elevado*, Av. Farrapos 63, F with hot shower, clean, very friendly, rec., both near bus station. *Glória*, Travessa Eng. Acelino de Carvalho 67, E, with shower, central, quiet, clean; *Savoy*, Av. Borges Medeiros 688, E, good value, *Santa Catarina*, Rua Gen. Vitorino 240, E; *Praca Matriz*, Praça Mal Deodoro, F; *Palácio*, Av. Vigário José Inácio 644, F, central, clean, friendly, hot water, rec.; *Ritz*, André da Rocha 225, E, friendly, central, helpful, Spanish spoken; next door is *Finks*, same price range; *Uruguay*, Dr. Flores 371, F, good; *Marechal*, Rua Andrade Neves 123, F, basic, clean (not far from Mercado Municipal). Two *Casas dos Estudantes* (for those with student cards), at Av. João Pessoa 41, and Rua Riachuelo 1355 (both not far from bus station), night free, breakfast and evening meals US$0.40, lunch US$0.60, if there's room. Youth hostel *Laçador*, Rua Aurora Nunes Wagner 148, Morro Santa Tereza, T 287717.

Camping Do Cocão, 10 km. out on Viamão road; Praia do Guarujá, 16 km. out on Av. Guaíba.

Restaurants (except on the *Everest Roof* and at the *Korote* and *Panarea* (US$10-20), the normal cost of dinner is US$8-12). General: *Everest Roof*, Duque de Caxias 1357; *Mosqueteiro*, Estádio Olímpico; *Rodo Ferroviária*, Rua Voluntários da Pátria 1177, good; at No. 509 same street, *Panorama Lancheria*, always open, good large meals; *Rancho Alegre*, Cristóvão Colombo 2168, good "gaúcho" music; also with folklore shows, *Bon Ami*, Av. Salgado Filho 360, good and reasonable; *Gaúcho* at Rodoviária is good, with live entertainment nightly; *Fogão de Chão*, Cavalhada 5200, for churrascos; *Tutty's*, Centro

---

Porto Alegre: Key to map

1. Parque Farroupilha; 2. Praça Senador Florência; 3. Praça 15 de Novembro; 4. Praça Mal. Deodoro; 5. Cathedral; 6. Prefeitura; 7. University; 8. São Pedro Theatre; 9. Government Palace; 10. Mercado Público; 11. Alfândega; 12. Júlio de Castilhos Museum; 13. Post Office, Embratel; 14. Telephone Office; 15. Epatur Tourist Offices (x2); 16. Touring Club do Brasil; 17. *Hotel São Luiz*; 18. *Hotel Vitória*; 19. *Hotel Palácio*.

PORTO ALEGRE
CENTRE NOT TO SCALE
35

TO GUAIBA BRIDGE

B

N

AVENIDA MAUÁ

AV. JÚLIO DE CASTILHOS

CARLOS CHAGAS

CHAVES BARCELLOS

COMENDADOR PEREIRA

CEL. VICENTE

11

AV. SEPÚLVEDA

C. NASCIMENTO

FRANÇA TRUDA

SIQUEIRA

URUGUAÍ

13

6

10

VOLUNTÁRIOS DA PÁTRIA

To AIRPORT

18

17

SÊTE DE SETEMBRO

2

ANDRADAS

GENERAL

GAL. ANDR. NEVES

URUGUAÍ

CARUNHAI

AV. BORGES DE MEDEIROS

15

3

PÇA DE ACÚ

JOSÉ INÁCIO

OTÁVIO ROCHA

VIG.

FLORES

DOS PASSOS

PINTO BANDEIRA

CEL. VICENTE

AV. ALBERTO BINS

AV. INDEPENDÊNCIA

ANDRADAS

RIACHUELO

8

9

14

AV. FLORIANO PEIXOTO

GAL. OR. VITURINO

IMIGUO SALGADO FO.

PROF. ANNES DIAS

JERÔNIMO COELHO

4

MARECHAL FLORIANO PEIXOTO

JOSÉ SEN.

VIG.

19

DUQUE DE CAXIAS

5

12

DUQUE DE CAXIAS

SARMENTO LEITE

AV. OSVALDO ARANHA

PAULO GAMA

CEL. ESPÍRITO SANTO

FERNANDO MACHADO

AV. DES. ANDRÉ DA ROCHA

AVAÍ

LUIS ENGLERT

7

DEMÉTRIO RIBEIRO

CEL. GENUÍNO

GAL. LIMA E SILVA

AVENIDA JOÃO PESSOA

SETEMBRINA

AVENIDA BORGES DE MÉDEIROS

AVAÍ

LEÃO XIII

SARMENTO LEITE

SOFIA

VELOSO

TRAV. GETÚLIO

TRAV. DO CARMO

RUA DA REPÚBLICA

16

1

JOÃO ALFREDO

PADUA

MARTINS COSTA

15

RUA DA REPÚBLICA

JOSÉ DO PATROCÍNIO

LUIS AFONSO

AVENIDA JOÃO PESSOA

AV. PRAIA DE BELAS

MIGUEL TEIXEIRA

BARONESA

TRAV. PESQUEIRO

JOÃO ALFREDO

LUIS AFONSO

LOPO

JOAQUIM

ALBERTO TORRES

GONÇALVES

NABUCO

OTÁVIO CORRÊA

VENÂNCIO AIRES

OLAVO BILAC

Comercial, Loja 15, Av. da Independência, rec.; *Churrascaria Quero-Quero*, Praça Otávio Rocha 47; *Panorâmico*, Correia Lima 1949; *Grumete*, 24 de Outubro 905; *Umbu*, Av. Farrapos 292; *Ipanema*, Av. Coronel Marcos 1645; *Korote*, Silva Jardim 16; *Ratskeller*, Cristóvão Colombo 1654; *Panarea*, Eça de Queirós 819; *Scherazade*, Av. Protásio Alves 3284; *Barranco*, Av. Protásio Alves 1578.

Vegetarian: *Aroma*, Rua Lima e Silva 292, 2nd floor; *Macrobiótico*, Rua Marechal Floriano Peixoto 72; *Ilha Natural*, Rua Andrade Neves, lunches only.

Chinese: *Palácio do Dragão*, Luciana de Abreu 471; *Chinatown*, Rua Andrade Neves (nr. *Metrópole* hotel), Chinese and other food, good value; *Gold Dragon*, Rua Dr. Valle 479; *Tai Seng Nhe*, Andradas 1097.

German: *Printz*, Protásio Alves 3208; *Steinhaus*, Paulino Teixeira 415; *Floresta Negra*, 24 de Outubro 905; *Germânia*, 24 de Outubro 945; *Franz*, Av. Protásio Alves 3250.

Portuguese: *Casa de Portugal*, João Pessoa 579; *Galo*, João Alfredo 904.

Italian: *Copacabana*, Praça Garibaldi; *Cantina do Peppe*, Getúlio Vargas 273; *Jardim Itália*, Av. Protásio Alves 3580; *Cantina Vila Romana*, Av. Carlos Gomes 1385.

Night Bars (beer and sandwiches, etc.) *Tivoli*, Av. Protásio Alves 766; *Hubertus*, Rua Professor Annes Dias 116; *Xuvisko*, Cristóvão Colombo 927; *Julius*, José de Alencar 480; *Bartok*, José de Alencar 173; *Barril*, Estádio Internacional; *Bar Occidentes*, Av. Osvaldo Aranha and Gral. João Telles, popular; *Bologna*, Av. Coronel Marcos 2359; *Dom Jayme*, Mostardeiro 112.

Electric Current 110-120 A.C. 50 cycles.

Bookshops *Livraria Kosmos*, Rua dos Andradas 1644 (international stock); *Livraria Lima*, Borges de Medeiros 539; *Livraria Globo*, Andradas 1416; airport bookshop. *Livres e Artes* bookstall in book market, Praça Senador Florêncio, new English books with front covers missing! Brasil-America Cultural Centre has free English library, next door used books are sold and exchanged.

Shopping *H. Stern* jewellers at Shopping Center Iguatemi and international airport. There is a street market (leather goods, basketware, etc.) in the streets around the central Post Office. Good leather goods sold on the streets. Sun. a.m. handicraft and bric-a-brac market (plus sideshows) Av. José Bonefacio (next to Parque Farroupilha). Very good food market.

Discotheques *Água na Boca*, *Discoate*, *Looking Glass*, *Maria Fumaça*. Av. Farrapos has an assortment of less reputable establishments.

Entertainments The old Hotel Majestic has become the **Casa de Cultura Mário Quintana**, at Rua dos Andradas 736: this is a lively centre for the arts, with exhibitions, theatre etc. Plays by local and visiting companies at the theatres of São Pedro (opposite Government Palace) free noon and late afternoon concerts Sat., Sun., art gallery, café, and Leopoldina (Av. Independência). Modern cinemas. Centro de Tradição Gaúcha has *gaúcho* shows every Sat., starting at 2200.

Sports The Jockey Club at which races are held on Saturdays and Sundays; the Country Club (picturesque 18-hole golf course).

Swimming from the beaches near or in the city is forbidden because of pollution. See "Beaches", below for out-of-town beaches.

Museums The **Museu Júlio de Castilhos**, Duque de Caxias 1231, has an interesting historical collection, and there is the **Museu do Trem** in the old railway station of São Leopoldo. **Museo de Arte do Rio Grande do Sul**, Praça Senador Florêncio (Praça da Alfândega), Tues.-Sun. 1000-1700, entry free, is interesting. **Varig airline museum**, open Wed. and Fri. 0900-1200.

Exchange on Av. Borges de Medeiros, good rate, cash only (e.g. Agência Platina, on corner with Andradas). Many câmbios in the centre will change travellers' cheques at parallel rates; e.g. Platino Turismo, Dos Andrades e Av. Borges de Medeira (only one to change travellers' cheques, Amex, but 6% less than cash), Exprinter, Sen. Salgado Filho 247 (best for cash); for other addresses consult tourist bureau brochure. Lloyds Bank, Rua General Câmara 249 (open 1000-1630). Banco do Brasil, Uruguai 185, 10th floor, good rates for travellers cheques. Citibank, Rua 7 de Setembro (open 1300-1700).

Cultural Institutions British Club, Av. Carlos Gomes 534 (Montserrat). Instituto Goethe, 24 de Outubro 122 (open Mon.-Fri., 0930-1230, 1430-2100). Instituto Cultural Americano Brasileiro, Mon.-Fri., 0800-2000 (Sats. 0800-1700).

Consulates **U.S. Consulate**, Genuino 421, corner of Mendeiros. **British Consulate** Rua Itapeva 110, Sala 505, Edif. Montreal Bairro D'Areia, T 41-0720; **Austrian Consulate**, Rua

7 de Setembro 1069, conj. 1714, Caixa Postal 1771, T 2460 77/85. **Argentine Consulate**, Rua Prof. Annes Dias 112, 1° andar, T 24-6799/6810/6786.

Dentist Ursula Finkenwerder, R. Quintino Bocaiúva 655, Sala 301, Mon.-Fri. 0830-1130.

Cables Embratel, Rua Siqueira de Campos 1245. T 41233.

Post For sending parcels abroad: Rua Araújo Ribeiro 100; bring parcel unopened.

Tourist Information Epatur, Travessa do Carmo 84 (head office), helpful as is branch in Praça 15 de Novembro. Branch offices: Salgado Filho airport; interstate bus station, very helpful (free city maps); Rua General Câmara 368; Av. Salgado Filho 366. CRTur (Companhia Riograndense de Turismo), Rua dos Andradas 1137, 6th floor. Epatur maintains information booths at the frontier towns. A monthly booklet is available. City bus tour US$5, Regional tour US$15, Spanish or Portuguese only. **Touring Clube do Brasil**, Av. João Pessoa 623.

Rail The only long-distance passenger service from Porto Alegre is the line W to (386 km.) **Santa Maria** (pop. 197,000, *Hotel Itaimbé Palace*, B, useful junction for road connections N to São Miguel mission ruins and Iguaçu, and S direct to Pelotas) and on to Cacequi, where the line branches for Uruguaiana (**see page** 365), for connections to Argentina, and for Santana do Livramento, for connections to Uruguay (by bus only, there are no longer passenger rail services in Uruguay). 6 days a week a standard train (no sleepers) leaves Porto Alegre at 2050 to Santa Maria, continuing to Cacequi, thence 3 a week to Uruguaiana and 3 a week to Santana do Livramento. There is also a suburban service from Mercado station (Av. Mauá) north to Sapucaia do Sul, serving Esteio and Canoas. The suburban train service (faster than the bus) links the centre, Rodoviária and airport (10 mins.).

Buses Bus to Rio, US$24 (*leito* 48), 26 hrs.; São Paulo, US$16.75 (*leito* 33.50), 18 hrs.; Uruguaiana, US$9, 9 hrs.; Santa Maria, 4¾ hrs., frequent service with Planalto; Santana do Livramento, 1230 and 2300, 8½ hrs., *leito* at 2330; to Pelotas, 8 daily, US$4.60, 3-4 hrs.; to Gramado, 8 daily, 2hrs.; to Canela, 5 daily, 2½ hrs.; to Caxias do Sul, almost hourly, 2 hrs., US$2.65, executivo service also. Florianópolis, US$5.50, 7 hrs. with Viação São Cristóvão (beware of overbooking and of stopping buses—e.g. Santo Anjo—on this route); Curitiba, US$10.50, 11 hrs.; Blumenau, US$8.50, 9 hrs.; Rio Grande, US$6, 8 per day, 0600 to 2000, 4½ hrs. Foz do Iguaçu, US$15, 15 hrs.; Londrina, 22 hrs. To Cascavel (Paraná) for connections to Campo Grande, Cuiabá and Porto Velho: daily except Sat. with Aguia Branca, 21 hrs., or Unesul, 19 hrs. To Jaguarão on Uruguayan border at 2400, 6 hrs., US$5.50.

Bus to Montevideo, with international buses TTL (daily 1730 and 2000) or Onda (daily 2200, not rec. as a/c is too cold and window blinds inadequate), 12 hrs., US$19; alternatively take bus to border town of Chuí at 0700 or 1200 daily, 7½ hrs., US$8.75, then Onda or Rutas del Sol bus to Montevideo (US$8, cheaper bought in Porto Alegre or Chuí than in Uruguay). Ouro e Prata operates a 2-3 times weekly service to Salto and Paysandú (Uruguay), via Santana do Livramento/Rivera. To Asunción with Unesul at 1900 daily via Foz do Iguaçu. Expresso Singer bus Porto Alegre-Posadas (Argentina) via Oberá, Alba Posse, Porto Mauá, departs 2100 on Tues., Thurs., and Sun. arriving following day at 1135. There are bus services to Buenos Aires (US$35) 19 hrs. (depending on border) with Pluma, 1400 or 1500, and 2300, route is Uruguaiana, Paso de los Libres, Entre Ríos and Zárate, or 22 hrs. with General Urquiza company, Mon., Thurs. N.B. take your passport when purchasing international bus tickets.

The new and excellent bus terminal on Av. Mauá with Garibáldi has good facilities, including a post office and long-distance telephone service until 2100. A regular bus runs from the Rodoviária to the airport, also the suburban train service (see above).

Roads Good roads radiate from Porto Alegre, and Highway BR-116 has a paved surface to Curitiba (746 km.). To the S it is paved (though some stretches are in poor condition), to Chuí on the Uruguayan frontier, 512 kms The new paved coastal road to Curitiba via Itajaí (BR-101), of which the first 100 km. is a four-lane highway, is much better than the BR-116 via Caxias and Lajes. The road to Uruguaiana is now entirely paved but bumpy.

Air Services There is a large modern international airport, Salgado Filho, 8 km. from the city, connected to the centre by train (see above). There are daily flights to Rio, São Paulo, Curitiba, Buenos Aires and Montevideo, and many other Brazilian cities. Vasp flies to Iguaçu and Brasília on Mon., Wed., Fri., and Sun. The airport is served by all Brazilian airlines, Pluna and Aerolíneas Argentinas. Taxi to centre US$60.

Excursion Cervejaria Brahma, Av. Cristovão Colombo 545, offers tours of its brewery (but not Dec.-March).

Beaches The main beach resorts of the area are to the north of the city. The towns of **Tramandaí** (126 km.) and **Torres** (209 km.) are the most popular, with lots of luxury (and more reasonable) hotels and motels, bars, restaurants, and other standard requisites associated with seaside resorts. The sea is dirty and most of the atmosphere has been lost to development. Picturesque walk along the shore to see basalt rock formations. To reach Florianópolis, take a bus to Ararangua and change. Between the two towns (buses leave Torres 0900 and 1500) are the small resorts of Arróio Teixeira (Camping Clube do Brasil site), Capão da Canoa (*Hotel Kolman*, R. Sepé 1718, youth hostel *Riviera di Fiori*, Av. Venâncio Aires 711, T 265944, swimming pool, rec., and others) and Atlântida, *Hotel Azul*; Arroio do Sal, *Hotel Itália*, on beach, F, open all year, highly rec; *Casa da Sogra*, good food. There is no lack of cheap accommodation, but hotels tend to be very full during the summer season. There are fully equipped campsites at both towns, and camping is also allowed on some beaches.

Torres Hotels *Dunasda Praia*, on beach, C-D; *A Furninha*, Rua Joaquim Porto 281, D, good service; *Farol*, Rua José A. Pirasol 240, D to B with full board; *Grande Hotel Torres*, Rua Júlio de Castilhos 124, D with bath, balcony and breakfast (off-season). On Av. General Osório, *Camping*, No. 450, E, clean, friendly, and *Mini-Torres*, E with breakfast and bath out of season; *Salth*, central, E with bath, friendly, clean; *Central*, F, clean and friendly; Dec-Feb *São Domingo Youth Hostel* in a school building, F, Jujio de Castilhos 875, T 664-1865, clean; Other hotels, E, bath and breakfast are available. Rec. restaurants: *A Furninha* for fish, and *Bom Gosto*, churrascaria.

Tramandaí Hotels *Samburá*, Av. Beira Mar. *Motel Junges*, on main street, D with bath and breakfast, friendly, German spoken. *São Jorge*, F, Aaral 19, T 661-1154,E, quiet, clean, bath, rec. Many more.

Exchange In Torres, Banco do Brasil and at Rodoviária.

Another popular beach area is south of Porto Alegre, around Cassino, near Rio Grande (**see page 365**). 40 km. to the south (towards Rio Grande) begins the Costa Doce of the Lagoa dos Patos; noted bathing points are Tapes, Barra do Ribeiro, Arambaré, São Lourenço do Sul (rec. camping site 1 km. out of town on lake shore) and Laranjal.

At **São Lourenço do Sul** is *Hotel Vilela*, Rua Almirante Abreu 428, family hotel, clean, friendly. The town is a good place to stop to enjoy the lake, the beaches, fish restaurants and water sports.

Inland is the pleasant Serra Gaúcha, the most beautiful scenery being around the towns of **Gramado** and **Canela**, about 130 km. from Porto Alegre (chocolate factory between the two towns). There is a distinctly Bavarian flavour to many of the buildings. In spring and summer the flowers are a delight, and in winter there are frequently snow showers. This is excellent walking and climbing country among hills, woods, lakes and waterfalls. There are many excellent hotels at all prices in both towns, but it is difficult to get rooms in the summer. Local crafts include knitted woollens, leather, wickerwork, and chocolate. Gramado has two fine parks, Parque Knorr and Lago Negro, and Minimundo, a collection of miniature models. The town is decorated and, on Sat., about one week before 24 Dec. there is outdoor Christmas music; book hotels in good time as the town is crowded.

Gramado Hotels *Hortensias*, Rua Bela Vista 83, T 286-1057, C; *Serrano*, Costa e Silva 1112, T 286-1332, C; *Serra Azul*, Rua Garibáldi 152, T 286-1082, C; *Pequeno Bosque*, Rua Piratina 486, D with bath, fridge, TV, good breakfast, located in wood close to Véu da Noiva waterfall; *Parque*, Leopoldo Rosenfeldt 818, T 286-1326, bungalows, good breakfast, friendly, maid will do laundry reasonably, D; *Ritta Höppner*, Rua Pedro Candiago 305, T 054-286-1334, D in cabins, very good value, friendly, good breakfasts, German owners, cabins have TV, fridge, pool and miniature trains in grounds. *Luiz*, Senador Salgado Filho 432, T 286-1026, E, good breakfast, clean, good value; *Tia Hulda*, Av. Borges de Medeiros 1653, T 286-1813, friendly, E; *Dinda*, Rua Augusto Zatti 160, T 286-1588, one of the cheapest, E; *Pousada Zermatt*, E, rec; try in the private house opposite the tourist office, not very friendly but very clean and comfortable, (E). *Planalto*, opp. Rodoviária, clean and friendly.

Restaurants *Saint Hubertus*, Rua da Caixa d'Água; *Nápoli*, Av. Borges de Medeiros, good Italian. Coffee shop, *Tia Nilda*, Av. Pres. Costa e Silva. *Pyp* yoghurt factory, Av. S. Diniz 1030, has snack bar serving health food sandwiches and yoghurt. The local speciality is *café colonial*, a 5 o'clock meal of various dishes, including meats, rec. at *Café da Torre* (order one helping for 2 or more people, very filling). Visitors should also sample hot pinhões (pine nuts) and quentão (hot red wine, cachaça, ginger, cloves, sugar and cinnamon, often topped with gemada—beaten egg yolks and sugar).

Tourist Office Corner of Borges de Medeiros and Coronel Diniz, Gramado (3 blocks from Rodoviária, no English spoken), good maps and hotel lists.

Canela Hotels *Laje de Pedra*, Av. Pres Kennedy Km. 3, T 282-1530, all amenities; *Vila Suzana Parque*, Theoboldo Fleck 15, T 282-2020, C, chalets, heated pool attractive. *Bela Vista*, Rua Oswaldo Aranha 160, T 282-1327, near Rodoviária, clean, good breakfasts, F (D with additional facilities). Cheap hotels: *Jubileu*, Oswaldo Aranha 223, F-G (acts as Youth hostel, T (054) 282-2133), reported unfriendly, and *Central*, E. Av. Júlio de Castilhos 146, clean, safe, rec.

Camping Camping Clube do Brasil, 6 km. from Canela, near waterfall in Parque do Caracol; excellent honey and chocolate for sale here. Sesi, camping or cabins, 2½ kms outside Canela, T (054) 282-1311/1697, clean, restaurant, rec.

Wine merchant in Canela, Joliment, Estrada de Morro, Calçado.

Electric Current 220 volts A.C.

Bus Several daily Canela-Caxias do Sul, 2 hrs., US$1.65. From Florianópolis, you have to go via Porto Alegre.

6 km. from Canela is the Parque Estadual do Caracol (bus marked "Caracol Circular" from outside Citral bus office at 0830, 1200 and 1700, US$0.20, 20 mins., return about ½ hour after departure time); a slippery path leads to the foot of the falls, which are 130 metres high (allow 1½ hrs. of daylight, it gets dark very quickly at the bottom in the forest). Good paths lead to smaller falls above Caracol; from the high point at Ferradura there is a good view into the canyon of the River Cai. Good views also from Moro Pelado, follow signs from behind the town (no bus, but nice walk through forest). 80 km. from São Francisco de Paula is the **Parque Nacional de Aparados da Serra**, where the major attraction is the 7.8-km. canyon, known locally as the Itaimbezinho. Here, two waterfalls cascade 350 metres into a stone circle at the bottom. Tourist excursions, mostly at weekends, from São Francisco de Paula. At other times, take a bus to Cambara, get off at the cruce, from where it is 15 km. to the park—walk or hitch hike if you're lucky. There is a free campsite and a restaurant, which has a few rooms, in the park. From the restaurant one can walk to the canyon of Malacara. For experienced hikers (and with a guide) there is a difficult path to the bottom of Itaimbezinho. One can then hike 20 km. to Praia Grande in Santa Catarina (**see page 367**).

24 km. W of Gramado (99 km. from Porto Alegre, 30 km. from Caxias do Sul) is *Nova Petrópolis* (bus US$0.40), another city with strong German roots; there is a Parque do Imigrante, an open-air museum of German settlement. (Hotels include *Veraneio dos Pinheiros, Recanto Suiço*, 3 star, Petrópolis, *Veraneio Schoeller*, one-star.) N of Nova Petrópolis is Jammerthal, a valley in the Serra Gaúcha with German farms, many of whose inhabitants still speak German (go to Joanette and walk from there).

Caxias do Sul (pop. 267,000) 122 km. from Porto Alegre, is the centre of the Brazilian wine industry. The population is principally of Italian descent, and it is an expanding and modern city. Vines were first brought to the region in 1840 but not until the end of the century and Italian immigration did the industry develop. The church of São Pelegrino has paintings by Aldo Locatelli and 5 metre-high bronze doors sculptured by Augusto Murer. Good municipal museum at Rua Visconde de Pelotas 586 (open Tues.-Sat., 0800-1200, 1400-1800), with displays of artefacts of the Italian immigration. The best time to visit is Jan.-Feb.

Hotels *Volpiana*, Ernesto Alves, 1462, C; *Cosmos*, 20 de Setembro 1563, D-C; *Alfred Palace*, Rua Sinimbu 2302, C; *Itália*, Av. Júlio de Castilhos 3076, D; *Real*, Rua Marquês de Herval 606, E; *Alfred*, Rua Sinimbu 2266, C; *Bandeira*, same street, No. 2435, E with T.V. and bath; *Santa Rita*, Os 18 do Forte 2149, E without breakfast, cheap; *Pérola*, corner Ernesto Alves and Marquês de Herval (No. 237), E, clean, good value; *Peccini*, Rua Pinheiro Machado 1939, E, shared bath, good breakfast. *Samuara*, 10 km. out on RS-25 road, D. Hotels fill up early p.m.

Good **restaurants**: *Fogo de Chão*, Os 18 do Forte 16, reasonably priced, live music (not touristy), "gaúcho"-style; also *Cantina Pão e Vino*, Rua Ludovico Cavinato 1757, Bairro Santa Catarina, Caxias, good value.

Camping Municipal campsite, 4 km. out on Rua Cons. Dantas; Palermo, 5 km. out on BR-116 at km. 118; Belvedere Nova Sonda, 38 km. out in the district of Nova Pádua. At Garibáldi, near the dry ski slope.

Tourist Office Praça do Centro Administrativo; kiosk in Praça Rui Barbosa, also in Ed. Bonifa, Júlio de Castilho 1634, 2nd floor.

Caxias do Sul's festival of grapes is held in February-March. One should not miss the opportunity to visit the many *adegas* (but do not always expect free tasting), and the neighbouring towns of Farroupilha (*Hotels Don Francesco*, Rua Dr. J. Rossler 88, 2 star; *Grande*, Júlio de Castilhos 1064) and Bento Gonçalves (hotels *Dall'Onder*, C, Rua Erny Hugo Dreher 197, T (054) 252-3555; *Vinocap*, D, Rua Barão do Rio Branco 245, T 252-1154/2566) and **Garibáldi**: hotels *Pietá*, D; *Estação de Esqui*, D in cabins without breakfast; dry ski slope and toboggan slope—equipment hire, US$2 per hour. There is a "wine supermarket" on the road between Bento Gonçalves and Caxias, a selection of 40 wines at low prices. A good *adega*, with free tasting, is Cooperativa Viti Vinícola Emboaba Ltda, in Nova Milano (bus to Farroupilha, then change—day trip). Good tour and tasting (6 wines) at Adega Granja União, Rua Os 18 de Forte 2346, US$0.25. That at Chateau La Cave (BR-116, Km. 143, Bairro São Ciro, bus from Sinimbu, US$0.15) is poor.

A restored steam train, Maria Fumaça, leaves Bento Gonçalves on Sun at 0900 for Jabuticaba; reserve in advance.

On the road north, 112 km. from Porto Alegre, is **Osório**, a pleasant town near sea and lakes, with a good cheap hotel, Big Hotel, E.

Rio Grande (pop. 164,000) at the entrance to the Lagoa dos Patos, 274 km. S of Porto Alegre, was founded in 1737. The city lies on a low, sandy peninsula 16 km. from the Atlantic Ocean. To-day it is the distribution centre for the southern part of Rio Grande do Sul. Its cattle and meat industries are important.

During the latter half of the 19th century Rio Grande was an important centre, but today it is a rather poor town, notable for the charm of its old buildings. (Museu Oceanográfico, US$0.30, 0900, 1400-1700 daily, interesting, 2 km. from centre; bus 59 or walk along waterfront.) At Praça Tamandaré is a small zoo.

Hotels *Charrua*, Rua Duque de Caxias 55, T 32-8033, rec. for good value, D; *Paris*, Rua Marechal Floriano 112, T 32-8746, E, old, charming; *Novo Mundo*, nearby, F; *Europa*, Rua Gen. Neto 165, main square,T 32-8133, D. Cheap hotels: *City, Iria*, both E (latter clean, friendly), on Rua Luís Loréa; *Ritter*, Silva Paes 373.

Restaurants *Porção*, Rua Dr. Nascimento 389, cheap churrascaria, good service; *Recanto Doce*, Silva Paes 370, cheap, friendly; Chinese restaurant on Rua Luís Loréa, good but not cheap; *Pescal*, for fish, fairly expensive and a long taxi ride from the centre; *Angola*, Benjamin Constant 163 e Luís Loréa, very good and reasonable; *Bar Brejeiro*, Andrades 193, jazz upstairs.

Exchange Hotel *Charrua* for US$ notes.

Cables Embratel, Rua Andrade Neves 94.

British Consulate Rua Francisco Marques 163, Caixa Postal 455, Centro, 96-200 Rio Grande, T 32-7788..

Tourist Office Rua Gral. Bacelar, near Cathedral; good map.

Transport Frequent daily buses to and from Pelotas (56 km.), Bagé (280 km.), Santa Vitória (220 km.), and Porto Alegre (US$6, 4½ hrs.). To Itajaí, 14 hrs., US$13. Road to Uruguayan border at Chuí is paved, but the surface is poor (5 hrs. by bus, at 0700 and 1430, US$4.50).

Boat Trip By boat across mouth of Lagoa dos Patos, to pleasant village of São José do Norte, US$0.25, every 40 mins from Porto Velho. In this vicinity is the recently created **National Park Lagoa do Peixe** (details from Rua Miguel Teixeira 126, Praia de Belas, Cidade Baixa, CEP 90.000, Porto Alegre).

Excursions To **Cassino**, a popular seaside town on the Atlantic Ocean, 24 km., over a good road. The Cassino beaches are populous, but have no restaurants, hotels or facilities (note the statue of Yemanjá); those further N are mainly used in summer.

Hotels *Atlântico*, Av. Rio Grande, 387, D, clean, refurbished, special rates for students; *Marysol*, Av. Atlântica 900, D, near beach, friendly. Private campsite on Avenida 33, on the way out to Rio Grande. Camping Clube do Brasil site near town.

The breakwater (the Barra), 5 km. E of Cassino, no bus connection, through which all vessels entering and leaving Rio Grande must pass, is a tourist attraction. Barra-Rio Grande buses, from E side of Praça Ferreira pass the Superporto. Very good fishing. The coastline is low and straight, lacking the bays to the N of Porto Alegre; unfortunately the beach is used as a roadway. One attraction is railway flat-cars powered by sail; the railway was built for the construction of the breakwater.

Pelotas (pop. 278,000), on the BR-116, 56 km. N of Rio Grande, is the second largest city in the State of Rio Grande do Sul, on the left bank of the River São Gonçalo which connects the Lagoa dos Patos with the Lagoa Mirim. Its proximity to Rio Grande has hindered the development of its own port. Pelotas is prosperous, with an array of shops and pleasant parks. Like Rio Grande, it is rather damp.

Within a radius of 60 km., say an hour's drive, there are numerous excursions into the hilly countryside. Simple and clean accommodation and cheap, good and plentiful food can be found on the farms of settlers of German descent.

Hotels *Estoril*, Rua Gen. Osório 718, T 25-2411, a/c, reasonable, D; *Rex*, Praça Pedro Osório 205,T 22-1163, E, friendly, dowdy; *Grande*, Praça Pedro Osório 51, T 25-8139, old, some rooms with electric shower, F; *Germano*, next bus station, owner speaks some German, E.

Camping 60 km. out at the Arco Iris waterfall, no facilities; *Cascata*, 25 km. out on the Cangussu road. Between Pelotas and Chuí, 1 km. S of junction with Rio Grande road, 1,200 metres from road at a working ranch, rec., clean, meals included.

Restaurant Tyrolean restaurant, opposite *Hotel Rex*, excellent, cheap. 29 km. out of town, on the road to Rio Grande, is an excellent restaurant owned by Tia Laura, who specializes in home cooking and café colonial.

Exchange Difficult to change travellers' cheques. Try Sr. Jesus Faria at 15 de Novembro 626 for good cash rate.

Communications Plane a day to Porto Alegre. Rodoviária is far out of town, with bus every 15 mins. to centre. Frequent daily buses to Porto Alegre, 244 km. (US$4.60, 3-4 hrs., paved road); Rio Grande, 90 min. (paved but in poor condition); Jaguarão, on frontier with Río Branco, Uruguay, paved; and inland to Bagé (*Hotel Medronha*, near bus station, E, without breakfast, clean) and other towns. The road to the Uruguayan frontier at Chuí (paved), has international bus service, but only a couple of daily buses Pelotas-Chiú Onda and TTL bus services (Montevideo-Porto Alegre) stop at the bus station for Montevideo (Ruas Chile and Venezuela); tickets must be purchased from agency during day. Bus to Buenos Aires (via Uruguaiana), US$28.75. From Bagé, the Uruguayan company Núñez runs buses 3 times a week to Melo, via Aceguá. Good direct road NW to Iguaçu via São Sepe (*Trevo Parque Hotel*, D, a/c, very friendly), Santa Maria (**see page 361**) and São Miguel mission ruins (see below).

The southern interior of the state is the region of the real gaúcho. Principal towns of this area include **Santana do Livramento** (pop. 70,000, bus and train, 3 a week, services to Porto Alegre) with its twin Uruguayan city of Rivera (**page 1032**) a great attraction of the latter being its casino. Rivera is considered to have the better hotels and better exchange facilities. Duty free shopping.

Hotels: *Portal*, Av. Tamandaré 2076, B, T 242-2533, garage, clean, rec.; *Jandaia* D, R. Uruguai 1452 T 242-2288, rec; *Piranga*, cheap and clean, E; *Uruguaiana*, E, close to bus station.

In the extreme west are **Uruguaiana**, pop 106,000, a cattle centre 772 km. from Porto Alegre (*Hotel Glória*, Rua Domingos de Almeida 1951, E, good; *Califôrnia* and *Pampa*, near the bus station, both D; *Moderno*, Rua Santana, E; *Palace*, Praça Rio Branco, E, without breakfast; *Fares Turis Hotel* may let you leave your bags while you look around town) and its twin Argentine town of Paso de los Libres, also with a casino (**see page 142**). A 1,400-metre bridge over the River Uruguai links the two cities; taxi or bus across about US$2. Buses connect the railway and bus stations, and centres of each city every half-hour; if you have to disembark for visa formalities, a following bus will pick you up without extra charge. There are train (3 times a week) and bus services to Porto Alegre.

The west of Rio Grande do Sul also contains the Sete Povos das Missões Orientais (**see page** 356). The only considerable Jesuit remains in Brazilian territory (very dramatic) are at **São Miguel** (church, 1735-45, and small museum) some 50 km. from **Santo Ângelo**. (*Hotel Nova Esperança*, behind bus station, F, without breakfast; *Hotel Turis*, R Antônio Manoel 726, T (55) 312-4055, helpful, rec; other cheap central hotels near old railway station). At São Miguel there is a *son et lumière* show, weekdays at 2000, weekends at 1930, but ends too late to return to Santo Ângelo; in São Miguel village is *Hotel-Churrascaria Brillante*, E. East of Santo Ângelo is Passo Fundo, "the most *gaúcho* city in Rio Grande do Sul", so much so that the town's square boasts a statue of a maté gourd and bombilla— otherwise not much of interest; *Hotel dos Viajantes* opposite bus station, F. Planalto buses run from Uruguaiana via Barra do Quaraí/Bella Unión to Salto and Paysandú in Uruguay.

Entering Uruguay Those requiring a visa face problems: a medical exam is required before a visa can be issued, cost approximately US$20 and US$10 respectively. All buses, except those originating in Pelotas, stop at customs on both sides of the border; if coming from Pelotas, you must ask the bus to stop for exit formalities. You must have a Brazilian exit stamp to enter Uruguay. The Brazilian immigration office (and tourist caravan) is about 2 1/2 km. from the border, on Av. Argentina; the bus from Porto Alegre stops here and the conductor hands over tourist cards to the officials. Make sure you get out to get your stamp, asking the driver to wait; or walk back from town at your leisure. The Brazilian border town, Chuí is much cheaper than its Uruguayan neighbour, so stock up with food and drink before crossing.

At Santana do Livramento all one need do is cross the main street, but the Uruguayan immigration is hard to find, in a side street. No customs formalities, but luggage is inspected on boarding bus for Montevideo, and there are checkpoints on the roads out of town. Bus to Montevideo, US$7. For motorists there are 3 customs offices in Santana do Livramento, about 1/2 hr. needed for formalities.

Entering Brazil from Uruguay, on the Uruguayan side, the bus will stop if asked, and wait while you get your exit stamp (with bus conductor's help); on the Brazilian side, the appropriate form is completed by the Rodoviária staff when you purchase your ticket into Brazil. The bus stops at Polícia Federal (Av. Argentina) and the conductor completes formalities while you sit on the bus. Buses run from Chuí to Pelotas (6-7 daily, US$4, 4 hours), Rio Grande (0700, 1400, 5 hrs., US$4.50) and Porto Alegre (1200, 2300, 7 1/2 hrs., US$7); also from Chuí to Santa Vitória nearby, where there are a few hotels and rather quicker bus services to the main cities. N.B. Change all remaining Uruguayan pesos into new cruzeiros before leaving Uruguay since not even black marketeers in Brazil want them. Also, if entering by car, fill up with petrol in Brazil, where fuel is much cheaper.

Chuí hotels *San Francisco*, Av. Colombia e Rua Chile, E, shower, clean, restaurant; *Cairo*, Av. Uruguai, T 65-1076 opp. Atlantic petrol station), D, shower, breakfast, clean, TV lounge; on Rua Chile, **Hospedagem Roberto** at No. 1631 and **Pensão** in private house at No. 767, F. *Atlantico*, Barra do Chuí, Km. 11; *Turismo* Av. Rio Branco 1078, T 63-1431, E. In Chuy (Uruguay), there is a **hospedaje** on Av. Brasil, opp. the Atlantic petrol station .

Exchange *Cambios* on Uruguayan side of Av. Brasil/ Av. Uruguay, between Calles L. Olivera and Gen. Artigas; best rates fro AmEx travellers' cheques at Val de Marne.

Post Offices Av. Uruguay, between Colombia and Argentina (Chuí); Av. Brasil, 4 blocks from Gen. Artigas (Chuy).

Telephones in Brazil, corner of Rua Chile and Av. Argentina; in Uruguay one block behind plaza, between Calles L. Olivera and Gen. Artigas.

Tourist Information On Av. Argentina (Chuí), 2 1/2 km. from border; Uruguayan office in middle of Av. Brasil/Uruguay, at Av. Argentina/Calle Gen. Artigas junction.

Santa Catarina

Further up the coast, in Santa Catarina (pop. 4,339,000), a group of Germans was settled at Lajes in 1822. In 1848 a new German-speaking settlement was founded at Blumenau. The Germans spread inland over the mountains from the port of São Francisco to Joinville. The Italians came later. Over northern Rio Grande do Sul and Santa Catarina the vast majority of people to-day can trace their origin to these immigrants.

In Santa Catarina, a state of small holdings, the farmer owns his land and cattle: the familiar European pattern of mixed farming worked by the family. Sixty per cent of the population is rural. There is coal in the S, and flourishing food processing and textile industries. Itajaí and São Francisco do Sul are the main ports, handling 90% of the trade. Except for the summer months of January and February, the beaches of Santa Catarina are pleasant and uncrowded.

386 km. NE of Porto Alegre is the small fishing port of **Laguna** (pop. 50,000; *Hotel Laguna Tourist*, first class; *Hotel Itapirubá*, 4-star with beach and pool; *Turismar*, Av. Rio Grande do Sul 207, view over Mar Grosso beach, C, TV; several others, medium-priced, *Grande*, opp. post office, clean, E, without breakfast), in southern Santa Catarina. At Laguna is the Anita Garibáldi Museum, containing documents, furniture, and the personal effects of the Brazilian wife of the hero who fought in the 1840s for the independence of Rio Grande do Sul and later helped to unify Italy (US$0.05). Laguna's beach, 2 km. from the centre, is not very good, but 16 km. away (by ferry and road) are beaches and dunes at Cavo de Santa Marta. South of Laguna is **Praia Grande**, on the Ilha de São Francisco (cheap hotel at bus station, F). Buses from Praia Grande to Araranguá and Laguna. Also from Laguna, take a Lagunatur or Auto Viação São José bus to Farol (infrequent, US$0.70). You have to cross the mouth of the Lagoa Santo Antônio by ferry to get to Farol; look out for fishermen aided by dolphins (*botos*). Here is a fishing village with the alleged third oldest lighthouse in the world (Farol Santa Marta)—guided tours available (taxi, US$8.25, not including ferry toll). No hotels, but it is possible to bargain with fishermen for a bed. (Bus to/from Porto Alegre, 5½ hrs., with Santo Anjo Da Guarda; same company goes to Florianópolis, 2 hrs., but you can't buy a ticket before the bus arrives in Laguna—as soon as it comes in, follow the driver to ticket office.) Another 32 km. to the north of Laguna is the port of **Imbituba**, where there is a carbo-chemical plant, from which air pollution is very bad. Imbituba sends the coal mined in the area between Araranguá and Tubarão in coastal vessels to Rio de Janeiro, where it is railed to the steel mills at Volta Redonda for coking. The rail link between Imbituba and Tubarão is one of the busiest steam services in South America (freight only). There are good beaches (those near Garopaba and Araçatuba have been particularly recommended), and bus services to Porto Alegre.

The coalfield towns of **Tubarão** (*Hotel Mossi*, in centre, E, excellent), Criciúma and Içara are interesting, and the nearby beaches are good.

From Tubarão one can visit the Termas do Gravatal. (There is one first class hotel, and two others: *Petit Village*, F, a/c, mineral pool, good value, quiet, good food.) Also, buses go inland to Lauro Müller, then over the Serra do Rio do Rastro (beautiful views of the coast in clear weather). At Bom Jardim da Serra there is an apple festival every April. A dirt road continues to São Joaquim (see page 370), and over Pericó to Urubici (*Pensão Anderman*, E, clean, friendly, big meals). A new paved road is being built, as far as Santo Amaro da Imperatriz. There are direct buses from São Joaquim to Florianópolis.

J. P. Monnickendam, of Elstree, writes: About 60 km. inland from Tubarão is **Orleães**. It has one of the most interesting and least known museums in the area, which has an original water-powered workshop and sawmill, complete with waterwheel. It dates from the original settlers (late 19th century), and is still in working order. To get there one must get off the bus at the junction about 3 km. from the town.

The festival of São João in June can be seen best in Santa Catarina at Campo Alegre, the first town on the road inland to Mafra. There are bonfires, a lot of (German) folk dancing, and large quantities of *quentão* (a hot drink made of red wine, cinnamon, ginger and *cachaça*) and *pinhões* (the nuts of the Paraná pine tree). It is a beautiful climb on the road from the BR-101 to Campo Alegre. The road continues through São Bento and Rio Negrinho to Mafra, from where a good road (the BR-116) goes to Curitiba.

124 km. N of Laguna is **Florianópolis** (founded in 1726, pop. 218,000) capital of the State, on the Ilha de Santa Catarina joined to the mainland by two bridges, one of which is Ponte Hercílio Luz, the longest steel suspension bridge in Brazil

(closed to all traffic in 1983). The newer Colombo Machado Salles bridge has a pedestrian and cycle way beneath the roadway. It is a port of call for coastal shipping, 725 km. from Rio de Janeiro and 420 from Santos. The natural beauty of the island, beaches and bays make Florianópolis a popular tourist centre (only January and February are very crowded and expensive). The southern beaches are usually good for swimming, the east for surfing, be careful of the undertow. It seems a pity that the waterfront, scene of a traditional market, has been filled in and reclaimed and that the city is not in general better maintained. The cathedral on Praça 15 de Novembro has a life-size sculpture in wood of the flight into Egypt, originally from the Austrian Tyrol. Forts include the Santana (which houses a Museum of Military Arms), São José da Ponta Grossa and Nossa Senhora da Conceição. There are three other museums, the Historical Museum in the old Palácio Cruz e Souza, on Praça 15 de Novembre (1000-1800, Tues.-Sun.), the Anthropological Museum at the Federal University and the Sambaqui Museum at the Colégio Catarinense, Rua Esteves Júnior 159 (last-named open 1330-1730 Mon.-Fri., others 0800-1200, 1400-1800, Mon.-Sat.). There is a look-out point at Morro da Cruz (take Empresa Trindadense bus). Carnival is recommended as beautiful.

Hotels *Florianópolis Palace*, Rua Artista Bittencourt and Rua dos Ilhéus 26, T 22-9633, best, B; *Royal*, Trav. João Pinto, T 22-2944, B, good; *Oscar Palace*, Av. Hercílio Luz 90, T 22-0099 C, watch the bill carefully; *Ivoram Palace*, same street No. 66, T 22-5388, E, discount in off season; *Valeiro*, Rua Silva Jardim 234, E with a/c and TV, new, rec., take Cidade Universitária bus; *City Hotel*, Rua Emílio Blum 31, F, very basic, friendly.
    Within 10 minutes' walk of the Rodoviária: Rua Felipe Schmidt, *Faial Palace*, No. 87, T 23-2766, C, good restaurant; *Valerim*, No. 74, T 23-3280, central, D with bath, E without (cheaper off season), fridge, radio, T.V., stove, but not rec.; *Sumaré*, No. 53, E, good, clean, good value but check rooms for ventilation; *Querência Palace*, Rua Jerônimo Coelho 1, T 22-2677, B, clean, good. On Conselheiro Mafra: *Colonial*, No. 45, basic, hot water, fair, safe, pleasant, F; *Felippe*, one block from 15 de Novembro at Rua João Pinto 25, D, friendly, small rooms, 10% off to Youth Hostel members. *Dormitória Estrela*, Rua Mafra, nr. Rua Bento Gonçalves, very basic but cheap.On the mainland: *Oasis*, Rua Gral. L. Bittencourt 201, E, with breakfast, clean, good (take bus 201 from here to bus terminal); *Bruggeman*, Rua Santos Saraiva 300 T 44-2344, (bus 236 or 226 from Terminal Urbano do Aterro), E for motel-type rooms and 2-star accommodations; *Noblis* and *Continental* in the same road are cheaper. Cheap hotels around Rodoviária reckoned less good than those of similar price on the mainland, close to the bridge, take bus 236, ask the driver to stop at Saraiva. To rent a room, contact Leny Saboia, Rua J. Colago 525, Jardím Santa Mônica, T 33-4684 (take a bus to Beira Mar Norte, alight at Santa Mônica supermarket).

Youth hostels on the island: Ilha de Santa Catarina, Rua Duarte Schutel 59 (T 22-3781); Barra da Lagoa (T 22-6746) and Fortaleza da Barra (T 32-0169), both on Estrada Geral da Barra da Lagoa; Praia do Campeche (T 22-6746) and Praia dos Ingleses (T 22-6746 also).

Camping Camping Clube do Brasil, São João do Rio Vermelho, near the lagoon, 21 km. out of town; also at Lagoa da Conceição, Praia da Armação, Praia dos Ingleses, Praia Canavieiras. "Wild" camping allowed at Ponta de Sambaqui. Beaches of Brava, Aranhas, Galheta, Mole, Campeche, Campanhas and Naufragados. 4 km. S of Florianópolis, camping site with bar at Praia do Sonho on the mainland, beautiful, deserted beach with an island fort nearby. Take bus to Laguna and walk or hitch to beach (5 km. from highway). "Camping Gaz" cartridges from Riachuelo Supermercado, on Rua Alvim with Rua São Jorge.

Restaurants *Braseiro*, R. Trajano 27 (behind Governor's Palace), crowded at lunch-time. *Dalton's*, Rua Trajano 29, first floor meals better than ground floor pizzas, etc.; *Divina Comedia*, next to Cathedral, excellent food, friendly, run by American lady; *Galerie*, Trajano 41, very good and reasonable; *Manolo's*, Rua Felipe Schmidt 71, near centre, good, but not cheap. *Lindacap*, Rua Felipe Schmidt 178 on outskirts (closed Mon.), rec., good views. All the above give a good meal and beer for around US$7. *Pim-Pão*, R. Marechel Deodoro, good cheap breakfast, lunches; *Von Pepé Pizza*, Almirante Lamego, giant helpings; *Snack Bar Doll*, R. Vidal Ramos, open 0900-1900; *Dom Dom*, Praça Pereira Oliveira 6, cheap, good; *Rotisserie Acapulco*, Rua dos Ilhéus 20, central, cafeteria-style, popular. Shrimp dishes are good everywhere. *Polly's*, Praça 15 de Novembro, good food and service, reasonable prices; *Macarronada Italiana*, Av. Beira Mar Norte 196, good. *Churrascaria Ataliba*, Rúa Jaú

Guedes da Fonseca s/n, 2 km. from centre at Coqueiros, excellent rodízio, US$3.75. Vegetarian: *Sol da Terra*, Rua N. Ramos 13, popular, *Vida*, Rua Visconde Ouro Preto 62, *Neu Sol*, Rua Vida Ramos 36 (all closed Sun.). *Padaria União*, R. Tenente Silveira, very good.

Electric Current 220 volts A.C.

Car Hire Auto Locadora Coelho, Felipe Schmidt 81, vehicles in good condition.

Exchange Banco do Brasil, Praça 15 de Novembro 20; Banco do Estado de São Paulo, Tenente Silveira 55; Banco Estado de Santa Catarina, Trajano 33. Turismo Holzmann, Rua Conselheiro Mafra 53, parallel exchange rate in adjoining room. Lovetur, Av. Osmar Cunha 15, Ed. Ceisa and Centauru Turismo at same address. Money changers on Rua Felipe Schmidt.

Post Office Praça 15 de Novembro 5, T 22-3188.

Cables Telesc, Praça Pereira Oliveira 20, T 23-3700 (interstate and international telephones).

Tourist Office Head office: Portal Turístico de Florianópolis (Setur), at the mainland end of the bridge, 0800-2000 (Sat., Sun. 0800-1800); Praça 15 de Novembro, 0800-1800 (2200 in high season); at bus terminal, very helpful and multi-lingual (0700-2200, 0800-1800 Sat., Sun.), and airport, 0700-1800, (0800 Sat., Sun.); maps available, free.

Transport Daily flights to Porto Alegre and São Paulo. There is a new bus terminal with helpful tourist information at the east (island) end of the Ponte Colombo Machado Salles; the Terminal Urbano do Aterro for the island nearby, between the Rodoviária and the Mercado Municipal, which serves the northern beach towns, the east coast and most of the southern ones, and a further terminal at the junction of Rua José da Costa and Av. Mauro Ramos which serves the other towns. All local bus destinations and schedules are clearly posted. Regular daily buses to Porto Alegre (US$5.50, 7 hrs.), São Paulo (US$11.65, Rio, US$16 ordinary, Brasília, 3 a week at 0300, US$23; Curitiba (US$5, 5 hrs.), Blumenau (US$3, 4 a day, 3 hrs.), Joinville (2½ hrs. direct, 3½ with stops) US$3 and other towns in the State. Also regular daily buses to Foz do Iguaçu (with Catarinense, US$10.50, continuing to Asunción), to Campo Grande, 28 hrs., US$42, 1400 daily, to most other Brazilian cities and to Montevideo, US$29, by TTL. The coastal highway (BR-101) is preferred as an alternative to the congested inland BR-116; it runs close to Florianópolis but it is bad in places and has many lorries.

Excursions There are 42 beaches around the island almost all easily reached by public buses from the centre (buses of the Empresa Canavieras go from Rua José da Costa, corner Av. Mauro Ramos to the northern towns and beaches, Empresa Ribeironense from next to the Rodoviária to the south-eastern ones, schedules from Tourist Office). The local buses (US$0.10) take you hourly to virtually every place on the island. To Lagoa da Conceição (Emflotur bus 403) for beaches, sand dunes, fishing, church of N.S. da Conceição (1730), boat rides on the lake (restaurants: *Oliveira*, excellent seafood dishes; *Miguelão*, Praça Pio XII 5, poor value; *Leca*, try *rodízio de camarão*, prawns cooked in a dozen ways; *Caminho das Índias*, Av. das Rendeiras 69, warmly rec.). Across the island at Barra da Lagoa is a pleasant fishing village and beach, with plenty of good restaurants, which can be reached by Emflotur bus 403 (US$0.10, every ½ hr., *Hotel Camping Duvalerim*, F, on beach, rec.). Bus 401 goes to beach at Joaquina (surfing championships in January, *Hotel Cris*, T 32-0380, D, luxurious, rec). At Barra da Lagoa, *Cabanas da Barra*, Rua Geral 23, D, good, German and English spoken. Hotel near Barra da Lagoa: *Gaivota* T 32-0177 (Familia Coelho), Praia do Moçambique, E, closed off season, excellent food; *Pousada Ale-Pris*, F; *Dormitório Beira Rio*, G. Also visit the "city of honey bees" with a Museo da Apicultura, closes 1600 Sat., and the Church of Sto. Antônio Lisboa, take Trinidadanse bus 331 or any bus going north, to the turn off, on the way to Sambaqui beach and fishing village. There is a pleasant fishing village at Ponta das Canas, walk 1 km. to Praia Braua for good surfing, and the beach at Canavieiras is good. In the north of the island, at Praia dos Ingleses (bus 602) is *Sol e Mar*, T 62-1271, D, excellent, friendly, rec. In the S of the island are Praia da Armação with, just inland, Lagoa do Peri (a protected area), Further south is Pantana do Sul, an unspoilt fishing village. *Pousada Sitio dos Tukanos*, E, Caixa Postal 5016, T 325084; take bus to Pantana do Sul, walk 6 kms or telephone and arrange to be picked up, German owner speaks English, warmly rec. Praia dos Naufragados and Farol beaches: take bus to Caieira da Barra do Sul and take 1-hr. walk through fine forests.

Excursions can be made on the mainland to the hot springs at Caldas da Imperatriz (41°C) and Águas Mornas (39°C); at the former are 2 spa hotels (*Caldas da Imperatriz*, C, meals and baths included, built in 1850 under the auspices of Empress Teresa Cristina, houses public baths; *Plaza Caldas da Imperatriz*, from B, with baths, swimming pools, very well appointed), at Águas Mornas, the *Palace Hotel* is on the site of the springs, A, baths open to public Mon.-Fri. a.m. only. Boat trips can be made from Florianópolis in the bay, T 22-1806, from

US$4.50-6.80.

From Florianópolis a poor road runs SW inland via São Joaquim (see below) to **Lajes** (pop. 143,000) a convenient stopping place on BR-116 between Caxias do Sul and Curitiba. Despite the poor road, however, this journey is perhaps the most interesting in the State (2 buses a day do this journey, via Alfredo Wagner, otherwise go via Blumenau). (*Grande Hotel*, good, but no heat; cheaper is *Presidente*, E; *Natal*, cheap, adequate; *Rodalar*, *Centaro*, both F, near bus station. Bus station is ½-hr. walk S.E. of centre. Voltage 220 A.C.)

On the coast N of Florianópolis there are many resorts. They include Porto Belo, a fishing village settled in 1750 by Azores islanders, with a calm beach and a number of hotels and restaurants (and wilder beaches reached by rough roads nearby: bus Florianópolis—Porto Belo with Praiana or Biguaçu, 8 daily, 4 on Sat., 3 on Sun.); Itapema (66 km., many hotels); **Camboriú** (86 km., beautiful beach, hotels *Dinamarca*, *Paraná*, *Motel San Carlos*, D, *Balneario de Camboriú*, central, on beach, D, friendly, clean; camping *Mag-Mar* is good; buses from Florianópolis, Joinville and Blumenau) a few kms south, at Lojas Apple, there is a museum, zoo and aquarium; and Meia Praia, which is quieter and cleaner than Camboriú. Between Itajaí and Camboriú is the beautiful, deserted (and rough) beach of Praia Brava.

São Joaquim, at 1,360 metres, the highest town in Southern Brazil, regularly has snowfalls in winter; very pleasant town with an excellent climate (Camping Clube do Brasil site). To the East of the town, in the Serra Geral is the **São Joaquim National Park** (33,500 hectares), with canyons containing sub-tropical vegetation, and araucaria forest at higher levels. The local IBDF office is at Av. Moura Ramos 187, Florianópolis (Caixa Postal 660, CEP 89.000). Hotels: *Nevada* (expensive meals) and *Maristela*, E (good breakfast) both on Rua Manoel Joaquim Pinto, 213 and 220 respectively (5 mins'. walk from Rodoviária). Bus to Florianópolis 0830 and 2230, 7½ hrs., US$6. To Caxias do Sul, 4½ hrs., US$4.

One hundred km. up the coast N of Florianópolis by the BR-101 paved road or by sea is the most important port in Santa Catarina:

Itajaí, at the mouth of the Itajaí river. It is well served by vessels up to 5½ metres draught, and is the centre of a district largely colonized by Germans and Italians. Main exports: timber, starch, tapioca, sassafras oil, and tobacco. Population, 64,000. Airport. You can walk to Cabeçudas beach, which is quiet and small.

Hotels *Balneário Cabeçudas*, at Cabeçudas beach, best, 6 km. out of town, C; *Grande*, Rua Felipe Schmidt 44, good value, E; *Maringá*, N of town, friendly, cheap and clean, with Shell service station next door, providing good food, open all night. *Rex*, *Cacique*, both on R. Asseburg, cheap, near market. Rec. **Bar**, *Trudys*, on riverfront at end of main street, a good place in changing cash.

Resorts north of Itajaí include Piçarras, with sandy beaches interspersed with rocky headlands (ideal for fishing), and Barra Velha (*Hotel Mirante*, E, good, cheap restaurant, and 2 dearer hotels).

There is a 61 km. paved road to **Blumenau** (pop. 192,000), 47 km. up the Itajaí river. It is in a prosperous district settled mostly by Germans; see Museo da Família Colonial, German immigrant museum, Av. Duque de Caxias 78, open Mon.-Sat., 0830-1130, 1330-1730, US$0.05. German Evangelical Church. Places of interest include the houses, now museums (open 0800-1800) of Dr Bruno Otto Blumenau and of Fritz Müller (a collaborator of Darwin), who bought the Blumenau estate in 1897 and founded the town, which is a notable textile centre. A "traditional" Oktoberfest beer-festival was started in 1984 here, and was expected to become the second largest in the world after Munich's. Visitors report it is worth attending on weekday evenings but weekends are too crowded. It is repeated, but called a "summer festival", in the 3 weeks preceding Carnival.

Hotels *Himmelblau Palace*, Rua 7 de Setembro 1415, T 22-5800, C; *Blumenau Tourist Hotel*, 200 m. from bus station, D, helpful; *Garden Terrace*, Rua Padre Jacobs 45, T 22-3544, C; *Grade Hotel*, Alameda Rio Branco 21, T 22-0366, D; *Glória*, Rua 7 de Setembro 954, T

22-1988, D, German-run, excellent coffee shop (all aforementioned hotels have heating in rooms); *Plaza Hering*, 5-star, 7 de Setembro 818, T 22-1277, B, heating and a/c; *Central*, Rua 7 de Setembro 1036, T 22-0570, basic, E with bath, F without, both without breakfast, clean, but not safe for luggage; *Herrmann*, central, Floriano Peixoto 213, T 22-4370, rec., E, a/c, shower, clean. *City*, Rua Ángelo Dias 263, T 22-2205, F. Many cheap hotels do not include breakfast. Most hotels and restaurants very clean. Youth Hostel at Rua Paraíba 66 (T 22-8420).

Camping Municipal campsite, 2 km. out on Rua Pastor Osvaldo Hesse; Paraíso dos Poneis, 9 km. out on the Itajaí road, also Motel; Refúgio Alpino, 11 km. out on Rua da Glória.

Restaurants Good German food at *Frohsinn* (panoramic view) and *Cavalinho Branco*, Av. Rio Branco 165, huge meals, but check the bill, international eating at *Moinho do Vale. A Cantina de Mai*, Rua R.C. Deeke 165, large helpings, good; *Blumental*, 15 de Novembro 962 and Av. Castelo Branco 671, good value; *Amigo*, Peixoto 213, huge cheap meals; *Caféhaus Glória*, in *Hotel Glória*, excellent coffee shop; *Rancho Alegre*. 7 de Setembro 1335, good value; *Deutsches Eck*, same street No. 432, rec., esp. carne pizzaiola; *Das Cafehaus*, serves huge, delicious cakes (tortas); *Gruta Azul*, Rodolfo Freygang, good, popular, not cheap.

Voltage 220 A.C.

Amenities Teatro Carlos Gomes is also exhibition centre; public library open 0800-1800; German bookshops, Librerias Alemãs, at bus station and Ruas 7 de Setembro and 15 de Novembro. Craft shop, Casa Meyer, 15 de Novembro 401.

Exchange At *Cambios*/travel agencies: *Vale do Hajaí Turismo e Cambio*, Av. Beira Rio 167, very helpful, German spoken; *International Turismo*, 1 block away. *President Turismo*, 7 de Setembro, 2nd floor; also *Turismo Holtzmann* nearby; *Ilhatur Turismo*, Rodolfo Freygang 5, 1st floor.

International Telephones Corner of Av. Brasil and República Argentina.

Tourist Office in town hall, Rua 15 de Novembro 420, corner of Rua Nereu Ramos, friendly, limited information; also kiosk on 15 de Novembro, good town map. Only Portuguese spoken.

Bus The Rodoviária for interurban travel is in the village of Fortaleza, US$0.10 by Rodoviária-7 de Setembro bus from the old bus station at Av. 7 de Setembro and Padre Jacobs (US$2.50 by taxi). Left luggage lockers at Rodoviária; tokens available in cafeteria on 2nd floor. Good bus connections in all directions from Blumenau. Blumenau to Caxias do Sul at 1930 only, arrives 0400, US$8; to Curitiba, 4 hrs., US$4.

Excursions By bus to Timbo and Pomerode (from riverside road opp. Prefeitura) past rice fields and wooden houses set in beautiful gardens. At *Pomerode*, 32 km., US$0.50 (*Hotel Central*, E, big lunches) there is an interesting zoo (US$0.60). Tourist office. The North German dialect of Plattdeutsch is still spoken here. The *Tortenparadies* serves excellent German cakes. Rex Bus goes to Iraguã from Pomerode; change for connection to Joinville, US$1.50. Boat trips down the River Itajaí, daily in season, Sat. and Sun. out of season, unspectacular. 1/2-day excursion to Gaspar to visit the cathedral set high above the river (Verdi Veli bus company from stop outside the huge supermarket on Rua 7 de Setembro in the centre).

To Iguaçu As an alternative to the direct Catarinense bus, daily from Florianópolis and Itajaí to Iguaçu via Blumenau, you can travel through rich and interesting farming country in Santa Catarina and Rio Grande do Sul, stopping at *Joaçaba*, a town of German immigrants (*Hotel Colonial*, at bus station, *Lotus*, across bridge, both F); Erexim (Hotel Rex, E, strong gaúcho influence), or *Iraí* Italian immigrant area, town with thermal springs (*Hotel São Luís*, E, with full board, town good for semi-precious stones), thence from any of these places to Pato Branco and Cascavel (**see page 378**for connections to Foz do Iguaçu). The Tourist Office has details of combined ticket to Iguaçu—bus to Curitiba, then flight to Iguaçu—for US$62.

São Francisco do Sul (pop. 23,000) 80 km. up the coast is the port for the town of Joinville, 45 km. inland at the head of the Cachoeira river. Most of the colonial architecture has been replaced by modern buildings. There are some excellent beaches nearby, such as Ubatuba, Enseada (hotels, pensions and 3 camp sites, Pascerella recommended) and Cápri. (At weekend trips to Ilha do Farol in port's supply boat.) Petrobrás oil refinery, but oil pollution has been reported, take mosquito repellant. *Hotel Avenida*, E with breakfast, clean, friendly; Zibamba, R. Fernandes Dias 27, central, C. The *Restaurante Franciscano*, on the Praia dos

Coqueiros, is recommended, so are the *Metralhas* and *Flutuante* (good seafood.) Bus terminal is 1½ km. from centre. Direct bus (Penha) daily to Curitiba at 0730, US$3, 3½ hrs. Train from Joinville leaves daily at 0810 and frequent buses. Men are not allowed to wear shorts here.

Joinville (pop. 303,000) the state's second largest city lies 2 km. from the main coastal highway, BR-101, by which Curitiba and Florianópolis are less than two hours away. To Guaratuba (**see page** 378) by bus, 1¼ hrs., US$1 (connections to Paranaguá).

See the Museum of History in the Prince of Joinville's mansion, which has a collection of objects from the original German settlement. The interesting Museo de Arte is in the old residence of Ottokar Doerfeu, Rua 15 de Novembro 1400 (open Tues.-Sun., 0900-1800). The Archaeological Museum has a collection of the Sambaquis period dating back to 5000 BC (open Tues.-Fri., 0900-1800, Sat., Sun., and holidays, 0900-1200, 1400-1800; US$0.20). Other museums are Museum of Immigration and Colonization, R. Rio Branco 229 (closed Mon.) and the Museum of the sculptor Fritz Act, Rua Aubé (closed Mon.)

At Expoville, 4 km. from centre on BR-101 (continuation of 15 de Novembro) is an exhibition of Joinville's industry and an industrial museum. The industry does not, however, spoil the considerable charm of the city. There is an annual flower festival in the first fortnight of September.

Hotels *Tannehof*, Visconde de Taunay 340, T 22-2311, 4 stars, restaurant on 14th floor; *Anthurium Parque*, São José 226, T 22-6299, C, colonial style, good value, English spoken, friendly; *Ideal*, Jerônimo Coelho 98, D, with excellent breakfast, friendly, clean; *Novo Horizonte*, at bus station, basic, clean; *Konig*, 15 de Novembro 937, E; same street No. 811, *Mattles*, E, T 22-3582

Camping Camping Clube do Brasil, Rua Saguaçu, Horto Florestal. Municipal site, same road, 1 km. from centre.

Restaurants *Petisqueira Pinheiro*, 7 de Setembro, is well worth a visit for excellent fish and shrimp dishes for about US$5. For meat or German specialities, *Churrascaria Rex*, *Churrascaria Ataliba*, near Expoville, *Bierkeller*, 15 de Novembro 497; *Dietrichs*, Rua Princesa Isabel, excellent beer and German food (especially cakes). *Pasteleria Japoneza*, R. Princesa Isabel, excellent pásteis; *Jerke*, a bar on Dr João Colin, has good empadas; *Padaria Brunkow*, 9 de Maio, good snacks. Vegetarian: *Cozinha Natural*, Rua Marinho Lobo 38. The cheapest place to eat is the *Sociedade Ginástica*, Rua Ginásticos—you don't have to be a member.

Banks Banco do Brasil. Open 1000-1630.

Tourist Office corner Praça Nereu Ramos with Rua Príncipe; no information on cheap hotels. Good exchange rates

Buses To Blumenau, US$2, 2¼y hrs. The bus terminal is 2½ km. outside the town (regular bus service).

Air Service Airport 5 km. from city. Daily flights to major cities.

Excursions Four daily buses go to Ubatuba beach, a week-end resort (see above under São Francisco do Sul). The Sambaqui site of Rio Comprido can be reached by Gideon Bus, but there is not much to see. It is a pleasant trip to Jaraguá do Sul, European, hilly landscape.

The State of Paraná

The Italians were first in Paraná, but apart from a few Germans most of the later settlers were of Slavonic origin—Poles, Russians, Ruthenians and Ukrainians. Paraná made astonishing progress until the past few years. It is now the leading producer of wheat, rye, potatoes and black beans, but its population, 8,308,000, no longer expands as quickly as it did, partly because of the displacement of rural workers following the uprooting of coffee plants in the more frost-prone areas and the turning of the land over to cattle. The recent boom crop, soya, also employs fewer workers throughout the year than coffee.

Curitiba, capital of Paraná state (pop. 1.5 million), is a modern city at 900 metres on the plateau of the Serra do Mar. The commercial centre is busy Rua 15 de Novembro (old name: Rua das Flores), which has a pedestrian area where there are Sat. morning painting sessions for children. Another pedestrian area is behind the cathedral, near Largo da Ordem, with sacred art museum, flower clock and old buildings, very beautiful in the evening when the old lamps are lit. Art market Sat. morning in Praça Rui Barbosa, and on Sun. morning in Praça Garibáldi (recommended), beside attractive Rosário church. The Civic Centre is at the end of Avenida Dr. Cândido de Abreu, 2 km. from the city centre: a monumental group of five buildings dominated by the Palácio Iguaçu, headquarters of the state and municipal governments. In a patio behind it is a relief map to scale of Paraná. The Bosque de João Paulo II behind the Civic Centre contains the Polish immigrants' museum: both are worth a visit. In contrast to the Civic Centre is the old municipal government building in French Art Nouveau style, now housing the Museu Paranaense in Praça Generoso Marques. Nearby, on Praça Tiradentes, is the Cathedral (1894). The most popular public park is the Passeio Público, in the heart of the city (closed Mondays); it has a good little zoo, a network of canals with boats, and a small aquarium. On the north east edge of the city is Parque do Barigui, take bus 450 "São Braz" from Praça Tiradentes. Near the shores of Lake Bacacheri on the northern edge of the city (R. Nicarágua 2453) is an unexpected Egyptian temple (the Brazilian centre of the Rosicrucians—visits can be arranged—take Santa Cândida bus to Estação Boa Vista, then walk). There are three modern theatres, the Guaíra for plays and revues (also has free events—get tickets early in the day), one for concerts and ballet, and the Teatro Paiol in the old arsenal. Many of the main streets have been widened and the city is being rapidly transformed.

Local Holidays Ash Wednesday (half-day); Maundy Thursday (half-day); 8 September (Our Lady of Light).

Hotels The following, in our category A, are rec.: *Caravelle Palace*, Rua Cruz Machado 282, T 223-4323, first class; *Lancaster*, R. Voluntários da Pátria 91, T 223-8953, tourist class; *Ouro Verde*, R. Dr. Murici 419, T 224-1633, standard class. *Mabu*, Praça Santos Andrade 830, T 222-7040, L; *Del Rey*, Ermelino de Leão 18, T 224-3033, A, good restaurants. *Tourist Universo*, Praça Gen. Osório 63, B, T 223-5816, good restaurant, rec.; *Climax*, Rua Dr. Murici 411, T 224-3411, good value, popular, C; *Palace*, Rua Barão do Rio Branco 62, E with bath, central, European atmosphere; *Regência*, Rua Alfredo Bufrem 40, T 223-4557, D, with breakfast, excellent; *Cervantes*, same street No 66, T 222-9593, F, rec. *Vitória*, Rua São Francisco, F, central, pleasant, clean, friendly, but security a problem.
   There are hotels in categories D downwards in the vicinity of the Rodoferroviária, but the cheaper ones are close to the wholesale market, which operates noisily throughout the night: *Nova Lisboa*, Av. 7 de Setembro 1948, E with breakfast, bargain for cheaper rates without breakfast, clean; *Condor*, No. 1866, D, a/c, TV, clean, breakfast, rec; *Itamarati*, Tibagi 950, 500 m. from Rodoferroviária, E, clean, with bath, fan, friendly; *Costa Brava*, Rua Francisco Torres 386, T 262-7172, D, well rec.; *Império*, Av. Pres. Afonso Camargo 367, D with bath, E without, small and poor breakfast, take insect repellent; next door, *Maia*, E with bath, incl. breakfast, clean and quiet; *Wang*, same street, No. 549, no sign, F, safe, clean, good value, but run down; *Jaguarã*, opposite station, very clean, noisy, good breakfast, rec. (but not the buffet supper) D; *Doral*, Mota 1144, T 222-1060, TV, frigobar in room, good breakfast, D; *Filadélfia*, Gen Carneiro 1094, T 264-5244, D, clean, good breakfast, private bath, 4 blocks from station through market; *Nalini*, Pedro Ivo 713, 1 block from bus terminal, F, helpful owner speaks German, T 234-1449, hot shower.
   Casa dos Estudantes, Parque Passeio Público, F, with student card. Youth hostels in Paraná state: Asociação Paranaense de Albergues de Juventude, Av. Padre, Agostinho 645, Curitiba PR, CEP 80.410; in the city, *Hans Staden*, Rua Pe. Agostinho 645.

Camping Official site 7 km. N of city, on São Paulo road, US$1 a night. Camping Clube do Brasil, 14 km. out on same road.

Restaurants *Ile de France* (French), Praça 19 de Dezembro 538; *Schwartze Katz* (German and international), Rua Francisco Torres 18; *Schwarzwald*, Claudino dos Santos 63, beerhaus/ restaurant, in centre (German); *Matterhorn*, Mateus Leme 575, centre. *Golden*

CURITIBA 36
(centre)
Not to Scale

N

1. Praça Tiradentes
2. Praça João Cândido
3. Praça Garibáldi and Flower Clock
4. Praça Generoso Marques and
   Museu Paranaense
5. Praça Santos Dumont
6. Praça Zacarias
7. Praça Carlos Gomes
8. Largo da Ordem
9. Cathedral
10. Rosário Church
11. Sacred Art Museum
12. Museum Guido Viário
13. Museum of Contemporary Art
14. Railway Museum
15. Post Office (x2)
16. Telephone Office
17. Tourist Kiosk
18. Hotel Lancaster
19. Hotel Tourist Universo
20. Cheaper hotels and wholesale
    market area

Chopp, Rua André de Barros (near corner with Rua Barão do Rio Branco), good value, rec.; *A Sacristia*, Rua João Manuel 197, restaurant, pizzeria, bar, very good; *Oriente*, Rua Ebano Pereira 26 (1st floor), excellent, huge Arab lunch. Good Arab food also at *Casa da Efina*, Cruz Machado 247, and *Cantina Árabe*, Al. Augusto Stellfeld 143. Local and Italian food and local red wine in nearby Santa Felicidade (10 km. out of town on road to Ponta Grossa), e.g. *Madalosso*, Av. Manoel Ribas 5875, Italian self-service, rec. Sukiyaki at *Yuasa*, Av. Sete de Setembro, cheap and good, rec.

Vegetarian: *Transformação* (macrobiotic, shop also), Al. Augusto Stellfeld 781; *Vegetariano*, Carlos de Carvalho 127, 13 de Maio 222; *Ao Natural*, Rua São Francisco 332 (lunch only, shop also); *Verde Jante*, Rua Pres. Faria 481, very good; *Super Vegetariano*, Rua Pres. Faria 121, Cruz Machado 217, Rua Dr. Murici 315, lunch and dinner Mon.-Fri., very good and cheap.

Paláchio, Barão Rio Branco, is all-night restaurant, good food and cheap; cheap food also near old railway station and a good meal in the bus station. Close to the Rodoferroviária is the market, where there are a couple of *lanchonetes*. Students can eat at University canteen (student cards required). Hot sweet wine sold on the streets in winter helps keep out the cold. Rec. tea house: *Chez Arnold*, Av. Manoel Ribas 526, in the Mercês district.

Electric Current 110 v. 60 cycles.

Bookshop *Livrarias Ghignone*, Rua 15 de Novembro 409, has good selection of English books.

Shopping Curitiba is a good place to buy clothes and shoes. *H. Stern* jewellers at Mueller Shopping Centre.

Local Transport The city has a very efficient bus system; all bus stops have maps. Express buses on city routes are orange: for example, from centre (Praça Rui Barbosa) take Leste bus marked "Villa Oficinas" or "Centenário" for Rodoferroviária (combined bus and railway station).

Museums Museu Paranaense, Praça Generoso Marques (open Tues.-Fri. 1000-1800, other days 1300-1800, closed first Mon. of each month). Museu David Carneiro, on Rua Comendador Araújo 531, Sat., 1400-1600. Museo Guido Viário, R. São Francisco 319, painter's house; Museum of Contemporary Arts, Rua D. Westphalen 16 (closed Sats., and Sun. morning). Casa Andersen, R. Mateus Leme 336, house of painter, open Mon.-Fri. Railway Museum, Av. 7 de Setembro, in the old railway station, open Tues.-Fri., 1300-1900, Sat.-Sun., 0800-1300; Second World War Museum, Casa Expedicionário, Praça do Expedicionário; Museo do Automóvel, Av Cândido Hartmann 2300 (Sat. 1400-1800, Sun. 0900-1200, 1330-1800), all worth a visit.

Exchange Best exchange rates at Jade travel agency, Rua Quinze de Novembro 477 (cash only); Triangle Turismo Travel, Praça General Osório 213, cash and travellers' cheques; Transoceania, R. Mal Deodoro 500, good rate for cash or cheques; Diplomata, Rua Presidente Faria 145 in the arcade.

Cultural Institutes Centro Cultural Brasil-Estados Unidos (Mon.-Fri., 0800-1200, 1400-2100); Sociedade Brasileira de Cultura Inglesa (British Council), Rua General Carneiro 679 (Caixa Postal 505). Instituto Goethe, Duque de Caxias 4, open Mon., Wed., Thurs., Fri., 1500-1900.

Austrian Consulate, Rua Marechal Floriano Peixoto 228, Edif. Banrisul, 17 andar, Caixa Postal 2473, T 22 46 795.

Laundry Rua C. Laurindo 63, next to theatre, US$3 for 5 kg.

Church services held in German at the Evangelical Church.

Post Office Main post office is at Marechal Deodoro 298; post offices also at Rua 15 de Novembro and Rua Pres. Faria. **Cables** Embratel, Galeria Minerva, Rua 15 de Novembro.

Tourist Office Av. Sete de Setembro 2077, CEP 80.050, Curitiba, maps and information in English. *Guía Turística de Curitiba e Paraná*, annual, US$4, on sale at all kiosks, has been rec. Paranatur has booths at Rodoferroviária, in the old rail car at Rua 15 de Novembro 141 and Ebano Pereira, and at airport, helpful, English spoken, but no maps. Free weekly leaflet, *Bom Programa*, available shops, cinemas, paper stands etc.

Transport Rodoferroviária at end of Av. 7 de Setembro, very efficient (bus to centre US$0.10); short-distance bus services (up to 40 km.) begin at old bus station at Rua João Negrão 340. Passenger trains to Paranaguá, see below.

Frequent buses to São Paulo, including night bus at 2320 (6 hrs., US$6; leito 12) and Rio de Janeiro (11 hours, US$13, leito 26). To Santos, 3 a day (leito at 2300), 6½ hrs., US$7. Buses to Foz do Iguaçu, 10 buses a day, 10 hrs., US$6 (3 leito buses at night, US$12); to Pelotas, US$17, 18 hrs; to Porto Alegre, 10 hrs; to Londrina via Ponta Grossa, 8 hrs.; to Guaíra, 0700, 1915 and leito 1930 (12 hrs). Itajaí, 4 hrs., US$3.50; Blumenau, 4½ hrs., US$4. Florianópolis, 4½ hrs, US$5 (leito US$10). TTL runs to Montevideo, 26 hrs., US$25, 0300 departure (leito) US$46. If travelling by car to Porto Alegre or Montevideo, the coastal highway (BR-101) is preferable to the inland road (BR-116).

Excursions The beautiful Ouro Fino estate (34 km.) is open to the public every day except Mon., Dec.-March, and every second Sunday the rest of the year. The nearest bus stop is 16 km. away at Campo Largo, so car is the best way to get there. Advance permission needed, from Rua Silva Jardim 167, Curitiba, T 232-7411, or phone Ouro Fino (041) 292-1913. On the first and third Sunday of each month, a steam train runs from Curitiba to Lapa (about 80 km. SW), returning after a tour of the town. Nearby there is a free, secure campsite from which the Groto do Monge can be visited.

20 km. from Curitiba (at Km. 119) on the road to Ponta Grossa on the Museu Histórico do Mate, an old water-driven mill where mate was prepared (free admission). On the same road is **Vila Velha**, now a national park, 97 km. from Curitiba: the sandstone rocks have been weathered into most fantastic shapes. There is a Camping Clube do Brasil site near Vila Velha, 85 km. from Curitiba. Alternatively, stay in Ponta Grossa (**see page** 378, from which buses leave for Vila Velha at 0900, 40 mins., last bus back at 1830). The park office is 300 metres from the highway and the park a further 1½ km. (entrance US$0.30—opens at 0800). If taking a bus from Curitiba, make sure it's going to the Parque Nacional and not to the town 20 km. away. Transport from the Park to a swimming pool (free—costumes can be rented for US$1.20), 2 km. away. Princesa dos Campos bus from Curitiba at 0730 and 0930, 1½ hrs., US$1 (return buses pass park entrance at 1500 and 1700). The Lagoa Dourada, surrounded by forests, is close by. Nearby are the Furnas, three water holes, the deepest of which has a lift (US$0.30—not always working) which descends almost to water level (the same level as Lagoa Dourada); entrance US$0.05. Bus from Vila Velha at 1310, 1610 and 1830, US$0.30, 4½ km. to turn-off to Furnas (another ¼y-hr. walk) and Lagoa Dourada (it's not worth walking from Vila Velha to Furnas because it's mostly uphill along the main road). From the turn-off buses to Curitiba pass 10 minutes before they pass Vila Velha. Allow all day if visiting all 3 sites (unless you hitch, or can time the buses well, it's a lot of walking). Since the afternoon buses which pass en route to Curitiba are often full, it may be advisable to go to Ponta Grossa and return to Curitiba from there.

Popular expeditions during the summer are by paved road or rail (4½ hrs.) to Paranaguá. Two trains a day do the journey, the most **spectacular railway** trip in Brazil. There are numerous tunnels,with sudden views of deep gorges and high peaks and waterfalls as the train rumbles over dizzy bridges and viaducts. Near Banhado station (Km. 66) is the waterfall of Véu da Noiva; from the station at Km. 59, the mountain range of **Marumbi National Park** can be reached: see below. The ordinary train leaves Curitiba at 0800 Mon.-Fri. and 0700 Sat. and Sun. only, arriving in Paranaguá at 1030 (US$1.50 one class, tickets on sale at 0600, except for Sun. train where on sale on Fri., no seat reservations—ticket office is closed on Sun.; sandwiches, chocolate and drinks for sale on board; in the off season the schedule may vary according to freight needs; do not trust printed schedules, ask at the station). Avoid the front coach. A modern air-conditioned rail-car (the Litorina, called the automotriz) leaves at 0830, arriving at 1100 (US$6 each way, reserved seats bookable 2 days in advance; latest reports say it only runs Wed., Sat. and Sun.) with recorded commentary (in Portuguese, French, Spanish and English) and stops at the viewpoint at the Santuário da N.S. do Cadeado and at Morretes (only a few minutes). Sit on the left-hand side on journey from Curitiba (in the automotriz, the seats, not the car, are turned round, so you sit the same side in each direction). If Litorina is full, take bus to Paranaguá, US$1.30, then take Litorina back: return journeys start at 1530 (Litorina) and 1630 (ordinary train) so remember that in winter part of the ordinary train's journey is covered in the dark (also, on cloudy days there's little to see on the higher parts). The train is usually crowded on Saturdays and Sundays. Many travellers recommend returning by bus (1½ hrs., buy ticket immediately on arrival), if you do not want to stay 4½ hrs. A tour bus meets the train and offers a tour of town and return to Curitiba for US$3.

You can also visit **Antonina** (not on main route) and **Morretes** (on main route), two sleepy colonial towns which can be reached by rail and also by bus on the old Graciosa road, which is almost as scenic as the railway. Bus Paranaguá to Morretes at 1830, US$0.60, to Antonina, stopping en route at Morretes, 6 a day, (US$1). 12 buses daily Morretes-Curitiba US$1; 20 buses a day Curitiba-Antonina. On Tues., 0700, a train runs from Curitiba to Morretes only (and does not take passengers on the return journey). Every fourth Sunday, a steam train runs from Antonina to Morretes to connect with the ordinary train from Curitiba.

Morretes hotel: *Nhundiaquara*, in town centre, beautifully located, F and up, good restaurant; good restaurants in town (try "barreado", beef cooked for 24 hrs, especially good in the two restaurants on the river bank) and a river beach. **Antonina hotels**: *de Lazer*, B, 3-star; *Christine*, F and up, clean. Antonina is a port, but there are no beaches. 14 km. N of Morretes is the beautiful village of São João de Graciosa, 2 km. beyond which is the flower reserve of the Marumbi Park. The Graciosa road traverses the park for 12 km., with 6 rest stops with fire grills, shelters and camping. The park is very beautiful; you can also hike the original trail which follows the road and passes the rest-stops. Take food, water and plenty of insect repellent. The Marumbi Park can be entered at a gate 3-4 km. from the BR-116 Curitiba-São Paulo highway.

Paranaguá (pop. 95,000), and chief port of the state of Paraná and one of the main coffee-exporting ports, was founded in 1585, 268 km. south of Santos. It is on a lagoon 29 km. from the open sea and is approached via the Bay of Paranaguá, dotted with picturesque islands. The fort of Nossa Senhora dos Prazeres was built in 1767 on a nearby island; one hour's boat trip. The former Colêgio dos Jesuitas, a fine baroque building, has been converted into a Museum of Archaeology and Popular Art (Tues.-Fri., 1000-1700, Sat.-Mon., 1200-1700; entrance US$0.10). Other attractions are a 17th century fountain, the church of São Benedito, and the shrine of Nossa Senhora do Rocio, 2 km. from town. There are restaurants and craft shops near the waterfront. The part of town between the waterfront, railway station and new bus station has been declared a historic area. Paranaguá is a free port for Paraguay.

The paved 116-km. road to Curitiba is picturesque, but less so than the railway (see above), which offers one of the most beautiful trips in Brazil.

Hotels *Santa Mônica*, Praia de Leste, 30 km. from town, on fine beach, C; *Auana*, Rua Correia de Freitas 110, T 422-0948, E-D, good value, rec. (but electric showers in the more expensive rooms). *Ribamar*, E, with breakfast; *Litoral*, Rua Correia de Freitas 66, F without breakfast, clean and comfortable; *Rio Mar* and *Mar de Rosas*, both on waterfront, E.

Camping Camping Clube do Brasil site at Praia de Leste, on the beach, 27 km. from Paranaguá.

Restaurants *Bobby's*, Faria Sobrinho 750, highly rec., esp. for seafood. *Danúbio Azul* 15 de Novembro 91, good, not cheap, view of river; *Churrascaria do Maneco*, Praça Eufrásio Correia 560, cheap. *Aquarius*, Av. Gabriel de Lara 40, good but not cheap seafood.

Tourist Information kiosk outside railway station.

Air Services Curitiba airport.

Bus Station All buses operated by Graciosa. To Curitiba, US$1.30, many, 1½ hrs. (only the 0745 in either direction and the 1500 to Curitiba take the old Graciosa road).

Excursions *Matinhos* is a Mediterranean-type resort, invaded by surfers in October for the Paraná surf competition; several cheap hotels, including Bolamar (F, basic, cheapest) and *Beira Mar*. 3 camp sites, but the municipal site is closed until November. Cruises on Paranaguá Bay by launch, daily from Cais do Mercado. Bus from Paranaguá at 1000, 1400 and 1615,

US$0.50. 6 buses a day to Guaratuba, US$0.60. **Guaratuba** (which is less built up than Caiobá) has *Pensão Antonieta*, E, clean, dangerous showers, and other hotels; campsite. All Guaratuba buses pass **Caiobá** (*Hotel Caiobá*, D, cheapest). Caiobá to Guaratuba by ferry, free for pedestrians, US$0.80 for cars, 10 minutes, frequent departures.

To **Ilha do Mel**, take bus to Pontal do Sul (many daily, direct from/to Curitiba, 1hr., US$1); turn left out of the bus station and walk 25 metres to main road, turn right for 1½ km. and bear left along a sandy road for 2 km. to fishermen's houses from where a ferry runs (US$0.75). On the island, which is well-developed for tourism, there are bars, holiday homes, etc. Camping is possible on the more deserted beaches. At Praia dos Encantados, one can camp or rent a fisherman's house—ask for *Valentim's Bar*, or for Luchiano; *Estalagem Ancourado*, nr. the lighthouse, F, shared facilities, clean, friendly, meals cooked if required. Dona Ana and Dona Maria sell bread and cakes, and meals if you ask in advance. The beaches, caves, bays and hill walks are beautiful. 4 hrs.' walk from the village is an old Portuguese fort, possible to hitch a ride in a fishing boat back. If camping, watch out for the tide, watch possessions and beware of the *bicho de pé* which burrows into feet (remove with a needle and alcohol) and of the *borrachudos* (discourage with Autum repellent). In summer and at holiday times the island is very crowded.

About 117 km. from Curitiba the road inland (which passes Vila Velha— see page 376) reaches **Ponta Grossa** (pop 223,000, 895 metres). It now calls itself the "World Capital of Soya" (as does Palmeira das Missões, in Rio Grande do Sul). Roads run north through Apucarana (Camping Clube site) and Londrina to São Paulo, and south to Rio Grande do Sul and the Uruguayan border.

Hotels *Vila Velha Palace*, Rua Balduino Taques 123, T 24-2200, C; *Planalto Palace*, Rua 7 de Setembro 652, T 24-2122, plain and clean, E; *Gravina*, Rua Cnel. Bittencourt 92, T 24-0503, E. *Sch a Fransky*, Rua Francisco Ribas 104, T 24-2511, D, very good breakfast; almost next door, same street No. 162, is *Central*, E, with fan and basin, good breakfast; *Luz*, bargain, near railway station. *Cristina*, F without breakfast, OK. *Esplanada*, in bus station (quiet, however), E with bath and breakfast, clean, safe. Try area around Praça Barão de Garaúna.

Camping Camping Clube do Brasil, 26 km. out at the entrance to Vila Velha.

Restaurants *Chopin*, for excellent churrascos. *Shanadu*, on main square, good value.

Buses Princesa dos Campos to Curitiba, 6 a day, 2 hrs., US$2; same company to Iguaçu, 4 daily, 11 hrs., US$7.50.

In Alto Paraná in the extreme NW of the State, connections have traditionally been with São Paulo rather than with Curitiba. Large new centres of population have risen in a short time. In 1930 four Japanese and two Germans arrived in **Londrina** (pop. 346,000), developed by a British company. Today it is a city with skyscrapers, modern steel and glass cathedral, and wide streets (*Hotel Coroados*, Sen. Souza Naves 814, T 23-7690, D, standard; *Hotel Aliança*, nr. bus station, E, very clean, good breakfast; *Hotel dos Viajantes*, F, Av. São Paulo 78, clean, quiet, safe, friendly; *Hotel Triunfo*, F, R. Prof João Cândido 39, T 23-5054, clean, friendly; *Hotel Cravinho*, F, R. Minas Gerais 88, clean, friendly. Youth Hostel, Rua Gomes Carneiro 315, centro Esportivo Moringão). **Maringá** (pop. 197,000, about a third Japanese) is 80 km. W of Londrina, founded in 1947. There is a small conical cathedral; Parque Ingá is shady, with a Japanese garden. (*Hotel Santos*, nr. bus station, F, basic, clean; others in this area. *São Carlos*, Joules de Carvalho 422, E, rec.) Londrina and Maringá are good points for connections between the south (Porto Alegre), Foz do Iguaçu and Mato Grosso do Sul (Campo Grande). Bus from Londrina to Porto Alegre takes 22 hours; to Campo Grande 11 hours, via Presidente Prudente (see page 354). A number of bus services from Paraná state to Porto Alegre (Aguia Branca, Unesul) and to Campo Grande, Cuiabá and Porto Velho (Eucatur) commence at **Cascavel**, further S on the Curitiba-Iguaçu road (hotels: *Vila Paraguaya*, F, clean, simple; *Grand Prix*, clean, good value).

The Paraná River

In the extreme SW of the State, on the Argentine frontier, are the **Iguaçu Falls**, approached by a good paved road from Curitiba, through Guarapuava and Cascavel, with frequent bus services. There is an international airport about 14 km. from the Falls, and 32 km. from the Falls is the city of Foz do Iguaçu, with excellent road connections with Argentina and Paraguay.

For a detailed description of the Falls as a whole, and the Argentine side in particular, together with an account of road links between the Argentine and Brazilian sides, **see the Argentine section, page** 136.

Ideally, one should first visit the Brazilian side to get some idea of the size and magnificence of the whole, and to take one's introductory photographs in the morning, and then cross to the Argentine side to see the details (quickest to get some australes on the Brazilian side), this can all be done in a day, starting at about 0700, but the brisk pace needed for a quick tour is very exhausting for the non-athletic in that heat. If one's time is very limited, then the Brazilian side, with its marvellous distant views, is the one to visit.

A 1½ km. paved walk runs part of the way down the cliff near the rim of the Falls, giving a stupendous view of the whole Argentine side (the greater part) of the falls. It ends up almost under the powerful Floriano Falls; a catwalk brought into use at the end of 1984 was closed again in 1989. Waterproof clothing can be hired although it is not absolutely necessary. An elevator (from 0800) hoists the visitor to the top of the Floriano Falls and to a path leading to Porto Canoa, if there is a queue it is easy and quick to walk up. Helicopter flight over Falls—US$30 per head—lasts 4 minutes. (There is pressure for the helicopter rides to stop: the noise is seriously disturbing the wildlife, especially the birds.) There is a small but worthwhile museum 5 km. from the Falls (1 km. from park entrance is side road to museum, look for sign) and opposite it are some steps that lead down the steep slope to the river bank. Beautiful walk. It can be misty early in the morning at the Falls. Entry to the Brazilian side of the Falls is about US$0.50, included in the bus fare out, or payable at the National Park entrance. If possible, visit on a weekday when the walks are less crowded.

From Foz do Iguaçu, Dois Irmãos buses (from local bus station—*Terminal Urbana*—on Av. Juscelino Kubitschek, opp. Infantry Barracks, 1½ blocks from Rodoviária— interstate bus station) marked Cataratas run the 32 km. to the falls every 2 hours from 0600 to 2100, past airport to *Hotel das Cataratas*, takes 40 mins. At weekends, holidays and other high seasons, frequency increases to every hour. Buses return 0700-1900, about US$0.80 one way. (The taxi fare is US$4.50, plus US$2 for each hour of waiting.) The tours of the Falls organized by the various hotels have been recommended in preference to taxi rides. At least 4 buses an hour from 0700 to 2100 (Transbalan, Viação Itaipu, Tres Fronteiras companies, about US$0.50) ply over the bridge between the *Terminal Urbana* and the bus station in Puerto Iguazú.

Be sure to get a stamp on your passport if intending to stay in Brazil. There is an entry tax on the Brazilian side for car passengers only, not for bus passengers. If driving into Brazil insist on visiting customs. You must get entry papers for your car here or you'll have serious problems later.

There are Brazilian immigration offices on the Brazilian sides of the bridges into Paraguay and Argentina; if you are just visiting Ciudad del Este (formerly Ciudad Stroessner) or Puerto Iguazú and the Argentine side of the Falls and returning to Brazil the same day, no need to have your passport stamped. There are Brazilian customs patrols looking for undeclared goods on the roads past the frontier. Note that if entering or leaving a country and you have to visit customs and immigration, buses won't wait; take a taxi instead.

Foz do Iguaçu is a rapidly developing and improving town of about 200,000 people, with a wide range of accommodation and good communications by air and road with the main cities of southern Brazil, and with Asunción, Paraguay.

Hotels On a height directly overlooking the Falls, 32 km. from Foz, is the *Hotel Tropical* (ex-*das Cataratas*), T 74 2666, Fax 74 1688, an attractive colonial-style building with nice gardens and a swimming pool not without insects. Much wildlife can be seen in the grounds at night and early a.m. Rates: L (but 30% discount for holders of the Brazil Air Pass). It is reported the money is exchanged only at the official rate, check before paying. Non-residents can have US$15 lunch here (midday and evening buffets, or else wait 45 minutes for *à-la-carte* dishes).

If you know which hotel you wish to stay in (and there are over 180), do not be put off by touts who say it no longer exists. Note also that touts quote room rates below what is actually charged.

Many out-of-town hotels on the Falls road state their address as km. from Foz. *Salvatti*, Rua Rio Branco 577, T 74-2727, B, all a/c (with restaurant and cinema); *Internacional*, Almirante Baroso 345, T 74-4855, L, good; *Rafahin Palace*, Br 277-Km. 727, T 73-3434; *Rafahin*, Mal. Deodoro 909,T 74-4455, B, good restaurant, pool, well spoken of. Rec.: *Foz Presidente*, Rua Xavier da Silva 918, T 74-5155,E in winter D in summer, shower, a/c, good restaurant, swimming pool, trips arranged to Falls, English spoken. On road to Falls (Rodovia das Cataratas) are the *Bourbon*, all facilities, (Km. 2.5), *Carimã*, B, (Km. 16), *Dom Pedro I*, B, (Km. 3, T 74-2011), *Panorama*, B, (Km. 12), *Belvedere*, C, (Km. 10.4). *Colonial*, (Km. 16.5), T 74-1777, A, near airport, swimming pool, fine location. *Continental Inn*, Av. Paraná 485, T 74-4123, A; *Lanville*, Jorge Schimmelpfeng 827, T 72-2211, B. On Av. Brasil: *Diplomata*, No. 678, T 74-3155, some a/c, D with shower, value for money, arranges taxi tours to Argentine side; *O Astro*, No 660, T 72-3584, F, clean, friendly, a/c; *City*, No. 938, T 74-2074, F, own bathroom, fan, hot water, clean; *Foz do Iguaçu*, No. 97, B, good laundry and breakfast, will look after luggage, fair; *Syaden*, No. 16, opp. Rodoviária, F, hot water, clean, comfortable, friendly. *Bogari Palace*, No. 106, D, excellent restaurant, swimming pool; *Cisne*, No. 144A, T 72-2488, D, good breakfast, clean, friendly, English spoken, fridge; *Imperial*, No. 168, T 74-2422, E with bath, clean; *Luz*, Almte Barroso, near rodoviária, E, clean, rec; *Turis*, Rua Xavier da Silva 699, T 74-4955, 2 blocks from bus station, E, fans, bathroom, noisy, excellent breakfast, comfortable, organizes tours; *San Remo*, Kubitschek e Xavierda Silva 467, T 72-2956, E, a/c; *Goya*, Kubitschek 969, T 74-3955, E; *Bastos*, Castelo Branco 216, T 74-5839, E, a/c with bath, clean, secure, helpful, rec.; *Hospedaria Antunes*, Av. República Argentina, 288, F with coffee, fans, friendly, clean, quiet, rec; *Tarobá*, Tarobá 878, T 73-5437, quiet, clean, E with bath, a/c, fans, rec; *Riviera*, Mal. Deodoro 559 with Bartolomeu de Gusmão, E, clean, friendly. *Hospedaria*, Rua Tarobá 501, Manuel Baiano, F, family atmosphere, breakfast in kitchen; *Trento*, Rebouças 665, T 74-5111, E, shared bath, clean, rec.; *Scaeli*, Alronso 256, F, basic; *Plaza*, Bartolomeu de Gusmão 376, T 74-2515, F, good, clean rec.; *Senhordo Bontin*, Almte Barroso 6, T (0455) 7-4540, F, clean, friendly; *Geny*, R. Tomé de Souza, F; *Hospedaria*, Floriano Peixoto 263, E with bath, F without, fridge, fan, clean, German spoken. Rec. accommodation: house of Laura Coivo, Rua Naipi 629, 4 rooms with bath, D, friendly, helpful; also house of Gertrudis Roth, Rebouças 907, pleasant, 3 rooms, deals fixed up with restaurants, exchange dealers etc; Evelina Navarrete, R. Mar Floriano 1327, T 74-3817, clean, excellent breakfast, helpful, rec, English, French and Spanish spoken. *IYHA* affiliated hostel, between immigration and the bridge, G. Be sure to leave hotels punctually, or you will be charged an extra day. Many hotels have a minibus service to the airport for guests for a small fee and also offer excursions to Falls. Sra Murro, at Estrada Velha das Cataratas, T 72-1808, rents rooms at her house, D, with fine breakfast, lovely atmosphere. Leave town on road to falls, drive 1 km. then on to road to Porto Meira for 1 km., then turn left for 3.4 km. at School of Agriculture; house is on left, painted red.

Camping (pretty cold and humid in winter) 8 km. from Foz, on road to Falls is the *Cataratas*, quite clean; 1 km. from *Churrascarias Boina Brasa* and (best) *Rafahin* on Route 277 (Paraguayan music) next to *Rafahin Palace Hotel*. By National Park entrance Camping Clube do Brasil, 17 km. from Foz, US$3 p.p. a night (half with International Camping Card), swimming pool, clean; park vehicle or put tent away from trees in winter in case of heavy rain storms, no restaurants, food there not very good, closes at 2300, there are cheaper sites nearer the town on the same road. Not permitted by hotel and Falls. Sleeping in car inside the park also prohibited. Avoid *Camping Internacional*, where several assaults have been reported, 5 km. from Foz centre.

Electric Current 110 volts a/c.

Restaurants Many open till midnight. *Rafahin* before the policia rodoviária post at Km. 533, with Paraguayan harp trio, good alcatra (meat), excellent buffet, but expensive, next to *Rafahin Palace Hotel* on Route 277, km. 727. There are two other establishments called *Rafahin*: one, *Rafahin Center*, at Av. Brasil 157 in Foz, good value, fast food, and a third at Av. das Cataratas Km. 7, between Foz and the airport, is a *churrascaria*. *Las Tres Fronteras*, Av. J. Kubitschek 393, Argentine owner, cheap and friendly; *Arandela*, Brasil 1179, Italian style, full meal, US$3.30, rec. The pizzas at Av. Brasil 1283, have been rec. *Churrascaria Cabeça de Boi*, Av. Brasil 1325, large, live music, dinner US$5, also for coffee and pastries. *Cataratas late Club* serves feijoada (Sat. and Sun., fish and other specialities, Av. Gen. Meira, opp. agricultural college. *Karvês*, Av. Kubitschek e Xavier de Silva, good food, large helpings, US$4. *Casa do Frango*, chicken specialities, also take-away, on Almte. Barroso, opp. *Hotel Basso*; *Star Foz* R. Alm. Barroso 330, good steaks, outstanding value. *Akitem*, vegetarian, Av. Brazil 531, rec. A fruit shop and restaurant are next to the Atlantic gasoline station, 2 blocks from the bus station, and one block behind the bus station is an excellent *churrascaria*, *Espetão*. *Italia*, behind bus station, cheap and popular, huge quantities; *Amigo John*, behind the bus station, cheapest in town, excellent value; *Supermercado Maringo*, lunch counter US$1.

Beware of overcharging at *lanches* (small restaurants)—sometimes three times the posted price; have the right change available.

N.B. There are increased reports of night-time assaults at Foz, with thieves carrying knives or guns.

Entertainment Discotheque *Whiskadão* with three different dance halls, Alm. Barroso 763, reasonable, lively at weekends. Fun fair, Centro de Diversões Imperial, on Av. Brasil.

Consulates Argentina, Rua Don Pedro II, close to Paranatur, open 0800-1300; **Paraguay**, Bartolomeu de Gusmão 777.

Health Translation offered, doctor arranged by Edgar Leiminger, R. Mal. Deodoro 233, T (045) 574-5650, Spanish, English, German spoken.

Post Office Praça Getúlio Vargas 72, next to Tourist Office.

Tourist Office Paranatur, very helpful, Almirante Barroso 485. Kiosk on Av. Brasil, by Ponte de Amizade (helpful), will book hotels.

Travel Agents and Currency Exchange Transatlântica Turismo, Av. Brasil 99, Waterfall Travels, Av Brasil 267, Caixa Postal 157 CEP 85 890, and others. Dicks Tours has been rec. for its all-day tour to the Brazilian side of the Falls, to Paraguay (Ciudad del Este) and to the Itaipú dam, US$12 with good lunch included. Recommended guides, Ruth Campo Silva, STTC Turismo Ltda, Av. Brasil 268, T 74-3122; Chiderly Batismo Pequeno, R. Almirante Barroso 505, Foz, T 74-3367, US$20 for a full day for 5 people. Very difficult to exchange on Sunday, but quite possible in Paraguay. Turismo Ortega, Av. Brasil 1140, also handles exchange; Cambio Iguaçu, Av. Brasil 268; Casa Jerusalém, Av. Brasil 1055, for new cruzeiros, australes, guaraníes, good rates. Frontur on Av. Brasil accepts travellers' cheques, so does Venson Turismo, next to *Hotel Foz do Iguaçu*; many street changers nearby, good rates also at the airport.

Excursions From Foz, you can make an excursion to the 12,600-megawatt **Itaipú dam** (see below), which Brazil and Paraguay have built nearby. The Sete Quedas Falls were flooded in 1982-83 under the project. Bus marked Canteira da Obra from Terminal Urbana goes every 40 minutes to the Public Relations office at the main entrance, visits free (but in groups only)—film in German, English or Portuguese and then the dam (only one stop for taking photos), ask in reception if you may see turbines. Tours (US$0.30) start at 0830, 1000, 1400, 1500; 0800, 0900, 1000, 1330 and 1430 on Suns, the first English tour starts at 0900. There are also an "executive" bus and agency tours but these are an unnecessary expense as the visit itself is free. If it's sunny, go in the morning as the sun is behind the dam in the afternoon and you will get poor photographs. You cannot go alone to the site as it is fenced in and guarded by its own security force. You can also visit the Paraguayan side, **see page 836**.

It is also possible to stay in Ciudad del Este (Paraguay) visiting both sides of the falls without immigration stamps; documents must be carried at all times, however. Take the Foz do Iguaçu bus to interstate rodoviária or walk over the Ponte de Amizade (Friendship Bridge), Brazilian post open until 0200, pay US$2 in dollars, guaraníes or new cruzeiros at the Paraguayan end) past Brazilian Customs and take Ponte-Cidade bus (US$0.05) to local bus station (10 mins. from Rodoviária) where buses go to the Falls or to Argentina. Taxi from Ciudad del Este to centre of Foz, US$10. It is not possible to change travellers cheques in Paraguay unless your passport is stamped.

Airport The Iguaçu international airport has daily flights from Río, São Paulo, Curitiba and Asunción, Paraguay, and good connections from other Brazilian cities. 3 flights a week to Buenos Aires. Taxis to town from the Brazilian airport 18 km from Foz, or about half-way between Foz and the Falls, are expensive (*comum*, US$5; *especial*, US$7); Dois Irmãos town bus for US$0.10, first at 0530, does not permit large amounts of luggage (but backpacks OK). Varig/Cruzeiro office in Foz: Av. Brasil 821, T 74-3344; staff speak foreign languages; Vasp, T 74-2999.

Buses Rodoviária, Av. Brasil 99, T 73-1525; has trustworthy baggage store. Foz is reached by many buses from Curitiba (9-11 hours, paved road, US$7, leito US$14 Sul America), from Guaíra via Cascavel only (5 hrs., US$4.25), and from São Paulo (15 hours, about US$15 with Pluma, leito US$26). Foz-Florianópolis, daily, 1900, US$10.50, 16 hrs., with Catarinense or Pluma. Porto Alegre-Foz US$10, direct buses daily, 14 hrs. with Unisul, book in advance. To Campo Grande, 15 hrs. by Maringá company (3 hrs. to Cascavel, and 12 from there to Campo Grande); Nacional Expresso to Brasília direct, 26 hrs. There are direct buses from Rio (US$18 one way pullman bus), 22 hours (return to Rio daily at 0900 with Pluma direct, or 1400 with Maringá, US$14; leito to Rio, 1900, US$30, good for sleeping).

Travel From Paraguay By daily plane from Asunción to Foz do Iguaçu, or by paved road from Asunción (book in advance to take the 0730 bus from Asunción, arriving at 1300 at the Brazilian border and at the bus terminal at 1500) about US$4. (If you wish to return to Asunción the same day, get a small bus to the falls and return at 1730 to the bus station, to be back at 2400.) Several bus companies ply the route: Nuestra Señora, Rysa, Pluma etc., fare US$4-6 according to quality, about 5 hrs.

In the far NW of the state, also on the River Paraná, were the tremendous waterfalls known in Brazil as Sete Quedas (the Seven Falls), and in Spanish Latin America as the Guaíra Falls; they were drowned by the filling of the lake behind the Itaipu dam in 1982. Guaíra (about 130 km. N of Iguaçu by air or road) will not be flooded, but much of its agricultural land and its clay beds will be. A train for **Presidente Epitácio** on the Paraná leaves São Paulo (Júlio Prestes station) daily at 1600 (900 km.), reaching the port at 1020 the next morning and leaving at 1530. It has sleepers and a restaurant car. Price for a double sleeper, US$35. Normal 1st class fare US$8.50 (this service is under threat of closure—check). An alternative to the 17½ hour train ride is a bus journey. Andorinha several daily, US$15. A luxury passenger vessel, the *Epitácio Pessoa*, sails twice monthly (weekly during holiday periods) on Wed. at 1700 downstream to **Guaíra**, 400 km. S, getting there at 1900 Thurs. evening. Return trips on Sat. at 1100, arrive at Pres. Epitácio at 2200 Sun., US$100. (Note: These schedules appear to be variable.) Prices per person using double cabin, including meals, US$170. Cheaper accommodation available on lower decks. Bookings should be made in advance with: Comércio e Navegação Alto Paraná Ltda., Praça da República 177, Loja 15, São Paulo, T 259-8255, Telex: 011-32400. Passages can also be purchased (subject to space available) at the office by the port in Presidente Epitácio, and in Guaíra from Ernst Mann, Americatur, Rua Alvorada 253. Alternatively it may be possible to obtain passage on a cargo boat.

The 4 km. from Guaíra to the lake can be walked or done by car (US$1.50 one way, return taxi up to US$10). Entrance to park US$0.30; small museum three blocks from Guaíra bus terminal, 0800-1100 and 1400-1700.

Presidente Epitácio Hotel *Haverá*, Curitiba 622, E, including breakfast, good value, near station.

Guaíra Hotels Near the bus station: *Palace Hotel*, Rui Barbosa 1190, T 42-1325, D; *Majestic*, opposite bus station, E with or without bath, with breakfast, good; also *Hotel Itaipu*, E with bath, hot showers, good food (restaurant closed Sun.); *Sete Quedas*, Otávio Tosta 385, E, with breakfast and sandwich lunch, not too clean; *Ichapena*, E, not very clean but very friendly; and others.

Camping Municipal site at Bosque do Kartódromo. 2 km. out of town on the road from the bus station; ask at the Prefeitura for details. Basic facilities at each.

Restaurants *Recanto da Costela*, churrascaria, all you can eat for US$4. *O Chopão*, pleasant. Cheap snacks at *Bar São José*. *Restaurant Otto* for fish dishes.

Buses Guaíra-Campo Grande: buy a ticket (US$18) at the Guaíra bus terminal, take ferry to Ponta Porã, then bus to Mondo Novo, change bus there for Campo Grande; morning and night bus, 12 hrs. in all. There is a bus service between Curitiba and Guaíra, US$12, 10 hrs.; bus to São Paulo, US$15, 16 hrs.; Guaíra to Presidente Epitácio, US$1.80. The road is surfaced throughout. Also a bus from Londrina (US$7.20, 7½ hrs.) and Cascavel (connecting with bus from Iguaçu). The direct route Iguaçu-Guaíra is very bumpy, but interesting, takes 5 hrs. in the dry, but buses may be cancelled in the wet, US$5, or US$6 via Cascavel. There are also flights.

Note If entering Brazil from Paraguay in the Guaíra region, make sure to get passport stamped at the nearest available location (probably Foz do Iguaçu)—there is no passport control when coming off the boat from Salto Guaíra, Paraguay. There is an hourly passenger ferry service from Porto de Lanchas and Porto Guaíra to Paraguayan side, US$0.50, and hourly car ferry from Porto Guaíra. There is a time change when you cross the Paraná.

THE NORTH-EAST (7)

The nine states of the north-eastern bulge of Brazil are best considered as one entity. They cover 2.6 million square km. and contain a third of Brazil's people. The birthrate is the highest in Brazil, but so is the infant mortality rate. The average annual income from subsistence farming is deplorably low. Despite the misery, both regional and state loyalty remain ineradicable.

There was a brief period of colonization from northern Europe in the NE, when the Dutch West India Company, based at Recife, controlled some seven captaincies along the coast. They gained control in 1630, when Portugal was subject to Spain. After 1640, when Portugal freed itself, the colonists fought the Dutch and finally expelled them in 1654.

The nine states are Bahia, Sergipe, Alagoas, Pernambuco, Paraíba, Rio Grande do Norte, Ceará, Piauí, and Maranhão. They by no means form a homogeneous unity, but may be roughly divided into three contrasting parts. One is the sugar lands of the Zona da Mata along the coast between Salvador (Bahia) and Natal, where the rainfall can be depended upon. This was the first part of Brazil to be intensively colonized; hence the number of 16th century buildings and the density of old settlements are way above the national average. Inland from the Zona da Mata is the Zona do Agreste, with less rainfall, but generally enough for cattle raising. Inland again is the true interior, the Sertão, where rainfall cannot be depended upon; there is a little agriculture where water allows it but the herding of goats, and occasionally cattle, is more important. There are few blacks in the interior; the inhabitants are mostly of Portuguese-Indian stock, one of the most distinctive in Brazil. They are known as the *flagelados*, the scourged ones.

When there is rain, food in the zone is plentiful and varied. Manioc is a basic food; in addition, there are goat's milk and cheese, beef, beans, and sweet potatoes. But in the years of drought, when the hot dry winds from Africa scorch the earth, the effects can be tragic. Migration towards the coast and the southern towns begins, and the people are exposed to castigation of yet another sort: exploitation by grasping labour contractors. But at the first news that there is rain, the *flagelado* heads for home.

The main export crops of the north-east are sugar, cotton and cacao. Sugar and cotton have long been in decline, and now the southern states grow more than half of the Brazilian total. But cacao is grown almost entirely in southern Bahia, inland from the port of Ilhéus.

Brazil's main oilfields are in the State of Bahia; there are also offshore wells in the coastal waters of Alagoas, Sergipe and Rio Grande do Norte.

South of Cape São Roque there is abundant rainfall, but in Pernambuco the zone of ample rain stretches only 80 km. inland, though it deepens southwards. São Luís in Maranhão also gets plenty of rain, but between eastern Maranhão and Pernambuco lies a triangle, with its apex deep inland, where the rainfall is sporadic, and occasionally non-existent for a year. Here the tropical forest gives way to the *caatinga*, or scrub forest bushes which shed their leaves during drought. In this area grow the palms that produce carnauba wax and babaçu nuts, and the tree that produces oiticica oil.

Cities of the North-East

Salvador (often known as Bahia), is the capital of the state of Bahia. It is the fifth largest city in Brazil with a population of 2 million. The population of the state is 14 million in an area about that of France. It rains somewhat all the year but the main rainy season is between May and September. The climate is pleasant and the sun is never far away. Temperatures range from 25°C to 32°C, never falling below 19° in winter.

Salvador stands on the magnificent Bahia de Todos os Santos, a sparkling bay dotted with 38 islands. The bay is the largest on the Brazilian coast covering an area of 1,100 sq. kms. Rising above the bay on its eastern side is a cliff which dominates the landscape and, perched on top, 71 metres above sea level, are the older districts of Salvador with buildings dating back to 17th and 18th centuries. The bay was discovered by Amérigo Vespucci on 1 Nov, 1501, All Saints Day. The first Governor General, Tomé de Sousa arrived on 23 March, 1549 to build a fortified city to protect Portugal's interest from constant threats of Dutch and French invasion. Salvador was the capital of Brazil until 1763 at which stage it was the most important city in the Portuguese empire after Lisbon, ideally situated in a safe, sheltered harbour along the trade routes of the New World.

The city's first wealth came from the cultivation of sugar cane and tobacco, the plantations' workforce coming from the West coast of Africa. For three centuries Salvador was the site of a thriving slave trade and this major influx is responsible for Salvador being described as the most African city in the Western Hemisphere, "Africa in Exile". The influence permeates the city: food sold on the street is the same as in Senegal and Nigeria, Bahian music is fused with pulsating African polyrhythms, men and women nonchalantly carry enormous loads on their heads, fishermen paddle dug out canoes in the bay, the pace of life is a little slower than elsewhere. The pulse of the city is *candomblé*, an Afro-Brazilian religion in which the African deities of Nature, the Goddess of the sea and the God of creation are worshipped. These deities (or *orixás*) are worshipped in temples (*terreiros*) which can be elaborate, decorated halls, or simply someone's front room with tiny altars to the *orixá*. *Candomblé* ceremonies may be seen by tourists—but not photographed—on Sundays and religious holidays. Contact the tourist office, Bahiatursa, or see their twice monthly calendar of events.

Salvador today is a city of 15 forts, 166 Catholic churches, 1,000 *candomblé* temples and a fascinating mixture of old and modern, rich and poor, African and European, religious and profane. It is still a major port exporting tropical fruit, cocoa, sisal, soya beans and petrochemical products. Its most important industry, though, is tourism; after Rio it is the second largest tourist attraction in the country, very popular with Brazilian tourists who see Bahia as an exotic destination.

The centre of the city is divided into two levels, the Upper city (or Cidade Alta) where the Historical Centre lies, and the Lower city (Cidade Baixa) which is the commercial and docks district. The two levels are connected by a series of steep hills called *ladeiras*. The easiest way to go from one level to the other is by the *Lacerda* lift which connects Praça Municipal (Tomé de Sousa) in the Upper city with Praça Cairu and the famous Mercado Modelo. There is also the Plano Inclinado Gonçalves, a funicular railway which leaves from behind the Cathedral going down to Comercio, the commercial district.

There is much more of interest on the Upper city. From Praça Municipal to the Carmo area 2 km. north along the cliff is the Historical Centre (Centro Histórico), now a national monument and also protected by Unesco. It was in this area that the Portuguese built their fortified city and where today stand some of the most important examples of colonial architecture in the Americas.

Dominating the Praça Municipal is the old Council Chamber building (1660), while alongside is the Palácio Rio Branco (1918), once the Governor's Palace now the headquarters of Bahiatursa, the state tourist board. Leaving the square with its panoramic view of the bay, Rua Misericôrdia goes north passing the Santa Casa Misericôrdia (1695—see the high altar and painted tiles) to Praça da Sé. This square with its mimosa and flamboyant trees leads into Terreiro de Jesus, a picturesque square named after the church which dominates the square. Built in 1692, the church of the Jesuits became the property of the Holy See in 1759 when the Jesuits were expelled from all Portuguese territories. The façade is one of the earliest examples of Baroque in Brazil, an architectural style which was to dominate the churches built in the 17th and 18th centuries. The whole church was built with Portuguese Lioz marble. The interior is particularly impressive, its vast vaulted ceiling and 12 side altars in Baroque and Rococco, framing the main altar completely leafed in gold. The tiles in blue, white and yellow in a tapestry pattern are also from Portugal. It houses the tomb of Mem de Sá and coloured marble and inlaid furniture. The church is now the city Cathedral and is open Tues. to Sun., 0800 to 1100 and 1500 to 1800. Across the square is the church of São Pedro dos Clérigos, while alongside is the church of the Ordem Terceira de São Domingos (Dominican Third Order), both rarely open to the public.

Facing Terreiro de Jesus is Praça Anchieta and the church of São Francisco. Its simple façade belies the treasure inside. The entrance is by a small door to the right of the main doors and leads to a sanctuary with a spectacular painting on the wooden ceiling, by local artist José Joaquim da Rocha (1777). The main body of the church is the most exuberant example of Baroque in the country. The cedar wood carving and later gold leaf was completed after 28 years in 1748. The cloisters of the monastery are surrounded by a series of blue and white tiles from Portugal. The church is open from 0800 to 1115 and 1400 to 1700. Next door (and with the same opening hours) is the church of the Ordem Terceira de São Francisco (Franciscan Third Order—1703) with its façade intricately carved in sandstone. Inside is a quite remarkable Chapter House with striking images of the Order's most celebrated saints.

Leading off the Terreiro de Jesus is Rua Alfredo Brito, a charming, narrow cobbled street lined with fine colonial houses painted in different pastel shades. This street leads into the Largo do Pelourinho. Considered the finest complex of colonial architecture in Latin America, it was once the site of a pillory where slaves were publicly punished and ridiculed. It was also the site of the slave market. Nossa Senhora Do Rosario Dos Pretos church, the so-called Slave Church, dominates the square. It was built by former slaves, with what little financial resources they had, over a period of 100 years. The interior is much simpler than the Cathedral of São Francisco, with side altars in honour of black saints. The ceiling tiles are also impressive, the overall effect being one of tranquillity in contrast to the complexity of the other two churches. A small entrance fee is charged.

At the corner of Alfredo Brito and Largo do Pelourinho is a museum to the work of Jorge Amado (Casa da Cultura Jorge Amado), who lived in, and set many of his books, in this section of the city. His works have been published in 47 languages. A good way to get a feel of the city and its people is to read *Dona Flor and her two husbands*. The Carmo Hill is at the top of the street leading out of Largo do Pelourinho. The Carmelite Third Order church (1709) houses one of the sacred art treasures of the city, a sculpture of Christ made in 1730 by a slave who had no formal training, Francisco Xavier das Chagas, known as O Cabra. One of the features of the piece is the blood made from whale oil, ox blood, banana resin and 2000 rubies to represent the drops of blood. Opening hours are 0800 to 1200 and 1400 to 1730.

South of the Praça Municipal, in the direction of the mouth of the bay, is the more modern section of the city with many skyscrapers. Rua Chile leads to Praça Castro Alves, with its monument to Castro Alves, who started the campaign which finally led to the Abolition of Slavery in 1888. Two streets lead out of this square, Avenida 7 de Setembro, a bustling street of shops and street vendors selling everything imaginable, and parallel to it, Rua Carlos Gomes. São Bento church (rebuilt after 1624, but with fine 17th century furniture) is on Av. 7 de Setembro. Both eventually come to Campo Grande (also known as Praça Dois de Julho). In the centre of the square is the monument to Bahian Independence, 2 July, 1823. The British Club is just off the square on Rua Banco dos Ingleses. Av. 7 de Setembro continues out of the square towards the Vitória area, indeed this stretch is known as Corredor da Vitória (Vitória Corridor). There are some fine homes along this street built during the last century as the city expanded in this direction. The "Vitória Corridor" comes to Praça Vitória and continues down Ladeira da Barra (Barra Hill) to Porto da Barra. The best city beaches are in this area. Also in this

Salvador: Key to Map

1. Lacerda Lift; 2. Gonçalves Funicular; 3. Cathedral; 4. Church of São Francisco; 5. Church of the Ordem Terceira de São Domingos; 6. Santa Casa da Misericórdia; 7. Conceição de Praia; 8. Church of the Ordem Terceira de São Francisco; 9. Church of São Bento; 10. Church of São Pedro dos Clérigos; 11. Church of Palma; 12. Church of Sant'Ana; 13. Nossa Senhora da Ajuda; 14. Convent of Lapa; 15. Convent of Santa Teresa/Museumof Sacred Art; 16. Afro-Brazilian Museum; 17. Museum of the City; 18. Museum of Santa Casa; 19. House of Rui Barbosa; 20. House of the Sete Mortos; 21. Archbishop's Palace; 22. Palace of Saldanha; 23. Council Chamber; 24. Berquió Mansion; 25. Fort of São Marcelo; 26. Customs House (Alfândega); 27. Government Palace (Rio Branco) and Bahiatursa Tourist Office; 28. Central Post Office; 29. Post Office; 30. Post Office; 31. Mercado Modelo.

district are the best bars, restaurants and nightlife. A little further along is the Santo Antônio Fort, 1580, built on the spot where Amérigo Vespucci landed in

1501. It is right at the mouth of the bay where Bahia de Todos Os Santos and the South Atlantic Ocean meet.

The promenade leading away from the fort and its famous lighthouse is called Av. Oceânica, which goes along the coast to the new beach suburbs of Ondina, Amaralina and Pituba. The road is also called Avenida Presidente Vargas, but the numbering is different. Beyond Pituba are the best ocean beaches at Jaguaripe, Piatã and Itapoan (take any bus from Praça da Sé marked Aeroporto or Itapoan, about one hour, sit on right hand side for best views). En route the bus passes small fishing colonies at Amaralina and Pituba where *jangadas* can be seen. A *jangada* is a small raft peculiar to the northeastern region of Brazil used extensively as well as dug out canoes. Near Itapoan is the Lagoa do Abaeté, surrounded by brilliant, white sands. This is a deep, fresh water lake where local women traditionally come to wash their clothes and then lay them out to dry in the sun. The road leading up from the lake offers a panoramic view of the city in the distance, the coast, and the contrast of the white sands and fresh water less than a kilometre from the sea and its golden beaches. Near the lighthouse at Itapoan there are two campsites on the beach. A little beyond the campsites are the magnificent ocean beaches of Stella Maris and Flamengo, both quiet during the week but very busy at the weekends. A good, lively Barraca on Stella Maris is *Padang*, very popular at weekends. Beware of strong undertow at these beaches.

See also the famous church of Nosso Senhor do Bomfim on the Itapagipe peninsula in the suburbs, whose construction began in 1745; it draws endless suppliants (particularly on Fri. and Sun.) offering favours to the image of the Crucified Lord set over the high altar; the number and variety of ex-voto offerings—often of parts of the body deemed to have been cured by divine intervention—is extraordinary. The processions over the water to the church on the third Sun. in January are particularly interesting.

Also on the Itapagipe peninsula is a colonial fort on Mont Serrat point, and at Ribeira the church of Nossa Senhora da Penha (1743). The beach here has many restaurants, but bathing from it is not recommended because of pollution (bus from Praça da Sé or Av. França).

Local Holidays 6 Jan. (Epiphany); Ash Wed. and Maundy Thurs., half-days; 2 July (Independence of Bahia); 30 Oct.; Christmas Eve, half-day. An important local holiday is the Festa do Nosso Senhor do Bomfim; it takes place on the second Sunday after Epiphany, but the colourful washing or *lavagem* of the Bomfim church takes place on the preceding Thurs. (usually mid-January). The Festa da Ribeira is on the following Mon. The most colourful festival of all is that of the fishermen of the Rio Vermelho district on 2 Feb.; gifts for Yemanjá, Goddess of the Sea, are taken out to sea in a procession of sailing boats to an accompaniment of *candomblé* instruments. The Holy Week processions among the old churches of the upper city are very colourful.

The **pre-Carnival festive season** begins towards the end of Nov. with São Nicodemo de Cachimbo (penultimate Sun. of Nov.), then comes Santa Bárbara (4 Dec.), then the Festa da Conceição da Praia, centred on the church of that name (open 0700-1130 normally) at the base of the Lacerda lift. (8 Dec. is the last night—not for those who don't like crowds!) The last week of Dec. is the Festa da Boa Viagem in the lower city; the beach will be packed all night on the 31st. On 1 January is the beautiful boat procession of Nosso Senhor dos Navegantes from Conceição da Praia to the church of Boa Viagem, on the beach of that name in the lower city. The leading boat, which carries the image of Christ and the archbishop, was built in 1892. You can follow in a sailing boat for about US$1; go early (0900) to dock by Mercado Modelo. A later festival is São Lázaro on the last Sun. in January.

Folklore Carnival in Salvador is particularly lively, with nearly everyone in fancy dress and dancing in the streets; parades are centred on Campo Grande (grandstand seats cost about US$5).

Visitors find carnival exciting and entertaining, but look out for the more violent elements and don't carry any valuables. For greater safety join an organised group, security guards hold ropes but there are no toilet facilities (Tietê VIPS, R Direita da Piedade next to Baita-Kão, US$60; Pike, R da Aragã 9, T 245-0934, US$120). The *blocos* (samba groups) can be seen practising at any time from end-

November; ask locals, Bene at *Zanzi-bar* or Bahiatursa for details. Many clubs have pre-carnival and Carnival dances; Baile das Atrizes has been recommended (always book tickets early). To make the most of carnival, arrive a week or two in advance and enjoy the festivities of the preceding week. In recent years the frenetic trio-electrico music has given way to the gentler African rhythms. The highlight of the Carnival are the *afoxés*, or Afro drumming groups who parade through the streets from mid-day to dawn. They can be seen practising from the end of November. Olodum practices on Suns., from 1800-2230 in the Largo do Pelourinho. Ilê Aiyê practices on Sat. from 2200-0400 in the Forte de Santo Antônio, Santo Antônio Além do Carmo, small admission fee.

The Bahianas—black women who dress in traditional 18th century costumes—are street vendors who sit behind their trays of delicacies, savoury and seasoned, made from the great variety of local fish, vegetables and fruits.

See *capoeira*, a sport developed from the traditional foot-fighting technique introduced from Angola by African slaves. The music is by drum, tambourine and *berimbau*; there are several different kinds of the sport. If you want to attempt *capoeira*, the best school is Mestre Bimba in Terreiro de Jesus, at Rua Francisco Muniz Barreto 1. Classes are held in evenings (if you want to get the most out of it, knowledge of Portuguese is essential). There are two more schools in Forte de Santo Antônio behind Pelourinho, but check addresses at tourist office. Exhibitions take place in the Largo do Pelourinho, very picturesque, in the upper city (cost: US$2). You can also see the experts practising outside the Mercado Modelo on most days and at Campo Grande and Forte de Santo Antônio on Sunday afternoons; they often expect a contribution. Negotiate a price before taking pictures or demands may be exorbitant. At the Casa da Cultura at Forte de Santo Antônio there is also free live music on Saturday night.

Warning Be very careful of your money and valuables at all times and in all districts. Avoid the more distant beaches out of season, when they are empty (e.g. Itapoan, Piatã, Placafor); on Sundays they are more crowded and safer. Conversely, the old city on Sundays is deserted and should therefore be avoided. At night, the historical centre (especially the Largo do Pelourinho), around and in the lifts, and buses are unsafe. On no account change money on the streets; this is a guaranteed way to be robbed. Leave valuables securely in your hotel (inc. cameras if possible), particularly at night. Parts of the centre to the NE of the Praça da Sé are run down and rather dubious, and one is warned not to walk down the Ladeira de Misericórdia, which links the Belvedere, near the Lacerda lifts, with the lower city. The civil police are reported to be very sympathetic and helpful.

Hotels Those listed below are in the categories L+, L, A and B. Prices are lowest available. A 10% service charge is often added to the bill. Some hotels may add a surcharge for payment by credit card if the rate of inflation is high. All have swimming pool unless indicated otherwise.

Name	Address	Phone	Sgl	Dbl	*
			US$		
Enseada das Lajes	Av. Oceânica 511, Rio Vermelho	237-1027	150	160	
Meridien	Rua Fonte do Boi 216, Rio Vermelho	248-8011	85	95	5
Quatro Rodas	Rua da Passárgada, Farol de Itapoan	249-9611	85	95	5
Salvador Praia	Av. Pres. Vargas 2338, Ondina (run down)	245-5033	64	67	5
Bahia Othon Palace	Av. Pres. Vargas 2456, Ondina	247-1044	58	64	5
Da Bahia (Tropical)	Praça 2 de Julho 2, Campo Grande	237-3699	54	60	5
Ondina Apart Hotel	Av. Oceânica 2500, Ondina		53	58	5
Grande da Barra	Av. Sete de Setembro 3564, Barra	247-6011	47	52	4
Farol	Av. Presidente Vargas 68, Barra	247-7611	42	47	4
Marazul	Av. Sete de Setembro 3937	235-2100	42	47	4
Praiamar	Av. Sete de Setembro 3577, Barra	247-7011	42	47	4
San Marco	Jardin da Praia de Armação, Boca do Rio		42	47	4
Pituba Plaza	Av. Manoel Dias da Silva, Pituba	248-1022	39	43	4
San Marino	Av. Pres. Vargas 899, Barra	235-4363	35	40	3
Ondina Praia	Av. Pres. Vargas 2275, Ondina	247-1033	33	38	3
Vela Branca‡	Av. Antônio Carlos Magalhães 585, Pituba	248-7022	34	38	3
Bahia do Sol‡	Av. Sete de Setembro 2009, Vitória	247-7211	34	38	3

Bahia Praia‡	Av.Presidente Vargas 2483, Ondina	247-4122	31	35	3
Golden Park	Av Manoel Dias da Silva 979, Pituba		32	35	3
Vilha Velha‡	Av. Sete de Setembro 1971, Vitória	247-8722	30	33	3
Itapuã Praia	Jardim Itapuã, Placafor	249-9988	28	32	3
Praia da Armação‡	Av. Otávio Mangabeira, Armação	231-2722	25	31	3
Ondimar	Av. Presidente Vargas 1843, Ondina	245-0366	27	30	3

‡ = No swimming pool.

Quatro Rodas is a complete vacation hotel, 22 km from the city, extensive grounds, peaceful but plenty of activities available, rec. *Chalé Enseada das Lajes*, 9 rooms in what used to be a private house, now Relais Château, antique furniture, excellent pieces of art, good food and 2service, ocean views, 2 mins. from beach. *Da Bahia*, 2 de Julho (Campo Grande), new, owned by Varig, so 15% discount if using Airpass. Also rec from above list: *Ondina Apart Hotel*, *Grande da Barra*, *Pituba Plaza*, *Ondina Praia* and *Ondimar*.

   Centre (includes old city and main shopping area): *Palace*, Rua Chile 20, T 243 1155, C, rec, much better value than *Chile* opp; *Bahia de Todos os Santos*, Av. Sete de Setembro 06 (Ladeira de São Bento), C, T 321 6344. *Paris*, Rua Ruy Barbosa 13, T 321 3320, E, a/c rooms more expensive, shared showers, breakfast, restaurant in same building, rec; also *Pousada da Praça*, at No. 5, T 321 0642, E, breakfast, rooms with and without bath, clean, friendly, rec. *São Bento*, Largo de São Bento 2, T 243 7511, E, friendly, good cheap restaurant. Cheaper hotels on Av. 7 de Setembro: *São José*, No. 847, T 321 4928, E-D, safe, rec.; *Imperial*, No 751, Rosario, T 321 1919, E, a/c, breakfast, rec; *Madrid*, No 186, Mercês, T 321 9505, F; *Mercês*, No. 46, Mercês, T 321 0676, F; *Pousada Pampulha*, No 76, 1st floor, São Pedro, 243 1240, F, breakfast, restaurant, laundry service, upstairs *Pousada Cosmé e Damião*, F, clean. *Internacional*, Rua Senador Costa Pinto 88, T 243 6151, E, clean, convenient, good value. *Joana Angélica* in street of same name, F, friendly, no breakfast.
   It is not recommended that you stay in the hotels near Praça da Sé as this is a dangerous area at night. There are many hotels in this area and many travellers do stay there. The following have been rec: *Pelourinho*, Rua Alfredo Brito 20, T 321 9022, D; Spanish is spoken in all of the following: *Solar São Francisco*, Cruzeiro de São Francisco, in front of São Francisco church, T 242 6015, G, breakfast available; next door is *Colon*, T 321 1531, G; *Solara*, Rua José Alencar 25, Largo do Pelourinho, F, with shower, toilet, breakfast, clean, laundry facilities; *Jequié*, off Praça da Sé at Ciné Liceu, G, clean, no breakfast, some rooms better than others; *Vigo*, Rua 13 de Maio 18, 2 blocks from Praça da Sé, F with bath and breakfast, fairly clean; *Ilheus*, Ladeira da Praça 4, 1st floor, T 243 2329, F, breakfast.
   Campo Grande/Vitória. This is a much safer area, quieter and still central and convenient for museums: *Mater Café Teatro*, Rua Marechal Floriano 5, Canela T 235 1958, E with breakfast, clean (but poor locks on doors) with good café/restaurant next door called *Café dos Artistas*, Spanish spoken; *Anglo Americano*, Av. Sete de Setembro 1838, Vitória, T 247 7681, E with breakfast and bath, cheaper without bath (F), safe, pay in advance, clean, good gringo hotel in pleasant district, some rooms with bay view, rec; *Caramuru*, Av. Sete de Setembro 2125, Vitória, T 247 9951, E, breakfast, very friendly, clean, safe parking, rec; *Do Forte*, Rua Visc. de São Lourenço 30, Campo Grande, T 321 6915, E, breakfast, bath; *Santiago* at No. 52, E, breakfast, bath, T 245 9293.
   Barra The best location to stay in: it is safe, has good beaches, is a short bus ride from the centre, has good restaurants in all price ranges and good nightlife. On Av. 7 de Setembro: *Barra Turismo*, No 3691, Porto da Barra, T 245 7433, C, breakfast, bath, a/c, TV, fridge, on beach, rec; *Solar da Barra*, No 2998, Ladeira da Barra, T 247 4917, C-D, some rooms with bay view; *Porto da Barra* No 3783, Porto da Barra, T 247 4939, C, friendly, clean, some rooms very small, on beach; *Pousada Malu*, No 3801, T 237 4461, E, small and friendly with breakfast, on beach. *Enseada Praia da Barra*, Rua Barao de Sergy 49, Porto da Barra, T 235 9213, C-D, a/c, or fan, good breakfast, clean, safe, friendly, money exchanged, laundry bills high otherwise good value, near beach; *Villa Romana*, Rua Lemos Brito 14, T 247 6522, C, pool, restaurant, individual safes, rec; *Barra Praia*, Av. Alm. Marqués de Leão 172, Farol da Barra, T 245 3437, C, a/c, clean, one street from beach, rec; *Hitz*, Rua Marqués de Caravelas 136, T 247 8459, E, a/c, bath, converted mansion, clean, friendly; *Seara Praia*, Rua Belo Horizonte 18, Barra Avenida, T 235 0105, D, good breakfast.

Atlantic Suburbs. This is the modern suburban area built along the coast from Ondina to Itapoan stretching for 12 miles towards the airport. The best beaches are in this area. *Ondina Plaza*, Av. Pres. Vargas. 3033, Ondina, T 245 8071, C, a/c, pool, good value, on beach, rec; *Amaralina*, Av. Amaralina 790, Amaralina, T 248 7822, D, a/c, near beach; *Pituba*, Av. Manoel Dias da Silva 1614, Pituba, T 248 5469, E, no breakfast; *Paulus*, Av. Otavio Mangabeira, Pituba, T 248 5722, C, a/c, pool; *Praia Dourada*, Rua Dias Gomes 10, Placaford,

T 249 9639, C-D, a/c, near excellent beach, rec; *Pituaçu Praia*, Jardim Iracema, Lote 27, Corsario. T 231 9139, C, a/c, 2 blocks from good beach; *Praia dos Coqueiros*, Av. Otavio Mangabeira, Placaford, T 249 9828, D, a/c, near excellent beach, rec; *Europa*, Rua Genibaldo Figuereido 53, Itapoan, T 249 9344, E, breakfast; *Grão de Areia*, Loteamento Jardim Piatã, Quadra 25, Lote 23/24, Itapoan, T 249 4818, D, a/c, pool, near good beach; *Pousada Glória*, Rua do Retiro 46, Itapoan, T 249 1503, F, with bath, no breakfast, near beach; *Pousada de Itapoan*, Av. D. Caymmi, V. dos Ex. Combatentes, Quadra 1, Lote 3, Itapoan, E, breakfast, laundry, parking.

Portal Da Cidade, Av. Antonio Carlos Magalhães, 4362, next to bus station, T 230 0099, a/c, pool, C.

Youth Hostels are called Albergues de Juventude and most were opened in 1988-89. They cost F p.p. incl breakfast but cheaper if you have a YHA membership card. *Casa Grande*, Rua Minas Gerais, 122, Pituba, T 248 0527; *CNEC do Salvador*, Rua Bicuiba, Loteamento Patamares, near beach out of town; *Dois de Julho*, Rua Areial de Cima 44, Largo 2 de Julho, Centre, T 243 9513; *Lagash*, Rua Visc. de Itaboray 514, Amaralina, T 248 7399; *Senzala*, Rua Florianopolis 134, Jardim Brasil, Barra, T 247 5678, good location; *Boca do Rio*, Av. D. Eugenio Sales 72, Lote 11, Boca do Rio, T 230 8371, near the popular Praia dos Artistas; *Solar*,. Rua Macapá 461, Ondina, T 235 2235, good location for beach and city; *Costa do Sol*, R Arquimedes Gonçalves 226, T 241-4744, quiet.

Pensionatos are places to stay in shared rooms (up to 4 persons per room) e.g. **Pensionato No. 20**, Av. Cerqueira Lima; part or full board available. Houses or rooms can be rented for US$5-35 a day from Pierre Marbacher, Rua Carlos Coqueijo 68A, Itapoan, T 249 5754 (Caixa Postal 7458, 41600 Salvador), he is Swiss, owns a beach bar at Rua K and speaks English, French and German. At Carnival its a good idea to rent a flat; the tourist office has a list of real estate agents (e.g. José Mendez T 237 1394/6).

Apart Hotels. These are self-contained apartments with fully equipped kitchen and a/c, with all the facilities of a hotel, which can be rented by the day; standards are generally high. *Jardim Paraiso*, Rua Contorno 7, Itapoan, T 249 3397, C, pool, near beach; *Bahia Flat*, Av. Pres. Vargas 235, Barra, T 247 4233, C, on beach, pool, sauna, rec; *Barra Apart Service*, Rua Marques de Caravelas 237, Barra, T 247 5844, D; *Flat Jardim de Alã*, Av. Otavio Mangabeira 4371, Armação, T 230 5288, B, beautiful location by beach, pool, sauna, rec; *Manhattan Residence Service*, Rua Maranhão 445 Pituba, T 248 9911, B-C, pool, gym, popular with businessmen; *Parthenon Farol da Barra Flat*, Av Oceânica 409, Barra, T 235 6281, B-C, pool, sauna, on beach, rec; *Pituba Apart Hotel*, Rua Paraíba 250, Pituba, T 240 7077, B, pool, sauna.

Camping Near the lighthouse at Itapoan, take bus from Praça da Sé direct to Itapoan, or to Campo Grande or Barra, change there for Itapoan, about 1 hr., then 1/2 hr. walk; two campsites, one Camping Clube do Brasil, at US$6 p.p. per night (members half price), and a cheaper one opposite. Camping de Pituaçu, Av. Prof. Pinto de Aguiar, Jardim Pituaçu. Sea bathing is dangerous off shore near campsites.

Bahian cuisine is spiced and peppery. The main dish is *moqueca*, seafood cooked in a sauce made from coconut milk, tomatoes, red and green peppers, fresh coriander and *dendê* (oil made from the crushing of the fruit of the dendezeiro palm tree). It is traditionally cooked in a wok-like earthenware dish and served piping hot at the table. Served with *moqueca* is *farofa* (mandioc flour) and a hot pepper sauce which you add at your discretion, it's usually extremely hot so try a few drops before venturing further. The dendê palm oil is somewhat heavy and those with delicate stomachs are advised to try the *ensopado*, a sauce with the same ingredients as the *moqueca*, but without the palm oil.

Nearly every street corner has a Bahiana (see above under **Folklore**) selling a wide variety of local snacks, the most famous of which is the *acarajé*, a bean dumpling fried in palm oil. To this the Bahiana adds *vatapá*, a dried shrimp and coconut milk paté, fresh salad and hot sauce (pimenta). For those who prefer not to eat the palm oil, the *abará* is a good substitute. *Abará* is steamed, wrapped in banana leaves.

Two good Bahianas are *Chica*, at Ondina beach (beside *Saveiro Hotel*) and *Gina* at Largo da Mariquita, Rio Vermelho. The Bahians usually eat *acarajé* or *abará* with a chilled beer on the way home from work or the beach at sunset.

Another popular dish is *Xin-Xin de Galinha*, chicken on the bone cooked in dendê, with dried shrimp and squash.

Restaurants Historial Centre. *Cantina da Lua*, Terreiro De Jesus sq, open daily 1100-2300, music nightly, legendary; *Salada De Frutas*, Alfredo B rito 5, Mon-Sat 0830-1800, very good juices, snacks and light meals, clean, friendly, rec. *Ibiza Bar*, Alfredo Brito 11 (upstairs), open Mon.-Sat., 1100-2330, Sun. 1800-2330 good food, cheap. *Casa Azul*, Praça José Alencar. (Largo do Pelourinho) Mon.-Sat. 0900-1830, good juice bar with wide range of light snacks, clean, *Senac*, Praça José Alencar 8, state run catering school, a selection of 40 dishes including local ones, buffet, lunch 1130-1530, dinner 1830-2130, both US$5, very popular, folkloric show in the evening at 2000. *Casa do Benin*, Praça José Alencar 29, Afro-Bahian restaurant, great surroundings, try the shrimp in the cashew nut sauce, closed Mon., open 1200-1600, 1900-2300, not cheap, highly rec. *Bar Banzo*, Praça José Alencar 6 (upstairs) Mon.-Sat. 1100 to 2300, Sun. 1800 to 2300, cheap, good view of streetlife in Largo do Pelourinho below, friendly. *Contos De Reis*, Rua Do Carmo, T 241-6401, Portuguese, wonderful view of the bay and the lower city, excellent service in peaceful setting, highly recommended.

Between Historical Centre and Barra At Praça Da Sé, *Café Brasil*, good breakfast. There are some good snack bars on Av. 7 de Setembro; *Kentefrio*, No. 379, the best, clean, counter service only, closed Sundays, rec; on same street, 600 block, *La Portuguesa*, good, cheap; *Casa D'Italia*, corner of Av. 7 and Visconde de São Lourenço, reasonable prices, good service; *Grao de Bico*, No. 737, very good vegetarian. *Frutos Da Terra*, Rua Carlos Gomes, 21, vegetarian, good, fine view of bay and lower city. Another good vegetarian restaurant nearby is *Nutrebem*, Av. Joana Ângelica 148. Also on same street is *Bela Napoli*, Italian, reasonable. *Casa Da Gamboa*, Rua da Gamboa, beautifully located in old colonial house overlooking the bay, good reputation, open Mon. to Sat. 1200-1500 and 1900-2300, not cheap. An excellent Japanese restaurant is *Gan*, Praça A. Fernades 29, Garcia, intimate atmosphere, Tues.-Sun. 1900 till midnight, recommended. The best churrascaria in Salvador is *Baby Beef*, Av. A.C. Magalhães, Iguatemi, top class restaurant, excellent service, extremely popular, not expensive, highly recommended, open daily 1200-1500 and 1900-2300.

At the bottom of the Lacerda Lift is Praca Cairu and the famous *Mercado Modelo*: on the upper floor of the market are two very good restaurants, *Camafeu De Oxossi* and *Maria De São Pedro*, both specializing in Bahian dishes, great atmosphere, good view of the port, daily 1130 till 2000, Saturday lunchtime particularly busy. At the base of the Lift is *Cinquenta Saladas*, not only salads, very reasonable. On Av. Contorno, *Solar Do Unhão*, beautiful manor house on the edge of the bay, lunch and dinner with best folklore show in town, expensive.

Barra Section *Xangai*, Avenida 7 de Setembro, 1755 (Vitória) Chinese, reasonable; *Hotel Anglo Americano*, across the street, fair, cheap; also restaurant at *Hotel Bahia Do Sol*, No 2009, on first floor, good, reasonably priced; at the bottom of Ladeira Da Barra is *Bar Do Chico*, good, cheap, no frills; *Restaurant Porto Da Barra*, Av. 7 de Setembro, 3713, very good regional dishes, big portions, recommended, open daily 1100-2300. *Sandwich Bar*, Rua Cezar Zama 60, great sandwiches, wide variety, open 1900 till 0200; *Kasbah*, Rua Barão do Sergy 67, Arab, rec, cheap, open 1200-1500 and 1900-2300, closed at weekends; three other good restaurants on same street are *Berro D'Agua*, No. 27 (upstairs, watch your head on stairway), good steaks, lively bar; *Alface e Cia*, wide range of salads and juices; *Cantina Roma* No 162, T 247-6973.

Near the lighthouse at the mouth of the bay (Farol Da Barra area) there are a number of good fast food places: *Micheluccio*, Av. Oceânica 10, best pizza in town, always busy, friendly, rec; next door is *Baitakão*, good hamburger and sandwiches; *Speed Lanches*, nearby, good snack bar. *Mon Filet*, Rua Afonso Celso, 152, good steaks, pastas, open 1830 till midnight; on same street, *Pastaxuta*, pizza, pasta, reasonable prices. The best Bahian restaurant in the area is *Frutos Do Mar*, Rua Marques De Leão 415. A very good vegetarian restaurant is *Rama*, Rua Lord Cochrane, great value.

Further along Av. Oceânica towards the Rio Vermelho district is *Sukiyaki*, No. 3562, an excellent Japanese restaurant, open 1200-1500, and 1900 till midnight, not cheap, rec. Also highly rec is *Extudo*, Largo Mesquita 4 T 237-4669, good varied menu, lively bar at night, attracts interesting clientele, open 1200 -1500 and 1900-0300, not expensive. *Marisco*, at Paciencia Beach nearby, good seafood, 1100-1500 and 1800-2100, good value. Next door is *Camburity*, good, wholesome regional food at a good price.

There is an interesting fish market at Largo Da Mariquita with a number of stalls serving food from noon until the small hours, recently built, clean, good atmosphere, popular with locals. A little further along a *MacDonald's* has recently opened at Amaralina.

Further along Avenida Oceânica at Jardim Armação are three very good restaurants: *Yemanjá*, excellent Bahian seafood, open daily from 1130 till late, very typical, always busy, reasonably priced, good atmosphere, highly rec. Nearby is *Tamboril*, busy seafood restaurant, 1200 to 1600 and 1900 till midnight. The very best Bahian restaurant in the city is *Bargaço*, open daily midday till 1600 and 1900 till midnight, great selection of starters, oyster, lobster, fresh water shrimp, crab meat, etc, highly rec, expensive but worth it. *A Porteira* at Boca do Rio specialises in northeastern dishes including carne do sol (beef dried in the sun), 1200 to 1600 and 1800 to 2300, seafood dishes also served. A popular bar/restaurant is *Casquinha De Siri* at Piatã beach, daily from 0900 until last customer leaves, live music every night, cover charge US$2. The beaches from Patamares to Itapoan are lined by Barracas, thatched huts serving chilled drinks and freshly cooked seafood dishes, ideal for lunch and usually very cheap. At Itapoan the road goes left towards the airport along Av. Dorival Caymmi. *Restaurant Uaua*, Av. Dorival Caymmi 46 specialses in northeastern dishes, meat based, seafood also served, open Thurs. to Sunday. Friday and Saturday are very busy with *forro* dancing till 0400.

Markets The Mercado Modelo, at Praça Cairu, lower city, offers many tourist items such as wood carvings, silver-plated fruit, leather goods, local musical instruments. Lace items for sale are often not handmade (despite labels), are heavily marked up, and are much better bought at their place of origin (e.g. Ilha de Maré, Pontal da Barra and Marechal Deodoro, **see page 406**). Cosme e Damião, musical instrument sellers on 1st floor, has been rec., especially if you want to play the instruments. Bands and dancing, especially Sat. (but very much for money from tourists taking photographs), closed at 1200 Sun.; two restaurants on top floor, large balcony provides good view over harbour; restaurants on ground floor are cheaper. Photograph exhibition of the old market in basement. (Many items are often cheaper on the Praça da Sé in the nearby Cidade Alta.) Largest and most authentic market is the Feira de São Joaquim, 5 km. from Mercado Modelo along sea front: barkers, trucks, *burros*, horses, boats, people, mud, all very smelly, every day (Sun. till 1200 only), busiest on Sat. morning; interesting African-style pottery and basketwork; very cheap. (Car ferry terminal for Itaparica is nearby.) Instituto Mauá at Porto da Barra and the Iguatemi Shopping Centre sells good handicraft items, it is run by the government so prices are fixed and reasonable. Every Wed. from 1700-2100 there is a handicrafts fair in the 17th century fort of Santa Maria at the other end of Porto da Barra beach. On Sun. from 1700-2100, there is an open air market of handicrafts and Bahian food in Porto da Barra, a popular event among the local young people. Daily market of handicrafts in Terreiro de Jesus in the old city from 1000-1800. Also many shops in the Pelourinho area. Mosquito nets from Casa dos Mosquiteiros Rua Pedro Sá 6F, Calçada, T 226 0715.

Bookshops *Livraria Brandão*, Rua Ruy Barbosa 4-B, Centre (opp. *Hotel Paris*), T 243 5383, secondhand English, French, Spanish and German books. *Livraria Civilizaçao Brasileira*, Av. 7 de Setembro 912, Mercês, and in the Barra and Iguatemi shopping centres have some English books; also *Graúna*, Av. 7 de Setembro 1448, many English titles. The bookshop at the airport has English books and magazines.

Shopping *H. Stern* jewellers at *Hotels Meridien*, *Othon* and *Bahia*, also at Barra and Iguatemi Shopping centres. Visit the stone-cutting workshops at *Breis* in the Largo do Carmo; best prices for cut stones and jewellery made to order in 24 hours with a genuine guarantee. The Barra and Iguatemi shopping centres are big, modern and a/c with big department stores; few typical souvenirs, although soulless, can be practical. **Camera repair**: Pepe, Rua da Ajuda, ed. Triunfo, first floor Centre.

Local Transport Taxi meters start at US$0.25 for the "flagdown" and US$0.10 per 100 metres. They charge US$5 per hour within city limits, and "agreed" rates outside. Taxi-drivers tend to overcharge, especially at night; the night-time charge should be 30% higher than daytime charges. Teletaxi (24-hr. service), 321-9988. Local buses US$0.20, air-conditioned *frescões* US$0.50. On buses and at the ticket-sellers' booths, watch your change and beware pickpockets. To get from the old city to the ocean beaches, take a "Barra" bus from Praça da Sé to the Barra point and walk to the nearer ones; the Aeroporto *frescão* (last 2130) leaves Praça da Sé, passing Barra, Ondina, Rio Vermelho, Amaralina, Pituba, Costa Azul, Armação and Boca do Rio, before turning inland to the airport.

Car Rental Avis, Av. Sete de Setembro 1796, T 237-0155, also at airport, T 249-2550; Budget, Av. Presidente Vargas 409, T 237-3396; Hertz, R. Baependi, T 245-2577, Unidas, Av. Sete de Setembro 4183, T 247-3224. If renting a car check whether credit card or cash is cheapest. National Car Rentals allow decision at the end of the rental.

Hitching out of Salvador, take a "Cidade Industrial" bus from the bus station at the port; it goes on to the highway.

Nightlife In the **historical centre** is *Bar Do Reggae*, Rua João De Jesus 32, Pelourinho, a hot spot in a city where Bob Marley still lives, daily 0700 to 2200. Tuesdays especially busy. See also **Restaurants**. Note: Most bars and restaurants in the Historical Centre close early for security reasons. it is recommended to come and go by taxi at night.

    Barra Section: *Mordomia Drinks*, Ladeira Da Barra, enter through narrow entrance to open air bar with spectacular view of the bay, very popular; *Volupia*, Av. 7 De Setembro 510, Porto Da Barra, nightly, highly recommended, most "Bohemian" of the bars in the area, always full, interesting people, owners speak English, great music and famous passion fruit or mango daikiris; nearby is *Bom Pescador*, lively, open till 0400. *Club 45*, Rua Barão do Sergy 13, live music every night, good late night bar, "pub" feel; *Bon Vivant*, Rua Barão De Itapoã 2, closed Sundays, upstairs, quiet bar with good view of the bay, in front of Santa Maria fort; *Habeas Corpos*, Rua Marques de Leão 172, famous street side bar, very popular; *Agua do Mar*, Av. Oceânica 639, open 24 hours a day, good snacks; *Barra Vento* across the street, popular open air bar on the beach front.

Further along the coast at Odina is the *Bahia Othon Palace Hotel* with a good disco called *Hippotamus*, busy at weekends, invitation. In **Rio Vermelho** district are *Zouk Santana*, Largo da Santana, new disco bar, good sound system, nightly, go early; US$2 to enter, rec. *Bar Canoa* at the *Meridien Hotel* has live music every night, jazz, popular Brazilian music, cover charge US$6, 2100 till 0100. Dancing at *Carinhoso*, Av. Otavio Mangabeira, T 248-9575; *Champagne* at *Salvador Praia Hotel*, T 245-5033; *New Fred's*, Av. Visc. de Itaboraí 125, T 248-4399. *Intermezzo Bar* at Teatro Maria Bethania at Largo da Mariquita is a relaxed, friendly, open air bar; *Bual Amour* disco at Boca Do Rio, open Tues. to Sat. 2200-0400; *Sabor Da Terra*, near Boca Do Rio for the best lambada dancing in town; *Concha Acústica*, Ladeira da Fonte. (behind Teatro Castro Alves, Campo Grande), concerts every weekend with best Brazilian musicians. rock, M.P.B. (popular Brazilian music), mainly during summer months, usually very cheap, open air, good venue.

Theatres Castro Alves, at Campo Grande (Largo Dois de Julho), closed until 1992; Teatro da Gamboa; Teatro Vila Velha; Senac; Instituto Cultural Brasil-Alemanha (ICBA): Teatro Santo Antônio, part of the Escola de Teatro da Universidade Federal da Bahia; Teatro de Arena, Alto de Ondina, Ondina (good folklore show, 2 hrs., US$4); and the Tenda dos Milagres in Amaralina.

Cinema Maria Bethania film theatre, Praça Colombo 4, Rio Vermelho, art and foreign films.

Museums The city has 27 museums. **The Museum of Contemporary Art**, converted from an old estate house and outbuildings off Av. Contorno, is only open for special exhibitions. The good restaurant(*Solar do Unhão*) is still there, and the buildings are worth seeing for themselves (take a taxi there as access is dangerous).

There is a remarkable **Museum of Sacred Art** in the 17th century monastery and church of Santa Teresa, at the bottom of the steep Ladeira de Santa Teresa, at Rua do Sodré 276. Many of the 400 carvings are from the Old World, but a number are local. Among the reliquaries of silver and gold is one of gilded wood by the great Brazilian sculptor Aleijadinho. Open Tues.-Sat. 1300-1700, US$0.40. Many of the treasures which used to be in an old mansion, the Casa de Calmon, Av. Joana Angélica 198, are here now. This important collection is well worth a visit.

The **Carmo Church** has a museum with a collection of icons and colonial furniture; closed for renovation until 1992. Next door is the Third Order of the Carmo Church and Museum, open daily 0800-1200, 1400-1800; don't miss the carving of Christ by Francisco Xavier das Chagas (see above), entry US$0.10. **Museu Abelardo Rodrigues**, in the Solar Ferrão, Pelourinho (Rua Gregório de Mattos 45, open Mon.-Fri. 1000-1200, 1400-1700, closed Tues., Sat.-Sun. 1100-1700), is another religious art museum, with objects from the 17th, 18th, and 19th centuries, mainly from Bahia, Pernambuco and Maranhão.

Museu Costa Pinto, Av. 7 de Setembro 2490, US$0.35 (1500-1900 except Tues.) is a modern house with collections of crystal, porcelain, silver, furniture etc. It also has the only collection of *balangandãs* (slave charms and jewellery), highly rec.

Museu de Arte da Bahia, Av. 7 de Setembro 2340, Vitória, Tues.-Sun. 1400-1800, poor.

Afro-Brazilian Museum, in former Faculty of Medicine building, Terreiro de Jesus, open Tues.-Sat., 0930-1130, 1400-1730, comparing African and Bahian Orixás (deities) celebrations, beautiful murals and carvings, highly rec. Medical and ethnographic museums in same complex.

Casa do Benin, below Igreja dos Pretos, shows African crafts, photos, video show on Benin and Angola, open Tues-Sat 1000-1800.

City Museum, Largo do Pelourinho (centre of old upper city), arts and crafts, old photographs, entrance free, Mon.-Sat. 0800-1200, 1330-1800. **Hydrographical Museum**, Forte de Santo Antônio, free (Tues.-Sun. 1100-1700).

Thirty-six km. from the city is the **Museu do Recôncavo** (Museu do Wanderley Pinho, 0900-1200, 1400-1700) in the old Freguesia mill—1552 (closed for refurbishing), in which one can find artefacts and pictures of three centuries of the economic and social life of this region. The Casa Grande e Senzala (the home of the landowner and the combined dwelling and working area of the slaves) is still intact. It is a peaceful way to spend an afternoon, but difficult to get to by public transport, the museum is 7 km. from main highway. The **State Geological Museum** is at Av. 7 de Setembro 2195, Vitória, open Mon.-Fri. 1000-1200,

1400-1800 and Sat. and Sun. 1400-1800. Opposite the Museum of Sacred Art is Tempostal, a private museum of postcards, open Tues.-Sat., 1000-1130, 1400-1730, at Rua do Sodré 276 (proprietor, Antônio Marcelino do Nascimento).

N.B. Many guides offer their services in museums, but their English is poor and their expectations of a tip high.

Electric Current 110-220 A.C., 60 cycles.

Exchange Do not be tempted to change money on the street (see above), especially in the Upper City (where rates are usually better). Lloyds Bank, Rua Miguel Calmon 22; Citibank, Av. Estados Unidos; Banco Holandês Unido, Praça da Inglaterra; and national banks. Banco Econômico, Av. 7 de Setembro 38, 5th floor. Banco do Brasil, Rua Rio de Janeiro 750 (4th floor). Banco Mercantil de São Paulo, Rua M. Calmon, near Mercado Modelo, and Banco Nordeste, close by, accept Master Charge cards, Banco Real, Rua Ourivés (Visa). Banco Mercantil do Brasil, Rua Portugal; open 1000-1630. Also exchange shops, e.g. Watt Representações, Rua Miguel Calmon 63, room 601; American Express, Kontik-Franstur, Praça da Inglaterra 2, 1st floor (Lower City); travel agency at Estados Unidos 4 (in the arcade of Edifício Visconde de Cayru) changes travellers' cheques; López e López, Rua Conselheiro Dantas 57, Edifício Paraguassu, Room 101. Catedral Corretora de Câmbio, Rua Miguel Calmon 382-5", in the Banco Francês e Brasileiro building; funeral parlours on Praça da Sé and Praça Anchieta give good rates. Carlos, Av. 7 de Setembro 1451, loja F, Campo Grande Sul, next to *Hotel Bahia*, T 245-3012/237-5331; Asta, Rua Dantas 22/24, edifício Pradesco. Good rates for cash (in small amounts) from manager of *Hotel Modelo*, at foot of Lacerda lift. Good rates also at Marquisa S.A. (Sr. Nelson), Rua Visconde do Rosário 04, Edifício Senador Dantas, Conjunto 101-106 (corner Rua Portugal).

British Club, Inglesa 20B, just off Campo Grande. **Associação Cultural Brasil-Estados Unidos**, Av. 7 de Setembro 1883, opp. *Hotel Anglo Americano*, has a library and reading room with recent U.S. magazines, open to anyone, and at No. 1809 on the same avenue is the German **Goethe Institut**, also with library and reading room with recent papers.

Consulates British Vice-Consulate, Av. Estados Unidos 4, Salas 1109/1113, Ed. Visc. de Cairu, Caixa Postal 38, Comercio, T 243-9222, Mon.-Fri., 0800-1200, 1400-1730. **USA**, Av. Antonio Carlos Magalhães, Ed. Cidadella Center 1, Bala 410, Itaigara, T 348 9195/359 9166, Mon.-Fri., 0830-1130. **W. Germany**, Rua Luzia 281, Rio Vermelho, T 247 7106, Mon.-Fri. 0900-1200. **Austria**, Rua Alm. Marqués do Leão 46, Apto 33, Barra, T 247 6013. **Belgium**, Centro Empresarial Iguatemi, Bloco B, Sala 809, Iguatemi, T 358 5431. **Denmark**, Av. Sete de Setembro 3959, Barra, T 247 9667, Mon.-Fri. 0900-1200, 1400-1700. **Spain**, Rua Marechal Floriano 21, Canela, T 245 9055. **Finland**, Jardim Ipiranga 19, Barra, T 247 3312. **France**, Trav. Francisco Gonçalves 1, Sala 805, Comércio, T 241 0168, Mon.-Fri. 0900-1200, 1300-1700. **Holland**, Rua da Belgica, 10, Sala 604, Comércio, T 242 1266, Mon.-Fri. 0800-1130, 1400-1730. **Italy**, Av. Sete de Setembro 1238, Mercês, T 245 8564, Mon., Wed., Fri., 1500-1700. **Norway and Sweden**, Rua Quintino de Carvalho 153, Apto. 601, Jardim Apipema, T 247 0528, Mon.-Fri. 0900-1200, 1400-1600. **Portugal**, Praça Piedade, Gabinete Português de Leitura, T 241-1756, Mon.-Fri. 0800-1400.

Clinic Barão de Loreto 21, Graça. Dr Argemiro Júnior speaks English and Spanish. First consultation US$24, second free. Dr Manoel Nogueira (from 1000-1200), Av. Joana Angâlica 6, T 241-2377, English-speaking. Yellow fever vaccinations free at Delegação Federal de Saúde, Rua Padre Feijó, Canela. Israeli travellers needing medical (or other) advice should contact Sr. Marcus (T 247-5769), who speaks Hebrew and is glad to help.

Hairdresser Edmea Penteados, Praça da Sé, Edificio Themis, 3rd floor, rec.

Laundry Lavanderia Lavalimpo, Rua do Pilar 31, Comércio, Mon.-Sat. 0800-1800.

Immigration (for extensions of entry permits), Policia Federal, corner of Ruas Polonia and Santos Dumont, Lower City. Show an outward ticket or sufficient funds for stay, visa extension US$7.

Post Office Main post office and poste restante is in Praça Inglaterra, in the Lower City, open Mon.-Sat. 0800-1800, Sun. 0800-1200. Other offices at Praça da Sé in Ed. Associaçao Bahiana de Imprensa on Rua Guedes de Brito 1, T 240-6222; Rodoviária, Mon.-Sat. 0800-1800 (till 1200 on Sun.); Mercado Modelo; airport.

Communications Embratel, Av. Estados Unidos, near Mercado Modelo. Cia. Rádio Internacional do Brasil, Rua Miguel Calmon 41. Telebahia has offices at Campo da Pôlvora, on Rua Hugo Baltazar Silveira (open always), Porto da Barra, airport, Rodoviária and Mercado

Modelo.

Tourist Office (with lists of hotels and pension stays in private homes) Bahiatursa, Palácio Rio Branco (former government palace, which may be viewed). Rua Chile on Praça Municipal, open 0800-1830. Visitors can obtain weekly list of events and itineraries (on foot or by car) planned by the city, well worth doing, but be warned that the itinerary goes through some very run down area of the city. Map, US$2, good; offices have noticeboard for messages. Also at bus station (good, English spoken), airport, helpful in finding hotels, in the Mercado Modelo, and other offices at Porto da Barra. Also details of travel throughout Sate of Bahia. Phone 131 any time for tourist information in English. **Maps** from Departamento de Geografia e Estatística, Av. Estados Unidos (opp. Banco do Brasil, lower city): also from newsstands; maps of Brazil US$1.50.

Bus tours are available from several companies: *L.R. Turismo, Itaparica Turismo* and *Alameda Turismo*: city tour (US$15 p.p.), Bahia by Night includes transport to Moenda restaurant, show and dinner (US$25 p.p.). All day boat trip on Bahia de Todos Os Santos from 0800-1700 including visit to Ilha das Frades, lunch on Itaparica (US$6 extra) US$20 p.p. *Tatu Tours*, Caixa Postal 1219, 40000 Salvador, BA., T 237 3161, run by two Irishmen, specialise in Bahia, give private guided tours and can make any necessary travel, hotel and accommodation arrangements. They are represented in London by Travellers Tree, 116 Crawford St., London W1H 1AG, T 935 2291.

Buses Bus station 5 km. from city but regular services to centre; bus RI or RII, "Centro-Rodoviária-Circular"; in centre, get on in lower city at foot of Lacerda lift; buses also to Campo Grande; journey can take up to 1 hr. especially in peak periods. Executive bus, quicker, from Praça da Sé runs to Iguatemi Shopping Centre from where there is a walkway to the bus station (take care in the dark). To Recife, US$12 (*leito*, 24), 13 hrs., 3 a day, 1800, 1930, 2100; plenty to Rio (28 hrs., US$25, *leito* 50, buy ticket 5 days in advance, 27 hrs. leaves at 1300), São Paulo (30 hrs.), US$30, *leito* US$60, Belo Horizonte 22 hrs, 2 normal (US$29), 2 *leito* buses (US$58); to Fortaleza, 19 hrs., US$18 at 0900 and 2100 with Viação Brasilia; Ilhéus, 7 hrs., US$6, several (e.g. Sulba at 2210 daily); Valença, 10 a day, 5 hrs., US$4; Porto Seguro, 2000, 2100, 12 hrs., US$6; Maceió, US$6, 4 a day, 9-10 hrs, road bad in places, book early (only service, Empresa Bomfim at 2000); Belém US$36, 37 hrs. There are daily bus services to Brasília along the new (fully paved) road, BR-242, via Barreiras; buses leave at 1200 and 2000, 23 hrs. (US$28). To Paulo Afonso, US$8, 10 hrs., leaving 0430, 2000, and 1910 on Sun., Wed. and Fri., partly paved road. (Travel agency Remundi, Rua da Grécia 8, 1° andar, Cidade Baixa, T 242-5286, sells bus tickets.)

Motorists to Rio can do the trip on the BR-116 highway in 3 days, stopping at **Vitória da Conquista** (524 km. from Salvador), *Hotel Bahia*, D, with huge meals; *Hotel Aliança*, D and *Hotel Livramento*, E, with restaurant; also Camping Clube do Brasil site at Km. 1,076; Teófilo Otôni, 946 km. **see page** 332; or Governador Valadares, 1,055 km. (**see page** 332), and Leopoldina (1,402 km.). There are also various motels; two in the State of Bahia are at Vitória da Conquista; and at Feira de Santana; also between Feira and Salvador. Fairly good hotels are also available in Jequié (*Itajubá, Rex*, and motels), and basic ones in Milagres. Stopovers on the BR-101 coastal road can be made at Vitória and Itabuna (or Ilhéus), and there are many other towns on or near the coast.

Rail From Salvador there are only local train services, though the tracks are continuous to Rio.

Air To Brasília, daily, 2 hrs, to Rio, about 2 hrs; also São Paulo, Recife, Belo Horizonte, Manaus, Belém, Fortaleza, São Luis and Porto Seguro. Dois de Julho airport is 32 km. from the city. Buses go between airport and city centre, bus "Aeroporto-Politeama" goes to Av. 7 de Setembro, US$0.10, 1 hr., or special taxi (buy ticket at airport desk) US$10. Bus service from Praça da Sé to Pituba and airport US$1.50.

Shipping National coastal vessels.

Excursions From the lower city the train (Trem do Leste) leaves Calçada for a 40 min. journey through the bayside suburbs of Salvador—Lobato, Plataforma (canoes and motor boats for Ribeira on the Itapagipe peninsula), Escada (17th century church), Praia Grande, Periperi and Paripe (take bus for 17th century church at São Tomé de Paripe). The same trip can be made by bus, less picturesquely. From Ribeira a small boat goes 25 km. to **Ilha da Maré** between 0900 and 1100, connecting the island's villages of Itamoaba, Praia Grande and Santana (US$0.70); boat returns next day from Santana at 0400-0500. Santana is a centre for lace making, Praia Grande for basket-weaving. None of the villages has a hotel, but there are restaurants and bars and camping is possible.

There are ferries to Vera Cruz on the island of **Itaparica**, on the other side of the bay from the city. Passenger ferries run next to the Mercado Modelo every half-hour, 50-min journey. US$0.20, last boat returns at 1700, more expensive Sun, good juices at landing stage, the car ferry leaves hourly from São Joaquim (bus from in front of Lacerda lift to São Joaquim) to Bom Despacho, 45 min. journey. At Vera Cruz there are good beaches, swimming, horses and bikes for hire, but to other parts of the island one has to take a taxi. From Bom Despacho buses go to other parts of the island. The island has beaches most of which are dirty, but good one at Ponta de Areia (1 hr. walk from Itaparica town), and at *Club Mediterranee*, of which some very poor reports; it has adequate hotels (*Grande Hotel de Itaparica*, near sea, *Icaraí*, Itaparica, D, fair food, run by Fernando Mesquita, very friendly and obliging, and one at Gameleira), but poor family accommodation and inadequate car parking. Restaurants are expensive (although *Santa Bárbara* on the main square is good and inexpensive), but there are food shops and a self-service restaurant at the Paes Mendonça shopping centre in Gameleira. Camping is worthwhile. The church and fortress of São Lourenço are in Itaparica town. **Mar Grande**, which can be reached direct by ferry from Mercado Modelo (first one at 0630, last back at 1700, every half-hour, but hourly after 1600, 45 mins.), US$0.50, or by VW *Kombi* or launch from Itaparica (0630, 0900, 1400, 1700— may not leave until full), is very unspoilt, but beach very dirty. To rent houses costs up to US$55 for one month. *Hotel Galeão Sacramento*, suites in four separate buildings, swimming pool and other sports facilities; *Arco Iris Pousada*, C, magnificent building and setting in mango orchard, overpriced hotel, good restaurant; next door is a campsite, same owners, filthy but shady, 1 block from beach and town centre. Another *pousada*, C, 4-star. Eat at *Philippe's Bar and Restaurant*, Largo de São Bento, good French and local food, local information in French and English, or at *O Pacífico*, Praça da Gamboa, local cuisine, rec., friendly and peaceful. There is a minibus service between Mar Grande and Itaparica. Bicycles for hire. At the southern tip of the island is Cacha Pregos (VW bus from Mar Grande, US$6.70); *Pousada Cacha Pregos*, next to supermarket, T 839-1594, E-D (bargain) with bath, fan, clean, no breakfast. Nice beaches across the bay, but you have to pay US$6.50 to get a boat across. From Bom Despacho on the island, trips can be made to the picturesque small colonial port of **Jaguaribe** and to Nazaré (see below), with its market (both on the mainland). Jaguaribe can be reached by boat from the Mercado Modelo, leaving Thursday and Saturday and returning Friday and Monday.

The Companhia de Navegação Bahiana provides excursions in the ship *Bahia de Todos os Santos*, from near the Mercado Modelo. An excursion along the city front (Tues., Thurs., Sat.), taking 3 hours, costs US$6; an all-day trip around the bay's islands, including a 3-hour stay at Itaparica, costs US$10 (Wed., Fri., Sun.). Small boats for trips round the bay may be hired privately at the fishing port (Porto dos Saveiros) at the W side of the Mercado Modelo. There is also an excursion to all parts of the city accessible by boat. For other excursions by boat contact agencies such as L. R. Turismo, Av. Sete de Setembro 3959; Grey Line, Av. Presidente Vargas 2456; Remundi, Rua da Grécia, 8 (1st floor); Kontik, Praça da Inglaterra, 2. For cheaper excursions to the bay's islands, watch for notices in lunch bars and in bank windows in the lower city bank district, put up by employees looking for people to go on trips (US$2.50-3.75, including a beer and sandwich).

Nazaré das Farinhas, 60 km. inland from Itaparica, and reached over a bridge by bus from **Bom Despacho**, is an 18th-century town celebrated for its market, which specializes in the local ceramic figures, or *caxixis*. There is an especially large market in Holy Week, particularly on the Thursday and Good Friday. 12 km. from Nazaré (taxi US$3, also buses) is the village of Maragojipinha, which specializes in making the ceramic figures. Bus from Salvador, 1530, takes 5 hours.

Feira de Santana (pop. 355,000), 112 km. NW of Salvador on both the coastal BR-101 and the inland BR-116 roads to Rio, the centre of a great cattle breeding and trading area; its Monday market, known as Feira do Couro (leather fair), said to be the largest in Brazil, attracts great crowds to its colourful display of local products. The permanent Artesanato market in the centre has a bigger selection, including leather, than the Monday market. Bus every half hour from Salvador, 2 hrs., US$1.60. (Bus station has a wall of painted tiles made by Udo-Ceramista, whose workshop is Brotas, Av. Dom João VI 411, Salvador.)

Hotels Half-way to Feira from Salvador is the turn off for the *Hotel Fazenda*, Alto da Ipê. At Feira: *Luxor Pousada da Feira*, Km. 1,470 on BR-116, B; *Vips Hotel Restaurante*, Rua Visconde do Rio Branco 367; *Flecha Motel Feira*, E, about 20 km. away at Km. 1,067 BR-101; *Hotel da Bahia*, Rua Visconde do Rio Branco 562; *Vitória*, Rua Marechal Deodoro, E, with breakfast; several cheap ones in Praça da Matriz and near the bus station, which is quite near the centre.

Bar Restaurant *A Kaskata*, Rua Presidente Dutra, good food, open terrace.

The Recôncavo The area around Salvador, known as the Recôncavo Baiano, was one of the chief centres of sugar and tobacco cultivation in the 16th century.

Leaving Salvador on the Feira road, at Km. 33 one forks left on the BR-324 to the **Museu de Recôncavo Wanderley de Pinho (see page 393).** Further W, round the bay, is São Francisco do Conde, 54 km. from Salvador, with a church and convent of 1636 and the ruins of Don Pedro II's agricultural school, said to be the first in Latin America.

At 60 km. from Salvador the BA-026 road branches off the BR-324 to Santo Amaro, Cachoeira and São Félix. Seventy-three km. from Salvador is **Santo Amaro da Purificação** (pop. 64,000) an old sugar centre sadly decaying, noted for its churches (often closed because of robberies), municipal palace (1769), fine main square, house of the poet and singer Caetano Veloso (his sister, the singer Maria Bethânia, is also from here), and ruined mansions including Araújo Pinto, former residence of the Barão de Cotegipe. Other attractions include the splendid beaches of the bay, the falls of Vitória and the grotto of Bom Jesus dos Pobres. Festivals in January and February (Santo Amaro and N.S. da Purificação) are interesting. Craftwork is sold on the town's main bridge. No good hotels or restaurants.

At 54 km. from Santo Amaro, and only 4 km. from the BR-101 coastal road, are the twin towns of **Cachoeira** (Bahia's "Ouro Preto"), and **São Félix**, on either side of the Rio Paraguassu below the Cachoeira dam. Cachoeira, recently declared a national monument, was twice capital of Bahia: once in 1624-5 during the Dutch invasion, and once in 1822-3 while Salvador was still held by the Portuguese. It was the birthplace of Ana Néri, known as "Mother of the Brazilians", who organized nursing services during the Paraguayan War (1865-70). There are beautiful views from above São Félix. Cachoeira's main buildings are the Casa da Câmara e Cadeia (1698-1712), the Santa Casa de Misericórdia (1734—the hospital, someone may let you see the church), the 16th-century Ajuda chapel (now containing a fine collection of vestments), and the Monastery of the Carmelites' Third Order, whose church has a heavily gilded interior. Other churches: Carmo (1548) and its Third Order (fine *azulejos* and gilding), the Matriz with 5-metres-high *azulejos*, and Nossa Senhora da Conceição da Monte. Beautiful lace cloths on church altars. All churches either restored or in the process of restoration. Ruined Jesuit seminary. Tourist office in the Casa de Ana Néri. Festivals: São João (24 June) "Carnival of the Interior" celebrations, well-attended by tourists, Boa Morte (early August), and a famous *candomblé* ceremony at the Fonte de Santa Bárbara on 4 December. Try the local dish, *maniçoba* (meat, manioc and peppers). Craftwork in ceramics and wood readily available. Buses from Salvador (Carnurujipe) every hour or so.

Hotels Cachoeira: *Pousada do Convento de Cachoeira* (run by Bahiatursa), T 724-1151, in newly restored 16th-century convent, C, good restaurant, *Pousada do Guerreiro*, 13 de Maio 40, T 724-1203, no restaurant; *Colombo*, basic, friendly, rec.; **Restaurants**: *Cabana do Pai Thomaz*, excellent Bahian food, good value; *Recanto de Oxum*, nearby, *Gruta Azul*, lunch only. São Félix: *Xang-hai*, F.

Excursion 6 km. from Cachoeira, on the higher ground of the Planalto Baiano, is the small town of Belém (turning 2½ km. on road to Santo Amaro). Church and seminary of Carmo. Healthy spot: people from Salvador have summer homes. We are told there is an 8 km. secret passage between the Carmo churches here and in Cachoeira, but have not seen it—reports welcome.

The tobacco centre of Cruz das Almas can also be visited, although transport is poor. The São João celebrations here (24 June) are not rec.: very dangerous games with fireworks are involved.

Maragogipe, (pop 41,000) a tobacco exporting port 22 km. SE of Cachoeira along a dirt road (BA-123), can also be reached by boat from Salvador. See the old houses and the church of São Bartolomeu, with its museum. The main festival is São Bartolomeu, in August. Good ceramic craftwork.

Inland from Salvador Motorists to Brasília can save a little time by taking the ferry to Itaparica, book in advance to avoid long queues, and then going across country to Itaberaba for the BR-242 highway. The journey can be broken at Itaberaba (*pousada*), Lençóis (see below), at Ibotirama on the River São Francisco; at Barreiras on the River Negro, where buses stop for 2-3 hrs. (*Hotel Vandelena*, D, full board); or at Alvorada do Norte (several poor-looking places), Sobradinho (*Hotel Alvimar*, D) or at Posse (Goiás). The road is paved from Salvador to Brasília, but it is poorly maintained.

400 km. W of Salvador on the BR-242 to Brasília is ***Lençóis*** (pop. 6,000) a town which is a historical monument and a colonial gem, founded in 1844 because of diamonds in the region (there are still some *garimpeiros*). It is the headquarters of the new (1985) **Parque Nacional da Chapada Diamantina**, of which the director is Roy Funch, who used to be a tour guide in the area. *Pousada de Lençóis*, T (075) 3341102, C, with breakfast, swimming pool, rec.; *Colonial*, T (075) 334-1114, E, *Tradição*, E with bath, breakfast, fridge, mosquito net, pleasant; *Pous Alegre*, Praça Aureliano Sá, T 334-1124, F with good regional breakfast, friendly, hot showers, good vegetarian restaurant; *Canto de Águas*, D, comfortable; *Pensão Diamantina*, Rua Miguel Calmon, E, *Casa dos Nomadies*, simple and reasonable, F p.p.); 2 campsites, one 2 km. before Lençóis, in the town centre (friendly, rec.). Restaurant: *Dom Ratão*, sometimes has armadillo, snake, toad, piranha and alligator included on the menu; *Laredo*, good food. The Parque Nacional contains 1,500 square km. of mountainous country, with waterfalls (including the Cachoeira de Glass, 400 metres, the highest in Brazil), large caves (take care, and a strong torch, there are no signs and caves can be difficult to find without a guide), rivers with natural swimming pools and good walking hours. Ask for English-speaking guide Luís Krug near the central campsite. There is also a Casa do Artesão, where children learn to fill bottles with patterns of coloured sand, a local speciality. There is a local liquor factory. 30 km. away is Morro de Pai Inácio with good views from the left-hand hill as you come up the gravel road, hard work scrambling down (bus from Lençóis at 0815, 30 mins., US$0.60); good prato comercial at the *churrascaria*. Paraíso bus from Salvador 0915 and 2030 (0900 and 2100 Sat.), US$6.30, Feira de Santana; buses also from Recife, Ibotirama, Barreiras or Brasília 16 hrs, US$10.

South from Salvador 271 km. from Salvador, on an asphalted road, is ***Valença*** (10 buses a day to Salvador, 5 hrs., US$4, and to Itabuna, Expresso São Jorge, 5 hrs., US$4, very slow, and Ilhéus), a small, attractive and bustling town at the mouth of the River Una (the quickest, cheapest way to get there is to take a ferry to Bom Despacho/Itaparica, from where it's 3 hrs. to Valença; the minor road shown on maps does not cross the estuary). Two old churches stand on rising ground above the town; the views from Nossa Senhora do Amparo are recommended. The town is in the middle of an area producing black pepper, cloves and *piaçava* (used in making brushes and mats). Other industries include the building and repair of fishing boats (*saveiros*). Tourist office opposite Rodoviária on other side of river, friendly. Valença and the beaches towards Ilhéus are being developed and are becoming less attractive to those wanting to get away from it all. The River Una enters an enormous region of mangrove swamps. The main attraction of Valença is the beaches on the mainland (Guabim, 14 km. N) and on the island of Tinharé.

Hotels *Rio Una*, T 741-1614, fairly chic, expensive, swimming pool; *Guabim*, Praça da Independência, T 741-1110, modest, E; good *Akuarius* restaurant; *Universal*, E, Marquês de Herval 98, clean, helpful, good breakfast, restaurant; *Cabana*, on road to Guabim, D, in high season, friendly, chaotic.

Tinharé is a large island (with good walking, beaches and camping, but no banks or exchange) separated from the mainland by the estuary of the River Una and mangrove swamps, so that it is hard to tell which is land and which is water. Boats (US$0.75) leave every day from Valença for Galeão (1½ hrs.) and also for Gamboa (1½ hrs.) and Morro de São Paulo (1½). The boat for the two last named leaves at 0800 and 1200 on weekdays, first on Sun. at 0700, first returning from Morro de São Paulo at 0600 (fishing boats will go to Morro de São Paulo for US$2 p.p.). May be fewer boats in winter. Boats can be arranged in p.m., but not after dark. **Morro de São Paulo** is very popular in summer, situated on the headland at the northernmost tip of the island, lush with ferns, palms and birds of paradise, dominated by the lighthouse and the ruins of a Dutch colonial fort (1630). The village has a landing place on the sheltered landward side, dominated by the old gateway of the fortress. From the lighthouse a path leads to a ruined lookout with cannon, which has panoramic views. *Pousada do Campo*, C, on top of the hill, individual chalets, restaurant, run by Stefano and Linda Starita; *Pousada Cio do Mar*, E with bath (D in season), fan, simple breakfast, lots of steps up to rooms; *Pousada Bora Bora*, F p.p., shared bath, OK; *Pousada Casa Rolã*, F with shared bath, has rooms for up to 4, near first beach; plenty of restaurants (*Gaúcho* good food, cheap; *Canto da Sereia*, excellent value, friendly; *Ilha de Saúde*, very good, esp. breakfast), bars, and small hotels and *albergues*, F (just ask by the fountain). The second beach is reported to be cooler at night, *Pousada Una*, T (021) 61-2128, friendly but not perfectly secure. Camping is possible, but not too safe on the beach to the S of the village; washing at the public fountain. Fish can be bought from the fishermen in summer, or borrow a pole and catch your own at sunset. Secondhand books (English, German, and others) sold almost opp. *Pousada Bora Bora* nightly (when not raining), will trade 2 for 1 if he's in the mood. The place is expensive December-March, crowded at holiday times, but cheaper during the rest of the year. All roads are unmade, but beaches are good.

Galeão is another village in the island, but has no beach, only mangrove swamps. The church of São Francisco Xavier looks imposing on its hill. (Another island worth visiting is Boipeba.) It is sometimes possible to get a direct boat from Salvador, 2-3 times a week in summer, 6-7 hrs, ask for Sr. Cacu and the *Natureza* at the fishing port next to the Mercado Modelo.

On the coast, south toward Ilhéus, is the picturesque fishing village of **Itacaré**. It is a beautiful area with a protected beach with crystal-clear water to the right of town; across the river there are beaches with good surfing. It is becoming a popular weekend spot, especially for surfers.

Hotels *Bom Jesus*, at bus station; *Sta. Bárbara*, Praça Izaac Soares 4, clean, good food. *Bela's Casa de Família*, nice rooms, F (next to *Hotel Santa Bárbara*); *Pousada Iemanjá*, near praça; *San Miguel*, 1 street from waterfront, nr. the cannon at N end of town, F, basic, uncomfortable; *Pousada da Paz*, nr. waterfront, S end of town. Camping site.

Restaurant *Marconi*, bar also, good, cheap, friendly.

Buses To Ilhéus (70 km.), 3-4 hrs., US$1.50; to Salvador, change at Ubaituba (3 hrs., US$1, several daily), 6 hrs. Ubaituba-Salvador, US$5, several daily.

Ilhéus (pop. 145,000), near the mouth of the Rio Cachoeira, 380 km. south of Salvador, serves a district which produces 65% of all Brazilian cocoa. Shipping lines call regularly. A bridge links the Pontal district (airport) to the mainland. The town is the scene of the famous novel by Jorge Amado, *Gabriela, Clove and Cinnamon*. The local beaches are splendid and the place is highly recommended for a short stay. Among the churches to visit: Nossa Senhora da Vitória, in Alto da Vitória, built in 17th century to celebrate a victory over the Dutch; São Jorge, in city centre; and the cathedral of São Sebastião on sea shore; Santana, in Rio de Engeho is one of the 3 oldest in Brazil. There is a cocoa museum near *Tio San Hotel*, open 1400-1800. Tourist office on Av. Soares Lopes, near cathedral.

Local Festivals include Festa de São Sebastião (17-20 January), Carnival, Festa de São Jorge (23 April), Foundation day, 28 June, and Festa do Cacau (October).

Hotels *Hotel Barravento* on Malhado beach, Rua N.S. das Graças, T 231-3223, ask for the penthouse—usually no extra charge, C, including bath, breakfast and refrigerator; next door is *Motel Barravento*, D. *Britânia*, T 231-1722, D, Rua 28 de Junho 16, and at 29 the *San Marino*, E, friendly, clean. *Lucas*, Rua 7 de Setembro 17, T 231-3772, D, central, O.K.; *Central*, Araújo Pinho 115, E with bath no breakfast, adequate; *Vitória*, Rua Bento Berilo

95, T 231-4105, E without breakfast, poor value; *Pontal Praia*, T 231-3033, Praia do Pontal, B, swimming pool; *Florida*, Rua General Câmara, E without bath; *Ilhéus Praia*, Praça D. Eduardo (on beach), T 231-2533, B, pool, helpful, rec.; *Real*, Rua General Câmara 102, E with breakfast, near beach, friendly. *Rio Cachoeira*, road to Itabuna, Km. 7, pool, also good without bath; *Illheus Praia*, Praça to Itabuna, Km. 7, pool, also good *churrascaria*. *Pousada G.G.*, Praça Cairu 18, E without breakfast (restaurant next door), clean, near beach. *Tio San*, R Antonio Levigne de Lemos, T 231-3668, *Pousada Cravo e Canela*, along beach F, clean, rec.; In Rua Carneiro da Rocha are *Tropical*, No. 129 and *Bahiano*, No. 94 (helpful, clean, friendly), each E, and two *dormitórios*. Plenty of cheap hotels near municipal bus station in centre.

Restaurants *Luanda Beira Bahia*, Av. Soares Lopes s/n, *Moqueca de Ouro*. *Cabana do Mirante*, Alto do Ceará, with good views. *Tokyo*, 2 de Julho, Japanese, very good, not cheap. At Pontal, *Cabana Cinco Estrellas*, excellent, cheap Bahian food. *O Velho Marinheiro*, on the waterfront, rec; *Come Ben*, nr. Praça Cairu, cheap and good; *Vesúvio*, Praça D. Eduardo, next to Cathedral, made famous by Amado's novel (see above), now Swiss-owned, very good but pricey. Local drink, coquinho, coconut filled with cachaça, only for the strongest heads! Also try suco de cacau at juice stands. *Carlos Twity's* in Una, 40 kms S, for shrimp muceca, which Michael de Lapa opines "will knock your socks off".

Buses Station is some way from centre, but Itabuna-Olivença bus goes through centre of Ilhéus. Several daily to Salvador, 7 hrs., US$6 (*leito* US$12, Expresso São Jorge); 0620 bus goes via Itaparica, leaving passengers at Bom Despacho ferry station on the island—thence 50-minute ferry to Salvador. To Itacaré, early a.m. and 1530, 4 hrs., US$2.50; to Eunápolis, 7 hrs., US$3. Insist that taxi drivers have meters and price charts.

Buses run every 30 mins. to **Itabuna** (32 km.; pop. 167,000), the trading centre of the rich cocoa zone. Bus from Salvador, 6½ hrs., US$4.50. Of the hotels, the *Principe*, *Lord* and *Itabuna Palace* (Av. Cinquentenário 1061, B, restaurant) are probably the best (*Rincão Gaúcho*, B, small, friendly, overlooking river; opposite Rodoviária is *Dormitório Rodoviária*, F, basic; several motels on the outskirts). The paved BA-415 links Itabuna to Vitória da Conquista (275 km.) on the BR-116. Ceplac installations at Km. 8 on the Itabuna-Ilhéus road show the whole processing of cocoa. Tours of cocoa plantations can be arranged through the *Ilhéus Praia* hotel; Jorge Amado's novel *The Violent Lands* deals with life on the cocoa plantations.

The beaches between Ilhéus and Olivença are good, e.g. Cururupe, and frequent buses run to Olivença. For the good beaches at Pontal, take "Barreira" bus and get off just past *Hotel Jardim Atlântico*. Hot baths (*balneário*) 18 km away, are reached by Viação São Jorge or Cana Vieiras buses.

About 400 km. south of Ilhéus on the coast is the old town of **Porto Seguro** (pop. 56,000), now developed for tourism (the airport has been enlarged to take jets). Direct buses from Rio, São Paulo and Salvador. (For the routes from Vitória **see page** 317 and from Belo Horizonte **page** 325). This is the capital of the *Lambada*, an energetic, sensual dance of African origin. At Brazilian holiday times, all transport north or south should be booked well in advance.

It was N of the site of Porto Seguro that Cabral first landed in 1500; a cross marks the supposed site of the first mass in Brazil on road between Porto Seguro and Santa Cruz Cabrália. From the roundabout at the entrance to the town take a wide, steep, unmarked path uphill to the historical core, three churches, the former jail and the cross; a peaceful place with lovely views. 23 km. to the N of Porto Seguro is Santa Cruz Cabrália (simple accommodation, good restaurant *Coqueiro Verde*—try *pitu*, a kind of crayfish); dugout ferry crosses the river, then a short walk to the beach at Santo André. Trips on the river can be made. Bicycles for hire at hardware shop, Dois de Julho 242, US$2 a day. In this area there are *borrachudos*, little flies that bite feet and ankles in the heat of the day; coconut oil keeps them off; at night mosquitoes can be a problem.

Across the Rio Buranhém (10 minutes, US$0.25, ferries take cars day time only, every ½-hr. day and night), and a further 5 km. (US$0.30 in bus), is the village of **Arraial da Ajuda**; about 15 mins. walk from the beach (better for camping than Porto Seguro). Pilgrimage in August to the shrine of Nossa Senhora da Ajuda (interesting room in church, full of ex-voto offerings). Ajuda has become very popular with tourists and there are many *pousadas*, bars and small shops.

Parties almost every night, on the beach or in the *Broadway*; at the *Jaboba* bar the famous lambada is danced. Beach protected by coral reef. At Brazilian holiday times it is very crowded, and with the coastline up for sale, it may become overdeveloped in a few years. The beaches in this neighbourhood are splendid, for instance Pitinga, also protected by coral reef.

25 km. to the S of Porto Seguro and 15 km. from Ajuda is **Trancoso**, reached by bus from the other side of the Rio Buranhém, 5 a day (US$0.80, 50 mins., last returns at 1530, more buses and colectivos in summer), by colectivo, hitch-hiking or by walking along the beach; the road bridges are not safe, bus passengers alight and walk across. The village is simple but also popular with tourists, some nude beaches and many Europeans have built or bought houses there. There are good restaurants around the main square. Trancoso has a historic church. Colectivos run from Trancoso to Ajuda (US$1.20). Between Ajuda and Trancoso is the village of Rio da Barra. Caraíva with beautiful beaches, no electricity, can be reached by boat, 4 hrs. from Porto Seguro, 2 hrs. from Trancoso, or by bus via Eunápolis and Itabela.

Porto Seguro Hotels *Porto Seguro Praia*, 3 km. N of city on coast road, T 288-2321, B; *Cabanas do Tio João*, BR-367, Km. 64, 2 km. N of Porto Seguro, T 288-2315, a/c, pool, retaurant, English and French spoken, rec.; *Vela Branca*, Cidade Histórica, T 288-2316, C, top of cliff, good; *Pousada Casa Azul*, 15 de Novembro, T 288-2180, D with bath, swimming pool; *Pousada Coroa Vermelha*, Getúlio Vargas 12, T 288-2132, D, with bath, no breakfast, friendly owners; a number of cheap *pousadas* on Av. Getúlio Vargas, most without breakfast; *Mar Azul* at No. 109, E with bath, clean, friendly; *Pousada São Luiz*, E, rec. *Pousada do Cais*, Portugal 382, T 228-2121, D with bath, colonial house on sea-front, good; several others on same street; *Pousada Rio do Prado* (No. 236), rec., E with big breakfast; *Porto Brasília*, Praça Antonio Carlos Magalhães 234, E with breakfast, F without, clean, friendly; *Pousada Vera Cruz*, Av. 22 de Abril 100, T 288-2162, E with bath, good breakfast, clean. *Pousada Navegante*, near port, rec. *Pensões* and *dormitorios* near the port are cheap; those near the bus station are dearer.

Ajuda Hotels *Pousada Le Cottage* (across ferry from Porto Seguro, but before Ajuda, T 288-2181), French owner, Sr. Georges, D with bath, C in chalet; also here *Pousada Ivonnet*, by landing stage, E, good, clean, safe, use of kitchen; *Pousada Canto d'Alvorada*, on road to Ajuda, C in season, D out of season, Swiss run, 7 cabins, restaurant, washing facilities; *Thaina Plage*, D, highly rec., reserved in São Paulo, T 011-533-5898, or in Paris T 43-26-31-41, and *Pousada Tororão*, D, rec.; *São João*, good set lunch, bungalows for rent, hot shower. *Brisas Chalets*, C-D, clean, panoramic views, T 288-2348; *Pousada Natur*, D and E, run by German environmentalist, clean, friendly, rec., English spoken T 288-2738; *Pousada do Campo*, D, R. do Campo; *Pousada dos Guaiamuns*, on road to Ajuda, E, very good, French owner is very knowledgeable; *Jardim Tropical*, hot showers, clean, good breakfast, E, rec.; also rec., *Flamboyant* and *Broadway*, E with bath, mosquito nets, breakfast, clean (on road to beach), and *Marimar*, F, garden, no breakfast, near church. Many rooms for rent (for days, weeks or months); best accommodation in private houses behind the church (F). Camping rec. at Arraial de Ajuda Praia, on beach, US$1 p.p.; also at Da Gringa, BR-367 (beach), and Mucugê, Ajuda.

Trancoso Hotels *Pousada Miramar*, next to church (good view, hammock space); several other *pousadas*, mostly in E/F range (of which Henry Giese's *Pousada do Bosque*, Rua de Cuba, and Bianca and Jurgen's oriental bungalow (E) and dinner (US$2) are rec.); private houses, also houses for rent. *Pousada do Brasil* may allow free camping if you use its restaurant, its rooms in D range (on beach).

Porto Seguro Restaurants *Cruz de Malta*, Av. Getúlio Vargas 358, good seafood; *Preto Velho*, Praça da Bandeira, 30 (small helpings); *Arrecife*, good. *Calda de Pau*, Av. Getúlio Vargas, rec.; *Umbertina*, same street, lunch only, good; *Anti-Caro*, Rua Assis Chateaubriand 26, restaurant (cheap and good) and antique shop; *Casa da Esquina*, very good, moderately priced. *Sambuca*, opp. bus station, good for pizza; *Travessia*, near ferry and bus station, Bahian food, OK, takes credit cards; bar opp. bus station very expensive; *O Circo*, good sandwiches. *The Lambada Club*, open every night, facing the beach.

Tourist Office Rua Dois de Julho 172, Porto Seguro, open daily 0800-2200, map available. **Public telephone**, same street, No.71. Better rates of **exchange** in Salvador.

Buses from Porto Seguro: Salvador, daily, 12 hrs., *Leito*, 15 hrs, 4 a week, US$6; Vitória, daily, 11 hrs, US$6; Ilhéus daily 0730, 5½ hrs., US$4; Eunápolis, many on paved road, 1½ hrs., US$1. For Rio direct buses (São Geraldo), leaving at 1745, US$17, 18 hrs. For Minas Gerais, take a bus to Nanuque on the Bahia MG border, then change to Teófilo Otôni. To São Paulo direct, 1045, 25 hrs. US$24; other services via Eunápolis or Itabuna (5 hrs., US$4). All now leave from terminal by boat dock.

Air Nordeste daily from Rio, 1 stop, 3 hrs, also Rio Sul twice a week via Campos; Nordeste daily also to Salvador, São Paulo.

North from Salvador

The paved BA-099 coast road from near the airport is known as the Estrada do Coco (coconut road) and for 50 km. passes some beautiful beaches. The best known from south to north are Ipitanga (with its reefs), Buraquinho, Jauá, Arembepe, Guarajuba, Itacimirim, Castelo Garcia D'Avila (with its 16th century fort) and Forte. Buses serve most of these destinations.

Some 50 km. to the north of Salvador is the former fishing village of **Arembepe**, now a quiet resort. *Pousada da Fazenda* on the beach, thatched huts, good seafood, not cheap; Pousada and restaurant *Mar Aberto*, T 824-1257, rec., food very good, English and French spoken. Best beaches 2 km. N of town. Bus from Terminal Francés, Salvador, every 2 hours, 1½ hrs., US$0.60, last one back at 1700; or from Itapoan. Buses from Salvador run to Praia do Forte (75 km.), where there are Hotels *Club Maritime* (5-star, L, sports facilities, good meals), *Praia do Forte*, L, and a few *pousadas* (e.g. *Ouxi Mari*, clean, good breakfast, shower). There is also a fishing village, a ruin and turtles.

247 km. N of Salvador, on BR-101, is Estância, with pleasant hotels: *Turista*, E, and *Dom Bosco*, opposite, E, slightly cheaper, bath and breakfast, both pleasant.

Monte Santo About 270 km. N of Feira da Santana, via the direct BR-116 road to Fortaleza, is the famous hill shrine of Monte Santo in the Sertão, reached by 3½ km. of steps cut into the rocks of the Serra do Picaraça (about 45 mins'. walk each way—set out early). This is the scene of pilgrimages and great religious devotion during Holy Week. The shrine was built by an Italian who had a vision of the cross on the mountain in 1765. One block north of the bottom of the stairs is the Museu do Sertão, with pictures from the 1897 Canudos rebellion. **Canudos** itself is 100 km. away; religious rebels led by the visionary Antônio Conselheiro defeated three expeditions sent against them in 1897 before being overwhelmed. These events are the theme of two great books: *Os Sertões* (Revolt in the Backlands) by Euclides da Cunha, and *La Guerra del Fin del Mundo* (The War of the End of the World) by the Peruvian writer Mario Vargas Llosa. The Rio Vaza Barris, which runs through Canudos has been dammed, and the town has been moved to Nova Canudos by the dam. Part of the old town is still located 10 km. West.

Hotels *Grapiuna*, Praça Monsenhor Berenguer 401 (T 275-1157), E-D, with bath (cheaper without downstairs), rec.; *Santa Cruz*, opp. Banco do Brasil, E, shared bath, basic but clean; pleasant bars. At Euclides da Cunha, on the BR-116 and 39 km. from Monte Santo, are *Hotel Lua*, simple and *Hotel Conselheiro*.

Buses Direct from Salvador and São Paulo (since the paving of BR-324).

Aracaju (pop. 360,000), capital of Sergipe (state pop 1,366,000), 327 km. N of Salvador, founded 1855, is a clean and lively town. It stands on the south bank of the Rio Sergipe, about 10 km. from its mouth, and can be reached from Maceió or Salvador by road. The city—unusually for Brazil—is laid out in the grid pattern. It has a beautiful park, clean streets (some in centre reserved to pedestrians); there is a handicraft centre, the Centro do Turismo, open 0900-1300, 1500-1900, in a restored colonial building in Praça Olímpio Campos, the cathedral square. A 16-km. road leads to the fine Ataláia beach: oil-drilling rigs offshore. There is an even better beach, Nova Ataláia, on Ilha de Santa Luzia across the river, reached by boat from the ferry station. On 8 December there are both Catholic (Nossa Senhora da Conceição) and Umbanda religious festivals.

Hotels *Parque dos Coqueiros*, A, Ataláia beach, T 223-1511, large pool, luxurious and attractive; *Brasília*, Rua Laranjeiras 580, T 222-5112, D, good value, good breakfasts; *Serigy*, Rua Santo Amaro 269 (T 222-1210), D, comfortable, no hot water in rooms; *Turista*, E, noisy, mosquitos, no hot water or breakfast, friendly; *Oasis*, Rua São Cristóvão 466 in centre, T 224-2125, E with good breakfast, rec.; *Guanabara*, noisy, cold water in rooms, Rua Florentino Menezes 161, E, good meals; *Amado*, F, R. Laranjeiras, fan, clothes washing facilities. Many cheap hotels in Rua Santa Rosa. New *Youth Hostel*, T 231-9166, F, on road to Ataláia (take bus Os Campos, from Centre), no card needed, clean, friendly.

Camping Camping Clube do Brasil site at Ataláia beach.

Restaurant *Tropeiro*, on boulevard, seafood and live music, highly rec.

Tourist Information Emsetur, Av. Barão de Maroim 593, maps of Aracaju, Laranjeiras, São Cristóvão. *Artesanato* interesting: pottery figures and lace particularly. Fair in Praça Tobias Barreto every Sun.

15 km. from Aracaju is **Laranjeiras**, reached by São Pedro bus, from old Rodoviária in centre, 30 mins-1 hr. A small pleasant town, with a ruined church on a hill, it has two museums (Museu Afro-Brasileiro and Centro de Cultura João Ribeiro), and the Capela de Sant'Aninha with a wooden altar inlaid with gold. *Pousada Vale dos Outêiros*, E, rec.

São Cristóvão (pop. 37,000), SW of Aracaju on the road to Salvador, an unspoiled colonial town, was the old state capital of Sergipe, founded in 1590 by Cristóvão de Barros. Worth visiting are the Museu de Arte Sacra e Histórico de Sergipe, the Assembly building, the Provincial Palace and five churches including Misericórdia and Nossa Senhora da Vitória (all closed Mon.). Outdoor arts festival in 2nd half of October. Buses (São Pedro) from Aracaju, from old Rodoviária in centre, 30 mins.-1 hr. (No hotels, but families rent rooms near the bus station.)

70 km. west of Aracaju is Itabaiana, which has a famous gold market on Saturdays. Between Aracaju and the next port to the north—Maceió—is the mouth of the São Francisco river, whose great Paulo Afonso falls upstream (**see page 407**) can be visited from Maceió or (if travelling from Aracaju to Maceió by bus) from Penedo by river and bus. The BR-101 between Aracaju and Maceió is now paved, crossing the São Francisco by bridge between Propriá and Porto Real do Colégio.

Penedo, in Alagoas near the mouth of the River São Francisco, 451 km. from Salvador (US$9, 10 hrs., by daily bus at 0830; 115 km. from Maceió), is a charming town, with a nice waterfront park with stone walkways and walls. Old churches include Convento de São Francisco and N.S. dos Anjos. Long two-masted sailing vessels cruise on the river (they can be rented for US$2.40 per hour, regardless of the number of people, possibly stopping to swim or visit beaches on islands in the river). Frequent launches across the river to Neópolis, 25 mins., US$0.45. Also half-hourly car ferry (US$0.50; take care when driving on and off). Daily street market. Good hammocks. Buses from Maceió, US$2, 4 hrs. One bus to Aracaju daily, 0600.

Hotels *São Francisco*, Av. Floriano Peixoto, T 551-2273, D, rec. except for poor restaurant; *Pousada Colonial*, Praça 12 de Abril 21, T 551-2677, E with bath, good cheap restaurant, most rooms with view of Rio São Francisco; *Turista*, Rua Siqueira Campos 148, T 551-2237, E with bath, rec., close to bus station; in same street *Majestic* and *Vitória*, both E; *Império*, Av. Floriano Peixoto, E. Good **restaurant**, *Forte da Rocheira*, Rua da Rocheira, good food, especially ensopada de jacaré (alligator stew).

Tourist Office in Casa da Aposentadoria, Praça Barão de Penedo, helpful.

Maceió (pop. 482,000), capital of Alagoas state (pop. 2,381,000), is about 287 km. NE of Aracaju by road, and 244 km. S of Recife. It is mainly a sugar port, although there are also tobacco exports and a major petrochemical plant. A lighthouse stands on an eminence built in a residential area of town (Farol), about one km. from the sea.

Two of the city's old buildings, the Government Palace and the church of Bom Jesus dos Mártires (covered in tiles), are particularly interesting, as is the recently restored Cathedral. The Associação Comercial has a museum, near the beach, in a beautiful, though deteriorating building. There is an enjoyable lagoon (Lagoa do Mundaú), 2 km. S at **Pontal da Barra**: excellent shrimp and fish at its small restaurants and handicraft stalls. It is a ten-minute taxi ride (US$2.50) from the town centre (or take "Ponta da Terra" bus) to Pajuçara beach, where there are a nightly craft market and several good hotels and restaurants. The beaches, some of the finest and most popular in Brazil, have in most cases a protecting coral reef a kilometre or so out, but it is said that underwater reef life is not plentiful, and visibility is poor. Good ones are Jatiúca, Cruz das Almas—both good for surfing, Jacarecica, Sete Coqueiros, Guaxuma, Mirante, Garça Torta, Riacho Doce, all within 30 mins. taxi ride from town; buses to the last two from terminal, US$0.65, or local "Fátima" bus, US$0.10. Beaches fronting the old city and between Salgema terminal and the modern port area (Trapiche, Subra) are too polluted for swimming.

Jangadas take passengers to a natural pool 2 km. off Pajuçara beach (Piscina Natural de Pajuçara), at low tide you can stand on the sand and rock reef (beware of sunburn). *Jangadas* cost US$2.15 per person per day (or about US$9.25 to have a *jangada* to yourself)—go early, 0800, by midday it is overcrowded, take mask or goggles (at weekends lots of *jangadas* anchor at the reef selling food and drink). From Maceió, a ferry crosses the lagoon to Coqueira Seca (30 mins., US$0.20), a small pretty fishing village.

Alagoas is one of the poorest and least developed states. Be prepared for delays, cancellations and changed opening times, Maceió, however, is a friendly city with a low crime rate and a Caribbean atmosphere.

Local Holidays 27 August (Nossa Senhora dos Prazeres); 16 Sept. (Freedom of Alagoas); 8 December (Nossa Senhora da Conceição); Christmas Eve; New Year's Eve, half-day.

Hotels It is better to stay on Praia Pajuçara than on Praias Avenida or Sobral: many hotels on Av. Dr Antônio Gouveia and Rua Jangadeiros Alagoanos, Pajuçara. *Othon*, Av. Antônio Gouveia 1113, Pajuçara, good cinema downstairs; *Verde Mar*, same street, No. 1, D with bath, a/c, hot water, TV, T 231-2669, very good; *Maceió Praia*, No 3, T 231-6391, D, highly rec. Good *pousadas* can be found in the Pajuçara beach district, not too expensive; *Buon Giorno*, Jangadeiros Alagoanos 1437, 1 block from beach, T 231-7577, D, a/c, fridge, clean, English-speaking owner, rec.; *Laguna Praia*, same street No. 1231, T 231-6180, clean, highly rec. also *MarAzul*, E; *Pousada Rex*, E with bath, clean, friendly, honest, helpful, highly rec. (esp. the breakfast); also *Pousada Saveiro* and *Pousada Tropical*, both E, on beach; *Pousada Sete Palmeiras Coqueteiras*, E, rec.; *Hotel do Mar*, Av. R. Kennedy 1447, T 231-3171, D, good. *Sol de Verão*, Rua Eng. Mário do Gusmão, Ponta Verde, E with bath, F in small rooms without, clean, friendly. **Youth hostel** *Nossa Casa*, Rua Prefeito Abdon Arroxelas 177, Ponta Verde, T 231-2246, F. *Jatiúca*, Lagoa da Anta 220, T 231-2555, L, a/c, on the beach, swimming pool, heavily booked, good breakfasts, but small rooms with thin walls; *Hospedaria de Turismo Costa Azul*, Av. João Darino and Manoel Gonçalves Filho 280, T 231-6281, E, clean, hot shower, fan, English spoken, discounts over a week. *Pousada Cavalo Marinho*, Rua da Praia 55, Riacho Doce, T 231-4580, rec.

Luxor, Av. Duque de Caxias 2076, T 223-7075, first class, 4 star, L; *Atlântico* is further along, E-F; behind is *Praia Avenida*, Artur Jucá 1250, 2 star, C, clean, comfortable; *Sobral Praia*, Av. Assis Chateaubriand 8022 (Praia do Sobral), T 221-6665, C, shower, a/c, excellent restaurant, pool, reductions out of season; *Beiriz*, Rua João Pessoa 290, T 221-1080, comfortable, E-C, good value (except for breakfast); pool; *Parque*, Praça Dom Pedro II 73, T 223-2399, D, a/c, good, central, comfortable; *Golf*, Rua Prof. Domingos Moeda 38A (near the Cathedral), clean, F; *Pousada Sol e Mar*, Av. Rosa da Fonseca s/n, T 221-2615, E with bath, helpful owners, safe, rec. Cheap hotels (mostly without windows) in Rua Barão de Ataláia, e.g. *Pajuçara*, F, clean, friendly; *Rodoviária* (friendly), F. *Sany*, next to bus station, F with shower and fan, clean; *Reencontro*, next door, F. *Maceió*, Rua Dr Pontes de Miranda 146, T 221-1883.

Camping There is a Camping Clube do Brasil site on Jacarecica beach, a 15-min. taxi drive from the town centre. Camping Pajuçara at Largo da Vitória 211, T 231-7561, clean, safe, food for sale, rec. Camping also possible on the Avenida beach, near the *Hotel Atlântico*.

Electric Current   220 volts A.C., 60 cycles.

Restaurants *Bem*, Praia de Cruz das Almas, good seafood and service; *Ao Lagostão*, Av. Duque de Caxias 1348, seafood, fixed price (expensive) menu; *O Gaúcho*, Av. Duque de Caxias 1466, good Brazilian food from all regions; *Pizza Nostra*, Av. João Davino, nr. Praia de Jatiúca, excellent pasta; *Pizzeria Sorrisa*, Av. Alagoana e J. Pessoa Imperador, very cheap, good food, popular with Brazilians; *Bar das Ostras*, Rua Cruzeiro do Sul 487, Vergel do Lago, expensive but good. *New Hakata*, Av. Assis Chateaubriand 3146, Praia do Sobral, Japanese, quite good; *Passaporte Santa Lucia*, Praia da Avenida, good cheap sandwiches, juices on beach. Vegetarian: *O Natural*, Rua Libertadora Alagoana (Rua da Praia) 112; *Nativa*, Osvaldo Sarmento 56, good views; *Chegança*, Rua do Imperador 342A; *Calabar*, Antônio Gouveia 293, Pajuçara, live music nightly after 2100; *O Dragão*, Antônio Gouveia 21, Pajuçara; *Paraíso*, Av. Antônio Gouveia 631, Pajuçara; at No. 1103 *Tempeiro Paulista*, typical food, good service, cheap. Italian and Arab cooking at *Comes e Bebes*, Antônio Gouveia 943; *Mello's Bar*, Rua Epaminondas Gracindo 194 (continuation of Jangadeiros Alagoanas, at Pajuçara), excellent food and value; many food stalls (barracas) on Praia Pajuçara, e.g. *Sete Coqueiros* and *Pedra Virada* for shrimp. At Ponto da Barra, on the lagoon side of the city, *Alipio*, and many others. Good eating places on the road to Marechal Deodoro and at Praia do Francês. Local specialities include oysters, pitu, a crayfish (now becoming scarce), and sururu, a kind of cockle. Local icecream, Shups, has been rec.

Entertainment Teatro Deodoro, Praça Marechal Deodoro, in centre; Cinema São Luiz, Rua do Comércio, in centre; the other cinemas tend to be fleapits. *Bar Chapéu de Couro*, José Carneiro 338, Ponto da Barra, is a popular music bar for young people. Many bars at end of Av. Roberto Kennedy by Parque de Sete Coqueiros, e.g. *Bar Lampião* (or *Tropical*), R. Kennedy 2585, food and *forró* every night.

Museums Instituto Histórico, Rua João Pessoa 382, good small collection of Indian artefacts and Lampião relics. Museu de Arte Sacra, same street (closed indefinitely). Museu Folclórico Theo Brandão, in the old University building, Mon.-Fri., 0800-1200, 1400-1700, Sat., 1400-1700, free, Av. Duque de Caxias 1490, interesting local artefacts.

Exchange Banco do Brasil, etc. Open 1000 to 1630. Aeroturismo, Rua Barão de Penedo 61 or Pajuçara Turismo on same road, which begins opposite Ferroviária at Praça Valente de Lima (but not named on all maps). Good rates at *Luxor Hotel*.

Cables Embratel, Rua João Pessoa 57, Praça Dom Pedro II 84. Telegráfico Nacional.

Tourist Information Ematur, Av. Siquera Campos (Estádio Rei Pelé), 2nd floor, T 223-6868; at Largo do Livramento, on Av. Senador Mendonça, and on ground floor of *Hotel Othon*. Also at airport and at Rodoviária. Helpful, has good maps.

Tourist Agencies Alatur, Duque de Caxias 1416; Dreamar Turismo, Av. Cons. Lourenço Albuquerque 261; Lysturismo, Duque de Caxias 1338.

Buses Rodoviária is 5 km. from centre, on a hill with good views and cool breezes. Luggage store. Take bus marked "Ouro Preto p/centro" or "Serraria Mercado" which has a circular route from centre to suburbs and bus terminal (taxi quicker—all local buses are very crowded, taxi to Pajuçara, US$2.15). Bus to Recife, 20 a day (but buses full), 4 hrs., US$3; to Salvador, 9-10 hrs., 4 a day (3 at night), US$6. **N.B.** If travelling to Salvador, or if booking through Bom Fim, check all details on your ticket; they are not reliable. To Penedo, several, 4 hrs, US$3.

Airport 20 km. from centre, taxi about US$8.50. Buses to airport from near *Hotel Beiriz*, Rua João Pessoa 290, signed "Rio Largo"; alight at Tabuleiro dos Matrices, then 7-8 min. walk to airport, bus fare US$0.25. Tourist flights over the city.

Excursion By launch or bus (22 km. South) past Praia do Francés to the attractive colonial town and former capital of Alagoas, **Marechal Deodoro**, with the fine old churches of São Francisco, Terceira Ordem (being restored) and Rosário. There is also the State Museum of Sacred Art, open Tues.-Sun., 0900-1700. The town is the birthplace of Marshal Deodoro da Fonseca, founder of the Republic; the modest house where he was born is on the Rua Marechal Deodoro, close to the waterfront, open Tues.-Sun. The cleanliness of this little town is exemplary: on Mondays everyone is required by local law to sweep the streets. The trip by launch, leaving from Trapiche on the lagoon, is very pleasant indeed. Good local lacework. *Restaurant São Roque*, simple but good. A recommended excursion is to take Real Alagoas bus from in front of Ferroviária to Marechal Deodoro (every hour, US$0.45, 1 hr.) then after visiting the town spend some time (beware the *borrachudos* behind the beach) at beautiful **Praia do Francês**, the northern half of the beach is protected by a reef, the southern half is open to the surf where Quatro Rodas is to build a new hotel (restaurant and guest house *Tortuga*, rooms E, on beach; recommended restaurants *Panela Mágica* and *Chez Patrick*; try *agulhas fritas* on the beach; many existing hotels including *O Pescador* and *Pousada das Águas*, both D; *Hotel do Francês*, D, further from the beach; *Água Prai*, E, good, clean. Return to Maceió by bus (last one leaves 1800) or *kombi* van, 20 mins. Further out from Maceió is the beach of Barra de São Miguel, entirely protected by reef, with *Pousada da Barra*, good, new, and *Village Barra Hotel*, T 272-1207, C-B, pool, restaurant, excursions to other beaches.

There are many interesting stopping points along the coast between Maceió and Recife, such as Barra de Santo Antônio, 45 km. N, a busy fishing village, with beach on a narrow peninsula, a canoe-ride away; *Peixada da Rita*, try prawns with coconut sauce, rec. Also Japaratinga (*Hotel Solmar*, F, 2 rooms, basic, good restaurant—bus from Maceió at 0515) and São José da Coroa Grande (*Hotel Lar Ana Luiza*, E, cheaper without breakfast; *The Pousada*, Av. Pedro Cavalcante 535, T 291-1112, F, rec.; a few families rent rooms); at low tide watch colourful fish in the rock pools on the reef. Along this coast, the protecting reef offshore prevents garbage and silt from being taken out to sea at high tide, so water is muddy and polluted. At Paripueira, 40 mins. bus ride from Maceió (Rodoviária) is the *Paripueira Praia Hotel*, E, good value, very clean, friendly.

The Falls of **Paulo Afonso**, once one of the great falls of the world but now exploited for hydroelectric power, are 270 km. up the São Francisco river, which drains a valley 3 times the size of Great Britain. There are 2,575 km. of river above the Falls to its source in Minas Gerais. Below the Falls is a deep, rock gorge through which the water rushes. The lands around are a national park, an oasis of trees and the lake amid a desert of brown scrub and cactus. The best time to visit the Falls is in the rainy season (Jan.-Feb.); only then does much water pass over them, as almost all the flow now goes through the power plant. The best view is from the northern (Alagoas) bank. The Falls are in a security area; no admission for pedestrians, so you need to visit by car or taxi (US$4.50 an hour). Admission is from 0800 onwards, but it depends on the availability of guides, without whom one cannot enter; go to the tourist information office in the centre of the town and sign up for a tour of the hydroelectric plant, 2 hrs., US$5.75 per car.

There are the *Hotel Casande* (B), *Grand Hotel de Paulo Afonso* (B, a/c, TV, pool) and a guest house (apply for room in advance) at the Falls. The town of Paulo Afonso (pop. 86,000) is some distance from the Falls, reached by paved road from Recife, bus, 7 hrs., US$5.50, from Salvador, bus (475 km., 160 paved, the rest bad), or from Maceió (306 km.) via Palmeira dos Índios, partially paved. Hotels *Guadalajara* and *Paulo Afonso*, friendly, cheap; *Belvedere*, T 281-1814, D, a/c, swimming pool and *Palace*, T 281-1521, D with bath, a/c, swimming pool, "best value in town", next door to each other on Rua André Falcão; *Hospedagem Lima*, very basic, F, near *Hotel Guadalajara*; *Hotel Dormitório*, F—all hotels within walking distance of bus terminal. Plenty of restaurants, e.g. *Kilanche*, next to Tourist Office. For information about Paulo Afonso and the *sertão*, ask the Italian fathers (Mario, Antonio and Riccardo) who are most helpful. Handicrafts (embroidery, fabrics) from Núcleo de Produção Artesanal, Av. Contorno s/n. It is possible, with plenty of time, to go upstream from Penedo (**see page 404**) to about Pão de Açúcar or Piranhas, but on to the Falls is complicated and involves non-connecting buses. **Piranhas**, 80 km. from Paulo Afonso (road almost completely paved, buses difficult), is a charming town with good beaches on the Rio São Francisco; it has picturesque houses and an old railway station which is now a *Pousada* (3-4 rooms, F, restaurant) with a small museum (photographs of the severed head of Lampião, the Brazilian "Robin Hood"). If you have a car, you can drive south from Paulo Afonso to Jeremoaba (76 km.), then west to Canudos (111 km.—**see page 403**).

Travel on the River São Francisco (see page 332). The river is navigable above the Falls from above the twin towns (linked by a bridge) of **Juazeiro** (62,000 people), in Bahia, and **Petrolina** (74,000), in Pernambuco (buses from Salvador, 6 hrs., also from Recife, Fortaleza, Teresina) to Pirapora in Minas Gerais, linked by road to the Belo Horizonte-Brasília highway. Like Pirapora, Petrolina is famous for the production of *carrancas* (boat figureheads, mostly grotesque) of wood or ceramic. River transport has changed rapidly in the past few years; for information telephone Juazeiro (075) 811-2465. On the road between Juazeiro and Feira de

Santana (BR-407 and 324) is Senhor do Bonfim, a busy market town with lots of life (also banks and post office).

John Hale writes: Juazeiro and Petrolina are thriving towns compared with many others on the upper São Francisco. Petrolina has its own airport and close to this is the small Museu do Sertão—relics of rural life in the North-East and the age of the "coronéis" and the bandit Lampião. *Hotel Newman*, Av. Souza Filho 444, T 961-0595, E; *Pousada da Carranca*, BR-122, km. 4, T 961-3421, D; *Espacial*, EF Leste Brasileiro km. 2, E; *Grande Rio*, Rua Padre Praga, B; and *Restaurante Rancho Grande*. *Restaurante Panorâmico*, the only one on the river front, is good. Juazeiro is the poorer of the two cities. Hotels: *Grande Hotel*, Rua Pititinga, T 811-2710, *Vitória*, T 811-2712, and *União* (rec.) and *Oliveira*, the last two in Rua Conselheiro Saraiva. *Hotel Pousada de Juazeiro*, 6 km. S on BR-407, T 811-2820, C with bath, a/c, pool, restaurant, bar, pleasant. Unique restaurant known as the *Vaporzinho* is high and dry on the river front, a side-wheel paddle steamer (poor food), the *Saldanha Marinho*, built at Sabará in 1852. Market on Fri. and Sat.

Margy Levine and Jordan Young (Lexington, MA) write:
There are three new wineries in the area: one in Casa Nova (Bahia); Ouro Verde in Lagoa Grande (Pernambuco); and Fazenda Milano in Santa Maria da Boa Vista (Pernambuco), on the north shore of the Rio São Francisco. Fazenda Milano (24 km. from Lagoa Grande, towards Santa Maria da Boa Vista) was the first winery in the north-east, and makes wine from European grapes, with 150 hectares of vines. Owned by Forestier, a winemaker from the south, they make red, white and rosé, blended and varietals. You can visit the winery on Thursdays, if you call in advance on (081) 961-4669 or, in Recife, (081) 251-2200. Wine can be bought at US$3 for 3 bottles. When you get to the Fazenda Milano sign on the Lagoa Grande-Santa Maria road, turn south towards the river, and drive 8 km. on a dirt road to the gate.

About 244 km. N of Maceió and 835 km. N of Salvador is

Recife Pernambuco (pop. 1,300,000), founded on reclaimed land by the Dutch prince Maurice of Nassau in 1627 after his troops had burnt Olinda, the original capital, is the capital of Pernambuco state (state population 7,106,000). It consists of three portions, all on islands: Recife proper, Santo Antônio, and Boa Vista. The three districts are connected by bridges across the rivers Capibaribe and Beberibe. Olinda, the old capital, is only 6 km. to the North (**see page** 415).

Churches The best of them are the churches of São Francisco de Assis (1612), on Rua do Imperador; São Pedro dos Clérigos in São José district (1782, for its façade, its fine wood sculpture and a splendid *trompe l'oeil* ceiling, open Tues.-Fri. 0800-1130, 1400-1630, Sat. 0800-1200); Santo Antônio (1753), in Praça da Independência, rebuilt in 1864; Conceição dos Militares, in Rua Nova (1708), grand ceiling and a large 18th century primitive mural of the battle of Guararapes (museum next door), open Mon.-Fri., 0700-1100, 1300-1600, Sat. 0700-1200; Nossa Senhora do Carmo, Praça do Carmo, (1675), open Mon.-Fri. 0800-1200, 1400-1800; Madre de Deus (1706), in the district of Recife, with a splendid high altar, and sacristy; the Pilar church (1680), Rua do Pilar; the Espírito Santo (1642), the original church of the Jesuits, in Santo Antônio district; Santo Antônio do Convento de São Francisco (1606; beautiful Portuguese tiles), in the Rua do Imperador; the Capela Dourada (Golden Chapel, 1697), in Rua do Imperador (the finest sight of all, 0800-1130 and 1400-1700, Sat. 0800-1130: no flash photography; it is through the Museu Franciscano de Arte Sacra); S. José do Ribamar (19th century), in São José. There are many others. Most of them are closed to visitors on Sunday, because of services.

A few km. S of the city, a little beyond Boa Viagem and the airport, on Guararapes hill, is the historic church of Nossa Senhora das Prazeres, open daily 0800-1700. It was here, in 1648-9, that two Brazilian victories led to the end of the 30-year Dutch occupation of the North-East in 1654. The church was built by the Brazilian commander in 1656 to fulfil a vow. Boa Viagem's own fine church dates from 1707.

Other Attractions Fort Brum (1626), is an army museum—open Tues.-Fri.,

1300-1800, Sat.-Sun. 1400-1800. Cinco Pontas fort (with Museu da Cidade do Recife—cartographic history of the settlement of Recife—open Mon.-Fri. 0900-1800, Sat.-Sun. 1400-1800, free), built by the Dutch in 1630 and altered by the Portuguese in 1677. Visit the city markets in the São José and Santa Rita sections. Go fishing on log rafts—*jangadas*—at Boa Viagem with a fisherman who charges US$2. Visit sugar plantations in interior (though few tour agencies offer such trips), try Sevagtur, T 341-3956, in Casa da Cultura.

Boa Viagem, now a southern suburb, is the finest residential and hotel quarter. The 8 km. promenade commands a striking view of the Atlantic, but the beach is crowded at weekends. The main square has a good market Sats., with *forró* being danced. Good restaurants along sea shore. Bus from centre, take any marked "Boa Viagem"; from Nossa Senhora do Carmo, take buses marked "Piedade", "Candeias" or "Aeronautica"—they go parallel to the beach all the way to Praça Boa Viagem (at Av. Boa Viagem 500). Back to centre take buses marked "CDU" from the main road one block from the beach.

The artists' and intellectuals' quarter is based on the Pátio de São Pedro, the square round São Pedro dos Clérigos (see under **Churches**). Folk music and poetry shows in the square on Fri., Sat. and Sun. evenings and there are pleasant little restaurants, with good atmosphere, at Nos. 44, 46 and 47, and No. 20 *Caldeira de Cana e Petisqueira Banguê*. The square is an excellent shopping centre for typical North-East craftware. Not far away is the **Praça do Sebo**, where the city's second-hand booksellers concentrate; this Mercado de Livros Usados is off the Rua da Roda, behind the Edifício Santo Albino, near the corner of Av. Guararapes and Rua Dantas Barreto.

The former municipal prison has now been made into a cultural centre, the Casa da Cultura, with many cells converted into art or souvenir shops and with areas for exhibitions and shows, and the Museu de Imagem e Som, open Tues.-Sun., 1300-1900 (also public conveniences). Local dances such as the *ciranda, forró* and *bumba-meu-boi* are held as tourist attractions on Mon., Wed. and Fri. at 1700 (but may not happen). Among other cultural centres are Recife's three traditional theatres, Santa Isabel (Praça da República, open to visitors 0800-1200, 1400-1700), Parque (Rua do Hospício 81, Boa Vista, newly restored and beautiful, open 0800-1200, 1400-1800) and Apolo (Rua do Apolo 121, open 0800-1200, 1400-1700).

The State Museum, Av. Rui Barbosa 960, Graças (closed Mon.), has excellent paintings by the 19th-century landscape painter, Teles Júnior. The Museu do Homen do Nordeste, Av. 17 de Agosto 2223 (open Tues.-Sun., 1100-1700), Casa Forte (open Tues., Wed., Fri. 1100-1700; Thurs. 0800-1700; Sat. Sun. and holidays 1300-1700) comprises the Popular Art Museum, containing ceramic figurines (including some by Mestre Vitalino and Zé Caboclo); the Museu do Açúcar, which contains models of colonial mills, collections of antique sugar bowls and much else; the Museum of Anthropology, the Nabuco Museum (at No. 1865) and the modern museum of popular remedies, Farmacopéia Popular. Take the "Dois Irmãos" bus (check that it's the correct one, with "Rui Barbosa" posted in window, as there are two—one for each brother, we suppose) from in front of the Banorte building near the Post Office on Guararapes, half-hour ride 10 km. outside the city to the zoo (US$0.20, not very good) and Botanical Gardens; it passes the museum complex, and together with the zoo they make a pleasant day's outing. Also the Museu do Trem, Praça Visconde de Mauá, small but interesting, especially the Garrett steam locomotive (open Tues.-Fri., 1000-1200, 1300-1700, Sat.-Sun., 1400-1800). The first Brazilian printing press was installed in 1706 and Recife claims to publish the oldest daily newspaper in South America, *Diário de Pernambuco*, founded 1825. Museu da Abolição (of Slavery), Rua Benfica 150, Madalena, is worth a visit, in an early 19th-century tiled house, once owned by the abolitionist João Alfredo, open Mon.-Fri., 1000-1200 and 1400-1700. You

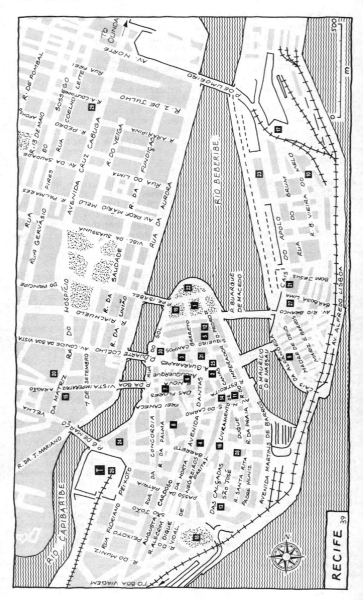

RECIFE 39

may like to visit Cerámica Brennand, a factory in the western suburbs at Várzea, 16 km. from the centre, on the Camaragibe road (take a taxi, or walk the 3 km. along Rua Gastão Vidigal—past hotels *Costa Azul* and *Tropical*—from the end of the bus line along Av. Caxangá). They make ceramic tiles, and one of the brothers is a sculptor of idiosyncratic works on display, for those interested in the wilder shores of artistic endeavour. Entry is free, and it is very friendly. They also have a shop at Av. Conselheiro Aguiar 2966, loja 4, convenient for Boa Viagem.

Local Holidays 1 January (Universal Brotherhood). 24 June (São João). 16 July (Nossa Senhora do Carmo, patron saint of the city). São João, though cancelled by the Pope, is still celebrated with bonfires and fireworks on 24 June all over the State of Pernambuco—and, indeed, throughout Brazil. 8 December (Nossa Senhora da Conceição).

Carnival The carnival groups dance at the doors of all the churches they pass; they usually go to the Church of Nossa Senhora do Rosário dos Pretos, patron saint of the slaves, before proceeding in procession into the down-town areas. A small car at the head bears the figure of some animal; it is followed by the king and queen under a large, showy umbrella. The *bahianas*, who wear snowy-white embroidered skirts, dance in single file on either side of the king and queen. Next comes the *dama do passo* carrying a small doll, or *calunga*. After the *dama* comes the *tirador de loas*: he chants to the group which replies in chorus, and last comes a band of local percussion instruments.

Still flourishing is the dance performance of the *caboclinhos*. The groups wear traditional Indian garb: bright feathers round their waists and ankles, colourful cockades, bead and animal-teeth necklaces, a dazzle of medals on their red tunics. The dancers beat out the rhythm with bows and arrows; others of the group play primitive musical instruments, but the dance is the thing: spinning, leaping, and stooping with almost mathematical precision.

There is a *pre-carnavalesca* week, followed by the main days Sunday to Tuesday; on the Saturday the *bloco* "Galo da Madrugada" officially opens Carnival (wild and lively), see local press for routes and times. The groups taking part are *maracatu*, *caboclinhos*, *trocas*, *blocos*, *ursos*, *caboclos de lança*, *escolas de samba* and *frevo* (the costumes are better than the music). Usually they start from Av. Conde da Boa Vista and progress along Rua do Hospício, Rua da Imperatriz, Ponte da Boa Vista, Praça da Independência, Rua 1° de Março and Rua do Imperador. During Carnival (and on a smaller scale throughout the year) the Casa de Cultura has *frevo* demonstrations where visitors can learn some steps of this unique dance of Pernambuco (check local press for details of "Frevioca" truck and *frevo* orchestras during Carnival in the Pátio de São Pedro). The best place to see the groups is from the balconies of *Hotel do Parque*.

In the "Festivais Juninos", the June *festas* of São João and São Pedro, the *forró* is danced. This dance, now popular throughout the North-East, is believed to have originated when the British builders of the local railways held parties that were "for all".

Hotels (for Olinda hotels **see page 415**)
Hotels in the **centre** and away from the beach: in Casa Forte, NW of centre, is *Pousada Casa Forte*, Av. 17 de Aposto 735, T 268-0524, B, 3-star; in the centre (Santo Antônio), *Grande*,

---

Recife: Key to map

1. Praça da República; 2. Praça da Independência; 3.Praça do Sebo; 4. Pátio de São Pedro and São Pedro dos Clérigos; 5. Capela Dourada; 6. Church of Santo Antônio; 7. Conceição dos Militares; 8. Nossa Senhora do Carmo; 9. Church of Madre de Deus; 10. Church of Pilar; 11. Church of Espíritu Santo; 12. Santo Antônio do Convento de São Francisco; 13. São José do Ribamar; 14. Nossa Senhora do Rosário dos Pretos; 15. Matriz de Boa Vista; 16. Nossa Senhora do Livramento; 17. Fort Brum; 18. Fort of Cinco Pontas/Museu da Cidade de Recife; 19. Teatro de Santa Isabel; 20. Teatro do Parque; 21. Teatro Apolo; 22. Governor's Palace; 23. New Municipality; 24. Casa de Cultura; 25. Diário de Pernambuco; 26. Museu do Trem and Central Metrô Station; 27. Banco do Brasil; 28. São José Market; 29. Empetur Tourist Office; 30. Post Office; 31. Telephone Office.

Av. Martins de Barros 593, T 224-9366, B, good service, friendly.

In the cheaper categories: *Recife*, Rua do Imperador 310, T 2240799, E with bath (cheaper without), central, pleasant; *Treze de Maio*, Rua do Hospício 659, E with breakfast; *Parque*, Rua do Hospício 51, good value, F with cooked breakfast, safe, good bars and restaurants nearby; *Lido*, Rua do Riachuelo 547, E, good breakfast, hot water, friendly, rec.; *Pousada Paris*, Rua do Riachuelo 630, Boa Vista, T 231-4627, E, good breakfast, fan, basic but pleasant. *América*, Praça Maciel Pinheiro 48, Boa Vista, 2-star, D with a/c (cheaper without), clean, quiet; *Palácio*, Rua Henriques Dias 181, Boa Vista, D, T 221-0222, breakfast, quiet, friendly, mangoes in the patio. *Nassau*, Largo do Rosário 253, E, clean, hot showers, but a bit noisy (breakfast only, served on 7th floor, with a balcony overlooking the city). *Sete de Setembro*, Matias de Albuquerque 318, E including breakfast, rec., but not very clean or quiet; *Central*, Av. Manoel Barba 209, D, clean; *Hospedaria Ysa* Praça 17, central, F, including breakfast, clean, fan, mosquito net. *Santini*, Rua Barão de Vitória 295, near railway station, E, with shower, reasonably quiet.

Hotels on or near the beach in **Boa Viagem**: *Recife Palace*, No. 4070, T 325-4044, L, 5-star; *Vila Rica*, No. 4308, T 326-5111, L, 4-star; *Internacional Othon Palace*, No 3722, T 326-7225, A, 4-star; *Savaroni*, No 3772, T 325-5077, A, 4-star; *Do Sol*, No. 987, T 326-7644, A, 4-star; *Jangadeiro*, No 3114, T 326-6777, A, 4-star; *Boa Viagem*, No. 5000, T 341-4144, A, 4-star, near beach. Also in Boa Viagem, *Miramar*, Rua dos Navegantes 363, T 326-7422, L, 5-star, near beach and on same street, *Park*, No. 9, T 325-4666, A, 3-star; on Rua Barão de Souza Leão, *Mar*, No. 451, T 341-5433, L, 5-star; and *Canto do Mar*, No. 400, T 341-4000, A, 3-star; *Casa Grande e Senzala*, Av. Conselheiro Aguiar 5000, T 341-0366, A, 3-star.

There are several cheaper hotels in Boa Viagem (check all prices carefully—beware of sudden price increases), *Marazul*, José Brandão 135, T 326-1900, D, comfortable, clean, friendly, pleasant, care with electric shower; *Aguamar Praia*, D, R dos Navegantes 492, a/c, TV, safe, helpful, good breakfast, highly rec; at No. 2661, *Aguas Mornas*, T 325-0469, D, clean, quiet, rec; *Pousada das Flores*, Rua Padre Leandro Carmelo 57, T 341-1989, D, German-owned, pleasant; *Pousada da Praia*, Alcides Carneiro Leal 66, D with bath, a/c (may be able to bargain lower rates for longer stays), mixed reports; *Solimar*, Rua Solidômo Leite 180, D, near beach, bath, warm water, a/c, good location, friendly but pricey for what's offered; *Saveiro*, R. Conselheiro Aguiar 4670 (T 326-6073), no pool, mosquitoes, but new and clean, a/c, D; *Pousada Aconchego*, Félix de Brito 382 (T 326-2989) D with bath, a/c, pleasant, swimming pool, good meals, English-speaking owner; *Praia e Sol*, Av. Boa Viagem 5476, T 341-0674, a/c, helpful, reasonable prices; *200 Milhas*, No. 864, D, safe, highly rec.; *Albergue Mandacaru*, Rua Maria Carolina 75, E, T 326-1964; stores luggage, English and German spoken, good breakfast, rec.; *Sea View*, Rua dos Navegantes 101, E, Dutch-owned (Dutch, English, French spoken), small, very friendly, rec.; *Guest House Pousada*, Luis Marques Teixeira 151, E, a/c, secure, proprietor Ricardo Teixeira is a Sevagtur guide, helpful, highly rec., English and German spoken; *Pousada Casuarinas*, D, Antonio Pedro de Figuereido 151, T 325-4708, family-run, very clean, fine garden, English spoken, warmly rec.; *Solarda Tia Cléo*, R. Joaquim Carneiro da Silva 48, T 326-3460/1090, no sign outside, F, fans, family atmosphere, rec.

Youth Hostel: *Albergue Arrecifes*, Padre Carapuceiro 132, Praia de Boa Vista, T 081-326-7549, friendly, clean, F, restaurant below rec.; *Albergue 909*, Rua dos Navegantes 909, E, cheaper for IYHA members, good breakfast and atmosphere. For longer stays, rooms may be rented in the centre for about US$20 a month, make inquiries on the streets. For example, contact Dr. Bezerra dos Santos, Rua Floriano Peixoto 85, Edif. Vieira da Cunha S/511, T 224-1098 (English-speaking dentist). Hotels near the bus station are not rec.; this area, especially Santa Rita, is dangerous at night.

During Carnival, private individuals rent rooms and houses in Recife and Olinda; Lins Turismo has listings as does the *Diário de Pernambuco*, or ask around the streets of Olinda. This accommodation is generally cheaper, safer and quieter than hotels, which inflate prices at Carnival.

Electric Current 220 volts A.C., 60 cycles.

Restaurants There are many good restaurants, at all prices, in the city, and along beach at Boa Viagem.

City: *Adega da Mouraria*, R. Ulhoa Cintra 40; *Panorâmico AIP*, Av. Dantas Barreto 576 (12°); *Pierre* (French), R. Ulhoa Cintra 102; *Faia*, R. Ulhoa Cintra 122; *Buraco da Otília*, Rua da Aurora 1231 (lunch only). *Rex*, Rua do Hospício, and next door, *Viena*, better value; *Le Buffet*, Rua do Hospício, good, helpful, friendly, English-speaking owner; *Fuji* (Japanese), R. do Hospício 354, economical, good tofu dishes; *Lisboa á Noite*, Hospício nr. Conde da Boa Vista, good, reasonable, open Sun. evenings (unlike many); *Leite* (lunches only), Praça

Joaquim Nabuco 147/53 near Casa de Cultura, old and famous, good service, meal for US$4. *Galo de Ouro*, Gamboa do Carmo 83, rec., US$3 for main course; *Dom Pedro*, Rua do Imperador 376, specializes in fish dishes. *Bar Esquina 17, Grande Hotel*, rec. *O Pirata*, on Av. 17 de Agosto (Casa Forte) near Museu do Homem do Nordeste. *O Vegetal*, Rua Cleto Campelo (2nd floor) behind Central Post Office, lunch only, less than US$2, highly rec. *Rosa de Ouro*, Rua das Flores 59, delicious food and cheap. *Café do Joca*, Av. Rui Barbosa 1071, local specialities, cheap, good. *Casa dos Frios*, da Palma 57, loja 5, delicatessen/sandwich bar, salads, pastries etc., very good. Good baker *Nabuco* opposite park at Rua do Sol and Rua Concórdia.

   Boa Viagem: Main hotels. *Canton* (Chinese), Rua Desembargador João Paes 123, rec; *Golden Dragon* (Chinese), Rua Barão de Souza Leão 691; *Maurício de Nassau*, Av. Boa Viagem 908; *Lobster*, Av. Boa Viagem 2612 and *Churrasco*, Av. Boa Viagem 1700, both rec.; *Canto da Barra*, 20 km. from centre at the far end of Candeias, the beach past the S end of Boa Viagem, very expensive, but excellent, live music (taxi from Boa Viagem US$4.30); *Ceia Regional*, Rua Prof. Andrade Bezerra 1462 (by Centro de Convenções) rec. for regional dishes. *Moenda*, Rua dos Navegantes 1417; *Baiúca*, Praça Boa Viagem 16; *Shangai* (Chinese), Av. Domingos Ferreira 4719, excellent, plenty of food; *Futuba*, on a tiny side street towards beach from Av. Conselheiro Aguiar 1313, Japanese, good; *Chinés*, Herculano Bandeiro (just after bridge, on Boa Viagem side), good value; *Prá Vocês*, Av. Herculano Bandeira 115, Pinas (town end of Boa Viagem beach), good but pricey seafood; *O Chocalho*, Av. Barão de Souza Leão 297, for local dishes; *Snack Bar Flamingo*, Av. Cons. Aguiar 542, good hamburgers and ice cream. *Bar Branco e Azul*, near bus station, good.

   (For Olinda restaurants see under Olinda, **page 416**). Be careful of eating the local small crabs, known as guaiamum; they live in the mangrove swamps which take the drainage from Recife's shantytowns (mocambos).

Bars The following are suggested: *Lapinha*, Praça Boa Viagem; *O Veleiro*, Primeira Jardim. Also try *Café Passacole*, Av. Visconde de Suassuna 871, Boa Vista, *Depois do Escuro*, Rua da Amizade 178, Graças, and the cafe/ice cream parlours *Fri-Sabor* and *Eskimo*, both close to Praça Boa Viagem. *O Beliscão*, Av. Boa Viagem, by Sea View Hotel, rec.; *Mustang*, Av. Conde de Boa Vista, Boa Vista, also rec. for a beer and watching the "movimento". *Highlander*, English pub at Av. Domingo Ferreira 2222, Boa Viagem.

Markets Permanent craft market in Casa da Cultura (old prison). Mercado São José (1875) for local products and handicrafts. Casa Amarela for a truly typical market on Sats. Sun. evenings: "hippy fair" at Praça Boa Viagem, on the sea front, life-sized wooden statues of saints (a good meeting place is the *Bar Lapinha* in the middle of the square). New Sat. craft fair at Sítio Trindade, Casa Amarela: during the feast days of June 12-29, fireworks, music, dancing, local food. On April 23, here and in the Pátio de São Pedro, one can see the *xangô* dance.

Hairdresser Dellos Cabeleireiros, Av. Visconde de Jequitinhonha 106, Boa Viagem, T 326-1600.

Bookshops *Livraria Brandão*, Rua da Matriz 22 (used English books and some French and German) and bookstalls on the Rua do Infante Dom Henrique. *Livro 7*, Rua Sete de Setembro 329 and Guararapes airport. *Ao Livro Técnico*, R. Princesa Isabel, has thrillers in English and beginners' readers. Also a great local character, *Melquísidec Pastor de Nascimento*, second-hand bookseller, at R. Bispo Cardoso Aires, 215; he also has a second-hand stall at Praça de Sebo (**see page 409**).

Discotheques tend to be expensive and sophisticated: *Esquina 90 Disco Club*, corner Av. Conselheiro Aguiar and Wilfred Shorto (Boa Viagem); *Misty*, Riachuelo 309, Boa Vista; *Caktos*, Av Conselheiro Aguiar 2328, Boa Viagem; *Disco 34*, Av. Boa Viagem 3114 (*Hotel Jangadeiro*); *Gaslight*, Rua dos Navegantes 363 (*Hotel Miramar*), Boa Viagem; *Skorpios*, Rua Barão de Souza Leão (*Mar Hotel*), Boa Viagem; *Aritana*, Rua José de Alencar 44, Loja 4, Boa Vista; *Leandro's*, Av. Conselheiro Aguiar 5025, Sobreloja, Sala 116, Boa Viagem.

Also visit a typical North-Eastern *forró* where local couples dance to typical music, very lively especially on Fridays and Saturdays. Among the best are: *Belo Mar*, Av. Bernardo Vieira de Melo, Candeias; *Casa de Festejo*, Praça do Derby; *Torre*.

Exchange Lloyds Bank, Rua do Fogo 22; Banco Internacional; Citibank. Open 1000-1600. For good advice on exchange, ask at one of the consulates. Amex office, R da Concórdia 278. Lins Câmbio, Rua da Palma corner with Guararapes, better rate than banks (but not as good as some others), but dollars cash only. Money changer hangs out at *Casa dos Frios* deli. next door. Edifício Bancomérica, 7th floor, Rua Matias de Alberquerque 223, takes cash and travellers' cheques. *Restaurante Leite*, Praça Joaquim Nabuco 147/53, good rates for travellers' cheques and cash. Good rates from Sr Manuel E. Cal Muinôs, Rua Santa Rita 290; Monaco men's clothing store, Praça Joaquim Nabuco.

British Council Domingos Ferreira 4150, Boa Viagem, 0800-1500, library with current English newspapers.

Consulates British, Domingos Ferreira 222, sala 203, Boa Viagem, T 326 3733, open 0800-1130. **Swedish**, Rua do Moeda 63, 1st floor, 50.000 Recife, T 224-1622/1329/1772. **West German**, Dantas Barreto 191, Edif. Santo Antônio, 4th floor. **U.S.**, Gonçalves Maia 163. T 221-1412.

Laundrette Av. Conselheiro Aguiar 1385, Boa Viagem.

Church Episcopalian, Rua Carneiro Vilela 569.

Post Office including poste restante, Central Correios, 50001, Av. Guararapes 250 (or American Express, Rua da Concórdia 278 for poste restante).

Cables Embratel, Av. Agamenon Magalhães, 1114, Parque Amorim district, T 221-4149; also Praça da Independência. Telex, public booth, Av. Guararapes 250.

International Telephones Rua Diário de Pernambuco, 38; also at airport (first floor), noisy.

Tourist Offices Empetur (for the State of Pernambuco). Main office, Av. Conde Boa Vista and Alençar; Casa da Cultura, Rua Floriano Peixoto (old prison), unhelpful, Mon.-Sat., 0900-2000, Sun. 1400-2000. Emetur (for Recife), Pátio de São Pedro, loja 10. At Carnival-time they have a full programme. Maps available: Empetur, US$0.33, who also publish walking tour schedules for Recife (one leaves Sun. 1500 from Santo Antônio church on Av. Dantas Barreto) and Olinda in several languages; also central map in monthly guide *Itinerário Pernambuco*. Offices at airport—24 hrs. (will book hotels, helpful, English spoken). Information trailer parked corner Av. Dantas Barreto and Av. Guararapes, 0800-1900.

Hours of opening of museums, art galleries, churches etc. are published in the daily newspaper *Diário de Pernambuco*.

Rail Recife is the centre of the Rede Ferroviária do Nordeste, with lines north to Paraíba and Natal (no passenger services), and a western route to Salgueiro (train every other Sat. 0700. Commuter services, known as the **Metrô** but not underground, leave from the Central station; they have been extended to serve the new Rodoviária at São Lourenço da Mata (frequent trains, 0600-2300, US$0.10). If going to Boa Viagem from the Rodoviária, get off the Metrô at Joanna Bezerra and take a bus from there.

Buses A new Rodoviária, mainly for long-distance buses, with 30-minute rail connection to the central railway station, entrance through Museu do Trem (opp. Casa da Cultura) (US$0.10), has been built 12 km. outside the city at São Lourenço da Mata (it is called Terminal Integrado dos Passageiros, or TIP, pronounced "chippy"); from Boa Viagem taxi US$12, bus US$0.25, 1 hr., from centre. The train to the centre is much quicker than the bus.

To Salvador, 13 hours, 3 a day (all at night) US$12 (*leito*, 24), 12 hrs. to Fortaleza, US$11, and 5 hrs. to Natal US$3.50. To Goiana, every ½ hr., US$0.90. To Rio, 38 hrs., US$34 (*leito* 68); to São Paulo, 40 hrs., US$42 (*leito*, 84); to Belo Horizonte, 36 hrs., US$32. To Teresina (Piauí), 19 hrs. (US$17), and further to São Luís, 26 hrs., US$24; to Belém, 34 hrs., US$30 (Boa Esperança bus rec.). To Paulo Afonso, US$5, 7 hrs. on completely paved road. To Lençois, 20 hrs, US$15, bus continues to Brasília. Good roads N to João Pessoa, Natal and Fortaleza, W to Arcoverde and Caruaru (and ultimately Belém), SW to Garanhuns and S to Maceió,

US$3, 4 hrs. (Maceió can be reached either by the main road or by the coast road "via Litoral"); in all 20 buses daily. **Local Buses** The Prefeitura issues a guide to routes. Buses to the nearby destinations of Igaraçu and Itamaracá leave from Avenida Martins de Barros; those to beaches beyond Olinda from Av. Dantas behind the post office.

Coastal Shipping Lóide Brasileiro ships run frequently between Brazilian coastal ports. They have several up-to-date vessels, some de luxe.

Air Services The principal international and national airlines fly to Guararapes airport, 12 km. from the city. Direct flights from Europe with Air France from Paris and Air Portugal from Lisbon. Bus to airport, No. 52, US$0.25, 30 minutes from N.S. do Carmo. Tourist taxis at the airport are twice as expensive as ordinary red taxis picked up on the main road.

Olinda (pop. 335,000), the old capital, founded in 1537 and named a "Patrimônio de Humandade" by Unesco in 1982, 6 km. to the north, is served by buses and taxis (US$3). This city, which has recently become very commercialized, contains many fine old colonial churches, monasteries and convents; tourist handout gives schedule of opening times (available in Casa da Cultura in Recife). Particularly interesting are the Prefeitura, once the palace of the viceroys; the monastery of São Bento, founded 1582, restored 1761, the site of Brazil's first law school and the first abolition of slavery, by the Benedictine monks (paintings, sculpture, furniture, open 0800-1100 and 1300-1700 daily) and the beautifully restored Rua São Bento; the convent of Santa Tereza (1687), the monastery of São Francisco, 1585 (splendid woodcarving and paintings, superb gilded stucco, and azulejos, in Capela de São Roque, open daily 0800-1130, 1400-1630); the Igreja da Misericôrdia, built 1540, open daily 0700-1700, fine tiling and gold work, and Académia Santa Gertrudes; the Cathedral (1537), the first church to be built in the city, of simple and severe construction; São João Batista dos Militares (1581), the only church not burnt by the Dutch; the Graças church (seminary) built 1582, no fixed visiting times; Nossa Senhora do Monte, built early 16C., likewise; the Carmo church (1588—under restoration), likewise, and the colonial public fountain, the Bica de São Pedro. There are some houses of the 17th century with latticed balconies, heavy doors and pink stucco walls, including a house in Moorish style at Praça João Alfredo 7, housing the *Mourisco* restaurant. There is a large colony of artists (as the superb graffitti at election times testify), and excellent examples of regional art, mainly woodcarving and terra-cotta figurines, may be bought in the Alto da Sé, the fine square on top of the hill by the Cathedral, or in the handicraft shops at the Mercado da Ribeira, Rua Bernardo Vieira de Melo (Vieira de Melo gave the first recorded call for independence from Portugal, in Olinda in 1710.) There is a Museum of Sacred Art in the beautiful Bishop's Palace (1696) at Alto da Sé 7, open Tues.-Fri., 0800-1200 and 1400-1800, Sat.-Sun. 1400-1800. At Rua 13 de Maio, in the old jail of the Inquisition, is the Museum of Contemporary Art; also the old slave market, where *capoeira* is practised on Suns, about 1800. A programme of restoration, partly financed by the Netherlands Government, has been undertaken in order to comply with the recently-conferred title of National Monument. The Regional Museum, Rua do Amparo 128, is excellent.

Hotels At Casa Caiada, Av. José Augusto Moreira 2200 (T 431-2955), is *Quatro Rodas* (L), with swimming pool, excellent restaurant, tennis courts, gardens, very good. *Quatorze Bis*, Av. Beira Mar 1414, T 429-0409, C, friendly, helpful, clean, run by Dutchman. *Pousada dos Quatro Cantos*, Rua Prudente de Morais 441, D-C, in a converted mansion, very good, highly rec. apart from alleged overcharging during Carnival, T 429-0220/1845; *Pousada São Francisco*, Rua do Sol 127, T 429-2109/0386/1469, up to B, clean, comfortable, pool, rec.; *Albergue da Olinda*, Rua do Sol 233, E, new, reasonable, clean, friendly, popular with gringos; *Pousadas do Mar* and *da Praia*, E-F, Av. Beira Mar 497 and 633, Bairro Novo, T 429-2883 for either, each has 16 rooms with bath, some a/c, cheaper for stay longer than 3 days. Also on Av. Beira Mar, *Portolinda*, No. 295, T 429-3198, opened 1987, E, warmly rec.; *Hospedaria do Turista*, No. 989, E, excellent, T 429-1847; *Coqueiro Verde*, No. 1173, F, family atmosphere, excellent breakfast; *Marolinda* (No. 1615), 2 star, D, rec., rooms at front very noisy at weekends; *Pensionato Beira Mar* (No. 1103, E) and *Hospedaria Olinda Beira*

Mar (No. 1473, E). *Flor da Manhã*, R. São Francisco 162, T 429-2266, E-F, clean, good food, beautiful views, friendly, safe, rec.; Several **youth hostels**: *Portalinda*, Av. Beira Mar 295, Bairro Novo, T 429-3198; *Da Praia*, same avenue, No. 633; *Bomfim*, Rua do Bomfim 115, Carmo, T 429-1674, F, rec; *Palanquim*, Prof. Cândido Pessoa 1833, Bairro Novo, T 222-1084.

At Carnival, the price of accommodation rises steeply. Houses or rooms may be rented at this time for 5-10 days (up to US$800 for a house, US$230 for a room, often without bed); try Maria da Silva, Rua Epitácio Pessoa Sobrinho, Bairro Umuaramê, T 429-0320, 2 rooms to let (US$50 a week each). Ask also at the AmEx office in Recife about lodging.

Camping   Olinda Camping, Rua Bom Sucesso 262, Amparo, T 429-1365, US$3 p.p., space for 30 tents, 5 trailers, small huts for rent, quiet, well-shaded, town buses pass outside, rec.

Restaurants   *L'Atelier*, Rua Bernardo Vieira de Melo 91, Ribeira, small converted workshop with beautiful view, run by Swiss tapestry artists, excellent international food, local dishes with reservation (necessary) T429-3099, open Wed.-Sun. *Mourisco*, Rua João Alfredo 7, calm and pleasant, discotheque attached; *Las Vegas*, Av. Beira Mar 1571, food good (watch the bill) but sanitary facilities not reliable; *Zé Pequeno* and *Samburá*, Av. Beira Mar (no number—both with terrace) rec. to try caldeirada, agulhas fritas (at former) and pitu (crayfish), also lobster in coconut sauce or daily fish dishes at latter, very good; *Churrascaria La Cabaña*, on beach, good, medium-priced; *Lanchonete Coqueiro Verde*, Av. Beira Mar 1173, good; same street, *Ouriço*, local food good; *Gouiaba*, charcoal grill, facing sea, good value, rec; *Cantinho da Sé 305*, lively, good view of Recife; *Chin Lee*, excellent Chinese food; many others, mostly for fish, along Av. Beira Mar; *Saúde*, Av. Prudente de Morais 411, serves vegetarian meals. *O Cachorrão* (lunch stand), Praia do Quartel, good cheap sandwiches. The traditional Olinda drinks, Pau do Índio (which contains 32 herbs) and Retetel, are both manufactured on the Rua do Amparo.

Discotheques   *Menphis*, Av Beira Mar 1051, Bairro Novo; *Restaurant Mourisco*; *Las Vegas*.

Entertainment   At Janga beach on Fri. and Sat., you can join in a *ciranda* at the bar-restaurant *Ciranda de Dona Duda*. For the less active, there is the *Casa da Seresta*, also in Janga on the beach side of the main road. On Praça do Carmo is *Cheiro do Povo*, a forró dance hall.

Beginning at dusk, but best after 2100, the Alto da Sé becomes the scene of a lively street fair, with arts, crafts, makeshift bars and barbeque stands, and impromptu traditional music. Street urchins try to tell you the history of Olinda (for a price). The fair becomes even more animated at Carnival.

At Olinda's **carnival** thousands of people dance through the narrow streets of the old city to the sound of the *frevo*, the brash energetic music which normally accompanies a lively dance performed with umbrellas. The local people decorate them with streamers and straw dolls, and form themselves into costumed groups to parade down the Rua do Amparo; Pitombeira and Elefantes are the best known of these groups.

Tourist Office   Mercado da Ribeira, R. Bernardo Vieira de Melo, helpful and friendly, has a map with a recommended walking tour of the sights, opening times, as well as churches, museums and other places of interest, and houses to stay during Carnival.

Transport from Recife   Take any bus marked "Rio Doce", No. 981 which has a circular route around the city and beaches, or No. 33 from Av. N.S. do Carmo, US$0.25 or "Jardin Atlântico" from beyond the central Post Office; from Boa Viagem, take bus marked "Rio Doce/Piedade" or "Casa Caiada/Piedade". From airport to Olinda by bus, take airport bus to Holliday (a Y-shaped building on Av. Conselheiro Aguiar, Boa Viagem), ask to be let off, and catch a "Rio Doce" or "Bairra de Jangada/Casa Caiada" bus to Praça do Carmo, Olinda. In all cases, alight in Praça do Carmo. Taxis between Olinda and Recife put their meters on to higher rates at the new Convention Centre (between the two cities), best to start a journey either way there.

Beaches   North from Olinda, there are beautiful, usually deserted, palm-fringed beaches beyond Casa Caiada, at Janga, and Pau Amarelo (though they are said to be dirtier than Boa Viagem, S of Recife). At many simple cafés you can eat *sururu* (clam stew in coconut sauce), *agulha frita* (fried needle-fish), *miúdo de galinha* (chicken giblets in gravy) and *casquinha de caranguejo* (seasoned crabmeat and *farinha de dendê* served in crabshells). Visit the Dutch fort on Pau Amarelo beach; small craft fair here on Sat. nights. A beautiful beach, reached by direct bus from Recife US$0.75, otherwise via the town of Nossa Senhora do Ó, 2 hrs., is Porto de Galinhas. It has cool, clean water, and waves. *Solar Porto de Galinhas*, on beach, D, good food, many facilities, beautiful place, warmly rec.; *pensão* of Dona Benedita in the street where the bus stops, very basic, clean; food at *Rang Bem* in same street.

Excursions   About 30 km. S of Recife, beyond Cabo, is the beautiful Gaibu beach, *Pousada Beto Qualhado*, cheap restaurants; Itapuama beach even more empty, both reached by bus from Cabo. **Cabo** (pop. 121,000), Pernambuco's main industrial city has interesting churches and forts and a Museu da Abolição, and at nearby Suape are many 17C. buildings and a Biological Reserve.

Biological Reserves For information on Pernambuco's two reserves, contact IBDF, Av. 17 de Agosto 1057, Casa Forte, CEP 50.000, Recife. They are **Saltinho**, which preserves some of the last vestiges of Atlantic Forest in the North East, and **Serra Negra**, which has some of the last remaining forest at higher altitude in the interior.

Igarassu (pop. 68,000), 32 km. N of Recife on the road to João Pessoa, has the first church built in Brazil (SS Cosme e Damião), the Livramento church nearby, and the convent of Santo Antônio with a small museum next door. The church of Sagrada Coração is said to have housed Brazil's first orphanage. Much of the town (founded in 1535) has been declared a National Monument; it is an attractive place, with a number of colonial houses and Brazil's first Masonic hall. Hotel: *Fazenda Praia da Gavoa*, Extrada do Ramalho, A; Camping Clube do Brasil has site nearby at Engenho Monjope, an old sugar estate, now a historical monument and interesting (it is 3 km. before Igarassu coming from Recife—bus US$0.30—alight at the "Camping" sign and walk 5-10 mins.). Igarassu buses leave from Av. Martins de Barro, Recife, 45 mins., US$0.35. N of Igarassu you pass through coconut plantations to Itapissuma, where there is a bridge to **Itamaracá** island, where, the locals say, Adam and Eve spent their holidays (so does everyone else on Sundays, now). It has the old Dutch Forte Orange; an interesting penal settlement with gift shops, built round the 1747 sugar estate buildings of Engenho São João, which still have much of the old machinery; charming villages and colonial churches, and fine, wide, clean beaches. Buses from Recife (Av. Martins de Barros opp. *Grand Hotel*) and Igarassu.

Itamaracá Hotels *Caravela*, T 224, C with shower, good restaurant, on beach; *Pousada*, T 297, C, pool etc., some minutes from beach; *Pousada Telhadão*, Av. Beira Mar 3, Quatro Cantos, D, clean, excellent restaurant, swimming pool, garden, warmly recommended; *Itamaracá Parque*, T 242, C.

Goiana, on the Recife-João Pessoa road, founded 1570, is one of the most important towns for ceramics. Carmelite church and monastery, founded 1719, impressive but poorly restored; San Benedito, needs restoring; Matriz do Rosário, only open for 1800 mass, Soledade convent (1755); Amparo church with Sacred museum; Misericôrdia church (1723). The uniformity of many of the dwellings is due to their construction, for his workforce, by the owner of a now-defunct textile factory. *Hospedaria Durma Bem*, open weekends only; ask at Prefeitura at other times. Visit the workshop of Zé do Carmo, opposite the *Buraco da Giá* restaurant (excellent seafood; owner has tame crab which will offer you a drink), R. Padre Batalha 100. Just north of Goiana is a sugar-mill, Usina Nossa Senhora das Maravilhas, which can be visited during the week; ask for Dr Jairo.

At the Pernambuco-Paraíba border, a 27 km. dirt road to the fishing village of Pitimbu, with *jangadas*, lobster fishing, surf fishing, lobster-pot making. No tourist facilities but camping is possible; food from *Bar do Jangadeiro*. Bus from Goiana, US$0.50.

Another possible excursion is by a slow railway or a good roads via Caruaru or Palmares to the city of **Garanhuns** (pop. 100,000), 243 km. SW of Recife. It claims to be the best holiday resort in the North-East, partly because of its cool climate—it stands at 890 metres, and has an average temperature of 21°C—and partly because of its mineral waters and beautiful landscapes and parks.

Hotels *Familiar*, Av. Santo Antônio 12. *Grande Hotel Petrópolis*, Praça da Bandeira 129, T 761-0543. *Tavares Correia*, B, Av. Rui Barbosa 296, T 761-0900. **Camping**, *Camping Treze*, BR-432, km. 105.

Tracunhaém (pop. 10,600), 30 km. from Recife, is a peaceful town where fine ceramics are made; there are two interesting early 19C. churches. To get there, turn off the Limoeiro road at Carpina, on to the road to Nasaré da Mata. Even the children are adept in working in clay.

Carpina, 54 km. from Recife, 65,000 people, is well-known for its Carnival and for the traditional Epiphany festival early in January, and also for the carpets made in nearby village of Lagoa do Carro. There is a historical museum. Hotels (*Pousada das Acácias*, BR-408, B; *São João da Escócia*, Av. João Alfredo 136, D) and restaurants.

Caruaru (pop. 191,000), 130 km. W of Recife by paved road (many buses, 2 hrs., US$3) and rail, has a big Fri. to Sun. market with a separate site across the river for leather goods, pottery and articles of straw, although it is disappointingly tourist-oriented now (smaller market on other days of the week). See the hand-painted textiles of Sr Valério Cristóvão, Rua 13 de Maio 94, 1st floor; he is very helpful and his work depicts local history. The little clay figures (*figurinhas de barro*) originated by Mestre Vitalino, and very typical of the North-East, are a local speciality; many local potters live at Alto da Moura 6 km. away, where a house once owned by Vitalino is open, but has no examples of his work. Bus, ½ hour, bumpy, US$0.30. Rodoviária is 4 km. from town. Bus to Maceió, 0700, 5 hrs., US$3.50. Bus to Fazenda Nova 1030, 1 hr., returns for Caruaru 1330. Train to Recife, 1700 Sunday.

Hotels *Do Sol*, T 721-3044, A (4-star) on hill outside town, good restaurant, pool; *Centenário*, 7 de Setembro 84, T 721-1932, E, clean, friendly, restaurant. Cheap *hospedarias* around central square, Praça Getúlio Vargas.

Restaurants *Mãe Amara*, R. São Paulo, for regional food. *Guanabara*, clean, cool, not too expensive. *Churrascaria São Luís*, Rua dos Guararapes 15, near Praça Getúlio Vargas, good and cheap; *Churrascaria Trêvi*, said to be good.

On the way to Caruaru is **Gravatá**, 60,000 people (*Hotel Fazenda Portal*, L, BR-232; *Grande da Serra*, BR-232, D; *Central*, Av. C.B. de Oliveira 301 (BR-232), D), known as the Switzerland of Pernambuco for its scenery and good hill climate.

During Easter Week each year various agencies run package tours to the little country town of **Fazenda Nova**, a few km. from Caruaru. Just outside the town is **Nova Jerusalém**, where from the Tuesday before to Easter Sunday, an annual passion play, suggested by Oberammergau's, is enacted. The site is one-third of the size of the historic quarter of Jerusalem, with 12 permanent stages on which scenes of the Passion are presented; the audience moves from one to another as the story unfolds.

Hotels in Fazenda Nova *Grande*, best; *Mansão Verde*; *Fazenda Nova*.

Camping Close to site.

Arcoverde (pop. 51,000), about 126 km. W of Caruaru, is a market town in the Sertão, market every Saturday, cool at night. Hotel: *Grande Majestic* (fair), E, with breakfast.

Triúnfo (pop. 28,000), about 200 km. W of Arcoverde via Serra Talhada, is a delightful small town in Serra de Borborema, good climate, with great variety of crops, flowers and fruits. There are also a sugar mill that can be visited (Engenho Boa Esperança), waterfalls, sounding rocks, the convent of São Boaventura, and the Museu do Cangaça, showing the lives and relics of the traditional bandits of the Nordeste. Stay at *Hotel-Orphanage Lar St. Elizabeth*, run by German religious sisters, D, with private apartment and 3 excellent meals. Two buses daily to and from Recife (6½ hrs.); trains run from Recife to Serra Talhada, *Hotel Municipal* on main square, F with breakfast.

Fernando de Noronha is a small archipelago 345 km. off the NE coast. It was declared a Marine National Park in 1989. Only one island is inhabited. It used to be an independent dependency under military control but is now part of the state of Pernambuco administered from Recife. The islands were discovered 1503 and were for a time a pirate lair. In 1738 the Portuguese built the Forte dos Remédios, later used as a prison in this century; remains still exist as well as a semi-deserted village nearby. Sea landing is difficult but an airport has been built. Twice daily flights from Recife at 0800 and 1200 on 13 and 17 seater planes by Nordeste, T 341-3187, US$50 each way, 1 hr. 40 mins. Special permission is no longer required to visit the archipelago. This has led to an influx of tourists. Many locals are now dependent on tourism and it can be difficult to find fish as the fishermen are busy taking tourists on boat trips. Most food is brought from the mainland and prices are about double. Repellent is not available for the many mosquitoes. The island, which is dominated by a 321 metre peak, has many unspoilt beaches, interesting wildlife and fishing; scuba-diving and snorkelling are excellent. It is now prohibited to swim with the dolphins but they can be seen from the beach.

Only hotel, *Pousada Esmeralda*, can only be booked as part of a 7-day package tour from Recife, departures Sat. and Sun. through Mubatur in Recife T 341-4519, or Quadratur in Rio T 262-8011; cost is US$800 p.p. Holiday camp type cabins, a/c is only on from 2200 to 0600 so better to take room with fan. Food is only reasonable. Beware of similar packages at lower prices in other "pousadas" because they turn out to be rooms in family homes. Aeroporto Turismo in Recife offers such "deals". Independent travellers can go much cheaper as many local families rent out rooms with full board, US$15 p.p. per day. The best known is that of Suzanna and Rocha, rooms with fan and bathroom, but they never refuse a reservation and farm people out to other families with much inferior levels of accommodation. Vanilda across the street has been highly recommended. Boat trips and jeep tours around the island are available; also possible to hire a jeep or beach buggy. You can hitch everywhere as everyone stops. Scuba-diving is organised by Aguas Claras in the hotel grounds, but staff are regarded as unhelpful and unreliable. There is only one restaurant, called *Ilha Encantado*, near the hotel. Bars: *Bar da Vila* in the village of Remédios, only open in the daytime; *Bar Idade* on the Çonceição beach, daytime only with loud rock music; *Mirante Bar*, near the hotel, with spectacular view over Boldró beach, has loud music and at night is an open-air disco and the only nightlife on the island. Take sufficient new cruzeiros as dollars are heavily discounted. The time is one hour later than Brazilian Standard Time.

It is a bus ride of 2 hours through sugar plantations over a good road from Recife (126 km.) to

João Pessoa (pop. 400,000), capital of the State of Paraíba (pop. 3,164,000), on the Paraíba River. Ocean-going ships load and unload at Cabedelo (pop. 21,600) 18 km. by road or rail. The old monasteries are worth seeing, and the 18th century church of São Francisco is a beauty (currently under restoration). Other tourist points include the Casa da Pólvora, an old gunpowder store which has become the city museum; the city parks; and trips on the River Paraíba. Airport for internal services. See the booklet *Relíquias da Paraíba*, by Padre Antônio Barbosa.

Hotels *Tropical* (ex-*Tambaú*), Av. Alm. Tamandaré 229, Tambaú, T 226-3660, A, comfortable, good service, rec., though sometimes they pretend no standard rooms are available when they are; *Gameleira*, Av. João Maurício 157, T 226-1576, opposite *Tropical*, E, good breakfast, rec., but noisy at night; *Costa Bela Praia*, Av. Négo 131, Tambaú, T 226 1570, C, rec., small; *Aurora*, Praça João Pessoa 51, central, T 221-2238, E with a/c and bath, clean, friendly; *Guarany*, Rua Almeida Barreto 181 e 13 de Maio, T 221-2161, E (more with a/c and TV), clean, central, safe, friendly, rec. as good value, good breakfast; *Pedro Américo*, Praça Pedro Américo, 109, E, clean, central (no breakfast on Sun.); *Motel Veraneio*, on BR-230; *Motel Fogeama*, Rua das Trincheiras (with restaurant); *Pousada do Conde*, BR-101 Sul (with churrascaria); cheap hotels near the old bus station, e.g. *São Pedro*, Rua Irineu Pinto 231, clean, basic, friendly, E. **Youth hostels**, on Av. das Trincheiras, at Palácio dos Esportes, T 221-7220/1, and *Cabo Branco*, Av. Pe-José Trigueiro 104, Praia de Cabo Branco, T 221-2903/226-6171.

Electric Current 220 volts A.C, 60 cycles.

Restaurants *Cabo Branco Clube* has two restaurants, one in Rua Peregrino de Cavalho and the other in the Miramar district. Two good restaurants on Tambaú beach are *Adega do Alfredo* (Portuguese) and *Wan Li* (Chinese); *A Caravela*, Quadra 3, Jardim Beiramar; *Badionaldo*, Praia do Poço (20 km. from centre) and also *Bardilucena*. *Itacoatiara*, near *Hotel Tropical*; *Pescador*, near Cabo Branco lighthouse; *O Luzeirinho*, Av. Vasco da Gama, Jaguaribe; *O Boiadeiro*, Av. Coração de Jesus; *A Gameleira*, Av. João Maurício, Tambaú. *Pavilhão do Chá*, pleasant, drinks, sandwiches, TV, open air, in centre.

Exchange Banco do Brasil, near Praça João Pessoa, 3rd floor, helpful.

Cables Embratel, Rua das Trincheiras 398.

Tourist Information PB Tur, Av. Getúlio Vargas 301, Centro João Pessoa; also bus terminal (helpful). Crafts at Casa do Artesão, R. Maciel Pinheiro near city bus station.

Tourist Agencies Planetur, Av. Miguel Couto 5, Loja 12, and *Hotel Tropical*. Agência de Viagens e Turismo Arnaldo von Sohsten, Rua Gama e Melo 100.

Bus Station is 10 mins. from centre; luggage store. To Recife, every 60 mins., US$1.50, 2 hrs. To Natal, every 2 hrs., US$2.50, 3 hrs.; to Fortaleza, 2000 only, 10 hrs., US$8. Warning: you will be refused permission to travel from João Pessoa Rodoviária wearing shorts, whether or not you arrived in shorts (Bermuda shorts are acceptable).

Excursions The principal beach and seaside resort is Tambaú, 7 km from João Pessoa, take a taxi or bus (No. 510 "Tambaú" from outside Rodoviária, or "Lagoa" from city centre, alight at *Hotel Tropical*); excellent bathing. The Centro Turístico Tambaú, Av. Almirante Tamandaré e Rua Sen. Ruy Carneiro (in shopping mall) is helpful, with an informative book on all Paraíba and maps. North of Tambaú is Manaira beach, but the section near *Hotel Tropical/Tambaú* is too polluted for bathing. Cabo Branco club on Tambaú beach, open to visitors: good food, beautiful views. 14 km. south down the coast is the Cabo Branco lighthouse at Ponta do Seixas, the most easterly point of continental Brazil and South America; there is a panoramic view from the cliff top. The beaches below are palm-lined but oil-polluted. Take bus 507 "Cabo Branco" from outside Rodoviária, or "Lagoa" bus from centre and get out at last stop; hike up to the lighthouse. At Cabedelo are the impressive walls of the 17th-century fortress of Santa Catarina. If you take a Cabedelo bus and alight at Jacaré, about 12 km from João Pessoa, there is an excellent beach with food stalls at weekends. In Jacaré, where the yachts tie up, is a bar run by an Englishman.

Campina Grande (pop. 280,000), the "Porta do Sertão", is 120 km. from João Pessoa (bus 2 hours), a rapidly growing centre for light industry and an outlet for goods from most of the North-East. There is a museum of modern art, and another of the cotton industry. Most genial climate. Near Campina Grande is Lagoa Seca, where the local craft is the making of figures in wood and sacking.

Hotels *Rique Palace Hotel* (excellent) is on the top floors of the tallest building in town, T 321-4207: the restaurant is on the 11th floor. Other hotels: *Ouro Branco*, E; *Barborema*, near old bus station, E, friendly. *Dormitório São Paulo*, also near bus station, F, cheap, clean. Many others near old bus station. **Restaurant** *Miura*, Rua Major Juvino 262, good steaks, and in old bus station.

W of Campina Grande the main highway, still paved, leads on through **Patos** (*Hotel JK*, E) to Ipaumirim (Ceará). Here a left turn leads to the twin towns of **Crato** (*Hotel Crato*, E) and **Juazeiro do Norte** (Ceará), oases of green in the dry Sertão. Mosquitoes can be a problem at night.

Juazeiro do Norte is a small pilgrimage town; it was the home of Padre Cícero, one of the unofficial saints of the North-East. A statue to him stands in the Logradouro do Horto, a park overlooking the town; either take the pilgrim trail up the hill or go by bus. **Hotels**: *Panorama*, D, good value; *Vieira*, corner of Rua São Pedro and Rua Santo Antônio, E, private bathroom and breakfast; and *Municipal*, E, rec.

Many beautiful fishing villages along the coast, often difficult to reach; one of the most popular is Baía Formosa in Rio Grande do Norte (daily bus from Natal, 2½ hrs.). No hotel; ask in town for accommodation in fishermen's houses, infinitely preferable to the overpriced accommodation at the *Miramar* bar.

Natal (pop. 510,000), capital of Rio Grande do Norte (pop 2,244,000), on the estuary of the Rio Potengi, is about 180 km. to the north of João Pessoa. It is served by weekly coastal vessels and there is a railway S through the State of Paraíba to Recife and Maceió (only suburban passenger services). There is a large airport 13 km. from the city (taxi US$6.50). The old part of the city is called Cidade Alta. The main square, the Praça João Maria, oblong in shape, has a traditional cathedral at one end and a fine modern bank building at the other. The city is centred on the Av. Rio Branco. The church of Santo Antônio, Rua Santo Antônio in the centre, dates from 1766, and has a fine, carved wooden altar. The Museu Câmara Cascudo, Av. Hermes de Fonseca 1398 (T 222-0923), has exhibits on archaeological digs, Umbanda rituals and the petroleum industry (open Tues.-Fri., 0800-1100, 1400-1600, US$1.40). The Forte dos Reis Magos (16th-century) on the coast at Rocas is open Tues.-Sun. 0800-1700; between it and the city is a military installation, and the walk along the beach road is not very safe. Best to go in a tour, or by taxi; it is worth it for the views (entry US$1.40). The Casa da Música Popular Brasileira has dancing on Friday and Saturday night and Sunday from 1700, very popular. The Marine Research Institute at the Praia da Areia Preta can be visited; bus marked "Areia Preta" from Av. Rio Branco. Good local craftware Sats. at Mercado do Alecrim, along Rua Quaresma near Rua Gonçalves. At Mãe Luiza is a lighthouse with beautiful views of Natal and surrounding beaches (take city bus marked Mãe Luiza; get key from the house next door. Some 20 km. from Natal is the rocket base of Barreira do Inferno, near Eduardo Gomes, which can no longer be visited by foreigners.

Hotels *Reis Magos*, Av. Café Filho, Praia do Meio, T 222-2055, facing sea, obligatory full board in high season, food not rec., B; *Marsol Natal*, Via Costeira 1567, km. 7, Parque das Dunas, T 221-2619, 3-star, new; Via Costeira is a good place to stay, but hotels mostly in A-B range; e.g. *Barreira Roxa Praia*, T 222-1093, clean, helpful, good. *Santo Antônio*, R. Santo Antônio 724, E, with breakfast, very clean and helpful; *Natal*, Av. Mar Floriano Peixoto 104, F, clean, friendly, English spoken; *Fenícia*, Av. Rio Branco 586, E (more with a/c) with breakfast and shower, friendly; *Casa Grande*, Rua Princesa Isabel 529, T 222-1513, E with a/c, F without bath, good breakfast, pleasant, excellent value; *Casa da Maçã*, near *Casa Grande*, good value, friendly; *Pousada Meu Canto*, Manoel Dantas 424, Petrópolis, E incl. good breakfast, clean, friendly, nice garden, trips organized; *Pousada O Caipira*, Manuel Maschado 354, E, clean, friendly, noisy at weekends, between beach and centre, take "Via-Tirol" bus; *Samburá*, Rua Prof. Zuza 263, T 221-0611, C, rec.; *Majestic*, Rua Dom Pedro I 20, clean, friendly, E; *Beira Mar*, Av. Pres. Café Filho, Praia dos Artistas, T 222-4256, on the beach front, D, with breakfast, but no a/c, small, good value, popular; *Praia do Meio*, Av. Beira Mar, D, a/c, clean, friendly, good value; *Pousada Bejo Tropical*, R. Valentim de Almeida 10, F, T 221-5361, clean, helpful, warmly rec.; *Farol*, Av. Gouv. Silvio Pedrosa 174 (on beach), T 222-4661, E with a/c; *Le Bateau*, Praia de Areia Preta, D, on beach front, clean, helpful, good breakfast, English and French spoken. Also on beach, *Praia dos Artistas*, clean, helpful, good breakfast, rec; *Tirol*, Av. Alexandrino de Alencar 1330, T 221-3223, D, good but noisy. *Pousadas* at Ponta Negra and Genipabu beaches, e.g. *Caminho do Mar*, nr. Ponta Negra beach, clean, very friendly. *Ponta Negra*, E, pool, friendly, rec; *Pousada do Mar*, T 236-2509, D, pool; *Miramar*, *Bella Napoli*, *Pousada do Praia* offer some reductions for single people in double rooms. Cheap accommodation at *Casa de Estudantes*, near the Tourist Centre (separate facilities for men and women), "Via Tirol" bus from Rodoviária to centre passes here, very crowded in Suns. **Youth hostel**, *Meu Canto*, Rua Dr. Manoel Dantas 424, Petrópolis, T 222-8351, highly rec.

Camping on the Praia do Forte beach, near the Forte dos Reis Magos, not rec. because unsafe. Camping Clube do Brasil site at Sítio do Jiqui, expensive. Vale das Cascatas, Ponta Negra beach, swimming pool, leisure facilities, US$4 p.p.

Electric Current 220 volts A.C., 60 cycles.

Restaurants *Casa de Mãe*, Rua Pedro Afonso 230, up hill from *Hotel Reis Magos*, regional food, rec.; Rua Princesa Isabel No. 717-C has *Bom Demais*, cheap, good; same street, *Casa Grande*, good value; *Casa da Maçã*, Av. Marechal Deodoro, central, beer and good, cheap dishes; *Pietro's*, same avenue, opp. cathedral, cheap, good; *Marinho*, Rua do Areial 265, 15 mins. walk from centre, clean, friendly, inexpensive; *Raizes*, Av. Campos Sales, with C. Mossoró, good regional dishes; *Tirraguso*, Av. Café Filho 27, good; *Rampa*, Rio Potengi, good for grilled fish but not service; *Café de Paris*, south end of Praia de Meio, very good and cheap. *Thin-San*, Mipibu 710, Petrópolis, Chinese, quite good, not expensive. Vegetarian (with shops): *Amai*, General Varela 624, and *A Microbiótica*, Princesa Isabel 524. Good, inexpensive lanchonetes on Rua Judas Tadéu, just off Rio Branco. For snacks try the stalls outside the *Hotel Reis Magos*; there are also various restaurants along the beach road nearby, where itinerant musicians play. Try the restaurants on the point that separates Praias dos Artistas and da Areia Preta (e.g. *Calamar*), for seafood.

Cables Embratel, Av. Duque de Caxias 99. T 1230. International phone calls, Telern, 2 blocks behind cathedral.

Exchange Cash advances against Visa card at Banco do Brasil only. *Hotel Luxor Natal* will change dollars cash and AmEx cheques, but not Thomas Cook.

Tourist Information Centro de Turismo (a converted prison with handicraft shops) Rua Aderbal de Figueiredo s/n, off Rua General Cordeiro, Petrópolis; Rodoviária and Aeroporto Augusto Severo. Natal is a very poor place to change money.

Tourist Agencies Aertur, Rua João Pessoa 219; Bradesco, Av. Rio Branco 692, 1°andar; Aparecida Turismo, Av. Rio Branco, Ed. Barão do Rio Branco.

Airport Augusto Severo, 15 km. from centre; flights to Belém, Brasília, Cuiabá, Fortaleza, Manaus, Recife, Rio, Salvador, São Paulo and other cities. Bus every half-hour from old bus station near centre US$0.35, taxi US$9.50.

Bus (terminal, with luggage store, is about 6 km. out of town, bus "Cidade de Esperança Av. 9", "Areia Preta via Petrópolis" or "Via Tirol" to centre). To Recife, 5 hrs., US$3.50; to Fortaleza, 8 hrs., US$5 (*leito*—freezing—US$12); to Maceio, buses of Real Alagoas go either direct, or via Recifé, 4-6 hrs.; to João Pessoa, US$2.50, 3 hrs.

At Pirangi, 25 km. S, or 30 mins. by bus from new Rodoviária, is the world's largest cashew-nut tree (*cajueiro*); branches springing from a single trunk cover an area of some 7,300 square metres. From Natal (Viação Campos), 5 times a day from 0630 to 1815, 3 on Sun., 0730, 0930, 1645; the snack bar by the tree has schedules of buses back to Natal. A number of good beaches and attractive villages may be found along this coast. North of Natal are extensive cashew plantations.

Beaches Natal has excellent beaches (for example Ponta Negra, with many new hotels and restaurants, 20 mins. by bus from centre), pleasant and "quaint" atmosphere, some on the far side of the Potengi river, for example Redinha and Genipabu—where you can toboggan down the sand-dunes—reached by direct bus from old Rodoviária, last bus back from Genipabu at 1730—N.B. muggings have been reported in Genipabu. Praia do Meio, however, is reported as depressing and treeless. You can hire buggies to get to the beaches for US$20-30 a day, or by the hour.

The state of Rio Grande do Norte (whose people are called "Potiguares" after an Indian tribe that now resides at Jacaré de São Domingos, municipality of Rio Tinto in neighbouring Paraíba state) has three main paved roads radiating from Natal: S to João Pessoa and Recife, SW to Caicó and W to Mossoró and Fortaleza. Between **Caicó** (*Hotel Guanabara*, rec., F) and **Mossoró** (pop. 158,000) (*Hotel Termas*, C, comfortable, with a hot, mineral water pool system, each pool on a terrace, with temperatures ranging from 54°C at the top to 30°C at the bottom; *Hotel Grand*, F, *Hotel Pax* next to market; *Hotel Zenilândia*, F, highly rec.) there is a turning to **Patu** with its huge basilica on a hillside, with passable "hotels", rather primitive. Trains run twice a week S from Mossoró to Sousa, via Patu. From Mossoró you can visit the salt pans at Grossos on the coast, but get written permission from the administrative offices in Mossoró. Bus Mossoró-Aracati at 0800 with Emp. Nordeste, 2 hrs., US$1.15.

Fortaleza (pop. 1,600,000), capital of the State of Ceará, is about 520 km. from Natal, NW along the coast (population of Ceará state 6,207,000). It is 1,600 km. by road from Belém and 885 km. from Recife. There are fair dirt roads throughout the State, and paved roads W to São Luís and SE to Recife; the federal highway S to Salvador (BR-116) is now largely paved but much is in poor condition. A fine tourist centre in the old prison on the waterfront (Av. Senador Pompeu 350) includes the Museu de Arte e Cultura Popular (open Mon.-Fri., 0800-1200, 1400-1800, Sat. 0800-1200, most interesting), shops and restaurants. Other museums: Museu Histórico e Antropológico do Ceará, Av. Barão de Studart 410 (open Tues.-Fri., 0730-1230, 1430-1730, Sat.-Sun., 0800-1200, 1400-1800; take bus marked "Dom Luís"); in the next street, the Museum of Ceará's Minerals, Rua

José Vilar 196 (open Mon.-Fri., 0700-1300), bus to centre, "Praia do Futuro" or "Serviluz". Museu das Secas, Pedro Pereira 683, 0800-1100, 1400-1700, collections of photographs and anti-drought equipment. Also visit Forte Nossa Senhora da Assunção, originally built by the Dutch. The mausoleum of President Castello Branco (1964-67), next to the state government building, may be visited. The new cathedral, in gothic style but built in concrete, stands oppsite the Mercado Central; it is beautiful stained glass windows. At night the centre of town is dead, but by day it is very busy with vendors and crowds. Still, it is not over-agitated or dirty.

Beaches are fine (take bus marked "P. Futuro" from Praça Castro Carreira, "Praia Circular" bus which does a circular route to Praia Futuro, or bus marked "Caça e Pesca", which passes all SE beaches on its route), and you can watch the boats coming in before sundown with their catch. The majority of high class hotels are on the beach from Praia de Iracema (which is the most popular beach, though now described as unsuitable for swimming; in the evenings everyone promenades along this beach and on Sunday a huge TV screen is erected on the beach close to *Hotel Beira Mar*—see and be seen!). Another near town is Barra do Ceará, where the Rio Ceará flows into the sea. Praia do Futuro is 8 km. to the SE, Praia de Icaraí 22 km. to the NW (it is under development); also Cumbuco where one can swim safely and there are palm trees (bus from Av. Tristão Gonçalves to Caucaia, then another bus). Iguape beach is recommended, but is at end of 90 min. bus ride—São Benedito bus marked "Iguape" from Praça F. de Melo (trips on *jangadas* for US$7). Beaches not suitable for bathing are Diarios, Meireles, Volta da Jurema and Mucuripe. The Serra de Maranguape with tropical growth and distant views back to the city is 30 km. inland. The local dance, *forró*, can be experienced at the *Clube dos Vaqueiros* out on the BR-116 road South, Wed. 2230; or at *Viva Maria*, Vieira e Estados Unidos, Sat. at 2200 (check by phone first).

Local Holidays 6 Jan. (Epiphany); Ash Wed.; 19 March (São José); Christmas Eve; New Year's Eve, half-day.

A festival takes place on the last Sunday in July, during which the traditional *jangada* (raft) races take place. On 15 August, the local Umbanda *terreiros* (churches) celebrate the Festival of Iemanjá on Praia do Futuro, taking over the entire beach from noon till dusk, when offerings are cast into the surf. Well worth attending (members of the public may "pegar um passo"— enter into an inspired religious trance—at the hands of a *pai-de-santo*). Beware of pick-pockets and purse-snatchers.

Hotels *Beira Mar*, on beach, T 224-4744, swimming pool, A; *Novotel*, Av. Pres. Kennedy 2380, T 244-1122, A; *Othon Palace*, 5-star, T 224-7777, beach front location; *Esplanada Praia*, Av. Presidente Kennedy 2000, T 224-8555, A; *Colonial*, 4-star, T 211-9644, pleasant, with best grounds and biggest pool, laundry service, reported to be somewhat run down (10 mins. walk from Av. Kennedy). *Nordeste Palace*, Rua Assunção 99 in centre, large rooms, friendly, good value; *Samburá Praia*, Av. Beira Mar 4530, T 224-8929, B, cheaper than most beach hotels; *Pousada Jardim*, run by Sr. Abelardo Bezerra at Ildefonso Albano 950 (T 231-7991) in Aldeota district, by Iracema beach, B, very clean, friendly, nice garden, excursions arranged, many languages spoken, warmly rec.; another on same street, No. 644, E, clean and friendly (T 226-9206); *Ondas Verdes*, Av. Pres. Kennedy 934, T 226-0871, D, fan, TV, shower, clean, rec.; *Cabana Praia*, at Rua João Lourenço 441 (224-2557) and at Av. Rui Barbosa 555, both D, small, friendly; *Excelsior*, Guilherme Rocha 172, T 211-0233, D, with good breakfast, no bath; *San Campio*, Guilherme Rocha 1156, a/c, D, quiet, friendly. *Chevalier*, Av. Duque de Caxias 465, T 231-4611, E with bath and fan, pleasant; *Blumenau*, Rua 25 de Março 705, T 221-1892, E, noisy, a/c, TV, friendly, helpful; *Lord*, Praça José de Alencar, T 231-6188, F and up, private bath, hot water, fan, large and clean but single rooms may be poor (restaurant not rec.). *Pousada da Praia*, Av. Mons. Tabosa 1315, Iracema, 2 blocks from beach, E, fan, valuables may be left in safe of English-speaking owner, rec., buses to centre stop at door; *Pousada Osvaldo Cruz*, R. Osvaldo Cruz, F, rec; *Pousada do Mar*, behind *Esplanada*, near Av. Mons. Tabosa, F, clean and friendly; *Pousada d'Antonietta*, Carlos Vasconcelos 660, T 224-3454, good breakfast, clean, quiet, 5 mins. from beach, buses to centre and other beaches nearby, E with bath; *Paraíso da Praia*, R. dos Pacajus 109, Iracema, small, on beach, helpful and friendly, good *trattoria* next door; *Apart-hotel, Aquidabá*, Av. Aquidabá 630, T 226-1405, at beginning of Praia Iracema, 20 mins.' walk from centre, F and up, with bath, pool and bar, clean, quiet; *Nossa Pousada*, Rua Ana Bilhar 123, Meireles, E without bath, near beach, friendly, helpful. Inexpensive hotels along Rua Senador Pompeu, e.g. No. 492, *Savoy*, E with breakfast (cheaper rooms without bath), basic, grubby but friendly; *Moreira*, No. 562, F with fan, central, good, clean, laundry; *Universo*, at No. 1152, F without breakfast, clean, friendly, may rent by the bed (i.e. single sex clients 3 to a room) some rooms have mosquito nets; No.725, *Tio Patinho 2*, F, less good than *Tio Patinho 3*. *Jacanã*, Rua 24 de Maio 845, E with breakfast; across street are *Tio Patinho 3* and *Dormitório Belo Horizonte*, both F. *Passeio*, Rua Dr. João Moreira 221, E with bath, fan, good breakfast, good value. *Caxambu*, General Bezerril 22 (T 231-0339), a/c, D with breakfast, and bath, clean, good value, but poor food, central (opposite Cathedral, in market area). Note that the central area is deserted at night. *Amuarama*, T 227-4744, D, pool, sauna, by Rodoviária (6 km. from centre), entrance by service station. Try student houses on Av. Universitários, cheap or even free. **Youth Hostel**: Rua Frei Mansueta 370, T 244-1254, IYHA card with photo necessary.

Camping Official site about 10 km south of city, 2 kms along a bumpy road off the highway, signposted, expensive US$3.50 p.p.

Electric Current 220 volts A.C., 60 cycles.

Restaurants Several good fish restaurants at far end of Av. Presidente Kennedy, where the boats come ashore between 1300 and 1500, for example, *Trapiche*, No. 3950 (expensive, but excellent except for wine list). At Praia de Iracema (Av. Kennedy 4616) are *Alfredo* (good fish) and, next door, *Peixada do Meio* (better). Italian are *La Trattoria*, Praia de Iracema between Tabajaras and Av. Kennedy, and *La Távola*, Aquidabá 393, good pizzas. *Sandras*, Av. Perimetral, Praia do Futuro, lobster from US$7 upwards, has been specially rec. *Rancho Gaúcho*, Praia Náutica (between *Novotel* and *Othon Palace*), good. *Churrascaria Tourão*, Av. Mons. Tabosa, all you can eat for US$4.50; *Opção*, Mons. Tabosa with Albano, good, inexpensive. Good restaurant in Clube Náutico. A short taxi ride from Clube Náutico is *O Ozias*, Rua Canuto de Aguiar 1449 (T 224-9067), good for seafood, but hard to find. Good Chinese: *HongKong*, Av. Pres. Kennedy 4544, Mucuripe, and *Tung Hua*, Av. Visconde de Mauá 81, Meireles. Vegetarian: *Caminho á Saúde*, lunch only, US$1.50, very good value, Barão do Rio Branco 1468; next door is *Alivita*, Barão do Rio Branco 1486, good, lunch only, US$1, Mon.-Fri.; *Céu da Boca*, Rua Franklin Távora 136, lunch and 1800-2000 Mon.-Fri., good and inexpensive. *Rio Lanches*, Almirante Barroso 1003, good sandwiches and fruit juice; *Caminho á Saúde* also has lanchonete and store at Mons. Tabosa 1326. *Kury*, Rua Senador Pompeu 959, good food at reasonable prices; opp is a good Chinese restaurant. Another good place in centre is *Belas Artes*, Major Facundo 82, just up from Passeio Público. Cheap meals at railway station. Emcetur restaurant, in old prison, good atmosphere. Good view of Fortaleza from *Restaurant Panorámico*, Rua Mirante, in Mucuripe district, near the lighthouse.

Shopping Fortaleza has an excellent selection of textiles at reasonable prices (among the cheapest in Brazil) and some handicrafts. Also good for clothes. The local specialities are lace (some hand-made) and embroidered textile goods; also hammocks (US$8-10—try Gerardo, Loja Cifa, Travessa Crato 28/32, in mall opp. Mercado central), fine alto-relievo wood carvings of North-East scenes, basket ware and clay figures (*bonecas de barro*). Bargaining is O.K. at the Mercado Central in the Praça da Sé, and the Emcetur tourist market in the old prison (more expensive). Every night (1800-2300), there are stalls along Av. Pres. Kennedy (the beach), lively but more expensive than the Mercado Central, where some stallholders will accept a better price if you're paying in dollars. The Centro de Artesanato Lucila Távora is decaying. Boutiques along Monsenhor Tabosa between Senador Almino and João Cordeiro. Cashew nuts at the Mercado Central are excellent.

Car Hire Beach buggies rentable for US$30 a day plus small km. charge, from Junna's Buggy, Av. Abolição 2480, T 244-7872.

Theatre Teatro José de Alencar, near railway station in centre, built 1810, building contains also newer theatre built 1910.

Exchange Lloyds Bank, Rua Barão do Rio Branco 862; and national banks. Open 0900-1630. Exchange at Tropical Viagens, Rua Barão do Rio Branco 1233, English spoken, or at Ari, Sapataria Brasileira, Rua Gen. Bezerril 142, or at the Zely shop in the old prison.

Post Office in centre. Parcels must be taken to Receita Federal office at Barão de Aracati

909, Aldeota (take "Dom Luiz" bus).

Telephone International calls from Emcetur hut on Iracema beach and from Teleceará offices (Rua João Moreira esq. Rua Floriano Peixoto).

Cables Embratel, Rua Castro e Silva 286/290.

Tourist Information Emcetur, in ex-municipal prison, helpful, has maps. Open 0700-1800, Sun. 0700-1200. Also on Iracema beach.

Tourist Agencies Mundiatur (helpful, English spoken), Turismo Viagens, Itala Viagens Turismo and Intertur. Advised that it is best to book beach trips through Emcetur.

Rail South to Baturité (tourist train round trip Sun.).

Air Service Direct flights to Belém, Recife, Rio and other cities in Brazil. Bus from airport to Praça José de Alencar.

Bus Service New bus station 6 km. from centre, bus to Praça José de Alencar marked Aguanambi 1 or 2 (and others); no luggage store, only lockers. The Expresso de Luxo runs daily to Recife (12 hrs., US$11, leave at night), also Rio de Janeiro, 48 hrs., US$45 (*leito* 90), São Paulo, 48 hrs., US$46 (*leito* 92), Crato, Parnaíba, and many other cities. To Brasília, Expresso Ipu-Brasília, same company to Belo Horizonte, 42 hrs. Salvador, 19 hrs., US$18; Natal, US$5, 8 hrs. (Nordeste has *leito* US$14, an *executivo* at noon, and 5 semi-leitos which make only 3 stops); Teresina, US$7, 9 hrs. (at least); São Luís, US$16, 18 hrs., 4 a day; Belém US$21, 5 buses a day, 23 hrs., (2 companies, Exp. Timbira good). To Piripiri, for Parque Nacional de Sete Cidades, US$5, 9 hrs.

Excursions *Caponga* beach, to the SE, is reached by direct bus from Fortaleza (2 a day) or by taking a bus from Fortaleza to Cascavel (80 mins., US$0.75) then a bus from Cascavel (20 mins., US$0.25); accommodation at *Caponga Praia*, on the beach front, simple cheap rooms and good meals, and at *Pousada Sereia*, very friendly, good, E. A ½-hour walk S along the deserted white-sand beach leads to a river mouth, offering a combination of fresh-and salt-water bathing. *Jangadas* set sail in the early morning (arrangements can be made to accompany fishermen on overnight trips); there is a fish market on the beach. 174 km. SE of Fortaleza is *Aracati* (bus every 2 hrs., US$1.70; bus to Natal, via Mossoró, 6 hrs., US$5). From this town take a VW Combi-Bus to *Canoa Quebrada* (US$0.50, from corner of Gen Pompeu e Tableau João Paulo—taxi US$3.50), a fishing village on a sand dune, 10 km. from Aracati. There are now many *pousadas* (*Pousada Cultural*, F, basic, clean, friendly; 2 rooms behind *Sol de Manhã* café on mainstreet, clean, with shower, F, good breakfast in the café; *Tenda do Cumbe*, at end of road on cliff, thatched huts E, restaurant, warmly rec.; also on cliff above beach, *Pousada Ao Nascer do Sol*, F, clean, shower, friendly, hammocks for rent) and villagers will let you sling your hammock or put you up for about US$1.50 (Brendan is rec., but his food is expensive, European books exchanged; Sr Miguel rents good clean houses for US$7.50 a day); bars and restaurants for food, vegetarian food in *Espácio Cultural*, cheap seafood (don't drink the water); only a few places have running water. Nowhere to change money. The village is famous for its *labirinto* lacework and coloured sand sculpture, for sand-skiing on the dunes, for the sunsets, and for the beaches, though beware of jiggers (*bicho de pé*), best to wear shoes. Canoa Quebrada has been "discovered" and is becoming a major tourist attraction; basic tours (no food) from Fortaleza, 12 hrs., US$10.

   40 km. from Fortaleza, along the coast, is *Prainha*, a fishing village and weekend resort (bus terminal in Fortaleza opp. Escola Normal at 1430 and 1700, return 1530 and 1800). You can see *jangadas* coming in daily in the late afternoon. The beaches are clean and largely empty. *Prainha Solex Hotel*, Rua Pericich Ribeiro 5, T 361-1000/01/02, ramal 156.7, D, pool, comfortable. Good fish restaurant, *O Leonção*, on same street. There are several small, cheap and good restaurants, where it is possible to see displays of the *carimbó*, the main local dance of Ceará. 87 km. from Fortaleza (too far for a day trip) is *Morro Branco* (4 km. from Beberibe, bus), with spectacular beach, craggy cliffs and beautiful views. *Jangadas* leave the beach at 0500, returning at 1400-1500; hotel-restaurants, E; *Cabana do Morro*, *Pousada do Morro*, E, clean, but mosquitoes, fan and shower, *Novo*, E, clean, noisy at weekends and *Recanto Praia*, F, clean, good breakfast, rec. (first two have swimming pool); *Pousada Sereia*, F, on the beach, clean, good breakfast, friendly, highly rec; or you can rent fishermen's houses; meals can also be arranged at beach-front bars (try *O Jangadeiro*). Double room for rent at *Bar São Francisco*, F, or 7-room house for rent. São Benedito bus from Fortaleza, US$1; 2½ hrs., 4 a day. To get to Natal, take 0600 bus to Beberibe, then 0800 bus (only one) to Aracati, US$0.50, then on to Natal. Town is very crowded at holiday time. No money exchange available.

   Two hours NW of Fortaleza by bus is *Paracuru*, a small fishing port (fish readily available), which is being developed as Ceará's carnival city (*Teto da Praia*, E, cooking facilities, close to beach; restaurant *Ronco do Mar*, good fish dishes also *Balança do Mar* and a pizzaria; breakfast at Dona Luci's *sitio*, No. 25 in the market; *Boca do Poço* bar is scene of *forró* at weekends). It has some lovely deserted white sand beaches with good bathing, and the people are very friendly. Some 7 hours from Fortaleza is the sleepy fishing village of **Almofala**, served by many buses. There is electricity, but no hotels or restaurants, although locals rent hammock space and cook meals (usually US$2 p.p., food and lodging). Bathing is better elsewhere, but the area is surrounded by dunes and is excellent for hiking along the beach to nearby lobster-fishing communities. In Almofala, the church with much of the town was covered by shifting sands and remained covered for 50 years, reappearing in the 1940s.

Nestled in the dunes near the border with the state of Piauí is the tiny fishing community of **Jericuacuara** (known as Serrote by locals). Described as one of Brazil's most secluded primitive beaches, it is becoming increasingly popular with travellers and Brazilians, crowded Jan. to March, despite the difficulty of getting there. There is no real road, so the trip is part of the adventure: take the bus from Sobral or Fortaleza to Gijoca at 0800 or 2000 (8 hrs., US$4), then a jeep meets the bus: Jericuacuara from Gijoca costs about US$2 per person for the hour-and-a-half journey. A direct journey from Fortaleza on a 2 or 3-day tour is possible in a VW Kombi, book through an hotel or T 244-5974, Maria do Carmo. You can also get there by boat "seasickness guaranteed", or bus from Camocim, *Hotel Lusitania*, F, (a little further west). Once there, the visitor is rewarded with towering sand dunes, deserted beaches with little shade, cactus-covered cliffs rising from the sea, and a chance to savour life in a sleepy, primitive fishing community. Pigs, chickens and donkeys roam the streets at will; there is no electricity and no running water (take your showers at the town pump). Fortunately, ice-cold beer is available in several tiny lantern-lit bars and there is *forró* on Fri. and Sat. nights. Many locals rent hammock space (US$0.50), hammocks, and cook food (about US$2 per day, room and board), and there are three *pousadas* (E): *O Alemão*, rec; *Pousada Natur* with a restaurant belonging to a very helpful German. There are several restaurants serving vegetarian and fish dishes (*Restaurante Central*, rec.). Fresh banana tart available most days at about 1300. Several shops sell basic provisions, so camping is possible. Returning, the bus leaves Gijoca for Fortaleza at midnight and 0630.

The pilgrimage centre of Canindé may be visited, 3-hour bus ride from Box 21 of the Rodoviária (Viação Nova Esperança). Large modern church on hill with carved baptistery doors, many ex-votos, interesting dry-land vegetation along route. (Hotels: *Plaza*, by basilica, food OK; *Santo Antônio*). Another inland town, Baturité, can be seen, 3 hrs. from Rodoviária (Box 45) by Redenção bus, mornings only, also a tourist train round trip Sundays.

The Ubajara cave in the **Ubajara National Park** is worth seeing; it is 18 km. off the road to Teresina, on a good paved road, 3 km. from Ubajara town. A cablecar used to descend the cliff to the cave entrance but has not been repaired since it broke down in 1985 and the visitors centre is closed. Ask for a guide at the park entrance (they leave at 0800 for the 6 km. round trip); a torch is necessary for the cave, which is an hour's walk down a rocky, wooded path (also take drinking water). The views of the *sertão* from the upper cablecar platform are superb. Here is the *Pousada Neblina*, E, near caves, with swimming pool, with breakfast and private shower, meals rec.; opposite is an unnamed hostel, G with bath, clean, friendly, rustic, restaurant, rec. In **Ubajara** town are *Hotel Gruta*, Rua 31 de Dezembro 74, F, basic, good breakfast, and *Hotel Churrascaria Ubajara*, Rua Juvêncio Pereira 370, E, clean and friendly, hot water, good breakfast, restaurant. Interesting Sunday morning market. Several buses a day to Fortaleza.

The road to Sobral and Teresina is paved, but in poor condition. To hitch-hike to Teresina, take a bus W to the BR-222, the Teresina road.

Sobral (pop. 112,000), the principal town in western Ceará and well-known for straw hats, has *Hotel Municipal*, E, meals available. South of Sobral is the remote town of **Crateús** (pop. 68,000), rail link, but no paved roads there, with the *Crateús Palace Hotel*, very reasonable and clean, F, with breakfast. Good restaurant, *Churrascaria Pequena Cabana*, at back of hotel. Bus service from Crateús over very bad road to Teresina, every two days. At Tianguá, 311 km. from Fortaleza on the Teresina road, is *Serra Grande* hotel, all amenities, D, good.

Between the states of Maranhão and Piauí runs the river Parnaíba. Near its mouth is the anchorage of Luís Correia, where ships unload for final delivery by tugs and lighters at **Parnaíba** (pop. 116,000) 15 km. up river, the collecting and distributing centre for the trade of Piauí: tropical products and cattle.

Hotels *Parnaíba Palace*; *Rio Parnaíba*. *Cívico*, E with bath and a/c, good breakfast, friendly, rec.; *Rodoviária*, F and other basic hotels in the centre.

Beaches at Luís Correia, which with Parnaíba has radioactive sands (good hotel at Luís Correia, F). Some 15 km. from Parnaíba is Pedra do Sal: dark blue lagoons and palm trees. At Lagoa de Portinho there are bungalows, a bar and restaurant and it is possible to camp; canoes for hire.

Teresina (pop. 475,000) about 435 km. up the Parnaíba river, is the capital of the State of Piauí, (pop 2,584,000) reputed to be the poorest in Brazil. There are paved road and rail connections with the neighbouring state capitals. The city itself is reputed to be the hottest after Manaus (temperatures rise to 42°C). The Palácio de Karnak (the old governor's palace), just South of Praça Frei Serafim, can be visited, Mon.-Fri., 1530-1730; it contains lithographs of the Middle East in 1839 by David Roberts R.A. There is an interesting open market by the Praça Marechal Deodoro and the river is picturesque, with washing laid out to dry along its banks. The market is a good place to buy hammocks, but bargain hard. Every morning along the river bank there is the *troca-troca* where people buy, sell and swap, but it is no longer spontaneous; an under-cover complex (Mercado Central do Artesanato) has been built at Rua Paissandu 1276 (Praça Dom Pedro II), open daily 0800-2200 (not weekends). Most of the year the river is low, leaving sandbanks known as *coroas* (crowns).

Hotels *Luxor Hotel do Piauí*, A, T 222-4911, and *Teresina Palace*, T 222-2770, luxury class; *Grande*, Firmino Pires 73, F, very friendly and clean; *Sambaíba*, Rua Gabriel Ferreira 230-N, 2-star, T 223-6711, C, central, good; *Victoria*, Senador T. Pacheco 1199, F, friendly, basic, clean; *São José*, João Cabral 340, T 223-2176, E, reasonable restaurant; *Fortaleza*, Felix Pacheco 1101, Prça. Saraiva, T 222-2984, F, fan, basic, rec.; many cheap hotels and *dormitórios* around Praça Saraiva. *Rex*, Rui Barbosa 36, E, central, clean, a/c, good breakfast; *Gurgueia*, Rui Barbosa 519, D, a/c; *Viana*, R. Senador T. Pacheco 899, F, cheap. Many cheap ones in Rua São Pedro: *Bom Clima*, No.890, E; *São Pedro*, No. 905, E; *Globo*, No. 861, E; and in Rua Alvaro Mendes, *Glória*, at 823 (clean, best); and at 860, 906, all E. No hotels at new Rodoviária as yet.

Restaurants *Churrascaria Gaúcha*, 12 km. W of newer river bridge, with all the meat you can eat for US$3.50. For fish dishes, *Pesqueirinho*, near the confluence of the rivers in Poti Velho district. Many eating places for all pockets in Praça Dom Pedro II. (*Típico do Piauí*, good value).

Shopping Supermarket on Praça Marechal Deodoro 937, clean, good, fresh food. Local handicrafts include leather and clothes.

Exchange For parallel market try Banorte Turismo, Av. Pacheco and Barbosa. Larger hotels may be helpful (e.g. *Luxor do Piauí*).

Laundry Tintoraria São Paulo, Rui Barbosa 431, nr. *Luxor Hotel do Piaui*.

Tourist Information Piemtur, Rua Alvaro Mendes 2003, Caixa Postal 36, information office at Rua Magalhães Filho s/n (next to 55 N -English spoken); kiosks at Rodoviária and airport.

Buses The bus trip from Fortaleza is scenic and takes 9 hrs. (US$7, *leito* at 2100, arr. 0600, US$14). Another road, very bad, leads inland to Porto Franco and Imperatriz on the Belém-Brasília highway (**see page** 430); daily bus takes 26-40 hrs. for the trip to Imperatriz (US$9), depending on the state of the road; these buses are very crowded. There are direct buses to Belém, but avoid the non-express (*parador*) service. The road to São Luís is quite good, bar a few potholes. Another main road, runs SE to Picos (*Hotel Picos*, E, basic, but a/c); from there a good road runs via Salgueiro (many *pousadas*) to Recife (800 km.) and another to Petrolina, on the River São Francisco opposite the Bahian town of Juazeiro. Bus, one or two a day, 15 hrs., US$10. Buses from Petrolina/Juazeiro (see page 407) SE to Salvador. Bus to Belém, about 16 hrs., US$12. To São Luís, bus takes 7 hrs., US$5.

Rail Teresina-Parnaíba, mixed train, once a week but often cancelled.

Air Flights to Recife via Fortaleza, to Brasília and Salvador.

Excursion Some 190 km. NE of Teresina and 12 km. from Piracuruca is the interesting 20-sq. km. Parque Nacional de **Sete Cidades** with its strange eroded rock formations, just off the Fortaleza-Teresina road. From the ground it looks like a medley of weird monuments. The inscriptions on some of the rocks have never been deciphered; one Austrian researcher in the

1920s suggested links with the Phoenicians, and the Argentine Professor Jacques de Mahieu, considers them to be Nordic runes left by the Vikings. There is plenty of birdlife. If hiking in the park, beware of rattlesnakes. IBDF guides drive round the park (2½ hrs.), you may be able to get around on their tractor, or else walk (takes all day, very hot). Small booklet with sketch map (not really good enough for walking), US$0.20; entrance US$0.30. There are camping facilities (US$0.60) and two natural swimming pools, although several years of drought have lowered their water level drastically. Local food is limited and monotonous: bring a few delicacies, and especially fruit.

6 km. from the park entrance is the hotel *Fazenda Sete Cidades*, C, with private bathroom, swimming pool, good restaurant and free bicycle or horse transport (it is at Km. 63 on BR-222, T (086) 261-3642); also has a free pick-up to the park (and a most unpleasant zoo). In the park is a IBDF (Forestry Institute) hostel, G p.p., rooms with bath, pleasant, good restaurant, natural pool nearby, rec.

A free bus service leaves the Praça in **Piripiri** (in front of Telpisa office), 26 km. away, at 0700, passing *Hotel Fazenda Sete Cidades* at 0800, reaching the park 10 mins. later; return at 1630, or hitch-hike. Taxi from Piripiri, US$8, or from Piracuruca, US$10. Bus Teresina-Piripiri and return, throughout the day 2½ hrs., US$2.10. Bus São Luis-Piripiri, 1200, 1630, 2130, 10 hrs., US$6.50. Several daily buses Piripiri-Fortaleza, 9 hrs. US$5. Bus Piripiri-Ubajara (see previous page), marked "São Benedito", with Itapemirim, 2½ hrs.; US$2, first at 0700 (a beautiful trip, although one dirt stretch will get your belongings dusty unless protected by plastic). Hotels in Piripiri: *Dos Viajantes*, G, basic and clean; *Piripiri*, both near bus offices and behind the church. Exchange at the bank only.

In the south of the state is **Oeiras**, old capital of Piauí, where the state government is restoring some of the old buildings, such as the bishop's palace and the church of Nossa Senhora da Vitória.

Maranhão state (pop. 4,978,000) is about the size of Italy; its land is flat and low-lying, with highlands to the S. The Atlantic coastline—a mass of sandbanks and creeks and sandy islands on one of which stands São Luís—is 480 km. long. A quarter of Maranhão is covered with *babaçu* palms, and by far the most important products are *babaçu* nuts and oil. Rice often takes second place, but well behind *babaçu*. There are salt pans along the coast. The huge Boa Esperança hydroelectric plant on the Parnaíba river now floods the State with energy, and some petroleum has been discovered. The main road from Teresina passes through the Maranhense town of Caxias, which has a good churrascaria, *Selva do Braz* (Av. Central 601), live music in the evening.

São Luís (pop. 560,000) the capital and port of Maranhão state, founded in 1612 by the French and named for St. Louis of France, is about 560 km. west of Fortaleza (1,080km. by road) and 400 km. SE of Belém (830 km. by road) in a region of heavy tropical rains, but the surrounding deep forest has been cut down to be replaced by babaçu palms. The city stands upon São Luís island between the bays of São Marcos and São José. The urban area extends to São Francisco island, connected with São Luís by three bridges. The old part, on very hilly ground with many steep streets, is still almost pure colonial (it has been restored with generally splendid results): the damp climate stimulated the use of ceramic tiles for exterior walls, and São Luís shows a greater variety of such tiles than anywhere else in Brazil, in Portuguese, French and Dutch styles. See the Governor's Palace (state rooms open Mon., Wed., Fri. 1500-1800, take passport, beautiful floors of dark wood (*jacarandá*) and light (*cerejeira*), marvellous views from terrace) and the old slave market. The best colonial churches to see—some of them rebuilt and not improved by it—are the Cathedral and the churches of Carmo, São João, Rosário, and Santana. On Largo do Desterro is the church of São José do Desterro, finished in 1863, but with some much older parts. The restored Fortaleza de Santo Antônio, built originally by the French in 1614, is on the bank of the River Anil at Ponta d'Areia. The Fonte do Ribeirão, Largo do Ribeirão, was begun in 1796. The Museu do Estado, in a fine early 19th century mansion (complete with slave quarters) at Rua do Sol 302, US$0.35, is open Tues.-Fri., 1400-1800, Sat.-Sun., and holidays, 1500-1800. Also on the Rua do Sol is the Teatro Artur Azevedo

(1816). The commercial quarter is still much as it was in the 17th century; best shopping area is Rua de Santana near Praça João Lisboa. Visit the Fábrica Canhamo, a restored factory now housing an arts and crafts centre, near Praia Grande. The Centro da Creatividade Odylo Costa Filho, Praia Grande, is an arts centre with theatre, cinema, exhibitions, music, etc., with a bar and café, a good meeting place.

Festivals On 24 June (São João), the "Bumba-Meu-Boi", a fantastic bull dance and masque with traditional words. For several days before the festival street bands parade, particularly in front of the São João and São Benedito churches. The São Benedito, at the Rosário church in August. Festival in October, with dancing, at Vila Palmeira suburb (take bus of same name).

Hotels *Quatro Rodas*, 8 km. from centre on Calhau beach, T 227-0244, A, excellent, with all facilities; *Vila Rica*, 5-star, Praça D. Pedro II, T 222-4455, A, central, many amenities; *Pousada Colonial*, Rua Afonso Pena, D-E, in beautiful restored, tiled house; *Lord*, E, Rua Joaquim Távora 258, T 222-5544 facing Praça Benedito Leite, comfortable, clean, rec., good breakfast; nearby is *Central*, Av. D. Pedro II 258, more expensive, but noisy at night with TV, D. *São Marcos*, D, Saúde 178, T 221-4761, restored colonial house, a/c, family-run, rec. More basic, but with excellent food, *Pousada Solar do Carmo*, Largo do Carmo, T 222-2455, D-E, pleasant, friendly, light and airy. Many cheap hotels in Rua das Palmas, very central, and Rua Formosa; *Klauss*, opposite *São Marcos* in side street off Rua Formosa, F, friendly, dirty; *Novo Nazaré*, Rua de Nazaré (extension of Rua do Sol), F, central, fair facilities and breakfast, reckoned the best of the cheap hotels by one who has tried them all; *Estrela* F, Rua da Estrela 370, Centro (T 222-1083) clean, safe, rec; *Globo*, E, with bath (F without) and breakfast, friendly, quite clean; *Casa do Estudante*, Rua do Passeio, 2 km. from centre. *Pousada da Praia*, R dos Magistrados 10, E, helpful owner, mosquitoes. At Ponta d'Areia: *Ponta d'Areia*, Av. dos Holandeses, Quadra 13 (T 227-2737), about 3 km. from centre, C, a/c, bath, hot water, TV, fridge, restaurant, pool; *Praia Mar*, on the beach, B, 5-star, all amenities, opp. *São Francisco*. **Youth hostel**: *O Cortiço*, Rua 14 de Julho 93, central; *Albergue da Juventude*, Rua 14 de Julho 88, T 222-6258, F, restaurant open for lunch to non-residents, rec.

Restaurants *Solar do Riberão*, Rua Isaac Martins 141, T 222-3068, good buffet lunch and seafood, good value but not cheap, regional cuisine, closed Sat. p.m. and Sun.; *La Bohème*, on same street, very good food, live music, expensive, popular; *Candelabro*, Rua do Egito, very expensive but excellent international cuisine; *Base de Edilson*, Rua Vila Bessa, centre, shrimp only, excellent; *Hibiscus* Av. dos Franceses, and *Tia Maria*, Av. Nina Rodrigues (Ponta d'Areia), seafood, rec.; *Base do Germano*, Av. Wenceslau Bras in Canto da Fabril district, excellent *caldeirada de camarão* (shrimp stew), about US$4 per head. *Panorama*, Av. Dom Pedro II, 206, good, nice views; *Atenas*, Humberto de Campos 175, good stew for US$2; *Aliança*, Praça Benedito Leite, good regional food. *Egito*, friendly, good food and atmosphere; *Ladeira*, massive portions, share. *Naturaleza*, Rua da Formosa, vegetarian, good, lunch only, Mon.-Fri.; *Naturalista Alimentos*, Rua do Sol 517, very good, natural foods shop and restaurants, open till 1900. *Marjuce* in Rua das Palmas, good value. Said to be more choice in new São Francisco district, just across bridge, e.g. *Oriental*, Av. Pres. Castelo Branco, good Chinese, *Agapê*, good pizzas and *Pizzaria Internacional*.

Exchange Travellers' cheques only at Banco do Brasil; Agetur, Rua do Sol 33.

Cables Embratel, Avenida Dom Pedro II 190. T 2500.

Portuguese Lessons Sra Amin Castro, T 227-1527. rec.

Tourist Offices Av. dos Franceses, good information on walks in city. Recent travellers report Maratur offices of little use. Taguatur, in *Hotel Central* building, good. Town maps from agencies. Funai shop at Rua do Sol 371. Centro do Artesanato in main street of São Francisco suburb, over bridge from the city.

Airport Internal flights only. 15 km. from centre; buses ("São Cristovão") to city until midnight, US$0.20. Flight to Belém, US$46 (US$32 at night).

Railway Three trains a week on Carajás railway to Paraupebas, 16 hrs., 890 km., leave São Luís 0800, Mon. Wed., Fri., return 0300, Tues., Thur., Sat. (crowded, take own food); for station take "Vila Nova" or "Anjo da Guarda" bus.

Road Bus station 12 km. from centre on airport road, "Alemanha" bus to centre. The Teresina-São Luís road is paved ("just about OK"), bus service, US$5, 7 hrs. Bus to Piripiri, US$6.50, 10 hrs.; Expresso de Luxo continues to Fortaleza. Bus to Fortaleza, US$16, four a day, 18 hrs. (road also paved). Also to Recife, US$24, 25 hrs.

To Belém Direct road via Santa Inês and Alto Bonito paved, in reasonable condition, with petrol stations not far apart (about 9 hrs. driving with stop for lunch). There is a bus service 12 hrs., US$11, three daily (no *leito*). There are occasional coastal ships of the Costeira line.

Excursions Calhau is a huge beach, 10 km. away, excellent *Churrascaria Pavan*; Ponta D'Areia is nearer to São Luís but more crowded. An hour's bus ride from São Luís is Raposa, a fishing village built on stilts; another fishing village is Ribamar, a half hour's bus ride from São Luís, from in front of the market.

To the East of the city, on the Atlantic Coast is the **Parque Nacional Lençóis Maranhenses**, 155,000 hectares of beaches, lakes and dunes, with very little vegetation and largely unstudied wildlife. For information, the IBDF office is at Av. Jaime Tavares 25, São Luis (Caixa Postal 276, CEP 65.000).

Some 22 km. away by boat is ***Alcântara*** (city population 4,000, municipality 20,000) the former state capital, on the mainland bay of São Marcos. Construction of the city began at the beginning of the seventeenth century and it is now a historical monument. There are many old churches (e.g. the ruined Matriz de São Matias) and colonial mansions (see the Casa, and Segunda Casa, do Imperador, also the old cotton barons' mansions with their blue, Portuguese tiled façades), the traditional pillory, the Pelourinho, in the Praça Gomes de Castro, also a small museum in the square (US$0.20) and the Forte de São Sebastião (1653) now in ruins. See also the Fonte de Mirititiva. Good beaches, good walking around the coast (can be muddy after rain), mosquitoes after dark. A rocket-launching site has been built nearby. Principal festival: Festa do Divino, at Pentecost (Whitsun).

Transport A boat service leaves São Luís daily at between 0700 and 0800, but check time at the dock the day before as departure depends on the tides. The journey takes 90 minutes, from close to the Governor's palace, for Alcântara, returning between 1300 and 1400, but check return time, US$1 plus US$0.25 each for boat to take you from ferry to Alcântara dock; sea can be very rough.

Hotels *Pousada do Pelourinho*, Praça Gomes de Castro, D, clean, friendly, good restaurant, communal bathroom; *Pousada do Imperador*, D, some rooms with bath; *Pousada do Mordomo Regio*, C, rooms with bath, TV, refrigerator, good restaurant. One can also stay cheaply in houses (e.g. Dona Maria, 3rd house on left on Rua Neto Guterres, near harbour, US$1.50 for hammock space and 2 meals). Try bargaining for hammock space in private houses. Children who offer themselves as guides can help arrange accommodation in private houses, friendly but no great comfort; provide your own mineral water.
    Restaurante Tijupa has very good home cooking but meals must be ordered in advance, owner Claudio is the best guide in town; *Bar do Lobato*, on the praça, is pleasant, with good, simple food, fried shrimps highly rec.

On the Eastern bank of the Rio Tocantins, at Maranhão's western border with Goiás, is ***Imperatriz***, a city serving a large cattle region. Go down Av. Getúlio Vargas and see the range of goods on offer. It is also in an area of violence over landholding; in 1986, a priest was shot in his church. To get to the ferry across the river, go along Rua Luis Domingues, which runs parallel to Av. Getúlio Vargas. **Hotels**: *Poseidon*, Rua Paraíba 740, T 721-4466, central, best, D, a/c, TV, swimming pool, rec.; *Anápolis*, BR-010, Km. 1345, T 721-2255, opp. Rodoviária, E, a/c, fridge, swimming pool, friendly; a lot of cheap hotels near Rodoviária. Restaurant *Bar Central* is OK. There is a good, expensive discotheque at Beira Rio, north of the ferry crossing, *Fly Back Disco Club*; it has two dance floors, one fast, one slow (for couples only). Telephone office on Rua Rio Grande do Norte, a side street off Av. Getúlio Vargas, near *Hotel Poseidon*. Lying on the Belém-Brasília highway, Imperatriz has bus connections with both cities; there is a slow, crowded bus service to Teresina. To get to Marabá on the Transamazônica, you can either take a Transbrasiliana bus direct, 7-10 hrs (starting on the Belém highway, the bus then turns west along a poorer road, passing finally through destroyed forest, new fazendas and unplanned cities), or, a faster route, involving taking a ferry across the river in the early morning (0600-0700) to catch a pick-up on the other side, takes about 5 hours, but is more expensive.

NORTHERN BRAZIL (8)

Northern Brazil consists of the states of Pará, Amazonas, Amapá and Roraima. The northern states of Rondônia and Acre are dealt with under Section 9, Southern Amazonia.

The area is drained by the Amazon, which in size, volume of water—12 times that of the Mississippi—and number of tributaries has no equal in the world. At the base of the Andes, far to the west, the Amazonian plain is 1,300 km. in width, but east of the confluences of the Madeira and Negro rivers with the Amazon, the highlands close in upon it until there is no more than 80 km. of floodplain between them. Towards the river's mouth—about 320 km. wide—the plain widens once more and extends along the coast south-eastwards into the state of Maranhão and northwards into the Guianas.

Amazonia, much of it still covered with tropical forest, is 56% of the national area, equivalent to two-thirds of Canada. Its jungle is the world's largest and densest rain forest, with more diverse plants and animals than any other jungle in the world. It has only 8% of Brazil's population, and most of this is concentrated around Belém (in Pará), and in Manaus, 1,600 km. up the river. The population is sparse because other areas are easier to develop; the rainfall is heavy, the humidity high and the climate hot; and the soil, as in all tropical forest, is poor.

Successive Governments have made strenuous efforts to develop Amazonia. Roads have been built parallel to the Amazon to the south (the Transamazônica), from Cuiabá (Mato Grosso) northwards to Santarém (Pará), and NE from Porto Velho through Humaitá to the river bank opposite Manaus. Agricultural settlements are being established along these roads, and great concern has been expressed at the wholesale destruction of the forest. The area is changing rapidly, especially under the impetus of major energy and mining projects for bauxite and iron ore now in progress. This is reflected in the burgeoning cities. Manaus now suffers from air pollution.

Anyone interested in the Amazonian development programme and its ecological, social, economic and political effects should read Richard Bourne's masterly *Assault on the Amazon* (London, Gollancz, 1978), *Dreams of Amazonia*, by Roger D.Stone (Penguin, 1986), or *Amazon* by Brian Kelly and Mark London (Harcourt Brace Jovanovich, New York, 1983).

Along the Transamazônica

The Transamazônica, about 5,000 km. in length, represents the greater part of a direct road connection between Brazil's furthest E and furthest W points. It skirts the southern edge of the Amazonian plain, linking the following places: Estreito (junction with the Belém-Brasília highway, N of Araguaína, **see page** 461), Marabá (on the Tocantins river), Altamira (on the Xingu), São Luís do Tapajós, near Itaituba (on the Tapajós), Jacarèacanga, Humaitá (on the Madeira), Rio Branco, and Japim, in the far W of the State of Acre. The road was officially opened in December 1973; parts are paved and buses are running along virtually the whole length; they are operating between Marabá and Humaitá and there are also services from Santarém to the Belém-Brasília road and to Cuiabá along a very bad road; it is frequently impassable and closed in the rainy season (October onwards) and it is dangerous to stay in small villages en route.

From **Marabá** (pop. 135,000) (*Plaza*, Nova Marabá, by rodoviária, T 321-1661, D with a/c pleasant, helpful, some English spoken; *Hotel São Félix, Hotel Hilda Palace*, E; *Norte-Sur*, F; *Pensão Nossa Senhora do Nazaré*, F, clean, near bus terminal; *Avenida*, F; *Churrascaria Beira Rio*; *Restaurant O Calmon* for fish) buses leave daily at 0430, 1200 and 1500 for Belém, for Santarém (34 hrs.) at 1730 and many daily for Imperatriz (7-10 hrs., US$5; there is also a pick-up to the bank of the Tocantins opp. Imperatriz, 5 hrs., but more expensive, US$6-8); buses can be caught going south at Toncantinópolis, opposite Porto Franco on the Belém-Brasília road. Also a bus can be taken to Araguaína, 12½ hrs., US$10; bus

Marabá-Goiânia (change at Araguaína), US$25. Bus to Santa Inês (Maranhão, on Belém-Terisina road), 1700, 19 hrs., US$12. On these bus trips take plenty of food and drink—local supplies are expensive. With the filling of the Tucuruí dam the town has been moved; even so it suffers from flooding. The bridge across the Toncantins at Marabá is now open. Banco do Brasil will not cash travellers' cheques; parallel market in larger stores.

To visit the **Serra Pelada** gold mines, now worked by individuals on a very diminished scale, hitch a lift from the road junction outside Marabáo. 11 km. before the town is a police post: search for weapons and alcohol (forbidden); second search at airport 2 km. from the mine. *Hotel Serra de Ouro*, E, all of wood, shower; good *Churrascaria* in main square near public TV set; juice bars and *DiscoTony* discotheque. No prior permission needed to visit the mines. The miners are usually friendly and like being photographed, but enquire about the conditions before going there.

From Marabá, or from São Luis or Belém, one can reach the Carajás iron mine (the largest mineral development in Brazil) by road or train (see under São Luis above, train can be caught at station 12 km. from Marabá, Mon. Wed., Fri. approx 2100; to São Luis Tues., Thurs., Sat. 0500). Plenty of Transbrasiliana buses daily Marabá-Carajás, 4-5 hrs, US$3; Military Police check for weapons and drugs at Curianópolis. Many unplanned towns along the road. To get into Carajás (checkpoint 35 km. from the project), you must have a permit, available from Companhia Vale Rio Doce (CVRD) in Marabá, São Luis, São Paulo or Rio (hotel bookings handled here too); apply in advance and have a good reason. There are flights from Brasília and São Luis by Varig and Vasp. Between Marabá and Belém, on the Tocantins river, is the Tucuruí hydroelectric scheme (which is causing much ecological damage), reached either by bus or by day and night riverboat from Belém. *Hotel Transamérica* best in Tucuruí; *Marajoara*, Rua Lauro Sodré 685, T 787-1776, E, simple but OK. Floating bar (light meals), *Fluente*, 1½ km. N, take a taxi or motorboat, or walk, popular. To go to the dam, take bus "V Temp. I II" or " Vila Temporávia". From Marabá to Tucuruí, take Transbrasiliano bus, 3 a day, 8 hrs., US$5, road good to Itupiranga, deteriorates thereafter; also boat from Belém (32 hrs.).

The Transamazônica crosses the river Xingu at Altamira (pop. 47,000); the crossing is by ferry. The town is served by jets and boats from Belém. *Garimpeiros* sift the waters of the river bend to the east. No organised trips but a boat can be hired, US$20 per day, for a trip up the Xingu. Many animals. The area is an Assurine Indian reservation and it is not allowed to enter villages; buy food in Altamira.

Rurópolis (Presidente Medici) lies at the junction of the Transamazônica and the Santarém highway. Hotel run by Incra, "by all accounts, like the rest of the place: cracked, empty, dreaming of a future that never came" (Kevin Healey).

At **Itaituba** (the jumping-off place for the **Amazonia national park**; see Father Paul Zoderer, who may help to arrange a visit, at church on waterfront—nearest IBDF office, Av. Cons. Furtado 1303, Belém, CEP 66.000) the Transbrasilina company has a bus station on the river Tapajós, near the ferry docks. Bus fare Itaituba-Marabá, US$17. At Marabá, a new bridge has been built over the river Itacaiunas.

In **Humaitá** there are several basic hotels on the eastern edge of town; *Hotel Humaitá*, F, basic but friendly; *Aquarius Palace*, E with breakfast, is also the Expresos Humaitá bus stop; a similar hotel is the Andorinha bus stop. The Soltur bus station is in the centre. Lots of military activity in Humaitá.

There is very little traffic on the Transamazônica between Itaituba and Humaitá (1,028 km.); local drivers may give lifts. A ferry crosses the Rio Aripuanã at Vila do Carmo. The road is good for about 350 km. from Humaitá, then it deteriorates badly. It is hilly, narrow, and the jungle usually grows over the side of the road. Expresos Humaitá depart at 1500 daily. It takes 24 hours from Humaitá to Jacarèacanga, 597 km. (the town is 8 km. off the highway). One must stay overnight and catch the Transbrasiliano bus to Itaituba (24 hours, schedule erratic; the bus is replaced occasionally by a truck). There are two insanitary and expensive hotels in Jacarèacanga (try the gas station on the Transamazônica near the Jacarèacanga turn-off, they may have hammock space). Bus fare Humaitá-Jacarèacanga, US$15.60; Jacarèacanga-Itaituba, US$8; travel time depends on the weather conditions, the condition of the bus, and whether the driver decides to stop somewhere for the night.

Up the Amazon River

The Amazon system is 6,577 km., long, of which 3,165 km. are in Brazilian territory. Ships of up to 4/5,000 tons regularly negotiate the Amazon for a distance of about 3,200 km. up to Iquitos, Peru. Regular passenger services as far as Manaus are operated by the State shipping line Enasa. Distances upstream from the river mouth to Manaus in nautical miles are:

Belém	80	Santarém	538
Narrows (entrance)	225	Óbidos	605
Narrows (exit)	330	Parintins	694
Garupa	334	Itacoatiara	824
Prainha	452	Manaus	930

What to wear Remember that some Enasa boats' restaurants do not permit shorts. Light cotton or poplin clothing for the day and, at night put on a sweater or coat, for it gets quite cold. From April to October, when the river is high, the mosquitoes at night can be repelled by Super Repelex spray or K13; protective clothing is advisable. Leather sandals fall apart in the wet, rubber ones are better, but proper shoes or boots are best for going ashore: there are many foot-attacking parasites in the jungle. (2 pairs of tennis shoes, so you always have a dry pair, is a good idea.) A hammock is essential on all but the most expensive boats; often too hot to lie down in cabin during day. Also take a hat and rain gear, such as a poncho with hood.

Health There is a danger of malaria in Amazonia. On the smaller boats sanitary standards are low and one is very likely to contract intestinal infections; take plenty of tablets (Colestase are the locally available brand), toilet paper, soap, water sterilization tablets (none available in Belém) and some plain biscuits. A good idea also to take oranges, mineral water, tea bags, seasonings, sauces and jam. A yellow-fever inoculation is strongly advised; it is compulsory in some areas.

N.B. If going in the smaller boats, be prepared for mechanical breakdowns that prolong the journey. If you have the choice, remember that the small boats often keep close to the banks; the patient watcher can see plenty of wildlife.

There has recently been much criticism of food and sanitary conditions on the Enasa boats, and travellers have recommended the smaller boats, despite their well-known disadvantages.

Joanna Burrill and Henry Perks (of Hornsea, E. Yorkshire) have sent us the following information on river travel: Most boats have two decks and are divided into three classes: 1st class cabins (upper deck), which can be very hot and cramped; 1st class hammock space on upper deck, seems best as this is pleasanter during daytime; 2nd class hammock space on the lower deck, can be cramped because of cargo, and hot and noisy from the engine. Food is ample but monotonous. Fresh fruit is a welcome addition. Fresh coffee available; most boats have a bar of sorts. Plates and cutlery may not be provided. A strong fishing line and a variety of hooks can be an asset for supplementing one's diet; with some meat for bait, *piranhas* are the easiest fish to catch. Negotiate with the cook over cooking your fish. "The sight of you fishing will bring a small crowd of new friends, assistants, and lots of advice—some of it useful".

Light cotton hammocks seem to be the best solution. Buy a wide one on which you can lie diagonally; lying straight along it leaves you hump-backed. Mosquito nets are not required when in motion as boats travel away from the banks and too fast for mosquitoes to settle, though repellant is a boon for night stops. Most boats begin their journeys in the evening, but stops en route come at any hour. If making connections en route it is easy to miss a boat in the night. On arrival at the final destination it is usually possible to negotiate with the captain to stay an extra night on the boat (perhaps more) for no extra charge. This can be useful if arriving in a town late.

Exchange facilities are sparse in Amazonia, outside Belém and Manaus. Bargaining with the masters of small boats may be greatly helped if one has some low-value dollar bills.

Food in Amazonia Inevitably fish dishes are very common, including many fish with Indian names, e.g. *pirarucu*, *tucunaré*, and *tambaqui*, which are worth trying. Also shrimp and crab dishes (more expensive). Specialities of Pará include duck, often served in a yellow soup made from the juice of the root of the manioc with a green vegetable (*jambo*); this dish is the famous *pato no tucupi*, highly rec. Also *tacaca* (shrimps served in *tucupi*), *vatapá* (shrimps served in a thick sauce, highly filling, simpler than the variety found in Salvador), *maniçoba* (a green vegetable mixed with cheaper cuts of meat). Avoid food from street vendors.

Belém (do Pará—population of city 1,120,000, of state 4,617,000), founded in 1616, 145 km. from the open sea and slightly S of the equator, is the great port of the Amazon. It is hot (mean temperature, 26°C), but frequent showers freshen the streets. There are some good squares and fine buildings. The largest square is the Praça da República; the main business and shopping area is along the wide Avenida Presidente Vargas leading to the river and the narrow streets which parallel it. The Teatro da Paz, one of the largest theatres in the country, is of neo-classical splendour, worth visiting (recently restored, open Mon.-Fri. 0800-1200, 1400-1800, tours cost US$0.40). There was much renovation of public places in 1985-87, but just as many old buildings are being replaced with ugly new ones.

Places to visit are the Bosque Rodrigo Alves (0900-1700 closed Mon.,) a public garden (which is really a preserved area of original flora), with a small animal collection, yellow bus marked "Souza" or "Cidade Nova"—any number—30 mins. from "Ver-o-Peso" market), and the Goeldi Museum. Both can be reached by bus from the Cathedral. The Goeldi Museum, Av. Magalhães Barata, takes up a city block and consists of the Museum proper (with a fine collection of Marajó Indian pottery, an excellent exhibition of Mebengokre Indian lifestyle), a zoological garden (including manatees), and botanical exhibits including Victoria Régia lilies; open 0900-1200, 1400-1700, all day Sun, closed Wed. Entry US$0.50, now renovated. The Murucutu ruins, an old Jesuit foundation, are reached by the Ceará bus from Praça República, through an unmarked door on the right of the Ceará bus station.

In the Belém market, known as "Ver-o-Peso" (see the weight) after the large scales on which the fish landed nearby were weighed, now has lots of gift shops with the charms on sale for the local African-derived religion, *umbanda*; the medicinal herb stalls are also interesting. In the old town, too, is the fort, which you can enter on request; the site also contains the *Círculo Militar* restaurant (entry US$0.75; drinks and *salgadinhos* served on the ramparts from 1800 to watch the sunset, restaurant is good). At the square on the waterfront below the fort the *açaí* berries are landed nightly at 2300, after picking in the jungle (*açaí* berries ground up with sugar and mixed with manioc are supposed to provide a balanced diet)—Mary Beath, NY. Visit the Cathedral (1748) with several remarkable paintings, and directly opposite the 18th-century Santo Aleixandre church (now being restored) noted for its wood carving. The 17th-century Mercês church, near the market, is the oldest church in Belém; it forms part of an architectural group known as the Mercedário, the rest of which was heavily damaged by fire in 1978 and is being restored. The Basílica of Nossa Senhora de Nazaré (1909), built from rubber wealth, is an absolute must for its beautiful marble work and stained glass windows.

Local Holidays Maundy Thurs., half-day; June 9, Corpus Christi; August 15, accession of Pará to independent Brazil; Our Lady of Nazaré, second Sun. and fourth Mon. in October, known as Cirio. Oct. 30, half-day; Nov. 2, All Souls Day; December 8, Immaculate Conception; Christmas Eve, half-day.

Cirio, the Festival of Candles in October, is a remarkable festival based on the legend of the Virgin of Nazaré, whose image is kept in her Basílica; it apparently was found on that site around 1700. To celebrate, on the second Sun. in October, a procession carries a copy of the Virgin's image from the Basílica to the cathedral. On the Mon., two weeks later, a further procession takes place, to return the image to its usual resting-place. There is a Cirio museum in the crypt of the Basílica, enter at the right side of the church; free. Exhibits from the celebrations of the past 100 years; enthusiastic guide. (All hotels are fully booked during Cirio.)

Lambada, the music and dance form which found international popularity in 1989, originated in Pará. Its fame spread via Salvador and France.

Hotels Expensive: *Hilton*, Av. Pres. Vargas 882, T 223-6500, L, swimming pool, sauna, restaurants; *Seltom*, 2 km. from airport, T 233-4222, A, swimming pool; *Novotel*, Av. Bernardo Sayão 4808, T 229-8011, L, with bath, a/c, TV, swimming pool, unprepossessing neighbourhood, far from centre (take Universidade bus); *Excelsior Grão Pará*, Av. Presidente Vargas 718, T 222-3255, B, fair breakfast, noisy a/c and internal rooms, reports vary, but good food; *Vitória Régia* restaurant, bars, swimming pool, sauna, Lusotur travel agency. Less expensive: *Vanja*, Av Benjamin Constant 1164, T 222-6688, B, good service, rec.; *Regente*,

Av. Gov. José Mulcher 485, T 224-0755, 3-star, modest, comfortable, friendly, good breakfast; *Sagres,* Av. Gov. José Malcher 2927, opp. bus station, T 228-3999, air conditioning, good meals, swimming pool, English-speaking manager, rec., C; *Zoghbi,* R Padre Prudencio 220, T 241-1800, C-D, modern, rec.; *Verde Oliva,* Boaventura da Silva 1179 (T 224-7682), 10 mins. from centre, D, a/c, TV, good value, rec.; *Cambará,* 16 de Novembro 300, esq. Tamandaré, T 224-2422, D, a/c, good, mosquitoes; *Executivo,* Av. Alcindo Cacela 866, T 223-0767, 20 mins. walk or US$1 taxi ride from centre, D, good. *Ver-o-Peso,* Castilhos Franco 214, T 224-2267, opposite Ver-o-Peso market, E, rooftop restaurant, TV and fridge in room, rec. *Central,* Av. Presidente Vargas 290 (T 222-3011), E without bath (D with bath and a/c), noisy, but friendly, clean, comfortable, good breakfast, a must for art-deco fans; *Vidonho,* same ownership, good, E-C with abundant breakfast, Rua O. de Almeida, 476, T 225-1444, in a side street opp. *Novo Avenida,* Av. Presidente Vargas 404, T 223-8893, C/D, central, some rooms better than others, no backpackers, good breakfast; *Plaza,* Praça da Bandeira, T 224-2800, 2-star, E-D, a/c, bath, fridge, restaurant good value; across square is *Lis,* Rua João Diogo 504 (old city), 1 star, E, with bath, a/ c, fridge, gloomy, short-stays accommodated, has good cheap restaurant; *Vitória Régia,* Frutuoso Guimarães 260, F, with breakfast, good, clean, friendly, convenient for Enasa boats, owner changes money and cheques at good rates; next door but not so good is *Fortaleza,* Frutuoso Guimarães 276, E, with fan, safe; *Palácio das Musas* nearby, G, clean, friendly; *Transamazônico,* Travessa Indústria 17, waterfront by docks, F, with breakfast, clean, will store luggage for short periods. Many cheap hotels close to waterfront, in old part of town, for example dormitory bed in *Pensão Canto do Rio* opposite the dock, a "classic and unspoilt waterfront dive", F; try bargaining for cheaper rate if you have hammock; next door is *Grajaú,* F with or without breakfast, reasonable.

Camping nearest at Mosqueiro, 86 km. away.

Restaurants All the major hotels have good but expensive restaurants. *Hotel Internacional,* Av. Lobo nr. Presidente Vargas, prato do dia US$2, rec. *Círculo Militar* rec. for Belém's best Brazilian food and situation in the grounds of the fort with view over river (good choice, expensive). *Churrascaria Sanambaia,* Quai Kennedy. Also rec.: *Inter,* turn off Av. Pres. Vargas at *Hotel Central,* good and reasonable; also *Trevu,* Pres. Vargas 396, good value, tasty meals; *Regatão,* Av. Senador Lemos 3273; *Marisqueira do Luiz,* Av. Senador Lemos 1063; *Marcilias,* Frutuoso Guimarães 329, good for fish; *Capitol,* Av. Presidente Vargas near docks; *Casa Portuguesa,* Rua Manoel Barata 897, good, inexpensive; *Lá em Casa,* Av. Gov. José Malcher 982, try menu paraense; *Miako,* Travessa 1 de Março 766, behind Praça de República (menu includes very good medium-priced oriental food); *Kyoto 294,* Trav. Dr. Morais 294, good Chinese; *Livorno,* Dr. Morais 314, good, mid-price; *Avenida,* Praça Justo Chermont 1294 (opp. Basilica), very friendly; *La Romana,* Av. Gentil Bittencourt 574 and *Pizzaria Napolitano,* Praça Justo Chermont 12 (in particular pizzas and Italian dishes); *Cantina Italiana,* Benjamin Constant 1401, very good Italian food; *Pato de Ouro,* Rua Diogo Móia 633 (next to *Sorveteria Santa Martha* ice-cream parlour); *Renasci,* Travessa José Pio 322 (in particular for regional dishes); *Churrascarias Linda Cap* and *Tucuravi,* both on the highway leading out of Belém. Vegetarian: *Nutribem,* Rua Santo Antônio (off Av. Pres. Vargas) US$2 for as much as you can eat, lunch only.

Specially rec. for tourists are also some very good snack-bars (mostly outdoors in Belém) where you can buy anything up to a full meal, much cheaper than restaurants: *Pappus,* Av. Conselheiro Furtado 637 (nr. Padre Eutíquio); *Garrafão,* Av. Serzedelo Correa (below Ed. Manuel Pinto); *Charlotte,* Av. Gentil Bittencourt 730, at Travessa Quintino Bocaiuva, for best salgadinhos in the city, also good desserts, very popular. *Bos's,* Av. Gentil Bittencourt/Travessa Quintino Bocaiúva (snacks, standing only); *Milano,* Av. Presidente Vargas, next to *Hotel Grão Pará* (especially for espresso, desserts, cakes); also a good bar next to *Hotel Central* on same street. *Só Delicias,* Nazaré 251, rec. for pastries, sweets, soft drinks. *La Crème,* snack bar on Praça Nazaré, sells exotic fruit ice creams, view of Basilica; *Sorveteria Cairu* in Umarizal has excellent ice creams, including 30 fruit flavours. *Casa dos Sucos,* Av. Presidente Vargas, Praça da República, serves 41 types of juice (including Amazonian fruits) and delicious chocolate cake (vegetarian restaurant upstairs). *Navegante,* R. Barata, *Tip-Top,* Trav. Pedro Catiquio and Rua Pariquis (40 mins'. walk from harbour), excellent ice cream. *Bar do Parque,* next to Municipal Theatre, excellent place for meeting local people. There are also many street and market vendors, who, although they should be viewed with care, often sell delicious local food.

Shops in Av. Presidente Vargas; also try the Indian handicrafts shop at Praça Kennedy, set in a garden with Amazonian plants and animals. Funai (Indian agency) shop, Av. Presidente Vargas 762, loja 2, near Casa dos Sucos, is highly recommended. We have been told that Belém is an even better place than Fortaleza to buy hammocks.

Entertainment *O Lapinha* discotheque/nightclub, good floor show, out of town, take taxi.

Exchange Lloyds Bank, Rua Quinze de Novembro 275, and Brazilian banks (open 0900-1630, but foreign exchange only until 1300). Dias Lopes e Cia, 5th floor Rua Santo Antônio 316, also photo shop, 15 de Agosto on Av. Presidente Vargas, Loja Morpho, Presidente Vargas 362, Orion Perfume Factory, Trav. Frutuoso Guimarães, Sr. Milo, Travessa Campos Sales 28. *Central* (cash only), *Ver-o-Peso* and *Victória Rêgia Hotels*.

Electric Current 110 A.C., 60 cycles.

Post Office Av. Presidente Vargas.

Cables Embratel, Travessa Quintino Bocaiúva 1186 (T 22-9099) or at the Post Office, Av. Presidente Vargas. For phone calls: Telepará, Av. Presidente Vargas.

Consuls Venezuelan: 2 blocks from Trav. Benjamín Constant (new address unknown at time of going to press), open 0800-1300, T 222 6396. (Venezuelan visa takes 3 hrs., latest reports indicate that a yellow fever vaccination certificate is not required but best to check in advance, free for Danes, US$0.70 for Swedish, Swiss, W. German and Canadian citizens, US$2 for US citizens, all others US$10). **British**, Rua Gaspar Viana 490, Caixa Postal 98, T 224-4822. **Swedish**, Rua Santo Antônio 316, mailing address Caixa Postal 111, 66.000 Belém, T 222-4788, open 1600-1800; **Danish** (Consul Arne Hvidbo), Rua Senador Barata 704, sala 1503, T 223-5888, (P.O. Box 826); **U.S.**, Av. Oswaldo Cruz 165. T 23-0800.

Health Clinic Clínica de Medicina Preventativa, Av. Bras de Aguiar 410 (T 222-1434), will give injections, English spoken, open 0730-1200, 1430-1900 (Sat. 0800-1100).

Tourist Office Municipal office, Detur, in airport and Rodoviária, good free map and guide. Hotel reservations made, including low-priced hotels. Paratur, Praça Kennedy on the waterfront, inside the handicraft shop; has a good map of Belém in many languages (but some references are incorrect). Town guidebook, US$2.75.

Travel Agent Ciatur, Av. Presidente Vargas 645, T 224-1993, good half-day tour on water and in forest (US$13) and 32-hour trip to Marajó (US$200).

Roads A good asphalted road leads E out of the city to the coast town of Salinópolis, some 228 km., at the extreme end of the eastern part of the Amazon Delta. Various paved roads branch off: 118 km. out of Belém one turns right on to the paved highway S to Brasília (2,100 km.). Straight on, the road leads to Bragança, the centre of an early, unsuccessful, attempt in the 1900s to transfer population to Amazonia. At Capanema (*Hotel São Luís*, F, good), on the road to Bragança, the road for São Luís, Teresina, Fortaleza and Recife branches right.

Bus Services The Rodoviária is located at the end of Av. Gov. José Malcher 5 km. from centre, take Aeroclube, No. 20 bus, or Arsenal or Canudos buses. It has a good snack bar and showers (US$0.10). There are four buses a day to Brasília (US$36), modern and comfortable, and also a *leito* bus— US$72, 36 hours. Belém-Imperatriz bus takes 10-12 hrs. (US$9). There are also direct buses from Belém to Marabá (16 hrs.), on the Transamazônica, via Porto Franco and Toncantinópolis, and then change to Santarém (Marabá-Santarém 34 hrs.). One direct bus Belém-Santarém once a week (US$36, more expensive than by boat and can take longer). To Salvador (US$36) and also to Recife (US$34), 1 daily, to each, 2000, 34 hrs. The trip to Recife can be broken at Teresina, Picos (*Picos Hotel*, F, with meals) and Ouricuri (*Hotel Independência*, E, with bath). To São Luís, 3 a day, 12 hrs., US$11; to Teresina, US$12, frequent (but avoid Transbrasileira unless you want to stop everywhere); to Fortaleza, 1,595 km. 23 hrs., US$21, 3 daily; to Rio, US$52; to Belo Horizonte, US$48.

Hitch-hiking Going south, take bus to Capanema, 3½ hrs., US$2, walk ½ km. from Rodoviária to BR-316 where trucks stop at the gas station.

Shipping Services Regular coastal services to Southern Brazil. Agency for international services, Agências Mundiais Ltda, Av. Pres. Vargas 121, T 224 4078.

Services to Manaus and Porto Velho by the **Government's Enasa boats** (office: Av. Presidente Vargas 41, T 223-3011 or 223-3572, Telex 2064, or Rua Uruguaiana 39, sala 1402, T 222-9149 or 224-7267, Rio de Janeiro) whose schedules are published the 20th for the next month: they leave for Manaus at 2200 on the same day of the week each month, normally Wed., but the day and frequency may change monthly, taking 5 days; they take cars and motorcycles (Sonave, Transnav, B. 15 de Novembro 226, T 222-9930/7025, and Jonasa are reportedly cheaper than Enasa; Envira also ship cars and have secure port facilities and showers.) You must show your passport when buying an Enasa ticket, at boat dock on Av. Castillo França (10-minute walk from centre). Ticket must be bought on Mon. for Wed. departure (but it is possible to buy on Wed. itself for an unofficial "fee"). Fare to Manaus,

US$11, hammock space only, terribly crowded (least crowded are the couples' and single women's sections). Sanitary conditions are appalling, but the 3 meals a day now not too bad (take your own cutlery to speed up the queuing). A hammock and rope are essential (easily bought for between US$5 and US$25, buy cotton ones); also useful is a light blanket. Arrive early (some say 8 hrs.) to ensure a good hammock space, chain belongings to a post in the hammock area (thieves abound) and don't drink from the drinking fountains on board: the small canteen sells mineral water, beer and soft drinks. Some advise sleeping outside, as it's cooler if the boat stops. For an inducement of say US$100, the captain may let you have a cabin. Enasa has a 10-day tourist service Belém-Santarém-Manaus-Santarém-Belém in new catamarans (*Pará, Amazonas*), leaving Belém every other Wed., Manaus every other Thurs., at 2000 with air-conditioned cabins, restaurant, swimming pool, bar, night club, with fares from US$150 per person in a 4-berth cabin, to US$430 internal double, US$520 external double cabin, US$1,300 special cabin. Also bookable through Soletur, Rua Visconde de Pirajá 500, Suite 1708, 22410 Rio de Janeiro (T 239-7145, Telex 212 3858, 213 0237 SOLE BR); can include at extra cost a night in Manaus or Belém, or a week in Rio. Belém-Manaus (about US$70 less to Santarém in 4-berth and double cabins).

Non-Enasa fare to Manaus US$50 in covered hammock space (cabins US$100)—take food and water; look after your equipment, especially at night and in port. Ask guards at the dock gate for permission to look for a boat. Two companies that are recommended are Rodomar for destinations close to Belém (office near cathedral) and Fe em Deus, Av. Bernardo Sayão 3590 (take bus to Cremacão), recommended to Santarém (US$20 in *Fe em Deus IV*, 1st class hammock space, basic, crowded, take fruit, mineral water, books, 3 days, 4 nights). Also recommended to Santarém, Santo Agostinho company, Evani (nr. Fe em Deus, and *Terra Santa I*, also from Doca 15, Av. Bernardo Sayão, US$22.25 hammock space, US$26.70 cabin space, 3 meals included. Also *Franz Rossy*, every second Thursday at 1800, 3 days, US$23 hammock space, US$26 cabin, from Armazem 09, Portão 15, Cais do Porto, but this service not rec. Take a bus 514 from the city centre to the intersection 10 mins. beyond the Cata textile factory, and ask directions from there to the *posto comercial* area.

There is an **Enasa ferry to Macapá** about once a month, US$12 for hammock space, US$54 for cabin; check at docks; boat goes through the channels of Marajó Island; *Idalino Oliveira*, sails approximately three times a month, departs Belém 0300 Weds., arrives Macapá 1000 Thurs., crowded, free chilled drinking water, good food and bar on board, passengers may embark at 2000 on night prior to sailing (tickets from Av. Castilhos 234), boat goes through the channels of Marajó Island; Representação do Governo do Território de Macapá ferry Belém-Macapá every 4 days or so, tickets from Av. Castillo França 234 (opp. Ver-o-peso), US$8 for hammock space, US$12 for cabin, 28 hrs. Enal, Av. Bernardo Sayão 1740, T 224-5210, sails Tues. and Sat., 36 hrs., hammock US$25 inc. food and water. Other non-regular sailings, *Príncipe do Mar* and *Príncipe do Mar II*, US$16 upper deck, US$14 lower, with food, 2 days. Also *Barco Souza*, every Friday, return Tuesday, US$12 for hammock space, US$13.50 for cabin (only 2), wait on board while cargo is loaded at Porto Santana; *São Francisco de Paula*, US$15, friendly, clean, food not too good, best to take some of your own. Weekly Enasa boat to Tucuruí on the Tocantins River at 1730 or later (with 5 stops, 32 hrs.; there are other boats to/from Tucuruí).

Warning Boat passengers arriving from Manaus (a free trade zone) may experience long delays at customs. Note that dress in Amazonia is often more conservative than further south.

Air Services Bus "Perpétuo Socorro-Telégrafo" or "Icoaraci", every 15 mins. from Prefeitura to airport, US$0.10. Taxi to airport, US$6 (ordinary taxis cheaper than Coop. taxis, buy ticket in advance in Departures side of airport). Airport has a hotel booking service but operated by, and exclusive to, 5 of the more expensive hotels, discounts offered. Regular flights N to Miami once a week by Varig, S to Brasília and other Brazilian cities, and W to Santarém and Manaus, the latter with connection for Leticia, Colombia. To Paramaribo, twice, and Cayenne several times weekly. To Oiapoque on French Guyane frontier by Taba (Rua O. de Almeida 408, T 223-8811). Travellers entering Brazil from Guyane may find it necessary to obtain a 60-day visa (takes two days) before airlines will confirm their tickets.

Tour Volker Filss, a German traveller, has sent us the following suggestion for a one-day sightseeing tour, subsequently revised by Philip A. Smith, recently of BOLSA, Belém: "Go to the Ver-o-Peso market early in the morning when the boats are coming in and watch the unloading of the fish and the vendors in the market. Take a bus marked Souza at the market and ask the driver to drop you at the Bosque (open 0800-1100 and 1400-1700). Take the same bus back and get off at the Museu Paraense (Goeldi) in Av. Magalhães Barata (formerly Independência). After visiting museum and gardens, walk down avenue to the Basilica (Nossa Senhora de Nazaré) and then on to the Praça da República (on the way the Tourist Office will be passed on the right). From the Edifício Manuel Pinto de Silva at this end of the Praça, you walk to the Teatro da Paz and along Av. Presidente Vargas. Before reaching the docks, turn left along, say, Av. Santo Antônio and Av. João Alfredo, through the shopping and commercial area (interesting narrow streets and open-fronted shops) to reach the harbour with its fishing boats and to the left the Prefeitura Municipal and Palácio do Governo. Beyond stand the Cathedral and the old fort (entry US$0.10) and *Círculo Militar* restaurant. Depending on your progress, lunch can be taken by the Basilica (e.g. *Avenida* restaurant directly opposite), or on the terrace of Edifício Manuel Pinto, or, say, at *Hotel Central* on Av. Presidente Vargas".

Excursions Travel agents offer short and longer visits to the rivers and jungle. The nearest beach is at **Outeiro** (35 km.) on an island near Icoaraci, about an hour by bus and ferry (the bus may be caught near the Maloca, an Indian-style hut near the docks which serves as a night-club). Further north is the island of **Mosqueiro** (86 km.) now accessible by toll bridge (US$0.20) and an excellent highway, with many beautiful sandy beaches and jungle inland.

Many hotels and weekend villas at the villages of Mosqueiro and Vila; rec. *Hotel Farol*, on Praia Farol, D, 1920s architecture in good repair, small restaurant, good views; *Hotel Murumbira*, on Praia Murumbira, C, pool, restaurant. Restaurants at Mosqueiro: *Ilha Bela*, Av. 16 de Novembro 460, rec. for fish, at Praia Chapeu Virado; under same management is *Marésia*; *Pizzeria Napolitana*; *Sorveteria Delícia*, Av. 16 de Novembro, good local fruit ice creams, owner buys dollars. At Praia do Farol (Mosqueiro) is *Bar-restaurant O'Stop* which has a shower and will let you leave luggage and hang your hammock. The traffic is heavy in July and at weekends, and hotels are full. Food at hotels US$3.50, but same quality costs US$2 at stalls along beach. Camping is easy. Buses Belém-Mosqueiro every hour from Rodoviária, US$0.75, 80 minutes.

Marajó Island is worth visiting for a weekend's water buffalo hunting (use a camera, not a gun). Boats to Marajó leave every Wed. and Fri. at 2000, Sat. 1400, return Thurs. 1700 and Sun. 1700 and Mon. a.m., 6 hrs., US$3 for a seat, US$20 for cabin for two (buy return ticket in Belém to ensure passage). Trips to the island are arranged by the *Grão Pará Hotel* and travel agents in Belém. Alternatively, a light aircraft may be hired to see Marajó from the air (with pilot, about US$80 for 2 hours) e.g. from Kovacs, Av. Dr. Freitas, opposite the airfield of the Aero Clube do Pará. (Cheap weekend flights were easier to find than boats.) The island was the site of the precolumbian Marajoaras culture.

At Soure, on the island, are *Hotel Soure*, (walk straight on from Enasa dock, then take 3rd street on left), E p.p. full board, good excursions arranged; *Pousada Marajoara*, and *Pousada Parque Floresta*, nearby, E, friendly and clean, good meals. *Pensão da Dona Maria* G, 2nd Street 575 (*Bar Guaraní*), simple rec. *Canecão*, Praça da Matriz, sandwiches, meals, rec. Changing money is only possible at very poor rates. Take plenty of insect repellent. There are fine beaches, Araruna (2 km.), do Pesqueiro (bus from Praça da Matriz, 1030, returns 1600, eat at *Maloca*, good, cheap, big, deserted beach, 13 km. away) and Caju-Una (15 km.).

Salinópolis (228 km.) about 4 hrs. by bus (US$3) on excellent highway, also worth a visit. Seaside resort with many small places where you can eat and drink at night by the waterfront, and fine sandy beach nearby (buses and cars drive on to the beach). Best during holiday month of July. Atalaya, opposite Salinópolis, is pleasant, reached by taxi (US$5) or with a fisherman.

Hotels *Solar*, Av. Beira Mar s/n, D with bath, best in town, good restaurant; *Salinas*, on beach, E; *Jeanne d'Arc*, E with breakfast.

There are ferries and daily flights from Belém to **Macapá** (pop. 168,000) a town on the northern channel of the Amazon Delta, which used to be decrepit but is now improving, particularly along the riverfront. (The ferries often go to Porto Santana, 30 km. from Macapá, to which there are frequent buses, US$0.30, and shared taxis US$2 p.p., boats readily hired to visit river communities). Macapá is the capital of Amapá (agriculture, gold, manganese, coal, timber), one-quarter the size of France but with only 234,000 inhabitants. Each brick of the Fortaleza de São José do Macapá, built 1764, was brought from Portugal as ballast. Interesting market behind the Fortaleza. A handicraft complex has been built next to the *Novotel*. The riverfront has been pleasantly developed. There is a monument marking the equator halfway between Porto Santana and Macapá, known as Marco Zero, with nightclub underneath and more nearby. Gold is sought by washing sand in the river, using a gallon kerosene can: if you find less than 5 grams of gold in a canful of sand you move on.

The popular local beach is at Fazendinha (take bus of same name), extremely lively on Sundays.

Hotels *Novotel* (formerly *Macapá*), French-owned, on waterfront, T 222-1144, small, 4-star, A, all rooms a/c, swimming pool, service and cleanliness strongly criticized as being far below acceptable standard; *Tropical*, Av. Antônio Coelho de Carvalho 1399, 20 mins. from centre, one star, T 231-3739, E with a/c (cheaper without), rec.; *Glória*, Leopoldo Machado 2085 (just round corner from *Tropical*, 20 mins. walk from centre), T 222-0984; *Excelso*, E, has been rec. *Santo Antônio*, Av. Coriolano Jucá 485, T 222-0226, near main square, E, very clean, fan, shower, good breakfast extra. *Meruno*, F, central, good value; *Amapaense Palace*, Rua Tiradentes 109, T 222-3366, E-D, 2 star, a/c, cold showers, comfortable, clean (*lanchonete* in same building, poor). The following are 10-mins. walk from port and from Praça São José (where bus from Porto Santana stops): *Palace*, Rua Cora de Carvalho 144, F with breakfast; *Mata*, Rua São José 2390, F with fan; *Mercúrio*, Rua Cândido Mendes, 1300 block (no sign), F.

Restaurants *O Boscão*, Hamilton Silva 997, no sign, quite good; *Portenho*, Hamilton Silva 1390; *O Paulistano*, Av. Henrique Galúcio 412, a/c, good; *Pizza San Carlos*, Cândido Mendes 1199, good for lunch; *Lennon*, good pavement café, no meals, at Rua Gen. Rondón esq. I.C.Nunes; *Lanchonete Zero Grau*, in city centre, rec. for food. Excellent ice cream sold in Macapá. e.g. *Sorveteria Amapaense*, nr. *Hotel Santo Antônio*, good, wide selection.

Exchange Banco do Brasil, near *Novotel*, or in *Novotel* itself, rates reported better than in Belém. Good rates also with gold merchants around Canal da Fortaleza.

Transport Ferries: Enal, Rua Machado de Assis 59, Porto Santana, T 632-6141/6196, to Belém Wed. and Sun., US\$25 inc food and water; Enasa about 10th of every month, US\$12 for hammock space, US\$54 for cabin. Check departures at Porto São Benedito, Av. Bernardo Sayão 868, T 222-6025, **see page** 437.) Four flights daily to Belém (including night flight), about 45 mins. with Cruzeiro do Sul (also to Santarém, Manaus daily) and Vasp. Taxi airport-town US\$2.25, about 4 km.

Rubber was almost the only product of the Territory until the 1950s, when manganese was discovered 150 km. NW of Macapá. A standard-gauge railway, 196 km. long, the only one in Brazil, has been built from the mining camp to Porto Santana, from which there is an excellent road. Malaria is rampant in Amapá; the illiteracy rate is 85%; smuggling goes on in a big way. But the mining area—Icomiland, pop. 4,000—is a startling exception: swimming pools, football fields, bowling alleys, supermarkets, dance halls, movies, a healthy oasis in the wilderness.

IBDF office, Rua Hamilton Silva 1570, Santa Rita, CEP 68.900, Macapá, has details on the **Cabo Orange National Park** in the extreme north of the Territory, and the **Lago Piratuba Biological Reserve**, neither accessible by road.

Sr João Batista de Oliveira Costa in Macapá is a good pilot who flies around the delta, particularly to the mouth of the Araquari river to see the *pororoca*, a tidal wave that travels upriver in the high tides of spring and autumn.

An unpaved road has been built from Macapá northward to the small town of *Oiapoque* (one hotel), on the coast near the French Guyane border; road completed halfway to Calçoene (government-owned hotel by bus stop E, expensive; free food in adjoining canteen; sleeping space advertised in a café on Oiapoque road, very cheap), via Amapá (*Tourist Hotel* and one other, E, clean, comfortable—one block from square towards docks, turn right, 2nd house on left). Amapá is better than Calçoene for travelling on. Macapá-Amapá bus, US\$6.50, 6 hrs.; daily Estrela de Ouro bus Macapá-Calçoene from Praça Veiga Cabral (timetable varies), US\$8, 7 hrs. (minimum), many delays, book at least 2 days in advance. 80 km. from Calçoene is Lourenço, the centre of the local gold rush. For the 216 km. from Calçoene to Oiapoque there is a bus scheduled for 0700, Mon., Wed., Fri. (US\$5), but it often does not run (also an unscheduled government lorry, which does not run in the rainy season, Jan.-Apr.); you can hitch from Macapá, take a private lorry (little traffic), costing US\$7 to 15, or hire a vehicle—for all means you will be overcharged. From Oiapoque a ferry goes to St. Georges (Fr. Guyane), US\$2—a bridge is being built; be sure to get exit and entry stamps on either side of the border: in Oiapoque the Federal Police station is past the church on the road to Calçoene, and in St. Georges visit the Gendarmerie Nationale (no customs). Accommodation in Oiapoque for US$2 p.p. near ferries, basic. It is impossible to get francs anywhere in St. Georges (try in Brazil). **Warning** Everyone must have a visa for entering French Guyane here, obtainable in Belém, but not Manaus. This is a most difficult border crossing for tourists: the authorities seem to believe that no-one other than Brazilians or Guyanais will want to make the attempt.

A government boat makes the trip from Macapá to Oiapoque once or twice a month, US$10. The boat service on its journey south stops at Calçoene (24 hrs., US$8.50, including food) and from there a trip can be made by lorry (US$5) to Macapá. There are Taba flights from Macapá to Oiapoque on Tues., Fri., Sat. (return Tues., Wed., Sat., continuing to Belém), US$52 (US$107 to Belém), unreliable service; Taba office in Oiapoque on the quay by the ferry, rarely open (flights usually booked up). Varig/Cruzeiro have 3 flights a day to Belém. It is possible, but hard, to fly Amapá-Oiapoque. (Taxi into Oiapoque US$4, bus US$1.25.) If using Paris-Cayenne route as a cheap way to South America, it is recommended to fly Cayenne-Belém, US$135, compared with five days of discomfort and delays overland from Cayenne to Macapá (you have to fly Cayenne-St. Georges anyway; the boat, *São Pedro*, from S.T.M.G., 136 Monnerville (opp. Market), Cayenne, T 311388, apparently does not run any more).

Belém to Manaus

A few hours up the broad river the region of the thousand islands is entered. The passage through this maze of islets is known as "The Narrows". The ship winds through 150 km. of lanes of yellow flood with equatorial forest within 20 or 30 metres on both sides. In the Furo Grande the vessel rounds a hairpin bend almost touching the trees, bow and stern.

After the Narrows, the first point of special interest is formed by the curious flat-topped hills, on one of which stands the little stucco town of Monte Alegre (airport), an oasis in mid-forest.

Santarém (pop. 250,000) 2-3 days upstream on the southern bank, stands at the confluence of the Tapajós River with the Amazon, just half-way between Belém and Manaus. It was founded in 1661, and is the third largest town on the Brazilian Amazon. The yellow Amazon water is mottled with greenish patches from the Tapajós; the meeting of the waters is said by some to be nearly as impressive as that of the Negro and Solimões near Manaus. There is now a road southwards to Cuiabá (Mato Grosso), meeting the Transamazônica at Rurópolis (**see page**). (The southward leg from the Transamazônica to Cuiabá begins about 90 km. W of this point, or 20 km. from Itaituba.) Timber, bauxite and gold discoveries have promoted very rapid growth of the city, which has become very expensive. It is the jumping off point for gold prospectors in the Mato Grosso territories to the South. It is reported that prospectors are exploited by high prices, and that lawlessness abounds in the goldfields. The unloading of the fish catch between 0500 and 0700 on the waterfront is an interesting scene. There are good beaches nearby on the river Tapajós.

Hotels *Santarém Palace*, close to city centre, Rui Barbosa 726, T 522-5285, good, C with bath and TV; *Tropical*, Av. Mendonça Furtado 4120, T 522-1533, B, de luxe, swimming pool seems to be unrestricted, friendly staff, good chef (but not "de luxe" cooking), meals for around US$5, excellent value; *San Rafael*, Rua dos Bares 222 (T 232-8335/8488), B, pleasant, rec., English and German spoken; *City*, Trav. Francisco Correia 200, T 522-4719, D with bath, a/c, TV, radio, frigobar, good; *Central Plaza*, Praça Rodrigues dos Santos 877, E, with bath and fan, run-down, friendly, *São Luís*, near market, E, good value, meals; opposite is *Horizonte*, Travessa Lemos 737, E, clean; *Brasil*, Travessa dos Mártires, 30, E, including breakfast, other good meals served, clean, basic; *Drink Hotel*, on waterfront, safe and friendly but rooms hot, E. *Equatorial*, F, good value, friendly.

Restaurants *Mascotinho* bar/pizzeria, on beach in front of *Hotel Uirapuru*, popular, good view, US$5 for pizza for 2; *Storil*, Travessa Turiano Meira, 2 blocks from Rui Barbosa, good fish (dinner about US$4.25), live music, takes credit cards; *Ritz*, Praça do Pescador, good, US$3 lunch; *Cisne*, rec; *Lanchonete Luci*, Praça do Pescador, good juices and pastries;

Sombra do Jambeiro, Trav. 15 de Novembro, Norwegian-owned bar and lanchonete, excellent meals; *Pirâmides*, good local fish dishes; good value restaurant beneath *Equatorial Hotel*. Good ice-cream at *Sorveteria Go-Go*, Siqueira Campos 431.

Banks Banco do Brasil changes foreign currency and travellers' cheques. It is reported that hotels are unwilling to change dollars at the tourist rate.

Health Dr Ihsan Youssef Simaan, T 522-3886/3982, speaks English and Spanish.

Travel Agents Amazon Tours, Trav. Turiano Meira 1084, T 091-522-2620, run by Steve Alexander (from Alaska), highly reasonable and recommended, has produced a useful guidebook on Santarém. He also has a property in the jungle for overnight tours, also highly recommended.Gil Serique, Caixa Postal 76, CEP 68100, T 522-5174, English-speaking guide, rec. Coruá-Una Turismo, 15 de Novembro 185-C, CEP 68100 T 522-6303/7421 offers various tours, Pierre d'Arcy speaks French, rec.

Airport 15 km. from town. Internal flights only. Buses to centre or waterfront, or taxis (US$10 to waterfront); *Hotel Tropical* has a free bus for residents; you may be able to take this.

River Services Small launches leave for Manaus 2-5 days, most days, e.g. Luciatur, US$20 including food, 3rd class. Other examples of fares to Manaus: US$37.50 1st class (upper deck cabin), US$20, 2nd class (upper deck hammock), US$18.50, 3rd class (lower deck). You may sleep on board (in hammock) days before departure. Enquire at the waterfront. Enasa, Trav. Agripina Matos 1089; T 522-1138. For Manaus, *Moreira da Sibra III*, US$12 with good meals for 1st class hammock space; *Rio Nilo*, US$16 for hammock space, also rec.; and *Onze de Maio*, has bar. For Belém, *Franz Rossy*, every second Thursday at 1200, 2-3 days, US$23 hammock space, US$26 cabin (not rec.); *Cidade de Teresina*, Wed. 1800, US$22 hammock space, cabin US$28, 2 nights, adequate. For Macapá (Porto Santana), 36-48 hrs., US$18, e.g. *São Francisco de Paula*, clean, efficient, friendly, good food, leaves Mons. at 1830. Boats, to Manaus or Belém, including Enasa, may leave from the waterfront in town, as well as from the "Cais do Porto" dock (where all boats arrive) about 4 km. from the centre; take bus marked "Circular" or "Circular Externo" (US$0.10), both of which go to Cais do Porto, and pass Rodoviária. Guards will allow you to enter the dock and look for boats, but you may have to wait several days for a cargo/passenger boat going in either direction. Along the river, closer to the centre, are numerous boats, usually leaving daily, for Itaituba (daily, 1800, arr. late next morning), Óbidos, Oriximiná, Alenquer or Monte Alegre. Do not buy tickets from touts.

Buses Rodoviária is on the outskirts, take "Rodagem" bus from the waterfront near the market, US$0.12. Santarém to Itaituba, 8 hrs. US$5.40; there connecting service east to **Marabá on the River Tocantins**, 28 hrs. (if lucky, can be 60 hours, or even 6 days), US$25, 1830 with Trans Brasiliana. Also to Imperatriz, 46 hrs., US$30, office on Av. Getúlio Vargas and at Rodoviária. (Beware of vehicles that offer a lift, which frequently turn out to be taxis.)

Excursion to Altar do Chão, a village set amid Amazonian vegetation on the river Tapajós, at the outlet of Lago Verde; hotel (D), comfortable; *Pousada* near the church, quiet, clean; luxury hotel to be built shortly; *Restaurant Mongote*, Praça 7 de Setembro, good fresh fish, huge portions; *Lago Verde*, try *calderada de tucunaré*; good swimming in the Tapajós from the beautiful, clean beach; bus from Mercado Municipal, Santarém, leaves 0500, 1100, 1600, 1½ hrs., returns 0630, 1230 and 1730 approx. (rugged, but fun). Also by 1000 bus to Porto Novo, 3 hrs. into jungle by a lake, bus returns 0330 next morning (you can sleep in it). Interesting wildlife on the lake; canoe can be hired.

37 km. S from Santarém on a dirt road is **Belterra** (pop. about 8,000), where Henry Ford established one of his rubber plantations, in the highlands overlooking the Tapajós River. Ford built a well laid-out new town; the houses resemble the cottages of Michigan summer resorts. Many of the newer houses follow the white paint with green trim style. The town centre has a large central plaza that includes a band stand, the church of Santo Antônio (circa 1951), a Baptist church and a large educational and sports complex. There is a major hospital which at one time was staffed by physicians from North America and attracted people from Manaus and Belém. There has been little replacement of old trees: extraction has been the only activity. As a result, the rubber forest is in bad condition since the late 1940s. (*Hotel Seringueira*, F, with about 8 rooms and pleasant restaurant).

Fordlândia was the Ford Motor Company's first rubber plantation, founded in 1926, but it was never profitable; it is a friendly town since there are few visitors. *Hotel Zebu*, in old Vila Americana (turn right from dock, then left up the hill); one restaurant, two bars and three shops on town square. There is a little pebble beach north of the town.

Bus from Santarém to Belterra (from unmarked *Café Amazonas*, Travessa Moraes

Sarmento between Rui Barbosa and São Sebastião), 1000 and 1230, Mon.-Sat., return 1300 and 1530, US$1, about 2 hrs.—note: one hour time difference between Santarém and Belterra so if you take the 1230 bus you'll miss the 1530 return bus). If driving, take Av. Santarém-Cuiabá out of town, which is paved for 8 km. At Km. 37 is a small Shell station; fork right and stop at the guardhouse; it's 15 km. into town, following the electricity cables. Boats from Santarém to Itaituba may stop at Fordlândia if you ask (leave Santarém 1800, arrive 0500-0600, US$5 for 1st class hammock space); ask the captain to stop for you on return journey, about 2300. Boats may stop for Belterra, but it's a walk of several km. from the river to town.

110 km. up-river from Santarém is **Óbidos** (pop. 45,000) a picturesque and clean city, located at the narrowest and deepest point on the river. For many kilometres little is seen except the wall of the great Amazonian forest. Small airport.

Manaus, the next city upstream, was at one time an isolated urban island in the jungle. This remote "free port" is, in fact, the collecting-point for the produce of a vast area which includes parts of Peru, Bolivia and Colombia. There is superb swimming in the natural pools and under falls of clear water in the little streams which rush through the woods, but take locals' advice on swimming in the river; electric eels and various other kinds of unpleasant fish, apart from the notorious *piranhas*, abound and industrial pollution of the river is growing.

Until recently Manaus' only communications were by river and air, but now a road SW to Porto Velho, which is already connected with the main Brazilian road system, has been completed and partly paved. Another, not yet fully paved, has been built due N to Boa Vista, from where other roads already reach the Venezuelan and Guyanese frontiers.

Manaus (1.1 million people) is the capital of the State of Amazonas, the largest in Brazil (1.6 million square km), with a population of 2.1 million. Though 1,600 km. from the sea, it is only 32 metres above sea-level. The average temperature is 27°C. The city sprawls over a series of eroded and gently sloping hills divided by numerous creeks (*igarapés*). Dominating the centre is a Cathedral built in simple Jesuit style on a hillock; nothing distinguished inside or out. Nearby is the main shopping and business area, the tree-lined Avenida Eduardo Ribeiro; crossing it is Av. Sete de Setembro, bordered by ficus trees. The area between Av. Sete de Setembro and the rear of *Hotel Amazonas* is now reserved for pedestrians. There is a modern air-conditioned theatre. Manaus is building fast; 20-storey modern buildings are rising above the traditional flat, red-tiled roofs. It was the first city in South America to instal trams, but they have now been replaced by buses.

The main attractions are the Botanic Gardens, the military zoo, the well stocked public library, and the legendary Opera House, the Teatro Amazonas, completed in 1896 during the great rubber boom following 17 years of construction and rebuilt in 1929. It seats 685 people and was restored in 1974. A further restoration was started in 1987 and has now been completed; for information on programmes and viewing times, T 233-0929/234-3525. Another interesting historic building is the Mercado Adolfo Lisboa, commonly known as the Mercado. It was built in 1902 as a miniature copy of the now demolished Parisian Les Halles. The wrought ironwork which forms much of the structure was imported from Europe and is supposed to have been designed by Eiffel. It was restored in 1978. Go early in the morning when it is full of good quality regional produce, food and handicrafts (open daily 0500-1800). See the two markets near the docks; best early in morning. In Rua Duque de Caxias is a rubber factory open to the public. There is a curious little church, the Igreja do Pobre Diabo, at corner of Avs. Borba and Ipixuna in the suburb of Cachoeirinha; it is only 4 metres wide by 5 metres long, and was built by a worker (the "poor devil" of the name); take Circular 7 Cachoeirinha bus from cathedral to Hospital Militar.

The remarkable harbour installations, completed in 1902, were designed and built by a Scottish engineer to cope with the up to 14 metre annual rise and fall

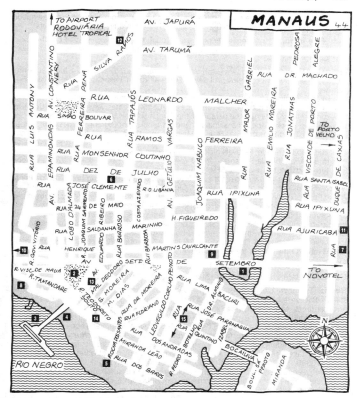

Key: 1. Government Palace, 2. Cathedral, 3. Floating Harbour, 4. Customs House, 5. Municipal Market, 6. Opera House/Teatro Amazonas, 7. Museu do Indio, 8. Museu do Porto, 9. Museu do Homem do Norte, 10. Instituto Geográfico Histórico (off map), 11. Rubber factory, 12.Tourist Office, 13. Post Office, 14. *Hotel Amazonas*, 15. Cheap hotel area.

of the Rio Negro. The large passenger ship floating dock is connected to street level by a 150-metre long floating ramp, at the end of which, on the harbour wall, can be seen the high water mark for each year since it was built. When the water is high, the roadway floats on a series of large iron tanks measuring 2½ metres in diameter. The material to build the large yellow Customs building near the harbour was brought block by block from Scotland as ballast. Tourists can visit the docks on Sun., 0600-1000.

Manaus has been a free trade zone, since 1967. All travellers are required to fill out a customs declaration on all articles bought there, which you are requested to pack in your hold luggage; in fact it is a good idea to declare goods of non-Brazilian origin such as cameras, radios, tape-recorders etc. on arrival in order to avoid any problems. It is only necessary to give information to Customs on goods already possessed if one is travelling into Brazil. You have to go through customs when leaving the Rodoviária. If flying from Manaus to a destination outside Brazil, no such documentation is required. Nor is it required of boat travellers.

Duty-Free Imports Travellers entering Brazil through Manaus may import from the zone, duty-free, foreign electrical or electronic goods and food products, up to maximum values that are often changed.

Local Holidays 6 Jan. (Epiphany); Ash Wed., half-day; Maundy Thurs.; 24 June (St. John); 14 July; 5 Sept.; 30 Oct.; 1 Nov., All Saints Day, half-day; Christmas Eve; New Year's Eve, half-day.

14 Jan., Anniversary of Praça 14 de Janeiro, commemorates the founding of the bairro; Samba Schools, street market, and fun fair. Feb., Carnival, dates vary—5 days of Carnival, Amazonense culminating in the parade of the Samba Schools, Avenida Djalma Batista. 3rd week in April Week of the Indians, Indian handicraft, talks, photographic exposition, various localities. First fortnight of June, Festival Marquesiano, three days of festival, regional and Afro-Brazilian dancing, Arabian, Russian and European folklore, held at the Campo da Amizade, São Raimundo; Festival Folclórico do Amazonas, second fortnight, Praça Francisco Pereira da Silva, Bola da Suframa. Second fortnight of Aug. Fair of the Amazonian Wood Furniture and Artefact Industry, SESI, Est. do Aleixo Km. 5. 10 Sept. Travessia Almirante Tamandaré, swimming race across the Rio Negro (8500 metres) leaving from Praia da Ponta Negra; also in Sept., Fair of the Amazonian Clothing Industry second fortnight, SESI, Est. do Aleixo Km. 5; Festival de Verão do Parque Dez, second fortnight, summer festival with music, fashion shows, beauty contests, local foods, etc., Centro Social Urbano do Parque Dez; Festival da Bondade, last week, stalls from neighbouring states and countries offering food, handicrafts, music and dancing, SESI, Est. do Aleixo Km. 5. Nov., Festival Universitário de Cultura (entire month) with music, art and book exposition, organized by the students on the University Campus. 8 Dec., Procissão de Nossa Senhora da Conceicão, from the Igreja Matriz through the city centre and returning to Igreja Matriz for a solemn mass.

N.B. Manaus time is one hour behind Brazilian standard time (2 hrs behind during October-March when rest of Brazil is on summer time).

Hotels Extremely crowded, especially in Jan.-Feb., when hotels often raise their prices steeply. Prices are high generally; we give high season prices, so reductions may be available at other times. Many hotels offer a special price for triple occupancy. 10% tax and service must be added to bills.

Tropical, Praia da Ponta Negra, T (92)234-1165, a lavish, 5 star Varig hotel 20 km. outside the city, L+, very expensive, *Restaurant Tarumã* open for dinner only, *churrascaria* by pool, open to non-residents on weekdays only (well-dressed non-residents may use pool on weekdays, take free bus from Rua José Paranaguá in front of Petrobras building esq. Dr. Moreira 0830, 0930, 1130 to Hotel, 1200, 1400, 1500, 1800 to town). It is rarely full, except in Jan-Feb. Parkland setting, pools when not being renovated, small zoo with animals in small cages, departure point for many river cruises, tennis. Do not exchange money here, official rate only; don't pay in dollars or with credit cards for same reason. Also away from centre, *Novotel*, Av. Mandii 4 in the Industrial Area, T 237-1211, L, 4 star, luxurious, pool, US$1.75 taxi ride from centre, reported markedly less good than *Tropical*; *Las Vegas*, Joaquim Nabuco 2235, D, restaurant, T 234- 0250.

Central hotels: *Amazonas*, Praça Adalberto Vale, T 232-2857, 4 star, L, the ground floor is not rec., but rooms are reasonable, hot water, a/c, and it's the best of a poor lot for business travellers; opp. *Amazonas* is *Ana Cassia Palace*, expensive, Rua dos Andradas 14, T 232-6201, A; *Lord*, Marcílio Dias 217/225,T 234-9741, L, some rooms a/c, expensive for what they offer, with good breakfast, good service; has a cheaper annex. *Premier*, Av. Eduardo Ribeiro 124, D some rooms with TV and fridge, friendly, good value; *São Rafael*, Rua dos Barés 222, T 232-8488, C, clean, safe, helpful, tours arranged, close to waterfront and market. In Av. 7 de Setembro; *Palace* (593), T 234-5764, old refurbished building, a/c but cramped, C; *Martins* (1429), D, with breakfast, stores luggage, friendly; *Monaco*, Rua Silva Ramos 20, T232-5211, 3 star, A, luxury rooms have good view, pleasant, rooftop restaurant/bar; *Nova Avenida*, Av. Pres. Vargas, D, helpful, rec.; *Janelas Verdes*, Leovegildo Coelho 216, T 233-1222, E, a/c, shower, TV, small, quiet (except Sun.), safe, T 233-1222; *Fortaleza*, Rua dos Bares 238, E with fan, reasonable, rec; *Dez de Julho*, Dez de Julio 679, T 232 6280, E, a/c, clean, rec.

In Rua G. Moreira: *Rio Mar*, (325, T 234-7409), incl. breakfast and bath C, clean, central; *Central* (202), T 232-7887, C, some a/c, quiet, very good value; *Internacional* (168), B-C (2-stars), T 234-1315, a/c, friendly, central, coffee most of the day, good exchange rates; *Nacional* (59), T 233-0537, C with bath, fridge, a/c, clean, rec. *Rey Salomão* (No. 119, T 234-7374), E, clean, breakfast.

In Av. Joaquim Nabuco: *Doral* (687), E, T 232-4102, a/c, friendly, excellent breakfast, rec.; *Pensão Sulista* (347), T 234-5814, E with fan, no breakfast, laundry facilities; *Aurora* (130), E with bath, a/c, friendly, clean, noisy TV; *Artêrio*, No. 471, near corner with R. Lima Bacuri, E with a/c or fan, clean, large rooms with bath; *Bela Vista*, No. 278, E without bath *Manauara*, No. 129, E with bath, a/c, fridge, coffee all day, friendly, has TV; *Hospedaria Paulista*, E with breakfast, fan, popular; next door is *Astoria*, E with breakfast, a bit run down; *Luz* and *Iguaçu* (Nos. 779 and 711 respectively) are better than most on this street: the former is singles only above a gym, clean, breakfast included at *Iguaçu*, both E. *Rio Branco*, Rua dos Andradas 484, E, rec., popular, friendly, clothes-washing facilities; *Dona Joana* No 553, same street, T 233-7553, E, a/c, clean, good value, rec.; other cheaper places in same area. *Nadie*, opp. Rodoviária, F.

O Explorador **Youth Hostel**, Rua Silva Ramos 685 (central, T 234-6796, P.O. Box 2890), F p.p. not inc. bedding or beakfast, non-IYHA members welcome, tours arranged; *Cetur* (Amazon Safari Club) doubles as youth hostel, at Km. 13. Rodovia Tarumã, 10 km. from airport (T 233-8658/1573), at Ponta Negra, described as a ripoff, D without breakfast, sheets extra, extra charge to use pool, US$1 pick up from airport, no bus service nearby. **N.B.** Lori Kornblum suggests keeping your room key, in view of reports of staff allowing bogus police officers into guests' rooms. **N.B.** also, when taking a taxi from the airport, insist on being taken to the hotel of your choice, and not to the one which pays the driver commission.

Camping There are no campsites in or near Manaus; it is difficult to find a good, safe place to camp wild. It is possible to camp wild on the bank of the Rio Negro near the *Hotel Tropical*; through outskirts of city via Tarumã bathing waterfalls to Ponta Negra bathing beaches, 20 km. Good swimming. Bus daily (US$0.15). Camping Praia Dourada, showers, toilets, restaurant, boat hire, good swimming, busy at weekends.

Electric Current 110 volts A.C.; some hotels 220 volts A.C., 60 cycles.

Restaurants *Novotel* serves a rec. feijoada completa on Sat.; *La Barca*, R. Recife 2235, wide variety of fish dishes, classy, popular, often has live music; *Fiorentina*, Rua José Paranaguá 44 (opposite Praça da Polícia), Italian, reasonably priced, good salad, pizza (government rating A); *São Francisco*, Blvd. Rio Negro 195, ½ hr. walk from centre (or bus 705), in Educandos suburb, good fish, huge portion, US$5.50, highly rec.; *Panorama* next door, No. 199 (also good for fish, cheap). *Caçarola*, Rua Maués 188, Cachoeirinha, T 233-3021, very good local fish dishes (take a taxi); *Casarão*, Joaquim Nabuco 497, good fish dishes. Japanese at *Miako*, Rua São Luís 230, also *Suzuran*, Blvd. Álvaro Maia 1683, Adrianópolis, good, closed Tues., taxi US$2; *O Gauchão*, Av. Castelo Branco 2009, fixed price of about US$5 for as much as you can eat, rec. Another churrascaria is *Rodaviva*, Av. Ajuricaba 1005, open air, all you can eat for US$4, also *Búfalo* Joaquim Nabuco 628, all you can eat (of high quality) for US$6, and *Churrascão*, Av. Castello Branco, Cachoeirinha. *O Vegetariano*, Rua Rui Barbosa 128, good, also take-away, open 1100-1430 Mon.-Fri.; another at Saldanho Marinho 429B; *Chapaty*, R. Costa Azevedo 105, vegetarian; *Sorveteria Pingüim*, Av. Eduardo Ribeiro, good, medium-priced; *Forasteiro*, R. Dr Moreira, No. 178, excellent fish dishes; *Mister Pizza*, R. José Paranaguá 104 (Praça da Polícia), good pizza and sandwiches, a/c, upstairs; *Fiorella*, R. Pará 640, good Italian; *Veneza*, Av. Getúlio Vargas 570, good Sat. feijoada; *Central*, Rua José Clemente, US$1.50; *Jangada Bar*, opp. *Hotel Amazonas*, good for snacks; good, but expensive snacks in *Hotel Amazonas* itself; *Alemã*, cafeteria, Rua José Paranaguá/Praça da Polícia, good for juices, sandwiches, cakes; good *pratos* at Brasileiros department store, Av. 7 de Setembro; *Lanchonete Bali*, Rua Marechal Deodoro 172, US$1.50 for prato comercial. *Arigato*, R. Guilherme Moreira and Av. 7 de Setembro, for American food. On river front at end of Av. Joaquim Nabuco are several floating restaurants serving fish very cheaply, less than US$1. Reasonable, but probably not completely hygienic. The floating retaurant in the harbour below the market building is rec. for best tucunaré fish. Many restaurants close on Sunday nights and Mondays. City authorities grade restaurants for cleanliness: look for A and B. Good juice bars along Av. Joaquim Nabuco: *Lanchonete Pigalle* particularly rec.

The fishing catch is brought to the waterfront between 2300-0100, including the giant pirarucu. Good fruit and vegetable market by the port.

Souvenirs Indian handicrafts in the *Museu do Indio*, R. Duque de Caxias (nr. Av. 7 Setembro) and at the Funai shop (R. Maj. Gabriel 592). The *Central Artesanato* Handicraft Centre (Rua Recife s/n, nr. Detran) has local craft work. A *Festa de Arte* is held on Sundays from 1700 in Praça de Saudade. *Casa de Beija-Flor*—The House of the Hummingbird (R. Quintino Bocaiúva) good and centrally located. *Selva Amazônica*, Mercado Municipal, for wood carvings and bark fabric. For hammocks go to R.dos Andradas where there are many shops.

Bookshop *Livraria Nacional*, stocks some French books, the *Livraria Brasília* has some English books.

Car repairs Mavel VW, highly recommended, English spoken.

Entertainment (including gambling): *Vogue Club* (jacket and tie obligatory), *Boîte Inglês*, *The In Crowd*, *Danielo's*. *Spectrum*, R. Lobo D'Almada 322. *Canoas*, Miranda Leão 167A, good live music, bar, expensive but rec. Cachoeirinha has a number of bars offering music and dancing, liveliest at weekends. *Superstar*, next to the terminal; *Orvalho da Noite*, R. Santalsabel 1000; *Nostalgia Clube*, R Ajuricaba 800; *Clube de Samba*, R Manicoré.

Clubs Ideal; Athletic Club of Rio Negro; Bosque (bathing pool, tennis courts).

Cinema The cinemas in Manaus are located in: R. José Clemente (opp. Teatro Amazonas); R. Joaquim Sarmento (corner R. 24 de Maio); Av. Eduardo Ribeiro (Manaus Shopping Centre); Av. Joaquim Nabuco (400m. north Av. 7 de Setembro); Av. Joaquim Nabuco (800m. north Av. 7 de Setembro); R. Jonathas Pedrosa (corner Av. 7 de Setembro). Most foreign films are shown with original soundtrack and Portuguese sub-titles. Afternoon performances are recommended as long queues often form for the evening performances.

Museums Museu do Indio (Indian Museum), kept by the Salesian missionaries, the museum's collection includes handicrafts, ceramics, clothing, utensils and ritual objects from the various Indian tribes of the upper Rio Negro, Rua Duque de Caxias (nr. Av. 7 Setembro); open Mon.-Fri. 0800-1200 and 1400-1700, Sat. 0800-1200, T 234-1422, US$0.30; **Museu do Porto de Manaus (Harbour Museum)**, kept by Portobras, the national harbour authority, holds various historical pieces, documents, letters, diaries and charts, Rua Vivaldo Lima 61 (nr. Harbour); open Mon.-Sat. 0700-1100 and 1300-1700, Sun. 1200-1700, T 232-0096; **Museu Tiradentes**, kept by the Military Police, the museum holds selected historical pieces and old photographs, Praça da Policia; open Mon. 1400-1800, Tues.-Fri. 0800-1200 and 1400-1800, T 234-7422; **Museu de Minerais e Rochas (Geological Museum)** contains a large collection of minerals and rocks from the Amazon region, Est. do Aleixo 2150; Mon-Fri 0800-1200 and 1400-1800, T 236-1582; **Museu do Homem do Norte (Anthropological Museum)** reviews the way of life of the Amazonian population; social, cultural and economic aspects are displayed with photographs, models and selected pieces, Av. 7 de Setembro 1385 (nr. Av. J. Nabuco); open Mon-Fri 0800-1200 and 1300-1700, T 232-5373; **Instituto Geográfico e Histórico do Amazonas**, located in one of the older districts of central Manaus, houses a museum and library of over 10,000 books which thoroughly document Amazonian life through the ages, Rua Bernardo Ramos 117 (nr. Prefeitura); open Mon.-Fri. 0800-1200, T 232-7077, US$0.20; **Museu de Ciências Naturais da Amazônia (Natural Science Museum)**, newly inaugurated, has a pavilion with insects and fish of the region, Est. Belém s/n (difficult to get to, best take a taxi), Tues.-Sun. 0900-1700, T 244-2799.

Jardim Botânico "Chico Mendes" The botanical gardens, now renamed after the murdered Amazonian rubber tapper and trade union leader, contain a collection of plants from the Amazon region. Unfortunately the plants are not well named. Av. André Araujo s/n (Buses Aleixo, Coroado). Daily 0800-1200 and 1400-1700.

Zoo Run by CIGS, the Brazilian Army Unit specializing in jungle survival. About 300 Amazonian animals are kept in the Gardens, panthers, tapirs, monkeys, alligators and various species of birds (latest description of the conditions for the animals is "appalling"). Est. Ponta Negra 750. Bus 205 or 217 (marked "Ponta Negra"), US$0.10, every 1/2 hr from Rua Tamandaré, opp. cathedral in centre, alight 400 metres past the 1st Jungle Infantry Barracks (a big white building). Open 0800-1700. Entrance for foreigners, US$0.75. Small zoo also at *Hotel Tropical*, see above. Instituto Nacional de Pesquisas Amazonas (INPA), Estrada de Aleixo, at km. 3 (any bus to Aleixo), has named trees and manatees (best seen Wed. and Fri. at 0830 when water is changed), caimans and giant otters; worth a visit and good for birdwatchers.

Exchange Lloyds Bank, Rua Guilherme Moreira 147; Banco do Brasil, Rua Marechal Deodoro (5th floor) and Airport (basement) changes dollars at tourist rate, efficient; many local banks. Open 0900-1600. Most offices shut afternoons. Foreign exchange operations 0900-1200 only, or close even as early as 1100. Reported that only Banco do Brasil and Lloyds will change US$ notes. It is possible to change US$ at the airport; open 24 hrs. per day. Exchange at the main hotels but not the *Tropical*, though, official rates only), at Souvenirs de Manaus shop and at Luciatur, Av. Eduardo Ribeiro 365, Minitur and Selvatur (good rates); try also bakery opp. *Hotel Rio Branco* for cheques, Francisco or Agostinho at 1st floor, Dr Moreira 105, in pedestrian shopping centre, and Sr. Ayoub, Av. 7 de Setembro 711. Canto Turismo, Rua Rui Barbosa, good rates. It is not safe to change money on the streets.

Consulates Most open a.m. only. **Peruvian**, Conjunto Aristocratais, Chapada, Rua A, Casa 19 (T 236-3666, open 0800-1400). **Colombian**, please note that apparently the Colombian consul (Rua Dona Libânia 62, near opera house, T 234-5777) has been advising travellers from Manaus to Leticia that if they are only visiting Leticia they do not require a tourist card. Either get your Colombian tourist card before reaching Manaus or tell the consul you are travelling further into Colombia, which will probably then require proof of money and return ticket. **Venezuelan**, Rua Recife 1620, T 236-0406 (bus Cachoeirinha Chapada, alight near Detran), 0800-1500; the Consul will give you a visa only if you have an air ticket into and out of Venezuela. **Bolivian**, Av. Eduardo Ribeiro 520, Sala 1410, T 237-8686.

British, Eduardo Ribeiro 520, Sala 1202 T 234-1018. United States, Rua Dr Machado 106 T 234 4546 (office hours) and 232 1611 (outside office hours), Mr. James F. Fish. Will supply letters of introduction for US citizens. **W. Germany**, Rua Barrosa 355, 1st floor, room A, T 232-0890; **Spain**, Instalação 124, T 234-0465; **Dutch**, Rua M.Leão 41, T 234-8719/223-6874; **Italy**, R. Belo Horizonte 240, T 234-8059; **Japanese**, Rua Ferreira Pena 92, T 232-2000; **Danish**, Rua M.Leão 45, T 233-6094; **Norway**, Rua Terazina 256, T 234-7073; **Belgium**, 13 qd D conj Murici, T 236-1452; **Portugal**, Rua Terezina 193, T 234-5777.

Hospital of tropical medicine, treatment free, some doctors speak a little English: take "Dom Pedro" bus from main terminal, about 20 min. ride. Dr Hank Koolen, T 234-5955, English-speaking, is sympathetic to sick gringos.

Laundromat Bd Álvaro Maia 1570, Mon.-Sat. 0800-2200, coin operated, take mini bus ROTA 05 from Av. 5 de Setembro.

Post Office Main office including poste restante in Marechal Deodoro (for American Express, Rua Saldanho Marinho 530). On the first floor is the philatelic counter where stamps are sold, avoiding the long queues downstairs. Staff don't speak English but are used to dealing with tourists. For airfreight and shipping, Alfândega, Av. Marones Santa Cruz (corner of M. Deodoro), Sala 106. For airfreight and seamail, Correio Internacional, Rua Monsenhor Coutinho e Av. Eduardo Ribeiro, downstairs (bring your own packaging).

Telephone TeleAmazonas on Rui Barbosa, opp. Banco do Brasil (most central); Av. Getúlio Vargas, about 7 blocks N of 7 de Setembro, or Rua Guilherme Moreira.

Tourist Information Emamtur, Praça 24 de Outubro, Rua Tarumã 379 helpful, airport and floating harbour. Town map from *Hotel Amazonas* or from Amazon Explorers, *Hotel Lord. Guide Book of Manaus*, US$3, available from *Hotel Amazonas* and other places, in English, useful. *A Notícia*, newspaper, lists local entertainments and events.

Tours There are many different kinds of tours: "luxurious", which are comfortable but "set up" for tourists; some aiming at seeing lots of animals, and others at seeing how the people in the jungle live. Be sure to ascertain in advance the exact itinerary of the tour, that the price includes everything (even drink and tips), that the guide is knowledgeable and he himself will accompany you, and that you do not want to kill anything rare. It is worth shopping around for the best service and bargaining may reduce prices. **N.B.** Guides must be officially registered with Embratur and must carry an identity card.

Bill Potter, resident in Manaus, writes: opposite Manaus, near the junction of the Rio Negro and the Rio Solimões, lies the Lago de Janauri, a small nature reserve. This is where all the day or half-day trippers are taken usually combined with a visit to the "meeting of the waters". Although many people express disappointment with this area because so little is seen and/or there are so many "trourist-trash" shops, for those with only a short time it is worth a visit. You will see some birds and with luck dolphins. In the shops and bars there are often captive parrots and snakes. The area is set up to receive large numbers of tourists, which may relieve pressure on other parts of the river. Boats for day trippers leave the harbour constantly throughout the day, but are best booked at one of the larger operators such as Amazon Explorers or Selvatour.

Those with more time can take the longer cruises and will see various ecological environments, but bear in mind that most tour operators will make a trip up the Rio Negro because it is easier to navigate, generally calmer and there are many fewer biting insects. There is also much less animal life in general, so to see any patience and luck and needed. On the Rio Solimões there is more wildlife, but you are less likely to see anything because you'll be constantly fighting the mosquitos and sandflies.

Another alternative is to go up river to one of the jungle hotels. From the base, you can then take short trips into the forest or along the river channels.

Taking a transport boat from Manaus is not a substitute for a tour as they rarely get near to the banks and are only interested in getting from A to B as quickly as possible. The passengers see very little of the forest. An exception to this rule is the Enasa tourist service to Belém, where the boat tries to take a route more interesting for tourists.

Amazon Explorers Manaus Ltda, run by Manoel (Bebê) Barros, Rua Quintino Bocaiúva 189, T 232-3052 his day's tour including "meeting of the waters", Lago do Januari and rubber collecting, US$20 including lunch, has been highly recommended by most users; 32-hour trips, require a minimum of 4 people; other tours available. Boat *Amazon Explorer* available for hire at about US$230 per day. *Kurt Glück*, Quintino Bocaiúva 224, Caixa Postal 361, offers a more personal service at US$100 day plus food and fuel; his shortest boat trips, which need to be booked as far in advance as possible, last five days in an open 5.5 metre canoe, and he explores many of the tributary rivers of the Amazon; maximum two persons. *Transamazonas Turismo*, Leonardo Malcher 734, T 232-1454/232-4326 (reservations through South American Turismo, Av. N.S. de Copacabana 788, T 255-2345, 22050 Rio de Janeiro), for parties of 10 or less offers a 3-days-plus stay at *Amazon Lodge*, a floating lodge on Lake Periquitão, 80 km. from Manaus, or *Amazon Village*, an hotel on dry land, about US$100 basic charge, inc. meals and transfers, + US$50 per night, recommended, book well in advance. *Windjammer Adventures Club*, owner and operator Hans Budig, multilingual, rec, Caixa Postal 541, AG.M. Coutinho 69000, T 234-6028/1580, USA T (212) 986-9191. *Ariaú Jungle Tower*, Rio Amazonas Turismo, at *Hotel Monaco*, Rua Silva Ramos 41, T 234-7308, 35 km from Manaus on a side channel of the Rio Negro, 16 rooms and penthouse, 35-metre high observation tower and a 1-km walkway across a swamp, trips to Anavilhanas islands, US$100 basic fee inc meals and transfers, plus US$50 per night, generally good, but US$5 surcharge for non-residents. The better hotels also arrange tours (ask for Joe Sears in *Hotel Tropical*), and so do *Selvatur* (office in *Hotel Amazonas*, T 233-2900), Rio Negro trip per person, US$10, 0800-1300, with lunch at *Janaurylândia* floating hotel, returning at 1500, US$30 or 2-day trip for US$200 p.p. *Jungle Trips*, R.Guilherme Moreira 281, 3-day jungle trip, all included, irrespective of numbers, for US$130; *Amazon Odyssey*, Rua Guilherme Moreira 286-A (T 234-2348/1147), run by Englishman, Richard Bryan, 2-3 day jungle trips (*Janauaca Jungle Lodge*—US$170), good value; *Safari Ecológico*, Av. Marechal Câmara 160, Sala 621, Caixa Postal 3321, CEP 20.010, Rio de Janeiro, T (021) 240-6785, has been recommended for its 3 and 6 day/night ecological tours on the Amazon, US$499 and US$899 (US$450 and US$815 April-May) respectively. (Manaus address: Rua Lima Bacury 204, T 233-6910, bookings also through Carretour du Brésil, Paris; Brazil Nuts, Fairfield CT, USA; Jolivac, Montreal. All tours are accompanied by guide, scientific adviser and doctor; boat is equipped with full safety equipment; jungle walks, fishing, visits to caboclo settlements and boatyards, swimming, nighttime excursions.

There appears to be an endless supply of guides: those listed below have been positively recommended by travellers: for trips on the Amazon and Rio Negro, Moacir Fortes, R. Miguel Ribas 1339, Santo Antônio, Manaus, T 232-7492 or through Amazonia Expeditions Ltd, Houston, T (713) 660-8115 (has his own 19-metre boat *Amazonia Expedition*), he speaks English and German (US$100 per day, plus fuel and food). Ernesto Carvalho, Cx. Postal 2890, Manaus, contactable through *Hotel Rio Mar*, does a 3-day, 3 night trip for US$100 per couple 80 km. up the Solimões to the Lagoa do Janauaca, using local boats. Also Gerry Hardy, contact through *Hotel Rio Branco*, or T (092) 2376981, or Paul Hardy, Rua Efigênio Sales, Cond. Jardim Vila Rica, Quadra B, Casa 6, 69060 Manaus, T 236 8734, English-speaking, 4 days US$70, min. 4 people, everything included. *FM Turismo* (director Pedro Neto), Rua Saldanha Marinho 700, T 232-8811/233-9428, Telex 092-1348 FMUR, English spoken, specializing in special interest and professional groups, rec, about US$100 p.p. per day. Margareth Rose Fernandes, *Jungle World Turismo*, Guilherme Moreira, rec.; Elmo de Morais López and Cássio Serra Vieira, Rua Henrique Martins 364, Centro, for 2-5 day tours, 2-4 people, sleeping in hammocks, US$100 a day per couple; Gentil Metelo, P.O. Box 2792, Manaus, T 236-5894/232-4876, has his own agency, 10-metre covered canoe, access to 14-metre, diesel-powered boat with crew, will arrange tours from 1 hour to 1 month, very knowledgeable, speaks Portuguese, English, French, Spanish and Italian; Marco Valério Teixeira, P.O. Box 2968, Manaus, T 234-1315/6, or contact through *Hotel Internacional*, offers a 3-day tour for US$80 p.p., involving a one-day canoe journey beyond the Lago do Janauaca, one day in a camp, then the final day returning by bus (along BR-319) and ferry. José Nunes is a guide who speaks fluent English and has a combi for general transport (T 233-5102); Gustavo, a Peruvian, 3-day tours for US$110 p.p. for 2 (less for more people), he speaks several languages, T 233-0958; *Cristóvão Amazonas Turismo*, Marechal Deodoro 89, Salas 605/1203, T 233-3231, experienced jungle guides, reasonably-priced tours for 1, 2 or more days, German, English, French, Italian, Spanish spoken, very helpful. Miguel M. Barbará (El Barón), Caixa Postal 1227, Manaus 69.000, operates the *Xarrua* for tours on the Rio Negro, US$100-120 for 4; Francisco Almeida, *Aventura Turismo*, Rua 10 de Julho 130, loja 2, P.O. Box 949, T 234-0197, also arranges tours on the Rio Negro; Aquinaldo Telex da Silva, contact via *Central Hotel*, R. Dr. Moreira 202, T 234-2197, personal tours, adventurous interesting and cheap, speaks English; Rubens Silva, Eduardo Ribeiro 420, has been recommended for his 3-day trip up the Rio Branco for 2-5 people, US$110 p.p.; Carlos Francisco Viana, Av. Epaminondas 751-9, US$60 p.p. for 3 days, all inclusive; Francisco da Silva Karaja, Rua Dapaz 189A, T 238-5592, speaks English and French; Luis Alberto Motta, Rua Carla Tupinambá Nobre, Quadra 22, Casa 30, Conjunto Belvedere (take bus "Alvorada 2", alight at Panificadora Belvedere). Motorized canoes can be hired from behind Mercado Municipal, US$50 for 6-hr. trip, takes 8, with navigator/guide, goes to inaccessible places.

For those prepared to spend around 10 days in the interior on a real expedition, contact Carlos Colares, Av. Atlântica 91, Raiz, 69.000 Manaus, T 092-237-1961, Telex 092-165 XPMNA, or P.O.Box 360, who conducts private excursions, with fishing, hunting and exploring in the more remote regions of the Rio Negro (max. 4 people—US$200). Carlos Colares speaks good English. Similar tours arranged by Sabrina Lima de Almeida, R. Boa Esperança 6, T 237-7359, Portuguese speaking only, rec.

Generally, between April and September excursions are only by boat; in the period October-March the Victoria Regia lilies virtually disappear. Fishing is best between September and March (no flooding).

Bird-watchers can see many kinds of birds in and around the grounds of the *Hotel Tropical* (for instance: fly catchers—kingbirds and kiskadees, swallows, yellow-browed sparrows, aracaris—member of the toucan family, woodpeckers, woodcreepers, thrushes, anis, three species of tanager, two of parrots—the dusky and blue-headed). Sloths and monkeys may also be seen. Bird-lovers anxious to pursue their hobby on the Amazon River and its backwaters should contact Moacir Fortes, see above for address and further details (we are grateful to John and George Newmark of Eastbourne for this information).

The enterprising go to the Capitânia do Porto and find out what boats are making short trips; e.g., Manaus-Itacoatiara, US$6 first-class. For swimming, it is possible to travel to Ponta Negra beach (no shade) by Soltur buses for US$0.25, though beach virtually disappears beneath the water in April-August and is now polluted. Good swimming at Bolívar Falls; in the river Tarumã, where lunch is available, shade, it is crowded at weekends, and not too nice; take Tarumã bus from Rua Tamandaré or Rua Frei J. dos Inocentes, 1/2 hr., US$0.15 (very few on weekdays), getting off at the police checkpoint on the road to Itacoatiara.

About 15 km. from Manaus is the confluence of the Solimões (Amazon) and the Rio Negro, which is itself some 8 km. wide. Here you can see the meeting of the blue-black water of the Rio Negro with the yellow-brown Solimões flood; the two rivers run side by side for about 6 km. without their waters mingling. Tourist agencies run boat trips to this spot, or if travelling on a tight budget you can get up about 0330 in Manaus, take a "milk boat" such as the *Capitão Braga* (try to arrange the day before) at about 0400. It returns about 1300, passing through the confluence. Also the *Joanne d'Arc* leaves the dock area around 0730 and returns late afternoon, and the *Castelo*, 0800 to 1500 to the confluence, US$2. Alternatively hire a motorized canoe from near the market for about US$10 per hr. (you'll need 3 or 4 hrs. to take in the experience properly). The simplest way is to take a taxi or "Vila Buriti" bus to the Careiro ferry dock, and take the car ferry across. The ferry goes at 0700, returning 0900, 1100, returning 1400, and 1500, returning 2000 (approx.). You can also take small private launches across, 40 mins. journey, about US$10 per seat. A 2-km. walk along the Porto Velho road from the Careiro ferry terminal will lead to a point from which Victoria Regia water lilies can be seen in April-September in ponds, some way from the road. If you continue over the Capitari bridge, you reach unspoilt jungle. There are several small restaurants on the S bank in Careiro, where the road SW to Porto Velho and the South begins.

Urs Bucher, of Zug, Switzerland, recommends a trip to Manacapuru, 84 km on AM-070 by bus 304 (30 mins.) at 0800, there is a special bus which is quicker, ferry from São Raimundo (30 mins.)and 2-hr. bus ride (bus every hour), to see a typical Amazon town (buy bus ticket before you get on the ferry: don't wait till you arrive at the other side). A small market town on the Solimões W of Manaus, with three basic hotels and *Il Maccarone* pizzeria, Av. Eduardo Ribeiro 1000, with its friendly Italian owner Mário. Another village one can visit is Araçá, a 3-hr bus ride from Rodoviária in the direction of Castanho; the journey includes a ferry crossing at the confluence of the Negro and Solimões (fare to Araçá US$0.70). The village is on the banks of the River Mamori; canoes can be hired for US$3-5 for a day (night trips also possible) and you may be able to sling your hammock in a private house. Plenty of wildlife close at hand. 3 buses a day return to Manaus. Helmut Zettl of Austria, recommends a trip from São Raimundo to Barcelos on the Rio Negro, in the boat *Emerson Madeiros*, 2 days, and a night an *Hotel Oasis*, where you can meet Tatunca Nara, a Brazilian von Daniken.

Roads To *Itacoatiara*, 285 km. E on the Amazon, with Brazil-nut and jute processing plants (bus service 8 a day, 4 hrs); now paved route AM-010, 266 km, through Rio Preto da Eva.

A mostly unpaved road in poor condition and closed in rainy season runs N from Manaus to Boa Vista (770 km.—see below).

The Catire Highway (BR 319) from Manaus to Porto Velho, which is supposedly paved with work continuing (in poor shape nonetheless throughout), sometimes closed March-May during the rainy season (868 km.). It is possible to ship a car down river on a barge. Bus, Manaus-Porto Velho, 0830 and 1400 with Eucatur, US$15, 24 hrs., best to book in advance. Bus to Humaitá; 679 km., where the Catire Highway crosses the Transamazônica, twice a day, 18 hrs. (including 5 ferry crossings), US$6; three buses a day from Humaitá to Porto Velho (3 hrs. with one ferry crossing, paved stretch), 257 km., US$3. If driving this highway, the following information may be useful (but note that conditions change greatly according to season): the first ferry (Careiro da Várzea) is pretty disorganized; at Km. 40 there is a bridge and a floating grocery store; ferry at Km. 42; at the town of Careiro (second place of this name), about Km. 80, third ferry, there is a service station where you can camp, and the US priest here (Father Jim) welcomes English speakers at his church on the square. At Km. 245, Sentinela dos Pampas, there is a ferry across the Igapó-Açu, petrol and camping; between this ferry and Km. 325, Hevelândia (service station, branch road AM-464 84 km. SE to Madeira river opp. Manicoré) the road deteriorates, but improves a little to Piquiá, Km. 500, where there is a clean restaurant with showers and toilets (service station also at Jutaí, Km. 370). If there is no petrol at Km. 500, there is another station at Km. 570. As the road approaches the turnoff to Humaitá (Km. 672), it improves. Between Humaitá and Port Velho there is a service station at Km. 700.

Bus station is 5 km. out of town at the intersection of Av. Constantino Nery and Rua Recife; take local bus from centre, US$0.30, marked "Aeroporto Internacional" or "Cidade Nova" (or taxi, US$4). Local buses to Praça 14 or airport leave from opposite *Hotel Amazonas* (take airport bus and alight just after Antártica factory) or take local bus to Ajuricaba. Hitch-hiking from Manaus can be very difficult. For Boa Vista, take a Tarumã bus to the customs building and hitch from there, or try at "posta 5", 2 km. beyond Rodoviária.

Air Services International flights: Varig to Iquitos twice a week, Bogotá, Panama and Miami once each; LAB twice weekly to La Paz, via Santa Cruz, Caracas and Miami. Manaus-Iquitos, Cruzeiro do Sul, once or twice a week (Sat./Wed.) US$270 one way, stopping at Tefé and Tabatinga for Leticia (separate Manaus-Tabatinga—US$90, Tabatinga-Iquitos—US$85 available and cheaper). To Georgetown, Guyana, Varig/Cruzeiro once a week stops at Boa Vista, otherwise to the Guyanas, connection must be made in Belém.

Internal flights: There are frequent internal flights with Varis, Vasp and Transbrasil. The most frequent routes are Brasília-Rio, Brasília-São Paulo and the N.E. Coast milk run Santerém-Belém-Sao Luís-Teresina-Fortaleza-Recife. Transbrasil tends to be cheaper than the others. For flights to other Amazon towns call Taba (232-0149). Taba flights can be irregular and often reservations cannot be changed. Return reservations cannot be made with Taba when purchasing ticket. Transbrasil's daily schedules (Jan. 1990): 0130 for Brasília (change here for Rio and Belo Horizonte) and São Paulo (change for Curitiba, Cuiabá, Porto Alegre and Florianópolis); 0745 for Brasília (change for São Paulo, Curitiba and Porto Alegre) and Rio; 1945 for Belém, São Luis and Fortaleza (change here for Recife, where connections for Maceió and Aracaju). In winter time, flights leave 1 hour later. Vasp flies to Santarém, Altamira, Belém, São Luís, Teresina, Fortaleza, Recife, Brasília, Goiânia, Belo Horizonte, Rio, São Paulo, Salvador, Rio Branco, Porto Velho, Vilhena, Cuiabá and Campo Grande.

The taxi fare to or from the airport is US$5, but settle price before journey or obtain a ticket that fixes flat-rate fares, or take bus 608 or hourly bus 201 marked Aeroporto Internacional from Rua Tamandaré near cathedral, US$0.20. Last bus at night to airport from R. Tamandaré at 2345; last from airport is 2330. (Taxi drivers often tell arrivals that no bus to town is available, be warned!) It is sometimes possible to use the more regular, faster service run by the *Tropical Hotel*. Check all connections on arrival. N.B. Check in time is 2 hours in advance. Allow plenty of time at Manaus airport, formalities are very slow, and there are queues for everything (try asking an official if you can queue-jump if you are a foreigner with no duty-free items to declare). The restaurant serves good à la carte and buffet food through the day, "certainly much better food than you are going to get on your flight." Local flights, such as Taba to Tabatinga, leave from airport terminal 2: make sure in advance of your terminal.

Shipping For details of Enasa services, **see page** 436. We are advised that it is better to travel Manaus-Santarém and Santarém-Belém in local boats than to use the normal Enasa service, though to Belém the direct trip by M.V. *Benjamin* is acceptable. Enasa to Belém once a week at 1800, the day is normally Thur., but day and frequency may change every month, but in any one month it's the same day of the week (buy ticket in advance, Enasa office closes 1130 on Sat. very crowded, board early); 4 days, one class, hammock space only, US$11; insanitary, with inadequate number of life jackets; bar on board (foreigners 1st class only fare comparable with night flight). Take your own cutlery and utensils, they are unobtainable after the first meal; it is preferable also to take own food. The address of the Enasa line is R. Mal Deodoro 172, Ed. Galeria Central, 6th Floor, Suite 601, T 232-7084. Taxi from centre to docks, US$1.20. Occasional German vessels.

Fairly frequent (irregular) river boats to Tefé (3 days, US$20, including food), and Benjamin Constant (see below). Boa Vista (not good), US$19, 60 hrs to Carcaraí then 3½ hrs by bus. Porto Velho (US$70 in 2-berth cabin, US$30 2nd class, 7 days, 3 days downstream at high water, rec. boat, *Clivia*). Buy a hammock (*rede*—pronounced "hedgie", best in Rua dos Andrades) if travelling 2nd or 3rd class, plenty of drinking water and plenty of books to read; often the boats only stop at night. Boats to Santarém almost every evening except Sun. (about 1800), from E end of dock, journey can be as little as 33 hrs.; prices vary, roughly US$14 lower deck, US$15 upper deck, US$37.50 cabin (Navio Motor Emerson); *Dejard Viera*, leaves Wed., 1800 37 hrs., US$16 lower deck, US$20 upper, US$28 cabin, US$12 by *Cidade de Natal*, well rec.; also rec. *Miranda Dias*, small, family-run, reasonable food and sanitary conditions, US$30 for hammock space and food; *Ayapua*, US$28 d, a/c cabin (cold at night) including meals, leaves Manaus every Fri. 1830 (no guaranteed connexion to Belém). Also rec. to Santarém, *Rio Nilo*, leaves Wed. 1800, clean, good food, US$16 for hammock space, US$28 cabin, 2 nights; also M.V. *Onze de Maio*, leaving each Tues. evening, its sister ship doing return at same time, good meals, top deck with chairs, tables. Shipping a car: either with Enasa (fortnightly), Envira, or Sonave Cia, Entrada do Bombeamento 20, Compensa, Manaus, T 234-4803/4302, telex 092-2463 SOCN, rec., driver free, one passenger and car US$250 plus US$30 tax at the port each end of the journey, weekly to Belém, inc. meals (no variety), sleep in car or hammock; cheaper if you load the car on to an empty truck (trucks are shipped on pontoons, so you may get your car on one of these). Other companies Transnav, Av. 7 de Setembro 1251, Room 612, T 234-1062/1570 (talk to Geraldo Brandão), and Jonasa, which leaves from Compensa, are somewhat cheaper than Enasa and Sonave for shipping cars to Belém. The Capitânia do Porto, Av. Santa Cruz 265, Manaus, has a list of all shipping (you won't be allowed in wearing shorts). All boats, when berthed, display destination and time of sailing so you can check facilities and costs. Boats for Belém and international shipping leave from west end of the docks (entrance at Capitânia do Porto), all others from east end, where a new pier is being built. The shipping agencies are beside the market halls on left of BR316, 1 km. before the landing point, also the cargo harbour.

N.B. Be careful of food on the boats; may be cooked in river-water. You may need a visa to travel to Peru; consulate address above. Those arriving from Leticia should go to the police for their immigration entrance stamp, but you should get this in Tabatinga. Departures to the less important destinations are not always known at the Capitânia do Porto. Be careful of people who wander around boats after they've arrived at a port: they are almost certainly looking for something to steal.

Passports For those arriving by boat who have not already had their passports stamped, the immigration office is on the first of the floating docks next to the tourist office. Take the dock entrance opposite the cathedral, bear right, after 50 metres left, pass through a warehouse to a group of buildings on a T section.

Tefé (pop. 26,000) lies approximately halfway between Manaus and the Colombian border. The waterfront consists of a light sand beach; waterfront market Mon. a.m.; the nuns at the Franciscan convent sell handicrafts and embroidery; there are three small hotels and five pensions (*Anilce*, Praça Santa Teresa 294, E, clean, a/c, do not leave valuables in your room; *Hotel Panorama*, rec., good restaurant), the restaurant *Au Bec d'Or* by the port, French/Amazonian cuisine, and an airport with connection to Manaus. Recommended boat, *Captain Noones* (safe food, plenty of space, drinks on sale). Also *Jean Filho*, leaves Manaus 1800 Sat. (arrives Mon. p.m.), leaves Tefé Tues. 1900 (arrives Wed. p.m. or Thurs. a.m.). US$19 first class with good food, bottled water, 2nd class and small cabins available.

For jungle tours, contact Joaquim de Jesus López, Rua Hermes Tupina No. 740, Barro Holaria, Tefé, not a professional guide, but he has been recommended for self-organized trips (cost for 4 for 1 week, US$200). No English spoken.

Benjamin Constant (pop. 15,000) on the frontier with Peru, with Colombian territory on the opposite bank of the river. Several hotels, including, *Benjamin Constant*, beside ferry, C, all a/c, some with hot water and TV, good restaurant, arranges tours, postal address Apartado Aéreo 219, Leticia, Colombia; store opposite exchanges cheques and cash at good rates. *Hotel São Jorge*, E, meal US$2, try bargaining, recommended; *Araponga*, C, run down; *Hotel Lanchonete Peruana*, F, good food; *Márcia Maria*, E with bath, a/c, fridge, clean, friendly, rec. Eat at *Pensão Cecília*, meals US$1.80 each; *Bar-21 de Abril* for less than US$1. Clothes shop on road reaching to port (left hand side) changes US$ cash. Boat services from Manaus, 7 days, or more, US$40, to Manaus, 4 days, or more, cabin (Wed. and Sat. evenings) US$50. Boats from Manaus to Benjamin Constant normally go on to Tabatinga, and start from there when going to Manaus. Prices do vary, try bargaining. Recommended vessels are *Almirante Monteiro*, US$24 with hammock space, US$28 in cabin; *Dominique* and *Cidade de Teresina*, cleaner than most, cabin US$33 p.p., hammock space US$28; *Clívia*, from Manaus every 2nd Sat., 6½ days, returns Wed., 3 days, cabins US$100 for 2 with fan, hammock space US$40 each, good food, clean; *Itaúna* leaves Wed. or Sat. at 1900, 72 hrs. to Manaus, US$33.30 inc. 3 meals, take fresh water; hammock space on the *Comandante Soares* costs US$35, but food is poor. The frigorífico *Conte Maciel* returns empty to Manaus every 10 days, comfortable, clean, good food, 3 days, US$22.50. It is wise to bring food to supplement the rice, beans, chicken and salt fish, and sterilized water (some boats sell chilled beer or Coca Cola); mosquito spray is a must when you are in port, all year round. Ferry (Recreio) to Leticia (Colombia) twice daily, US$1.30, 1½ hrs., ferry calls at **Tabatinga** (pop. 19,000), only 4 km. from Leticia. (*Hotel Miraflores*, E, clean, safe; *Halley*, F, reported dirty, *Residencial Aluguel Paji*, F with bath, fan, clean, unfriendly; *Solimões*, run by the military—close to the airport—E with breakfast, other meals available if ordered in advance, excellent value, clean—some taxi drivers are unaware that this hotel accepts non-military guests, but there is a VW colectivo minibus from the barracks to town centre, harbour and Leticia; excellent *Tres Fronteiras* restaurant. Better accommodation is available in Leticia, there are no border formalities if you go no further into the country. Hammock (good) will cost US$12 in Tabatinga (try Rei de Redes on main road) or Benjamin Constant. It is difficult to change travellers' cheques in Tabatinga (try Casa Branca, Casa Verde or Casa Amarela on main road, or general manager of the main shopping centre), and far harder to purchase Peruvian intis than in Leticia. See under Manaus for flights Manaus-Tabatinga on route to Iquitos. Airport to Tabatinga by minibus, US$0.40. The Port Captain in Tabatinga is reported as very helpful and speaking good English. N.B. The port area of Tabatinga is called Marco. Mosquito net for hammock essential if sailing upstream from Tabatinga; much less so downstream.

Entering Brazil from Colombia Cross frontier between Leticia and Tabatinga. Boats to Manaus also depart from Benjamin Constant (see preceding paragraph and below). Brazilian exit/entry formalities at Marco (Tabatinga) are essential: walk through docks and follow road to its end, turn right at this T-junction for one block, white immigration building is opp. *Café dos Navegantes*, ten minutes' walk from docks, Mon.-Fri., 0800-1200, 1400-1800 (immigration also at airport, may not be open every day), proof of US$500 or exit ticket may be required. This is a frontier area: carry your passport at all times, but travel between Leticia and Tabatinga is very informal. Taxi to Leticia, US$4, colectivo US$0.25. Brazilian Consulate in Leticia, Calle 8, No. 8-71, Mon.-Fri., 1000-1600, requires two black-and-white passport photos and 36 hrs. for visa (best to get your visa beforehand); go there if you have entry problems coming from Peru into Brazil.

Entering Brazil from Peru Boats from Iquitos to the Brazilian border stop at Islandia, a mud-bank anchorage off Benjamin Constant (passengers are ferried by canoe between the two: Peruvian boats are not allowed to stop at Benjamin Constant). You must have a Peruvian exit stamp (obtained on the boat, or at Peruvian consulate in Leticia, or at Puerto Alegría practice seems to vary so check first in Iquitos), and you must get an entry stamp in Tabatinga (yellow fever certificate needed); without either you will be sent back to Peru. Don't wear shorts in the Brazilian immigration office. Take one of the ferries from Benjamin Constant to Tabatinga (1½-2 hrs., US$1, or hire a canoe, US$3), get off at first stop, walk 1 km. to the main road, police offices are on the right, the larger will stamp your passport. To get on to the ferry in Tabatinga it is necessary to walk the plank, narrow muddy and without a handrail. Tans flies Islandia to Iquitos (US$12.75), but there are no guarantees of flights.

To Peru and Colombia N.B. Exit stamps in Tabatinga are given at the airport, whether you are leaving by air or by boat (see above for Leticia in town); you are permitted one week in transit; Tabatinga-Iquitos flights available on Wed. and Sun (US$80); get your Brazilian exit stamp at the airport. Entering Colombia from Brazil, you must have a tourist card to obtain a stamp to go beyond Leticia, but there appears to be no problem in staying in Leticia without a stamp (but you cannot change travellers' cheques without a stamp); check these details on arrival. Colombian consulate on unnamed street opp. Restaurant *El Canto de las Peixadas*, open 0800-1400. Frequent sailings from Peruvian border jetties (Santa Rosa/Islandia) to Iquitos, US$15, 3 days. Peruvian tourist cards obtained from Puerto Alegría, 2 hours up river where boats stop for police checks (these formalities may change).

It is possible to get a launch up the Rio Negro, but there are hardly any villages of more than a few houses; these places are important in terms of communications and food resources. It is vital to be self-sufficient in food and to be able to speak Portuguese or have a Brazilian guide who can negotiate with the locals. Nova Airão, on the west bank of the Negro, is about two days upstream from Manaus. It has a large boat-building centre at the south end, and a fish and vegetable market at the north end. Ice and bread can also be purchased here. The town has many similar houses of wood and corrugated-iron construction. It has a telephone (from which calls to Europe can be made—after a fashion). Airão is the starting point for the **Parque Nacional Jaú** (IBDF office in Manaus, BR-319, Km. 01, Distrito Industrial, Caixa Postal 185, CEP 69.000). Moura is about 5 days upstream from Manaus; it has about 120 people based around the military-run granite quarry. There are basic medical facilities and the military base has an airstrip (only usable September to December) and telecommunications. About a day further upstream is Carvoeira, almost opposite the mouth of the Rio Branco; although small, it has a vibrant festival in the first week of August. A great distance further upstream is São Gabriel da Cachoeira, from where you can continue to Venezuela (see Venezuela section). São Gabriel is near the **Pico de Neblina National Park** (Pico de Neblina is the highest mountain in Brazil, 3,014 metres, IBDF office in Manaus, see above); in São Gabriel, Tom Hanly, an Irish Salesian brother, is helpful, friendly and informative. The town has one hotel, cheap, clean, good food (ask for it), shops and, in the river, rapids for 112 km.

About two days up the Rio Branco is Santa Maria de Boiaçu, a village of about 30 families. There is a military airstrip which is in use in July and August, very basic medical facilities and an indirect radio link with Manaus. There are three small shops selling basic necessities (but they aren't often open), and several tiny, but lively churches. The Rio Branco is yellowish in colour, and less acidic than the Negro. Therefore, biting insects and their associated diseases are more prevalent outside the wet season. The river is better for fishing, though, and there is more wildlife to see. (We are grateful to Marianne Evans of Northampton, for much of this information).

River traffic on the Rio Branco connects Manaus with **Caracaraí**, a busy, but unattractive river port with modern installations. When the Manaus-Boa Vista road is washed out, this is the only route through to Venezuela. There is a passenger boat once a fortnight, or you can ride on the barges which take trucks and their drivers (not recommended for single women). In the rainy season, transport is quite easy to arrange (bargain for your fare, and sling your hammock under a truck); it's an interesting journey, 96 hours upstream, 48 down. The river banks are closer, so there is more to see than on the Amazon and stops in the tiny riverside settlements are fascinating. Bus on from Caracaraí to Boa Vista costs US$3, 3 hrs.

Hotels *Márcia*, F, next to bus stop, a/c, breakfast, clean; *Roraima*, F, cold shower, basic. *Pizzeria Delícia*, good, English spoken.

N.B. The Perimetral Norte road marked on some maps from Caracaraí E to Macapá and W to the Colombian frontier does not yet exist; it runs only about 240 km. W and 125 km. E from Caracaraí, acting at present as a penetration road.

The road which connects Manaus and Boa Vista (BR-174 to Novo Paraíso, then the Perimetral, BR-210) is of rough dirt, except for the last 60 km. to Boa Vista, which are paved. It is often closed in the wet season owing to flooding; the best chance for bus travel is after September. For drivers on this route, some advise being defensive with regard to lorry drivers (who drive for too long, haul too much and drink); others say they are very helpful to anyone in difficulties. There are service stations with toilets, camping, etc., every 150-180 km., but all petrol is low octane; take a tow cable and spares. At Km. 100 is Presidente Figueiredo, with shops and a restaurant. About 100 km. further on is a service station at the entrance to the Uaimiri Atroari Indian Reserve, which straddles the road for about 120 km. Traffic may not stop in daytime except for emergencies or fuel; this part of the road is hilly, with virgin forest and real jungle sounds. There is a police checkpoint and service station at the other end (Km. 325). At Km.359 there is a monument to mark the equator. At Km. 434 is the clean and pleasant *Restaurant Goaio*. The road junction 65 km. further on is a popular stopping place, with petrol, restaurant and showers. Beyond here, large tracts of forest have been destroyed for settlement, but already many homes have been abandoned. The road, built up with poor bridges, then enters a region of dense vegetation. 12 km. before Carcaraí, there is a ferry across the Rio Branco;

continue then to Boa Vista. (If you do not want to go through the hassle of driving this route, you can try to have your vehicle taken by truck.)

Boa Vista has road connections with the Venezuelan frontier at Santa Elena de Uairen (237 km., a rough road, often closed and very slippery when wet, the only gasoline 110 km. south of Santa Elena) and Bomfim for the Guyanese border at Lethem.

Boa Vista (pop. 69,000), capital of the extreme northern State of Roraima (pop. 116,000), is 759 km. N of Manaus. Mount Roraima, after which the Territory is named, is possibly the original of Sir Arthur Conan Doyle's "Lost World". There is swimming in the Rio Branco, 15 mins., from the town centre (too polluted in Boa Vista) reachable by bus only when river is low. This town has a modern functional plan, which often necessitates long hot treks by the traveller from one function to another. It is an expensive place because of nearby goldmining; the influx of *garimpeiros* in the W of the state is threatening the existence of the Yanomami Indians, whose reserves have been violated. Industrial estate S of town. New government district is being built on the NW edge of town. Interesting modern cathedral; also a museum of local Indian culture (poorly kept). Taxi from airport should cost no more than US$3.50 (45 min. walk) and will assume you want *Hotel Tropical* unless you indicate otherwise.

Hotels Generally expensive and heavily booked. *Praia Palace*, A, on river, with beach, hard beds but service friendly, T (095) 224-4147 (good food in restaurant next door); *Eusébio's*, C-D, always full, book ahead, demand single if on your own, very good restaurant, swimming pool, free transport to bus station or airport, recommended; *Paraíso*, Getúlio Vargas e Araújo Filho, D with bath, popular with Guyanese shoppers (reportedly a centre for narcotics trading, not clean, "arrogant and overpriced"); *Roraima*, Av. Cecília Brasil e Benjamin Constant, E-D with bath, not very good value; *Imperial*, E, Benjamin Constant, clean; *Colonial*, Ajuricaba 532, near Consolação church, D, a/c with bath and breakfast, clean; *Brasil* in Rua Benjamin Constant 331 W near Drogafarma, E (do not confuse with sleazy *Hotel Brasa* in same street), also *Lua Nova*, F without, E with a/c, English spoken, often full. *Casa Nova*, Av. Sebastião Diniz, D with a/c, E with fan; *Ideal*, E, mixed reports. *Rodoviária*, at bus station about 1½ km. from town centre, F, communal rooms, clean, shower, clean, friendly, rec.; *Pensão* at grocery at Rua Benito Brasil 566, F. *Tres Nações*, Av. Ville Roy 1885, also close to bus station, E, some rooms a/c, others more basic, reported to be dirty. There are also two missions who offer hospitality to those in need. If all else fails, sling your hammock in the trees around the Rodoviária.

Camping Rio Caviné, 3 km. N of town.

Restaurants *Eusebio's Hotel*, very good; *Senzala*, Av. Castelo Branco 1115, where the town's high society eats; *Casa Grande*, Av. Villa Royo, good; *Churrascaria Venezuela*, bus station; *Bigode*, on waterfront, fish, music at weekends; *Café Pigalle*, just off central square, next to *Eusébio's*, good food, drinks and atmosphere, open till all hours; *Góndola*, Benjamin Constant and Av. Amazonas, good; restaurant and bar in Parque Anana, near airport. Snacks at *Top Set*, Av. Jaime Brasil, *Catequeiro*, Araújo Filho with Benjamín Contant, rec. prato feito. Good prato feito at the restaurant by the petrol station opp. *Hotel Brasil*.

Exchange US$ and Guyanese notes can be changed in Boa Vista; try Ramiro Silva, Rimpex, Av. Jaime Brasil. Travellers' cheques in Banco do Brasil. There is no official exchange agency and the local rates for bolívares are low: the Banco do Brasil will not change bolívares. Best rate for dollars, Casa Pedro José, Rua Araújo Filho 287, T 224 4277; try the chemist/drugstore on main square for dollar exchange or the Compra e Vende Ouro shop on Av. Araújo Filho, or the gold dealers in front of *Hotel Paraíso*.

Bus (See also Border Crossings below). To /from Manaus, by Eucatur, US$14, 22 hrs., advisable to book because sometimes buses are fully booked days in advance, check times. Breakdowns are frequent and the road is poor. Buses often run late, and the night bus has to wait up to 4 hrs. for the Rio Branco ferry. Service may be suspended in the rainy season. Boa Vista-Caracaraí US$3, 3 hrs. To border, see below. Rodoviária is on town outskirts, 3 km.; taxi to centre, US$2.30, bus US$0.30 (marked "13 de Setembro" to centre). Local bus terminal is on Av. Amazonas, just off central praça. Note that it is difficult to get taxi or bus to Rodoviária in time for early morning departures; as it's a 25 minute walk, book a taxi the previous evening.

Hitch-hiking from Boa Vista to Manaus is fairly easy on the many trucks travelling to Manaus;

try from the service station near the Rodoviária. You may have to change trucks at Caracaraí. At the ferry crossing over the Rio Branco there is usually a long queue of waiting hikers; try to arrange a lift on the ferry. Hitching to Santa Elena, Venezuela, is not easy; either wait at the bridge and police checkpoint on the road to the border, or try to find a Venezuelan driver on the square. Drivers often charge for hitches—maybe as much as a bus fare.

Air Travel   To and from Manaus (US$50, night flights US$30). Varig flies to Puerto Ordaz, Venezuela, once/twice a week US$128. Aircraft maintenance, baggage checking and handling are unreliable; Guyanese come to Boa Vista to buy goods unavailable in Guyana—make sure your luggage is not among the excess that has to be taken off the plane. Also to Lethem. No left luggage facilities at airport, and no public transport other than taxis.

Border Crossing, Guyana   Get exit stamp at police station in Lethem, Guyana, then take rowing-boat over border river Tacutu. No car ferry, but river can be forded in dry season. Once in Brazil, register at military camp at Bomfim (hotels: *Blessing*, F, and *Bomfim*) and get entry stamp (closed for lunch). Phone Bomfim 2290 (for one G$) for car to take you to Boa Vista (US$45), or if lucky, take a colectivo (US$15, 3 hrs.) or daily bus at 0800. The bus leaves Boa Vista for Bomfim at 1600 only (according to latest reports, schedules change), US$10, 3½ hrs.; luggage is checked at the Ministério da Fazenda checkpoint, before Bomfim, from where a jeep takes travellers to the Brazilian immigration post (US$1) and then walk the short distance to the river, 5 km. in all. To cross the river, yell "Boat" and a motor boat will come. It is very difficult to hitch between Boa Vista and Bomfim. From Bomfim to Boa Vista the road is acceptable (1 bus daily), but subject to washouts; bridge over Rio Branco. There is another border crossing at Iaramonta from where it is a hard, but rewarding walk to the Guyanese town of Orinduik. A weekly jeep connects Iaramonta with Boa Vista (US$25), also flights once a week, US$84 to Georgetown, often fully booked. A good rate for new cruzeiros is reported in the Guyana border area. New cruzeiros can be changed into G$ in the shop at Brazilian immigration post; Bomfim is a much better place for exchange, but Boa Vista is best. If you need visa to enter Guyana, you must get it in Brasília or São Paulo; no consulate in Boa Vista.

Border Crossing, Venezuela   Everyone who crosses the border from Boa Vista, regardless of nationality, requires a visa (passport must be valid for 1 year). These can be obtained (allow 2-3 days) from the Venezuelan Consulate in Boa Vista, Av. Benjamín Constant 525E (T 095-224-2182, open Mon.-Fri. 0830-1300 but may close earlier—no shorts allowed); the only requirements are one passport photograph and an onward ticket (not an MCO). Health requirements are reported to have been relaxed: a malaria test certificate, yellow-fever vaccination certificate and certificate of medical checkup are no longer necessary, but be prepared for them anyway. It is much simpler to get a visa for Venezuela in Belém (**see page 436**), or maybe even Rio (check in advance); if you have no alternative but the consulate in Boa Vista, you can ask for Embassy in Caracas to telex Boa Vista to prove that you are a bona fide tourist. Border officials may also insist on US$20 a day—however, regulations state that a visa is sufficient. Trucks leave for Venezuela from Rua Benjamin Constant, drivers are not officially supposed to take passengers. Andorinha runs a daily bus between Santa Elena and Manaus, via Boa Vista, US$26. Buses leave Boa Vista for Santa Elena at 0600 (direct) and 0800, US$13.50 (stopping at all check points), in front of *Hotel Fronteras*, rough and dusty, take water, journey 8-10 hrs. Boa Vista-Ciudad Bolívar direct Thur. Border search is thorough (there are also road checks in Venezuela). Entry stamp can be obtained only in Santa Elena; border closes at 1700. There are a bank and a basic hotel, *Pacaraima Palace*, on Brazilian side and you can camp. The road from the frontier is well-maintained and is being paved; it passes through some very scenic countryside.

SOUTHERN AMAZONIA (9)

Porto Velho (1985 pop. 202,000, but growing at an estimated 20,000 a month), capital of the State of Rondônia with a population of 862,000 in 1985, but at least 1.2 million by the end of the decade. The city stands on a high bluff overlooking a curve of the River Madeira; at the top of the hill is the cathedral, built in 1950. The principal commercial street is Av. Sete de Setembro, which runs from the railway station and market hall to the upper level of the city, past the Rodoviária. Parks are under construction. Rondônia is the focus of experimental development in agriculture, with concomitant colonization of the area. At the same time, much of the state is being reserved for Indians and national forests. Porto Velho is expensive because of the local gold rush. About 20 km. from Porto

Velho, the Samuel hydroelectric scheme is under construction, with a new town to house the workers. When it comes on stream in the 1990s, it will be insufficient to provide power for the states of Rondônia and Acre as was originally intended. The population has grown too rapidly. Malaria is common. With the growth in population, crime has increased in the city and outside.

The Madeira is one of the major tributaries of the Amazon. The four main rivers which form it are the Madre de Dios, rising a short distance from Cuzco (Peru); the Beni, coming from the southern Cordillera bordering Lake Titicaca; the Mamoré, rising near Sucre, Bolivia; and the Guaporé, coming out of Mato Grosso, in Brazil.

Hotels *Rondón Palace*, B, Av. Jorge Teixeira with Jacy Paraná, about 4 blocks to the left of bus station, T 221-3166, a/c, hot water, rec.; *Samaúma Palace*, Rua Dom Pedro II, 1038, T 221-3737, B, nice rooms but said not too friendly (221-3159); *Vila Rica*, Av. Carlos Gomes 1616, T 221-2286, L, tower block, "flashy, flamboyant and mechanically efficient"; *Floresta*, Prudente de Morais 2313, T 221-5669, C, a/c, good breakfast, swimming pool, which non-residents may use for the price of a drink or two. *Aliança*, 7 de Setembro 1160, C, a/c, rec. Hotels within sight of the Rodoviária: *Libra*, *Avenida Palace*, 2-star, *Porto Velho Palace*, 2-star; *Príncipe da Beira*, Rua Getúlio Vargas 2287, D (221-6135). From Rodoviária, take bus No. 301 "Presidente Roosevelt" (outside *Hotel Pontes*), which goes to railway station at riverside, then along Av. 7 de Setembro, passing: *Yara*, Gral. Osório 255, E; *Guaporé Palace*, 7 de Setembro 927, E, a/c, restaurant; *Nunes*, 7 de Setembro 1195, F, probably best value among cheapest hotels; *Sonora*, 7 de Setembro 1103, E, clean, fan, clothes washing facilities; *Rio*, Av. Joaquim Nabuco 2110, F, basic, good breakfast, friendly, fairly good cheap meals; *Laira*, Joaquim Nabuco 2005, F with fan; *Brasil*, Av. Pres. Kennedy, 15 mins. from Rodoviária, clean, cheap, breakfast; *Tres Irmãos*, Av. Nações Unidas 30. Hotels often full.

Electric Current   110 volts A.C., elsewhere in Rondônia 220 volts.

Restaurants   At hotels: *Tarantella*, Av. Joaquim Nabuco with 7 de Setembro, fairly good pizza; *Caravela de Madeira*, R. Ariquemes 104, excellent fish, good atmosphere; *Remanso do Tucunaré*, Av. Brasília 1506, popular, cheap; *Carioca*, R. Prudente de Morais 2450, "a hole in the wall", pleasant service, very cheap.

Shopping   Bookshop *Livraria de Rosa*, off Av. 7 de Setembro, near the port, a few English paperbacks; manageress speaks English. Indian handicrafts at *Casa do Índio*, Rua Rui Barbosa 1407.

Car hire   Silva Car, Rua Almirante Barroso 1528, CEP 78.900, Porto Velho, T (069) 221-1423/6040, Telex (069) 1129 SLVL. US$30/day.

Exchange   Banks; try *Hotel Vila Rica* (Carlos, the doorman, for cash), *Hotel Floresta* (cash), *Hotel Rio*, Varig/Cruzeiro office. Local radio news and papers publish exchange rates; try local businesses too. Difficult elsewhere in Rondônia.

Travel Agent   Rotur, near *Hotel Floresta*. Guaporetur, Av. 7 de Setembro 925, Helga speaks English and German.

Air Services   Airport 8 km. W of town. Daily flights to Manaus, Brasília, Cuiabá, Rio Branco, Corumbá, Cruzeiro do Sul, via Rio Branco, Mon. Taba flies Mon., Wed. and Fri. about 1300 to Guajará Mirim, US$25.

River Services   Manaus, 1st class, with passable food; 2nd class very crowded US$30. Journey takes 3-4 days when river high; as much as 7 days when low. The boat leaves on Thurs. and Sat. at 1800. 1st class means upper deck, with more hammock-hanging room, or, if lucky, one of two 2-person cabins (US$70). Advantages to 1st class: more room, better view, coffee with milk, meals served first. Food is safe to eat, though monotonous; water-purifying tablets or bottles of sterilized water strongly recommended. Wait at the Capitânia do Porto in the centre of town for a possible passage on a cargo boat; these boats leave from Porto Bras, down river from Porto Velho. Porto Velho-Humaitá US$6.66 (boat *Dois de Junho*).
    Six days a week a boat leaves at 1800 for Manaus from Manicoré, at the confluence of the Rivers Madeira and Manicoré, US$32 for two nights, and one day's journey, including food; boats from Porto Velho to Manicoré on Mon., Wed. and Sat. (1800, arr. 0200, but you can sleep on the boat), connecting with Manicoré-Manaus boats. *Manicoré* (about 10,000 people) is a pleasant town; the Praça de Bandeira is at the corner of Av. Getúlio Vargas and Av. Pedro Tinoco (one block to left of road that goes up from the dock). *Hotel Manicoré*, 4 blocks left from Praça on Av. Vargas, just before the big church; *Restaurant Tapuia*, 1 block

from Praça in opp. direction to river on Av. Tinoco; slow but good restaurant at floating dock. Fruit market on Av. Vargas.

Buses New Rodoviária on outskirts of town, Av. Pres. Kennedy. Bus to Manaus, 1600, and 2000 normal (US$15), 1700 and 1800 (*leito* US$30), 24-26 hrs. (up to 4 days in the rainy season); to Humaitá, US$2; to São Paulo, change at Cuiabá, sixty-plus hrs., US$42; to Cuiabá, 23 hrs. US$17, take plenty of food and drink. To Guajará-Mirim, see below. To Rio Branco, twice daily, 12 hrs., US$15. Daily bus with Eucatur from Cascavel (Paraná, connections for Foz do Iguaçu) via Maringá, Presidente Prudente, Campo Grande and Cuiabá to Porto Velho. To Cáceres for the Pantanal, Colibri, 18 hrs., US$12. To Vitória, daily, 61 hrs. Hitching difficult, try at the *posto* 2 km. out of town. For Manaus try at the ferry crossing just outside town (may be impossible in the rainy season).

Roads to Cuiabá (BR-364—Marechal Rondon Highway, 1,450 km., fully paved; **see page** 469); Rio Branco, 490 km., following Madeira-Mamoré railway, paved as far as the Acre border; to Humaitá (205 km.) on the Madeira river (fully paved), connecting with the Transamazônica Highway, and on to Manaus (877 km.), not completely paved and in poor condition. Road journeys are best done in the dry season, the second half of the year; the Manaus road (Catire Highway) is sometimes closed in the rainy season.

A result of the paving of BR-364 is the development of towns along it: Ariquemes (159 km. from Porto Velho, municipal pop. 200,000, buses hourly from 0600, 3-4 hrs., Banco do Brasil, some hotels, *Valerius Palace*, E); Nova Vida (200 km.), Jaru (257 km.), Ouro Preto d'Oeste (297 km.), **Ji Paraná** (337 km., municipal pop. 200,000—bus to Porto Velho, US$7, 14 hrs.; to Cuiabá, 15 hrs., US$11, 22 *leito*; hotels *Horizonte*, E, rec. with reasonable restaurants, *Sol Nascente*, F with *churrascaria*, *Hotel Transcontinental*, B, rec.; trips to frontier towns possible, e.g. Nova Colina), Presidente Médici (373 km., 50,000 people), Cacoal (404 km., 200,000 people, Hotels *Cacoal Palace* (D) and *Amazonis*), Pimenta Bueno (440 km., pop. 50,000) and Vilhena on the Rondônia-Mato Grosso border (658 km. from Porto Velho, 170 km. from Cuiabá; *Diplomata Hotel*, D, near bus station; *Rodoviária*, F, rec.; *Gastão*, F). At Vilhena proof of yellow-fever inoculation required: if no proof, new shot. Two cities have grown without prior planning: Rolim de Mouro, W of Pimenta Bueno, with a population of over 60,000 and a *Transcontinental Hotel*, and Itarua do Oeste, 91 km. S of Porto Velho, at what used to be a bus waiting station (population about 5,000).

The **Pacaás Novos National Park**, 765,800 hectares, lies west of the BR-364; it is a transitional zone between open plain and Amazonian forest. Details from IBDF, Av. Gov. Jorge Teixeira, CEP 78.900, Porto Velho; also enquire here about the Jaru and Guaporé Biological Reserves in the State.

Porto Velho was the terminus of the Madeira-Mamoré railway of 367 km. (closed 1971), Brazil's price to Bolivia for annexing the Acre territory during the rubber boom. It cost a life for every hundred sleepers, 6,208 in all, during construction. The line, built 1907-12, by-passed the 19 rapids of the Madeira and Mamoré rivers, and gave Bolivia an outlet of sorts to the Atlantic. It was supposed to go as far as Riberalta, on the Rio Beni, above that river's rapids, but stopped short at **Guajará Mirim** (pop. 41,000). 3 locomotives operate out of Porto Velho. The railway expert will enjoy the ancient steam locomotives in the railway station and on a siding 2 km. away. There are still two engines in working order, which run Sunday excursion trains as far as Santo Antônio, 7 km. away (US$0.10). Small railway museum at station has been moved so that the station can accommodate passengers on the newly restored line. (The conductor on the Sunday train, Silas Shockness, who also runs the shop where the locomotives are being repaired, is from Grenada; his brother Denis runs the museum.) The railway is now replaced by a fair road, which uses its bridges (in poor condition); the 370-km. bus ride (8 buses a day, US$7, takes 7 hrs. or more depending on season—road, in poor condition south of Abunã, is often closed March-May) is far faster than the train was. The Bolivian town of Guayaramerín is across the Mamoré river (speedboat service or ferry, which is free for foot passengers); it is connected by road to Riberalta, and there are air services to other Bolivian cities. An ancient stern wheeler plies on the Guaporé; 26-day, 1,250 km. trips (return) can be made on the Guaporé from Guajará Mirim to Vila Bela in Mato Grosso, fare including food, is US$5. 170 km. from Guajará Mirim, on the Guaporé river, is the Forte Príncipe da Beira, begun in 1777 as a defence of the border with Bolivia. The fort, which is being restored, can be reached from Costa Marques (20 km. by road), which can only be reached by air or by river.

If travelling by road between Porto Velho and Guajará Mirim, two possible stops are at Maluca dos Índios, from where you can visit villages of gold prospectors by the Madeira river; the other is from the railway bridge just before Vila Murtinho where you can see gold panners, and, walking a few hundred metres, the rapids on the Mamoré river.

Guajará Mirim Hotels *Comercial*, E; *Mini-Estrela*, Av. 15 de Novembro 460, E; *Fénix Palace*, Av. 15 de Novembro 459, E; *Hudson*, Av. Marechal Deodoro s/n, E, rec. *Alfa*, Av. Leopold de Mattos; *Camponés*, F.

Restaurant Best is *Oasis*, at Posto Nogueira service station, Av. 15 de Novembro 837, US$5 with drinks.

Museum Museu Municipal at the old railway station beside the ferry landing—small, with railway memorabilia and a few specimens of regional wildlife.

Exchange Banco do Brasil (foreign exchange a.m. only). Loja Nogueira, Av. Pres. Dutra, esq. Leopold de Matos (cash only). There is no market in Brazil for bolivianos.

Note If you need a visa to enter Brazil, apply to the Brazilian Consul at Guayaramerín (Bolivia), open 1100-1300, before crossing the Rio Mamoré into Brazil. If the Policia Federal are not on duty at the waterfront, you must get passport stamped at their office in town, address below. Similarly, before crossing into Bolivia you may need a visa (free) from the Bolivian consul in Guajará Mirim (2 photos needed) in Av. Lepoldo de Mattos, the same buildings as *Hotel Alfa*. Western Europeans can cross river and visit the Immigration Office; which closes at 1100 on Sat. You will need a Brazilian exit stamp from Policia Federal, Av. Antônio Correia da Costa 842.

From Abunã, 220 km. from Porto Velho (*Hotel Ferroviário*, E, including meals, however town is best avoided if at all possible) the road from Porto Velho continues W to **Rio Branco**, (pop 45,000) the capital of the State of Acre, (pop. 385,000, 1985 figure). Hotels always crowded: *Pinheiro Palace*, C, Rui Barbosa 91, T 224-7191, a/c, pool, friendly, rec; *Cuzco*, near airport, new; *Lux Palace*, R. Quintino Bocaiuva 397, T 224-7340, F, clean, friendly (20 mins from centre); *Inacio's*, C, overpriced, dirty, fair restaurant; *Rio Branco*, C, on park, nice but simple; *Amazonas*, *Fontes* (best of a dark bunch of budget hotels, F, not clean), *Fortaleza*, all on left bank. On right bank, *Sucessor*, F, showers, fan, clean, comfortable, friendly. Cheap meals at *Dos Colonos* near market. *Marayina*, for pizzas, sandwiches, cakes, ice cream, popular at night; *Casarão*, also popular; *Churrascaria Triângulo*, near airport, as much charcoal-grilled meat as you can eat, rec.; *Churrascaria Modelo*, Rua Marechal Deodoro 360, less good. There is a park with a military post on one side; beyond is the Governor's palace and another park leading to the market on the bank of the Acre river. There is a bridge across the river, which is only navigable to Manaus in the wet season. The city has a cathedral, an airport and an agricultural research centre. Trips to see rubber tapping, or the religious colony at Colonia Cinco Mil, can be arranged by the travel agent in *Hotel Rio Branco*.

Warning The road from Porto Velho to Rio Branco should be travelled with caution; the area is seriously affected by malaria. We have also received reports of lawlessness on the BR-364 after dark; to be safe, be in a city before nightfall.

At Rio Branco the Transamazônica Highway meets the road from Brasília and goes on to Cruzeiro do Sul and Japim; it is expected to reach the Peruvian frontier further W when completed; it is hoped that it will be continued by the Peruvians to Pucallpa. It is very difficult to get from Rio Branco to Cruzeiro do Sul by road because there is no bus service, and the occasional lorry goes mainly in the dry season; the road is frequently impassable. There is a plane (Cruzeiro do Sul) every Tues., Fri. and Sun. at 0735 to Cruzeiro do Sul (originating in Manaus).

Cruzeiro do Sul (pop. 59,000) an isolated Amazonian town, is situated on the river Juruá; cheap excursions can be made on the river, for example to the village of Rodrigues Alves (2-3 hrs., return by boat or by road, 15 km.). In the jungle one can see rubber-tapping, and collecting the latex into "borrachas" which weigh up to 45 kg. Hotels: *Sandra's*, D; *Novo do Acre*, F, rec., a/c, clean; *Hospedaria Janecir*, F; *dos Viajantes*; *Flor de Maio*, F, facing river, clean, showers, full board available. Restaurant *O Laçador*, good food. Money changing is very difficult; none of the banks will change dollars. Try the airline staff (poor rates). From Cruzeiro do Sul to Pucallpa one can go either by air: Sasa, US$37.50, 50 mins.,—details from Blvd. Taumaturgo 25 (no phone), flies only when plane is full, it seats 5; undertake all formalities at Policia Federal before leaving. Alternatively one can go by boat when river is high (Nov.-Feb.): only for the hardy and well-equipped; journey takes about 10 days: 4 by boat to Tamburiaco, on rivers Juruá and Juruá-Mirim, then 2 days' walk through the jungle to the Peruvian border at Canta Gallo, then 3-4 more days by boat on the rivers Amonia and Abojao to Pucallpa. The regional airline Taba have a permit to fly to Eirunepé on the Juruá river from Manaus and Tabatinga; Eirunepé is a small town near Carauari, where Dutch missionaries live.

A road from Rio Branco (the BR-317), paved as far as Xapuri (the location of the Fundacão Chico Mendes in memory of the environmentalist and union organiser murdered in 1989), goes to Brasiléia (bus twice daily, 6 hrs., US$4, basic hotel, Federal Police give exit stamps), opposite the Bolivian town of Cobija on the Acre River, and finally to Assis Brasil where the Peruvian, Bolivian and Brazilian frontiers meet; across the Acre River are Iñapari (Peru) and Bolpebra (Bolivia). There is no public transport, and little else, beyond Brasiléia to Iñapari. In Assis Brasil, there is one small hotel (a dormitory, basic but clean, friendly), one snack bar, a bank which does not change US dollars (the hotel owner may be persuaded to oblige) and river transport only, which is dependent on the seasons.

N.B. Rio Branco time is one hour behind Manaus time; this means two hours behind Brazilian Standard Time.

THE CENTRE-WEST (10)

The so-called centre-west of Brazil is occupied by the states of Goiás, Mato Grosso and Mato Grosso do Sul (divided from Mato Grosso in 1977) . Goiás is one of Brazil's most rapidly developing agricultural areas, producing cattle, coffee, soya and rice. The Federal District of Brasília (**see page** 274) was subtracted in 1960 from the territory of Goiás, which has been further split to form the new State of Tocantins in the north.

Goiânia (pop. 925,000) 202 km. SW of Brasília, the second (after Belo Horizonte) of Brazil's planned state capitals, was founded in 1933 and succeeded Goiás Velho as capital of the State of Goiás (pop. 4,765,000) in 1937. Goiânia is a spacious city, with its main avenues excellently lit and ornamented with plants; tourists can enjoy the Parque Mutirama with its planetarium on the city's eastern side and the Horto Florestal, with good zoo and anthropological museum in the west; there are a racecourse and a motor racetrack. The Jaó Club on the edge of a reservoir provides for sun bathing and water skiing. Every Sunday morning there is a handicrafts fair in the city's central square, the Praça Cívica, where there is a small museum of local handicrafts, animals and Indian artefacts.

Hotels *Castro Park*, T 223-7766, A, new, warmly rec.; *Samambaia*, Av. Anhanguera 1157, T 261-1444; *Bandeirantes*, same street, No. 3278, T 224-0066; *Umuarama*, Rua 4, No. 492, T 224-1555; *São Conrado*, Rua 3, No. 652, T 224-2411; *Augustus*, Praça Antônio Lizita 702, T 224-1022 (all good D-C). Many cheap hotels e.g. *J. Alves*, opp. Rodoviária; *Santo Antônio*, Av. Anhanguera 6296, F.

Restaurants *Jaó Club; Long Feung*. Goiânia is much cheaper for eating and sleeping than Brasília. Restaurant at the Rodoviária for good food at very low prices, and plenty more eating places nearby.

Bookshop on Rua 4 has some secondhand English books; will exchange.

Banks National banks.

Tourist Office Goiastur, in the football stadium (Estádio Serra Dourada), very friendly: it's rather remote!

Travel Agents Cardealtur, Av. Goiás 382; Incatur, Av. Goiás 151; Transworld, Rua 3, 560, in Galeria Central. All good for exchange.

Airport Nearby, with daily flights to main cities.

Roads and Buses To Cuiabá (Mato Grosso) paved, 4 buses a day, US$12, 13 hrs.; continues to Porto Velho (Rondônia) and Rio Branco (Acre). To Brasília (about 17 a day, 2½ hrs., US$3) and São Paulo (bus services, US$19, 14 hrs.); Campo Grande 18 hrs. US$15. To Goiás Velho, 136 km. Distances by road (km.): Belém, 2,017; Brasília, 202; Campo Grande, 1,212; Corumbá, 1,641; Cuiabá, 934; Foz do Iguaçu, 1,232; Manaus, 3,222; Porto Alegre, 2,025; Recife, 2,505; Rio, 1,354; Salvador, 2,301; São Paulo, 918.

Anápolis, 61 km. nearer Brasília, with a population of 161,000, is an important trading centre.

Hotels *Itamarati; Príncipe; Central Palace; Anápolis*. Many cheap ones around bus station, e.g. *Serra Dourada*, Av. Brasil 375, E, good value.

Goiás Velho (25,000 population), a picturesque old gold-mining town founded in 1727, was capital of the State of Goiás until 1937. There is a regular bus service between Goiânia and Goiás Velho. The city has seven baroque churches, the oldest being São Francisco de Paula (1761).

Museums The Museu da Boa Morte in the colonial church of the same name has a small but interesting collection of old images, paintings, etc. The Museu das Bandeiras is in the old town hall and prison (Casa da Câmara e Cadeia), by the colonial fountain. The old Government Palace, with fine rooms, is now open to the public, next to the red-brick Cathedral in the main square. A local tradition is the Fogaréu procession in Holy Week.

José Joaquim da Veiga Valle, who was born in Pirenópolis in 1806, was the "Aleijadinho" of Goiás. Many of his works are in the Boa Morte museum.

Hotels *Vila Boa*, T 371-1000, large, C, pool, views; *Municipal*, simple, F; *Minas Goiás*, F incl. small breakfast, clean, in Rua Dr Americano do Brasil; *Araguía*, F.

Restaurants *Pito Aceso*, grills; *Hotel Vila Boa*; *Pedro's Bar*, good cold beef. Try the local meat pie, empadão goiano.

Shopping Centro de Tradições Goianas, in *Hotel Vila Boa*.

Excursion Centro de Gemologia de Goiás, Quadra 2, Módulo 13, Daia, about 10 km. by bus from Anápolis, will show visitors how real and synthetic gem stones are distinguished; you can also buy stones. Cachoeira Grande, 7 km. from Goiás Velho on the Juçara road, has bathing place and snack bar.

Pirenópolis, another colonial town, is 128 km. from Goiânia, 220 km. from Brasília. There is a regular bus service between Anápolis and Pirenópolis (66 km.). **Hotels**: *Rex*, E, *Central*, F (for the desperate).

Chapada dos Veadeiros This national park is about 200 km. N of Brasília, reached by paved road to Alto Paraíso de Goiás (buses from Brasília 1000 and 2200, US$3) and gravel road from there W towards Colinas. The park entrance is on a side turning from the Colinas road, just before the village of São Jorge. Bus from Alto Paraíso to São Jorge leaves 1600. The park's main attraction is a series of waterfalls on the Rio Negro, 7 km. from São Jorge by rough track; there are other falls about 2 km. from the park entrance. Camping is permitted; difficult to reach without a car, take food. There is an hotel, E, by the bus station in Alto Paraíso and a *dorimitório* (take a sleeping bag or hammock) in São Jorge. By jeep it is possible to cross from Alto Paraíso to the BR-242 Salvador-Brasília road, a very slow but beautiful journey of 150 kms.

Caldas Novas (pop. 12,500), 187 km. SE of Goiânia (many buses; best reached via Morrinhos on the BR-153 Goiânia-São Paulo highway is a newly-developed thermal resort with good hotels and camp sites with hot swimming pools. Daily bus from Morrinhos, US$0.50, 1½ hrs. There are three groups of springs within this area: Caldas Novas, Fontes de Pirapetinga (7 km. from the town) and Rio Quente (25 km. from the town, bus from Caldas Novas; the *Pousada Hotel* (5 star) has lots of pools, entry US$20); water temperatures are 37-51˚C.

Hotels 48 in all. *Tamburi*, R. Eça de Queirós, OK. Very fashionable is *Hotel Turismo* (5-star, T 421-2244, L, full board, a/c) at Rio Quente and, sharing some of its facilities (inc. phone), *Pousada do Rio Quente*, 3-star, A, full board, but not a/c. (The *Turismo* has a private airstrip; flights from Rio and São Paulo with agencies.) *Parque das Primaveras*, R. do Balneário, T 453-1355, A, rec. by locals, cheaper than the Rio Quente places. *Serra Dourada*, Av. Correia Neto 574, T 453-1300, D, rec. *Goiás*, E with breakfast, rec. Camping at Esplanada, and Camping Clube do Brasil site on the Ipameri road, 1 km. from the centre. Many other "Clubes e Campings": *Tropical*, US$1 p.p., 2 sites in town, can use both in 1 day, others mostly US$1.30 a day, all have snack bars; *Berro d'Água* in Bairro do Turista rec.

Two other natural attractions in Goiás are the Cachoeira do Salto (160 km. from Brasília) and the thermal waters of the Lagoa de Aporé on the border with Mato Grosso. At Cristalina (120 km. from Brasília) there is a waterfall; also semi-precious stones for sale (**see page 282**). The River Araguaia, forming the border between Goiás and the two Mato Grosso states, provides many sandy beaches and good fishing: 1,600 km. of the river are navigable by boat.

A dirt road connects Goiás Velho with Aragarças (on the Goiás side) and **Barra do Garças** (on the Mato Grosso side) on the River Araguaia (Barra can also be reached by a more southerly route from Goiânia). Barra has various hotels on Av. João Alberto, e.g. *Avenida*, clean, E; *churrascarias* near main bridge and on Av. João Alberto; pleasant river beach with bars and snacks; campsite on island in river; night-time entertainment by the port. A road to the north of Barra extends as far as São João do Araguaia; where this road crosses the Rio das Mortes is the town of **Xavantina** (*Hotel Xavantina*, F, basic; *Churrascaria Arca de Noé*, highly rec.). The road is paved as far as Serra Dourada (160 km. N of Barra). Anti-malaria precautions are recommended for the Rio Araguaia region. June-Oct. is said to be the best time to visit the region; low water allows camping on beaches and islands. Avoid July, when the fishermen and their families all come. Boats and guides can be hired in Aruanã, Britânia or Barra do Garças.

The BR-153, Brasília-Belém road, runs north through the heart of Goiás and Tocantins states. At Guaraí the road forks, one branch continuing west into Pará, then turning north to Marabá on the Transamazônica and onto Belém. The other branch goes to Araguaína, whereafter the BR-226 goes to Estreito in Maranhão, from where the BR-010 runs north through Imperatriz to Belém.

Araguaína (pop. 90,000) in the new state of Tocantins, is on the Brasília-Belém road (Brasília, 1,102 km.; Belém 842 km.; Imperatriz, 174 km.). Several hotels near Rodoviária including *Esplanada*, F p.p., may have to share a room, friendly, clean, fan, no breakfast, good; *Líder*, *São Jorge*, *do Norte* and *Goiás* (all F). Bus leaves Araguaína for Marabá 0700 and 1400. Ordinary bus to Goiânia takes 24 hours: try to get an express. If travelling to Belém or Brasília by bus, reservations are not normally accepted: be at the terminal 2 hrs. before scheduled departure as buses tend to leave early; as soon as bus pulls in, follow the driver to the ticket counter and ask if there are seats. Buses also to Santarém. Varig flights twice a week from Brasília.

Off the Brasília-Belém road are fast-developing frontier regions between the lower Araguaia and Xingu rivers. Kevin Healey writes: There is now a soaring concrete bridge spanning the Araguaia just south of Conceição do Araguaia, although the road connection to the Belém highway at Guaraí is still gravel and nasty in the wet. (This is the only bridge across the Araguaia between Barra dos Garças and Marabá.)

North and west of Conceição are many new townships and ranches. Places like Redenção and Xinguara are raw, dusty and not very salubrious for tourists. At Xinguara (pop. 20,000 already) is the *Hotel Rio Vermelho*, F, pretty grotty, pigsty outside windows, orange water in taps, bed legs in cans of paraffin to discourage ants and termites. To the west, Cumaru is a *garimpeiro* settlement, from where the local military governor keeps "law and order" over the gold mining centres near the Rio Fresco. Here, the miners and prospectors are already on the edge of the Gorotiré Indian Reserve and a road is poised to enter the Indian land. To the south is Campo Alegre (pop. 6,000), the centre of cow country, with a huge new slaughterhouse serving the corporate ranches around the region (e.g. the experimental ranch of Cristalino, owned by VW Brasil). This is a perfect place to see the destruction of the rainforest and the changing climate pattern.

At **Conceição do Araguaia** the best hotel is the *Taruma Tropical* (E), each room a concrete cell, soft and squishy beds, ant parades along the walls, but clean and functioning bathrooms; a/c—when it works; the hotel is well-patronised by ranchers and absentee landowners from Brasília. The town has a frontier atmosphere, although mudhuts are being replaced by brick: cowboy hats, battered Chevrolet pick-ups, skinny mules and a red light district. Airport 17 km. SW. Conceição would be a useful base for visiting the Ilha do Bananal.

Douglas Trent, of Tropical Tours, Belo Horizonte (see page 324), writes: **Bananal** is the world's largest river island, located in the state of Tocantins on the northeastern border of Mato Grosso. The island is formed by a division in the south of the Araguaia River and is approximately 320 km. long. The entire island was originally a national park (called **Parque Nacional Araguaia**), which was then cut in half and later reduced to its current size of 562,312 ha. (of an original 2 million). The island and park are subject to seasonal flooding and contain several permanent lakes. The island, and especially the park, form one of the more spectacular wildlife areas on the continent, in many ways similar to the Pantanal. The vegetation is a transition zone between the *cerrado* (woody savanna) and Amazon forests, with gallery forests along the many waterways. There are several marshlands throughout the island.

The fauna is also transitional. More than 300 bird species are found here, including the hoatzin, hyacinthine macaw, harpy eagle and black-fronted piping guan. The giant anteater, maned wolf, bush dog, giant otter, jaguar, puma, marsh deer, pampas deer, American tapir, yellow anaconda and South American river turtle also occur here. The island is flooded most of the year, with the prime visiting (dry) season being from June to early October, when the beaches are exposed. Unfortunately, the infrastructure for tourism aside from fishing expeditions (the island is a premier spot for big fish) is very limited. Access to the park is through the small but pleasant town of **Santa Teresinha** (pop. 6,000) which is north of São Felix (see below), and is the gateway to the park. A charming hotel is the *Bananal*, Pça Tarcila Braga 106, CEP 78395 (Mato Grosso), B with full board. There is room only for 10; make your reservations well in advance. Reservations can be made by mail, allowing several months for the mail to get through, or through Focus Tours, T (031) 223-3811 Tlx. (031) 3823 RAPT BR.

Permission to visit the park should be obtained in advance from Sr. Levi Vargas, Director of the Park, IBDF, Rua 229, No. 95, Setor Universitário, 74.000 Goiânia. There is some simple accommodation for scientists at the park, which can sometimes be reserved at the address above or from IBDF, the National Parks department in Brasília. Bring your own food, and the severely underpaid but dedicated staff would appreciate any extra food or financial help, although it will not be solicited. A boat to the park can be lined up at the *Hotel Bananal*.

São Félix do Araguaia (pop. 15,000) is a larger town with more infrastructure for fishing. A very simple hotel with the best view in town is the *Mini Hotel Araguaia*, Av. Araguaia 344, T (065) 522-1154, E with breakfast. They have a/c rooms, not rec., electricity is turned off at night and the closed-in room gets very hot. Another hotel, *Xavante*, is in the city centre. A good restaurant is the *Pizzaria Cantinho da Peixada* on Av. Araguaia, next to the Texaco station, overlooking the river. *Bar Paralelos* has live music. Many Carajás indians are found in town; a depot of their handicrafts is between the *Pizzaria* and *Mini Hotel* on Av. Araguaia.

Bananal can be visited from São Félix (with permission from Funai in the town) by crossing the river to the Carajá village of Santa Isabela de Morra and asking to see the chief, Aruiana, who can tell you the history of the tribe. The island can be crossed from São Félix to São Miguel de Araguaia by taking an 8-hour trip (departures twice a week) with Zico in his van (contact him at the *Bar Beira*), US$8 p.p. From São Miguel a 5-hour bus trip brings you to Porangatu (*Hotel Mauriti*, F, shower, restaurant) on the Belém-Brasília highway.

Access to both Santa Teresinha and São Félix is by Brasil Central/TAM flights, and to São Félix by bus from Barra do Garças, 17 hours, and from Marabá. The service is unreliable and, as the planes hold just 15 passengers, it is common to get held over for a day or two. In Sta. Teresinha look out for a man in a yellowish taxi who kindly offers a free ride and then tries to collect outrageous sums from foreigners. There are legitimate taxis available—use them. Mosquito nets are highly recommended: high incidence of malaria.

In the far SW of Goiás are the **Emas National Park**, about 130 km. from Mineiros, a town just off the Brasília-Cuiabá road. Father Herbert Hermes (US) at the São José convent, Mineiros, can arrange permission to visit (necessary, or from IBDF address above), also Sr. José Roberto Carvalho at Prefeitura. A 3-day, 4-night visit to the Park costs about US$50. The park, of 1,300 sq. km., contains rolling prairies with numerous termite mounds, savanna-type woodland and forested rivers. Among the mammals encountered are armadillos, giant anteaters, marsh and pampas deer, the maned wolf and the rare giant otter. Birds include rheas, king vulture and crested screamers (seriema). It is reported that half the park was destroyed by fire in 1987.

To the west of Goiás are the states of Mato Grosso and Mato Grosso do Sul, with a combined area of 1,231,549 sq. km. and a population of only about 3.5 million, or under three persons to the square km. The two states are half covered with forest, with a large swampy area (220,000 sq. km) called the Pantanal (roughly west of a line between Campo Grande and Cuiabá, between which there is a direct road), partly flooded in the rainy season (**see page** 467). East of this line the pasture plains begin to appear. The Noroeste Railway and a road run across Mato Grosso do Sul through Campo Grande to Porto Esperança and Corumbá, both on the River Paraguay; much of the journey is across swamps, offering many sights of birds and other wildlife.

Campo Grande (pop. 384,000) the capital of the State of Mato Grosso do Sul is a pleasant modern town. It was founded in 1899 and became state capital in 1979. Because of the *terra roxa* (red earth), it is called the "Cidade Morena". In the centre is a shady park and nearby the Casa do Artesanato (Av. Calógeras and Afonso Pena) has a good collection of Indian jewellery and arrows on sale. There is a market (Feira Livre) on Weds. and Sats. Mato Grosso do Sul (pop. 1,729,000) is a good region for buying cheap, good leather shoes.

Regional Indian Museum (Museu Regional Dom Bosco), Rua Barão do Rio Branco 1843 (open daily 0700-1100, 1300-1700, T 383-3994), has interesting exhibits and handicrafts of the Pantanal and Mato Grosso Indians. There is also a collection of animals and birds (particularly good and well-preserved, if not well labelled) from the Pantanal, and a fossil collection.

Hotels *Jandaia*, Rua Barão de Rio Branco 1271, T 384-4081, well located, best, A. *Campo Grande*, Rua 13 de Maio 2825, T 384-6061, a/c, luxury, B. *Concord*, Av. Calógeras 1624, T 382-3081, very good, swimming pool, a/c, B. *Fenícia*, Av. Calógeras 2262, T 383-2001, a/c, D. *Iguaçu*, T 384-4621, opposite bus station but quiet, modern, clean, pleasant, D, rec.; *Gaspar*, Av. Mato Grosso 2, T 383-5121, opp. railway station, E with bath, ask for quiet room, good breakfast, clean. *Rio*, Marechal Rondón 1499, in city centre, E, with bath, breakfast, a/c, good value in rooms with bath (communal baths serve too many rooms), friendly, good restaurant; *Anache*, same street No. 1396, T 383-2841, E; many cheap and shabby *pensões* on Avs. Calógeras and Mato Grosso within a few blocks of railway station; also *Estaçao* and *Priape*, similar location. *Cosmos*, Dom Aquino 771, T 383-4271, 1 block N of bus station, E, good value; *União*, E, Calógeras 2828, 1½ blocks from the station, good breakfast, clean, ask for quiet room, friendly; *Continental*, Rua Maracaju 229, 2 blocks from railway, 5 from bus terminal, F, clean, comfortable; *Plaza*, same street, F, clean, unfriendly; *Paulista*, Antônio Maria Coelho 1085, F, basic but adequate facilities, cheap café (on the street behind *Gaspar*); *Tupi*, between bus and railway stations, cheap, basic, also *Estaçao* and *Priape*, similar location; (*Califôrnia* at Rodoviária is F, but very basic and dirty); *Nacional*, Rua Dom Aquino 610, near bus station, E, basic, shabby but friendly, clean; *Rocha*, Barão do Rio Branco 343, 1 block from Rodoviária, E without breakfast, fan, clean, T 383-6874; *Turis Rodoviária*, Av. Barão do Rio Branco 342, close to bus station, E, good, friendly. *Caçula*, Av. Calógeras, F, cheap, safe, clean, washing facilities, 300 m. from railway station, 700 m. from Rodoviária. Some hotels near bus station both seedy and dear, best go into town (*Presidente*, opp. Rodoviária, is F, OK; *Dormitório*, F, is basic).

Restaurants *Cabana Gaúcha*, Av. Afonso Pena, 1919, rec., live music evenings; *Vitório*, next door, slightly cheaper, also live music evenings; *Churrascaria do Papai*, at bus station, huge meal; *Carinca*, SE corner of main *praça*, modern, clean, good plain food. *Shanghai*, Rio Branco 1037, rec.; *Hong Kong*, Rua Maracaju 131, centre, good Chinese food; *Lanchonete Arabe* rec. *Cafeteria Lojas Americanas*, Marechal Rondón 1336, in a supermarket; *El Café*, R. Dom Aquino 1248, both good. *Nutre Bem*, vegetarian, Pedro Celestino 1696, good. Plenty of good, cheap places in Rua Barão de Rio Branco, e.g. *Sabor e Artes*, No. 1016.

Exchange Banco do Brasil changes travellers' cheques. Parallel rate hard to find, try at Rodoviária, *Hotel Caranda*, 1 block from Rodoviária; Sr. Abdala in the clothes shop at 14 de Julho 2581; or try in Las Vegas billiard hall, Barao Rio Branco 1130.

Post Office on corner of R. Dom Aquino and Calógeras. **Telephone** Dom Aquino e Rui Barbosa.

Health Yellow and Dengue fevers are both present in Campo Grande. There is a clinic for both at the railway station, but it's not very hygienic (take precautions in advance).

Tourist Information, maps, etc. at MSTur, Rua Antônio Maria Coelho 2802, T 382-3811. Extremely helpful. Empresa de Turismo do Mato Grosso do Sul, Av. Afonso Pena 3149, T 382-3091. Town information in pedestrian area of Av Barão do Rio Branco.

Tourist Agency Tainá Turismo, Rua Mal. Rondon 1636,T 384-6544, Telex 067-2607; Dallas, Rio Branco 1454. Vax Tour, Ruy Barbosa 3014, English spoken.

Roads Distances in km. from Campo Grande: Belém, 3,299; Brasília, 1,405; Corumbá, 429; Cuiabá, 712; Foz do Iguaçu, 1,141; Goiânia, 1,212; Manaus, 3,006; Porto Alegre, 1,786; Recife, 3,708; Rio, 1,475; Salvador, 2,935; São Paulo, 1,046.

Buses Rodoviária at Rua Barão do Rio Branco e Rua Joaquim Nabuco, T 383-1678, all offices on 2nd floor; 2 long blocks' walk from town. Fun fair next to bus station. (Taxi to Rodoviária, US$1.75.) São Paulo, paved road, US$14.50, 16 hrs. 6 buses daily, 1st at 0800, last at 2100, *leito* buses at 1600 and 2000. Cuiabá, US$9, 10 hrs., 12 buses daily, *leito* at 1700 and 2200. To Brasília, US$23 (Motta rec.), 23 hrs. at 0900. Rio de Janeiro, US$32, 21 hrs., 4 buses daily, *leito* at 1745. Corumbá, with Andorinha 4-8 buses a day, US$12, 6 hrs., on paved road. Campo Grande-Corumbá buses connect with those from Rio and São Paulo, similarly those from Corumbá through to Rio and São Paulo. Ponta Porã, 5½ hrs., Expresso Queiroz, US$5, 5 ordinary buses a day, 2 executive buses, US$7.50, 8 buses daily, 1st at 0630, last at 2130. Dourados, same schedule as Ponta Porã, 4 hrs., US$3. Beyond Dourados is Mundo Novo, from where buses go to Ponta Porã (0530) and to Porto Frajelli (many between 0420 and 1900, ½ hr.); from Mundo Novo ferries for cars and passengers go to Guaíra for US$0.20. Buses Campo Grande-Mundo Novo, 0900, 10 hrs. in dry weather, US$4.20, return 0730 and 1800; buses Dourados-Mundo Novo, unpaved road, four a day. No direct service to Foz do Iguaçu, though you can buy a through ticket; journey takes 15 hrs. with Maringá company via Cascavel, with good connections, US$15.50.

Air Daily flights to São Paulo, Rio, Corumbá, Cuiabá, Brasília, Manaus, Porto Velho. Reduction of 12% on VASP night flights to Rio and São Paulo. City bus No. 116, "V. Popular," stops outside airport. Taxi to airport, US$3.

Trains The railway station is 5 blocks from the bus terminal. Ponta Porã, slow train (9 hrs.) daily at 1000 (not Sun.; lone females are advised to sit on left-hand side since, 1 hour before Ponta Porã, is a predominantly male factory town where you may get some unwanted attention). Ponta Porã to Campo Grande at 0845, US$4 1st class, US$2.25 2nd class on the train (this service is under threat—check). To Corumbá: train leaves Tues, Thur and Sat, many timetable changes so check in advance, at 0840, arriving 2000, meals served at seats, US$3. Fares US$4 1st class, US$3 2nd class (no advance ticket sales, office open 1 ½ hrs before train departs, a very tiring journey. Thefts and drugged food reported on this journey, especially in July when trains are very crowded. Latest reports indicate that the only **trains to Bauru** are those which originate in Corumbá, leaves 1830, Mon, Wed and Fri (i.e. no local Campo Grande-Bauru train); best to check in advance if possible. First class fare to Bauru is US$5.70.

The Campo Grande—São Paulo journey can be broken at **Tres Lagoas** near the Paraná river and on the railway, and 10 hours by road to São Paulo (bus Campo Grande—Tres Lagoas, 6 hrs., US$8, dep. 0800, 1200 and 2230, a bumpy, interesting journey). *Novo Hotel* near bus station, F. friendly.

The road from Campo Grande to the Paraguayan border passes through **Dourados** (*Hotel Alphonsus*, C, Av. Pres. Vargas 603). Good bus connections to Campo Grande, Ponta Porã and Mundo Novo (see under Campo Grande, Buses, above).

A road and railway run SW from Campo Grande to **Ponta Porã** (pop. 50,000) on the Paraguayan border opposite the town of Pedro Juan Caballero.

Hotels *Pousada do Bosque,* very nice motel type with a/c, restaurant and swimming pool, Av. Pres. Vargas, out of town, T 431-1181, C. *Barcelona,* Rua Guia Lopes, maze-like building, pool, restaurant, a/c, D-E. *Internacional,* Rua Internacional 1267,T 431-1243, E with a/c, F with bath or without, hot showers, clean, good breakfasts, rec.; *Francia,* E, opposite *Barcelona,* bath, clean, friendly, restaurant, US$3 for big meal. *Grande,* Av. Brasil 1181, E. *Alvorada,* F, clean and pleasant. *Dos Viajantes,* across park opp. railway station, F, very basic, clean.

Restaurants *Top Lanches,* beside *Hotel Barcelona,* cheap and friendly. *Chapão,* good food at reasonable prices. *Pepe's Lunch e Pizzeria,* good, fairly cheap; *Karina Lanches,* near Federal Police office, good, cheap; *Santa Antônia,* rec.

Electric Current 220 volts A.C.

Exchange Banco do Brasil changes travellers' cheques. Several *cambios* on the Paraguayan side, but none deal in cheques. Many in the centre of town (but on Sun. change money in hotels or the gambling hall beneath Livraria Sulamérica).

The border post at Ponta Porã normally closes at 1700 (it is also closed on national holidays). The Federal Police office is in a new white building shared with an engineering supply company in the same block as the Expresso Queiroz Rodoviária; open 0800. To reach Paraguayan control, follow the Rua Guia Lopes 4 blocks into Paraguay. If crossing into Paraguay some nationalities require visa from Paraguayan consulate next door to *Hotel Internacional,* Rua Internacional (check requirements advised).

A new area of tourist interest in Mato Grosso do Sul is being established in the municipalities of Bonito (hotels: *Bonanza, Alvorado, Florestal,* all F; campsite at Ilha do Padre, 10 km. N of Bonito, very pleasant, no regular transport; restaurant, *Tapera*) and Aquidauana (several hotels around railway station, including *Fluminense,* F with fan and breakfast, a/c more expensive), where cave formations comparable to those found in the Lagoa Santa region of Minas Gerais are encountered. Two of the first to be opened are the **Lago Azul and N.S. Aparecida** (Sérgio Gonzales in Prefeitura of Bonito controls entry), both 26 km. from Bonito (no buses) and 320 km. from Campo Grande. Lago Azul has a lake 150 metres long and 70 metres wide. It is best visited in Jan.-Feb., 0700-0900 for the light, but there are no organized visits as yet, so Brazilian holiday times are best. Bus Bonito-Campo Grande, US$4, 3 hrs, 0545 and 1600. Also possible by changing at Jardim. Daily bus between Bonito and Aquidauana, about 3 hrs. on dirt road. From Bonito there is a road to **Puerto Murtinho** where a boat crosses to Isla Margarita in Paraguay. Hotels *Eldorado*, F, friendly, clean, good food; *Beira Rio*, F, basic; *Caicaras*, F; *Americano*, F, 2 *lanchonetes*, *Churrascaria Gaspão*, Elia, taxi driver, will change money.

Corumbá (pop. 80,000) on the River Paraguai, with Bolivia on the opposite bank and beautiful views of the river, has millions of mosquitoes in Dec., Jan. and Feb., but is a pleasant place nevertheless. River boats ply occasionally between it and Buenos Aires. The Forte Junqueira, the city's most historic building, which may be visited, was built in 1772. In the hills to the south is the world's greatest reserve of manganese, now beginning to be worked. From the Bolivian border town of Quijarro a 650-km. railway is open westwards to Santa Cruz de la Sierra, and there is a road of sorts. The Campo Grande-Corumbá road, via Aquidauana, crosses the Paraguai (now mostly paved, gasoline near the Rio Miranda bridge). The scenery between Campo Grande and Corumbá is most interesting, the road and railway follow different routes, but the train is more reliable than the bus (though slower). Corumbá is the best starting point for the southern part of the Pantanal, with boat and jeep trips and access to the major hotel/farms.

Warning Police have very strict controls on drug-trafficking in Corumbá; there are many drug-runners, searches are very thorough.

Climate Hot and humid (70%); cooler in June-July, very hot from Sept. to Jan.

Hotels *Santa Mônica*, R. Antônio Maria Coelho 369, T 231-3001, a/c, D, good restaurant; *Alphahotel*, next door, F, clean, tours arranged. *Nacional*, R. América 934, C, good pool, T 231-6868; *Santa Rita*, Dom Aquino 860 (unsigned), T 231-1525, E, with bath, F without, bathrooms dirty otherwise clean but basic, noisy, good meals in restaurant, reported not safe for luggage; *La Siesta*, Dom Aquino 47, good, helpful, restaurant; *O Laçador*, R. América 482, T 231-6933, D without breakfast, rec; *Victoria Régia*, R. Ladário 271, F, clean, rec; *Moderna*, R. Delamaré 909, E, restaurant; *Schabib*, Rua Frei Mariano 1153, E, basic but clean, owner friendly, multilingual and helpful; *Nova Horizonte*, F, on steep street down to port, friendly and clean. *Esplanada*, opp. railway station, F, clean, cold shower, basic; *Cóndor*, R. de la Mar, F; *Modfull*, next door, F; other small clean hotels: *Irure*, Rua 13 de Junho 776, *Campus*, R. Antônio João, *Caçula* and *Madrid* on Rua Cuiabá, *Lincoln*, Rua 15 de Novembro, and *Pousada de Marieta*, América 243.

Restaurants *Churrascaria Gaúcha*, R. Frei Mariano; *Tarantella* (Italian), R. Frei Mariano and América, large helpings, not cheap, but rec. *Barril de Ouro*, R. Frei Mariano; *Peixaria de Lulu*, R. Antônio João, nr. centre, good fish; *El Dorado*, on waterfront, good for fish; *Churrascaria Rodeio*, very good, R. Antônio Maria Coelho. *Casa Mia*, Rua Dom Aquino; on the waterfront you can eat good fish at *Portal do Pantanal* and *El Pacu*, run by a German, Hermann, and his Brazilian wife. Good beer in *Xaraes*, Rua Gen. Rondon; Bolivian snacks in '*Sslato*, Rua Dom Aquino.

Museum Museu Regional do Pantanal, Praça da República 0800-1100, 1400-1800; Sat. and Sun closed. Arts and Crafts Centre, Rua Dom Aquino Correa, in a converted prison.

Exchange Banco do Brasil changes travellers' cheques (open a.m. only). Many money changers at the border—cash only. Street traders in shopping street between Rua Delamaré and Post Office.

Tourist Office Rua Delamaré 1557, T 231-6030, Portuguese only spoken, not very helpful.

Travel Agents *Evidência Turismo*, Rua Cuiabá 861, T 231-3840, Telex 67-7060, specializes in 1-day trips (English, French, Spanish spoken); *Melgatur*, Ladeira Cunha e Cruz 8, T 231-2523, Telex 67-7084, 2-8 day tours in N and S Pantanal, ecological trips, helpful (English and German spoken); *Receptivo Pantanal*, Rua Frei Mariano 502, T 231-5795, helpful (1-day tour US$50, 3-day US$100, 4-day US$130; *Pantanal Tours*. R. Manoel Cavassa 61, T 231-4683, fishing trips by hotel boat; *Pérola do Pantanal Viagens e Turismo*, R.Manoel Cavassa 219, T 231-1460, good one-day river tour with *Lancha Pérola*. *Turismo Sandino*, R. Firmo de Matos, T 231-3345, rec. tours, good food; *Pantur*, R América 969, T 231-4343 helpful.

Shipping No regular passenger service to Asunción (see **Paraguay** chapter). It may be possible to get a boat to Porto Esperança and continue from there. Seek information at travel agents, *El Pacu* restaurant, or from small cargo boats at the waterfront. (**See page 469**, under Cáceres.)

Air VASP daily to Campo Grande and on to São Paulo; VASP also daily to Cuiabá, Brasília, Goiânia, Belo Horizonte, and Rio de Janeiro. TAM US$45, Tues., Sat., LAB US$52, Mon., Wed., Sat., to Santa Cruz. Airline office at Pto. Suárez or 3 hrs. before flight at airport. Daily private flights to Santa Cruz, Bolivia, especially in rainy season, US$100 per person—cheaper to travel overland to Asunción and fly from there.

Trains and Buses The day train from Corumbá to Bauru, via Campo Grande and with very poor connections to São Paulo, leaves Mon., Wed. and Fri., at 0700, arriving in Campo Grande at 1830 (US$4 in 1st class, US$3 in 2nd), and Bauru the next afternoon at 1600, US$17.25, (very crowded and tiring). TAM Campo Grande only, Tues., Thur., Sun. 1900, 11 hrs, double cabin US$22, single US$14, reclining seat US$9. All trains serve food. These times have been subject to frequent changes, check in advance (T station 231-2876). Tickets can only be booked as far as Bauru (tickets can be bought from 1300 on previous day) Buses from Campo Grande to São Paulo are quicker, but dearer. The Corumbá-São Paulo bus journey takes at least 22 hrs. (US$18). As there is no fixed timetable the year round, confirm bus times in advance (T 231-3783); it is best to go Corumbá-Campo Grande, 6 hrs., US$12, 4-8 buses a day, then make a connection to all parts of Brazil. Two buses (Andorinha, rec) to Rio daily 0800 and 2300, US$22, 28 hrs., with change Campo Grande, US$21. To Cuiabá, 18 hrs, US$15; São Paulo 22 hrs; to Ponta Porã, for Paraguay, daily, 12 hrs. Bus station is on Rua Porto Carrero, next to the railway station and 1 block from town centre (also for Andorinha buses; Viação Motta bus terminal is nearby). Taxis from both stations to centre are extortionate. Don't rely on getting a supply of new cruzeiros in Bauru; exchange is difficult there. Stock up in Corumbá.

There are four train services to Santa Cruz in Bolivia, the *ferrobus*, *rápido*, *omnibus* and *mixto*; all leave from Quijarro, the Bolivian frontier station, not from Corumbá. The schedule of each appears to change frequently so check on arrival in Corumbá. There is a Bolivian railway office at Corumbá railway station for all details. Tickets must be purchased in Quijarro on day of departure, go as early as possible (it may be best to stay in Quijarro to get a good place in the queue; 2 or 3 F hotels opp. station, basic). If the ticket office has "sold out", ask around on the platform as people buy up tickets and sell them for a few bolivianos more: the money-exchange women know all about it. Quijarro-Santa Cruz *ferrobus*, about 3 times a week, Pullman US$14.50, special US$13.50; *rápido* Quijarro-Santa Cruz, perhaps daily; *omnibus* (stopping train), twice a week; *mixto* also twice a week; fares on last 3, Pullman US$12, first US$10, second US$6 (all converted from bolivianos). If immigration is closed, buy your train ticket before going there. It is worth buying a 1st class seat, which is much more comfortable on night trips than the 2nd class, but these are often mysteriously "sold out". 2nd class is on the baggage van floor, is crowded and there are no toilet or water facilities. Stops at stations are brief; take your own water; journey time 19½ hrs (not rec.). Colectivo Corumbá-Quijarro, US$1.50, from in front of Dona Aparecida's store, *A Favorita*, R. Antônio Maria Coelho (Dona Aparecida changes money outside banking hours; bargaining recommended). Also taxis, US$12 per taxi; colectivo border—Quijarro US$1. The railway to Santa Cruz is liable to flood damage.

Going to Bolivia Immigration and emigration formalities are constantly changing so check procedure in advance. Have passport stamped by Brazilian Policia Federal at Corumbá bus station (open often at variance with published opening hours, 0700-1130, 1500-1600, 1900-2000, Sat. and Sun. 0700-0830, 1000-1200, 1800-1930). Take bus from port end of Rua Antonio Maria to Bolivian border (15 mins.), walk over the bridge to the Bolivian border post (white building), go through formalities, then take colectivo to Quijarro for train (US$0.90 p.p.). At the border Bolivian police stamp passport free. At the frontier, it is not necessary to pay any money to anyone. Show ticket at border to return to Corumbá. Money changers at the border and in Quijarro offer same rates as in Corumbá. Bolivian Consulate in Corumbá: Rua Antônio Maria Coelho 825 (colectivos may be caught nearby for frontier), Mon.-Fri., 0700-1100, 1500-1730, Sat. and Sun. closed. They tell everyone a visa is necessary, but this may not be true: check Bolivian section "Information for Visitors". Those who need a visa must pay US$5; a yellow fever vaccination certificate is required. Alternative to train: Bolivian LAB or TAM flights, see above.

Coming from Bolivia If you arrive at the border when the Bolivian offices are closed (e.g. at night) and you therefore have no exit stamp, be prepared to be sent back for an exit stamp by Brazilian officials in Corumbá (the Bolivian border post opens at 0700). If you arrive in Brazil without a yellow fever vaccination certificate, you must go to Rua 7 de Setembro,

Corumbá, for an inoculation. When travelling from Quijarro, take a taxi (bargain fare) or walk to the Bolivian border, go through formalities (US$0.15), outside office take bus to Corumbá Rodoviária (US$0.10). Find a hotel then take a taxi or walk to railway station for Brazilian formalities (some buses go direct to the station): if you're in luck the office will be open.

Pantanal This vast swampy area, located between Cuiabá, Campo Grande and the Bolivian frontier, is one of the world's great wildlife preserves, slowly being opened up to tourism. The flora and fauna are similar in many ways to those of the Amazon basin, though because of the more veldt-like open land, the wildlife can be viewed more easily than in the dense jungle growth. Principal life seen in this area are over 650 species of birds, in the main, waders and water fowl, storks (the *tuiuiu* or jabiru stork is almost 1.2 metres tall), herons, coots, ducks, as well as pheasants, quails and parrots. There are some 230 varieties of fish, from the giant *pintado*, weighing up to 80 kilos, to the voracious *piranha*. Fishing here is exceptionally good. Animal life is represented by deer, ocelot, puma, boar, anteaters, tapir, and the ubiquitous *capivara*, a species of giant aquatic guinea-pig. Probably the most impressive sight is the *jacaré* (Brazilian alligator). The extraordinary thing is that man and his domesticated cattle thrive together with the wildlife with seemingly little friction. Local farmers protect the area jealously. (Only one area is officially national park, the Biological Reserve of Cará-Cará in the municipality of Poconé, 135,000 hectares of land and water, only accessible by air or river. Permission to visit at Delegacia Estadual do IBDF, Av. Jaime Figueredo 550, CPA de Cuiabá, CEP 78.000, Cuiabá.) Hunting in any form is strictly forbidden. Fishing is allowed with a licence (enquire at travel agents); it is not encouraged in the breeding season Oct-Jan. The International Union for the Conservation of Nature is concerned at the amount of poaching, particularly of *jacaré* skins and *capivaras*. Recently, the Forestry Police have built control points on all major access roads to the Pantanal.

There are two distinct seasons. In the rainy season (wettest in February), most of the area floods, and cattle crowd on to the few islands remaining above water, while the wild animals have long since left the area, at this time an experienced guide and a 4-wheel drive vehicle are essential. The dry season (July to October) is the nesting and breeding season. At this time the birds form vast nesting areas, with hundreds and thousands crowding the trees creating an almost unsupportable cacophony of sounds. At this time the white sand river beaches are exposed, where *jacarés* bask in the sun.

The Pantanal is not easy to visit. The best starting points are Cuiabá, Corumbá and Campo Grande, from where one finds public transport all around the perimeter, but none at all within. Hitching is not advised because of the amount of drug smuggling in the area. Litter is becoming a problem; don't contribute to it. Wild camping is possible if you have your own transport.

There are several lodges with fair to good accommodation, some only approachable by air or river; most are relatively expensive. The best plan is to hire a car and check accommodation for yourself. Following is a list of those presently operating:

From Cuiabá: Focus Tours of Belo Horizonte (**see page** 324) is specializing in tours in this part of the Pantanal. Ametur, Samariana and Confiança off day tours by car (US$40), along Transpantaneira to Fazenda Pixaim. *Hotel Fazenda Santa Rosa* reservations at the Samariana Turismo in Cuiabá, 250 km. from Cuiabá near Porto Jofre. A, with full board, an old *fazenda*, under new management, good food, service and trips, breakfast-eating parrot, rec. Buses run from Cuiabá to **Poconé** (a large town, 100 km., US$2.50) from where one can hire a car from *Hotel Skala*, E, in the main square or hitch (not rec.) to Porto Jofre (just a gas station), or hire a vehicle to get there, around US$150, the road from Poconé can be impassable (see under Cuiabá). Poconé also has *Pousada Pantaneira*, F, good restaurant, European-run, clean and simple, on Transpantaneira road, T 721-1220; *3 Poderes Restaurant*, Rua Beri, cheap good food. At Km. 30 on the Transpantaneira is *Hotel das Araras*, 10 rooms with bath, good food, home-made *cachaça* (hotel itself has no phone, but T 065-321 6754), rates L with full board (reservations at Samariana Cuiabá or Melgatur, Corumbá). Where the road crosses the river Pixaim is *Hotel Beira Rio*, 3 rooms with several beds in each, no electricity, good home-grown food (expansion is planned). *Fazenda Pixaim*, D, 170 km. from Cuiabá, halfway between Poconé and Porto Jofre; taxi US$27 from Poconé. *Hotel-Fazenda Cabanas do Pantanal*, A, 142 km. from Cuiabá, 50 km. from Poconé by the rivers Pixaim and Cuiabá, on the northern edge of the Pantanal, 10 chalet bedrooms with bath, restaurant, boat trips (few in dry season), horse-riding, fishing, helpful proprietor and staff, everything except boat trips and bar drinks included in price (booking: Confiança, Cuiabá). Boats ply between Porto Cercado (near *Cabanas do Pantanal*) via Porto Jofre to Corumbá (48 hrs.) about once a week, e.g. *San Antônio* and *Elza*. Expeditours or Melgatur in Cuiabá can book a journey by car from Cuiabá to Porto Jofre, then hotelboat to Corumbá (or vice versa), 4 days.

Baráo de Melgaça, 150 km. from Cuiabá (twice daily bus, US$3) on Rio Cuibá, is the starting point for the *Pousada Passar Gada*, programmes from 3 days up, full board, boat, car and trekking expeditions, transport from Baró de Melgaço. Owner speaks English and French; reservations in Baró de Melgaço on riverside, or through Melgatur, Corumbá. *Pousada do Baráo*, 6 chalets with bath, swimming pool, 1st class, boat and trekking expeditions (book through Melgatur). *Baráo Tour Hotel*, in the town, apartments with a/c, restaurant, boat trips and excursions (T Cuiabá 322-1568, or Melgatur.)

From Corumbá: One day river trips available on river boats with a capacity of 80 passengers, US$20, transfers and hot fish meal inc. Tickets at travel agents. *Pousada do Pantanal*, 125 km. from Corumbá near the Campo Grande road at Fazenda Santa Clara (still a working cattle ranch), very comfortable, but some complaints that trips into the jungle are too short, easy access by bus, reservations from all agencies in Corumbá; US$50 p.p. for groups of 4-6 for 3 days/2 nights, good food, with horseback, car and boat excursions, guides included, canoes, simple fishing gear, motor boats for rent (try bargaining in the off-season for reduced rates). *Fazenda Santa Blanca*, on the Rio Paraguai, 15 mins. by boat S of Porto Esperanza, C, full board, very clean and friendly, good kayak excursions, horseriding, (US$5), information from Rua 15 de Novembro 659, 79300 Corumbá, T 067-231-1460, or Flins Travel (Walter Zoss), Rua do Acre 92, 6th floor, 602, CEP 20.081, Rio de Janeiro, T (021) 253-8588/0195, Telex 021 32971 ATDA or Safári Fotográfico, R. Frei Mariano 502, Corumbá, T 231-5797 Highly recommended is *Fazenda Leque*, Roberto Kassan (contact through Rua América 262, Corumbá, T 231-1598): US$65 p.p. for 3 days, 6 per group, US$5-10 p.p. per day if you want to stay longer; take mosquito coils; unlimited use of horses and boats, on small lake behind the farm, good food; plenty of wildlife to be seen. *Ilha do Santo Antônio*, farm, rooms with bath, restaurant with good food, clean, boat, horse and trekking trips (reservations through Evidéncia or Melgatur); *Rancho no Paraíso* (Berenice), 180 km from Corumbá in the middle of one of the most interesting section of the Pantanal (Ñecolândia), very simple but clean, horse trekking, photo safaris, adventure programme (enquiries: Melgatur); *Pousada do Paraíso*, farmhouse now used as a hotel (booking as for *Santo Antônio*). The going rate for a 3-day photosafari by jeep is US$60 p.p. for 4-6 people (e.g. through Melgatour); also fishing trips for 4 days with Hotelboat for 8 (e.g. *Pérola do Pantanal* and *Pantanal Tours*, Corumbá—must be booked in advance). Hotels specialising in fishing, all reached from Corumbá by road: *Pesqueiro do Lontra*, D, T (067) 383-4532, 180 km from Aquidauana on the corumbá road. *Pesqueiro Tarumã* and *Pesqueiro Paraíso do Dourado* (contact Evidência Turismo). José Paraguaio, r. Manoel Cavassa 331, T (067) 231-1721, 3 day tours to *Fazenda São Joaquim*, US$60, rec.

Julie Williams (Muswellbrook, NSW) writes: On arival in Corumbá you will be met by private tour guides offering a tour on the spot. The tours are of 3-4 days, costing US$50-60 (includes all food, accommodation and transport). There is fierce competition between guides who provide similar services in the Ñecolândia region. Travel is in the back of a pick-up (good for seeing animals), up to a maximum of 6. Accommodation is in a hammock under palm thatch on a fazenda. Food is good. If you want flushing toilets, showers or luxury cabins, approach an agency. Guides provide bottled mineral water, but you must take a hat, sun screen and mosquito repellent. Gather a group together, shop around and "one of these tours could be the highlight of your travels". Guides who have been recommended include Joaquin, Katu, Armando or Rodríguez, ask in *Hotel Schabib*. Rey Tur, Manoel Cavassa 127, guide Ico, knows area well, rec.

Camping out is preferable to staying in *fazendas* because less driving (which scares animals) is involved, and you can see the wildlife at its greatest period of activity—dawn and dusk (protection against mosquitoes essential). In the wet season, access to the Pantanal from Corumbá is only by boat. Tues. boat Corumbá-Poconé, 36 hrs., US$12. Boats can be hired for US$35 a day. Cattle boats will take passengers on their round trips to farms in the Pantanal, 3 days, US$6.50 but take your own food—it is not possible to disembark. Ask at Bacia da Prata, 10 mins. out of Corumbá on the Ladário bus (the gatekeeper is unhelpful). Road trips from Corumbá into the Pantanal US$35 for 6 hours per vehicle.

From Campo Grande: *Hotel dos Camalotes*, Porto Murtinho, 440 km. from Campo Grande; access by bus long, tedious, bumpy and dusty; best access by air taxi. 4-star luxury hotel on the shores of the Paraguai river, favoured by wealthy Paulistas, A, with full board. *Cabana do Pescador*, 50 km. from Aquidauana on the Miranda river, access by bus to Aquidauana, and local bus to Bonito, possible to visit the impressive Bonito Caves, A, includes breakfast. *Pousada Agua Pek*, near Aquidauana, farmhouse hotel, horseriding, boat trips, trekking, full board, friendly and clean; *Pousada Caiman*, near Miranda, first class, full board, excursions, book in advance (Evidencia, Corumbá); *Fazenda Solabra*, T (067) 242-1162, 6 km. from Miranda, which is 209 km. from Corumbá, 198 from Campo Grande, is rec., A, including all meals; it is by the Rio Salobra (clear water) and Rio Miranda, with birds and animals easily seen. Take bus from Campo Grande to Miranda, and alight 50 m. from the bridge over Rio Miranda, turn left for 1,200 m to the *Fazenda*; by train, coming from Campo Grande, get out one stop after Miranda, 250 m. to the *Fazenda*. There is a good camp site 30 km. past Miranda. Alternatively, hire a car in Corumbá and drive to Miranda, but note that the dirt road is bad after rain (consequently not much traffic and more wildlife can be seen). Car with driver can be hired at Salobra for US$25.

A suggestion from Stephen L. Meredith, London SW19, is to take the 0715 train from Corumbá to Agente Inocêncio, where you change for the local train to Porto Esperança, a 10-minute journey. There you may be able to hire a boat for a 2-3 hr. trip on the River Paraguai (about US$15, but bargain). The return train connects with the main line train at 1718. You can walk back along the track, but this is dangerous on the bridges, which have gaps between the sleepers.

Tours to N or S Pantanal arranged in Rio de Janeiro by Pelajo Turismo, Av. Rio Branco 52, 16th floor, T 296-4466 or 233-5085: from 4 to 8 days; also Excursões Soletur, and many others. In São Paulo Evidência Turismo, Rua Dr. Costa Júnior 390, Perdizes, T 864-0400, Telex 11-82650. Most tours last 4 to 15 days, and are based at Corumbá. 20% discounts are offered in December, but this is the wet, and mosquito, season.

River trips from Cuiabá to Corumbá are very difficult since boats on the Cuiabá river are few and irregular. You can get to Corumbá by river from **Cáceres** (pop. 70,000), on the banks of the Rio Paraguai, 250 km. west of Cuiabá, very hot but clean and hospitable. There is a yacht club, with swimming pool, volley ball and children's playground. Annual cattle fair at the airport. Hotels: *Comodoro*, Praça Duque de Caxias; *Charme*, Col. José Dulce; *Ipanema*, Rua Tiradentes 403, good restaurant; *Fênix*, C-D, fridge, a/c, TV; *Santa Terezinha*, Rua Tiradentes 485, F with fan, breakfast, not clean, friendly. Many other cheap hotels, e.g. *Hispano*, F, clean. *Hotel Barranquinho*, outside Cáceres, book in advance through Ametur, Cuiabá. Good restaurants: *Corimba* on main square (fish specialities); *Bisteção*, on the waterfront. Change money elsewhere: travellers' cheques take 10 days to change at the banks, Soteco by the main square changes cash at the official rate. For information on boat sailings, ask at the Capitânia dos Portos, on the corner of the main square at the waterfront. If possible phone in advance to Cáceres, Posto Arrunda, 221-1707 to find out which boats are going. Also Portobrás on the outskirts at the waterfront (T 221-1728), you may (with a lot of luck) be able to get passage on a boat; 3 days to Corumbá (8 the other way). These boats are officially not allowed to take passengers. You may have a better chance of getting a boat in Corumbá since there are more head offices and river traffic. Bus Cuiabá-Cáceres, US$5, 10 a day (book in advance, very crowded), 3½ hrs. now that the road is paved, one stop in the jungle at a restaurant. At the waterfront you can hire a boat for a day trip (US$25).

From Cáceres to the Bolivian border: Get passport stamped by the Federal Police then take the 1600 bus to San Matías, Bolivia, where you must have your passport stamped (*Residencial Génova*, F, rec.); military flights on Fri. and Sun. to Santa Cruz via Roboré—book in advance).

Cuiabá (pop. 370,000, 1989) the capital of Mato Grosso state, (pop 1,660,000) on the Rio Cuiabá, an upper tributary of the River Paraguai, has an imposing government palace and other fine buildings round a green main square. Alt.: 165 metres; There is a paved road to Campo Grande (712 km.), on the Noroeste railway to São Paulo, and the 2,400 km. BR-364 road from Brasília to Porto Velho and Rio Branco passes through Cuiabá; it is paved all the way between Brasília, Cuiabá and Porto Velho. The more direct road to Brasília through Barra do Garças and Goiás Velho (the BR-070) is paved also. Several paved feeder roads connect the BR-070 and BR-364. The Transpantaneira Highway, originally projected to connect Cuiabá with Corumbá, goes only as far as Porto Jofre on the Cuiabá River. Work has been suspended indefinitely because of difficulties, costs and ecological considerations. It is very hot; coolest months for a visit are June, July, and August, in the dry season. Good fishing in the Cuiabá and smaller Coxipó rivers (fish and vegetable market, picturesque, at the riverside); wildlife for photography, and the Aguas Quentes hot springs, 90 km. (*Hotel Aguas Quentes*) can be visited. The University of Mato Grosso has an attractive museum of Indian objects (closed Sat. and Sun.), and also has a small zoo.

Hotels *Santa Rosa Palace*, Av. Getúlio Vargas 600, T 322-9044, A, overpriced; *Colorado Palace*, Jules Rimet 22, opp. bus station, a/c, good range of room prices. *Mato Grosso*

Palace, Joaquim Murtinho 170 (T 322-9254), 4-star, A with bath and breakfast; *Aurea Palace*, Gen. Melo 63, T 322-3377, B, pleasant rooms, restaurant, swimming pool, good; *Fenícia*, Av. Getúlio Vargas 296, T 321-5122, D, with a/c, breakfast, shower, clean, central, good. *Real Palace*, Praça Ipiranga 103, D with shower, a/c, TV, good breakfast, helpful, good value; *Abudi Palace*, Coronel Escolástico 259, T 322-7399, good; *Bandeirantes*, Av. Coronel Escolástico 425, T 321-0920, D, a/c, out of centre; *Almanara*, Av. Coronel Escolástico 510, T 322-2241, D, opposite *Bandeirantes* and better. *Mato Grosso*, Rua Comandante Costa 2522 (T 321-9121), 2-star, almost opposite the *Fenícia* and down a side street, small, clean, restaurant, good value, D-E. *Santiago*, Av. General Mello 115 (Centro), F, very friendly, clean, laundry, meals. *Samara*, Rua Joaquim Murtinho 150, central, E, cold shower, fan, basic but good, clean, friendly; *Presidente*, Av. Getúlio Vargas 119, central, fans in rooms, F p.p. Cheap clean hotel near old bus station, *Cidade Verde*, F. *Dormitório Cézar*, near bus terminal, F p.p.; others in same area.

Youth hostel Albergue da Juventude, Rua Cel. Otilis Moreira 445, T 319-1231; also contact Amilton Martins da Silva, Praça de República s/n, C.E.P. 78015, T 322-5363, or Rua Duque de Caxias 19, Barrio Alvorada, C.E.P. 78070, T 319-1231, he also runs reasonably-priced tours to the Pantanal (only speaks Portuguese and a little Spanish, contact him through Turimat).

Restaurants *Regionalíssimo*, Rua 13 de Junho nr Handicraft shop, regional food; *Beco do Candieiro*, Rua Campo Grande 500; *Churrascaria Recanto do Bosque*, Rua Cândido Mariano; *Bierhaus*, Isaac Póvoas 1200; *A Integral*, Rua Antônio João s/n; *Hong Kong*, Av. Gen. Melo 639, Chinese; *Sachimi*, Av. Ipiranga 740, Japanese. On Av. C. P.A. are many good restaurants and small snack bars.

Electric Current 110 volts A.C., 60 cycles.

Entertainment Cuiabá is quite lively at night; *Pino's Ball* bowling alley, on Av. C.P.A.

Souvenirs Handicrafts in wood, straw, netting, leather, skins, Pequi liquor, crystallized *caju* fruit, compressed *guaraná* fruit (for making the drink), Indian objects on sale at airport, bus station, and craft shops in centre, interesting; Funai (Indian Foundation) shop, poor stock, Rua Barão de Melgaço 3900, opposite Shopping Cuiabá.

Money Exchange, Ametur, R. Joaquim Murtinho.

Car Hire Unidas, Av. Isaac Póvoas 720, T 321-4646; Nobre, at airport, T 381-1651; Localiza, Av. Dom Bosco 963, T 321-0846; A VW Beetle costs about US$30 a day. (Beyond Poconé on the Transpantaneira, diesel and gasoline available in Porto Jofre, alcohol available in Pixaim.)

Tourist Information Turimat, state tourist authority (T 322-5363), Praça República, next to Post Office building. Good maps, friendly, helpful regarding hotels and car hire. Ramis Bucair, Rua Pedro Celestino 280, is good for detailed maps of the region.

Travel Agents *Confiança*, Mariano 434, T 321-4142, very helpful travel agency, but tours to Pantanal are expensive. Also recommended *Expeditours*, Av. Gov. Ponce de Arruda 670, T 381-4959/5674, sightseeing, fishing trips for 4-5 days by boat; *Ametur*, Rua Joaquim Murtinho 242, T 321-4948, very helpful, advice on Pantanal tours (also run their own tours, from 12 hours—US$30—to 5 days, not cheap); *Samariana*, Rua Campo Grande 423, T 341-7947; *Melgatur*, Barão de Melgaço, Av. Augusto Leverger 38. All these agencies arrange trips to the Pantanal; for longer or special programmes, book in advance.

Excursions To *Chapada dos Guimarães*, 68 km. from Cuiabá (3 hotels and some apartments available *Hotel Turismo*, F, 1 block from Rodoviária, clean, good food, friendly, rec), a pleasant ride into the mountains (Rubi bus from Cuiabá US$0.80—8 a day, or hire a taxi, US$20. Take insect repellent.) See the 70-metre Véu de Noiva waterfall (12 km. from Chapada, get bus to drop you off after Buruti; there is a short route, or a longer route through forest to the falls, recommended, small restaurant), strange rock formations, canyons, and the beauty spots of Mutuca, Salgadeira (camp and waterfall), Rio Claro, Portão do Inferno viewpoint, and the falls of Cachoeirinhas (small restaurant)—all unspoilt. Chapada itself is a small village with the oldest church in the Mato Grosso, Our Lady of Santana (1779), a huge spring-water public swimming pool, a good *churrascaria*, and restaurant (*Nivio's*, opp. church); it is still inhabited mainly by *garimpeiros* (diamond-seekers), but a craft community is being established, complete with health food shops. Just outside the town is the official Geodesic Centre of South America, marked by a plaque on a plateau which offers panoramic views of the surrounding plains.

To the Pantanal by the Transpantaneira Highway to Porto Jofre. Guides available at Cuiabá airport; Carlos Wolff de Arruja and Vinícius de Albuquerque Maranhão (through Wildlife

Tours/Geotur, Rua Cel. Benedito Leite 55-Porto Cuiabá, T (065) 321-2639) both rec. A 2½-day tour with Vinicius Maranhão costs US$300 for everything except drinks; he has his own jeep, speaks excellent English and is very knowledgeable. Also recommended is Joel Souza, whose tours are good value and informative; he speaks fluent German and English. Another guide is Amilton Martins da Silva (see above under **Youth Hostel**). Excursions by bus to Poconé, and hitch-hike to Porto Jofre (see section on Pantanal, **page** 467). Very little traffic on this road, except at weekends. Watch out for park rangers, who can be very helpful and friendly, after you have persuaded them you are not poachers or hunters. The research station 40 km. from the end of the Transpantaneira is for Brazilian scientists only. There are buses (TUT) from Cuiabá Mimosa to Barão de Melgaço.

Transport By air to Corumbá, São Paulo, Manaus, Campo Grande, Goiânia, Brasília, Rio de Janeiro, Belo Horizonte and Porto Velho. Comfortable buses (toilets) to Campo Grande, 719 km., 10 hrs., US$9, 12 buses daily, *leito* at 2000 and 2100. To São Paulo, 24 hours, US$18, Rio de Janeiro, 32 hrs., US$28. Goiânia, 14 hrs., US$12; direct to Brasília, São Luiz company, 24 hours, US$22. Direct São Luiz bus to Belo Horizonte, 2000, 26 hrs., US$25; from Belo Horizonte bus passes through Ituiutaba (*Hotel São Luiz*, E, rec.), Nova São Simão (a new dam nearby), and Jataí. Now 4 buses daily (including one *leito*) to Manaus, via Porto Velho, around 80 hrs. To Porto Velho, 10 buses a day, US$17 (Colibri said to be better than São Luiz). Spectacular scenery between Cuiabá and Porto Velho, road newly paved, 1,450 km., bus journey takes 21 hrs. (Andorinha 1700 bus São Paulo-Cuiabá connects with Porto Velho service). (Eventually a paved road from Brasília to Caracas is envisaged). Hitch-hiking from Cuiabá to Manaus is possible—ask truck drivers for lifts at the roadside eating places. The road due N to Santarém has been completed and is paved to Colíder, where the paving diverts to Alta Floresta: daily bus at 2000. Yellow fever inoculations insisted on when travelling this route. Rodoviária at Cuiabá is now on outskirts: bus link (No. 117) with centre costs US$0.15.

Road Distances (km.): Belém, 2,955; Brasília, 1,127; Campo Grande, 712; Corumbá, 1,141; Foz do Iguaçu, 1,849; Goiânia, 934; Manaus, 2,294; Santarém, 1,777 km.; Porto Alegre, 2,356; Recife, 3,430; Rio, 2,118; Salvador, 3,226; São Paulo, 1,758.

From **Rondonópolis** (pop. 101,000 many cheap hotels, such as *Dormitório Beija Flor*, near bus station, or *Sumaré*, clean but unfriendly, both E) about 215 km. SE of Cuiabá on the road to Goiânia, a paved road branches southwards to Campo Grande and thence to the western parts of the State of São Paulo.

Buses from Rondonópolis Brasília, US$12, 14½ hrs.; Goiânia, US$10, 11 hrs.; Campo Grande, US$5, 6½ hrs.; Presidente Epitácio, US$4; Presidente Prudente, US$6. Beware of overbooking on Viação Motta buses.

Airport, for internal flights.

Indians The Bororo tribe, on a reservation three hours by truck from Rondonópolis, have long been "civilized". It may be possible to visit the Xavantes at one of the Reservas Indígenas along the BR-158, N of Barra do Garças (**see page** 460). Funai is reluctant to permit travellers to visit Indian reservations on their own.

A journey along the Porto Velho road from Cuiabá (BR-364) demonstrates the amount of development along Brazil's "Far West" frontier, **see page** 457. A side road off the BR-364 goes to Vila Bela on the Guaporé River, which used to be the capital of Mato Grosso. It has a ruined church, cannon balls lying around, and is very interesting.

N.B. When travelling N of Cuiabá, yellow fever vaccination is obligatory; if you do not have a certificate, you will be (re)vaccinated.

INFORMATION FOR VISITORS

Documents Consular visas are not required for stays of up to 90 days by tourists from Western European (except for French nationals) or Latin American countries, Finland, Morocco and the Philippines. For them, only the following documents are required at the port of disembarkation: valid passport (or *cédula de identidad* for nationals of Argentina, Chile, Paraguay and Uruguay) and adequate proof that you can pay your way and your return fare, subject to no remuneration being received in Brazil and no legally binding or contractual documents being signed. (Some consulates, e.g. Santiago, ask to see an onward ticket, persistence, adequate money and showing a credit card may overcome this). 90-day renewals are easily obtainable, but only within 15 days of the expiry of your 90-day permit, from Policia Federal, open till 1600: the procedure is, buy 3 DARF forms from a *papeleria* and take them back to a bank; pay US$2 tax; then go to Policia Federal who will stamp the extension in your passport after they have seen onward flight tickets, receipt from the bank for the tax, and proof of sufficient funds for your continued stay. For longer stays you must leave the country and return (immediately if you wish) to get a new 90-day permit. US, Canadian and French citizens and people of other nationalities, and those who cannot meet the requirements above, *must* get a visa before arrival, which may, if you ask, be granted for multiple entry. Do not lose the emigration permit they give you when you enter Brazil. Leaving the country without it, you may have to pay up to US$100 per person.

Officially, if you leave Brazil within the 90-day permission to stay and then re-enter the country, you should only be allowed to stay until the 90-day expires. Usual practice, though, is to give another 90-day permit, which may lead to charges of overstaying if you apply for an extension.

You must always carry identification when in Brazil; it is a good idea to take a photocopy of the first 5 pages of your passport, plus that with your Brazilian immigration stamp, and leave your passport in the hotel safe deposit. Always keep an independent record of your passport details. In Rio it is a good idea to register with your consulate to expedite document replacement if yours gets lost/stolen.

Airport Tax US$10 is charged for international flights and US$1 (or US$0.50 for 2nd-class airports) for local ones. Tax is waived if you stay in Brazil less than 24 hrs.

How to Get to Brazil: By Air Brazil is connected with the principal cities of Europe by Air France, KLM, Scandinavian Airways, Lufthansa, Alitalia, Iberia, Swissair, Aerolíneas Argentinas, Varig and TAP. Varig flights from London to Rio (three times a week) take only 11½ hrs. British Airways flies thrice weekly, non-stop London to Rio and on to São Paulo. Cheap carriers to Europe are Pluna and LAP (non-IATA) from Rio to Madrid. Varig fly to Salvador from Frankfurt, Rome and Paris. Royal Air Maroc from Brussels is reported to be cheapest.

Brazil is connected to the USA direct by Varig, Pan American, American Airlines, Aerolíneas Argentinas and Japan Airlines (Varig—4 times—and Japan Airlines twice a week, fly Tokyo-Los Angeles-Rio, and Pan Am, LA-Rio). The cheapest route is probably from Miami. Non-stop New York-Rio by Pan-Am or Varig is 9 hrs. 20 min. Lloyd Aéreo Boliviano (non-IATA) flies twice weekly between Miami and Manaus/Rio; book through Monark Turismo, Visconde de Pirajá 207, Ipanema, Rio (T 287-9746).

All South American capitals are connected by air services to Rio. Caracas, 4 weekly (Varig, Viasa); Bogotá, 4 weekly (Varig, Avianca); Lima, 6 weekly (AeroPerú, Varig); La Paz, 3-4 weekly (Cruzeiro; also LAB to São Paulo); Quito/Guayaquil, once a week with Varig; Asunción, daily with Varig, also LAP, Iberia and Ladeco; Santiago, several daily (LAN-Chile—also daily from São Paulo, Ladeco, Varig and others); Montevideo, about 20 weekly (inc. Varig, Pluna); Buenos Aires, several daily; Paramaribo, once a week each by Cruzeiro do Sul and Suriname Airways to Belém; Cayenne-Belém by Cruzeiro do Sul (twice a week), Suriname Airways, Air France (three times a week) heavily booked. Iquitos, Peru, via Tabatinga (on the Brazilian border with Colombia, a few km. from Leticia) to Manaus by Cruzeiro on Wed and/or Sat.

For many travellers flying to Rio de Janeiro from Europe via South Africa, there is little difference in air fares compared to the direct route. Varig and SAA have one flight each per week between Rio and Johannesburg, and Capetown. Varig has a weekly flight from Rio to Luanda and to Lagos. Airline tickets are expensive in Brazil, buy internal tickets with new cruzeiros. External tickets must be paid for in dollars or proof shown that new cruzeiros were bought at the official rate.

N.B. Regulations state that you cannot buy an air ticket in Brazil for use abroad unless you first have a ticket out of Brazil.

By Sea For shipping lines that carry passengers to Brazil, see **Introduction and Hints. N.B.** There is an 8% tax on international shipping-line tickets bought in Brazil.

By Car To drive in Brazil you need either a translation of your home driving licence, or an international licence. There are agreements between Brazil and border countries (Uruguay, Paraguay, Argentina and Bolivia, and probably now Venezuela) whereby a car can be taken into Brazil (or a Brazilian car out of Brazil) for a period of 60 days; an extension of up to 60 days is granted by the customs authorities on presentation of the paper received at the border; some reports suggest this may be done at most customs posts.

This now applies to cars registered in other countries; the requirements are proof of ownership and/or registration in the home country and valid driving licence (international or from home country). It is better to cross the border into Brazil when it is officially open (from 1300 to 1800 Mon. to Fri.) because an official who knows all about the entry of cars is then present. The motorist should in any case insist on getting the correct paper "in accordance with Decree No. 53.313/63", or he might find it impossible to get the 60-day extension. You must specify which border station you intend to leave by, but application can be made to the Customs to change this. If you want to leave by ship the Touring Club in Rio (possibly also elsewhere, but this is less definite) will arrange it for about US$60; you can also arrange the paper yourself by taking your car away by ship, but it takes about two days and costs about US$15 in port and police charges; the Touring Club provides information on how to go about it. (Klaus Elgner, of Hannover, reports this can be done with a letter in Portuguese saying you wish to leave by ship plus passport number, vehicle number, entry forms data plus an *ordem de embarque* supplied and stamped by the shipping agent. These should be presented to the Customs.) Crossing by a land border is, in any case, easier and probably cheaper. The law allowing for free entry of tourist vehicles applies only to vehicles entering from Argentina, Uruguay, Paraguay and Bolivia; a large deposit is still required if shipped from other countries.

Any foreigner with a passport can purchase a Brazilian car and travel outside Brazil if it is fully paid for or if permission is obtained from the financing body in Brazil. Foreigners do not need the CPF tax document (needed by Brazilians—you only have to say you are a tourist) to purchase a car, and the official purchase receipt is accepted as proof of ownership. There are second-hand car markets on Sun. mornings in most cities—but don't buy an alcohol-driven car if you propose to drive outside Brazil. At a garage, a decent secondhand car will cost about US$1,000 (Jan. 1990); a specialized agent will arrange the paperwork for about US$10. Brazilian cars may not meet safety regulations in N. America and Europe, but they can be easily resold in Brazil.

Customs Clothing and personal articles are free of import duty. Such articles as cameras, movie cameras, portable radios, tape-recorders, typewriters and binoculars are also admitted free if there is not more than one of each. Tourists may also bring in, duty-free, 2 litres of spirits, 2 litres of champagne, 3 litres of wine, 600 cigarettes, 25 cigars, 280 grams of perfume, and 700 grams of toilet water. Duty free goods may only be purchased in foreign currency.

Air Internal air services are highly developed. A monthly magazine, *Guia Aeronáutico*, gives all the timetables and fares. All four national airlines—Varig, Vasp, Cruzeiro and Transbrasil (said to be rather cheaper)—offer excellent service on their internal flights (although Varig has been criticised recently for overbooking, losing baggage, delays and giving poor information to passengers). Between 2400 and 0600, internal flights cost 30% less than daytime flights. On some flights couples can fly for the price of one-and-a-half.

Varig/Cruzeiro offer a 21-day Airpass, which costs US$440. The Airpass must be purchased outside Brazil by holders of an international flight ticket to Brazil, routes must start in either Rio or São Paulo, no journey may be repeated, it may not be used on the Rio-São Paulo shuttle. The airpass is limited to 5 coupons, to which a maximum of 4 may be added (purchased outside Brazil) at US$100 each. No sector may be repeated in the same direction; the itinerary may be changed in Brazil. Make sure you have two copies of the Airpass invoice when you arrive in Brazil; otherwise you will have to select all your flights when you book the first one. Remember that domestic airport tax has to be paid at each departure. Hotels in the Tropical and Othon chains, and others, offer discounts of 10% to Airpass travellers; check with Varig, who have good hotel reservation service. We have been told that it is advisable for users of the Airpasses to book all their intended flights in advance or on arrival in Brazil, as so many internal flights are full these days, especially around summer holiday and Carnival time. Converting the voucher can take some hours, do not plan an onward flight immediately. Cost and restrictions on the Airpass are subject to change. An alternative is to buy an internal flight ticket which includes several stops.

The small feeder airlines have been formed into scheduled domestic airlines, and now operate Brazilian-built *Bandeirante* 16-seater prop-jets into virtually every city and town with any semblance of an airstrip. It has been reported that Cruzeiro do Sul and Varig may combine their flights, with consequent last minute changes in flight time and/or number. **N.B.** Internal flights often have many stops and are therefore quite slow. Foreigners are not allowed to travel on Brazilian air force flights. Most airports have left-luggage lockers (US$0.30 for 24 hours).

Road Transport There is no lack of transport between the principal cities of Brazil; few are connected by railway, but almost all are by road. Ask for window seats (*janela*), or odd numbers if you want the view. Brazilian bus services have a top speed limit of 80 kph (buses are supposed to have governors fitted). They are extremely comfortable (many have reclining seats and toilets), stopping fairly frequently (every 4-5 hrs.) for snacks; the cleanliness of these *postos* has greatly improved, though generally less good in the poorer regions. Buses only stop at official stops. Take something to drink on buses in the North. The bus terminals are usually outside the city centres and offer fair facilities in the way of snack bars, lavatories, left-luggage stores, local bus services and information centres. *Leito* buses ply at night between the main centres, offering reclining seats with foot and leg rests, toilets, and sometimes in-board refreshments, at double the normal fare. For journeys over 100 km., most buses have chemical toilets. Air conditioning can make *leito* buses cold at night, so take a blanket or sweater (and plenty of toilet paper); on some services blankets are supplied; others have hostess service. Bus stations for interstate services and other long-distance routes are usually called *rodoviárias*. It is not easy to sell back unused bus tickets. Some bus companies have introduced a telex system enabling passengers to purchase return tickets at point of departure, rather than individual tickets for each leg. Buses usually arrive and depart in very good time; you cannot assume departure will be delayed. In the South East and South a *Horário de Ônibus* is available at *rodoviárias* (not available for North or North East). Many town buses have turnstiles which can be inconvenient if you are carrying a large pack. Urban buses normally serve local airports.

Taxis Taxi meters are out of date. Drivers have a list of price alterations which should be consulted: make sure it's not a photocopy as that is a well-known minor swindle! Make sure the meter is cleared and shows tariff 1, except 2300-0600 and in Dec. when 2 is permitted. Check that the meter is working, if not, fix price in advance. The radio taxi service costs about 50% more but cheating is less likely. Taxis have a 40% surcharge on Sundays.

Motoring Most main roads between principal cities are now paved. Some are narrow and therefore dangerous.

Car Hire It is reported that car hire is more cheaply arranged outside Brazil. It is essential to have a credit card in order to hire in Brazil. Avis is found only in the major cities and have only a time-and-mileage tariff. National, i.e. Localiza, is represented in many places, often through licencees. Head office: Av. Bernardo Monteiro 1563, Belo Horizonte, T (031) 800-2360; connected with InterRent/Europcar in Europe, will accept credit cards from InterRent/Europcar and offers unlimited mileage if booked in advance from Europe on a fixed US$ rate.

Note It is virtually impossible to buy premium grades of petrol/gasoline anywhere. Fuel in Brazil costs US$0.18 per litre (alcohol), but you need about 50% more alcohol than regular gasoline. Larger cars have a small extra tank for "gasolina" to get the engine started; remember to keep this topped up. Fuel is only 85 octane (owing to high methanol content), so be prepared for bad consumption and poor performance and starting difficulties in non-Brazilian cars in winter. Diesel fuel is cheap and a diesel engine may provide fewer maintenance problems for the motoring tourist. Service stations are free to open when they like, but have mandatory opening hours of Mon.-Sat. 0600-2000.

Motor Spares Volkswagen spares in Brazil are not always interchangeable with German VW spares, but in the main there should be no problems with large components (e.g. gears).

Hitch-hiking Information on hitch-hiking (*carona* in Portuguese) suggests that it is difficult everywhere. Try at the highway-police check points on the main roads (but make sure your documents are in order) or at the service stations, or *postos*. Large increases in the price of gasoline and restrictions on its sale have diminished the amount of road traffic, especially pleasure traffic at weekends.

Rail Trains are appreciably slower than buses. The sleeper services between Rio and São Paulo, and Rio and Belo Horizonte, can be recommended. There are services in the state of São Paulo and between Campinas and Brasília. There is a service between Porto Alegre and the Argentine and Uruguayan frontiers at Uruguaiana and Santana do Livramento. More and more services are being withdrawn; travellers are normally advised to go by air or road. Timekeeping is good on the whole. To obtain the Amerailpass (see Introduction) one is theoretically required to purchase the ticket in new cruzeiros equivalent to US$120 (16 days), US$140 (23 days), US$175 (30 days), US$260 (60 days), exchanged at the official rate. The Ministry of Transport, Esplanada dos Ministerios, Bloco 9, DF 70 062 Brasília, or Praça Mauá 10, Rio, insist on seeing the exchange receipt; Fepasa, Praça Júlio Prestes 148, São Paulo (T 011-233-7211) do not insist on the receipt. However, a number of travellers have suggested that, as rail travel in Brazil is so cheap, the Amerailpass is not good value for money.

Hotels The best guide to hotels in Brazil is the *Guia do Brasil Quatro Rodas* (although it does not list the cheapest places), with good maps of regions and towns. Motels on the outskirts of cities are primarily used by very short-stay couples. The type known as *hotel familiar*, to be found in the interior—large meals, communal washing, hammocks for children—is much cheaper, but only for the enterprising. Usually hotel prices include breakfast; there is no reduction if you don't eat it. In the better hotels (our category D and upwards) the breakfast is well worth eating: rolls, ham, eggs, cheese, cakes, fruit. Normally the *apartamento* is a room with a bath; a *quarto* is a room without bath. The service stations (*postos*) and hostels (*dormitórios*) along the main roads provide excellent value in room and food, akin to truck-driver type accommodation in Europe, for those on a tight budget. The star rating system for hotels (five-star hotels are not price controlled) is not the standard used in North America or Europe. Low-budget travellers with student cards (photograph needed) can use the Casa dos Estudantes network. **Warning** Hotel safe-deposits are not always secure: take a substantial part of your funds in travellers' cheques. Leave rooms in good time so frigobar bills can be checked; we have received reports of overcharging in otherwise good hotels.

Business visitors are strongly recommended to book accommodation in advance, and this can be easily done for Rio or São Paulo hotels with representation abroad. Varig has a good hotel reservation service, with discounts for its customers.

N.B. Taxi drivers will try to take you to the expensive hotels, who pay them commission for bringing in custom. Beware!

Camping Members of the Camping Clube do Brasil or those with an international campers' card pay only half the rate of a non-member, which is US$8 p.p. (US$6 for meals). The Club has 43 sites in 13 states and 80,000 members. For enquiries, Camping Clube do Brasil, Divisão de Campings, Rua Senador Dantas 75—29° andar (T 262-7172), Rio de Janeiro. For those on a very low budget and in isolated areas where there is no camp site, service stations can be used as camping sites; they have shower facilities, watchmen and food; truck drivers are a mine of information; some have dormitories. There are also various municipal sites; both types are mentioned in the text. Campsites often tend to be some distance from public transport routes and are better suited to those with their own transport.

Good camping equipment may be purchased in Brazil and there are several rental companies: Rentalcenter, Av. Brig. Luís Antônio 5088, São Paulo (T 852 0081 and 853 5147) and Av. Bernardino de Campos 661, Santos (T (0132) 41489); Camping Service, Rua Tibiriçá 115, Brooklyn, São Paulo. For special jungle equipment, Selva SA, Rua do Carmo 65-3° andar, Rio de Janeiro (T 242 9695); for equipping camping vans, Camp Car, Rua Piauí 375, Todos os Santos, Rio de Janeiro. It may be difficult to get into some Camping Clube campsites during the high season (Jan.-Feb.). *Guia de Camping* is produced by Artpress, Rua Araçatuba 487, São Paulo 05058; it lists most sites and is available in bookshops in most cities. Quatro Rodas publishes a *Guia de Áreas de Camping* annually.

Food The food can be very good indeed. The most common dish is *bife* (*ou frango*) *com arroz e feijão*, steak (or chicken) with rice and the excellent Brazilian black beans. The most famous dish with beans is the *feijoada completa*: several meat ingredients (jerked beef, smoked sausage, smoked tongue, salt pork, along with spices, herbs and vegetables) are cooked with the beans. Manioc flour is sprinkled over it, and it is eaten with kale (*couve*) and slices of orange, and accompanied by glasses of *aguardente* (unmatured rum), usually known as *cachaça* (booze), though *pinga* (drop) is a politer term. Almost all restaurants serve the *feijoada completa* for Saturday lunch (that means up to about 1630). Bahia has some excellent fish dishes (**see note on page** 390); some restaurants in most of the big cities specialize in them. *Vatapá* is a good dish in the north; it contains shrimp or fish sauced with palm oil, or coconut milk. *Empadinhas de camarão* are worth trying; they are shrimp patties, with olives and heart of palm. A mixed grill, including excellent steak, served with roasted manioc flour (*farofa*; raw manioc flour is known as *farinha*) goes under the name of *churrasco* (it came originally from the cattlemen of Rio Grande do Sul); normally served in specialized restaurants known as *churrascarias* or *rodízios*; good places for large appetites. Minas Gerais has two splendid special dishes involving pork, black beans, *farofa* and kale; they are *tutu á mineira* and *feijão tropeiro*. A white hard cheese (*queijo prata*) or a slightly softer one (*queijo Minas*) is often served for dessert with bananas, or guava or quince paste. Meals are extremely large by European standards; if your appetites are small, you can order, say, one portion and one empty plate, and divide the portion. Unless you specify to the contrary many restaurants will lay a *coberto opcional*, olives, carrots, etc., costing US$0.50-0.75.

NB The main meal is usually taken in the middle of the day; cheap restaurants tend not to be open in the evening. **Warning** Avoid mussels, marsh crabs and other shellfish caught near large cities: they are likely to have lived in a highly polluted environment.

For vegetarians, there is a growing network of restaurants in the main cities, where a main meal is unlikely to cost more than US$2. In smaller places where food may be monotonous try vegetarian for greater variety. We list several. Most also serve fish. Alternatives in smaller towns are the Arab and Chinese restaurants.

There is fruit all the year round, ranging from banana and orange to strawberries (*morango*), pineapple (*abacaxi*) and avocado pear (*abacate*). More specialized fruits include mango (*manga*), pawpaw (*mamão*), custard-apple (*fruta do conde*) and guava (*goiaba*). One is especially recommended to try the *manga de Uba*, a non-fibrous small mango. Also good are *mora* (a raspberry that looks like a strawberry), *jaboticaba*, a small black damson-like fruit, and *jaca* (jackfruit), a large yellow/green fruit.

The exotic flavours of Brazilian ice-creams should be experienced. Martin Crossland recommends readers to try *açaí, bacuri, biribá, buruti, cupuaçu* (not eveyone's favourite), *mari-mari, mucajá, murici, pajurá, pariri, patuá, piquiá, pupunha, sorva, tucumá, uxi* and others mentioned below under "drinks".

If travelling on a tight budget, remember to ask in restaurants for the *prato feito* or *sortido*, a money-saving, excellent value *table-d'hôte* meal for US$2.50 or less. The *prato comercial* is similar but rather better, costing up to US$3. *Lanchonetes* are cheap eating places where you must pay before eating. *Salgados* (savoury pastries), *coxinha* (a pyramid of manioc filled with meat or fish and deep fried), *esfilha* (spicey hamburger inside an onion-bread envelope), *empadão* (a filling—e.g. chicken—in sauce in a pastry case), *empadas* and *empadinhas* (smaller fritters of the same type), are the usual fare. Hamburgers are referred to as "X" (pronounced "shees"—often spelt on menu-boards "cheese"), e.g. *X-Salada*. In Minas Gerais, *pão de queijo* is a hot roll made with cheese. A *bauru* is a toasted sandwich which, in Porto Alegre, is filled with steak, while further north has tomato, ham and cheese filling. *Cocada* is a coconut and sugar biscuit.

Drinks Imported drinks are expensive, but there are some fair local wines. Chilean and Portuguese wines are sometimes available at little more than the cost of local wines. The beers are good and there are plenty of local soft drinks. *Guaraná* is a very popular carbonated fruit drink. There is an excellent range of non-alcoholic fruit juices, known as *sucos: caju* (cashew), *pitanga, goiaba* (guava), *genipapo, graviola* (= *chirimoya*), *maracujá* (passion-fruit), *sapoti* and *tamarindo* are recommended. *Vitaminas* are thick, mixed fruit or vegetable drinks, often with milk. *Caldo de cana* is sugar-cane juice, sometimes mixed with ice. Remember that *água mineral*, available in many varieties at bars and restaurants is a cheap, safe thirst-quencher (cheaper still in supermarkets). Apart from the ubiquitous coffee, good tea is grown and sold. N.B. If you don't want sugar in your coffee or *suco*, you must ask when you order it.

Among the better wines are Château d'Argent, Château Duvalier, Almadén, Dreher, Preciosa and Bernard Taillan. The red Marjolet from Cabernet grapes, and the Moselle-type white Zahringer have been well spoken of. It has often been noticed that a new *adega* starts off well, but the quality gradually deteriorates with time. Greville Brut champagne-type is inexpensive and very drinkable. A white-wine *Sangria*, containing tropical fruits such as pineapple and papaya, is worth looking out for. The Brahma and Antárctica beers are really excellent, of the strong lager type, and are cheaper by the bottle than on draught. Buying bottled drinks in supermarkets, you may be asked for empties in return.

Some genuine Scotch whisky brands are bottled in Brazil; they are very popular because of the high price of Scotch imported in bottle; Teacher's is the most highly regarded brand. Locally made gin, vermouth and campari are very good. The local firewater, *aguardente* (known as *cachaça* or *pinga*), made from sugar-cane, is cheap and wholesome, but visitors should seek local advice on the best brands; São Francisco, Praianinha, Maria Fulô, "51" and

Pitu are recommended makes. Mixed with fruit juices of various sorts, sugar and crushed ice, *cachaça* becomes the principal element in a *batida*, a delicious and powerful drink; the commonest is a lime batida or *batida de limão*; a variant of this is the *caipirinha*, a *cachaça* with several slices of lime in it. *Cachaça* with Coca-Cola is a *cuba*, while rum with Coca-Cola is a *cuba libre*.

Tipping is usual, but less costly than in most other countries, except for porters. Hotels and restaurants, 10% of bill if no service charge but small tip if there is; taxi drivers, none; cloakroom attendants, small tip; cinema usherettes, none; hairdressers, 10-15%; porters, fixed charges but tips as well; airport porters, about US$0.50 per item.

Best Buys Jewellery (especially in Minas Gerais), costume jewellery, and articles made of gemstones, such as lamps; ornamented articles of jacaranda and other tropical hardwoods; clay figurines from the North-East; lace from Ceará; leatherwork; strange pottery from Amazonia; carvings in soapstone and in bone; tiles and other ceramic work, African-type pottery and basketwork from Bahia. Good general shops for those with little time to search are "Folclore" shops in Copacabana next to *Rio Othon Palace* and also in Ipanema. Brazilian cigars are excellent for those who like the mild flavours popular in Germany, the Netherlands and Switzerland.

Indian artefacts are perhaps best obtained from the Funai shops: *Brasília*, bus station and airport; *Rio de Janeiro*, airport and Museu do Indio; *São Paulo*, Galeria Ouro Velho, Rua Augusta 1371; *Cuiabá*, Rua Pedro Celestino 305; *Manaus*, Praça da Matriz; *Belém*, Galeria do Edifício Assembléia Paraense, Avenida Presidente Vargas. Also recommended purchases are musical instruments, e.g. guitars made of fine, exotic woods, other stringed, and percussion instruments. A shop worth visiting is Pro-Musica, Av. Copacabana 435, Lojas M e N, Posto 2, T 237-2688, Rio de Janeiro.

Security As pointed out in the chapters on Rio de Janeiro and Salvador, personal safety in Brazil has deteriorated of recent years, largely because of the economic recession of the early 1980s. The situation is now improving, with a larger police presence in tourist areas.

Apart from the obvious precautions of not wearing jewellery, do not travel alone (this applies especially to women), do not camp or sleep out in isolated places and if you are hitch-hiking, never accept a lift in a car with two people in it. Money belts are safer than bags for your valuables. If you are held up and robbed, it is worth asking for the fare back to where you are staying. It is not uncommon for thieves to oblige. Do not leave valuables in hotel rooms. Overcharging is rife; Ted Stroll of San Francisco advises, "temper your legitimate exasperation at minor rip-offs: remember that economic privation has many Brazilians close to the edge, and that those with a sense of honour are probably as ashamed of exploiting you as you are angry at being exploited". The corollary is be generous to those who give you a good deal.

Warning Most houses and hotels outside the large cities have electric showers operated by water pressure, delivering a supply of tepid to warm water. Despite electrical earthing, these showers are potentially dangerous. Care must be exercised in their use. Do not touch the appliance with wet hands or when the water is turned on.

Health Vaccination against smallpox is no longer required for visitors, but vaccination is necessary against yellow fever if you are visiting Amazonia, or are coming from countries with Amazonian territories, e.g. Bolivia, Colombia, Ecuador. Poliomyelitis vaccination is required for children from 3 months to 6 years. It is strongly recommended to have a yellow fever inoculation before visiting northern Brazil since those without a certificate will be inoculated on entering any of the northern and centre-western states, probably in unsanitary conditions. If you are going to Amazonia, or to other low-lying forested areas, malaria prophylaxis is advised (this can be difficult to obtain in some areas) and water purification tablets are essential. Dengue fever is now endemic in Brazil, and Rio is one of the worst places: protect yourself against mosquitoes. Also, in the Amazon basin, sandflies abound; take a good repellent and get inoculations against hepatitis and typhoid. Be very careful about bathing in lakes or slow rivers anywhere in Brazil: harmful parasites abound (including the snails that carry schistosomiasis—this disease is rampant in Minas Gerais and most of central Brazil). South of the Amazon beware of *borrachudos*, small flies with a sharp bite that attack ankles and calves; coconut oil deters them. Water should not be drunk from taps unless there is a porcelain filter attached or unless you have water sterilizing tablets ("Hydrosteril" is a popular local brand); there is mineral water in plenty and excellent light beer, known as "chopp" (pronounced "shoppi"), and soft drinks. For those who have been in Brazil for a while, *água gelada* (chilled water) is usually safe to drink, being filtered water kept in a refrigerator in most hotels, restaurants and stores. Avoid ice in cheap hotels and restaurants; it is likely to be made from unfiltered water.

Yellow fever (**see page** 471) and some other vaccinations can be obtained from the Ministério da Saúde, Rua Cais de Pharoux, Rio de Janeiro. Less common vaccinations can be obtained at Sande de Portos, Praça 15 de Novembro, Rio de Janeiro.

An excellent hospital, supported by the American and British colonies in São Paulo, is Hospital Samaritano, Rua Conselheiro Brotero 1486, São Paulo (T 51-2154). Good Brazilian medical service is dear. If staying in Brazil for any length of time, it is recommended to take out Brazilian health insurance; Banco Econômico and Citibank are reported to provide good advice on this matter.

Climate and Clothing Conditions during the winter (May to September) are like those of a north European summer in Rio de Janeiro (including periods of rain and overcast skies), but more like a north European autumn in São Paulo and the southern states. Summer-weight woollens can be worn without discomfort in winter in Rio de Janeiro (temperatures vary at this season from 14°C to the high 20s), but further south something heavier is often required. It can get very cold in the far South. In São Paulo, which is in the Highlands, light-weight clothing is only required in the summer; the climate can be treacherous, however, with large temperature changes in a brief space of time. It can get surprisingly cold S and W of Rio, and on high ground anywhere in Brazil, at night; warm clothes are needed. The season of heavy rains is from November to March in Rio and São Paulo, January to April in the north, and from April to August around Recife.

Summer conditions all over the country are tropical, but temperatures of 40°C are comparatively rare. On the coast there is a high degree of humidity. The luminosity is also very high; sunglasses are advisable.

Casual clothing is quite cheap to buy; indeed we are advised that even fashionable clothing is cheap by London and Paris standards. In general, clothing requirements in Brazil are less formal than in the Hispanic countries. It is, however, advisable for men visiting restaurants to wear long trousers in Rio and Manaus (women in shorts are also likely to be refused entry), trousers and jackets or pullovers in São Paulo (also for cinemas). As a general rule, it is better not to wear shorts in official buildings, cinemas and inter-state buses. Trousers and long-sleeved shirts are advisable for visits to government offices.

Best Time for a visit is from April to June, and August to October, inclusive. Businessmen should avoid from mid-December to the end of February, when it is hot and people are on holiday. These are not good months for tourism either, because hotels, beaches and means of transport tend to be crowded. July should also be avoided: it is a school holiday month. The climax of the soccer season is in Nov. and Dec.

British Visitors are referred to "Hints to Exporters: Brazil", obtainable from Dept. of Trade, Export Services Division, Sanctuary Bldgs, 16-20 Great Smith Street, London SW1P 3DB.

Hours of Business are 0900-1800 Mon. to Fri. for most businesses, which close for lunch some time between 1130 and 1400. Shops are open on Sat. till 1230 or 1300. Government departments are open from 1100-1800 Mon. to Fri. Banks 1000-1500, but closed on Sat. The British and American embassies' hrs. are 0830-1245 and 1415-1700 Mon. to Fri. The consular section's hrs. are 0830-1230; 1330-1630 Mon. to Fri.

National Holidays are 1 January (New Year); 3 days up to and including Ash Wed. (Carnival); 21 April (Tiradentes); 1 May (Labour Day); Corpus Christi (June); 7 September (Independence Day); 12 October, Nossa Senhora Aparecida; 2 November (All Souls' Day); 15 November (Day of the Republic); and 25 December (Christmas). The local holidays in the main cities are given in the text. Four religious or traditional holidays (Good Fri. must be one; other usual days: 1 November, All Saints Day; 24 December, Christmas Eve) must be fixed by the municipalities. Other holidays are usually celebrated on the Mon. prior to the date.

Time Brazilian Standard Time is 3 hrs. behind GMT; of the major cities, only the Amazon time zone, Manaus, Cuiabá, Campo Grande and Corumbá are different, with time 5 hrs. behind GMT. The State of Acre is 4 hours behind GMT. Clocks move forward one hour in summer for approximately 5 months, (usually between October and February or March) but times of change vary. This does not apply to Acre.

Currency The currency unit is the new cruzeiro, which in March 1990 replaced the new cruzado, itself introduced in January 1989 to replace the cruzado. The new cruzado and the March 1990 cruzeiro are identical in value. At the time of going to press there were in circulation all sorts of notes dating from four currency revisions, some overstamped. Be very careful to check what you get. Any amount of foreign currency and "a reasonable sum" in cruzeiros can be taken in; residents may only take out the equivalent of US$4,000.

Money sent to Brazil is normally paid out only in Brazilian currency, so do not have more money sent to Brazil than you need for your stay in the country itself. Tourists cannot change US$ travellers' cheques into US$ notes, nor can they obtain US$ travellers cheques on an American Express card.

From 1989, banks were permitted to exchange foreign currency at a new tourist rate, which was set close to the black, or parallel rate (which was illegal). In March 1990 the exchange rate was unified. Nevertheless, at the end of the month, three rates were still quoted; the trade rate (Cr 42:$1), the tourist rate (Cr46:$1) and the parallel rate (Cr 61:$1). The Banco do Brasil in most major cities will change cash and travellers' cheques; also Lloyds Bank (ex-BOLSA) branches. For the latest rate, see **Economic Indicators** near end of book. If you keep the exchange slips, you may convert back into foreign currency one-third of what you changed into cruzeiros. This applies to the official markets only; there is no right of reconversion unless you have an official exchange slip. The parallel market "mercado paralelo" is so common that travellers use it without problems (as far as we have been told). It is to be found in travel agencies, exchange houses and among hotel staff. Loiterers outside hotels will direct you to money changers—they will expect a tip. It is also possible to change money on the street, but this is very dangerous, especially in the Upper City in Salvador, where conmen abound. Finding the parallel market where there are no exchange houses may involve a lot of walking; ask around in imported goods shops, chemists, souvenir shops or big hotels. The best rates are to be found in the tourist centres. If you want to use the parallel market, take plenty of US dollars in cash, and be prepared to haggle (note, however, that travellers' cheques are a safer way to carry your money, but also that rates for cheques are usually lower than for cash). Wherever possible in the text, we quote prices converted from cruzeiros to dollars at the parallel rate; travellers should bear this, and subsequent fluctuations in both the exchange and inflation rates, in mind when working out budgets. Black market and official rates are quoted in the papers and on TV news programmes. While inflation is high, change only what you need for a few days at a time, except when travelling in remote areas. Look in the daily press for advance warning of hikes in transport or other prices as a result of inflation.

Credit cards are widely used; Diners Club, Master Card and American Express are useful. Visa-Elo is the Brazilian Visa but many places will not take overseas Visa. Master Charge/Access is accepted by Banco Econômico and Banco Real and some airline offices, overseas credit cards need authorisation from São Paolo, this can take up to 2 hrs, allow plenty of time if buying air tickets. Banco do Brasil handles money forwarded on Visa card. Credit card transactions are charged at the official rate, so are expensive. Cash advances on credit cards will only be paid in cruzeiros at the tourist rate, incurring a 1½% commission. Automatic cash dispensers are becoming common in Brazil: you need only a passport and address to open an account with a large Brazilian bank, and you can then draw cash from a machine as required.

Cost of Living There has been heavy inflation in Brazil for some years. Good rates of exchange on the parallel market, especially in Rio, have made Brazil inexpensive for travellers, except for high-class hotels and restaurants. Since this chapter was prepared at a time of major economic revision prices may have changed at the time of the book's use.

Weights and Measures The metric system is used by all.

Postal charges are high (we do not publish rates owing to the rapid changes caused by inflation). Air mail takes 4 to 6 days to or from Britain or the U.S.; surface mail takes some 4 weeks. "Caixa Postal" addresses should be used when possible. Leaflets on postal rates are not issued; ask at the post office. Some post offices will not accept picture postcards unless enclosed in an envelope. Postes restantes usually only hold letters for 30 days. Letters from abroad may be subject to random checks by Brazilian officials. You can buy charge collected stamps, Compraventa de Francamento (CF) for letters only, to be paid on delivery. The Post Office sells cardboard boxes for sending packages internally and abroad (they must be submitted open); pay by the kilo; you must fill in a list of contents; string, but not tape, provided. Postal services are reported to have deteriorated because of the theft of stamps for resale (franked and registered letters are more secure). Some post offices have installed posting machines, stamps are not needed. It may be easier to avoid queues and obtain higher denomination stamps by buying at the philatelic desk at the main post office. Poste Restante for AmEx customers efficiently dealt with by the AmEx agents, Kontik-Franstur, with offices in most large towns.

Telephone The system has been greatly improved. There is a trunk-dialling system linking all parts: for the codes look up DDD in the telephone directory. There are telephone boxes at airports, post offices, railway stations, hotels, most bars, restaurants and cafés, and in the main cities there are telephone kiosks *for local calls only* in the shape of large orange shells, for which *fichas* can be bought from bars, cafés and newsvendors; in Rio they are known as *orelhões* (big ears). Phone calls are half-price after 2000 until 0400 and all day Sun. Phone calls abroad are US$4 for first 3 mins. to Europe. Note that Brazil is now linked to North America, Japan and most of Europe by trunk dialling (DDI). Codes are listed in the telephone directories. AT and T offers a service to USA subscribers, for information call 1-800-874-4000. For collect calls from phone boxes (in Portuguese: "a cobrar"), dial 107 and ask for the *telefonista internacional*. No collect calls available to New Zealand, though to Australia is OK. It is useless trying to dial long-distance from hotels or orange *orelhões*, as a blocking device is installed on those lines. There are special blue *orelhões* for long-distance DDD calls; for these you need to buy *fichas interurbanas* from telephone company offices. Making phone calls abroad from hotels is very expensive.

Fax service operates in main post offices in major cities, charges are cheaper than telephone if messages are short and on one sheet of paper.

Cables Cables are listed under cities. Cable facilities are available at all post offices, the main ones have public telex booths. Post offices are recognizable by the ECT (Empresa de Correios e Telégrafos) signs outside. There is a 40% tax added to the cost of all telegraphic and telephonic communications, which makes international service extremely dear. Local phone calls and telegrams, though, are quite cheap. Make sure that hotels equipped by telex facilities can send outgoing telexes; some are unable to do so, or only at certain times of day.

Press: Rio *Daily Post/Brasil Herald*, the only English-language daily in Brazil, Rua do Resende 65, Rio de Janeiro 20231, T 221 2772. Not published Mons. The main papers are *Jornal do Brasil, O Globo*, and *Jornal do Commércio*. **São Paulo** Morning: *O Estado de São Paulo, Folha de São Paulo, Gazeta Mercantil* and *Diário de São Paulo. Daily Post/Brasil Herald* (except Mons.) Evening: *A Gazeta, Diário do Noite, Ultima Hora*. A monthly publication, *Jornal de Turismo* (Largo do Machado 29, Rio), gives notes on tourism, hotel prices, timetables, etc. There is a similar monthly magazine in English, *Rio Visitor* (Rua Marquês de São Vicente 52, Loja 318, Gávea, Rio).

English-language radio broadcasts daily at 15290 kHz, 19m Short Wave (Rádio Bras, Caixa Postal 04/0340, DF-70 323 Brasília).

Language The language is Portuguese. Efforts to speak it are greatly appreciated and for the low-budget traveller, Portuguese is essential. If you cannot lay your tongue to "the language of the angels", apologize for not being able to speak Portuguese and try Spanish, but note that in remoter parts you may well not be understood, and you will certainly have difficulty in understanding the answers.

One important point of spelling is that words ending in "i" and "u" are accented on the last syllable, though (unlike Spanish) no accent is used there. This is especially important in place names: Parati, Iguaçu. Audioforum, 31 Kensington Church Street, London W8 4LL, T

937-1647 does cassette course on Brazilian Portuguese.

Working in Brazil Work-permit restrictions are making it harder to find work as an English language teacher than it used to be, though many people do it unofficially and leave Brazil every 90 days in order to re-enter as tourists. One's best bet would be in a small language school. Charges: private, US$5 per hr.; school, US$2 per hr. Or advertise in the Press.

Information All Brazil's States, and most cities and towns have their own tourist information bureaux. They are not usually too helpful regarding information on very cheap hotels, tending to imagine that no foreign tourist should consider staying in anything of that kind. It is also difficult to get information on neighbouring states. *Quatro Rodas*, a motoring magazine, publishes an excellent series of guides in Portuguese and English at about US$5 each. Its *Guia do Brasil* is a type of Michelin Guide to hotels, restaurants, sights, facilities and general information on hundreds of cities and towns in the country, including good street maps. The same company also publishes a camping guide and more specialized guides to Rio, São Paulo, Salvador and the South, with other cities and areas in preparation. These guides can be purchased at street newspaper vendors throughout the country. Quatro Rodas Guides may be bought in Europe from Distribuidora Jarim, Quinta Tau Varais, Azinhaga de Fetais, Camarate 2685, Lisbon, Portugal, T Lisbon 257-2542. There is also the "Transbrasil Guide to Attractions and Services" with maps, in Portuguese, English and French. A new publication in 1990 is *Backcountry Brazil* by Alex Bradbury (Bradt Publications), with chapters on the Pantanal, the Amazon and the Nort East Coast, as well as practical tips.

Many of the more expensive hotels provide locally-produced tourist information magazines for their guests. Travel information can be very unreliable and it is wise to recheck details thoroughly.

We wish to offer our grateful thanks for updating the Brazilian chapter to Sylvia Brooks. We thank also Michael Wooller of Lloyds Bank Economics Department for currency information. Also to the following residents and travellers: R.B.L. Gordon (Guarujá), Georgia Kaufmann (Belo Horizonte), Stephen Newcomer (Centerville, Iowa), Sean O'Flynn and Conor O'Sullivan (Salvador), Bill Potter (Manaus), Wolfgang Thiel (Porto Seguro), Franck Abadie (Megève, France) and Marianne Joelius (Stockholm), Tam Agosti-Gisler (Anchorage, Alaska), Karl Alchorn (Oromocto, NB), Dean A. Alper (Mill Valley, CA), Martin Anderle, Susanne Riller and Tilo Timmermann (Fürth, W. Ger.), Stan Anderton (Preston, Lancs.), Lucie Armstrong (Ithaca, NY), Adriana Bacheschi (São Paulo), Ronen Barak and Yehuda Corcos, Ofra Hazrati, Yoram Hazrati (Israel), Peter Bench (Hertford), Paul Beppler, Momik Bernaerts (Amsterdam) and Thomas Hartmann (Copenhagen), Stefan Berther (Geneva), O. Blane, Marcela M. Bonilla (Bogotá), Dorothea Bornholdt (Lutzhorn, W. Ger.), Erez Boyarsky (Nazzareth Ilit, Israel), Tom Brandt (Buenos Aires), Sara Braune (Stroud), Lucy Broadbent and Rick Palmer (Palmerston North, NZ), Fiona Brown (Thornton Heath), R.J. Brown (London SW4), Peter Bruhbühler (Switz.) Felicity and Charles Buchan (Fraserburgh), David M. Butler (Belmont, Victoria), Ken Chitty (Rochester, Kent), Paul Stacey (London) and Ione Christiansenand (Denmark), Lucinda Coates (North Ryde, NSW), Jane Coburn and Philip Barnes (Thirroul, NSW), A.N. Cottam (Buntingford), David S. Cousens and Antonia E. Melvin (London E18), Kate Craik (Edinburgh), Mark Crathorne (Woking), Joanne Cross and Frank Pinelli (Oak Park, IL), Gary Curtis (Port Lincoln, S. Aus.), Louis-François Debêtaz (Concise, Switz.), Michael D. Delapa (Monterey, CA), Christian Delbrouck (Freiburg, W. Ger.), Bill Dixon (Flitwick, Beds.), Hermien Don (Amsterdam), Rosetta Drioli, Joy Jarvis, Dorothy Mitchell and Anneli Soininen (Waverton, NSW), Sonia and Tzvi Dugan (D.N. Eilot, Israel), Jennifer Eberle (Westwood, NJ), Kate Edwards (Freeport, Grand Bahama), Fred and Marianne Emery (London SE26), Bert Ernste (Rio de Janeiro), Maarten Feteris and Charlotte Geerards (Leiden, Neth.), Volker Filss (Oberhausen, W. Ger.), Mo Fini (Bath, Avon), Elisabeth Fischer and Thomas Winter (München 40), Alexandra Fisher (London W8), Bernadette Fitzsimons (Varig, London), Bruce Fitzwater (Portland, OR), Olivier and Paloma Foro (St-Moritz), Paul Forte (London NW1), D. Friend (Melbourne), John N. Fugelso (Durham NC), Roman Füglister (Alpnach Dorf, Switz.), Katy Gardner (Liverpool 8), Schömig Gerold (Würzburg, W. Ger.), Theodor A. Gevert (Barueri, SP, Brazil), Tony Gowers (Bristol), Rudolf Graf (Genthod, Switz.), Jacqueline Greig (Cuckfield, E Sussex), Pilou Grenié (Antibes), Christian Gurney (Thornhill, Ont.), Simon Gustafson (Taby, Swe.), Erich Gysling (Zürich).
    John Hale (London N3), Astrid Hansen (Aars, Dnmk) and Jane Harfeld (Hornsyld, Dnmk.),

Jim Hardy (Waukesha, Wis.), Lucy Harper, Wayne Harvey (South Australia), Kevin Healey (Melbourne, Vic.), Judith and Stephen Adler Hellman (Toronto), Olav Holger Helø (Copenhagen), David W. Heumann (Los Angeles, CA), Ursula Hochuli (Switz.) and Vincent Choblet (Paris), Thomas Hodel (Kaufdorf, Switz.), Anders Holm (Gothenburg), Hans-Jürgen Holst (Tostedt, W. Ger.), Bob Horsfall and Judi Johnson (Auckland, NZ), Ulrich Hummel (Stuttgart 1), Edward Hutt (Stowmarket), Richard A. Jacobsen (Bloomington, Minnesota), Volkmar E. Janicke (München 40), Lennart Wedel-Jarlsberg (Ramnes, Norway), Simon Jeffreys (Peterborough), Roland Johnsson (Danderyd, Swe.), Martina Jost and Heinz Eisenhauer (Darmstadt), Norunn Kalgraff (Landås, Norway), V. Kenyon (Oxford), Rosi Kerler (München 40), Marcel Kersten (Roosendaal, Neth.), Justin Koprowski (High Wycombe), Thomas Krauss and Petra Fadi (Glasgow 12), Brad Krupshaw (Silver Springs, Maryland), Karen Kuebel and George Georgiadis (São Luis), Daniel Küng (Wohlen, Switz.), Rudi Lamparter (Gaechingen, W. Ger.), Remo Legnazzi (Bern), Jo Lerner (Grimbergen, Belg.), John Lewis (London NW2), Henri van Ligten (Arnhem, Neth.), Ariel and Tally Lofsky (D.N. Habikaa, Israel), Kirsten Lührs (Stuttgart, 1), Mika Määttänen (Tampere, Fin.), Susan MacCallum and Peter Hedvlin (Sydney, Aust.), Jan Madsen (Agedrup, Dmk.), Malle Mallmann (Herten), S.D. Manley (London E12), Asa, Martina and Lena (Swe.), Trevor J. Mason (Winchester), Nelly Matthey (Lausanne), Kirk Mayer and Barbara Pearce (Macclesfield), Brigit McCarthy (Rome), Dean McCauley (San Francisco, CA), David McDonnell (London N13), Ralph-Peter Mechnik (Nürnberg 1), Barbara Meier and Thomas Ester (Essen 15, W. Ger.), John Messenger (Braddan, Isle of Man), Guy Middleton (Liverpool 4), Alan I. Mishael (Coral Gables, FL), Valerie and Bob Mitchell (Cottesloe, Western Australia), Ortelli Visalakshi Moreno (Italy), Daniel Morgan (Wellington, NZ), Dr Boris Moro (North Carolina State University), Dimitri Moursellas (Manhattan Beach, CA), Richard Müller (Gümligen, Switz.), David, Christine, Philip and Catherine Mylan (Worksop), Melanie Newman (with John Pritchard, Ros Harris, Danial Taylor, Carol Finn and Finn Bangshaad Jensen—London W9), Steve Newman and Wendy Chilcott (Bahía Blanca), Jonas Noreús (Varberg, Swe.), Claus Nrgaard and Bitten Pedersen (Silkeborg, Dmk.), Dave Nutting (Melbourne), N. Nyffenegger (Bern), John O'Heron (Tampa, Florida), Bryan F. O'Leary (Redondo Beach, CA), Justine O'Keefe and David Couper (N Z), Barry Oldham (Plymouth, Devon), Shawn and Jeff Olsen (St Paul, Minnesota), Karl Olson (New York, NY), Karin Ottiger (Ottikon, Switz.), Lucy Paine and William Petrie (Watlington, Oxon), John and Jane Parkinson (Ilkley), Barry M. Pell and Judith L. Katz (Brookline, MA), Jeff Perk (Carbondale, IL), Sarah Parry (Southampton), Wulf Peters (Querenhurst, W. Ger.), Sandrine Pétremand and Gilles Maitre (Bevaix, Switz.), Bill Porter (Herford, W. Ger.), Michelle Portman (Haifa, Israel), Ortrun Poettering (Rio de Janeiro), Robert Jan Prenger and André Kuipers (Amsterdam), Bernd Proissl (Wernau, W. Ger.), Tsafrir Rabinovitz (Israel), John M. Raspey, Renate and Ralf, Jörg Retzluff (Aurich, W. Ger.), George Riuggeler (Landringen, W. Ger.), Miranda Roberts (London SE3), Dr Edith Rockenbauer (Puerto de la Cruz, Tenerife), Marvin and Pat Rosen (New York), Yves Rougeaux (Montreuil, France), Dafna and Yoram Rozy (Tel-Aviv), J. Rushton (Calgary), Louise Santamera (Liverpool 3), Rick and Su Sareen (Thailand), Kate Scanlon (London N1), Piero Scaruffi (Redwood City, CA), Alex Scherer (Brugg, Switz.), Kathrin Schildknecht and Jürg Schmutz (Bern, Switz.), Andrea Schneiber (Herborn, W. Ger.), Jolanda Schneider (Malans, Switz.), Rolf Schneider (Effretikon, Switz.), Henrique Schoenacher (Tainá Turismo, Campo Grande), Leon van der Schoor (Den Bosch, Neth.), Horst H. Schulz (Hamburg), Karen Schulpzand and Rudy Cruysbergs (Dilbeek, Belgium), von Schubert (Kehl, W. Ger.), Sidney .A Schwartz (Rio de Janeiro), Colin Sears and Caroline Richard, Vivienne Shave (Truro), Irene Singer and Leonel Lurua (Buenos Aires), Dr A.E. Smith (Formoor, Oxford), Bette Smith and James Amidon (Winter Park, CO), John Spraos (London NW11), Dietrich Stahl (Bridgewater, Nova Scotia), M. Stead (British Consulate-General, Rio de Janeiro), Ted Stroll (San Francisco, CA), Christian Stückle (Ingolstadt, W. Ger.), Joseph Syfrig (Riehen, Switz.), Raquel Rotnes Thalenberg (Brazil) and Guiora Thalenberg (Israel), Martin and Susanna Theander (Malmö), Trevor Toone (Burnaby, BC, Canada), Douglas B. Trent (Focus Tours, Belo Horizonte), Levy Venanzius (Disentis, Switz.), Maarten van Vlerken (Amsterdam), Thomas Walbaum (Steinheim, W. Ger.), T.C. Walker (Chobham, Sy.), Ingrid Walter and Norbert Eisinger (Schnelldorf, W. Ger.), Ignaz Wanders (Haarlem), Rob Ward (Sutton, Sy.), Jonathan Weiland (Philadelphia, PA), Roland Weitkamp (Braunschweig, W. Ger.), Maks Westerman (New York), Robert Westra (São Paulo), Regina Wetzer and Richard C. Brusca (San Diego, Ca), Michael R. White (Birmingham, B14), Urs Wigger (Menznau, Switz.), Julie Williams (Muswellbrook, NSW), Oliver Williams (London W10), F Worthington (Leicester) and Helmut Zettl (Ebergassing, Austria).

CHILE

INTRODUCTION

CHILE, with an area of 756,626 square km., is smaller than all other South American republics save Ecuador, Paraguay and Uruguay. Its territory is a ribbon of land lying between the Andes and the Pacific, 4,329 km. long and, on average, no more than 180 km. wide. Of this width the Andes and a coastal range of highland take up from a third to a half. Chile contains within itself wide variations of soil and vast differences of climate; these are reflected, from area to area, in the density of population and the occupations of its almost 13 million people.

In the extreme north Chile has a frontier with Peru running ten km. north of the railway from the port of Arica to the Bolivian capital of La Paz. Its eastern frontier—with Bolivia in the far north and with Argentina for the rest of its length—is along the crest of the Andes, gradually diminishing in height from Santiago southwards to the southern seas, where the Strait of Magellan lies, giving access to the Atlantic. Chile's western and southern coastline is 4,500 km. long.

Down the whole length, between the Andes and the coastal range, there runs a valley depression, though it is less well defined in the north. North of Santiago transverse ranges join the two massifs and impede transport, but for 1,044 km. south of the capital the great longitudinal valley stretches as far as Puerto Montt. South of Puerto Montt the sea has broken through the coastal range and drowned the valley, and there is a bewildering assortment of archipelagos and channels.

From north to south the country falls into five sharply contrasted zones:

1. The first 1,250 km. from the Peruvian frontier to Copiapó is a rainless hot desert of brown hills and plains devoid of vegetation, with a few oases. Here lie the nitrate deposits and several copper mines.

2. From Copiapó to Illapel (600 km.) is semi-desert; there is a slight winter rainfall,

The desert North.

Copiapó to Illapel.

The Heartland and Santiago.

South through the central valley.

Forest Chile: Temuco to Puerto Montt.

Archipelagic Chile.

Chilean Patagonia.

0 100 200 300 400 500
km

CHILE

but great tracts of land are without vegetation most of the year. Valley bottoms are here cultivated under irrigation.

3. From Illapel to Concepción is Chile's heartland, where the vast majority of its people live. Here there is abundant rainfall in the winter, but the summers are perfectly dry. Great farms and vineyards cover the country, which is exceptionally beautiful.

4. The fourth zone—Forest Chile—between Concepción and Puerto Montt, is a country of lakes and rivers, with heavy rainfall through much of the year. Cleared and cultivated land alternates with mountains and primeval forests.

5. The fifth zone, from Puerto Montt to Cape Horn, stretches for 1,600 km. This is archipelagic Chile, a sparsely populated region of wild forests and mountains, glaciers, fjords, islands and channels. Rainfall is torrential, and the climate cold and stormy. There are no rail links S of Puerto Montt, but the Carretera Austral Presidente Pinochet now provides almost unbroken road access for more than 1,000 kilometres S of that city. Chilean Patagonia is in the extreme south of this zone. To make the most of this trip, read Darwin's *Voyage of the Beagle* beforehand.

A subdivision of the fifth zone is Atlantic Chile—that part which lies along the Magellan Strait to the east of the Andes, including the Chilean part of Tierra del Fuego island. There is a cluster of population here raising sheep and mining coal. Large offshore oilfields have now been discovered in the far South, and the area is developing rapidly.

History A century before the Spanish conquest the Incas moved south into Chile from Peru, moving across the desert from oasis to oasis at the foot of the Andes. They reached the heartland and conquered it, but were unable to take the forest south of the Río Maule; there the fierce Mapuches (Araucanians) held them. In 1537 Diego de Almagro, at the head of a hundred Spaniards and some thousands of Indians, took the Inca road from Peru south to Salta and across the Andes. Many of the Indians perished, but the heartland was reached; bitterly disappointed at not finding gold they returned to Peru. The next *conquistador*, who took the desert road, was Pedro de Valdivia; he reached the heartland in 1541 and founded Santiago on February 12. Reinforced by fresh colonists from Peru and Spain, Valdivia widened his conquest and pushed S into Mapuche land, but was able to hold only the settlement to which he had given his name. The Mapuches fought desperately—they soon mastered the use of the horse—and in 1554 they captured Valdivia himself and killed him. Fighting continued for three centuries, and it was not until 1881 that peace was made, and immigrants were able to settle in the Mapuche lands.

The colonial period was greatly troubled by constant wars against the Mapuches and by internal dissensions, particularly between the landowners and the priests, who strongly objected to a system of Indian serfdom—the Indians were constantly in revolt. There have been, too, natural disasters in the form of earthquakes and tidal waves which have wiped out the cities again and again. From the end of the 16th century British and French pirates frequented the coasts. From the first, Chile formed part of the Viceroyalty of Peru; it was controlled from Lima, and trade was allowed only with Peru. This led to uncontrolled smuggling and by 1715 there were 40 French vessels trading illegally along the coast. It was not till 1778 that trading was allowed between Chile and Spain.

In 1810 a group of Chilean patriots, including Bernardo O'Higgins— the illegitimate son of a Sligo-born Viceroy of Peru, Ambrosio O'Higgins, and a Chilean mother—revolted against Spain. This revolt led to seven years of war against the occupying troops of Spain—Lord Cochrane was in charge of the insurrectionist navy—and in 1817 General José de San Martín crossed the Andes with an army from Argentina and helped to gain a decisive victory. O'Higgins became the first head of state: under him the first constitution of 1818 was drafted. But there was one thing which was dangerous to touch in Chile: the interests of the dominant landed aristocracy, and O'Higgins's liberal policies offended them, leading to his downfall in 1823. A period of anarchy followed, but in 1830 conservative forces led by Diego Portales restored order and introduced the authoritarian constitution of 1833. Under this charter, for almost a century, the country was ruled by a small oligarchy of landowners. It was during this period, from 1879 to 1883, that the War of the Pacific was fought against Peru and Bolivia; all three contestants were claiming the new nitrate wealth of the desert in the north. Chile emerged victorious—even Lima was occupied—and for 40 years thereafter it drew great wealth from the nitrate fields. One unexpected result of the war was that the Chilean land workers or *inquilinos*, after a taste of liberty, were unwilling to return to the bondage of the big estates; the demobilized soldiers migrated to the cities, and later pushed south into the new lands beyond the Bío-Bío recently opened by pressure on the Mapuches. The free labourer had made his appearance.

The rule of the Right was challenged by the liberal regime of President Alessandri in 1920. Acute economic distress in 1924, linked to the replacement of Chile's natural nitrates with artificial fertilizers more cheaply produced in Europe, led to army intervention and some reforms were achieved. The inequalities in Chilean society grew ever sharper, despite the maintenance of political democracy, and gave rise to powerful socialist and communist parties. President Eduardo Frei's policy of "revolution in freedom" (1964-70) was the first concerted attempt at overall radical reform, but it raised hopes it could not satisfy. In 1970 a marxist coalition assumed office under Dr. Salvador Allende; the frantic pace of change under his regime polarized the country into Left- and Right-wing camps. Gradually increasing social and economic chaos formed the background for Allende's deposition by the army and his death in September 1973. A military regime, led by Gen. Augusto Pinochet Ugarte, succeeded him. In its early years particularly, it suppressed internal opposition by methods which were widely condemned. Despite economic prosperity and efforts to make the regime more popular, President Pinochet's bid to be chosen for a further eight years in office after 1989 was rejected by the electorate in 1988.

A Christian Democrat, Patricio Aylwin Azócar, was elected President in 1989 and took office on 11 March 1990 in a peaceful transfer of power from military dictatorship to a constitutional, democratically-elected civilian government. The new Congress began work by suspending many laws passed by the military, prior to revising them. These included the anti-terrorist law, the death penalty, the budget, tax and labour legislation, curbs on freedom of expression and a plethora of laws decreed by the junta in its final months.

The People There is less racial diversity in Chile than in most Latin American countries. There are about 150,000 pure blooded Mapuche Indians, 95% of whom live in the forest land around Temuco, between the Bío-Bío and Toltén rivers. A fifth is European; the rest is *mestizo*, a compound of bloods. The stock has been much less modified by immigration than in Argentina and Brazil. The German, French, Italian and Swiss immigrants came mostly between 1846 and 1864 as small farmers in the forest zone S of the Bío-Bío. Between 1880 and 1900 gold-seeking Serbs and Croats settled in the far S, and the British took up sheep farming and commerce in the same region. The influence throughout Chile of the immigrants is out of proportion to their numbers: their signature on the land is seen, for instance, in the German appearance of Valdivia, Puerto Montt, Puerto Varas and Osorno.

The population (12,961,000 in 1989) is far from evenly distributed: Middle Chile (from Copiapó to Concepción), 18% of the country's area, contains 77% of the total population. The Metropolitan Region of Santiago contains, on its own, about 39% of the whole population. The rate of population growth per annum—1.7%— is slightly under the average for Latin America.

The birth rate is highest in the cities, particularly the forest zone. The death rate, 6.7%, is highest in the cities. Infant mortality is 22.8 per thousand live births; it is highest in the rural areas. There are 300 hospital beds per 100,000 population and 1,038 inhabitants per doctor. Life expectancy is 71. Of the total population, only 7.5% are illiterate.

Today, there is in process an intense urbanization of the populace. The cities are expanding, partly because so many people have left the land, and some 83% now live in the towns. Housing in the cities has not kept pace with the increased population; many Chileans live in slum areas called *callampas* (mushrooms) in the outskirts of Santiago and around the factories.

The Economy   Chile is endowed with a diversified environment, allowing the production of all temperate and Mediterranean products. Agriculture, however, supplies only about 10% of gdp, employs 20% of the labour force and contributes about 16% of merchandise exports. Given the country's topography, only 7% of the land is devoted to crop production, while 14% is used for pasture. Traditional crops, such as cereals, pulse, potatoes and industrial crops (sugarbeet, sunflowerseed and rapeseed) account for about 37% of the value added of agriculture, and vegetables for about 25%. The area showing fastest growth is fresh fruit. Another area of expansion is forestry. Chile has over 9 m hectares of natural forest of which planted forests cover 1 m hectares, with more than 90% planted with insignis radiata pine, a species which in Chile grows faster than in other countries. Chile is the most important fishing nation in Latin America and the largest producer of fishmeal in the world. Industrial consumption absorbs about 93% of the fish catch; fresh fish and fish products contribute about 11% of merchandise exports.

The dominant sector of the economy is mining. Chile has been the world's largest producer of copper since 1982 and also produces molybdenum, iron ore, manganese, lead, gold, silver, zinc, sulphur and nitrates. Chile has a quarter of the world's known molybdenum ore reserves (3m tonnes), and is believed to have around 40% of the world's lithium reserves. Mineral ores, most of which is copper, account for half of total export revenue. Fluctuations in world prices for minerals therefore have a great impact on the balance of payments.

Chile is fortunate in possessing reserves of oil, natural gas and coal, and abundant hydroelectricity potential. About 60% of its energy requirements are met by oil and gas, 15% by coal, 24% by hydroelectricity and the balance by biomass. Almost all the country's hydrocarbon reserves are in the extreme south, on Tierra del Fuego, in the Strait of Magellan and the province of Magallanes. Oil reserves are estimated at 736 m barrels, 188 m of which are offshore.

Manufacturing has been particularly vulnerable to changes in economic policy: nationalization during the Allende administration in the early 1970s; recession brought about by anti-inflationary policies in the mid-1970s; increased foreign competition resulting from trade liberalization in the early 1980s, and greater exports together with import substitution in the mid-1980s. The contribution of manufacturing to total gdp fell from 25% in 1970 to 21% in 1989 although its share of exports rose. Activity is mostly food processing, metalworking, textiles and fish processing.

High rates of inflation were recorded in the first half of the 1970s, but were brought down from over 500% at the end of 1973 to less than 10% by end-1981, largely because of fiscal balance and an overvalued currency. Following the freeing of the exchange rate in 1982 inflation accelerated somewhat, but was successfully moderated by tight monetary control and a lower public sector borrowing requirement. Monetary policy was formulated to cope with high domestic indebtedness in the light of restrictive IMF programmes. IMF involvement was sought following a sharp fall in international commercial lending in 1982 and a decline in Chile's terms of trade. The average annual rate of growth of external debt fell from 32% in 1978-81 to 6% in 1982-84. Chile has successfully negotiated several debt refinancing packages with commercial banks and with the Paris Club of creditor governments. In the second half of the 1980s, Chile's foreign debt declined as the Government introduced schemes whereby debt could be converted into equity in Chilean companies.

Constitution and Government After the deposition and death of President Salvador Allende on 11 September, 1973, Chile was ruled by a military president, Gen. Augusto Pinochet Ugarte, and a 4-man-junta with absolute powers. The pre-1973 constitution was replaced by a new one, which was approved in a plebiscite held on 11 September, 1980 and put into effect on 11 March, 1981. Under this Constitution, President Pinochet was to remain in office until the end of the decade. In 1988 a plebiscite was held to determine whether he should remain in office for a further 8 years. A large 'no' vote resulted in direct presidential and congressional elections being called in 1989, with a new president to take office in 1990. The Constitution provides for an eight-year non-renewable term for the President of the Republic, a bicameral Congress and an independent judiciary and central bank. Patricio Aylwin Azócar, a Christian Democrat and candidate of the Coalition of Parties for Democracy (CPD), won the presidential elections with 55.2% of the vote, while the CPD won 71 of the 120 seats in the Chamber of Deputies. The coalition won only 22 seats in the 47-seat Senate, its majority wiped out by nine seats held by Pinochet appointees, who could block constitutional reform. President Aylwin took office on 11 March, 1990. Gen Pinochet remained as Army Commander although other armed forces chiefs were replaced.

In 1974 Chile established thirteen regions to replace the old system of 25 provinces. The regions (now named) are subdivided into 51 new provinces.

Communications   Chile's difficult topography—archipelagos, forests, mountains, deserts—makes communications other than by air a formidable problem. It would be much more serious if 90% of the Chilean population did not live in the compact central rectangle, with good roads and adequate railways, between La Serena and Puerto Montt. Only a short distance along one river—the estuary of the Bío-Bío—is navigable.

Railways There are 10,100 km. of line, of which most are state owned. Most of the privately owned 2,130 km. of line are in the desert north, where the northern terminal is Iquique. From the longitudinal Iquique-Puerto Montt trunk line branches run westwards to the ports and seaside resorts, and eastwards to mines and mountain resorts. The main gauge on the Valparaíso and southern lines is 5 ft. 6 in. (1.676 metres). Passenger services on N of Santiago have virtually ceased except for the international routes to La Paz.

Four international railways link Chile with its neighbours. There is a local line between Arica and Tacna, linking Chile with Peru. There are two railways to Bolivia: between Arica and La Paz (448 km.), and from Antofagasta via Calama to La Paz. Between Chile and Argentina there is only one line now in operation, between Antofagasta and Salta, in the Argentine north-west. There is no international service on this line. The Transandine Railway linking Santiago with Buenos Aires is disused on the Chilean side. The Ferrocarriles del Estado publish an annual *Guía Turística*, available in various languages from the larger stations.

CHILE
RAILWAYS ++++++
MAIN ROADS ++++++

48

Roads About one-half of the 88,000 km. of roads can be used the year round, though a large proportion of them are unimproved and only about 9,700 km. are first class. The region round the capital and the Central Valley are the best served.

The Pan-American (Longitudinal) Highway runs from Arica through Santiago to Puerto Montt and recently extended by the Carretera Austral to beyond Cochrane; from Llay-Llay a branch goes to Los Andes and over La Cumbre (Uspallata) pass to Argentina. Another main international road in the Lake District goes from Osorno across the Puyehue pass to Argentina. The Longitudinal Highway, vital to the Chilean economy, is paved throughout, but many sections are in a bad state.

Chile has an extensive system of protected natural areas, 7 million hectares in all. The areas, managed by Conaf (the Corporación Nacional Forestal), are divided into 30 national parks, 36 forest reserves and 10 natural monuments. Of the 76 areas, 46 have public access, and details of the majority are given in the text.

THE DESERT NORTH (1)

		Population ('000)	
Regions	Provinces	1982	1987
I (Tarapacá)	Arica, Parinacota, Iquie	273	324
II (Antofagasta)	Tocopilla, El Loa, Antofagasta	341	371
III (Atacama)	Chañaral, Copiapó, Huasco	183	196

The 1,250 km. between Arica and Copiapó are desert without vegetation, with little or no rain. The inhospitable shore is a pink cliff face rising to a height of from 600 to 900 metres. At the bottom of the cliff are built the towns, some of considerable size. The far from pacific Pacific often makes it difficult to load and unload ships. The nitrate fields exploited in this area lie in the depression between Pisagua and Taltal. Copper, too, is mined in the Cordillera; there are two large mines, at Chuquicamata, near Calama, and at El Salvador, inland from Chañaral.

Life in the area is artificial. Water has to be piped for hundreds of km. to the cities and the nitrate fields from the Cordillera; all food and even all building materials have to be brought in from elsewhere. Only the small populations of the oases, such as Calama, are self-supporting.

There is some difference of climate between the coast and the interior. The coast is humid and cloudy; in the interior the skies are clear. The temperatures on the coast are fairly uniform; in the interior there is often a great difference in the temperature between day and night; the winter nights are often as cold as -10°C, with a cruel wind. Drivers must beware of high winds and blowing sand N of Copiapó.

Chile's most northerly city, 19 km. S of the Peruvian border, is **Arica**, with a population of 145,415, built at the foot of the Morro headland and fringed by sand dunes. The Andes can be clearly seen from the anchorage. The Morro, with a good view from the look-out park on top (an hour's walk along the road from town, ½ hr. by footpath from the south end of Colón, or 10 mins. by taxi), was the scene of a great victory by Chile over Peru on 7 June, 1880.

There is no rain, winter or summer. The average, daytime winter temperature is 19°C, and the average summer temperature 24°C. It is frequented for sea-bathing by Bolivians as well as the locals. The attractive cathedral church, San Marcos, built in iron by Eiffel and fitted with bright coloured windows, is in the Plaza de Armas. It was brought to Arica from Ilo (Peru) in the 19th century, before Peru lost Arica to Chile, as an emergency measure after a tidal wave swept over Arica and destroyed all its churches. Eiffel also designed the customs house. A 63-km. railway connects the town with Tacna, in Peru, and another (448 km.) with La Paz, the capital of Bolivia; the old steam locomotive (made in Germany in 1924) once used on this line can be seen outside Arica station. In the station is a memorial to John Roberts Jones, builder of the Arica portion of the railway.

It is this railway, over which today flow about half the imports and exports of Bolivia, that makes Arica important; it will become more important now that the international highway to Tambo Quemado, Bolivia, is completed for normal traffic. An oil pipeline runs from Bolivia. There are large fishmeal plants.

The Free Zone in the First Region now imposes customs duties on many articles, but vessels, aircraft and other transport still enter the Zone without payment of customs dues and other charges. Because of the free zone, overland travellers heading south are subject to baggage checks, the first at the bus terminal.

Local Festival Fiestas for the Virgen de las Peñas at the Santuario de Livircar in the Azapa Valley (see below) are held on the first Sunday in October and a lesser festival on 7-9 December (on 8 Dec. the festival moves to Arica). Take a bus from Av. Chacabuco y Vicuña Mackenna, then walk 12 km. from where it stops to the sanctuary. The December festival is not particularly outstanding but it takes place in a part of the valley not normally accessible.

Hotels *Hostería Arica* Av. Cdte. San Martín 599 (T 231201), best, A-L depending on season, new wing being built, accommodation is good value but all other services expensive (inc. breakfast, set lunch for US$6, free pisco sour on arrival) about 2 km. along shore, reached by frequent bus service along front (Nos. 7, 8), hotel has lava beach (not safe for swimming), but there are two public beaches nearby, to left and right; *El Paso*, bungalow style, pleasant gardens, swimming pool, Av. Gral. Velásquez, 1109, T 231965, B with breakfast, good set meals US$6 inc wine; *Central*, 21 de Mayo 425 (T 252575), new, central, nicely decorated, C; *Res. Las Vegas 120*, Baquedano 120, T 231355, F p.p., clean, hot water, safe, central, English spoken, rec; *Príncipe de Asturias*, Capitán Avalos 2041 (T 222289), C, new, motel-style; *King*, Colón 376 (T 232094), D, with bath, overpriced; *Motel Azapa*, attractive grounds but several km. from beaches and centre: G. Sánchez 660, Azapa, T 222612, B, but cheaper cabins available, fair restaurant 1/2 km. away; *Diego de Almagro*, Sotomayor 490, T 232927, D, clean, rec, will store luggage; *Savona*, Yungay 380, T 231000, D; *Lynch*, Lynch 589, T 231581, D, cheaper without bath or hot water, clean, rec; *Residencial Chungara*, Lynch 675 (T 231677), E with bath, clean, quiet; *Residencial Las Condes*, Vicuña Mackenna 628, T 251583, E, helpful, hot water, prices negotiable if staying a few days, rec; *Residencial Puerta del Sol*, 21 de Mayo 480, E, 12 rooms, shared bath, meals available, clean, quiet, excellent service; *Residencial Blanquita*, Maipú 472, T 232064, clean, hot water, F p.p.; *San Marcos*, Sotomayor 367 (T 232149/232970), clean, helpful, D; *Residencial Madrid*, Calle Baquedano 685 (T 231479), clean, good value but awful beds, F, communal toilets and showers (hot water), theft from washing line reported, acts as Youth Hostel; *Residencial Venecia*, Baquedano 739, T 252877, F, spotless, rec., hot water, small rooms; *Pensión Donoso*, Baquedano y Maipú, F, friendly, cheap, rec; *Residencial Patricia*, Maipú 269, F p.p., basic, safe, friendly, but tiny rooms and poor beds, no hot water; *Residencial Maipú*, Maipú 479, T 252157, F p.p., hot water, clean, safe, old, good; *Residencial Núñez*, Maipú 516, T 252457, F, basic, cell-like rooms, not rec. *Residencial Leiva*, Av. Colón 347, T 232008, F, incl. breakfast, shared bath, hot water a.m. only; *Residencial Universo*, Colón 662, F, T 232652, no hot water, in cheap rooms, unfriendly, unhelpful, not rec; *Residencial Velásquez*, Velásquez 669 (T 231989), good, clean, hot water, laundry available, F p.p.; on same street *Res. Alondra*, No. 704, T 252482, G p.p. and *Res. Chillán*, No. 719, T 251677, F p.p. Private house, at Av. D.Portales 885 (Barbino Guajardo C.), room for rent in F range (opp. bus station, friendly); also Velázquez 721, F, rec., safe, good breakfast. Sra. Leony Vidiella, Gonzálo Cerda 1030, close to bus station, F p.p. with breakfast, shared bath, cooking facilities, clean, safe, tepid water.

Camping On beach at S end of town, past fishmeal factories. Interesting shoreline; caves, waves, blow-holes and birdlife.

Restaurants *Acuario*, Máximo Lira, Terminal Pesquero, good food and atmosphere, in the same area, *El Gallo Cojo*; *El Rey de Mariscos*, corner Colón and Maipú, 2nd floor, cheaper, rec.; underneath are plenty of seafood lunch places in the market; *El Arriero*, 21 de Mayo y Colón, good; *890*, pizzeria, 21 de Mayo; also at Blanco Encalada 402; *El Padrino*, 18 de Septiembre 332, rec. pizzeria; *Bavaria*, Colón 611, good, cheap, with delicatessen and expresso coffee, repeatedly rec.; *Centro Español*, Bolognesi 311, good and cheap. *Naturista Vegetarian Restaurant*, Bolognesi y 21 de Mayo, good value; *El Sitio*, Centro Comercial Parque Colón, Chacabuco y Colón 2nd floor. On Baquedano, good *chifa* in 600 block, fresh seafood, in Chinese Association building (built 1923), and *Americano* in 700 block for cakes and expresso coffee. Good eating at fire station, *Casino de Bomberos*, on Colón; good ceviche and juices in market; good cheese empanadas at Arturo Gallo 449. *Il Molino Vecchio*, 18 Septiembre y Lynch, excellent delicatessen and bread. Bread from Maipú 510.

PAN-AMERICAN HIGHWAY
NOATH: TO PERU
ALSO TO AIRPORT
LAUCA NATIONAL PARK
BOLIVIA

RIO SAN JOSE

1. San Marcos Church, 2. Municipality,
3. Eiffel Customs House, 4. Casino,
5. Taxis to Tacna, 6. Railway station for
La Paz, 7. Railway station for Tacna,
8. Harbour, 9. Tourist Office and
Post Office, 10. Entel (Telephones),
11. Bolivian Consul, 12. Peruvian Consul,
13. Market.

J.A. RIOS
M. BLANCO ENCALADA
AV. SANTA MARIA
ANDAMOS
CEMENTERIO
GRAL VELASQUEZ
UNIVERSIDAD DE CHILE
INDEPENDENCIA
J. WAIDELLE
LARCO HERRERA
SALVO
AV. B VICUÑA MACKENNA
A. LATORRE
LASTARRIA
JUAN NOE
CHACABUCO
O'HIGGINS
BAQUEDANO
P. LYNCH
MAIPU
GRAL LAGOS
18 DE SEPTIEMBRE
PAN-AMERICAN HIGHWAY SOUTH TO AZAPA
ARTURO GALLO
GRAL VELASQUEZ
A. PRAT
COLON
M. BLANCO ENCALADA
SAN MARTIN
BOLOGNESI
21 DE MAYO
SOTOMAYOR
SAN MARCOS
YUNGAY
7 DE JUNIO
P. MON MAXIMO LIRA
EJERCITO
MORRO
FALDEOS EL MORRO
CAMINO AL MORRO
TO LA LISERA AND BEACHES SOUTH EL MORRO

ARICA
49

N.B. In this area, pensión means restaurant, not hostel.

Cafés *La Tranquera*, 21 de Mayo 431; *Café Scala*, Pasaje Bolognesi y 21 de Mayo, good juices, sandwiches and fruit salads; *Shop 18*, 18 de Septiembre, good, cheap sandwiches; *Café Suceso Inn*, 18 de Septiembre 250.

Night-Clubs Casino, Gral. Velásquez 955, open all year, but not to everyone's taste.

Cinemas Colón, 7 de Junio 190; Rex, 21 de Mayo 570.

Shopping Handicrafts: *Pueblo Artesanal Arica*, Rotonda Libertador Bernardo O'Higgins; *Cema-Chile*, Baquedano 311; *Hugali*, Pasaje 10, No. 932; *Casa Martínez*, 21 de Mayo 423; *Feria Sangra*, Sangra 350; *Feria Dominical*, Av. Costanera, Sun. a.m. only; *Poblado Artesanal*, Plaza Las Gredas, Hualles 2825 (local 2, especially good for musical instruments); Mercado Central, Sotomayor, 0800-1500 daily. Fruit, vegetable and old clothes market at Terminal Agropecuario at edge of town; take bus marked "Terminal Agro".

Laundry Lavandería Americana, Patricio Lynch 651, reasonable, 48 hr service; Lavandería Moderna, 18 de Septiembre between Colón and Lynch, 24 hr service. All expensive, charge per item.

Shoe Repairs and leather goods, Calzado El Eléctrico, Maipú y Baquedano.

Taxis Within city limit, US$0.25 p.p. on fixed distances.

Car Hire Viva Rent a Car, 21 de Mayo 821, T 251121; Hertz, *Hotel El Paso*, Gral Velázquez 1109, T 252543, cheaper.

Automóvil Club de Chile Chacabuco 460, T 232780.

Car Service Shell, Panamericana Norte 3456; Esso, Av. Diego Portales 2462; Shell Cánepa, Chacabuco, San Martín. Volkswagen/Michelin, very helpful for repairs and assistance.

Museums At San Miguel, 12 km. along road towards Azapa Valley, small but good for pathological analysis of mummies, including one dating from 5000 BC if you are feeling strong. Open Mon.-Fri., 1100-1800, Sat., Sun. and holidays 1300-1800, US$0.35; much of the information is in English. Colectivo with "Azapa" sign, from Calles Lynch y Maipú, passes museum (US$0.40 one way). Anthropological Museum, University of Tarapacá Saucache Campus, Av. 18 de Septiembre 2222 (just beyond stadium), Mon.-Fri. 0900-1300, 1500-1800; Museo Histórico Salitre, Calle Sotomayor 415, voluntary contributions expected; free Pacific War Museum on the Morro.

Exchange Many banks and money changers on 21 de Mayo and its junction with Colón. Banco de Santiago will exchange travellers' cheques for dollars cash, but at US$12 per transaction, daily limit US$500; no others will cash travellers' cheques. Fincard (Visa and Mastercard), 21 de Mayo 252, Mon.-Fri. 0900-1400, 1600-2100, Sat. 1000-1400, only pesos given, at varying rates. Also at tourist office on main square. When banks closed money can be changed at *Hotel International*, *Hotel King*, or at the exchange houses (Tacora, 21 de Mayo 171, good rates for cash; Yanulaque, Colón 380 or 21 de Mayo 175), which stay open until 2000 but closed all day Sun.

Consulates **Honorary British Consul**, Sra Gladys Hulse (the only one in Chile north of Valparaíso) Baquedano 653, T (080) 31960, Casilla 653, and Instituto Británico reading room, opposite *Restaurant Aduana*, also on Baquedano, between 21 de Mayo and Sotomayor. **Argentina**, M.Rodríguez 144, Depto. 41 (in a cul-de-sac, entrance at approx. A. Prat 550), T 231322, Mon-Fri. 0900-1300, Consul Sr Daniel Azzi Balbi, very helpful, onward ticket required, preferably out of Argentina, to obtain visa (US$15); **Belgium**, Sotomayor 504; Bolivia, Bolognesi 344; **Costa Rica**, Sotomayor 802; **Denmark**, 21 de Mayo 399; **Peru**, Yungay and Colón; **Italy**, Chacabuco with San Martín; **France**, Santa María 2860; **Spain**, Santa María 2660; Instituto Cultural Chileno Norteamericano, San Marcos 581.

Post Office Arturo Prat 375. To send parcels abroad, contents must be shown to Aduano (under main post office) between 1500 and 1700. Your parcel will be wrapped, cheaply, but take your own carton.

Telephones 21 de Mayo and Baquedano, open 0900-2200.

Tourist Office National office: Calle Arturo Prat 375, 2nd floor; post-office complex, open Mon.-Fri. 0830-1300, 1430-1830. T 232101. Very helpful, English spoken, sells good map, US$3, but not all information is accurate. Also kiosk in main square (Nuestra Sra. del Carmen) part way up to Cerro Moro. Closed weekends.

Travel Agencies Turismo Payachatas, Prat 372, T 251514, rec.; Jurasi, Bolognesi 360 A., T 232635, will hold mail, helpful, good city tour for US$8.75, ½ day; Kijo Tour, Bolognesi 359, T 232245; Huasquitur, Sotomayor 470, helpful, English spoken, will cater for individual itineraries; and many others.

Bathing Olympic pool beyond Parque Brasil, 2 km. N of centre, Tues.-Sat. 0900-1800, US$0.50; take No. 5 bus, the pool looks like a football stadium. Take No. 2 bus to beaches south of town, or walk along seaside promenade. For swimming, better La Lisera than El Laucho (very rocky); Playa Chinchorro receives mostly good reports; Playa Brava (surf beach) to south with fine, white sands; Playa Arenillas Negras, 3 km. to south; Playa Corazones, 15 km. to south (no buses, take taxi or hitch), rec. not for swimming but picnics and fishing.

Airport Chaculluta, to town costs US$13 for taxi, US$3 sharing. Lan-Chile office, 7 de Junio 14.8. Flights to La Paz (Mon. and Fri., also with LAB), Iquique, and Santiago. Ladeco, 18 de Septiembre 370, T 232596, fly to Santiago direct once a week, or via Iquique and Antofagasta or El Salvador.

Rail To La Paz by Arica-La Paz Railway (**see page 217**) either direct by *ferrobus*, Wed. and Sat. (maybe 2nd and 4th Tues. and Fri. as well in summer) 0930, arrive 2000, US$48 with meals, good trip and views. One Chilean (Payachatas, US$48) and one Bolivian (Coche Motor, US$35) company operate *ferrobuses*; ask in advance what food and drink is included in the price as refreshments are offered all day and a bill is presented at the end. A connection can also be made at Charaña, reached by colectivo, bus (Martínez, P. Montt 620, Tues., Fri., 1000, 9 hrs., US$8.50, or Charaña, P. Montt 662) or occasional train from Arica, then ferrobus to La Paz (leaves next day, spend night in Charaña, *Alojaniento Aranda*, G), or bus, for which the wait is shorter; very cold change over, waiting on the track for tickets. Change money in the market or on the train.

The line from Arica skirts the coast for 10 km. and passes into the Lluta Valley, whose vegetation is in striking contrast with the barrenness of the surrounding hills. From Kilometre 70 there is a sharp rise of 2,241 metres, in 42 km. The line is racked for 48 km., but the rack is no longer used. At Puquios station, Kilometre 112, the plateau is reached. The altitude here is 4,168 metres. In the distance can be seen the snowcapped heights of Tacora, Putre, Sajama, and their fellows. The greatest altitude is reached at General Lagos (4,247 metres). The frontier station of Visviri is at Kilometre 205, with a custom house. Beyond, the train enters Bolivia and the station of Charaña. Tourist train (in summer at least) to the pampa and back, Sat. and Sun. 0930, return 1800.

To Tacna, Peru, by rail costs US$1.85, daily 1300, 1700 and 1900, 1½ hrs. (exit stamp obtainable at station, but allow ½ hour for this—it is preferable to relying on the Town Hall); it is best to avoid Sats. because of crowds and delays at the border. Check times in advance, schedules change.

Road Services Terminal at corner of Av. Portales and Santa María, T 41390, bus or colectivo No. 8 (US$0.10, or US$0.25), 10 mins. from Maipú y Baquedano (US$0.50 to use terminal; public showers; extensive baggage search prior to boarding). The Longitudinal (Pan-American) Highway S is mostly good, fast, 2-lane, concrete with hard shoulders and well signposted and served. All buses are modern, clean and air-conditioned, but ask carefully what meals are included. To Antofagasta, Flecha Norte, US$10, 10-11 hrs., via Tocopilla, not a comfortable trip; other lines, some more expensive. Some services to destinations between Antofagasta and the capital involve a change in Antofagasta. To Calama and Chuquicamata, 6 a day all between 0800-1000, 10 hrs., US$10, plus Tramaca at 2130 most days, 9¾ hrs., rec. To Iquique, daily, US$4.50, 4½ hrs. To Viña del Mar, US$30. To Santiago, 28 hrs., a number of companies, e.g. Carmelita, US$30, Flecha Dorada, Ramos Cholele and Fénix, US$37, Flota Barrios, US$37.50 pullman, US$63 *salón cama*, Fichtur, US$50 *salón cama*; most serve meals and the more expensive, the more luxurious, student discounts available. To La Serena, daily at 1400, 18 hrs. and others.

To Arequipa, Peru, with Ormeño, 3 a day, US$12.50, supposedly 6 hrs.

To La Paz, Bolivia, via Tambo Quemado: Litoral bus, Chacabuco 454, journey to La Paz via Chungará takes at the very least 20 hrs. (involving very cold change at border—take blanket/sleeping bag, food, water and sense of humour), leaves on Tues. and Fri. (or Mon. and Thurs., days vary), in either case at about 2400, US$23. US$ cash only can be exchanged with the Bolivian Immigration Officer at Tambo Quemado.

Colectivo taxis run to and from Tacna for about US$3 p.p. (telephone Arica 31376 or Tacna 2288) one way and take about an hour for the trip (drivers take care of all the paperwork—it's a fairly uncomplicated border crossing). Colectivos leave from Chacabuco and Vicuña Mackenna. Bus costs US$1.75 and leaves from the bus station, as does Taxibus, 2 hourly,

US$2. Money-changing at frontier, but reported better rates in Tacna.

Drivers are required at the Chile-Peru frontier to file a form, *Relaciones de Pasajeros* (7 copies, no carbons), giving details of passengers, obtained from a stationery store in Tacna, or at the border in a booth near Customs. You must also present the original registration document for your car from its country of registration. The first checkpoints outside Arica on the road to Santiago also require the *Relaciones de Pasajeros* from drivers. If you can't buy the form details on a piece of paper will suffice or you can get them at service stations. The form is *not* required when travelling south of Antofagasta.

N.B. Remember that between October and March, Chilean time is 1 hr. later than Bolivian, 2 hrs. later than Peruvian time October to December (1 hr. vis-à-vis Peru the rest of the year).

Several checkpoints on the Longitudinal south from Arica. It is illegal to take fruit S from Arica; there is a checkpoint for fruit at Cuya (Km. 105); 20 km. further on are petroglyphs to the right (signposted), a checkpoint for buses and lorries at Huara (Km. 234, hotel), and customs and fruit control at Quillagua on Río Loa (Km. 430, where there is a museum of local Indian artefacts—key held by lady in telephone exchange). A sense of humour is required during fruit searches, especially on night buses. **N.B.** If driving S, en route to Quillagua there are some steep ascents and descents best tackled in daylight (at night, sea mist, *camanchaca*, can reduce visibility).

Service stations between the Peruvian border and Santiago can be found at: Arica, Cuya, Huara, Iquique, Pozo Almonte (also hotel), Oficina Vitoria, Quillagua, Tocopilla, Oficina María Elena, Chuquicamata, Calama, Carmen Alto, Antofagasta, La Negra, Agua Verde, Taltal, Chañaral, Caldera, Copiapó, Vallenar, La Serena, Termas de Soco, Los Vilos, and then every 30 km. to capital.

Before proceeding further, we offer the following advice on travelling off the beaten track in this region, kindly supplied by vulcanologist Dr. Lyndsey O'Callaghan. In all of the mountain areas of the North of Chile, it is important to note that weather and road conditions are very variable. The *carabineros* and military are very active trying to control the borders with Bolivia and Argentina, so they know about the conditions and are quite willing to tell, but only if asked.

In many villages it is possible to rent a small unfurnished house, if you are planning to stay for a while. Ask for the schoolmaster (or mayor in larger villages). It may also be possible to stay in the small clinics (e.g. at Socaire or Chiu-Chiu).

If you plan to stay in the mountains for any length of time, it is advisable to take small gifts for the locals: tea, sugar, coffee, salad oil, flour make very acceptable gifts. It is often possible to get people to bake bread etc. for you every day, but you need to supply flour, yeast and salt. If you are planning to do much cooking, then a good pressure cooker is indispensible (remember water boils at only 90 degrees at these altitudes). You may also get problems with kerosene stoves, petrol ones, though rather dangerous, are much more reliable.

Moreover, anyone travelling in this region should consult the *Turistel Norte* guide (see **Tourist Information** in Information for Visitors).

Excursions To the fruitful Azapa valley by colectivo (US$1), from Patricio Lynch and Maipú, or taxi, US$13; book through tourist agency. To the Lluta valley, 10 km. to north, figures built with stones on sandy hills, and to the wild desert and mountain scenery at the foot of the Andes.

Lauca National Park A visit to the Parque Nacional Lauca, some 120 km. E of Arica, is highly recommended. It is in the Altiplano (so beware of *soroche*, if you are not coming from Bolivia); the scenery shows snowy volcanoes reaching to over 6,500 metres, blue cold lakes swarming with waterfowl, and much mammalian life including vicuñas, pumas and vizcachas. The Park is maintained by the Corporación Nacional Forestal (Conaf), Sotomayor 216, 3rd and 4th floors, Arica (T 231559, closed weekends), and it is advisable to obtain their advice before making the visit; they may also give you a lift. At *Putre* (a scenic village at the Park entrance) is a Conaf hut, not suitable for sleeping, and 2 hotels: *Hostería Las Vicuñas*, 3 classes of room, bungalow-type, B, excellent restaurant; *Hostería San Martín*, E, Baquedano y O'Higgins. At both hotels, groups of 15 or more get one person accommodated free; ask for Sr. Krause, the owner, for flights Arica-Putre. Putre is a good base for acclimatisation for the Park. There are 2 refuges in the Park which allow sleeping, but check in advance if they are open: at **Parinacota** (need sleeping bags, plenty of space, only 4 beds though, US$1, fully equipped kitchen—there is supposed to be oxygen for those suffering from *soroche*, but it is often not available, beware) 4,392 metres up, at the foot of the Payachatas volcano (interesting 17th-cent. church—rebuilt 1789—with wall paintings and churchyard statuary; local resident Lorenza de Calle will knit alpaca sweaters for US$18-20; weavings of wildlife scenes also available), and at Lake Chungará (8 beds and floor space, sheets and blankets provided (but take sleeping bag for warmth) 2 bathrooms with cold water, cooking facilities) one of the highest lakes, a must (4,600 metres above sea-level, 196 km. from Arica). Limited possibilities of purchasing food at Chucuyo, a village just beyond the police control 30 km. from Putre, better to take your own (enough for yourself and the Park guards). Trips can be arranged with Turismo Payachatas, Huasquitur, or Jurasi (addresses above, US$17.50 p.p. with breakfast, lunch and oxygen, generally recommended although some find the minibuses cramped and dusty. For 5 or more, the most economical proposition is to hire a vehicle; petrol is available in Putre, ask at the shop, take at least one spare fuel can.

Public transport to Lauca: The Arica-Bolivia road passes through the Park. Lorries leaving port of Arica early in the morning will often give lifts to the Park on their way to La Paz. Best place to wait is at the Pocón Chile control point on the road through the Valle de Lluta, about an hour out of Arica on the Putre road. From Parinocota you can hitch to Visviri on Tues. with lorries going to meet the train; catch the train to La Paz at Charaña. Hitching is good every second Sunday when trucks go to the international market at Visviri. Flota Paco buses leave from Germán Riesco 2071, Arica, for Putre on Tues., Thurs., Sat. at 0630 (returning Tues., Thurs., Sun. at 1200), US$3, then take daily "Vialidad" truck at 0700 into the Park, or hitch. On Tues. at 1000 and Fri. at 2200 Martínez buses leave Arica (P. Montt 620) for Visviri on the Bolivian border (to connect with the La Paz train, see above); they pass Parinacota after 6-7 hrs., US$5 on Tues., US$8 on Fri.; buses return Wed. and Sat. at 1800, passing Parinacota about 2400. Lake Chungará is on the road route to La Paz, it is a 1 hr. walk to the border (Tambo Quemado), which opens at 0800; trucks pass infrequently, or you may be lucky and get on the Litoral bus which will charge full Arica-La Paz fare. The road into Bolivia is terrible, especially in the wet.

Dr. Klaus Busch, of Osnabrück, describes driving in the Park (he used a Toyota Landcruiser): "The road can be managed with a city car. Leave Arica via Panamericano North/Aeropuerto. After 9 km. turn off right; at 39 km. you will reach Pocón Chile, the control point for cars, and at 62 km. Molinos. Zapahuira, at 3,270 metres, marks the end of the paved road, with a marvellous view over the mountains. Later, at 152 km., at the turn off to Putre, you can see the Nevado de Putre (5,825m.) The track to Chucuyo and back to Zapahuira is not even suitable for 4-wheel cars, or at least must be taken very slowly."

South of Lauca is the beautiful **Reserva Nacional Las Vicuñas**, at 4,300 to 5,600 metres, which is suitable for "adventure tourism", to use Conaf's phrase. Be prepared for cold, skin burns from sun and wind, etc; there is no public transport. Administration is at Guallatiri, reached by turning off the Arica-La Paz road onto the A147 to Las Cuevas and Cerro Capitán. In the summer wet season, the road is only passable with four-wheel drive; take spare fuel. Open March-November. The same road leads into the **Monumento Natural Salar de Surire** (4,200 metres), which is open for the same months and for which the same conditions apply. Administration is in Surire, 7 hours from Arica.

Detours off the Pan-American Highway: to Tignamar (take a turning E about 20 km. S of Arica, 100 km. to the village) and Codpa (road E about 70 km. S of Arica), both interesting villages. The latter is an agricultural community in a deep gorge with interesting scenery. Codpa is 40 km. from the Pan-American Highway on a good dirt road.

At Zapiga (184 km. S of Arica on the Pan-American Highway) there is a cross-roads. One branch leads west for 41 km. to the run down nitrate exporting port of Pisagua. There is little left of this place, though some of the ruins of the nitrate port are still standing. There are a few quite good fish restaurants in the town and it makes a pleasant stop for a meal.
     However, the branch which leads east is much more interesting, though the road is not in very good condition, with deep sand and dust causing problems. After 67 km. there is the

picturesque village of Camiña where there is a basic hostal. 45 km. further on is the Tranque de Caritaya, a dam which supplies water for the coastal towns set in splendid scenery with lots of wildlife and interesting botany (especially *llareta*). Travelling further east along mountain roads (not in very good condition) leads through magnificent volcanic scenery to *Isluga* (120 km. from Caritaya). This remote area, the **Parque Nacional Volcán Isluga**, contains some of the best scenery in northern Chile. Conaf wardens are at Enquelga in the Park. Isluga has a traditional, Andean walled church and bell tower. It is, in theory, possible to drive north from Isluga through the Salar de Surire (see above) via Guallatiri to the Parque Nacional del Lauca, and from there to Bolivia, or via Putre and Poconchile to Arica or Peru.

The best way to return to the Pan-American Highway, if going south, is via the road to the village of Cariquima (35 km. south of Isluga), and take the road via the thermal springs at Chuzmisa (100 km. from Cariquima). It is possible to stay in a basic hotel at Chuzmisa. The water here is bottled and sold throughout northern Chile. Chuzmisa lies about 3 km. down a side road, but it is signposted. From Chuzmisa a good dirt (last part paved) road leads to Huara on the Pan-American Highway (80 km.). The round trip from Zapiga to Huara is about 540 km., and fuel is not available between Cuya (80 km. N of Zapiga) and Huara.

Humberstone, at the junction of the Pan-American Highway and the road to Iquique, is a large nitrate ghost town; ancient Indian drawings are to be seen and there is an interesting British cemetery 10 km. to the north. 2 km. beyond the junction to Humberstone is the Oficina Santa Laura, an impressive early nitrate plant, through which you can walk.

Iquique, the capital of the First (Tarapacá) Region and one of the main northern ports, is 304 km. by road south of Arica. The name of the town is derived from the Aymará word *ique-ique*, meaning place of "rest and tranquillity". It was founded in the 16th century on a rocky peninsula sheltered by the headlands of Punta Gruesa and Cavancha. The city was partly destroyed by earthquake in 1877. It has some old wooden houses, gaily painted, in a Victorian style (especially along Baquedano), an outstanding square, Plaza Prat, with a clock tower and bell, and wide avenues bordered by trees. One, Av. Balmaceda, runs along the coast. The Museo Regional, Baquedano 951, open Mon.-Fri. 0800-1300, 1600-2100 and Sat., 1000-1300, small but well displayed, includes a section on minerals and a shop selling goods made by Chilean Aymarás (entry US$0.25, Thurs. free). At the seaward end of Calle Esmeralda is a Naval Museum concentrating on the 1879 sea battle—see below (entry US$0.10, open Mon.-Sat. 0930-1230, 1430-1800, Sun. and holidays 1000-1300). The Palacio Astoreca on Calle O'Higgins 350 esq. Lynch, built in 1903, formerly the Intendencia and now a cultural centre, has fine pinewood architecture and exhibitions of shells and on the history of the nitrate industry (open Tues.-Fri. 1000-1300, 1600-2000, Sat. and Sun. 1000-1300 US$0.35). Population: 140,300. There are checkpoints on the road N to Arica, on the road S at Quillagua, and on the road inland (to Mamiña).

The harbour is well protected and ships tie up to load at modern docks. Sealions and pelicans can be seen from the harbour. To get closer to the sealions, ask at the shipyard if they'll let you cross the yard; you may get a guide, a helmet and even a boat. It was at Iquique that the *Esmeralda* and another wooden ship, under Captain Arturo Prat, resisted the attack of the Peruvian ironclad ship *Huáscar* on May 21, 1879, during the War of the Pacific (**see page 555**). The main exports are fishmeal, fish oil, canned fish and salt.

Iquique has a Free Zone (Zofri), at the north of town: it is worth a visit (much better value than Punta Arenas), goods from Hong Kong and Taiwan, reasonably priced cameras, electronics and cheap Ektachrome films are sold.

Local holiday During the ten days before 16 July there is a religious festival, "La fiesta de Tirana", at a village 70 km. E of Iquique (near Pica, see next page). Over 100 groups dance night and day, starting on 12 July, before making their pilgrimage to the church of the Virgen del Carmen. All the dances take place in the main plaza in front of the church; no alcohol is served. Accommodation is impossible to find, other than in organized camp sites (take tent) which have basic toilets and showers.

Hotels *Hostería Cavancha*, Los Rides 250, T 21158, L, south of city, on water's edge; *Primeras Piedras*, street of same name, T 21358, 3 km. from city, B, good food, friendly;

Playa Brava, Playa Brava 3115, T 22705, B with breakfast, good, new wing built; *Tamarugal*, Tarapacá 369, T 24365, central, clean and modern, C, good restaurant. *Camino del Mar*, Orella 340 (T 20465), restored building, clean, simple, D-C; *Arturo Prat*, Av. Aníbal Pinto 695, T 21414, facing Plaza Prat, B; *Barros Arana*, Barros Arana 1330 (T 24420), clean, modern, good value, D; *Inti-Llanka*, Obispo Labbe 825 (T 26383), good, D; *Durana*, San Martín 294 (T 28085), good, D; *Phoenix*, Aníbal Pinto 451 (T 21315) room with bathroom, breakfast, old but nice, D; *España*, Tarapacá 465, near Plaza Condwell, F, shared bath, friendly, warm water, dirty. *Res. Li Ming*, B. Arana 705, near Thompson (T 21912), and *Res. Nan-King*, Thompson 752 (T 23311), both E; *Res. Danny*, Vivar 1266, T 21676, E, not central but may have room when others are full. *Residencial Catedral*, Obispo Labbe 253, T 23395, D, clean, friendly, but breakfast expensive; *Residencial Marclaud*, Juan Martínez 753, F, rec., quiet, clean, motor-cycle parking (good cheap restaurant at the corner); *Residencial Norte del Sol*, Juan Martínez, F, clean, airy rooms, courtyard, shared showers and toilets, laundry facilities, rec; *Condell*, Thompson 684 esq. Vivar, nice, clean, quiet, E; *Casa de familia*, Bulnes 1110, F with breakfast, clean, friendly.

Restaurants *Las Urracas*, Avenida Balmaceda 551, on seafront regarded as best place for fish; *Don Lolo*, Thompson 930, good, cheap, tasty food. *Club de la Unión*, reasonable lunch. Also, the *Sociedad Protectora de los Empleados de Tarapacá* (Plaza Prat) is open to tourists and has reasonable prices. *Club Español*, on main square, excellent meals well served in cool, Moorish decorated 100-year-old rooms; attractive. *Rapa Nui*, Amunátegui 715, for good, cheap, local food. Several good, inexpensive seafood restaurants can be found on the second floor of the central market, Barros Arana with Latorre; also café's opp the bus station, on the wharf, sell good, cheap fish lunches. *Bahía*, on seafront, cheap, good fish; *Portofino*, Thompson 650, 3 courses for US$2. Yacht Club at the harbour serves inexpensive lunch. *El Pescado Frito*, Bulnes y Juan Martínez, very nice local place with good and cheap seafood dishes. *Chifa Fu-Wa*, Barros Arana 740, rec, Chinese.

Cafés *Salón de Té Chantilly*, Tarapacá 520 and Barros Arana 716; *Café Diana*, Vivar 836; *El Mastique*, Thompson 728; *La Tentazione*, Sargento Aldea 749; *Ciocolatta*, Aníbal Pinto 487.

Car hire Hertz, Juan Martínez 2040, T 26316.

Theatre Teatro del Norte at Sotomayor 728.

Cables Post and Telegraph Office, Calle Bolívar y P.Lynch; telex available.

Exchange National banks; black market in the Free Zone (Zofri). Fincard (Visa and Mastercharge), Serrano 424, open Mon.-Fri. 0900-1400, 1600-2100, Sat. 1000-1400.

Tourist Information Aníbal Pinto 436. T 21499; another office on Plaza Prat, corner Thompson, open when other office is closed. Offices provide details on car hire. **Automóvil Club de Chile**, Serrano 154, T 22422.

Travel Agencies Iquitour, Tarapacá 465B, Casilla 669, T 22009, tours to Pintados, La Tirana, Humberstone, Pica, etc., 0900-1900, lunch included, US$20, a lot of time spent eating and bathing. Flonatur, Sgto. Aldea 786B.

Fishing Broadbill swordfish, striped marlin, yellowfin tuna, oceanic bonito, March till end of August. In the harbour there are hundreds of sea lions (for a closer look you can hire a boat for a few dollars).

Bathing Balneario Cavancha (good) and Huaiquique, reasonable, November-March. Restaurants at Cavancha. Piscina Godoy, fresh water swimming pool on Av. Costanera at Aníbal Pinto and Riquelme, open p.m., US$1.

Buses To Arica, 6 daily, US$4.50, 4½ hrs., comfortable in spite of various checkpoints. To Antofagasta, daily 2000, US$10, a dusty, hot 8-hr. drive through the desert, relieved by the occasional oasis. To Calama and Chuquicamata, daily at 2100, 2130 and 2200, 8 hrs. to Calama (US$7). To La Serena, Carmelita bus at 2030, 10-11 hrs., US$20. To Santiago, 28 hrs. Carmelita are the cheapest, about US$25 incl. meals; others (Ranos Cholele, Flota Barrios) charge US$30-35 (US$61 for Barrios *salón cema*). All buses leave from terminal at N end of Obispo Labbe, except Tramaca, which has own terminal on B. O'Higgins; bus offices are at corner of Sargento Aldea and B.Arana.

Airport Diego Aracena international airport, 35 km. S at Chucumata. Taxi from outside *Hotel Prat*, Plaza Prat, US$3, T 26184. Free airport bus to city centre. Lan-Chile, Av. Aníbal Pinto, next to *Hotel Prat*, T 22526; Ladeco, Aníbal Pinto 444, T 24794 (Santiago-Iquique daily; to Calama, 1715, US$32, en route to Antofagasta and Santiago). To Antofagasta, Arica and Santiago daily by Lan-Chile.

Excursions Hire a car and drive south along the Pacific coast to see sealions, *guano*, fishing settlements and old salt works, including the ghost town of Guanillos, complete with castle. Good roads run to the nitrate fields, which are 900 metres above sea level. A road runs NE to the hot mineral springs in the mountains at Termas de **Mamiña** (2,700 metres), where there is an interesting church (1632) and good accommodation for tourists (*Hotel Termas de Salitre*, D, full board, thermal pool in each room, electricity till midnight, swimming pool open 0930-1300; *Residencial Ipla*, D, cheapest, 4 others). The rainy season in Mamiña is mainly in January and is called *Invierno Boliviano* (Bolivian winter). Near Mamiña, 5 km. SW, is an Inca village with lots of pottery lying around.

The Iquique-Mamiña bus trip (130 km.) takes 2½ hrs.; Iquique-Mamiña, Mon.-Fri. 1600, from Mamiña same days, 0900, US$2. (The police control point just outside Iquique requires registration by foreigners, but the bus waits.) The road is well paved for the first 50 km., but from Pozo Almonte onwards is unpaved and very bad. There is a large ravine, Quebrada Dubliza, where no vehicle can pass another, but as it is located slightly on a bend it is easy to avoid trouble.

The Pan-American Highway continues South: 13 km. after the turn-off to Iquique is a detour to La Tirana (10 km.—see above) and the fertile oasis of **Pica** (2,750 metres), famous for its citrus groves and two natural springs. Hotels: *O'Higgins*, T 741322, E; *San Andrés*, E, T 741319, D, both on Baquedano; 2 motels. Campsite US$0.85 p.p. Carmelita/Julita bus leaves Iquique from near market, Mon.-Fri. 1700, from Pica at 0700, 2 hrs., US$1.75; Flonatur leaves 0900, returns 1800, US$3 one way (also near market, check if running at weekends). 4 km. before Pica is the oasis of Matilla, whence a road in poor condition returns to the Pan-American Highway. There are well-preserved petroglyphs 2-4 km. W of Pintados, which is 43 km. S of Pozo Almonte.

La Tirana and Pintados fall within two of the three areas which make up the **Reserva Nacional Pampa del Tamarugal**, the third part is some 60 km north of Pozo Almonte, straddling the Pan-American Highway.

Tocopilla

Tocopilla, 195 km. S of Iquique, exports nitrate and iodine from two famous nitrate fields—María Elena (68 km.), and Pedro de Valdivia (85 km.). Population: 22,600. There are two sports stadiums and two good beaches: Punta Blanca and Caleta. In the centre is the copper concentrate plant of Cía. Minera de Tocopilla. There is a sporting 18-hole golf course and fine deep sea fishing if you can find a boat and a guide. There are two paved roads out: a 185-km. coast road S to Antofagasta via Mejillones (see below) and the other E up the narrow valley 72 km. to the Pan-American Highway (with a short spur to María Elena and Pedro de Valdivia nitrate mines) and on to Chuquicamata. From Tocopilla to Chuquicamata is poor, particularly the eastern half which is eroded by the heavy lorries which use it (requires careful driving). A new coastal road runs N to Iquique.

Hotel *Chungará*, 21 de Mayo 1829, D, comfortable, clean, rec., no restaurant; *Hostal Bolívar*, Bolívar 1332, T 811903, E, clean, friendly.

Cables All America Cables & Radio, Inc., Calle Serrano 1180.

Automóvil Club de Chile 21 de Mayo 1377, T 811059.

Bus To Santiago, Tues. and Sat. To Antofagasta daily, 0730 and 1730, US$6.

The coast road Tocopilla-Antofagasta is paved all the way, but deteriorates after 78 km., there is no fuel. The route runs at the foot of 500-metre cliffs, behind which are mountains which are extensively mined for copper, often by *piquineros* (small groups of self-employed miners). There are larger mines, with the biggest concentration inland of Michilla (80 km. S). The treatment plants use the "tin can" process, hence the heaps of rusting cars and metal junk. Despite the unprepossessing appearance, this is a good place to stop for a meal.

A zig-zag road (very steep) winds up the cliffs to the mine at Mantos de la Luna about 35 km. S of Tocopilla. At the top there are rather dead-looking groves of giant cactus living off the sea mist which collects on the cliffs. Wildlife includes foxes (*zorros*).

The coast is rocky though there are good beaches at Poza Verde (70 km. S of Tocopilla) and Hornitos (104 km., town is dead except at week-ends). There is also the Tocopilla Yacht Club (45 km.) and Punta Blanca (25 km.), which have bars and restaurants.

The main interest is the ruins of Cobija, the coastal end of the silver trail from Potosí. This town was destroyed by an earthquake in 1877, and captured by the Chileans in the War of the Pacific two years later. Mud brick walls, the rubbish tip (right above the sea) and the wreckage of the port are all that is left of the town. There is an amazing ransacked cemetery about 1 km. from the ruins on the approach road. 15 km. further down the coast are the atmospheric ruins of Gatico.

Mejillones, 64 km. N of Antofagasta (130 km. S of Tocopilla), has a good natural harbour protected from westerly gales by high hills. Since the export of tin and other metals from Bolivia ceased, Mejillones lives solely by fishing. The town comes alive after 1700 when the fishermen prepare to set sail. There is a Museo del Mar in the old customs building (1866) on Aníbal Pinto. The sea is very cold because of the Humboldt current. Population: 3,820.

Hotels *Hostería Luz de Luna*, A. Goñigg 99, T 582, D, with restaurant; *Residencial Elisabeth*, Alte. Latorre 440, T 568, F, friendly, restaurant. *Juanito Restaurant*, Las Heras 24.

Antofagasta is 1,373 km. N of Santiago and 700 km. S of Arica. It is the capital of the Second (Antofagasta) Region, and its population of 190,000 makes it the largest city in northern Chile. It exports the nitrates of the area and the copper of Chuquicamata. A huge anchor stands high in the mountains, and was used as a navigational aid by ships. The main historical interest lies in some ruins at the edge of town, and a Bolivian silver refinery dating from 1868 (Huanchaca, now a military zone—you may visit, but not take photos), but it is lively and attractive, with a university of high standing, quite good parks and public gardens, an interesting waterfront, a clock tower on the main plaza donated by the British community, and very expensive shops. There is a small museum near the university, which has an interesting handicraft shop; museum opens Tues.-Fri., 0900-1200; 1500-1900; Sat. 0900-1200; Sun. 1100-1300. There is also an archaeological museum on Pasaje López (Prat 482 y Latorre), Mon.-Fri. 1530-1900, Sun. 1030-1300; Museo Regional (formerly Universidad del Norte museum in Iquique) on Balmaceda y Bolívar is also interesting about the history of the area from the arrival of the Spanish (Tues.-Sat. 1000-1300, 1600-1900, Sun. 1000-1300, US$0.50). The modern sports stadium is close to the most popular beach (S end of city) where there is also a restaurant-pool-discotheque complex. The Balneario Municipal (take bus No. 10 S of the city) is good. The climate is delightful (apart from the lack of rain); the temperature varies from 16°C in June/July to 24°C January/February, never falling below 10°C at night. The tap water is not potable.

Local Holiday 29 June, San Pedro, patron saint of the fishermen: the saint's image is taken out by launch to the breakwater to bless the first catch of the day.

Festivals On the last weekend of October, the foreign communities put on a joint festival on the seafront, with national foods, dancing and music.

Hotels *Antofagasta*, Balmaceda 2575, T 224710, run-down, garage, swimming pool, lovely view of port and city, B with breakfast (discount for Automóvil Club members, but still not very good value), beach; *Diego de Almagro*, Condell 2624, T 222840, C, good for the money but a bit tatty; *San Martín*, Calle San Martín 2781, T 221749, ½ block from main plaza, D, poor value; *San Antonio*, Condell 2235, T 225086, D, clean, good but noisy from bus station; *Residencial La Riojanita*, Baquedano 464, F, good, use of kitchen permitted, washing facilities; *Rawaye*, Sucre 762, T 225399, shared bathroom, clean, friendly, F, good; *Residencial Paola*, Prat 766, T 222208, F, excellent value, friendly; *Residencial Familiar*, Baquedano 539, F, dark rooms; *Res. Cobre*, Prat 749, T 225162, F, shared bath (E with bath), hot water, clean, 2 blocks from bus station (acts as youth hostel, no cooking facilities); *Plaza*, Baquedano 461, T 222058, C, modern, noisy, clean, comfortable; *Residencial Vargas*, Condell 2342, F without bath or windows, but clean and friendly. *Res. O'Higgins*, Sucre 773, F, big, old, dirty, no hot water. *Tatio*, Av. Grecia 1000, T 225707, D, out of old town on the beach, has buses converted into caravans, friendly, beautiful views, acts as youth hostel, no cooking facilities.

Camping Las Garumas, 16 km. on route to Coloso, US$10 for tent, US$15 for cabins; hot water, showers and beach (reservations Av. Angamos 601, casilla 606). 2 other sites on same road, *7 cabañas*, T 221988 and Rucamóvil, T 226734. All open year-round. Official campsite at S end of beach beyond university.

Restaurants *Apoquindo*, Prat 616, reasonable, good, as is *Club Náutico*, Pinto 3051; *Centro Español*, Prat 430; *Grill Bar Americano*, Malta 621; *Tío Jacinto*, Calle Uribe, by Tramaca terminal, friendly, good seafood; *El Arriero*, good grills, Spanish-style, Condell 2632; *Bavaria*, J. S. Ossa 2428, excellent meat and German specialities; *Chifa Wai Lin*, Sucre 721, average Chinese food. The al fresco luncheons at the *Auto Club* are fashionable both in summer and winter. *Club de la Unión*, Calle Prat 470 (quite good). *Societá Italiana*, next to *Residencial Paola* on Prat, rec. Difficult to find any coffee, etc., before 0900. *Café Express* and *Café Haiti*, next to each other on Prat, good coffee; *Café Roma*, Sucre 717, good breakfasts and lunches; *Chico Jaime* above the market, seafood, US$3 p.p. incl. wine. Many eating places in the market.

Clubs Club de Tenis Antofagasta, Av. Angamos 906, connected with Av. Brasil; Yachting Club, Calle Balmaceda.

Market Municipal market, corner of Matta and Uribe.

Car Rental Rent-a-Car, Prat 810, T 225200; Avis San Martín y Bolívar, T 221668 (small car US$250/week, inc. tax, insurance, free km.; Suzuki jeep suitable for Altiplano roads US$350/week); Budget, A. Prat y Balmaceda (pick-up, US$50/day); Hertz, Balmaceda 2646 (T 223549), offer city cars and jeeps (group D, Toyota Landcruiser) and do a special flat rate, with unlimited mileage, if you hire the car for over a week.

Bookshop Multilibro, Baquedano 522.

Cinemas Gran Vía, Av. Angamos; Nacional, Sucre 735; Arte, Copiapó 1125; Colón, San Martín 2755 (2 for the price of 1 on Thursdays); Teatro de la Barra, Baquedano y Condell (cine and live theatre).

Exchange Banks in main square will not buy or sell Argentine or Bolivian money, and only change dollars at poor rates and 5% commission. Fincard (Visa and Mastercard), Prat 461, oficina 401, 24 hrs a day, T 251775. It is hard to get good rates for travellers' cheques. Good rates at Farmacia Rimassa, Prat 656, for cash; also in travel agency at Latorre 2563, and Licorería San Marcos at Latorre y Baquedano. At weekends, try Licores Mitjans, Baquedano y Latorre. N.B. There is practically no official opportunity to change currency S of Antofagasta until you reach La Serena.

Swimming Olympic pool at Condell y 21 de Mayo, US$1.20, open till 1800, best to go in a.m.

Post Office Washington 2623; **Telephones**, Uribe 746.

Travel Agent Tatio Travel, Latorre 2579, T 225698/223192, Telex 225242 TATIO CL, English spoken, tours arranged for groups or individuals, highly rec. Turismo Cristóbal in *Hotel Antofagasta*, helpful. Alex Joseph Valenzuela Thompson, Edif. Vaticano, Prat 548, oficina 701, T 243322/251504, FAX 222718/222818, Aptdo Postal 55, offers to guide German speakers around the area.

Tourist Office at Baquedano 360 (one block from sea front), T 223004; also Prat y Matta, T 224834, and Airport. **Automóvil Club de Chile**, Condell 2330, T 225332.

Customs Agent Luis Piquimil Bravo, Prat 272, oficina 202, excellent, fast service, efficient.

Roads To Tocopilla, 187 km.; to Mejillones, 62 km.; to Pedro de Valdivia, 168 km.; to María Elena, 193 km.; to Taltal, 307 km.; to Calama, 196 km.; to Chuquicamata, 206 km. **N.B.** the Pan-American Highway between the N and S exits to Antofagasta; beware of flying stones from lorries. This route does avoid Antofagasta and the long climb out. Fuel at La Negra, then no more for 200 km. (Aguas Verdes) is not paved (22 km.) (Caracoles and La Negra respectively).

Buses The main bus terminal is at S end of town, Av. Argentina y Díaz Gana; all buses call here but each company has its own office in town (some quite a distance from the centre) and leaves from it. Some, like Tramaca, go only from their own terminal. To Santiago, 20 hrs., (luxury double decker/sleeper coach, Flota Barrios, US$50 including drinks and meals, pullman US$24; 30% reduction on Inca Tramaca, and Geminis buses for students, but ask after you have secured a seat; many companies: fares range from US$21, Carmelita, to US$25, Ramos Cholele, Fénix, US$36, Geminis, US$43, Fichtur, book 2 days in advance). If all seats to the capital are booked, catch a bus to La Serena (US$14 or 25 with lunch and supper, go by day to see the scenery) or Ovalle and travel to Santiago from there. To Valparaíso, US$17.50. To Arica, US$10 (Flecha Dorada), 13½ hrs., Tramaca 2100, US$11.40. (It is forbidden to take fruit south from Antofagasta because of fruit-fly control.) To Chuquicamata, Flecha Dorada leaves at 0700, returns at 1900, as well as many others. To Calama, several companies, US$2.50-3.20 (Tramaca, 3 hrs.). Direct to Copiapó on Thurs. and Sat. at 2230, US$10.50. Frequent buses to Iquique; US$10, 8 hrs., checkpoints near Iquique for foreigners. To Mejillones, twice a day from Latorre 2700. Bus station has a left luggage office.

Empresa de Transportes Atahualpa (Uribe 936) runs a Sat. bus service to Argentina, as does Geminis (Díaz Gana 1074, T 225494—better), Wed., both US$30; via Calama, immigration check at San Pedro de Atacama, then on to high Cordillera (very cold) and to San Antonio de los Cobres; change bus at Salta. There is nowhere to change Chilean pesos en route. (No service July-September.)

If hitching to Arica or Iquique try at the beer factory a few blocks N of the fish market on Av. Pinto, or the lorry park a few blocks further N. If hitching S go to the police checkpoint/restaurant/gas station La Negra, about 15 km. S of the city.

N.B. There are no more railway passenger services from Antofagasta. The famous journey to Bolivia now starts from Calama (see below), and the line into Argentina has been closed to passengers for some years.

Air To Santiago, Lan-Chile (US$103) and Ladeco (Prat 242, T 222860) fly daily. Ladeco flies once a week to La Paz, Bolivia. Lan-Chile, on Balmaceda, opp. *Hotel Antofagasta*; bus from this hotel to airport US$1, check at office for schedule. Taxi to airport US$7, but cheaper if ordered from hotel.

Excursions There are two favourite spots for picnics: near the town of La Chimba, and the fantastic rock scenery at La Portada, the symbol of the Second Region (16 km. north) taxi fare, US$1.50 (if you have a bike, go at dusk); it's easy to hitch to the sign, from where it is 2 km. to the beach and rocks. Alternatively, ask the driver of the airport bus No. 20, which leaves from Plaza de Armas by the Cathedral, to drop you at the junction for La Portada; goes every 2 hrs., US$0.35. Last bus back leaves at 2030. Excellent seafood restaurant and café at La Portada. A number of bathing beaches are within easy reach, including La Portada. Oficina Chacabuco is a military camp and "off limits"; in 1938 it was a town with 7,000 inhabitants (at junction of Antofagasta-Calama and María Elena roads). 50 km. from Antofagasta at Juan López is a windsurfers' paradise. Buses leave from Latorre 2723 (Sat. and Sun. only). For those with their own transport, follow the road out of Juan López to the beautiful cove at Conchilla. Keep on the track to the end at Bolsico. The sea is alive with birds, including Humboldt penguins, especially opposite Isla Santa María.

215 km. NE of Antofagasta is the oasis town of **Calama**, population 100,365, at an altitude of 2,265 metres. The Cía. Sud Americana de Explosivos manufactures high explosives. The town is modern, expensive and has a developed commercial centre. 2 km. from the centre on Av. B.O'Higgins is Parque Loa, with an exhibition of pre-cordillera life, 2 museums, a zoo, craft shops and a copy of Chiu Chiu church; open Tues.-Sun. 0930-1230, 1430-1700, US$0.40.

Travellers by car coming from the N can drive via Chuquicamata, although the road is quite poor on either side of that town, or, from the S, by a paved road (94 km.—police checkpoint at Baquedano, also meals available) leaving the Pan-American Highway 98 km. N of Antofagasta at Carmen Alto (petrol and food). This road passes interesting industrial archaeological sites at the abandoned nitrate mines (*oficinas*); look for the rubbish dumps of old bottles, shoes and other articles.

Sierra Gorda is the centre of a concentration of small copper and silver mines, 63 km. before Calama. If you are interested in minerals, ask in the café with the tree growing out of its centre to see the owner's collection of exotic copper minerals and fossils. Just after Sierra Gorda, there is a turning to the east along a good dirt road (which gradually deteriorates) leading to a network of tracks connecting old silver workings most of which closed at the end of last century. These are good places for collecting bottles etc., and are much less turned over than the nitrate oficinas. Water is available at the top of the pass on the main road NE of Sierra Gorda. There is a police checkpoint at Dupont, just before Calama.

Hotels *Hostería Calama,* Latorre 1521, T 211511, B, comfortable, good food and service; *Alfa*, Sotomayor 2016, T 211565, B, reasonable; *Topotel*, Camino Aeropuerto 1392, T

212208, 274-67701 in Santiago, A, first class, swimming pool, popular, bar and restaurant; *Lican Antai*, Ramírez 1937, T 212970, A with breakfast, good service and restaurant, TV, phone, safe, travel agency, car hire, rec.; *Atenas*, Ramírez 1961, T 212666, new, clean, shared baths, E; *Quitor*, Ramírez 2116, T 211716, B, good. *Casablanca* on Plaza, Sotomayor 2160, T 211722, C; *Residencial Internacional*, Gral. Velázquez 1976, T 211553; hot water, E, friendly but noisy; *Residencial Casa de Huéspedes*, Sotomayor 2073, clean, noisy, shared hot shower, E; *Res. Splendid*, Ramírez 1960, T 212141, E with bath, cheaper without, clean, hot water, breakfast US$1; *Res. John Keny*, Ecuador 1991, T 211430, D, modern, clean, friendly; *Prat*, Vivar 1970, F, cheap, cold water; *Res. Toño*, Vivar 1973, next to Kenny bus, E, shower, "a bit of a dive"; *Los Andes*, Vivar, next door, F, basic, cold shower, friendly, stores luggage; *Capri*, Vivar, E, friendly but dirty, hot water, not rec.; *Residencial El Tatio*, P. L. Galo, 1987, T 212284, F, basic, friendly, noisy, clean, reasonable.

Restaurants　*La Nueva Florida*, Calle Vargas 1975, cheap, *Bavaria*, Sotomayor 2095, modern, clean, good coffee and delicatessen; *Fuente de Soda Moltis*, Ramírez 2120, good bar with cakes; good eating at market and fire station (*Casino de Bomberos*). *Nueva Victoria*, Albaroa, serves early breakfast, good, other meals. Yugoslav club, Plaza de Armas, serves good lunches, US$2. *Mariscal JP*, Felix Hoyos 2127, 4 houses from Tramaca bus, good seafood. Good ice cream at *Flor di Gelalo*, Plaza de Armas.

Car Hire　Comercial Maipo S.A., Barrio Industrial, sitio 14, T 212204, take taxi—½ hr. out of town; Hertz, Latorre 1510 (T 211380); Comercial Automotriz Miranda, Granaderos 2625, T 211175, helpful. American's, Latorre 1512, T 211220, Maxso, Abaroa 1100, T 212194, jeep US$80/day. Budget, cheapest. A hired car, shared between several people, is an economic alternative for visiting the Atacama region, and is much cheaper than hiring one in San Pedro de Atacama.

Cinemas　Central on Latorre and another on Ramírez, near plaza.

Exchange　La Media Luna dry goods store, Ramírez 1992, *Hotel Los Andes*, Copper Tour, Sotomayor 2016, for travellers' cheques and cash, *Hostería Calama* (fair rates); Banco de Crédito e Inversiones will only change cash (but not dollars). Fincard (Access and Visa), Latorre 1751, oficina 207, Mon.-Fri. 0900-1400, 1600-2000, Sat. 1100-1300. Money changers selling Bolivian money for Chilean can be found outside the railway station (last chance before Oruro or La Paz). If arriving from La Paz by train on Sat. p.m. without pesos, you may find nowhere to obtain them, but try Tramaca bus office or *farmacias* (poor rates); better to get some before leaving Bolivia.

Consul　The Bolivian Consulate (Vicuña Mackenna 1896) is open 0900-1230 and 1530-1830, Mon.-Fri., friendly, helpful.

Laundry　Ramírez 2216; Ramírez 1867, English spoken (Mon.-Sat. 0900-2100, not cheap); Sotomayor 1984, both expensive.

Travel Agents　*Copper Tour* (address above); *Talikuna*, Gral. Velázquez 1948; tours to Atacama region when enough people want to go, very long day's travel, better to go from San Pedro.

Tourist Office　José La Torre and Mackenna, T 211314. Map of town, arranges car hire and details for tours to El Zatio geysers, Salar de Atacama, US$30 p.p., minimum 6 people. Open Mon.-Fri. 0900-1300, 1430-1900 Sat.-Sun. 0900-1300. **Automóvil Club de Chile**, Av. Ecuador 1901, T 212770.

Buses　Daily bus services to Santiago (23 hrs., fares from US$26, Tramaca 4 a day, US$38.70, Geminis, to US$53.35 Flota Barrios *salón cama*), Arica—often involves a change in Antofagasta (Geminis, 2130 and Tramaca, 4 until 1730 daily, may be more in summer, US$8.15), Iquique (US$7) and Ovalle. Also to San Pedro daily, with Tramaca on Félix Hoyos y Granaderos (see below for fares and schedules), Morales bus continues to Toconao Tues., Thurs., Sat.; to Chuquicamata (see below). Antofagasta, 3 bus., several companies, e.g. Tramaca, hourly on the half-hour till 2130, US$3 and Libac, US$2.50 (cheapest). Bus to Salta, Argentina, Wed., a.m. and Sat. p.m. (2), 17 hrs., US$27. 2 companies: Geminis (Av. Granaderos) and Atahualpa.

Air　Lan-Chile (Latorre 1499) and Ladeco (Mackenna 2020, T 211355) flights to Antofagasta and Santiago leave daily—except Sat. Taxi to town US$3 (courtesy vans from Hotels *Calama*, *Alfa* and *Lican Antai*).

Rail　Antofagasta (Chile) and Bolivia Railway to Oruro (no longer to La Paz, apparently—1989) starts at Calama now. Bus leaves Antofagasta (Uribe 936) Wed. a.m. to connect with train leaving Calama at 1245 (check in advance), via Ollagüe (2300 with a 1-2, maybe 10, hr. wait in the bitter cold for the Bolivian train, and 3 hrs. at customs) and Uyuni, arriving in Oruro sometime on Thurs. (all times are "pure fantasy"). No sleeping cars available from Calama to Oruro so take blankets or sleeping bag. The frontier is the scene of considerable palaver with smugglers throwing their gear on and throwing others' off. There is a change of trains at the border (just after Ollagüe); your ticket is supposedly valid for both, but ensure that it is stamped with a reservation for the second, and be quick at the changeover. It is cheaper, though, to buy a ticket to the border, then another into Bolivia. Fare from Calama to Oruro US$15; to Uyuni US$10; scenery beautiful but journey crowded, very slow and uncomfortable. On certain days a freight train goes to Ollagüe with one or two passenger cars attached; no fixed schedule, ask at station, buy ticket a few hours before departure, US$2, not crowded. No passengers are allowed to cross the border on the train, so you have to walk 15 km. to the Bolivian station if there's no connecting train or persuade an engine driver to take you if an engine is going. Get on a freight train in Bolivia for Uyconi, US$10, again, no schedule. Take warm clothes, food, blankets and plenty of time. This is the only way to see the Salar de Uyuni by train in day light.

Bus Calama-Ollagüe on a widened road in good condition, Trans. Abaroa, Vivar 1962, US$7.50, leaves Tues. night, heavily booked in advance. After Oruro, go on by bus to La Paz (3 hrs., US$3). For Potosí and Cochabamba change trains at Río Mulato and Oruro respectively; note that the connection is not always assured. Note that before leaving you must visit (a) the Bolivian consulate for visa if needed, and (b) the railway station. It is advisable, but not necessary, to visit the railway office at Bolívar 255, Antofagasta (open Tues. 0900-1300 and 1500-1630, and Wed. 0900-1230) to make sure if there is a seat, but they can be purchased (with luck) at Calama (office opens Tues. 1500 and Wed. a.m.). You must have your passport with you when buying ticket. It can be very cold at night (-15°C) and into the day. Meals available at Ollagüe and Río Mulato (only for the conditioned).

Calama, 2,255 metres above the sea, is a useful point at which to stay for a day or two to get used to the altitude before going higher. The summit is reached at Ascotán (3,960 metres), and the line descends to 3,735 metres at Cebollar, where it skirts a great borax lake, 39 km long. The Bolivian frontier is crossed a short distance beyond (444 km.) Ollagüe station (a change of trains—very cold—be quick to get your seat), from which there is a 77 km. spur to the copper mines of Collahuasi. For the next 174 km. to Uyuni the line maintains an almost uniform level of 3,660 metres.

Uyuni, the junction with the branch of 90 km. to Atocha, gives rail access, via Villazón on the Argentine border, to Buenos Aires, a route which is not interrupted by snowstorms. Río Mulato is the railway junction for Potosí, but it may be better to go to Oruro for transport to Potosí and Sucre, Cochabamba and La Paz (details in Bolivian chapter). After crossing the Bolivian border you need bolivianos to buy food on the train, so if you have no bolivianos make sure you have some small dollar notes for changing into bolivianos at the first stop in Bolivia. Money can be changed at Ollagüe (Chilean Customs) and Oruro. **Watch baggage** at Oruro; the thieves are notorious, even grabbing bags through open windows.

N.B. Remember, if arriving from La Paz between October and March, then Chile is 1 hr. later than Bolivia.

Excursion As the road enters Calama (from Antofagasta), there is a turning to the left to Ojos de Opache (signposted). It passes through the market garden supplying Calama and ends at a petrifying spring, where objects put in the water become encrusted with dissolved minerals.

At *Chuquicamata*, 16 km. from Calama at 2,800 metres, is the world's largest open-cast mine, a state-owned copper mine that used to belong to a U.S. firm. It is an astoundingly large hole. All the processes can be seen; there are guided tours with a film show three times a week on Mon., Wed. and Fri. at 1000, or 1300 (reports—all from Feb. 1990—vary) from the Public Relations Office, near Puerta Una, taking 2½ hrs, US$0.70 (very interesting but only given in Spanish—be in good time because space is limited; photographing the smelting plant is not permitted). Register at Gate No. 1 an hour beforehand; passport essential. You must wear a long-sleeved garment (shorts and skirts not allowed) if you wish to see the industrial plants; children under 12 are not normally allowed to enter. Buy postcards before the tour as the office closes before the tour ends.

Good fixed menu at the tour office cafeteria, US$2 for 4 courses. The clean, modern and pleasing town has about 30,000 people. (Guest house at east end of Plaza, nice, but book at Santiago or Antofagasta; overnight accommodation may be difficult.) There is a country club with a golf course at Río Loa.

Bus marked "Chuqui" from main plaza in Calama to Chuquicamata, US$0.60, ½ hr., frequent, then colectivo (marked "Local Chuqui") to mine, US$0.25. To Arica at 2200 (weekends at 2300), US$9, 9 hrs. To Antofagasta, ten a day, US$6 single. To Iquique at 2300. To Santiago at 1400, US$26, 24 hrs.

Within 40 km. of Calama there are several small towns and villages nestling in remote oases in the Andean massif. Just E is the village of **Chiu Chiu**, with a very interesting old church and nearby a unique, perfectly circular, very deep lake. An ancient fortress and rock carvings are to be found in the Río Loa valley. This excursion is only possible by private or hired car. Due E of Chuquicamata, 37 km. on the way to Ayquina (**see page** 508), are the pre-Incaic ruins of **Lasana**, a national monument, with explanatory tablets (soft drinks and beer on sale). They are arguably the most impressive in Chile.

From Calama to Ollagüe you can go via Chiu-Chiu and Lasana, direct via Lasana, or direct via Conchi (take the turning signposted Lasana from the Calama-Chuquicamata road, then turn left/north). At **Conchi**, there is a spectacular view from the bridge over the Río Loa, but it is a military zone, so no photographs allowed. Access to the river is by side tracks, best at Santa Bárbara; interesting wildlife and flower meadows, trout fishing in season (permit from Gobernación in Calama).

Estación San Pedro (16 km. from Conchi) has quite an interesting old village and small gorge, away from the railway station. Possible to camp at the station (ask the station master). There is a *carabinero* checkpoint at Ascotán, the highest point of the road at 3,900 m. After Ascotán the road becomes worse, especially where it crosses the Salares de Ascotán and Ollagüe (ask at Ascotán or Ollagüe about the conditions, especially in December/January or August). There are many llama flocks along this road and flamingoes on the salars. **N.B.** The desert to the eastern side of the road is extensively covered with minefields.

5 km. before Ollagüe is the sulphur mining camp of Buenaventura. It is possible to camp here. If you want to go to the summit of Ollagüe volcano, ask for a lift on the mine truck to the mine at 5,800 m. (only 150 m. short of the summit). Amazing views of volcanoes and salt flats.

419 km. from Antofagasta, at 3,690 metres, on the dry floor of the Salar de Ollagüe near the Bolivian border, is **Ollagüe**, surrounded by a dozen volcanic peaks of over 5,000 metres. Population: 500. **N.B.** There is no petrol between Calama and Uyuni in Bolivia. If really short try buying from the *carabineros* at Ollagüe or Ascotán, the military at Conchi or the mining camp at Buenaventura. The only real answer is to take enough. A 77-km. spur railroad of metre gauge runs to the copper mines of Collahuasi, and from there a 13-km. aerial tram to the highest mine in the world: the Aucanquilcha, at 6,100 metres. Its sulphur is taken to Amincha, a town at the foot of the volcano, to be refined. The highest passenger station in this spur is Yuma, at 4,400 metres. A train can be taken from Calama on Wed. at 1255, US$3.30 to Ollagüe, but if you stop off, you will have to hitch back, the daily freight trains are not allowed to take passengers. Bad unmade road from Ollagüe into Bolivia (**see page** 242).

At this altitude nights are cold, the days warm and sunny. Minimum temperature at Ollagüe is -20°C, and at the mine, -37°C. There are only 50 mm. of rain a year, and water is very scarce.

An interesting excursion can be made N from Ollagüe to the village of Coska with its traditional agriculture and herds of llamas and alpacas.

The main stock animals are llamas and alpacas, whose principal forage is the *ichu* bunch-grass covering the lower slopes. There is no timber. *Taqui*—dried llama dung— and *tola* scrub are used for cooking fires, but the main fuel is *yareta*, a resinous moss growing in pillow-like masses in rocky outcrops from 3,500 to 5,000 metres high. Its calorific value is half that of bituminous coal. It apparently is an Ice Age relic, growing very slowly but now worked out in this area. Across the border in Bolivia there is plenty, which is used as fuel for the Laguna Verde sulphur mine. It is claimed, like mineral land, and broken up with dynamite into chunks for transport.

103 km. SE of Calama by a good road is **San Pedro de Atacama**. There is no fuel, food or water on the road. At the top of the pass half way to San Pedro is a turn to the left which leads (unmade) through interesting desert scenery to the small, mud-brick village of Río Grande. Look out for vicuñas and guanacos on the pass. The paved road skirts the Cordillera de la Sal about 15 km. from San Pedro. Spectacular views of sunset over to the Western Cordilleras. The old unmade road,

which crosses the new road several times traverses this range through the Valle de La Luna (see below), but is effectively blocked by sand dunes, allowing no passage to San Pedro. This road is partly paved with salt blocks. Along the road are various archaeological remains.

San Pedro de Atacama, at 2,436 metres, is a small town (pop. 1,600) more Spanish-Indian looking than is usual in Chile, well worth a visit. Both Diego de Almagro and Pedro de Valdivia stopped in this oasis (Valdivia's house on the main square may be visited by knocking at the green door next to it and asking for the key). A most impressive archaeological museum now under the care of the Universidad del Norte (Mon.-Fri., 0800-1200, 1400-1800; Sat., and Sun., 1000-1200, 1400-1800, entry US$0.30) is a fascinating repository of artefacts, with an insight into hundreds of years of Atacameño culture, as well as the contents of the study of the late Father Le Paige, who used to run the museum. Labels on displays are good and there is a comprehensive booklet in Spanish. The anthropologist Héctor Garcés is a mine of information at the museum. Graham Greene tells us that "the striking feature of the museum is . . . the mummies of Indian women with their hair and dresses intact dating from before the Conquest, and a collection of paleolithic tools which puts the British Museum in the shade".

The Valle de la Luna, with fantastic landscapes caused by the erosion of salt mountains, is traversed by a road 13 km. before reaching San Pedro; the San Pedro-Calama bus does not pass through the valley but passes the old road which used to cross it (most bus drivers know where it is and will let you out—the sign is not visible if coming from Calama). From here it is a stiff 5-hr. walk back to San Pedro and can only be done in the middle of the day. Far better is to walk from San Pedro on the old road, 3 hrs. there, 3 hrs. back (don't expect a lift), aim to get there just before sunset. Take water, hat, camera and torch. There are no signs for the return to San Pedro, but the road is straight all the way. If worried about coming back in the dark a trip can be arranged through Hostería San Pedro (US$4), Residenciales Florida and Chiloé, Nuevo Extremo Expediciones (NEX) at Takha-Takha camping, or Turismo Ochoa. A recommended guide is Roberto Sánchez (he speaks German); Caracoles s/n, his name is on the door, T 40. To hire a 4-wheel-drive vehicle with driver costs US$25. Driving through the Valle de la Luna at sunset, with the Licancábur volcano, 5,916 metres, in the background, is a superb experience. If you are in your own car (4-wheel drive essential to cope with sand dunes), make the detour on your way south (i.e. from Calama), as from N drifting sand makes uphill driving difficult. There are also some pre-Conquest, Indian ruins about 3 km. from San Pedro at Pucará, and a fine sandstone cave nearby. Pucará can be reached on foot by following the river bed (or crossing it, 3-5 times going upstream, if there is water in it), or US$1.20 for pick-up truck, seats 6. The best places to see the sunset are Pukará, or the football pitch (cancha). The archaeological site at Tulor, 4 km. from San Pedro, is a stone-age village; worth a visit on foot (you can sleep in two reconstructed huts), or take a tour, US$5 p.p.

Hotels *Hostería San Pedro,* on Solcor, recently refurbished, C, rec., Australian joint proprietors Luis Hernández and Mrs. Bobbee Andrews have prepared a short guide to the area in English, German, French, Spanish and Japanese; the *hostería* has a swimming pool (US$1.40 for non-residents for a day), shop and a Copec petrol station, tents for hire, US$3 for 2 people, camping in grounds, US$0.75 p.p., 2 cabins with 6 and 3 beds, hot water, electricity 1800-2300, restaurant (good lunch US$8.75) and bar, "Llamaroo" supermarket, T 21-1511. *Residencial Chiloé,* Domingo Atienza, F, good, hot water (if possible the Sra. will cook for vegetarians), T 17; *Residencial Solcor,* Domingo Atienza s/n, 2 blocks from plaza, G p.p., friendly, good meals; *Pukará,* E, Tocopilla 28, cold water, mixed reports; *Pensión Florida,* on Tocopilla, good, F, hot water, shared baths, safe, fleas; *Pensión y Restaurant Porvenir,* F, good value and excellent food (only one self-contained room with toilet), rec.; *Hostal-camping Takha-Takha,* on Tocopilla, F p.p. (G camping), hot water, good sanitary facilities, some tents for rent, friendly and clean, restaurant (owner Quenie Quezada Lima). If arriving after "lights out" and there is nowhere to stay (e.g. on Atalmalpa bus from Salta), ask the police if they will let you stay in their office.

Restaurants *Juanita's,* reasonably priced, adequate (some rooms to let); *Cobreloa.* Don't drink the tap water, it contains a high level of arsenic.

Exchange Best done elsewhere, no cheques, poor rates for cash. If stuck try Almacén El Chagüito, Tocopilla 28.

Swimming Pool Pozo Tres, 3 km. outside village, was drilled in the late 1950s by Unesco as part of a mineral exploration project, US$0.50 to swim, sometimes empty. Worth asking around before walking there. Camping US$0.55.

Electricity   Only from 1 hour after sunset till 2300-2400, depending who is on duty, what film is on TV, or so they say.

Tours   Turismo Ochoa, opened by Héctor Ochoa, rec.; Roberto Sánchez, NEX (see above); Sra María Luisa Baron, chief archaeologist of the area, arranges trips to the Salar and geysers. Contact her through *Residencial Chiloé*, US$15 p.p. to the Salar, US$17 p.p. to geysers (max 8 passengers); similar prices from *Pensión Florida* (trip to Salar not so good, evening departure, 4-hr. trip).

Buses   There are Tramaca buses daily at 1100, from Calama, extra buses Jan.-Feb., especially at weekends, 1½-2 hrs., US$3.50 (US$6 return, if possible book in advance), returning from the plaza at 1800 (1845 Sat.-Sun. in Jan.-Feb.); the bus goes on to Pozo Tres before coming back to San Pedro at 1700.

An interesting route from San Pedro de Atacama to Calama is to go north on a maintained road which passes the Baños de Puritama (27 km., truck drivers leaving from behind the police station for the sulphur mine at 0500 may give you a lift and collect you on return), then to the geysers at El Tatio. The geysers, at an altitude of 4,500 metres, are at their best 0630-0830. There is no public transport, so if going in a hired car, make sure the engine is suitable for very high altitudes and is protected with antifreeze; 4-wheel drive is preferable. If driving in the dark it is almost impossible to find your way: the sign for El Tatio is after the turn off coming from San Pedro de Atacama. Near El Tatio is a workers' camp which is empty apart from one guard, who will let you sleep in one of the huts in a bed. Give him a tip and take your own food. If you stay here, you can hike to surrounding volcanoes if adapted to altitude. Hitching to El Tatio is impossible; the police advise against it. Tours arranged by those mentioned above. Also ask the army outside San Pedro, who may give groups of 10-12 people a lift in a truck (US$3 p.p.);.beware, it gets very cold in the truck. From Calama, trips for El Tatio leave at 0300, continuing to San Pedro and the Valle de la Luna, arriving back at 2000 (US$30 p.p.).

There are 3 alternative routes between El Tatio and Calama: direct, on an atrocious track, to Caspana, beautifully set among hills, with an interesting museum. Between Caspana and Toconce are pampas grass filled valleys with llama herds. It is proposed to make the area north of San Pedro, including El Tatio and Caspana, a national park.

N of El Tatio to Linzor; here you can turn W to Toconce, which has extensive prehispanic terraces set among interesting rock formations. If visiting Toconce, check in with the *carabineros* in the square. Then to Calama via Lasana and Chiu Chiu, or via **Ayquina**, in whose ancient church is enshrined the statue of the Virgin of Guadalupe. Her feast-day is 8 September, when pilgrims come from far and wide. There is day-long group dancing to Indian rhythms on flute and drum. Towards sunset the Virgin is carried up a steep trail to a small thatched shrine, where the image and the people are blessed before the dancing is renewed at the shrine and all the way back to the village. The poor people of the hills gather stones and make toy houses all along the route: miniatures of the homes they hope to have some day.

With a detour, the thermal waters and ruins of Baños de Turi may be visited and, 35 km. north, Cupo, which has a *fiesta* on 19 March (San José). Between this village and Turi is a large, ruined prehispanic settlement at Paniri with extensive field systems, irrigation canals (including aqueducts) and a necropolis. Some of the fields are still in use. The area around Cupo is one of the best for seeing the Atacama giant cactus (*Notocereus atacamensis*). Flamingos can be seen on the mudflats. The Vegas de Turi is an important site for the llama and sheep herders, who believe it has curative properties. At several times in the year, herders from a wide area congregate with their flocks, especially in September.

The third alternative is to continue North from Linzor to Inacaliri and the Ojo de San Pedro saltflat. Follow the road along the Río San Pedro Valley and cross the Río Loa at Conchi. The Río San Pedro has been a route for herders and silver caravans for centuries and there are many sites of interest, although access is on foot. For details on Conchi, Lasana and Chiu Chiu, **see page 506** above.

A well-surfaced road south of San Pedro runs through groves of acacia and pepper trees to Toconao (40 km.). There are many tracks leading to the wells (*pozos*) which supply the intricate irrigation system. Most have thermal water but bathing is not appreciated by the local farmers. The groves of trees are havens for wild life especially rheas (ñandu) and Atacama owls.

About 4 km. before you reach Toconao, there are some vehicle tracks heading east across the sand. They lead to a hidden valley 2 km. from the road where there is a small settlement called Zapar. Here are some well-preserved pre-hispanic ruins on the rocky cliffs above the cultivated valley. The sand is very soft and 4-wheel drive is essential. **Toconao**, with some 500 inhabitants is on the eastern shore of the lithium-salt lake Salar de Atacama. All houses are built of bricks of volcanic stone, which gives to the village a very characteristic appearance totally different from San Pedro. Its colonial clock tower is modelled in the same volcanic stone by the local craftsman and it has an attractive oasis called Quebrada de Jérez. The quarry where the stone (sillar) is worked can be visited. Worth visiting also are the vineyards which produce a unique sweet wine, and the tree-filled gorges with their hidden fields and orchards. Hitch from San Pedro (most traffic at weekends). Tours arranged in San Pedro. Camping possible along river bank of Quebrada de Jérez.

Ask the jefe de carabineros in San Pedro or Toconao for a chance to go with police patrols to the Bolivian or Argentine border areas (paying your share of fuel).

From San Pedro de Atacama one can cross into Argentina over the pass of Laguna Sico (4,079 metres) to San Antonio de los Cobres. Travellers by car should make careful enquiries into road conditions (often impassible in rainy season, 1 Jan. to mid-March, and blocked by snow in winter); gasoline may be bought in Calama or at Hostería San Pedro. Passport control and customs clearance must be undertaken in San Pedro.

The first village reached is Toconao (see above; cars registered at the entrance to the village); the Atacama desert can be seen in the distance. The road heads south through the scenic villages of Camar (where handicrafts from cactus may be bought) and Socaire (which has domesticated llamas, knitwear for sale). 20 km. S of Socaire is the beautiful Laguna Miscantí where wildlife abounds, including 3 types of flamingo: Andean, Chilean (white and pink, no black) and James (small, with yellow legs). After Socaire the road goes on to the mine at Laco (one poor stretch below the mine), proceeding to Sico, which has replaced the higher, more northerly Huaytiquina pass (4,295 metres) to Catúa and San Antonio de los Cobres.

10 km. S of Toconao the old road branches E towards Huaytiquina. In a deep quebrada below Volcán Láscar is the small agricultural settlement of Talabre, with terracing and an ancient threshing floor. Above the quebrada is an isolated, stone-built cemetery. Large flocks of llamas graze where the stream crosses the road below Láscar. After a steep climb, you reach the Laguna Lejía (4,190 metres), where flamingoes abound. You then pass through the high plains of Huaytiquina (4,275 metres), where only a few herdsmen are found. This crossing is not open for road traffic to Catúa, the first Argentine settlement, after which the road crosses the railway, descends into the ghost-like town of Agua Castilla, and after 8 km. reaches San Antonio de los Cobres. It is a further 3½ hours by car to Salta.

60 km. further south from Toconao, on a road that branches initially W between Camar and Socaire, is the attractive village of **Peine**, which is the site of the lithium extraction company. There is also a pool filled by thermal springs where you can swim. Woollen goods and knitwear are made here. To the east of the village lies a group of beautifully coloured hills (colours best at sunset) with good views over the Salar de Atacama. It is worth asking if a visit access road can be used to visit the Salar de Atacama's spectacular salt formations.

Other villages worth visiting include Tilomonte and Tilopozo, S and W of Peine. The road can be followed to Pan de Azúcar where it joins the road to Argentina via the Portezuelo de Socompa. It is possible to stay at Pan de Azúcar (hot showers and water). From Pan de Azúcar a good road leads back to San Pedro de Atacama along the western side of the Salar.

Pan de Azúcar is on the road which leads from the Pan-American Highway, 50 km. S of Antofagasta to Socompa on the Argentine border. The road passes the mining centre at La Escondida (owned by RT2) and continues, after Pan de Azúcar, in bad condition to Monturaqui. This is the source of the green onyx which is much used for carving in northern Chile. Formalities for crossing into Argentina are completed at Socompa. The road carries on to San Antonio de los Cobres and Salta.

If coming into Chile by train on the Salta-Socompa line, cross into Chile immediately and ask about freight trains to Baquedano (you may have to wait days—the staff at the railway and customs offices are helpful, but officially the freight trains are not allowed to carry passengers. Trains may go only as far as Victoria, where there is a mining camp from which you can get a pick-up to Antofagasta, or to Baquedano if you want to go to Calama (bus from Baquedano police control point).

Some 175 km. S of Antofagasta there are ruined nitrate mines at Oficina Alemania and Oficina Flor de Chile (just off the Pan-American Highway). Mining tracks lead off to the E, but there are no real signs. A good one leads East from Aguas Verdes (fuel) to Plato de Sopa, a camp built into caves above a salt flat.

The next important port to the south is **Taltal**, 309 km. S of Antofagasta, connected with it by the Pan-American Highway and a poor but scenic road along the coast. It is a nitrate and copper ore centre with 8,275 people. There is an airport, but few flights.

Hotels Several *residenciales*, e.g. *Verdi* and *Ramírez* on Ramírez (Nos. 345 and 519), E, *Viña del Mar*, Serrano 762, F. "The water supply is random, and the Salón de Te has no tea" (J. D. H. Smith).

Buses Three a week to Santiago; several to Antofagasta.

Chañaral, a neglected looking port and town with wooden houses perched on the hillside and beset by water shortages, is 100 km. S of Taltal and 400 km. S of Antofagasta by sea or Pan-American Highway. Population, including Potrerillos and Caleta Barquito: 39,225. Anchorage is very near jagged rocks which rear out of the sea all round.

Hotels *Jiménez*, (E); *La Marina*, both on Merino Jarpa (Nos. 541 and 572), latter F without bath, clean; *Hostería Chañaral*, Miller 268, T 80055, C with evening meal.

Buses All companies on Merino Jarpa; 3 a day to Santiago; to Antofagasta at 0930 and 2100.

Excursions North of Chañaral is the **Parque Nacional Pan de Azúcar**, which consists of the Isla Pan de Azúcar on which Humboldt penguins and other sea-birds live, and some 43,700 hectares of coast whose vegetation, mainly cacti, is nourished by frequent sea mists (*camanchaca*). There are some fine beaches in the park (popular at weekends). Access by secondary road from Chañaral (22 km. to Caleta Pan de Azúcar), or more easily from the Pan-American Highway (45 km. N, then side road 20 km. W). After rain in some of the gullies there are tall purple lilies. Conaf office, Atacama 898, Copiapó, T 3404/2571; wardens in the park.

12 km. E of Chañaral is a paved road to the mine of El Salvador. This follows a valley which contains the outflow of the mine purification process. All along it there are people extracting metal ore from the water by building primitive settling tanks. Climb above El Salvador to *Hostería Louis Murray*, no booking possible, just turn up. Daily flights from Santiago to El Salvador.

Copiapó, 240 km. S of Chañaral, capital of the Third (Atacama) Region, is an inland town in a ribbon of farms and orchards about 150 km. long on the river Copiapó, the river generally regarded as the southern limit of the Atacama desert. It is an attractive mining centre with an important mining school, and a population of 72,165. There is a monument to Juan Godoy, a pioneer of the mining industry. The plaza is interesting, with an unusual church and piped music on Sundays. The best mineralogical museum in Chile is at Colipí y Rodríguez, 1 block from Plaza de Armas (east), no fee; Tues.-Sat. 1000-1300, 1600-2000, Sun. 1000-1300. Many ores shown are found only in the Atacama desert. Also Museo Regional Atacama Copiapó; entrance US$0.35, interesting. Open Sat. 1530-1800. The museum at the railway station is dull, but an early steam locomotive can be seen at the university on the northern highway. Airport.

Hotels *Hostería Las Pircas*, Av. Kennedy s/n, T 213220, B, bungalows, pool, dining room, good apart from service, out of town; *Inglés*, Atacama 337, T 212797, D; *Residencial Rodríguez*, Rodríguez 528, T 212861, F; *Carrera* (small rooms round courtyard), Los Carrera 525, T 3255, D, reasonable value, good dining room; *Derby*, Yerba Buena 396, T 212447, D, clean.

Restaurants 5 km. from *Las Pircas*, *La Carreta*, on Carretera de Copayapu, ranch-style, very good meat and fish; *Willy Beer* restaurant, Maipú 386, has fancy hot-dogs, hamburgers and entertainment. *El Corsario*, Atacama 245, good restaurant; *La Chispa*, Chacabuco 157, opp. bus station, good, cheap; *Bavaria Restaurant*, on main square, excellent but not cheap.

Car Hire Av. Kennedy 310, T 2964.

Exchange Fincard (Visa and Access), Chacabuco 389, open Mon.-Fri. 0900-1400,

1630-1930, Sat. 1030-1300.

Tourist Office Los Carrera 691, T 2838.

About 70 km. W of Copiapó is the port of **Caldera**, which has a pier of 230 metres; 1½ km. to the S there is a terminal for the loading of iron ore. There is a fruit inspection for all passing through Caldera going South; this applies to bus passengers, whose luggage is searched.

Hotels *Costanera*, Wheelwright 543, D inc. tax, takes credit cards, unwelcoming; *Hostería Puerta del Sol*, Wheelwright 750, T 315205, C inc. tax, cabins with bath and kitchen, view over bay; *Portal del Inca*, Carvallo 945, T 315252, C inc. tax, shower, cabins with kitchen, English spoken, restaurant not bad, order breakfast on previous night; *Pucará*, Ossa Cerda 460, T 315258, D; *Los Andes*, Edwards 360, F. Excellent fish **restaurant** at the beach by the fishing quay.

Camping Bahía Inglesa, 6 km. W of Highway, 3 km. S of Caldera; 2 campsites, 2 cabin/hosterías, a shop and one good restaurant. Swimming in the Pacific; beautiful beach but can get crowded. There are other beaches within walking distance.

50 km. S of Copiapó is a signposted turning to Chañarcillo. This was one of the 19th century's richest silver mines. The tips are being reworked and this has destroyed much of the ruins.

A road runs NE through the pass of San Francisco in the Andes to Tinogasta, in Argentina (suitable only for 4 wheel-drive vehicles, often closed by landslides). South of the pass rises the Ojos del Salado mountain, believed to be the second highest peak in the Americas; its height is now thought to be in the range of 6,875-6,887 metres. There is fumarolic activity 300 metres below the summit of Ojos del Salado, which makes it a contender with Cotopaxi in Ecuador for the title of the world's highest active volcano.

COPIAPO TO ILLAPEL (2)

The second geographic zone, lying between the valleys of the Copiapó and the Aconcagua, contains the southern half of the Third (Atacama) Region and the whole of the Fourth (Coquimbo) (population at 1982 census, 419,956; 1987, 459,400). The zone is about 600 km. long.

This is a transitional zone between the northern desert and the fruitful heartland. S of Copiapó the central valley is cut across by transverse spurs of mountain which link the Andes and the coastal *cordillera*. Between these spurs several rivers flow westwards. Southwards the desert gives way slowly to dry scrub and bush interspersed with sand dunes. This desert is of little interest except after rain. Then it is covered with a succession of flowers, insects and frogs, in one of the world's most spectacular wildlife events (graphically shown in Michael Andrews' *The Flight of the Condor*, episode 2, BBC TV). Rain, however, is rare: there is no rain in summer; in winter it is light and lasts only a short time. It is about 115 mm. at Copiapó and 500 mm. at Illapel. In the river valleys under irrigation, fruit, vines, and barley are grown, and some alfalfa for cattle. There are many goats.

Vallenar (airport), inland up the Huasco valley, is 144 km. S of Copiapó; it is the second city of the Third (Atacama) Region, with a population of 42,000. Good wines are produced in the Huasco valley, in particular a sweet wine known as Pajarete. A road runs down the valley to **Huasco**, an interesting port. 1½ km. S of Huasco is a terminal for loading iron ore from the deposits at Algarrobal, inland 35 km. N of Vallenar. Population: 7,065.

Vallenar Hotels *Hostería Vallenar*, Alonso de Ercilla 848, T 611847, A (good—also Hertz car hire office); *Cecil*, Calle Prat 1059. T 611272, E with bath and hot water, clean, rec.

130 km. S of Vallenar there is a turning to the old mines at El Tofo. Some trees have a precarious hold on life as a result solely of fog. Follow the road to the sea for some spectacular scenery and wildlife.

La Serena, on the coast 187 km. S of Vallenar, 480 km. N of Santiago (95,400 people), is the capital of the Fourth (Coquimbo) Region, an attractive town built on a hillside, which has become a major tourist resort. It was remodelled in the 1950s and is now one of the pleasantest towns in Chile, with many colonial-style buildings, pretty gardens and a lot of *azulejos*, or coloured tiles. It has a Cathedral, 29 churches and several old convents. Many rodeos are held, and Chilean independence is celebrated on 20 September with a huge open-air picnic on the sands at nearby Coquimbo. The most popular nearby beaches are Peñuelas, half way to Coquimbo, and La Herradura. The climate is often damp and rarely hot. Market on Sun. New market (La Recova) on Cienfuegos, cheap food and souvenirs.

History La Serena was founded by Juan de Bohón, aide to Pedro de Valdivia, in 1544, destroyed by Diaguita Indians in 1546, rebuilt by Francisco de Aguirre in 1552, and sacked by the English pirate Sharpe in 1680. Legends of buried treasure at Guayacán Bay, frequented by Drake, persist.

The Archaeological Museum, in a colonial-style building, has an interesting collection of Diaguita and Molle Indian exhibits, especially of most attractively decorated pottery, at corner of Calles Córdovez and Cienfuegos. It is open Mon.-Sat. 0900-1300, 1600-1900, Sun. 1000-1300, entrance, US$0.35. There is a mineralogical museum in the Technical University, Calle A. Muñoz between Benavente and Infante (for geologists, open Mon.-Fri. 0930-1230, free).

Hotels *Mediterráneo*, Córdovez y Cienfuegos 509, Casilla 212, T 215233, A including good breakfast, rec. (Las Brisas supermarket next door, Archaeological Museum opposite); *Francisco de Aguirre*, Córdovez 210, T 222991, B inc. tax and breakfast, shower, good rooms, reasonable restaurant; *Londres*, Córdovez 566, T 211906, E, fair restaurant; *Pucará*, Balmaceda 319, T 211966, C with bath and breakfast, good; *Alameda*, D (less without bath), Av. de Aguirre 450, T 213052, clean and comfortable, towels supplied; *Residencial Brasilia*, Brasil 555, T 212263, D, good, friendly; *Res. Chile*, Matta 561, T 211694, D, basic, clean, hot shower, breakfast, rec. *Residencial El Loa*, Bernardo O'Higgins 362, E with shower, good inexpensive home cooking (US$2.50-3 per main meal), friendly; *Residencial Petit*, Edo de la Barra 586, T 212536, E, basic; *Res. Norte Verde*, Cienfuegos 672, T 213646, F, dirty, not rec; *Residencial Carreras*, Los Carrera 682, T 51-213646, E, clean, comfortable, cheapest; unnamed *residencial* at Los Carrera 880, F, OK. Family pensión of Isabel Ahumada Rolle, Eduardo de la Barra 315, F. *Casa del Turista*, Colón 318, E, clean, hot water, friendly. **Motel Les Mouettes**, Av. de Mar, T 214216, B, good; several more motels along the beach. In fact, the road from La Serena to Coquimbo is full of accommodation, from hotels to *cabañas* and campsites, and restaurants.

Campsite Maki Payi, 153 Vegas Norte, about 5 km. N of La Serena, near sea, friendly, rec., self-contained cabins available; US$3.10 per tent and US$9.50 p.p. for chalet. Also by Playa El Pescador, Hipocampo, T 214276.

Restaurants *Club Social*, Córdovez 516, unpretentious but excellent. *Restaurant Galeón*, Brasilia, good seafood; *La Barca*, Av. del Mar, good seafood; *Cirio's*, Francisco de Aguirre 431, T 213482, good lunch, US$5, rec.; *Mi Casa*, Av. Aguirre 596, 2nd floor, cheap *almuerzos*; *Café Milan*, Balmaceda 655, good pastries. *Rapsodia*, Arturo Prat 470, tea house with good cakes; *Torreón*, Prat 545, good coffee. Good selection of cheap meals on 1st floor of market hall. Copec gas station an S-bound side of Pan-American Highway, excellent food.

Car Hire Hertz, Francisco de Aguirre 0225, T 213955/212639, Automóvil Club de Chile, Eduardo de la Barra 435, T 211504, small car US$250/week (inc. tax, insurance, free km.) or US$870/month, pick-ups and jeeps US$300-350/week.

Discotheques Oriente, Balmaceda 677.

Exchange Fincard (Visa and Mastercard), Balmaceda 391, Local 217, Mon.-Fri. 0900-1400, 1600-2030, Sat. 1000-1400.

Italian Vice-Consulate Plaza de Armas, Los Carrera 446, also Alitalia representative.

Post Office Plaza de Armas.

Tourist Office Prat y Malta, 1st floor, T 213134 (open Mon.-Fri. 0830-1300, 1430-1800); kiosk in market area (Cienfuegos y Prat) and in bus terminal (helpful in finding accommodation).

Transport Bus terminal, El Santo y Amunátegui, in Coquimbo direction. Buses daily to La Calera and Santiago, several companies, 8 hrs, US$8.35-10; to Arica, US$20; to Calama, US$17, 16 hrs. To Valparaíso, 7 hrs., Pullman at 1300 and 2315, Incabus at 1300, US$8. By bus to Antofagasta takes 13 hrs., US$10-14 and to Iquique 20 hrs, US$20. Bus to Vicuña, Transportes Via Elqui, Calle Peni y Benavente, 9 daily; *colectivo* to Vicuña, Empresa Nevada del Sol de Elqui, Domeyko 550, T 21450, US$1.50, others from Calle Aguirre; to Coquimbo, from Av. Aguirre, US$0.25.

The Agua Negra pass, on the road between La Serena and San Juan in Argentina is in very bad condition and to all intents and purposes impassable. There is no public transport and the route and private vehicles do not attempt this crossing.

Excursion La Serena is at the mouth of the Elqui river valley, where the Nobel Prize-winning poet Gabriela Mistral was born. She described the valley as "confined yet lofty, many-sided yet simple, rustic yet a mining area". The road up the valley has been rebuilt and paved as far as Vicuña; "its branches all lead to fertile nooks, to shady vegetation, to dense groves, to gardens fed by the very sap of the hills". Except for Vicuña, most of the tiny towns have but a single street. Of the *elquinos*, the people of the valley, she says that "even the most taciturn of them come out with witty and charming remarks". There are still a few descendants of the Diaguitas, the tribe that inhabited the valley at one time.

Vicuña (66 km.) capital of the valley, is on the way to Rivadavia at an altitude of 600 metres and has a population of 19,395. Beautiful hand-woven rugs may be purchased at the village of Chapilca (25 km. from Vicuña). There are mines, vineyards and orchards in the district, which produces pisco and dried fruits. Vicuña is picturesque, fairly clean and friendly; it is within reach by car (120 km.) of Termas del Toro in the mountains. A small Gabriela Mistral Museum has been opened. Her grave is at Monte Grande, 20 km. S of Rivadavia. Good cinema, on plaza on San Martín, open on Fri., Sat. and Sun. Post office in public services building on same plaza. Tourist Office kiosk on main square will also arrange a visit to the Pisco distillery, Capel, between 0800-1200 and 1400-1800. Alternatively, you can walk there; walking in farmland around Vicuña, for instance to Peralillo (7 km. along Route 41), is delightful. Good views from Cerro La Virgen, N of town.

Hotels *Hostería*, Sgto. Aldea 101, T 411301, B, swimming pool; **Gran Hotel Jasna**, Gabriela Mistral 542, T 411266, E with bath (cheaper without), hot water, charming, clean, safe restaurant; *Residencial Moderna*, at No. 718 same street, F, full board available, no hot water, nothing modern about it, but quiet, clean, very nice; also **Gabriela Mistral**, same street, F, basic; camping at airstrip a few km. from town (ask police).

Restaurants *Halley*, Gabriela Mistral 404, not cheap but good; **Club Social** on same street; **Café Cecilia** (opens 1800); 2 or 3 good bakers and **Frutería Guayaquil** on Gabriela Mistral.

Buses Last bus Vicuña-La Serena at 1815, others in day, US$1.25, colectivo US$1.50; 2 buses a day to Santiago, one a.m., one 2200, US$5.50.

The road to Rivadavia continues up the valley, in which there are orchards and orange groves. Beyond Rivadavia the road runs to the small towns of Paihuano and Pisco Elqui (*Hotel Plaza*, F) (34 km.), where you can visit old-fashioned pisco distilleries. Table wine is made at Pisco Elqui.

Up the Elqui valley, beyond Monte Grande, on the road to El Colorado, are several Ashram places, some of which welcome visitors (e.g. Rama Mission, 12 km. from Monte Grande); one can camp ("a firm belief in UFOs is a help"—Quentin Crewe). Bus from Vicuña plaza to Monte Grande US$1.20, from Monte Grande you can walk or take a pick-up if one is running to a self-contained community where you can stay up to 4 days (take sleeping bag and food); ask for Gladys or Juanita. May be possible to go with transport to El Indio mine to get higher up the valley.

The La Serena district is one of the astronomical centres of the world. On a peak about 35 km. S of Vicuña is the new Cerro Tololo Inter-American Observatory, which has a 400-cm. (the largest in the Southern Hemisphere), a 150-cm., a 100-cm., a 90-cm. and two 40-cm. reflecting telescopes. Visits only on Saturdays and Sundays at 0900 and 1300 and permission must first be obtained from the AURA office in La Serena (near new University) or write to Observatorio, Cerro Tololo, Casilla 603, La Serena in English or Spanish. In peak season book a week in advance. No transport provided, takes 1½ hrs. by car from La Serena, or take taxi from Vicuña, hitch, or Vicuña bus from La Serena to AURA sign (about 1 hr.), walk 3 km. to entrance, then wait for other visitors. On Cerro La Silla, 100 km. NE, is the European Southern Observatory, with 13 more large telescopes, the largest of which is 360 cm. Visiting with permission from ESO, Av. Alonso de Córdoba 3107, Las Condes, Santiago (take metro to Los Leones, then bus to Vitacura, get off at Av. Vitacura y Alonso de Córdoba, then walk north

200 metres), or AURA in La Serena; free excursion first Sat. of every month.

Only open on first Saturday of the month, 54 km. from La Silla, are three large telescopes, a 250 cm., and a 100 cm. run by the Carnegie Institution of Washington, and a 61-cm. telescope run by University of Toronto. Permission to visit must be obtained from office at Colina El Pino, La Serena.

Coquimbo, 11 km. S of La Serena and on the same bay, is a port of considerable importance and with several industries. The city has one of the best harbours on the coast. A pleasant walk is along Aldunate, past the port and fishmeal factory to view a guano covered rock, 50 metres offshore, with many seabirds, penguins and an occasional sealion (binoculars a help). Population: 92,105.

Hotels (generally cheaper and less full than La Serena) *El Bucanero* at La Herradura, on Guayacán Bay, 1½ km. from Coquimbo port, T 312231, B, listed "de luxe" but is not; *Ibería*, Lastra 400, T 312141, E, safe; *La Valle*, F, in front of bus station. Cheap hotels near bus terminal at south end of Aldunate, e.g. *Castex*, No. 473, a rambling barn with large rooms, F. Many more hotels, *cabañas* and motels.

Campsites Guanaqueros, at km. 43 on the Pan-American Highway, 34 km. S of Coquimbo. Camping also available at Morrillos (several sites), km. 442 on the Pan-American Highway. Both are beside clean beaches. There are also several campsites between Coquimbo and Los Vilos.

Restaurants *La Barca; Mai Lan Fan* (excellent Chinese cuisine), *Don Pepe* (seafood).

Museum In 1981 heavy rain uncovered 39 ancient burials of humans and llamas which had been sacrificed. A small museum has been built behind the Post Office to exhibit these.

Excursions Good beaches to the S at Totoralillo (good swimming), Guanaqueros (30 km.) and Tongoy (56 km.). If motoring, watch the fuel gauge; the nearest service station is at Coquimbo. In the suburb of Guayacán there is one of Eiffel's steel churches.

From here to Santiago, the Pan-American Highway mainly follows the coastline, passing many beautiful coves, alternatively rocky and sandy, with good surf, but the water is very cold, as is the air. The last stretch before Santiago is through green valleys with rich blue clover and wild artichokes. Beware, the green caterpillars crossing the road in November sting!

From La Serena or Coquimbo, 51 km. SE by road, is the little town of **Andacollo**. (colectivo, US$2.40; bus, US$1.70—last 20 km. of road very bad). Here, on 24 to 28 December, is held a most picturesque religious ceremony. The pilgrimage to the shrine of the miraculous Virgen del Rosario de Andacollo is the occasion for ritual dances dating from a pre-Spanish past. The church is huge. Alluvial gold washing and manganese and copper mining in the area. No hotel, but some *pensiones*; during the festival private houses rent beds and some let you pay for a shower. Colectivos run to the festival from Calle Benavente, near Colocolo, in La Serena, but "purists" walk (torch and good walking shoes essential). 2 villages are passed on the route, which starts on the paved highway, then goes along a railway track and lastly up a steep, dusty hill.

Ovalle is S of Coquimbo in the valley of the Limarí river, inland from the sea. There are bus services from Coquimbo and La Serena (US$1.10, about 5 a day, 2 hrs.). It is the centre of a fruit, sheep-rearing, and mining district. Market days are Mon., Wed., Fri. and Sat., till 1600; the market is by the railway on Benavente (*feria agrícola*). Population: 72,765. 115 km. S by gravel road is the town of Combarbalá, where there is a TB sanatorium. Campsite. A 30 km. road runs NW to the small port of Tongoy, which has become quite popular among the locals for their summer break. The Paloma dam, at the confluence of the Grande and Huatulame rivers, SE of Ovalle, is one of the largest in Chile.

Hotels *Hotel de Turismo*, Victoria 295, T 620159; *Quisco*, Maestranza 161, T 620351; *American Hotel*, V. Mackenna 169, T 620722, on Libertad, *Buenos Aires*, No. 136, E, no locks on doors, O.K.; *Francia*, No. 231, T 620828, E; *Venecia*, No. 261, T 620968, also E; **Restaurant** *El Bosco*, Benavente 88, good, cheap; *La Económica*, also on Benavente, good.

Museum Museo Regional, Calle Independencia, open Tues.-Sun. 1000-1600, has 3 rooms, information on petroglyphs and a collection of Diaguita artefacts.

Buses 2 a day to Santiago, at 0930 and 0030, 6½ hrs., US$7, Empresas LAN and Chispa.

Excursions The **Monumento Nacional Valle del Encanto**, about 22 km. from Ovalle, has Indian petroglyphs as well as dramatic boulders, its own microclimate, cacti and lizards. No local bus service; you must take long distance bus and ask to be dropped off—3 km. walk to the valley; may be necessary to hitch back. Camping facilities are being upgraded. The **Parque Nacional Fray Jorge** (40 km.) has interesting forest land, which contrasts with the otherwise barren surroundings (very poorly signposted). Round trip in taxi, US$30. 2 km. N of Ovalle along Monte Patria road is Balnearia Los Peñones, on a clean shallow river. NE is the **Monumento Nacional Pichasca**, which has archaeological remains and petrified tree trunks. Daily bus from Ovalle to Río Hurtado pass the turn off 42 km from the city.

Termas de Socos, 35 km. S of Ovalle, has fine thermal springs (entrance US$1.30), a good hotel (C, T Ovalle 1373, Casilla 323) and a campsite (about US$1.50 p.p.) nearby. Bus US$2.

About 165 km. S of Ovalle by road, and 59 km. by new paved road from Los Vilos, is *Illapel*, in the basin of the river Choapa (Hotel). Population: 25,600. Fruit, grains and cattle are raised in the valley.

Los Vilos, 280 km. S of Coquimbo, is a small seaside resort with frequent launches to the off-shore Isla de La Reina and a beautiful nearby beach (26 km. S) at *Pichidangui*. On the pier at Los Vilos are some old, British-manufactured railway engines; the pier is only used now for fishing from. Good fresh seafood is available near the harbour.

Hotels in Los Vilos *Cabañas Antulanquen*, B (negotiable during off season), good service, own porch, kitchenette, rec.; *Hostería Puquen*, good restaurant, clean, honest, D, good restaurant; *Hostería Arrayán*, clean, E; *Lord Willow*, Hostería 1444, overlooking beach and harbour, E with breakfast and bath, pleasant; *Bellavista*, Rengo 20, F, shared bath, hot water, clean. The *Panamerican Motel* is right on the highway, Km. 224, and is a convenient stopping place between La Serena and Viña del Mar or Santiago; it claims to be American style, which will surprise Americans, but is quite good. Campsite on Av. El Bosque. **In Pichidangui**: *Motel El Bosque*, rec.; *Motel Pichidangui*, Francis Drake s/n, C, swimming pool; various other hotels and *pensiones* in every price range. Restaurants tend to be pricey although there is a food shop. Only 1 bus daily Pichidangui-Santiago, but N-S buses on the Highway are in walking distance of the beach.

Just south of Pichidangui is Los Molles, a small town where many wealthy residents of Santiago have their summer homes. There are two small hotels, one down at the beach and the other on the cliff overlooking the beach. *Restaurant La Pirata Suiza*, excellent European-style cooking, run by a Swiss couple.

See page 496 for list of service stations between Santiago and the Peruvian border.

SANTIAGO AND THE HEARTLAND (3)

(From the River Aconcagua to the River Bío-Bío)

Nearly 70% of the people of Chile live in the comparatively small heartland. The capital, Santiago, is here, and so is the largest port: Valparaíso. The rural density of population in the area is exceptional for Latin America: it is as high as 48 to the square km. in the Central Valley running S from Santiago to Concepción.

Region	Provinces	Population ('000) 1982	1987
V (Valparaíso)	Petorca, Los Andes, San Felipe de Aconcagua, Quillota, Valparaíso, San Antonio, Isla de Pascua	1,205	1,336
Metropolitan	Santiago, Chacabuco, Cordillera, Maipo, Melipilla, Talagante	4,295	4,913
VI (O'Higgins)	Cachapoal, Colchagua, Cardenal Caro	585	628
VII (Maule)	Curicó, Talca, Linares, Maule	723	805
VIII (Bío Bío)	Ñuble, Concepción, Arauco, Bío-Bío,	1,517	1,626

CHILEAN HEARTLAND AND SANTIAGO
52

From a third to half of the width of the area is taken up by the Andes, which are formidably high in the northern sector; at the head of the river Aconcagua the peak of Aconcagua, the highest in the Americas, rises to 6,964 metres. S of Talca, and to the W of the main range, there is a series of active volcanoes; the region suffers from earthquakes. There is a mantle of snow on the mountains: at Aconcagua it begins at 4,300 metres; at Curicó at 3,350; at Bío-Bío at 1,980. The lower slopes are covered with dense forests. Between the forest and the snowline there are alpine pastures which narrow towards the S; during the summer cattle are driven up to these pastures to graze.

The coastal range takes up another third of the width. It is lower here than in the northern desert, but the shoreline is still unbroken; it is only at Valparaíso, San Antonio and Talcahuano (the port for Concepción) that good harbourage is to be found. The coastal range is over 2,130 metres high in the N, but it falls gradually to about 600 metres near Concepción.

Between the coastal range and the Andes lies the Central Valley; most rivers cross it at right angles and cut their way to the sea through narrow canyons in the coastal range, but the Maule and the Bío-Bío have broad valleys along the whole of their courses. The valley of the Aconcagua is separated by a mountainous spur from the valley of the Mapocho, in which Santiago lies, but from Santiago to Concepción the Central Valley is continuous. The land here is extremely fruitful.

There is rain during the winter in the heartland, but the summers are dry. The rain increases to the S. On the coast at Viña del Mar it is 483 mm. a year; at Talcahuano it is 1,168 mm., but is somewhat less inland. Temperatures, on the other hand, are higher inland than on the coast. There is frost now and then in the Central Valley, but very little snow falls.

Santiago, founded by Pedro de Valdivia in 1541, is the fifth largest city in South America, with 4m people, and one of the most beautifully set of any, standing in a wide plain, 600 metres above the sea. The city is crossed from E to W by the Río Mapocho, which passes through an artificial stone channel, 40 metres wide, spanned by several bridges. Public gardens, laid out with admirable taste, are filled with flowers and kept in good order. The magnificent chain of the Andes, with its snow-capped heights, is in full view for much of the year, rain and smog permitting; there are peaks of 6,000 metres about 100 km. away. More than half the country's manufacturing is done here; it is essentially a modern capital, full of bustle, noise, traffic, smog (tables for which are published in the daily papers) and skyscrapers.

The centre of the city lies between the Mapocho and the Avenida O'Higgins. From the Plaza Baquedano (Plaza Italia), in the E of the city's central area, the Mapocho flows to the NW and the Avenida O'Higgins runs to the SW. From Plaza Baquedano the Calle Merced runs due W to the Plaza de Armas, the heart of the city; it lies 5 blocks S of the Mapocho. On the eastern and southern sides of Plaza de Armas there are arcades with shops; on the northern side is the Post Office and the City Hall; and on the western side the Cathedral and the archbishop's palace. The Cathedral, much rebuilt, contains a recumbent statue in wood of St. Francis Xavier, and the chandelier which lit the first meetings of Congress after the liberation; it also houses an interesting museum of religious art and historical pieces. In the Palacio de la Real Audiencia on the Plaza de Armas is the Museo Histórico Nacional (see **Museums**, below). A block W of the Cathedral is the Congress building; the Congress, which held no sittings after 1973, has now been moved to Valparaíso to a purpose-built building for the two houses of government. A commission is studying the possibility of congress returning to Santiago, but for the time being, Valparaíso will remain the seat of government. The original Congress building is at present the Ministry of Foreign Affairs. Nearby are the law courts. At Calle Merced 864, close to the Plaza de Armas, is the Casa

Colorada, built in 1769, the home of the Governor in colonial days and then of Mateo de Toro, first President of Chile. It is now the Museum of the History of Santiago.

The Avenida O'Higgins (usually known as the Alameda) runs through the heart of the city for over 3 km. It is 100 metres wide, and ornamented with gardens and statuary: the most notable are the equestrian statues of Generals O'Higgins and San Martín; the statue of the Chilean historian Benjamín Vicuña Mackenna who, as mayor of Santiago, beautified Cerro Santa Lucía (see **Parks and Gardens** below); and the great monument in honour of the battle of Concepción in 1879.

From the Plaza Baquedano, where there is a statue of General Baquedano and the Tomb of the Unknown Soldier, the Alameda skirts, on the right, Cerro Santa Lucía, and on the left, the Catholic University. Beyond the hill the Alameda goes past the neo-classical National Library on the right, which also contains the national archives. Beyond, on the left, between Calle San Francisco and Calle Londres, is the oldest church in Santiago: the red-walled church and monastery of San Francisco. Inside is the small statue of the Virgin which Valdivia carried on his saddlebow when he rode from Peru to Chile. Beside the church is the Museum of Colonial Art. On the left, a little further along, is the University of Chile; the Club de la Unión is almost opposite. The Municipal Theatre is on Calle Agustinas with Calle San Antonio 149, and nearby on Calle Nueva York is the Bolsa de Comercio.

N of Plaza de la Libertad, hemmed in by the skyscrapers of the Civic Centre, is the **Palacio de la Moneda** (1805), containing historic relics, paintings and sculpture, and the elaborate "Salón Rojo" used for official receptions. Until 1990 at least, written permission was required to visit the Moneda, and that was difficult to obtain. The Moneda was damaged by air attacks during the military coup of 11 September 1973; repairs are now completed and the presidential offices have been restored. In front of the Palace is the statue of Arturo Alessandri Palma, who was President of the Republic for two terms.

The Alameda runs westwards to the Planetarium and, opposite it on the southern side, the Estación Central (or Alameda), the railway station for the S. On Avenida Matucana, running N from here, is the very popular Parque Quinta Normal. About seven blocks west of the Estación Central is the southern bus terminal.

Four blocks north of the Plaza de Armas is the interesting Mercado Central, at Puente 21 de Mayo. The building faces the Parque Valenzuela, on which is the Cal y Canto metro station, the northern terminus of Line 2, and, at its western end, the former Mapocho railway station. No trains run from the station, which is being converted into a cultural centre; exhibitions are already being held there. The centre is planned to include the prison which is beside it (currently in use). Four blocks west of Mapocho station is the northern bus terminal. If you head east from Mapocho station, along the river, you pass through the Parque Forestal (see below), before coming back to Plaza Baquedano.

Between the Parque Forestal, Plaza Baquedano and the Alameda is the Lastarria neighbourhood (Universidad Católica metro). For those interested in antique furniture, objets d'art and old books, the area is worth a visit, especially the Plaza Mulato Gil de Castro (Cale José V. Lastarria 305). Occasional shows are

Santiago Orientation: Key to map

1. Plaza de Armas; 2. Cerro Santa Lucia; 3. Plaza de la Libertad; 4. Plaza de la Constitución; 5. Plaza Baquedano; 6. Parque Forestal; 31. Airport bus; 32. Parque O'Higgins; 33. Plaza Ercilla; 34. Parque Quinta Normal, and Museo del Ferrocarril; 35. Museo de Historica Natural; 36. Museo de la Aviación; 37. Cerro San Cristóbal; 38. Funicular; 39. Virgen; 40. Observatory of the Catholic University; 41 Teleférico; 42. Jardín Zoológico; 43. Museo de los Tajamares/Parque Balmaceda; 44. Providencia district; 45. Bellavista district; 46. Los Leones; 47. Former Mapocho station; 48. Market; 49. Sernatur; 50. Conaf; 51. Palacio Cousiño.

put on in the square, on which are the Museo Arqueológico de Santiago in a restored house, a bookshop (*Librería Latinoamericana*), handicraft and antique shops, and art gallery, the Instituto de Arte Contemporáneo and the *Pergola de la Plaza* restaurant. Nearby, on Lastarria, are the Jardín Lastarria, a cul-de-sac of craft and antique shops (No.293), *Gutenberg, Lafourcade y Cía*, an antiquarian bookseller (No.307), the Ciné Biógrafo (No. 131) and, at the corner with Merced, the Instituto Chileno-Francés (see below).

On the north bank of the Mapocho from Plaza Baquedano is the Bellavista district, stretching from Calle Loreto to Calle Concha. At the foot of Cerro San Cristóbal (see below), this area is full of restaurants and cafés, theatres, entertainments, art galleries and craft shops (especially those selling lapis lazuli, a semi-precious stone found only in Chile and Afghanistan).

East of Plaza Baquedano, the main east-west axis of the city becomes Avenida Providencia which heads out towards the residential areas, such as Las Condes, at the eastern and upper levels of the city. It passes the new headquarters of Sernatur (the national tourist board), the modern shopping, office and restaurant areas around Pedro de Valdivia and Los Leones metro stations (collectively known as Providencia), to become Avenida Apoquindo at Tobalaba metro.

Parks and Gardens

Cerro Santa Lucía, bounded by Calle Merced to the north, Avenida O'Higgins to the south, Calles Santa Lucía and Subercaseaux is a cone of rock rising steeply to a height of 70 metres. It can be scaled from the Caupolicán esplanade, on which, high on a rock, stands a statue of that Mapuche leader, but the ascent from the northern side of the hill, where there is an equestrian statue of Diego de Almagro, is easier. There are striking views of the city from the top (reached by a series of stairs), where there is a fortress, the Batería Hidalgo (the platform of which is its only colonial survival—the building is closed). Even on smoggy days, the view of the sunset is good; the Cerro closes at 2100. It is best to descend the eastern side, to see the small Plaza Pedro Valdivia with its waterfalls and statue of Valdivia. The area is famous, at night, for its gay community.

The great Parque O'Higgins (Parque O'Higgins metro station on Line 2, or bus from Parque Baquedano via Avs. Mackenna and Matta), is about 10 blocks south of Avenida O'Higgins. It has a small lake, playing fields, tennis courts, swimming pool (open from 5 Dec.), an open-air stage for local songs and dances, a discothèque, the racecourse of the Club Hípico, an amusement park, Fantasilandia, admission US$1.50 (open on weekends only in winter, and not when raining), kite-fighting contests on Sunday, and a group of about twenty good "typical" restaurants, some craft shops, the Museo del Huaso, an aquarium and a small insect and shellfish museum at El Pueblito. Cars are not allowed in the Parque.

In the large Parque Quinta Normal, north of the Estación Central, are four museums, details of which are given below.

There are several other parks in Santiago, but perhaps the most notable is the

---

Santiago centre: Key to map

1. Plaza de Armas; 2. Cerro Santa Lucia; 3. Plaza de la Libertad; 4. Plaza de la Constitución; 5. Plaza Baquedano; 6. Parque Forestal; 7. Cathedral; 8. Archbishop's Palace; 9. San Francisco Church and Museo de Arte Colonial; 10. Santo Domingo; 11. Palacio de la Moneda; 12. Municipalidad; 13. Museo Histórico Nacional; 14. Congress; 15. Palacio de la Justicia; 16. Museo de la Santiago/Casa Colorada; 17. Museo de la Merced; 18. Museo de Arte Precolombino; 19. Museo de Bellas Artes; 20. Biblioteca Nacional; 21. Teatro Municipal; 22. Bolsa de Comercio; 23. Universidad de Chile; 24. Club de la Unión; 25. Plaza de Mulato Gil de Castro/Lastarria neighbourhood; 26. Argentine Embassy; 27. Post Offices; 28. CTC Telephone Office; 29. Entel Telephone Office; 30. Federación de Andinismo; 31. Airport bus.

Parque Forestal, due N of Santa Lucía hill and immediately S of the Mapocho. The Museo Nacional de Bellas Artes is in the wooded grounds and is an extraordinary example of neo-classical architecture (details below). The Parque Balmaceda (Parque Gran Bretaña), E of Plaza Baquedano, is perhaps the most beautiful in Santiago (the Museo de los Tajamares is here).

The sharp, conical hill of San Cristóbal, the Parque Metropolitano, to the NE of the city, is the largest and most interesting of the city's parks. A funicular railway goes up the 300-metre-high hill from Plaza Caupolicán at the northern end of Calle Pío Nono every few minutes from 1000-1900 Mon.-Fri., 0900-1930 Sat. and Sun. (closed for lunch 1330-1430); US$1, US$1.15 return. The funicular passes on its way up Jardín Zoológico (open 1000-1300, 1500-1800 weekdays, 1000-1800 Sat., Sun. and holidays, US$1.25 in week, US$1.40 weekends). The zoo is small, but clean, and the animals are well-cared for. A *teleférico* ascends from Estación Oasis, Av. Pedro de Valdivia Norte (only taxis go there, although it is not a long walk from Pedro de Valdivia metro station), via Tupahue to the summit, a short way from the funicular's upper station. The fare from Oasis is US$1.80 to the top, US$1.15 to Tupahue and US$1.80 return to Tupahue. A combined funicular/*teleférico* ticket is US$2. The *teleférico* runs 1000-1930 at weekends, 1500-1830 weekdays (in summer only), so to get to Tupahue on weekdays out of season you must take the funicular up and walk down from the summit (or drive, or take a taxi). An open bus operated by the *teleférico* company runs to Tupahue and the summit from the Pío Nono terminal with the same schedule as the *teleférico* itself.

On the hill's summit stands a colossal statue of the Virgin, which is floodlit at night; beside it is the astronomical observatory of the Catholic University which can be visited on application to the observatory's director. The hill is very well laid out around the Tupahue station, with terraces, gardens, and paths; in one building is a good, expensive restaurant with a splendid view from the terrace, especially at night, and an Enoteca, or exhibition of Chilean wines and tastery. (You can taste one of the three "wines of the day", US$0.30, and buy if you like.) The Casa de la Cultura has art exhibitions and free concerts at midday on Sundays. There are two good swimming pools: one at Tupahue, US$2.20 (US$2.70 at weekends); the other, Antilen, can be reached from the road that starts below the Enoteca. Also in the Tupahue vicinity are the Botanical Gardens, with a collection of Chilean native plants, beautifully laid out, guided tours available (recommended).

Things to do Ballet is popular. During the summer, free performances are given in the city parks, but seats are usually hard to get. The theatre (houses are listed below) is more active than in most Latin American capitals. Daily lists of events in *El Mercurio* and *La Epoca* should be consulted; *El Mercurio's Wikén* magazine on Friday has the most comprehensive listings.

During November there is a free art fair on the banks of the Mapocho River flowing through Parque Forestal, lasting a fortnight. In October or November there are a sumptuous flower show and an annual agricultural and industrial show (known as Fisa) in Parque Cerrillos. Religious festivals and ceremonies continue throughout Holy Week, when a priest ritually washes the feet of 12 men. The image of the Virgen del Carmen (patron of the Armed Forces) is carried through the streets by cadets on 16 July.

Climate In the central region (including Santiago and Valparaíso) the climate is Mediterranean: temperatures can reach 29°C in January, but fall to 13°C (3°C at night) in July. Days are usually hot, the nights cool.

Museums

Note, almost all museums are closed on Monday.

Museo Historico Nacional, Plaza de Armas 951, covers the period from the Conquest until 1925 (well worthwhile); open Tues.-Sat. 1000-1730, Sun. and holidays 1000-1345 (Sunday free, but donation welcome).

Museo de Santiago, Casa Colorada, Merced 860, history of Santiago from the Conquest to modern times, excellent displays and models, guided tours; open Tues.-Sat., 1000-1800,

Sun. and holidays (free), 1000-1300, free.

Museo Chileno de Arte Precolombino, Bandera 361, in the former Real Aduana, recommended, representative exhibition of objects from the precolombian cultures of Central America and the Andean region; open Tues.-Sat. 1000-1800 (US$0.35), Sun. (free) 1000-1400. Booklet, US$0.35.

Museo Iglesia de la Merced, MacIver 341, colonial religious art and archaeological collection from Easter Island; Tues.-Fri. 1000-1300, 1500-1800, Sat. 1000-1300.

Museo de Arte Sagrado, in the Cathedral, open Monday only, 1030-1300, 1530-1900, free.

Museo Arte Colonial, Londres 4, beside Iglesia San Francisco, religious art, including one room with 54 paintings of the life of St Francis; in the cloisters is a room containing Gabriela Mistral's Nobel medal; also a collection of locks; Tues.-Sat. 1000-1800, Sun. 1000-1400, US$0.25.

The Palacio de la Alhambra, Compañia 1340 (with Amunátegui) is a national monument sponsored by the Society of Arts; it stages exhibitions of paintings as well as having a permanent display; open Mon.-Fri. 1100-1300, 1700-1900, T 80875.

Biblioteca Nacional, Moneda 650, temporary exhibitions of books, book illustrations, documents, posters, etc.

At Calle Dieciocho 438, some 5 blocks S of the Alameda, is the **Palacio Cousiño**, a large elaborate mansion amongst crumbling buildings and shanties; it contains some good oriental rugs and 19th-century European furniture. It is run by the Corporación Cultural as a museum; open Tues.-Sun. 1000-1300, free, but donations welcome. Visitors must be accompanied by a guide and wear cloth bootees to protect the floors.

Museo Nacional de Historia Natural, in the Parque Quinta Normal, has exhibitions on zoology, botany, mineralogy, anthropology, ethnography and archaeology; open Tues.-Fri. 1000-1230, 1400-1730, Sat.-Sun. 1000-1730 (Sunday free). The **Museo Ferroviario** is also in the Quinta Normal; it has 13 steam engines built between 1884 and 1953 (open Tues.-Sun. 1000-1300, 1400-1730, Sat., Sun. and holidays, 1100-1400, 1500-1800). The **Museo Aeronáutico**, by the Parque Quinta Normal (Av. Portales 3530) is also worth a visit; Tues.-Sun. 1000-1800, free, T 90888. Also in the Quinta Normal is the **Museo Ciencia y Tecnología**, open same hours as **Ferroviario**. Nearby, at Av. O'Higgins 3349, is the excellent **Planetarium**, open Weds.-Fri. 1900, Sat.-Sun. 1700, 1900 and 2030, T 762624.

Museo Arqueológico de Santiago, in Plaza Mulato Gil de Castro, Lastarria 307, temporary exhibitions of Chilean archaeology, anthropology and precolombian art; open Tues.-Sat., 1100-1400, 1600-2000, Sun. 1100-1400, free.

In the Parque Forestal is the **Museo Nacional de Bellas Artes**, which has a large display of Chilean and foreign painting and sculpture, and contemporary art exhibitions are held several times a year (Tues.-Sat. 1000-1800, Sun. and holidays 1000-1330; free on Sunday). In the west wing of the building is the **Museo de Arte Popular Americano**, a collection of North and South American folk art (this wing is awaiting renovation, so only a small part of the exhibition is on display). Similarly, the **Museo de Arte Contemporáneo** is on limited view as it is normally housed in the west wing.

Museo Tajamares del Mapocho, Parque Balmaceda, Av. Providencia 222, an exhibition of the 17th and 18th century walls built to protect the city from flooding by the river, and of the subsequent canalization; Tues.-Sat. 1000-1800, Sun. 1000-1330.

Museo Benjamín Vicuña Mackenna, Av. V. Mackenna 94, recording the life and works of the 19th century Chilean historian and biographer; occasional exhibitions.

In Parque O'Higgins, at Pueblito: **Museo del Huaso**, a small, interesting collection of criollo clothing and tools; Tues.-Fri. 1000-1300, 1430-1715, Sat., Sun. and holidays 1000-1800, free; **Municipal Aquarium** at Local 9, Tues.-Fri. 1000-2000 (till 2100 Sat., Sun., holidays—small charge); **Museo de Insectos y Caracoles**, Local 12, a collection of indigenous items, same hours as the aquarium but open till 2200 at weekends and holidays.

Museo de la Escuela Militar, Los Militares 4500, Las Condes, with displays on O'Higgins, the Conquest and the Pacific War, Mon.-Fri. 0930-1230, 1500-1800, Sat. 1500-1800, Sun. 1000-1300, free.

Museo de Artes Decorativos, Casas Lo Matta, Av. Presidente Kennedy 9350, Vitacura, a new, beautiful museum containing Don Hernán Garcés Silva's bequest to the nation: antique silverplate from South America and Europe, 16th-18th century Spanish colonial and European furniture, 15th century Books of Hours, housed in an 18th century country mansion. Guided tours available; by bus, take Intercomunal No.4 from Mapocho station, or take a taxi; in either case ask to be let out at "Casas lo Matta".

The house of Pablo Neruda, the poet, **La Chascona**, is at F. Márquez de la Plata 0192, Bellavista, now restored after earthquake damage in 1985 and headquarters of the Fundación Pablo Neruda. For an appointment to visit the poet's library, art and photo collections, T 778741 (see also page 542).

Hotels Check if breakfast anf 16% tax is included in the price quoted.

Hotels in the upper price brackets in the Providencia area are: *San Cristóbal Sheraton*, Av. Santa María 1742, T 745-528, FAX 223-6656, L+, with all facilities, also *Sheraton Towers*, slightly cheaper; *Santa María*, Av. Santa María 2050, T 232-6614, A; *Los Españoles*, Los Españoles 2539, T 232-1824, A; all three north of the Río Mapocho. *Orly*, Pedro de Valdivia 27, close to Pedro de Valdivia metro station, T 232-8225, A, but has smaller, cheaper rooms with less comfort, small, comfortable hotel but reported unreliable over reservations, has apartments for rent on Juana de Arco, just off Av. Pedro de Valdivia, 3 blocks S of Av. Providencia, good, US$70 a day (reductions may be possible). *Posada del Salvador*, Av. Eliodoro Yáñez 893, nearest metro Salvador, T 492-072, C with bath, friendly, English, French, German, Italian spoken.

Expensive hotels in the central area: *San Francisco Kempinski*, Alameda 816, T 392-832, FAX 397-826, Lufthansa affiliated, 5-star, L-L+, good; *Holiday Inn Crowne Plaza*, Av. B. O'Higgins 136, T 381-042, FAX 336-015, L-L+, all facilities, also good; also in L range, *Carrera*, Teatinos 180, T 698-2011, *El Conquistador*, Miguel Cruchaga 920, T 696-5599, *Galerías*, San Antonio 65, T 384-011, and *Tupahue*, San Antonio 477, T 383-810. *City*, Compañía 1063, T 724-526, B, clean, hot water, rec.; *Conde Ansúrez*, Av. República 25, T 698-3779, B, convenient for central station and southern bus terminal, clean, helpful, safe, luggage stored (100 metres from metro República); *Libertador*, Av. O'Higgins 853, T394-212, B, helpful, rec., will store luggage, good restaurant, bar, roof top pool; *Panamericano*, Teatinos 320 y Huérfanos, T 723-060, B, comfortable, serves popular business lunch between 1230 and 1530; on Huérfanos, *Don Tito*, No.578, T 391-987, A, good, English spoken; *Santa Lucía*, No. 779, 4th floor, T 398-201, garage 2 blocks away, B, clean, comfortable, front rooms a little noisy and tatty; *Gran Palace*, No. 1178, T 712-551, B, with shower, clean, noisy rooms facing street (others quiet), good restaurant. *Hostal del Parque*, Merced 294, just across from Parque Forestal, T 392-694, L, excellent; *Foresta*, Subercaseaux 353, T396-262, A, and *Monte Carlo*, Subercaseaux 209, T 339-905, both at bottom of Santa Lucía, the latter rec., modern, restaurant, with heating, B-A.

C-D range hotels in the centre: *Apart-Hotel Agustinas*, Agustinas 1990, T 711-002, clean, quiet at back, C, rec., secure parking; *Du Maurier*, Moneda 1512, T 724-257, C, handy for catching early (0630) Aerobus Tour Express; *Residencia Alicia Adasme*, Moneda 2055, T 6960787, hot water, friendly, with breakfast, C; *Imperio*, O'Higgins 2879, near central station, T 97774, C with bath, good restaurant; *Vegas*, Londres 49, C, clean, TV/radio, decent-sized rooms, more with breakfast; *Hotel Turismo Japón*, Almte. Barroso 160, T 698-4500, C, helpful, manager speaks English, rec.; *España*, Morandé 510, T696-6066, D/E without bath, hot water, clean, friendly; *Cervantes*, Morandé 631, D, T 96-5318, good value but noisy; *Residencial Tabita* (Tabita Gutiérrez), Príncipe de Gales 81 (cul-de-sac off Moneda between Amunátegui and San Martín, T 715-700), D with breakfast, clean, safe, central, temperamental hot showers upstairs, popular; *São Paulo*, San Antonio 357, T 398-031/2/3, D with bath, clean, good value.

Cheaper central hotels: *Residencial Londres,* Londres 54, T 382-215, near San Francisco Church, former mansion, Victorian furniture, some gloomy rooms, otherwise rec. repeatedly, E, more with bath (often full after 1000—don't confuse with *Hotel Londres* opp., which is not rec.), breakfast US$0.65 extra; *París,* Calle Paris 813, nearby, E with bath, quiet, clean, also short-stay; *Residencial Mery,* Pasaje República 36, off 0-100 block of República (T 696-8883), big green building down an alley, E, hot showers, quiet, rec.; *Res. Alemania,* República 220 (no sign), T 712-388, nr. Metro República, E, hot water, clean, pleasant atmosphere, good cheap meals available, rec. *Res. Santo Domingo,* Santo Domingo 735, near MacIver, central, E with full board, good cheap lunches Mon.-Fri.; *Indiana,* Rosas 1339, T714-251, convenient for buses to centre, only front rooms with bath, hot water, back rooms poor, basic but OK, E; *Gran,* Morandé y San Pablo, F-E (with bath), simple but OK, short and long stay.

Convenient accommodation for southern bus terminal and Estación Central: *Antiguo Palace,* San Alfonso 24, 2 blocks E of Central Station, 1 metro stop from southern bus station, F, good value, clean. Those on República (see above) are only 2-3 metro stops away. On F. Reich, 100-200 block, behind the bus terminal are *Roma* and *México,* both F. Sra Isaura Tobar Urra, Federico Scott 130, N side of Alameda opp. bus terminal, G p.p. without breakfast, good meals available, hot water, clean, good. *Marconi,* O'Higgins 2532, F without bath, clean, cheap rooms on Avenida, very noisy, 15 mins. from bus terminal.

Around the northern bus terminal, *Caribe,* San Martín 821, F p.p., clean, basic, hot showers, convenient to centre and bus station, safe to leave luggage but mainly short-stay; many on Mackenna, e.g. *San Felipe* in 1200 block (rec.), most are basic, but are between the bus terminal and Cal y Canto metro. **N.B.** Many hotels on Morandé, Gen. Mackenna, San Martín and San Pablo are convenient for northern bus terminal, but are in the red light district and are therefore cheap in both senses of the word.

As the above list shows there is little good accommodation under US$10 a night. Travellers can find comfortable guesthouse lodging through *Amigos de Todo el Mundo,* Av. Bulnes 285, dept. 201, PO Box 52861 Correo Central, T 726-525, Sr Arturo Navarrete, prices from US$6 with breakfast, other meals extra, monthly rates available, rec. Sra Marta, Amengual 035, Alameda Alt. 4.400, T 797592, lado Norte (metro Ecuador), F p.p., good family accommodation. **Casa del Estudiante Americano,** Huérfanos 1891, G p.p., good dormitory accommodation—acts as youth hostel out of season, must be in bed by 2200 and out by 1000 (Metro Los Héroes—7 blocks from centre over motorway).

For longer stay accommodation, read the classified ads in *El Mercurio,* flats, homes and family *pensiones* are listed by district. A small studio can cost from US$50 a month, a house much more; staying with a family is an economical and interesting option for a few months. A recommended estate agent is Sra. Carmen Martínez Jara, Av. 11 de Septiembre 2155, Ed. Panorámico, Torre B, oficina 502, T 251-7331/231-5955. Providencia and Las Condes are residential districts, but the latter is some way from the centre; the area west of Plaza Baquedano, east of Cerro Santa Lucía and south of Parque Forestal is good and central; or you could try Bellavista, but not Calle Pío Nono where the nightlife goes on until 0300.

Youth Hostel information available from Av. Providencia 2594, oficina 421 (between metros Los Leones and Tobalaba), T 231-5649 (worth getting list of YH addresses around country as these change year by year—even in Santiago). Hostels in the capital, Grajales 2013, metro República, T 726100, and Almte. Latorre 449, T 698-8315, same metro, both G p.p.

Camping The campsite on San Cristóbal hill has been closed because of muggings. Alternatives are the Farellones road near the river; or S of Santiago near Puente Alto (take Av. J. Pedro Alessandri S to Las Vizcachas and La Obra where there is a small park on left side of road). At Km. 25 S of city on Panamericana, Esso garage offers only a vacant lot near highway. Club Camping Maki, and Casino Camping, both 70 km. from Santiago, **see page** 534. Rec. camping at Tenis Centrum Alemán, Parcela 68, Santa Ana de Chena, Camino Lonquén, run by Dieter and Myriam Mittelstaedt (take Panamericana Sur for 9 km., turn right at blue and white water tower, then 4.5 km. on road to Los Espejo, look for sign, then 4 km. on right); 5 good courts, hot showers, small restaurant, US$1.50 p.p. per day. Standard camping gas cartridges can be bought at Unisport, Providencia 2503, or Santo Domingo 1079. Other equipment for camper-vans from Bertonati Hnos, Manuel Montt 2385. Caravans (US model Tioga) can be rented from Castanera Turismo, Av. Providencia 1072, local 14 D. Tent repairs: Juan Soto, Silva Vildosola 890, Paradero 1, Gran Avenida, San Miguel, Santiago, T 555-8329. Reinaldo Lippi, Toesca 2171, makes tents, sleeping bags, back packs, etc., and does repairs, most helpful. Camping goods from Club Andino and Federación de Andinismo (see page 535 below): expensive because these articles are imported. Cheaper boots from Edvobal, Paseo Las Palmas 2242, metro Los Leones, T 251 5488.

Restaurants In addition to those at the main hotels and those in Parque O'Higgins there are, in the centre of the city: *Pinpilinpausha*, Matías Cousiño 62, good, cheap; *Da Carla*, MacIver 577, Italian food, very good; also Italian, *San Marco*, Huérfanos 618, serving seafood and vegetarian as well, not cheap (US$12 p.p. with drinks) but excellent; *Le Due Torri*, San Antonio 258, expensive, closed Sun.; *Les Assassins*, Merced 297, French, rec.; *La Omelette*, Agustinas near AmEx, clean and good, closes 2100. *Gran Parrillada la Brasileña*, San Diego 265, huge portions, rec.

Seafood: *Don Lucho, Rey del Pescado*, Banderas 848, good food but poor atmosphere; *Atelier*, Tenderini 171, rec., good, but expensive; *El 27 de Nueva York*, Nueva York 27, central, good; *Savory Tres*, Ahumada 327, good and reasonable, particularly seafood. Some of the best seafood restaurants are to be found in the Mercado Central (by Cal y Canto metro), or on the other side of the Mapocho from there.

For mainly local food in the centre: *Chez Henry*, on Plaza de Armas, excellent empanadas, parrillada de mariscos a speciality, dining room at back of butcher's shop has live music and dancing, a/c is cold (also does take away meals), also has a delicatessen at Alameda 847, which is highly rec.; *Marco Polo* in Plaza de Armas, local dishes, clean; also in Plaza de Armas, *Raison d'Or*, good pastel de choclo, pleasant place to have a drink and watch the world go by; on Phillips, the small street off the east side of the Plaza is *La Zanahoria*, clean, good lunches. *Silvestre*, Huérfanos 956, open 0800-2400, good buffet-style, US$3; *Mermoz*, Huérfanos 1048, good; *Bar Nacional No. 1*, Huérfanos 1087, good restaurant; *Guima*, Huérfanos y Teatinos, good, reasonable prices; *Café Dante*, Merced 801 y San Antonio, for pastel de choclo; *Bar Central*, San Pablo 1063, typical food, rec.; *Verdijo*, Morandé 526, good food, noisy, cheap and popular; *Bar-restaurant Inés de Suárez*, Morandé 558, cheap and good; *El Lugar de Don Quijote*, café, and *Parrilladas de Don Quijote*, restaurant, good, corner Morandé and Catedral; two doors away is *Congreso*, popular at lunchtime. *Café Amazonas*, 21 de Mayo 784, round corner from Mercado Central, good, inexpensive, English/German owned, popular meeting place with notice board. *Los Adobes de Argomedo*, Argomedo 411 y Lira, hacienda-style, Chilean food and spectacular floor show including cueca dancing, salsa and folk, Mon.-Sat., only place in winter which has this type of entertainment on a Monday. There are many cheap places along Paseo Ahumada, between the Plaza de Armas and the Alameda.

Oriental in the centre: *Guo Fung*, Moneda 1549, rec.; *Yuet Wong Chan*, Agustinas 715, delicious food; *Chifa Kam Thu*, Santo Domingo 769 y 21 de Mayo, good value; *Pai Fu*, Santa Rosa 101 y París, good; all Chinese.

In the Lastarria and Bellavista neighbourhoods: *La Pergola de la Plaza* in Plaza Mulato Gil de Castro, but better still, and close by, is *Quiche Lorraine* in the Instituto Chileno-Francés, Merced 298 y Lastarria, highly rec. for food, drink and ambience. *Café Universitario*, Alameda 395 y Victoria Subercaseaux (near Sta. Lucía), good, cheap almuerzos. *Eladio*, Pío Nono, nr. foot of San Cristóbal funicular, good steaks, but expensive; also near the funicular station on Pío Nono are *La Puña* and *Los Ladrillos*, popular, lively; *Café del Cerro*, Ernesto Pinto Lazarrigue 192, T 778-308, with live music (check *El Mercurio* for programme), US$2 door charge, highly rec. *Karim*, Pío Nono (Arabian); good; *Zingarrella*, Pío Nono, Italian, good.

Outside the centre, in the Providencia: *La Pizza Nostra*, Providencia 1979, sells good Italian food as well as pizzas, real coffee, pricey; *da Renato*, Mardoqueo Fernández 138 (metro Los Leones), Italian, good; *El Parrón*, Providencia 1188, parrilladas, the local dice game of "dudo" is played in the bar; *Gatsby*, Providencia at Pedro de Valdivia, American food, as-much-as-you-can-eat buffet US$8, lunch/dinner US$10, snack bar open till 2400, tables outside in warm weather, good; *Tung Kung*, Providencia 1091, Chinese; *Danubio Azul* (Chinese), Reyes Lavalle 3240 (near Metro El Golf). *del Centro Catalá*, Av. Suecia 428 near Lota, good, reasonably-priced. Recommended places on El Bosque Norte, Providencia: *München*, No. 204, German, *Angus*, No. 0111, international.

Many first-class restaurants out of the centre can be found in the Las Condes district, including grills, Chilean cuisine (often with music), French cuisine and Chinese. They tend to be more expensive than central restaurants. Good examples are *El Alero de Los de Ramón*, Av. Las Condes 9889 (Chilean cuisine and music, expensive but really excellent in both departments); *Canta Gallo*, Av. Las Condes 12345 (ditto); *La Querencia*, Av. Las Condes 14980, not dear for the quality; *Seriatutix*, Av. Colón 5137, restaurant and disco, live music, café, great atmosphere; *Praga*, Vitacura 3917, Czech; *Mexicano*, Vitacura 2916, Mexican; *Martín Carrera*, Isidora Goyenechea 3471, good nouvelle cuisine.

Vegetarian restaurants: *La Huerta*, café, Orrego Luco 54, (Providencia), metro Pedro de

Valdivia, and *El Huerto*, restaurant, next door, rec., open daily, live music at the restaurant, Fri. and Sat. evenings; *El Naturista*, Moneda 846, rec., also has a branch in Providencia, Orrego Luco Sur 42; *El Vegetariano*, Huérfanos 827, Galería Victoria, expensive, mixed reports; *Eos*, Av. Francisco Bilbao 3008, Providencia (metro Tobalaba), excellent, "no smoking, no alcohol"; *Govinda*, MacIver 531.

Cafés and Bars Many bars (some serve snacks) on Pedro Valdivia, very popular. *Café Paula*, several branches, e.g. Estado at entrance to Galería España, excellent coffee and cake, good breakfast, also on San Antonio opp. the Teatro Municipal. *Bar-Restaurant Casa Suiza*, Huérfanos 640 local 5 (Metro Sta. Lucía), good Swiss and Chilean food. *Café Santos*, Huérfanos 1011 y Ahumada, popular for "onces" (afternoon tea). Try *Café Haití* and *Café Caribe*, both on Paseo Ahumada for delicious coffee. *Tip-Top Galetas* rec. for freshly baked biscuits, branches throughout the city, e.g. Merced 867. *Salón de Té Tavelli*, Drugstore precinct, Providencia 2124, rec. *Café de la Dulcería Las Palmas*, Antonia López de Bello 190 (Bellavista), good pastries and lunches; *La Casona de San Ysidro*, Alameda 151, T 334-046, student-type café with Chilean folk music Fri. and Sat. night, rec.; *Bob Bon Oriental*, Merced 345, superb Turkish cakes.

Geo Pub, Encomenderos 83, owner Francisco Valle speaks English, pub and restaurant with travel films once a week in winter, music occasionally, popular with travellers, rec.; *Phone Box Pub*, Providencia 1670, T 496627, slightly more expensive; *Violín Pub*, Providencia 1684, good lunch; *Cross Keys Pub*, Las Bellotas 270 local 5, opp. *La Mia Pappa*, near Los Leones metro, English, with darts, pints, etc., good value. Note that almost all hotel bars are closed Sun.

For snacks and excellent ice cream, try *Coppellia*, Av. Providencia 2211, *Bravissimo*, same avenida No. 1406, and *El Toldo Azul*, at No. 1936.

Clubs Ñuñoa (T 223 7846), with swimming pool, tennis courts and school; Polo y Equitación San Cristóbal; Chess Club, Alameda O'Higgins 898, Mon.-Sat. 1800, lively.

Shopping *El Almacén Campesino*, Purísima 289, Bellavista, handicrafts from all over Chile. Best bargains are handicraft articles, black pottery (best bought in Pomaire, 50 km. away, **see page** 534) and beautiful wrought copper and bronze. The best place for handmade tapestries is Talleres Artesanales, Lyon 100, in a subway near Los Leones metro, Providencia. Good shops for local copper work are Bozzo, at Ahumada 12 in the centre, and at Av. Providencia 2125. The gemstone lapis lazuli is best bought in the numerous outlets on Bellavista (shop around), but is cheaper around the market. *H. Stern* jewellery shops are located at the *San Cristóbal Sheraton* and *Carrera* hotels, and at the International Airport. *Cema-Chile* (Centro de Madres), Portugal 351 and at Universidad de Chile metro stop, *Artesanía Popular Chilena*, Av. Providencia 2322 (near Los Leones metro), and *Artesanía Chilena*, Estado 337, have a good selection of handicrafts, and so do *Cema-Chile* branches in the provinces. *Talleres Solidarios*, 1st floor Vicaría de la Solidaridad, on Plaza de Armas (next door to the Cathedral). *Pel y Pel*, Pedro de Valdivia 20, fur and leather articles, good. Antique stores in Plaza Mulato Gil de Castro and elsewhere on J.V. Lastarria (Merced end).

Beside and behind the Iglesia de los Dominicos, on Av. Nueva Apoquindo 9085, is *Los Graneros del Alba*, or *El Pueblo de Artesanía*, open daily except Mon., 1130-1900; all types of ware on sale, classes given in some shops. *Restaurant El Granero* is here. To get there, take a small, green Los Dominicos bus from Av. Providencia, or Apoquindo bus, as long as either is marked "Camino del Alba", or take an Apoquindo bus, similarly marked, from Metro Escuela Militar; get out at the children's playground at the junction of Apoquindo y Camino del Alba, at the foot of the hill leading up to the church, and walk up.

Mercado Central, between Puente y 21 de Mayo by the Río Mapocho (Cal y Canto metro) is excellent but quite expensive; there is a cheaper market on the opposite bank of the river. Centro Artesanal Santa Lucía, on Av. B. O'Higgins (Santa Lucía metro) has a wide variety of woollen goods, jewellery, wood, etc.; there are other craft markets in an alleyway, 1 block S of Av. B. O'Higgins between A. Prat and San Diego, and at Pío Nono y Av. Santa María, Bellavista. The shopping arcade at the Central Station is good value, likewise the street market outside. Many charity clothes shops around Bandera 600 block, good for winter clothes for travellers who need them. There is a good outside fruit market at Puente 815, by Frutería Martínez. There is an antique fair on Sun. (1400-1400) in the summer and a Fiesta de Quasimodo on the first Sunday after Easter at Lo Barnechea, 30 min. by bus from Santiago.

Bookshops Book prices tend to be high compared with Europe. *Librería Albers*, Merced 820, local 7 and Av. Tobalaba 032 (Spanish, English and German—good selection, cheaper than most); *Librería Altamira*, Huérfanos 669; *Feria Chilena del Libro*, Huérfanos nr. McIver, and in Drugstore precinct, Providencia 2124; *Librería Inglesa* (*Librería Kuatro*), Pedro de

Valdivia 47, English books, sells *South American Handbook*. There are many bookshops in the Pedro de Valdivia area on Providencia. Second-hand English books from arcade at San Diego 121, 1½ blocks south of Alameda and *Librería El Patio*, Providencia 1652, nearest Metro stop Pedro de Valdivia; exchange for best deal. Also, from Henry at Metro station, Los Leones and *Books*, behind *Phone Box Pub*, Providencia 1670. *Librairie Française*, books and newspapers, Calle del Estado 337. As well as the antiquarian bookshop mentioned above in the Lastarria district, there are other good antiquarian bookshops on Merced around the corner from Lastarria, e.g. *América del Sur Librería Editorial*, No. 306, *Libros Antiguos El Cid*, No. 344. Many stalls on Paseo Ahumada/Huérfanos sell foreign newspapers and journals.

Camera Repairs Harry Müller, Ahumada 312, oficina 402, rec.; speaks German and English. For Minolta and Canon repairs, Nueva York 52, Of.302, rec. Developing (Fuji), Reifschneider Laboratory, Ahumada 100 y Huérfanos, 1 day service, rec. Full color, on Ahumada, is to be avoided, but many others on this street offer good 24-hr service (eg Reifschneider).

Buses and Taxis There are three kinds of buses: the small fast kind called *liebres* (hares) which cost US$0.25-0.35 a ride; the regular buses at US$0.25, and the large buses marked Expreso. At present charges are slightly higher at night and on Sun. Taxis are now abundant (black with yellow roofs), and not expensive, with a minimum charge of US$0.40 (50% surcharge on basic rate after 2230). At bus terminals, drivers will charge more—best to walk a block and flag down a cruising taxi. Large blue taxis do not have meters. There are also colectivo taxis to the suburbs. Visitors going outside the city should arrange the charge beforehand. The private taxi service which operates from the bottom level of *Hotel Carrera* has been rec. (same rates as city taxis).

Underground Railway The first line of the underground railway system (Metro) runs west-east between San Pablo and Escuela Militar, under the Alameda, and the second line runs north-south from Cal y Canto to Callejón Ovalle. The connecting station is Los Héroes. Line 3 is to be constructed between Buen Pastor and Vivaceta. The ticket for Line 1 costs 50 pesos; save queuing by buying a ten-ticket booklet (450 pesos). The ticket for Line 2 costs 40 pesos, but is good for Line 1. The trains are fast, quiet, and full. The first train is at 0630 (Mon.-Sat.), 0800 (Sun. and holidays), the last about 2245. Metrobus services connects with the underground railway at Lo Ovalle for southern Santiago and Escuela Militar for Vitacura, Las Condes and Apoquindo.

Car Hire Hertz, Avis and Budget available from airport. Hertz (Av. Costanera 1469, T 225-9328, and airport, T 601-9262) has a good network in Chile and cars are in good condition. Avis also at Eliodoro Yáñez 869, T 495-757. Automóvil Club de Chile car rental, Marchant Pereira 122, Providencia, T 274-4167/6261, discount for members and members of associated motoring organizations (rate for a Nissan Sunny, US$39/day with 150 km., or US$242/week, unlimited km., insurance US$6.35/day). A credit card is usually asked for when renting a vehicle. Tax of 16% is charged. If possible book a car in advance. Note that in the capital driving is restricted according to licence plate numbers; look for notices in the street.

Theatres Teatro Municipal, Agustinas y San Antonio, stages international opera, concerts by the Orquesta Filarmónica de Santiago, and the Ballet de Santiago, throughout the year; on Tues. at 2100 there are free operatic concerts in the Salón Claudio Arrau; tickets range from US$7 for the cheapest seats at the ballet to US$80 for the most expensive opera seats. Teatro Universidad de Chile, Plaza Baquedano, is the home of the Orquesta y Coro Sinfónica de Chile and the Ballet Nacional de Chile; prices from US$1.25-3.50 for concerts to US$1.25-13.50 for ballet.

There are a great number of theatres which stage plays in Spanish, either in the original language or translations, e.g. La Comedia, Merced 349, Abril, Huérfanos 786, Camilo Henríquez, Amunátegui 31, Centro Arrayán, Las Condes 14891, El Galpón de los Leones, Av. Los Leones 238, El Conventillo, Bellavista 173. Four others, the Opera, Huérfanos, California, Irarrázaval 1546, Humoresque, San Ignacio 1249 and Picaresque, Recoleta 345, show mostly Folies Bergères-type revues. Outdoor rock concerts are held at the Estadio Nacional, Av. Unión Latino Americana (metro of same name), at the Teatro Teletón, Rosas 325 (excellent sound system), and elsewhere.

Cinemas "Ciné Arte" (quality foreign films) is very popular and a number of cinemas specialize in this type of film: El Biógrafo (Lastarria 181), Normandie (Av. B. O'Higgins 143), Camara Chile (Miraflores 544), Espaciocal (Goyenechea y Vitacura), Tobalaba (Providencia 2563), Microciné del Barrio (López de Bello 083) and others, full details are given in the press. Other cinemas tend to show "sex, violence and war". Seats cost about US$1.25 with reductions on Wed. (on Thur. elsewhere in the country).

Night Clubs Some of the restaurants and cafés which have shows are given above. Listings are given in *El Mercurio*, or *La Epoca*. *La Cucaracha*, Bombero Núñez 159 (Bellavista) is very popular, floorshow at 2330, US$3.50 cover charge, orchestras, dancing. *Gato Viudo*, on Vitacura, very popular, live music, cheap, fun, pleasant area in the daytime, "alternative" at night.

Discotheques *Gente*, Av. Apoquindo 4900, also *Baltas*, both expensive, but good, US$10 p.p. Many more, mainly in the Providencia and Las Condes areas.

Swimming Pools Antilen (closed Mon.) and Tupahue, better, open daily 1000-1500 (Mon.-Fri., US$2, Sat.-Sun. US$3), both on Cerro San Cristóbal (check if they are open in winter, one usually is). In Parque O'Higgins, same prices. Olympic pool in Parque Araucano (nr. Arauco Shopping Centre, closest Metro E.Militar), open Tues.-Sat. 0900-1900 November-March.

Running The Hash House Harriers hold runs every other week; information through the British Embassy and Consulate.

Tennis Santiago Tennis Club; also, Club de Tenís Jaime Fillol, Rancho Melnichi. Par.4. See also Tenís Centrum Alemán, under **Camping** above.

Bowling Bowling Center, Av. Apoquindo 5012.

Racecourses Club Hípico, racing every Sun. and every other Wed. afternoon (at Viña del Mar, January-March); Hipódromo Chile every Sat. afternoon; pari-mutuel betting.

Exchange Banco Central de Chile, one block from Plaza Constitución, demands the minimum of formalities, although there is usually a commission charge for most transactions. Banco O'Higgins, Av. Agustinas, will change travellers' cheques into dollars with US$12 commission on transactions between US$100-1,000 (Mastercard or AmEx cheques). American Express, Agustinas 1360 (No. 1173 for travel information and mail collection), does not charge commission. Citibank, Ahumada 40 (10% commission) and Afex, Agustinas 1360, will change travellers' cheques into US dollars for up to US$500 with US$15 commission. Banks, open from 0900 to 1400, but closed on Sat.
   Official daily exchange rates are published in *El Mercurio* and *La Epoca*. Parallel market rate can be obtained at corner of Agustinas and Ahumada and around the Moneda; agents on the street take you to exchange offices (bargain with them before going to the office, but it is better to go to the office direct). Travellers' cheques attract a worse rate than cash on the street. Financiera Ciga, Agustinas 1287, Casa de Cambio Blancas, opp. *Hotel Orly* on Pedro de Valdivia, and Exprinter are rec. for good rates, low commission, also Inter, Moneda 940, upstairs office at Ahumada 131 (oficina 103), Cambios Andino, Ahumada 1062 and Teletour, Bandera 191. Most exchange houses are on Agustinas and Huérfanos and some, such as Husa, Providencia 1990 (Metro Pedro de Valdivia), are open on Sat. mornings. Sr. Fernando Sáez (travel agent), M. Cousiño 150, Oficina 322, T 382885, for good exchange rates (and australes). Casa de Cambio, Calle Bombero A. Ossa 1010, Of. 214 (near Ahumada/Agustinas), open 0900-2200 (Mon.-Sat.), 1000-1600 (Sun.). General Holley 66, Providencia, also gives good rates. Ideally, be introduced to someone who will change dollars at optimum rates. Mastercard and Visa at Fincard, Morandé 315, T 698-4260/2465-67/699-2632, offers its full range of services (even lost or stolen cards are replaced in a couple of days); open 24 hrs. Mastercard also at Intercambio, Edif. Santiago Center, Moneda 940, local 221, official rates for cash against the card.

Cultural and Trade Institutions Instituto Chileno Británico de Cultura, Santa Lucía 124, 0930-1900, except 1330-1900 Mon., and 0930-1600 Fri., has English papers in library (also in Providencia, Dario Urzúa 1933, and Las Condes, Renato Sánchez 4369), runs language courses; British Chamber of Commerce, Bandera 227, Casilla 536, T 698-5266; British Council, Av. Eliodoro Yáñez 832, nr. Providencia, T 694-6005. The British community maintains the British Commonwealth Society (old people's home etc.), the interdenominational Santiago Community Church, at Av. Holanda 151 (Metro Tobalaba), Providencia, which holds services every Sunday at 1045. English Schools: The Grange, Redlands, Santiago College, Craighouse and The Brandford School, all coeducational.
   Instituto Chileno Francés de Cultura, Merced 298, in a beautiful house (see also under **Restaurants** above); Instituto Chileno Alemán de Cultura, Goethe-Institut, Esmeralda 650; German Chamber of Commerce, Ahumada 131. Instituto Chileno de Cultura Hispánica, Providencia 927; Instituto Chileno Italiano de Cultura, Triana 843; Instituto Chileno Israeli de Cultura, Moneda 812, oficina 613; Instituto Chileno Japonés de Cultura, Providencia 2653, oficina 1902.
   Instituto Chileno Norteamericano de Cultura, Moneda 1467, good for US periodicals,

The South Pacific Mail

Established in Valparaiso, 1865

Why you won't see The South Pacific Mail on the table in your banker's waiting room

BECAUSE it's on his desk. Quite possibly it's locked up inside it.

The South Pacific Mail is much too expensive to leave lying around.

"This spectacular...Thing!", as Mario Vargas Llosa called it on a visit to Santiago, was founded in Valparaiso 125 years ago in the days when Valpo was the first stop round Cape Horn.

The National Library in Santiago has a complete file from 1909 onwards. And that includes today's editions. By law, and a very good one, too.

But they are the only free ones around.

The South Pacific Mail covers Chile. It is in Chile. It gets its information straight from the horse's mouth.

We spend most of our time out in the mines, in the fishing ports, at the logging camps and pulp mills, on the farms and at the packing stations where Chile's business is based today.

We are also, of course, at the stock-jobbers'offices, the insurance companies and at the ministries in downtown Santiago.

Then there's the bank HQs, the lawyers' inns of court, the accountants'pens and the HQs of the big corporations.

All these serve as lobby bases for the government offices around which they revolve. The South Pacific Mail is there, too. Ahead of the game because we're thinking about what's happening, not just reporting it after the event.

That's why we are able so frequently to predict what's going to happen.

Our main group of subscribers is in Santiago itself, where the CEOs and CFOs of the major companies are concentrated.

An increasingly large group of subscribers is in Tokyo, New York, Washington, Buenos Aires, London, Frankfurt, Moscow, Helsinki, Madrid, Johannesburg, Singapore, Honk Kong, Sydney, Auckland, Montreal, Paris, Rome, Sao Paulo, Lima, Caracas.

And so on.

If you feel you have to know what's happening in Chile, what's going to be happening in Chile, you might as well sign up.

Because sooner or later you're going to have to. The kind of info you pick up in the South Pacific Mail, and only in the SPM, will change your view of Chile, whether you've been here for 50 years or five hours.

We warn you, we tip you off, we give you ideas. We get it right.

Above all, we provide you with focus.

Send me your card, or fax me - (562) 225-8922 - your name on some headed notepaper.

That's all there is to it. You're in.

Part of the deal is that our registered subscribers are free to consult with us, from here or from abroad. Give me a call.

Nicholas Asheshov, Editor.
The South Pacific Mail, Salvador 60, Santiago. Postal Address: <u>Central de Correo, Casilla 4068, Santiago.</u> Phone: (562) 225-3847. FAX: (562) 225-8922.

cheap films on Fri.; also runs language courses.

Instituto Cultural del Banco del Estado de Chile, Alameda 123, regular exhibitions of paintings, concerts, theatrical performances; Instituto Cultural de Providencia, Av. 11 de Septiembre 1995 (metro Los Leones), art exhibitions, concerts, theatre; Instituto Cultural Las Condes, Av. Apoquindo 6570, near beginning of Av. Las Condes, also with art exhibitions, concerts, lectures, etc. Academia Chilena de la Historia, Clasificador 1349, Correo Central, for information and help on archaeology.

Embassies and Consulates **Argentine Embassy**, Vicuña Mackenna 41 (T 222-8977), Australians need letter from their embassy to get visa here, open 0900-1400 (visa US$15, free for US citizens), if you need a visa for Argentina, get it here or in the consulates in Concepción, Puerto Montt of Punta Arenas, there are no facilities at the borders; **Brazilian Embassy**, McIver 255, 15th floor; **Bolivian Embassy**, Av. Santa María 2796 (T 232-8180, Metro Los Leones); **Panamanian Embassy**, Bustos 2199 (open 1000-1330); **Paraguayan Consulate**, Burbos 245, Las Condes (metro Alcántara); **Peruvian Embassy**, Andrés Bello 1751 (T 490045).

U.S. Embassy, Agustinas 1343 (reported to be relocating soon); **U.S. Consulate**, T 710133, Merced 230 (visa obtainable here); **Canadian Embassy**, Ahumada 11 (prints a good information book). **Australian Embassy**, Gertrudis Echeñique 420, Las Condes. **New Zealand Embassy**, Av. Isadora Goyenechea 3516, Las Condes (T 487071). **South African Embassy**, Av. 11 de Septiembre 2353, Edif. San Román, 16th floor. **Thai Consulate**, Suiza 1553, visas while you wait, US$20 multiple entry, open 0900-1300.

British Embassy and Consulate, La Concepción 177, 4th floor, Providencia 1800 (metro Pedro de Valdivia), Casilla 72-D, will hold letters (also reported to be planning to relocate); **West German Embassy**, Agustinas 785 (T 693-5031/ 693-5035); **Netherlands Consulate**, Calle Las Violetas 2368, T 223-6825, open 0900-1200; **Austrian Embassy**, Av. Pedro de Valdivia 300, Barros Errázuriz, 3rd floor. **Italian Embassy**, Triana 843. **Spanish Consulate**, Av. Providencia 329, 4th floor; **Swedish Embassy**, Dario Urzúa 2165, Casilla 55-D, T 495052; **Swiss Embassy**, Av. Providencia 2653, 16th floor, T 232-2693, open 1000-1200 (metro Tobalaba).

Policia Internacional for lost tourist cards, etc., Olivares 1229, 2nd floor, metro Los Héroes or La Moneda.

Laundry Very few wet-wash places in the centre: there is one at Monjitas 510, but there are plenty of dry-cleaners, e.g. Merced 494. Wet wash also at Portugal 71, Torre 7, local 4, US$2.50, open Sun., can leave washing and collect it later. In Providencia there are many more laundries, e.g. Diagonal Paraguay 371, about US$0.65/kg., quick, rec., open till 1930; Marva, Carlos Antúñez 1823 (Metro Pedro de Valdivia), wash and dry US$8; Providencia 1039, full load, wet wash, US$5, 3 hrs. At the corner of Providencia and Dr. Luis Middleton there are several self-service dry cleaners (Metro Pedro de Valdivia, 11 de Septiembre exit).

Health Emergency hospital at Marcoleta 377 costs US$12. For a yellow fever vaccination Hospital San Salvador, Salvador 420, T 2256441. Arrive at correct time, Tues. 0900-1000, or you have to pay for a whole capsule (enough for 20!) Also Vaccinatoria Internacional, Hospital Luis Calvo, Mackenna, Antonio Varas 360. **Emergency Pharmacy**, Portugal 155 (T 382439).

Post Office Agustinas 1137, Plaza de Armas, poste restante well organized (though only kept for 30 days), list of letters and parcels received in the hall of central Post Office; also has philatelic section, for stamp collectors. Another office at Moneda 1155. If sending a parcel, the contents must be checked at Post Office; parcel is then sealed for US$0.75.

Cables and Telephones Compañia de Teléfonos de Chile, Moneda 1145. International phone calls also from: Entel, Huérfanos 1132, Mon.-Fri. 0830-2200, Sat. 0900-2030, Sun. 0900-1400, calls cheaper 1400-2200; Fax upstairs. Fax also available at CTC offices, e.g. Mall Panorámico, 11 de Septiembre, 3rd level (phone booths are on level 1). There are also phone offices at some metro stations, e.g. La Moneda and Pedro de Valdivia for local, long-distance and international calls. International telex service, Bandera 168. Local calls require 3 10-peso coins.

Tourist Information Servicio Nacional de Turismo (Sernatur—the national tourist board), Av. Providencia 1550 (Casilla 14082), T 698-2151, Telex SERNA CL 240137, between metros Manuel Montt and Pedro de Valdivia, next to Providencia Municipal Library, open Mon.-Sat. 0900-1700. English spoken and maps (road map US$1.50), brochures and posters are available. Information office also at the airport, open 0900-2100 daily. N.B. Many tourist offices outside Santiago are closed in winter, so stock up on information here.

A recommended guide book is *Turistel*, published annually in three parts, *Norte*, *Centro*, and *Sur* (or in a combined edition), sponsored by the CTC telephone company, with information and a wealth of maps covering the whole country, in Spanish only. Each whole volume costs about US$4, but buying the whole set is better value; they can be found in CTC offices, bookshops, but best of all in the news stands in the centre of the city. There is also a *Turistel* camping guide. The publisher is Impresora y Comercial Publiguías S.A.

Excellent road maps (US$1.75) and information may be obtained from the **Automóvil Club de Chile**, Vitacura 8620, T 212-5702/3/4/7/8 (a US$6 taxi ride from the centre), which also gives discounts to members of affiliated motoring organizations. Geophysical and topographical maps are available from **Instituto Geográfico Militar**, at their sales office, Alameda 240 (Universidad Católica metro) or main office Dieciocho 407 (opposite Palacio Cousiño, Toesca metro), closed in the holiday season. **Conaf** (Corporación Nacional Forestal), General Bulnes 259, oficina 206 (main office at No.285), T 696-0783/3801, has little written information for visitors to take away, but there are documents that can be consulted about the national park system. Walkers' maps are not available outside Santiago. Write to the Departamento de Estudios Vialidad Nacional, Morandé 59, oficina 344, Santiago, to see if their set of 14 maps of the country (scale 1:500,000—border areas 1:1,000,000) is available. Maps on sale from news kiosks: Esso road and town plans, Copec, Inupal and others.

Travel Agencies Wagons-Lits Cook (Calle Agustinas 1058, Casilla 1534), Turismo Cocha (American Express representatives with mail service), Agustinas 1173 (check also AmEx bank at Agustinas 1360 for mail). Agency Pudahuel, Paseo Ahumada 312, oficina 1024, highly rec. For local tours: Tour Service, Teatinos 333, 10th floor, T 6960415/727166, and at same address Sportstours, T 696-8832/698-3058, German-run, are helpful (offices also at Hotels *Carrera*, and *San Cristóbal*); Ace Turismo, O'Higgins 949, T 6960391, city tour, $12 for ½ day. Altue Expediciones, Encomenderos 83, T 232-1103, for wilderness trips, rec. (above *Geo Pub*). Climbing and adventure tours in tenth region and elsewhere, Antu Aventuras, Casilla 24, Santiago, T 271-2767, Telex 440019, RECAL CZ. Turismo Cabo de Hornos, Agustinas 814, Of. 706, T 338480/1, for DAP flights (Punta Arenas-Puerto Williams) and Tierra del Fuego/Antártica tours. Ugarte International, Huérfanos 1178, Loc.A, very helpful. All Travels, Huérfanos 1160, local 10, T 696-4348, good for flight tickets, ask for Vivian Zuvanich de Selamé; MTK Tours, Huérfanos 752, has been recommended for cheap flights, also Beach Tours Huérfanos 1052, local 34, T 710-806/715-368. Blanco, Pedro Valdivia near Providencia, good for flight information and exchange. Rapa-Nui, Huérfanos 1160, specializes in trips to Easter Island. Turismo Grace, Victoria Subercaseaux 381, T 693-3740, good service.

Airport Arturo Merino Benítez (at Pudahuel), 26 km. from Santiago with a speed limit. Airport taxi, about US$15, fixed taxi fares on board by cab rank, but confirm fare before entering taxi. Pullman service by Aerobuses Tour Express to and from city centre, Moneda 1523, T 717380 (US$0.90) buses every ½hr., 0630-2115, ½-¾ hr. journey (service from airport after 2115 to meet incoming flights); plenty of luggage space; Flota LAC from central reservation of Alameda at Metro Los Héroes, returns from airport to La Moneda, US$0.70, half-hourly service. Internal flights by Lan-Chile and Ladeco operate from the International Airport. For schedules, see under individual towns. On arrival, get entry card from desk at entrance to arrivals hall before proceeding to immigration, otherwise you will be sent back. Bank and Afex *cambio* (better rates) outside customs hall; Sernatur office in same area will book accommodation. There are some shops, but they are very expensive, as are the bar and restaurant. Buy your wine etc. in town.

Airline Offices Lan-Chile, Agustinas 1197 y Morandé, T 723-523; Ladeco, Huérfanos 1157, T 698-1258 and Pedro de Valdivia 0210, T 251-7204; Aerolíneas Argentinas, Moneda 756; Viasa, Agustinas 1141, 5th floor; Varig, Miraflores, between Agustinas and Moneda; South African Airlines, Moneda 970, 17th floor, next to Lufthansa. LAP, Agustinas 1141, 2nd floor.

Rail International service to Buenos Aires suspended. No passenger trains to northern Chile nor to Valparaíso and Viña del Mar. All trains leave from Estación Central at Alameda O'Higgins 3322. Buses from northern bus terminal to Estación Central, Nos. 34 and 45, 10 mins., US$0.30, or take metro and change at Los Héroes. The line runs to Rancagua, San Fernando, Curicó, Talca, Linares, Parral and Chillán, thereafter services go to 1) Concepción, 2) Temuco and Valdivia, 3) Temuco, Osorno and Puerto Montt. Schedules change with the seasons, so you must check timetables before planning a journey. See under destinations for fares and notes on schedules. *Expreso* services do not have sleepers; some *rápidos* do (in summer *rápidos* are booked up a week in advance). *Dormitorio* carriages were built in Germany in 1929/35, bunks lie parallel to rails in 1930's, US-Pullman-style (washrooms at each end, one with shower-bath—visit early before the hot water has run out); an attendant for each car; bar car shows 3 films—no cost but you must purchase a drink ticket in advance. There is also a newer, *Gran Dormitorio* sleeping car (1984), with private toilet and shower,

US$10 extra for 2, rec. For the *expresos* there are no reservations (get your ticket the morning of the day the train leaves and sit on the train as soon as you can get on; otherwise you'll stand for the whole journey). Free hot water supplied, so take own mug and coffee. Also a car-transporter service to Concepción, Valdivia and Puerto Montt. Trains are still fairly cheap (though none too reliable), although 1st class is generally dearer than bus; meals are good though expensive. Check for family service, senior citizen and student discounts. Trains can be cold and draughty in the spring. Booking offices: for State Railways, Alameda O'Higgins 853 in Galería Hotel Libertador, T 301818/330746, Mon.-Fri. 0830-1900, Sat. 0900-1300; or Metro Esc. Militar, Galería Sur L-3, T 228-2983; central station, open till 2230, T 699-5718/699-1682; for Antofagasta-La Paz, Ahumada 11, Of. 602, T 698-5536. Left luggage office at Estación Central.

Buses There are frequent, and good, interurban buses to all parts of Chile. (**NB** Many leave early because of tight competition: arrive at bus station early.) Check if student rates available (even for non-students), or reductions for travelling same day as purchase of ticket; it is worth bargaining over prices, especially out of the summer season. Also take a look at the buses before buying the tickets (there are big differences in quality among bus companies); ask about the on-board services, many companies offer drinks for sale, or free, and luxury buses have meals and wine, colour videos, headphones. Reclining seats are common and there are also *salón cama* sleeper buses. Fares from/to the capital are given in the text. On Friday evening, when night departures are getting ready to go the terminals are murder.

There are 3 bus terminals: 1) Terminal del Norte, Gral. Mackenna y Amunátegui, T 712-141, about 5 minutes' walk from Cal y Canto metro station (Line 2); from here buses leave for northern destinations, and some international services (see below). 2) Terminal de Buses Sur, Av. B. O'Higgins 3878, T 791-385, nearest metro Universidad Técnica/Universidad de Santiago (both names are used); buses from here go to southern destinations. 3) To Viña del Mar/Valparaíso, Bus and Pullman Tur-Bus have their own terminal on Al. B. O'Higgins 3712, next to Estación Central, metro Estación Central or Universidad de Santiago, Línea 1. Varmontt buses, who run an expensive service to Puerto Montt, have their own terminal at Av. 21 de Septiembre 2212 (office on 2nd floor), metro Los Leones; many companies have offices away from the terminals, at which their buses call.

See the note under *Taxis* about not taking expensive taxis parked outside bus stations. Also, do not change money at the bus terminals; if coming from Argentina, try to get some pesos before you arrive.

International Buses Long distance: to Buenos Aires, from southern and northern terminals, US$37-45, 22 hrs.; also to Montevideo, several companies, most involving a change in Mendoza, e.g. El Rápido, US$50, 28 hrs., meals included; Caracas (Tues. and Fri. 0900); Lima 51 hrs., it is cheaper to take a bus to Arica (US$30 and up), another to Tacna (US$1.75), thence bus to Lima. Bogotá (7 days); São Paulo and Rio de Janeiro (US$76 and 80 respectively); Asunción (US$80); Guayaquil; and Quito. Tramaca, from northern terminal, runs a *combinación* service which links with the train from Calama to Uyuni and Oruro in Bolivia. Geminis, also from northern terminal, goes on Tues. to Salta, Argentina, changing in Calama, US$55. Short distance: there are frequent bus and *colectivo* taxi services from the Terminal del Norte over the Andes to Mendoza, 6 hrs., or so, about US$13.35 on either; taxis also go from the southern terminal, touts will approach you. All buses now go through the Cristo Redentor tunnel, and it is no longer possible to go to the Cristo Redentor statue from the Chilean side. TAS-Choapa, from northern terminal, has been rec., US$17.65; Cata is not rec. Many *colectivos* for Mendoza go from the 800/900 blocks of Morandé, more expensive than the buses, but with shorter waiting time at customs: Chi-Ar taxi company, Morandé 890, rec., leaves at 0800 and charges US$16 for Santiago-Mendoza—Chile-Bus, Morandé 838, at 0830, US$15.50; Cordillera Nevada, Morandé 870, T 698-4716, or Local 61 at southern terminal, drive very fast. Have some small change available for tipping Argentine porters at the border.

Shipping M/n *Tierra del Fuego*: Puerto Montt to Puerto Natales and return, reservations accepted for all classes, and M/n *Evangelistas*: Puerto Montt-Puerto Chacabuco, Navimag, Miraflores 178, piso 12, T 696-3211, Telex 341234 NISA CK (or contact Turismo Cocha, Agustinas 1173, T 6983341, for 1st class; also Agentur, see below). Transmarchilay, Agustinas 715, oficina 403, T 335959, Telex 340334 MARCHI CK, for services between Chiloé and the mainland, ferry routes on the Carretera Austral and on Lake General Carrera. M/n *Skorpios*: luxury cruise out of Puerto Montt to Laguna San Rafael, Constantino Kochifas C., MacIver 484, 2° piso, Oficina 5, Santiago T 336-187, Telex 340592 NATUK CK, FAX 336-752. M/n *Quellón*: cruise out of Puerto Montt to Laguna San Rafael, early December to late March, Agentur, Huérfanos 757, oficina 601, T 337118, Telex 645387 AGENT CT. Enquire at Agentur for trips to Antarctica and for Empresa Marítima del Estado, Empremar. Navimag, Transmarchilay and Empremar also sail to the Laguna San Rafael in summer.

Hitch-hiking to Valparaíso, take Metro to Pajaritos and walk 5 minutes to W—no difficulty. Or, take bus "Renca Panamericana" from MacIver and Monjitas. To hitch south, take Metro to Estación Central, then Buses del Paine at Calle Borja as far as possible on the highway to the toll area, about US$1, 75 mins.

Excursions from Santiago On the NE outskirts in Las Condes is the Santuario de la Naturaleza Yerba Loca, administered by Conaf, open September to April (small entrance fee). Several small resort towns are easily reached by car from the capital. Peñalolén, 16 km., a beautiful view of the city if there's no smog (bus in front of Mapocho station at Av. Independencia and Balmaceda, some hiking possibilities); Colina (915 metres), an attractive, popular spa in the mountains 32 km. to the N (bus from Av. La Paz and Juárez, US$0.50 one way), *Hotel Termas de Colina*, E p.p., T 844-1408, thermal baths, US$3.70, swimming pool, US$2.70 (crowded at weekends), last return bus at 1900; San José de Maipo, some 80 km. to the SE (return journey by car: 3 hrs., buses every 15 mins. from N end of Parque O'Higgins, return fare US$1.75), particularly beautiful in spring; just beyond is the mountain town of Melocotón (*Millahue Hotel*, D p.p.). Just past Melocotón between San José de Maipo and El Volcán is San Alfonso, in the Callejón del Maipo (*Hostería Café Cordillera*, C, full board, warmly rec., ring 72-4082 in Santiago, also others). Buses at hourly or 2-hour intervals from Parque O'Higgins, Santiago. Beautiful mountain-river area, with vineyards. Three buses a day (US$2) run from Parque O'Higgins (same metro) to El Volcán in the Andes, 77 km. to the SE (1,400 metres); there are astounding views, but little else (the village was wiped away in a landslide). (Bus, 0800 Sat. and Sun., to Puente Alto.) From El Volcán the road runs 12 km. E and then N to the *Refugio Alemán Lo Valdés*, A-frame chalet accommodation, clean, cold water, no electricity, D p.p. with full board, good food, rec., a good place to stay for mountain excursions, open all year. A splendid region which deserves the journey required to get there. 12 km. away are hot natural baths, Baños Morales; open from October (bus leaves daily from Parque O'Higgins at 0730, arriving at Baños Morales 1100, US$2 each way; returns at 1800—buy return on arrival to ensure seat back). By Baños Morales is **El Morado National Park** with a glacier. Drinks can be obtained from Negro José nearby. The Lo Valdés area is popular at weekends and holiday times, but is otherwise deserted.

S of Santiago is the **Reserva Nacional Río Clarillo**, reached by Micro No. 32 to El Principal, 1 km. from the entrance. It is in the precordillera and can be visited at any time of year for its landscapes.

The small towns in the Aconcagua Valley to the N—San Felipe, Jahuel and Los Andes—are described in the section "To Buenos Aires across the Andes", page 536.

The National Votive Temple of Maipú, of fine modern architecture and stained glass, 30 min. by car (or about 45 mins. by bus from corner of Calle Teatinos and Av. Bernardo O'Higgins) from Santiago, commemorates O'Higgins' battle; interesting (open daily 0800-2100, also daily mass at 1830, 1730 Sat., 1000-1400, 1600-2000 Sun. and religious holidays), and so is the attached Museo del Carmen of carriages, furniture, clothing and other colonial and later items, Sat. 1600-2000, Sun. and holidays, 1100-1400, 1600-2000.

Campsites Excellent facilities about 70 km. from Santiago at Laguna de Aculeo, called **Club Camping Maki**. Facilities include electricity, cold water, swimming pool, boat mooring, restaurant, US$2 p.p. daily, but only available to members of certain organizations. An alternative site is El Castaño camping (with casino), 1 km. away, on edge of lake, US$2 for 2 per night (beware of overcharging). Very friendly, café sells fruit, eggs, milk, bread and kerosene. Good fishing. No showers, water from handpump.

Pottery is best bought in *Pomaire*, a little town about 80 km. from Santiago towards the coast, where the artists can be observed at work. The area is rich in clay and the town is famous for its cider (*chicha de uva*, 3 strengths: *dulce, medio* and *fuerte*) and Chilean dishes; try *Restaurant San Antonio*, welcoming, semi-outdoor, good food and service. Pomaire may be reached by Melipilla bus from Calle San Borja, Santiago, bus station behind Estación Central metro station, every few minutes, US$0.85 each way, Rutabus 78 goes on the motorway, 1 hr., other buses via Talagante take 1 hr. 25 mins. (alight at side road to Pomaire, 2-3 km. from town, colectivos every 10-15 mins.); en route, delicious *pastel de choclo* can be obtained at Restaurant *Mi Ranchito*. Both Pomaire and Melipilla have been rebuilt after the 1985 earthquake, although the former is said to have lost some of its character.

Vineyards Another agreeable excursion is to the vineyard of Concha y Toro at Puente Alto, 40 km. south of Santiago. Tours of the *bodega*, and wine can be bought direct from vineyard. Pirque vineyard of Concha y Toro, entry free, bus from San Francisco and Tarapacá, ¾ hour, US$0.50. The Undurraga vineyard at Santa Ana, south-west of Santiago, also permits visits on weekdays (tours given by the owner-manager, Pedro Undurraga). Take a Melipilla bus (but not Rutabus 78—see above) to the entrance.

Horse-Breeding A specially rec. excursion is to **Los Lingues**, a private *hacienda* 120 km. S of Santiago, where it is said the best horses in Chile are bred. Rosie Swale was lent two of them for her epic ride from Antofagasta to Cape Horn, described in *Back to Cape Horn* (Collins, London, 1986). Visits can be arranged to the C.17 house, a gift of the King of Spain, at Hacienda Los Lingues, Torre C. de Tajamar, Of. 205, Santiago, T 223-3518, Telex 340200 STORE CK. To 6060 LINGUE. A one-day tour costs US$35 p.p. including transport, rodeo and lunch; vacations (all inclusive) cost US$125 per day p.p. (the Hacienda is a member of the French Hotels et Relais de la Campagne).

Skiing There is an excellent ski centre at **Farellones**, 51 km. E of Santiago at 2,470 metres, and reached by car, bus, or truck in under 90 min.: *Motel Tupungato* (Candelaria Goyenechea 4750, Santiago, T 211-7341), Refugio Club Alemán Andino (D p.p., El Arrayán 2735, Santiago, T 232-4338, 1800-2000 May- June) and *Posada Farellones*. Most skiers stay in the two *refugios* belonging to Santiago's universities (full board D p.p.). High season: June to September/October, weather depending. An excellent network of five ski-lifts. There are excursions for a day from Santiago at US$15, including ski-lifts ticket; enquire Ski Club Chile, Goyenechea Candelaria 4750, Vitacura (north of Los Leones Golf Club), T 211-7341. In season, small buses leave from Av. Apoquindo (El Faro shopping centre), Sat. and Sun. between 0800 and 0900, but it is easy to hitch from the junction of Av. Las Condes/El Camino Farellones (petrol station in the middle): take a Las Condes bus from Calle Merced almost to the end of the line. Alternatively, go by ordinary bus which leaves at 0800, weekdays, from front of Omnium building, Av. Apoquindo (Escuela Militar metro), US$5 return (buy ticket day before, office open until 2000). Beautiful views for 30 km. across ten Andean peaks. Incredible sunsets. Large restaurants. No telephone, only communication is by radio. Five min. away by car (6 km.) is the village of La Parva with twelve lifts, 0900-1730 (*Condominio Nueva Parva*, good hotel and restaurant, reservations in Santiago Roger de Flor 2911, T 231-3411, or T 220-8510), where the runs are a little easier. In summer, this is a good walking area. Lift ticket, US$12, and equipment rental, US$7-10 depending on quality. Two skiing areas close by, both of which are undergoing massive investment, are El Colorado (accommodation in *Edificios Los Ciervos* and *Monteblanco*, T Santiago 333564 or 393908, San Antonio 486, of. 151), with 3 triple chairlifts and a ski lodge, and Valle Nevado (owned by Spie Batignolles of France). Valle Nevado aims to be the largest ski resort in South America by 1992; its hotel is incredibly expensive (L+ and then some), but the resort is very highly regarded. Casa Valle Nevado, Gertrudis Echeñique 441, T 480-839/484-995, Fax 487-525. There are 8 runs, 2 chairlifts, 6 skilifts and many more are planned. Sunglasses are a must for skiers.

Other skiing and mountaineering clubs: **Club Andino de Chile**, Enrique Foster, 29, ski club (open 1900-2100 on Mon. and Fri.). **Federación de Andinismo de Chile**, Almirante Simpson 77 (T 232 4338), open daily; has a small museum (1100-1330, 1500-2000, free), sells equipment and guides to the mountains around Santiago (US$2.50) and the extreme south (e.g. Paine, US$4.35). Little other information available, apart from the addresses of all the mountaineering clubs in the country, it has a mountaineering school. Club Alemán Andino, Arrayán 2735, open Tues. and Fri., 1800-2000. Also try Skitotal, Apoquindo 4900, Oficina 32,33,43, T 246-0156, for one-day excursions.

Portillo, 145 km. from Santiago and 62 from Los Andes, is the greatest centre for skiing and winter sports in Chile. The weather is ideal, the snow conditions excellent, the runs many and varied; 12 lifts carry skiers up the slopes. The season is from June to September/October, weather depending. Cheap package can be arranged at the beginning and out of the season. On three sides the mountains soften into snow-clad fields and finally slope gently into the Laguna de Inca, 5½ km. long and 1½ km. wide; this lake, at an altitude of 2,835 metres, has no outlet, is frozen over in winter, and its depth is not known. Out of season this is another good area for walking, but get detailed maps before setting out.

Portillo is easily reached from Santiago by daily bus services (except in bad weather). In summer, ask the bus driver to stop, as it is not a routine call and on the way down you may have to hitch to the customs station with your baggage. In summer take a bus to Los Andes (US$2.25), then to Río Blanco (US$0.70), then hitch (see page 537). The train service from Santiago no longer operates.

Hotels *Hotel Portillo* (L+), including a cinema, night club, swimming pool, sauna baths and medical service, on the shore of Laguna de Inca. Rates include meals, tax and service; accommodation ranges from lakefront suites to family apartments to bunk rooms without or with bath (much cheaper, from D up). A fabulous view, and parking charges even if you go for a meal; jacket and tie must be worn in the dining room. Self-service lunch, US$12 p.p. Lift charges are US$12 per day. Open all year. Reservations, Roger de Flor 2911, T 231-3411, Telex 440372 PORTICZ, Santiago. Cheaper food available at *Restaurant Yuly* across the road, and *Restaurant Los Libertadores* at the customs station 1 km. away. *Hostería Alborada*, A, including all meals, tax and service. During Ski Week (last in Sept.), about double normal rate, all included. Reservations, Agencia Tour Avión, Agustinas 1062, Santiago, T 72-6184, or Calle Navarro 264, San Felipe, T 101-R.

There are boats for fishing in the lake; but beware the afternoon winds, which often make the homeward pull 3 or 4 times as long as the outward pull. There are some gentle ski slopes for beginners near the hotel. The major skiing events are in August and September. Mules for stupendous expeditions to the Cristo, to the glacier at the head of the valley or of the Cerro Juncal, to the pass in the west side of the valley.

Lagunillas is a favourite ski-resort only 50 km. from Santiago, 2 hours by gravel road along the beautiful Maipo valley road to the Ojo de Agua area. Accommodation in the lodges of the Club Andino de Chile (bookings may be made at Ahumada 47, Santiago).Tow fee US$12; long T-bar and poma lifts; easy field.

To Buenos Aires across the Andes The Pan-American Highway runs north from Santiago to the rich Aconcagua Valley, the so-called Vale of Chile. The transandine route to Argentina branches east just after Llay-Llay.

San Felipe, the capital of Aconcagua Province, is 96 km. from Santiago and 128 km. from Valparaíso; it is an agricultural and mining centre with 42,000 inhabitants, 635 metres above sea level, with an agreeable climate. Part of the Inca highway has recently been discovered in the city; previously, no traces had been found further south than La Serena. A paved highway (13 km.) runs N from San Felipe to the old town of Putaendo.

Hotel *Hostería San Felipe*, Merced 204, T 510508, D.

Termas de Jahuel (hotel, T 511240, L), is high in the Cordillera (1,190 metres) 18 km. by road from San Felipe. The hill scenery includes a distant view of Aconcagua. Good roads in the neighbourhood.

Curimón, between San Felipe and Los Andes, has a historic church, with a small museum attached.

Sixteen km. SE of San Felipe is ***Los Andes***, in a wealthy agricultural, fruit-farming and wine-producing area. There are monuments to José de San Martín and Bernardo O'Higgins in the Plaza de Armas, and a monument to the Clark brothers, who built the Transandine Railway (much of which is now either disused or pulled up). Good views from El Cerro de la Virgen. Trail starts at the municipal picnic ground on Independencia (easy to climb taking approx. 1 hr.). It is 77 km. to Santiago by road. See also under Valparaíso **Rail** for train service to the coast. Population: 30,500. Altitude: 730 metres.

Hotels *Continental*, Esmeralda 211, T 421013, D; *Plaza*, Esmeralda 367, T 421929, C, good but restaurant expensive. *Central*, Esmeralda 278 (1 block from bus station) T 421275, F, reasonable and very friendly (excellent bakery opposite, try the empanadas). *Baños El Corazón*, at San Esteban, T 421371, with full board, A, use of swimming pool but thermal baths extra; take bus San Esteban/El Cariño (US$0.50). *Restaurante Círculo Italiáno*, near bus station, rec.

Beyond Los Andes the Pan-American Highway passes into the Cordillera and winds along the Río Aconcagua for 34 km. until it reaches the village of **Río Blanco** (1,370 metres), set at the confluence of two rivers which go to form the Río Aconcagua: the Blanco and the Juncal. There is a fish hatchery with small botanical garden at the entrance of the Andina copper mine. *Hostería Luna*, 4 km before Río Blanco on road from Los Andes, good value, clean, helpful, good food. *Hostería Guardia Vieja*, expensive but untidy, 8 km. beyond town. Possible to camp. Buses run daily from Los Andes; from Santiago, Bus Ahumada, at 1930 daily, direct, 2 hrs., US$2.

(Do not wait around at Los Andes for bus transport to Argentina as the local buses only go as far as Río Blanco; much better from Santiago. Hitch-hiking over Andes possible on trucks from Aduana building in Los Andes).

Beyond Caracoles (Customs post; long delays; no fruit can be taken across) the highway over La Cumbre (Uspallata) pass rises by steep grades to the Redentor tunnel. The tunnel is open from 0800 to 1800, Chilean time. Toll US$0.50. The top of old pass, with the statue of Christ the Redeemer, at an altitude of 4,200 metres, is 8 km. beyond the tunnel and can be reached only by a good, unpaved road from Las Cuevas on the Argentine side (no access from Chilean side). However, if you leave your passport at the Chilean border post, you can walk further on to just before the tunnel into Argentina. Take the old road up to Cristo Redentor for superb views, and even better views from the hill on the left of the pass; start early in the morning because clouds often come up in the afternoon. Take food and windproof jacket and cap. The frontier is crossed at the foot of the statue, which is dwarfed by the scenery. The mountain views (including Aconcagua) are stupendous; as are the wild flowers in late January and early February. On the far side of the Andes the road descends 203 km. to Mendoza, where there are road and rail connections for Buenos Aires. The road from the tunnel to Mendoza is in fair condition, all of it paved.

Valparaíso, the principal port of Chile and capital of the Fifth (Valparaíso) Region, is built on the shores of a sweeping bay and on a crescent of hills around it. With the construction of a new congress building, it is now the seat of the Chilean government. Seen from the ocean, the city presents a majestic panorama: a great circle of hills is backed by the snow-capped peaks of the distant Cordillera. Population, 277,220.

There are two completely different cities. The lower part is the business centre, with fine office buildings on narrow, winding streets. This area is known as "El Plano". Above, in the hills, is a fantastic agglomeration of tattered houses and shacks, scrambled in oriental confusion along the littered back streets. *Ascensores*, or funicular railways, stairs, and winding roads connect the lower and the upper cities.

The climate is good, for the summer heat is tempered by fresh breezes and sunshine mitigates the unkindness of a short winter. (The mean annual temperature is 15°C, with -1°C and 31°C as the extremes.) The city was founded in 1536, but not many antiquities have survived the sequence of pirates, tempests, fires and earthquakes. A remnant of the old colonial city remains in the hollow known as El Puerto, grouped round the low-built stucco church of La Matriz. The last devastating earthquake was in 1906, and most of the principal buildings date from that time. Until recently, all buildings were low, as a precaution against earthquakes, but during the last few years modern multi-storey blocks have appeared. There was another serious earthquake in July 1971 and, most recently, in March 1985.

The main business quarter stands on land reclaimed from the sea. A further large tract has been regained for the port works, which are partially protected by a sheltering mole; but there is always a high swell, particularly when a north wind blows. Mail and passenger vessels moor alongside.

The Plaza Sotomayor is opposite the passenger landing pier (handicraft shops on pier). It has a fine statue to the "Heroes of Iquique"; the Palacio del Intendencia

(Government House) is across the way. Near the landing pier is the railway station, from which passenger services run on the metropolitan line to Los Andes. The streets of El Puerto run N and S from Plaza Sotomayor. To the N Calle Cochrane runs for 7 blocks to the Plaza Echaurren, on which stands the old church of La Matriz. A block beyond rises the bold hill of Cerro Artillería, crowned by the huge Naval Academy and a park. To the W of the Cerro the Avenida Playa Ancha runs to a stadium, seating 20,000 people, and to Playa Ancha park. From the western base of the hill the Avenida Altamirano runs by the sea to Las Torpederas, a picturesque bathing beach.

Leaving Plaza Sotomayor by the Calle Serrano and Plaza Echaurren, the Plaza Aduana is reached, where there is a public lift for the Paseo Veintiuno de Mayo, a terrace on Cerro Artillería giving views of the bay and the hills. The New Year is celebrated by a firework display on the bay, which can be seen from this and the many other terraces on the surrounding hills (arrive early for a good place).

Sightseeing Launches run trips around harbour from Muelle Prat, 30 mins., US$0.65; other boats for hire for fishing. **N.B.** Don't photograph naval ships or installations (be prepared to show documents for taking pictures). The Camino Cintura is the only road which connects all the hills above Valparaíso; it affords constantly changing views, perhaps the best being from Plaza Bismark. No. 9 company "Central Placeres" bus gives fine scenic drive over hills to the port; also bus "Mar Verde" (O.) from Av. Argentina near the bus terminal to Plaza Aduana.

Warning Pickpockets operate in El Puerto around La Matriz.

Hotels *Prat*, Calle Condell 1443, T 253082, 220 beds, B, restaurant; *Residencial Dinamarca*, Dinamarca 539 (take Subida Bellavista), E, excellent value; *Residencial Maureen*, Edwards 700, F, hot water, comfortable. Many cheap hotels on Cochrane and Blanco Encalada, S of Plaza Sotomayor, but very few are recommendable, one that is O.K. is *Residencial Lily*, Blanco Encalada 866, T 255995, 2 blocks from Plaza Sotomayor, F, clean, safe (despite no locks on doors), hot water. *Residencial Gemini*, Pedro Montt 2062, T 255537, F, good, clean, and *Gemini II*, Condell 1386, T 215544; *Reina Victoria*, Plaza Sotomayor 190, T 212203, F, with small breakfast, hot shower, clean and central but noisy. *Copihues*, Chacabuco 2883, behind bus terminal, friendly, E; *Residencial Mi Casa*, opp. bus terminal, F, friendly, safe, cheap. María Pizarro, Chacabuco 2340, Casa No. 2, highly rec., E p.p. Many of the "cheap" hotels in the Chacabuco area are for short-term occupation only. Youth hostel office at Edwards 695, 3rd floor, will extend membership; nearest hostel in Viña del Mar.

Restaurants *Krill*, Errázuriz 210, across street from docks, rec. for seafood; *Bar Inglés*, Cochrane 851 (entrance also on Blanco), good food and drink, traditional, rec., not cheap; *Café Riquet*, O'Higgins, by Plaza Anibal Pinto, also traditional, comfortable, good coffee and breakfast, rec.; *Marisquería La Sureña*, Valdivia 169, near market, lunch only, very good; in municipal market, good seafood stalls on second floor, for lunch. *Hamburg*, O'Higgins 1274, German management, German beer, and reasonably-priced food. *Bote Salvavidas* on the harbour, good, at Muelle Prat; *Café Express Delmónico*, Av. Prat (near Plaza Sotomayor), good, cheap lunches, popular; *Natur-in*, Francia 549, 2nd floor, vegetarian; fresh juices at *Salud*, Condell 1678; *Bernal Fuente de Soda*, Esmeralda 1140. *Casino Social de Pescadores*, 1 km. N of university in Valparaíso, good, cheap fish meals; the "casino" of the Asociación de Clubs de Regata, on the waterfront, is rec. for good seafood. *La Tentazione*, Av. Pedro Montt 2484, good, cheap; *Café Apollo*, Av. Argentina 179, cheap and sustaining. Chocolate from the factory and retail store, Hucke on Gral. Cruz 824, rec.

Bookshop *Librería Universitaria*, Esmeralda 1132, good selection of regional history.

Transport Taxis are more expensive than Santiago: a short run under 1 km. costs US$0.50. Public transport good. Trolleybuses still run, also extensive bus routes. Fares within city limits US$0.20.

Museums Museo Municipal de Bellas Artes, with Chilean landscapes and seascapes and some modern paintings, housed in Palacio Baburizza, Paseo Yugoeslavo, a fine old house overlooking harbour (free), open Tues.-Sun. 1000-1300, 1500-2000; take *Ascensor El Peral* from Plaza Sotomayor opposite Law Courts. Museo del Mar Almirante Cochrane, in Lord Cochrane's house overlooking city, take *ascensor* from Calle Serrano, which leads off Plaza Sotomayor, to Cerro Cordillera; at the top, Plazuela Eleuterio Ramírez, take Calle Merlet to the left. Museo Naval, Paseo 21 de Mayo, Tues.-Fri. 0930-1230, 1430-1800, Sat., Sun. and holidays 1030-1800, US$0.35 (take *ascensor* from Plaza Aduana).

Exchange National banks. Open 0900 to 1400, but closed on Sat. Rate of exchange at Banco de Santiago (Prat 816) and Banco de Crédito e Inversiones (Cochrane 820) good. Parallel market outside Exprinter, Prat 895 (the building with the clocktower at junction with Cochrane), good rates, no commission on travellers' cheques (open 0930-1400, 1600-1900); Cambinter (good) exchange house, close to railway station, on corner of Errazúriz 627.

Addresses British Pro-Consul, Mrs Moira Macauliffe, Edif. Kenrick, Errázuriz 730, T (032) 256117, Casilla 82-V; YMCA, Blanco 1113; YWCA, Melgarejo 45; Chilean-British Cultural Institute, Blanco 725, T 2828; Valparaíso Seamen's Institute, Blanco 394, T 2717; Instituto Chileno-Norteamericano, Esmeralda 1061.

Cables Transradio Chilena, Esmeralda 932.

Tourist Office at bus terminal (good map available), helpful, open Fri.-Wed. 0900-1300, 1600-2000; small kiosk on Muelle Prat. For day trips around Valparaíso and Viña del Mar, Turismo Continental T 6992807.

Airlines Lan-Chile, Esmeralda 1048, T 51441; Ladeco, Blanco 951, T 251001.

Rail Regular service on the Valparaíso metropolitan line, *El Porteño*: Valparaíso, Viña del Mar, Quilpue, Limache, Quillota, La Calera, Llay-Llay, San Felipe and Los Andes (and intermediate stations); trains that run the entire route at 1800 daily, 1430 Mon.-Fri. (not holidays), 0805, 1200 and 1445, Sat., Sun. and holidays, fare Valparaíso-Los Andes US$10.20. There is talk of extending the line to the Argentine border as a "tourist resource".

Buses Excellent and frequent bus service runs between Valparaíso (Av. Brasil)/Viña del Mar (25 min.) and Chorrillos; fare US$0.25. To Santiago, 2 hrs., US$2 Tur Bus and Pullman Bus, others US$1.85 (returns to the capital heavily booked on Sun. p.m.); to Concepción, 11 hrs., US$10. La Serena, 7 hrs., 1000. Terminal Rodoviario is on Pedro Montt 2800 block, corner of Rawson, 1 block from Av. Argentina; plenty of buses to/from Plaza Sotomayor.

If driving from Santiago there are two tunnels, toll of US$2.25 paid at the first; several other tolls.

Hitch-hiking to Santiago is easy from service station on Av. Argentina.

Lighthouse The Faro de Punta Angeles, on a promontory just beyond the Playa Ancha, was the first on the West Coast; you can get a permit to go up. On another high point on the other side of the city is the Mirador de O'Higgins, the spot where the Supreme Dictator exclaimed, on seeing Cochrane's liberating squadron: "On those four craft depends the destiny of America".

National Park About 25 minutes from Valparaíso, on the road to Santiago (Ruta 68) is the Reserva Nacional Peñuelas, surrounding the artificial Lago Peñuelas. Access is permitted for walking and fishing; administration at park entrance.

If driving from Valparaíso to the Argentine border, Route 62 runs through Viña del Mar, climbs out of the bay and goes through (16 km.) *Quilpue*, 1½ km. from El Retiro, a popular inland resort with medicinal springs. It crosses a range of hills and reaches the Aconcagua Valley at **Limache** (40 km. from Valparaíso); population 22,511. Between Quilpue and Limache is Peñablanca, the town of the white windmills. 8 km. from Limache is Olmué, beyond which is **Parque Nacional La Campana**, an area of native woodland, including the Chilean palm (*Kankán*), much varied birdlife, and the Cerro La Campana which Darwin climbed in 1836. There are extensive views from the top, but a guide may be necessary because there are a number of ascents, some of which are very difficult. Route 62 joins Route 60 just before **Quillota**, an orchard centre (Balneario El Edén, 5 km out of town, good swimming), continuing to La Calera (88 km. from Valparaíso), where it joins the Pan-American Highway; turn SE and E for Llay-Llay, San Felipe, Los Andes and the pass over the mountains to Mendoza.

Laguna Verde, a couple of hours' dusty walk over the hills (or a short road journey, buses from Calle Buenos Aires) to the W of Valparaíso, is a picturesque bay for picnics. Camping site *Los Olivos*, good facilities, well run and friendly. Further S still is Quintay where there is camping; 45 km. from Viña del Mar, turn left at Peñuelas on the main Santiago-Valparaíso road.

Pleasure Resorts near Valparaíso

Viña del Mar, one of the foremost South American seaside resorts, is 9 km.

from Valparaíso by one of the innumerable express buses, which run along a narrow belt between the shore and precipitous cliffs. Halfway, on the hill of Los Placeres, is the Universidad Técnica. The popular bathing resort of El Recreo is passed, then Caleta Abarca with its crowded beaches, floral clock and big *Hotel Miramar*. Beaches are often closed because of pollution.

At the entrance to Viña del Mar there is a steep bluff, worth climbing for the views over Viña from its *paseos*. Here also is Cerro Castillo, the summer palace of the Presidents of the Republic. Below, to the left, is the lagoon of the Marga Marga, crossed by a bridge which leads direct to the Casino, built in the 1930s and set in beautiful gardens, US$2.40 to enter, jacket and tie for men required (open all year). Population: 259,300 (1982).

One of the sights is the municipally owned Quinta Vergara, set in superb gardens with a double avenue of palms; it houses a collection of pictures (Museo de Bellas Artes) and an art school (T 680618). Take bus to El Salto. Part of the grounds is a children's playground, and there is an outdoor auditorium where concerts and ballet are performed in the summer months, and an international song contest is held every February.

"The Song Festival is recommended as a fascinating experience not to be missed, but make sure you have a place to stay before going to Viña! It may be better to watch for the first 3 nights on the television (to familiarize yourself with the songs and performances), and then to attend in person the last two nights. Pay the extra money and sit down near the Quinta Vergara stage (reserved seats and much better views). Otherwise, for the economy seats, you will have to arrive several hours in advance. Doors open at 1700 (except for the last night, when they open at 1500)—show doesn't start until 2130, so bring a hat for sun protection, snacks and something to read!" (Richard Crowe, Univ. of Toronto).

The Teatro Municipal is on Plaza Vergara. Near the Valparaíso Sporting Club with its racecourse and playing fields are the Granadilla Golf Club and a large stadium. In the hills behind a large artificial lake, the Tranque Sausalito, is frequented by picnic parties, and popular with waterskiers; not far away is the Salinas golf course and the football ground of Everton, named by the former British Community.

Festival El Roto, 20 Jan., in homage to the working men and peasants of Chile.

Hotels Many in A-B range, some with beach. *San Martín*, Av. San Martín 667, T 972548, A with breakfast; *José Francisco Vergara*, Calle Dr. von Schroeders 367, T 664122, B, has garden houses for up to 5; *Alejandra*, 2 Poniente 440, T 974404, with shower and breakfast, C (D in low season, breakfast included); *El Escorial*, two places: one at 5 Poniente 114, the other at Poniente 441 (T 975266), D with breakfast, shared bath, clean, central. *Residencial Blanchait*, Valparaíso 82F, T 974949, clean, E with breakfast, hot water, clean, good service; *Residencial Magallanes*, Arlegui 555, T 685-101, with breakfast, clean, friendly, run by a family, good meals, C. There are a great many more places to stay.

Motels Several at Reñaca (6 km. from Viña del Mar).

N.B. It is cheaper to stay in Valparaíso and commute to the Viña beaches.

Youth Hostel Agua Santa 153, US$3 p.p. a night for YHA card holders, breakfast included, other meals available, no cooking facilities; family rooms available. Open Jan.-Feb.

Camping At the *Aku-Aku* at Reñaca, T 970763 also *Camping Reñaca*, Santa Luisa 401. Unofficial site in woods behind Quinta Vergara park. Camping gas and similar articles for sale at Valparaíso 464.

Restaurants At hotels; *Cap Ducal*, also on beach near Naval Museum, expensive, highly rec. *Casino Chico*, Valparaíso 99, Chilean and international dishes; *Salòn de China*, 5 Poniente y 4 Norte; *Han's Dragón*, Libertad y 8 Norte; *Sen San*, opp. Ciné Rex on Valparaíso, Chinese, good. *Mapuche*, San Martín 529, excellent. Many restaurants on Av. Valparaíso, try in the Galerías (arcades, e.g. *Café Big Ben*). Many smaller ones along the sea front. *Terminal Pesquero*, 1st floor, interesting.

El Poncho at Reñaca, good seafood and service; also at Reñaca, overlooking the sea, are *Anastasia*, excellent international menu, expensive; *Hotel Oceanic*, very good, expensive; *Mirador Cochoa*, good, pricey; *Cura Nurín*, not so good but pricey.

Market At intersection of Av. Sporting and river, open Wed. and Sat.

Museums The Museum of Naval History, in the Castillo Wolff, good, next door is a small Aquarium. Institute of Oceanography, in Montemar, worth seeing; Quinta Rioja, built at turn of century by a prominent local family and now used for official municipal receptions, main floor open to visitors during season, Museum on a lower floor, Quillota 214 (T 972802). Nearby is an Archaeological Museum, Calle 4 Norte 784, with objects from Easter Island and Mapuche silver, open Mon.-Fri. 1000-1800, Sat.-Sun. 1000-1400. In the centre of town is an Easter Island statue.

Cultural Associations North American Institute, in fort off Avenida Alvarez; British, Calle 3 Norte. Goethe Institut, 3 Norte 599, T 976581, in plaza opposite station; Instituto Chileno-Francés, Alvarez 314, T 685908.

British Community The community here maintains two schools: St. Margaret's and Mackay. There is also an Anglican church, with a resident English chaplain, postal address Casilla 561.

Exchange Fincard (Visa, Mastercard), Ecuador 259. In travel agencies.

Tourist Office Av. Marina esq. Puente Libertad, T 883154. Arrangements may be made at the Tourist Office for renting private homes in the summer season. **Automóvil Club de Chile** 1 Norte 901, T 971815.

Bus to Santiago, US$2-3; to La Serena, 6 daily, 7 hrs., US$8; to Antofagasta, 20 hrs., US$20. Terminal at Av. Valparaíso and Quillota.

Excursions In the eastern suburbs, beyond El Salto, is the Jardín Botánico Nacional, a national park in the Parque del Salitre. Beyond Reñaca beach (6 km. N, very popular with young people) is Cochoa with its large sealion colony, 100 metres offshore.

Resorts N of Valparaíso There is a very fine drive N of Viña del Mar along the coast (many motels being built) through Las Salinas to Concón, then inland to Quintero. Las Salinas, beach between two towering crags, is very popular. **Concón**, on the NE point of Valparaíso Bay, is 16 km. further (take bus 9 from Av. Libertad between 2 and 3 Norte). Main attractions: tennis, bathing, fishing, and riding. Main eyesore: an oil refinery (not visible from beach). Near the Concón beach there is a very interesting pelican colony. There is also a new inland road, much faster than the coast road, between Viña del Mar and Concón.

Concón Hotels *Playa Amarilla*, T 811915, and several motels. Good seafood empanadas at bars. *Vista al Mar*, Av. Borgoño 21270, T 812-221, good fish restaurant, US$7 per plate.

Campsite Las Gaviotas. Camping Mantagua Playa.

Horse riding Horses for hire from Ernesto Farias Usario, Las Encinas 55, Las Romeras, Concón Alto (last bus stop on route 9 or 10 from Viña del Mar or Valparaíso), US$2/hour. Rides in forest or along sand dunes.

Another 16 km. to the N of Concón over the new bridge is the resort of **Quintero**, the naval aviation centre. **Hotels** *Isla de Capri*, Av. 21 de Mayo 1299, T 930117; *Hotel Yachting Club*, Luis Acevedo 1736, T 930061, B. A number of residenciales at the resort.

Horcón, set back in a cove surrounded by cliffs, is a pleasant small village, mainly of wooden houses. Vegetation is tropical with many cacti on the cliff tops. Seafood lunches with the catch of the day rec. The resort is best avoided in Jan.-Feb. when it is packed out. **Hotels** *Horcón*, *Aranciba* and *El Faro*, all on beach. Restaurant *El Ancla* rec.
From Las Ventanas the road continues N to the fashionable resort of **Zapallar** and the once fashionable **Papudo**. Road is paved from Zapallar to the Pan-American Highway. No cars are allowed on the Zapallar seafront. Excellent bathing, but water is cold. Hotels are 3rd class. **Hotels** at Zapallar: *Motel Aguas Claras*; *César*, T 711313, A, very nice but dear, good, reasonably-priced food in *Restaurant César* (different management), on seafront; hotels are relatively expensive for what is offered. At Papudo: *Moderno*, E; *Di Peppino*, T 711482; many more.

Excursions There is a fascinating drive to Cachagua, where a colony of penguins may be viewed from the northern end of the public beach.
Several excellent sea beaches are frequented by people from Santiago: some lie N of Valparaíso (already described), and some at the mouth of the Río Maipo. The railway (no passenger services) runs to the port of **San Antonio**, 113 km. from Santiago and 112 km. south of Valparaíso. A motorway, extending from that which goes from Santiago to Melipillai (**see above, page 535**), is due for completion in 1991. Its shipping shows a considerable growth, mostly at the expense of Valparaíso. The port exports copper brought by railway from the large mine at El Teniente, near Rancagua. Population: 60,826. Itself a popular resort

(although the sea is polluted), it is also the centre for other resorts to the N and S: **Cartagena**, the terminus of the railway 8 km. to the N (occasional passenger trains in summer), an old town, is a great playground for Santiago residents. N of Cartagena there are several small resorts—Las Cruces, *Residencial La Posada*, E, good birdwatching; El Tabo, **El Quisco** with a beautiful white sand beach, and particularly **Algarrobo** (the most chic) with its yacht club, marina and penguin colony, access to colony by fishing boat—landing not permitted. On the road between El Quisco and Algarrobo is the town of Isla Negra where the house of the Chilean poet Pablo Neruda is located. The beautifully-restored **Museo Casa Pablo Neruda** can be visited by groups of up to 5 with prior reservation from the Fundación Neruda (see under Santiago **Museums**); to get there by public transport, take a bus to San Antonio/Cartagena. **Llolleo** (a famous resort for those who suffer from heart diseases, 4 km. S of San Antonio), and **Maipo**, at the mouth of the Río Maipo, are other resorts. Near Llolleo are many beautiful places, including La Boca. **Santo Domingo**, with good hotels is about 10 mins. by road S of San Antonio. It has a golf course, and is by far the most attractive place on this coast; it is also not too crowded in high season.

Hotels At San Antonio: *Jockey Club*, 21 de Mayo 202, T 31302, D. At Cartagena: *Biarritz*; *La Bahía* both on Av. Playa Chica (T 32246 and 31246), both D. At Llolleo: *Oriente*, Inmaculada Concepción 50, T 32188, E p.p.; *Residencial El Castillo*, Providencia 253, T 373821. At Santo Domingo: *Rocas de Santo Domingo*, La Ronda 130, T 31348, C. At El Tabo: *Hotel El Tabo*, T 33719, quite nice, and *Motel El Tabo*, next door (overfull in Jan.-Feb.). At El Quisco, *Hotel El Quisco*, Av. Isidora Dubournais 166, E p.p. with breakfast, clean; others on this avenue; *Motel Barlovento* Calle El Quisco 0520, T 81030, D; *Cabañas Pozo Azul*, Capricornio 234, SE of town, quiet, E; *residenciales* 100-200 m. from beach in E range. Excellent seafood restaurant *La Galleta* on beach. At Algarrobo, there are restaurants and *residenciales* on beach (e.g. *Vera*, Av. Carlos Alessandri 1521, T 81132, E with breakfast, good).

N.B. This entire coastal area, and especially San Antonio, was damaged in the severe earthquake of March 3, 1985.

THE CHILEAN PACIFIC ISLANDS (4)

Juan Fernández Islands, some 650 km. W of Valparaíso, were discovered by Fernández in 1574. They are now a national park administered by Conaf. One of them was the home (1704-09) of Alexander Selkirk (the original of Defoe's *Robinson Crusoe*), whose cave on the beach of Robinson Crusoe island is shown to visitors. The main island has 550 people housed in simple wood frame houses, who fish for *langosta de Juan Fernández* (a pincerless lobster) which they send to the mainland. The village of San Juan Bautista has a church, schools, post office, and wireless station. The official names of the three islands are: Robinson Crusoe (previously Más a Tierra), Alejandro Selkirk (previously Más Afuera) and Santa Clara (the smallest island).

The climate is mild, the vegetation rich, and there are plenty of wild goats—and some tourists, for the islands are now easily reached by air. There are no beaches to speak of. The boat service, about every three weeks from Valparaíso on the *Río Baker* and *Charles Darwin*, is for cargo and passengers, modest accommodation, 36-hour passage; Empremar, Almirante Gómez Carreño 49, Valparaíso (T 258061) or Agentur, Huérfanos 757, oficina 601, T 337118, Santiago. There is an air taxi daily in summer (subject to demand) from Santiago (Los Cerrillos airport, US$370 round trip), by Taxpa, Nueva York 53; also from Valparaíso. The plane lands on an airstrip in the W of the island; passengers are taken by boat to San Juan Bautista (1½ hrs., US$2 one way). In summer, a boat goes once a month between Robinson Crusoe and Alejandro Selkirk if the *langosta* catch warrants it, so you can visit either for a few hours or a whole month.

The anvil-shaped peak, El Yunque, is the highest peak on Robinson Crusoe and it was upon this hill that Selkirk lit his signal fires. A tablet was set in the rock at the look-out point by British naval officers from HMS *Topaze* in 1868, to commemorate Selkirk's solitary stay on the island for 4 years and 4 months.

RAPA NUI
EASTER ISLAND
55

Selkirk, a Scot, was put ashore from HMS *Cinque Ports* and was taken off by a privateer, the *Duke*. The look-out (Mirador de Selkirk) is the only easy pass between the north and south sides of the island. During the First World War, two British destroyers, HMS *Kent* and *Glasgow* sank a German cruiser, the *Dresden*, in the bay upon which the village is located. The ship (which was actually scuttled) is still on the bottom; a monument on shore commemorates the event and, nearby, unexploded shells are embedded in the cliffs.

Each February, a yachting regatta visits the islands; it originates in Algarrobo, sails to Robinson Crusoe, thence to Talcahuano and Valparaíso. The bay is full of colourful and impressive craft, and prices in restaurants and shops double for the duration. (Thomas G. Lammers, Miami University, Department of Botany).

Hotels *Hostería Robinson Crusoe*, B (US$30-35 d, full board, plus 20% tax), about 1 hour walk from the village. *Daniel Defoe Hotel*, A, at Aldea Daniel Defoe; *Hostería Villa Green*, good. Lodging with villagers is difficult. T Valparaíso 81573.

Easter Island (Isla de Pascua, Rapa Nui) is just S of the Tropic of Capricorn and 3,790 km. W of Chile; its nearest neighbour is Pitcairn Island. It is triangular in shape, 24 km. across, with an extinct volcano at each corner. Its original inhabitants called the island Te Pito te Henua, the navel of the world. The population was stable at 4,000 until the 1850s, when Peruvian slavers, smallpox and emigration (encouraged by plantation-owners) to Tahiti reduced the numbers. Now it is about 2,500, of whom about a quarter are from the mainland, mostly living in the village of Hanga Roa. Just north of Hanga Roa, there is a reconstructed site with a temple, houses and a ramp leading into the sea. Further along, there is a mediocre museum (Mon. to Sat., 0900-1200, 1400-1700, Sun. 0900-1500). About half the island, of low round hills with groves of eucalyptus, is used for sheep and cattle, and nearly one-third constitutes a National Park. The islanders, of Polynesian origin, have preserved their indigenous songs and dances, and are extremely hospitable. Tourism has grown rapidly since the air service began in 1967. Paid work is now more common, but much carving is still done. The islanders have profited much from the visits of North Americans: a Canadian medical expedition left a mobile hospital on the island in 1966, and when a US missile-tracking station was abandoned in 1971, vehicles, mobile housing and an electricity generator were left behind. The unique features of the island are the 600 (or so) *moai*, huge stone figures up to 9 metres in height and broad in proportion. One of them, on Anakena beach, was restored to its (probably) original state with a plaque commemorating Thor Heyerdahl's visit in 1955. Heyerdahl's theories, as expressed in *Aku-Aku, The Art of Easter Island* (New York: Doubleday, 1975), are not as widely accepted as they used to be, and South American influence is now largely discounted (see below). Other *moai*, at Ahu Tepeu and Ahu Tahai, have since been re-erected. The rainy season is from February to the end of August. Useful information is contained in David Stanley's *South Pacific Handbook*, and there is a very thorough illustrated book by J. Douglas Porteous (a frequent, and valued, correspondent of ours), *The Modernization of Easter Island* (1981), available from Department of Geography, University of Victoria, BC, Canada, US$6.

David Bulbeck, an anthropologist from Adelaide, writes: Far from being the passive recipient of external influences, Easter Island shows the extent of unique development possible for a people left wholly in isolation. It is believed to have been colonized from Polynesia about AD 800: its older altars (*ahu*) are similar to those of (French) Polynesia, and its older statues (*moai*) similar to those of the Marquesas Islands. The very precise stone fitting of some of the *ahu*, and the tall gaunt *moai* with elongated faces and ears for which Easter Island is best known were later developments whose local evolution can be traced through a comparison of the remains. Indigenous Polynesian society, for all its romantic idylls, was competitive, and it seems that the five clans which originally had their own lands demonstrated their strength by erecting these complex monuments. The *moai* were sculpted at the Rano Raraku quarry and transported on wooden rollers over more or less flat paths to their final locations; their red topknots were sculpted at and brought from the inland quarry of Puna Pau; and the rounded pebbles laid out checkerboard fashion at the *ahu* all came from the same beach at Vinapu. The sculptors and engineers were paid out of the surplus food produced by the sponsoring family: Rano Raraku's unfinished *moai* mark the end of the families ability to pay. Over several centuries from about AD 1400 this stone work slowed down and stopped, owing to the deforestation of the island caused by roller production, and damage to the soils through deforestation and heavy cropping. The birdman cult represented at Orongo is a later development after the islanders had lost their clan territoriality and were concentrated at Hanga Roa, but still needed a non-territorial way to simulate inter-clan rivalry.

Things to See The visitor should see the crater of the volcano Rano Kau with its reed-covered lakes; best for photographs in the afternoon. The adjacent ceremonial city of Orongo with its petroglyphs (entrance US$1.50, pamphlet in Spanish extra) is famous for the birdman cult and gives good views of Motu Nui, Motu Iti and Motu Kaokao, the so-called bird islets. The volcano Rano Raraku; the statues at Ahu Tahai; the beaches of Ovahe and Anakena (Thor Heyerdahl's landing place, also restored *moai*); and the *ahu* and *moai* at Vinapu, Akivi/Siete Moai, Pitikura, Vaihu and Tahai. Ahu Tongariki, once the largest platform, was badly damaged by a tidal wave in 1960. Cave paintings at Ana Kai Targata. Music at the 0830 Sun. mass is "enchanting". Museum near Tahai, US$0.40, disappointing, most objects are reproductions.

Handicrafts Wood carvings, stone moais, best bought from the craftsmen themselves, such as Antonio Tepano Tucki, Juan Acka, Hipolito Tucki and his son (who are knowledgeable about the old culture). The municipal market, east of Tahai, will give you a good view of what is available—no compunction to buy. There is a Cema-Chile store; the airport shop is expensive. Good pieces cost between US$30 and 150. Souvenirs at *Hotu Matuu's Favorite Shoppe* have been described as "top dollar and she will not bargain", but she does have the best T-shirts.

Accommodation and Food A comprehensive list of all accommodation available is displayed at the airport information desk. Note that room rates, especially in *residenciales* can be much cheaper out of season and if you do not take full board. *Hotel Hanga Roa*, Av. Pont (L) including all meals (120 beds), does not take credit cards, breakfast included, T 299; *Hotel Otai*, Te Pilo Te Henua, T 250, B, comfortable, friendly, run by a family, rec.; *Hotel

Victoria, Av. Pont, T 272, A, friendly, helpful owner Jorge Edmunds arranges tours; *Iorana Hotel*, on Ana Magara promontory (5 mins. from airport), T 312, 14 rooms, friendly, excellent food, convenient for visiting Ana Kai Targeta caves; *Topo Ra'a*, Atamu Kekena, T 225, A, 5 mins. from Hanga Roa, very good, helpful, excellent restaurant; *Easter Island Hotel*, Av. Policarpo Toro, Hanga Roa, B, breakfast and dinner (excellent restaurant), good service, nice garden (T 294). Homes offering accommodation and tours (rates ranging from US$18 to US$35, including meals): Yolanda Ika's (*Residencial Taire Ngo Oho*, T 259), B with breakfast, rec., modern; Krenia Tucki's *Residencial Kaipo*, Av. Pont, B, small, clean, friendly with hot water; *Residencia Hanga Roa Reka*, T 276, B full board, good, friendly, camping US$5; María Georgina Hucke, of Tiki Tours, C with half board, rec.; *Residencial Pedro Atán* (A, full board, T 329, Av. Policarpo Toro); Sophia Gomero and María Luisa Pakarati. *Res. El Tauke* (Clementina Riroroko Haoa), T 253, same rates as *Hanga Roa Reka*, excellent, airport transfers, tours arranged; *Res. Taheta One One*, T 257, same rates, ask here for cheap motorbike rental, US$8/day; *Res. Apina Nui*, Hetereki, T 292, A (D-C low season), good food, helpful; *Res. Holiday Inn* (Viviane Tepano), T 337, C p.p. with breakfast and one meal, excellent food, hot water, rec; *Inn at Tahai* (María Hey), A full board, rec.; María Goretti, rooms E with breakfast, camping US$6; Sra. Inez Pateñarez, Calle Make Make, Hanga Roa, private house accommodation. Emilio and Milagrosa Paoa, B with full board, rec. accommodation and tours. Some families (such as Anakena and Raraku) and *Residencial Pedro Atán* will rent their gardens to travellers with a tent, US$7, with meal; the lack of natural water makes this uncomfortable. On arrival at the airport, visitors are met in force by guest-house keepers, drivers, horse-hirers, etc. Unless it is a particularly busy season there is no need to book in advance; mainland agencies make exorbitant booking charges.

Kopa Kabana restaurant, quite good; another opp. municipal market (which does not sell food). There are a couple of expensive supermarkets, cheapest is ECA on main street. Local produce which can be found free (but ask) includes wild guava fruit, fish, "hierba Luisa" tea, and wild chicken. Food, wine and beer expensive because of freight charges, but fruit and bread are cheap, and fish bought from the fishermen is good value. Average prices: coffee/tea US$0.35, meals about US$6, snacks US$0.80, beer/cola US$0.90 in most bars and restaurants. Bring all you can from the mainland (and remember that wine, whisky, watches, clothing—especially army surplus gear and tennis shoes—are good items for barter). Vegetarians will have no problems on the island. There are two discotheques in Hanga Roa. Both are popular, but drinks are expensive: a bottle of pisco costs US$5, canned beer US$1.20. *Porifico*, the original island disco, is open Thur. 2100-2400, Fri.-Sat. 2300-0300, entrance free, good entertainment. Beware of extras such as US$3 charge for hot water.

Camping Free in eucalyptus groves near the Ranger's house at Rano Raraku, and at Anakena. Officially, camping is not allowed anywhere else, but this is not apparently strictly enforced. Several habitable caves around the coast: e.g. between Anakena beach and Ovahe.

Warning The water on the island is not safe to drink; its high magnesium content may make you sick: drink only boiled or iodized water. Ask for the local herbal infusion which is a remedy for sickness. Bottled water costs US$2 for 1½ litres. Also, although the islanders are very nice about getting you a horse—they will get you *any* horse, so beware.

Transport on Easter Island There are no taxis and the only *colectivo* is often off the road. Lan-Chile office in *Hotel Hanga Roa* provides tours of the island. A horse can be hired for US$10 a day or less, and is the best way to see the island as long as you are in good shape for riding. Another good way of getting around is by bicycle, but none is available for rent; buy or rent a robust one in Santiago (Lan-Chile transports bikes free up to a limit of 20 kg.). After 4 days you can sell a bike on the island. Aku-Aku Tours arrange accommodation with islanders and excursions around the island, US$25 per person for full day, US$13-14 for half-day. Krenia Tucki of *Residencial Kai Poo* will also organize jeep tours, US$25 per day, as will Michel Fage. Some islanders, including Fernando and Marcelo León (Pai Tepano Rano, rec.) and Hugo Teave (good English, well-informed, polite) also provide tours. Charles Wilkins, Agencia de Viajes Mahinatur Ltda, T 20, English-born guide, rec., as is Victoriano Giralde, Kia-Koe Tours: provides transport for groups, arranges various activities and owns a local supermarket. Others may provide internal transport at a discount but be discreet, as an islander so doing is subjecting himself to social disapproval. The English of other tour guides is often poor. Good maps are available on the island. For instance that of Antoni Pujador Iti, 2nd edition 1988; Motu Iti "Ediciones del Pacifico Sur", Hernando de Aguirre 720, Depto. 63, Providencia, Santiago. Cheaper if bought outside Chile.

For **hiking**, allow at least a day to walk the length of the island, one way, taking in all the sites. It is 5 easy hours from Hanga Roa to Rano Raraku (camp at ranger station); 5 hrs. to Anakena (camp at ranger station, but ask first). You can hitch back to Hanga Roa, but there aren't many cars. Anyone wishing to spend time exploring the island would be well-advised to speak to Conaf first (T 236); they also give good advice on special interests (biology, archaeology, handicrafts, etc.).

Vehicle Rental If you are hiring a car, you should do the sites from south to north since travel agencies tend to start their tours in the north (also a high-clearance vehicle is better-suited to the roads than a normal vehicle). Cheapest jeep hire at Sunoco service station, Vaihu, T 325 or 239, on airport road, US$8/1 hr., US$16/4 hrs., US$30/8 hrs. There is no insurance available, drive at your own risk (be careful at night, many vehicles drive without lights). Motorbikes may be rented for about US$30 a day including gasoline (Suzuki 125 rec. because of rough roads). Rentals from Av. Policarpo Toro, T 326.

Bank at Tahai, open 0900-1400 daily. Bank charges 10% commission per cheque. Prices are quoted in dollars, but bills can be paid in pesos; there is an island-wide conversion rate about mid-way between the mainland official and parallel rates. AmEx credit cards are accepted on the island, and while most places accept travellers' cheques, cash dollars are expected. Best rates of exchange at Sunoco service station. Kia-Koe Land Operator, *Hanga Roa Hotel*, changes AmEx cheques. **Post Office** 0900-1700.

Tourist Office Kia-Koe, at *Hanga Roa Hotel*, excellent range of excursions which include all the island's sites in 2½ days (to see it all you must start with the 1530/1600 tour on the day you arrive).

Travel Agency Mahinatur Ltda, will make your car reservations in advance.

Medical There are a 20-bed hospital, 2 resident doctors and 2 dentists on the island.

Time Zone Easter Island is always 2 hrs behind the Chilean mainland, summer and winter time.

How to Get There Lan-Chile fly three times a week the year round, Sun., Wed., Fri. (1990), 5 hrs. Return to Santiago is Mon., Thur., Sat. (Mon., Wed. and Sat. out of season). Lan-Chile's office on the island is at *Hotel HangaRoa*, T 79; do not fly to Easter Island unless you have a confirmed flight out (planes are less crowded to Tahiti, to which Lan-Chile's flights continue, than back to Santiago). For details of Lan-Chile's air passes which include Easter Island and which must be purchased outside Chile, see **Information for Visitors**. It may be cheaper to buy a simple return with pesos exchanged on the parallel market. The fare in late 1989 was US$469 return, but out of season it may be reduced; confirm and reconfirm all bookings as flights are heavily oversubscribed. Students studying in Chile eligible for 30% discount. If flying to, or from Tahiti, check if you can stay over till another flight or even if there is time for sightseeing before the flight continues (in either case it won't be long enough to take it all in properly. Don't take pesos to Tahiti, they are worthless in French Polynesia. The airport runway has been improved. A US project to extend the airfield, to provide an emergency landing for space shuttles, has been completed.

Airport tax Flying from Santiago to Easter Island incurs the domestic tax of US$3.50; if flying to Tahiti without stopping on Easter Island you pay the international departure tax of US$12.50. The airport tax for international flights from Easter Island to Tahiti is US$5.

Dr. R. H. Webber writes: "It is possible to walk around the main part of the island in two days, either camping at Anakena or returning to Hanga Roa and setting out again the next day (but most correspondents agree that this is far too quick). From Hanga Roa, take the road going past the airport and continue northeast until you come to a right turn at a wireless station. Continue along the south coast, past many *ahus* to Rano Raraku (20 km.). The statues have been pushed over in some places, exposing the hollow chambers where human bones are still to be found.

"There are also many temple sites in the Hanga Nui area nearby; the road goes past "the trench of the long-ears" and an excursion can be made to Poike to see the open-mouthed statue that is particularly popular with local carvers. The jeep-track continues to Ovahe, passing many temple sites and conical houses. At Ovahe, there is a very attractive beach with pink sand and some rather recently carved faces and a cave.

"From Ovahe, one can return direct to Hanga Roa or continue to Anakena, site of King Hotu Matua's village. From Anakena the coastal path is variable in quality, but there are interesting remains and beautiful cliff scenery. At Hanga o Teo, there appears to be a large village complex, with several round houses, and further on there is a burial place, built like a long ramp with several ditches containing bones.

"From Hanga o Teo, one can venture inland to Aku Akivi, where there are several other sites and a cave at Tepahu. Near here there is a trail to Puna Pau; a track near the church leads to the top of the volcano.

"Rano Kau, south of Hanga Roa, is another important site to visit; one finds the curious Orongo ruins here. One final place not to be missed is Vinapu, where the *ahu* masonry work rivals that of the Incas."

A shorter walk is from Hanga Roa to Ahu Akivi, down to the South West coast, and back to Hanga Roa (8 km. one way).

Recommended reading, *Islas Oceánicas Chilenas*, edited by Juan Carlos Castillo (Ediciones Universidad Católica de Chile, 1987), contains much information on the natural history and geography of Juan Fernández and Easter Islands.

SANTIAGO SOUTH TO TEMUCO (5)

Road and railway run S through the Central Valley, one of the world's most fruitful and beautiful countrysides, with the snowclad peaks of the Andes delimiting it to the E. Most of Chile's population lives in this valley.

The railway has been electrified from Santiago to just S of Temuco. Along the road from Santiago to Temuco there are several modern motels. From Santiago to San Fernando, the highway is dual carriageway, with two tolls of US$2 to pay.

Rancagua, the capital of the Sixth (Libertador General Bernardo O'Higgins) Region, 82 km. S of Santiago (1 hr. 10 mins bus, US$2.10), is an agricultural centre with a population of 140,000, where a battle was fought in 1814 by O'Higgins against the Royalists. Its Merced church is a national monument; it also has a historical museum. El Teniente, the largest underground copper mine in the world, is 67 km. to the E, at 2,750 metres; a permit to visit may be obtained in Santiago only (Huérfanos 1270). 28 km. E from Rancagua by road, are the thermal springs of Cauquenes.

Festivals at Rancagua The national rodeo championship is held there at the end of March. Festival del Poroto (Bean Festival), 1-5 Feb.

Hotels *Turismo Santiago*, Av. Brasil 1036, T 225060, C; *España*, San Martín 367, T 223963, D with bath, less without, central, hot water, pleasant, clean; *Rancagua*, San Martín 85 y Cáceres, T 232663, D with bath, quiet, clean, secure parking, rec. *Termas de Cauquenes*, T 297226, A, quiet, clean, expensive but excellent food (colectivo from Rancagua market, US$1.10). Many hotels do not accept guests before 2000 hrs., or may charge you double if you arrive in the afternoon. Some 50 km. south is *Hacienda Los Lingues*, see page 535.

Exchange Fincard (Visa, Mastercard), Astorga 485, Mon.-Fri. 0900-1400, 1530-1930, Sat. 1000-1300.

Tourist Office Germán Riesco 277, T 225777, helpful, English spoken. **Automóvil Club de Chile**, Ibieta 09, T 223575.

Rail Trains from Santiago, at least 4 a day, about 1 hr. 10 mins., US$2 *económico*, US$2.65 *superior*.

To the south west of Rancagua, in the valleys of rivers Cachapoal, Claro and Zamorano, the land is given over to fruit growing (including the estates of Viña Concha y Toro). Towns such as Doñihue, San Vicente de Tagua Tagua and Peumo have their roots in an Indian past which has been replaced by the *huaso* (cowboy) and agroindustry. West of Peumo is Lago Rapel, the largest artificial lake in the country (camping, water sports, etc. at Bahía Skorpios). The lake feeds the Rapel hydroelectric plant, best reached from Melipilla.

San Fernando, founded in 1742, capital of Colchagua Province, with 44,500 inhabitants, is 51 km. S of Rancagua. It stands in a broad and fertile valley at a height of 340 metres. A road (buses) run W to the seaside resort of Pichelemu. A road runs E towards the Cordillera and bifurcates: the northern branch runs to the Termas del Flaco, near the Argentine frontier (camping, *cabañas* and hotels), the southern branch goes to the resort of Sierra Bella Vista, a private *fundo* where many Santiago businessmen have holiday houses. Cowboy rodeos in October and November.

Hotels On Av. Manuel Rodríguez: *España*, No. 959, T 711098, C; *Marcano*, No. 968, T 712917, E; and *Imperio*, No. 770, T 712322.

From San Fernando a road runs to the seaside resort of Pichilemu (120 km., 86 paved), with beaches, camping and a great many hotels and *residenciales*.

Curicó, 60 km. S of San Fernando and 192 km. from Santiago, is in the heart of the wine country; population: 74,000. The surroundings are picturesque and the town's main Plaza de Armas is one of the finest in the country. In the plaza there are lovely fountains with sculptures of nymphs, black-necked swans and a monument to the Mapuche warrior, Lautaro, carved from the trunk of an ancient beech tree. The church of San Francisco, a national monument on the plaza, contains 17th century sculptures from Spain. At the junction of Carmen and Av. San Martín is the imposing Iglesia del Carmen. The Centro Cultural, Merced 437, is worth a visit; it has an art gallery, cinema, auditorium for concerts and an excellent cheap café. Overlooking the city, the surrounding countryside and with views to the distant Andean peaks is Cerro Condell (100 metres); it is an easy climb to the summit where there are a number of walks. The fine, broad and tree-lined Avenida Manso de Velasco leads to Parque Balmaceda, in which is a bust of the poet, Gabriela Mistral.

There is a toll (US$2) on the Longitudinal Highway south of Curicó. The city has a good road connection with Argentina, via Paso Vergara (Paso del Planchón, 92 km. from Curicó) to San Rafael (transport schedules from Turismo Bucalemu, Yungay 621). (We are grateful to Simon Watson Taylor for much new information on Curicó.)

Hotels *Luis Cruz Martines*, Prat 301 y Carmen, T 310552, C, breakfast extra, elegant, comfortable, good; *Comercio*, Yungay 730, T 311516, also C but a little cheaper, similar facilities and likewise rec.; *Prat*, Peña 433, near Plaza de Armas, F p.p., not all rooms have windows, but clean, hot water, heated lounge and good value; opp. is *Residencial Rahue*,

No. 410, similar rates, meals extra, hot water, annex rooms have no ventilation, but otherwise acceptable. On the outskirts of town, at Km. 190 on the Panamericana is *Hostería y Restaurante Agua Negra*.

Restaurants *El Fogón Chileno*, Yungay 802, excellent for meat and wines; *Villota*, Merced 487, popular, especially for lunch, very good value; *American Bar*, Yungay 647, coffee, pizzas, good sandwiches, pleasant atmosphere, open early a.m. to late p.m. inc. weekends, rec.; *Café-Bar Maxim*, Prat 617, light meals, good coffee, beer and wine. Many good, cheap restaurants in the streets around the Plaza de Armas.

Exchange Fincard, Carmen 498, for Visa and Mastercard.

Laundry/Dry Cleaners Limpiabien, Prat 454 (and other branches), quick, efficient.

Tourist Office Municipalidad building, 2nd floor, Plaza de Armas, helpful, has street map. **Automóvil Club de Chile**, Chacabuco 759, T 311156.

Buses To Santiago, US$3, companies have their own terminals, also for other interprovincial destinations. Rural bus terminal, O'Higgins y Prat, one block from railway station; buses to coastal towns from outside railway station.

Rail Station is at the end of Prat, 4 blocks west of Plaza de Armas. To/from Santiago, US$3 *económico*, US$3.65 *superior*.

Excursions A road runs W to Licantén, 26 km. from the popular sea beaches of Iloca. North of Iloca is another popular resort, Llico, reached either by a coastal route or by an inland road which branches off the road to Licantén. Just before Llico are Lago Vichuquen (hotels, camping at Bahía Mansa, and watersports) and **Laguna de Torca**, a natural sanctuary for wildlife (there are *miradores* for birdwatching, the administration is 4 km. away at Llico, open September-April). Daily buses run Curicó-Llico. From Curicó you can also visit the **Siete Tazas National Park**, where a river flows through seven rock bowls, each with a pool emptying into the next by a small waterfall. The river then passes through a canyon, 15 metres deep but only 1½ metres wide, which ends abruptly in a cliff and a beautiful waterfall. Go to Molina from where buses run to the Park, daily in Jan. and Feb., twice weekly in March, and Oct.-Dec., once a week at other times. The park is open October to March. Camping may be permitted at the park or at Parque Inglés 5 km. away.

Talca, 56 km. S of Curicó (258 km. from Santiago) is the most important city between Santiago and Concepción and an important maufacturing centre; it is the capital of the Seventh (Maule) Region, and has a population of 300,000. It was founded in 1692, and destroyed by earthquake in 1742 and 1928; it has been completely rebuilt since 1928. Chilean independence was declared in Talca on 1 January, 1818. The market is near the bus station, where there are also stalls selling cheap food. A 175 km. road runs E through the pass of Pehuenche (2,490 metres) to San Rafael (Argentina). Near the border is Lake Maule (2,130 metres). The road passes through some of the finest mountain scenery in Chile, but permission to visit this area must be obtained from the Vice Comandancia del Regimiento de Infantería No. 16, Calle 3 Oriente, Talca (T 38159). There is no transport, accommodation or food there. A visit to an old estate at Villa Cultural Huilquileru is rec., 10 km. away.

Hotels *Plaza*, 1 Poniente 1141, T 231515, B, good commercial standard; *Claris*, 1 Sur 1026, T 232202, D; *Alcázar*, 2 Sur 1359 and 7 Oriente, F, breakfast and meals available, rec. as reasonable and clean. Also, *Cordillera*, 2 Sur 1360, T 233078, F p.p., near new bus terminal. *Café-bar El Gobelino*, on Plaza de Armas, English-style pub.

Museum Museo O'Higginiano, 1 Norte 875 y 2 Oriente, entrance US$0.35, open Tues.-Sat. 0930-1300, 1500-2000, Sun. 1000-1300; interesting.

Tourist Office Edificio Intendencia (at the town hall), T 33669. **Automóvil Club de Chile**, 1 Poniente 1267, T 223-2774.

Bus Terminal, corner 12 Oriente and 2 Sur. To Chillán, frequent service, US$2; also frequent to Constitución, 2 hrs., US$1.20.

Train Station at 2 Sur y 11 Oriente. Most trains from the capital to Concepción, Chillán, Valdivia and Puerto Montt stop here (Talca is the first stop on the Rápido Puerto Montt, 3 hrs. 20 mins. from Santiago, 17 hrs. 15 mins. to Puerto Montt); fare from Santiago, US$3.65

económico, US$5 *superior*.

Excursion To *Vilches*, the starting point for the climb to the volcanoes Quizapu and Descabezado (3,850 metres) 2 buses a day, US$1.50, 2-2½ hrs., leave Talca 1300 and late p.m., leave Vilches 0700 and 1730. *Hostería Rancho Los Canales* has log cabins, D p.p. bed and breakfast, use of kitchen, hospitable, knowledgeable family (postal address: Clasificador 28, Correo de Talca). 2 km beyond the town is the **Area de Protección Vilches**, with 20 km. of beautiful walks; visit the lakes Los Patos, La Encantada and El Toro, and the Piedras Tacitas, a stone construction supposedly made by the aboriginal inhabitants of the region. The administration is near the *Hotel Altos de Vilches*; there is a visitors' centre in the park (2 daily buses from Alto Vilches).

Constitución, 105 km. from Talca by rail, and also reached by paved road from San Javier, is the centre of a prosperous district producing grain and timber, but its main attraction is as a seaside resort. The beach, an easy walk from the town, is surrounded by very picturesque rocks. There are good views from Cerro Mutrún, at the mouth of the river (access from Calle O'Higgins). The nearby scenery is attractive, despite nearby factory. There are plenty of hotels and *pensiones*, but accommodation is difficult from January to March, and bookings must be made well in advance.

Hotels *Hostería Constitución*, Echeverria 460, T 671450, B, best; *Residencial Bulnes*, Bulnes 673, F with breakfast, hot water, clean.

Restaurants *Colonial*, good but expensive; *Portales*, good, cheaper; both on Portales.

There are two **Reservas Nacionales** south of Constitución, in the vicinity of Chanco: **Los Ruiles**, protecting woods and flowers (open October-March, daily buses from Constitución or Cauquenes, on the road to the coast from Parral), and **Federico Albert**, ½ km. from Chanco (bus), which covers a marginal zone of woods and encroaching sand (visitors' centre, 4 paths of 5 km., open October-March).

About half-way between Talca and Chillán is the road and rail junction of Parral, 342 km. S of Santiago, celebrated as the birthplace of the Nobel Prize-winning poet Pablo Neruda.

Chillán, 105 km. S of the road junction for Linares, was the birthplace of Bernardo O'Higgins. In Chillán Viejo (SW of the centre) there is a monument and park in his honour; it has a 60-metre long mural depicting his life (an impressive mosaic of various native stones), and a Centro Histórico y Cultural, with a gallery of contemporary paintings by regional artists (park is open 0900-1300, 1500-1900). (Chile's naval hero, Captain Arturo Prat, was born 50 km. from Chillán, at Ninhue.) It is an important agricultural centre, capital of Ñuble province, with a population of 121,000. When the city was destroyed by earthquake in 1833, the new city was built slightly to the N; that, too, was destroyed by earthquake in 1939 and there was a further earthquake in 1960. It is a pleasant city with a modern cathedral. The Mercado y Feria Municipal (covered and open markets) sells regional arts and crafts, and has many cheap, good restaurants, serving regional dishes; open daily, Sun. until 1300. Murals by David Alfaro Siqueiros, the great Mexican artist, in the library of Escuela México (Av. B. O'Higgins between Vega de Saldias and Gamero).

Hotels *Gran Hotel Isabel Riquelme*, Arauco 600, T 223664, B; *Rucamanqui*, Herminda Martín 590 (off Plaza de Armas), T 222927, C, clean, spartan; *Cordillera*, Arauco 619, on plaza, T 225222, D, 3-star, small, all rooms with heating and bath, good; *Quinchamalí*, El Roble 634, T 223381, D, central, quiet, clean, hot water, heated lounge. On Libertad: *Libertador*, No. 85, T 223255, E, large rooms, clean, hot water; *Real*, No 219, T 221827, E, good; *Ruiz de Gamboa*, O'Higgins 497, T 221013, D with bath, E without, good value; these three are a few minutes' walk from the railway station and are much better than the closer hotels such as *Chillán*, Libertad 65, *Santiago*, next door, and *Bahía*, opp. station, reported clean but basic, F; *Claris*, 18 de Septiembre 357, T 221980, 2 blocks from plaza, friendly, F p.p., good value, hot water; *Residencial Su Casa*, Cocharcas 555, T 223931, cheap, clean (owner is a dog- and rose-lover), parking.

Restaurants *O'Higgins*, Constitución 199, good almuerzo; *Centro Español*, on Plaza, adjacent to Cathedral, almuerzo US$4.50, dinner US$10, bar with snacks in separate room,

SOUTH-CENTRAL CHILE

good. *Fuente Alemána*, on Arauco, just to left of plaza, for churrasco; opposite is *Café París*, expresso coffee. *Club Comercial*, Arauco 745, popular at lunchtime, good value almuerzo, popular bar at night; *Quick Lunch*, El Roble 610, open 0800-2400 for good value meals with good service. 2 good Chinese: *Jai Yang*, Libertad 250 and *Taipe* at No. 285. On the plaza: *La Copucha*, 18 de Septiembre y Constitución, inexpensive meals and sandwiches, *El Cafetín*, good for coffee and breakfast (closed Sat. and Sun.); *Café Madrid*, 5 de Abril 608, also good for coffee, open weekends; *La Masc'a*, 5 de Abril 544, excellent cheap meals, *empanadas de queso*, drinks, rec. In Chillán Viejo, *Los Adobes*, on Parque O'Higgins, good food and service, reasonable prices.

Exchange Both Banco de Concepción and Banco Sudamericano give poor rates. Better rates at *Café París* on Arauco. Fincard (Visa and Mastercard), El Roble 553.

Tourist Office In Gobernación building on main plaza, central courtyard, left-hand gallery; street map of city, leaflets on skiing, Termas de Chillán, etc. Another office reported at Av. O'Higgins 250, Parque O'Higgins, Chillán Viejo, T 223272 (long way from centre). **Automóvil Club de Chile**, O'Higgins 677, T 222550.

Train T 222424 for station, which is on Av. Brasil opp. Calle Libertad, 5 blocks from plaza. To Santiago, at least 5 daily, 5½ hrs., *Salón* US\$7-7.35 depending on the service, *económico* US\$5-5.35. Check times in advance. To Concepción, either by train or bus link, 4 a day, US\$2, 2 hrs.

Bus Terminal at Maipon and Sgto. Aldea for local buses (4 blocks from centre). For Santiago, 7 hrs, US\$7.50, buses leave from the interprovincial terminal at Constitución 10 y Brasil (opp. railway station). Tegualda 860 and Barrios Arana 90, bus to Concepción, every ½ hr.

Excursions 27 km. SW of Chillán is **Quinchamalí**, a village famous for the originality of its craftsmen in textiles, basketwork, black ceramics, guitars and primitive paintings (all on sale in Chillán market). Its ferry, at Confluencia, 5 km. away, powered by the flowing river and manned during daylight hours, except 1200 to 1400, is a must for enthusiasts of alternative technology; in summer, when the current is weak, it runs on human power. To the thermal baths, **Termas de Chillán**, 82 km. E, 1,850 metres up in the Cordillera, reached by a good road all the way. Season: middle December to the end of March (no public transport at other times, except from *Hotel Isabel Riquelme* at weekends). Here the Ski Club de Chile has a tourist centre with hotel (L, full board, T 223887 Chillán, Casilla 247, office at Arauco 600, or Santiago T 251-5776, Av. Providencia 2237, locales 42-4) and ski-lifts. There is excellent ski-ing on the slopes and views of the Chillán volcano, E of the Termas. Cheaper than centres nearer Santiago; packages available. This ski resort is to be expanded. On the road to the Termas, 70 km. from Chillán are *Hotel Los Pirineos*, T 222462 and *Parador Jamón, Par y Vino*, T 222682, Casilla 22, Chillán (Don Emilio Chamorro), or in Santiago, 18 de Septiembre 661, oficina 23, T 744577. The latter arranges recommended horse riding expeditions (accommodation in our A range).

From Chillán there are various road routes to Concepción: (1) SW to Penco and S along the coast—there is a scenic railway; (2) along the Longitudinal Highway to Bulnes, where a branch road goes SW to Concepción; or (3) along the Highway past the Salto del Laja to Los Angeles, from which a main road and a railway run NW to Concepción.

Concepción, the capital of the Eighth (Bío-Bío) Region, 15 km. up the Bío-Bío river and 515 km. from Santiago, is the most important city in southern Chile and the third city of the Republic. Its port, Talcahuano, is 15 km. away. Population: 240,000 (with Talcahuano: 468,000).

The climate is very agreeable in summer, but from April to September the rains are heavy; the annual average rainfall, nearly all of which falls in those six months, is from 1,250 to 1,500 mm. Concepción has been outstandingly unfortunate in the matter of earthquakes; it was founded in 1550, but its site has had to be moved more than once during its history.

In the attractive Plaza de Armas at the centre are the Intendencia and the Cathedral. The old arcades have given way to a new shopping area. In the Parque Ecuador (on Victor Lamas, at the foot of Cerro Caracol), there is a craft fair every February. At the edge of the park, between Angol and Lincoyán, is the Galería de la Historia, covering both Concepción and the region, open Tues.-Sun.

1000-2000, entrance free (worth a visit).

Cerro Caracol can easily be reached on foot starting from the statue of Don Juan Martínez de Rozas in the Parque Ecuador, arriving at the Mirador Chileno after 15 minutes. There are two other sets of steps up the hill. Chile's largest river, the Bío-Bío, and its valley running down to the sea lie below. On the far side of the river you see lagoons, the largest of which, San Pedro, is a water-sport centre. On the city side, among cypress trees, is the modern Barrio Universitario. A stroll through the grounds, which are beautifully kept with geese, ducks, swans, hummingbirds and a small enclosure with *pudu-pudu* (miniature deer) is rec.; the Casa del Arte here contains a fine allegorical mural, 35 by 6 metres, the *Presencia de América Latina*, by Jorge González Camerena (closed Monday). There is a golf club on the road to Coronel, La Posada, by the side of a picturesque lake.

There are striking massive rock formations along the banks of the Bío-Bío estuary. Concepción is linked with Talcahuano, on the bay, by railway (no passenger services) and 2 good roads, half-way along one of which is the Club Hípico's racetrack. Races are held on Sun. and holidays. A branch road leads to good beaches, including Penco with two good seafood restaurants. It passes through the Parque de Hualpén, which can be reached by bus in summer (US$1) and taxi all the year (US$10). In it, on a farm, is a small museum containing curious local and Mapuche Indian items. Nearby is the strikingly set beach of Desembocadura del Río. Two other beaches are Las Escaleras (a private club)—a flight of natural stairs down a sheer 53-metre sea cliff leads to it—and Ramuntcho, named after a novel by a visitor in 1875: Pierre Loti.

Concepción is one of Chile's industrial centres. It has plenty of the most important industrial raw material, water, and good port facilities at Talcahuano and other places in the bay. It is near the coalfields, has ample sources of hydroelectric power, good rail and road communications with the consuming centres further N, and plenty of room to expand.

Hotels *El Araucano*, Caupolicán 521, T 230606, A; *Cruz del Sur*, Freire 889, T 230943 (not very friendly), B-C; *Ritz*, Barros Arana 721, T 226696, C, reasonable; *El Dorado*, Barros Arana 348, T 229400, Telex 260031 DORAL CI, B; *Alborada*, Barros Arana 457, Casilla 176, T 228226, A; *Tabancura*, Barros Arana 790, 8th floor, T 226927, C, clean, highly rec.; *Alonso de Ercilla*, Colo Colo 334, T 227984, C; *Residencial Antuco*, Barros Arana 741, flats 28-33 and *Residencial San Sebastian*, Barros Arana 741, flats 34-35, both D, both rec. **Res. Colo Colo**, Colo Colo 743, F p.p., central, spartan, hot water, heated lounge, pleasant, welcoming, rec.; apart from this one, good budget accommodation is hard to find; *Residencial Central*, Rengo 673, E (F over 3 nights), very unfriendly; **Res. Metro**, Barros Arana 464, F p.p., hot shower, but basic, overpriced, rooms without windows; **Res. Concepción**, Freire 552, across from the market, run down; **Res. O'Higgins**, Av. O'Higgins 457, central, E, pricey, grubby, cold, poor breakfast; *Youth Hostel*, Colo Colo 354, draughty but O.K., closed in winter.

Restaurants *El Rancho de Julio*, Barros Arana 337, Argentine parrillada, good value; *Piazza*, Barros Arana 327, good pizzas; *Rincón de Pancho*, Cervantes 469 (closed Sun.), excellent for meat, mainly, but also pasta and congrio, good service and ambience; *Tagore*, Lincoyán 660, grills, seafood and excellent vegetarian main dish, small, intimate, good service and value, open till late inc. Sun.; *Novillo Loco*, Portales 539, good food, efficient service. *Le Château* (French), Colo Colo 340, for seafood and meat, but overpriced and closed Sun. Oriental: *Yiet-Xiu*, Angol 515, good, cheap; *Ta-Tung*, Lincoyán 540, similar value and quality, Cantonese; *Chung Hwa*, Barros Arana 270. **Hotel Concepción** restaurant, Barros Arana 101, is good value; *Big Joe Saloon*, O'Higgins 808, just off plaza, popular at lunchtime, closed Sun. a.m. but open in p.m., good breakfasts, vegetarian meals, snacks and pizzas. *Saaya 1*, Barros Arana 899, excellent panadería/pastelería/rotisería, highly rec. Vegetarian: *Naturista*, Barros Arana 244, good fresh juices, soups and other dishes, live guitar music at lunchtime. Many *fuentes de soda* in centre; *Fuente Alemana*, Av. O'Higgins, rec.; those on the Plaza de Armas include *Café El Dom*, Caupolicán side, open Sun. 0900, *Café Haiti*, Plaza end of Caupolicán, also open Sun. a.m., and *Café Status*, on first floor, pleasant, reasonable lunches; *Royal Pub*, O'Higgins 796, not a pub but a rather posh snack bar serving fat sandwiches, all named after famous Britons, go to look at the menu if nothing else, try to puzzle out the relationship between the fillings and who they are named after (closed Sun. a.m., opens Sun. 1900); *Salón Inglés*, next door, is an English tea shop, "good for expats longing for a cuppa"; *Nuria Café Bar*, Barros Arana 736, serves very good breakfasts and lunches, good value; good sandwiches at *Entrepanes*, Caupolicán, between B.Arana and Freire. The market place, bounded by Freire, Caupolicán, Maipú and Rengo, has excellent seafood and the best pastel de choclo, also good for fruit, vegetables, cheese and sausages (closes 2000, 1400 on Sun.). (Thanks are due to Simon Watson Taylor for his extensive research for the improvement of this section.)

Clubs Concepción at Los Copihues; Alemán; Aliance Française, Colo Colo y V. Lamas, library, concerts, films, cultural events; Chilean-British Cultural Institute, San Martín 531 (British newspapers, library); Chilean-North American Institute, Caupolicán 301 y San Martín, has library ; Chileno-Italiano, Barros Arana. Country Club, Pedro de Valdivia, outside swimming pool, tennis.

Car Hire Hertz, Lord Cochrane 862, T 223121; Avis, T 235837.

Museum Museo de Concepción, near Barrio Universitario, Tues.-Sat. 1000-1300, 1400-1700, Sun. 1430-1730; entrance US$0.30; interesting on history of Mapuche nation. See above for Galería de la Historia.

Exchange Cambios Fides, Barros Arana 565, local 58, Galería Internal, lower ground floor behind *Hotel Araucano*, best rates for travellers' cheques; Fincard (Visa, Mastercard), O'Higgins 402, open 24 hrs. Banks such as Banco Concepción charge high commission on travellers' cheques.

Post Office and telex, O'higgins y Colo Colo. There is a CTC **telephone** opposite, also at Barros Arana 673, local 2. Entel, Caupolicán 567, 2nd floor.

British Consul Dr. John F. Pomeroy, Castellón 317, T (041) 225655, Casilla 452.

Laundry Many laundries and dry cleaners in the centre.

Tourist Office Aníbal Pinto 460 on plaza, T 223272. Will advise on the more expensive hotels and *residenciales*. **Automóvil Club de Chile**, San Martín 519, T 226554, for information and car hire.

Travel Agent Pawulska Tour, Tucapel 340, 3rd floor, B, T 236850, Telex 360165, arranges tours, flights, translation, interpretation, and welcomes travellers for a chat.

Air In the summer, flights daily to and from Santiago (in winter, only four a week) and connections to Temuco, Puerto Montt and Punta Arenas. The new jet airport is by the fast road from Talcahuano and Concepción. Lan-Chile, Barros Arana 541, T 25014; Ladeco, Barros Arana 451, T 225872.

Rail 3 regular daily trains to/from Santiago, one (No. 1019) non-stop, 9 hrs.; in summer the service is increased: *salón* US$8-8.65 depending on service, *económico* US$6-6.35, sleeper from US$12 to US$33.35 for *departamento*. Connections by rail or road to Chillán; no regular, direct services to Temuco (a seasonal service runs once a day), or Puerto Montt. Station at A. Prat with Barros Arana. Ticket office Galería Alessandri, local 6, T 225286, or T 226-925 for station.

Buses Long distance terminal on outskirts, on Av. Gen. Bonilla, next to athletics stadium; buses from Av. Maipú in centre. To and from Santiago, 8½ hrs., US$7 (cheapest is Sol del Pacífico, US$4, not very comfortable but OK); to Loncoche, 7 hrs., US$6.50; to Puerto Montt several companies, US$7.50-9, about 12 hrs., only one ½ hour stop so take food and drink with you; to Pucón, 8 hrs., US$7.35. Igi-Llaima, to Temuco, 5 hrs., US$4.25, and other companies. To Los Angeles, US$1.50. Best direct bus line to Chillán is Línea Azul, 2 hrs., US$2, at 0700. For a longer and more scenic route, take Costa Azul bus which follows old railway line, through Tomé, Coelemu and Ñipas on to Chillán (part dirt-track, takes 5½ hrs.). Frequent service to Coronel (US$0.45). For Arauco and Bío-Bío region (including Cañete) buses leave from railway station on Av. Prat. To Contulmo, 0745 and 1545, US$2.55. To Lota, from Carrera y Prat, every 15 mins., 1 hr., US$0.50 (ask tourist office for details of all services).

Excursion To the Museo y Parque Hualpen, a house built around 1885 (now a national monument) and its gardens, donated to the city by Pedro del Río Zañartu; it contains beautiful pieces from all over the world, 2 hr. visit, rec. (open Tues.-Sun. 0900-1230, 1400-1800, free). Take a city bus to Hualpencillo, ask driver to let you out then walk 40 mins, or hitch. You have to go along Av. Las Golondrinas to the Enap oil refinery, turn left, then right (it is signed). To Lirquén, a small, old, pretty town of wooden houses with a good beach (walk along railway to reach it). Recommended. Plentiful cheap seafood for sale (try *Casa Blanca*, on Calle Manuel Rodríguez). At Penco, near the beach, is *Casinoriente*, another good seafood place, and *Hotel La Terraza*, Penco 20, T 451422, E. Local buses from Av. Prat 484 take 20-30 mins., US$0.40.

16 km. further along is Tomé, 1½ hrs., US$0.70, another picturesque village; *Restaurante Piña*, main Plaza (owner speaks English); *Hotel Roxy*, Sotomayor 1077, T 378, E, and *Linares*, Serrano 875, T 538, F. An interesting cemetery, Miguel Gulán Muñoz, is set on a cliff overlooking the ocean. **Dichato**, a 1-hr. bus ride away, is also worth visiting: it is a beautiful fishing village and has the oceanographic centre of the University of Concepción. In summer it is a holiday resort. *Hotel Chicki*, P. L. Ugalde 410, T 681004, E; *Montecarlo*, Ismael Valdés 685, F; *Residencial Santa Elena*, on beach, G, clean, cold water; *Restaurant Monte Carlo*, on beach, good. Private Museo del Mar, by Benjamín Ortega, interesting, free. Take a local bus to the tiny village of Cocholgüe.

Between Concepción and Lota (see below) are the Lagunas San Pedro Chica (swimming) and Grande (water sports), just across the Bío-Bío river. Nearer Lota are Playa Negra (small, few people, black sand) and Playa Blanca (bigger, bars, cafés, crowded, white sand, free campsite), both on the Bahía de Coronel (see below).

Talcahuano, on a peninsula jutting out to sea, has the best harbour in Chile. It is Chile's main naval station; its dry docks accommodate vessels of 30,000 tons. Population: 228,000. 1½ km. away the steel plant at Huachipato has its own wharf to unload the iron ore shipped from the N. "Base Naval" bus from main plaza in Concepción, going W on O'Higgins.

Hotel *Res. San Pedro*, Manuel Rodríguez 22, T 542145, E. **Restaurants** *Bentoteca*, on seafront, a row of four restaurants sharing one window facing the harbour, superb fish and seafood in each one, rec., reasonable prices. *El Alero de los Salvo*, Colón 3396; *La Aguada*, shellfish dishes; *Domingo Lara Lara*, Aníbal Pinto 450, seafood specialities, excellent.

The *Huáscar*, a relic of the War of the Pacific, is in the naval base. On 21 May, 1879, at the beginning of the war, the Peruvian Navy's huge ironclad, the *Huáscar*, and a small one arrived at Iquique. Chile sent two small wooden ships under Captain Arturo Prat to challenge them. Prat fought with ferocity. When his broken vessel, the *Esmeralda*, was rammed by the *Huáscar* Prat called upon his men to follow him, boarded the enemy and continued fighting until he was killed. Chile later captured the *Huáscar* at the battle of Angamos, Mejillones, on 8 October, 1879. The ship is open daily 1030-1630, but the schedules do change. Photography is permitted, but passports must be handed in at main gate.

A railway to Curanilahue links Concepción with the coal-producing districts to the south. It crosses the Bío-Bío by a 1,885-metre bridge, the longest of its kind in Chile. A new road bridge, which passenger traffic uses, has been built. The town of **Coronel**, in the heart of the coal area, is 29 km. from Concepción. Coronel was the scene of a British naval defeat in 1914 (the *Good Hope* and *Monmouth* were sunk by the *Scharnhorst*—a monument was dedicated in November 1989), which was later avenged at the Falklands with the destruction of the German squadron. The coast is very picturesque, the country wooded.

Buses Buses to Concepción every hour. Bus to Lota US$0.25.

Lota, 8 km. S of Coronel, is a coal-mining centre with 52,000 inhabitants. To the west of the town, on a promontory, is the famous Parque de Lota (Cousiño Isidora), laid out with views of the sea by an English landscape architect in the last century. It contains many flower gardens, romantic paths, and peafowl and pheasants roaming freely. (Admission US$0.60, no picnicking; open 1000-1800 daily, till 2000 in summer.) The Cousiño mining company runs an excellent ceramic factory. The road is paved beyond Lota as far as the seaside resort of Laraquete (an hour's run by car from Concepción), where there are miles of golden sands, and on to Arauco (*Hotel Plaza*, Chacabuco 347, T 551265, E; *Hostería Arauco*, P. de Valdivia 80, T 551131, B), past the Celulosa Arauco wood-pulp plant.

Hotel Third house (blue, no numbers) in Calle Condell rec., F. Bus drivers from Agencia Miramar stay there. *Residencial Central*, Cousiño 656, F. **Hotels in Laraquete** *Laraquete*, on Gabriela Mistral, main street, F, friendly, small rooms, baths in poor repair. Several *residenciales* close to beach.

Buses to Coronel (20 min.), and Concepción (1½ hrs., US$0.50). No rail services.

From Curanilahue, 96 km. from Concepción, a 32 km. road runs to Los Alamos, where a bus (26 km.) can be taken W to **Lebu**, a fishing port and coal washing centre with a population of 17,000 (*Hoteles Central*, Pérez 183, T 511904, D and some cheaper rooms, and *Rocha*, Pérez 309, T 511939, F; *Res. Alcázar*, Alcázar 144, G with breakfast, cold water, friendly). It lies at the mouth of the Río Lebu, and is the capital of Arauco province (buses S leave from Los Alces, next to train station). The lower river reach and the beach are popular with tourists in summer. The views from the hill behind the town are majestic.

13 km. S of Los Alamos, is **Cañete,** a small town on the site of Fort Tucapel where Pedro de Valdivia and 52 of his men were killed by Mapuche warriors in 1554. Museo Mapuche de Cañete, half-hour walk from town in direction of Contulmo. Open, Tues.-Sun. 1000-1230, 1400-1800. Entrance US$0.60. Interesting for its architecture, landscape, gardens with flowers cultivated by the Mapuches. Ask for Sr. Mauricio Rivera Osorio.

Accommodation *Hotel Nahuelbuta*, Villagran 644, T 611251, main street near plaza, F, private parking; *Alonso de Ercilla*, opposite, No. 641, T 611974, F, clean; *Derby*, Nariñan 680, T 211621, F, central, clean, friendly, good restaurant. Some shops rent rooms, F. Mormons in Calle Condell offer accommodation, free and friendly.

Buses 3 night buses to and from Santiago, 12 hrs. Buses to Purén, US$1.50; sit on right-hand side to get good views of Lake Lanalhue. To Concepción, 3 hrs., US$2.50.

From Lebu or Los Alamos you can go to Puerto Peleco on the highly picturesque Lake Lanalhue, 63 km. S of Lebu (buses S leave Los Alces, next to train station). 3½ km. S of Peleco, the road forks, the west branch running parallel to the coast (from this road, a dirt road goes along the south side of the lake to *Hostería Lanalhue*—16 km. from Peleco. A nice location—and continuing to Contulmo bus terminal, taxi US$14, negotiable). By taking the west branch of the road for about 25 km. and then asking the way to Contulmo, you can reach the south-eastern end of the lake after crossing a high ridge from which you can see both the ocean in the W and the snow-capped Andes to the E. In **Contulmo** *Hotel Contulmo* is highly recommended, E (Millaray 116, Eduardo Videla and family love to break out the wine and guitar with visitors); *Hotel Central*, Calle Millaray no sign, also E and very hospitable. Taxi from Contulmo to lake beach US$2; good swimming, but fishing not so. Bus Contulmo-Temuco, Thiele company, 3 a day, US$3, at least two a day to Concepción, US$2.55 (check times in advance).

Travelling S from Chillán on the Longitudinal Highway, the next major centre is **Los Angeles**, capital of Biobío province, a town of 106,000 inhabitants in a wine, fruit and timber district. Founded in 1739 as a fort, it is now a pleasant, expanding city, with a large Plaza de Armas; Colón is the main shopping street. There is a good daily market.

Hotels *Gran Hotel Müso*, Valdivia 222 (Plaza de Armas), T 323163, C, good restaurant open to non-residents; *Mariscal Alcázar*, Lautaro 385 (Plaza de Armas), T 321275, B; *Mazzola*, Lautaro 579, T 321643, D. *Res. Winser*, Colo Colo 335, F; *Res. Santa María*, Caupolicán, next to bus station, E, hot shower, TV, breakfast extra. Private house at Caupolicán 651, F, basic but OK. Youth hostel: *Complejo Turístico Los Manantiales*, Caupolicán 332, camping and cabins, open 1 March to 31 December.

Restaurants *El Arriero*, Colo Colo 235, T 322899, good parrillas and international dishes; *Julio's Pizzas*, Colón 452 and *Rancho de Julio*, Colón 720, excellent parrilla; *Brasilia*, Colón 431. *Brisa Mamina*, Mercado Central Local 22, Villaquán 599, good, check bill.

British Cultural Institute Vicuña 648.

Post Office on Plaza de Armas.

Tourist Office Av. Caupolicán and Villagrán; also kiosk on Plaza de Armas. **Automóvil Club de Chile** Villagrán y Caupolicán, T 322149.

Bus to Santiago, 9 hrs., US$7.50. To Viña del Mar and Valparaíso 10 hrs., US$8.25, 4 daily to Concepción, US$1.50, 2¼ hrs. Hourly buses to Temuco. To Curacautín, daily at 0600, 3 hrs., US$2.25.

Excursion The **Salto del Laja** is a spectacular waterfall in which the Laja plunges 47 metres over the rocks. It costs a few pesos to enter the "parque" and walk up to the falls, or to walk on the hotel side. There is a good motel (the *Motel Salto del Laja*, C, address: Casilla 562, Los Angeles) with fine restaurant, 2 swimming pools and chalet-type rooms on an island overlooking the falls. Also at or near the falls are *Camping Los Manantiales* and Motels *El Pinar* and *Los Coyuches*. It is 6 hrs. drive from Santiago (by bus, US$7.25). To see the falls, buy bus ticket (Bus Sur or Bio Tal) from Los Angeles (32 km., US$0.60, ½ hr.—fairly frequent buses back to Los Angeles) or Chillán (Carretera US$2).

A road runs to the **Parque Nacional Laguna de Laja** past the impressive rapids of the Laja river. A car can take about 3 hours to get to the lake, where there is stark volcanic scenery of scrub and lava, dominated by the Antuco volcano and the glacier-covered Sierra Velluda. Take a bus to Abanico, 20 km. past Antuco (US$1.35, 2 hrs., 5 a day but only 0845 in a.m., return 0715), then 4 km. to park entrance, passport retained by guards till you leave (details from Conaf in Los Angeles, José de Manzo 275, 0800-1300, 1430-1800 Mon.-Fri.). *Cabaña y Camping Lagunillas*, 50 m. from the river, 4 km. from the ski slopes, campsite US$1.65 p.p. or US$4.65 for 3 or more. Camping not permitted on lake shore. 21 km. from the lake is the *Refugio Chacay* offering food, drink and bed (B, T Los Angeles 222651); two other *refugios*: *Digeder*, E, and Universidad de Concepción, both on slopes of Volcán Antuco, for both T Concepción 221561, office O'Higgins 734. Following the road one reaches the Club de Esquí de los Andes with two ski-lifts, giving a combined run of 4 km. on the Antuco volcano (season, May-August). There is swimming in the Río Duqueco, ten minutes away by bus, US$0.80.

The road continues from Los Angeles to Santa Bárbara on the Bío-Bío river, and then via Collipulli (campsite), Victoria, Púa and Lautaro to Temuco.

From Collipulli and Los Angeles paved roads run W to **Angol** (25,000 people), capital of the Province of Malleco (Ninth Region), founded by Valdivia in 1552, seven times destroyed by the Indians and rebuilt. Bus from Los Angeles, US$1.20. Worth seeing are the Vergel experimental fruit-growing station, the Dillman S. Bullock regional museum with stone-age Indian artefacts (open Mon.-Sat. 1000-1230, 1500-1800, Sun. 1500-1800; free, a 5 km. bus-ride from town) and the San Francisco church. 22 km. W is the **Parque Nacional Nahuelbuta**, in the coastal mountain range, reached by bus to Vegas Blancas, 0700 and 1600 Mon., Wed., Fri., 1½ hrs., US$1, 27 km. from Ayol, then walk (or possibly hitch) 7 km. to park gate, and a further 7 km. to the campsite (US$0.70 to enter park, US$0.70 to camp—there are many free campsites on the way to the entrance). The park has many araucaria trees (monkey-puzzles) and viewpoints over both the sea and the Andean volcanoes. Rough maps are available at the park entrance for US$0.25. Roads run W to Los Sauces and Purén. Bus to Temuco, US$2.15.

Hotels *Millaray*, A. Prat 420, T 711570, D; *Olimpia*, Lautaro 194, T 711517, D; *El Parrón*, O'Higgins 345, T 711370, F; *Residencial Olimpia*, Caupolicán 625, T 711162, E.

Mulchén, a small, old-fashioned town, 32 km. to the south of Los Angeles, has few cars, no concrete and is a glimpse of a world gone-by.

A small town which has hot springs nearby, **Curacautín**, is 56 km. SE of Victoria (on the Longitudinal Highway, Ruta 5) by paved road; bus from Los Angeles or Temuco.

Curacautín Hotels *Turismo*, Tarapacá 140, T 116, F, clean, good food, comfortable, best value; *Plaza*, Yungay 157, T 56, E.

The beautiful pine-surrounded Termas de Tolhuaca, with hot springs, are 37 km. to the NE of Curacautín by unpaved road, or 57 km. by unpaved road from just N of Victoria. (*Hotel Termas de Tolhuaca*, B with full board, use of baths, and horse riding included, good; *Residencial Roja*, F, hot water, food; camping near the river, good.) It is about 9 km. from the hotel to the **Parque Nacional Tolhuaca**, in which are the waterfalls of Malleco and Culiebra, and Lake Malleco; superb scenery and good views of volcanoes from Cerro Amarillo (the park is open Nov.-March). SE of Curacautín (32 km. by road) are the hot springs and mud baths of Río Blanco (hotel), at 1,046 metres on the slopes of the Sierra Nevada and near Lake Conguillo (bus to Conguillo National Park—see below—only at 1800). 18 km. from Curacautín (direction Lonquimay) are the Termas de Manzanar, reached by bus from Temuco and Victoria (*Hotel Termas*, C, but also has simple rooms with bath but not luxurious; *Hostería Abarzua*, F, simple, friendly).

THE LAKE DISTRICT

14/57

The nearby Lonquimay volcano has the Puelche ski-run, season May-November. The volcano begun erupting on Christmas Day 1988; the new crater is called Navidad. To see it, access is made from the village of Malalcahuello, half-way between Curacautín and Lonquimay town. In Malalcahuello, the teacher at the school charges US$8.50 for the car to drive up to the volcano and collect you later; Sra. Naomi (Saavedra at *Residencial Los Sauces* also arranges lifts (E full board, or G p.p. with use of kitchen, hot water, good value). You can also stay at a refuge in the **Reserva Nacional Malalcahuello-Nalcas** on the slopes of the volcano (E, hot showers); this is 10 km. from the bus stop where the driver lets you off, 5 km. from the volcano. The bus to take is Erbuc, Temuco-Lonquimay, US$2 to Malalcahuello, 4 a day, 4 hrs., 5½ to Lonquimay town, US$2.80. There is accommodation in Lonquimay, but little transport to the volcano. The road Curacautín-Lonquimay town, 57 km., passes the Salto del Indio (Km. 14), before which is a turnoff to Laguna Blanca (25 km. away, take fishing gear, ask Sernatur about trucks), and Salto de la Princesa, just beyond Manzanar. The next village is Malalcahuello which, besides the services mentioned above, has a steam-powered carpenter's shop, with oxen hauling logs.

THE LAKE DISTRICT (6)

		Population ('000)	
Region	Provinces	1982	1987
IX (Araucanía)	Malleco, Cautín	698	755
X (Los Lagos)	Valdivia, Osorno, Llanquihue, Chiloé	848	903

South from the Bío-Bío river to the Gulf of Reloncaví the same land formation holds as for the rest of Chile to the N: the Andes to the E, the coastal range to the W, and in between the central valley. The Andes and the passes over them are less high here, and the snowline lower; the coastal range also loses altitude, and the central valley is not as continuous as from Santiago to Concepción. The climate is cooler; the summer is no longer dry, for rain falls during all the seasons, and more heavily than further N. The rain decreases as you go inland: some 2,500 mm. on the coast and 1,350 mm. inland. This is enough to maintain heavy forests, mostly beech, but there are large clearings and an active agriculture; irrigation is not necessary. The farms are mostly medium sized, and no longer the huge *haciendas* of the N. The characteristic thatched or red tiled houses of the rural N disappear; they are replaced by the shingle-roofed frame houses typical of a frontier land rich in timber. The farms raise livestock, fruit and food crops, and the timber industry is being encouraged.

About 20,000 pure blooded Mapuches live in the area, more particularly around Temuco. There are possibly 150,000 more of mixed blood who speak the Indian tongue, though most of them are bilingual.

A Mapuche music festival (plus market) is normally held mid-February in Villarrica. Enquire at the Santiago or Temuco tourist office.

Between parallels 39° and 42° S is found one of the most picturesque lake regions in the world. There are some 12 great lakes of varying sizes, some set high on the Cordillera slopes, others in the central valley southwards from Temuco to Puerto Montt. Here, too, are imposing waterfalls and snowcapped volcanoes. Anglers revel in the abundance of fish, the equable climate, and the absence of troublesome insects (except for enormous horseflies between mid-December and mid-January). The season in the lake district is from mid-December to mid-March, when prices are higher and it is best to book well in advance. It is a peaceful area, with fewer tourists than across the border in the Argentine lake district.

The Lake District proper does not begin until we reach Chile's newest city, Temuco, founded 1881 after the final treaty with the Mapuches.

1. Parque Nacional Cerro Ñielol
2. Visitors' Centre
3. Cerro Conun Hueno
4. Plaza de Armas
5. Museo de la Araucania
6. Livestock Market
7. Municipal Market
8. Other Markets
9. Terminal Rural (Buses)
10. JAC Buses
11. Tourist Office
12. Conaf
13. Post Office
14. Entel Telephone Office
15. CTC Telephone Office
Hotels
16. *Turismo*
17. *Nuevo de la Frontera*
18. *Continental*
19. *Nicolás*
20. *Espelette*

TEMUCO
NOT TO SCALE 59

Temuco, 676 km. S of Santiago, has 220,000 inhabitants. It is the capital of the Ninth (Araucanía) Region, and one of the most active centres in the S. Wheat, barley, oats, timber and apples are the principal products of the area. The cattle auctions in the stockyards behind the railway on A. Malvoa, Mon. (1200, sheep and pigs) and Thurs. (cattle) are interesting; you can see the *huasos*, or Chilean cowboys, at work. Also, cattle sales at Feria Agroaustral, just outside Temuco on road to Nuevo Imperial, on Fri. (take bus 4 from Calle Rodríguez), auction starts at 1400, and at Nuevo Imperial, 35 km. away, on Mon. and Tues. The Municipal Cultural Centre at the intersection of Balmaceda, Caupolicán and Prat houses the municipal library, a theatre, and art galleries. About 100 metres away, at Caupolicán y Balmaceda is the Cema-Chile shop for Mapuche arts and crafts. Both are worth a visit. Temuco is the Mapuches' market town and you may see some, particularly women, in their typical costumes in the produce market next to the railway station (Lautaro y Pinto). (If you wish to take photographs, ask first; you may be asked for money.) The best places to look for Mapuche textiles, pottery, woodcarving, jewellery etc. are the indoor municipal market in centre of town (corner of Aldunate and Diego Portales—it also sells fish, meat and dairy produce); or, for textiles, early in the morning, near the rural bus station (Pinto y Balmaceda—also selling produce). There is a grand view of Temuco from Cerro Ñielol, a national park, where there is a fine array of native plants in the natural state, including the national flower, the *copihue rojo*. There is also a bathing pool (US$0.40) and a restaurant. On Cerro Ñielol is also La Patagua, the tree under which the final peace was signed with the Mapuches in 1881.

Hotels *Turismo*, slightly run-down restaurant, good value, C with bath, D without, good service, Claro Solar 636, T 232348, near main square; *Nuevo Hotel de la Frontera*, A, Bulnes 726, T 236190, excellent; *Nicolás*, Mackenna 420, T 235547, B with shower and heating, restaurant, poor all round; *Espelette*, Claro Solar 492, T 234255, C with bath, D without, breakfast US$1, excellent, clean, friendly; *Continental*, A. Varas 708, T 231166, C, popular with business travellers, and the bar is popular with locals in the evening, cheaper rooms without bath, rec.; *Casa de huéspedes Centenario*, Aldunate 864, E, with breakfast, hot water, clean; *Oriente*, M. Rodríguez 1146, D-E, clean, rec.; *Residencial Méndez*, Matta 382, F, hot water (doesn't work), mixed reports. Many cheap *residenciales* and *pensiones* near railway station in market area. Also *Rupangue*, Barros Arana nr. Igi-Llaima terminal, 2 blocks from Terminal Rural, E, hot shower, clean, helpful, good value; *Omega*, Av. Pinto 91, corner of Miraflores, opp. rural bus terminal, overlooking market, near train station, F p.p., hot shower, clean, friendly but thefts reported, not a salubrious area; *Flor Acoca*, Lautaro 591, F, hot water, breakfast, clean. Unnamed *hospedaje* at Pedro Lagos 576, F p.p., meals, good, friendly; another *hospedaje* at Claro Solar 483. Sra. Veronica Kiekebusch, Av. Alemania 0649 (T 32079), E with breakfast, rec., buses No. 1 or 9 for train and rural bus stations; also Alemania 035, F p.p., hot water, pleasant; Casa familiar Mirtha Lagos de Concha, Zentano 525, E with breakfast, nice, clean. Private house, Blancolat 959, corner of San Martín, F p.p., use of kitchen, rec., but only open for tourists in summer (student hostel in winter); also G. Cruz 212, 2nd floor, E, breakfast, clean, friendly, good value; Bulnes 995, E; Claro Solar 151, E with breakfast; Bello 886, E. Ask in Tourist Office for accommodation in private houses.

Restaurants *Nueva Hostería Clei*, Bulnes 902, next to LIT terminal, excellent; *Kim Long*, Portales 1192, Chinese, excellent; *Café Mariel*, in mall between Prat y Bulnes, excellent coffee; *Café Istanbul*, Bulnes 563, good, especially for coffee; also on Bulnes: *Dino's*, No. 360, branch of a chain of good restaurants; *Julio's Pizza*, No. 778, wide variety, not cheap; *Del Mayo*, good; *Centro Español*, Bulnes 483. *Club Alemán*, Senador Estebáñez 772, away from centre. Plenty iof good eating places inside the municipal market. *Rincón Naturista*, Prat 425, vegetarian meals, snacks, fresh fruit juices, yoghurts, health food shop, bookstore, rec. Outside town: *Hostería La Estancia* (dancing), highly rec., on Longitudinal Norte; *La Cumbre del Cerro Ñielol* (dancing), on top of Cerro Ñielol.

Museum Museo de la Araucania, Alemania 084, a well-arranged collection devoted to the history and traditions of the Mapuche nation. Open Mon.-Sat. 0930-1300, 1500-1830; Sun. 0930-1300, US$0.50.

Camera Shop Ruka, Bulnes 394, helpful, owner speaks German.

Car Hire Hertz, Bulnes 726-733, T 236190/231226. Budget, Montt 498, good value; Automóvil Club de Chile, Bulnes 763, T 231283; Puig, on Portales, cheap.

Exchange Turcamb, Claro Solar 733; Turismo Money Exchange, Bulnes 655, Galería Arauco, local 1, on plaza; Inter-Santiago, Bulnes 443, local 2. All deal in dollars and australes. Fincard (Visa, Mastercard), Claro Solar 922.

Laundry Lavajet, Claro Solar 574; Caupolicán 110, Nos. 4 and 5, open 0900-2100 daily; Portales 1185, expensive.

Telephones Centro de Llamadas CTC, A. Prat just off Claro Solar and plaza, Mon.-Sat. 0800-2400, Sun. and holidays 1030-2400. Entel, Bulnes 307, casi M. Rodríguez, daily 0830-2200.

Post Office at railway station and Prat y Portales.

Tourist Office on main square, at Calle Bulnes 586, esquina Clara Solar, T 34293. Open 0830-2030, all week in summer, Mon.-Fri. in winter. Has full list of places to stay. Also at Balmaceda and Av. Prat. **Automóvil Club de Chile**, Bulnes 763. **Conaf**, Bilbao y Caupolicán, T 34420.

Rail Station at B. Arana and Lautaro, T 226925. Daily to Puerto Montt, No. 1023 "Rápido Puerto Montt", leaves in early morning, 8 hrs., also an *expreso* service, *económico* about US$5, *salón* US$6.60; to Concepción once a day, but not all year. To Valdivia: once a day in winter (3½ hrs.), twice a day in summer. To Santiago: 2 *rápidos* a day, both with sleepers, leaving after 2030 (times change through the year) and one *expreso*, also leaving in evening; trains from Santiago as for Valdivia or Puerto Montt; *económico* US$6, *superior/salón* US$10-11 (depending on service), sleeper US$16.65-23.35, compartment US$51.50. Ticket office at Bulnes 590, T 233522, open Mon.-Fri. 0900-1300, 1430-1800, Sun. 0900-1300 as well as at station.

Air Airport 6 km. from the city. Lan-Chile, Bulnes 667, 3 times a week to Santiago and Puerto Montt, once to Concepción. Ladeco (Bulnes 396, T 236739) has several flights a week to Valdivia, Osorno and Santiago; also one to Concepción. Varig and Pan Am agent at Salfa vehicle showroom, Mackenna y Bello.

Bus to neighbouring towns from Terminal Rural at Pinto and Balmaceda. Flota Erbuc (also at Miraflores y Bulnes, and Balmaceda 1415), to Curacautín, US$1.35, 7 daily, 2¾ hrs; also to Lonquimay, 4 daily, 5½ hrs., US$2.80, Laguna Captren Mon. and Fri. 1645, 4 hrs., US$2.20; Santiago, 2100, US$5. Long-distance buses leave from individual company terminals. Buses Cruz del Sur from V.Mackenna 671, 3 a day to Castro, 10 a day to Puerto Montt (US$5.25, 5½ hrs.), to Valdivia US$2; to Osorno US$3.30. Other buses in 600 block of V. Mackenna (nr. Claro Solar): ETTA, Longitudinal Sur, Thiele (for Lebu and Contulmo, 0745, 1310, 1600, 3½ hrs. to Contulmo, US$3, change here for Cañete and Concepción), and JAC for Santiago. JAC's main terminal is at Mackenna y Bello for all other services except to Argentina (see below): Villarrica and Pucón many between 0705 and 2045, 1½ hrs., US$1.25 and 2 hrs., US$1.60 respectively, Coñaripe, 3 hrs., and Lican Ray (2 hrs.). Several other companies on Claro Solar, 500-600 blocks, e.g. LIT at No. 694. Fenix, Pedro Lagos y Claro Solar, to Arica (2200 and 2245, arrives 1400 2 days later, US$45 or US$60 *cama*), Iquique, Antofagasta (US$35), La Serena and Santiago, also Pucón and Valdivia. Power, Bulnes 174 and Balmaceda 1438 to Villarrica and Pucón 0730 (US$1 and US$1.35), and Panguipulli at 0730, 2 hrs., US$1.65. Also to Panguipulli, Pangui Sur, Miraflores 871, 10 a day between 0700 and 1915, 3 hrs., US$2, also to Loncoche, Los Lagos, Mehuin in summer only. Most companies have a service to Santiago (try also Unión del Sur, Bonanza in the arcade at Balmaceda y Pinto), charging about US$10, usually overnight (book in advance). Bío Bío bus to Concepción (US$4.25), six daily.

Buses to Argentina JAC from Terminal Rural to Junín de los Andes (US$8.15), San Martín de los Andes (same price) and Neuquén (US$16), Wed. and Fri. 0400; Igi Llaima and San Martín both go three times a week to San Martín; Nar Bus from Terminal Rural to San Martín and Neuquén, Mon.-Fri., US$16.50 each (San Martín buses go via Villarrica and Pucón when the Tramen Pass is open); Ruta Sur, Miraflores 1151, to Zapala (US$11.65) and Neuquén (US$15), Wed. and Sat. 0400; La Unión del Sud, Miraflores 1285, same destinations Wed., Fri. and Sat. Fenix (address above) to Buenos Aires, US$52, and Mendoza, US$22.50. Buses on the Zapala route go via the Pino Hachado pass, not Icalma.

Excursions A road and railway run W to (55 km.) Carahue. About 30 km. further, at the mouth of the navigable River Imperial, is **Puerto Saavedra**, where there is a stretch of beach with black volcanic sand. It comprises 3 distinct towns: the first administrative; the second, 2 km. away, the fishing port with one poor *residencial*; the third, a further 2 km., the tourist area with many *hosterías* in E-F category. It is reached from Carahue by car (1 hr.), or by bus from Temuco Terminal Rural (Nar Bus, 0730, 0800, 0930, 2½ hrs., US$1.20).

From Puerto Saavedra there are interesting excursions to Nehuentue, on the other side of the river, or to Lakes Budi and Trovolhue, both well worth seeing. Trovolhue is reached by a specially chartered launch which takes 4 hrs. to go up the Moncul River. Puerto Domínguez, on Lake Budi, a picturesque little place famous for its good fishing, is reached by dirt road from Carahue (40 km.). From Puerto Saavedra beach or fishing port, walk 1 hr. to Balsa Budi from where a raft goes to Isla Huapi. A further 3 hrs.' walking leads to a ferry for Puerto Domínguez.

" Another pleasant trip through Mapuche country is to take a minibus from the Central Market to the country town of Chol-Chol, 30 km. to the north-west. There are daily buses (Huincabus from Terminal Rural, 1 hr., 4 times between 1100 and 1430, US$0.60, or García/Gangas from same terminal at 1000), laden with corn, vegetables, charcoal, animals, as well as the locals. The trip traverses rolling countryside with panoramic views. On a clear day it is possible to see five volcanoes. Nearer Chol-Chol, the traditional round houses made of thatch (*rucas*) can be seen. There is not much to see in Chol-Chol itself, but it does have a delicious wild west flavour somehow. " (Ian H. Dally, Iglesia Anglicana de Chile). For an overnight stay and information, contact Sra. Lauriza Norváez, Calle Luzcano (s/n), who prepares meals, and is very helpful. You can continue from Chol-Chol to Imperial and Puerto Saavedra, but bus connections few and slow (stay overnight in Puerto Saavedra).

The 3,050-metre Llaima volcano has at its foot one of the prettiest skiing resorts in Chile: **Llaima**, at 1,500 metres, 80 km. E of Temuco. It stands in the middle of two large **national parks**, **Los Paraguas** (named for the umbrella-like araucaria pine trees—best visited August-October according to Conaf) and **Conguillio** (open 20 Nov.-13 March). The latter, too, is full of araucaria forests and contains the Laguna Conguillio and the snow-covered Sierra Nevada. It is one of Chile's most popular parks, but is deserted outside the Jan./Feb. season. The best way to get to the park is to drive yourself, preferably in a high-clearance vehicle and with clear instructions on which roads shown on maps are suitable and exist. There are three routes, on all of which there is public transport, via Curacautín, via Melipeuco or via Cherquenco. Take a bus from Temuco to Curacautín (**see page** 557) then a bus at 1830, Mon. and Fri. towards the park, 1 hr., US$1, or hitch, to Conaf hut (you can camp nearby). It is then 10 km. to Laguna Captren situated in araucaria forest, where you pay a park entrance fee of US$0.50; campsite (US$4 including firewood but no other facilities), good hiking. 6 km. further on is Laguna Conguillio (take the Sendero de los Carpinteros), with a visitor's centre, campsites (US$6 per site, hot water, showers, firewood; *cabañas*, summer only, US$20, sleep 6, no sheets or blankets, gas stove) and café/shop, from where you can hike into the Sierra Nevada. At Laguna Verde in the Park is a free campsite without facilities. 15 km. beyond Laguna Conguillio, mostly across deserted lava fields, is the other entrance to the park, and then it is 13 km. though farmland to the village of Melipeuco (*Hotel Central*, F, good; *Hostería Hue-Telén*, Pedro Aguirre Cerda 1, D, good; Nar Bus from Temuco Terminal Rural to Melipeuco, 5 daily, 0900-1830, 3 hrs., US$1.30, last back to Temuco at 1630). Transport can be arranged from Melipeuco into the park, but in summer buses from Temuco go, via Melipeuco, right through the park (3 a week). The third alternative is to go to Cherquenco (road paved to Vilcún, the road very poor for the last 40 km., high clearance essential. Daily buses Temuco-Cherquenco). It is then a 2-3 day hike around Volcán Llaima to Laguno Conguillio, dusty, but beautiful views of Laguna Quepe (good camping spot), then on to the Laguna Captren *guardería*.

For details of these excursions visit the Corporación Nacional Forestal, IX Región, Caupolicán y Bulnes, Temuco. For best touring, hire a 4-wheel drive vehicle in Temuco.

The way from Temuco to Villarrica follows the paved Longitudinal Highway as far as Freire (24 km.), then (also paved) runs 63 km. SE. A road to Villarrica from the S runs substantially parallel with the old railway line from Loncoche. Wooded Lake

Villarrica, 21 km. long and about 7 km. wide, is the most beautiful in the region, with snow-capped Villarrica volcano (2,840 metres) in the background.

Villarrica, pleasantly set at the extreme SW corner of the lake, was founded in 1552 but destroyed by the Indians in 1602; the present town (24,000 population) dates from 1882.

Festival   Festival Cultural Mapuche in second week of February.

Hotels   *Yachting Club*, Gen. San Martín 802, pleasant atmosphere, terraced gardens, swimming pool, restaurant, boating and fishing, rec., B, but cheaper rooms in motel annex; *Hotel El Ciervo*, Gen. Koerner 241, T 411215, B, German-run, also rec.; *Hostería Kiel*, Gen. Koerner 153, T 411631, C, lakeside, clean, friendly; *Hotel y Cabañas El Parque*, 3 km. out of Villarrica on Pucón road, T 411120, Casilla 65 (or T Temuco 235872), lakeside with beach, tennis courts, C without breakfast, good restaurant set meals, highly rec.; *Residencial Puchi*, Valdivia 678, T 411392, E, hot water, good restaurant; *Casa San Jorge*, Calle Catedral, F, is a Scouts' hostel, good value dormitory accommodation. Youth hostel, *Residencial San Francisco*, Julio Zegers 646, G p.p. in shared rooms. Also, rooms in private homes, e.g. Calle Francisco Bilbao 969, run by Tom Funk, F; at No. 827 and also V. Letelier 702 (open throughout the year).

Camping   2 sites just outside town on Pucón road, *Los Castaños* and *du Lac*. Many more on S side of Lake Villarrica, see under Pucón (below). Also 25 km. south of Villarrica (1 hour, US$1 bus), at Lican-Ray on Lake Calafquén (see below). Bus leaves from near tourist office. Summer houses available in Dec.-Feb.

Restaurant   *Club Social*, on main street, good, Henríquez 379, for snacks and ice-cream dishes. Also *Yandally*, Camilo Henríquez 401. *Panaderías*, at Gral. de Aldunate 632 and 635.

Exchange   Banco de Osorno will change travellers' cheques; also Carlos Huerta, Anfión Muñoz 417, for cheques and cash (dollars and australes—rec. that only men deal with him). Grocery shop opp. *Residencial* on Valdivia changes australes.

Laundry   Lavandería y Lavaseco Villarrica, Andrés Bello 348, T 411449.

Post Office   Anfión Muñoz esq. General Basilia Urrutia, open 0830-1230, 1400-1800 (Mon.-Fri.), 0830-1230 (Sat.). Telex service also available. Entel, Reyes 721.

Tourist Office   Next to museum and library at Valdivia and Acevedo, will give information and maps (open all day all week in summer).

Buses   To Santiago, US$10. To Pucón, ½ hr., US$0.60; 4 a day, 3 on Sun., to Valdivia (JAC, Reyes 616), US$2, 3-5 hrs.; daily service to Panguipulli at 0700, US$2, scenic ride. To Coñaripe and Liquiñe at 1600 Mon.-Sat., 1000 Sun. Temuco, US$1.25. To Loncoche (road and railway junction), US$1.15. N.B. JAC has 2 terminals: long distance at Reyes y Montt, local on Reyes between Henríquez y Muñoz. To Argentina at 0615 on Tues., Thurs. and Sat. with Empresa San Martín (Av. A. Muñoz 417) and at 0730 on Mon., Wed. and Fri. with Igi-Llaima, US$12, but passes can be blocked for four months by snow. If Tromen Pass is closed, buses go via Panguipulli instead of Pucón.

Pucón, a most attractive little town on the south-eastern shore of Lake Villarrica, can be reached by bus from Villarrica (26 km.) or Temuco, not by water. Pucón has a good climate and first-class accommodation. The black sand beach is very popular for swimming and watersports on the lake (prices given below). Queen Elizabeth II stayed there during her visit in 1968. The season is from 15 December to 15 March, when the town is extremely crowded and very expensive. Off season it is very pleasant but many places are closed. There is a pleasant walk to La Península for fine views of the lake and volcano, pony rides, golf, etc. (private land, you must get permission first). Launch excursion from the landing stage at La Poza at end of O'Higgins at 1500 and 1900, US$4 for 2 hours. There is a large handicraft centre where you can see spinning and weaving in progress. The town is scheduled for major development, with plans to build on La Península and around La Poza, the yacht harbour. A Centro de Ski is under construction so that Pucón may become a winter sports centre. Some predict that by the mid-1990s Pucón will be a second Viña del Mar.

Pucón Hotels In summer, December to February, add 20% to hotel prices. State owned *Gran Pucón*, Holzapfel 190, T 441001 (9-hole golf course), open mid December to April, L, disappointing, accessible in off season for entrance fee; *Interlaken*, A, Caupolicán on lakeside 10 minutes from town, T 441276, Swiss run, chalets, rec., will exchange travellers' cheques (only open December to February); *Antumalal*, luxury class, 30 metres above the shore, 2 km. from Pucón, T 441011, very small (18 rooms), picturesque chalet-type, with magnificent views of the lake (take lunch on terrace), expensive and excellent (the Queen stayed there), A, with meals (open year round; good beach, and good fishing up the river. *La Posada*, Valdivia 191, T 441088, open Dec.-Feb., B with bath, cheaper without, full board available; *Hostería Suiza*, O'Higgins 112, T 441945, D, clean, has a small café which is cheap and serves excellent empanadas; *Turista*, O'Higgins 136, T 441153, D (E low season), with bath, friendly, clean; *Gudenschwager*, Pedro de Valdivia 12, T 441156, classic Bavarian type, D (C with bath), views over lake, volcano and mountains, attentive staff, comfortable, excellent restaurant, rec. (open in summer only). *Araucarias*, Caupolicán 243, T 441286, B, clean, comfortable but not luxurious; *Saint John*, hostería and campsite, 2 km. on Villarrica road, open Dec.-March, rooms E p.p., camping US$7.50-11 for 5, full board available, Casilla 154, T 441165/90; *Residencial Lincoyán*, Av. Lincoyán, T 441144, E with bath, F without, clean and comfortable; *Hostería Viena*, summer only, cabins for 6 only, clean and pleasant; *Hostería El Principito*, Av. Gral. Urrutia and Fresia, T 441200, D, with bath, very friendly, rec.; *Salzburg*, O'Higgins 311, T 441907, D with bath and breakfast (summer only), rec, German spoken, some rooms with view over volcano (possible to borrow crampons). *Hospedaje El Fogón*, O'Higgins 472, T 441267, F, good value, good breakfast, next to JAC buses; *Hostería Milla Rahue*, Av. O'Higgins 460, T 441904, E, clean, good restaurant, convenient for JAC. Familia Acuña, Palguín 233 (ask at *peluquería* next door), good, F without breakfast, hot water, use of kitchen and washing facilities. Juan Torres, Lincoyán 445, T 441248, good, clean, cooking facilities (log fires in winter), very friendly, F p.p. including breakfast, use of kitchen, home-made marmalade, information on climbing Villarrica and the Huerquehue National Park; Lincoyán 485 (Sonia), E, warm showers, use of kitchen, has a notebook listing all the good places to stay in Chile, T 441269, friendly, rec.; *Casa de Familia*, Don Juan, Lincoyán 815, cooking facilities (information on climbing Villarrica); *El Refugio*, Lincoyán 348, vegetarian menu, limited but good; Sra. Lucía Sandoval, Lincoyán 565, F p.p., good; family at Perú 720 has accommodation at F, use of kitchen, will help organize excursions to Volcán Villarrica and Huerquehue National Park; also Roberto y Alicia Abreque, Perú 170, F, clean, rec., has information on excursions; *Don Pepe*, Urrutia 592, F p.p. inc. breakfast, good, restaurant is quite cheap; Lucila Oliva y familia, Pasaje Chile, nr. petrol station, rec., F p.p. bed and breakfast, kind, use of kitchen. Also ask in bars/restaurants, e.g. next to garage opp. *Gran Hotel Pucón*.

Camping Next to lake, 20 mins. walk from town, US$7 for two. There are several campsites between Villarrica and Pucón: *Acapulco*, *Playa Linda* (Villarrica), *Suyay*, *Lorena*, 10 km. from Villarrica; *Huimpalay*, 12 km. from Villarrica; *Millaray*, 7 km. S of Pucón; *Trancura* and *Saltos del Molco*; *Albergue Juvenil*, US$1 p.p./night, tent provided, sleeping bags required, 2 km. out of town. In fact, there are so many establishments along the lake's southern shore that you cannot get to the water's edge unless staying in one. On the road to Tromen Pass, *Cabañas El Dorado*, US$18 for 2, good site, poorly maintained. Cheaper sites en route to Caburga.

Restaurants *Pizzería Che Thomas*, Palguín 465, good value, small place run by Jorge; *El Fogón*, O'Higgins, next to JAC office, good meat (*hospedaje* behind); *Il Ristorante*, O'Higgins 323, Italian, fresh pasta, rec., moderate prices; *El Refugio*, Lincoyán 348, *Le Demago*, Lincoyán 361 (plus *Pub Naf-Naf*); *Carnes Orlando*, bar/restaurant/butcher's shop, Ansorena near Urrutia; *Pastelería Suiza*, next to *Hostería Suiza* on O'Higgins; *Café Brasil*, Fresia, good, especially pancakes.

Exchange Good rates at the big supermarket on O'Higgins. Banco del Estado de Chile, O'Higgins casi Lincoyán (new).

Car Hire Hertz, Fresia 220, US$65 for cheapest car (inc. tax, insurance, and 200 km. free); same prices per day at *Gran Hotel*. **Bicycle Hire** Taller de Pollo, Palguín, US$5/day.

Watersports Water-skiing, sailing, windsurfing at the beach by *Gran Hotel* and La Poza beach end of O'Higgins (more expensive than hotel, not rec.); hotel rates: waterskiing US$10 for 15 mins., Laser sailing US$5/hour, US$25/day, sailboards about the same, rowing boats US$1.50/hr.

Laundry on Colo-Colo, good.

Telephone International service at O'Higgins 170.

Travel Agents On O'Higgins: Nieve y Sol (esq. Lincoyán, also at *Grán Hotel Pucón*), Altue, No. 371, Nacional Travel Club, No. 323, and Expediciones Chonos (Sr Ricardo Vázquez). All arrange trips to thermal baths, trekking to volcanoes, whitewater rafting, etc. and are exceedingly good value. (Altue prices, 1990: rafting, US$12 for 1½-2 hrs., 3 trips a day; climbing Villarrica, US$32, 12 hrs., equipment provided; mountain bike tours to glaciers, waterfalls, etc, US$22, all day. Nacional volcano climb, US$20); Sergio Catalán, T 441269 (office) or 441142, Gerónimo Alderete 192, tours, excursions and taxi service all year round. Taxi excursions from O'Higgins y Ansorena.

Tourist Office Av. Caupolicán and Av. Brasil, very helpful, ask here about all types of accommodation; Cema-Chile shop at same location. If closed, Municipal at O'Higgins and Palguin will provide information and sells fishing licences (US$1/month).

Bus JAC terminal: O'Higgins 478 for Villarrica, Temuco (US$1.60, about 20 a day) and Valdivia (0630, 1545, 1845, US$2.50), better to change in Valdivia than in Temuco for Puerto Montt, JAC to Santiago, US$10 from O'Higgins 480. At Palguín 383, agency for Servi-Tur, Tur-Bus—sleeper bus US$20 to the capital, Inter Sur, Fénix Power and Igi-Llaima. LIT, for Temuco and Santiago, O'Higgins y Palguín. Cordillera, Av. Miguel Ansorena (nr. O'Higgins, next to minimarket) for Paillaco and Lake Caburga—see below. Colectivos to Villarrica from O'Higgins y Palguín.

Pucón and Villarrica are celebrated fishing centres, for the lake and the very beautiful Lincura, Trancura and Toltén rivers. The fishing is now reported to be even better further S, in Lake Ranco (**see page •••**) for example. Local tourist office will supply details on licences and open seasons etc.

Excursions from Pucón may be made to the active **Villarrica** volcano in a **National Park** 8 km. S of the town for the grand view (no bus from Pucón, either hitch, or take a taxi to national park entrance, US$4.30, to volcano, US$16.50; Miguel, at O'Higgins entre Lincoyán y Fresia, blue and white Naturista house, charges US$3.50 for round trip to the park; national park entry US$0.75, or US$1.50 to camp). There is a refuge without beds 4 km. inside the Park, insecure and in desperate need of renovation (which is due to start soon). Campsite with drinking water, toilets, below refuge. The volcano can be climbed up and down in 8-9 hrs. (go in summer when days are longer), good boots, iceaxe and crampons, and sun block essential—beware of sulphur fumes at the top; taking a guide is highly rec., it is not an easy hike, ask the park guards about conditions before attempting the climb. If you don't go with a guide, go in a group of at least 3. Guides: Alvaro Martínez, Cristóbal Colón 430, also Juan Carlos, at Lucila's *pensión*, or his pool room on main street; Joaquín, who lives in Calle Brasil, contact him at Sonia's *residencial* (he used to be a rescue worker, very experienced). Many others, all with equipment; ask at the tourist office, average fee is US$20 p.p. inc. transport to foot of volcano. Crampons, ice axe, sunglasses can be rented for US$3.60/day from the Taller de Pollo bicycle shop on Calle Palguin, Pucón, near fire station—a cloth mask moistened with lemon juice helps to filter the sulphur fumes at the summit.

To Lake Colico to the N and volcanic Lake Caburgua, very pretty, to the NE, both in wild settings (row-boats may be hired, US$1.50 per hour). Lake Caburgua is unusual for its beautiful white sand beach whereas other beaches are black sand of volcanic origin (campsite, T 236989, expensive in season, US$2.50 car, US$6.50 tent, but cheap out of season, US$2.50 for tent). Visit also the Ojos de Caburgua, beautiful pools fed from underground. Cordillera bus departs 1230, returns 1400, 2nd bus leaves 1700 and returns next morning (US$1 single), but there are colectivos or you can try hitching. No shops, so take own food. Three more beautiful lakes are Verde, Chico and Toro in the **Huerquehue National Park**, W of Lake Caburgua; there is a well-signed track to them from the car park at Lake Tinquilco (it is more-or-less straight uphill, 2 hrs.—sign says 5 km., but worth it). In Huerquehue there are 20 lakes in all and they keep changing. For Huerquehue, take Cordillera bus to Paillaco, beyond Caburgua, 1½ hrs., US$1, from where it's 7 km. (3 uphill, 3 down, 1 along Lake Tinquilco) to park entrance, where there is a campsite. 2 km. before the Huerquehue Park entrance, the Bratt family (German spoken) take in guests and let people camp for US$1.50; they also rent rowing boats on the lake. Park open officially only Jan.-March, but you can get in at other times. Warden very helpful; people in park rent horses and boats. To protect against horse flies, do not wear dark clothes.

Outside the Huerquehue Park are the Huife thermal baths (T 441222, PO Box 18, Pucón), US$3.20, including use of one pool, "very upmarket, but pleasant". Termas de Quimaico can be reached from the road to Huife: new, less ostentatious than Huife, camping allowed, 2 cabins and *hosteria* (*centro turistico* under construction). To the thermal baths of San Luis, N of the road to Argentina, 25 km. from Pucón, small hotel, ½ hr. walk to Lago del León and

Palguín, S of the same road (*Hotel*—address, Casilla 1D, Pucón—D full board, F in small huts with bath, German-speaking owner, cool swimming pool, baths US$1.75, lots of hikeable waterfalls in the area, e.g. Salto El León, entry US$0.30, slippery walkways). A new complex is being built at Palguín, which is 36 km. from Pucón. At the entrance is the entry to the Villarrica national park; the road goes back 6 km. to the park (high clearance vehicle necessary, horses best), free camping in the park, *refugio* at first campsite. Ask rangers for the route to the other entrance.

Two excursions from Pucón close to Lake Villarrica: 2-km. walk along the beach to the mouth of the Río Pucón, with views of the volcanoes Villarrica, Quetrupillán and Lanín. To Quelhue, across the Río Pucón: walk 7 km. or take a taxi (US$1.35) to the two-stage ferry across the river, the first stage is river-powered, the second a rowing boat, both free but tip the boatman (ferry operates 0800-1300, 1400-1800 Mon.-Fri., 0800-1200, 1400-1800 Sat.). La Reducción de Quelhue is supposed to be a Mapuche village, but no traditional dress, language or customs are used, and the children ask for money. The walking is pleasant, though, towards the N shore of the lake, towards Caburgua, or up into the hills through farms and agricultural land, with views of the three volcanoes and, higher up, of the lake. You cannot go too far up into the hills without meeting gates by a bridge.

There is a road from Pucón to the Argentine town of Junín de los Andes. The route is past the volcanoes of Villarrica and Quetropillán and round Lake Quilleihue, a gem set between mountains at 1,196 metres above sea level. On the border, to the S, is the graceful cone of Lanín volcano (3,747 metres), and beyond the border is Lake Tromen, much visited by Argentine tourists. Conaf campsite 5 km. from border, on a good dirt road by Lake Tromen, no amenities. The Argentine road from the border to Junín de los Andes goes on to San Martín de los Andes, and via Lago Hermoso and Villa Angostura (a beautiful drive) to Bariloche. There is a more direct road from San Martín de los Andes to Bariloche but it is not so interesting (see under Argentina, **page** 150).

About 25 km. S of Villarrica and 125 km SE of Temuco is **Lican-Ray**, with 2 good beaches, on Lake Calafquén, full of islands and good for fishing. Boats can be hired from the beach. The resort is very crowded in season. Several buses daily from Villarrica (JAC—7 a day, 3 on Sun.— and García, Reyes y Henríquez) and, in Jan.-Feb., there are frequent direct buses from Santiago and Temuco. 4 km. away to the E is the river of lava formed when the Villarrica volcano erupted in 1971. Buses Mon.-Sat. at 0730 from Lican-Ray to Panguipulli.

Hotels (most closed out of season) *Bellavista*, Cacique Punulef 240; *Refugio*, B, Mr and Mrs Jack Douglas Feka, Canadian couple, with North American standards, on Playa Grande, open all year, has a Travellers' Exchange Library for English-language books, all donations of paperbacks (in reasonable condition) welcome, please send to Jack D. Feka, Casilla 299, Temuco—for information contact the hotel. *Cabinas Los Pinos*, 3 blocks from lake, F, nice; *Río Negro*, Gerónimo 776, F; several motels (e.g. at *Cabañas El Eden*, Huenuman 105, D for a chalet for 6 with hot water; *El Conquistador*, Cacique Millaqueo s/n), *hosterías*, and camping sites. *Café Ñaños*, Gral. Urrutia 105, very good, reasonable prices, helpful owner.

A road, 14 km., runs SE from Lican-Ray to **Coñaripe**, at the eastern end of Lago Calafquén. At first sight, the village is dusty and nondescript, but its setting, with a black sand beach surrounded by mountains, is very beautiful. There is a good walk from the left-hand side of the beach back through the fields to Coñaripe. This is a popular Chilean tourist spot; *Hotel Antulafquen*, F p.p., homely; cheap campsites near private houses. A road around the lake's southern shore leads to Lago Panguipulli (see below).

The Longitudinal Highway (Ruta 5) runs from Loncoche (81 km. S of Temuco, good place for hitchings) through Lanco to Paillaco and Osorno. At San José de la Mariquina, a road branches off Ruta 5 to Valdivia, 42 km. from the Highway (bus Lanco-Valdivia, Chile Nuevo, US$0.85), 4 a day, fewer at weekends). The road from Valdivia to Ruta 5 going S is not in very good condition; the Highway is rejoined by Paillaco.

Panguipulli, on the W bank of the lake of the same name, is in a beautiful setting, with roses planted in all the streets (the name is Mapuche for "hill of lions"). It is reached by paved road from Lanco, with buses from Santiago, Temuco and Valdivia; there are also road connections to Lake Calafquén and Villarrica. Excursions can be made to Lakes Panguipulli, Calafquén, Neltume and Pirehueico, and south to the northern tip of Lake Riñihue at El Desagüe (*Hostería Riñimapu*, T 388, B, excellent). There is a new 30-km. road around the lake to Choshuenco, a beautiful coastline, wooded, with cliffs and sandy beaches. Buses leave daily at 1530 and 1630 along the North bank of the lake, but it is not possible to return from Choshuenco on same day. (Bus returns from Choshuenco at 0645 and 0700.) Choshuenco volcano is at the SE end; on it Club Andino de Valdivia has ski-slopes and a *refugio*. For fishermen, daily excursions on Lake Panguipulli are recommended. The waterfalls of Huilo-Huilo are most impressive; the river channels its way through volcanic rock before thundering 100 metres down into a natural basin. They can be reached by the Choshuenco bus, get off beyond Choshuenco about 1 km. from Neltume and walk 200 metres to the falls, or at *Alojamiento Huilo Huilo*, where the road crosses the Huilo Huilo river. From here it is a 1½ hr. walk the following day to the falls. Alternatively, walk from Choshuenco along Puerto Fuy road for 3½ hrs. and turn right at sign to the falls. It's 22 km. from Choshuenco to Puerto Fuy, an interesting 5-hour walk. Another road S from Choshuenco goes to the turn off for the Club Andino *refugio* on Volcán Choshuenco and to Enco, at the eastern end of Lago Riñihue (**see page** 572). A scenic road runs through rainforest around the Choshuenco volcano from Puerto Fuy to the river Pillanleufú, Los Llolles and Puerto Llifén on Lake Ranco (see below); in 1989 this road was reported closed to the public, enquire at the lumber mill at Neltume (Sr. Thomas Morefield), 5 km. from Neltume, 3 km. from Puerto Fuy.

A boat crosses Lake Pirehueico Tues., Thurs., Sat. at 1700, US$3, 2-3 hrs. from the Argentine side to Puerto Fuy; bus daily to Panguipulli at 0600, 3 hrs., US$2, except Sun. when it runs at 1700 from Neltume, 7 km. from Puerto Fuy. Ferry returns to Pirehueico at 0900: a beautiful boat trip.

Hotels   At **Panguipulli**: *Central*, clean, hot water, E, not very friendly, good breakfast; *Hostería Panguipulli*, F; *Hostería Quetropillán*, Etchegaray 381, T 348, E, comfortable, food; also, private house opposite; Sra. Pozas, Pedro de Valdivia 251 (E, clean, clothes washing extra); Sra. Eva Halalr, Los Olmos 62, G p.p., English spoken, friendly, good. *Las Brisas* restaurant, has rooms to let, E; *Restaurante Valparaíso*, rec.; *Café Central*, Martínez de Rosas 880; few places to eat in Panguipulli. At **Liquiñe**: *Hostería Termas de Liquiñe*, C p.p.; private houses, F. At **Choshuenco**: *Hotel Choshuenco*, F, good meals; various *hosterías*, including *Hostería Rayen Trai* (former yacht club), María Alvarado—s/n, good food, rec.; Sra. Elena Arrigada, Padre Vernave 198, F, rec.; free camping. At **Pirehueico**: beds available for US$1 or so in private houses. You can stay in white house by the ferry dock.

Campsite   Chollinco, on Lake Ranco, 8 km. from Futrono. Municipal campsite at Panguipulli 3 km. outside town, US$3 with all facilities, rec; free camping on lakeside at Panguipulli possible. Also, at Los Molinos; and at Choshuenco on the lake shore (food shops in the village), and Puerto Fuy on the beach (take your own food, none available to buy).

Tourist Office   in plaza next to police station.

NB   No foreign exchange facilities.

Bus   to Santiago daily at 1845, US$9; 14 daily (Sun. only 4) buses (several lines) from/to Valdivia, 2 hrs., US$1.50 and 9 daily to Temuco (e.g. Power at 1800, 2 hrs., US$1.65, or Pangui Sur, 10 a day, US$2, 3 hrs.) To Calafquén, 3 daily at 1200, 1545 and 1600. To Choshuenco 1530, US$2, return 0630. To Lican Ray (lovely journey) and on to Villarrica at 1530, 2 hrs., US$2. Bus to Villarrica leaves from depot in Calle Etchegaray, 100 yards uphill from *Hostería Quetropillán*.

There is a road from Panguipulli to Coñaripe, on Lake Calafquén, which offers superb views of the lake and of Villarrica volcano, whether you are travelling on foot or by bus. Some buses continue to Lican Ray. It is not possible to travel by bus from Villarrica to Choshuenco on a Sunday; you have to stay overnight in Coñaripe, then take a bus to Panguipulli and make a connection there.

Rail   To Puerto Montt at 0730, change at Antilhue, arrive 8 hrs. later; a long, slow trip but

VALDIVIA 58

1. Plaza de la Republica
2. Municipality
3. Museum
4. Botanical Gardens
5. Universidad Austral
6. Muelle Fluvial (dock)
7. Tourist Office
8. Post Office
9. Market
10. *Hotel Pedro de Valdivia*

worthwhile for the scenery around the lake.

Valdivia, a pleasant city standing where two rivers join to form the Río Valdivia, is 18 km. from the port of Corral and the Pacific Ocean. It is the capital of Valdivia Province and has a population of 140,000. It is 820 km. by rail or road (about 16 hrs.) from Santiago.

The city is set in a rich agricultural area receiving some 2,300 mm. of rain a year; it was founded by Pedro de Valdivia in 1552. Lord Cochrane's greatest victory for Chilean independence was at Valdivia, when he took the forts at Corral, Amargos and San Carlos (the Niebla fort surrendered—see below). From 1850 to 1860 a comparatively small number of German colonists settled in the area; their imprint in terms of architecture and agricultural methods, order, education, social life and custom is still strong. In particular they created numerous industries, most of them on Teja Island (5 by 2 km.) facing the city. The Universidad Austral de Chile was founded in Valdivia in 1954. On the tree-lined, shady Plaza de la República, a new cathedral is under construction. Avenida Prat (or Costanera) runs around the bend in the river, from the bus station to the bridge to Teja Island, the boat dock and the riverside market, which is fascinating.

Hotels *Pedro de Valdivia,* Carampangue 190, T 212931, B with bath, good; *Naguilán,* Gen. Lagos 1927, T 212851/52/53, B, clean, quiet; *Palace,* Chacabuco 308 y Henríquez, T 213319, C, good, comfortable; *Raitúe,* Gral. Lagos 1382, T 21503, D with bath; *Villa del Río,* B with bath, Av. España 1025, T 216292, restaurant expensive (try salmon in almond sauce), rents apartments with kitchen; *Melillanca,* rec. but pricey, B, Av. Alemania 675, T 212509. *Villa Paulina,* Yerbas Buenas 389, T 216372/212445, C, hot showers, clean, pool, parking, highly rec. On Picarte, *Hostal Montserrat* (No. 849), D with breakfast, clean, comfortable; the Salvation Army (US$1.50); *Residencial Anilebu,* No. 875 (nr. bus station) and *Residencial Germania,* No. 873, T 212405, clean but no heat in rooms, D with breakfast; cheaper hotels in same street include Nos. 979 and 1005 (no hot water); hospedaje (no name—one of 2 white *hospedajes* opp. bus terminal) at No. 953, E with breakfast, good value, clean, heated lounge; the other white hospedaje, No. 1151, is also good. *Hospedaje Turismo,* Gral. Lagos 874, T 215946, old German house, pleasant family atmosphere, rec. (the *Schuster,* Maipú 60, T 213272, a popular old Victorian-type German hotel was "temporarily closed" in 1990); *Unión,* Prat 514, T 213819, E, central; *Hospedaje* at Arauco 905, F, clean, friendly. Student *pensiones* include Arauco 852. The house at Aníbal Pinto 1335 (T 3880) is friendly and cheap; *pensión* of Sra. Armida Navarrete Uribe, Calle A.R. Phillippi 878, E/F, full board if desired, hot water, good value; Hospedaje de Señora A. de Prussing, opp. bus terminal, A. Muñoz 345, F p.p. with breakfast, clean, friendly; Sra. Segovia, A. Muñoz 353, opp. bus station, E, breakfast, hot water, rec.; and Sra. Paredes, García Reyes 244, F with breakfast, hot water, rec. For houses offering lodgings in E-F range in summer, leave bus station and turn right into Calle Anwandter (e.g. No. 624, F p.p., with breakfast, comfortable, friendly), or left into Av. Picarte. Casa de Orielle Hermosillo, Carlos Anwandter 400, G p.p., very good.

Campsite Quillín, between Ranco and Valdivia. Also in Parque Saval, Valdivia. White gas impossible to find, other than in pharmacies/chemists.

Restaurants *Centro Español,* Calle Henríquez, good; *Club de la Unión,* on Plaza, serves a large lunch US$2 p.p.; *Sociedad Protectora E.E. de Comercio,* Independencia y Libertad, near Plaza, good and cheap; *El Conquistador,* on plaza at O'Higgins, glass fronted, on 1st floor, good food, reasonable prices; *Dino,* good, Plaza de la República (Maipú y P. Rosales); *Palace,* Arauco y P. Rosales, popular, good atmosphere, reasonable prices; *Delicias,* Camila Henríquez 372, T 213566, rec. for meals and cakes (open Sun. a.m.); *Selecta,* Av. Ramón Picarte 1093, clean, good fish and meat; *Café Haussmann,* O'Higgins 394 (good tea and cakes); *Bomba Bar,* Caupolicán 594; *Phoenix Haus,* Av. Viel s/n, on Teja Island; restaurant on house boat in the dock, good seafood; several restaurants on the Costanera facing the boat dock, have good food and good atmosphere. *Pizza Trattoria la Nonna,* Chacabuco 325, mixed reports, cheap. *Cafetería* at Chacabuco 423 has simple, cheap food; *Café Paula,* Pérez Rosales 633-45, good lunch; *Entrelagos,* Pérez Rosales 622, ice cream and chocolates. Bakery: *La Baguette,* Libertad 110, Picarte 813 and Caupolicán 435, French-style cakes, brown bread. Health food shop and restaurant; *La Vie Claire,* Caupolicán 435A (next to *La Baguette*), good light meals, juices, yoghurts, muesli, etc, rec.

Clubs Chilean-North American Institute, Calle Beauchef; Santa Elvira Golf Club (9 holes);

tennis, sailing, motor, and rowing clubs like Phoenix on Teja Island; also Club Español.

Museum   run by University on Teja Island, free in off-season, US$0.70 in summer, cartography, archaeology, history of German settlement (including cemetery), local Indian crafts, etc. Open Tues.-Fri., 1000-1300, 1500-1800. Also on the island, near the library in the University, a botanic garden and arboretum with trees from all over the world. "Lago de los Lotos" in Parque Saval on the island—has beautiful November blooms.

Festival   Semana Valdiviana, 12-18 Feb.

Car Hire   Hertz, Picarte 624, T 215252; Turismo Méndez, Gral Lagos 1249, T 3205.

Exchange   Banco del Estado at Arauca y Camilo Henríquez, also Banco Osorno, P. Rosales 585, and Banco Concepción, Picarte 370, will change cash and cheques, but slightly better rates at Turismo Cochrane, Caupolicán 544, rec. for changing pesos to australes and for travellers' cheques. Fincard (Visa, Mastercard), Galería Los Castellanos, oficina 18, Mon.-Fri. 0900-1400, 1500-1930, Sat. 0900-1330.

Tourist Office   Calle Arturo Prat 555, by dock. Good map of region and local rivers. Helpful kiosk in bus station next to the news stand. **Automóvil Club de Chile**, Caupolicán 475, T 212378, also for car hire. **Conaf** Ismael Valdez 431.

Rail   Station at Ecuador 2000, off Av. Picarte, T 233522; information and booking office at Arauco 220, T 213574. Daily to Santiago, Rápido Calle-Calle, No. 1026 (No. 1025 from Santiago), with sleepers, 16 hrs., leaves Valdivia in afternoon, leaves the capital mid-evening; also an *expreso* service: *económico* US$11, *Superior* US$14, sleeper US$16.65-23.35, compartment US$51.50. In early 1990 there was a daily service at 1240 to Osorno and on to Puerto Montt; if this is not running you have to change at the main line at Antilhue. No train services to Pucón.

Bus   Terminal is at Muñoz and Arturo Prat, by the river. To Santiago: Pullman daily, leaving 2100, arriving next morning at 0830, about US$10-13.75. Pullman daily to and from central and southern towns. Half-hourly buses to Osorno, 1 hr. 40 mins., several companies, about US$1.65. To Lanco, US$2. Thrice daily to Llifén, US$2.50. 15 buses daily to Panguipulli, US$2. Many daily to Puerto Montt, US$2.50, 3 hrs. To Puerto Varas, ETC bus, 3 hrs., US$2.35. To Frutillar, on Pullman Sur Temuco-Puerto Montt bus, US$2.75, 3 hrs. To Villarrica, by Bus JAC, 3-5 hrs., US$2, daily at 0700, 1100 and 1600. For Pucón change at Villarrica, to Bus JAC. To Bariloche via Osorno (10 hrs.) with Bus Norte and Tas Choapa, 5 a week. Twice daily to Riñihue, Mon.-Sat., 1630 and 1830, Sun. 1945 and 2015.

Air   Lan-Chile and Ladeco (Caupolicán 579, local 18, T 213392) to Santiago every day except Saturday.

Excursions   The district has a lovely countryside of woods, beaches, lakes and rivers. The various rivers are navigable and there are pleasant journeys to Futa, Putabla, and San Antonio, behind Teja Island and through the Tornagaleanes, the Isla del Rey (these journeys can only be made in a rented motor boat). Among the waterways are countless little islands, cool and green.

At the mouth of the Río Valdivia are remains of the fortifications built by the Spanish to defend the entry to Valdivia. There are two centres for visiting the area, **Niebla** on the north bank and **Corral** on the south. In all there are the ruins of 17 forts but the principal ones to see are the Fuerte de la Pura y Limpia Concepción de Monfort de Lemus, a substantial earthwork fort on a promontory W of Niebla; opposite it, in Corral, the Castillo de San Sebastián with a battery of 24 guns and a view upriver to Volcán Llaima in the distance; Castillo San Luis de Alba in Amargos, 20 minutes' walk along the coast from Corral; and, in midstream, the Castillo de San Pedro de Alcántara on Isla Mancera. This last has the most standing buildings; all are national monuments. Niebla is also a bathing resort with seafood restaurants and accommodation (*Hosterías Riechers*, E, and *Santa Clara*, F); information and telephone office by the fort. Further round the coast is Los Molinos, a seaside resort on the ocean. The fishing port of Corral has several restaurants (e.g. *Español* opp. the dock, good seafood), and *Residencial Mariel*, Calle Arica, F. 4 km. along the coast from Corral is San Carlos, with its *Hostería los Alamos* (F), a delightful hideout for those seeking a quiet life. The coastal walks are splendid. Isla Mancera is a pleasant place to stopover on the boat trips, but it has no restaurants and gets crowded when an excursion boat arrives.

The tourist boats (*Neptuno*) or *Calle-Calle*) to Isla Mancera and Corral, including a guided half-day tour (US$11.50 with meals—cheaper without) leave the Muelle Fluvial, Valdivia (behind the tourist office on Av. Prat 555), at 1330 and return at 1830. Cheaper boats to Corral leave 5 times a day, from 0800, from Muelle Fluvial, Valdivia and return between 0800 and 1900, 1¼-hour journey; only at 1200 in winter; they usually go out via Niebla (ferry dock is 20 mins. walk from the fort, near the Copec station) and call at Isla Mancerra (if you want to stop en route, yo u must first pay full fare, US$0.70 then US$0.50 for each "leg"; some boats make a 1¼-hr. stopover on Isla Mancera en route back to Valdivia). The river trip is beautiful, but you can also take a bus to Niebla from Calle Yungay (river end), Valdivia, roughly twice an hour between 0715 and 1945, 20 mins., US$0.45 (bus continues to Los Molinos, US$0.55, students US$0.10), then cross to Corral by boat (US$0.50) and return to Valdivia by river. Colectivo Valdivia-Niebla, US$0.50. There are occasional buses from Valdivia to Corral.

Mehuin, on the coast, 2 hrs. bus ride north from Valdivia through San José de La Mariquina; post office, good sea bathing and several hotels: *Hostería Millalafquen*, T 279, *Hotels Mehuin* and *Playa*. Queule, 6 km. from Mehuin, has two simple *residenciales*. Good beach but bathing dangerous at high tide because of undercurrents; safer to bathe in the river near ferry.

A road runs from Valdivia along the River Calle Calle to Los Lagos (61 km.), and on to the beautiful **Lake Riñihue** (39 km.). The road around the southern edge of the Lake from Riñihue to Enco is now closed (except to jeeps in summer only), so Choshuenco at the SE end of Lago Panguipulli can only be reached by road from Panguipulli or Puerto Fuy. Riñihue, a beautiful but very small and isolated village, is worth a visit. Campsite by the lake; *Restaurant del Lago* has rooms, E (no meals).

Access from the Longitudinal Highway to lovely, island-starred Lake Ranco and, beyond it, to **Lake Maihue** is made from Los Lagos, or from a point 18 km. S of Los Lagos, 11 km. N of Paillaco. These two roads join to meet the road around the lake some 5 km. W of Futrono at the northern shore. The road curves round the north of Lake Ranco to **Llifén**, a picturesque place on the eastern shore. From Llifén, a visit can be paid to Lake Maihue (Cordillera Sur bus Valdivia-Llifén twice daily, once Sun.).

Hotels *Hostería Chollinco*, 3 km. out of town on the road towards Lake Maihue, B, overpriced, poor food, limited electricity, swimming pool; *Hostería Lican*, D; *Hostería La Cascada*, Torremolinos 357, A; *Huequecura*, Casa 4, A, including meals and fishing services. 4 campsites in the vicinity.

On the south side of Lake Ranco is Lago Ranco, an ugly town (several small hotels and *residenciales*, houses to let in summer, campsites—bus from Osorno, see below) and Riñinahue (*hostería*, B); the road is terrible (lots of mud and animals, including oxcarts), but is worth taking to see an older lifestyle, the beautiful lake, waterfalls and sunsets on the distant volcanoes (if walking, beware the numerous guard dogs in the area). There is excellent fishing on the S shore of the lake. On the western shore is Puerto Nuevo (hotel of same name, A, very good, watersports, fishing on the Río Bueno). Roads from Puerto Nuevo and Lago Ranco run W to La Unión (*Hotel Unión*, Letelier 497, T 2695, E), which is bypassed by the Longitudal Highway.

Río Bueno is at the crossroads of the Lago Ranco-La Unión road and the Highway (Ruta 5). Some 42 km. S of this point is Osorno, another centre for exploring the Lakes.

Osorno, 911 km. from Santiago and 105 km. N of Puerto Montt (103,000 people) was founded in 1558. It was destroyed shortly after its foundation, and was later settled by German immigrants, whose descendants are still of great importance in the area. The city has some old wooden buildings mixed in with the new (e.g. on Calle Mackenna). On the large Plaza de Armas stands the modern, concrete cathedral, with many arches, repeated in the tower, itself an open, latticed arch with a cross superimposed. Behind the new railway station is the Fuerte Reina Luisa, constructed 1793, restored 1977, with only the river front walls and end turrets standing. The old railway station, down the line from the new, is almost derelict, but its forecourt is used by some buses and shops.

The Argentine town of Bariloche is reached by a road E through Puyehue pass (paved most of the way on the Chilean side, large sections now paved on Argentine side, for buses see below) or via the lakes of Todos los Santos and

Laguna Verde, both crossed by ferries. The trip via the lakes takes at least a whole day; maybe 2-3 in winter (April-Nov.). The road via Puyehue (120 km.) is more reliable, and still a very beautiful trip.

Hotels *Waeger*, Cochrane 816, T 233721, P.O. Box 802, Fax 237080, A, 4-star, restaurant, comfortable, rec; *Del Prado*, Cochrane 1162, T 235020, swimming pool, garden, good meals, well-located, charming, A; *Villa Eduviges*, Eduviges 856, T 235023, D; *Inter-Lagos*, Cochrane 515, T 234695, B; *Gran* (good restaurant), main square, O'Higgins 615, T 232171, C, with bath; *Tirol*, Bulnes 630, T 233593, C, with bath; *Residencial Hein*, Cochrane 843, T 234116, E p.p., breakfast US$1.80, pleasant; *Residencial Riga*, Antahuer 1058, T 232945, D, highly rec. but heavily booked in season. *Residencial Schulz*, Freire 530, E with breakfast, hot water, other meals extra. *Residencial* at Amunátegui 520, run by Sra. Gallardo, near bus terminal, good, E; *Residencial Ortega* (strongly rec.) Colón 602, nr. Errazúriz, 1 block from bus terminal, toilet facilities limited, F; others near bus terminal: at A. Pinto 1758, F p.p. inc. breakfast and hot water, T 238024; *Residencias/Restaurantes La Paloma* (Errázuriz 1599), *Richmond*, (Lastarria 500 block) and *Ver-Mar* (Errázuriz y Lastarria, T 234429), these places are fairly basic. *Germania*, Rodríguez 741, F p.p., no hot water, cooking facilities. Youth hostel: *Residencial Stop*, Freire 810, G p.p. in shared rooms, or contact Secretaria Provincial de la Juventud, Bilbao 850. Private houses at Germán Hube, pasaje 1, casa 22, población Villa Dama, E, hot water, clean, use of kitchen, rec.; Lynch 1306 (1 block from bus station, use of kitchen).

Restaurants *German Club*, O'Higgins 563; *Bahía*, Ramírez 1076, rec. for quality and economy; good ice cream at Ramírez 939. *Peter's Kneipe*, M.Rodríguez 1030, excellent German restaurant; *La Casona*, Juan MacKenna 945, service and cuisine excellent, price moderate. *Café Dino*, on the plaza, restaurant upstairs, bar/cafeteria downstairs, good. *Luca's Pizzas*, Cochrane 551, pizzas, pastas, burgers, etc., fair. Good restaurant in the bus station. *Hostería Socavi*, 25 km. S on the Longitudinal Highway, excellent roast chicken. Try chicha (cider) or local pisco sour.

Shop Reinares and Thone, Ramírez 1100, for good fishing gear.

Museum Museo Histórico Municipal, Matta 809. Entrance in Casa de Cultura, free; some old photos, archaeology and anthropology, history, black and white reproductions of old masters.

Garage Automotriz Salfa Sur SA, Fco. Bilbao 857; Automotriz Amthauer, Amthauer 1250. **Car Hire**, Hertz, Bilbao 857, T 235402.

Laundry Av. Arturo Prat 678 (allow at least a day).

Exchange Fincard for Visa and Mastercard, Mackenna 877, Mon.-Fri. 0900-1400, 1530-1900, Sat. 0930-1330. For parallel rates try Cambio Tur, Mackenna 1010, T 4846; Frontera Ltda., Ramírez 949, local 5 (Galery Catedral).

Post Office O'Higgins 645, also Telex. **Phone Office** Ramírez at central plaza and Juan Mackenna y Cochrane.

Tourist Office Provincial government office, on O'Higgins, 1st floor, left, s/n. **Automóvil Club de Chile**, Bulnes 463, T 232269, information and car hire.

Club Andino Juan Mackenna esq. Manuel Bulnes, 3rd floor.

Buses Most leave from the bus terminal 1 block from municipal market at Errázuriz 1400. Left luggage at terminal open 0730-2030. Bus from centre, US$0.30. Frequent buses to Santiago, US$11, 16 hrs. Cruz del Sur to Santiago US$18 pullman, US$36 *cama*, to Puerto Montt US$1.65, to Castro US$4.65, to Concepción, US$7.65, to Temuco, US$3.35, to Punta Arenas, US$27. Other services to Punta Arenas: Sur, Mon. and Sat., Turisbus, Mon. and Thurs., Eurobus and Bus Norte. Varmontt buses every ½ hr. (from about 0700 to 2200) to Alto Frutillar (US$1.25), Llanquihue, Puerto Varas and Puerto Montt (US$2). To Puerto Octay, US$1.50, Vía Octay company 6 daily between 0815-1930 (return 0830-1930) Mon.-Sat., Sun. 5 between 0800 and 2000 (4 return buses). Buses to Valdivia, every half hour, 1½-2½ hrs. journey depending on company (e.g. Trans Norte, Etta, Cruz del Sur), US$1.50 and up. To Lago Ranco, Buses Ruta 5, 6 a day from 0810, 2 hrs., US$1.50. To Entre Lagos, Puyehue and Aguas Calientes, Buses Puyehue from the municipal market; to Entre Lagos, 4 a day, 0915-1500, return 1600, 1800, 1900, 1 hr., US$1; Puyehue and Aguas Calientes, 0915, 1130, 1530, return 1230 and 1730 (1600 also on Sat., in theory), 2 hrs., US$1.35 (US$2.35 return). Local bus to Anticura (Chilean customs post) leaves at 1620, 3 hrs., 22 km. from border.

Buses to Argentina Cruz del Sur, Sun. 1215, US$16.65, to Bariloche; Turismo Lanín, also to Bariloche, Tues., Wed., Fri., Sun. 1000, US$20; Tas Choapa daily to Bariloche, 1120, and to Mendoza, US$21.65, to Buenos Aires, US$52, Montevideo, US$62, Rio de Janeiro, US$88. Buy tickets for international buses from the bus terminal, not through an agency.

Rail Station at Juan Mackenna 600, T 232992. To/from Santiago one Rápido daily, "Rápido Puerto Montt" with sleepers, also *expreso* service in summer, 16½ and 20 hrs.: *económico* US$12.50, *salón* US$16.50, sleeper US$21–29, compartment US$64. Rail services S may be suspended in winter; buses connect with Santiago trains.

Air Lan-Chile, Mackenna 1100, T234355, Ladeco, Mackenna 975, T 236102. Ladeco operates flights Osorno-Santiago Mon., Wed., Fri., Sun. Lan-Chile Mon.-Fri.

Excursions E to the Pilmaiquen waterfall, and on to Lake Puyehue and the thermal waters at **Termas de Puyehue** (US$3.50 p.p. for bathing, 0900-2000); 2 hrs. by car, 2½ by bus (schedule under Osorno **Buses**). The bus does not stop at the Lake (unless you want to get off at *Gran Hotel Termas de Puyehue* and clamber down), but goes 4 km. further to **Aguas Calientes** (later one goes to Anticura and Argentine border). Aguas Calientes has the headquarters of the **Puyehue National Park**, an open air swimming pool with hot thermal water beside the Río Chanleufú, open 0830-1900, US$1.35, children US$0.85 and a very hot indoor pool, open Mon.-Fri. 0830-1230, 1400-1800, Sat., Sun. and holidays 0830-2030, US$2.15, children US$1.50-1.65. There is a Conaf campsite with private sites (US$8.35 per site), cabin type accommodation (in our C range, take food if you want to cook) and a café. In the Puyehue National Park is surviving temperate rain-forest. Three marked paths can be followed: Los Rápidos, 1,000 metres to falls on the Río Chanleufú (the trail starts at the entrance to the outdoor pool, if you don't want to swim, just say you're going to Los Rápidos); El Recodo, a continuation of Los Rápidos up the river bank; El Pionero, 1,800 metres up to a viewpoint (good for the exercise before you bathe). The trees are lovely: listen to the birds and watch for kingfishers by the river.

The road from Aguas Calientes continues 18 km. to Antillanca through a lovely region of small lakes and fairytale forests. (*Hostería Antillanca*, T 235114/232297, C p.p., at foot of volcano, 4 km. from crater, excellent hotel/restaurant/café, with pool, sauna and small ski resort, 2 ski lifts.) The views from Antillanca are breathtaking, with the snow-clad cones of Osorno, Puntiagudo, and Puyehue forming a semicircle. The tree-line on Antillanca is one of the few in the world made up of deciduous trees (southern beech). It is possible to hike from Antillanca to Volcán Casablanca for even better views of the surrounding volcanoes and lakes; no path, information from Club Andino in Osorno. No public transport from Aguas Calientes to Antillanca, try hitching—always difficult, but it is not a difficult walk.

Hotels at Lake Puyehue *Gran Hotel Termas de Puyehue* has a hot-springs swimming pool (T Osorno 232157), large and well kept, B p.p. (cheaper May to mid-Dec.), main meals and breakfast expensive, generally overpriced, in beautiful scenery, heavily booked Jan.-Feb. (Telex 273146, SOTERCL). In **Entre Lagos**, a pleasantly-located small town at the E end of Lake Puyehue, *Pub del Campo*, highly rec. restaurant, reasonable prices, owner is of Swiss descent; *Villa Veneto*, Gral. Lagos 602, T 203, E p.p.; *Hostería Entre Lagos*, Ramírez 65, lake view, T 647225, E. On the S lakeshore are: *Chalet Suisse*, Ruta 215, Km. 55 (Casilla 910, Osorno, T Puyehue 0647-208, Osorno 064-234073), *hostería*, restaurant with excellent food; a few km. beyond, *hospedaje y cabañas* at Almacén Valenciana; *alojamiento* at Shell station after Km. 60, before *Motel Ñilque*, T 232356, or (0647) 218, cabins, A-L, half-price May-October, fishing trips, watersports, car hire. *Hostería Isla Fresia*, located on own island, C, transport provided.

Camping *El Manzano*, Route 215, Km. 58; *Camping No Me Olvides*, Km. 56; *Playa Los Copihues*, Km. 59 (hot showers, good), all on S shore of Lake Puyehue; *Camping Playa Puyehue*, 25 km. E of Entre Lagos, near turning to Termas de Puyehue; and a site at Anticura beside Río Gol-Gol, also restaurant and *cabañas* in summer. Wild camping allowed at Aguas Calientes fortunately, the Conaf site is very expensive (see above); ask the rangers.

A further excursion can be made to the S shore of Lake Rupanco (65 km.) taking the road to

Puerto Octay and turning E after 33 km. This lake is very beautiful and much less developed than most of its neighbours. At the eastern end of the lake is *Hotel Bahia Escocia*, run by Ian and Alice Hamilton (Casilla 1099, T 0647-254, Telex 273002 BOOTH CL), beautiful setting, most hospitable, hot water, good meals, warmly rec.; tennis, boating, walking. Access by car only, 40 km. of dirt road. Bus from Osorno, Piedras Negras at either *Minimarket El Capricho*, Mackenna y Colón, or from Estacion Viejo (old railway station), leaves 1645, 1545 on Sat., returns from Piedras Negras midway along the southern shore at 0700.

Drive or take bus (US$0.60, frequent) N to Río Bueno, celebrated for its scenery, to La Unión, and to **Trumao**, a river port on the Río Bueno, whence a launch may be taken to La Barra on the coast; leaves Wed. and Sat. only at 0900, 5 hrs., US$6; returns Sun. at 0900.

The sea beaches at Maicolpue (60 km. from Osorno—*Hosteria Millor*, on the beach, E, clean, good service, rec.) and Pucatrihue (*Hosteria Incalcar*, summer only) are worth a visit in the summer (daily bus service).

From Osorno it is 106 km. S to Puerto Montt, including 25 km. along the shore of **Lake Llanquihue**. Across the great blue sheet of water can be seen two snowcapped volcanoes: the perfect cone of Osorno (2,680 metres) and the shattered cone of Calbuco, and, when the air is clear, the distant Tronador (3,554 metres). Lake Llanquihue covers over 540 square km. and is the third largest natural lake in South America. There is a road, 187 km. long, around it.

At the northern tip of the lake is **Puerto Octay**, just 56 km. SE of Osorno. It is a small town in a lovely setting (buses daily). 5 km. away is the Peninsula of Centinela with lodging, camping, a launch dock, bathing beaches, water sports. From the headland are fine views of the volcanoes Osorno, Calbuco, Puntiagudo and the Cordillera of the Andes; a very popular spot in good weather. 7 km. E of Puerto Octay is Playa Maitén, "highly recommended, nice beach, marvellous view to the Volcán Osorno, no tourists". Further on is Las Cascadas, surrounded by picturesque agricultural land, old houses and German cemeteries. The small settlement at Las Cascadas also has vacation houses. For a circuit by car from Osorno, follow the road from Puerto Octay along the lakeside, with the Osorno volcano on your left, to Ensenada, a short distance up the road (20 mins.) is Petrohué with its beautiful falls, and the Osorno volcano again in the background, and Lake Todos los Santos; continue to Puerto Varas, then along the W side of the lake to Octay and back. Note that the road round the north and east sides of the lake is poor, necessitating speeds of 20-30 kph at best in places. *Café Kali* on main square at Octay, Amunátegui, is recommended.

Hotels Puerto Octay *Haase*, Pedro Montt 344, T213, very pleasant, C (rooms with and without bath), US$70 for rooms, breakfast and supper for family of 6; *Posada Gubernatis*, Calle Santiago s/n, lakeside, clean, comfortable, D. **Centinela** (3 km. S): *Hotel Centinela*, Casa 114, Península de Centinela, T 22 (Pto. Octay), D (rooms with or without bath), meals US$6 with wine, nice setting, friendly staff, rooms in a dreadful state; *Hostería La Baja*, Península de Centinela. **Las Cascadas** *Centro de Recreación Las Cascadas*, T 235377; *Hostería Irma*, on lake, 2 km. past Las Cascadas, F, run by 3 Marías, good food, very pleasant.

Camping *Centro de Recreación Las Cascadas* and Villa Las Cascadas picnic area (free); at Playa Maitén, rec.; Centinela municipal site, US$4 per group.

About half-way down the west side of the lake is **Frutillar**, in fact two towns: Alto Frutillar, with a railway station, just off the main highway, and Bajo Frutillar on the lakeside, 4 km. away. It is 5 minutes by colectivo between the two towns, US$0.25.

Bajo Frutillar is possibly the most attractive town on the lake. A beautifully kept town, it offers a highly-regarded classical music festival in late January to early February (accommodation must be booked well in advance). The Museo Colonial Alemán, including watermill, a model of a German colonial house, a blacksmith's shop, and a *campanario* (circular bar with agricultural and dairy machinery and carriages inside), gardens and handicraft shop, is well worth a visit. Open 1000-1200, 1500-1800, closed Tues., US$0.40 (maintained by the Universidad Austral de Chile).

Accommodation and Food *Hotel Frutillar*, on stilts above lake, T 277, B, best, good restaurant and bar, Andina del Sud travel agency in reception; *Casona del 32*, C with bath and breakfast, comfortable old house, central heating, English and German spoken, T 369, Caupolicán 28, P.O. Box 101; *Hospedaje Costa Azul*, Philippi 1175, T 388, mainly for families, good breakfasts, E; also on Philippi: *Hospedaje Vivaldi*, No. 851-5, T 382, Sra. Edith Klesse, E p.p., quiet, comfortable, excellent breakfast and lodging, also family accommodation, rec.; *Winkler*, No. 1155, T 388, D; *Las Rocas*, No. 1227, T 397, E with breakfast; *Hospedaje Trayen* at No. 1285, T 205. Many more in the lower town. *Frutillar Alto*, Calle Principal 168, F, clean.

Restaurants The *Club Alemán* has a good restaurant, on the square; there is a Bar Restaurant upstairs at the Fire Station, opp. *Hotel Frutillar. Bierstube*, A. Varas, open 1600-2400. Many German-style cafés and tea- rooms on Calle Philippi (the lakefront, e.g. *Salón de Te Frutillar*, No. 775). *Der Volkladen*, O'Higgins y Philippi, natural products, chocolates and cakes, natural cosmetics. *Café Hermosa*, good breakfast (view of lake and Volcán Osorno). Budget travellers should eat at *Bar/Restaurant Colonial*, Winkler 420, Alto Frutillar, US$3.35 for excellent 3-course meal, "country" cooking.

Camping *Playa Maqui*, 7 km. N of Frutillar, fancy, expensive; *Los Ciruelillos*, nr. Frutillar, T 9123, most services.

Services and Transport Toilet, showers and changing cabins for beach on O'Higgins. Cama-Chile shop, Philippi y O'Higgins. Tourist Office on lakeside opp. *Club Alemán*, helpful; Viajes Frutillar in Alto Frutillar (Richter y Alissandre) run tours. Bus every half hr. from Varmontt terminal on San Francisco, Puerto Varas to Alto Frutillar, US$0.65. In summer, buses back to Puerto Varas from Av. Philippi (between O'Higgins and Montt) in Bajo Frutillar every ½ hr.; also to Puerto Montt. Out of the summer season, buses leave from Alto Frutillar, every ½ hour. Varmontt bus from Puerto Varas continues to Osorno, 1¼ hrs., US$1.25.

Puerto Varas, a beauty spot of about 23,300 inhabitants, is on the shore of Lake Llanquihue, with standard roses grown along the streets. It is 1,046 km. from Santiago and only 26 by rail or 24 by paved road from Puerto Montt. Parque Philippi, on top of hill, is a pleasant place to visit; walk up to *Hotel Cabañas del Lago* on Klenner, cross the railway and the gate is on the right. The views are a bit restricted by trees and the metal cross at the top is unattractive (so is the electric clock which chimes the quarter-hours in town). Casino charges US$2.65 entry, including first drink.

Hotels *Puerto Varas*, Klenner 351 (*Gran Hotel Turismo*), T 2524, C, luxury class with casino, a huge, ugly place; *Cabañas del Lago*, Klenner 195, T 2291, cabins, B, adequate, but unhelpful staff; *Bellavista*, V. Pérez Rosales 60, T 20211, B, cheerful, rec., no restaurant, but breakfast service, overlooking lake; *Hospedaje Loreley*, Maipo 911, T 2226, D, rec., homely, quiet, good restaurant; under construction, *Los Alerces*, in medium price range; *Licarayén*, San José 114, T 2305, small, B with bath, highly rec., book in season; *Residencial Hellwig*, San Pedro 210, E, rooms and bathrooms clean and neat, water usually tepid, not welcoming; *Grand Hotel Heim*, San Pedro and San José, basic, but good food, E. *Asturias*, Del Salvador 322, T 2446, B, friendly, discounts for cash, fine restaurant; *Hostería La Sirena*, Santa Rosa 710, E, incl. breakfast, comfortable, good restaurant, on hill overlooking the town. Also cheap *residenciales* opposite bus station and in Plaza de Armas. *Motel Ayenteno*, V. Pérez Rosales 950, clean, comfortable cabins, friendly, T 2270; *Motel Altué*, Av. V. Pérez Rosales 01679, T 2294, C, incl. breakfast; *Motel Sacho*, San José 581, T 2227, D. Residencial at Salvador 423, D, run by a German lady, rec., as is María Schilling Rosas' *hospedaje* at La Quebrada 752; Sra. Elly. A. Prat 151, F p.p. with breakfast; *hospedaje* at Santa Rosa y Mirador, E with breakfast. Familia Niklitschek-Pozas, Calle Imperial 8 (opp. *Motel Trauco*), highly rec.

Camping On S shore of Lake Llanquihue starting at Puerto Varas: Km. 10, Playa Hermosa (T Puerto Varas 8283, Puerto Montt 252223), fancy, expensive; Km. 11, Playa Niklitschek, full facilities; Km. 20, Playa Venado; Km. 49, Conaf site at Puerto Oscuro, beneath road to volcano, very good.

Restaurants *Club Alemán*, San José 413, best, dinner, expensive; *Mercado*, next to market, excellent food, good service, not cheap but good value; *Café Asturias*, San Francisco 302, good empanadas and other food (same management as hotel of same name); *Ibis*, Pérez Rosales, next to *Motel Ayentemo*, rec.; *Central*, San José 319, good coffee, cakes, pies and breakfast, opens early. *Costa Azul*, Av. Pérez Rosales 01071, 2 km. from town towards Puerto Chico, in wooden building (expensive motel restaurants just beyond it aren't worth visiting).

①

© John Bartholomew & Son Ltd., 1983

These maps are for interest only and are not of political significance

KEY TO
MAP SECTIONS

ON THE SAME SCALE

⑦

1:16M

Tropic of Capricorn

400 miles
600 km.

BAHIA

SERGIPE

Salvador (Bahia)

Rio de Janeiro

São Paulo

MINAS GERAIS

GOIÁS

MATO GROSSO

MATO GROSSO DO SUL

PARANÁ

ESPÍRITO SANTO

⑪

A T L A N T I C

O C E A N

1:16M

miles
0   100   200   300   400   500

0   200   400   600 km.

ON THE SAME SCALE

South Georgia

Shag Rocks

C. Alexandra   Grytviken

C. Disappointment

FALKLAND ISLANDS
ISLAS MALVINAS

Jason Is

West Falkland   C. Dolphin   Stanley

Falkland Sd   *East Falkland*

Weddell   *Beauchene Is*

Golfo
San Matías

Maquinchao   C. de   Pto Piramides
Pto Madryn
S. Carlos de   Pto Punta Delgada
Bariloche   El Bolsón   Pto Lobos
Norquinco   Gastre   Camarones
Esquel   C. Dos Bahías

Ancud   Las Plumas   Rawson
I. de Chiloé   Castro   Gaimán
Castro   Trelew

Golfo
Comodoro Rivadavia   San Jorge
Coihaique   Caleta
Balmaceda   Olivia
Pen.   L. Buenos Aires   Colonia Las Heras
de   Deseado
Taitao

Archipiélago
de las
Chonos

Campana   L. San Martín   C. Tres Puntas
Esmeralda   Pta Medanosa
Madre de Dios   Sta Cruz
Arch. de la   Bahía Grande
Reina Adelaida   Río Gallegos
Desolación   Río Grande
Santa Inés   Tierra del
Fuego   Ushuaia
Hoste   C. de Hornos
Londonderry   Navarino
Wollaston
C. San Diego
I. de los Estados

⑫

TRINIDAD 1:4M

Toco
Arima
Princs Town
Guayaguayare
Port of Spain
Gulf of Paria
San Fernando
Bonasse

TOBAGO 1:4M

Charlotteville
Plymouth
Scarborough

JAMAICA 1:4M

Montego Bay
St.Ann's Bay
Annotto Bay
Falmouth
Brown's Town
Spanish Town
Kingston
Blue Mtn.Pk. 2256m
Port Antonio
Port Morant
Mt.Denham 966m
Mandeville
May Pen
Savanna la Mar
Black River
Portland Point

ATLANTIC OCEAN

Leeward Islands
Virgin Is.
Anguilla
St. Martin
Barbuda
ANTIGUA
Point-à-Pitre
Guadeloupe
Montserrat
St. Kitts
Nevis
St. Croix
DOMINICA
Roseau
Martinique
Fort-de-France
Windward Islands
LESSER
ANTILLES
ST. LUCIA
Castries
ST. VINCENT
Kingstown
GRENADA
St.Georges
BARBADOS
Bridgetown
Tobago
TRINIDAD
& TOBAGO
Port of Spain
La Asunción
I. Margarita
La Tortuga

San Juan
Ponce
PUERTO RICO
Mayaguez
Mona Passage

NETHERLAND ANTILLES
Aruba
Curaçao
Bonaire
Pto. Fijo
Willemstad
G. de Venezuela
Coro
Uribia
Pta Gallinas
Riohacha

CARIBBEAN SEA

Hispaniola
Santiago
DOMINICAN REPUBLIC
Cap-Haïtien
Gonaïves
HAITI
Santo Domingo
La Romana
Azua
Port au Prince
Les Cayes
Windward Passage
Mona Passage

Santa Marta
La Guaira
Cúmana

THE BAHAMAS
Nassau
Eleuthera I.
Cat I.
Andros Is.
Long I.
Acklins I.
Caicos Is.
Gt.Inagua I.
Turks Is.

Straits of Florida

La Habana
Matanzas
Santa Clara
Sagua la Grande
Cienfuegos
Sancti Spiritus
Camaguey
Holguin
Bayamo
Santiago de Cuba
Turquino 2005m
C.Cruz
Guantánamo
GREATER ANTILLES
Cayman Is.
I. de la Juventud (I.de Pinos)
pinar del Rio

JAMAICA
Montego Bay
Spanish Town
Kingston
Savanna la Mar

1:16M

0   100   200   300   400 miles
0   200   400   600 km.

HONDURAS
L.de Caratasca
C. Gracias a Dios
Puerto Cabezas
Prinzapolca
NICARAGUA
Bluefields

Rio Atlantica Suite Hotel. A touch of Switzerland, right on Copacabana Beach.

Setting new standards on Rio's hotel scene.

■ Conveniently located in the heart of Copacabana, right on the Beach.

■ Minutes away from the city's financial/business center and shopping district makes the Rio Atlantica convenient for businessmen and tourists.

■ 18 floors with 228 suites and rooms, most featuring ocean view. Our suite accommodations are cost competitive with the standard rooms of hotels of the same category.

■ Round-the-clock security. Featuring in-room safety-deposit boxes and wet bars.

■ 2 restaurants serving the finest in Brazilian, international and Swiss cuisine ("Ao Ponto" and "Helvecia").

■ Ample facilities for business meetings and functions. 68-seat fully equipped auditorium.

■ Rooftop swimming pool, solarium, health club with saunas, exercise room and deck bar for the exclusive use of guests.

■ Drugstore/newsstand, boutiques, jewelry and gift shops.

■ Accommodations for handicapped available.

■ The newest and only hotel under Swiss management.

Management by

CEM
CASPAR E. MANZ
HOTELS & RESTAURANTS
SWITZERLAND

rio atlantica
SUITE HOTEL

Av. Atlántica, 2964 · Copacabana
22070 · Rio de Janeiro · RJ · Brazil
Tel: (021) 255-6332 Tlx: (21) 36 893
Fax: (021) 255-6410
P.O. 43060

El Molino, an excellent coffee house in an old mill, on road to Ensenada about 27 km. from Pto. Varas.

Exchange Turismo Los Lagos, Del Salvador 257 (Galería Real, local 11), open daily 0830-1330, 1500-2100, Sunday 0930-1330. Better rate of exchange for travellers' cheques obtained in Puerto Montt.

Phone Office Salvador y Santa Rosa.

Tourist Agent Graytur; Andina del Sur (Del Salvador 243, T 511) offer trips for US$42 to Lake Todos los Santos, Peulla, Cerro Tronador and return, plus other excursions, good. Also Turismo Nieve (on San Bernardo, rec.), Turismo Puerto Varas, Turismo Casoria Alemana, Turismo Llancahue, ACE Turismo and Varastur (San Francisco 272).

Tourist Office Del Salvador 328, helpful, will find cheap accommodation; also art gallery.

Buses To Santiago: Igi-Llaima (office San Francisco 516) leaves from Salvador at 1830, arrives 1130 (US$11.50). To Puerto Montt every ½ hr. from Varmontt station (San Francisco 600 block), 30 mins., US$0.65; same company, same frequency to Frutillar and Osorno.

To Bariloche, Andino del Sur, daily at 0900, arrives 2130 (by boat and bus), US$35 (same company has excursions to Peulla and Petrohué). You can hitch, or take a cheaper bus to Petrohué en route to Bariloche, but you must spend the night there before catching the ferry. It is not possible to go by private car from Puerto Varas direct to Bariloche, as the ferry on the Argentine side does not take cars; one must go via Osorno.

Excursions Buses from Puerto Montt run every day on the southern side of the lake between Puerto Varas and (50 km.) Ensenada, in the south-eastern corner of the lake, continuing to Ralún, Cochamó and Río Puelo (see below and **Excursions** from Puerto Montt). In summer, buses go daily from Puerto Montt and Puerto Varas in the morning to Ensenada, Laguna Verde, Petrohué Falls and Lake Todos Los Santos, US$5, good value. The drive around the lake is very picturesque. On the northern road are Puerto Octay and Centinela (**see above**).

Puerto Varas is within easy reach of many famous beauty spots—Desagüe, Totoral, Frutillar, Los Bajos, Puerto Octay (direct bus only from Osorno), Puerto Chico, Puerto Fonck, La Poza, the Loreley island, the Calbuco volcano, La Fábrica, Puerto Rosales, Playa Venado, Ralún and Río Pescado. The Falls (Salto) of Petrohué should not be missed. The whole countryside with its primeval forest, deep blue rivers and snowcapped volcanoes is very beautiful; interest is added by the timber-frame buildings with shingle roofs—even the churches.

La Poza is a little lake to the S of the main lake and reached through narrow channels overhung with vegetation; a concealed channel leads to yet another lake, the Laguna Encantada. The motor-boats that tour Lake Llanquihue stop at Loreley Island, very beautiful and well worth a visit.

It is only 16 km. by a scenic paved road from **Ensenada**, a lovely spot at the eastern end of Lake Llanquihue to Lake Todos Los Santos, a long irregularly shaped sheet of water, the most beautiful of all the lakes in southern Chile. The ports of **Petrohué** at its western and **Peulla** at its eastern ends are connected by boat, costing US$8; it leaves Petrohué at 1100, Peulla at 1530, some reports say 1600 on Sun. and that there is a boat at 0800 Mon.-Sat. (2½ hrs.—most seating indoors, no cars carried). This is the only public service on the lake and it connects solely with the Andina del Sud tour bus. If you prefer to go walking, ask for the park guard, Hernán, who organizes expeditions from Petrohué in the summer months. Peulla is a good starting point for hikes in the mountains. Trout and salmon fishing at Petrohué are excellent. The waters are emerald green. There is a shop in Petrohué; bread is sold by Sra. Marci González every morning, ask at the post office. The Salto de Petrohué (entrance, US$0.35) is 4 km. from Petrohué, 10 km. from Ensenada (only worth a visit in summer, when the sun is out, and it's much nicer to walk from Petrohué). At the other end, the Cascadas Los Novios, signposted above the *Hotel Peulla*, are a steep walk, but are stunning once you reach them; don't forget to turn round to see the views. The falls, Lake Todos Los Santos and the surrounding areas to the borders with the Puyehue National Park and Argentina fall within the **Parque Nacional Vicente Pérez Rosales.**

Petrohué and Peulla are infested by *tavanos* (local horseflies) in Jan. and Feb. Cover up as much as possible with light-coloured clothes.

Hotels At **Ensenada**: *Hotel Ensenada*, T 2888, B with bath, olde-worlde (closed in winter) good view of lake and Osorno Volcano; *Cabañas Brisas del Lago*, E p.p., chalets for 6 on beach, good restaurant next door but one, highly rec. for self-catering, but bring your own food; *Hostería Los Pumas*, 3 hrs. up the hill also highly rec., in season only, D; *Ruedas Viejas*, T 312, D for room, E in cabin, about 1 km. from Ensenada, fairly basic, has popular restaurant, good value; about 2 km. from town is *Pucará*, D, also with good restaurant (the steaks are rec.); opp. is *Hospedaje Opazo*, F with breakfast, no hot water, friendly; *Hospedaje Arena*, on same road as *Ruedas Viejas* but nearer police station, D with breakfast, rec.; *hospedaje* above Toqui grocery, F p.p., use of kitchen, beach in the back yard, rec. Ensenada has little more than the hotels, restaurants (*Canta Rana* rec. for bread and kuchen) and a few pricey shops; bring your own provisions. At **Petrohué**: *Hostería Petrohué*, C, with bath, E p.p. b and b (reports vary), built for Queen Elizabeth; *Familia Küscher* on other side of river, F p.p., meals available for US$3, cold water, camping possible; *Refugio* above being repaired. At **Peulla**, on the opposite shore: *Hotel Peulla*, A (cheaper out of season), beautiful setting by the lake and mountains, restaurant and bar, poor beds, cold in winter, often full of tour groups (tiny shop at back of hotel); *Residencial Palomita*, 50 metres W of Hotel, E half board, family-run, simple, comfortable but not spacious, separate shower, this is the only accommodation, advertised as such, apart from the Hotel, but *Restaurant Rabinito*, D half-board, has one small double room, clean, hot shower, lunch available, reasonable food, and we have been told that Elma Hernández Maldonado, close to the bridge has beds available, F p.p. with breakfast, clean. Homemade marmalade, dulce de leche available from Mrs. Gisela Schwitzgaeble, Ruiz Moreno 938. Otherwise food hard to find in Peulla, so take your own.

Bus Bohle bus Puerto Montt-Petrohué US$5, 1230, with stops for views and lunch, rec.; a bus returns from Petrohué at 1700, via Ensenada and Puerto Varas. There are day return bus and boat tours to Peulla from Puerto Montt, with possibility of continuing to Bariloche. If planning to go to Bariloche in stages, book through to Bariloche in Petrohué, not Peulla because onward connections from Peulla may be full and the accommodation is not so good there. Fare Petrohué-Bariloche US$35 (Andina del Sud—same as from Puerto Montt).

Market On Tues. and Thurs. mornings; a number of lorries sell food, wine and clothes.

Camping At Peulla, opp. Conaf office, US$1.50; at Petrohué, a National Parks Environment Centre for the Parque Nacional Vicente Pérez Rosales with display and slide show (camping US$4 p.p.), near *Hotel Petrohué*; an unofficial one by lake shore 1 km. beyond *Hotel Ensenada* at Playa Larga, basic.

A good hike from Ensenada goes to Laguna Verde, with a beautiful circular trail behind the lake (take first fork to the right behind the information board), and then down the road to a campsite at Puerto Oscuro on Lake Llanquihue. The site is quiet and secluded, a good spot for a picnic. It is about a 45 minute hike from *Hotel Ensenada*.

A paved road runs 31 km. SE from Ensenada along the wooded lower Petrohué valley to **Ralún**, on the salt-water Estuario de Reloncaví. Here is the *Hotel Ralún*, at S end of the village, a magnificent timber building to a fine modern design by Cristián de Groote, with a choice of rooms or cabins, warmly rec., A (25% more in summer than rest of year) plus US$35 p.p. full board (cabins rented at US$80 a night). Telex 240048 Santiago; address Casilla 678, Puerto Montt. *Restaurant El Refugio*, 1 km. N of *Ralún*, rents rooms, F; also *Navarrito*, restaurant and lodging, F; *Posada Campesino*, F for simple room; *El Encuentro*, village shop and post office, with telex, F. Bus from Ensenada, US$0.70, daily 1015; more easily reached by bus from Puerto Montt. (Buses Bohle, 5 a day from 1000-1930, 4 on Sat., return 0700-1830, US$1.85).

In 5 hours you can hike from Ralún to Lago Cayutúe, then a further 3 to the town of Cayutúe. At the 5-6 houses in Ralún before you cross the big bridge you can buy bread, honey and cheese. Follow the main road to the first turning on left which goes up a valley. The dirt road ends at a farm, ask directions to a track which is 100 metres to the right. Continue to another farm, where the track goes right, round a fence. Good views of the valley behind you from the top of the pass; descend to Lago Cayutúe, set between two mountain ranges with forest around it. Good camping and swimming at the lake (Aad Bol, Poelijk, Neth., and Trish Clements, Faulconbridge, Australia).

Lake Todos los Santos has no roads round it; the shores are deeply wooded and several small islands rise from its surface. A boat trip to Isla Margarita on the lake costs US$3, ½ hr. each way, with ½ hr. on the island where there is a beautiful crater lake (leaves Petrohué 1500, run by Cruz del Sur in Puerto Montt). Private launches can be hired for other trips, for instance to Cayutué (about US$30) on a southern arm of the lake.

In the waters of the lake are reflected the slopes of **Osorno volcano**. Only experienced climbers should attempt to climb right to the top, ice climbing equipment required: there are many deep crevasses, the weather can change suddenly, never go alone, and set off early in the morning; there is a shelter for hikers. Antu Tours organize a one-day hike to the summit for a reasonable fee (rec.). They can be contacted through their postal address: Casilla 24, 29 Santiago 29; T 2712767, Telex 440019 RECAL CZ.

The Club Andino Osorno (address under Osorno) has three shelters (US$3 p.p.) at La Picada (84 km. from Osorno, 24 km. from Las Cascadas on Lake Llanquihue), on the ski slopes on the Osorno volcano at 950 metres and on a road off the main road between Octay and Ensenada; *Las Pumas* on the Volcán Osorno at 900 m., with plenty of beds at US$2 p.p. and cooking facilities, very friendly guards (apply at the Oficina de Turismo de Osorno). At 1,200 metres is **Refugio Teski Club**, E, 4 hrs. walk from *Hotel Ensenada* (where you should check if the *refugio* has food), bleak site above the tree line; not open all year (usual ski season is June to September). If you wish to climb Volcán Osorno, ask first at Las Pumas or Refugio Teski for advice. To reach Volcán Osorno, take bus to Ensenada from Puerto Varas then walk 12 km. to Las Pumas. A ski resort is under construction on Volcán Osorno.

Beyond the hilly shores to the E are several graceful snow-capped mountains, with the mighty Tronador in the distance. To the N is the sharp point of Cerro Puntiagudo (2,278 metres), and at the north-eastern end Cerro Techado (1,720 metres) rises cliff-like out of the water.

Puerto Montt, capital of the Tenth (Los Lagos) Region, 1,080 km. from Santiago, is the terminus of the railway. The first German colonists arrived in 1852; they have remained to this day a small but influential percentage of the 106,000 inhabitants. The houses are mostly faced with unpainted shingles; here and there stand structures in the Alpine manner, all high pitched roofs and quaint balconies. The little fishing port of Angelmó, 2 km. from the centre of town, is noted for its seafood restaurants and handicrafts. It has become a tourist centre and the market area there is being refurbished. Costanera bus along D. Portales costs US$0.15, but it's an easy stroll past the handicraft stalls which line the road between the ferry terminal and Angelmó (woollen items from Chiloé are cheaper in Ancud and Castro, but there's greater choice in Angelmó).

The port is much used by fishing boats and coasting vessels, and it is here that passengers embark for the island of Chiloé, for Aysén, and for the long haul S to Punta Arenas. A paved road runs 55 km. SW to Pargua, where there is a ferry service to Chiloé.

Hotels Check Tourist Office. *Vicente Pérez Rosales*, Antonio Varas 447, T 252571, Telex 270056, A, with bath and breakfast, some rooms noisy, excellent restaurant, seafood and tourist information, rec.; *Le Mirage*, Rancagua 350, T 255125, C, quite good but cheaply built, T 255125; *Punta Arenas*, Copiapó 119, T 253080, C with bath, a bit tatty, restaurant decaying but good table d'hôte; *Colina*, Tacna 81, T 253502, B with bath, expensive, clean, some rooms with sea view, breakfast extra, restaurant, bar, car hire; *Burg*, Pedro Montt and Portales, T 253813, modern, central heating, centrally located, good, B (being remodelled in 1989); *Montt*, Av. Varas and Quillota, T 253651, C, with bath, D without, poor water supply but clean, friendly, good value (good restaurant); *Hostal Panorama*, San Felipe 192, T 254094, D, steep climb up steps to get there, some rooms with bath, some with view, crowded meeting place for Europeans and Americans, watch belongings, good restaurant; *Millahue*, C, T 253829, Copiapó 64, good food; *Residencial Urmeneta*, Urmeneta 290, T 253262, D, with bath, F p.p. without, clean, comfortable, good breakfast, rec.; *Royal*, Quillota 136, T 252602, D with breakfast, near railway station, run down, chilly, fairly basic, good meals. *Miramar*, Andrés Bello 972, T 254618, D, breakfast US$1, hot water, across Av. Diego Portales from museum and bus terminal; *Residencial Embassy*, Calle Valdivia 130, E,

PUERTO MONTT

1. Plaza de Armas   4. Tourist Offices
2. Cathedral   5. Post Office
3. Museum   6. Hospital

clean, breakfast US$1 extra, will store luggage, few bathrooms and some rooms lack windows, but otherwise good; *Residencial Talquino*, Pérez Rosales 114-116, T 253331, near bus terminal, E, hot water, clean; *Residencial Calipso*, Urmeneta 127, T 254554, E, with breakfast, shared bath, hot water, clean and friendly (acts as youth hostel); *Residencial El Turista*, Varas esq. Ancud 91, E with and without bath, with breakfast, friendly; *Residencial Sur*, San Felipe 183, E (poor breakfast extra), basic, clean; *Residencia Punta Arenas*, J. J. Mira 964, F with breakfast, hot water, basic but clean. Many private homes give you a bed for US$3.50-5, look for signs in windows, particularly rec. is *Casa Haraldo Steffen*, Serrano 286 (T 253823), E, with breakfast, excellent, homemade bread and jam, free transport to/from bus station; *Uncle Renato*, Guillermo Gallardo 621, US$1 with own sleeping bag, popular, packed in summer, boiled water for coffee available; *casa de familia*, G. Gallardo 552, F p.p. with breakfast, E with bath, cooking facilities, clean, comfortable, pleasant. There are also several inexpensive hostels in Calle Huasco, e.g. at No. 16, E, with breakfast (hot water), but much better is No. 126, F, friendly. Also J. J. Mira 1002, F, excellent, breakfast included; Aníbal Pinto 328, E with breakfast, friendly, popular, can do laundry, rec.; Ancud 117, F, bed and breakfast, hot water, good; Sr. Raúl Arroyo at Concepción 136 (go to the "inland" end of Concepción, turn right to end of alley), F p.p. with breakfast, cooking facilities, Sra. Arroyo does laundry, hot water, Navimag agency, meets people at bus station, helpful, some English spoken, often packed (rec.); also Concepción 120, F, good; *Hospedaje*, Balmaceda 300, F p.p., with breakfast, clean, friendly; Sra. Olivia, A. Prat 412, F p.p bed and breakfast; *Residencial Familiar*, Egaña 538, picturesque wooden house, friendly, breakfast only; Familia Turra, Calle Regimiento 842, Población Lintz, F with breakfast, excellent but for nearby noisy disco; and Balmaceda, esq. Vial 754, Ida Soto de Arras, F, very friendly, good breakfast, safe; **Sra. Egla J. de González**, Av. España 15, next to train station, E with breakfast, family accommodation, use of kitchen, warmly rec. Near Puerto Montt *Cabañas Los Abedules*, Calle Pto Montt 55, Pelluco (see under **Excursions**), T 254231, D, comfortable, completely furnished incl. cooking facilities (sleep 2-6 people): Mailing address—Casilla 338, Pelluco, Puerto Montt.

Camping At Chinquihue, 10 km. W of Puerto Montt (bus service), about US$1.50 p.p. Open October-April US$8 per site, for any size of tent. Each site has table, two benches, barbecue and plenty of shade. Toilets and showers. Small shop, no kerosene. Good camping shop, "Winkler", on Calle Varas, will buy used gear. "Wild" camping possible along the front. 4 km. E of Puerto Montt, Copec have a network of 18 "Rutacentas" between Quillagua and Puerto Montt, which, apart from selling petrol and oil, have good shower (US$0.25) and toilet facilities and restaurants. At Los Alamos on the road to Panitao and Calbuco.

Restaurants *Embassy*, Ancud 106 and Pelluco, is rec. for reasonably priced seafood; *Club de Yates*, good, Av. J.S. Manfredini, on waterfront beyond railway station; *Centro Español*, on Quillota (2nd floor), moderate prices; *Super Yoco*, Urmeneta 478, good value; *Nettuno*, Illapel 129, cheap Italian food, good atmosphere; *Rapanui*, Benavente 550, good, reasonable prices; *Café Real*, Rancagua 137, near main plaza, good for empanadas, congrío frito, hot dogs, coffee and cakes; *Café Central*, Rancagua 117 and A. Varas, good atmosphere, food and pastries. *Restaurant Café Dino*, Varas 550, excellent restaurant upstairs, snacks and delicious pastas downstairs (try the lemon juice). *La Llave*, by the sea, in railway station, good. *Patts Pizza*, Pedro Montt 65, excellent, clean, good service; *Café Amsel*, Pedro Montt y Portales, good variety and quality; *Plato's*, Av. Diego Portales 1014, Galería Comercial España, cheap, good. Excellent and cheap food at the central bus depot (all credit cards accepted). Restaurants in market at Angelmó, and on the road there, highly rec. for fish (not so good for hygiene but food can be trusted, ask prices first as there is no menu. Try picoroco al vapor, a giant barnacle whose flesh looks and tastes like crab; curanto, a regional dish (seafood, chicken, sausages and potatoes). In Angelmó, *Rancho Patache*, Pasaje Martí, on corner, 2nd floor, T 252974, very good, simple, informal. Bakery: *La Estrella*, Gallardo 174, self-service, good.

Shopping Woollen goods and Mapuche-designed rugs. Cheaper at roadside stalls between port and Angelmó (see above) than at tourist shops in town (cheaper still on Chiloé). Las Brisas supermarket opp. bus station, very good, open 0900-2200 daily; local produce on sale opp. bus terminal.

Museum Museo Juan Pablo II at Avenida Diego Portales opp. Ancud, interesting. Open Mon.-Fri. 1000-1300, 1500-1900; Sat., Sun. 1100-1900; US$0.35.

Car Hire Hertz, Urmeneta 1036, T 55000/52122; Automóvil Club de Chile, Cauquenes 75, T 252968, and several at airport. Others are Avis, Benavente 878; Budget, San Martín 200; Dollar (Rosse Turismo), Varas 447; Sport, Benavente 531, 4th floor; First, Varas 437.

Exchange You are advised to change money here if visiting Chiloé as reports indicate that it is difficult on the island. Banco del Estado and Banco Chile (cash only) and Turismo Latinoamericano, Urmeneta 351, offer good rates. Fincard (Access and Visa), A. Varas 575, open Mon.-Fri. 0845-1400, 1530-1900, Sat. 0930-1300. *Hotel Pérez Rosales* will change money at parallel market rate. Varas Tours change travellers' cheques at a good rate without commission (they also run good excursions). Also Turismo Los Lagos, Varas 595, local 3. La Moneda de Oro at the bus terminal will exchange Latin American currencies. Try also *Café Real*, Calle Rancagua 137, or Rosse Turismo, Varas 445.

Consulates **Argentine**, Cauquenes 94, 2nd floor, T 253996; **German**, Chorrillos 1582, T253001; **Spanish**, Rancagua 113, T252557; **Dutch**, Seminario 350, T 253428.

Laundry Opposite Banco O'Higgins on Pedro Montt; Center at Varas 700, and Unic at Chillán 149.

Post Office Rancagua 120, open 0830-1900 (Mon.-Fri.), 0830-1200 (Sat.-Sun.).

Telephone Office on Pedro Montt between Urmaneta and A. Varas, and at Chillán 98.

Tourist Office Sernatur has opened a new office on Quillota, almost at the junction with A.Varas, diagonally across from *Hotel Montt*. The headquarters is at Edificio Intendencia Regional, Av. Décima Región 480, T 254580, Telex 270008. Open 0830-1300, 1430-1730 Mon.-Fri. Also near main plaza, a kiosk run by Sernatur, the municipality and the hotel association, open till 1800 on Sat., good. Town maps available. Telefónica del Sur and Sernatur operate a phone information service (INTTUR), dial 142 (cost is the same as a local call). Dial 149 for chemist/pharmacy information, 148 for the weather, 143 for the news, etc. The service operates throughout the tenth region. Sernatur in Puerto Montt has a reciprocal arrangement on information with Bariloche, Argentina.

Rail Station at San Felipe 50, T 254908. Daily to Santiago, via Osorno and Temuco. Daily *expreso* to Santiago in summer only leaves at 0900, 23 hrs. (US$11 and US$9.50). Rápido at 1600, 19 hrs., US$64 for sleeper compartment; *salón* US$16.50, *económico* US$12.50. Ticket office opens 0830-1130, 1300-1700.

Bus Service Bus station on sea front, at Av. Diego Portales and Av. Lota, has telephones, restaurants, *casa de cambio* (left luggage, US$0.20 per item for 24 hrs.). To Puerto Varas (US$0.45), Llanquihue (US$0.65), Frutillar (US$1) and Osorno (US$2) every 30 min. between 0750-2050 (2120 Sun.), 1½ hrs. with Varmontt, either from main terminal or own terminal at Copiapó y Varas. To Santiago, express 15 hrs., average fare US$12, US$20 *cama*; Varmontt are the most expensive, double-decker bus (US$35 including cocktails, cold dinner, breakfast). Bus service to Punta Arenas, Bus Norte, Turibus, Fernández Sur, Eurobus, Victoria Sur and Ghisoni, each twice a week in summer, once in low season, about US$35 (bus goes through Argentina, but you don't need australes because the bus company purchases meals, etc., and you pay the driver's assistant), 38 hrs. Many buses daily to Temuco US$4.65-7, to Valdivia, US$3-4; Concepción, US$7.50-9. For services to Chiloé, **see page 585**.

Empresa Andina del Sud, very close to central tourist kiosk, Varas 437 (Casilla 15-D, T 253253/254692/357797) sells a daily tour at 0830 (not Sun.) to Puerto Varas, Parque Nacional V.Pérez Rosales, Petrohué, Lake Todos los Santos, Peulla and back (without meals, US$13, with meals US$21, with overnight at *Hotel Peulla*, US$23), and to other local sights. Varastur in the same building runs tours to Petrohué (US$12 with lunch), rec., Puyehue, Frutillar, or Ancud (US$13.30).

To Argentina To Bariloche, US$20 with Bus Norte via Puyehue (daily 0830, or night bus, change in Osorno); Tas-Choapa, US$15, three times a week direct 0930, three times via Lake Todos los Santos 0900; Lanín, US$18 via Osorno, 4 times weekly 0800, no toilets, plenty of stops. Andina del Sud to Bariloche via the lake, US$35 all inclusive, Mon.-Sat. 0900, rec., longer but less tiring than the road route, also shorter customs checks. Mercedes bus to Bariloche, 9 hrs. with lots of breakdowns we are told (see also routes to Argentina given below). Laníin also goes to Neuquén, as does Igi Llaima (also to Zapala).

Hitch-hiking is difficult and may take as long as four days between Puerto Montt and Bariloche. When driving north out of Puerto Montt (or out of Puerto Varas, Frutillar, etc.), look for signs to "Ruta 5".

Air Service Ladeco run 3-5 flights a week to Coyhaique/Balmaceda, and daily flights to Santiago and Punta Arenas. In January, February and March you may well be told that the plane to Punta Arenas is booked up; however, cancellations may be available from the airport. There are air force flights to Punta Arenas about once every two weeks; seat availability is only known when plane arrives from Santiago, price about US$35 compared with US$80

Lan-Chile, which has daily flights to Santiago. ASA, Fokker 27, run twice daily service to Chaitén and Coyhaique (will stop at Puerto Aysén if 6 or more passengers want to get off there). El Tepual airport is 16 km. from town, bus to bus terminal, ETC, US$0.85, 20 mins. Lan-Chile bus to centre of town, US$0.70 (check with Lan-Chile for schedule). Lan-Chile, San Martín 200, T253141 and Ladeco offices at Benevente 350, T 253002.

Shipping Service Taxi from centre to ferry terminal, US$1.35. The roll-on/roll-off vehicle ferry m/n *Tierra del Fuego* of Navimag (Naviera Magallanes S.A.) runs about every nine days or so (double check times) throughout the year to Puerto Natales, taking 3 days and 2 nights. First class accommodation ("gran turismo") comprises 6 cabins (all double with bath); tourist class 34 bunks; and third class ("pionero") 120 reclining seats. The first class fare is US$195-625 depending on cabin and number of occupants; tourist class bunks cost about US$115 p.p. but truck drivers take most of these; third class fare is US$85-100 (2 types of seat). All fares include 3 meals (not very good, take your own); all drinks cost extra (beer US$0.75, wine US$2), take your own, they may run out. Book in advance. Reservations handled in Santiago (**see page** 533). Priority is given to lorry drivers for tourist class tickets which go on sale at the last minute (4 hrs. before departure, perhaps earlier). The dramatic 1,460 km. journey first goes through Seno Reloncaví and Canal Moraleda. From Bahía Anna Pink along the coast and then across the Golfo de Peñas to Bahía Tarn it is a 12-17 hrs. sea crossing, usually rough. The journey continues through Canal Messier, Angostura Inglesa, Paso del Indio and Canal Kirke (one of the narrowest routes for large shipping). The only regular stop is made off Puerto Edén (1 hr. south of the Angostura Inglesa), where the local Alacalufe Indians come out to sell their shellfish.

The roll on/roll off vehicle ferry m/n *Evangelistas*, also of Navimag, runs twice weekly to Puerto Chacabuco (80 km. to the east of Coyhaique), Wed. and Sat., returning from Puerto Chacabuco on the following day. From 31 December to 31 March the schedule changes to include a Sunday-Tuesday trip from Puerto Chacabuco to Laguna San Rafael, so Pto. Montt to Pto. Chacabuco is Wed. and Sat., but return to Pto. Montt is Tues. and Thurs. The cruise lasts about 24 hrs. First class accommodation include 2 cabins with bath (US$80-210 depending on which cabin and number of occupants); tourist class, 14 bunks (about US$100 inc. meals); and third class, 400 reclining seats (US$13.35). Fare to Laguna San Rafael US$97, reclining seat, or US$150 in tourist bunk, US$170-450 in cabin. First class reservations must be made in advance at the Santiago offices. There are canteens and bars on board.

The m/n *Calbuco* of Empremar (Empresa Marítima del Estado) leaves Puerto Montt every Tuesday for Puerto Chacabuco. Arrives on Fridays at 0800, and returns to Puerto Montt on Sundays at 0900. From late December through early March she sails from Puerto Chacabuco on Thursdays at 2000, stays Saturdays 0900 to 1900 at Laguna San Rafael, calls again at Puerto Chacabuco on Sundays at 0800 and returns to Puerto Montt on Tuesdays at 0800. She is a simple ship with only 4 berths in 2 cabins plus 36 seats in tourist class and 53 seats in 3rd class. The fare from Puerto Montt to Puerto Aysén is US$30 first class, US$19 tourist class; to Laguna San Rafael US$105 first class, US$65 tourist class (food on board poor, advisable to supplement with own provisions). Sailing dates are published in *El Mercurio* newspaper.

Between August and May, the m/n *Quellón* of Empremar leaves Puerto Montt on Saturdays at 1130, calling at Melinka, Puerto Aguirre, Pto. Chacabuco (with a shore excursion to Coyhaique), Laguna San Rafael, returning to Puerto Montt via Río Cisnes, Puyuguapi, Castro, arriving back on Fridays at 0800. This journey is sold on a round-trip basis only by Empremar's agent in Santiago (address under **Shipping**) and Puerto Montt. There are three classes of cabin and three pricing seasons; fares range from US$342-539 (April-May) to US$526-781 (Dec., Jan. Feb.).

It has been reported that the ship has tiny cabins, many without washbasin, insufficient toilet and shower facilities, small public room and bar, but we must add that we have received a number of satisfactory comments.

Empremar also run a service on the *Río Cisnes* from Puerto Montt to Laguna San Rafael every Friday at 1600 between September and April. Primarily for motorists, the route is: Pto. Montt-Chaitén by boat; Chaitén-Río Cisnes overland; Río Cisnes-Laguna San Rafael-Pto. Chacabuco by sea; Chacabuco-Coyhaique-Río Cisnes overland; Río Cisnes-Quellón (Chiloe) by sea, then overland (plus ferry) to Puerto Montt. The ship has one vehicle taking 8 passengers. Fares include transport of your vehicle, bar and lodging in Puyuguapi: low season US$800 for two (Sept.-Nov., March-April), US$1,000 for two (Dec.-Feb.). The boat claims to lower lifeboats at the glacier but does not appear to.

The m/n *Skorpios 1* and *2* of Constantino Kochifas C. leave Pto. Montt on Saturdays at 1100 for a luxury cruise with stops at Melinka, Laguna San Rafael, Quitralco, Castro (each ship has a slightly different itinerary) and returns to Puerto Montt on Fridays at 0800. The fare varies according to season, type of cabin and number of occupants: a double ranges from US$770-US$3,300 on *Skorpios 2*, which is the more comfortable of the two. It has been reported that there is little room to sit indoors if it is raining on *Skorpios 1*, but generally service is excellent, the food superb and that, at the glacier, you chip your ice off the face for your whisky.

Transmarchilay Ltda. runs a ferry service from Chonchi to Chaitén in summer (2 Jan.-15 March, see under Chonchi); the rest of the year it runs Pargua-Chaitén and back, Thur. p.m. and Mon. a.m. returning Mon. and Fri. both p.m., 9 hrs., US$4.65 p.p. Its vessel *El Colono* sails Chonchi-Puerto Chacabuco in summer (see under Chonchi) and the rest of the year from Pargua every 3-4 days, 27 hrs., US$13.35 *turista*, US$21.35 *popa*. For sailing dates, their timetable should be consulted. Ticket availability better at the ports than at head office.

See also under Chaitén for passenger services on Terminales Marítimos Chilenos.

Shipping Offices in Puerto Montt: Navimag, Terminal Transbordadores Angelmó, T 253318/253754/253204, Telex 370055 NAMAG CK. Empremar, Av. Diego Portales 1450, Tel. 252548, Telex 370001 EMAR CK. Constantino Kochifas C., Angelmó 1660 y Miraflores (Castilla 588), T 252952, Telex 370161 NATUK CL. Transmarchilay Ltda., A. Varas 215, T 254654, telex 370043 Marchi CK.

Excursions The wooded island of Tenglo, close to Puerto Montt and reached by launch, is a favourite place for picnics. Magnificent view from the summit. The island is famous for its *curantos*, a local dish. Chinquihue, W of Angelmó, has many seafood restaurants, with oysters as a speciality. East of Puerto Montt, Chamiza, up the River Coihuin, has fine fishing. There is a bathing beach (polluted) at Pelluco (*Gran Papa*, opposite ETC bus terminal, good chicken; *Fogón Criolla*—meat, *Jahuel*, and *Pazo*—curantos, all rec.; *Restaurant Juan Pazos*, rec.), a fair walk from Puerto Montt. Isla Guar may be visited by boat from Angelmó harbour (1600, 2 hrs.); boat returns from other end of island at 0730. The north shore is rocky. Accommodation, if lucky, at the church; best to camp.

The (cargo) launch trip from Angelmó jetty up the Reloncaví estuary (8 hrs.) is very beautiful, fjords, sealions, dolphins, local colour, and rec. The estuary is the northernmost of Chile's glacial inlets. At **Cochamó**, at the end of the estuary, there is the *Hotel Cochamó*, basic but clean, F, friendly, good meals, rec., and a large number of *pensiones* (just ask), e.g. *Mercado Particular Sabin*, F p.p., Calle Catedral 20 (Sra. Suni, next to *Hotel*), Sra. Flora Barrientos offers floorspace in her bar/restaurant/drugstore, same street No. 16, F; also *Restaurant Copihue* and *Residencial Gato Blanco*, both F; cheapest accommodation in same street, No. 2, by the pier (floor space only). Cochamó itself is pretty but limited; a side trip is to the Termas de Sotomó, but this requires an affinity for mud. Boats as far as Cochamó from Angelmó jetty only leave once a week, US$4, taking up to nine hours (tip the locals who row you to the launch), returning to Puerto Montt next day (advisable to take warm clothes and plenty of food). Since a good road has been built to Cochamó via Ralún (**see page** 578) (Buses Bohle's 1300 and 1700 services from Puerto Montt to Ralún continue to Cochamó Mon.-Fri.; also Buses Río Frío.) Most boats up the estuary go only as far as Río Puelo, a small settlement 3 km. walk from Puelo. Rowing boats and a barge for cars cross the river; on the other bank buses go to Puerto Montt at 0700 and 1700. The road will soon be completed to Puelo. At Puelo, lodging is available with Roberto and Olivia Telles, simple, clean, no bath/shower, meals on request, beverages inc. beer and wine can be bought a few houses away. This is a most peaceful place. It is 5-6 hours from Angelmó to Río Puelo (advisable to take warm clothes, food and seasickness pills if windy). Among the boats that go is *Rosita Carmen*, Captain Juan Carlos; book a seat and ascertain departure time 2-3 days in advance. Information is available from a booth in the harbour at Angelmó.

There is a beautiful 2-day hike from Cochamó through forests to Cayutué, a quiet, peaceful village (see the Bradts' book, *Backpacking in Chile and Argentina*, for route); the settlement is on Lake Todos los Santos and occasional boats go to Petrohué—US$30 to hire one (**see page** 577); you can camp by the lake.

The Maullin River, which rises in Lake Llanquihue, has some interesting waterfalls and good fishing (salmon). The little old town of **Maullin** (*Motel El Pangal*, 5 km. away, T 244, B), at the mouth of the Maullin River, is worth a visit. **Calbuco**, centre of the fishing industry, with good scenery, can be visited direct by boat or by road. Puerto Montt is a good centre for excursions to the lakes via Puerto Varas. From Puerto Montt to Puerto Varas by the old (dirt) road is a short but beautiful journey.

Chiloé island is 250 km. long, 50 km. wide, 9,613 sq. km., and has a population of 116,000. There are two main towns, Ancud and Castro (airport), and many fishing villages. Seaweed is harvested for export to Japan. Typical of the island are substantial wooden houses (*palafitos*) built on stilts over the water. The hillsides in summer are a patchwork quilt of wheat fields and dark green plots of potatoes. Inland are impenetrable forests. There has recently been appreciable development, and power and water shortages and poor sanitation are now things of the past. Though the weather is often cold and foggy, the island is extremely beautiful when the sun is out. Sweaters and woollen caps are good purchases. Music is popular, with many players in the waterfront cafés in Castro. The local sailing sloops, *lanchas*, are fast being replaced by diesels, very few can be seen now. The islanders of Chiloé were the last supporters of the Spanish Crown. When Chile rebelled the last of the Spanish Governors fled to the island and, in despair, offered it to Britain. Canning turned the offer down. The island finally surrendered to the patriots in 1826, the last remaining Spanish possession in South America.

From Puerto Montt buses run 15 times a day (US$1.50) to Pargua (55 km., 1 hr.) on the Straits of Chacao. (At Pargua, *Hotel La Ruta*, on A. Prat. At Chacao, *Pensión Chiloé*, F; *Hospedaje Angelino*, F.) There are two ferry terminals in Pargua, one in town, one down a dusty road from town; check which when you get there. Most buses go right through to Ancud and Castro (e.g. Trans Chiloé at 0810, 1220 and 1820, Varmontt at 0800, 1230 and 1830, Bus Norte at 1115, but the company with most services is Cruz del Sur, 10 a day to Ancud and Castro, 5 to Chonchi and Quellón. Fares from Puerto Montt: Ancud, US$2 (Trans Chiloé US$1.65), Castro US$3.15 (Trans Chiloé US$3), Chonchi, US$4, Quellón, US$5.15. Note that there are direct bus services from Osorno, Valdivia, Temuco and Los Angeles to Chiloé. Buses drive on to ferry across the Chacao Strait to Chiloé (passengers can get out of the bus). Transmarchilay run frequent ferries (two vessels in summer) and Cruz del Sur runs ferries for its buses; the buses have priority, but cars are also taken. There are 24 trips a day to Chiloé by the ferry (US$0.50); cars US$4 one way (20 mins. crossing). The Tourist Office in Ancud has a number of brochures of different circuits on Chiloé which are very useful (e.g. Circuito Histórico Cultural, Circuito Mitológico, Excursión al Sur de Chiloé), all are free.

Ancud Beautiful views, Spanish fort (Fuerte San Antonio) and powder magazine restored, a good regional museum on the Plaza de Armas open 0900-1230, 1430-1830 (Mon.-Fri.), 0930-1230, 1430-1800 (Sat.), 1000-1200, 1430-1730 (Sun.) (entry, US$0.25), the tourist office, Libertad 665 (T 2800), and craft shops (speciality is basketwork). Buses every day to Mar Brava and Playa de Pumillahue, 20 km. west of Ancud.

Hotels *Quintanilla*, Libertad 751, rec., B, with bathroom and breakfast, open in summer only; *Hostería Ancud*, San Antonio 30, T 2340/350, Telex 275002, A with bath and hot water, very comfortable, friendly and helpful, but meals overpriced; *Polo Sur*, Av. Costanera 630, T 2200, C with bath, hot water, good seafood restaurant, not cheap; *Hostería Ahui*, Av. Costanera 906, C with bath and breakfast, modern, clean, good views, T 2415; *Lydia*, Chacabuco 630, T 2990, D-C with bath and restaurant, overpriced; *Montserrat*, Baquedano 417, T 2957, C with bath, hot water, breakfast; *Cabañas Las Golondrinas*, end of Baquedano, T 2823, C with bath, hot water and kitchenette; *Moteles Huaihuén*, A. Pinto 1070, T 2554, C; *Residencial Montenegro*, Blanco Encalada 531, T 2239, F, fair, no hot water; *Residencial* on Aníbal Pinto 515, good, F. *Hospedaje Miranda*, Mocopulli 753, cheap, friendly, hot water; *Residencial Weschler*, Cochrane 480, T 2318, D, clean, friendly, comfortable, view of bay; private house at Bellavista 449, E, with sleeping bag on floor much cheaper, no hot water; Edmundo Haase Pérez, Ramírez 299, F, breakfast, clean, basic, good value; also Ramírez 396, T 489, Sra. Edith Hualibota, E, nice; Elverrez 442, G p.p. with breakfast, cold water; Pudeto 357, E, fair, next to watch shop; Elena Bergmann at Aníbal Pinto 382 (5 rooms in private house), clean, friendly, F p.p.; Sra. Lucía, San Martín 705, G;

Familia Reuter-Miranda, Errázuriz 350, T 2261, F with breakfast, clean, spacious, hot showers, rec. In summer, the school on Calle Chacabuco is open for lodging, US$1.30 p.p.

Camping Camping Playa Larga Huicha, 9 km. N of Ancud, E per site, bath, hot water, electricity.

Restaurants Excellent. Seafoods, especially king crabs (very cheap), almejos and cheese in market area. *Balai*, Pudeto 119, seafood, meat, sandwiches; *Carmen*, Pudeto 145, Chilean cooking, pasteles; *Coral*, Pudeto 346, good, cheap; *Jardín*, same street No.263; *Macaval*, Chacabuco 691; *El Tirol*, A. Prat; *El Trauco*, Blanco y Prat, seafood; *Lydia*, café-restaurant, Pudeto opp. *Jardín*, Chilean and international; *El Cangrejo*, Dieciocho 155, seafood highly rec.

Travel Agent Turismo Ancud, Galería Yurie, T 2235, Telex 97700 ANCD CL.

Bus Ancud-Castro, US$1.50; frequent buses daily on both routes, 1½ hrs. No direct Sunday bus from Ancud to Dalcahue, need to stay in Castro. To Puerto Montt, Cruz del Sur 11 times between 0710 and 2000, office on Chacabuco nr. Pudeto, Varmontt 3 a day from *Hotel Polo Sur*, Trans Chiloé also 3. Local buses leave from terminal at Pto. Montt 538.

Shipping Transmarchilay has offices in Ancud, Libertad 669 (T 23172279, Telex 375007 MARCHI CK.).

Walk from Ancud along the beach towards Faro Corona (34 km. to Punta Corona), good views, interesting birdlife, dolphins can be seen, but the beach is not suitable for swimming. A side road from the Ancud-Castro highway leads to Chepu on the west coast, famed for its river and sea fishing.

Castro Capital of the Province and a very friendly town, 88 km. from Ancud (NB if driving between the two, watch out for humps and hollows in the road). There is a tremendous variety of styles in housing, including houses on stilts (*palafitos*) above the water, on the northern side of town and by the bridge over the Río Gamboa. Cheap woollen articles (hats, sweaters, gloves) can be found at Feria, or Mercado Municipal de Artesanía on the waterfront; they are the best value in the Tenth Region, especially if you bargain. *Palafito* restaurants have been put up behind the market. The large cathedral (1906) with excellent wooden interior on the Plaza de Armas, was built by Italian architect, Eduardo Provosoli. One-room museum (Calle Serrano) contains history, folklore, handicrafts and mythology of Chiloé. Very good views of the city from Mirador La Virgen on Millantuy hill above the cemetery, which is legendary. Tourist office in main square only open in summer, not very helpful. Conaf at Gobernación, 3rd floor, Plaza de Armas.

Hotels *Hostería Castro*, Chacabuco 202, T 2301, C with bath and breakfast, but 16% VAT on top, hot water, good restaurant, interesting building (in summer coach and boat trips are organized to other places on the island); *Cabañas Centro Turístico Nercón*, 5 km. S, rooms with bath, hot water, heating, restaurant, tennis court; *Gran Alerce*, O'Higgins nr. Mistral, C with bath and TV, excellent rooms and breakfast; *Residencial Mirasol*, San Martín 815, good, F, next to bus station, noisy; *Hospedaje Angie*, San Martín 747, F p.p., small rooms, clean, pretty; also near bus terminal, *Hospedaje Chiloé*, F, breakfast, clean, rec. *La Bomba*, Esmeralda 270, T 2300, E, without bath, decent, hot water, 3 course menu (US$4). *Quinta Niklitschek*, Panamericana Norte 331 (3 km. north), better inside than out, D; *Unicornio Azul*, Pedro Montt 228, T 2359, A in summer, good but expensive for what is offered; *Residencial Lidia*, Blanco Encalada 276, T 2331, F, clean, cold shower, good; *Res. Inés de Banen*, Blanco Encalada 266, F, OK, breakfast US$1; *Costa Azul*, F, Lillo 67, T 2440, friendly, hot water, bed bugs, but restaurant poor value; also on Lillo, *Res. El Gringo*, G, O.K.; *Plaza*, Blanco 366, T 5109, C with bath, D without, rec. on 3rd floor, breakfast included, 2 fair *comedores*, expensive food; *Moteles Auquilda*, on way to Aeropuerto Gamboa, T 2458, D. *Hospedaje* at Las Delicias 287, E, hot shower, nice family and place; Serrano 488, above TV shop, F p.p. with breakfast,rec.; Esmeralda 233, with bath; Adriana Gutiérrez, Freire 758-9, E, breakfast, clean, good value; also good, Freire 497; Maruja Vera, O'Higgins 841, O'Higgins 446 (hot water, clean), Chacabuco 449 (no hot water), and *El Rusgo*, San Martín 700, all E; La Torre 212, F, friendly, clean, good breakfast with homemade bread. Private house at Luis Espinoza 380, G p.p. with sleeping bag, friendly, washing and cooking facilities; also San Martín 879 (Sra. Judith Mancia), F, quite good.

Camping Camping Pudú, Ruta 5, 10 km. N of Castro, cabins, showers with hot water, sites with light, water, children's games.

Restaurants *Krill Café* and *La Amistad* (seafood), Feria Campesina Lillo (local 26), very good food and value, on stilts over the sea, and others here behind the market; many more across the road from the market; *Chilo*, San Martín 419, pleasant; *Lidia*, Blanco 276, good, friendly (café, pastelería, restaurant and residencial—see above); *Sacho*, Thompson 213, good food, not too dear, clean; *Brisas del Mar No. 1*, good, and others, like *Palafito*, on the waterfront behind the Feria. *Chilo's Café*, San Martín 419, rec., good lunches. *Don Octavio*, Lillo 67, T 2440, seafood incl. curantos. In the market, try "milcaos", fried potato cakes with meat stuffing; also "licor de oro", like Galliano.

Shopping See above for market. Cema-Chile outlet on Esmeralda, opp. *Hotel La Bomba*. *Libros Chiloé*, Serrano y Blanco, books in Spanish on Chiloé.

Exchange Banco del Estado de Chile on main square accepts travellers' cheques (at a poor rate).

Post Office On O'Higgins, W side of square; **phone office** O'Higgins y Ramírez, 3 blocks N of square.

Doctor Muñoz de Las Carreras, near police station, surgery 1700-2000 on weekdays, rec.

Tours Pehuén Expediciones, Lillo 119, T5254, Telex 297805, Fax (0657) 2432, day trips around the island. **Ladeco** agency on Serrano, opp. *Hostería Castro*.

Buses The Municipal Terminal is on San Martín, 600 block, before Sgto. Aldea. From here, Trans Chiloé to Ancud and Puerto Montt, 0740, 1320, 1620; Bus Norte to Ancud, Puerto Montt, Osorno and Santiago (1815), Wed. to Puerto Montt and Punta Arenas, and daily to Puerto Montt at 0830 with connection to Bariloche; Bus Sur, Mon., Sat. 0630 to Punta Arenas; Eurobus to Puerto Montt, Punta Arenas and Coyhaique; also Ghisoni, Victoria Sur and Varmontt. Local buses: Arroyo to Cucao Tues., Thur. 1130, Sun. 0900, return 1300-1400, Sat. 1800, no advance sales, fight for a seat; to Chonchi and Huillinco, Mon., Wed., Fri. 1130, 1630; Cárdenas to Dalcahue; buses to Puqueldón and Queilén.

Cruz del Sur buses (T2389) and buses for Achao leave from the terminal behind San Francisco cathedral: Cruz del Sur to Ancud and Puerto Montt 11 a day (0700-1930—last bus to ferry at 1830), also to Osorno, Valdivia, Temuco, Concepción, Santiago (1545 Pullman, 1600 *cana*); 7 a day to Chonchi and Quellón (0700-1845). At least 4 buses daily to Achao (0700-1700) via Dalcahue and Curaco de Vélez. Turibus for Concepción and Santiago next to *La Bomba*; Trans Chiloé on square; Varmontt, Balmaceda 289, T 2776, next to *Hotel Plaza*.

Dalcahue 21 km. N of Castro, the wooden church dates from 1858, on older foundations. Market on Sundays, from 0700 to 1300 in this picturesque village (better value in Castro or Puerto Montt). Good choice early on, but better bargains in late morning. Tourist kiosk in season. Bus from Castro, 40 mins., US$0.75. Colectivos also available. (*Pensión Montaña*, M. Rodríguez 9, F, basic; *Pensión San Martín*, San Martín 1, T 2207, F, better; many private houses offer accommodation). Further N still, on the east coast is Quemchi, with *Gran Hotel Alerce*, O'Higgins y Gabriela Mistral, B with bath, heating, sauna and restaurant. Tenaún, 56 km. NE of Castro, is an interesting fishing village with a good 18th-century church, as has Vilpulli, 20 km. S of Castro. Quilquico, between Castro and Rilán, has a wooden church dating from 1767.

From Castro, buses every day in summer, 3 a day (but none Tues. and Thurs.) otherwise, 2 hrs. US$2 (via Dalcahue and Curaco de Vélez de Achao and a ferry (US$3 return) takes one to **Achao**, 39 km. away on the Isla de Quinchao (*Hotel Splendid*, F, hot water; *Hotel Sao Paulo*, Serrano 52, F, reasonable, hot water; *Hotel Delicia*, Serrano y Delicias, F, clean, friendly, small restaurant; *Restaurant Central*, Delicias, simple, cheap, good; *Restaurant La Nave*, Prat y Sargento Aldea, good seafood, by beach; *Cocinería Insular*, F, friendly, rec. excellent breakfast; *Restaurante Cristina*, excellent seafood), a quiet, pretty fishing village with a lovely old wooden church, built in 1730, which inspired most other churches in the area (2-roomed museum close to church). It is possible to return to Castro same day.

Chonchi, 25 km. S of Castro (bus US$0.75, paved road), is a picturesque fishing village with rambling shingled houses painted in many colours and a lively wharf for fishing (neo-classical wooden church, 1850). Visit Opdech (oficina Promotora del Desarrollo Chilote), on waterfront, which has a weaving cooperative. *Posada Antiguo Chalet*, Irarrazával, T 221, winter C, summer B, charming, beautiful location, very good; *Hospedaje Chonchi*, O'Higgins 379, T 288, D, full board available, very nice; *Pensión Turismo*, F. Rooms available in *Hostería* next to *Provisiones Magallanes*, G p.p. in shared room, or floor space, use of kitchen; at

Almacén la Patagonia and with Sra. Gamín Chacón, Calle Andrade, corner Alvarez and Manuel Gómez, baker at P.J. Andrade 184, G with breakfast. *Restaurant La Parada*, on left half way down hill from centre to quay, very good value.

A visit to the island of Lemuy is rec.; 90 sq. km., quiet, with good walking through undulating pastures and woodland. Daily ferry service from Chonchi; terminal 4 km. from Chonchi, then, once across, 8 km. (no bus) to the main town, Puqueldón which offers basic accommodation, clean, F, good food, in Calle J. M. Carrera. *Restaurant Lemuy* is next to the municipal offices and *Café Amancay* opposite (bus from Castro). Good walks to Lincay, 5 kms., or Lincura, one-day expedition.

Southeast of Chonchi is Queilén beach; daily bus from Castro, US$1.35.

In summer only (2 Jan.-15 March), the Transmarchilay ferry *Pincoya* sails from Chonchi to Chaitén on the mainland, Tues., Wed., Thurs. at 0800, 6 hrs. crossing, US$26.50 per car, US$4 p.p. Transmarchilay's *El Colono* sails Chonchi-Puerto Chacabuco Wed. and Fri., again in summer only, 22 hrs., US$52.50 per car, US$15 with seat, US$13.35 p.p. (*económico*). From 15 March to 29 Dec. ferries go only from Pargua to Chaitén and Puerto Chacabuco. Transmarchilay office, Av. Costanera s/n, T 319. *Mercedes* ferry of Somarco leaves Chonchi for Chaitén, Sat. 1200 (approximately), office at Agroser *farmacia veterinaria* on the harbour. The ship gives absolute preference to trucks, but foot passengers may be taken, without accommodation. Enquire first.

Cucao, a village 40 km. west of Chonchi and one of two settlements on the West coast of Chiloé, can be reached by road. There is an immense 15 km. beach with thundering Pacific surf. Nearby is the **Chiloé National Park** (opened in 1984), with reception centre, small museum, helpful staff, guest bungalow available for visiting scientists (apply to Conaf, through your Embassy, stating environmental interests). The forests in the park are vast and impenetrable; ask at Conaf for directions or guides. There is a 15 km. walk from Cucao to Cole Cole in the national park, a good hike with great views. The first *refugio* is 24 km. along the coast and there are 3 others (access difficult). Many houses rent horses for US$1/hour, US$5/day. Camping, US$2.50 at entrance, free wood, no car access, 15 min. walk from bridge in village (wild camp here in camper van). Accommodation, F, with full board or *demi-pension* at *Provisiones Pacífico* (friendly), Sra. Boreuel or with Sra Luz Vera, next to school (rec.); one shop. For buses from Castro see above; hitching is very difficult. Taxis can be rented for about US$20; for a bit more Alfredo Alvarez will drive out from Castro, wait for several hours and take you back. Half way between Castro and Cucao is Huillinco, a little town on a large lake, a charming place to stop on the way to the ocean (one *hostal*, G p.p. with good food, or stay at the Post Office).

Quellón Southernmost port on Chiloé; 92 km. from Castro, fishing boats built at wharf, pleasant beaches (*Hotel Playa*, P. Montt 255, T 298, E, good, clean, hot water, restaurant; same street, No. 217, *Hostería Quellón*, T 250, E, basic; *Pensión Vera*, A. Gómez García, casi P.Montt, F, good, clean; *La Pincoya*, La Paz 64, T 285, E; *Restaurant Las Brisas* on seafront, good). Daily service from Castro to Quellón, US$2, 2 hrs.

ARCHIPELAGIC CHILE From Puerto Montt to Cape Horn (7)

		Population ('000)	
Region	Provinces	1982	1987
XI (Aysén)	Aysén	67	76
XII (Magallanes)	Magallanes and Antarctic Territory	131	146

South of Puerto Montt lies a third of Chile, but its land and its climate are such that it has been put to little human use: less than 3% of the country's population lives here. There is no real dry season. On the offshore islands and the western side of the Andes it is frequently wet and windy, particularly south of the Río Baker. North of that river, the summers are drier than the winters, but to the south, summers are windier and marginally wetter. Impenetrable forest covers much of the land, although in many parts there is stark evidence of the felling of trees which began in the nineteenth century. Wood is used for construction, fencing and fuel; in this last respect it is in such demand in population centres like Coyhaique that it costs as much as petrol in winter.

It is only the northern part, as far south as Coyhaique, and the far S that are inhabited. S of Chiloé, for 1,100 km., there is a maze of islands—the tops of submerged mountains—separated by tortuous fjord-like channels, a veritable topographical hysteria. It is fortunate for shipping that this maze has a more or less connected route through it: down the channel between Chiloé and the mainland, about 290 km. of open sea beyond the southern tip of Chiloé and then down the Moraleda, Mesier, Inocentes and Smyth channels into the Straits of Magellan. In some places along this route the tide levels change by 12 metres. In one particular place two sharp-cut walls, 900 metres high, enclose the constricted channel which leads to Puerto Natales; here the waters are deeper than the cliffs are high and slack water lasts for 30 mins. only. The Smyth Channel enters the Straits of Magellan at Cape Thamar. January and February are probably the best months for a trip to this region.

With the opening of the **Carretera Austral Presidente Pinochet** (Southern Highway) in 1988, the Pan-American Highway has been extended a further 1,013 km. through southern Chile to Cochrane. The highway is divided into three major sections: Puerto Montt-Chaitén (242 km.) with three ferry crossings; Chaitén-Coyhaique (435 km.), and Coyhaique-Cochrane (336 km.). By early 1990, the road had been extended some 40 km. beyond Cochrane; the eventual goal is Puerto Yungay, a further 85-km. to the south west.

Although the section from Puerto Montt to the border between the Tenth (Los Lagos) and Eleventh (Aysén del General Carlos Ibáñez del Campo) Regions does not strictly belong to Archipelagic Chile, we deal with the Carretera Austral as a single entity.

Puerto Montt to Chaitén Before setting out on this section, it is imperative to check when the three ferries are running, normally only from December to March, and to make a reservation for each if travelling by car. Book passage in Puerto Montt, rather than Santiago, at the Transmarchilay office, Antonio Varas 215, T 254654.

The road (Ruta 7) heads east out of Puerto Montt, through Pelluco, the city's black sand beach, and after an initial rough stretch follows the shore of the Seno Reloncaví to the first ferry across the Reloncaví estuary at Las Arenas. Allow 1 ½ hours to get there. The last part of this section passes the southern end of the **Parque Nacional Alerce Andino** which contains tall trees (alerces), some up to a thousand years old, and waterfalls. Park wardens are at the northern end of the park, at Correntoso (35 km. east of Puerto Montt) and Lago Chapo (46 km.); there are buses from Puerto Montt; also campsites.

Ferry Las Arenas-Puelche: ½-hr. crossing, US$4.65 for a car, at 0745, 0945, 1445, 1845 and 2045. Roll-on roll-off type.

61 km. from Puelche is **_Río Negro_**, also called Hornopiren after the volcano above it. Electricity 1900-0100; when the ferry is running there is a daily bus service (Fierro) from Puerto Montt. Río Negro is at the head of a fjord at the mouth of which is Isla Llancahué, good for hiking in the forests amid beautiful scenery. _Hotel Termas de Llancahué_ charges D p.p. full board (excellent food), hot spring at the hotel. To get there, broadcast a message on Radio Reloncaví in Puerto Montt (US$0.50) asking to be picked up at Río Negro at a specified time. The hotel will send an open boat for you; the one-hour crossing affords views of dolphins and fur seals.

Hotels at Río Negro: _cabañas_ at Copec service station, **_Perlas del Reloncaví_**, clean, pleasant, good restaurant (may not have fuel); the cabins are usually taken before the rooms in the two other hotels, the **_Holiday Country_**, on the road to Pichanco, E p.p., hot shower, restaurant, and the **_Hornopiren_**, at the water's edge, next to the sawmill.

Leave Río Negro at 0600 to drive the 35 km. for the 0800 ferry at Pichanco (there is little opportunity to camp at Pichanco and just one small stand offering food and drinks). This is a 2-hour crossing the length of the Fiordo Comau to Leptepu. There is one other crossing at 1500 (fare is US$11.50 per car; reverse on to the ferry to cope with the steep slope from the dock at Leptepu). Soon after the ferry sets out it passes a narrow channel to the left; in here the German battle cruiser *Dresden* hid from the British fleet in 1915. The crew was protected by the local German community. After disembarking from the morning ferry at Leptepu, try to get away quickly to Fiordo Largo, the next ferry, 10 km. away. This boat has about half the capacity of the previous one so if you miss it you will have to wait 2 hours for its return. It runs every two hours between 0800 and 2000, ¾-hour crossing Fiordo Reñihue to Caleta Gonzalo, US$4 per car (reverse on).

After Caleta Gonzalo there is a steep climb on a coarse gravel surface to Laguna Blanca. After 44 km. is Caleta Santa Bárbara, a black sand beach with nice camping and swimming. It is a further 12 km. to Chaitén.

Chaitén to Coyhaique The port of *Chaitén* has grown in importance because of the military camp and the new road. The town is quite well-laid out, but is a typical transit place, either full or empty, depending on the movements of the ferries from Pargua or Chonchi. Fuel is available in Chaitén.

Hotels and services *Hotel Continental*, Juan Todesco 18, T 202, D, no heating nor private bath, but good meals, very helpful and friendly, rec.; *Restaurant/Hotel Mi Casa*, Av. Norte, T 285—on a hill—rec., C with bath, water heaters in rooms, negotiable, the owners prefer you to eat in their restaurant; *Hostería Schilling*, C, Av. B. O'Higgins 243, T 295, on waterfront, with bath and heating (hot water is turned on or off on the intuition of the landlady, check your shower before entering), no restaurant; *Hotel/Restaurant Cordillera*, Todesco y O'Higgins, D. *Residencial Astoria*, Av. O'Higgins 442, T 263, F p.p. with breakfast, shared bath, clean, bar downstairs; *Pensión* at Juan Todesco 205, F (G for floor space), hot water and meals extra, free use of kitchen; large youth hostel, F, sleep on floor; free campsite 4 km. N, with hot showers and close to sea. *Café-restaurante Flamengo*, Av. O'Higgins 218, T 314, excellent, popular with travellers; *Restaurante Mahurori*, Independencia 141. Shopping and most facilities. Phone office in supermarket next to *Hostería Schilling*.

Transport Transmarchilay ferry from Pargua, 15 March-29 Dec. Sun. late p.m., returning Mon. late p.m., and Thur. returning Fri. From 2 Jan. to 15 March the ferry runs between Chaitén and Chonchi on Chiloé, Mon. 1700, Tues. and Wed. 1500, from Chaitén, 6 hrs., US$4 p.p., US$26.50 per car. Check in advance for exact times; office is two doors from *Hostería Schilling* at Av. O'Higgins 243, T 272. There is also a ferry to Puerto Montt for trucks, Terminales Marítimos Chilenos, which will also take passengers but with no shelter, Mon., Wed., Fri. and Sat., 2000, 12 hrs. Office is in a hardware store (*ferretería*) on Juan Todesco. Similar service by Somarco on the *Mercedes* to Chonchi on Fri.; schedule unknown.

Flights Puerto Montt-Chaitén-Puerto Montt with ASA, Mon., Wed., Thur., Sat., leaves Puerto Montt 1545, Chaitén 1630, US$23.50 one way; T Puerto Montt 254364/4471. Fierro bus twice a week from Puerto Montt in summer season only, US$8.35.

Two companies run microbuses between Chaitén and Coyhaique, Aerobus twice a week (US$21.50) and Artetur, twice a week in winter, three times in summer (US$20) 12-14 hrs. The service depends very much on demand and in winter especially may not run all the way (i.e. only to La Junta). On the full service, the bus stops overnight in La Junta in winter but only briefly in summer. Other stops on request, but it is easier to go right through than pick up a bus on route. Hitching the whole route takes about a week, but you must be prepared for a day's wait if you find yourself out of luck.

There is superb salmon fishing in the rivers, and the local people are very friendly. 25 km. S of Chaitén is Amarillo (accommodation in village bar, F, breakfast US$1); 5 km. from the village are thermal baths (2 wooden sheds with very hot pool inside, US$1.50 p.p.), camping possible and one cabin for hire with woodstove and bath, sleeps 4, C (accommodation is being extended). From the thermal baths it is possible to hike along the old trail to Futaleufú, 4-7 days, not for the inexperienced, be prepared for wet feet all the way. The trail follows the River Michinmawida (passing the volcano of the same name) to Lake Espolón. A sporadic ferry crosses the lake taking cargo only to Futaleufú. Campsite at this end of the lake also has bungalows (see below).

At Puerto Cárdenas 46 km. S of Chaitén, on the northern tip of beautiful Lago Yelcho (out of 10 houses and a police post, there are 2 places to stay, inc.

Residencial Yelcho, full board available); beautiful setting. Free campsite 3 km. after the river crossing, ask the owners in a little white house near the lake. An elderly, free ferry crosses the Río Yelcho at Puerto Cárdenas (all day till 1800 in winter, 2000 in summer, stops 1230-1330 for lunch). A bridge is under construction. At Km. 60, on the western side of Lago Yelcho is a free Conaf campsite (limited facilities) from which it is a 2 hour walk to the glacier which can be clearly seen from Puente Ventisquero on the road. At *Villa Santa Lucía*, 31 km. from Puerto Cárdenas, a road branches east to Argentina. Santa Lucía has 30 houses, a military camp, one small shop, bread from a private house, and accommodation on main street at No.7 (Sra. Rosalía Cuevas de Ruiz, basic, meals available), No. 13, breakfast US$1, and No. 16, not bad, all G p.p., none has hot water.

The road to the border is single track, gravel, passable in a regular car, but best with a good, strong vehicle; the scenery is beautiful. Accommodation can be found at La Cabaña, Puerto Piedra (Camping y Cabañas, T 280) and Puerto Ramírez (*Hostería Río Malito*—Sr. Soto—nearby, rooms, camping, fishing), whence there are two roads to the Argentine border at **Futaleufú** and **Palena** (several *pensiones*, Expreso Yelcho bus from Chaitén twice a week). 6 km. before Futaleufú, turn left to Lago Espolón for campsite and cabins, F per bed, US$3.75 for a motorhome; gorgeous lake, warm enough for a quick dip (take care with the current); superb rainbow trout fishing, ask for the Valebote family's motorboat. Aníbal, who owns the campsite, sells meat, bread, beer and soft drinks and will barbecue lamb. The area around Espolón and Futaleufú has a microclimate, 30° C in the day in summer, 5° at night.

Hotels and transport Futaleufú Res. Carahue, O'Higgins 322, E; **Hotel Continental**, Balmaceda 597, F, basic, hot water, clean, rec., cheap restaurant. A microbus runs from Chaitén to Futaleufú on Tuesday, at least. At the small grey store, Kitty, at the school corner on Balmaceda, ask about bus Futaleufú to the border, Tues. and Fri. 1300 approx., US$1.25. The bus is met at the ferry across the river: half-hour to border, 1 hour at border crossing, half-hour for ferry, then bus to Esquel, US$3, 2 hrs. Esquel is the starting point for several Argentine national parks.

Coming from Argentina, it is 2 km. from the free, hand-winched ferry across the Río Grande to the border (allow 1½ hrs. for formalities); continue from Futaleufú to Puerto Ramírez, but don't go into Ramírez, take the unsigned right turn to Chaitén (left goes to Palena). **N.B.** Only transit visas are issued at border points, so you must either leave within 10 days or renew your entry stamp at an immigration office.

Between Villa Santa Lucía and La Junta are two, free, water-driven ferries (0800-2200 in summer, 0800-1900 winter). *La Junta* (where the buses stop) is at the confluence of Río Rosselot and Río Palena, 151 km. from Chaitén, 270 km. from Coyhaique. It is a drab, expensive village, but the fishing is good and the walks to Lake Rosselot beautiful. 3 *hosterías*, *Residencial Copihue*, Antonio Varas 611, E p.p., few rooms but nice, shared bath, hot water, good meals; another one at Antonio Varas 33, F, breakfast US$1.50, use of kitchen. Fuel is available at La Junta.

Puerto Puyuguapi (also spelt Puyuhuapi), about half way, at the end of the Puyuguapi Canal, is an intriguing town founded by Germans in 1935. There is a famous carpet factory in the village. 18 km. southwest of the village, accessible only by jeep and boat, there are several springs with 50°C water filling two pools near the beach (rent a boat for a group, for US$15 p.p., baths cost US$4.75 p.p., children under 11 half price, take food and drink). The *Hostería Termas*, T 2741515, has accommodation in our C range p.p. **Parque Nacional Queulat** nearby is, according to legend, the place where the rich town of Césares once was. The Ventisquero (glacier) Colgado can be seen in the park, about 25 km. S of Pto. Puyuguapi, very beautiful, camping possible; also the Salto del Cóndor waterfall. The Portezuelo Queulat is the highest pass on the Carretera.

Accommodation and services *Residencial Alemana*, Av. Otto Uebel 450, C, a large wooden house on the right-hand side of the road which leads from the quayside through the village, 150 metres before the police post, owned by Sra. Ursula Flack Kroschewski, very good board and lodging; *Hostería Ludwig*, on the road south, D, excellent, often full;

Hospedaje Tita, D, basic; *pensión* of Sra. Leontina Fuentes, Llantureo y Circunvalación, F p.p., clean, hot water, good breakfast for US$1; 300 metres south at Sur Rolando, stay at Sra. Sophía's house; *pensión* at Tureo 18, F. There is a dirty campsite by the sea behind the general store. The store is behind the service station, which sells fuel until 2100. There are 2 bars. Transport out of Puyuguapi is very scarce; bus offices of Aerobus, Artetur and Suray.

At **Puerto Cisnes** along the Seno Ventisquero (33 km. from the main road), you can buy food and find accommodation (*Posada Gaucho*, E p.p. with breakfast, dinner available, welcoming, hot water, *pensión* at Carlos Condell y Dr. Steffen, E p.p., with breakfast, hot shower, friendly; also a youth hostel and campsite). There are buses Wed. and Sun. at 1100 to Coyhaique with Litoral, 5½ hrs, US$8, Mansur on Tues., US$8, and with Pudú Mon. and Fri. at 0830.

The Río Cisnes is rec. for rafting or canoeing; 160 km. of grand scenery, with modest rapids except for the horrendous drop at Piedra del Gato; there is a 150 metre cliff at Torre Bright Bank. Good camping in the forest. At Cisne Medio (no hotel, restaurant or telephone), there is **a road to La Tapera** and to the Argentine border. A few km. N of Cisne Medio provisions and lodging can be found at Villa Amengual. 10 km. S of here is the **Reserva Nacional Lago Las Torres**, a wonderful lake with good fishing and a small Conaf campsite (free).

Villa Mañihuales, 20 km. S of El Tocqui copper mine, is connected by bus with Coyhaique (Trans. Mañihuales, one a day except Sun., US$2). There are at least 3 *pensiones*, inc. *Pensión Bienvenido*, F p.p., clean, friendly, and restaurant *Villa Mañihuales*, F, friendly, breakfast US$0.75 (both right-hand side of road going S at south end). After Mañihuales the road forks west to Puerto Aysén, east to Coyhaique. At Villa Ortega on the Coyhaique branch, the *Restaurant Farolito* takes guests, F, rec.

The Eleventh Region (Aysén) lies between Chiloé and Magallanes. Its original inhabitants were Tehuelches (Tzónecas, or Patagones), who lived on the pampa hunting guanacos, ñandúes (rheas) and huemules (a large indigenous deer, now almost extinct), and Alacalufes (Kaweshour, or Canoeros), who were coast dwellers living off the sea. The arrival of the Spaniards, who called the region Trapananda, led to little more than exploration of the coast by navigators and missionaries. Inland exploration in the nineteenth century was greatly helped by Fitzroy's cartographical surveys; George Charles Muster, Enrique Simpson Baeza and Juan Steffen led the main expeditions, travelling up the rivers. Colonization followed the first commercial enterprises (timber extraction, cattle farming) on an east-west axis, from Argentina or the sea, with Puerto Aysén-Coyhaique becoming the most important route.

Puerto Aysén used to be the region's major port, but it has been replaced by Puerto Chacabuco, 15 km. to the west. They say it rains 370 days a year in Puerto Aysén (pop. 13,050), quite an attractive town for all that at the meeting of the rivers Aysén and Palos. There are few vestiges of the port left, just some boats high and dry on the river bank when the tide is out and the foundations of buildings by the river, now overgrown with fuschias and buttercups. To see any maritime activity you have to walk a little way out of town to Puerto Aguas Muertas where the fishing boats come in. There is a good walk to Laguna Los Palos, 2 hours. Folklore festival in 2nd week of November. A new bridge over the Aysén and paved road lead to **Puerto Chacabuco**; a regular bus service runs between the two. The harbour is a short way from the town and is a dreary place to hang around waiting for the ferry, especially on a wet evening (a new passenger waiting area is being built). Services given below are in Puerto Aysén unless stated otherwise.

Accommodation hard to find, most is taken up by fishing companies in both ports. In Puerto Aysén: *Motel Imperio y Gastronomía Carrera*, Cochrane 465, T 332551, C with breakfast, new and smart; *Hotel Aisén*, Chacabuco 130, T 332672, C; *Residencia de lo Nene*, Av. Serrano Montaner 57, T 332725, E, clean, full board available; *Roxy*, hotel and restaurant, Aldea 972, T 332704, F p.p.; *Plaza*, O'Higgins 237, T 332784, E without breakfast; *Residencial Marina*, Aldea 382, F, clean, only cold water; *El Fogón*, Aldea 355, both with *comedor*; unnamed *pensión* at Aldea 1026, G p.p. with sleeping bag; *Café-Restaurant Yaney Ruca*, Aldea 369, E, clean, friendly. No campsite but free camping easy.

In Puerto Chacabuco: *Parque Turístico Loberías de Aysén*, J. M. Carrera, T 115, B; *Hotel Moraleda*, O'Higgins, T 332784, F p.p.

Exchange on Plaza de Armas will only change cash, not travellers' cheques.

Post Office on other side of bridge from Plaza de Armas; **telephone office** on south side of Plaza de Armas, next to *Café Rucuray*, which posts boat information.

Tourist Office in Municipalidad, Arturo Prat y Sgto. Aldea, 1 Dec. to end-Feb. only; helpful.

Bus to Puerto Chacabuco, Las Cascadas on Montaner Serrano, to left of Sgto Aldea (main street) walking away from Plaza de Armas, 6 a day between 0800-1730, 30 mins, US$0.50, return 0830-1800; colectivo US$1.35 p.p.
Las Cascadas to Coyhaique, 3-4 a day between 0830-1900 (Sun. and holidays between 0845 and 1930), US$1.35; Transaustral, Sgto. Aldea next to No.348, 3 a day; Don Carlos taxi-bus, 5 a day, US$2.50. When a ferry is in, buses to/from Coyhaique go to Puerto Chacabuco, details at bus offices.

Shipping Offices Empremar, Teniente Merino 728, T 332725, or Agemar, Teniente Merino 909, T 332726, Puerto Aysén; Navimag, Sargento Aldea 398, T 332699, Puerto Aysén; Transmarchilay, Av. O'Higgins s/n, T 144, Puerto Chacabuco. It is best to make reservations in these companies' offices in Puerto Montt, Coyhaique or Santiago (or, for Transmarchilay, in Chaitén, Ancud or Chonchi). For trips to Laguna San Rafael, see below; out of season, they are impossible to arrange.

Ferry Services Transmarchilay's *Colono* runs from Puerto Chacabuco via the Canal Moraleda to Chonchi on Chiloé on Mon., and Thur. at 1500 and takes 22 hours (seats US$13.35, car US$52.50); meals are available. This service operates 2 Jan. to 15 March only, and in this season the ship makes an excursion to Laguna San Rafael each Saturday (fares from US$90-170, ranging from economy class to cabin). For the rest of the year the *Colono* goes to Pargua, 27 hours, about 3 times a week, seats US$13.35-21.35. Navimag's *Evangelistas* sails each Thur. and Sun. from Puerto Chacabuco to Puerto Montt, taking about 24 hours (fares under Puerto Montt, the *pionero* seats are quite spacious and comfortable and there is a cafeteria selling burgers, sandwiches, soft drinks, beer, hot beverages, etc.); it too diverts from its schedule in summer to run a trip to Laguna San Rafael (Sunday, returning Tuesday), US$96.65 for a seat, cabins from US$150 shared bath to US$270 d with bath.

The paved road from Puerto Aysén to Coyhaique passes through the **Parque Nacional Río Simpson**, with beautiful waterfalls and good views of the river. There is a campsite near the turning to Santuario San Sebastián.

Coyhaique (population, 40,000), the administrative and commercial centre of the region, is located in a large green valley surrounded by mountains. The town provides a good base for hiking and skiing excursions in the area and has a good Museo Regional de la Patagonia Central in the Liceo San Felipe Benicio on the pentagonal square (in term time, if the museum is closed, ask the secretaría for the key; in holidays it should be open, US$0.15, small but interesting with photos of early settlers, history, paleontology, fauna and archaeology). When entering Coyhaique from the airport, look left from the bridge over the Río Simpson for the Piedra del Indio, a rock outcrop which looks like a face in profile. Petrol is available in Coyhaique, several stations.

Hotels In summer rooms are in very short supply; the tourist office has a full list of all types of accommodation, but look out for notices in windows since any place with less than 6 beds does not have to register with the authorities (several on Baquedano and Almte. Simpson).
Chible, José de Moraleda 440, T 221643, C; *Hostería Coyhaique*, on La Onsa, T 221137, A, poor beds, unreliable hot water, good restaurant; *Los Ñires*, Baquedano 315, T 222261, B with breakfast, pleasant; *Residencial Puerto Varas*, Serrano 168, T 221212, F p.p., check which of the bathrooms has hot water, restaurant and bar, basic, tatty; *Residencial Navidad*, Baquedano 198, F p.p. without bath or breakfast (which is US$1.25 extra), comedor; *Hospedaje* at Baquedano 20, T 222520, Patricio y Gedra Guzmán, room in family home (also 3 comfortable flats), F p.p., use of kitchen, breakfast with homemade bread, tent sites with bathroom and laundry facilities down by the river, English spoken, most hospitable; *Residencial Carrera*, 12 de Octubre 520, F p.p. without breakfast; *Residencial* at Cochrane 532 (no sign), F, quite nice except for bathroom; *Res. La Pastora*, Prat 553, E, no hot water, meals available. *Pensión América*, 21 de Mayo 233, G p.p., dirty, basic, not

```
1. Square
2. Museum
3. Piedra del Indio
4. Fish Farm/
   Piscicultura
5. Colectivos
6. Artetur buses
7. Navimag
8. Transmarchilay
9. Tourist Office
10. Post Office
11. Telephone Office
12. Brautigam
    Supermarket
13. Hostería Coihaique
14. Hotel los Ñires
15. Hotel Chiiié
16. Residencial Puerto
    Varas
17. Giobbi bus for
    Argentina
18. Conaf
```

COYHAIQUE

NOT TO SCALE   G1

rec. Other *hospedajes* and family accommodation (usually about US$5): Ignacio Serrano, T
222287, Manuel Torres de la Cruz, good breakfast, cheap, rec.; Ignacio Serrano 91, Sra. Berly
Pizarro Lara, T 220522, E full board; Colón 203, F p.p., pleasant, use of kitchen, Sr. Fidel Pinilla
arranges tours; Colón 495, F p.p. without breakfast (more with), hot water, clean; Ignacio
Serrano 391, T 221408, E with breakfast, not as good; Carrera 33-A, rec.; *Hospedaje* with
restaurant at Baquedano 444, another at No. 102, also Freire 554. Youth hostel in summer
at one of the schools (it changes each year), G p.p. with sleeping bag.

Camping about 3 km. north, up a steep bumpy road off the Chaitén road, rec. More
campsites in Coyhaique are expected to be ready for 1991.

Restaurants *Loberías de Chacabuco*, Barroso 553, good seafood; *Mi Pub*, Prat y Dussen,
pizzas and sandwiches; *Estancia*, José Carrera y Moraleda, also rents rooms (G p.p., hot
water) and allows use of kitchen; *Café Oriente*, Calle 21 de Mayo y Condell, good bakery,
tea; *Café Kalu*, A. Prat 402, serves good set meals, hamburgers. *Café Ricer*, Calle Horn,
good; *Los Colonos* in an arcade on Horn; *Cafetería Alemana*, Condell 119, nice; *Café
L'Express*, in mall at Condell 140; *Pollo Listo* (fast food) F. Bilbao 234 and *Todo Pollo*, 21

de Mayo 552.

Shopping Feria de Artsanía on the square; Cema-Chile on square, between Montt and Barroso. Large well-stocked supermarkets: Brautigam, Horn, Prat y Bilbao (closed Sun.), Central, Magallanes y Bilbao, open daily till 2230; 2 small ones on Prat, Nos. 480 and 533, open Sun. Dehydrated camping food available. Food, especially fruit and vegetables, is more expensive than in Santiago.

Car Hire Automóvil Club de Chile, Bilbao 583, T 221847, rents Suzuki jeeps, about US$25/day, plus fuel. Hertz, Moraleda 420, T 223456.

Taxis US$5 to airport (US$1.65 if sharing); fares in town US$1.35. To Puerto Ibáñez US$60, to Puerto Chacabuco US$40, to Puerto Aysén US$34. 50% extra after 2100. Colectivos congregate at Prat y Bilbao, average fare US$0.35.

Post Office Cochrane 202, open Mon.-Fri. 0830-1230, 1430-1800, Sat. 0830-1200.

Telephone office at Barroso 626, open till 2200, opens on Sun. about 0900. **Telex**, 21 de Mayo 472.

Exchange Prat 340, oficina 208, T 223342, and Turismo Prado, 21 de Mayo 417, T 221271, both will change travellers' cheques. For australes, dollars and cheques go to Lavaseco on Gral. Parra. Fincard (Visa and Mastercard), A. Prat 340, local 1, T 223202, Mon.-Fri. 0900-1400, 1530-1900, Sat. 0930-1330.

Travel Agents Turismo Prado, address above; Expediciones Coyhaique, Bolívar 94, T 222300, FAX 222500. Both offer tours of local lakes (US$20) and other sights (e.g. US$56 to Ventisquero Colgante), arrange Laguna San Rafael trips, etc. Prado does historical tours, while Expediciones does fishing trips and excursions down the Río Baker.

Tourist Office Cochrane 320. Conaf office, Ogana 1060. Maps (photocopies of 1:50,000 IGM maps) from Dirección de Vialidad on the square.

Shipping Transmarchilay, 21 de Mayo 417, T 221971, Telex 377003 MARCHI CK. Navimag, Dussen 340, T 223306.

Buses Terminal at Lautaro y Magallanes; most buses leave from here, but not all. Puerto Aysén-Coyhaique, Transaustral, 5 a day, 4 on Sun., US$1.35; La Cascada, 3-4 daily, US$1.35, and Don Carlos taxi-bus US$2.50, 4-6 a day, the route is extended to Puerto Chacabuco, US$1.65, if there's a boat in. Puerto Cisnes Pudú Sun. and Thur., Mansur, Wed., Litoral Tues. and Sat. at 1100, US$8. There are daily buses to Mañihuales (not Sun.), Trans Mañihuales, US$2 and to Balmaceda, Libertad (at Simpson y Magallanes), US$1.35. Empresa del Norte at the terminal runs a round trip service to Villa Simpson (US$0.85), Villa Frei (US$1), Seis Lagunas, Lago Atrevesado (all US$1.15), Coyhaique, Mon., Wed., Fri. 0730 and 1730, 2 hours there and back.

In summer Pudú runs twice a week to Puerto Ibáñez on Lake Carrera, the Chilean section of Lake Buenos Aires (US$4.50), to connect with *El Pilchero* ferry, see below; Transaustral also connects with *El Pilchero*, Mon. and Fri. 1630, US$5. In winter, colectivos connect with *El Pilchero*, leaving Mon. 1730 (stay overnight in Pto. Ibáñez) and Sat. 0700, from Calle Prat, beside *Res. La Pastora*/Farmacia Regional, No. 553, 3 hrs., US$6.65.

Buses on the Carretera Austral: north, with Artetur, Baquedano 1347, T 223368, Wed. 0700, Sat. 0800, US$20, may be an extra services in summer, in winter may go only as far as La Junta; Aerobus, at bus terminal, T 221172, Mon. and Thur. to Chaitén at 0800 (but check), US$21.65. South, also with Aerobus to Cochrane (in minibus), Mon., Wed., Fri., 1000, arrive 1730, lunch stop at Río Tranquilo (returns Tues., Thur., Sat.). Pudú, at terminal, T 221008, to Cochrane Tues. and Sat. at 0900, returning Wed. and Sun. 0900, US$13.35 in a standard bus taking longer than Aerobus because it stops in all the settlements on the way (e.g. Guadal, US$11.65, Murta, US$7.65).

Travel to Argentina To Comodoro Rivadavia, Giobbi, Bolívar y Barroso, T 222067, Tues., Thurs., Sat. 0830, US$20, 12-13 hrs. via Coyhaique Alto, Río Mayo and Sarmiento. Another route is via Balmaceda (bus from Coyhaique, Ladeco flights from Santiago via Temuco and Puerto Montt), but there is no through transport. Alternatively, the routes south of Lago General Carrera, via Chile Chico (public transport—see below), or through Villa Chacabuco and Paso Roballos, north of Cochrane (no public transport, road passable in summer, but often flooded in spring). Beware, many border posts closed at weekends. If looking for transport to Argentina it is worth going to the local Radio Santa María, Bilbao y Ignacio Serrano, and leave a message to be broadcast.

Air Airport, Teniente Vidal, about 5 km. from town including a steep climb up and down to the Río Simpson bridge. Lan-Chile flies daily from Santiago (not Sun.), with stops in Concepción and Puerto Montt; Ladeco flies daily via Puerto Montt, Valdivia and Los Angeles or Osorno. A quicker route is to fly Santiago-Puerto Montt direct, then change to ASA, daily 1100, return to Puerto Montt 1400. Ladeco office at Gral. Parra 215, T 221188. ASA, Lillo 315, T 222981 to Chile Chico (Tues., Thur., Sat.), US$21, and Cochrane (Mon., Wed., Fri., US$31.50, 45 mins., rec. only for those who like flying, with strong stomachs, or in a hurry).

Excursions Excellent views of the Río Simpson valley from the hill, 4 hrs. walk north of town, at **Reserva Forestal Coyhaique**. To the lakes Elizalde, Atrevesado, Frío, Castor and Pollux. Skiing at El Fraile in winter (it's rather a bleak place out of the ski season). **Reserva Forestal Mañihuales**, 76 km. from Coyhaique, was largely destroyed by forest fires in the 1940s, but the views are good. **Monumento Natural Dos Lagunas**, lakes Toro and Bonito, 21 km. on the Coyhaique Alto road, is worth a visit.

The Carretera Austral continues south of Coyhaique, a road junction just short of Villa Cerro Castillo. A branch south leads to Puerto Ibáñez. 35 km. S of Coyhaique is El Blanco, a hamlet with *pensión* at *Restaurant El Blanco* (or *El Nuevo*—G, breakfast US$0.75). At **Puerto Ibáñez**, on Lake Carrera, there are three *residenciales: Ibáñez*, Bertrán Dixon 01 (clean, warm, hot water) and, next door, *Mónica*, good meals (both F p.p.), and *Hostería Bajada Río Ibáñez*, E. Petrol/gasoline available at Luis A. Bolados 461 (house with 5 laburnum trees outside); it's sold in 5-litre containers. 6 km. away are some grand waterfalls on the Río Ibáñez.

To reach **Chile Chico** (population 2,200), a quiet, friendly but dusty town on the southern shore of Lake Carrera, one can either go by boat from Puerto Ibáñez or go through Argentina. The region prides itself in having the best climate in Southern Chile with some 300 days of sunshine; much fruit is grown as a result. Rainfall is very low but strong winds are common. Annual festival at end-January. The lake itself, a beautiful azure blue, covers 2,240 sq. km.; the Chilean end is predominantly Alpine and the Argentine end (Lake Buenos Aires, 881 sq. km.) dry pampa.

Hotels at Chile Chico: *Aguas Azules*, Rodríguez 252, T 320, E full board (F without), rec. *Residenciales Frontera*, O'Higgins 332, T 314, F, good food, clean rooms, rec., except for bathrooms. Private house, Blest Gana 240, basic but nice, F; turquoise house at O'Higgins 332, F, clean, rec.; also O'Higgins 43, F p.p., good meals. Youth hostel at Blest Gana 320, from Jan. to end Feb. (just an empty house, no electricity or furniture, US$0.80 p.p., ask next door). *Casa Quinta/No me Olvides* (María Sánchez de Campaña), F p.p. just by Puerto Márquez on road to Argentine border, clean, cooking facilities, warm, no hot water, honey, eggs, fruit for sale, rec. Free campsite at Bahía Jarra, 15 km. east. **Restaurants** Apart from *residenciales: Cafetería Elizabeth y Loly* on Plaza serves coffee and delicious homemade cakes; will prepare meals if asked (expensive), also has rooms at E; *La Cabañita*, typical, cheap; *Rapa Nui*, cheap and good. Supermarket on B. O'Higgins, buy your own wine here. It is very difficult to change dollars (*Café Elizabeth y Loly* changes dollars at bank rate in small amounts); change australes in shops and cafés on main street (very poor rates). Ask at the Municipalidad or at the tourist office on O'Higgins for help in arranging tours.

Regular service by Transmarchilay car ferry, *El Pilchero*, across the lake, leaves Puerto Ibañez for Chile Chico 0800 Tues. and 1100 Sat. (check all times on arrival—2½ hrs, each way: US$2 p.p., US$26 for car; offices in Santiago, Puerto Montt, Chaitén, Chonchi, Ancud, Puerto Chacabuco or Coyhaique). The Sat. boat from Puerto Ibañez goes only to Chile Chico, returning on Sun. at 1600 (1400 in winter); the Tues. service continues from Chile Chico to Fachinal, Cristal, Mallín Grande, Puerto Sánchez and Río Tranquilo, arriving back in Puerto Ibáñez on Wed. This schedule operates 2 Jan.-15 March (when extra service may be put on). From 15 March to end Dec. only the Tues. service runs regularly, the Sat. one goes according to demand. Buses and jeeps meet the ferry in Puerto Ibáñez for Coyhaique. Number of passengers limited to 70; locals given preference, no reservations possible. Jeeps run from Chile Chico to Los Antiguos, the Argentine border, US$1.70; from here connections can be made to Perito Moreno.

Chile Chico is connected by road along the S shore of the lake only as far as Fachinal (50 km.—people will let you stay for free, take sleeping bag). From here there is a trail to Mallín

Grande, 18 km., takes all day; we have no direct proof of this trail, only reports. Mallín Grande is a ferry jetty and little else, although people will put you up for free if you have a sleeping bag. A road runs to Puerto Guadal (shops, post office, 3 lodgings: Sr. Félix Elías, no sign, near port in big, old brown building, F p.p., hot water, meals available, rec., at Quemel "Sade" Guerrero—1st shop you see from jetty, No. 382 on corner of Los Pinos—and one other; *Restaurant La Frontera*, Los Lirios y Los Pinos). Pudú has a bus service between Guadal and Mallín Grande on Tues. and Wed., US$2 each way, the only traffic otherwise is on Tues. when the ferry calls. The road continues from Guadal to El Maitén on the Carretera Austral. If you wish to take *El Pilchero* to see Lago General Carrera from the water and then connect with the Pudú bus service (or Aerobus at Río Tranquilo, see below) for Cochrane or Coyhaique, an overnight stop in Mallín Grande or Río Tranquilo may be necessary and careful checking of schedules in advance will be essential.

The country to the S and W of Chile Chico provides good walking for the mountaineer. The weird rock formations and dry brush-scrub give a "wild west" feel to the country. The northern and higher peak of Cerro Pico del Sur (2,168 m.) can be climbed by the agile from Los Cipres (beware of dogs in farmyard). You will need a long summer's day and the 1:50,000 map. Follow the horse trail until it peters out, then navigate by compass or sense of direction until the volcano-like summit appears. After breaching the cliff ramparts at an obvious point, there is some scrambling and a 10-foot pitch to the summit: indescribable views of the Lake and Andes. (Brian Spearing)

The Carretera Austral branches off the Coyhaique-Puerto Ibáñez road 97 km. S of Coyhaique. It goes through Villa Cerro Castillo (small supermarket, basic *residencial* on main street), named after the fabulous nearby mountain, which looks like a fairytale castle, with pinnacles jutting out of thick snow. This and other peaks in the northern wall of the Río Ibáñez valley, are in the **Reserva Nacional Cerro Castillo** (*guardería* on the Senda Ibáñez, opposite Laguna Chinguay, open Nov.-March). The Carretera climbs out of the valley, passing the aptly-named Laguna Verde and the Portezuelo Cofré. It descends to the boggy Manso valley, with a good campsite at the bridge over the river, watch out for mosquitoes, then goes on to Bahía Murta (the village, just off the Carretera on the northern tip of the central "arm" of Lago General Carrera, has *Res. Patagonia*; *Res. y restaurante Lago Gen. Carrera*, welcoming; free camping by lake, good view of Cerro Castillo). The road follows the lake's western shore; the colour of the water is an unbelievable blue-green, reflecting the mountains that surround it and the clouds above. At Río Tranquilo, where the buses stop for lunch at *Residencial Los Pinos* (G p.p., basic), fuel is available at the ECA store for a large drum (no sign). The Carretera continues to skirt the lake to its southwestern tip at El Maitén (turn off for Guadal). It then becomes steeper and more bendy (in winter this stretch, all the way to Cochrane, is icy and dangerous).

Just past Puerto Bertrand, a good place for fishing, is a sign to the Nacimiento del Río Baker, with the most abundant water of any Chilean river. Note how the colours of the rivers and lakes change in this region. The road climbs up to high moorland, passing the confluence of the Ríos Neff and Baker, before winding into Cochrane. The scenery is splendid all the way; in the main the road is rough but not treacherous. Watch out for cattle on the road and take blind corners slowly.

Cochrane (1,500 people) sits in a hollow a little distance west of Lago Cochrane. It is a simple place, sunny in summer, good for walking and fishing. Northeast of the town is the **Reserva Nacional Tamango**, administered by Conaf in two sectors (Tamango, 9 km. by dirt track, and Húngaro, 4 km., which reaches down to Lago Cochrane). In the Húngaro sector are a few remaining huemules (deer—two radio-tagged); there are also guanaco in the pampa part, foxes, lots of birds including woodpeckers and hummingbirds and lenga forest. It is inaccessible in the four winter months. Ask in the Conaf office on the square about visiting because some access is through private land and tourist facilities are still in the planning stage. The views from the reserve are superb, over the town, the nearby lakes and to the Campo de Hielo Norte to the west.

Accommodation, food and services *Hostería Wellmann*, Las Golondrinas 36, T 171, D p.p., hot water, comfortable, warm, good meals, rec.; *Residencial Sur Austral*, Sra. Sonia Salazar, A. Prat s/n, T 150, E with full board, hot water, very nice; *Residencial Rubio*, Teniente Merino 04, T 173, Sra. Elva Rubio, also very nice, D full board, F bed only, breakfast US$1.65, lunch and dinner US$3.25 each; *La Tranquera* restaurant and residencial, Av. San Valentín 651, at entrance to town, F p.p., hot water, friendly, poor food. In summer it is best to book rooms in advance. Restaurants: *La Sota de Oro*, Tte. Merino; *Café Lematin*, Merino y Maitén; *El Viajero*, Maitén.

Pudú bus office is in *Bottillería Quiaco*, Tte Merino (bus leaves 0915, arrives in Coyhaique 2030); Don Carlos office is in *Residencial Sur Austral*. Petrol is available, if it hasn't run out, at the Empresa Comercial Agrícola (ECA) until a filling station has been completed. Horses can be hired for excursions in the surrounding countryside, ask around, e.g. at *Hostería Wellmann*.

The Carretera is being constructed further south of Cochrane with a view to reaching Puerto Yungay. It will bypass Tortel, a village built on a hill above the sea. It has no streets, no proper plan, only wooden walkways ("no hay ni una bicicleta"). It trades in wood with Punta Arenas and fishes for shellfish (such as *centolla* and *loco*). Access is either by Don Carlos plane, or by horse, several days journey from Cochrane.

Some 150 nautical miles south of Puerto Aysén is the **Laguna San Rafael** glacier, 30 metres above sea level, and 45 km. in length. It calves small icebergs, carried out to sea by wind and tide. The thick vegetation on the shores, with snowy peaks above, is typical of Aysén. The glacier is one of a group of four that flow in all directions from Monte San Valentín. This icefield is part of the **Parque Nacional Laguna San Rafael** (1.35m. hectares), regulated by Conaf. The only way there is by plane or by boat: Air Taxi from Coyhaique (Don Carlos), US$100 each if party of 5; some pilots in Puerto Aysén will fly to the glacier for about US$85, but many are unwilling to land on the rough airstrip. The glacier is best seen from the sea: there are 9 official cruises: Empremar's *Calbuco, Río Cisnes* and *Quellón* (see under Puerto Chacabuco and Puerto Montt); *Skorpios I and II* (under Puerto Montt); Navimag's *Evangelistas* and Transmarchilay's *Colono* (see under Pto. Chacabuco); Mar del Sur, 21 de Mayo 417, 2nd floor, T 221271, Coyhaique, or Matias Cousiño 82, oficina 1106, Santiago, T 6985100/6984784, Fax 698589, fares from US$280 to US$360 p.p., or US$2,542 + tax to charter; *Odisea*, a motorized sailing boat, from 7 Nov.-29 April, US$680 for cruise (flight with Ladeco Santiago-Coyhaique extra), T 330883 Santiago (*Hotel Crowne Plaza*), or Sgto. Aldea 679, Puerto Aysén, T 332879. Local fishing boats from Chacabuco/Puerto Aysén take about 18-20 hrs. each way, charging the same as the tourist boats. Ask for Jorge Prado at the port (he takes a minimum of 7, more expensive than others); Andino Royas, Cochrane 129; Justiniano Aravena, Dr. Steffen 703; Rodrigo Azúcar, Agemar office, T 716; or Sr. Ocuña, ask at the port. These unauthorized boats may not have adequate facilities.

The *Calbuco* of Empremar, a government supply ship, leaves Chacabuco on Thurs. at 2000, returning from the Laguna on Sat. at 1800, arriving Chacabuco on Sun. at 0800, two lifeboats make the trip to the glacier (bring food as you may be left at the glacier for 3 hours). Operates to San Rafael only between December and March, book in advance in Aysén in Jan./Feb. season (all year round the *Calbuco* runs from Puerto Montt to Puerto Chacabuco). Fares given under Puerto Montt **Shipping**. (On the return journey you can continue to any of stops back to, and including Puerto Montt, 48 hrs.) Rooms can be hired for US$1.50 p.p. at the old hotel administered by Conaf (bring a week's supply of food: unless lucky enough to hitch back on another boat, you'll have to wait for the *Calbuco*; also bring anti-mosquito cream and candles—no electricity. Water can be scarce and the hot shower only works when water is plentiful, 2 very cold waterfalls nearby if necessary—take biodegradable soap). At the glacier there is a small ranger station. The rangers are willing to row you out to the glacier in calm weather, a 3-hr. trip. Robert af Sandeberg (Lidingö, Sweden) describes this journey as follows:

"The trip in the rowboat is an awesome venture. At first it is fairly warm and easy to row. Gradually it gets colder when the wind sweeps over the icy glacier (be sure to bring warm clothes—a thick sweater, and waterproof jacket are rec.—Ed.). It gets harder to row as small icebergs hinder the boat. Frequently somebody has to jump onto an icefloe and push the boat through. The glacier itself has a deep blue colour, shimmering and reflecting the light; the same goes for the icebergs, which are an unreal, translucent blue. The glacier is very noisy; there are frequent cracking and banging sounds, resembling a mixture of gun shots and thunder. When a hunk of ice breaks loose, a huge swell is created and the icebergs start rocking in the water. Then great care and effort has to be taken to avoid the boat being crushed by the shifting icebergs; this is a very real danger."

In the national park are puma, pudu pudu (minature deer), foxes, dolphins, occasional sealions and sea otters, and many species of bird. Walking trails are limited (about 10 km. in all) but a lookout platform has been constructed, with fine views of the glacier.

N.B. If you plan to go to Laguna San Rafael by boat, check first with the Gobernación Marítima in Puerto Aysén that the boat is licensed for the trip.

CHILEAN PATAGONIA (8)

The Twelfth Region (Magallanes), which includes the Chilean part of Tierra del Fuego, has 17.5% of Chile's total area, but it is inhabited by under 1% of Chile's population. In summer rains are frequent. In winter snow covers the country, except those parts near the sea. The country is then more or less impassable, except on horseback. Strong, cold, piercing winds blow, particularly during the spring, when they reach a velocity of 70 to 80 km. an hour. During the winter they do not blow all that hard, and from May to August a strong wind is almost exceptional. The dry winds parch the ground and prevent the growth of crops, which can only be cultivated in sheltered spots.

Until the discovery of oil—Tierra del Fuego and N of Magellan Strait produce all Chilean oil—the most important industry was the breeding of sheep. At one time there was a large British colony there; it has been diminishing steadily of late. Coal has been discovered on the Chilean side of the frontier, at Pecket, but the mine is considered uneconomic; miners still cross into Argentina to work at Río Turbio.

Punta Arenas, the most southerly city in Chile, and capital of the Twelfth Region, 2,140 km. S of Santiago, is on the Straits of Magellan at almost equal distance from the Pacific and Atlantic oceans, 1,432 nautical miles from Valparaíso, and 1,394 from Buenos Aires. The population is about 113,500. Most of the smaller and older buildings are of wood, but the city has expanded rapidly, and practically all new building is of brick or concrete. All the main roads are paved and the country roads are of gravel; when driving in Patagonia, some form of windscreen protection is absolutely essential. Punta Arenas is a busy little city somewhat neater looking than the average Chilean town. The cemetery, at Av. Bulnes 929, is even more fantastic than the one at Castro (Chiloé), with a statue of Indiecito, the little Indian, and many memorials to pioneer families and victims of shipping disasters (open 0800-2000 daily). Walk up Calle Fagnano to the Mirador Cerro La Cruz for a view over the city.

Punta Arenas is the centre of the sheep farming industry in that part of the world and exports wool, skins, and frozen meat. Besides the export of oil and gas, there is the regular carriage of crude between the Strait oil terminals and the refineries in central Chile. Good roads connect the city with (240 km.) Puerto Natales in Ultima Esperanza and Río Gallegos in Argentina. There are no railways. Punta Arenas has certain free-port facilities; the Zona Franca is 3½ km. N of the centre (shops open 1000-1200, 1500-2000 Mon.-Sat.). (The restaurant is open at lunch time on Sundays.)

There is an excellent modern museum in the Colegio Salesiano, "Mayorino Borgatello" dealing with the Indians, animal and bird life of the region, and other interesting aspects of life in Patagonia and Tierra del Fuego, at Av. Bulnes 374, entrance next to church. Open Tues.-Sat. 1100-1600, Sun. 1100-1300, hours seem to change frequently (entry US$0.25). Museum of regional history, Braun Menéndez, Calle Magallanes 949, off Plaza de Armas, located in a mansion built by one of the early millionaires, is well worth visiting. Part is set out as room-by-room regional history, the rest of the house is furnished and visitors are taken round in groups by a guide. Closed Mon., otherwise open 1100-1600, till 1300 on Sun. (entry US$0.50). The Instituto de la Patagonia, Av. España y Los Flamencos (opp. the University), open Mon.-Fri. 0900-1200, 1500-1700, has an open air museum. The British School on Waldo Seguel, and St. James' Church next door, are wooden, in colonial style. N.B. Calle Pedro Montt runs East-West,

Map legend:

1. Plaza de Armas
2. Cathedral
3. Cemetery
4. Museo Braun – Menéndez
5. Bus Sur
6. Bus Fernández
7. Lan-Chile
8. Ladeco
9. Tourist Office
10. *Hotel Cabo de Hornos*
11. *Hotel Los Navegantes*

while Calle Jorge Montt runs North-South.

Hotels *Cabo de Hornos*, Plaza Muñoz Gamero 1025, T 222134, A, excellent, rec.; *Los Navegantes*, José Menéndez 647 (Casilla 230, T 224677), A, excellent restaurant, slightly cheaper than *Cabo de Hornos*; *Savoy*, same street, No. 1073, T 225851, C, pleasant rooms but some lack windows, good place to eat; *Mercurio*, Fagnano 595, T 223430, B with breakfast, bath, TV and phone, good restaurant and service, rec.; *Cóndor de Plata*, Av. Colón 556 (T 227987/224301), B, very good; *Hostal de la Patagonia*, O'Higgins 478, T 223521, C with bath, excellent; *Turismo Plaza*, José Nogueira 1116 2nd floor, T 221300, C (cheaper without bath), pleasant; better value is *Residencial París*, J. Nogueira 1116, T 223112, 4th floor, D, rec., heating, though some rooms are without windows. *Monte Carlo*, Av. Colón 605, T 223448, D with bath, E without, with breakfast, clean, rec.; *Ritz*, Pedro Montt 1102, T 224422, D, fine; *Residencial Villegas*, Boliviana 238, E with meals; *Residencial Central*, Balmaceda 545, D, with breakfast; *Chalet Capital*, Armando Sanhuesa 974 (Casilla 213, Mirtha Mansilla Giner), E, good, comfortable, welcoming; *Residencial Roca*, Calle Roca 1038, T 223803, F p.p., clean; *Casa Deportista*, O'Higgins y Errazúriz, T 222587, F p.p. with breakfast, several bunks to a room, noisy; *Residencial Internacional*, Arauco 1514 (esq. Boliviana, T 223677), F, highly rec., hot water, large meals, use of kitchen, popular. Private house, Sra. Carolina Ramírez, at Paraguaya 150, F, nice and friendly, no heating, breakfast included, safe motorcycle parking; Sra. Angela Hernández, Rómulo Correa 0370, Barrio Prat, G, with or without breakfast; Nena's, Boliviana 366, friendly, F with breakfast, highly rec. but won't take everyone; Mireya Cárdenas, Boliviana 375, E with breakfast, use of kitchen, good meals, rec.; also Boliviana 238, rec., F, a bit noisy. Youth hostel-style accommodation at Calle Bella Vista 577, G p.p., kitchen, hot showers, clean; Sra. Inés Ojeda de Alvorado, Av. España 1291 y Balmaceda, F, heaters, shared bath with hot water, pleasant; or ask for private house accommodation at tourist office. **Camping** in Reserva Forestal Magallanes, 8 km. from Punta Arenas (check with Tourist Office for directions).

Restaurants Main hotels. *El Mercado*, Mejicana 617, T 227415, open 24 hrs., reasonably-priced lunch, expensive dinner; *Club de la Unión*, Plaza Muñoz Gamero 716, accepts non-members for meals, and is reported to be very good. *Centro Español* is excellent, above Teatro Cervantes on Plaza de Armas; *Trovador*, Pedro Montt 919, German-run, cheap, runs excursions to Puerto Hambre and Fuerte Bulnes, US$2.50, often folk music at night; *Garage*, Pedro Montt 988, good decor but expensive. Seafood at *Sotitos*, O'Higgins 1138, good service and cuisine, expensive; also good on O'Higgins, *El Fogón* (parrillada) and *Beagle*, Magallanes 875 (accepts Visa). *Dino's Pizza*, Bories, cheap, good, big pizzas; *Café Garogha*, Bories 817, open Sun. p.m., pleasant but busy at night. *Asturias*, Navarro 967, T 223763, good food and atmosphere; *Don Quixote*, Navarro 1087, good café; *Café Monaco*, Bories y Menéndez, cheap snacks and drinks. *Sayonara*, Errázuriz, good value bar. Restaurant above fish market offers centolla and oysters, but slow service and expensive. Cheap fish meals available at stalls near the fishing cooperative near the docks. The bakeries on Calle O'Higgins are well worth a visit, with excellent rye bread sold on Mons. and Thurs. Also, *Pancal*, 21 de Mayo 1547, good bread and cakes. Try Polar beer. Lobster has become more expensive because of a law banning fishing them with nets, allowing only lobster pots.

Bookshop *Fenix Libros*, Lautaro Navarro 1125, good selection on regional history.

Night Club *Normita* discotheque, Balmaceda, downmarket, all night, free on Fri. and Sat.

Sport 9-hole golf course 5 km. from town on road to Fuerte Bulnes.

Car Hire Hertz, Lautaro Navarro 1064, T 222013; Avis, nearby on same street. Autómovil Club, O'Higgins 931, T 221888, Budget is opposite; Avips, Mejicana 730, US$40 for 1 day, with 250 km., tax extra; Turismo Pehoé, 21 de Mayo 1464, T 224223/224506; Turismo Cabo de Hornos, Plaza Muñoz Gamero 1039, T 225599.

Exchange National banks. Open 0900 to 1400 but closed on Sat.; but the Casa de Cambio Andino, Roca 886, Office 25 is open until 1900 on Fri. Banco O'Higgins good for exchange. Argentine australes can be bought at *casas de cambio*. Good rates at Cambio Gasic, Lautaro Navarro 549, T 222396, La Hermandad, same street No. 1099, T 223991, Cambio Taurus, 21 de Mayo 1502, and at Bus Sur office on Menéndez 565, T 224864 and Lautaro Navarro 1001, T 225656 (accepts travellers' cheques). Kiosco Redondito, Mejicano 613, T 227369. If banks and *cambios* are closed, exchange is available at *Hotel Los Navegantes*, José Menéndez 647, or *Hotel Cabo de Hornos* (worse rates than *cambio* in same building).

British Vice-Consul Mr Roderick Matheson ask at hotels for his whereabouts, Casilla (P.O. Box) 327, helpful and friendly. **Argentine Consulate** Av. 21 de Mayo 1878, open

1000-1400. Visas take 24 hrs., US$15. Other consulates: **W. German**, Independencia 865 (T 223781), **Danish**, Bories 911 (T 221850), **Dutch**, 21 de Mayo 1243 (T 224275), **Swedish**, Errazúriz 891 (T 224107), **French**, Colón 399 (T 224482), Italian, Balmaceda 357 (T 223518), **Norwegian**, Mejicana 916 (T 222156).

British School founded 1904, co-educational.

Laundry   Lavasol, self-service, O'Higgins 969, Mon.-Fri. 0900-2200, weekend 1000-2000, US$3.35 per machine, wash and dry; Lavaseco Josseau, Pinto 766.

Dentist   Dr. Hugo Vera Carcamo, España 1518, T 227510, rec.

Post Office   Carlos Bories y J.Menéndez, open 0830-1230, 1400-1830 (Mon.-Fri.), 0830-1230 (Sat.), closed on Sundays.

Telex   Bories 911. Fax and Telex, VTR, Bories 801, T 225600. **Telephones** Nogueira 1116, Plaza de Armas, 0800-2200, international and local.

Tourist Office   Sernatur, Waldo Seguel 689, Casilla 106-D, T 224435, at the corner with Plaza Muñoz Gamero, 0830-1230, 1430-1830. English spoken. Kiosk on Colón between Bories and Magallanes (ask for Juanita Cofré, who has room to let at Boliviana 533, F with breakfast, and is helpful on travel on supply boats and planes to Antarctica). Turistel Guide available from kiosk belonging to *Café Garogha* at Bories 831. **Conaf**, J.Menéndez, between Montt and Quilota.

Travel Agents   Skartour and Cabo de Hornos Tur, Plaza Muñoz Gamero 1013 and 1039. Ventistur in lobby of *Hotel Las Navegantes*, T 223795, competent, run by Sr. Ernesto Fernández de Cabo, helpful and excellent for arranging tours to Patagonia. Turismo Aventour, J. Nogueira 1255, T 224926, English spoken, helpful, organizes trips from Punta Arenas to Puerto Williams by plane, with 2-3 days visiting glaciers around Tierra del Fuego by boat (US$500-600). Austral Adventure Services (Lautaro Navarro 975, T 228159, Telex 380090 AASPA CK) arranges tours and adventure expeditions in the region (they also provide information on boat trips to glaciers and the southern Patagonian icecaps). And others.

Shipping   The *Tierra del Fuego* sails between Puerto Montt and Puerto Natales although it will sail to Punta Arenas if there are problems at Pto. Natales (as in 1989-90). Navimag, office at Independencia 840, T 226600 and 222593, Telex 380060-NAVIN CK; buy tickets at Comapa, Magallanes 970. Tourist tickets are not sold in the off-season, so try truck companies, or truck drivers at the dock (male passengers only should try this). Fares given under Puerto Montt. Government supply ships are recommended for the young and hardy, but take sleeping bag and extra food, and travel pills. Empremar's *El Navarino* to Puerto Edén, Chacabuco and Valparaíso sometimes sells passenger tickets. Ask at Tourist Office for details or enquire at Empresa Marítima del Estado (Empremar), Lautaro Navarro 1338, T 223015/225238. For transport on navy supply ships to Puerto Williams, enquire at Tercera Zona Naval, Calle Lautaro Navarro 1150, or ask the captain direct. All tickets on ships must be booked in advance Jan.-Feb..

Ferries   Regular services between Punta Arenas and Puerto Porvenir (Tierra del Fuego) in *Melinka*, leaving Tres Puentes (5 km. from Punta Arenas) at 0900 daily (1000 on Sun.), depending on tides, US$2 p.p., US$2 per bike, US$25 per vehicle. Buy tickets on board, or at Agencia Broom, Roca 924. It returns from Porvenir (Sampaio 302) at 1400 (1500 Sat.) 2¾ hrs. each way. Bus to ferry at either end is US$0.25, take "Tres Puentes" bus to within 250 m. of ferry at Punta Arenas, or take colectivo No. 14 or 15 (US$1.50) all the way.

Air Services   Lan-Chile and Ladeco run daily flights to Puerto Montt (sit on right for views) and Santiago (night flight at 0330, bus from office at 0200, flight costs US$100). With Lan-Chile flights there is a free bus service to Ancud and Castro on Chiloé. Lan-Chile, Lautaro Navarro 999, T 223460; Ladeco, Roca 924/Lautaro Navarro 1061, T 224927/226100. Aerovías DAP, Carrero Pinto 1022, T 223958, fly to Porvenir daily (US$15), and to Puerto Williams Tues. and Sat. (US$110 return), plus other irregular flights, with a Twin-Otter aircraft. (Heavily booked so make sure you have your return reservation confirmed.) Aerovías DAP established a fortnightly charter service from Punta Arenas to Port Stanley on the Falkland Islands/Islas Malvinas in May 1990. Military (FACh) flights approx. twice a month to Puerto Montt; information and tickets from airforce base at the airport; need to book well in advance. Reserve passages in advance in January and February. Bus from airport, US$1.50; colectivos run from Colón y Magallanes. Lan-Chile, DAP and Ladeco have their own bus services from town. The airport restaurant is good.

Bus Service   To Río Gallegos, daily, 4 companies (at least 2 a day except 1 on Sun. and

Mon.—e.g. El Pingüino, Lautaro Navarro 549, T 222396/228448 (one bus daily), and Viajes Vera, 21 de Mayo y Boliviana (Thurs. 0900, Sun. 1000); English spoken, helpful; all leave before 1300), US$10, officially 5 hrs., but can take up to 8, depending on customs, 15 mins. on Chilean side, up to 3 hrs. on Argentine side, including ½ hr. lunch at km. 160. All customs formalities now undertaken at the border, but ask before departure if this has changed. Puerto Natales, 4 hrs. with Fernández, Chiloé 930 (rec., coffee served) and Buses Sur, José Menéndez 556, each twice a day. Several companies run a service through Argentina to Puerto Montt and Santiago (most do not run in winter); svereal companies including Bus Norte, Ghisoni, Fernández, Turibus, Victoria Sur, Eurobus, Bus Sur. Fare to Puerto Montt US$35, to Santiago US$50. Trans Chiloé, Bus Sur, Eurobus and others also run to Castro, Chiloé via Puerto Montt.

Skiing Cerro Mirador, only 9 km. west from Punta Arenas, one of the few places in the world where one can ski with a sea view. Transtur buses 0900 and 1400 from in front of *Hotel Cabo de Hornos*, US$3, return. Daily lift-ticket, US$4.50; equipment rental, US$6 per adult. Mid-way lodge with food, drink and equipment. Season June to September/ November, weather depending. Contact the Club Andino (on the hill, not far from Las Minas Reserve) about crosscountry skiing facilities. Also skiing at Tres Morros.

Excursions Within easy reach are Puerto Hambre and Fuerte Bulnes, a reconstructed, old fort, a 56-km. trip (*Peña Trovador*—see **Restaurants** above)—run tours each afternoon). At Río Penitente is Morro Negro, a large rock outcrop. The trip can be done in a day. 7½ km. west of town is the **Reserva Forestal Magallanes** (follow Independencia right through town and up the hill). In the reserve is the Mirador de la Garganta del Río Las Minas, with views over Punta Arenas and Tierra del Fuego. There is a botanical trail (US$0.30); there are sandcliffs which one can descend with care to the Río Las Minas valley, but beware of boggy ground, and thence back to Punta Arenas. Another reserve on the Brunswick Peninsula is **Laguna Parrillar**, 53 km. from Punta Arenas, protecting the lake and the vegetation around it (no public transport, open Oct.-April). A small penguin colony can be visited 60 km. N of Punta Arenas; tours from agencies start at US$4 p.p. Taxis also run for US$12.50 for 1¼ hrs. (in windy weather the birds go underground so there is nothing to see).

The most interesting excursions are to the Ultima Esperanza region (see below under Puerto Natales) and so to the Torres del Paine National Park. Ventistur offer excursions from Fri. night to Sat. night; Turismo Pehoé, 21 de Mayo 1464, goes to Paine for US$200; Cabo de Hornos Tur organize tours with station wagons. Sr. Mateo Quesada, Chiloé 1375, T 222662, offers local tours in his car, up to 4 passengers.

The fjords and glaciers of Tierra del Fuego (70 km. by schooner) are exceptionally beautiful. Once a fortnight there is a 22-hr. 320-km. round trip to the fjord d'Agostino, 30 km. long, where many glaciers come down to the sea. A three-day tour to Puerto Natales, the glacier, Balmaceda and Torres del Paine can be arranged from Punta Arenas with meals and accommodation included. Empresa Buses Fernández, Calle Chiloé 930, runs this excursion and also afternoon excursions to Club Andino and the Fuerte Bulnes (US$15), and to the penguin hatchery and fine scenery on Otway Sound (US$15). They also run a 3-day, Puerto Natales/Cueva Milodón/Paine trip for US$110 with food and lodging (at *Hotel Eberhard*, Puerto Natales); the trip is quite flexible and variations in itinerary or duration can be accommodated. Aiketour, Menéndez 750, Oficina 6 (T 226916), also goes to the penguin colonies.

Antarctica Punta Arenas has become the number one starting point for visits to Antarctica. The following possibilities exist: Turismo Cabo de Hornos, Plaza Muñoz Gamero (Casilla 62-D), Punta Arenas, T 222599, Telex 280342 HORNO CL, now offers in March and October six-day packages, which include three nights accommodation at the *Hotel Estrella Polar* at the Teniente Rodolfo Marsh base on King George Island in the South Shetlands. Air transport is by Chilean Air Force (FACh) C-130 Hercules aircraft. Cost US$2,500. Lindblad Travel, P.O. Box 912, Westport CT 06881, USA, T (203) 226-8531, has made cruises to Antarctica with the luxury chartered Chinese ship m/v *Yao Hua* of 10,151 grt. Fare range US$2,490-15,325 for land/cruise arrangement. Telex 643443 LIND UR.

Society Expeditions Cruises, 723 Broadway East, Seattle WA 98102, T (206) 324-9400, (800) 426-7794, Telex (910) 444-1381, using the luxury small cruise ships *World Discoverer* of 3,153 grt and *Society Explorer* of 2,367 grt (formerly *Lindblad Explorer*), have made cruises to Antarctica, fare range US$4,750-17,775. In addition, the *World Discoverer* has made an Antarctica Circumnavigation from

Ushuaia, Argentina to Wellington, New Zealand. Fare range US$8,900-23,900.

Adventure Network International, 200-1676 Duranleau St., Vancouver, BC, Canada V6H 3S5, T (604) 683-8033, Telex 0636-700-749 MBX CA leads climbing and skiing expeditions to Antartica. Local contacts: Calle Jorge Montt 747, T 225370, Punta Arenas, may be able to secure a seat on a flight for US$600, return same day; Hugh Macleary, Casilla 0124, Punta Arenas, T 224484, Telex 380076 LANAS CK; Javier Lopetegui, Portales 780, San Bernardo, Santiago, T 028593081. *Hotel Cabo de Hornos* arranges trips to Antarctica in October. Depending on the number of travellers, the price ranges from US$800 to US$2,200 for a 2-day visit.

Joe and Cristina Kessler of New York write: "From Punta Arenas we went with the Chilean Navy to Antarctica. To say it was an exceptional trip is a vast understatement. We went from Punta Arenas through the southern canals to Puerto Williams, then S past Cape Horn, across the Drake Passage to the Antarctic Peninsula. We traversed back and forth between 5 Chilean bases including Deception Is. The furthest south we went was the American Palmer station at 65° S." To secure a place on board ask the ship's captain direct. The Antarctica flotilla consists of two ships: the *Piloto Pardo* which sails from Valparaíso (US$80/day) and the *Yelcho* from Punto Arenas (US$40/day with food, US$20 without food—but men only in the latter cabins). If tourist accommodation is full, crew berths may be offered; check it out before accepting. The trips take place at the beginning of the year, but space is limited. Knowledge of Spanish is essential; trip takes about 20 days, stopping at up to 12 bases. About 40 hours of open sea can be very rough. Information, in person only, from Tercera Zona Naval, Calle Lautaro Navarro 1150, Punta Arenas.

Puerto Natales (17,000 people) is 247 km. N of Punta Arenas and close to the Argentine border at Río Turbio. It stands on the Ultima Esperanza gulf amid spectacular scenery, and is the jumping-off place for the magnificent Balmaceda and Paine national parks.

Hotels *Eberhard,* Pedro Montt 25, T 411208, A, excellent views, good; *Juan Ladrilleros,* Pedro Montt 161, modern, A with bath and breakfast, good restaurant, clean, T 411652; *Natalino,* Eberhard 371, T 411968, clean and very friendly, D, breakfast included, rec. (tours to Milodón Cave arranged); *Palace,* Ladrilleros 105, T 411134, B, good food; *Austral,* Valdivia 955, T 411593, clean, friendly, good food, run by Eduardo Scott, E, without bath, D with bath and breakfast, hot water. *Residencial Temuco,* Ramírez 202, T 411120, friendly, reasonable, good food, F p.p.; opp., next to *zapatería* at Bulnes 810, is Elba Edita Solo Pérez, T 411026, F p.p., breakfast US$0.50; homemade bread and jam, clean, hot water, laundry, use of kitchen, will store luggage; *Residencial La Busca,* Valdivia 845 (no sign outside), F, run down, cheap food available; *Res. Termas de Puyehue,* O'Higgins (nr. hospital), F, clean, friendly, dinner extra; *Pensión Magallanes* on Calle Magallanes (no sign), F, hot water; many mountaineering parties stay here, the owner's son runs day excursions to Lake Grey. *Residencial Grey,* Bulnes 90, F incl. breakfast, hot water, some rooms with heating, very friendly, clean, good but expensive dinners; *Residencial Bulnes,* Calle Bulnes 407, T 411307 (no sign), beside police station, good, F, stores luggage; *Casa de Familia Dickson,* Bulnes 307, T 411218, F p.p., good breakfast, other meals available to order, clean, rec.; *Garahue,* Bulnes 370, F p.p., breakfast and hot water, nice; *Casa de familia Elsa Millán,* Philippi 405, G p.p., breakfast US$1, homemade bread, hot water, warm, friendly, cooking facilities; similar at O'Higgins 70, 431 and 484 (rec.) and Perito 443; *Casa de familia* at Galvarino 846, F with breakfast, rec.; Sra. Nelly, Uvaldo Segero (opp. hospital), F, friendly, clean, use of kitchen; private house at Magallanes 1, G p.p. with breakfast, friendly, cheap meals; Sra. Bruna at Don Bosco 41, clean, friendly, F, meals on request; Ana y Ernesto, Baras Arana 175, small and cosy. Sra. Elsa, A. Prat 15, with breakfast, cooking facilities, G. Sra. Teresa, Esmeraldas 463, F with breakfast, good value, cheap meals extra, quiet, friendly, rec.

　　Hotels in the countryside and around include: *Hostería Llanura de Diana,* Km. 220 Road 9 Sector Río Tranquilo, T 222350, on road to Punta Arenas (hidden from the road), B, highly rec.; *Posada de Cisne de Cuello Negro,* a former guest house for meat buyers at the *frigorífico,* B, friendly, clean, reasonable, all rooms with bath, excellent cooking, new owners, 5 km. from Puerto Natales at Km. 257 Road 9 Sector Puerto Bories; *Patagonia Inn,* B, Km. 257 Road 9 Sector Dos Lagunas, T 222599, 23 km. from Puerto Natales, open only in summer, from November to March; *Hostería El Pionero,* Cerro Castillo, Km. 315 Ruta 9, C with basin but not bath, country house ambience.

Restaurants *Nikol's,* Barros Arana 160, seafood and salmon very good; *Socorro* is also rec. as is *Don Alvarito,* Blanco Encalada 915; *La Ultima Esperanza,* opp. *Hotel Natalino,* rec. for salmon, seafood; *Midas,* Rogers 169, both good, clean. *Café Tranquera,* Bulnes

579, good coffee, meals, snacks. *Centro Español*, Magallanes 247, reasonable restaurant. *Club de Pesca y Caza Río Serrano*, Eberhard 261, excellent food, take away lunches, moderate prices; cheap meals at *Club Deportivo Natales*, Eberhard 332.

Car Hire Andes Patagónicos, Blanco Encalada 226, US$85 per day inc. insurance and 350 km. free; others US$80 a day, or US$85 with driver. Best to have international driving licence here; national licence may restrict insurance cover.

Fishing Tackle for hire at Andes Patagónicos, Blanco Encalada 226, US$3.50/day for rod, reel and spinners; if you prefer fishing with floats, hooks, split shot, etc., take your own. Other companies up to 5 times as expensive.

Exchange *Casas de cambio* on Blanco Encalada 226 (Andes Patagónicos) and 266 where australes (and sometimes US$—former will change cheques into dollars cash at 3% commission) can be changed. Cambio Stop, Baquedano 380, good for cash (also arranges tours). Another two at Bulnes 683 and 1087 (good rates). Australes are accepted everywhere and can be bought in *cambios*.

Museum Museo De Agostini, Tierra del Fuego fauna.

Laundry at *Tienda Milodón*, on Bulnes.

Travel Agents Turismo Paine, Calle Eberhard. Urbina Tours, Eberhard 554 (contact either here or at Tourist Office in Punta Arenas, Telex 282009 CL), tours to Paine National Park, Milodón Cave, in 11-seater Toyota; also tours tailored to individual requirements. Lago Grey, Bulnes 622, not very helpful.

Tourist Office in kiosk on waterfront, Av. Pedro Montt y Phillipi, helpful; maps for US$1 from Eberhard 547, reasonable. **Conaf**, Encalada, between O'Higgins and Chorillos.

Buses to Punta Arenas, 4 times daily, 4 hrs. US$10. Bus Fernández, Eberhard 555 (0900 and 1830) and Bus Sur, Baquedano 224.
　　To Argentina: Thrice weekly to Río Gallegos (Argentina): Alvaro Gómez, Baquedano 244, Wed. and Fri. 0730, Sun. 1030, met at border by San Caferino bus, US$10.70; hourly to Río Turbio (Argentina), US$1.50, 2 hrs. (depending on Customs—change bus at border). 1000 bus to Río Turbio arrives in time for 1300 El Pingüino bus to Río Gallegos. To Calafate, in summer Bus Sur goes daily at 0630 for US$30; Luís Díaz, Patricio Lynch 170, T 411050, US$20 (trips also to Torres del Paine, Punta Arenas, camping equipment for hire); Empresa Gómez runs a minibus direct to Calafate, Argentina, for US$36, Mon., Wed. and Fri. (Nov.-March). Scott Turs, at *Hotel Austral*, goes to Calafate for US$20, but no regular schedule. The cheapest route is to take El Pingüino bus from Río Turbio to La Esperanza and wait there (no more than an hour) for a Río Gallegos bus to Calafate, US$14.
　　If driving, note that there is no petrol between Puerto Natales and Calafate.

Shipping The m/n *Tierra del Fuego* of Navimag runs the 1,460 km. between Puerto Natales and Puerto Montt and carries passengers (**see page** 583). Navimag office: Independencia 840 Punta Arenas, T 222593, 226600, Telex 380060 NAVIN CK, and Pedro Montt 380, Terminal Marítimo, T 411287/411642, Puerto Natales (direct telex with Punta Arenas office, which is better). Tourist tickets only available in off-season if not enough truck drivers turn up.

Excursions A recommended walk is up to Cerro Dorotea which dominates the town, with superb views of the whole Ultima Esperanza Sound. Take Río Turbio bus and alight at jeep track for summit. 25 km. NW of Puerto Natales the **Monumento Natural Cueva Milodón** can be visited. It now contains a plastic model of the prehistoric ground-sloth whose bones were found there in 1895. (Free camping once entrance fee has been paid.) Fernández bus is cheapest, going on Fri. and returning Sun., mid-Nov. to mid-March only; at other times, take a taxi (US$15 return). A cutter, the *21 de Mayo*, sails from the pier to **Balmaceda National Park** 2-3 times a week, if enough passengers book, US$20 (all travel agents handle the trip). *21 de Mayo* is operated by Juan C. Alvarez, Ladrilleros 171, T 411-176; max 50 passengers. The boat has life jackets and modern communications and navigation equipment. An interesting trip, viewing glaciers and the rugged mountains at the S end of the Patagonian ice cap. On the trip one may see dolphins, sea-lions (in season), black-neck swans, and the quaint steamer ducks.

145 km. NW of Puerto Natales is the **Torres del Paine** National Park, covering 1,630 sq. km., a "must" for its wildlife and spectacular scenery. Along the (gravel) road it is common to spot the Andean condor and herds of *guanaco*. The Torres and Cuernos del Paine are oddly shaped peaks, surrounded by glaciers, which fall straight down to the valleys, now covered with beautiful lakes at 50 to 200 metres above sea level. The glaciers Grey, Dickson and Zapata are three of the main ones branching off the huge mass forming the Patagonian icecap.

There are about 250 km. of well marked hiking trails and nine National Park shelters; bring food, a tent, sleeping bag and cooking gear. Allow a week to ten days to see the park properly. The area is very popular in summer and the shelters often crowded, and in poor condition.

The park is administered by the forestry department (Conaf) with a centre at the southern tip of Lake Pehoé and seven guardhouses located throughout the park. There the friendly wardens (*guardaparques*) give advice and one should register with them before setting out for a hike.

The scenery in the Park is spectacular. Walking along the trails one is constantly rewarded by changing views of fantastic peaks, ice-fields, vividly coloured lakes of turquoise, ultramarine and grey and quiet green valleys. Wild life abounds: one can expect to see *guanaco*, hares, foxes, condors, black-neck swans and many other birds. Apparently the park has a micro-climate especially favourable to plants and wild life. The Park is open all year round, although snow may prevent access in the winter: best time is January-April.

The most popular hike starts from either the administration building at the south end of Lake Pehoé or the Park entrance, and takes seven days going from *refugio* to *refugio* past the spectacular Grey Glacier and round the back of the Cuernos and Torres del Paine. It is tough, the longest lap being 30 km., but not too steep. (Note that the main footbridge to Grey Glacier was washed away by floods in 1983 and that there is no access from the circuit to the northern shores of Lakes Dickson or Paine—except at Refugio Amarga—for a similar reason.) To walk from the administration just to Grey Glacier takes at least 3 hours to the *refugio* at the N end of Lake Pehoé (no firewood nearby), then 6-10 hours there and back to Grey Glacier (where the *refugio* has been burnt down). Ask at the park administration about a boat trip to Laguna Grey glacier, at least 8 people required, US$14 inc. sandwiches, cake, coffee and pisco, a stunning trip.

Another recommended walk is to Ventisquero (glacier) del Francés, 2 hrs. from Pehoé to the Río Francés, 5 hrs. on to Campamento Británico (the path is hard to find, and involves crossing the hazardous Río Francés at the snout of the glacier). Also recommended is the walk to Lake Pingo (plenty of wildlife, icebergs in the lake), with *refugios* half way and at the Lake.

The walk to the Torres Base is recommended: from the Park entrance it is 2 hrs. to the *refugio* and campsite at Laguna Amarga, then 1½ hrs. to an *estancia* where you can camp. From here it's 3½ hrs. to the lake, a well-marked path, but the last ½ hr. is up the morraine; it's well worth humping camping gear up and spending the night.

Descriptions of several walks in the Torres del Paine area are found in *Backpacking in Chile and Argentina* (Bradt Publications).

Refugios cost US$0.50, and an entrance fee to the Park (US$1) is charged. Most of the *refugios* have good areas, so take your own food (beware of mice!) as it is expensive to buy and limited in the Park. In most cases a tent is preferable to the *refugios* and is essential if doing a complete circuit. Also essential are protective clothing and strong footwear. Maps (US$0.50), are obtainable at Conaf offices in Punta Arenas or Puerto Natales, but beware inaccuracies: some of the trails marked peter out and bridges get washed away); better maps can be bought from *Hotel Austral*, Puerto Natales, or try at the tourist kiosk (not Sernatur) in Punta Arenas. The Visitor Information Centre, an old *estancia*, has a good slide show on Sat. and Sun. at 1900; guards will store luggage and arrange transport back to Puerto Natales. Wardens know how many people are on each route so you can find out which *refugios* are likely to be full. Horses may be rented from Brigitta Buhofer (nr. *Posada Río Serano*) for US$18, 6 hrs. with guide; horses for beginners and experienced riders available.

Accommodation *Posada Río Serrano*, C, some rooms with bath, some with shared facilities, breakfast extra, 2 km. from park administration, with expensive restaurant and a shop. (Reservations advisable: Serco Ltda., Casilla 19-D, Punta Arenas, T 223395). *Hostería Pehoé*, B, 60 rooms, private facilities, 5 km. S of Pehoé guardhouse, 11 km. N of park administration, on an island with spectacular view across the Lake to Paine Grande and

Cuernos del Paine, runs a boat up to Grey Glacier, good meals, welcoming. (Reservations: Turismo Pehoé, 21 de Mayo 1464, T 224223 in Punta Arenas or Nataniel 31, office 68, T 718709, Telex 240875 PEHOE CL in Santiago).

Camping Pehoé (32 lots, hot shower US$4.65 p.p.) and Camping Río Serrano (25 lots) are operated by Serco Ltda., Camping Laguna Azul (10 lots) and Laguna Amarga (15 lots) by Conaf (all except Pehoé US$3.50). Camping and lighting fires are permitted outside official campsites (e.g. at Lago Grey), but only where indicated by park wardens. You can camp outside *refugios*, but firewood is hard to find in their vicinity.

Bus Sur (addresses above) runs a daily service to Paine National Park between December and March (till Easter Sunday, not on Mon., depart 0630, returns 1100, 1430 Sun., US$6). Out of season they go twice weekly if there are 5 or more passengers (US$13.50).

To go from Torres del Paine to Calafate (Argentina) either return to Pto. Natales and go to Río Turbio for bus to La Esperanza, or hitch from the park to Cerro Castillo (106 km. S of the administration), the Chilean border point, cross to Paso Cancha de Carreras (Argentina) and try to link with the Río Turbio-La Esperanza-Río Gallegos bus schedule, or hitch. (Note that it is easier to visit this region on a circuit Ushuaia-Torres del Paine-Calafate than vice versa.)

Tours For all-in trips from Punta Arenas **see page 607. Eduardo Scott, who speaks English, can be contacted at his hotel,** *Austral*, Valdivia 955, Puerto Natales (T 411593), he runs tours of the Park in a 8-seater bus (about US$30 p.p.—highly rec. by many, others have not been satisfied). Also José Torres of Sastrería Arbiter in Calle Bulnes 731 (T 411623). Enap weekend tours in summer cost US$45 including accommodation and meals. Taxi costs US$80 per day, run by Sergio Zaley (Arturo Prat 260), but may be cheaper if you catch him when he's going to the Park anyway. A minibus can be hired for about US$50 at Puerto Natales, to take a party of up to 8 to a *refugio* in the Paine National Park. After mid-March there is no public transport and trucks are irregular.

Hiring a pick-up from Budget in Punta Arenas is an economical proposition for a group (up to 6 people): US$415 for 4 days. If driving yourself there, the first 61 km. from Pto. Natales to Cerro Castillo is poor with too much gravel, the next 60 km. to the entrance better, then in the Park, the roads are narrow, bendy with blind corners, use your horn a lot; it takes about 3½ hrs. from Pto. Natales to the administration. Petrol may not be available in the park.

Tierra del Fuego is the island off the extreme south of South America. It is surrounded by the Magellan Strait to the north, the Atlantic Ocean to the east, the Beagle Channel to the south—which separates it from the southern islands—and by the Whiteside, Gabriel, Magdalena and Cockburn channels etc. which divide it from the islands situated to the west. The western side belongs to Chile and the eastern to Argentina. It produces most of Chile's oil.

In Chilean Tierra del Fuego the only town is **Porvenir**, with a population of 4,500, several hundred from Yugoslavia. There is a small museum, the Fernando Cordero Rusque, Samuel Valdirieso 402, mainly Indian culture.

Porvenir Hotels *Los Flamencos*, Teniente Merino, T 580049, best, B; *Rosas*, O'Higgins 296, T 580088, D with bath, hot water, heating, restaurant and bar, rec.; *Residencial Cameron* (ask at bar called *Somos o no Somos*), E, for shared room, "friendly folk", good meals, sleep on dining-room floor for US$1; *Central*, Phillipi 298, T 580077, D, hot water; *Residencial* at Santos Mardones 366, F (E with full board), clean, friendly, heaters in rooms, hot water, good; *Res. Colón*, Damián Riobó 198, T 580108, E p.p.; many good *pensiones*, E, with full board. *Yugoslav Club* does wholesome and reasonable lunch (about US$5), also *Restaurante Puerto Montt* for seafood. Many lobster fishing camps where fishermen will prepare lobster on the spot.

Other hotels on Chilean Tierra del Fuego: *Hostería de la Frontera*, on the Chilean side of the border, E in the annex which is 1 km. away from the more expensive main building. There is a friendly *hostería* at Cerro Sombrero, F.

Exchange at *Estrella del Sur* shop, Calle Santos Mardones.

Buses on Tierra del Fuego Two a week between Porvenir and Río Grande (Argentina), Wed. and Sat. 1400, US$12.50 (buy ticket early on the day of travel). Bus from Rio Grande arrives 1300, two to Punta Arenas leaves 1400; from terminal to ferry, taxi US$2.75, bus (if running) US$1, ferry US$2; trip takes 7-8 hrs. depending on border crossing. Beware: taxis are not allowed to cross the border. If you go to the police station and ask for a ride to the border on a truck, you can save the fare to Río Grande. Hitch-hiking elsewhere is difficult as there is so little traffic. Argentine time one hour ahead of Chilean time. N.B. If crossing from Argentina, Chile does not allow entry of fruit, vegetables, dairy produce or meat. All stocks will be confiscated.

Bus from Calle Manuel Señor, Porvenir, Mon. and Fri., 1700, US$10, to Cameron, from where a road runs SE to Estancia Vicuña. Before Vicuña is a scenic fishing-ground; beyond Vicuña a horse trail leads across the Darwin Range to Yendegaia. From there you can either retrace your steps, or cross the unmanned border to Ushuaia (get permission from the Argentine consul in Punta Arenas first).

Puerto Williams is a Chilean naval base on Isla Navarino, S of the Beagle Channel, the most southerly place in the world with a permanent population (about 1,500-1,800. Position 54° 55' 41" South, 67° 37' 58" West). It's a small, friendly, remote place. The island is totally unspoilt and beautiful, with a chain of rugged snowy peaks, magnificent woods and many animals, including beaver. The *Hotel Patagonia*, on the edge of Lauta bay, T 223571, with attractive locally-made furniture and soft furnishings, roaring log fire in lounge, is now owned by the Navy (but run by Ladeco), L in summer, much less in winter, meals US$16 (monthly rates available); 2 km. out of town, splendid walks. Hotel can arrange car trips to the beaver dams, cascades, and other sights (the Ubika Village, 2 km. east of town, the place where the last descendants of the Yamana people live; the local *media luna* where rodeos are held). *Residencial Onashaga* (run by Señor Ortiz—everyone knows him), E plus meals, which are good, pleasant, helpful, full board available; bakery next to *Café Beagle*, E, full board; you can also stay at private houses. Ask where you can eat king crab (*centolla*) pizza. *Restaurant Beagle* on coast, excellent. There is a supermarket. You can camp near the *Hosteria*: collect drinking water from the kitchen, bring food from Punta Arenas as it is expensive on the island, but you can buy gasoline for stoves at the *Hosteria*. Aeropetrel will charter a plane, if a sufficiently numerous party is raised, to Cape Horn. Near Puerto Williams there is a *centolla* canning factory which is well worth a visit (closed Feb.-March).

Museum Excellent Martín Gusinde museum in Puerto Williams, full of information about vanished Indian tribes, local wildlife, and voyages including Charles Darwin and Fitzroy of the *Beagle*. Open 1000-1300, 1500-1800 (Tues.-Fri.); 1500-1800 (Sat.-Sun.), Monday closed. Admission free.

Offices Post Office, telephone, telex, Aerovías DAP, Lan-Chile, Ladeco in the centre of town (maps available). Tourist Office (closed in winter) near the museum. Ask at the yacht club on the off chance of hitching a ride on a private yacht.

Transport to Tierra del Fuego For ferry services from Punta Arenas, **see page 608. There are two ferries running across the Primera Angostura (First Narrows) between Delgada** (*Hosteria Tehuelche*, D with restaurant) and Espora points, 170 km. NE from Punta Arenas, schedule varying with the tides. Reservations at the ferry. Price US$1 p.p. and US$12 per car, one way. There is no ferry between Ushuaia and Puerto Williams, but see under Ushuaia (Argentina) for possibilities of boat crossings (e.g. on the *Barracuda*). By air from Punta Arenas—weather and bookings permitting, Aerovías DAP (Ignacio Carrera Pinto 1022, T 223958 Punta Arenas and Oficina Foretic, T 80089, Porvenir) fly twice daily to Porvenir, but not Sat., US$15 to Porvenir, and Tues. and Sat. to Puerto Williams, US$110 return; cheaper are Cabo de Hornos (TACH), Montt 687, T 223335 (Señoret 408, Porvenir), also twice daily to Porvenir, Mon. and Fri. to Puerto Williams, US$80 return. Heavily booked so make sure you have your return reservation confirmed. The flight to Puerto Williams is beautiful, with superb views of Tierra del Fuego, the Cordillera Darwin, the Beagle Channel, and the islands stretching S to Cape Horn. Also army flights available (they are cheaper). Boat Punta Arenas-Puerto Williams: *Ñandú* or Ultragas leaves on a fixed schedule every 10 days, about 2400, arrives 1700 each way, reclining chairs, no food, US$45 one way. Enquire at the office, Independencia 865, next to service station.

INFORMATION FOR VISITORS

Travel Documents Passport and tourist card only are required for entry by all foreigners except citizens of France, New Zealand, Mexico, Guyana, Haiti, Suriname, Kuwait, African countries and the Communist countries, who require visas. National identity cards are sufficient for entry by citizens of Argentina, Brazil, Paraguay, and Uruguay. The tourist card is valid for 90 days and is renewable for 90 more; it is available from Chilean consulates, immigration office at the Ollagüe land frontier, as well as at Arica, airline offices and most aircraft bound for Chile;

it will be surrendered on departure. If you wish to stay longer than 180 days (as a tourist), it is easier to make a day-trip to Argentina and return with a new tourist card, rather than to apply for a visa, which involves a great deal of paperwork. An onward ticket is officially required but is seldom asked for. On arrival you will be asked where you are staying in Chile. Visa is required for French passport holders, US$5.25; valid for no more than 90 days, strictly one entry only. This can create problems if you wish to travel overland to or from Tierra del Fuego since the Argentine-Chilean border is crossed more than once, requiring multiple entry. A student card is very useful for obtaining discounts on buses, etc.

All foreigners who wish to work in Chile must obtain visas. Smallpox vaccination and health certificates no longer required.

Airport Taxes 3,700 pesos, or US$12.50 for international flights; US$3.50 for domestic flights. There is a tourist tax on single air fares of 2%, and 1% on return fares beginning or ending in Chile; also a sales tax of 5% on all transport within Chile.

How to get there by Air From Europe: Air France from Paris (3 per week), Iberia and Lan-Chile from Madrid (2 each), KLM (2), Lufthansa (2), Swissair (1) and Alitalia (1) fly to Santiago. Some flights go via Rio/São Paulo, Montevideo and Buenos Aires; others via New York, Lima and/or other points in northern S. America. Also, Varig, Aerolíneas Argentinas, Viasa and Avianca offer services between Europe and Santiago, with connections via Rio, Buenos Aires, Caracas and Bogotá respectively.

From North America: American Airlines has taken over Eastern's service from Miami, but schedules, routes and connections with other US cities were not known at the time of going to press. Lan-Chile has 3 flights per week from New York and Miami and 4 other flights from Miami alone, 3 of them non-stop. Also from Miami, Ladeco flies both non-stop and either via Bogotá and Guayaquil or Bogotá and Arica; Pan Am 5-6 per week. Also from Miami fly Viasa, Ecuatoriana and LAB with connections in Caracas, Guayaquil or La Paz. From Los Angeles there are flights with Lan-Chile, Ecuatoriana and Avianca (none non-stop). From other US cities, connect with Lan-Chile flights in Miami, New York or Los Angeles. CP Air have 2 flights per week from Toronto, with which connections are made from Montreal/and Vancouver. Lan-Chile flies twice a week from Montreal (via Miami). Lan-Chile flies once or twice a week, depending on season, between Tahiti (making connections from Japan, Australia and New Zealand) and Santiago; they stop over at Easter Island. For excursion fares between Australia/New Zealand and Chile, the stopovers at Easter Island now carry a surcharge of about US$125.

Within South America: from Buenos Aires (about 40 per week) by Lan-Chile, Ladeco, Ecuatoriana, Aerolíneas Argentinas, Aeroperú, Avianca, CP Air, Air France, Iberia, KLM, Alitalia, Swissair or Pan Am; from Mendoza by Aerolíneas Argentinas or Ladeco twice a week each. From Montevideo (5 per week) by Lan-Chile, Iberia, KLM; from Asunción (seven times a week) by Lan-Chile, Pluna, Avianca or KLM; from Rio/São Paulo, non-stop by Lan-Chile, Ladeco, Varig, Lufthansa or by several other European airlines via Buenos Aires; from La Paz (5/6 per week) by Lloyd Aéreo Boliviano (LAB), Lan-Chile; from Caracas, Lan-Chile and Viasa (one Lan-Chile flight is non-stop); from Lima (10 per week) by Aeroperú and Lan-Chile; from Bogotá (6 per week) by Avianca and Ladeco; from Ecuador: Ecuatoriana from Quito via Guayaquil, Ladeco non-stop from Guayaquil.

To Arica, from La Paz (6 per week) by LAB and Lan-Chile.

From Neighbouring Countries by land. There are railways from La Paz (Bolivia) to Calama for Antofagasta, and to Arica. All passenger services have been suspended on the lines between Chile and Argentina. Roads connect Santiago with Mendoza, and Osorno and Puerto Montt with Bariloche, in Argentina. Less good road connections N and S of Santiago are described in the main text. The roads connecting N Chile with Bolivia are poor.

Customs Allowed in free of duty: 500 cigarettes, 100 cigars, 500 grams of tobacco, 3 bottles of liquor, camera, and all articles of personal use. Fruit, vegetables, flowers and milk products may not be imported. It has been reported that bringing a video recorder into Chile involves a great deal of paperwork.

Internal Air Services Lan-Chile and the private airline Ladeco both fly between Santiago and Arica, Iquique, Antofagasta, Calama, Copiapó, La Serena, Concepción, Temuco, Los Angeles, Osorno, Puerto Montt, Coyhaique and Punta Arenas. In addition, Lan-Chile flies to El Salvador, and Ladeco to Valdivia and Balmaceda. Try and sit on the left flying S, on the right flying N to get the best views of the Andes. Lan-Chile and Ladeco usually have a bus service from airport to town, check at the desk on arrival.

Small airlines which operate on a regional basis are given in the text.

Lan-Chile offers a 21-day "Visit Chile" ticket; 4 prices: US$349, valid for mainland Chile; Pacific 1, US$499, Santiago-Easter Island-Santiago; Pacific 2 and Pacific 3, both US$520, valid for a trip to Easter Island and either northern Chile, or southern Chile. It must be purchased abroad and reservations made well ahead since many flights are fully booked in advance. **N.B.** The ticket cannot be changed, though reservations can, so it is worth including as many destinations as possible. It is also possible for the route Santiago-Antofagasta-Arica-Santiago to take a coupon ticket which allows greater flexibility.

Surface Transport Buses are frequent and on the whole good. Apart from holiday times, there is little problem getting a seat on a long-distance bus; most have toilets, serve drinks (sometimes free) and sandwiches. Stops are infrequent. Prices are highest between Dec.-March. Since there is lots of competition between bus companies, fares may be bargained lower. Students generally get discounts.

Trains in Chile, which now run only on the lines S of Santiago, are moderately priced, and not as slow as in other Andean countries, but dining car food is expensive. There is a railway information office at O'Higgins 853 (at end of arcade), Santiago, for all lines except the Antofagasta-Bolivia (Ahumada 11, Oficina 602, T 698-5536). English spoken.

Shipping information is given in the text under Santiago and all the relevant southern ports. Local newspapers are useful for all transport schedules.

Taxis have meters, but agree beforehand on fare for long journey out of centre or special excursions. A 50% surcharge is applied after 2100 and Sun. Taxi drivers rarely know the location of any streets away from the centre. There is no need to tip unless some extra service, like the carrying of luggage, is given.

Motoring in Chile Car drivers require a *Relaciones de pasajeros* document, available at borders, and must present the original registration document of their vehicle, as must motor cyclists. The Carta Caminera from the Dirección de Vialidad is the most detailed road map (series of twenty-six) but is only available at Vialidad, Marsende and Alameda, Santiago. Reasonable road maps may also be obtained from the Automóvil Club de Chile, Av. Vitacura 8620, Santiago; or other regional offices. Members of foreign motoring organizations may join the Automóvil Club de Chile, and obtain discounts at hotels. Town maps from the Automóvil Club and Copec service stations. The *Turistel* Guides are very useful for roads and town plans, but note that not all distances are exact and that the description "ripio" (gravel) usually requires high clearance; "buen ripio" should be OK for ordinary cars. Hydrographic maps from Instituto Hidrográfico, Malgarejo 59, Valparaíso. Gasoline costs US$1.80 a gallon; it becomes more expensive the further north you go. Diesel fuel is only available along Longitudinal Highway. Spare car parts available from many shops on Calle Diez de Julio, Santiago. Yamaha motorcycle spares are sometimes available.

Car drivers should have all their papers in order and to hand since there are frequent checks, but fewer in the south. When driving in the south (on the Carretera Austral particularly), and in the desert north, always top up your fuel tank and carry spare petrol/gasoline. Tyres need to be hard-wearing (avoid steel belt); it is recommended to carry more than one spare.

Car Hire Many agencies, both local and international, operate in Chile. Vehicles may be rented by the day, the week or the month, with or without unlimited mileage. Rates do not normally include insurance (about US$6.50/day) or 16% VAT. A small car, with unlimited mileage costs about US$300 a week, a pick-up US$500. Note that the Automóvil Club de Chile has a car hire agency (with discounts for members or affiliates) and that the office may not be at the same place as the Club's regional delegation.

Hitch-hiking is easy and safe, but in some regions traffic is sparse.

Walking Serious walkers are advised to get *Backpacking in Chile and Argentina*, edited by Clare Hargreaves (Bradt Publications) 1989 edition. Also recommended: *Chile and Easter Island: A Travel Survival Kit*, by Alan Samagalski (Lonely Planet).

Andean Project For those interested in the Andean region of Chile, the Directors of the Andean project will be very pleased to give information. Contact Mrs P. Vincent, Los Españoles 2420, Dpto. 24, Providencia, Santiago.

Hotels On hotel bills service charges are usually 10%, and taxes on bills are 16%. Whether or not the 16% is added to bills in hotel restaurants that are signed and charged to the hotel bill depends on the policy of the establishment. When booking in make certain whether meals are included in the price or only breakfast or nothing at all, and don't rely on the posted sheet in the bedroom for any prices. Small *residenciales* are often good value. If you are looking for a motel, ask for a *motel turístico*; most motels are short stay.

Youth Hostels There are youth hostels throughout Chile; average cost about US$2.50-3 p.p. Hostels are open only from Jan. to the end of February and a Chilean membership card is necessary (US$3.50). They are usually crowded and noisy, with only floor space available. An additional stamp costing US$4 enables one to use the card in Argentina, Uruguay and Brazil. This can be obtained from the Asociación Chilena de Albergues Turísticos Juveniles, Providencia 2594, oficina 420-421, Providencia, Santiago, T 231-5649; together with a useful guidebook of all Youth Hostels in Chile, *Guía Turistica de los Albergues Juveniles*. If you carry an IYHF card you can stay in summer in makeshift hostels in many Chilean towns, usually in the main schools.

In almost every town, private houses offer *alojamiento* (bed, breakfast and often use of kitchen) for about US$2.50-4.25 p.p. (bargaining may be possible).

Camping is easy but no longer cheap at official sites. A common practice is to charge US$10 for up to 5 people, with no reductions for less than 5. "Camping Gaz International" stoves are recommended, since green replaceable cylinders are available in Santiago.

Local Dishes A very typical Chilean dish is *cazuela de ave*, a nutritious stew containing large pieces of chicken, potatoes, rice, and maybe onions, and green peppers; best if served on the second day. Another popular Chilean dish is *empanadas de horno*, which are turnovers filled with a mixture of raisins, olives, meat, onions and peppers chopped up together. *Pastel de choclo* is a casserole of meat and onions with olives, topped with a maize-meal mash, baked in an earthenware bowl. *Prieta* is a blood sausage stuffed with cabbage leaves. The popular *empanada frita*, a fried meat pasty, is delicious. A normal *parrillada* is a giant mixed grill served from a charcoal brazier. The *pichanga* is similar but smaller and without the brazier. Goat cheese is a delicacy of the Fourth Region, but can be a source of food poisoning.

What gives Chilean food its personality is the seafood. The delicious conger eel is a national dish, and *caldillo de congrio* (a soup served with a massive piece of conger, onions and potato balls) is excellent. *Paila Chonchi* is a kind of bouillabaisse, but has more flavour, more body, more ingredients. *Parrillada de mariscos* is a dish of grilled mixed seafood, brought to the table piping hot on a charcoal brazier. Other excellent local fish are the *cojinoa*, the *albacora* (swordfish) and the *corvina*. An appetizing starter is the shellfish *loco* (known to Australians as abalone), and in the S one should try the *centolla* (king crab). *Cochayuyo* is seaweed, bound into bundles, described as "hard, leathery thongs". Avocado pears, or *paltas*, are excellent, and play an important role in recipes. The *erizo*, or sea-urchin, is also commonly eaten. Make sure whether vegetables are included in the price for the main dish; menus often don't make this clear. Always best, if being economical, to stick to fixed-price *table d'hôte* meals or try the local markets. A *barros jarpa* is a cheese and ham sandwich. *Luche* is a black cake, like "flakey bread pudding". Ice cream is very good; *lúcuma* and *chirimoya* are highly recommended flavours.

Lunch is about 1300 and dinner not before 2030. *Onces* (Elevenses) is tea taken at 1700 often accompanied by a couple of fried eggs. The cocktail hour starts at 1900. Waiters are known as *garzón*—never as *mozo*. Good, cheap meals can usually be found in Centros Españoles or Casinos de Bomberos. By law restaurants have to serve a cheaper set meal at lunchtime; it is called *colación* and may not be included on the menu.

It seems impossible to get real coffee unless you go to expresso bars and specify *café-café, expresso*. If you ask just for *café*, you get soluble coffee. The soluble tea should be avoided. If you order "*café*, or *té, con leche*", it will come with all milk; to have just a little milk in either, you must specify that. After a meal, instead of coffee, try an *agüita*—hot water in which herbs such as mint, or aromatics such as lemon peel, have been steeped. There is a wide variety, available in sachets, and they are very refreshing.

Drinks Imported whisky and other spirits are still cheap, but are increasing relatively in price. The local wines are very good; the best are from the central areas. Among the good *bodegas* are Cousiño Macul, Santa Carolina, Undurraga, Concha y Toro, Tocornal, San Pedro and Santa Helena. Santa Elena (no H) is less good. The bottled wines are graded, in increasing excellence, as *gran vino, vino especial* and *vino reservado*. Champagne-style wines are also cheap and acceptable. A small deposit, US$0.30, is charged on most wine bottles. Beer is quite good and cheap; the draught lager known as *Schop* is good; also try Cristal Pilsener or Royal Guard. Malta, a brown ale, is recommended for those wanting a British-type beer.

Good gin is made in Chile. Reasonably good brandy, *anís* and crème de menthe are all bottled in Chile. *Vaina* is worth trying, and so is the traditional Christmas drink, *cola de mono*, a mixture of *aguardiente*, coffee, milk and vanilla served very cold. *Pisco* is worth sampling, especially as a "Pisco Sour" or with grapefruit or lemon juice. *Manzanilla* is a local liqueur, made from *licor de oro* (like Galliano); *crema de cacao*, especially Mitjans, has been recommended. *Chicha* is any form of alcoholic drink made from fruit; *chicha cocida* is 3-day-old fermented grape juice boiled to reduce its volume and then bottled with a tablespoonful of honey. Cider (*chicha de manzana*) is popular in the South. *Chicha fresca* is plain apple juice.

Tipping Standard is 10% in hotels and restaurants and 20% in bars and soda fountains. Railway and airport porters: US$0.10 a piece of luggage. Make a deal with dock porters. Cloakroom attendants and cinema usherettes: US$0.05. Hairdressers: 10% of bill. Taxi-drivers are not tipped.

Shopping There is an excellent variety of handicrafts: woodwork, pottery, copperware, leatherwork, Indian woven goods including rugs and ponchos in the South. Good quality at the Cema-Chile shops (Av. Portugal 351, Santiago, and main provincial cities).

Health
Tap water is fairly safe to drink in the main cities but bottled water is safer on trains and away from the larger centres. Hotels and restaurants are usually clean. Inoculation against hepatitis and typhoid is a wise precaution. Travellers should not eat salads, strawberries or ground-growing food; hepatitis and typhoid are all too common as the result of the use of untreated sewage for fertilizer (Check extra precautions against typhoid are necessary e.g. 3-pill preventative treatment, available locally.)

Clothing Warm sunny days and cool nights are usual during most of the year except in the far S where the climate is like that of Scotland. Ordinary European medium-weight clothing can be worn during the winter (June to mid-September). Light clothing is best for summer (December to March), but men do not wear white tropical suits.

Seasons The best time for a visit to Santiago is between October and April when fine weather is almost assured, but business visits can be made any time during the year. During the holiday season, between January and March, it is sometimes difficult to make appointments.

Hours of Business Banks: 0900-1400, but closed on Sat. Government offices: 1000-1230 (the public is admitted for a few hrs. only). Business houses: 0830-1230, 1400-1800 (Mon. to Fri.). Shops (Santiago): 1030-1930, but 0930-1330 Sat. British business visitors are advised to obtain "Hints for Exporters: Chile" from the Department of Trade, Sanctuary Bldgs, 16-20 Great Smith Street, London SW1P 3DB.

Public Holidays 1 Jan., New Year's Day; Holy Week (2 days); 1 May, Labour Day; 21 May, Navy Day; 15 Aug., Assumption; 18, 19 Sept., Independence Days; 12 Oct., Discovery of America; 1 Nov., All Saints Day; 8 Dec., Immaculate Conception; 25 Dec., Christmas Day.

Time GMT minus 4 hrs.; minus 3 hrs. in summer. Clocks change on second Sat. in October and March.

Currency and Exchange
The unit is the peso, its sign is $. Notes are for 500, 1,000, 5,000 and 10,000 pesos and coins for 1, 5, 10, 50 and 100 pesos.

Travellers' cheques are widely accepted at reasonable rates if exchanging them for cash, they must be changed before 1200 in banks, but this limitation does not apply in exchange shops (*cambios*) and hotels, which give better rates than banks (rates tend to worsen after the banks close and at weekends). Travellers can buy pesos on the parallel (black) market, which is tolerated, at slightly better rates. *El Economista* quotes rates, and you can get fairly close to the *paralelo* nowadays in *cambios* and hotels (rates tend to fall around Christmas and the New Year). Rates are usually better in Santiago than elsewhere in the country. Changing travellers' cheques can be time-consuming and has become difficult in most towns apart from Arica, Antofagasta, Santiago and Puerto Montt. Traveller's cheques can be changed into dollars, but check if a commission is charged as this practice seems to vary. Foreigners may no longer exchange pesos for dollars when leaving the country. Diners' Club, Visa and Mastercharge are common in Chile (Bancard, the local card, is affliated to the last two—offices, called Fincard, can be found in most cities and will give cash against the cards), but American Express is less useful (use in American Express banks does not incur commission).

Living Conditions and Cost Shops throughout Chile are well stocked and there is a seasonal supply of all the usual fruits and vegetables. Milk in pasteurized, evaporated, or dried form is obtainable. Chilean tinned food is dear. Food is reasonable, but food prices vary tremendously. Santiago tends to be more expensive for food and accommodation than other parts of Chile. Southern Chile can be expensive between December 15 and March 15.

The **metric** system is obligatory but the quintal of 46 kilos (101.4 lb) is used.

Electric Current 220 volts A.C., 50 cycles

Posts Airmail takes 3-4 days from the UK. Seamail takes 8-12 weeks. There is a daily airmail service to Europe with connections to the UK. Poste restante only holds mail for 30 days; then returns to sender. Lista de Correo in Santiago, Central Post Office, is good and efficiently organized. On no account send anything of value through the postal service, letters are frequently opened, or go astray, both entering and leaving the country. Astonishing how throughout Chile one post office official will charge rates different from the next, and they are all "right".

Telephones International telephone and telegraph communications are operated by Entel and CTC (Compañía de Teléfonos de Chile), both have offices throughout the country and their rates are slightly different. Calls may be made collect, but with difficulty to some places (e.g. West Germany). Cheap rates on international calls at Entel are all day Sat., Sun. and holidays to all destinations except Japan, Australia and E Asia (0700-1859), Mon.-Fri. 1900-0659 to North and South America, 1400-0459 to Europe, Africa and W Asia and 0700-1859 Japan, Australia and E Asia. 3 minute call to Europe costs US$10.35 (US$7.25 cheap rate); to Australia US$14 (US$7.25 cheap rate, Entel); cheap rate to N and S America US$6, but US$5 to Argentina and Uruguay. Phone abroad from a private line is cheaper after 1800.

New telephone boxes, accepting coins, can be used to make local, long-distance and overseas calls, for making collect calls and receiving calls. For local calls from a public booth you need 3 ten-peso coins, or *fichas* bought from kiosks.

Fax is operated by Entel and VTR, who have offices throughout the country. VTR also operate telex services. Amex Card holders can often use telex facilities at Amex offices free of charge.

Media Santiago daily papers *El Mercurio*, *La Nación*, *La Epoca* (liberal/left), *La Segunda*, *La Tercera* and *La Quarta*. *Las Ultimas Noticias*, *El Cóndor*, weekly in German.

Weekly magazines; *Hoy*, *Qué Pasa*; *Análisis*, *Ercilla* and *Panorama Económico* are best economic journals. Monthly: *Rutas* (official organ, Automobile Association).

Sports Sernatur will give all the necessary information about sport. **Skiing** Season from June to September/October, weather depending. For information write to: La Federación de Ski de Chile, Casilla 9902, Santiago. Horse racing is also popular and meetings are held every Sunday and on certain feast days at Viña del Mar, Santiago and Concepción throughout the year; horseback riding is also popular. Santiago and Valparaíso residents fish at the mountain resort of Río Blanco, and some of the the world's best fishing is in the Lake District. The licence required can be got from the local police or sport angling associations as the Asociación de Pesca y Caza, which gives information on local conditions. Other popular sports are football and basket ball. Viña del Mar has a cricket ground; on Saturdays there are polo matches at Santiago.

Language The local pronunciation of Spanish, very quick and lilting, with final syllables cut off, can present difficulties to the foreigner. See also Argentine section, **page 193**.

Tourist Information The national secretariat of tourism, Sernatur, has offices throughout the country (addresses are given in the text). City offices provide town maps, leaflets and much useful information. In addition, a much-used series of guide books is that called *Turistel*, details of which are given under Santiago.

The Editor would like to thank the following for their help and hospitality in November 1989: in Santiago, Jaime and Patricia Duhart, Alan Holmes, Nicholas Asheshov of *The South Pacific Mail*, Patricia Pohl (Librería Inglesa), la periodista Ana María of the public relations office, and Verónica Campillo, both of Sernatur, Pedro Araya, Conaf, and Alan and Clare White at the British Embassy; in Melipilla, Mike and Jeannette Sargent; in Coyhaique, Patricio and Gedra Guzmán, Luis Pérez and María Antonieta Mayorga Trueba of Sernatur, Baldo Araya Uribe, Justo Beroiza (Radio Santa María), John Hoyle; in Cochrane, Gerardo Vera of Conaf; in Puerto Montt, Patricio Yáñez Strange of Sernatur, and Raúl Arroyo; in Temuco, Jack and Gloria Feka; in Pucón, Erna Avello Aedo of Sernatur. Our warmest thanks are also due to Francisco González Rojas, Director Regional de Turismo, Región de los Lagos, Puerto Montt; Lyndsey O'Callaghan and Simon Watson Taylor, all of whom have provided most useful new material and corrections for this edition. We are grateful to the following travellers: Helen Fell (Punta Arenas), Thomas Thanner (München 40), John Edmonds (Harpenden, Herts), Tam Agosti-Gisler (Anchorage, Alaska), F.R. Allemann and Xenia V. Bahder (Kleinrinderfeld), Rick Ansell and Paulette Milego (Porto Alegre), Haz Arad, Lucie Armstrong (Ithaca, NY), Hans and Verónica Liechti-Avaneda (Santiago de Chile), Brian Bass (Clun/Craven Arms, Shropshire), Maarten Beeris (San Pedro de Atacama), Erik Bernesson (Båstad, Swe.), Momik Bernaerts (Amsterdam) and Thomas Hartmann (Copenhagen), Christine Blenntoft (Santiago), Aad Bol and Trish Clements (Poelijk, Neth. and Faulconbridge, Australia), Rop Bomer and Wilhelmien ter Haar (Mexico DF), Jens Borchers and Michael Frantz (W. Ger.), Dorothea Bornholdt (Lutzhorn, W. Ger.), B. A. Bošnjak (Los Alamitos, CA), Alex Brand (Heidelberg 1), Sara Braune (Stroud), Michael Brooke (Saffham Bulbeck, Cambs.), Kirsten Bruun and Jesper Juel Rasmussen (Copenhagen), Felicity and Charles Buchan (Fraserburgh), Daniel Buck and Anne Meadows (Washington DC), Kathryn Bullock (London SE8), Bain Chadsey (Corrales, NM), Tage Christensen and Palle Kangstad (Århus, DMK), Jim Cilek (Twin Falls, ID), Lucinda Coates (North Ryde, NSW), Jane Coburn (Thirroul, NSW), W.J. Coppock (Ukiah, CA), Andrew Cresswe.ll (Worcester), G.G.A. Cumming (Viña del Mar), Jörg Cusker (Ushuaia), Karen Dahl (Hamden, Conn), Daniel Darwish (Oxford), Patrick Debergh (Cressier, Switz.), Larry Dolan (Helena, MT), Sonia and Tzvi Dugan (D.N. Eilot, Israel), Frank Dux (Detmold 18, W. Ger.), Jennifer Eberle (Westwood, NJ), Barbara Egger and Betti Müller (Fahrwald, Switz.), Julie Eisenberg and Andy Daitsman (Santiago), Russell A. Eisenberg (Milwaukee, WI), Dag K. Ellingsen (Oslo 2), Mary Eschbach (Rockledge, FL), Anthony Feeny (London EC1), Maarten Feteris and Charlotte Geerards (Leiden, Neth.), Bruce Fitzwater (Portland, OR), Harry Floyd (London W8), John N. Fugelso (Durham NC), Katy Gardner (Liverpool 8), Don and Anne Garman (Buckingham), Theodor A. Gevert (Barueri, SP, Brazil), Tony Gowers (Bristol), Rudolf Graf (Genthod, Switz.), Jon and Julia Gruffydd (Lima) Rupert Hafner (Vienna), Ellen Hansen and Morten Volden (Saupstad, Norway), Jim Hardy (Waukesha, Wis.), Lucy Harper, Roy and Joan Harris (Nanaimo, BC), Wayne Harvey (South Australia), John Hayes, Richard Murison and Colin, Kevin Healey (Melbourne, Vic.), Dr Paul Heaton (London NW6), Etai Heled, Ronit Glazer (Kibbutz Hokuk, Israel) and Ami and Sary Saranga (Menahamia, Israel), Frank Hermann (Nauheim), Ursula Hochuli (Switz.) and Vincent Choblet (Paris), Mary Hodgson (Sydney, NSW), Robin Holloway and Fiona Butler (Birmingham), Hans-Jürgen Holst (Tostedt, W. Ger.), Simon J. Hughes (Hertford), Jeff Inglis (Seattle), Volkmar E. Janicke (München 40), Simon Jeffreys (Peterborough), Allan Jensen and Vibeke Nageh (Munke-Bjergby, Dnmk.), Martin Jung (Tübingen), Tobias Kämpf (Rupperswil, Switz.), Gil Kats (Haifa), Bill Kauffman (Sydney, NSW), Marcel Kersten (Roosendaal, Neth.), Ingeborg Knottek-Hecht (New York), Peter Kocan (Summit, NJ), Jürgen Kölbl (Frankfurt/Main), Justin Koprowski (High Wycombe), Lucy, Ian and Laura Krause (Newcastle-upon-Tyne), Karen Kuebel and George Georgiadis (São Luis), Thomas G. Lammers (Oxford, Ohio), Antony and Elisabeth Lancaster (Lima 18), Toby Lanzer (Santiago de Chile), Herbert S. Levi (Buenos Aires), John Lewis (London NW2), Udo Lichtenthäler (Berlin 21), Gaston Luk (Valparaíso), Mika Määttänen (Tampere, Fin.), Herbert Malinow (London W1), Bill Manley (Boulder, CO), Dean McCauley (San Francisco, CA), A. Mckenzie Brockman (Deux-Montagnes, Quebec), Barbara Meier and Thomas Ester (Essen 15, W. Ger.), Karssen Mengel and Birgit Borkholm Nielsen (Langeskov, Dnmk.), Shelia Misdorp (Salta), Alistair and Liz Mitchell (São Paulo), Helene Monsme (Leiden, Neth.), Daniel Morgan (Wellington, NZ), Matthias Müller (Berlin 31), Hallam Murray (London SW11), H. and G. Netsch (Sainte-Foy, Quebec), Dr Hannes Neuhauser (München 70), Stephen Newcomer (Centrevill, Iowa), R.H. Newton (Puerto Natales), Jörg Niggli (Trimbach, Switz.), Jonas Noreús (Varberg, Swe.), Dave Nutting (Melbourne), Bryan F. O'Leary (Redondo Beach, CA), Ingrid Østergaard (Vestervig, Dnmk.), Mark Ottaway (London W11), Lucy Paine and William Petrie (Watlington, Oxon.), Barbara E. Pawulska de Pinto (Concepción), Angus Pelham Burn (Banchory, Kincardineshire), Jérôme De Perlinghi and Rosa Gobien (Brussels), Mirco and Cristina Perot (Grüt, Switz.), Sandrine Pétremand and Gilles Maitre (Bevaix, Switz.), Ortrun Poettering (Rio de Janeiro), Louis Prefontaine (St Malo, Manitoba), Bernd Proissl (Wernau, W. Ger.), Antoni Pujador (Barcelona, Spain), Suzanne Riesenburger and Robert Snelinski (Winnipeg), Antonio Righetti and Daniela Wenger (Bern), Andrew Robinson (Guildford), Gisele Rochat (Neuchâtel, Switz.), Marvin and Patricia Rosen (New York), Richard and Yvonne Ruming (Bathurst, NSW), Silvia Salzmann (Mettmenhasli), Louise Santamera (Liverpool 3), Rick and Su Sareen (Thailand), J.J. Schat (Zoetermeer, Neths.), Chr Scherlenzky (Bendorf, W. Ger.), Kathrin Schildknecht and Jürg Schmutz (Bern, Switz.), Ueli Schlatter (Hemmental, Switz.), Jolanda Schneider (Malans, Switz.), Rolf Schneider (Effretikon, Switz.), Karen Schulpzand and Rudy Cruysbergs (Dilbeek, Belgium), Guenther Schwerin (Moeglingen, W. Ger.), Manfred Sengl (München 5), Eleanor Sepora (New Zealand), Vivienne Shave (Truro), A.F. Siraa (Miami), Hans and Ina Stoffregen (Celle, W. Ger.), W. de W.W. Symons (Bovingdon, Herts), Richard Tinnerello (Flower Mound, Texas), Karen Uemura (Hollister, CA), Alex Joseph Thompson Valenzuela (Antofagasta), Mark D. Viner and Kim Hutchings (Bromley, Kent), Hugh J. Wade (Anchorage, Alaska), Thomas Walbaum (Steinheim, W. Ger.), T.C. Walker (Ensenada), William Walker (Washington DC), Andrew Wallace and Michelle Still (Teddington), Anne H. Walton (US Embassy, Buenos Aires), Ingrid Walter and Norbert Eisinger (Schnelldorf, W. Ger.), Roland Weitkamp (Braunschweig, W. Ger.), Urs Wigger (Menznau, Switz.) and Helmut Zettl (Ebergassing, Austria).

COLOMBIA

INTRODUCTION

COLOMBIA, with 1,138,618 square km., is the fourth largest country in South America and has the third largest population (30.5 millions). It has coast lines upon both the Caribbean (1,600 km.) and the Pacific (1,306 km.). Nearly 55% of the area is almost uninhabited lowland with only 4% of the population; the other 96% are concentrated in the remaining 45%, living for the most part in narrow valleys or isolated intermont basins, or in the broad Caribbean lowlands. The population is infinitely varied, ranging from white, Indian, and black to mixtures of all three.

The 620,000 square km. of almost uninhabited land in Colombia lie E of the Eastern Cordillera. Near the foot of the Cordillera the plains are used for cattle ranching, but beyond is jungle. Islands of settlement in it are connected with the rest of the country by air and river, for there are no railways and very few roads: communication is by launch and canoe on the rivers.

In the populous western 45% of the country four ranges of the Andes run from S to N. Between the ranges run deep longitudinal valleys. Of the 14 main groups of population in the country, no less than 11 are in the mountain basins or in the longitudinal valleys; the other three are in the lowlands of the Caribbean.

The first 320 km. along the Pacific coast N from the frontier with Ecuador to the port of Buenaventura is a wide, marshy, and sparsely inhabited coastal lowland. Along the coast N of Buenaventura runs the Serranía de Baudó. E of this range the forested lowlands narrow into a low trough of land; E of the trough again rise the slopes of the Western Cordillera. The trough—the Department of the Chocó—is drained southwards into the Pacific by the Río San Juan, navigable for 200 km., and northwards into the Caribbean by the Río Atrato, navigable for 550 km.; there are vague plans to link the two rivers by canal. The climate is hot and torrential rain falls daily. The inhabitants are mostly black.

From the borders of Ecuador two ranges of mountain, the Western Cordillera

COLOMBIA
65

1 Bogotá.
2 Bogotá to Cúcuta.
3 The Llanos and Leticia.
4 The North coast and Islands.
5 Up the Magdalena River.
6 The central cordillera: Medellín and Manizales.
7 The Cauca valley.
8 Southern Colombia

and the Central Cordillera, run N for 800 km. to the Caribbean lowlands. Five peaks in the Western Cordillera are over 4,000 metres but none reaches the snowline. The Central Cordillera, 50-65 km. wide, is much higher; six of its peaks, snow clad, rise above 5,000 metres and its highest, the volcano cone of Huila, is 5,439 metres. There is hardly any level land, but there are narrow ribbons of soil along some of the rivers.

Between the two ranges, as they emerge from Ecuador, lies a valley filled in the S to a height of 2,500 metres by ash from the volcanoes. Not far from the frontier there is a cluster of self-subsisting Indians around Pasto. Further N between these two ranges lies the Cauca valley; in its northern 190 km., roughly from Popayán N past Cali to Cartago, there is an important agricultural region based on a deep bed of black alluvial soil which yields as many as five crops a year. This valley, which is at a height of about 1,000 metres and up to 50 km. wide, is drained northwards by the Cauca river. Cali is the business centre of the valley, and a road and railway run from Cali over a low pass of less than 1,500 metres in the Western Cordillera to Buenaventura. Sugar cane was the great crop of this valley in colonial times, but has now been varied with tobacco, soya, cotton, pineapple, and every other kind of tropical fruit. There is still some cattle raising. Coffee is grown on the Cordillera slopes above 600 metres. A " Tennessee Valley " scheme of development to drain the swamps, control floods, irrigate parched areas, improve farming, and produce electric power has been applied in the Cauca Valley since 1956.

At Cartago the two Cordilleras close in and the Cauca valley becomes a deep gorge which runs all the way to the Caribbean flatlands. In the Cordillera Central, at an altitude of 1,540 metres, is the second largest city and industrial centre in Colombia: Medellín. Much of the coffee and 75% of the gold comes from this area. N of Medellín the Cordillera Central splits into three ranges, separated by streams flowing into the Caribbean.

Near Latitude 2°N, or about 320 km. N of the Ecuadorean border, the Eastern Cordillera, the longest of all, rises and swings N and then NE towards Venezuela. About Latitude 7°N it bifurcates; one branch becomes the western rim of the Maracaibo basin and the other runs E into Venezuela, to the S of the Maracaibo basin.

Between this Eastern Cordillera and the Central Cordillera runs the 1,600 km. long Magdalena river, with the Caribbean port of Barranquilla at its mouth. There are more intermont basins in the Eastern Cordillera than in the others. Some of its peaks rise above the snow line. In the Sierra Nevada del Cocuy (just before the Cordillera bifurcates) there is a group of snowy peaks, all over 5,200 metres; the highest, Ritacuba Blanca, reaches 5,493 metres. The basins are mostly high, at an altitude of from 2,500 to 2,750 metres. In the Lower Magdalena region the river banks are comparatively deserted, though there are a few clearings made by the descendants of black slaves who settled along the Magdalena after their emancipation. There are oilfields in the valley, particularly at Barrancabermeja.

In a high basin of the Eastern Cordillera, 160 km. E of the Magdalena river, the Spaniards in 1538 founded the city of Bogotá, now the national capital. The great rural activity of this group is the growing of food: cattle, wheat, barley, maize and potatoes.

Roads run N from Bogotá to the basins of Chiquinquirá and Sogamoso, over 160 km. away. Both are in the Department of Boyacá, with Tunja, on a mountain between the two, as capital. Both basins, like that of Bogotá, produce food, and there are emerald mines at Muzo, near Chiquinquirá.

There are other basins in the N of the Eastern Cordillera: in the Departments of Santander and Norte de Santander at Bucaramanga and Cúcuta, and a small one at Ocaña. Movement into these basins by Europeans and *mestizos* did not take place until the 19th century, when chinchona bark (for quinine) rose into high demand. By 1885 this trade was dead, but by that time coffee was beginning to be planted. In Bucaramanga coffee is now the main crop, but it has been diversified by cacao, cotton and tobacco, all grown below the altitude suitable for coffee.

There is one more mountain group in Colombia, the Sierra Nevada de Santa Marta, standing isolated from the other ranges on the shores of the Caribbean. This is the highest range of all: its snow-capped peaks rise to 5,800 metres within 50 km. of the coast.

To the W of this Sierra, and N of where the Central and Western Cordilleras come to an end, lies a great lowland where three groups of population on its Caribbean shores; at Cartagena, Barranquilla and Santa Marta. The rivers draining this lowland (the Magdalena, Sinú, Cauca, San Jorge and César) run so slowly that much of the area is a tissue of swamps and lagoons with very little land that can be cultivated. Indeed the whole area E of the channel of the Magdalena is under water at most times of the year. When the floods come, large areas of the land W of the Magdalena—the plains of Bolívar—are covered too, but during the dry season from October to March great herds of cattle are grazed there.

History Before the coming of the Spaniards the country was occupied by Indians, most of whom were primitive hunters or nomad agriculturists, but one part of the country, the high basins of the Eastern Cordillera, was densely occupied by Chibcha Indians who had become sedentary farmers. Their staple foods were maize and the potato, and they had no domestic animal save the dog; the use they could make of the land was therefore limited. Other cultures present in Colombia in the precolumbian era were the Tairona, Quimbaya, Sinú and Calima. Exhibits of their and the Chibcha (Muisca) Indians' gold-work can be seen at the Gold Museum in Bogotá, the one total "must" for all visitors to the city (**see page 632**).

The Spaniards sailed along the northern coast as far as Panama as early as 1500. The first permanent settlement was by Rodrigo de Bastidas at Santa Marta in 1525. Cartagena was founded in 1533. In 1536, Gonzalo Jiménez de Quesada (who wrote a full account of his adventures) pushed up the Magdalena river to discover its source; mounting the Eastern Cordillera in 1536, he discovered the Chibchas, conquered them, and founded Santa Fe de Bogotá in 1538. In the meantime other Spanish forces were approaching the same region: Pizarro's lieutenant, Sebastián de Benalcázar, had pushed down the Cauca valley from Ecuador and founded Pasto, Popayán and Cali in 1536. Nicolás de Federmann, acting on behalf of the Welser financiers of Germany, who had been granted a colonial concession by Charles V, approached from Venezuela. Benalcázar reached Bogotá in 1538 and Federmann got there in 1539. As in Peru, the initial period of settlement was one of strife between contending *conquistadores*. The royal Audiencia de Santa Fe set up in 1550 gave the area a legislative, judicial and administrative entity. In 1564 this was followed by a **presidency of the kingdom of Nueva Granada** controlling the whole country and Panama, except Benalcázar's province of Popayán. The Presidency was replaced in 1718 by a viceroyalty at Bogotá which controlled the provinces now known as Venezuela as well; it was independent of the Viceroyalty of Peru, to which this vast area had previously been subject.

The movement towards independence from Spain was set going in 1794 by a translation into Spanish by the *criollo* Antonio Nariño of the French Declaration of the Rights of Man. The movement was given point and force when, in 1808, Napoleon replaced Ferdinand VII of Spain with his own brother Joseph. The New World refused to recognize this: there were several revolts in Nueva Granada, culminating in a revolt at Bogotá and the setting up of a *junta* on 20 July, 1810. Other local juntas were established: Cartagena bound itself to a *junta* set up at Tunja. Late in 1812 the young Bolívar, driven out of Venezuela, landed at Cartagena. In a brilliant campaign in 1813 he pushed up the Magdalena to Ocaña, and from there to Cúcuta, and obtained permission from the *junta* at Tunja to advance into Venezuela. In 90 days he marched the 1,200 km. to Caracas over mountain country, fighting six battles, but he was unable to hold Caracas and withdrew to Cartagena in 1814.

Napoleon fell in 1815, and the Spanish Government immediately set about reconquering, with some success, Venezuela and New Granada. General Pablo Morillo took Cartagena after a bitter siege of 106 days—Bolívar had withdrawn to Jamaica—and was later "pacifying" Bogotá with a "Reign of Terror" by May 1816.

Bolívar had by now assembled an army of Llaneros, fortified by a British legion recruited from ex-servicemen of the Peninsular wars, in Venezuela at Angostura, or Ciudad Bolívar as it is called today. In the face of incredible difficulties he made a forced march across the Andes in 1819. After joining up with Santander's Nueva Granada army, he defeated the royalists at the battle of the Swamps of Vargas in July and again at Boyacá on 7 August. He entered Bogotá three days later.

Bolívar reported his success to the revolutionary congress sitting at Angostura, and that body, on 17 December, 1819, proclaimed the Republic of Gran Colombia, embracing in one the present republics of Venezuela, Colombia, and Ecuador. A general congress was held at Cúcuta on 1 January, 1821, and here it was that two opposing views which were to sow such dissension in Colombia first became apparent. Bolívar and Nariño were for centralization; Santander, a realist, for a federation of sovereign states. Bolívar succeeded in enforcing his view for the time being, but Gran Colombia was not to last long; Venezuela broke away in 1829 and Ecuador in 1830. The remaining provinces were named Nueva Granada; it was not till 1863 that the name Colombia was restored.

Almost from its inception the new country became the scene of strife between the centralizing pro-clerical Conservatives and the federalizing anti-clerical Liberals. The Conservative president Tomás Cipriano de Mosquera (1845) encouraged education, began building roads, adopted the metric system, and put steamers on the Magdalena. The Liberals were dominant from 1849 for the next 30 years of insurrections and civil wars. In 1885 the Conservatives imposed a highly centralized constitution which has not been modified in this respect to this day. A Liberal revolt in 1899 turned into a civil war, "the War of the Thousand Days". The Liberals were finally defeated in 1902 after 100,000 people had died. It was in 1903 that Panama declared its independence from Colombia, following U.S. pressure.

After 40 years of comparative peace, the strife between Conservatives and Liberals was re-ignited in a little-publicized but dreadfully bloody civil war known as *La Violencia* from 1948 to 1957 (some 300,000 people were killed); but this was ended by a unique political truce. It was decided by plebiscite in 1957 that the two political parties would support a single presidential candidate, divide all political offices equally between them, and thus maintain political stability for sixteen years. In 1978 the agreement was ended, though some elements of the coalition— representation of the main opposition party in the Cabinet, for instance— were allowed to continue until 1986. Sr. Belisario Betancur, the Conservative president from 1982-86, offered a general amnesty to guerrilla movements in an attempt to end violence in the country. Following an initial general acceptance of the offer, only one of the four main guerrilla groups, the FARC, upheld the truce in 1985-7. In May 1986, when the Liberal candidate, Sr. Virgilio Barco, won the presidential elections, FARC's newly-formed political party, the Unión Patriótica, won 10 seats in congress; the Liberal party took the majority. Right-wing groups, unwilling to accept the Unión Patriótica, began a campaign of murder against UP's elected representatives. By the begining of 1990, 1,040 party members had been killed since the UP was formed in 1985. This, together with continuing left-wing, and drugs-related, violence, provoked civil instability into the 1990s. During the campaign for the 1990 presidential and congressional elections violence brought the assassination of the Liberal Party and the UP presidential candidates. Luis Carlos Galán and Bernardo Jaramillo. President Barco pledged to crack down on the drugs barons and an international effort was launched to bring them to justice, but opposition to extradition of suspects to the USA stymied progress.

In the March 1990 parliamentary elections, the Liberal Party won 60% of the seats, against 37% for the Conservatives. Presidential elections were held on 27 May, 1990. The Liberal Party candidate and eventual winner was César Gaviria, a former Finance Minister and Interior Minister, who won a clear majority in the March primaries after taking up the candidacy of the murdered Luis Carlos Galán.

The People of Colombia The regions vary greatly in their racial make-up: Antioquia and Caldas are largely of European blood, Pasto is Indian, the Cauca Valley and the rural area near the Caribbean are African or *mulatto*. No colour bar is legally recognized but it does exist in certain centres. Colombia has 19 cities with over 100,000 people. Total estimated population in 1988 was 30,568,000, with an annual growth rate of 2.1%.

About 70% live in the cities, with 34% of the work force engaged in agriculture, pastoral and forest pursuits, hunting and fishing. Gdp per capita is US$1,220. The birth and death rates vary greatly from one area to the other, but in general infant mortality is very high (53.3 per 1,000 live births; the mortality rate is 7.7 per 1,000). The birth rate (1980-85) was 31.0. Hospitals and clinics are few in relation to the population. About 66% of the doctors are in the departmental capitals, which contain 12% of the population, though all doctors now have to spend a year in the country before they can get their final diploma. Deplorable *barrios clandestinos* (shanty-towns) have sprung up around Cali, Barranquilla, Cartagena and Buenaventura.

The Economy Agriculture is the most important sector of the economy, contributing about 22% of gdp and employing 34% of the labour force. It is also the largest earner of foreign exchange, with over 57% of total legal exports. The traditional crops are coffee, sugar cane, bananas, rice, maize and cotton. Colombia is the leading producer of mild Arabica coffee and second to Brazil in world production. Output has declined since 1984 as the Government has encouraged diversification, but coffee remains the dominant export item with up to 50% of total revenues.

Manufacturing contributes almost as much to gdp as agriculture, with agricultural-related activities such as food processing, drink and tobacco accounting for 35% of the sector's value added. Textiles and clothing are also important, and provide an outlet for home-grown cotton. Heavy corporate indebtedness in the first half of the 1980s affected the growth of manufacturing and led to a decline in employment to only 15% of the total labour force. In the second half of the decade, however, strong growth was shown by chemicals, textiles and clothing, transport equipment, cement, metalworking and paper and unemployment fell.

Although contributing only 2% of gdp, mining, mainly oil and coal, was the most dynamic sector of the economy in the 1980s, with growth rates of over 20% a year. With the exception of a few major projects, mining is concentrated in the hands of small scale producers with little technology or organization. Much of their output remains outside the formal economy. Colombia is, however, the largest producer of gold and platinum in Latin America, and these two metals, together with emeralds, have traditionally dominated the mining sector. Mining of precious metals, including silver, is primarily in the Departments of Antioquia and El Chocó; huge gold deposits have also been discovered on the borders of the Departments of Cauca and Valle, while others have been found in the Guainía, Vaupés and Guaviare regions near the Brazilian border. In 1984, Colombia became self-sufficient in energy. Rising production of hydrocarbons moved the oil trade into surplus for the first time in ten years and by 1988 oil imports had virtually ceased. Development of energy sources has been given high priority to satisfy domestic requirements and to diversify exports. Most of the oil production comes from the Magdalena basin, but these are older fields which are running down. The discovery of the Caño Limón field near Arauca has raised output to around 450,000 barrels a day. As well as oil and gas, Colombia has the largest coal reserves in Latin America, which partial surveys have put at 16.5 bn tonnes. The largest deposits are in the Cerrejón region, where a huge project has been set up to mine and export steam coal from a new port at Bahía de Portete. Hydroelectricity now accounts for 70% of installed generating capacity. It has an advantage over thermal power because 75% of the nation's hydroelectric potential is in the central zone, where 80% of the population live. Total potential is said to be 100,000 MW, of which only about 5% is harnessed.

Current account surpluses in the late 1970s during the coffee price boom were turned into large deficits in the first half of the 1980s, reaching over US$3bn in 1982 and 1983, because of lower export receipts and rapidly rising imports. However, Colombia was able to avoid having to reschedule its foreign debts, and took steps to adjust its external accounts. The devaluation of the peso was speeded up, reinforced by import restrictions and export incentives. The fiscal accounts were also turned around and the public sector deficit was reduced from 7.5% of gdp in 1984 to 2.0% in 1986 while economic growth remained positive throughout the 1980s. The World Bank and the IMF endorsed the Colombian economic strategy and commercial banks continued to lend to the country to refinance loans falling due.

Constitution and Government Senators and Representatives are elected by popular vote. The Senate has 112 members, and the Chamber of Representatives has 199. The President, who appoints his 13 ministers, is elected by direct vote for a term of four years, but cannot succeed himself in the next term. Every citizen over 18 can vote.

Administratively the country is divided into 22 Departments, 5 Intendencias, 5 Comisarias, and the Special District of Bogotá.

Liberty of speech and the freedom of the press are in theory absolute but in practice more limited. The language of the country is Spanish. Its religion is Roman Catholicism. There is complete freedom for all other creeds not contravening Christian morals or the law.

Education The literacy rate is 82%. Education is free, and since 1927 theoretically compulsory, but many children, especially in rural areas, do not attend. There are high standards of secondary and university education, when it is available.

Communications A major problem still facing the country is that of surface transport. Its three Cordilleras, separated by valleys often no more than 1,500 metres above sea-level, make internal communications extremely difficult. The 3,700 km. of narrow-gauge railways and the 38,200 km. of roads have eastern and western systems, with inter-communicating laterals (see maps and text). Only about 10% of the road system is paved. Given these difficulties it is natural that Colombia, which ran the first airline in South America, has taken ardently to the air.

BOGOTA (1)

Bogotá, capital of the Republic and a city of 5.3 million people, is on a plateau at 2,650 metres. The average temperature is 14°C (58°F). It is built on sloping land, and covers 210 square km. The central part of the city is full of character and contrasts: colonial buildings stand side-by-side with the most modern architecture. For the most part the houses are low, with eaves projecting over the streets; they are rarely brightly painted. The traffic is very heavy.

Visitors should not be too active for the first 24 hrs. Some people get dizzy at Bogotá's altitude. Be careful with food and alcoholic drinks for the first day also.

There is a very good view of the city from the top of Monserrate, the lower of the

BOGOTÁ
Orientation Map
Main Streets Only
NOT TO SCALE   67A

1. Parque Santander
2. Parque de la Independencia
3. Parque Nacional Olaya Herrera
4. Parque Simón Bolívar
5. Monserrate
6. Teleférico station
7. Quinta Bolívar
8. National Museums
9. Chapinero
10. El Campin Stadium
11. Ciudad Universitaria and Instituto Agustin Codazzi
12. Centro Administrativo Nacional
13. Inderena
14. DAS
Area of detailed map

CIRCUNVALACIÓN

CRA. 5
CRA. 7
AV. 19
CRA.

CARRERA 7

TO VILLAVICENCIO

CARACAS
C. 63
C. 53
C. 45
C. 34
AV. 22
AV. JE. GAITÁN

TO THE NORTH

AV. CIUDAD   DE QUITO
CIUDAD DE LIMA
JIMÉNEZ QUESADA
AV. 30

TO THE SOUTH

CALLE 26
TRANS 39
DIAG 53
AV. DE LAS
CRA. 48
CRA. 50
AV. DE LOS COMUNEROS

CALLE
CALLE 13
AMÉRICAS
AV. 3

AV. DEL ESPECTADOR
AV. 68

TO THE NORTH

DORADO
AV. EL

TO MEDELLIN ON AV. 81

AV.   BOYACÁ

AV. CENTENARIO
TO FACATATIVÁ

N

two peaks rising sharply to the E. It is reached by a funicular railway and a cable car. The new convent at the top is a popular shrine. At the summit, near the church, a chairlift (US$0.20) and a platform give a bird's-eye view of the red-roofed city and of the plains beyond stretching to the rim of the Sabana. Also at the top are a Wild West-style train for children, several restaurants and snack bar (good *tamales*, US$1), and the Calle del Candelero, a reconstruction of a Bogotá street of 1887. Behind the church are popular picnic grounds. The fare up to Monserrate is US$1.60 adult return (US$0.80 child), four trips per hour. The funicular works only on Sun. and holidays (expect to have to queue for an hour if you want to go up before about 1400, and for coming down); the cable car operates 0900-1800 weekdays, 0600-1800 on Sun.

The neighbourhood can be dangerous though there is a police station nearby. At weekends, especially Sundays which is a local day of pilgrimage, there are so many people that it is usually safe to walk up and down Monserrate. However during the week, muggings are frequent even in daylight. Take a bus or taxi to the foot of the hill Mon.-Fri., and never be tempted to walk down from the top. Taxi to foot, allowing 1 hour at the top, US$5.30.

At the foot of Monserrate is the Quinta de Bolívar, a fine colonial mansion, with splendid gardens and lawns. There are several cannons captured at the battle of Boyacá. The house, once Bolívar's home, is now a museum showing some of his personal possessions and paintings of events in his career. (Open 1000-1700, Tues.-Sun.; its address is Calle 20, No. 3-23 Este; charge US$0.50.)

The Plaza Bolívar, with a statue of the Liberator at its centre, is at the heart of the city; around the Plaza are the narrow streets and massive mansions of the old quarter (known as the Barrio La Candelaria), with their barred windows, carved doorways, brown-tiled roofs and sheltering eaves. The district is popular as a residential area and has an artists' community. Most of the mansions and best colonial buildings are in this district: the Palace of San Carlos, the house of the Marqués de San Jorge (housing an archaeological museum), the Municipal Palace, the Capitol, and the churches of San Ignacio, Santa Clara, San Agustín, and the Cathedral.

The Calles (abbreviated "Cll.", or "C") run at right angles across the Carreras ("Cra." or "K"). It is easy enough to find a place once the address system, which is used throughout Colombia, is understood. The address Calle 13, No. 12-45 would be the building on Calle 13 between Carreras 12 and 13 at 45 paces from Carrera 12; however transversals and diagonals (numbers with letters appended) can complicate the system. The Avenidas, broad and important streets, may be either Calles (like 19) or Carreras (like 14). Av. Jiménez de Quesada, one of Bogotá's most important streets, owes its lack of straightness to having been built over a river-bed. Carrera 7, one of the main shopping streets, is now closed to motor traffic on Sundays.

The street map of Bogotá on **page** 625 is marked with numerals showing the places of most interest for visitors. Each place will be described under the numeral for it in the map.

1. The Plaza Bolívar, heart of the city, coeval with the city's foundation. On the eastern side is the Archbishop's Palace, with splendid bronze doors. To one side of it is the colonial Plazuela de Rufino Cuervo. Here is the house of Manuela Sáenz, the mistress of Bolívar. On the other side is the house in which Antonio Nariño printed in 1794 his translation of "The Rights of Man" which triggered off the movement for independence.

See the Casa del Florero or 20 de Julio museum in a colonial house on the corner of Plaza Bolívar with Calle 11. It houses the famous flower vase that featured in the 1810 revolution and shows collections of the Independence War period, including documents and engravings. Entry fee US$0.40, open Tues.-Sat., 0915-1830. On the northern side of the Plaza is the spectacular Palace of Justice, wrecked in a guerrilla attack in 1985. A new Palace of Justice is under construction.
2. The Cathedral, rebuilt in 1807 in classical style. Notable choir loft of carved walnut and wrought silver on altar of Chapel of El Topo. Several treasures and relics; small paintings

BOGOTÁ
NOT TO SCALE 67

attributed to Ribera; banner brought by Jiménez de Quesada to Bogotá, in sacristy, which has also portraits of past Archbishops. There is a monument to Jiménez inside the Cathedral. In one of the chapels is buried Gregorio Vásquez Arce y Ceballos (1638-1711), by far the best painter in colonial Colombia. Many of his paintings are in the Cathedral.

3. The beautiful Chapel of El Sagrario, built end of the 17th century. Several paintings by Gregorio Vásquez Arce.

4. The Municipal Palace.

5. The Capitol, an imposing building with fine colonnades (1847-1925). Congress sits here.

6. The church of Santa Clara, another colonial church, is now a religious museum and concert hall.

7. San Ignacio, Jesuit church built in 1605. Emeralds from the Muzo mines in Boyacá were used in the monstrance. Paintings by Gregorio Vásquez Arce.

8. The Palace of San Carlos, where Bolívar lived. He is said to have planted the huge walnut tree in the courtyard. On September 25, 1828, there was an attempt on his life. His mistress, Manuela, thrust him out of the window and he was able to hide for two hours under the stone arches of the bridge across the Río San Agustín. Santander, suspected of complicity, was arrested and banished. Now the Presidential Palace, with a huge banquet hall used for state affairs. The guard is changed—full-dress uniform—every day at 1700.

The Museum of Colonial Art, across from the Palace of San Carlos (Carrera 6, No. 9-77) is one of the finest colonial buildings in Colombia. It belonged originally to the Society of Jesus, and was once the seat of the oldest University in Colombia and of the National Library. It has a splendid collection of colonial art and paintings by Gregorio Vásquez Arce, all kinds of utensils, and 2 charming patios. Open Tues. to Sat. 0930-1830; Sun. and holidays, 1000-1700. Entry fee US$0.40 for adults; students US$0.20.

9. Church of María del Carmen, with excellent stained glass and walls in bands of red and white.

10. **Colón Theatre**, Calle 10, No. 5-32 (operas, lectures, ballets, plays, concerts, etc.), late 19th century with lavish decorations. Seating for 1,200, and very ornate. Cheap concerts on Fri evenings and Sat mornings.

11. The Mint (Casa de la Moneda), built in 1720, is at Calle 11, No. 4-93; contains a museum of religious paintings and numismatics. Open Mon.-Sat. 0900-2100, Sun. and holidays, 0900-1800. In the same street, No. 4-16, is the Banco de la República's Luis Angel Arango library, one of the best endowed and arranged in South America, with 3 reading rooms, research rooms, an art gallery and a splendid concert hall. There are free concerts and exhibitions. The architecture is impressive and the lavatories are recommended.

12. Palacio de Nariño (1906), the presidential palace. Spectacular interior, fine collection of modern Colombian paintings. Free tours Sat. morning with guide, 0930 in Spanish, 1000 in English, though not on a regular basis (enquire). It is not open to the public any other time.

13. Church of San Agustín, strongly ornamented (1637). Fine paintings by Gregorio Vásquez Arce and the Image of Jesus which was proclaimed Generalísimo of the army in 1812.

14. Santa Bárbara church (mid-16th century), one of the most interesting colonial churches. Paintings by Gregorio Vásquez Arce.

15. Church of San Juan de Dios, well worth a visit.

16. Parque Mártires (Park of the Martyrs), with monument, on the site of the Plaza in which the Spanish shot many patriots during the struggle for independence.

17. Palace of Communications (postal and telegraph), built on the site of the old colonial church of Santo Domingo.

18. The Banco de la República, next to Parque Santander. Next to the Bank is the wonderful Gold Museum (**see page 632**). In Parque Santander there is a bronze statue of Santander, who helped Bolívar to free Colombia and was later its President.

19. Government Palace of Cundinamarca Department, almost as imposing as the Capitol. Corinthian style.

20. San Francisco church (mid-16th century), with notable paintings of famous Franciscans, choir stalls, and a famous high altar (1622). Remarkable ceiling is in Spanish-Moorish (*mudéjar*) style.

21. Church of La Veracruz, first built five years after the founding of Bogotá, rebuilt in 1731, and again in 1904. In 1910 it became the National Pantheon and Church of the Republic. José de Caldas, the famous scientist, was buried along with many other victims of the "Reign of Terror" under the church. Fashionable weddings.

22. La Tercera Orden, an old colonial church famous for its carved woodwork, altars, and confessionals.

23. Las Nieves, old colonial church, has been demolished and replaced by an ugly modern church.

24. Planetarium, Natural History Museum and Museum of Modern Art, in Parque de la

Independencia. Two daily showings of best foreign modern painters, US$0.30. (see also page 631)

25. *Tequendama Hotel*. Nearby (on Carrera 7 and Calle 26) are the church and monastery of San Diego, a picturesque old building recently restored. The Franciscan monastery with fine Mudéjar ceiling was built in 1560 and the church in 1607 as its chapel. It is now used as a crafts shop by Artesanías de Colombia. SE of the *Tequendama Hotel* is the National Library, with entrance on Calle 24.

Warning The old part around Plaza Bolívar and from Calle 28, extending to the centre and South (i.e. declining Calle numbers) is less dangerous than it was, with increased police patrolling. The central area is less safe at weekends after 1900. Mugging, however, may occur in other parts of the city. Around Carrera 16, Calle 16 is unsafe at night and taxi drivers may refuse to let tourists out in this area.

Under state-of-siege legislation police may shoot and kill a suspect during any narcotics operation and it will be automatically classified as self-defence. A large number of would-be drug traffickers have been killed in this way.

The Judicial Unit for Tourism (Tourist police) offers 24-hour service for tourists at Carrera 7, No. 27-42, T 283-4930. If you are robbed of documents, contact police at Calle 46 y Carrera 14, of valuables, police at Calle 40, No. 8-09.

Hotels Book hotels in advance whenever possible. The following expensive hotels are recommended: *Bogotá Royal*, Av. 100, No. 8A-01, T 2183261, L, said to be one of the best in South America; *Tequendama*, Cra. 10, No. 26-21, T 2861111, L; *Charleston*, Cra. 13, No 85-46, T 2180590, L; *El Belvedere*, Tr. 18, No. 100-16, T 2577700, A; *Continental*, Av. Jiménez, No. 4-16, T 2425901, C; *Nueva Granada*, Av. Jiménez, No. 4-77, T 2816121, B. Other luxury and 5-3 star hotels: *Hilton*, Cra. 7, No. 32-16, T 2329898, L+; *La Fontana*, Diagonal 127A, No. 21-10, T 2747868, L; *Bogotá Plaza*, Calle 100, No. 18A-30, T 2364940, L; *Bacatá*, Calle 19, No. 5-20, T 2432210, A; *Dann*, Calle 19, No. 5-72, T 2840100, A; *El Presidente*, Calle 23, No. 9-45, T 2435020, B.

Aparta-Hotel América, Carrera 8, No. 65-89 (Aptdo Aéreo 59859, T 212-81-10, 212-44-90, 212-42-09), A for apartment for one to four persons, clean, comfortable, quiet; *Country*, Calle 85 with Carrera 15, apartments with kitchen, very clean, close to a good supermarket, reservation necessary; *Nuechatel*, Calle 90, No. 7A-66, A, old-fashioned, safe district, good restaurant but poor plumbing; *Las Terrazas*, Calle 54, No. 3-12, C, 2-star, T 2555777, very clean, "rustic charm", nice view of city; *Monserrat*, Av. Caracas, 18-08, D, rec., clean, impeccable service; *Regina*, Carrera 5, No. 15-16, D, with private bath, TV, phone, friendly, good; *Bogotá Internacional*, Carrera 7A, No. 21-20, T 343898, D, very central, comfortable, clean, restaurant and bar, highly rec.; *La Hostería de la Candelaria*, Calle 9, No. 3-11, T 286-1479/242-1727, Aptdo. Aéreo 15978, D, highly rec. for comfort, atmosphere and service (good for longer stays).

On Calle 14 near Carrera 4 are: *Dann Colonial*, No. 4-21, C; opposite is *Santa Fe*, No. 4-48, hot shower, good service, E, quiet, clean, friendly, safe, warmly rec.; *Residencias Florián*, Calle 14, No. 4-67, F. *Hotel la Candelaria*, Carrera 4, No. 14-87, E with bath, heating, good value; also rec., *Residencia Aragón*, Carrera 3, No. 14-13, clean and safe, F, friendly and honest, no hot water, warmly rec. (cheap taxi to airport can be arranged); *Residencias Las Vegas*, Calle 13, No. 3-81, F, clean, central.

De Lujo, Carrera 13, No. 22-46, T 242-8849, D, with bath, clean, safe, friendly, recommended; *San Diego*, Carrera 13 y Calle 24, D, T 2842100, friendly, clean, large rooms, good value; *Del Duc*, Calle 23, No. 9-38, T 2340080, D, friendly, clean, good French restaurant; *Centro International*, 3-star, Carrera 13, No. 38-97, friendly, small rooms, D; *Avenida 19*, Avenida (Calle) 19, No. 5-92, D, with shower, good price considering its central location, clean, very helpful service; *Hostal Residencias Moreno*, Transversal 33 No. 95-28, T 257-9127, D inc. two meals, two house taxi drivers, nearby frequent bus service to town centre, very friendly, safe for left luggage, quiet, comfortable, hot water, highly rec.

Pensión Alemana, Carrera 14, No. 25-15, E, safe, rec.; *Regis*, Calle 18, No. 6-09 (also known as *Residencias María*), E (C with shower), sometimes hot water, old-fashioned, run down but safe, clean; *Hollywood*, Calle 18, No. 8-68, E, clean but small rooms with bath; *El Turista*, Av. Jiménez, between Cras. 4 and 5, E with bath, hot water, safe, small establishment, rec.; opp is *Zaratoga*, E with bath, quite nice; *Internacional*, Av. Jiménez, nr. *Nueva Granada*, E, hot water, safe, friendly; *Vas*, Calle 15, No. 12-30, E, with bath, safe, clean and friendly; *Residencias Schlief*, Calle 33A, No. 14-38, E, with breakfast, no twin beds, pleasant; *María Luisa*, Carrera 14, between Calles 15 and 16, hot water, very reasonable and food is good; *Residencia Dorantes*, Calle 13, No. 5-07, very clean, E (cheaper without bath), hot water, reasonable, safe, rec.; *Residencias Elis*, Calle 14, between Carreras 14 and 15, good and cheap; *Residencias Ya*, Calle 24 y Carrera 14, E, clean, secure garage;

Residencias Ambala, Carrera 5, No. 13-46, T 2412376, E, cheap, clean, friendly and central. *Fiesta Avenida,* Carrera 14, No. 47-28, T 2853407, F, rec; *Residencias Panamá No. 2,* Carrera 16, No. 16-88, T 241-04-05, F, friendly, clean, safe, hot shower (unsafe area). *Alcron,* Calle 20 y Carrera 5, F, simple, safe; *Residencias Americana,* Calle 13 and Carrera 16, clean, G, safe, but only cold water; *Residencias El Hogar,* Calle 16, No. 15-87, clean, small rooms, warm water, F (gringos pay a US$1 surcharge). *Camelia,* Calle 16, No. 15-20, F, clean, safe, hot water, good value, T 243-4131; *Asturias,* next door (No. 15-36), T 242-0931, F, same standard but no hot water; *Residencia Bucamaranga,* Calle 15, No. 16-68, G with bath, cold water, basic; many other cheap hotels in this area, which is dangerous especially for women alone.

We are informed that from Calle 12 southwards, Carrera 13 westwards is not salubrious: visitors are therefore advised to pick hotels in streets NE of Calle 12, with higher numbers. There are certainly many hotels between Calles 13 and 17 and Carreras 15 and 17, many of which are cheap, some of which are clean. Private vehicles should be parked in lockable, guarded parqueaderos.

Youth Hostel Association   Alcom, Apartado Aéreo 3220, Carrera 7, No. 6-10, T 280-3041/280-3202, Fax 280-3460; IYHA member, has a full list of 18 hostels around the country. In the capital there is a hostel in La Candelaria. In Cundinamarca Department there is a hostel at *Centro Vacacional La Esperanza,* 79 km. from Bogotá and two on the road to Melgar (see **Excursions South-West**).

Restaurants   10% value-added tax is now charged. *Refugio Alpino,* Calle 23, No. 7-49, is an excellent international restaurant; *Casa San Isidro,* on Monserrate, good, not cheap; *Tramonti,* Vía La Calera Km. 1½ (Cra. 1, No. 93-80, approached via Carrera 7 and Calle 84), in hills to NE of city, beautiful views, open fires, parking, luxurious, open daily 1200-2400; *Eduardo,* Carrera 11, No. 90-43, international and expensive; *Las Acacias,* Carrera 11, No. 65-46, for typical Colombian food; *Verners,* Calle 25, No. 12-23 (very good German food); *Casa Vieja del Claustro,* Carrera 3, No. 18-60, typical food; *El Café de Rosita,* Carrera 3, No. 8-65, connected with *Hostería de la Candelaria,* breakfast, lunch, bar and tapas, concerts Thurs. and Fri., rec.; *Casa Vieja,* Av. Jiménez 3-73, traditional Bogotá food, live music, atmosphere better than the food; close by on Av. Jiménez is *La Guayacana,* Colombian food, reasonably priced lunches; *El Zaguán de Las Aguas,* Calle 19, No. 5-62, local dishes, atmosphere and national dancing in evening, but expensive and poor cooking and drinks (beer and soft drinks not available) very expensive; good cheap local food at *Doña Lilia,* Calle 17 No. 14-33; also *Regia,* Calle Pallau (next to Gold Museum); *Los Sauces,* Carrera 11, Calle 69, also has traditional music and dancing, expensive with cover charge; *Donde Canta la Rana,* Carrera 24-C, No. 20-10 Sur, a few km. from centre, is refreshingly local and unspoilt, open 1400-1900. *Doña Bárbara,* Calle 82, corner of Carrera 11, dinner costs US$4-7, excellent latino jazz played: *Temel,* Carrera 19 at Calle 118, good steaks, expensive; *Giuseppe Verdi,* Calle 58, No. 5-85, excellent pasta; *Petit Paris,* Carrera 4 and Calle 74, expensive French food; *Jeno's,* Carrera 15, near Calle 85, serves good, though not cheap, pizzas, another outlet at Calle 19, near Cra. 6; *Berlín,* Carrera 15 and Calle 74, German food; *Chalet Europa,* Carrera 9, No. 16-91, 4-course meals for US$5; *Cafetería Romano,* Av. Jiménez, between Carrera 6 and 7, all meals, very clean and reasonable, good pasta, excellent breakfast menu, well rec., as is its sister restaurant *Salerno,* Carrera 7, No. 19-43, good value; *Punta Roja,* Carrera 7 y Calle 24, good 3-course meal for US$2; *Barra Llanera,* Carrera 9, No. 21-45, open weekends and rec. for cheap fish. *Robin Hood,* near *Hotel Nueva Granada,* very good, three-course weekday lunch for US$4, there are other branches. Also on Avenida Jiménez, *Balmoral,* No. 4-92, good food, reasonable prices, open Sun. and holidays, and *Restaurante Briceño,* 5-19, large portions, cheap. *Tierra Colombiana,* Carrera 10, No. 27-27, good, expensive food, evening floor show. There are two restaurants called *Sandricks,* one on Carrera 16, No. 91-25, the other on Carrera 15, No. 79-92; they are run by two brothers and are highly rec., though not cheap (US$6-9 for a main dish). There is a small chain of restaurants called *La Sultana:* the best is at Carrera 7, No. 20-86; *Doña Hertha,* Calle 19, No. 8-13, 3-course meal US$3, specialty is goulash.

Ranch Burger, Centro El Lago, on Carrera 15, serves hamburgers; *Burger King,* Cra. 7 with Calle 34 next to *Hilton,* also *Centro Granahorrar,* Av. Chile with Cra. 9, in Chapinero at Carrera 13 with Calle 64, and more; several *Wimpy Bars* on Cra. 7, good burgers and grills but not cheap; *Dominó,* a chain of good, fairly cheap, typical food restaurants, at Calle 19 with Cra. 3, Cra. 11 with Calle 71; another chain is *Crepes y Waffeles,* good value; *La Gran Barilla,* Carrera 4, with Calle 13, cheap, rich meals; *Parrilla de Oro,* Carrera 4, No. 17-94, excellent inexpensive typical food; *El Ranchito China,* Carrera 4 between Calle 15 and 16, cheap and open late; *Delphi,* opposite Teatro Gaitán, Carrera 7 No. 22-66, rec. for cheap meals; *Trattoria Bistro,* Calle 59, No. 8-50, with branch at Unicentro (Local 2-45), not cheap, but good food, must book at weekends; for US$1.20 a two-course meal can be had in the cafeteria of the Ley and Tía supermarkets; also Cafam, Calle 17 y Carrera 9 (Centro Colseguros).

El Vegetariano, Calle 22, No. 8-89, set meals for US$1, rec. (the restaurant on 3rd floor with only a small sign); there are other branches at Calle 18, No. 5-74, Calle 14, No. 5-00, and Carrera 8, No. 21-39, self-service, not as good as the others, but open on Sun., none is open in the evening; *El Trópico*, Carrera 8, No. 17-72, vegetarian restaurant, good food (especially the fruit cake) and whole wheat loaves for US$1.20 (4-course meal, US$3); *El Vegetariano Fleber*, Calle 17, No. 10-49, good; *Vegetariano de Sol*, Calle 63, No. 10-62 with Yoga Institute in Plaza de Lordes. *Jugos Cali*, Carrera 11, No. 64-60, mostly juices, with pastries. 4 rec. vegetarian restaurants, all with the same owner, are: *El Champiñón*, Transversal 20, No. 122-05 (T 213-2278), near Unicentro, *Samovares*, Carrera 11, No. 69-89 (T 249-4549—lunch only, fixed menu, US$6, nice atmosphere), Carrera 11, No. 67-63 (T 249-6515) and Av. Caracas No. 32-64 (T 285-6095). *El Integral Natural*, Carrera 11, No. 95-10, health food shop with a few tables at street level, restaurant downstairs, fixed menu US$1.50; *Los Vegetarianos*, Calle 41, No. 8-65 (good) and another location with courtyard, very nice; *Acuarius*, Carrera 16, No. 43-30 and also at Calle 18, good vegetarian food, rec. Vegetarian food, excellent, at Calle 74, No. 12-30.

El Dorado, Carrera 15, No. 16-39, good meal for US$2.60; *Freddy*, Carrera 15, No. 16-55, good, budget, popular. *Monte Blanco*, Carrera 7a, No. 17-31, and other branches, very good. *Diana*, Calle 8 with Carrera 6. Good pizzas are served at branches of *Little John's*; *Tío Tim's*, Carrera 13, Calle 67, for pizza, beer and mechanical bull (owned by a Welshman); *Pizzería*, Calle 33, No. 15 (opp. *Hotel María Isabel*), excellent food, atmosphere and music; *La Candelaria*, Calle 11, No. 3-89, 3-course meal for US$2; *Residencias Lido*, Carrera 11, No. 8-79 (just off Plaza Bolívar) serves good, cheap, complete meals; *La Fregata*, Calle 15, No. 9-30 and Calle 77, No. 15-36, expensive but excellent for sea food. Spanish food at *El Mesón de la Paella*, Calle 69, No. 12-14. French food at *La Reserva*, Calle 39 and Carrera 15, expensive (dinner for 2, US$30), good food and service in an old house with open fire. For Italian food, *Il Piccolo Café*, Carrera 15, No. 96-55, very good. *Longaniza*, Carrera 15, No. 92-73, very good for meat, with salad bar. For Chinese food, *Nanking*, Calle 23, between Carreras 6 and 7; and *Pagoda China* on Calle 69, Cra. 6. Japanese and Korean dishes at *Restaurant Arirang*. For excellent inexpensive Arab food, *Ramses*, Carrera 7, No. 18-64. For the traveller on a budget, *bandeja* (the local *plato del día*) can cost US$1.50- 2 for a 2-course meal at the right places. *Mi Ranchito*, Calle 21, No. 5-77, good cheap bar, drinks only. Good ice cream at *Yeti Helados*, Carrera 11 with Av. Chile. *El Fogón de la 5a*, Carrera 5 No. 14-24, rec. for good cheap fruit salad. On Sunday nights it is difficult to find anywhere open; try Calle 22 (the entertainment district).

All along Carrera 15 in El Chicó are shops, bars and restaurants, many of which have tables out on the pavement. *Pimm's*, Carrera 15, Calle 83; *Tony Roma's*, Carrera 15 esq. Calle 77 and Calle 93, No. 13-85, good quality food and excellent service. Also on Carrera 15, 85-42, interior 7, is *Academia de Golf* which has a good beef/fish and salad restaurant, as well as golf driving and putting ranges, and equipment for sale. *Quiebracanto*, 2 locations, Carrera 5 near Calle 16, and next to University of Los Andes, Calle 18 and Carrera 2, student places with recorded music, occasional films, talks, etc.; *Café Libre*, Carrera 15, near Universidad Católica, bar with live music, also serves lunches; *Café Oma*, Carrera 15, Calle 89/90, good food and coffee, nice atmosphere, open till 0100; *Café Omo Lago*, Carrera 15, No. 82-60. *Chicanos*, Carrera 11, No. 78-70, good value and quality (about US$15-20 for 2), excellent juices and cocktails; *Shamua*, Calle 85, No. 11-69, good cocktails, small selection of well prepared food, US style. Many small, popular bars and cafés around Calle 82, Carreras 12, 13, 14, frequented by young people, not cheap. For those visiting the Centro Administrativo Nacional (CAN, on Av. El Dorado near airport), a good restaurant nearby is *La Casa de Fernando*, Transversal 42, Diag. 40, No. 43-22; others nearby.

Tea Rooms Benalcázar, near Plaza de las Nieves on Carrera 8, No. 20-25, excellent pastries and quite all right for women alone; *La Suiza*, Calle 25, No. 9-41, excellent pastries. *Fábrica del Pan*, Av. Jiménez at Carrera 8, good for breakfasts, teas, snacks, reasonably priced. A chain of *Cyranos* throughout the city offers good pastries.

Clubs Anglo-American Club, Country Club (golf, polo, swimming), Magdalena Sports Club (tennis), San Andrés Golf Club, Club de Los Lagartos (social; with a pool heated by hot springs, water-skiing, a golf course and tennis courts), Club Campestre Fontanar (tennis), America Tennis Club, Lions' Club, Bogotá Sports Club (cricket, football, tennis, squash, rugby and hockey). Both the Lagartos and the Country Club have beautiful gardens designed by Enrique Acosta.

Shopping 10% value-added tax on all purchases. *Artesanías de Colombia* (state-owned), Almacén San Diego, in the old San Diego church, Cra. 10, No. 26-50, Almacén Las Aguas, next to the Iglesia de las Aguas, Carrera 3A, No. 18-60, has good selection of folk art and crafts, at fair prices. A good place for handicrafts is *El Lago*, Carrera 7, No. 16-81. Another good place is *El Balay* on Carrera 15, No. 75-63, rather expensive, and, of course, there is the shop in the Museo de Artes y Tradiciones Populares, which is recommended. *Artesanía* shop at Carrera 15, No. 83-30 often has cheap objects. *Lana Lana Cuero Cuero*, Cra. 15, No. 74-47, moderate prices. See *H. Stern's* jewellery stores at the International Airport, *Hilton Hotel* and *Tequendama Hotel*. A street market on Avenida Jiménez and Carrera 14 (Avenida Caracas) sells cheaper *ruanas*, blankets, leatherware, etc. Good *ruanas* can be bought at *Tipicentro*, Calle 17, No. 5-46 and No. 5-37, with better prices at the smaller shop although bargaining can bring them down a bit further. Shopping centre at Chapinero, Carrera 13, Calles 55-60, specializes in men's shoes and leather. Women's shoes are found on Calle 18 between Carrera 7 and 9. Boutiques are to be found in El Chicó on Carrera 15, Calles 76-100. Permanent crafts markets at Calle 100, Carrera 15 and Carrera 7 opp. *Hotel Tequendama*. There is another market, at Christmastime only, which is good for handicrafts, at Carrera 10, Calle 10. Another seasonal market is held at Carrera 7 and Calle 72. High-quality leather goods on Calle 18, between Carreras 4 and 7, also at *Todo en Cuero*, Calle 19, No. 6-56, next to the Museo de Oro Calle 16 Carrera 64, and Carrera 10, between Calles 13 and 19. Also the *Boots and Bags* and *Pecarí* chains for high-quality leather. *Galería Cano*, Edificio Bavaria, Carrera 7, Bogotá Hilton, Unicentro, Loc. 218, Airport, sells gold and gold-plated replicas of some of the jewellery on display in the Gold Museum. *Mitus* (in *Hotel Tequendama*) also sells reproduction jewellery from its own workshop, and Indian pottery. *Galería 70*, Avenida 13, No. 70-14, exhibition of and shop selling hand-woven textiles and rugs. For hammocks, try Pasaje Rivas, Carrera 10, No. 10-54, big choice, good quality, bargain prices. Primitive paintings are often on show in the *Galería El Callejón*, Calle 16, No. 6-34, as well as old maps and prints. Banco de Fotografías Movifoto, Calle 15, No. 4-66, has a very large selection of postcards from all over Colombia. There are several antique shops around Calle 66 and Carrera 11; check yellow pages for precise addresses. Antiques also at *Hijos de Antonio Cancino* on Plaza Bolívar.

The pavements and cafés along Av. Jiménez, below Carrera 7, Parque de los Periodistas, and Calle 16 and Carrera 3, are used on weekdays by emerald dealers. Great care is needed in buying: bargains are to be had, but synthetics and forgeries abound. (Beware of stones that seem too perfect or have a bluish colouring.) Three shops selling good emeralds at reasonable prices are: *Joyería Frida*, Carrera 7, No. 18-31; *Willis F. Bronkie*, Carrera 9, No. 74-08, oficina 801; *Jewelry Prado*, Carrera 7, No. 16-50. Also *El Palacio de la Esmeralda*, Carrera 10, No. 26-7, Int. 126, reasonable prices, certificates given. Also jewellery shops in the basement of *Hotel Tequendama*, and on Calles 12 and 13, between Carreras 7 and 9. Modern textiles and knitwear can be bought at low prices at *Unicentro*, a large shopping centre on Carrera 15 at Calle 127A (take "Unicentro" bus from centre, going N on Cra. 10—takes about 1 hr.). *Cafam*, Av. 68 with Calle 72, is said to be cheaper than Unicentro. *Centro Granahorrar*, Av. Chile (Calle 72) between Carreras 10 and 11 is another good shopping centre; also *Metropolis*, Calle 68 y Carrera 68 (with *Exito* supermarket opposite), and *Boulevard Niza*, Av. Suba, Calle 11-127. *Técnica*, Carrera 7A, No. 16-13 (first floor) will put gold lettering on leather goods quickly and cheaply.

Bookshops *Librería Buchholz*, Carrera 7, No. 27-68 (opp. *Hotel Tequendama*), also at Calle 59, No. 13-13 (Chapinero); useful advice in a number of languages, low prices. *Librería Aldina*, Carrera 7, Calle 70-80, most helpful on books and Bogotá alike, excellent stock of English-language books, open 0930-1930, Sat. 0930-1700. *Librería Nacional*, Carrera 7, No. 17-51 (has small selection of English bestsellers). *Librería Francesa*, Calle 65, No. 9-07. *OMA* Cra 15, Calle 75, good art and literature books. *Librería Lerner*, Av. Jiménez, No. 4-35 (no English books). *Ateneo*, Calle 82, No. 13-19, in the north of the city, good selection of Colombian titles, knowledgeable staff; *Librería Tercer Mundo*, Carrera 7, No. 16-91, knowledgeable; *Librería Cultural Colombiana*, Calle 72, No. 16-15; *Casa de Libro*, Calle 18 between Cras. 7 and 6. Books in Colombia are generally expensive. Book Exchange Stalls, Calle 19, between Carreras 7 and 10. English novels secondhand at Carrera 10 y Calle 21.

Photography Cheap film for sale, e.g. Fuji 135-36 for US$2, and good quick developing at Foto Rapid, Calle 14 No. 6-05 (Plazoleta de Rosana). Developing film at the local Kodak laboratory was reported as of disappointing quality and not recommended in 1989.

Taxis have meters (although newer ones are reported not to have them); insist that they are used. Starting charge, US$0.35, plus US$0.07 for every 90 metres, minimum charge US$0.85. Additional charge of US$0.35 after 2000 and on public holidays and Sun. (a list of legal charges should be posted in the taxi).

Tan and green tourist taxis can be rented by the hour or the day through the *Tequendama Hotel*, most of the drivers speak English and are very helpful. Taxis are relatively cheap, so it is worthwhile taking one if you are carrying valuables, or at night. Taxi tours with Jaime Carvajal (Spanish spoken only), T 203-1063.

Travel in Bogotá Bus stops in centre by red and yellow "Paradero" boards; otherwise flag buses down. Bus fares are US$0.10, *busetas* charge US$0.15. Green buses with letters TSS (i.e. unsubsidized) cost US$0.12. There are some "super-executive" routes with plush seats and videos, at US$0.30-0.50 (if traffic is heavy you might see the whole film). Urban buses are not good for sightseeing because you will be standing as likely as not. A metro is planned.

Car Rental Dollar Rent-a-Car, airport and Cra. 13, 82-28; Hertz, at airport, and at Carrera 10, No. 26-35; National, Carrera 7, No. 33-27; Hernando Zuluaga & Cía, Carrera 7, No. 20-80; Aquilautos Ltda., Carrera 7, No. 34-81. Avis, Calle 79, 53-70, Cra 10, 27-79 and at airport.

Night Life Monserrate Room at the *Tequendama*; *Unicorn*, Calle 94, No. 7-75, expensive and spectacular; *Noches de Colombia*, show 2100-0030, typical dances and songs from various parts of the country, not dear; *Son de Grillos*, near bullring, intellectual salsa place; *La Teja Corrida*, also next to bullring, need to reserve table at weekends, good lively salsa; *Ramón Antigua*, rather quieter than Teja Corrida, but they dance on the tables at weekends; *San Líbero* bar, in Candelaria district, open till 0400, highly recommended; opposite San Líbero is *Goce Pagano*, also good. (Information from Angela.) Many popular bars and dancing places on Carrera 5 with Calle 25, entrance between US$2-3, relatively safe area.

Theatre Many of the theatres are in the Candelaria area. Colón Theatre details on **page 626**. The following are the equivalent of the British fringe theatre: La Candelaria, Calle 12, No. 2-59; Sala Seki Sano, Calle 12, No. 2-65; Teatro Libre de Bogotá, Calle 13, No. 2-44.

Cinema Cinemateca Distrital, Carrera 7 No. 22-79. Good films, US$0.85. Also on Carrera 7: Teatro Municipal, No. 22-53, Metro, No. 21-78, Tisquesa, No. 27-29. Av. Chile shopping centre cinema, Calle 71, between Carreras 11 and 13 (usually prize-winning films). Consult *El Tiempo* for what is on; frequent programme changes. Admission, US$0.70.

Sports Bull fighting on Sats. and Suns. during the season at the municipally owned Plaza de Santamaría, near Parque Independencia. (Local bullfight museum at bullring, door No. 6.) Boxing matches are held here too. Horse races at Hipódromo los Andes, on Autopista Norte, races at 1400 (entrance US$1 and US$0.35), and at the Hipódromo del Techo, in the SW, on Sats., Suns. and public holidays. Nearby is the Municipal Stadium, which can hold 50,000 spectators. Football matches are played here. See also under **Clubs** above.

Football Tickets for matches at El Camplin stadium can be bought in advance at *Cigarrería Bucana*, Calle 18, No. 5-92. But not normally necessary to book in advance, except for local Santa Fe-Millionarios derby. Take a cushion; matches Sun. at 1545, Weds. at 2000.

Museums (all closed on Mondays) The **National Museum**, on Carrera 7, No. 28-66, the Panóptico, an old prison converted into a Museum (to the NE of the map), founded by Santander in 1823. Its top floor houses a fine art section, comprising national paintings and sculptures. Open Tues.-Sat. 0930-1830, Sun. 1000-1700, US$0.55. Many of its pre-conquest exhibits have been transferred to the **Archaeological Museum** at Carrera 6, No. 7-43, see below. See map: 8 for **Museum of Colonial Art**, under 1 for **Museo 20 de Julio** and 11 for the Banco de la República's Luis Angel Arango library.

The **Museum of Modern Art**, Calle 24, No. 6-55, entry US$0.28 (open Tues.-Sun. 0900-1900). It has a programme of films. The **Planetarium** and **Natural History Museum**, Calle 26 with Carrera 7, open Tues.-Fri. 0900-1800, Sat., Sun., and holidays, 1000-1800 (see map, no. 24).

The **Museo Mercedes de Pérez**, formerly the Hacienda de El Chicó, a fine example of colonial architecture, is at Carrera 7, No. 94-17. It contains a world-wide collection of mostly 18th century porcelain, furniture, paintings, etc. Open Tues.-Sun., 0930-1230, 1430-1700.

The **Museum of Popular Art and Tradition** is at Carrera 8, No. 7-21 in an old monastery and exhibits local arts and crafts. It has a shop, selling handicrafts at higher prices than Artesanías de Colombia, and a reasonably-priced bar and restaurant (dishes typical of different regions of Colombia served in colonial setting, usually with regional traditional music). Open 0900-1730, Tues.-Sat., Sun. and holidays 1000-1400. The shop is not open on Sun. and holidays. Entry fee US$0.25.

Museo Siglo XIX, Carrera 8, No. 7-91, founded by the Banco Cafetero, has a collection of 19th-century painting, clothes and furniture. Open Mon.-Fri., 0900-1800, Sat., 1300-1700. US$0.28.

The **Museo Arqueológico** (belonging to the Banco Popular) is a fine and extensive collection of precolumbian pottery, assembled in the restored mansion cf the Marqués de San Jorge, Carrera 6, No. 7-43. The house itself is a beautiful example of 17th century Spanish colonial architecture. US$0.60 entry. Open: 1000-1700, Tues. to Fri.; 1000-1300, Sat.-Sun. There is a restaurant.

Museum of Urban Development, Calle 10 No. 4-21 (open Tues.-Sat., 0900-1800, Sun. and holidays, 1000-1800), interesting maps and photos of the development of Bogotá in an attractive colonial house near the Palacio San Carlos.

Military Museum, Calle 10, No. 4-92, history of Colombian armed forces and good collection of weapons.

Quinta de Bolívar (Simon Bolívar museum), Calle 20, No. 3-23 Este, open Tues.-Sun., 1000-1700, his residence in Bogotá with documents, period rooms, nice garden.

Casa-Museo Jorge Eliécer Gaitán, Calle 42, No.15-52, is former residence of the populist leader whose assassination in April 1948 triggered the infamous "Bogotazo", at the outset of La Violencia.

Instituto Nacional de Investigaciones Geológico-Mineras has a library and pleasant museum at Diagonal 53, No. 34-53. Entrance US$0.10.

Museo de los Niños, Carrera 48, No. 63-97, natural sciences explained for children, created by Sra. Ximena Rosas with funding from industry.

Museo del Oro (the Gold Museum), is in splendid premises at the Parque de Santander (corner of Calle 16 and Carrera 6-A, see No. 18 on map). This collection is a "must", for it is unique. No less than 30,000 pieces of precolumbian gold work are shown. Open: Tues. to Sat., 0900-1600; Sun. and holidays, 0900-1200. (People in shorts not allowed). Charge, US$0.60 (US$0.10 on Sat., US$0.35 for children). Do not miss seeing the collections kept in a huge strong-room on the top floor. Several film shows a day; at 1200 and 1530 they are in English.

The ancient gold objects discovered in Colombia were not made by the primitive technique of simple hammering alone, but show the use of virtually every technique known to modern goldsmiths.

The **Universidad Nacional** (about 13,000 students) is off our map, to the NW. The fine buildings are coated with political graffiti, and foreigners are not usually welcome on the campus. The oldest centres of learning are in the old centre: oldest of all is the Colegio Nacional de San Bartolomé (C 10, No. 6-57), in the same block as the Chapel of El Sagrario (3 on map), founded 1573. The second oldest, founded on December 18, 1653, is the Colegio Mayor de Nuestra Señora del Rosario (C 14, No. 6-25); its beautiful colonial building is well worth a look.

Banks Banco de la República, the only bank permitted to exchange travellers' cheques in denominations of less than US$50 (up to 1500 Mon.-Thurs., to 1630 Fri., no commission charged), will give cash on American Express card, but not Visa, which is accepted at most other banks; leave plenty of time. Banco Anglo Colombiano, Carrera 8, No. 15-60, and eleven local agencies. Banco Royal de Colombia, Av. Jiménez with Carrera 8, will change cheques for US$50 but charges commission; Banco Internacional de Colombia; Banco Francés e Italiano de Colombia; Banco Franco Colombiano, and other Colombian banks. Open 0900-1500 Mon. to Thurs. and 0900-1530 on Fri. Closed on Sat.; also closed at 1200 on last working day of month.

Exchange American Express, Tierra Mar Aire Ltda, edif. Bavaria Torre B, Local 126, Carrera 10, No. 27-91, T 283-2955, Telex 41424 BOGCL. International Money Exchange, Carrera 7, No. 32-29, open till 1600 on Sats., check all transactions carefully; exchange at Av. 19, No. 15-35. Exprinter on Av. Jiménez and Carrera 6. Inside you can only get pesos and no travellers' cheques are exchanged, but the black market operates on the pavement outside, or try the kiosk right there, Peruvian and Ecuadorean currencies available (rates generally little different from official rates). Check the rate first, though, and if you use it, be extremely careful. Normally, the best rates you will get are at the Banco de la República.

Cultural Institutions British Council, Calle 87, No. 12-79, T 236-25-42/257-96-32. Has a good library and British newspapers. Anglo-Colombian School, Transversal 30, No. 152-38. Postal address: Apartado Aéreo 52969, Bogotá 2. English School, Calle 170, No. 31-98 (T 254-1318 or 254-8874), Apartado Aéreo 51284, Bogotá. American School, Colegio Nueva Granada, Carrera 2E, No. 70-20, T 212-35-11. Centro Colombo Americano, Calle 109A, No. 17-10, T 2144960, Spanish courses, rec.

Embassies and Consulates Venezuelan Consulate, Avenida 13, No. 103-16, T 256-3015, hrs. of business 0900-1230, 1300-1500, visa free, but allow 3 days (if they don't merely send you to Cúcuta for all paperwork). **Panamanian Consulate**, Calle 87, No. 11A-64, T 236-7531; Mon.-Fri., 0900-1300 (take "Usaquén" bus going north from centre, US$0.15). **Costa Rican Consulate**, Carrera 15, No. 80-87, Mon.-Fri. 0900-1300. **Guatemalan Consulate**, Transversal 29A, Calle 139A, No. 41, T 2745365, Mon.-Fri., 0900-1200, visa takes 48 hrs., US$10 (cash only), one photo, one airline ticket (does not have to be return), tourist visa free for Canadians; takes 48 hours. **Mexican Consulate**, Calle 99, No. 12-08, Mon.-Fri., 0900-1300. **Bolivian Embassy**, Calle 78, No. 9-57, T 2118962.

U.S. **Embassy**, Calle 38, No. 8-61 (mailing address: Apartado Aéreo 3831, Bogotá 1, D.E.), T 285-1300/1688. **Canadian Embassy**, Calle 76, No. 11-52; T 217-5555, open 0800-1630 (mailing address: Apartado Aéreo 53531, Bogotá 2, D.E.).

British Embassy, Calle 98, No. 9-03, 4th floor, T 218-5111, postal address: Apartado Aéreo 4508. **W. German Embassy**, Carrera 4, No. 72-36, 6th floor, T 212-0511. **French Embassy**, Avenida 39, No. 7-94. **French Consulate**, Carrera 7, No. 38-91, T 285-4311. **Finnish Embassy**, Calle 72 No 8-56, 7th floor, T 212-6111. **Norwegian Consulate**, Carrera 13, No. 50-78, Oficina 506, T 235-5419. **Swedish Embassy**, Calle 72 No. 5-83, T 255-3777. **Danish Embassy**, Calle 37, No. 7-43, 9°, Bogotá 2, T 232-6753/93. **Swiss Embassy**, Carrera 9, No. 74-08, oficina 1101, T 255-3945, open Mon.-Fri. 0900-1200. **Israeli Embassy**, Edificio Caxdac, Calle 35, No. 7-25, piso 14, T 2877783/808/962.

DAS Immigration office, Carrera 28, No. 17A-00, open 0730-1530, T 277-9211.

Laundry La Solución No. 2, Carrera 5, 21-84, 0800-1200, 1400-1900, US$0.75 for 1 kg. Piccadilly, Calle 63, No. 7-10; Auto Servicio Burbujas, Edificio Procoil, Avenida 19, No. 3A-37, open Mon.-Sat. 0730-1930. Panorama, Carrera 7, Calle 67. Drycleaners: *Lavaseco*, Av. Jiménez, No. 4-30.

Sauna Los Andes, Carrera 4, No. 16-29, good service, US$3.20, open daily 1000-2200. Sauna San Diego, Carrera 7 near Calle 25, turkish bath and sauna US$2.50 to enter, US$2.50 massage, rec.

Health Cruz Roja Nacional, Avenida 68, No. 66-31, T 250-661/231-9027/231-9008, open 0830-1800. Centro Médico La Salud, Carrera 10, No. 21-36, 2nd floor, T 243-13-81/282-40-21. Clínica Bogotá, Carrera 17, No. 12-65 (not a safe area to walk in), discourages travellers from having gamma-globulin shots for hepatitis. Walter Röthlisberger y Cía Ltda., Calle 25A, No. 13A-28, T 2836200, imports medicines, including Vivotif for typhoid and gamma globulin, and stores them correctly; trade prices. The US Embassy will advise on doctors, dentists, etc. Profamilia, Calle 34, No. 14-46, for contraceptives. For health information, T 15; emergency medical service (TAS), T 277-6666. Clínica Marly and Clínica del Country are well-equipped private hospitals. Dr. Arturo Corchuelo at Calle 89, No. 12-21, T 2188710, recommended for orthopaedic problems.

Postal Services Main airmail office and foreign *poste restante* in basement of Edificio Avianca, Carrera 7, No. 16-36, open 0700-2200 Mon. to Sat. closed Sun., and holidays (0830-1200, 1530-1700, Mon. to Fri. for *poste restante*, letters kept for only a month). At weekend the Post Office only franks letters; stamps for postcards are not sold. Pharmacies and newsagents in Bogotá have an airmail collection. Parcel post, Calle 13 and Carrera 8, US$1.50 to US$4 per kilo to overseas destinations.

International Telephone Calls from several Telecom offices in centre of Bogotá (e.g. Calle 23, No. 13-49); all close 2000.

Travel Agents recommended: *Lands of Colombia*, Carrera 16, No. 72A-16, friendly (helpful, English-spoken). *Tierra Mar Aire*, Cra. 10, No. 27-91, is Amex agent; does city tours from *Hotel Tequendama* (T 286-1111). Similar tours of the City (4 hrs.) can be arranged from *Hotel Nueva Granada*, much better value than tours to Zipaquirá (each costs about US$14). *Viajes Don Quijote*, Carrera 10 No. 27-51, also organizes tours of the city, 3½ hrs. by day, and 4 hours by night in a country-type bus (*chiva*) with musicians on the back seat. *Expedición Colombia*, Edificio KLM, piso 9, Calle 26, No. 4A-45, T 284-8284/8456, runs tours to the Llanos by private, chartered plane.

Tourist Offices Corporación Nacional de Turismo (CNT), Calle 28, No. 13A-15, T 283-9466, Edificio Centro de Comercio Internacional (the name at the top of the building is Banco Cafetero) T 283-9466 (Mon.-Fri., 0900-1300, 1400-1700, and Sat. 0900-1200, take passport); they will tell you which parts of the country are unsafe, good maps of major cities available; at Eldorado Airport and new bus terminal (both helpful, will book hotel rooms). Municipal tourist office, *Alcadia* offices on Plaza Bolívar (Carrera 8, No. 10-65, 1st floor, S side of Plaza), and Carrera 35, No. 26-18 (Edif. Lotería de Bogotá). The Coordinadora de Turismo de Bogotá (Carrera 13, No. 27-95) has daily tours of the city with interpreters. For information on 24-hr. chemists (pharmacies), events, attractions, etc., T 282-0000.

Inderena, the National Parks Office, is on Diagonal 34, No. 5-84, T 2851172, for information and permission to visit the parks (very helpful), some permissions may take a day or two. Good maps of Bogotá and road maps of Colombia can be purchased in the drugstore nearest the main road in the *Hotel Tequendama* arcade. Hiking **maps** from Instituto Geográfico, Agustín Codazzi, Carrera 30 y Calle 45, US$0.75 each (topographical details are generally accurate, but trails and minor roads less so). Esso road maps from service stations, US$0.40.

Thefts Most hotels charge US$0.10 a night for insurance against theft. If you have something stolen go to the Corporación Nacional del Turismo for help and collect the insurance; this will probably take a few days of strenuous effort, but it has been known to work.

Airport The airport at El Dorado has the world's second largest landing field. "Tourist Guide" policemen have white armbands. The taxi fare from airport to city is usually about US$4 (30% more at night and early a.m.). There are colectivos (US$0.30 plus luggage p.p.) from airport to centre; also buses, US$0.10. In the city centre buses and colectivos leave from Calle 19, between Carreras 3 and 10, then turning right down Carrera 10 to airport; buses marked "Aeropuerto" or "Universitaria Dorado"; colectivos marked "Aeropuerto". Make sure you get a registered taxi, where a policeman notes the numbers and gives you a paper stating fares, found at left (from inside) side of main terminal or Avianca terminal (drivers try to overcharge all the same). Unofficial taxis not advisable. Watch belongings outside airport, especially at night. Airport shops are beautiful, and there is a restaurant. Free Colombian coffee inside the customs area, between gates 2 and 3. Many snack bars and restaurants on first floor. There are luggage lockers at the airport. Hotel reservations can be made at the airport but their hotel rates are often out of date. The cheapest is in our Category D. Exchange rates are marginally lower than in the city, but pesos cannot be changed back into dollars at the airport without receipts. Airport bank may not change travellers' cheques. N.B. If flying from Colombia to Mexico and you do not need an exit ticket from Mexico, you may have difficulty persuading Avianca staff otherwise.

For internal flights, which serve all parts of the country, **see page** 715. For domestic shuttle flights to Medellín/Montería, Cali/Pasto, and Barranquilla, go to Puente Aéreo terminal, 1 km. before main terminal on Av. El Dorado. To Leticia, 1¾ hrs.; to Medellín; to Cúcuta US$45. 45 mins.; to Cali, 40 mins. Avianca international flights also use this terminal (usually Miami and New York). It is more comfortable but there is not as much duty-free shopping (there is a 100 pesos tax payable at this terminal). You have to cross eight busy lanes of traffic to get a bus into town, and negotiate two drainage ditches. As a rule, all flights are overbooked, so book well in advance. The Avianca office is at Carrera 7, No. 16-36, T 266-97-00. Satena, Avenida 19, 13A-18, T 283-55-57/282-55-57, military airline, best for comfort and delays. SAM office is in the shopping arcade next to *Tequendama Hotel*. Many international airline offices are closed on Sat. and Sun. **See page** 715 for procedure to obtain refunds on unused tickets.

Rail Although there are 3,700 km. of railways (metre gauge) in Colombia, the only long-distance route carrying passengers from Bogotá is to Santa Marta, called the Tayrona, which runs once a week, only between December and March. For the rest of the year you must go to La Dorada to take the Expreso del Sol train to Santa Marta, and that only goes twice a week. Luggage is checked into locked compartments, so you need to have light clothing available before journey starts. Sit on right to avoid afternoon sun. Station is at Calle 13 and Carrera 20. "Germania" bus goes from railway station to the city centre. Special excursions on steam trains go to Zipaquirá and Nemocón, Sat. and Sun., 0900, returning 1800, US$6 return (details under Nemocón **page** 637) to Facatativá each Sun. and holiday, US$2.50 return; to Parque Duque, a pleasure park on the road to Tunja, Sun. and holidays, US$3 return, leave 1000, return 1830.

Buses There is a long-distance bus terminal on Av. Boyacá between El Dorado (Av. 26) and Av. Centenario (Calle 13). There is also access from Carrera 68. To get to the terminal take bus marked "Terminal" from "Terminal Transportes" bus stop at corner of Av. Jiménez de Quesada and Cra. 15, or colectivo taxi from Av. 13 y Av. Caracas, US$0.35 (this is the only method in the evening, no buses). To get into town take Route No. 1 or No. 3 at the terminal and get off at Carrera 13 esq. Calle 13, closest to the centre (from this junction "Germania" bus goes to the centre). A *buseta* (US$0.05) runs from Carrera 68 to the terminal and back. Taxi US$2.50 (plus US$0.15 at night—could give price slip; avoid the unofficial taxis, normally touting for particular hotels), or take colectivo from beside Ruta 3 bus stop, US$0.30. The terminal is well-organized, comfortable and safe; free self-service luggage trolleys are provided. There are shops and restaurants. There are showers at the terminal (between Nos.

3 and 4), US$0.40, soap and towel provided. Companies are grouped according to routes. Buses to: Cali, 12 hrs., about US$10; Medellín, 12 hrs., on new autopista (often washed out), US$13; Manizales, 8-9 hrs., US$7-8.50; Honda, 4 hrs., US$3; Tunja, 2½ hrs., US$3; Villa de Leiva, US$3.50; La Dorada, 5 hrs., US$4; Popayán, 16 hrs., US$15; Florencia, US$19.50; Neiva, 5 hrs., US$5.50; Girardot, US$2.70; to Sogamoso, US$4, 4 hrs. (US$5 by executive minibus, 3 hrs.); Bucaramanga, 10-11 hrs., US$9; Cúcuta, 18 hrs., US$15 (the daily service by Berlinas del Fonce, 2 stops, 1600, rec., US$2 extra for *cochecama*); Cartagena, 23-28 hrs., US$23; Santa Marta US$20, 4 a day, 22 hrs., check if bus is going to Santa Marta, those continuing to Barranquilla may drop you short of town; direct bus to Barranquilla, US$20 also; Pereira, 9-10 hrs., US$6.50, via Girardot, Espinal, Ibagué, Cajamarca, Armenia (fly if you wish to avoid the Quindío pass, 25 mins.); San Agustín, 12 hrs., US$10, only Coomotor, 4 daily, not a good service; Villavicencio, 4 hrs., US$2.75; Ipiales, 24 hrs., US$20, only gets crowded at Cali (the bus stops for an hour in Cali; it leaves from a different level of the terminal from that on which it arrived—don't lose your bus!); Pasto, 23 hrs., US$19.50. Velotax busetas are slightly quicker and more expensive, as are colectivos, which go to several long-distance destinations. For an early morning start to Neiva (approx. hourly), Pitalito (0730 and 1030) and San Agustín take Taxis Verdes who will pick you up at your hotel. Buses can be caught along Av. Caracas, north of Calle 26, and can be stopped at street corners for: Zipaquirá, 1¼ hrs., US$0.45; Guatavita, 2-3 hrs., US$1.25; Chía, US$0.30.

Bus to Venezuela It is better not to buy a through ticket to Caracas with Exp. Berlinas as this does not guarantee a seat and is only valid for 2 Venezuelan companies; moreover no refunds are given in Cúcuta. Sometimes the border with Venezuela is closed because of illegal immigration; in this case, tickets can be refunded in Bogotá. Ideally, if you have time make the journey to Cúcuta in two stages to enjoy the scenery to the full. Bus connections from San Antonio de Táchira in Venezuela to Caracas are good.

Excursions from Bogotá

If you have a car, drive round the Av. Circunvalación for splendid views. The salt mines of Zipaquirá are described on **page 637**. Other excursions are to the beautiful artificial lake of Muña, formed by a dam; to **Sopó**, in the Sabana (63 km.), where they venerate an image of the Saviour which has appeared in an eroded stone; the paintings of angels in the church are very strange and worth seeing (ask at the Casa Cural for entry to church—give a tip); in Sopó a restaurant (previously *Nicolás*) serves good local dishes. Nearby are the Alpina yoghurt factory (no free samples) with another restaurant, *La Embarrada*, opposite, which specializes in cooking meat in clay dishes on coals; Parque Puerto de Sopó (with artificial lake) at km. 32.5 on Autopista Norte, and an amusement park a few km. N. For the Falls of Tequendama, **see page below**. For Tunja (2 hrs. over first-class road), and Guatavita Nueva, **see page 639**. Bogotanos like to warm up at weekends: popular destinations are Melgar (**see below**) and Girardot (**page 680**). About half-way to Girardot, near Fusagasugá (**see below**) is *Hotel Miramonti*, C, Italian-run family place, very quiet. To the east of Bogotá is **Choachí**, an attractive village set in a valley, where there are hot springs (good food at *El Colonial*, 1½ blocks from main square). Flota Macarena bus, Av. 17, No. 23-96, T 277-3900, several a day. A turnoff from the Choachí road brings one to the Santuario de San Francisco, with better views of Bogotá than one can get from Monserrate.

Hiking "Salsipuedes" is a hiking group based in Bogotá, hiking 15-40 km. every Saturday on trails in Cundinamarca; a very friendly group which welcomes visitors. Contact Alfonso Gamboa, Diagonal 123, No. 50-30, Bogotá, T 2839980 office, 2536228 home.

Longer excursions are taken in four main directions, which are dealt with in the following pages. They are to the south-west (Fusagasugá, Melgar), the north-west (Facatativá, Guaduas, Villeta), the north (Chía, Zipaquirá) and the north-east (along the Cúcuta road). A fifth direction, east to the Llanos, will be dealt with separately.

South-West: The Simón Bolívar Highway runs from Bogotá to Girardot (**see page 680**); this 132-km. stretch is extremely picturesque, running down the mountains within 5 km. of the Salto de Tequendama.

At the **Salto de Tequendama**, the water of the Río Bogotá or Funza falls 132 metres over the lip of the Sabana; the water is dirty with sewage but the falls are still a spectacular sight though the smell can be most unpleasant. The site is 31 km. from Bogotá in an amphitheatre of forest-clad hill sloping to the edge of a rock-walled gorge. There is a good bus service from Bogotá.

After the Tequendama Falls turning is **Fusagasugá** which lies in a rich wooded valley famous for its fruits. A few kilometres beyond is the *Hotel Catama*. Fusagasugá is noted for its good climate and Sunday market. Population: 22,460, with an admixture of the wealthier families from Bogotá during the summer. A visit should be paid to the Jardín Luxemburgo for its splendid orchids, best flowering Nov.-Feb. but it is a long walk out of town; the Jardín Clarisa for orchids, and that at the Casa de la Cultura are pleasant. There are bathing spots on the Sumapaz river. Altitude: 1,740 metres. From Bogotá, Autos Fusa (Carrera 22, No. 14-27) and Cootransfusa (Carrera 14, Calle 10), US$1.

Hotels *La Scala*, F, rec.; *Castillo*, E, rec. There are many luxury hotels on the road to Melgar.

From Fusagasugá, a bumpy 1½ hr. bus ride will take you to **San Bernardo**, a pretty little town. The cemetery has a macabre attraction; looking through a window near the central "altar" you see mummified figures, including a woman and child, assembled in the dimly lit cellar.

From Boquerón, beyond Fusagasugá, a side road goes about 10 km. to **Pandi** where there is a park with ancient stones. Nearby, on the road to Incononzu, is a famous natural bridge in a spectacular and very deep gorge through which runs the Sumapaz river.

Melgar, near Girardot, is a popular weekending place for Bogotanos who like a little warmth. There are lots of hotels in the area most of which have swimming pools; it is best to try whichever you like the look of and move on to another if it is full; the *Esmeralda, Plaza Crillón* (D) and *Nuevo Guadaira* have been recommended; there are also camping sites and the state-subsidized Cafam vacation centre, best visited in mid-week. Toll at 14 km. S of Fusagasugá, US$0.50, and 20 km. S of Bogotá, US$0.40.

Between Bogotá and Melgar are 2 youth hostels: *Centro Vacacional Los Guaduales* at Chinauta (Km. 68), and *Parador Camping El Laurel* at Silvania. Details from Alcom; see under Bogotá.

North-West: The Sabana of Bogotá is dotted with white farms and groves of eucalyptus. The road passes through two small towns, Fontibón and Madrid. **Fontibón**, 10 km. from Bogotá, has a good colonial church, and about 3 km. outside the town are stones with Indian pictographs; nearby, on the road from the old Techo airport to Bogotá, there are replicas of San Agustín statues.

Facatativá, a town of 22,460 people, is 40 km. from Bogotá. Some 3 km. from Facatativá, on the road to the W, is the Piedras de Tunja, a natural rock amphitheatre of enormous stones; it has numerous Indian pictographs and has now been established as a park with an artificial lake. A road goes SW from Facatativá through Tocaima to Girardot. From **Tocaima**, a small, attractive holiday town (several hotels; *Bella Vista*, D, clean, friendly, good simple food, swimming pool, no hot water), a road runs through beautiful mountain country, via La Mesa, to Mosquera on the road between Madrid and Fontibón. This is a good alternative to the Simón Bolívar highway from Girardot to Bogotá.

71 km. from Facatativá is **Villeta** (9,700 inhabitants), which has become a popular weekend resort for the Bogotanos. Not far away are the waterfalls of Quebrada Cune. Hotels: *Pacífico* and *Mediterráneo* (both have swimming pools and are expensive); less expensive is the *Colonial Plaza*, Carrera 4, No. 6-07 (corner of main square), good restaurant, with swimmimg pool, pleasant. Nearby is *Llamarade* restaurant, good value; many good ice cream parlours around the

square. The road continues to Honda (**see page 678**).

Midway between Villeta and Honda is **Guaduas**; in the main square is a statue of the liberator Policarpa Sala Varrieta. Also in the main square is a delightful colonial hotel. Public swimming pool in town. There is a Sunday market. Best local dish is *quesillos*. Bus to Honda, US$1.20, 1 hr. The surrounding countryside is beautiful, including waterfalls at Versalles (10 km.). Hotel: *Tacuara*, swimming pool, riding, *cabañas*, B; *Cacique*, 1 km. outside village, and *Real Agrada*, in resort area.

North: An interesting trip from Bogotá can be made to the salt mine of Zipaquirá and to the large centre of population around Chiquinquirá. Bogotá is left by an *autopista*, a northern extension of Avenida Caracas and Carrera 13. The *autopista* ends after 24 km. at an intersection where a road leads off left at a right-angle for Chía and Zipaquirá. Taking this road you soon come to a fork which takes you left to Chía and right to Zipaquirá. At the beginning of the road to Zipaquirá is the *Restaurant Arrieros*, where *antioqueño* food is served by waiters in the appropriate dress and *antioqueño* music is sometimes played.

Chía has a graceful colonial bridge and a typical Sunday market. Near Chía is Terijo, whose metalworks is famous. On the way there you pass through Fonqueta, where tapestries are made. Walk, or take a bus to La Barbanera church on a hill overlooking the *sabana* of Bogotá. Good restaurant just outside Chía, *Andrés Carne de Res*.

From Chía (via Cájica, 22,000 pop., pleasant town with good shopping) to **Zipaquirá** (40,850 people), centre of a rich cattle farming district, and famous for its rock salt mine, which has enough salt to last the world 100 years, though it has been exploited for centuries. The church in the attractive central Plaza is also worth a visit for its stonework (despite its external appearance, it has a modern interior).

The immense black galleries of salt gleaming under electric lights are most impressive and a little eerie. A road has been opened into the galleries but because of damage cars are no longer allowed to drive in. You can walk its whole length in 15 mins. An underground cathedral dedicated in 1954 to Our Lady of the Rosary (patron saint of miners) is about 4 mins. on foot from the entrance and very impressive. The roof is 23 metres above the floor and the main altar table is a block of salt weighing 18 tons. It took ten years to complete. To photograph the interior you need a strong flash *and* a fast film. Entry (adults US$0.75, children US$0.37, open Tues.-Sun. 1000-1600) is on a hill, which is a 20 mins. walk from the Plaza. Many buses from Avenida Caracas, Bogotá, US$0.45 each way, 1¼ hours. The Zipaquirá bus station is 15 minutes' walk from the mines and cathedral. Tours are also arranged by some of the Bogotá hotels and cost about US$15. Zipaquirá can also be reached from Tunja (**see page 639**), by taking a Bogotá-bound bus and getting off at Alcaro for connection to Zipaquirá, US$2. Leave plenty of time for the return journey as it can be difficult to stop Bogotá-Tunja buses at Alcaro. Minibus Zipaquirá- Chiquinquirá, US$2.75, 2 hrs.

The *Hostería del Libertador*, near the mine, good food, but no longer a hotel. *Hotel Colonial*, E, without bath, clean and friendly. Restaurants on main square, *El Mesón del Zipa*, good, cheap food, US$1.50-2.00; *Los Pijaos*, pleasant.

Not far from Zipaquirá, at **Nemocón**, there are salt mines and a church, but the mines are sometimes closed to visitors, following accidents. A side (dirt) road connects with the Bogotá-Cúcuta highway.

A steam-hauled *tren turístico* on Saturday and Sunday at 0900 from the main station in Bogotá, calling at a halt at Calle 100 and Carrera 15 at 0927, going to Zipaquirá and Nemocón: 2 hrs. 20 mins. to Zipaquirá, 2 hrs. 45 mins. to Nemocón, where the train is met by the town band. At Nemocón there is time to have lunch and look around before train returns, leaving at 1510, back in Bogotá at 1800. Tickets in Bogotá from Tierra Mar Aire travel agency. You are advised to book in advance. Restaurant in Nemocón, *El Colonial*, 100 metres from the station.

Ubaté is 48 km. by road to the N. On Sunday, the market in the big plaza has nothing of interest for the tourist. It is the cheese-making centre of the Sabana; the church is being refurbished. Here a branch road runs E to Lenguazaque (6,125 people). Close by, at Chirbaneque, is a worked-out emerald mine in lovely scenery. A spur from this road branches left to Guachetá, 21 km. from Ubaté, and slightly larger than Lenguazaque. Nearby is the Laguna de Fúquene (Devil's Lake, hotel), about 4,850 hectares of water with four cultivated islands.

Chiquinquirá, 50,000 people, 134 km. by road from Bogotá, is on the W bank of the Suárez river at 2,550 metres. It is a busy commercial centre and the focus of a large coffee and cattle region. In December thousands of pilgrims honour a painting of the Virgin whose fading colours were restored by the prayers of a woman. In 1816, when the town had enjoyed six years of independence and was besieged by the Royalists, this painting was carried through the streets by Dominican priests from the famous monastery, to rally the people. The town fell, all the same.

Hotels *Moyba*, Carrera 9, No. 17-53, facing square, F, with bath (cheaper without); *Residencias San Martín*, Carrera 9, No. 19-84, F, basic; *Residencias Viajero*, G, opposite Banco de Colombia, good, cheap meals. Many others.

Restaurant *El Escorial*, good but expensive.

In the shops of Chiquinquirá are displayed the toys made by local Indians: some ceramics painted in gay colours and others white and porous as they come from the kiln; tops and teetotums and other little things carved from tagua nuts; orange-wood balls to catch on a stick; the most durable tambourines in the world; shining, brightly coloured gourds; diminutive nine-stringed guitars on which children try the first measures of the *bambuca*; many scapularies; but better than anything else, the little pottery horses from Ráquira, or, by the same Indian craftsmen, little birds that whistle, hens with their chicks, and enchanting little couples dancing to an orchestra of guitars and mandolins.

Bus from Chiquinquirá to Villa de Leiva takes 1¾ hr., US$1.70 (**see page 640**). Bus to Tunja, 3 hrs., US$3.25; to Zipaquirá, US$2.75; to Bogotá, 2½ hrs., US$3 (last returns at 1730); all from bus station.

Excursion A road runs 105 km. SW to *Muzo*, on the banks of the Río Carare, 600 metres above sea-level. Population: 5,000. Sixteen km. away a famous open-cast emerald mine has been worked since 1567, and long before that by the Muzo tribe of Indians. In 1989 it was reported that police permission is needed to visit the mine, and it has become a dangerous area.

There are roads from Chiquinquirá to Tunja, the capital of the Department, and to Barbosa. Both are on the Bogotá-Cúcuta highway and are described below. On the Tunja road a short branch right at Tinjacá leads to *Ráquira*, where Indians make the pottery described above (sold in about 10 shops on the main street, including branch of Artesanías de Colombia). There's nowhere to stay, not much to eat. Market day Sunday. 30 minutes' walk along a very rough road is a beautiful 16th-century monastery, the Convento de la Candelaria, with anonymous 17th-century paintings of the life of St. Francis; they sell honey to finance the monastery. Also nearby are some waterfalls. The old colonial town of Villa de Leiva is also on this road. Ráquira is best reached from Tunja although there are direct buses from Bogotá (Rápido El Carmen, 0545, 0715, US$2.50, 6 hrs., returning 1300) on an appalling road. Last bus to Tunja 1330. If stuck after 1330, walk 5 km. to Tres Esquinas on Villa de Leiva-Chiquinquirá road (70 km.), where buses pass between 1530-1630, mostly going E.

BOGOTA TO CUCUTA (2)

A 618-km. road runs NE from Bogotá to Cúcuta, near the Venezuelan border, through Tunja, Moniquirá, Barbosa, Socorro, San Gil, Bucaramanga and Pamplona. It runs through some beautiful scenery, and is good most of the way. Toll points 10 km. N of Bogotá, US$0.40, and at La Cara, S of Tunja, US$0.40. The railway via Tunja to Duitama and Sogamoso is now for freight only. The road out of Bogotá is the *autopista* to near Chía (**see page 637**), then follow Tunja signs.

At Sesquilé you can take a minor road to the right, to Guatavita Nueva.

Guatavita Nueva This modern town, 75 km. from Bogotá, was built in colonial style when the old town of Guatavita was submerged by a hydroelectric reservoir. Although the blend of old and new is fascinating, Guatavita Nueva has failed as a social experiment. All the country folk have left and it is now a week-end haunt for Bogotanos and tourists. (During the week the town is empty.) Cathedral, artisan workshops, museum, and small bull-ring for apprentices to practise Sun. afternoons. Sun. market best in morning, before Bogotanos get there. Bus from Bogotá (Flota Valle de Tenza, Carrera 25, No. 15-72, recommended; Flota Aguila, Carrera 15 No. 14-59), US$1.25, 2-3 hrs., departures 0730, 0800 and 0930; last return bus at 1730. You can walk (or ride, US$7 per horse) from the town to the Laguna de Guatavita (also called Lago de Amor by locals), where the legend of El Dorado originated, but it is a long (2-3 hr.) walk. It is easier to approach the lake from a point on the Sesquilé-Guatavita Nueva road (the bus driver will let you off at the right place) where there is a sign offering "Alpina Yoghurt" and a kiosk. It is a 2 hr. walk along a dirt track from the main road to the lakeside. This track can be driven to the lakeside (in the dry season, in a good car); turn right near the barn with the red door, and right again opposite small lake. Beside the lake are houses of rich Bogotanos.

There are no hotels in Guatavita Nueva, although rooms are sometimes to be found.

The basis of the El Dorado (Gilded Man) story is established fact. It was the custom of the Chibcha king to be coated annually with resin, on which gold dust was stuck, and then to be taken out on the lake on a ceremonial raft. He then plunged into the lake and emerged with the resin and gold dust washed off. The lake was also the repository (as with the *cenotes* in Yucatán, Mexico) of precious objects thrown in as offerings; there have been several attempts to drain it (the first, by the Spaniards in colonial times, was the origin of the sharp cut in the surrounding hills) and many items have been recovered over the years. The factual basis of the El Dorado story was confirmed by the discovery a few years ago of a miniature raft with ceremonial figures on it, made from gold wire, which is now one of the most prized treasures of the Museo de Oro in Bogotá. Part of the raft is missing; the story is that the gold from it is now reposing in one of the finder's teeth! (Read John Hemming's *The Search for El Dorado* on the subject.)

Beyond Chocontá (15,300 inhabitants), 88 km. from Bogotá, the route is across the western slopes of the Eastern Cordillera to Tunja, 137 km. from Bogotá.

Tunja, 180,000 inhabitants, capital of Boyacá Department, stands at 2,820 metres in an arid mountainous area. The climate is cold; mean temperature, 12°C. One of the oldest cities in Colombia, it was refounded as a Spanish city by Gonzalo Suárez Rendón in 1539. It was then the seat of the Zipa, one of the two Chibcha kings. The old city has been compared with Toledo, but the modern city is far less attractive. Of the many colonial buildings the most remarkable is the church of Santo Domingo, a masterpiece begun in 1594; the interior is covered with wood most richly carved. Another is the Santa Clara chapel (1580), now the hospital of San Rafael, with some fine wood carving. In Parque Bosque de la República is the adobe wall against which three martyrs of the Independence were shot in 1816. The Tourist Office in the Casa del Fundador (see below), on the main square, Plaza Bolívar, is helpful. Market open every day (good for *ruanas* and blankets). Bus from Bogotá, 2½-4½ hrs., US$3 (Duitama, Cotrans, and others). The bus station is a steep 500 metres from the city centre. Friday is market day.

The house of Don Juan de Vargas has been restored as a museum of colonial Tunja (0800-1200, 1300-1800). The Casa del Fundador Suárez Rendón, Plaza Bolívar, dates from 1540-43 and is one of the few extant mansions of a Spanish *conquistador* in Colombia; open as a museum (except Mon. and Tues.); see the unique series of plateresque paintings on the ceilings. The church of Santa Bárbara is full of colonial woodwork, and in the nearby parish house are some notable religious objects, including silk embroidery from the 18th century. Some houses still have colonial portals. There are some fine colonial buildings on Plaza Bolívar opposite the Cathedral. Also impressive is the church of San Ignacio.

The city formed an independent Junta in 1811, and Bolívar fought under its aegis during the campaign of the Magdalena in 1812. Six years later he fought the decisive battle of Boyacá, nearby (see below). For the Piedras de Tunja see under Facatativá **page** 636.

Hotels *Hostería San Carlos*, colonial style, good restaurant, highly rec.; *Pensión Suárez Rendón*, Plaza Bolívar (good food, D, friendly but basic); *Centenario*, hot water, good restaurant, D; *Res. Lord*, Calle 19, No. 10-64, F, small rooms but hot water, clean, friendly; *San Francisco*, Carrera 9, No. 18-90, on Plaza Bolívar, near cathedral, E, clean, friendly, check bill; **Don Camilo** on Plaza Bolívar, F, clean and friendly; **Príncipe**, F with hot water, small rooms but clean, near bus station, 5 mins. from Plaza Bolívar, rec.; **Americano**, on Carrera 9 near Plaza Bolívar, F, good. Fairly cheap is **Dux**, off the plaza, F, quaint, basic; **Conquistador** on the corner of Plaza Bolívar, F, has hot water, is safe and clean, but many rooms don't have outside windows; **Granada**, three blocks from Plaza Bolívar, basic, friendly. Area around bus station said not to be safe at night.

Restaurants Good cheap meal at **Bolo Club** and at **El Pasaje** through an archway leading off the Plaza opposite the cathedral; **La Fonda**, US$1.50 for a big meal; **San Ricardo**, Calle 19, No. 8-38, good; **Surtipan**, Calle 20, No. 12-58, good cakes and coffee; **Estar de Hunzahúa**, Calle 20, No. 11-20 (2nd floor), good food and value, rec.; **Bodegón de los Frayles**, beside the church of San Ignacio, one block from the Plaza Bolívar, rec. as friendly with good food. On Carrera 10, there is a restaurant in a converted Jesuit church.

Bank Banco de la República, Carrera 11, No. 18-12.

Excursions from Tunja The battle of Boyacá was fought about 16 km. south of Tunja, on the road to Bogotá. On the bridge at Boyacá is a large monument to Bolívar. Bolívar took Tunja on 6 August, 1819, and next day his troops, fortified by a British Legion, the only professional soldiers among them, fought the Spaniards on the banks of the swollen Río Boyacá. With the loss of only 13 killed and 53 wounded they captured 1,600 men and 39 officers. Only 50 men escaped, and when these told their tale in Bogotá the Viceroy Samao fled in such haste that he left behind him half a million pesos of the royal funds. There is now a huge modern restaurant overlooking the site.

On a hillside outside Tunja is the carved rock throne of the Chibcha king, the Zipa; ask for directions from the Tourist Office.

At **Paipa**, between Tunja and Duitama, there are municipal thermal baths, US$0.75, 30 mins. bus ride from Tunja, US$1. *Hotel Sochagota*, overlooking the lake, has a swimming pool fed by hot springs, C, cabins for hire, with 2 bedrooms, bathroom, log fires and private hot spring pools. Other places to stay include *Casona El Salitre* and *Panorama* (C, meals US$2.50, huge swimming pool, Turkish bath, sauna), *Cabañas El Portón*, *Hotels Victoria* and *La Posada*, *Posadero La Casona*, *Las Palmeras*, *Residencias Daza*, and *Minihotel Familiar* (all F p.p.). There are 7 restaurants: it's a popular centre for Colombians.

Villa de Leiva, an extremely pretty place, is reached by a branch road, left, at Arcabuco. (Toll at Arcabuco, US$0.40.) The drive affords some beautiful views and, at Km. 20 from Villa de Leiva, turn left for the **Iguaque National Park** (3 km.) run by Inderena, which is the site of interesting oak woods, flora, fauna and several lakes. There is a tourist centre with accommodation for 60 and a restaurant. There are guided paths and a marked trail to Lake Iguaque, a walk of 2½ hours. (Camping is allowed and safe.) The town dates back, like Tunja, to the early days of Spanish rule, but unlike Tunja, it has been declared a national monument so will not be modernised. The first president of Nueva Granada (**see page** 619), Miguel Venero de Leiva, lived in the town. There are two colonial houses which are worth a visit: the house in which Antonio Nariño lived (Carrera 9, No. 10-39, open Tues.-Sun. 0900-1230, 1400-1800)—he translated the *Rights of Man* into Spanish—and the building in which the first Convention of the United Provinces of New Granada was held. Also worth a visit is the restored birthplace of the independence hero Antonio Ricuarte. A palaeontological museum has been opened 15 mins. walk N of the town on Carrera 9. The shops in the plaza have an excellent selection of Colombian handicrafts, while the Saturday market, not yet geared to the tourist trade, still offers many bargains. On the Plaza Mayor is the Casa-Museo Luis Alberto Acuña, housing fascinating examples of Acuña's work (recommended, entry US$0.70, extra to take photographs). The Monasterio de las Carmelitas has one of the best museums of religious art in Colombia, open Sat. and Sun. 1400-1700.

The mountains around Villa de Leiva abound in fossils. 5 km. along the road to Chiquinquirá can be seen the complete fossil of a dinosaur now housed in a room, entry US$0.30, there are road signs to it, ask for *El Fósil* (open 0800-1200, 1300-1500); the children sell fossils and rough emeralds. 2 km. from El Fósil along this road is the turning for (1 km.) the archaeological site known as El Infiernito, where there are several huge carved stones believed to be giant phalli and a solar calendar. 3 km. after the Infiernito turning, and one hour by bus (one per day) from Villa de Leiva is the Monastery of Ecce-Homo (founded 1620), which is worth a visit. The road goes through the desert of La Candelaria, a beautiful, highly-eroded countryside. Note the rectangular cromlech with 24 menhirs. Tourist Office just N of main square (Carrera 9, No. 13-01) most helpful. The town tends to be full of visitors at weekends and bank holidays.

N.B. It is better not to visit Villa de Leiva on Mondays or Tuesdays as almost everything is closed. Also there are few services in Villa de Leiva, buy fuel etc. in Tunja. The houses are closed Monday-Friday out of season, but the trip is worth while just for the views. In any event, the town and surrounding hills are excellent for long, peaceful walks.

Hotels *El Molino la Mesopotamia,* Calle del Silencio, which used to be a colonial mill, very good, C, meals US$4, breakfast US$3, including all meals (US$12.50), 10% rebate for booking 10 days ahead (closed during the first weeks of January), home cooking, excellent food, beautiful gardens. *Mesón de la Plaza Mayor,* Calle 79, No. 10-11, C (B full board), beautifully restored *hospedaría,* owner, Mauricio Ordóñez, speaks English, helpful; *Los Llanitos,* 5 min. walk from main plaza, D, quiet, hot water, very friendly, good food; *El Marqués de San Jorge,* D, pleasant, on Calle 14, No. 9-20; *Hospedaje El Mesón de Los Virreyes,* Carrera 9, No. 14-51, D, with bath, good restaurant; *Cabaña Jequeneque,* opposite *La Mesopotamia,* D, with breakfast, open only at week-ends but rec. Unnamed *residencia* on Plaza Bolívar (the only one), F, hot water, pretty. *Hospedería Convento de San Francisco,* E, one of the cheaper hotels, quiet, spartan rooms, helpful staff, swimming pool not always filled; *Hospedería Duruelo,* C, above the town, magnificent view, good cooking, horse riding, rec., high standards. Accommodation with Señora Carmen Castaneda, Calle 14, No. 7-51, 4 rooms, all giving onto a flower-filled patio, E, clean, friendly; also Familia Fitata, Calle 12, No. 7-35, E (F in week), breakfast extra, friendly, clean, safe. The telephone connection from Bogotá is poor and most hotels have reservation numbers in Bogotá. Information from the Tourist Office. Booking essential during holidays, and advisable at weekends (try bargaining Mon.-Thurs.) Accommodation also in *Hostería La Roca,* Calle 13, No. 9-54, F, hot water, clean and pleasant, with rooms overlooking main square and reasonable breakfast, noisy at night because of bar music; cheap rooms available in bar-cum-bus-agency at entrance to town, also at restaurant *hospedaje* on the corner of the plaza near the Caja Agraria on the road out to Chiquinquirá, but some beds only have blankets, not mattresses over the springs. **Camping** at Los Olivares near village of Sáchica, 4 km. from Villa de Leiva (no services).

Restaurants On the main square try *Pueblito Viejo, Lino's Pizzeria,* very good, but expensive; several in and opposite the bus station. *La Parrilla,* Carrera 9, No. 9-17 and *Los Kioskos,* Carrera 9, No. 11-52; *El Estar de la Villa,* Calle 13, No. 8-89, good; *Nueva Granada,* Carrera 9, No. 13-69, good value; *Los Balcones,* just off plaza, cheap, early breakfasts; *Freilon,* recently opened nearby; *El Parrilón de los Caciques,* W side of town on Carrera 9, No. 9-05, warmly rec., good value. Visit the shop of Marcos A.Buitrago set in tropical gardens on El Paraíso de los Sachos, near the main square—he likes to talk to visitors.

Post Office in Telecom building, Calle 13, No. 8-26.

Transport Buses to Leiva from Tunja, 1 hr. 5 mins., US$1 with Flota Reina or Valle de Tenza company. (From Bogotá to Villa de Leiva, via Tunja, takes 4 hrs.) Colectivo taxis leave the bus station in Tunja for Villa de Leiva every hour and return from the main square. Leiva bus station in 8th block of Carrera 9. It is recommended to book the return journey on arrival. If driving from Tunja, watch out for rockfalls. Another way of getting to Villa de Leiva is via Sáchica, either directly from Tunja or, coming from Bogotá, turning left (W) at the Boyacá monument, via Samacá.

From Tunja there are two possible routes to Cúcuta; the main road, almost entirely paved, goes via Bucaramanga, but the other via Duitama and Málaga, rejoining the main road at Pamplona, is also interesting, though there are few filling stations N of Duitama. In *Duitama* there is the interesting tourist complex Punta Larga, close to a furniture manufacturer. (*Hospedería D'la 18,* Carrera 18, No. 18-60, clean, quiet, F; many others nearby). About 3 km. from Duitama, on the road to Belencito, there is another hotel, also in an old *hacienda,* the *Hostería San Luis de Ucuenga.* Bus Duitama to Bucaramanga at 0900, 9 hrs., US$9. At Duitama turn right for *Sogamoso,* where a good museum of archaeology has been opened on the site of the centre of the precolumbian city. It is possible to camp in the museum grounds if you ask permission. A museum of religious art is open on the road from Duitama to Sogamoso (its most valuable exhibits were stolen in 1981). *Hotel Hacienda Suescún,* E, nearby in old *hacienda*, excellent service (but food not too good); many hotels near bus station e.g. *Hostal Aranjuez*, G, basic, safe, very helpful, *Santa Marta*, F, not rec. E of Sogamoso the churches of Mongua (a pleasant colonial town, 20 km.) and Topaga are worth a visit, and so is the mountain-ringed **Lago de Tota** (3,015 metres above sea level), south of Sogamoso. The *Refugio el Pozo Azul*, on the lakeside, is a private club run by Gary Clements and his Colombian wife, who will extend membership to readers of *The South American Handbook*; an excellent place to stay, in D price range, also has cabins for up to 7 people, US$40. Good food, fresh trout caught in the lake, suitable for children, very friendly atmosphere. Boats and fishing tackle for hire; good walking, and bird-watching country; recommended to book in advance, postal address: Apartado Aéreo 032, Sogamoso, Boyacá (or through Gladys García, Representative, Calle 80, No. 12-37, Bogotá, T 255-8682). Also on the lake is *Las Rocas Lindas*, D with bath and hot water, US$2.50 for each extra person, 2 cabins for 7 (US$30) one for 8 at Playa Blanca across the lake (US$40), boats for hire, dining room, bar, fireplaces, recommended. The owner, Sr. Mauricio Moreno Arenas, is very friendly. **Aquitania**, a cold, expensive town on the lake, is a centre of onion growing, with a nice camp ground called Playa Blanca nearby, with services and cafeteria. It is reached by bus from Sogamoso, US$0.75, 1 hr.; bus from Bogotá (Rápido Duitama), via Tunja and Sogamoso, goes round the lake to Aquitania, passing Cuitiva, Tota and the *Rocas Lindas* and *Pozo Azul* hotels (3 hr. wait in Aquitania). In Aquitania, *Residencia Venecia*, Calle 8, No. 144, F, with restaurant *Lucho* below, reasonable.

Just before the descent to the Lago de Tota, a road branches left, leading in 4 hours to **Yopal**, capital of the Intendencia of Casanare in the Llanos. (Pop. 10,000.) The road passes through *páramo* and virgin cloud forest. A fine waterfall can be reached in one hour's walk from the DAS checkpoint just above Pajarito. The best *residencias* in Yopal are usually full; direct buses from Sogamoso. **N.B.** Casanare and Arauca beyond are centres of guerrilla activity.

NE of Duitama, on the road to Málaga, is the turning at Belén for Paz de Río, where Colombia's national steelworks is sited; visitors can see over it. The road goes N to **Soatá** (*Residencias Colonial*, excellent, good restaurant; *Hotel Turístico*, E, swimming pool) and then descends to the very dry, spectacular valley of the Río Chicomocha.

By the bridge over the river at Capitanejo is the turning to the very attractive **Sierra Nevada del Cocuy** in the Eastern Cordillera. The Sierra extends in a half circle for 30 km., offering peaks of rare beauty, lakes and waterfalls. The area is good for trekking and probably the best range in Colombia for rock climbers. The most beautiful peaks are Cocuy (5,100 m.), Ritacuba Negra (5,200 m.), Ritacuba Blanca (5,200 m.) and El Castillo (5,400 m.) The area is good for trekking. The main towns are **Cocuy**, on one side of the sierra, reached by Paz de Río bus from Bogotá, Av. 6, Carrera 15 (13 hrs., US$10), tourist office on Carrera 3, No. 8-06, *Residencia Cocuy*, F, cold water, laundry; and **Guicán**, on the other side, one hotel, F, good meals (extra), cold water. Both towns are 1-1½ hrs. drive by jeep from the mountains, so it is recommended to stay higher up. Above Guicán, you can stay at some farms or, at 3,600 metres, 3 tourist cabins have been built (each with 9 beds, well-furnished, open fires, electrically-heated showers, good meals included in room price, horses for hire), from which it is 3 strenuous hours' walk to the snowline on Ritacuba Blanca. This would also be the best base for the 2-3 day walk round the N end of the Sierra and into Ratoncito valley, which is surrounded by snow-capped mountains. At Panquera is *Hospedaría El Portón de la Sierra*, owned by Jorge Ibáñez, who runs tours and has horses for hire, nice meals. Above Cocuy, accommodation is available at Estadero Don Pastor and, probably, Hacienda La Esperanza. Horses can be hired at both places. La Esperanza is the base for climbing to the Laguna Grande de la Sierra (3-4 hours), a large sheet of glacier-fed water surrounded by 5 snow-capped peaks, and also for the 2-day walk to the Laguna de la Plaza on the E side of the Sierra, reached through awesome, rugged scenery. Permission to camp can easily be obtained from the friendly people. It takes 1 to 2 days to walk between the two towns; maps available in Cocuy and at La Esperanza. It takes 8-10 days to trek from one end to the other through a central rift, but equipment (crampons, ice pick, rope etc.) is necessary. The perpendicular rock mountains overlooking the Llanos are for professionals only. The area can also be reached by bus from Pamplona and Bucaramanga. The best weather is from December to April.

The area around **Málaga** is very picturesque: pretty red-tiled villages, horsemen in ponchos and cowboy hats, and mountains (some covered in flowering trees). The roads are twisty but spectacular. In Málaga there are several hotels (including *Príncipe*, near main square, F, shared bathroom, clean, friendly, good meals) and restaurants. Good bus services to Duitama (6 hrs.), Bucaramanga and Pamplona.

The main road from Tunja goes on to **Barbosa** (*Hotel Príncipe*, clean rooms with private bath; youth hostel at *Parador Turístico Barbosa*; *El Palacio del Pollo*, good, simple roadside restaurant), 64 km. NW in the Department of Santander. Eleven km. from Barbosa, at Puente Nacional, is *Agua Blanca*, a splendid hotel with a swimming pool (also acts as youth hostel).

A road runs NW from Barbosa to the Magdalena at Puerto Olaya, opposite Puerto Berrío. Eighteen km. from Barbosa is **Vélez**, a charming little town where horses and mules are raised. (*Hotel Galés*, G.)

The road (toll at Santana, US$0.40) goes NE for 84 km. to **Socorro** (23,500 people), with steep streets and single storey houses set among graceful palms. It has a singularly large and odd stone church. The local museum, La Casa de la Cultura, is worth seeing, as is the market which is open every day.

At Socorro, in 1781, began the revolt of the peasant *comuneros*: not a movement for independence but a protest against poverty. It was led at first by a woman, Manuela Beltrán, and then, when other towns joined, by Juan Francisco Berbeo. They marched as far as the salt town of Zipaquirá, N of Bogotá; rebel terms were accepted by the Spaniards, and sworn to by the Bishop of Bogotá, but when they had returned home troops were sent from Cartagena and there were savage reprisals. Another woman from Socorro, Antonia Santos, led guerrillas fighting for independence and was captured and executed by the Spaniards in 1819; her statue is in the main square. The Casa de Cultura museum (opening hours vary according to season) has disappointingly little information on these local heroines, but is still worth a visit.

Hotels *Tamacara*, swimming pool, new, B-C, *Venezia*, F, with shower, has dining room, nice old rooms, good value (single women beware peeping toms); *Sucre*. **Restaurant** *Chanchón*; *Panadería Imperial*, Calle 14 y Cra. 13, very good, simple; avoid the local hamburger joint.

From Socorro, a road leads N and W to Barrancabermeja. 21 km. along is **Barichara**, a beautiful colonial town at 1,336 metres, population 8,400, founded in 1714 and designated as a national monument to preserve its character. There are many places of historical interest, the most important being the house of the former president Aquiles Parra (the woman next door has the key). An interesting excursion is to Guane, a town 9 km. away by road, or 1½ hrs. walk by trail, where there is an archaeological museum in the priest's house, large collection of coins and a mummified woman (admission, US$0.25).

Hotels *Corata*, Carrera 7, No. 4-02, F, with private bath, restaurant and lovely cathedral views. *Posada Real*, Carrera 7, No 4-78, F; *Santa Barbara*, Carrera 9, Calle 5, E.

Restaurant *La Corsona*, Calle 6, Carreras 5-6, cheap, good food, friendly.

Another 20 km. N of Barichara is **Zapatoca** a sleepy town which at one time controlled the traffic between highland Santander and the Magdalena. Local products include juicy sweets (*cocadas*) and *pauche*, a balsa type wood painted and carved into many forms. There is also a small "rather goofy" museum. The road continues to Barrancabermeja, see page 677.

About 21 km. beyond Socorro, NE on the main road to Bucamaranga, is **San Gil**, an unspoilt and friendly colonial town with a good climate, which has the tourist attraction of El Gallineral, a riverside spot whose beautiful trees are covered with moss-like tillandsia. Good view from La Gruta, the shrine overlooking the town (look for the cross). Bus to Bogotá, US$6; to Bucaramanga, US$1.90; to Barichara from Calle 12, US$0.75, 1 hr. You can fly to Bogotá (US$25) and Málaga (US$6).

Hotels *Bella Isla* (swimming pool), C, a good stopover on the Bogotá-Cúcuta run (locked parking); *San Gil*, Calle 11, F, showers, clean, friendly; *Alcantuz*, Calle 11, No. 10-15, E, clean, free coffee, good location, pleasant but noisy facing street; *Residencias Royal*, Calle 10 y Carrera 10, F with bath but no a/c; *Residencias Guananta*, Calle 11 (same block as *Hotel Bogotá* and *Colombia*), F, small, clean, hard beds, noisy in daytime; *Pensión Victoria*, E, motorcycle parking, clean and friendly; *Residencia Abril*, Cra. 10, Calle 8, E, secure parking, refrigerators in rooms (contents overpriced), relatively quiet; *Residencias Señorial*, Calle 10, Cra. 8, E, pleasant and quiet; *Nacional*, G, very basic but friendly.

Restaurants Just outside Pinchote on the road from Socorro to San Gil is the *Mesón del Cuchicote*, which specializes in dishes from the Santander region. A good restaurant in San

Gil is *Herberduc*, US$2-5; *Central*, Calle 10, No. 10-70, good and cheap; *Antojos*, Carrera 9, No. 11-19, good juices; also good and cheap is *Santandereano*; *La Palma*, across from *Residencias Abril*, rec.; *Bambi*, Cra. 10—at night it is a discotheque; *El Turista* is adequate; *Dusi's King*, on plaza, fast food.

A road runs E from San Gil to Onzaga (bus), through Mogotes and San Joaquín, dropping from high mountain ridges to tropical valleys. From Onzaga it is 20 km. to Soatá (see previous page); no regular public transport, if walking make sure you take the right road. 1 hour east of San Gil is Charalá, which has a beautiful plaza with a statue of José Antonio Golán, leader of the 1781 Comunero revolt. Also an interesting church and Casa de la Cultura; very attractive lush scenery.

About 24 km. beyond San Gil, a little off the road, is the picturesque village of Aratoca, with a colonial church. Ten km. further on, the descent from the heights along the side of a steep cliff into the dry canyon, with spectacular rock colours, of the Río Chicamocha is one of the most dramatic experiences of the trip to Cúcuta, but, if driving, this is a demanding and dangerous stretch.

Bucaramanga, 420 km. from Bogotá, is the capital of Santander Department. It stands at 1,018 metres on an uneven plateau sharply delimited by eroded slopes to the N and W, hills to the east and a ravine to the S. The city was founded in 1622 but was little more than a village until the latter half of the 19th century. The metropolitan area has a population of 700,000, which has expanded rapidly because of the success of coffee, tobacco and staple crops. The Parque Santander is the heart of the modern city, while the Parque García Rovira is the centre of the colonial area. Just off Parque García Rovira is the Casa de Cultura. Casa Perú de la Croix, Calle 37, No. 11-18, is a beautiful colonial mansion (closed, temporarily it is hoped, in 1989). There is a pleasant park where the market next to the bus station used to be. The city's great problem is space for expansion. Erosion in the lower, western side topples buildings over the edge after heavy rain. The fingers of erosion, deeply ravined between, are spectacular. The Club Campestre is one of the most beautifully set in Latin America. There is an amusement park, Parque El Lago, in the suburb of Lagos I, SW of the city on the way to Floridablanca. On the way out of the city NE (towards Pamplona) is the Parque Morrorico, well-maintained with a great view. There is a sculptured Saviour overlooking the park, a point of pilgrimage on Good Friday.

Average maximum temperature is 30°C; average minimum, 19.4°C. Rainfall is about 760 mm., and humidity is high (68% to 90%).

The annual international piano festival is held here in mid-September in the Anditorio Luis A. Calvo at the Universidad Industrial de Santander, one of the finest concert halls in Colombia.

Hotels *Chicamocha*, luxury, Calle 34, No. 31-24, A, a/c, clean; *Bucarica*, spacious, on main plaza, C, private bathroom, telephone, exceptionally good value, good restaurant and snack bar; *Andino*, Calle 34, No. 18-44, D, private bath; *Ruitoque*, nr. plaza, D, nice, colour TV; *Carolina*, near bus terminals, E, private bathroom, no hot water, some air-conditioned rooms; *Zulima*, Calle 36, Carrera 22, E, with bath, no hot water, also has an annex on Calle 31; *Balmoral*, uphill from centre, Calle 35, Carrera 21, E, with bath; *El Pilar*, Calle 34, Carrera 25, E (bargain), clean, hot water, quiet, highly rec.; good service and food; *El Edén*, Calle 31, No. 19-25, one block from bus station, E, clean, safe; *Tamana*, Carrera 18, No. 30-31, E with bath, F without, clean, friendly, rec. A few blocks uphill from the bus terminal are several *residencias*; one is *Residencias Colonial*, rec., D, with hot shower and w.c., T.V., bar, expensive; *Residencias Tonchala*, Calle 56, No. 21-23, F, with bath, good; *Amparo*, Calle 31, Carrera 20, E, with bathroom, good; *Hostal Doral*, Calle 32, No. 21-65, G, family business, clean, safe, several nice tiny rooms; *Pasajeros*, F with bath, clean, comfortable, near bus station. *Morgan*, Calle 35 y Carrera 19, E-F, 2 blocks from bus station, central, old and new wings, O.K. Wide variety of hotels on Calle 31, between Carreras 18-21. *Residencias Real*, Calle 33 y Carrera 19, clean, friendly but noisy early a.m. Accommodation at the *Club Campestre*, E, is good, but you must have an introduction; try the mayor's office or Chamber of Commerce. **Note**: Since Bucaramanga is the site for numerous national conventions, it is sometimes hard to find a room.

Camping Half-an-hour drive S of Bucaramanga, on left of dual carriageway, with swimming pool and waterside restaurant.

Restaurants *La Carreta*, Calle 27, No. 42-27, excellent, not cheap, delightful surroundings, music at times; *Mi Bodequín*, Carrera 17, No. 31-77, also good; good food at *Club del Comercio* (by invitation or introduction). *Di Marco*, Calle 48, Carrera 29 esquina, excellent meat; *La Casa de Spagheti*, Calle 33, Cra. 32, cheap and good; *La Brasa*, Carrera 33, No. 34, good typical meals; *La Tranquera*, Carrera 33, Calle 40, good Baby Beef, US$6; *Corcobado*, on hill overlooking town Km. 4 road to Pamplona (another branch in Cabecera), slow service, but good, expensive; *La Puerta del Sol*, Carrera 30, No. 62-304 and *La Fonda*, Vía Girón Km. 4, serve typical dishes; *El Maizal*, Calle 31, No. 20-74, and *Consulado Antioqueño*, Carrera 19, No. 33-81, both serve Antioquian food; *Portofino*, Calle 37, No. 13-13, good; *Fujiyama*, Calle 38, No. 33-34, Chinese; *Oriental* and *Tokio*, both on Carrera 18, between Calles 35 and 34; in same area, *Aldana*, good grills; *Pesquera*, Carrera 33, for seafood; *Krakus*, Carrera 33, No. 38-02, Colombia's only Polish restaurant, good; pizzas at: *Piz Pan Pum*, Carrera 33, No. 31-107 (next to Cinema Rivera), *Oskar's* and *Alero del Castillo* in Centro Comercial Cabecera, also *Super Pizza*, Centro Comercial Cabecera (pizza by the slice, hamburgers, etc.). *Lonchería La 36*, Calle 36, No. 13-02, very good savoury pasties and snacks; *Desayunadero La 18*, opposite the Copetran terminal, cheap, friendly, English spoken, open every day till late; good snack bars including *Mucho Pinchos* (Calle 54, No. 31-07), *Mar Villa* (in the centre and at Centro Comercial Cabecera); *Almuerzo Colonial*, Carrera 33, No. 38-33, good fixed price lunch only; *Los Arrayanes*, Calle 32, No.29, good value, especially lunchtime; *El Tony*, Carrera 33, No. 33, very popular, live music late at night; *Gran Gastby* (correct spelling! Carrera 33, No. 30-30).

Vegetarian: *Genesis*, Calle 35 y Carrera 25, good; *El Toronjil*, vegetarian at Carrera 33, No. 52-123, a bit dear; *Govinda*, Indian vegetarian, Cra. 20, Calle 35/36, excellent lunch US$2.50; *Berna*, Calle 35, No. 18-30, best pastries in town. Try the *hormigas* (large black ants), a local delicacy mainly eaten during Holy Week. Service in Bucaramanga's many restaurants is slow, so be warned.

Shopping Camping equipment, *Acampemos*, Calle 48, No. 26-30, last place in Colombia to get camping gas cartridges before Venezuela. Handicrafts in Girón (expensive—see below) and typical clothing upstairs in the food market, Calle 34 y Carreras 15-16. Similar articles (*ruanas*, hats) in San Andresito. *Feria de artesanías* in first 2 weeks of September, usually near the Puerta del Sol.

Discotheques On road to Girón are *El Pulpo* and *Capricornio*; *Ulisses 2000*, Av. Quebrada Seca y Carrera 28, gay. Many on Carrera 33, try *Silver Rose*.

Transport Taxis do not have meters but the fare within the city is US$0.70 (US$0.75 at night). Buses charge US$0.10.

Museums Museo de Arte Moderno Calle 37, Cra. 26, new, US$0.20. Also Casa de Bolívar, Calle 37, No. 12-15, an interesting museum (0900-1200, 1400-1700, free, closed Sat. and Sun.).

Banks Banco Anglo Colombiano, Calle 36, No. 20-04, and agency on Carrera 15. Banco de la República, Carrera 19, No. 34-93, is the only bank authorized to cash travellers' cheques. Long queues (cheques and passports have to be photocopied). Many other banks. Open Mon.-Fri. 0800-1130, 1400-1600, and last working day of month, 0800-1030. Closed Sats.

Tourist Office On main plaza in *Hotel Bucarica* building, friendly and knowledgeable. City maps for sale.

Airport Palonegro, on three flattened hilltops on other side of ravine S of city. Spectacular views on take-off and landing. 3 Avianca flights to Bogotá, regularly overbooked; also to Cúcuta. Flights to Medellín are better value and less hassle than going by bus. Taxi, US$3-4; colectivo, US$1. Buses are scarce despite the fact that some bus boards say "Aeropuerto" (direction "Girón/Lebrija" from Diagonal 15).

Roads To the Magdalena at Barrancabermeja, 174 km.; to Cúcuta, 198 km.; to Bogotá, 420 km.; to Medellín, 1,010 km.; to Santa Marta, 550 km., all paved.

Buses Bus terminals are mostly around Diagonal 15, S of the centre, until the new terminal on the Girón road has been completed. To Bogotá, 8-11 hrs., US$9 (Pullman) with Berlinas del Fonce, Carrera 18, No. 31-06 (this journey is uncomfortable, there are no relief stops, and it starts off hot and ends cold in the mountains, come prepared), Copetran, Calle 55, No. 17B-57, recommended for advance bus reservations, has 3 classes of bus to Bogotá including Pullman, 10 hrs, US$10; Expreso Brasilia runs to Bogotá but they sell tickets only half an hour before departure. Tunja, 9 hrs., US$5.10; Barranquilla, 9 hrs. (US$13.50 first class with Copetran); Cúcuta, 6 hrs., US$4.25 (Pullman), Berlinas buses often arrive full from Bogotá,

Cotran also to Cúcuta; colectivo to Cúcuta, US$6; Santa Marta, 9 hrs., maybe more according to season, US$15 with Copetran; Barrancabermeja, 3 hrs., US$1.90, a scenic ride with one rest stop permitted; this road is now paved. Hourly buses to San Gil, US$1.90. To Berlín, US$1. Other companies with local services to nearby villages on bad roads, e.g. the colourful folk-art buses of Flota Cáchira (Calle 32, Cra. 33-34) which go North and East.

Excursions The suburb of **Floridablanca**, 8 km. SW, has the famous El Paragüitas gardens, belonging to the national tobacco agency, reputed locally as "a replica of the Garden of Eden"; you can get a free pass (two needed if you want to visit both a.m. and p.m.) to the gardens from the Tourist Office in town. The gardens have been recently reconstructed and open at weekends (1000-1130 and 1500-1630 only). It's a 2-hour walk from Bucaramanga to Floridablanca, but not very interesting; there are plenty of buses. Take the Cotandra bus (US$0.25) from Carrera 22, Bucaramanga, either Florida Villabel which goes by El Paragüitas, or Florida Autopista (continuation of Carrera 33) which goes direct to the square in Florida and you have to walk about a km. Toll on road to Floridablanca, US$0.20. *Rincón Santanera* restaurant, Cra. 8, No.4-41, good local food.

Lebrija (20,400 people), 17 km. to the W, is in an attractive plain. Rionegro (36,750 people) is a coffee town 20 km. to the N with, close by, the Laguna de Gálago and waterfalls. **Girón** (27,500 people) a tobacco centre 9 km. SW of Bucaramanga on the Río de Oro, is a quiet and attractive colonial town, filled with Bumangueses at weekends, with a beautiful church. The buildings are well preserved and the town unspoilt by modernization. By the river are *tejo* courts and popular open air restaurants with *cumbia* and *salsa* bands; in the square at weekends, sweets and *raspados* (crushed ice delights) are sold. (Hotels: *San Juan de Girón*, B, outside town on road from Bucaramanga, swimming pool; *Río de Oro*, in centre, F, make sure you get a lock for the door. Restaurant: *Mansión del Fraile* on the square, in a beautiful colonial house, good food—Bolívar slept here on one occasion, ask to see the bed.) Take the bus from Carrera 15 or 22 in Bucaramanga, US$1.45. In **Piedecuesta**, 18 km. SE of Bucaramanga (bus from Carrera 22, US$0.35, 45 mins.), you can see cigars being hand-made, furniture carving and jute weaving—cheap, hand-decorated *fique* rugs can be bought. There are frequent buses to all these places; a taxi costs US$5. Corpus Christi processions in these towns in June are interesting. They are all dormitory towns for the city, so there is plenty of public transport.

Another excursion is to **California**, about 60 km. NE of Bucaramanga, where there are gold mines that tourists can visit.

The road (bad and narrow) runs E to Berlín, and then NE (a very scenic run over the Eastern Cordillera) to Pamplona, about 130 km. from Bucaramanga.

Berlín has been recommended to the hardy camper as challenging and rewarding. The village lies in a valley at 3,100 metres, the peaks surrounding it rise to 4,350 metres and the temperature is constantly around 10°C, although on the infrequent sunny days it may seem much warmer. The scenery is awesome. The inhabitants are tolerant of visitors; ask a farmer for permission to camp in his field. There are no hotels, but there are several basic eating places. It has been recommended as an ideal place to appreciate the grandeur of the Eastern Cordillera and the hardiness of the people who live on the *páramo*.

Pamplona, Department of Santander del Norte, lies amid mountains at 2,200 metres. Population, 40,000. The climate is cold and uninviting, but the town is definitely worth seeing. Founded in 1548, it became important as a mining town but is now better known as a university city. Few modern buildings have as yet broken its colonial harmony. Cathedral in the spacious central plaza. The earthquake of 1875 played havoc with the monasteries and some of the churches: there is now a hotel on the site of the former San Agustín monastery, but it may still be possible to visit the ex-monasteries of San Francisco and Santo Domingo. The Iglesia del Humilladero, adjoining the cemetery, is very picturesque and allows a fine view of the city. Museum of religious art at Calle 5 y Carrera 5. See the Casa Colonial archaeological museum, Calle 6, No. 2-56, open Tues-Sat., 0900-1200, 1400-1800; Sun., 0900-1200. The town's Easter celebrations are famous throughout Colombia.

Hotels *Cariongo*, Carrera 5, Calle 9, D, very good, excellent restaurant (locked parking available); *Montaña*, Carrera 6, No. 8-02, E; *Residencias Doran*, Carrera 6, No. 7-21, E with bath (F without), large rooms, good meals, US$1.50; *Anzoátegui*, F with bargaining, for dinner, bed and breakfast. *Orsua*, on main square, F, clean, friendly, cheap, good food also available; *Lincoln*, on the Plaza, F, simple, but good beds, private bath and hot water; *Llanos*, Calle 9 y Carrera 7, F, motorcycle parking, rec. Hotel accommodation may be hard to find at weekends, when Venezuelans visit the town.

Restaurant *El Doran*, meals for US$1.60. *El Maribel*, Calle 5, No. 4-17, cheap lunch; *La Casona*, Calle 6, No. 6-57, limited but good menu; *El Gran Duque*, on main square, student-run, good music. *Los Bucaros*, close to main square, good value set meal US$2.

Shopping Pamplona is a good place to buy *ruanas*. Good indoor market.

Banks do not change dollars or travellers' cheques in Pamplona.

Tourist Office Calle 5 y Carrera 6, on main plaza.

Buses To Bogotá, US$11.50, 13-16 hrs.; to Cúcuta, US$1.65; to Bucaramanga, US$2.75, 4 hrs.; to Málaga, 0930 8 hrs. in dry weather, beautiful but very hard journey; to Tunja, US$9, 12 hours (leaving at 0600). To Berlín, US$1.75.

It is a run of 72 km. from Pamplona through sparsely populated country, descending to an altitude of only 215 metres, to **Cúcuta**, capital of the Department of Santander del Norte, and only 16 km. from the Venezuelan frontier, was founded 1734, destroyed by earthquake 1875, and then rebuilt, elegantly, with the streets shaded by trees, and they are needed for it is hot: the mean temperature is 29°C. Population: 600,000. Coffee is the great crop in the area, followed by tobacco. There are also large herds of cattle.

Cúcuta, because it is the gateway of entry from Venezuela, was a focal point in the history of Colombia during the wars for independence. Bolívar captured it after his lightning Magdalena campaign in 1813. The Bolívar Column stands where he addressed his troops on February 28, 1813. At El Rosario de Cúcuta, a small town of 8,000 inhabitants 14½ km. from Cúcuta on the road to the frontier, the First Congress of Gran Colombia opened on May 6, 1821. It was at this Congress that the plan to unite Venezuela, Ecuador, and Colombia was ratified; Bolívar was made President, and Santander (who was against the plan) Vice-President. (Santander was born at a *hacienda* near El Rosario which is now being developed as a tourist centre.) The international bridge between Colombia and Venezuela is a few km. from El Rosario; just beyond it is San Antonio del Táchira, the first Venezuelan town, and 55 km. on is San Cristóbal.

Hotels *Tonchalá*, Calle 10, Av. 0, B, good restaurant, swimming pool, air conditioning, airline booking office in hall; *Tundaya*, Av 7 y Calle 8, 1-star, E, clean, safe, very good restaurant, breakfast US$10; *Victoria Plaza*, Calle 8, No. 2-98, D; also D are *Frontera*, Calle 12, No. 7-36 and *Sol*, Calle 10, No. 7-51; *Lord*, nearby, E, nice rooms, good restaurant and service, safe; *Casa Blanca* (swimming pool), D, good, reasonable meals, rec.; *Aurora*, Calle 11 No. 3-52, F, central, friendly, good cheap restaurant; *Residencias Los Rosales*, near bus station, Calle 2, 8-39, fan and private bath, good, F; *Imperial*, Av. 7, No. 6-28, F with bath, clean, secure, highly rec.; *Residencia Mary* at bus station, E, with bath (cheaper per person in triple room), good. Also near the bus station are *Zulia*, F, with bath, clean; and *Residencias Catacumba*, F, good value. *Residencias Los Dos Santanderes*, Calle 1 between Av. 9 and 10, F; *Amaruc*, Av. 5, No. 9-37, E, with fan, private bath, no hot water. Private *Residencia*, Av. 6A, No. 0-24 N, Barrio La Merced, T 41984, F, run by family Mogollón de Soto, private bath, clothes washing, free coffee all day, rec. **Youth Hostel** at El Rosario de Cúcuta in *Hotel El Saman*, with bar, restaurant, disco and pools. Details from Alcom in Bogotá.

Restaurants *"M"*, also called *Chez Esteban*, on road to Venezuela, very good; *Bahía*, just off main square, pleasant; other good restaurants at reasonable prices are *El Pollo Especial*, *El Jarrón de Baviera*, *Cantón* (Chinese) and *Las Acacias*, Avenida 5, rec.

Shopping A good range of leather goods at possibly the best prices anywhere in Colombia. Cuchitril, Av. 3 No. 9-89, has a selection of the better Colombian craft work.

Exchange A good rate of exchange for pesos is to be had in Cúcuta, at the airport, or on the border. There are money changers on the street all round the main square and many shops advertise the purchase and sale of bolívares. The price is usually better than at the Banco de la República, Diagonal Santander, Avs. 3E y 4E. Change pesos into bolívares in Cúcuta or San Antonio—difficult to change them further into Venezuela. AmEx and Citicorp travellers' cheques can be exchanged only in Banco de la República.

Tourist Office Calle 10, No. 0-30, helpful, has maps, etc. At airport. Other maps obtainable from Instituto Geográfico, Banco de la República building, in the main plaza.

Airports At Cúcuta for Colombian services (to Bogotá, at least twice a day, US$40 if paid in pesos, with Avianca; less with Satena, and with Aerotal). Airport 10 minutes by taxi, US$1.70. To Barranquilla and Cartagena, 1 flight per day US$46 (US$72 if you buy your ticket in Venezuela). Also at San Antonio, Venezuela (30 minutes) for Venezuelan domestic lines. At latter, be sure all baggage is sealed after customs inspection and the paper seals signed and stamped.

Note Cúcuta is a great centre for smuggling. Be careful.

Transport To San Cristóbal colectivo, US$2; bus, US$1 (Bolivariano); to San Antonio taxi US$6; bus US$0.30. Bus to Bogotá, hourly, 17-24 hrs., US$15, Berlinas del Fonce 1400, 2 stops, including 15 mins. with free refreshments in Bucaramanga, or Bolivariano, 20 hrs., often delayed at check points. There are frequent buses, even during the night. To Bucaramanga, US$4.25, 6 hrs, with Berlinas del Fonce Pullman, several departures daily; from there a connection to Barranquilla can be made. To Tunja, US$9. The road is bad for the first part of the journey. Bus station: Avenida 7 and Calle O (a really rough area). Taxi from bus station to town centre, US$2.

Warning All travellers report that the bus station is overrun with thieves and conmen. You must take great care, there is little or no police protection. Watch out for dubious money changers, ticket sellers and security officers claiming to be from the tourist office. These "officials" ask travellers to declare, for "insurance purposes", the amount of money they are carrying. The money is placed in plastic envelopes and returned for you to secrete about your person. Should the bus be robbed later, you are told, the company will reimburse you. In fact, you will have lost part of your money before you even board the bus. Resist this larceny as strongly as possible. Don't put your valuables in bus company "safety boxes"; you'll get out half what you put in (Berlinas del Fonce is the most trustworthy company). Make sure tickets are for buses that exist; tickets do not need to be "stamped for validity". For San Cristóbal, only pay the driver of the vehicle, not at the offices upstairs in the bus station.

There are good roads to Caracas (933 km. direct or 1,046 km. via Mérida), and to Maracaibo (571 km.). Bus to Caracas, 14 hrs., Expreso Occidente, two daily, US$13; taxi colectivo US$15.75.

From Venezuela to Colombia It is cheaper to fly Caracas-San Antonio (US$30 approx.), take a taxi to Cúcuta (US$6), then take an internal Colombian flight, than to fly direct from Caracas to Colombia. It will, of course, take longer. The airport transfer at San Antonio is well organized, with taxi drivers calling at necessary immigration offices, and at exchange places, the trip taking 25 mins. You do not have to buy your Colombian ticket in Cúcuta, you can make a reservation and purchase a ticket in a travel agency in Venezuela some days in advance (check exchange rates to see whether it is better to pay in Venezuela or Colombia). With a computer (*localizador*) reference number, you can avoid queues.

If arriving by bus, make sure bus stops at border for Venezuelan exit formalities. If you need one, obtain your Colombian tourist card at the border, and entrance stamp from the DAS in Cúcuta. It is essential to obtain entry stamps (passport and/or tourist card) at the border. You will otherwise have problems with police checks, banks and leaving the country. You can also be fined. Border checks in Cúcuta are very strict. Air travellers can undertake all Colombian formalities at Cúcuta airport.

From Colombia to Venezuela All visitors need a visa and tourist card to enter Venezuela. There is a Venezuelan Consulate at Cúcuta (Av. O, Calle 8—open 0800-1300, Mon.-Fri.) which supplies these—same applies at Venezuelan Embassy in Bogotá (may send you to Cúcuta for visas, etc.). You must also provide one photograph for a visa; evidence of onward transportation out of Venezuela, often with a date, is officially required (but often not asked for in Cúcuta—it is necessary in Bogotá), and proof of funds is sometimes requested. In 1989 applicants had to pay from US$2 to US$10 into a bank (open until 1130 only), then take the receipt back to the Consulate. The process is pretty pushy, be pushy and start early in the day. You are strongly advised to obtain visa and card from the Venezuelan embassy in your own country, if you know in advance when you will be arriving at the frontier. (Just to visit San Antonio de Táchira in Venezuela, no documents are required.) As there are no Colombian exit/entrance formalities at the international border bridge, it is necessary to obtain a DAS exit stamp before leaving the country from the offices in Cúcuta (open 0800-1200, 1400-1800, Mon.-Fri.; Avenida Primera, No. 28-57 Barrio San Rafael, 2 km. from centre); open 7 days a week, or you can go to the DAS office at the airport. If you do not, you will be turned back by Venezuelan customs officials, and the next time you enter Colombia, you will be subject to a fine of US$7.50.

Entering or leaving Colombia by car, you must have your passport stamped at the DAS in town and the car papers stamped at the Customs (Aduana) office on the road to the airport—watch hard for the small sign. At the Customs Office is a restaurant serving excellent, large meals for US$2. Venezuelan car documentation is checked at the border post in San Antonio.

7 km. from Cúcuta is Zulia (Petróleo *buseta*), worth a visit if waiting for a Venezuelan tourist card.

The Andes chain N of Cúcuta is the branch which sweeps north to the Guajira Peninsula after the bifurcation of the Eastern Cordillera near Cúcuta: the other branch crosses into Venezuela. This western branch is the Sierra de Perijá y Motilones, in which live the Motilones Indians, the only Indians in Colombia who have refused to accept absorption into the larger nation. Little is known of them; they have killed many of the missionaries sent to convert them, and the anthropologists sent to study them.

THE LLANOS AND LETICIA (3)

A spectacular 110-km. road (due for improvement) runs SE from Bogotá to **Villavicencio**, capital of Meta Department in the Llanos at the foot of the eastern slopes of the Eastern Cordillera. Population: 300,000. Rice is now grown near Villavicencio and milled there for transport to Bogotá. Altitude: 498 metres. The town fills up at weekends. It is also full of military police owing to guerrilla activity to the SE.

Hotels *Villavicencio*, in town, D, suites available, a/c, hot water, very comfortable, good restaurant, tell them if you don't want extras—TV, telephone, newspaper—and you won't be charged; *Centauros*, in centre, E, reasonably clean and quiet, small rooms; *Inambú*, E plus extras, Calle 37A, No. 29-49, central; *Savoy*, Carrera 31, No. 41-01, E, with shower and air conditioning, clean and friendly; *Carimagua*, F, shower, rec. *Residencias Medina*, Calle 39D, 28-27, F, common shower, fair, washing facilities; *Residencias Don Juan*, Carrera 28, No. 37-21 (Mercado de San Isidro), attractive family house, E, with bath and fan, sauna, safe, rec. *El Nogal*, F, clean, comfortable, good value. *Residencias Myriam* (off main square), F, fairly clean, check roof for leaks.

Restaurants On main square: *Palace*, rec.; *La Brasa*. One Chinese; others, some with swimming pools, on road to Puerto López.

Tourist Office on main square (Plaza Santander), helpful.

Airport Flights to Miraflores and Mitú for those who want to see "uncommercialized" jungle. To Puerto Carreño: Urraca, a freight service with some seats, 0630, Mon., Wed., Fri., arrive early to get a seat, 1½ hrs. Taxi to town, US$2; bus US$0.30.

Buses La Macarena and Bolivariano run from Bogotá about every half-hour, US$2.75, 4 hrs.; alternatively there are colectivos (e.g. Velotax, US$3.50, or Autollanos who run every hour, US$5.25). Be prepared to queue for tickets back to Bogotá.

Villavicencio is a good centre for visiting the Llanos and jungles stretching 800 km. E as far as Puerto Carreño, on the Orinoco, with Venezuela across the river. Cattle raising is the great industry on the plains, sparsely inhabited by *mestizos*, not Indians. The cattle town of San Martín to the south of Villavicencio may be visited by bus, 1½ hrs., US$1.20 each way.

A good asphalt road has been built E from Villavicencio to **Puerto López** on the Meta river, a port of call for large river boats. Hotels: *Tío Pepe*, D, with swimming pool; *Marichal*, E, fans but no a/c, swimming pool; two good *residencias: Doña Empera*, F, and *Popular*, F, cheaper, friendly, every bed with mosquito net, good meals. Good food also at *Restaurante Yamiba*. Armando Mildenberg, at *Res. Popular*, speaks German, some English and French, is helpful; he may be able to arrange tours in the *llanos*, or trip to Puerto Carreño. The road E (unpaved and poor, but reported to be about to be improved) continues for another 150 km. through Puerto Gaitán, where there are hotels and restaurants, and San Pedro to Arimena. Here the road branches: one road goes N to the Río Meta at El Porvenir, where a ferry (dry season only) takes you across the river to the Orocue tourist centre, E, swimming pool, excursions. The main road, now degenerated to a rough track impassable in the wet season, continues E through Vichada to Puerto Carreño.

Puerto Carreño (population about 5,000) has two banks (one of which changes travellers' cheques); shopkeepers will exchange Venezuelan bolívares. The DAS office and Venezuelan Consulate are on the Plaza Bolívar. Passports are checked at the waterfront, then you must go to the DAS office and insist on having your passport stamped on entry. You may encounter problems over documents; the military are active in the area and frequently demand permits and proof of how much money you have, and carry out spot checks. There is a Satena office; next to it is *Residencias Mami*, F; *Hotel Samanare*, Av. Orinoco No. 1-67, F p.p. more expensive with fan, clean, meals US$3; *Residencias La Vorágine*, F, friendly, clean, safe, good; the *residencia* on the waterfront doubles as a brothel.

N.B. The rainy season is April/May to September when it is humid, flooded and accessible only by air.

For boats to Puerto López, be prepared to wait 4-5 days; check with Ulises, a bar owner on the river front by the moorings (he gives free coffee to those prepared to help with his son's English lessons). Between December and May, a bus runs on Thursday between Puerto López and Puerto Carreño at 0500, taking 2 days, night spent at La Primavera, US$25 (Flota La Macarena).

Air Services To Villavicencio and Bogotá with Satena on Wed. and Sat., about US$53 to Bogotá, 2 hrs. 50 mins.

To Venezuela Launches take about 25 minutes to cross to Burro, stopping at Puerto Páez, from which Caracas can be reached by road. *Por puesto* service is available to Puerto Ayacucho. Both Puerto Páez and Puerto Ayacucho are connected to Caracas by air. It is possible to cross from Puerto Ayacucho to **Casuarito** in Colombia by ferry across the Orinoco. Duty free shops, modest restaurants few or no formalities. Casuarito appears to have no road connection with the rest of Colombia.

For fishing excursions from Puerto Carreño, contact Jairo Zorro, owner of the *Samanare Hotel* (15% discount to *South American Handbook* owners, refer to "Klaus El Alemám, amigo de Juancho"). He will arrange trips up the Ríos Meta, Vita, Tomo or De Agua, depending on time available. The rate for a canoe with guide is about US$50; count on US$20-30 a day for fuel; to hire fishing gear costs US$5 a day (bring your own). Equipment can be bought in Puerto Carreño or Puerto Ayacucho. The trips are rough, sleeping in hammocks on the river bank (lots of mosquitoes), but great adventure with unforgettable sunsets, alligators, *babillas* (small alligators) and jaguars. (Klaus Brandl, Buenos Aires.)

The road S from Villavicencio is surfaced as far as San Martín. It runs on to **Granada** (*Hotel Yali; Tío Pepe Motel*, very clean) and from there deteriorates rapidly. **Vistahermosa** (Macarena bus from Bogotá, 0845, US$5, 9 hrs.), situated near the break-point between the Llanos and the jungle, lies further S along this road (*Residencias Royal* is cheap and comfortable; *Lilian's* restaurant). It is normally a good place from which to visit the Sierra de la Macarena, a Tertiary outcrop 150 km. long by 35 km. broad. Its vegetation is so remarkable that the Sierra has been designated a national park exclusively for scientific study, although latest reports suggest that the flora are rapidly being destroyed by colonization, with much marijuana and coca being planted, and the area has in any case been occupied by guerrillas since about 1982. The road from Vistahermosa to the Sierra de la Macarena is very muddy in the wet season (March-Nov.). For the energetic, a worthwhile trip is to the Sardinata or Cañones falls. Both can be reached from Maracaibo, which is a day's walk from Vistahermosa. In present conditions, as will appear from these lines, a visit to the Sierra de la Macarena is not recommended.

To the SE of Villavicencio, along the river Vaupés, and near the border with Brazil, is **Mitú**, which can be reached by air from Villavicencio and Bogotá (Satena, about US$40). On arrival in the town you must fill in an entry card at the police station. Several anthropological studies are being carried out in the Mitú area and trips can be made from the town to Indian villages. The cost of a trip down river to visit an Indian village where you stay overnight is approximately US$10, plus the cost of the fuel, at US$1.60 a gallon, used by the boat. Take your own food. Recommended guides in 1989: Hilario Gondura, his son José Ignacio, Jacinto Ortis, Orlando Morena. Good local buys are baskets and bark paintings.

Hotels *La Vorágine*, E, shower, fan, clean, owned by Sr. León who will help you to arrange trips; *JM*, F, friendly, helpful, morning coffee, next to Satena office. Plenty of restaurants around, recommended: **Restaurant de la Selva**, a meeting place of the pilots who fly into Mitú.

A gold mine, the Taraira mine, has been worked since 1986 near the Brazil border. Make friends with the pilots if you wish to visit.

You can get a good away-from-it-all holiday in the Llanos. Plenty of reserve gasoline should be carried when travelling by car, as there are few service stations. Take food with you, unless you can live by gun and rod. Everybody lets you hang up your hammock or pitch your tent, but mosquito nets are a must. "Roads" are only tracks left by previous vehicles but easy from late December till early April and the very devil during the rest of the year. More information on the Llanos can be obtained from the office of the Gobernación del Departamento de Meta, Calle 34 and Carrera 14, Bogotá.

Leticia, 3,200 km. up the Amazon on the frontiers with Peru and Brazil, a fast-growing community of 15,000, is a clean modern town. It is rapidly merging into one town with neighbouring Marco in Brazil. There is a modern, well equipped hospital. The best time to visit the area is in July or August, the early months of the dry season. Tourist services are better than in Tabatinga or Benjamin Constant (Brazil). Small Amazonian zoo (huge anacondas) and botanical garden on road to airport.

Hotels *Parador Ticuna*, B, has 19 apartments (all with bathrooms which have hot and cold running water, which can each sleep up to 6. The hotel has a swimming pool (uncleaned), bar and restaurant, and is a little run down. The owners of the *Ticuna* also operate the *Jungle Lodge*, on Monkey Island, 2 hrs' boat ride from Leticia (see below). They also operate the *Colonial*, 16 double rooms and one triple, all with airconditioning or fans, power and water unpredictable, swimming pool, cafeteria, noisy, unhelpful staff, B, US$6 per additional person, not including tax and insurance (not rec. at present). Cheaper accommodation: *Residencias La Manigua*, E, with bath, dirty. *Anaconda*, C, overpriced, no hot water; there is a restaurant (beware overcharging) which serves meals for about US$6, swimming pool; *Residencias Marina*, Carrera 9 No. 9-29 (T 7201/2), D/E, TV, some a/c, cold water, good breakfast and meals at attached restaurant, clean; *Residencias Ferrando*, Carrera 9 No. 8-80, E, well equipped but electricity only at night, clean, rec.; *Residencia Leticia*, Calle 8, No. 11-93, F, very friendly (not possible to sling hammock), good value, laundry facilities, clean, use of kitchen, warmly rec.; *Residencia Familiar*, Calle 8, cheap, F, friendly, laundry facilities; *Primavera*, Calle 8 between Cras. 9 and 10, F with bath and fan. (*Parador Ticuna* and *Hotel Colonial* boil water.)

Restaurant *Tres Fronteras* (across from *Hotel Colonial*), good. Several small sidewalk restaurants downtown with set meals at around US$1. Restaurant opposite *Residencia Leticia* serves good lunches and dinners, and *Señora Mercedes*, 3 doors from *Residencia Leticia*, serves good, cheap meals until 1930. *Heladería Bucaros* offers empanadas, sandwiches, juices, etc. Cheap food (fried banana and meat, also fish and pineapples) is sold at the market near the harbour. Also cheap fruit for sale. The campsite also has a good restaurant.

Museum Recently set up by Banco de la República, covers local ethnography and archaeology.

Leticia is a good place to buy typical products of Amazon Indians, but the growth of Leticia, Tabatinga, Marco and Benjamin Constant has imposed an artificiality on the immediately surrounding Amazon territory.

Exchange The *cambio* next to the *Anaconda Hotel* has good exchange rates for dollars, cruzeiros or intis. The street money changers and *cambios*, of which there are plenty, give a better rate of exchange than the banks, which charge a 15% levy on travellers' cheques, except Banco de la República on American Express. Travellers' cheques cannot be changed at weekends, and are hard to change at other times.

Brazilian Consulate very efficient and helpful; 2 black and white photos needed for visa (photographer nearby).

Tourist Office Calle 10, No. 9-86. **DAS** office, Carrera 8 (between Calles 9 and 10), near Brazilian consulate. Make sure you get an entry stamp here before going to the airport for flights into Colombia. If you need a visa, but not a tourist card, to visit Colombia, don't be bullied into purchasing one of the latter.

Excursions If you choose to go on an organized tour, do not accept the first price and check that the supplies and equipment are sufficient for the time you will be away. It is cheaper and better to find yourself a local guide. You can hire a dug-out for about US$3 a day. Motorboats cost much more (e.g. US$54, 8 hrs, for 10 people). *Turamazonas, Parador Ticuna*, Apto. Aereo 074, T 7241, offers a wide range of tours including day visit to Yagua and Ticuna Indians, jungle walk and stop at **Monkey Island** (rec.); provisions and bedding for overnight safaris are supplied by the agency, whose staff are all expert, at Monkey Island. You can also stay at the *Jungle Lodge*, though visitors in 1989 found it little used and run down. There are not many monkeys on Monkey Island now, those left are semi-tame. Turamazonas has US representation at 855A, U.S. 19S, Tarpon Springs, FL 33581, T (813) 934-9713. The Inderena office, Centro de Visitantes Yewae, Leticia, will plan a trip for you and put you in touch with guides. (Rec. as reliable in 1989: Fernando Martínez, Jugaluis Valencia, Gervite Rodríguez, Ángel Mejía, Miguel Mejía.) You can also stay at their centre in the **Parque Nacional Amacayacu** US$8 for full board. Other reputable tour companies are *Amaturs* (in lobby of *Hotel Anaconda*) and *Kapax*. The following tours are available: to Benjamin Constant to see a rubber plantation, 8 hrs.; to Monkey Island to see Ticuna and Yagua Indians, overnight trip, with full board. Turamazonas offers tours up the river to visit Indian communities, 3 days (price depends on number of people in group), recommended. Recommended tours from Leticia to Puerto Nariño are run by *Punto Amazónico*, Carrera 24, No. 53-18, 2° piso, Bogotá, T 249-3618 (guides Fernando and José), including fishing, visits to Indians, alligator watching for 4-5 days, about US$375 including flights and hotel accommodation. Many independent guides can be found on the river front; for one day excursions to Yagua Indians (gifts of food and provisions much appreciated), Victoria Regia waterlilies, Monkey Island and more. A recommended guide is Luis Daniel González, Carrera 8, No. 9-93 (he can either be found at the airport, or contacted through *Hotel Anaconda*; he runs a variety of tours, is knowledgeable and speaks Spanish, Portuguese and English; a one-day tour, inc. meal and fuel costs US$110.) Another recommended is Daniel Martínez, speaks good English and is knowledgeable about the jungle and the Indians. Make sure the guides bring rubber boots as it can be quite muddy. Cheap guides do not have the experience or first aid equipment of the main tour companies, and there have been many instances of boats breaking down and guides getting drunk and abandoning their clients. If you choose to go on a night excursion to look for cayman make sure the boat has powerful halogen lights.

When going upstream remember that the slower and dirtier the boat, the more mosquitoes you will meet. (You can swim in the Amazon and its tributaries, but do not dive; this disturbs the fish. Also do not swim at sunrise or sunset when the fish are more active, nor when the water is shallow in the dry season, nor if you have a wound, however slight, which might open up and bleed.)

Transport Avianca flies to Leticia (Tabatinga airport if Leticia's is closed) from Bogotá, Mon., Wed., Fri., Sat., Sun., US$140 return; Leticia to Bogotá, departs 1420, arrives 1605; to Cali (via Bogotá), US$85; Satena has flights on Thurs. afternoon, US$50; it is possible with some persuasion to return to Bogotá by freight plane, but you have to sit with the cargo, often refrigerated fish. Check with Satena crew, who stay in the *Hotel Colonial*, if there is a seat available, or at the airport. (From Bogotá by freight plane, you have to be at the halls of the cargo companies—all at the same place—at 0400, and ask which company is flying.) Líneas Aero Caribe cargo flights twice a week; flight time 3½-4 hrs. Cruzeiro do Sul flies Manaus-Tabatinga (for Leticia)-Iquitos and back on Wed. and Sat. (there is a connection on Wed. for Pucallpa from Iquitos). Taba operates three flights weekly Manaus-Tabatinga-Manaus. It is also possible to get a seat on a Petrobrás plane to Manaus. This leaves every Friday, and can be arranged with the crew, who stay at the *Anaconda Hotel*. A letter of recommendation helps. Taxi to airport, US$1.90. Expect to be searched before leaving Leticia airport, and on arrival in Bogotá from Leticia. If arriving in Leticia by plane with a view to leaving for Brazil or Peru, get your exit stamp at the airport while you are there.

The cheapest way to get to Leticia is by bus to Puerto Asís, and then by boat (**see page 711**). There are twice-daily ferries between Leticia, Tabatinga and Benjamin Constant, Brazil (US$5, 1½-2 hrs., US$15 in private launch); if leaving Brazil by this route, disembark at Tabatinga and obtain exit stamp from office which is 1 km. from dock: turn right one block at main street, office is on the left. There is a Colombian Consular Office near the border on the road from Tabatinga, where Colombian tourist visas are issued on presentation of 2 passport photographs. Most boats down to Manaus take passengers—all leave from Benjamin Constant, perhaps Tabatinga—none from Leticia. Departure times are uncertain, and the boats tend to be overcrowded. The trip takes at least 4½ days; there is a better selection of provisions in Leticia, but purchases are much cheaper in Benjamin Constant. Boats to Peru from Tabatinga wharf La Ronda sail daily at 1800 and take passengers and cargo. For boats travelling on the Brazilian and Peruvian Amazon (to Manaus and Iquitos), see under the relevant sections of the Brazil and Peru chapters. Remember to get your passport stamped by the DAS office near the church, just off main square in Leticia before you leave the area;

there are no customs formalities for everyday travel between Leticia and Tabatinga in Brazil, taxis cost US$5.65 from a rank (or US$7.55 if you want to stop to change money, immigration, etc. en route to harbour), or US$0.70 as colectivos (N.B. colectivos increase their charges after 1800); bus, US$0.20; 24-hour transit stamps can be obtained at the DAS office for one-night stays in Leticia, although it appears that these are not necessary if you are not going beyond Leticia—best to check, though; also see below.

N.B. Robert Smith and Geoffrey Dempsey tell us that if entering Colombia at Leticia, from Brazil en route to Peru, you should try to get your tourist card before Manaus because the Colombian consul there will tell you that a card is not needed just for passing through Leticia. This is not true: you must have a card. If you do have to see the consul in Manaus tell him you are going further into Colombia—you may have to show an onward ticket, or money—this may get you a card.

It is reported that for travellers interested in Amazonian wild life the Putumayo is more accessible than Leticia; it is best reached from Pasto (**see page** 710).

THE NORTH COAST AND THE ISLANDS (4)

The climate is much the same for the whole area: the heat is great—ranging from 26° to 36°C, and there is a difference of only 2° between the hottest and coolest month. From November to March the heat is moderated by trade winds.

Character, like climate, seems to change in Colombia with the altitude. The *costeños* (the people of the coast) are gayer and more light-hearted than the more sober people of the highlands. (The contrast is sharply drawn in the great modern Colombian novel, *Cien Años de Soledad*, by Gabriel García Márquez.) The coastal people talk very fast, slurring their words and dropping the final s's.

N.B. In this region hotel prices are subject to high and low season variations: high season is 15 December-30 April, and 15 June-31 August.

Barranquilla, with almost 2 million people, is Colombia's fourth city. It lies on the western bank of the Magdalena river, about 18 km. from its mouth, which has been deepened and the silted sandbars cleared so that it is now a seaport (though less busy than Cartagena or Santa Marta) as well as a river port. Those who know the people say they are the most friendly in Colombia.

Barranquilla is a modern industrial city with a dirty central area near the river, and a good residential area in the north-west, beyond Calle 53. The principal boulevard is Paseo Bolívar; there is a handsome church, San Nicolás, formerly the Cathedral, in Plaza San Nicolás, the central square, and before it stands a small statue of Columbus. The new Catedral Metropolitana is at Carrera 45, No. 53-120, opposite Plaza de la Paz. This was visited by the Pope in 1986. There is an impressive statue of Christ inside by the Colombian sculptor, Arenas Betancourt. The commercial and shopping districts are round the Paseo Bolívar, a few blocks N of the old Cathedral, and in Calle Murillo. The colourful and vivid market is between Paseo Bolívar and the river, the so-called Zona Negra on a side channel of the Magdalena. Good parks in the northern areas, the favourite one is Parque Tomás Suri Salcedo on Calle 72. Stretching back into the north-western heights overlooking the city are the modern suburbs of El Prado, Altos del Prado, Golf and Ciudad Jardín, with the German-run *El Prado Hotel*. There are five stadia in the city, a big covered coliseum for sports, two for football and the others cater for basketball and baseball. The metropolitan stadium is on Av. Murillo, outside the city.

Festivals Carnival, lasting four days, parades, floats, street dancing and beauty contests.

Hotels *El Prado,* the social centre, swimming pool and tennis courts, B, good restaurant, sauna, some distance from the centre (Carrera 54, No. 70-10); in same district; ***Royal,*** Carrera 54, No. 68-124, T 35-78-00, B, good service, with swimming pool, modern; ***Davega,*** Calle 72 y Carrera 44, T 359020, D (incl tax), good value, rec.; ***Génova,*** swimming pool, Calle 44, No. 44-66, 10 blocks from centre, C; ***Arenosa,*** Carrera 48, No. 70-136, C, with bath, TV, pleasant staff and surroundings; ***Villa Venecia,*** Calle 61, No. 46-41, T 414107, D, clean, TV, a little noisy but rec.; *Majestic*, Carrera 53, No. 54-41, out of city centre, C, very good; *Cadelia*, Calle 75, No. 41-79, D; *El Golf*, Barrio El Golf, Cra. 59b, No. 81-158, D; *Dann*, Cra. 51b, No. 19-246, opened in 1989. *Los Angeles*, Calle 41, E with bath, safe, clean, friendly; *Zhivago*, Plaza Bolívar, very good, E, without bath; *Horizonte*, Calle 45 y Carrera 44, F with bath, clean, quiet, fan, rec.; *Apartotel Salerno*, Calle 45 down from Brasilia bus station, cheap, good and safe. *Embajador*, Calle 34 (Paseo Bolívar), No. 40-66, F with bath and phone, very good; *Real*, Paseo Bolívar, next to Plaza, D, clean, friendly, English and German spoken. **Note**: hotel prices may be much higher during Carnival. Watch for thieves in downtown hotels.

Restaurants *La Puerta de Oro*, Calle 35, No. 41-100, central, a/c, good for meals (inc. breakfast); *Fonda Antioqueña*, local dishes, friendly; *Jardines de Confucio*, Cra. 54, No.75-44, good Chinese food, nice atmosphere; *El Calderito*, also local, tropical garden atmosphere; *Los Techos Rojos*, steak-house; various Lebanese (*Baalbek, Biblios, Tripoli*) with belly-dancers; several Chinese and *pizzerias*. *El Mesón de Morgan*, excellent sea-food, good service, but very expensive; *El Famoso Chino*, Paseo Bolívar, good and cheap self-service, clean.

Clubs Barranquilla; Anglo-American; German; Italian; Centro Israelita.

Market San Andrecito, or "Tourist Market", Vía 40, is where smuggled goods are sold at very competitive prices; a good place to buy film. Picturesque and reasonably safe. Any taxi driver will take you there.

Bookshop *Librería Nacional*, Carrera 53, English, French and German books. Maps from Instituto Agustín Codazzi, Calle 36, No. 45-101.

Local Transport Taxis within the town cost US$1.40.

Entertainments Theatre, Amira de la Rosa. **Night Life** *La Cabaña* at *Hotel El Prado*. Famous disco *Agua Sala* at beach.

Museum Small archaeological collection, Calle 68 No. 53-45 (Mon.-Fri. 0900-1200, 1400-1700), with big physical relief map on front lawn. Also, Museo Romántico, Cra. 54, No. 59-199, history of Barranquilla.

Zoo There is a well-maintained zoo with some animals not often seen in zoos, but many are in small cages, Calle 74, Cra. 50 (bus "Boston/Boston" or "Caldes/Recreo"), entrance US$0.60, students US$0.30, 0830-1200, 1400-1800. All the trees are labelled.

Exchange Banco Royal de Colombia; Banco Anglo Colombiano, Calle 34, No. 44-43, with agency on Calle 72; Banco Internacional de Colombia. Open: Mon.-Thurs, 0800-1130, 1400-1600; Fri. 0900-1130, 1400-1630; last working day of month 0800-1130. *Casa de cambio* El Cacique, Calle 34, No. 43-108, T 326392, reliable. American Express agency at Tierra Mar Aire, downtown.

Consulates **Venezuelan Consulate**, Calle 70, No. 53-74 (Centro Financiero El Prado, 4° piso), T 580048/582832, 0800-1500 (take "Caldas/Recreo" or "Boston/Boston" bus), visa issued same day, but you must be there by 0915 with photo and US$10 cash; onward ticket may not be requested, not a helpful office. **US Consulate**, Centro Comercial Mayorista, Calle 77, No. 68-15, opposite zoo (Apartado Aéreo 51565), T 45-70-88 or 45-71-81 (visas obtainable only in Bogotá). **British Consulate**, Cra 44, No. 45-57, T 326936; **W. German Consulate**, Calle 80, near Vía 40 (ask for Herr Schnabel). **Dutch Consulate**, Carrera 42H, No. 85-33, T 341282; **Spanish Consulate**, Calle 51, No. 37-64, T 313694.

Police (for declarations of theft, etc.), Policía F2, Calle 47 y Carrera 43.

Tourist Information at main hotels and at Calle 72, No. 57-43, of. 401, T 45-44-58 or 33-66-58. CNT is at Carrera 54, No 75-45, T 454458. A recommended taxi-driver/guide to the city is Henry Robinson, T 35-37-14; he speaks English. Locals will show you beautiful beaches off road to Cartagena.

Airport Ernesto Cortissoz airport is 10 km. from the city; there is plenty of transport of all types. City bus from airport to town, US$0.10 (US$0.15 on Sunday). Taxi to town, US$4.50 (taxis do not have meters, fix fare in advance). Special bus from outside the airport, US$2.50 (to town, take only buses marked "centro"); the bus to the airport (marked Malambo) leaves from Carrera 44 up Calle 32 to Carrera 38, then up Calle 30 to Airport. Taxi to Cartagena, US$40. Avianca to Aruba and Curaçao as well as Colombian destinations; Lacsa to Caracas, Panama, San José and San Juan (Puerto Rico), and connections to Mexico City, other Central American capitals and Los Angeles.

Buses Most bus companies operate from Calle 34 and Carrera 45 (Brasilia at Calle 45 y Carrera 35). To Santa Marta, US$1.80, Pullman (or US$1.60 in non-a/c, Coolibertador), about 2 hrs., also direct to Santa Marta's famous Rodadero beach; to Montería, US$9.25, 8 hrs.; to Medellín by Pullman, US$16, 16hrs.; to Bucaramanga, US$13.50 with Copetran, air-conditioned, first class, departures at 1130 most days, arriving 2030; to Bogotá, 20 hrs., US$20 direct; to Caucasia, US$9, 11 hrs. To Maicao US$6.50, 5 hrs. (with Brasilia, every ½ hour from 0100-1200); to Cartagena, 3 grades of bus, 3 hrs. (US$2.25 with Transportes Cartagena, US$2.75 with Expreso Brasilia, by Brasilia Van Tours mini-bus, US$2, from their downtown offices as well as the bus terminals), 2 hrs. by colectivo, US$2.50.

Warnings When leaving by air for the USA, you may be searched by drug squad police; they are very civil, but acquisitive—check your belongings afterwards. Tourist Police can be very rough when searching foreigners. Beware also of people claiming to be ships' officers who say they can arrange a passage if you pay in advance; buy a passage only in a recognized shipping office or agency. If shipping a car into Barranquilla allow 2 days to complete all paperwork to retrieve your car from the port.

Roads Regular buses from Paseo Bolívar and the church at Calle 33 and Carrera 41 to the attractive bathing resort of **Puerto Colombia**, 19 km. (US$0.50, ½ hr.). Beach clean and sandy, water a bit muddy. S along the Magdalena to the little town of Palmar de Varela. On this road, 5 km. from the city, is the old colonial town of **Soledad**, with 16,000 inhabitants. The cathedral and the old narrow streets round it are worth seeing.

Barranquilla-Cartagena, a good paved road but driving is violent, and cyclists have reported muggings. From Baranoa a branch road runs to Usicurí (72 km. from Barranquilla), known for its medicinal waters and for the grave of the popular Colombian poet, Julio Flores. The main road goes on via Sabanalarga (50 km. from Barranquilla) to Cartagena. From Sabanalarga an all-weather road continues to Puerto Giraldo, a port on the Magdalena River linked by ferry with the small town of Salmina (ferry 0500 to 1800). A spectacular new bridge over the River Magdalena gives a fine view of Barranquilla and the river. An all-weather road leads to Fundación, on the Atlántico Railway, and a junction point with the road from Santa Marta to Bucaramanga and Bogotá, which is now paved throughout, though surface somewhat uneven.

Cartagena, old and steeped in history, is one of the most interesting towns in South America. Its population is 700,000. An arm of the river, 145 km. long, canalized in 1650 by Spain—the Canal del Dique—from Calamar to Cartagena allows free access for ships from the up-river ports.

What interests the visitor is a comparatively small part of Cartagena, the old walled city almost completely surrounded by the Caribbean sea on the W, the waters of the Bay of Cartagena on the S, and lakes and lagoons to the N and E. Cartagena was one of the storage points for merchandise sent out from Spain and for treasure collected from the Americas to be sent back to Spain. A series of forts protecting the approaches from the sea, and the formidable walls built around the city, made it almost impregnable.

Cartagena was founded by Pedro de Heredia on 13 January, 1533. There were then two approaches to it, Bocagrande, at the northern end of Tierra Bomba Island—this was a direct entry from the Caribbean—and Boca Chica. Bocagrande was blocked after Admiral Vernon's attack in 1741, and thereafter the only approach was by the narrow channel of Boca Chica from the S. Boca Chica leads into the great bay of Cartagena, 15 km. long and 5 km. wide. The old walled city lies at the head of it.

Entering Boca Chica by sea, the island of Tierra Bomba is to the left. At the tip of a spit of land is the fortress of San Fernando (entrance fee, US$0.60; guide, US$1.50 for one to five people); boat trips out (1 hr.) are worth while. Opposite it, right on the tip of Barú island, is the fortress of San José. You can paddle your own canoe from San Fernando to San José. The two forts were once linked by heavy chains to prevent surprise attacks by pirates. North of Barú island stretches Manga island, much larger and now an important suburb. At its northern end a bridge, Puente Román, connects it with the old city. This approach was defended by three forts: San Sebastián del Pastelillo built between 1558 and 1567 (the Club de Pesca has it now) at the north-western tip of Manga Island; the fortress of San

Lorenzo near the city itself; and the very powerful fortress of San Felipe inland on a height to the E of the city. Yet another fort, La Tenaza, protected the walled city from a direct attack from the open sea. The huge encircling walls were started in 1634 and finished by 1735. They were on average 12 metres high and 17 metres thick, with 6 gates. They contained, besides barracks, a water reservoir.

In spite of its daunting outer forts and encircling walls Cartagena was challenged again and again by enemies. Sir Francis Drake, with 1,300 men, broke in successfully in 1586. The Frenchmen Baron de Pointis and Ducasse, with 10,000 men, beat down the defences and sacked the city in 1697. But the strongest attack of all, by Sir Edward Vernon with 27,000 men and 3,000 pieces of artillery, failed in 1741 after besieging the city for 56 days; it was defended by the one-eyed, one-armed and one-legged hero Blas de Lezo, whose statue is at the entrance to the San Felipe fortress.

Cartagena declared its independence from Spain in 1811. A year later Bolívar used the city as a jumping-off point for his Magdalena campaign. After a heroic resistance, Cartagena was retaken by the royalists under Pablo Morillo in 1815. The patriots finally freed it in 1821.

The old walled city was in two sections, inner and outer. Much of the wall between the two was razed a few years ago. Nearly all the houses are of one or two storeys. The houses in El Centro were occupied by the high officials and nobility. San Diego (the northern end of the inner town) was where the middle classes lived: the clerks, merchants, priests and military. The artisan classes lived in the one-storey houses of Getsemaní in the outer city.

The streets are narrow and rarely straight. Each block has a different name, a source of confusion, but don't worry: the thing to do is to wander aimlessly, savouring the street scenes, and allow the great sights to catch you by surprise. Our map is marked with numerals for the places of outstanding interest. The most attractive streets have been given a star (*). Most of the "great houses" can be visited.

The numbers stand for the following places:
1. The Puente Román, the bridge which leads from the island of Manga into the Getsemaní district. Visitors should on no account miss seeing the *casas bajas* or low houses of Getsemaní, but be careful; it is not a very safe neighbourhood.
2. The Chapel of San Roque (early 17th century), near the Hospital of Espíritu Santo.
3. The Church of Santísima Trinidad, built 1643 but not consecrated till 1839. The plaza in which it stands is most interesting. North of the church, at number 10, lived Pedro Romero, the man who set the revolution of 1811 going by coming out into the street shouting "Long Live Liberty".
4. The Monastery and Church of San Francisco. The church was built in 1590 after the pirate Martin Côte had destroyed an earlier church built in 1559. The first Inquisitors lodged at the monastery. From its courtyard a crowd surged into the streets claiming independence from Spain on the morning of 11 November, 1811. The Church of the Third Order is now the Colón Theatre.
   Immediately to the N is Plaza de la Independencia, with the landscaped Parque del Centenario just off it. At right angles to the Plaza runs the Paseo de los Mártires, flanked by the busts of nine patriots executed in the square on 24 February, 1816 by the royalist Morillo when he retook the city. At its western end is a tall clock tower. Passing through the tower's arches (the main entrance to the inner walled city) we get to
5. The Plaza de los Coches. Around almost all the plazas of Cartagena arcades offer refuge from the tropical sun. On the W side of this plaza is the famous Portal de los Dulces, a favourite meeting place.
6. Plaza de la Aduana, with a statue of Columbus and the City Hall.
7. Church of San Pedro Claver and Monastery, built by Jesuits in 1603 and later dedicated to San Pedro Claver, a monk in the monastery, was canonized 235 years after his death in 1654. He was called the Slave of the Slaves: he used to beg from door to door for money to give to the black slaves brought to the city. His body is in a glass coffin on the high altar, and his cell and the balcony from which he sighted slave ships are shown to visitors. Entry, US$0.50. Guides charge US$1.
8. Plaza de Bolívar (the old Plaza Inquisición), very pleasant, and with a statue of Bolívar. On its W side is
9. The Palace of the Inquisition, established in 1610, but the building dates from 1706. The stone entrance with its coats of arms and well preserved and ornate wooden door is very notable. Indeed the whole building, with its overhanging balconies, cloisters and patios, is a fine example of colonial baroque. There is a very pleasant historical museum at the Palace,

and a library. Entry charge US$0.40; good historical books on sale. Open Mon-Fri, 0800-1130, 1400-1730.

On the opposite side of the Plaza to the Palace of the Inquisition, the Museo del Oro y Arqueológico has been installed in an old building. Gold and pottery, very well displayed.

Entrance free.

In the NE corner of Plaza de Bolívar is

10. The Cathedral, begun in 1575 and partially destroyed by Francis Drake. Reconstruction was finished by 1612. Great alterations were made between 1912 and 1923. A severe exterior, with a fine doorway, and a simply decorated interior. See the guilded 18th century altar, the Carrara marble pulpit, and the elegant arcades which sustain the central nave.

11. **Church and Convent of Santa Teresa**, founded 1609, now occupied by the police.

12. The Church and Monastery of Santo Domingo, built 1570 to 1579 and now a seminary. The old monastery was replaced by the present one in the 17th century. Inside, a miracle-making image of Christ, carved towards the end of the 16th century, is set on a baroque 19th century altar. Most interesting neighbourhood, very little changed since the 16th century. In Calle Santo Domingo, No. 33-29, is one of the great patrician houses of Cartagena, the Casa de los Condes de Pestagua, now the Colegio del Sagrado Corazón de Jesús. North of Santo Domingo, at

13. Calle de la Factoria 36-57 is the magnificent Casa del Marqués de Valdehoyos, now owned by the tourist authority and containing a Tourist Office; open to visitors.

14. The Church and Convent of La Merced, founded 1618. The Convent—a prison during Morillo's reign of terror—is now occupied by the Law Courts and its church is the Municipal Theatre.

15. The Monastery of San Agustín (1580), now the University. From its chapel, now occupied by a printing press, the pirate Baron de Pointis stole a 500-pound silver sepulchre. It was returned by the King of France but the citizens melted it down to pay their troops during the siege by Morillo in 1815. Adjoining the University is the Edificio Ganem, which offers a good, free view of the city from the 9th floor.

16. The Church of Santo Toribio de Mongrovejo. Building began in 1729. In 1741, during Admiral Vernon's siege, a cannon ball fell into the church during Mass and lodged in one of the central columns; the ball is now in a recess in the W wall. The font of Carrara marble in the Sacristy is a masterpiece. There is a beautiful carved ceiling (*mudéjar* style) above the main altar. Opens for Mass at 0600 and 1800, closed at other times.

17. Casa del Consulado (Calle Sargento Mayor) was one of the great houses but has now become a teachers' college.

18. Church and Monastery of Santa Clara of Assisi, built 1617-21, now the Hospital of Santa Clara.

19. Plaza de las Bóvedas. The walls of Las Bóvedas, built 1799, are some 12 metres high and from 15 to 18 metres thick. Cars can drive along the rampart, from which there is a grand view of the harbour. At the base of the wall are 23 dungeons, now containing tourist shops. Both a lighted underground passage and a drawbridge lead from Las Bóvedas to the fortress of La Tenaza on the sea shore.

20. Casa de Núñez, just outside the walls of La Tenaza in El Cabrero district opposite the Ermita de El Cabrero and 5 minutes from the old bullring; here lived Rafael Núñez, president (four times) and poet (he wrote Colombia's national anthem). His grandiose marble tomb is in the adjoining church.

Three of the sights of Cartagena are off our map. One of them is the Fortress of San Fernando, already mentioned.

The Fortress of San Felipe, across the Puente Heredia (21) from the outer walled city, stands on the hill of San Lázaro, 41 metres above sea-level. Building began in 1639 and it was finished by 1657. Under the huge structure are tunnels lined with living rooms and offices. Some are open and lighted; visitors pass through these and on to the top of the fortress. Baron de Pointis, the French pirate, stormed and took it in 1697, but Admiral Vernon failed to reach it in the abortive attack of 1741. Entrance fee US$0.85. Guide US$1.50 for one to five people.

A lovely road leads to the summit of La Popa hill, nearly 150 metres high, from which there is a fine view of the harbour and the city (entry US$0.85). Here are the church and monastery of Santa Cruz and restored ruins of convent dating from 1608. In the church is the beautiful little image of the Virgin of La Candelaria, reputed a deliverer from plague and a protector against pirates. Her day is 2 February. For nine days before the feast thousands of people go up the hill by car, on foot, or on horseback. On the day itself people carry lighted candles as they go up the hill. The name was bestowed on the hill because of an imagined likeness to a ship's poop. It is dangerous to walk up on your own; either take a guided tour, or take a public bus to Teatro Miramar at the foot of the hill (US$0.50), then bargain for a taxi up, about US$2.50 (or US$5 from centre of town). The Tourist Office recommends a guided tour from an agency opposite the *Hotel Playa* in Bocagrande, for US$5.50, which also takes in San Felipe and San Pedro Claver. You can tour the old town and Bocagrande in a *chiva*, a brightly coloured wooden seated bus with a live band in the back.

Feasts The other great feast, apart from Candlemas, is on 11-14 November to celebrate the independence of Cartagena. Men and women in masks and fancy dress roam the streets, dancing to the sound of *maracas* and drums. There are beauty contests and battles of flowers and general gaiety. This festival tends to be wild and can be dangerous.

Caribbean Music Festival For 5 days in March, groups from all over the Caribbean region and beyond perform salsa, reggae, etc., etc.; loud and fun. There is a **film festival** at the end of April.

Warnings Carry your passport (or, safer, a DAS-approved photocopy of it) at all times. Failure to present it on police request can result in imprisonment and fines. Regarding sea passages, see warning under Barranquilla (**page** 655). In addition, if offered a job on a ship to the Galápagos or to New York, insist on full documentation at the Seamen's Union office and do not make any arrangements on the street.

Beware also of self-appointed tourist guides who charge very highly for their services, and can turn nasty if thwarted. Bus travellers are met by people offering to recommend a hotel; their services are not necessary and may lead to "coincidental" theft later. Expert pickpockets reported in crowded areas in town and on the beaches.

Hotels On Bocagrande beach, 10 mins by bus from city: *Cartagena-Hilton*, El Laguito, L, T 50666 (Apto. Aéreo 1774); *Capilla del Mar*, B, Calle 8, Carrera 1, T 51140, excellent French restaurant, swimming pool on 4th floor, be careful of their travel desk and check any reservations they make for you, no connection with restaurant of same name ½ km. away; *Las Velas*, Calle Las Velas, No. 1-60, T 80000, C, opposite *Caribe Casino*, warm water all day, showers, good restaurant; *Hotel del Caribe*, Cra. 1, No. 1-114, T 50155, B, all rooms a/c, older half nicer, administration could be better, nice grounds, swimming pool in the (expensive) restaurant, pancakes rec.; *India Catalina*, Carrera 2, No. 7-115, T 55392, C, very good, with a/c, safe, clean (acts as youth hostel); *Residencias Internacional*, Av. San Martín 4110, T 50-675, C, with bath and a/c, clean, safe, friendly; opposite at No. 5-86 is *Flamingo*, C (D in low season), T 50301, with bath and a/c, clean, helpful, pleasant, eat on the terrace, highly rec.; *Succar*, Carrera 2, No. 6-40, D, clean, helpful. *Playa*, on Av. San Martín, T 50552, C, all rooms with private bathroom, very clean, open air bar, restaurant (breakfast, US$1), swimming pool, noisy disco next door, Av. 2a, No. 4-87; *Residencias Bocagrande*, D, with shower, no hot water, clean and friendly, but noisy, try to get a room with a balcony and a view over the sea, good restaurant; *Leonela*, Carrera 3a, 7-142, D, quiet, comfortable; *Residencias Astoria*, D, bath, fan (air conditioning 25% extra), friendly, breakfast US$1.50, good, not actually on beach, but nearby *Residencia Punta Canda*, Calle 7 between Cras 2 and 3, E, reasonable and everything works. On Carrera 3, there are plenty of small, pleasant *residencias*, for instance Carrera 3, No. 5-29, D in season, clean and friendly. Apartments may be rented from Apartments Intercontinental, Diagonal 1 y Calle 1, e.g. US$40 a day for 6, on Bocagrande next to *Hilton*.

In town: *Del Lago*, Calle 34, No. 11-15, T 44192, D, no hot water, phone, no singles, reasonable; *Montecarlo*, between Av. Urdaneta Arbeláez and Av. Venezuela, T 45013, D, good value, big neon sign on the roof, good reliable laundry next door. *Veracruz*, Calle San Agustín, opp. San Agustín church, E, clean, safe, with or without a/c, helpful but noisy from disco on ground floor; *Bucarica*, San Agustín 6-08, F, quite popular with travellers, but rooms vary a lot and acts as a brothel; *Residencial Pacoa*, Calle Pacoa, F, noisy, uncomfortable but friendly; *Magdalena*, same street, F with bath, cold water, fan, clean but small rooms; *Monterrey*, Camellón de los Mártires (opposite the clocktower), F, clean, safe, friendly, central; *Real*, Calle Espíritu Santo 29-70, E with shower, basic, mice, laundry service, not very safe area; *Residencias Familiar*, Calle Espíritu Santo 29-197, T 648374, F, family owned, safe, friendly, rec.; *San Francisco*, Plaza Independencia opp. Parque Centenario, E, quiet; *Plaza Bolívar*, Plaza Bolívar No. 3-94, T 40431, D, good, nice restaurant, accepts dollars cash and credit cards; *Carisma*, Cuartel y Soledad, F, clean, safe, but unfriendly, not rec. *Residencias Venezia*, Calle del Guerrero No. 29-108, F, friendly, rec. some rooms with fan, clean and secure; *Doral*, Media Luna, friendly, nice, fan, large rooms, E, good cheap restaurant; *Hostal Valle*, Calle Media Luna, F, very friendly, hot water, some rooms with private bath, free coffee, discounts for long stay, helpful owners, the Guzmans. *Media Luna*, Media Luna y Centenario, F without bath, clean, good value; *San Felipe*, Media Luna 943, with rooms in F range, and good cheap meals; many cheap hotels on Calle Media Luna are brothels; area not advisable for women on their own. On the road to the airport are several hotels and *pensiones*, particularly at Marbella beach (e.g. *Bellavista*, Av. Santander, D, clean, nice patio, English-speaking owner, Enrique Sedó, secure; *Playa Blanca*, Av. Santander, E, very nice; *Miramar*, D, with toilet and shower, clean, secure).

N.B. Hotel prices tend to go up by as much as 25 per cent in December each year (i.e. increase

Bocagrande hotels by a letter in our range at this time; in town nothing is below E); hotels tend to be heavily booked right through to March. Either book well in advance yourself, or avoid the city at this time. For hotel insurance, add 5%, plus US$0.05 p.p. per day.

Camping In a secure walled garden at *Hotel Bellavista*, Av. Santander, on the beach, US$2.50 p.p.; camper vans also welcome (price in E range). People camp on the beach, but may be troubled by thieves—and the police.

Restaurants *Nautilus*, facing the statue of La India Catalina, seafood; another *Nautilus* (same menu and service) on road to airport in Marbella; and yet another *Nautilus*, Carrera 3, Bocagrande, good but expensive; *Capilla del Mar*, rec., sea food dinner for 2, US$20-30; all-you-can-eat buffet on Tues. (shrimp) and Fri. (seafood) for US$15. Also in Bocagrande, Av. San Martín, *Da Marisa*, pizzas; *Fontana di Trevi*, Italian, rec.; *Alexander*, German food; *El Arca de Noé*, very good steaks; *El Patio de la Atarraya*, good fish restaurant overlooking the sea; *Rincón Argentino* for good steaks (US$4); *La Olla Cartagenera* and *La Petite Sensation*, both on Carrera 2, very good, but not cheap; *La Fonda Antioqueña*, Cra. 2, No. 6-161, traditional Colombian, nice atmosphere; *La Piragua*, Carrera 2, an open-air bar with live music, pleasant; *La Heladería Arabe*, Carrera 3, good ice cream; *Little Chicken*, Americanized Colombian food, clean, good food and juices (US$4 for steaks), English spoken by Ivan, helpful manager; *La Hormiga*, Calle Bocagrande, good, cheap; *Kokoriko* is a chain of barbecued chicken restaurants, US$6 for a whole chicken. Many good juice bars in Bocagrande.

Away from Bocagrande: *Club de Pesca*, at the Fuerte del Pastelillo: you can dine in the open air in a lovely setting, expensive (taxi, US$3.50-4.50); *Marcel Hostería Sevillana*, Malecón 70, near *Residencias Ligia*; *El Candilejo*, more expensive than it looks, but good food (in Candilejo). *Loon Foon*, Chinese, good, on first street into city from the statue of La India Catalina; *Kon-Nam*, Calle San Pedro Claver, good Chinese cuisine; good, cheap Chinese restaurant in C. Estanco de Tabaco; *Nuevo Oriente*, near Santo Domingo, Chinese, good; *Wing Wah*, Calle Ayos, good Chinese, rec.; *El Ganadero*, Calle Media Luna, good food, friendly; *Paco's Restaurant* on Plaza Santo Domingo, pleasant atmosphere, excellent food, not cheap; *Bodegón de la Candelaria*, Calle de las Damas (T 47251), excellent food and service, but expensive; *El Rinconcito*, near Plaza Fernando de Madrid, good cheap meals; also *El Pollo Dorado* on Calle Ricuarte, opposite Banco de Bogotá. *La Langosta*, Av. Venezuela, just outside old city walls, good food, reasonable prices; *Nuevo Mundo*, Calle 30, No. 8B-62 serves typical menu, cheap, good sized servings; *Americano*, near central post office, good meals for US$1.50; *Bar La Vitrola*, rec. for its atmosphere; *La Fragata*, in old town, two blocks behind *Hotel Bolívar*, French maître d'hôtel, German cook. Many restaurants around Plaza Independencia have meals for about US$2. Restaurants in Calle San Andrés cost about US$1.30, with plenty to eat; cheap meals at *San Martín*, Calle de las Damas, and in a restaurant on the corner of Plaza de los Coches. Vegetarian restaurant and health food shop, *Santísimo*, lunch under US$1. *Panificadora la Española*, Calle 8, No. 7-61, fresh bread and pastries; *Heladería Almirante Vernón*, a block from San Pedro Claver church towards Plaza Bolívar, has hearty, reasonable meals and good fruit juices; *Heladería Cecilia* for good ice-creams. *Juguería Dino* (near the clocktower at entrance on landward side to the city walls) for fruit juices, good. At cafés try the patacón, a biscuit made of green banana, mashed and baked; also in Parque del Centenario in early morning. *Stella Maris*, near the harbour in Barrio Manga, used mainly by seamen, is a bar and shop, selling stamps (0900-2300) and souvenirs, administered by the Salvation Army.

Market There is a new market out of town, which is disappointing; bus from Av. Urdaneta Arbeláez. The fish market is in the SE suburbs of the old city.

Shopping A good selection of *artesanías* on Plaza Bolívar, but in general (except for leather goods) shopping is much better in Bogotá. Woollen *blusas* are good value, US$8-12; try the *Tropicano* in Pierino Gallo building in Bocagrande. Also in this building are reputable jewellery shops. *H. Stern* has a jewellery shop in the Pierino Gallo shopping centre and at the *Hilton Hotel*. Suntan oils and lotions can vary in price as much as 100%—shop around. Comercial Centro Getsemaní, Calle Larga between San Juan and Plaza de la Independencia, a large new shopping centre has many establishments.

Gambling Casino Turístico, Av. San Martín and Casino de Caribe at Pierino Gallo shopping centre, Bocagrande.

Car Rental National and Hertz at airport; Avis at *Hilton Hotel*.

Local Transport Within the city large buses (with no glass in windows) cost US$0.05, short-wheelbase type (with glass windows), US$0.10. **Taxis** from Bocagrande to the centre should be less than US$1; to the airport US$2.20; centre to airport, US$2 (more at night). Try to fix price for journey before committing yourself. A horse-drawn carriage can be hired for US$9, opposite *Hotel El Dorado*, Av. San Martín, in Bocagrande, to ride into town at night (romantic but rather short ride).

Sport Fishing; yachting. Windsurf rental, Bocagrande, US$6.50 per hour. Also bullfights and cockfights. The former take place mainly in January and February in the new Plaza de Toros on Av. Pedro de Heredia away from the centre; the latter throughout the year on Sat., Sun. and holidays. On Sat. and Mon. at 1500 cockfighting takes place at the Gallerita Popular de la Quinta and on Sun. at 1600 at Club Gallístico Pedro Rhenals in El Bosque.

Beaches Take bus from Plaza de la Independencia to Bocagrande, which has good beaches (although dirty and often crowded). The Boca Chica beach is also dirty, and the boat service there unreliable. Boats leave from Plaza de la Independencia; the round trip can take up to 2 hrs. each way. *Ferry Dancing*, US$2 about half the price of luxury boats, carries dancing passengers; the much faster launches cost US$3.50. For about US$1.50 you can take a tour round the fort of San Fernando in a dugout canoe. There are boats from the city; the last return trip is at 1230. Swimming is good. Boats taking in Boca Chica and San Fernando are US$5 return without lunch or US$10.50 with lunch (children under 12, half price); Alcatraz run a daily trip from the Muelle Turístico leaving at about 1000, returning at 1530. There is a daily cruise to **Islas del Rosario**, US$14.50 including lunch (possible to bargain in low season), with Alcatraz, leaving 0630, returning 1630. The boat may stop at the San Fernando fortress (entrance US$0.60) and Playa Blanca on the mainland for 1 hr. (bargain with boatman to leave you for a day, camp on the beach, and continue the cruise next day—Playa Blanca is crowded a.m., but peaceful after the tour boats have left.) At the Islas del Rosario is an aquarium in the sea, worth visiting, entrance US$1 not included in the boat fare. There are cheaper boats to the islands, shop around. Marbella beach, just N of Las Bóvedas (the locals' beach, and therefore quieter than Bocagrande) is good for swimming, though subject at times to dangerous currents.

Art Gallery and Museum Contemporary Latin American paintings, Banco Ganadero, Plaza de la Aduana. Nearby is the Museo de Arte Moderno (open Mon.-Fri., 0900-1200, 1500-1800, Sat., 1000-1200), opposite the San Pedro Claver church.

Exchange Banco Anglo Colombiano. Banco Royal changes American Express travellers' cheques up to a maximum of US$300, with US$10 commission. Banco de la República, on Plaza Bolívar, changes American Express and Thomas Cook cheques, with commission, fingerprints and photo taken. There are many *cambios*; the only one we've heard of changing travellers' cheques is *Caja de Cambio Caldas*, Av. San Martín, No. 4-118, Bocagrande. Be sure to count the pesos yourself before handing over your dollars. Never change money on the street, they are nearly all crooks and will short-change you. American Express (Tierra Mar Aire), Bocagrande, Carrera 4, Calle 8, is a travel agency only. Travellers' cheques can be changed Sat. a.m. (arrive early) at Joyería Mora, Román 5-39, in the old city.

Anglican Church Calle Ricuarte, services in English can be arranged.

Post Office beside Avianca office between Avs. Venezuela and Urdaneta Arbeláez.

Venezuelan Consulate Carrera 12, No. 557 Bocagrande, no visa issued without onward ticket, minimum wait 24 hrs. Better try elsewhere. **DAS** just off Av. Crisanto Luque, near La Ermita at foot of La Popa, T 64649 (take "Socorro" bus), very helpful. **Canadian Honorary Consul** (for emergencies only), Calle de la Inquisición con Santo Domingo, esq., No. 33-08, Apto. 201.

Tourist Office Carrera 3, No. 36-57 (Plaza Bolívar, T 43400); also at Casa del Marqués de Valdehoyos, Calle de la Factoría (T 47015/9). Also, at the airport, but you will only be given information on the more expensive hotels. Recommended guide, Fernando Vargas Osorio, Calle de Magdalena, No. 7-52.

Shipping There are modern wharves. It is possible to ship a car from Cartagena to Panama. Interoceánica, Centro Carrera 4a, No. 31-14, T 45976/ 44047; cargo ships. Comar agency for Lykes Line, formalities take 3 days; Lykes sails to New Orleans, taking passengers (more expensive than flying). Cargo ships are not allowed to take passengers to San Andrés; some may risk it, charging about US$25. You have to ask the captain; ships leave from Embarcadero San Andrés, opp. Plaza de la Aduana. There are boats leaving most days for points south along the coast and up the river Sinú to Montería, and the Atrato as far as Quibdó. For the trip to Quibdó see page 692.

Airport Crespo, 1½ km. from the city, reached by local buses from Blas de Lezo, SW corner of inner wall. Bus from airport to Plaza San Francisco US$0.10. Taxi to Bocagrande US$2.20, to town US$2, less if you share. Commuter flights to Barranquilla. Tourist information desk gives list of taxi prices. Good self-service restaurant. No exchange facilities. SAM and Avianca offices both near the post office. From December to March all flights are overbooked—even reconfirming and turning up 2 hours early doesn't guarantee a seat; don't book a seat on the last plane of the day.

Buses All long-distance buses leave from Calle 32, with Av. Pedro Heredia, near foot of San Felipe fortress (any bus marked "E-Villa" goes to the old city and Parque Centenario). Pullman bus from Cartagena to Medellín 665 km., US$14 (1st class). Several buses a day, but book early (2 days in advance at holiday times), takes 13-16 hrs. The road is now paved throughout, but in poor condition with 4-5 checkpoints. To Santa Marta, US$4.75 (with Brasilia, Calle 32, No. 20D-55), 4 hrs., also cheaper lines, US$3.50. To Barranquilla US$2.25 with Transportes Cartagena, 3 hrs., or US$2.75 with Expreso Brasilia pullman or La Costeña, US$2.60, 3 hrs. To Bogotá via Barranquilla and Bucaramanga with Expreso Brasilia pullman, four a day, US$23, may take 21-28 hrs., depending on number of check-points. To Magangué on the Magdalena US$4, 4 hours with Brasilia. To Valledupar with Expreso Brasilia, pullman US$8.50 (with a 1/2 hour stop in Barranquilla), for Sierra Nevada and Pueblo Bello. To Riohacha, US$7.50. Bus to Maicao on Venezuelan frontier US$4.75 (with Expreso Auto Pullman, Expreso Brasilia at 2000, or Unitrasco, Av. Pedro Heredia), 12 hrs.; the road is in good condition, except for 30 km.

Excursions from Cartagena To the little fishing village of *La Boquilla*, E of Cartagena, about 20 mins. past the airport. One small hotel, *Los Morros* (E, clean, good food) and campsite. On Sat. and Sun. nights people dance the local dances. Go there by taxi, US$3 (there is a reasonable bus service, and Carlos drives a green Dodge regularly to the bus terminal, US$0.50); can be dangerous for pedestrians and cyclists. Visit the mangrove swamps nearby to see the birds. To *San Jacinto*, 1 1/2 hrs. by road S of Cartagena, good place for local craft work (*residencial*). To *Turbaco*, 24 km. SE by road (Botanical Garden, 1 1/2 km. before village on the left, student guides, worth a visit for 1/2-day excursion; one *residencial*).

Ninety-six km. S of Cartagena along the coast is *Coveñas*, the terminal of the 420-km. crude oil pipeline from the Barco oilfields to the N of Cúcuta, on the Venezuelan frontier (*Hotel y Motel Fragata*, on the beach, reported overpriced, fleas). 20 mins. away, E, is *Tolú* village (*Residencias Manuelito*, F, and *Residencias El Turista*, very friendly, has own generator, F; *Residencias La Cabaña*, at western end of beach road, F, no running water, friendly; many fish stalls along the beach) whose beaches are not as nice as those at Coveñas, which are unsigned—ask to be let off the bus. W. of Coveñas are beautiful beaches at Porvenir, no food available, afternoon buses infrequent. Coveñas is 40 minutes from

Sincelejo, capital of Sucre Department, a cattle centre 193 km. S of Cartagena on the main road to Medellín (population, 109,000). It is well known for the dangerous bull-ring game, likened to the San Fermín festivities in Pamplona, Spain, in which bulls and men chase each other. Also at Eastertime there is the "Festival del Burro" where they dress up donkeys and prizes go to the best and the funniest. A big party for three days. The town is hot and dusty and power cuts are a factor of life.

Hotels *Majestic*, Carrera 20, No. 21-25, E; same range are *Palace*, Calle 19, No. 21-39, and *Marcella*, Calle 21, 23-59; *Finzenu*, Carrera 20 and Calle 22, D, with a/c and some good basic eating; *Sincelejo*, Plaza Santander, F with shower, clean, friendly, fair restaurant. *Panorama*, Carrera 23, 23-108, E, with air-conditioning.

Near Sincelejo is the finca of José Gonzalo Rodríguez Gacha, the notorious "drug baron" where he was caught and killed by the security forces in December 1989.

127 kms of Sincelejo is *Planeta Rica*, 60 km. beyond which there is a camping site in the grounds of the *Parador Chaubacá* (US$4 per tent); next door is the *Mesón del Gitano*. Fifty km. further on is *Caucasia*, which makes a good stopping point if you want to break the journey from Cartagena to Medellín. *Auto Hotel*, new, best, quiet, heavily booked; *Hotel Playa Mar*, F, good food available, friendly, but noisy; *Hostería Horizontes*, D, calm, spacious, two swimming pools, good restaurant. *Residencias San Francisco*, Carrera 49 esq. Calle 45, E, with bath, good value. Chinese restaurant, 3 doors up, good cheap food. A nice place to visit, Jardín Botánico, entrance fee US$0.25. About half way between Caucasia and Medellín is *Valdivia* with a spectacular bridge over the Cauca. The road continues to Yarumal (see page 690).

Montería, capital of Córdoba Department, on the E bank of the river Sinú, can be reached from Cartagena by air, by river boat, or from the main highway to Medellín. (Bus from Cartagena—dual carriageway almost completed, US$5.25, 5 hrs., with Brasilia, has own terminal in Montería.) It is the centre of a cattle and agricultural area turning out tobacco, cacao, cotton and sugar. Present population is 144,000. Compared with other Caribbean cities there is little to attract the tourist except for the one fine church, picturesque street life and the extremely friendly people. Average temperature: 28°C. Road to Planeta Rica (airport).

Hotels *Sinú*, Carrera 3, Calle 32, C, a/c and swimming pool, watch out for short changing in the restaurant; *Alcázar*, Carrera 2, No. 32-17, F, comfortable and friendly, restaurant not always open; *Embajador*, F, fan, OK; lots of cheap dives in the neighbourhood; *Pensión Rincón*, F, reasonable, clean, meals, US$1; *Residencias Imperial*, Carrera 2, F; *Santa Rosa*, F, with water, good.

Warning There is a high risk of kidnapping in rural areas of Sucre and Córdoba departments; tourists are advised not to stray from the beaten track.

On the Gulf of Urabá is the port of ***Turbo***, now a centre of banana cultivation, which is booming. It is a rough frontier community; not too law-abiding, tourists are advised to be very careful. Turbo may be reached from Cartagena and from Medellín (6 buses a day, a gruelling 13-16 hrs., US$7.50; 4-wheel drive to Montería, 5 hrs., US$6, rough dirt track between Turbo and Valencia, several army checkpoints). Hotels: *Playa Mar*, D, the best; *Sausa*, D, running water in early morning only, helpful owners, pleasant dining room; *Residencia Sandra*, F, good; *Residencia Turbo*, *Residencia Marcela*, both F and best value; good rooms are hard to find, most hotels are brothels; in Playa district: *Miramar*, *Rotitom*, both D. No banks are open for exchange of travellers' cheques on Monday or Tuesday, either don't arrive then, or have dollars in cash with you.

186 km. S of Turbo, on the road to Antioquia (**see page** 690), is Dabeiba (*Residencia Diana*, on main street, F, simple, clean, very helpful, free morning coffee).

To visit the **Los Katíos National Park** (**see below**), go first to the Inderena office in Turbo, where all necessary information is available (recommended trip). A description of routes by boat and overland from Colombia to Panama will be found below; note that if going from Colombia to Panama via Turbo you should get an exit stamp from a DAS office. The nearest we have heard of is at Apartadó, 30 km. from Turbo (40 mins. in colectivo, US$0.80, closed Sat. and Sun.) but even this may now be closed. If leaving Colombia, check the facts in Cartagena (or any other place with a DAS office); if arriving from Panama, you can either go to the police in Turbo for a letter stating your arrival date, then go to DAS in Montería or Cartagena, or just go straight there and explain yourself in full. We have also been informed that the immigration office at the Panamanian port of Puerto Obaldía can be extremely obstructive. Think twice about taking a trip in a small boat between Panama and Colombia: the majority are contraband, even arms runners and if stopped, you will be in trouble. (Even if not stopped you will have difficulty obtaining a DAS entry stamp because the captain of the boat must state officially that he is carrying passengers into Colombia.) If taking a reputable cargo boat be sure to arrange with the captain the price and destination before departure. Boats may also be stopped outside Turbo for medical checks: yellow fever inoculations will be given (free) to all without a certificate.

From Colombia to Panama

The simplest way is to fly from Barranquilla, Bogotá, Cali, Cartagena, Medellín or San Andrés. There are also various routes involving sea and land crossings around or through the **Darién Gap**, which still lacks a road connection linking the Panamanian Isthmus and South America. Descriptions of these routes are given in the *Mexico and Central American Handbook* (although in the direction Panama-Colombia), and a more detailed account is given in *Backpacking in Mexico and Central America* (Bradt Publications—new edition due in 1991). While maps of the region are available, there is no substitute for seeking informed local advice. In all cases, it is essential to be able to speak Spanish.

One route is from Bahía Solano or Jurado in Chocó Department (Jurado can be reached by plane from Turbo). Canoes go from both towns to Jaqué, 50 km. N of the Colombian border, from where you can fly to La Palma, capital of Darién in Panama (one *pensión* F, cooking and laundry facilities, English spoken). Launches and dugouts go from La Palma to Puerto Lardo on the Río Sabanas, from where it is a 2-hour walk (or hitch on a truck) to Santa Fe on the Panamá-Yaviza road. (Bus Santa Fe-Panamá 6-8 hrs.)

On the Caribbean side, the starting point is Turbo on the Gulf of Urabá. From Turbo boats with no fixed schedule sail to Acandí, Zapzurro (in Colombia) and Puerto Obaldía (Panama), from where boats go to Colón, planes to Panama City. If your papers are not in order on arrival in Puerto Obaldía you will be sent back to Colombia. There is an overland route from Puerto Obaldía which involves a 4-hour walk to the foot of the Darién range (guide essential, US$10), crossing the hills to the Río Tuquesa (3 hrs.) and following the river downstream with a great many crossings and one night camping out, to Maranganti (immigration post). From here a dugout can be taken to B. Vigía; walk to the next village, Villa Calleta, where two US missionaries, Doug and Ernie, work (take care with directions on this stretch). From Villa Calleta you walk along the Río Chucucanaque to join the Yaviza-Panama City road near La Pinita. Note that locals on this route are very wary of foreigners (much illegal immigration). We are grateful to Jamie Butler of Petersfield, Hants., for this information.

Two alternative routes from Turbo cross the Gap to Paya, from where there is a well-trodden route to Yaviza: Paya-Pucuro, 5-6 hrs. on foot; Pucuro-Boca de Cupe, by dugout, US$15-30; Boca de Cupe-Pinogana, also by dugout, US$15 p.p., plus a walk, 2 hrs. in all; Pinogana-Yaviza, walk and ferries/dugouts. From Yaviza (one hotel, *Three Américas*, E, basic) buses can be caught to Panama City, US$15, 10 hrs., road subject to wash-outs.

The first route to Paya: motorboat Turbo-Cacarico/Puerto América (US$10 if scheduled, US$130 to hire a boat); then another boat to Bijao (3 hrs., US$30). From Bijao you have to get by boat to Cristales in the Los Katios National Park; the Inderena rangers may take you for about US$10. At Cristales there is an Inderena hut; 7 hrs. through the Park on foot is Palo de los Letras, the frontier stone, from where it is 4-6 hrs. to Paya.

The **Katios National Park** (**Warning**: entry by motorized vehicle is prohibited), extending in Colombia to the Panamanian border, can be visited with mules from the Inderena headquarters in Sautatá (rangers may offer free accommodation, very friendly). In the park is the Tilupo waterfall, 125 metres high; the water cascades down a series of rock staircases, surrounded by orchids and fantastic plants. Also in the park are the Alto de la Guillermina, a mountain behind which is a strange forest of palms called "mil pesos", and the Ciénagas de Tumaradó, with red monkeys, waterfowl and alligators.

The second route to Paya: take a boat from Turbo across the Gulf of Urabá into the Río Tarena to Unguía (accommodation, restaurants). From here it is 3-4 hours to the frontier, then 3 hours to the Río Paya. You then hike down the Paya river through dense jungle to Paya itself (about 12 hours). Do not attempt the Unguía-Paya route without a guide.

Dr Richard Dawood, author of *Travellers' Health: How to Stay Healthy Abroad*, and photographer Anthony Dawton, crossed the Darien Gap at the end of the wet season (November). We are pleased to include Dr Dawood's health recommendations for such a journey: **Heat** Acclimatization to a hot climate usually takes around 3 weeks. It is more difficult in humid climates than in dry ones, since sweat cannot evaporate easily, and when high humidity persists through the night as well, the body has no respite. (In desert conditions, where the temperature falls at night, adaptation is much easier.) Requirements for salt and water increase dramatically under such conditions. We had to drink 12 litres per day to keep pace with our own fluid loss on some parts of the trip.

We were travelling under extreme conditions, but it is important to remember that the human thirst sensation is not an accurate guide to true fluid requirements. In hot countries it is always essential to drink beyond the point of thirst quenching, and to drink sufficient water to ensure that the urine is consistently pale in colour.

Salt losses also need to be replaced. Deficiency of salt, water, or both, is referred to as heat exhaustion; lethargy, fatigue, and headache are typical features, eventually leading to coma and death. Prevention is the best approach, and we used the pre-salted water regime pioneered by Colonel Jim Adam and followed by the British Army; salt is added to all fluids, one quarter of a level teaspoon (approx 1 gram) per pint—to produce a solution that is just below the taste threshold. Salt tablets, however, are poorly absorbed, irritate the stomach and may cause vomiting; plenty of pre-salted fluid should be the rule for anyone spending much time outdoors in the tropics.

Sun Overcast conditions in the tropics can be misleading. The sun's rays can be fierce, and it is important to make sure that all exposed skin is constantly protected with a high factor sun screen—preferably waterproof for humid conditions. This was especially important while we were travelling by canoe. A hat was also essential.

Food and Water Diarrhoea can be annoying enough in a luxurious holiday resort with comfortable sanitary facilities. The inconvenience under jungle conditions would have been more than trivial, however, with the added problem of coping with further fluid loss and dehydration.

Much caution was therefore needed with food hygiene. We carried our own supplies,

DARIÉN

Rough Sketch; not to be used as walking map.

M173B

which we prepared carefully ourselves: rather uninspiring camping fare, such as canned tuna fish, sardines, pasta, dried soup, biscuits and dried fruit. In the villages, oranges, bananas and coconuts were available. The freshly baked bread was safe, and so would have been the rice.

We purified our water with 2 per cent tincture of iodine carried in a small plastic dropping bottle, 4 drops to each litre—more when the water is very turbid—wait 20 minutes before drinking. This method is safe and effective, and is the only suitable technique for such conditions. (Another suggestion from Peter Ovenden is a water purifying pump based on a ceramic filter. There are several on the market, Peter used a Katadyn. It takes about a minute to purify a litre of water – Ed.) It is also worth travelling with a suitable antidiarrhoeal medication such as Arret.

Malaria Drug resistant malaria is present in the Darien area, and antimalarial medication is essential. We took Paludrine, two tablets daily, and chloroquine, two tablets weekly. Free advice on antimalarial medication for all destinations is available from the Malaria Reference Laboratory, T (071) 636 8636 in the UK. An insect repellent is also essential, and so are precautions to avoid insect bites.

Insects Beside malaria and yellow fever, other insect-borne diseases such as dengue fever and leishmaniasis may pose a risk. The old fashioned mosquito net is ideal if you have to sleep outdoors, or in a room that is not mosquito-proof. Mosquito nets for hammocks are widely available in Latin America. An insecticide spray is valuable for clearing your room of flying insects before you go to sleep, and mosquito coils that burn through the night giving off an insecticidal vapour, are also valuable.

Ticks It is said that ticks should be removed by holding a lighted cigarette close to them, and we had an opportunity to put this old remedy to the test. We duly unwrapped a pack of American duty-frees that we had preserved carefully in plastic just for such a purpose, as our Indian guides looked on in amazement, incredulous that we should use these prized items for such a lowly purpose. The British Army expedition to Darien in 1972 carried 60,000 cigarettes among its supplies, and one wonders if they were for this purpose! The cigarette method didn't work, but caused much amusement. (Further discussion with the experts indicates that the currently favoured method is to ease the tick's head gently away from the skin with tweezers.)

Vaccinations A yellow fever vaccination certificate is required from all travellers arriving from infected areas, and vaccination is advised for personal protection.

Immunization against hepatitis A (with gammaglobulin) and typhoid are strongly advised.

Attacks by dogs are relatively common: the new rabies vaccine is safe and effective, and carrying a machete for the extra purpose of discouraging animals is advised.

In addition, all travellers should be protected against tetanus, diptheria and polio.

You can get some food along the way, but take enough for at least 5 days. Do take, though, a torch/flashlight, and a bottle of rum for the ranger at Cristales. It is highly recommended to travel in the dry season only, when there is no mud and fewer mosquitoes. If you have time, bargains can be found.

Taking a motorcycle through Darién is not an endeavour to be undertaken lightly, and cannot be recommended. Ed Culberson (who, in 1986 after two unsuccessful attempts, was the first to accomplish the feat) writes: "Dry season passage is comparatively easy on foot and even with a bicycle. But it simply cannot be done with a standard sized motorcycle unless helped by Indians at a heavy cost in dollars...It is a very strenuous, dangerous adventure, often underestimated by motorcyclists, some who have come to untimely ends in the jungle".

San Andrés and **Providencia**, two small and attractive, but very expensive, islands in the Caribbean Sea, have belonged to Colombia since 1822. They are 400 km. SW of Jamaica, 180 km. E of Nicaragua, and 480 km. N of the Colombian coast. Henry Morgan had his headquarters at San Andrés. A road circles the island, of coral, some 11 km. long rising to 104 metres. The original inhabitants, mostly black, speak some English, but the population has swollen with unrestricted immigration from Colombia. The population in 1988 was put at 35,000, but it could now be about 65,000. Main products: coconuts and vegetable oil. Main problem, deteriorating water and electricity supplies (in most hotels the water is salty—a desalination plant was installed in 1987). Places to see: the beautiful Keys, like Johnny Key with a white beach and parties all day Sunday (US$1.90 return, you can go in one boat and return in another), and the so-called Aquarium (US$2 return), off a Key where, using a mask and wearing sandals as protection against sea-urchins, you can see colourful fish. Boats to these places all leave a.m.; none p.m. Snorkelling equipment can be hired on San Andrés for US$4-5, but it is better and cheaper on the shore than on the island. The Hoyo Soplador is a geyser-like hole through which the sea spouts into the air most surprisingly when the wind is in the right direction. Less spoilt parts of the island are San Luis, Sound Bay and the west side (but no beaches this side). Buses (which circle the island all day) US$0.25. Bicycles are a popular way of getting around on the island and are easy to hire, e.g. opposite *El Dorado Hotel*—usually in poor condition, choose your own bike and check all parts thoroughly (US$1.10 per hour, US$6 per day); motorbikes also easy to hire, US$3.60 per hour. Cars can be hired for US$15 for 2 hours, with US$6 for every extra hour. Pedalos can be hired at US$4 per hour. Diving trips to reef cost US$50 with Pedro Montoya at Aquarium diving shop.

The islands are a customs-free zone; they are very crowded with Colombian shoppers looking for foreign-made bargains. Although alcoholic drinks are cheap, essential goods are extremely costly, and electronic goods are more expensive than in the UK. In July and August, it is very difficult to get on flights into and out of San Andrés; book in advance if possible. Checking in for flights can be difficult because of queues of shoppers with their goods. There is a customs tax of 15% on some items purchased if you are continuing to mainland Colombia.

Only cruise ships and tours go to San Andrés; there are no other passenger services by sea. To ship a vehicle costs US$900 with bargaining (officially US$1,300). To ship a vehicle to Panama costs US$400-450. Interoceánica cargo ships, T 6624-6625. Beware of offers of tickets on ships to/from San Andrés, or of a job on a ship, these are con tricks. Officially, ships may not carry passengers to the mainland; if you want to leave by sea, speak only to the ship's captain.

There are Panamanian and Costa Rican consulates on San Andrés.

Airport Flights to most major Colombian cities: to Bogotá and Medellín with Aces, SAM (you can arrange a 72-hr. stop-over in Cartagena) and Avianca (dearer); to Cartagena, with SAM or Avianca, US$50; to Barranquilla (SAM, Avianca); SAM and Avianca also fly to Cali (US$85) and Pereira. Also to Guatemala City, San José (both daily), Tegucigalpa, Panama. Avianca flies to Miami once a week. Note that Panama, Costa Rica and Honduras all require onward tickets which cannot be bought on San Andrés, can be in Cartagena. Care: SAM will not issue one way tickets to Central America. You buy a return, and SAM office on the mainland will refund once you show an onward ticket. The refund (less 15%) may not be immediate. Sunday flights are always heavily booked. 15 mins. walk to town (taxi US$2.50 p.p.). All airline offices in town, except Satena at airport. SAM offers hotel packages as well as the airfare.

Carry your passport (or photocopy) at all times.

Hotels *Gran Internacional*, Av. Colón, No. 2-77, B, a/c, swimming pool, decrepit; also on Colón, *Galaxia*, C with breakfast, bath, fan, smelly; *Mediterráneo*, Av. Los Libertadnes, D, clean, friendly; *Nueva Aurora*, Av. de las Américas, B, fan and private bath; *Bahía Marina*, Carretera San Luis, B, swimming pool, the largest on San Andrés, and good restaurant; *El Dorado*, Av. Colombia, No. 1A-25 (casino, swimming pool), C; *Abacoa*, Av. Colombia, B, with bath and a/c; also *Royal Abacoa*, A, on same avenue at No. 2-41, with good restaurant; *Isleño*, Av. La Playa, C, great sea view; *Bahía Sardina*, Av. Colombia, across the street from the beach, a/c, TV, fridge, good service, comfortable, clean, no swimming pool; *Europa*, Av. 20 de Julio, No. 1-101, C, with bath, clean; *Capri*, Av. Costa Rica, No. 1A-110, B, with bath and a/c, good value; *Cacique Toné*, Av. Colombia, Cra. 5, A, deluxe, a/c, pool, on sea-front; *Tiuna*, Av. Colombia, No. 3-59, A, a/c, swimming pool; *Las Antillas*, Av. 20 de Julio, No. 1A-81, D with bath and fan, clean, safe, good water (inc. for drinking), good value; *Turista Natania*, in front of Coliseo, B; nearby are *Coliseo*, friendly, noisy, good restaurant, C, and *Malibú*, restaurant, B. *Residencia Restrepo*, "gringo hotel", near airport—turn left to beach, then left, second left at fish restaurant and it's a hundred metres on left (no sign), noisy ("share a room with a Boeing 727"—till midnight), F or G for a hammock in the porch, clean, some rooms with bath, breakfast US$0.50, other meals US$1.50, good place for buying/selling unwanted return halves of air tickets to/from Central America or the Colombian mainland; *Astor*, D inc. 3 meals; *Residencias Hernando* Henry, D, restaurant, fan, clean, good value, on road from airport. Campsite at South End said to be dirty and mosquito-ridden.

Restaurants *Oasis* (good); *La Parrillada* (Argentine), good meals at US$4; *Popular*, on Av. Bogotá, good square meal for US$4; comida corriente at *Don Joaco's* for US$2, good fish.

SAN ANDRES

NOT TO SCALE

M158A

1. Tourist Office
2. Telephone Office
3. Banco de la Republica
4. Hospital
5. Coliseo
6. Airport Terminal
7. Avianca and Airmail Post Office
8. SAM
9. Sahsa
10. Boats to Johnny Cay

11. Fisherman's Place

Hotels:
12. Cacique Toné
13. Bahia Sardina
14. Nueva Aurora
15. Europa
16. Capri
17. Royal Abacoa
18. Residencia Restrepo
19. Residencias Hernando Henry

Mercapollo, good value; *San Andrés* and *High Seas* are also rec. for cheap, typical meals; *Fonda Antioqueña Nos. 1 and 2,* on Av. Colombia near the main beach, and Av. Colombia at Av. Nicaragua, best value for fish; *Miami,* special for US$3; excellent fruit juices at *Jugolandia,* Calle 20 de Julio; *Jugosito,* Av. Colombia, 1½ blocks from tourist office towards centre, cheap meals; *Mundo Acuático,* snacks of fresh fish and papaya for US$1, cheaper beer, soft drinks and mangoes. *Fisherman's Place,* in the fishing cooperative at N end of main beach, very good, simple. Good ice cream next to *Hotel Gran Internacional. The Barboat,* a floating bar, off the beach between the Centro Comercial Dann and Club Náutico, English and German spoken, waterskiing and windsurfing rental, also instruction available, water taxi to the Keys. Fish meals for US$2.50 can be bought at San Luis beach.

Taxis round the island, US$8; to airport, US$3; in town, US$0.60; *colectivo* to airport, US$0.50.

Exchange Banco de la República (Mon.-Fri., 0800-1300) will exchange dollars and travellers' cheques; Banco Cafetero will advance pesos on a Visa card. Aerodisco shop at airport will change dollars cash anytime at rates slightly worse than banks, or try the Photo Shop on Av. Costa Rica. (Rates are lower than in Bogotá.) Many shops will change US$ cash; it is impossible to change travellers' cheques at weekends. (Airport employees will exchange US$ cash at a poor rate.)

Tourist Information, Avenida Colombia No. 5-117, in front of *Hotel Isleño,* English spoken, maps, friendly, helpful.

Providencia, commonly called Old Providence, 80 km. back to the NNE from San Andrés, is 7 km. long and is more mountainous than San Andrés, rising to 610 metres. There are waterfalls, and the land drops steeply into the sea in places. It is also an expensive island. The 3 main beaches are Manchincal Bay, the largest, most attractive and least developed, South West Bay and Freshwater Bay, all in the South West. Most of the accommodation is at Playa Agua Dulce (Freshwater): *Cabañas El Recreo* (Captain Brian's), E, p.p.; *Cabañas El Paraíso, Cabañas Aguadulce* and *Hotel Royal Queen; Ma Elma's* rec. for cheap food; at Santa Isabela on the N end of the island, *Flaming Trees Hotel,* E, clean, restaurant, good value, but a long way from the beach; at Smooth Water Bay, *Dutch Inn* (C full board) and several houses take in guests. Camping is possible at Freshwater Bay. Truck drivers who provide transport on the island may be able to advise on accommodation. The sea food is good, water and fresh milk are generally a problem. Horse riding is available, and boat trips can be made to neighbouring islands such as Santa Catalina (an old pirate lair), and to the NE, Crab Key (beautiful swimming), day trip from 1000 to 1500, about US$7 p.p. Superb views can be had by climbing from Bottom House or Smooth Water to the peak. Day tours are arranged by the Providencia office in San Andrés, costing US$35 inclusive. SAM fly from San Andrés, US$30, 25 mins., up to 5 times a day, bookable only in San Andrés. (Return flight has to be confirmed at airport. Tourist office at airport.) Boat trips from San Andrés take 8 hours, but are not regular.

Santa Marta, capital of Magdalena Department (pop. 350,000), the third Caribbean port, is 96 km. E of Barranquilla, at the mouth of the Manzanares river. It is best reached from Barranquilla by the paved road along the coast, which passes salt pans and skirts an extensive and most interesting lagoon, the Ciénaga de Santa Marta, in which all types of water birds, plants and animals may be seen. (There has been an ecological disaster there, as a result of cutting off the egress to the sea to build the coast road.) There is a paved road S to Bucaramanga (**see page 644**) and Bogotá.

Santa Marta lies on a deep bay with high shelving cliffs. The climate ranges seasonally from hot and trying to hot but pleasant in February and March; occasionally one can see snow-clad peaks of the Sierra Nevada to the E, less than 50 km. away and 5,800 metres high.

Its sandy beaches stretch from the Simón Bolívar airport to Punta Aguja across the Rodadero de Gaira and the little fishing villages of Villa Concha, surrounded by meadows and shady trees, and Taganga (see below). A jutting rock—the Punta de Betín—rises from the sea in front of the city and is topped by a lighthouse. Rugged Moro Island, 3 km. off Santa Marta, completes the panorama. Rodadero Bay is the most fashionable and tourist-oriented part of Santa Marta, though it lies some distance W of the city (local bus service, taxi, US$1.80) It is extremely dangerous to wander off the beaten track at Rodadero: correspondents have been robbed at gunpoint. Many of the buses coming from Barranquilla and Cartagena stop at Rodadero on the way to Santa Marta. There is also a dirty, unsafe beach with a seaside promenade close to the centre of town.

Santa Marta was the first town founded (1525) by the *conquistadores* in Colombia. Founder: Rodrigo de Bastidas. Most of the famous sea-dogs—the brothers Côte, Drake and Hawkins—sacked the city in spite of the two forts built on a small island at the entrance to the bay. It was here that Simón Bolívar, his dream of a Great Colombia shattered, came to die. Almost penniless he was given hospitality at the *hacienda* of San Pedro Alejandrino, 5 km. to the SE. He died on 17 December, 1830, at the age of 47, and was buried in the Cathedral, but his body was taken to the Pantheon at Caracas 12 years later. The simple room in which he died and his few belongings can be seen today (admission, US$0.10, open Tues.-Sat. 1330-2000): take the "Mamatoca" bus from the waterfront (Carrera 1C) to the *hacienda*, US$0.20.

Warning The north end of town, beyond the railway station, is very dangerous and travellers are advised not to go there alone. If you arrive by bus, beware taxi drivers who take you to a hotel of their choice, not yours (no doubt for a commission). Also beware of "jungle tours" sold by street touts in Santa Marta and avoid the trail to Pueblito.

Hotels In town: *Residencia Park Hotel*, Carrera 1C, No. 18-63, on sea front, D with shower, reasonable; *Tairona*, Carrera 1, No. 11-41, T 32408, D, with fan, bath, clean and safe; *Dos Virreyes*, Calle 12, No. 1-34, near waterfront, can be bargained to E, only 5 rooms, with fan and shower, friendly, rec.; *Miramar*, Calle 10C, No. 1C-59, F with fan (cheaper rooms without), "gringo hotel", very friendly, safe, 2 blocks from railway station and beach (not to be confused with **Hotel Residencias Miramar**, Carrera 1C, No. 18-23); several others nearby, e.g. **Res. Marinas**, Calle 10, No. 1C-83, F, clean, friendly, fan, bath; **Hotel Residencias Yarimar**, Carrera 1A, No. 26-37, E, clean, fan, noisy; *Yuldama*, Cra. 1, No. 12-19, C, clean a/c, reasonable food; *Residencias Adelita*, Calle 24 and Carrera 8, D; many on Calle 22. *Andrea Doria*, 300 m. from seashore, E, friendly, clean. *Residencias Costa Azul*, E, with bath and shower, rec. as impeccably clean with good mattresses, fan and window on to courtyard, in town, very friendly. **Youth Hostel** *Hotel Nabusimake*, details from Alcom in Bogotá.

At Rodadero Bay: *Tamacá* (best, Carrera 2, No. 11A-98, C, good service, fine pool); *Irotama*, L (km. 14, between airport and Rodadero Bay; has bungalows); *Residencias Edma*, Carrera 3, No. 5-188, Rodadero, D, a/c, new, clean, cafeteria, run by two ladies, welcoming; *La Sierra*, Carrera 1, No. 9-47, B, disorganised, not currently rec., though relatively inexpensive restaurant; *Residencial Bastidas*, Cra. 2, F, shower, friendly, laundry facilities; *Valladolid*, E, Carrera 2, good value, large clean rooms, helpful, rec.; *Puerto Galleón*, at km. 18 (difficult to reach by taxi at night); *Santa Mar*, at Km. 8, D. Cheapest is *Toronto*, E, clean, friendly, 2 blocks from sea. In season, it is difficult to find a single room for less than US$4. Apartments: *Patuca*, on beach, US$40 for 8. Bungalows for 8 for rent from Isidro Ramos, casa 5, Manzana G, Rodadero del Mar, Santa Marta.

Motels *El Rodadero*, Calle 11, No. 1-29, D, swimming pool, English-speaking manageress (Marino Salcedo), very helpful; *Taboga*; and *Lilium*, secure parking.

Restaurants *Grill Venecia*, in roof garden of Posiheuica building, facing the bay; the *Pan American*, on the beach walk, is pleasant; good food and service; *Vegetariano*, Calle 12, No. 6-18, good breakfast; *Yarimar*, Carrera 1A, No. 26-37, next to hotel of same name, good seafood; opp. is *La Terraza Marina*, also rec. for seafood. *Madrid*, Calle 11, 100 metres from seafront, cheap and good; *El Platanal*, Calle 13, No. 1-33, good cheap food, good service. *La Gran Muralla*, Carrera 5, No. 23-77 and *Oriental*, Calle 22, No. 3-43, both good Chinese. A good breakfast in *Colonial*, on corner of *Park Inn. Bermuz*, Calle 14, No. 4-08, good, cheap; *Toy San*, Calle 22, Chinese, good, big portions.

At Rodadero: *La Bella Napolés*, first class; *Pacabuy*, on seafront, highly rec.; *Porto Fino*, three blocks from *Tamacá*, good food, not too expensive; *Restaurante Karey*, highly rec., seafood excellent, but not cheap; *Pekin*, Calle 22, between Carreras 4 and 5, good value.

Museum Casa de la Aduana, Calle 14 y Carera 2, displays an excellent archaeological collection, including a large number of precolombian gold artefacts. Open Tues.-Sat., 0800-1200, 1400-1800, Sun. 0800-1200, during the tourist season, Mon.-Fri., 0800-1200, 1400-1800, the rest of the year; entry US$0.15.

Exchange Change money at the Banco de la República, on Carrera 5, No. 17-04; open 0800-1100 and 1400-1530. *Casas de cambio* in 3rd block of Calle 14, many others on this street. In Rodadero, Apto. 201, Carrera 1, No. 9-23.

Tourist Office in the former Convent of Santo Domingo, Carrera 2, No. 16-44. There is also an office at Rodadero, Calle 10, No. 3-10. Inderena office, Carrera 1C, No. 22-77, and at the Quinta de San Pedro Alejandrino.

Train Expreso del Sol leaves on Mondays and Thursdays at 0700 for La Dorada; 24 hrs. (US$10), long delays possible. One class only; meals at US$1.50 each, quite good. From La Dorada, one can also take a bus to Bogotá (**see page** 677). The Tayrona runs to Bogotá once a week between December and March only. The Nutibara runs once a week from Santa Marta to Medellín during the same months; connects with the Tayrona at Grecia.

Buses Terminal is at Calle 24 and Carrera 8 (take a taxi or walk to Calle 22, then take "Playa" bus to centre, passing waterfront—Carrera 1C). The Copetran bus to Bucaramanga takes about 9 hrs. (US$15). Journey time will be affected by the number of police checks. There is a good meal stop at Los Límites. From Bucaramanga the buses take 8 hrs. to Bogotá (11 minimum by 2nd class). Buses to Barranquilla, 2 hrs. (US$1.60-1.80); to Cartagena, 4 hrs. (US$3.50, or US$4.75, Brasilia). To Riohacha US$2.85, 3 hrs.; Pullman to Maicao, US$5.75. The buses stop at the Venezuelan border on the way to Maracaibo for exit and entry stamps, usually better organized than at Cúcuta. There are three buses a day (Brasilia) direct to Rodadero Beach from Barranquilla, taking 2 hrs. and costing US$1.50. They return to Barranquilla at 1300, 1530 and 1730. Fastest service to Barranquilla and Cartagena reported to be Transportes la Costeña.

Airport Simón Bolívar, 20 km. from city; bus, US$0.20, taxi from Santa Marta, US$7, from Rodadero, US$2.40. During the tourist season, get to the airport early. Note, planes are full, book well ahead.

Port It can take up to 4 working days to get a car out of the port, but it is usually well guarded and it is unlikely that anything will be stolen.

Sightseeing Tours in air-conditioned jeeps run by Airline travel agency at centre. Launches leave Rodadero beach every hour for the Aquarium, modest, not as good as the one at Islas del Rosario near Cartagena, US$3 return (includes admission). From the Aquarium, one can walk (10 mins.) to the Playa Blanca (White Beach) where one can swim in less crowded conditions than elsewhere—food available at the beach. Small Indian figures are sculpted at José Pertuz, Calle 38, Carrera 17. They cut stone with traditional instruments and will chisel animals etc. to order. They are sold on Rodadero beach.

Excursions Close to Santa Marta (bus US$0.10, 30 mins. taxi US$2, 10 mins.) is the fishing village and beach of **Taganga**, with hotel *La Ballena Azul*, D, most attractive, friendly, comfortable, clean, restaurant, also run boat tours to secluded beaches, ask Mauricio about tours, horses for hire (postal address: Aptdo Aéreo 799, Santa Marta, Telex 38886 CCSMT CO). One can stay with Joselito Guerra on the beach, G for hammock space, secure for luggage, or rent houses on beach (not secure). Restaurants expensive, but a good one is *Tibisay*, seafood. Swimming good, especially on Playa Grande, 25 mins'. walk round coast, but thieving is common there. Taganga is quiet during week, but trippers from Santa Marta pour in on Sun. On the E shore of the Ciénaga de Santa Marta, is **Ciénaga**, a town of 75,000 people. Cotton, bananas, tobacco and cacao are grown in the area. Hotels in Ciénaga: *Tobiexe*; Naval. (Granturismo tours to Ciénaga are not recommended; much too fast). South of Ciénaga, just before Fundación, is **Aracataca**, birthplace of Gabriel García Márquez, fictionalised as Macondo in some of his stories (notably *One Hundred Years of Solitude*). His home, called a museum, may be seen in the backyard of La Familia Iriarte Ahumada—just ask for directions. There are *residencias* (G), but it is better to stay in Fundación. Best hotel is *Caroli*, Carrera 8, No. 5-30, Fundación, F (E with a/c); others all in this price range. Do not walk between Aracataca and Fundación at night, otherwise it is safe. Bus Fundación-Aracataca, US$0.15; Fundación-Ciénaga, US$0.75; Fundación-Barranquilla, US$3.50. Banana growing in the area has now been replaced almost entirely by African palm plantations.

To go to the **Ciudad Perdida**, discovered in 1975, permission is required from Inderena, Carerra 1a, No. 22-77, Santa Marta, T 36355; it is not always given because the area is dangerous. The site covers 400 hectares, at 1,100 metres altitude, near the Río Buritaca; comparisons have been made with Machu Picchu.

Ettore Grugni, of Roddi, Italy, writes: Ciudad Pedida was founded between 500 and 700 A.D. and was surely the most important centre of the Tairona culture. It stands on the steep slopes of Cerro Corea, which lies in the northern part of the Sierra Nevada de Santa Marta. It consists of a complex system of buildings, paved footpaths, flights of steps and perimetrical walls, which link a series of terraces and platforms, on which were built cult centres, residences and warehouses.

You can reach Ciudad Perdida by helicopter from Santa Marta in about 20 minutes. Ask at Helicol, at the airport, or at Corporación Nacional de Turismo, Carrera 2a, No. 16-44 (T 35773). Price: about US$290 there and back with a 3 hour stay.

More adventurous trekkers can reach Ciudad Perdida in a six/eight days' excursion, leaving about 0700 from Santa Marta market, at the corner of Carrera 11 and Calle 11.

Toyota jeeps go up to La Tagua (about 3 hours), where it is possible to rent mules and pay local guides (but see below). You can go on alone, but route finding is difficult. You need to take hammock, plenty of protection against mosquitoes, sleeping bag, warm clothing for the night, plastic bags to keep everything dry, and strong footwear. Check conditions especially information on river crossings and ensure you have adequate food before you start. The first day's walking is about 7 hours, through fine wild scenery. The first night will be spent in a hammock in a typical farmhouse. They are very hospitable, but you need to take your own food. The second day will bring you up to the heights of Alto de Mira where, after 8 hours' walking, you will stay the night in a hammock in a typical "bohío", where a group of archaeologists is still working. With their permission, you may be able to stop for a day to visit the excavations. The third day will bring you down to the Buritaca river and then, through impressive scenery, up to the steps which bring you to the archaeological site of Ciudad Perdida. The visit to the town will take you the fourth day; there is nowhere to stay as yet. The return to Santa Marta will take you three days.

Archaeologists and army guards will ask you for your permit. Don't forget that Ciudad Perdida is a National Park: it is strictly forbidden to damage trees and collect flowers or insects.

One week trips organized by the tourist office in Santa Marta cost US$200, but can be bargained much lower: price includes mules, guide and food, 3 days' hike there, 1 day at site, 3 days back. Hotels in Santa Marta or Taganga may charge up to US$400 p.p. Recommended guides: Frankie (ask at the tourist office about him), Joselito (see above under Taganga) and his cousin Pacho. Also Jairo Garciá, who lives at the *Residencia Miramar*, in Santa Marta, rec; cost US$120 for 6 days (1989).

Jim Lindsay of the Australian Embassy in Caracas recommends a circuitous route to the site, which can be arranged through *Hotel La Ballena Azul* (above). It costs about US$250 p.p. for the 6-day round trip, all inclusive. Its advantage is that it avoids all settlements, especially in the drug-growing lower valleys and Kogui villages which may not welcome foreigners. He also recommends Juan Mayr's book, *The Sierra Nevada of Santa Marta*(Mayr y Cabal, Apartado Aéreo 5000, Bogotá) which deals beautifully with the Ciudad Perida.

The **Tairona** national park, 35 km. E of Santa Marta in the Riohacha direction, wild woodland on the coast, is beautiful and unspoilt. Take a Maicao or Riohacha bus to the park entrance (US$0.70), then walk or hitch 5 km. to beach at Cañaveral (a safe place to visit). Alternatively, there is a tour bus at 1000 from *Park Inn* in Santa Marta, direct to Cañaveral, return at 1500, US$3 (not long enough). Bathing not recommended as there is heavy pounding surf and the tides are treacherous. The place is not without thieves, but a most attractive spot for camping; the beach is less crowded and cleaner than Rodadero. (There are splendid and deserted sandy beaches, to which you have to walk, about 5 km. E of Cañaveral.) Relics of ancient Tairona culture abound. A taxi to Cañaveral and back from Santa Marta costs US$14. A guided tour round the Pueblito archaeological site is free, every Sat. or as arranged, under escort of a park guard (a full tour from *Hotel Irotama*, including transport and guide, costs US$55). Camping in the Park at Cañaveral costs US$5 per site. Many camping and hammock places on the path from the Park to Pueblito. The camp at Cañaveral has facilities but there is only one restaurant (expensive) with a tiny store, so take all supplies. There are plenty of mosquitoes. Good camping at Arrecife (US$1.75 for tent, US$1.10 for hammock space, US$2 to hire hammock, US$2.85 for hut), fresh water shower and toilets at campsite, one good restaurant (but not cheap), soft drinks available (e.g. from Alberto), beautiful beach nearby (sea dangerous). Avoid, if possible, camping at Finca Martínez—dirty, narcotics centre; Finca Bermúdez (on the road to Pueblito) has better camping, for US$1 p.p. Walking in the park, it is 1 hour from the entrance to Cañaveral, then another hour to Arrecife; follow the beach for ¼ hour to Rancho Viejo from where a clear path leads S to Pueblito (1½ hrs.). At the site there are Indians; do not photograph them. From Pueblito you can either return to Cañaveral, or continue for 2 hours to Calabazo on the Santa Marta-Riohacha road. It is advisable to inform park guards when walking in the park as it is a marijuana-growing area; also wear hiking boots and beware of bloodsucking insects. You will see monkeys, iguanas and maybe snakes. In the wet, the paths are very slippery.

You need to obtain permission from Inderena to camp in the park if you are not staying in Cañaveral, but this is normally forthcoming if you specify where you intend to stay.

Riohacha, capital of Guajira Department, 160 km. E of Santa Marta, is a port of 75,000 people at the mouth of the Río César: low white houses, sandy streets, no trees or hills. It was founded in 1545 by Nicolás Federmann, and in early years its pearling industry was large enough to tempt Drake to sack it (1596). Pearling almost ceased during the 18th century and the town was all but abandoned. (It is best to travel from Riohacha in a luxury bus, early a.m. as these buses are less likely to be stopped and searched for contraband.)

Hotels *Campestre* (state-owned); *Gimaura,* (also state-owned), on beach, D, including breakfast, they allow camping (free) in their grounds, with outside shower; *Los Delfines,* E, clean, friendly, one block from sea and central plaza, two from Venezuelan consulate. *Hostal* opposite the bus station, E, fan, clean, friendly, expensive food; *Nelly,* F, basic but convenient for bus stations on the edge of town; *Residencia Yatoonia* (or *Yalcarón*), Carrera 7, No. 11-26, T 73-487, F, private bath, clean, safe, helpful, half way between beach and bus station.

Many small restaurants along sea-front including *Europa,* German run. *Tizones,* opp. *Los Delfines,* Carrera 2 y Carrera 10, rec. for food and juices (takes Visa and Diners Club); *Golosinas,* café near the beach, good food, friendly service. All accommodation and food is expensive (no hotel or *pensión* costs less than US$5). You can sling your hammock for free at the police station. There are an airport, a cinema, a tourist office on the beach front and a bank, which changes dollars cash, but not if you're in your beachwear. The best place for buying mantas and other local items is La Casa de la Manta Guajira, Carrera 6, No. 9-35, be prepared to bargain. At the weekend, Riohacha fills up, and bars and music spring up all over the place. The sea is clean, despite the red silt stirred up by the waves.

Venezuelan Consulate Calle 7, No. 3-75 (hours 0900-1300, and closed from 1500 Fri. to 0900 Mon.). With two passport photographs and an exit ticket most can get a visa on the same day, but be prepared for an interview with the consul himself; visas cost US$10 for all but Danish citizens (free), US, West German and Swiss (US$0.70).

Tourist Office Carrera 7, No. 1-38. **DAS Office** (immigration) Calle 1 y Carrera 6, T 72407.

Going south from Riohacha on an alternative road to Maicao and the Venezuelan frontier, you come to Cuestecita (*Hotel Turismo; Restaurant La Fogata*), where you can turn southwest to **Barrancas.** Here a large coal mine (one of the largest in the world—El Cerrejón) has recently come into operation (1986). A good dirt road and an industrial railway (no passengers) have been built between the mine and the new Puerto Bolívar in the Bahía Portete, many millions of tons of coal are being exported annually. Visitors are apparently welcome, but it would probably be best to make arrangements first at the El Cerrejón main office in Barranquilla.

Continuing on this road, which takes you either round the Sierra Nevada to Barranquilla and Santa Marta via Fundación (see above) or south to Bucaramanga, you come to **Valledupar,** capital of César Department, said to be an unfriendly town, population 202,000. Bus from Santa Marta, 8½ hrs., from Cartagena, US$8.50 (with Expreso Brasilia); to Bucaramanga, 8 hrs US$12. You can fly to Bogotá.

Valledupar claims to be the home of the *vallenato* music, in which the accordion features prominently. Each year there is a *vallenato* festival from 29 April to 1 May in the town.

Hotels *Vajamar,* C, Carrera 7, Calle 17, pool, expensive food; *Sicarare,* two-star, Carrera 9, No. 16-04, D; cheaper 2-star hotel is *Kurakata,* Calle 19C, No. 7-96; *Residencial El César 1,* Calle 18 No. 9-39, *El César 2,* Calle 18, No. 11-58, both F with bath, clean; another opp. *El César 1; Central,* basic, E. *Residencia El Triunfo,* Carrera 7, No. 19-31, F with bath, fan, clean, good, but slightly dubious part of town; next door is *Hotel/Restaurant Nutibara,* excellent cheap meals and breakfast, excellent fruit juices; several other hotels in this street.

The Sierra Nevada, covering a triangular area of 16,000 sq. km., rises abruptly from the sea, or from lowlands which nowhere reach over 300 metres above sea-level. "Indeed, the north slope is one of the most striking anywhere, lifting from the Caribbean to 5,800-metre snow peaks in about 45 km., a gradient comparable with the south face of the Himalaya, and unequalled along the world's coasts. The interior is made up of some eight E-W ranges with their intervening valleys. The lower parts of these interior valleys are flanked by forests—the homes of primitive Indians as well as of pumas, jaguars, and a variety of snakes and birds—but for the most part the Sierra is almost lunar in its sterile grandeur, bleak *páramos* leading to naked crag and scree and glacier, where only an occasional questing condor moves. In the rocky heart of the area are a large number of small, beautiful lakes, many in cirques." —Frank F. Cunningham, in an excellent illustrated article on exploring the Sierra in *The Geographical Magazine*. The rainy season in these mountains ends November; January is best month for a visit.

It is necessary to obtain a safe-conduct pass from the Casa Indígena (45 minutes out of town) and the police in Valledupar before visiting the Sierra Nevada, if you are going further than San Sebastián. From Valledupar the best route is along the Guatepurí valley. Jeeps and buses run from Valledupar, Carrera 7A, Calle 18, Nos. 37-55, to Pueblo Bello, 2 hrs. US$1.50. In Pueblo Bello (*Hotel El Encanto*, F, good meals US$1, friendly; *El Hogar de Mamí*, E, very clean; *El Hogar de Mercedes*, F), enquire for jeeps to San Sebastián de Rábago, the central village of one of the four tribes of Indians living in the Sierra, the Arhuacos (jeep owners Quico and Gudar Neader are the only ones who go frequently, US$20 per vehicle, or US$3 per seat, 2-2½ hrs.). It is set in beautiful surroundings, is the epitome of an Indian village; the jeep driver may be able to arrange for you to stay on a farm; Doña Inés recommended, F, clean, friendly, good food. Also recommended is Ñoco, a mestizo who has lived in the valley for 30 years; he has floor space and rents mules for trips in the Sierra (US$7 per mule and per guide, per day). Ñoco himself may act as guide if he is free (he runs a grocery store); he is very knowledgeable. Camping is also permitted in the valley.

Before hiking in the Sierra, visitors must pay a "tourist tax" to the Arhuaco chief in San Sebastián (at the police HQ); this ranges from US$7 to US$15, depending on what you want to do. (Do not leave litter or disrespect the Indians' sacred grounds.) **The Indians of the Sierra** distrust strangers (stay on paths; do not stray on to private land) and do not take kindly to being photographed, especially without permission. However they like to be given sea-shells which can be ground into powder and mixed with coca leaves and such a gift may improve their reaction to strangers and cameras. Those interested in the Arhuaco culture should seek out Celso Domingo, a dentist in Pueblo Bello, himself an Arhuaco. **N.B.** The Sierra Nevada is a marijuana-growing area—take care.

A recommended guide to the Sierra Nevada is Mauricio Guevera (T Bogotá 213-7002), who organizes treks (but not all year). You need to be fit for his 12-day hikes through the villages, valleys alive with butterflies, flowers and waterfalls, and to the lakes and the snowfields and summit of Pico Colón at 5,750 metres (Jim Lindsay, Australian Embassy, Caracas). It is also possible to hike on the coastal side of the Sierra, but it is absolutely essential to take a guide through the marijuana districts. Recommended is Juancho, at *Restaurant Pilón de Gaira*, at Rodadero, Santa Marta, or at the village of Bonda, half an hour from Santa Marta by taxi. Juancho is an ethnologist (formerly of Medellín) who has lived with Kogui Indians for 13 years, owns a farm and speaks the different dialects. You need to be fit for his treks too. US$130 p.p. for a week, maximum 6 people, minimum 4.

From Valledupar on to Codazzi is asphalted, but not beyond until the road joins the paved Bucaramanga-Santa Marta highway. There is a possible overnight stay at Curumaní (*Hotel Himalaya*), or at Aguachica, just off the road.

Beyond Riohacha to the E is the arid and sparsely inhabited Guajira Peninsula. The Indians here live primitively, collecting dividivi, tending goats, and fishing. To visit a small part of the Peninsula you can take a pick-up truck from Riohacha (they leave twice a day from the Indian market) to Manaure for US$1.50, or a daily bus, 0830 from bus station, which may be safer. It is an uncomfortable 3-hr. drive through fields of cactus but offers glimpses of the Indians. Manaure, which is known for its salt flats, has a *residencia*—restaurant (G). From Manaure there are trucks to Uribia (one basic *residencia*, no running water, but fresh water is a problem throughout the Guajira) and thence to Maicao. In Uribia you can buy handicrafts intended for local, not tourist, use by asking around. Sometimes it is possible to get a lift to Cabo de la Vela, further round the coast, where the lagoons shelter vast flocks of flamingoes, herons and sandpipers. There are fine beaches and, in Cabo de Vela, a basic but friendly, Indian-run hotel (rooms, hammock veranda, showers, good meals—excellent fried fish). Sunsets in the Guajira are magnificent. There is a paved road from Riohacha to Maicao near the frontier. The Caribbean coastal highway, now paved, runs direct from Santa Marta along the coast to Riohacha, and the Riohacha-Maicao road (also paved) has been greatly improved. Now that there are no flights from Barranquilla to Maracaibo, taxi or bus to Maicao, and colectivo to Maracaibo is the most practical route.

Maicao is full of Venezuelan contraband, and is still at the centre of the narcotics trade. Its streets are unmade and it has a considerable reputation for lawlessness; most commercial premises close before 1600 and after 1700 the streets are highly unsafe. If at all possible travellers should avoid Maicao and the road services that go there, which are liable to ambush. Also, all isolated areas of César and Guajira Departments are unsafe for tourists.

Entering Venezuela, everyone needs a visa; a transit visa will only suffice if you have a confirmed ticket to a third country within 3 days. The Venezuelan Consul in Maicao is reluctant to grant visas, given the area's reputation: much better to get a visa in Barranquilla or Riohacha; with all the right papers, border crossing is easy. Entering Colombia, immigration is at the border.

Hotels in Maicao *Maicao Juan Hotel,* C, the only safe one; *Residencia Gallo,* E, private bath and pool; *Hotel Hilda,* C, reasonable; *El Parador.*
 If stuck in Maicao, seek out Francisco Agudelo at ARA, Carrera 9, No. 13-16, T 8133, who can make arrangements with Guajira Tours, Riohacha, and help with transport, money changing, etc.

Buses (basic): Maicao-Riohacha, US$1.10; Maicao-Santa Marta, US$5.75; Maicao-Maracaibo, US$3.25 (Expreso Maicao, 0400-1800); Maicao-Barranquilla, US$6.50. Maicao-Cartagena, US$4.75-7.50. There are bus services along the Caribbean coastal highway, and also **flights** Barranquilla-Maicao (Aces). Colectivo, Maicao-Maracaibo, US$4.50 p.p.

UP THE MAGDALENA RIVER (5)

Passenger travel by the lofty paddle boats on the river has now come to an end, though the adventurous traveller may still find an occasional passage by cargo paddle boat. But in general the only way of getting from one place to the other along the river is by motor launch (*chalupa*), and this is more expensive. Insect repellants should be taken, for mosquitoes are a nuisance. Guerilla activity has been reported in the Magdalena valley away from the river and the main roads.

The Magdalena is wide but shallow and difficult to navigate because of surface eddies, and there are little whirlpools over submerged rocks. Away to the NE, in the morning, one can see the high snow-capped peaks of the Sierra Nevada de Santa Marta.
 At Tenerife Bolívar had his first victory in the Magdalena campaign. At Zambrano, a cattle centre 96 km. beyond Calamar, there are tobacco plantations. Population, 4,000. There is a road W to the N-S Cartagena-Medellín road, and a trail E to the oil fields at El Difícil. Near Pinto the river divides: the eastern branch, silted and difficult, leads to ***Mompós,*** an old town of 20,000 people: cattle farming and tobacco, and the scene of another victory for Bolívar: "At Mompós", he said, "my glory was born." Mompós was founded in 1537 and, thanks to its comparative isolation, preserves its colonial character more completely than any other town in Colombia. Old buildings are the Casa de Gobierno, once a home of the Jesuits, and the Colegio de Pinillos. There are 7 churches and the Easter celebrations are said to be among the best in Colombia. The town is well known in Colombia for handworked gold jewellery. Airport. Malaria is endemic in the surrounding countryside.

Mompós Hotels *Residencias Unión,* Calle 18, No. 3-43, F, with bath and fan; *Hostal Doña Manuela,* Calle Real del Medio, 17-41, D, a converted colonial house, quiet and peaceful but run down; with cockroaches, nearby *Residencias Aurora,* F, shower, fan, nice and friendly; also *Residencias Solmar,* Calle Carrera 18-22, near main square, F, clean, friendly, basic; *Tropicana,* Núñez.

Restaurant *La Brasa,* facing river.

Bus From Cartagena with Unitransco and Brasilia daily, 4 hrs., US$4, but you can only book as far as Magangué; you pay a second time from there. From Magangué you have to take a launch to an island in the Río Magdalena, 1½ hours, US$12.60, and thence a jeep to Mompós. Connections can be unreliable if the incoming bus misses the ferry. Plenty of willing hands to carry your luggage to the launch—for an outrageous fee! It is cheaper and quicker to Cartagena by shared taxi to La Bodega, US$1, 1 hr., then motor boat to Magangué, US$0.85, 20 mins. From Magangué, buses also go to Barranquilla and Sincelejo.

CENTRAL
COLOMBIA

72

Most vessels go by the western arm of the loop to **Magangué**, a town of 40,800, the port for the savannas of Bolívar. To El Banco the charge is US$3, by *chalupa* 2¼ hrs. A road runs W to join the N-S Cartagena-Medellín highway. 5 hotels inc. *Mardena*; 10 *residenciales*, cheapest *Londres*, *Brasil* or *Hotel Medellín*, all G p.p.

Beyond Magangué, the Río San Jorge, 379 km. long, 240 km. of it navigable, comes in from the Western Cordillera. Later the Río Cauca, 1,020 km. long, comes in from the far S. Its Caribbean end is navigable for 370 km., and it is navigable again for a distance of 245 km. in the Cauca Valley above the gorge.

At **El Banco** (*Residencias Las Delicias*, Calle 9 near jeep terminal, F, basic; *Residencia Ocaña*, cheaper, G p.p., basic, clean, noisy; about a dozen others), 420 km. from Barranquilla (airport, one flight each weekday US$27), the river loops join. This is an old, dirty and beautiful town of 10,250 people. Along the river front are massive stone stairways. The Cordilleras are in the distance, a blue range on either side of the valley. Pink herons and blue macaws much in evidence. There are many sandy islands in the river to complicate navigation. A difficult trail leads N of El Banco to the small town of Chimichagua (5,000 inhabitants), on the shores of the large lake of Zapatosa. Continuing upriver are the small towns of Gamarra (3,700 inhabitants) and Puerto Wilches (5,600). Daily buses from El Banco to Bucaramanga, US$7, Cúcuta and Valledupar. *Chalupa* service El Banco-Barrancabermeja with Cootransfluviales, 0800, 7 hrs., US$10.

Some 30 km. above Puerto Wilches is **Barrancabermeja** (usually referred to as Barranca), so called because of the reddish-brown oil-stained cliffs on which it stands. With a population of 66,400, the town is an important oil centre; it is a warm, humid place with an interesting indoor market, but the oil refinery is prominent. *Chalupa* to Puerto Boyacá, 0845, 6 hrs., US$10. In 1989, this city was reported to be "incredibly violent", and best avoided by travellers.

Hotels *Residencias Ferroviario*, G with bath, opp. railway station, friendly. *Santa Fe*, in town, G, clean and friendly; many more around the train station and in town. A shop at Calle 19, Avs. 18 y 19 sells good bread and muesli. *Iris*, just up road from port, F, clean, friendly.

Rail 4 to 6 trains a week to Santa Marta, 2 to Bogotá, daily to Medellín, according to the timetable in 1989, but check carefully. Time to Medellín, 12 hours but "not too exhausting".

Puerto Berrío (airport; 12,750 inhabitants) is on the W bank 100 km. above Barrancabermeja and 756 km. from Barranquilla. It is the river port for Medellín and the rich Antioquia Department. A railway from Medellín runs down the slopes of the Cordillera Central and over a low pass to Puerto Berrío, where it connects with the Bogotá-Santa Marta line. Bus to Barbosa, 10 hrs., US$4.50.

Hotels at Puerto Berrío *Hotel Magdalena*, pleasant, on a hilltop near river, E; *Residencias El Ganadero*, F, with bath, clean, modern, with ceiling fans. Many other hotels, *residencias* and *apartamentos*. **Restaurants**: *Tabrona*; *La Buena Mesa*, good big meals; *Heladería Joi*, good ice cream and sundaes.

Rail To Santa Marta, Bogotá and Medellín, check days and times at Grecia station, 4 km. from the town and hotels, taxi service only.
    Note: to get to El Banco or Mompós from a Santa Marta-bound train, get off at Palestinos, 8 hrs. north of Puerto Berrío, then a shared taxi to Tamalameque (US$1; *Residencia Tamalameque* and restaurant, F, basic), or Puerto Boca, 2 km. further on (no accommodation), then take a motor boat.

River Transport From Puerto Boca, *chalupas* run from 0500 till dusk; Cootrafturmag has a service to Barrancabermeja, Gamarra, San Pablo, La Gloria, El Banco (US$2.25, 45 mins.), Mompós (changing at El Banco). Don't be bullied into taking an *expreso* service, or you'll pay for all the empty seats.

75 km. upriver (5 hours by road) from Puerto Berrío is **Puerto Boyacá**. The road is mostly unpaved, passing zebu *fincas*, swamps and oil fields. There are army checkpoints on the road, owing to guerrilla activity in the area. (Hotels: *Residencias Lusitania*; *Santa Fe*; *Hotel* and *Heladería Embajador*.) Rápido Tolima has regular buses to Honda (3 hrs., US$1.50) and a daily 1100 bus to Puerto Berrío, US$3.50.

It is 151 km. up river from Puerto Berrío to **La Dorada** (6,000 people) on the W bank, but only 134 km. by rail (7½ hrs.) along the W bank. (Hotels: *Rosita*, Calle

17, No. 3-28, T 72301, F, with bath, friendly, pleasant, rec.; *Departamental*; on highway to Honda, *Magdalena Motel*; others near railway station; youth hostel at *Centro Vacacional La Magdalena*, 3 km. from La Dorada—details from Alcom in Bogotá—*Parador Turístico* next door). This railway crosses the Magdalena by a bridge from La Dorada to **Puerto Salgar**, on the E bank, from which the Cundinamarca Railway (198 km.) goes up the slopes of the Eastern Cordillera to Bogotá. Bus La Dorada-Bogotá, US$4, La Dorada-Medellín, US$4.25. Train La Dorada-Santa Marta twice a week; to Bogotá, the Tayrona (from Santa Marta) passes once a week, Dec. to March only. Hotels: *Salgar; Residencia Antioquia*, G, with fan. The Lower Magdalena river navigation stops at La Dorada as there are rapids above, as far as Honda. Cargo is taken by railway to Honda, where it is re-embarked. The Upper Magdalena is navigable as far as Girardot.

Honda (airport) on the W bank of the river, is 32 km. upstream from La Dorada (149 km. from Bogotá). It is a pleasant old town with many colonial houses. The streets are narrow and picturesque, and the town is surrounded by hills. El Salto de Honda (the rapids which separate the Lower from the Upper Magdalena) are just below the town. Population: 31,600. Average temperature: 29°C. Altitude 230 metres. Several bridges span the Magdalena and the Guali rivers, at whose junction the town lies. In February the Magdalena rises and fishing is unusually good. People come from all over the region for the fishing and the festival of the Subienda, as the season is called.

Hotels *Ondama*, D, swimming pool, run down; *América*, with pool; *Río Ritz*, good restaurant; *Campestre El Molino*, 5 km. from Honda on Mariquita road, D, swimming pools, fans in rooms, friendly; **Residencias Las Mercedes**, E, with bath, clean and friendly; **La Piscina**, E, fan, swinmming pool, clean, friendly, arranges safe parking at reasonable rates with neighbours, rec.; *Las Villas*, F, clean, pleasant; *Residencias Katty*, F; *Los Puentes*, next to cinema, a bit run down, across river from **La Cascada**, F.

Restaurants **La Cascada**, overlooking river, a good meal for US$3. There is a good *panadería* at the entrance. Good ice cream (La Campiña brand) at *heladería* next to Teatro Unión; *Fuente Mar* for yoghurt and ice cream. There is a row of good cheap restaurants across the Magdalena River bridge in Puerto Bogotá.

Buses from Bogotá by Velotax US$4, and Rápido Tolima, US$3. Manizales, US$3. Rápido Tolima run half-hourly buses to La Dorada (1 hour), and beyond, to Puerto Boyacá (3 hrs.), US$2.25. To Puerto Berrío, 8 hrs., departures at 0300 and 0800 with San Vicente. The new Bogotá-Medellín highway passes round the town.

West from Honda a paved road goes 21 km. to **Mariquita** (13,000 people; *Hotel Bocaneme* and others; campsites), the centre of a fruit-growing country. Buses depart from Honda every half hour, US$0.30, ½ hr. with Rápido Tolima. On the way is the clean and pleasant bathing pool of El Diamante. On again is the Club Deportivo: private, but visitors are welcome to its swimming pool, a blessing in this climate. There is another, El Virrey, in Mariquita. The town has several old houses and buildings: a mint, the viceroy's house, the parish church. Here José Celestino Mutis lived for 8 years during his famous Botanic Expedition towards the end of the 18th century (when he and his helpers accumulated a herbarium of 20,000 plants, a vast library, and a rich collection of botanical plates and paintings of native fauna). The collection was sent to Madrid, where it remains. Mariquita was founded in 1551, and it was here that the founder of Bogotá, Jiménez de Quesada, died in 1579. From Mariquita a road runs W up the slopes of the Central Cordillera to Manizales.

Motel *Las Acacias*, outside Mariquita, on the Armero road.

Fresno, in the heart of a big coffee growing area, is 30 km. from Mariquita. The road to Honda is appalling. Bus to Manizales (83 km.) US$2.80 (Rápido Tolima).

From Mariquita the road turns S to (32 km.) Armero, which used to be a cotton growing centre. This town and surrounding villages were devastated by the eruption of the Nevado del Ruiz volcano (**see page** 695) in November 1985. (Armero can be reached by colectivo from Honda; no lodging in Armero, nearest at Lérida, 12 km. S, a "really nasty village"—Hotels *Central*, F, cheapest, not too clean, unfriendly, *Colonial*, *Tundama*, F p.p.—,Mariquita or possibly Guayabal; no drinks available in Armero, either, only icecream and flowers; there are lots of mosquitoes, though). A branch road runs 35 km. W **to Líbano**, 29,700 inhabitants. (Hotels: *Cumanday; Rex*.) Coffee is the great crop here, with potatoes in the uplands. Away to the W looms the peak of Nevado del Ruiz, which before its eruption was the second highest in the Cordillera Central. Bus from Líbano to Ibagué, US$2.25, 4 hrs.

From Armero a branch road runs down to the Magdalena past Gambao to **Ambalema** (Hotels: *Barcelona; Nariño*). (At Gambao the river is crossed for the road to Bogotá.) The main road from Armero goes direct for 88 km. to Ibagué.

Ibagué, capital of Tolima Department, is a large city (350,000 inhabitants), lying at the foot of the Quindío mountains at 1,250 metres. It is cooler here (22°C) than in the valley. Parts of the town are old: the Colegio de San Simón is worth seeing, and so is the market. The Parque Centenario is very pleasant. The city specializes in two things; hand-made leather goods (there are many good, cheap shoe shops) and a local drink called *mistela*. There is an excellent Conservatory of Music.

The National Folklore Festival is held during the third week of June. The Departments of Tolima and Huila commemorate St. John (24 June) and Sts. Peter and Paul (29 June) with bullfights, fireworks, and music.

Hotels There are many hotels of reasonable quality which are quite comfortable. *Ambala*, Calle 11, No. 2-60, C, not good value, slow service, no hot water; *Suiza*, D, but not very clean; *Italia*, cheap, reasonable; *Athabasca*, D, with restaurant; *Bram*, E, Calle 17 and Carrera 4, convenient, clean, secure, and insect-free; *Acapulco*, same station, E, hot water, shower, clean and pleasant, but noisy; *Ambeima*, Carrera 3 No. 13-32, E; *Raad*, E, next door; both good. *Residencia Puracé* (opposite Tolima bus station), E; *Montserrat*, Calle 18, Carrera 1 y 2, G p.p., clean, quiet.

Restaurants *Parador Los Cristales*, S side of town, reasonable; *Casino Chamaco*, with excellent, typical tamales at weekend. *Toy Wan*, Carrera 4, Chinese. 24 hr. restaurants include *Punto Rojo*, in the shopping precinct on Carrera 3, and *Punto Fácil*, Calle 15 y Carrera 3. Vegetarian, *Govinda*, Carrera 2 y Calle 13.

Tourist Office Carrera 3, between Calles 10 and 11; helpful; closed Sat. and Sun. The Instituto Giográfico Agustin Codazzi has an office at Calle 14A, No 3-14, 3rd Floor, for maps.

Just outside, on the Armenia road, a dirt road leads to the slopes of the Nevado del Tolima. Gerhard Drekonja of Vienna writes: For climbing the Nevado del Tolima (5,215 metres) take in Ibagué at 0600 the *mixto* train to Juntas and El Silencio (2 hrs.). From there half-an-hour walk to the primitive but fabulous thermal waters (90°C) of El Rancho (simple sleeping accommodation and food available). The climb starts from El Rancho. It takes 8 to 10 hours to the top; equipment (crampons and pica) indispensable. The final climb has to be done at sunrise because clouds and mist invariably rise around 0800. From the top a breathtaking view across the other snowcapped mountains of the Cordillera Central. For information contact Cruz Roja Colombiana in Ibagué, Zona Industrial El Papayo, near the east entrance to the city, T 646014, who can put you in touch with a climbing group, Asociación Tolimense de Montañistas y Escaladores. Nevado del Tolima is the southernmost "nevado" in the **Parque Nacional Natural Los Nevados** which extends up to Nevado del Ruiz overlooking Manizales (see under Manizales and Pereira). A local mountain guide with some Himalayan experience and well rec. is Manolo Barrios, Barrio La Francia, Casa 23, Ibagué, T 646726.

There is a road to Girardot, 79 km. E on the Magdalena, going on to Bogotá which is 224 km. by road from Ibagué. On this road is the village of **Gualanday**, with *Hotel Rozal*, F, clean, friendly, safe for motorcyclists and 4 good roadside restaurants (*Dona Eva's* also has accommodation). *Espinal*, pop.: 80,000, is an important agro-industrial town, but of little interest to the tourist. A 2-star hotel is being built outside the town. Restaurant *Parador Rokoko*, on the main street is costly but has decent meals; *El Maestro*, being built. Mobil station on W side of main street, cheap and good. Bus to Ibagué, 1 hr., US$0.75, just flag one down; bus to Neiva, US$2. Toll between Ibagué and Espinal, US$0.50; between Espinal and Girardot, US$0.40. W of Ibagué the road runs over the 3,350-metre high Quindío Pass to Armenia,

105 km. from Ibagué across the Cordillera Central. The bus trip to Pereira takes 4 hrs. and costs US$2.55. To Cali, on Flota Magdalena pullman, 7 hrs., US$5.75; ordinary buses US$4; Velotax US$5. To Bogotá, 4½ hrs., US$3.75 with Velotax, US$3.50 by bus. Bus to Popayán, US$6.75.

Between Ibagué and Armenia, on the E side of the Quindío Pass, is **Cajamarca**, a friendly town in a beautiful setting; *Residencia Central*, G; *Nevado*, expensive, somewhat noisy; both on same street, friendly and clean. Interesting market on Sunday.

Girardot (airport) is on the Upper Magdalena. Altitude, 326 metres; population, 70,000. The climate is hot and there are heavy rains. Here the navigation of the Upper Magdalena ends, although in dry weather boats cannot get this far; walk across the fine steel bridge to see merchandise being loaded and unloaded—coffee and hides are the main items, although shipments of the former have declined considerably. Launch rides on the river can be taken, starting from underneath the bridge. A 1-hour trip to Isla del Sol is rec. (US$4). Large cattle fairs are held on June 5-10 and December 5-10. There is a two-storey market, at its best in early morning but nevertheless good all day, and another good market on Sun. mornings. Bogotanos come down here at weekends to warm up.

Hotels *El Peñón*, on site of former *hacienda* just outside town, fashionable bungalow complex, casino, huge pool, lake, B per bungalow. *Bachué*, Carrera 8, No. 18-04, C, modern large cooled pool, excellent, rooms a/c with bath and TV, restaurant; *Los Angeles*, on main plaza, D, clean, friendly, rec.; *Canala*, comfortable and reasonable; *Waldorf*, on market square, F, clean, showers; *Residencias La Paz*, Carrera 1 E, No. 11-3. Opp. new bus terminal, *Maroti*, F, and *El Cid*, F with fan; *El Dorado*, G, shared bath, basic.

Restaurants *Laresa*, Carrera 8a, US$2-3 for a meal; *Club 60*, across the bridge, US$3-8. There is a good food market.

Banks Only the Banco de la República will change travellers' cheques in Girardot.

Roads To Bogotá, 132 km., bus costs US$3, about 3½ hrs.; bus to Neiva, US$2.55, 3½ hrs.; to Ibagué, 78 km. To Fusagasugá, US$1.65.

Another centre of population in the Magdalena Valley lies upstream from Girardot, with Neiva as its capital. Coffee and tobacco are grown on the slopes here, and cattle are raised in the valley.

The road, and its short branches E and W, runs through a number of small towns of under 25,000 people. One of these, 35 km. from Girardot, is **Guamo**, with 21,000 inhabitants. Just before Guamo is a marked turn off to La Chamba, where internationally famous pottery is made and sold. The pottery is fired in the afternoon; lots of mosquitoes here. Eight km. beyond Guamo is **Saldaña**, where there are irrigation works that have made 15,000 hectares available for rice, sesame and cotton.

Hotel at Guamo *Lemayá*, modern, swimming pool, best in region. At El Espinal, before the road to La Chamba is *Hotel Yuma*, new. At **Saldaña**, *Hotel Saldaña*, not too good.

A pretty spot is the reservoir located near **Prado**, Tolima. Turn off the Ibagué-Neiva road at Saldaña for 25 km.; it is well signposted. There is a dirt road for the last 12 km. past Purificación, where you cross the Magdalena. Buses can be caught in Bogotá, Ibagué and all intermediate towns. A pleasant government hotel is at the lake (D, B for cabin for 6-10, free camping on the shoreline, water-skiing US$2.50, short trip with a boat). The pretty part of the lake is hidden from the end of the road and must be seen from a boat. Official boat trips to the islands are about 3 times cheaper than those of "sharks" operating here; the official mooring-point is down the slope at the end of the road. Swimming is good and the water is warm, but wading is not advisable because of the presence of the fresh-water stingray. Cheap hotels are available in Prado, 4 km. from the lake. There are restaurants of questionable quality in town. Excellent food can be obtained at the end of the road in the boat-dock area, but sanitation leaves something to be desired.

A little beyond the 50 kilometre stone from Neiva you can turn to the left, cross a fence, and see the Piedra Pintada de Aipe, a stone not in fact painted but carved by precolumbian Indians with designs akin to the shapes of some of the gold pieces in the Museo del Oro at Bogotá.

Neiva, capital of Huila Department, has a population of 150,000. It was first founded in 1539, when Benalcázar came across the Cordillera Central from

Popayán in quest of El Dorado. It was soon after destroyed by the Indians and re-founded in 1612. It is now a pleasant, modern city. There are rich coffee plantations around Neiva, for here the valley bottom is high enough to be in the coffee zone. The cathedral was destroyed by earthquake in 1967. There is a large and colourful market every day. Tourist information is given at the cultural centre with museum and gallery on the main square. Altitude: 470 metres; very hot.

Fiesta from 18 to 28 June, when the Bambuco Queen is elected, with folklore, dances and feasting.

Hotels *Hostería Matamundo,* in old *hacienda* 3 km. from centre, on road to Garzón and San Agustín, C, a/c, swimming pool, good meals, US$2.50-7, but slow and poor service, disco (does not accept Visa card; will not put extra beds in room for children); *Tumbaragua,* Calle 5A, No. 5-40, C, no swimming pool or hot water but nevertheless rec.; *Americano,* Carrera 5, No. 8-65, D, clean, swimming pool; *Plaza,* Calle 7, No. 4-62, D, swimming pool, fan, pleasant but food expensive and not reliable; *Central,* Cra. 3, No. 7-82, E, meals US$1 each, near market, good value. *Cali,* F, basic, reasonable, next door is *San Jorge,* F, cheaper, clean, adequate. *Res. San Agustín,* near bus station, F, basic, clean; nearby, *Gloria,* G, adequate; *Res. Nena,* across from back of Coomotor terminal, F, clean, quiet, friendly. Several cheap hotels are to be found off the square where the bus companies are centred. Many small boys meet the buses and suggest accommodation.

Restaurants *Hostería Los Cerros,* Calle 11, No. 32-39; *El Caimo,* Calle 8, No. 7A-22; *Los Gauchos,* Carrera 15, No. 5-12; *Neiva Viejo,* Calle 9, No. 6-49.

Exchange Banco de la República, Carrera 5, No. 5-73, including AmEx cheques.

Airport La Marguita, 1½ km. from city. Aires and Satena fly from Bogotá (Aires to Bogota daily, US$30; to Cali, US$33; to Medellín, either direct or via Ibagué, US$34). Satena flies to Leguizamo, via Florencia daily. Taxi to bus terminal about US$0.85 (overcharging probable).

Bus No central bus station. To Bogotá (331 km., paved road), 5½ hrs., US$5. Regular bus service with Autobuses Unidos del Sur (Carrera 2, No. 5-32) and Coomotor to San Agustín, US$4, 5½ hrs. (US$4.50 by colectivo). To Garzón, US$3; to Pitalito, US$4.35. To La Plata, for Tierradentro, 3 hrs., US$2, good road except for stretch between Nataguima and Aipe. To Pasto, US$9; to Popayán, US$7.75, ordinary bus at 0330, 1000, 1930, to Florencia, US$6.50. Long-distance buses leave from Carrera 2, Calles 5 and 6.

Warning At the bus stations in Neiva, Garzón and especially Pitalito, theft is rife.

Excursions To Rivera, a ½ hr. drive S, with thermal springs and swimming pools to cool off; to the Tacacoa desert to the N, past Tello and Villavieja, where there is a museum showing prehistoric finds in the area; to the Betania dam project with boat trips on the lake formed by the dam, from the village of Yaguará.

Beyond Neiva lie the plains of Huila Department, arid, but still capable of supporting cattle, and dominated by the snow-capped Nevado del Huila to the NW. The road runs S from Neiva, past (92 km.) **Garzón**, a pleasant cathedral town set in mountains with roads W across the Cordillera to Popayán and SE to Florencia, capital of the Intendencia of Caquetá (**see page 685**), and is paved past Pitalito to San Agustín. **Pitalito** (72,000 people), has little to offer the tourist. See map of area, **page 707.**

Hotels at Garzón: *Damasco,* D, colonial building, rec., good meals for US$3; *Cecil,* near bus station, E, with private bath; *Miami,* E, good. The *Abeyma,* a state hotel, is rec., D; it is possible to camp in the grounds, US$1. *Residencias Pigoanza,* on main square, E, rec. 32 km. before Garzón, at El Gigante, is *Posada,* E, swimming pool, hot shower, restaurant (breakfast overpriced); good views between El Gigante and Garzón. At **Pitalito** there is a *Hotel de Turismo.* There are 2 hotels with swimming pools: the *Calamó,* C, hot water, and the *Timanco,* a 3-star hotel; *Residencia Pitalito,* F, without shower, reasonable, Calle 5 round corner from police station; *La Laroyano,* on main street, cheap, adequate; *Residencial El Globo,* main street, F, clean, basic. *Grand Hotel,* F, bath, good food. *Restaurant Cando* rec.; also *Napolitano,* good, cheap.

Transport If you hitch you'll find it fairly easy to Garzón; slower on to San Agustín, but plenty of buses and colectivos (US$1). Buses in Pitalito go from Calle 3a; Taxis Verdes from the main square (US$9 to Bogotá). Aires fly from Bogotá to Pitalito, via Neiva, on Fri. and Sun. at 1500,

1¾ hrs, US$50, returning to Bogotá at 1745 same days, but the plane only goes if there are enough passengers (confirm tickets 24 hrs. in advance).

South of Pitalito is the **Cueva de los Guácharos** National Park; take a bus to Palestrina, US$1, 1 hour, and then walk for 6 hours along an eroded, muddy path. Between December and June swarms of oilbirds (*guácharos*) may be seen; they are nocturnal, with a unique radar-location system. The reserve also contains many of the unusual and spectacular cocks-of-the-rock. The rangers are particularly friendly, providing tours and basic accommodation; permission to visit the park must be obtained from the Inderena offices in Pitalito, Neiva or Bogotá.

The way to the remarkable Tierradentro underground burials in man-made caves painted with geometrical patterns is given on **page 705**; they can be reached by Popayán bus from San Agustín, Pitalito or Garzón, with a change at La Plata, or at the Cruce San Andrés de Pisimbalá.

San Agustín (altitude 1,700 m.) is 27 km. from Pitalito (all paved). Here, in the Valley of the Statues, are some hundreds of large rough-hewn stone figures of men, animals and gods, dating from roughly 3300 B.C. to just before the Spanish conquest. Nothing is known of the culture which produced them, though traces of small circular bamboo straw-thatched houses have been found. Various sculptures found here are exhibited in the National Museum at Bogotá, and there are some life-sized copies of San Agustín originals along the highway from Bogotá to the superseded Techo airport, near Fontibón. There are about 20 sites; information can be obtained from the tourist office, Calle 5, No. 15-47, T 73019, open 0830-1230, 1330-1730, Mon.-Fri., 0900-1200, 1300-1700, Sat. and Sun., Sr Joaquín Emilio García is most helpful in all matters. Free maps to the area can only be obtained here or in Bogotá. It is recommended that visitors arriving in San Agustín should go initially to the tourist office which has a list of all hotels, their prices and quality, and a price list for guides, taxi rides and horse hire.

The nearest sites are the Parque Arqueológico and the Bosque de las Estatuas (open 0800-1600 daily, entrance to both costs US$0.45 students), both about 2½ km. from San Agustín town, 1½ km. from the *Hotel Yalconia*, and less than 1 km. from the *Hotel Osoguaico*. The statues in the Parque are *in situ*, though some have been set up on end and fenced in with wire; those in the Bosque (a little wood) have been moved and rearranged, and linked by gravel footpaths. Of particular interest are the carved rocks in and around the stream at the Fuente de Lavapatas in the Parque, where the water runs through the carved channels (visitors should not miss the Cerro de Lavapatas, above the Fuente, which has an extensive view, closes at 1600); refreshment stands at "Fuente" and on the way up to Lavapatas. There is a museum in the Parque which contains pottery and Indian artefacts (entry included on Parque ticket, closes at 1700 and on Mondays). You can get a very good idea of the Parque, the Bosque and the museum in the course of three hours. The whole site leaves an unforgettable impression, from the strength and strangeness of the statues, and the great beauty of the rolling green landscape. The further sites are a very long walk away: use of a jeep or a horse appears advisable.

Rainy season April-June/July, but it rains somewhat during most of the year, hence the beautiful green landscape; the driest months are Nov.-March. The days are warm but sweaters are needed in the evenings; average temperature 18°C.

The *fiesta* of Santa María del Carmen is held in mid-July (not on a fixed date) in San Agustín. Two festivals in June are San Juan (24th) with horse races and dances, and San Pedro (29th) with horse races, dances, fancy dress, competitions and other events. In the last week of October, the Casa de Cultura celebrates La Semana Cultural Integrada, with many folklore events from all parts of the country. There are cockfights in San Agustín on Sundays at 2030.

Hotels *Yalconia*, outside town, B full board, some rooms with hot water, very pleasant, swimming pool, T (980) 73001 (camping allowed next door, sheltered tents available). Between San Agustín and the Parque Arqueológico is the *Osoguaico*, friendly, warm water, very clean, restaurant, E, laundry; swimming pool, camping site, US$1 p.p. *Central*, Calle 3,

No. 10-32, near bus offices, E, with bath (F, in the 3 rooms without bath, or G if you want a room just to dump your luggage in during day's visit), good meals at US$1.50, it is possible to do laundry here (but keep an eye on your clothes), clean and friendly, secure motorcycle parking, will hire horses, English and French spoken. *Colonial*, Calle 3, No. 10-54, F, shower, clean, pleasant, good restaurant, rec.; *Residencias Náñez*, Calle 5a with Carrera 16, F, singles may have to share room, hot water (usually), friendly and clean; guests may use the kitchen; also the owners have horses for rent (US$5 for 5 hrs., check them first) and will act as guides to the archaeological sites. *Mi Terruño*, Calle 4, No. 15-85, 5 rooms, F, colonial house, some rooms with bath, hot water, friendly, morning coffee, rec., owner Carlos Arturo Muñoz also has 3 cabins, *Los Andaqui*, for rent. *Residencias Luis Tello*, Calle 4a, No. 15-33, run by a teacher, hot water, pleasant and friendly, good value, G; also *Residencias Cosmopólita*, Cra. 16, No. 4-91, clean, safe, friendly, E, rec. *Residencias Eduardo Motta*, Calle 4, No. 15-71, has five rooms, friendly, clean, hot water, F, hard beds, but with morning coffee, quiet, rec, similar establishment run by Luis who runs the post office, F; *Residencia Familiar*, Calle 3, No. 11-14, one block down from Coomotor-Autobuses Unidos del Sur office, 7 rooms, hot water extra, laundry, friendly, G p.p., book meals in advance, horses for hire; *Residencias La Gaitana*, Calle 6A, No. 14-47, F with bath, warm water, clean, friendly management, rec. Small boys (and thieves **beware**) will meet you off the bus with offers of such accommodation; they are also remarkably competent guides in many languages. There is accommodation in private houses for about US$2 p.p., which is often preferable (ask, for example, for Sra. Elena Rojas de Llanos, "La Gorda", near the church, whose house is clean, safe, but no hot water). Ask at Tourist Office about cabins for rent for about US$4, with hot showers and cooking facilities. Accommodation at the farm of Constantino Ortiz is rec., 3½ km. from town, bordering on the Parque Arqueológico, 4 rooms, meals and horses available, peaceful, inexpensive, good cooking, plenty of morning coffee, also has camping; reservations at Calle 5, 1113 in town.

Camping *El Camping* and *Camping Ullumbe* both provide tents or charge per site, both good. Next to *Yalconia* is Rafael Gómez's campsite, clean, pleasant, toilets, lights, laundry service, horse hire (see below).

Restaurants *Brahama*, Calle 5, No. 15-11, vegetarian meals and comida including soup and drink (also meat dishes), good fruit salads, rec. (has horses and jeeps for rent); *Superpollo*, Diagonal a la Iglesia, US$2 for half chicken, good; *Pandi's* does European-style food at reasonable prices; *El Paraíso*, Calle 3 and Carrera 11, good; *Arhuac*, Calle 3, No. 12-22, pricey, not good value; *La Martina/Las Negras*, very good local food, only Sat. p.m., all day Sun. and Mon.; *Los Idolos*, good also; *La Negra*, Carrera 12, No. 3-40, good tamales; *Copacabana*, Carrera 14, good and cheap; *Nayn*, Cra. 11 y Calle 3, across from bus offices, good comida; *Palacio de Jugos*, Carrera 13, No.3-32, excellent fruit juices; also at *Heladería de Turista*, Calle 3, No. 10-20, friendly, excellent fruit juices with at least a half glass refill on request; *El Ullumbe*, opp. *Hotel Yalconia* pleasant, nice salads, friendly owner, not cheap, has rooms to let. Also opp. *Yalconia*, *Villadolly*, local and international food, rec. Further on, *Casa Blanca*, opp. *Hotel Osoguaico*, good cheap breakfast. Tap water is not safe to drink.

Shopping Bring lots of film (you can't buy it in the town). Leather goods are beautiful and priced reasonably. Many local shops make boots to your own design for about US$27.50 (double-check the price beforehand); *Calzado Líder* is highly recommended, or *Artesanías El Viajero*, Calle 3 no. 11-33, T 73102. Recommended handicraft shops are *Intillay*, Calle 5, No. 14-28 (wood and stone sculptures, weavings, jewellery), and *Nevay*, Calle 5, No. 15-04, bronze, ceramic, basket and leather ware. Don't buy artefacts on the street; if they are not fakes, their sale is illegal. Market day in San Agustín is Mon.

Exchange Travellers are warned to change travellers' cheques before arriving in San Agustín; the Tourist Office and the small shop opp. police station will exchange cash only, at a poor rate; the Banco de Colombia will not change money but does give cash on Visa cards; 0800-1300 Mon. to Fri., 0800-1000 Sat.

Transport San Agustín may be reached directly from Bogotá by taxi (Taxis Verdes have one service a day, leaving at 0500, US$12, 10-12 hrs. will pick you up at your hotel in Bogotá—ticket must be bought one day in advance or by bus (Coomotor, from new bus terminal, 4 a day, US$10, 12 hours). Alternatively there are frequent services from Bogotá to Neiva (US$7, 6 hrs.) as well as some to Pitalito (Taxi Verde costs US$9, leaving Bogotá at 0730). From Neiva there are 6 buses a day to San Agustín, taking 6 hrs. and costing US$4. To Neiva with Autobusco, US$5, 6 a day (1000 bus arrives in time for 1630 flight to Bogotá). The journey from Pitalito takes 1½ hrs., costs US$1 by jeep. To Popayán and Cali, Coomotor daily via Pitalito, Garzón and La Plata, US$9 to Popayán, US$14 to Cali. The bus stops at La Plata (for Tierradentro), 5 hrs; La Gaitana also leaves for Popayán at 0530 (tickets from *Res. Familiar* and La Plata at 1600 (5 hrs., US$4.50), same company continues to Tierradento at 0500, 2½ hrs. **See also page** 703.

A new 135-km. direct route has been opened between **Popayán and San Agustín (via Isnos** and the Puracé National Park); it is unpaved, with one stretch of 20 km. single track, suitable only for jeeps and trucks. There is also a frequent bus service, daily from 0530, with Cootranshuila (office on Calle 3 opp. *Hotel Central*), slow, 6 hrs., US$5.50, very scenic—check these services in advance. (For information ask in the tourist office.)

There is good riding in the neighbourhood. The rate for hiring horses works out at between US$1.50-2 per hour; US$8.50 for a full day. (Check the horses carefully before you hire them—they do not all, for instance, have shoes.) You must pay for the guide's horse, plus usual tip equivalent to the cost of one horse for the trip you have made. Good horses are hired out by Sra. Luz Angélica de Martínez, Calle 7, No. 14-16. For horses without guides there is a place on the road to the Archaeological Park by the football pitch. There are 3 types of guide: *Baquianos* (white identity cards), permitted only to accompany visitors to sites reached on horseback; *Alquiladores*, who own horses, but may not explain the statues or enter the Archaeological Park; and qualified, *Guiatur* guides (orange cards) who are fully trained, may explain all the sites, and charge US$6 to explain the Archaeological Park, US$12 for full day's guidance. Always ask to see a guide's identity badge; if you have any problems, ask at the Tourist Office or seek a tourist police officer. Recommended guide: Sra. Luz Omayra González, employee of the Corporación Nacional de Turismo. Rafael Gómez (next to *Hotel Yalconia*) hires good horses, and will act as a guide for a little extra. Jorge Palacios, who has a handicrafts shop opposite *Hotel Yalconia*, has also been recommended as a horseback guide. Lucas Peña at *Hotel Central* will act as guide on treks in the area; he also provides information on money exchange, etc. "Jerry" Luis Alfredo, Cra. 12 No. 2-78, speaks English, French and a little German, good guide, but check horses carefully; Lucás Garzón, Calle 3, No. 11-55, has also been recommended for information, horses, etc. Another recommended guide for the longer excursions (4 days, Puerto Quinchana-Valencia and return) is Sr. Segundo Arsenio Guzmán (see below).

Alternatively, jeeps may be hired and about 8 people can fit in one! Prices vary according to the number of sites to be visited, for example: the tourist office runs tours by jeep (5 people) to Alto de los Idolos, Alto de las Piedras, and Mortiño, for US$15; trip lasts 5 hrs., departure at 0900, book the day before. A full day visiting 4 sites costs US$25. The *Hotel Central* offers a one-day excursion by jeep to Alto de los Idolos, Alto de las Piedras, and the 2 waterfalls. When hiring a jeep, be clear about what you are to be shown before setting out, don't be rushed, don't let the driver pick up people *en route*, and don't let the driver charge more than the tourist-office-approved rate.

The area offers excellent opportunities for hiking, although some trails to remote sites are not well marked. Two sites easily reached on foot are El Tablón (5 statues) and La Chaquira (figures carved on rocks and good view of Río Magdalena). At the site of La Pelota, two painted statues were found in 1984 (well worth a visit, a 3-hr return trip, 6 hrs. if you include El Tablón and La Chaquira, 15 km. in all). The latest archaeological discovery (1986) in the area is a series of at least 30 stones carved with animals and other designs in high relief; they are on the right bank of the Río Magdalena, near the Estrecho (narrows) to which jeeps run. The leaflets given out by the Tourist Office disagree about distances to the sites. For accurate route information, seek advice from Joaquín Emilio García at the office. Probably best for several people to organize their trips together; prospective horseriders and jeep passengers tend to congregate at the health-food restaurant near the Tourist Office.

The best books on the subject are *Exploraciones Arqueológicas en San Agustín*, by Luis Duque Gómez (Bogotá, 1966, 500 pages) or *San Agustín, Reseña Arqueológica*, by the same author (1963, 112 pages); a leaflet in English is obtainable from tourist offices. The Colombian Institute of Archaeology has published a booklet (English/ Spanish), at US$1.80, on San Agustín and Tierradentro (**see page** 705), available at museums in San Agustín and San Andrés (also available at the Tourist Office, free).

The visitor with time to spare should visit Alto de los Idolos, or about 10 km. by horse or on foot. Inexperienced riders should be warned that the path is very steep in places. On foot it is a lovely (if strenuous) walk via Puente de la Chaquira, but 27 km. by road via San José de **Isnos** village (which is 5 km. from Alto de los Idolos), and to which a bus can be taken, US$1, 0500 on Sat. return bus at 1100, 1300, or catch a bus from the *cruce* on the Pitalito road or hitch, well signposted (the site is open until 1600, entry US$0.20). Here on a hill overlooking San Agustín are more and different statues known as *vigilantes*, each guarding a burial mound (one is an unusual rat totem). The few excavated have disclosed large stone sarcophagi, some covered by stone slabs bearing a sculpted likeness of the inmate. Alto de las Piedras, 6 km. from Isnos, has a few interesting tombs and monoliths, including the famous "Doble Yo". The Director of the Parque (Don Hernán Cuéllar Muñoz) can arrange transport and guide to outlying sites. Only less remarkable than the statues are the orchids growing nearby. There is the *Parador de los Idolos* (3 rooms), ½ km. from Alto de los Idolos, new, D. From San Agustín the Bordones waterfalls can be visited; best with a car; there is a 13-room *Parador* right by the falls, E, clean and pleasant (reservations at San Agustín Tourist Office).

From Isnos many of the sites can be visited by road. As you come S into Isnos from Popayán, turn left just after the bridge (sign Salto de Bordones). 6 km. on right is Alto de las Piedras, and 8 km. further is Bordones village. Turn left at end of Bordones and there is (½ km.) parking for the falls. Coming S through Isnos, turn right off main street to Alto de los Idolos (5 km.). From Isnos it is about 20 km. to San Agustín; after 7 km. turn left (½ km.) to Salto del Mortiño, 300-metre falls.

Market day is Sat. in Isnos (*Hospedaje Nueva*, F)—bus at 0500 from San Agustín.

It is possible to walk from San Agustín to the Lago Magdalena, involving a bus ride or 6-hour walk the first day, 7-hour walk the second, and 8-10 hours walking on the third, either to the lake and back to the second *refugio*, or on to Valencia. Good bases for this excursion are *Residencias El Paraíso*, at Puerto Quinchana, 30 km. away on the road to the source of the Río Magdalena, 2 km. from the Cementerio Indígena de Quinchana, owned by Sr. Arsenio Guzmán, F, friendly, peaceful, restaurant; *Residencias El Páramo* at Juntas on same road, beautiful countryside, owner Alvaro Palechor, F, clean, safe, friendly, restaurant.

Caquetá

Lying to the E of the Cordillera Oriental is the Intendencia of Caquetá, reached by air, or by road from Neiva or Garzón. This region, although still sparsely populated is an area of intensive settlement. The population has trebled since about 1965 ; people have been moving down from the highlands to turn the area into a productive livestock region. The natural forest cover around Florencia, the capital of the Intendencia, has been cleared and for a radius of 10-15 km. lie well-established, undulating pasturelands, dotted with tall palms—the fruits of which are a delicacy for grazing cattle. To the SE, beyond the cleared lands, lie little-touched expanses of tropical forest inhabited by indigenous tribes and wide varieties of Amazonian flora and fauna.

The road Neiva-Florencia is 260 km.: possible in one day, but it is recommended that travellers should try to complete the last 100 km. over the mountains into Florencia by daylight. From the Garzón-San Agustín road, the only route for vehicles into Caquetá branches off at Altamira. Here the surfaced road ends and becomes a single-track dirt road, originally engineered in 1932 during the Leticia dispute between Colombia and Peru. The climb up over the mountains passes through a region of small farms (some of their cultivated fields appear to be on almost vertical valley sides), through sugar-cane cultivation and up into cloud at the higher points of the route. Here there is rain-forest, sporadically cleared for farms. Soon after the summit, and on a clear day, there are extensive views out over Caquetá and then the road winds down through substantial forests—ablaze with the colours of tropical flowers in the dry season (Jan.-March) and into the lowlands. The lower section of the road into the lowlands is prone to frequent landslides (or *derrumbes*) because of weak geological structures.

The roads in Caquetá run from Florencia along the foothills of the Cordillera; eventually a road is planned to run from Puerto Asís through Florencia to Villavicencio, skirting the foothills of the eastern Andes. Other routes are difficult and seasonal (although tracks, or *trochas*, are laid out as part of the settlement scheme, financed by the World Bank) and the main lines of communication into the lowlands are by boat along the rivers Caquetá and Guayas and their tributaries.

Florencia (pop. 78,000) is the capital of the region and the centre for settlement in Caquetá, originally established in 1908. The square contains sculptures, fountains, a large forest tree (*saba*) and flower beds. When the road to Garzón is obstructed by landslides, petrol supplies are limited.

Fiesta The local Saint's day is on 16 July, when there is a candlelight procession in the evening around the town.

Hotels *Plaza*, Carrera 1, No. 30-70, C; *Apartamentos Capri*, E, with bath, clean and safe; those located around the central square are reputed to be more salubrious, and charge about US$3-4 per night. *Residencia Cordillera*, E.

Cafés, Restaurants Plenty, but prices tend to be high because much food is trucked in. For good value try *Tocarema*, 4-course meal US$2, large portions. Vegetarian restaurant on main street for good patacones.

Bank Cash cheques at the Banco de la República.

Car parking Overnight, cars are best left in the care of the fire-station (US$0.20 a night).

Buses There are regular services from Neiva (US$6.50, 7 hrs.), Garzón and Altamira to Florencia (bus Altamira to Florencia, US$3.15) and frequent services as far as Puerto Rico and Belén. Bus to Bogotá costs US$19.50.

Air Services To Puerto Asís, with Satena, on Mon., Wed., Fri., daily to Neiva (Satena and Aires) and to Leguizamo, San Vicente del Caguán and Solano, with Satena. Several planes a day to Bogotá.

Excursions From Florencia down the Orteguaza river: take a morning bus to Puerto Lara or a bus to San Antonio (US$3.25) where there is a cheap hotel; you can visit Indian villages.

From Florencia the road runs northeastwards as far as Puerto Rico: it is paved for 34 km. to La Montañita and then unsurfaced, passing through El Paujil (2,750 pop.), where the *residencias* are unnamed and are situated alongside the road into the town. A dry-weather road runs from here for 21 km. towards Cartagena before giving way to a mule track. Then, on the Puerto Rico road, comes El Doncello (5,500) a very pleasant town, overlooked by the church which has a brightly painted steeple. The *Residencias Americanas* is highly recommended, F. Popular Sun. market. Next comes Esmeralda, a small settlement located on a ford that is too deep for cars, although trucks and buses may cross, and there is a wooden suspension bridge over the river for which the toll is US$0.20. The hotel there provides a very plain but excellently cooked breakfast.

Puerto Rico (4,950) is at the end of the road—which is interrupted by the River Guayas. It is possible to cross the river by ferry (US$0.08) and travel by bus as far as San Vicente where a mule-track goes over the Cordillera to Algeciras in Huila Department. Puerto Rico is a river port; ferries travel downstream to Río Negro (1½ hrs.) and Cartagena (4½ hrs.). Houses built down by the river are raised on stilts above possible flood levels. River boats are made and repaired by the riverside. **Hotels** and *residencias* are full on Sat. nights—book a room early in the day. *El Gran Hotel*, despite its name, provides basic amenities. *Hotel Almacén* is the only place in Puerto Rico serving fresh fruit juices.

The road southwest from Florencia to San José is unsurfaced. At Morelia there is a poor branch road S to the River Pescado, where a ferry will take you across the river to the town of Valparaíso (1,175). *Hotel Ceilán* is cheap and friendly; there is also the *Hotel Turista*. From Valparaíso mule tracks go further into the lowlands. If travelling to Valparaíso by car, make sure it is left well away from the river when catching the ferry as, during times of flood, the river may rise rapidly overnight. Morelia to Belén de los Andes is an unsurfaced road, passing through some very interesting scenery, and crossing very clean, fast-flowing rivers by metal bridges. For some reason prices are higher in **Belén** (2,235) than in other towns in Caquetá. Hotels fill up very quickly, and mosquito nets are not always provided, although they are needed. In the area are a group of co-operative farms, and an oil palm plantation. From Belén an unsurfaced road runs to Albania (1,075) which is a small frontier settlement with only one hotel. A semi-surfaced road runs from here for 11 km. further towards the new areas of settlement.

Anyone wanting to look at wildlife in Caquetá must travel beyond the settlement area. Toucans, monkeys, macaws etc. are kept as pets, but there is little wild-life. Boats and canoes are easily hired, but horses and mules are more difficult, especially in the dry season when they are needed to transport the harvest.

THE CENTRAL CORDILLERA: MEDELLIN AND MANIZALES (6)

The Central Cordillera lies W of the Magdalena River. In it are two of the most important cities in Colombia: Medellín, the third largest city in the country, and Manizales. Manizales can be reached by a road (309 km.) passing through Facatativá and Honda; or through Girardot to Ibagué, then over the high crest of the Quindío pass via Armenia. (For the road from Manizales to Medellín, **see, page** 693.) Medellín can be reached from Bogotá by road three ways: the highway opened in 1982 (**see page** 690); the old direct road (478 km.) with a 207-km.

unpaved stretch from La Dorada to La Unión; and the third via Manizales.

The town of Antioquia was founded in 1541, but the Spaniards, eager for gold, were not interested in the hinterland, which was then very sparsely inhabited by nomadic Indians who made very poor agricultural labourers. But during the 17th century a new wave of settlers came to Colombia from Spain; many of them were Jewish refugees who were deliberately seeking isolation, and found it in the little valley of the Río Aburrá, where they founded the city of Medellín in 1616. They were farmers with their families rather than *conquistadores*: they had an extraordinarily high birth rate; they intermarried very little with either Indian or black; and they divided the land into small farms which they worked themselves. Their exports were small: a little gold and silver from their streams. They lived on the food they themselves produced: maize, beans, sugar-cane, bananas, fruit.

In the early 19th century the settlement began to expand and to push out in all directions, particularly to the S. The settlers followed the forested slopes on the western side of the Central Cordillera and occupied all the cultivable land. Manizales, 120 km. S, was founded in 1848. In the second half of the century new lands were occupied further S.

It was coffee that brought stability to this expansion, but they were slow to adopt it. Coffee appeared in the Magdalena Valley about 1865, but none was being exported from Antioquia before the end of the century. It was the 1914-18 war that suddenly gave a fillip to the industry: within 20 years the Departments of Antioquia and Caldas were producing half the coffee of Colombia, and they are by far the most important producers today. The industrialization of Medellín followed the coffee boom. There has been little immigration since the original settlement, but the natural growth in population has been extraordinary.

Medellín, capital of Antioquia Department, is a fast growing city of 2.5 million people, at an altitude of 1,487 metres. It could hardly be less advantageously placed, for it faces forbidding mountain barriers in nearly all directions. Its climate alone, that of an English summer day (21°C), is in its favour, despite a certain amount of smog. Yet Medellín is one of the main industrial cities of Colombia, and seethes with energy. The first looms arrived in 1902. Today the city produces more than 80% of the textile output of the country, and textiles account for only half its industrial activity. A metro is planned for the city. Excellent views from Cerro Salvador (statue on top), SE of city, and from Cerro Nutibara, S of city, where there are an outdoor stage for open air concerts, miniature village, souvenir shops and restaurants.

Medellín is a well-laid-out industrial city. There are four universities, together with other higher educational institutions. The old colonial buildings have nearly all disappeared, but there are still some 17th century churches left: the old Cathedral on Parque Berrío and the churches of San Benito, La Veracruz, and San José. The new Cathedral of Villanueva (Catedral Metropolitana), one of the largest brick buildings in the world, is on Parque Bolívar, an attractive place. Below the statue of Bolívar in the park are inscribed the words of the conquered Indian leader Choquehuanca to his visitors: "With the centuries, your glory will grow as the shadows grow when the sun sets". Three churches of the 18th century survive: San Ignacio, in Plaza San Ignacio, San Juan de Dios, and San Antonio. The city's commercial centre, Villanueva, is interesting for its blend of old and modern architecture, including many skyscrapers. There is a fine sculpture, Monumento a la Vida, next to the Edificio Seguros Suramericana on Calle 50, where exhibitions of work by leading South American artists are held on the ground floor. The cattle auctions on Tues. and Thurs., held in specially built cattle yards on the outskirts, are interesting. There is a zoo, **Zoológico Santa Fe**, in the southern section of the city, mainly of South American animals and birds; reached by the Guayabal bus (US$0.07; admission US$0.80). In the zoo grounds is a Historical Museum (closed Mon. and Tues.), costing an extra US$0.20 to enter. Christmas illuminations are very good, in Parque Bolívar and Cerro Nutibara.

Travellers should take the same safety precautions as they would in any large city, particularly at night, but remember that Medellín has been the centre of narcotics, and anti-narcotics operations. You are advised to check conditions before going.

Hotels *Intercontinental*, the best, some distance from the centre, A, excellent; *Amaru*, Carrera 50A, No. 53-45, A, central, quiet, good, expensive restaurant with excellent service; *Ambassador*, Carrera 50, No. 54-50, C, in connection with *Veracruz*, Carrera 50, No. 54-18, B, with bath, swimming pool, very good, restaurant on 11th floor gives fine view over city; *El Balcón*, near *Intercontinental*, in Transversal Superior, A, beautiful view of the city, good meals, US$6 p.p.; *Nutibara* (casino and swimming pool), Calle 52A, No. 50-46, A; *Residencias Nutibara*, an annex facing hotel of same name, slightly cheaper with all the same facilities; *Europa Normandie*, Calle 53, No. 49-100 (T 41-99-20), C, restaurant, cafeteria, sauna, disco, central, fair; *Horizonte*, Carrera 47 No. 49A-24, C, good and popular restaurant; *La Montaña*, Calle 48, No. 53-69, E, with shower, good meals available, in the dangerous market area; *Eupacla*, Carrera 50, No. 53-16, C, central, noisy, mosquitoes, but helpful staff; *Comercial*, Calle 48, No. 53-94, E, friendly, clean, hot water available in some rooms, the best of which are on the top floor, doors barred to all but residents after 1800, meals US$2; *Holiday*, Carrera 45, No. 50-25, E, with bath, clean, 5 mins. walk from centre; *Residencias Hotel Gladys*, Carrera 48 and Calle 45, E, modern, clean, friendly and helpful, but rather noisy; all rooms face street; *Linton*, Cra. 45, No. 47-74, E with bath and hot water, very clean. *Príncipe*, Bolívar and Carrera 51, E, clean and friendly; *Nuevo*, Calle 48 and Carrera 53, E, with bathroom, noisy but clean, good meals for US$1; *San Francisco No. 2*, Carrera 54, No. 48-44, F, good and clean, friendly but noisy; *Samaritano*, Carrera 45, No. 45-25, E, clean and friendly, but noisy; *Casa Blanca*, Carrera 45, No. 46-09, E, safe but noisy; *Internacional*, La Playa No. 46-56, F, secure, clean, good value; *Gómez Córdoba*, Carrera 46, No. 50-41, F, basic, safe; *Romania*, Av. Echeverri, Calle 58, No. 50-46, F with bath, clean, a bit noisy. Many *residencias* on Carreras 54 and 55, but this is not a safe area; a safer area for accommodation is around Carrera 43. An excellent private house to stay in is on Carrera 58, No. 53A-36, 3rd floor, US$3 a night, very safe. Calle 45 is said to be an unsafe street.

Restaurants *Cacique Nutibara*, on Cerro Nutibara, offers excellent views of the city and good, reasonably-priced food; *Hato Viejo*, opp. *Intercontinental Hotel*, good local cuisine (another branch on Carrera Junín); *Aquarius*, on road past *Intercontinental Hotel*, first class; on same road, and good also, *Las Sombrillas, La Yerra, Los Cristales*. Roast chicken is provided at the four branches of *Kokoriko*, for US$3; good steaks at *Texas Steak House*, Calle 44 and Carrera 80; good arroz con pollo from *Los Alejos* in Centro Comercial Boyacá. *Finale*, Av. El Poblado with Calle 8, bar serving excellent food, art gallery upstairs, manager speaks English, very friendly; also in El Poblado, *Bar-Pizzería Julio's* (T 46-04-37) open till 0300. Other restaurants in El Poblado, all near Parque Poblado: *Arepizza* on Calle 10 (local food, juices, cheap); *Che's*, Calle 9, good steaks; on Av. 43B, one block from Parque, *Frutos del Mar*, good seafood; *La Crêperie*, opposite, French; *La Torre de Pizza*, good. On Av. Poblado (Av. 43A), *Presto* hamburgers and 2 good chicken restaurants; *Piemonte* and *La Bella Epoca*, very good and expensive, both on road to Envigado, as are *La Mesa* and *Isla Verde* (good, but expensive); *El Boquerón*, on the mountain top; *Aguacatala* and *La Posada de la Montaña*, both outside off road to Envigado, good, Colombian food, expensive; *Noche y Día*, Carrera Junín, between Maturín and Amador, good meals for US$0.80; in fact there are several of these round-the-clock cafés in the vicinity which serve cheap meals. *La Vida*, round corner from *Hotel San Francisco No. 2*, US$1.60 for comida, excellent fruit juices, friendly, also, 2 doors from this hotel, *Popular*, is good. Two good self-service restaurants are *La Estancia*, Carrera 49, No. 54-15, on Plaza Bolívar, and *Contenalco*, Calle la Playa, between Av. Oriental and El Palo, clean, cheap, very busy in rush hours. *Cirus*, Calle 53, meals for US$1, good value. *Palma Sola*, Carrera 51 and Calle 48, comidas for US$1.50. Many good, cheap restaurants on Carrera 49, e.g. *Versalles*, on pedestrian precinct between Av. La Playa and Plaza Bolívar. Good cheap meals at *Helados Sayonara*, opp. Parque Bolívar, and at *Refugio*, Cra. 45 y Calle 47, across from *Residencias Doris*. For hamburgers and sandwiches, *Mr Ham*, *Hardy's*, four of each in the city. Excellent pastries at *Salón de Té Astor*, Carrera 49, No. 53-39. Many cheap cafés near bus station.

Clubs Campestre (good food, rooms, golf, tennis, swimming pool); Ejecutivos (lunch club in centre).

Shopping Silver seems cheaper than in Bogotá. Poor selection of handicraft shops in the city, but there are *artesanía* shops on the top of Cerro Nutibara. Cercado San Alejo, Parque

Bolívar, open on the first Saturday of every month (handicrafts on sale). Carrera 47 has 3 antique shops. Many of the textile mills have discount clothing departments attached where good bargains can be had; ask at your hotel. *La Piel*, at Calle 53, No. 49-131, has an excellent selection of leather goods at very reasonable prices (the selection and price of leather goods in Medellín is better than in Bogotá). *Supermarket Exito* is reaonable for cheap leather bags. There are 2 new shopping centres, San Diego and Oviedo.

Bookshop Librería Continental, Junín No. 52-11, sells foreign-language books.

Taxis Pay what is on the meter plus US$0.90. From airport, about US$2.70.

Discotheque Delfos (in *Hotel Europa Normandie*); others in central hotels, and in El Poblado district.

Music Monthly concerts by the Antioquia Symphony Orchestra. Band concerts in the Parque Bolívar every Sun. at 1130. Open air concerts, on Sundays, of Colombian music on Cerro Nutibara.

Museums Museo Etnográfico Miguel Angel Builes, Carrera 81, No. 52B-120, has an extensive collection of artefacts housed in beautiful new building. The **Museum of the Missionary Sisters of Mother Laura** has a good collection of indigenous costumes and crafts from Colombia, Ecuador and Guatemala. **Museo El Castillo**, Calle 9 Sur, No. 32-269, formerly a landowner's home, has interesting objects and beautiful grounds; entry US$1.20; take bus to Loma de los Balsos, El Poblado (US$0.07), then walk 1 km. up the hill until you see the road lined with pine trees to the right. Open 1300-1700, closed Sun. The **Museo de Antioquia**, Carrera Cundinamarca and Diagonal Carabobo, opp. main post office, shows contemporary pictures and sculptures, including works by Fernando Botero, Colombia's leading contemporary artist (now living in U.S.A.) US$0.50. **Museum of Modern Art**, Carrera 64B, No. 51-64, small collection, open Tues.-Fri., 0900-1300, 1500-1800. The **Museum of the Chamber of Commerce**, Carrera 46, No. 52-82, (exhibitions of modern art). **Casa Museo Maestro Pedro Nel Gómez**, Carrera 51B, No. 85-24, T 332633/440725, house of the contemporary painter and sculptor. **Museo Antropológico** at University of Antioquia (new campus). (In the old University of Antioquia building, beside San Ignacio church, is a **Museo Histórico**.) **Philatelic Museum** in Banco de la República building. Most museums are closed on Mondays.

Botanical Gardens Joaquín Antonio Uribe gardens, near the new campus of the University of Antioquia, which include an aviary, are open daily, 0900-1730, US$0.40 entrance, well worth a visit (some of the plants are named); there is a restaurant, pleasant but not cheap. There is also a zoo (**see page 687**); take Marinilla bus from centre. Also visit El Ranchito, an orchid farm between the towns of Itagüí and La Estrella (entry US$0.50; April to June is the best time to visit).

Bullfights at the bull-ring of La Macarena in February.

Exchange Banco de la República, Calle 50 (opp. Parque Berrío), changes travellers' cheques, but your photo will be taken; has other branches; Banco Anglo Colombiano, Calle 50 (Bolívar), No. 51-06; agency on Calle 45, No. 55-65 and two others; Banco Internacional, Banco Royal, Banco Francés e Italiano de Colombia, and various other Colombian banks. Open: Mon.-Thurs. 0800-1130, 1400-1600; Fri. 0900-1130, 1400-1630; last working day of month 0830-1100. Main hotels will cash travellers' cheques for residents when banks are closed. (The owner of *Café Arturo* is reported to cash cheques.)

British Consulate Calle 9, No. 43-893, T 246-3114.

Post Office Main airmail office in Avianca building, Carrera 52, Calle 51A, Mon.-Sat., 0700-2200.

Telecommunications Pasaje Junín and on corner of Calle 49 and Carrera 50.

Travel Agents Tierra Mar Aire (American Express agents), Calle 52, No. 43-124, helpful. Viajes Marco Polo, Calle 48, No. 65-94, T 230-5145, recommended; also Terra Nova, Calle 5A, No. 39-114, T 266-5000, who run an excursion by train to Cisneros, 3 hrs. journey, with 3-4 hours for a picnic and swim (US$5.20). Viajes Turandina, Calle 53, No. 49-80, T 455815.

Tourist Office Calle 57 No. 45-129, in bus station (some English spoken, helpful), and in airport (will book hotel rooms), and Turantioquia, Carrera 48, No. 58-11, T 254-3864, has good maps, good information on Antioquia and owns 5 good hotels in the Department. For a cheap tour of the city take any "Circular" bus, for US$0.06.

DAS T 239-5076; **Tourist Police** at airport, T 260-1212, ext. 3052; police T 12; general information T 13.

Airport A new airport, José María Córdoba, 38 km. from Medellín and 13 km. from Rionegro, has been opened; *Presto* restaurant. Taxi to town US$7, colectivo US$3, *buseta* to centre, via bus terminal, US$1.25, frequent service, about 1 hr. journey, sit on right going to town (catch bus in town by *Hotel Nutibara*). To Rionegro, bus US$0.15, taxi US$8.50. By air to Bogotá, 45 mins. with Avianca, on shuttle flight, every ½ hour between 0730 and 1630. Copa office, Carrera 45B, No. 33-24. Daily flight to Panama with SAM or Copa, but you will have to buy a return unless you have another exit ticket out of Panama. **See page** 715 regarding transport of motorcycles by air to Medellín.

Rail Apart from a daily train to Barrancabermeja (check in advance) and the Medellín-Santa Marta train, called the "Nutibara", in December to March, there are no regular passenger services from or to Medellín. The Nutibara connects with the Bogotá-Santa Marta "Tayrona" at Grecia. For the tourist train from and to Cisneros, see above under Travel Agents.

Buses The new bus terminal for all long-distance buses is about 3 km. NW of the town centre, with shops, cafeterias, left luggage (US$0.30 per day) and other facilities. Quite safe. Bus service to city centre, US$0.15, buses to station from Calle 50, marked: "Terminal de Transporte". To Bogotá, 9-12 hrs. US$13, every 40 minutes or so, with 5 companies, to La Dorada, US$4.25. Frequent buses for Cali, Flota Magdalena US$11, 10-13 hrs. Frequent buses to Manizales, 6 hrs. (US$6.50 1st class, 4.50 2nd, by Empresa Arauca). To Cartagena, Brasilia, 17-20 hrs., or 14 hrs., by Pullman bus, US$14; road paved throughout but poor. To Barranquilla, US$16 by Pullman, 16 hrs. To Cartago, 8 hrs., Flota Magdalena, US$5. To Pereira, 8 hrs., US$6.25 by Flota Occidental Pullman. To Sincelejo, 9½ hrs. To La Dorada, 9 hrs. To Popayán, US$13.25, 16 hrs. To Turbo, US$7.50.

Roads The new **Medellín-Bogotá highway** has been completed, but beware of landslides in wet weather. The road is totally paved but there are potholes, waterfalls and detours between Medellín and Honda. There are many campgrounds along the route, for example 130 km. and 150 km. from Medellín. On the way from Honda to Medellín is **Doradel** with a large zoo called Hacienda Nápoles and several hotels, e.g. *La Colina*, C, pool, rec. 10 km. beyond Doradel, a dirt road to the left (badly signposted) leads to **La Danta** where there is a cave with *guácharos* (oilbirds). Village boys will lead you there for a tip, take torches. At **Marinilla** 40 km. from Medellín, there is a reservoir in picturesque surroundings, swimming possible, accommodation nearby.

A paved road, 665 km. long, goes N to Cartagena, and another S to Manizales, which provides an alternative route to Bogotá. There are two other important roads: one, 383 km. NW through Antioquia to Turbo, on the Gulf of Urabá; and another, 478 km. SE from Medellín through Sonsón and La Dorada and on to Bogotá. The latter is paved as far as Rionegro, but from Rionegro to Sonsón is in a bad state of repair. The scenery compensates for this to some extent. Also attractive is the road to Quibdó through coffee, tobacco and pineapple plantations.

Excursions A run N along the Cartagena road to (132 km.) **Yarumal** (with 61,250 people and many hosterías; *Restaurante La Nena*), or NW (many hotels and resort areas, crowded weekends) to (80 km.) **Antioquia** (13,275 people) will give a good idea of the very beautiful countryside, excellent walking. Antioquia lies just W of the Cauca river; it was founded as a gold mining town by the Spaniards in 1541, the first in the area, and still retains its colonial atmosphere, with interesting Christmas/New Year fiestas. Until 1826 it was the capital of the Department. The fine old Cathedral is worth seeing, as is the church of Santa Bárbara. There are two small museums close to the church. There is an interesting wooden bridge, 300 metres long, 3 km. downstream from the steel bridge which the buses use—ask for directions or take a taxi. Hotels: *Mariscal Robledo*, D, 37 rooms, swimming pool, good; *Hostería Real*, 2 km. from town, C full board, good food, pool; *Del Río*, also outside, *San Pedro* in resort area, or you can stay en famille with Marta Merizalde de Roldán, Cra. 11, No. 9-39, very friendly and informative, pretty garden. There is good food in the main square US$1 for a full meal. Bus from Medellín US$1.50 (Flota Urbara or Transporte Sierra), 2½ hrs. The road goes on to Turbo (daily bus at 0900), on the Gulf of Urabá (see page 663).

Another interesting excursion from Medellín is along the Sonsón road SE to (39 km.) the town of **Rionegro**, in a delightful valley of gardens and orchards. Here was born one of Bolívar's generals, José María Córdoba, the hero of the battle of Ayacucho. Medellín's new airport has been built 13 km. away. The Casa de Convención (where the 1863 Convention took place) is now an archive museum, entry US$0.20. The cathedral, with its gold and silver altar, deserves a visit. A museum of religious artefacts is behind the altar (entry US$0.20) and you can climb up behind the Virgin donated by Philip II to look down into the cathedral. There are processions in Easter Week. Many interesting pottery and ceramics factories in Rionegro area, hardly mechanized, as well as leather working; they welcome visitors and explain the processes. A day trip can cost US$15, but the Medellín-Rionegro *rápido* taxi service is very cheap. Bus to Rionegro, from Calle 44, No. 44-43, US$0.75, one hr.; bus back to Medellín from plaza every ½ hr. Prices of leather goods are high. 10 km. from Rionegro (15 minutes by colectivo, leave when full from plaza, US$0.50; buses every 2 hrs., US$0.15) is **Carmen de Viboral**, well-known for its pottery; there are several factories just N of the market place.

Rionegro Hotels *Aymará*, E, hot showers, meals available; *Rionegro*, E, friendly, dark rooms, cold water; *residencia* on main square; *Gutier*, central, D with restaurant; *Oasis*, Carrera 50, No. 46-23, D, with restaurant, bar, laundry, TV in rooms. *Residencias Onassis*, F with bath, good value; *Residencias David*, same price, both near market. **Restaurants** Pizza at *La Mansarola* and *Capuccino*; *Kokorico* on main square for chicken.

Beyond Rionegro to the east is El Peñol, a precipitous, bullet-shaped rock which towers above the surrounding hills and lakes. It has been eroded smooth, but a spiral staircase has been built into a crack which extends from the base to the summit. Entrance to rock, US$0.30. A snack bar has been built at the summit, and the views are very fine (meals available only in holiday seasons). Cabins can be rented at the foot of the rock for about US$28 per day (sleep six, everything except food provided), T Medellín 234-6966, Santamaría y Cía; architects, Calle 81A, No.51-79. Bus to the rock and to the pretty town of Guatapé with Cía. Fco. López, US$1.20. Back to Medellín is harder to catch; best take a colectivo to town of Peñol and bus from there. From Rionegro, take a colectivo to Marinilla (US$0.25, leaves from near market), then wait for the San Rafael bus which passes El Peñol (US$1.20); from Marinilla you can also take a colectivo to the new town of Nuevo Peñol (US$0.70), then another to El Peñol (US$0.50)—in all about 2 hrs., either route.

On the road to El Retiro is Fizebad, an old estate house, restored with original furniture and artefacts, and a display of flowering orchids; entry, US$1.75. In El Retiro itself is a small colonial church and an even older chapel which is seldom open: ask for the caretaker. On the road to La Ceja, have lunch in *Parador Tequendamita*, in a beautiful setting by a waterfall. The route is through splendid scenery, and one can see typical Antioquian life and costume. (To Fizebad by bus, catch a La Ceja or El Retiro bus).

La Ceja, also on the Sonsón road, is well worth a visit. Transportes La Ceja cover the route; the journey takes 1¾ hrs. For the energetic, any one of the surrounding hills affords an excellent view of the area. *Hotel Primavera* and one other, both delightful, have rooms (F). Youth hostel at *Centro Vacacional La Montaña*, details from Alcom in Bogotá. At **Sonsón**, there are the *Tahami* (F, very good value) and *Imperio* (F) hotels.

At **Bello**, 6½km. N of Medellín (pop. 153,000), is the hut in which Marcos Fidel Suárez, President 1918-1922, was born. It is completely covered in with glass for its preservation.

A good trip is by car to **Hatillo**, 32 km. along a road which parallels the railway to Puerto Berrío, and then another 80 km. along a new road to Caldas. There are many restaurants along this road.

To the SW of Medellín, the towns in the coffee-growing district (Fredonia, Jericó, Jardín, Venecia) are worth visiting; all have basic inns. The scenery is beautiful.

At **Envigado**, 10 km. S of Medellín, craftsmen have for generations turned out the traditional *antioqueño* pouch called *carriel*, carried by the men. Now used for money, its original use was for coffee samples.

55 km. S of Medellín is **Santa Bárbara**, at 1,857 metres on a green hill top, with stunning views in every direction of coffee, banana and sugar plantations, orange-tiled roofs and folds of hills. *Hotel Palomares* on main square, F, clean, well-maintained; restaurants and cafés also on square, as is the large church. Bus to Medellín, US$1. 140 km. S of Medellín is **Supia**, a pleasant little town with new plaza, no sign, F with bath, clean and good. Supia is 13 km. N of Riosucio (see page 693).

Quibdó, the capital of Chocó Department, is a small, very friendly jungle town (41,000; *Hotel Citará*, D; *Dora Ley*, F without, rooms vary greatly in quality, meals available; *Pacífico*, E, good, with bath, its restaurant, *Club Náutico*, on 2nd floor has good food and views; several *residencias* including *Del Río* and *Darién*; Restaurant *El Paisa* rec.; *Chopán* bakery, good pastries and coffee.). There is a good museum at the Normal School. Sunday market is attended by many Indians, some painted, who arrive by canoe. Boats can be hired for river trips; try Ruffo at the sawmill, US$20 an hour. Quibdó can be reached (1) by bus from Medellín, 12 hrs.; (2) from Buenaventura by boat up the Río San Juan to Istmina and on by road (**see page 700**); (3) by plane from both Medellín and Cali and (4), much the best, by the **Río Atrato**: small speedboats go to and from Riosucio, US$40 p.p., large cargo boats go from Quibdó to Riosucio, Turbo and Cartagena (one week, US$35 p.p. inc. meals, warm clothes and blankets necessary at night, wash in river water, stops allow enough time to disembark and look around).

Chocó Department, thickly wooded and mountainous, is impressive; travel is rough but the rewards are high. A road is planned from Quibdó to the Pacific Coast at Bahía Solano, good for skin-diving; *Cabañas El Almendral*, 40 mins. by decrepit taxi from Bahía Solano, rec. for its setting on the Pacific, for river trips and accommodation. E p.p., book through Aces which runs the airlink (**see page 664** for boats to Panama). 2 Youth hostels at Bahía Solano, details from Alcom in Bogotá.

Manizales is dominated by its enormous (still unfinished) concrete Cathedral and the Nevado del Ruiz volcano, which erupted so catastrophically in November 1985. The city was founded in 1848 by settlers from the Department of Antioquia; it has a population of 450,000 and is the capital of the small Department of Caldas, which originally (until 1965) contained what are now the new Departments of Quindío and Risaralda. The old Department, now known as Viejo Caldas, produces about 30% of all Colombian coffee and picturesque coffee farms abound.

Manizales, at 2,153 metres above sea level, rides its mountain saddle uncompromisingly, the houses falling away sharply from the centre of the city into the adjacent valleys. The climate is extremely humid—average temperature is 17°C, and the annual rainfall is 3,560 mm.—and frequently the city is covered in cloud. The best months of the year are from mid-December through to early March, and early in January the Fair and Coffee Festival is held, with bullfights, beauty parades and folk dancing. The city looks down on the small town of Villa María, "the village of flowers", although with the rapid expansion of Manizales, Villa María is now almost a suburb.

The architecture is predominantly modern with high-rise office and apartment blocks, although traditional architectural styles are still seen in the suburbs and the older sections of the city. The departmental government building, the Gobernación, opposite the Cathedral in the Parque Bolívar, is an imposing example of neo-colonial architecture; the bull-ring built 25 years ago is an impressive copy of the traditional Moorish style. The suburbs stretch away North (with best shopping around Calle 59) and South of the city centre and are reached by a four-lane highway lined with flowers—marguerites—which grow to enormous proportions (as also the geraniums) because of the damp and the altitude. Chipre, a recreational park, provides a good view of the city (well-visited on Sundays); El Tanque, near Chipre, is another vantage point.

Hotels N.B. in January, during the fiesta, hotel prices are grossly inflated. *Carretero*, B, good (T 33206); *Fundadores*, C, good (T 22333); *Las Colinas*, Carrera 22, Calle 20 (T 29400), three-star, two bars, good restaurant, very comfortable, C; *Bonaire*, above Ley supermarket, not too noisy, spacious, very clean, hot water, D, shared rooms cheaper, rec.; *Europa*, Av. Centenario, No. 25-98 (T 22253), near the bull-ring, restaurant for breakfast only, comfortable and clean, D; *Rokasol*, Calle 21, No. 19-16, near bus station so noisy, hot water, clean, all rooms have bathrooms, E, good restaurant, set meal US$2; *Villa Kempis*, on road to Pereira, about 2 km. past bull-ring, old religious retreat house, beautiful view over the valley, very quiet, hot water a.m. only, restaurant and bar, good food at moderate prices, T 32961/30187, D; *Tama Internacional*, Calle 23, No. 22-43, next to Cathedral, E, with bath, meals US$1, clean and cheap, but noisy. Cheaper: *Residencias Nueva York*, Calle 18 between Cras. 22 and 23, extremely clean, hot water, clothes-washing facilities, some bar noise in front but rec., F; *Residencias Monaco*, near bus station, F, adequate, English spoken; *Residencias Caldas*, Carrera 19, No. 22-45, near bus station, F, US$1 surcharge on holidays, hot water, quiet, good; *Cosmos*, opp. bus terminal, F, clean but overpriced, hot water with luck.

La Rochela hotel in the "hot country" about 30 km. W from Manizales on the road to Arauca, large swimming pool for adults and smaller one for children, E, for a room for six; no smaller accommodation, family holiday atmosphere, good food at moderate prices; in process of building separate cabins. *Hotel Termales Arbeláez*, 25 km., from Manizales on the road to the Nevado El Ruiz, D, hot swimming pool, private bathrooms, restaurant.

Restaurants Two well-known places in the Chipre area of town overlooking valleys: *Los Arrayanes* has plain food at moderate prices; *Las Torres*, local specialities, more expensive. *El Cable*, so-called because it stands beside the remaining tower of a disused cable-way for coffee, good food; *Las Redes*, Carrera 23, No. 75-97, predominantly sea food, good but pricey; *Vitiani*, Carrera 23, No. 25-32, Italian and European food, quite smart, food and wine fairly expensive, has good trout and excellent crab-claws (muellas de cangrejo); *El Dorado Español*, moderate prices, good food, carne a la parrilla highly rec., on road to Chinchiná; *Holandesa*, Carrera 19, good, plentiful meals; *El Pilón*, moderate prices, plato montañero and sopa de mondongo rec.; *Hong Kong*, opp. *Hotel Carretero*, good Chinese; *Chung-Mi*, Chinese, does take-away meals; *La Suiza*, Carrera 23, No. 26-57, good fruit juices and cakes; *Caballo Loco*, Calle 21, No. 23-40, expensive pizzas; *Domo*, modern-type hamburger joint and pizzeria, moderate prices; *Picaflor*, very good food at moderate prices; *El Ruiz*, Carrera 19, No. 22-25, filling 3-course meal.

Teatro de los Fundadores is a modern cinema-theatre auditorium. Interesting wood-carved mural by local artist, Fernando Botero, who also has murals in the entrance hall of the Club Manizales and *Hotel Las Colinas*. Events held here and at other locations during Theatre Festival in first two weeks of September.

Museums Bellas Artes, anthropology museum with interesting selection of findings from Indian tombs (and a marvellous view of the Nevado El Ruiz), open in the afternoon (erratically) after 1400. Banco de la República, Carrera 23, No. 23-06, gold and anthropology museum open during banking hours, classical music every afternoon in the Bank. Universidad de Caldas, natural history museum open every day from 0800 to 1200 and 1400 to 1800 (take a "Fátima" bus to the University). La Galería del Arte, Av. Santander at Calle 55, exhibitions of work by local artists, pictures can be bought.

Bank Banco Anglo Colombiano, Carrera 22, No. 17-10, and other banks. Open 0800-1130, 1400-1600, Mon. to Thurs., 0900-1130, 1400-1630 Fri. only. Last working day of the month 0830-1130.

Tourist Office Parque Bolívar, opposite Cathedral, well-organized.

Airport Manizales has a small airport, La Nubia, and the regional airline Aces provides an efficient and punctual service to Bogotá, Medellín, and Cali.

Buses New terminal with good restaurant. Buses to Medellín: Autolegal via Neira and Aguadas, 6 hrs., US$4.50; Empresa Arauca via Anserma, 10 hrs., 1st class, US$6.50 ordinary, US$4.50; colectivo to Medellín, US$8.55. Both routes offer impressive scenery, but the shorter route is largely unpaved between Aranzazu and La Pintada. Bus to Bogotá, 8-10 hrs. by Expreso Bolivariano Pullman, US$7, 9 hrs.; 7½ hrs. by Flota El Ruiz *buseta*, US$8.50—beautiful scenery. To Honda, US$3 (Expreso Bolivariano). Cali by bus Expreso Palmira, 5½ hrs., US$4.50 ordinary; Pullman 6 hrs., US$6. To Cartago, 4 hrs., every 20 mins., US$1.25; Pereira, Expreso Palmira, Expreso Trejos, hourly, 1¼ hrs., excellent road, beautiful scenery, US$1 ordinary. Armenia, Expreso Palmira, 3 hrs., US$2. **N.B.** Unlike in other places, town buses stop only at bus stops.

Excursion To see the full process of coffee growing, apply to the Comité Departmental de Cafeteros de Caldas, Carrera 22, No. 18-21, T 41706; recommended.

Parque de los Nevados national park includes **El Ruiz, Santa Isabel, El Cisne** and **Tolima**—all snow-capped peaks. Contact Inderena (National Conservation Institute) for details. To climb El Nevado del Ruiz, see Pereira, and under Ibagué for El Nevado de Tolima. We should be grateful for more information about Santa Isabel and El Cisne. Also La Laguna del Otún, where there is trout fishing by permission of Inderena. To reach park take Bogotá road, then branch road leads to (22 km.) viewpoint for Nevado del Ruiz. La Esperanza is the point to leave the main road for excursions towards the volcano.

Roads To Medellín direct, 265 km. via the winding mountain road through the picturesque towns of Salamina (*Residencia Puerto Nuevo*, F, opp. bus office, clean, good meals), Pácora and Aguadas, all perched on mountain ridges, to La Pintada (*Hostería Los Farallones*, C, ice pool, meals fair), but further if we go West across the Cauca river via Arauca, Anserma, **Riosucio** (a delightful old town with fine mountain views all round and a large colonial church next to the Arauca bus terminal; many restaurants, bars and shops); and then on to La Pintada. Manizales-Honda-Bogotá: all paved but in poor condition. The road climbs to 3,000 metres, with most superb scenery and little traffic. First accommodation is in Padua, then Fresno (cheap hotels), Mariquita and Honda. (**See page** 678).

THE CAUCA VALLEY (7)

From Manizales a road runs S to Pereira (fine scenery) and then to Cartago, at the northern end of the rich Cauca Valley, which stretches S for about 240 km. but is little more than 30 km. wide. The road goes S up this valley to Cali and Popayán, at the southern limit of the valley proper. There it mounts the high plateau between the Western and Central Cordilleras and goes through to Ecuador. From Cali a railway (no passengers) and a road run W to the Pacific port of Buenaventura. The Valley is one of the richest in Colombia. From Cartago S the river Cauca is navigable by barges up to Cali.

Pereira, capital of Risaralda Department, 56 km. SW of Manizales, stands overshadowed by green mountains, at an altitude of 1,476 metres, above the Cauca Valley. Population, 450,000; a centre for coffee and cattle. It is a pleasant modern city, founded in 1863, with an undistinguished cathedral and four parks: the best is the Parque del Lago, with an artificial lake; a fountain is illuminated several times a week. (Good Christmas illuminations, too.) There is a lively market. Matecaña airport is 5 km. to the S (bus, US$0.05). Outside it is a good zoo (bus from town centre to zoo, US$0.06.)

Hotels *Meliá Pereira*, Carrera 13, No. 15-73 (T 50-770/53-970, Apartado Aéreo 4050), 5-star, A (taxes not included), restaurant, bars, swimming pool; *Soratama*, main plaza, C; *Gran*, Calle 19, No. 9-19, C, restaurant, bar, travel agency, etc.; *Residencias Bolívar*, opp. Cathedral, F, friendly but plumbing suspect, meals available; *Res. Metropolitana*, Cra. 7 No. 17-21, E, hot water, TV, friendly, some noise; *Cataluña*, E, clean and friendly, good set meal in dining room; *Royal*, Calle 16, No. 7-56, F, with bath and hot water, clean, highly rec.; *Residencia Edén No. 1*, Calle 15, Carrera 10, near market, F, clean, friendly. Plenty of *residencias* in Calle 19, e.g. *Savoy*, F with bath. Youth hostel, *Centro Vacacional Viejo Caldas*, 10 mins. by car from Pereira, details from Alcom in Bogotá.

Restaurants *El Pollo Campestre* (near airport), *La Ricura*, Carrera 8, No. 22-21, very good meal, US$1.50; *El Manolo*, Calle 20, No. 8-22, which has good meals for over US$4 near the market; good self-service restaurant on main square; vegetarian restaurant *Naturista No. 2*, Calle 19, No. 5-73, good. *Pequeña Italia*, Fiducentro, Carrera 12, Calle 19, run by Mike Homyak, expat American, Italian and international good; *El Mirador*, on a hill overlooking the town (ask Tourist Office for directions), good food and views.

Clubs *Club Rialto; Club Campestre*, 5 km. from town.

Banks Banco Anglo Colombiano, Carrera 9, No. 17-48. Banco Internacional. Open 0800-1130, 1400-1600, Mon.-Thurs., 0900-1130, 1400-1630, Fri. Last working day of month, 0800-1030.

Transport New bus terminal, clean, with shops, outside city centre. Bus to Armenia, 1 hr., US$1, a beautiful trip. SAM and Avianca flights to and from Bogotá, Cartagena, Cúcuta, Medellín and San Andrés. Bus to Cali, US$3.50, 4½-5 hrs.; Manizales, US$1, 1½ hrs.; to Armenia, US$1; to Bogotá, US$6.50, 7 hrs., rough journey, not recommended for motorbikes.

Excursion 15 km. away, at Santa Rosa de Cabal, a poor 11-km. road branches off to Los Termales, where waters from a hot spring cascade down a mountain into a swimming pool. There are also cold showers fed from a natural spring. The hotel (B) is overpriced and food in the restaurant is disappointing. Bus Pereira-Santa Rosa, US$0.20; then bargain for a jeep ride, US$4, to the springs. Package tours from Santa Rosa to Los Termales, including meals and one night's lodging, are available, but an afternoon excursion is the best value.

From Pereira, a 2-day excursion to the Ucumari Park is recommended. This is one of the few places where the Andean spectacled bear survives (but you won't see one). Above 4,000 metres in the park are spectacular *frailejón* plants. Hikes can be made to the Nevado del Ruiz (5,399 metres). Park guards run an excellent *refugio* (La Pastora, US$2 in bunk bed, good meals, US$1.20, hot shower, very good). Take a bus from Pereira (Transportes Florida, Calle 12, No. 8-82) at 0900 and 1440, to El Cedral (1½ hrs.—return at 1130 and 1630), then walk 2 hours to the *refugio* through lush forest. Reservations for the *refugio* must be made in advance at El Lago, piso 12, Calle 25 between Carreras 7 and 8. We have no clear information on whether **Nevado del Ruiz** is safe to climb after the 1985 eruption which, apart from ejecting millions of cubic metres of dust, devastated the town of Armero to the east, killing over 25,000 people. Approximately 10% of the ice core melted, a major cause of landslides and mudflows.

Armenia, capital of Quindío Department, is in the heart of the Quindío coffee district; population 350,000; altitude 1,838 metres; mean temperature 19°C. This modern city, founded in 1889, is the seat of Quindío University. The Bogotá-Armenia-Cali road is fully paved, but slow through the mountains; fog at night, reckless drivers and stray animals make the Quindío Pass (3,350 metres) a hazard at night. A newer, more direct road from Armenia to Cali, joining the Panamericana S of Zarzal, has heavier traffic than the old road.

Hotels *Palatino*, Calle 21 at Cra. 14, E-D, central, comfortable; *Izcay*, Calle 22 with Cra. 14, D; *Residencial El Viajero*, opp. bus station, but 15 blocks from the centre of town, E; *Pensión Nueva York*, Carrera 19, No. 23-52, basic but clean and cheap, G; *Moderno Aristi*, Calle 18, Carrera 20, E, with bath, hot water, clean; opposite is *Superstar*, F.

Restaurants *La Fogotá*, near university; *Frisby*, Carrera 16, No. 20-22, good pizza or fried chicken; *El Pollo Campestre*, near Country Club. Vegetarian: *Manjar*, Calle 18, No. 15-52 and *Rincón*, Carrera 16, No. 18-28, closed Sun.

Archaeological Museum Calle 21, No. 16-37; closed Sun.

Airport El Edén, 13 km. from city. Fog often makes air services unreliable.

Bus New terminal. To Neiva, Flota Magdalena, 0100, 0400, 2230, US$4.75. To Ibagué, US$2. To Bogotá: Velotax bus, US$6, hourly, 9 hrs.; Velotax colectivo, US$8, 7 hrs.

Before the road drops into the Cauca Valley, between Armenia and Buga is **Sevilla**; *Hotel Estelar Sevilla*, good, B/C; *Residencias Soratama*, Cra. 49, No. 51-48, F, secure parking; others similar. Restaurant: *Chicken Loco*. 30 minutes' bus-ride from Armenia is Montenegro, a coffee centre (ask at FNC office on Plaza Bolívar about visits to *fincas* in the district); Plaza Bolívar is heavily wooded.

Cartago, 64,830 people, about 17 km. SW of Pereira, is on a small tributary of the Cauca river before it takes to the gorge separating the two *cordilleras*. Coffee, tobacco and cattle are the main products. Founded in 1540, it still has some colonial buildings, particularly the very fine Casa de los Virreyes. Visit the cathedral, with the cross apart from the main building.

Hotels Around Plaza Bolívar: *El Gregorio*, Carrera 5 y Calle 10, D, swimming pool, a/c; *Central*, Carrera 6, No. 11-51, G, basic; *Residencias El Dorado*, Carrera 6, No. 11-16, G. *Villa del Río*, F, rec. *Residencial Paraíso*, Carrera 9, No. 8-99, F, cold showers only, clean, Sat. noisy at night. Many others in same area, i.e. around bus terminals (Carrera 9) and railway station (Carrera 9 y Calle 6); those in the same block as Flota Magdalena office are better value than the others.

Restaurants *Mullipán*, Carrera 6 y Calle 12, good cheap meriendas; *El Portal*, Carrera 6 y Calle 11, OK.

Post Office on Plaza Bolívar.

Cinema Roblero, Calle 11 between Carreras 5 and 6 (opp. *Hotel El Gregorio*).

Transport Local train service to Cali via Zarzal, Tuluá (vegetarian restaurant *Vivamejor*, Carrera 26, No. 31-64, good), Buga, Palmira: *tren ordinario* at 0450 and 1405, US$2; *ferrobus* at 0625 and 1635, US$3 (crowded), 4-6 hrs., occasional derailments; on weekends and holidays, El Expreso Caleño at 1245. Bus to Cali, US$3.50, 3½ hrs.

About 27 km. S of Cartago is **La Victoria** (the Pan-American Highway bypasses it to the east), a pleasant, small colonial town with a shady plaza. There is a *Hotel Turista* (F, family atmosphere, clean and friendly, will change US$ cash), one block from the plaza, and several restaurants. La Victoria is in the centre of a scenic area where cattle are raised, and cotton, sorghum, maize and soya are grown. You can cross the Cauca River by turning right off the road going to the south (good fishing Jan., Feb. and July) and 10 km. (paved road) further on is **La Unión** at the foot of the mountains on the west side of the valley. La Unión is a small agricultural town, a centre for grape production. *Residencia Los Arrizos*, and *Residencia El Cacique*. The countryside around offers good walks. Just south of La Unión is Rondanillo, a small town in the hot Cauca Valley, with a museum of paintings by the Colombian artist, Omar Rayo. A road runs E to the main highway at Zarzal.

About 50 km. S of Cartago is Zarzal, and 71 km. S again is **Buga**, an old colonial city of 75,220 people and a centre for cattle, rice, cotton, tobacco and sugar cane. Founded in 1650, and its modern Cathedral contains the image of the Miraculous Christ of Buga to which pilgrimages are made. N of Buga, at Uribe (50 km.), is the junction of the road S from Medellín with the one from Bogotá and Venezuela. Bus to Cali, US$1.50. Toll 22 km. S of Buga, US$0.40.

Hotels *Guadalajara* (swimming pool), D, rec., cabins for family groups, excellent restaurant and self-service cafeteria; *La Casona*, E, good; *Capacari*, E, with bath, clean (swimming pool), but overpriced, poor restaurant; *residencias* around Cathedral better value. *Res. Palermo*, Calle 9, No. 9-82, G with bath, clean.

Excursion If you take the road from Buga to Buenaventura you come to the man-made Lake Calima. Taking the southern route round the lake, 42 km. from Buga is the *Hotel del Lago Calima* (D) set in very pleasant surroundings on the edge. There is no swimming pool, but some brave people swim in the lake, which is cold at about 16°C, and a kilometre deep. Closer to Buga on this road, before the Río Cauca, is the Laguna de Sonso Reserve, which is good for birdwatching.

47 km. from Buga is **Palmira**, in the Department of Valle; population, 163,000. Good tobacco, coffee, sugar, rice and grain are grown, and there is a College of Tropical Agriculture. The Pan-American Highway runs direct to Popayán via Pradera, but the road through Cali is preferable. The best road S is from Palmira through Candelaria and Puerto Tejada, avoiding Cali, to Popayán; paved, straight, not much traffic. (Taxi connection with Cali, 29 km. south, US$5.55; bus US$0.45, Transportes Palmira, terminal on Calle 30, near Cra. 33)

Hotels *Las Victorias*, C; *Palmira*, E; *El Dorado*, D without bath, clean; *Residencias Belalcázar*, F, with bath, G without, clean, friendly, good value. *Escorial*, F, and many other cheap places.

Restaurants *La Fonda*, good; *Grill Caña de Oro*, nice; *Paradero los Parrales*, good breakfast, good service, clean loos.

At La Manuelita, 5 km. N of Palmira, is a famous sugar estate. Beyond La Manuelita any of 3 roads running E will reach, in 12 km., the fine restored colonial *hacienda* of El Paraíso, where the poet Jorge Isaacs (author of *La María*, a Colombian classic) lived and wrote. Entry US$0.50; there is a café. To visit the *hacienda*, take a bus from Palmira, corner of Cra. 25 and Calle 26, at 1230 (another in a.m.), which passes the *hacienda* 1/2-an-hour later (US$0.55); returns about 1515. 9 km. from El Paraíso is a sugar cane museum in the Hacienda Piedechinche (open 0930-1600, closed Mon.; admission, US$0.20). 42 km. from Cali, take a bus to Palmira, then taxi, or take bus from Cali to Amaime, a small place on the road to Cartago, US$0.60, then wait for bus to Santa Elena, which passes the turn off to the Hacienda. You can walk from Amaime: take the turning marked "El Paraíso" and walk for one hour to the turn off to the Hacienda (marked "Museo de Caño"), then it's another 1/2 an hour. There is no public transport connection between the two *haciendas*. Tours of this and Hacienda El Paraíso arranged by Comercializadora Turística Ltda, Carrera 4, No. 8-39, local 101, Cali (US$10, including transport, entrance fee, guided tour and lunch).

Cali, capital of Valle Department (2 million people), is the third largest city in Colombia, set in an exceptionally rich agricultural area producing sugar, cotton, rice, coffee and cattle. Altitude: 1,030 metres; average temperature: 25°C, hot and humid at mid-day but a strong breeze which blows up about 1600 hrs. makes the evenings cool and pleasant. It was founded in 1536, and until 1900 was a leisurely colonial town. Then the railway came, and Cali is now a rapidly expanding industrial complex serving the whole of southern Colombia. South of Carrera 10 are many one- and a few two-storey houses, tiled and wide-eaved. Through the city runs the Cali river, a tributary of the Cauca; with grass and exotic trees on its banks. On one overlooking mountain, from which the best views are obtained, there is a statue of Christ visible for 50 km. and there are three large crosses on another mountain. The statue of Benalcázar, the city's founder, is worth a look, beautiful views of the city. It is also worth while going up the skyscraper Torre de Cali, for good strong coffee and a view of the city. Two nearby *haciendas*, El Paraíso (see above under Palmira) and Cañas Gordas, have important historical associations.

The church and monastery of San Francisco are Cali's best buildings. Inside, the church has been renovated, but the 18th century monastery has a splendidly proportioned domed belltower. The 18th century church of San Antonio on the Colina de San Antonio is worth seeing and there are fine views. Cali's oldest church, La Merced (Calle 7, between Carreras 3 and 4), has been well restored by the Banco Popular. The adjoining convent houses two museums: Museo de Arte Colonial (which includes the church) and the Museo Arqueológico with precolumbian pottery (US\$1, but well worth it). More Indian pottery can be seen in the Sociedad de Mejoras Públicas, across the street from La Merced; this collection belongs to the Universidad del Valle. Another church worth seeing is La Ermita, on the river between Calles 12 and 13. The orchid garden along the Río Aguacatal, near the centre, is well worth seeing.

The city's centre is the Plaza de Caicedo, with a statue of one of the independence leaders, Joaquín Caicedo y Cuero. Facing the square are the Cathedral, the Palacio Nacional and large office buildings. Across the river, which is 2 blocks from the Plaza de Caicedo, is the Centro Administrativo Municipal (CAM) and the main post office.

Warning Cali has recently become a centre of both guerrilla and counter-insurgency activity and drug and anti-drug operations. It is best not to arrive after dark and to keep off the streets after midnight. Carry your passport (or photocopy—DAS approved) at all times and be prepared for frequent police checks.

Fair Held during December; bullfights, masquerade balls, sporting contests. National Art Festival in June (painting, sculpture, theatre, music, etc.). Also in June Feria Artesanal at Parque Panamericano, Calle 5, handicrafts and excellent leather goods.

Hotels A *Hilton* is under construction, on Av. Colombia, Carrera 10 Oeste. *Intercontinental*, Av. Colombia, No. 2-72, recently extended, tennis and pool, rec., good barbecues, A (weekend discounts); *Americana*, for businessmen, B, a/c, Carrera 4, No. 8-73; *Dann*, opposite *Intercontinental*, A, (with weekend discounts), service could be improved, but good; *Don Jaime*, Av. 6, No. 15N-25, B, good, restaurant rec.; *Menéndez*, Av. Colombia, No. 9-80, D, all rooms have own bath, good, reasonably priced meals available, nice old colonial building, popular with Colombians; *del Puente*, Calle 5, No. 4-36, D, with bath, clean, will store luggage, rec.; *Aristi*, Carrera 9, No. 10-04, 3-star, C, but weekend discounts, rec., large and old by Cali standards, turkish baths, rooftop pool, restaurant; *New York*, Calle 12, No. 3-62, D, clean, hot water, basic, near bus station and market; *Los Angeles*, Carrera 6, No. 13-109, E, good; *La Merced*, Calle 7, No. 1-65, D, swimming pool, pleasant young staff are very helpful, restaurant expensive, English spoken, rec.; *Hotel Residencias Stein*, Av. 4N, No. 3-33, B, full board, C, bed only, friendly, very good, quiet, excellent food, dinner for non-residents US\$5, French, German and English spoken, Swiss-run, swimming pool; *Residencial Paseo Bolívar*, Av. 3 Norte, No. 13N-51 (T 68-50-67) and *Paseo Bolívar II*, Av. 3N, No. 13N-43 (T 68-28-63), both F, cold water, clean (cheaper rates for long stay); *Mónaco*, Calle 14 No. 2-13, F, central and friendly but on edge of unsavoury area; *Bremen*, Carrera 6, No. 12-61, T 761998, some rooms with bath, F; *del Río*, Carrera 2 N, No.24-82. G p.p.; *Amoblador Bolívar*, Calle 25, No. 2N-47, near bus terminal, F, basic, safe, highly rec. for friendly atmosphere (the owner collects foreign coins); *Amoblador las Américas*, Calle 25, 2N-31, E with bath, F without, cold water, clean, safe; *Amoblador Belmonte* in same block; *Casa del Viajero*, Calle 15 Norte, No. 4-44 (T 621477), F or E, but you are not given keys to rooms and your belongings are not safe, two *amobladores* next to it; *Arca de Noé*, on road leading up to the Cristo Rey, D, fabulous views, marvellous gardens, good food in restaurant, poor service but worth the effort. It is possible to rent a furnished apartment in Cali for about US\$45 per month.

Restaurants Cali is a good place for eating, as the attached list attests (but restaurants close early, and many close on Sun.): *Don Carlos*, Carrera 1, No. 7-53, excellent seafood, elegant and expensive; *Hostería Madrid*, Calle 9, No. 4-50, European specialities, good service, above-average price; *Canarias*, Calle 8, between Carreras 3 and 4, rec. for cheap meals; *Restaurante Suizo*, Carrera 30 y Diagonal 29, Swiss, excellent fondue bourguignonne, pleasant atmosphere, reasonably priced; *Los Farallones*, at *Hotel Intercontinental* on 9th floor, is Cali's most atmospheric restaurant, with shows starting at about 2230-2300; try their Chateaubriand for two with drinks and desserts, less than US$25 including tips, a real buy; also their weekday noontime buffet at about US$6.50 a head is very reasonable, eat all you want; *El Quijote*, Carrera 4, No. 1-64, atmospheric, European dishes, expensive; *Simonetta*, Diagonal 27, No. 27-117, pleasant, reasonable, Italian dishes; *El Rancho*, S end of Av. 6, near municipal building, good local food, draught beer, pricey, closed Sun.; *Dominique*, Av. 6N, No. 15N-25, good Italian food and service, reasonable; *La Terraza*, Calle 16, No. 6N-14, elegant, music and dance, nice atmosphere; *El Cortijo Andaluz*, Carrera 38 and Calle 53, atmospheric (converted residence), Spanish food; *Los Girasoles*, Av. 6N, Calle 35, steaks, other meat grills, good atmosphere; *Los Gauchos del Sur*, Calle 5 about Carrera 60, Argentine-style grilled meat, dancing, excellent food, very reasonable; *China*, Av. 6N, No. 24-52, excellent food and service, pleasant atmosphere, large servings for reasonable price; *Shanghai*, Av. 8N, No. 17-33, Chinese, excellent food in utilitarian setting, takeaway, very reasonable; *Embajada Antioqueña*, Av. Roosevelt, Antioquian regional food, relatively cheap; *Cali Viejo*, in the Bosque Municipal, about US$10 p.p. for very good local food in pleasant surroundings, music, try their tamales, also good is *La Cazuela*, Avenida Roosevelt, 26-30; *Los Panchos*, Carretera a Meléndez with Autopista Sur, very good Colombian food, a favourite of Caleños; *Gloria*, Carrera 6, Calle 14, good and cheap; *Eduardo VIII*, piano bar, attempt at English pub atmosphere, good food, well-stocked bar; *Mauna Loa*, Centro Comercial del Norte, seafood a speciality, reasonably priced, Lebanese food too; *Mac Club*, Centro Comercial Imbanaco (Calle 5a and Carrera 39), hamburgers and hotdogs, excellent, cheap, good hamburgers also at *Primos*, near Calle 5, Carrera 34; *Sears Cafeteria*, open 0930-1930, excellent food, rather expensive but large servings. *Kokorico*, places all around town, spit-roasted chicken; *La Calima*, Carrera 3, No. 12-06, good meal US$1.30, always open; *El Galeón*, Calle 8a, No. 1-27, very good seafood and atmosphere, expensive; *Jino's Pizza*, held to be Cali's best pizzas, reasonably priced; *La Veda*, near bus station, good gaucho food. At least 10 eating places in the bus station, *Doble Vía* is the best.

Vegetarian: *Centro Naturista*, Calle 17N, No. 6-39.

You can find lots of European-style side-walk places along Av. 6 at good prices. Cheaper are the *fuentes de soda*, mostly with Colombian-style cooking, a decent meal for US$3-4. There are also *Masserna* on Carrera 7 between Calles 10 and 11 and *La Sultana*, Calle 10, on the corner with *Hotel Aristi*. Try their buñuelos (cheesy fritters) and the pandebono (cheesy buns) next door at *Montecarlo*. Cafés and ice-cream parlours abound near the university, across the river from the main part of town.

Clubs Club Colombia; Club de Tennis de Cali; Club San Fernando, modern and luxurious; Club Campestre, as good as any club anywhere, with a magnificent golf course, tennis courts and swimming pool; Club La Ribera y Náutico.

Shopping *Platería Ramírez*, Carrera 11b, No. 18-64, for gold, silver, brass, jewellery, table settings, etc. *Artesanías de Colombia*, Calle 12, No. 1-20 and for larger purchases Av. 6 N, No. 23-45. For leather goods and shoes, try *Boots and Bags*, *Carlo's* and *Clogs*, all in the same precinct. For boots and shoes *Chaparro* (*Botas Texanas*), Av. 6, No. 14N-14, T 651007, good, owner Edgar speaks a little English. Best shopping district: Av. 6N, from Río Cali to Calle 30 Norte.

Bookshop *Librería Nacional*, on main square, has a café.

Taxis Black taxis are the most reliable; ensure that meters are used. Prices, posted in the window, start at US$0.11. On holidays an extra charge is made.

Nightclubs Locally known as "Grills". The ones along the Av. Roosevelt and along Calle 5a are safest and best known. *Arca de Noé*, *Farallones* at the *Intercontinental* and *El Peñol* on the Buenaventura road are probably Cali's best (and most expensive).

Entertainments Experimental Theatre, Calle 7, No. 8-63, T 781249; films Wed. nights at Centro Colombo-Americano (see below).

Sports Within its Villa Olímpica in San Fernando, Cali has three stadia: the Pascual Guerrero Stadium, holding 50,000 people, the Olympic Stadium, holding 7,000 people and the Piscinas Olímpicas, 3,000. Another stadium holding 18,000, the Monumental de Cali, is 10 minutes from the city on the road to Meléndez. Outside the city also is the new, first-class bull-ring.

Museums Museo de Arte Moderno La Tertulia, Av. Colombia, No. 5-105 Oeste (10 mins. from centre) has an exciting exhibition of S. American art, open Tues.-Sat. 0900-1300, 1500-1900, Sun. and holidays, 1500-1900. Museum of Natural History, Cra 2 Oeste, No. 7-18, pre-Colombian exhibits as well as biological specimens from the area, similar opening hours. Two other museums are mentioned in the introduction above.

Parks and Zoos Lovely walks and parklands stretch along both sides of the river Cali. There is a zoo on the South bank some distance from the centre, entrance US$0.50. There is an orchid garden, Orchideorama, Av. 2N, No. 48-10, T 643256.

Exchange Banco Anglo Colombiano, Calle 11, No. 4-48 (Plaza de Caicedo), and agencies on Avenida Roosevelt and Av. 6; Banco Internacional; Banco Royal de Colombia, Calle 3; Banco Francés e Italiano; Banco Colombo Americano and other national banks. Open: Mon.-Thurs., 0800-1130, 1400-1600; Fri., 0900-1130, 1400-1630. Last working day of month, 0800-1130. Closed Sats. Money can be changed at Almacén Stella, Carrera 8, No. 9-64 (by *Hotel Aristi*) open 0800-1200, 1400-1800, or at travel agents.

Consulates Swiss: Carrera 5, No. 8-50. US Consul from Bogotá visits monthly at the centro Colombo-Americano, Calle 13N, No. 8-45, T 67-35-39. British, Ed. Garcés, Calle 11, No. 1-07, No. 409, T 783-2752.

Post Office Adpostal for national service, Calle 10, No. 6-25; Avianca for international service, Calle 12N, No. 2a-27.

Tourist Office Corporación Nacional de Turismo, Calle 12N, No. 3-28 (T 686972); regional office, Carrera 3, No. 8-39 (closed Sat. and Sun.). Maps, posters and general information.
DAS office, Av. 3N, No. 50N-20 (T 643809). Also co-operative for shopping. There is a Thomas Cook office at Wagons-Lits, Cra. 4 No. 8-20. Good street map from municipal building just N of river at Calle 11.

Rail No passenger service, except to Cartago (US$3, 4 hrs.).

Buses New bus terminal (connected by tunnel to railway station) is at Calle 30N, No. 2A-29, 25 mins. walk from the centre (leave terminal by the taxi stands, take first right, go under railway and follow river to centre). Hotel information available. *Casa de cambio*, bank only. Showers on second level (US$0.40). There are plenty of local buses between the bus station and the centre, which charge US$0.06. Taxi from centre to bus station, US$2. Buses to Popayán, US$3, 2½-3 hrs., also colectivos. To Pasto, US$10, 9 hrs.; to Ipiales (direct), US$11, 12 hrs. or by Bolivariano Pullman, US$9, departures at 0400 and 0615 and 0800; Coomotor have a direct service to San Agustín via Popayán, US$12; to Cartago, 3½ hrs., US$3.50; to Ibagué, US$6, 7 hrs.; to Buenaventura, US$3.15, 4 hrs.; to Manizales, US$4.50, 5 hrs.; to Medellín, US$11, 11-15 hrs.; to Bogotá, 10-15 hrs., by Magdalena (rec.) and Palmira, US$10. *Busetas* (Velotax and others) charge about 50% over bus prices but save time; taxi-colectivos about 2½ times bus prices and save even more.

Airport Palmaseca, 20 km. from city, has *casa de cambio*. International standard, with good *Hotel Aeropuerto Palmaseca*. Frequent services to Bogotá, Medellín, Pereira, Ipiales (US$40), Cartagena (US$70), Barranquilla, San Andrés, Leticia (Mon., Wed., Fri., US$85). Minibus from airport to bus terminal (2nd floor), every 10 minutes, approx. 30 mins., US$0.75. Colectivo to city about US$1; taxi, US$6. One flight a week to Quito; direct flights (Avianca) to Panama; also to Miami and New York.

145 km. by road from Cali (4 hrs.) over a pass in the Western Cordillera is **Buenaventura**, Colombia's only important port on the Pacific. It was founded in 1540, but not on its present site. It stands on the island of Cascajal, 16 km. inside the Bay of Buenaventura. Port works are in progress. Beaches such as La Bocana, Juanchaco and Ladrilleros (many small hostels and restaurants) may be reached by motor launch, but they are not very safe. Trips to beaches cost between US$10-40 for 10-person launch (rate per launch, not per person).

Buenaventura is 560 km. by sea from Panamá, 708 km. by road from Bogotá. Population, 122,500, mostly black. Mean temperature, 27° C. It rains nearly every day, particularly at night; the average annual rainfall is 7,400 mm. (relative humidity 88%). There are still problems with malaria. The port handles 80% of Colombia's coffee exports, and 60% of the nation's total exports, including sugar and frozen shrimp.

The toll road to Cali is fully paved; the toll is about US$0.40 for cars and US$0.10 for motorcycles. The ordinary road is not paved. (Both give beautiful views of mountains and jungle, and from the old road you can reach the Parque Nacional Farallones. To reach the park, take the dirt road S from the plaza in Queremal, at 1,460 metres, about 1 hr. from Cali, 3½ hrs. from Buenaventura.)

There are plenty of buses to Cali, US$3.15 each way, 3 hrs. Colectivos run at half-hourly intervals to Cali, US$4.75 p.p.

The commercial centre is now entirely paved and has some impressive buildings, but the rest of the town is poor, with steep unpaved streets lined with wooden shacks. It is more expensive than Cali and it is difficult to eat cheaply or well. Festive atmosphere every night. S of the town a swampy coast stretches as far as Tumaco (see page 709); to the N lies the deeply jungled Chocó Department, where the most important gold and platinum mines are found.

Hotels *Estación*, B, good restaurant; on Carrera 3 with Calle 3, *Del Mar*, C, restaurant, TV, phone in rooms, and *Balmoral*, E with bath. Several F and G hotels on Carrera 5, e.g. *Comfort*, a/c; *Colombia*, fan, *Felipe II*, a/c, D with bath, restaurant. *Bahía*, Calle 3, F, clean, friendly. *Gran*, E with bath; *Continental*, Carrera 5, No. 4-05, E with bath; opposite is *Europa*, F without bath.

Camping With the permission of the commandant, it is safe to camp in the police compound at the docks while awaiting your ship.

Restaurants *Los Balcones*, Calle 2 y Carrera 3, very good, but expensive. Self-service restaurant on main plaza, clean, modern, open 24 hrs. *La Sombrita de Miguel*, on road to El Piñal, good seafood, reasonable prices. Chinese restaurant in street leading NE from telephone building. Good seafood at Pueblo Nuevo market, but not very cheap.

Exchange Do not change money in Buenaventura, but in Cali.

Tourist Office Calle 1, No. 1-26, Mon.-Fri., 0800-1200, 1400-1800. Cámara de Comercio nearby is also helpful; has plan of city.

Air Services Local airport only; flights to Cali.

Grace Osakoda from Hawaii tells us that you can get from Buenaventura to Quibdó (see page 691) on the Río San Juan, but that boats are scarce out of Buenaventura (lumber boats from El Piñal only go about a day and a half upstream, and port authorities are strict about allowing passengers on cargo boats). One way is to take a bus from Pueblo Nuevo, Buenaventura, to San Isidro on the Río Calima (28 km., 6 hrs., terrible road), then a motorized dugout (panga) to Palestina on the Río San Juan. From there take a dugout going upstream; they rarely go as far as Istmina, which is connected by road and bus to Quibdó. Try to get as far as Dipurdú (no hotels, but friendly locals who offer sleeping space, shops with tinned goods), from where daily boats go to Istmina.

Shannan Shiell, from Glasgow, recommends a visit to the island of **Gorgona** which is about 150 km. down the coast from Buenaventura. Until a few years ago, it was Colombia's high security prison (a sort of Alcatraz), convicts were dissuaded from escaping by the poisonous snakes on the island and the sharks patrolling the 30 km. to the mainland. However, now it is a nature reserve, controlled by Inderena. All visitors, research students, scientists and tourists must obtain a (free) pass to go there. Facilities on the island are run by Inderena employees. It is virtually unspoilt with deserted sandy beaches and an abundance of birds (pelicans, cormorants, geese, herons) that use the island as a migration stop-over. There are paths to follow to see monkeys, iguanas, and a wealth of flora and fauna. Collect your own coconuts. You can stay in cabins on the island (US$5) and there is a restaurant with (naturally) a mainly fish menu. You can take your own food but all non-biodegradable items must be taken off the island.

To get there, apply for a pass at the office of Inderena in Buenaventura (their offices elsewhere in Colombia will advise you). There is a fair amount of paperwork, but persevere. Boats leave every 2/3 days in the evening from the El Piñal dock in Buenaventura. The trip, US$23 return, takes up to 10 hours depending on conditions. You can book a bunkbed in advance. You may be able to make arrangements in **Guapi** on the mainland to make the 1 hour boat trip free to Gorgona Island, and Guapi can be visited from Gorgona with Inderena staff going to the market.

Local basket-weaving is on sale, as are musical instruments such as the guaza (a hollow tube filled with seeds) and the marimba (about US$15). The only passable place to stay in Guapi is the *Hotel El Río* run by Pedro Arroyo, who speaks a little English, and his brother Camilo. The only way out of Guapi is by boat or by plane to Cali, US$36.

The paved Pan-American Highway (142 km.) runs S through the Cauca Valley from Cali to Popayán. (Toll, US$0.40.) It takes 2½-3 hrs. by bus through splendid scenery. At first we pass through a land of rich pastures interspersed with sugar-cane plantations. To left and right are the mountain walls of the two Cordilleras. The valley narrows and we begin to climb, with occasional glimpses E of the Nevado del Huila (5,750 metres).

Warning All of rural Valle Department off the main roads is unsafe because of guerrilla activity. Similarly, Cauca Department E of the Highway is not recommended for tourists.

Popayán is in the valley of the Pubenza, at 1,760 metres, in a peaceful landscape of palm, bamboo, and the sharp-leaved agave. (Pop. 250,000.) The early settlers after setting up their sugar estates in the hot, damp Cauca valley, retreated to Popayán to live, for the city is high enough to give it a delightful climate. To N, S, and E the broken green plain is bounded by mountains. To the SE rises the snowcapped cone of the volcano Puracé (3,960 metres).

Popayán was founded by Benalcázar, Francisco Pizarro's lieutenant, in 1536. After the conquest of the Pijao Indians, Popayán became the regional seat of government, subject until 1717 to the Audiencia of Quito, and later to the Audiencia of Bogotá. It is now the capital of the Department of Cauca. The equestrian statue of Benalcázar on the Morro de Tulcán overlooks the city; it is worth climbing this hill, which is the site of a pre-Columbian pyramid, or even better the one with the three crosses on top, for the views. The streets of two-storey buildings are in rococo Andalusian style, with beautiful old monasteries and cloisters of pure Spanish classic architecture. Look for the Puerto Chiquito, a colonial bridge constructed in 1713 (Calle 6, Cra 2). it is said that Simón Bolívar marches over this bridge.

In March 1983, an earthquake devastated the city. Following restoration work, Popayán has come fully back to life and has managed to retain its colonial character. The Cathedral (Calle 5, Cra. 6) and the following churches are now open again: San Agustín (Calle 7, Cra. 6), Santo Domingo (Calle 4, Cra. 5, used by the Universidad del Cauca), La Ermita (Calle 5, Cra. 2), La Encarnación (Calle 5, Cra. 5), San Francisco (Calle 4, Cra. 9), El Carmen (Calle 4, Cra. 3). The town centre has been fully restored. Walk to Belén chapel, which is also open (Calle 4 y Cra. 0), seeing the statues en route, and then continue to El Cerro de las Tres Cruces if you have the energy, but best not to go alone (there are plenty of guides offering their services). Popayán was the home of the poet Guillermo Valencia; it has given no fewer than eleven presidents to the Republic.

The scientist Francisco José de Caldas was born here in 1771; it was he who discovered how to determine altitude by variation in the boiling point of water, and it was to him that Mutis (of the famous *Expedición Botánica*) entrusted the directorship of the newly founded Observatory at Bogotá. He was a passionate partisan of independence, and was executed in 1815 during Morillo's "Reign of Terror".

At weekends you will find people playing "sapo", see under **Sports** in **Information for Visitors**. A good place is along the La Plata road near Belén Church. During the week, the open markets are interesting—Bolívar market, Calle 1N, Cra. 5 is best in the early morning—local foods such as *pipián*, *tamales* and *empanadas*.

Festivals Easter processions, every night of Holy Week until Good Friday, are spectacular; the city is very crowded. The childrens' processions in the following week are easier to see. The children assume all the rôles of the official processions to the delight of parents and onlookers. As at Pasto (but less violent), there are the Día de los Negros on 5 Jan. and Día de los Blancos on 6 Jan.; drenching with water is not very common, but 6 don't walk under windows when you see people on the first floor.

Hotels *Monasterio*, Calle 4, No. 10-50, in what was the monastery of San Francisco, lovely grounds, swimming pool, C, very good, T (939) 22191-6 with shower, pool open to non-residents, US$1.20. *Los Balcones*, Calle 3, No. 6-80, D, hot water, Spanish-style restaurant for breakfast and lunch (often closed), good, will change travellers' cheques; *Veraneo El Bosque*, 5 km. N of city, 1 km. off Cali road (turn left opposite service station) C, very quiet, good restaurant; *Chayaní*, Panamericana Calle 17 Norte, D, travellers' cheques accepted, and change given in US dollars; *Camino Real*, Calle 5, No. 5-59, T 21546/21254,

P.O.Box 248, C, good service, excellent restaurant (try their 6 course dinner US$7), friendly, rec.; *Viajero*, Calle 8, No. 4-45, F, with bath, hot water, quiet, helpful, modern, highly rec; *El Príncipe*, Calle 8, No. 4-35, F with shower and hot water, rec; *El Gran Hotel*, on Plaza, F, room for up to 5 persons; *Hostal Santo Domingo*, Calle 4, No. 5-14 (T 21676), D, with bath, friendly, good value, in recently restored colonial building; *Residencia Comercio*, Calle 6, just off Carrera 17, clean, friendly; *Casa Grande*, Cra. 6, No. 7-11, T 22225, E, family run, hot water, convenient, will store luggage, highly rec.; *La Casona del Virrey*, Calle 4, No. 5-78, E, hot water, big rooms with bath, friendly, nice colonial house, warmly rec; *El Viti*, F, clean, with bath, no hot water, near old bus station; *Casa Suiza*, Calle 4, No. 7-79, E, pleasant, hot water, clean but cockroaches; *Residencias El Castillo*, Carrera 4 esq. Calle 1, D, bath and hot water, clean, very friendly, cafeteria and bar; *Residencias Bolívar*, Carrera 5, No. 7-11, F, clean, pleasant, good restaurant, parking across street; nearby *Residencia Panamá*, G, good, hot water, good food, rec, doors close at 2200; *Residencias Cataluña*, Cra. 5, No. 8-27, F, clean, quiet, friendly; *Casa Familiar*, Carrera 5, No. 2-41, F, clean, good breakfast for US$1, hot water, family-run, no sign, highly rec.; there are many others (E) on Carrera 5 e.g. *Venicia*, No. 7-45, *Manizales*, No. 7-55, *Viena*, No. 7-56, *Cecilia*, No. 7-60. *Residencias San Agustín*, Cra. 6, No. 1N-15, behind the old bridge, clean, good beds, washing facilities; *Residencia San Diego*, just around the corner (turn right off Carrera 6), F, no hot water, but clean and safe, noisy from disco next door; *Plaza Bolívar*, Carrera 6N-12, F with bath, hot water, clean, safe, good value; many others in this area (around Parque Bolívar and market).

Restaurants *La Castellana*, Carrera 6, No. 6-47 (meal and soft drinks for two, good and cheap at US$4.50); *El Mesón del Arriero*, Carrera 6, No. 7-37, good value but limited menu; *El Danubio*, Calle 8, No. 5-33, good, open till midnight; *Delicias Naturales*, Calle 6A, No. 18-21, good, cheap, vegetarian; *Mei Chow*, Carrera 10A, No. 10-81, good but not cheap; *Café El Alamo*, Calle 3, No. 5-65, nice colonial atmosphere and good coffee; *El Pasaje*, Calle 3, Carrera 2, good, reasonably priced typical food; *Pizzería El Recuerdo*, Carrera 6 Vía Cauca, cheaper, but better pizzas at *Don Sebastián*, Calle 3, No. 2-54, and *Nuevo Italiano*, Calle 4, No. 8-83, who also cater for vegetarians. For good lunches (US$1) *Los Olivares*, Carrera 4, No. 7-37; and *Punto Aparte*, Carrera 9, No. 6-09; cheap lunches at *Bogotá*, Carrera 5, No. 6-57; *La Oficina*, Calle 4, No. 8-01, friendly, good value; *Pollo Pío Pío*, Carrera 6, No. 8-11 open, till 0300, good. On the continuation of Cra. 6 across the bridge from centre there are many cafeterias, bars and discos (good café: *Pitufos*, cheap, large menu). *La Brasa*, Calle 6, Cra. 6, has a set lunch and evening meal for US$1.20. *La Fontana*, Calle 6, between Carreras 7 y 8, excellent bakery with café serving meals and sandwiches. *El Bambo*, restaurant with swimming pool, on outskirts on road from Cali, friendly, camping permitted (US$0.50 for 2). Also on road to Cali (5 km.) is *El Rancho*, excellent.

Bars For music try *Taberna La Tolda*, Calle 6, No. 7-73, friendly, student type place; *El Muro*, Calle 7, Cra. 6, or *Anarkos*, Calle 6, Cra. 5 for salsa. *El Trapiche 2* and *Maxim's* on the road out to Cali are the best nightclubs.

Taxis No meters; normal price within city is US$0.50, or US$0.60 at night.

Museums Now open (but not on Mondays): Museo Negret, Calle 5, No. 10-23, US$0.40, with works, photographs and furniture of Negret. Museo Guillermo Valencia, Cra. 6 y Calle 3, birthplace of the poet; Casa Museo Martínez, Calle 3 out of town; Museo Casa Mosquera, Calle 3, No. 5-14; Museo de Historia Natural, Cra. 2, No. 1A-25. Small collection in Banco de la República. All others damaged and closed.

Cinemas Teatro Popayán, Calle 4, Carrera 8/9, best; Teatro Anarkos, Carrera 5, Calles 6/7. Teatro Bolívar, Calle 7, Cra. 3, shows black and white classics.

Exchange Banco de la República, Calle 6, No. 2-78, is the only one that changes foreign currency and travellers' cheques, but will not give dollars change if changing a portion of a large bill. (Open 0800-1130; 1400-1600, Mon.-Thur., until 1630 on Fri.) However, the *Hotel Monasterio* will accept travellers' cheques when you pay your bill and will give you change in pesos. There is also Salvador Duque at Diana shop on the main plaza, near the cathedral. For US$ notes, change them with Don Carlos Castrillón, owner of *Hotel Los Balcones*, Calle 3, No. 6.80, for the best rate.

Post Office Carrera 7, No. 5-77. **Telephone Office** Telecom, Carrera 4 y Calle 3.

Tourist Office Carrera 6, No. 3-69, between Puente del Humilladero and Plaza Mayor (T 22251), has good maps of the city, prices of all hotels and pensions, and bus schedules and prices. Ask for Sra. Haydée Gasca de Varela about accommodation. They are very friendly and helpful, giving information on places of interest, will tell you where horses may be hired for exploring, and will store your luggage. In addition to normal hours, they are open Suns. until 1200. Ask at the Tourist Office about which areas of the city are unsafe. They also offer coffee, and sell local crafts; telephone and mail service. The Tourist Office and the Colegio Mayor de Cauca have details on art exhibitions and concerts. Try also the Casa de la Cultura, Calle 5, No. 4-33, for information on cultural events.

Travel Agent Avialoi Ltda, Calle 4, No. 7-59, good prices for air tickets bought with cash dollars.

Buses Popayán has a new bus terminal, next to the airport, 15 mins. walk from the centre (Ruta 2-Centro bus, terminal to centre, US$0.10, or taxi, US$0.50). Luggage can be stored safely (receipt given); there is a charge to use the toilets, and a US$0.07 departure tax. From the bus station, turn left to statue of Bolívar, then take second right to Parque Bolívar; here are the market and cheap hotels. To Bogotá, US$15. To Cali, US$3, 2½-3 hrs., or Velotax microbus, US$4.25, colectivos leaves from the main plaza (US$3.50); to Pasto, with Coop de Nariño, Carrera 6, No. 2-16, 1130, Cootranar (best and cheapest), Flota Magdalena, Exp. Bolivariano and Supertaxis del Sur, US$5, 5-8 hrs., spectacular scenery (sit on right); to Medellín, US$13.25, 16 hrs.; to Ipiales, something runs every hour; Supertaxis at 1230, US$6, or bus, US$7 (Transportes Ipiales at 0700, Bolivariano at 0530 or 0900, the best), 7½-10 hrs. To **San Agustín**, La Gaitana, 11 hrs., at 0900 and 2000, Coomotor, 13 hrs., US$9 each once a day. Cootranshuila buses run over the new road via Isnos to San Agustín from bus terminal, several daily, US$5.50, 6 hrs. To Tierradentro (Cruce de Pisimbalá), with Sotracauca, 5 a day between 0500 and 1500 (T 26-46), US$3, 4-6 hrs.; and goes to La Plata. Best to take the 0500 or 1000 bus, as the 1300 and 1500 will land you at the Cruce when it's dark, leaving you with a long unlit walk. Flota Magdalena to La Plata, US$3.75, 5 hrs., also Unidos del Sur (not via Tierradentro). To Puracé, US$1, 2 hrs. (Pullman is slightly more, Sotracauca at 0600, La Gaitana 0700, Coomotor later in a.m.) To Silvia (see below), daily Coomotorista *buseta* at 0800 (US$1.30) or: take Expreso Palmira bus to Piendamó on Cali road, every ½ hour, US$0.60; from there, colectivo to Silvia, US$0.70. On market day (Tuesdays) buses leave directly to Silvia at 0600.

Air Services Airport is 20 mins. walk from the centre. Service to Bogotá with Aires, usually daily at 0925. Daily flight to Ipiales US$18 with Intercontinental, 20 mins. flight at 0745 (office on main plaza). Avianca office for airmail, Carrera 7, No. 5-77.

Excursions A favourite is the drive northeast to Silvia, at 2,521 metres, one way through Totoró (partly paved) and the other through Piendamó (paved) two beautiful routes. In Piendamó there is *Hotel Central* behind the former railway station (E, clean, quiet, but has seen better days).

Silvia lies in a high valley. It is no longer an Indian town; the Indian market on Tues. mornings seems to be full of Otavalo Indians from Ecuador and their goods—more expensive than in Otavalo. The market is at its best between 0600 and 0830. Not much to buy, but very colourful. Guambiano Indian farms can be reached by local bus: ask for the "paradero de los Guambianos". A typical Indian settlement, La Campana, is ½ hour on the bus; 1½ hours' walk downhill back to Silvia. The Indians wear their typical blue and fuchsia costumes, and are very friendly and communicative. It is not safe to park cars in the street at night in Silvia, and guerrilla activity has been reported in the area. Horse hire from Sr. Marco A. Mosquiro, under US$1 per hour. On market days you can take a bus to Totoró (on the Popayán-Tierradentro road), departs 1200, US$0.50, and then a bus from Totoró to Tierradentro, US$1.25.

Hotels *Casa Turística*, E, helpful, good food; *Cali*, an old house, with good craft shop, E, including food, a little primitive, but very pleasant. *Silvia*, F, simple; *Ambeina*, F (3 beds per room), clean, friendly, efficient, rec., good meals; *Residencias La Villa*, about 200 metres up main road, G, basic but friendly, negotiate your price; *Cali*, F, good meals but poor plumbing. **La Parrilla**, F, water supply erratic, basic, restaurant has reasonable, cheap food. *Taberna El Buho*, friendly, with live music Sats. p.m.

For those who like to go off the beaten track, Sr. Camilo Arroyo (address: Carrera 3, No. 4-65, Popayán) arranges trips towards the coast, W of Popayán, for birdwatching or gold-panning (his family has a *finca* on the coast). He charges about US$50 a day p.p., depending on the length of the trip, size of the party, etc. His trips into the mountains are reported as less interesting—obtain full details before embarking on one.

Road to Neiva (page 680) from Popayán across the Central Cordillera, which is paved from Puerto Seco to Neiva, has interesting sights off it (best seen from left-hand side of the bus). Drive 37 km. along it (or take 0400, 0900 or 1100 bus, US$1) to the small town of **Puracé**, which has several old buildings. *Residencias Cubina*, F, clean, safe, friendly, cold showers, secure parking, no restaurant in the town but two stores will prepare meals on request. Drive to the Escuela and walk 5 mins. to see Chorrera de las Monjas waterfalls. About 11 km. E of Puracé towards Neiva a road branches S from the main road; 1 km. along this road is another fork at El Cruce de la Mina (bus 0530, US$0.50), the right branch leads to the Puracé sulphur mines (3,000 metres) 5 km. away; 1 km. along this road is a left fork to Pilimbalá, signed "Piscinas" (1½ km.) where are the Puracé National Park office, 5 warm sulphur baths in stone pools (which can be smelt a km. away), and a path leading to Puracé volcano. The Park is open all the week, but reduced service on Mondays. The volcano is steep; loose ash makes footholds difficult. It takes up to 5 hours to get to the top (4,646 metres). Close to the main road (which continues to La Plata), and more easily reached from El Cruce de la Mina are Laguna San Rafael (10 km. from Pilimbilá), the Cascada de Bedón (15 km), the Cueva de los Guácharos (26 km.), and the Termales de San Juan (17 km., but only 700 metres from the main road; cafeteria; entry US$0.10; 2 hrs. by bus from Popayán). 112 hot sulphur springs combine with icy mountain creeks to produce spectacular arrays of multi-coloured mosses, algae and lichens—a must if you are in the area. Buses on the Popayán-La Plata route go near Pilimbalá and will drop you near any of these places (fare from Popayán about US$1.50). The Tourist Office in Popayán will supply full information. The Park's fauna include the spectacled bear and mountain tapir. The only accommodation in the Park is at the thermal baths of Pilimbalá—cabins with up to six beds, D per cabin, up to 4 persons E, make reservations at Popayán Tourist Office (very cold, blankets and wood for the fire provided—rooms for 2 in the cellar can be hired at F rates); power goes off at 2200, but candles are provided. Camping costs US$3 p.p. and there are an expensive, but good restaurant/bar and a picnic area.

N.B. There has been some guerrilla activity in the areas traversed by this road.

Take warm clothes (and a sleeping bag) if climbing the volcano or visiting the baths; the nights are cold and blankets in the mountain cabins are thin. The weather is best, especially for climbing the volcano, in July and August, or between December and March. The highest point on the road is Quebrada Honda, at 3,340 metres above sea level.

Ute Lindner (of Freiburg) tells us that one may stay at a *finca* called Merenberg, 5 km. from Santa Leticia, on the road between Popayán and La Plata; the owners speak English and German. Take your own food (Santa Leticia is the only town in the mountains with shops); a good centre for walking.

Coconuco, at 2,734 metres, has beautiful landscapes. Turn to the right off the Popayán-Neiva road after 21 km. (16 km. short of Puracé); then 7 km. along is Coconuco (*Hotel de Turismo*; *Casa Familiar*, G, basic). There are good thermal baths near the village (camping US$1.50). Drive on 12 km. to the impressive scenery of the Paletará highland, where you can traverse vast areas of primeval forest; a bus to the village of Paletará takes 1 hour and costs US$0.40. Bus to Popayán, US$1, 1 hr. The direct 130-km. road from Popayán to San Agustin (**see page 684**) through Coconuco was opened in March 1985.

The Tierradentro Archaeological Park, (see below), can be reached from Popayán, or San Agustín via **La Plata** (20,000 people), 147 km. from Popayán, 210 km. from San Agustín. Direct bus service with Coomotor from La Plata to Bogotá, 10 hrs., at 0900 and 2100.

Hotels *Berlin*, by church on square, 4 blocks from the bus office, E with bath, F without, friendly, but unappealing toilets; next door is *Residencias Tunubalá*, F, OK, friendly;

Brooklyn, clean, F, and *Norteño,* in the same price range; *Pensión Murucuju,* basic place to sleep and eat; *Residencias Nariño,* F, *Viajero,* F, convenient; *La Familia,* F, dirty, unfriendly.

Restaurants *Es Aquí,* good meals for US$2; *Noche y Luna,* just off main square, very good. There is a café in the house where Bolívar stayed in 1829. *Patolandia,* good, cheap fruit juices. There is a cinema (2030).

From La Plata drive 35 km. NW to Guadualejo where one road goes N to Belalcázar (12 km.—a dusty drive). Another road continues NW to

Inzá (17 km.); hotels *Inzá* and *Ambalá.* Nine km. before Inzá is the Cruce de Pisimbalá, sometimes known as the Cruce de San Andrés, where a road turns off to San Andrés de **Pisimbalá** (4 km.), the village at the far end of the Tierradentro Park.

At Pisimbalá there is a unique and beautiful colonial church with a thatched roof; for the key ask behind the church. Some few km. before reaching Pisimbalá you pass the Tierradentro Museum, hours: 0700-1100 and 1300-1700, entrance US$0.40, camping is not allowed. Make sure you see both parts of the museum.

At Pisimbalá hire horses (US$2 an hr.)—or you can walk—for visiting the **Tierradentro** man-made burial caves painted with geometric patterns. There are four cave sites—Segovia, El Duende, Alto de San Andrés and El Aguacate. The main caves are now lighted, but probably as well to have your own torch. If you don't have one, try to borrow one from the park administration office. Entry US$0.15. The surrounding scenery is splendid. It is very crowded at Easter-time.

For people on a one-day visit: go to Segovia, which has over 20 tombs, 5 of which are lit (these 5 are not opened until 0800-0900). Nos. 9, 10 and 12 are best decorated; Nos. 8 and 28 are also impressive. The site is a 20 min. walk uphill from the administration building. El Duende (two of the four tombs are very good), is 15 mins. beyond Segovia. El Aguacate is a 2 hrs. hike one way (reported in disrepair in 1989), and one can return via El Alto de San Andrés (Nos. 1 and 5 tombs the best—the guards at Segoria and El Alto are very helpful).

At El Tablón in the Parque there are 8 stone statues. There are several more in the new plaza at Inzá. A beautiful area for walking. From behind El Tablón, you can walk back to the museum via El Duende and Segovia in 2½ hrs. The surroundings have spectacular natural beauty; see small Indian villages in the mountains, e.g. Santa Rosa, 2 hours' hard walk beyond El Duende (get exact directions before setting out).

The Páez Indians in the Tierradentro region can be seen on market days at Inzá (Sat.), Pisimbalá (Wed.), and Belalcázar (Sat.); all start at 0600. The second floor of the museum at Pisimbalá is dedicated to their work: not to be missed. Take bus (US$0.50) from Tierradentro to Inzá market, on Sat. (buses leave from 0200); best to go into Pisimbalá and out again to be sure of getting a seat. On Saturdays there is plenty of transport going to and from Inzá on the Tierradentro road.

Hotels at Tierradentro A short way up from the museum, state-owned *Albergue de San Andrés,* E, good, restaurant and swimming pool (also available to non-residents, US$0.80). Houses on either side of the Albergue offer accommodation, F, meals for US$1.50; green house next to museum, 2 rooms available, G, clean, friendly, rec.; *Residencia Turista,* in the village, basic, clean, F p.p., insufficient bedding; *Hospedaje El Viajero,* Sra. Marta de Angel, F, friendly, meals US$1.20 excellent; between Pisimbalá and museum, *hospedaje* of Sra Pola Angel de Velasco, Carmelita's house (*Hospedaje Lucerna*) next to museum, clean and friendly, F, showers, quiet, free coffee and fresh orange juice on request, highly rec. Other cheap accommodation in village: *Residencial Pisimbalá,* "opposite the museum and up a bit", F, good, clean, set meal; *Residencias El Viajero* (Marta Veláquez), F, meals US$1, clean, friendly, rec. *Residencia El Bosque,* F, cold showers, cheap meals, friendly dueña collects coins, rec.; *Residencias Murujuy,* F (breakfast, US$0.65, lunch and dinner, US$1); *Residencias Las Veraneras,* F p.p. 2 houses, 300 metres from Archaeological Park, rent rooms for US$2 p.p., clean, run by friendly young couple, new beds (1989), restaurant, attractive garden and murals painted by locals. *El Gauchito* in Pisimbalá village, F, clean, pleasant, family atmosphere, meals available, rec.; camping.

Restaurants *Pisimbalá*, good food, cheap, rec.; good fruit juices at the *Fuente de Soda y Artesanía* store. The house of Nelli Parra de Jovar, opposite the museum with the long antenna, is rec. for abundance; you must book meals in advance. She can also give up to date information on accommodation. At Dalia's home, *Su Repuesto*, almost opp. *Hosp. Lucerna*, good meals for US$1.25, again best to arrange in advance.

Transport The road from Popayán to Tierradentro is difficult and narrow, but this is compensated by the beautiful scenery. Sotracauca buses from Popayán, US$3, 4-6 hrs. to Cruce Pisimbalá; take one of two morning buses as the two afternoon ones land you at the Cruce after dark. Walk (about 2 km.) from there to the museum. The village is another 20 mins. walk from the museum. Bus Cruce Pisimbalá-Popayán, 0600 (unreliable), 0800 and 1300, 5 hrs. If you want to go to Silvia, take this bus and change to a colectivo (US$1) at Totoró. There are buses on market day, or trucks (US$1). Buses from Tierradentro to La Plata leave at 0900 and 1500 (unreliable) from the Cruce, US$2, 3 hrs.; if you cannot get a direct Cruce-La Plata bus, take one going to Belalcázar (US$1), alight at Guadualejo from where there is a more frequent service to La Plata; or one can hitch. On Fri. only, a bus leaves from Pisimbalá village for La Plata at 0400. Similarly, on Fri. only, a bus from La Plata to Pisimbalá goes at 1200, otherwise the only La Plata-Tierradentro bus (La Gaitana) leaves daily at 0500 for Inzá; alight at Cruce (2½ hrs.). Private jeep hire La Plata-Tierradentro, US$18 after bargaining, or less if you agree to pick up other passengers. The road follows the spectacularly beautiful Páez valley. Buses from La Plata to Neiva and Bogotá.

From San Agustín, take Coomotor at 0600 to La Plata, 5 hrs., US$3.50, or La Gaitana at 0530 or 1600. Next morning, take the 0500 La Gaitana bus from La Plata to Cruce de Pisimbalá, arrives 0800 (continues to Inzá and Popayán). Alternatively, on arrival in La Plata, take a pick-up to Guadualejo (US$1), then hitch, or try to get a bus going past Tierradentro (about 3 per day). Buses from La Plata to San Agustín at 0700, 0900 and 1500.

Another site of archaeological interest is **La Argentina**, best reached from La Plata (some direct buses), 8 km. off the La Plata-Popayán road. Gillian Handyside writes; It is set in beautiful surroundings but is largely ignored by the archaeological authorities and the tourist board. The Museo Arqueológico de la Platavieja contains statues and ceramics as interesting as those found at San Agustín. Ask for Sr. Carlos Hernández, who runs the museum almost singlehanded and is extremely knowledgeable about the archaeological aspects of the area. (He also keeps bees, and sells honey.) The Universities of Los Andes, Cauca and Pittsburg run an archaeological project at La Argentina during the dry season: contact Carlos Hernández for details.

SOUTHERN COLOMBIA (8)

The Pan-American Highway continues S from Popayán to Pasto. The entire road is now paved, but poor in parts. After El Bordo (*Residencias Confort*, on main road, F, simple but recommended) the road takes a new route and the 294-km. drive takes 5 hrs. The express bus takes 7 hrs. in ordinary conditions, though landslides often block the road. 93 km. S of Popayán is a tourist complex including hotel, swimming pool and campsite.

If one has time, the old route via La Unión and Mercaderes can be done by bus; enquire at Popayán or Pasto bus terminals. There are three basic hotels at La Unión (beware of overcharging at the *Hotel Nevada*). In El Bordo, the *Aquí Jaramillo* restaurant serves good Colombian dishes (US$3 per head).

143 km. S of Popayán is **Mercaderes**, a small town with a pleasant climate. Hotels (F) are good and the *Restaurante Tropical* is recommended. 30 km. before Pasto is Chachagui, where the *Hotel Imperio de los Incas* is recommended, E with bath, friendly, swimming pool, 2 km. from Pasto airport. Toll N of Pasto US$0.30.

Pasto, capital of the Department of Nariño, stands upon a high plateau (2,534 metres) in the SW, 88 km. from Ecuador, with a population of 370,000. The city, which retains some of its colonial character, was founded in the early days of the conquest. Today it is a centre for the agricultural and cattle industries of the region, which exports little. Pasto varnish (*barniz*) is mixed locally, to embellish the strikingly colourful local wooden bowls. A visit to the church of Cristo Rey (Calle 20 y Carrera 24) near the centre is recommended. Also La Merced, Calle 18, is

UPPER MAGDALENA

worth seeing for its rich decoration and gold ornaments. From the church of Santiago (Carrera 23 y Calle 13) there is a good view over the city to the mountains, San Felipe (Calle 12 y Carrera 27) has green tiled domes. The interior courtyard of the municipal building on the main square (corner of Calle 19 and Carrera 24) has 2 tiers of colonnaded balconies. Do not visit Pasto on a Sunday: nearly everything is closed.

During the new year's *fiesta* there is a Día de los Negros on 5 Jan. and a Día de los Blancos next day. On "black day" people dump their hands in black grease and smear each other's faces. On "white day" they throw talc or flour at each other. Local people wear their oldest clothes. Things can get quite violent. On 28 December and 5 Feb., there is also a Fiesta de las Aguas when anything that moves—only tourists because locals know better—gets drenched with water from balconies and even from fire engines' hoses. In Pasto and Ipiales (see page 712), on 31 December, is the Concurso de Años Viejos, when huge dolls are burnt; they represent the old year and sometimes lampoon local people. On Suns. a game of paddle ball is played on the edge of the town (bus marked San Lorenzo) similar to that played in Ibarra, Ecuador.

During the wars of independence, Pasto was a stronghold of the Royalists and the last town to fall into the hands of the patriots after a long and bitter struggle. Then the people of Nariño Department wanted to join Ecuador when that country split off from Gran Colombia in 1830, but were prevented by Colombian troops.

Hotels *Morasurco*, Avenida de los Estudiantes, B, rec., reasonable restaurant; *Zorocán*, Calle 18, No. 22-33, C, bath, TV, a/c, indifferent restaurant; *Sindagua*, Calle 20, No. 21B-16, D, rec.; *Cuellar's*, Carrera 23, No. 15-50, D, roomy, well-furnished, new, some noise from bowling centre underneath, but rec.; *Res. Santa Ana*, Carrera 25, 16-45, E with bath, F without, top floor rooms are quiet; *El Duque*, Carrera 20 between Calles 17 and 18, E, including TV and shower, comfortable, rec.; *Mayasquer*, Av. de las Américas, 16-66, E, with bath, clean, friendly, restaurant; next door at No. 16-40 is *Juanambú*, E, friendly, clean, safe, F for rooms without bath, rec. *Hostería Imperio de los Incas*, at Chachagui near the airport, E with shower, dubious electrics, noisy (near Panamericana), beware overcharging in taxis to town. *Isa*, Calle 18, No. 22-33, E with bath, clean, helpful, safe, 100 metres from bus station; *Residencias Colón*, Carrera 22, No. 19-61, F, clean, friendly, hot water; *Mallorca*, Calle 18, 21a-45, F, pleasant, hot water a.m.; *Nueva York*, Carrera 19 bis, 18-20, F, clean rooms, dirty toilets, hot shower, friendly, near Magdalena bus company, the only place in the town where you can put a motorcycle inside; *María Belén*, Calle 13, No. 19-15, new, clean, safe, quiet, friendly, hot water; near bus station are *Líbano* (O.K., hot water), *San Juan* (D, clean, friendly, but rather expensive), *Las Pensas* (quiet, no hot water), *Cartagena* (cheap, adequate), *Jordán*, and others in F price range; *Manhattan*, Calle 18, 21B-14, F, clean, pleasant, hot water old-fashioned, big rooms, rec.; *Residencia Indi Chaya*, Calle 16, No. 18-23 (corner of Cra. 19 and Calle 16), T 4476, F, good value, clean, good beds, carpets, hot water, safe; *Residencias Galeras*, Calle 17, nr. bus station, F, hot water, communal bath, clean, safe; *Residencia Santa Isabel*, Calle 19, No. 20-39, F, clean, close to bus station. *Viena*, clean, Carrera 19B, No. 18-36, G, cheap and near bus station.

Restaurants *El Chalet Suizo*, Calle 20, 41-80 (T 4419), high class food; *La Esquina del Barril*, Calle 19, No. 28-12, good; *Viena*, opposite *Hotel Nueva York*, good, cheap; *Parma*, Carrera 25, good, large meals; *Pollorrico*, Carrera 25, 17-50, good. *Pollo Listo*, opp. *Agualonga Hotel*, cheap, good chicken dishes; *Mister Pollo*, Calle 17 y Cra. 26, central, good, clean fast food. *Punto Rojo*, Calle 17, No. 21B-38, self service, 24 hours, good choice of dishes; *Rancho Grande*, Calle 17, No. 22-03, cheap and open late; *La Picantería*, Calle 19, cheap, good food; *Alberto's*, Calle 17, No. 27-26, friendly; *Bar Concorde*, Calle 17, Carreras 26 and 27, French and English music, pleasant. *El Encinar*, Calle 16, No. 13-48, US$0.80, good value, rec. A cheap but good place to eat is the self-service cafetería at the Amorel shopping centre. *Riko Riko*, near bus station, good fast food; similar *La Espiga* close by. Most restaurants on main street are OK. *Moreno's* on the Panamericana, local dishes, excellent, live music some evenings. In the nearby village of Catambuco (15 mins. drive), the restaurant *Catambuey* is rec. if you like guinea pig.

Shopping *Artesanías de Colombia* have a branch on Carrera 25. *Casa del Barniz de Pasto*, Calle 13, No. 24-9, *Artesanías Nariño*, Calle 26, No. 18-91; *Artesanías Mopa-Mopa*, Carrera 25, No. 13-14, for *barniz*. See *Colegio Artesanías*, run by a government institute (Sena), 5 km. N on road to Popayán. Visitors welcome. Leather goods are cheaper here than in Bogotá, Ecuador or Peru. Most of the shops are on Calles 17 and 18. Also try the municipal market for handicrafts. *Mercado Campesino*, southern end of Calle 16, esq. Carrera 7. *Supermercado*

Confamiliar de Nariño, Calle 16b, No. 30-53, recommended, and, more convenient, Ley on Calle 18, next to Avianca postal office. On main square (Calle 19 y Cra. 25) is a new shopping centre with many types of shops and restaurants.

Drycleaners Calle 18 y Carrera 27.

Cinema Carrera 25 and Calles 17 and 18, good.

Exchange For changing travellers' cheques, Banco de la República on the main square. Banco Anglo Colombiano, Calle 17, No. 21-32, and at Amorel, and other national banks. Open Mon.-Thur., 0800-1130, 1400-1600; Fri., 0900-1130, 1400-1630; closed Sat. Last working day of month, 0800-1100. If going to Tumaco, this is the last place where travellers' cheques can be cashed. A *cambio* off the main square will change sucres into pesos, but the Banco de la República will not, though it does change Amex cheques without charging commission. An optician/pharmacist on the main square changes sucres into pesos (good rates).

Airmail Carrera 23, 18-42 and Calle 18, 25-86.

Telephones Long distance calls from Telecom, Calle 17 y Carrera 23.

Ecuadorean Consulate Calle 17, No. 26-55, 2nd floor. Four photos needed if you require a visa (but this office is not very knowledgeable about requirements for visas).

Tourist Office Just off the main square, Calle 18, No. 25-25, friendly and helpful. It will advise on money changing. **Maps** of Colombia and cities from Instituto Geográfico Agustín Codazzi, Calle 18, No. 23-36, 1st floor (Banco del Occidente building). The **DAS** office in town will give exit stamps if you are going on to Ecuador.

Buses Most buses leave from Calle 18. To Bogotá, 23 hrs., US$19.50 (Bolivariano Pullman). To Ipiales, 2 hrs., US$2.45, Cooperativo Supertaxis del Sur; by bus, US$1.50. To Popayán, ordinary buses take 10-12 hrs.; expresses take 5-8 hrs., cost US$5. To Cali, US$10, expresses, 8½-10 hrs. To Tumaco, 11 hrs. by bus, 10 hrs. by minibus, US$6.50. To Puerto Asis, 11 hrs., US$4.75 with Trans Ipiales or Bolivariano (both Calle 18), 0500 and 1100. To Mocoa, 8 hrs, US$4.

Air Services Daily to Popayán, 20 mins., and Bogotá; to Cali with Avianca at 0800, and to Ipiales by Avianca on Fri. Aerotal, Pasto to Cali, daily at 0800; to Medellín. Avianca to Leticia via Cali, US$95. The airport is at Cano, 40 km. from Pasto; by colectivo (beautiful drive), 45 mins. US$1.90 or US$11.35 by taxi. There are no currency exchange facilities, but the shop will change US$ bills at a poor rate.

Excursions There are some gold mines in the area. The volcano, Galeras (4,276 metres), overlooks Pasto to the W. Quiescent since 1934, it began erupting again in 1989. Check at the tourist office on whether it is safe to climb on the mountain and whether you need a permit. A highway traversing all kinds of altitudes and climates has been built round it; the trip along it takes half a day. A rough road goes to the summit where there is an army post guarding a TV relay station; you can scramble down into the crater. A taxi (arrange previous day, if possible) will take you to about 200 metres from the top; there is a fine view and the soldiers are glad to see people. If you can't get a taxi, take a bus to the village of San Vicente, then hitch as far up as you can, which will probably leave a 3-hour, but pleasant walk to the top. On it lies the village of **Sandoná** where Panama hats are made; they can be seen lying in the streets in the process of being finished. Sandoná market day is Saturday. (It is a worthwhile trip to Sandoná, 4 buses daily, the last back to Pasto is at 1700.)

Tumaco Region

The 250-km. road W from Pasto to Tumaco is paved for 20 km. beyond Túquerres, but is then unsurfaced (it was under reconstruction in 1988/89) and subject to landslides—check in Pasto. The region is very different from highland Colombia, with two-storey Caribbean-style wooden houses and a predominantly black population. Small farms are mixed with cattle ranches, rice farms and oil-palm plantations. Cocoa is grown. The coastal area around Tumaco is mangrove swamp, with many rivers and inlets on which lie hundreds of villages and settlements; negotiate with boatmen for a visit to the swamps or the beautiful, newly-developed island tourist resort of **Boca Grande**, US$7.50 minimum, the trip takes 30 mins.; ask for Señor Felipe Bustamante, Calle Comercial, Apto. 224, T 465, who rents canoes and cabins, has a good seafood restaurant and owns *Hotel Los Manglares* on the island, where water and electricity supplies are irregular.

Tumaco has a population of about 100,000; the unemployment rate is very high, the living conditions are poor, and the services and roads in the town are not good. It is in one of the world's rainiest areas; the yearly average temperature is in the 25°-35°C range. The movement of the tides governs most of the activities in the area, especially transport. A natural arch on the main beach, N of the town and port, is reputed to be the hiding place of Henry Morgan's treasure. Swimming is not recommended from the town's beaches, which are polluted; stalls provide refreshment on the beach. Swimming is safe, however, at El Morro beach, north of the town, only on the incoming tide (the outgoing tide uncovers poisonous rays). Hotels are well subscribed and of varying quality: it is advisable to get a bed early in the day. The northern part of the town is built on stilts out over the sea. Visit it during the daylight as it is reported to be dangerous at night, and not just because you could fall through the holes in the wooden pavements into the sea. There is an airport, and the area is also noted archaeologically for the finds associated with the Tumaco culture. The town has problems with water and electricity supplies. There is one cinema. There are no money exchange facilities (except in some shops that will buy dollars and sucres at a poor rate; change money in Cali or Pasto).

Hotels *Villa del Mar*, D, Calle Sucre, modern, clean, with shower, toilet and fan, no hot water, good café below; *Claudia*, Calle Mosquera, E, with restaurant; *Residencias Don Pepe*, near water-front and *canoa* dock, friendly but basic; *Porvenir*, G, far from luxurious, most of the family friendly. Children meet arriving buses to offer accommodation; most cheap places are in Calle Comercial, many houses and restaurants without signs take guests—nearly all have mosquito nets. Try opp. Trans Ipiales, under Cootranor sign, or 2 doors from Trans Ipiales (Barbería Nueva), both F. **Food** The main culinary attraction of the town is the fish, in the market and restaurants, fresh from the Pacific. A number of good restaurants on the main streets (Calles Mosquera and Comercial): *La Tropicana, La Tortula, La Brasa*. **N.B.** Be very careful of food and water because there are many parasites.

Transport Tumaco to Pasto, 11 hrs. (10 hrs. by minibus), US$6.50, with Supertaxis del Sur or Trans Ipiales (better), 4 a day, very rough but interesting ride. An alternative is to catch a bus from Ipiales to Espino (US$0.60, colectivo, US$0.90) and there change buses for Tumaco (US$4, 7½ hrs., rough ride). There are no hotels in Espino. There are daily flights to and from Cali with Aces (US$40 one way) and on Wed., Fri. and Sun. with Satena (US$35), 1 hr. Flights also to Pasto.

To Ecuador It is possible to travel to Ecuador by water, but only by motorized canoe. Part of the trip is by river, which is very beautiful, and part on the open sea, which can be very rough; a plastic sheet to cover your belongings is essential. Take suncream. Daily service at 0800 to San Lorenzo, 7 hrs. (but can take 14) US$6.50, Coop. de Transportes, tickets from Calle Comercial (protective plastic sheeting provided). Señor Pepello, who lives in the centre of Tumaco, owns two canoes: he leaves on Wed. and Sat. at 0700 for San Lorenzo and Limones in Ecuador—book in advance. Also enquire for Señor Lucho, or ask around the water-front at 0600. DAS stamp for leaving Colombia should be obtained from the DAS office in Tumaco, Calle Sucre, No. 6-13, office open on weekdays only. Visas for Ecuador (if required) should be obtained in Cali or Pasto. Entry stamps for Ecuador must be obtained in the coastal towns.

120 km. from Tumaco is Junín where you can turn north, and in 57 km. come to the interesting town of **Barbacoas**, a former Spanish gold-producing centre which still retains the remains of an extensive water-front, a promenade and steps coming down through the town to the river. Gold is still panned from the rivers by part-time prospector-farmers. *Hotel Telembi*, F, basic, friendly; *Residencial*, F, poor, unfriendly. Restaurant *Telembi* on the river front, good food. Problems with water and electricity supplies. River trips on the supply boats are possible, about US$6.75 for 8 hrs. Bus to Pasto, US$6, rough trip. The road to Barbacoas is limited to one-way traffic in places— enquire at the chain barring the road at Junín and the operator will telephone down the line to see if the route is clear for you to pass.

The *Putumayo*

One hour E of Pasto, on the road to Mocoa (capital of the Intendencia of Putumayo) is **Laguna La Cocha**, the largest lake in S Colombia (sometimes called Lago Guámez). By the lake is the Swiss-run *Chalet Guámez*, D, well recommended, particularly for the cuisine, cabins sleeping up to six can be hired, US$23; free van-camping allowed. Rafael Narváez has cheap, basic rooms to let. The chalet will arrange a US$22 jeep trip to Sibundoy, further along the road. Boats may be hired for US$2.20 per hour. La Cocha may be reached by taking a bus to El Encano and walking the remaining 5 km. Or walk 20 mins. from the bus stop to the fishing village of El Encano, where you can enjoy trout at very low prices at one of the many small restaurants, and from here take a *lancha* to the chalet for US$2-3. There is also a government hotel nearby, *Sindamanoy*, C, chalet style, good views, inviting restaurant with good but expensive food, free van-, and tent camping allowed with manager's permission. From the hotel you can take a 10-minute boat trip to the Isla de la Chorota nature reserve; interesting trees, but little wildlife. Taxi from Pasto, US$11.

The road from Pasto to the Putumayo deteriorates rapidly after El Encano. It is dangerous between Sibundoy and El Pepino and care should be taken, but there is a magnificent view out over the Putumayo by a large statue of the Virgin, just before the final descent.

Sibundoy There is a beautiful church on the main plaza, completed in 1968. About a quarter of the valley is now reserved for Sibundoy Indian occupation. Market Sunday. Best handicraft shop is Fudak, Calle 16 No. 16-73, a cooperative run by the Kamza Indians. Also Marcelino Chindoy, Carrera 18, 18-66, who travels a lot around Colombia and can normally be found at handicrafts fairs in Bogotá. Roasted guinea-pig (*cuy*) may be eaten in the restaurant here. Bus from Pasto (3 hrs., US$2.25), passing through Colón (*residencias*) and Santiago.

Hotels and Restaurants *Hotel Turista*, F, clean; *Oriente*, F, pleasant, with restaurant, best value in town; better meals at *Hotel Sibundoy*, also F; *Restaurant Viajero*, just off main street. You can camp in the hills, where there are lovely walks and you can see all kinds of flora and fauna.

Mocoa, the administrative capital of the Intendencia of Putumayo, is small (21,000 people), with a number of hotels (*Viajero*, D; *Central*, off main plaza, F, very clean and friendly) and *residencias*, e.g. *Residencia Colonial*, Carrera 6, No. 8-10, G, spartan but safe. The town has a very modern square, new offices and modern developments. Sugar-cane is grown in the area. The road to Puerto Asís is good, passing through a recently cleared area supporting cattle ranching. 8-12 hrs. by bus to Pasto. Bus from Sibundoy, US$2, 5 a day, continuing to Puerto Asís; a few police checks, a bit hair-raising in places, but stunning scenery between Sibundoy and Mocoa ("some of the best in Colombia").

Puerto Asís is the main town and port of the Putumayo. River traffic is busy. All boats that leave for Leticia (with connections to Manaus) are cargo boats, and only sail when they have cargo. Those carrying gasoline (and most do) are forbidden to take passengers. Only one company, Navenal, normally takes passengers, and it can be weeks between their sailings. One can also try the army for a passage. Fares are about US$100; at least 8-10 days; it is best to see the Jefe de la Marina, or the Oficina de Transporte Fluvial, about a passage. Another possibility is to take a *canoa* to Leguizamo (see below), and try for a passage there. By boat to Leguizamo takes 2-3 days, US$4.50, food US$2.50 per day. For those interested in flora and fauna it is necessary to travel down river, beyond new areas of settlement. Boats will not go unless the rivers are high; sometimes, they get stuck halfway.

There are regular flights to and from Puerto Asís three times a week by Satena to Bogotá, via Florencia. Flights to Florencia are on Mon., Wed. and Fri. at 1000 with Sarpa, who also fly to Leguizamo. Occasional flights to Leticia.

N.B. Puerto Asís is a marketing centre for cocaine.

Hotels *Residencias Nevado*, Carrera 20, close to the airport, well kept and comfortable, air-conditioning optional, F, without board. *Residencias Liz*, Calle 11, F, with bath, very friendly; *Residencia Volga*, Calle 10, No. 23-73, F, basic, safe; *Residencias Patiño*, G, rec.; *Residencias Gigante*, Calle 10, 24-25, F, clean. There are plenty of cheap hotels in the port, but it is hard to find a room late in the day.

Buses may be taken to Pasto (a 10 hr. journey, at 0500, 0600 and 0900 daily, on mostly mountainous roads, US$4.50, be prepared for military checks). Bus Sibundoy-Puerto Asís, US$3.25. Five buses a day to San Miguel near the Ecuadorean border (US$3) where the Sun. market provides a meeting place, and where *canoas* may be hired to visit villages 2-4 hrs. away on the river.

San Miguel There are several very basic hotels, e.g. *Mirador*, F, safe and *Residencias Olga* which has 6 single rooms. Accommodation away from the river is non-existent, except in

Orita, W of Puerto Asís, a small town on the oilfield. You can cross to Ecuador from here, get your exit stamp from the DAS office in Puerto Asís or Mocoa. The boat trip up the San Miguel river via Puerto Colón to La Punta takes ½ hour and costs US$1.50. There is a bus to Lago Agrio (US$0.60).

Leguízamo, downstream from Puerto Asís, can also be reached by air from Florencia, with Satena, daily, flight originates in Neiva. A national park (**Parque Nacional de Paya**) has been established between Puerto Asís and Leguízamo, but so far in name only. There are boats to Leticia and to Peru, but transport on all boats carrying gasoline is forbidden. For information go to Naval at the port, Transporte Fluvial Estrella del Sur (Carrera 27, off Calle 10) or Transporte Fluvial Amazonas (Carrera 20, 14-59—English spoken). Hotels: *Leguízamo*, *Madrago*, *Marlene*, *Viajero*, *San Pablo* and *Caucaya*, all G, basic. *Caucaya* is reported comfortable with very nice owners. Further downstream are El Encanto and the nearby village of **San Rafael**, which is a good place to see the Huitoto Indians, a four day trip by launch, the most important of the many tribes which live along the Putumayo river. At San Rafael there is a mission at which it is possible to stay.

It is possible to carry on down the Putumayo which now forms the boundary between Colombia and Peru, then crosses into Brazil, becoming the River Içá to join the Amazon at Santo Antônio. Leticia is 300 km. upstream on the Amazon towards Peru. From El Encanto to Leticia is about 10 days, but getting a passage beyond the Brazilian border is problematical. The border town is **Tarapacá** (airport). There is a basic *Residencial*, plenty of spiders and mosquitoes. It can be quite cold at night.

We are informed that travellers interested in Amazonian plants, birds and animals will find Putumayo more accessible, with more abundant wild life, than Leticia. Restaurant food in the Putumayo region is often uninspiring; take some canned goods for variety. There is a road of a sort from Mocoa to Puerto Limón, on the Río Caquetá (see Caquetá section, **page** 685).

South to Ecuador

Passing through deep valleys and a spectacular gorge, buses on the paved Pan-American Highway cover the 84 km. from Pasto to Ipiales in 1½-2 hrs (toll US$0.40). The road crosses the spectacular gorge of the Guaitara River near El Pedregal, 40 km. from Pasto. A detour via Túquerres (part unpaved) and its plain takes over an hour more; it reaches 3,050 metres at Túquerres, dropping to 2,440 at Guachucal, and rising again to 2,740 metres at **Ipiales**, "the city of the three volcanoes", with about 30,000 people; famous for its colourful Sat. morning Indian market. The Catedral Bodas de Plata is worth visiting. San Luis airport is 6½ km. out of town. "Intercontinental" flights to/from Bogotá daily, US$55.

If you have time, a visit to the nearby Sanctuary of the Virgin of **Las Lajas** is definitely recommended. On days set apart for religion, dazzlingly clean Indians come down from the hills in their traditional bright colours. Seen from afar the Sanctuary is a magnificent architectural conception, set on a bridge over the canyon; close to, it is very heavily ornamented. The altar is set into the rock face of the canyon which forms one end of the sanctuary. There are great pilgrimages to it from Colombia and Ecuador (very crowded at Easter) and the Sanctuary must be second only to Lourdes in the number of miracles claimed for it. The Church recognizes one only. Colectivo from Carrera 6 y Calle 4, Ipiales, US$0.30 p.p., taxi, US$5 return (it's about a 1½-hour walk, 7 km.); 3 basic hotels and a small number of restaurants at Las Lajas.

Hotels *Mayasquer*, 3 km. on road to frontier, D, modern, nice restaurant, very good, swings for children, discothèque, T (9304) 2643; *Pasviveros*, bright and clean, E, with bath and hot water; *Central*, Carrera 6a, 14-48, E, pleasant, clean; *Las Lajas*, E, hot water in the morning, good restaurant; *Buchue*, F, clean, comfortable, very good; *Nueva York*, Calle 13, No. 4-11, near main square, G, run down, friendly; *Colombia*, Calle 13, No. 7-50, F, hot water, mice but otherwise quite clean; opp. at No. 7-59 is *Valparaíso*, F, hot water; *Korpawasi*, Carrera 6, No. 10-47, E, good food, plenty of blankets; *India Catalina*, Carrera 5a, No. 14-88, G, new, hot shower, good value, 2 blocks from main plaza; *Oasis*, Cra. 6, No. 11-34, 1 block from main plaza, G, hot shower, clean, helpful; *Rumichaca Internacional*, E, clean and comfortable with good basic restaurant; *Residencial Belmonte* (Hotel B), Carrera 4, No. 12-111 (near Transportes Ipiales), F, very clean, hot water, rec., but crowded; *Residencia Tequendama*, Carrera 5, No. 14-08, F, family atmosphere, very basic; *San Andrés*, Carrera 5, No. 14-75, F, clean, TV, hot water; same street, No. 14-25, *Residencias Santa Fe*, F. Young travellers can expect to be questioned and searched by police soon after checking in to a hotel.

Camping Possible above the bus parking lot, or free behind last Esso station outside town on road north.

Restaurants *Don Lucho*, Carrera 5, No. 14-13 (antioqueño); *Bar D'Albert*, small, quiet, on main road from Bolivariano bus station to centre; *Greenhouse*, Carrera 6, No. 16-73, good, reasonable prices. *India Catalina*, 24-hour café in centre, useful for late-night arrivals and departures. Plenty of cheap restaurants. Meals in Almacenes Ley cost US$1. Many good bakeries on Carrera 6, or *Panadería Galaxia*, Calle 15, No. 7-89, for a good cheap breakfast.

Cinemas 2 on Calle Principal on road to Las Lajas.

Museum Small, recently set up by Banco de la República.

Exchange It is possible to cash travellers' cheques only at the Banco de la República, a few blocks from the main square (closed 1100-1400); you will have to show two different pieces of identification and may have to recite passport number from memory. *Casa de Cambio* at Carrera 6, No. 14-09. There are money changers in the street and on the border, but they may take advantage of you if the banks are closed. Better rates are to be had in Quito. There is an agency of Banco Anglo Colombiano, Carrera 6, 3 blocks from main square.

Frontier Ipiales is 2 km. from the Rumichaca bridge across the Carchi river into Ecuador. The frontier post stands beside a natural bridge, on a new, concrete bridge, where the customs and passport examination takes place from 0800 to 1800.

You obtain your Colombian exit stamp from the DAS at the frontier post. You have to get your entry stamp and tourist card for Ecuador at the frontier; if the border office is closed, you must go to the police station just before Tulcán. This applies at weekends, closed 1200-1400; taxis on the fast road to the border do not pass the police station. There is an Ecuadorean consulate on Carrera 6, Ipiales, one block from the main square, above Banco Cafetero, open weekdays. Ecuadorean officials do not usually give more than 30 days for visiting the country, but extensions are easy to obtain, from Amazonas 2639, Quito and the Migración offices in provincial capitals. Motorists have their *carnets* stamped at the border (very efficient). You may be required by Ecuadorean customs to show that you have enough money for your stay in the country. There can be long queues crossing into Ecuador.

Colombian customs have the same basic requirement of US$20 a day (US$10 for students), though you are not always required to show that you have this amount. Entering Colombia, tourist cards are issued at the frontier, and there is no need, if driving your own vehicle, to go through Tulcán: take the road signed Rumichaca. If entering Colombia by car, the vehicle is supposed to be fumigated against diseases that affect coffee trees, at the ICA office at the border; the certificate must be presented in El Pedregal, a village 40 km. beyond Ipiales on the road to Pasto. (This fumigation process is not always carried out.) There is a duty-free shop about ½ km. from the border. There are frequent police checks on the buses going to Popayán and neighbouring areas.

Transport From Ipiales to Tulcán: colectivo from main park (waits till all seats are full), US$0.20 to the frontier. Colectivo from frontier to Tulcán also US$0.20; to go to bus terminal, take blue bus from central plaza, US$0.05. Bus from small market 2 blocks from main car park to Rumichaca commercial centre, about ½ km. from border, US$0.10. Taxi to border, US$2 after bargaining; from border to Tulcán, US$2. From Ipiales airport to the border by taxi, about US$5.50; to centre of Ipiales US$3.25. From Tulcán's modern bus terminal buses go to Quito throughout the day; a beautiful five-hour Andean trip.

Bus to Popayán, Expreso Bolivariano, US$7, 7½ hrs., hourly departures, 0430-2030; Transportes de Ipiales, US$7 (neither on main square, best to take taxi from border), Super Taxis and Cootranar *busetas*, US$6, beautiful trip. Bus to Cali, US$11, 12 hrs. To Pasto with minibus from main square, US$2.45 (frequent police checks); Flota Bolivariano buses every hr., US$1.50, 1¼ hrs. Buses to Bogotá leave every other hour between 0500 and 0830, US$20.

TAME (of Ecuador) has flights to Quito from Tulcán. Mon.-Fri. at 1245.

INFORMATION FOR VISITORS

Documents A passport is always necessary; an onward ticket is officially necessary, but is not always asked for at land borders. Nationals of the following countries do not need visas or tourist cards: Argentina, Austria, Barbados, Belgium, Brazil, Costa Rica, Denmark, Ecuador, West Germany, Finland, Holland, Ireland, Italy, Japan, Liechtenstein, Luxemburg, Netherlands Antilles, Norway, Peru, Portugal, St. Vincent and the Grenadines, South Korea, Spain, Sweden, Switzerland, Trinidad and Tobago, UK, Uruguay. All other countries need visas or tourist cards (free). Normal validity for either is 90 days; extensions for a further month can be obtained in Bogotá (DAS, Carrera 27, No. 17-00, or any other DAS office; cost US$10, can take up to 3 days). Whether you need a tourist card or visa depends on your nationality, so check at a Colombian consulate in advance. Tourist cards are issued by CNT offices (in New York, or Caracas, for instance), or by Colombian airlines or authorized foreign carriers. Visas are issued only by Colombian consulates. A visa is required by U.S. and Israeli citizens (for example), who must be prepared to show 1 photograph, an onward or return ticket, as well as a passport (allow 48 hours). Alternatively, in the USA only, Avianca issues tourist cards (transit visas), valid for 15 days, costing US$10—these cards are renewable only by leaving the country. In Miami insist at the Consulate, as they will assume that you can work it all out through the airline. U.S. citizens who arrive in Colombia by air from a third country without a visa must get a tourist card on the plane, otherwise they will be fined. Citizens of Asian, African, Middle Eastern and socialist countries (including Cuba, Nicaragua and East Germany), must apply at least 4 weeks in advance for a visa. You may find that your onward ticket, which you must show before you can obtain a visa, is stamped "non-refundable". If you do not receive an entry card when flying in, the information desk will issue one, and restamp your passport for free. Visitors are sometimes asked to prove that they have US$20 for each day of their stay (US$10 for students). Note that to leave Colombia you must normally get an exit stamp from the DAS (security police). They often do not have offices at the small frontier towns, so try to get your stamp in a main city, and save time.

N.B. It is highly recommended that you have your passport photocopied, and witnessed by the DAS (about US$0.20). A rotary can also do this. This is a valid substitute, and your passport can then be put into safe-keeping. Also, photocopy your travellers' cheques and any other essential documents. For more information, check with DAS or your consulate.

Airport Taxes There is an airport exit tax of US$15, from which only travellers staying less than 24 hours are exempt. When you arrive, ensure that all necessary documentation bears a stamp for your date of arrival; without it you will have to pay double the exit tax on leaving (with the correct stamp, you will only be charged half the exit tax if you have been in the country less than 30 days). Visitors staying more than 30 days have to pay an extra US$15 tax, which can only be avoided by bona-fide tourists who can produce the card given them on entry. There is a 15% tax on all international air tickets bought in Colombia for flights out of the country (7% on international return flights). Unfortunately it is no longer possible to avoid the purchase tax by buying tickets outside the country, as the charge is included automatically. Do not buy tickets for domestic flights to or from San Andrés island outside Colombia; they are much more expensive. When getting an onward ticket from Avianca for entry into Colombia, reserve a seat only and ask for confirmation in writing, otherwise you will pay twice as much as if purchasing the ticket inside Colombia.

Travel by Air British Airways has a twice weekly service from London to Bogotá, via Caracas. Airlines with services from continental Europe are Air France, Alitalia, Iberia, and Lufthansa. Avianca, the Colombian national airline, flies from Frankfurt via Paris and Madrid.

Frequent services to and from the U.S. by Avianca and American (latter's schedule unknown at time of going to press). The cheapest flight from Miami to Bogotá is via Panama with a couple of hours' stopover with Air Panama. Another cheap route is Miami-San Andrés, then take a domestic flight to your Colombian destination. You can save up to US$50 this way going from Miami to Bogotá. Other flights from Miami: Avianca to Cartagena, Barranquilla, Pereira, Medellín, Cali, and San Andrés; Ladeco to Bogotá.

From Neighbouring Republics Lacsa flies from San José to San Andrés and Barranquilla. To Mexico City with Avianca and Varig from Bogotá. Sahsa flies to San Andrés from Honduras and Panama, 4 times a week. SAM flies from Bogotá and San Andrés, to San José, and Guatemala City daily. Fares between Central America and Colombia are cheaper with a change in San Andrés, rather than direct.

If flying from Guatemala to Colombia with SAM, via San José and San Andrés, you have to purchase a round-trip ticket, refundable only in Guatemala. To get around this (if you are not going back to Guatemala) you will have to try to arrange a ticket swap with a traveller going in the other direction on San Andrés. There is, however, no difficulty in exchanging a round-trip ticket for a San Andrés-Colombian ticket with the airline, but you have to pay extra. Lacsa, Copa, Air Panama, Avianca, SAM and others fly from Panama to Colombia; do not be persuaded by SAM desk at Panama airport to buy an onward ticket out of Colombia—this may not be needed—if you fail, SAM in Bogotá will give refunds: first you must go to the DAS, Extranjería section, show your passport and ticket and obtain a permit for a refund; then go to the SAM office. **Medellín-Panama** with Copa: one may not enter, or obtain a visa for, Panama without a return or onward ticket, so you must buy a return ticket and then sell half in Panama once you have purchased a flight ticket out of Panama. **Motorcycles** may be taken as luggage with Copa; remove oil, petrol, battery and anything breakable. Insist on supervising loading and unloading. Medellín customs take more than a day and you have to go from the airport to the *aduana interior*, in town; six copies of relevant papers have to be completed and delays can be experienced in getting hold of your property at Medellín. Officials, however, are helpful and friendly, despite the bureaucratic nightmare. The cheapest way to fly to Quito is to fly to Ipiales (Intercontinental from Bogotá), cross the border by road and take another 'plane at Tulcán. Avianca, Iberia, Lufthansa, Air France Aeroperú, Viasa, Ladeco and Ecuatoriana go S from Colombia. Avianca, Viasa and Ecuatoriana fly Bogotá-Caracas.

For a cheap means of flying from Venezuela to Colombia, **see page 648**.

For a cheap means of flying from Venezuela to Colombia, **see page 648**.

Customs Duty-free admission is granted for portable typewriters, radios, binoculars, personal and cine cameras, but all must show use; 200 cigarettes or 50 cigars or 250 grams of tobacco or up to 250 grams of manufactured tobacco in any form, 2 bottles of liquor or wine per person.

Internal Air Services are flown principally by Avianca, SAM, Aces, Aires, Satena and Intercontinental. They serve the whole country, the larger towns and cities receiving flights usually daily, the smaller places perhaps only once a week. Avianca offers a round ticket (*Conozca a Colombia*) giving unlimited domestic travel for 30 days on Avianca or SAM; conditions are that it allows up to ten stops, it must be bought outside Colombia in conjunction with an international air ticket, children up to 12 pay 50%, infants are free, the Air Pass is non-refundable unless the whole has been unused, one may not pass through each city more than once (except for transfers), and a proposed itinerary (not firm) must be submitted when buying the ticket (Leticia and San Andrés may be included). There are three prices:

US$325, available all year, not open to Colombians or residents abroad, may be used in conjunction with any transatlantic carrier; US$224, available all year, open to Colombians legally resident abroad, passengers must fly Avianca transatlantic; the third pass, US$190, is available for 8 days use only, and cannot be used in June, July, August or December, open to Colombians legally resident abroad, Avianca must be the transatlantic carrier. For single flights, the army airline Satena tends to be cheaper than Avianca. Avianca's domestic shuttle flights (Puente Aéreo) go from Bogotá to Medellín/Montería, Cali/Pasto and Barranquilla; for example to Medellín every ½ hour between 0730-1630. But it is best to book a ticket as for an ordinary flight: just turning up will involve a long wait. Stand-by tickets are available to Barranquilla, Cali, Medellín; known as PET, *pasajero en turno*. Domestic airports are good, though the tourist facilities tend to close early on weekdays, and all Sundays. In-flight service and airline services on the ground tend to be poor.

Buses Travel in Colombia is far from dull. The buses are generally fairly comfortable. Air-conditioned buses are often very cold (so take a sweater), or very hot (because the a/c has broken down, and the windows cannot be opened). The curtains may be down to keep the bus cool and/or to allow passengers to watch the video (so not much good for sightseeing); if you are not keen on crime thrillers, or Rambo, take a walkman, or insist on finding a bus without a video, or where it is broken—there usually is one! The luggage compartment is normally locked, but it is wise to keep an eye on your bags. Breakdowns are many. In all parts, police checks on buses are frequent. Note that meal stops can be few and far between, and short; bring your own food. Be prepared for climatic changes on longer routes. A full colectivo, such as a "Taxi Verde", costs only twice as much per person as a bus seat. The excellent minibus (*buseta*) services of Velotax have been recommended. If you entrust your luggage to the bus companies' luggage rooms, remember to load it on to the bus yourself; it will not be done automatically. There are few interdepartmental bus services on holidays. Always take your passport (or DAS-approved photocopy) with you: identity checks on buses are frequent.

Taxis Whenever possible, take a taxi with a meter, and ensure that it is switched on, otherwise you will be overcharged. All taxis are obliged to display the additional legal tariffs that may be charged after 2000, on Sundays and fiestas. If a taxi has a meter, do not haggle the price; if it does not (and most taxis on the N coast do not), fix a price beforehand. Don't take a taxi which is old; look for "Servicio Público" on the side. Women do not travel alone in taxis at night. If the taxi "breaks down", take your luggage out if you are asked to push, or let the driver push; it may be a trick to separate you from your luggage.

Motoring Roads are given in the text. Motor fuel: "premium" 95 octane (only in large cities), about US$0.70 per US gallon; "corriente" 84 octane, US$0.55 per US gallon. Diesel prices are similar. Roads are not always signposted. If driving yourself, avoid night journeys; vehicles are unlighted and it can be dangerous. The roads are often in poor condition, lorry- and bus-drivers tend to be reckless, and stray animals are often encountered. Police checks are frequent, keep your documents handy. In town, try to leave your car in an attended car park (*parqueadero*), especially at night. If you are planning to sleep in your car, it is better to stop in a *parqueadero*; you will be charged a little extra. In many guarded carparks, only the driver is allowed in; passengers must get out at the entrance.

National driving licences may be used by foreigners in Colombia, but must be accompanied by an official translation if in a language other than Spanish. International drivers licences are also accepted. To bring a car into Colombia, you must also have a valid, third-party insurance policy, documents proving ownership of the vehicle, and a tourist card/transit visa. These are normally valid for 90 days and must be applied for at the Colombian consulate in the country which you will be leaving for Colombia. Details of length of stay and car specifications will be sent to Bogotá and customs at the border, where the document should await your arrival. Carry driving documents with you at all times.

Car hire is very expensive in Colombia. Even if you are paying in cash, a credit card may be asked for as proof of identity (Visa, Mastercard, American Express), in addition to passport and driver's licence. Main international car rental companies are represented at principal airports but may be closed Saturday p.m. and Sundays.

Hitch-hiking (*autostop*) seems to be quite easy in Colombia, especially if you can enlist the co-operation of the highway police checkpoints outside each town. Truck-drivers are often very friendly, but be careful of private cars with more than one person inside, especially if you are travelling on your own; they may be unmarked taxis. There have been many reports of muggings of cyclists in the Caribbean coastal area.

Climbing For information ask at the Centro Nacional de Montaña, Transversal 10, No. 106-35, Bogotá, T 2140884. Maps can be obtained at the Instituto Geográfico (see under Bogotá, Tourist Offices). If you have a guide or are invited on a mountain tour, make certain costs/charges are clear before you start. For specific area details, see under Sierra Nevada del Cocuy, Valledupar, Ibagué, Manizales and Pereira.

Hotels There is a tourist tax of 5% on rooms and an insurance charge, but no service charge, and tipping is at discretion: 10% is generous. The more expensive hotels and restaurants also add on 10% VAT (IVA). Food is not expensive. A good lunch costs about US$5-6. A restaurant meal that business people might give to prospective customers would cost from US$6 to US$12 p.p. In many hotels outside the main cities you can only stay (very cheaply) at *en pension* rates and no allowance is made for missing a meal. The Colombian tourist office has lists of authorized prices for all hotels which are usually at least a year out of date. If you are overcharged the tourist office will arrange a refund. Most hotels in Colombia charge US$1 to US$6 for extra beds for children, up to a maximum (usually) of 4 beds per room. On the Caribbean coast and San Andrés and Providencia, high season is 15 December-30 April, 15 June-31 August. Although most hotels, except the very cheapest, offer private WC and shower as a matter of course, hot water often comes only in the more expensive hotels or in colder zones. Wash basin plugs are universally in short supply. Prices are normally displayed, if not, bargain.

Camping Sites are given in the text. Colombian Tourist Office has a list of official sites. Permission to camp is readily granted by landowners in less populated areas. Those in camper vans may camp by the roadside, but it is not particularly safe.

Colombia is one of the few countries which sell "white gas" for camping stoves etc., so stock up here.

Food Colombia's food is very regional; it is quite difficult to buy in Medellín, say, a dish you particularly liked in Bogotá. Restaurants in smaller towns often close on Sundays, and early on weekday evenings: if stuck, you will probably find something to eat near the bus station.

Locro de choclos is a potato and maize soup so rich and nourishing that, with salad and coffee, it would make a meal in itself. Colombia has its own variant of the inevitable *arroz con pollo* (chicken and rice) which is excellent. For a change *pollo en salsa de mostaza* (chicken in mustard sauce) is recommended. *Ajiaco de pollo* is a delicious chicken, maize, manioc, cabbage and potato stew served with cream and capers, and lumps of avocado; it is a Bogotá speciality; another Bogotá speciality is *sobrebarriga* (belly of beef). *Bandeja antioqueña* costs US$3 in most places and consists of meat grilled and served with rice, beans, potato, manioc and a green salad; the simpler *carne asada* may be had for as little as US$2. *Mazamorra*, boiled maize in milk, is a typical *antioqueño* sweet, and so is *salpicón*, a tropical fruit salad. *Lechona* (sucking pig and herbs) is a speciality of Ibagué. Cartagena's rice with coconut can be compared with rice *a la valenciana*. In Nariño, guinea pig (*cuy*, *curí* or *conejillo de Indias*) is typical. *Tamales* are meat pies made by folding a maize dough round chopped pork mixed with potato, peas, onions, eggs and olives seasoned with garlic, cloves and paprika, and steaming the whole in banana leaves (which you don't eat); the best are from Tolima. A baked dish of squash, beaten eggs and seafood covered with sauce is known as the *souffle de calabaza*. *Magras* is a typical Colombian dish of eggs and chicken baked together and served with a tomato sauce. *Sancocho* is a filling combination of all the tuberous vegetables, including the tropical cassava and yam, with chopped fresh fish or any kind of meat, possibly chicken. From stalls in the capital and the countryside, try *mazorcas* (roast maize cobs) or *arepas* (fried maize cakes). On the Caribbean coast, eat an egg *empanada*, which consists of two layers of corn (maize) dough that open like an oyster-shell, fried with eggs in the middle, and try the *patacón*, a cake of mashed and baked plantain (green banana). *Huevos pericos*, eggs scrambled with onions and tomatoes, are a popular, cheap and nourishing snack for the impecunious—available almost anywhere. *Pandebono*, cheese-flavoured bread is delicious. A good local sweet is the *canastas de coco*: pastry containing coconut custard flavoured with wine and surmounted by meringue. *Arequipe* is very similar to fudge, and popular (it is called *manjarblanco* in other parts of South America). *Almojábanas*, a kind of sour-milk bread roll, are delicious if fresh: "one day old and they are a disaster". There is, indeed, quite an assortment of little fruit pasties and preserves. Then there are the usual fruits: bananas, oranges, mangoes, avocado pears, and (at least in the tropical zones) *chirimoyas*, *papayas*, and the delicious *pitahaya*, taken either as an appetizer or dessert and, for the wise, in moderation, because even a little of it has a laxative effect. Other fruits such as the *guayaba* (guava), *guanábana* (soursop), *maracuyá* (passion fruit), *lulo* (*naranjilla*), *mora* (blackberry) and *curuba* make delicious juices, sometimes with milk added to make a *sorbete*—but be careful of milk in Colombia, and *sorbetes* are best left alone. Fruit yoghurts are nourishing and cheap (try *Alpina* brand; *crema* style is best). *Tinto*, the national small cup of black coffee, is taken ritually at all hours. Colombian coffee is always mild. (Coffee with milk is called *café perico*; *café con leche* is a mug of milk with coffee added.) *Agua de panela* is a common beverage (hot water with unrefined sugar), also made with limes, milk, or cheese.

Drink Many acceptable brands of beer are produced. The local rum is good and cheap; ask for *ron*, not *aguardiente*, because in Colombia the latter word is used for a popular drink containing aniseed (*aguardiente anisado*). Try *canelazo*—cold or hot rum with water, sugar, lime and cinnamon. Local table wines include Santo Tomás; none are very good. General food and wine tips: wine is normally about US$3.50-4.50 in restaurants for an acceptable bottle of Chilean or Argentine; European wines are very expensive.

Warning Great care should be exercised when buying imported spirits in shops. It has been reported that bottles bearing well-known labels have often been "recycled" and contain a cheap and poor imitation of the original contents. This can be dangerous to the health, and travellers are warned to stick to beer and rum. Also note that ice is usually not made from potable water.

Tipping Hotels and restaurants 10%. Porters, cloakroom attendants, hairdressers and barbers, US$0.05-0.25. Taxi-drivers are not tipped.

Best Buys Emeralds in Bogotá; handworked silver (excellent); Indian pottery and textiles. The state-run Artesanías de Colombia for craft work (see under Bogotá). In Antioquia buy the handbag—*carriel antioqueño*— traditionally made from otter skin, but nowadays from calf skin and plastic trimmed at that. At Cartagena crude rubber is moulded into little dyed figurines: odd but attractive. Clothing and shoes are cheap in Medellín. The Colombian *ruana* (poncho) is attractive and warm in any cool climate, and comes in a wide variety of colours; it may, however, be cheaper in Ecuador. Silver and gold work is cheaper than in Peru. Good duty-free shop at Bogotá airport. Leatherwork is generally good and not expensive especially in southern Colombia.

Security Most travellers confirm that the vast majority of Colombians are honest and very hospitable. Sadly, reports of crime, sometimes violent, are still received. In addition to the general advice given on page 678 of the **Introduction and Hints** section, the following local conditions should be noted. The warning against accepting cigarettes, chewing gum, sweets or any other type of food from fellow bus-passengers cannot be emphasized too strongly. This crime is particularly common between Popayán and San Agustín, and Bogotá and Ipiales. We have received a number of reports confirming this practice. That said, the southern area from Popayán to the Ecuadorian border is generally safer, and freer from thieves, than points further north.

Colombia is part of a major drug-smuggling route. Police and customs activities have greatly intensified and smugglers increasingly try to use innocent carriers. Travellers are warned against carrying packages for other people without checking the contents. Penalties run up to 12 years in none too comfortable jails, and the police sometimes behave very roughly towards those they choose for a spot check at airports; complaints have been made in this connection to the Colombian authorities. All young travellers are suspect, so be very polite if approached by policemen. If your hotel room is raided by police looking for drugs, try, if possible, to get a witness to prevent drugs being planted on you. Colombians who offer you drugs may well be setting you up for the police, who are very active on the north coast and San Andrés island, and other tourist resorts.

In 1989/90 much publicity has been given to the attempts by the authorities to tackle the "drug barons". Generally travellers have not been affected and simple robbery is a much greater problem. When travelling by bus, try to get a window seat on the side where your luggage is stowed, so you can check what luggage is taken from the bus. Many bus companies give luggage tags (like airlines). Try to avoid having your luggage put on top; you won't be allowed to jump out of the bus at every stop to check it's still there. In town buses, do not open windows so wide that belongings can be snatched; beware of pickpockets by the doors. Small *busetas* are marginally safer than buses because there is only one door for escape. Travelling by car, always keep an eye on your petrol cap, windscreen wipers and hub caps. Thieves tend to be particularly active in and around bus and railway stations. It is socially acceptable for women to keep banknotes in their bras.

Avoid money changers on the street who offer over-favourable rates of exchange. They often short-change you or run off with your money, pretending that the police are coming. Beware of counterfeit dollars and pesos.

If someone accosts you on the street, saying he's a plain-clothes policeman or drugs officer, and asks you to go to his office, offer to go with him to the nearest policeman (the tourist police where possible) or police station, or to your hotel if it's dark. He may well be a "confidence man" (if he doesn't ask to see your passport, he almost certainly is). These conmen usually work in pairs. The best advice at all times is to take care, and above all to use your common sense.

Also be prepared for frequent bus stopping and searches which are conducted in a rather haphazard and capricious manner. Travellers in private cars are also stopped often, but not necessarily searched. Some roads are more heavily policed than others, and you can expect to be stopped several times when travelling to or from the Caribbean coast and when coming from Ecuador into Colombia. There is some guerrilla activity in Colombia: the departments near Venezuela have been mentioned, also the Pasto, Tierradentro and San Agustín areas; the Magdalena Valley in Santander and the Turbo/Urabá region. Police and army checks are common in this respect also. All luggage is searched leaving Leticia airport and most tourists are checked arriving in Cartagena from the airport. It has been reported that the police charge 10% of the value of stolen articles for making out a declaration for insurance claims.

Health Emergency medical treatment is given in hospitals: if injured in a bus accident, for example, you will be covered by insurance and treatment will be free. Bogotá has well-organized sanitary services, and the water may be safely drunk. Take sterilizer with you, or boil the water, or use the excellent mineral waters, when travelling outside the capital. Choose your food and eating places with care everywhere. Fruit drinks made with milk should be avoided. Hepatitis is common; have a gamma-globulin injection before your trip. Mosquito nets are useful in the coastal swampy regions. There is some risk of malaria and yellow fever in the coastal areas and the eastern llanos/jungle regions; prophylaxis is advised. The local insect repellant, Black Flag, is not reliable.

Climate and Clothing Climate is entirely a matter of altitude: there are no seasons to speak of, though some periods are wetter than others. Tropical clothing is necessary in the hot and humid climate of the coastal fringe and the eastern llanos. In Bogotá medium-weight clothing is needed for the cool evening and night. Medellín requires light clothing; Cali lighter still; Manizales very similar to Bogotá. A dual-purpose raincoat and overcoat is useful in the uplands. Higher up in the mountains it can be very cold; woollen clothing is necessary.

The **best time for a visit** is December, January and February: the driest months. But pleasure—it happens sometimes—is in conflict with duty, because most business people are then on holiday. There is heavy rain in many places from June to September.

Hours of Business Mon. to Fri., commercial firms work from 0800 to mid-day and from 1400 to 1730 or 1800. Certain firms in the warmer towns such as Cali start at 0700 and finish earlier. Government offices follow the same hours on the whole as the commercial firms, but generally prefer to do business with the public in the afternoon only. Embassy hours for the public are from 0900 to noon and from 1400 to 1700 (Mon. to Fri.). Bank hours in Bogotá are 0900 to 1500 Mon. to Thurs., 0900 to 1530 on Fri. except the last Fri. in the month when they close at 1200; banks in Medellín, Cali, Barranquilla, Bucaramanga, Cartagena, Pasto, Pereira and Manizales open from 0800 to 1130 and 1400 to 1600 on Mon. to Thur.; on Fri. they are open until 1630 but shut at 1130 on the last Fri. in the month; banks in Popayán, Cúcuta, Neiva, Tunja, Ibagué and Santa Marta open from 0800 to 1130 and 1400 to 1530 on Mon. to Fri. and 0800 to 1100 on Sat. and the last day of the month. Shopping hours are 0900 to 1230 and 1430 to 1830, including Sat.

British Business Travellers should consult "Hints to Exporters: Colombia", from Room CO7, Export Services Branch, Department of Trade, Sanctuary Bldgs, 16-20 Great Smith Street, London SW1P 3DB. Similar U.S. publications may be obtained from the Department of Commerce, Washington, D.C. Also, *Colombian News Letter*, published monthly by the Colombian American Association Inc., 150 Nassau Street, New York, N.Y. 10038.

Public Holidays are on the following days: 1 January: Circumcision of our Lord; 6 January: Epiphany*; 19 March: St Joseph*; Maundy Thursday; Good Friday; 1 May: Labour Day; Ascension Day*; Corpus Christi*; Sacred Heart*; 29 June: SS. Peter and Paul*; 20 July: Independence Day*; 7 August: Battle of Boyacá; 15 August: Assumption*; 12 October: Discovery of America*; 1 November: All Saints' day*; 11 November: Independence of Cartagena*; 8 December: Immaculate Conception; 25 December: Christmas Day. When those marked with an asterisk do not fall on a Monday, or when they fall on a Sunday, they will be moved to the following Monday.

Time Zone Colombia is 5 hours behind GMT.

Currency The monetary unit is the peso, divided into 100 centavos. There are coins of 50 centavos (rare) and of 1, 2, 5, 10, 20 and 50 pesos; there are notes of 50, 100, 200, 500, 1,000, 2,000 and 5,000 pesos. Large notes of over 1,000 pesos are often impossible to spend on small purchases as change is in short supply, especially in small cities, and in the morning. There is now a limit of 500 on both the import and export of pesos. To change pesos back into dollars on departure (to a maximum of US$100), you need to keep the exchange slips received from banks. Travellers' cheques are not easy to change in Colombia; the Banco de la República prefers to change those of no more than US$20. Owing to the quantity of counterfeit American Express travellers' cheques in circulation, travellers experience great difficulty in cashing these cheques except in main cities, where the procedure is often slow, involving finger printing and photographs. The best advice we can give is to take Thomas Cook's or a US bank's dollar traveller cheques in small denominations. Sterling travellers' cheques are practically impossible to change in Colombia. The few, legitimate *casas de cambio* give rates slightly worse than the banks, but are much quicker. Also in circulation are counterfeit US dollar bills in denominations of US$50 and US$100; US$20 bills are therefore more readily accepted. It is generally dangerous to change money on the streets, and you are likely to be given counterfeit pesos. The safest way to obtain black market rates is at the border in a neighbouring country.

As it is unwise to carry large quantities of cash, **credit cards** are widely used, especially Diners' Club and Visa; Master Charge is less common, while American Express is only accepted in high-priced establishments in Bogotá. Many banks (e.g. Banco Cafetero) advance pesos against Visa, and Banco de Occidente and Banco Industrial de Colombia give cash advances against Mastercard, though there is talk of a possible government charge.

Weights and Measures are metric, and weights should always be quoted in kilograms. Litres are used for liquid measures but US gallons are standard for the petroleum industry. Linear measures are usually metric, but the inch is quite commonly used by engineers and the yard on golf courses. For land measurement the hectare and cubic metre are officially employed but the traditional measures *vara* (80 centimetres) and *fanegada* (1,000 square *varas*) are still in common use. As in many other countries food etc. is often sold in *libras* (pounds), which are equivalent to ½ kilo.

Electric Current 120 volts AC., is general for Colombia. Transformer must be 110-150 volt A.C., with flat-prong plugs (all of same size). Be careful with electrically heated showers.

Mail There are separate post offices for surface mail and airmail. Send all letters by airmail, for surface mail is very unreliable. Avianca controls all airmail services and has offices in provincial cities. Correspondence with U.K. is reported to be good. It costs US$0.25 to send a letter or postcard to the U.S., and US$0.27 to Europe; a 1 kg. package to Europe costs US$13 by air (Avianca). Note that the AmEx agent, Tierra Mar Aire, does not accept mail to be held for AmEx customers.

Telecommunications Empresa Nacional de Telecomunicaciones has offices in all main cities.

Telephone systems have been automated; the larger towns are interconnected. Inter-city calls must be made from Telecom offices unless you have access to a private phone. Long-distance pay 'phones are located outside most Telecom offices, also at bus stations and airports. They take 20 peso coins. 1 peso coins for ordinary 'phones may be bought in 20 peso packets from Banco de la República. From the larger towns it is possible to telephone to Canada, the U.S.A., the U.K., and to several of the Latin American republics. International phone charges are high (e.g. US$33 for 3 mins to Australia, US$22 to Europe) but there is a 20% discount on Sun., a deposit is required before the call is made which can vary between US$18 and US$36 (try bargaining the deposit down), US$1 is charged if no reply, for person-to-person add an extra minute's charge to Canada, 2 minutes' to UK; all extra minutes' conversation costs ⅓ more. Collect, or reversed-charge, telephone calls can be made from El Dorado airport (enquire) but otherwise are only possible from private telephones; make sure the operator understands what is involved or you may be billed in any case.

Press Bogotá: *El Tiempo, El Espectador* (both Liberal); *La República* (Conservative), *El Siglo* (extreme Conservative). Medellín: *El Mundo*; Cali: *El País, Occidente, El Pueblo*, all major cities have daily papers. Magazines are partisan, best is probably *La Semana*. U.S. and European papers can be bought at a stall in Bogotá on Av. 19 between Carreras 7 and 8.

Sport The game of *tejo* is still played in Cundinamarca, Boyacá and Tolima. In Pasto and Popayán it is played under the name of *sapo* (toad). This is the Spanish *juego de la rana*, in which a small quoit has to be thrown from an improbable distance into a metal frog's mouth. There are bullrings at Bogotá, Cali, Manizales, Medellín, Sincelejo and Cerete. Polo is played at Medellín and Bogotá. Most of the larger towns have stadia. Association football is the most popular game. American baseball is played at Cartagena and Barranquilla. Cockfights, cycling, boxing and basketball are also popular.

Fishing is particularly good at Girardot, Santa Marta, and Barranquilla; marlin is fished off Barranquilla. There is good trout fishing, in season, in the lakes in the Bogotá area, particularly at Lake Tota, in the mountains.

Tourist Information The Corporación Nacional de Turismo (CNT), with its headquarters at Bogotá, has branches in every departmental capital and other places of interest. They should be visited as early as possible not only for information on accommodation and transport, but also for details on areas which are dangerous to visit. CNT also has offices in New York: 140 East 57th St., T 688-0151; Caracas: P.B. 5 Av. Urdaneta Ibarras a Pelota, T 561-3592/5805; Madrid: Calle Princesa No. 17 Tercero Izquierda, T 248-5090/5690; and Paris: 9,

Boulevard de la Madeleine, 75001 Paris, T 260-3565. For details on National Parks, go to the Inderena Office in Bogotá (address on **page 634**).

The Automobile Club in Bogotá has offices on Avenida Caracas, No. 46-64 (T 2451534 and 2452684). Branches are at Manizales, Medellín, Cali, Barranquilla and Cartagena. It supplies Esso, Texaco and Mobil maps: good, but not quite up-to-date; a full set of Hojas de Ruta costs US$2.50. The Texaco map has plans of the major cities. Even the Shell series lacks detail. Maps of Colombia are obtainable at the Instituto Geográfico Militar, Agustín Codazzi, Carrera 30 y Calle 45, open 0800-1530, Bogotá, or from their office in Pasto. Drivers' route maps are available from the CNT. Buchholz and Central bookshops have a few country and Bogotá maps. Editorial Colina publish a series of books with colour photographs on different parts of Colombia (Cartegena, Antioquia, San Agustín) which have been recommended. Some of the photographs can be obtained as postcards.

This section has been updated by Peter Pollard to whom we are most grateful. Thanks are also due to the following residents and travellers: Shannon Shiell (Glasgow), Dr Barry D. Adam (Windsor, Ontario), Lindsay Adam (Forest Row, W. Sussex), May Berkouwer (Mantinge, Neths.), Momik Bernaerts (Amsterdam) and Thomas Hartmann (Copenhagen), Marcela M. Bonilla (Bogotá), J.N. Bowden and K.E. Badgery (Plymouth), Klaus Brandl (Buenos Aires), Dirk Von Braunmuehl (Bonn 1), Lucy Broadbent and Rick Palmer (Palmerston North, NZ), Michael Brooke (Swaffham Bulbeck, Cambs.), Remo Bulgheroni (Killroergen, Switz.), Peter Caesar (Bogotá), Susan Carroll (Bearwood, W. Midlands), John Charles (Washington, DC), Bryan Crawford (Beauly, Inverness-shire), Jan Van Dalfsen and Tineke Puister (Neths.), Alan and Audrey Davies (Bogotá), James Derry (Courtenay, BC), Barbara Evans and Hugh O'Donnell (London), Dr Dietz Evers (Krumesse), Harry Floyd (London W8), Olivier and Paloma Foro (St-Moritz), Sharon Franklet (Lima 18), Monika Friedhoff (Frankfurt) and Ignaz Utz (Biel, Switz.), D. Friend (Melbourne), Rüdiger and Renate Funk (Laubach 1, W. Ger.), Tony Gowers (Bristol), Rudy Graf (Geneva), Andrew Grassie and Sara Gilbert (Lewes, E. Sussex), D. Graves (Brooklyn, NY), David W. Hamblin (Provo, UT), A.M. De Boer-Van Hamel (Amstelveen), Astrid Hansen (Aars) and Jane Harfeld (Hornsyld, Dnmk.), Jim Hardy (Waukesha, Wis.), Wayne Harvey (South Australia), Dr Paul Heaton (London NW6), Peter and Elaine Hebard (Alamogordo, NM), Sylvio Hellemann (Bonn 2), Uli Herbert (Stuttgart 75), Susan Holze and Astrid Brombosch (Heidelberg), Lennart Wedel-Jarlsberg (Ramnes, Norway), Simon Jeffreys (Peterborough), Ursula Jenny (Bottmingen, Switz.), Michel Joly (Orchamps-Vennes, France), Tobias Kämpf (Ruppersil, Switz.), Birgit Kastner and Hans Lindenthaler (Salzburg, Austria), John Kissack (Bogotá), Rita Kränzlin (Luzern, Switz.), Rudi Lamparter (Gaechingen, W. Ger.), Jochen Langheim and Thomas Reckhorn (Aachen, W. Ger.), Fabrice Leonard (Bergisch-Gladbach, W. Ger.), David Lewis (Willowdale, Ontario), Raymond Lloyd (London WC1), Ole W. Lund (Oslo 3), Helena van Maanen (Velp, Neths.), Judith Martínez (Leticia), Nelly Matthey (Lausanne), Andreas Mietzsch (Braunschweig), Wolfgang Meusburger (Dornbirn, Austria), Martha van Mil and Monica van Eysden ('s-Hertogenbosch, Neths.), Alan I. Mishael (Coral Gables, FL), Helene Monsme (Leiden, Neths.), Daniel Morgan (Wellington, NZ), Steve Morris (Saint John, NB, Canada), Margrit Mosimann and Philipp Strässle (Switz.), Matthias Müller (Berlin 31), Stephen Newcomer (Centrevill, Iowa), Jonas Noreús (Varberg, Swe.), Bryan F. O'Leary (Redondo Beach, CA), Karl Olson (New York, NY), C.A. Ospina (Bogotá), Carlo Ottavio (Potenza, Italy), Sandrine Pétremand and Gilles Maitre (Bevaix, Switz.), Eduardo Carranza Ramírez (Director General, Albergues de Colombia Para El Mundo), Geoff Richardson (Scarborough), Jenny Rowlands and Huw Owen (London), Kathrin Schildknecht and Jürg Schmutz (Bern, Switz.), Ueli Schlatter (Hemmental, Switz.), Thorsten Schüller (Aschen, W. Ger.), F.A. Scire (Leeds), Matthew Shugart (San Diego, CA), Ann Simon (Saffron Walden, Essex), Irene Singer and Leonel Lurua (Buenos Aires), Bob Snyder (Norwich, Ontario), Hans and Ina Stoffregen (Celle, W. Ger.), Richard Stoller (Durham, North Carolina), Kay Stricker (Unterseen, Switz.), The Loving Team (London), Levy Venanzius (Disentis, Switz.), Maarten van Vlerken (Amsterdam), Betsy Wagenhauser (South American Explorers Club, Quito), Andrew Wallace and Michelle Still (Teddington), Alon Warburg and Katy Ostrovska (Cali), Markus Weder (Binningen, Switz.), Simon Weidmann (Bern, Switz.), Roland Weitkamp (Braunschweig, W. Ger.), Dr Ferdinand Welch (Quito), Urs Wigger (Menznau, Switz.), Emma Williams (Teddington) and Paul Newman (Dublin), Huw Williams (Sutton Abinger), Alison Wood (Rotherham) and Heidi Ziernhöld (Richterswil, Switz.).

ECUADOR

INTRODUCTION

ECUADOR is bounded by Colombia to the north, Peru to the east and south and the Pacific Ocean to the west. Its area is about 283,520 square km., which makes it the second smallest republic in South America.

The Andes, running from the Colombian border in the north to the borders of Peru in the south, form a mountainous backbone to the country. There are two main ranges, the Eastern Cordillera and the Western Cordillera, separated by a 400-km. long trough, the Central Valley, whose rims are from 40 to 65 km. apart. The rims are joined together, like the two sides of a ladder, by hilly rungs, and between each pair of rungs lies an intermont basin with a dense cluster of population. These basins, which vary in altitude between 1,800 and 3,000 metres, are drained by rivers which cut through the rims to run either west to the Pacific or east to join the Amazon. The whole mountain area is known as the Sierra.

Both rims of the Central Valley are lined with the cones of more than thirty volcanoes. Several of them have long been extinct, for example, Chimborazo, the highest (6,310 metres), Cayambe (5,790 metres), standing directly on the equator, Illiniza (5,263 metres) and Altar (5,319 metres). At least eight, however, are still active; Cotopaxi (5,897 metres), which had several violent eruptions in the nineteenth century; Tungurahua (5,016 metres), which had a major eruption early this century; Antisana (5,704 metres), which showed signs of activity in the 1960s; Pichincha (4,794 metres), which erupted in 1981, and Sangay (5,230 metres) one of the world's most active volcanoes, continuously emitting fumes and ash. Nowadays all the main peaks except for Altar and Sangay, which are less accessible, are climbed fairly regularly.

East of the Eastern Cordillera the forest-clad mountains fall sharply to the plains—the Oriente—through which meander the tributaries of the Amazon. This eastern lowland region makes up 36% of Ecuador's total territory, but is only sparsely populated by native Indians and agricultural colonists from the highlands.

ECUADOR

0   50   100
km

To Cali

Tumaco

C O L O M B I A

San Lorenzo
Limones
Esmeraldas
Atacamés
Muisne
Cojimies
Pedernales
Jama
Bahia de
Caráquez
Manta

Tulcán
Ipiales
Pasto
Puerto Asis
Puerto
Colón
San
Miguel
Ibarra
Otavalo
Cayambe
Lago
Agrio

Santo Domingo
de los Colorados

1 QUITO

Baeza
Coca

Portoviejo
Jipijapa
Puerto López
Manglaralto

Saquisilí
Quevedo
Ambato
Guaranda
Cajabamba
Babahoyo

Latacunga
Tena
Baños
Shell-Mera
Riobamba
Puyo

Misahuallí

Guayaquil
Durán
Salinas
Playas
Posorja

Bucay
Alausi
Sibambe
Ingapirca

Macas

Cuenca
Machala
Santa Rosa
Huaquillas
Zaruma

Sigsig
Saraguro
Loja
Zamora

Gualaquiza

Tumbes
To
Trujillo
and Lima
Macará

Sullana

P E R U

1 Quito.
2 North of Quito.
3 North and West
Lowlands.
4 Guayaquil.
5 The Southern
Lowlands.
6 Guayaquil to Quito.
7 Southern Sierra.
8 The Oriente.
9 (Off map) The
Galápagos.

In total, the region has only 5% of the national population, but colonization is now proceeding rapidly in the wake of an oil boom. There are substantial oil reserves in the northern Oriente near the Colombian border, and exports began in 1972.

Between the Western Cordillera and the Pacific lies the Costa, 685 km. from north to south and some 100 km. wide. It is from this area that Ecuador draws the majority of its agricultural products for export. Guayaquil, the main city of this region, is 464 km. from the capital, Quito, which lies high in a northern intermont basin.

The Sierra   There are altogether ten intermont basins strung along the Sierra from north to south. There is little variation by day or by season in the temperature in any particular basin: temperature depends on altitude. The basins lie at an elevation of between 2,100 and 2,750 metres, and the range of shade temperature is from 6°C to 10°C in the morning to 19°C to 23°C in the afternoon. Temperatures can get considerably higher in the lower basins. There is one rainy season, from November to May, when the average fall in Quito is 1,270 mm; the skies are mostly cloudy or overcast at this time and there are frequent rainfalls during the afternoons and nights. Over half the area is now grassy *páramo* on which cattle and sheep are raised and subsistence crops grown. What crops are grown is determined by altitude, but the hardiest of them, the potato, cannot thrive above 3,800 metres or so. The intermont basins produce livestock, poultry, wheat, barley, oats, maize, quinoa, fruit and vegetables, some of which find their way down to the coastal plain.

Some 47% of the people of Ecuador live in the central trough of the Andes, and the majority are pure Indians. Most of the land is held in large private estates worked by the Indians, but some of it is held by Indian communities. With the limited application of an agrarian-reform programme, the *huasipungo* system whereby Indians were virtual slaves on the big highland *haciendas* is now disappearing, and co-operatives are proliferating. Though many Indian communities live at subsistence level and remain isolated from national centres, others have developed good markets for products using traditional skills in embroidery, pottery, jewellery, knitting, weaving, and carving.

The Costa   Most of the Costa region is lowland at an altitude of less than 300 metres, apart from a belt of hilly land which runs west from Guayaquil to the coast and trends northwards. In the extreme north there are two rainy seasons, as in Colombia, and a typical tropical rain forest. But the two rainy seasons soon merge into one, running from December to June. Further south, the later the rains begin, the sooner they end: at Guayaquil the rains normally fall between January and April. The forests thin out too in the more southerly lowlands, and give way to thorn and savanna. The Santa Elena Peninsula and the south-western coast near Peru have little or no rainfall.

The main agricultural exports come from a small area of lowland to the SE and N of Guayaquil. It lies between the coastal hills and the Andes; rains are heavy, the temperature and the humidity high: ideal conditions for the growth of tropical crops. One part of this Guayas lowland is subject to floods from the four rivers which traverse it: bananas, normally accounting for half the exports of the lowland, are grown here, as well as rice. Cacao too is farmed on the natural levees of this flood plain, but the main crop comes from the alluvial fans at the foot of the mountains rising out of the plain. High on these same alluvial fans excellent coffee is also grown; cacao, bananas, coffee and sugar, whether processed or unprocessed, are about 30% of the exports by value. Cotton is developing. Add to this that the Guayas lowland is a great cattle-fattening area in the dry season, and its importance in the national economy becomes obvious. A good network of paved roads now links Guayaquil with the major zones of agricultural production, and the once thriving river-ports have now declined. Along the northern coast, the main areas of population are at Esmeraldas, along the highways inland, in the irrigated lands of northern Manabí, and near Manta, Montecristi, and Jipijapa.

Two areas of the coastlands have experienced spectacular rises in population and agricultural production: El Oro Province in the extreme south, centred on the town of Machala, and the Quevedo-Santo Domingo zone along the Andean fringe to the north of Guayaquil. In both areas, highland settlers have mixed with coastal entrepreneurs to produce a particularly progressive agriculture. Irrigation in El Oro has produced a thriving zone of very intensive banana plantations. In the Quevedo-Santo Domingo area, large areas of forest have been cleared; bananas used to be the main crop, but are now being replaced by African palm. Further north, in Esmeraldas Province, there still remain large areas of land which could be cleared and developed for farming, although the fertility of this zone is reputedly much lower than that of the Quevedo, Guayaquil and Machala areas.

History The Incas of Peru, with their capital at Cuzco, began to conquer the Sierra of Ecuador, already densely populated, towards the middle of the 15th century. A road was built between Cuzco and Quito, and the empire was ruled after the death of the Inca Huayna Capac by his two sons, Huáscar at Cuzco and Atahualpa at Quito. Pizarro's main Peruvian expedition took place in 1532, when there was civil war between the two brothers. Atahualpa, who had won the war, was put to death by Pizarro in 1533, and the Inca empire was over.

Pizarro claimed the northern kingdom of Quito, and his lieutenants Sebastián de Benalcázar and Diego de Almagro took the city in 1534. Pizarro founded Lima in 1535 as capital of the whole region, and four years later replaced Benalcázar at Quito by Gonzalo, his brother. Gonzalo later set out on the exploration of the Oriente. He moved down the Napo river, and sent Francisco de Orellana to prospect. Orellana did not return: he drifted down the river finally to reach the mouth of the Amazon: the first white man to cross the continent in this way.

Quito became an *audiencia* under the Viceroy of Peru. For 280 years Ecuador more or less peacefully absorbed the new ways brought by the conqueror. Gonzalo had already introduced pigs and cattle; wheat was now added. The Indians were Christianized, colonial laws and customs and ideas introduced. The marriage of the arts of Spain to those of the Incas led to a remarkable efflorescence of painting, sculpting and building at Quito. In the 18th century black slave labour was brought in to work the plantations near the coast.

There was an abortive attempt at independence in the strongly garrisoned capital in 1809, but it was not until 1822 that Sucre, moving north from Guayaquil, defeated the Spanish at Pichincha and occupied Quito. Soon afterwards Bolívar arrived, and Ecuador was induced to join the Venezuelan and Colombian confederation, the Gran Colombia of Bolívar's dream. On 26 and 27

July, 1822, Bolívar met San Martín, fresh from liberating Lima, at Guayaquil. What happened at that mysterious encounter is not known, but San Martín left it silently for a self-imposed exile in France. Venezuela separated itself from Gran Colombia in 1829, and Ecuador decided on complete independence in August, 1830, under the presidency of Juan Flores.

Ecuador's 19th century history was a continuous struggle between pro-Church conservatives and anti-Church (but none the less devotedly Catholic) liberals. There were also long periods of military rule from 1895, when the liberal General Eloy Alfaro took power. During the late 1940s and the 1950s there was a prolonged period of prosperity (through bananas, largely) and constitutional rule, but the more typical pattern of alternating civilian and military governments was resumed in the 1960s and 1970s. Apart from the liberal-conservative struggles, there has been long-lasting rivalry between Quito and the Sierra on one hand and Guayaquil and the Costa on the other.

The country's eastern jungle territory has been reduced from that of the old Audiencia of Quito by gradual Peruvian infiltration, which means that the country's official claim to be a "país amazónico" has little relation to present reality. This process reached an acute phase in 1941 when war broke out with Peru; the war was ended with the Rio de Janeiro Protocol of 1942 which allotted most of the disputed territory to Peru. Ecuador has denounced the Protocol, and the country's official policy remains the recovery of all the territories of the Audiencia of Quito. Border skirmishes occur at times although there has been no serious incident since 1981.

The first presidential and congressional election under the 1978 constitution took place on 29 April, 1979. Prior to then there had been military rule for seven years, attended by growing oil-based prosperity, until 10 August, 1979 when President Jaime Roldós Aguilera was inaugurated for a five-year term. His policy was to follow a programme of gradual reform. In May 1981, President Roldós was killed in an air crash and was succeeded by the vice-president, Osvaldo Hurtado Larrea. In 1984 President Hurtado handed power over to his elected successor and political opponent, the conservative Sr. León Febres Cordero, the first time in 23 years that such a transfer of power had occurred. President Febres Cordero's free market orientation was rejected by voters in the 1988 presidential and congressional elections. Rodrigo Borja, leader of the centre left Izquierda Democrática, was inaugurated as president on 10 August, 1988.

Population About 40% of Ecuador's 10,204,000 (1988) people are Indians, 40% *mestizo*, 10% European; the remainder are black or Asian. Roughly 48% live in the Costa region west of the Andes, and 47% in the Andean Sierra. Migration is occurring from the rural zones of both the coast and the highlands to the towns and cities, particularly Guayaquil and Quito, and agricultural colonization by highlanders is occurring in parts of the coastal lowlands and the Oriente. The population growth rate, 1980-83, was 2.9%; birth rate, 1980-85, 36.8. The mortality rate per 1,000 inhabitants is 8.1, while infant mortality per 1,000 live births is 69.6. About 15% of the inhabitants over 15 years of age are illiterate. 54% of the population is urban (living in a cantonal or provincial capital—urban growth rate 1981-88, 4.7%), and 46% is rural. National average population density is 30 per square kilometre, the highest in South America. Average income per head has risen fast in recent years like that of other oil-exporting countries, but the distribution has not improved and a few citizens are spectacularly wealthy.

The Economy In the early 1970s, Ecuador underwent a transformation from an essentially agricultural economy to a predominantly petroleum economy. From 1972 when substantial domestic oil output began, economic growth has largely followed the fortunes of the oil market, except in 1983, when freak weather conditions resulted in large crop losses. Agriculture's contribution (including fishing) to gdp has dwindled from over 22% in 1972 to less than 14% although it still employs a third of the labour force. The major export crops of bananas, coffee and cocoa are grown on the coast. Ecuador is the world's largest exporter of bananas, although it is not a member of the Union of Banana Exporting Countries (Upeb). Production is being promoted with increased plantings of high-yielding varieties and provision of technical assistance and quality control. Coffee is the most extensive of Ecuador's cash crops, accounting for over 20% of total agricultural land, but it is also the lowest yielding crop. Cocoa production has been increased by a rehabilitation programme after the 1983 floods, but although yields have trebled, output of 498 kg per hectare is still well below Brazil's 914 kg/ha.

Fishing is a growing industry, offering lucrative export potential. As well as tuna, sardines and white fish, shrimp is being caught in increasing amounts and is the most valuable catch. Shrimp farming is booming along the coast and has provided much-needed jobs for agricultural workers. Mining has been relatively unimportant historically, but the discovery of about 700 tonnes of gold reserves around Nambija (Zamora) in the southeast created intense interest in precious metals and over 12,000 independent miners rushed to prospect there. A new mining law was in preparation in 1990 designed to attract larger scale investment and introduce effective environmental controls over mining regions.

Although Ecuador's share of total world oil production is small (0.65%), foreign exchange earnings from oil exports are crucial to the economy. The main producing area is in the northern Oriente, and a 495-km. trans-Andean pipeline carries the oil to Esmeraldas on the coast, where it is refined and/or exported. There are also reserves of natural gas, mainly in the Gulf of Guayaquil, but these have not yet been fully developed. Hydroelectric potential is estimated at 90,000 MW, but generating capacity in the mid-1980s was only 2,000 MW. New projects on the Paute, Pastaza and Coca rivers could raise capacity to 12,000 MW by the end of the century.

Ecuador's foreign debt rose sharply in the 1970s when oil exports began and in the 1980s it joined other debtor nations in refinancing its external obligations. Adherence to free market economic policies in IMF programmes brought international approval and by 1985 Ecuador was widely acclaimed as a model debtor with sufficient creditworthiness to return to the voluntary market for loans. However, in 1986 oil prices crashed, cutting Ecuador's oil receipts by half, followed in 1987 by an earthquake which destroyed part of the trans-Andean pipeline and damaged other oil installations, causing a cessation of oil exports. It was clear that huge amounts of finance would be necessary for reconstruction of economic infrastructure and villages which had been destroyed. The effects on public finances were considerable, resulting in a higher rate of inflation. Subsequent loss of confidence in the Government's economic management resulted in a massive demand for dollars and a heavy devaluation of the sucre. Arrears on debt payments to all creditors built up in 1987 and 1988, and it was only in 1989 that the Government felt able to regularize some payments and begin negotiations with both official and private creditors.

Government There are 20 provinces, including the Galápagos Islands. Provinces are divided into cantons and parishes for administration.

Under the 1978 constitution, the vote was extended to include all literate citizens over the age of 18. The president and vice-president are elected for a five-year term. The president may not stand for re-election. The legislative branch consists of a single Chamber of Representatives of 71 members, which meets for two months of the year.

QUITO (1)

Quito (2,850 metres), with a population of 1,200,000, is within 25 km. of the equator, but it stands high enough to make its climate much like that of spring in England, the days warm or hot and the nights cool. Because of the height, visitors may initially feel some discomfort and should slow their pace for the first

24 hours. Mean temperature, 13°C, rainfall, 1,473 mm.; rainy season: Sept. to May with the heaviest rainfall in April, though heavy storms in July are not unknown. The day length (sunrise to sunset) is constant throughout the year.

Few cities have a setting to match that of Quito, the second highest capital in Latin America. The city is set in a hollow at the foot of the volcano Pichincha (4,794 metres). It was an Inca city, refounded by Sebastián de Benalcázar, Pizarro's lieutenant, in 1534. The city's charm lies in its colonial centre, where cobbled streets are steep and narrow, dipping to deep ravines. Through this section hurries the Machángara river, nowadays too polluted to wash clothes in. Westwards the valley is closed by Cerro Panecillo; from its top, 183 metres above the city level, there is a good restaurant and a fine view of the city below and the encircling cones of volcanoes and other mountains. There is a new statue on the hill to the Virgen de las Américas; Mass is held in the base on Sundays. There is a good view from the observation platform up the statue.

Warning On no account should you walk up the series of steps and paths to the Virgin which begin on García Moreno (where it meets Ambato) as assaults are very common: take a taxi up and leave your valuables behind.

The heart of the city is Plaza Independencia, dominated by a somewhat grim Cathedral (open 0800-1000, 1400-1600) with grey stone porticos and green tile cupolas. On its outer walls are plaques listing the names of the founding fathers of Quito, and inside are the tomb of Sucre (tucked away in a corner) and a famous Descent from the Cross by the Indian painter Caspicara. Beside the Cathedral, round the corner, is El Sagrario, originally built as the Cathedral chapel, now being restored. Facing the Cathedral is the old Archbishop's Palace, which has been renovated and now houses shops. On the northeast side is the new concrete Municipal Palace which fits in quite well, despite its material. The low colonial Palacio de Gobierno, on the northwest side of the Plaza, is silhouetted against the great flank of Pichincha (open 0900-1200, 1500-1800, free but you can only see the patio); on the first floor is a gigantic mosaic mural of Orellana discovering the Amazon, and the President's offices are on the second floor. The balconies looking over the main square are from the Tuilleries in Paris; a gift of the French government shortly after the French Revolution.

The best way to see old Quito is to walk its narrow streets. Wander down the Calle Morales, main street of La Ronda district (traditionally called Calle Ronda), one of the oldest streets in the city, past Plaza Santo Domingo to Carrera Guayaquil, the main shopping street, and on to shady Parque Alameda, which has the oldest astronomical observatory in South America (open Sat. 0900-1200). There are also a splendid monument to Simón Bolívar, various lakes, and in the NW corner a spiral lookout tower with a good view. The traditional colonial area is being preserved, with the buildings painted white and blue, but other parts of the city are being radically altered as a result of road improvements.

From Plaza Independencia two main streets, Carrera Venezuela and Calle García Moreno, lead straight towards the Panecillo to the wide Av. 24 de Mayo, at the top of which is a new concrete building where the Indians are supposed to do their trading since the street markets were officially abolished in 1981. Street trading still takes place, however, and there are daily street markets from Sucre down to 24 de Mayo and from San Francisco church west up past Cuenca.

Plaza San Francisco (or Bolívar) is west of Plaza Independencia; on the north-western side of this plaza is the great church and monastery of the patron saint of Quito, San Francisco, the earliest religious foundation in South America (1535), see below. Plaza Santo Domingo (or Sucre), to the south-east of Plaza San Francisco, has to the SE the church and monastery of Santo Domingo, with its rich wood-carvings and a remarkable Chapel of the Rosary to the right of the main altar. In the centre of the square is a statue to Sucre, pointing to the slopes of Pichincha where he won his battle against the Royalists. The modern University

City is on the NW side of the city, on the lower slopes of Pichincha by the Avenida de las Américas.

There are altogether 86 churches in Quito. The fine Jesuit church of **La Compañía**, in Calle García Moreno, one block from Plaza Independencia (open 0930-1100, 1600-1800) has the most ornate and richly sculptured façade and interior. See its coloured columns, its ten side altars and high altar plated with gold, and the gilded balconies. Several of its most precious treasures, including a painting of the Virgen Dolorosa framed in emeralds and gold, are kept in the vaults of the Banco Central del Ecuador and appear only at special festivals. Not far away to the north-east is the church of **La Merced**. In the monastery of La Merced is Quito's oldest clock, built in 1817 in London. Fine cloisters entered through door to left of altar. La Merced church contains many splendidly elaborate styles; note the statue of Neptune on the main patio fountain.

The church of **San Francisco** (open 0600-1200, 1430-1930), Quito's largest is said to be the first religious building constructed in South America by the Spanish and is rich in art treasures. The two towers were felled by an earthquake in 1868 and rebuilt. A modest statue of the founder, Fray Jodoco Ricke, the Flemish Franciscan who sowed the first wheat in Ecuador, stands at the foot of the stairs to the church portal. See the fine wood-carvings in the choir, a magnificent high altar of gold and an exquisite carved ceiling. There are some paintings in the aisles by Miguel de Santiago, the colonial *mestizo* painter. His paintings of the life of Saint Francis decorate the monastery of San Francisco close by. Adjoining San Francisco is the **Cantuña Chapel** with sculptures.

Many of the heroes of Ecuador's struggle for independence are buried in the monastery of **San Agustín** (Flores and Mejía), which has beautiful cloisters on 3 sides where the first act of independence from Spain was signed on 10 August, 1809. The church of **El Carmen Moderno** has a fine collection of Quito ceramics. In the recently restored monastery of **San Diego** are some unique paintings with figures dressed in fabrics sewn to the canvas -a curious instance of our present-day "collage". Ring the bell to the right of the church door to get in, entrance US$0.75, 0900-1200, 1500-1700, all visitors are shown around by a guide. Also **La Concepción**, Mejía and García Moreno; **San Blas**, Guayaquil and 10 de Agosto. The **Basílica of Guápulo** (1693), perched on the edge of a ravine SE of the city, is well worth seeing for its many paintings, gilded altars and the marvellously carved pulpit. Take bus 21 (Guápulo-Dos Puentes) from Plaza de Santo Domingo. Notice also the curious new "French Gothic" basilica under construction (since 1926) on a hill in the centre of the town. (You go up Carrera Venezuela to see it, puffing all the way, but it's worth while to see the local sculptors and stonecutters at work, if you can get friendly with the administrator.)

Note   A number of churches were temporarily closed after the 1987 earthquake and were still being restored in 1989. There are fears for the survival of La Compañía, El Sagrario and El Carmen Bajo, where the threat of subsidence from long term structural faults was compounded by earthquake damage.

Houses   The house of Sucre is at Venezuela 573, a beautiful restored house, open daily, entry free. The house of Benalcázar is on Olmeda with Benalcázar, a fully-restored colonial house. The house of Camilo Egas, a recent Ecuadorean artist, on Venezuela, has been restored by the Banco Central; it has different exhibitions during the year, entrance US$0.75.

Modern Quito extends northwards into a wide plain; it has broad avenues, fine private residences, parks, embassies and villas. Av. Amazonas, from Av. Patria to about Av. Colón, and the adjoining streets comprise Quito's modern tourist and business area: travel agencies, airlines, hotels and *residenciales*, exchange houses, moderate to expensive restaurants—several with sidewalk cafés, arts and crafts

Quito New City: key to map

1. Parque Andrade; 2. Plaza Rocafuerte; 3. Plaza Mantilla;4. Plaza Paul Rivet; 5. Iglesia Sta. Clara de San Millán; 6. Iglesia El Girón; 7. Iglesia Santa Teresa; 8. Iglesia El Belén; 9. Ministry of Public Works; 10. Ministry of External Relations; 11. Universidad Católica (museums); 12. Ministry of Finance; 13. Cultural Library; 14. Casa de la Cultura; 15. Nuevo Hospital Militar; 16. Colegio Milita; 17. Palacio de Justicia; 18. Palacio Legislativo; 19. Instituto Panamericano Geografía e Historia; 20. Instituto Geográfico Militar (IGM); 21. Ministry of Public Health; 22. Maternity Hospital; 23. Colegio Mejía (museum); 24. Consejo Provincial de Pichincha; 25. Astronomical Observatory; 26. Banco Central (museums); 27. DITURIS (Tourist Office); 28. Ecuadorian Tours (Amex); 29. Turismundial; 30. TAME; 31. SAETA and Red Cross; 32. Banco Holandés Unido and Dutch Consulate; 33. Lloyds Bank; 34. Casa de cambio "Rodrigo Paz"; 35. United States Embassy; 36. *Hotel Colón*; 37. *Alameda Real*; 38. *Tambo Real*; 39. *Residencia Los Alpes*; 40. *Hotel Embassy*; 41. *Inca Imperial*; 42. *Coral Internacional*; 43. *Libri Mundi*.

QUITO
NEW CITY
NOT TO SCALE   81

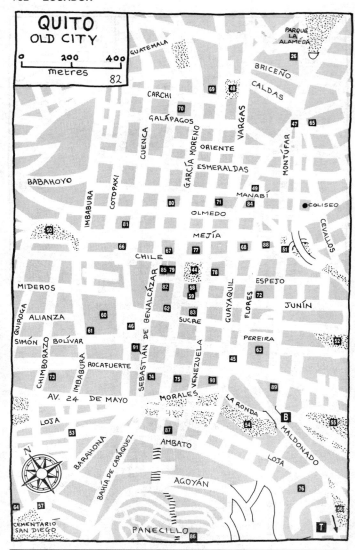

Quito Old City: key to map

44. Plaza Independencia; 45. Plaza Santo Domingo; 46. Plaza San Francisco; 47. Plaza de San Blas; 48. Plaza de Basílica; 49. Plaza del Teatro; 50. Plaza Hermano Miguel; 51. Plaza San Martín; 52. Plaza Lucinda Toledo; 53. Plaza Victoria; 54. Plaza M. Sáenz; 55. Plaza Santa Rosa;

stores and stalls, jewellery stores, book stores, car rental agencies, and pastry shops are all clustered in this neighbourhood. Av. Amazonas has British-style double-decker buses running along it and on to the airport, it is also open to private cars. On Sun. La Alameda and El Ejido parks are filled with local families.

Museums Quito prides itself on its art. Check museum opening times in advance. The **Casa de la Cultura Ecuatoriana**, a large circular building at the east side of Parque El Ejido, has good collection of Indian costumes, a picture gallery, the Natural History Museum previously in the Eloy Alfaro military college, an exhibition of Ecuadorean books, and a unique museum of musical instruments. Several of these museums were temporarily closed in 1989. (Normal opening hours: 0900-1230, 1500-1815, Tues.-Fri., 0930-1600 Sat.) There is a good collection of Ecuadorean sculptures and painting at the **Museum of Colonial Art**, on the corner of Cuenca and Mejía. The **Museo de San Francisco** has a fine collection of religious art, open 0900-1130, 1500-1730, entrance US$0.35, while the **Museo de Santo Domingo** has a further collection open Mon.-Fri., 0800-1100, 1500-1700, but not of quite the same quality. Similar collection in **Museo de San Agustín**, Chile y Guayaquil, open Mon.-Sat. 0830-1230, 1430-1800, interesting exhibition of restoration work (closed for reconstruction in 1990). The **Museo Jijón y Caamaño**, now housed in the Catholic University library building, has a private collection of archaeological objects, historical documents, portraits, uniforms, etc., very well displayed. Open 0900-1200, 1500-1800. Admission: US$0.30. There is also a Shuar ethnographic museum at the university. There are two first class museums in the Banco Central (Av. 10 de Agosto), the **Archaeological Museum** on the fifth floor (open Tues.-Sun. 0930-1500) with beautiful precolumbian ceramics and gold and a video film on Ecuadorean culture and the different Indian tribes, and the **Museo Colonial y de Arte Religioso** on the 6th (open Tues.-Fri. 0900-1700). There are guided tours in English, French and German—Entrance fee is US$0.75 for foreigners, US$0.35 for Ecuadoreans, US$0.20 for students, but free on Sunday. There is a fine museum in Bella Vista north east of Quito, **Museo Guayasamín**: as well as the eponymous artist's works there is a precolumbian and colonial collection; open Mon.-Fri. 0900-1230 and 1500-1830, Sat. 0900-1230, free admission. Works of art may be purchased. The museum is near the Channel 8 TV station, take Batán-Colmena bus no. 3 marked Bella Vista. Other museums: **Municipal Museum of Art and History**, Espejo 1147, near main plaza, was the old municipal offices, free; underneath is the cell where the revolutionaries of 1809 were executed (waxwork), cell reported closed indefinitely in 1987; **Museum of Ethnology**, Departamento de Letras, Ciudad Universitaria, Tues. to Fri. 0900-1230, Wed. and Fri. 1500-1700, Tues. and Thurs. 1500-1830; **Museo Histórico Casa de Sucre**, the beautiful house of Sucre on the corner of Venezuela and Sucre, open 0900-1200, 1300-1600, Tues.-Sat., closes 1500 Fri. **Museo de Artesanía**, 12 de Octubre y Madrid, and the **Museo de Arte Moderna**, 6 de Diciembre y Patria. The **Museo-Biblioteca Aureliano Polit** at the former Jesuit seminary beyond the airport has a unique collection of antique maps of Ecuador. Open Mon. to Fri. 0900-1200 and 1500-1800. Take the Condado minibus from the Plaza San Martín in Av. Pichincha. **Cima de los Libertadores**, museum at the site of the 1822 Battle of Pichincha, splendid view (open 0900-1200, 1500-1800). The Tourist Office recommends taking a taxi there as the suburbs are dangerous, but you can take a bus to the south of the city and walk up.

Note Quito has become a tourist centre and unfortunately, theft is on the increase, especially in parts of the old city. **N.B.** also: throughout Ecuador, you must carry your passport (not a copy) at all times.

Festivals A New Year *fiesta*, the Inocentes, from 28 Dec. to 6 Jan., fills the streets with people; much bitter satire on the politicians on 31 Dec., very entertaining and good-humoured (New Year's Day itself is very quiet, everything is shut). Another festival, for week ending 5

56. Plaza La Recoleta; 57. Plaza San Diego; 58. Cathedral; 59. El Sagrario chapel; 60. San Francisco church, monastery and museum; 61. Catuña chapel; 62. Iglesia de la Compañía; 63. Iglesia de Santo Domingo (museum); 64. Iglesia San Diego (convent and museum); 65. Iglesia de San Blas; 66. Basílica de la Merced; 67. Iglesia de la Concepción; 68. Iglesia de San Agustín (and museum); 69. The Basílica; 70. Iglesia San Juan; 71. Iglesia de Carmen Bajo; 72. Iglesia de Santa Catalina; 73. Iglesia San Roque; 74. Convent of Carmen Alto; 75. Hospital Chapel of San Juan de Dios; 76. Iglesia San Sebastián; 77. Archbishop's Palace; 78. Municipal Palace, including Tourist office; 79. Government Palace; 80. Instituto Ecuatoriano de Cultura Hispánica (Casa de Benalcázar); 81. Museum of Colonial Art; 82. Municipal Museum of Art and History; 83. Casa de Sucre (museum); 84. Teatro Sucre; 85. General Post Office; 86. Panecillo lookout and restaurant.
Hotels: 87. *Gran Casino*; 88. *Viena International*; 89. *Grand*; 90. *Caspicara*; 91. *Sucre*

Dec., celebrates foundation of city. Hotels allowed to charge extra. Bullfights, and music in streets. On 11 Dec., there is a children's day festival.

Carnival at Shrovetide is celebrated, as elsewhere in the Andes, by throwing plastic bags of water at passers-by (especially tourists), so you need a raincoat and umbrella at that season. The Good Friday processions are most impressive. Fancy-dress parades for Hallowe'en, celebrated last Sat. in October, along Av. Amazonas.

Hotels Note that major hotels change their prices daily in line with the devaluation of the sucre. In these establishments foreigners are expected to pay in dollars. *Quito*, González Suárez, with pool, A, meals dear, often room on weekdays as business travellers prefer the more central *Colón Internacional*, Amazonas y Patria, L, excellent food, good discotheque, shopping arcade, casino and many useful services, non-residents should dress neatly for best service. The *Colón* is in the **New City**, others in this part of Quito are: *Alameda Real*, Amazonas y Roca, L, can be booked through KLM airline, all rooms are suites and many have kitchenettes, rec.; *Oro Verde*, 12 de Octubre y Cordero, L, Swiss-run, pool, casino, restaurants.

Tambo Real, 12 de Octubre y Patria opp. US Embassy, C, rec., ideal for business visitors, casino, restaurant slow and extras can mount up; *Chalet Suisse*, Calama 312 y Reina Victoria, B, good except for restaurant; *Residencia Los Alpes*, Tamayo 233 y Washington, B, behind US Embassy, popular with Americans, "alpine" interior, clean, friendly, comfortable, water pressure poor on third floor, rec.; *Hostería Los Andes*, Muros 146 behind British Embassy, D, spotlessly clean, hot water, cable TV, family run, all speak fluent English, rec.; *Dan*, Av. 10 de Agosto 2482, E, a/c, private bathrooms, noisy rooms on Avenida, good food, services and laundry, rec. *Ambassador*, 9 de Octubre 1046 y Colón, C with bath, partially renovated, clean, friendly, rec; *9 de Octubre*, 9 de Octubre 1047 y Colón, E, shower, sporadic warm water, quick laundry service, safe deposit; *Res. Dapsilia*, 9 de Octubre 650 nr. Dávalos, T 550-529, E, good, hot showers, clean, parking, meals, rec.; *Residencial Italia*, Av. 9 de Octubre 237, G, clean, rather cold at night, family-run, rec.; *Residencial Cumbres*, Baquedano 148 y Av. 6 de Diciembre, D, good value, clean, helpful, large breakfast; *Royal Inn*, 6 de Diciembre 2751, E, comfortable, helpful owner; *Residencial Los Angeles*, Luis Cordero y 6 de Diciembre, F, popular with Peace Corps, often full. *Pickett*, Pres. Wilson near J.L. Mera, E, reliable hot water; *Embassy*, Pres. Wilson 441 y 6 de Diciembre, D, highly rec., clean, well furnished, showers, parking, good French restaurant; *6 de Diciembre*, Av. 6 de Diciembre 1230, D, private bath, quiet, comfortable. *Residencial Santa Clara*, Gustavo Darquea Terán 1578, F, just off 10 de Agosto, clean, laundry service, will store luggage, rec., some English spoken; *Residencial Carrión*, Carrión 1250 y 10 de Agosto, E, 20 rooms with bath, restaurant, bar, good value; *Majestic*, Mercadillo 366 y Versalles, E, has seen better days but clean, quiet and friendly; *Residencial St. James*, Versalles 1075 y Carrión, E, clean, friendly, rec.; *Residencial Indoamericano*, Pérez Guerrero 477 y Versalles, E, clean. Further north are *República*, Av. República y Azuay, D, clean, reasonable; *Zumay*, Av. 10 de Agosto y Mariana de Jesús, D, clean, hot showers, no water after midnight, laundry service; and *Res. Román*, Av. Tomás de Berlanga 531, near airport, T 248-289, parking.

In between the new and old cities are: *Coral Internacional*, Manuel Larrea 164, E, spacious, popular with families, clean, cafeteria, open 0730-2200; *Inca Imperial*, Bogotá 219, D with bath, hot water, Inca style with lavish decor, excellent value, restaurant variable, laundry service expensive, car park; *Hostal El Ejido*, Juan Larrea 535 y Riofrío, E, clean, hot water, overpriced; *Residencial Portoviejo*, Portoviejo y Av. América, G, clean, free luggage store, rec.; *Residencial Dorado*, 18 de Septiembre 805, F, intermittent water, basic, higher standard, dearer wing across the street; *Residencial Marsella*, Los Ríos 2035, G, clean, safe, friendly, good rooftop terrace with views over Parque La Alameda, top floor rooms rec., luggage store, laundry facilities, good breakfasts, convenient location; *Atahualpa*, Manuel Larrea y Riofrío, G, convenient location, basic, no hot water, clean, safe, friendly. *Oriente*, Yaguachi 824 y Llona (nr. Instituto Geográfico Militar), T 546157, F, with bath and kitchen, safe, family-run, discounts for longer stays.

In the **Old City**: *Real Audiencia*, Bolívar 220, D, spacious, well furnished rooms, front rooms a bit noisy, TV, laundry service, baggage stored, highly rec., restaurant; *Benalcázar*, Plaza San Francisco, friendly, safe, laundry facilities, rec.; *Sucre*, Plaza San Francisco, G, friendly, helpful, water tepid, laundry facilities, free luggage store, roof top views; *Quitumbe*, Espejo 815 y Flores, F, clean, secure, rec. but not enough bathrooms, street-facing rooms noisy; *Gran Casino*, García Moreno y Ambato, F, famous gringo hangout, rooms and beds have seen better days, dirty and noisy but a popular meeting place, sauna, cheap laundry service and cheap restaurant, theft from rooms reported, you either love it or hate it; round the corner, same owner, better quality is *Gran Casino Internacional*, 24 de Mayo y Bahía, E, clean, luggage store, good restaurant, own travel agency which sells trips to the Galápagos and Oriente (see under Travel Agencies); *Viena Internacional*, Flores y Chile, D, English spoken, hot water in mornings, phone, laundry, good meals, safe, opposite is *Viena*, F, clean, hot water, friendly, safe, rec.; *San Agustín*, Flores 626 y Chile, E with bath, clean, hot water, rooms expensive, restaurant variable; *Canarias*, Flores 856, F, rec.; *Huasi Continental*, Flores y Sucre, F, hot water, quiet, clean, friendly, good value; *Montúfar*, Sucre 162, F, clean, safe, highly rec.; *Hogar*, Montúfar 208, F, parking, luggage store; *Rumiñahui*, Montúfar 449 y Junín, E, safe, laundry facilities, excellent restaurant, good value; *Italia*, Junín y Flores, G, new, clean, basic, hot showers, safe, quiet, thin mattresses, friendly, family-run; *Yumba Imperial*, Guayaquil near Plaza Santo Domingo, F, clean, safe, friendly, quiet, laundry facilities, top rooms overlook old city, rec.; *Santo Domingo*, Plaza Santo Domingo, G; *Venezia*, Rocafuerte y Venezuela, G, clean, water tepid, often full.

In the vicinity of the Terminal Terrestre: *Grand*, Rocafuerte 1001 (T210192/519756), F, clean, safe, friendly, restaurant, highly rec.; *Caspicara*, Rocafuerte, corner of Plaza, G, clean, big rooms, hot water, good value, noisy, friendly, but watch your belongings; *Juana de Arco*, Rocafuerte 1311 y Maldonado, F, only back rooms with shower, front rooms cheaper but noisier, good restaurant next door. Many cheap hotels on Calle Morales, e.g. *Cumandá*, No. 449, E, comfortable, showers, rec., clean, safe, noisy from proximity to bus station but quieter at the back; *Syris*, G, hot water, safe, laundry; *Pensión Ramírez*, No. 781. On Maldonado: *Colonial*, No. 3035, F, G without shower, hot water (most of the time), clean, safe, quiet, laundry, cheaper annex; *Amazonas*, No. 915, F, safe, cold water, restaurant (often closed); *Indoamericano*, No 3022, F, tepid water in a.m., well furnished, clean, washing facilities; *Ingatur*, No 3226, F, hot water, clean, washing facilities, safe; opposite is *Capitalino*, G, pleasant, hot water; *Guayaquil No.1*, No. 3248, F, hot water, will store luggage for small fee, safe, basic. Many also on Loja in the red light district.

If you prefer not to stay in a hotel, Rolf Hebling, Veintimilla 531, T 233013, provides accommodation in his house, US\$5, rec. *Casa Paxi*, F, Pasaje Navarro 364 y Av. La Gasca, T 542-663, complete with cooking facilities, telephone and roof terrace, owned by Dutch guide Pieter van Bunningen; *Denmark House*, Ulloa 1710 y Cuero y Caicedo, T237-195, G p.p., cooking facilities, good information.

For longer stays with room, kitchen, TV, laundry service etc., the following have been recommended: *Suites Ejecutivos*, 10 de Agosto 4032 y Rumibamba, F, US\$150 a month; *Apartamentos Colón*, Leonidas Plaza 326, Casilla Postal 2103, T 230360, US\$320 a month for two people; *Apartamentos Calima*, Luis Cordero y 10 de Agosto, US\$140 a month for two people. Rates depend on length of stay and number of people. *Aparthotel El Sol* has suites for two people, Av. Orellana 1757, between 10 de Agosto y 9 de Octubre, T 524150, also suites for between 1 and 5 people. A self-contained flat with 4 bedrooms, kitchen, bathroom, laundry service, is available for rent from Sra. Blanca Espinales T., Lugo 115 y Laobrón de Guevara T 560601. Apartments for rent are advertised in *El Comercio*, though it is difficult to rent for under 6 months.

Note Those travelling by car may have difficulty parking in the centre of Quito and are therefore advised to choose the less central hotels.

Restaurants There are few restaurants in the Old City, although these tend to be cheaper, with more local and fast food types, than in the New City, where more foreign styles can be found. It is difficult to find places to eat in the Old City in the evenings, especially after 2200.

Many restaurants throughout the city close on Sun. **N.B.** Prices listed are often inaccurate. Restaurants with stickers indicating acceptance of credit cards do not necessarily do so. Check first. The following list is by type; all restaurants are in the New City unless otherwise stated.

International Excellent food at *Hotel Colón Internacional* for non-residents, Sun. buffet rec., US$6; cheaper in snack bar, 3-course lunch US$4, buffet breakfast US$4.50, excellent pastry shop too in the *Hotel Quito*, *Techo del Mundo* restaurant and *Cayambe* coffee shop are good; *Rincón La Ronda*, Belo Horizonte 400 y Almagro, excellent food but expensive, often has folklórico shows in evenings. *Excalibur*, Calama 380, expensive; in the north of the city is *La Vista Real*, Sun. buffet US$4 p.p.

Ecuadorean and General In the Old City: *Viena*, Chile y Flores; *Oasis*, Espejo 812, large helpings, good vegetables, clean, cheap, quick but can get very busy; *El Criollo*, Flores 825, clean, big helpings, very cheap, no alcohol, specialities; *Inti*, Mariana de Jesus y Hungría, typical, good service; *Monaco*, García Moreno y 24 de Mayo, cheap; *Gran Plaza*, Espejo y Guayaquil, huge meals for US$1.50, tasty, good value, rec.; *Los Olivos*, near Santo Domingo church, Ecuadorean, clean, good service, economical; *Café Madrillón*, Chile 1270 y Benalcázar, rec.; *Cafetería Dominó*, Venezuela y Mejía, cheap lunches, snacks, juices especially naranjila, good for breakfast and coffee; cheap meals in the market behind the shoe shops on Flores y Olmedo, 1130-1400. In the New City: *Mamá Clorinda*, Reina Victoria y Calama, Ecuadorean, cheap; *Cafetería Matrioshka*, Pinto 376 y Juan León Mera, good food and value; *La Choza*, 12 de Octubre y Cordero, typical Ecuadorean food; *Terraza del Tártaro*, Veintimilla 1106 y Amazonas (no sign), top of building, good views, good value, pleasant atmosphere; *El Padrino*, Bossano y 6 de Diciembre, clean, good Ecuadorean food, cheap; *El Peñón*, 10 de Agosto, popular with locals, mixed reports (avoid chicken).

French *Rincón de Francia*, Roca 779 y 9 de Octubre, highly rec., reservation essential; *Le Bistrot*, González Suárez, good steak Chateaubriand, live music at 2100, closed Sun.; *Fondue Bar*, Juan Rodríguez 175, fondues and French, reasonable prices, closed Sun., Mon. *La Marmite*, Mariano Aguilera 287, good food; *La Peche Mignon*, Belo Horizonte 338 y 6 de Diciembre, expensive but good; *Rincón de Borgoña*, Eloy Alfaro 2407, run by former waiters of *Rincón de Francia*, excellent; *Chantilly*, Roca 736 y Amazonas, restaurant and bakery, good and reasonably priced; *La Fite*, La Niña 559 y J.L. Mera, good; *La Belle Epoque*, Whimper 925 y 6 de Diciembre, very good. *Chalet Suisse*, Calama 312 y Reina Victoria, good steaks and some Swiss dishes, expensive but very good; **German** *El Ciervo*, Dávalos 270 y Páez, good food but slow service, German newspapers available; *Taverna Bavaria*, Cordero y Juan León Mera, good food, friendly atmosphere but not cheap, German, French and English spoken, tours to mountains, Oriente and Galápagos arranged; *Der Rhein*, 6 de Diciembre 3467 y Bélgica, German owner, very clean, good service, excellent food but expensive.

Middle-eastern *Chawarma*, Amazonas 1215, excellent; *Scherezade*, Calama 329, Arabian food, excellent salad bar, reasonably priced.

Spanish *La Rana Verde*, Juan León Mera near Veintimilla, good tapas and more, reasonably priced; *Costa Vasca*, 18 de Septiembre 553, entre Páez y 9 de Octubre, good food and atmosphere; *Casa Española*, Calama entre J.L. Mera y Reina Victoria, similar, flamenco on occasions; *El Hobo*, Amazonas 3837, steaks and paella, English spoken. In the Old City, *Las Cuevas de Luis Candela*, Benálcazar y Chile and Orellana y Coruña, not cheap, closed Sun. *El Limonar*, Juan Rodríguez 228 y Reina Victoria, good food, excellent value; *La Vieja Castilla*, La Pinta 435 y Amazonas, very good; *La Paella Valenciana*, República y Almagro, good value; *La Puerta de Alcalá*, Lizardo García y J.L. Mera, very good and cheap.

Italian *La Gritta*, Santa María 246, entre La Rábida y Reina Victoria, home made pasta, very good; *Trattoria del Veneziano*, Roca 562 y J.L. Mera, good, but wine expensive; *La Bettola*, Cordero 11-87 y J.L. Mera, rec.; *Taberna Piemonte*, Av. Eloy Alfaro, above stadium, excellent, expensive; *La Trattoria de Renato*, San Javier y Orellana, nice atmosphere, expensive, *Vecchia Roma*, Roca 618, good food and atmosphere, pricey; *Via Margutta*, Salazar 1093 y 12 de Octubre, expensive, pretentious; *Michele*, Páez 259 y J. Washington, very good; *Marina Yate*, Calama 369 y J.L. Mera, good, medium price. *Pizza El Hornero*, Amazonas 853, excellent pizzas cooked over wood, highly rec.; *Roy's Cervecería y Pizzería*, Amazonas nr. Orellana and in Centro Comercial Naciones Unidas, good; *Farina Pizzería*, Carrión, entre J.L. Mera y Av. Amazonas, very good; *Pizza Nostra*, Amazonas 252 y Washington, not cheap. In Old City, *Pizza Hut*, on Espejo down hill from Plaza Independencia, very friendly service but not cheap; *Master Pizza*, Amazonas between Robles and Roca, good; *Exxus Pizzas*, Los Shyris near Parque La Carolina, good pizzas with large-screen video.

Latin American and US *Churrasqueria El Toro Partido*, Amazonas y Veintimilla, cold buffet and meat at US$2 for as much as you can eat, good; *La Guarida del Coyote*, Carrión 619 y Amazonas, and at Jápon 542 y Naciones Unidas, good Mexican food, pleasant atmosphere; *Bom Bocado Paratí*, Pinto y Amazonas (opposite Varig office), small restaurant with best Brazilian dishes in town; *Churruscaría Tropeiro*, Veintimilla 564 y 6 de Diciembre, Brazilian-style, good salad bar; *Tex Mex*, Reina Victoria 225 y 18 de Septiembre, closed Sun., good food, lively; *Rincón Ecuatoriano Chileno*, 6 de Diciembre y Oriano, delicious, rec. *Rincón Cubano*, Amazonas 993 y Veintimilla, Cuban, rec. *Hyatt*, Juan León Mera y Bruna, southern US menu, very select; *Adam's Rib*, Juan León Mera, American ribs, good atmosphere, small portions, expensive, jazz concerts from 2200 on Fri. *Bentley's*, J.L. Mera y Robles, expensive.

Fast Food *Self-service Americano*, 10 de Agosto 666 y Chota, clean, pleasant setting; there is an imitation *MacDonalds* on Av. Amazonas y Cordero; *Dimpy* on Amazonas and in most shopping centres, quick service, hot dogs, sandwiches, etc.; *Manolo's Churrería*, Amazonas 420 y Robles, reasonable but snacks; *Mario's*, Amazonas 410 y Roca, good hamburgers and coffee, popular; *Tom Pollo*, 6 de Diciembre, good, inexpensive; *Bocadillos*, Luis Cordero, just west of Amazonas, good sandwiches and juices; *Super Papas*, 6 de Diciembre 1329 y Roca, delicious stuffed baked potatoes, some vegetarian, excellent cakes, takeaway service, inexpensive, highly rec. *Tip Top*, basement of Ecuatoriana building, Reina Victoria y Colón, good breakfasts and tasty lunches, inexpensive; *Pym's*, Calama just off Amazonas, good hamburgers, wide menu, cozy; next door is *Dickens*, hamburgers, steaks, cheeses and snacks. In the Old City: *Kentucky Fried Chicken* opp. Post Office on Plaza Santo Domingo and on Benalcázar; *Pollo Gus*, 24 de Mayo 1246 y Moreno, self-service chicken and meat cooked on open fire, waitress service downstairs; *Pollo Broster*, Sucre 258 y Venezuela, good also for ice cream, bread and pastries. Other inexpensive spit-roasted chicken places throughout Old City, e.g. *Piko Riko*.

Steak *Casa de mi Abuela*, J.L. Mera 1649, steak and salad, rec.; *Columbus* steak house, Colón 1262 y Amazonas, good value, popular. *Papy Zuko's*, Colombia y Luis Sodiro (near Parque La Alameda), excellent steaks, modern restaurant with video, good value; *El Toro House*, Washington 885 y Páez, all the meat you can eat, great salads. **Seafood** *Moby Dick*, Amazonas 272; *La Jaiba*, Reina Victoria y Colón; *Los Redes de Mariscos*, Amazonas 845 y Veintimilla, excellent food, lovely atmosphere, wines expensive, highly rec. (closed Sun. p.m.); under same management but more upmarket, *Mare Nostrum*, Foch 172 y Tamayo, excellent. *El Cebiche*, J.L. Mera 1232 y Calama, and on Amazonas, delicious seafood, best ceviche in town.

Oriental *Chifa Feliz*, Carrión 661 y Amazonas, specializes in vegetarian (tofu) dishes, excellent, friendly; *Pekin*, Bello Horizonte 197; *Chifa Gran Pino*, Colón y Juan León Mera, good; *Kontike*, Whimper 1094 y Diego de Almagro, Hawaiian, very good; *Chifa Mayflower*, 6 de Diciembre y Robles, good Chinese food; *Chifa El Chino*, Bolívar y Guayaquil in Old City, good cheap lunch.

Vegetarian *La Cabaña*, Cordero 1489 y Amazonas, friendly, excellent food, but expensive; *El Márquez*, Veintimilla 315 y Plaza, good; *Herbal Centro Vegetariano*, Colón 1485, good lunches; *Govinda* (Hare Krishna), Versalles 1738 y Colón, good; *Girasól*, Oriente 581 y Vargas, cheap. The British Council does a good vegetarian lunch.

Pastry Shops/Bakeries The *Pastelería* in the *Hotel Colón* building is excellent; *Casa de Pan*, Rocafuerte y García Moreno, described as best bakery in Old City; *El Cyrano*, Portugal y Shyris, highly rec., French owner also runs ice cream shop *Corfu* next door. *El Túnel*, Amazonas 1036 y Pinto, excellent; *Panadería Sevilla*, Edificio Torre Reina, Luis Cordero, try the sweets; *Baguette*, Amazonas y Mariana de Jesús, sells good pasteurized cheeses; good cheeses and meats at *Delicatessen Español* next to Libri Mundi, Juan León Mera y Veintimilla; *Panadería Nap*, Colón, just N of Amazonas, good, wide selection, several branches; *Pastelería Frederica*, 10 de Agosto 679, rec. for very fresh cachos. *Top Cream*, Naciones Unidas, nr. Amazonas, and on 6 de Diciembre, for high-quality ice cream; *La Frutería*, Colón 958, serves the "best fruit salad in Ecuador". In **Old City**, *El Torreón*, on Plaza del Teatro, good for cakes, juices, ice creams and sandwiches, though a little more expensive than usual.

Bars In New City: *Rumors*, Juan León Mera at Veintimilla, popular with Peace Corps, good atmosphere, not cheap; *Caento*, J.L.Mera, jungle theme, English spoken, pool table, popular; *El Pub*, opp. *Hotel Quito*, English menu, including fish and chips. In Old City, Teatro Bolívar has a good wine bar.

Bookshops *Libri Mundi*, Juan León Mera 851 y Veintimilla and at the *Hotel Colón Internacional*, Spanish, English (some second-hand available), French, some Italian books, international magazines, records, Ecuadorean maps when in stock, has a notice-board of what's on in Quito; very highly recommended. *Librería Universitaria*, García Moreno 739; *Su Librería*, books in English and German, García Moreno 1172 y Mejía; *Librería Científica*, Av. Colón y Juan León Mera; *Librería Cima*, Av. 10 de Agosto 285 y Sta. Prisca, good selection in Spanish; *Pomaire*, Av. Amazonas 863 (Spanish mainly). *Ediciones Abya-Yala*, 12 de Octubre 14-36 (T 562-633). The United States Information Service has an excellent library. *Biblioteca Luz*, Vargas 218 y Esmeraldas, runs a book exchange (mainly Spanish) charge US$1. Foreign newspapers at newsstand in *Hotel Colón* which also has a comfortable reading room open to non-residents.

Shopping Articles typical of Ecuador can be bought in the main shopping districts centred on Avenidas Amazonas and Guayaquil or at the two main markets. One of these, Mercado Ipiales, on Chile from Imbabura uphill, is where you are most likely to find your stolen camera for sale. The other is on 24 de Mayo and Loja from Benalcázar onwards. There are carved figures, plates and other items of local woods, balsa wood boxes, silver of all types, Indian textiles, buttons, toys and other things fashioned from tagua nuts, hand-painted tiles, hand-woven rugs and a variety of antiques dating back to colonial days. Panama hats are a good buy; *Eljuri*, Chile 1062. Indian garments (for Indians rather than tourists) can be seen and bought on the north end of the Plaza Sucre and along the nearest stretch of the nearby Calle General Flores. *Ocepa*, at Carrión 1336 y Versalles, good selection, government-run, also Jorge Washington 252 y Amazonas, near *Hotel Colón*, Amazonas 2222 and *La Granja*, and in Old City on Espejo y Venezuela; branches also in Guayaquil and Cuenca. Near *Hotel Quito* at Av. Colón 260 is *Folklore*, the store of Olga Fisch, a most attractive array of handicrafts and rugs, but distinctly expensive, as accords with the designer's international reputation; also at *Hotel Colón* and *Hotel Quito*.

Productos Andinos, an artisans' co-operative, Urbina 111 y Cordero, good quality, reasonably priced, recommended; there is a smaller branch store at Robles 900 y 9 de Octubre. After it in quality is *Artes*, Av. 6 de Diciembre 1118 y Veintimilla. *La Bodega Exportadora*, Juan León Mera 614 y Carrión, is recommended for antiques and handicrafts, and so is *Renacimiento*, Carrión y Mera. *Galería Latina*, next to Libri Mundi at J.L.Mera 823 y Veintimilla, has fine selection of handicrafts from Ecuador, Peru and Bolivia; *Centro Artesanal*, Juan León Mera 804, *El Aborigen*, Washington 536 y J.L. Mera and *Ecuafolklore*, Robles 609 entre Amazonas y J.L. Mera, have all been recommended. *Coosas*, Juan León Mera 838, the factory outlet for Peter Mussfeldt's attractive animal designs (bags, clothes etc.). Goldwork from *Antigüedades el Chordeleg*, 6 de Diciembre y Cordero. *Artesanías El Jaguar*, Juan León Mera 234 and 18 de Septiembre, behind *Hotel Colón*, souvenirs especially from the Oriente, the owner, Gladis Escobar, paints balsawood birds in colours of your choosing (not cheap). Ceramics made by Shirma Guayasamín at *Tierra y Fuego*, 6 de Diciembre y Veintimilla. *Handicrafts Otavalo*, Calle Sucre 255 and García Moreno, good selection, but expensive.

On Av. Amazonas, NE of *Hotel Colón*, are a number of street stalls run by Otavalo Indians, who are tough but friendly bargainers. Bargaining is customary in small shops and at street stalls. Recommended shops include *Hamiltons*, for jewellery, *El Huaquero*, Juan León Mero, good jewellery, not cheap, and *Bonita Fashions* where you can have a leather jacket made to order in 48 hours. Leather goods at *Chimborazo*, Amazonas (next to Espinal shopping centre) and *Aramis*, Amazonas 1234; *Camari*, Marchena 260, is a direct sale shop run by an artisan organisation. See *H. Stern's* jewellery stores at the airport, *Hotel Colón* and *Hotel Quito*. Recommended watchmaker, Sr. Torres, *Relojería Patek Phillipe*, Mejía 329. *La Guaragua*, Washington 614, sells *artesanías* and antiques, excellent selection, reasonable prices; *Joe Brenner* sells folk art and handicrafts at reasonable prices at Galería Sul, Pontevedra 698 y Salazar near *Hotel Quito*, recommended for quality and price. *El Scarabejo Azul*, Portugal 948 y Shyris, near southern end of La Carolina, Indian handicrafts and works by modern craftsmen using indigenous materials. Rainproof ponchos at shops along Flores between Espejo and Bolívar. *Casa de los Regalos*, Calle Mañosca 456, for souvenirs and antiquities. "Typical" articles tend to be cheaper outside Quito.

Supermaxi supermarkets offer 10% discount on purchases if you buy a Supermaxi card; this is available at the main counter. There are Supermaxi stores at the Centro Comercial Iñaquito and at the Multicentro shopping complex on Av. 6 de Diciembre y La Nina, about two blocks N of Colón, open 0830-1230, 1530-1900. Multicentro on Amazonas on the way to the airport; buy masks and snorkels for the Galápagos here. El Feria supermarket on Calle Bolívar between Venezuela and G.Morena sells good wines and Swiss, German and Dutch cheeses. Cheap food at Frigorífico Los Andes, Calle Guayaquil. Casa Americana, on Venezuela, inexpensive department store.

"*Bluet Camping Gas*" is reported to be easily obtainable: try Importadora Vega opp. Banco Central, or Deportes Cotopaxi, 6 de Diciembre y Baquedano, or Globo, 10 de Agosto, sometimes have it in stock but it's expensive. For primus stoves and parts, Almacenes Jácome, Chile 955 (nr. Guayaquil). For hiking boots, Calzado Beltrán, Cuenca 562. For mosquito nets, hunting and climbing gear: Capitán Peña, Flores 200 y Bolívar.

Camera Repairs and Equipment Foto Gómez, Olmedo 827; Gustavo Gómez, Asunción 130 y 10 de Agosto, Ed. Molina, 1st floor; Maxi Color, Amazonas 1700 y Orellana, one hour processing service, English spoken; Kodak, Orellana 476 y 6 de Diciembre, also at 10 de Agosto 4150 y Atahualpa; Fujicolor, Roca y Gutiérrez; Kis Colour, Amazonas 1238 y Calama, will develop and print 36 exposure film for US$7. Several places for cheap processing on Plaza Santo Domingo. Interfoto, Juan León Mera 1567, and Foto Estudio Gran, Simón Bolívar 140 y Plaza Santo Domingo for repairs and parts. Film is reportedly cheaper than in neighbouring countries but only ASA100 and 200 available.

Local Transport Standard fare on local buses and *busetas* is US$0.06, slightly more after 1900 and at weekends. The British style double-decker bus running along Áv. Amazonas to the airport costs US$0.10. Other buses are allowed along Av. Amazonas only before 0830. All tickets are bought on the bus; correct fare is sometimes expected. Standard **taxi** tariff in the city is US$0.60 to US$2 and not more than double by night; no increase for extra passengers; by the hour, US$4 up. Although the taxis now have meters and are required by law to use them, drivers sometimes say they are out of order, particularly at the airport. Insist on the meter being used, it is always cheaper! If they have no meter, it is imperative to fix fare beforehand. After dark meters do not apply: negotiate fare first. For trips outside Quito taxi tariffs should be agreed beforehand: usually US$30-32 a day. Outside main hotels cooperative taxi drivers have a list of agreed excursion prices which compare favourably with tourist excursion prices; most drivers are knowledgeable and speak some English.

Car Rentals All the main car rental companies (Hertz, International Avis, Ecuacar, Budget, Dollar and Carros Diligentes) are at the airport, with some having small offices in the city. It is best to ignore these and catch bus directly to the airport. Ecuacar has been particularly recommended. **Land Rover** specialists at Calle Inglaterra 533, Talleres Atlas. Also Luis Alfredo Palacios, Iturralde and Av. de la Prensa, T 234341 and Expo, Av.América 1116 y Bolivia. 24-hour filling station where Baeza road enters Quito.

Night Clubs *Licorne*, at *Hotel Colón Internacional*; discos at *JK*, Amazonas 541, *Mamma Rosa*, Amazonas 553, *Tobujas*, Amazonas y María, *La Diligencia*, 9 de Octubre 158, *Luis XVI*, Cordero 994 y Foch, rec.; *Castaway*, mainly for couples, Colón y Amazonas; *Gato Son*, Carvajal y Aldama, salsa, popular, bohemian atmosphere; *Salsa Bar*, Carrión y Reina Victoria, salsa disco. *Salsoteca*, Salazar, but relocating in 1990, good salsa disco, friendly; *Candela*, J.L. Mera, salsa; *Club 330*, Whimper y Coruña, "only for the cool". *Tulsa*, República 471 next to Ciné República, is a dance hall frequented by US expatriates (country and western and some salsa).

Local folk music is popular and the entertainment is known as a *peña*. Places include *Lira Quiteña*, Amazonas y Orellana; *Rincón Sentimental* and *Pan y Canto*, both at Veintimilla y 6 de Diciembre; *Peña del Castillo*, Calama 270 y Reina Victoria; *Billy Cutter*, Cordero 1952; *Guayusas Bar*, Juan León Mera 555, good music, reasonable prices, rec., but small, T 553-274; *Peña del Chino*, and *Ñucanchi Llacta*, both at Rodríguez y Almagro; *Las Jarras* and *Inti Illimani*, both at Baquedano y Reina Victoria. Most places do not come alive until 2230.

Theatre Teatro Sucre, Calle Flores with Guayaquil, the most elegant (box office down side-street, Montúfar, and is unmarked—brown door). Weekly concerts during the rainy season, but buy tickets in advance. Symphony concerts are free. Teatro Prometeo adjoining the Casa de la Cultura Ecuatoriana, 6 de Diciembre y Tarqui. Agora, open-air theatre of Casa de la Cultura (12 de Octubre y Patria) stages many concerts. Also, plays at the Patio de Comedia, 18 de Septiembre, between Amazonas and 9 de Octubre. Good music at Teatro Equitorial Experimental; check posters in Plaza Teatro for details. Centro Cultural Afro-Ecuatorian (CCA), Calle José Luis Tamayo 985 y Lizardo Garúa, Casilla 352, Sucursal 12 de Octubre, T 522318, sometimes has cultural events and published material (useful contact for those interested in the black community). Many cultural events, usually free of charge; see the listings section of *El Comercio* for details.

Cinema The Colón (10 de Agosto y Colón), República (Av. República) and Universitario (Av. América, Plaza Indoamérica, Universidad Central) usually have the best films, the former often has documentaries with Latin American themes. There are many others, especially in the Old City; usually there is a standard entry charge (US$1 or less)—stay as long as you like.

Sport A local game, *pelota de guante* (stone ball), is played, Saturday afternoon and Sunday, at Estadio Mejía. Football is played Sat. afternoons (1200 or 1400) and Sun. mornings (maybe as early as 0800) at Estadio Atahualpa (6 de Diciembre y Naciones Unidas, any northbound bus on 6 de Diciembre marked "Estadio" goes there), and basketball in the Coliseo. The first week of December is the main bullfighting season. Tickets are on sale at 1500 the day before the bullfight; an above-average ticket costs US$2.70 but you may have to buy from touts. There is a cold spring-water swimming pool on Maldonado beyond the Ministry of Defence building (US$0.10), hot shower (US$0.10); a public heated pool is in Villaflora, at the end of Calle Universitaria, you must take towel and soap to be admitted. Rugby is played at Colegio Militar on Sun. 1000. Inquire at *El Pub*.

Climbing Nuevos Horizontes Club, Venezuela 659, T 215135, on Pasaje Amador near Plaza Independencia, meets evenings (1900 or 2000), will advise on **climbing Chimborazo and Cotopaxi**, including purchase or hire of crampons, ice axes etc., but does not hire them (best to have with you). Non-members may go on the club's trips if these are not fully-booked. Padre José Ribas of Colegio San Gabriel is helpful. **Sr. Enrique Veloz** of Riobamba arranges

trips to Chimborazo (**see page 779**). Useful climbing equi[p, information) are Equipo Cotopaxi, 6 de Diciembre 1557, Altamc [...]
y Armero, Campo Abierto, 6 de Diciembre y Roca (closed weeker. [...]
de Diciembre 1329 y Roca, T 232149 or home 261873. Usual charg[...]
is US$1-2 per item per day, plus US$60 deposit in cash or cheques; store [...]
equipment. Freddy Ramírez, who runs Sierra Nevada, highly rec. as a moun [...]
and his brother Milton speak English and French and also do jungle tours. F. [...]
drive Toyota jeep for rent. Other clubs for climbers: Sadday, Manab[...]
Independencia; the Club de Andinismo of the Universidad Católica in Quito n[...]
Tuesday at 1930 and welcomes visitors. Those needing a professional climbing guic[...] [...]ry
Alan Cathey (T 230-847) who is fluent in English, Spanish and German and can also a[...]ange
ice climbing trips. Marco Cruz, guide for Sierra and Selva, can be contacted through
Metropolitan Touring. A Dutch guide, Pieter van Bunningen, Pasaje Navarro 364 y La Gasca,
T 542663, Quito, takes small parties on mountain and jungle treks at reasonable rates, he is
an experienced walker and climber and speaks Spanish, English and German. Rolf Helbling,
Gral. Veintimilla 531 y Av. 6 de Diciembre, Quito, T 233-013, for information on climbing,
transport and accommodation at his house; he speaks German, Spanish and some English.
Camilo Andrade, Pres. Wilson 643-apto. 135, Tel.:520-263 (speaks 7 languages),
recommended for climbing expeditions, trekking equipment rental; he has a Land Rover for
transportation. Nelson de la Torre, La Cumbre 189, Sector 32, Quito, T 242704, is a climbing
guide and can organize climbing and trekking tours; he is fluent in English. The agencies offer
climbs up the Illinizas (2 days, US$125), Cotopaxi (3 days, US$230), Tungurahua (4 days,
US$260). For climbing the volcanoes, proper equipment and good guidance are essential.

Exchange Lloyds Bank, Av. Carrión y Amazonas, with Torres de Colón, Jipijapa and San
Agustín agencies, quick service, rec.; Citibank, Reina Victoria y Patria (own cheques only);
Banco Holandés Unido, 10 de Agosto 911; Bank of America, Patria y Amazonas; Filanbank,
10 de Agosto, opposite Archaeological Museum, provides cash against Visa at 15%
commission; Banco Internacional, opposite Bank of America, notes only; Banco de Pichincha,
Amazonas y Colón branch, good exchange rates for cash; Banco Guayaquil, Colón y Reina
Victoria, arranges cash advances on Visa without commission or limit; Banco Popular,

o, good service; Banco del Pacífico, García Moreno near Plaza Independencia, ico Consolidado, Guayaquil y Olmedo, good rate for cash but does not accept ..eques. Good rates at Banco de la Producción, Amazonas, opp. Ecuadorian Tours. Open 0900-1330. Closed Sat. Master Card, Amazonas y Veintimilla, in Banco Pacífico building. Bank open all day Sat. and Sun. a.m. in departure lounge at airport. The American Express representative is Ecuadorian Tours, Amazonas 399, T 560-488. AmEx cheques available at Lloyds Bank, Amazonas branch. Ecuacambio, Av. de la República 192 y Almagro, Thomas Cook agents.

Exchange Houses: Rodrigo Paz, Venezuela 659, and Av. Amazonas 370, will change travellers' cheques into US$ cash up to US$300 for US$0.50 commission, plus all major currencies. Jaramillo Arteaga, Mejía 401 y Venezuela, and Colón y Amazonas, will change cheques into US$ cash, no limit, commission charged. Multicambio, Venezuela 689, no commission charged. The airport *cambio* and the *Hotel Colón* are the only places you can change money on Saturdays and Sundays (*Hotel Colón*, Sat. 0900-1800, Sun. 0900-1200, quick service, no commission). If you have trouble cashing American Express or Thomas Cook's travellers' cheques, try the Banco Popular. You are advised only to buy a few Peruvian intis in Ecuador for getting into Peru; you will get a much better rate in Peru.

Language Courses at the *Universidad Católica*, Av. 12 de Octubre 1076 y Carrión, *Instituto de Lenguas y Lingüística*, T 529-240: 6-week Spanish courses, US$100, large classes; courses in Quechua. They will provide student cards, valid for reductions in Peru. Quito has become the major centre in South America for language schools catering for foreigners. We have received favourable reports on the following: *Academia De Español Quito*, Marchena 130 y 10 de Agosto, T 553647, Casilla 39-C; *Academia Español Los Andes*, Pérez Guerrero 441 y Versalles, T 565856; *Centro Ecuatoriano de Español*, Queseras del Medio 778 y 12 de Octubre, T 237762, Casilla 737-A; *Instituto Infraitel*, Venezuela 1018 y Mejía; *Academia Español "One to One"*, Ed. Reina Victoria, Reina Victoria y Patria, T 541864, Casilla 209-A; *Academia de Español Pichincha*, América 3384 y Mariano de Jesús, 2 piso, T 523447, Casilla 936-A Sucursal 3, also at Matovelle between Vargas and San Luís in the Edificio El Conquistador; *Edinburgh Linguistic Centre*, Leonidas Plaza 1133 y Cordero, T 564466, Casilla 586 Sucursal 12 de

Octubre; *Escuela Israel*, Olmedo 552 y Flores; *South American Spanish Institute*, Italia 169 y Eloy Alfaro, T 545818, Casilla 21-373; *New Life Spanish School*, Venezuela 121 y Manabí, Casilla 2518, *Academia Equinoccio*, Ed. M.M. Jaramillo 913, Gran Colombia 242, T 517718, Casilla 2782; *Superior Spanish School*, Versalles y Carrión; *Summit Institute of Languages*, Foch 635 y Reina Victoria; *Spanish School Suiza*, Bolívar 343.

Schools usually offer courses of 7 hours or 4 hours tuition per day, either in groups or on a one-to-one basis. Several correspondents have suggested that 4 hours a day is normally sufficient. Charges range between US$1.40 and US$2.50 per hour for group classes, but beware of extras which may not be mentioned in the initial quote. Schools can arrange accommodation with families for about US$60 a week full board.

British Council Amazonas 1615 y Orellana, T 236-144, postal address: Casilla 1197. There is a library, open Mon.-Fri., 0800-1245, 1500-1915, which stocks back copies of British newspapers and a good café with cheap bacon and eggs.

Embassies **Colombian Consulate**, Av. Amazonas 353, insists on a ticket to leave Colombia before issuing a visa. **Peruvian** and **Brazilian Consulates** both in Edificio España, Av. Colón y Av. Amazonas. **Venezuelan Consulate**, Coruña 1733 y Belo Horizonte, visa US$10, takes 3 working days.
U.S.A., Av. Patria y 12 de Octubre, T 562-890. (The US embassy does not hold mail for US citizens.)
U.K., Av. González Suárez 111 (opposite *Hotel Quito*), letters to Casilla 314, T 560-309/669/670/671. **West Germany**, Av. Patria y 9 de Octubre, Edificio Eteco, 6th floor, T 232-660. **Austria**, Av. Patria y Amazonas, Edificio Cofiec, 11th floor, T 545-336. **Denmark**, Ed. Las Cámaras, Av. Amazonas y Av. de la República, No. 3, T 458585/786; **Sweden**, Ed. Las Cámeras, 2nd floor, Av. República y Amazonas, Apartado 420-A, T 454-872/452-010 (a.m. only). **Switzerland**, Catalina Herrera 120Y Av. Amazonas, Edificio Xerox, 2nd floor. **Canadian Honorary Consul**, Ed Banco Popular, 6 de Diciembre y República. **Honorary Dutch Consul**, 10 de Agosto y Buenos Aires, behind Banco Holandés Unido (a.m. only). **Honorary Irish Consul**, T 235-713 (a.m. only). **Israeli Embassy**, Av. Eloy Alfaro 969 y Amazonas, P.O. Box 2138, T 565-509/510-2. **Belgium**, Austria 219 y Irlanda, T 434-631.

Immigration Office Independencia y Amazonas 877. For visa extensions, Av. Amazonas 2639, open 0800-1200 and 1500-1800; take bus 15 or double-decker bus along Amazonas; go early and be prepared to wait; service more reliable a.m. in Extranjería, Reina Victoria y Colón, Mon.-Thurs., 0830-1230, for visas other than tourist.

Police Criminal Investigations, Calle Montúfar.

Medical The British embassy has telephone numbers of English-speaking doctors; other embassies provide similar information. Hospital Voz Andes, next to Voz Andes radio station, Villalengua 263 (T 241-540), emergency room, quick, efficient, rec., fee US$4, some English spoken (American-run), has out-patient dept., reached by No. 1 bus to Iñaquito; the new American hospital, the Metropolitan, has also been rec. Among health centres recommended are Centro Médico Alemania (Dr Klier speaks German), Eloy Alfaro y Alemania. Clínica Pichincha, Veintimilla 1259, amoebic dysentry tests, results within hours, US$2.50; Clínica Americana Adventista (some English spoken) 10 de Agosto 3366, 24 hrs., US$5. Clínica San Francisco, 6 de Diciembre y Colón, 24 hrs, x-rays. For amoebic dysentery tests, Análisis Médicos Automatizados, Alpallana 477 y Whymper, Ramírez Dávalos 202, T 545-945; for gamma gobulin prescriptions and injections, Clínica Santa Cecilia, Veintimilla 1394 (nr. 10 de Agosto); also Centro Médico Martha Roldas, Plaza Teatro, Hepatitis B injections for US$0.30, but buy own syringe, needle and phial from *Fybeca* chemist (see below). Dr. Rosenthal, La Rábida 160, German spoken. Dr Vargas Uvidia, Colombia 248, T 513152, speaks English and French; Dr Pancho, República 754 y Eloy Alfaro, T 553206, speaks German. **Dentist**: Dra. Rosa Oleas, Amazonas 258 y Washington (T 524-859); Dr. Fausto Vallejo, Madrid 744 (1 block from end of No. 2 Camal/Colón bus line), rec., very reasonable; Dr Roberto Mena, Tamayo 1255 y Colón, speaks English and German. All-night **chemist**, *Farmacia Alaska*, Venezuela 407 y Rocafuerte (T 210-973); *Droquería Doral*, on Amazonas, is a well-stocked, inexpensive pharmacy/chemist; also *Fybeca* on Guayaquil in the Old City (sells typhoid/paratyphoid pills—Vivatif, Swiss). For injections and prescriptions, Rumipampa 1744 y Vasco de Contreras, opp. Coliseo de Colegio San Gabriel (old city), T 457-772.

Public Baths Montúfar 534 (Old City), no sign, 0730-1930, cheap, good.

Laundromat Lavanderías Modernas, can take 2 days, Av. 6 de Diciembre 24-00 y Orellana (US$0.37 per 450 grams). Lavandería América, Venezuela 264 (48 hours service); Lava Duplex, Reina Victoria y Carrión. Dry-cleaning, Martinizing, Av. Colón y Mera (same day).

Anglican Church Joint Anglican/Lutheran service is held (in English) at the Advent Lutheran Church, Isabel la Católica 1419, Sun., 0900.

Charity The Centro del Muchacho Trabajador, or Working Boys' Centre, run by the Christ of the Andes Mission, is a charitable organization which welcomes visitors who wish to see the progress it is making in improving the conditions of the shoe-shine boys. It is located on one side of the Plaza San Martín coming down the Calle Chile from the Plaza de la Independencia. Handicrafts made by the boys are on sale at Caperucita Roja in the Palacio Arzobispal, Calle Venezuela with Chile, shop 12 and at some *artesanías*.

Post Office The main post office is at Eloy Alfaro between 9 de Octubre and 10 de Agosto. Post office in old city is at Benalcázar 769 y Chile (this is the only post office open on Sat. mornings). Post Office also at Reina Victoria y Av. Colón. *Post Restante*, at the post offices at Benalcázar and at Eloy Alfaro: all *post restante* letters are sent to Benalcázar 769 unless marked "Correo Central, Eloy Alfaro". For parcels service **see page** 815. Philatelic service, 3 de Octubre 354 y Eloy Alfaro, 7th floor.

Telecommunications International and interprovincial calls are only possible from the Ietel offices at Av. Colón y 6 de Diciembre, open until 2200, in *Hotel Colón* and at the Terminal Terrestre. Fax service available through Intimexpo, Amazonas 877 y Wilson, Oficina 306, T 568617, Fax 568664 (Mon-Fri 0830-1800).

South American Explorers Club Toledo 1254 y Luís Cordero, T 566076, Mon.-Fri. 0930-1700, provides a wide range of information on South America through its resource centre and quarterly journal as well as selling guidebooks, maps and equipment, both new and used. Annual membership US$25. Write to Apartado 21-431, Eloy Alfaro, Quito.

Tourist Office Dirección Nacional de Turismo (Dituris) at Reina Victoria 514 y Roca (T 239-044) and the new Palacio Municipal, Plaza Independencia, open Mon. to Sat., 0800-1630 (T 514-044); provide maps and other information. Dituris also has a kiosk on the corner of Amazonas and Carrión. Some staff speak English. Their information on bus departure times is reported as being extremely inaccurate, so check at bus stations.

Maps Instituto Geográfico Militar on top of the hill at the eastern end of El Ejido park, on corner of Patria. Opposite the entrance to the Casa de Cultura on 12 de Octubre, running SE up the hill is a small street, Jiménez, which becomes Paz y Miño, follow this up and round to the IGM on the right. You have to exchange your passport for a visitor's pass. Map and air photo indexes are all laid out for inspection. The map sales room (helpful and efficient) is open 0800-1600, Mon.-Fri.

Tourist Agencies *Ecuadorian Tours* (American Express agent), Av. Amazonas 399, T 560-488 (Poste Restante can be sent for clients, Aptdo. 2605, Quito); *Metropolitan Touring*, helpful for information for non-customers, Amazonas 235, T 524-400; also downtown and at *Hotel Quito*; general agents for Galápagos Cruises and Transturi; runs tours to the Galápagos, also arranges climbing, trekking expeditions led by world-known climbers, as well as tours of Quito, generally rec., *Transturi*, part of Metropolitan Touring, operate a cruise ship, the *Flotel Francisco de Orellana*, in 4-5 day trips from Coca along the jungle rivers. *Turismundia*, friendly, Av. Amazonas 657 (reservations to Galápagos). *Seitur*, for the Galápagos and elsewhere, Pinto 525 y Amazonas, helpful, fluent English. *Yanasacha*, Av. República 189 with Diego del Almagro, T 528-964, arranges trips to the Galápagos and Oriente as well as mountaineering expeditions. *Viajes Americanos*, Amazonas y 18 de Septiembre, highly rec., including to Galápagos. *Samoa Tours*, Ramírez Dávalos 151 y Amazonas, T 239892/524135, very friendly, trips to Galápagos have been rec.; *Coltur Travel*, Páez 370 y Robles, T 545777, Casilla 2771; *Sierra Nevada*, 6 de Diciembre 1329 y Roca, helpful, provides information and sells tours to Galápagos and Oriente, also specialises in climbing; *Napo Tour*, Patria y 10 de Agosto (7th floor) has been rec. as efficient and cheap, it is better value to book Napo's *Anaconda Hotel* (near Misahuallí) in Quito than to book in Misahuallí (it is also cheaper to make your own way there than to go with Napo Tour). *Alpa Tours*, Amazonas 631 y Carrión, rec., very helpful. *Etnotur*, Juan Léon Mera y L. García, helpful, English and German spoken, jungle, mountain and Galápagos tours. *Latin Tour*, office at airport, organizes various trips around the country in a jeep, English speaking and very friendly staff, frequently rec. Pablo Prado, Rumibamba 730 y Av. de la República, T 446954/542142, for tours in 4-wheel drive vehicle, especially for photographers. The *Hotel Gran Casino Internacional* sells tours to the Galápagos (although many complaints and unfavourable reports received, others are fully satisfied) and sometimes sells cheap airfares to Galápagos with TAME.

Galasam Cia. Ltda., Pinto 523 y Av. Amazonas, operates Economic Galápagos Tours as well as Condor Tours, Uniclán, Yanasacha, Sol Mar Tours and their tours can be purchased in Switzerland: Artou, 8 rue de Rive 1204, Geneva; France: Delta Voyages, 11 Rue Edouard Jacques, Paris 75014; Italy: Nouvelles Frontières, Vicolo del Divino Amore 180, 00186 Rome; Peru: Top Tours, A. Miró Quesada 247, Of. 704, Lima and El Punto, Av. Nicolás de Piérola 742, Lima 1; USA, Latin American Student Travel, 43 Millstone Road, Randallstown, MD 21133, T (301) 922 2409; Canada, Galapagos Tour, 745 Gerrard Street East, Toronto, M4M 1Y5 T (416) 469 8211, exclusive representatives, prices are the same as in Ecuador. For other agencies organizing tours to the Galápagos, see page 806.

Airport Mariscal Sucre Airport. Taxi (yellow) to centre US$1.50-2 (beware of black taxis which charge at least double). From airport catch bus 16 to go to Plaza Santa Domingo. The No. 1 Iñaquito and Aeropuerto buses go to the airport, look for a sign "*Aeropuerto*" on the windscreen; also No. 43, Marím-Carcelén. Double decker buses run all the way along Av. Amazonas to the airport. Beware of self-styled porters: men or boys who will grab your luggage in the hope of receiving a tip. There are no facilities for long-term left luggage at the airport, but there are at *Hotel Aeropuerto*, just outside the terminal, US$2 per day. Watch out for thefts by security officials when searching your bags; it has been reported that while you walk through the metal detector they remove money from your hand baggage. There are three duty-free shops in the international departure lounge; they sell few appliances and no film.

A monthly booklet, *Transport Junior*, supplement to *Revista Transport*, 150 sucres, gives details of all international and national flights, and phone numbers of all airlines in Quito and Guayaquil.

Internal Flights There are about 14 flights a day to and from Guayaquil, book in advance for daytime flights, US$14 (TAME, Saeta, SAN) and 3 to Cuenca (US$18). There are daily flights to Esmeraldas (US$10), Manta, Tulcán, Loja (except Sun., US$20), Lago Agrio and Coca, and the Galápagos; daily flights to Portoviejo and 2 a week to Macas; flights to Machala (US$12) Mon.-Fri. only. TAME, Reina Victoria y Colón (T 524-023) another TAME office is at Av. 10 de Agosto 239); Saeta, Av. Colombia y Elizalde (T 502-706 national).

The Icaro flying school will organize trips in a light plane along "Avenue of the Volcanos", 4-5 people, US$25 each. (US$30 an hour for lessons.)

Buses Most main roads are paved, so interurban buses are fast and tend to be reliable. The Terminal Terrestre, at Maldonado and Cumandá (near Plaza Santo Domingo), enlarged in 1986, handles all long-distance bus services. From Terminal Terrestre to Av.Amazonas area take red and white bus "Colón-2-Camal". Take No. 10 bus marked "*terminal terrestre*" from city, No. 1 Bartolo-Miraflores from Plaza Santo Domingo, or a taxi (US$1.50). Most buses marked "*terminal terrestre*" do not go right to the bus station but stop 300-500 metres away, which is awkward if you have luggage. There are company booking offices but staff shout destinations of buses leaving; you can pay them and get on board. To Santo Domingo de los Colorados, 2½ hrs., US$1; to Quevedo via Santo Domingo, US$2, 4 hrs.; Esmeraldas, US$2.50, 6 hrs. by Trans Esmeraldas; Trans Ibarra much quicker, or by Aerotaxi minibus, 5½ hrs., 8 a day (for which you need a reservation), US$2.10, 12 passengers. Buses to Otavalo, every 20 mins, 1¾—2½ hrs., US$1, 9 a day (Transportes Otavalo goes into Otavalo; Transportes Andina by-passes the centre). Some buses pass *Hotel Colón* and will pick up passengers there. To Ibarra, 2-2½ hrs., US$1.25 or US$2 by minibus (Taxis Lagos de Ibarra), to Tulcán, 4 hrs. (Velotaxi, Espejo), US$2, every ½ hr. Buses to Guayaquil, 8 hrs., US$2.75 with Trans Ecuador or Aerotaxi, ½ hourly between 0100-2400. Ambato, US$1, 2 hrs.; Cuenca, 10 hrs., US$3.75 (Turismo Flota, Imbabura), minibus, 8 hrs., US$4.50; to Latacunga, 1½ hrs., US$0.75; to Riobamba, 3½ hrs., US$1.50 (Transportes Chimborazo, 6 hrs., US$1.40). To Baños 3 hrs., US$1.30 (Trans. Baños. ½ hourly). To Huaquillas, 12 hrs., US$4; to Machala, US$4.50 first class, 12 hrs. (Also minibuses.) For buses out of Quito it is often advisable to reserve the day before as they may leave early if they are full. To Oriente: Lago Agrio, US$4, 9½ hrs.; Coca, US$5, 0700 and 1400 daily, 10 hrs. Puyo, US$2, 7 hrs. (US$2.50, 9 hrs. via Baeza); Tena, US$2.50, 6½ hrs. (US$3, 8 hrs. via Ambato). Panamericana, Maldonado 3077, runs an "international" bus to Bogotá, but this involves many changes and greater expense; it is better to take a bus to the border and change. There are now no direct through buses to Peru so take a bus to Huaquillas via Machala, cross the border and catch one of the Peruvian long-distance buses from Tumbes on to Piura, Trujillo and Lima, complete trip about 36 hrs. The alternative route for crossing the Peruvian border via Loja and Macará takes much longer than the Machala route. Tepsa has an office at Pinto 539 y Amazonas but avoid buying Peruvian bus tickets here as they will be half the price in Peru; tickets also sold for other S.American destinations.

Drivers should note that there is now a ring road around Quito, and a by-pass to the S, the Carretera de Amaguaña.

Railway station is two km. S of centre, along continuation of Calle Maldonado, reached by buses along that street (e.g. No. 1 or Colón-Camal, No. 2). The ticket office at the station is frequently closed. Severe rains and flooding destroyed much of the track in 1983. Trains to Riobamba provide spectacular views along the "Avenue of the Volcanoes". Conflicting reports about services: there is usually a daily *autoferro* (bus mounted on train chassis) at 1500, 5 hrs., tickets on sale from 0500, but there may be a train at 0800—if so, take it because on the 1500 service you miss the best views owing to cloud and nightfall. Buy tickets in advance. Services are liable to alteration, cancellation or delay especially in the rainy season: enquire in advance; train information T 266144. Metropolitan Touring does 2-day tour: down to Riobamba by train on Tues. or Sat., overnight Riobamba, back by bus, US$131.

Cruz Loma and Rucu Pichincha Cruz Loma is one of the two antenna-topped peaks overlooking Quito from the west (it has two antennae, its neighbour one). On a clear day you can see about 50 km. down the central valley and to the east. Do not try to walk up from Calle 24 de Mayo in central Quito as this is extremely dangerous (frequent attacks reported—on no account go alone): if walking go up Av. La Grasca to Highway Occidental—then take the track which begins at the "Doom" gate just past the eucalyptus forest (beware of dogs—take a stick). To save time and energy take a taxi or bus, e.g. No. 14, to Toctiuco, to the upper reaches of the city and start from there (allow at least 3 hrs to reach the summit). There are roads up to both peaks, but traffic is sparse. Try hitching early in the morning, but remember that it is difficult to hitch back after about 1730 and you will have to walk in the dark. The road to the northern hill is better for hitching; it leads to the radio station at the top of the hill; take bus no. 5 from Calle Gabriel García Moreno. No water is available so be sure to carry adequate supplies, especially if going on to Rucu Pichincha. **Rucu Pichincha** (4,700 metres) cannot be seen from Quito, but can be climbed either via Cruz Loma or via its neighbour. The path to its foot runs due west over and around hummocks on the rolling, grass-covered *páramo*. The climb up to the peak is not technical, but it is rocky and requires a bit of endurance. About half an hour beyond Rucu Pichincha, is a second peak, Paso de Muerte. From Cruz Loma to Rucu Pichincha peak takes about 4 hrs. and the return about 2. Take rainproof and cold-weather gear just in case. (*Note:* please pick up your flotsam; the area is rubbish-strewn enough as it is.)

Guagua Pichincha A recommended route for climbing Guagua Pichincha volcano is to take a bus to Lloa, from where a 4-wheel-drive track goes to a *refugio*, maintained by Defensa Civil, at the crater rim (if walking allow 6 hrs). The descent into the crater is scree and sand, and very steep; use of a rope is not strictly necessary but advisable (not for the novice): following the route is difficult despite the occasional route markers. There are fumaroles and thermal springs at the bottom, and the ground shakes under you. Allow 2 hrs. for the descent and another hour to reach the thermal springs.

Excursions 23 km. N of Quito is the Equatorial Line Monument at an altitude of 2,483 metres. The exact equatorial line here was determined by Charles Mane de la Condamine and his French expedition in 1735. The monument forms the focal point of a park and leisure area with restaurants, gift shops, etc., and has a museum inside (open Tues.-Fri., 0900-1500, Sat.-Sun., 1000-1600). Admission to the monument free, to the museum US$0.35. The museum is run by the Central Bank; a lift takes you to the top, then you walk down with the museum laid out all around with different Indian cultures every few steps. A paved road runs from Quito to the Monument, which you can reach by a "Mitad del Mundo" bus (US$0.20, 1 hr.) from the Parque Hermano Miguel; beware of pickpockets on the bus. Two minutes' walk before the Monument is the restaurant *Equinoccio*, good food, not cheap, live music. Available at the restaurant are "certificates" recording the traveller's visit to the Equator. Other restaurants are now being opened.

A few km. beyond the Monument is the Pululagua crater, well worth visiting, and there is now a paved road. Continue on the road past the Monument towards Calacalí. After a few km. (1 hr. walk) the road bears left and begins to climb steeply; the paved road to the right leads to the rim of the volcano and a view of the farms on the crater floor. Buses to Calacalí (infrequent) will drop you at the fork, from where it is a ½ hr. walk. Plenty of traffic at weekends for hitching a lift. There is a rough track down from the rim to the crater, to give an impression of the rich vegetation and warm micro-climate inside the crater. Also in the vicinity of the Monument, 3 km. from San Antonio beyond the Solar Museum, is the ruined Inca fortress of Rumicucho. Restoration poor, but situation magnificent (investigations under the auspices of the Museum of the Central Bank, entry US$0.15). Start early if you want to visit all these in one day.

Before San Antonio, on the road to Calacalí, is the village of Pomasqui, near where was a tree in which Jesus Christ appeared to perform various miracles, El Señor del Arbol, now enshrined in its own building. In the church nearby is a series of charming paintings depicting the miracles (mostly involving horrendous road accidents); well worth a visit. You may have to find the caretaker to unlock the church (we are grateful to Hilary Bradt for this information).

Martin Cooper writes from La Paz: For the naturalist, the best place in Ecuador to see the cock-of-the-rock is in the protected woodland near the village of **Mindo** to the west of Pichincha volcano (Bus San Pedrito leaves *terminal terrestre*, Quito, twice a week for Mindo). Mindo has a clean *pensión* in the square (G) and two rockpockets. The reserve has a hut where visitors can stay, but take food. Ask for Don Pedro Peñafiel in the village who will act as a guide.

The Equator line also crosses the Inter-American Highway 8 km. south of Cayambe, where there are a concrete globe beside the road and a mark on the road itself. Midday by the sun, incidentally, is between 1200 and 1230. Take Cayambe bus (2 hrs., US$0.80) and ask for Mitad del Mundo.

The Parque Pasochoa, 45 mins. by car from Quito, is a subtropical natural park set in mountain forest, run by the Fundación Natura, 6 de Diciembre 5043 y El Comercio, T 454962, who provide further information, a map of suggested walks and guided tours. Camping is permitted in the park (US$20 for 2 nights); take all your own equipment, food and water as there are no shops and take your rubbish away with you. From Quito buses run from the centre of Villaflora district to Amangua (ask the driver to let you off at the "Ejido de Amangua"); from there follow the signs for the Bosque Natural Pasochoa, about 7 km. walk, not much traffic for hitching.

According to the vulcanologists, the best hot springs in Ecuador are the Baños de **Papallacta**, 80 km. E from Quito, 1 km. from the road to Lago Agrio. There are 4 thermal swimming pools and one cold pool fed by a river, open 0600-1800. You can camp in the pastures up towards the baths. There are showers, toilets and changing rooms. The restaurant is open daily. The farm next door sells milk and cheese. Buses from Quito: take a bus to Lago Agrio or Baeza (drivers charge full fare), or take a local bus from the Partida de Tumbaco, on 6 de Diciembre just north of Av. República to Pifo, from where it is a 1½ hr walk to Papallacta (hitching easy at weekends). In the valley of Chillos (SE, 1 hr. by car) are the thermal pools of Alangasí and El Tingo. A few km. from El Tingo is La Merced, which has thermal baths. Camping is allowed in the vicinity. Further on from La Merced is Ilaló, a semi-private swimming club, admission US$2 but clean, fewer mosquitoes and people.

Another interesting trip is to **Sangolquí** about 20 minutes away by bus. There is a colourful Sun. market (and a lesser one on Thurs.), with Indians in traditional costumes and few tourists, and there are thermal baths nearby (pop. 18,000). At Laguna Mica, at 4,000m., near Hacienda Pinantura close to Píntag, condors can quite often be seen.

Day tours via Cotopaxi to Indian fairs at Pujilí and at Saquisilí (**see page** 785), about 93 km. each way, or to Cotopaxi itself.

NORTH OF QUITO (2)

A railway (no passengers) and the Pan-American Highway run north-east from Quito to Otavalo (121 km.) and Ibarra (145 km.). At Ibarra, the railway and Highway separate. The railway goes north-west to the Pacific port of San Lorenzo, a very spectacular trip, passenger services only from Ibarra: the highway runs north for another 108 km. to Tulcán and on to Ipiales in Colombia. The Pan-American Highway is now paved for the whole stretch Quito-Tulcán.

Calderón, 30 km. N of Quito, is the place where miniature figurines are made of bread; you can see them being made (not on Sun.), and prices are much lower than in Quito. Especially attractive is the Nativity collection. Prices range from about US$0.10 to US$4 (excellent value). See the Indian cemetery on 1-2 November, when the graves are decorated with flowers, drinks and food for the dead. Corpus Christi processions are very colourful. Many buses from Quito (corner of Colón and 10 de Agosto). Take food as restaurants are reported to be poor.

The road for the north traverses the Indian area around Calderón, descends the spectacular Guayllabamba gorge and climbs out again to the fertile oasis of Guayllabamba village, noted for huge avocados and chirimoyas. Further north the road runs through dry, dusty land before irrigated land is reached again at **Cayambe** (pop. 14,168); *Pensión Cayambe*, G, clean dominated by the snow-capped volcano of the same name. This area of rich dairy farms produces a fine range of European-style cheeses. Cayambe is the Agrarian Reform Institute's showplace; its only major project. The monastery of the Salesian fathers in Cayambe has a superb library on indigenous cultures.

Between Guayllabamba and Cayambe, before entering Tabacundo, a narrow dirt road to the left leads to Tocachi and further on to the Estancia **Cochasqui** national archaeological site; the whole area is covered with hills of pyramid shapes and ramps built between 900 and 1500 AD by Indians of the Caras or Caranquis tribe. Festivals with dancing at the equinoxes

and solstices. Note the spectacular wind-eroded rocks. Students offer free, 20-min. guided tours which are recommended. The only bus to pass the turn off to Cochasqui is Transportes Lagos' Quito-Otavalo route via Cayambe; ask driver to let you out at the sign; from there it's an 8 km. walk (if you arrive at the sign between 0900-0930, you should get a lift from the site workers). Taxi from Cayambe US$8 round trip.

Rob Rachowiecki writes that about 1 km. before Cayambe is an unmarked cobbled road heading right for 26 km. to the Ruales-Oleas-Berge refuge at 4,400 metres, opened in 1981. It costs US$2.50 p.p. a night and provides beds (bring sleeping bag), but no equipment. It is named after three Ecuadorean climbers killed by an avalanche in 1974 while pioneering a new route up the Cayambe volcano from the west. This has now become the standard route, using the refuge as a base. The climb is heavily crevassed, especially near the summit, and is more difficult and dangerous than either Chimborazo or Cotopaxi. Cayambe (5,790 metres) is Ecuador's third highest peak and the highest point in the world which lies directly on the Equator.

The road forks north of Cayambe: to the right a cobbled road, the very scenic *carretera vieja*, runs through Olmedo, Zuleta and Esperanza, to Ibarra; to the left, the main paved road crosses a *páramo* and suddenly descends into the land of the Otavalo Indians, a lively and prosperous group who have been making commercial woollens for over fifty years. The men are recognizable by their white, bell-bottomed, mid-calf-length trousers (whitened by using a special reed in washing), long braided hair and blue ponchos. Although some work on *haciendas* between San Pablo and Ibarra, most of the scattered homes in the fields belong to Indians.

An alternative route from Quito to Otavalo is via San Antonio (Inca ruins of Rumicucho) and San José de Minas. The road curves through the dry but impressive landscape down to the Río Pita, then climbs again, passing some picturesque oasis villages. After Minas the road is in a very bad condition and a jeep is necessary for the next climb (beautiful views; at both junctions on this stretch, take the left fork) and then descent to join the Otavalo-Selva Alegre road about 15 km. from Otavalo. The journey takes about 3 hours altogether and is rough but magnificent.

Otavalo (population 18,000) is at 2,530 metres in beautiful countryside which is worth exploring for 2 or 3 days. In the Plaza Bolívar is a statue of Rumiñahui, a local leader who successfully resisted the Incas; Otavalans argue that they are the only pure Ecuadorean Indians. The town is notable for its colourful Indian fair on Sat. The fair is a "must" for tourists. There are 3 markets in different places: (a) textiles and *artesanías*, 0600-1330 in Plaza de Ponchos; (b) livestock, 0530-1000, outside town in the Barrio San Juan at Cotocachi turnoff; (c) produce, 0700-1300, in Plaza 23 de Mayo. The market is rated highly for woollen goods, though it is now rather highly organized and touristy and prices are not low; very little of the traditional weaving is now to be seen and many of the ponchos are made of orlon (these are easily recognizable). The earlier you get there the better; prices tend to be higher after 1100 when the organized trips from the *Hotels Quito* and *Colón* arrive. Bargaining is essential, but difficult. All the same, Otavalo is the best place in Ecuador to buy a man's woollen poncho. Your chances of being allowed to photograph Indians will improve if you buy something first, then ask politely. Watch out for pickpockets and bag slashers in the market. (Goods sold in the market can also be bought in local shops, sometimes cheaper and with less bargaining.) There are also small markets on Sun. and Wed.

The Otavalo Indian weavers come from the villages of Peguche, Iluman, Carabuela and Quinchuqui, close to Otavalo. They are very friendly and will indicate where you can buy their products more cheaply from the loom. For a tour contact Rafael Perugachi, Calle Sucre 12-16; or Zulaytour, Sucre y Colón. Otavalo textile shops include *Tejidos y Artesanías Atahualpa*, Bolívar 1015, and *Coop. Indígena de Tejidos Peguche*, Bolívar 910. **Note**: If planning a spending spree, bring plenty of cash; Otavalo can be as expensive as Quito, and the exchange rate is very unfavourable, even in the bank. Banks are open until 1330 on Sat.

OTAVALO
Not to Scale 84

To Cotacachi

To Ibarra

LOS CORAZUS

Estados Unidos

COLLAHUAZO

MACKENGARA

QUITO

MIGUEL EGAS

RICAURTE

DE OCTUBRE

QUIROGA

SALINAS

MORALES

BOLIVAR

ROCA

RIO

To Cascadas de Peguche

EL TEJAR

MODESTO JARAMILLO

OCOLON

AV. ABDON CALDERON

EUGENE

JUAN MONTALVO

GARCIA MORENO

PIEDRAHITA

ATAHUALPA

GUAYAQUIL

Bypass

RIO

To Lagunas Mojanda

OLMEDO

MEJIA

ROCAFUERTE

ESTEVES MORA

TO IMBABUELA

To Laguna de San Pablo

OLD ROAD

TO QUITO

To Quito

1. Parque Central
2. Plaza de Ponchos
3. Produce Market
4. Animal Market, Barrio San Juan
5. Instituto Otavaleño de Antropología
6. Museo Arqueológico/*Pensión Los Andes*
7. Cockpit
8. Tourist Office and Municipality

9. Zulaytour
10. Post Office
11. Ietel Phone Office

Hotels
12. *Yamor Continental*
13. *Otavalo*
14. *Sami Huasi*
15. *Riviera y Sucre*
16. *Residencia El Indio*
17. *Isabelita*
18. *Peña Amauta*

We have received many reports of stealing from Otavalo hotel rooms; you are advised to ensure that your door is always locked, even if your absence is very brief.

Hotels May be full on Fri. nights, before fair, when prices go up. *Yamor Continental*, at northeast end of town, D, comfortable, some small cabins, water intermittent and only occasionally warm, lovely building, swimming pool, restaurant expensive; *Otavalo*, E-D, hot water, cheaper rooms without bath or outside window, clean, fine old building with attractive patio, rec., the new part across the street is clean but noisy, Indian music on Fri. nights, nice restaurant, set menu with infrequent changes (homemade ice cream in the *Golden Eagle* coffee shop but pizzas are not rec.); *Residencial El Rocío*, Morales, E, clean, safe, friendly, the owner, Sr. Cobos offers expeditions to surrounding villages in his truck, 0830 departure, highly rec; *Riviera y Sucre*, Moreno y Roca, G, hot water, laundry facilities, good breakfasts, table tennis, book exchange, clean, safe, friendly, English, French and Dutch spoken by the owner, who is an expert on the area, highly rec.; *Residencial El Indio*, Sucre 12-14, F, also has suites with sitting room and balcony, F for 3 people, rec., hot water, clean, restaurant, reports of theft from rooms. *Pensión Los Andes*, Roca y Montalvo, G, grimy (see under Museums below). *Residencial Centenario*, Pasaje Saona y Jaramillo, F, clean, good parking; *Isabelita*, Roca 1107 y Quiroga, G, quiet, hot water, laundry facilities, very clean, helpful, parking space, rec. *Pensión Otavalo*, G p.p., basic, noisy from disco behind, showers, laundry facilities, friendly; opp. is *Colón*, F; *Residencia Santa Marta*, G, on Calle Colón, pretty courtyard, large rooms, ask for hot water, clean, safe, popular; opp. is *Colón*, F; *Residencia Santa Ana*, Colón, big clean rooms, hot water, nice garden, good breakfasts. House rental from *El Sandwich Viajero*, Sucre 10-02, weekly or monthly.

Restaurants *Sumak Mikuy*, Jaramillo y Pasaje Saona, criollo food; *El Triunfo*, Moreno y Jaramillo, good breakfast early, English spoken. *Ajadero Crystal*, Bolívar, clean, noisy jukebox. *Tuparima*, Bolívar y Calderón, friendly atmosphere, open fire, local dishes, "cheapest beer in Ecuador", rec; *Ali Mikuy*, vegetarian food, cheeseburgers, juices, beer, not cheap but good value, avoid the soyaburgers; *Guacamayo*, Sucre y Colón, clean, good food, pricey, lovely garden for lazy afternoons, popular; *Jatun Pacha*, Morales 410 y Sucre, vegetarian, open all day, good wholemeal bread and lovely jams, inexpensive; *Mama Rosita*, Sucre, 1 block from plaza, prepares vegetarian meals if you order them in a.m. *La Portada Vieja*, good 3-course meal for US$3; *Casa de Korea*, opposite *Hotel Otavalo*, Oriental food, good and cheap; *Chifa Tien An Men*, near Moreno and Bolívar, reasonable, generous portions, tasty food, inexpensive; *Copacabana*, Montalvo y Bolívar, basic, clean, reasonable, set meal about US$1, good for breakfast; *Cafetería Shanandoa*, Salinas y Jaramillo, good pies, milk shakes (expensive) and ice cream, expensive but good, rec. for breakfast; *Tapiz Café*, Sucre 12-03, good, friendly, breakfast highly rec; *Snack El Sandwich Viajero*, Sucre 10-02, friendly owners; *Centro Latino*, Sucre y Calderón, good fried chicken and grills; *Royal*, on main plaza, clean (even the toilets), meal with cola about US$1.40.

Entertainment *Peña Amauta*, Modesto Jaramillo y Salinas, the best, mainly foreigners, US$0.60 entrance fee; *Peña de los Chaskis*, Jaramillo y Salinas; *Peña Yamar*, Atahualpa y Olmedo; *Peña Tucano*, Morales 5-10 y Sucre. Peñas normally only on Fri and Sat from 2200. 2 cinemas: *Apolo*, on Bolivia. There is also a cockpit (*gallera*), at 31 de Octubre y Montalvo, fights Sat. and Sun. 1500-1900, US$0.50.

Games and Festivals Near the market, a ball game is played in the afternoons. It is similar to the game in Ibarra described below except that the ball is about the size of a table-tennis ball, made of leather, and hit with the hands, not a bat. From 24 to 29 June, at the Fiesta de San Juan, there are bullfights in the plaza and regattas on the beautiful Lago de San Pablo, 4 km. away (bus to Espejo, US$0.20) and there is the *Fiesta del Yamor* from 3 to 14 September.

Museums Instituto Otavaleño de Antropología, exhibition, on Panamericana Norte; Museo Arqueológico César Vásquez Fuller, at *Pensión Los Andes*, Roca y Montalvo (free if staying there); Museo Jaramillo, Bolívar, off Parque Central.

Tourist Agencies *Zulaytour*, Sucre y Colón 1014, English spoken, information, map of town, slide show, horse-riding, tours, good value, repeatedly recommended (N.B. there is another Zulaytour, which is not a legal operation); *Intipungo Touring*, Sucre 11-06, T 920391, run adventure tours, climbing expeditions, horse-riding and local tours; *Inca Tours*, Calderón 402 y Bolívar, T 902446, also organise local tours. The original Zulaytour and Intipungo are the only officially recognized tour operators in Otavalo. All these agencies run tours with English-speaking guides to artisans' homes and villages, which usually provide opportunities to buy handicrafts cheaper than in the market. All-day tour US$3-6 p.p. We have received favourable reports on all, especially Zulaytour.

OTAVALO Environs
ROUGH SKETCH
84A

Transport There is no bus station, though one is planned for 1991. Bus to Ibarra, every 15 mins., US$0.15, 1/2 hr. From Quito by taxi takes 11/2 hrs. (US$20); by minibus (Transportes Andinas) from 18 de Septiembre and Av. Guerrero, 11/2 hrs., US$1.75; by bus (Cooperativa Otavalo, Coop Las Lagos) 13/4-21/2 hrs., US$1, every 20 minutes, last bus about 1800. The Tourist Office in Quito will help with reservations; the organized tour sold by hotels is expensive. Travelling on Friday is rec. as the best prices and best goods are found early on Saturday morning before the tourist bus arrives. Train service between Otavalo and Ibarra, slow, but beautiful views.

Excursions At the Lago de San Pablo is the Club de Tiro, Caza y Pesca where one can rent canoes. It is worth walking either to or back from Lago de San Pablo for the views, the walk back via the outlet stream from the lake (staying on the right hand side of the gorge), taking 2-3 hrs., is particularly recommended. The new 13-roomed *Hotel Chicapán*, C, on the lakeshore is recommended; from the restaurant there is a fine view of the lake and Imbabura mountain. *Cabaña del Lago*, on the lakeside, E, has cabins with bunk beds, clean, good food. Boats and pedalos for hire, pony rides etc. Also in San Pablo del Lago (half-hourly buses from Otavalo) is *Hostería Cusín* in a converted *hacienda*, D, but often open only Fri.-Sun. (run by an Englishman, Mr Creighton, who grows roses). Pleasant setting. There are also other restaurants. From San Pablo del Lago it is possible to climb the Imbabura volcano, 4,900 m and almost always under cloud—allow at least 6 hrs to reach the summit and 4 hrs for the descent. Easier, and no less impressive, is the nearby Cerro Hearmi Imbabura, 3845 m.

It is also possible to hike much further south to the Lagunas Mojanda, 15 km from Otavalo and also accessible by car (take a tent and food, no accommodation). From Laguna Grande de Mojanda (also called Caricocha) the route continues south about 5 km. before dividing: the left-hand path leads to Tocachi, the right-hand to Cochasqui (**see page 748**): both are about 20 km. from Laguna Grande and offer beautiful views of Quito and Cotopaxi (cloud permitting). On the shore of Laguna Grande is a basic mountain hut from which you can climb Fuya Fuya (4,259 m.) and Yanaurco (4,289 m.).

There is a network of old roads and trails between Otavalo and the Lago San Pablo area, none of which takes more than an hour or two to explore. To reach the Cascadas de Peguche follow the old railway track through the woods until the track drops away to the left and a dirt path continues up the hill towards the waterfall—allow 1½ hrs. each way. Four km. from Otavalo are cold ferrous baths at the Fuente de Salud, said to be very curative (John Streather) but opening hours very irregular. Zulaytour and Intipungo Touring offer tours to many of these places.

Off the road between Otavalo and Ibarra is **Cotacachi**, where beautiful leather goods are made and sold; credit cards widely accepted. Frequent buses run from Otavalo. (Hotels: *El Mesón de las Flores*, E-D, converted ex-hacienda off main plaza, good meals; *La Mirage*, E-D, ex-hacienda ½ km. from town, beautiful garden, pool and gymnasium, very good rooms and food, good excursions, rec; and others.) A few km. before Cotacachi (turn off at Quiroga), at an altitude of 3,070 metres lies Lake **Cuicocha**, which has been developed for tourism (entrance US$0.15 to the nature reserve). This is a crater lake with two islands, although these are closed to the public for biological studies. The Ministry of Agriculture also maintains a research station/visitors' centre on the lake shore, open 0800-1600 every day. The restaurant on the lake shore, *Muelle*, has a dining room overlooking the lake, clean, moderate prices. Nearby is *El Mirador* with food, excellent view. Motor boats can be hired for groups of five or more. There is a path around the lake, which takes at least 6 hrs. (best to go anticlockwise), and provides spectacular views of Cotacachi, Imbabura and, occasionally, glacier-covered Cayambe peaks (best views in early morning). Hilary Bradt adds: Although it's perfectly possible—and exciting—to walk round the lake, the path does not follow the rim all the way because of deep ravines. The second half (if you walk anticlockwise) is very difficult and many people lose the path and end up floundering through thick scratchy vegetation on the steep hillsides. Best to go to the halfway look out point, then return the same way by the service road. This will take two to three hours, depending on how often you stop to admire the view or the orchids that grow in profusion near the trail.

The slopes of Cerro Cotacachi, N from the lake, are a nature reserve. From Otavalo or Ibarra take Cotacachi bus (US$0.10), and try to get a truck or colectivo to Lake Cuicocha from Cotacachi, US$1.60, one way; they await the buses from Otavalo. A taxi costs US$2 one way from Cotacachi. The 3-hr. walk back to Cotacachi is beautiful; after 1 km. on the road from the park entrance, turn left (at the first bend) onto the old road. You can also walk from Otavalo (Instituto Geográfico 1:50,000 or 100,000 maps recommended).

Warning Many people have been badly poisoned by eating the blue berries which grow near the lake. They are *not* blueberries; they render the eater helpless within 2 hrs., requiring at least a stomach pump.

Also off the main road between Otavalo and Ibarra is **San Antonio de Ibarra**, well known for its wood carvings, most of which are now reported to be either "cheap and nasty or expensive and tasteless". For the exceptions, visit the workshop of Moreo Santacruz, and the exhibition of Osvaldo Garrido in the Palacio de Arte. Luís Potosí's gallery on the main square has some beautiful carvings. (Buses from Ibarra, 13 km., ten mins.)

John Streather recommends a visit to **Apuela**, in the lush tropical valley of the Zona del Inca (*Pensión Apuela*, G, grim; small restaurant) for the thermal baths of Nungulví nearby (1 hr. walk). Apuela buses from Otavalo on a good new road (6 a day) pass Nungulví, where the swimming pool is emptied for cleaning on Tues. and Fri. Near Apuela, the Hacienda La Florida offers full board for $25 p.p. per day and a wide range of nature walks, horseriding and excursions. Write to Casilla 18, Otavalo, Imbabura, Ecuador. About 2 hrs. drive (bumpy track) from Ibarra are the clean, hot mineral swimming pools of Cachimbiro in the parish of Tumbariro. Buses from Ibarra 5 a day (2½ hrs.).

Ibarra, founded 1606, at 2,225 metres, population 80,000, is a pleasant colonial town with some good hotels. Local festival, Fiesta de los Lagos, last weekend of September, Thurs.-Sun.; also 16 July, Virgen del Carmen. Some interesting paintings are to be seen in the church of Santo Domingo and its museum.

Hotels   The better class hotels tend to be fully booked during Holy Week. *Hostería San*

Agustín, 1 km. south of the bus station on Quito road, D, beautiful location, clean, friendly, good service, hot water, good food; 1 km. further south is *Hostería Chorlavi*, set in a converted hacienda, D, US$2.50 for extra bed, also cabins, excellent buffet and folk music and crafts on Sun, discotheque at weekends, good value restaurant, pool open to non-residents US$0.30; *Ajavi*, between town and bus station, C, pool and very good restaurant; *El Dorado*, Oviedo y Sucre, D, clean, good restaurant; two *Residencial Madrids*, at Olmedo 857 y Oviedo, E, clean, comfortable, good views from upper rooms; and at Moncayo y Sánchez, E, clean; *Residencial Imperio*, Olmedo 8-62 y Oviedo (T952-929), F with bath, hot water, TV, a bargain; *Hotel Imbabura*, Oviedo 9-33 y Narváez, G, cheap, friendly; *Residencial Imbabura*, Flores y Narváez, G, hot showers, pretty garden, rec.; *Residencial Familiar*, Moncayo 726 y Olmedo, E, clean and good; *Los Alpes*, E, Velasco 732 y Bolívar, clean with private bath; *Pensión San Lorenzo*, Olmedo 1056, F, no hot water, clean; *Residencial Astoria*, G, Velasco 809, safe, can store luggage, friendly, basic, not very clean, upper rooms have beautiful view, large terrace, laundry facilities; *Residencial Colón*, Narváez 5257 y Velasco, G (more with bath), hot water, pleasant, clean, friendly, laundry facilities, will change money. *Residencial El Príncipe*, Sánchez y Cifuentes 882, G, basic but clean, restaurant. Several others, F and G, along Bolívar, Moncayo and Olmedo.

Restaurants *Hostería Chorlavi* restaurant rec. (but it is crowded with tour buses on Sat. lunchtime), likewise *Hotel Ajavi*. *El Chagra*, Olmedo 7-48, rec., reasonable prices; *Marisquería Las Redes*, Oviedo 638 y Sucre, seafood, clean, good, breakfast for US$1, accept US$ at top rate. Good breakfast and excellent bread at *Café Pushkin*, Olmedo 7-75 and at *Mejor Pan*, Olmedo 7-52. *El Caribe*, Flores 757, chicken and local food, excellent three-course set meal for US$0.60. *Chifa Muy Buena*, Olmedo 723, does a good Chaulafan; "muy buena"; *El Dorado*, Oviedo y Sucre, seafood, good, expensive, snacks; *Portón de Sevilla*, Oviedo 764, seafood; *Caldera del Diablo*, G. Moreno 443, expensive but good value; *Koco Rico*, Olmedo 724, and *Asadero a las Doradas*, Oviedo 720, both chicken; *Luchino's*, on main plaza, pizzas, slow service; *La Estancia*, García Moreno 7-66, very good grill but not cheap. *Salud y Vida*, Mosquera y Bolívar, vegetarian, cheap. *Los Helados*, Calle 27, near main plaza, for good ice cream; also *Heladería La Nevada*, Velasco 837 and *Crema Jugetoña*, Colón 721 y Bolívar, good coffee, ice-cream and fruit salads. Local specialities are sweets made from walnuts, blackberries (arrope de mora) and other fruits, and nougat (nogada).

Exchange Banco Continental, Cifuentes y Moncayo, changes travellers' cheques. *Las Redes* restaurant, *Residencial Colón* and Farmacia Sudamericana, Olmedo 864 y Moncayo will change US$ notes.

Immigration Olmedo y L.F.Villamar (T 951-712), very quick for extensions.

Tourist Office Dituris, Liborio Madero y Flores (Radio Punto building). Also, travel agency, Itipungo, Rocafuerte y García Moreno and Bolívar 4-43, friendly.

Things to Do Museo Fray Pedro (open 0900-1200, 1500-1800, US$0.15, closed Sun.), Santo Domingo church, religious art, also has a zoo. Balneario Primavera, Sánchez y Cifuentes 323, pool, sauna, turkish bath. Peña Folklórica at Poncho Libre, Olmedo 935; Peña Pedregal, near football stadium; Casa Cultural, near Terminal Terrestre, Piano bar, *El Encuentro*, Olmedo 953. A unique form of paddle ball is played on Sat. and Sun. near the railway station, also on way from bus station to centre, on left, just before the built-up area. The players have huge spiked paddles for striking the 2 lb. ball. On weekdays they play a similar game with a lighter ball.

Bus to Quito 2-3 hrs., US$1.25, about 50 departures a day. Colectivo taxis for about US$2, taxis US$16. To Yahuarcocha, US$1. To Tulcán, US$1, 2½ hrs. To Otavalo, ½ hr. Bus station (Terminal Terrestre) is 1 km. S of town, reached by bus No. 2 from centre.

Excursions Alexander Tkany, of Karlsruhe, recommends a visit to Guachara, NW of Ibarra, reached by bus from Ibarra railway station (US$0.10), or by train from Ibarra to Carchi and then bus. Tourists unknown, people friendly, mountains beautiful and hitch-hiking very possible. A pretty village to visit close to Ibarra, 10 km. directly south on the road to Olmedo, is **La Esperanza**, in beautiful surroundings with an Inca road which goes to Cayambe. Accommodation: Casa Aída, F, basic, Aída speaks some English and cooks vegetarian food. (Bus from Ibarra passes *Aída*.) Eugenio makes leather clothes cheaply to measure; e.g. US$60 for trousers. One particular lady does extremely fine embroidery; ask in village for her house. You can climb Cuilche volcano in 2 hours from La Esperanza for beautiful views; from the top you can walk down to Laguna de San Pablo. You can also climb Imbabura volcano more easily than from Lago San Pablo; allow 8 hrs. round trip.

At edge of **Lake Yahuarcocha** are *Parador El Conquistador*, 8 rooms, D, large restaurant, rec., run by Dituris, and *Hotel del Lago*, no accommodation, only refreshments.

It is possible to walk to Lake Yahuarcocha (4 km.)in about 1½ hrs. Follow Calle 27 to the end of town, cross the river and walk to the right at the first junction. At the end of this road, behind 2 low buildings on the left, there is a small path going steeply uphill. There are beautiful views of Ibarra and then from the top of the hill over the Lake surrounded by mountains and the village of the same name. Yahuarcocha, "bloody lake" in Quechua, named because legend says that the water turned red when the Incas threw in the bodies of the defeated Otavalo Indians. There are frequent buses back to Ibarra from the village. The beauty of the lake has been disfigured by the building of a motor-racing circuit round its shores.

Laguna Puruanta, 45 km. SE of Ibarra on Río Pisque, can be visited by bus to Pinampiro (US$0.40, 1 hr.), then walk to San Francisco de Sigsipamba (15 km.) and on trails from there to the Laguna. Return to Ibarra via Mariano de Acosta to complete 2-day excursion.

A 193 km. railway runs from Ibarra to the port of San Lorenzo (**see page** 766), N of Esmeraldas. An *autoferro* runs at least once a day at 0600 (check the day before), taking from 9 to 12 hrs. (US$1.75). The train is very crowded. Thieves are very active at the station and on the train; take as little luggage as possible, but you will need food and drink (aggressive beggars, dressed in banana leaves and coconut-shell masks, are reported to stop the train demanding money—ignore them). You must queue up at 0500 for the tickets and push like mad. Sit on the right side of the train: the track is on the left side of the valley down to San Lorenzo. The track is in very poor condition and lengthy delays and derailments are common.

Leaving Ibarra, the train descends past Salinas into the narrow gorge of the Río Mira (called Chota upstream) inhabited by blacks growing fruit and sugar cane, who sell fruit at the station (the train stops for 15 mins. for breakfast). After three hours the valley widens near Collapi (730 metres) and the land becomes better watered and has been more recently colonized. Lita (460 metres) is reached after five hours and a stop is made for refreshment (train returns from here at 1300—all foreigners' passports are checked at Lita). Through the lowlands cultivated land becomes commoner until we reach San Lorenzo.

North of Ibarra the Pan-American Highway goes past Lake Yahuarcocha, and descends to cross the Chota valley. The Highway divides in the valley, and you can go to Tulcán either via El Angel over a long stretch of *páramo* or, like most of the heavy vehicles, further east over eroded hill sides via San Gabriel (see below). On the El Angel road at the village of Chota and on the San Gabriel road at El Juncal, the highway descends to a mere 1,520 metres; in the tropical Chota valley you can buy excellent fruit from the local blacks, descendants of slaves brought from Africa in the 17th century by Jesuits to farm their estates. The El Angel route is still heavy going; the San Gabriel route is a good paved road but is subject to landslides, when the traveller is taken over poorly marked or unmarked dirt roads.

About 20 mins. to the west, off the El Angel road, is the town of **Mira** (pop. 5,000; bus from Ibarra, US$0.55, 1 hour; from Tulcán, 1600, 1½ hrs, US$1). Some of the finest quality woollens come from this part of the country; there are two women in Mira who produce them for export and a cooperative which sells in the town at export prices. There are two carnivals held each year, on 2 February, and 18 August, with fireworks and free flowing Tardón, the local *aguardiente*. There is a clean *residencia* (*Mira*, G, basic but good beds), but very few restaurants; the best is the *Bar Latino*. Stretches of virgin rain and cloud forest along the River Mira are accessible to the adventurous.

John Streather writes: **San Gabriel** (pop. 13,000) is a good place from which to visit the **Gruta de la Paz**, about 10 km. to the south, on the way to Bolívar. (Buses from Ibarra, Mira—US$0.50, 1hr.— and Tulcán; *Residencial Montúfar*, G, basic.) (If you are driving, the road branches off the Panamericana at the village of La Paz. The sign says 7 km. to "Grutas", but it is more like 4 km., on a cobblestone road which leads down into mosquito country, but with beautiful views and at least two thundering waterfalls.) There is a huge hotel, but it only opens sporadically and unpredictably—mainly for religious conferences. Buy tickets (US$0.20) for the hot showers and warm swimming pool from the convent before going down to the grotto, near which are the showers and the pool, which is only open from Thur. to Sun. inclusive. There is a restaurant of sorts on the bridge above the grotto. To get back to the main road, cadge a lift!—very long walk. There is a weekly excursion to the Gruta de la Paz from Tulcán.

Tulcán is a chilly town of 33,000 people at an altitude of 2,960 metres, the centre of a rich farming area. It is not particularly interesting for the tourist except for the famous cemetery, where the topiarist's art reaches its apogee; bushes are trimmed into fantastic figures of animals, plants, geometrical shapes etc. Camera essential (take bus from terminal). Ecuador's unique form of paddleball is played every afternoon by the south side of the cemetery.

The migration office is situated at the border at Rumichaca, so all exit formalities are carried out there. The office and the border are open 0600-2000 with skeleton staff at lunch-time (if not closed till 1400). Visas and tourist cards to enter Colombia can be obtained at the Colombian Consulate, Bolívar 54-076 y Junín (Mon.-Fri. 0830-1200, 1400-1600—better to get visas in Quito). See the Colombia Information for Visitors section, **Documents**, for which nationalities need which. Two photos for a visa and an onward ticket or MCO for visa or tourist card are needed. Colombian entry stamp is given at the border. Because of the high volume of local traffic, border crossing is fairly relaxed. Coming from Colombia into Ecuador, entrance stamp is given at the border. If entering Ecuador by car, fumigation costs US$1.50 and *carnet de passages* (essential) must be stamped at the border. When leaving Ecuador by car, some travellers have not needed to go into Tulcán, whereas others have had to return to the town for customs formalities. Immigration office is at the border. A new 4-km. highway leads from Tulcán to the border. The old road descends tortuously for 6½ km. through the mountains to the River Carchi, on the border, which is crossed by the natural bridge of Rumichaca (*Parador de Rumichaca*, D, pool, restaurant, casino, discotheque) and a new concrete bridge. Ipiales is 1½ km. beyond the bridge. *Colectivos* Tulcán-border and border Ipiales US$0.20 each. Taxi to border US$2, to Ipiales US$4. Airport between Tulcán and border, Mon.-Fri. TAME flight to Quito at 1245 (usually fully booked) there is a TAME office in Tulcán in the basement of *Hotel Azteca*, Bolívar y García Morena.

Hotels *Frailejón*, Sucre y Rocafuerte (T 980-129/981-149), E with bath, hot water, T/V, good but expensive restaurant; *Quito*, Ayacucho 450, G, clean, central; *Pensión Minerva*, G, 10 de Agosto y Bolívar, clean but cold; annex in centre, F, overpriced; *Residencial Carchi*, G, Sucre 576 y Pichincha, friendly, no hot water; *Residencial Oasis*, F, 10 de Agosto 395 y Sucre, private showers; *El Paso*, F, Sucre y Pichincha, communal shower sometimes has hot water. *Res. Ecuador*, opp. bus station, F, hot water, clean but poor bathrooms; *Avenida*, also opp. bus station, G, no hot water, clean; *Mallorca*, F, two blocks north of main plaza, friendly, hot water, but thin walls. If all are full (which they tend to be at weekends), try police station.

Restaurants *Avenida*, Bolívar y Ecuador, opp. bus station; *Terminal*, in bus station, reasonable. Many along Sucre: *Restaurant El Paso*, Chinese, good; and other *chifas*. *Parrilladas*, Roberto Sierran y Bolívar, good typical food, near cemetery; *Max Pan* for good breakfasts. Good cheeseburgers at *Café de la Rueda* just off main square.

Camping Possible at the sports field next to the cemetery.

Transport Bus, if you can get one, is cheaper, US$0.15. Bus to Quito 4 hrs., US$2, every ½ hr. with Velotaxi or Espejo; to Ibarra, 2½ hrs., US$1. Otavalo, US$1.40, 3 hrs. (make sure bus is going to Otavalo; if not get out on the Highway at the turn off), or take bus to Ibarra and then collective taxi. To Guayaquil, 20 a day, 11 hrs., US$5. Plenty of colectivos also. Bus terminal is long uphill walk from centre; best to take taxi or little blue bus.

Exchange There are many money changers who will exchange cash on both sides of the border. Travellers' cheques are reportedly difficult to exchange, but try Rodríguez Paz Casa de Cambio, on Ayacucho in front of *Hotel Quito*, or Carlos Burbano, Bolívar y Junín. For those arriving in Ecuador, change only what you need to get to Quito, where the rate is better. Banco de los Andes, Sucre y Junín, is the only bank which will undertake foreign currency transactions (cash only).

Excursions Weekly minibus trips with Cooperativa 11 de Abril, US$2 return, from opp. *Hotel Carchi*, to Gruta de la Paz (see above) at 0800 on Sats., and to Aguas Hediondas at 0800 on Suns. (leaves only if enough passengers). There are 3 daily buses from opp. Colegio Tulcán, near the cemetery, 0600, 0630, 0900, to Maldonado, passing Tufiño, 1 hr. From Tufiño walk 2 km. to turnoff for Aguas Hediondas, then 6 km. to springs themselves. You can probably hitch back to Tufiño. (Taxi Tulcán-Aguas Hediondas, US$6, including one hour wait.) John Streather tells us that Aguas Hediondas (stinking waters) is a pool of boiling sulphurous mineral waters in a wild, impressive, lonely valley. An ice-cold stream of melted snow water passes nearby—one needs to direct it into the pool to make it cool enough to enter! These waters are said to cure spots, rheumatism, etc. If one takes one's passport one can walk from Tufiño over the border to the various hot, warm and cold mineral baths, with a restaurant (friendly and cheap) about 2 km. away in Colombia (the public baths are free but not very clean, the private ones are clean and cost only US$0.20). One can spend the morning at these baths and return to Ecuador for the 1400 bus back to Tulcán, so long as the passport is shown at the border (a rope over the village street). There are five pools at Tufiño—the top, hot, one is good for liver and kidneys, the one below the restaurant for the nerves and rheumatism. The cold pool is some distance from the four others which are all close together. The landscape and the plants on the way up to Aguas Hediondas are really marvellous.

Another, longer but rewarding, trip from Tulcán is to go down to the hot jungle riverside town of Maldonado—same bus as for Tufiño—small *pensiones*, good swimming. The road to Maldonado passes the foot of the trail to the Chiles volcano. On the way up you see many Frailejón plants (related to the Puya Raimondii of Peru and found also in Venezuela).

THE NORTHERN AND WESTERN LOWLANDS (3)

From Quito, a scenic bus trip can be taken to (129 km. US$1.05, 2½ hrs.) **Santo Domingo de los Colorados**, in the W lowlands (pop. 66,661). There is a small daily market and a large Sun. market, but very few Indians now come to the town so both it and the market itself are unexciting and scruffy. You would do better to hire a taxi and go to their villages to see the Colorados (about US$10 for 1½ hrs.). Very few of them now wear the traditional hair dress. Santo Domingo, now the hub of roads radiating to Quito, Guayaquil (by bus 5 hrs.), Esmeraldas (bus, 4 hrs.—the road is very bad N of Rosa Zárate) and Manta, once had the boom town air of the American west a century ago, but is now dusty, noisy, and decaying. Shops in the town are open Tues.-Sun., and banks Tues.-Sat. There is a cinema.

Carnival water throwing is particularly vigorous in Santo Domingo.

Hotels Out of town: *Zaracay*, C, 2 km. out of town on the road to Quito, restaurant, casino, gardens and a swimming pool, good rooms and service, best available, advisable to book (T 750-023), especially at weekend. Nearby is *Hotel del Toachi*, just W of *Zaracay*, D, good showers, swimming pool. On the same road, 20 km. from Santo Domingo, is *Tinalandia*, pleasant and small, A, with its own golf course, and excellent food. Many species of birds, flowers and butterflies in the woods behind the *hostal* (open to non-residents for US$3 a day). Poorly signposted, take small road between Km. 16 and 17 from Santo Domingo on the right (for cheaper accommodation near *Tinalandia*, *Florida* in Alluriquín, 7 km. away on main road, F, with swimming pool).

In town: *Caleta*, Ibarra 137, E, good restaurant, private bath, good; *Colorado*, 29 de Mayo y Quinindé, F, a bit noisy; two *Hostales Turistas*, *No. 1* at 3 de Julio y Latacunga and *No. 2* at Ambato y 29 de Mayo, both F with bath (hot water); *No. 2* basic, noisy, no windows; *Hostal San José*, G, Latacunga y 3 de Julio, run down and dirty; *Pensión Don Pepe*, Calle Quito, F, clean, friendly, quiet. *Amambay*, quite good, water on demand; *Residencial Madrid*, G, Av. 3 de Julio 438, good and clean but used as a brothel and many rooms without windows.

Restaurants *Parrilladas Argentinas*, Chilenas, on Quevedo road Km. 5, for good barbecues. *Mocambo*, Tulcán y Machala, good; *La Fuente*, Ibarra y 3 de Julio, good; *Rico Pollo*, Quito y Río Pove, for chicken; two *chifas*, *Nuevo Hongkong* and *Nueva China*, on the Parque Zaracay; *Corea*, 3 de Julio y San Miguel. Several snackbars and pizzerias. *La Hacienda*, 13 km. along the road to Chone, good food, pleasant surroundings.

Exchange Banco Internacional, Esmeraldas y Quito.

Immigration Camilo Ponce (police station), T 750-225.

A busy paved highway connects Santo Domingo de los Colorados with Esmeraldas to the North (**see page 763**). On this road is Quinindé (Rosa Zárate), where *Residencial Paraíso* is clean and quite good, water 24 hrs. a day. Another highway goes S to **Quevedo** (78,000 people) 1½ hrs. by bus. Set in fertile banana lands and often flooded in the rainy season, Quevedo is known as the Chinatown of Ecuador, with a fair-sized Chinese colony. It is a dusty, noisy, crowded town which has grown exceptionally rapidly over the last 25 years.

Hotels None offers a quiet night. *Olímpico*, Bolívar y 19a, D, good restaurant, near stadium; *Ejecutivo Internacional*, E, 7 de Octubre y Calle Cuarta, modern, large rooms, a/c, private bath, good value, clean, the least noisy; *Guayaquil* opposite is a brothel, basic, G. *El Cóndor*, E with a/c, F without; *El Turista*, F; *Continental*, F, basic; *Charito*, Bolívar 720, F. All are on, or near Av. 7 de Octubre and the plaza.

Restaurants *Hotel Olímpico*, best. Most others along 7 de Octubre: *Rincón Caleño* (Colombian), 1103; *Chifa 51* (Chinese), 928; other *chifas* at 806, 809 and 707; *Tungurahua* (local food), 711. Snackbar, *Quevedo City*, Bolívar y 4a.

Roads and Buses Quevedo is an important route centre. The old paved highway from Latacunga in the highlands to Portoviejo and Manta in the lowlands carries very little traffic, but for a leisurely traveller it is the most beautiful of the routes connecting the highlands with the coast. (Bus, Quevedo-Latacunga, Cotopaxi line, 6 hrs., US$1.50. Bus (*chiva*), Quevedo-Portoviejo, from 7 de Octubre and Calle 8, 5 hrs., US$1.40, uncomfortable, watch your possessions.) On this road is the *Selva Negra* hotel, basic accommodation, but excellent food.

Quevedo is connected with Guayaquil by two paved highways (bus, 3 hrs., US$1.25), one through Balzar and Daule, one through Babahoyo (41,000 people). The roads give a good idea of tropical Ecuador, with its exotic birdlife and jungle and plantations of cacao, sugar, bananas, oranges, tropical fruits and rice. To Quito, 4 hrs., US$1.80.

Popular beach resorts of the Western lowlands can be reached along a paved highway (toll) from Guayaquil. The road divides at Progreso (63 km.). One branch leads to Villamil, normally known as **Playas**, the nearest seaside resort to Guayaquil (2 hrs. by frequent bus—US$1). Its old charm as a fishing village has gone, although every day single-sailed balsa rafts can still be seen among the motor launches returning laden with fish. These rafts are unique, highly ingenious and very simple. The beaches shelve gently, but have been destroyed by hotel construction. As an alternative to the main beach take the unsurfaced road going north which leads to a long sandy beach backed by salt flats and giant cactus. Ecuadoreans flock to the sea from January to April and traffic is very heavy along the coastal roads. Anyone who goes to the beach in May-December will have it largely to himself, except on Sundays.

Hotels *Residencial Cattan*, sea view, D with good food, E without; *Miraglia*, F, run down but clean, sea view, seawater showers, fresh drinking water; *Playas*, E, beach hotel with seawater showers and plain rooms without fans or a/c, good restaurant; *Rey David*, E, sea view; *Acapulco*, F, clean, friendly, restaurant, sea view; *El Galeón*, E, beside the church, friendly, clean, mosquito nets, water all day, cheap restaurant with excellent seafood attached; *Turístico*, F, just off square, clean, mosquito nets; *Hostería La Gaviota*, 500 metres out on Posorja road, D, colour TV, a/c, but rooms shabby with cockroaches, friendly, good clean restaurant. *Residencial California*, and *Restaurant Jalisco* nearby, good cheap food. *Hostería Costa Verde*, cheap, clean, F. Camping at S end of beach. Casino.

There is a water shortage all along the coast; drinking water has to be brought by tanker from Guayaquil and no hotel can guarantee water in the rooms at all times. There are showers on the beach.

An interesting place to visit, a walk or short drive from Playas, is the little village of El Morro. There is a picturesque wooden church and a large rock formation known as El Muerto. Beyond Playas lies **Posorja**, at the mouth of the Guayas estuary, home to a large commercial fishing fleet and fish processing plants. The ocean front is rubbish-strewn and muddy. Posorja and other coastal towns are receiving a population influx because of the economic boom caused by shrimp farming. Local people catch young shrimp in the sea and estuaries and sell them to large commercial ponds where they are grown to market size. From Esmeraldas to Machala, the ocean front is being transformed by shrimp farming. Native mangrove swamps are being destroyed rapidly; heavy construction equipment can be seen everywhere.

West of Progreso the road to Salinas runs through a vast area of arid thorn-scrub land whose inhabitants look very Indian and produce little besides charcoal. At **Santa Elena** the road forks. To the left, south, we pass a petroleum refinery and enter the busy port and regional market centre of **La Libertad** (*Hotel Villa Maria*, G, very run down, on Malecón, as are *Lido* and *Seven Seas*, both G, mediocre; *Hostería Samarina*, E, Dituris-run, some bungalows, swimming pool, restaurant, coffee shop, bar; *Hotel Turis Palm*, Av. 9 de Octubre, F, fan, bath—G without, older place and a bit run down, next door and similar is *Reina del Pacífico*). Buses every hour to Manglaralto, Puerto López and Jipijapa from near market.

A few km. further on, surrounded by miles of salt flats, is **Salinas**, the self-styled best resort in Ecuador (population, 21,000, buses from Guayaquil, US$1, at the new Terminal Terrestre about 2½ hrs.; return journey, go to La Libertad by bus or colectivo and take bus from terminal there). The beaches are not good and the town is becoming increasingly more developed; it is very quiet outside the holiday season (Dec.-Easter and July-Sept.). The best time for swimming is Dec.-May. The flat-topped hill at Punta Santa Elena dominates the landscape. Good deep-sea fishing and water-skiing. Pesca Tours, on the seafront, rents boats for US$250; four lines from the boat, you may keep any dorado you catch but Pesca Tours keeps the marlin. Car racing at the Autódromo.

Hotels *Salinas,* D, modern, off Malecón, restaurant reported good; *Miramar,* with casino, B, with bath and telephone. *Samarina,* C, or US$32 bungalow with 6 beds, acceptable; *Cantábrico,* D, lines of hammocks outside, 4-course set meal; *Yulee,* D, with own bath (but try bargaining), clean, excellent food, friendly, well placed for beaches; *Residencial Rachel,* 2 blocks from beach, E, mosquito nets inadequate.

Restaurants *Saavedra* rec. for large portions of well cooked fish for about US$1.50. *Mar y Tierra,* close to *Hotel Miramar,* expensive but excellent seafood, especially lobster; also near the *Miramar* is *Flipper,* cheap, simple, clean and friendly. Discothèque, *El Caracol.* Night club, *Che Papusa* (near town hall), normally known after its owner as *Donde el Roy.*

Exchange It is not possible to change travellers cheques' in Salinas. Not all banks change cash; you can change cash at the supermarket and the *Hotel Salinas* but the rate is bad.

Cables Ietel public telex booth at Radio Internacional.

At Baños San Vicente, about 7 km. E. of La Libertad, just off the main road to Guayaquil, Dituris has opened a large tourist complex, where for US$0.30 admission you have use of the whole facility, including swimming pools, thermal baths and a mud hole to cure assorted ailments. There is still more construction work to be done; a hotel is planned when finance is available.

Punta Carnero is on the S shore of the Santa Elena peninsula. Magnificent 15-km. beach with wild surf and heavy undertow, virtually empty during the week. To the E of Punta Carnero, along the coast, lies Anconcito, a picturesque fishing port at the foot of steep cliffs, but nowhere at all to stay; further on is Ancón, centre of the declining local oilfield.

The northward fork of the road at Santa Elena leads us along the coast (past Ballenita, pleasant beach, surfing with two good *ceviche* restaurants, cottages can be rented) as far north as La Entrada. Manta can be reached by going inland from La Entrada via Jipijapa. Part of the road is along the beach and therefore fast, but care should be taken as the tide rises fast and suddenly. La Entrada can be reached in less than 5 hrs. from Guayaquil, and because of this a number of attractive fishing villages along this stretch of coast contain the modern bungalows of Guayaquileños. Almost all the villages have good beaches, and there is particularly good swimming near the attractive fishing villages of Palmar and Ayangue (only hotel is *Hostal Un Millón de Amigos,* clean, friendly, good food, rec.; village very crowded at weekends). Many kinds of cactus are found in this area because of the dry climate (fewer than five days of rain a year). A typical dish from this region is *sopa de bola de verde,* made from several kinds of vegetable: green *plátano* is crushed, kneaded and formed into balls filled with green peas and diced carrots.

At Valdivia, a small port, is the site of the supposed Japanese-Jomón culture contact, via fishermen, about 3000 B.C. Little for the visitor to see; the little museum is closed; most artefacts discovered at the site are in museums in Quito and Guayaquil. A visit to the archaeological dig at Salango, 5 km. south of Puerto López, is recommended. Some beautiful artefacts have been found, all of which are housed in a museum around which the mainly English archaeologists (voluntary and qualified) are happy to show travellers. There are two new restaurants in the village, and nearby a complex of bamboo houses.

Manglaralto, the main centre of the region north of Santa Elena, is reached by bus from Guayaquil (change at La Libertad) as well as by numerous trucks. 3 km. N, at Montañita beach, reported best surfing in Ecuador, cottages to let (Gabriela rents tents), 1 hr., US$0.70, by bus or truck from La Libertad or Santa Elena.

Hotels *Alegre Calamar*, N end of town, F, good seafood restaurant; *Corona del Mar* restaurant has rooms, F, shared bath, and a bungalow for rent. Sra. de Arcos' house next to post office; also *Habitaciones* next to post office, F with bath, clean, friendly. It is a nice place to stay and bathe, with a good, quiet, clean beach, but little shelter. *Comedor Familiar* has meals weekends only; also *Comedor Florencia*, cheap and friendly.

North of Manglaralto the rainfall increases and at La Entrada the road peters out in the wet season (Dec.-Feb.; July-Sept.). A bumpy ride takes one from Manglaralto through lush tropical scenery via Puerto Rico and Salango (interesting archaeological museum) to Puerto López, set in an impressive bay with hills on either side. Near Puerto Rico is *Alandaluz*, an ecological/tourist centre, E full board, good base for exploring nearby villages. The main attraction in **Puerto López** is the arrival of the fishermen at 0800 and again at 1630. The whole town seems to assemble on the beach to greet the hordes of small boats and buy the fish. It seems to be easy to go out with the fishermen in their boats. Next to the sports field is a small museum with information on the nearby Parque Nacional Machalilla.

Lodging and food *Residencial El Pacífico*, F, on sea front, clean, basic, but insecure; *Residencial Soroya*, one street W, G; *Restaurant Viña del Mar* rents rooms next door, F, good, cheap food. Restaurant on sea front, next to *Carmita* (now closed), serves good ceviche and cold beer; *Acapulco* restaurant on main street, video shows nightly at 1930.

Buses 1½ hrs., US$1, hourly to Jipijapa. To La Libertad, 1 hr. US$1; to Manglaralto, 1 hr., US$1.

Further north of Puerto López is Puerto de Cayo (one hotel, E, several restaurants, nice beaches).

Offshore are the Islas de la Plata, which can be reached by small boat; plenty of seabirds, including the Galápagos albatros, can be seen, and there is also precolumbian pottery.

A new dirt road has been made from Manglaralto to the main Guayaquil-Manta road. This road climbs into the humid hills of S Manabí, then descends to the dry savanna scrub around **Jipijapa** (27,500 inhabitants), an important centre for the region's farmers, trading cotton, fruit and kapok (from the fat-trunked ceiba tree). (*Pensión Mejía*, F, 2 blocks from plaza, clean, basic, noisy. Bus from Manglaralto, 2½ hrs., US$1.75.) Thirty-two km. across dusty hills is **Montecristi** (8,190 people), below an imposing hill, high enough to be watered by low cloud which gives the region its only source of drinking water. The town is also famous for its Panama hats which, along with cane-work products, are much cheaper than in Quito.

Soon after, we reach **Manta** (100,000 people), the main commercial centre of western Ecuador, a noisy, busy, and dirty town with a few steep streets and a fine wooden church. By all accounts it has nothing to recommend it. The area around is denuded and poor, with many shanty towns. With its twin town, Tarqui, reached by a road bridge, it has the largest population W of Guayaquil. The Tarqui beaches are reported to be not as bad as those at Manta, which are filthy and smelly. Fishing boats are built on the beach. The Banco Central museum, Calle 9 y Av. 4, has interesting specimens of the Huancavilca-Manteña culture (AD 800-1550); open during banking hours, curator speaks English and French. Sites can be visited from Bahía de Caráquez. All streets have been given numbers; those above 100 are in Tarqui. Most offices, shops and the bus station are in Manta.

Hotels Wider selection of hotels in Tarqui. *Las Gaviotas*, Malecón y Calle 106, E, on beach, dirty, a/c, poor restaurant, tennis; *Manta Imperial*, D, Calles Playa y Murciélago, on beach, a/c, poorly maintained, not up to standard in either accommodation or restaurant, pool, private parking, disco and dancing; *Las Rocas*, Calle 101 y Av. 105, D, a/c, private parking, restaurant poor; *Panorama Inn*, Calle 103 y Av. 105, E, a/c, bath, TV, rec., swimming pool and restaurant. Also on Tarqui beach, *Residencial Eugenia*, Malecón y Calle 105, F, safe, comfortable, hot water, laundry facilities, clean; *Miami*, Malecón y Calle 107, F, private bath, good; *Residencial Niza*, Malecón y Calle 103, G, restaurant, shared bath, clean, pleasant. *Residencial Capri*, near bus station, G, good value. *Americano*, Av. 106 y Calle 105, E; *El Inca*, Calle 105 y Malecón, G.

Restaurants Cheap restaurants by Tarqui market, Av. 108 y Calle 102; and on the nearby beach. *El Ceibo*, in the centre, is rec. *El Boulevard* on Tarqui beach near the Plaza Tarqui, good fish and seafood, reasonably priced; *La Cascada*, Av. 105 y Calle 103, cafeteria with swimming pool; *Georgie*, Calle 16 y Av. 7, good fish, cheap. *Pelícan*, Malecón y Calle 105; *La Tebanda*, Playa y Murciélago, on beach, good food, chairs for children; *La Tortuga*, on seafront, food good but service poor; *Santa Ana*, 2 blocks inland from Malecón, good cheap meals.

Post Office above Banco de Pichincha; **Telephone** Ietel on road to the beach.

Tourist Office Dituris, Edificio Emapa. **Travel Agents** Ecuadorian Tours, at Av. 2 y Calle 13; Metropolitan Touring at Av. 3 y Calle 12.

Immigration Av. 4 de Noviembre y J-1 (police station).

Exchange *Casa de Cambio* Zanchi, Banco de Pichincha and Banco del Pacífico change travellers' cheques. Filanbanco accepts Visa.

Air Service Eloy Alfaro airport nearby. Every day by TAME to Quito, US$12, every day except Sun. to Guayaquil, US$9.

Buses To Quito, 8 hrs., US$3; Guayaquil, 4 hrs., US$2; Esmeraldas, 8 hrs., US$3; Santo Domingo, 6 hrs., US$2.10; Portoviejo, ½ hr., US$0.30; Jipijapa, 45 mins., US$0.45; Bahía de Caráquez, 3 hrs., US$1. All from bus station.

24 km. inland from Montecristi is **Portoviejo** (101,771 inhabitants), a major commercial centre with connections by road with Quito (bus, 7 hrs. with Reina del Camino, US$2.75) and Guayaquil.

Hotels *Ejecutivo*, B, very good, very expensive, extra charge for the guard, but unfriendly, does not accept Visa despite sign outside. *París*, off main plaza, E; *Residencial Maroles*, 2 Av./Calle 1, F, friendly, noisy. *Cristal*, Calle Ricaurte 106, F; *San Marcos*, Olmedo y 9 de Octubre; The restaurant *Chifa China* on the plaza has a clean, cheap hotel upstairs. Other restaurants: *Mariano*, Morales y Sucre, good food; good Chinese restaurant at bus terminal.

From Portoviejo a road goes E to Quevedo (147 km). At Calderón, branch NE for Calceta, Chone (36,000 people) and on to Santo Domingo de los Colorados. From Calceta and Chone paved roads run 50 km. to **Bahía de Caráquez** (18,000 people), a tranquil town in a pleasant setting on the seaward southern end of an inlet; the river front is attractively laid out, but there are water shortages except in the hotels with their own supply. Smart new homes fringe the seaward side. The town is a centre of banana and other agricultural exports as well as shrimp farming. On Isla de los Pájaros in the bay are many seabirds (hire a launch, US$3 per hour); launches can also be hired to visit mangrove islands.

Hotels *La Piedra*, Malecón, C, pool, good restaurant; *Herradura*, Bolívar y Malecón (beach), D, good restaurant; *Centro Vocacional "Life"*, Dávila y García Moreno, D, full board; *Americano*, Ascazubi y Morales, C with a/c and bath; *Manabí*, nearby, G, clean and friendly; *Residencial Vera*, Ante y Malecón, F, noisy, own water; *Palma*, Bolívar y Arenas, G, clean; cheap but dirty restaurant next door; *Residencial Tamarindos*, G, clean, friendly.

Restaurants *Brisas del Mar*, Bolívar y Malecón, good fish, cheap; *Los Helecheros*, cafeteria, good and clean, Bolívar y Malecón; *Chifa China*, cheap, good, Bolívar y Ascazubi. *Los Mellizos*, near hospital, excellent fish, very cheap; *El Galería*, Bolívar, expensive; *Miramar*, Malecón, overpriced; good *comedor* next to *Hotel Vera*.

Exchange Only at Banco Industrial, Malecón (very poor rate), or try the manageress at Banco Central (be nice to the security guards).

Tourist Office Dituris, Malecón, opposite Ietel building.

Bus from Bahía de Caráquez to Quito, 8 hrs., US$3.20, Esmeraldas, 8 hrs., and Portoviejo, 2 hrs., with Reina del Camino. To Guayaquil, 5½ hrs., US$2.80; to Manta, 3 hrs., US$1.

Airport at San Vicente (see below): Air Transportes Bahía flies twice a day to Guayaquil, US$14, with connections to Pedernales (US$5.50).

Those interested in exploring the coast further north can take the ferry (every 15 mins., US$0.13, also car ferry) from Bahía de Caráquez to **San Vicente**, on the far side of the Río Chone, a thriving market (*Hotel Vacaciones*, E, restaurant, TV in rooms; about 3 km. from San Vicente are *Cabañas La Playa*, US$20 for beach chalet sleeping 5, good food in restaurant; other *cabañas* on beach), and on by bus, truck or car north along the beach to Canoa, thence inland, cutting across Cabo Pasado through the more humid pasture-lands to the small market centre of **Jama** (small *pensión*).

From there the road runs parallel to the beach past coconut groves, inland across some low hills and across the Equator to **Pedernales**, another small market town on the coast, bus from San Vicente (4 daily), 6 hrs., US$3.50; several houses where you can stay (*Hotel Turismo*, F, basic, clean, helpful; *Cabañas Cañaverales*, F; *Playas*, F with bath, TV, friendly, clean; *Residencial Comedor El Gitano*, F, meals, friendly) and 2 or 3 eating places. A rough new road has been finished between Pedernales and El Carmen (thence to Sto. Domingo and Quito)—the two towns are expected to become booming tourist resorts—and on to Cojimíes (enquire if passable in rainy season).

Buses—one or two a day—use the beach at low tide, take 7 hrs. from San Vicente (US$3.50), 45 mins. from Pedernales (truck US$0.50) to **Cojimíes**: *Residenciales España*, G, shabby, no water; *Mi Descanso* and *Cojimíes*—all look the same; *Hotel Coco Solo* is 14 km. before Cojimíes, D, overpriced, nice but no services and no choice in restaurant. Flower-decorated house on same street will serve meals at any hour; other houses serve food; one restaurant, *El Caracol*, good but expensive. Cojimíes was a major pre-conquest centre; little of this is noticeable now, although many artefacts are still dug up, it is being continually eroded by the sea and has been moved about three times in as many decades. A boat leaves at high tide every Sat. for Esmeraldas, stopping at Chamanga (US$4, 7 hrs.) and one from Esmeraldas on Sat. as well. There is a boat to Manta on Wed. and a direct canoe to Muisné (US$4) at 0600, 2 hrs. The entry into Cojimíes and Muisné is treacherous and many boats have been thrown into the shallows by swell.

North of Cojimíes is a rich banana-growing region. **Muisné**, an island reached by road from Esmeraldas (bus US$1, 3 hrs., and a canoe over to the island), is the centre and main outlet of this area; through it some 50,000 stems of bananas a month are exported via Esmeraldas. On the Río Sucio, inland from Muisné and Cojimíes, is an isolated group of Cayapa Indians, some of whom visit the beaches on Sun. All hotels F, but women should avoid *Residencial Narcisita*; we have been warned of sexual attacks by the owner; *Galápagos*, on far side of town from docks, closest to beach, safe, F, rec; *Sarita*, F, clean, private bathroom; you can also rent small huts on the beach, G p.p., few if any have electricity or water, beautiful setting; *Cabañas Ipanema*, 200 m. from beach, rec. There are several simple seafood *comedores*. Also *Delicias del Mar*, Australian-run, good food, good service; *Mario's Bar*, open late(ish). No meals after 1900. The beaches 10-15 mins. walk from town, are large at low tide but practically disappear at high tide. There is a lot of litter and wood lying around and hordes of mosquitoes. In the wet season there are boats between Muisné and Cojimíes, mostly early a.m., US$3, 2 hrs. buy ticket at bus stop, take water proofs. Cargo boats ply between Muisné and Manta. A new road has been built between Muisné and Bolívar inland, behind the beaches; easier but less scenic. Be careful on the beaches; we have received reports of rape and violent attacks. If staying in huts on the beach beware thieves who may remove the roof to enter

Esmeraldas (117,000 people) is reported dirty and overpriced. The electricity and water supplies are still inadequate. The main street is closed to traffic from 1930 to 2130 nightly. Gold mines nearby, tobacco and cacao grown inland, cattle ranching along the coast, timber exported, and an oil pipeline from the Oriente to an ocean terminal at nearby Balao; an oil refinery has been built nearby. A new road bridge over the river at San Mateo upstream from Esmeraldas gives a direct road link to the General Rivadeneira airport. Las Palmas, just N of Esmeraldas, is being developed as a resort: several hotels have been built and restaurants opened. There is a broad sandy beach but it is reported as unsafe (theft) and dirty. White people have been advised to avoid the shanty-town on the Malecón. Even the water is muddy as it is close to a naval harbour and people use the beach as a speedway. Buses to Las Palmas (US$0.05, taxi US$1) leave regularly from the main square in Esmeraldas.

Mosquitoes and malaria are a serious problem throughout the province of Esmeraldas in the rainy season. All the beaches have mosquitoes that come out in hordes at night and bite through clothing. Take plenty of insect repellant because the Detán sold locally does not work well. Most *residencias* provide mosquito nets (*toldos* or *mosquiteros*); don't stay anywhere that does not. Best to visit in dry season, June-December.

Hotels Best in Esmeraldas are *Apart Hotel*, Av. Libertad 407 y Ramón Tello, D, excellent, good restaurant, and *Roma*, E, Olmeda y Piedrahita, with its *Restaurant Tres Carabelas*; *La Pradera*, 7½ km. S on Atacames road, D, a/c, swimming pool, tennis courts, restaurant, and *Europeo*, D, between Esmeraldas and Las Palmas, no a/c, but the restaurant is very good, German-owned but under Chilean management. *Galeón*, Piedrahita y Olmedo, D, bath, a/c; *Korea*, Mañizares y Bolívar, F, rec., private shower, fan; *Americano*, Sucre y Piedrahita, F with fan and bath, good value; *Diana*, Mañizares y Sucre, good, private showers, safe, F. *Hostal Domínguez*, G, on Sucre near Plaza Central, noisy, hot water, open all night; *Valparaíso I*, Libertad y Pichincha, G, very basic but good value, cheap restaurant. *Turismo*, Bolívar 843, F with bath and fan, clean and friendly. Other cheaper hotels include *Bolívar*, F and cheaper still, *Central*, F, and *Asia*, F, both are basic but clean. Generally, hotels in the town centre are not up to much and you are rec. to stay in the outskirts. Some hotels are not keen to take single travellers.

Las Palmas offers the best hotels along Av. Kennedy: *Cayapas*, D, a/c, showers and hot water in all rooms, overpriced, good restaurant; *Hotel del Mar*, D, on sea front, modern. *Colonial*, Platat y L. Tello, D; *Chimborazo*, G, cheap and noisy.

Restaurants In Esmeraldas: *Chifa Restaurante Asiático*, Mañizares y Bolívar, Chinese, excellent; *Pelican*, Malecón, very good, popular, vegetarian dishes, expensive but worth it. *La Marimba Internacional*, Libertad y Lavallén, has been rec.; *Daruma*, Olmedo y Mejía, is Japanese and local. *Café Congenita*, near *Hotel Americano*, for iced tea, milk shakes; other soda fountains at Olmedo y Piedrahita. In Las Palmas, *Atenas Tiffani*; Kennedy 707, good food but expensive; *Bayardo*, on the Malecón, good food, lively host, cheaper than *Tiffani*. *Artrang*, main plaza, good food, good value; *Las Redes*, main plaza, good fish, cheap; *Budapest*, Cañizares 214 y Bolívar, Hungarian-run, clean, pleasant. There are numerous typical restaurants and bars by the beach selling ceviches, fried fish and patacones, etc.

Throughout Esmeraldas province a cheap meal is the *comida típica*, fish, rice, boiled *plátano*, sometimes beans (*minestre*), called *tapao*. There is also *cocado*, fish, crabs or shrimp cooked in coconut cream served with rice and *plátano*. There is a soup made of shellfish and coconut milk which is very good. *Cocada* is a sweet made of brown sugar and grated coconut; *conserva* is a paste of guava, banana and brown sugar, wrapped in banana leaves.

Shopping   There is a Cayapa basket market across from the Post Office, behind the vegetables. Also three doors down, Tolita artefacts and basketry. **Exchange** at bank until 1200; at Botica Koch, Sucre y 9 de Octubre, good rates.

Entertainment In Esmeraldas, *El Portón* peña and discotheque, Colón y Piedrahita; *El Guadal de Ña Mencha*, 6 de Diciembre y Quito, peña upstairs, marimba school at weekends; good *Bar Asia* on Bolívar by main Parque. *Los Cuervos*, discotheque. In Las Palmas, *El Náutico* and *Déjà Vue* on the Malecón, a/c, discotheques. Cockfights, Eloy Alfaro y 9 de Octubre, weekends.

Music   Esmeraldas has been called "the capital of rhythm". The people prefer the livelier sound of Caribbean *salsa* to the *cumbia* heard in the sierra, and have retained the African-influenced marimba, usually accompanied by a bomero, who plays a deep-pitched bass drum suspended from the ceiling, and a long conga drum. Where there is a marimba school you will also find dancers, and the women who are too old to dance play percussion and chant songs handed down the generations, many with Colombian references, but the best marimba can only be seen in the backwoods of the province on Sundays and holidays as that in Esmeraldas is only for tourists. Centro Cultural Afro-Ecuatoriano (CCA), Calle Sucre y Catedral, Casilla 65, T 710603.

Cinema   *Ciné Bolívar*, Bolívar y 9 de Octubre, is the best, with a/c and upholstered seating. Three other cinemas offer more basic accommodation with bats and rats.

Immigration   Av. Olmedo y Rocafuerte, T 720-256.

Tourist Information   The tourist office (Dituris) is in the Edificio de la Alcaldía, Bolívar 517 y 9 de Octubre, 2nd floor, half a block from the main square, singularly unhelpful.

Buses   Terminal Terrestre planned for 1991. To Quito, US$2.50, 8 hrs., 30 a day, good paved road, Trans-Esmeraldas, Av. Piedrahita 200, rec., or by Occidental; by Aerotaxi (small bus), 5 hrs., 12 passengers, reserved seats, office on main square. To Santo Domingo, US$1.40, 4 hrs.; to Ambato, 5 times a day with Coop. Sudamericana, 8 hrs., US$2.50; to Guayaquil, hourly, US$5, 7 hrs.; to Portoviejo and Manta, US$2, to Quevedo, 6 hrs. To La Tola (road good to Río Verde), 2 daily, US$1.60, 5 hrs.; to Muisné, 28 daily with La Costeñita, US$1, 3½ hrs. To Súa (road reasonable) and Atacames every half hour from 0630 to 2030, US$0.30, 1-1½ hrs.

Boats to Limones and San Lorenzo: service irregular; ask at Port Captain's office at Las Palmas. Combined boat/bus service leaves for San Lorenzo at 1330.

Airport General Rivadeneira Daily flights to Quito with TAME, US$10; taxi to centre about US$1.60 (Esmeraldas), US$8 to Atacames.

Atacames, a beach resort 25 km. S of Esmeraldas, is still attractive, and the palm trees on the beach (washed away in 1983) are growing again. Atacames is famous for its black coral and the local people make handicrafts from it. Most accommodation has salt water in the bathrooms; fresh water is not always available and not very good. *Hotel Jennifer*, E, cold shower, fan, clean; *Hotel Tahiti*, with shower, F, dirty, theft from rooms reported, serves breakfasts, good restaurant, try the prawns, but check your bill carefully, also has bungalows, F; *Hostería Los Bohíos*, C, prices cheaper (F) in low season (June, July, August), for a bungalow, safe, clean; *Hostería Cayapas*, beach huts, F, cooking and barbecue; *Casa Blanca*, Urbanización Iñaquito, cabins for 6, with bathroom, kitchen, F p.p., on beach; *San Sebastián* and *Marbella*, beach huts for 5, both F; *Residencial Sol de Oriente*, F, clean, near beach. *Castel Nuovo*, 3 km. N on road to Esmeraldas, C with bath and fan, swimming pool, on beach, rec.; *La Pradera*, 4 km. along Esmeraldas road, pool, restaurant, good value. *Edén*, cabins in F range, good location on beach, rec. Tents or beach bungalows can be hired at under US$1 a night; no facilities but can arrange with hotels. *Lumbaye* bungalows are rec., cheaper off-season. Beach bungalows with showers at *Cabañas Costa del Sol*, D, good breakfast and seafood; *Cabañas Arco Iris*, D, shower, fridge, clean, rec., charming, N end of beach, T Quito 525544 for reservations; *Cabañas South Pacific*, F, clean, American owner, fresh water showers. Rats are common in all these beach huts, and insect repellant is essential.

Restaurants on beach are reasonable, mostly seafood; try *Comedor Pelícanos*, fresh fish, chicken, *ceviche*, occasionally music, rec.; also *Cafetería Pelícanos*, best, includes vegetarian dishes and salads; *Comedor Popular*, good Italian and criollo cooking, order special requests in advance. 2 discotheques on beach. *Cocada*, a sweet made from different nuts, brown sugar, cocoa, etc., is sold in the main plaza. **Warning**: It is reported that there have been many assaults on campers and late-night beach strollers. The sea can be very dangerous, there is a powerful undertow and many people have been drowned.

Súa, another beach resort a little S of Atacames, is quiet, friendly, with a beautiful bay with pelicans and frigate birds, but the sandy beach is very dirty. *Pensión Palmar*, G, cabins; *Residencial Quito*, G; *Mar y Sol*, G, washing facilities poor. The hotels along the seafront vary little in standard but quite significantly in price. *Hotel Súa*, French-run, clean, friendly; *Motel Chagra Ramos*, on beach, F, clean, fan on request, good restaurant. Insect repellant is essential along this coast. Beyond Súa is Playa de **Same**, quiet, with a beautiful, sandy beach lined with palms; one hotel, *Club Casablanca*, A, restaurant, tennis courts, swimming pool, luxurious (reservations Wagons-Lits Turismo, Ed. Galicia, Diego de Almagro 1822 y Alpallana, Quito, T 554933/4/7, Telex 22763 VALEJO ED); and 5 places for rental of *cabañas*, *Centro Turístico Manila*, 8 cabins for 4 people, restaurant (reservations Wagons-Lits Turismo); *La Terraza*, 5 cabins for 3-4, good restaurant (reservations *Restaurante La Bettola*, Quito, T 239396); *Cabañas Isla del Sol*, 12 cabins for 4-6, bath, comfortable, safe, good restaurant, rec., stoney beach front, reservations T 731-151, Atacames, or telegram to Casilla 358, Esmeraldas; *Complejo Turístico Las Canoas*, 21 cabins, 2-6 people, restaurant (Reservations Wagons-Lits Turismo); *El Acantilado*, 8 cabins for 6-8, cooking facilities, on hill by the sea, no palm trees. All cabins about US$5 p.p. with water and electricity; booking advisable at holiday times and weekends. **Tonchigüe**, 1 hr. S from Esmeraldas beyond Súa, is also lovely during the rainy season (Dec.-May).

There are no good beaches for swimming north of Esmeraldas. Río Verde, where the paved road ends, has a dirty beach and one hotel, *Paz y Bueno*, F, basic (N side of river). It was the setting for Morriz Thompson's book on Peace Corps life, *Living Poor*. Beyond Río Verde is **Rocafuerte**, recommended as having the best seafood in the province, including oysters and lobsters. At **La Tola**, where one catches the boat for Limones and San Lorenzo, the shoreline changes from sandy beaches to mangrove swamp. The wildlife is varied and spectacular, especially the birds. La Tola is 3½ hrs. (US$1.50) from Esmeraldas, by bus, four daily a.m., dusty, uncomfortable, buses often get stuck. Four boats go daily from La Tola to San Lorenzo via Limones, 2 hrs., US$1.50 (beware overcrowding); seem to connect with boats from Esmeraldas. Try to avoid staying overnight in La Tola; take a raincoat.

Mangrove coastlands stretch north into Colombia, and have only two towns of note in Ecuador: Limones and San Lorenzo.

Limones, the main commercial centre, largely a saw-mill town, is the focus of traffic down-river from much of northern Esmeraldas Province where bananas from the Río Santiago are sent to Esmeraldas for export. The Cayapa Indians live up the Río Cayapas and can sometimes be seen in Limones, especially during the crowded weekend market (uninteresting), but they are more frequently seen at Borbón.

Limones has two good shops selling the very attractive Cayapa basketry; selection includes some items from Colombia. The first is opposite *Restaurant El Bongó* and the second by the dock opposite Banco de Fomento.

Two hotels, both execrable. Limones is "the mosquito and rat capital of Ecuador". A hired launch (6 pers. US$1.40 p.p., 1½ hrs.) provides a fascinating trip through mangrove islands and passing hundreds of hunting pelicans. Information on boat journeys from the Capitanía del Puerto, Las Palmas, reached by bus No. 1 from the main square in Esmeraldas. From Limones you can also get a canoe or boat to Borbón. Better to stay at San Lorenzo.

Borbón (*Residencial Capri*, F, with marimba dance hall next door; *Panama City*, G, modern, friendly, clean, mosquito nets, rec.), with population almost entirely black, is on the Río Cayapas past mangrove swamps. Buses to Esmeraldas, US$1.40, 4 hrs; to Limones and San Lorenzo at 0730 and 1100. Upstream are Cayapa Indian villages. From Borbón hire a dugout to Boca de Onzole one hour upstream, which is the confluence of the Cayapas and Onzole rivers. There is a fine lodge built by a Hungarian (for advance bookings write to Stephan Tarjany, Casilla 187, Esmeraldas), E with full board, good value, clean, warm showers. Water skiing available on request. You can hire a dugout with him for US$50 to Santa María (board and lodging with Sra. Pastora at missionary station, F, mosquito nets, or at the *Residencial*, G, basic, will prepare food but fix price beforehand, owner offers 5 hr. jungle trips to visit Cayapa villages) and on upstream to San Miguel. Alternatively, a supply boat goes several times a week between Borbón and Santa María, which sometimes takes passengers, US$4 p.p. return. You pass Zapallo Grande, a friendly village with many gardens, where the American missionary Dr Meisenheimer has established a hospital, pharmacy, church and school. You will see the Cayapa Indians passing in their canoes and in their open long houses on the shore. San Miguel is the last outpost of civilization with a church and a few houses, beautifully situated on a hill at the confluence of two rivers. From there you go back 5 hrs. downstream to La Tola where you can pick up the bus from Esmeraldas or go on to Limones and San Lorenzo.

San Lorenzo is relatively more attractive than Limones. There is a beach nearby at San Pedro (no facilities), reached by boat, Sat. and Sun. at 0800 and 1400. The best places to see *marimba* are two schools, one Esmeraldeña and one Colombiana. The latter practice on Calle 24 de Mayo between *Residencial Pailón* and *Residencial Ibarra*; you can't miss the sound. The former practice Wed. and Sat. nights, are more disciplined, better musicians and dance more. They have toured the continent and are led by a woman called Lydia who can make marimbas to order. *Marimba* can be seen during the local fiesta on 30 Sept. San Lorenzo is an expensive town, with a poor water supply.

Hotels *Wilma*, F, basic, ask for rooms 15 or 16, they are newer and bigger; *Residencial Margaritas*, F, friendly, clean, good showers, Imbabura y Ortiz; *Pailón*, Ayora y 24 de Mayo, satisfactory, G; *Ecuador*, Alfaro y 10 de Agosto, F, restaurant OK, basic, laundry facilities, mosquito net provided; *Residencial Vilmar*, Imbabura y Mariano, G, near the station. *San Lorenzo*, Alfaro y 10 de Agosto, G, rec. for meals, but not so good to stay; *Residencial Ibarra*, Coronel y 24 de Mayo, possibly the best, G, some rooms with fan, clean, friendly. **Restaurants**: *Cabaña del Sol*, rec. for good, cheap fish, Ayora y Alfaro. *El Fogón*, Garces, near railway station, excellent camarones. *Rumory's* marimba and discotheque at Imbabura y 10 de Agosto. Insect repellant is a "must" in San Lorenzo. Be sure to check your bedding for scorpions.

Train The *autocarro* (motor rail-coach) leaves daily (but not Thur.) from the station 10 mins. from town centre (usually overcrowded; reserve day before travelling, if possible, otherwise be there at 0600. The train journey gives an excellent transect of Ecuador (**see page** 756). To Ibarra, US$1.75, up to 12 hrs., departing at 0700. The train can get very crowded and angry passengers unable to board have been known to beat up the driver! Because of heavy rains, roadworks and landslides, delays and derailments are frequent.

Boats Dugouts, with motors, to La Tola (5 a day from 0630, 2 hrs., US$1.50) and Borbón (3 hrs, US$2), via Limones, US$1. Boats leave daily at 0730 and 1400 (stops at Tambilla and Limones en route), bus from there to Esmeraldas, through ticket US$2.75. Beautiful journey but dusty bus trip. Launch to Esmeraldas at 0500 and 0730; plane to Quito at 0930, tickets at airport at 0800.

From San Lorenzo there are occasional boats to Tumaco in Colombia, but gringos are not normally welcome as passengers because contraband is being carried. When arriving in San Lorenzo from Tumaco, the customs office run by navy personnel is in the harbour, but you have to get your passport stamped at the immigration office in Ibarra or Esmeraldas because the immigration police in the *Hotel Imperial* office do not handle passports. Problems may arise if you delay more than a day or two before getting an entry stamp, as the immigration police in Ibarra are less easy-going.

Nancy Alexander, of Chicago, writes that about 75% of the population of Limones, Borbón and San Lorenzo has come from Colombia in the last fifty years. The people are mostly black and many are illegal immigrants. Smuggling between Limones and Tumaco in Colombia is big business (hammocks, manufactured goods, drugs) and there are occasional drug searches along the N coastal road.

GUAYAQUIL (4)

Guayaquil, the chief seaport and commercial city, founded in 1537 by Francisco de Orellana, stands on the west bank of the Guayas river, some 56 km. from its outflow into the Gulf of Guayaquil. Its population of 1,600,000 makes it the largest city in the Republic. The climate is at its best from May to December with little or no rain and cool nights, though the sky is overcast more often than not. The heat and humidity during the rainy season, January to April, are oppressive. The Puerto Marítimo, opened in 1979, handles about 90% of the country's imports and 50% of its exports.

The city is dotted with small parks and pleasant gardens. A waterfront drive, known as the Malecón, runs along the shore of the Guayas river. Here are the splendid Palacio Municipal and the severe Government Palace. From the landing pier of the Yacht Club the drive is known as the Paseo de las Colonias. The main street, Avenida 9 de Octubre, runs due west from a central pier; there are 11 piers in all, 6 to the north of 9 de Octubre, 4 to the south. About half-way along it is the Plaza Centenario, the main square of the city, where stands the large liberation monument set up in 1920. On Calle Pedro Carbo, between Vélez and 9 de Octubre, the restored interior of the colonial church of San Francisco is beautiful. At La Rotonda, on the waterfront near the beginning of Av. 9 de Octubre, is a statue commemorating the famous and very mysterious meeting of Bolívar and San Martín in 1822. The dazzling white cemetery, north of the city at the foot of a hill, is worth seeing, but best to go on Sundays when there are plenty of people about. The snow-capped peak of Chimborazo can sometimes be glimpsed from Guayaquil.

The city is bustling and prosperous, and much cleaner than it used to be. The locals are much livelier and more open than the people of Quito. There are clubs for golf, tennis, yachting, and a race track set in delightful surroundings some 5 km. outside the city: there are a football stadium and an enclosed coliseum for boxing, basketball, etc. The pleasant suburb of Urdesa, NW of the city, contains some of the best restaurants and places of entertainment.

One of the oldest and most interesting districts is Las Peñas, at the foot of Cerro Santa Ana, by the river. Here is the city's first church, Santo Domingo (1548). Nearby is an open-air theatre, the Bogotá. Then, up the hill, there is a flat space where two cannon point riverward, a memento of the days when pirates sailed up the Guayas to attack the city. Here begins a curving, narrow colonial street, Numa Pompilio Llona. Paved with huge stone slabs, and lined with many fine houses which used to be an artist's colony, it is picturesque but somewhat neglected. To reach Las Peñas, turn left at end of Av. 9 de Octubre and carry on along the Malecón, to its end. It is a picturesque but still poor area; even the locals say it is unsafe and you are advised not to walk up the adjacent streets on Cerro Santa Ana.

The pride of Guayaquil is the enormous River Guayas bridge linking the city with Durán, the rail terminal on the east bank of the Guayas River. About half an hour is saved in comparison with the ferry journey, which costs US$0.06 and leaves every 15 min. from Muelle 5. From Durán, paved highways fan out to Babahoyo, Milagro, Riobamba (pass 4,120 metres high on the way), Cuenca and Machala.

Guayaquil: Key to Map

1. Parque Centenario; 2. Parque Bolívar; 3. Parque Rocafuerte; 4. Parque Pedro Carbo; 5. Parque de la Madre; 6. Cathedral; 7. Iglesia San Francisco; 8. Basílica de la Merced; 9. Iglesia San Agustín; 10. Iglesia San Alejo; 11. Placio Municipal; 13. Palacio de Gobernación and Immigration; 14. Supreme Court; 15. Casa de la Cultura; 16. Biblioteca Municipal and Musuem; 17. La Rotunda and Bolívar/San Martín monument; 18. Clock Tower; 19. Banco Central; 20. Lloyds Bank; 21. Bank of America; 22. TAME; 23. Ecuatoriana; 24. Tourist Office; 25. Post Office/Ietel; 26. Yacht Club; 27. Red Cross; 28. Librería Científica; 29. Unicentro Shopping Mall; 30. Central Market; 31. Other Markets; Hotels: 32. *Gran Guayaquil*; 33. *Unihotel/Plaza*; 34. *Palace*; 35. *Alexanders*; 36. *Continental*; 37. *Italia*; 38. *Residencial Pauker*.

Warnings Guayaquil has many thieves and pickpockets, especially outside the hotel entrances and on the waterfront, often working in pairs, and the area south of Calle Ayacucho is generally unsafe. Except in the best hotels, there is a chronic water shortage. Dengue fever has been reported.

Local Holidays 9 and 12 October. 24 and 25 July, Bolívar's birthday, and Foundation of the City; Carnival is in the days before Lent: watch out for malicious throwing of water balloons, mud, ink, paint etc.; women are prime targets. In contrast New Year's Eve is lots of fun, there is a large exhibition of tableaux, featuring *Años Viejos*, along the Malecón, children begging for alms for their life-size *viejos*, families with cars taking their *viejos* for rides through the centre of town, and a vast conflagration at midnight when all these figures are set on fire and explode.

Museums The Museo Municipal is housed in the Biblioteca Municipal, at Sucre with Pedro Carbo (near the *Hotel Continental*) where there are paintings, gold and archaeological collections, a section on the history of Guayaquil and also a good newspaper library. The museum (which contains Shuar heads) is open Wed.-Fri. 0900-1200 and 1500-1800; Sat. 1000-1500, Sun. 1000-1300. Entrance US$0.15 for Ecuadoreans and US$0.40 for foreigners (free on Sat., but passport must be left at desk). The Central Bank's anthropological museum is at José de Anteparra 900 and 9 de Octubre, open Mon.-Fri. 1000-1800, Sat. and Sun. 1000-1300. There is an impressive collection of prehistoric gold items at the museum of the Casa de la Cultura, together with an archaeological museum, Av. 9 de Octubre 1200 and Moncayo, open Mon.-Fri. 0900-1200 and 1500-1830, Sat. 0900-1600. There is a small zoo, open Sun., at the Colegio Nacional.

Hotels Hotel prices, which are higher than in Quito, are set by the Tourist Board and should be posted inside hotel. Rooms are much in demand in better hotels, the cheap ones being pretty basic, and singles seem very hard to find. All tend to be heavily booked, particularly in the week before July 24, the *fiesta*.

The best hotel is probably *Oro Verde*, 9 de Octubre y García Moreno, L, restaurants, bar, disco, pool, also good are *Unihotel*, Clemente Ballén 406 y Chile, L, good restaurant; *Grand Hotel Guayaquil*, Boyacá 1600 y 10 de Agosto, L, restaurants, swimming pool, sauna, etc.; *Continental*, Chile y 10 de Agosto, T 329270, Fax 325454, L (a KLM Golden Tulip hotel), rec.; *Apartamentos Boulevard*, 9 de Octubre 432, A, rec.; *Palace*, Chile 214 y Luque, C, restaurant, being completely refurbished (1990); *Plaza*, Chile 414 y Clemente Ballén, T 324195, B-C, unfriendly, some cheaper rooms; *Doral*, Aguirre y Chile, D, a bit run down, good restaurant; *Italia*, 10 de Agosto 115 y Pichincha, D, reasonable, convenient, quiet, a/c, rooftop restaurant; *Alexanders*, Luque 1107 y Pedro Moncayo, D, very comfortable but noisy and restaurant poor; *María del Cisne*, Chile y Chiriboga, E, quiet, safe, clean, a/c, no hot water or breakfast; *Residencial Cervera*, E, Gral. Córdoba 1036, a/c, clean, some rooms with bath; *Residencial Metropolitana*, V.M. Rendón 120 y Panamá, E, large rooms, laundry facilities, a/c, clean, friendly, safe for luggage; *Los Andes*, Garaycoa y Aguirre, D, poor service, noisy, windowless rooms; *Residencial Embajador*, Chimborazo 1106, F, clean but shower rarely works; *Pensión Pauker*, Baquerizo Moreno 902, F, English spoken, rooms on street side noisy, safe for luggage, mixed reports, beware cockroaches; *San Juan*, Vélez y Boyacá, E, own bathroom, no a/c, acceptable but most rooms without windows; *Sanders*, Pedro Moncayo 1100 y Luque, E, with bath, phone and fan (D a/c), central, good; *Victoria*, Moncayo y Colón, F, shower, clean but noisy; *Santa María*, E, Villamil 102, central, adequate, restaurant; *Orchidea Internacional*, Centro Comercial at Villamil 210, E, good, clean, TV, a/c, hot water; *Libertador*, Parque Centenario, G with bath, no glass in windows, good value, friendly; *Colonial*, Rumichaca y Solano, F, clean, safe, rec.; *Hotel USA*, Rumichaca y Quisquis, F, basic but bright, clean, good value; *Ecuatoriana*, Sucre y Rumichaca, F, clean, but some rooms with no window, safe, rec; *Delicia*, Clemente Ballén 1105, G, clean, fair, try to get room away from street. Sra Greta Portugal at Imbabura 214 y Rocafuerte, Aptdo 4-2, lets rooms at price category D, rec. Total tax of 20% on all hotel rates.

Restaurants Centre: *El Fortín* restaurant in the *Hotel Continental* won the Gran Collar Gastronómico Internacional competition worldwide and has excellent food (but poor service); the cheaper *La Canoa* has local food. *1822* restaurant at the *Grand Hotel Guayaquil*, expensive, but pleasant surroundings, high quality cuisine with good daily outdoor barbecue at pool-side. Good dining in *Le Gourmet* and *La Fondue* in *Hotel Oro Verde*, its coffee shop, *El Patio*, has nice and reasonably priced platos típicos. *The Steak House*, García Moreno 811, opposite *Hotel Oro Verde*, pleasant atmosphere, good food and service. Good food at other hotels. *El Parque*, top floor of Unicentro, highly rec. (US$10-12 p.p.), buffet lunch (US$3 for as much as you can eat), overlooks Parque Bolívar. Well-known and expensive *Caracol Azul*, 9 de Octubre 1918 y Los Ríos, wonderful seafood and meats (US$10-12 p.p.).

For good ice cream and cheap lunches, *Crema*, Chimborazo y 9 de Octubre.

Also on 9 de Octubre: *San Remo*, No.737, varied menu, Italian and Ecuadorean, well prepared; *La Rotonda*, No.432, 1st floor of casino, good large portions, not cheap; *Pizzería Italia*, No.706, expensive; *Bavaria*, No.1313, German run, good meat; also on this street, lots of US-style snack bars, quite expensive, and the usual fast food at *Burgerking* and *Kentucky Fried Chicken*. Also central: *Don Vito*, Carchi 803 y 9 de Octubre, disco and bar, closed Sun; *El Pirata*, riverboat, good food, reasonable prices, "good place to watch the river life go by"; *Anderson*, 810 y Hurtado, good, French, closed Sun.; *Pique y Pase*, Alejo Lascano 16-17 y Carchi, typical; *Pizzalandia*, Carchi y 1° de Mayo, good pizza. Local food at *Clérico*, Junín 213 y Panamá; *Muelle 5*, Malecón opp. Roca, expensive; *El Camino*, Pedro Ycaza y Córdova, economical, best at lunchtime, owned by English-speaking Jaime Mendoza. Many good *chifas*, including *Himalayas*, Sucre y Chile, cheap, good food; *Gran Chifa*, Pedro Carbo 1018, ornate, reasonable prices. Best ice cream at *Il Gelato Italiano*, 9 de Octubre y Carchi, also in Urdesa. *Submarine* sandwich shop, 9 de Octubre y Chile, excellent; *Galleta Pecosa*, 10 de Agosto y Boyaco, cakes and cookies.

Restaurants outside the centre are mostly in Urdesa and Kennedy suburbs. Urdesa: *Juan Salvador Gaviota*, Boloña 603 y Décima, good seafood, closed Sun.; *Il Fiorentino*, Datiles y V.E. Estrada, international, closed Mon. *Trattoria Da Migliorini*, La Primera 604 y Las Monjas, opposite Ietel, very good Italian food, service excellent; *Costa Brava*, Catalan food, Las Monjas 303 y Cuarta; many others of all kinds along V.E.Estrada. Kennedy: several on Francisco Boloña and Av. Kennedy. Tax on restaurant bills 20%.

Shopping Guayaquil has four shopping centres, the Policentro, the Unicentro, the Centro Comercial Urdesa and the Albán Borja shopping centre. To buy handicrafts, the best places are Madaleine Hollander's shop in the *Oro Verde*, (expensive), and *Manos* (offshoot of *La Bodega* in Quito) at the *Grand Hotel Guayaquil* and also in Urdesa, e.g. *Coosas* on V.E. Estrada, same quality as in Quito. Every day except Sun., Otavalan Indians sell their handicrafts under the arcades along Calle Chile between 9 de Octubre and Vélez. Beware of newly manufactured "Inca relics" and "Jívaro shrunken heads" sold in souvenir shops. *Artesanías del Ecuador*, 9 de Octubre 104 y Malecón, are good and reliable, and so are *Ocepa*, V.M.Rendón 405 y Córdova. The prices here differ little from those in the towns where the goods are made. Good shops include *Inca Folklore* in the Edificio Gran Pasaje, Av. 9 de Octubre 424, *Arte Folklore Otavalo*, 9 de Octubre 102 y Malecón; *Artesaniás Cuenca*, Vélez 110; and *Artesanías Mariel*, Vélez y Chile. There is an *H. Stern* jewellers shop at the airport. Stands in street near Post Office, and a small market in Calle Chile, between 9 de Octubre and Vélez, next to San Francisco church, open daily. Camera repairs at Calle Aguire 714, 2nd floor.

Everyone in Guayaquil, rich, poor and in-between, does their shopping at the Bahía, or black market, located along Pichincha, S of Colón and along Olmedo. A wide selection of shoes, appliances, TVs, radios and houseware can be found along Pichincha. Clothing is along Pedro Carbo and Olmedo. There is a food market ("bahía") in a covered area on Huancavelica near Pichincha, behind the Cepe gasoline station. Watch your valuables; however the area is generally safe, lots of police. Most name-brand goods will probably be counterfeit. Camping gas at Casa Maspons, corner of Ballén 517 y Boyacá.

Books *Librería Científica*, Luque 223 and Chile, good for field guides to the flora and fauna of South America and the Galápagos. *Librería Selecta*, Aguirre 717. *Librería Cervantes*, Aguirre 606A. *Su Librería* at Chimborazo 416. Book Exchange at *Nuevos Horizontes*, 6 de Marzo 924.

Local Transport Buses and colectivos about US$0.06 (most visitors dare not try them, but they are not lethal although once on it is difficult to get off). The *busetas*, or minibuses, are cheap and safe to ride. Ruta 15 will take you from the centre to Urdesa, 13 to Policentro, 14 to Albán Borja. *Buseta* passengers and drivers have been occasionally robbed by armed thieves, but generally in the poorer areas of the city. For more roomy travel the *Servicio especial* buses marked with blue and white diagonal stripes are clean and convenient. To get off at your stop, yell *pare*. Taxis: short runs, US$0.50; to Policentro or Urdesa, US$0.08; to the airport US$1, city centre to Terminal Terrestre, US$1; by the hr. US$1.50. To Durán, across bridge, US$4.50; also ferry. Taxis are notorious for overcharging; check on fare before entering.

Car Hire Hertz, Avis, Budget, Dollar at airport, town centre offices and main hotels, prices around US$30 a day, inc. insurance and tax, for a small car. Dollar offers competitive prices but the cars are often reported in poor condition.

Entertainment Discos and bars in the good hotels. Also *El Corsario*, Los Ríos y Piedrahita; *Buccaneer* and *Flashdance* in centre; *Cuartito Azul*, Luque y Garaycoa; *Zebras*, Los Ríos y 9 de Octubre. There is a *peña* (folklore show) at *Rincón Folklórico*, Malecón 208 y J.Montalvo. Casinos at *Oro Verde*, *Unihotel* and *Boulevard* hotels. See *El Universo* for cinemas and other entertainments.

Horse-Racing Hipódromos Buijo and Río Verde in Salinas. Parimutuel betting. Amazingly low standard.

Exchange Lloyds, Pichincha 108-110 and Merado and Urdesa agencies, advances money on Visa card. Banco Holandés Unido, P. Ycaza 454 y Baquerizo Moreno, T 312900; Citibank, Av. 9 de Octubre, Citicorp cheques only; Bank of America, Elizalde 100. Open 0900-1330. Closed Sat. US$ cash on Visa, no commission; Banco del Pacífico recommended, advances money on Master Card and changes Thomas Cook travellers cheques into dollars cash for small commission (San Francisco 300 building, 9th floor, next to Plaza San Francisco, enter either from Pedro Carbo or Gen. Córdova). Banco Popular, Pedro Carbo y 9 de Octubre, changes Amex travellers' cheques into cash dollars, commission 1%.

There are several *Casas de Cambio* on Av. 9 de Octubre, also many on Av. Pichincha, between Aguirre and 9 de Octubre. All the *cambios* in the centre will exchange Amex travellers' cheques, though the banks generally offer better rates. Cambiosa, 9 de Octubre 113 y Malecón, rec.; also Cambitur, near *Pensión Pauker*. Most open 0900-1900, shut on Saturday. Wander Cambios at airport open 7 days a week (poorer rates than in town).

Consulates Peru, Av. 9 de Octubre 411, 6th floor, T 512-738. 0900-1330. **Bolivia**, P. Ycaza 302 of. 601, T 304260. **Uruguay**, V. M. Rendón 1006, T 513-461. **Brazil**, La García 103, T 362-772. **Argentina**, Aguirre 104. USA, 9 de Octubre y García Moreno, T 323-570. **Austria**, Av. 9 de Octubre 1310, T 392307. **Netherlands**, Av. 9 de Octubre 2309, 5th floor. T 366410. **Switzerland**, 9 de Octubre 2105. **Italy**, 9 de Octubre y Baquerizo Moreno. **W. Germany**, 9 de Octubre 109; **Canada**, Ed. Torres de la Merced, 4th floor, office 11, Córdova 800 y Rendón (T 313747/303580); **France**, Boyacá 1215.

Telecommunications and post Instituto Ecuatoriano de Telecomunicaciones (Ietel). Telephone company and post office share same block, Pedro Carbo y Aguirre. Public telex booth. Many kiosks in arcades all round it, each with the flag and name of a different country, plenty of stationery.

Medical Dr. Angel Serrano Sáenz, Av. Boyacá 821, T 301-373, English speaking. Dr. Alfonso E. León Guin, Centro de Especialidades, Av. Boyacá 1320 y Luque, T 528-179/517-793; open 1100-1300 and 1400-1900 and Sat., also English speaking. The main hospital used by the foreign community is the Clínica Kennedy, T 396-963. It also contains the consulting rooms of almost every kind of doctor.

Churches Episcopalian Church of USA; Lutheran Church; Anglican Church, Luis Urdaneta y Malecón del Salado, Urdesa.

Schools US and German. School year, May -mid-January. The Inter-American Academy (US system), August-May.

Immigration Av. Pichincha y Aguirre (Gobernación), T 514-925/516-789, for visa extensions.

Tourist Bureau Dituris, Malecón 2321 y Av. Olmedo, first floor; T 518-926, 526-241. Enthusiastic, English spoken by some staff, open 0900-1600, Mon.-Fri. Map of Ecuador. A Policía de Turismo man can be hired for a guided tour of Guayaquil. Cost will be about US$4 per hr. for taxi (2 hrs. will do) and US$3 to the Policía de Turismo.

Travel Agents Reportedly, none is open at weekends. *Galasam Cía Ltda.*, Edificio Gran Pasaje, sala 1107, Av. 9 de Octubre 424, T 306-289; their Galápagos programme is called Economic Galápagos Tours; see Galápagos section (**page 804**) for details. *Metropolitan Touring*, Pichincha 415 y Aguirre. *Machiavello Tours*, 9 de Octubre y Anteparra (rec.). *Galápagos Cruises*, Los Ríos 0-80, T 390-893. *Gordon Tours*, 9 de Octubre 2009, rec. *Ecuadorian Tours*, 9 de Octubre 1900 at corner of Esmeraldas, is agent for American Express, T 397-111.

Rail Service to Quito suspended in 1983. Travellers arriving in Durán and ferrying to Guayaquil land on the Malecón Bolívar about 10 blocks N of the Palacio de Gobernación. The first ferry is at 0600, the last at 2130 but buses run later. Accommodation in Durán, *Pensión La Paz*, near station, F. From **Durán to Alausí**, services are subject to alteration: there is a daily train leaving at 0620 or 0900, 12 hrs, US$0.50. It is important to check details in advance. The train usually stops for some hours at Bucay, leaving there about 6 hrs. after departure from Durán; you can take a bus to Bucay, 2 hrs., and catch the train there.

Bus Services The new bus station (Terminal Terrestre) is near the airport, just off the road to the Guayas bridge (no left luggage depot, but well-organized). Several companies to Quito, US$2.75, 8 hrs. To Cuenca, US$2.65, 6 hrs.; Riobamba 5 hrs., US$2.15. Santo Domingo de los Colorados, 4¾ hrs., US$2. Manta 3 hrs., US$2; Esmeraldas 7 hrs., US$5; to Portoviejo, 3½ hrs., US$2, and to Bahía de Caráquez, 5½ hrs., US$2.80. Machala (for Peru) 3½ hrs., US$2, frequent, or by minibus 2½ hrs., leave at 20 minute intervals between 0600 and 1900, 10 kg. baggage limit. For the Peruvian border, to Huaquillas, avoiding Machala, US$2.50, 5 hrs.; via Machala, 6 hrs. To Ambato, US$2.50, 6½ hrs. To Alausí, 4 hrs., US$2. Regular and frequent buses to Playas (2¼ hrs., US$0.90) and to Salinas (2½ hrs., US$1). Colectivos are not rec. for journeys to the Sierra, they drive too fast and are dangerous. Town buses 2, 66, 69, 70, 71 and 76 from new bus station to centre, US$0.06, taxis not metred (to city centre US$1). **Trucks** carry freight and passengers, slower, bumpy, cheaper than buses, and you see better. Inquire at Sucre 1104.

Simón Bolívar Airport, near the centre. US$0.12 for bus (sometimes allow backpacks on board), No. 2 from Malecón, No. 3 from Centro Cívico, No. 69 from Plaza Victoria, US$1 for taxi from centre, but if you are arriving in Guayaquil and need a taxi from the airport, walk ½ block from the terminal out to Av. Las Américas, where taxis and *camionetas* wait for passengers. The fare will be about half of what you will be charged for the same trip by one of the drivers who belong to the airport taxi cooperative. Dituris advises that visitors should not pay more than US$2.50 for taxis from the airport to town. There are several car hire firms at the airport; an information desk; Dituris office; a *cambio*.

Air Services About 14 flights daily to and from Quito, US$14 (TAME, Saeta, SAN; ensure seats are confirmed, not standby). Sit on the right side for the best views. There are flights to Cuenca (1 a day except Sat. US$14), Manta (1-2 a day, US$9), Loja (1 a day, US$9), and Ambato 3 a week. Daily to Galápagos (**see page** 804). Commuter flights are also available on small 5 or 7 seater planes with Cedta and Lansa from the Avioneta terminal on the city side of the international terminal; weekday flights to the Peruvian frontier, to Bahía de Caraguez and Pedernales. TAME, 9 de Octubre, Edif. Gran Pasaje (T 305-800); Saeta, Escobedo 1114 y 9 de Octubre (T 303-024). Flights to Lima: Aero Perú (9 de Octubre). Andes Airlines will ship vehicles to Panama.

Excursions To Playas, Salinas and the Santa Elena peninsula (**see page** 759).

THE SOUTHERN LOWLANDS (5)

On the southern shore of the Gulf of Guayaquil is **Puerto Bolívar** (Hotels: *Pacífico* (restaurant) and *Jambelí*, both basic, G), built above a mangrove swamp and backed by jungle. Approximately one million tonnes a year of banana exports pass through this port. It serves (6½ km.) **Machala**, a growing agricultural town of 122,000 with an annual banana fair in September. The area is an unattractive (mosquitoes) but prosperous irrigated banana zone. It is also a centre for pond shrimp production. From Machala paved roads run inland to Pasaje (26 km.; *Hotel Pasaje*, F with bath), and Arenillas (76 km.), and NE from Puerto Bolívar via Pasaje and Girón to Cuenca. An all-weather road runs SE through Arenillas to Loja (161 km.).

Buses run every 10 min. from Puerto Bolívar to Machala (20 mins. journey), and taxis are available. The airport is about 1 km. from town centre, beside local prison; in late 1989 it was closed owing to the poor state of the runway. There are rumours of impending repair work. Cedta flies from Guayaquil to Santa Rosa, which is closer to the Peruvian border than Machala.

Machala Hotels *Encalada*, Tarqui y 9 de Octubre, D, T 920681, restaurant, bar, cafetería, disco; *Rizzo*, Guayas y Bolívar, D, T 921511, a/c, T.V., suites available, slightly worn luxury, pool, casino, cafetería, restaurant, rec. for breakfast as well as dinner; *El Oro*, Sucre y Juan Montalvo, D, T 922408, refurbished, good, excellent but very expensive restaurant; *Perla del Pacífico*, Sucre 603 y Páez, D, T 920915, T.V., a/c, no hot water; *Inés*, Montalvo y Pasaje, E, T 922301, good restaurant; *Gran Hotel Machala*, Juan Montalvo y Rocafuerte, E, clean, no fan, T 920530; *Residencial El Oro*, 9 de Mayo y Bolívar, G, basic but OK; *Las Cuevas de los Tayos*, F, clean, parking, rec.; *Residencial Internacional*, Guayas y Sucre, F, clean, friendly, fan, rec; *Hotel Ecuatoriano*, 9 de Octubre y Colón, E, bath, a/c. A mosquito net may be needed for sleeping.

Restaurants *Cafetería San Francisco*, Sucre block 6, good filling breakfast; *Pepe's Parrillada*, Av. 9 de Octubre y 9 de Mayo, food and service rec., but not cheap, specializes in kebabs and steaks, bife better than lomo; *Parrillada Sabor Latina*, Sucre y Guayas, steaks and grills; *Pío Pío Rico Pollo*, Av. Guayas, chicken; *Norberto's*, near town centre, very good; *Chifa China* and *La Peña*, both 9 de Octubre y Guayas; two branches of *Kingburger* offer good hamburgers, clean; *La Fogata*, near telephone office, for good chicken. In Puerto Bolívar, *El Acuario* offers excellent value in seafood dishes (on main street which runs back from the pier). A good spot for a beer and toasted sandwich or ceviche is the *Miramar* bar at the pierhead.

Cinemas There are several, of which *El Tauro* is the best, a/c, cushioned seats, good sound. The *Teatro Municipal* has wooden benches and rats, US$0.32 a seat.

Sport A development just outside Machala on the Pasaje road has two large outdoor swimming pools. The Machala tennis club has three clay and two concrete courts, a swimming pool and a club house. It is situated on the left-hand side of the Santa Rosa road just after the roundabout where the Pasaje road branches off, about 5 km. from Machala. Cockfighting takes place every Saturday afternoon at the cockpit on Calle 9 de Octubre.

Exchange Banco del Pacífico, Rocafuerte y Tarqui, changes travellers' cheques and notes; the *casas de cambio* do not change cheques.

Peruvian Consulate At the NW corner of Colón y Bolívar, 2nd floor.

Post Office Bolívar y Montalvo; telephone and cable office, **Ietel**, 9 de Octubre near stadium.

Travel Agent Ecuadorian Tours, Bolívar y Guayas.

Tourist Office Dituris, Tarqui y Primera Constituyente; maps are in the basement.

Buses The bus companies Occidental, Panamericana, Ecuatoriano Pullman and Rutas Orenses (the best safety record) have depots in the town with direct services to Quito (12 hrs., US$4.50), Guayaquil (3½ hrs., US$2), Esmeraldas (11 hrs., US$3.70), Loja (7 hrs., US$2.75). Hourly (a.m.) service to Cuenca by Empresas Pullman Sucre, Sucre block 7, US$2.70, 5 hrs., "exciting ride guaranteed" along a winding road. Major construction work on roads in the area may cause delays.

Excursions From the old pier on the Puerto Bolívar waterfront motorized canoes go to the tourist beach at Jambelí, on the far side of the mangrove islands which shelter Puerto Bolívar from the Pacific. The beach is long and safe but there is no shade. Canoes cost US$12 return (arrange return time with boatman) or there is a regular boat service (US$1 p.p.), 1000 and 1300 returning 1500 and 1700 on weekdays, more frequent at weekends. A trip to the quieter beach at La Bravita can be arranged, but there are no facilities and again no shade, so take drinks, etc. If arranging a trip to the beach at Costa Rica (2 hrs.) be sure to carry passport as a military post has to be passed. This beach is pleasant but the waves and currents can be dangerous. The trip through mangrove channels is interesting, especially for bird watchers. All the above locations suffer from ferocious mosquitoes after about 1630 and it is better not to stray off the sand at any time as the driftwood is infested with biting insects. The gold mines at Zaruma can be visited. Frequent buses to Zaruma, Transportes TAC, Colón y Rocafuerte.

Crossing the Border into Peru

The normal route overland to Peru is via Machala. Buses run 8 times a day (US$0.50, 1¾ hrs.) to **Huaquillas**, the Ecuadorean border town, something of a shopping arcade for Peruvians (all shops close about 1730), described by one traveller as a "seedy one-horse banana town full of touts with black briefcases". Travellers who haven't obtained their Peruvian tourist cards in Guayaquil or Quito can get them at the border.

Hotels at Huaquillas *Parador Turístico* Huaquillas, E, at N of town, Dituris-operated, swimming pool, restaurant and bar; *Residencial Huaquillas*, Córdovez y 9 de Octubre, G, basic, clean; *Residencial San Martín*, opp. Customs on main street, G, dirty, noisy, mosquito nets, convenient; *Guayaquil*, opposite Customs, G, clean, mosquito nets, noisy, rec; *Mini*, Av. República, G, mosquito net, adequate, reasonable restaurant downstairs.

Restaurants Best at *Parador Turístico*; also *Rapa Nui*, on ground floor of *Residencial Mini*, and *Sinqi*, Av. de la República, good. Expect bananas with everything here. There appear to be no set meals.

Complete Ecuadorean formalities at customs and immigration, Av. de la República y Portovelo, in Huaquillas, then walk along the main street and across the bridge. At the bridge, the police check passports. The Peruvian immigration and customs post is about 60 m. past the bridge; from here colectivos and buses run to Tumbes, US$0.70 (taxi to Tumbes, waiting at border for formalities, US$5). The border is officially open 0800-1800, but long lunches are common (Ecuadorean lunch 1200-1400). It is often best to cross just after lunch when the officers are still sleepy and do not pay you much attention. Peruvian time is one hour earlier than Ecuadorean in Jan., Feb. and March. From Tumbes (or from the border), fast long-distance buses run to Lima.

Border practices tend to vary, so check to make sure what the authorities require. For example, Australians need a consular visa (US$2, available in Machala) from Peru's consular office near the main plaza, but much quicker in Quito.

Warning Officially, a ticket out of Peru is necessary for entry into the country. Although rarely asked for, some agencies reportedly still sell cheap tickets for non-existent runs out of Peru. (Tepsa sells tickets in Quito at twice the price they are in Peru). If you are required to show a ticket, you can buy a Miscellaneous Charges Order, valid one year, minimum US$150, but remember there is a 10% tax on all tickets bought in Ecuador. (We have been told that one traveller's MCO was not accepted by Peruvian officials as an exit ticket.) Peruvian customs and police have asked for bribes at this crossing.

The Peruvian inti has been greatly devalued recently, so verify the rate with travellers leaving Peru. Avoid changing near either of the immigration posts; in general the rates at the border are very poor, the best rate is usually for cash dollars. Be sure to count your change carefully; the money changers (recognizable by their black briefcases) are positively dishonest, and clever. Travellers leaving Peru should get rid of their intis inside Peru, and buy sucres on the Ecuadorean side. At Huaquillas, better rates are obtained in the town (though not at the bus terminus) than in the vicinity of the border post when buying sucres, though it is difficult to change travellers' cheques.

Coming from Peru into Ecuador; take a bus to Tumbes and a colectivo from there. Some travellers crossing border from Peru to Ecuador at Huaquillas report being required by the Ecuadorean authorities to show an exit ticket (a bus ticket will do) but this is now less common.

Buses There are a few direct buses from Huaquillas to Quito each day, 14 hrs., US$4; most go via Quevedo, but if you get a slower one via Riobamba and Ambato you may see all the great volcanoes. To Guayaquil about 5 hrs., including several stops at military check points, US$2.50. If in a hurry to reach Quito or Guayaquil, it may be advisable to change buses in Machala. Ecuatoriano and Panamericana have a reciprocal arrangement regarding tickets across borders and onwards, but there are few through bus services between Ecuador and Peru. (Direct bus at 1500 from Huaquillas to Piura, US$5, 6 hrs, and Trujillo.) To Cuenca several daily, 7 hrs., US$3.10. To Loja, 4 daily, 7 hrs., US$2.50. The road is completely paved going up the coast towards Guayaquil and then turning inland at El Triunfo; a circuitous route but quicker than taking the more direct road (10 hrs.) via Girón which is still under reconstruction.

An alternative point for crossing Peruvian border is Macará in Loja Province (**see page** 793).

FROM GUAYAQUIL TO QUITO (6)

Note to Motorists There is a 3¼-km. bridge from Guayaquil across the river to Durán. A good paved road from there (summit at 4,120 metres) connects with the Andean Highway at Cajabamba, near Riobamba (**see page** 776).

The floods in 1983 closed the Guayaquil-Quito railway for through traffic. Contracts for repair work were awarded in 1985 but it will be several years until normal service can be resumed. The Riobamba-Quito service (223 km.) is in operation. Service on the Alausí-Guayaquil (142 km.) section was resumed in 1987 (**see page** 771). The lowland section is in very poor condition. We have retained the description of the full journey in the hope that the complete service will be restored.

The 464-km. railway line (1.067 metre gauge), which was opened in 1908, passes through 87 km. of delta lands and then, in 80 km., climbs to 3,238 metres. At the summit, at Urbina, 3,609 metres is reached; it then rises and falls before debouching on to the Quito plateau at 2,857 metres. The line is a most interesting piece of railway engineering, with a maximum gradient of 5.5 per cent. Its greatest achievements, the Alausí loop and the Devil's Nose double zigzag (including a V switchback), are between Sibambe and Alausí, on the reopened section.

Leaving the river the train strikes out across the broad, fertile Guayas valley. It rolls through fields of sugar cane, or rice, past split cane houses built on high stilts, past sugar mills with their owners' fine homes. Everywhere there are waterways, with thousands of water-birds.

The first station is **Yaguachi**. On 15 and 16 August more than 15,000 visitors pour into this little town to attend the feast day celebrations at the church of San Jacinto, who is honoured in the region for having put an end to many epidemics.

The first stop of importance is **Milagro**, a large but uninteresting town of 77,000 people (*Hotel Viker*, F, no food, communal washing facilities; *Hotel Marta*, F; *Restaurant Topo-Gigio*, nearby, good, cheap food). Women swarm about the train selling pineapples which are particularly sweet and juicy. About 87 km. from Durán the train stops at **Bucay**, at the base of the Andes (*Pensión Turismo*, G, clean, basic; market Sunday), where a steam engine is attached. Buses run parallel to the train between Bucay and Guayaquil, but take only 2 as opposed to 4 hrs.

The landscape spreads before you in every shade of green; row on row of coffee and cacao trees, with occasional groves of mango and breadfruit trees, banana plantations, fields of sugar cane, tobacco, and pineapple. The train follows the gorge of the River Chanchán until it reaches **Huigra**. By road Bucay to Huigra is still rough going. After leaving Huigra the train crosses and recrosses the River Chanchán, and then creeps along a narrow ledge between the mountain and the canyon. Here begins the most exciting part of the trip. The first mountain town reached is Chanchán, where the gorge is so narrow that the train has to pass through a series of tunnels and bridges in its zigzag course. Next is **Sibambe** (no hotels), the junction for trains to Cuenca. A train leaves Sibambe at 0500 for Cuenca (service resumed), arrives at 1100. There is also a daily *autoferro* for tourists to Cuenca run by Metropolitan Touring. Shortly after leaving Sibambe the Quito train starts climbing the famous Nariz del Diablo (Devil's Nose), a perpendicular ridge rising in the gorge of the Chanchán to a height of 305 metres. This almost insurmountable engineering obstacle was finally conquered when a series of switchbacks was built on a 5.5 per cent grade. The air is chilly and stimulating.

Next comes **Alausí**, an old and colourful village (Sunday market), in the mountains on the Pan-American Highway, popular with Guayaquileños (at present the end of the railway line from Durán: daily train at 0900, tickets on sale from 0800): *Residencia Tequendama*, F, clean, friendly, hot water, rec.; *Hotel Europa*, opposite, E, safe parking in courtyard. *Hotel Panamericano*, G, clean, food poor; *Hotel Gampala*, F, basic, clean, friendly, breakfast available, check restaurant bill carefully. Restaurants: *Paradero Chumpisti, Salón Oriental*. By road Alausí is best reached from Riobamba; the Cuenca and Guayaquil road links are less good. Bus Alausí-Quito at 0400 and 0800, 5½ hrs, US$1.75, often have to change in Riobamba; to Cuenca, 4 hrs; to Ambato hourly, 3 hrs., US$1, from main street. All buses stop in front of *Hotel Panamericano*. You can walk on the railway track to Chunchi, a friendly village with a Sunday market, 15 km. An Inca trail to Ingapirca (**see page 791**) can be followed: it starts at **Achupallas**, 25 km. from Alausí. **N.B.** There are no trains at present on the following section. After crossing the 120 metre long Shucos bridge, the train pulls into Palmira, on the crest of the first range of the Andes crossed by the railway. The train has climbed nearly 3,350 metres in less than 160 km. Precipitous mountain slopes covered with temperate-climate crops such as wheat and alfalfa gradually change to a bleak, desolate *páramo* (moor) where nothing grows except stiff clumps of grass. Now and then the drab landscape is brightened by the red poncho of an Indian shepherd watching his sheep. One by one the great snow-capped volcanoes appear: Chimborazo, Carihuairazo, Altar, Tungurahua, and the burning head of Sangay. They seem very close because of the clear air.

Guamote is another point on the Pan-American Highway, three hours by car from the capital. There is an interesting market on Thursdays and some good half day walks in the area. There is a *pensión*, F, near the railway station and also some places to eat nearby. There have been reports of finds of Inca pottery and gold in the area. The train skirts the shores of Lake La Colta, before reaching the fertile Cajabamba valley. A road is being built to Macas (**see page 802**).

Cajabamba is a small, rather poor town. In 1534 the original Riobamba was founded on this site, but in 1797 a disastrous earthquake caused a large section of the hill on the north side of the town to collapse in a great landslide, which can still be seen. It killed several thousand of the original inhabitants of Riobamba and the town was moved almost twenty kilometres north-east to its present site. The new Riobamba has prospered, but Cajabamba has stagnated. Indian market on Sun., small but uncommercialized and interesting (easily reached by bus from Riobamba, 25 mins., US$0.10). There are no hotels and few restaurants.

Cajabamba is connected to Riobamba and Quito by a good paved highway and there is another paved highway from Cajabamba to Bucay and Guayaquil. A fairly good dirt road leaves the Pan-American Highway soon after Cajabamba, to the west; it is one of the oldest of the coast-Sierra routes and links Cajabamba with Guaranda and Babahoyo.

Riobamba (2,750 metres) is the capital of Chimborazo Province. It has 148,000 inhabitants, is built on a large flat site and has broad streets and many ageing but impressive buildings. Altogether, it seems a quiet, dignified place, with the nickname "Sultan of the Andes". Riobamba has many good churches and public buildings, and magnificent views of three of the great volcanic peaks, Chimborazo, Altar and Tungurahua. Four blocks NE of the railway station, along Calle Juan de la Valle, the Parque 21 de Abril affords an unobstructed view of Riobamba and environs; the park also has a colourful tile tableau of the history of Ecuador and is especially fine at sunset. Another good viewpoint is La Loma de Quito.

Riobamba has a new market building, but only a small part of the activity at the Saturday market takes place there. Buying and selling go on all over town. The "tourist" market in the small plaza south of the Convento de la Concepción museum is particularly fascinating and a good place to buy local handicraft—*ikat* shawls (*macanas*), embroidered and finely woven belts (*fajas*), blankets, embroidered dresses and shirts, Otavalan weavings and sweaters, *shigras*. Indian women come to the plaza each week with sacks full of bead and coin necklaces, old belts and dresses, blanket pins (*tupus*), and much more. Since Indian-style clothing is also sold here, the plaza is full of colourful Indians from different parts of Chimborazo province, each group wearing its distinctive costume. Two blocks east, there is a huge produce market in another plaza, also pottery, baskets, hats. All the streets in this area are filled with traders. There are also 2 markets on Weds.: Mercado La Condamine and Mercado San Alfonso. A variety of *pelota* games can be seen on Sunday afternoons. On Saturdays at 2100 there are cockfights on the corner of Tarqui with Guayaquil, entrance US$0.25. Open-air restaurants do a flourishing business in that Andean delicacy, roast *cuy* (guinea-pig). Hotel prices rise during independence *fiestas* around 20 April, and rooms are difficult to obtain during the November basketball tournament. There are three cinemas.

The Convento de la Concepción, Orozco y España, has been carefully restored by the Banco Central and now functions as a religious art museum, open Tues.-Sat. 0900-1200 and 1500-1800, Sun. 0900-1230. Admission: US$0.60 for Ecuadoreans, US$1 for others. The guides are friendly and knowledgeable (tip expected). The priceless Custodia de Riobamba Antigua is the museum's greatest treasure, one of the richest of its kind in South America. Well worth a visit.

Hotels *El Galpón*, A/B, Argentinos y Zambrano, pool, sauna, in decline, dirty, food poor (pleasant location on hill overlooking city); next to it is *Chimborazo Internacional*, D, spacious rooms, fully carpeted, noisy discotheque, restaurant with fair food at reasonable prices; *Hosteriá La Andaluza*, 10 km. from Riobamba at the foot of Chimborazo, D, friendly, good restaurant; *Hostería El Troje*, 4½ km. on road to Chambo, D, pleasant, tourist centre, restaurant; *Liribamba*, Pichincha y Primera Constituyente, E, only serves breakfast, rec.; *Humboldt*, Av. Daniel León Borja 3548, E without breakfast, clean, with bath; *Segovia*, Primera Constituyente 2228, E, friendly, safe, hot water, ask for front room, rooftop view of the volcanoes. *Los Shiris*, 10 de Agosto y Rocafuerte, E, with private bathroom, clean, nicely furnished, friendly, noise from nearby disco, restaurant good; *Imperial*, Rocafuerte 22-15 y 10 de Agosto, E, a good quality hotel, hot water, private or shared bathroom, laundry facilities, can store luggage, friendly and comfortable, but loud music from bar on Fri. and Sat. nights. *Whymper*, Av. Miguel Angel León 23-10 y Primera Constituyente, T 964575, E, private bath, cafeteria; *Zeus*, Borja 4139, E with bath, clean, friendly, good restaurant, English spoken; *El Altar*, Km. 2 on Ambato road, F, good; *Americano*, G, dirty, above restaurant of same name on Borja near station; *Colonial*, G, clean, usually hot water, hard beds; *Venecia*, Dávalos 2221 y 10 de Agosto, G, hot water; *Metropolitano*, Borja y Lavalle, F with or without bath, a pleasant, central, traditional hotel; *Residencial Camba Huasi*, 10 de Agosto 2824, G, laundry facilities, clean, dormitory beds, hot water, spacious, friendly, owner is a mountaineer and organizes trips to Chimborazo, safe parking in courtyard; *Residencias Villa Ester*, Unidad Nacional y Lavalle, F, hot shower, basic; *Puruhua*, F, near bus station at Eplicachima 2076 y

Borja, friendly, fairly clean, but noisy; nearby is *Monterrey*, Rey Cacha y Eplicachima, F with or without bath, clean, good.

Restaurants *Chuquiragua*, 2 km. out on Quito road, typical restaurant; *El Mesón*, Veloz 4199 y Los Sauces, some way out, good, high-class; *Steak House*, Magdalena Dávalos y Veloz, good food, expensive; *El Rodeo*, 10 de Agosto y García Moreno, a bistro, not cheap but good; *Alexander*, Falconi y Brasil, bistro style, reasonable; *Cabaña Montecarlo*, García Moreno 2410, good food, friendly service, popular with tourists; *León Rojo*, Primera Constituyente 2625, German-run, very clean, good food, not cheap; *Hilton*, Av. Borja, good steaks; *Candilejas*, 10 de Agosto, good, clean, cheap lunches; *Chifa Joy Sing*, Guayaquil near station, cheap, excellent; *Chifa Pale Hua*, García Moreno y 10 de Agosto, vegetarian dishes, good value; *Chifa China*, León Borja opp. *Hotel Puruhua*, good, cheap; *Chifa Internacional*, Veloz y Dávalos, Chinese food, good; *Chifa Chung Wah*, 10 de Agosto 2558, good food; *Café Paola*, Calle Pichincha (between Guayaquil and 10 de Agosto), good breakfast, empanadas and hamburgers; *Valentín*, 10 de Agosto, "average pizzas but liveliest bar in town"; *Pato Juan*, España y 10 de Agosto, snack bar, pleasant. Many other snackbars along 10 de Agosto, of which *Pollo Gus*, simple chicken and chips, but cheap and tasty.

Entertainment *Peña*-restaurants *Media Estocada*, Borja y Duchicela, and *Parrillada Gaucha*, Unidad Nacional. *Peñas* at *Taquí Huasi*, Orozco y 4a Transversal, and *La Casa Vieja*, Orozco y Tarqui. Disco, Thurs.-Sun, at *Zero*, Km. 1½ on road to Cajabamba.

Note In Riobamba jail is a British citizen who welcomes visitors. You must hand in your passport at the gate and your bags will be searched.

Exchange Banco Internacional, 10 de Agosto y García Moreno.

Immigration Tarqui y 10 de Agosto.

Post Office Primera Constituyente between García Moreno and España (second floor).

Tourist Office Dituris, Calle Tarqui 2248 y Primera Constituyente (very helpful). Open Tues.-Sat. 0800-1200, 1430-1700. Addresses for hirers of climbing equipment. Souvenir shops on 10 de Agosto between Carabobo and Rocafuerte.

Transport All trains to Guayaquil were suspended in 1983 after heavy rains destroyed much of the track. A daily train runs to Quito, 0500, US$0.50, check details and buy tickets in advance. For Guayaquil, take the 0430 or 0530 bus for Cuenca, which arrives in Alausí after 1½ hrs. in time to catch the 0900 train (you may have to pay fare to Cuenca to be sure of a seat). A tourist train runs to Quito on Sun. and Wed. a.m. (details from Metropolitan Tours or other travel agencies). **Buses** to Quito, US$1.40-1.50, 3½-6 hrs., about every 30 mins; to Guaranda, US$0.80, 2 hrs., beautiful views; to Ambato, US$0.40, 1 hr; to Cuenca, 6 a day via Alausí, 7 hrs., US$3.15. A more popular route to Cuenca, entirely on paved roads, is via El Triunfo, on the Guayaquil bus US$2 to El Triunfo, where you change buses, then US$2.50 to Cuenca; mostly good roads and scenery. Bus to Santo Domingo, US$2, 5 hrs; to Baños, US$0.50, 1 hr; to Puyo, US$1.10, 3½ hrs. direct. There are 2 buses (US$3.50, 10 hrs.) to Huaquillas every evening (1915 and 2100), which avoid Guayaquil; book the day before, arrive early and be prepared to fight for your seat. Bus to Guayaquil, about 35 a day, US$2.15, 4½ hrs.; the trip is really spectacular for the first two hours. There are pirate buses which charge more than the regular lines and do not sell tickets in the bus station, first come first served, they can be useful when all the others are full up. There is a well-run Terminal Terrestre on Eplicachima y Av. D. L. Borja for buses to Quito, Guayaquil, Ambato, etc., but buses to Baños and the Oriente leave from the Terminal Oriental, Espejo y Baños.

Excursions Two are of great interest: the first, to *Guano*, an attractive hemp-working and carpet-making town of 6,000 inhabitants 10 km. to the north, with prehistoric monoliths on a nearby hilltop; there are frequent buses but nowhere to eat. You can have rugs made to your own design. After Guano you can take the bus on to Santa Teresita from where it is a 1 km. walk downhill to Balneario Las Elenas: 3 pools, 1 tepid, 2 cool. The second is to Baños, scenic route along Chambo River (see page 781).

Climbing To climb Chimborazo contact Enrique Veloz Coronado, mountain guide and technical adviser of the Asociación de Andinismo de Chimborazo, Chile 33-21 y Francia, Riobamba (T 960916). He will provide all the necessary equipment; you must agree on a fee with him for the trip you want to make (see page 780). He is best reached after 1500 and is very helpful even if you don't need his services as a guide. Also recommended is Marcelo Puruncajas, Espejo 24, who rents equipment and is a cheap guide. For Sangay, take a taxi to Alao and hire guides or carriers of food, tents, etc. there; remember you have to pay for and organize the food for your porters separately, otherwise you have to pay them a lot more.

Make sure the fee covers the return journey as well. Also Expediciones Andinas (Marco Cruz), Argentinos 3860 y Zambrano, T 964-915 (office), 962-845 (house), recommended (he is a certified guide of the German Alpine Club).

To the crater of **Altar**: Travel to Penipe by bus (bargain for the price) from Baños or Riobamba/Ambato, then to Candelaria by truck, or bus which passes between 1200 and 1400. Walk out of the village, cross the bridge and go up to Hacienda Releche on your left (about 2 km.). There is a *refugio* (US$1.10) with beds, warm water, shower, cooking facilities and friendly keeper, about 1 km. from Candelaria, a light and dark green building at the turning for the Hacienda, marked by a Sangay National Park sign. It is not always open, ask in Riobamba beforehand at the Ministry of Tourism or the Sangay National Park office, Primera Constituyente y Pichincha, Ministry of Agriculture. In Penipe ask for Ernesto Haro, who will take you to the *refugio* in his jeep (US$3 one way) and pick you up from there at a pre-arranged time. The track to the Altares leads on past the Hacienda, but it is best to ask someone to point out the faint track which branches to the left about 30-40 minutes after the Hacienda and leads up a hill to a ridge where it joins a clear track. This goes south first and then turns east up the valley of the River Collanes. It is about 8 hrs. to the crater which is surrounded by magnificent snow-capped peaks. It is possible to camp in the crater, but better still, about 20 mins. before you turn into the broad U-shaped valley leading up to the crater there is a good-sized cave, the floor of which is lined with dry rushes; there is a fire ring at the entrance. Guides to Altar can be hired for about US$3.50 a day, and horses are US$3.50 each a day. Because of damage done to the track by mudslides the route is hazardous and you would be unwise to do it alone. Consult the National Park Office about conditions, they are in radio contact with the Guardería at Candelaria.

From Riobamba to Quito the road is paved. Between Riobamba and Cevallos the railway reaches its highest point at Urbina (3,609 metres). At the pass, there are fine views in the dry season (June is probably the first safe month) of Chimborazo and its smaller sister mountain, Carihuairazo. Then the railway and the Pan-American Highway wind down towards the Ambato basin. Between Riobamba and Ambato is Mocha, where guinea-pigs (*cuy*) are raised for the table; you can sample roast *cuy* at stalls by the roadside. The valley's patchwork of fields gives an impression of greater fertility and prosperity than the Riobamba zone. The houses seem larger and better built, and almost universally, a small crucifix crowns the roof, where figurines of domestic animals are also found. Large areas of apple orchards and onion fields are passed before Ambato is finally reached.

Ambato (population 140,000) was almost completely destroyed in the great 1949 earthquake. The modern cathedral faces the attractive Parque Montalvo, where there is a statue of the writer Juan Montalvo (1833-1889) who is buried in a memorial in a neighbouring street. His house (Bolívar y Montalvo) is open to the public; entrance free (T 821-024). In the Colegio Nacional Bolívar, at Sucre y Lalama, there is a museum of stuffed birds and other animals and items of local historical interest (US$0.05, closed Sat. and Sun.). The Quinta de Mera, an old mansion in gardens in Atocha suburb, open 0900-1200, 1400-1800, can be reached by bus from Espejo y 12 de Novembre. Out along the River Ambato (a pleasant walk) is the prosperous suburb of Miraflores. Ambato has a famous festival in February, the *Fiesta de frutas y flores*, during which it is impossible to get a hotel room unless you book ahead; similarly in Riobamba, Baños and Latacunga. The town has the unique distinction of prohibiting water-throwing at carnival, making it safe for tourists at this time! It is an important centre for the manufacture of rugs and has some excellent tourist shops in the centre, e.g. Artesanías Montalvo, Eguez y Cevallos: look for colourful and good-quality cloth shoulder bags. Leather clothes can be specially made quite cheaply. On a clear day Tungurahua and Chimborazo can be seen from the city.

The main market is held on Mon., and smaller markets on Wed. and Fri.; they are interesting, but have few items for the tourist.

Hotels *Ambato*, Guayaquil y Rocafuerte, C, best, clean, restaurant, casino, squash, highly rec.; *Florida*, Av. Miraflores 1131, D, pleasant, clean, set meal good at US$3; *Villa Hilda*, E, in Av. Miraflores, German spoken, rec., laundry, restaurant good, limited menu but lots to eat, big garden. Buses from the centre stop outside the *Florida*. *La Lira*, Montalvo y Cevallos, E, good, cheaper for long stay; *Cumandá*, 12 de Noviembre 2494, F with bath, clean, safe, basic, water supply erratic in this area; *Carrillo*, F, Av. de las Américas, clean, basic water supply, sometimes used as a brothel, near bus station, restaurant; *Residencial Americano*, Plaza 12 de Noviembre, G, basic, hot water; *Surtrek*, Los Syris y Cordero, F, owner speaks German and English, is an experienced guide and organises mountain and jungle tours, bicycles also for hire. *Executivo*, Espejo y 12 de Noviembre, E, hot water; *Vivero*, Mera 504 y Cevallos, E, good. There are a lot of cheap *pensiones* and hotels on Calle Juan León Mera; *Residencial Laurita* has been rec.

Restaurants *Cabaña del Negro*, Av. Miraflores 263, good seafood; *El Alamo*, Swiss-owned, excellent meals, now three restaurants, one at Sucre 660, *El Alamo Júnior*, self-service, for snacks, and the *Gran Alamo*, round the corner at Montalvo 520. *La Borgoña*, 13 de Abril y Mera, French; *Chambord*, Quito y Rocafuerte, international; *El Pollo Loco*, Lalama y Sucre, chicken, likewise *Pollo Rico*, Alfaro 521; local cooking at *Rincón Criollo*, Eguez y Bolívar. Seafood at *Monarca*, Bolívar y Eguez (best), *Los Sauces*, Mera y Bolívar, and *El Tiburón No. 2*, Primera Imprenta y 5 de Junio. Oriental at *Chifa Nueva Hongkong*, Bolívar y Martínez, and *Chifa Internacional*, 12 de Noviembre y Aillón; also along Cevallos (e.g. *Chifa Jao Fua* at No. 540, popular). Grills: *La Brasa*, Montalvo y Olmedo, *El Gaucho*, Bolívar y Castillo, and *El Faraón*, Bolívar y Lalama. Many good cafeterias and snackbars. *Mama Miche*, Centro Comercial, open 24 hrs. For rockbottom prices with rather dubious hygiene, try the markets. *Happy Chicken*, next to *Hotel Vivero* for clean, cheap, fast food.

There is a *peña* on Fri. and Sat., Peña del Tungurahua, in block 2 of the Centro Comercial.

Exchange Only Citibank travellers' cheques can be changed at Citibank, Calle Sucre; Banco del Pacífico changes notes only. Cambiaria Pichincha, Dárquea y Sevilla, accepts travellers' cheques; *Cambiato*, Bolívar 686, changes Visa cheques; money exchange at *Café Español*, Montalvo 607, Mon.-Sat., 0900-1800.

Immigration Av. Fermín Cevallos y Juan León Mera, T 820-000.

Tourist Office Dituris is next to the *Hotel Ambato* on the 900 block of Calle Guayaquil. Open 0830-1230, 1430-1830, Mon.-Fri.

Travel Agents Metropolitan Touring, Bolívar 471; Coltur, Cevallos 536; Ecuadorian Tours (American Express) Bolívar 678.

Buses To Quito, 2 hrs., US$1. To Guayaquil, 6½ hrs., US$2.50. To Cuenca, US$4, 7 hrs., to get to Cuenca in daylight take a morning Guayaquil bus to El Triunfo and pick up a Guayaquil—Cuenca bus, or take a bus to Biblián and change there. (There can be some discomfort from descent to under 200 metres and subsequent climb up to 2,600, and you may have a long wait at El Triunfo; this route is 2 hrs. slower than the direct one.) To Baños, paved road, lovely scenery, 45 mins., US$0.40. To Latacunga, 30 mins. US$0.50. To Santo Domingo de los Colorados, 4 hrs., US$1.60; to Tena, US$2.20, 6 hrs. To Puyo, US$1.10, 3 hrs. To Esmeraldas, US$2.50, 8 hours. Main bus station is 2 km. N from centre, near the railway station; town buses go there from Plaza Cevallos in the city centre.

Ambato is connected by the excellent paved Pan-American Highway south to Riobamba and north to Latacunga and Quito. To the west, a narrow, winding road (now paved) leads up the valley of the Ambato river, over a high area of desert called the Grande Arenal, past Carihuairazo and Chimborazo, and down through the Chimbo valley to Guaranda. This spectacular journey takes about three hours.

Excursions To Salasaca (see below); to Picaihua by frequent bus to see the local work from *cabuya* fibre, and to Pinllo to see the leather work.

Chimborazo, 6,310 metres: there are two routes up the mountain:

1) The South West face: there are no direct buses so take a taxi (US$25 for one day, US$30 return next day or later, US$15 one way) from Riobamba to the Edward Whymper refuge, which takes 1½ hrs., 47 km., or a bus to San Juan village and hitch from there. The road ends at 4,800 metres, where there is a new refuge, or you can walk up to the Edward Whymper refuge at 5,000 metres which is at the foot of the Thielman glacier. There should be two keepers at this refuge, which provides water and a bed (US$1 p.p. a night). Beware of thieves if you leave anything in the refuge or even in your car at 4,800 metres. From the refuge to the summit the climb is 8-9 hrs and the descent about 4 hrs. There are three routes depending on your experience and ability. Recommended to start at 2400 or 0100. There is a road from San Juan to Pogyos round Carihuairazo, making a round trip by jeep, Riobamba-Chimborazo-Ambato, possible.

2) The North West face, or Pogyos route: Take the Guaranda bus from Ambato along the new paved road or a truck along the spectacular old road (50 km.) to the valley of Pogyos. At Pogyos (4,000 metres) there is a house with a metal roof where you can hire mules for US$4 each to carry your luggage. (Beware of pilfering from your bags on ascent.) Walk about 3 hrs. to the Fabián Zurita refuge (4,900 metres) which is uninhabitable. From the refuge to the summit is about an 8-hr. climb and 3-4 hr. descent. Advisable to start at 0100. Take tents and water (obtainable at Pogyos, containers in Ambato). (We are grateful to Enrique Veloz Coronado—**see page 740**—for much of this information.)

Dr Sverre Aarseth writes that in order to climb this mountain it is essential to have at least one week's acclimatization above 3,000 metres. The best season is December and June-September. Sr. Héctor Vásquez at Colegio National Bolívar, Ambato, has helped many expeditions with travel arrangements and information; he is a top-grade mountaineer. The original Whymper route is harder than the Pogyos route, but it is more accessible and there are more climbers in case of difficulty; the afternoon descent is particularly hazardous owing to stones rolling from the scree (the upper part is quite straightforward with two or three on a rope). Previous parties will most likely have left marker flags; these are often needed for descent in a cloud. Very soft snow between first and second summit but usually there will be a good path from previous parties (otherwise snow shoes might be needed). The ascent to the summit is very steep and partly exposed (falling could be fatal). No one without mountaineering experience should attempt the climb, and rope, ice-axe and crampons must be used. Carihuairazo (5,020 metres) is a spur of Chimborazo.

The Fiesta de las Nieves is celebrated near the Whymper shelter on the second Sun. in December—music and dancing at 4,800 m. Trucks leave Riobamba around 0700; hitch back.

Guaranda (14,000 inhabitants) is the capital of Bolívar Province. It is a beautiful, clean, quiet town which, because it is built on seven hills, proudly calls itself "the Rome of Ecuador". Carnival is very enjoyable. Market day is Sat. The daily *paseo* in the main square is from about 1800 to 2100 exactly. Guaranda is connected by a new paved road to Ambato (several buses) and Babahoyo, and a poor, narrow road to Riobamba. It is the main centre for the wheat and maize-growing Chimbo valley, but has long stagnated since newer, faster routes replaced the old Guayaquil-Quito road through Babahoyo and Guaranda. A water-powered grist mill on the river welcomes visitors.

Hotels *La Colina*, high up on Av. Guayaquil, D, well kept, good value; *Cochabamba*, García Moreno y 7 de Mayo, F with bath, best in town; *Pensión Ecuador*, opposite, F; *Residencial Bolívar*, Sucre y Rocafuerte, F, very good, hot showers; *Matiaví*, Av. Eliza Mariño, F, clean, next to bus station; *Residencial Acapulco*, 10 de Agosto y 9 de Abril, G, basic.

Restaurants *Rumipampa*, Parque Simón Bolívar, best in town, try churrasco; *La Choza*, 10 de Agosto between Sucre and Pichincha, good tacos. *Hotel Cochabamba*, variable, limited selection, not cheap; *Guaranda* soda bar on G. Moreno y Pichincha.

Buses Bus station on road to Ambato. To Ambato, US$1.20, 3¼ hrs.; Riobamba, US$0.70, 2½ hrs.; Guayaquil, US$1.75, 3½ hrs; Quito, several a day US$1.75 or take bus to Ambato and change.

Excursion North of Guaranda, 1½ hrs. by taxi along poor roads, is Salinas (de la Sierra), pop. 5,000, noted for its cheeses and sweaters, which are also sold in Quito. No buses except maybe on Sat.; hitching is difficult.

To the east of Ambato, an important road leads to Salasaca, Pelileo, and Baños and then on along the Pastaza valley to Mera, Shell Mera, Puyo and Tena in the Oriente (**see page 801**). It is paved to Puyo.

Salasaca is a small modernized village 14 km. (½ hr.) from Ambato, at the centre of the Salasaca Indian zone. The Salasacas wear distinctive black ponchos with black trousers and broad white hats; this is said to reflect perpetual mourning for the death of their Inca, Atahualpa. Most of them are farmers, but they are best known for weaving *tapices*, strips of cloth with remarkable bird and animal shapes in the centre. A co-operative has fixed the prices on the *tapices* it sells in its store near the church. Throughout the village the prices are the same, and no cheaper than in Quito. If you have the time you can order one to be specially made; this takes four to six weeks, but is well worth the wait. You can watch the Indians weaving in the main workshop opposite the church.

Pelileo, 5 km. beyond Salasaca, is a lively little market town which has been almost completely rebuilt on a new site since the 1949 earthquake. In all, Pelileo has been destroyed by four earthquakes during its 400-year history. The new town springs to life on Saturday, the main market day. The ruins of Pelileo Viejo can be seen about 2 km. east of the present site on the north side of the road to Baños. *Fiesta* on 15 August. Regular buses from Baños, 15 min.

From Pelileo, the road gradually descends to Las Juntas, the meeting point of the Patate and Chambo rivers to form the Pastaza river, and where the road from Riobamba comes in. It then continues along the lower slopes of the volcano Tungurahua to Baños (25 km. from Pelileo). The road gives good views of the Pastaza gorge and the volcano.

Baños (1,800 metres) is a holiday resort with a supposedly miraculous Virgin and hot springs; very busy at weekends and increasingly touristy. The central Basilica attracts many pilgrims; the paintings of miracles performed by Nuestra Señora de Santa Agua are worth seeing. There is a *fiesta* in her honour in October with processions, bands, fireworks, sporting events and a lot of general gaiety. The Basilica of Baños has a museum (stuffed birds, Nuestra Señora's clothing). There is another civic *fiesta* on 15 December to celebrate the town's anniversary when each *barrio* hires a *saka* band and there are many processions. The following day there is a parade in which spectators are outnumbered by participants. There is a zoo off the road to Puyo on the left, about 1 km. from town, run by the Church authorities, US$0.20 entrance, cages far too small and excessive loudspeaker noise. The Pastaza river rushes past Baños to the Agoyán falls 10 km. further down the valley, marred by engineering works connected with the construction of a hydroelectric scheme. The whole area between Pelileo and Baños has a relaxing sub-tropical climate (the rainy season is usually from May to October, especially July and August). It is here that Ecuador's best *aguardiente* is made. Street vendors sell *canelazo*, a sweet drink of *aguardiente*, lime, water and cinnamon, also jawsticking toffee (*tafi*) made in ropes in shop doorways, and painted balsa-wood birds (see *El Chaguamango* shop by Basílica). Two sets of thermal baths are in the town: the main set is by the waterfall close to the *Hotel Sangay*; the Santa Clara baths are about ½ km. further W, up against the mountain, and the third, the Salado, which is pleasanter (but very busy so go early), is 1½ km. out of town on the Ambato road (entrance to each, US$0.25). There are regular buses every 30 mins. between the Salado baths and the Agoyán Falls, passing by the centre of town. All the baths can be very crowded and the water not very hot. **Interesting side trips** are possible from the main Pelileo-Baños highway across the main valley, north to Patate, or up the Chambo valley to Penipe and Riobamba, or take taxi to Puente Vendas, 2 hrs., US$2.20, beautiful ride.

Note Baños is a good meeting place to form a group to visit the Oriente, more interesting than Misahuallí, if you have to wait a few days.

Hotels *Sangay*, D, with bath, beautifully situated close to waterfall, restaurant (rec.), sauna and pool all open to non-residents, tennis and squash courts, accommodation in chalets reported better than in rooms (same price), rec. Information and some equipment for expeditions to the jungle and volcanoes may be provided by the hotel. *Villa Gertrudis*, Montalvo 2975, good situation on edge of town, with lovely garden, D, demi-pensión, reserve in advance, rec.; *Cabañas Bascún*, on edge of town (nr. El Salado hot springs), D, quite comfortable, pool, sauna (US$1.50 to non-residents), tennis, restaurant; *Paraíso (Humboldt)*, Ambato y Haflans, D with board or F without food, bath, clean, beautiful view from front rooms; *Palace*, opposite *Sangay* (even closer to waterfall), old-fashioned, friendly, good value, restaurant, breakfast US$1, dinner US$3. *Residencial Magdalena*, Oriente y Alfaro, E with bath, clean, warm water, rec.; *Hostal Los Helechos*, E, on Parque Central, close to Post Office and Ietel, restaurant, noisy but rec.; *Timara*, near plaza (ask for *Tienda de Mariposas*—butterfly shop), G, hot showers, clean, laundry facilities, use of good kitchen, good breakfast, rec, owner's son takes tours to Oriente (US$15/day); **Pensión Patty**, Eloy Alfaro 556, near market, G, rec., clean, basement rooms poor, otherwise good facilities, use of kitchen, laundry, comfortable and quiet, family-run, the helpful owner is a mountaineer and can offer good, free advice, sell maps and hire equipment; **Residencial Los Pinos**, Rocafuerte y Maldonado, F, clean, friendly, ask for front room with view, preferably on second floor; **Residencial Baños**, F, Ambato y Alfaro, good, washing facilities; **Residencial Teresita**, Parque de la Basílica, G, cooking facilities, hot water, prices vary; **Alborado**, on the plaza opposite **Teresita**, F with shower, modern, clean, friendly, rooms have balconies overlooking the square; **Americano**, G, 12 de Noviembre y Martínez, basic but friendly, cooking facilities available, thin walls. **Flor de Oriente**, Ambato y Maldonado, E, very good, lots of choice in restaurant, rec. There are two **Residenciales Las Delicias**, **1**, on the Parque Central, F, front rooms have lovely view, but are noisy, friendly; **Las Delicias 2**, Ambato y Haflans, is newer, both reported dirty; **Residencial Olguita**, overlooking plaza, G, basic, O.K.; **Agoyán**, F, opposite Basilica, clean, good, ask for front room overlooking square; **Anita**, Rocafuerte y 16 de Diciembre, F, behind the market, clean, friendly, quiet, use of kitchen; **El Santuario** above Banco del Pacífico, F with bath, hot water on request, good value; **Chile**, in nearest square to bus station, clean, comfortable, private bath; **Santa Clara**, 12 de Noviembre y Montalvo, G, use of kitchen possible, washing facilities, noisy, nice garden, rec.; **Pensión Guayaquil**, on Parque de la Basílica, G, old and picturesque, good food, but no private baths; **El Castillo**, Martínez y Santa Clara, G, quiet, clean, hot water, restaurant; **Charvic**, near Terminal Terrestre, F, clean, rec. Several near corner Ambato with Alfaro. Houses for rent on a weekly basis: the owners of **El Paisano** restaurant have three houses, US$24 for the most expensive. **Casa Familiar**, 2 blocks behind clocktower, rooms, F, and vegetarian restaurant, use of kitchen, laundry facilities (Danish and Ecuadorean owners). Camping is not recommended on the mountainsides as several people have frozen to death.

Restaurants Many close by 2130. **El Marqués No. 1**, on Montalvo, just beyond Hotels **Sangay** and **Palace**, in old house, closes early, good steaks for US$2, quiet and friendly. **El Marqués No. 2**, 16 de Diciembre y Rocafuerte, international food; **Monica's**, Alfaro y Espejo, well-prepared and interesting menus, popular gringo meeting place, good, but be careful with overcharging, very slow service; **Donde Marcelo**, Ambato nr. 16 de Diciembre, good, inexpensive, friendly gringo bar; **La Petite Restaurant**, Eloy Alfaro 2-46 y Montalvo, excellent French cuisine, friendly, good value; next door Christian sells fresh sourdough bread (and rents horses); **Chifa Oriental**, Ambato y Alfaro, fair food, low prices, friendly; **Chifa Come Bien**, nr. main square, friendly, cheap; **Hostal Los Helechos**, good food, wide selection, slow service; **Salón Latino**, Parque de la Basílica, good seafood, clean, slow but worth waiting; **El Paisano**, rec., Martínez y Santa Clara, on road to **Sangay** hotel, vegetarian, but meat also served, also good for breakfast, with yoghurt; **Rincón de Suecia**, opposite **Acapulco**, pizzas, good, Swedish and English spoken; **Reguies**, 12 de Noviembre y Montalvo, is a German café, good breakfasts, good cakes, good meeting place, very popular, excellent Irish coffee; **La Fuente**, on main street, good set meal; **Lucerno**, also on main street, clean, friendly, good value set meal; **Country Kitchen**, Martínez 615 y Haflans, one block behind main square, mostly vegetarian, good value (American owned); **Edén**, nr. bus terminal, good food, large breakfasts, cheap, slow service; **Cafetería Chushi**, on Maldonado opp. bus station, good breakfast and snacks, has guidebooks for consultation and book exchange (small fee); **Hotel Humboldt** rec. for breakfast, in main street; **Pan de Casa**, next to market, good breakfasts, hot bread, rec.; **Pan Rico**, Parque Central, cheap breakfasts, hot bread.

Entertainment Cockfighting, Coliseo, Sun. 1400-1800. Peñas La Burbuja and Agoyán (near main baths), Fri. and Sat. Hard Rock Café, Eloy Alfaro near market, beer, cheap drinks, "good old rock, favourite gringo hangout".

Bank Banco del Pacífico, Carrera 3 y Calle 2, changes all travellers' cheques and foreign currency, but only from 1100-1330.

Spanish Classes given by Norwegian Jörgen Grönneberg, Corinca, 16 de Diciembre y Martínez, 5th floor, rec. Also offers guided tours by car of volcanoes and local sites.

Book Exchange J.Urquizo (local artist), 12 de Noviembre y Ambato.

Laundry Clothes can be washed at the municipal washhouse next to the main baths for US$1.20 a bundle.

Warning Many people have been bitten by dogs in Baños, there are hundreds of strays. If you are bitten, report to the hospital where you will be treated, free of charge, and passed on to the public health inspector who will find out whether the dog concerned is rabid (**but see warning on page** 815).

Tourist Office on Parque Central (Haflans y Ambato) open Tues.-Sat., 0800-1200, 1400-1800; near bus terminal, friendly but not very helpful.

Buses To Quito, via Ambato, US$1.30, 4½ hrs.; to Ambato, ¾ hr., US$0.40; to Riobamba, 1 hr., US$0.50; to Latacunga, 2½ hrs., US$0.60; to Puyo, 2 hrs., US$0.80 (road has been reopened after 1987 earthquake damage); for Macas, change at Puyo, 0830, US$1.30, 6 hrs., magnificent scenery, sit on right; to Tena, 5½ hrs., US$1.80 by bus (more leg room) with Coop. Riobamba, or US$2 by *buseta*, only three direct buses Baños-Tena, but frequent passing buses from Riobamba and Ambato (or change at Puyo); seat reservations rec. (but buses don't always leave); to Misahuallí, change at Tena, buses leave every 20 mins., US$0.30, 1 hr.; or at the Río Napo crossing, **see page 799**. The bus station is on the Ambato-Puyo road a short way from the centre, and is the scene of vigorous volleyball games most afternoons.

From Baños it is possible to climb **Tungurahua** (5,016 metres—part of Sangay National Park); follow road opposite police control on Ambato side of town, then first mule track to right of store and follow the path to Pondoa; do not follow the road up to the baths. If you are driving to Pondoa, take the main Ambato road and turn off to the left about 1 km. from the town centre. The road runs parallel to the main road for several km. before turning east into the mountains. Park the car at the shop in Pondoa. The walk from the shop to the beginning of the trail takes 30 mins. *Pensión Patty* in Baños arranges equipment, guide (min. US$32 a day for two climbers and US$16 for each extra one), and jeeps to Pondoa Tues., Thurs., Sat. 0830, US$1 p.p. (return 1600-1700 next day); there is also an occasional bus from Baños to Pondoa, and a milk truck leaves at 0800 daily from *Pensión Patty*. It returns from Pondoa at 1400. It takes 3-5 hrs. walking from the park entrance to reach the Santos Ocaña *refugio* (3,800 metres—US$1, purchase ticket either at the shop in Pondoa, where sketch map of route can be obtained, or at the refuge) situated 3-4 hrs. below the snowline, then about 4 hours from the *refugio* to the summit early next morning (about 0330). Leave summit about 0930 as clouds come down later in the day: allow 2 hours for descent to *refugio* and leave *refugio* by 1400 in order to get back to Baños on same day. Take a sleeping bag and food; there are cooking facilities at the *refugio*, but no eating utensils and rarely any lighting, no heating and it can be cold. For a guide and pack animals enquire at Baños tourist office or Pondoa shop; guide and mule for 1 pack US$5, for 2 packs, US$7. Horses can be hired for US$0.90 an hour (see Julio Albán, Segundo Sánchez or Víctor Barriga near the Plaza Central or through tourist office). A tiring but rewarding climb; requires little experience and, depending on season, crampons for the summit (check in Baños beforehand). Best season is December to March.

There are many interesting walks in the Baños area. You can cross the Pastaza by the San Francisco suspension bridge across the main road from the bus station. Short hikes include San Martín shrine, 3 hrs., which overlooks deep rocky canyon with the Pastaza River thundering below; beyond the shrine is a path to the Iñes María waterfall; along the old road to Ambato to Lligua, a flowery little village straddling the Lligua River at its junction with the Pastaza; to Runtún, a village of a dozen mud dwellings, two sporting a billiard table, from which there is a splendid view of Tungurahua (3½-4 hrs.). Cold drinks sold at the billiard hall, no food. There are two paths from Baños to Runtún, one from south end of Calle 9, the other from Calle 6.

20 km. from Baños on the Puyo road are the Río Verde falls; a bus goes from the Baños terminal, ¾ hr., US$0.12. Cross river and take path to right of last house on right, take immediate left fork, trail down to suspension bridge with view of falls.

Guides in Baños: apart from Carlos at *Pensión Patty*, whose trips cost US$14 a day, there is Sebastián Moya, who can be found either at *Country Kitchen* or Tsantse Tours (*Pensión Patty*—T 740202). He is a Shuar Indian who will lead tours anywhere for US$13 a day (careful planning needed to minimize travelling time), food not included. You may have to wait some weeks for him to be free. Also contactable through *Pensión Patty* is mountain guide Carlos Alvarez, who takes climbs in both the Sangay and Cotopaxi National Parks. Marco Bermeo Velástegui of Cruceros Fluviales Misahuallí (T 740599) organises tours to the Oriente (very mixed reports). Geovanny Romo, small agency on Maldonado opp. bus station, jungle tours, experienced, US$25 p.p. per day for trips originating in Coca; also arranges horseback tours from Baños. Christian, a German, also has good horses for rent, rec., has a sign outside his house on Alfaro, just S of Martínez, next to *La Petite Restaurant*. We have received some critical reports of tours out of Baños, especially of Ayahuasca Tours. Beware also of a guide called Ernesto or El Jefe.

Horses to hire on the square in front of the Post Office, US$0.75 per hour, without guide, for trekking in the mountains.

North from Ambato the railway and Pan-American Highway (many buses) pass through **Salcedo**, good Thurs. and Sun. markets (*Hostería Rumipamba de las Rosas*, D, restaurant, swimming pool, exchanges US$ notes; *Hostal Las Piedras*, G, on Parque; *Residencial Las Vegas*, Bolívar y Paredes, F, hot water, private showers; *Restaurant Ritz*, Bolívar y Sucre, chicken) to Latacunga, the capital of Cotopaxi Province.

Latacunga, with 30,000 inhabitants, is a place where the abundance of light grey lava rock has been artfully employed. Cotopaxi is much in evidence, though it is 29 km. away. Provided they are not hidden in the clouds, which unfortunately is all too often (try the early morning), as many as nine volcanic cones can be seen from Latacunga. The central plaza, Parque Vicente León, is a colourful and beautifully maintained botanical garden, where the shrubs are sculpted into various shapes (e.g., fans, globes, wedding cakes). There are several other gardens in the town including Parque San Francisco and Lago Flores. The colonial character of the town has been well preserved.

Just off the Parque Vicente León is the Pasaje Catedral, a colonial building converted into an arcade of shops, offices, and a small art gallery that features a 17th-century aerial view painting of Latacunga (open Tues.-Sat. 0830 to 1800). Casa Cultural, the Museo Etnográfico (closed Sun. and Mon.). There is a Sat. (also, but smaller, on Tues.) market on the Plaza de San Sebastián; goods for sale include *shigras* (fine woven, colourful straw bags) and homespun wool and cotton yarn. Tourist Office at Quito 73-12.

Festival The Fiesta de Nuestra Señora de la Merced (22-24 Sept.) is celebrated with dancing in the streets. Some of the masks and costumes used are on display in the Casa Cultural. Mama Negra festival, colourful costumes, headdresses and masks, in November.

Hotels *Copitaxi*, on main square, E, with bathroom, good, safe for luggage, clean, parking, hot water after 0700, rec., ask for view over plaza (these rooms noisy at weekends); *Estambul*, Belisario Quevedo 7340 y Salcedo, G, clean, quiet, soap, toilet paper, rec., trips to Cotopaxi National Park; *Latacunga*, on main Quito road, E with bath, TV, friendly, restaurant rarely open at weekends. *Jacqueline* is G, but bad. Also **Costa Azul**, G, unfriendly, good meals; this and the *Residencial Los Andes* (F) are along the Ambato road. Accommodation is not abundant.

Restaurants *Los Copihues*, in *Hotel Cotopaxi*, Chilean, best in town; *La Carreta*, Quito 150, good 4-course lunch; *Cyrano*, 2 de Mayo 7674, chicken; *Chifa Tokio*, Guayaquil 45-58, moderate prices, good value; *Chifa Yut Wah*, Quinchero y Ordóñez 6973, good, cheap; nearby on same street, *Chifa Formosa*, cheap, good value; *Salón Coseñita*, Echeverría 1143, good cheap meals; *El Estudiante*, Antonio Vela 78, lunch US$0.50. *Pollo Dorado*, 5 de Junio y Vela, good value, US$1.30; milkshakes and real coffee recommended at *Pingüino*, Quito y Salcedo; *Los Alpes*, opposite the *Cotopaxi*, good, cheap. *Pollos Gus*, cheap roast chicken, on Ambato road. Ice cream store off main square, Salcedo y Quito. Superb bread at *Hector's*, opposite *Pingüino*. Difficult to eat after 2000 and difficult to find breakfast.

Exchange Banco de Pichincha on Plaza, cash and travellers' cheques.

Post Office on Belisario Quevedo, near *Hotel Estambul*.

Buses to Quevedo, 6 hrs., US$1.60; to Quito, 2 hrs., US$0.75; to Ambato, ½ hr., US$0.40; to Guayaquil, US$2.50, 6 hrs. Day trips to Cotopaxi (**see page** 786) can be arranged with a taxi for about US$16.

A fine paved road leads west to **Pujilí** (good Sun. market; also, but smaller, on Wed.; beware local illicit liquor and pickpockets, 15 km. away (bus, US$0.18) and then on over the Western Cordillera to Zumbahua, Macuchi and Quevedo.

Zumbahua, a cluster of 40 houses by an old *hacienda*, 1 km. from main road, 65 km. from Pujilí, has a fine Sat. morning market (a local market for produce and animals, not tourist items, but rated as one of the most interesting and colourful in Ecuador and not to be missed) with llamas on view (two basic *residenciales* on the main plaza, both G, no water, no light, dirty; only restaurant is on main road outside village). Buses US$0.60 from Latacunga depart from Panamerican Highway outside the town, but the best for continuing to Quilotoa, 0630, leaves from corner of *Hotel Turismo*, 2 hrs., beautiful ride. Bus drivers on the Latacunga-Quevedo line often do not want to take tourists to Zumbahua as they want to fill up the bus with people going to Quevedo. Car hire has been rec. A taxi can cost the same as the bus. Many interesting crafts are practised by the Indians in the neighbouring valley of Tigua: skin paintings, hand-carved wooden masks, baskets.

Zumbahua is the point to turn off for a visit to **Quilotoa**, a volcanic crater filled by a beautiful emerald lake, to which there is a steep path from rim. From the rim of the crater several snowcapped volcanoes can be seen in the distance. It is reached by a dusty road which runs north from Zumbahua (turn right and over the bridge at the fork in the road, there are no road signs and the crater can only be recognized when you are on top of it) to Quilotoa and on to Chugchilán (this last stretch is the worst). At the crater itself, expect to be besieged by persistent beggars. It's wise to carry some food or small bills to buy them off, and take a stick against dogs on the road. Also be prepared for sudden changes in the weather. The walk to Quilotoa is 9-10 km., or about 2-3 hrs. hike from Zumbahua; take water as that from the lake is quite sulphurous and water is generally hard to find. Alternatively, you can get a bus on Saturdays, US$0.15, but it will only go part of the way, leaving you with a ½ hr. walk to the crater. Trucks go up after the Saquisilí market on Thurs. p.m. During the wet season, the best views are in the early morning so those with a tent may wish to camp. Alternatively, hitch a truck (which is easy on market day); you will be dropped close to the volcano; trucks back from Zumbahua leave about midday on market day, and a bus goes to Latacunga at 1300. Vehicles bound for Chugchilán drop the traveller 5 mins. from the lagoon, about 40-min. walk north. Hitching a return trip should not be left till late in the afternoon.

The Sat. trip to Zumbahua market and the Quilotoa crater is one of the best excursions in Ecuador, despite the poor accommodation in Zumbahua (see above). Macuchi, on the main road to Quevedo some way beyond Zumbahua, is a mining centre for gold and various non-ferrous metals. The mines were developed in the 1930s by an American company, and now they are almost abandoned.

It is 20 km. from Quilotoa crater to **Chugchilán**, a beautiful but tiring walk along the edge of a canyon. Water is available from small streams, but take a purifier. One bus leaves Zumbahua for Chugchilán at 1400; return buses (3) between 0300 and 0330 (also at this time on Thurs. to Saquisilí). In Chugchilán, a very poor village in one of the most scenic areas of Ecuador, you can buy an evening meal in a private house, and sleep on the bus till it leaves. It is an interesting journey back as local people board with their animals and produce for market.

About 45 min. by bus north-west of Latacunga is the small but very important market town of **Saquisilí**. Its Thurs. (0700-1100) market is famous throughout Ecuador for the way in which all eight of its plazas and most of its streets become jam-packed with people, the great majority of them local Indians with red ponchos and narrow-brimmed felt hats. The best time to visit the market is between 0900 and 1000 (0700-0800 for the animal market); be sure to bargain, prices may be inflated. Rated the best market in Ecuador by a traveller who has visited them all, but less good for textiles than Otavalo. Saquisilí has colourful Corpus Christi processions.

Dan Buck and Anne Meadows write: Tightly woven decorated baskets plentiful but expensive, though somewhat cheaper than in Quito. Bargain hard, there is a lot of competition for your custom. Livestock market hectic and worth a visit. Some animal buyers set up small corrals in which they collect their purchases. Trucks brimming with oranges and yellow and red bananas; reed mats, fans, and baskets; beef, pork and mutton parts piled on tables; Indian women hunkered down beside bundles of onions, radishes, and herbs, and little pyramids of tomatoes, mandarin oranges, potatoes, okra, and avocados; cabuya and maguey ropes and cords laid out like dead snakes; and a food kiosk every five feet offering everything from full almuerzos to tortillas de papa.

Accommodation Pensión Chavela, main plaza, G, basic, good views, billiards and gambling hall downstairs, noisy; Salón Pichincha, Bolívar y Pichincha, G, good restaurant-bar below, friendly, not very clean, secure motor cycle parking. Some basic restaurants can be found in the same district (at the entrance to the village).

Transport The Saquisilí and Cotopaxi bus companies have frequent services between Latacunga and Saquisilí (US$0.10, ½ hr.) and several buses a day run to Saquisilí from Quito (catch them in Quito bus terminal, US$0.65, 1½-2 hrs.). Alternatively you can catch an Ambato bus from Latacunga, ask the driver to let you off at the junction for Saquisilí and get a passing pick-up truck (US$0.25) from there. The Hotel Quito and the Hotel Colón in Quito both organize efficient but expensive taxis for a 2-hr. visit to Saquisilí market on Thurs. Bus tours cost about US$17.50 p.p., taxis can be found for US$35, with 2 hr. wait at market.

North of Latacunga, the railway and the Pan-American Highway cross one another at Lasso, a small village with a milk bottling plant and two recommended cafés serving dairy products. Just north of Lasso, east of the highway, is the San Agustín hill, thought to be a prehistoric pyramid.

The area around San Agustín is owned by the Plaza family, which has two large *haciendas* and breeds bulls for the bull-fights in Quito in December. One of the two *haciendas* is actually at the base of the San Agustín hill and includes some converted Inca buildings.

About 2 km. off the road from Latacunga to Quito, near Lasso, is the *Hostería La Ciénega*, a good restaurant also operating as a small hotel (C) in an old *hacienda* with outstanding gardens, an avenue of massive, old eucalyptus trees to the hacienda and a small private chapel; accommodation is very good, service in the restaurant very slow, but it is also a good place for lunch or a drink after visiting Saquisilí market (reserve accommodation in advance at weekends); horse-riding US$1.50 per hour. It used to belong to the Lasso family when their land spread from Quito to Ambato (T Quito 549126). Take the bus from Quito to Ambato and get off 2 km. south of Lasso.

A little beyond San Agustín, a poor road leads off towards the Cotopaxi volcano, at the Parque Nacional de Cotopaxi sign. National Park authorities are breeding a fine llama herd on the lower slopes. Just north of Cotopaxi are the peaks of Sincholahua (4,893 metres), Rumiñahui (4,712 metres) and Pasochoa (4,225 metres).

Cotopaxi (6,005 metres). Rob Rachowiecki writes: There are two entrances to the Cotopaxi National Park: the first is near a sign for the NASA satellite tracking station, from where one can walk (no vehicle access) the 3 km. to the NASA station (army-run now, can be visited with preauthorization from Instituto Geográfico Militar, 4th floor, oficina Clirsen, in Quito) and then continue for over 30 km. more along a signposted dirt road, past two campsites, through the National Park gates, past Lake Limpio Pungo, past the old Armada Nacional refuge and on to the parking lot (4,600 metres) where the road ends. From here it is 30 mins. to 1 hr. to the José Ribas refuge (4,800 metres). The second entrance, about 6 km. further south, is marked by a small Parque Nacional de Cotopaxi sign. It is about 28 km. from here to the refuge. Nearly 1 km. from the highway, turn right at a T junction and a few hundred metres later turn sharp left. Beyond this the road is either signed or you take the main fork; it is shorter and easier to follow than the first route which you join just before the Park gates.

The ascent from the refuge takes 6-11 hrs, start climbing at 0100 as the snow deteriorates in the sun. Equipment and experience are required. Climb the sandy slope above the hut and head up leftwards on to the glacier. Getting on to the glacier is the steepest and technically hardest part of the climb. The route then goes roughly to the right of Yanasacha and on to the summit. Allow 2-4 hrs. for the descent.

Dr. Sverre Aarseth writes that the best season is December-April; strong winds and clouds in August-December but still possible for experienced mountaineers. The route is more difficult to find on Cotopaxi than on Chimborazo (see page 779); it is advisable to seek information from Quito climbing clubs (Nuevos Horizontes is the best). The snow and ice section is more heavily crevassed than Chimborazo and is also steeper; however it is less climbing time.

Visitors to the Parque Nacional de Cotopaxi must register when entering the park. The park gates are open 0700-1800 with lunch 1200-1400. The refuge (US$0.85 p.p. a night) has a kitchen (you may use the stove for a small charge), water, and beds. Bring sleeping bag and mat, also padlock for your excess luggage when you climb. There are many campsites in the Park (a good spot is Laguna Limpiopungo). If you have no car, the best bus to take from Quito is the Latacunga bus and get off at Lasso. Do not take an express bus as you have to get off before Latacunga. Trucks are available from Latacunga for about US$25 round trip—ask at the *Hotel Estambul*.

At Cotopaxi the road and railway begin to dip into the Quito basin. In a valley below the bleak *páramo* lies the town of **Machachi**, famous for its mineral water springs and very cold swimming pool (US$0.35). The water, "Agua Güitig", is bottled in a plant 4 km. from the town and sold throughout the country. Machachi produces a very good cheese. Cockfights on Sun. *Pensión El Tiempo*, F, clean; *Restaurante Moderno*, round corner, very good. Bus to Quito US$0.35. Taxi to Cotopaxi, US$16 per car.

Machachi is a good base for climbing **Illiniza**. Illiniza Norte can be climbed without technical equipment; for Illaniza Sur (4 hr. ice climb) experience of ice climbing is essential. The rock is very crumbly, so caution is advised. There is a *refugio* on the saddle between the two.

THE SOUTHERN SIERRA (7)

The Pan-American Highway and railway S of Sibambe to Cuenca run through mountainous country and high above the valleys of the west-bound rivers. The countryside is poor, dry, chilly and wind-swept, and the Indians small, withdrawn and wrapped-up. Near Gun and Cañar, more Indians, dressed in black, are seen. At Gun an all-weather road runs to Cochancay in the coastal lowlands, from where there are paved roads to Guayaquil and Machala. Towards Cuenca the road loses height and the land is more intensively farmed. There are excellent roads linking Quito-Guayaquil and Guayaquil-Cuenca, which meet at El Triunfo on the coastal plain. Some transport goes this way rather than using the direct road, although there the scenery is magnificent; there are often detours which lead to deep ravines and precipitous peaks. The main road south divides at Cajabamba into two equally respectable-looking paved roads to Cuenca and Guayaquil; the paving of the Cuenca road is complete except for 12 km. around Alausí which are still terrible (**see page** 775). On this route, near Alausí, is Chunchi, a small, welcoming village with a Sunday market.

Cañar, 65 km. N of Cuenca (36 km. N of Azogues), is famous for its double weaving and is a good area for walking; it is close to the Inca ruin of Ingapirca (**see page** 791). Market on Sun. (*Residencia Mónica*, main square, G, only hotel, 10 rooms, clean, hot water, laundry facilities, owner offers tour service to Ingapirca; *Flamingo Restaurant*, Bolívar 106, dirty; restaurants close about 1830.) Bus every 30 mins. to the Terminal Terrestre in Cuenca, US$0.60; also to Quito and El Tambo.

Azogues (14,452) is 31 km. N of Cuenca (1 hr. by bus) and a centre of the panama hat industry, though good quality hats for sale only at the large Sat. market (*Hotel Charles*, F, in centre, friendly; *Residencial Tropical*, G, showers sometimes electrocute guests). Both Azogues and nearby Biblián have attractive churches overlooking the towns from neighbouring hillsides.

Cuenca (2,595 metres), with 201,500 people, was founded by the Spaniards in 1557 on the site of the indigenous settlement of Tomebamba. The climate is spring-like, but the nights are chilly. The city has preserved its colonial air, with many of its old buildings constructed of the marble quarried nearby. On the central square, Parque Calderón, are the old cathedral and a fine new cathedral, completed in 1885 (containing a famous crowned image of the Virgin), the work of the German architect Padre Johannes Baptista Stiehle, who also designed many other buildings in the Cuenca area. The University is now on the other side of the Tomebamba river. Part of the Padre Crespi collection can be seen at the Banco Central "Pumapungo" museum (open Mon. 1300-1600, Tues.-Fri. 0930-1600, Sat. 0900-1200, free), Calle Larga y Huayna Capac, on the edge of town at the Tomebamba site (excavation continuing). It is often shut if the exhibition is being changed. Padre Crespi (died June 1982) used these artefacts to support his theory that the Phoenicians reached Cuenca via the Amazon. The Instituto Azuayo de Folklore, also at the "Pumapungo" museum (open Mon.-Fri. 0830-1230, 1430-1830) has an excellent exhibition of popular art, with a few items on sale. Museo del Monasterio de los Conceptos, Hermano Miguel between Pres. Córdova and Juan Jaramillo, well-displayed collection of religious and folk art, extensive collection of lithographs by Guayasamín. There is a municipal museum at Calles Sucre y Talbot (modern art and Indian artefacts, closed for renovation in 1989) and a small museum in the Casa de la Cultura, Luis Cordero y Sucre (second floor). A pleasant walk is upstream along the river.

The churches which deserve a visit are the old Cathedral, which has a fine organ (under restoration in 1989); La Concepción (convent founded 1599, religious art museum) San Blas, San Francisco, Santo Cenáculo, and Santo

Domingo. Inca ruins have been found on the banks of the river: about 300 metres from the Pumapungo site, at Larga 287, there are excavations at the Todos Los Santos site, which reveal ancient traces of Inca and Cañari (pre-Inca) civilizations (open Mon.-Fri., 0800-1600).

The main market is on Thursday when pottery, clothes, guinea pigs and local produce, especially baskets, are sold in the Plaza Rotary. There is also a colourful daily market. Be careful of pickpockets in the market. If you are robbed, however, contact the police, their efficiency has been praised by one traveller who had most of his money returned to him after paying them a small fee.

Many tourists now visit Cuenca, but the city is not yet well organized for tourism; many places of interest are closed at weekends and many churches are open only at irregular hours. Police searches of tourists' luggage at their hotels are not unknown.

Festivals On Christmas Eve there is a parade; children and adults from all the *barrios* and surrounding villages decorate donkeys, horses, cars and trucks with symbols of abundance: strings of dollar bills, bottles of Cinzano, strings of lemons and peppers, bunches of bananas, whole roasted chickens with banknotes in their beaks, toys etc. Little children in colourful Indian costumes or dressed up as Biblical figures ride through the streets accompanied by Indian musicians. The parade starts between 1000 and 1100 and ends in the Plaza de Armas, which is a good place to watch it, 2-3 hours later. Travellers in Cuenca over New Year's Eve report that the festivities include the parading and burning of effigies (some political, some fictional) which symbolize the old year; there is also much water throwing and tourists are a prime target. The festivities seem to go on all through January. The burning of straw puppets (*el hombre viejo*) takes place at the moment of the New Year throughout Ecuador. There are also festivals on 10-13 April (Foundation of Cuenca) and 3 November (Independence). There are also festivities involving the throwing of buckets of water at Carnival time before Lent and around Easter, and tourists in Cuenca and throughout southern Ecuador can expect to be thoroughly soaked. Visitors are welcome at the water plant, with its gardens.

Warning There is a short, dark, pudgy man who asks lone female travellers to write letters for him to non-existent friends, and then invites them out. He is a known rapist and dangerous, but seems to have close relations with the police. Avoid him. Also (and this may be the same man), a man, who claims to be a businessman travelling abroad, who asks women to answer questions and then go with him to meet his "sister", or a "woman friend", by way of thanks.

Hotels Hotels are reported to be relatively expensive in Cuenca. *El Dorado*, Gran Colombia y Luis Cordero, T 831390, B, night club, the best in town, good restaurant, good view; *La Laguna*, Ordoñez Lasso, Swiss-run, on lake in outskirts of town, A, T 831200, pleasant rooms, but service not equivalent to cost, quick laundry, small pool which is in shade most of p.m. restaurant "pretentious and expensive"; *Hostería El Molino*, D, Km. 8.5 on road Azogues-Cuenca, pleasant position between road and river, Spanish run, typical Ecuadorean dishes, pool, rustic style, rec., advisable to book; *Crespo*, Calle Larga 793, T 827857, C, with good restaurant overlooking river, very clean, a lovely building, construction work in 1990; *Crespo Annex*, D, comfortable, nice, good value, Cordero 422 y Larga; *Alli-Tiana*, Córdova y Aguirre, T 831844, E, clean, hot water unreliable; *La Fuente*, F, Av. 12 de Abril, nr. Teatro Carlos Cueva, T 835344, hot shower, but suspect plumbing, unfriendly, garden; *Hurtado de Mendoza*, Sangurima y Huayna Capac, T 831909, E, good, restaurant; *Las Américas*, Mariano Cueva 13-59 y Vega Muñoz, T 831160, D, English spoken, carpets, hot water, telephone, noisy, dirty, helpful, good cheap restaurant next door; *El Conquistador*, Gran Colombia 665, T 831788, D, without breakfast, sauna, good, friendly, good restaurant but slow service; *Presidente*, Gran Colombia, T 831066, D, good value, comfortable, convenient, good 9th floor restaurant; *Tours Cuenca*, Borrero 1069, large rooms, TV, central, D with bath, clean; *Catedral*, Padre Aguirre 8-17 y Sucre, T 823204, E, overpriced but cheaper rates for Peace Corps and other service organizations, spacious, modern, but not very warm. English-speaking manager, safe, laundry service, good food; *Gran Hotel*, Torres 9-70 y Bolívar, T 831934, E, clean, hot water, laundry service, good restaurant, beautiful patio; *Tomebamba*, T 831589, E, quiet, clean, hot water, good breakfast. *Internacional*, Benigno Malo 1015, F, cheerful, good value for set meal; *Pichincha*, Gral. Torres y Bolívar, T 823868, F, clean, spacious, helpful, hot water, luggage stored; *Milán*, Pres. Córdova 989 y Aguirre, T 835351, E, friendly, helpful, reliable for storing luggage, good breakfast, warmly rec.; *Residencial Niza*, Mariscal Lamar 4/51, F, clean, water not too hot; *Residencial Atenas*, Cordero 1189, F, clean, comfortable, helpful, but not safe for left-luggage; *Residencial*

Norte, Mariano Cueva 11-63 y Sangurima, F, clean, hot showers; *Residencial Sánchez*, G, Muñoz 428 y Mariano Cueva, T 831519, set meal rec.; *Emperador*, F, Gran Colombia 1077, T 825469, clean, front rooms noisy; *Siberia*, G, Gran Colombia 531, hot water, bargain for room rates, laundry facilities, central and convenient; *Residencial Colombia*, Mariano Cueva 1161, T 827851, G, clean but noisy, overlooking market, hot showers, thieving staff. In the vicinity of the bus terminal are: *Residencial Tito*, Sangurima 149, T 829734, F, safe but rooms are very dark, restaurant very good value; *Residencial España*, Sangurima 117, T 824723, F, with bath and TV, friendly, laundry facilities, hot water, good restaurant, safe parking for motor cycles; *La Ramada*, Sangurima 551, F, friendly, clean and pleasant but noisy; *El Galeón*, Sangurima 240, T 831827, F, large, modern rooms, own bathroom, hot water, parking; *Los Alamos*, F, modern, communal hot shower, clean, rec., Av. España, opposite main bus terminal.

Furnished two-bedroom apartments are available; *El Jardín*, Av. Pumapungo y Viracochabamba, US$5 p.p. per day plus tax, cooking facilities and parking, T 804-103, or write to address above, Casilla 298.

Restaurants Foreign styles *El Jardín*, Presidente Córdova 7-23, lovely, superb food, nouvelle cuisine (closed Sun.), allow US$10 p.p.; *Rancho Chileno*, España y Elia Liut, good steak and seafood, slow service, pricey; *Los Copihues*, Bolívar 6-31, Chilean empanadas, juices, coffee; *Tupahue*, 12 de Abril 1107 (near Vergel church), also Chilean. **Italian** *La Tuna*, on Gran Colombia, good pizzas, popular; *Pizzería*, Calle Colombia 8-80. **Criollo** *El Escorpión*, Malo y Largo, rec.; *El Dorado Hotel*, good buffet Sun. from 1100, reasonably priced. *Balcón Quiteño (Nos 1 and 2)*, Sangurima 649 near market, popular, quick service; *Nutibara*, Sangurima y Luis Cordero, inexpensive, limited menu; *D'Bernardo*, Antonio Borrero 9-68, excellent food, lovely atmosphere; *El Bucanero*, Sangurima 617, set meals, clean, small helpings; *El Túnel*, Gral. Torres, good; *La Cantina*, Borrero y Córdova, refurbished mansion delicious food, good value. **Vegetarian** *El Paraíso*, Ordóñez 1023, 3rd floor; *El María*, Mariscal Lamar 1269 y Tarqui; *Primavera*, Borrero 5-29, whole food shop, also at Mariano Cueva 9-58; good one at Gran Colombia y Tomás Ordena. **Seafood** *El Cangrejo*, Av. 12 de Abril (just beyond El Vergel church, near hospital), for lunch; *Marisquería La Mona* Huayna Capac, delicious, cheap, huge helpings; *El Acuario*, Huayna Capac 138; *El Calamar*, Pizarro 148 y España. **Oriental** *Chifa Pack How*, Presidente Córdova 9-89 y Aguirre, rec; *Chifa China*, Hermano Miguel 9-40, good food, fair prices. **Snackbars, bakeries, etc.** *Los Pibes*, Gran Colombia y Cordero, good; *Trattoría Césare*, Cordero y Larga, clean; *Pity's*, Gran Colombia 2087, hamburgers, rec.; almost next door, *Pollos Gus*, Gran Colombia y Unidad. *Picadilly*, bar with snacks, Pres. Borrero entre Sucre y Córdova, nice. *Heladería Holanda*, Larga 8-89 with Benigno Malo, ice cream, sandwiches, sweets, excellent breakfasts, real coffee; *Helados Honey*, Mariscal Lamar 4-15, clean, cheap, rec. milkshakes; *Capuchino*, Bolívar y Aguirre, good real coffee; *Monte Bianco*, Bolívar near San Blas church, good cakes, ice cream; *Top Cream*, Gran Colombia, ice cream; *Mi Pan*, Pres. Córdova 842 and General Torres y Gran Colombia, cakes, tarts, doughnuts, good breakfast; *El Trigal*, Cordero 9-38, good fresh bread. *Dulce Día*, Av. España near Terminal Terrestre, good doughnuts.

Bars *Picadilly Pub*, Borrero 7-30 y Pres. Córdova, up market, clean, relaxing; *La Barra*, Pres. Córdova, local brew.

Shopping Many craftware shops along Gran Colombia, near *El Dorado* hotel, and on Benigno Malo. These include *Ocepa*, *Productos Andinos*, *Artesanías Atahualpa*, *Arte Artesanías*, *Arte del Pacífico* and *Artesanías Paucartambo*. *Bazaar Susanita*, Benigno Malo 1092, for good woollen sweaters at reasonable prices. Good souvenirs are carvings, leather, basketwork, painted wood, onyx, woven stuffs (cheapest in Ecuador), embroidered shirts, etc. On Bolívar, between Mariano Cueva and A. Miguel, are two shops side-by-side which sell excellent sweaters. For leather goods try *Cuero y Turismo*, Cordero 11-53. *Artesa*, Presidente Córdova 6-96 y Borrero, sells modern Ecuadorean ceramics at good prices. Expensive shops on Borrero, behind old cathedral. *Joyería Guillermo*, owned by Leonardo Crespo, at Gran Colombia 9-31, has been recommended; he will let wholesale buyers tour his factory. Jewellery prices are reported as high: shop around. High quality Panama hats are made by *Homero Ortega*, Vega Muñoz 9-33, T 823-429, who exports all over the world; panama hats also at Tarqui 6-93 y Córdova and on Benigno Malo. Interesting market behind new cathedral. A Centro Comercial has opened in the industrial park, with interesting shops.

Taxis US$0.40 for short journey; US$0.50 to airport; US$1 per hr. Local buses US$0.05.

Entertainment Discos at Hotels *Conquistador* and *Alli-Tiana*, and *Las Galaxias*, Núñez de Bonilla 239. *Peñas* at *Hotel la Laguna*, outside town. Many cinemas.

Exchange Citibank, Gran Colombia 749 (charges commission, no cheques), and local banks. Filanbanco reportedly won't change Visa cheques despite being Visa agents. Cambidex on Luis Cordero are helpful. Cambistral in City Hall on Sucre 664 y Malo; Cambiosur, Borrero 8-20 y Sucre; another at Sucre y Pres. Borrero, good rates for cheques and cash, no commission, rec. Generally the rates are very variable.

British Honorary Consul Sr. Teodoro Jerves, Av. España y Chapetones, T 831996.

Post Office and **Ietel** on corner of Calles Gran Colombia and Borrero.

Immigration Bolívar y Luis Cordero (Gobernación), T 824-020.

Laundry Service *La Química*, Borrero y Bolivar, US$2, takes a few days.

Tourist Office Dituris, Miguel 686 y Córdova, open Mon.-Fri. only, 0800-1200, 1430-1830, helpful. Maps of Cuenca US$0.20. Map of the city also available from major hotels. Local maps are not very accurate.

Travel Agents *Yroo Tours*, Larga y Malo, English spoken, recommended; *Santa Ana Tours*, Presidente Córdova y Borrero (T 832340) run day tours by train to San Pedro, bus to Ingapirca and return. Also *Metropolitan Touring* and *Ecuadorian Tours*, both at Sucre y Malo. A recommended guide for the Cuenca area is Vicente López Cárdenas, T 823-790, well-informed on local flora and culture, Spanish speaking only.

Buses The Terminal Terrestre is on Av. España, a 20-min. walk northwest of the city centre, or take a minibus, US$0.05. To Riobamba 7 hrs., US$3.15, scenic. Ambato, US$4, 7½ hrs. (travel during day because scenery is magnificent, the road, not all paved, goes from 2,600 metres to under 200 and up again); Baños, from 12 de Noviembre, Turismo Baños; Quito, 10½ hrs., US$3.75. To Loja, 8 hrs., US$2.65, major construction work on this road, long delays; Machala, 4 hrs., US$2.70; to Guayaquil, 5 hrs., US$2.65 (road now entirely paved)—shop around for most comfortable bus. To Huaquillas, 6 hrs., US$3.10, at 2100—sit on left (the bus sometimes stops for 2 hrs. in Machala, it is often better to get a local bus from there to Huaquillas). The evening bus arrives in Huaquillas at 0300, but passengers sleep on the bus till daylight. Be prepared for frequent police checks on the way. To Azogues, US$0.25, leaves when full. To Saraguro, US$2, 6 hrs. To Macas, 11 hrs., US$1.80.

Trains The train service to Sibambe, leaving daily at 1300, has been restored. A pleasant round trip by train and bus can be made to El Tambo and back, to see Ingapirca (see below). There is also a special tourist *autoferro* to Sibambe run by Metropolitan Touring, daily service. Check beforehand as all services are liable to alteration.

Air Service The airport is 5 mins. walk from the Terminal Terrestre. Local buses run along the road outside. Daily connections with Quito (US$18) and Guayaquil (US$14) with TAME (office at airport) and SAN.

Excursions There are sulphur baths at Baños, with a beautiful church in a delightful landscape, 5 km. S of Cuenca. Two separate warm baths, of which the lower one is better (US$0.80 for private bathroom, US$0.40 for swimming pool), the upper one is rather dirty (US$0.40). There are *Residenciales Baños* and *Rincón de Baños*, both F with bath, on the main road, and the *Hostería Durán*, D, rec., with restaurant, pool and amenities, at the baths. Buses from Cuenca (Calle Larga), US$0.05, taxis US$1.80.

About 40 km. NE of Cuenca in the beautiful Paute Valley is the *Hostería Uzhupud*, C, deluxe, good rooms (those at back have best views), swimming pool, very good food, excellent value, highly rec., despite being touristy, Casilla 1268, Uzhupud, Paute, T Cuenca 821-853 (taxi from Cuenca US$5-7, bargain hard); also *Residencial Cutilcay*, G.

E to **Gualaceo** (Sun. market), 45 mins. by bus every ½ hr., on a recently-paved road, US$0.25 (leave from corner of Terminal Terrestre) pretty town in beautiful landscape, with charming plaza and fine new church with splendid modern glass; embroidered goods sold from private home above general store on main square; hotels: *Hostería Rivera*, E; *Gran Hotel Gualaceo*, F; *Residencial Gualaceo*, F; and *Español*, basic, G; restaurant *Manabí* on main road to Cuenca. Good shoes made locally; splendid bargains. To **Chordeleg** by colectivo (plenty), or by local bus, US$0.10 from Gualaceo market square, every ½ hr. (direct bus from Cuenca, 1 hr., US$0.30), a village famous for its crafts in wood, silver and gold filigree and pottery, also panama hats, although it is very touristy nowadays. Watch out for fake jewellery. Joyería El Brillante has been found to sell gold-plated silver for solid gold. Joyeria Puerto del Sol, on Juan B. Cobos y Eloy Alfaro, has been recommended. The church is interesting. Try *Restaurante El Turista*. Chordeleg has a small Museo de Comunidad of fascinating local textiles, ceramics and straw work. The walk between the two towns is a good uphill one from Gualaceo to Chordeleg, and a very pleasant hour downhill in the other direction. With your own vehicle (4WD advisable), you can drive back to Cuenca through San Juan and San Bartolomé (2 small mines affect this village welcome visitors).

Ingemar Tholin of Västerås, Sweden, recommends taking a bus (US$0.50, 1½ hrs.) from Cuenca to Sígsig (S of Gualaceo, 83 km. from Cuenca, *residencial*, G), and from there another to Chiqüinda (stay overnight with Sr. Fausto, the teacher). A trail from Chiqüinda goes to Aguacate (4-5 hrs. walking), a village of 70 people. Sr. Jorge Guillermo Vásquez has a *hospedaje*, horses can be hired for trekking to caves. There are shops, electricity at night only, and good *fiestas* at Christmas and New Year, and carnival in February (very popular). From Aguacate either walk or hire a horse to continue SE to Río Negro, a friendly village, from where daily buses at 1300 and 1600 go to Gualaquiza (1 hr., US$0.35—**see page 803**). A road is being built between Sígsig and Gualaquiza, along a beautiful and unspoilt route; the trail can be hiked by the intrepid but is not yet passable by wheeled vehicles; take a minimum of luggage.

NW of Cuenca, **El Cajas** is a national park with over 200 lakes, 2½ hr. bus trip (one daily, except Thurs., between 0600 and 0630 from the San Sebastián church, bus back between 1400 and 1600, US$1, arrive early as the bus can get very full, hitchhiking difficult, little traffic). Ideal but strenuous walking, 4,200 metres altitude. It is best to arrive in the early morning since it can get very cloudy after about 1300. Obtain a permit for entry to the park from the Cuenca office of the Ministry of Agriculture above the Banco Azuay, Bolívar 6-22 y Miguel, 3rd floor, US$0.35, or pay US$2.50 at park entrance. They are supposed to provide maps, but these are unreliable and usually unavailable. There is a refuge with four bunks and cooking facilities in the park which you can book at the Ministry. The park is easy to miss; avoid being carried 8 km. further to the village itself. Camping possible but you need good equipment, sleeping bag, warm clothing and waterproofs as it can get very wet; it is not possible to hire equipment in Cuenca. Take also food, water, stove and gas (no firewood available). There are organized tours to the lakes from Cuenca, but these tend to be expensive, up to US$34. Alternatively, hire a private truck, US$16 with driver.

To the **Laguna de Surucucho**: catch the bus at the Plaza Santo Domingo to Sayausi (US$0.05) and walk from there; about 2 hrs. from Sayausi take a dirt road to the left and walk a further 20 minutes. There is good trout fishing in the lake and the river.

A beautiful hour-long bus trip on the Machala road from Cuenca takes one to the town of Girón, whose beauty is spoiled only by a modern concrete church. From there trucks take passengers up a winding road to the hamlets of San Gregorio and Chumblín. Friendly inhabitants will act as guides to three lakes high in the *páramo* where excellent trout-fishing is to be had. Take camping gear.

Ecuador's most important Inca ruin, **Ingapirca**, can be visited from Cuenca. You can take a taxi for the 5-hr. round trip from Cuenca bus terminal (US$35), or take any Guayaquil, Quito or Cañar bus. On the first two, ask to be let out at Tambo, 2 km. past Cañar (and 11 km, 3 hrs walk from the site, hitching reported possible), thence take a bus, colectivo, or truck to Ingapirca (US$0.20 maximum). From Cañar to Tambo a bus costs US$0.10. There is also a route from 2 km. before Cañar at a very bad side road to the right, 14 km. from Ingapirca. A third route is to go to San Pedro by bus or train, where there is a municipal *hospedería* where travellers can stay free of charge (although difficulties have been reported in obtaining the key); a 3 km. dirt road leads to the ruins. On Fri. there is an Indian market at Ingapirca. There is a good co-operative craft shop next to the church. Camping at the site is possible. There is no hotel at Ingapirca, but there are 2 basic restaurants at the entrance, and a third, *Inti Huasi* (good), in the village; the *refugio* has benches, table and fireplace but no beds. Ask at the museum for a key (if one is available) and for permission to stay overnight, included in museum fee of US$0.85 (you may have to surrender your passport at 0900 only).

Ingapirca is commonly known as a fortress complex although this is contradicted by archaeologists. The central structure is an *usnu* platform probably used as a solar observatory. It is faced in fine Inca masonry, and it is interesting to note that the length is exactly three times the diameter of the semicircular ends. This may have been connected with worship of the sun in its morning, midday and afternoon positions. (John Hemming). Nearby is the "face of the Inca", an immense natural formation in the rock looking over the landscape. There is a good museum (open Tues.-Sat. 0900-1700), which sells a good guide book (US$0.80), and will look after belongings.

Warning   Be careful of overcharging by truck drivers.

There is a 3-4 day hike to Ingapirca from Achupallas (**see page** 775—take Coop. Chunchi or Coop. Patria bus from Riobamba to La Moya, then truck to Achupallas or a direct truck from Alausí). It is a spectacular walk through valleys and on vestiges of an Inca trail; the locals are very friendly; take a fishing rod if you have one—the route is described in Rob Rachowiecki's *Climbing and Hiking in Ecuador*.

From Cuenca, the Pan-American Highway runs S to La Y, about 20 km. away near the village of Cumbe. Here the road divides into two all-weather gravel roads: one continuing the Pan-American to Loja (beautiful views on both sides) and the other, which is faster (or less slow), running to Pasaje and Machala. (One traveller reports that on a night trip on this route, the bus driver stopped before beginning the descent, made a collection from the passengers and having made the sign of the Cross, apparently tossed the money over the edge of the cliff.) Santa Isabella and Pasaje (pop. 27,000), the main towns along the route, have little to recommend them. Most buses travel NW to El Troncal and then S down the coast road to reach Machala and Huaquillas for the Peruvian border (**see page** 773).

The Pan-American Highway climbs S from La Y and rises eventually to the 3,500 metre Tinajillas pass. The road descends sharply into the warm upper Jubones valley past cane fields and rises again near the small town of Oña (*Pensión Central*, G, very basic, poor sanitary installations). From there it weaves through highland *páramo* pastures and then descends towards Saraguro. Here we meet Indians once more, the most southerly Andean group in Ecuador, dressed all in black. They wear very broad flat-brimmed hard felt hats: the men are notable for their black shorts (sometimes covered by a whitish kind of divided apron) and a particular kind of double bag, the *alforja*, and the women for their pleated black skirts, necklaces of coloured beads and silver *topos*, ornate pins fastening their shawls. They have entered the money economy with vigour: many now take cattle across the mountains east to the tropical pastures above the Amazonian jungle.

The road runs through **Saraguro** (picturesque Sun. Indian market—the Indians wear black, the men with a long plait of hair), over the mountain and then makes a long, very tortuous, descent towards Loja. The direct Cuenca-Loja road is under reconstruction and when the widening is completed it will be one of the most beautiful and breathtaking in Ecuador without the discomfort offered by the longer, alternative route via Arenillas.

In Saraguro, two pensions, *Nueva York* over the *farmacia*, F, friendly, family-run, freezing shower, and the other, unsigned, on main street opp. church to S, No. 03-5, G, clean, laundry facilities. Restaurant: *Salón Cristal*, behind the church. The restaurants are poor, but cheap food in the market. It is a very cold town.

Loja (2,225 metres, 71,130 inhabitants), lies near the Oriente. There are crude but original paintings on the patio walls of many of the old houses. There are two universities, with a well-known law school. Some of the Universidad Nacional buildings have good murals. The cathedral and San Martín church have painted interiors. Museum on main square, by bank, 0900-1500. The town, encircled by hills and pleasant countryside, can be reached by air from Quito or Guayaquil to La Toma and then 35 km. by paved road. There is a market on Sat. and Sun. Souvenir and craft shops on 10 de Agosto between Kennedy and 18 de Noviembre.

Hotels *Vilcabamba*, on waterfront, D, clean; *Residencial La Rivera*, Universitaria y 10 de Agosto, E, good; *Hostal Quinara*, opp. *La Rivera*, E, also good; *Saraguro Internacional*, Universitaria 724, E, hot water, TV, restaurant open Mon.-Fri.; *Ejecutivo Sudamérica*, Universitaria 1076, F, good, also "video club"; *Metropolitano*, 18 de Noviembre y Colón, F with bath and TV, hot water, clean; *París*, 10 de Agosto 1637, clean with electric hot showers, F, bargain for good rate, near food market, rec.; *Hostal Carrión*, Colón 1630, G, basic, clean, safe; *Primvera*, Colón 1644, G, clean, cold shower; *Miraflores*, 10 de Agosto 1656, G, can bargain, clean; *Londres*, Sucre y 10 de Agosto, F, constant hot water, clean, reports of theft from locked rooms; *Acapulco*, Sucre 743, G, clean, pleasant, private bathroom, safe for leaving luggage, rec. Basic *residenciales* in G range for instance on Rocafuerte; also

Alborada, Sucre 1279 y Lourdes, F with shower, clean.

Restaurants *Mesón Andaluz*, Bolívar y Eguiguren, best in town; *Suizo Lojano*, Guerrero y Eguiguren, international; *Palace*, Eguiguren y Sucre, local food; *Trece*, Universitaria y Colón, also Eguiguren 1468, good. Other criollo places are *Ocaso*, 10 de Agosto 1639; *Cordillera*, 10 de Agosto 1419; *La Choza*, Sucre y Riofrío. *La Casona*, 18 de Noviembre near Imbabura (the better of 2 branches), near Cuenca bus terminal, good, rec. Chicken at *Rico Pico*, 18 de Noviembre y Colón. Seafood at *Pescadería Pacífica*, Bolívar 931; and *Doscientas Millas*, Bolívar y Eguiguren (evenings only). Vegetarian: *Acuarius*, Mercadillo 15-45, Sucre y 18 de Noviembre, 2nd floor. *Chifa 85* on main plaza, clean, good quality food, including Chinese dishes. Chinese also at *Chifa Feliz*, Eguiguren y 18 de Noviembre. Good *Unicornio* piano bar on main square. Good snacks, pastries and yoghurt at *Pastelería Persa* (2 locations—one at Rocafuerte 14-58). *Helados de Paila*, Av. Kennedy, nr. market, good icecream and snacks.

Exchange Filanbanco, changes cheques, other banks do not. No *casas de cambio*; good rate for US$ in gift shop in front of *Hotel Acapulco* (El Universo agent changes money at weekends at poor rate).

Tourist Office Dituris is on the corner of Bolívar and Eguiguren.

Buses To Cuenca, 7 hrs., 7 a day, US$2.65 with Viajeros (18 de Noviembre e Imbabura), the only company which leaves at 0500; Machala, 10 a day, 7 hrs., US$2.75. Cooperativa Loja (10 de Agosto y Cuarto Centenario) runs many buses in all directions, including Quito, 4 a day, US$5 (Trans. Santa to Quito, 12 hrs., US$5), and Guayaquil, 5 a day, 11 hrs., US$4.40, and two nightly buses to Huaquillas at 2030 and 2230; Macará, at 1000, 7 hrs., US$1.50.

Excursions The entrance to the *Podocarpus National Park*, spectacular walking country and good for bird-watching, is about 15 km. south of Loja on the Vilcabamba road. Permits from the Ministerio de Agricultura office, on Ríofrío just off Bolívar, 2nd floor, in Loja who provide a somewhat adequate map. Take a Vilcabamba bus, park entrance is 20 mins. from Loja, then 6 km. hike to guard station. Direct transport by taxi only., US$10 round trip, can arrange later pick up for guard station. Camping possible.

    Vilcabamba is a 1½ hr bus ride. Sur Oriente, Calle Azuay and Av. Kennedy, hourly (US$0.50) from Loja. People here were reputed to live to over 100 as often as not; recent research has eroded this belief, but it's still a very pleasant and healthy valley, with an agreeable climate, 17°C min., 26°C max. There is the attractive *Parador Turístico*, E, with restaurant and bar; *Hotel Valle Sagrado*, G, on main plaza, basic but clean, friendly, hot showers rarely work; there are 4 restaurants on the plaza, including *Cabañita*. *Madre Tierra*, cabins, E p.p. full board, reductions for a long stay, health food (home made, home grown), horses to rent (about US$14 per day), mud treatment, private sun bathing, beautiful setting about 2 km. before village, English and French spoken; the Mendoza family make travellers very welcome. They also offer intensive Spanish classes at US$15 p.p. per day; write in advance to Jaime Mendoza, P.O. Box 354, Loja, Ecuador. A small and peaceful farmhouse, owned by Sra. Leticia Jiménez de Macanchi, may be rented; very pleasant for a long stay. About 40 minutes from Vilcabamba, in the Capamaco valley at Yamburara Alto, is the ranch of René and Sabina Sangolqui, where you can camp, rent a cabin (US$30 irrespective of number of guests) and hire horses for excellent expeditions (prices from US$30 for 1 day to US$110 for 4 days, min. 2 people): recommended (Spanish, English and French spoken). With advance notice, they will meet you at Loja airport. Postal address: Casilla 812, Loja; in UK, contact David Hickmet, Southways, Lowfield Heath, Nr. Crawley, Sussex, RH10 2TQ, T (0293) 552743, Telex 878447.

    The scenic road to Zamora (40 km.) is narrow but in good condition. You can carry on from there into the Oriente.

Most road travellers enter and leave Loja via Machala (**see page** 772). There are two routes from Loja to Machala, one of which goes through Piñas and is rather bumpy with hairpin bends but has the better views, the other is paved and generally quicker (depending on the driver). Machala can be avoided, however, if you take a Machala bus to the Huaquillas crossroads, called La Avanzada, and there catch another one straight to Huaquillas, the border town. There is also a road into the Oriente, at Zaruma (on this road), where there are interesting carved wooden houses. The old Portovelo gold mines at Zaruma are worth a visit.

    An alternative, more scenic route to Peru is, however, available from Loja via **Macará**, a dusty town on the border, in a rice-growing area, with road connections to Sullana near the Peruvian coast. (Population 8,000; altitude 600 metres.)

Hotels *Paradero Turístico*, E, best, pool, restaurant may not be open, not far from centre; *Residencial Paraíso*, F, Veintimilla 553, new and clean, laundry facilities, highly rec; *Guayaquil*, F, with shower, not rec., fleas, large cell-like rooms; *Internacional*, G, by Loja bus office and *Amazonas*, Rengel 418, G, friendly, clean, basic, on same street. Restaurants *Colonial Macará*, Rengel y Bolívar (helpful, but food not too good), and *Macará*, opposite, a cafetería; *Soda Bar Manolo* for breakfast.

Leaving Loja on the main paved highway going westward, the airport at La Toma is reached after 35 km. (If flying to or from La Toma, stay at Catamayo, nearby, *Hotel El Turista*, Av. Isidro Ayora, F, shared bath; *Hotel San Marcos*, on plaza; taxi to airport US$0.50). At La Toma (where you can catch the Loja-Macará bus), the Pan-American Highway divides into two branches, one, the faster, via Velacruz (paved to here) and Catacocha (4 hotels, *Res. Patense* cheapest; *Restaurante Sidoney*, good, cheap), and the other going to Macará via Cariamanga. The road is unpaved but fair, offering lovely views. The bank at Macará does not change money, so change sucres through the *ambulantes* to give you enough intis to last you until you reach Sullana (Peru). A Peruvian tourist card can be obtained from the Peruvian Hon. Consul in Macará, if he is available, or at the border if not already obtained in Quito or Guayaquil. There is a 2½ km. walk or taxi ride (US$1, US$0.55 in a pick-up from Macará market—less if more passengers) to the international bridge over the Río Macará. Border crossing formalities (0800-1800) can last about 1 hr. Peruvian officials may ask to see an onward ticket out of Peru. A colectivo (US$2.20, 3-4 hrs.) is then taken from La Tina on the Peruvian side to Sullana from where it is ½ hr. to Piura, a better place to spend the night. No hotels, and only food stalls, in La Tina. Buses leave Sullana from Av. Buenos Aires in early a.m.; if none running, there are plenty of *camionetas* to the border. There are many military checkpoints along the route but these are not usually a problem. Coop Loja runs four buses a day from Macará to Loja (6 to 8 hrs., US$1.50), at 0700, 1000, 1300, and 1800, so the whole journey can be done in a day if you arrive at the border at noon. The Loja-border journey takes only 3½ hrs. by car. There is less likelihood of bureaucratic hassle or drug-pushing at Macará than at Huaquillas, but since not many travellers go by this route, be prepared for extensive, but generally good-natured searches by bored officials. Also, officials are not above acquiring things, or asking for a bribe if you do something unusual, such as crossing the border after 1800 and returning the next day to get your passport stamped. If you are asked to pay, ask for a receipt and note the official's name and number in full view of him.

THE ORIENTE (8)

Ecuador's eastern tropical lowlands can now be reached by four different road routes, from Quito, Ambato, Cuenca or Loja. These roads are narrow and tortuous and subject to landslides in the rainy season, but all have regular, if poor bus services and all can be attempted in a jeep or in an ordinary car with good ground clearance. Their construction has led to considerable colonization by highlanders in the lowland areas. Several of the towns and villages on the roads can be reached by air services from Quito, Cuenca and Guayaquil, and places further into the immense Amazonian forests are generally accessible by river canoe or small aircraft. The country is particularly beautiful, and some of the disadvantages of other parts of Amazonia, such as the inadvisability of swimming in the rivers, are here absent. Anti-malaria tablets are recommended, however, and be sure to take a mosquito net and an effective repellent. A yellow fever vaccination is recommended for travel into the Oriente.

Travel agencies (e.g. Metropolitan Tours of Quito, *La Selva*—see under Coca) do trips to the Oriente or to the Napo River, with meals, flights, lectures included. Going by bus and/or boat you can do a round trip much more cheaply, but you should allow a week. The Oriente also has an unpredictable air service provided by army planes; passengers pay insurance, US$1-2; apart from that, fares are low and the flights save a lot of time. Frequent military checks; always have your passport handy. You may be required to register at Shell-Mera, Coca, Misahuallí, Puerto Napo and Lago Agrio.

The Route from Quito From Quito, through Pifo, the road is paved for 50 km. It is being graded in preparation for paving to Baeza, near where it worsens. A new road was built in 1987, following the earthquake which destroyed the old road to Coca. It crosses the Eastern Cordillera at an altitude of 4,064 metres at a

pass just north of the extinct volcano **Antisana** (5,704 metres, which, according to Cliff Cordy, gets vast quantities of snow, has huge glaciers and is the hardest peak in Ecuador to climb), and then descends via the small villages of Papallacta (**see page 748**), and Cuyuja to the old mission settlements of Baeza and Borja. The trip between the pass and Baeza has beautiful views of Antisana, high waterfalls, tropical mountain jungle, *páramo* and a lake contained by a glacial moraine almost on the equator.

Baeza is a small town in the beautiful setting of the Quijos pass, recommended for long scenic walks (beware trucks passing) with many waterfalls (the town is about 2 km. off the main road—get off Lago Agrio bus at the police checkpoint and walk up the hill; Tena bus goes through the town). The old Spanish cobblestone trail can be found if you go past the hospital and cemetery; the path goes up over the hill (a beautiful walk). Because of the climate, *ceja de montaña*, orchids and bromeliads abound. Trout in the rivers. (See the books of Padre Porras Garcés, Centro de Investigaciones Arqueológicas, Pontífica Universidad Católica del Ecuador, Quito on archaeological remains in the area).

Hotels *Nogal de Jumandy*, G, English spoken, basic, parking, friendly, laundry facilities, near church, on main Tena road. *Oro Negro*, residencial and restaurant, at Tena/Lago Agrio junction, rooms with bath and cold water.

Restaurants *Gina*, and *Lupita*, good, opposite each other on Calle Chimborazo. Everything closed by 2030.

At Baeza the road divides: one branch heads S to Tena, with a newly constructed branch road going directly to Coca (7 hrs.). The other goes NE to Lago Agrio, following the Quijos river past the villages of Borja, a few km. from Baeza (small hotel on roadside; *residencial* on corner of plaza, clean, cold shower, meals provided; basic restaurant *Costa Azul*) and El Chaco (hotel and eating places all reported as dirty) to the slopes of the still active volcano Reventador, 3,485 metres. (At the village of Reventador there is a *pensión*, *Las Orquídeas*, F, and a restaurant.) The road winds along the north side of the river, past the impressive 145-metre San Rafael falls (to see them, get off bus at Inecel sign about 2½ hrs from Baeza, walk down side road, and then down a steep path, for 45 mins. to a bridge; ask people working there to let you pass, then it's a further 15 mins. walk—camping possible, but take all equipment and food). The road then crosses the watershed between the Coca and Aguarico rivers. A ferry operates 0600-1800 across the Aguarico river until the bridge is rebuilt. The road runs along the north bank of the river to the developing oil towns of Santa Cecilia and Lago Agrio.

Lago Agrio is growing rapidly: it is still a rough place but the infrastructure is improving; excursions into the jungle can be made. Virtually everything in the town is along the main road, Av. Quito.

Hotels *El Gofán*, E, a/c, best, good restaurant; *La Mexicana*, F, reasonable, mosquito nets; *Willigram*, F with own bath, clean, rec.; *Putumayo*, F, shared bathroom; *Hilton*, *Oro Negro*, *Chifa China* (restaurant) and *Chimborazo*, all G with shared bathrooms. *Comercial Calvopeña* is the best place to buy groceries and supplies.

Exchange Several *casas de cambio* on Av. Quito, good rates for notes.

Transport Several daily TAME flights to Quito at 1200, US$9. Buses to Quito (US$4, 9½ hrs.), Baeza (US$2.10, 6 hrs.), Coca (US$1.10, 3 hrs.) and Tena (US$3.20, 9 hrs.).

From Lago Agrio it is possible to take a bus to Chiritza and then a 2 hour boat ride to San Pablo de Kantesiya, a small village on stilts where one hut where visitors can stay. There are buses north to La Punta (US$0.40, 1¼ hrs., make sure you get an exit stamp from Migración in Lago Agrio, Quito 111—police station, T 125), where you get a boat across the Río San Miguel to Puerto Colón, in Colombia. There are canoes along the river to the village of San Miguel in Colombia and from there you can catch a bus (5 hrs.) to Puerto Asís (border formalities). For permission to go downriver on the Aguarico (as opposed to an exit stamp) go to the Brigada (military post) rather than Migración because the store owner there will give you permission to go anywhere as long as you buy something from his shop.

At Lago Agrio, a temporary ferry crosses the Aguarico River (bridge washed away), then the road heads south to **Coca** (officially named Puerto Francisco de Orellana—pop. 16,000), a river port at the junction of the Coca and Napo rivers; described as a typical oil town, dirty, noisy, with heavy drinking. All foreigners have to register with the police. The bank will not change travellers' cheques, but Sr. Londoño (at Almacén Londoño) may change them at a fair rate. Food and supplies are reportedly less expensive in Coca than in other parts of the Oriente. At Carnival, water and petroleum throwing is the sport. There is usually no electricity after midnight.

Hotels *Auca*, F, comfortable, clean, electricity in p.m., big garden with monkeys roaming free, reasonable food but crowded, manager speaks English; *Florida*, on main road from airport, F with fan, good; *Residencial Rosita*, G, noisy, cold water unsafe, not rec. *Tungurahua*, F, favourite with oil workers, rooms OK, but dirty toilets and showers and 3 basic *residenciales*: *Turingia*, *Lojalita* (F) and *Camba Huasi*.

Restaurant *Doña Erma's* set meal is cheap and filling; *Venecia*, good food, away from main market area; *Mama Carmen*, good for early breakfast; *El Buho*, good food, reasonably priced; *King Burger*, cheap, good chicken and chips, friendly, ask for Braulio Llori Pugachi, a recommended, good value jungle guide.

Tours Coca is now the most logical place from which to arrange tours into the jungle. Many of the guides who previously operated in Misahuallí have moved to Coca. All guides out of Coca charge about US$15-20 p.p. per day, but you may have to bargain down to this from US$25. You are strongly advised to check what precisely is being offered, and that the price includes equipment such as rubber boots, tents, mosquito nets, cooking equipment and food, and transport. Trips which do not go beyond the Río Napo itself are not worth taking since you will see nothing. Among the guides who have moved from Misahuallí are Carlos Lastra, who has been recommended as knowledgeable, cheerful and a good cook (he does not speak English), Wymper Torres, and Wilson Vasco (also good, but no English spoken). Canoes and guides for jungle trips can be hired from Fernando Silva, who lives at the end of the riverside lane next to the bridge. Kevin Johnsrude warns "Insist that there be no hunting or dynamite fishing or the only animals you will see will be in your soup!" More expensive is Fluvial Tours (minimum 4 people). Pedro Grefa offers 5-day jungle tours on the Río Tiputini: take the 1200 Ranchero bus of Coop. de Coca from Coca to the bridge over the Río Tiputini (2½ hrs., US$0.50); his is the small, wooden house at left side of bridge. (Shell has a camp here, drinks only available.) Allow a day for the trip to be organized, ask for fruit and vegetables to be included in the provisions, take a torch and insect repellent, and ask Pedro (or his nephew Carlos—also rec. as leader) not to throw litter away in the jungle.

Transturi of Quito (Orellana 1810 y 10 de Agosto, T 544963) do trips from Coca into the jungle on a floating hotel, *Flotel Orellana*, US$200 (3 days) per person in double cabin, US$375 (4 days) or US$465 (5 days) including Quito-Coca air fare and all meals, guides, etc. and visits to Limón Cocha, Monkey Island, *Hacienda Primavera*, and Pompeya Catholic mission. *Hacienda Primavera* is 2 hours downstream from Coca and is open to those not on Transturi's tours. There are clean, basic rooms available (E p.p.), or you can camp (US$0.50). Meals cost US$2.50, bring bread. There is a generator but candles are used for after-generator hours. Excursions are not cheap (e.g. US$30 for 2 to Limón Cocha) and there is not much wildlife to see apart from birds, but it is supposed to be possible to hire canoes from the *hacienda* to visit other places along the Napo. The *Flotel Orellana* stops here for a visit. It has been reported that independent travellers to *Primavera* have experienced overcharging and dishonesty on transport back to Quito, and to/from Coca, and difficulties in arranging independent activities.

La Selva, a jungle centre 3 hrs. down the Napo from Coca, has been frequently recommended for the quality of its accommodation and food, and its interesting excursions into the jungle; 4-night packages from Quito including all transport, lodging, and food, not cheap, but worth it. Book at *La Selva*, 6 de Diciembre 2816 y James Orton, P.O. Box 635/Suc. 12 de Octubre, Quito, T 550995/554686, Telex 2-2653 JOLEZ ED, Fax 563814 or through most travel agencies in Quito.

Transport Bus to Quito (twice daily), 9 hrs., US$5; to Lago Agrio, 3 hrs., US$1.10; to Tena, 10 hrs., US$4.20; to Misahuallí, 14 hrs; to Baeza, 9 hrs., US$3.25.

Flights to Quito with TAME, reserve one day in advance, Mon.-Sat and two flights on Mon., Wed. and Fri. There are military flights to Tena and Shell-Mera from Coca on Mon., Wed. and Fri. Cepe and Texaco oil companies also fly Quito-Coca and sometimes take travellers on board their small planes. **NB** Do not walk or ride from the airport to town up the side street which leads to *Hotel Auca*, the police make very thorough, and acquisitive searches of arriving passengers here.

For passenger boats out of Coca, ask at the military post in the marina. There are no regular passenger boats to Misahuallí now that a road has been completed from Coca to the Baeza-Tena road. Canoes only go if there are 8 or more passengers, taking about 14 hours, if it is not reached before nightfall, the party will camp beside the river. For a price, of course, the willing traveller can hire his own canoe with owner and outboard motor to take him anywhere along the Napo. (To Misahuallí the charge is about US$120. Take a cushion and waterproofs for self and luggage.)

Canoes (irregular service, best to hire your own) pass Coca carrying passengers and cargo down-river to Limón Cocha (where *Flotel Orellana* has a lodge, closed to guests other than their own tour parties), the Capuchin mission at Pompeya with a school and museum of Napo culture, and Nueva Rocafuerte. Local tours can be hired from Limón Cocha and also canoes to return to Coca. Halfway between Coca and Nueva Rocafuerte is Pañacocha (*Pensión*, G, friendly, but watch out for jiggers in the mattresses), near which are the magnificent lagoons of Pañacocha and Pihuallicocha on the Panayacu River.

In **Nueva Rocafuerte**, the missionaries and Sra. Jesús let rooms; there are no restaurants. There is a Monday boat from Coca to Nueva Rocafuerte but you must get a military permit to enter the area. The officer has to write exactly the area you wish to visit and you have to leave your passport. The boat takes 24 hrs. at least (hammocks provided) US$5.50. You can stay overnight at the mission in N. Rocafuerte. It is possible to hire boat and guide, but it would be wise not to add tourism to the pressures to which the Waorani Indians are already subjected (e.g. oil exploration on their land). It is not possible to cross from Nueva Rocafuerte into Peru. There is a boat back on Mon. but it doesn't always run and you may have to wait until Fri. To Coca it is a 2-day ferry ride (US$9) with an overnight stop at Sinchichieta and a meal stop at Pañacocha.

Roads from both Baeza and Coca go South to Archidona, a village (*Residencial Carolina*, F; *Residencial Regina*, pleasant and friendly) centred around its mission and an extraordinary church and luxuriant square, and **Tena**, 10 km. further S, the capital of Napo Province. Both settlements have good views of Sumaco, an extinct volcano to the north (3,807 metres), and both have a large lowland Quechua Indian population living in the vicinity, many of whom are panning for gold in the rivers. These Indians are unlike the Indian groups further into the Oriente forests. "They are Quijos, of Chibcha stock, and their old territory extended in pre-conquest times from Puerto Napo up the Quijos pass to Papallacta and from there down to Coca. Their forthright character, bravery and their inherent honesty have not changed since the days when they held the Spaniards back from their efforts to find "El Dorado'." (Jay Louthian, Florida). From Tena or Archidona, a visit can be made to the famous Jumandí caves by the Río Latas, 10 km. N. of Archidona (taxi, or bus from Archidona, ½ hr.). It is necessary to go with a guide; take good boots and a strong torch. It is very muddy (sometimes full of water) so it can be useful to take spare clothes. The side ducts of the caves are extremely narrow and claustrophobic. There are several colonies of the vampire bat (*Desmodus rotundus*) in the caves. Before going, make full enquiries about routes and conditions.

Hotels *Mol*, E, with bath, clean, restaurant closed, garage, rec.; *Tena*, G, noisy at night, due to restaurant below; *Amazonas*, G, clean, near main square; *Jumandy*, G, clean, friendly, breakfast from 0600; *Enmita*, G, near bus station, reasonable restaurant; *Res. Hilton*, F, good and clean; *Res. Alemania*, F, good and clean, own bath. *Hostal Baños*, near bus station, G, very basic, clean; *Res. Alexander*, F, 2 rooms with bathroom, near bus station. A modern resort-style hotel is *Auca*, E, on the river out of town, 1½ km. on road to Archidona, Dituris-run, restaurant and bar, nice grounds, discotheque, casino, swimming in river, electricity and water unreliable.

About 30 km. from Tena is a new tourist centre, *Aliñahui*, cabin accommodation and food US$10 p.p. per day, German-managed, boat trips on Napo River, jungle trips and riding can be arranged. Contact Centro Turístico Aliñahui, Casilla 6064, C.C.I., Quito (T 524 177/479831).

Restaurants In Tena, *Don Quiño*, good, reasonable; *Niagara*, *Oriental*, reported as hostile to gringos; *Tena*. Throughout the Oriente there are small, set-menu restaurants, about US$1. It is difficult to find a meal if you arrive on a late bus and you may prefer to go hungry rather than eat what is on offer.

Buses Quito (via Baeza), 5 daily (Coop. Baños, and 1 each Amazonas and Pelileo), US$2.50, 5 hrs., book in advance; Baeza, US$1, 3 hrs.; Ambato (via Baños), 10 a day (several companies), US$2.20, 6¼ hrs.; Riobamba (via Puyo and Baños), 5 daily. Archidona every 20 mins., US$0.08, 15 mins.; Misahualli every 20 mins., US$0.35, 1 hr. (via Puerto Napo, US$0.08, 15 mins.) to Coca, 6 a day, 2 companies; Jumandy at 1800 to Lago Agrio; Puyo, US$1, 3 hrs.

Flights to Shell-Mera with the Air Force, Mon., Wed., Fri., at about 1100, US$3.50, 20 seats, rec.

Jatun Sacha (quechua meaning "big forest") is a biological station of about 180 hectares of land, 80% of which is primary forest. Located 45 minutes outside of Tena, it is an area set aside by its founders Alejandro Suárez, David Neill and Michael McColm for biological field research. Sleeping facilities for 20 in open air cabins is provided along with cooking facilities (bring own food). Equipment for collecting and drying plant specimens is available. Fee is US$5/day. Reservations can be made by writing Casilla 2177, Quito, Ecuador.

From Tena the main highway (unpaved) runs southward to Puyo. The whole area is a large-scale producer of sugar cane, yuca and *naranjillas* (an orange fruit related to the tomato, used for making a delightfully refreshing fruit drink). Puerto Napo, a few km. south of Tena, has a bridge across the Napo river (2 hotels near the bridge). Here is the turn-off for Misahuallí; if travelling N from Puyo, avoid going into Tena by getting off the bus here.

On the north bank, a road leads eastwards to **Misahuallí**, about 17 km. downstream, a small port (pop. 1,000) at the junction of the Napo and Misahuallí rivers. From the **Napo bridge** you can get a ride in a truck, US$0.50, or colectivos. At the *Hacienda Popoyal*, half way between Puerto Napo and Misahuallí, the owners welcome travellers. Misahuallí used to provide one of the best opportunities to visit the jungle, being one of the easiest places to get to, as it is only 7-8 hrs from Quito and 5 hrs. from Baños. However, there is not a great deal of wildlife around Misahuallí, although butterflies are plentiful, and for animals and birds you are advised to go further into the jungle to Coca (which is overtaking Misahuallí as a tour centre) or to take an excursion lasting several days; the one to three-day trips have been described as disappointing. Oil exploration in the area is also diminishing chances of seeing wildlife. There is a fine, sandy beach on the Río Misahuallí, but don't camp on it; the river can rise suddenly and unexpectedly.

Hotels *Anaconda*, B, on Anaconda Island in the Río Napo, about 1 hr. by canoe, US$1.20 downstream from Puerto Misahuallí; consists of three bungalows of bamboo and thatch, with space for about 48 guests, no electric lights, but flush toilets and cold showers, with water available most of the time. Watch out for thieving monkeys. The meals are good. Canoe and hiking trips arranged, US$50 for 4 days, meals and guides inc., guides only speak Spanish. Opposite, on the river bank at Ahuano, is *Casa del Suizo* (Swiss, Ecuadorean-owned), D p.p. full board, cheaper with shared bath, highly rec. for hospitality, food (but little scope for vegetarians) and location, electricity till 2200, animal sanctuary, trips arranged (for further information contact Gulliano Bonello, Koescherruetistr. 143, 8052 Zuerich, Switzerland, T 01-302-37-27). No public canoes from Misahuallí on Sun. p.m., only private hire, US$30, but there are buses Tena-Almano, US$1.50, ask to be dropped at ferry point. *Hotel Jaguar*, 1½ hrs. downstream from Misahuallí, congenial atmosphere, C p.p., with full board, good value, reservations from Quito, Ramírez Dávalos 653, T 239400, a full tour (3 days) including transport from Quito, all meals and good excursions into the jungle costs US$170 p.p. (US$70 from Misahuallí) with an extra charge of US$32 for each additional day. Avoid paying in US$ as they give you a very bad rate (independent canoe journey there costs US$30, except by public canoe at 1100).

In Misahuallí are *Cabañas Aliñahui*, D with full board p.p., new, good, private bath, good views, German and Cuban owners both speak English. Also, in the F price range (or G where stated): *El Paisano*, clean, washing facilities, hammocks, nice garden, rec., eight rooms behind restaurant, good breakfast; *Fifty-Five (55)*, on main square, G p.p., communal baths, good, clean, friendly, vegetarian restaurant; *Milca Isca*, on main square, friendly, clean, cheap, good restaurant, English spoken; *Sacha*, owned by Héctor Fiallos, basic, bamboo walls, noisy, at point where rivers meet, dirty, apes in the garden, path to hotel floods when rains heavy, buy souvenirs of the Oriente here, cheaper than in Baños or Quito; *El Albergue Español*, owned by Dr. José Ramón Edesa and Cristina Olsen (same ownership as *El Popoyal*—see above), G p.p. meals US$1.50, new, all rooms with bath, information of tours, horse-riding planned; *Balcón del Napo*, G, basic, central, meals available, clean, friendly, noisy from disco at weekends; *Amazonas*, on riverbank nr. square, clean, friendly, basic, 2 rooms with bath, reasonable; *Etsa*, F with or without bath, owner is guide Carlos Cordero. Douglas Clarke now provides basic accommodation in bamboo huts with bunk beds behind the restaurant, showers available. Beware of thieves poking hooks through the floor.

Restaurants Douglas Clarke's *Restaurant Dayuna* is reasonably good and cheap, as is *El Paisano*, mostly good vegetarian food (but meat should be treated with caution), poor service, popular meeting place for gringos, hence its nickname *Restaurant Paleface*.

Exchange at the general store on the plaza, US$ cash only, poor rates.

There are many guides available to take parties into the jungle for trips of 1 to 10 days, seeing river and jungle flora and fauna, the Cuyabeno National Park and other jungle locations, all involving canoeing and varying amounts of hiking. Note that guides are moving to Coca, where it may be easier to get a tour party together; another good place to collect a group is Baños, rather than Misahuallí itself. The going rate is between US$20 and US$25 p.p. per day, depending on season and length of trip. This should include food and rubber boots, which are absolutely essential (but see below). Overnight tours are recommended only for the hardy. Héctor Fiallos, of Fluvial River Tours (information in Quito T 239044), arranges one-day outings, and it is possible to make 3- and 4-day tours. A 6-day tour takes in the Cuyabeno National Park (special permit needed and may be difficult to get) and the Aguarico River. A 10-day tour goes down the Napo to Nuevo Rocafuerte and up the Aguarico to the Cuyabeno National Park. Reports have reached us, however, that Héctor is less conscientious than he used to be and does not accompany his parties, leaving them in the care of less experienced guides: Domingo, Enrique and Bolívar have been recommended but not others. We have received very mixed reports of trips arranged by Cruceros Fluviales Primavera (also based in Baños). Julio Los Angeles is very knowledgeable on the flora and fauna. His two-day trip includes one day of fairly rigorous hiking and one day of light hiking and canoeing down river, but he will arrange anything you wish to do; his 4-day tour on Río Tiputini to see animals is the minimum time (you can see very little in a shorter time); his cooking is good; a 6-day tour includes floating downriver on balsa rafts made by Julio, highly recommended by those who like peace and quiet and offering the opportunity of sighting wildlife undisturbed by motor launches. Adonis Muñoz of Caiman Tours has also been warmly recommended as good English-speaking guide (and cook). He was born in Limón Cocha and studied biology in the U.S.A. Douglas Clarke (speaks English), who runs the *Restaurant Dayuna*, and his sister, Billy, arrange trips with other guides. Their one-and two-day walks are recommended, but expensive. Also trips to Coca, to smaller rivers and lagoons, Limón Cocha, and longer ones into the jungle of up to ten days, similar to those organized by Héctor Fiallos but reportedly slightly more expensive. At *Hotel Balcón del Napo* contact Galo, who does 7-day jungle tours, or Carlos Sevilla, whose tours are up to 18 days, both are well recommended. (Carlos Sevilla can also be contacted via his sister in Quito, T 241981). Another tour operator is Walter Vasco, of Experiencia en Selva y Río, who has 2 or 3 canoes for fairly inexpensive trips. Luis Duarte has been recommended as very knowledgeable, but unless you insist otherwise, you will dine on products of his hunting: cayman, monkey, piranha fish and turtle eggs! He too can be contacted at the *Balcón del Napo*. Other good guides: Elías Arteaga, office on main square, good meal at his house afterwards; Fernando Alomia, maximum 4 people, lives at **Residencial La Posada** on corner of square by road leading to the river; Sócrates Nevárez, runs 1-10 day tours including trips further down Napo River, well-organised.

Some tours have been criticized for too much walking for too few rewards, so make sure your guide knows enough to make your effort worthwhile; an inexperienced guide can mean a boring, or even distressing, walk. Remember that, however good your guide is, organization may be bad, resulting in delays. If short of time, think twice about taking a tour. Consider also the harmful effects of visiting Indian villages. Travellers into the Oriente must have their passports stamped at the naval office, which is clearly marked at the canoe embarkation point. Fees for chartering a canoe are open to bargaining; fares on excursions are fixed. Every canoe pilot is supposed to have his passenger list checked before going downstream but this is not always done. For your own safety ensure that the authorities have a record. Essential items for a trip of any length are rubber boots (or, if you prefer, two pairs of suitable light shoes—keep one pair dry), sleeping bags, rain jackets, binoculars, insect repellant, sun tan lotions, mosquito net, water-purifying tablets, sticking plasters. The cautious might also take a tent, stove, extra food and playing cards. Wrap everything in plastic bags.

Transport Direct bus to Quito, 3 daily, 10 hrs.; none direct Misahuallí-Baños. Buses to Puerto Napo, Tena and Coca.

Owing to the completion of the road to Coca, there are no regular boat services to Coca, Limón Cocha and Nueva Rocafuerte; canoes ply this route but only when there are 8 passengers or more (out of season this may be once or twice a week). During and after heavy rainfall there are obviously no services, nor are there any services during a long dry period.

Puyo is the most important centre in the whole Oriente and the junction for road travel into the southern Oriente and for traffic taking the **route to/from Ambato** via Baños (**see page** 781). The pioneer fringe has now left Puyo far behind, and its wooden buildings are giving way to concrete and cement. The electricity supply is turned off promptly at midnight. There is a cinema, Coliseo, the Ñucaloma discotheque, and a cock-pit (cockfights Sun. 1400). Immigration office in Gobernación handles visa extensions.

The road from Puyo to Baños has been reconstructed. It is a dramatic journey with superb views of the Pastaza valley and a plethora of waterfalls. From Baños to Ambato is paved. **Shell-Mera** (a few km. W of Puyo, 50 km. from Baños, 1½ hrs, Hotel Esmeraldita, Residencial Azuay) has an army checkpoint where foreigners must register if coming from Ambato, and an airfield.

Hotels Hostería Turingia, Orellana y Villamil, D, small huts with bath, in tropical garden, comfortable but noisy, restaurant quite expensive but good; Europa, F, with bath, good value and good restaurant, also newer Europa Internacional, E (bright, pleasant, good restaurant), and California, F, slightly cheaper, noisy, all on Calle 9 de Octubre; Grenada, Calle 27 de Febrero y Orellana, G, dirty; Pensión Susanita, 9 de Octubre y Orellana, E, cafetería, rec. Some other pensiones F or G.

Restaurants Hostería Turingia, set meals, poor service; Europa (next to Hostal) 9 de Octubre y Marín, good; Rincón Ambateño, on river front, follow 29 de Julio, restaurant and pool complex; Delicia (local), Ejecutivo, Viña del Mar and El Delfín (both seafood), all on Marín; Chifa China, 9 de Octubre y 24 de Mayo, clean. Mistral, Atahualpa y 9 de Octubre, good for breakfast; Pan Selecto, Marín y 9 de Octubre, good, fresh bread.

Buses to Baños, US$0.80, 2 hrs.; Ambato, US$1.10, 3 hrs.; Quito, US$2, 7 hrs.; Tena, US$1, 3½ hrs. (fight for a seat, rough road). Riobamba, US$1.10, 3½ hrs. Most buses leave from the new Terminal Terrestre on the outskirts of town (10-15 mins. walk). Buses for Macas leave from small station near new market at far end of Atahualpa, past Amazonas (sign says Transportes Amazónicas), leaves daily 0500, 0900 and occasionally in p.m.

Flights Air Force to Tena; Macas via Taisha, good views. Shell-Mera can also be reached by military flight from Quito, ½ hr.; also flights to Macas. Military flights from Shell-Mera to Montalvo and Tiputini.

Betsy Wagenhauser writes: "The first leg of the Puyo-Macas bus (US$1, 3 hrs.) goes as far as Chuitayo, a small settlement at the junction of the Upshin and Pastaza rivers. There is no bridge, so travellers cross on a home-made catamaran (US$0.25) powered by outboard motors. When the river is low this is no problem, but during the rainy season, it could be treacherous. The current is swift, and debris swept down from upriver could cause the "ferry" to overturn. Another crossing option is a heavy cable stretching the width of the river connected to high platforms on either shore. Attached to the cable is a cage-like contraption, large enough to hold 2. You climb the platform, enter the cage, then release the catch. The cage swings along the cable, high over the river, to the other side. Definitely an interesting ride!

On the opposite shore, a bus arrives to carry passengers the rest of the way to Macas (US$1, 3 hrs.). It stops often at small settlements, mostly inhabited by Shuar descendents. The ride is slow and rough, the road hard packed dirt, full of potholes. The jungle which borders this road is beautiful."

Macas, the capital of Santiago-Morona province, is developing rapidly thanks to nearby oil deposits. Its environs are very beautiful and the surrounding hills give excellent views of the volcano **Sangay**, 5,230 metres, within the Sangay National Park, entrance US$10, reached by bus to village of 9 de Octubre, Wed. and Sun. 1600, then walk. You can cross the River Upano (footbridge) and take bus (½ hr.) to the Salesian Sevilla-Don Bosco mission. Good swimming. The whole settlement area has been developed for beef production. In Taisha, a village E of Macas, the *Casa Morocho* rents a few basic rooms, G; on the road to the mission there is a small stream in which you can swim or wash clothes. Malaria precautions essential.

Macas Hotels *Peñon del Oriente*, most modern, F, rec, clean, secure, hot water (electric showers, but not problematic), good views from roof; *Orquídea*, 9 de Octubre y Sucre, F, with bath, cold water, if any; *Peñón del Oriente*, Domingo y Amazonas F p.p., clean, good, firm beds, electric showers; *Hostería del Valle*, 5 km. out on Sucúa road, self-contained cabins, F. Others are all G: *Residencial Macas*, clean and friendly; *Hotels Splendit* (run down), *Amazonas*, *Residenciales Emperatriz* and *Elvira* (over liquid gas store); *Pensión Turismo*, basic.

Restaurants *Fredy*, below *Resid. Macas. Chifa* below *Peñon del Oriente*; *Chifa Perla Oriental*, *Mesón Dorado* and bus station restaurant, all on 10 de Agosto. *Rincón del Miguel*, Soasti y 10 de Agosto, Chifa menu, wide variety, rec.; *Eros Café*, Amazonas y Tarqui, good for snacks, breakfast, friendly owners.

Cinema next to Ietel, 24 de Mayo y Sucre, weekends only.

Transport Flight to Quito, TAME, Mon., Wed., Fri. 1400, US$12, sit on left for best views of Sangay. Bus to Cuenca, 11 hrs., US$1.80; hourly to Sucúa, 1 hr., no regular service on Thurs.

Sucúa 23 km. from Macas, 9 hrs. from Cuenca is of particular interest as the centre of the now-civilized branch of the ex-head-hunting Shuar (Jívaro) Indians; their crafts can be seen and bought but it is tactless to ask them about head-hunting and shrinking. You can contact the Shuar Federation at Domingo Comín 17-38 (Calle Tarqui 809) for information about visiting traditional villages, though they tend to be somewhat resistant to tourists.

Hotels *Oriente*, clean, friendly, but run down, restaurant; *Cuhanda, Colón, Rincón Oriental*—friendly, good set meals, all F; *Cuenca*, G, small rooms, basic, clean but toilets filthy; *Hostal Alborada*, F, clean, cheap, good restaurant. Bar/restaurant *Sangay*, opp. *Rincón Oriental*.

There are an interesting bookshop and (ten minutes walk from the town centre) a small museum in the Centro de Formación.

Nearby is the Río Upano, 1½ hrs. walk, with plenty of Morpho butterflies; also the Río Namangoza, 15 mins. walk, with rapids, good swimming, but be careful after rain.

From Sucúa, the road heads south (2 hrs.) to (Santiago de) Méndez (*Pensión Miranda, Residencia Medina*, both G, basic). Here a newly constructed road goes east into the jungle (9 hrs.) to the village of Morona, located on the Morona river just at the (disputed) Peruvian border (no accommodation, camping possible). No border crossing is permitted. At this time the area is newly opened and not set up for tourists, no accommodation available. However, it is virtually unexploited, and the wildlife and primary forest abundant. With the opening of the road, colonists and exploitation will shortly follow, but until then, for the more adventurous, an attempt to arrange a jungle excursion from Morona could prove to be an incredible experience.

Along the Méndez-Morona road is the junction of the Zamora-Coangos rivers. East of the confluence, at the village of Santiago, a canoe can be hired (about US$30) to a point from where you can walk in 2½ hours to the Cueva de Los Tayos, a huge cave, 85 metres in depth. The trail is obscure, and a guide is necessary; Mario Cruz, in conjunction with Metropolitan Touring in Quito, organizes treks from the capital.

2 hrs, 50 km. S of Méndez is Limón, official name General Leónidas Plaza (*Res. Limón*, G, clean, modern, basic; *Res. Paraiso*, G, basic; *Restaurante Rico Pollo Turco*). Buses, all from Calle Quito, go to Cuenca, Macas and Gualaquiza. It is some distance N of the turn-off for the **route to Cuenca**. From Limón, the road to Cuenca (132 km.) passes through Gualaceo and El Descanso; it is a longer route (Macas-Cuenca) than from Quito, but just as spectacular; there are several beautiful stretches.

A round trip by car Cuenca-Gualaceo-Limón-Sucúa-Macas-Mera and onwards to Quito will be possible once a bridge across the Pastaza River is completed (scheduled for late 1991). Quicker access to Quito will be given by the construction of a road between Macas and Riobamba; it has reached 9 de Octubre, N of Macas, and from the mountains is being built out of Guamote (**see page** 775). If travelling by public transport on this route enquire at the bus stations in Macas or Puyo about the condition of the roads and river crossing.

From Limón, it is 3-4 hrs. to Gualaquiza on the route from Loja to the Oriente.

From Loja The road to the Oriente (**see page** 792) crosses a low pass and descends rapidly to **Zamora**, an old mission settlement about 65 km. away at the confluence of the Rivers Zamora and Bombus cara. There is an entrance to the Podocarpus National Park here (see above under Loja). The area has scarcely been affected by tourism yet. For the mission at Guadelupe, take a La Paz bus, which goes up the Yacuambi valley. You can also visit gold mines on the Río Nambija (try your luck yourself).

Hotels *Maguma*, E, best; *Res. Venecia*, G, shared bathroom; *Zamora*, F, clean; *Amazonas*, F. **Restaurants** in *Hotel Maguma* (best), *GranRitz*, good, and *Comedor Don Pepe*.

Buses All leave from Terminal Terrestre. To Loja, 4 a day, 2½ hrs; to Cuenca, 1 daily via Loja, over 10 hrs; to Yantzaza and La Paz, 6 a day.

From Zamora, the road follows the Zamora river to **Gualaquiza**, a pioneer town off the tourist track. It is surrounded by densely forested mountains, in which are interesting side trips. Very little can be purchased here so take your own supplies (and don't forget your antimalarials). If you intend to explore the area, bring tent and sleeping bag. Among the excursions are: caves near Nuevo Tarqui, the Salesian mission at Bomboisa; Tutusa Gorge (3 hrs. walk, 2 hrs. by boat, take a guide, e.g. Sr. José Castillo); Aguacate, 6 hrs. walk, near which are precolumbian ruins, presumably Inca (food and bed at Sr. Jorge Guillermo Vázquez); and Yumaza, 40 mins. walk, for more precolumbian ruins, possibly Inca (2 sites). The valley produces large quantities of *naranjillas* and some sugar cane, maize, bananas and yuca.

Hotels *Turismo*, G, good value, restaurant; *Residenciales Estambul* and *Amazonas*, both G, basic. *Restaurante Gualaquiza* is best of a mediocre lot.

Buses to Cuenca (0700, 2000 and 2100), 6 hrs; Loja (0300 and 2200); Macas (1800), 10 hrs.

We are most grateful to Betsy Wagenhauser of the South American Explorers Club for help in updating the Oriente section, and to G.R. Leitner for much useful information.

GALAPAGOS ISLANDS (9)

Lying on the Equator, 970 km. west of the Ecuadorean coast, the Galápagos consist of 6 main islands (San Cristóbal, Santa Cruz, Isabela, Floreana, Santiago and Fernandina—the last two uninhabited); 12 smaller islands (Baltra, with an airport, and the uninhabited islands of Santa Fe, Pinzón, Española, Rábida, Daphne, Seymour, Genovesa, Marchena, Pinta, Darwin and Wolf) and over 40 small islets. The islands have a total population of just over 6,000. The largest island, Isabela (formerly Albemarle), is 120 km. long and forms half the total land area of the archipelago. Its notorious convict colony was closed in 1958; some 650 people live there now, mostly in and around Puerto Villamil, on the S coast. San Cristóbal (Chatham) has a population of 2,321 with the capital of the archipelago, Puerto Baquerizo Moreno. Santa Cruz (Indefatigable) has 3,154, with Puerto Ayora, the main tourist centre; and Floreana (Charles) fewer than 50. The group is quite widely scattered; by boat, Puerto Baquerizo Moreno and Puerto Ayora are 6 hours apart.

The islands are the peaks of gigantic volcanoes, composed almost exclusively of basalt. Most of them rise from 2,000 to 3,000 metres above the seabed. Eruptions have taken place in historical times on Fernandina, Isabela, Pinta, Marchena, Santiago and Floreana. The most active today are Fernandina, Isabela, Pinta and Marchena, and fumarolic activity may be seen intermittently on each of these islands. There have been recent eruptions on Volcán, Sierra Negra, Isabela and Fernandina.

The Galápagos have almost certainly never been connected with the continent. Gradually, over many hundreds of thousands of years, animals and plants from over the sea developed there and as time went by they adapted themselves to Galápagos conditions and came to differ more and more from their continental ancestors. Thus many of them are unique: a quarter of the species of shore fish, half of the plants and almost all the reptiles are found nowhere else. In many cases different forms have evolved on the different islands. Charles Darwin recognized this speciation within the archipelago when he visited the Galápagos on the *Beagle* in 1835 and his observations played a substantial part in his formulation of the theory of evolution. Since no large land mammals reached the islands, reptiles were dominant just as they had been all over the world in the very distant past. Another of the extraordinary features of the islands is the tameness of the animals. The islands were uninhabited when they were discovered in 1535 and the animals still have little instinctive fear of man.

The most spectacular species to be seen by the visitor are the giant tortoise (species still survive in 6 or 7 of the islands, but mostly on Isabela); marine iguana (the only seagoing lizard in the world and found throughout most of the archipelago; it eats seaweed); land iguana (on Fernandina, Santa Cruz, Santa Fe, Isabela, Seymour and Plaza); Galápagos albatross (which nests only on the island of Española, it leaves in December and returns in late March-early April); Galápagos hawk, red-footed, blue-footed and masked boobies, red-billed tropic-bird, frigate birds, dusky lava gulls, mockingbirds, 13 species of Darwin's finches (all endemic and the classic examples of speciation quoted by Darwin); Galápagos sea-lion (common in many areas) and the Galápagos fur-seal (on the more remote and rocky coasts). Santiago and Plaza islands are particularly interesting for students of these species.

There is a National Park Tax which every visitor has to pay; in January 1990 it was US$40, payable only in sucres, US$ cash or travellers cheques. The number of tourists to the island is controlled by the authorities to protect the environment. Limits have been increased and may be increased again, but tourism infrastructure remains fairly basic.

Alban Johnson and Luci Montesinos Aguilar write: The most-visited islands (and main attractions) are Plaza Sur (many birds flying close to the cliff top), Santa Fe (land and sea iguanas, sea-lions), Seymour Norte (magnificent frigate birds, blue-footed boobies), Rábida (sea-lions, flamingoes, pelican rookery), and Santiago (James Bay for fur seals; Sullivan Bay and Bartolomé Island for fantastic lava fields and maybe a few penguins). On a tour of these islands it may be possible to go also to Punto García on Isabela to see flightless cormorants (it takes at least a full day to climb up one of the volcanoes to see the tortoises). Daphne Island with very rich birdlife may be visited by each boat only once a month (a permit is required).

More distant islands are Española (blue-footed boobies, masked boobies, waved albatross, brightly-coloured marine iguanas), Genovesa (red-footed boobies, frigate birds and many others) and Fernandina (penguins and many other birds). Floreana, San Cristóbal and Baltra have little wildlife, and on Santa Cruz it is worth visiting the Darwin Station, Tortoise Reserve and Tortuga Bay. All the other islands are closed to tourists.

Tours generally leave from Puerto Ayora, but can finish at Baltra for the airport. Take some chocolate and biscuits with you; you will certainly miss them if you don't. Boat operators tend to underestimate the amount of drinking (mineral) water (they may not supply any, see below) and overestimate the amount of Coca Cola that foreigners drink. Food can be good if they catch fish, poor if not.

In 1959, the centenary of the publication of Darwin's *Origin of Species*, the Government of Ecuador and the International Charles Darwin Foundation established, with the support of Unesco, the Charles Darwin Research Station at Academy Bay 1½ km. from Puerto Ayora, Santa Cruz, the most central of the Galápagos islands, open Mon.-Fri. 0700-1300, 1400-1600, Sat. 0700-1300. A visit to the station is a good introduction to the islands as it provides a lot of information. Collections of several of the rare races of giant tortoise are maintained on the station as breeding nuclei, together with a tortoise-rearing house incorporating incubators and pens for the young. The Darwin Foundation staff will help bona fide students of the fauna to plan an itinerary, if they stay some time and hire a boat. Avoid visiting in July and especially August (high season).

Travel to the Islands There are 2 airports, one at Baltra, across a narrow strait from Santa Cruz, the other at Puerto Baquerizo Moreno, on San Cristóbal. The two islands are 96 km. apart with regular boat services only twice a week. When booking make sure your flight goes to the island of your choice. There are flights with SAN to Puerto Baquerizo Moreno (San Cristóbal) from Guayaquil and connecting flights from Quito (on Mon., Wed. and Sat.). The round trip in 1989 cost US$324 from Guayaquil, and US$365 from Quito (though there are no direct flights from Quito and it is cheaper to book separate flights from Quito to Guayaquil and Guayaquil to Galápagos). One-way tickets are available and it is now possible to buy an open-ended ticket (valid one year—e.g. from Manatours, Av. Amazonas, Quito). SAN will change dates for return to mainland. TAME flies daily, except Sunday, to Baltra, and offers 25% reductions on flights originating in Quito to holders of International Student Identity Cards (details from office at Edificio Pichincha, Amazonas y Colón, Quito); return to Guayaquil is permitted. Beware of "temporary" fare increases, e.g. in December; buy your ticket in

November. Tour operators still buy up blocks of seats in advance and they always try to sell you one of their excursions. For this reason, if time is limited, it is probably advisable to go for a package tour. If you cannot get a flight within a week, try going to the airport to get a seat on stand-by.

The Air Force flights, known as *logísticos*, are handled at the Departamento de Operaciones of the Air Force at the Ministry of Defence, Av. Maldonado y la Exposición, Quito. To enter the office, leave identification, but not your passport. Latest reports (1990) indicate that foreigners, no matter what their qualifications or requirements, are not allowed on these flights. Foreigners need the special authorization of the general commander of the Air Force, but this is not being granted, even to those with the support of their embassy and letters of introduction from a recognized educational/research institution where they work or study. (Note: UK Embassy charges £25 for a letter.)

There are now many travel agencies operating tours of the Galápagos Islands. Their quality and price varies considerably so shop around. Prices are no longer significantly cheaper in the low season (Feb.-May, Sept.-Nov.) but ask if an agency has 1-3 spaces to fill on a cruise; you can sometimes get them at 20% discount.

We have received persistent reports that tour operators, whether contacted on the mainland or the Galápagos, are unreliable in sticking to their agreed programme, and that some of the guides deviate from the scheduled route, wasting time in port and leaving out some islands. Insist on a written itinerary or contract prior to departure as any effort not to provide this probably indicates problems later (written contracts seem to be ignored, none-the-less). The South American Explorers Club (Quito: Toledo 1254 y Cordero, T 566076—Apartado 21-431, Quito; Lima: Av. Rep. de Portugal 146, Breña, T 314480—Casilla 3714, Lima 100; USA: P.O. Box 18327, Denver, CO 80218, T 303-320 0388) has produced a useful, brief guide to the Galápagos which includes a specimen contract for itinery and living conditions. Ensure that not more than a half-day is spent on either Santa Cruz or San Cristóbal for restocking of provisions. Count your money regularly and don't leave your beach gear unattended if other boats are in the vicinity when you are ashore. If you have problems afterwards, take your contract to the Capitanía (port captain).

In Guayaquil, **Galasam** (Economic Galapagos Tours), Av. 9 de Octubre 424, Edificio Gran

Pasaje, 11° piso (T 306 289/ 313 724, Telex 42680 GALASA ED, Fax 313351) sell flights as well as their own tours and can sell air tickets for their tours at a discount by using the free market. If you buy your air ticket from their office they throw in one night and lunch at a hotel in Puerto Ayora even if you do not purchase their tour. If you book the SAN flight to San Cristóbal with them, they throw in the Ingala boat trip to Santa Cruz free. In Quito, Galasam is at Pinto 523 y Av. Amazonas, T 550094. The Galasam 8-day tours, Mon. departure, normally cost about US$500, on 3 small boats each taking 8 people, on which conditions are fairly spartan; the *Yolita* (tourist class); two 16 passenger boats are more comfortable (US$700 for an 8-day tour), and have specially trained bilingual guides; the *Dorado* is more luxurious still. In 1991 Galasam will introduce two first-class yachts with diving facilities. Galasam say the guides on the smaller boats are English-speaking, but their knowledge of English may be very limited. It has also been alleged that their boats sometimes travel in convoy and that prices on board are exorbitant.

Metropolitan Touring, Av. Amazonas 239, Casilla 2542, Quito (represented in the USA by Adventure Associates, 5925 Maple, Suite 116, Dallas, Texas 75235), T 524-400 offers 7-night cruises on the M.V. *Santa Cruz* (90 passengers), about US$250 a day, said to be the best boat, very professional service, with multilingual guides. They also have five yachts for private charters. Macchiavello Tours of Guayaquil (Anteparra 809 y 9 de Octubre, T 392-892) is ordering two new boats from Italy.

Other recommended agencies with tours to/in the Galápagos are: Galápagos Cruises, Los Ríos 0-80, Guayaquil, T 390-893, Telex 3610 ETICAG; Coltur, Robles y Páez 370, Quito, T 545-777, Telex 2302, with an office in Puerto Ayora; Nuevo Mundo, Av. Amazonas 2468, Quito T 552-617, Telex 2484; Castro Turismo, Vélez 205, Guayaquil, T 512-174; Famitur, Veintimilla 928 y Amazonas, Quito, T 529-742; Samoa Tours, Victoria 907 y Wilson, Quito, T 551597; Ceviar, 9 de Octubre, Guayaquil. The *Hotel Gran Casino* in Quito, Av. 24 de Mayo y Bahía, arranges 8-day tours for US$350; reports on their reliability have not always been favourable. Kayaking trips in the Islands are organized by Northern Lights Expeditions, 5220 NE 180th, Seattle, WA 98155, USA.

There are cargo ships making the trip, but dates are irregular, the chances of a passage remote and some interesting but remote ports are missed. Check with the naval port authorities on the Malecón in Guayaquil, or with the boats themselves several days prior to departure. *Iguana* leaves on the 7th of each month, *Congal* on the 17th and *Piquero* on the 27th. None is reported to be reliable. We have received reports of a ban on passengers travelling on cargo ships, but it may still be worth trying.

From Britain, inclusive tours can be booked through Twickers World, 22 Church Street, Twickenham, TW1 3NW, or through the Coltur representative in London, Cecilia Irivalo, T 071-221 0968. David Horwell, naturalist and author of *Galápagos, the Enchanted Isles*, London, Dryad Press, 1988 (£7.95), arranges tailor-made tours to Ecuador and the Galápagos islands. For further details write to him at Galapagos Adventure Tours, 29 Palace View, Bromley, Kent, BR1 3EJ, England.

From the airport on Baltra, one takes a combination of bus (US$1), ferry (US$0.20) and bus (US$1.50) to Puerto Ayora, Santa Cruz. The whole process takes at least 3 hours. Airport buses leave Puerto Ayora (Pyky supermarket) at 0800 and 0830 for Baltra (best buy ticket night before—not possible for Sat. bus though). TAME office in Puerto Ayora closes Sat p.m. and Sun. Hotel may make prior arrangements.

Travel between the Islands There are official (Ingala) sailings on Tues. and Sat. from Santa Cruz at 1200 to San Cristóbal (US$10.50), returning at 1200 from Mon. and Wed. The Ingala office in Puerto Ayora is next to the hospital on the road inland from the waterfront. Get your name on the list here as early as possible on the day before sailing, buy ticket for San Cristóbal on day of departure between 0800 and 1000 and be at the quay at 1100. The Ingala office in Puerto Baquerizo Moreno is up the hill on the road leading inland, on the edge of town.

The best centre from which to visit the Islands is **Puerto Ayora**, Santa Cruz. Here you can hire boats (lists available from National Park Service) and a two-week sojourn will allow you to see most of the Islands. If you only have a short time, the northern islands are the more scenic with the more interesting wildlife. Reservations are strongly recommended for June-August and December-April. For cheaper tours it is generally recommended that you form a group of six to ten people once you reach the Islands, talk to people about the boats they may have used and then talk to the boat owners (known as *dueño*), not the captains, about what you wish to do. Bargain over the route and the price, and get a firm commitment from the owner on dates and itinerary, leave a deposit "to buy food" and get a receipt; however, prices have risen sharply and boat owners have made several attempts to form a cartel so that it is now difficult to find a small boat taking six to eight people for less than US$45-50 p.p. per day for a full load (small boats are essentially for travellers who do not mind a lack of privacy and facilities). Some boats travel by night (check if they have radar) which allows much more time for visiting the islands. If travelling to the more distant islands, night sailing should be standard, and should not incur extra expense. Try to make sure you have a full itinerary for the last day—otherwise the boat may bring you back at around 1500. Larger, more comfortable boats can cost twice as much, especially if they have bilingual guides. Each boat has to be accompanied by a Park-trained guide, either a naturalist (who will be English-speaking, more knowledgeable and therefore more expensive), or an auxiliary; this is arranged by the boat owner. Most boats operate 4-8 day cruises, it appears that only the 50-berth *Isabela*, owned by Etica, can be booked for longer—up to 3 weeks. The *San Juan* is recommended for its speed, which allows you to see as much in 7 days as some do in 10; it is also one of the cheaper boats. Also recommended is the *Golondrina*; friendly crew, knowledgeable guide and excellent food. Gil and Anita De Roy have been highly recommended for tours on their yacht *Inti*, which accommodates 4 to 5 passengers besides two crew; they speak French, German, English and Spanish, are experienced naturalists and guides and serve excellent food. Eduardo García has been recommended as one of the best guides. The *Aida Maria*, which sails at night, is highly rec; contact the owner at the Aida Maria pharmacy in Puerto Ayora. Coltur (see above) has been recommended for visits to North Seymour and Caleta Tortuga Negra on the north coast of Santa Cruz. Their representatives can arrange tours on the *Pirata* (Augusto and Georgina Cruz), which has been recommended for its friendly and helpful staff and good cooking; Georgina Cruz is English.The *Angelito* has been highly recommended, partly because the captain navigates by night so that you have more time on the islands by day. Others recommended in this category are *Española* (8 passengers), *Sulidae*, also 10 passengers, *Lobo del Mar* (10 passengers), *Dorado* (15 passengers), *Daphne* and *San Antonio* (8). The trimaran *Wind Shadow* (slow if there's no wind), owned and sailed by Richard Núñez, costs US$320 per day (maximum capacity 4); Sr. Núñez is knowledgeable and speaks English. It must be stressed, however, that a boat is only as good as its crew and when the staff change, so will these recommendations. Check that the small boats can carry enough food and supplies for the length of journey so you do not waste a day restocking. Many boats require you to provide your own drinking water: check this when you make arrangements. It may be possible to travel on a fishing-boat, though this will be to a predetermined destination—try the Ingala office and the Capitanía del Puerto for information, though the latter may not be very helpful as fishing boats are not supposed to take passengers. Priority on fishing boats tends to go to Ecuadoreans. It may also be possible to travel on supply ships—ask the crew.

Note: If not booking a cruise in advance, it can take several days to arrange a tour, so allow yourself plenty of time (up to a week in high season). If you do get stuck, the Tourist Office in Puerto Ayora offers one-day tours (US$36 p.p. with lunch; departure 0600-0800) to Seymour Norte, Plaza Sur or Santa Fe. These smaller islands have a good sample of animal species (although fewer in numbers) and, together with sightseeing on Santa Cruz, can be a worthwhile experience for the tourist with only limited time. There is excellent swimming with the sealions at Santa Fe. Never miss the chance to do a bit of snorkelling, and enquire carefully about the likelihood of sharks (*tiburones*—not all are dangerous).

Byron Rueda offers day trips for 10 in his dinghy *Santa Fe* to Santa Fe and to the Plaza islands (US$18). His office is on the Ninfa dock and he also represents other boats (open 0800-1800).

The Cost of Living in the Galápagos is very high, particularly in the peak season (December, July and August). Most food has to be imported although certain meats, fish, vegetables and fruit are available locally in the Puerto Ayora market.

Hotels at Puerto Ayora Hotel space is limited (more are being built) and reservations are strongly rec. in high season. *Galápagos*, L (local class 1), bungalows with private bathroom, hot water, ocean-view, laundry service, generator, restaurant with fixed menu, price and time, fruit and meat from hotel farm, near Darwin Research centre, reservations can be made through Ecuadorean travel agencies, day excursions can be made from hotel in Pedro and Sally García's own dinghy for 10, the *Fernandina*. *Delfín*, on far side of Academy Bay, with lovely beach, D (1), meals extra, well rec., accessible only by boat, write to Mrs Sievers. *Residencial Angermeyer*: about 20 beds, F, cooking facilities, described as very simple, and idiosyncratic; Mrs Angermeyer keeps the place spotlessly clean and is a mine of information, for guests, on good and bad boats. There is a peña next door. *Sol y Mar*, 20 beds (double, triples and quadruples) in cabins; D (1), without meals; B, with 3 meals; 10% discount for stays of 2 nights or more; reservations can be made by writing to the owner (Sr. Jimmy Pérez), or Macchiavello Tours, Casilla 318, Guayaquil. *Castro*, D (2), with private bath, owned by Sr. Miguel Castro, he arranges 7-day inclusive tours, including Friday TAME flight, rec. He is an authority on wildlife and his tour includes one or two nights away visiting the islands of Plazas and Santiago, and a day-trip to Santa Fe, with visits to the tortoise reserve and the Darwin Institute. *Colón*, 22 beds (doubles) in third class rooms; F (3), without food; D, including 3 meals. Write to Sra. Piedad Moya. *Elizabeth*, F with bath (3), reasonable, now remodelled, has running water; *Las Ninfas*, D, very close to harbour, clean, comfortable, restaurant, has its own boat at reasonable price for day trips and Fernando Jiménez is helpful with arrangements; *Lobo de Mar*, E (2), 30 beds, modern, clean; *Gloria*, G (3), 12 beds, simple, Sr. Bolívar very friendly, clean, you can cook your own food over a wood fire, mosquito repellant needed; *Darwin*, E, with bath, clean, restaurant (order meals in advance), rec. but don't leave valuables in your room; *Las Palmeras*, E (2), private bath, cafeteria, laundry facilities, pleasant, clean; *Salinas*, opposite, also F, 20 beds. *Santa Cruz*, F (3).

Restaurants at Puerto Ayora *Rincón del Mar*, near the plaza, best, good food, reasonable prices; *Don Enriques*, main road, local dishes; *Los Gemelos*, near the school, good value; *La Garrapata*, open air, on road to research station, popular meeting place for travellers, pizzas, hamburgers, cakes, morning and evening but not Sun.; *Fausto's*, between Gloria and Angermeyer hotels, good pizzas, friendly owner speaks English, exchanges paperback books and changes cheques; *Four Lanterns*, facing Pelican Bay, good, Italian/vegetarian, reasonable (dinner US$1.50); *Pastry Shop* (in front of hospital) for snacks and drinks; *Ninfa Dock Bar/Restaurant*, on dock, excellent grilled lobster, changes money, meeting place; nearby is *Pasty Pan* for bread and cakes (not open Sun.) *La Terraza*, main street, bar and restaurant; *Chifa Asia* on main street, decent; *Viña del Mar*, on main street, basic, O.K. *Henri's Snack Bar*, main street, German run, good meeting place, good breakfasts; *Snack Bar Popeyes*, in the plaza, Chilean run, empanadas and the best fruit juices in town; *Carmen's* pastry shop rec., good coffee and sweets; *Fragata Bar*, good, on road to research station, as is *Galaps Pizzería*. *Pelikano*, good value breakfast, and *Pastik-Shock* cafeterias. *Banana Bar*, near Angermeyer hotel, serves delicious banana flambée. Restaurants serve lobster dinners at US$5; *merienda* costs between US$1.50-2.

Entertainment Three discos (*La Terraza*, *Five Fingers* and *Disco Light*) and one *peña-disco*

(*Peter Cheese*) in Puerto Ayora.

Hints For boat charters and camping trips most basic foodstuffs generally can be purchased in the islands (e.g. Pyky supermarket in Puerto Ayora), although occasionally there are shortages. However, no special items (dehydrated or freezedried foods) are available other than a few common ones such as oatmeal and dried soups. Fresh milk available in Puerto Ayora from Christine Aldaze, 0930, on main road (24 hrs. notice appreciated). There is a shortage of drinking water on Santa Cruz; some travellers have warned against drinking water, but mineral water is expensive and often unavailable. Take your own water bottle with you: there is a purification plant at the *pizzería* next to the *Hotel Gloria* and you can buy water there.

Medicines, sun lotions (only up to factor 4 available in Ecuador), mosquito coils, film, and other useful items are either not available or cost a lot more than on the mainland. It may be advisable to take sea-sickness tablets; the waters south of Santa Cruz are particularly choppy. Take plenty of film with you; the birds are so tame that you will use far more than you expected; a telephoto lens is not essential, but if you have one, bring it. Snorkelling equipment is particularly useful as much of the sea-life is only visible under water. There is a souvenir shop next to Angermeyer's hotel, Galápagos Souvenirs, and a camera repair place next to the cemetery near the Darwin Station. Artesanías Bambú, near *Hotel Galápagos*, sells local handicrafts, printed T-shirts, etc.

Warning: Valuables should be watched.

Some of the prices charged are exorbitant. There is a cinema at Puerto Ayora—each evening at 2015. Information and retrieval of lost property from Radio Santa Cruz, next to Catholic Church. Short-stay camping permitted at the Caseta in the highlands and at Tortuga Bay.

There is a hospital in Puerto Ayora; consultations are free, medicines reasonably-priced.

Exchange It is advisable to take plenty of cash; there are few facilities for cashing cheques in Puerto Ayora, and rates are about 5% less than for cash. Some boats accept US$ while others only accept sucres; take plenty of sucres, you can always sell them to other travellers. The *Hotel Sol y Mar* and *Ninfa* restaurant will change notes and cheques, but at a poor rate. There is a bank at Puerto Ayora but it gives a poor rate of exchange and will not accept credit cards. Several shops change US$ notes. Good rates for cheques and cash at *Fausto's Pizzería*.

Immigration The police will extend visas with a little persuasion for those who overstay their visa or tourist card; but such extensions are reportedly not valid.

British Consul David Balfour, C/o Etica, Barrio Estrada, Puerto Ayora.

Tourist Office Dituris, near the pier, open Mon.-Fri. 0800-1200, 1500-1800. Information also available at the boat owners' cooperative office nearby.

Excursions on Santa Cruz From Puerto Ayora buses leave the main square frequently from 0800 to 2100 for Santa Rosa, Bellavista and Baltra (fare for all destinations US$1). There are also trucks (cheaper). On roads to the main sites hitching is easy but expect to pay a small fee. Walk to Tortuga Bay. A new, shorter track, 2 km. long (1½ hours) has been opened: turn at *Hotel Elizabeth* off main road, then left at *Hotel Santa Cruz*. Take drinking water.

Hike to the higher parts of the island called Media Luna, Puntudo and Mt. Crocker. Trail starts at Bellavista, 7 km. from Puerto Ayora. Round trip from Bellavista is 4 to 8 hrs., depending upon distance hiked, 10-18 km. (permit and guide not required).

There are two natural tunnels (lava tubes) 1 km. from Bellavista (on private land, US$0.70 to enter, torch provided—it takes about ½ hr. to walk through the tunnels).

Hike to the Chato Tortoise Reserve; trail starts at Santa Rosa, 22 km. from Puerto Ayora. Horses can be hired at Santa Rosa, US$6 each, guide optional US$6.50 extra. Round trip takes one day. The Puerto Ayora-Bellavista bus stops at the turnoff for the track for the reserve (US$0.50). It's a hot walk; take food and drink. From Santa Rosa, distance to different sites within the reserve is 6-8 km. (permit and guide not required).

Two sinkholes, Los Gemelos, straddle the road to Baltra, beyond Santa Rosa; if you are lucky, take a *camioneta* all the way, otherwise to Santa Rosa, then walk (4-5 mins). A good place to see the Galápagos hawk and barn owl.

Visit the giant Galápagos tortoises in pens at the Darwin Station, a short distance from Puerto Ayora. Small tortoises in rearing pens may be observed. The Station has a museum (explaining the geology and natural history of the islands) and a library. There are also public lectures (details from Dituris office near the pier).

Puerto Baquerizo Moreno, on San Cristóbal island to the E, is the capital of the archipelago, with a new airport with flights Mon., Wed. and Sat. by SAN. The island is being developed as a second tourist centre and, to encourage tourists, in mid 1989 SAN was offering two free nights at the *Grand Hotel* included in the price of a Monday flight from Quito or Guayaquil. Three Ingala boats a week to Puerto Ayora (US$10.50); fishing boats also take passengers (US$7 to Puerto Ayora). Be warned that it can take several days to find room on a boat to Puerto Ayora or Santa Cruz.

Hotels *Grand Hotel Cristóbal*, owned by SAN, opp. a white beach to E of town, A with bath (not inc. tax), good restaurant; *Mar Azul*, on road from airport, D with bath, restaurant; *Residencial Northia*, E with bath; *Cabanas Don Jorge*, close to beach, F p.p., clean, friendly, "not luxurious"; *Res. Miramar*, F, good value, clean restaurant, good; *Pensión Gloria*, pleasant family, but leaky roofs, new rooms are being added; *Res. Flamingo*, F, basic, clean, friendly; *Hotel San Francisco*, E, good, clean, friendly. *Delfín*, G, basic but cheap.

Restaurants *Rosita*, best in town; *Chatham*, good; *Laurita*, fair; *La Terraza*, on beach; *Fragata*, on road to airport. *Cafetería Tagu*, cheap.

Excursions Bus (shuttle) to El Progreso, then short walk to El Junco lake, tortoises may be seen on the way. From El Progreso (eating places), a trail crosses the high lands to Cerro Brujo and Hobbs Bay; also to Stephens Bay, past lakes. 2 buses go to the crater lake in the middle of the island, and may continue to the other side. SAN organizes a day trip (ask at *Grand Hotel*) to Point Lobo, reported as disappointing, and another to Española; the latter is often cancelled because the sea is too rough for their small boats.

The Galápagos Climate can be divided into a hot season (January to April), when there is a possibility of heavy showers, and the cool or *garúa* season (May to December), when the days generally are more cloudy and there is often rain or drizzle. Daytime clothing should be lightweight. (Clothing generally, even on "luxury cruises" should be casual and comfortable.) At night, however, particularly at sea and at higher altitudes, temperatures fall below 15°C and warm clothing is required. Boots and shoes soon wear out on the lava terrain. A good supply of sun block and skin cream to prevent windburn and chapped lips is essential. A hat is also recommended. Apart from Tortuga Bay, there are no beaches on Santa Cruz, but several on San Cristóbal.

Information The *Galápagos Guide* by Alan White and Bruce White Epler, with photographs by Charles Gilbert, is published in several languages; it can be bought in Guayaquil in Librería Científica and the airport, Libri Mundi (US$5) in Quito, or at the Charles Darwin station. *Galápagos, the Enchanted Isles*, by David Horwell (**see page 807**). Highly rec. is *Galápagos: a Natural History Guide* by Michael H. Jackson (US$20 from Libri Mundi, Quito), used by all the guides. A must for birdwatchers is *Field Guide to the Birds of the Galápagos* (US$20). A map of the Galápagos, drawn by Kevin Healey and illustrated by Hilary Bradt, is published by Bradt Enterprises (who also sell a range of books on subjects related to the islands—41 Nortoft Road, Chalfont St. Peter, Bucks SL9 0LA, England, T 02407-3478, Fax 734-509262). The National Park now publishes a good guide in English and Spanish, with plans of all the places where visitors are allowed to land: *Guide to the Visitor Sites of Parque Nacional Galápagos*, by Alan and Tui Moore, US$3.30. National Park Office, Puerto Ayora, Santa Cruz, Mon.-Fri. 0800-1200, 1400-1800, Sat. 0800-1000. For more information write to the Director of the Charles Darwin Research Station or the Superintendent of the Galápagos National Park Service, Isla Santa Cruz, Galápagos (correspondence in English.)

INFORMATION FOR VISITORS

Documents Passport (valid for at least six months required on arrival at Quito airport), and a tourist card valid for 90 days (tourists are now allowed only 90 days in any one calendar year) obtainable on arrival. You are required to say how many days you intend to stay and the card will be stamped accordingly; most travellers are given 15 or 30-day stamps irrespective of their requests (at Huaquillas, Macará and Tulcán), and travellers arriving by air may be given a stamp valid for only 10 days (transit pass) unless they request otherwise. It is therefore better to overestimate as you can be fined on leaving the country for staying too long. An extension can be routinely obtained at the Department of Immigration in Quito or Guayaquil, or at the Gobernación offices of several provincial capitals (addresses in the text); make sure the extension is given an official stamp. Evidence of sufficient funds (see below) is sometimes required. A visa is required for French nationals (US$10), New Zealanders (US$7) and Australians (free) and for business people and students who stay longer than 90 days (3 photos required), application to be made in home country, and they must get an exit permit with both tax and police clearance.

The procedure for obtaining a student visa involves taking a letter from the school at which you will be studying to the Ecuadorean consulate, a letter from your bank and a ticket out of Ecuador (or South America), plus a fee of US$30 in cash (only dollars, wherever paid): it is illegal to study on a tourist visa.. There are many other essential procedures, for which at least 6 passport photos will be required (4 face, 2 profile). Holders of student visas do not have to pay the Cuoto de Compensación Militar on leaving, although business visa holders do. Verify all details at the Consulate before departure.

Tourists crossing from Colombia or Peru may be asked for evidence that they possess US$20 p.p. for each day they propose to spend in Ecuador. Theoretically you must have an onward ticket out of Ecuador, but this is almost never enforced if you are travelling overland. However, travellers arriving from Miami with Ecuatoriana have been refused entry without a ticket and an MCO may not be sufficient. For a car a *carnet de passage* is required; failing that a bond equal to the value of the car will be demanded.

Warning Always carry your passport with you (a notarized photocopy will *not* do); if it is not in your possession you will be taken to prison.

Air Taxes There is a 10% tax on international air tickets for flights originating in Ecuador, regardless of where bought, and 12% on domestic tickets, and a tax of US$25, payable only in dollars, on all passengers departing on international flights.

How to Get There By Air Air France flies weekly from Paris to Quito. Iberia flies from Madrid to Quito via San Juan, Puerto Rico, and Bogotá, twice weekly. KLM flies weekly from Amsterdam to Guayaquil via Curaçao and Quito. Lufthansa flies from Frankfurt twice weekly via Bogotá. Viasa flies from Caracas with connecting flights to several European destinations.

There are flights from New York with Ecuatoriana, the national company, which also flies to Chicago, Miami and Los Angeles. Saeta also flies to Miami.

Ecuatoriana flies to the following Latin American destinations: Buenos Aires (Quito and Guayaquil—also Aerolíneas Argentinas, Guayaquil only), Bogotá, (also Avianca, Iberia and Lufthansa from Quito; Aerolíneas Argentinas and Ladeco from Guayaquil), Caracas, Lima (Quito and Guayaquil), Mexico City, Panama, Santiago de Chile (Quito and Guayaquil—also Ladeco from the latter).   AeroPerú has an overnight flight from Miami to Guayaquil; the plane goes on to Buenos Aires via Lima and Santiago. From Brazil weekly Varig flights to Guayaquil and Quito from Rio and São Paulo. There are no direct flights from Paraguay, Bolivia, or Uruguay. Varig/Ecuatoriana/Lacsa (using Varig aircraft) fly to San José, Costa Rica. Connections to other Central American capitals in Panama City. For all international connecting flights into/out of Ecuador, consult the monthly *Transport Junior* booklet, 150 sucres.

Customs Personal effects, a litre of spirits and a reasonable amount of perfume are admitted free of duty. No foreign cigarettes are allowed to be brought into Ecuador.

Internal Air Travel The local airlines Saeta, SAN and TAME operate internal flights between the main cities. TAME and SAN fly to the Galápagos; both have received favourable reports on reliability and baggage control. Also local airline Cedta operating Santa Rosa, near Machala-Guayaquil. Ecuavia operates charter flights. There are air taxis (Cessnas or Bonanzas) to anywhere you want to go to, also helicopters. On internal flights passengers may have to disembark at intermediate stops and check in, even though they have booked all the way to the final destination of the plane. Seats are not assigned on internal flights.

Railway Travel The railways are not too comfortable or reliable. The total track length is 1,043 km., but the system is not yet completely restored following the 1983 floods. The Quito-Riobamba, Guayaquil-Alausí, Sibambe-Cuenca and Ibarra-San Lorenzo stretches are in operation for passengers.

Road Travel Bus travel has improved greatly and is generally more convenient, and cheaper, than in other Andean countries. Since most buses are small they fill up and leave at frequent intervals. Half the 17,700 km. of road are open the year round. The length of paved highway is developing rapidly, including Quito-Guayaquil, Quito-Riobamba, Quito-Tulcán, Guayaquil-Cuenca, Guayaquil-Riobamba, Riobamba-Baños, Ambato-Puyo and the lowland (Costa) road Huaquillas-Machala-Guayaquil-Babahoyo-Santo Domingo-Esmeraldas. When touring by car, beware the bus drivers, who often drive very fast and rather recklessly (passengers also please note).

Car Rental Cars are available at US$33 per day, but there is a minimum three-day rental period. Impossible to hire with unlimited mileage, but on extended rentals you may receive a limited daily amount free (e.g. 100 km. per day, with US$0.10 and up per additional km.). Insurance is US$5, and tax is 6 per cent on the total transaction. Some car hire firms do not have adequate insurance policies and you will have to pay heavily in the event of an accident. Be sure to check the car's condition, not forgetting things like wheelnuts. Also make sure it has good ground clearance because not all roads have been repaired after 1983 flood damage on the coast. Beware of large potholes and crevices in any road. Always carry your passport and driving licence; there are police checks on all the roads leading out of main towns and you can be in serious trouble if you are unable to present your documents. The lack of road signs can be a nuisance. Gasoline costs US$0.50 per US gallon for 80 octane and US$0.60 for 92 octane (only in the main cities). Gasoline shortages are common, so fill up where you can. Diesel costs US$0.42 per gallon.

The Instituto Geográfico Militar, on top of the hill at the E end of El Ejido Park, Quito (**see page** 745), produces a 1:1,000,000 map of Ecuador which is quite good, but large. A comprehensive road map (1989 edition) is also available as well as various other maps, US$0.50-$0.80 apiece. Maps of the Oriente take a day to be photocopied. There are also road maps issued as a small booklet (US$2) with 26 partial maps published by Nelson Gómez, Editorial Camino.

Hitch-hiking on the main roads is reported to be easy in the north, but nearly impossible south of Riobamba, and it can be very cold in the mountains in the back of a truck (when hitching, it is common to pay a small sum). In the arid S the unpaved roads are dusty; use a wet cotton handkerchief to filter the air you breathe. Whether hitching or driving always take plenty of drinking water.

Walking Walkers are advised to get Rob Rachowiecki's book (see next para.).

Climbing can be arranged through climbing clubs in Quito and other cities, or those associated with universities. Recommended guides to climbing: *Climbing and Hiking in Ecuador*, by Rob Rachowiecki (published by Bradt Enterprises—currently out of print, but a new edition due in 1991) and *The Fool's Mountaineering for Ecuador and Peru* (from the South American Explorers' Club in Quito or Lima, US$3.50). Edward Whymper's, *Travels among the Great Andes of the Equator* (published by Gibbs M. Smith, Salt Lake City) is available from Libri Mundi. The quality of hired equipment needs scrutiny.

Accommodation outside the main towns; almost standard prices are charged of US$1.50-2 p.p. (without bath) in a *pensión, residencial*, or hotel (where this is the minimum charge). One can bargain at cheaper *pensiones* and *residenciales*.

Outside the provincial capitals and the resorts of Salinas and Playas, there are few higher-class hotels. Service of 10% and tax of 10% are added to 1st and 2nd class hotel and restaurant bills. The cheaper hotels charge at most 5%, generally. Hotel owners tend to try and let their less attractive rooms first, but they are not insulted if you ask for a bigger room, better beds or a quieter area. The difference is often marked.

Camping   White gas, like US Coleman fuel, is virtually impossible to find. Campers should be sure that their stove will either burn kerosene, or regular car gas/petrol. For stoves, kerosene is known as "kerex" and is available where gasoline is sold (e.g. CEPE stations). Pure alcohol fuel is sold in hardware stores. See also page 738.

Food Well worth trying are *humitas tamales* made of sweet maize), *llapingachos* (fried mashed potatoes with cheese), and *locro* (a soup of stewed potatoes and cheese topped with an avocado), served, with a beer, at bars. Local food is usually unspiced, though you may add *ají* (red pepper) sauce to make it (very) hot. *Tamales de moracho* (not unlike Venezuelan *hallaca*) and *empanadas de moracho* are delicious (same insides, breadcrust outside); *fanesca*, a kind of fish soup with beans, meat, and more, sold in Easter Week, is filling and rich. A typical food (but a matter of taste) is roast *cuy* (guinea pig). Hamburger meat is not always safe in Ecuador. *Cacho*, a croissant-like pastry, is cheap and filling. If economizing ask for the set meal in restaurants, *almuerzo* at lunchtime, *merienda* in the evening—very cheap; it costs between US$1 and US$2. There are interesting *encocada* (coconut) dishes on the coast. The fruits are magnificent: try *mamei colorado*, a fruit of the avocado family. A good sweet is *quimbolito*, a sweet sponge pudding made with maize flour.

Drink The local wines, often made from bananas, are safe but sickly, and cannot be recommended. Argentine and Chilean wines are cheaper than European or US ones. The best fruit drinks are *naranjilla, taxo* and *mora* (blackberries), but note that fruit juices are often made with unboiled water. Main beers available are Pilsener and Club. International drinks, when they can be had, are costly. Good *pisco, aguardiente* (Cristal is recommended), *paico* and *trago de caña*. The usual soft drinks, known as *colas*, are available. Instant coffee or liquid concentrate is common, so ask for *café puro* if you want real coffee.

Tipping Hotels and restaurants, 10% usually in the bill (in cheaper restaurants, tipping is uncommon—but obviously welcome!). Taxi, nil. Airport and railway porters, US$0.08-0.20, according to number of suitcases; cloakroom attendants, US$0.04, hairdressers, 20%.

Security Although Ecuador is generally one of the safer countries in the region, there have been reports of increased problems as a side effect of the drug situation in Colombia: police searches are now more frequent. If your luggage is searched, make sure that you are present during the search: women travelling alone, especially in Otavalo, should beware of police officers who ask to look at their passport and then insist on taking them to police station.

Health Amoebic dysentery is a danger. Visitors should drink mineral water (Güitig or Manantial), avoid uncooked vegetables or salads, and be inoculated against typhoid. Hepatitis (jaundice) is a very real risk and should be inoculated against with gamma globulin; see "Health Information" in front of book. Travellers in the Oriente and the Costa are advised to take anti-malaria tablets; chloroquinine and Fansidar (Falcidar) are both available in chemists/pharmacies without prescription. Mosquito netting is also useful, a good mosquito repellant essential (not a local one—they don't work). Also recommended is an anti-itch cream in the Oriente. Yellow-fever vaccination is recommended for travel into the Oriente. Cholera vaccination is not available. There are excellent hospitals both in Quito and Guayaquil. Climbers are warned to undergo a period of acclimatization before attempting to scale the volcanoes.

It has been reported that the free rabies vaccine given out in Ecuador is made from mouse brain and is said to be dangerous, if not fatal. Human diploid vaccine (the correct type) can be ordered from USA through the US Embassy, but it is expensive. You are recommended to get a rabies vaccination at home, in which case a booster-type injection is all that is needed if you are bitten (note that the initial vaccine is very costly).

Clothing Spring clothing for Quito (mornings and evenings are cold). In Guayaquil tropical or light-weight clothes. Laundering is excellent, but dry cleaning expensive.

The **best time for a visit** is from June to October, during the dry season, though September can sometimes be wet. The coastal area is extremely hot and wet from December to May.

Information for business travellers is given (1) in "Hints to Exporters: Ecuador", available from Department of Trade, Sanctuary Buildings, 16-20 Gt. Smith Street, London SW1P 3DB; (2) the Ecuadorean-American Association, Inc. (55 Liberty St., New York, NY 10005) issues monthly bulletins and a free sample copy may be requested. Telephone directories in Ecuador have "green pages" giving useful tourist information, sometimes in English. Business travellers may wish to consult the *Ecuadorean News Digest*, published by the Ecuadorean American Association, 150 Nassau St., New York, NY 10038.

Public Holidays New Year's Day; 6 January; Monday and Tuesday before Lent (Carnival); Holy Thursday; Good Friday; Holy Saturday; 1 May-Labour Day; 24 May-Battle of Pichincha; 24 July-Birthday of Bolívar; 10 August-Independence of Quito, Opening of Congress, 9 October-Independence of Guayaquil, 12 October-Discovery of America; 1 November-All Saints' Day; 2 November-All Souls' Day; 3 November-Independence of Cuenca; 6 December-Foundation of Quito; Christmas Day.

Local Time is 5 hrs. behind GMT (Galápagos, 6 hrs. behind.)

Currency The sucre, divided into 100 centavos, is the unit of currency. Bank notes of the Banco Central de Ecuador are for 5, 10, 20, 50, 100, 500, 1,000 and 5,000 sucres; there are nickel coins of one sucre, 50, 20 and 10 centavos. The one sucre coin is also sometimes called an *ayora*.

There is no restriction on the amount of foreign money or sucres you can take into or out of Ecuador. It is said to be easier to cash Bank Americard cheques than American Express cheques. It is very easy to change US$ cheques into US$ notes at the *cambios*; the commission varies so it is worth shopping around and *cambios* sometimes run out of US$ notes. Rodrigo Paz *cambios* are recommended as reliable, with only 0.5% commission, but may offer a slightly lower rate than banks. M. M. Jaramillo is also recommended and you can try to bargain for a better rate than shown on the blackboard. Many *cambios* ask to see the receipt for travellers' cheques purchased abroad. US$100 notes may be difficult to change, many banks regard them with suspicion. Ecuador is the best place in South America to have money sent to. All major **credit cards** are widely accepted in banks and cambios, but note that although many hotels and restaurants have signs indicating acceptance of credit cards, this is often not the case; always check first. It is quite difficult to change US$, whether cheques or bills, outside the main towns, especially in the Oriente.

Weights and Measures The metric system is generally used in foreign trade and must be used in legal documents. English measures are understood in the hardware and textile trades. Spanish measures are often used in the retail trade.

Electric Current 110 volts, 60 cycles, A.C. throughout Ecuador.

Posts Many post offices away from Quito may not know the foreign rates (10g air-mail to the Americas US$0.20, Europe about US$0.35) and give incorrect ones. For a small extra charge you can certify your letters and parcels; ask for "con certificado" when you buy stamps, so that they are stamped separately (US$0.12 extra). The only post office (probably in all Ecuador) which deals in International Reply Coupons is in Quito, at Eloy Alfaro y 9 de Octubre (new city). **For sending parcels:** up to 20 kg. maximum dimensions permitted is 70 X 30 X 30 cms. Take contents and packaging (unpacked) to the Correo Maritimo Aduana, Davalos y Ulloa (next to the Santa Clara Market) (Mon.-Fri. 0830-1600) for customs inspection. Parcels can also be sent from the post office at Reina Victoria y Colón, though the staff are reported to be unhelpful. Rates vary according to weight and destination. There is no surface mail service. Packages under 2 kg. can be sent "certificado" (US$2 per kg. to USA, US$3 per kg. to Europe) from the post offices at Benalcázar 769 and at Eloy Alfaro. Transpak (also called STAIR), Amazonas y Veintimilla, will ship out packages for about US$4 per kg. to USA, minimum charge about US$50. Letters for Europe bearing the correct postage can be dropped off at the Lufthansa office, 6 de Diciembre 955 y 18 de Setiembre, to be sent in the next international bag.

N.B. The postal service is reported to be highly unreliable, with frequent thefts and losses. Some correspondents report that parcels and letters sent "certificado" are more vulnerable to theft and that packages should be marked as "used clothing" and the value declared as US$0.00. Even if not certifying your mail, watch to see that the stamps are franked (then they at least, cannot be stolen).

Telecommunications All the principal towns have long-distance telephone facilities.

Telephone call to Europe is US$17 for first 3 min. and US$5 per min. thereafter (there is no signal to indicate that your time is up). For international operator dial 116, normally only 5-20 minute wait for call to UK. All collect calls were suspended in February 1990; previously this service was only available to the USA and to Canada from the Ietel office in Quito but not to Australasia or Northern Europe. A charge is made for person-to-person calls even when the person is not there. Telegrams, ordinary US$4.30 first 7 words and US$0.57 per word thereafter, nightletter US$0.20 per word. There are public telex booths in the best hotels in Quito and Guayaquil (US$13.50 for 3 mins.), and at Cuenca.

Newspapers The main newspapers are El Comercio, Hoy, Tiempo, and Ultimas Noticias, in Quito; Expreso, El Telégrafo, El Universo (with good international news), La Prensa, La Razón and Extra (an afternoon paper), in Guayaquil; El Mercurio, in Cuenca; La Opinión del Sur, in Loja; and El Espectador, in Riobamba. Newspapers cost more outside their town of publication, up to double the price in the Oriente.

Sport The Sierra country is excellent for riding, and good horses can be hired. Quito, Guayaquil and Riobamba have polo clubs. There are golf clubs at Guayaquil and Quito and on the Santa Elena Peninsula. There is excellent big-game fishing for bonito and marlin off Playas, Salinas and Manta. Bull fighting is rarely seen at Guayaquil, but there is a well-known bullfight festival on Dec. 6 at Quito. A favourite sport is cock fighting; every town has its pits, but association footbal l is fast taking over as the national sport. Baseball, volleyball and basket-ball are also popular. There is Sunday horse-racing at Guayaquil.

Wild Life includes the jaguar, puma, tapir, several kinds of monkey, the armadillo, ant-bear, squirrel, porcupine, peccary, various kinds of deer, and many rodents, including the guinea pig. There are also tortcises, lizards and iguanas. Among the birds are condors, falcons, kites, macaws, owls, flamingoes, parrots, ibises, cranes, and storks. Unhappily, every type of insect is found in the coastal towns and the Oriente. The Galápagos Islands have their own selection of nearly tame wildlife.

National Parks All foreigners have to pay to each national park, the charge for the Galápagos is now US$40.

We are most grateful to Charlie Nurse for doing the updating of this chapter. We should also like to thank Betsy Wagenhauser of the South American Explorers Club, Quito and Ann K. Rodzai (Quito); also the following residents and travellers: Bernard Van den Doof (de Lier, Neth.), Roy and Joan Harris (Nanaimo, BC), Chris Larson (Oakleigh, Vic, Australia), Jean Mercier (Quito), Jane Nimmo (Swansea), The Loving Team (London), Franck Abadie and Marianne Joelius (Megève, France and Stockholm), Dean A. Alper (Mill Valley, CA), Stan Anderton (Preston, Lancs.), Dr Eugen Baldas (Freiberg, W. Ger.), Prof Fabrizio Bartaletti (Turin), Catharine Beamer (Claremont, CA), Sue Bennett (Kendal), May Berkouwer (Mantinge, Neths.), Momik Bernaerts (Amsterdam) and Thomas Hartmann (Copenhagen), Ivo Boeni and Friends (Switz.), Mark van den Boer (He Tilburg, Neths.), Dorothea Bornholdt (Lutzhorn, W. Ger.), J.N. Bowden and K.E. Badgery (Plymouth), Robert G. Brands (Amsterdam), Dirk Von Braunmuehl (Bonn 1), Sara Braune (Stroud), Rachel Bridgeman (Harpenden), Lucy Broadbent and Rick Palmer (Palmerston North, NZ), Karen A. Brown (London SW5), John Buckrell (Byfleet), Remo Bulgheroni (Killroergen, Switz.), Susan Carroll (Bearwood, W. Midlands), Martin Cooper (La Paz), Joanne Cross and Frank Pinelli (Oak Park, IL), G.G.A. Cumming (Viña del Mar), Jan Van Dalfsen and Tineke Puister (Neths.), James Derry (Courtenay, BC), Kate Edwards (Freeport, Grand Bahama), Dag K. Ellingsen (Oslo 2), Gennaro Escobedo (Milan), Humphrey Evans (London N7), Dr Dietz Evers (Krumesse), Alexandra Fisher (London W8), Olivier and Paloma Foro (St-Moritz), Petra Franke (Gundelsheim, W. Ger.), Sharon Franklet

(Lima 18), Ursula Gaedke (Konstanz, W. Ger.), Nancy H. Gage (Greenbrae, CA), Diane Garetz (Escuintla, Guat.), Theodor A. Gevert (Barueri, SP, Brazil), Jens Gjerlev (Bodøn, Norway), David Goodings (Hamilton, Ont.), Tony Gowers (Bristol), Rudolf Graf (Genthod, Switz.), Rudy Graf (Geneva), Andrew Grassie and Sara Gilbert (Lewes, E. Sussex), D. Graves (Brooklyn, NY), Thomas Gray (Houston, TX), Karl Gugler and Konstanze Mittendorfer (Vienna), Jim Hardy (Waukesha, Wis.), Wayne Harvey (South Australia), Olav Holger Helø (Copenhagen), Paul Herron (Austin, TX), Susan Holze and Astrid Brombosch (Heidelberg), Bob Horsfall and Judi Johnson (Auckland, NZ), David Horwell (London SE1), Edward Hutt (Stowmarket), Jeff Inglis (Seattle), David Jeffcock (Worthing), Simon Jeffreys (Peterborough), Ursula Jenny (Bottmingen, Switz.), Allan Jensen and Vibeke Nageh (Munke-Bjergby, Dnmk.), Joan and Patrick (San Francisco, CA), Tobias Kämpf (Rupperswil, Switz.), Birgit Kastner and Hans Lindenthaler (Salzburg, Austria), Bill Kauffman (Sydney, NSW), Marcel Kersten (Roosendaal, Neths.), Peter Knight (Quito), Carsten Kolbe (Marburg, W. Ger.), Lucy, Ian and Laura Krause (Newcastle-upon-Tyne), Loren Lacelle (Willits, CA), Jiri Lambert (Göttingen, W. Ger.), Rudi Lamparter (Gaechingen, W. Ger.), G. Langsdale (North Miami), Jochen Langheim and Thomas Reckhorn (Aachen, W. Ger.), Toby Lanzer (Santiago de Chile), Meg Laughlin (Miami) and Bob Moorhead (New Zealand), John Lewis (London NW2), Udo Lichtenthäler (Berlin 21), Helena van Maanen (Velp, Neths.), M.C. Majano (Spanish Embassy, London), Joe Mark (Edmonton), Nelly Matthey (Lausanne), Andreas Mietzsch (Braunschweig), Wolfgang Meusburger (Dornbirn, Austria), Cindy Miller (Vancouver, BC), Martha van Mil and Monica van Eysden ('s-Hertogenbosch, Neths.), William Milliken (Royal Botanic Gardens, Kew), Alistair and Liz Mitchell (São Paulo), Valerie and Bob Mitchell (Cottesloe, Western Australia), Barbara Monkiewicz (Kodiak, Alaska), Helene Monsme (Leiden, Neths.), Ortelli Visalakshi Moreno (Italy), Daniel Morgan (Wellington, NZ), Martin Mowforth (Tavistock), Matthias Müller (Berlin 31), Jonas Noreús (Varberg, Swe.), Max Nussbaumer (Köln 41), Martin Oehlen and Petra Pluwatsch (Köln 41), John and Jane Parkinson (Ilkley), Sandrine Pétremand and Gilles Maitre (Bevaix, Switz.), Penny Plostra (Neths.), Ian Powell (Stafford) and Judy Proctor (London), M. Rademater (Köln, 60), Gene Rainone (Cuenca), Alan Riddell (Edinburgh), George M. Ridenour (Albuquerque, NM), Marvin and Patricia Rosen (New York), Yves Rougeaux (Montreuil, France), Thomas Roztocil and Marie Gomez (Geneva), Chr Scherlenzky (Bendorf, W. Ger.), Kathrin Schildknecht and Jürg Schmutz (Bern, Switz.), Ueli Schlatter (Hemmental, Switz.), Elizabeth B. Schmidt (Belmont, MA), Andrea Schneiber (Herborn, W. Ger.), Hans Schoch (Stans, Switz.), Isabelle and Heinz Scholl-Kalt (Zürich), Thorsten Schüller (Aschen, W. Ger.), Daniel Schweimler and Claudia Ricca (London E7), Mary Shiner and Martin Walsh (Manchester 20), Julie Skippon (West Vancouver, BC), W.J.D. Smith (Leicester), Bob Snyder (Norwich, Ontario), Hadas Spector (Israel) and Celina Peres (Argentina), Barbara Springer and Franz Schalk (Kreuzlingen, Switz.), Hans and Ina Stoffregen (Celle, W. Ger.), Kay Stricker (Unterseen, Switz.), Fredi Suter (Goldau) and Claudia Räber (Oberkirch, Switz.), Eileen Synnott and Paul Gurn (Waterbury, CT), Martin and Susanna Theander (Malmö), Frederic Turcotte and Caroline Senneville (Quebec), Karen Uemura (Hollister, CA), Mrs Egide, Mrs Julia Vanbesien and Mrs Licue Passchyn (Grimbergen, Belgium), Julio C. Velasco (Edinburgh Linguistics Institute, Quito), Maarten van Vlerken (Amsterdam), Andrew Wallace and Michelle Still (Teddington), Peter Warren (Mitcham, Vic.), Arielle Webb (Stratford-on-Avon), Simon Weidmann (Bern, Switz.), Roland Weitkamp (Braunschweig, W. Ger.), Lorraine Westerink (Old Toongabbie, NSW), Urs Wigger (Menznau, Switz.), Patrick de Wilde (Huldenberg, Belgium), W. Wollenheit (Oregon), Alison Wood (Rotherham), Tim Woodward (Tottenham, N15), James Woolf (London SW7), Maryan van Woorselaer (Gent, Belgium), S.L. Wyatt, Joel Zanger (Jerusalem) and Heidi Ziernhöld (Richterswil, Switz.).

WILL YOU HELP US?

We do all we can to get our facts right in the **South American Handbook.** Each chapter is thoroughly revised each year, but South America covers a vast area, and our eyes cannot be everywhere.

Your information may be far more up-to-date than ours. If your letter reaches us early enough in the year it will be used in the next edition, but write whenever you want to, for all your letters are used sooner or later.

Thank you very much for your help.

Trade & Travel Publications Limited
6 Riverside Court, Lower Bristol Road, Bath BA2 3DZ, England.

PARAGUAY

INTRODUCTION

PARAGUAY is entirely landlocked, encircled by Argentina, Bolivia and Brazil. Its total land area is put at 406,752 square km., cleft into two quite distinct parts by the great river Paraguay. It has over 4.0 million people (roughly 41% living in towns). It has not as yet fully developed its potential, partly because it was deeply involved in two out of the three major wars staged in Latin America since independence.

To the W of the Paraguay river is the Chaco (246,950 square km., nearly 61% of the country's area), a sparsely inhabited tract of flat and infertile country. E of the river is Paraguay proper (159,800 square km.), a rich land in which almost all the population is concentrated. Paraguay proper is itself divided into two contrasting areas by a high cliffed formation which runs almost due N from the Alto Paraná river, W of Encarnación, to the Brazilian border. E of this cliff lies the Paraná plateau; W of it, as far as the Paraguay river, lie gently rolling hills and flat plains.

Paraguay's southern boundary with Argentina from the confluence of the Río Paraguay to that of the Río Iguazú is the Alto Paraná river. From the Iguazú Falls, the Itaipú Lake and the Alto Paraná form the eastern border with Brazil; from Guaíra Falls (now flooded) the northern boundary with Brazil runs north-westwards across the land mass to the confluence of the Apa and Paraguay rivers. From Resistencia as far N as Asunción the Río Paraguay is the western boundary with Argentina. From Asunción as far N as the confluence with the Apa, the river divides Paraguay into two. For some distance N of the entry of the Apa, the Paraguay river is the Chaco's eastern boundary with Brazil. The S border of the Chaco with Argentina is along the Río Pilcomayo; its W and N borders are with Bolivia.

The Paraná Plateau, ranging from 300 to 600 metres in height, has comparatively heavy falls of rain and was originally forest. Across the plateau, much of which is in Argentina and Brazil, runs the Paraná river. West of the high cliff which forms the western edge of the plateau lies a fertile plain stretching to the Paraguay river. This plain is diversified by rolling, wooded hills. Most of Paraguay's population is concentrated in these hilly lands, stretching SE from Asunción to Encarnación.

Much of the flat plain is flooded once a year; it is wet savanna, treeless, but covered with coarse grasses. On this plain, rice, sugar, tobacco, grains, soya and cotton are grown. Several heavily forested rivers drain the plain and hill lands into the Paraguay.

The Chaco, lying W of the Paraguay river, is mostly cattle country or scrub forest. Along the river there are grassy plains and clumps of palms, but westwards the land grows drier and more bleak. Much of the north-western area is almost desert. The marshy, unnavigable Pilcomayo river forms the boundary with Argentina. Apart from Mennonite colonies, small settlements on the river banks, and a number of *estancias* in the SW, only a few nomadic Indian tribes live in the vast region. (The average density is less than 1 person to the square km..) The *quebracho* (axe-breaker) tree, the world's principal source (with mimosa) of tannin, comes from the scrub forests of the Chaco and of the Paraná river.

Some 51% of the country is covered with forest, 39% is pastoral, 5.4% is agricultural. In eastern Paraguay the land supports only 11 people per square km.

Climate The climate is sub-tropical, with a marked difference between summer and winter and often between one day and the next throughout the year. Summer (Jan.-March) is hot (and humid in Asunción). Temperatures range from 25 to 43°C. The autumn (April-June) is mild, but nights are cold. During winter (July-Sept.) the temperature can be as low as 5°C, though it can equally well be much higher. Temperatures below freezing are rare, and it never snows. The heaviest rains are from October to April, but some rain falls each month.

History The original inhabitants of the area of Paraguay were the semi-nomadic Guaraní Indians; they had spread by the 16th century to the foothills of the Andes, along the coast of Brazil, and even into the basin of the Amazon. They did not contest the coming of the Spaniards, the first of whom, under the navigator Diego de Solís, arrived at the River Paraguay in 1524. A member of Solís's expedition, Alejo García, the discoverer of the Iguazú falls, was the first European actually to enter Paraguay; he was also the first European to fight against the Incas, as his career included an attack on them with a Guaraní army of 2,000. He set out through the Chaco in search of El Dorado in 1525. The main expedition, led by Juan de Ayolas, came from Buenos Aires, where the earliest Spanish settlement was planted in 1536. Finding no gold, and harassed by the hostile Indians of the Pampa, they pushed north along the river, seeking a short route to the gold and silver of Peru. They reached the friendly Guaraníes in 1537 and a member of the party, Juan de Salazar de Espinosa, is generally credited with founding Asunción on August 15.

Asunción became the nucleus of Spanish settlement in southeastern South America. Spaniards pushed NW across the Chaco to found Santa Cruz, in Bolivia, eastwards to occupy the rest of Paraguay, and southwards down the river to re-found Buenos Aires in 1580, 43 years after they had abandoned it.

During the colonial era one of the world's most interesting experiments in dealing with a native population was carried out, not by the conquerors, but by their missionaries, over whom the civil power had at first little control. In 1609 the Society of Jesus sent missionaries to Paraguay to civilize the Indians. During the 158 years until they were expelled in 1767, the Jesuits formed 30 "reductions", or settlements, run along theocratic-socialist lines. They induced the Indians to leave the forests and settle in townships, where they helped build magnificent churches, employing unsuspected native skills in masonry, sculpture, and painting. Selected natives were even given a sound classical education. The first reductions were further north, but they were forced to abandon these because of attacks by the *bandeirantes* of São Paulo, Brazil. They settled finally in Misiones; parts of the area of settlement are now in Argentina and southern Brazil. After the expulsion of the Jesuits, the reductions fell to pieces: the Indians left, and were reduced to peonage under other masters. Most of the great churches have fallen into ruin, or been destroyed; the few that remain are dealt with in the text.

Paraguay got its independence from Spain, without bloodshed, on May 14, 1811. Gaspar Rodríguez de Francia, known as "El Supremo", took power in 1814 and held it until 1840. His policy of complete isolation was a response to the landlocking of Paraguay by the *porteños* of Buenos Aires who wished to annex it: no one might leave the country, no one might enter it, and external trade was not permitted, but Paraguay achieved a high level of self-sufficiency. Rodríguez de Francia was followed as president by Carlos Antonio López, who ruled until his death in 1862. He reversed Rodríguez de Francia's policy of isolation and in 1854 began the building of the Central Paraguayan Railway from Asunción to Encarnación. He was followed by his son, Marshal Francisco Solano López, who saw himself as the Napoleon of South America and is today the most venerated of Paraguay's heroes. His Irish mistress Madame Eliza Lynch, who encouraged him in his ambitions, is also held in high esteem. In 1865 he became involved in the war of the Triple Alliance against Brazil, Argentina and Uruguay. His motive was that Uruguay, with whom Paraguay had a treaty of reciprocal help, had been occupied by Brazil and Argentina and forced to oppose Paraguay. The war was disastrous for the Paraguayans, who held out against overwhelming odds until Marshal López was killed at Cerro Corá in 1870, when the war ended. Out of a population of 800,000, only 194,000 were left alive after the war, and of these only 14,000 were male (only 2,100 of whom were over 20); out of 400,000 females at the beginning of the war, 180,000 survived. Paraguay was occupied for eight years during which time it was deprived of all its gold reserves, many national treasures and 156,415 square km. of territory. (Brazil took 62,325 square km., Argentina 94,090 square km.; previously Paraguayan were the Iguazú Falls and the town of Posadas, once called San José del Paraguay.) (For further reading on the origin and aftermath of the War of the Triple Alliance, see *Paraguay: un destino geopolítico*, by Dra Julia Velilla Laconich de Aréllaga; *Genocídio Americano: a Guerra do Paraguai*, by Júlio José Chiavenalto; *Women on Horseback*, by William E Barrett.) After 1870 a certain number of European immigrants arrived; their descendants are still influential in the social life of Paraguay. Various religious communities were among them; the Mennonites, mostly of German descent, who are largely responsible for the development of the Chaco, are the most notable.

The country's history since the "National Epic" of 1865-1870 has been the story of a recovery from disaster, but this process received a severe setback in the wars with Bolivia which broke out intermittently between 1929 and 1935 over the Chaco. The Paraguayans, fighting with their customary courage and tenacity, triumphed, and were given a large area of the Chaco in the final settlement. Bolivia was given an outlet, of little use, to the Paraguay river.

After the Chaco War, Paraguay endured several years of political dictatorship, followed by disorder. This period was ended by the seizure of power in 1954 by General Alfredo Stroessner, soon appointed President. Thereafter he gained the support of the Colorado Party (founded in 1888), which was an integral part of his regime. He held power through repeated reelection until he was deposed in 1989 (surpassing El Supremo's 26-year tenure by 9 years) by General Andrés Rodríguez. On 1 May, 1989, Gen. Rodríguez, also of the Colorado Party, won a presidential election unopposed, and he promised to hand over the presidency to an elected successor in 1993. The apparent commitment to greater democracy permitted opponents, who had previously boycotted, or been banned from elections, to gain an unprecedented number of seats in the legislative elections of the same date.

The People of Paraguay Because the proportion of Spanish blood is smaller than elsewhere, the people of Paraguay today are bilingual, speaking both Spanish and Guaraní. Outside Asunción, most people speak Guaraní by preference. There is a Guaraní theatre, and books and periodicals are published in that tongue, which has official status as the second national language. There are about 39,000 pure-bred Indians left: two-thirds of them are in the Chaco, and one-third in the southern part of Paraguay proper.

Population: 4.04 m (1988 estimate). Annual growth: 3.2%; urban growth: 3.9%; . Life expectancy at birth: 66 years. Infant mortality: 53 per thousand. Some 41% live in towns. Over 47% work on the land, nearly 14% in industry. 25% of all Paraguayans live abroad.

The Economy Paraguay is essentially an agricultural country; farming employs 50% of the labour force, and accounts for 26% of gdp. Agricultural exports earn over 93% of Paraguay's foreign exchange with normally about 80% coming from cotton and soya. Cattle raising and meat exports used to be the principal agricultural activities, but their importance has declined as a result of uncompetitive pricing policies and import restrictions in potential markets. Fluctuations in the value of exports characterize the performance of Paraguay's main commodities, since they are so subject to the weather and world prices. Other major products are timber, tobacco, tung and other industrial oilseeds, essential oils (mainly petit grain) and *quebracho*. Self-sufficiency in wheat has been achieved since 1985, and the country now grows most of its basic food requirements.

Industry has traditionally been dependent upon agriculture: for instance, cotton ginning, sugar milling, textiles, meat packing, timber processing and extraction of *quebracho*, industrial and essential oils. The country industrialized fast in the 1970s and early 1980s, and manufacturing now accounts for 16% of gdp. On the back of hydroelectric development, Paraguay has its own cement industry and a steel plant opened in 1986. Both these, shipbuilding and the distillation of alcohol for fuel and other purposes, are state-owned. 14% of the workforce are employed in manufacturing, 8% in construction.

The massive hydroelectric scheme undertaken by Brazil and Paraguay at Itaipú on the river Paraná is reported to be the largest of its kind in the world. Both the total cost, of about US$15.3bn, and the final capacity, of 12.6m kilowatts, are to be shared equally between the two countries. Paraguay's share already exceeds domestic requirements and the surplus energy is being sold to Brazil now that a high-tension line to São Paulo is in place. Paraguay is cooperating with Argentina on the construction of the Yacyretá-Apipé plant, also on the river Paraná, with capacity of 2.7m kilowatts. A third Argentine-Paraguayan hydroelectric project, Corpus, has been postponed until the turn of the century at the earliest. Paraguay has its own hydroelectric facility at Acaray.

Until 1983, Paraguay managed to offset its current account and trade deficits with capital inflows for Itaipú. Since the completion of civil works, the overall balance of payments has fallen into deficit, with a consequent drain on international reserves. In 1986, the situation was exacerbated by the World Bank and the Inter-American Development Bank refusing to disburse loans until a more realistic exchange rate was adopted.

When General Stroessner was ousted at the beginning of 1989, the new administration moved quickly to introduce economic reforms, including freeing the exchange rate and lifting many controls. This had the effect of dramatically improving registered foreign trade flows; previously about half of all exports and imports were contraband. Dwindling reserves led to restructuring of Paraguay's debt to Brazil, its major creditor, and bilateral deals were expected with others, to spread out maturities on the estimated US$2.6 bn foreign debt.

Government There was a new Constitution in 1967. Executive power rests with the President, elected for five years. There is a two-chamber Congress. Voting is secret and obligatory for all citizens over 18. Uniquely in Latin America, the Constitution permits the immediate reelection of the President.

Communications The only practicable water route is by the Paraná to the Plate estuary, and Buenos Aires is 1,450 km. from Asunción. So difficult is the river that communication with Buenos Aires was mainly by road before the railway to Asunción was opened in 1913. Most freight is now moved to Buenos Aires, or to Santos or Paranaguá in Brazil, by good paved roads, though river barges still ply along the Paraná. For major roads, **see page** 830.

There are more than 600 km. of public railways, and 732 km. of private industrial lines, mostly forest lines of metre gauge or narrower. The standard-gauge railways are the 370 km. from Asunción to Encarnación, the 200 km. from Puerto La Victoria into the Chaco, and 64 km. from Borja (on Asunción-Encarnación line) to Abaí.

N.B. After the fall of President Stroessner, it was understood that all references to his name throughout the country would be removed. Ciudad Presidente Stroessner has been officially renamed Ciudad del Este; the airport, too, has been given a new title, Silvio Pettirossi (named after a pioneer of flying in Paraguay).

ASUNCION (1)

Asunción, the capital and largest city in Paraguay, is built on the shores of a bay cutting into the eastern bank of the Paraguay river, almost opposite its confluence with the Pilcomayo. Its population is 600,000 (excluding suburbs). The city, built on a low hill crowned by the large modern church of La Encarnación, is laid out in the colonial Spanish rectangular manner; many avenues are lined with beautiful trees, including orange, rubber and jacaranda. The central plazas of the city are drenched in colour during July-August with the prolific pink bloom of the *lapacho* trees, which grow everywhere. The oldest part is down by the water's edge, but none of the public buildings is earlier than the last half of the 19th century. Dwelling houses are in a variety of styles; new villas in every kind of taste have replaced the traditional one-storey Spanish-Moorish type of house, except in the poorer quarters.

You see most public buildings by following Calle El Paraguayo Independiente from the Customs House. The first is the Government Palace, built during the Triple Alliance War in the style of the Louvre (easy to walk around and take photographs now). In Plaza Constitución stands the Congressional Palace (debates can be attended during the session from April to December, on Thursdays and Fridays), with the Cathedral at the corner of the square. Two blocks SW, along Calle Chile, is Plaza de los Héroes, with the Pantheon of Heroes, based on the Invalides in Paris, begun during the Triple Alliance War and finished in 1937. It now contains the tombs of Carlos Antonio López, Marshal Francisco Solano López, two unknown Paraguayan soldiers, and Marshal Estigarribia, the victor of the Chaco War in the 1930s. The national cemetery, which resembles a miniature city, with tombs in various architectural styles, is on Av. Mariscal López, 3 km. from the centre.

The best of several parks are Parque Carlos Antonio López, set high and with a grand view (doctor and sports supervisor in attendance); Parque Caballero; and Parque Gaspar Rodríguez de Francia. The Botanical Gardens are 6 km. out, on Av Artigas with Primer Presidente at Trinidad, quickly reached by bus (Nos 2, 6, 23, and 40, US$0.15, about 35 mins; outward they can be caught on Luis A Herrera, or Nos. 24, 35 or 44B from Oliva or Cerro Corá). They lie along the Paraguay river, on the former estate of the López family, and have an enormous range of plants (poorly maintained), an eighteen-hole golf course, and a little zoo (animals kept in appalling conditions). Entrance fee US$0.10, or US$0.60 for 2 persons and a car. The Gardens temporarily housed the Maca Indians when they were moved from their reservation across the river; they were moved again in 1985 to very poor conditions (if you wish to photograph the Indians, bargain with them first). The López residence is in the Gardens; a typical Paraguayan country house with verandahs, which has become a natural history museum and library. The beautiful white church of Santísima Trinidad (on Santísimo Sacramento, parallel to Av Artigas), where Carlos Antonio López was originally buried, dating from 1856 with paintings inside, is well worth a visit.

N.B. Plaza Constitución is often referred to as Plaza de la Independencia; it should also be noted that Plaza de los Héroes is called Plaza Independencia on some sources. Av España

ASUNCIÓN

originally extended as far out as Av San Martín, but the section between Av Kubitschek and Av Santísimo Sacramento was renamed Av Generalísimo Franco (not to be confused with Presidente Franco) and the remaining section between Av SS Sacramento and Av San Martín was renamed Av General Genes. Many people still use the name Av España for the whole of its original length, ignoring the renamings.

Hotels Hotel prices are given at the financial exchange rate at the time of going to press. Outside Asunción: 12 km. from town, at Itá Enramada, on its own beach on the River Paraguay is *Hotel del Yacht y Golf Club Paraguay*, L, 3 restaurants, super luxury, with pool, gym, golf, tennis, airport transfers, etc.; many extras free. The *Hotel y Casino Itá Enramada*, 7 km. S of Asunción, A/B, with breakfast (rec.), free bus link with town, 7-hectare park, swimming pools, sauna, tennis, mini-golf, water-skiing on river, reservations through KLM, or Hugen Int, Fort Lauderdale, Fla (T 1-800-327-8571), fishing nearby, "Honeymooners get 20% off", T 33041/9.

   In Asunción: *Excelsior*, L/A, Chile 980 between Manduvirá and Piribebuy, telex 5192, T 95632/5, best, new 175-room tower, another under construction, conference facilities, etc.; *Chaco*, Caballero y Mariscal Estigarribia, A, parking one block away (but no garden), rooftop swimming pool, good restaurant, T 92066/9; *Cecilia*, rec., Estados Unidos 341, T 91271/3, A, very smart, good restaurant; *Guaraní*, Oliva e Independencia Nacional, T 91131/139, recently renovated, efficient, courteous, clean, A, good value, reasonable restaurant with good buffet; *Internacional*, Ayolas 520, T 94113, A, new, rec.; *Husa* (a Brazilian chain hotel), 15 de Agosto 420 y Estrella, B, 1st class, all rooms a/c, TV, swimming pool, restaurant, rec. cafeteria, bars, laundry service; *Presidente*, Azara 128, B, with breakfast and a/c, restaurant, has seen better days; *Gran del Paraguay*, C, Residente y Padre Pucheu, out of town, in a park, with swimming pool and a night club on Fridays, was the palace in which López lived; the recommended restaurant with floral murals, was the private theatre of Eliza Lynch; an air-conditioned annex has been built in the gardens, breakfast. *Touring 25*, 25 de Mayo 1091, C, small, modern, includes breakfast. *Amalfi*, D, Caballero 877, comfortable, modern; *Paraná*, Caballero y 25 de Mayo, D with breakfast, central, secure, discounts negotiable, short-stays catered for too; *Córdoba*, Oliva 1275, D with bath, friendly, clean, 1 km. from centre (take taxi); *Sahara*, Oliva 920 nr. Montevideo, C with breakfast, a/c, good, small pool, interesting garden; *Gran Renacimento*, Chile 388 y Estrella, central, B, a/c, friendly service, but poor value with poor breakfast in room; *Señorial*, colonial style (Mcal. López 475 y Perú), C, with breakfast, a/c, swimming pool, parking, strongly rec.; *Azara*, Azara 850 (T 49754), E with bath and a/c, less with fan, recommended by Auto Club and travellers, most rooms face a shady patio and pool

   Residencial Ideal, Azara 1549, E (F without breakfast), clean, quiet, very friendly; opposite is *Daniel*, F with bath and fan; *Española*, Herrera y Yegros, F, laundry, with meals, friendly; *Ambassador*, Montevideo 111, F, with bath, very old (rooms overlooking the Palacio del Gobierno must close their windows during working hours – fear of snipers – makes rooms very hot); *Lord*, Tacuary 576, E with bath (electric showers), meagre breakfast, Korean owner, going downhill and noisy; *Hispania*, Cerro Corá, F, Korean-run, watch bill carefully, friendly, recently refurbished, front rooms noisy; *Stella d'Italia*, Cerro Corá 945, F without bath (popular with Peace Corps volunteers), parking; *Lago Ypoa*, Azara 1161, small, rec., F, used by Peace Corps volunteers, as is *El Lapacho*, Kubitschek, near Mcal. López; *Oasis*, Azara 736, F without breakfast, friendly, Korean owned; *Ñandutí*, Presidente Franco 551, D with bath and breakfast, clean, comfortable, friendly; *Residencia* (also Restaurant) *Japón de Kikoyo Uchiyamada*, Constitución 763 (T 22038), E, management prefers Orientals, good meals; *Cardel*, Ygurey 1145 esq Av Dr. Eusebio Ayala, modern, clean, quiet, D, near Pettirossi market, excellent breakfast; *Casa Menonita*, República de Colombia 1050, E, friendly, German spoken, plain food (bus stop here for Filadelfia). Specially for German-speaking travellers: *Pensión Alemana Castillo*, Cruz del Chaco 925-959, E, German-owned, clean and friendly, T 650356; *Ayuda Social Germano-Paraguaya* (hospice attached), Av España 202, near railway station, E, including breakfast, central, clean, most rooms a/c, nearly always full, friendly, T 49485; also *Deutsche Pensión*, E, Milano 222, T 43217, clean, friendly,

---

Asunción: Key to Map

1. Government Palace; 2. Congressional Palace; 3. Customs; 4. Cathedral; 5. Encarnación Church; 6. San Roque Church; 7. Pantheon of the Heroes; 8. Casa de la Independencia Museum; 9. Nacional Archive and Museum of Fine Arts; 10. Railway station; 11. Tourist Office; 12. Post Office; 13. Centro Paraguayo del Diagnóstico; 14. British Embassy; 15. Lloyds Bank; 16. Citibank; 17. Finamérica; 18. American Express; 19. Deutsche Bank; 20. Casas de cambio; 21. Compañía Marítima; 22. Police Station; 23. Hotel Chaco; 24. Hotel Guaraní 25. Hotel Husa; 26. Hotel Plaza; 27. Hotel Presidente; 28. Hotel Lord.

owner's name Federau. *Hospedaje El Viajero*, Antequera 451, noisy, clean and friendly, F. *América*, Montevideo 160, F, clean, fans, mosquito nets, rec.; *Ipiranga*, Av México 489 with Cerro Corá, F, with bath and breakfast, friendly, clean; *Miami*, México 449, T 444950, E, clean; *Residencial Rufi*, Cerro Corá, near Antequera, F, no breakfast, friendly, clean, helpful; *Rosa*, 25 de Mayo 350, F with bath, not too clean, rec. although used for short stay, good book exchange; *Hosp Hollywood*, Azara 722, F, central, clean, very friendly, good basic restaurant; *Margarita*, Paraguarí y Azara, F without bath and breakfast, more with bath, clean, good, basic. Unnamed *pensión* at Tacuary 348, near Plaza Uruguaya, cheap, washing facilities, use of kitchen. *Residencial Nuevo Horizonte*, Calle Eligio Ayala, F with breakfast, clean, comfortable; *Hotel Residencial Cadi*, Piribebuy 150 (T 96901), also F, rec.; *Residencial Milagros*, Nuestra Señora 1053, E with breakfast and bath, business travellers from neighbouring countries, good food opposite at *Bar Chaconí*; *Residencial Itapúa*, E, Calle Fulgencio R Moreno 943, quiet, comfortable, decent breakfasts, lunch available. Two hotels at the railway station, one is *Plaza*, simple but acceptable, E, the other is not good. *Residencial Familiar*, Eligio Ayala 843 near railway station, F, without breakfast, friendly, clean, will do washing. *Hospedaje El Sol*, Lapacho 185 (2 mins from bus station), Korean-run, E, good, but rooms very small; *Hospedaje San Pablo*, nr. bus terminal, F with bath, noisy rooms on courtyard. There are two motels, *San Martín*, Av San Martín 889, F, and *La Cuesta*, Bogado y Cacique Lambaré, E. Family *pensiones* are expensive, in the D range.

The hotel bill does not usually contain a service charge. It pays to tip when you arrive as well as when you go, say US$1 to the table waiter at both ends of a week's visit. A tip of 10% is enough for non-residents, at hotels and in restaurants. Many hotels have electric showers.

Camping The pleasant site at the Botanical Gardens now charges a fee, US$1.20 per car plus US$0.30 per person, US$0.60 p.p. plus tent, cold showers and 220v electricity. If camping, take plenty of insect repellant and beware large (but harmless) toads. You can camp at rear of *Restaurant Westfalia*, T 31772, owner speaks English, French, German, very knowledgable, 5 km. out on Itá Enramada road, US$1 per night for car, cold showers, noisy, animals.

Restaurants Most closed Sunday. Average price of a good meal in quality restaurants, US$9-15. *La Preferida*, Estados Unidos and 25 de Mayo 1005 T 91126, rec. (part of *Hotel Cecilia*); *Talleyrand*, French, reported best in town, Estigarribia 932, T 41163; *La Pergola del Bolsi*, Estrella 389, good, wide choice of wines; under same ownership, *La Pergola Jardín*, Perú 240, good food and service. *Le Grand Café*, Oliva 476, French-owned, good value set lunch. You can get a fantastic view of the city from the *Panorámico*, 14 de Mayo 150, 13th floor, expensive, but good; *Hermitage*, 15 de Agosto 1360, food is good, mostly international, as is the music, moderately expensive, cover charge; *Munich*, Eligio Ayala 163, good German food, excellent value; *Hostería del Caballito Blanco*, Alberti 631, Austrian-run, good food and service; *Trevi*, on Palma, excellent; *Deutscher Ecte*, near the university, good value, German food; *San Roque*, Eligio Ayala esq Tacuary, traditional and German, rec.; *Germania* in Cerro Corá, rec., reasonable prices; *Bayern-Stuben*, Av Sucre 2689, excellent German (Bavarian); *Westfalia*, Bavarian style, see above under **Camping**.

La Taberna, Franco, excellent, Spanish; *Chalet Suizo*, Av Kubitschek 975 (Ethiopian Goulash rec.). *Mastropiero* has 130 types of pizza at Av España 1372 (T 60160); another Italian restaurant is *La Bettola*, rec. at C del Maestro 1698, off the Av San Martín; *La Piccola Góndola* is very good for Italian (and other) food, so is *Buon Appetito*, 25 de Mayo near Av Mariscal López y Juan Motta. *El Encuentro*, Azara 548, entre México y Paraguarí, good food, value and service. Good cheap lunches (try puchero) at *Copetín El Oro*, Benjamin Constant 473, behind central post office.

Da Vinci, Estrella 695, disco upstairs, rec.; *Asunción*, Estrella y 14 de Mayo (opp Deutsche Bank), bar and restaurant very good, service a bit slow; *Pizzería Cábala* Estrella 602 y 15 de Agosto, good cakes too; *Pizzería Vecchio*, San Martín 535 y Bertoni, T 601053, good; *Antica Trattoria Alpina*, Sucre 1645 y San Martín, T 601254, English and Italian spoken. Plenty of good, cheap places on Colón, south of Estrella. *Castel Blanc*, on Pacheco, T 66079, very good; *Bistro*, part of *Hotel Husa* at 15 de Agosto y Estrella, good and reasonable; *Lucho*, Estados Unidos y Cerro Corá, good local food, cheap. *Rincón Chileno*, Estados Unidos 314, friendly, excellent empanadas; *Bar de la Estacíon*, at railway station, Eligio Ayala 587, cheap, friendly, popular locally; *Tío Toms*, quiche and pizza, Av Perú y Estigarribia; *El Molino*, Calle España near Brasil, good service and food (particularly steaks); nearby is *Casa Nostra*, good pizza. *American Fried Chicken*, on Plaza de los Héroes (open Sunday). *Subito*, 500 block of Palma, a/c, rec. for empanadas. For good roast chicken try *Nick's Restaurant*, on Azara near Iturbe (open Sunday). *Don Vitos* is well known for empanadas, San José 585.

There are many good oriental restaurants including: *Green*, Dr. Franco 150 e Yegros, very good Chinese; *Gran Oriente*, Brasil nr. Luis Herrera; *Celestial* (ex *Taiwan*), Herrera 919, highly rec.; *Sinorama*, Av Próceres 265; *Chino Embajador*, Ed V Haedo 668; *Hoy*, Azara 830; *Noodle House Pynong-Ynong*, Perú y Francia, excellent; *Suki Yaki*, Constitución 763 y Pettirossi, authentic Japanese; *Hiroshima*, also authentic, on Chóferes del Chaco; and others. Plenty of Korean places around Perú y Francia.

Vegetarian restaurant on Díaz, nr. Montevideo; *Restaurant 2000*, Colón, good vegetarian food, Brazilian run; *Krunch*, Estrella 716, vegetarian lunches; *Superpán*, 25 de Mayo 845, "pan integral" and good sweets. *Wagner*, Presidente Franco 828 y Ayolas, excellent bread and sweet shop; good icecreams next door. Excellent fast food at *Bar Lido*, Plaza de los Héroes, corner Palma y Chile. Various ice cream parlours and fast food outlets are to be found in Av Brasilia, near Av España e.g. *Heladería París*, Brasilia y Siria, is very popular. The *Liverpool Bar*, Pte Franco 590, and the *Taurina*, at No 583 are reasonable bars; *Bar Victoria*, corner of Chile and main Plaza, has good food.

Paraguayan harp music, bottle dancing, good food and service at *Jardín de la Cerveza*, Av República Argentina y Castillo, US$10, strongly rec. (but sometimes they ask extra money for the music), and *Yguazú*, Chóferes del Chaco 1334 (San Lorenzo) US$30 for two, good meat, both some distance from centre. About 20 mins out of town on bus route 26 or 27 is the *Ñandutí Parrillada* (T 24643), an open-air restaurant with good atmosphere, highly rec., on Av Eusebio Ayala y Bartolomé de las Casas. Good Paraguayan harp/guitar group at *Churrasquería Sajón*, Av Carlos A López, bus 26 from centre, and *Yaci Morotí* bar on Humaitá, near Chile, at weekends. A rec. typical restaurant is *La Paraguayita*, Brasilia y Siria.

Shopping Calle Colón, starting at the port, is lined with good tourist shops, and so are Calles Pettirossi, Palma and Estrella. *Casa Arnoldo*, Calle Palma 640, is worth a try for hand-embroidered blouse lengths. *Catedral*, at Eligio Ayala e Yegros, manufactures shirts or dresses in 3 days. *La Asunceña*, Palma 766, leatherware; *Galería Colón*, good for leather, near port; *Boutique Yrene*, Montevideo y Oliva, also rec. for leather goods. Calle Franco for handmade furniture. For wooden articles and carvings go to *Artes de Madera* at Ayolas (222), Palma y Pte Franco. Also *Artesanía Raity* at Pai Pérez 778, woodcraft, prints and paintings, rec.; *Arte Popular*, 25 de Mayo 1138 and *Casa Vera* at Estigarribia 470 for Paraguayan leatherwork, cheap and very good. Other recommended shops, *Artesanía Kuarajhy*, Pte Franco 663; *Casa Overall*, Mcal. Estigarribia, nr. Plaza Uruguaya, good selection. On Rioja near the main park for all local handicrafts and imported items (4 floors). *Pistilli* has a fine selection of canework and furniture, Estados Unidos esq Azara. Check the quality of all handicrafts carefully, lower prices usually mean lower quality. A small but excellent fruit and vegetable market is to be found at San José behind the España supermarket. The markets are worth a visit, especially the Pettirossi (food and ordinary clothes). There is a daily market on Av Dr. GR de Francia, and a Saturday one on Plaza de la Independencia, where the nuns from Villeta sell their hand-made clothing for children. Supermarkets are usually well stocked, especially with imported liquor. Outside Asunción, visit Luque (musical instruments and jewellery – **see page 831**) and Itauguá (lace) – **see page 834**. Cameras can be bought cheaply in Paraguay; the selection of all types of consumer goods is better in Ciudad del Este.

Bookshops *Librería Internacional*, Oliva y Alberdi, Estrella 723 y Juan O'Leary and Palma 595 y 15 de Agosto, good for maps; also "*Books*" at Mcal. López 3971, at Villa Morra shopping centre, also carries English stock (at 3-4 times UK prices); magazine/newspaper kiosk *El Lector* on Plaza Uruguaya and 25 de Mayo has a selection of foreign material. *Librería Alemana*, Av Luis A de Herrera 292, warmly rec. Booshop at Gral. Díaz 350 exchanges English books.

Taxis Minimum fare in Asunción is US$0.40 plus US$0.10 for every 100 metres. The average journey costs about US$2. (Check if there is an extra charge for luggage, and that the meter has not been speeded up). Hire by the hour; about US$4. Tip 10%.

Trams (Streetcars) One line, the No 5, still runs through the centre, along Calles Palma (one way) and Estrella (the other).

City Buses The system is extensive, running from 0600-2400; buses stop at signs before every street corner. Journeys within city, US$0.25, including from the centre to the new bus terminal, e.g. No 8 (not much fun with bulky luggage). Keep your ticket for inspection until you leave bus.

Night Clubs and Discotheques *Kaktus*, Teniente Vera y San Martín; *Musak*, Bertoni y José Ocampos; *J y C*, Boggiani y O'Higgins; *Fantasio*, Av Bogado and Felicidad, in front of Radio Primero de Marzo; *Piper's*, in the centre, good disco, drinks not expensive, popular;

Torremolinos, Costa Azul Urbanización, 2001; and one in the *Hotel Casino Itá Enramada* (open every day in summer, Saturdays in winter).

Municipal Theatre, Pte Franco, nr. Alberdi, has an extensive winter programme of concerts and ballets (entry US$4). Cinema programmes are given in the press; some offer 3 films at one price (US$1). Art gallery and dance studio (Taller de Movimiento Creativo), 15 de Agosto 530, English-speaking owner. Concerts are given at the Teatro de las Américas, J Bergés 297.

Museums National Museum of Fine Arts (closed for an extended period). Asunción Seminary Museum has some "mission" art. At the Museum of Fine Arts (in Archivo Nacional building, Calle Palma W of Plaza Uruguaya), the paintings are very badly displayed; it has a Murillo and a Tintoretto and collections of Acevedo (about 1910) caricatures. In the Botanical Gardens are the Museo de Historia Natural and the Museo Etnográfico, both open Mon.-Sat. 0730-1130, 1300-1700, Sun. 0600-1200, 1300-1700, neither in good condition. In the Casa de la Independencia (14 de Mayo y Presidente Franco) is an interesting historical collection; entry free. Pantéon Nacional de los Héroes, esq Palma y Chile, open every day. Historical and military museum at Ministry of Defence, Mariscal López esq Gen. Santos. Museo Dr. Andrés Barbero, 200 block of España (near Estados Unidos), open Mon.-Fri., 0800-1100, anthropological, free, good. Most museums are small and basic.

Exchange Lloyds Bank, Palma y O'Leary (and six agencies in Greater Asunción – will give US dollars); Finamérica (ex-Bank of America), Oliva esq Chile; Citibank, Estrella y Chile (will change Citibank travellers' cheques into dollars cash for a small commission); Banco Corporación (ex-Chase), VE Haedo e Independencia Nacional; Banco General (ex-Boston), Chile y Haedo (will give US dollars); Bank of Commerce and Industry, Caballero esq Eligio Ayala, also gives dollars; Interbank, 14 de Mayo 339; Deutsche Bank, Estrella y 14 de Mayo (charges 2% commission on money sent from W Germany – very fast service, 2 days – paid by cheque which can be cashed into dollars at Cambio Guaraní for small commission); Banco Sudameris (ex-Francés e Italiano), Oliva e Independencia Nacional. Banco Holandés Unido, Independencia Nacional y VE Haedo. Also Argentine, Brazilian and local banks. Banco Unión branch at Estrella y Alberdi (and throughout the country) will give quick cash advances on guaraníes on Visa or Mastercard in about 15 minutes, English spoken, friendly, only between 0800-1100.

Several *casas de cambio* on Palma (open Mon.-Fri. 0730-1200, 1500-1830, Sat., 0730-1200; rates for neighbouring countries' currencies usually good, except bolivianos), Deutsche Marks can be changed at good rates, and all rates are better than at the various frontiers. Be careful to count money received from street exchange-sellers (Palma and surrounding area – their rates are less good when banks and *cambios* are closed). *Casas de cambio* do not like changing sterling travellers' cheques, the only one that will do it is Cambio Paraná on Palma. Some will change one type of dollar travellers' cheque. Cambio Guaraní, Palma 449, between 14 de Mayo and Alberdi, T 90032/6, is good, will change dollar cheques into dollars cash, but charges 2% commission for this. German spoken at Cambios Menno Tour, Azara 532. Cambios Yguazú (Palma) is OK. (Thomas Cook, but can't deal with stolen cheques). See **Currency** section in Information for Visitors.

Embassies and Consulates Brazilian Consulate, in Banco do Brasil building on main square (open 0800-1200, Mon.-Fri.), Nuestra Señora de la Asunción y Oliva (may charge US$10 for visa); **Argentine Consulate**, in Banco de la Nación Asunción, also on main square, open 0700-1100, visas processed in 1-2 hours, photograph needed (will only give transit visas unless you can prove, with a letter from your consulate, that you are a bona fide tourist). **Chile**, Guido Spano 1740, T 660344; **Bolivian Consulate**, Eligio Ayala 2002, T 22662; **Peruvian Consulate**, Estrella 451, piso 3, T 41741; **Uruguay**, Av Brasil y Siria, T 44242 (visas processed immediately if exit ticket from Uruguay, overland travel to Uruguay and onward country visas can be shown); **Mexico**, Edif Ytá Ybate, esq Cerro Corá y Juan O'Leary.

US Embassy and Consulate, Av Mcal. López esq Kubitschek, T 201041.

Great Britain, Presidente Franco 706, esquina O'Leary, 4th floor (Casilla 404), T 49146; **Switzerland**, O'Leary 409 esq Estrella, T 48022; Spain, Calle 25 de Mayo 175, esq Yegros; **Swedish Consulate**, Bogado 1039-47, T 205561/9; **Dutch Consulate**, Franco y 15 de Agosto; **Austrian Consulate**, Nuestra Señora de la Asunción 764, T 25567. **W German**, José Bergés 1003-1007; **France**, Av España 676, T 23111; **Israel**, Ed Líder, piso 3, O'Leary y Gen. Díaz; **South Africa**; Banco Sudameris, piso 4, esq Cerro Corá e Independencia Nacional.

Cultural Institutions The US-Paraguay cultural centre has a good library at España 352 (open Mon.-Fri. 0900-2000, Sat. 0900-1200, also has snack bar); Peace Corps, address from US embassy. Instituto Anglo-Paraguayo, España 457, where you can acquire much useful

ASUNCIÓN SURROUNDINGS
NOT TO SCALE   93A To Encarnación

information and read English newspapers. Goethe Institut behind Goethe school, small library with a few newspapers, open 1600-2000. Alianza Francesa, Mcal. Estigarribia 1039, T 210382.

General Post Office Alberdi, Benjamín Constant y El Paraguayo Independiente. T 48891, 0700-2000, but closed for lunch. Also philatelic museum, open 0700-1800, Mon.-Fri.; 0700-1200, Sat. Post boxes throughout the city carry address of the nearest place one can purchase stamps. Register all important mail; you must go to main PO for this. *Poste Restante* charges about US$0.10 per item collected. There are sub-offices at the railway station and at the docks.

Telephone Antelco, E. Ayala, nr. Cathedral, for international calls; also Manuel Domínguez y Gral. Bruguez, both 24 hrs.

Non-Catholic Churches Anglican Church: St Andrew, on España with Uruguay; Synagogue at Gen. Díaz 657.

Police, T 46105.

Laundry Lavamático, Yegros 808 y Fulgencio Moreno. Lava Pronto, Azara 850, T 45147, good, quick service. Lavafácil, México y Moreno, good, cheap, fast.

Photographic Repairs: Panatronic, Benjamín Constant 516. Rodolfo Loewen, Camera Service, Blas Garay y Morelo, T 23807. Slide film costs US$3, print film US$2.50 (35 mm.). Good place for buying cameras, *Casa Fanny*, Mcal. Estigarribia 144.

Travel Agencies (all very helpful) *Inter-Express* (Amex), Yegros 690; *Maral* on 25 de Julio y Caballero; *Continental*, Benjamín Constant 777. *American Tours*, Independencia Nacional, under *Hotel Guaraní*, both German and English spoken. *Grupo Cataldi*, Estrella 876, T 90458, can occasionally pick up at airport; real estate agents (German run) with good contact in hotels and apartment accommodation. *Menno Tour*, Azara 532, is also staffed by Germans and will book buses to Foz etc. To hire a car and driver from an agency costs US$32 p.p.

Tourist Office 2nd floor, building on 25 de Mayo between Alberdi y 14 de Mayo (maybe temporary). Open Mon.-Fri. 0700-1200, 1500-1800. T 45306, 49521, 47865. Helpful, free map, also one available for sale in bookshops. There is a display of lace and handicrafts.

Airport Silvio Pettirossi, 15 km. NE of centre. There is a desk where you can book a taxi to your hotel, US$5. Bus 30A to the centre (Calle Oliva-Cerro Corá) (US$1.14) stops every 15 minutes just outside the airport perimeter at the road fork, 300 metres from the main entrance. Ask to be set down at road fork. (Do not walk on the grass outside the airport or the police will fine you). Buses 30 and 18 to the bus terminal. Buses only recommende outside rush-hours, with light luggage. Líneas Aéreas Paraguayas (LAP) has its own colectivo, which collects from hotels, US$3.10 p.p., as does TAM. Enquire at airline offices. LAP office at Oliva 467; Eastern at Independencia Nacional y Azara.

A new airport terminal has been built (duty free facilities, small *casa de cambio* – turn left as you leave customs and immigration, but rates poor – handicraft shop and restaurant), 1 km. from the old building. There is a helpful tourist office on the ground floor at the airport; they will book for the Varig flights to Foz do Iguaçú, as well as arranging transport into town (minibus arrives and leaves from Iberia Office), finding accommodation and changing money at poor rates.

Rail Presidente Carlos Antonio López Railway to Encarnación and Buenos Aires (1,510 km.) journey of 44 hours, Tues. (better to take bus to Encarnación and catch train in Posadas). To Encarnación: with wood-burning steam locomotive, Tues. and Fri. 1800, at least 14 hrs. (first 12 hrs. in the dark), US$3, 1st class (rec.—no sleeper), US$1.90 2nd class; tickets on sale 2 hrs. before departure (Tues. train has through coach to Buenos Aires). Good hot food can be ordered for US$1.50, drinks US$0.30. In dry weather dust, and in wet weather rain, gets into 2nd-class carriages. Track liable to flooding. (Trains may be cancelled on public holidays, such as Christmas.) See under Excursions for a trip to see the woodburning locomotives. At the station is a steam engine called *Sapucai*, built in 1861. The platform is too short for trains, which block Calle Bogado when loading.

River Boats To Concepción (26 hrs.) with Flota Mercantil del Estado (FME), Estrella 672-682 (tickets from here only). Weekly (every Tues., 0800—returns on Sun. 1200), US$14 1st class, US$10 2nd class (4 beds to a cabin, men and women not segregated, comfortable, but 2nd class food is not recommended – take food with you), US$7 3rd class (wooden benches on upper deck, bring hammock and mosquito repellant). Restaurant on board; said to be good. Boats are modern, elegant and comfortable. Other boat lines work this route, but they are less comfortable, although cheaper, with no regular sailings; enquire at the small boat dock to the right of the main dock; you will have to take your own food. Ferries sail thrice weekly to Balletín one day's journey N of Concepción, 2 day's journey in all (seats and cabins).

When conditions permit FME sails to **Corumbá, Brazil**, on Friday at 0800, arriving Tuesday 1200, 2nd class costs US$37, 3rd class US$27. When the boat does not go to Corumbá, it stops at Bahía Negra, close to the frontier. **See also page 833**.

Ferry to Puerto Pilcomayo (Argentina) about every 20 minutes (US$0.50, 5 mins) from Itá Enramada (Paraguayan immigration), take bus 9 from Asunción (Argentine immigration closed at weekends for tourists). Compañía Marítima Paraguaya SA, Presidente Franco 199 esq 15 de Agosto, for all shipping enquiries.

Roads There is a 32 km. road NW to Villa Hayes (bridge) and on through the Chaco (Route 9) to Filadelfia (paved to here) and Bolivia, 805 km. (an account of a direct journey from Bolivia by this road will be found on **page 840**. Route 8 is now paved N from Coronel Oviedo, 100 km. to San Estanislao (see also under Coronel Oviedo, page 835), where it becomes successively Routes 3 and 5 (being paved for about 100 km.) and runs 305 km. N and then NE, to Pedro Juan Caballero on the Brazilian frontier. Also paved are the long-distance Route 1 to Encarnación (372 km.), and Route 2 to Coronel Oviedo, which leads to Route 7 to Ciudad del Este (formerly Ciudad Presidente Stroessner) and the Iguazú falls (362 km.). A round trip Asunción-Ciudad del Este-Encarnación-Asunción is easily done. The roads are described in the text.

Buses All buses leave from the bus terminal, out of town at República Argentina esq Fernando de la Mora. Take local bus numbers 8, 10, 25, 31, 38, on Oliva, Haedo, or Cerro Corá in the centre for Terminal Nuevo; from the terminal to the city, get off the bus at the corner of General Díaz and Chile. The terminal has tourist information desk (reported unfriendly), restaurant (quite good), café, shops, and lots of noisy televisions. Hotels nearby: turn left from front of terminal, 2 mins' walk. Taxi from down town, rec. if you have luggage, US$2 p.p. or US$4 per taxi. Many bus companies still maintain ticket offices around Plaza Uruguaya.

To Ciudad del Este, about 20 buses a day, 3-7 hrs., most with toilet, with the following companies: Sirena del Paraná, Rápido Caaguazú, Nuestra Señora de la Asunción and Rysa

(Rápido Yguazú, has an office on Plaza Uruguay, Ayala y Antequera), US$4.25 (last 2 the best). Nuestra Señora and Rysa, with the Brazilian companies Pluma and Unesul, continue to Foz do Iguaçu (Paraguayan buses all advertise that they go to Foz, but very few do—check); all luxury bus fares to Foz are US$5, 5-7 hrs., six direct buses a day in all. Seat reservations recommended; take the 0100 bus (easy to sleep), which arrives at Foz at 0700 if you want to visit the Brazilian side of the Iguaçu Falls in one day; take 1200 bus from Falls to bus station, then 1430 bus back to Asunción – remember to buy new cruzeiros in Asunción.

Bus to Encarnación (for Posadas in Argentina), many, 5 hrs., Alborada SRL, Rápido Yguazú, Flecha del Oro (7 a day); Nuestra Señora de la Asunción, and La Encarnaceña, rec., US$4. To Villarrica, La Guaireña, US$1.50, La Yuteña, US$0.85. To Concepción, US$4.50, 10 hrs., La Encarnaceña (0100), San Jorge (1950, 2400),US$5; San Jorge runs to Guaíra for US$3.70, and to Pedro Juan Caballero for US$5-12 (direct, La Santana), or US$4 (Amambay also to PJ Caballero). Bus to Filadelfia, Nasa, Colombia 1050, T 26059 daily at 1400 (stopping at the main bus terminal at 1430), 8-10 hrs., US$6.50. San Bernardino, US$ 0.45; Itauguá, US$0– dry season only – .30; Yaguarón US$0.45; Caapucú (on Encarnación road), US$0.50.

To Uruguay and Brazil   COT runs to Montevideo, 0800, Sat. and Wed., 20 hrs., US$30 Brújula runs other days (the route is Clorinda, Resistencia, Reconquista, Santa Fe, Paraná, Colón, Paysandú). To Curitiba, US$24 with Pluma, buses daily, 17 hrs.; to São Paulo, Rápido Yguazú, Pluma and Brújula, US$24 (*leito*, US$48). Pluma to Rio de Janeiro, US$30. Unesul run to Porto Alegre on Thurs. and Sun., Nacional Expresso to Brasília 3 times a week.

To Argentina   There is a 10 km. road N from Asunción (passing the Botanical Gardens on Primer Presidente) to a concrete arch span bridge (Puente Remanso – US$1 toll) which leads to the border at Puerto Falcón and then to Clorinda in Argentina. The border is open 24 hours a day; last bus from Falcón to the centre of Asunción at 1830. The colectivo fare from Asunción to the border (at Falcón) is US$0.80; from Falcón to Clorinda costs US$0.25. There is a good bus service to Resistencia and Buenos Aires from the Argentine side, by Empresa Godoy.

Buses Asunción-Buenos Aires (20 hrs.) daily with La Encarnaceña (0900), Nuestra Señora de la Asunción (0830, 1330, US$38), Rysa (US$35), Godoy (US$53), via Rosario and Santa Fe, also with Brújula and La Internacional, each 6 times a week. To Resistencia (US$8) and Formosa (US$6), 3 a day, Brújula and Godoy; Brújula and Cacorba to Córdoba, each twice weekly.

Excursions   At Barrio San José Obrero (follow the river bank north) is the local brick works with about 20 kilns. Everything is still done by man and horse power. From the FME dock a ferry leaves Sat. and Sun. across to the Rowing Club, many facilities, welcoming people. To **Villeta** (27 km., 5,232 people), on the E bank, which has undergone a rapid economic expansion; it is well known for good river-fish restaurants and for the fine children's clothing hand-made by nuns at a local convent. A little North is a park at Ytororó where trenches used in the war of the Triple Alliance can still be seen. The town of **Luque** (population, 24,917), close to Asunción, is famous for the making of Paraguayan harps, difficult to find though (Guitares Sanabria is one of the best-known firms, Km. 13, T 023-2291), and for fine filigree work in silver and gold (ask around for Alberto Núñez). There are also many fine musical instrument shops on the road to Luque; get off the bus – No 30 – from Asunción just before the major roundabout. Marshal López' house may be visited. 8 km. from Luque is Balneario Yukyry, with an artesian well, springs, swimming pools, football pitches and a snackbar; for details and reservations, T 23731 (closed in winter, but pleasant trip anyway).

Parque Nacional **Ybicuy** is reached by bus two to three times daily US$1.85, 4 hours. Good walks, a beautiful camp site (hardly used in the week, no lighting, some facilities may not be available) and lots of waterfalls; it is one of the few areas of protected forest in the country. At the entrance is a well-set out park and museum as well as the reconstructed remains of the country's first iron foundry (La Rosada). The only shops (apart from a small one at the entrance selling drinks, eggs, etc.) are at Ybicuy, 30 km. away (*Hotel Pytu'u Renda*, E/F, good food, clean, cooking facilities, friendly; *Pensión Santa Rosa* and *San Juan*, both F). Bus from Ybicuy at 0430 and 1120, returning 0700 and 1345, goes as far as camp site, 2 km. beyond the museum. Crowded on Sundays but deserted the rest of the week.

The most popular trip is east to Itauguá, and San Bernardino and Aregua on Lake Ypacaraí (**see page 834**).

A short steam train trip to Aregua leaving Asunción station at 1200 daily, takes 1 hrs., US$0.15. The engine burns exotic tropical hardwoods; Ian and Carol Martin of Falmouth, tell us that this is the only train they know of where passengers lower the windows, to sample the aromatic smoke (but watch out for cinders). Bus for return trip via Itauguá, or take a boat frp, Aregua to San Bernardino and then return: a good outing. For a longer look at the countryside, hire a car with driver for US$12 from any travel agent (pick-up at your hotel –

cheaper with private drivers) to drive the "Circuito Central" also called "Circuito de Oro": Asunción – San Lorenzo – Itá – Yaguarón – Paraguarí – Chololó – Piraretá – Piribebuy – Caacupé – San Bernardino – Ypacaraí – Itauguá – Aregua – Capiatá – Asunción. Some 200 km. on paved roads, 7 hrs. Lions, at Alberdi 454, 1, T 90.278, run a full service of trips. Beware of the Argentine Hugo, otherwise OK. Alternatively, from San Lorenzo, take Route 1 towards Encarnación and at Km. 28 (LP Petrol station) turn right to Guarambaré, a sleepy town in the sugar area with many Peace Corps trainees. From May to November bullock carts and trucks take the cane to the factory, 1 km. past the electricity sub-station. After your visit continue to Guarambaré (bus Asunción-Guarambaré, 45 mins, US$0.15, every 10 mins from terminal). Take the second dirt road on the right after the Plaza and for about 10 km. continue through typical farmlands and citrus orchards. The road then continues through Ypané, Nemby and back to Asunción via Lambaré. In Lambaré, near the *Itá Enramada Hotel*, is Lambaré hill with very good views.

A 3-hour colectivo ride from Asunción is Sapucay, 88 km. away, where the main workshops for the wood-burning steam locomotives are located. There are cheap *hospedajes* in Sapucay; either stay there, or take the Asunción-Encarnación train which passes through Tues. and Fri. at 2130.

NORTH FROM ASUNCION (2)

A boat trip up the Paraguay to Concepción, about 312 km. N of Asunción, is one of the easiest ways of seeing more of the country. The winding river is 400 metres wide, with a lot of traffic, for in the absence of a direct road between Concepción and Asunción (though there are roads via the Chaco and by Coronel Oviedo) this is the main trade route for the products of northern Paraguay: cattle, hides, *yerba mate*, tobacco, timber and *quebracho*. Nevertheless, for passengers there is a weekly boat, but not all year round.

Concepción (22,866 inhabitants), a free port for Brazil, lies on the E bank. This pleasant, friendly, quiet and picturesque town is the trade centre of the N, doing a considerable business with Brazil. There is an interesting market. A new bridge across the Río Paraguay is now open.

Hotels *Victoria*, Franco y Caballero, E without breakfast, cheap and clean, private bath with hot water, rec., has new annex; on same street, *Center*, F with breakfast, and *Concepción*, F with bath and breakfast. *Francés*, Presidente Franco 1016, E with bath and a/c, F bath and fan, cheaper without bath, no breakfast, restaurant, recently renovated, clean and friendly. *Paraguay*, F, restaurant excellent, good food at low prices. Also F, *Boquerón*, dirty, noisy, mean. *Cosmos* (clean, fan, breakfast included) and *Bar Estrella del Norte* (near port), both F, basic but possible.

Restaurants *Copetín Chino*, A F de Pinedo 1188, fair. *Bar Victoria* under *Hotel Victoria* serves excellent empanadas. *Candilejas*, Mcal. Estigarribia 744, good food and music (Fri. and Sat.). Bread shop at Mcal. Estigarribia 229. Prices may rise rapidly during Brazilian tourist seasons, but at other times can be negotiated downwards.

Exchange Bancopar, Garay y Franco, open a.m.

Consulate Brazilian, Presidente Franco 945, open Mon.-Fri. 0800-1200.

Communications The bus station is on the outskirts: from Pte Franco, with your back to the port, it's 8 blocks up Gral. E. A. Garay (to the left). Arriving in town by bus, get out in town centre, don't wait for bus station. There is a bus from Concepción to Horqueta, 56 km. to the E (1 hrs., US$0.55), a cattle and lumbering town of 10,000 people. There is a dry-season road – frequently closed – from Concepción W across the Chaco, to Pozo Colorado on the Transchaco highway, 146 kms. Efforts are being made to improve the road, parts are now paved but it can take 3 days in the rain to drive. Bird life is spectacular. The Concepción-Pozo Colorado bus normally takes 2 hours, US$2.75, but it is difficult to get onward connections. Once a week the "Camioneta Cristo Rey", a jeep belonging to the Anglican Church, goes across the Transchaco highway. Concepción-Asunción via Chaco takes 9 hours, US$6.50 (departure 0700, 0730, 1300), road impassable with heavy rains; to Coronel Oviedo, bus departs at 0700, 1800 and 1900, bad road, rains often delay departures. Bus to Pedro Juan Caballero, 4 hrs., several, US$2.50.

Air Service Asunción-Concepción flights are operated by LATN, Aeronorte and TAM (which tends to be cheapest). TAM to Asunción daily at 0800, US$14, book as early as possible (only 25 seats), free colectivo from TAM office on main street to airport. On Fridays TAM flies from Asunción and Concepción to Vallemí, Fuerte Olimpo and Bahía Negra, all three villages to N of Concepción on the Río Paraguay. Air services to these places are irregular because runways are sometimes flooded or muddy. From Puerto Casado, 210 km. N of Concepción, a 200 km. railway runs W into the heart of the Chaco (used mainly by Mennonite settlers, and soldiers). There is no direct air connection between Concepción and Pedro Juan Caballero.

NB Unless you already have an exit stamp (obtainable in Asunción or Concepción), you cannot go upriver to Bolivia or Brazil by small boat from Bahía Negra; no-one there is authorized to give you an exit stamp. In any case, very few boats pass these frontiers.

Shipping To Asunción, Weds. 1400, US$14 1st class, US$10 2nd class (no segregation, no locks on doors), US$7 3rd class, 19 hrs., also Sun. 0300 (*Cacique II*), board Sat. 2300. To Balletín, once a week, 24 hrs. To Fuerte Olimpo, Mon. only; contact Agencia Marítima Ramón Velázquez, Presidente Franco 2, near dock. None of these sailings is guaranteed.

You can enter Brazil, as long as you have a Paraguayan exit stamp, by taking a boat from Asunción or Concepción to Isla Margarita, where you can get a ferry to Porto Murtinho, Brazil. (You cannot get a Brazilian entry stamp there: for that you must go to Cáceres, Corumbá or Campo Grande.)

When it is not possible to go by boat to Corumbá, Brazil (i.e. when the river is in flood), FME sails from Asunción to **Bahía Negra**, from where it returns 1 hr. after arrival. Bahía Negra has neither hotel nor bank, but the policeman is very helpful, although he will require you to obtain all entry and exit stamps. Sra. Ferreira will change money, at a poor rate. It is possible to hire a small boat to Porto Coimbra (Sr. Ferreira or Sr. Silva), about US$80, and from there go by boat to Porto Esperança, from where you can catch a train to Corumbá (US$1). Entry at Porto Esperança requires a yellow fever certificate and much red tape because the official, Sr. Sanitário, is not used to the unexpected. Since local river traffic is sparse, this trip is recommended only for the adventurous and patient.

There is a 215 km. road (Route 5 - first 112 km. unpaved but moderate, last 100 km. paved) to the Brazilian border. The road is very scenic, passing through the Cordillera de Amambay. About half way between **Yby Yaú** (junction with road to Coronel Oviedo, fuel, restaurants) and Pedro Juan Caballero is a short road to the **National Park of Cerro Corá**, which is the site of Marshal Francisco Solano López' death, with a monument to him and other national heroes; the site is constantly guarded. It has hills and cliffs (some with petroglyphs), camping facilities, swimming and hiking trails. Administration office is at Km. 180 on Ruta 5, 5 km. past the main entrance towards Pedro Juan Caballero.

The border town of **Pedro Juan Caballero** (pop: 37,331), opposite Ponta Porã, Brazil, which has a road and railway to São Paulo and the Atlantic coast. The two towns are divided only by a road (Rua Internacional) and the locals come and go as they please. To cross into Brazil officially, first obtain a Paraguayan exit stamp (ask around: the office was last reported in a private house in Calle General Brughez), then report to Brazilian federal police in Ponta Porã. If you need a Brazilian visa go first to the Brazilian consul (closed 1200-1400) opposite the *Hotel La Siesta* in P J Caballero. From P J Caballero there are daily flights to Asunción (they may be suspended after heavy rain, at which time buses may not run to Asunción either, though colectivos, which cost about 25% more than buses, may run when buses do not). Much cheaper here than Asunción for most purchases. A good shopping street is Mcal. López, cheap liquor and electronics. It has been reported that some caves have recently been discovered nearby and maybe visited.

Hotels *Peralta* (F) and *Holiday* (E) on the same street as the TAM offices. *Eiruzú*, D, with breakfast, clean, modern, rec., swimming pool, good restaurant; *La Siesta*, modern, luxury, good restaurant, close to border with Ponta Porã; *Paraguay*, D, with breakfast, good, friendly. *Corina*, very clean with breakfast, F, rec.; *Guavira*, F, no breakfast, clean and comfortable.

Buses Several to Concepción US$2.50, 4 hrs. To Asunción, La Santana at 1200, 1900 and 2130 (direct), 8-9 hrs., US$5 (US$12 deluxe sleeper) and slower buses, 11-12 hrs. (indirect) at 0900 and 1700, US$4.

Exchange Bancopar, Banco del Paraná for exchange. At least 6 *casas de cambio*. For travellers' cheques you can go to the *casas de cambio*, or to *Hotel Eiruzú*, one block behind the *casas de cambio* (also deal in the European currencies). Reports vary as to which gives the better rates, you may have to show receipt for purchase of travellers' cheques (if you don't have it, try *Cambio Amambay*, near *Hotel Eiruzú*). There are many street changers.

EAST FROM ASUNCION (3)

Route Two   The Mariscal Estigarribia Highway leaves Asunción past typical markets, reached by 26 bus from Asunción. At km. 12 is **San Lorenzo** (pop: 74,359), an industrial town with the National School of Agriculture (Universidad de Agronomía – it has an extensive insect collection; also excellent Museo de las Indígenas, by the Cathedral, handicrafts for sale at reasonable prices, non-profit-making organization run by Catholic Relief Services). Here is the Balneario El Tigre, with swimming pool and shady trees. (*Hotel San Lorenzo*, Gral. Caballero y Cerro Corá, T 2261, F with breakfast, excellent). At Km. 20 is **Capiatá**, founded in 1640, where there is a fine cathedral with remarkable 17th century sculpture made by Indians under the tutelage of the Jesuit Fathers. Here there is a left turn sign-posted to Lake Ypacaraí via an inexpensive toll road, 7 km. to the lake, worth a visit.

Km. 30, **Itauguá** (5,369 inhabitants), founded in 1728, is where the famous *ñandutí*, or spiderweb lace, is made. The blocks of uniform dwellings in the broad plaza, with their reddish tile roofs projecting over the sidewalk and their lines of pillars, are very close to the descriptions we have of Guaraní Jesuit settlements. The church and the market are worth seeing, and the town looks most attractive with the *ñandutí* work spread or hanging outside the houses; you can buy the most beautiful hammocks, tablecloths, shirts, hats and dresses locally made. There is a 3-day festival in mid-July, including processions and the crowning of Señorita Ñandutí. Accommodation poor (there is only one *pensión*, F), but Itauguá is only 45 mins by bus from Asunción, US$0.30.

At km. 40 a branch road, 5 km. long, leads off to **San Bernardino**, on Lake Ypacaraí, by bus from Asunción (Route 2, 56 km., 1 hrs., US$0.45) or partly by rail. The lake is 24 km. by 5. Crowded from December through February. Facilities for swimming and water sports, with sandy beach, but water is a bit dirty (*Hotel Casino San Bernardino*, with swimming pool and restaurant, a/c, T (0512) 391; *Restaurant Siddartha* is good).

Aregua, a pretty town on the far shore (church and convent across from railway station), is also a resort, with interesting ceramics cooperative. An increasing number of houses are being built around the lake. Riding is possible.

Hotels *del Lago; Acuario*; IPS (the Medical Social Service of Paraguay) has a first-class hotel, open for tourists. *Santa Rita*, E, bed and breakfast, friendly (good German food, and Paraguayan folk music at weekends). It is possible to find rooms in private houses.

Camping   At Km. 43 is Casa Grande Camping Club with all facilities. For information, Corfín Paraguaya, Ayolas 437 y Estrella, T 92360/1, Asunción, or direct, T (0511) 649. It is possible to camp right on the lake but there are many mosquitoes, inadequate sanitary facilities and not much safety for your personal belongings; also possible to camp in disused walled sports ground.

At Km. 54 is **Caacupé**, a popular resort and religious centre with 9,105 inhabitants. Its sights include the beautiful Basilica of Our Lady of the Miracles. Her day is 8 December, when pilgrims come to the town from far and wide. The old church has been demolished, but a small replica has been built about 5 blocks away. The very beautiful new basilica, with copper roof, stained glass and polychrome stone esplanade, was consecrated by the Pope in 1988. There is an interesting market next to it, where one can buy pottery, etc., and swimming pools in the streams nearby. Parque Anka, outside town on the Asunción road, has a swimming pool, tennis courts, ponies, a Disneyland, camp site and good restaurants.

Thousands of people from Paraguay, Brazil and Argentina flock to the shrine. Besides fireworks and candle-lit processions, pilgrims watch the agile gyrations of Paraguayan bottle-dancers; they weave in intricate measures whilst balancing bottles pyramided on their heads. The top bottle carries a spray of flowers and the more expert dancers never let drop a single petal.

Hotels *Gran Hotel Victoria*; *El Uruguayo*, F, with good restaurant, friendly service; *San Blas I*, F.

Camping Club de Camping Melli, all facilities, Km. 53, close to Caacupé, T (0511) 313.

Excursions Poor roads lead to several interesting churches. One is at Tobati, a tobacco centre, with local pottery and woodwork, 16 km. to the N. At Km. 64 beyond Caacupé a paved road runs 13 km. SE to **Piribebuy** (pop: 5,902, *Pensión Santa Rosa*, F, basic; *Restaurant Rincón Viejo*, reasonable), founded in 1640 and noted for its strong local drink, caña. In the central plaza is the church (1640), with fine sculptures, high altar and pulpit. Near the town are the attractive small falls of Piraretá. The road goes on to Cholóló, with good views from a hill, and you can visit the Cholóló falls (motel); it reaches Route 1 at Paraguarí, 22 km. from Piribebuy.

At Km. 132, but off the main road (buses drop passengers at El Cruce – a roundabout), is **Coronel Oviedo**, an important road junction (21,782 people; *Hospedaje Juancito*, 1 de Marzo y Carmelo Peralta, F with bath, mosquito net, nice garden, rec.; *Hotel Ramírez*, E, clean and good; *El Rey*, E, clean, modern, breakfast included; *Pensión Ñanda Roga*, F, without breakfast, basic but friendly; on main road to the West, *Hotel Alemán*, rec., or in centre, *El Sueño Feliz*, F, clean and friendly). Here the road branches: one branch, Route 8, is paved for 42 km. S to Villarrica and continues S (unpaved) through Caazapá to Boquerón.

Villarrica, 173 km. by road or rail from Asunción and 219 from Encarnación, with 21,203 people, is delightfully set on a hill rich with orange trees. It has a fine cathedral, and a public, open-air swimming pool. Museum behind the church has a foreign coin collection; please contribute. Products of the region are tobacco, cotton, sugar, *yerba mate*, hides, meat and wine produced by German settlers. Horse-drawn taxis.

Hotels *Ybytruzu*, on main street E p.p. with breakfat, new, better than most; *Guaíra*, F, near bus terminal, shower, fan, a/c, noisy, not rec. Also F: *Hospedaje Restaurant San Miguel*, Natalicio Talavera, and *Pensión el Toro*. Eating places are hard to find (except plenty of ice cream parlours): *El Mesón III*; *La Casa Vieja*, good, simple, some distance from main road (ask); poor café at bus terminal (closes 1800).

Bus to Coronel Oviedo US$1.50; to Asunción, US$2; also direct service (Empresa Guaireña) to Ciudad del Este, 4 daily. By train from Asunción, Tues. and Fri. 1800, US$1, arrive Villarrica at midnight.

Excursions About 30 km. from Villarrica there are some petroglyphs worth visiting. The taxi drivers know the way (US$12 return including an hour at the site) and a nearby farmer's children will guide you to them.

There are three German colonies near Villarrica. At Colonia Independencia, *Hotel Tilinski*, E, full board, peaceful, good German food, German spoken, swimming pool (filled with river water), and Señora Bürg has two rooms for about US$6, full board; very good food, fresh milk, lemon juice. Makes a good stop, especially for German-speaking travellers, who can also visit the German cooperative farms. Direct bus to Asunción, three daily (US$1.60, 4 hrs.), as well as to Villarrica.

The other branch, the paved Route 7, runs 195 km. from Coronel Oviedo through cultivated areas and woods and across the Caaguazú mountain to the spectacular 500-metre single span "Friendship Bridge" across the Paraná (to Brazil) at **Ciudad del Este** (formerly Ciudad Presidente Stroessner) , where there is a grass-strip airport. This was the fastest growing city in the country (83,000 inhabitants) until the completion of the civil works of the Itaipú hydroelectric project, for which it is the centre of operations. Ciudad del Este has been described as the biggest late-night shopping centre in Latin America, with little to excite the tourist (except the prices for electrical goods, watches, perfumes, etc.; shop around and bargain hard) – but watch the exchange rates if you're a short-term visitor from Argentina or Brazil; hotels and restaurants tend to be dearer than elsewhere in Paraguay. The leather market is well worth a visit, be sure to bargain. The nearby towns of

Hernandarias (pop: 32,000; *Hotel El León*, E, clean, quiet) and Puerto Presidente Franco (pop: about 24,000) have also had a tremendous increase in population and activity.

Hotels (incl. breakfast) *Hotel de la Tour* at Paraná Country Club, superb, A, Swiss-owned, excellent restaurant (US$12-16 p.p.), swimming pool, gardens, beautiful view; *Acaraí Casino*, B, a/c, with swimming pool and casino, quiet; *Catedral*, C, a/c, with swimming pool, restaurant; *Mi Abuelo*, Adrián Jara 128, highly rec., F, including breakfast, good value, shared shower, fan; *Tres Monedas*, D, on the main street, decent breakfast. *Puerto del Sol*, D with bath, a/c, clean, just off main street; *Viena*, next door, above restaurant, E with breakfast, clean, German family. *Tripolis*, E, a/c, friendly, clean; *Munich*, rec. Other cheap ones near market. *Executive*, Av Adrián Jara y Curupayty, T 8981/8982, B (incl. breakfast – restaurant rec.); also in this class are *Floresta*, Av Teniente Cabello y C.A. López, T 8255/8197, and *Santo Domingo*, Emiliano R. Fernández y Alejo García, T 2505, superb.

Restaurants *Mburucuyá*, with music, at Alejo García y A. Jara; *Hostería del Lago* at the same address; *Cary-Bar* at Nanawa y Monseñor Rodríguez; *Tripolis* for good moderately-priced meal. *Tai Fu*, Chinese, very good value, on 8th floor above *Casa Mona Lisa*, good views. *Coreio*, Av San Blas 125, T 60448, good Korean food, meal about US$5; *New Tokio*, Jara 202, very good, authentic Japanese meal for US$3; opposite is *Mi Rancho*, quite good. *Dolíbar*, clean and fair value. Cheaper ones in market.

Exchange Banco Holandés Unido; Lloyds Bank agency; local banks (open Mon.-Fri. 0730-1100). Dollars can be changed into new cruzeiros in town, but exchange may be better and easier in Foz do Iguaçu; note that money changers do not operate at the Brazilian end of the Friendship Bridge.

International Phone Antelco, near centre on road to bus terminal.

Communications The road links with the Brazilian road system at Foz do Iguaçu across the bridge, from where another 32-km. road leads to the Iguazú Falls. Passengers disembark on each side of the bridge. The international bus then goes to the inter-city depot, behind Av Brasil, at the edge of Foz do Iguaçu. Crossing from Paraguay to Brazil other than on the international bus, you just pass through Paraguayan customs etc., walk across, visit Brazilian immigration, then take a bus to the city terminal (*terminal urbana*), US$0.05, just outside Foz, opposite a military training camp. There is a local bus from the Ciudad del Este bus terminal to Foz, which drops you off at Brazilian immigration; keep your ticket and continue to Foz free on the next bus. Remember to put your watch forward 1 hr. From the *terminal urbana*, buses run to the Falls; if only visiting the Brazilian side of the Falls, immigration procedure on the Paraguayan and Brazilian sides of the Friendship Bridge is minimal, even for those normally requiring a visa to visit Brazil. If in doubt, though, obtain all necessary exit and entrance stamps. If entering Paraguay, sit next to the bus exit so you can alight to visit Brazilian immigration for your exit stamp. Travellers report this crossing is very busy at weekends and not all buses stop at immigration.

Direct journeys to Argentina may be made by launch from Puerto Presidente Franco to Puerto Iguazú, US$0.50, about every 2 hours.

Many buses (US$4) and colectivos (up to US$5) run to Asunción, 3-7 hrs. Nuestra Señora and Rysa reported to run the best buses. Bus to Encarnación, along fully paved road, 4 hrs., US$3.50.

The *Monday* falls, 10 km. from Ciudad del Este, are worth visiting by taxi. There is good fishing below the falls.

The huge Itaipú hydroelectric project is close to Ciudad del Este, and well worth a visit. Take a bus from Terminal Urbano to the Visitors' Centre, open 0730-1200, 1330-1700, Sun. and holidays 0800-1200, 1330-1630. Free conducted tours of the project include a film show half an hour before bus tour, starting at 0900, 1030, 1430, 1530 Mon.-Sat.; on Sundays and holidays they are at 0830, 0930, 1030, 1400, and 1500 (check times in advance). Take passport. If you don't like guided trips but still wish to visit the project, apply to head office in Asunción.

Another paved road from Coronel Oviedo runs N to San Estanislao (5,538 people, small historical museum), then (Route 10) NE for 323 km. to the Itaipú dam area, past numerous "colonies" where the jungle is being cleared at an alarming rate.

At Mbutuy, S of San Estanislao, a dry-weather road branches eastwards through Curuguaty to where the Salto del Guaira waterfalls used to be (now under Itaipú lake). There is now a ferry from Puerto Guaira to Brazil. There are daily buses from Asunción (14 hrs.). A wide, dry-weather road runs N from Hernandarias, via Itaquyry to the Coronel Oviedo – Salto del Guaira road at Cruce Guaraní.

A rough road runs N from San Estanislao to Yby Yaú (**see page** 833), via Lima (*Hospedaje Mburucuya*, G, basic; *Restaurant La Delicia*). 40 km. N of Lima, a road suitable for 4-wheel-drive vehicles only goes east, through patches of beautiful jungle, to Capitán Badó.

SOUTHERN PARAGUAY (4)

South from Asunción

A trip down river can be made to **Pilar** (13,135 inhabitants), 306 km. S of Asunción, opposite the confluence of the Paraguay and the Bermejo, coming in from the Argentine Chaco. A road (Route 4) is open E to San Ignacio Guazú, on the Asunción-Encarnación highway; in the other direction, it continues to the extreme SW tip of Paraguay, near Humaitá, the site of a heroic siege during the War of the Triple Alliance. Flights from Pilar to Asunción and Resistencia, Argentina, on Mon. and Thurs. by LAP.

Hotels *Gardel*; *Prinquelli*.

South-East from Asunción

Route One runs through some of the old mission towns to Encarnación, 370 km. away, on the Alto Paraná.

Km. 37, **Itá** (9,308 inhabitants), an old town turning out rustic pottery (by Rosa Britez as you enter village). At Carapeguá there is a turn off Route 1 to Ybycuy; 18 km. away is one of the more accessible National Parks (**see page** 831). Km. 48, **Yaguarón**, founded in 1539, was the centre of the Franciscan missions in colonial times. It is set on a river at the foot of a hill in an orange-growing district, and has a famous church, begun by the Franciscans in 1640 and finished in 1720, and reconstructed in 1885. (Open 0700-1100, 1400-1900.) The tints, made by the Indians from local plants, are still bright on the woodcarvings. Stations of the Cross behind the village lead to a good view of the surroundings. Most of Paraguay's petit-grain comes from the area. (For the by-road to Caacupé **see page** 834.) Buses every 15 mins or so from Asunción (US$0.45). (*Hotel Silva*, *Bar Elsi*, both F.)

"The corridor, or outside walk under a projecting roof supported by pillars, is a typical feature of Paraguayan churches. Generally it runs all the way round the church, forming an entrance portico in front. An excellent example is the church at Yaguarón. It is the prototype of the mission sanctuaries of the early 18th century, when the structure was built with a sturdy wooden skeleton and the walls – simple screens of adobe or brick – had no function of support. The belfry is a modest little wooden tower somewhat apart from the church; in the missions it also served as a *mangrullo*, or watch tower." – Paul Dony.

Museum   Museo Doctor Francia, 700 metres from church, with relics of Paraguay's first dictator, "El Supremo". Open Tues., Thurs., Sat. 1500-1700; Sun. and holidays 0930-1130; 1500-1700.

Km. 63, **Paraguarí**, founded 1775, the N entrance to the mission area, is on the railway (5,724 people), set among hills with many streams. Its church, though cruder, is reminiscent of the famous church at Yaguarón. It has a curious bell tower.

Hotels *Paraguarí*; *Domínguez*. *Pensión San Luis*, F, cheapest, on edge of town.

24 km. north of Route 1 from Eusebio Ayala (pop: 5,316) is the **Vapor Cué National Park**,

with peaceful swimming and fishing in the river in the middle of fertile cattle country. It contains the remains of seven steamships sunk during the War of the Triple Alliance. Several boilers and one ship have been reconstructed. Camping is permitted, public transport runs to within 4 km. of the site. Transport can be hired in the village.

Just before Km. 141 where the Tebicuary river is crossed by bridge (toll) is Caapucú (*Hotel Misiones*, F). At Km. 161 is **Villa Florida**, an ideal holiday resort for sailing, fishing and relaxing, with first-class hotel, 2 *paradores*, camping near the river (good fishing); also at **Centú Cué**, 5 km. away, on the banks of the Tebicuary river, there are hotels (*Parador Centú Cué*, D full board, pleasant, peaceful) and camping facilities, for reservations either at, T Asunción 206570 or directly to Centú Cué 083219. At San Miguel (Km. 178), all types of woollen articles are on sale (blankets, shawls, ponchos, hammocks, etc.). The delightful Jesuit town of **San Juan Bautista**, about half-way between Asunción and Encarnación, is worth a stop (population 6,872, *Waldorf Hotel*).

Km. 226, San Ignacio Guazú; there is a superb museum of Guaraní carvings in the old Jesuits' house. 12 km. to the NE (up a muddy side road) is the new church of Santa María de Fe, with some 60 to 70 Guaraní sculptures in the chapel. From San Ignacio Guazú a road, 156 km., runs W to Pilar (**see page 837**). At Santa Rosa (Km. 248), the Casa de Loreto has a beautiful Annunciation group and the remains of frescoes of the flight of the Holy Family's house from Nazareth to Loreto in Italy (poorly restored; ask for the priest from Louisiana to open it up). A road at Km. 262 leads 52 km. SW to Ayolas, associated with the Yacyretá hydroelectric scheme (*Hotel Nacional de Turismo*, D with shower, poor breakfast, otherwise OK; *El Dorado*, E, with good restaurant). Coronel Bogado (5,180 people), Km. 319, is the southern limit of the mission area. Turn off Route 1 just before Coronel Bogado to reach the Jesuit ruins of **San Cosme y Damián** (343 km. from Asunción) – church, refectory, etc. (A great variety of birds can be seen from this road.) Route One reaches the Alto Paraná at Carmen del Paraná, Km. 331, 40 km. W of Encarnación, the terminus of the railway from Asunción.

Encarnación (pop 27,632), a busy port on the Alto Paraná, is connected by ferry to the Argentine town of Posadas; the bridge between the two was complete in January 1990, but was still not carrying traffic. The town is the centre for the construction of the Yacyretá-Apipé dam to be shared by Paraguay and Argentina. Encarnación exports the products of a rich area: timber, soya, *mate*, tobacco, cotton, and hides; it is fast losing its traditional and very rural appearance. (Travellers should be prepared for cold weather, despite the latitude). The upper part of the town is not especially interesting, although prices here are lower than downtown near the river. The lower, older part of the colonial town will be flooded when the Yacyretá dam is completed. The cost of living is higher in Encarnación than in most other parts of Paraguay, and souvenir prices are much the same as in Posadas. The road along the Alto Paraná to Ciudad del Este is now paved.

Hotels *Novohotel Encarnación*, A, first class, Route 1, km. 2, T 071-5120/24; *Repka*, Arquitecto Pereira 43, a small grey house in pretty garden, private baths, very good home cooking, E, bed and breakfast; *Viena*, Calle Caballero 568 (T 071-3486), nr. bus station, beside Antelco, E with bath and breakfast, German-run, good food, garage; *Paraná*, E without breakfast, satisfactory; *Central*, Mcal. López 542, E, includes private bath and meals, German spoken; *Viera*, a/c, good location, E (F with fan), Estigarribia and 25 de Mayo, gambling, private bath; *Hospedaje Liz*, Estigarribia 1767, F with shower, fan, hot water, clean, good patio; *Hospedaje San Cayetano*, F, near station, clean, fan, hot shower, good restaurant downstairs; *Rueda*, F, near bus station, hot water, clean, fan, mosquito repellant required. *Suizo*, Mcal. Estigarribia 562, just below bus terminal, F without bath, E with, breakfast, clean; others near railway station, all F (basic). *Pensión Vila Alegre*, Antequera 951, F, very basic but the people are pleasant and the food excellent.

Restaurant *Ara-Mi*, centrally located in the upper town, good food, pleasant. *Rubi*, Chinese, Mcal. Estigarribia 519, near railway, excellent; and **Restaurant Paraná**, international cuisine, on Mcal. Estigarribia (main street) and Memmel. *Bar-Restaurant Imperial*, Iturbe, corner Estigarribia, good and cheap; *Rosita*, Mcal. Estigarribia 1109, good meal, US$3.50; *Karanday*, Gral. Caballero, good grill but poor wines; *Confitería Tokio*, Estigarribia 484, good. Two good cheap ones on square by bus station.

Taxis Horsedrawn (about US$0.25), but prices tend to be high if drivers suspect you don't know the distance you want to travel. Some motor driven ones for those in a hurry. Horse-drawn taxi from railway station US$1.25 (compared with US$3.75 by car).

Exchange Lloyds Bank, agency at Villarrica y Mariscal Estigarribia, open Mon.-Fri. 0730-1100. Many money-changers at the Paraguay side but will only change notes – better rates for australes here than in Argentina. *Casas de cambio* for travellers' cheques on Mariscal Estagarribia: Guaraní at No 301, and Comercio at No 1404 (Thomas Cook cheques preferred); it is difficult to change money at weekends.

International Phone Antelco, 0700-2200, unfriendly.

Tourist Office Kiosk on the ferry pier.

Consulate Argentine, at Cabañas y Mallorquín.

Transport Bus to Asunción, about 6 hours, US$4 with Rysa, colectivo with Halcones. (Bus terminal is above the town, up the main street; good cheap snacks at the terminal.) Train to Asunción, 18 (can take 24) hours, US$3, 1st class (no sleepers), US$1.90, 2nd class, Sun. at 1530, Wed. at 1530. Bus to Trinidad, US$0.40, 30 mins, every hour. Bus to Ciudad del Este US$3.50, several daily, 3 hrs. Buses also to Villarrica. Boats to Asunción leave Wed. 1600.

Passenger ferry to Posadas, 4 a day (last at 1720), including Sat. and Sun., US$1, baggage extra; car ferry 4 times a day. Taxi from dock to bus terminal, US$0.75. The bridge linking Encarnación with Posadas will be open for cars and trains.

Warning On arrival, foreign travellers may be searched at the ferry terminal (principally for "communist" literature). Entry card costs US$3, payable in dollars, australes or guaraníes.

Beyond Encarnación, the road goes on 28 km. to Trinidad, and then to the thriving German settlements of Obligado and Bella Vista (another, Colonia Hohenau – reported dirty – is due E of Trinidad on the Alto Paraná); this road continues N, fully paved, as Route 6, paralleling the Alto Paraná, to meet Route 7 near Ciudad del Este (long stretches without petrol). About half way, at the village of Santa María Auxiliadora, is *Hospedaje La Norma*, G, basic. 71 km. from Encarnación is the Japanese Colonia Pirapó.

At **Trinidad** there is a great Jesuit church, once utterly in ruins but restoration should be finished soon and a museum set up. The church was founded in 1706 by Padre Juan de Anaya; the architect was Juan Batista Primol. For information, or tours of the ruins, contact Sr. Augusto Servián Goana, Ruinas Trinidad, Itapúa, Encarnación; a US$3 booklet by Clement MacWaspy is available at the site. A visit to the church and museum is recommended (hours of opening 0730-1130, 1330-1730), also for the surrounding countryside. Next to the ruined church at Trinidad is a small modern church; it contains a large carved wooden statue of the Deity, so hollowed at the back that a priest in hiding could simulate the resounding voice of the Eternal Father to impress the Indians of the mission. Bus Encarnación-Trinidad 0600, 0800 and 0830. You can stay at the Centro Social, food and shower available, take sleeping gear; camp behind the souvenir stall.

Ten km. N of Trinidad, at Jesús, there is another ruined church, which is also being restored (frequent but irregular minibuses between Trinidad and Jesús, same opening hours in theory, man who has the key lives 2 km. from the ruins, ask at the village square). Bus service to Encarnación hourly from 0630 (US$0.25, 3/4-hr. journey).

Twenty km. before Encarnación on the highway from Trinidad is *Hotel Tirol del Paraguay* (Capitán Miranda, Ruta 6, km. 20), with 3 swimming pools, chalets with private terrace, bath, TV, a/c for 40 people and a landing strip.

THE PARAGUAYAN CHACO (5)

Michael Wigan writes: The Paraguayan Chaco covers 24 million hectares, but under 100,000 people live there. A single road, the Transchaco Highway, runs in a straight line north-west to the Bolivian border 20 km. beyond Nueva Asunción. It begins as an excellent asphalt top turning (N of the Mennonite colonies) into a levelled earthen road of average quality. It seldom rains but if it does all vehicles slither about hopelessly: you cannot move till it dries. The elevation rises very gradually from 50 metres opposite Asunción to 450 metres on the Bolivian border.

The Chaco is divisible into 3 terrains. The first, the Low Chaco, leaving Asunción, is open palm forest and marshes, much of which is permanently beneath shallow water. The lack of slope and the impermeable clay hardpan mean the water hardly moves. The palm forest is used for cattle ranching of the most extensive type, some *estancias* lying several hundred km. down tracks off the highway. The cattle are very mixed – English Herefords, Indian Brahmins, and Brazilian. Most *estancias* are chronically overstocked and overgrazed; calving rates are very low. Remote *estancias* have their own airfields, and all are equipped with 2-way radios.

The Middle Chaco, around the capital, Filadelfia, has been settled by Mennonites, latterday Baptists chiefly of German extraction who arrived in Paraguay from 1930 onwards. They set up three distinct colonies: Menno (from Canada and Mexico, but originally from Russia); Fernheim (the first group directly from Russia) and Neuland (the last group to arrive, also from Russia, after 1945). The Mennonites speak "plattdeutsch" – a cross between Dutch and German, and normal "hochdeutsch"; very few speak Spanish. Altogether there are 118 villages with a population of about 10,000 Mennonites, 10,000 Indians and a very small number of other immigrants. The natural cover is scrubland with a mixture of hardwoods, and more cactus further north. The bottle-tree with a pear-shaped, water-conserving, trunk, and the *quebracho* (axe-breaker), used for tannin, are native.

The Mennonites, who run their own banks, schools, hospitals and a cooperative agricultural system, are the only organized community in the Chaco. They are mainly crop-farmers (though they also run dairy cattle and make cheese and butter) and grow grapefruit, lemons, groundnuts, sorghum and cotton.

From Filadelfia an alternative route goes north and into the north-west Chaco where most of the remaining jaguars are found. This road is very rough, but the main highway remains negotiable by car although it narrows. In the western sector scattered military outposts are the only human presence. The whole area is under military jurisdiction; the visitor may find a letter of authorization or military introduction useful.

The north-western part, the High Chaco, is a low thorn forest, an impenetrable barricade of hard spikes and spiny branches resistant to fire, heat and drought. Occasional tracks lead off the highway for a short distance. Towards Bolivia cactus becomes more concentrated. There are a few *estancias* further south, where the brush is bulldozed into hedges and the trees left for shade. In summer it is very hot. The animal life – wild hog, puma, jaguar, tapir – congregates around the water-holes at night. The whole area is a national park.

The primeval character of the Chaco is reflected in the 1975 discovery of a kind of wild hog, formerly thought extinct since the Pleistocene era, now listed as Wagner's peccary. When camping out fires should be kept up to deter the local fauna; the greatest danger is from several species of poisonous snakes. Grass round the tent should be cut. The highway is a smuggling route from Bolivia, so it is unwise to stop for anyone in the night. In the High Chaco there is almost no traffic.

The Chaco's Indian population is nomadic and Guaraní-speaking, and sets up little brushwood and mud villages wherever there is a plentiful food-supply. The Indians eat everything, bird and mammal, and even the poisonous snakes. The great delicacy is armadillo. Anthropologists have found the Indians' social structures, marriage and death rites as inscrutable as the surrounding countryside. They are friendly and peaceful, and periodically work on the *estancias*.

No expedition should be without supplies of water, food and fuel. Although there are service stations in the Middle and Low Chaco self-sufficiency is advised. Ill-equipped expeditions have had to be rescued by the army or have come to grief. In winter temperatures are warm and comfortable by day, cooler by night. In summer heat and mosquitoes make it very unpleasant (pyrethrum coils – *espirales* – are available throughout the region). The Low Chaco is one of the foremost bird habitats in the world, and although bird-life may be enjoyed from the road it is still comparatively unknown and rarely visited. Until recently entry into the Chaco was by plane only. The rapid development of the Highway will surely open it up before long; land purchases, especially by foreigners, and oil exploration are on the increase.

A bus ride to **Filadelfia** (472 km.), in the Chaco, from Asunción, costs US$6 with Nasa (one or more buses each day). At Km. 270 is Pozo Colorado (turning for Concepción, **see page** 832). Then after a further 80 km., one starts seeing the Mennonites' neat little homes with painted wooden shutters, surrounded by flowering plants and orchards. A good place to eat on the Transchaco is at Km. 415, called Cruce Loma Plata; fuel also available. The centres are Filadelfia and Loma Plata, clean modern agricultural communities with wide unpaved streets. The Unger Museum at Filadelfia gives a good idea what this industrious people had to go through to make this rich area what it is today (ask at the Information Office, two doors left of *Hotel Florida*, for opening times). Some Indian tribes live nearby, but have been "civilized", seemingly to their disadvantage.

The Mennonite bus company, Chaco Boreal, leaves from the colonies for Asunción daily, US$5; Nasa leaves Filadelfia for Asunción at 1900, make reservations early; the bus from Asunción stops at all 3 communities and ends at Neuland (US$6.50). There is a travel agency, the Reiseburo, close to *Hotel Florida*.

Hotel *Florida*, in Filadelfia, new wing with a/c and private bath, D, very comfortable, old section, fans and shared bath, F (uncomfortable, beetles), sells excellent German cakes. **Restaurants**: *La Estrella* recommended for good ice cream and asados; another good restaurant *La Girasol*, opposite; *Remi*, on same street, pizzas and good ice cream. Plenty of good ice cream parlours (you need them in the heat), but no bars. 2 km. south-east is the Parque Trébol, a charming public park, with facilities where one can camp. Lots of frog noise at night, however.

Nearby is **Loma Plata** (*Hotel Loma Plata*, E/F, with restaurant, can be booked from the Mennonite centre in Asunción). Good hotel in the village of Neu Hallestadt, Neuland, is *Boquerón*, E with breakfast. Ask around in Filadelfia for people to drive you round the Mennonite communities (US$0.15 per km.).

To Bolivia From Filadelfia to the Bolivian border at General Eugenio A Garay is 304 km. Best to fill up with fuel at Filadelfia; well-stocked supermarkets in Filadelfia and Loma Plato. There are sparse facilities (cafés, fuel) until Mariscal Estigarribia (*Hotel Alem-án*, F with breakfast, friendly). Thereafter only military outposts or *estancias* may offer food, fuel and perhaps a bed for the night. At Km. 662 a Centro Urbano Rural is under construction, with motel and service station, at Estancia La Patria. Trucks travel all the way to Bolivia. You can try to hitch. Frequent Army identity checks are inevitable. It is important to have photographs on documents which are a good likeness to the bearer. Backpackers need expect no special difficulties. Take plenty of food and water since even the smallest amount of rain can cause delays.

INFORMATION FOR VISITORS

Documents A passport is required. Visitors are registered on arrival by the immigration authorities and get their documents back immediately. Visas are normally not required for a stay of up to 90 days, by visitors who hold tourist cards, which are issued to non-visa holders on arrival by air or land; they cost US$3 (payable in dollars or guaraníes – cheaper). If you do not complete formalities you can be turned back at the border, or have trouble when leaving Paraguay. This concession does not apply to citizens of France and the communist countries, who need visas (US$8); Canadians also need visas (US$5), as do citizens of Finland. Visitors from those countries who do not have visas, or with Soviet, Cuban and Nicaraguan entry stamps in their passports may have to surrender their passports and undergo interrogation by the police in Asunción before getting them back; there appears to be no hard and fast rule so a lot depends on the official's mood or even your appearance. (Restrictions on Asians are being applied for immigration purposes.)

Airport Tax is US$5, payable in US$ or guaraníes (tends to be cheaper).

Flights from Europe Iberia has one weekly flight to Asunción from Madrid, via Rio and São Paulo. Líneas Aéreas Paraguayas (LAP – now a member of IATA) has a twice-weekly service from Frankfurt, via Brussels and Madrid (once a week with a refuelling stop in Dakar, Senegal). From other points in Europe, slow connections can be made via Rio or São Paulo (Varig or LAP). Routes from Europe via Brazil offer greater ticketing flexibility than other options.

From North America American/Eastern operates three times a week Miami-Panamá-Lima-La Paz-Asunción. LAP also operates flights from Miami to Asunción. Alternatively from New York, connections every day via Rio, but Varig's connecting flights are slow. From California, connections via Lima or Miami.

Within South America From Montevideo (3 flights a week) by Líneas Aéreas Paraguayas (LAP) or Pluna; from Buenos Aires by Aerolíneas Argentinas (from Aeroparque domestic airport via Corrientes), or LAP (from Ezaiza international airport); from Santiago (6 a week) by Ladeco (Chile) and LAP; from Lima (5 a week) by LAP or Eastern; from La Paz (twice a week) by Eastern, or via Santa Cruz (2 a week) by LAP or LAB (also stopping at Cochabamba); from Rio, São Paulo and Iguazú Falls (daily) by Varig; from São Paulo and Rio de Janeiro thrice weekly by LAP; from Río and São Paulo, without stop at Iguazú, two Ladeco (Chile) and one Iberia flight per week.

By Sea from Europe   for freight, the only regular all-water direct service is Europe-Paraguay Line from Grangemouth, Rotterdam, Bremen, Hamburg, Antwerp and Bilbao, owned by Hamburg Süd Eggert & Amsinck, Ost-Weststrasse 59, Hamburg 11, and van Nievelt, Goudriaan & Co, BV, Veerhaven 2, 3016 CJ Rotterdam. Agent: Belserve/Belgian Maritime Services, Antwerp (T 03-232 25 44).

By Land/River from Argentina   The international rail route from Buenos Aires to Posadas is given on **page 830**. There is a paved road from Buenos Aires via Santa Fe to Clorinda and then on new paved roads via the borders at Puerto Pilcomayo and the new Remanso Castillo suspension bridge to Asunción: 1,370 km., about 23 hrs.; also via Posadas to Encarnación. Good bus services on these routes. After the border at Puerto Falcón, before the Remanso Castillo bridge, a road forks to the Paraguayan Chaco (paved part of the way) and on to Bolivia. Boat services on the River Paraná between Buenos Aires and Asunción are irregular, depending on the level of the river.

To/From Brazil   The headwaters of both the Paraguay and the Alto Paraná are in Brazil. There are unscheduled boat services from Asunción northward along the Paraguay river to Porto Esperança, Brazil (from which there is a railway to São Paulo), and scheduled services to Corumbá (1,220 km. – **see page** 830), which is connected by road, rail and air with Bolivian and Brazilian cities. The normal means of surface communications are by road between Foz do Iguaçu and Ciudad del Este, and between Pedro Juan Caballero and Ponta Porã. Frontier with Brazil is officially closed at weekends but it is worth checking as sometimes passports will be stamped on Sunday.

International Bus Services   See under Asunción, page 830.

Customs   "Reasonable quantities" of tobacco products, alcoholic drinks and perfume are admitted free of duty. Travellers' books are vetted, in case they're subversive.

Travel in Paraguay: By Air   There are scheduled services to most parts of the country by Líneas Aéreas de Transporte Nacional (LATN) and to Concepción, Vallemí, Bahía Negra and Fuerte Olimpo by Transportes Aéreos Militares (TAM). Planes can be chartered.

By Rail   Passenger services are very slow. There are police on all passenger trains; make sure you are carrying your documents.

By Road   Buses ply on the main roads. For motorists, there are sufficient service stations in Paraguay, except in the Chaco area. Motorists should beware stray cattle on the road at night. Diesel fuel is US$0.25 per litre in Paraguay; gasoline users should use only *super* (Shell Spark Aider Super is recommended), US$0.45 per litre (which is 93 octane; regular gas, *alconafta*, contains 10-15% alcohol at US$0.40 per litre). It is highly recommended that drivers in Paraguay (and neighbouring countries) use diesel-powered vehicles as almost all the locals do: not only is diesel usually cheaper than gasoline, but a diesel engine will not stop in water, has no ignition/carburettor problems, and will not encounter the corrosive effects of alcohol in the fuel. Motor fuel and oil are sold in Paraguay by the litre. The documents needed in Paraguay for private cars are *carnet de passages en douanes*, international car registration and driver's licence. Border police charge US$11 to stamp *carnet* on entry and exit. **Warning**: beware of traffic police claiming that an International Driving Licence is not valid, or some other vague charge, and then demanding an "on-the-spot fine" of US$5 (at the very least). For entry into Brazil the only document necessary is the title to the car (or other proof of ownership). Touring y Automóvil Club Paraguayo has a good map. It is essential to drive at walking pace through military areas and stop completely if a flag ceremony is in progress.

Car Hire Hertz offers unlimited mileage for reasonable rates, free delivery to airport, minimum rental 3 days, but no insurance whatsoever. You will be responsible for any accident, damage or theft.

Motor Repairs A recommended mechanic is Lauro C. Noldin, Dr. Moleón Andreu 493 y 4ta Proyectada, Barrio Santa Librada, Asunción, T 33933; he repairs Land Rover, Range Rover, Jaguar and all makes of British, European, American and Japanese cars, diesel and petrol engines, motorcycles, power generators for motor homes. Bosch Garage Office, Chispa SA, Carios y José Rivera, Asunción, T 553315/7. Recommended garage, especially for Volkswagen repairs: Rodolfo Stecher, Av Fernando de la Mora 920, Asunción. Caravan and camper repairs at Metalúrgica Anahí SRL (Sr. Julio Schmidt), República de Colombia 261, Km. 7, Fernando de la Mora, Asunción, T 503335. For diesel service, MBT service garage at Av Eusebio Ayala y Lapacho Km. 4, T Asunción 553318. Land Rover body repairs at Taller San José of José Escobar at Battilana, casi Santo Domingo; T 203311. A recommended Land Rover parts source is Repuestos Agromotor at Herrera 604, Asunción. Good mechanics at Premetal Alemán, near crossing Eusebio Ayala with Rep. Argentina (T 64131). Spares are available in Paraguay for all makes of car (European, North American, Asian); also available are most makes of tyre.

Food and Drink Typical local foods include *chipas* (yuca bread flavoured with egg and cheese), *chipa soo* (maize bread with meat filling) and *sopa paraguaya* (a kind of dumpling of ground maize and cheese). *Soyo* is a soup of different meats and vegetables, delicious; *albóndiga* a soup of meat balls; *bori bori* another type of soup with diced meat, vegetables, and small balls of maize mixed with cheese. *Palmitos* (palm hearts) should not be missed; the beef is excellent in better class restaurants (best cuts are *lomo* and *lomito*). Paraguayan *chorizos* (sausages) are good. *Parrillada completa* is recommended. *Surubí*, a Paraná river fish, is prepared in many different ways, and is delicious. Sugar-cane juice, greatly beloved, is known as *mosto*. Fruit is magnificent. Very typical of Paraguay is *tereré* (cold *mate* with digestive herbs) for warm days and hot *mate* to warm you up on cold days. The national wine is not recommended (better is imported from Chile), but the local lager beer is acceptable and the cane-sugar spirit, *caña* is good (the best is "Aristocrat"; ask for "Ari").

Tipping Hotels, restaurants, 10%. Railway and airport porters US$0.15 a suitcase. Porters at docks US$0.40 a suitcase. Cinema usherettes are not tipped.

What to Buy The famous *ñandutí* lace, made exclusively by the women of Itauguá (**see page 834**). The local jewellery is also attractive. Handmade *ahopoi* (fine cloth) is suitable for shirts and blouses, and there are cotton thread belts in all colours. The best place to buy these items is Villarrica. Tourists are often attracted by the leather articles, the pottery and small wooden articles made from Paraguayan woods. Some of these are exhibited, and sold, at the Inter-Express Travel Agency's shop, Galería del Turista. See also "Shopping", under Asunción (**page 827**). Imported goods, especially cameras and film, are cheaper in Paraguay than in most other Latin American countries (although prices in the UK, for instance, are cheaper).

Warnings The prejudice against "hippie-looking" people carrying rucksacks seems to have diminished. The proverbial "official-looking" letter is, however, still useful. Searches for "communist" literature are made at land borders. Since President Stroessner was deposed the political atmosphere is more relaxed. Avoid provocation however, e.g. taking pictures of "military" installations. Backpackers entering via Clorinda may have problems crossing the International Bridge; it is therefore recommended that they enter Paraguay via Puerto Pilcomayo or Ciudad del Este. Apparently, hitch-hiking is still illegal, although possible in rural areas.

Health Tuberculosis, typhoid, dysentery, and hepatitis are endemic. Hookworm is the most common disease in the country, and there is much venereal disease, goitre and leprosy. Visitors should be inoculated against tetanus, typhoid, and paratyphoid. Be very careful over salad and tap water. Local mosquito repellant, *Repel*, and pyrethrum coils are effective. Denegue fever (**see page 36**) has recently been reported. Medical fees and medicine costs are high. The Centro Paraguayo del Diagnóstico, Gral. Díaz 975 y Colón, Asunción, is recommended as inexpensive, foreign languages spoken. Clínica Integral de Mujer, Mcal. Estigarribia 1085 y Brasil, Asunción, T 94722, has been recommended as a good gynaecological clinic. Dentists can be found either at the centre, or at Odontología 3, Mcal. Estigarribia 1414 y Pai Pérez, T 200175, Asunción.

Business Visitors Foreign business is transacted in Asunción, Ciudad del Este and Pedro Juan Caballero (with retail outlets particularly in the last two). From May to October is the best time for a visit. British business travellers are advised to get a copy of "Hints to Exporters: Paraguay", obtainable from the Department of Trade, Sanctuary Buildings, 16-20 Gt Smith Street, London SW1P 3DB.

Clothing In summer, January to March, tropical clothing, sunglasses and an umbrella are needed. The best time to visit is from May to September, when the heat is not too oppressive.

Business Hours Paraguayans are up early and many shops, offices and businesses open between 0630 and 0700. *Siesta* (generally observed during the hot season) is from 1200 to 1500. Commercial office hours are from 0730 to 1100 or 1130, and 1430 or 1500 to 1730 or 1900. Banks: from 0730 to 1100, closed on Saturday and Sunday. Government offices are open 0630 to 1130 in summer, 0730 to noon, in winter, open on Sat.

Official Holidays 1 Jan., 3 Feb., 1 March, Maundy Thursday, Good Friday, 1 14, 15, May, Corpus Christi, 12 June, 15, 25, Aug., 29 Sep, 12 Oct., 1 Nov., 8, 25 Dec.

Time Zone 3-4 hours behind GMT (clocks go on 1 hour in local summer time).

Currency The Guaraní (plural Guaraníes) is the unit of currency, symbolized by the letter G (crossed). There are bank notes for 100, 500, 1,000, 5,000 and 10,000 guaraníes and coins for 1, 5, 10 and 50 guaraníes. It is possible to buy US dollar bills in Asunción (**see page 828**), and rates for all foreign currencies, except bolivianos, are reasonable. Get rid of all your guaraníes before leaving Paraguay; there is no market for them elsewhere (except in some *cambios* in Buenos Aires or Montevideo). *Casas de cambio* will cash travellers' cheques for US dollars in Asunción for a 1% commission; they sometimes want to see customers' records of purchase before accepting travellers' cheques. **N.B.** In 1989 reports suggested that it was increasingly difficult to change travellers' cheques; visitors are advised to check on the situation in advance. Visa and Mastercharge cash advances are a possibility in Asunción. Street dealers operate from early in the morning until late at night, even at weekends or public holidays. In Asunción their rates are marginally better than the *casas de cambio* during business hours only, but they are not recommended at Ciudad del Este. Many cheap hotels will neither accept nor change travellers' cheques although they may accept credit cards.

Visa and Mastercharge credit cards are widely accepted even for small purchases. Foreign-issued Visa cards may not always be accepted though a phone call will often resolve the problem; Visa is displayed as Unioncard. Credit card transactions are subject to a 10% tax.

Cost of Living is generally cheap. Hotels in our G range are hard to find although there are many good ones in our F-E ranges, with breakfast, private shower and toilet. Hotels near the hydroelectric construction sites are often more expensive and require booking.

Weights and Measures The metric system is used except by carpenters, who use inches.

Electricity Nominally 220 volts AC and 50 cycles, but power surges and voltage drops are frequent.

Postal and Telegraph Services Postal services are cheap and efficient. A normal airmail letter to Europe costs US$0.25 and a registered air letter US$0.35. Register important mail if you want it delivered. Parcels may be sent from main post office on El Paraguayo Independiente, Asunción. Rates: up to 5 kg, US$4 by surface, US$10 by air; 15-20 kg, US$10 by surface, US$35 by air. Packages under 2 kg should be handed in at the small packages window, not "encomiendas". Customs inspection of open parcel required.

The telephone service (few telephone boxes) links the main towns, and there is a telephone service with most countries, operated by Antelco. Collect calls are difficult, charge US$0.30 extra. A phone call to Europe, Australia, and South Africa costs US$2.50 a minute; USA, Canada, US$2 a minute; Spain, US$1.50 a minute. A telex message to Britain is US$5 (1 minute). There is a US$2.50 tax charged by the Post Office for all telexes sent or received in Paraguay.

Newspapers El Diario; Hoy, La Tarde, Ultima Hora, El Diario Noticias and El Pueblo are published daily in Asunción. English-language papers from Argentina and Brazil are available the following day at corner of Estrella and Chile.

Sports Football is very popular. Tennis and horse-racing are popular. There are two rowing and swimming clubs of some 2,000 members, and a motor-boat club with 150 members, in Asunción. Swimming in the Río Paraguay is not recommended: beware stinging starfish where there is mud on the islands and beaches. Golf is played in the Botanical Garden, and there is a Paraguayan Aviation Club. There are two boxing rings. Fishing, basketball and rugby football are popular.

Tourist Information The Dirección Nacional de Turismo has an office in Asunción on the 2nd floor in a building on 25 de Mayo between Alberdi y 14 de Mayo (this appeared to be temporary in 1990). Information about weather and roads from Touring y Automóvil Club Paraguayo (TYACP) at 25 de Mayo y Brasil (who also produce an excellent road map), and the office of the traffic police in Asunción. The best map is available from Instituto Geográfico Militar, Av Artigas (on the way to the zoo), price US$4.50, take passport. Small national maps, made by Army, can be bought from shop across street from Tourist Office. The USAID office has a good booklet on Paraguay. Other books: Así es el Paraguay (with maps and very useful information) and Paraguay, Land of Lace and Legend (reprinted 1983, available from bookshops and Anglo-Paraguayan and US-Paraguay cultural institutes in Asunción); also Green Hill, Far Away, by Peter Upton.

We are most grateful to the following travellers: Karl Alchorn (Oromocto, NB), Martin Anderle, Susanne Riller and Tilo Timmermann (Fürth, W. Ger.), Hans and Verónica Liechti-Avaneda (Santiago de Chile), Erik Bernesson (Båstad, Swe.), Gordon Bethell (St Leonards On Sea), Fearon and Richard Blair (Kamloops BC, Canada), Rop Bomer and Wilhelmien ter Haar (Mexico DF), Jens Borchers (Herzberg/Harz, W. Ger.) and Michael Frantz (Sieber, W. Ger.), Alex Brand (Heidelberg 1), Sara Braune (Stroud), Ken Chitty (Rochester, Kent), Frank Dux (Detmold 18, W. Ger.), Daniel K. Erdin (Gansingen, Switz.), René Erhardt and Lorena Ibáñez (Berlin and Caracas), Anthony Feeny (London EC1), Margaret Fleming (Karlsfeld, W. Ger.), Michael Frantz and Jens Borchers (W. Ger.), Theodor A. Gevert (Barueri, SP Brazil), Martin Gorst (London W13), Rudolf Graf (Genthod, Switz.), Christian Gurney (Thornhill, Ont.), Simon Gustafson (Taby, Swe.), Knut Per Hasund (Stockholm), Jeff Inglis (Seattle), Volkmar E. Janicke (München 40), Rosi Kerler (München 40), Daniel Küng (Wohlen, Switz.), Jo Lerner (Grimbergen, Belg.), John Lewis (London NW2), Mika Määttänen (Tampere, Fin.), Daniel Morgan (Wellington, NZ), Dimitri Moursellas (Manhattan Beach, CA), Richard Müller (Gümligen, Switz.), David, Christine, Philip and Catherine Mylan (Worksop), Stephen Newcomer (Centrevill, Iowa), Steve Newman and Wendy Chilcott (Bahía Blanca), Lauro C. Noldin (Asunción), Barry Oldham (Plymouth, Devon), Karl Olson (New York, NY), Mark Pangbourne (Hastings), Dave and Laurie Parker (Pedro Juan Caballero), Barry M. Pell and Judith L. Katz (Brookline, MA), Jeff Perk (Carbondale, IL), Wulf Peters (Querenhurst, W. Ger.), Rick and Su Sareen (Thailand), Chr Scherlenzky (Bendorf, W. Ger.), Kathrin Schildknecht and Jürg Schmutz (Bern, Switz.), Ueli Schlatter (Hemmental, Switz.), Andrea Schneiber (Herborn, W. Ger.), von Schubert (Kehl, W. Ger.), Daniel Schweimler and Claudia Ricca (London E7), Christian Stückle (Ingolstadt, W. Ger.), Douglas B. Trent (Focus Tours, Belo Horizonte), T.C. Walker (Chobham, Sy.), Patrick Wallerand (Liège, Belg.), Ignaz Wanders (Haarlem), Rob Ward (Sutton, Sy.) and Helmut Zettl (Ebergassing, Austria).

PERU

INTRODUCTION

PERU, the third largest South American country, with an area of 1,285,216 sq. kms (over twice the size of France) presents formidable difficulties to human habitation. The whole of its western seaboard with the Pacific is desert on which rain seldom falls. From this coastal shelf the Andes rise steeply to a high Sierra which is studded with massive groups of soaring mountains and gouged with deep canyons. The highland slopes more gradually eastwards; the mountains in its eastern zone are deeply forested and ravined. Eastward from these mountains lie the vast jungle lands of the Amazon basin.

The coastal region, a narrow ribbon of desert 2,250 km. long, takes up 11% of the country and holds 44% of the population. When irrigated, the river valleys are extremely fertile. Almost 600,000 hectares are watered today, creating 40 oases which grow cotton throughout the country, sugar-cane and rice in the N, and grapes, fruit and olives in the S. Petroleum comes from the N and Amazonia. The coastal zone is the economic heart of Peru; it consumes most of the imports and supplies half of the exports. Climate is determined by cold sea-water adjoining deserts: prevailing inshore winds pick up so little moisture over the cold Peruvian current that only for five months, from June to October, does it condense. The resultant blanket of cloud and sea-mist extends from the S to about 200 km. N of Lima. This *garúa* dampens isolated coastal zones of vegetation (called *lomas*) and they are grazed by livestock driven down from the mountains. The Peruvian coastal current teems with fish, and Peru has had the largest catch in the world; however, in recent years, the *anchoveta* shoals have moved southward into Chilean waters. At intervals during December-April a current of warm water, known as "El Niño", is blown S from the equator over the cold offshore waters and the surface temperature rises, the fish migrate, and evaporation is so great

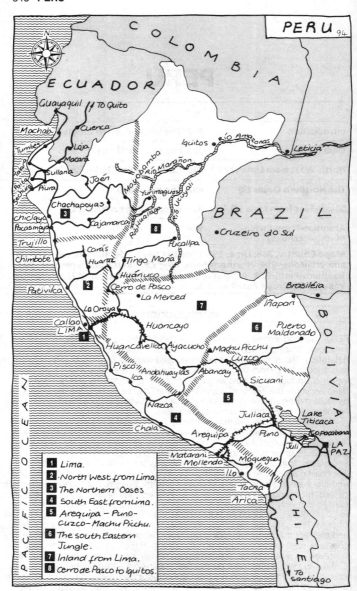

PERU 94

1 Lima.
2 North West from Lima.
3 The Northern Oases.
4 South East from Lima.
5 Arequipa – Puno –
   Cuzco – Machu Picchu.
6 The South Eastern
   Jungle.
7 Inland from Lima.
8 Cerro de Pasco to Iquitos.

that the desert is deluged with rain which creates havoc (most recently in 1983).

In the Sierra, at an average altitude of 3,000 metres, which covers 26% of the country, live about 50% of the people, an excessive density on such poor land. This high-level land of gentle slopes is surrounded by towering groups and ranges of high peaks. Ten are over 6,000 metres; the highest, Huascarán, is 6,768 metres. There are many volcanoes in the S. The continental divide is the western rim of mountains looking down on the Pacific. Rivers which rise in these mountains and flow towards the Amazon cut through the cold surface of the plateau in canyons, sometimes 1,500 metres deep, in which the climate is tropical. Pastoral farming is possible on about 13 million hectares of the plateau; the deep valley basins contain the best land for arable farming.

The plateau, mountains and canyons are inhabited mostly by Indians. There are 5,000 Indian communities but few densely populated settlements. Their literacy rate is the lowest of any comparable group in South America and their diet is 40% below acceptable levels. Nearly 99% of the rural population and 60% of the town dwellers have no running water or drainage. About two million Indians speak no Spanish, their main tongue being Quechua, the language of the Incas; they are largely outside the money economy.

A mostly Indian labour force of over 80,000 is engaged in mining, and mineral exports from the Sierra represent half of total exports. Minerals are extracted as far up as 5,200 metres. Some of the sheep-farming areas are at altitudes ranging up to 4,250 metres.

The wide areas of high and wind-swept Altiplano in S Peru are near the limit of agriculture—though some potatoes and cereals (*quinoa* and *cañihua*) are grown—but the Indians use it for grazing llamas, alpacas and sheep; it cannot support cattle. The pastoral Indians of the area live off their flocks; they weave their clothes from the wools, eat the meat, use the dried dung for fuel and the llamas for transport. They are, in short, almost entirely self-supporting.

The **Montaña**, or **Selva**, the forested eastern half of the Andes and the land beyond covered with tropical forest and jungle, is 62% of the country's area but holds only about 5% of the population. Its inhabitants are crowded on the river banks in the cultivable land—a tiny part of the area. The few roads (given in the text) have to cope with dense forest, deep valleys, and sharp eastern slopes ranging from 2,150 metres in the N to 5,800 metres E of Lake Titicaca. Rivers are the main highways, though navigation is hazardous and the draught of the vessels shallow. The area's potential is enormous: immense reserves of timber, excellent land for the production of rubber, jute, rice, tropical fruits and coffee and the breeding of cattle. Few of these products come out by road to the W; most of them converge by river on Iquitos, which is 11,250 km. from Callao via the Panama Canal and the Amazon but only 1,010 km. as the condor flies.

Oilfields have been discovered southwards from the Ecuadorean border and estimates indicate that about 80% of Peru's oil reserves are in the jungle area.

The Nor Peruano oil pipeline links the Amazon area with the coast.

Climate The climate of the highlands is varied: the W side is dry, but the northern and eastern parts get very heavy rains from October to April, and are heavily forested up to a limit of 3,350 metres: the grasslands are between the forest line and the snowline, which rises from 5,000 metres in the latitude of Lima to 5,800 metres in the S. Most of the Sierra is covered with grasses and shrubs, with Puna vegetation (bunch grass mixed with low, hairy-leaved plants) from N of Huaraz to the S.

Pre-History Two Harvard archaeologists, Michael Moseley and Robert Feldman, concluded, following excavations at coastal sites at Ancón, Supe, etc., that an early civilization sprang up on the coast on the basis of a fishing economy and was well developed by 2100 BC. (This is in complete contradiction of one of archaeology's basic tenets that development of agriculture must invariably precede civilization.) The key site is Aspero near Supe, where low mounds facing the shore revealed stone walls, plaster clap-board shaped friezes, wall niches, a trapezoidal doorway (predating the Incas by 3,500 years) and unbaked clay figurines. One of the mounds is bisected by a gigantic looters' pit which gives an interesting cross-section across the mound, showing at least fifteen different occupation levels defined by floors and bands of ash and burnt rocks (heated and dropped into gourds or tightly-woven baskets to cook fish before the days of cooking pots). The hypothesis of Moseley and Feldman has, however, been seriously questioned by further study such as that of David J. Wilson of the University of Michigan. He argues that a mixed agricultural-maritime economy based primarily on plant cultivation is evident at coastal sites such as El Paraíso and Aspero, and that El Niño conditions must be taken into account as a recurring and biologically devastating phenomenon creating critical lean periods in the diet of maritime-oriented coastal populations at all levels in the food chain.

This early start on the coast developed into a *huaca* (mound)-building culture of whose works the easiest to visit is Garagay, within sight of Lima airport and identified easily by an electricity pylon built on top. It is a U-shaped complex of three mounds with magnificent adobe friezes (not open to the public as there is no way of preserving them) half way up the main mound, dated by Dr. Roger Ravines to 1000 BC. In the huge plaza enclosed by the mounds a circular subterranean plaza has been found with symmetrical staircases. This is an important find, as a similar circular plaza was found recently at Chavín. The Chavín culture flourished mainly in the highlands near the coast from Piura S to Pisco, from about 800 to 200 BC. Whether it had origins on the coast or in the highlands is a matter for debate because it is unknown where the fusion of styles which characterized the Chavín cult took place. Its centre was Chavín de Huantar, which was a cross-roads of trade between coast, Sierra and jungle; the University of San Marcos has an interesting museum including a collection of Chavín pottery. It influenced heavily the Paracas culture of the S at about 200 BC to AD 200 (see under Nazca), the high Nazca culture (AD 400-800) the more primitive culture around Lima in the centre, and the Mochica culture in the N which had its beginnings just before the Christian era—some say as early as 300 BC—and lasted until the sixth century AD, characterized by realistic moulded pottery, sculptured wood and worked metals and by the huge adobe pyramids of the Moche valley (see under Trujillo). About AD 600, the Huari empire, based at Huari near Ayacucho, came to prominence; at its greatest its influence spread from Cajamarca and the Chicama valley in the North to almost the Titicaca basin and the Ocaña valley on the South coast. It overlapped with the Tiahuanaco culture, which was possibly an indigenous development, even if complementary to Huari and the Nazca culture. The classical Tiahuanaco culture, whose great monument is the ruins of Tiahuanaco, E of Lake Titicaca in Bolivia, dominated the coast until the 9th century. Possibly towards the end of the 11th century, the Incas had begun to rise in the Cuzco basin; their conquest of Peru and Ecuador was only completed around 1450. (Their civilization is briefly described under Cuzco, **page 950**.)

History A short time before the Spaniards arrived Peru was being ruled from Cuzco by the Inca Huáscar and from Quito by his half-brother Atahualpa, who was victorious in the civil war between the two. When Francisco Pizarro and Diego de Almagro landed a tiny force in Peru in 1532, Atahualpa, no doubt anxious for allies, allowed them to reach the Sierra. Pizarro's only chance against the formidable imperial army he encountered at Cajamarca was a bold stroke. He drew Atahualpa into an ambush, slaughtered his guards, promised him liberty if a certain room were filled with treasure, and finally killed him after receiving news that another Inca army was on its way to free him. Pushing on to Cuzco, he was at first hailed as the executioner of a traitor: Atahualpa had killed Huáscar after the battle of Huancavelica two years previously. Panic followed when the *conquistadores* set about sacking the city, and they fought off with difficulty an attempt by Manco Inca to recapture Cuzco in 1538. (For the whole period of the Conquest John Hemming's *The Conquest of the Incas* is invaluable; he himself refers us to Ann Kendall's *Everyday Life of the Incas*, Batsford, London, 1978.)

In 1535, wishing to secure his communications with Spain, Pizarro founded Lima, near the ocean, as his capital. The same year Almagro set out to conquer Chile. Unsuccessful, he returned to Peru, quarrelled with Pizarro, and in 1538 fought a pitched battle with Pizarro's men at the Salt Pits, near Cuzco. He was defeated and put to death. Pizarro, who had not been at the battle, was assassinated in his palace in Lima by Almagro's son three years later. For the next 27 years each succeeding representative of the Kingdom of Spain sought to subdue the Inca successor state of Vilcabamba, N of Cuzco, and to unify the fierce Spanish factions. Francisco de Toledo (appointed 1568) solved both problems during his 14 years in office: Vilcabamba was crushed in 1572 and the last reigning Inca, Túpac Amaru, put to death. For the next 200 years the Viceroys closely followed Toledo's system, if not his methods. The Major Government—the Viceroy, the High Court (*Audiencia*), and *corregidores* (administrators)—ruled through the Minor Government—Indian chiefs put in charge of large groups of natives: a rough approximation to the original Inca system.

The Indians rose in 1780, under the leadership of an Inca noble who called himself Túpac Amaru II. He and many of his lieutenants were captured and put to death under torture at Cuzco. Another Indian leader in revolt suffered the same fate in 1814, but this last flare-up had the sympathy of many of the locally-born Spanish, who resented their status, inferior to the Spaniards born in Spain, the refusal to give them any but the lowest offices, the high taxation imposed by the home government, and the severe restrictions upon trade with any country but Spain. Help came to them from the outside world: José de San Martín's Argentine troops, convoyed from Chile under the protection of Lord Cochrane's squadron, landed in southern Peru on September 7, 1820. San Martín proclaimed Peruvian independence at Lima on July 28, 1821, though most of the country was still in the hands of the Viceroy, La Serna. Bolívar, who had already freed Venezuela and Colombia, sent Sucre to Ecuador where, on May 24, 1822, he gained a victory over La Serna at Pichincha. San Martín, after a meeting with Bolívar at Guayaquil, left for Argentina and a self-imposed exile in France, while Bolívar and Sucre completed the conquest of Peru by defeating La Serna at the battle of Junín (August 6, 1824) and the decisive battle of Ayacucho (December 9, 1824). For over a year there was a last stand in the Real Felipe fortress at Callao by the Spanish troops under General Rodil before they capitulated on January 22, 1826. Bolívar was invited to stay in Peru, but left for Colombia in 1826.

Important subsequent events were a temporary confederation between Peru and Bolivia in the 1830s; the Peruvian-Spanish War (1866); and the War of the Pacific (1879-1883), in which Peru and Bolivia were defeated by Chile and Peru lost its southernmost territory. A long-standing legacy of this was the Tacna-Arica dispute, which was not settled until 1929 (see under Tacna).

A reformist military Junta took over control of the country in October 1968. Under its first leader, Gen. Juan Velasco Alvarado, the Junta instituted a series of measures to raise the personal status and standard of living of the workers and the rural Indians, by land reform, worker participation in industrial management and ownership, and nationalization of basic industries, exhibiting an ideology perhaps best described as "military socialism". In view of his failing health Gen. Velasco was replaced in 1975 by Gen. Francisco Morales Bermúdez and policy (because of a mounting economic crisis and the consequent need to seek financial aid from abroad) swung to the Right. Presidential and congressional elections were held on May 18, 1980, and Sr. Fernando Belaúnde Terry was elected President for the second time. His term was marked by growing economic problems and the growth of the Maoist guerrilla movement Sendero Luminoso (Shining Path). Initially conceived in the University of Ayacucho, the movement now gets most of its support from highland Indians and migrants to urban shanty towns. Its main target is Lima-based authority and its aim is the overthrow of the whole system of government. The activities of Sendero Luminoso and another guerrilla group, Túpac Amaru, frequently disrupt transport and electricity supplies.

The April 1985 elections were won by the APRA party leader Alán García Pérez, who took office as President on July 28, 1985. During his populist, left-wing presidency disastrous economic policies caused increasing poverty and civil instability. In presidential elections held over two rounds in April and June 1990, Sr. Alberto Fujimori of the Cambio 90 movement defeated the novelist Mario Vargas Llosa, who belonged to the Fredemo (Democratic Front) coalition. Both candidates were entering national politics for the first time and the victor did not have an established political network behind him. He failed to win a majority in either the senate, where Cambio 90 won a sixth of the seats, or the lower house, where it gained a third. Fredemo, with a third of each house, and Apra with a third of the senate and a quarter of the lower house, were the dominant political forces with whom he would have to negotiate.

Population 21.3m. (1988 estimate), growing at an annual rate of 2.6%. Just under 70% of the population is urban, and the urban growth rate in 1981-88 was 3.5%. Birth rate, 36.7 per 1,000 (1980-85); death rate 10.7 per 1,000 (1980-85). Infant mortality per 1,000 live births between 1980 and 1985 was 98.6. The literacy rate is 86%. Gdp per capita is US$1,503 (1988).

The Economy Revitalization of agriculture, which accounts for 14% of gdp and 37% of employment, is a government priority. While the Costa (which occupies 11% of the land area) has traditionally been the dominant economic region, with excellent crops of cotton, rice, sugar and fruit where the coastal desert is irrigated, the Sierra is being given preferential treatment with a view to restoring the self-sufficiency in food production of Inca times. Irrigation of the coastal region using Andean waters is the key to improved yields of the main export crops, sugar and cotton. The other main export crop is coffee.

Although employing only 2% of the workforce, mining contributes 10% of gdp and the six major minerals and metals account for 40% of total export value. These are copper, iron, silver, gold, lead and zinc. Copper and iron deposits are found on the southern coast, but the principal mining area for all minerals is the Sierra. Low world prices, particularly for zinc and lead, strikes in the copper industry, rising costs an uncompetitive exchange rate have contributed to considerable losses for both public and private mining companies, and to reduced real output.

Peruvian oil accounts for 50% of domestic energy consumption. The northeastern jungle produced an average of 115,500 b/d in 1986, on and off the northwestern coast 55,000-65,000 b/d, while fields in the southern jungle are being explored. No major new reserves have been found since 1976. Local funds for investment fell in the 1980s, hence the need for foreign companies to invest in exploration, but in 1985 the García Government rescinded the operating contracts of three major foreign firms, adversely affecting investment prospects, despite subsequent new agreements. By the end of 1989 total oil production had fallen to 105,000 b/d.

Manufacturing contributes 23% of gdp, employing 10% of the workforce. After high growth rates in the early 1970s, industry slumped to operating at 40% of its total capacity as purchasing power was reduced, and the cost of energy, raw materials and trade credit rose faster than inflation. A consumer-led recovery in 1986 led to most of industry working at full capacity, but the boom was followed by a severe slump in 1988-1990. Similarly, construction returned to growth in 1986 as a result of government projects, after three years of recession, but declined heavily in 1988-1990.

Fishing, which accounts for 1% of gdp, suffered a dramatic decline in 1983 as the Niño current forced out of Peruvian waters the main catch, anchovy, whose stocks were already seriously depleted by overfishing in the 1970s. From being the world's leading fishmeal exporter, with exports accounting for 14% of the country's total, fishmeal sales fell to 4% in 1985, recovering in 1986 to 8%. The García government partially reversed its predecessor's policy of closing fishmeal plants, in conjunction with promoting fish as a domestic food source.

Growing fiscal deficits in the 1980s led to increasing delays in payments of principal and interest on the foreign debt, which was estimated at US$20.4 bn. at the end of 1989. As arrears accumulated to both multilateral agencies and commercial banks, the IMF declared Peru ineligible for further credits in 1986. On taking office, President García limited public debt service payments to 10% of foreign exchange earnings in order to maintain reserves to promote development. The need to import food, the low level of exports and the fall in disbursements of foreign capital in fact caused international reserves to fall. By 1987 the country was bankrupt after the free spending policies at the beginning of the administration and inflation soared as the Government resorted to printing money.

Government Legislation is vested in a Congress composed of a Senate (60 seats) and a Chamber of Deputies (180 seats). Men and women over 18 are eligible to vote; registration and voting is compulsory until the age of 60. The President, to whom is entrusted the Executive Power, is elected for five years and may not be re-elected until after one presidential term has passed. A new Constitution was approved in July 1979. In 1987 Congress approved a change in the administration of the country and a system of 13 Regions replaced the previous 25 Departments (divided into 150 Provinces, subdivided into 1,321 Districts). Elections for these Regions were held in 1989 and 1990.

Education is free and compulsory for both sexes between 6 and 14. There are public and private secondary schools and private elementary schools. There are 32 State and private universities, and two Catholic universities. A new educational system is being implemented as too many children cannot complete secondary school.

Communications Several roads and two railways run up the slopes of the Andes to reach the Sierra. These railways, once British owned, run from Lima in the centre and the ports of Matarani and Mollendo in the S. There are in all 2,740 km. of railway. There are three main paved roads: the Pan-American Highway runs N-S through the coastal desert and sends a spur NE into the Sierra to Arequipa, with a partially paved continuation to Puno on Lake Titicaca which then skirts the lake to Desaguadero, on the Bolivian frontier, a total of 3,418 km.; the Central Highway from Lima to Huancayo, which continues (mostly paved) to Pucallpa in the Amazon basin; and the direct road from Lima N to Huaraz. Both roads and railways are given in the text and shown on sketch maps.

LIMA (1)

Lima, capital of Peru, was the chief city of Spanish South America from its founding in 1535 until the independence of the South American republics in the

Key to Map.
1. Plaza de Armas. 2. Palacio de Gobierno. 3. Cathedral. 4. Union Club. 5. Plaza San Martín. 6. Torre Tagle Palace. 7. Plaza 2 de Mayo. 8. Plaza Bolognesi. 9. Plaza Grau. 10. Palacio de Justicia. 11. National Museum of Art. 12. Museum of Italian Art. 13. Panteón de los Próceres. 14. Museum of Peruvian Culture. 15. Las Nazarenas Church. 16. National Library. 17. *Hotel Bolívar.* 18. *Hotel Crillón.* 19. *Hotel Riviera.* 20. *Hotel Savoy.* 21. *Hotel Maury.* 22. Municipal Theatre. 23. Teatro Segura. 24. *Hotel Continental.* 25. *Hotel Sheraton.* 26. Civic Centre. 27. City Hall. 28. Parque Universitario.

N.B. A good map of Greater Lima may be bought at the Jorge Chávez airport and in the main shopping streets; it has street references and the main bus routes on the back (US$2).

early 19th century. It is built on both sides of the Río Rímac, lying at the foot of the Cerro San Cristóbal. From among the traditional buildings which still survive soar many tall skyscrapers which have changed the old skyline out of recognition. The city, which is now very dirty and seriously affected by smog for much of the year, is surrounded by "Pueblos Jóvenes," or shanty settlements of squatters who have migrated from the Sierra; much self-help building is in progress. There are still signs of damage after the disastrous 1970 earthquakes nearby, especially in the Rímac section of the city. Many of the hotels and larger business houses have moved to the plush seaside suburbs of Miraflores and San Isidro.

Half of the town-dwellers of Peru now live in Lima. The metropolitan area contains six to seven million people, nearly one third of the country's total population, and two-thirds of its industries.

In the older part the way the streets are named may confuse the visitor. Several blocks, with their own names, make up a long street, a *jirón* (often abbreviated to Jr.). The visitor is greatly helped by the corner signs which bear both the name of the *jirón* and the name of the block. The new and old names of streets are used interchangeably: remember that Colmena is also Nicolás de Piérola, Wilson is Inca Garcilaso de la Vega, and Carabaya is also Augusto N. Wiese. The city's urban motorway is often called "El Zanjón" (the ditch).

Only 12° S of the equator, one would expect a tropical climate, but from June to at least October the skies are grey; it feels chilly, clothes take ages to dry, and a damp *garúa*, or Scotch mist, is common. The rest of the year is mild and pleasant with temperatures ranging from 10° to 27°C (15° to 30°C in summer)

History The University of San Marcos was founded in 1551, and a printing press in 1595: among the earliest of their kind in S. America. Lima's first theatre opened in 1563. The Inquisition was introduced in 1569 and was not abolished until 1820. For some time the Viceroyalty of Peru embraced Colombia, Ecuador, Bolivia, Chile and Argentina. The city's wealth attracted many freebooters and in 1670 a protecting wall 11 km. long, which was demolished in 1869, was built round it. Lima's power was at its height during the 17th century and the early 18th, until the earthquake of 1746 destroyed all but 20 houses and killed 4,000 inhabitants. There were few cities in the Old World that could rival its wealth and luxury. It was only comparatively recently, with the coming of industry, that Lima began to change into what it is today.

Sightseeing The heart of the city, at least in plan, is still what it was in colonial days. A single block S of the Río Rímac lies the Plaza de Armas; the Desamparados Station of the Central Railway is quite near. Most of what the tourist wants to see is in this area. The newer parts of the city are based on Plaza San Martín, S of Jirón de la Unión, with a statue of San Martín in the centre. One and a quarter km. W is the Plaza Dos de Mayo. About 1 km. due S of this again is the circular Plaza Bolognesi, from which many great *avenidas* radiate.

The Jirón de La Unión, the main shopping street, runs to the Plaza de Armas; it has been converted into a pedestrian precinct (street theatre, street vendors, etc., in the evening). Later the pedestrian area will be extended to cover the southern half of Jirón de la Unión, from Plaza San Martín to Plaza Grau. In the two northernmost blocks of Jr. Unión, known as Calle Belén, several shops sell souvenirs and curios: the nearer the shops are to the best hotels the dearer the souvenirs are. Around the great Plaza de Armas stand the Government Palace, the Cathedral (**see page 856**), the Archbishop's Palace, the City Hall and the Unión Club. The Central Post Office is opposite the visitors' entrance to Government Palace. Running along two sides are arcades with shops: Portal de Escribanos and Portal de Botoneros. In the centre is a bronze fountain dating from 1650.

The **Palacio de Gobierno** (Government Palace) was built from 1921 to 1938, on the site of and with some of the characteristics of Pizarro's palace. Visitors' entrance is on Jirón de la Unión. Guided tours at 1230, but you must present your documentation on previous day (Mon.-Thur. only). Under state-of-siege regulations it is difficult to get in at other times. The ceremonial changing of the guard behind the gates of the palace is worth watching, most days 0800 and 1245-1300 (check with the Tourist Office).

The **Municipalidad de Lima**, built 1945, has a picture gallery (open 0800-1500 Mon.,-Fri., free).

Near San Pedro, at Jirón Ucayali 363, is **Torre Tagle Palace**, the city's best surviving specimen of secular colonial architecture: a Sevillian mansion built in 1735. Now occupied by the Foreign Ministry, but visitors are allowed to enter courtyards to inspect fine wood-carving in balconies, wrought iron work, and a 16th-century coach complete with commode. During working hours Mon.-Fri,. visitors may enter the patio only.

A short taxi ride across the Río Rímac takes you to the Convent of Los Descalzos (**see page 857**) and the Quinta de Presa (incorrectly reputed to be the house of La Perrichola), now the Viceregal Museum (Museo Virreynal— **see page 858**), closed at present for repairs.

La Perrichola—real name Micaela Villegas—was a beauty, wit, actress, and mistress of Viceroy Amat (1761-1776). Legend says he installed her in this mansion, but the house the Viceroy built for her was torn down last century. She has inspired plays, an opera (by Offenbach) and many books, the best known of which is Thornton Wilder's *The Bridge of San Luis Rey*.

The Puente de Piedra, behind the Presidential Palace, is a Roman-style stone bridge built 1610. Hundreds of thousands of egg whites were used to strengthen its mortar.

Other important mansions worth visiting are the **Casa Pilatos**, opposite the San Francisco church at Jirón Ancash 390, now the Casa de Cultura, open 0830-1645, Mon.-Fri.; **Casa de la Riva** at Jirón Ica 426, now the German Institute; **Casa de Oquendo** at Conde de Superunda 298 has been reopened after restoration, and stages art exhibitions; **Casa Negreiros** (a restaurant), at Jirón Azángaro 532; and **Casa de las Trece Monedas** (also a restaurant), at Jirón Ancash 536. The **Casa Aliaga**, at Unión 224, is still occupied by the Aliaga family and has recently been opened to the public; Vista Tours has exclusive rights to include the house in its tours (T 27-6624, or any travel agent). The house contains what is said to be the oldest ceiling in Lima and is furnished entirely in the colonial style. Don Jerónimo de Aliaga was one of the 13 commanders to arrive with Francisco Pizarro, and all 13 were given land around the main square to build their own houses when Lima was founded in 1535. The house of the author Ricardo Palma is open to the public, Mon.Fri. 1000-1230, 1600-1900 (a.m. only Sat.), small entrance fee, Gral. Suárez 189, Miraflores—a 19th-century middle-class residence.

Other old mansions worth seeing: **Museo Berckemeyer** (art and bullfighting), Jr. Lima 341, a typical 17th-century *limeño* house—one of the few left; T 270025 for an appointment to visit, Mon.-Fri., 0830-1300. **Casa Barbieri**, Jr. Callao, near Jr. Rufino Torrico—a fine old 18th-century town house in the Sevillian style; ring bell in entrance hall for permission to look at the patios. **Casa Museo Prado**, Jr. Cuzco 448, visitable when Sr. Prado is in residence, a beautifully maintained house with early 19th-century front and, apparently, a 17th-century patio. **AAA Theatre**, Jr. Ica 323, is in a lovely 18th-century house. **Casa de la Rada**, Jr. Ucayali, opposite Palacio Torre Tagle—an extremely fine mid-18th-century town house in the French manner; patio and first reception room open occasionally to the public (now belongs to a bank).

Churches

The Cathedral (open to visitors 0930-1200, 1400-1700 every day) is on the Plaza de Armas. See the splendidly carved stalls (mid-17th century); the silver-covered altars surrounded by fine woodwork; mosaic-covered walls bearing the coats of arms of Lima and Pizarro and an allegory of Pizarro's commanders, the "Thirteen Men of Isla del Gallo"; in a small chapel, the first on the right of the entrance, are remains in a glass coffin originally said to be those of Pizarro, but later research indicates that his remains lie in the crypt. Museum of Religious Art in the cathedral, guided visits, ask to see picture restoration room, all-inclusive entrance ticket, US$0.90. The Archbishop's Palace was rebuilt in 1924, with a superb wooden balcony.

Four notable churches are quite near the Plaza de Armas: **La Merced** (open 0700-1230, 1600-2000 every day) and its monastery (open 0800-1200 and 1500-1730 daily) are in Plazuela de la Merced, Jirón de la Unión, two blocks from the Plaza de Armas. The first mass in Lima was said on this site. Very fine restored colonial façade, and attractive cloister. See the choir stalls and the vestry's panelled ceiling. At independence the Virgin of La Merced was made a Marshal of the Peruvian army. **Santo Domingo**, built 1549, is in Jirón Camaná (first block). In an urn in one of the altars are the remains of Santa Rosa de Lima (1586-1617), the first saint of the New World: 30 August is her day. Pope Clement presented, 1669, the alabaster statue of the Saint in front of the altar (entrance, US2.75, students US$1.25, open 0700-1300, 1600-2000 daily; monastery and tombs open 0930-1230, 1530-1730 Mon.-Sat.; Sun. and holidays a.m. only). The main hall has some interesting relics. **San Francisco**, open 1000-1300 and 1500-1730, in first block of Jirón Lampa, corner of Ancash, is a baroque church with Arabic influences, finished 1674, under reconstruction (but a great deal has been done). See carved "Sillería Coral" (1622), gold monstrance set with jewels made in Cuzco (1671), and José de Rivera's paintings (1672). The monastery is famous for Sevillian tilework and panelled ceilings in the cloisters (1620). Catacombs under church and part of monastery, well worth seeing; entry charge is US$2, by guided tour only, Spanish and English, last groups start at 1245 and 1745 daily. **San Pedro** (open 0700-1300, 1740-2030 every day), 3rd block of Jirón Ucayali, finished by Jesuits in 1638, has marvellous altars with Moorish-style balconies, rich gilded wood carvings in choir and vestry, and tiled throughout. Several Viceroys buried here; the bell called La Abuelita, first rung in 1590, sounded the Declaration of Independence in 1821.

Santuario de Santa Rosa (Av. Tacna, 1st block), small but graceful church. A pilgrimage centre; here are preserved the hermitage built by Santa Rosa herself, the house in which she was born, a section of the house in which she attended to the sick, her well, and other relics. Open 0930-1245 and 1530-1830 daily; entrance to grounds free.

Las Nazarenas Church (Av. Tacna, 4th block, open 0700-1130 and 1630-2000 daily), built around an image of Christ Crucified painted by a liberated slave in 1655. This, the most venerated image in Lima, and an oil copy of El Señor de los Milagros (Lord of Miracles), encased in a gold frame, are carried on a silver litter—the whole weighing nearly a ton—through the streets on 18, 19, and 28 October and again on 1 November (All Saints' Day).

San Agustín (Jirón Ica, 251), W of the Plaza de Armas, is a much changed old church, but its façade (1720) is a splendid example of churrigueresque architecture. There are carved choir stalls and effigies, and a sculpture of Death, said to have frightened its maker into an early grave. Open 0830-1200, 1530-1730 daily, ring for entry. Since being damaged in the last earthquake the church has been sensitively restored, but the sculpture of Death is in storage.

Fine 18th century carving also in gilt altars of **Jesús María** (Jirón Moquegua, 1st block), and in **Magdalena Vieja** (1557, but reconstructed in 1931), with altar pieces, of gilded and carved wood, particularly fine; it should be seen during visit to the Museum of Archaeology, Plaza Bolívar (in Pueblo Libre). Another church worth seeing for its two beautiful colonial doors is **San Marcelo**, at Av. de la Emancipación, 4th block.

The **Convent of Los Descalzos** on the Alameda de Los Descalzos in Rímac contains over 300 paintings of the Cuzco, Quito and Lima schools which line the four main cloisters and two ornate chapels. The chapel of El Carmen was constructed in 1730 and is notable for its baroque gold leaf altar. The museum shows the life of the Franciscan friars during colonial and early republican periods; the cellar, infirmary, pharmacy and a typical cell have all been restored. The library has not yet been incorporated into the tour. The convent is open Mon.-Sat. 0930-1300, 1400-1730, entrance US$1. Guided tour only, 45 mins. in Spanish, but worth it.

The church of **Santo Tomás** is now a school (Gran Unidad Escolar "Mercedes Cabello de Carbonera", on corner of Junín and Andahuaylas); it is said to have the only circular cloister in the world apart from St. Peter's in Rome, and a fine 17th-century Italian-designed baroque library. The headmistress is glad to show people round.

Note: Churches are open between 1830 and 2100 unless otherwise stated.

Museums

Museum of National History, Plaza Bolívar, Pueblo Libre, in a mansion built by Viceroy Pezuela and occupied by San Martín (1821-1822) and Bolívar (1823-1826). Exhibits: colonial and early republican paintings, manuscripts, portraits, uniforms, etc. Paintings mainly of historical episodes. 0900-1730, except Sat. Admission US$0.50. Bus 12 from corner of Tacna and Emancipación, minibus 2 from Rufino Torrico, bus 21, 42, 48 from Parque Universitario.

The Gold Museum (Museo Miguel Mujica Gallo), is in 7th block of Prolongación Av. Primavera (Av. de Molina 1110), Monterrico, several km. from centre (T 352919); bus 76 from Av. Alfonso Ugarte, or bus 2 from Plaza San Martín to Miraflores (corner of Avenida Arequipa and Angamos), then change to colectivo 112 which passes the door (call out "bajo en el museo"); alternatively, take any of the buses (such as 55) going up Angamos, they go past the side road to the museum—bus 59b goes from Parque Unversitario to Angamos (get out after the bridge under Panamericana Sur), orange bus marked "Monterrico/Covina" from Plaza 2 de Mayo; by taxi, with 2½ hrs. at the museum, US$10 (US$3 without wait, 45 mins. from centre, 30 mins. from Miraflores). It is still privately owned. An underground museum contains items which have been exhibited in the world's leading museums. The collection includes precolumbian metals (99% pre-Inca), weavings, mummies and a remarkable arms collection. Well worth seeing, despite being poorly displayed and explained; catalogue costs US$9. Open daily (incl. Sun. and holidays) 1200-1900. Admission: US$5, students (with card) half price. No photography allowed. Good copies of ancient pottery are on sale and there are high quality craft shops in the garden.

National Museum of Art, Paseo Colón 125, in the Palacio de la Exposición, built in 1868 in Parque de la Exposición. More than 7,000 exhibits, giving a chronological history of Peruvian cultures and art from the 2,000-year-old Paracas civilization up to today. Excellent examples of 17th and 18th century Cuzco paintings, a beautiful display of carved furniture, heavy silver and jewelled stirrups, also precolumbian pottery. During the autumn and winter seasons, starting in April, there are guided tours, lectures and films every Friday evening (see also under **Cinemas** below). Several good, English-speaking guides. 0900-1700 Tues.-Sun. Admission US$2. Recommended guide: José Luis Vilches, who speaks English and French, and is most helpful and informative. English books for sale and exchange in the bookshop.

Museum of the Inquisition, Plaza Bolívar, Calle Junín 548, near corner of Av. Abancay. The main hall, with splendidly carved mahogany ceiling, remains untouched. Court of Inquisition held here 1569-1820; until 1930 used by the Senate. In the basement there is an accurate re-creation *in situ* of the tortures. A description in English is available at the desk. Students offer to show you round for a tip; good explanations in English. The museum was closed in 1989.

Museum of Anthropology and Archaeology, Plaza Bolívar (San Martín with Antonio Pola), not in the centre but in Pueblo Libre (T 611312—not Av. José de la Riva as shown on Cartografía Nacional map), a museum for exhibition and study of art and history of aboriginal races of Peru. Most interesting textiles from Paracas and ceramics of Chimú, Nazca, Mochica and Pachacámac cultures, and various Inca curiosities and works of art. See the Raimondi stella and the Tello obelisk from Chavín, and the marvellous Mochica pottery, and a reconstruction of one of the galleries at Chavín. An impressive model of Machu-Picchu in the Sala Inca. Easily the most interesting museum in Peru. Open Mon.-Sun., 1000-1830. Admission US$1.60 (students half price), plus US$1 to take photographs with flash. Students guide you around for no charge, but give a tip. Guide book in English US$4.50; gift shop next door. Bus 12 from corner of Tacna and Emancipación, Bus 41M from Cuzco and Emancipacíon, Minibus 2 from Rufino Torrico, also bus 21, 24, 41 or 42 from Parque Universitario. Direction "Avenida Brasil", alight at General Vivanco.

There is also an archaeological museum at Puruchuco (see page 877), and at the excavated mound of Santa Catalina, Parque Fernando Carozi in La Victoria (an insalubrious district); minibus 1 or 46 from Plaza 2 de Mayo.

Museo de la Nación, Javier Prado Este 2465, San Borja, anthropological and archaeological exhibits from pre-Inca and Inca times, with a section on costume and weaving. Open Tues.-Fri. 0900-2100, Sat., Sun., and holidays 1000-1900, entry US$3. Take bus or colectivo from the centre or Miraflores to Javier Prado, then bus 13, 12 or colectivo to the museum (block 24).

Museo Banco Central de Reserva, Av. Ucayali and Lampa (one block from San Pedro Church, on same side as Torre Tagle Palace). Large collection of pottery from Vicus or Piura culture (AD 500-600) and gold objects from Lambayeque, as well as 19th and 20th century paintings. Both modern and ancient exhibitions highly recommended. (Don't be put off by the sombre bank exterior!) Tues.-Fri. 1000-1700. Photography prohibited.

Museo Etnográfico de la Selva, Av. Tacna 120 (4 blocks NW of Plaza de Armas), houses cultural and household objects from Madre de Dios; run by Dominicans, open every day (except Mon.) until 1900, US$0.10 (under reconstruction 1988/89).

Museum of Peruvian Culture, Av. Alfonso Ugarte 650, showing pots and popular art, and costumes worn by Indians in various parts of Peru, includes exhibition of *mate burilado* (carved gourds); open 1000-1700, Mon.-Fri., 0900-1700, Sat. Admission US$0.20 (students half price); US$0.70 to take photographs.

Rafael Larco Herrera Museum, Av. Bolívar 1515, Pueblo Libre, is the Chiclín pottery museum brought from Trujillo. The greatest number of exhibits stem from the Mochica period (AD 400-800). The Cupisnique period, dating back to 1000 BC, and the Nazca, Chimú, and Inca periods are also well represented. There is an erotica section in a separate building. This is a museum for the pottery specialist; it is more like a warehouse than a museum, but the general visitor will enjoy the excellent collection of precolumbian weaving, including a sample of two-ply yarns with 398 threads to the inch. Also several mummified weavers buried with their looms and a small display of gold pieces. Admission US$3 (US$1.50 student-card holders), open Mon.-Sat., 0900-1300, 1500-1800, Sun. and holidays, 0900-1300. Photography not permitted. Bus 23 from Avenida Abancay, or minibus 37 from Av. Nicolás de Piérola (Colmena) or taxi (US$2).

Museum of the Viceroyalty (Quinta de Presa), is a fine 18th century mansion. Exhibits: colonial portraits, furniture, dresses, candelabra, and so on; one of the Viceroy's carriages is shown. Closed since 1986 for repairs.

Museo Histórico Militar (Real Felipe Fortress, Callao), has interesting military relics: a cannon brought by Pizarro, a cannon used in the War of Independence, the flag that flew during the last Spanish stand in the fortress, portraits of General Rodil and of Lord Cochrane, and the remains of the small Bleriot plane in which the Peruvian pilot, Jorge Chávez, made the first crossing of the Alps from Switzerland to Italy: he was killed when the plane crashed at Domodossola on Sept. 23, 1910. Open 0900-1200 and 1500-1700, Tues., Wed., Thurs.; 1400-1730, Sat., Sun. Entrance free. Closed April-August. Bus No. 63 from Post Office in Jirón Lima. The **Museo Miguel Grau**, Calle Lezcano 170 (near Basílica La Merced, just off Jr. Unión), is the house of Admiral Grau and has mementoes of the War of the Pacific. **Museo Morro de Arica**, Cailloma 125, Tues.-Fri., 1130-1900, gives the Peruvian view of the famous battle. **Museo Naval** (Av. Jorge Chávez, off Plaza Grau, Callao), open 0900-1230, 1500-1730 on Mon., Wed., Fri. and Sat. Admission free.

Museo Hospital Dos de Mayo open 0900-1800 daily, admission US$1.25.

Museo Peruano de Ciencias de la Salud, Jr. Junín 270 (just off Plaza de Armas), houses a collection of ceramics and mummies, showing precolumbian lifestyle; divided into five sections: *micuy* (Quechua for food), *hampi* (medicine), *onccoy* (disease), *hampini* (healing) and *causay* (life). Minibus Nos. 35 or 42 from Miró Quesada. Open: Wed.-Sat., 1000-1600, very interesting indeed. Admission, US$2. A guide is available in Spanish; signs in English and Spanish.

Pinacoteca Municipal (Municipal Building, Plaza de Armas), contains a large collection of paintings by Peruvian artists. The best of the painters is Ignacio Merino (1817-1876). Rooms and furnishings very ornate. Open: Mon.-Fri., 0900-1300.

Museum of Italian Art (Paseo de la República, 2nd block), is in a building, Italian renaissance style, given by the Italian colony to Peru on the centenary of its independence. Open Tues.-Sun., 0900-1900, but 0900-2000 on Fri., US$1. Large collection of Italian works of art, but most of the paintings are reproductions, including lithographs and etchings. Now also houses Institute of Contemporary Art, which has many exhibitions.

Museum of Natural History (Av. Arenales 1250) belongs to University of San Marcos. Exhibits: Peruvian flora, birds, mammals, butterflies, insects, minerals and shells. Prize exhibit is a sun fish (more plaster than fish)—only two other examples known, one in Japan and another in New Zealand. Open Mon.-Fri. 0830-1530, Sat. 0830-1200, 0900-1300; admission US$0.25. Bus No. 54A or minibuses 13 and 73 from Av. Tacna.

Philatelic Museum (Central Post Office, off Plaza de Armas). Open 0800-1330, 1400-1600, Mon.-Fri., 0800-1330, Sat., 0900-1200, Sun. Incomplete collection of Peruvian stamps and information on the Inca postal system. There is a stamp exchange in front of the museum every Sat. and Sun., 0900-1300. You can buy stamps here as well (shop hours: Mon.-Fri., 0800-1200, 1400-1500).

Bullfight Museum (Hualgayoc 332, Plaza de Acho, Rímac). Apart from matadors' relics, contains good collections of paintings and engravings— some of the latter by Goya. Open 0900-1300, 1500-1800. Closed Sat., Sun. and holidays in the afternoons. Admission US$0.20.

Contemporary Folk Art Museum, Saco Olivero 163, between Arenales and 3rd block of Arequipa, recommended. Shop in museum grounds. Open Tues.-Fri., 1430-1900; Sat. 0830-1200.

Amano Museum (Calle Retiro 160, Miraflores). A very fine private collection of artefacts from the Chancay, Chimú and Nazca periods owned by Mr. Yoshitaro Amano—one of the most complete exhibits of Chancay weaving. Particularly interesting for pottery and precolumbian textiles, all superbly displayed and lit. Open Mon.-Fri. Guided tours 1400, 1500, 1600, 1700. T 412909, at least one day in advance, for an appointment; try to get a small group (under 10) first. Admission free (photography prohibited). Bus No. 73 or Santa Cruz minibus (no. 13) from Av. Tacna, get out at Av. Angamos. Calle Retiro is unmarked: it is the street on your right as you stand with your back to the Pacific on the 11th block of Angamos.

Pedro de Osma Museum (Av. Pedro de Osma 421, Barranco). A private collection of colonial art of the Cuzco, Ayacucho and Arequipa schools. T 670019 for an appointment. No. 54A bus from Av. Tacna. (Apparently this museum is now closed.)

Numismatic Museum, Banco Wiese, 2nd floor, Cuezo 245, T 275060 ext. 553, open Mon.-Fri., 0900-1300, free admission. Peruvian coins from the colonial era to the present day.

Museum of Mineral Specimens at Krystal S.A., León Velarde 537, Lince, Lima 14 (T 710713, 711379).

Museo Miniatura de la Plaza de Armas del Siglo XIX in the house of Dr. César Revoredo, Salaverry 3052, is a private small scale reproduction of the Plaza de Armas in the last century. Dr. Revoredo also has a fine collection of prints by Rancho Fierro, the 19th century *costumbrista* watercolour artist.

Casa Galería de Esculturas de Sra. Marina Núñez del Prado, Antero Aspillaga 300, Olivar de San Isidro, another private collection, of fine sculpture; phone for an appointment on Weds., or Sats. Two more private collections that are occasionally open to visitors on application by telephone are: the collection of precolumbian artefacts belonging to Sra. Elsa Cohen, Esquina Larraburre Unánue 392 (Bus 54A, or minibus 13 from Tacna) and, at Parque

Hernán Velarde 199, the collection of rural handicrafts (pottery, engraved gourds, etc.) belonging to Sra. E. Luza (bus 13, Tacna with Emancipación, or bus 2 from corner of Plaza San Martín).

Galería Wari 69, Cailloma 630, exhibits the tapestries of the Sulca family of Ayacucho; traditional designs and techniques are used in their beautiful work.

For those interested in modern Peruvian art, a gallery has been opened at Independencia 812, Miraflores, T 451058, by Gaston Garreaud, who speaks English and French and will kindly guide you if you make an appointment. Admission free.

Note Some museums are only open between 0900 and 1300 from Jan. to March, and some close altogether in January. Many are closed at weekends and on Monday. When electricity supplies are cut, many museums close.

Parks and Gardens

Lima and its suburbs have many parks and gardens. **Alameda de los Descalzos**, at the foot of the Cerro San Cristóbal, was laid out as early as 1610; it is a walk shaded by ancient trees and fenced by a wrought-iron grille. It was once a haunt of Lima's aristocracy. The marble statues, each representing a month of the year, and the marble seats date from 1856. Nearby is another walk, the **Paseo de Aguas**, created by the Viceroy Amat in the 18th century to please his mistress, La Perricholi. The great arch with cascades was rebuilt in 1938. This walk is in extremely poor condition.

Campo de Marte (Plaza Jorge Chávez and Av. Salaverry), a large open park, reportedly full of thieves and drug-pushers now. In the centre is a huge monument to the Peruvian soldier. The National Symphony Orchestra plays in the auditorium on the W side during the summer.

Parque Universitario, where the old San Carlos Jesuit church was turned into a **Pantheon of the Heroes** (Panteón de los Próceres) on the 100th anniversary of the Battle of Ayacucho. A graceful 18th century church with a circle of famous tombs under the rotunda. General Miller, the Englishman who fought in the wars of independence, and whose memoirs contain an excellent picture of the time, is buried here, and so is Admiral Guise, of Gloucestershire, who was killed at Guayaquil. Also the poet and composer who wrote the Peruvian national anthem. Next to the church is the former building of San Marcos University, which has now been restored and is used for meetings and conferences. Worthy of a visit are the beautiful patio and the small archaeological museum. In the centre is the clock tower presented by the German colony on the centenary of Peruvian independence. On the far corner of the park is the tall Ministry of Education building.

Between Paseo Colón and Av. 28 de Julio is **Parque de La Exposición**, a quiet place shaded by trees; several of the main avenues border it. It was opened for the 1868 International Exhibition. The great Palace of the Exhibition, facing Paseo Colón, is now the Museum of Art. South of the Parque de La Exposición is the **Parque Japonés**, which has a small admission fee.

Parque de la Reserva (Av. Arequipa, 6th block). In the middle is a statue of Sucre; of the other two statues, one is of Tangüis, who selected the famous cotton. By the park is the Edificio El Pacífico-Washington (British and Israeli embassies).

Parque las Leyendas, between Lima and Callao, is arranged to represent the three regions of Peru: the coast, the mountainous Sierra, and the tropical jungles of the Montaña, with appropriate houses, animals and plants, children's playground. Elephants and lions have been introduced so the zoo is no longer purely Peruvian (not recommended at weekends, too crowded). The Park is open 0900-1700 (closed Mon.), entrance US$0.35. There is a handicrafts fair (Feria Artesanal) at the entrance to the park; particularly good insect specimens can be bought here. Buses from Paseo de la República, in front of *Sheraton*, 23 and 57 from Plaza dos de Mayo; also minibus 75 from Jirón Azángaro goes direct to the park.

Note The centre of Lima has been refurbished and conditions have improved for the visitor. You are, however, recommended to consult the general **Security** section in the **Information for Visitors** and see also under **Buses** and Miraflores beaches below. Many visitors base themselves in San Isidro, Miraflores or Barranco (see **suburbs** below), rather than in the historic centre.

Festivals 18 January, Founding of Lima. The whole of February is Carnival, with plenty of water-throwing, especially on Sundays; if you don't want to get wet, stay in your room. If you don't mind (and it's quite refreshing), enjoy it and carry your own water balloon (some "jokers" mix paint, oil, etc. with the water, so watch out). 28 July, Independence, with music and fireworks in Plaza de Armas on evening before; last week of August, Cañete; October, month of Our Lord of the Miracles with impressive processions (see *El Comercio* for dates and routes); November (every other year), Pacific International Fair.

Hotels Prices very negotiable outside peak July-August holiday season. There is a 12% tax on hotel rooms, and a service charge of 13% is usually added (neither is included in prices below). In cheaper hotels water may be scarce in the middle of the day. The more expensive hotels charge in dollars according to the parallel rate of exchange at midnight.

Accommodation in **Miraflores**: *Miraflores César*, La Paz y Diez Canseco, (T 441212), L, luxury, very nice but expensive; *El Pardo*, Av. Pardo 420, (T470283), L; *María Angola*, Av. La Paz 610, (T 441280), A, rec; *Country Club*, Los Eucaliptos, San Isidro, T 404060, A; *Ariosto*, Av. La Paz 769 (Tel:441416, Telex: 21195), B, rec.; *El Condado* (close to *César*), L, deluxe. *José Antonio*, 28 de Julio 398, T 456870, A, clean, friendly, good restaurant, rec.; *Hostal Residencial Esperanza*, Esperanza 350, T 442411/444909, Fax 440834, B, with bath, TV, phone, pleasant; *Suites Larco*, Apart Hotel, San Martín 481, of. 202 (corner of 7th block Av. Larco), T 461461/461970, B for 3-room suite with kitchen, TV, phone, cleaning, guarded property; *Pensión Lucerna*, Calle Las Dalias 276 (corner Av. Larco), B with breakfast, friendly, clean, T 457321, rec.; *Grand Hotel Miraflores*, Av. 28 de Julio 151, very pleasant, T 479641.

Residencial 28 de Julio, 28 de Julio 531, T 470636/473891, C, with breakfast, parking, café and bar, phone and bathroom with each room, secure, rec.; *Hostal El Ejecutivo*, Av. 28 de Julio 245, T 476310, D, including bath and breakfast, clean, tariff negotiable for long stay, safe, luggage can be left; *Pensión Alemana*, Arequipa 4074, T 456999, C, comfortable, clean, excellent breakfast (triple rooms available), book in advance, laundry service extra;, Arequipa 4074, T 456999, C, comfortable, clean, excellent breakfast (triple rooms available), book in advance, laundry service extra; *Hostal La Alameda*, Av. José Pardo 930, D with limited breakfast, friendly, quiet, safe, clean, rec.; *Hostal Residencial Torreblanca*, Av. José Pardo 1453, T 479998, C, including breakfast and tax, (pricing a bit haphazard), quiet, friendly, clean, helpful, rec.; *Ovalo*, Av. José Pardo, Plaza Morales Barros, T 465549, C, quiet, good, breakfast served; *Colonial Inn*, Cmdte. Espinar 310, T 466666, C, room service, TV, parking; *Hostal El Patio*, Diez Canseco 341 (next to *Miraflores César*), C with reductions for long stays, clean, comfortable, friendly, English and French spoken; *Hostal La Castellana*, Grimaldo del Solar 222 (3 blocks E of Larco, between Schell and Benavides), T 443530, 444662, C (D off season), with bath, pleasant, good value, nice garden, safe, cafeteria, laundry, English spoken; *Hostal Señorial*, José González 567 (T 459724/457306), C, 60 rooms all with bath, including tax and breakfast, rec., clean, friendly, well-appointed, garden; *Hostal Palace*, Av. Miraflores 1088, C, very clean, comfortable, friendly; *Winnie's Bed and Breakfast*, La Calera de Monterrico, M-13, Lima 34 (close to Miraflores), T 455864, C, run by Winnie Reyes de Espinosa of VIP Travel Service, warmly rec. *Hostal Huaychulo*, Av. Dos de Mayo 494, T 451195, C, safe, helpful, excellent (German owner-manager, speaks English too); *Hostal Benavides*, Av. Benavides, block 22 (out of centre of Miraflores), D, good for longer stays; *Hostal Residencial Kimari*, Pasaje Los Pinos 156, piso C, Edificio El Comodoro, T 422266/422177, D for stays of more than week, clean, modern, safe, friendly; *Pensión José Luis*, Fco. de Paula, Ugarriza 727, San Antonio district, T 441015, D, use of kitchen, laundry facilities, very friendly English-speaking owner; *Hostal Catalina*, Toribio Polo 248 (½ block W of Av. Ejercito blocks 7/8), D negotiable, friendly, English spoken, bath, good transport connections, T 410192/424037; *Concorde*, Av. Ricardo Palma, D, modern and clean; *Hostal Miraflores*, Av. Petit Thouars 5444, D, leave valuables at desk, English and German spoken.

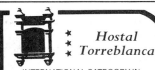

Bailiwick's Lodge, Colón 577-79, T 471749 (no sign), E, English spoken, clean; Sra Emilia, Porta 264, T 473953, D with breakfast, friendly, clean and safe. *Pensión San Antonio*, Paseo de la República 5809, T 475830, E, shared bathroom, clean, comfortable, friendly, helpful, ask for hot water; *Imperial Inn*, Av. Bolognesi, E, clean, but noisy and run-down; *Pensión Yolanda Escobar*, Domingo Elias 230 T 457565, E, clean, facilities for preparing own breakfast, dueña speaks fluent English, rec. Visitors with vehicles are recommended to stay in Miraflores, since parking is difficult in the centre.

Accommodation at **San Isidro**, *Hostal San Isidro Inn*, Av. Pezet 1761, just off Salaverry; *Hostal Limatambo*, Av. Aramburú 1025, B, T 419615, 24-hour snack bar, won the "América-86" award for good service and quality; *Residencial Beech*, Los Libertadores 165, T 40-5595, C, with bath, including breakfast, rec.; *Garden*, Rivera Navarrete 450, T 421771, rec., A, good, large beds, shower, small restaurant; *Hostal Santa Mónica*, Av. Pezet 1419, D, T 419280, rec.; *Hostal El Golf Inn*, Av. A. Miro Quesada, round corner from Cuban Embassy, D with bath, E without, swimming pool, safe, friendly, hard beds; *Residencial Los Petirrojos*, Petirrojos 230, Corpac (Sra. Miri), D, T 416044, clean, spacious, breakfast included; *Hostal Callacocha*, Coronel Andrés Reyes 100, C, very good; *Hostal El Olivar*, Raymundo Morales de la Torre 385, T 417745, C with bath, friendly, garden, nice restaurant; *Hostal Firenze*, Chinchón (2 blocks from Las Camelias), T 422382, D, clean, family-run, hot water, English and Italian spoken, highly rec.; *Pensión Doratina*, Los Cedros 285, D, excluding food (which is pricey), very good; *Sans Souci*, Av. Arequipa 2670, T 226035, towards Miraflores, B with bath, clean, gloomy, noisy; *Residencial Javier Prado*, Av. Javier Prado Este 461, C with bath, toilet and breakfast (front rooms noisy), good, 4 blocks from colectivo to centre, transport to airport US$8; *Hostal Antarki*, Chacarilla 250, clean, quiet, helpful, E.

In **Santa Beatriz**, between San Isidro and Centre, *Hostal Mont Blanc*, Jr. Emilio Fernández 640, T 247762/737762, D (negotiable) with bath, comfortable, clean, good service, café, bar, highly rec., 15 mins' walk or 5 mins' by minibus to centre, owner arranges excursions.

In **Barranco**, *Barranco*, Malecón Osma 104, converted mansion above the cliffs, rooms from E to B, safe, family atmosphere, helpful, rec., swimming pool, access to beach, good views of sunset from the garden (clarify all payment arrangements in advance); *Armendariz*, Av. Armendariz (between Miraflores and Barranco), E, on convenient 2 bus line, cable TV, rec.

In **Magdalena del Mar**, *Los Cóndores*, Domingo Ponte 874, Magdalena Mar, C with bath, cheaper rooms available, safe, warm water, clean, free transport from airport, tour guide (Alfredo) operates from here. Also in Magdalena del Mar, *De Klomp*, Jr. Libertad 1439, T 612153, owned by a Dutch/Peruvian couple, cosy, clean, good, dormitory rooms at G p.p., bus stop for all directions round the corner. In **Lince** is *Hostal Ambassador*, Julio C. Tello 650, clean, safe, hot water, E, changes money for guests, highly rec.

In **central Lima**: Rec. in the upper price brackets: *Lima Sheraton*, Paseo de la República 170, T 328676, L, *La Pascana*, coffee shop good; *Grand Bolívar*, Unión 958, Plaza San Martín, T 276400, Telex 25201 PECP, L, good ambience, helpful, excellent restaurant, have a pisco on the terrace overlooking plaza, highly rec; *Crillón* Colmena 589, T 283290, Telex 25274PE, L, good food and service in *Skyroom*; *Plaza*, Nicolás de Pierola 850, T 286270, B, good restaurant, safe for luggage (cheaper in low season); *Gran Maury*, Ucayali 201, C/D, good bath, breakfast, helpful staff; *Savoy*, Cailloma 224, T 283520, B; *Columbus*, Av. Arequipa 1421, T 710129, C.

Hostal Los Virreyes, Jirón Cañete 826, C, comfortable, clean, hot water, central position, a bit noisy, rec.; *Hostal Renacimiento*, Parque Hernán Velarde 52, D, cheaper at the back, in a quiet cul-de-sac 2 blocks from central bus station, 10 mins walk from centre, not all rooms with bath but clean, helpful, T 318461/ 324821; *Pensión* at Hernán Velarde 72, run by Pablo W.See, T 246352, C, very good, 5 mins. by bus from centre. *Hostal del Sol*, Rufino Torrico 773, C, with shower, helpful, fairly quiet, clean, safe, rec.; *La Casona*, Moquegua 289 (nr Jr. Cailloma and No. 56 bus route from airport), clean, secure, friendly; *Hostal San Martín*, Av. Nicolás de Piérola 882, 2nd floor, Plaza San Martín, T 285377, rec., good value, C inc. taxes, a/c, with bath, breakfast served in room, helpful, money changing facilities, Japanese run, good restaurant, good service; *Hostal Eiffel*, Jr. Washington 949, T 240188/249181, C, expensive but breakfast inc., very clean, hot water, safe, cheaper taxis to airport; *Granada*, on Huancavelica 323, T 279033, D without breakfast, clean, safe, hot water, English spoken, friendly; *Grand Castle*, Av. Carlos Zavala Loayza 218, opp. Ormeño bus station, D, including breakfast (poor), hot water, comfortable, good service, Japanese restaurant, rec.; *Residencial Santa Rosa*, Camaná 218, D, with bath, quiet, some hot water, laundry service.*Hostal El Tambo*, Av. Bolognesi 373, D, including breakfast, laundry, dry cleaners and supermarket all nearby.*Hostal Colombia*, Av. Colombia 137 (with Av. Brasil), D, beware overcharging, with breakfast, clean, friendly, good; *Residencial Francia*, Samuel Velarde 185, Av. Ejército, T 617054, D including taxes and breakfast, bath, hot water, laundry facilities, swimming pool, gardens, very friendly and helpful, 20 min. bus ride from centre; *Hostal Belén*, Belén 1049, just off San Martín, Italian spoken, F, very popular, basic breakfast extra, hot water, friendly, music groups practising.

Asociación de Amistad Peruano Europea, Jirón Camaná 280, 7th floor, F, dormitory (16 beds), one shower, clean, friendly, laundry facilities, will store luggage. *El Dorado*, N. de Piérola, E with bath, clean and friendly, some rooms rented by the hour; *Hostal Niza*, N. de Piérola 206, F (triples available), breakfast, friendly, central, clean but not so the toilets, basic, noisy; *Hostal San Sebastián*, Ica 712, T 23-2740, run by Nellie de Viana, F (G p.p. in dormitory), clean, friendly, English spoken, popular, gringo place, safe to leave luggage, bit noisy on street corner, rooms on top floor mixed reports, restaurant, book exchange and laundry facilities (runs taxi service to airport); *Residencial Roma*, Jr. Azángaro 105, F (cheaper in dormitory) in a restored house in old Lima, hot water 0600-2300, family run, English spoken, secure, can leave luggage, vegetarian café on top floor, rec.(next door are a good pastry shop and Roma Tours, a small travel agency); *Hostal España*, Ica 326, E, hot water, safe to leave luggage, quiet, basic but clean, rec., often full, breakfast restaurant on roof; *Pensión Ibarra*, Av. Tacna 359, Apt. 162, 15th and 16th floors, no sign, E, including breakfast (less if staying several days), clean, friendly, very helpful owner, full board available;*Hostal Tairo*, Av. Tacna, F, clean, rec., 20 metres from airport colectivo terminal; *Hostal El Paraíso*, Jirón Unión 428, down a passageway, past bookshop, F, hot water all day, but erratic water supply, safe, dormitory and communal bathroom; *Hostal Samaniego*, Av. Emancipación 184, Apto. 801, near Plaza San Martín, G, rec., 15 spaces available (4 per room), hot water, friendly, safe, will store luggage for foreigners; *Casa de Hospedaje*, Pasaje Acisclo Villarán 365, no sign, central, E, F without breakfast, clean, homely, good; *Familia Rodríguez*, Av. N. de Piérola 730, 2nd floor, T 236465, F with breakfast, clean, friendly, will store luggage, dormitory accommodation with only one bathroom.

La Granja Azul, in B range, Carretera Central (turn off between Km. 13 and 14 of Carretera Central, buses from Parque Universitario every 15 minutes; last bus back leaves 2000 but a minibus leaves the hotel for Lima at 2200), restaurant specializing in exotic cocktails and chicken dishes, dancing every night, rec.

If arriving by air, especially at night, a visit to the tourist office at the airport (beyond passport control) is helpful if you want to arrange a hotel room. **Hotel reservations** for Lima and elsewhere in Peru can be made through Centro de Reservaciones, Av. Panamericana 6251, San Antonio/Miraflores, T 466-895.

Youth Hostel *Albergue Juvenil Internacional*, Av. Casimiro Ulloa 328, Miraflores, T 465-488, F, basic cafeteria, travel information, laundry facilities, double rooms and dormitories, swimming pool often empty, "spacious, clean and safe". Open to non-members of the Youth Hostel Association, ten minutes walk from the beach. Transhotel bus between airport and Plaza San Martín passes, so does Ikaros bus (Av. Benavides stop), so does bus No. 2 from Av. Tacna to Miraflores, 30 mins. to centre; taxi to centre, US$6. Albergue Juvenil Karima, Chancay, F p.p. in dormitory, inc. breakfast, clean, friendly.

Camping Under no circumstances camp on or near beach at Miraflores, theft and worse is rife in these areas. Propane gas in heavy iron gas bottles available from Delta-Gas, Av. Benavides (former Colonial) 5425, Lima. Camping gas (in small blue bottles) available from Trekking and Backpacking Club Peruano (address below) and from Técnica Import, Dávalos Lisson 323, nr. Washington, 0900-1300 and 1400-1700. Oechsle sell butane gas cartridges. N.B. Airlines do not allow the carriage of gas bottles.

Baths Baños Pizarro, Unión 284, steam rooms, US$3, cold showers only, café and swimming pool. Windsor Turkish Baths, on Miguel Dasso, San Isidro, separate facilities for men and women, steam, sauna, cold pool and whirlpool, US$4.

Restaurants In **Miraflores** we recommend the following: *Dom Beta*, José Gálvez 667, excellent seafood, moderate prices; *Rosa Náutica*, built on old British-type pier (Espignon No. 4) in Lima bay, near Miraflores, not to be missed, delightful opulence, finest cuisine (US$30 p.p.), sunset rec.; *El Jibaro II*, Av. Elmer Faucett 1718, Bellavista, rec. for seafood; *Vivaldi*, Ricardo Palma 258, US$5-7 p.p., also for drinks and snacks, nice atmosphere; Italian restaurant at Benavides 346, good; *Café Restaurant Strauss*, Benavides 400, rec. for Peruvian and seafood dishes in German style at moderate prices; *El Faisán*, Diez Canseco 10, for traditional food; *Las Tejas*, Diez Canseco 340, good anticuchos and seafood at reasonable prices; *Parrillada en la Parque*, Av. Petit Thouars (N end), good steaks, expensive; huge steaks at *La Tranquera*, Av. Pardo 285; *Casiopeia Bar* at Centro Comercial Aurora, Swiss and Peruvian dishes, Swiss-owned; *El Dorado* (Chinese), Av. Arequipa, good food, expensive; *Kuo Wha*, Paseo de la República 5046; *Ajinomen*, Calle Los Pinos (between Benavides and Schell), Chinese, good; *Lau's Chifa*, Ricardo Palma 322, good and cheap Chinese food; *La Costa Verde* (on Barranquito beach, excellent food and wine, but expensive). *Rincón Gaucho* on Parque Salazar, T 474778, and *El Gaucho*, not far away on Av. Larco, two of the best steak-houses in Peru, both serve superb steaks imported from Argentina; *Café Lusitania*, Av. Larco, good international cooking; *Haiti*, Av. Benavides, good food, cheap, rec. *La Colina*, Schell 727, cheap and good; *Kentucky Fried Chicken*, also Av. Schell. *Salad House*, Av. Grau 164, 42 different salads, very good, open (except Mon.), 1230-1530, 1930-2300. Typical Peruvian restaurants can be found at the end of Avenida Brasil, including *Gran Chifa Brasil*, opposite Av. Javier Prado.

Vegetarian restaurants are *Bircher Berner*, Av. Schell 598, good value, *Govinda*, Schell 630, *Productos JJGC*, Manuel Bonilla 178 (off Larco, opp. Cine Pacífico), nondescript storefront, but excellent food (try crema de choclo), and *Koricancha*, Petit Thouars 2686, 3rd floor.

Try also *Carlín*, Av. La Paz 644, excellent, expensive, seafood specialities, good coffee; *Le Bistro*, in El Suche pedestrian mall, small, French, expensive; also in El Suche, *El Condado*, rec., and among other restaurants (and good shopping) in same area is *La Crêperie*, delicious filled pancakes; *Manolo*, Larco 608, good food, meals US$2, popular, rec.; *The Brenchley Arms*, Atahualpa 174, T 459680, English pub serving English food, English speaking, informal and relaxed, tourist information. *Friday's Pub*, on Benavides just S off Av. Larco, rec.; *Café Suisse*, main square, for cakes, coffee, European-style food and delicatessen. *La Tiendecita Blanca*, opp. *El Pacífico*, tea rooms/delicatessen, good cakes, sandwiches, coffee. Good ice cream at *Lamborghini*, Av. Larco, *Helados Sabores*, Av. Larco, *Heladería Italiana*, Angamos Oeste 408 (really excellent); *Pastelería Sueca*, Av. Larco 759, good hamburgers, pastries and salads. Good pisco sours at *El Estribo*, Av. Larco; just off Av. Larco are *Vivaldi*, Ricardo Palma 258, T 471636, expensive but good and *Liverpool*, good food, Beatles music and décor.

In **San Isidro** these restaurants are rec.: *Aquarium* (at the *Country Club Hotel*); the restaurant formerly called *La Barca*, Av. del Ejército 2195, excellent but expensive sea food; *Los Condes de San Isidro* (Av. Paz Soldán 290—an 18th-century mansion—T 222557) excellent; *Génova*, Av. Petit Thouars 3865, good, reasonable; *Valentino's*, Calle M. Bañón (near Camino Real and Av. Javier Prado), excellent food and service; *Don Adolfo*, Manuel Bañón 295, excellent food, helpful, friendly; *Los Cántaros de Darío*, Guillermo Prescott 337, excellent seafood in colonial-style setting, reasonable. *Micasa*, Augusto Tamayo 150 (Japanese); *Fredo*, very busy and good, on Conquistadores. *Blue Room* at Las Begonias 379; *Steak House*, Las Camelias 870, open 1200-2400, serves Argentine steak (about US$20 for 3 courses).

In **Barranco**, *El Otro Sitio*, Sucre 317, excellent Creole Buffet US$4-5, live music; *El Buen Gusto*, Av. Grau 323, good atmosphere and service, good selection of meat dishes, rec; *El Puente*, below Puente de los Suspiros; *Karamaduke*; *La Casa de Florentino*.

In **Magdalena**, *José Antonio* (Peruvian food, music after 2200), Monteagudo 210 B, strongly rec.

In **Monterrico**, near the Gold Museum, *Pabellón de la Caza*, expensive, but very good food and service, "sumptuous gastronomic treat". Also *Puerto Fiel*, Av. Primavera 1666, 3 blocks from Gold Museum, rec., seafood.

In **central Lima**:*L'Eau Vive*, Ucayali 370, across from the Torre Tagle Palace, run by nuns, open Mon.-Sat., 1245-1430, 2030-2230, fixed-price US$4 lunch menu (+ taxes and couvert), Peruvian-style in interior dining room, or à la carte in either of dining rooms that open on to patio, excellent, profits go to the poor. *Las Trece Monedas*, in an old colonial mansion off Av. Abancay (Ancash 536), excellent, local food, insist on an itemized bill; *Domino*, in an arcade off Unión, near San Martín, good, Swiss-owned, expensive, rec. *Goyescas*, Plaza S. Martín, good food (full meal including drinks, US$6.20 p.p.); *Parrilladas San Martín*, Plaza San Martín (opposite *Bolívar*), rec. (especially the anticuchos and sauces) US$5-8; *1900*, Belén 1030, very good, US$15 for dinner, drinks and salads in patio, live music from 1930. *La Reserva*, Emilio Fernández 330 (near Parque de la Reserva), very good, expensive. *Balcón Colonial*, intersection of Jr. Cuzco and Camaná, open 1130-1530, good lunches. *Las Papas Fritas*, Av. Colmena, good meals for US$10; *Lukyi*, Callao 300, good Chinese, reasonable; another *chifa* in 6th block of Jirón Ica, friendly, food highly rec.; also *Wah Shing Chifa*, Ica almost opp. *Hostal San Sebastián* good and cheap; *Chifa Santos*, N. de Piérola, opp. *Hotel Colmena*, rec. *Mario's*, N. de Piérola y Tacna, Argentine, cheap, relaxing;*Giannino*, Rufino Torrico 899 (good Italian food); *Rincón del Pescador*, opposite *Hotel Crillón*, excellent but expensive, US$20 per head; *Chalet Suisse*, Av. Nicolás de Piérola 560, rec., international and

Peruvian cuisine. **Rosita Ríos**, Av. El Altillo 100, Rímac, for highly seasoned Peruvian food at reasonable prices, to and from centre by bus No. 10; **Mesón La Ronda**, in the bullring, has an excellent bullfight museum. **Raimondi**, Miró Quesada 110, excellent, not too expensive. Cheaper restaurants include: **Jerry's Restaurant and Coffee Bar**, Carabaya 336, simple, clean, cheap, open Sun. p.m.; **Cordano**, Ancash y Carabaya, near Desemparados station, 1920s décor, good, popular, rec; **Rincón Toni**, Nicolás de Piérola, friendly service, rec., main dishes US$3 (German and Swiss food, good); **El Torreón**, Jirón Camaná 571, good, US$1.50 p.p.; **Ciervo de Oro**, Jr. Ica 322, good empanadas and cakes; **Las 4 Estaciones**, Ica y Jr. Unión, pizzeria, good juices; **Pizzería Romana**, Av. Sucre near hospital, good Italian food and pizzas, near Pueblo Libre museums; **El Barroco**, Jr. Cañete 349, good and reasonable; **Don Juan** (off Plaza de Armas), good and cheap, open from about 1000, but not open late or on Sundays. Rec. is **Casa Camaná** on Camaná, south of N. de Piérola. Also try Rímac district, over Puente de Piedra, for cheaper food, e.g. the chicken restaurants on Av. Trujillo. There are several inexpensive restaurants on Av. Venezuela, and good snack-bars on Unión, particularly **Las Vegas**, western-style, good, cheap. On Jirón Ancash and Av. Abancay (near Buena Muerte church) there are restaurants serving good lunches. **Machu Picchu**, Azángaro 142, good, cheap, popular, also Jr. Ancash, next to **Hostal San Francisco**.The church of San Francisco (Jr. Laupe) has beautiful garden restaurant, good food at reasonable prices.

Vegetarian restaurants at Carabaya 744, where a meal costs US$1.05, excellent; **Govinda**, Av. Callao 200 block, good value lunch; **El Meson**, Moquegua 204, menú US$1.20, good; **Casa Naturista**, Abancay 839, cheap but not too good; **Avigail**, Av. Bolivia y Paseo de la República, expensive; **Centro Aplicación Naturista Sebastián Kneipp**, Jr. Loreto 379, Rímac, highly rec.; **Comedor Vegetariano Nuevo Mundo**, Camillo Carrillo 159, Jesús María, cheap, acceptable; **Natur**, Moquegua 132, rec., some English spoken.

For students, **Comedor Universitario Congallo**, filling meal for US$0.20. **Soda Bar La Esquina del Sabor**, Junín 500 and Moreno, rec.; decor basic but typical food good. A good coffee bar for snacks and sandwiches is **Googies** in Plaza San Martín; also **Tívoli** bar, Nicolás de Piérola 820; **Sandwich Tacna**, Tacna 327, popular and crowded at lunchtime. There are good cheap fish restaurants near Parque Universitario. **El Rinascate**, NW corner of Parque Universitario, good and cheap. **Colonial** on Emancipación by Cailloma; **La Buena Muerte**, Jr. Paruro 394, corner Ancash, seafood, popular, open Mon.-Sat. 1200-1400. **El Abuelo**, Jr Camaná, spit-roast chicken, moderately clean; **Snack-bar Koala**, Camaná, Italian and Peruvian food, good, friendly, clean. **Alemania** pastry shop (near **Pensión Ibarra**, Swiss-run) is good, as is **Munich Cakehouse**, Cailloma 329 and Ica. Cake shop at Camaná 284 (1 block from Plaza de Armas) has been rec; good coffee at **Café de Paso**, Carabobo y Cuzco (stand-up coffee shop). Good bread rolls at corner of Moquegua and Unión. **Pastelería Lobatón**, Jr. Unión 672, good churros; **El Pan Nuestro**, Jr. Ica 265, clean, good service, big portions.

N.B. Most restaurants now have 20% added to the bill: 15% for tip and 5% for taxes (although this can vary according to the restaurant; some show no extra charges at all).

Clubs Phoenix Club, Av. Nicolás de Piérola 1014, 3rd floor (Plaza San Martín). Lima Cricket and Football Club, Justo Vigil 200, Magdalena del Mar, T 610080/ 614030; anyone with a Commonwealth, US and possibly other foreign passport can become a temporary member (for a small fee)—ask the staff to phone a committee member. The club has extensive sports facilities, as well as football, rugby (training at 1700 on Thurs., May-October) and cricket, squash, swimming, snooker, etc. (Rugby players and cricketers are always welcome). Also cheap restaurant, pub and friendly place to meet people.

Shopping Silver and gold handicrafts of all kinds; Indian hand-spun and hand-woven textiles; manufactured textiles in Indian designs; llama and alpaca wool products such as ponchos, rugs, hats, blankets, slippers, coats, sweaters, etc.; *arpilleras*, appliqué pictures of Peruvian life (originated in Chile with political designs), made with great skill and originality by women in the shanty towns; fine leather products mostly hand made. The *mate burilado*, or engraved gourd found in every tourist shop, is cheap and a genuine expression of folk art (cheaper in villages near Huancayo). For handicrafts produced by cooperatives, with benefits going directly to the producers, contact the non-profit organization **Minka**, Barcelona 115, Lince, PO Box 14-0359, T 222132, open Mon.-Fri. 0900-1600 (nr. Clínica Lozada, Av. Javier Prado y Salaverry). There is an exhibition room displaying the whole range of Peruvian handicrafts and the regions in which they originate. Minka also provides information and addresses about producer groups throughout Peru; it will arrange for purchases made outside Lima to be transported to the capital and posted abroad. For further information contact Norma Velásquez.

Silvania Prints, Colmena 714 (near *Hotel Bolívar*), Conquistadores 905 (San Isidro) and in lobby of *Miraflores César Hotel*, sell modern silk-screen prints on Pima cotton with precolumbian designs. *Plaza México*, jewellery in precolumbian designs. On Av. Nicolás de Piérola vendors sell oil paintings of Andean scenes, bargains abound. One of the best selections of folk art, but not the cheapest, will be found at the *Artesanías del Perú* shops in Lima. *Cerámica Los Reyes*, Av. Nicolás de Piérola. Ground floor of *Hotel Bolívar* for all metal, pottery, woollen and handicraft items, reasonably priced, credit cards accepted. *Artesanía Huamanqaqa*, Belén 1041 between Hotels *Sheraton* and *Bolívar*, the best store for high-quality weaving (but very expensive), specializes in Indian weaving from San Pedro de Cajas. Next door is a permanent exhibition with a century-old loom. Also try the 24 stores in *Restaurant 1900*, Belén 1030, very good arpilleras. *EPPA (Empresa Peruana de Promoción Artesana)* government store for Peruvian handicrafts in San Isidro (Av. Orrantia 610). *Antisuyo*, Jr. Tacna 460, Miraflores, an Indian cooperative run by an Englishwoman, sells high-quality handicrafts from all regions, reasonable prices, T 472557. *Art-Andina*, Belén 1045, good selection of Indian weaving and rugs at very reasonable prices. Precolumbian textiles can be bought from the *Casa de Antigüedades*, Av. de Emancipación 253. On Unión is *Casa Mas*, with a wonderful display of gold and silver handicrafts, and antiques. In Miraflores, lovely shopping arcade *El Suche*, at La Paz 646, but high prices in the woollen goods, ceramics and leather shops. Antiques available in Miraflores on Calle La Paz. Vicuña is unobtainable for the time being in Peru and Bolivia alike. See *H. Stern's* jewellery stores at Hotels *Miraflores César*, *Bolívar* and *Sheraton*, and at the International Airport. (Note: It is better to buy pullovers in the Sierra. However, although Lima is more expensive, it is often impossible to find the same quality of goods elsewhere.) Alpaca cloth for suits, coats, etc. (mixed with 40% sheep's wool) can be bought cheaply from factories: Cirsa, Av. Argentina 2400, microbus 93, 70 or 84 from Plaza Castilla; Lanificio, Alberto del Campo 285, bus 59 from Av. Abancay (gives 10% discount to foreigners attached to their embassies). Alpaca wool for knitting or weaving from Alpaca lll, Av. Larco 859, Miraflores. Made-to-measure cotton shirts in 24 hrs. from Sr. Hurtado, "Sir", Jr. Carabaya 1108. A good tailor is Navarro Hermanos, in Belén, below the Tourist Office. There are bargains in clothing made from high quality Pima cotton. Records: *Discos del Mundo*, Unión 779, allows you to listen, in sound-proof booth, before you buy.

Markets Parque Diagonal/Kennedy, Miraflores (by *Restaurant Haití*): jewellery, sandals made to measure, paintings and other handicrafts, Dec.-June, Wed. to Mon., in winter Sat. and Sun. only; Feria Artesanal, Av. de la Marina 790 and Av. Sucre westwards, in Pueblo Libre (take bus 2, 7, 10, or 48 on Av. Abancay, but watch your possessions, as thieves are numerous): extensive market selling woollen goods, leatherwork, bric-a-brac and Peruvian goods and souvenirs; sidestreets off Lampa: hardware; sidestreets off Av. Colmena: books; Parque Universitario: bargains; Plaza San Martín, behind *Hotel Bolívar*: ambulantes (money-changers). Polvos Azules, behind Central Post Office, 1 block from Plaza de Armas: sells just about anything, small handicraft section (ask directions), beware pickpockets. There is an interesting flower market with enormous arrangements near Plaza George Washington, on the way to the Gold Museum. Good Indian market on Avenida de la Marina, San Miguel, bus No. 10 from Miraflores.

Bookshops Fair selection of foreign-language books at *Librería Delta*, N. de Piérola 689, Todos shopping area, Galax commercial centre (Todos and Galax are the largest stores), Miraflores and Jorge Chávez airport. *ABC Bookstores* also sell foreign-language books (including *South American Handbook*). *Librería Studium*, Plaza Francia 1164 (also on N. de Piérola), sells history/travel books in English. *Studium* and *Librería de la Universidad de San Marcos* give student discounts. Tourist books in English, French and German also available from *Librería Ayra*, Jirón Unión 560, rec., will supply works in Quechua. *Librería Internacional*, Jirón Unión (corner of Plaza San Martín) has a wide selection of books on South America in all languages. Good English selection at *Epoca*, on Belén in the centre and on José Pardo in Miraflores. Bookshop on the plaza in Barranco has good selection, with a gallery and coffee shop. The *Book Exchange* at Ocoña 211a (near Plaza San Martín), open 1400-1900, is best place in centre for foreign-language books; will exchange them (mainly science-fiction, detective and porn) if bought there; also offers money transfer and postal service! *Librería El Pacífico* in Miraflores has the best selection of English books in Lima. Rare books, many shops on Av. Azángaro. French bookshop, *Plaisir de France*, Colmena 958. International newspapers, from newstands, Block 6, Av. N de Piérola.

Secondhand books (mostly in English) from dark blue/green both on Plaza San Martin, esquina N de Piérola, and along Tacna, between Moquegua y Arequipa.

Film Agfa distributor at Av. Tomás Marsano 390; for cheap film try at the black market at Feria Polvos Azules, at Puente de Piedra. Foto Mare, Belén 1047. Many developers using Kodak equipment offer same-day service; all at similar prices. Many on Jr. Unión and Plaza San Martín; also Av. Larco, Miraflores. Fujicolor offer a free film with developing. Quality tends to be poor, although Profot, Av. Juan de la Fuente 760, San Antonio, Miraflores, 0900-1300, 1400-1700, is rec. for both slide and print developing. **Camera Repairs** Casa Hindú, Jr. Unión, between Plazas de Armas and San Martín, repairs Olympus cameras. Camera House, Larco 1150, Office 39, 2nd floor, Miraflores, Mon-Fri 1530-1900, ask for Clemente Higa, who is often there later in pm. Frankitec, Sr. Max Bürkli, Jr. Lampa 1115-104, Lima 1, T 284 331, repairs all cameras (Swiss technician).

Pharmacy Botica Inglés, Jirón Cailloma 336, sells Dr. Scholl foot supplies for those contemplating or recovering from the Inca Trail. Deza, Conquistadores, San Isidro (1 block from Ovalo Gutiérrez), modern, like a US drugstore. Tampons reported only available in Miraflores.

Local Buses Standard fares in Lima: buses and minibuses, US$0.10, sometimes half price with student card, not very reliable. The main routes, such as from Plaza San Martín down Av. Arequipa to Miraflores and on to San Isidro, are also served by colectivos, US$0.15, which continue late at night after many buses stop.

Taxis No taxis use meters, you must bargain the price beforehand and don't give in to demands for payment in dollars, unless you get a bargain! Also, insist on being taken to the destination of your choice, not the drivers', from about US$0.50 for short journeys up to US$2.50 from the centre to the suburbs (within the city US$1.25 on average). After 2400 and on holidays, 35%-50% surcharge. Be careful of black "pirate" taxis; they usually charge 50% more. Paco, T 616394, is dependable for phone hiring.

Drivers don't expect tips; give them small change from the fare. If hiring a taxi for over 1 hour agree on price per hour beforehand. To Callao, La Punta, San Miguel, Magdalena, Miraflores (should be US$1.50), Barranco, Chorrillos, by agreement, basis US$5 per hour. Rec, knowledgeable driver, Hugo Casanova Morella, T 857708 (he lives in La Victoria), for city tours, travel to airport, etc.

Car Rental Cars can be hired from Hertz Rent-a-Car, Ocoña 262 (beside *Hotel Bolívar*), T 289477; Budget Rent A Car, Airport, T 528706 and Miraflores; Graf Automóviles Seleccionados, S.A. (Avis), Av. Petit Thouars 915, Miraflores, T 233486; Turamérica, Ocoña 164 (beside *Hotel Bolívar*), T 276413, or Nicolás de Piérola 590 (opp. *Hotel Crillón*), T 278970. The condition of vehicles is usually very poor. Beware of deep street potholes. Make sure that your car is in a locked garage at night. Russian-made four-wheel drive Niva vehicles are often rented; they are up to the conditions of Andean driving, but Lada saloon cars are not.

Motor Parts International Motors S.A. in Lima is the only Land Rover agent in Peru. Some BMW parts seem to arrive in Lima.

Night Clubs International cabaret—*Sky Room* at the *Crillón Hotel* (folk shows—disappointing, US$7), *Embassy* in the Plaza San Martín and *Yorkas* on Av. Nicolás de Piérola.

Folklore Every Sunday at the Coliseo Cerrado, Av. Alfonso Ugarte. AAA Theatre, Ica 323, has folklore evening every Tues., 2015, admission US$3. Also at the Teatro Municipal, Jirón Ica (tickets US$0.60-3.60), Tues. 2000 and at the Teatro La Cabaña. Cooperativa Santa Elisa, Cailloma 824 (3rd floor) has a folk group every Wed., 2000. The Museo de Arte has seasons of Peruvian folklore on Weds., at 2000, US$1.20 entrance. Many *peñas* have opened in recent years; these are generally cheap, tavern-like places with Peruvian music, much dancing and audience participation, *Hatuchay Peña*, Trujillo 228 (across the bridge past the Post Office), Fri., Sat., 2100, entrance US$2.20, inexpensive, crowded, good, but best to phone for taxi late at night; *La Peña de Pocho Ugarte* in Miraflores; *Las Brisas de Lago Titicaca*, just off Plaza Bolognesi, US$0.30, rec.; *Peña El Ayllu*, Jr. Moquegua 247, open every night, entrance free, rec. *La Palizada*, Av. del Ejército 800, Miraflores; *Las Guitarras*, in Miraflores and *Wifala* on Calle Cailloma have been rec. Many others in Barranco around Plaza Grau and Puente de los Suspiros, e.g. *1900* above a bookshop on Plaza Grau and *Los Balcones* on Av. Grau; *La Estación de Barranco*, at Pedro de Osma 112, good, family atmosphere, varied shows, and *Latinoamericano* on same street; *Nosferatu* next to Puente de los Suspiros.

Bars (with music) *Charlie's Peppermint Bar*, Av. Corpac, *Percy's Candlelight Room*, Todos shopping centre, San Isidro. *Satchmo Jazz Bar*, Av. La Paz 538, Miraflores, good. *La Taverna*, Barranco, live folkloric or western music; *Juancito's Bodega Bar*, Barranco, rec for local colour.

Discotheques Ebony 56 in San Isidro. *Las Rocas* in San Isidro is good and not expensive. *Keops* disco, San Isidro, is very popular with young Limeños. Good nightlife in Miraflores near Parque Diagonal and Av. Larco, with discos, video-pubs and pizzerias. Recommended in Miraflores, *Video Club*, just off Av. Diagonal; *La Miel*, min. consumption US$5.50 (pay as you go, don't wait for a big bill), and *Arizona*, US$4 (not very authentic, but good enough for a night out). *Unicorno del Mar* at Herradura beach in summer. *La Caverna*, Aviación 2514, San Borja.

Theatre Most professional plays are put on at the Teatro Segura, Teatro Municipal (Jirón Ica, 300 block—also orchestral and ballet performances); Teatro Arequipa and Sala Alzedo; Teatro Marsano, Av. Petit Thouars, Miraflores. Others are produced by amateur and university groups. Teatro Cabaña in the Parque de la Exposición puts on a strong programme of progressive theatre, especially for Institutos shows, local and cheap, take student card. Theatre Workshop, Jirón Ica 323. See the newspapers for announcement; the Sunday edition of *El Comercio* publishes all cinema and theatre details.

Cinemas Tickets cost about US$0.65 in Lima. Good films can be seen cheaply at the Cooperativa Santa Elisa, Cailloma 824, Thurs., Fri., Sat., and Sun. each week, Tel: 322641. Museo de Arte, Paseo Colón 125, has good international films, ask for monthly programme, rec; Alianza Francesa (every Tues.), Av. Garcilaso 1550, as well as at the British and North American-Peruvian Culture Associations (usually Thurs.) Ciné Pacífico Miraflores, in central Miraflores, most films in English with Spanish subtitles.

Sports There are two bullfight seasons, one in October-November and a short one in March. They are held in the afternoons on Sun. and holidays. Tickets at 2nd block of Calle Huancavelica, or at the Plaza de Acho bullring early on the day of the *corrida*. Famous *toreros* practise in the Lima ring, the oldest in the Americas, and fighting bulls are of Spanish stock. Cockfights are frequently organized and advertised: the Plaza de Gallos at Calle Sandía 150, near Parque Universitario, is recommended, US$6 for best seats. Horse racing, Hipódromo Monterrico, on Tues. and Thurs. evenings (1900) and Sat. and Sun. (1300) in summer, and in winter on Tues. evening and Sat. and Sun. afternoons. Colectivos on race days leave from the Plaza San Martín, fare US$0.10. The popular stand is not recommended. Pelouse and Primera stands US$0.60. Tourists may enter the members' stand on production of their passports. For Paso horses, which move in four-step amble, extravagantly paddling their forelegs, National Paso Association, T 476331. The Lima, Inca, Granja Azul and La Planicie golf clubs and the Country Club de Villa all have 18-hole courses. The Santa Rosa, Cruz de Hueso and Huampani golf clubs have 9-hole courses. (Contact Gerard Astruck of Sudex S.A., T 28-6054, for particulars.) Polo and tennis are also played. Boxing or all-in wrestling (Sat. night) at the Coliseo Nacional.

Association football matches and various athletic events take place at the National Stadium, seating 45,000, in the centre of the city on ground given by the British community on the 100th anniversary of Peru's Declaration of Independence.

Exchange Banco de la Nación (e.g. Av. Abancay 491). Citibank, Las Begonias 580, San Isidro, charges 3% on its own travellers cheques, open 0830-1245 in summer. Bank of America, Augusto Tamayo 120, San Isidro; will change Bank of America travellers' cheques into intis, 1.5% commission. Interbanc on Unión changes cash and travellers' cheques. Peruvian banks: Banco de Crédito, good rates and low commission on Thomas Cook travellers' cheques at Larcoy Schell branch, Miraflores, sometimes changes travellers' cheques into dollars, 5% commission. Open: Jan. 1 to March 31—0830 to 1130; April 1 to Dec.31—0915 to 1200. Closed Sat. except Banco de la Nación at Rufino Torrico 830 (opposite *Hotel Crillón*), which is open Sat. 0900-1200 (for changing dollar bills only—poor rate) and also open in the afternoons 1600-1830; small and crowded, it can be quicker elsewhere. Visa (Banco de Crédito) Jr. Lampa 499, 0900-1200, 1630-1830. Mastercard, Banco Continental, Seminario 320, 6th floor, San Isidro. Always check your money in the presence of the cashier, particularly bundles of pre-counted notes. Thomas Cook office reported unhelpful; lost cheques only replaced in Santiago de Chile or Quito.

The gold dealers near the *Hostal Kimari* on Pasaje Los Pinos, Miraflores, give good street rates. Many money changers at corner of Plaza San Martín and Jirón Unión, and in the streets behind *Hotel Bolívar*, identified by their calculator and hiss of "dollars", change money at the very profitable (for you) parallel rate; some change other South American currencies (beware, many forgeries in circulation, street changers also short change you, often a hassle). Best not to change money at your hotel: rates are usually better on the street. The optician opposite the *César* hotel gives a good rate. *Casas de cambio* are the recommended places to change, around Av. Ocoña and a few in Marafores; they are safe, good value and will give US$ cash for travellers' cheques, but you must bargain hard (e.g. *Cambio* nr. *Hotel Gran Bolívar*).

British Schools Markham College, for boys, is one of only four Headmasters' Conference Schools outside the Commonwealth. Colegio San Andrés, for boys, run by the Free Church of Scotland. Colegio San Silvestre, a school for girls at Miraflores, is represented in the Association of Headmistresses. Colegio Peruano-Británico, San Isidro, co-educational. In La

Molina, Colegio Newton offers the international baccalaureate.

American Schools Colegio Franklin Roosevelt, the American School of Lima, Monterrico, co-educational: Villa María, La Planicie (for girls); María Alvarado, Lima (girls).

Cultural Institutions Peruvian-British Cultural Association, Av. Arequipa 3495, San Isidro, with reading room and British newspapers (bus 1, 2, 54A). For other offices, library and film shows, Jirón Camaná 787, T 277927, classes only; theatre, Av. Benavides 620, Miraflores, T 454326. British Council, Alberto Lynch 110, San Isidro 27, T 704-350. Teatro Británico (amateur productions of plays in English), Calle Bella Vista, Miraflores. Peruvian North American Cultural Institute, Cuzco 446, in centre, with library; branch at Av. Arequipa 4798, Miraflores. Language tuition, US$30 for 4 weeks. American Chamber of Commerce, Juan de Arona, San Isidro. The American Society of Peru, Av. Angamos 1155, Miraflores. Tel: 414545. Goethe-Institut, Jr. Nazca 722, Jesus María, Lima 11, Mon.-Fri., 1100-2000, library, theatre, German papers, tea and cakes. Alliance Française, Avenida Garcilaso de la Vega 1550, also in Miraflores.

Spanish Classes Centro de Idiomas de Lima, P.O. Box 772, Lima 100 (Av. Manuel Olguín 215, Monterrico, T 35 0601/5970), 4 grades of tuition, US$8/hour, classes suited to students travelling schedules, accommodation with families can be arranged (room with bath, about US$150 a month). Euroidiomas, Juan Fanning 520, Miraflores 4, 6 and 8 week residential courses (US$480, 890, 1200).

Embassies/Consulates Argentine Consulate, Pablo Bermúdez 143, 2nd floor, Jesús María, T 245984/28172, open 0800-1300.Bolivian Consulate, Los Castaños 235, San Isidro, T 228231 (0830-1330). Brazilian Consulate, Cmdte. Espinar 181, Miraflores, T 462635. Chilean Consulate, Javier Prado Oeste 790, San Isidro, T 407965. Ecuadorean Consulate, Las Palmeras 356, San Isidro, T 228138. Colombian Consulate, Natalio Sánchez 125, 4th floor, T 12074, Mon.-Fri. 0900-1230. Venezuelan Consulate, Av. Salaverry 3005, San Isidro, T 415948.

U.S. Embassy, Av. Inca Garcilaso de la Vega 1400, Lima, T 338000; Consulate: Grimaldo del Solar 346, Miraflores, T 443621/443921. (NB if registering your passport, you have to leave a photograph). Canadian Embassy, Av. Libertad 132, Miraflores, T 444015. Australian Consulate, contact Canadian Embassy. New Zealand Embassy, Av. Salaverry 3006, San Isidro (Casilla 5587), T 621890, open 0800-1600 Mon-Thurs., 0800-1300 Fri (no direct bus there). South African Consulate, contact Swiss Embassy.

British Embassy and Consulate, Edificio Pacífico-Washington, Plaza Washington, corner of Av. Arequipa (5th block) and Natalio Sánchez 125, 11th floor (Casilla de Correo 854), T 334738. In case of emergency, the embassy duty officer can be contacted through his bleeper service, T 320982/320053, extension (anexo) 216.(Yellow bus No. 2 passes the Embassy.). Irish Consulate, Carlos Povias Osores 410, San Isidro, T 230808. Austrian Embassy, Av. Central 64, 5th floor, San Isidro, T 428851. West German Embassy, Av. Arequipa 4210, Miraflores, T 459997. French Consulate, Arequipa 3415, San Isidro, T 704968. Belgian Consulate, Angamos 380, Miraflores, T 463335. Swiss Embassy, Av. Salaverry 3240, San Isidro, Lima 27, T 624090. Swedish Embassy, Las Agatas 189, La Victoria, T 406700/722425. Norwegian Consulate, Canaval Moreyra 595, T 404048. Finnish Embassy, Los Eucaliptos 291, San Isidro, T 703750. Danish Consulate General, Jr. Lampa 946, 2nd floor, Lima, T 283620. Netherlands Consulate, Av. Principal 190, San Borja, T 72865/721548, open Mon-Fri 0900-1200. Italian Embassy, Av. G. Escobedo 298, Jesús María. Israeli Embassy, Natalio Sánchez 125, 6° piso, Santa Beatriz, Aptdo 738, T 334431.

N.B. During the summer, most embassies only open in the morning.

Useful Addresses Tourist Police, T 714579. Dirección General de Migraciones, Paseo de la República 585; if passport stolen can provide new entry stamps. Intej, Av. San Martín 240, Barranco, can extend student cards, T 774105. PSNC: Nicolás de Piérola 1002-06, Plaza San Martín. T 283250. YMCA: Carabaya 664. New building with more facilities on Avenida Bolívar in suburb of Pueblo Libre. Biblioteca Nacional, Av. Abancay (cuadra 4) y Miró Quesada.

Doctor Dr. Manfred Zapff-Dammert (German), Av. Monte Grande 109, of. 208, Chacarilla del Estanque, Lima-33, Monterrico, T 361532 (office), 350292 (private), highly recommended. Malaria pills from Dr. León on 3rd floor of Ministerio de Salud, Av. Salaverry.

Hospitals Anglo-American Hospital, Av. Salazar, 3rd block, San Isidro. T 403570 (rec. for injections; stock gamma globulin). Hospital de Niñas, Av. Brasil, vaccination centre at the side. Anti-rabies centre, Chacra Ríos.

Laundry Continental, Cailloma 430, same-day and next-day laundry and dry-cleaning, good, but expensive. Miraflores, Tarapacá 199 and Inclán, Miraflores; insist on an itemized receipt.

Autoservicio, Porta 198, Miraflores, fast, US$1.20 per machine. Burbujitas, Porta 293, Miraflores, 4 kg. wash and dry for US$1. Av. Petit Thouars 3139, Miraflores, US$2 wash and dry. Lava Velox, Atahualpa 175, Miraflores, US$2 a load, good. Lava Center, Víctor Maurtúa 140, San Isidro, T 403600, US$0.50 per kg. Businessman, A. N. Wiese, fast. Good dry cleaning, but not cheap, at Forty Minutes, Jirón Lampa 1180 in centre.

Non-catholic churches The Union Church of Lima (Interdenominational), Av. Angamos 1155, Miraflores, Worship Service Sun. 1030, T 41-1472. Trinity Lutheran Church of Peru, Las Magnolias 495, Urb. Jardín, San Isidro. Church of the Good Shepherd, Av. Santa Cruz 491, Miraflores (Anglican) T 45-7908, Sun. 0800 Holy Communion, 1000 morning service. International Baptist Church of Lima, Coronel Inclán 799, Miraflores, T 75-7179, Worship Service Sun. 1000. Christian Science Society, 1285 Mayta Capac (near Av. Salaverry), Jesús María. English Benedictine Monastery, Jirón Olivares de la Paz, Las Flores (57M minibus from Plaza de Acho); Sunday Mass 0900, weekdays 1900. **Catholic Mass in English**, La Iglesia de Santa Maria Reina, Ovalo Gutiérrez, Av. Santa Cruz, Miraflores T 24-7269, Sun. 0930.

Post Offices Central office is on Jirón Junín, west of the Plaza de Armas, hours: Mon.-Sat., 0800-1915, Sun., 0800-1200. On Av. Nicolás de Piérola, opp. *Hotel Crillón*. *Poste restante*, Camaná 195 (letters held for 2 months). Also on Av. Petit Thouars in Miraflores (1 block from intersection of Angamos and Arequipa), open 6 days a week. Express letters can only be sent from the Post Office at the airport. Be careful with the rates charged at this Post Office, they sometimes try to charge more than in the city. For parcels **see page 1011, Mail.**

Telecommunications International **phone** calls from Entel office in Edificio Sudamérica on Plaza San Martín. Cables Hotels *Bolívar, Crillón, Miraflores César,* and *Country Club*, also Jirón Lampa 667 and San Isidro. Public telex booths.

Air Freight Emery, in Callao, T 52-3643: to USA US$50 plus US$3 per kg.

Tourist Offices The Fondo de Promoción Turística (Foptur), Unión (Belén) 1066, T 323559 (open Mon.-Fri., 0900-1800, Sat., 0900-1200), highly recommended, many languages spoken, knowledgeable and helpful to budget-minded travellers, sells maps and has free brochures, Cuzco, Puno, Iquitos, etc. Head Office, Andrés Reyes 320, San Isidro, T 700781, Telex 21363 PE FOPTUR. Enturperú, which administers the State Tourist Hotel chain, is at Av. Javier Prado-Oeste 1358, San Isidro (a 15-min. taxi ride from the centre), open Mon.-Fri., 1000-1900, Sat., 0900-1300 (T 721928/728227/228094, telex. 20394; P.O. Box 4475), very helpful; rooms in the *hoteles de turistas* may be booked in advance. There are two tourist offices at the airport, which have lists of hotels and will ring to reserve rooms for travellers, or will book taxis—check whether prices are on the free or official rate; will also change money, very helpful staff. Ask for the helpful, free, *Peru Guide* published in English by American Express.

The Ministerio de Industria y Turismo, Calle 1 Oeste, Corpac, Lima 27, is very helpful regarding complaints and problems connected with travel agencies and touring.

Maps A good map of the whole country is available from street sellers in N. de Piérola and Plaza San Martín (published by Lima 2000, US$3.50). Newstands sell a bus transit map for US$0.75. The Instituto Geográfico Militar (Av. Aramburu 1190, Surquillo, Lima 34), sells a standard map of Peru (1:2,200,000), US$1.15, department maps, US$0.85 and a 4-sheet map of Peru, 1: 1,000,000, US$8.70, good value, but only available as separate sheets at Av. Aramburu, black-and-white aerial photos available; passport may be required; they are open

0900-1600, Mon.-Fri.; Av. Aramburu open for map sales Mon.-Fri., 0800-1230, 1400-1530. Maps of N and S border areas are not sold. If you submit a letter to the IGM, giving your credentials and adequate reasons, plus a photocopy of your passport, you may be able to obtain maps of the border regions. No accurate maps of the jungle regions have yet been prepared. The Instituto Nacional de Planificación, Avenida República de Chile, also sells a large atlas of Peru, US$25. Petroperú maps for town centres recommended.

South American Explorers' Club Av. Rep. de Portugal 146 (Breña—in the 13th block of Alfonso Ugarte), T 31-4480, is a non-profit, educational organisation which functions primarily as an information network for Peru and South America. Membership is US$25 a year, which includes subscription to its quarterly journal, *The South American Explorer*, and numerous member services such as access to files of travel information, equipment storage, personal mail service, trip planning, etc. Open 0930-1700 Mon. to Fri.; non-members are welcome, but asked to limit their visits, staff very helpful. The clubhouse is attractive and friendly; it is not necessary to "explore" to feel at home here. They will sell used equipment on consignment (donations of used equipment, unused medicines etc., are welcome). Their map of the Inca Trail is good (US$4), and they sell an excellent map of the Cordillera Huayhuash. Other useful dyeline trekking maps include the Llanganuco-Santa Cruz trek in the Cordillera Blanca, and the Cordillera Vilcanota (Auzangate). There is a good library and they sell travel books and guides (at a discount to members), and some excellent handicrafts. For further information, and the most recent views on where and how to travel safely, write to: Casilla 3714, Lima 100, Peru; PO Box 18327, Denver, CO USA (T (303) 320-0388); or Apartado 21-431, Eloy Alfaro, Quito, Ecuador (T 566-076). (Also see the Bradts' *Backpacking* book, listed in "Information for Visitors"; all Bradt publications are on sale at the Club.)

Trekking and Backpacking Percy Tapiá, Casilla 3074, Lima 100, leads treks for groups on the Inca Trail, Cordillera Vilcabamba and Cordillera Blanca. Club Andino Peruano, Amatistas 263, La Victoria, Lima 13, also helpful; meetings on Thur., 1930-2130. Instituto Nacional de Recreación, Educación Física y Deportes (Inred), have an Andean specialist, César Morales Arnao, at the Estudio Nacional, Tribuna Sur, 3rd floor, T 329177. Trekking and Backpacking Club Peruano, Jr. Huáscar 1152, Jesus María, Lima 11 (T 22515), also at Huaraz; free information on Peru and South America, storage and gas cylinders available. Issues a magazine, *El Trekkero*, write for information. Open Mon.-Fri., 1730-1900, phone first at weekends.

The Peruvian Touring and Automobile Club Av. César Vallejo 699 (Casilla 2219), Lince, Lima (T 403270), offers help to tourists and particularly to members of the leading motoring associations. Good maps available of whole country; regional routes and the S. American sections of the Pan-American Highway available (US$2.10).

Tourist Information Best guide to archaeological sites is *Manual de Arqueología Peruana*, by Kaufmann Doig, on sale from stalls and most bookshops, published in Spanish, US$8; an abridged version, *El Perú Arqueológico*, US$2, covering pre-Inca remains, is also available. *Cut Stones and Crossroads: A Journey in Peru*, by Ronald Wright (Penguin Travel Library) is an excellent, modern travel book. Booklet *Lima, City of Treasures and Traditions* by Frances E. Parodi (published by the American Woman's Literary Club, Lima). *Guía "Inca" de Lima Metropolitana* is invaluable for finding less well known, but interesting, parts of Lima, as is the *Guía de Transportes de Lima Metropolitana* (US$1.75) for getting to them. For those interested in architecture, *Itinerarios de Lima*, by Héctor Velarde (in Spanish and English), and *Guía Reparaz del Perú*, by Gonzalo Reparaz Ruiz (Spanish, English and French) are very useful. Also useful is *Guide to Lima* by J. E. Maguiña and *The City of Kings: A Guide to Lima*, by Carolyn Walton (available from major bookshops). Spanish and English news in the lobby of the *Sheraton Hotel*. *Lima Times* publishes a monthly *Peru Guide* and sells some other travel books.

Professional archaeologists should contact the Instituto Nacional de Cultura, Casilla 5247, Lima, or Centro de Investigación y Restauración de Bienes Monumentales del Instituto Nacional de Cultura, Jirón Ancash 769, Lima.

Travel Agents There are many, around Plaza San Martín and Av. Nicolás Piérola (Colmena). *Sudex S. A.* (Gerard Astruck), Sudamérica building, Carabaya 933, Of. 310-317; *Lima Tours*, Belén 1040, just off Plaza San Martín, American Express agent, slow for money changing, publishes a tourist guide (T 276624). *Coltur S.A.*, Jr. Camaná 868, rec.; *Creditio S. A.*, Schell 319, Oficina 706, Miraflores (T 444200/444727), efficient, helpful, English spoken; *Spazio Tours*, Juan Fanning 179, Miraflores, T 476451, or PO Box 18-5497, Lima, very helpful, highly rec.; *Viajes Universal*, Av. Arequipa 2885, San Isidro (T 421111/421112), helpful, contact María del Rosario Berio; *Explorandes*, Av. Bolognesi 159, Miraflores, rec.; *Key Tours* (Jorge

Gonti Angeles), Av. Nicolás de Piérola 677, Of. 9, T 284311 rec. for swift and efficient arranging of tours throughout Peru and to La Paz. *Aventours*, Av. La Paz 442, Miraflores, Lima 18, T 441067, trekking, rafting, wildlife tours and more (office in Cuzco, Av. Pardo 505, T 237307).*Chávez Tours* will arrange drivers to take small groups (or individuals) on trips for US$22 per day. *Machu Picchu Tours*, Washington 949 (*Hostal Eiffel*), Sarela Pumarica, T 249181/240188, good for flight tickets; *Majestic Tours*, Centro Comercial Centro Lima, Blvd 196-M (near *Sheraton*), will arrange virtually any itinerary, rec. *Tour Peruana S.A.*, Miguel Dasso 138, San Isidro, T 220751/221639, ask for Sigiario Carrizales, good for flight arrangements; *Nouvelles Frontières*, N. de Piérola, for cheap flights to Europe. *Cecilia Toso Stagi*, *Turispa*, Av. La Paz 1101, Miraflores (T 474903), rec. Julio E. Figueroa Cubas, Fco. Sarmiento de Gamboa 289, Urb. La Colonial, Callao, T 514748, private guide, rec. particularly for non-Spanish speakers, Lima tours, US$5 per hour; also Alfredo Hiromoto, T 312-709 (home), or 441-799 (*Hotel Diplomat*). A good archaeological tour guide is Rolando Peceros, T 276720. To contact the Lima Association of Guides, T 245131. **N.B.** A commission is charged for booking tickets, 20% usual, 50% complained of, ask before booking.

Airport The Jorge Chávez airport is 16 km. from the centre of Lima. Taxi, about US$10 to centre, US$15 to Miraflores (negotiate price before leaving, hang on to your bag if surrounded by taxi touts—if you walk 100 metres outside the airport gate you can probably bargain a much cheaper price from taxis not working the airport route—but not recommended at night). Airport bus to centre (and also colectivos; look for big brown sign) leaves from right-hand end of building as you step out of the door. Municipal blue bus 35 (US$0.10) and colectivo (outside the Air France office), to and from Plaza Dos de Mayo in the day-time, US$0.50 p.p. and per item of luggage. Minibus every 20 mins., US$0.75, from Calle Serrano, opposite Iberia office. Also, 15 and 35 from the Plaza Dos de Mayo leave for the airport; service about every 30 mins. No. 56 from airport enters Lima along Av. Emancipación. There is a cheap colectivo service from corner of Av. Tacna with Colmena (N. de Piérola) 733, from 0400 to 2000, colectivos wait until they have 5 passengers, US0.50 p.p., and US$0.25 for luggage. Buses go from Trans Hotel, Camaná 828 (T 275697, 289812), supposedly 24-hour service, will also collect passengers from hotels (fares range from US$1.75 p.p. with one bag leaving from Camaná office or a hotel nearby, to US$6 if they pick you up from a hotel away from the centre and from airport to town at night). Passengers report being let down by this service. Also from Miraflores (Avenida Ricardo Palma 280), every 20 min., US$2 p.p. (buses will collect travellers from private houses, US3.20), T 469872. If using this service, book well in advance at Trans Hotel. At airport, T 518011; after leaving Arrivals turn right and go to desk at the end of the hall. The big hotels also have their own buses at the airport, and charge about the same. There is a duty-free shop but no duty-free cigarettes. Only official Corpac porters are allowed in the customs area. Avoid getting left with intis at the airport when leaving; changing them back into dollars at Banco de la Nación can take a lot of time, and you need to show the official exchange slips. Car rental booths in airport may buy intis. Left luggage costs US$2 per day, US$0.40 per hour per item. Foptur office at airport open daily 0830-1430, 2100-0200 (T 524416) in international area, 0600-1830 (T 333664) in national area. The Prohotel agent at the airport is very helpful with hotel bookings of all classes; there is a second hotel booking agency. Taxi drivers also tout for hotel business, offering discounts—don't let yourself be bullied. Safe to stay all night in 24-hour expresso-snack bar.

Be prepared for extensive searches; have your money ready counted, the notes bundled together and the amount written on the outside.

Internal Air Services To Andahuaylas, Arequipa, Ayacucho, Bellavista, Cajamarca, Chiclayo, Chimbote, Cuzco, Huánuco, Iquitos, Juanjui, Juliaca, Moyobamba, Piura, Pucallpa, Puerto Maldonado, Rioja, Tacna, Talara, Tarapoto, Tingo María, Trujillo, Tumbes and Yurimaguas. Prices (Feb. 1990 tourist, in dollars) and other details are given in text, under names of destinations, but note that tourist prices are double those for Peruvians - see *Information for Visitors.*

Air Lines Most international airlines have moved out to San Isidro and Miraflores. Faucett (Garcilaso de la Vega 865, Lima centre, T 338180; office in Miraflores Av. Diagonal 592, T 462031), Aeroperú (Plaza San Martín; more helpful than offices at airport, T 317627, or Av. Pardo 601, Miraflores, T 478333); 24-hr. reconfirmation service T 478333). Office hours are 0900-1800, Mon.-Sat.

Rail Central Railway of Peru maintains passenger and freight service to La Oroya (with an extension N to Cerro de Pasco) and SE to Huancayo (with an extension to Huancavelica): Desamparados station, behind Presidential Palace. (For description of line **see page 976**). Train to La Oroya and Huancayo departs 0700 daily except Sun., arriving La Oroya 1300 and Huancayo 1600 (schedules published in *El Comercio,* service may be cut to Mon., Wed., Sat each way). The train from La Oroya to Cerro de Pasco also runs daily, but one cannot buy a through ticket from Lima because the Cerro de Pasco train leaves La Oroya at 1330 before the train from Lima has arrived. If not wishing to go beyond La Oroya, colectivo back to Lima costs US$5.50, 5 hrs., you can make a day trip of it, being back by 2000. You can also return by bus, 7½ hrs., for railway enthusiasts especially. The return from Huancayo is at 0700, arriving Lima 1603. Single, 1st class, US$2.50, 2nd class, US$1.50; good cheap breakfast and lunch (US$1) served. 1st class and buffet seats can be reserved for US$0.50—take a torch for the long, dark tunnels; ticket office opens 0830-1200, 1300-1600 Mon.-Fri., 0700-1100 Sat.; tickets can only be bought one day in advance in Lima; in the high season, tickets are often sold out for 1st class by 1200. Sit on the left; remember that the train changes direction at San Bartolomé, so you will be sitting on the right to begin with. Guard your possessions very carefully against pickpockets at the station (heavy police presence on the train). Only ticket holders are allowed on the platform. The station is closed on Sundays.

Bus Companies Coastal buses are usually good although liable to delays. Buses in the Sierra, in view of the road surfaces, often break down. The services of the Ormeño group, are generally recommended throughout Peru; Cruz del Sur are also generally well thought of. Tepsa, Paseo de la República 129 (T 731233) run N and S on the coast and to Pucallpa and Arequipa; they use older, more run-down buses than some other companies, but we are told they still tend to drive too fast for safety. Expreso Continental (Ormeño) to Trujillo, Piura and Tumbes, rec.; Chinchay-Suyo (northwards), Apurímac 391 and Av. Grau 525; also going north, Perú Express, Pacífico El Norte (to Chimbote), Atahualpa, Jr. Sandía 266, T 275838/287255 (to Cajamarca, Celendín, etc.), good; Sudamericano buses (Av. Nicolás de Piérola 1117) to Tumbes are variable and its service to Nazca is unreliable; Roggero are unreliable and slow. Along the South coast route, Ormeño, Av. Carlos Zavala 177, T 27-5679/28-8453, reliable, also to Arequipa and Cuzco (terminal at Calle Oyazaca, best go there by taxi, especially at night); Cruz del Sur, Paseo de la República corner with Almirante Grau (also go to Santiago). To Cuzco: via Arequipa, Cruz del Sur; via Nazca and Puquío, Ormeño, El Cóndor. To Huancayo, Compresa Cáceres, Av. 28 de Julio 2195, and Comité 22 colectivo, Av. Ayacucho 997, T 289082. To Huánuco: León de Huánuco, Av. José Gálvez 1734 (also to Pucallpa not rec., buses in bad condition); Nor Oriente, Luna Pizarro 365. Arrellano, for Huánuco and Tingo María, to be avoided because terminal is in dangerous La Victoria district. Expreso Intersa, Av. Nicolás de Piérola, 1631; El Trome, Montevideo 949. Colectivos leave for all parts of Peru from Parque Universitario. For prices of routes and more details, see under individual cities in pages following.

International Buses Tepsa runs a twice weekly service to Santiago, Chile (3 days, 3,500 km.) leaving Lima on Thurs. and Sun. at 1645, also Pul Bus Norte; Ormeño to Santiago, 2½ days, US$70 inc 3 meals, and to Buenos Aires, US$140 inc 3 meals, rec. El Rápido, Av. Carlos Zavala Loayza 218, T 283181, weekly to Mendoza (US$130) and Buenos Aires (US$140), fare includes meals and one night in a hotel, takes 4 days. Connecting twice weekly services to Guayaquil and Quito (although there are no through buses; you can buy through tickets but they are very expensive and give no priority), leaving Lima on Wed. and Sun. at 0845. The trip takes 2½ days; often long frontier delays.

The international trips are much cheaper if one is prepared to take buses to frontier posts only, walk across frontiers, and buy tickets as one goes along (going to Ecuador, it is also possible that a Huaguillas—Quito bus booked in Lima will not exist). To enter Peru, a ticket out of the country may be required. If you have to buy a bus ticket, be warned: they are not transferable or refundable.

Warning The area around the bus terminals is very unsafe; thefts and assaults are more common in this neighbourhood than elsewhere in the city. You are strongly advised to consider taking a taxi to and from your bus. Make sure your luggage is well guarded and put on the right bus. It is also important not to assume that buses leave from the place where you bought the tickets.

In the weeks either side of July 28/29 (Independence), and of the Christmas/New Year holiday, it is practically impossible to get train or bus tickets out of Lima.

Suburbs of Lima The Avenida Arequipa connects the centre of Lima with Miraflores. Parallel to this is the Vía Expresso, a 6-lane highway carrying fast traffic to the suburbs. At **San Isidro** is El Olivar, an old olive grove turned into a delightful park (best visited in daylight). Beyond this is the Lima Golf Club where the Country Club is found, primarily a hotel, which incorporates the Real Club with swimming pools, tennis courts, etc. This is an 8 km. taxi ride from the centre of Lima. There are many good hotels and restaurants in San Isidro; see main Lima lists, hotels page 862 and restaurants 865. Between San Isidro and Miraflores is the Pan de Azúcar, or Huallamarca, a restored adobe pyramid of the Maranga culture, of about AD 100-500 (Calle Nicolás de Rivera 201, small museum, open daily, 0900-1700, bus 1 from Av. Tacna, or minibus 13 or 73 to Choquechaca, then walk).

The road reaches the sea at **Miraflores**, the largest, most important suburb of Lima, with well stocked shops and many first class hotels and restaurants (see main Lima lists: hotels **page 861**, Youth Hostel, **page 864** and restaurants, **page 864**). There is a handsome park in the middle of the shopping centre and at the end of Avenida Mariscal Benavides, which is commonly called Av. Diagonal, you can get the best view of the whole Lima coastline from Chorrillos to La Punta.

The Mariscal Necochea clifftop park overlooks the Waikiki Club, a favourite with Lima surfers. Near Parque Kennedy is the artists' and craftsmens's quarter of L'Ovolo. On no account camp on Miraflores beach; it is extremely dangerous as well as pebbled and dust-blown because of cliff erosion. (In fact, any of the beaches near Miraflores are unsafe regarding theft, especially during school holidays.) You can see sealions at close quarters, but the fishing seabirds are not so numerous as they were.

Buses to Miraflores No. 2 from Plaza de Armas or Plaza San Martín, Nos. 2 and 53 from Emancipación and Tacna; others from Tacna and Huancavelica (US$0.10); buses to Miraflores run down Tacna, Garcilaso de la Vega and Arequipa. Taxi-colectivos recommended, Quilca and Garcilaso de la Vega, 2 blocks from Plaza San Martín US$0.15.

The road passes through **Barranco** (not to be confused with Barranca, 200 km. N of Lima), with an attractive plaza and nearby the interesting *bajada*, a steep path down to the beach, where many of Lima's artists live and exhibit their work; many old houses are under restoration. (Take bus No. 2 to Miraflores and Barranco beaches from Plaza San Martín, for US$0.15.) The next development on the coast is at **Chorrillos**, a fashionable resort (*Café Suizo* overlooking beach) with a cliff promenade, and boating. At Hacienda La Villa, an old Spanish *hacienda* worth visiting, there is occasionally open air dancing to *salsa* music. Near Chorrillos is the Playa de los Pescadores with seafood stalls, Playa Agua Dulce (a clean beach), and the Club Regatas de Lima. Beyond Chorrillos is **La Herradura**, another bathing resort with several restaurants. The private Club Unicornio is open to tourists. A beach road runs round the entire bay; the main access to it is either at the end of the Paseo de la República in Barranco or by the Bajada de Balta, which is at the end of Av. Diagonal in Miraflores.

Avenida Costanera passes through a run down seaside resort, **Magdalena del Mar**, served by a separate road and bus route from Lima. A little inland, along this route, is **Pueblo Libre**, where the Museum of Anthropology and Archaeology, the Museum of the Republic and the Rafael Larco Herrera Museum are found (see under Museums, **page** 857, as well as the old church of Magdalena Vieja (1557), which was unfortunately heavily damaged in the 1974 earthquake.

N.B. Bathing is not recommended at any of the beaches around Lima; the water is dangerous and contaminated (the municipality bans swimming at most beaches for this reason).

Callao Passengers coming to Peru by sea usually land at Callao (now contiguous with Lima). It handles 75% of the nation's imports and some 25% of its exports.

Callao's maritime terminal or inner harbour covers 100 hectares, and the largest vessels go alongside. Population, 545,000. San Lorenzo island, a naval station, protects the roadstead from the S; inland stretches the Rímac valley. It is a commercial place with no architectural beauty. Lima is reached by road (20 mins. by car or bus, US$0.12). Passengers are expected to be on board half-an-hour before the vessel's departure. (Some have been attacked and robbed just outside the dock gates.) There are some interesting shops in the area between Calle Constitución and Av. Sáenz Peña, and a market between Sáenz Peña and Buenos Aires. "The Club", the oldest English club on the W coast, is at Pasaje Ronald, Calle Constitución, Callao; there is an English cemetery.

History Drake and others raided Callao in the 16th century. An earthquake wiped it out in 1746. On November 5, 1820, Lord Cochrane boarded and captured, after a bloody fight in which he was wounded, the Spanish frigate *Esmeralda*. The Real Felipe fortress (1774), last stronghold of the Royalists in S. America, withstood a siege of a year and finally surrendered after terrible sufferings in 1826. It is still a military post, and tourists are allowed to visit it. The Military Museum (**see page** 858) is in the old barracks. The railway to Lima, opened May 17, 1851, was one of the first in S. America.

Leading Restaurant *El Chalaquito*, Calle Constitución. A number of good fish restaurants can be found on Av. Sáenz Peña. There are a number of reliable bars in the Pasaje Ríos and Calle Constitucíon.

Taxis In Callao use taxis recommended by U.S. Embassy or port authorities—for safety's sake. About US$15 for 3 hrs.

Addresses British Vice-Consulate, Sáenz Peña 154. P.S.N.C., Calle Independencia 150 (Casilla 368), T 299040.

Cables Pasaje Ronald y Constitución 258. Sáenz Peña 160; T 29-0117 (Public Telex booth).

Tourist Office Foptur, Terminal Marítimo-Guardia Chalaca s/n, T 299210.

The Naval College is at **La Punta**, just beyond Callao, served by municipal buses and colectivos through Callao from Lima. La Punta is on a spit of land stretching out to sea; once a fashionable beach, but water is cool. A new yacht club has been built on the N side. The walk along the seafront between Callao and La Punta has its charms.

The road from Callao to Lima is lined by factories. Shipyards, far from sea, load the fishing vessels they build on huge lorries and launch them into the ocean at Callao. San Marcos University (founded 12 May, 1551) has now been transferred to a new University City, near the Naval Hospital.

On Avenida Marina between Lima and Callao, a turn-off opposite the entrance to the Feria del Pacífico grounds leads to the Parque Las Leyendas (**see page** 860).

There are bathing, tennis, and a yacht club at **Ancón**, 30 km. NW of Lima, reached by a double-lane asphalted highway. Colectivo from Plaza 2 de Mayo in Lima, US$0.50, returns 1 block from Ancón Cathedral. It is the only real seaside resort in Peru, but no hotels apart from *Restaurant Cinco Luches*, which has rooms, E. Beaches are very small. Crowded Jan.-March holidays, good for fish (recommended restaurant, *Los 5 Tenedores* on the Corniche). On the way to Ancón is the pleasant Santa Rosa beach (entrance fee). Beyond Ancón is a Chancay cemetery, from which has come much Chancay weaving and pottery (as seen in the Amano Museum). There are also Inca ruins at Maranga and Chuquitanta, near Lima; unfortunately the latter cannot be visited at present.

Excursions **Pachacámac** is in the Lurín valley, 31 km. from Lima. When the Spaniards arrived, Pachacámac was the largest city on the coast. The ruins encircle the top of a low hill, the crest of which was crowned with a Temple of the Sun, a large pyramid built in 1350 of sun-baked bricks. (There are also a reconstructed Temple of the Virgins and the ancient temple of the Creator God.) Hernando Pizarro, brother of Francisco, came to Pachacámac in 1533; he destroyed images, killed the priests and looted the temples. The setting is marvellous, but the restoration has been criticized and vandals have been at work. Bus or colectivo from Lima, caught from Av. Montevideo, near Petro Perú station in 800 block. The buses (US$0.25, 1 hr.) and colectivos (US$0.50) go by way of Miraflores and Chorrillos, but tell the driver you are going to the *ruinas* or he will land you in Pachacámac town further on. Taxi, 3 hr. trip, US$40. Closed Mon. and 1 May, open 0900 to 1700. Entrance US$0.40.

Pucusana, 50 km. from Lima, Silencio, Santa María and Cerro Azul, 90 km., are fishing villages with beaches that are much cleaner than those near Lima. Robbery is common on the beaches and you are advised to sit on your clothes and other possessions. Do not leave anything unattended when swimming.

Also to the South, up the Omas valley beyond Coalla are the Inca adobe structures at Los Gentiles (on the right, well before Omas) and, nearer Omas, Pueblo Viejo, Yampa and Viracocha. Take a colectivo from Plaza Santa Catalina, Jr. Puno (2 blocks from Av. Abancay), Lima to Mala, then hitch, or taxi, via Asia to the sites.

A second excursion is to Chosica, 40 km. up the Rímac valley. In the residential district of **Chaclacayo**, just before Chosica, are the *Huampani Hotel*, C, modern, attractive, good meals, swimming pool (US$0.40), run by the Government's hotel chain, and *Residencial La Casa de los Olivos*, at Los Ficus 373 y Los Olivos, with restaurant and ten rooms. An excellent chicken meal at the *Granja Azul* (take bus 88M or 204 from Parque Universitario) and there are several other places on the road from Lima to Chosica. The *Hotel El Pueblo* has swimming pool, horse riding, tennis, a beautiful garden, entrance, US$3, used heavily for conventions. Try restaurant and campground of *Puerto del Sol*, owned by Sr. Italo de Neqzi Herreros. A delightful place for dinner and dancing is the restaurant *Fiesta*, at km. 6 on the Central Highway. At km. 33 is *El Bosque* Country Club (anyone may enter on payment of US$85), private lake, 4 swimming pools, tennis and ball courts, riding stables, bull ring, etc. Colectivos for Chosica leave from just W of Parque Universitario, near the Ministry of Education building. Buses, 204, 1M.

On the way to Chosica a diversion may be made at Km. 4½ to **Puruchuco**, to see the reconstructed palace of a pre-Inca Huacho noble; with small museum (ceramics, textiles, etc., from the lower Rímac or Lima valley) and a selection of indigenous plants and animals, open 0900-1700, Tues.-Sun. (closed 1 May and 28 July). Entrance US$1; Chosica bus or colectivo from Parque Universitario. One km. from Puruchuco are Huaquerones and Catalina Huaca sites now being restored. Nearby, at Chivateros, is a quarry said to date from 10,000 BC. The large adobe pre-Inca city of **Cajamarquilla** may also be visited, for which the turnoff (left, at Huachipa) is about 6 km. on from the Puruchuco turn. The site is difficult to find—you can't see it from the road—but look for a sign "Zona Arqueológica" in the middle of a brick yard. Keep on driving through the yard, and you will find Cajamarquilla at the end of an ill-kept dirt road. Open every day, 0900-1700. Beyond the Huachipa turn-off for Cajamarquilla, along the main road, there are precolumbian ruins at San Juan de Pariache and Huaicán-Tambo, 13½ and 16½ km. respectively from Lima.

Chosica (40 km.), the real starting place for the mountains, is at 860 metres, and is a popular winter resort because it is above the cloudbank covering Lima from May to October. One train a day and frequent buses and minibuses. Beyond the town looms a precipitous range of hills almost overhanging the streets. Up picturesque Santa Eulalia valley off the Rímac valley are the Central Fruit Culture Nurseries. There is some dramatic scenery on the road up the valley, fairly good as far as the hydroelectric station at Callahuanca, but the road is afterwards quite nasty in places, narrow and rocky. Population: 31,200.

Hotels *Residencial Chosica*, D; *Residencial San Jorge*, Av. Lima Sur 401, with hot water, rec., restaurant and bar.

Bus from Lima, No. 204, from 18th block of Calle Ayacucho (US$0.50); also 1M. Colectivos leave from near Education Ministry, just W of Parque Universitario and from Calle Montevideo around the corner from the Ormeño building in the centre.

Beyond Chosica, near the Santa Eulalia river (80 km. from Lima), is **Marcahuasi**, a table mountain about 3 km. by 3 km. at 4,200 metres, near the village of San Pedro de Casta (accommodation in a cold shelter only, less than US$1). The *meseta* has been investigated by Daniel Ruzo: there are 3 lakes, a "monumento a la humanidad" (40 metres high), and other mysterious lines, gigantic figures, sculptures, astrological signs and megaliths which display non-American symbolism. Ruzo describes this pre-Incaic culture in his book, *La Culture Masma*, Extrait de l'Ethnographie, Paris, 1956. Others say that the formations are not man-made, but the result of wind erosion. Truck to San Pedro de Casta from Chosica, 3 hrs., colectivo 2 hrs (US$1.70). Trail starts behind the village of San Pedro bending to the left—about 2 hours to the *meseta* (guides about US$3 a day, advisable in misty weather). Buses available for US$1.85 from San Pedro de Casta to Lima. Take food as no-one lives on the *meseta*, although there is a hut which provides good basic shelter; nights are cold. Srta. Paquita Castillo, T Lima 275251, arranges group tours.

Beyond Casta is San Juan de Iris, a tiny village, outside of which impressive ruins have been discovered (bus or truck from *Restaurant 41* in Chosica at 0900 if you're lucky, 7 hrs.).

There are the ancient (from 1500 BC) ruins of a small town on the hill of San Pedro de Casta, a fortress on the hills of Loma de los Papas (daily bus from Chosica at 0800), the ruins of Tambo Inca, and an ancient cemetery to the South.

The Central Highway to La Oroya (**see page** 976) opens up possibilities of excursions by car with attractive stopping places like Matucana (1 hr.), San Mateo and Río Blanco (2 hrs.). The trip to La Oroya takes over 5 hrs., and crosses the Andean divide at 4,843 metres. An excursion may be made to Infiernillo ("Little Hell") Canyon, beyond Matucana, which is well worth seeing. The Lima-Chosica-Santa Eulalia-Huanza-Casapalca trip is the most impressive in the environs of Lima, and can be done in one day.

To the North, up the Chillón valley is Cantamarca. "Beyond Cantamarca one comes (writes John Streather) to the beautiful Abra de la Viuda pass, where one passes through the Bosque de Piedras (rocks in extraordinary shapes and sizes) and the Junín pampa to Cerro de Pasco." In the Chancay valley are Chiprac, Rupac and Añay. John Streather writes: "These extraordinary ruins are very little visited, especially the last two which are more or less perfectly preserved. They have roofs on them and are extraordinarily well built. For Chiprac and Rupac, go with food, tent and sleeping bag to Huaral on the coast (bus from Lima from the Plaza de Acho, by the bullring, over the Puente de Piedra— beware of thieves). From Huaral, get a lift or a bus (one a week) to San Juan up beyond Acos. Best go first to Acos where there is a restaurant and accommodation and wait at the road junction a few km. out of the village for a lift up to San Juan. Chiprac is high above the village and can be reached on one's own;

it is a good day's walk there and back with time to take photographs and eat. In San Juan, a man called Chavelo will act as a guide to Rupac, which can be reached via the pretty and deserted town of Pampas—also a day there and back. For Añay, go to Hurial as for the other ruins, then get transport to Huayopampa (basic accommodation) or La Perla whence the visit to the ruins can easily be made; get a guide to show you up from either village." Further on are **Sayán, Oyón and Churín** (near here, at Chinchín, is *Albergue San Camilo*, C, excellent; bus from Lima, US$5 with Espadín y Hnos at Ormeño terminal to Churín, Oyón and Huamahuanca); at Churín, there are hot, sulphurous baths. From Chinchín, there are buses to nearby villages, such as Huancahuasi, where one can buy woven goods, see interesting churches, and spot *vicuña* in lovely surroundings.

NORTH-WEST FROM LIMA (2)

From Lima to Chimbote Between Lima and Pativilca there is a narrow belt of coastal land deposited at the mouths of the rivers, but from Pativilca to the mouth of the Río Santa, N of Chimbote, the Andes come down to the sea. Between Lima and Pativilca cotton and sugar-cane are grown, though the yield of sugar is less than it is further N where the sunshine is not interrupted by cloud. Cotton is harvested from April to September by Indian migrants from the basins of Jauja and Huancayo. Much irrigated land grows vegetables and crops to supply Lima and Callao. Cattle are driven down from the Highlands to graze the *lomas* on the mountain sides when the mists come between June and October.

The Pan-American Highway parallels the coast all the way to the far N, and feeder roads branch from it up the various valleys. Just N of Ancón, the Pasamayo sand dune, stretching for 20 km., comes right down to the seashore. The old road which snakes along the base beside the sea is spectacular, but is now closed except to commercial traffic. The new toll road (US$0.85), which goes right over the top, is much safer and you get spectacular views over the nearby coast and valleys. **Chancay**, on the coast (no bathing, sea both dangerous and heavily polluted), suffers from severe water shortages, but there is a fresh water source on the beach; *Hostal Villa de Arnedo*, D, clean and friendly, pool and restaurant, rec.; *Hostal Chancay*, F, safe, friendly, can wash clothes; *Restaurant Rebeca*, good.

Turn right 5 km. along road to Sayán where there is a national reserve, Loma de Lachay, which has thousands of snail shells, locust-trees and much bird life. Or continue north, dual carriageway to Km. 101, to the small port of **Huacho**, 132 km. from Lima. It is the outlet for cotton and sugar grown in the rich Huaura valley; a branch road runs up it to Sayán and beyond to Churín and Raura. There is a cemetery near Huacho where mummies may be found. There are cotton-seed oil and other factories. Port and sea are sometimes alive with monstrous jellyfish. Pop.: 35,900.

Hotels *El Pacífico*, F, safe, dirty, water problems, inadequate clothes-washing facilities; *Italia*; *Grace*; *Hostal Maury*, E, basic but friendly. Camping is possible at El Paraíso beach.

The journey inland from Huacho is splendid (Lima to Huacho by bus: Transportes América S.A., Av. Colonial 129, Lima). Beyond Sayán are terrific rock formations, then the road passes through subtropical vegetation around Churín (**see page** 879), which is visited for its mineral springs. There are coal mines. Above 4,000 metres is a chain of lakes which reflect the Cordillera Raura (up to 5,800 metres). Road ends at Raura mine.

About 25 km. beyond Huacho is Medio Mundo, with a lake between the village and the sea. It is a good camping spot, with tents for rent; bring food and water. The turnoff is outside the village on the Pan-American Highway, to the left, look for the sign, "Albufera de Medio Mundo". It is hot and busy in summer.

Just across the river is **Huaura**, where the balcony is still preserved from which San Martín declared the country's independence from Spain. Try *guinda*, the local cherry brandy. We pass from the wide valley of Mazo through the irrigated valley of San Felipe. There is more desert and then the cotton-fields of San Nicolás lead to **Supe**, a small busy port shipping fishmeal, cotton, sugar and minerals (*Hostal*

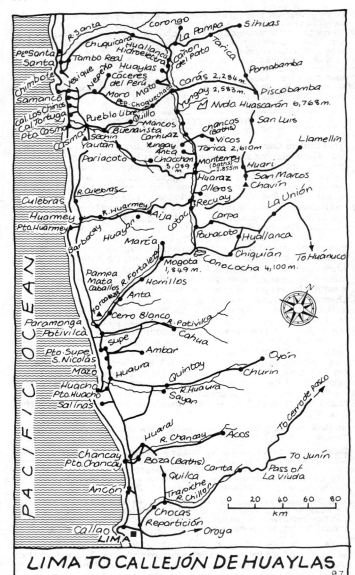

LIMA TO CALLEJÓN DE HUAYLAS

97

Supe, G; better is *Hostal Grau*, basic, G, clean, safe, comfortable, laundry, good value, next to which is a good restaurant: *El Norteño*. At Aspero, near Supe, is one of the earliest prehistoric sites in Peru (see History section, **page** 851). We pass through the town of **Barranca** (*Hotel Chavín*, F with bath, warm water, clean, good value, rec, front rooms are noisy, also restaurant on first floor for lunch and dinner (try *arroz con conchas*), breakfast bar and café opens onto street by main entrance; *Pacífico*, F with bath, clean, good value; *Colón*, Jr. Gálvez 407, G, friendly, basic; *Jefferson*, Lima 946, F, clean, friendly; *Hostería Central*, F, basic; many others on main street, and plenty of bars and restaurants, e.g. *Chifa*). The beach is long, not too dirty, though windy. Buses stop opposite the service station (*la grifa*) at the end of town. Americano to Lima, 3 hrs., US$2.50. Next is the straggling town of **Pativilca**, at Km. 203, which has a small museum (bus from Lima US$4, 2½ hrs.—*Restaurant Cornejo*, good and cheap) from which a well-paved road turns off for the Callejón de Huaylas and Huaraz (**see page** 886). The road is paved to Conacocha (4,080 m.) then in very poor condition to Catac and on to Chavín. 4 km. beyond the turn-off, beside the Highway, are the well preserved ruins of the Chimú temple of **Paramonga**. Set on high ground (view of the ocean), the fortress-like mound is reinforced by 8 quadrangular walls rising in tiers to the top of the hill (admission US$1.20, well worth visiting, taxi from Paramonga and return after waiting, US$4.50, otherwise hitch from Barranca). Not far from the fortress, the Great Wall (La Muralla) stretches across the Andes. Paramonga is a small port, 3 km. off the Pan-American Highway, 4 km. from the ruins and 200 km. from Lima, shipping sugar.

Hotel There is no hotel at Paramonga. There are several in Barranca; as bus companies have their offices there, buses will stop there rather than at Pativilca or Paramonga. No buses run to the ruins, only to the port.

Bus from Lima to Paramonga, Compañía Fortaleza or Empresa América recommended. From Lima to Barranca, 3 hrs. US$2.50, Empresa América, very comfortable. 1st class from terminal on outskirts; Compañía Fortaleza and Comité Cinco (2nd class) go to Barranca from Parque Universitario in Lima. Buses cover the 7-8 km. from Barranca to Paramonga. Bus from Barranca to Casma US$1; Ancash bus to Huaraz, 4 hrs., US$3. Truck, Pativilca-Huaraz, 5-6 hrs., US$1.70; many buses, first at 1030.

Between Paramonga and Chimbote (225 km.) the mountains come down to the sea. The road passes by a few very small protected harbours in tiny rock-encircled bays—Puerto **Huarmey** (small *Hotel de Turistas*, D, clean and good service, but noisy, being on Pan-American Highway, rebuilt and reopened after earthquake, at Huarmey town, not port), Puerto Casma, and Vesique. Tepsa bus Lima-Huarmey, US$5.10, US$8.50 by colectivo, from Parque Universitario. From Casma a road runs through the **Callán pass** (4,224 metres) to Huaraz. A difficult but beautiful trip. Not all buses take this route, so check before leaving. From Casma to the pass (apart from the paved first 30 km.), the road is appalling (many land-slides), but once the Cordillera Negra has been crossed, the road is better (gravel, wide) with spectacular views. About 40 km. before Casma, at Km. 330, is *Restaurant San Miguel*, good and clean, used by Tepsa as meal stop.

Casma The town was largely destroyed by the 1970 earthquake, but has since been rebuilt. A good new food market, but not much else to recommend.

Hotels *Hostal El Farol*, E, ask for cheaper rate in low season, good, with bathroom (no hot water), breakfast and dinner available (and sandwiches and coffee), pleasant garden setting; *Hostal Central*, on plaza, G p.p., dirty, basic, but helpful; *Hostal Madeleine*, Plaza de Armas, F, very basic. *Indoamericano*, F with bath, hot water, clean, good; *Chifa Tío Sam*, good, off plaza.

Bus From Parque Universitario, Lima, colectivo to Casma, US$8.80. Bus to Lima leaves 1100 daily (Tepsa) US$4.25 also Chinchay-Suyo, on main street, and Turismo Chimbote (main road opp. road on which *Hostal El Farol* is located), 4 a day, US$3.40 (truck, US$3). Tepsa to Barranca, US$2.25, 2 hrs. Bus to Huaraz, Chinchay-Suyo, 2300, daily and Moreno, 0700, 10 hrs., US$3.40. It is well worth making this trip in daylight to get the view of the Cordillera Blanca. Bus to Trujillo, Tepsa and Chinchay-Suyo, US$2, 3 hrs. Most buses pass Casma in the morning.

Excursions From Casma, take a truck going to San Rafael and ask for Castillo (departures all day from the garage opposite Huaraz bus stop). After alighting, walk 2 km. uphill to a cemetery with pottery on the ground, and a Chimú castle of 4 concentric rings, with 3 towers in the middle, the Castillo de Chanquillo. Further on is a large wall with 13 towers on a ridge. Take water with you. The trucks return all day up to about 1600. There are several other sites around Casma: Sechín Alto, Pallka, Tokán, Mojeque, La Cantina, Tokachi and Huanchay.

Sechín At Km. 370 on Pan-American Highway, shortly before reaching Casma from Lima, watch for a large concrete sign to Sechín on the right. Follow the road indicated for about 2 km. until you reach the ruins (about one hour's walk). Three sides of the large stone temple have been excavated and restored. You cannot see the adobe buildings inside the stone walls, which belong to an earlier period. They were later covered up and used as a base for a second storey which unfortunately has been completely destroyed. Some experts think the temple and surroundings were buried on purpose. Others believe it was engulfed by natural disaster. The latter theory is supported by finds of human skeletons. Tombs have been found in front and at the same level as the temple. A wall of a large adobe building under excavation can be seen and runs round the sides and back of the temple. The site is open to tourists, 0800-1700 (US$3.40, children half price); ticket also valid for Pañamarca (**see page 883**), and there is an attractive, shady picnic garden. The Max Uhle Museum opened in 1984 by the ruins: interesting display of Sechín artefacts. It is quite easy to walk to the ruins from Casma. One must walk about 3 km. S to a well posted sign showing a left turn, then simply follow the road for 2 km. to the ruins. (Frequent colectivos from in front of market in Casma, US$0.30 p.p., but leave early in the morning; no buses.) 2 km. further along there are two pyramids of the late Chavín period, but these have not yet been excavated.

Sechín is one of the most important ruins on the Peruvian coast. It consists of a large square temple completely faced with carved stone monoliths—probably over 500 of them—which depict gruesome battle scenes: men being eviscerated, heads with blood gushing from eyes or mouths, dismembered legs, arms, torsos, ears, eyes and vertebrae. The style is unique in Peru for its naturalistic vigour. Within the stone temple is an earlier, pre-ceramic mud temple with painted walls. The temples are pre-Chavín, about 1500 BC. (John Hemming)

Chimbote, 420 km. from Lima, is one of Peru's few natural harbours, ample in area and depth of water. Rapidly growing population of 185,000; a new port has been built to serve the national steel industry: iron ore from Marcona field is shipped from the port of San Juan, 547 km. S of Lima; anthracite comes by railway from the hinterland, and power comes from the hydroelectric station in the Cañón del Pato, 129 km. inland. The steel industry creates heavy pollution; also Chimbote is Peru's largest fishing port; fishmeal is exported and the smell of the fishmeal plants is very strong. Bathing is forbidden on the beach near the hotel. Flocks of brown pelicans and masked boobies may be seen from the beach. Shanty towns have burgeoned around. Small airport, but no commercial flights. Public swimming pool at Vivero Forestal.

Hotels *Turistas* now a State Tourist Hotel (D, with bath, meals US$3.50, uninspiring), Chimbote's cleanest snack bar, there are some cheaper but noisier rooms at the back, must ask, safe parking; *Presidente* (3 star), E, with bath, clean, friendly, hot showers, safe parking, poor snack bar, rec.; *Carabelle*, F, round corner from *Presidente*, hot water doesn't work, but good value; *Rivera*, E, good, clean, hot water, restaurant on top floor with good view but poor food; *María Isabel*, F, dingy, helpful; *El Santa*, E, with bath, clean and good; *Venus*, F, near Roggero and Moreno bus stations, useful if you arrive at 0200; in same district *Augusto*, Aguirre 265, F, with shower and toilet, overpriced, clean, front rooms noisy, water intermittent as everywhere in town, *Huáscar*, G p.p. very basic, clean rooms, filthy toilets, and *San Felipe*, F; *Felic*, Av. José Pardo, 552, F, noisy.

Restaurants *Pollo Gordo*, Prado y Aguirre, good chicken and cold beer; *San Remo*, Pardo y Villavicencio, seafood, good and cheap, good pisco sours; *Buenos Aires*, Aguirre near beach, popular lunch place; *Marisquito*, Bolognesi near Palacios, good local food, disco at night; *Franco* and *Venecia*, same block, good seafood. You can eat well and cheaply (US$0.50) in the market.

Tourist Office Av. Bolognesi 465.

Buses To Lima, best is Turismo Chimbote on Pardo, US$4.50, 6-7 hrs. The Santa valley road via Huallanca to the Callejón de Huaylas and beyond has been rebuilt, but is still hair-raising (scenery is superb). Bus leaves Chimbote for Huaraz daily at 0700 and 2000, via Caraz and Cañon del Pato, US$4.40, sit on left. (Transportes Moreno, Jr. Manuel Ruiz 288, T 321235, book the previous day, open from 0630, but not in evening), 8 hrs. (12 hrs. in rainy season). Road is unsurfaced to Caraz (bus to Caraz, US$3.65, 6 hrs., daily); bus to Huallanca, US$3.25. Bus Chimbote—Huaraz via Casma at 0700 and 1900; colectivo to Casma, 0700 and 0830 daily, US$1.25. Buses run Chimbote to Trujillo, US$1.50 (Empresa El Aguila, José Gálvez 317, hourly from 0600-2000), Tepsa at 1600; Colectivo to Trujillo, US$2, 2 hrs.

Warning Thefts are common around the Moreno bus station.

John Streather tells us that about 25 km. S of Chimbote a paved road leads E to the Nepeña valley, where a sculpted precolumbian tomb and the temple of Cerro Blanco may be found; also ruins at **Pañamarca** (pre-Mochica temple), 10 km. from the crossroads. Pañamarca is a town from the Mochica culture, where buildings and animal sculpture remains can be seen. 20 km. from Pañamarca is the site of Paredones with the "Puerta del Sol", and a stone carving, the "monolito de siete huacas".

From Chimbote a road branches off to the NE and, joining another road from Santa, goes up the Santa valley following the route, including tunnels, of the old Santa Corporation Railway. This used to run as far as **Huallanca**, 140 km. up the valley, but the track was largely destroyed by the 1970 earthquake. At Huallanca is an impressive hydroelectric plant, built into a mountain, which can not be visited. *Hotel Huascaran*, good, friendly; everything closes early. At the top of the valley the road goes through the very narrow and spectacular **Cañón del Pato** (where the road is closed to private vehicles because of fears of guerrilla attacks on the hydroelectric plant, but buses still ply) before reaching the Callejón de Huaylas and going on S to Caraz and Huaraz. From Caraz to Santa (200 km. unpaved) can be driven, in normal times, in 5 hours. The road up the Santa Valley is not recommended for cyclists owing to its poor condition.

Daniel Morgan, of Wellington, N.Z, writes: "At its mouth, the Santa Valley is fertile, being well-irrigated from the river. Further up it becomes barren. There is only rock, scree slides, exposed shale strata at angles up to the vertical (a must for geologists). The colours are fantastic: greys, blues, purples, oranges, reds, browns. The beauty is accentuated by the bright sun throwing jet black shadows, highlighting, contrasting, hiding.

"After Huallanca, the road clings to the side of a cliff as water thunders below and rock faces climb vertically on each side. Again light and shadow interplay, creating a fantastic vista like abstract art. Beyond the dam the valley flattens out. The walls are no longer vertical and you come back to Planet Earth. It is a hot, dusty, bumpy, and awesome trip."

Caraz, is now almost totally restored after the 1970 earthquake, and is reported a good centre for walking; splendid views of Huandoy and Huascarán. Information on mountaineering obtainable from the director of the Huascarán National Park in Huaraz, or the Tourist Office in Yungay. Excellent views of the northern *cordilleras* in July and August; in other months, mountains are often shrouded in cloud. One has to cross a river by cable (20 mins.) and go to Pueblo Libre to climb Tunaspampa. Caraz has a milder climate than Huaraz and is more suited to day excursions but it is difficult to change money there. There is a zoo, SE of town; take food for the animals.

Hotels *El Cafetal*, friendly, clean, hot water; *Hostal Carás*, Calle Sucre, F, dirty, hot showers; *Chavín*, just off Plaza, F with bath, new, clean, good value (but no views), said to be "best of a poor bunch"; *Hostal Suizo Peruano*. San Martín 1133, G with bath (cheaper without) clean and friendly. *Ramírez*, above Moreno terminal, G p.p., dirty, basic, helpful; *Morovi*, just outside town on Yungay road, F, clean, friendly, helpful, with bath and hot water; *Herrera*, F.

Restaurants *Jeny*, on plaza, good food and prices; *La Capullana*, excellent local dishes; *Juventud*, rec.; *La Punta Grande*, on corner of turn-off to Lake Parón, inexpensive local meals. Also, *Esmeralda*, Av. Alfonso Ugarte, cheap, good local food, friendly; *Djurjuri*, good food and atmosphere; *Chifa Lorena*, Jr. Sucre 1021, cheap and local and Chinese food; unnamed restaurant at Sucre 1003, good, English spoken. About 1 km. S of Caraz, open-air *Restaurant Palmira,* serves excellent trout, reasonably priced (open 1200-1800); follow the sign for trout off the main road and go through German-owned carnation farm.

Buses Bus to Lima 14 hrs., direct 1500, via Huaraz (to which the 67-km. road is now paved) 0600. Also frequent buses to and from Huaraz, US$1.20 (last at 1900), 2 hrs., to Yungay, US$0.20. Bus to Chimbote, daily, 1000, 2200, 7 hrs., through the Santa Valley, US$3.65; Transportes Expreso Moreno, Jr. Daniel Villar 407, T 2014, through the Cañon del Pato, sit on right for views, US$2, 0930, 7 hrs; to Chimbote via Huaraz and Casma (US$3) at 0600 and 1800, with one hour stop in Huaraz, continuing at 0900 and 2100 respectively. Chinchay-Suyo to Trujillo at 1730, stops for dinner at Huaraz, US$10.

From Caraz a narrow, rough road branches E to Lake Parón, nestling right under the snow-capped peak of Huandoy; the water level has been lowered, and the lake is to be used for the Cañon del Pato hydroelectric scheme. Latest reports indicate that some of the lake's beauty has been lost, but that the gorge leading to it remains spectacular. For the best views you have to climb up unstable moraine. Taxi from **Caraz,** US$20 return, will wait all day at the lake, pick-up US$3 approx., bargain hard; Nevado Huáscaran Tours from Huaraz, full day inc. 30-40 mins. at lake, US$2. One can stay at a lodge by the lake, US$1.60 p.p. (unguarded, and therefore may not be possible, at weekends), or at the houses 1-2 km. before the lake, US$1 p.p.

For hikes in the Cordillera Negra, a truck leaves from Caraz market at 1000 to Huata (dirty hotel, F; 2,700 metres) from where one can climb to the Quebrada de Cochacocha (3,500 metres) at the top of which is the Inca ruin of Cantu, and on to the Inca lookout, Torreón Andino (5,006 metres; also reached from Rocracallán, US$1 by truck from Caraz). Take water, food and tent with you. 6 km. down a track off the Caraz-Huata road are the Inca ruins of Chonta. Alternatively, Prof. Bernardino Aguilar Prieto (former teacher), San Martín 1143 (T 2161—rooms to let, G), close to *Hotel La Suiza Peruana,* Caraz, can advise in evenings on 2-3-day hikes in the Torreón Andino area. One can visit his apiary and sample the honey (sold at his town house) as well as camp for free at his farm, La Fronda (run down), 7 km. from Caraz, rooms G but you must bring bedding/food/candles etc., colectivo from Caraz, US$0.15. N of Caraz are hot springs at Shangol. The ruins of Pashash Cabana and Huandoval are reached from Chuquicara, about halfway along the Santa Valley road.

See following page for access from Caraz to the Llanganuco—Santa Cruz hike; see also page 890 for notes on walking in this area.

John Streather writes: A spectacular circuit may be made to Chavín (page 889) from Caraz (or Huaraz). Take a Morenos Hnos. bus to Tres Cruces or Yuracmarca on the other side of the Cañon del Pato. A detour from Yuracmarca is along a frightening road to Corongo (0530 bus from Caraz, Empresa Callejón de Huaylas from the main square once a week), but only go in summer, or else you may be stuck for months. Eat at the baker's shop on the square; the baker is very helpful with information about ruins in the area. From Tres Cruces (basic friendly restaurant, but no accommodation) one can take daytime lorries to Pomabamba, passing pre-Inca *chullpas,* Yanac, Tarica (**see page 886**), the mining town of Pasacancha (hotel and restaurant) and the Callejón de Conchucos. The road continues through cold, wild mountains and valleys to Andaymayo and Palo Seco to Pomabamba, "city of the cedars"—where I saw not one cedar tree.

Pomabamba is worth a visit on several counts. There are very hot natural springs there, the furthest are the hottest and the best. The lady of the house also sells delicious orange-blossom honey from her own garden; however, fresh vegetables may be in short supply. Various hotels; the best is in a nameless house on the hill going down to the bridge over which lie the hot springs and the path to Yaino. *Hostal Pomabamba,* on main square, F, basic, safe for luggage; *Altamayo,* plaza, basic; *San Martín de Porras,* off the smaller plaza, basic. The restaurant on the corner of the main square is friendly and good (cold though); *Canela,* rec. There is a small museum opposite which the people in the courtyard offices will open free on request. Victor Escudero, who speaks English, runs One Pyramid Travel, Huaraz 209, T 721283; he specializes in archaeological tours, including some little known, unspoilt places, rec. Several good walks into the Cordillera Blanca start from nearby: via Palo Seco or Laurel to the Lagunas Safuna, from which one can go on, if hardy, to Mt. Alpamayo ("the most beautiful mountain in the world") and down to Santa Cruz and Caraz—several days' hard walking. Up to the quite large and extensive, though sadly dilapidated, ruins of **Yaino** on top of a very steep mountain and visible from the main square of Pomabamba—though still a good 4½-5 hours walk away. Ask directions in the village and on the way too. If in doubt, veer left after about two hours of going fairly straight uphill. The ruins, when one reaches them, are certainly worth the effort. The walls are beautifully built and there are two very large buildings, a square one and a circular one. The site commands far and majestic views of the many peaks of the Cordillera. Again, the hardy could continue their walk (several days) to the two lakes of Llanganuco and so to Yungay in the Callejón de Huaylas, or down to Santa Cruz and Caraz on the other side. The walk to Yaino and back to Pomabamba can be done in a day if one starts early. Take a good lunch, and lots of juicy fruit—one gets very dehydrated climbing and perspiring in the thin dry air. It's also very cold high up if the sun goes in, so go with warm, waterproof clothes.

Cóndor de Chavín and Peruano Andino buses run S to Chavín and on to Lima, all at night. Buses to and from Lima via Chimbote are Empresa Marino (Ayacucho 1140, Lima), leaving Lima at 0800, Sun. and Wed., and Pomabamba at 0600 on the same days, 20 hrs.

The main road goes on to **Yungay**, which was completely buried by the 1970 earthquake—a hideous tragedy in which 20,000 people lost their lives. The survivors are housed just north of the old town, which is now recovering, with houses and a concrete market (Thurs. and Sun.). A new church is being built. The site now has a few monuments and a field of rose bushes.

Bed and Board A hotel without a signboard is on the left of the Carhuaz road (F); *El Señor Blanco's Hotel* (past maternity hospital), G, breakfast and dinner US$1.40, hot water, rec., mixed reports on security, and women need to beware of Sr. Blanco's overfriendly attitude; *Hostal Gledel*, Av. Arias Graziani (owned by Sra. Gamboa, who is hospitable and a good cook), F, clean, good, nice courtyard, rec.; *Hostal Yungay*, on plaza, F, clean; *Alojamiento Acuña*, F, clean, meals available. There is also private accommodation. Good food and drink can be found in the new market, and there is a good restaurant run by the local co-operative; also *Comedor Yungay* (good) and *El Portal* (fair). Provisions for trekking (e.g. tinned fruit, bread, vegetables, eggs, drink sachets, pasta, etc.) can be bought in Yungay.

Tourist Office on the plaza (rarely open); opposite is *Café El Palmero*, which offers simple accommodation, F. Moreno bus, Fitzcarrald 109, to Huaraz, US$0.60. There are several trucks which leave from the café for Lake Llanganuco (provided there are at least 10 passengers, US$2 single or return). A return allows only about an hour at the lake. Times of departure always change, so check at the Tourist Office. A tourist minibus to the lake leaves at 0800 on Sat., 2 hrs.

For trekkers, one of the finest walks (trees, flowers, birds, midges) is over the path by Huascarán and Lake Llanganuco (2 lakes: Orkoncocha and Chinancocha) from Yungay to Piscobamba (Yungay to Lake Llanganuco, trucks on Mon., Wed., Fri., at 0400, US$3, and Sun. from Huaraz, no trucks will go unless there are enough passengers, and departure is often delayed; trucks to Llanganuco continue on the new road to the Portachuelo Pass at 4,750 metres, beautiful views of Huascarán; return to Yungay at 1000). It is a 5-6 day hike over a well-travelled route, but don't try it unless you are properly equipped. After 3-4 days you reach Llumpa on the Chavín-Piscobamba road (basic accommodation, unfriendly people), from here there are 2 buses per week to Piscobamba, and 2 per week to Chavín. After Llumpa, the trek to Piscobamba becomes rather boring and tiring. There are 2 buses per week between Piscobamba, Pomabamba (see page 884) and Huaraz. Advice and registration for mountain hut at Llanganuco from National Park office. N.B. If making an excursion to photograph Huascarán and Huandoy, note that they are usually hidden by cloud after midday.

Deservedly the most popular walk in the Cordillera Blanca is from Llanganuco through the Portachuelo Pass to Colcabamba, and then through the Punta Unión (4,750 metres) to Cashapampa, Santa Cruz and Caraz. This hike takes 3-5 days and is well-signed. Guides useful, US$5-8 a day, will catch trout for you. Entrance to the National Park costs US$1.20 a day for foreigners to stay overnight (for a one-day visit US$0.60—overnight fee for Peruvians US$0.20). Some of the route is on Inca roads (see pages 999-1000). The mountain flowers and humming birds at these altitudes are magnificent. The road to the lake (full of trout) continues up to the tongue of the glacier of Cerro Chopicalqui (not suitable for cars, 4,830 metres)—insect repellant needed; take food, warm clothes, tent, sleeping bag and a stove. The early morning trucks from Yungay on a new road running from Llanganuco over the Portachuelo Pass go to Vaquería, the first settlement after the pass; get off the truck at the tin shacks on the left after Vaquería; from there the trail descends on S side of stream to Colcabamba (3 hrs.), or crosses a stream below thatched farmhouse to join Colcabamba-Punta Unión trail above Colcabamba. At Yanamá, on the eastern side of the Cordillera Blanca (beyond Colcabamba—and not on the trail), there is lodging and food; a day's hike to the ruins above the town affords superb views (truck Yungay-Yanamá, US$2.50—ask at plaza in Yungay). At Colcabamba, the Calonge family welcome travellers with good meals and basic accommodation (G), and small shop, but very little on offer. Cashapampa, the first village at the bottom of the Santa Cruz valley, is at the end of the path and where the dirt road begins; it has basic accommodation; meals at the house of Sra. Zenaida Pajuelo. Above Santa Cruz (the next village, very basic accommodation—dirty and for midgets!) are hot springs at Huancarhuás, which are being "developed". Footpath Santa Cruz to Caraz.

Transport Bus Yungay—Colcabamba (or 150 m. above it), Wed. a.m., perhaps daily in season, US$1.75, or pick-up from square if 8 passengers, US$2.20 p.p. About 4½ hrs. to top of Postachuelo Pass (cold, have sweater accessible); the road is not for the faint-hearted, but great views. Trucks Colcabamba-Yungay most mornings except Sun., US$2 p.p., 4-6 hrs; best to get on in Colcabamba, they don't like stopping en route. From Caraz, colectivos go to Lake Llanganuco, US$2, or taxi US$15-20; pick-ups to Cashapampa at 0900-1100, US$0.75 p.p., bus Cashapampa-Caraz at 0500, US$1; pick-up Santa Cruz-Caraz on Sat. at 1500 or 1900.

After Yungay, the main road goes to Mancos at the foot of Huascarán (*Hotel Mancos*, F, lovely setting, but bathroom dirty, water rationing) and on to **Carhuaz** (daily bus service to Huaraz, and to Huallanca via the Cañón del Pato), with fair hotels (*Perú*, F, good restaurant; and *Gran Hotel*, E, pleasant, no hot water; *Hospedaje La Merced*, F, excellent, clean, friendly, hot water, rec.; *Restaurant Palma*, good value) and very good walking in the neighbourhood; precolumbian baths at Vicus and La Merced, ruins at Cuntuyoc, Hualcan, Huacoy, Torojirca, Tuyo and Huamanvilca. Carhuaz has a *mestizo* festival on October 24, followed eight days later by an Indian festival. Before Huaraz the road goes to Marcará (bus to Huaraz, US$0.50), where there is a branch road 3 km. to **Chancos**, another thermal resort (*Hotel Chancos* closed but you can camp in the neighbourhood, 2 restaurants, minibus from Huaraz). Further up the Huandoy valley is Vicos, set in superb surroundings with views of Nevados Tocllaraju and Ranrapalca. From Vicos, one can walk through the Quebrada Honda to Chacas (*Hostal Pilar*); a road has been built to Chacas. From Chacas you can get transport to San Luis (**see page 1000**). The main road goes to Tarica (*Hostal Sterling*, G, no hot water, food, friendly).

The valley's focus is **Huaraz** (population 80,000), capital of the Department of Ancash, at 3,028 metres, 398 km. from Lima. The city was half destroyed in the earthquake of May 1970. Reconstruction is well advanced; the Plaza de Armas has been rebuilt, except for the Cathedral, which is being resited elsewhere. The setting, with the peaks of Huascarán, Huandoy, and San Cristóbal in the background, is tremendous. Good panoramic views are to be had from the *mirador* at the cross (visible from Huaraz) one hour's walk from the town (turn left past the cemetery and head uphill through a small forest). Huaraz is becoming a very lively place, popular with young gringos and Peruvians alike. Market day is Thursday.

Festival Patron saints' day, 3 May, parades, dancing, music and fireworks; much drinking and overcharging. Prices shoot up at time of Independence celebrations, end-July. Semana del Andinismo end of May, international climbing and skiing week.

Hotels *Termas de Monterrey*, 7 km. N (½ hr. in bus), run by State Tourist Hotel chain, rec. for walking, swimming in warm springs, C (accepts American Express), with bath, good meals US$3, swimming pool. Rock climbing behind hotel, but don't be vigorous at the start; it's over 2,750 metres up. *El Patio*, near **Hotel Termas**, E incl. breakfast, friendly, no restaurant, nicely laid out, rec. In town, *Hotel de Turistas*, Av. Centenario (T 2696), C, large rooms, clean, restaurant poor; *Marañón*, E, new, clean, near market, hot water limited; *El Tumi I*, San Martín 1122, E, with bath, good restaurant, fairly good; *Tumi II*, beside *Tumi I*, F with bath, good value; *Hostal Huandoy-Cusco*, F (triple rooms available), communal bathrooms, good; *Hostal Andino* (*Chalet Suisse*) C, Jr. Pedro Cochachín 357 (some way from centre), best hotel, clean, meals served (fondue expensive), safe parking, Swiss run, rec., beautiful view of Huascarán, climbing and hiking gear for hire; *Hostal Colomba*, Calle Francisco de Zela 210, bungalow, rooms D, plus 21%, family-run (German), garden, friendly, safe car parking, English spoken; *Cataluña*, Av. Raymondi 622, T 72117, F with bath, less without, cheaper accommodation in dormitory, restaurant, somewhat expensive, clean, safe, noisy, tepid water; *Raymondi*, Av. Raymondi 820, F, central, bath, hot water (a.m. only in ground floor shower), comfortable, unfriendly, charges for left luggage, with café serving good breakfast; **Yanett**, Av. Centenario 106, E, friendly, hot water, clean, large rooms, rec., restaurant for breakfast; **Edward's Inn**, Av. Bolognesi 121, T 722692, E, clean, hot shower, laundry, friendly, food available, highly rec., popular, Edward speaks English and knows a lot about trekking and rents gear; under same ownership, **Alojamiento de Quintana**, Juan de la Cruz Romero 593, F, hot shower, laundry facilities, clean, hard beds, popular with trekkers. **Hostal Premier**, Av. Luzuriaga 651-53, T 721954, E with bath (cheaper without), not very hot showers, clean, modern, English spoken by owners' son, helpful, informative, rec.; **Landauro**, on Plaza de Armas, F, cheap, clean, basic, friendly, good breakfast place downstairs; **Hostal Colonial**, Av. Fitzcarald 368, F, owner is Swiss-trained mountain guide, will arrange treks, hot showers; **Hostal Continental**, 20 de Julio y Luzuriaga, G, clean, hot water, friendly, cafetería, rec.; **Hostal Los Andes**, Av. Tarapacá 316, (G p.p. low season), hot water, clean, friendly, with laundry, attractive but noisy, hard beds and prices shoot up in the peak season; **Albergue El Tambo**, Confraternidad Internacional—Interior—122 B, F, clean, clothes washing, 3 rooms with 12 beds, and cooking facilities, nice people; **Alpamayo**, same street No. 126, F with bath, G without, clean, quiet, rents camping eqpt., laundry (or do it yourself), rec. **Pensión Maguiña**, Av. Tarapacá 643, opposite Rodríguez bus terminal, noisy a.m., F, hot water, rooms single to 4-bed, clothes-washing facilities, breakfast available, rucksack store, clean, English and French spoken, helpful in arranging trekking and equipment hire, rec.; **Hostal Alfredo**, Jr. Victor Vélez (go N on Al. Fitzcarrald, cross bridge and take 2nd on right, 10 metres on right), F with shower, good; **Alojamiento Galaxia** (de Inés Herrera) Jr. Romero 638, limited hot water F, friendly, laundry facilities, rec.; **Hostal Oscar**, Morales, F with bath, hot water, cheap breakfast, rec.; **Familia Estella**, Jirón Nueva Granada 519, F, hot water very intermittent, friendly, safe, rec.; **Casa de Señora López** (ask near Estadio just off Avenida Bolognesi at Santa river end), F, luke-warm showers, safe, washing facilities for clothes, patio, very friendly, rec. **Familia Sánchez** Jr. Carás 849, G, clean, basic, warm water, helpful, cheap breakfast; **Alojamiento San Martín de Porras**, Las Américas, T 721061, F, clean, friendly, rec.; **Alojamiento Líder**, Fitzcarrald 233, G, hot showers, friendly, safe, rec. **Albergue Juvenil Los Capulíes**, Jr. Los Capulíes 160, Centenario—Huaraz (15 mins., walk from the centre—information from the owner's bodega at San Martín 618), F, clean, friendly, showers, cooking and washing facilities, rec. **Albergue Juvenil Copa**, Jr. S. Bolívar 615, F, good, hot water, washing facilities. There are usually people waiting at the bus terminals offering cheap accommodation in their own homes.

Hot Public Showers on Av. Raymondi 904, US$0.20.

Restaurants Restaurant and bar at **Ebony 86**, Plaza de Armas, friendly, clean. **Tabariz**, Av. Centenario y Av. Raymondi, good food. On 28 de Julio is **Oja-Yo**, Chinese, good. **Samuel's**, off Luzuriaga, "very rich salads, wide variety, inexpensive, excellent, serves breakfast, but check your bill". **La Familia** at Luzuriaga 431, popular with gringos, vegetarian dishes, impersonal; **Leñador**, Luzuriaga 979, good coffee, snacks, German books. Good breakfast at **San Miguel**, San Martín 1001. **La Cabañita** is also good and cheap, as is **Rivioli**, Av. Guzmán Barrón 244. **Francos Parrilladas**, Luzuriaga 410, good grills; **Pepe's Place**, Raymondi 622 (upstairs from **Hostal Cataluña**), expensive but good; **Tic-Toc**, Raymondi 639, good breakfasts; **Ticino**, Luzuriaga 651, pizzas and pastas; **La Posada**, Luzuriaga, good pizzas and lasagne, nice atmosphere; **Pizzería Mamma Mía**, Luzuriaga 808, excellent and cheap. **Créperie Patrick**, Luzuriaga y Raymondi, excellent crêpes, but not cheap; **Ebenezer**, opposite **Mamma Mía**, good local food, clean and cheap. **Las Puyas**, Morales 535, good cheap meals and breakfasts, popular with gringos; **Pío Pío**, Av. Centenario 329, rec.; **Amadeus**, next to Plaza, good breakfast and reputed best coffee in town. **Tasco bar**, Lucar y Torre, popular with climbers. **Sandy**, Av. Centenario y Raymondi, good, cheap, popular, rec.; **Paccha'k Pub**, Centenario 290, folklore shows, local and international food, travel information.

Entertainment There are discotheques at **Tabariz**, **Bodega**. **Peña El Rizzo**, Luzuriaga 455, shows Thurs., Fri., Sat.; **Imantata**, Luzuriaga 424, disco and folk music; **Tambo**, José de la Mar, folk music daily, rec.

Museum Museo Regional de Ancash, Instituto Nacional de Cultura, containing stone monoliths and *huacos* from the Recuay culture has been set up in the *Casa de Cultura*, well labelled and laid out. Open 1000-1700, Tues.-Sun., US$0.60, pay to take photographs.

Camping Several shops of the trekking agencies sell camping gaz cartridges. Bodega Santillana, Centenario 417, good for all supplies. Andean Sport Tours, Av. Luzuriaga 571, T 721612, German-owned, rents or sells camping equipment, incl. camping gaz cartridges; treks, climbing, donkeys for hire, US$2 a day, guides, US$5, tents, US$1.50 a day. Tent hire for five days about US$13. All prices standard, but not cheap, throughout town; US$100, or airline ticket, deposit usually demanded. All require payment in advance and will only give 50% of your money back if you return gear early.

Shopping Daily market (1600-2000) in covered sidewalks of Luzuriaga for local sweaters, hats, gloves, etc., wall hangings; good value.

Car Hire Empresa de Transporte Turismo Huascarán, Av. Raymondi 870, T 310099; VW Beetles for US$18 a day, plus US$0.18 per km., vehicles not up to much.

Exchange Banco Internacional changes travellers' cheques; also behind Banco de la Nación on Plaza de Armas, open till 1800. Quite good rates from travel agents. Street changers on Luzuriaga.

Laundry Fitzcarrel, Fitzcarrald, close to bridge; Lavandería El Amigo, Bolívar y Sucre.

Tourist Office Foptur, Av. Luzuriaga 459 on main Plaza beside post office, T 721031, for Chavín tour and treks; ask there for Miguel Chiri Valle, English speaking, maps available, good for backpacking in the Cordillera Blanca. Also Pomabamba 415, 1st floor, and ground floor of Palacio Municipal, Plaza de Armas. **Trekking & Backpacking Club**, San Martín 995 (Casilla 112), issues magazine *El Trekkero*, maps and library at office, also hires equipment and organizes tours. Better maps of the area are available in Lima. However, the Instituto de Geología y Minería (Av. Guzmán Barrón 582, open a.m. only) sells useful maps for hikers; *Hostal Andino* also sells IGM maps.

Travel Agencies *Explorandes*, 28 de Julio y Luzuriaga, adventure travel, good. *Pablo Tours*, Luzuriaga 501 and *Chavín Tours*, Av. Luzuriaga 502, organize trips to Chavín (US$6, all day), Llanganuco and the Huascarán park, the latter is more expensive. *Azul Tours*, Av. Luzuriaga 658, helpful, friendly staff, hires good quality trekking equipment, rec. *Montrek*, Luzuriaga 640, good for rafting on Santa river, US$12 (in dollars), including transport to/from Huaraz, 2-hour raft trip. Marco Ugarte, Unasam, Av. Centenario s/n, offers tours to Chavín (US$7 for day) and treks (US$35 per day, inclusive), he is a professor of English, and his services have been recommended. With companies apart from those rec. above, beware overcharging and unreliability. In the main, US$5-10 tours to sites other than Chavín are too short; private arrangements with taxis are preferable.

Climbing and Trekking Huaraz, which is the climbing centre of Peru, particularly between May and October, is the headquarters of the Huascarán National Park (entrance US$1 per day). The office is on Av. Centenario 912 (Prolongación Av. Raymondi—5th block), behind the Ministry of Agriculture building, open 0700-1415, helpful staff. For **organized treks**, contact Percy Tapiá, Casilla 3074, Lima 100: prices range from US$26 (16-20 people), to US$40 (under 8 people) daily. One should also contact Andes Adventures, Jr. Simón Bolívar 925, Casilla Postal 925, T 721646, Telex 46502 PE CP, Huaraz, run by a Belgian, efficient, Spanish, English, French, German and Dutch spoken, reasonably-priced; also Eudes Morales Flores (speaks fluent English) at Pyramid Adventures, Casilla 25, office: Av. Luzuriaga No. 530, Huaraz, T 721864, rec. On the second floor of the *Hotel Residencial Cataluña*, Av. Raymondi, T 72117, José Valle Espinosa, "Pepe", hires out equipment (pricey), organizes treks and pack animals, sells dried food, and is generally helpful and informative. Carlos Rodríguez, *Tasco Bar de Lucho*, PO box 111, Huaraz, for climbing and trekking in the Cordillera Blanca.

 Casa de Guías, one block from Luzuriaga, behind Banco Internacional between Sucre y Morales, houses the guide association of Huaraz, provides climbing and trekking information and maintains a list of porters/arrieros/guides available for expeditions. Dormitory-style rooms, a small restaurant serving good breakfasts and apple pie, and a good meeting place for climbers; there is a notice board for messages.

Buses, Lima Ormeño (address in Lima section, book 12 hrs. in advance); Transportes Rodríguez, 3 a day, leaves from office at Roosevelt 354, Lima (timekeeping and maintenance criticized), and Tarapacá 622, Huaraz; Expreso Ancash, 4 a day (rec.), Av. Carlos Zavala 177, Lima, and Raymondi 845, Huaraz; Arellano-Intersa, Colmena 1635, Lima, and Raymondi 408, Huaraz; El Trome, Montevideo 1049, Lima, and Raymondi 422, Huaraz (not rec.); Empresa Huaraz, Leticia 655 (T 275260), Lima, and Raymondi 601, Huaraz, not rec; Empresa Callejón de Huaylas, Leticia 626 (leaves at 0730); Co-op. de Transportes Huaraz Ltda, Prolongación Leticia 1059, Lima, and Raymondi 680, Huaraz (neither too good). Transportes Tadeo, Arenillas 139, Act. Cda. 4, Av. Zarumilla, San Martín de Porras, Lima (an extremely dangerous area of Lima) and Raymondi 450, Huaraz. Return from Huaraz to Lima mostly in evenings, 8-10 hrs., average price US$4.50. Taxi to Lima, US$70 for 5.

Other Buses To Casma (150 km.) 6¼ay hrs. US$3.40. Bus to Chimbote (Moreno, Av.

Fitzcarrald 309) at 0800, 2000, US$4.40, 9½ hrs. via Cañón del Pato, overcrowded, often delayed, day travel advised for both safety and views, sit on the right for best and scariest views; via Casma 0900 and 2030. Bus to Marcará, US$0.50. Colectivos take visitors to see the Cordillera, and there is also a trip to the Chavín site, Huari and Huascarán. To Trujillo, US$6, only with Chinchay Suyo (Gamarra 736) departs 2030 and 2200, 10 hrs. via Pativilca. Truck to Pativilca on coast, 5 hrs., US$2.75, or buses Intersa (old, poor service) and El Trome. To Barranca, Ancash, US$3, 4 hrs. Bus to Carás, US$1.20, 2 hrs. (Ormeño) colectivo frequent; to Yungay US$1 hourly. Buses Huaraz-Carhuaz-Yungay-Caraz run every ½ hr.

N.B. You are advised to take buses which arrive in Huaraz in daylight given the growth of terrorism in the area.

Excursions   About 8 km. into mountains is **Willcawain** archaeological site (entrance, US$0.60, students US$0.30), the ruins of a Tiahuanaco-style temple, dating from about AD 1000. The site is now signposted; walk down Av. Centenario and take the signed right turn 1 km. out of town, 2½ hrs. uphill walk; for better views on return, take right fork when passing the school, the main road is reached after 2 km. Alternatively, take a colectivo towards Yungay or Monterrey, get out 2 stops past the *Hotel de Turistas*, turn right and then left at a house for "pirotécnicas" (fireworks). Bring torch. There are more ruins at the end of the track, which goes on 27 km. to Laguna Llaca, but taxis reluctant to go there because track is very poor. Excursion by taxi to the Parque Nacional de **Huascarán** costs about US$15; in the park, puya plants, which flower only once at the end of a hundred-year lifetime, usually May-August, reach heights of 10 metres; they grow in the Quebrada Pachacoto valley, some 57 km. S of Huaraz and 26 km. E of the road; there is no sign for the Park: the turning is 3 km. before Catac and the signpost is marked Huanzala. Carpa can be reached on foot, by truck, or by San Cristóbal bus from Catac (continuing to La Unión). You can see the Park cheaply by getting the early Huaraz-Lima bus to Pachacoto crossing, then hitch a ride on the road through the Park. Chavín Tours and others (all much the same) to the Huascarán Park include a visit to the glacier on the Quebrada Pachacota and to ice caves; take gloves and food, rec., 7½ hrs., US$6.50 p.p. in low season (negotiate), more in high (you also have to pay park entrance fee of US$0.60). Punta Callán, on the Cordillera Negra between Huaraz and Casma, may be reached (3 hrs.) by truck from the football stadium; spectacular views of the Cordillera Blanca. Hitch, or walk virtually straight down, 2-3 hrs. Inca ruins in the Huaraz vicinity include Jongopampa, Canray Grande, Llasha, Pallasca, and Quequepampa. To the hot springs and sauna at Chancos (**see page 886**); minibuses and trucks go there.

S of Huaraz, off the main road, is **Recuay**, a provincial capital (*Hotel Santa*, G, clean, friendly, basic) where unusual pottery is sold. There are a museum and the Pueblo Viejo de Catac ruins here. Many buses run from Recuay to Huaraz and Catac (for Chavín).

Chavín   The Chavín de Huantar ruins, of a fortress temple built about 600 BC, are about 3½-7 hrs. drive (depending on the bus, 109 km., avoid back seats) from Huaraz, reached by a rough and rocky spectacular road branching E from the main Huaraz-Catac road. Unesco has proposed that the site be designated a worldwide cultural heritage. Entry US$1, students US$0.50, camera permit US$0.75. The 1970 earthquake destroyed many of the underground structures and now only the first few levels can be toured, but work is now in progress to excavate and light the tunnels closed by the earthquake as well as other temple mounds so far unexplored. Open 0800-1600, 1000-1600, Sun. and holidays. The main attraction is the marvellous carved stone heads and designs in relief of symbolic "gourd" figures. The carvings are in excellent condition, though many of the best sculptures are in Huaraz and Lima. The famous Lanzón dagger-shaped stone monolith of 800 BC is found inside the temple tunnel. **N.B.** Entrances to the temple buildings are locked: you must either hire a guide at the gate or get a child from the caretaker's house to open them for you. Sr. Chiri, Foptur, can arrange permission to enter. You cannot rely on the chambers being lit; if they are not, ask for the guard—but anyway take a torch.

John Streather writes: There is only one carved head *in situ* on the walls of Chavín now. The best things are the finely drawn stone reliefs of condors, pumas and priest warriors— by far the finest work in stone of any Peruvian, or indeed any Andean, culture of any period. The lines are outstanding for their fluidity, sinuousness, complexity and precision. Nothing like them seems to have existed either before or after them: the earlier Sechín art is clearly a fount of inspiration, but is very clumsy when compared with the delicate exactitude of the Chavín. In many ways it resembles early Chinese art more than anything Andean—in its spirit and manner, though not in its symbolism, which is entirely Andean and American.

There are hot sulphur baths about 2 km. S of Chavín (US$0.15 for a bath, reported filthy; camping possible here). Beware of thieves in Chavín village; children try to sell fossils and stonework, or swap them for ballpens. Electricity 1800-0600.

Hotels *Gantu*, F (not rec.) and *Inca*, F, bathrooms filthy, basic but friendly; also *Monte Carlo*, main plaza, F, fairly clean, warm at night; *Monterrey*, F; *Casa de Alojamiento Geminis*, Jr. Túpac Yupanqui, F, fork left after bridge just past ruins, basic (no bath or shower, toilet in outhouse), but clean and friendly, all meals extra; *Albergue de Turistas*, D, with bath, modern, clean, breakfast expensive, beautiful setting, 1 km. from the town on road to Huari; *Alojamiento Chavín Turist Shelter*, 17 de Enero-Norte 831, F, basic, clean and friendly.

Restaurants Good one 1½ blocks from ruins, on road to them. *La Ramade*; *Chavín Turístico*, cheap and friendly; *Montecarlo*, very slow, indifferent food; *Comedor de Cooperativa de Chavín*, behind church, good but difficult to get in, closed between mealtimes. All eating places appear to close after 1830. (Better hotels in Huari, 44 km. further on.) Nowhere to change money in or near Chavín.

Bus to Chavín Huascarán from Huaraz, 1000 daily, returns 1000, US$2 (tickets available from the *Comedor El Sol*). A magnificent 6-hr. scenic journey, if frightening at times, passing through the mountains and along the River Mosna gorge; spectacular views of the Yanamarey peaks and of many snow-fed waterfalls, road surface very poor. Trucks US$1.25, 7 hrs., but very cold. Several from Catac, early a.m. and late p.m. Chavín Tours, Pablo Tours and Corazón de Jesús (tours, generally preferable to public transport, about US$6) make daytime excursions to Chavín and other places of interest; collection from hotels at 0900. Taxi, Huaraz-Chavín, US$15, 3-4 hrs. return. Direct bus Chavín to Lima, 13 hrs. Peru-Andino, Av. Grau 525, Lima, Tues. at 1400, Sat. at 1300 to Huaraz, returning Mon. and Thurs. The Lima-Chavín bus goes on to Pomabamba or Huari. From Barranca, every second day by truck, US$1.50, 17 hrs., trip is very bumpy and cold.

Hiking For the active, there is the possibility of a 4-day walk from Olleros, reached by bus or truck from the *frigorífico* in Huaraz (US$0.25). The Olleros village carpenter, on the square, has a room where one can stay. Enquire at National Park Office about necessary equipment for walk. A good map of the route is available from the Instituto Geográfico Militar in Lima, or the Trekking and Backpacking Club in Huaraz, line maps from Don Pepe at *Hotel Cataluña*, Huaraz (ask directions from anyone you meet along the way). The first day you go half-way along the meadows to the next, nameless Quebrada; on the second, you climb the first pass and sleep in the next valley; on the third, you pass Punta Yanashallash and camp in the valley somewhere after it, but before Jato; on the last day you reach Chavín. The area is isolated, so be sure to take good camping equipment, extra food and plenty of warm clothing. A longer walk may also be made to the Laguna Verdecocha, a glacier lake; this is recommended for experienced climbers only. On the first day of the walk, one reaches the Quebrada Quilloc: the second day, the Quebrada Otuto and the Punta Yanashallash (altitude: 4,680 metres); several Inca remains may be seen en route. On the third day, the trail dips and rises like a roller coaster, passing through the River Shongo valley (spectacular views of the Huachecsa gorge), finally reaching Chavín. A two-day walk from Huaraz to the Laguna de Churup (4,250 metres) a beautiful blue lake in a crater beneath a mountain peak beyond the small village of Pitec is possible; a guide is necessary for the inexperienced (ask for Victor, US$6 per day), or a very good map to find the Laguna. A pick-up is supposed to go half-way there, but it is hard to find. It is 18 km. from Huaraz, of which the first 15 km. are easy, in the valleys (locals will advise on the route)—follow Av. Raymondi E out of Huaraz. Just before Pitec, turn right at a fork, and in Pitec, turn left, just before a mountain stream. From here it is very hard going, initially with no path, then occasional trail markers—the general direction is NE towards the snow-covered peak. The hike can be done in a day, with an early start; take sun cream and food.

Warning The Callejón de Huaylas has, in the past 2 years, been the target of many military/terrorist confrontations. The Cordillera Huayhuash, due to its remoteness, has been infiltrated by terrorist groups. Treks and climbs to this area have virtually ceased, and may even be prevented by the authorities. In the Cordillera Blanca, however, climbing and trekking is still possible, but the visitor should be aware that conditions could change overnight. Check with guides, agencies, locals before going into an area. It is a good idea to hire a

Quechua-speaking *arriero* or porter to accompany you on long treks. Don't hike alone. Avoid staying overnight in remote villages, and *do not*, under any circumstances, involve yourself with the politics or in any political demonstration or military confrontation. If you can't leave the area immediately, remain silent and unobtrusive. Tourists in the Callejón de Huaylas have encountered hostility from local people and dogs (a stick is most useful— otherwise, throw stones).

Advice to Climbers: The height of the Cordillera Blanca and the Callejón de Huaylas ranges and their location in the tropics create conditions different from the Alps or even the Himalayas. Fierce sun makes the mountain snow porous and the glaciers move more rapidly. The British Embassy advises climbers to take at least six days for acclimatization, to move in groups of four or more, reporting to Club Andino or the office of the guide before departing, giving date at which search should begin, and leaving telephone number of Embassy with money. Rescue operations are very limited and there are only eight guides with training (by the Swiss). Insurance is essential, since a guide costs US$40-50 a day and a search US$2,000-2,500 (by helicopter, US$10,000).

Robert and Ana Cook (formerly of Lima) write of the **Callejón de Huaylas**: The heavy rainy season lasts from Jan. to Mar., while the dry season is from May to Sept. The mean daily temperature is determined by the altitude and hardly varies throughout the year. For instance, at 3,000 metres (the altitude of Huaraz) the mean temperature is 14°C.

Apart from the range of Andes running along the Chile-Argentina border, the highest mountains in South America are along the Callejón and perfectly visible from many spots. From the city of Huaraz alone, one can see over 23 snow-crested peaks of over 5,000 metres, of which the most notable is Huascarán (6,768 metres), the highest mountain in Peru. Although the snowline now stands at the 5,000 metres level, it was not long ago (geologically speaking) that snow and ice covered the Callejón at 3,000 metres. Despite its receding snowline, the Cordillera Blanca still contains the largest concentration of glaciers found in the world's tropical zone. From the retreating glaciers come the beauty and the plague of the Callejón. The turquoise-coloured lakes which form in the terminal moraines are the jewels of the Andes and visitors should hike up to at least one during their stay. At the same time these *cochas* (glacial lakes) have caused much death and destruction when a dyke has broken, sending tons of water hurtling down the canyons wiping out everything in their path. Now government engineers combat this problem by monitoring water flows and dyke stability.

Hilary Bradt writes: The Cordillera Blanca offers the most popular backpacking and trekking in Peru, with a network of trails used by the local people and some less well defined mountaineers' routes. Most circuits can be hiked in five days. Although the trails are easily followed, they are rugged and the passes very high—between 4,000 and nearly 5,000 metres—so backpackers wishing to go it alone should be fit and properly acclimatized to the altitude, and carry all necessary equipment. Essential items are a tent, warm sleeping bag, stove, and protection against wind and rain (climatic conditions are quite unreliable here and you cannot rule out rain and hail storms even in the dry season). Trekking demands less stamina since equipment is carried by donkeys. There are various trekking companies in Huaraz.

The South American Explorers' Club publishes a good map with additional notes on the popular Llanganuco to Santa Cruz loop, and the Instituto Geográfico Militar has mapped the area with its 1:100,000 topographical series. These are more useful to the mountaineer than hiker, however, since the trails marked are confusing and inaccurate. Recommended guides through the Cordillera Huayhuash are Catalino Rojas and Cerillio Zambrano, both from the village of Llamac; also Alejandro Kayupe in Chiquián. "Jefe", who sells maps and key chains in Chiquián, is to be avoided.

Apart from the book by Hiliary Bradt (see "Information for Visitors"), the only useful guide to the area currently in print is *Peruvian Andes* by Ph. Beaud (which costs US$24), available through Cordee in the UK, some shops in Huaraz and The South American Explorers' Club.

Probably the best way to see the Santa Valley and the Callejón de Huaylas, which contain some of the most spectacular scenery in Peru, is to take the paved road which branches off the coast road into the mountains just N of Pativilca (**see page 881**), 187 km. from Lima. (About 15 km after the turnoff is *Restaurant El Viajero*, Panamericana Norte, Km 185, good.) This route also gives a more spectacular view of the Cordillera Blanca. In 120 km. it climbs to Lake Conococha (delicious trout available in Conococha village), at 4,100 metres, where the Santa River rises. After crossing the high level surface it descends gradually for 87 km. to Huaraz, and goes on to the Callejón de Huaylas, where it runs between the towering Cordillera Negra, snowless and rising to 4,600 metres, and the snow-covered Cordillera Blanca, whose highest point is the 6,768 metres high Huascarán. Farms appear at about 4,000 metres, but most of the farming is around Huaraz. The inhabitants grow potatoes and barley at the higher and maize and alfalfa at the lower altitudes. The valley has many picturesque villages and small towns, with narrow cobblestone streets and odd-angled house roofs. (At weekends and holidays beware of reckless Lima drivers on the roads.)

The alternative routes to the Callejón de Huaylas are via the Callán pass from Casma to Huaraz (**see page** 881), and via the Cañón del Pato (**page** 884).

There are two spectacular transandine routes from Huaraz to La Unión (and on to Huánuco for Cerro de Pasco, La Oroya, etc.; **see page** 986). The first is by twice weekly direct bus or bus leaving Huaraz at 1100 (Señor Huascarán) to Conococha and from there another bus, via Chiquián to La Unión. At **Chiquián** (*Hostal San Miguel*, clean, simple) one can walk into the Callejón de Huayhuash. There are two poor bus services Lima-Chiquián: Landano, Ayacucho 1040, Lima, Mon., Wed., Sat. at 1100, returning to Lima Mon., Fri., 1100; Tubsa, Leticia 633, Lima, Mon., Wed., Fri., 1900 to Chiquián, and in both directions Tues., Thurs., Sat., 1400 (bus Huaraz-Chiquián from Av. Tarapaca 133, at 1130; then Chiquián-La Unión with Tubsa, Mon., Wed., Fri. at midnight). Or one can take a truck from the crossroads at Lake Conococha (a very cold place). The second is to take a Comité 5 bus to Catac (US$0.85, 1 hr., frequent service from 0630); ask to be set down at garage on the edge of Catac. Take a taxi or walk the 5 km. to Pachocoto (2 cafés with accommodation if stranded). If you cannot get a truck Pachocoto-La Unión (9 hrs., US$2.30), wait for a truck from Lima going to the mines at Huansalá (take warm clothes). The road passes through the Huascarán National Park and ascends to a high section with most rewarding views of gigantic geological features. From Huansalá, bus, truck or walk to Huallanca (8 km.) and take transport on to La Unión "through an entertaining gorge by a demanding gravel road" (Friedrich Dürsch). There are occasional trucks Huaraz-La Unión. Bus Huaraz-Huallanca, 3½ hrs., US$2.80.

THE NORTHERN OASES (3)

N of the mouth of the River Santa the Andes recede, leaving a coastal desert belt of from 8 to 16 km. wide containing the three great oases of Northern Peru—the areas of Trujillo, Chiclayo and Piura.

N of Chimbote we cross the valleys of Chao and Virú, coming after 137 km. to the first great oasis of northern Peru, Trujillo. In the valley there is an abrupt line between desert and greenery; cultivation requires irrigation ditches which take their water from far up in the mountains. The area's port is **Salaverry**, exporting sugar and minerals, importing consumer goods and machinery. There is an 8 km. road to Trujillo.

The Quiruvilca copper mines are 120 km. inland by road from Salaverry. The concentrating plant at Shorey is connected with the mines by a 3 km. aerial cableway, and with its coal mine by a further 8 km. The ore is then taken by a 40 km. cableway to Samne, whence it is sent by road to Salaverry.

Trujillo, capital of the Department of La Libertad, disputes the title of second city of Peru with Arequipa. Population 750,000. The traveller entering Trujillo is delighted with its surrounding greenness against a backcloth of brown Andean foothills and peaks. Founded by Pizarro, 1536 (and named after his native town in Spain), it has moved with the times, but still retains many old churches, graceful colonial balconies and windows overhanging its modern pavements, of homes built during the reigns of the viceroys. Besides the Cathedral it has 10 colonial churches as well as convents and monasteries. Its University of La Libertad, second only to that of San Marcos at Lima, was founded in 1824.

Near the Plaza de Armas is the spacious 18th century house in which General Iturregui lived when he proclaimed the city's freedom from Spain in 1820. It is now the exclusive Club Central and Chamber of Commerce, at Pizarro 688 (may be visited in mornings). Two other beautiful colonial mansions on the Plaza have been taken over by the Banco Central and Banco Hipotecario, which maintain as museums the parts they do not need as offices (they may be visited a.m.). Certain other mansions, still in private hands, may occasionally be visited with the help of Trujillo Tours; they include the magnificent Orbegoso house at Pizarro 316 and the one at Junín 682; also the Casa de los Condes de Aranda, Bolívar y Gamarra; the Casa del Mariscal de Orbegoso in the 5th block of Calle Orbegoso; Casa del Mayorazgo; Casa Ganoza Chopitea, 4th block of Independencia (which has a private museum that can be seen when Sr. Ganoza is in residence); Casa Madalengo, Pizarro y Gamarra; Casa Baanante, in Grau near Almagro.

The focal point is the spacious Plaza de Armas, with a sculptured group to the heroes of the Liberation (note the short legs on the statue, reportedly the result of the Church's plea that it should not be taller than the Cathedral). Fronting it is the Cathedral, with the old palace of the Archbishop next door; the *Hotel Trujillo*; the building in colonial style of the Sociedad de Beneficencia Pública de Trujillo; and the Municipality building. Many churches damaged in the 1970 earthquake. One of the best, La Merced at Pizarro 550, with picturesque moulded figures below the dome, is being restored, but part of the dome has collapsed because of building work next door. El Carmen church and monastery, described as the "most valuable jewel of colonial art in Trujillo", has reopened to the public after the earthquake. Other old churches include La Compañía, near Plaza de Armas; San Francisco on 3rd block of Gamarra; Belén on 6th block of Almagro; Santa Clara on 4th block of Junín; San Agustín on 6th block of Mariscal Orbegoso; Santa Ana on 2nd block of same street; Santo Domingo on 4th block of Bolognesi. There are also two markets, one on Gamarra and the Mercado Mayorista on Calle Roca. The city's water supply is generally poor.

Archaeological Museum, normally open 0800-1400 in Jan.-March and 0800-1200, 1500-1800 the rest of the year, Pizarro 349 (entrance, US$0.60), recommended; it has an interesting collection of pottery. Another place to visit in Trujillo is the basement of the **Cassinelli** garage on the fork of the Pan-American and Huanchaco roads; it contains a superb private collection of Mochica and Chimú pottery. Be sure to ask for a demonstration of the whistling *huacos*; entry, US$0.85, open 0830-1130, 1530-1630. Sr. Cassinelli has plans to construct a larger museum. The University has a Zoological Museum, San Martín, corner with Bolognesi (0745-1300, 1500-1900).

Fiestas Second half of September or first half of October transport and hotels booked. Other busy periods are around Mothers' Day (in March/April) and the last week of January. The Nacional Marinera contest is held each September (dancing by all ages, public participation and viewing welcomed).

Warnings As with all Peruvian cities, Trujillo is troubled by theft—beware of robbers working in pairs, especially beyond the inner ring road, Av. España, towards the hill and in the Sánchez Carrión district at night.

Hotels *Turistas*, Plaza de Armas, C with bath (cheaper without), accepts American Express, full of character, rooms on street are noisy, meals US$4, excellent buffet lunch on Sun. Tour Peruvian S.A. travel agency in foyer for local trips; *Los Jardines*, 4 km. from centre, bungalows in garden, buses to town, D; *San Martín*, in 7th block of San Martín, F, with bath, good value, clean but some rooms damp, has more than 100 rooms, no restaurant. *Opt Gar* (5th block Grau), C, with bath, good, friendly, rec.; excellent restaurant (try sea food) and snack bar; *Los Escudos*, Orbegoso 676, T 243523, E, with bath and hot water, breakfast, small garden, rec.; *Continental*, Gamarra, opp. market, E, clean, good, safe, occasional hot water, restaurant, overpriced; *Hostal Monterrey*, Av. Los Incas 256, T 241673, open 24 hrs., F, friendly, comfortable, but not very clean (close to Tepsa, good for late arrivals); 3 blocks down is *Hostal Rayers*, G with bath, hot water, friendly but dirty; *Primavera*, Nicolás de Piérola 872, E, noisy on the street side, modern and cool; *Hostal Americano*, Pizarro 764, is a vast, old building, F, with bath (G without), rooms without bath are noisy (back on to cinema), most rooms without window, (Nos. 134 and 137 have windows, balconies and good views) basic, comfortable, many gringos, parking; *Vogi*, on Ayacucho, E with bath, clean, highly

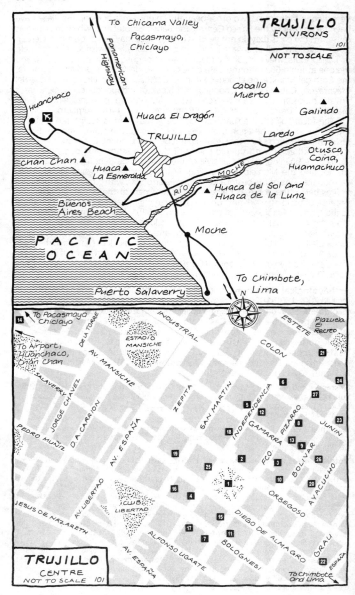

TRUJILLO
ENVIRONS

NOT TO SCALE

To Chicama Valley
Pacasmayo,
Chiclayo

Panamerican Highway

Caballo
Muerto

Galindo

Huanchaco

Huaca El Dragón

TRUJILLO

Laredo

To Otusco,
Coina,
Huamachuco

chan Chan

Huaca
La Esmeralda

RIO MOCHE

Huaca del Sol and
Huaca de la Luna

Buenos
Aires Beach

Moche

PACIFIC
OCEAN

Puerto Salaverry

To Chimbote,
N Lima

To Pacasmayo
Chiclayo

INDUSTRIAL

ESTETE

Plazuela
El Recreo

To Airport,
Huanchaco,
Chán Chán

DE LA TORRE

ESTADIO
MANSICHE

COLON

21

AV. MANSICHE

SALAVERRY

JORGE CHAVEZ

D.A. CARRION

ZEPITA

SAN MARTIN

INDEPENDENCIA

GAMARRA

PIZARRO

6

24

27

5

12

8

13

23

JUNIN

BOLIVAR

PEDRO MUÑIZ

AV. ESPAÑA

18

19

FCO.

2

3

9

26

25

10

ORBEGOSO

AYACUCHO

16

4

1

20

AV. LIBERTAD

CLUB
LIBERTAD

15

DIEGO DE ALMAGRO

GRAU

JESUS DE NAZARETH

17

7

11

GRAU

22

ESPAÑA

AV. ESPAÑA

ALFONSO UGARTE

BOLOGNESI

To Chimbote
And Lima

TRUJILLO
CENTRE
NOT TO SCALE 101

rec. *Estmar*, César Vallejo 134, G without bath, cold water, basic. *Hostal Lima*, Ayacucho 718, popular with gringos, F without bath, baths terrible; similar standard is *Hostal Central*, Ayacucho 728; *Paris* and *Perú*, opp each other on Ayacucho, G p.p., usually full; *Acapulco*, Gamarra 681, G with bath, sauna upstairs. Hotel next to Chinchay Syyo bus, F with bath, clean; *Hostal Marco Polo*, Jr. Moche 613, G, clean, quiet. *Hostería Recreo*, Astete 647, T 246991, F, clean, friendly, safe, restaurant, rec.; *Hostería El Sol*, E, opened by the late Dr. Kaufmann of Coina (**see page 900**) and now run by his family, castle-shaped, 55 beds, very clean and quiet, 10 mins. from centre by bus to Santa Inés or Huanchaco (US$0.50 by taxi), at Calle Los Brillantes 224, in front of the Parque Ramón Castilla, in Urbanización Santa Inés. For a private *pensión* contact the family Bravo Díaz, Huayna Capac 542, Urb. Sta. María, T 243347, very friendly, cheap (Clara Bravo Díaz is a tour guide), Familia Moreno, Huáscar 247, F, near centre, clean, quiet, safe, or Catrina Castillo, Pedro Muñiz 792. See also under Huanchaco, **page 898**.

Restaurants *Hotel Opt Gar*, lunch only except for guests, rec.; *Chifa Oriental*, Gamarra 735, rec.; *El Pesquero*, Junín 118, good fish; *Morroco*, Av. Bolívar, smart and cheap; *Santa Inés*, Calle Los Robles, good fish, try the corvina; *Grau* (on Grau), lunch only, good Criollo food.

Vegetarian restaurants: *El Sol*, Pizarro 660, excellent, cheap, filling; *Naturista*, Pizarro 671, very cheap and filling; *Gran Fraternidad Universal*, Bolívar y Colón.

Pollos Bolívar, Bolívar 577, chicken and salad. Excellent local dishes at *Pedro Moriallas* in nearby seaside resort of Buenos Aires. Good Argentine-style food at *Parrillada El Gaucho*. *24 Horas*, Jr. Gamarra, reasonably priced meals for about US$1, always open, as the name implies; *ABC*, on Orbegoso, good for chicken; *De Marco*, Pizarro 725, good, especially the ice creams, set menu for US$1, desserts and cakes. *La Calesa*, Pizarro 716, good snack bar; *Romano*, opp. *Hotel Americano*, at Pizarro 747, good menu, highly rec.; *El Mesón de Cervantes*, Pizarro, bar-restaurant, polite, good cheap food; *Ceviche del Rey*, Av. Mansiche opposite clinic, seafood, open only until 1800. *Pizzería Valentino*, Orbegoso block 2, very good; another on Pizarro, near *Hotel Americano*, very good. *Subterráneo*, Plaza Murillo, set lunch US$1. New bar, *Las Tinajas*, on Plaza, good. *La Pileta* (next to Tepsa bus office, Astete 472, strongly rec. for good local food) and *El Recreo*, Bolívar 879, good for breakfast. *La Miel*, Jirón Bolívar 600, good breakfasts, poor coffee, friendly. Wholewheat bread at *Panadería Chalet Suizo*, Av. España e Independencia. Cheap meals in the market at Grau y Gamarra. It's difficult to find a meal before 0800.

Note Tourists may be approached by vendors selling *huacos* and necklaces from the Chimú period; the export of these items is strictly illegal if they are genuine, but they almost certainly aren't.

For old car freaks, look for the funeral director's premises, just off the main square, where there are hearses as old as a 1924 Ford; the proprietor is happy to show you around.

Taxis Town trip, US$0.45. Chan Chan, Huanchaco, US$1.30. Taxi driver Jorge Enrique Guevara Castillo, Av. del Ejército 1259, Altos 1, rec. By the hour, in town, US$3, outside US$4.

Night Club Granja Azul—country club. *Billy Bob's* for drinking. Discotheques: *Las Rocas*, *The Drive Inn.*

Peruvian-North American Cultural Institute Húsares de Junín y Venezuela, T 245832, 232512.

Honorary British Consul Jesús de Nazareth 312, T (044) 235548.

Laundry Rapilavo, Grau 337, good and cheap.

Camera Repairs Laboratorios de Investigación Científica, San Martín 745, over Fuji shop opp. *Hotel San Martín*, good.

Post Office Corner of Independencia and Bolognesi. Entel for international phone calls: Calle de la Puerta Aranda 680.

Trujillo: Key to map

1. Plaza de Armas; 2. Cathedral; 3. La Merced; 4. La Compañia; 5. San Francisco; 6. Santa Clara; 7. Santo Domingo; 8. Casa Iturrégui; 9. Casa de los Condes de Aranda; 10. Casa del Mariscal Obregoso; 11. Casa del Mayorazgo; 12. Casa Ganoza Chopitea; 13. Casa Madalengo; 14. Museo Casinelli; 15. Archaeological Museum; 16. Zoological Museum; 17. Post Office; 18. Foptur, Tourist Office; 19. Immigration; 20. Central Market; 21. Tepsa Office; 22. Tepsa buses; 23. Chincay-Suyo office; 24. Buses Díaz; 25. *Hotel Turistas*; 26. *Hotel Continental*; 27. *Hostal Americano.*

Hospital Anglo-American Hospital, good, reasonable fees.

Exchange Banco de Crédito, Gamarra, changes travellers' cheques and cash without commission (also cheques into dollars cash). Banco NorPerú, recommended for changing cheques and cash with no delay, good rates. Banco Popular del Perú, Gamarra, for cheques (a protracted operation, poor rates). América Tours, Plaza de Armas, cash dollars only at good rates; Ghia Tours, near Plaza, changes travellers' cheques outside banking hours, but double check the rates offered. Street changers around the market offer good rates; shop around.

Tourist Office Foptur, Independencia 628, T 24-1936; Pizarro 402, very helpful, and at airport. Maps and information also from Touring and Automobile Club, and from Gira Tours on Calle Independencia; maps from Librería Ayacucho, Ayacucho 570. Tourist Police have an office at Pizarro 422 on the corner of Plaza de Armas; they wear white uniforms and are extremely helpful; will even help lone travellers to visit Chan Chan safely.

Travel Agents Sra. Carmen Melly, *Trujillo Tours*, Gamarra 440 (T 233-069), recommended for knowledgeable guides (Napoleon speaks good English and Italian) and efficient service. *San Valentín Tours*, Orbegoso 585 (T 232-812), ask for Sr. Jorge Sánchez, good local tours, very reasonable.

Guides Pedro Puerta, an English speaking expert on Chan Chan and former college librarian, who has an office at Km. 560 on the Panamericana Norte, 2½ km. from the Plaza de Armas, offers interesting tours to Chan Chan, Huaca El Dragón, and Huaca La Esmeralda. He charges US$3 per hour for a 6-7 hr. tour, not including taxi hire and lunch for him and the taxi driver. He also sells prints of Chan Chan reliefs and Mochica pottery motifs, beautiful but expensive. He gives a slideshow at 2000 nightly at the *Hostal Americano*, free but you may be expected to buy one of his prints. Sr. Puerta is not an official guide, but is experienced and rec. The tourist office has a list of official guides (favourable reports received). Other experienced guides are Oscar, Trujillo Tours, Clara Díaz Bravo (address under **Hotels**, rec., tours from US$4-6 depending on number of sites covered) and Gustava Prada Marga, Miguel Grau 169, Villa del Mar, US$10 for 5 hrs, plus US$16 for taxi. All other guides should be treated with suspicion.

Immigration Edificio Demarco, 3rd floor, Diego de Almagro 225. Gives 90-day visa extensions (proof of funds and onward ticket required). Involves taking forms to Banco de la Nación, and waiting for papers to be stamped.

Air Transport Faucett, Pizarro 532, and AeroPerú, Junín 537, daily flights from Lima, 1 hr., US$51, Faucett from Tumbes. AeroPerú fly to Cajamarca (Mon., Fri., low season), 25 mins. Tarapoto and Juanjui (Tues. and Sat.). Faucett and AeroPerú to Iquitos, change at Tarapoto. Flights by Faucett to Cajamarca, Chiclayo and points N and to a multitude of small jungle towns. Taxi to airport, US$2.50; or take bus to Chan Chan and get out at airport turn-off.

Buses To Lima, 551 km., colectivo, 7-9 hrs., US$11, or by bus, 8-10 hrs. US$6 with Tepsa (3 a day—station in Trujillo, Av. Almagro, between Avs. España and Grau, tickets Astete 482), Peru Express, Chinchay-Suyo (5 a day, González Prada 337, insist on ticket before you board or you may get charged extra for luggage), Expreso Continental (part of Ormeño), US$6, or Roggero; mostly at night. To Lima, Roggero departs at 0930, Chinchay-Suyo at 1000 and Panamericana at 1100, 2200 and 2330. Try to book your bus to Lima a day in advance: they fill up quickly. Buses to Lima quite frequent but difficult to go north as buses booked for days; try Emtrafesa (Av. Miraflores with España) N to Pacasmayo (US$1, 2½ hrs.), Chiclayo (US$2, 3 hrs.), Piura, Tumbes. To Huaraz (via Pativilca) with Chinchay-Suyo, US$6, 10 hrs., depart 2030, daily (Jirón Bolívar 720, book ahead). To get to Huaraz by day without spending the night in malodorous Chimbote you will have to find transport to get you to Chimbote before the Moreno bus leaves at 0700. Bus to Chimbote US$1.50, 2 hrs., Empresa Cajamarca, Av. España 2023-27, Empresa El Aguila, Av. Nicaragua y Moche, hourly (book in advance in high season). Empresa Chinchay-Suyo leaves 1300; Chinchay-Suyo and Tepsa have buses to Casma, 3 hrs., US$2, and to Tarapoto, departing at 1200 daily. Empresa San Pedro, Av. Moche, 3rd block, every 2 hrs.; colectivo to Chimbote, 2 hrs., US$2. Colectivo to Cajamarca US$5, 1100, 6½ hrs., office at Ayacucho 896, reserve day in advance, at least 3 passengers required; Empresa Cajamarca (very old buses), 2100, US$3.20, 2300 with Díaz bus, Av. N. de Piérola 1059, US$3, El Cóndor buses (Pizarro 789) at night, 6-9 hrs., US$4.50 (also Etucsa block 20 of Av. España, 2200, rec.); to Cajamarca in daylight, take Chiclayo bus to La Cruz, turn-off for Cajamarca, and wait there for a colectivo to Cajamarca US$3, 8 hrs. Chinchay-Suyo and Tepsa have buses to Casma, 3 hrs., US$2 and to Tarapoto, departing at 1200 daily. Colectivo to Piura, 1000 daily, US$10; bus to Piura (Tepsa, 2000, Chinchay-Suyo 1300 and at night),

US$5, 6½-9 hrs.; to Chiclayo, US$3, 3-4 hrs. Tepsa to Tumbes, daily at 1930, US$5 and up, Expreso Moderno and Sudamericano (Jr. Montevideo 618), 12 hrs. Bus to Sullana, Sudamericano, also Chinchay-Suyo at 2300, arrive about 0800, The road is paved till just after Sullana, then poor till within 50 km. of Tumbes.

Excursions from Trujillo About five km. to the crumbling ruins of **Chan Chan**, imperial city of the Chimú domains and largest adobe city in the world. The ruins consist of nine great compounds built by Chimú kings. The nine-metre high perimeter walls surrounded sacred enclosures with usually only one narrow entrance. Inside, serried rows of storerooms contained the agricultural wealth of the kingdom, which stretched 1,000 km. along the coast from near Guayaquil to Paramonga. Most of the compounds contain a huge walk-in well which tapped the ground water, raised to a high level by irrigation higher up the valley. Each compound also included a platform mound which was the burial place of the king, with his women and his treasure, presumably maintained as a memorial. The Incas almost certainly copied this system and transported it to Cuzco where the last Incas continued building huge enclosures and although they are still standing, many of the interesting mouldings are closed to visitors. The Ciudadela of Tschudi has been reconstructed (15 min. walk from the road), open 0830 to 1600 (but it may be covered up if rain is expected).

A ticket which covers the entrance fees for Chan Chan, the Huaca El Dragón and the Huaca La Esmeralda (for 2 days, but only 1 visit to Chan Chan permitted) costs US$4. Minibuses leave from José Gálvez 394, corner of Los Incas, near market, or corner of España and Orbegoso/Mansiche, or from Salaverry, US$0.15, last one returns about 1200; Trujillo-Huanchaco bus, US$0.10 to Chan Chan entrance; these buses are worked by teams of pickpockets; taxi, US$1.30, rec.

Warning If you walk to the ruins from the main road, keep to the path. Do not go to Chan Chan alone or in couples; it is preferable to go with a guide. White shirted, armed police are in evidence. Sgto. José Soto Ríos, T 251489, is a good guide, speaks English. Do not walk on Buenos Aires beach near Chan Chan as there is serious danger of robbery, and being attacked by dogs.

The restored temple, Huaca El Dragón, dating from the Mochica empire of between 800 and 100 BC, is also known as Huaca Arco Iris (rainbow), after shape of friezes which decorate it. It is on the W side of the Pan-American Highway in the district of La Esperanza; taxi costs US$1; open 0800-1700.

The Caballo Muerto ruins, about 11 km. inland up the Moche valley, are now forbidden to visitors, and the sculptures have been re-buried to protect them from robbers.

The poorly restored Huaca La Esmeralda is at Mansiche, between Trujillo and Chan Chan, behind the church. Buses from Pasaje Agustín, between Obregoso and Gamarra, 2 blocks from Plaza (not a friendly district).

A few km. south of Trujillo are the huge Moche pyramids, the Huaca del Sol and the Huaca de la Luna (open all the time, entry free, a police hut is manned from 0700 to 1300), taxi US$3-6 return, (ask around all the drivers for best rate) colectivo from the Av. de los Incas y Suárez, US$0.25, marked Moche El Alto or La Compiña if at all, leaves 0800 and 1300, stops right in front of the ruins, alternatively bus marked Salaverry, El Alto or La Compiña, US$0.15 from corner of Zela near Mercado Mayorista, get out at Bodega El Sol on the right hand side of the road; opposite is a huge Sprite sign. Here starts a path to Moche, about an hour's walk; it is inadvisable to walk unless in a large group. The pyramids consist of millions of adobe bricks and are the largest precolumbian structures in South America (the interior passageways of the Huaca de la Luna are not open to visitors; the site is under the control of the tourist police). An interesting feature of the site is the innumerable number of ancient pottery shards lying around on the ground.

The fishing village of **Huanchaco** is worth visiting to see the narrow pointed fishing rafts, known as *caballitos*, made of tortora reeds and used in many places along the Peruvian coast. Unlike those used on Lake Titicaca, they are flat, not hollow, and ride the breakers rather like surfboards (you can rent one on the beach). These craft are depicted on ancient Mochica and Chimú pottery. The village, now developed with the beach houses of the wealthy of Trujillo, is overlooked by a huge church from the belfry of which are superb views. Children sell precolumbian *objets d'art* and beads; beware of eating fish in the hut-like restaurants as they aren't very hygienic. Bus to Huanchaco (marked with a "B"), US$0.12, from corner of Av. España and Av. Mansiche (regular ringroad bus, every 10 mins.), or, after 1830, Pasaje Agustín, Trujillo, 2 blocks from Plaza about one an hour; taxi US$4. Fiestas throughout January and February.

N.B. The strength of the sun is deceptive; a cold wind off the sea reduces the temperature, but you can still be badly sunburned.

Hotels *Hostal Sol y Mar*, Jirón Ficus 570, E, with bath and balcony (some rooms without), kitchen facilities, friendly owner, garden, rec.; *Hostal Bracamonte*, Los Olivos 503, F, comfortable, good, chalets with private bath, or converted caravans, pool, own water supply, emergency generator, rents bicycles, secure, bar nearby, good pies and cakes (beware of monkey when eating lemon meringue pie, he's very fast), English spoken, highly rec.; *Hostal Huanchaco*, Larco 287 on Plaza, also F with hot shower, clean and friendly, swimmimg pool, cafeteria with home-made cakes and other good meals, video, pool table, highly rec.; *Hostal Las Palmeras*, Calle Las Palmeras, G-F, 6 rooms, hot water in bathrooms, cooking facilities, clean, American owner has extensive folk-art collection; *Barraca*, F, private showers; *Caballitos de Totora*, F, swimming pool, friendly, nice garden, but rooms not too clean, the owners are to open a vegetarian restaurant and hold cultural events at the hotel; cheap accommodation at the house of Señora Consuelo, about US$0.50 p.p. Accommodation, inc. food, with families, easy to find, US$2-3 a day.

Restaurants Good fish restaurants on the sea front *La Casita de la Playa*, owned by Walter (an American), meals for US$1.25, highly rec; others on seafront tend to overcharge; *Viña del Mar, El Peón, El Erizo* rec.; *Violetta*, a private house near the plaza (good meals provided) and Familia Flores, popular; *El Tramboyo*, near the pier, good, helpful, friendly. *Lucho del Mar*, excellent sea food; *Piccolo*, 5 blocks from plaza, cheap, friendly, sometimes live folk music; *Colonial Club*, main square, run by Belgians, fish, chicken or meat, good, but not cheap. Try picarones, people come from Trujillo at weekends especially to eat them.

About 20 mins from Trujillo by bus, 15 by taxi (US$0.30 and US$2 respectively) is Las Delicias,

NORTHERN PERU

with a clean beach and good surf. *Hostal Zlang* here is recommended, small, clean, F, quiet, shared baths, breakfast in *Bar-Café* attached, other meals available from other members of the family, owner very knowledgeable and his son offers tours of Chan Chan. Good restaurant serving traditional food around the corner (US$1.50-2.50).

A visit may be made from Trujillo to one of the sugar estates, say the Hacienda Cartavio, in the Chicama valley (43 km.). At Laredo (bus from Trujillo, near central market, 7 km.), a sugar refinery can be visited—the tour is free; apply to public relations office in administration building; there are also interesting ruins at Galindo, near Laredo. One of the biggest sugar estates in the world, also in the Chicama valley, is the Casa Grande cooperative. It covers over 6,000 hectares and employs 4,000 members. Visits (guided) are only possible before 1200; US$0.70 by bus. The Chiclín museum, once famous for items from Chan Chan, now contains interesting collection of colonial religious paintings and statuary. Ruins in the Chicama valley: Huaca Prieta and Chiquitoy; colectivos from Av. España, change at Cartavio.

    132 km. E from Trujillo is the village of **Coina**, at 1,500 metres in the Sierra Alto Chicama, where the late Dr. Kaufmann, from Germany, opened a hospital for Indians and built the *Hostería El Sol*, with glorious views, E, for full board, F, bed only. Walking. English, French and German spoken. Information from the *Hostería El Sol*, at Calle Los Brillantes 224, Santa Inés, Trujillo (T 231933). Mail can be forwarded to Apartado 775, Trujillo.

To the NE of Trujillo is Cajamarca, which can be reached either from Trujillo or from Pacasmayo (paved throughout). The old road from Trujillo is terrible and (for cyclists especially) lonely, taking 12-15 hours (as opposed to 8 hrs. via Pacasmayo), but it is more interesting, passing over the bare puna before dropping to the Huamachuco valley. Off it lies **Otusco**, an attractive Andean town with an imposing but unfinished church and narrow cobbled streets. In Agallpampa there is one, unsigned *hostal* ("less than basic, no light, bath, toilet or water, and tries to overcharge"). Further on, at the mining town of Shorey, a road branches off to **Santiago de Chuco**, birthplace of the poet César Vallejo, where there is the annual festival of Santiago El Mayor in the second half of July. The main procession is on 25 July, when the image is carried through the streets. Close to Yancabamba is *Hostería El Viajero* and in Quiruvilca there is one hotel. The road runs on to the colonial town of **Huamachuco**, 181 km. from Trujillo, which has a huge main plaza and a controversial modern cathedral. There is a colourful Sunday market. A 2-hr. walk (take the track which goes off to the right just after crossing the bridge on the road to Trujillo) takes you to the extensive ruins of hilltop pre-Inca fortifications, Marcahuamachuco (car US$5 p.p.).

Huamachuco Hotels *Hostal San Francisco*, Sánchez Carrión 380, F, clean, hot shower; *La Libertad*, G, not rec., rooms and bathrooms filthy; *Fernando*, G, Bolívar 361, good value, clean; also *Sucre*, G. Rec. restaurants: *Caribe*, quite good, and *El Sol* (both on main square), *El Cairo*, Sánchez Carrión 754, good food and service, rec. and *Danubio*. Good snacks at *Salón Venecia*, Carrión near main plaza.

Buses Transportes Quiroz from Trujillo, US$5, 12 hrs., at 1530, 1700, 1800, take warm clothing; Antisuyo to Trujillo three daily, US$4, 10 hrs. There are also colectivos from Trujillo. Buses to Cajamarca, US$1.50; to Casa Grande, US$0.85. Direct bus to Lima, 24 hrs.

From Huamachuco buses (Empresa Huancapata which start in Trujillo) run to Tayabamba (important ruins nearby), on the far bank of the Marañón, passing through the old gold-mining centres of Pataz province, such as Parcoy and Buldibuyo. This journey takes a good 18 hours in "normal" conditions. Not far, but a time-consuming journey on mule-back, from Pataz itself (a friendly gold-mining town, about 100 km. from Huamachuco) are the unique circular ruins of El Gran **Pajatén** (pre-Inca); ask at Tourist Office in Cajamarca for details. A national park, Río Abiseo, incorporating Gran Pajatén, four other sites—La Playa, Las Papayas, Los Pinchudos and Cerro Central—and the surrounding cloud forest, is scheduled to open for visitors in 1991; until then you need a permit (hard to get) from the Instituto Nacional de Cultura in Lima. Also worth seeing in the Huamachuco area are Laguna Sausacocha (with Inca ruins, similar to those of Vilcashuamán, near Ayacucho, nearby) and *haciendas* Yanasara and Cochabamba, deep down in the valley of the river Chusgón, about 2-3 hrs. by truck east of the town. Yanasara, noted for its fighting bulls, is still in the hands of its long-term owner, Francisco Pinillos Montoya, a well-known local character. There is a guest house at Cochabamba, which used to be the Andean retreat of the owners of the Laredo sugar plantation, near Trujillo. The climate, at about 2,300 metres, is mild.

There is a 2-day walk from Bolívar in the NE to Huamachuco, parts of which follow an Inca trail used by Túpac Yupanqui (**see also page** 999). One walks from Bolívar to Bambamarca, then down the stone steps leading to the Calemar trail, which crosses the River Marañón. At Pallar, there are trucks to Huamachuco. Be sure to take food, water, a small kerosene cooker and a compass; this is an arduous trip and not recommended for beginners.

From Huamachuco the road runs on 48 km. through impressive eucalyptus groves to **Cajabamba**, which lies in the high part of the sugar-producing and once malaria-infested Condebamba valley. It has an attractive Plaza de Armas. Several buses daily to Huamachuco; Quiroz, Antisuyo, about 3 hrs., US$1.75, also trucks and lorries. Two direct buses a day from Trujillo, 12 hrs.

The best hotel is the *Flores* (F, with toilet, friendly, clean) on the Plaza de Armas; *Hostal Bolívar*, F, including fleas but without bath; also *Ramal*, F, friendly; *Restaurant Gloriabamba* good.

Cajabamba can also be reached in a strenuous but marvellous 3-4 day hike from Coina (see above). The first day's walk brings you to Hacienda Santa Rosa where you stay overnight. Then you cross the mountains at about 4,000 metres, coming through Arequeda to Cajabamba. The ruins at Huacamochal may be seen en route; the scenery is spectacular. It is advisable to hire a guide, and a donkey to carry the luggage. The cost for both is about US$4 a day. A map of the route is available from the Post Office in Coina.

The road continues from Cajabamba through **San Marcos** (3 hotels; *Nuevo*, G p.p. with bath, water shortages, but clean and quiet), important for its Sunday cattle market, to Cajamarca. Bus to Cajamarca (124 km.), Atahualpa and Empresa Díaz leaving early in the morning, takes 6 hrs., US$3.

Pacasmayo, port for the next oasis northward, is 100 km. N. of Trujillo on the Pan-American Highway running N to Chiclayo (bus, 2 hrs., US$0.75). Population: 12,300.

Hotel *Ferrocarril*, F, on seafront, quiet and clean, no hot water (ask for water anyway); *Panamericano*, Leoncio Prado 18, F, with private cold shower, good value, friendly, clean, safe, reasonable restaurant downstairs; *San Francisco*, opp. *Panamericano*, F, basic, OK. Several cheap restaurants on the main street.

Pacasmayo is the best starting point for visiting Cajamarca. The new paved 180 km. road to it branches off the Pan-American Highway soon after it crosses the Jequetepeque River. The river valley has terraced rice fields and mimosas may often be seen in bloom, brightening the otherwise dusty landscape. A few km. to N on other side of River Jequetepeque are the ruins of Pacatnamú—pyramids, cemetery and living quarters of nobles and fishermen, possibly built in Chavín period. Evidence also of Moche tribes. Where the Pan-American Highway crosses the Jequetepeque are the well-signed ruins of Fartan (separate from those of Pacatnamú, but probably of the same period). At the mining town of **Chilete**, a worthwhile diversion is to take the road N to San Pablo; 21 km. from Chilete are the stone monoliths of the Kuntur Huasi culture, which resemble those of San Agustín in Colombia. There are occasional buses from Chilete to the site, 1½ hrs., then 20 mins.' walk (no signs; you must ask locals), then a long wait for transport back, best to hitch. In Chilete, hotels *Amazonas* and *San Pedro*, G, filthy bathrooms, rooms hard to find on Tues. because of Wed. market; restaurant *Montecarlo* serves cheap *cuy* and other dishes. Truck to Chilete from the police control 1 km. from main plaza in Cajamarca, US$0.85. On the road to Cajamarca is Yonán, where there are petroglyphs.

An alternative route from Trujillo to Cajamarca, via Contumazá, passes through the cane fields and rice plantations of the Chicama valley before branching off to climb over the watershed of the Jequetepeque. From Contumazá, an attractive little town, trucks can be taken to Cajamarca, via Chilete.

Cajamarca (pop. 70,000, 2,750 metres), is a beautiful old colonial town and most important town in the northern mountain area. Here Pizarro ambushed and captured Atahualpa, the Inca emperor. The Cuarto de Rescate (not the actual ransom chamber but in fact the room where Atahualpa was held prisoner—closed on Tues. and after 1200 on Sat. and Sun.) can be seen (US$2, ticket also valid for nearby Belén church and nearby museums); a red line purporting to be the height of Atahualpa's hand was only recently painted in. (The room was closed to the public for centuries, and used by the nuns of Belén hospital). The chamber also has two interesting murals. The Plaza where Atahualpa was ambushed and the stone altar set high on Santa Apollonia hill where he is said to have reviewed his subjects are also shown (small entrance fee). There is a road to the top, or you can walk up from Calle 2 de Mayo, using the steep stairway. The Plaza das Armas has a 350-year old fountain, topiary and gardens (but little peace from the beggars and shoeshine boys). The Cathedral (San Francisco, seventeenth century, with catacombs) and Belén churches (handicrafts for sale in the cloisters) are well worth seeing; so are San Pedro (Gálvez and Junín), San José (C. M. Iglesias and Angamos), La Recoleta (Maestro and Casanova) and Capilla de La Dolorosa, close to San Francisco. Many belfries were left half-finished in protest against a Spanish tax levied on the completion of a church. The Cathedral, which took 350 years to build, was completed in 1960; it still has no belfry. Next to the Belén church (closed on Tues.) is a hospital (1774) for men and women. The women's hospital is an interesting musuem, one section with well-displayed archaeological finds, pots and textiles, and the other showing modern arts and crafts.

Points of interest include the Bishop's Palace, next to the Cathedral, and many old colonial houses with garden patios, and 104 elaborate carved doorways: see palace of the Condes de Uceda, now occupied by the Banco de Crédito on Jr. Apurímac 719; the house of Toribio Casanova, Jr. José Gálvez 938; the house of the Silva Santiesteban family, Jr. Junín 1123; and the houses of the Guerrero and Castañeda families. The Education Faculty of the University has a museum on Jirón Arequipa with objects of the pre-Inca Cajamarca culture, not seen in Lima; the attendant knows much about Cajamarca and the surrounding area. Open 0800-1200, 1500-1700, in winter, and 0800-1200 in summer, US$0.20 (guided tour). The University maintains an experimental arboretum and agricultural station. The Museo de Arte Colonial, at the Convento de San Francisco, is also worth a visit.

The town is a favourite among Peruvians for holidays, and has an interesting market with some crafts, especially noted for cotton and wool saddlebags (*alforjas*). Bargains of hand-tooled leather goods can be bought from the prisoners at the jail beyond the white arch on Calle Lima (7 blocks from Plaza de Armas). All museums are closed on Tuesdays (shops take a long lunch) but open at weekends. The rainy season is Dec.-April.

Festivals Plenty. Corpus Christi is a favourite. The pre-Lent Carnival has been revived; it is spectacular but includes much throwing of water, oil and paint, which can develop into fights between local youths and gringos. 28/29 July, Independence: *fiesta*, with bullfight and agricultural fair; prices shoot up. In Porcón, 16 km. to the NW, Palm Sunday processions are remarkable.

Warning Beware of pickpockets in the Plaza de Armas and in cinemas.

Hotels *Turistas* (60 rooms) in the Plaza de Armas, D, with private bath, helpful, laundry service, 2 restaurants, bar, ask to see room before booking. *Continental*, off Plaza, very clean, hot water, D, rec.; *Laguna Seca*, at Baños del Inca, D, in pleasant surroundings, clean, private hot thermal baths in rooms, swimming pool with thermal water, horses for hire, food average. *Sucre*, Amalia Puga 815, near Plaza de Armas, G, with toilet and wash basin in each room, water a.m. only, good value, sometimes noisy, not very safe, poor restaurant upstairs;

Cajamarca: Key to map

1. Plaza de Armas; 2. Santa Apollonia hill; 3. Cathedral; 4. Belén church and hospital; 5. San Francisco Convent and Museo de Arte Colonial; 6. San Pedro; 7. La Recoleta; 8. Cuatro de Rescate; 9. Casa Silva Santiesteban; 10. Museum of Education Faculty; 11. Post Office; 12. Foptur, Tourist Office; 13. Central Market; 14. *Hotel de Turistas*; 15. *Hostal Cajamarca*.

CAJAMARCA ENVIRONS 102

Porcón

RÍO PORCÓN

To Hualgayoc and Bambamarca

Cerrillo

▲ Ventanillas de Combayo

Ventanillas de Otusco

To Celen dín and Chachapoyas

CAJAMARCA

Layzón ▲

▲ Las Torrecitas

▲ Baños del Inca

RÍO CHONTA

Cumbe Mayo ▲

Ayllambo

Llacanora To cajabamba

NOT TO SCALE

To Pacasmayo

Pariamarca La Colpa

N

CAJAMARCA CENTRE 102

JOSE GALVEZ

PISAGUA JUNÍN

TARAPACÁ

LA MAR

APURIMAC

UNION

ATAHUALAPA

CAJAMARCA

HUANUCO

SAN MARTIN

LIMA

AMALIA PUGA

LA MAR

APURIMAC

AREQUIPA

JOSE SABOGAL

S. SALVADOR

TO AIRPORT

DOS DE MAYO

BELLAVISTA

BELEN

AMALIA PUGA

ETEN

AMAZONAS

PEATEROS

STA APOLONIA

SAN PABLO

DESAMPARADOS

GUILLERMO URRELO

GUADALUPE SILVA SANTISTEBAN

CINCO ESQUINAS

SOLEDAD

AYACUCHO

ROMERO

LA ESPERANZA

TO CUMBE MAYO

NOT TO SCALE

TO BAÑOS DEL INCA

nas, Jirón Amazonas 528, modern, F, clean, no hot water, friendly. *Casa Blanca*, Plaza de Armas, E, room service, clean, safe, nice building and garden, good; *Gran Hostal Plaza*, Plaza de Armas 631, F, old building with handmade wood furnishings, private bath and balcony (G without bath), hot water but poor water supply, pleasant, rec (especially room 4) with new annex (dirty but is open at 0200 when bus arrives); *San Francisco*, Jr. Belén 570, F, "a bit dirty, but friendly"; *Jusovi*, Amazonas 637, F, comfortable, all rooms with private baths but hot water only in communal bathroom, safe, rec.; *Becerra*, Jr. Arequipa 195 (unsigned), F, intermittent tepid water, rec.; *Hostal Cajamarca*, E, in colonial house at Dos de Mayo 311, clean, hot water, rec. as the best hotel, food excellent, good local guitarists, musicians welcome. The owners also run *Albergue San Vicente*, outside the town, in an old hacienda. *Hostal José Galves*, E, thermal water; *Hostal Atahualpa*, E, private bath, clean, good value, but hard beds, rec. *Hostal Prado*, Calle Lamar, G without bath, rec. Try to get a room in the sun, no heating for the cold nights.

Restaurants *El Sitio*, Jr. Dos de Mayo 311, in *Hostal Cajamarca*, local specialities, friendly, informal, rec., peña in the evening. *Arlequín*, corner of Plaza de Armas, good; *Salas*, on Plaza, not expensive, good local food, best tamales in town; *El Zarco*, Plaza de Armas at Arequipa 170, very highly rec., much frequented by local residents, inexpensive, try the sopa fuchifú, humitas de maíz, also has short chifa menu; *La Namorina*, on edge of town on road to Baños del Inca, opposite Ché service station, renowned for its speciality, cuy frito (fried guinea-pig); *La Taverna*, Plaza de Armas, good variety, but food cold as in most places, reasonable prices, *Super Pollo* on Plaza, rec. for its jugo especial (made from algarrobina); *Playa Azul*, good food, clean, in Magdalena (about 1 hr. from Cajamarca by car); *Capri*, Jirón Lima, good ice cream; *Rescate* has been rec. for its cuy. *Cajamarqueña*, Amazonas 770, very good, not cheap, tables in garden of colonial building; *Petit Café*, nr. Belén church, good, sometimes live music at night; *El Cumbe*; *Taverna Johnny*. For early breakfasts go to the market.

Tea Rooms *Café Florida* on Plaza de Armas.

Food Specialities *Queso mantecoso* (full-cream cheese); *manjar blanco* (sweet); *humitas* (ground maize with cheese); *cuy frito*; eucalyptus honey (sold in the market on Calle Amazonas; said to be a cure for rheumatism). Try the flaky pastries filled with apple or *manjar blanco* from the street sellers. The area is renowned for its dairy produce; many shops sell cheese, *manjar blanco*, butter, honey, etc, or go to La Cajamarquiña factory and shop on Amazonas.

Shopping Handicrafts are cheap, and good leather items at the prison, but bargain hard. Items can be made to order.

Exchange Banco Nor Perú, corner of Lima and Tarapacá, exchanges dollars for 1% commission. Banco de Crédito will not even change cash. Some of the hotels and restaurants, e.g. *Hotel Casa Blanca*, *Rest. Cajamarqueña*, may help out with travellers' cheques if you're eating there. Street changers on Arequipa just off Plaza de Armas.

Addresses Post Office, Jr. Lima 406; Entel Perú, Jr. San Martín 363; Telephone office for international calls, on Plaza de Armas; Hospital, Av. Mario Urteaga; Guardia Civil, Plaza Amalia Puga.

Tourist Information Foptur, Santisteban 144, T 92-2228, good maps (open 0830-1300, 1430-1700). Ask here for car hire.

Travel Agents *Cajamarca Tours*, Dos de Mayo 323, guides do not speak English, despite what they claim. A group of local guides has formed *Cumbemayo Tours* (Amalia Puga 669 T 922938, or 2nd floor *Hostal Plaza*), and *Inca Atahualpa Tours*, (Jr Junín 1288, Aptdo 224, T 922495, or Jr. Amalia Puga 695), and do good economical trips, e.g. to Cumbe Mayo itself (US$3 p.p.), the pottery workshop at Ayllambo, 3½ km. out, and the Palm Sunday celebrations at Porcón. *Aventuras Cajamarca*, enquire at *Hotel Casa Blanca*, trips to Kuelap, Jorge Caballero, rec. Several travel agenices around the Plaza de Armas offer trips to local sites (see below) and further afield (eg Kuelap).

Air Service AeroPerú flights to Lima via Trujillo on Tues., Thurs., Sat. mornings (US$75). Cheaper to pay for each stage separately. **Warning**: Delays at Cajamarca are all too frequent.

Buses Daily buses and colectivos to Lima (bus, US$13), Trujillo (7-8 hrs., US$3-4.50 by bus); Chiclayo (US$5, 6-7 hrs. by Empresa Díaz, Ayacucho 758 y Amazonas, 1400 and 2100, with El Cumbe, near El Che filling station (*grifo*) about 1½ km. from centre, 1100 and 1500, US$3, at 1100 and 1500, with Atahualpa—best—at 1430, US$2.50, Comité de Autos 2, and Chinchay-Suyo). Tepsa leaves for Trujillo and Lima at 1400 and 1700, 17 hrs; Empresa Díaz for Trujillo at 2000, for Chimbote, for Lima at 1800 (1730 from Tourist Hotel, "Presidential service" non-stop) and for Celendín at 1200 4½ hrs, US$2. No day time buses to Trujillo, only colectivos, ask at tourist office. Expreso Cajamarca, Amazonas 807, Comité de Autos 12 and 40 also go to Trujillo. Atahualpa to Lima, 15 hrs., US$9, overnight, rec.; to Celendín daily at 1200 (also to Cajabamba, Chota, Cutervo). Also daily to and from Cajabamba (Empresa Díaz, who also go to Bambamarca, or Atahualpa at 1000), US$3, 6 hrs. (milk trucks will also take passengers to Cajabamba).

Excursions To Ayllambo, 1½ hr. walk, 3½ km., from Av. Independencia, a village which specializes in ceramics. You can visit the *Escuela/Taller* where children learn pottery, open Mon.-Fri. 0730-1200, 1300-1700, Sat. 0730-1230. The warm sulphurous thermal springs known as Los Baños del Inca, where there are a public pool and private rooms (US$0.10, excellent) are 6 km. away. Atahualpa tried the effect of these waters on a festering war wound. Nearby can also be seen La Collpa, a *hacienda* which is now a cooperative farm of the Ministry of Agriculture with bulls for breeding and a lake and gardens. At 1400 the campesinos can be seen handmilking the cows, some of which come when called by name. There is a minibus service from the main square, US$0.10.

The surrounding countryside is splendid. Look out for the local building method called Tapial, made of compressed adobe alternating with layers of stones or wood. Other excursions include Llacanora, a typical Andean village in beautiful scenery and Ventanillas de Otusco, part of an old pre-Inca cemetery (minibus from town, US$0.10), with a gallery of secondary burial niches (US$2.20 entry for foreigners, but can be photographed from road with ease). A good walk, 10 km., is from Baños del Inca on Celendín road to Ventanillas de Otusco (start from the bridge and take the path along the brook), through beautiful countryside. A new road continues to Ventanillas de Combayo, some 20 km. past those of Otusco; these are more numerous and more spectacular, being located in a rather isolated, mountainous area, and are distributed over the face of a steep 200-metre-high hillside. A one-day round trip can be made, taking a bus from Av. Arequipa to Ventanillas de Otusco (½ hr.); walk to Baños del Inca (1½ hrs, 6 km.); walk to Llanacora (1 hr., 7 km); then a further hour to La Collpa.

Cumbe Mayo, mountain village (20 km. SW of Cajamarca but no bus service; it is dangerous to go alone, take a guided tour, prices vary between US$1.50 and US$4; taxi US$12). An aqueduct can be followed for several km., very remarkable; also, be sure to take a strong torch; alternatively you can walk and ask local passers-by the way. The trail starts from the hill of Santa Apollonia (Silla del Inca), and goes to Cumbe Mayo straight through the village and up the hill; at the top of the mountain, leave the trail and take the road to the right to the canal. The walk takes 3 hours, but is not difficult and you do not need hiking boots. The Indians use the trail to bring their goods to market. On the way to Cumbe Mayo is the Layzón ceremonial centre, the same period as Huacaloma. Other Inca ruins in the area include Tantarica, Torrecitas, and San Pedro de Pacopampa.

North of Cajamarca is Hualgayoc (**see page** 915). Trip with fantastic scenery. There is excellent trout served in restaurant on the way there; easy to find as it is the only place for a long way. Order on your way there to eat on the way back.

South of Cajamarca, through Santa Catalina and Trinidad, are the Inca and pre-Inca ruins of Tantarica, near Cholol.

Cajamarca is the starting point for the northern route to Iquitos. From Cajamarca there are several buses daily to **Celendín** (4½-5 hrs., 112 km., US$2), where there are several hotels off the main plaza (*Amazonas*, G with toilet, clean, friendly, helpful, rec.; *Hostal Celendín*, F, with bath, check room is clean before booking, good restaurant; *José Galves*, G, basic, dirty toilets, humid rooms, but plenty of character; *Restaurant Jalisco* on Plaza de Armas, simple, not cheap, also *Salazar* and *Buen Amigo*, Calle 2 de Mayo, next to *José Galves*, or eat at market; cinema and cock fighting Sunday night in the local arena. Festival July 16 (Virgen del Carmen). There is also an interesting local market on Sunday. The town has electricity from 1800 to 0100. The road follows a winding course through the northern Andes, crossing the wide and deep canyon of the River Marañón at Balsas after 55 km. (2½ hrs.). The road climbs steeply with superb views of the mountains and the valleys below. The fauna and flora are spectacular as the journey alternates between high in the mountains and low in the rain forest. After rain, landslides can be quite a problem. There are some interesting Inca ruins on the road between Celendín and Leimebamba (146 km.).

Bus to Chachapoyas from Jr. Salaverry 595 (private house) Sun. 1900, 12-14 hrs., US$4.50 (11 hrs. to Tingo, US$3.75); on other days you must try your luck to find a truck to Chachapoyas, US$4, 14-16 hrs., take food on all journeys. Don't take a *buseta* or *camioneta* from Celendín to Chachapoyas. They charge US$9.25 and you'll be "dead on arrival." All transport is difficult in the rainy season. Ask at the police checkpoint what transport is going.

Leimebamba is a pleasant town with 2 hotels, the better of which is *Escobedo*, G, friendly owner has lots of local information, toilets, cold shower; 3 restaurants, including *Oasis*, just off Plaza de Armas, and *El Caribe* on the Plaza. Trucks park in main square, leave 0300-0600 for Celendín and Chachapoyas; buses run daily to Celendín; daily bus Leimebamba—Chachapoyas 0500, returning after lunch, also pick-ups in p.m. from Chachapoyas. Of the ruins in the area **La Congona**, a Sachupoyan site, is 2½ hrs. walk away, take the trail at the end of the street with the hotels and climb up (next to police station). The trail levels out and follows round the mountain, then down into a little valley. La Congona, a system of 3 hills can be seen: aim for the right-hand (easterly) conical hill with a visible small cliff. The trail does not go all the way up the hill; you must cross a field and climb through moss forest. This is the best preserved of 3 sites, with 30 decorated round stone houses (some with evidence of 3 storeys) and a watch tower. The other hills have been levelled. It is worth following the trail along the crest beyond these hills, and then to the left, down through rain forest (muddy), eventually to join the main trail. (A good day's walk—Haydn Washington, Australia.)

The road on to Chachapoyas is poor (dry weather only), but the scenery is magnificent. Food and warm clothing are necessary; usually only chicken and rice is available in the villages. Gasoline may be available in Leimebamba but cannot be relied on. If you want to go through to Iquitos, better to fly.

Chachapoyas, population 50,000, altitude 2,400 m., is the capital of the Department of Amazonas and has been called the friendliest town in Peru. If you have any problems contact the Guardia Civil (green uniforms), very friendly and more helpful than P.I.P. (Amazonas), in the town and countryside. Archaeological and anthropological information can be sought from the local anthropologist, Carlos Torres Mas, who is the head of the Instituto Nacional de Cultura, in the 1200 block of Libertad, also advises about walks in the area (will store luggage). Those interested in the abundant archaeological sites in the area should read Gene Savoy's *Antisuyo* (British edition: *Vilcabamba*). There is also a Tourist Office on Calle Amazonas, a few blocks from the Plaza de Armas, the director, Don Segundo Pastor, and Cortés Domínguez Bobadillo are helpful, luggage can be stored here (there is a small but good museum in the same building).

Hotels *El Dorado*, Ayacucho 1062, F, hot water, clean, helpful, rec.; *Johumaji*, Jr. Ayacucho 711 (T 138), F, with bath, cheaper without, some rooms have hot water, safe for luggage; *El Danubio*, Junin 572, F, clean, hot water, safe for luggage, rec., son of owner works for P.I.P.; *Casa Blanca*, F; *Hostal Kuelap*, Jr. Chincha Alta 631, G with bath, cheaper without, hot water extra (electric showers); *Continental*, Jr. Ortiz Arreta 441, G. A new tourist hotel is planned at Laguna Pomacocha, 3 hrs. by bus from Chachapoyas.

Restaurants *Chacha*, on Plaza de Armas, clean, good for bistec apanado, friendly; *Oh Qué Bueno*, limited menu; good pastries also at *Patisserie*, Jr. 2 de Mayo 558; *Kuelap*, same street as *Johumaji*, good; *Chifa El Turista*, Amazonas 575 near post office, is reasonable, friendly and helpful; *Café Bar Mary*, 2 blocks SE of Plaza de Armas, clean, good, cheap; *Monte Carlo*, opp. market entrance, cheap, friendly; *Mio Mio*, near Post Office, good value chicken restaurant; good fruit juices at stall 67 in the market; *Los Michitos*, Jr. de la Merced 604.

For leatherwork, Zapatería "El Cairo": a pair of boots costs US$27.

Buses To Chiclayo 3 times per week (Olano, US$15, 1000, 1100, on Sat., none on Sun.) via Bagua and Jaén (18-25 hrs.); trucks more frequent to Bagua (see below). Several buses a week, 12-14 hrs., US$4.50, to Celendín 230 km. (not for those without a head for heights), trucks run, 16 hrs., US$4. You can alight in Tingo, for Kuelap. Some trucks will take passengers to Moyobamba or Bagua, or Tingo in afternoon; remember most trucks do shortish runs and be prepared to change trucks frequently. **Bagua** (no hotels reported) is a good place to reach by truck (US$3 from Chachapoyas) as Cruz de Chalpón runs an overnight bus service (US$6) from there to Chiclayo. There are two Baguas, Grande and Chica, with about 20 km.

between them; each sells half the available bus tickets. Bagua Chica has the better eating places.

Air Service A new airport has been built; AeroPerú, office on main square (open 0800-0900, if closed go directly to airport), fly Lima-Chiclayo-Chachapoyas on Mon. and Thur. arriving 0900 and 1200 respectively (plane returns immediately to Chiclayo), frequent delays and protestations that flight is fully booked. *Camioneta* from AeroPerú office to airport 0700 (20 mins.), or truck from Plaza de Armas up to 2 hrs. before flights leave, US$0.25. Also Wed. flights to Rioja and weekly to Selva. Aeronorte fly to Chiclayo Fri. Flights are not reliable and are often cancelled.

Guide Martín Antonio Oliva, Jr. Amazaonas 557 (or *Bar Chacha*), Chachapoyas, acts as a guide to most of the sites described below.

Excursions Huancas, which produces unique pottery, can be reached by a 2-hour walk on the airport road; also Inca and pre-Inca ruins.

The road is now open via Chachapoyas to **Mendoza**, a hair-raising five-hour journey from Chachapoyas by *camioneta*, daily at 1000, US$1 (return 0200, sometimes 0700). Mendoza is the starting point for an ethnologically interesting area in the Guayabamba Valley where there is a high incidence of very fair people. Some maintain that these people are descendants of Vikings who reached South America (Kaufmann Doig, Dr Jacques de Mahieu of Buenos Aires), others that they are a local group (called by Morgan Davis the Cloud People), while they themselves say they are descended from Conquistadores (which is unlikely since the Spanish chronicler Garcilaso de la Vega describes them resisting the Incas before the conquest). The region is in the *selva*, very remote, and can be reached on foot from Mendoza or Limabamba (2 hrs. by *camioneta* from Mendoza), but a road is under construction. Seek all advice locally (we are grateful to Helmut Zettl of Ebergassing, Austria, for this information).

"Two hours by truck on the road to Mendoza is Molinopampa, which marks the starting point of an adventurous five-day hike to Rioja. Only experienced hikers should attempt this journey, which is very difficult. Food supplies for the whole journey should be purchased at Chachapoyas and a guide, absolutely essential, hired at Molinopampa for about US$5. The steep trail leads through waist-high unbridged rivers, over the cold, high Sierra and then for three days one follows the muddy trail down to the dense and humid jungle. We were accompanied by exotic butterflies, and never a quiet moment with the chattering of birds and monkeys. The whole magic of the jungle—trees, birds, animals and insects—can be seen untouched in their natural surroundings." (Katrina Farrar and Andy Thornton).

Tingo (1,800 metres), 37 km. from Chachapoyas, is reached by driving S up the Utcubamba valley from Chachapoyas; several pick-ups, at 0630-0700 from Chachapoyas, but be in Tingo by 1500 to ensure you get one to Chachapoyas, US$1, 1½ hrs. in dry, up to 3½ hrs in wet (trucks infrequent from Celendín US$4—leave at 0300, 12 hrs., driver collects you from hotel); buses Tingo—Leimebamba and Cachapoyas daily (from Leimebamba in a.m., returning p.m.). There is a new *hostal* over the bridge on left as you enter from Celedín, with water, clean, basic bathrooms, good meals and a cheap *pensión*, at the entrance to the village painted blue and white, F, mouldy, good restaurant; *Restaurant Viajero* on main road has rooms, G, good breakfast, clean, reasonable prices, and can arrange horses, US$1 per day, to go to Kuelap; *Hotalito Tingo*, G, friendly, basic, rec.; no electricity in Tingo. Sunday market.

A 3-4 hr. steep walk uphill (take waterproof, food and drink, and start early a.m.), leads to **Kuelap** (3,000 metres), a spectacular pre-Inca walled city. Its massive stone walls are as formidable as those of any precolumbian city. Some reconstruction has taken place, mostly of small houses and walls, but the majority of the main walls on both levels are original, as is the cone-shaped dungeon. There are a number of defensive walls and passageways, many houses, but virtually no carvings of any type. An interesting feature is that all the buildings are circular. Entrance fee is US$1.80 (the ruins are locked; the proprietor, Gabriel Portachero, has the keys and accompanies visitors, he's very informative). Kuelap is very remote: you are advised not to try to visit the site unless you have a week to spare: the roads are bad and the public transport spasmodic. The new road from Tingo to Kuelap is very circuitous (1½ hrs. by car from Tingo). A truck may be hired in Chachapoyas for the day; also donkeys can be hired for US$1 per day. If walking from Tingo, follow the path upstream on the right-hand side of the river and take the path to the right before the bridge, after ½ an hour there is a sign to Kuelap, the track is steep. In the rainy season it is advisable to wear boots; at other times it is hot and dry. After 2 hours the track passes a stream; purify this water if you need to drink it. After another hour you reach a cluster of houses. Red arrows mark the path. Soon the walls of Kuelap become visible at the top of the hill. The last house to the right of the track offers accommodation (bed US$0.20, good meals, friendly, helpful); a bit further on the left is an area of flat land outside the Project Kuelap office. At the archaeologists' research station you can hire cot and bedding for US$1 a night and leave luggage safely. There is also a camping area.

The whole area is full of largely unexplored remains; some of them have been studied by the Swiss archaeologists Henri and Paula Reichlen (who surveyed 39 sites in 1948—see *Récherches archaeologiques dans les Andes du haut Utcubamba*, in *Journal des Américanistes*, which includes an accurate map), and the American archaeologist Gene Savoy (who went further than the Reichlens-see his book *Antisuyo*); Kaufmann Doig refers to them as the "12 Cities of the Condors"; his map showing their location is in his *Arqueología Peruana*. See also the booklet on Kuelap, available at the Tourist Office in Chachapoyas, very informative.

Mark Babington and Morgan Davis write: Kuelap, discovered in 1843, was the last outpost of a lost white race, known variously as the Sachupoyans or the Chachas, who were in retreat from the advancing Inca around the years 1450-1470. Up till now Kuelap and La Congona were the only Sachupoyan ruins to have been explored in any detail whatsoever. The fact is that Kuelap was the final refuge of the Sachupoyans in a region which must have supported at least one million people before the arrival of the Inca. The known area inhabited by the Sachupoyans extends north from Leimebamba to Chachapoyas, and west as far as the Marañón.

  "In 1977 a team of three Americans explored the area between the Marañón and Utcubamba Rivers; they were the first to do so. They left an account of their journey in the American magazine *Outside*. Inspired by their account the two of us decided to retrace their steps. This is surely a region which overwhelms even Machu-Picchu in grandeur and mystery. It contains no less than five lost, and uncharted cities; the most impressive of which is Pueblo Alto, near the village of Pueblo Nuevo (25 km. from Kuelap). It was discovered some 60 years ago by the father of a local farmer, Juan Tuesta, with whom we stayed. By far the majority of these cities, fortresses and villages were never discovered by the Spaniard; in fact many had already returned to the jungle by the time the Spaniard arrived in 1532. The sites are situated in the tropical rain forest, and on the upper slopes of the *puna*. Furthermore many of them are to be found on or near the trails which today still provide the only medium of transport in this heavily populated and agricultural region. On a recent map of the area, with which we were provided in Chachapoyas, no less than 38 sites can be counted; but Ojilcho and Pueblo Alto, for example, are not charted on this new 1977 map in spite of their enormous dimensions. If all this sounds a bit exaggerated and inaccessible, we must add that the local farmers are conversant with the ruins, whether charted or not. It is among these people that one must look for information, provision and hospitality and, most important of all, guides and mules. The area, though well populated, provides virtually no facilities for the traveller. One should be cognizant of the difficulties ahead before attempting this journey, though this is not to say the trip is beyond the ability of most. Hiking gear is essential: sleeping bags, tents and canned goods (and a machete—Ed.). Small gifts are also much appreciated by the local people in return for their hospitality. (Take money in small notes as villagers do not have change for larger.) Water is no problem, unless it is the rainy season (Feb.-May). Travelling at this time is not advised as the mountain passes are shin-deep in mud.

  Oscar Arce Cáceres based at "El Chillo" 4½ km. outside Tingo, who owns a farm and knows the area very well, will help the traveller. The trek into this area, like the walk up to Kuelap, starts from Tingo; the way is all mule track. In Magdalena (a 15-minute walk from Tingo), Abram Torres will be happy to provide one with his services as guide, and his mule, for the first leg of the journey as far as Choctamal, about 4 hours away.

Levanto is 2 hrs by new road (*camioneta* at 0600-0700, no scheduled return) or 6 hrs. walk from Chachapoyas by the road, or 3½ hrs by mule track, ask in Chachapoyas market if anyone returning to Levanto will guide you for a small fee (it is also possible to walk from Tingo—see below). Levanto was the first Spanish capital of the area and the Spaniards built directly on top of the previous Sachupoyan structures. Although, not many years later, the capital was moved to Chachapoyas, Levanto still retained its importance, at least for a while, as it had been one of the seven great cities of the Sachupoyans as described by Cieza de León and Garcilaso de la Vega. The Kuelap East-West Highway starts at Levanto and links with the Inca military highway at Jalca Grande. Nowadays Levanto is a small, unspoilt, and very beautiful colonial village set on flat ground overlooking the massive canyon of the Utcubamba river. Kuelap can, on a clear day, be seen on the other side of the rift. Levanto is a good centre for exploring the many ruins around, being the centre of a network of ancient ruins, fortified redoubts, residential areas and many others.

Very close to Levanto are the ruins of **Yalape**, recently cleared under the supervision of Sr César Torres Rojas, a resident of Levanto. Yalape seems to have been a massive residential complex extending over many hectares and including many well-preserved examples of typical Sachupoyan architecture and masonry with quite elaborate and beautiful friezes. Its scale, like that of Kuelap, can be only described as titanic. In fact the whole area is covered in ruins, almost every prominent hilltop in the immediate vicinity has at least a watchtower of some sort.

To walk from Tingo to Levanto, head up to Magdalena, then down to the bridge at Cundechaca (1/2 hr); walk for 1 hr. on the main road to Teya until the end of the valley and the bend in the road from E to S; here look for the path which leads down into a small gorge, crosses the river and passes the little farm which is visible from the main road. From there it's a steep, 3-hr walk on the well-defined Inca road on a ridge between two gorges into Levanto. (You can add 2 1/2 hrs to this walk by starting at Kuelap—possible in a day.) As yet there is no official accommodation as such in Levanto, although plans are being made to build a small *alojamiento*. However, small groups of travellers are very welcome and beds and bedding are provided in the mayor's office and village meeting hall. Sr Torres Mas, in Chachapoyas, will put the traveller in touch with César Torres Rojas, in Levanto, with regard to all the above. César is entertaining and very friendly, as well as being the official guardian and archaeological supervisor of Levanto. There is one small shop and bar in the village (selling coffee and Pepsi, but little food). Using Levanto as a staging point, many beautiful and interesting walks can be done in the area. Taxi from Cachapoyas to Levanto and back, including driver waiting while you look around, US$20.

About 65 km. SW of Chachapoyas, the largest ruined complex yet discovered in South America, **Gran Vilaya**, was found in 1985 by Gene Savoy. There are 80 inter-connected city-type layouts, comprising some 24,000 structures. It faces the Río Marañón at 2,850 metres.

Another Sachupoyan site is **Cerro Olán**, reached by colectivo to San Pedro (near Tingo), then a 1/2-hr. walk; here are the remains of towers which some archaeologists claim had roofs like mediaeval European castles.

40 km. from Chachapoyas are the pre-Inca ruins of **Monte Peruvia** (known locally as Purunllacta), hundreds of white stone houses with staircases, temples and palaces (2 hrs. from the town of Lamud). Colectivos leave Lamud for Chachapoyas at 0600, returning around 1200, 2 hrs. One hotel in Lamud, *Kuelap*, G. Nearby, in Luya, are the Pueblos de los Muertos of the same culture, with fantastic burial figures high on a cliff (daily bus from Chachapoyas). "8 km. from Monte Peruvia is Puente de Conica, where you can see precolumbian burial figures in niches on the cliffside, known as the Purumachus de Aispachaca" (John Streather).

From Chachapoyas the next stretch of the road is 2-3 hrs. through more of the beautiful river canyon (US$.20, pick-up truck, about 0830, or when full) to a small crossroads, **Pedro Ruiz**, where you continue on to Yurimaguas or return to the coast. Plenty of trucks in Pedro Ruiz go to the Selva and to Chiclayo (via Bagua not Celendín). There is basic accommodation (*Hostal Marginal* with good, cheap restaurant, and one other, both F), but advisable to stay the night if you arrive late as most trucks to Rioja leave at 0500-0700. Pedro Ruiz to Rioja is about 14 hrs., US$5, on an appalling piece of road; in the rainy season, this and the continuation to Moyobamba and Tarapoto can be very bad.

An hour before Rioja on this road is the new town of Nueva Catamarca (a few thousand inhabitants, *Hotels Puerto Rico*, on main road, and *Perú*, off to the right towards Rioja). There is a large market for local produce. Hourly colectivo to Rioja, US$0.80, 45 mins; colectivo to Chachapoyas US$10, 10-12 hrs.

From **Rioja** (an attractive, friendly town, 3 hotels, *Hostal San Martín*, Gran 540, *San Ramón*, Jr. Faustino Maldonado 840 and *Carranza*, Jr. Huallanga, all basic, and *Restaurante Los Olivos* rec.) there is a road to Naranjillo and Aguas Verdes, with a 5-hr. walk to Venceremos, a pleasant way to see the jungle in good weather (don't attempt otherwise). An excursion can made to the Cueva de los Huácharos, unexplored caves, take a torch; by truck to La Unión (45 mins.), walk 40 mins. to Palestina then 50 mins. more to the caves, ask locals for directions.

A road with plenty of transport (about ½ hr.) runs to **Moyobamba**, capital of San Martín district (ruins of Pueblo de los Muertos nearby) (915 metres, 14,000 people). Tourists must register with the P.I.P; tourist office on plaza. Moyobamba is a pleasant town, in an attractive valley. Mosquito nets can be bought cheaply.

Hotels *Turistas*, D with breakfast, 1 km. from centre, fine situation, pool, good restaurant; *Hostal Inca*, E with bath, new, clean, good but noisy; *Hostal Cobos*, F with bath, good; *Hostal Country Club*, F, clean, comfortable, friendly, nice garden, rec.; *Hostal Los Andes*, F, clean; *Monterrey* and *Mesía*, both basic and cheap. **Restaurants** *El Sol del Norte*, good and cheap; several others.

Exchange Viajes Turismo Río Mayo, Jr. San Martin 401.

Flights AeroPerú flights from Lima to Chiclayo stop at Rioja (Wed. and Sun.).

Excursions Puerto Tahuiso in the town's harbour, where locals sell their produce at weekends. From Morro de Calzada, there is a good view of the area; truck to Calzada, 30 mins, then walk up, 20 mins. Baños Termales (4 km. from Moyobamba on Rioja road), worth a visit. The more adventurous can hike to the Jera waterfalls in the jungle near Moyobamba. Take a truck in the direction of Tarapoto; alight at the restaurant at km. 218. Take a good path through a well-populated valley (cross 2 bridges), then along the river, through dense jungle, with 3 more river crossings (no bridges—dangerous). A local guide is necessary to find the falls. Information is available from the Instituto Nacional de Cultura, Jr. Benavides, 3rd block. Guides: Emigdio Soto, an expert on trips to native communities in the Alto Mayo area, contact him at the Projecto Especial Alto Mayo; Orlando Peigot Daza, for jungle trips (no English), at Yurayacu village. There have been guerrilla and drug activities in this region; take good care.

The road is paved for a short way out of Moyobamba, then deteriorates to **Tarapoto** (colectivo from Moyobamba, 3½ hrs., US$7.50, truck, 5 hrs., US$5), is a busy town with several hotels. Good local market 1½ blocks from Plaza de Armas on Av. Raimondi. The journey from Rioja to Tarapoto costs about US$5.75 and it is best to carry food because of endless delays and road problems. A through bus service (Chinchaysuyo) runs to Chiclayo, via Moyobamba, Rioja, Bagua and Olmos; and same company runs to Trujillo, US$11, at least 36 hrs. Rioja, Moyobamba and Tarapoto are growing centres of population, which much small-scale forest clearance beside the road after Balsapata. The road is heavily used by trucks, with fuel and meals available. When/if the road is improved, the area will surely boom. Until then, food and accommodation will remain expensive.

Hotels *Turistas* (D, with bath, excellent meals US$3.50) 1 km. out of town, non-residents can use the swimming pool for US$1; *Tarapoto*, E with fan, clean; *Las Palmeras*, just off Plaza, F; *San José*, 4 blocks from Plaza, clean and friendly, restaurant; *Juan Alfonso*, F, with shower, noisy, Jr. Pedro de Urzúa. *Hostal Residencial Grau*, Plaza de Armas, G, communal, cheap (in both senses of the word), shower. *Edinson*, Av. Raimondi, 1 block from Plaza de Armas, E with bath (less without), cold water, clean and comfortable; *Hostal Americano*, F, fan and private bath with each room. *El Sereno*, E with shower, clean. Plenty of others.

Restaurants *Río de Janeiro*, *Sadel*, *Tiveli*, *Chalet Venecia*, *La Pascana* and *Achín* good; *Heladería Tip Top* and *Cream Rica* for ices. *Las Terrazas*, good, rec. Many others. Coconut water is recommended as coconuts abundant. Jirón Gregorio Delgado 268 sells excellent liquor at US$0.50 a glass (uvachado and siete raices).

Exchange Banco de Crédito, Maynas 134, efficient, no commission on travellers' cheques.

Tourist Office Foptur, Gregorio Delgado 240, T 2753.

Air Transport US$1.75 per taxi airport to town (no bus service, but no problem to walk). Flights by Faucett and AeroPerú to Lima (US$50, 50 mins.), Iquitos, Juanjui and Yurimaguas, but book in advance, particularly in rainy season. Those visiting Tarapoto and Iquitos would be advised to visit Tarapoto first, as aircraft leaving Iquitos tend to overfly Tarapoto; possible to be stuck there for days. AeroPerú flies to Tarapoto from Lima, Iquitos, Chiclayo, Trujillo, Juanjui and Yurimaguas. Faucett has similar routes, and daily flights to and from Trujillo and

Chiclayo. Many smaller airlines operate flights to Yurimaguas e.g. Aerotaxi Ibérico: turn up at airport at 0700-0800, wait for it to open, wait for people to turn up, wait for a list for your destination to be drawn up and you should get away later in the morning, US$17.50 to Yurimaguas, 50 min. flight (US$6 with Grupo Ocho—Air Force).

Excursions La Mina de Sal, salt mine outside the city; Laguna Sauce, 3 hrs. by truck; Laguna Venecia.

Between Tarapoto and Moyobamba a road leads off to **Lamas** (colectivo from Tarapoto, US$1.20, 35 km.), where there is a picturesque Indian community completely unspoilt by tourism; also a small museum, with exhibits on local Indian community (Lamistas), ask at the café opposite if museum shut, and a new restaurant en route, *El Mirador*, recently opened by Tom, an American, and his Peruvian wife. Market in the early morning. Interesting journey also from Tarapoto to Tingo María (**see page** 989), not advisable in the rainy season. From Tarapoto to Yurimaguas (136 km.) (**see page** 990), the road can be very bad in the wet season, taking at least 13 hrs. for trucks (at 0800 or earlier, US$6), also colectivos, US$8. There is also a daily bus (10 hrs.). Truck/pick-up leaves for Yurimaguas (usually 0800-0900, and in p.m.) from Jorge Chávez 175, down Av. Raimondi 2 blocks, then left 5 blocks along Av. Pedro de Uruaz (pick-ups from this street to other destinations). About 14 km. from Tarapoto on this road are the 50-metre falls of Ahuashiyacu, which can be visited by tour from Tarapoto (US$12 incl. lunch) or by hiring motorcycle from Grand Prix, corner Shopajo and Raimondi, US$2.50 an hour. A restaurant nearby serves reasonable food and has 2 rooms to rent (G p.p., basic but OK). The road continues for 10 km. through lush vegetation to a small village (with restaurant). Once the plains are reached, the road improves and there is more habitation. 55 km. from Tarapoto is the village of El Pongo (2 restaurants, electricity, no hotel). At km. 40, 96 km. from Tarapoto (US$6, 7 hrs.) there is a bridge over the Shanusi river and the small village of Shanusi. It is possible to leave your truck here and take a boat ride down the river, meeting the Huallaga at Yurimaguas. There is no accommodation at Shanusi, take a hammock, and no electricity. Canoe leaves daily at about 0600 for Yurimaguas, US$1.75, 4½ hrs., plenty of birdlife and river traffic to be seen. From Yurimaguas on the Huallaga River, launches ply to Iquitos.

Pacific Coast North of Trujillo

When Spanish conquistadores first encountered the broad, north Peruvian coastal valley oases, they marvelled at the creativity and sophistication of these desert farmers and fishermen. Early 16th century accounts describe enormous precolumbian settlements and sacred places, now impressive monumental ruins.

Today the rural population has its centre at Chiclayo, the bustling city and capital of the department of Lambayeque, a melting pot of ancient and modern traditions and tastes. Recent archaeological discoveries nearby have attracted tourists and scientists to northern Peru, which is also blessed with a balmy, rainfree climate the year round.

Ruins of a splendid past are not the only treasures Lambayeque offers. Today's rural peasantry are also inheritors of many of the customs and technologies of their Moche forebears, who were master craftsmen in many fields. Artisan markets, primitive ocean going vessels, folk curing sessions and colourful religious "fiestas" enliven any visitor's stay. In addition, the north sports Peru's finest beaches for bathing and surfing, again all year round.

Sandwiched between the Pacific Ocean and the Andes, Lambayeque is one of Peru's principal agricultural areas, and its chief producer of rice and sugar cane. Even so, archaeological studies indicate that prehispanic people here cultivated some 25% more land than farmers today; the extensive irrigation canals and reservoirs of north Peru constitute one of the major technological achievements of ancient America.

N from Trujillo are three ports serving the Chiclayo area. The more southerly is **Etén**, an open roadstead 21 km. by road from Chiclayo; Panama hats are local industry; festival of the Divine Child of the Miracle, 2-17 June. **Pimentel**, N of Etén, is larger, a favourite summer bathing place, with a broad sandy beach (very crowded on Sundays). The surfing between Pimentel and the Bayover Peninsula is excellent. Reached from Chiclayo (14½ km.) by road branching off from the Pan-American Highway. Sea-going balsa rafts (*caballitos de totora*) are used by fishermen and may be seen here and at Santa Rosa. Also worth seeing is **Santa Rosa**, situated between the two groups of totora reed boats (*caballitos*) and *bolicheros* (pastel-painted boats which line the shore after the day's fishing)—a pleasant, 1-hr walk from Pimentel. Small hotel, *Perú*, restaurant *Bello Horizonte*. The seafood is superb: two specialities are *tortilla de rayo* (manta ray) and *chingurito*, a ceviche of little strips of dried guitar fish (chewy, but good). The 3 ports may be visited on a pleasant ½ day trip. A red bus leaves Chiclayo market place every ½ hr. for Pimentel and Santa Rosa. Colectivos run frequently from Pimentel to Santa Rosa, and on to Etén and back to Chiclayo (10 mins. from Santa Rosa, 15 mins. from Pimentel). To avoid paying excess luggage charges for weight above 15 kg, buy ticket in advance, and catch bus outside terminal (no scales!).

Chiclayo was founded in the 1560s as a rural Indian village by Spanish priests. It now has a population of over 260,000 and has long since outgrown other towns of the Lambayeque Department, of which it is the capital. A major commercial hub, Chiclayo also boasts distinctive cuisine and musical tradition (*marinera*, *tondero* and afro-indian rhythms), and an unparalleled archaeological and ethnographic heritage (see **Excursions**). A walking tour in the centre reveals the mixture of creole, Spanish and Indian architecture along curving, narrow streets, once precolombian canals now filled and paved with cobble stones.

On the Plaza de Armas is the 19th century neoclassical cathedral, designed by the English architect Townsend, whose descendants can still be identified among the town's principals. The Palacio Municipal (Municipal Palace) and private Club Unión line Balta street, the major avenue. Continue five blocks north on Balta to the Mercado Modelo, one of northern Peru's liveliest and largest daily markets. Don't miss the colourful fruits (including enormous 2lb avocados), handicrafts stalls (see "*Monsefú*") and the well-organized section (off Calle Arica) of ritual paraphernalia used by traditional curers and diviners (*curanderos*). James Vreeland, an American anthropologist living in Chiclayo, considers the Chiclayo *mercado de brujos* (witch doctors' market) to be one of the most comprehensive in South America, filled with herbal medicines, folk charms, curing potions, and exotic objects used by *curanderos* and *brujos* to cure all manner of real and imagined illnesses. (Note: As in all markets, don't let your enthusiasm cloud your common sense; take good care of your belongings.)

Hotels *Turistas*, Villareal 135, D, with bath; E, without, meals included, helpful, but service can be wanting, some distance from business centre, but there is much traffic noise, swimming pool often empty, safe car park; *Garza*, Bolognesi 756, nr. Balta, owned by beer company of same name, with bath, hot water, takes credit cards, convenient, excellent restaurant, *El Cazador*, highly rec, swimming pool, car park, tourist office in lobby provides maps, information in English, Land Rovers, jeeps and minibuses for hire; *Obby*, Francisco Cabrera 102, T 231074, Fax 51-074-229282, E-D, good value, English spoken, rec; *Costa de Oro*, Balta 399, E, central, poor, but good restaurant *Ebony* downstairs; *Inca*, L. González 662, E with bath, clean, new and good; *Paraíso*, Pedro Ruiz 1064, near market, good value, E; *Oriental*, Arica 825, nr. market, good Chinese-style food downstairs; *Sol Radiante*, Izaga 392, central, small, comfortable, no restaurant, but friendly owner will provide breakfast; *Royal*, Plaza de Armas, F, cheaper without bath, old, clean, poor beds, smelly toilets, basic, restaurant downstairs is good value; *Miami Beach*, Tte. Pinglo 169, popular, but fading; *Hostal San Ramón*, Héroes Civiles, F, friendly, clean, comfortable, restaurant, car park; *Europa*, Elías Aguirre, F with or without bath, good value, clean, friendly, restaurant, some hot water; *Lido*, on same street, F with bath, clean; *Leguia*, Leguia 105, G p.p., very clean, a bit noisy. Several cheap hotels on Calle Balta, near bus offices. Some hotels prohibit clothes-washing in rooms because of the high cost of water.

Restaurants *Fiestas*, Av. Salaverry 1820 in Ocho de Octubre suburb, local specialities, first class, not cheap, but worth it; *Le París*, M.M. Izaga 716, excellent, international and creole food, very expensive. First-class and very reasonable food (usually good breakfast—watch

INDIANA TOURS
a cultural tour operator in northern Perú

TOURS   Archaeological, ethnographic, ecological, arts, crafts and special interest tours with professional, bi-lingual guides, pre-Columbian canals and highways, shamanism and mysticism

SIPAN - TUCUME - BRÜNING MUSEUM - KUELAP

ADVENTURE	Desert, mountains, jungle, beaches and exploration
SPORTS	Surfing, hiking, camping, horse-back riding
INFORMATION	Maps, books, post cards and travel consultation
VEHICLE RENTALS	Car, jeep, microbus and bus, with experienced drivers
CRAFTS	Fine hand-made artisan products, natural fibers with traditional and pre- Columbian techniques, including weaving, ikat, pottery, gourds, silkscreen prints, silver and gold jewelry

INDIANA TOURS

Main office	M.M. Izaga 774, Chiclayo
	Perú tel. 24-0833
Counters	*Regional airport, Chiclayo
	*Garza Hotel, Bolognesi 756
	*Tourist Hotel, Villareal 115
	*Sipan Hotel, L. Gonzales 241
Postal address	Apartado 596, Chiclayo - Perú
Communications	tel (51-74)24-0833
	tel / fax (51-74)240833
	telex 42003 pe-pb

prices of drinks, though) at *Roma,* Balta 512, popular with locals; *Bristol* on Balta, good and cheap, with a *comedor municipal* next door to *Ebony,* also *El Tauro,* reasonable prices, and *Cruz de Chalpón* (good breakfasts) on same street; *Imperial,* and others on Balta, choose according to outward cleanliness; *Che Claudio,* Bolognesi, parrillada with reasonable empanadas and house wine; *Snack Bar Elias,* Aguirre 830, just off Central Pláza, small, efficient, quite clean, good apple pie, lomo sandwiches and sweets at reasonable prices; *Chifa Cantonés,* Juan Cuglievan 470, wide variety of traditional chifa/Chinese food, dining room on 2nd floor; *Fuente de Oro,* Cabrera 1213, excellent seafood at reasonable prices: *Men-Wha,* 5th block of Pedro Ruiz, delicious, large helpings, Chinese.

Local Food and Drink Ceviche and chingurito (see above); *cabrito,* spiced stew of kid goat; *arroz con pato,* paella-like duck casserole; *humitas, tamale-*like fritters of green corn; *King Kong,* baked pastry layered with candied fruit and milk caramel; *chicha,* fermented maize drink with delicious fruit variations.

Folklore Peñas at *Brisas del Mar,* Elías Aguirre; *Los Hermanos Balcázar,* Lora y Cordero 1150; *El Embrujo,* Vicente de la Vega.

Exchange Change travellers' cheques at Banco del Norte. Be prepared to wait. The travel agency next to *Hotel Royal* will change cash or cheques at reasonable rates out of banking hours. Several street changers on 600 block of Balta and on Plaza de Armas.

Post Office on Aguirre, 6 blocks from Plaza.

Doctor Dr José Gálvez, Clínica de la Concepción, Av. Santa Victoria, rec. as good general medical practitioner.

Tourist Office Foptur, San José 867, oficina 201, helpful. Touring y Automóvil Club de Perú, Huancavelica 280, of. 406.

Travel Agent Indiana Tours, M.M. Izaga 774, T 240833, highly rec. for trips to Sipán, Thor Heyerdahl's Kon Tiki museum in Túcume, Brüning Museum in Lambayaque and a variety of other excursions; very knowledgeable about the archaeology of the region.

Air Service Coronel Ruiz airport 2 km. from town. Daily Faucett (a.m.) and AeroPerú (p.m.) jet flights from Lima, US$140 return; flights to Rioja (Aero Perú, Weds., and Sat., 1000 via Chachapoyas) Tarapoto, and to Iquitos and intermediate stops. AeroPerú flies to Chachapoyas Mon., Wed., Fri (30 mins. compared with 24 hrs by bus).

Buses and Colectivos To Lima, Nor Pacífico, 2100, US$10 (most companies leave from 1600 onwards). To Trujillo, Empresa Emtrafesa on Av. Balta, 6 blocks from plaza, leaves hourly from 0530 until 1430, then 6 between 1500 and 2000, US$2, 3 hrs. Bus to Piura, US$3, 3½ hrs., about 20 a day. *Micros* to Lambayeque leave from 200 block of San José, US$0.10, frequent. Direct bus to Cajamarca, Empresa Díaz, 1200 (old buses, frequent breakdowns) and El Cumbre (much better), US$5, several daily. To Chachapoyas, D. Olano company (Vicente de la Vega 101, T 236310), US$15, 1300, except Sun., 18-25 hrs. depending on breakdowns; goes via Olmos and Jaén (see below), thereafter road is appalling to Pedro Ruiz, then O.K. to Chachapoyas. To Tarapoto, Chinchay-Suyo runs via Olmos, Bagua, Rioja (US$14.50) and Moyobamba. Bus to Huancabamba leaves Tues. and Fri., 1500, arrives 0530 next day, US$7.75 (Civa and Tepsa office, Balta 114b)—very rough ride, impossible to sleep. Tepsa to Tumbes, 0100 daily, US$5, 9½ hrs.; also Continental (Ormeño), Roggero (1930), Olano (rec.), and others (Nor Pacífico not rec.), all night buses US$6, 12 hrs., some continue to Aguas Verdes, on the border. Trucks going in all directions leave from Calle Pedro Ruiz 948 and from the market.

Local Festivals Some of the towns mentioned here are described in **Excursions** below: 6 January, Reyes Magos in Mórrope, Monsefú and other towns, a recreation of a medieval pageant in which precolumbian deities become the Wise Men; 4 February, Túcume devil dances; Holy Week, traditional Easter celebrations and processions in many villages; 27-31 July, Fexticum in Monsefú, traditional foods, drink, handicrafts, music and dance; 5 August, pilgrimage from the mountain shrine of Chalpon to Montupe, 90 km. N of Chiclayo, the cross is brought down from a cave and carried in procession through the village; 24 September, Virgen de los Mercedes in Incahuasi, 12 hrs. by truck E of Chiclayo (Indians still sing in the ancient Mochica language in this post-harvest festival); Christmas and New Year, processions and children dancers (*pastorcitos* and *seranitas*) in many villages, e.g. Ferreñafe, Mochumi, Mórrope.

Excursions A short distance from Chiclayo rises the imposing twin pyramid complex of **Sipán**, where excavations have brought to light a cache of funerary objects considered to rank among the finest examples of precolumbian art. Peruvian archaeologist Walter Alva, leader of the dig, continues to probe the immense mound that has revealed no less than five royal tombs filled with 2,000-year-old offerings worked in precious metals, stone, pottery and textiles of the Moche culture. In the most extravagant Moche tomb discovered, El Señor de Sipán, a priest was found clad in gold (ear ornaments, breast plate, etc.), with turquoise and other valuables. The find is currently being studied in West Germany and is due back at the Brüning Museum in Lambayeque in 1992. In another tomb were found a priest, aides, llama and a dog, together with bronze decorations. The excavations are being sponsored by the National Geographic Magazine, but are closed to the public. You can wander around the previously excavated areas to get an idea of the construction of the pyramids. For a good view, climb the large pyramid across from the Sipán excavation. Part of the same complex is the Huaca Rajada. Nearby is the Pampagrande site.

The colonial town of Ferreñafe, NE of Chiclayo, is worth a visit, as are the traditional Indian towns of Mórrope, on the new Pan-American Highway N of Chiclayo, where pottery and textiles are made, Monsefú, SW, also for handicrafts, and Etén (see above). 51 km. S are the ruins of the town of Saña, destroyed by floods in 1726; 5 colonial churches can be seen.

A minor road runs to **Chongoyape** (bus from Chiclayo, US$0.85, 1½ hrs., leaves from Leticia, just off Balta on N. of Plaza de Armas; hotel, F, near Plaza de Armas, without restaurant; *Restaurant Cascada*, main street, limited menu), a quaint old town 60 km. to the E (3 km. west are the Chavín petroglyphs of Cerro Mulato). Nearby are the vast Taymi precolumbian and modern irrigation systems. Also near Chongoyape are the aqueduct of Racarrumi, the hill fort of Mal Paso and the ruins of Maguín. **Batán Grande**, a site 50 km. from Chiclayo consisting of nearly fifty adobe pyramids where many precolumbian gold artefacts, notably the 915-gram Tumi, were found, is reached by a branch turning left off the Chongoyape road after Tumán, about 30 km. from Chiclayo (colectivos, US$1.20, from Pedro Ruiz—12th block—and Juan Cuglievan, go first to the museum in Lambayeque and get an "order" from the director, Dr Alva, before visiting, then to the *algarobina* cooperative (in which the ruins are set) from where you must get permission to visit the site, Mon.-Fri. only; directions hard to come by at the cooperative, seek sound advice before you go). The road goes to **Chota**, an attractive town with a fine Sunday market (several hotels, F, *Plaza* the best, clean; *Continental*, poor; *Hostal Elisabeth*, on plaza, cheap rooms with balcony, dirty bathrooms. *Restaurant San Juan*, good) where weavings are cheaper than in Cajamarca: cheap, friendly shops at 27 de Noviembre 144 and 246. Daily bus to Chiclayo a.m., 12-14 hrs.; bus to Cajamarca Wed., Fri., 9-10 hrs., return Tues. and Thurs. Occasionally buses, and many trucks, run on to **Bambamarca** (*Hotel Bolívar*, best; *Hotel Velásquez*, G, *Hotel Perú* has bugs; *Restaurant Pollos a la Brasa*, very good) which has an attractive Sunday morning market (truck from Chota US$1; Empresa Díaz to Cajamarca daily at 0600, 9 hrs., frequent stops, US$4, on Sun, there is a 2 hr. stop in Bambamarca for the market, some days also with Peregrino). Two buses a day pass through Chongoyape to Chota, 8 hrs., US$4. From there it goes on to **Hualgayoc** (a beautifully unspoilt, quaint old mining town) and Cajamarca; a very interesting and beautiful journey, but few buses. The stretch from Bambamarca, about 90 km., to Cajamarca is exhilarating; the road climbs to about 4,000 metres through the Andean highlands with beautiful scenery of a *puna* landscape, nearly uninhabited, no fuel supply; it takes about 6 hrs. in a 4-wheel drive car. The whole trip between Chongoyape and Cajamarca takes about 2 days in a car, the road is particularly bad between Chongoyape and Chota, max. speed 25 kph. The Chiclayo—Chota bus passes through Cochabamba (no hotels, not a friendly place, police searches for drugs), 34 km. from Chota, from where you can hitch in a truck to **Cutervo**, a town of 6,000 people at 2,800 metres in green meadows. Cattle and vegetables are raised here. Hotels: *San Juan* on plaza, cheap but has bugs; nicer one by Ciné San Juan, several more. Restaurants: *Salón Azul*, very good; *Central*, very dirty. A very friendly town which tourists rarely visit—don't be surprised if the local radio station wants an interview. Many trucks to Cutervo, Tues.-Sat., return Mon.-Fri., bus from Chiclayo Sat., returns Sun. 2000. Local market Thurs. and Sun.

Ten km. to the N of Chiclayo is **Lambayeque**, population 20,700, worth a visit. The narrow streets are lined by adobe houses, many retaining their distinctive wooden balconies and wrought iron grill-work over the windows. The town has an old church and early Spanish colonial chapels. Its most interesting feature is the well-known, recommended Brüning Museum, relocated in an impressive modern building. It specializes in Cupisnique, Lambayeque and Vicus cultures, has a fine collection of Mochica and Chimú ceramics, household implements, and gold artefacts. The magnificent treasure from the tomb of a Moche warrior priest, found at Sipán in 1987, has also been displayed here (see above), open 0830-1245 and 1500-1730 on weekdays, 0900-1300, Sat., Sun. and holidays. Admission, US$0.60. A hotel is soon to be opened. Try the famous Alfajor King-Kong (a sweet).

The old Pan-American Highway to Piura (which skirts the Eastern edge of the Sechura desert) passes two major precolumbian sites, within easy reach of Chiclayo. About 45 km. north of Chiclayo lies the archaeological site of **Túcume**, ruins of a vast city built over a thousand years ago. A short climb to a hillside "mirador" offers the visitor an unparallelled panoramic vista of 26 major pyramids, platform mounds, walled citadels and residential compounds flanking a ceremonial centre and ancient cemeteries. Excavations in the heart of this fascinating site, led by Norwegian explorer-archaeologist, Thor Heayerdahl of *Kon-Tiki* fame, are quickly challenging many conventional views of ancient Peruvian culture.

Some suspect that it will prove to be a civilization centre greater than Chan Chan. There is also evidence that the people of Túcume were intrepid seafarers. A 10-year excavation project is under way; visitors are welcome, but are asked to go in the afternoon only, leaving the morning free for uninterrupted excavation. Colectivos go from Chiclayo, Pedro Ruiz y Luis González, or Manuel Prado y L. González; walk from the town to the ruins. Alternatively, contact Indiana Tours. At Apurlec, 60 km. N, is stone wall surrounding hill and pyramids dating from Tiahuanaco period, as well as irrigation canals and reservoirs; the system was enlarged during Mochica, Chimú and Inca occupation of the site.

Branching off the old Pan-American Highway at **Olmos** (885 km. from Lima, a tranquil place—*Hospedaje San Martín*, G, very dirty, bargain hard; a better place exists) is a poor road (being improved) which runs eastwards over the Porciulla Pass (2,150 metres); at km. 257 is a restaurant, but there are better ones at Jaén and Bagua Chica. A road branching from Chamaya, N of Hualgayoc, leads to the towns of Jaén and Bellavista. N of Chamaya, travelling via Aramongo and Oracuza, one finds a symmetrical hill of niche tombs.

Jaén (population: 3,600), an old settlement, has recently been revived as a rice-growing centre. The annual festival of the patron saint, Our Lord of Huamantanga, is on 14 September. Hotels at Jaén: *Danubio*; *Hostal Lima*, not rec. A road has been built N from Jaén to San Ignacio (114 km.), near the frontier of Ecuador. It crosses the valley of the Chinchipe, renowned for its lost Inca gold. San Ignacio has a *fiesta* on August 31. Another branch road from Jaén has been built SE to Chachapoyas, 263 km. from Olmos (see page 906), and has now been completed another 359 km. to Yurimaguas, on the Huallaga River (see page 990). A road also goes to Aramongo (280 km.), on the Marañón; it has been extended to Nazareth. From Nazareth two roads branch: one to Oracuza, via Puente Huabico and Puerto Delfus, and the other to **Sarameriza**, the most westerly point on the Marañon with a regular boat connection to Iquitos—it is 1 hr. downstream from Puerto Delfus. To reach Sarameriza, take a bus to Bagua (see page 906) from Chachapoyas or Chiclayo, US$5.50, 12-15 hrs., from where pick-ups run twice daily to Imasa. Get out at Campamento Mesones Muro, 15 mins. before Imasa (US$2.55, 7 hrs.), where you must register with the police (this can take time). For 150 km. from Mesones Muro to Sarameriza, you must wait for a pick-up (one should be along in 3-6 days) and then be prepared for a 2-3 day journey because of poor roads and missing bridges. The m/n *Fernández* makes the journey from Sarameriza to Iquitos every second week: downstream US$26 (inc. meals), 4 days, only a few cabins (US$2.50 extra), so take a hammock; upstream, US$30, 6 days. If you can't wait for the boat, it is possible with local help to make a raft and sail downstream, camping at night, until the *Fernández* catches you up (Peter Legaard Nielsen and Niels Pedersen, Copenhagen).

At Lambayeque the new Pan-American Highway branches off the old road and drives 190 km. straight across the desert to Piura. There are a few restaurants along its length. There is also a coast road, narrow and scenic, between

Lambayeque and Sechura via Bayovar.

A large area of shifting sands—the Sechura Desert—separates the oasis of Chiclayo from that of Piura. Water for irrigation comes from the Chira and Piura rivers, and from the Olmos and Tinajones irrigation projects which bring water from the Amazon watershed by means of tunnels (one over 16 km. long) through the Andes to the Pacific coast. They will eventually water some 400,000 hectares of desert land. The northern river—the Chira—has usually a superabundance of water: along its irrigated banks large crops of Tangüis cotton are grown. A dam has now been built at Poechos on the Chira river, to divert water to the Piura valley. In its upper course the Piura—whose flow is far less dependable—is mostly used to grow subsistence food crops, but around Piura, when there is enough water, the hardy long-staple Pima cotton is planted. In 1983 the Niño current brought heavy rains and turned the Sechura desert into an inland sea. Damage to crops, roads, bridges and buildings was estimated at around US$1bn.

Piura, an oasis in the parched desert, is a proud and historic city, 264 km. from Chiclayo. Population, 1,125,800. Founded in 1532, three years before Lima, by the *conquistadores* left behind by Pizarro (whose statue is in the Parque Pizarro). There are two well kept parks, Cortés and Pizarro, and public gardens. Old buildings are kept in repair and new buildings blend with the Spanish style of the old city. Three bridges cross the Río Piura, the oldest from Calle Huancavelica, for pedestrians, the second oldest from Calle Sánchez Cerro, and the newest from Calle Bolognesi, used by most traffic. Its special dish is the delicious *natillas*, made mostly of goats milk and molasses; its local drink is *pipa fría*, chilled coconut juice drunk from the nut with a straw. The winter climate, May-September, is very pleasant although nights can be cold and the wind piercing; December to March is very hot.

A few blocks from the Plaza de Armas, where the cathedral stands (gold covered altar, paintings by Ignacio Merino), is the San Francisco church, where the city's independence from Spain was declared on January 4, 1821, nearly 8 months before Lima. The colonial church of Las Mercedes has ornately carved balconies, three-tiered archway, hand-hewn supports and massive furnishings. San Sebastián, on Tacna y Moquegua, is also worth seeing. Birthplace of Admiral Miguel Grau, hero of the War of the Pacific with Chile, whose house Casa Museo Grau, on Jirón Tacna opposite the Centro Cívico, has been opened as a museum; it contains a model of the *Huáscar*, the largest Peruvian warship in the War of the Pacific, which was built in Britain. Interesting local craftwork is sold at the Model Market. Museo Complejo Cultural, with archaeological and art sections, is open on Huánuco, between Loreto and Sullana, 1 block from bus station.

Cotton has been grown mainly on medium-sized properties, which have changed hands frequently in recent years and which now form communal or co-operative farms, sponsored by the agrarian reform programme. Worth seeing as an example of a fine old plantation is the former Hacienda Sojo, in the lower Chira valley, which was the centre of the properties of the Checa family.

Hotels *Turistas*, D, faulty air conditioning, food and service poor, the city's social centre, swimming pool being added, facing Plaza de Armas. *Cristina*, Jr. Loreto between Plaza Grau and Jr. Ica, one block from Plaza, E, pleasant; *Hostal Esmeraldas*, opp. colectivo stop on Loreto, good rooms, E; *Perú*, clean, reasonably priced, E, rec; *Hostal Las Palmeras*, Jirón Loreto, E with bath, fan, clean, highly rec., English owner; *San Jorge*, F with bath, clean and good value, Jr. Loreto, 3 blocks from Plaza Grau, rec.; *La Terraza*, Av Loreto, 2 blocks from Grau monument, F with bath, G without, hot water, clean, fan or a/c, small rooms; *Hispaniola* on Ica, F, is similar; *Hostal Ica*, Ica, G, very cheap; *Tambo*, E, good, clean; *Continental*, Jr Junín 924, F without bath, clean; *California*, same street, same category, clean, pleasant; *Palermo*, F, with bath, clean, rec.; *Bolognesi*, E with private bath, near Roggero bus terminal, good. On Pan-American Highway are *El Sol*, Sánchez Cerro 411, E, bath, snack bar, will change travellers' cheques at official rate; *Vicus*, D, with bath, quiet, restaurant poor. *Oriental*, F without bath, E with, clean but very noisy, with TV in reception, Jr. Callao. Over the river in Castillo, *Tacna*, G p.p., modern, and *Atenas*, G p.p., dirty, bargain for cheap price. Cheaper *hostales* behind *Las Palmeras*, e.g. *Amanta*, Apurímac y Cuzco, F, clean; also cheap, *Lalo* and *Hispano*, both G. It is extremely difficult to find a room in the last week of July because of independence festivities. The city suffers from water shortages and there are reports that no hotel has hot water.

Restaurants and Night Clubs *Tiburón*, 2 km. out of Piura on Panamericana Sur. *Ganso Azul*, a group of steak houses just out of town, rec. (but not a safe area at night). In town: *Puente Viejo*, Huancavelica 167, T 32-1030 (close to *Hotel Turistas*), excellent seafood, reasonable, rec; *Carburmer*, in Centro Comercial, very good but not cheap. *Las Tradiciones*, Ayacucho 579, high quality, reasonable prices, good service; *La Taverna*, Av. Loreto between Av. Grau and Jr. Ica, excellent for fish; *Ferny's*, next to *Hotel San Jorge*, good food, clean, on Loreto; *La Cabaña* serves pizzas and other good food; *Café Concierto*, Cuzco 933, pleasant, popular, not cheap; *Las Redes*, Apurímac between Tacna y Libertad, pizzas, good atmosphere; *Brasil*, Huancavelica y Junín, good for breakfast and lunch, US$2; *Snack Bar*, Callao 536, good fruit juices. Good little cheap restaurants on Jirón Junín: *Chalán del Norte* at 722, *Bianca* at 732, *El Capri* at 715. A good ice cream shop is *Venezia*, Libertad y Apurímac. *La Huerta*, Libertad 801 on corner of Plaza de Armas, sells 19 fresh juices, quesillo con miel (cream cheese and honey) and natillas.

Shopping Fuji film readily available. Good delicatessens around main square, selling local sweets; *natilla* factory on Sánchez cerro, Miraflores, 4 blocks from bridge, sells *natilla* and *algorrobina* fruit drink. Market on Sánchez Cero, good for fruit.

Exchange Banco de Crédito recommended, changes travellers' cheques, open 0900 but exchange from 1000. Banco Continental, Plaza de Armas, changes travellers' cheques with commission.

Honorary British Consul Casilla 193, T (074) 323532.

Post Office on Plaza de Armas, very helpful.

Tourist Offices Foptur, Ayacucho 377, Plaza de Armas, next to Municipalidad, T 333720, has city maps and lots of information; and at airport. Touring y Automóvil Club del Perú, Sánchez Cerro, 1 block from bus station for Chiclayo, in small building by a parking lot, good maps of Peru for US$1.25.

Air Faucett (0830) and AeroPerú (1700) daily jet flights to and from Lima (US$82). Taxi to airport, US$1.25.

Buses Tepsa, Roggero and other buses leave daily to Lima, average fare US$6.50, coming from Tumbes. To Trujillo, 6 hrs., buses run day (not a.m.) and night, US$5 (Chinchay-Suyo on Calle Libertad 1117-27, leaves at 2200 and 2400, also at 1300 to Chiclayo- Trujillo-Chimbote-Huaraz). To Trujillo in daylight, take through Chinchay-Suyo bus, or 0800 Empresa Chiclayo bus to Chiclayo (US$3, 3 hrs.) then change to Empresa Emtrafesa. To Tumbes, US$4.50 (El Dorado, Sánchez Cerro, 4 a day, Compañía Petrolera, same location, 2130, continues to Aguas Verdes, or Empresa Chiclayo), with Tepsa, leaving at 1200 (coming from Lima, no reservations), or Sudamericana at 0400 (cheaper), colectivo US$9.50; to Chiclayo, US$3.50, 3½ hrs., leave 1400; colectivo to Chiclayo US$5. To La Tina for Ecuadorean frontier, take an early bus to Sullana (start at 0630, every 20 mins), then a truck, no buses. **N.B.** To the north of Piura, buses are subject to military checks.

Excursions 12 km. to the SW of Piura is the village of **Catacaos** (colectivos leave from Plaza Pizarro, US$0.35, bus US$0.25) famous for its *chicha* (maize beer, be careful, quality not always reliable), *picanterías* (local restaurants, some with music, *La Casa de Tales*, rec.), tooled leather, gold filigree jewellery, wooden articles, straw hats (pricey) and splendid celebrations in Holy Week. Also from Piura, one can visit **Sechura**, a coastal town with a fine 17th-century cathedral (splendid west front-under renovation for a long time, normally closed to the public) and the *Hospedaje de Dios* (usually full of workmen from the oil terminal at Bayovar--forbidden to visitors). One can visit the coastal villages (no accommodation in any of them) of San Pedro (with a huge lagoon, edible crabs, flamingos - if you're lucky, a superb beach and a fierce sun—best visited in the week, no facilities whatsoever; take bus or colectivo to the right fork past Vice, about 10 km. from Sechura then hitch); Yacila, a picturesque fishing village with a few fish restaurants, church on the beach (reached also by *camioneta* for Paita); Los Cangrejos beach nearby, where you can rent an apartment from Sr. Belcázar, but little food available, motel open in summer, no facilities in winter), La Tortuga, Parachique, Matacaballo (which has the best beach of these four places); Chullachay (the nearest beach to Sechura), Los Puertos and Angostura. Balsa reed-boats are common on the coast.

Chulucanas, 50 km. SE of Piura and 10 km. off the Pan-American Highway, is the centre of the lemon and orange growing area. *Hotel Ica*, Ica 636, F; *Restaurant Cajamarquino*, Ayacucho 530, good. **Canchaque** (*Hostal Don Félix*, central square, F, just tolerable;

otherwise simple clean accommodation for about US$2 on right hand side of church), is a delightfully-situated small centre for coffee, sugar-cane and fruit production. Foreigners have to register here at the Policía de República. The difficult and tiring road, impossible for ordinary vehicles in the wet season, continues over a pass in the Andes of more than 3,000 metres to **Huancabamba** (Hotel El Dorado, F, good, clean, informative owner, with restaurant, on the main square; also a couple of others on the Plaza. Local specialities: *rompope*, a rich and strong drink made of egg, spices and *cañazo* (sugar-cane spirit); roast *cuy* (guinea-pig); and local cheeses. This very pretty town in a wonderful setting has three claims to fame. First, the predominance of European features, due to the fact that it was an important Spanish settlement in colonial times. Second, it is called "the walking town, *la ciudad que camina*", as it is built on irregularly slipping strata which cause much subsidence. Evidence for this includes the fall of the bridge over the Río Huancabamba some years ago. Third, and by far the most remarkable element, it is the base for reaching Las Guaringas, a series of lakes at about 4,000 metres. Around here live the most famous witchdoctors of Peru, to whom sick people flock from all over the country and abroad. Buses to the lakes at 0400 from main square.

Horses to the lakes can be hired, US$5; village of San Antonio below Lake Carmen, village of Salalá below Lake Shumbe (*Hotel San José*, G, very basic, take own food). Ignacio León, who owns a *bodega* opposite *El Dorado* runs an early pick-up service to outlying villages and takes trips at negotiable prices.

A bus from Piura to Canchaque and Huancabamba leaves daily at 0900 and 1000, at least 10 hrs. (and returns from Huancabamba 0700 and 1000), US$10, from the Civa office, Av. Ramón Castilla 155 (buy ticket early on day before travelling). Truck US$9.50. If driving, take the Pan-American Highway south of Piura for 66 km. where there is a signpost to Huancabamba. Canchaque is 78 km. along this same road, at first paved, then dirt, and then there are 69 km. more of steep and winding road to Huancabamba.

By lorry from Piura, or bus from Sullana, is **Ayabaca**. John Streather writes: In the Andean summer—roughly the end of May till mid-September—it is worth making the long trip by lorry or bus (about 0600 from Piura market square, enquire the day, or days, before) to Ayabaca, whence many trips can be made to surrounding ruins, caves, petroglyphs and lakes. Mules are usually essential as guides; mules about US$4 per day, guides the same. The man to contact in Ayabaca is Sr. Celso Acuña Calle, Jr. Cáceres 161. Buy food and medicine in Piura (enough for the guides too) before leaving, as it is in short supply in Ayabaca. The little town is near the Ecuadorean border in a lovely situation, but is unfortunately a centre of cocaine smuggling. Therefore be sure to carry passport and visa on all trips (in a waterproof bag) and, of course, stop whenever asked to by police. In summer one can usually get a lift to the village of Yanchalá where most trips begin. It is a long muleback journey from there to the petroglyphs of Samanga (booklet purchasable at Piura Catholic University), and another long muleback ride to the Inca fortress town of Aypate—large but very overgrown. Other places of interest are: the pre-Inca cemetery of Hualcuy, Inca ruins and good view from Cerro Granadillo; pre-Inca ruins of Potrero de los Chaves; mummies in the pre-Inca cave cemetery of Potrero de los Jiménez at Cerro Pajonal; 4 or 5 days by mule to the Cuatro Lagunas Sagradas—all different colours. Near Chicuate is the Ciudad Encantada which still awaits explorers or indeed any visitors at all, as it is in a very isolated region, beyond Laguna Shimbe, and the few locals are frightened to visit it. It is said to be a ruined Inca town. There are at least three hotels in Ayabaca; the best, nameless, is in the first street parallel to the square and directly behind the Banco de la Nación (which will almost certainly refuse to change money). Various restaurants too: the *Trébol* is probably the best of a mediocre bunch. A torch is essential for trips outside Ayabaca, as there is no electric light in the region. No one should attempt to journey outside Ayabaca without a guide: there is danger from drug smugglers as well as of getting lost in the trackless bush. The way to the lost Inca city of Chicuate is particularly dangerous: lightning in the pass that gives access, and thick fog descending over the 100 metres of narrow road that lead between two lakes. Easier to reach from Chulucanas (see above) is Frías, where there is a pre-Inca cemetery and more caves can be reached if you have enough time (few locals know of them), rough road, no facilities, beautiful countryside.

The port for the area is **Paita**, (no public transport)50 km. from Piura (colectivos and buses near Plaza Grau, US$1.50), which exports cotton, cotton seed, wool and flax. Population 51,500. Built on a small beach, flanked on three sides by a towering, sandy bluff, it is connected with Piura and Sullana by paved highways. Several colonial buildings survive, but they are in poor condition. The Paita-Piura road is now good, buses hourly from Parque Cortés, Piura, 45 mins. (get tickets from office on Av. Sullana, facing the park, US$1.50). Fishing, fishmeal and whaling (at Tierra Colorada, 6½ km. S of Paita) are prosperous industries.

Hotels Best is *Las Brisas*, Av. Ugarte, E with bath but scant, cold water, safe; *El Mundo*, 300 block of Bolívar, not bad but short-stay; *Miramar*, opp. Credicoop Paita, an old wooden mansion on seafront, looks expensive, but is filthy; *Ceci*, above pharmacy, F; *Pacífico* and others, none recommendable. Most are full anyway.

Restaurants *El Mundo*, Jr. Junín, quite good; much better is the restaurant on 2nd floor of Club Liberal building, Jorge Chávez 161, T 2141, good fish, seafood and crêpes, good value; others on Plaza de Armas.

Exchange Credicoop Paita, Jr. Junín 380 for dollars cash; helpful guard.

On a bluff looming over Paita is a small colonial fortress built to repel pirates. 25 km up the coast is **Colán**, a summer resort, reached by driving down a large, sandy bluff (no public transport); near the base is a striking and lonely church over 300 years old (it's in very poor condition). There is a good beach, but Colán is rather derelict since the agrarian reform; it used to be the favourite resort of the estate-owners.

Bolívar's mistress, Manuela Sáenz, lived the last 24 years of her life in Paita, supporting herself until her death in 1856 by weaving and embroidering and making candy after refusing the fortune left her by her husband. The house may be visited if you ask the people living in it, but there's not much to see.

Sullana (population 151,000), 39 km. N of Piura, is built on a bluff over the fertile Chira valley. It has a long market on the main avenue; a busy, modern place. **Warning** Robberies of travellers are common.

Hotels *Sullana* (rooms with bath), E; *Hostal y Restaurant San Miguel*, opposite bus companies, E (G in shared rooms), helpful, good showers; staff will spray rooms against mosquitoes; *Chifa Cantón*, next door, serves good food cheaply, but smaller portions than in *San Miguel*; *Hostal Aypate*, Av. José de Lama, E, comfortable, showers; *Buenos Aires*, G p.p., Av. Buenos Aires, 15 mins. from city centre, friendly but bathrooms dirty; *Res. Wilson*, Tamaraya, G p.p. large rooms, dirty facilities. *Hostal La Siesta*, Av. Panamericana 400-04 (T 2264), at entrance to town (direction Talara), D, 3-star, hot water, swimming pool, café, laundry.

Exchange On main street, near Bata shoe shop, usual touts, *cambio* upstairs changes travellers' cheques, but wait till after 1100 for today's rate.

Bus to Tumbes, US$2.10. Piura, 45 mins., US$1 bus, US$1.40 colectivo (if you have time, it is worth continuing to Piura rather than staying in Sullana); Chiclayo, Tepsa, 4 hrs., US$3. Trujillo, 8 hrs., Sudamericano (US$2.50), Ormeño (US$2.10), plenty. To Lima with Sudamericano, Tepsa (*presidencial*, US$10, 1820, ordinary, US$7.50, 1830, 16-17 hrs.), Panamericana, US$5, Roggero. Colectivos to Paita, Colán and Esmeralda leave from the main road parallel to the market; buses to Máncora and Talara (Empresa EPPO) from market area.

To Ecuador At Sullana the Pan-American Highway bifurcates. To the E it crosses the Peru-Ecuador frontier at La Tina and continues via Macará to Loja and Cuenca; the road is paved to Las Lomas (75 km.), but thereafter is poor, though marvellously scenic. Many trucks and other vehicles leave at 0630 to the border at La Tina, US$2 p.p., 5 hrs, return from border to Sullana 1030 or when full; taxis also go, US$3 per seat, 3-4 hours. No accommodation at La Tina (in El Suyo, 14 km. from La Tina, is a small hotel). At the border the officials try to get extra payments from those entering Peru, stand your ground if possible—the Peruvian can be found at the nearby *cevichería* if not at his desk—walk over the bridge, pick-ups run from the border to Macará. A bus leaves the Ecuadorean side at 1300 for Loja, so you can go from Sullana to Loja in one day.

The better route is the W road which passes through Talara and Tumbes, crossing the border at Huaquillas and on via Machala to Guayaquil; it is asphalted and has excellent bus services. All but a section of this road between Talara and Los Organos (20 km.) has been rebuilt since the heavy floods in January 1983.

The main centre of the coastal oil area is **Talara** (135 km. from Piura, 1,177 km. from Lima), in a desert oasis, which has a State-owned 60,000 barrel-a-day oil refinery and a fertilizer plant. Water is piped 40 km. from the Chira River. The city is a triumph over formidable natural difficulties, but was badly damaged in the 1983 floods and has many shanty districts. Population 44,500. La Peña beach, 2 km. from Talara, is still unspoilt.

Hotels There are 4 hotels, all overpriced and usually full by early afternoon because of the number of oilmen in the town. *Hostal Talara*, clean comfortable, E. If in trouble finding a bed, enquire at the police station.

Restaurants *La Colmena; Club de Golf.*

Transport Airport with daily flights to Lima by Faucett and AeroPerú (not Sat.). AeroPerú has a direct route to Miami; leaves Tues. at 1035, arriving 1500. Return flight departs Miami Tues. at 0130, arriving at 0550.

Paved highways connect the town with the Negritos, Lagunitos, La Brea and other oilfields. Of historical interest are the old tarpits at La Brea, 21 km. inland from Punta Pariñas, S of Talara, and near the foot of the Amotape mountains. Here the Spaniards boiled the tar to get pitch for caulking their ships. Buses run to **Máncora** (wayside fish restaurants superb, including lobster: *César*, rec.), a small attractive resort with good beaches, water warm enough for bathing, surfing (best No.v-March). Punta Ballena, E p.p., full board, clean, friendly, rec.; *Bamboe*, next to Tepsa on main street, basic, cheap (pay in advance), clean, G; 3 km. S, *Las Pocitas*, 9 rooms, attractive, friendly, fishing and harpooning trips, balsa rafts, food excellent US$9 for main meal, cheaper for full board (C). Punta Sal about 20 km. to the north has *Punta de Sal Club Hotel*, B p.p. full board, attractive, good beach, rec., watersports, pool, comfortable, relaxing (in Llma T 425961). Aqua Explorer arranges undersea activities, fishing, sailing and horseriding. Camping is reported to be safe along the beach between Talara and Tumbes, Punta Negra, etc. Bus Máncora-Tumbes, 2 hrs., US$2.

N of Talara, 51 km., is the small port of **Cabo Blanco**, famous for its excellent sea-fishing; scenery spoilt by numerous oil installations. Camping permitted free of charge at Cabo Blanco, by the Fishing Club Lodge, overlooking the sea (at least in the off-season June-December). Fishing Club, B, clean, attractive, rec., restaurant, pool, watersports, likely to be full in New Year period. Hemingway wrote *The Old Man and the Sea* here.

Tumbes, about 141 km. N of Talara, and 265 km. N of Piura, is the most northerly of Peruvian towns; it is a garrison town with 34,000 inhabitants (do not photograph the military or their installations—they will destroy your film and probably detain you). There is a long promenade, the Malecón Benavides, beside the high banks of the Tumbes River. There are some old houses in Calle Gran, and a colonial public library in the Plaza de Armas with a small museum. The cathedral is 17th century but restored in 1985. There is a sports stadium; cockfights in the Coliseo de Gallos, Av. Mcal. Castilla, 9th block, Sun. at 1500, special fights 28 July and 8 Dec. The main products are bananas and rice. The water supply is not good.

Hotels *Turistas*, C, clean, restaurant, good food and service, parking, has nice garden, provides some tourist information; *César*, E with bath, clean, secure; *Continental*, E; *Roma*, Plaza de Armas, basic, simple, few services, E; *Amazonas*, E, Av. Tumbes 333 (old name Tnte. Vásquez), clean, friendly, showers; *Córdova*, J. R. Abad Puell 777, F, with bath, no hot water, safe, clean, friendly; *Hostal Estoril*, 2 blocks from main square, F, good, friendly; *Lourdes*, one block from main square, E with bath, clean, friendly, rec.; *Italia*, Grau 733, E, cold showers, friendly, good; *Florián*, E, near El Dorado bus company, clean, fan, private bath, rec.; opposite is *Hostal Elica*, F with bath, clean, good; *Hostal Tumbes*, Grau 614, F with bath, cold water, clean. *Hostal Patty*, Huáscar 513, G, clean, water for 2 hrs. in a.m. Many other cheap hotels. Hotels are often fully booked by early afternoon, so try to arrive early, and at holiday times it can be very difficult to find a vacant room.

Restaurants *Bolívar*, cheap, rec. *Pez Espada*, good for fish, as is *Curich* in the Plaza de Armas. *La Blanquita* rec. For criollo dishes, *Pekos* acceptable; *Europa*, off main square, is rec., particularly for omelettes. *El Quarique*, Huáscar 319, small, friendly, shell decoration; *Samoa*, Av. Bolívar 235, nr. plaza, good, big portions; *El Brujo*, 7 de Enero 320, good value; *Chifa D'Koko*, Piura y F. Navarete, rec; *Mini Chifa*, Av. Tumbes Tte. Vásquez, good local and chifa dishes. There are other inexpensive restaurants on the Plaza de Armas and near the markets. *Heladería La Suprema*, Paseo Libertadores, good ice cream, sweets and cold drinks. Try bolas de plátano, soup with banana balls, meat, olives and raisins, and sudado, a local stew.

Exchange Only in Banco de Crédito, opp. Banco Popular which is in a new building on the edge of the main square, poor rates. Bad rates at the airport. Money changers on the street (on Bolívar, left of the Cathedral) give a much better rate than banks or *cambios*, but don't accept the first offer you are given. None changes travellers' cheques.

Post Office San Martín 240; Entel **Telephone** office, San Martín 242.

Tourist office Foptur, Edificio Majestad, Alfonso Ugarte y Mayor Bodero, T 5054, helpful. Further information from Ricardo Pérez Saavedra, Pueblo Nuevo, Casilla 204, archaeologist, author, works for the Instituto Nacional de Cultura (ask to see his collection of figurines); Carlos Sáenz, Urb. Fonavi 4-16, T 523412, coordinator of Fundación Peruana para la Conservación de la Naturaleza (details on national parks); Luis Alvarez Saldariaga, Tarata 132, a fisherman who organizes trips on the Río Tumbes (US$20 - also contact him through Doris Guerra at Foptur).

Buses Daily to and from Lima, 1,330 km. by Sudamericano, 1600, 1900, US$9 (overbooked, often subject to long delays); Expreso Continental (Ormeño group), new buses, 1130, 1600, 1800, 22 hrs, US$10 also Tepsa, US$11.50 (often full, leaves 1100, 1800, 1900), 26 hrs., comfortable, rec.; for other companies, ask around (e.g. Roggero, not rec.); cheaper ones usually leave 1600-2100, dearer ones 1200-1400, fare to Lima US$8 and up. All buses to Lima are very slow because of repeated police checks—no chance of sleep overnight. On the bus to Lima try to get a seat on the right hand side in order to have a good view of the coast. One can get tickets to anywhere between Tumbes and Lima with little difficulty, although buses are often booked well in advance; Piura is a good place for connections. To Sullana, poor road, except for first 1.50 km. from Tumbes, US$2.10. To Talara, 176 km., US$1.50 with El Dorado (colectivo US$7). To Piura, 276 km., US$4.50 with Tepsa, Empresa Chiclayo, 6 hrs. Colectivo, US$8.10. To Chiclayo, 548 km., US$5 (Tepsa). To Trujillo, 758 km., 5 a day, 12 hrs. from US$6. To Chimbote, 15 hrs., US$8 with Sudamericano, 16 hrs. Most buses leave p.m. from Av. Tumbes (formerly Tnte. Vásquez). Frequent buses to Aguas Verdes, 23 km., from market at 0600 onwards, colectivo, US$1, 20 minutes. Bus to Machala (Ecuador), US$4. Colectivo to Huaquillas (Ecuador), US$0.50. Taxi to Lima US$30 per seat. Hitching slow.

N.B. Travellers who hold a Tumbes-Huaquillas-Guayaquil ticket with Panamericana Internacional (bought outside Peru as an onward ticket) should note that Panamericana does not have an office in Tumbes. However, this ticket can be used for a colectivo (but not a taxi) to the border, caught at corner of Piura and Bolívar; if colectivo is full, you will be transferred to another company. Connection with bus at the border.

Air AeroPerú and Faucett, Lima to and from Tumbes daily 0840, US$91. Essential to reconfirm flights 24 hrs. before departure. Taxi to airport, US$1; taxis meet flights to take passengers to border, US$1.20, 2 mins.

Excursions Río Tumbes is navigable by small boat to the mouth of the river, an interesting 2 hr. trip with fantastic birdlife and mangrove swamps.

This is the only part of the Peruvian coast where the sea is warm all year. Two good beaches near Tumbes: one at Caleta La Cruz 16 km. SW, where Pizarro landed in 1532. The original Cruz de Conquista was taken to Lima. Easy to get to with regular colectivos (US$0.60 each way); *Motel*, E. **Zorritos**, 35 km. S of Tumbes, heavily damaged by the 1983 flooding but with a good beach (the water is not oily), *Hotel de Turistas*, E (reported closed for renovation), also *Punta Sal Chica*, 2 stars; the better of the 2 restaurants is *Arriba Perú*. Camping recommended. The first South American oil well was sunk here in 1863. Just north of Tumbes is **Puerto Pizarro**, a small fishing beach at the southern limit of the mangrove swamps. Take a boat across the lagoon to reach a good clean sandy beach (about 10 minutes journey, bargain hard). Festival of St Peter and St Paul, 29-30 June; colectivo No. 6 from Tumbes (US$0.30). *Puerto Pizarro Motel*, D, no hot water, restaurant dear and slow but food good, swimming pool, which is usually empty, watersports; *Restaurant Venecia*, seafood cheap, beware shellfish which may cause stomach upsets. Plenty of fishing and swimming; ideal for windsurfing and water-skiing but few facilities. The mangrove swamps are full of pelicans and a few tame ones beg for fish on the beaches. Three islands, Isla Hueso de Ballena, Isla del Amor, Isla de los Pájaros may be visited by boat, bargain hard, good for swimming and picnics, take food and water. Remains of Cabeza de Vaca abode cult centre of the Tumpis Indians can be found at Corrales, 5 km. S of Tumbes. They were heavily damaged by 1983 rains; Museo de Sitio nearby. Bosque Nacional de Tumbes (75,000 ha.) wildlife includes monkeys, nutria and crocodiles; Parque Nacional Cerros de Amotape (91,000 ha.) is a dry tropical forest with jaguars and anteaters, a guide essential. Mosquito repellant is a must for Tumbes area.

To Ecuador Small buses and colectivos (some marked "Puente Internacional") leave about every 20 min. and take 30 min. to get to **Aguas Verdes** on the Peruvian side of the international bridge (the Peruvian departure office opens at 0830, is closed 1200-1400 and after 1800; try not to arrive within 1/2 hour of the border closing). On the way most of them pass by the airport. By taxi it costs about US$4, colectivo fare is US$1.50 and bus fare US$1. If entering, they may refuse to accept a return ticket from another country as proof of intended exit from Peru; this is an invitation to bribery, be courteous but firm. Colectivos do not wait at customs. Some bus companies from Chiclayo and beyond go to the border. At Aguas Verdes a walkway leads to Peruvian Immigration; beware of dishonest money changers lingering outside. Get your exit stamp and proceed across the bridge into Huaquillas; 100 metres up is the Ecuadorean Immigration on the left. Change money with the men near the end of the bridge (they have briefcases on their laps and sit under umbrellas). They are not entirely scrupulous, so it helps to have your own calculator. With a pass from the authorities at the border you can spend the day in Huaquillas, the Ecuadorean border town, as long as you are back by 1800. There is nothing much to see there, but Peruvians hunt for bargains. It is a thoroughly unscrupulous border, with chaotic opening hours. Tepsa leave from the border for Lima daily at 1000, 22-5 hrs., US$14; Tepsa to Tumbes at 1300 and later. A bus leaves Huaquillas at 1500 for Piura and Trujillo (US$5, 6 hrs. to Piura). Entering Peru, it may be easier to take a colectivo to Tumbes and then a bus south, rather than get on a bus from the border to a southern destination. These buses are usually full of shoppers and their goods and involve long stops at checkpoints.

Warnings Porters on either side of the border charge exorbitant prices: don't be bullied. The money changers on the Ecuadorean side give a better rate than the banks in Tumbes (but not at the airport on the Ecuadorean side); always try to check the rate beforehand. If you are going to change cheques into Ecuadorean sucres in Huaquillas, make sure you cross the border in the morning because the bank is closed after lunch. Do not change money on the minibus to Aguas Verdes, their rates are very poor. Relations between Peru and Ecuador are not good: Ecuadorean Customs tends to confiscate guidebooks and maps of Peru because they show as Peru's certain areas claimed by Ecuador.

Checks for goods smuggled into Peru are carried out, especially at Tepsa bus station as well as at Aguas Verdes. Checks are thorough, both of luggage and body. Checks also intermittently on road to Piura.

N.B. In Jan., Feb. and March, Peru is one hour ahead of Ecuador, but dates of time-change are different each year.

SOUTH-EAST FROM LIMA (4)

The group of oases south from Lima grow Pima cotton, sugar-cane and vegetables for Lima and Callao, but the more southerly valleys specialize in vines—Ica in particular is well known for this and its port, Pisco, has given its name to the well-known brandy sold all along the coast. The Pan-American Highway runs S from Lima through all the places now to be described to Tacna and Chile, it is 4 lane to Km. 116 and there are extensive repairs and new building as far as Km. 135. There are battery chicken houses all along the beach. At Km. 200 the *garúa* lifts.

The first 60 km. from Lima are dotted with a series of seaside resort towns and clubs, including **Pucusana,** which is a charming fishing village (*Hotel Bahía*, good seafood). Excellent panoramas from the cliffs above the village. Hire a boat for an hour (fix price beforehand and stick to it); don't go in the direction of the only, smelly factory, but to the rocks where you can see seabirds close at hand.

Resort town of **Santa María**, 40 km. from Lima, beautiful *Santa María Hotel*, A, meals included. Taxi to Santa María: US$30 per day.

Cañete (hotels and restaurants), about 150 km. S of Lima, on the Río Cañete, is a prosperous market centre amid desert scenery. There is a road (no buses) to Huancayo (**see page 977**).

At Cerro Azul, 13 km. N of Cañete, is a unique Inca sea fort known as **Huarco**, now much damaged. *La Malla* is an excellent fish restaurant.

35 km. N of Pisco, near Chincha Baja, is **Tambo de Mora**, with nearby archaeological sites at Huaca de Tambo de Mora, La Centinela, Chinchaycama and Huaca Alvarado. Chincha itself is a fishing village where the negro/criollo culture is still alive. Their famous festival,

Verano Negro, is at the end of February. On old *hacienda*, San José (1769), is just outside Chincha (need your own transport); it operates as a hotel, with pool, restaurant, garden, small church, colonial crafts, C full board, book through Foptur.

Pisco, population 82,250, the largest port between Callao and Matarani, 237 km. S of Lima, serves a large agricultural hinterland. The town is divided into two: Pisco Pueblo, colonial-style homes with patios and gardens; and Pisco Puerto, which has been replaced as a port by the deep-water Puerto General San Martín, beyond Paracas. In Pisco Pueblo, half a block W of the quiet Plaza de Armas, with its equestrian statue of San Martín, is the Club Social Pisco, the H.Q. of San Martín after he had landed at Paracas Bay. There is an old Jesuit church hiding behind the new one. You can book for trips to the Ballestas Islands (see below) at agencies around the main square, or through a hotel. Pisco is an alternative airport when landing is not possible at Lima. A 364 km. road has been built to Ayacucho, with a branch to Huancavelica (see Tambo Colorado, next page).

Hotels *Pisco*, on Plaza, E, shared showers, basic, breakfast good but quite expensive, friendly, clean, disco until 2400 some evenings, can book (hotel provides sandwiches) for Ballestas Islands, near Ormeño bus station. *Hostal Belén*, Plaza Belén, E, clean, comfortable, electric showers. *Embassy*, E with bath, clean, noisy, security reported suspect, nice bar on roof, has disco in Jr. Comercio just off Plaza de Armas, good, cheap trips to Ballestas Islands; *Hostal San Jorge*, Juan Osores 267, E, hot water, friendly, very clean, rec., arranges excursions; *Cesar*, 2 de Mayo, F; *Colonial*, clean, quiet, no private baths but good value; *Comercial*, F, dirty rooms but good restaurant. *Hostal Angamos*, Pedemonte 134, tiny rooms but good beds, clean, friendly, F, economical with water and light. Mosquitoes are a problem at night in the summer. The town is full at weekends with visitors from Lima. At Pisco Puerto, *Portofino*, F, basic, friendly, clean, in slum area on sea front, good seafood, arranges day excursion to Paracas, but avoid the nearby peña which is poor and can be dangerous.

Restaurants *La Rinconada* rec. but expensive; *As de Oros*, on the Plaza de Armas, good restaurant, reasonable prices, closed Mons.; *Las Vegas*, on Plaza, very popular; *Roberto's*, always busy, near Plaza, rec. for seafood; *Candelabra*, next to *Hotel Embassy*, quite expensive; *Bill More* near *Hotel Embassy*, good, cheap seafood, also at restaurant of *Hotel Portofino*; *Turistas*, good cheap food. *Bar Piave*, on Plaza, excellent pisco sours, but lone women should beware of the owner; *La Fontana*, Lima 355, good food and pisco sours. *Piccolo-Bar*, near Plaza, good breakfast and coffee; *El Norteño*, off Plaza de Armas, good, cheap, clean; a number of restaurants around M. de Mancera 160. Seafood restaurants along shore between Pisco and San Andrés, and in San Andrés (buses from Plaza Belén, near *Hotel Perú*) there are *La Estrellita*, rec., *Olimpia* (Grecia 200), and *Mendoza*, for fish and local dishes, all rec. Good fried chicken place opposite Ormeño: save your foreign cigarette packets for their mural! *Mendoza 2*, in Pisco Puerto, excellent simple fish restaurant.

Exchange Banco de Crédito on Plaza de Armas gives good rates, but only for Amex and cash.

Tourist Office on Plaza, next to **Hotel Pisco**; poor information.

Transport Bus to Lima, Ormeño (500m. from main plaza), US$2, recommended, 4 departures, 4 hrs., San Martín, Callao 136, 4 a day, rec.; Roggero, US$2, twice a day. To Ayacucho, US$7.80 with Ormeño, 12 hrs., 1730, often delayed, wear warm clothes as the road reaches 4,600 metres near Castrovirreyna and is very cold at night; Oropesa (Calle Comercial) to Huancavelica, US$7, 0800 daily, 13 hrs., very tiring, many stops; colectivo to Ica US$1, bus to Ica, US$0.80, 2 hrs. (Ormeño, Roggero). To Arequipa direct 1220 with Ormeño, arrive 0300, US$10.75. To Nazca by bus, US$2, Roggero, 1430 (3-4 hrs.), Ormeño, 5 daily, rec. (3½-4 hrs.), colectivos reported to be more reliable. Reservations can be made here at Nazca Tours for flights over the Nazca lines for US$40 n.p.p.

Fifteen km. down the coast from Pisco Puerto is the bay of **Paracas**, sheltered by the Paracas peninsula. (The name means "sandstorm"—they can last for 3 days.) The peninsula is a National Park (entrance US$3 for 2 days, no less), ask permission to camp, no water (don't camp alone, robberies are common); it is one of the best marine reserves, with the highest concentration of marine birds, in the world. There are archaeological and natural history museums about 90 mins'. walk from the residential area along an isolated stretch of beach (no bus—take water and sun hat), but contents reported less interesting than the Ica museum. A monument on the sands marks the spot where San Martín set foot in Peru. The area has been developed as a resort: a beautiful bay, good sands, bathing (some pollution from local fishing industry, and beware of jellyfish) and fishing and excursions by boat to offshore islands. The Paracas necropolis, the burial place of a civilization which flourished here between 700 and 300 BC, has been buried by shifting sands and archaeologists can no longer visit it. About 17 km. from the museum is the precolumbian Candelabra traced in the hillside, at least 50 metres long, best seen from the sea, but still impressive from the land. Hitch along paved road which leads to Punta Pejerrey, get off at left fork and you will see a trail (1½ hrs. walk to Candelabra). La Mina, a small beach 2 km. from Lagunilla, and Punta El Arquillo are also worth visiting.

On the southern side of the peninsula there is a colony of sealions, with many species of birds (such as cormorants, gannets, gulls, terns, pelicans). On the northern side, in the bay, there are flamingoes (in June and July mainly)—only reached on foot from Paracas. Condors may be seen from the (bad) road between Paracas and Laguna Grande. Trips to the **Ballestas Islands** for US$5 upwards can be arranged at the agencies on the main plaza in Pisco, or (dearer) with the main hotels in Pisco and Paracas (e.g. US$17 from *Hotel Paracas*, 3½ hrs. in safe boat, minimum 8 passengers, take warm clothing). Blue Sea Tours, Calle Chosica 320, Pisco, has been recommended as giving the longest tours, with least disturbance of the wild life, US$5 p.p. Negotiate for a good price. The trip to the islands, which are now a national reserve, takes about 5 hrs. all together, and is highly recommended (although some boats do not have life jackets, and are very crowded). You will see thousands of inquisitive sealions, guano birds, pelicans (the book *Las Aves del Departamento de Lima* by Maria Koepcke is useful); the boat returns past the Candelabra to the bay of Paracas where flocks of flamingoes and pelicans can be seen.

Taxi from Pisco to Paracas (return) US$5, but more if arranged by a hotel. Colectivo, one way, US$0.50 or less if you change at San Andrés. Small buses leave frequently from the market place in Pisco to Paracas (US$0.25, US$0.40 with stop at J. C. Tello museum; last bus from museum at 1630). A yellow bus for Enapu workers leaves Pisco main square 2300 for Paracas National Park; it may give you a lift. Good walking in Paracas peninsula, details available from Park Office or ask for "Hoja 28-K" map at Instituto Geográfico Militar in Lima (it is not safe to walk if alone). The Mirador de los Lobos is a cliff overlooking sealion beaches, 20 minutes by car from *Hotel Paracas*—no public transport and the road peters out after a while (make sure your car is in good repair), crossing salty sand flats and mountains. To see the park properly you need a vehicle; try hitching with a tour group.

Hotels *Paracas*, B, check your bill carefully, good hotel, bungalows on beach (T Pisco 2220 or Lima 464865) good food, not cheap, good buffet lunch on Sun., US$6 low season, US$9 high, fine grounds facing the bay, is a good centre for excursions to the Peninsula and flights over Nazca; it has tennis courts and an open-air swimming pool (US$2 for non-residents); it also houses the Masson ceramics collection (worth seeing). *Hostería Paracas*, C, clean, safe, pool, very good restaurant; *El Mirador*, E, at entrance to Paracas, no hot water, O.K., boat trips arranged, meals available. *As de Oros*, Plaza de Armas, excellent tortuga. Excellent fried fish at open-sided restaurants by the fishing boats, e.g. *Rancho de la Tía Fela*, in Lagunilla, where one can sleep for free on the floor. Camping is possible on the beach near the *Hotel Paracas*.

Up the Pisco valley, 48 km. from Pisco on the road to Huaytará and Ayacucho, is **Tambo Colorado**, one of the best-preserved pre-Inca ruins in coastal Peru (entrance US$0.60); apparently a palace with ancillary buildings; the wall paintings have survived from Inca times. Buses from Pisco, 0800, Oropesa US$0.50 (3 hrs.). Alight 20 mins. after stop at Humay; the road passes right through the site. Return by bus to Pisco in afternoon; for bus or truck back to Pisco wait at the caretaker's house (he will show you his small collection of items found on the site), as the area is dangerous. Taxi from Pisco US$19.50. From Humay, go to Hacienda Montesarpe, and 500 metres above the hacienda is the line of holes known as "La avenida misteriosa de las picaduras de viruelas" (the mysterious avenue of smallpox spots) which stretches along the Andes for many kilometres (its purpose is still unknown).

Huaytará, on the Pisco-Ayacucho road, contains Inca ruins and baths, and the whole side of the church is a perfectly preserved Inca wall with niches and trapezoidal doorways.

From Pisco the Pan-American Highway runs 93 km. S to **Ica**, on the Ica river, population 147,000. The image of El Señor de Lurén in a fine church in Parque Lurén draws pilgrims from all Peru to the twice-yearly festivals in March and October (15-21), when there are all-night processions. The San Jerónimo church at Cajamarca 262 has a fine mural behind the altar. Ica is famous for its *tejas*, a local sweet of *manjarblanco* (sold behind Lurén church); it is also Peru's chief wine centre and has a harvest festival in March. The Bodega El Carmel (on the right-hand side when arriving from Lima) can be visited; it is a pisco distillery and has an ancient grape press made from a huge tree trunk. The Vista Alegre wine and pisco distillery can be also be visited (Spanish essential) and its shop is recommended. Local bus drops you at the entrance, or 10-15 mins. walk on the other side of the river. 10 km. outside Ica, in the district of Subtanjalla, is José Carrasco González, *El Catador*, a shop selling home-made wines and pisco, and traditional handicrafts associated with winemaking. In the evening it is a restaurant-bar with dancing and music; best time to visit is during harvest, late Feb. to early April. Open daily 0800-1800, take a bus from 2nd block of Moquegua, roughly hourly. *Cachina*, a very young white wine "with a strong yeasty taste", is drunk about two weeks after the grape harvest.

The waters of the Choclacocha and Orococha lakes from the eastern side of the Andes are tunnelled into the Ica valley and irrigate 30,000 hectares of land. The lakes are at 4,570 metres. The tunnel is over 9 km. long.

Hotels *Las Dunas*, A plus 13% tax and service, about 20% cheaper on weekdays, highly rec., in a complete resort with restaurant, swimming pool, horseriding and other activities, own airstrip for flights over Nazca, 50 mins.; Lima offices: Ricardo Rivera Navarrete 889, Oficina 208, San Isidro, Casilla 4410, Lima 100, T 424180; *Turistas*, large and modern, with swimming pool, C, with private bath, meals (US$4.50); *Colón*, Plaza de Armas, E with bath, F without, basic, dirty, old, noisy, restaurant; *Siesta II*, Independencia, E, clean, ask for quieter back room, rec.; *Lima*, Lima 262, basic but quiet, F; *Confort*, Lamar 251, 4 blocks from square, F, clean; *Presidente*, E, with bath, clean, good; *Royal*, and *Ica* (basic, noisy), both friendly, clean, F or G, and on 100 block of Calle Independencia; *Europa*, Independencia 258, G p.p., clean and friendly; *Hostal Viña*, diagonally across from Entel, G, shower, safe, helpful. Several good hotels on Castrovirreyna, *Las Brisas*, D and *Silmar*, D. *El Carmelo*, on the Pan-American Highway S of turn-off for *Las Dunas*, swimming pool. Hotels are fully booked during the harvest festival and prices rise greatly.

Restaurants *Sergio*, *San Remo*, *Flor de Canela*, and *La Casona*, good and reasonable, all along Lima; *Siesta*, Independencia 160; *Venecia*, just off plaza, is the best. *Macondo*, Jr. Bolívar 300, fish good, rec. *El Fogón*, Municipalidad 276, good and cheap. Good one at Ormeño bus terminal. *El Eden*, *Casa Naturista*, vegetarian at Bolivar 387, menú US$0.75.

Warning Beware of thieves, for instance in the market, even in daylight.

Museo Regional Bus 17 from Plaza de Armas, open 0745-1900, Mon.- Sat.: Sun. 0900-1300 (US$0.50). Houses mummies, ceramics, textiles and trepanned skulls from Paracas, Nazca and Inca cultures; a good, well-displayed collection of Inca counting strings (*quipus*) and clothes made of feathers. Good and informative displays with maps of all sites in the Department. Behind the building there is a scale model of the Nazca lines with an observation tower, a useful orientation before visiting the lines. The attendant paints copies of motifs from the ceramics and textiles in the original pigments (US$1), and sells his own good maps of Nazca for US$1.65.

The museum on the Plaza de Armas, run by Dr. Javier Cabrera, has a collection of several thousand engraved stones. Open Mon.-Sat. 0930-1230 and 1730-2000 and sometimes open Sun. If visiting in a group T 234363. We are informed that some of these stones are fakes: people have talked to the craftsmen concerned. If authentic, the stones suggest the existence of a technologically-advanced people contemporary with the dinosaurs, but the archaeological establishment seems very reluctant to study them. If interested, contact Ms. Sophia Afford, Le Petit Canadeau, Le Plan du Castellet, Le Beausset, 83330, France, T 94

987241, a geologist who has written several articles on the subject. (There are so many stones that it is impossible to believe they are all fakes. Most are in a recognisably pre-Inca style, but, for instance, kangaroo and a giraffe in the style of a modern children's story book, strain the visitor's credulity. However, Dr Cabrera is an interesting character, worth a visit. Ed.)

Exchange No travellers' cheques.

Tourist Office Av. Grau 148, T 235247, very helpful and courteous. Touring y Automóvil Club del Perú, Manzanilla 523.

Buses To Lima, Ormeño (Lambayeque 180) and Tepsa, US$4.20, 5 hrs.; Roggero 4 a day; colectivo to Lima, US$8.15. Several buses daily in the evening to Nazca, US$1.75, 2-3 hrs. Colectivo to Nazca, US$2.15; to Pisco, US$1; bus to Pisco, US$0.80 (Ormeño or Roggero). Bus to Arequipa, US$10.25 with Ormeño (a very popular route at weekends). Ormeño go to Cuzco Wed. and Fri., leaving 1700, 30 hrs., US$17.25. To Abancay with El Cóndor de Aymaráes at 1600, US$12.20, 20 hrs. (take blankets). Several departures to Tacna, e.g. 1700, arrive 0900.

5 km. from Ica, round a lake and amid impressive sand dunes, is the attractive summer resort of **Huacachina**, flourishing again after some years of decline. The *Hotel Mossone* (4 hours' drive from Lima), D, full board, is at the eastern end of the lake. Another good hotel is the *Salvatierra* (under renovation). Sleeping in the open is pleasant here, and swimming in the lake is beautiful, but watch out for soft sand. Local bus from the square in Ica to Huacachina, US$0.20, 10-15 mins.

The southern oases, S of Ica to the Chilean frontier, produce enough to support themselves, but little more. The highlands grow increasingly arid and the coast more rugged. There are only thin ribbons of cultivable lands along valley bottoms, and most of these can be irrigated only in their upper reaches. However, there are a few exceptions: the cotton plantations between Ica and Nazca, the orange-growing centre at Palpa, the large and well-watered oasis with Arequipa at its centre, and the smaller oasis of the river Moquegua further S. In several places the Highway is not protected against drifting sand and calls for cautious driving.

Nazca, 141 km. S of Ica by the Pan-American Highway, is a town of 30,000 people set in a green valley amid a perimeter of mountains, 444 km. from Lima. Its altitude of 619 metres puts Nazca just above any fog which may drift in from the sea: the sun blazes the year round by day and the nights are crisp. **Warning** Beware of thieves if you arrive early in the morning off a bus.

The Nazcas had a highly developed civilization which reached its peak about AD 800. Their decorated ceramics, wood carvings and adornments of gold are on display in many of Lima's museums. The Nazca municipality's own museum, on the main plaza, has a small but fine collection (entry, US$0.25, open 0945-1300, 1345-1815). The valley about 35 km. S of Nazca is full of ruins, temples, and cemeteries; the last-named are quite difficult to find, but taxis do excursions for about US$20 per car. The trip should be made by all who have time: mummies, bones, pottery shards and scraps of textiles may be seen lying in the desert sun, although the best pieces have of course been taken by grave robbers and archaeologists. At the edge of the town is the reservoir of Bisambra, whose water was taken by the Nazcas through underground aqueducts—many still in use—to water the land.

Hotels *Turistas*, C, with bath (less without), clean, rooms with private patio, hot water, peaceful, rec., good meals US$2.75, safe car park, swimming pool (US$1.20 for non-guests), rec. *Hostal Don Agucho*, Paredones y San Carlos (T 209), E, clean, friendly, rec.; *Nazca*, Calle Lima 438, F, warm showers (electric—beware), clean and friendly, parties in courtyard at night, luggage store, helpful (only hotel with good information on tours, they also run cheap tours); rec; *Montecarlo*, Jr. Callao, E with hot water (ask for it), F without, all rooms with bath, bungalows at back D, offers flights over the Lines plus one night's lodging but not all year round, mixed reports; *Lima*, basic but rather good, F; *Konfort*, Calle Lima 587, G,

SOUTHERN PERU

small, clean, safe, intermittent water (as elsewhere), indifferent manager; **San Martín**, Arica 116, G, basic, electric showers; **Hostal El Sol**, E, basic but friendly, hot showers, small, on Jirón Tacna at Plaza de Armas; **Internacional**, Av. Maria Reiche, E, with bath, clean, quiet, cheap, hot water (if they ask for 10% tourist tax, they won't insist if you refuse to pay), rec. but be careful with belongings. **Hostal Alegría**, Jirón Lima 166, T 62, near bus station, F without bath, clean, hot water, helpful, manager (Efraín Alegría) speaks English, rec, tours and flights arranged, reductions for IYHA members, swimming pool, washing facilities, restaurant (flight inc. tax, taxi to airport and 1 night in hostal US$30); **Posada Guadalupe**, San Martín 480. Hostales opp. airport, **Maison Suisse**, rundown, food expensive, owned by Aeroíca, **Nido del Cóndor**, only for Aerocóndor passengers, but **Hostal Alegría** will get you a pass to use the pool. **La Borda**, nr. airstrip, B, old hacienda, surrounded by cottonfields, swimming pool, excellent restaurant, quiet, helpful, rec., but about 5 km. from town, English-speaking manageress.

Camping *Wasipunko*, Panamericana Sur, Km 450.

Restaurants *Selva Alegre*, Lima, unfriendly service; *Oasis*, Arica 213, quite good and cheap; *La Esperanza*, good set lunch, Lima 594; *La Pascana*, Morzesky y Lima, rec.; *Cañada*, Lima 160, friendly, good seafood, reasonable; *Los Angeles*, half-block from Plaza de Armas, good, cheap, try sopa criolla, and chocolate cake, similar is *Concordia*. *Chifa Orlando*, on Lima, not original Chinese but cheap and good, 1¼ blocks from *Hotel Nazca* (direction Roggero); *La Taberna*, Jr. Lima 326, excellent seafood, bar, live music, friendly, popular with gringos, worth a look just for the graffiti; also *El Dorado*, Lima, near *Hotel Nazca*, good sopa criolla; *Mister Tiburón II*, Jr. Callao 195, next to *Hotel Montecarlo*, clean, good food. *Fuente de Soda*, near cinema, good *almuerzo*; at Cruz del Sur bus terminal, gringo restaurant, changes dollars, expensive food. Seafood is cheaper than beef. Do not drink the water, but the pisco sours are recommended as the best in Peru.

Exchange Difficult to change travellers' cheques, impossible at weekends; bring cash. Banco de la Nación exchanges at poor rate: better from Chinese-owned paint shop opposite Banco del Crédito.

Post and telephone office Lima 816; **police** Av. Los Incas, T 36.

Tourist Office Bolognesi 397. They will organize local tours for you and they sell books about the lines.

Buses To Lima, about US$5, 8 hrs., Tepsa 1600, Ormeño, opp. *Turistas* and *Montecarlo* hotels about 8 a day, cheaper (best to take a morning bus, 0900, to arrive in daylight). Colectivo to Lima, Comité 3, Montevideo 581, US$8.80. To Arequipa (if possible, travel by day as there have been a number of hold ups), Ormeño, 7 a day (recommended as seats can be reserved, but dearer, and buses coming from Lima may be delayed), Sudamericano also OK (2030, 0300), all companies take about 12 hrs, US$4.50-6.50, Tepsa US$6.25, delays possible out of Nazca because of drifting sand across the road. Book ticket on previous day. Ormeño to Pisco, leaves at 0900, 1130, 1400, rec.; Roggero to Pisco, US$2. Colectivo to Ica, US$2.15. Bus to Ica, US$1.75, 3-4 hrs. Ormeño, 0900, 1830, Tepsa, 2200, Roggero, 2030. Colectivo to Marcona, US$2. Bus to Tacna, US$9; Ormeño leaves at 1730, 2000 and 2300. Lima-Nazca-Cuzco takes 40 hours (can take 70 hrs.); the route is done by Ormeño twice a week, also Hidalgo. Cruz del Sur, Ormeño, Nazca-Cuzco, US$12, 30 hrs.; El Cóndor de Aymaráes to Abancay, Tues., Thurs., Sat., Sun., 21 hrs., from there take bus or colectivo to Cuzco. **N.B.** The Nazca-Cuzco route, through the Department of Ayacucho, is not safe at present.

Excursions The Fernández family, who run the *Hotel Nazca*, also have details of the Asociación de Guías de Turismo, a group of six guides trained by the Peruvian Ministry of Tourism. They offer three 2-hr. tours to the *mirador* on the pampa, cemetery at Chauchilla and nearby Inca ruins (e.g. the Estanquería—astronomical sighting posts) and aqueducts (US$4 each tour), rec. Also available is a tour to the pyramids of Cahuachi (17 km. W of Nazca on a very bad road), US$6 p.p. Tours only run if 4 people or more. Profesor Josué Lancho, Callao 771, T 327, offers tours in his car and gives lectures. Mario Raúl Etchebarne, T 85, is a well-informed guide with a car; also Juan Tohalino Vera, Jirón Lima 438, T Nazca 85, an official guide, rec. Recommended taxi-guides are Armando Denegri, office on Plaza de Armas by Aeroíca office, and José Barahona Calle, Jr. Bolognesi 282. All guides must be approved by the Ministry of Tourism: ask to see an identity card.

Nazca Lines About 22 km. N of Nazca, along the Pan-American Highway, are the famous Nazca Lines. Cut into the stony desert are large numbers of lines, not only parallels and geometrical figures, but also some forming the shape of a dog, an enormous monkey, birds (one with a wing span of over 100 metres), a spider and a tree. The lines can best be appreciated from the air; it is now forbidden to walk or drive on them. The German expert, Dr Maria Reiche, who has studied the lines (mostly from a step ladder!) for over 40 years, lives in the *Hotel de Turistas*; she maintains that they represent some sort of vast astronomical pre-Inca calendar.

The lines are thought to have been etched on the Pampa Colorada sands by three different groups: the Paracas people 900-200 BC, Nazcas 200 BC-AD 600 and the settlers from Ayacucho at about AD 630. For years Dr Reiche presented a free lecture in the hotel every evening, but she has handed this over to her sister, Dr Renate Reiche. In 1976 she had a platform put up at her own expense, from which three of the huge designs can be seen—the Hands, the Lizard and the Tree (taxi, US$12 return). Her book, *Mystery on the Desert*, is on sale for US$10 at the hotel, or it may be obtained for US$10 from Dr. R. Reiche Grosse, Kohlgarten 7, 8726 Hohenpeisserberg, W. Germany. Another good book is *Pathways to the Gods: the mystery of the Nazca Lines*, by Tony Morrison (Michael Russell, 1978), obtainable in Lima. Another theory is that the ancient Nazcas flew in hot-air balloons; this is based on the fact that the lines are best seen from the air, that there are burn (launching?) pits in many of the figures, and that there are pieces of ancient local pottery and tapestry showing balloonists, and local legends of flying men (which would be supported by the engraved designs on stones in Ica—see page 926) if these are proved authentic. See *Nazca, the flight of Condor 1*, by Jim Woodman, Murray, 1980 (Pocket Books, N.Y. 1977.) Georg A. von Breunig (1980) discounts both the above theories, claiming that the lines are the tracks of running contests. He bases his argument on the asymetrical surface level at curves in the designs and on the triangular fields which accord with human running characteristics, and with a number of runners starting from a straight line, then becoming an extended string of contestants. A similar theory was proposed by the English astronomer Alan Sawyer. Other theories are that the Nazca designs represent weaving patterns and yarns (Henri Stirlin) and that the plain is a map demonstrating the Tiahuanaco Empire (Zsoltan Zelko). *The Nazca Lines—a new perspective on their origin and meaning* (Editorial Los Pinos, Lima 18), by Dr Johan Reinhard, brings together ethnographic, historical and archaeological data on the lines, including current use of straight lines in Bolivia. Taxi-guides to the lines, 0800-1200, cost US$4 p.p., or you can hitch, but there is not always much traffic. Ormeño bus leaves for the lines at 0900 (US$0.60); hitch back, but have patience. Go by an early bus as the site gets very hot. Better still, take a taxi and arrive at 0745 before the buses.

Small planes take 3-6 passengers to see the Nazca Lines; reservations can be made at the airport for flights with Aerocóndor: small planes, 3 passengers, good view (office opposite *Hotel de Turistas*, or can be booked at *Hotel Nazca*), or Aero Montecarlo (from hotel of that name; new planes and experienced pilots, and good). Aeroíca in Jirón Lima and at the airport, also fly over the lines. Price for flight US$40, but it may be possible to negotiate a lower price, US$25-28 at quiet times, plus US$2 airport tax. Travellers' cheques accepted; or apply at the Aerocóndor office in Lima (basement of *Hotel Sheraton*, T 329050, ext. 150-117; 471253; 453305, 460296). Sra. Fernández from *Hotel Nazca* can arrange flights by joining single travellers into group parties. Flights should last from 30 to 45 minutes, but are sometimes cut to 20, and are bumpy with many tight turns—many people are airsick. Aerocóndor offer the following round trips: Lima-Nazca-Lima, US$144; Lima-Nazca-Ica (lunch at *Las Dunas*) US$100 for 3; Pisco-Nazca-Pisco, US$98; Ica-Nazca-Ica, US$60; all include a flight over the Lines, and other sights of interest (those from Lima involve a change of plane). The best time to fly is early in the morning, or 1500-1600 (in October at least) to benefit from the horizontal light. (Taxi to airport, US$1.10, bus, US$0.07). Many air companies (especially Aerocóndor) overbook early flights, then keep you waiting until later in the day when the light has deteriorated. For photographs, be careful you do not find yourself in a middle seat (small planes are best—a roll of 36 should allow 2-3 shots per figure). Nanaska Tours does a tour of the Nazca lines on land, operated by Sr. Carlos Santa Cruz and Sr. Josué S. Lancho (both students of ancient culture), recommended.

Nazca to Cuzco (see warning under **Buses** above.) A very rough 470 km. road (can be driven in private car in 18 hrs.' driving time) cuts off through Puquío and NE to Abancay (**page 983**) on the Ayacucho-Cuzco road. Many buses from Lima to Cuzco take this route, which is now being paved; it is mostly narrow with a very bad 25-km. stretch between km.187 and 212 from Abancay, but offers wild scenery; the journey may be broken at **Puquío** (159 km. from Nazca, *Hotel Los Andes*, F, with garage, "grim"; *Hostal Espinosa*, F, basic), although the town has little to recommend it and is freezing cold at night. Further on is Chalhuanca (*Hostal Zegarra*, dirty and cold, and *Hostal Porvenir*). After the dusty ascent from Nazca, you reach the research station at Pampa Galera, 89 km. E from Nazca, which controls a vicuña reserve currently containing about 37,000 animals; visitors are welcome, accommodation available (3 rooms). From Puquío to Abancay is very hard for private cars: after the ascent from Puquío you reach the pampa and lakes where you can see flamingoes. About 160 km. from Abancay, you descend to the Pachachaca valley, which is followed to Abancay.

From a point 40 km. beyond Nazca along the Pan-American Highway a branch road (39 km.) runs to the ports of San Juan and San Nicolás, built to ship iron ore from the Marcona field, 29 km. inland, and Acarí, 53 km. E again, where a copper deposit is also being worked. San Juan, 553 km. S of Lima, has a beautiful deep-water bay.

After Nazca the Highway returns to the coast at Lomas (*Hotel Machora* with only 3 rooms and *Restaurant Melchorita*; *Capricho de Verano*) and passes by Chala, Atico (*Alojamiento*, G, good and clean) and Ocoña, to Camaná (392 km. from Nazca).

Chala, 173 km. from Nazca, is a fishing village with beaches where condors may be seen. Good fresh fish available in the morning and possibilities of fishing with the local fishermen. Electricity all day. Between Chala and Camaná a missing bridge causes traffic delays on the highway.

Hotels *Otero*, F, friendly, basic, clean; *Hostal Chala*. No good restaurants.

Excursion 10 km. N of Chala there are the large precolumbian ruins of Puerto Inca on the coast. Go 6 km. N on the Pan-American; at Km. 603 take the unpaved road on left. Follow this for 2 km., then take right fork another 2 km. to sea (bay with cliffs). Graf Rudolf of Geneva tells us that, on their discovery in the 1950s, the ruins were misunderstood and thus neglected. It is now recognised that this was the port for Cuzco. A French archaeologist runs a small hotel and restaurant on the beach, while studying the ruins. The site is in excellent condition: the drying and store houses can be seen, on the right side of the bay is a cemetery, on the hill a temple of reincarnation, and the Inca road from the coast to Cuzco is clearly visible. The road was 240 km. long, with a staging post every 7 km. so that, with a change of runner at every post, messages could be sent in 24 hrs.

Camaná is a picturesque little town, 222 km from Chala, with a good food market and pleasant beaches 5 km. away at La Punta (hourly buses from Camaná); good bathing but little shade. Rice is the principal crop.

Hotels *Turistas*, E, poor; *Central*, F, just off main square, adequate; *Lider*, F with bath, clean, good restaurant; *Villa Mar*, F, basic.

Restaurant *Hong Kong*, Plaza de Armas, good. The fresh-water shrimps are delicious.

Camaná sends its products to the small port of Quilca, S on the Río Quilca, in colonial times the unloading point for goods imported via Arequipa to Potosí (now in Bolivia). Now a seedy harbour. The village of Quilca is further along, perched on a cliff overlooking the Siguas river.

The Pan-American Highway swings inland from Camaná and runs along the top of a plateau with strange crescent-shaped dunes (**see page 934**). The sudden descents into the canyons of the Siguas and Víctor rivers are interesting. Before Repartición a branch to the left leads to Aplao and the valley of the Majes river. From there continue past Coropuna, the highest mountain in southern Peru, to Andagua, a village lying at the head of the valley of the volcanoes (bus from Arequipa, Sun., Wed., Fri., 1530, with Empresa Delgado; basic accommodation at the mayor's house in Andagua). The Arequipa-Andagua bus goes on to Orcopampa, from which the thermal springs of Huancarama can be visited. A mining lorry leaves Orcopampa for Cailloma on the 12th and the last day of each month; this enables one to make a round trip from Arequipa.

At Repartición, 134 km. from Camaná, the Highway bifurcates: one branch runs through Arequipa into the highlands (near Arequipa is a new 39 km. toll road, US$0.25, Camaná-Arequipa, 172 km.); the other leads S to the Chilean border.

From this latter road a branch leads off from La Joya W to Mollendo and Matarani.

Mollendo, 14,650 people, has now been replaced as a port by ***Matarani***, 14½ km. to the NW. Port workers still live mostly in Mollendo, where the main customs agencies are. Three beautiful sandy beaches stretch down the coast, small beach nearest town is safest for swimming (swimming pool on the beach open Jan.-March). Mollendo now depends partly upon the summer attraction of the beaches and partly upon the 15,000 hectares of irrigated land in the nearby Tambo valley. On the coast, a few km. SE by road, is the summer resort of Mejía.

Mollendo Hotels *Salerno*, 30 rooms, all with bath, excellent seafood. *Aller*, Arequipa 681, E; *Hostal Cabaña*, Comercio 240, F, clean, good; *Royal*, Tacna 155, basic, clean; *Moderno*, Tacna 179, F; *Verana*, Arequipa 337, cheap.

Restaurants *Salerno Bar*, good, excellent food; *Marco Antonio*, good; *Pizzería*, many gringos; *Sea Room*, Pasaje San Francisco, overlooking the Pacific; *Venezia*, Comercio 188; *Chifa Tun Fong*, good and cheap.

Bus to Arequipa (Empresa Agarón), 2 hrs., US$2 twice daily; colectivo to Arequipa, US$2.95. To Tacna, 3 hrs., US$3.40.

The Pan-American Highway runs S from La Joya through Moquegua to Tacna and Arica (Chile). ***Moquegua*** (200 km. from Arequipa), population 10,460, described as "calm and clean", is a small town of winding cobblestone streets at 1,370 metres in the narrow valley of the Moquegua river. The plaza has llama-shaped hedges. The roofs are built with sugar-cane thatch and clay. Most of the valley below the city grows grapes and the upper part grows avocados (*paltas*), wheat, maize, potatoes, some cotton, and fruits. Climate: subtropical. Interesting cacti at Torata, nearby.

Hotels *Turistas* (1 km. from town), swimming pool, D, clean, friendly, hot water, restaurant fair, telephone calls expensive; *Limoñeros*, E, old house, basic rooms, showers, pretty garden, swimming pool (usually empty); *Hostal Comercio*, one block from Plaza, G, safe and friendly.

Restaurants *La Sirena*, rec. for seafood and chicken dishes.

Buses Moquegua-Ilo, US$1, leaves at 1100. Returns from Ilo at 1700. Moquegua-Tacna, 0500, 3 hrs., US$1.25; Moquegua-Puno, San Martín, daily, about 10 hrs., US$5.

Moquegua's exports—avocados and wine—go by an excellent 96-km. road to the port of ***Ilo*** (population 95,000: *Hotel Turistas*, D, with or without bath, meals US$3.20).

There are three Ilos: Ilo Viejo, in ruins after the earthquake of 1868; Ilo Nuevo, the present town, dirty, with a fishmeal factory, oil tanks, and dusty and sometimes cobbled streets and "half-door" saloons; and the spick and span village built by the Southern Peru Copper Corporation (hospital, cinema, playgrounds, etc.) for its engineers and their families.

The Southern Peru Copper Corporation is exploiting its copper property at Toquepala, at an altitude of 3,050 metres, and is developing its property at Cuajone nearby (good view of valley, which is full of cacti). All exports are through Ilo, along the 183-km. railway and road from Toquepala. The SPCC smelter is on the coast, 18 km. from the port of Ilo. Some 70 km. S of Moquegua a sign points to the Minas de Toquepala (64 km. by a good road); bus service from Tacna. ***Toquepala*** village, in a hollow, has a guest house (swimming pool), a church, club house and an American school, and is a pleasant place; however, it is a private mining community, and permission from the management must be obtained in advance to visit the village. A nearby cave contains paintings believed to date from 8000 BC, but it is very hard to find. Helio Courier planes reach it from Moquegua (12 min.) and Ilo (26 min.). Taxis from Ilo. In the desert between Moquegua and Tacna, John Streather tells us that engraved stones dating from 10,000 BC have been discovered.

Tacna, at 550 metres, backed by the snow-capped peak of Tacora, is 156 km. S of Moquegua by Pan-American Highway, 42 km. from the Chilean frontier, and 64 km. from the international port of Arica, to which there is a railway. Above the city, on the heights, is the Campo de la Alianza, scene of a battle between Peru and Chile in 1880. Tacna is 1,292 km. from Lima by road, 987 by air.

Tacna was in Chilean hands from 1880 to 1929, when its people voted by plebiscite to return to Peru. There are good schools, housing estates, a stadium to seat 10,000 people, an airport suitable for jet planes, many military posts and one of the best hospitals in Peru. Population: 46,250.

Around the city the desert is gradually being irrigated. The local economy includes olive groves, vineyards and fishing. The waters of Laguna Aricota, 80 km. N, are now being tapped for further irrigation and hydroelectric power for industry. The cathedral, designed by Eiffel, faces the main square, Plaza de Armas, which contains huge bronze statues of Admiral Grau and Colonel Bolognesi. The interior is austere but the round stained glass windows, each with a different motif, accentuate the fine, clean lines. The bronze fountain is said to be the duplicate of the one in the Place de la Concorde (Paris) and was also designed by Eiffel. The Parque Locomotiva (near city centre) has a British-built locomotive, which was used in the War of the Pacific. There is a very good railway museum at the station (0900-1500, US$0.10); the museum in the Casa de la Cultura has precolumbian pottery and war relics (very good, free, 1500-1800).

Hotels *Turistas*, Av. Bolognesi, gardens, small swimming pool, tennis court, safe car park, D, with bath, meals expensive, but good breakfast for US$2, large rooms, clean, can make telephone bookings for other Tourist Hotels; *Central*, C with bath, near Plaza; *Holiday Suite*, with swimming pool and safe car park, 10 minutes' walk from centre, follow Av. Bolognesi to the University, from where it's one block to the left; *Don Quijote*, Leguía 940, E with shower, secure, clean, pleasant, near Chasquitur office for colectivos to Arica; *Camino Real*, D, restaurant OK, discotheque, modern; *Lima*, on main square, E, with bath, bar, good restaurant, friendly, stores luggage; *Hostal Junín*, Junín, F, old house, hot water, good beds, clean. Cheaper hotels rec. are the *Gruta*, E, and *Hostal Comercio*, *Lido*, Calle San Martín 876, near Plaza, good, F; *El Dorado Hospedaje*, Calderón de la Barca 476, *Tacna*, *Las Vegas*, and *San Cristóbal*, all F. Accommodation is hard to find in the centre, especially at Christmas-time, because of Chileans on shopping sprees.

Restaurant *Sur Perú*, Ayacucho 80, rec. *Viejo Almacén*, one of the best in Tacna; *Los Tenedores*, San Martín 888, good, clean, expensive; *Hostal Lido*, San Martín 876 A, good value; *Pizzeria Italiana*, Libertad ½ block from San Martin, good; *El Sameño*, Arias Aráguez, near Ormeño bus terminal, good value fish restaurant. *Helados Piamonte*, 1 block from *Hotel Turistas*, good ice cream.

Club Unión de Tacna. There is an exclusive Casino.

Tourist Office Foptur, San Martín 405, T 71-5352 (good map); Av. Bolognesi 2088 and Complejo Fronterizo Santa Rosa. Touring y Automóvil Club del Perú, Av. 2 de Mayo 55.

Air Faucett daily jet flights to Lima, many cancellations; AeroPerú on Mon., Wed., and Sat. (US$86). Taxi to town US$1.50 approx., but beware overcharging. No transport direct to border; cheapest way is taxi to town first, then take colectivo.

Buses New bus station in operation on Hipólito Unanue, to N of city. Only Tepsa and Ormeño use their own terminals. Tacna-Arequipa, US$3, Ormeño, about 5 hrs., 6 a day, from Aráguez 698 y Grohman. Berrios to Arequipa very slow, 5-6 police stops en route; better companies are harassed less, e.g. Ormeño. Colectivo to Arequipa, US$10 (at official rate), 6 hrs., leave from plaza, opposite church. Expreso Tacna, San Martín 201, T 2642, will collect from hotel. Several to Lima, tickets can be purchased several days before departure; many passport checks; Tepsa (Leguía 981) at 1700, Ormeño 5 a day, cheapest is Hermanos Flores, US$12; all take 21-23 hrs. Bus to Ilave, US$5, about 16 hours; Gironda (the best), Río Blanco and Ponce companies, all leave about 1700. Plenty of minibuses from Ilave to Puno. To Nazca, US$10.65. Bus Moquegua-Tacna, US$1.25, 3 hrs, Ormeño 7 a day, Sur Peruano. To Arica, see below.

The road E to Bolivia—via Tarata (where Inca terraces are still in use) and Challapalca to Ilave, where it connects with the Puno-La Paz highway—is gravel, not too bad in the dry season, though difficult in the rains.

N.B. Soon after buses leave Tacna, passengers' passports and luggage are checked, whether you have been out of the country or not. Train to Arica, 0800 and 1400, US$0.30, customs at station, you must purchase a ticket after getting your exit stamp. Delays are common, journey takes 1½ hrs. Buses to Arica, e.g. Empresa Adsublata rec. (US$1.50). Plenty of colectivos to Arica, which will deliver you to a hotel; 2 hrs., US$4 drivers present all documents to officials), Empresa Chasqui and Chiletur, which stop at both Peruvian and Chilean immigration; they leave from terminal area on Calle Coronel Mendoza. If going direct from the Tacna bus terminal, take a colectivo to this point, not to immigration, because you won't get a colectivo to Arica there. Despite what the Prefectura says, colectivos will take you across at weekends as well as during the week. Peruvian formalities are quick, Chilean ones take an hour. We are told that passport-holders in buses can only cross the border between 0900 and 1300; the rest of the day only border-pass holders (residents of Tacna and Arica) can cross. Coming into Peru from Chile, you can only change pesos into intis with street money changers in Tacna (Banco de la Nación will not); the street rate is bad. Money changers line Av. Bolognesi. Better when leaving Peru to change intis to dollars at Banco de la Nación in Tacna and then buy pesos with dollars. You probably get a better rate for intis here than in Chile, but the money changers give a poor rate for pesos. Border closes at 2200, and Peruvian immigration is shut on public holidays. Entering Peru here, travellers are rarely asked for a return or onward ticket.

For those travelling by car between Peru and Chile, ask the taxi drivers at the rank beside the Tourist Hotel for details of border formalities, and buy *relaciones de pasajeros* (official forms) from a bookshop or from booth close to Customs; you will need eight (8) copies.

AREQUIPA—PUNO—CUZCO—MACHU-PICCHU (5)

The Southern Railway no longer carries passengers between Mollendo and Arequipa, but there is a well-paved road from Mollendo to Arequipa via Matarani, about 130 km.

The **ash-grey sand dunes** near La Joya, on the Pan-American Highway and almost half way from the coast to Arequipa, are unique in appearance and formation. All are crescent shaped and of varying sizes, from 6 to 30 metres across and from 2 to 5 metres high, with the points of the crescent on the leeward side. The sand is slowly blown up the convex side, drifts down into the concave side, and the dunes move about 15 metres a year.

Arequipa, with about 850,000 people, 1,030 km. from Lima by road, stands at 2,380 metres in a beautiful valley at the foot of El Misti volcano, a snow-capped, perfect cone, 5,822 metres high, guarded on either side by the mountains Chachani (6,096 metres), and Pichu-Pichu (5,669 metres). The city has fine Spanish buildings and many old and interesting churches built of *sillar*, a pearly white volcanic material almost exclusively used in the construction of Arequipa. It was re-founded on August 15, 1540, by an emissary of Pizarro, but it had been an Inca city. It is the main commercial centre for the south, and its people resent the general tendency to believe that everything is run from Lima; business travellers should know this. The climate is delightful, with a mean temperature before sundown of 23°C, and after sundown of 14½°C. The sun shines on 360 days of the year. Annual rainfall is less than 150 mm.

Because of the danger of earthquakes the churches are low, the houses have one storey only, patios are small with no galleries. Roofs are flat and windows are small, disguised by superimposed lintels or heavy grilles. In recent years, higher buildings with large windows have been constructed.

Points of Interest The twin-towered Cathedral on the Plaza de Armas, founded 1612, largely rebuilt 19th century, remarkable for having its façade along the whole length of the church; La Compañía church, whose main façade (1698) and side portal (1654) are striking examples of the florid Andean *mestizo* style: see the Royal Chapel to the left of the sanctuary, and its San Ignacio chapel with a beautiful polychrome cupola (admission, US$0.10, open 0900-1130, 1500-1730, recommended); Puente Bolívar, designed by Eiffel. Arequipa has several fine seignorial houses with large carved tympanums over the entrances. The Gibbs-Ricketts house (now offices, open to public 1700-2000), with its fine portal and puma-head waterspouts, and the Casa del Moral, or Williams house (Banco Industrial, with museum) are good examples, as is the Casa Govaneche, Merced 201, now an office of the Central Bank (ask the guards who will let you view the courtyard and fine period rooms). One of the oldest districts is San Lázaro, a collection of tiny climbing streets and houses quite close to the *Hotel de Turistas* at Selva Alegre. Behind the cathedral there is a very attractive alley with more handicraft shops. Churches are usually open 0700-0900 and 1800-2000. The

AREQUIPA
107

NOT TO SCALE

N

SELVA ALEGRE

TO AIRPORT CHIVAY, CUZCO

AV. BOLOGNESI

AV. DEL EJÉRCITO

PUENTE GRAU

RIVERO

RECOLETA

RÍO CHILI

VILLALBA

UGARTE

AYACUCHO

MELGAR

ZELA

JERUSALEM

SANTA CATALINA

SAN FRANCISCO

SANTA MARÍA

MORAL

BOLÍVAR

SANTA MARÍA

SAN AGUSTÍN

SAN JOSÉ

PERAL

AV. SIGLO

PUENTE

BOLOGNESI

MERCADERES

COLÓN

O. MUÑOZ N.

PALACIO VIEJO

CRUZ VERDE

SUCRE

VALDIVIA

MORÁN

STO. DOMINGO

TO JULIACA AND PUNO

CONSUELO

SAN JUAN DE DIOS

SAN CAMILO

LIMA

PIZARRO

SAN MARTÍN

LA MERCED

TRISTAN

N. DE PIÉROLA

ALTO

PERÚ

DE LA LUNA

PIZARRO

AV. JORGE CHÁVEZ

EJERCICIOS

28 DE JULIO

TO THE SOUTH

AV. ALFONSO UGARTE

SALAVERRY

AV. TACNA

JUNÍN

QUIROZ

HUÁSCAR

T

1. Plaza de Armas	12. Casa del Moral
2. Cathedral	13. Casa Gibbs-Ricketts
3. Santa Catalina Convent	14. Tepsa and other
4. La Compañía	bus offices
5. San Francisco	15. Tourist Office
6. San Agustín	16. Post Office
7. La Merced	17. Intel, Telephone
8. Santo Domingo	Office
9. La Recoleta	18. San Camilo
10. Municipal Museum	Market
11. Archaeological Museum	19. Hotel de Turistas
at San Agustín	20. Hostal Guzmán
University	

churches of San Francisco, San Agustín, La Merced and Santo Domingo are all well worth seeing. Opposite San Francisco is a handicraft centre, housed in a beautiful former prison. Next door is the municipal museum with much war memorabilia, open 0900-1730, interesting, US$0.40. The archaeological museum at the San Agustín University has a good collection of ceramics and mummies (it is being restored and a donation is expected for entry); apply to Dr. E. Linares, the Director. La Recoleta, a Franciscan monastery on the other side of the river, is well worth visiting, with museums; open 0900-1300, 1500-1700, entry US$0.60 (guide is not recommended). It contains several cloisters, a religious art museum, an Amazon museum and a library with many rarities. The church itself is open only 0700-800, 1900-2000.

By far the most interesting visit is to Santa Catalina Convent, opened in 1970 after centuries of mystery, the most remarkable sight in Arequipa; excellently refurbished, very beautiful, period furniture, kitchen utensils, and paintings. It is a miniature walled colonial town of over two hectares in the middle of the city; about 450 nuns used to live there in total seclusion, except for their women servants. The few remaining nuns have retreated to one section of the convent, allowing visitors to see a maze of cobbled streets, flower-decked cloisters and buttressed houses. These have been finely restored and painted in traditional white, browns and blues. Open 0900-1700, but entrance till 1600, admission US$2, daily, including Sun.; the free tour they offer you at the entrance is worthwhile. The many pictures of the Arequipa and Cuzco schools are worth seeing. There is a small café, which sells cakes made by the nuns.

The flowered Plaza de Armas is faced on three sides by colonial arcaded buildings, and on the fourth by the Cathedral. The central San Camilo market (between Perú, San Camilo, Piérola and Alto de la Luna) is also worth visiting. At Selva Alegre there is a shady park in front of the *Hotel de Turistas*, which is within easy walking distance of all the famous churches and main plaza. Arequipa is said to have the best-preserved colonial architecture in Peru, apart from Cuzco. A cheap tour of the city can be made in a Vallecito bus, 1½ hrs. for US$0.30; a circular tour going down Calles Jerusalén and San Juan de Dios.

Festivals Interesting Holy Week ceremonies, culminating in the burning of an effigy of Judas on Easter Sunday and the reading of his "will", containing criticisms of the city authorities. Another festival at end-April and beginning-May fills the hotels. On 14 August, eve of the city's anniversary, there is a splendid firework display in the Plaza de Armas and a decorated float parade. On Sundays at about 1030 there is a civic and military parade on the Plaza de Armas.

Warning Thieves are very active in Arequipa. Beware particularly in market area, especially after dark, and in Calle San Juan de Dios between Plaza and bus offices; keep baggage secured in restaurants. Women travelling without men can expect much harassment here. However, the police have been complimented as friendly, courteous and efficient.

Hotels *Turistas*, Selva Alegre, C, with bath (less without bath), unsafe area, swimming pool (cold), gardens, good meals, pub-style bar, cocktail lounge, tennis court, Wendy house for children; *Portal*, C, Plaza de Armas, excellent, wonderful views, expensive but food and service disappointing, roof top swimming pool. *Posada del Puente*, Av. Bolognesi 101, T 21-74-44, D, good, restaurant, rec.; *Maison Plaza*, Plaza de Armas, D, with breakfast, bathroom and TV, clean, friendly, good value; *Villa Baden Baden* (Sra Bluemel de Castro), Manuel Ugarteche 401, Selva Alegre (T 222416), 6 rooms, D (F p.p.), breakfast included, German, French, English spoken, very informative about city's environs and climbing, rec.; *Arequipa Inn*, Rivero 412, modern hotel, D, with bath (US$4.60 for extra bed in room), garage, T 226077, slow service, owner unsympathetic; *Viza*, 3-star, Perú 202, all rooms with bath and phone, reports please.

Jerusalén, Calle Jerusalén 601 (T 222502/3), E, will change dollars, comfortable, modern with restaurant; next door at No. 605 is *Hostal Florentina*, F, hot water, good but washrooms a bit smelly; *Crismar*, Calle Moral 107, opposite main Post Office, E, with shower, modern, central, civilized, food good; *Hostal Las Mercedes*, end of Calle Consuelo, P.O. Box 417 (T 213601), E, clean, safe, restaurant, highly rec. (but do not confuse with *Hostal La Merced*, in Calle La Merced, which is not); *Hostal Premier*, 50 rooms, Av. Quiroz 100, 2-star, E with bath, will store luggage, restaurant, garage (T 221-791); *Casa de Mi Abuela*, Jerusalén 606, E, very clean, friendly, safe, hot water, laundry, self-catering if desired, English spoken, breakfast on patio or roof terrace, beautiful garden, highly rec.; *El Conquistador*, Mercaderes 409, E, T 212916, clean, safe, lovely colonial atmosphere, credit cards accepted, owner speaks English; *Hostal Selva Alegre*, Los Geranios 104, reasonable, clean; *Residencia Niza*, Calle Siglo Veinte 122, E (rooms, cabins and apartments), meals served, friendly; *Hostal Tumi de Oro*, San Agustín 311A, Cercado, 2½ blocks from Plaza de Armas, F p.p., hot water, breakfast on request, rooms with and without bath, rec.

Guzmán, Jerusalén 408 (T 227142), F, hot water irregular, friendly, small café, laundry, very helpful, a bit run down; and *Hostal Núñez*, Jerusalén 528 (T 218648), F, hot water, laundry, safe, clean, both crowded and opinions vary. *Excelsior*, Mercaderes 106, T 215241, F, clean, 6 rooms with private bath, warm electric shower, central, some rooms noisy, laundry facilities, safe for luggage and person, owner speaks German and English; *Mirador* (on Plaza de Armas), clean bedrooms but sagging beds, F, good, secure for luggage, friendly, some English spoken, hot water 0900-1700, bathrooms not too clean, but rec.; *Hostal Parra Residencial*, Av. Parra 97, T 223787, 5 mins. from station, clean, friendly, laundry facilities, F (some rooms with shower, US$1 more), rec.; *Le Foyer*, Ugarte 114, T 214658, F, hot water, washing facilities, clean, comfortable, central, very popular, discounts at travel agents downstairs; *Hostal Santa Catalina*, E or F, near Convent, clean, hot water, friendly, light bulbs in short supply (take your own); *Residencial Rivero*, Rivero 420, F, clean, with bath but not always hot water, friendly, helpful, washing facilities; *Crillón Serrano*, Calle Perú 109, G, with bath, hot water a.m., friendly to Germans, mice; *Americano*, Calle Alvarez Tomás (also called Ejercicios on maps), 4 blocks from the plaza, F, hot shower at any time, clean, beautiful geraniums; *Gran Hostal*, Alvarez Tomás, friendly. On San Juan de Dios are *Hostal Royal*, F, hot showers but not enough (some rooms without water), very noisy but clean and friendly; *San Francisco*, F, good, hot showers, washing facilities, clean; and *Hostal Florida*, E (cheaper without bath), clean, modern, good beds, rec. *Hostal Tradicional*, Sucre 113, F, family-run, cheap breakfasts downstairs, order hot water in advance, washing facilities, clothes drying on roof, safe, clean, peña in p.m. *Hostal Sucre*, Sucre 407, G without bath, friendly, clean; *Hostal Fernández*, Quesada 106, E, 10 mins. from centre, beautiful garden with parrot, views of El Misti, family affair, breakfasts, hot water, clean, rec.; *César's*, Consuelo 429, F with bath, clean, good, friendly, safe.

Restaurants Many tend to close early—2030 or 2100. *Le París*, Mercaderes 228, good international food and local seafood, quite expensive but good, excellent washrooms; *The Royal Drink*, Centro Comercial Cayma, T 20-20A, clean, good local and Italian dishes; *Manolo*, San Francisco 135, clean, good, expensive; *Central Garden*, San Francisco 127, good food and value; *Astoria*, Calle Santo Domingo, local dishes, good service; *Monza*, Santo Domingo 1½ blocks from Plaza, good set meal and breakfast; *Chopería*, vaguely German, beer good, on road to airport, quite expensive; *André de París*, Santa Catalina 207, good food, holds peñas twice a week; *El Quinqué*, opp. Santa Catalina, meals and peñas, all week in season, otherwise weekends; *Las Delicias del Carbón*, Villalba 317, near Santa Catalina, good grills, friendly atmosphere; *Rodeo*, on O.M.Najar, Argentine-style grill, rec. *1900 Pub Pizzería*, behind the cathedral, excellent pizzas; *Balcón Arequipa*, good view over Plaza, popular with locals, good breakfasts and fruit juice, slow service, corner of Merced and Bolognesi; *El Fogón*, Santa Marta 112, good; *Pizzería San Antonio*, Jerusalén y Santa Marta, excellent; *La Rueda*, in side street off Jerusalén, US$3 for excellent parrillada; *Bonanza*, Jerusalén 114, one block from Plaza de Armas, excellent fish and local food, but poor service, peña group Fri. evenings; *Sol de Mayo*, Jerusalén, good, reasonable prices, beautiful garden, open till 1800; *Bagatelle*, Jerusalén, good snacks and sandwiches, courtyard to eat in; *La Nueva Mundial*, Jerusalén 522, popular, local dishes, band playing; *La Gran Vía*, Calle Bolognesi, cheap and friendly; *Chifa Liura*, Plaza de Armas, rec. Also Pasaje Catedral, 101, *La Chimenea*, simple, good food. *La Pizza Nostra*, on Plaza de Armas (open for breakfasts), safe dishes but no local ones. We have received a number of reports of robberies at *El Cerrojo*, Portal de San Agustín 111, Plaza de Armas.

Vegetarian: *Comedor de Gran Fraternidad Universal*, Jerusalén 400, cheap, friendly; *Govinda*, good, bread and honey, small, friendly, but slow service, Jerusalén 402; *Come y Vive Mejor*, Calle Nueva 410A, cheap and good. *La Zanahoria*, Salaverry 203, not too good; *Secretos y Virtudes de la Naturaleza*, Peral 321, good and cheap; *Mathesis*, Jerusalén 224, a bit more expensive than others; *Rainbow Community Diet System*, San José 1126; *Madre Natura*, Grau 310. Excellent natural yoghurt at Jerusalén 517, US$0.45 per litre.

Rec. café *Monaco*, Calle Mercaderes, cheap and good; *Hospedaje Cuzco*, corner of Plaza, balcony for drinking and watching the world go by, excellent (especially vegetable) tortillas but avoid the *ceviche*; *Aurelius*, San Francisco 125, cheap and friendly. *Harumi* snack bar, San José 216, Chinese, US$1 for set menu. Excellent bread and cakes at *La Canasta*, Jerusalén 115. *Dairy Room*, Plaza de Armas, cakes and pastries, very good coffee; *Dolce Vita*, Plaza de Armas, good pastries; *Salón de Té*, Mercaderes, good coffee, cakes, ice-cream; *La Esquina*, Morán and San Juan de Dios, café with good pisco sours; cheapest good pisco sours at *Jumbo Jet*, Colon 221. *Nenovi*, San Juan de Dios 301, good coffee; *Ice Palace*, Mercaderes 230 and Cruz Verde 213, excellent, ice cream.

A score of picanterías specialize in piquant foods; try one called *El Pato*; rocoto relleno (hot stuffed peppers), cuy chactado (seared guinea-pig), papas con ocopa (boiled potatoes with a hot yellow sauce) and adobo (pork stew). Try them in Yanahuara suburb. Arequipeño food also at San Camilo market. Good cheap places down San Juan de Dios, but dodgy area for tourists. A good local speciality is Mejía cheese; try also the queso helado (frozen fresh milk mixed with sugar and a sprinkling of cinnamon), the chocolate (*La Ibérica*), the toffee (e.g. at *San Antonio Pizzería*), and the fruit drinks called papayada and tumbada, local specialities in the market and restaurants.

Current 220 volts A.C., 50 cycles.

Clubs Club Arequipa; Golf Club; North American Cultural Institute; International Club; Club Hípico Los Leones (riding club).

Shopping *Casa Secchi*, Mercaderes 111, sells good arts, crafts and clothing; also *Artesanías Peruanas*, Puente Bolognesi 147. *Empresa Peruana de Promoción Artesanal (EPPA)*, General Morán 120. The covered market opposite the Teatro Municipal in Calle Mercaderes is rec. for knitted goods, bags, etc. Market around Valdivia and N. de Piérola. Sweaters and woollen goods can be better value than in Juliaca or Puno. Arequipa is noted for its leather work; the street of saddlers and leather workers is Pte. Bolognesi. The handicraft shop in the old prison opposite San Francisco is particularly good for bags. At *Fundo del Fierro* shop 14, on Plaza San Francisco, alpaca-wool handicrafts from Callalli in the Colca canyon are sold. *El Zaguán*, Santa Catalina 120A, good for handicrafts. Three antique shops in Calle Santa Catalina. Chocolate factory on Jerusalén (NE of Plaza de Armas) gives tours on weekdays only. Supermarkets nr. market sell good bread and yoghurt.

Photography Sr. Fernando Delange, N-10 Urbanización Adepa, T 233120, repairs all kinds of electrical equipment as well as cameras. Foto Esperanza S. R. Ltda, Mercaderes 132-2, English spoken, cameras mended.

Bookshop *Librerías ABC* has a branch in Calle Santa Catalina 217, between the convent and the Plaza de Armas, *Codersa*, San Francisco 131, has *Handbook*.

Laundry Lavandería Cayro, Jerusalén 311 and Ejercícios 442. Lavendería del Pueblo, Ejercícios 558.

Taxi Fares US$0.75 a trip, US$2 an hr. within the town, US$0.30 minimum; US$2.10 in the country; US$1.50 airport to city (can be shared). US$1 railway station to centre.

Car Hire National, Bolívar 25; Avis (cheaper), Puente Bolognesi nr. plaza, US$35/day + US$0.10/km over first 200 km for a VW.

Entertainment Bar *Romie*, Plaza San Francisco, tiny bar with live music, Mon., Tues., autóctono, Wed.-Sat., peña. Excellent *peña El Sillar* in the cloisters of La Compañía church, minimum charge of US$0.50, plus US$1 for the music, 1930-2300; *Peña Waykopac*, Jerusalén 204, good atmosphere, Fri. and Sat. *Peña Chunenea*, Pasaje la Catedral 4. Watch out for the local folk-music group Chachani, said to be one of Peru's best.

Sports Two public stadia, a racecourse, several swimming pools, tennis courts and golf links (18 holes). The Arequipa Golf Club welcomes visitors from abroad. Riding is very popular. There are bullfights, and elaborate occasional firework displays (especially on 14 August).

Climbing Club de Andinismo de Arequipa. Chanchari Tours, Tristán 224, PO Box 2480, T 213186, hires climbing equipment, can provide guide and transport, rec. Sr Zárate, who also runs a camera repair shop, is very helpful with maps and advice.

Exchange Banco Internacional, Mercaderes 217, exchanges Citicorp dollar cheques. Banco de Crédito accepts Visa Card and gives good rates, no commission, recommended. Others include Banco Popular, Banco Continental (will not change travellers' cheques) and Banco del Sur del Perú (Calle Jerusalén, close to Post Office, will change travellers' cheques, 2-3% commission, accepts Master Charge). Lima Tours, Santa Catalina 120 (American Express agent but will not change any travellers' cheques). Via Tours, Santo Domingo 114, good rates. Diners Club, San Francisco 112. Parallel market down Calle Santo Domingo, Jerusalén near Plaza de Armas, and at Morán y San Juan de Dios.

Spanish Course Silvana Cornejo, 7 de Junio 118, Cerrito Los Alvarez, Cerro Colorado, T 225308, about US$1.50/hour, rec., she speaks German fluently.

British Consul Mr. Roberts, Calle Quesada 107, Yanahuara, T (054) 211961.

English Library at Peruvian-North American Cultural Institute, Melgar 109.

French Consul and Library Alianza Francesa, Santa Catalina 208.

Chilean Consulate Mercaderes 212, 4th floor, entrance to lift 30m. down passageway down Mercaderes on left, open 0900-1300, present passport 0900-1100 if you need a visa.

Post and Cables At central Post Office, Moral 118 opposite *Hotel Crismar*. The central Post Office also provides a telex service. Letters can only be posted at the Post Office during opening hours. Telephone and fax: Intel, San Francisco y Valdivia.

Doctor Dr Julio Postigo, Independencia 225; Dr Jorge A. del Carpio Alvarez, Santo Domingo 123, of 303, T 215483, rec, only Spanish spoken. **Dentist** Dr José Corrales, San Juan de Dios 216.

Tourist Information Foptur, Portal Municipal 112, Plaza de Armas, south side, T 213101. Complaints and suggestions are welcomed, information not always accurate but they try to be helpful, open 0730-1500, free street plans. The Librería at Jerusalén 109 sells maps. Police may be contacted for information by phone: 226549, but not at all hours; Tourist Police, Jerusalén 317, and at the bus station, are also helpful. Touring y Automóvil Club del Perú, Calle Sucre 209.

Travel Agencies Tony Holley takes small private groups by 12-seater Land Rover to interesting places in the area such as the Salinas borax lake, Chivay, the slopes of El Misti, cave drawings at Sumbay, the volcanoes Ubinas and Chachani, Caylloma where the Amazon rises, and rural Arequipa. Excursions cost from as little as $20 per person, providing there is a minimum of 6 people on tour. With fewer passengers the cost rises proportionally. Passengers are insured. Mr. Holley's postal address is Casilla 77, Arequipa, and his home address is Urb. Tahuaycani F-28, Umacollo, Arequipa (T 212525, Mon.-Fri. 0730-1600; 224452 daily after 1700, 24 hrs. Sat., Sun., and feast days.) When not on tour, Mr. Holley's car may be found near Santa Catalina between 0715 and 1230.

Turandes, Mercaderes 130, T 22962, specializes in tours, guides and equipment for climbing El Misti and other mountains, and trips to other local places of interest. They have very good maps. Continental Tours, Calle Jerusalén 402, good value, English and French-speaking guides. Conresa Tours, Jerusalén 409, Casilla 563, T 211847/223073/215820, specializes in trips to the Colca Canyon, and to the Toro Muerto petroglyphs (US$20 p.p.), Las Salinas and Mejía lakes, and city tours, *South American Handbook* users welcome. Several agencies offer tours (1 or 2 days) to the Colca Canyon: Vlado, Merced 408, cheaper than most; Expreso Turismo y Confort, Peral 304 (US$15); Condor Tours, on Ugarte across from entrance to Santa Catalina; and Santa Catalina Tours, buses with large windows, recommended. Many agencies, including Happy Travels, Santa Catalina 106, offer tours of the city and surrounding area, T 218592; English spoken. Local office of Lima Tours reported reliable.

Buses Most companies have their offices in Calle San Juan de Dios (5-6 blocks from Plaza de Armas). To Lima, 1,030 km, colectivos take 19 hrs., rain damage to the road can cause delays; fare US$12.75 or more. Warning: need to book in advance to and from Lima in Jan.-March holiday season. Buses, de luxe Pullman, air conditioned with hostess, many daily, 16 hours or more, up to US$15.75: Cruz del Sur, Arequipeño, Tepsa (toilet on board), Ormeño rec.; Sudamericana is cheapest. Few buses stop at Pisco. Trucks to Lima take 3-4 days. To Puno and Cuzco roads and buses are generally bad; the train is better; buses run only at night to Puno, US$4, San Cristóbal cheapest, up to 17 hrs., uncomfortable, cold; colectivo, heavily booked, some by day (1000), fare US$10. To and from Cuzco by bus (680 km.), San Cristóbal, 1600 (18 hrs.) US$8; Cruz del Sur, 21 hrs., US$8.50, 1600, Jacantaya at 1800. Colectivo-taxi to Cuzco US$20. Colectivo to Juliaca US$8.15 (office on Calle Salaverry) leaves 0900. Bus to Juliaca 8½-9½ hrs., US$4.90. Bus to Tacna (about 20 a day), Cruz del Sur (rec.), Ormeño, US$3, 6 hrs.; also Flores Hnos. Colectivo to Tacna, Expreso Tacna, San Juan de Dios 537, T 213281, will collect at hotel, rec., US$4.75, 6 hrs. Moquegua by Angelitos Negros, leaves in the morning, US$2, interesting journey. Buses must be booked 24 hrs. in advance. Bus to Nazca, Sudamericana, 3 a day, US$7, Ormeño, 7 a day, 10 hours, US$6; also with Roggero and Tepsa.

Air Rodríguez Ballón airport, 7 km. from town. To and from Lima, daily air service by Faucett and AeroPerú, US$75. No direct flight to Iquitos; all go via Lima. To Miami via Lima and Panama; leaves on Wed. at 2340, arrives Miami 2155 following day. Return flight from Miami on Wed. at 0130 arriving 1045. To Cuzco, US$40, by Faucett and AeroPerú, daily at 0815 (except Sun.); to Puerto Maldonado with air force (Grupo 8), usually Friday. To Juliaca by AeroPerú daily except Sun. and Faucett, about US$25, 20 mins. (book well ahead). The plainclothes police at the passport desk may arrange a taxi for you. Buses marked "Zamacola" go to about ½ km. from the airport. The offices of both Faucett and AeroPerú are on the Plaza de Armas. Taxes: US$5 state tax; US$3 airport tax.

Rail To Puno, at 2100, with connections to Cuzco via Juliaca; day train suspended. Fares: 1st class US$6, 2nd class US$4. Only the Pullman cars, US$4 extra, are heated—important above 4,000 metres—do not wear too much clothing; the doors are locked. If not travelling Pullman, take a blanket. If travelling 2nd class take a cushion as well. Rail trip to Puno and Cuzco is safer in the rainy season than by road. The train arrives in Juliaca after about 7 hrs, there is then a 2 hr. wait; if going to Cuzco you have to change trains here. Fare to Juliaca is US$8 pullman, US$4 first class, US$2.50 second class; to Cuzco, US$6 first class, US$4 second class; best to travel in buffet car, which costs US$20 for tourists; food good. The ticket office is open 0730-1200, 1500-1800, 2000-2100, Sat. 0800-1200, 1500-1800, Sun. 0900-1200, 1500-1800; queue at 0400 for 1st class tickets on day before departure. Sr. Guzmán of *Residencial Guzmán*, Jerusalén 408, may be able to help with tickets, for a fee US$0.35; Continental Tours and others charge US$2 extra to book for you. If you have difficulty buying train tickets, try in the shops opposite the station, or even ask a policeman at the station. Train schedules and ticket office hours change frequently.

If you feel bad on train ask for the oxygen mask at once.

Warning On the Arequipa-Juliaca-Puno or Cuzco rail route, beware of thieves at every station, especially at night. Wait until everyone else has left the train and then till everyone else has left the platform, or (at Arequipa) ask at the police office if they will let you out of their exit. If not travelling in the locked "turismo" pullman coach, padlock your bag to the luggage rack, tie all your belongings to you and keep pockets empty. It's best to take only one large bag which cannot be thrown through a window. The lighting may not always work, or may be sabotaged by thieves: take a torch. Latest reports indicate that the least secure part of the trip is the wait at Juliaca, "the theft stop". Police may escort foreigners who have to go to the Juliaca ticket office, but watch your bags all the same.

Excursions The hillside suburb of **Cayma**, with delightful 18th century church (open only until 1600). It also has many old buildings associated with Bolívar and Garcilaso de la Vega and is the home of contemporary Arequipeño poet, Manuel Gallegos Sanz. The Candelaria festival on February 2 is colourful. Many local buses marked Cayma. **Yanahuara**, also a suburb, with a 1750 *mestizo*-style church (opens 1500), with magnificent churrigueresque façade, all in *sillar*; the Tiabaya valley; thermal baths of Jesús (1/2 hour by car, on the slopes of Pichu-Pichu), open 0500-1230. **Yura**, 29 km. from Arequipa (bus every 3 hours from San Juan de Dios, US$0.30) in a small, interesting valley on the W slopes of Chachani (*Yura Tourist Hotel*, D, wth bath, meals US$3, and an unsigned hotel opposite, F, good), has thermal baths open Tues.-Sat., morning only. **Socosani** (1 1/2 hrs. by rail and road), now a spa owned by a mining consortium, can only be visited by appointment, 40 km. from Arequipa, in a beautiful small valley SW of Chachani, with a modern hotel providing meals and Socosani water, sports in Socosani include tennis, bowls. **Tingo**, which has a very small lake and 3 ill-kept swimming pools, should be visited on Sun. (bus 7), US$0.15) for local food; *anticuchos* and *buñuelos*. 3 km. past Tingo on the Huasacanche road is *La Mansión del Fundador*, originally a Jesuit foundation but later a *hacienda*, restored as a museum with original furnishings and paintings, entrance fee US$0.75, with cafeteria and bar (and soon to provide accommodation); it is beside the Sabandía river. Molino de Sabandía, built 1600, entrance fee US$0.50, swimming bath and countryside, well worth seeing (taxi, US$6.50 round trip); Yumina (adjoining Sabandía), many Inca terraces which are still in use. The interior of the church at Chiguita is well worth seeing.

Up a passable dirt road running through Cayma, Sumbay (4,150 metres) and Viscachani, between Misti and Chachani, is the village of **Chivay** (regular buses 5 hrs.) lying in the spectacular terraced **Colca Canyon**. A charge of US$0.35 is made to enter the canyon at Chivay. Local, very distinctive, costumes still worn by women, and there is a swimming pool fed by hot springs (US$0.40, clean, rec.). Water from this river is currently being diverted through a series of tunnels and canals to the desert between Repartición and Camaná, to irrigate the Siguas and Majes pampas. Further down the Colca Canyon, on both sides (bridge—Puente del Inca—at Chivay only) unspoilt Andean villages are to be found, overlooked by the two volcanoes, Hualca-Hualca and Ampato. At one of these, Yanque (good church, where two nuns from the Bronx sell handicrafts), walkers can cross the canyon by a colonial bridge (no vehicles)— reached from the main square in Yanque via Av. Santa Rosa) and walk to villages on the other side: Coporaque and Ichupampa (about 2 hrs.), also with good churches; beyond Ichupampa is Lari, also with a fine church. On the opposite side of the river from Lari is Maca, whose church has an interesting interior. Beyond Maca is **Cabanaconde**; festivals: 25 May: horseriding, dancing; 14-18 July: bullfighting, dancing. There is a path to the Colca Canyon from the main square, 4 hours' walk; it is possible to cross and go up to Tapay. A longer hike, 4 days, crosses the pass (5,000 m.) and reaches

Madugal through a red walled valley. 10 km. before Cabanaconde, you reach the Cruz del Cóndor viewpoint, spectacular scenery, condors to be seen early a.m. and late p.m. (take 0400 bus from Cabanaconde). If hiking, which is strenuous but worth it, buy food in Arequipa, and maps from the Instituto Geográfico Militar in Lima, take water sterilizer. **N.B.** Robbery in the Colca Canyon has been reported; if hiking seek advice on local conditions.

The Colca (or Majes) Canyon, said to be twice as deep as the Grand Canyon, was discovered from the air in 1954 by Gonzalo de Reparaz; the first descent was made in 1978 and the first descent by raft and canoe was made in 1981. AeroPerú and Aerocóndor have flights over it. It is possible to visit the canyon in one day, but you will reach Cruz del Cóndor by about 1300, when there will be no condors around, and the return to Arequipa is very long. A short circuit from Arequipa goes via Chivay, Yanque (more thermal baths), Achoma, Maca, Cabanaconde, then on to Huambo and back to Arequipa. A longer route involves going to Callalli (beautiful alpaca-wool work at Centro Artesanal) from Viscachani, instead of to Chivay, then to Sibayo (possible detour to Cailloma), Tuti, and then to Chivay. This route adds an hour to the circuit, permitting views of fine landscapes with vicuña, Andean duck and llama, and a glance at the churches of Callalli and Tuti.

Accommodation Chivay: *Hotel Moderno*, G, basic, noisy, upstairs rooms best, no hot water, restaurant below OK, sanitation unmentionable, friendly; *Hostal Anita* on plaza, G, clean, friendly, hot shower; best food at unnamed restaurant at Calle Siglo 20 107, just off the plaza. The *Aldea Turística de Colca* (rec., E, bungalows for 6 are C) at Achoma, half an hour from Chivay along the Cabanaconde road, offers breakfast US$1.50, other meals US$2.50, only electricity, heating and hot water in valley; book through Receptur in Lima or Arequipa or Ricketts Turismo, Mercaderes 407, Arequipa, T 225-382, open April-Nov. only. In Cabanaconde: *Hotel de la Colca*, G, friendly; *Cruz del Cóndor*, basic but clean, good meals, F, horse hire to Cruz del Cóndor, 2-3 hrs. there, 1 back, impressive ride; *Alojamiento Bacilia*, G p.p., unwelcoming; several small restaurants—look for "cerveza Arequipeña" sign.

Travel to Colca Canyon Buses to Cabanaconde from Arequipa via Chivay: Transportes Delgado (rec.), leave Arequipa 0600 and Cabanaconde 0500 daily, 7½ hours. Transportes El Chasqui Transandino, San Juan de Dios 515, goes as far as Maca, 0530. Transportes Sur Colca, San Juan de Dios 537, direct to Cabanaconde daily at 0500, US$3, 5-6 hours. Via Huambo with Transportes Jacantaya, Víctor Lira 108, T 23258 leaves Arequipa at 0900, and Cabanaconde at 0700, not daily. Setrasur at 0600 to Cabanaconde, return 0500, US$30. Buses leave Chivay for Cabanaconde at 1100, US$0.60, return from Cabanaconde to Chivay 0500. Alternatively a taxi can be hired for a day tour (US$80 for up to 5 make sure no more are carried, too uncomfortable otherwise) at Expreso Chivay (Comité 10), Calle San Juan de Dios (if going by rented car, ask for an extra fuel can; no fuel in Canyon except at Chivay).

Arequipa travel agencies run day tours to the Canyon for about US$17 (avoid agents who overcharge), but the one-day trip (0400-2400) is very tiring and the viewing stops are short. Among the companies are Conresa Tours, Jerusalén 409 (Casilla 563, T 215820/223073), Condor Tours on Ugarte, Santa Catalina Tours, Receptur, General Morán 118, of. 13, T (054) 212989, Arequipa, ask for Mónica who speaks English, or Marco Elias Rebaza Merino (bookable in Linca through Coltur, Av. Pardo, Miraflores), and Colca Tours; Vlado, at Merced 408, is cheaper than most. Puci Tours, Av. Arequipa, Miraflores, Lima, organize a tour to Chivay with a 2/3 night stop over in Achoma, rec. Canyon best visited April-November, after rainy season, but never travel in mountains after dark. Whether travelling independently or on a tour, always take warm clothing or a blanket.

El Misti volcano may be climbed. Start from the hydroelectric plant (first register with the police there), then you need one day to the Monte Blanco shelter (4,800 metres). Start early (take water) for the 4 hrs. to the top, to get there by 1100 before the mists obscure the view. If you start back at 1200 you will reach the hydroelectric plant by 1800. (Erick and Martine Perruche, of Montargis, who took this route, have left a map in the *Hotel Guzmán*). Alternatively, buses leave Arequipa for Baños Jesús, then on to Chiguata, where one can walk to the base of El Misti. Be sure to take plenty of food and water, it takes 2 days to reach the crater, guides may be available at Cachamarca.

The world's largest field of petroglyphs (hard to find on your own) at Toro Muerto (off the Majes canyon) can be reached by taking a bus (San Antonio, Lima 119, 0700, returns Arequipa at 1400 and 1700) to Corire, 3 hrs., US$4 return; get out 2 km. before Corire and walk 1 hr. to Toro Muerto (entry US$0.15). Guide for US$3. The higher you go, the more interesting the petroglyphs; take plenty of water and protection against the sun, including sunglasses. There are several restaurants around the Plaza de Armas in Corire; one hotel: *Hostal Willys*, F, clean, good, intermittent water supply.

The railway from Arequipa winds its way up the valley towards Juliaca. Skirting

Misti and Chachani the train climbs steadily past Yura, Socosani and Pampa de Arrieros; after another 80 km. it reaches Crucero Alto, the highest point on the line (4,500 metres). Lakes Lagunillas and Saracocha are very pretty lying on opposite sides of the railway, which passes their margins for nearly an hour. As the descent continues streams become more plentiful. The scene changes in a few hours from desolate mountain peaks to a fertile pampa carrying a fairly populous agricultural community. (Since there is no day train, much of this scenery is not visible en route.)

The rough road from Arequipa to Juliaca reaches its highest point at Alto de Toroya, 4,693 metres. Train is more comfortable than bus.

Juliaca, 289 km. from Arequipa, at 3,825 metres (cold at night), has a population—mostly Indian—of 100,000. It is reported to be very poor and run down, and therefore lawless; you can buy good alpaca clothing here very cheaply, in the plaza in front of the railway station; fleeces can be purchased at about US$2.50 per kilo, but they sell very fast. On the huge Plaza Melgar (good place to meet local students), several blocks from the main part of the town, is an interesting colonial church. Large market in the square on Mondays, reported cheaper than Cuzco and Puno; there is another daily market in the square outside the railway station, which is more tourist oriented. Tupac Amarú market, on Moquegua 7 blocks E of railway line, cheap black market. A first class hospital is run by the Seventh Day Adventists.

Warning Beware of pickpockets and thieves, especially at the station, where they get on the train.

Hotels *Turistas*, good, D, but water turned off 2300, meals US$3; *Hostal Royal*, San Román 158, E, clean, decent accommodation, rec., restaurant good. *Hostal Perú*, on main square, D, with bath, E, without, clean, comfortable, hot water sometimes; 3 cheap, fairly safe, unnamed hotels around plaza; *Victoria*, F, cold water, clean but simple. *Yasur*, E with bath, F without, clean, safe, friendly, 500 metres from station, rec., small bar and restaurant in evening. *Alojamiento San Antonio*, G, basic but clean. In Juliaca water is available generally only between 0700 and 1900.

Restaurants *Royal Hotel* (best); *Ressi*, San Martín, good, but not cheap; *El Comedor del Sur*, adequate; Hole-in-the-wall breakfast parlour at corner of plaza opposite station, good. *El Trebol*, vegetarian restaurant, Pasaje Santa Isabel (off San Ramón, ½ block from station square).

Transport Rail to Cuzco, US$20 "turismo" pullman in buffet car where good, reasonably-priced lunches are served, US$3, 1st class, US$2, 2nd class; trains leave Mon.-Fri., 0850, Sat., 0930, 8½ hrs. Ticket office for first class tickets to Cuzco opens at 0630—tickets are hard to get. Trains to Arequipa daily at 2155, Tues. and Thurs. at 0835, Sat. at 1055. See above for warning, under Arequipa **Rail**.

Also watch your belongings on the Cuzco line at stations like La Raya and Sicuani. Jacantaya bus service, which is half the price of other buses, 11 hrs., to Arequipa. Bus to Cuzco, 3 companies, 12 hrs., US$5.50. **Colectivo to Puno** (from plaza outside rail station), US$1.50; US$0.50 bus. Taxi to Puno via Sillustani, US$15 per car. Daily bus to Moho, on east side of Lake Titicaca, from where it is possible to hitch into Bolivia. A private car can get to Cuzco in 7 hrs.

Air To Lima (US$90), via Arequipa, with Faucett, 2 a day; AeroPerú, daily, except Sun. 20 mins. to Arequipa. Taxi to airport, US$1 (negotiate), to Puno US$12, 45 mins. inc. photo stops.

Excursion to thermal springs at village of Putina, 90 km. from Puno. Bus from Juliaca, US$0.50. About 32 km. NW of Juliaca (76 km. from Puno) is the unspoiled little colonial town of **Lampa**, known as the "Pink City", with splendid church, La Imaculada, containing a copy of Michelangelo's "Pietà", and Kampac Museo, Ugarte 462, musuem with sculptures and ceramics from Lampa and Juli areas, owner lives next door, interesting. The area also has a chinchilla farm and a grove of *puya* plants. About 114 km. NE of Juliaca is the old town of **Azángaro** with another famous church, La Asunción, filled with *retablos* and paintings of the Cuzco school. Stone monoliths may be seen at Taraco and at Hatuncolla. The sheep farm of San Antonio, between Ayaviri and Chiquibambilla, owned by the Prime family (descendants of British emigrants), may be visited by those with a day to spare.

Puno, capital of its Department, altitude 3,855 metres, population 80,000 (with 8,000 at university), on the NW shore of Lake Titicaca, has a fine main square and an interesting, but dirty, lakeside quarter, largely flooded since the rise in the lake's water level. The austere Cathedral was completed in 1657. Puno gets bitterly cold at night: in June-August the temperature at night can fall to -25° C, but generally not below -5° C. Some guerrilla activity; hotels close at midnight, restaurants at 2200. the provinces of Melgar and Azángaro in Puno Department have seen terrorist acitivity; seek advice before visiting them.

N.B. The people who invade buses and trains when they arrive seem to have the hotel business sewn up, so don't shrug them off: you may need their help.

Festival 1-8 February, the very colourful Fiesta de la Virgen de la Candelaria, bands and dancers from all the local towns compete on the Sunday; better at night on the streets than the official functions in the stadium. Check in advance on actual date because Candelaria may be moved if pre-Lentern carnival coincides with it. 3 May, Invención de la Cruz, exhibition of local art; 29 June, colourful festival of San Pedro, procession at Zepita (**see page 946**). Also 20 July. 4-5 November, pageant on founding of Puno and emergence of Manco Capac from waters of Lake Titicaca.

Hotels *Isla Esteves* (Tourist Hotel), T 724, A, spacious, good views, cold site (you can ask for an electric fire), on an island linked by a causeway 5 km. NE of Puno (taxi US$1.75), is built on a Tiwanaku-period site, with bath, telephone, bar, good restaurant, discotheque, good service, electricity and hot water all day, poor rate of exchange, check bill carefully, camping allowed in car park; *Motel Tambo Titikaka*, B, with half-pension, at Chucuito on the lakeside, 17 km. S of Puno; electricity only between 1800-2300, poor heating, rooms icy after sunset, food indifferent and bill charged in dollars, wonderful view, book in advance (travellers need own transport, local transport is scarce and expensive); *Sillustani*, Jr. Lambayeque 195, T 351881, C, including breakfast and dinner (mixed reports), good service, clean, friendly, cold rooms but hot water. *Ferrocarril*, Av. La Torre 185, T 409, opposite station, is modern, D (reservation may be necessary), plenty of hot water, food good (except for breakfast), but good rooms, noisy, live folk music from 1915 in restaurant (food overpriced), central heating adequate, annex (F, not so good) no hot water (accepts many credit cards and changes Bolivian currency); *Don Miguel*, Av. Torre, T 177, D (negotiable), with shower, does not always honour reservations, comfortable, clean with restaurant, clean, service good, water intermittent; *Hostal Real*, Av. El Sol (½ block S of Av. Titicaca), E-D, very nice, hot water all day; *Hostal Nesther*, Deústua 268 (T 321), E (also 3-bedded rooms) with bath, hot water, 0730-0900, clean rec., except for safety; *Internacional*, Libertad 161, T 25, E, with shower (extra bed US$1.50), hot water, clean, secure, central, reservations not always respected. *Roma*, La Libertad 115, F, is passable. *Hostal Embajador*, E, los Incas 289 (T 592), overpriced, but clean, quiet, hot water, fairly friendly; *Hostal Tumi*, Cajamarca 237, Tel.:147, E (less in low season), negotiable, clean, safe, helpful, hot water limited (1830-2100), noisy from 0600; *Continental*, Alfonso Ugarte 161, F, cold water, dirty, friendly; *Bolognesi*, Bolognesi, E-F, friendly, good; *Hostal Monterrey*, Lima 447A, T 343, F, "gringo hotel", reasonable, some rooms with bath, better than those without, a/c, hot water after 1800 (supposedly), fairly clean, secure for luggage (has colectivo service to La Paz); *Hostal Lima*, Lima, E, popular, hot water twice a day, mixed reports on cleanliness; *Hostal Inti*, Av. La Torre, opp. station, G, clean, basic, hot water sometimes, small. *Hostal Italia*, Teodoro Valcarcel 122 (T 640), E-D (negotiable), with shower and breakfast, good, safe, rec.; hot water except in rooms on ground floor, good food, clean, electric heater, staff helpful, esp. Mario Alvarado, and Rubén, who arranges tours to the Uros islands and Sillustani, US$10 each. *Los Uros*, Calle Valcarcel 135, T 644, F, cheaper without bath, hot water at night, plenty of blankets, breakfast available, quiet, small charge to leave luggage (but reports of armed robbery on hotel received), friendly, often full, close to station and market; *San Carlos*, F, near railway station, no hot water, no bath but nice room; *Europa*, Alfonso Ugarte 112, G, "gringo hotel", luggage may be stored, but don't leave valuables in rooms, hot water in the common bathrooms in the evenings, quite clean; *Hostal Posada Real*, Av. Titicaca 156, T 738, F, good, central, clean, warm water, rooms overlooking lake are also nearest to disco close by, minibus to station. At Av. Circunvalación 470, good accommodation, F, in house of local priest run by Macericio and Nelly Rodríguez. Hotel rooms are difficult to find after trains arrive as everyone else is also looking. Clean public showers near the football stadium. Puno suffers from power and water shortages.

Restaurants Try *Sale Caliente*, Tacna 381, or any of the pollo (chicken) places: ¼ chicken and french fries, US$1. *Ambassador*, Lima 347, cheap and varied food, not all dishes of same standard; reasonable *Bar Café Delta*, good for snacks, on La Libertad, try flan de chocolate; *Hotel Ferrocarril* for pizzas and pasta; *Itos*, Plaza de Armas, good food, US$1, rec.; *Café Internacional*, Libertad 161, 2 blocks from Plaza, "gringo", meals huge and cheap but service variable, thieves around, "take waders if you want to go to the toilet", reasonable prices; *Café Restaurant Dorado*, Lima 361, good lunch, breakfast, quick service; *Peña Hostería*, Calle Lima, good music, serves only pizzas. *Club 31* on Moquegua, good cheap café; *Paititi*, Valcarcel 158, vegetarian, excellent; *Las Rocas*, on same street, good but slow; *Samaná*, Puno 334, inconsistent service, sometimes has live folk music from 2100, open fire and snacks and drinks (no minimum charge). *Ayllu*, Puno, good sandwiches, pastries; *Cafetería Chimú*, Jr. Lima 517, excellent breakfast and cakes, closed p.m., run by very friendly German lady, highly rec.; *La Sirena*, in the lakeside quarter, for cheap breakfasts; *Kimano*, Calle Lima one block from Plaza, very good cakes, good (safe) yoghurt; *Café Copacabana*, Melgar y Av. del Sol, good pastries. Good coffee shop next to *Hotel Monterrey*, Grau y Lima. *Restaurant Monterrey*, behind hotel, good fish, only drink is pisco. *Café Juthma*, Moquegua 153, open 0630, excellent cheap breakfast.

Shopping In the covered part of the market (mostly fruit and veg.) there are model reed boats, and attractive carved stone amulets and Ekekos (Bolivian household gods). Market on railway between Av. Los Incas and Lampa is one of the best places in Peru for llama and alpaca wool articles, but bargain hard, especially in p.m., many are still hand-made, unlike in Cuzco. *Artesanías Puno*, on Calle Teodoro Valcarcel, has good quality alpaca goods with sizes for large gringos. *Uros* on same road, higher quality alpaca, but more expensive. Food and clothing market next to stadium. For good *artesanías*, take a bus to km. 20, Chinchera, where the *Trenza de Oro* has very good quality goods.

Museums The Municipal Museum has been combined with the private museum of Sr. Dreyer, Conde de Lemos 289, open Mon. to Fri. 0700-1800, entrance US$0.50.

Exchange Very difficult to use credit cards anywhere: best not to try. Souvenir shop opp. *Hostal Monterrey* (closed 1300-1500). Good rates in *Cambio*, Lima 447, and *Hotel Uros*. Many street changers near bus and tourist agency offices.

Post Office Jirón Moquegua 267. **Telephone** Entel, Arequipa y Moquegua, long waits for international calls.

Bolivian Consulate Jr. Arequipa between Parque Pino y Jr. Deza; may send you to consulate in Yunguyo for visa.

Laundry Lavandería América, Jr. Moquegua 169; Lavandería Lava Clin, Deustua 252, El Sol 431 and Teodoro Valcarcel 132.

Tourist Information Government Tourist Office, Foptur, Jr. Arequipa 314, betweeen Lambayeque and Arbulu, T 353804 (above Farmacia Central), open Mon.-Fri., 0830-1300 (has maps). Check for details of village festivals. Touring y Automóvil Club de Perú, Arequipa 457. The booklet by Pedro Sueldo Nava on Puno, Arequipa and La Paz is informative and reasonably priced (includes maps), also available in Cuzco.

Travel Agencies *Viajes El Sol*, Jirón Arequipa 401, T 684, Sr. Ronald Zárate; *Puno Travel Service*, Tacna 254, rec.. *Cooperativa de Transportes Turísticos Dos de Febrero*, Libertad 111, has received mixed reports. *Turismo Titicaca*, Libertad, rec.; *Suri Tours*, Av. Teodoro Valcarcel, highly rec. for getting train tickets and service; *Kinjyo Travel Service*, Calle Arequipa 401. *Turpuno* next to *Hotel Sillustani* on Lambayeque rec.; also Andrés and Samuel López at *Hotel Don Miguel*. *Air Travel Services SRL*, Oquendo 250 (Sr. Jorge Oliart García), rec. for travel arrangements. The agency next to *Hotel Ferrocarril* is not rec. Beware of high commissions charged on tours and tickets.

Railways There is a 386-km. railway from Puno to Cuzco, via Juliaca. When the Puno-Juliaca section of line is closed, Puno passengers are taken to and from Juliaca by colectivos which leave from Jirón Pardo, 0630, US$1.50 (or by bus, US$0.25), arriving in good time to get Cuzco tickets in Juliaca station. When running, the Puno to Cuzco train leaves 0600 daily except Sun., arriving at 2030, tourist coach US$22 (good service, meals and drinks), 1st class US$6. Tickets are on sale only an hour before departure, or you can buy them the day before (which is the only way to get them), after the train to Arequipa has departed (ticket office hours are very irregular—check in advance). Tour companies often buy up all the available tickets and you either have to queue for hours (or ask a young boy to do this for you, paying him half in advance), or pay the companies a premium (from 20% to 100%). A magnificent run, with shopping possibilities at stations. Sit on right side on Puno-Cuzco train for best views. Hotel representatives join train near Cuzco to find customers.

Puno to Arequipa leaves 1900, Mon., Wed., Fri., sometimes withdrawn. Pullman US$10 (with blankets, heating, no vendors allowed), lunch, US$3.20, 1st class US$6, 2nd class US$4 (no lighting), 8 hrs. Tickets can be booked in advance, get to the station early to queue (0700 for 1000 opening of office); if short of time get them through a travel agent (20% commission, sometimes more). Beware of supposed Turismo class at an exhorbitant price which is actually 1st class.

See **Warning** under Arequipa **Rail**, page 940.

A good idea in Puno, Juliaca and other Andean towns, when moving about with heavy baggage, is to hire a 3-wheel cycle cart (about US$0.20 per km.)

Roads and Buses To Arequipa, road improved: more bridges have been built. Several bus companies leave in the early morning. Transportes San Cristóbal, cheapest, not recommended, 19 hrs. Jacantaya, El Sol 590, opposite the stadium, leaves at 0830, 10-11 hrs., US$4. Sur Peruano leaves at 1000, door-to-door service, about a 10-hr. journey by road. Colectivo (Comité 31 rec.; also Comité 3 Juliaca Express, Jirón Tacna) takes 9 hrs, US$8.50. To Cuzco, 14 hrs., road first 44 km. (to Juliaca) and last 85 km. paved, other 260 km. very bad (the stretch Juliaca-Sicuani is appalling and very demanding for drivers of private cars), again several bus companies cover the route (Ambassador rec.), from US$5, Sur Peruano, Transportes San Cristóbal. Cruz del Sur, El Sol 565, (1730), US$6.50, 11 hrs. Colectivo to Cuzco, US$10.75. To Lima, 18 hours, several companies. To Moquegua, for Chile, San Martín bus, US$5, 1800, 10 hrs., very cold, bad road.

Excursions from Puno The walk from Jirón Cornejo following the Stations of the Cross up a nearby hill (with fine views) has been recommended. Motorboats charging upwards of US$3.25 p.p. take tourists to the **Uros** "floating islands"; prices should not be over US$6. Those furthest from Puno are most worth seeing, but latest indications are that the islands have been totally spoilt by tourism. Boats go about every 1/2 hour from about 0630 till 1000, or whenever there are 10 or more people to fill the boat, and take 3-5 hrs. Local boats may also be hired. Out of season there are no regular boats, either get a group together and pay US$10 for the boat, rent a boat at US$1-2 p.p. or pay an agency US$15-20. (Be careful where you walk on the floating islands.) The Uro Indians on the islands have intermarried with the Aymará and no pure Uros exist. The temptation to move ashore may soon deprive the floating islands of all residents. The present Puno Bay Indians still practise some Uro traditions, but Aymará influence predominates. Many tourists report that though the people are friendly, they are very poor and consequently there are constant requests for money (less persistent out of season). Rather than giving the children money, give them fresh fruit, pencils and paper, and buy their little reed boats.

A much more interesting island to visit (quiet and hospitable, except at the height of the tourist season) is **Taquile**, some 45 km. from Puno, on which there are numerous pre-Inca and Inca ruins, and Inca terracing (described by Jane Coburn as "lots of local colour, but pricey due to all the gringos watching the local colour"). On the N side of the island is the warmest part of Lake Titicaca. Plentiful accommodation can be found in private houses but best to take warm clothes and a sleeping bag. No previous arrangements can be made; on arrival you walk up a steep path for 30 mins., are greeted by the Indians, sign the guest book and if wishing to stay are "assigned" a family to stay with (G p.p.); some families offer dinner and breakfast for about US$3.50 extra. Boats to Taquile leave daily (get ticket in harbour office ½ hr. in advance, 500 metres before boats, tour companies charge extra) at 0800 and 0915 (subject to change), but in low season there is only one a day, at 0830, return 0800, US$3.20 return, 4 hrs. (organized tours can cost double, but ask around), a day return is not recommended if you want to see the island fully, yet 3 hrs. of serenity are still very nice if time is short. Boats usually stop at one of the floating islands on the way to Taquile, for about 20 mins.; if you ask after the boat's started, they won't charge extra. An entire boat can be hired for about US$50 to take 5-7 people to Taquile: 3 hrs. there, 3 back, 3 hrs. on island, so day trip possible this way. A sailing boat can be taken to Taquile for about US$1.50 p.p., departure time depends on the wind. There is a cooperative shop on the square that sells exceptional woollen goods, not cheap but very fine quality (cheaper in the market at Puno). There are several small restaurants on the island (e.g. *El Inca* on main square); fish is plentiful and the island has a trout farm, but meat is rarely available and drinks often run out. Meals are a little more expensive than on the mainland. You are advised to take with you some food, particularly fruit (welcomed by the local children), bread and vegetables, water, plenty of small-value notes and a torch. Take precautions against sunburn. 7 June, mid-July (2 weeks, Fiesta de Santiago), 1 and 2 August are the principal festival days with many dances in between. Ask for Sr. Agustín, a dressmaker, who is very knowledgeable about the island.

Another island supremely well worth visiting, is **Amantaní**. It is very beautiful and peaceful and like Taquile, has 6 villages and ruins on both of the island's peaks, Pacha Tata and Pacha Mama: there are temples and on the shore there is a throne carved out of stone. On both hills, a fiesta is celebrated on 15 January. The Indians make beautiful textiles and sell them quite cheaply at the Artesanía Cooperativa; the people are Quechua speakers, but understand Spanish. There are no hotels but you are assigned to stay with local families, who like postcards, and fruit and vegetables: take some. Accommodation, inc. 3 meals, is in our G range. Families who have been recommended include: the Borda family, good food, also Benedicto Guli Calsin, nr. the windmill; for an insight into subsistance living, the shy but interesting Amadeus family, just outside the main village, turn left along beach from port, be sure to pay a fair price for their wicker work, they are liable to undercharge. Ricardo Quispe Mamani, who has bar/restaurant on main square has been recommended, F plus food. There is one restaurant, *Samariy*. Boats go to and from the island most days at 0800 (a one day trip is not possible), the cooperatively owned boat *Atún*, will take you for about US$7.50 (4 hours each way). Victoriano Calsín Guispe (Casilla 312, Amantaní) of the cooperative crosses in his boat *Rey Marino*. Also recommended is Benito, who may be found at the docks (establish a price before leaving the dock). The boat *Picaflor* has not received good reports. Buy ticket the day before at the harbour, or on the boat; agencies charge about US$11, some hotels US$9. The festivities in January have been reported as spectacular, very colourful, musical and hard-drinking. Another fiesta is the Aniversario del Consejo (of the local council). If you wish to visit both Taquile and Amantaní, go to Amantaní first, from there a boat goes to Taquile, but it is not possible to take a boat from Taquile to Amantaní.

Anybody interested in religious architecture should go from Puno along the western shore of Lake Titicaca to the churches of **Juli**, **Pomata** and **Zepita**. The church at Pomata, which is being restored, is spectacular, with beautiful carvings, in Andean *mestizo* baroque, of vases full of tropical plants, flowers and animals in the window frames, lintels and cornices, and a frieze of dancing figures inside the dome (which is unusual in Peru), and alabaster windows (John Hemming). On the road to Juli is **Ilave**, where the road for Tacna branches off.

(The Tacna road is unpaved, but in good condition and a worthwhile journey, not only in terms of scenery, but also because road conditions are better than on the alternative Juliaca-Arequipa route to the coast from Lake Titicaca.) Ilave is typical of a gaunt *altiplano* town; has a good Sun. market (woven goods—beware bag slashers). Many buses go there from Puno (US$1.15); Ilave-Tacna, US$6.50, 13 hrs., leaves at 1400 and 1700 (Transportes Ponce, best, and Transportes Gironda). You pass these places when travelling by road between Puno and La Paz. Near Juli there is a small colony of flamingoes and many other birds can be seen from the road.

Juli Hotels   Only one, *Hostal Tréboles*, G, cold, dirty—best not to arrive in Juli at night looking for somewhere agreeable to stay. Bus Puno to Juli at 1430 from the market.
  "Juli has four churches, two of them in ruins, that the visitor should see. The keys to two of these (Santa Cruz and San Juan Bautista) are kept by the couple who look after San Juan Bautista. San Pedro is now designated as the Cathedral. Juli's fourth church is La Asunción, now abandoned and its fine bell tower damaged by earthquake or lightning. The Peruvians have established a school of picture restoration at Juli to restore its mass of paintings" (John Hemming.)
  All the Juli churches are being renovated. San Pedro has been extensively restored, it contains a series of superb screens, some in ungilded mahogany and others taken from other churches; also fine paintings, and a collection of coloured objects in the sacristy. San Juan Bautista has two sets of 17th century paintings of the lives of St. John the Baptist and of St. Teresa, contained in sumptuous gilded frames. San Juan is now a state museum, open a.m. only (US$0.15); it also has intricate *mestizo* carving in pink stone. Santa Cruz is another fine Jesuit church, partly roofless, so that it is easy to photograph the carvings of monkeys, papayas and grapes. La Asunción has an archway and atrium which date from the early 17th century.

Minibus Puno-Juli, 0800, US$1.80 (Colectur). A hydrofoil at 0800 from Juli to Bolivia operates most days as part of a Puno-La Paz package tour. Juli-La Paz costs US$115, lunch included, from Transportes El Sol (Sr. Ronald Zárate).

Pomata Hotel   *Puma Uta*, F, water, electricity.

There are other excursions, near Puno, to the *chullpas* (precolumbian funeral towers) of **Sillustani** (admission, US$0.30) in a beautiful setting on a peninsula in Lake Ayumara, 32 km. (excellent road) from Puno. (Colectivo US$7 p.p. for 3 hrs.; mini bus from Puno, Tranextur, Jr. Puno 525, Plaza de Armas, 1400, US$3, 1 hr. at site, taxi, US$15 wait and return or take morning bus to Juliaca from Corrego y La Torre, get off at Sillustani turn, hitch a ride to Atuncolla, traffic frequent, walk 4 km., return in the afternoon by tourist bus US$0.50-1, negotiate. Take water, food and sunscreen.) Museum, reception area and restaurant now built. "Most of the towers date from the period of Inca occupation in the 15th century, but they are burial towers of the Aymará-speaking Colla tribe. The engineering involved in their construction is more complex than anything the Incas built—it is defeating archaeologists' attempts to rebuild the tallest "lizard" *chullpa*. Two are unfinished: one with a ramp still in place to raise blocks; the other with cut stones ready to go onto a very ambitious corbelled false dome. A series of stone circles to the east of the site are now thought to be the bases of domed thatch or peat living huts, rather than having any religious meaning. The quarry near the towers is also worth seeing."—John Hemming. There are local indians at the site, in costume. Take small change or chocolate, matches etc., as small presents if you wish to photograph the indians. Camera fans will find the afternoon light best; desert country, but impressive. There are Inca ruins at Tancatanca and Caluxo and an Inca sundial may be seen near the village of **Chucuíto** (which has an interesting church, La Asunción, a small museum in the church of Santo Domingo, and houses with carved stone doorways); cave paintings at Chichiflope.

Peru to Bolivia   (See also under Bolivia, page 225). Migration tax (50 intis) payable in intis at border.
  By Road: 1. The most remote route is along east side of Lake via Huancané and Puerto Acosta (Bolivia), rec. only on weekends when there is more traffic; after Puerto Acosta, the road is very bad.
  2. The most direct route is the Puno-Desaguadero road (paved) passing through Chucuíto, Ilave, Juli and Pomata. Desaguadero is a miserable place (*Alojamiento Internacional*, dirty, F). Many buses to La Paz e.g. Chaski Andina (Sun., 0930). Bus from Titicaca 165 leaves 2000, arrives Desaguadero 0200. Bus from border to La Paz at 1130; advisable to check the day before when buses are running (US$4 in total by bus). Puno-Desaguadero by colectivo,

US$4, leaving between 0600-0730. Colectivo, Juliaca Express, Puno-La Paz, twice daily, US$15. Offices: Puno, Tacna 298; Arequipa, Salaverry 111; **Cuzco, Ruinas 407**; Juliaca, San Román 129.

3. Transturin of La Paz runs a costly, luxury service Puno-La Paz, for US$80, including hydrofoil and lunch, leaves Puno 0630, arrives La Paz 1800 on Mon. to Fri. stopping at Copacabana. Transturin has offices in both Puno (Jirón Tacna 201, T 737) and Cuzco (Portal de Panes 109, Of.1, Plaza de Armas, T 222332) where tickets can be booked in advance. There is also a bus-hydrofoil-bus route from Puno to La Paz run by Crillón Tours (the hydrofoil crossing from Juli to Copacabana, calling at the Island of the Sun), leaves Puno 0800, arriving La Paz at 1830. Expensive (US$150, or US$200 with overnight stay and additional sightseeing); all luggage and formalities taken care of.

4. Puno-Yunguyo-Copacabana-La Paz: by far the pleasanter journey. Colectivos, leaving Puno 0800, ply to La Paz via Copacabana for US$7.50, but often ask you to pay ferry fare, US$0.20, in addition. You can take a bus Puno-Yunguyo (e.g. Cruz del Sur, leaving 0800, arriving 1030, US$1, colectivo, US$1.15), then bus (irregular service, US$0.30), truck, colectivo (plenty) or 11 km. walk to Copacabana for Immigration. There are three buses a day Copacabana-La Paz and you must book one or two days in advance (e.g. Pullman, US$2.50, reserve seats at *Hotel Ambassador*). Alternatively local buses and trucks go from Yunguyo to Copacabana, stopping at the frontier, for US$0.30. There are also direct buses from Yunguyo to La Paz, which stop at the border for both authorities to stamp passports. On Sun. there are many trucks carrying people between the markets. **Yunguyo** itself has a privet hedge on main square showing good examples of topiary. *Hotel Amazonas*, G, *Hostal Yunguyo*, also G, clean, but often no water or electricity. Parallel exchange market good in main plaza (the first you come to from Bolivia), better rates than border, and good for changing bolivianos. In the 2nd plaza are the buses and colectivos for Puno. Passport sometimes stamped at Yunguyo, walk across bridge to Kasami—1 km., where passport must be stamped.

A few agencies in Puno, for example Colectur (Jr. Tacna 232, T 697), Tour Latino, Tacna 300, offer minibus services to the Bolivian border, with a lunch stop in Copacabana, stops at all necessary official posts, and at money changers in Yunguyo, with connection to La Paz, for US$7 up (the less expensive do not include lunch, US$2); depart Puno at 0800, arriving in La Paz between 1500 and 1600. The average agency price is US$6-8, Puno-La Paz; it is not uncommon for the service to deteriorate once you have crossed the border (in either direction) and have changed bus in the new country. You may not be dropped at the hotel of your choice. Most agencies make you pay the US$0.20 to the Tiquina crossing. Colectur/Turisbus runs a luxury bus service Puno-La Paz (to *Residencial Rosario*, who give 10% discount for passengers) for US$12; you don't have to change bus, breakdowns not unknown. If you wish you can break your journey in Copacabana (US$1 bus, US$2.50 daily colectivo—you have to change buses at Copacabana regardless) and make a connection to La Paz next day. Coming into Peru at this point you can get an overnight truck to Puno for about US$1, though these are cold and uncomfortable. Many colectivos leave from the Laykakota market. La Paz-Copacabana-Yunguyo-Puno is possible in one day as a bus (2 de Febrero company) leaves La Paz at 0800 for Copacabana, leaving you time to catch an onward bus to Yunguyo and bus or colectivo to Puno. The road is unpaved from Yunguyo to Straits of Tiquina.

N.B. Delays and consequent expenses have been reported by travellers going from Puno to Bolivia by car. On the **Yunguyo-Copacabana route** immigration, customs and police offices are all at different places on both the Peruvian and Bolivian sides: failure to check in at each usually means several hours wasted. When crossing Peru to Bolivia get an entry stamp in Copacabana (exit stamp in Peru of course). Bolivian authorities may want proof that you have US$10 for each day you intend to spend in Bolivia. There is no need to go to the Bolivian Consul in Yunguyo—he charges US$5 for a 10 day visa, whereas, at the border, a 90 day visa is free. If you go via Desaguadero, there are two Peruvian offices to visit (colectivo drivers know where they are) and three Bolivian—at the frontier. Peruvian customs close from 1200-1400. Tuesday and Friday are bad days to cross because they are days for the peasants on both sides of the border to exchange "national natural produce". Smugglers' paradise: keeps the Customs very busy.

By Ferry: 5. In 1985 the passenger ferry service across Lake Titicaca was suspended; in 1989, the ferry and the rail continuation from Guaqui to La Paz were running for freight only.

Note Apart from January to April, Peruvian time is one hour behind Bolivian time.

Puno to Cuzco On the way from Puno to Cuzco there is much to see from the train, which runs at an average altitude of 3,500 metres. At the stations, Indians sell food (roast lamb at Ayaviri and stuffed peppers at Sicuani) and local specialities such as pottery bulls at Pucará; fur caps, furs and rugs at Sicuani; knitted alpaca ponchos and pullovers and miniature llamas at Santa Rosa.

There is a research station for high-altitude animals, ten km. after La Raya, the highest spot (164 km. from Juliaca; 4,321 metres—unless staying, do not leave the train here, it stops very briefly; small boys throw snowballs into the train if they can!). It is run by the University of San Marcos, Lima (whose permission is required); llamas, alpaca and vicuña may be seen here, and accommodation is available in the dining room at the research station, US$2.50 p.p. (there is an excellent hot-bath house). Up on the heights breathing may be a little difficult, but the descent along the river Vilcanota is rapid. Get out of the train at Aguas Calientes, the next station (4 km. from La Raya)— first class fare from Puno, US$3. To the right of Aguas Calientes station are steaming pools of hot water in the middle of the green grass; a startling sight. The temperature of the springs is 40°C, and they show beautiful deposits of red ferro-oxide. At Maranganí, the river is wider, the fields greener, with groves of eucalyptus trees.

N.B. If cycling from Juliaca to Cuzco, a suitable path runs beside the railway line for 200 km. from Tirapata; it is preferable to the road, and there is no danger from trains—only one a day in either direction.

Sicuani, 38 km. beyond the divide (250 km. from Puno—a very tiring road— 137 km. from Cuzco—Oriente Sur bus, US$1.90), is an important agricultural centre, and an excellent place for items of llama and alpaca wool and skins; they sell them on the railway station and at the excellent Sun. morning market. Also known for its mineral baths at Uyurmiri.

Hotels *El Mirador*, E, basic, clean; *Raqchi*, F, basic; *Quispe*, G, basic, no shower, friendly; *Turistas*, D, is cold but best hotel in town (some way from centre), reported renamed *Centro Vacacional*, being modernised, rec.

Restaurants *Elvis* and *Vilcanota* in centre of town, rec.

On the right, a few kilometres past the San Pedro stop, is the so-called Templo de Viracocha, grandiose, though almost unknown, with Inca baths 180 metres to the E. (For more information about various places between Sicuani and Cuzco, see page 962.)

Branch roads from S and N of Sicuani lead to a road past the Tintaya mines which forms an alternative route Cuzco-Arequipa. The surface is very bad in places, but it is a spectacular journey. Only one bus a day (Chasqui) passes, usually full. From Sicuani, a pretty lake is passed, then one climbs to a radio-transmission antenna; a few km. from the road is Yauri (primitive accommodation), isolated on a plateau by a canyon; the road leads to the Majes irrigation scheme and on to the Arequipa-Juliaca road.

The Vilcanota plunges into a gorge, but the train winds above it and round the side of the mountain. At Huambutío the railway turns left to follow the river Huatanay on the final stretch to Cuzco. The Vilcanota here widens into the great Urubamba canyon, flanked on both sides by high cliffs, on its way to join the Ucayali, a tributary of the Amazon.

Cuzco stands at 3,310 metres, a little lower than Puno. Its 143,000 inhabitants are mostly Indian, and the city is remarkable for its many colonial churches, monasteries and convents, and for its extensive Inca ruins. Respect the altitude; two or three hours' rest after arriving make a great difference; eat lightly and drink little alcohol, but suck glucose sweets the first day, and remember to walk slowly. To see Cuzco and the surrounding area properly—including Pisac, Ollantaytambo, Chinchero and Machu-Pinchu—you need 5 days to a week, allowing for slowing down because of altitude.

Almost every central street has remains of Inca walls, arches and doorways. Many streets are lined with perfect Inca stonework, now serving as foundations for more modern dwellings. This stonework is tapered upwards; every wall has a perfect line of inclination towards the centre, from bottom to top. The stones are "battered", with each edge and corner rounded. The circular stonework of the Temple of the Sun, for example, is probably unequalled in the world.

History Cuzco was the capital of the Inca empire—one of the greatest planned societies the world has known—from its rise during the 11th century to its death in the early 16th century. (See John Hemming's *Conquest of the Incas* and B.C.Brundage's *Lords of Cuzco* and *Empire of the Inca*.) It was solidly based on other Peruvian civilizations which had attained great skill in textiles, building, ceramics and working in metal. Immemorially, the political structure of the Andean Indian had been the *ayllu*, the village community; it had its divine ancestor, worshipped household gods, was closely knit by ties of blood to the family and by economic necessity to the land, which was held in common. Submission to the *ayllu* was absolute, because it was only by such discipline that food could be obtained in an unsympathetic environment. All the domestic animals—the llama and alpaca and the dog—had long been tamed, and the great staple crops—maize and potatoes—established. What the Incas did—and it was a magnificent feat—was to conquer enormous territories and impose upon the variety of *ayllus*, through an unchallengeable central government, a willing spiritual and economic submission to the State. The common religion, already developed by the classical Tiahuanaco culture, was worship of the Sun, whose vice-regent on earth was the absolute Sapa Inca. Around him, in the capital, was a religious and secular elite which never froze into a caste because it was open to talent. The elite was often recruited from chieftains defeated by the Incas: an effective way of reconciling local opposition. The mass of the people were subjected to rigorous planning. They were allotted land to work, for their group and for the State; set various tasks—the making of textiles, pottery, weapons, ropes, etc.—from primary materials supplied by the functionaries, or used in enlarging the area of cultivation by building terraces on the hill-sides. Their political organization was simple but effective. The family, and not the individual, was the unit. Families were grouped in units of 10, 100, 500, 1,000, 10,000 and 40,000, each group with a leader responsible to the next largest group. The Sapa Inca crowned the political edifice; his four immediate counsellors were those to whom he allotted responsibility for the northern, southern, eastern and western regions (*suyos*) of the empire.

Equilibrium between production and consumption, in the absence of a free price mechanism and good transport facilities, must depend heavily upon statistical information. This the Incas raised to a high degree of efficiency by means of their *quipus*: a decimal system of recording numbers by knots in cords. Seasonal variations were guarded against by creating a system of state barns in which provender could be stored during years of plenty, to be used in years of scarcity. Statistical efficiency alone required that no one should be permitted to leave his home or his work. The loss of personal liberty was the price paid by the masses for economic security. In order to obtain information and to transmit orders quickly, the Incas built fine paved pathways along which couriers sped on foot. The whole system of rigorous control was completed by the greatest of all their monarchs, Pachacutec (1400-48), who also imposed a common language, Quechua, as a further cementing force. After him the Incas conquered all Bolivia, northern Argentina, northern and central Chile, and Ecuador. The empire grew too large to be easily controlled from one centre, and the last of the great emperors, Huayna Capac, made the fatal mistake of dividing his realm between his two sons, Atahualpa reigning from Quito and Huáscar from Cuzco; the civil war that ended just before the Spaniards' arrival resulted in Atahualpa's victory but weakened the empire. Resistance to the Spaniards was reduced by the fact that Huáscar's faction at first looked on the invaders as allies; the struggle was in any case a most unequal one because of the Spaniards' superiority in equipment, though Manco Inca almost recaptured Cuzco in 1536 and the Inca successor state of Vilcabamba, centred near Espíritu Pampa in the jungle foothills N of Cuzco, was held against the Spaniards until 1572.

Churches (Many are closed to visitors on Sunday.) The heart of the city, as in Inca days, is the Plaza de Armas. Around the square are colonial arcades and four churches. To the N is the **Cathedral** (early 17th century, in baroque style), built on the site of the Palace of Viracocha. The high altar is solid silver; the original altar *retablo* behind it is a masterpiece of native wood carving. In the sacristy are paintings of all the bishops of Cuzco and a painting of Christ attributed to Van Dyck. The choir stalls, by a 17th-century Spanish priest, are a magnificent example of colonial baroque art. The elaborate pulpit and the sacristy are notable. Much venerated is the crucifix of El Señor de las Temblores, the object of many pilgrimages and viewed all over Peru as a guardian against earthquakes. (The Cathedral is open until 1000 for genuine worshippers— Quechua mass

0500-0600, and thereafter 1000-1200, 1500-1800 with the combined entrance ticket—see below). The tourist entrance is through El Triunfo, which has a fine granite altar and a statue of the Virgin of the Descent, reputed to have helped the Spaniards repel Manco Inca when he besieged the city in 1536. It also has a painting of Cuzco during the 1650 earthquake (the earliest surviving painting of the city) in a side chapel. Doors from the Cathedral open into Jesús María.

On the E side of the plaza is the beautiful **La Compañía de Jesús**, built on the site of the Palace of the Serpents (Amaru-cancha) in the late 17th century. Its twin-towered exterior is extremely graceful, and the interior rich in fine murals, paintings and carved altars. The cloister is also noteworthy (closed in 1990).

Three outstanding churches are La Merced, San Francisco, and Belén de los Reyes. **La Merced**, almost opposite the *Tambo Hotel*, first built 1534, rebuilt late 17th century, attached to a very fine monastery with an exquisite cloister; open 0830-1200, 1430-1730 (admission US$0.50, students US$0.35). Inside the church are buried Gonzalo Pizarro, half-brother of Francisco, and the two Almagros, father and son. Their tombs were discovered in 1946. The church is most famous for its jewelled monstrance, on view in the monastery's museum during visiting hours. The superb choir stalls, reached from the upper floor of the cloister, can be seen by men only (but you must persuade a Mercedarian friar to let you see them). **San Francisco** (3 blocks SW of the Plaza de Armas), is an austere church reflecting many Indian influences. Its monastery is being rebuilt (the first of the cloisters is now open to the public 0900-1200, 1500-1700—see the candelabra made from human bones and the wood carving). **Belén de los Reyes** (in the southern outskirts), built by an Indian in the 17th century, has a gorgeous main altar, with silver embellishments at the centre and goldwashed *retablos* at the sides (open 1000-1200, 1500-1700 except Thurs. and Sun.). **Santa Catalina**, on the street of the same name, is a magnificent building; the church, convent and museum are included on the tourist ticket, closed in 1989. Delicious marzipan is sold next to the museum by the nuns through a revolving wooden door, US$1 for 200 grams. **San Pedro** (in front of the market) was built in 1688, its two towers from stones brought from an Inca ruin (open Mon.-Sat. 1000-1200, 1400-1700). The nuns' church of Santa Clara is unique in South America for its decoration, which covers the whole of the interior (but virtually impossible to visit). The smaller and less well-known church of **San Blas** has a fine carved *mestizo* cedar pulpit.

Santo Domingo (SE of the main Plaza) was built in the 17th century on the walls of the Temple of the Sun and from its stones; visit the convent to see the ancient walls of the Temple of the Sun, now restored. (Model of the Temple upstairs: ask to see it.) Current excavation is revealing more and more of the five chambers of the Temple of the Sun, which shows the best Inca stonework to be seen in Cuzco. The Temple of the Sun was awarded to Juan Pizarro, the younger brother of Francisco, who willed it to the Dominicans after he had been fatally wounded in the Sacsayhuamán siege. Open 0900-1200, 1500-1700.

The baroque cloister has been gutted to reveal four of the original chambers of the great Inca temple—two on the west partly reconstructed in a good imitation of Inca masonry. The finest stonework is in the celebrated curved wall beneath the west end of Santo Domingo (rebuilt after the 1950 earthquake, at which time a niche that once contained a shrine was found at the inner top of the wall). Below the curved wall was a famous garden of gold and silver replicas of maize and other plants. Excavations now in progress have revealed Inca baths below here, and more Inca retaining walls. The other superb stretch of late Inca stonework is in Calle Ahuacpinta outside the temple, to the east or left as you enter (John Hemming).

Much **Inca stonework** can be seen in the streets and most particularly in the Callejón Loreto, running SE past La Compañía de Jesús from the main plaza: the

Key to map of Cuzco

1. Church of San Cristóbal; 2. Almirante Palace; 3. Church of San Antonio; 4. Cathedral;
5. Museum; 6. Church of Santa Catalina; 7. *Hotel Cuzco*; 8. Church of the Society of
Jesus; 9. House of Garcilaso de la Vega; 10. Church of La Merced; 11. Church of Santo
Domingo; 12. Convent of San Francisco; 13. Church of Santa Clara; 14. Church of San
Pedro.

walls of the House of the Women of the Sun are on one side, and of the Palace
of the Serpents on the other. There are ancient remains in Calle San Agustín, to
the NE of the plaza. The temples of the Stars and of the Moon are still more or
less intact. The famous stone of 12 angles is in Calle Triunfo (Calle Hatun Rumioc)
halfway along 2nd block from the square beside the Cathedral, on the right-hand
side going away from the Plaza. The Religious Art Museum in the former
Archbishop's Palace is nearby.

San Sebastián, an interesting church with a baroque façade, is in the little
village of San Sebastián, 6½ km. from Cuzco.

Visitors' Tickets It is not possible to purchase individual entrance tickets to the churches
and ruins in and around Cuzco; one must purchase a combined ticket for US$10 (US$5 for
student with identification), said to be payable only in US$ (but try intis—could be cheaper),
valid for five days, which allows entry to: the Cathedral, San Blas, Santa Catalina, Santo

Domingo-Coricancha, Museo de Arte Religioso, Sacsayhuamán and the 3 ruins (Kenko, Puku Pukará and Tambo Machay—see below) on the way to Pisac, Pisac itself, Chinchero and Ollantaytambo. The tickets can be bought at any of the places mentioned or at the tourist office (0900-1500), said to be renewable at Oficina del Boleta Turística, first block of Av. Sol. Students can pay per individual site, as can others with a lot of insistence (but you may be charged US$5 per site). If time is short, go to Machu Picchu first, stop in Ollantaytambo on the way back and buy your visitors' ticket there before seeing the sites nearer Cuzco. **N.B.** All sites are very crowded on Sun.

Palaces and Mansions The Palacio del Almirante, just N of the Plaza de Armas, is impressive. Nearby, in a small square, is the colonial House of San Borja, where Bolívar stayed after the Battle of Ayacucho. The Concha Palace (on Calle Santa Catalina), with its finely carved balcony, is now used by the Guardia Civil. The Palace of the Marquis of Valleumbroso (3 blocks SW of the Plaza de Armas) was gutted by fire in 1973 and is being restored. The Archbishop's Palace (two blocks NE of Plaza de Armas) was built on the site of the palace occupied in 1400 by the Inca Roca and was formerly the home of the Marqueses de Buena Vista; it has been opened to the public and contains a fine collection of colonial paintings and furniture, including the paintings of a 17th century Corpus Christi procession that used to hang in the church of Santa Ana. Well worth visiting. Above Cuzco on the road up to Sacsayhuamán, one finds the church of San Cristóbal, built to his patron saint by Cristóbal Paullu Inca and, N of it, the eleven doorway-sized niches of the great Inca wall of the Palace of Colcampata where Paullu Inca set up home. Further up, to the left, is a private colonial mansion, once the home of the explorer (and murderer) Lope de Aguirre. Also visit the palace called Casa de los Cuatro Bustos at San Agustín 400 (which is now the *Libertador-Marriott Hotel*) and the Convento de las Nazarenas, Plaza de las Nazarenas (alias *Casa de la Sirena*). See the Inca-colonial doorway with a mermaid motif.

Archaeological Museum House of Jerónimo Cabrera, Plaza de las Nazarenas, 150 m. behind Cathedral, first-rate precolumbian collection, contains Spanish paintings of imitation Inca royalty dating from the 18th century, as well as an excellent collection of textiles. Visitors should ask to see the forty miniature pre-Inca turquoise figures found at Pikillacta and the golden treasures, all kept under lock and key but on display. Closed in 1990 for relocation.

Religious Art Museum at old Archbishop's Palace in Calle Hatun Rumioc (constructed over temple of Inca Roca), with religious paintings of the Cuzco School and Colonial furniture in beautiful rooms. Open Mon.-Sat., 0930-1200, 1500-1800. Sun. 1500-1800.

Regional History Museum, in the Casa Garcilaso, Jirón Garcilaso y Heladeros tries to show the evolution of the Cuzqueño school of painting. Open Mon.-Fri., 0900-1200, 1500-1800, Sat., 0900-1200. Contains Inca agricultural implements, colonial furniture and paintings and mementos of more recent times. Note the pillar on the balcony over the door, showing a bearded man and a naked woman. Closed after earthquake damage, April 1986.

Festivals 24 June; pageant of Inti Raymi (Indians outnumber tourists) enacted at 1300 at the fortress of Sacsayhuamán. (Try to arrive in Cuzco 15 days before Inti Raymi, there are many festivals, and get to Sacsayhuamán at about 1030 as even reserved seats fill up quickly.) Tickets for the stands can be bought a week in advance from the Town Hall, and cost US$25, but standing places on the ruins are free (but be early and defend your space). Travel agents who try to persuade you to buy a ticket for the right to film or take photos are being dishonest. On Corpus Christi day statues and silver are paraded through the streets; colourful, everyone gets drunk by 1000. The Plaza de Armas is surrounded by tables with Indian women selling *cuy* and a mixed grill called *chiriucho* (*cuy*, chicken, *tortillas*, fish eggs, water-weeds, maize, cheese and sausage). One week before the Inti Raymi, there is a dance festival in the village of Raqchi (**see also page** 962). On the Monday before Easter is the procession of the Lord of the Earthquakes, starting at 1600 outside the Cathedral. A large crucifix is paraded through the streets, returning to the Plaza de Armas around 2000 to bless the tens of thousands of people who have assembled there. On 8 September (day of the Virgin), there is a colourful procession of masked dancers from the church of Alundena, at the SW edge of Cuzco, near Belén, to the Plaza de San Francisco. There is also a splendid fair at Alundena, and a free bull fight on the following day (tourists should be very discreet at these celebrations, as they are not welcome—avoid pickpockets, too). Carnival at Cuzco very basic; flour, water, cacti, bad fruit and animal manure thrown about in streets. **N.B.** Prices shoot up at end-July—Independence celebrations. December 8 is Cuzco day: church and museums close at 1200.

Warning Thieves are numerous and persistent. Do not wear jewellery, watches or carry credit cards, leave valuables with hotel management. Be careful when you change money on the streets. Be especially careful in the railway and bus stations, the bus from the airport, the market (otherwise rec.) and at out-of-the-way ruins. Beware also of cocaine hustlers who will offer you drugs but who, in reality, are setting you up for "fines" from the police (genuine or otherwise). More police patrol the streets and stations than in the past, but one should still be on the lookout.

Hotels Book more expensive hotels well in advance through a good travel agency, particularly for the week or so around 24 June when the Inti Raymi celebrations take place (prices are greatly increased at this time). Prices given are for the high season in June-August. On the Puno-Cuzco train there are many hotel agents for medium-priced hotels; prices can often be negotiated down to F category, but best to pay agent for one day only and then negotiate with hotel. Rooms offered at Cuzco station are usually cheaper than those offered on the train. Agents also provide transport to the hotel, which can be invaluable when arriving at the dimly-lit station and since taxis are not supposed to enter the station yard. It is cold in Cuzco, many hotels do not have heating. It is worth asking for an "estufa", a space heater which some places will provide for an extra charge.

Best is *Libertador-Marriott* (5-star), in colonial palace (Casa de los Cuatro Bustos) at Calle San Agustín 400, T 232601/231961, A, plus 28% tax, good, especially the service, but in July and August rooms in the older part of the hotel are cold and dark, restaurant poor and overpriced; *Royal Inka*, Plaza Regocijo 299, A, 3-star, bar, dining room, good service, rec., arranges trips to Machu Picchu; *Cusco*, A, Heladeros 150, administered by Sociedad de Beneficencia Pública del Cusco, hot water, largest and best known, "old fashioned, not cheap and a little fusty", central; *Alhambra*, Av. Sol, A, modern, very good, prices negotiable, but cold, limited hot water, and food disappointing; *Savoy*, Av. El Sol 954, A, group rate B, recently upgraded to Peruvian 5-star, food poor and expensive, no coffee or food served after 2200, disappointing, not a safe area at night; *Marqués de Picoaga* on Calle Sta. Teresa, A, 70 rooms, central heating, private bathrooms, dining room, information in Lima T 286 314; *Conquistador*, Santa Catalina Angosta 149, T 233661, A, clean, safe, good; *San Agustín*, Maruri y San Agustín, T 222322, A, fine interior, clean, friendly, very hot water, restaurant expensive;

B category: *Hostal Inti Raymi*, Matará 260, T 228401; *Espinar*, Portal Espinar 142, B (bargain for less in low season), rec. but food poor, clean and helpful, *Hostal El Dorado* (4-star) on Av. Sol, good but can be noisy in a.m., food good but expensive. *Hostal Garcilaso*, Garcilaso de la Vega 233, B with bath, but in off-season can be negotiated lower (E), safe for luggage, clean, helpful, "historic charm, but service poor", laundry expensive, noisy disco until 0300, overpriced in season, friendly; *Garcilaso III* in same street, C high season, E low, less good (make sure which one you want to go to if dealing with a tout).

C/D category: *Tambo*, Ayacucho 233, C, central, tatty rooms, hot water (intermittent), restaurant fair; *Viracocha*, Plaza de Armas, corner of Mantas, C, clean, hot water, restaurant opens at 0600, good breakfast (Casilla 502), Luis Guillén Pinelo, an employee here, is a good guide; *Hostal Matheos*, formerly *Tecsecocha*, Calle Tecsecocha, 490, T 223324, D, with breakfast, café, bar, restaurant, clean, a bit cold, but well furnished, English spoken, good, friendly; next door, *Hostal Carlos*, T 223091, C with breakfast; *El Inca*, Quera 251, D, F in low season, good, clean, musty, heating, may have to ask for hot water after 0900 and before 0600, breakfast overpriced, Wilbur speaks English, and is helpful; *Colonial Palace*, Quera 270, C (E in low season), "has potential", but poor service, colonial courtyard; *Samaná*, Nueva Baja 472, D, colonial mansion, recently redecorated, good rooms with heaters and private baths, plumbing unreliable, safe for luggage, helpful staff, laundry, restaurant slow but good, food must be ordered day before, rec.; *Hostal del Sol*, San Francisco, C in high season, D/E low, clean, rec.

Los Marqueses, Garcilaso 252, E, with bath, heaters extra, early colonial house, very helpful and comfortable, but not well kept, has a masseur, Douglas Chapman, rec., clean and convenient; *Hostal Corihuasi*, Calle Suecia, E, 4-room suites, colonial house, laundry arranged, hot water, quiet, rec.; *Qorichaska*, Nueva Alta 458, close to centre, F, clean, safe, hot water, rec. *Qoricancha*, opposite *Inti Raymi*, F, hot shower, rec.; *Internacional* (near San Pedro station), E, with bath (out of season, more expensive in season), good, clean, safe; *Suecia*, Calle Suecia, F, shared rooms, cosy, clean, hot showers, safe, will store luggage, highly rec., can use their bulletin board to arrange groups for the Inca trail; *Suecia* annex, Calle Tecseccocha (blue door, no sign), E without bath, rooms also with, good beds and blankets, clean, same recommendations as for parent hotel, beautiful building; *Huaynapata*, Huaynapata 369, small rooms, F p.p., very safe, family-run, hot water (problematic), stores luggage, friendly. *Trinitarias*, Trinitarias 263, near San Pedro station, E, clean, hot water in shower, friendly, secure for left luggage; *Hispaniola*, Trinitarias, nearby, G, good, safe; also near San Pedro station, *Milán*, Trinitarias 237, F, with unreliable hot water in evening, safe, clean, friendly, a bit noisy; *Imperio*, Calle Chaparro, comfortable new extension, run by Elena and family, also near station, F, hot water, friendly, clean, safe to leave luggage; *Palermo*, San Agustín 287, F, some Inca walls, good breakfast; *Hostal Cabillado*, E with or without bath, worth bargaining here, safe; *Hostal El Arqueólogo*, E (rooms or dormitory), Ladrillos 425 not far from Sacsayhuamán (T 232569), run by a Frenchman, hot water, highly rec., clean, with store luggage, cafeteria (expensive) and kitchen; accommodation in *Convento Santo Domingo* (down an alley, behind the church), G, a sleeping bag p.p. in double rooms, hot showers, clean, friendly, safe to leave bags, must be in by 2200; *Hostal Familiar*, Saphi 661, E, with bath, F without, cold, attractive flower-filled patios, with good rooms around them (other rooms are not as good), can leave luggage here, with café (owner's sister Gloria works with Kantu Tours), rec., but reported casual with reservations. *Hostal San Cristóbal*, Quiscapata 250, near San Cristóbal, G/F, cooking and clothes-washing facilities, very nice people, if everywhere full, Sra. Ema de Paredes will let you spread a sleeping bag on the floor, rec.; *Alamo*, Av. Antonio Lorena 18, F, with bath and hot water if you ask for it, reasonably cheap, needs maintenance; *Hostal Cáceres*, Plateros, 1 block from Plaza de Armas, G, safe, luggage store, hot water, quiet, helpful, mixed reports on cleanliness; *Hostal Familiar Las Esmeraldas* (Sra. Vega de Pineda), Av. de la Infancia 433, E, full board available, clean, hot showers, highly rec.; *Hostal Corona Real*, F, Av. Huáscar 226-228, clean, friendly; *Hospedaje El Peregrino*, Calle del Medio off Plaza, E with bath, clean, secure, quiet. *Raymi*, Pardo 954, E, hot water, carpeting, safe; *Hostal Bellavista*, Av. Santiago 100, F, hot water, very friendly, safe (10 mins. walk from centre, not a safe area at night), breakfast available, will store luggage, rec. (particularly, rooms with view towards Estación San Pedro), Carlos here takes guided trips on the Inca Trail, about US$3-4 p.p./day; *Hostal Cahuide*, Saphi 845, E, discount for long stay, clean, good laundry service, helpful, café, convenient for centre; *Hostal Bambú*, on Av. Tullumayo near San Cristóbal bus station, F, hot water, laundry facilities, quiet, clean; *Hostal San Blas*, Cuesta San Blas 526, T 225781, E, basic, a/c, friendly, secure for luggage; *Hostal Sapantiani*, Pumacurco 490, F without bath, safe, clean, pleasant, family run; *Mantas*, Calle Mantas 115 (near Plaza de Armas), E, rec., friendly, can leave luggage, has laundry service, good meals; *Posada del Corregidor*, Portal de Panes 151, Plaza de Armas, T 232632, E throughout year, pleasant, clean, central; *Hostal Granada*, Teatro, F, modern rooms on patio better but more expensive, will wash clothes. *Loreto*, Pasaje Loreto 115, Plaza de Armas, E-D (triples available—always full), will look after luggage while you go to Machu-Picchu (can arrange taxi to outlying stations on Cuzco-Machu Picchu line, and Lucio is a good guide), clean, very friendly, rooms with Inca walls and electric heaters rec, but dark; *Antarki* Siete Cuartones 245, F, simple but clean and quiet, stores luggage; *Residencial Las Rejas*, above main tourist office on Plaza de Armas, good value, hot water; *Tambo Real*, Av. Belén, E with bath and hot water, friendly but noisy (not to be confused with *Hotel Tambo*); *Hotel del Procurador*, F, good beds, clean, hot water, secure, will mind luggage, rec. *Hostal Residencial Rojas* (ex-*Hotel Tigre*), Tigre 129, F, good value, friendly, safe, clean, hot water. Sra. Rosa de Calderón rents 2-3 rooms for E, full board and warm water, Almagro 131, 2 blocks from Plaza de Armas, very friendly and helpful. Hortensia de Velasco, Av. Pardo, Pasaje España, private accommodation in F range. Also Irma Rodríguez de Alarcón, Zarumilla 2A-101, 15-20 mins'. walk from Plaza de Armas, 2 rooms sleeping 4 people, safe, breakfast, rec.

Camping   Not safe anywhere in the Cuzco area, but is permitted on hill above Cuzco museum, about ½ km. past museum on left; also permitted near Sacsayhuamán ruins, but arrive late and leave early so as not to interfere with the sightseeing. Travel agencies (see below) rent equipment (check tents carefully, and some sell camping gaz). If you use a spirit stove, "alcohol para quemar" can be bought in most pharmacies (bring your own bottle).

Restaurants   *Mesón de los Espaderos*, Espaderos y Plateros, parrilladas, good; *Roma*, on Plaza de Armas (good food, folk music nightly without extra cost). *Paititi*, Plaza de Armas, live music, good fish and also local food, US$7, complimentary pisco sour. For a good meal and décor try *Inti Raymi* in the *Libertador-Marriott*, à la carte dinner for US$13. *Korikancha*, opposite Calle Loreto, rec.; *El Fogón de las Mestizas*, Ruinas 463, local food, best in the afternoon less good at night, has roast guinea-pig (cuy, known in Cuzco as conejo—rabbit).

Vegetarian restaurants *Govinda* (Hare Krishna), Espaderos 128, just off W corner of Plaza de Armas, generally good, always busy, you can buy bread here which will keep for days, ideal for Inca Trail (but order a day in advance), also samosas, cheese, ensalada de frutas, etc. *Inca*, vegetarian, Garcilaso 270, cheap; *Café Shantam*, Plateros 334, quiet, friendly, good food, cheap (vegetarian), Japanese owner; *Comedor Vegetariano*, Av. Sol 555, lunch only; *Qhaliama Warí*, Torda, part of a natural health centre. *Café Varayoc*, Espaderos 142, good meeting place, Dutch connection (excellent coffee, pizzas and cakes). Good juice bar at Sta. Catalina Ancha 427.

There is a good restaurant with stained glass lamps on Procuradores; same street at 365, *Chez Maggy*, good atmosphere, popular with tourists, music Wed. and Sun., pasta, soups, pizzas freshly baked in wood-burning oven, service sometimes slow; also reasonable restaurants, (e.g. *Qarawantana* at 347, *Maximum*, good meal for less than US$1; *Bar Kukuli*, cheap food (order in advance) and interesting local drinks, slow service, good music, and *Los Almarios*, good food, nice atmosphere. *Bucaro*, Av. Sol 567, fair, reasonable service. *Pizzería America*, on Plateros, highly rec.; *Royal Qosco*, Plateros, cheap, good 3-course set meals; *Bilboquet*, Herrajes 171A, French crèperie, good meeting place, rec.; *Piccolo Bar*, Plaza de Armas, popular and good; *Ayllu*, Portal de Carnes 208, also on Plaza de Armas, Italian, classical/folk music, good atmosphere, has a superb range of milk products and wonderful apple pastries, try lecheasada, good breakfast, quick service; *Chef Victor*, Plaza de Armas, very good food and coffee, good value; *Lamborghinos*, next door on Plaza de Armas, nr Plateros, good cheap pastas, garlic bread, rec. for banana split; *Café Cuzco* on Plaza for breakfast. *Trattoria Adriano*, Calle Mantas y Av. Sol (just off SE corner of Plaza de Armas), Italian food, open for breakfast at 0700, friendly and helpful; *El Truco*, on Plaza del Cabildo (Regocijo 247), excellent stuffed green peppers, good trout, folklore some evenings (at 2030, an extra US$1.20 will be added to your bill), expensive; *Tip-Top*, Palacio 122, good food, reasonable prices; also restaurant of *Hotel Palermo*, San Agustín 287, cheap. *Chifa HongKong*, Av. Sol, good, reasonable prices; *La Cabañita* and *Comedor Nacional*, off the Plaza, good cheap food; *Café Restaurant Rick*, opposite *Hotel Conquistador*, dish of the day US$1. *Café-Restaurant Garcilaso*, Garcilaso 265, no sign, rec. for juices and lemon pie, good music and atmosphere in evening; *Hora Antiqua*, Garcilaso, log fire, friendly bar, reasonable prices; *Royal Inn*, Plaza San Francisco, good, cheap, enormous cakes; *Café Citera*, Espaderos, good capuccino and cakes, nice atmosphere, not cheap; *Focarela*, Saphi 478, good pizzeria, reasonable prices, rec; *Pizzería Michaelangelo*, San Agustín 171, rec.; *Los Candiles*, Calle Plateros near Plaza, excellent set meals; *Pucara*, Plateros 309, highly rec, good meals throughout the day, pleasant atmosphere, pottery for sale.; *Café Haylliy* on Plateros, popular meeting place, especially for breakfast, has good snacks and "copa Haylliy"—fruit, muesli, yoghurt, honey and chocolate cake. *El Tacho*, near San Pedro railway station, for local food, especially soup; *Paraíso*, Av. Sol 441, restaurant snack bar, reasonable prices, varied menu, small, friendly; *La Calesa*, Plateros 396, excellent, cheap bar; *Bazar-Cafetín Minka*, Huaynapata 331, craft shop and café (good) run to benefit disadvantaged women, has lots of German books and a free English; *Posada*, on Plaza de Armas, good. Several restaurants on Plateros do cheap 3-course set lunches (US$0.50). *Cross Keys Pub*, Plaza de Armas, 1st floor, run by a Mancunian, darts, great atmosphere; may not be open all year. You can eat cheaply in the market; a saltado (a mixture of meat and vegetables) costs about US$0.25, but be careful. Also cheap juices in market opp. San Pedro station. Street vendors at night on Plaza de Armas sell food: stuffed potatoes (papas rellenas) rec.

Local Specialities Roast stuffed guinea pig (*cuy*). Order in advance at one of the *quintas* (inns in the suburbs). *Quinta Zárate*, Calle Tortera Paccha, rec. A good cheap picantería-chichería is *Mi Casa*, on 100 block of Choquechaca. Also *Quintas Eulalia*, Choquechaca 384. Very rich and exotically spiced. The yoghurt is excellent. *La Chola*, Calle Palacio, uphill from the Nazarenas, local specialities, atmosphere, good chicha. Also try *Quinta Tejada* and *Quinta Country Club*. Try the anticuchos (roast beef hearts) cooked in side streets. The local drinks, herb tea with caña and hot milk with pisco, very warming in the cold evenings.

Folklore Shows Regular nightly folklore show at Qosqo Native Art Centre, Av. Sol. 604, at 1830 hours, for US$5 (students US$3), also Amanta Dances, Calle Unión 117, and Qoricancha Dances, San Juan de Dios 285 (US$4), 1830-2000. *La Taverna* bar on Plaza de Armas has folklore music nightly from 2100-0200, very crowded. Folk-dancing and music in the cellar of *Hotel Ollanta*, Av. Sol, nightly, US$2.50 p.p., 1845-2000. Also nightly at *Hotel Savoy*. Folk dancing at Teatro Central, US$4 and at Teatro Inti Raymi, Saphi 605, US$2 (nightly 1845, tickets sold by students in Plaza de Armas). Student group Intiraqui plays nightly in Calle Plateros. There are good peñas at *Qhatuchay*, Portal Confituría 233 on Plaza, very pleasant (2100), *Peña Do Re Mi*, also on Plaza, opp. La Compañía, and folk music at *Restaurant Roma*, evenings. *Cafir*, Saphy 605, daily 1845, excellent **N.B.** The Centro de Difusión Cultural Wasapay organizes "folklore evenings" in various restaurants which are supposed to be free, but which will be included as 15% extra on the bill—watch out for this if you don't want a more expensive meal.

Discotheques *El Muki* (opposite *Hotel Conquistador*) rec. *Kamikaze*, many gringos, entrance fee US$1, on San Juan de Dios, nr. Sta Teresa (upstairs), rec. *El Molino Rojo*, Av. de la Cultura; *El Gran Prise*, Av. Antonio Lorena 14; cheap local bars. Also, *Las Quenas* in the basement of the *Hotel Savoy*, rec.

Local Crafts In the Plaza San Blas and the surrounding area, authentic Cuzco crafts still survive. Wood workers may be seen in almost any street. Leading artisans who welcome visitors include: Hilario Mendívil, Plazoleta San Blas 634 (biblical figures from plaster, wheatflour and potatoes); Edilberta Mérida, Carmen Alto 133 (earthenware figures showing physical and mental anguish of the Indian peasant); Víctor Vivero Holgado, Tandapato 172 (painter of pious subjects); Antonio Olave Palomino, Siete Angelitos 752 (reproductions of precolumbian ceramics and colonial sculptures); Maximiliano Palomino de la Sierra, Triunfo 393 (festive dolls and wood carvings); Santiago Rojas, near San Blas (statuettes). Museo Inca Art Gallery of Amílcar Salomón Zorrilla, Huancaro M-B—L8, T 231232 (P.O. Box 690), Telephone between 0900 and 2100. Contemporary art.

Shopping Market opposite Estación San Pedro (which also has the name Santa Ana) is the best Indian market for a variety of goods, but although less self-conscious and less expensive than Pisac is not very interesting (best value at closing time or in the rain). *Empresa Peruana de Promoción Artesanal (EPPA)*, Plateros 359, and another good market on the corner of San Andrés and Quera. For handicrafts produced by cooperatives, with benefits going to the producers, go to the non-profit organization *Cosart*, Palacio 116 (1 block N of Plaza de Armas); ask for Antonio or Koki for information on local groups and women's committees.

Cuzco is the weaving centre of Peru, and excellent textiles can be found at good value. *Alpaca*, Calle Ruinas, genuine, 100% alpaca goods, but not cheap. *Artesania La Paloma*, Cuesta San Blas 552 and Plazuela Sta. Catalina 211, good but expensive; *Rafael Salazar Sucesores*, Plateros 305, for good quality alpaca. *Sr. Aller*, Plaza Santo Domingo 261, sells interesting antiques. *Josefina Olivera*, Santa Clara 501, sells old ponchos, without usual haggling. There is a good jewellery store beside the Cathedral in the Plaza de Armas and art shop at *Instituto Americano de Arte*, Av. Sol. Arto Ovaska from Finland and his Peruvian wife Edith have opened *Snow Shop*, Procuradores 347, for *artesania*, posters, music etc. The *Bazar-Cafetín Minka*, Huaynapata 331, sells craft-work made by people with special needs, and also runs a good café (home-made cakes). However, be very careful of buying gold and silver objects and jewellery in and around Cuzco; we have received many reports of sharp practices.

Sacks to cover rucksacks are available in the market by Estación San Pedro for US$0.75.

Bookshop Plaza Merced (Mantas 191), a small shop sells used English, French, German and Spanish paperbacks—not cheap, poor selection, but will trade paperbacks 2 for 1. Librería Studium, Mesón de la Estrella 144, stocks guide books. Los Andes, Portal Comercio 125, Plaza de Armas, large boxes of postcards, low prices.

Taxis Large cars parked in Plaza are more expensive. Railway-town, US$0.50; per hour in town, US$2.25, out of town, US$3. For many excursions, taxis have a fixed rate; ask the driver for a price list. A rec. taxi driver (also school teacher) is José Cuba, Urb. Santa Rosa, Pasaje R. Gibaja 182, T 226179, who is a guide and can organize tours; accommodation as necessary, he speaks English; he parks at the airport during flight times, and at the station to await train arrival. Another is Angel Salazar, Saguán del Cielo B-11, T 224597 to leave messages, Cuzco, English speaking, highly rec. helpful, arranges good tours; also José G. Valdivia Díaz, T 222210, not an official guide, but rec. as knowledgeable and helpful; Ferdinand Pinares Cuadros, Yuracpunco 155, Tahuantinsuyo, T 225914, English, French and German spoken, rec., reasonable prices.

Car Rental Avis, Av. Sol 900, Volkswagens and Toyotas (poor reports on maintenance). Also, National Rentacar, Calle Santa Catalina near main plaza (cheaper). Never leave anything in a hired car, thieves have keys and may strike the same car again and again.

Exchange Photocopy of passport sometimes required for changing travellers' cheques. Banco de Crédito, Av. del Sol, is good for changing travellers' cheques (same rate as cash). Banco de los Andes has the best rates and is quickest for international money transfers. Many travel agencies also change money at favourable rates and remain open during civil disturbances. No bank in Cuzco will give out cash on credit cards and their use is not rec.: surcharges are imposed and your account will be charged at official rate. Lavamatic laundry on Procuradores gives good rates as does Original Travels, Portal Comercio 141, Plaza de Armas; cash better than travellers' cheques, and Alpha Tours, Av. del Sol, in Centro Comercial Ollantaytambo, No. 104. Money changers on Plaza, or Av. Sol give a better rate than travel agents. *Casas de cambio* in and around plaza charge about 3-5% commission in changing cheques into intis, 7-10% into dollars. Beware of people watching you when you change money.

Spanish Classes Exel, Plaza San Francisco 303, T 235-298.

Consulates **US Agent**, Olga Villa García, Apartado 949, Cuzco, T 222183. **West German**, Sra Maria-Sophia Jürgens de Hermoza, San Agustín 307, T 235459, Casilla Postal 1128, Correo Central, Mon., Wed., Fri., 1100-1300, appointments may be made by phone. **French**, Calle Espinar (in a French-run hotel—may let French people leave luggage if going to Machu-Picchu).

Medical Hospital Regional, Av. de la Cultura, rec. If lab tests needed, Lab. Pasteur, Tullumayo 768 is rec. Dr. Oscar Tejada Ramírez (P.O. Box 425, Cuzco, T 233836 day or night) is a member of the International Association for Medical Assistance to Travellers and is prepared to help any visitor in emergency, 24-hr. attention; he charges according to that organization's scales. Dr Gustavo Garido Juárez, Clínica Paredes, Av. Matará 410, or at home, Av. Pardo 510 T 228613, rec.

Sauna corner of San Bernardo and Quera Almagro, dry sauna, Mon.-Sat. 0900-2000, Sun. 0900-1300, US$0.90.

Laundry Service at Lavamatic, Procuradores 354, min. US$3.50 for 5 kg. (charges per item), 4 hrs. Lavanderías Splendor, Suecia 328, just off Plaza de Armas (US$1.50 for 2 kg.), will also dry clean items such as sleeping bags, rucksacks etc. There is one on Plateros, reported cheaper and better. Also Lavanderías Superchick (Ana M. Velarde), Pumacurco 435, San Cristóbal, T 235629, US$3 for 5 kg., washed, dried and ironed in 24 hrs.

Post Office Principal one on Av. Sol, hrs.: 0800-1900, 0800-1200 Sun. and festivals. Stamps available and letters can be posted at Procuradores 340, off Plaza de Armas. Telephone and telegrams at Empresa Nacional de Telecomunicaciones, Av. Sol 386. To send packages over 2 kg., go first to Customs, Calle Teatro near Plaza San Francisco, open 0900-1200; buy sacking nearby to sew up the package, and then go to main post office. Packages over 2 kg. must be despatched by customs (more expensive).

Police Tourist police, Portal de Belén 115, next to Cathedral on Plaza de Armas (T 221961). If you are robbed and the thief has personal items of no commercial value but important to you, go to **Radio Tawantinsuyo**, Av. Sol 806, and place an *anuncio* offering an unspecified reward for their return. Tell the respondent to go through the radio station; do not reveal your hotel. The *anuncio* costs about US$1 a run and about ten times is standard. They will help you write it; there is a standard etiquette (items are "strayed" never "stolen"). The local TV station will also broadcast the *anuncio* a few times free; enquire at your hotel or at the Policía de Turismo. If you need a *denuncia*, a crime report for insurance purposes, the Policía de Turismo will tell you what documents to buy (stamped paper) at the Banco de la Nación. The police now investigate your complaint; you may have to spend 2 days looking for your things around likely spots, with a policeman, before the police will issue a *denuncia*. Stolen cameras often turn up in the local market and can be bought back cheaply; remember the man selling them is not the thief and has got them at about fourth-hand.

Tourist Office Foptur (very helpful), Portal Belén 115, Plaza de Armas, T 237364, 0830-1900, English spoken; at airport (until 1200) and on Av. Sol. Check all train information carefully. Maps available of Cuzco and Inca Trail to Machu-Picchu. Gives opening hours of churches in Cuzco. Other good guides to the area are the booklets by Víctor Angles (*Machu-Picchu, Ollantaytambo, Sacsayhuamán*) in Spanish and the Uniclam *Machu-Picchu* in French. Another office at Tecsecocha 474, 0745-1300 Mon.-Fri.

   Motorists beware; many streets end in flights of steps not marked as such. Very few good maps of Cuzco available; that of Cuzco and Puno Region by Zoila L. Vergara Valenza, available on train to Machu Picchu, is reasonable. The map of the Cuzco-Puno-La Paz route sold at the station can be bought more cheaply (US$0.50) in bookshops.

   The book *Exploring Cusco*, by Peter Frost, is very good; new edition available in Cuzco bookshops. Also rec. *Cusco Peru Tourist Guide*, published by Lima 2000 at US$3.50. *Apus and Incas*, by Charles Brod, describes cultural walks in and around Cuzco, and treks in the Cordilleras Vilcabamba, Vilcanota and Urubamba, plus the Manu National Park (2nd edition, Inca Expeditions, 2323 SE 46th Avenue, Portland, OR 97215, USA, US$10.95 plus US$1.50 postage, or from bookshops in N. America, Europe and Peru).

   Automóvil Club del Perú, Av. Sol, useful for maps.

Travel Agencies Shopping around will always save money. *Lima Tours* at Av. Sol 567, next to Faucett office (American Express agent). Cooks around the corner from the *Hotel Cusco*.

Andean Adventures, Portal de Panes 137 (T 236201), but may be relocating, friendly, reliable; trips to Tambopata and Manu Reserves, Inca Trail, mountains (Aurelio is highly rec. mountain guide, Raul Medina also rec.) also rent equipment, as do *Walking Tours*, Portal Confituría 257, Plaza de Armas. *Expediciones Mayoc*, Procuradores 354, Apartado 596, Cuzco, T 232666 organizes river-running and trekking expeditions on the Urubamba, Apurímac, Inanbari rivers, to the National Parks near Cuzco and weekly departures to walk the Inca Trail, also treks to sites round Cuzco on horseback. *Tambo Treks* organize 7-21 day tours in the region (to Paucartambo, Pongo de Mainique, Salcantay, with local weavers) from US$490. For information write to Tambo Treks, Casilla 912, Cuzco. *Aventours*, Av. Pardo 545. T 237307 (see also under Lima Travel Agents), highly rec. for rafting on the Urubamba, US$45 p.p. inc. lunch, ask for Gonzalo or Lucas in Cuzco, who also arrange mountain treks. *Turismo Inkaiko*, Av. El Sol 526 (T 224789. also Lima, Av. Garcilaso de la Vega 911, of. 404, T 281041), for local arrangements; *International Service* is a small, friendly organization with tours in and around Cuzco, including Machu-Picchu, their office is at Garcilaso 285, oficina 213. *Peru-Bolivian Tours*, Santa Catalina Angosta 149 arranges daily trips Cuzco-La Paz via Copacabana or via Desaguadero. *Kantu Tours*, Portal Carrizos 258, rec. for local tours, competitive, Gloria Hermosa Tapiá speaks good English. You can pay extra for English-speaking guides. Sigui Tours, Portal de Panes 123, rents camping equipment, sells maps, rec. *Snow Tours*, Portal de Panes 109, office 204, run by Arto (Finnish) and Edith Ovaska, local tours, camping equipment hired cheaply (check tents carefully); *Peruvian Andean Treks*, Av. Pardo 575, rec.; *Señorial Travel* at *Hotel Colonial Palace* has been rec.; *Sumac Tours*, Ayacucho 236, small, offers good personal attention; *APU Expediciones*, Portal de Carnes 236, P.O. Box 24, T (084) 235408/232743, Fax 241111, Telex 54051 PE, arranges river rafting on the Urubamba, mountaineering expeditions, trips to Manu and the Inca Trail, helpful, English spoken; *Luzma Tours*, Plaza de Armas, Portal de Harinas 191, rec. for white water rafting, English spoken. *SAS Travel*, Plaza de Armas 109, helpful and efficient; *Rio Bravo*, Almagro 120 (off Av. Sol), white water rafting and alternative routes to Machu-Picchu; *PeruLand Tours*, Portal Confituría 273 (Rosa Morote, English-speaking), rec.; *Milla Turismo*, Ayacucho 161, Aptdo Postal 348, T 231710, Telex 52018, run by Don Carlos Milla Vidal, mixed reports. *Explorandes*, Procuradores, rec, good equipment for hire; *Chincheros Tours* (registered at the Cuzco Tourist office) is recommended for the Pisac-Urubamba-Ollantaytambo-Chinchero round trip; also *Pisac Tours* on Plaza de Armas (US$4 for Sacred Valley tour). *Transvaal Tours*, Triunfo 122, T 236750, rec. *Valicha Tours*, Plateros 364, helpful and reliable for tickets and tours; *Dalphi*, Plateros 354, T 222300, will arrange tickets for Machu Picchu train, but mixed reports. Enrique Mercado, at *Peruvian Travel y Turismo*, San Agustín 371, is helpful and speaks good English.

Sra. Luisa Bueno Hermosa offers tours of the Cuzco area at reasonable prices (in Spanish); Sr. Luis Vargas, Calle Triunfo 374, also is a rec. guide. Srta. Juana Pancorbo, Av. Los Pinos D-2, T 227482, is a guide who speaks English, rec. Marco Bustamante, Casilla 720, T 225391, rec. David Choque, T 224-327, English-speaking, good, but insist on itinerary first. Haydee and Tomás Oblitas, Av. Ramón Castilla J-5, Urbanización Bancopata (15 mins.' walk from centre, or take taxi) have been particularly rec. as guides in and around Cuzco, Tomás speaks English, flexible tours, reasonably priced. The potter Nicolás Torre is also a good guide US$2 p.p. Raúl Castelo H., Calle Saphi 877B, Interior No. 6 (flute player at *El Truco*) is a good guide, using his own car. José Huaquina Pacheco, Saphi 635, patio 3, trustworthy guide for the Inca Trail, he has a good tent and stove, highly rec.

N.B. Equipment hire prices are often in dollars, so important to agree on exchange rate at time of hire. For river rafting tours, take bathing suit, T-shirt, rain gear, change of clothes and towel; life jackets should be provided.

Minibuses in front of tourist office take tourists to see the "Sacred Valley" (Pisac—make sure driver takes you to the ruins, not just the market, Ollantaytambo and Chinchero), 0800, all-day tour, US$3.50, drivers are competent guides; also Sacsayhuamán, Quenco and Tambo Machay, 1400, half-day, US$2.50. Other minibuses to these places, and further afield, from Av. Recoleta. An even cheaper "Sacred Valley" trip is given by César Silva Guzmán, T 226-627, who is often to be found in front of the tourist office on the Plaza de Armas.

Roads and Buses To Juliaca, Puno, La Paz, road in poor condition especially in the wet season, many parts are unsurfaced. Cruz del Sur, to Puno, leave at 1900 US$5, 12 hrs., rec., but very cold (book at least 1 day in advance in busy season). To Sicuani, Oriente Sur, Huáscar 244, US$1.90. Bus to Juliaca at 0900, US$5.50. To Lima (1,180 km.), road via Abancay, Andahuaylas, Ayacucho, Huancayo and La Oroya is rec. for magnificent scenery and interesting towns, but sometimes closed by guerrilla action. The road is appalling in places and takes from 3 to 6 days by successive buses or colectivos; take a rug for the cold nights, and extra food. Approx. times of journeys from Cuzco: Abancay 8 hrs.; Andahuaylas 14 hrs.; Ayacucho 24 hrs.; Huancayo 36-45 hrs.; Lima 2-3 days. Through fare Cuzco-Lima about US$23. An alternative road to Lima goes SW from Abancay through Puquío and Nazca; this road is narrow, unpaved but spectacular. Ormeño (office at Plaza de Armas 177, depot, Av. Huáscar 128) to Lima via Abancay and Nazca, Mon., Thurs. 0700, to Abancay 7 hrs., Puquío 22 hrs., Nazca 27 hrs., US$12, Lima 34-45 hrs. (US$22), also Hidalgo (Tullumayo 826). Señor de Anima, Belén 537, to Lima via Abancay and Nazca, US$14, advertised as 13 hrs., more like 40, poor meal stops and often stop at night in Abancay (as do Ormeño), Tues., Wed., Fri., Sun., 0600. By bus to Lima via Arequipa, 1,838 km., 3 days non-stop but the stretch Juliaca-Arequipa is poor, passing through a high arid plain at 4,700 metres before descending into Arequipa valley. Cruz del Sur, Av. Tullumayo, daily at 1800 to Lima via Arequipa, daily at 1900 to Puno, US$7, 11 hrs.; Señor de Anima, 50-55 hrs., US$9, good meal stops; San Cristóbal buses are less good (old and overcrowded), US$8, leave Cuzco at 0900, arrive Juliaca about midnight and depart Juliaca at 1000 for Arequipa next day. Ormeño to Arequipa via Tintaya, 18 hrs., Mon. and Thurs. 0800, US$15. Better to take a more expensive minibus from one of the companies on the Plaza de Armas. For buses to nearby towns and villages, see below under their entries.

No direct buses run from Cuzco to Ayacucho, you have to take a bus to Abancay (several between 0530 and 1000, US$4.75-6.50, 7 hrs.), then bus Abancay-Andahuaylas (0630 only, US$4.50, 8 hrs.; book seat as soon as possible), and bus Andahuaylas-Ayacucho (1400, US$6.40, 18 hrs. in the dry, forever in the wet, several companies, but don't always run). If taking a truck Andahuaylas-Ayacucho, take a powerful one; the road is terrible after Ocros. Many Guardia checkpoints, and military at Ocros; transport may also be stopped by Sendero Luminoso.

Rail To Juliaca and Puno from Av. Sol station, daily, except Sun., at 0800 (though delays common and schedules change) arriving at Juliaca 1900 and Puno 2030, sit on lefthand side. **To Juliaca,** 1st class, US$3. **To Puno,** tourist car US$22, 1st, US$6, can be purchased on day before leaving, 2nd, US$2, can be booked, tickets on sale before, or from 0630. Meals on train cost US$3, good value, second serving reported better than first. The advantage of the buffet car (if you can get on it: group tours sometimes book the whole car) is that no one is allowed into it without a reserved seat ticket. Usually at stations the attendant keeps out vendors and doors are locked for security, although you are allowed out if you want to buy something. **N.B.** Check ticket very carefully if booking to Puno, or you may find the ticket only covers the train to Juliaca, although paid for to Puno. Beware agents on train offering accommodation in Puno, pay no money.

To Arequipa, 0800 daily, 23 hrs., 1st class US$6, 2nd class US$4, heated buffet car, US$20. Train to Sicuani leaves at 1510, arriving at 2120 (US$3). To Lima, cheaper to go via Arequipa (bus from there to Lima) but make sure that your carriage does not detach at Juliaca. It is reported that the Juliaca-Puno stretch is sometimes closed; colectivos meet the train at Juliaca. See **Warning** on page 940, under **Arequipa Rail.**

To Anta, Ollantaytambo, Machu-Picchu and Quillabamba, **see pages 965, 969 and 971.**

Machu-Picchu trains leave from Estación San Pedro, opposite the market. Check all times as they change frequently, and that trains are running.

Air A new airport at Quispiquilla is in use. Taxi to airport, US$1, bus US$0.10, leaves from Tourist Office on Plaza de Armas (returns from airport to old market, dangerous after dark). To Lima, Faucett has daily flights (1200). AeroPerú also has 2 morning flights. From Lima, AeroPerú flies at 0630 and 0705, and Faucett at 0645, 1 hr., US$83. There is a Sat. and sometimes Thurs. military flight to Lima, ask for next scheduled flight with Grupo Ocho de la Fuerza Aérea; book at airport several days in advance, be at airport at 0830 for 1000/1100 departure, US$20, unpredictable in the extreme. Cuzco-Juliaca (for Puno), Fri. AeroPerú and Faucett fly daily to Arequipa, US$40, often delayed. AeroPerú also flies to Iquitos (and on to Miami) Faucett flies to Iquitos, Tues., Thurs., Sat., 0730, US$104, calling at Pucallpa, 2½ hrs. N.B. in summer all flights to Iquitos go via Lima. LAB Cuzco-La Paz-Cuzco Wed. and Sat., cheaper from La Paz (US$11 inc. tax, 2-way excursion in 1990, US$149 from La Paz). To Puerto Maldonado: AeroPerú daily; Faucett Tues., Thurs., Sat. (US$36); airforce (Grupo 8) Thurs., US$18, enquire at office of Grupo Ocho de la Fuerza Aérea in airport. Book return well in advance, especially in the busy season and reconfirm 24 hours before departure. Flights between Lima and Cuzco tend to be heavily booked between 29 July and 11 August because of school holidays. Shop around for seats at travel agencies, especially Lima Tours, if the airlines say they are full. The AeroPerú office is on Av. Sol; Faucett office is at Av. Sol 567. There is no facility for buying tickets at the airport. There is a limited hotel booking service at the airport, which will give you inflated US$-based prices: better to negotiate with hotels yourself. In emergencies, for flights to Lima, try Sra Rossi at Lima Tours, Plaza de Armas. **N.B.** There is no air service between Cuzco and Ayacucho.

Warning   Cuzco-Lima, high possibility of cancelled flights during wet season; tourists sometimes stranded for several days. Possible for planes to leave early if bad weather. Sit on right side of aircraft for best view of mountains when flying Cuzco-Lima; it is worth checking in early to get these seats. Both Faucett and AeroPerú are unreliable on bookings: you must reconfirm your tickets personally in the last 24 hrs. (don't trust an agency to do this for you) but even then you cannot be sure of a seat. Baggage is often lost en route. Airport taxes: US$5 security tax; US$2 airport tax.

There is some magnificent walling in the ruined cult centre of **Sacsayhuamán**, on a hill in the northern outskirts, which is within walking distance (about ½ hr. walk, tiring because of the altitude). Take steps to San Cristóbal church (shorter than via Calle Saphi). The Incaic stones are bigger and even more impressive than at Machu-Picchu; huge rocks weighing up to 300 tons are fitted together with absolute perfection; three walls run parallel for over 360 metres and there are 21 bastions. Sacsayhuamán was thought for centuries to be a fortress, but the layout and architecture suggest a great sanctuary and temple to the Sun, which rises exactly opposite the place previously believed to be the Inca's throne—which was probably an altar, carved out of the solid rock: broad steps lead to it from either side. The hieratic, rather than the military, hypothesis was supported by the discovery in 1982 of the graves of priests: they would have been unlikely to be buried in a fortress. Zig-zags in the boulders round the "throne" are apparently "*chicha* grooves", channels down which maize beer flowed during festivals. Up the hill is an ancient rock slide for children: the Rodadero; near it are many seats cut perfectly into smooth rock.

The temple and amphitheatre of Kenko (Quenco), with excellent examples of Inca stone carving, especially inside the large hollowed-out stone that houses an altar, are along the road from Sacsayhuamán to Pisac, past a radio station. On the same road are the Inca fortress of Puku Pukará and the spring shrine of Tambo Machay, which is in excellent condition; water still flows by a hidden channel out of the masonry wall, straight into a little rock pool traditionally known as the Inca's bath, but he would have had to be a pygmy to have used it as such. It seems much more likely that the site was a centre of a water cult.

The gates are manned from about 0700 but you can get in earlier if you wish and definitely try to get there before midday when the tour groups arrive. Carry your multi-site ticket, there are roving ticket inspectors. After seeing 3 sites you can catch truck back along road, 9 km., for US$0.25. Preferably, take the Pisac bus (from Calle Saphi) to Tambo Machay and walk back (downhill) to Cuzco, or taxi US$0.50 to Tambo Machay (to walk from Cuzco to Tambo Machay takes over an hour, but it's pleasant). If you walk back, don't take short cuts through farmland; you may get chased by packs of dogs. Between Kenko and Puku Pukará is Cusillyuioc; caves and Inca tunnels in a hillside (take a torch/flashlight). Taxis to Inca sites outside Cuzco for 3 hrs. cost US$14, not including entry to the sites, and may be hired in the Plaza de Armas. A tour bus to all 4 sites costs US$4. Another good way to see these ruins is on horseback, arranged by travel agents.

Cuzco is at the W end of the gently sloping Cuzco valley, which stretches 32 km. E as far as Huambutío. This valley, and the partly isolated basin of Anta, NW of Cuzco, are densely populated. Also densely populated is the Urubamba valley, stretching from Sicuani (on the railway to Puno, at 3,960 metres) to the gorge of Torontoi, 600 metres lower, to the NW of Cuzco. There are several ruins of Inca buildings and fortresses in the Cuzco valley itself, especially at **Pikillacta** (also pre-Inca Huari—8th century) on the road to Andahuaylillas (45 mins. by bus from Av. Huáscar and Av. Garcilaso, US$0.10—ask driver to drop you off at the turning, or take bus from Urcos where there are 2 basic *alojamientos*), the monkey temple (Templo de los Monos) NW of Pikillacta, the amphitheatre at Moray (three "colosseums", one large, two small, used by the Incas as a sort of plant breeding and acclimatization centre; remote, beautiful and worth visiting—by car to Maras, then 1½-hrs.' walk, or a bumpy 20-km. drive from Chinchero—Urubamba road; it is a 3½-hr. walk from Urubamba), the administrative and storage centre of Colcampata, and Rumicolca, on the shores of Lake Lucre. Interesting textile mill at Lucre village.

Andahuaylillas is a village 32 km. S of Cuzco, with a particularly fine early 17th century church; beautiful frescoes, splendid doorway and a gilded main altar (ask for Sr. Eulogio, good guide, Spanish only). Taxis go there as does Oropesa bus (Av. Huáscar, Cuzco) via Tipón, Pikillacta and Rumicolca. There are other unexcavated ruins just beyond Andahuaylillas.

John Streather has most kindly given us information about more places south of Cuzco with interesting Inca remains and colonial buildings:
   Tipón ruins, between the villages of Saylla and Oropesa, include baths, terraces and a temple complex, accessible from a path leading from just above the last terrace. **Oropesa** church contains a fine ornately carved pulpit. **Huacarpay**: ruins of the Inca town of Kañaracy, well-preserved, are nearby, reached from a path behind the Albergue. Also nearby are the ruins of Piquillacta, the monkey temple and the wall of Rumicolca. At Lucre, 3 km. from Huacarpay, there are many unexplored ruins; ask the local history teacher, Sr. Hernán Flores Yávar, for details. About 3 km. from Huacarpay is *El Dorado Inn*, in a converted monastery, some of the rooms in a remarkable style, very good service, but expensive at C. **Tinta**, 23 km. from Sicuani, has a church with brilliant gilded interior and an interesting choir vault. Hotel: *Casa Comunal*, dormitory accommodation, F, clean with good food. Frequent buses and trucks to Cuzco. **Huaro** has a church whose interior is covered entirely with colourful mural painting. **Cusipata**, with an Inca gate and wall, is where the ornate bands for the decoration of ponchos are woven; close by is the Huari hilltop ruin of Llallanmarca.

Raqchi is the scene of the region's great folklore festival in mid-June. A special train leaves Cuzco early in the morning, or take a truck, US$1, 4 hours. At this festival dancers come to Raqchi from all over Peru; through music and dance they illustrate everything from the ploughing of fields to bull fights, reported to be most enjoyable. John Hemming adds: The Viracocha temple is just visible from the train, looking from the distance like a Roman aqueduct. What remains is the central wall (adobe above, Inca masonry below) of what was probably the largest roofed building ever built by the Incas. On either side of the high wall, great sloping roofs were supported by rows of unusual round pillars, also of masonry topped by adobe. Nearby is a complex of barracks-like buildings and round storehouses. This was the most holy shrine to the creator god Viracocha, being the site of a miracle in which he set fire to the land—hence the lava flow nearby. There are also small Inca baths in the corner of a field beyond the temple and a straight row of ruined houses by a square. The landscape is extraordinary, blighted by huge piles of black volcanic rocks. (San Cristóbal bus to Raqchi from Av. Huáscar, Cuzco every hour, US$0.90, 4 hrs. Nearest hotel is in Tinta).

Pacarijtambo is a good starting point for the 3-4 hr. walk to the ruins of Mankallajta, which contain good examples of Inca stonework. From there, one can walk to Pumaorco, a high rock carved with steps, seats and a small puma in relief on top; below are more Inca ruins. From Pumaorco walk back to the nearby hamlet of Mollepata (bus from Cuzco, US$1) and ask the schoolteacher the way to Pacarijtambo (a 2-3 hr. walk). One may seek lodging for the night in Pacarijtambo at the house of the Villacorta family and leave for Cuzco by truck the next morning. On the way back, one passes the caves of Tambo Toco, where the legend says that the four original Inca brothers emerged into the world.

Acomayo is a pretty village (*Pensión Aguirre*), which has a chapel with mural paintings of the fourteen Incas. From Acomayo, one can walk to Huáscar and from there to Pajlia; a climb which leads one through very impressive scenery. The canyons of the upper Apurímac are vast beyond imagination, great cliffs drop thousands of metres into dizzying chasms and huge rocks balance menacingly overhead. The ruins of Huajra Pucará lie near Pajlia; they are small, but in an astonishing position. John Hemming adds that the church at Checacupe is very fine, with good paintings and a handsome carved altar rail.

Pisac, 30 km. N of Cuzco, is at the bottom of the Urubamba valley; high above it, on the mountainside, is a superb Inca fortress (admission by combined entrance ticket, **see page 952**, the ruins close at 1700). The masonry is better than at Machu-Picchu, the terraces more extensive and better preserved. When you climb it (a must), remember that there are 3 hill fortifications, but the third is the fortress proper, in which the actual temple is built: so go on to it and get the glorious view from the top. There is a 10-km. motor road up to the level of the ruins, upstream from Pisac town and then up a valley to the S of the spur containing the ruins. From the parking lot, enter along Inca roads and through Inca gates, seeing the fine view of terraces (which can be reached quite easily from the town by a footpath, local boys will guide you US$0.50 per couple). Quite a lot of walking is involved. The central part of the ruins is the Intihuatana group of temples and rock outcrops in the most magnificent Inca masonry. Above on the hilltop reached by a path along a vertiginous cliff are residential groups; there is a large Inca cemetery in caves on the valley opposite to the north; the curving group of houses called Pisallacta below the Intihuatana group; and more buildings, some with curious round towers, others of good Inca adobe, on the steep hillside above the town. It takes about 25 minutes to walk down. There is a path going right round the mountain, behind the main ruins; it has two tunnels. It takes 2½ hours to walk from the parking lot back to Pisac. Taxi to ruins US$2.

Pisac has a Sun. morning market, described as touristy and expensive after the arrival of tourist buses around 1000; it starts at 0900 and is usually over by 1500. There are picturesque Indian processions to a Quechua Mass. Pisac has another, less crowded, less expensive market on Thurs. morning. You can take in the market, then take taxi up to ruins, explore them, walk down and get last bus or truck back to Cuzco by 1630. It is reported that transport to the ruins is not always available for those not in a tour group. You can continue the Sun. morning tour to Pisac along the Urubamba to Ollantaytambo, with lunch at the Tourist Hotel in Urubamba (US$4.25) but tours from Cuzco usually allow only 1½ hours at Pisac: not enough time to take it in. Splendid scenery. Apart from Sun. when Pisac is crowded, there are very few tourists. An alternative for lunch is the restaurant on the square in **Yukay** (open-air, good buffet and local dishes). On the N side of the square is the adobe palace built for Sayri Túpac (Manco's son) when he emerged from Vilcabamba in 1558. A pleasant old hotel, the *Alhambra 3*, B, is in Yukay, rather overpriced but very pretty and old. In Yukay monks sell fresh milk, ham, eggs and other dairy produce from their farm on the hillside. The tour by taxi costs US$40-45. Good walks along river to Inca terraces.

Pisac Hotels *Albergue Chongo Chico*, F, basic, slightly decayed, electricity and water unreliable, friendly; camping allowed in garden. *Turistas*, E, pleasant, English spoken, meals US$5. The woman who owns the flour mill rents rooms for US$1.30 p.p. *Roma*, near the bridge by the Kodak sign, F, basic, quiet, cold shower, dreadful; camping allowed in its grounds for US$0.45 p.p. Reasonable restaurant on the plaza, but better to take a packed lunch from Cuzco. Fresh bread available from the oven *(el horno)* just off the plaza.

Buses Cuzco-Pisac road is paved. Early morning buses on Sunday, every ten min., from 0540 to 0700, 1 hr. (queue early in road opposite Puno station or catch them on Huáscar, halfway down 1st block on right-hand side looking downhill, before they fill up); several—bus Cuzco-Pisac from Recoleta y Tacna, 1½ hrs, US$0.25. Bus Pisac-Cuzco hourly on weekdays until 1700-1800. Colectivos to Pisac from Cuzco; they return all afternoon until 1715 and are always full, be prepared to return by truck. Fare US$0.70; try and book the previous day if possible. Tourist minibus leaves Cuzco Plaza de Armas outside Cathedral daily for Pisac and Ollantaytambo if there are more than five passengers, US$5 return. Minibus tours also Cuzco, Pisac, Urubamba, Ollantaytambo, US$10; taxi for this route, including Chinchero, US$40. Colectivos to Pisac and Ollantaytambo leave when full from Calle Recoleta, from 0600, Cuzco (past Calle Pumapaccha), to Pisac 45 mins., US$0.60, to Ollantaytambo, 2½ hrs., US$1. Return fare by truck, US$0.40, over 1 hr. Taxi fare (return) from Cuzco to the fortress costs US$8 and includes a visit to the market. Tours by agencies to Pisac on Thurs. and Sun. (market days) only. Two buses daily to Urubamba. Bus stops in Pisac are brief, make sure you get on or off the bus quickly. Try hitching opposite the police checkpoint.

Calca is 18 km. beyond Pisac (Hotels: *Alojamiento Grau*, basic; *Alojamiento Alvarez*; Alojamiento Central, F, basic. Restaurants: *Sondar, Bolívar*, on Plaza; *Moreñitas* and *Café Calqueñita*, near post office). Mineral baths at Minas Maco (½ hr. walk along the Urubamba) and Machacancha (8 km. E of Calca). If one continues past Minas Maco, one bears right up a small footpath leading by a clump of trees; the first house one comes to after crossing a small stream and climbing a hill is a precolumbian ruin. 3 km. beyond Machacancha are the Inca ruins of Arquasmarca. The ruins of a small Inca town, Huchuy Cuzco, are across the river Vilcanota, and up a stiff climb. There are a two-storey house, paved with flat stones, and a large stone reservoir at Huchuy Cuzco. Bus to Pisac, or to Urubamba, US$0.50; bus to Cuzco, US$0.30. Market day: Sun. It is a two-day hike from Cuzco to Calca, via Sacsayhuamán, Kenko, Puka Pukará, Tambo Machay and Huchuy Cuzco; there are many places to camp, but take water. Between Calca and Quillabamba the road is narrow and subject to landslides.

Zurite is a little-known village north of Cuzco; Inca terraces of Patapata are only about an hour's walk from the village's main square. The construction of these terraces represents a Herculean effort as all of the earth is said to have been brought from elsewhere. A canal was built to bring water from the mountains. (John Streather.)

   Chinchero; with an attractive church built on an Inca temple; recent excavations there have revealed many Inca walls and terraces. (On combined entrance ticket, **see page 952**.) It has become very tourist-oriented but nonetheless the Sunday market and Indian mass are more authentic than at Pisac (there is a small market on Thurs.). *Hotel Inca*, F, with restaurant; *Albergue Chinchero*, F, basic, clean, friendly. At the market, there is a varied selection of handicrafts, including weaving, pottery and alpaca goods (nothing is cheap). Celebrations are held in Chinchero on September 8 (the day of the Virgin).

A new road Cuzco-Urubamba has been completed, which has cut the travelling time to Chinchero to 40 mins. from Cuzco by bus, leaving about 0700 from Av. Arcopata on Sun. mornings, US$0.25. Also colectivos from Av. Arcopata. Taxi, US$20 for 5-hr. trip. There is also a scenic path to Chinchero from Urubamba, about 4-5 hrs.

76 km. from Cuzco on the Abancay road, 2 km. before Limatambo (accommodation in *Albergue*, **F**; nice restaurant hidden from road by trees), at Hacienda **Tarahuasi**, a few hundred metres from the road, is a very well-preserved **Inca temple platform**, with 28 tall niches, and a long stretch of fine polygonal masonry. The ruins have grandeur, enhanced by the orange lichen which give the walls a beautiful honey colour. 100 km. from Cuzco along the Abancay road is the exciting descent into the Apurímac canyon, near the former Inca suspension bridge that inspired Thornton Wilder's *The Bridge of San Luis Rey*. Also, 153 km. along the road to Abancay from Cuzco, near Carahuasi (restaurant on main road into town; camping possible on the football pitch, ask police), is the stone of Sahuite, carved with animals, houses, etc., which appears to be a relief map of an Indian village. (Unfortunately, "treasure hunters" have defaced the stone.) There are other interesting carvings in the area around the Sahuite stone.

For US$40 a taxi can be hired for a whole day (ideally Sun.) to take you to Cachimayo, Chinchero, Maras, Urubamba, Ollantaytambo, Calca, Lamay, Coya, Pisac, Tambo Machay, Kenko and Sacsayhuamán. If you wish to explore this area on your own, Road Map (*Hoja de ruta*) No. 10 from the Automóvil Club del Perú is an excellent guide.

Urubamba is N of Chinchero, on a new direct road from Cuzco via Chinchero; pleasant country surroundings. The Machu-Picchu tourist train can be caught at Pachar, about 20 minutes' drive away, at 0830; no fare reduction. Bus Cuzco-Urubamba, US$0.50 from Av Huáscar, 2½ hrs. Urubamba-Ollantaytambo, colectivo, US$0.25, 30-45 mins., 19 km.

Hotels and restaurants *Hotel de Turistas*, E, clean, hot water, poor service, bungalows with neglected garden and swimming pool; the *Centro Vacacional Urubamba*, cabins (some with kitchen, must take own stove), sports facilities, 2 pools, E and F; *Hostal*

Naranjachayoc, C, with antique furniture and swimming pool, 20 mins. walk from town, rec., friendly, accommodating, will help with any problems, very clean and well-stocked restaurant and bar, even in low-season, car can be parked in locked patio, *Hotel Urubamba*, F, pleasant; *Hostal Reymada*, F, basic, clean, friendly, outdoor pool, rec.; *Hostal Vera*, beyond the Tourist Hotel; and *Hotel Retamanioj*, and *Restaurant Quinta los Geranios*, excellent lunch for US$3 with more than enough food; *Restaurant Norteñito*; *Comedor Aries* and *Andes*, both on Plaza. *Quinta Galu*, close to Plaza, large, reasonable, friendly, good.

Joanna Codrington writes: 6 km. from Urubamba on the Ollantaytambo road is the village of **Tarabamba**, where a footbridge crosses the Río Vilcanota. If one turns right after the bridge one comes to Piychinjoto, a tumbled-down village built under an overhanging cliff. Also, just over the bridge and to the left of a small, walled cemetery is a salt stream. If one follows this (there is a footpath) one comes to Salinas, a small village below which are a mass of terraced Inca salt pans, still in operation. A very spectacular sight. Darrell High, from Ware, writes: **Moray** is well worth a visit: it is quite beautiful. Wait for pickup on bridge on Chinchero road. This will take you near to Maras; walk to Maras (½ hr.) and on through it, bearing left a little, and ask directions to Moray (walk 1½ hrs.). Hitching back to Urubamba is quite easy.

The Cuzco-Machu Picchu train reaches the heights N of the city by a series of switchbacks and then descends to the floor of the Anta basin, with its herds of cattle. (In **Anta** itself, *Restaurant Dos de Mayo* is good; bus to Anta, US$0.25., felt trilby hats on sale). The railway goes through the Anta canyon (10 km.), and then, at a sharp angle, the Urubamba canyon, and descends along the river valley, flanked by high cliffs and peaks.

The railway and a 53-km. road go on to **Ollantaytambo**, 70 km., a clean and friendly little town (alt.: 2,800 metres) built on and out of the stones of an Inca town, which is a fine example of Inca *canchas* or corral enclosures, almost entirely intact. The so-called Baño de la Ñusta (bath of the princess) is of grey granite, and is in a small field between the town and the temple fortress. Some 200 metres behind the Baño de la Ñusta along the face of the mountain are some small ruins known as Inca Misanca, believed to have been a small temple or observatory. A series of steps, seats and niches have been carved out of the cliff. There is a complete irrigation system, including a canal at shoulder level, some 6 inches deep, cut out of the sheer rock face. The flights of terraces leading up above the town are superb, and so are the curving terraces following the contours of the rocks overlooking the Urubamba. These terraces were successfully defended by Manco Inca's warriors against Hernando Pizarro in 1536. Manco Inca built the defensive wall above the site and another wall closing the Yucay valley against attack from Cuzco, still visible on either side of the valley. Visitors should also note the Inca masonry channelling the river and the piers of the bridge of Ollantaytambo. Entering Ollantaytambo from Pisac, the road is built along the long wall of 100 niches. Note the inclination of the wall: it leans towards the road. Since it was the Incas' practice to build with the walls leaning towards the interiors of the buildings, it has been deduced that the road, much narrower then, was built inside a succession of buildings. The site opens at 0700.

The temple itself was started by Pachacuti, using Colla Indians from Lake Titicaca—hence the similarities of the monoliths facing the central platform with the Tiahuanaco remains. The Colla are said to have deserted half-way through the work, which explains the many unfinished blocks lying about the site. Admission by combined entrance ticket, which can be bought at the site. If possible arrive very early, 0700, before the tourists. The Sunday following Inti Raymi, there is a colourful festival, the Ollantay-Raymi. The guide book *Ollantaytambo* by Víctor Angles Vargas is available in Cuzco bookshops, and Peter Frost's *Exploring Cuzco* is also useful.

Accommodation *Parador Turístico*, off main street between Plaza and ruins, for groups by reservation but will sometimes take other groups or couples if not booked up, E-F, good meals at US$2-3; offers travel info. and horseback/walking tours; for reservations write to María S. Martínez, Parador Turístico de Ollantaytambo, Cuzco, Peru or get your Cuzco hotel to phone the Ollantaitambo exchange as the Parador has no phone as yet. Russ Bentley writes: "a veritable oasis of comfort and excellent food (superb Italian cuisine)". *Hostal Miranda*, F with shower, basic, friendly, clean; *Hostal Alcázar*, F with shower, basic, good food, clean; *El Tambo*, also known as *Alojamiento Yavar*, 1½ blocks from main square, G (if full, will let you sleep on the floor free), basic, friendly, has information on riding in the area, horses for hire at US$3 a day; *Hotel Panificadora*, G, tantalizing smell of fresh bread, very hard beds, basic, between main plaza and ruins. *Miramar*, G p.p., clean, basic, hot water available for a fee. Hotel next to station, no sign, door in garden wall, access via footbridge over stream, F p.p., shared amenities, comfortable.

Camping possible in eucalyptus grove, ½ km. from town, and along the river between the town and the railway station.

Horses can be hired for US$3 per day; a rec. trek is to La Marca, a gentle day's ride along the beautiful river valley; ask in the square for details.

Restaurants *Restaurant Ollantay* on Plaza de Armas. *Café Alcázar* opposite *Parador Turístico* good, cheap food, slow service if full; *El Parador*, in converted barn, down from main square towards ruins, good pasta and garlic bread; *Restaurante Tanta Wasi*, by railway, has two rooms to let, run by Jaime and Pilar Paz. In restaurants, check your bill carefully.

Transport For those travelling by car, it is recommended to leave the car in Ollantaytambo (or the station previous on the road from Cuzco) for a day excursion by train to Machu-Picchu. Park car in front of the local police station at Ollantaytambo. Much safer there than parked in Cuzco for US$1 a day. Check in advance the time trains pass through here. The tourist train stops here, as do local trains (0730 or 1600, depending which is running). Station is 10-15 mins. walk from centre. Hourly bus from Calle Recoleta, Cuzco, 2½ hrs., US$1.15, to Urubamba, then colectivo to Ollantaytambo, also to Pisac. Beware of theft when queuing in Cuzco for the Ormeño bus to Ollantaytambo; if the bus goes down the company's alley to turn, get on there, if it doesn't, either don't rush for a seat, or queue with no valuables or possessions, push on, and reserve 2 seats for yourself and your friend with the gear. Many colectivos to Pisac on Sunday for market from 0600, 70 mins. Bus to Cuzco on Sat. at 0800 and 1200. Tourist minibus from outside Cuzco Cathedral to Pisac, Ollantaytambo, Cuzco, daily if over 5 passengers, US$10 (taxi tour costs US$40). Taxi to Cuzco, US$12. Bus to Urubamba, US$0.50 (truck US$0.15), from where one can return to Cuzco via Calca.

A major excavation project has been carried out since 1977 under the direction of Ann Kendall in the **Cusichaca** (Qucsichaca) valley, 26 km. from Ollantaytambo (only 9 km. passable by ordinary car) at the intersection of the Inca routes. (The Inca fort, Huillca Raccay, was excavated in 1978-80, and work is now concentrated on Llactapata, a site of domestic buildings).

From Ollantaytambo one can walk to the Inca Trail in about 5 hrs.: follow the railway in the direction of Machu Picchu until you come to a village where you can cross the river; climb up to a path that runs parallel to the river. This is an original Inca trail (still in use) that leads to Llactapata on the Inca Trail. **Warning** Best not to pass a night on this trail: thefts are common because you have to sleep near villages.

Pinculluna, the mountain above Ollantaytambo, can be climbed with no mountaineering experience, although there are some difficult stretches—allow 2-3 hours going up. The path is difficult to make out; best not to go on your own. Walk up the valley to the left of the mountain, very beautiful and impressive, Inca terraces after 4 km.

The **Inca Trail** hike to Machu-Picchu, about 33 kms., makes a spectacular 3 to 5 day hike (take it slowly to appreciate it fully). It runs from Km. 88, Qoriwayrachi (about 2,600 metres), a point immediately after the first tunnel 22 km. beyond Ollantaytambo station. A sturdy suspension bridge has now been built over the Urubamba River. An entrance ticket (US$11) for the trail (which also gives entry to Machu-Picchu if you get it stamped there) must be bought at Km. 88. The trail is rugged and steep (beware of landslides), at one stage traversing a 4,200-metre high pass, but the magnificent views compensate for any weariness which may be felt. It is cold at night, however, and weather conditions change rapidly, so it is important to take not only strong footwear and warm clothing but also food, water, insect repellant, a supply of plastic bags, coverings, a good sleeping bag, a stove for preparing hot food and drink to ward off the cold at night. A stove using paraffin (kerosene) is preferable, as fuel can be bought in small quantities in markets, whereas camping gas is expensive and scarce. **A tent is essential** (if hiring in Cuzco, check carefully for leaks) because walkers who have not taken adequate equipment have been known to die of exposure; caves marked on some maps are little better than overhangs, and are not sufficient shelter to sleep in. The trail is crowded in July and August. In the wet season (November-April) you don't have to worry about taking drinking water. At Puyopatamarca, on the Trail, there is a "tourist bathroom" where water can be collected (but purify it before drinking). Next place with water is Wiñay-Wayna (where there is a newly-built "tourist complex" with bunk beds (G p.p.), showers and a small restaurant, food and drink expensive), and then none till Machu-Picchu, where water supplies are turned off at 1530. A little-used variation to the Trail is to get off the train at Chilca, some 12 km. beyond Ollantaytambo, cross the bridge and walk 10 km. along the Urubamba River to join the trail at a point above Km. 88. This adds a day to the journey, but has the advantage of giving the body an opportunity to acclimatize itself before the very strenuous climb to the top of the first pass (medication for *soroche* may be necessary for some). Camping is possible on the bluff overlooking Llactapata (watch your belongings closely) and Km. 88 and this is an ideal starting point for the climb to the first pass, putting several hours between you and the other hikers who reach Km. 88 by train after 0900. **Warning** We have had a number of reports of armed robbery on the Inca Trail, mostly on the first night, the culprits being variously described as Sendero Luminoso or organized gangsters from Cuzco. For this reason alone, do not go singly or in couples (official advice: no fewer than four—post a guard at night), and if possible stay close to a tour group; avoid the July-August high season and the rainy season from November onwards. Camp away from the sites on the main trail, and leave all valuables back in Cuzco.

Train to Km. 88 Only the local train stops at Km. 88; the tourist train does not stop here. While the policy exists of deterring tourists from taking the local train (see below), it is difficult to get to the start of the Trail. Unless you can travel on the local train, the simplest method is to go to Ollantaytambo and start walking from there, adding 8 km. to the Trail. If you do manage to catch the stopping train, be ready to get out at Km. 88, it's easy to pass it.

All the necessary equipment can be rented; see page 958 under **Travel agencies**. Good maps of the Trail and area can be bought from Walking Tours, the tourist office, at the Club Andino, or at Copias Vélez, Plaza San Francisco, Cuzco. Try to get the map prepared by the curator of Machu-Picchu Museum; it shows best sleeping places and drinking water. The guide Alberto Miori from Inca Trails is recommended, with many good reports. Remember there are no houses you can rush to if you get into difficulties; check carefully all equipment you hire before starting out.

Susan Whittlesey and Michael Young have prepared an excellent booklet on the Inca civilization and the Inca Trail (including a superb map), which is available for US$4 from Cin Co., 2912 E. 5th Avenue, Denver, Colorado 80206, USA.

The walk to Huayllabamba, following the Cusichaca river, needs about 3 hrs. and isn't too arduous. If planning a 2-4 day trip, carry on past Huayllabamba, which has become notorious for robberies. There is a camping place about an hr. ahead, at Llulluchayoc and another before the ascent to the first pass, Warmiwañuska, about 4 hrs. on in a meadow (highly recommended) 1½-2 hrs. from the summit. From Huayllabamba to the meadows is often discouragingly steep. Following the right path demands intuition more than orienteering knowhow, and the forest is occasionally very thick—but you should emerge towards 1600 hrs.

Leave early next day. The ascent to the first pass (4,200 metres) is the most taxing part of the walk. Afterwards take the path downhill, along left side of valley. You could camp by a stream at the bottom; it is no longer permitted to camp on the way up to the second pass (a much easier climb) at Runkuracay (3,800 metres), an Inca ruin, where there are huts and caves. Magnificent views near the summit in clear weather. Good overnight place is past the Inca ruins at Sayajmarca (3,600 metres), about an hr. on after the top of the second pass.

Muddy jungle terrain leads gently up to the third pass, only about 2-2½ hrs.' walk, the gradient blissfully gentle. Near the top there's a spectacular view of the Urubamba river and the valley to the right. You descend to Inca ruins at Puyopatamarca, well worth a long visit.

From there steps go downhill to Wiñay-Wayna, reached by forking off to the right (it's marked by a sign) near the pylons, 3-4 hrs. or so on from Puyopatamarca. A tourist complex has been built at the fork: there is no road. There is a shop selling drinks and nearby there is a dormitory, F (no electricity). The ruins at Wiñay-Wayna, a village of roofless but otherwise well-preserved Inca houses, are in an impressive location. The path from this point goes more or less level through jungle. You need about 2 hrs. to walk to the Intipunku (3 camping sites on right of track, just before ruins.), where there's a magnificent view of Machu-Picchu, especially at dawn, with the sun alternately in and out, clouds sometimes obscuring the ruins, sometimes leaving them clear. Get to Machu-Picchu as early as possible, preferably before 0830 for best views but in any case before the tourist train arrives at 1030.

Four days would make a comfortable trip (though much depends on the weather) and you would not find yourself too tired to enjoy what you see. Walking the Trail has the advantage of putting Machu-Picchu in its true context: not a "lost city", but an integral part of a heavily populated valley. By the same token Machu-Picchu loses some of its uniqueness; the architecture and scenery are often finer at several points along the trail. **N.B** It is not allowed to walk back along the trail, though you may pay US$1.50 at Intipunku to be allowed to walk back as far as Wiñay-Wayna, and you may not take backpacks into Machu-Picchu.

It is no longer possible to walk back from Aguas Calientes to Km. 107 and cross the swing bridge to go to Wiñay-Wayna by a switch-back path, thence to Machu-Picchu. The terrorist threat to the electricity power station has forced the authorities to close this route.

Littering along the Trail is a serious problem as 5,000 people are now using it each year. The Earth Preservation Fund now sponsors an annual cleanup July-August: volunteers should write to EPF, Inca Trail Project, Box 7545, Ann Arbor, Michigan 48107, USA.

Machu Picchu, 42 km. from Ollantaytambo by rail (2,280 metres), is a complete city, set on a saddle of a high mountain with terraced slopes falling away to the Urubamba river rushing in great hairpin bends below. It is in a comparatively good state of preservation because the Spaniards never found it. For centuries it was buried in jungle, until Hiram Bingham stumbled upon it in 1911. It was then explored by an archaeological expedition sent by Yale.

The ruins—staircases, terraces, temples, palaces, towers, fountains, the famous sundial and the Museo de Sitio below the ruins—require at least a day—some say two (take an insect-repellant). The mountain overlooking the site, Huayna Picchu (on which there are also some ruins), has steps to the top for a superlative view of the whole but it is not for those who get giddy (don't leave the path); the walk up takes about 60 minutes but the steps are dangerous after bad weather (it is only possible to walk up in the morning—start early as there is shade then—and you must register at a hut on the trail; guards prevent you after 1300). The other trail to Huayna Picchu, down near the Urubamba, via the Temple of the Moon, in two caves, one above the other, with superb Inca niches inside (sadly blemished by idiots' graffiti), can only be undertaken with a guide to the

Temple of the Moon, leaving Machu-Picchu at 0900; he will clear the path and kill poisonous snakes. For the trail to the Temple of the Moon: from the path to Huayna Picchu, take the second trail to the left (both are marked "Danger, do not enter"). The danger is in the first 10 minutes, after which it is reasonable, although it descends further than you think it should. After the Temple you may proceed alone to Huayna Picchu; round trip about 4 hours. An almost equally good view can be had from the trail behind the Tourist Hotel. Before doing any trekking around Machu Picchu, check with an official which paths may be used, or which are one way.

From Machu-Picchu one can take the Inca Trail, which climbs up behind the Tourist Hotel, back to (2 hours' walk) the Inca settlement of Wiñay-Wayna (see above under the Inca Trail). On the way, you will have to pay US$1.50 for entry to the Trail. About 30 mins. along a well-marked trail on the other side of Machu-Picchu ruins is the famous Inca bridge. Both walks give spectacular views of the Urubamba River and the thickly wooded mountains, and the butterflies and flowers are beautiful. When going to the Bridge, "don't dwell on just why the path stays where it does" (Kirk Mayer). The tombs at Chaskapata, near Machu-Picchu, have recently been opened.

Gillian Handyside, of Harefield, Mx., tells us that another Inca site was discovered in 1987 opposite Machu-Picchu. An archaeologist, Moisés, who works on the project stays in the *Albergue* in Aguas Calientes and sometimes shows slides on the subject.

Transport N.B. "Machu Picchu" is the official name for Aguas Calientes station; that for Machu Picchu is "Ruinas". The most convenient way of seeing the ruins is to pay US$75 to Foptur, at the station, or an agency (which may add commission) for a *boleto único*, which includes: transfer hotel-station, return train ride in a locked car, bus to Machu Picchu site, entry and lunch. There are 2 trips a day, at 0630 and 0800 enabling tourists to arrive at Machu-Picchu at about 0945 and 1130, visit the ruins and leave Machu-Picchu at 1545 and 1730, arriving in Cuzco about 3½ hrs. later. The tourist trains stop at Ollantaytambo, but not at Aguas Calientes unless requested in advance. The later train out involves going to Ollantaytambo by coach to catch the train; passengers on the early train back are taken from Ollantaytambo to Cuzco by coach. At the San Pedro station you can book a single tourist ticket for US$20, which does not include entry or buses to the ruins. Tickets may be bought one day in advance (returns available); office open 0600-0820, 1000-1100, 1500-1700; make sure you buy a single if staying overnight, or returning on a different type of train.

Local trains from Cuzco, en route to Quillabamba, pass through Ollantaytambo, Aguas Calientes ("Machu Picchu") and Machu Picchu ("Ruinas"). It is imperative to check departure times in advance; they leave Cuzco at 0530, or 1400, or both, arriving at Aguas Calientes at 1000 or 1830, respectively. A tourist Pullman car is sometimes attached to the local train, with a fare of US$10 single. (Ticket office hours: 0800-1200, 1600-1700, Mon.-Fri.; 0500-0600, 1200-1430, Sat.; 1200-1430, Sun.). The local train returns at 0800 and 1600, but is unreliable. If the 0530 from Quillabamba is running to Cuzco, it passes Machu Picchu at 0815. Take a drinking mug on the train. **Note**: In the rainy season trains are often delayed by landslides.

Tourists are normally refused tickets for the local trains to "Ruinas", but in low season they may be allowed on at a tourist price (about US$12). Many cannot afford the tourist prices (as opposed to the local fare of about US$1.20 on the "Indian train"), so various alternatives have been worked out by foreigners. None is straightforward. 1) Take a taxi to El Arco, outside Cuzco, where the train stops briefly; the guard may let you on, for a fee. 2) Go to Ollantaytambo one way or another and buy a tourist ticket (cheaper than in Cuzco), or ask a local to buy a local ticket for you (not possible in Cuzco because identification has to be shown). 3) Persuade station officials that you are going to Quillabamba, not Machu Picchu, then get off at Machu Picchu (which may be difficult). 4) An agent in Cuzco may purchase a local ticket for you, with a hefty mark-up. 5) Buy a single tourist ticket to Machu Picchu from Cuzco, then take the local train back. This is not a problem since residents in Aguas Calientes will help you get a local ticket if you cannot get one yourself (they are angry at tourist prices which discourage independent travellers from going to Machu Picchu.)

Beware of thieves on the local train (bag-slitting is extremely common), particularly at the switch-backs when they can jump on and off the train, and on the Urubamba stretch where there are many short tunnels. Police presence has been stepped up at the stations and on the trains.

Buses from the station to Machu-Picchu start at 0700 (0630 buses for workers only) and meet both local and tourist trains, and charge US$3 each way for the 15-minute trip to the ruins and back. There are theoretically enough seats on the buses for all the train passengers, but in practice you will have to wait for a seat (beware of drivers asking inflated prices). Last bus down to station goes at about 1700 (if you wish to stay longer, demand a single bus ticket). You can walk up in 1½ hrs. to 2 hrs., and down in 1 hr., if you have no luggage; there is a short-cut for walkers, the Camino de Herradura, said to take 45 mins. to 1 hr., some of it almost rock climbing (take an extra T-shirt because it can be chilly at the top and, after sweating on the walk up, you may catch cold). Luggage can be deposited safely at the site entrance (for US$0.10, open 0800-1500, there is a self-service restaurant) but not at the station, nor at the museum (on opposite side of river from station, open Tues.-Sun. 1030-1530). Cost of entry to the ruins, US$10 in intis, per day, they are open 0630-1700. Only holders of Peruvian student cards get a discount. Post Office at Machu-Picchu station has special franking marks.

Permission to enter the ruins before 0630 to watch the sunrise over the Andes, which is a spectacular experience, may be obtained from the Instituto Nacional de Cultura in Colegio San Bernardo, Cuzco (near La Merced), but it is often possible if you talk to the guards at the gate. Sr. Quispe, a guard for many years (and of royal Inca descent), is friendly and informative.

Mon. and Fri. are bad days because there is usually a crowd of people on guided tours who are going or have been to Pisac market on Sun., and too many people all want lunch at the same time. Food is available around the station.

Camping Not permitted on the site, nor on Huayna-Picchu; official campsite at Ruinas, US$2 per tent, per night; may be possible on football field downstream of the station, or Aguas Calientes. Beware of thieves.

Accommodation and Food In season the Tourist Hotel at the ruins is heavily booked during the week (best rooms for the view are 10, 16, 18, 20, 22); try Sunday night as other tourists find Pisac market a greater attraction. Book well in advance, through a reliable agency, or at the Enturperú office in Lima or Cuzco: in this way you can spend 24 hrs. at the site. Often, however, though reportedly booked up weeks in advance, there are cancellations and you can obtain a room on arrival. Rooms with shower and breakfast (no singles) A, US$10 for meals in poor self-service cafeteria. There is electricity and water 24 hours a day. Service and honesty not always good, but as they state in the English version of the rules card: "The grandeur of nature is such, that the conniving of man is overcome." The Tourist Hotel often does not have intis for exchange, make sure you have enough before setting out for Machu-Picchu; but the hotel will accept American Express travellers' cheques at the official rate. Only hotel residents may eat in the restaurant; others have to use the expensive self-service counter outside. It is recommended that you take food and soft drinks with you; prices are very high compared with Cuzco

The cheapest options for staying overnight are at **Aguas Calientes**, 1½ km. back along the railway (the town has electricity 24 hrs a day). If you need to phone Aguas Calientes, the number is T 109. The *Albergue Juvenil*, constructed by Copesco, the state tourism agency for the region, has 200 beds in dormitories and private rooms, and dining facilities (US$3 for a poor meal), for travellers and family groups, dirty bathrooms reported, comfortable, noisy with students, laundry, rec., F p.p. (no IYHA card needed). *Hostal Caminantes*, with bath, G, basic, but friendly and clean; *Hostal Qoñi Unu* (known as Gringo Bill's), third house to left of church, F, clean, cheap, usually has hot water, laundry, money exchange, meals served, luggage stored, new huts built (upstairs rooms better value); *Hotel Sucre*, F, cheap and dingy; *Hostal Machu-Picchu*, F, clean, safe, quiet, friendly (esp. Wilber, owner's son, with travel info.), hot water, nice balcony over the Urubamba, grocery store, rec.; *El Refugio*, cheap, good food, slow service, also *Aiko*, rec.; *Waiki*, good cheap food, breakfast. At the *pizzería*, very slow service, but reasonable food; *El Mirador*, run by Manuel, "the prince of the primus", near station, friendly staff and cat, open 0500 for early starters to Machu-Picchu, opposite is a fruit stand which will make drinks without water if asked. *Chez Maggi* restaurant here nothing like as good as its namesake in Cuzco; *Huayna Picchu*, good value restaurant beside railway line; *Machu Picchu*, restaurant on hill up to hot baths, good, friendly; cheap, unnamed restaurants at Aguas Calientes station. Despite reports that the standard of food and hygiene has improved, you are warned to be careful about what you eat and if in doubt about your constitution, take your own food. It may be difficult to get a room, so be prepared to sleep on a floor. Two new swimming pools have been built. The thermal baths (a communal pool), a 15-minute walk from the town, are particularly welcome to those who have walked the Inca Trail; officially they close at 2000 (US$0.80 per bath, bathing suits required, baths murky, but reported cleaner in morning, showers for washing *before* entering baths allow soap and shampoo, bar).

Note Advisable to buy paperback edition of *Lost City of the Incas* by Hiram Bingham, in Lima or Cuzco (more expensive), or *A Walking Tour of Machu-Picchu* (rec.) by Pedro Sueldo Nava, available in Cuzco. Choice of guide books in Cuzco much improved. The Tourist Hotel also sells guides, although at a rather inflated price. (The South American Explorers' Club in Lima has detailed information on walks here, and so have Hilary Bradt's and Charles Brod's books.)

The railway goes on 79 km. through Chaullay to **Quillabamba** (24,000 people) in the Urubamba Valley at 1,054 metres, where there is a Dominican mission.

The train follows the Urubamba River much of the way from Machu-Picchu, and the improvised station at Quillabamba is right on the river. One crosses a foot bridge put up by the Lions Club and then climbs up a 100-odd flight of stairs to reach the town. Many *heladerías*, much needed in the heat, the best on the northwest corner of the square. Not many attractions for the tourist, but a place to bask in the sun or take a swim in the river, though ask the locals where the safe stretches are, as the current is quite rapid in places. Clean market building, and a football stadium.

Hotels *Don Carlos*, D-E, good, friendly, good, if limited meals, transport to station extra; *Hostal Alto Urubamba*, F, on Dos de Mayo, clean, good, with bath, or without, restaurant; *Quillabamba* (unmarked entrance next to Autoservicio behind market), roof terrace restaurant, rec., D; *Urusayhua*, near market, F; *Progreso*, near market, F; *Comercio*, Libertad, D, with bath; *Hostal San Antonio*, cheap; *San Martín*, dirty, F; *Thomas*, cheap; *Barrenechea*, cheap; *Turistas* expensive, though nice and modern, opposite the market, without sign. The best restaurants are to be found on Plaza de Armas.

Transport The morning train from Quillabamba leaves at 0530 and arrives at Machu-Picchu about 0815, giving you 2½ hours at the ruins before the invasion from Cuzco starts with the arrival of the tourist train. If you can get on the 0530 train from Cuzco to Quillabamba, or can catch it at 1000 at Aguas Calientes, you can go down to Quillabamba and return to Aguas Calientes or Cuzco the same day because it is the same train that leaves Quillabamba at 1300, 6½ hrs. to Cuzco. Tickets must be bought one day in advance, from Enafer office off main plaza. Minibus leaves Cuzco a.m. when full, from Calle General Buendía near Macchu-Picchu station; also trucks go in the daytime, US$2. The road between Ollantaytambo and Quillabamba passes through Peña, a place of great beauty with snowy peaks already appearing on either side of the valley (taxis are very reluctant to go there). Once out of Peña, the climb to the pass begins in earnest—on the right is a huge glacier. Soon on the left, Salcantay begins to appear in all its huge and snowy majesty. After endless zig-zags and breathtaking views, one reaches Puerto Málaga (rudimentary *pensión*). The descent to the valley is alarming, highlighted by a series of dangerous curves. The hillsides are covered in lichen and Spanish moss. At Chaullay, the road meets the railway to Quillabamba, Machu-Picchu and Cuzco. One can drive from Chaullay to Santa Teresa (hot springs, ask the locals) from where the railway goes to Machu-Picchu, and can hike to Lucma and the village of Vilcabamba, from where one can descend to the valley of the River Concebidayoc where one comes to Espíritu Pampa, the site of the Vilcabamba Vieja ruins, a vast pre-Inca ruin with a neo-Inca overlay in deep jungle at 1,000 metres (the disputed last capital of the Incas); the site is reached on foot or horseback from Pampaconas. From Chaullay, take a truck to Yupanca, Lucma or Pucyura: there rent horses or mules and travel through superb country to Espíritu Pampa. Then continue to Cosireni, from where trucks go to Quillabamba.

A permit from the National Cultural Institute is required to visit this area. Without one, you will be turned back at Pucyura. The Institute is not issuing passes (since Aug 87) to visit the area between the Ríos Urubamba and Concebidayoc because of guerrilla activity there, but travel to Chaullay, Quillabamba and Kiteni is permitted.

One can also go by boat to Kiteni and then by truck to Quillabamba (at 0400). There are no buses from Quillabamba to Kiteni, but *camiones* leave between 0700-1000, US$2, 7-10 hrs. (*Hotel Kiteni*, F, basic, several restaurants). At Kiteni you must register on arrival with the police station. Take torch, no electricity. Irregular boats to the Pongo de Maynique, where the river goes through the mountain with a rock wall of several hundred meters on either side, before descending into jungle, where you can see many varieties of animals, birds, butterflies, snakes etc. 2 days, from Quillabamba to Pongo. This journey is only possible between April and August (too dangerous at other times). Between Kiteni and Pongo, on the river, is the village of Israelitos, whose inhabitants have been convinced by a missionary that they are New Israelites and that the Messiah will arise there. You can stay in a small hut next to the synagogue, but bring food and supplies—also gifts—from Kiteni. From Pongo you can get down through the jungle to Pucallpa if there is the right amount of water in the river; boats can be arranged at Kiteni. Price varies for number of people in the party, approximately US$15-20 p.p. Beware of overcharging. En route to Pucallpa it is possible to go to Camisea and Sepahua (near where Yaminavak Indians can be visited; they live in constructions made of mud, but have a mini-hotel for passers-through). To hire a car in Cuzco for this area costs about US$50 per day, including insurance, mileage and fuel for about 250 km.

Paucartambo, on E slope of Andes, is NE of Cuzco by a good road (one way on alternate days). In this remote though now popular tourist town is held the Fiesta of Carmen, usually on July 16, 17, 18, with masked dances. (*Fiesta* dates should be checked in Cuzco.) Hotels: *Quinta Rosa Marina*, near bridge, basic, G; *San Martín*, G, dirty, even more basic. Private car hire for round trip on July 16: US$25, or the Tourist Office in Cuzco arranges an overnight trip (you sleep in the bus) for US$10. Minibus from Av. Huáscar, Cuzco, every other day, US$3, 3-4 hrs. (alternate days Paucartambo-Cuzco).

From Paucartambo, in the dry season, you can go 44 km. to Tres Cruces, along the Pilcopata road, turning left after 25 km.; Sr. Cáceres in Paucartambo will arrange trip. Tres Cruces gives a wonderful view of the sunrise in June and July and private cars leave Paucartambo between 0100 and 0200 to see it; they may give you a lift. One can walk from Paucartambo to the *chullpas* of Machu Cruz in about an hour, or to the *chullpas* of Pijchu (take a guide). You can also visit the Inca fortress of Huatojto, which has admirable doorways and stonework. A car will take you as far as Ayre, from where the fortress is a 2-hour walk.

The **Manu National Park** is the biggest nature reserve in Peru, covering 1.5 million hectares of jungle around the river Manu (an area half the size of Switzerland). Charles Munn, a zoologist from Wildlife Conservation International, writes that "No other park on earth can compare with Manu in terms of sheer variety of life forms." Giant otters, crocodiles, tapirs, jaguars and ocelot, and many other animals and birds may be seen. A gold rush, prospecting for oil and gas on the Park's western borders, and the arrival of colonists all pose a threat to this unique reserve. The dry season runs from April to October; July, August and September are the driest months when animals stay close to the river and are most easily seen. Information is available from Asociación y Conservación para la Selva Sur (ACSS), Av. Sol 627, 3rd floor, Cuzco.

The following companies offer 3-8 day tours: Expediciones Manu EIRL, Procuradores 372, Cuzco, T 226671/233190, Telex 52052PE; Manu Nature Tours EIRL, Av. Sol 627-B, oficina 401, Cuzco, T 231549/234793, Telex 52003/4, which owns *Manu Lodge*, the most remote of the 4 lodges in or near the park; it is highly recommended, both for comfort and as an experience of "pure magic" (it's also expensive).

Individual trips can be arranged by the hardy and adventurous. First obtain a permit (free) from the park's office, Calle Laderos, Cuzco, who may send you to Salvación for it (see below). Buy all supplies in Cuzco: camping gear, fishing tackle, food (for the boatmen as well) and gasoline; take finely-woven, long-sleeved and -legged clothing and effective insect repellent (that on sale in Cuzco is no good). On Mon., Wed. and Fri. a truck leaves Calle Huaruropata, Cuzco, supposedly at 0600, for Shintuya, 250 km. through wild scenery, US$5, minimum 30 uncomfortable hours (much longer in the rainy season as there are no bridges; recommended trucks are Augel Riarz, Taodora and Castilla). The priest in Shintuya will let you stay in the dormitory rooms at the mission, or you can camp. One restaurant only.

In Shintuya, hire a boat and guide to go down the Madre Dios river and up the Manu (the 4 Moscoso brothers are recommended). A six week trip will cost a minimum of US$350, after bargaining, maximum 10 people, but fewer are better as jungle clearings are small.

At Tres Cruces in the Park there is an empty bungalow that may be used for the night; it has no window-panes, water or electricity. The National Park office at Salvación can also arrange your entry permit and with luck you might catch a lift in with park staff, or they will know of other people going in (Hostal Salvación, F, clean, basic bathrooms, swimming pool). Transport to Shintuya infrequent but possible although most boats are already fully laden and rarely carry tourists. Quinta Erika, small jungle lodge run by Sra. Gerlach, a German woman who has lived in the jungle since 1951, tranquil, few bugs, good food, animals, boat trips can be arranged with prior notice, transport from Cooperativa landing, 3 km. from Salvación.

From Shintuya, it is 5½ hrs by boat to Boca Manu, then 4½ hrs to Romero where there is a park checkpoint and a park entry fee of US$10 is charged. Three lakes (cochas) can be visited from Romero, Wasi, Otorongo and Salvador. After your trip you can return to Cuzco via Shintuya, or take a colectivo boat from Boca Manu to Colorado (US$6—6 hrs.), then another to Laberinto (US$4—12 hrs.), then to Puerto Maldonado (US$1.50—1½ hrs.).

THE SOUTH-EASTERN JUNGLE (6)

From Urcos, near Cuzco (bus US$0.50), a spectacular 484-km. road has been constructed over the Eastern Cordillera to Puerto Maldonado in the jungle. No buses, but several trucks do the journey every day. 47 km. after passing the snow-line Hualla-Hualla pass (4,820 metres) the **super-hot thermal baths** (US$0.05) of Marcapata provide a relaxing break. From here the road continues its descent through a tropical rain forest well stocked with orchids. 82 km. from Urcos, at the base of Mount Ausangate (6,600 metres), is the town of **Ocongate**, which has two hotels on the Plaza de Armas. Beyond Ocongate is Tinqui, the starting point for hikes around Mount Ausangate and in the Cordillera Vilcanota. Trucks leave Cuzco for Tinqui daily between 0600-0900 from beside the railway station, taking 9 rough, cold hours. From Tinqui, you can hire horses for a 3- or 5-day hike passing lakes, ice caves and beautiful scenery. Take tent, food and warm clothing. Guides can also be found in Tinqui.

The air force (FAP) provides a weekly air service from Cuzco and Puerto Maldonado to **Quincemil**, 240 km. from Urcos, a centre for alluvial gold-mining with many banks (Hotel Toni, F, friendly, clean, cold shower, good meals); ask the food-carriers to take you to visit the miners washing for gold in the nearby rivers. Quincemil marks the half-way point and the end to the all-weather road. Gasoline is scarce because most road vehicles continue on 70 km. to Masuco, another mining centre, where they fill up with the cheaper gasoline of the jungle region. Thirty more km. of sloshing mud and cascading waterfalls brings one out of the mountainous jungle and into the flat plains, for the 141 km. straight run to Puerto Maldonado.

Owing to the present gold rush on the Madre de Dios river, there are many trucks from Cuzco to Puerto Maldonado: 50-55 hr. journey; US$8-11 in the back, US$13 up front. As trucks pass each other, watch out for the exchanges of fire with fruit as the ammunition. The road has been widened. Times by truck: Urcos—Ocongate 6 hrs. (US$2), Ocongate—Quincemil 12 hrs. (US$5), Quincemil—Masuco—Puerto Maldonado 15-20 hrs. (US$5).

Puerto Maldonado is capital of the jungle Department of Madre de Dios. (Altitude, 250 metres.) Overlooking the confluence of the rivers Tambopata and

Madre de Dios, this frontier town is the centre for development of Peru's southern jungle. The Plaza de Armas is very pleasant, and nearby is a new Banco de la Nación built to accommodate (and reflect) the prosperity that gold has brought. However, Puerto Maldonado is an expensive town and because of the gold mining and timber industries, much of the jungle (including most of the mahogany trees) has been destroyed. The temperature normally is between 30°-37°C during the dry season (May to October) and 28°-33°C in the rainy season (November to April); but *friajes* (cold winds that roll northwards along the foothills of the Andes from the South Atlantic region) can send the temperature plummeting, to about 7°C. Insect and reptile activity is greatly reduced; warm-blooded animals survive. Because of this climatic phenomenon, the fauna of the Madre de Dios include many unusual species not found in other jungle areas. Also unique to this area is the *rayo blanco* (white rainbow) seen at sunset on the Madre de Dios River.

Madre de Dios has three superb jungle reserves, among the best in the world: Manu National Park, 1.5 million hectares to the N of the department (**see page** 972); Río Heath Pampas Sanctuary, 100,000 hectares between the Río Madre de Dios and the Río Heath; Tambopata Wildlife Reserve, 5,500 hectares, 40 km. up the Río Tambopata. The Tambopata Reserve, like Manu, has an incredible diversity of animal, bird, insect and plant life, but, because it is so small, its survival is at risk. Logging rights around the reserve have been sold, settlers are moving in in large numbers, and the government has provided little protection up to now. A pair of binoculars is essential equipment for this area.

Hotels *Cuzco Amazonic Lodge* (*Albergue Cuzco Amazónico*), A, 45 mins. by boat down the Madre de Dios River, jungle tours and accommodation for 3 days, 2 nights, good food negotiable out of season; avoid in February when everyone goes on holiday including the mechanic. (Book at Av. Arequipa 4964, Lima, T 462775, or Procuradores 48, Cuzco, T 5047.) *Explorers Inn* (book through Peruvian Safaris, Garcilaso de la Vega 1334, Casilla 10088, T 313047 Lima, or through Peruvian Safaris, Plaza San Francisco 168, T 235342 Cuzco—post to Puerto Maldonado is very bad but local office is Fitzcarrald 136 or Teletours, Antero Aspillaga 240, El Olivar, San Isidro, Lima 27, T 403594, Av. José Pardo 182, piso 2, Miraflores, Lima 18, T 469046/464577), A, located in middle of Tambopata wildlife reserve, 58 km. from Puerto Maldonado: a 4 hr. ride on Tambopata river (2 hours return, in early a.m., so take warm clothes), take food and drink for the journey, one of the best places in Peru for seeing jungle birds (547 species have been recorded here), butterflies (1,100-plus species), dragonflies (over 150 species) as well as tree species and mammals (including a giant otter), but you probably need more than a 2-day tour to benefit fully from the location, guides are students; US$150 for 3 days, 2 nights (depending on season, 1 day spent actually in the reserve), extra day US$45, flight from Puerto Maldonado not included; naturalists' programme at US$45 a night (minimum 6 nights, mixed reports in 1989). *Tambo Lodge*, bungalows 8 km. out on opposite bank of Río Madre de Dios, 2, 3 and 4-day jungle programmes available, poor reports of service and food in 1989, book through Cusco-Maldonado Tour, Portal de Panes 109 (T 222-332), Cuzco. *Turistas*, on the bank of the Tambopata River, D(private bath), electricity and water sometimes cut, restaurant quite good.

In town: *Wilson*, D with bath, E without, well run, clean, no hot water, trucks coming from airport stop here; *Rey Port*, F with shower, insecure; *Cross*, clean, generally rec.; *Royal Inn*, F; *Toni*, *Central*, F and *Moderno*, G, (very clean but noisy, safe for luggage, no hot water). *Tambo de Oro*, F. As there are many miners in Maldonado, so rooms can be scarce.

Restaurants There are several good restaurants in town. The unnamed restaurant opposite the AeroPerú office has been rec.; so has *Rulman*, good Chinese food and large selection of other dishes, rec. apart from poor addition, round the corner from *Hotel Wilson*. *Kalifa*, Piura, some regional specialities, rec. Look for *pensiones* where meals are served at fixed times (lunch is at 1300). *Café Danubio Azul* on Plaza de Armas is good for information.

Typical Foods *Castañas* (Brazil nuts), try them, chocolate- or sugar-coated. *Patarashca*, fish barbecued in banana leaves. Try *pescado sudado* as an appetizer. *Sopa de motelo*, turtle soup cooked and served in its own shell. *Mazato*, an alcoholic drink prepared from yuca and drunk by the Indians at their festivals. *Sangre de grado*, a thick deep-red sap collected from trees deep in the jungle which is a highly prized cure-all throughout Peru.

Excursions Motorcycles can be hired for local trips for US$4 an hour. Bargain for reductions for longer. A very worthwhile one-or two-day excursion by motorcycle is to boat across the Madre de Dios River and follow the trail towards Iberia (*Hotel Aquino*, F). Along the trail are picturesque *caseríos* (settlements) that serve as collecting and processing centres for the Brazil nut. Approximately 70% of the inhabitants in the Madre de Dios are involved in the collection of this prized nut. The beautiful and tranquil Lake Sandoval is a 1-hr. boat ride along the Madre de Dios River and then a 2-km. walk into the jungle. For fishing Lake Valencia, 60 km. away near the Bolivian border, is unsurpassed (2 days). Many excellent beaches and islands are located within an hour's boat ride; however, make sure you have a ride back at the end of the day. For the adventurous a one-or two-day trip can be planned to visit Indians still relatively unaffected by civilization; the Indians living nearer Puerto Maldonado, like those near Iquitos and Manaus, are strictly tourist Indians. Boats may be hired at the port for about US$30 a day to go to Lake Sandoval or visit the Indians. Bargain hard, and don't pay the full cost in advance. Mosquitoes are voracious. If camping, take food and water. Barbara de Cárdenas from San Francisco and her Peruvian husband, Guillermo, organize interesting trips for photography, bird watching and fishing. They can be contacted at Puerto Tambopata, behind the Tourist Hotel (write to Correo Central, Puerto Maldonado). Tambopata Expeditions offer 2-day tours to Lago Sandoval and longer trips, owner is guide, speaks English and is knowledgeable; take binoculars. A recommended guide is Arturo Balarezo Revilla, who charges US$30 p.p. per day for a boat trip; contact him at his house near the Plaza de Armas, at the *Café Danubio Azul* or at the airport. Another recommended guide is Victorio Suárez, Apartado 177, who charges US$25 p.p. per day, all included, and will tailor the trip to his clients' requirements. Contact Sr. Gombringer, who lives beside the plaza (well known) who runs excursions from his house on Lake Victoria, 7 hrs. down river by boat, very good and reasonable, much wildlife. For guides meeting the plane, US$8-10 p.p. per day is a normal fee. Héctor is recommended. Beware of price changes and be prepared to negotiate with guides. **N.B.** All hunting in Amazonia is illegal.

For those interested in seeing a gold rush, a trip to the town of **Laberinto** (one hotel, several poor restaurants) is recommended. The bus leaves Puerto Maldonado at 0900, 1000 and 1100 and returns in the afternoon daily.

Transport It is possible to travel overland from Cuzco (4-5 days). Take a truck from the social security hospital to Pucapata (lodgings basic), or if possible direct to Shintuya; boats leave most mornings for Colorado (10 hrs.); next day take a canoe to Laberinto (8-12 hrs.), from where there is a dirt road to Puerto Maldonado (bus US$1.50, 1½ hrs.). Take food. Flying is cheaper and quicker but not so interesting.

Taxi to airport US$1.70. The airport has a paved runway; flights are often cancelled because of rain. Faucett to and from Lima and Cuzco, Tues., Thurs., Sat., AeroPerú on the other days; flights to Lima US$194 return, to Cuzco US$36; AeroPerú may cancel flights in Cuzco if not enough passengers. Once a week to Lima and Cuzco (usually Thursday) there is an air-force flight (Grupo Ocho) that goes in all but the worst conditions via Iberia and Iñapari, fare to Cuzco, US$18, to Iñapari, US$10. A weekly flight Arequipa-Puerto Maldonado (US$18 one way) is run by the air force, usually Friday, if demand is sufficient. Office of Grupo Ocho is in the airport at Cuzco. Open 0800-1200.

Flight to **Iñapari** (½ hr.) on the Brazilian frontier, Thursday; this is a cargo flight and you must see the captain about a seat on the day of the flight. From the landing field it is 7 km. to the village (one hostel) where you must seek out the police for border formalities. Wade across the river to Brazil, to the village of Assis Brasil. Private boats can be contracted for travel into Bolivia; to Puerto Heath, at the border (US$28, one day); to Riberalta (US$90-120, 4 days). The trip by boat to Riberalta is very difficult, especially in the dry season. Boats are very few and far between. Some boats only go as far as Puerto Pardo (a Peruvian military post opposite Puerto Heath) for US$2.20, or US$52-64 *expreso*. From here one can cross to Puerto Heath, a Bolivian naval post, but boats into Bolivia are just as infrequent here. It should be noted that waiting for sailings in either Puerto Heath or Puerto Maldonado can take a lot of time. In Puerto Pardo you can sleep at the military post, or in empty huts in the village; there is no accommodation in Puerto Heath. Take food with you. It may be possible to take a boat from Puerto Pardo to *garimpeiro* settlements (gold diggers) around Puerto América, 24-hr. journey, US$12, but chances depend on whether gold has been found. Planes go from Pto. América to Riberalta (Bolivia) for US$30 p.p.

Before leaving for Bolivia from Puerto Maldonado, one must first get a Bolivian visa (if needed) from the consulate (on Jirón Cuzco; very helpful), then a Peruvian exit stamp, before one can get a Bolivian entry stamp. Similarly if going to Brazil; if you have not obtained an exit stamp from the P.I.P. in Puerto Maldonado, you will be turned back at either border. The immigration office is opposite the *Hotel Moderno.*

Books *An Annotated Check List of Peruvian Birds*, by Theodore A. Parker, Susan Allen Parker and Manuel A. Plenge, published by Buteo Books, Vermillon, South Dakota, is particularly useful in this area. Also, *The Birds of Venezuela*, Princeton University, and *The Land Birds of South America*, by John Dunning.

INLAND FROM LIMA (7)

The Central Railway from Lima to La Oroya and on to Huancayo (335 km.) is one of the wonders of Latin America. It reaches its greatest altitude, 4,782 metres, inside the tunnel between Ticlio and Galera, 159 km. from Lima. The ruling grade is about 4½°. Along the whole of its length it traverses 66 tunnels, 59 bridges, and 22 zig-zags where the steep mountainside permits no other way of negotiating it. It is by far the most important railway in the country, and the views during the ascent are beyond compare. **N.B.** If you alight to take photos at Ticlio or Galera, be quick because the train stops for a very short time. This masterpiece was the project of the great American railway engineer, Henry Meiggs, who supervised the construction from 1870 until his death in 1877; it was built by the Pole Ernesto Malinowski, with imported Chinese labour, between 1870 and 1893. Railway buffs may like to know that the last Andes type 2-8-0 steam locomotive No. 206, is still in working order, although usually locked in a shed at Huancayo. It was built specifically for this route in 1953 by Beyer Peacocks of Manchester. The course of the railway is more or less paralleled by that of the Central Highway between Lima and Huancayo.

For a while, beyond Chosica (**see page 878**), each successive valley seems to be greener, with a greater variety of trees and flowers. At **San Bartolomé** (Km. 57, 1,513 metres), the platform is often crowded with local fruit sellers. The train reverses, then passes through tunnels and over bridges to the next canyon. Sometimes the train seems airborne over the valley and the road far below.

Matucana, Km. 84, at 2,390 metres, is set in wild scenery, where there are beautiful walks. At Tamboraque (3,009 metres) is the first of the mountain mines, with its overhead cables and smelter down a gorge. Climbing always, we pass San Mateo (Km. 107, 3,215 metres), where the San Mateo mineral water originates. From San Mateo a spectacular side-road branches off to the Germania mine. Beyond San Mateo is Infiernillo (Little Hell) Canyon, to which car excursions are made from Lima, 100 km. (Hotels: *Ritz*, F, fair, *Grau*, cheap.) Following Infiernillo (only a glimpse seen between tunnels) the train proceeds in rapid zigzags. Between Río Blanco and Chicla (Km. 127, 3,733 metres) the Inca contour-terraces can be seen quite clearly.

Casapalca (Km. 139, 4,154 metres) has more mines; its concentrators are at the foot of a deep gorge. A climb to the dizzy heights beyond ends in a glorious view of the highest peaks. Soon we see a large metal flag of Peru at the top of Mount Meiggs, not by any means the highest in the area, but through it runs Galera Tunnel, 1,175 metres long. Ticlio, the highest passenger station in the world (Km. 157, 4,758 metres), at the mouth of the tunnel, is on one side of a crater in which lies a dark, still lake. At Ticlio the line forks, one through the tunnel to La Oroya; the other line goes 14½ km. to Morococha, where there are important mines. The highest point, 4,818 metres, is reached on this latter line at La Cima. A siding off this line reaches 4,829 metres.

Beyond the tunnel zig-zags bring us down to Yauli (4,142 metres). Left is the ugliness inseparable from mining; right are mountainsides and moors with cold, small mountain tarns and herds of sheep, very few llamas. After La Oroya the railway follows the valley of the polluted river Mantaro.

La Oroya (Km. 208), the main smelting centre, with its slag heaps is full of vitality and here the train fills up. Population: 36,000. It is at the fork of the Yauli and Mantaro rivers at 3,755 metres, 187 km. from Lima by a road which although officially paved throughout, is in poor condition, particularly between the Anticona Pass at 4,843 metres and La Oroya. (For places to the E and N of La Oroya, **see pages** 983 **and** 986 respectively.)

Hotels *Hostal San Martín,* F, clean, friendly, no heating but plenty of blankets; *Wilson*; *Lima.*

Restaurants *Las Vegas,* rec. *Huánuco,* good, cheap food. *Central,* rec. *El Tambo,* 2 km. outside La Oroya, good trout and frogs.

Railway N to Tambo del Sol and Cerro de Pasco; SE to Jauja and Concepción (**see page** 979), Huancayo and Huancavelica; SW to Lima and Callao. Train to Cerro de Pasco leaving 1330 and arriving 1716; no connection with train from Lima. To Lima at 1005 and Huancayo at 1300. (Local train to Huancayo on Sun.)

Roads and Buses SE to Huancayo, Ayacucho, and Cuzco, paved to Huancayo; N to Cerro de Pasco (US$0.75) and on to Pucallpa; 25 km. north along this road fork E for Tarma (US$1.50 by bus, US$1.85 by colectivo), San Ramón, the Perené colony, and Oxapampa; SW to Lima (6 hrs. by bus, US$2.50, 5 or less, US$4, by colectivo). Take taxi from bus terminal in Lima, which is in a dangerous area.

Huancayo, capital of Junín Department, is the main commercial centre for inland central Peru; alt. 3,271 metres; pop. 359,000. The Indians flock in from far and wide with an incredible range of food, and rugs and blankets of llama and alpaca wool, for sale; fleeces can be bought (alpaca, US$2.50 per kilo), but arrive early before 1000, Av. La Marina, 700 block. The Sun. market, Jr. Huancavelica, 3 km. long and 4 stalls wide, sells typical clothes, fruit, vegetables, hardware, handicrafts but especially traditional medicines and goods for witchcraft. Huancayo is a good place to buy carved gourds, reputedly the lowest prices in Peru. Very impressive Good Friday processions. The colourful annual fiesta of the Virgin of Cocharcas starts on 8 September at Orcotuna, and there are a big early morning market and an afternoon bullfight on the same day as the parade of the Virgin; the feasting and dancing last a week. Costumes and dances are then at their best. In Huancayo, ponchos and various alpaca woollen goods are quite cheap, but often factory-made; most goods are reported to be cheaper than in Lima, particularly silver jewellery. Displays of folklore at the Coliseo, Calle Real, certain Sundays. For woven alpaca goods and other *artesanías,* much cheaper, go to outlying villages, such as San Jerónimo, or Hualhuas, 11 km. north of Huancayo (2 km. off the Huancayo-Jauja road, try Familia Meza, Jr. 28 de Julio 293); minibus from Huancayo, US$0.15 from Church of the Immaculate Conception (see Excursions below).

Warning Huancayo has a bad reputation for thieves, especially in the market and at bus stations.

Hotels *Turistas,* D, with bath, old building, some rooms small, quiet, good meals for US$3.50; *Presidente,* Calle Real 1138, T 231736, D, clean, friendly, helpful, safe, breakfast only, rec.; *Confort,* Calle Ancash 298, F, private bath, basic but clean, good; *Santa Felicidad*, Plaza de Armas, F, good; *Hostal Dani,* Giráldez 486 (T 235645/232762), F, small private hotel, hot water, clean, friendly, clothes-washing and cooking facilities, safe, English-speaking landlady Sra. María Carmela Barraza de Babilón, goes out of her way to help travellers with problems, even if they are not staying at her hotel, someone from hotel meets the Lima train; *Acolla,* corner of Antonio Lobato and Real, Tambo district, F, private toilet, hot shower. *Residencial Inca Wasi,* Federico Villareal 106, clean and friendly, F (owner meets Lima train with car); *Residencia Huancayo,* Av. Giráldez, near railway station, G, all rooms with wash basin, hot showers; *Inca,* Calle Loreto, F, with bath (cold water), clean, but noisy; *Pensión Huanca,* Pasaje San Antonio 113, San Carlos T 223956, small sign (owner's daughter meets Lima train), F, 8 rooms, English spoken, hot water, friendly, breakfast extra, laundry and kitchen facilities, good food, typical Huancayo dishes, rec.; *Residencia Baldeón,* Amazonas 543, G, with European-style breakfast, hot water, friendly; *Kiya,* Giráldez 107, Plaza de Armas (known nowadays as Constitución), E, with bath, hot water, restaurant does not serve breakfast, 'phones in rooms (avoid noisy rooms on Av. Real); *Universal,* opp. railway station, F, reasonable. *Hospedaje Suizo,* Huancas 473, T 231732, G p.p., 10 mins. walk from railway station, comfortable, hot water, family atmosphere, warmly rec. Luis Hurtado (**see page** 979) has 2 rooms (G including breakfast), with hot water, washing and cooking facilities.

N.B. Prices may be raised in Holy Week.

Restaurants *Inca,* Calle Puno 530, rec. On Av. Giráldez (Plaza de la Constitución) are

Olímpico, Lalo's, and *Café Giráldez,* all good, Peruvian dishes at *Olímpico,* Av. Giráldez 199, rec. as the best in town. *Bianca* (opposite *Hotel Prince*) is good, as is *Saloon. Caramba,* good for barbecues. *Marisquería Mar Azul,* Ancash 578, excellent cheap seafood, opened 1986. Street vendors sell delicious apple turnovers, and other delights, for about US$0.10. On Calle Real are *Santa Rosa, La Caravana,* for barbecued chicken and the *Panadería-Pastelería Imperial,* all rec. *Chifa Perú,* Puno 518, good and cheap; *Chifa Porvenir,* Jirón Real 417, clean, reasonable. *Restaurant Florida,* Calle Ayacucho, reasonable, good for fish; *Comedor Vegetariano,* cheap. Also vegetarian *Hare Krishna.* Calle Real 356, cheap, good, clean, friendly. *Koky's,* Av. Huancavelica 109, English-speaking owners Adán and Gladys Camargo, good drinks, food, music, friendly, 10% discount to "South American Handbook" owners, information on sightseeing and travel, rec. *José Antonio,* Av. Cuzco, average. Excellent pastries at *Chalet Suizo,* Huancas 473, closed Mon.

Peruvian-North American Cultural Institute, Jirón Guido 740. Intensive Spanish courses, 1, 2 or 4 weeks living with Indian families in villages or Huancayo, organized by Luis Hurtado and Beverly Stuart (see below).

Museum at the Salesian school has over 5,000 pieces, including a large collection of jungle birds, animals and butterflies, insects, reptiles and fossils.

Country Club (very rural) is open to all, in very pleasant surroundings near the Mantaro River, to the north of town.

Crafts Craft market, Calle Piura, behind the Municipalidad, open every day, good but smelly, also sellers along Calle Real in the evening. Visit *Kamaq Maki,* "the creating hand", Centro Regional de Artesanías (the best craft centre in the area), Jirón Brasilia 200 in San Carlos, about 2 km. from centre, an artesans' cooperative (formerly the workshop of Sra. Francisca Mayer), selling woven goods, ceramics, carved gourds and much more; open Mon.-Fri., 0800-1200, 1400-1730, Sat.-Sun., 1500-1700 (P.O. Box 609, T 226961). Take minibus 5, 6, 13 to corner of San Carlos with P. Aurora, then walk. Woven goods available from Arequipa 463. For carved gourds visit Hermanos Leoncio y Pedro Veli Alfaro, Cochas Chicas, Km. 9, also Florencio Sanabria Osores, excellent quality, high prices, Huancayo (Apartado 402); and Nicanor Sanabria Osores, Cochas Grandes, Km. 10, Huancayo (see under Excursions below). Also visit Izcuchaca, 3-4 hrs. from Huancayo by train or truck to see pottery made. Hotel in main square, F, basic. Back-strap weaving of beautiful *fajas* (belts) can also be seen at Viquez, on the road past Wari-Wilka, 20 mins. S of Huancayo by colectivo from near the Mercado Modelo (go in a.m.)

Discotheques *El Molino,* Calle Huancas, good; *El Dorado* (more Peruvian), *San Diego,* off Tambo (less good). In El Tambo district, three together, *Alpha 2001, El Infinito, El Rincón de los Recuerdos* ("boring romantic music and oldies").

Exchange Banco de los Andes, near main plaza. For travellers' cheques, Sr. Miguel Velit, Calle Real 552, or Sr. Jung (*Chalet Suizo,* no commission).

Tourist Information Foptur information office, Concejo Provincial, 1st floor, Plaza Huamanmarca, very helpful. Huancayo Tours, Calle Real 543, organize tours of the surrounding countryside with English-speaking guides; they handle AeroPerú and Faucett reservations. Emturce, Ancash 475, good service. Touring y Automóvil Club del Perú, Calle Ancash 603. Luis Hurtado (see next page) also gives information at his house; if he's on tour, his New Zealand wife Beverly will help. He has maps, photographs of local crafts, slide shows every Sunday, 1900, and travellers may use his phone for national or international calls.

Rail Train to Huancavelica narrow guage 3 ft., daily except Sun. *autovagón* US$2.30, 3½ hrs. 0700 and 1330, tickets from 0600, make sure to get off at second (smaller) station in Huancavelica (Sub Estación), since it is closer to Plaza; ordinary trains leave every day except Sun. 0730 (6½ hrs.). Both leave from Chilca station, which is not the station for Lima. Train from Huancayo to Lima 0700 daily except Sun., (may be reduced to Mon., Wed., Sat.) 9-12 hrs., 1st class US$2.50, 2nd class US$1.50, lunches in 1st class and buffet, US$1 (arrive early to ensure getting a seat, best on right hand side), 1st class and buffet are bookable one day in advance for US$0.50 extra; ticket office open 1000-1200, 1430-1700.

Road Transport Bus to Lima, Etucsa—not recommended although their terminal does have a waiting room (several daily, US$4, 10 hrs.) Mariscal Cáceres (US$5, 8 hrs.), and other lines, all leave in evening. Comité 30 and 22 colectivo to Lima, Av. Loreto 351, five a day, US$9, 5-7 hrs. (takes 5 passengers); also Comité 12 (Calle Montevideo 736, T 271283, Lima; Loreto 425, Huancayo), with services to Huanta. N.B. A new road to Lima is under construction, which will shorten the journey time. There is only one morning bus to Ayacucho (Empresa

Ayacucho, 0700, not every day, US$5.50, 16-19 hrs.); evening buses go via Pampa; they are run by Molina (1700 and 1800, book in advance), Empresa Ayacucho (1800, 1830) and Etucsa (not rec.) Mon., Wed., Fri. 1630, US$4.50, 12 hrs. if weather is good; if not can be 20 hrs., bus waits until daylight to cross pass. Colectivo to Ayacucho, US$20 p.p. (Comité 30). Daily bus with Nor Oriente (Calle Huancavelica) to Cerro de Pasco and Huánuco at 1500; same company Mon., Wed., Fri., to Tingo María and Pucallpa at 1600. Ucayali bus company for Huánuco, Loreto 973. Direct buses to Tarma (**see page** 984; the departure point for La Merced) twice daily, US$2.40. Note: Huancayo and other towns in the area have a *fiesta* in January when it is impossible to get a colectivo to Ayacucho and buses are fully booked. If driving to Ayacucho, be careful with direction. Only three signposts, all to totally unknown villages.

Buses to Cuzco can be something of a problem; get a seat on a truck if stuck, lovely scenery. This road is often closed during wet season or the journey can take up to three days. Book as far ahead as possible, as buses tend to be heavily overbooked. They also frequently break down. Trucks are cheaper and offer better views—but take blankets against the cold on the mountains. The trip gives a fine view of the Sierra; one passes the site of the last battle against the Spaniards, near Ayacucho; some distance before Abancay one passes a bridge built by the Spaniards. The canyon of the Río Tomás is recommended for a visit. Those who have made this journey describe it as one of the most beautiful in Peru, but the road may be closed if guerrillas are active in the Ayacucho area. Do not leave the main road to visit more remote villages, or take photographs.

Excursions W of Huancayo, past Chupaca (good Sat. market) and between Pilcomayo and Huayo is the Geophysical Institute of Huayo on the "Magnetic Equator" (12½° S of the geographical equator). Here meteorological, seismic and cosmic-ray observations are made. Six km. (standard taxi fare US$1.50) S of Huancayo the shrine of Wari-Willka (written "Warivilka" on buses), of the Huanca tribe of Inca times, has been reconstructed in a corner of the main plaza of **Wari** (often written "Huari"). Bus to Wari from Calle Real, US$0.10. Museum in the plaza, of deformed skulls, and modelled and painted pottery of successive Huanca and Inca occupations of the shrine. Open 1000-1200 and 1500-1700, US$0.15 admission. *Hotel Central*, G, good; *Hotel Sol*, G. Take a minibus to Cerrito de la Libertad, walk up hill to Torre Torre to see impressive eroded sandstone towers on the hillside (beware of begging children on the way up). Not far from here is a large park with a depressing zoo but also a beautiful, clean swimming pool (US$0.10, showers and changing rooms).

Another interesting excursion is to Cochas Chicas (beautiful views of Valle de Mantaro) or Cochas Grandes, where gourds are carved, highly recommended. Buses leave Huancayo every ½ hr. from Church of the Immaculate Conception, for 9 km. journey. In the hills beyond Cochas back-strap weaving of *mantas* for carrying babies can be seen. S of Huancayo by colectivo from near the Mercado Modelo. There is a beautiful drive to **Cañete (see page** 923); the road crosses mountain landscape before following the Cañete river basin with its spectacular gorges (see the Instituto Geográfico Militar map). No bus service, trucks only.

Lucho (Luis) Hurtado at Huancas 209, San Carlos (Apartado Postal 510, Huancayo, T 22-23-95), organizes 5-day and 7-day excursions, using local transport, to Indian villages in the low-lying jungle, with the possibility of living with the Indians, or to his father's farm near Chanchamayo in the high *selva*. He also organizes walking trips of 3 or more days into the mountains, to live with Indians. Trips cost about US$20 a day. Students can also study weaving, the pan flute and Peruvian cooking (US$350 for a month). He has been highly and repeatedly recommended as a guide. Contact him only at his home (impersonators make been operating). He is English-speaking, has a New Zealand wife, and takes groups of between two and eight people. Take old tennis shoes or something similar for walking in rivers; no other equipment necessary. He is proposing to set up a similar organization in Cuzco, with Inca Trail trekking and weaving, flute and cooking courses; T 228475, Matará 274.

22 km. NW of Huancayo is the village of **Concepción** (3,251 metres), which has a market on Sun. as well as a colourful bullfight later in the day during the season. Colectivos to Concepción from near *Hotel Turistas*, US$0.50, 30 mins. Other hotels, *El Paisanito*, 9 de Julio 641, G, clean; *Royal*, on Plaza, warm shower, G, pleasant; *Hotel Huaychulo* is near Concepción and a 2 hr. walk from Ingenio where there is a government trout farm; good restaurants, especially for pastries. From Concepción a branch road (5 km.) leads to the **Convent of Santa Rosa de Ocopa**, a Franciscan monastery in beautiful surroundings established in 1724 for training missionaries for the jungle, open 1000-1200 and 1500-1700; closed Tues. Tour costs US$0.65 (students US$0.25). It contains a fine library with over 20,000 volumes and a biological museum with animals and insects from the jungle. The convent has a guesthouse, US$2.50 each, hot water. There is also a good restaurant. Bus from Huancayo (change at

Concepción) takes 1½ hrs., US$0.35. Near Concepción is the village of **San Jerónimo**, renowned for the making of silver filigree jewellery (Wednesday market). The work of Sra. Nelly Vásquez, Calle Arequipa, 2 blocks from the Plaza de Armas, is particuarly recommended; opposite is Sra. Porras, who also produces good pieces. Its fiesta is in August. There are ruins 2-3 hrs. walk above San Jerónimo, but the hike is dangerous in places. Buses from Plaza Amazonas, Huancayo, US$0.10. 45 mins'. walk from San Jerómino is Hualhuas where beautiful tapestries of alpaca and sheeps' wool are made on rustic looms. (Luis Hurtado arranges day tours to these places, US$3 p.p., not incl. transport and food.)

18 km. beyond Concepción, on the road to La Oroya, is the old town of **Jauja** (3,552 metres), Pizarro's provisional capital until the founding of Lima, where an interesting festival (San Fermín and San Fabián) begins on January 20 and lasts several days, enjoyable (but lone tourists should be careful). Also, a very colourful Wed. and Sun. market. Jauja is a friendly, unspoilt town, in the middle of a good area for walking, with ruins near a lake 3½ km. away. It has the best archaeological museum in the Mantaro valley for the Wari culture. A modernised church retains 3 fine 17th-century altars. The Cristo Pobre church is claimed to have been modelled after Notre Dame and is something of a curiosity. On a hill above Jauja there is a fine line of Inca storehouses, and on hills nearby ruins of hundreds of circular stone buildings from the Huanca culture (John Hemming). Bus from Huancayo, US$0.50, many daily, also colectivos (US$1). (*Hotel Jauja* and *Hotel Pizarro*, both E; *Hostal Santa Rosa*, on the square, F, some rooms with bath, poor water supply, restaurant, and on north side, *Turistas*, E, near pleasant Laguna de Paca.) Wood carving is practised in the nearby town of Molinas. At Aco, 1½ hrs. walk from Mito on road to Jauja, large ceramic pots are made, take fruit as a gift if you do not intend to buy. The road to Satipo branches off near the Convento de Sta. Rosa de Ocopa; the village of Paca (2 km. further on) is very pleasant; easy to catch a taxi to Jauja; spectacular scenery, snow-capped mountains in the Paso de la Tortuga, followed by a rapid drop to the Caja de Silva in Satipo. (See Page 829)

Huancavelica, capital of its Department (altitude, 3,680 metres; population, 37,500), a friendly and attractive town, was founded over 400 years ago by the Spanish to exploit rich deposits of mercury and silver; it is predominantly an Indian town, and is still a major centre for mining. It is possible to visit the old mercury mine on the hill above the town—a stiff walk, or hire a car. There are beautiful mountain walks in the neighbourhood. The cathedral, located on the Plaza de Armas, has an altar considered to be one of the finest examples of colonial art in Peru. Also very impressive are the five other churches in town: the church of San Francisco has no less than 11 altars. (Sadly most of the churches are closed to visitors.) Lectures on precolumbian history and archaeology are given in the museum, 2nd floor.

Bisecting the town is the Huancavelica River. South of the river is the main commercial centre where fine leather and alpaca products can be purchased (especially on Calle Virrey Toledo). North of the river on the hillside are the thermal baths (US$0.15). There is a daily market. At the Sunday market, the men wear all black, with multicoloured woollen pom-poms dangling from their skull-caps, waists and knees; these are also used to decorate the livestock.

Hotels *Turistas*, D, for room with private bath, reasonable; *Perú*, near railway station, G, clean, good; *San Francisco*, G, basic; *Savoy*, G, clean rooms, adequate bathrooms, but not safe for women alone; *Tahuantinsuyo* near Plaza de Armas, F, clean and well maintained; *Santo Domingo*, F; *alojamiento* at Santa Inés. Little water in cheaper hotels in evenings.

Restaurants *Hotel de Turistas*, food is expensive and only fair. *El Padrino*, expensive, not rec. *Olímpica*, Virrey Toledo 303, good and cheap; good *chifa* in main street; *Cynthia*, cheap; *Fidel. Snake Bar Joy*, also *Ganso de Oro*.

Tourist Office In Correo building on Plaza da Armas, go up stairs from an entrance on the left-hand side of the building.

Transport Daily (except Sun.) to Huancayo (146 km.) are one train (0730, 7 hrs.) and two *autovagones* (US$2.30, 0700 and 1300, 3½ hrs.), and buses (7 hrs. Expreso Huancavelica leaves at 1700, Hidalgo, 0600 and 1500, US$2.50); sit on the right side for the best views. To Lima via Huancayo, US$5.75 (Expreso Huancavelica, 1700). To Pisco (267 km.), buses only, daily, US$7, 14 hrs. (Oropesa service leaves at 0600, but be there by 0530 to get a seat, tickets can be bought the day before); route is via Santa Inés (4,020 metres), where there are ten restaurants. Half-an-hour's walk from Santa Inés are Lakes Choclococha and Orcococha, where llama herds can be seen; beautiful views; be prepared for sub-zero temperatures a.m. as bus passes snowfields, then for temperatures of 25-30°C as bus descends to coast p.m.

Getting to Ayacucho (296 km.) is a problem particularly in the rainy season. Take a bus (Oropesa) to Santa Inés, 0600, 4 hrs., US$2.20, then catch the Ormeño bus from Lima (Santa Inés-Ayacucho, 8 hrs., US$3). Alternatively catch a pick-up truck to Pilpichaca, via Santa Inés, 1330-1730, US$1.50, then a truck from Pilpichaca to Ayacucho, 2000 to 0500, US$2, very cold. The road (very bad) is the highest continuous road in the world, rarely dropping below 4,000 metres for 150 km. Out of Huancavelica one climbs steeply on a road that switchbacks between herds of llamas and alpacas grazing on rocky perches. Around Pucapampa (km. 43) is one of the highest habitable *altiplanos* (4,500 metres), where the rare and highly prized ash-grey alpaca can be seen. 50 km. beyond Santa Inés, the rocks are all colours of the rainbow, and running through this fabulous scenery is a violet river (all caused by oxides). Eleven km. later one encounters Paso Chonta (4,850 metres) and the turnoff to Huachocolpa. By taking the turnoff and continuing for 3 km. one discovers the highest drivable pass (5,059 metres) in the world. Continuing on to Ayacucho one passes some very cold, fish-filled lakes before the road branches to Pisco at km. 77. Seventy km. later the high (4,750 metres) Abra Apachenta is reached, leaving a 98-km. descent into Ayacucho.

Ayacucho, capital of its Department, was founded on January 9, 1539. This old colonial city is built round Parque Sucre with the Cathedral, City Hall and Government Palace facing on to it. The city is famous for its religious processions and its splendid market. There are no less than 33 churches—some long deserted and most closed—and a number of ruined colonial mansions. A week can be spent there and in the surroundings, which include La Quinua, site of the battle of Ayacucho, December 9, 1824, which brought Spanish rule to an end in Peru. Ayacucho has a very active student life. Altitude: 2,440 metres, with gently rolling hills around. A 364-km. road has been built to Pisco on the coast. Population: 75,000.

Visitors are advised to see the 17th century Cathedral (with Museum of Religious Art, closed indefinitely) and churches of San Francisco de Asís, La Compañía de Jesús, Santa Clara, Santo Domingo, and Santa Teresa, all with magnificent gold-leafed altars heavily brocaded and carved in the churrigueresque style. There is a small but surprising Museo Histórico Regional, in the Centro Cultural Simón Bolívar, at the outskirts of town, US$0.35 (many Huari artifacts). Tombs of the Huari nobles are being excavated along the road from Ayacucho to Quinua. The University, founded 1677, closed 1886, was reopened in 1958.

Festivals Semana Santa begins on the Friday before Holy Week with the procession of the Virgen de los Dolores (very beautiful, but the suffering is "symbolised" by the custom of flinging pebbles from slingshots, aimed mainly at youngsters, but also foreigners). A charming Palm Sunday procession, beginning at 1600, of palm-bearing women and children accompanies a statue of Christ riding on a white donkey. There follows one of the world's finest Holy Week celebrations, with candle-lit nightly processions, floral "paintings" on the streets, daily fairs (the biggest on Easter Saturday), horse races and contests among peoples from all central Peru.

Warning Because of guerrilla (Sendero Luminoso) activity in this region, visitors are advised to seek information in advance and check whether a curfew is in force. Entry into the area has on occasion been prohibited for visitors and it is unwise to go outside the city at night.

Hotels *Turistas*, 9 de Diciembre, E, with bath, comfortable (meals, US$3.20, mediocre); *Colmena*, Jirón Cusco 140, just of Plaza de Armas, F, a beautiful building, nice rooms with table, clean, wardrobe, good but no hot water, not secure, noisy, good restaurant below; *Samari*, Jirón Callao, F, with toilet, very clean, friendly, rec.; *Hostelería Santa Rosa*, Jirón Lima 140, F, with bath, hot water mornings and evenings, friendly, car park, restaurant, rec. *Imperio*, Plaza de Armas, F, 4-bedded rooms; *Wari*, G, hot showers, clean and friendly; *Ayacucho*, just off the Plaza, G, cheap, with shower, basic; *Crillonesa*, near market, G, hot showers, clean, good value; *Magdalena*, F, next to Etucsa bus station, clean, hot water; *Santiago*, near market (1½ blocks from Hidalgo bus), F, rec. *La Sixtina*, Jirón Callao, F, basic but friendly, clean, clothes washing facilities; and the private home of Sra. Ayala de Ruiz, Libertad 539, hot water, laundry facilities, personal attention. It is extremely difficult to find accommodation at Easter.

Restaurants *La Fortaleza*, Lima 169, 3 courses for US$1.20, very good coffee, reasonable meals; *Chalán*, on same street but not as good; *Clarita*, Jirón Grau 221, cheap, clean, good;

good coffee and cakes at *El Turco*; *Tradicional*, San Martín 406, popular, good variety and value; *San Agustín Café Turístico*, Plaza de Armas, good food and lemon meringue pie; *El Alamo* (next to *Hotel Colmena*), reasonable, folk music some evenings, and *El Agullo de Oro* for fish. *Tradición*, Vivanco, rec.; *La Casona* behind *Turistas*, rec. Many good small cafés, one inside University buildings; *Cevichería* on block 500 of Grau, behind market, good fish dishes. On the Plaza, *Savory* café and *Los Portales* are good (live, local music at the latter). The airport offers a good breakfast. Try mondongo, a soup made from meat, maize and mint, also ponche, a hot drink made of peanuts, coconut and cinnamon.

Handicrafts Local craftsmen produce filigree silver, often using *mudéjar* patterns; others make little painted altars which show the manger scene, make carvings in local alabaster, manufacture harps, or carry on the pre-Inca tradition of carving dried gourds. However, the most famous goods are carpets and *retablos*. Best quality woven carpets can be bought in the Santa Ana district where you can watch them being made. Edwin Sulca Lagos, Plaza Santa Ana 82, offers weaving courses. His family are internationally renowned and his rugs sell for at least US$90; only natural colours are used. Other weavers are Gerardo Fernández Palomino, Jr. París 105, Santa Ana, Pomataylla on same street and Saturino Oncebay, same street (No. 60). For handicrafts produced by cooperatives, including good quality tapestries at reasonable prices, *Rasuwillka*, Jirón Grau 112, P.O. Box 176; ask for Sr. Monner for details on visiting weavers' houses. *Retablos* are wooden boxes containing three-dimensional scenes in papier maché; the Jiménez family in Santa Ana, or César Urbano Ch., Av. Perú 308-318, La Libertad, are worth seeking out. In both weaving and *retablos*, scenes of recent political strife have been added to more traditional motifs.

Sport There are public tennis courts in Ayacucho, and games may be booked at the police station.

Exchange Ayacucho Tours. Try *Hotel de Turistas*, *Hostelería Santa Rosa* (good rates), AeroPerú, Morocucho Tours (Plaza de Armas).

Tourist Information Foptur, Portal Municipal 46, on Plaza de Armas next to church, good information, friendly, T 912997. Also available from Ayacucho Tours, San Martín 406, near market, or from the AeroPerú office (Plaza de Armas, changes US$). Also rec., for information and excursions, Wari Tours. State Tourist Information Office, Asamblea 138, has good free leaflets on Ayacucho. The journalist, Sr. Ylpidio Vargas, Jirón 2 de Mayo 309, T 912987, is very knowledgeable on the department and on recent events there. He is willing to show visitors around in safety.

Air To Lima by AeroPerú, 35 minutes, daily at 0720 or 1005; flights Ayacucho-Cuzco with Faucett 4 a week. Much military scrutiny at airport. In the rainy season expect cancellations. Taxi to airport, US$0.50 p.p., buses from 0600 from Plaza de Armas.

Buses Bus Ayacucho-Huancayo, none by day; via Pampas, Etucsa, 16 hrs., US$4.50, very cold and uncomfortable. Ordinary bus goes at night (1500 and 1800 daily), no wc on board; Ayacucho Transport, Etucsa and Molina, Calle Grau, do the journey. Bus to Pisco (and Ica), US$7.80 with Ormeño (Jr. Libertad 257), 12-13 hrs.; to Lima (1300, 1900), US$10.75, also Hidalgo (San Martín 330), at least once a day. No direct buses between Ayacucho and Cuzco, you must take Ayacucho-Andahuaylas bus (Molina, 19 hrs. daily at 0900, US$6.40, beautiful scenery) and change in Andahuaylas for Abancay and again for Cuzco.

Excursions Inca ruins at *Vilcashuamán*, to the S, beyond Cangallo; "there is a five-tiered, stepped *usnu* platform faced in fine Inca masonry and topped by a monolithic two-seat throne. The parish church is built in part of the Inca sun temple and rests on stretches of Inca terracing. Vilcashuamán was an important provincial capital, the crossroads where the road from Cuzco to the Pacific met the empire's north-south highway" (John Hemming). Taxi trips can be arranged with Ayacucho Tours and Morocucho Tours, US$30 p.p., alternatively stay overnight; market day is Wed. A good road going N from Ayacucho (trucks from Calle Salvador Calvero) leads to Wari (**see page 979 Huari**), dating from the "Middle Horizon", when the Huari culture spread across most of Peru (US$0.50 by public transport). Trips can be arranged by Ayacucho Tours, rec., who do a tour to Wari, La Quinua village and battlefield for about US$4.65. **La Quinua** village has a charming cobbled main square and many of the buildings have been restored; there is a small market on Suns. There is a huge obelisk to commemorate the battle of Ayacucho. Handicrafts are recommended, guitars and, especially ceramics; most houses have miniature ceramic churches on the roof. San Pedro Ceramics, at foot of hill leading to monument, and Mamerto Sánchez, Jr. Sucre should be visited. The village's festival is celebrated around 7-8 October, lasting 3 days. Beautiful 18 km. walk downhill from La Quinua to Wari, where trucks leave for Ayacucho until about 1700.

San Francisco in the jungle on the Apurímac River (3 basic hotels, *Suria*, E, the best but dirty) can be reached by bus from Ayacucho (junction of Av. Centenario and Av. Cavero) on Sat. (return Mon.), 10-12 hrs. on a very bad road often impassable in the wet season (very cold at night). Trucks travel daily leaving at about 0700 (wait at police control near airport), US$5 in driver's cabin, US$3 on back, or private cars, twice the price, bargain hard. From San Francisco you can take a morning canoe to *Luisiana*, about 2 hrs. upstream, to stay in Sr. Parodi's *Jungle Hotel*, Centro Vacacional de Luisiana, with swimming pool, C, on his large *hacienda*; trips are organized in the jungle but it is only open for 3 months in the dry season and Sr. Parodi is not always there. There is an airstrip at Luisiana with daily connections to Ayacucho, for over five passengers, US$29 single. Details in the Ayacucho Tourist Office. From San Francisco you can make excursions to nearby villages on cargo canoes, but it is very difficult to find transport all the way to Pucallpa unless you have a large group of people and are willing to pay handsomely.

From Ayacucho to Cuzco (Because of guerrilla activity and army counter-measures, public transport is scarcer than it used to be, but travellers will be allowed through if they do not stray from the main road and do not take photographs.) The road to Cuzco goes through *Andahuaylas*, in a fertile, temperate valley of lush meadows, cornfields and groves of eucalyptus, alders and willows. It offers few exotic plants, no comfortable accommodation (you must register with the army as a condition for getting into a hotel), poor transport, but beautiful, largely undiscovered scenery. Buses (supposedly daily) Ayacucho-Andahuaylas stop between 2100 and 0530 if there is a curfew (very cold on board). From Ayacucho to Ocros, the road is terrible (mudholes and marshes), can take 20 hrs. for 80-100 km. In Ocros is an unfriendly military checkpoint; innumerable Guardia checkpoints thereafter, but the road is not too bad to Andahuaylas. Also be prepared for stoppages by Sendero Luminoso. No direct buses Andahuaylas-Cuzco; you must take the only daily bus or a colectivo to Abancay, then a bus to Cuzco. The road crosses three mountain ranges and is very rough in places but is definitely worthwhile. *Abancay* is first glimpsed when you are 62 km. away by road, nestled between mountains in the upper reaches of a glacial valley (registration with army required, as at Andahuaylas). From Abancay a 470 km. road runs SW through Chalhuanca and Puquío to Nazca on the Pan-American Highway (see page 930).

Trucks and a bus leave Andahuaylas for Abancay at 0630-0700, take 8 hrs., US$4.50. Book at least 2 days in advance for a seat on the bus from Ayacucho to Andahuaylas. Several bus companies from Abancay to Cuzco US$4-6.50 (196 km., 12 hrs.), minibus from near the market takes 7 hours to Cuzco, leaving 1200, colectivos also leave around 0800, arriving 1700, dramatic scenery especially in Apurímac valley, but most of the road between Abancay and Cuzco is very bad. See page 964 for sites of interest between Abancay and Cuzco, 10 hrs. Abancay to Machu-Picchu: take a truck to Izcuchaca (US$1.75) where the train can be caught to Machu-Picchu.

Andahuaylas Hotels *Turistas*, Jirón Dias Bárcenas 500, D with bath (E without), meals US$3 extra (no money exchange or credit cards accepted); *Gran*, Plaza de Armas, G, basic, and *Restaurant Las Palmeras*, meal for US$0.25, is possible; *Hermanos Chipuna*, G, basic, near bus station; *Delicias*, G, hot showers, basic but rec., only 7 rooms, ask for extra blankets, cold at night; *28 de Julio*, cheap, G, adequate.

Abancay Hotels Discrimination against foreigners reported. *Turistas*, D, with bath, food good, US$3, comfortable, old-fashioned house, safe car park, camping permitted at US$3; *Gran Hotel*, G, with bath, clean; *Abancay*, F; *El Misti*, G, fair. *Alojamiento Centenario*, F. **Restaurant**: *Elena*, on same street as bus companies, good, plentiful and cheap portions.

Ronald Berg, of Cambridge, Mass., writes: Around Andahuaylas the old road by the river to Talavera offers some pleasant scenery. San Jerónimo is another picturesque town nearby. Most worth seeing is Pacucha, an hour's ride by truck from Andahuaylas. Pick-ups leave from the centre of Andahuaylas daily, most frequently on Sun., which is market day. Pacucha (pop. 2,000) is the largest of six villages on the shores of a large scenic lake, with a view of mountains to the NW. In the plaza, where the trucks stop, women sell bread, coffee and hot lunches, the only food for 16 km. There are dirt roads around the lake and the circumference can be done in an afternoon (but be back in Pacucha before dark to ensure transport back to Andahuaylas). The wildlife includes many types of wild duck and other birds, sometimes including flocks of green parrots and swallows. Opposite Pacucha, some 2km. past the lake, are the ruins of a Chanka fortress called Zondor. The trails into the jungle beyond the lake are not recommended: the area is very desolate. Except for Andahuaylas itself, this is a mainly Quechua-speaking region. It is one of the poorest parts of Peru, but as long as you do not display your wealth or eat in public, the people tend to be friendly to foreigners.

East of La Oroya The 60-km. surfaced road to Tarma follows the Cerro de Pasco road for 25 km., then branches off to rejoin the old road quite near Tarma, which is 600 metres lower than La Oroya.

Tarma, population 105,200; altitude 3,050 metres, was a nice little flat-roofed town, founded in 1545, with plenty of trees. It is now growing, and there are garish modern buildings, but it still has a lot of charm. Semana Santa celebrations are spectacular, with a very colourful Easter Sunday morning procession in main plaza; Indians make fine flower-carpets. The cathedral is dedicated to Santa Ana; at *Hostal Central*, Calle Huánuco, there is an observatory. The surrounding countryside is beautiful.

Hotels *Turistas*, D, with and without bath, acceptable meals US$3.20, rather run down; medium-priced hotels are on the plaza, e.g. *Tuchu* and *Internacional*, both reasonable; cheaper places around the market, such as *Anchibaya*, *Tarma*, *Central*, and *Córdova*, all basic.

Restaurants *Tradición*, Jr. Moquegua 350, also good. *Acobamba*, outside Tarma, rec.; *Chavín Café*, beneath *Galaxia* hotel, on square, trout rec; several on Lima, including a vegetarian place. The manjarblanco of Tarma is famous; also pachamanca, mondongo and picante de cuyes.

Tourist Office Jr. Dos de Mayo 77, T 2945.

An Englishman, Mr. V. J. Barnes, an authority on the area east of Oroya, would welcome visitors seeking information at his home in Lima (T 287800).
    Direct bus service, Huancayo-Tarma, twice daily 0600 and 1600, US$2.15. Daily colectivos from Jirón Huánuco 439 run almost hourly to Huancayo, US$2.40, 2½ hrs, bus to Oroya, US$1.50, colectivo, US$1.85; bus to La Merced, US$1.45; colectivos often leave for Chanchamayo, US$2.15. Passes over high limestone hills with caves.

Visit the Grutas de Guagapo, 4 km. from town of Polcamayo—bus twice daily from Tarma US$0.80 (2 hrs). The caves, which are a tourist attraction especially in Easter week, can be entered for about 300 metres. Cave guide, Modesto Castro, lives opposite caves and is very informative. His wife cooks trout and potatoes for visitors; you can camp outside his house. The precolumbian ruins of Tarmatamba, Shoguemarca, Yanamarca, Huayipirca, Cachicachi, Pichgamarca and Huancoy also lie nearby.

Eight km. from Tarma (bus US$0.15, or pleasant 2 hrs' walk), the small hillside town of **Acobamba** has the futuristic Santuario de Muruhuay, with a venerated picture painted on the rock behind the altar. It also has fine *tapices* depicting the Crucifixion, made in San Pedro de Cajas. Festivities all May.

Hotels Two *alojamientos* (Doña Norma's near plaza, G, is basic but clean and friendly). Daily buses to Tarma, La Oroya (US$0.50) and Huancayo; 3 buses a week direct to Lima (Coop. San Pedro).

Dr. David Snashall writes: A road from Tarma via Acobamba goes through the village of Polcamayo to the Gruta de Guagapo (*la boca que llora*: the cave that weeps). Even without a guide you can penetrate the cave for some way with a torch. The road continues from Palcamayo (no buses, 3-hr. walk) to **San Pedro de Cajas**, a large village whence most of the coloured sheep-wool weavings for sale in Lima come. You can buy them here for half the price from the weavers themselves. *Hotel Comercio*, Calle Chanchamay0, G; 2 restaurants; no shops. The road continues on to rejoin the one from La Oroya to Cerro de Pasco below Junín.

Beyond Tarma the road is steep and crooked but there are few places where cars cannot pass one another. In the 80 km. between Tarma and La Merced the road, passing by great overhanging cliffs, drops 2,450 metres and the vegetation changes dramatically from temperate to tropical. A really beautiful run.

Some 11 km. before La Merced is **San Ramón** (population 7,000). Ask at the airport about journey to Pampasilva and Puerto Ubirique (see below).

Hotels *Chanchamayo*, fairly cheap, *Selva*. *Conquistador*, E, with shower, parking, on main street. There is a rec. *chifa* on the main street, and the *Hawaii* is good for juices. *La Estancia*, Tarma 592, local specialities.

La Merced, population 10,000, lies in the fertile Chanchamayo valley. Sometimes Campa Indians come to town selling bows and arrows, and there is a small but interesting market selling snake skins, hides, armadillo shells, etc. Festival in the last week of September.

Hotels *Rey* and *Christina*, good, E, with bath; *San Felipe*, F, dirty; *Chuncho*, basic; *Cosmos*, opp. police station, E, fair, probably quieter than others; *Hostal Mercedes*, F, with bath, hot water, clean, rec.; *Romero*, Plaza de Armas, T 2106, F, good but noisy and water in evenings only. Best **restaurant** is *Shambari-Campa*, off Plaza de Armas; *Hong Kong*, restaurant; plenty of bars patronized by the coffee workers, who spend 6 months in the mountains each year.

Note that San Ramón and La Merced are collectively referred to as **Chanchamayo**. Many buses, both from Lima (e.g. Transportes Chanchamayo, best, Av. Luna Pizarro 453, La Victoria, Lima; Los Andes, Arellano, good, 10 hrs., US$4.85) and from Tarma (US$1.45, 3 hrs.). Bus La Merced-Puerto Bermúdez, 8 hrs., US$4, 1000 (Túpac Amaru). To get to Pucallpa, take a launch from Puerto Bermúdez to Laurencia (8 hrs., or more, US$4.50, be prepared for wet luggage), then truck to Constitución, 20 mins., thence colectivo to Zungaro, 1½ hrs., US$2. From Zunzaro, colectivos take 4½ hrs., to Pucallpa, US$3. Alternatively, you can take a truck from La Merced to Pucallpa, 3 days, but between 0830 and 1400 each day you will probably be drenched by rain.

From La Merced you can take the Carretera Marginal de la Selva (a grandiose edge-of-the-jungle project of the mid-1960s, of which some parts have been built) to the jungle town of **Satipo** (Lobato or Los Andes buses from La Merced US$4.50 at 0800; *Hostal Majestic*, D, with bath, no clothes-washing facilities, electricity 1900-2300 only; *La Residensial*, 4 rooms, F, clean, garden, swimming pool, rec., many smaller hotels, all very basic, the best being *Palmero*, E, with bath, not very clean. Try *Dany's Restaurant*, surprisingly good food for such an out-of-the-way place). A beautiful trip. Halfway between La Merced and Satipo is Pichinaki, which has a good hotel, F, ideal for breaking one's journey (bus La Merced-Pichinaki, US$2.15). There are daily buses direct from Satipo to Huancayo (check whether tunnels are open) and Lima at night, very cold, US$6, 12 hrs.; Los Andes and Lobato, so no need to return from Satipo via La Merced. Satipo can also be reached from Concepción, following the Santa Rosa de Ocopa road (**see page 979**), and from Pucallpa by air.

About 22 km. beyond La Merced is San Luis de Shuaro, but 3 km. before it is reached a road, right, runs up the valley of the Perené river. The Perené colony, a concession of 400,000 hectares, nine-tenths of it still unexplored, has large coffee plantations. The altitude is only 700 metres. Saturday and Sunday are colourful market days for the Indians. Beyond San Luis de Shuaro a branch road runs right to Villa Rica. It is no longer possible to take motorized canoes from Pampasilva on the River Perené to Puerto Ubirique, since the building of the new road.

The road has been extended from San Luis de Shuaro over an intervening mountain range for 56 km. to **Oxapampa**, 390 km. from Lima, in a fertile plain on the Huancabamba river, a tributary of the Ucayali. Population, 5,140; altitude, 1,794 metres. Logging, coffee, cattle are local industries, colectivo service from La Merced. A third of the inhabitants are descendants of a German-Austrian community of 70 families which settled in 1859 at **Pozuzo**, 80 km. downstream, and spread later to Oxapampa. There is much livestock farming and coffee is planted on land cleared by the timber trade. 25 km. from Oxapampa is Huancabamba, from where it is 55 km. to Pozuzo; the whole road between La Merced and Pozuzo is very rough, depending on the season, 30 rivers to be crossed. Sr. Luis Orbeza's *mixto* leaves from Oxapampa, opposite *Hotel Bolívar*, to Pozuzo at 0300, returning 1200, Tues., Thurs., Sat. Downstream 40 km. from Pozuzo is Nuevo Pozuzo (local air service, or two-day walk); Padre Pedro has a collection of insects, weapons and stones in his office. There is a family near Padre Pedro's house who welcome guests for dinner (US$1), German spoken.

Oxapampa Hotels *Bolívar*, basic, good restaurant; *La Isabela*, F, cheap and clean, opposite church.

Pozuzo Hotels *Hostal Tirol*, E, full board, clean, rec.; *El Oriente*, basic.

There is an "air-colectivo" service from La Merced to **Puerto Bermúdez** on the Río Neguachi, US$10.50 single, 10 kg. baggage allowance, US$5 per kg. of excess luggage. The service continues to Atalaya, Satipo, Puerto Inca (**see page 994**) and Pucallpa. Bus service, La Merced-Puerto Bermúdez (see below). Air-colectivos go to Lima and to most places in the jungle region where there is an airstrip; flights are cheap but irregular, and depend on technical factors, weather and good will. Aero-taxis can be chartered (*viaje especial*) to anywhere for a higher price, maximum five people, you have to pay for the pilot's return to base. In Puerto Bermúdez there is accommodation (*Hostal Tania*, opposite dock where motorized canoes tie up, F, clean), an eating house opposite the airstrip; boat passages possible from passing traders.

North of La Oroya A railway (also a paved road) runs 130 km. N from La Oroya to Cerro de Pasco. It runs up the Mantaro valley through narrow canyons to the wet and mournful Junín pampa at over 4,250 metres, one of the world's largest high-altitude plains: an obelisk marks the battlefield where the Peruvians under Bolívar defeated the Spaniards in 1824. Blue peaks line the pampa in a distant wall. The wind-swept sheet of yellow grass is bitterly cold. The only signs of life are the youthful herders with their sheep and llamas. The line follows the E shores of Lake Junín. The town of **Junín**, with its picturesque red-tiled roofs, stands beside its lake, whose myriads of water birds have made it famous for its shooting. At Smelter, the coal washing plant, the track branches to Goyllarisquisga, while the main line goes to the long-established mining centre of **Cerro de Pasco** (population 29,810, altitude 4,330 metres), 130 km. from La Oroya by road. It is not a pleasant town, having many beggars and thieves and much unemployment. The nights are bitterly cold. Copper, zinc, lead, gold and silver are mined here, and coal comes from the deep canyon of Goyllarisquisga, the "place where a star fell", the highest coal mine in the world, 42 km. N of Cerro de Pasco. A fine new town—San Juan de Pampa—has been built 1½ km. away (*Gran Hotel*, noisy, no hot water, poor service). A recommended excursion is to the precolumbian funeral towers at Cantamasia, reached on muleback. At Morococha (alight from train at Tuctu) is the Centromín golf course, welcoming to playing visitors, which at 4,400 metres disputes the title of the world's highest with Malasilla, near La Paz, Bolivia.

Hotels *Gran Hotel Cerro de Pasco*, Av. Angamos in San Juan suburb, E, shower, little hot water, poor service, noisy; *América*; *Centromín Hotel*, emergency only; *El Viajero*, on the plaza, F, clean but no hot water; *Santa Rosa*, F, basic, very cold; *Restaurant Los Angeles*, near market, rec. Local specialities, trout and fried frog.

Train Through tickets to Cerro de Pasco can no longer be bought at the Desamparados Station in Lima; there is no longer a connection on the same day at La Oroya. The train leaves La Oroya for Cerro de Pasco at 1330; it arrives at 1716. The return train for La Oroya leaves at 0500 from Cerro de Pasco station, which is 20 min. out of town on foot; on the return journey there should be a connection at La Oroya: the train from Cerro de Pasco arrives there at 0825 and the train for Lima leaves at 1006. The *churrasco* served for breakfast on the train is a welcome defence against the cold.

Buses Bus to Lima, departs 0830 and 2000, 9 hrs., US$5. To La Oroya, bus from Plaza Arenales, 0900 and later, US$0.75; cars go when there are passengers, US$6. To Huancayo, US$2.95. Colectivos to Huánuco, US$4.50, from the central plaza. Buses to Huánuco leave between 0800 and 0900 from Plaza de Armas (5 hrs., US$1.20). A bus, connecting with the train from Lima, to Huánuco takes 3 hrs., at night.

CERRO DE PASCO TO IQUITOS (8)

The Central Highway There are two roads from Lima to Cerro de Pasco. One goes via **Canta** (3 buses daily to and from Lima, US$2.25—El Canteño company, San Román 151-153, Lima). Two hotels and one good restaurant in Canta, from where one can visit the pre-Inca ruins of **Cantamarca**—many of the buildings still have roofs, supported by pillars; it is a 2-3 hour walk up to the ruins, from where there are extensive views. Continuing through the beautiful high pass of

La Viuda (4,748 metres), one goes to the mines of Alpamarca (truck from Canta, 0200, take warm clothes, blanket, camping gear, food). From here there are 2-3 buses per week to Huallay, where there is the Bosque de Piedras (an outcrop of weathered limestone pinnacles which look from a distance like plantations of conifers). Thence to Cerro de Pasco.

The other road, the Central Highway, accompanies the Central Railway, more or less, over the Anticona Pass (4,843 metres) to La Oroya. From there it crosses the Junín pampa to Cerro de Pasco (130 km.), never far from the railway. From Cerro de Pasco it continues NE another 528 km. to Pucallpa, the limit of navigation for large Amazon river boats. The western part of this road (Cerro de Pasco-Huánuco) has been rebuilt into an all-weather highway (**see map, page 988**, for its contour). Buses run daily between Lima and Pucallpa, 847 km., taking 32 hrs., but ask about the state of the road during the rainy season from November to March, when the trip may take a week.

The sharp descent along the nascent **Huallaga River** (the road drops 2,450 metres in the 100 km. from Cerro de Pasco to Huánuco, and most of it is in the first 32 km.) is a tonic to travellers suffering from *soroche*, or altitude sickness. From the bleak vistas of the high ranges one drops below the tree line to views of great beauty. The only town of any size before Huánuco is Ambo; ask at the *dulcería* for Ricardo, who speaks English; he can arrange to take you to the beautiful village of Huacar where Sr. Tiburcio has a water-mill and distillery and keeps a small zoo.

Huánuco, on the Upper Huallaga (population: 82,240), is an attractive Andean town with an interesting market and the two old (but much restored) churches of San Cristóbal and San Francisco (16th century paintings). There is a small but interesting natural history museum at General Prado 495, called Museo de Ciencias; many of the displays have multiple language signs. Entrance, US$0.50. Watch locals catch fish from the river in their teeth! Visit ruin 5 km. on road to La Unión: **Kotosh**, the Temple of Crossed Hands, the earliest evidence of a complex society and of pottery in Peru (from 2000 BC). You must ford a stream to get there, and beware of the vicious black flies. The ruin has been sadly neglected since the original excavation in 1963. Main industry: sugar and rum; take Cisne bus from Jirón Ayacucho, 15 mins., in a.m. to visit Cooperativa Vichaycoto, rum for sale. Altitude 1,812 metres.

Hotels *Turistas*, D, with bath, no hot water, meals US$6; *Hostal Residencial Huánuco*, Jirón Huánuco (near Plaza de Armas) T 2050, F, with bath, hot water, more expensive than others in this range but excellent value, highly rec.; *Las Vegas*, on plaza, rec., has good restaurant; *Real*, on Plaza, C, overpriced, has expensive café; *Nacional*, cheap but adequate; *Bella Durmiente*, near market square, cheap; *Cuzco*, near market, F, with bath, no hot water, expensive restaurant; *Astoria*, F, cheap and clean; *Imperial*, Ayacucho 581, F, with cold shower (intermittent water), reasonable value, clean, quiet; *Kelin*, F, clean; *La Cabaña*, F, friendly, safe but bathrooms dirty; *Internacional*, F, hot water in the common bathroom in the morning, good, clean and cheap. Hotels are often fully booked; arrive early.

Camping Camp by river, near stadium.

Restaurants *Las Palmeras*, good and cheap. *Tokio* and *El Imán*, off main square, both good. *El Café*, in the plaza is cheap and good. Chinese restaurant also in plaza.

Tourist Information Foptur, General Prado 714, Plaza de Armas, opp. Post Office, T 522124. Huánuco Tours, Jirón General Prado 691.

Buses To Lima, US$7 with León de Huánuco, 10 hrs., 3 a day in early evening, slow; colectivo to Lima, US$12.75, leaves 0400, arrives 1400; book the night before at General Prado 607, one block from the main square, rec. Etposa also runs to Lima. Daily buses to Cerro de Pasco, La Oroya and Huancayo, 0830, 1600, with Nororiente or Ucayali, Constitución 638, 11-12 hrs., US$4.60. "Mixto" Huánuco-Cerro de Pasco, half bus, half truck, departs 0400, 3 hrs., US$2.25; colectivo 1 or 12, US$4.50 at 0500. Frequent buses and colectivos to Tingo María, 3 hrs. (colectivo, US$2, many start from near river bridge, two blocks from main plaza). Bus to Pucallpa, US$7, La Perla del Oriente (Etposa), 0800 and 1600, rec. 10 hrs. plus; buses make

LA OROYA TO PUCALLPA

115

0 20 40 60 80
km.

stops for meals but some of them are widely spaced; in any case it is wise to take your own food in case of breakdowns. To Huancayo, 10 hrs., US$3.

Air Huancapallac airport, 8 km. from town; AeroPerú (office at the Tourist Hotel) flights to and from Lima, 4 days a week.

To the north-west of Huánuco is **Tantamayo** (3,600 metres), a farming village in the Central Sierra; it is surrounded by precolumbian ruins which can be reached on foot (3-4 hrs., guides available) called Piruru, Susupillu, Japallan, and Castilla de Selinin; pictures and information from Huánaco Post Office. Hotel: *Turística*, where Don Cristián Ocaña and his Swiss wife, Theresa, offer full board, D (F without food), they are very helpful, and Sra. de Ocaña speaks German, French, Italian and English. Bus from Huánuco, US$4.25, 12-14 hrs., departs 1800; returns at night. Tantamayo can also be reached by taking a truck to Tingo Chico, US$1.70, then another to Chavín de Pariarca (US$0.75) where there is a basic hotel (US$0.75 p.p.) and restaurants, then walk. This route, like the walks to the ruins, is arduous; take warm clothing, a hat, suntan lotion.

From Huánuco, a road leads to **La Unión**, capital of Dos de Mayo district a friendly town, but electricity can be a problem (it gets very cold at night); 2 buses daily between 0700 and 1000, including Acosta, 2 blocks from the market, returns to Huánuco about midnight, US$3, 8-9 hrs.; truck, 10½ hrs., leaves late morning. La Unión-Tingo Chico, US$1.70. *Hostal Turista* and *Hostal Dos de Mayo*, at La Unión (G). Neither safe for left luggage. *Restaurant El Danubio*, near market, good home cooking, lots of garlic.

On the pampa above La Unión are the Inca ruins of **Huánuco Viejo**, a 2½ hr. walk from the town, a great temple-fortress with residential quarters. To get there, take the path starting behind the market and climb towards the cross, which is at the edge of a plateau. Continue straight through the village on the wide path (the locals are friendly, but some of their dogs are nasty); the views of the pampa, surrounded on all sides by mountains, are beautiful. Seemingly at the foot of a mountain, in front and to your right, is a silvery metalic roof of a little chapel, behind which are the ruins (about a 20-min. walk through herds of cattle). Take warm clothing and beware of thunderstorms. (Karin Kubitsch, West Germany).

Bus to Lima daily, crowded. Also possible to get to Callejón de Huaylas by taking 1600 bus to Conococha (US$3.25, 9 hrs.) and waiting there for a truck to Huaraz (2-3 hrs.— **see page 886**). The wait is very cold, at 4,100 metres. La Unión-Huaraz direct is very difficult because most transport does the route La Unión-Chiquián-Lima. You can take a truck from La Unión to Huansalla, then another to Pachacoto (some wait till 0100 for passengers), and from there it's 1 hr. to Huaraz. The San Cristóbal bus to Lima at 1100 goes a few km. S of Catac; from there connections are easy to Huaraz (1 hr.) and Chavín (via Catac). Salazar bus to Lima (3 a week at 1000-more like 1100), takes 9 hrs. To Conococha, US$4; this is supposed to connect with a Lima-Huaraz bus at 1900-2000; if you miss it, hitch in the cold and dark (2 hrs., US$1.50 to Huaraz). A night bus from Lima passes at 0300, but the restaurant at the Conococha crossroads closes at 2230. Check local political conditions before taking this route.

The journey to Tingo María, 135 km., is very dusty but gives a good view of the jungle. Some 25 km. beyond Huánuco the road begins a sharp climb to the heights of Carpish (3,023 metres). A descent of 58 km. brings it to the Huallaga river again; it continues along the river to Tingo María. (The road is paved from Huánaco to Tingo María, including a tunnel through the Carpish hills, but is reported to be in very bad condition.) Landslides along this section are frequent and construction work causes delays.

Tingo María is on the middle Huallaga, in the Ceja de Montaña, or edge of the mountains, isolated for days in rainy season. Climate tropical; annual rainfall 2,642 mm. Population, about 20,560 and very mixed. The altitude (655 metres) prevents the climate from being oppressive. The Cordillera Azul, the front range of the Andes, covered with jungle-like vegetation to its top, separates it from the jungle lowlands to the E. The mountain which can be seen from all over the town is called La Bella Durmiente, the Sleeping Beauty. The meeting here of Sierra and Selva makes the landscape extremely striking. Bananas, sugar cane, cocoa, rubber, tea and coffee are grown. The main crop of the area, though, is coca, grown on the *chacras* (smallholdings) in the countryside, and sold legitimately and otherwise in Tingo María—there have been several shoot-outs between the police and the drug entrepreneurs. As in many other places in Peru, watch out for gangs of thieves around the buses and do not leave luggage on the bus if you get off.

Although the town itself is safe, it is not permitted to leave it at night; it is also inadvisable to take a bus through the area at present.

A small university outside the town, beyond the *Hotel Turistas*, has a little museum-cum-zoo, with animals of that zone, and botanical gardens in the town, entrance free but a small tip would help to keep things in order. 6½ km. from Tingo is a fascinating cave, the Cueva de las Lechuzas. There are many nocturnal parrots in the cave and many small parakeets near the entrance. It is reached by car via the new bridge (or colectivo from garage, US$0.80); take a torch, and do not wear open shoes; also take a tape recorder "for your own private horror-movie soundtracks" when the birds leave the cave. The Cave can be reached by boat when the river is high. 13 km. from Tingo is the small gorge known as Cueva de las Pavas (no caves or turkeys, but good swimming).

Hotels *Turistas*, D, with and without bath, meals US$6 extra, including taxes, very good, swimming pool US$0.75, some way out of town; *Viena*, F, good value with private bathrooms, clean, near *Café Rex*; *Royal*, E, bed and private showers; *Marco Antonio*, F, dirty, insecure in the cheaper rooms, laundry service; *Imperial*, E, with bath, pleasant; *La Cabaña*, G, the cheapest, tolerably clean, good restaurant; *Cuzco*, G, clean and good; *Raimundo*, G (not to be confused with *Raimondi*, which is dirty, flea-ridden, and not rec.); *Palacio*, G, shower, but basic and not very clean; *Gran Hotel*, G. Hotels are often fully-booked. Rooms available at Av. Benavides 263, F, also meals; *Pensión* at Jr. Monzón 284, with 3 meals a day for US$1.50.

Restaurants *Pensión González*, expensive, but nice setting; *Café Rex*, Avenida Raimondi 500, cakes and ice cream, but rather run down; *Gran Chifa Oriental*, Chinese restaurant, on main street, cheap. Also 2 other restaurants of the same name elsewhere in the town—beware, they're not so good. Restaurant at *La Cabaña Hotel* good.

Transport Flights from Tingo María to Lima. Normally 3 flights a week to Tingo María by AeroPerú, but times often change. 4-seater plane flies to Juanjui, US$17.20 p.p. + US$0.35 for every kilo of luggage over 10 kilos. From Tingo María on, several transport services are run; the road is narrow and stony. Landslides and mud can be a problem. Some construction work is going on. Many Lima-Pucallpa buses go via Tingo, for example, Arellano, Av. Raimondi, whose buses leave between 0700 and 0900 (their terminal in Lima is in La Victoria, a very dangerous area). Bus takes 18 hrs. From Tingo to Pucallpa, US$5, 8 hrs. Seats are hard to get on buses to Pucallpa; there are 4 booking offices: Huallaga, Tepsa, Arellano, Nororiente. Bus to Aguaytía, 3 hrs., US$1.70. León de Huánuco bus Tingo María-Huánuco takes 5-6 hrs., 0930, US$1.40; colectivos take 3 hrs. but beware of unauthorized colectivos, which charge the same as authorized ones but are smaller, slower and sometimes get into trouble with the police, US$2.

The Huallaga river winds northwards for 930 km. The Upper Huallaga is a torrent, dropping 15.8 metres per kilometre between its source and Tingo María. The Lower Huallaga moves through an enervation of flatness, with its main port, Yurimaguas, below the last rapids and only 150 metres above the Atlantic ocean, yet distant from that ocean by over a month's voyage. Between the Upper and Lower lies the Middle Huallaga: that third of the river which is downstream from Tingo María, upstream from Yurimaguas. The valleys, ridges and plateaux have been compared with Kenya, but the area is so isolated that less than 100,000 people now live where a million might flourish. The southern part of the Middle Huallaga centres upon Tingo María; down-river, beyond Bellavista, the orientation is towards **Yurimaguas**, which is connected by road with the Pacific coast, via Tarapoto and Moyobamba (**see page 910**). There is a fine church of the Passionist Fathers, based on the Cathedral of Burgos, Spain, at Yurimaguas; population 25,700. Market from 0600-0800, colourful, full of fruit and animals. Tourist information from Consejo Regional building on main Plaza. Interesting excursions in the area include the gorge of Shanusi and the lakes of Mushuyacu and Sanango. Moped hire US$2.35/hour including fuel. **Warning**: there has been guerrilla activity in the Yurimaguas region; visitors can expect attention from the police.

Hotels *Yurimaguas*, E, with shower, toilet and fan, clean, reliable; *Estrella*, F, and shower, rec.; *Floríndez*, E, shower, air conditioning US$1.50 extra; *Camus*, no sign, Manco Capac 201, F, cheap; *Mache*, F, with bath and fan, rec.; *Leo's Palace*, F, Plaza de Armas 104-6, good, friendly, reasonably-priced, restaurant; *Heladería*, round corner from *Estrella*, serves good cheap lunch and dinner. Rec. restaurants, *Leo's Palace*, *El Aguila*, *Chifa Coni*.

Exchange Interbanc or travel agents; poor rates.

Air AeroPerú flies Lima-Trujillo-Yurimaguas-Iquitos Thurs. and Sun. Faucett flies Lima-Tarapoto-Yurimaguas on Wed., and to Yurimaguas on Fri. When Yurimaguas-Tarapoto road is impassable, Grupo Ocho flies for civilians. Flights also to Juanjui. Planes may not land in rain.

River Travel Yurimaguas-Iquitos by regular ferry *Jasmin* 60 hrs., US$15 on upper deck with meals (upstream takes longer). *Madreselva* and *Gardenia* are two large ferries to Iquitos, US$16.50, plus US$3 for a cabin; a smaller ferry is the *Oty*, US$14, bring your own hammock, takes 2 days and 2 nights, take fruit and drinks, police inspections at each end of the trip; similar is *Vencedor*. To buy a hammock costs US$10 in Yurimaguas. Ask at the harbour for smaller boats, which can take up to 10 days.
  You can break the journey at **Lagunas**, 12 hrs. by boat from Yurimaguas: *Hostal La Sombra*, Jr. Vásquez 1121, G with shared bath, basic, friendly, good food); *Hotel Montalbán*, Plaza de Armas, no sign, 2 clean rooms, friendly owner, Sr. Inga, 20-mins. walk from jetty, also accommodation at the Farmacia. You can ask the local people to take you on a trip into the jungle by canoe; you will see at very close range crocodiles, monkeys and a variety of birds, but only on trips of 4 days or so. Edinson Saldaña Gutiérrez, Sargento Flores 718 is a good guide; also Hopp and Genaro (ask at *La Sombra*), who charge US$80 for 5-day trip inc. basic food, with fishing and hunting; Juan Huaycama (Jáuregui 689), highly rec., price p.p. for 5 days, US$11, mostly on the river, sleeping in hammocks, fishing. Typical cost for party of 5 for 12 days is US$200, with 2 guides and 2 boats. One person for 5 days with one guide is charged US$45. Take water purifier and mosquito repellant on excursions that involve living off the land. The 45-foot river launch *Constante* plies to Lagunas 2-3 times a week, 12 hrs. downstream from Lagunas; from there US$10 to Iquitos if you can get a connection. A boat, *La Rosita*, runs regularly but stops at every village of any size. *Alfert* has been rec., cabins, good food. Times of boats to Iquitos and Pucallpa very vague (confirm departures the day before by radio). The boats pass by the villages of Castilla and Nauta (*Residencial Olguita*, basic), where the Huallaga joins the Ucayali and becomes the Amazon. You need a hammock, mosquito net, water-purification tablets, extra food and a good book.

At Tulumayo, soon after leaving Tingo María, a road runs N down the Huallaga past La Morada, successfully colonized by people from Lima's slums, to Aucayacu (*Hotel Monte Carlo*, E with bath; one other hotel, both poor) and Tocache (accommodation at *Hostal San Martín*, F; *Hostal Sucre*, F; one other). The road is paved to 20 km. past Aucayacu, thereafter it is good gravel. Colectivos run; Tingo-Tocache US$8.25 (4½ hrs.) or bus US$6 (6 hrs.). The road has been pushed N to join another built S from Tarapoto (Tarapoto-Tocache, US$4.65 by colectivo) and has now been joined at Tarapoto to the Olmos-Bagua-Yurimaguas transandine highway to the coast at Chiclayo. Colectivos and taxis run from Tocache to Yurimaguas (serviceable unpaved road); daily camioneta Tarapoto-Yurimaguas, US$4.90, 6 hrs. The Juanjui-Tocache road has five bridges, but the last one across the Huallaga, just before Juanjui, was washed away in 1983 to be replaced by an efficient ferry (US$9.20 per vehicle); Juanjui-Tarapoto by colectivo US$7.80. For the river journey, start early in the morning if you do not wish to spend a night at the river village of Sión. No facilities, but night is not cold. The river runs through marvellous jungle with high cliffs. Boats sometimes run aground in the river near Sión. Take food and water purifier. Many rafts of balsa wood. Also, a small plane flies between Tocache and Juanjui, US$16 (25 mins).
  From Tingo María to the end of the road at Pucallpa is 288 km., with a climb over the watershed—the Cordillera Azul—between the Huallaga and Ucayali rivers. When the road was being surveyed it was thought that the lowest pass over the Cordillera Azul was over 3,650 metres high, but an old document stating that a Father Abad had found a pass through these mountains in 1757 was rediscovered, and the road now goes through the pass of Father Abad, a gigantic

gap 4 km. long and 2,000 metres deep. At the top of the pass is a Peruvian Customs house; the jungle land to the E is a free zone. Coming down from the pass the road bed is along the floor of a magnificent canyon, the Boquerón Abad: luxuriant jungle and ferns and sheer walls of bare rock punctuated by occasional waterfalls into the roaring torrent below. E of the foot of the pass the all-weather road goes over flat pampa with few curves to the village of **Aguaytía** (narcotics police checkpoint; gasoline; *Hostal San Antonio*, F, clean; 2 restaurants). On to Pucallpa (160 km.—5 hrs. by bus, US$2.70); the last half has no service stations.

Pucallpa, a rapidly expanding jungle town, is on the Ucayali River, navigable by vessels of 3,000 tons from Iquitos, 533 nautical miles away. Population has increased to about 90,000 (district 130,000). It is the capital of the new Department of Ucayali. The newer sections have paved streets, sewers and lights, but much of the frontier town atmosphere still exists. Small but attractive zoo at the brewery (tours on Sat. but far out of city). The economy of the area is growing fast; sawmills, plywood factories, a paper mill, oil refinery, fishing and boat building are all thriving; timber is trucked out to the Highlands and the coast. A newly constructed floating dock for freight promises a great expansion in trade. Large discoveries of oil and gas are being explored, and gold mining is underway nearby. The local drugs problem is becoming serious. The Ganso Azul oilfield has a 75-km. pipeline to the Pucallpa refinery. From Tingo María, 286 km. (gravel road); from Lima, 847 km.

All jungle towns are expensive, but bargains can be found. The floating port of La Hoyada and Puerto Italia are worth a visit to see the canoe traffic and open-air markets. Care should be taken when arranging jungle trips from street vendors in Pucallpa or at the ports. The climate is tropical: dry season in July and August, rainy seasons October-November, February-March; the town is hot and dusty between June and November and muddy from December to May. The centre of Pucallpa is now paved, but both the port and new commercial harbour, about 5 km. away, are reached along dirt roads. Expect plenty of police searches as this is a narcotics area. Also expect plenty of thieves.

Hotels *Turistas*, C with bath (taxes included), swimming pool, good restaurant; *Mercedes*, E, good, but noisy with good bar and restaurant attached, swimming pool; *Inambu*, C, with good value restaurant, a/c; *Komby*, E, comfortable, swimming pool, excellent value; *Sun*, Ucayali, F, without bath, clean, good value next to *Komby*; *Comfort*, E, clean, *Sisley*, E, adequate, both on Coronel Portillo; *Perú*, Raymondi, E (try bargaining), dirty and not rec., basic; *Europa*, at river end of 7 de Junio, F, dirty, unsafe; *Barbtur*, F, Raymondi 670 (T 6377), friendly, clean, central, opp. bus stop, good beds; *Alex*, F, private bath, dirty; *Hostal Mori*, Jr. Independencia 1114, G, basic; *Hostal Los Angeles*, on Ucayali, E, clean, communal shower, but noisy; *Tariri*, Raymondi, G, dirty, basic, food cheap and good, Coronel Portillo, near Calle Frederico Basadre. If holidaying, better to stay at Lake Yarinacocha (see below).

Restaurants Two *chifas* (Chinese restaurants) downtown, both said to be good: *Chifa Pucallpa* and *Chifa Hongkong*, Raymondi 650. *Jugos Don José*, quite cheap; *Restaurant San Isidro* rec., also *Sabores Perú*, good food, poor service; *Jaricho*, under *Hotel Sun*, good; *Escorpión Cebichería*, Jr. Progreso, good, eat in rear garden; *Los Rosales*, expensive; *Puerto de Carlos*, best in the downtown area, expensive; *Jíbaros*, near *Hotel Amazonas*, good food and value; *Embutidos La Favorita*, Cnl. Portillo, good, cheap, friendly, US$1 for all 3 meals; *El Establo*, steak house on road to airport, excellent; *Sandwich Roma*, corner of Portillo and Ucayali, good snack bar. *La Baguette*, good bakery, cheap bottles of pisco. The local beer "San Juan" has been rec.

Small **motorcycles** for hire from Jr. Raymondi 654 and 7 de Junio 864, about US$1.50 per hour plus gasoline.

Bookshop Librería La Verdad has a collection of English books on loan; a boon for stranded travellers.

Exchange Banco Continental, no commission. Importaciones Gutiérrez Padilla, Jr. Ucayali, Raymondi 601 (also good ice cream). Try also the owner of the *Barbtur Hotel*, and Textiles Universales, Postillo y Ucayali.

Tourist Office Foptur, Saénz Peña 298, T 5008.

Air AeroPerú and Faucett to and from Lima daily in the afternoons, 1 hr. 3 flights a week to Iquitos with AeroPerú, 1855, try different agencies for lower price ticket (e.g. Pucallpa Tours, Jr. Coronel Portillo 747, T 6081); Some seats are assigned, you need to arrive early. Departures must be confirmed 24 hrs. in advance. Reconfirmation of tickets can only be done with any certainty at the office in town. Float plane, Aero San Martín, from the airforce base at Yarinacocha, Sat, 0900 to Iquitos (check in Fri., be there at 0700), US$20; will only go if there are enough passengers each end, otherwise one has to pay for additional seats. Grupo Ocho fly to Esperanza, San Ramón, Sepahua, Atalaya, with passengers—office in Pucallpa. The road to Brazil has not yet been opened. For connections by river see **Brazil** section. SASA fly to **Cruzeiro do Sul, US$35, minimum 4 passengers, if plane has no passengers booked for return, you'll have to pay US$70, very unreliable. Airport to town, bus US$0.25; taxi US$3.60.**

N.B. Before entering Peru at Pucallpa by air from Cruzeiro do Sul check thoroughly that immigration facilities have been set up at Pucallpa. If you arrive and cannot get a stamp, the PIP in Pucallpa will (or should) send you back to Brazil; if they don't, you'll be in for a lot of hassles further on in Peru, including the possibility of arrest. To leave Peru from Pucallpa, you must get a special exit visa from the PIP in town or at the airport.

Buses Much of the Pucallpa-Lima road is now paved (rough stretch for 80 km. E of Tingo María) and there are regular bus services to Lima (check in advance that the road is open and what political conditions are). Huallaga, Arellano, Perla del Oriente and León de Huánuco (at 1730) from Lima to Pucallpa (US$10, 24 hrs. in good weather) via Huánuco (10 hrs., US$7 with León de Huánuco (slow)—1300 from Pucallpa, US$6.50 with La Perla del Oriente, 1200). From Pucallpa Nororiente goes to Tingo María, US$5, 10-11 hours, also Amazonia Express, on Raymondi (controls at Aguaytía and about 40 km. from Tingo María). Advised to take blankets as the crossing of the Cordillera at night is bitterly cold. Try to pick a bus crossing the mountains by day as the views are wonderful. It is also possible to get to Lima by truck.

Excursions The Hospital Amazónico Albert Schweitzer, which serves the local Indians, and Summer School of Linguistics (callers by appointment only) for the study of Amazon Indian languages are on picturesque Lake **Yarinacocha**, the main tourist attraction of the area. Yarinacocha is 20 mins. by colectivo or bus (line 6) from the market in Pucallpa (US$0.25), 15 mins. by taxi (US$3.60). The Indian market of Moroti-Shobo is a must. Hotel La Cabaña, C (by appointment only, price rises in high season), same Swiss owner as Mercedes in Pucallpa, good service and food, excellent guide, Isabel, for short expeditions, plane excursions (for instance to Indian villages). Next door to La Cabaña is La Perla lodge, good and much cheaper, German-Peruvian owned, English and German spoken, homely atmosphere. Los Delfines, F, rooms with bath, clean, noisy; El Pescador, in Puerto Callao, F, cheap, friendly, restaurant, best for budget traveller, but mixed reports recently. Some small houses for rent on weekly basis. Restaurants: El Cucharón, good food; Grande Paraíso, good view; local specialities include tamales, humitas (maize patties with meat and herbs), junies (rice with chicken and spices), tacutacu (banana and sauces).

Here is bathing in clean water, but there is a lot of weed. It is a pleasant change after the mud of Pucallpa and the Amazon; you can camp, though there are no facilities and it is hot and insect-ridden. Motor canoes can be hired for about US$17 a day with guide, but guide not mandatory for lake trips. Trips into the canals and out to the river need a guide (Sr. Antonio has been rec.). Two types of excursions down river, recommended three days, can be arranged from the port in Yarinacocha directly with the boat owners, prices vary but approximately US$20 per boat a day, you buy food and some supplies. Boats hold up to 8 at reduced price. Recommended boats: Veloz, Akito (of the García family, who also have accommodation, rec., trustworthy), Thierry Giles, good English, has two boats called Delfín, rec. Beware, many boats are used for drug-running and tourists have come to grief. Recommended guides Daniel Saavedra (B/M Progreso), Roberto C. Cenepo, Jorge Rucoba (navigator), who offer fishing, hunting, walks in the jungle along the rivers Aguaytía, Callena and Ucayali, and rivers and canals (especially the Chanchaguaya region of Contamaná). Also special excursions to Iquitos from Pucallpa. None of them speaks English, but they can be found at Lake Yarinacocha, Puerto Callao, ask for B/M Progreso, prices are competitive. Also rec. for tours, Jorge Matos Grijalva of Selva Tours, also an English teacher and bar owner, great local character and most helpful, Coronel Portillo, next to Hotel Amazonas. Local guide, Gonzalo Vargas Cárdenas, c/o Aéro San Martín. **Note**: down-river trips visit numerous villages but much of the jungle is cultivated; up-river trips visit fewer villages but mostly virgin jungle.

Certain sections of Lake Yarinacocha have been designated as a reserve. The Botánico Parque Turístico of Francisco Montes-Shuna is worthy of a visit. It is a collection of jungle plants, well-laid out and labelled, by Lake Yarinacocha, including a part of the smaller Lake

Ormiga. Sr. Montes Shuna will demonstrate the uses of the plants, is very knowledgeable, and speaks English. To visit is free, but a donation is welcome. To get there take a boat to just past *La Cabaña*, then walk 12 minutes along a path: all details from Francisco Montes-Shuna, Jr. L.M. Sánchez Cerro 465, Pucallpa (turn off Guillermo Sisley Medina, the road from Yarinacocha to central Pucallpa, by Mercado 3), or contact Lenín Mera Rengifa, Elmo Tours, Jr. 7 de Junio 767, T 6798.

River Service Bus Line 1 to the port, La Hoyada. In the dry season boats dock 3 km. from the bus stop, along dusty walk, taxi US$2. To Iquitos, some better than others; only 3 boats with cabins, but don't count on getting one (hammocks are cooler): *Madre Selva*, clean, friendly, rec.; US$10 with cabin, 6 days. Travellers to Iquitos may need confirmation from the PIP that their documents are in order, this must then be signed by the Capitanía otherwise no passenger can be accepted on a trip leaving Pucallpa. No such clearance is necessary when returning to Pucallpa. Passenger services are in decline owing to competition by air and priority for cargo traffic; it may be better to make journeys in short stages rather than Pucallpa-Iquitos direct. There's a risk of illness on the river, and public transport can be extremely uncomfortable. River water is used for cooking and drinking: tinned food, mosquito netting, hammock and fresh water are necessary purchases, fishing line and hooks advisable. Take lots of insect repellant (local brand, Black Flag, is not effective), water purifier and tummy pills. The smaller boats call often at jungle villages if you want to see them, but otherwise because the river is wide, the shores can only be seen at a distance. Average time: 5 days. Boats leave very irregularly. When conditions are bad they leave in convoy: none may leave afterwards for 4 to 6 weeks. Avoid boats that will be loading en route, this can take up to 6 days. The fare is about US$20 a head with "cabin", (bargain), rice, meat and beans. It is possible to hire a small boat from Pucallpa to Iquitos for US$89. Try at the north section of the port, but take care not to hire a boat running drugs. Further down the Ucayali river are Contamaná (with frontier-town atmosphere) and Requena, from which launches sail to Iquitos, taking 12 hrs., US$7. Roroboya, a small Shipibo Indian village about 12 hrs. downstream from Pucallpa, should not be missed, as most other villages down to Iquitos are *mestizo*. You can go to Puerto La Hoyada and Puerto Italia (smaller boats) to find a boat going to Iquitos; the Capitanía on the waterfront may give you information about sailings, but this is seldom reliable. Do not pay for your trip before you board the vessel, and only pay the captain. (Captains may allow you to live on board a couple of days before sailing.) Boats going upstream on the Amazon and its tributaries stay closer to the bank than boats going down, which stay in mid-stream.

From Pucallpa to Cruzeiro do Sul overland requires plenty of time and money to organize, and even then is difficult. You can take a boat to Abojao (10 days), then walk to Brasiléia, from where buses go to Rio Branco. Boats and guides are very expensive.

You can take a colectivo from Pucallpa S to Zungaru (US$3), where a boat (30 mins.) can be taken to **Puerto Inca** on the Río Pachitea, about 120 km. N by air from Puerto Bermúdez (**see page** 985) and close to the Carretera Marginal (under construction). It is a gold-rush town, expanding quickly, with two hotels (Don José's *Alojamiento*, G, clean, safe, laundry, big rooms, rec.).

Iquitos, capital of the Department of Loreto and chief town of Peru's jungle region, is a fast-developing city of 350,000 people on the W bank of the Amazon, with Padre Isla island (14½ by 3 km.) facing it in midstream. It has paved streets and plenty of vehicles (including taxis) but roads out of the city go only a little way: Iquitos is completely isolated except by air and river. Some 800 km. downstream from Pucallpa and 3,200 km. from the mouth of the Amazon, it has recently taken on a new lease of life as the centre for oil exploration in Peruvian Amazonia. As one might expect from its use by the oil industry and its remoteness, it is an expensive town, but compensates by being a friendly place.

There is an iron house in the Plaza de Armas, designed by Eiffel for the Paris exhibition of 1898. It is said that the house was transported from Paris by a local rubber baron (the rubber boom lasted until 1912); it is constructed entirely of iron trusses and sheets, bolted together and painted silver.

Belén, the picturesque, friendly waterfront district, is lively, but not safe at night. Most of its huts are built on rafts to cope with the river's 10-metre change of level during floods. *Pasaje Paquito* is a bar with typical local drinks, as is *La China*. The main square has a bandstand made by Eiffel. (Canoes may be hired on the waterfront to visit Belén, US$3 per hour; do not try paddling yourself as the current is very strong.) See in the city the Market, at the end of the Malecón, or riverside walk. Note that the principal street Jirón Lima has been renamed Jirón Próspero. Recommended guide with a good car and two boats is Jorge Chávez, T 231532 or through *Hostal Caravel*.

The University of Amazonia of Loreto (1962) specializes in engineering and agriculture. Of special interest are the older buildings, faced with *azulejos* (glazed tiles). They date from the rubber boom of 1890 to 1920, when the rubber barons imported tiles from Portugal and Italy and ironwork from England to embellish their homes. Werner Herzog's film *Fitzcarraldo* is a *cause célèbre* in the town; Fitzcarraldo's house still stands on the Plaza de Armas, and Herzog's boats are moored in the port.

A short drive S of the city is beautiful Lake **Quistococha** in lush jungle, with a fish hatchery at the lakeside. Recommended is a visit (US$0.60) to the Parque Zoológico de Quistococha (with aquarium) on the lake (closed Mon.). At the entrance are pictures and texts of local legends, the tourist office will supply a map of the zoo. Take bus (tends to be crowded and dirty) from corner of Próspero and Gálves; also a truck (with pink frame, not green) from Abtao and Grau to the zoo and Quistococha, US$0.20; taxi US$3 for 4 people, with 2 hrs. wait. We have heard that the animals (and particularly the fish) often depend on food from visitors to survive. The monkeys roam freely, some cages are small, but the zoo attracts mixed reactions. See particularly the *paiche*, a huge Amazonian fish whose steaks (*paiche a la loretana*) you can eat in Iquitos' restaurants.

Warnings As elsewhere, beware of thieves, especially of handbags, watches, jewellery, etc. Secondly, locals sell necklaces made with red and black rosary peas (Abrus pecatorius), which are extremely poisonous. Do not give them to children. They are illegal in Canada, but not in the U.S.A. If possible, avoid visiting Iquitos around Peruvian Independence Day (27 and 28 July) and Easter as it is very expensive and crowded and excursion facilities are overloaded. Avoid the "headhunters" at the airport who try to steer you to travel agents for a commission (the tourist police at the airport help to avoid this practice): cheaper to go straight to the agents, who are all on Calle Putumayo near the Plaza.

Festivals Founding of Iquitos, 5 January; Carnival, February-March; tourist week, third week in June; San Juan, 24 June; Immaculate Conception.

Hotels *Amazonas*, previously *Holiday Inn*, on Abelardo Quiñónez, 3 km. out of town (taxi US$1.75), A, plus 19% tax and service, swimming pool (free bus service hourly from airport), designed for air conditioning but not working, a 5-star hotel only in price; *Turistas*, Malecón Tarapacá, C, with bath, meals US$4.50, with many good air-conditioned rooms US$1.50 extra (a few second-hand English books available in reception), does not accept travellers' cheques; *Hostal Caravel*, Próspero, B, a/c, very clean, friendly; *Hostal Acosta*, Ricardo Palma 252, A, hot and cold running water, shower, air conditioning, refrigerator in room, very good café, central, rec.; also *Acosta 2*, C, almost same standard plus good restaurant and swimming pool; *Isabel*, Brasil 174, E with bath, very good, clean (but plug the holes in the walls!), secure, often full; *Hostal Safari*, Napo 126, E, a/c, hot showers, restaurant; *Hostal La Pascana*, Pevas 133, F with cold shower, basic, fan, clean, breakfast available, rec.; *Lima*, Próspero 549, F (triple rooms available), with bath and fan, cold water, towel, soap and toilet paper provided, café good, and good breakfast 2 doors to the right; *Perú*, Próspero 320, F (triples available), fan, clean, bathroom, café downstairs, good value; *Hostal Residencial Alfert*, García Sanz 03, E, with bath, basic, friendly; *María Antonia*, Próspero 616, C, clean, air-conditioned, noisy; *Hostal Europa*, Brasil 222, very good, very helpful, D, a/c (cheaper with fan), shower; *Hostal Tacna*, Tacna 516, T 232839, F, rec.; *Hostal Residencial Ambassador*, Pevas 260, C, with shower, air-conditioning and snack-bar, rec.; *Hostal Residencial Loreto*, Jr. Próspero 311, E, with shower and air-conditioning (cheaper without air conditioning, noisy, poor water supply); *Hostal Karina*, Av. Putumayo 467, F, good value, central, friendly, laundry, cheap food, but poor water supply; *Maynas*, Próspero 388, E (triples available), with private shower and fan, very clean and friendly; *Residencial Wagner*, Coronel Portillo 687, opposite the Capitanía, F, friendly, cheap meals available, jungle tours of up to 6 days with groups of 4-6 people, US$40 p.p. a day. Cheapest: *Hostal Económico*, Moore 1164, G, very clean, good water supply, quiet, rec. *Excelsior* Arica, 3 blocks from Plaza de Armas, F, a/c, cold shower, safe, breakfast extra, friendly.

Restaurants The best are on or near Plaza Veintiocho (28) de Julio, e.g. *El Dorado Inn*, Calle Huallaga, good value and good menu; *Gran Chifa Wai Ming*, San Martín 462/6, good but quite expensive; *El Tropical*, Av. Quiñónez 39, 1½ km. from centre, owned by Paul Hitschler (German), reasonable, rec.; *El Shupihui*, Calvo de Araujo y Castilla, typical restaurant, highly rec.; *El Mesón*, Jirón Napo, fish rec.; *La Terraza*, Maldonado y Napo on waterfront, with frogs hopping between tables, good; *Maloca*, opposite *Hotel Turistas* on riverbank, excellent, average meal US$5, good fish, really good view, highly rec. Chinese restaurants include *Gran Chifa Central*, Av. Almirante Grau 1133; *Gran Chifa Chung Wa*, on the corner of Arica and San Martín, average. *Chifa Pekin*, Av. Almirante Grau 837. *La Favorita*, Próspero Morona; *Ebony*, on Próspero, good and cheap; *Chicken Broaster*, Próspero, 3 blocks from Plaza de Armas, good for paiche a la Loretana as well as chicken; *Tucunaré*, Putumayo 157, good for fish (try paiche); restaurant of Kaya Tours at Putumayo 139, good; the *Cocoroco* chain has a *Pollo a la Brasa* restaurant on the corner of Plaza Veintiocho de Julio. Café beneath *Res. Internacional*, Jr. Próspero, good, cheap. *Snack Jungle Bar*, Próspero 283, good value. Pineapples are good and cheap. Try the local drink chuchuhuasi, made from the bark of a tree, which is supposed to have aphrodisiac properties, and jugo de cocona, and the alcoholic vete bajando, cola de mono, rompe colzón and siete raices (aguardiente mixed with the bark of 7 trees and wild honey). You can eat cheaply, especially fish, at the three markets. Palm heart salad (chonta) excellent; also try inchicapi (chicken, corn and peanut soup) and cecina (fried dried pork).

Current 220 volts, A.C.

Clubs Club Social Iquitos, overlooking Plaza de Armas; Military Casino, for all classes; Centro Internacional.

Shopping *Artesanías del Perú*, Putumayo 128; Mercado Artesanal de Productores, 4 km. from the centre in San Juan district, take colectivo; *La Cocamita*, Putumayo 120; *Mocahua Juárez*, Arica 1083. All sell handicrafts. Pharmacies: *Tacna*, Tacna 450; *D'Onadio*, Próspero 541; *El Loretano*, Próspero 361-3. Secondhand English books at the travel agent on Próspero 184 (1 for 1 exchange, free).

Cinemas On Plaza 28 de Julio, another on Próspero.

Discotheques The best are said to be *Puma's Club* (*Amazonas Hotel*) or *Tropicana Club*, both in Putumayo. *La Pantera Rosa*, Moore 434; *Pax*, Napo y Condamine; *Acuario*, Napo 1st block; *St Chomas*, Condamine.

Motorcycle Hire US$15 a day, Carlos del Prado Bawer, Brasil 530, T 239147.

Museum Municipal Museum (1st block of Tawara), has a large, old collection of stuffed Amazonian fauna which is rather disappointing. It has been incorporated into the Parque Zoológico.

Exchange Banco Popular cashes travellers' cheques. Banco de Crédito, Plaza de Armas, good rates. Banco Amazónico changes cheques at the official rate without charging a commission or asking for a copy of your passport. Importaciones Lima on Próspero, and shops selling foreign electrical goods offer good rates of exchange. Many money changers on Próspero in the 3 blocks S of Plaza de Armas.

Consulates Brazilian, Sgto. Lores 363; Colombian, Malecón Tarapacá 260; Spanish, Moore 249.

Immigration Arica 477, T 235371.

Medical Services Clínica Loreto, Morona 471, T 23-3752, 24-hour attention, recommended, but only Spanish spoken.

Post Office corner of Calle Arica with Morona, near Plaza de Armas. **Entel**, Arica 276.

Tourist Office Foptur, on W side of Plaza de Armas, T 238523 (used to have an office at Próspero 163, Pinasco House, on Plaza de Armas); and at airport: useful town maps, maps of the Quistacocha zoo and literature from the main jungle tour operators. Town map also from Librería Mosquera, Jr. Próspero.

Travel Agencies Good information from Edith (speaks English and French), Three Roses Travel, Próspero 246, very helpful. Other agencies recommended for city and surroundings Belén Viajes y Turismo, Arica 1233, and Fénix Viajes, Pevas 216.

Jungle Tours All agencies are under control of the local office of the Ministry of Tourism, Calle Arica 566: if you think you're being overcharged, ask for Sra. Lastenia Rodríguez, who will show you the operator's file, in which route and price must be recorded. (Not worth while for booking bus or air tickets). They arrange one-day or longer trips to places of interest with guides speaking some English; package tours cost up to US$180 for three days when booked in Lima; it is cheaper to book tours in Iquitos, about US$40 per day. Launches for river trips can be hired by the hour or day (prices are negotiable, about US$10-15 per hour); many tour operators are located on Jirón Putumayo near the Plaza de Armas. *Explorama Tours* (rec. as the most efficient), Putumayo 150 (Box 446, Telex 91014, T 51-94-235471, Fax 51-94-234968; in USA, Selective Hotel Reservations, T 800-223-6764, MA (617) 581-0844), has three sites: *Explorama Inn*, 40 km. (1½ hrs.) from Iquitos, hot water, comfortable bungalows in a jungle setting, good food, attractive walks, rec. jungle experience for those who want their creature comforts, US$115 for 2 nights, 1 day, US$50 for additional night (1-2 people); *Explorama Lodge* at Yanamono, 60 km. from Iquitos, US$210 for 2 days/1 night and US$60 for each additional day; *Explornapo Camp* at Llachapa, 140 km. from Iquitos (better for seeing fauna), US$1,000 for 1 person, 5 nights/4 days, US$80 extra night (all prices include transfers, advance reservations, etc., local rates much lower). *Queens Tours*, Arica 297, 4-day trips to Amazon River camp and to Indian village, (guides don't speak much), interesting; good for flights. *Amazon Lodge Safaris*, Putumayo 165, owns the *Amazon Lodge*, clean, excellent food; special tours for fishermen, also a smaller lodge for the more adventurous. *Paseos Amazónicos Ambassador*, Putumayo 124, operates the *Amazon Sinchicuy Lodge*; they also organize visits to Lake Quistacocha and the zoo; *Jungle Amazon Inn*, about 10 km. further downstream from the *Amazon Lodge*, tour operators on ground floor of Eiffel-built house on corner of Plaza de Armas with Putumayo. *Lima Tours* offers 3 day, 2 night tours to Iquitos and the Amazon from Lima for US$250 p.p., flight included. *Amazon River Tamshiyacu Lodge*, S.A., Putumayo 184 or Los Carolinas 121, Miraflores, Lima T 476919, ask for Lucho de Cossio who runs *Tamshiyacu Lodge*, small, friendly, highly rec., swimming, jungle walks, night-time canoe rides, the guide, Antonio is very good, 1-day excursion, with lunch at the *Lodge*, US$19, 5 hrs in all; their trips include the Yarapa River Inn, Tambo Inn and wilderness expeditions; tourists are met at the airport by Sr. Pedro Alava with information. A new ornithological garden is opening at Tamshiyacu Lodge, entrance US$5. *Amazonia Expeditions*, Putumayo 139 (Carlos Grández), owns Yarapa river camp near confluence of Marañón and Ucayali 140 km. from Iquitos, warmly rec., experienced guides, strong conservationist inclinations, reductions in low season (make sure sufficient food is provided, but take your own fruit, chocolate and insect repellent). *Amazon Selva Tours*, Putumayo 133, highly rec.; they use *Selva Lodge* on Río Momón, and *Yarapa Lodge*, excellent food and able guides, *Amazon Camp Tourist Service*, Putumayo 196, or 1013 S Central Ave., Glendale, CA 91204, T (818) 246-4816, (800) 423-2791 (outside CA), P.O. Box 39583, Los Angeles, CA 90039, Fax (818) 246-9909, Lodge itineraries to 42-room *Amazon Camp*, or 20-bungalow *Camp Amazonia*, cruises on M/V *Arca*, 2 days/1 night at *Amazon Camp* US$65 p.p., at *Club Amazonia* US$92, cruises start at US$295 single for 3 days, longer stays/cruises available. For those who are tough, Freddie of Amazon Adventure Tours, Sgto. Lores 220, T 235151, organizes survival courses in the jungle and you learn to build your own camp, find your own food etc. Be warned, however: he has to approve of you and your level of fitness and stamina, not you of him. He speaks fluent English (US$400 for 3 for 5 days; longer would be better). *Amazon Village* was opened in 1981; tours there are operated by Exprinter; for details contact Amazon Village, c/o Amazon Hotel Iquitos, Miguel Dasso 167A, San Isidro, Lima, T 404-559. It is located on the Río Momón, some hours away from the Amazon itself, so difficult river conditions can easily prevent visits to the Amazon. At the Village there are clean, well-ventilated bungalows and good food. *Amazon botanical Gardens*, 56 km. from Iquitos on the Amazon (PO Box 105, Jirón Tacna 516, Iquitos, Telex 91003/91002 PBPE IQT, or 4301 Main St., Suite 14, PO Box 10025, Kansas City, Mo. 64111, T 816-931-2840), 3 days, 2 nights, US$175 (or less if more than 1 person), longer stays available. Arturo Díaz Ruiz, Sargento Lores 240 (registered guide no. 036) specializes in botanical tours; he is an experienced guide.

It is advisable to take a waterproof coat and shoes or light boots on such trips, and a good torch, as well as *espirales* to ward off the mosquitoes at night—they can be bought from drugstores in Iquitos. The dry season is from July to September and September is the best month to see flowers and butterflies. A recommended tour with a difference is the jungle survival excursion of Moisés Torres Viena, *Expediciones Jungle Amazónica*, Soledad 718—as taught to Peruvian soldiers—not cheap, but you will learn much about jungle botany and how to live off the plants; all the guides used are good, but the pace can be quite quick. Launches may do cruises to Leticia (Amazon Lodge Safaris have a 6-day trip to Leticia on the m/n *Adolfo*).

Excursions To the beach at Nanay, white sand, and small boats for hire to see the meeting of the Nanay and Amazon rivers; bus from Jr. Próspero US$0.10, boat US$0.20. By bus to the village of Santo Tomás, about 20 km., a favourite week-end retreat of inhabitants of Iquitos; the village has a good restaurant and canoes may be hired. Launches also leave Iquitos for the village of Indiana; get off at the "Varadero de Mazán" and walk through the banana plantations to the River Mazán. A trail leads from the village of Mazán through the jungle to Indiana (hotel), about a 2-hr. walk (steamy). Catch the launch back to Iquitos at 1300.

Naturalists should note that the area 50 km. around Iquitos is too inhabited to support much large wildlife; the Napo or Ucayali rivers have more to offer. Similarly the areas around the Lodges; however there is plenty of scope for seeing small fauna and learning about the flora. Trips to see Yagua Indians offer little but a chance to see "a way of life which is not so much in transition as abandoned." (John C. O'Conor, Arlington, Va.)

Air International airport, Francisco Secada Vigneta, T 231501, 233094. Taxi to the airport costs US$2.50 (US$5 at night); *motocarro* (motorcycle with 2 seats), US$1.50; bus, US$0.15, goes to market area, about 12 blocks from Plaza de Armas, taxi from there US$1.50. Automatic 60-day visa given on arrival on international flights. Airport tax on international flights, US$10, plus US$5 security tax and US$2 municipal tax (these two must be paid on local flights). Faucett (Próspero 630, T 239195) and AeroPerú (Próspero 248, T 231454) between them have two daily jet flights to Lima, both Faucett flights direct, one of AeroPerú's via Pucallpa or Tarapoto on alternating days, plus via Yurimaguas and Trujillo on Thur. and Sun. Fare to Lima, US$83. Iquitos-Cuzco via Lima only, No flights Iquitos-Ecuador. Faucett flies Sat. to Miami. TANS offices: Grupo 42 (for Brazil, Colombia), Sargento Lores 127, T 233512; Grupo 8 (for Lima US$35, Trujillo US$30, Yurimaguas and Tarapoto US$19), Castilla 353, nr Plaza Sargento Lores; these flights are less than the cost of the commercial flights. TANS also has a flight to Cabo Pantoja and other villages. TANS to Leticia (Tabatinga), but often booked up 2 months ahead for the aquaplane. Varig/Cruzeiro has two weekly flights on Sat., at 1100, between Iquitos, Leticia (Tabatinga airport) and Manaus. Varig/Cruzeiro office, Arica 273, T 234381; fare to Tabatinga US$92 inc. tax, you have to disembark at Tabatinga, pay US$1 tax in cruzeiros, check luggage (which comes off the plane and goes on again), get a new boarding pass and luggage tickets, and then fight for a seat. It is also possible to fly from Tefé (Brazil—**see page** 451) to Iquitos, stopping at Tabatinga for border formalities. (Mark your luggage "Iquitos" or it will be unloaded at Tabatinga.) Iquitos flights frequently delayed. (Be sure to reconfirm your flight in Iquitos, as they are often overbooked.) Peruvian Air Force flies Pucallpa-Iquitos, US$20, but unreliable as seats in that plane may be requisitioned at short notice, and Iquitos-Leticia, US$12. The Air Force also flies to Andoas, an oil town in the jungle, on the river Pastaza. TANS hydroplane flies NNW along the river to Peneya, opposite Leguizamo in Colombia, or Gueppi, the military frontier post from where you can get to Puerto Asís (Colombia) by boat. On this flight, locals take precedence.

Aircraft for Hire Ask at airport; normal rate US$300 an hour for plane taking 5.

Shipping Upstream. River boats to Pucallpa (2 boats a week in rainy season) or Yurimaguas, at least 4 days (longer if cargo is being carried, which is usually the case), cheap, but beware of overcharging gringos; fastest boat to Yurimaguas is *Jasmin*, 4 days or so. Information on boats for Pucallpa obtained on wharves, or at Meneses (Jirón Próspero), Bellavista (Malecón Tarapacá 596), Hurtado (Av. Grau 1223) and Casa Pinto (Sargento Lores 164). Cabins are 4 berth and you have to buy both a first class ticket, which entitles you to food (whether you want it or not) and deck space to sling your hammock, and a cabin ticket if you want the "luxury" of a berth. Adequate washing and toilet facilities, but the food is rice, meat and beans (and whatever can be picked up en route) cooked in river water. Stock up on fruit and tinned food in Iquitos. There is a good cheap bar. Take plenty of prophylactic enteritis tablets; many contract dysentery on the trip. Also take insect repellant; one sold locally, called Black Flag, is not effective. *Campeón* to Pucallpa, US$30 with food, 7 days; *Rosa* to Pucallpa, US$19, 7 days.

Downstream. Communications with Manaus by river are unreliable and the journey takes about 15 days (two boats doing this journey are *Clivia*, frequent, good food, and *Almirante Monteiro*, clean, reasonable food). The Hertzog boat, *Juliana*, is the most beautiful; friendly captain, US$15 to Islandia. Best go first to Leticia, or Islandia, opposite Tabatinga; Islandia itself is just a mud bank with an exchange shop on the Peruvian side of a narrow creek just a few yards from Benjamin Constant in Brazil. No boats from Iquitos go to Benjamin Constant, but all boats for Manaus start from there and a new hotel (*Benjamin*) has been built. Boats Iquitos-Islandia 36 hrs. (2 days in other direction), about US$10, inc. food, US$2 extra for cabin. On all boats, hang your hammock away from lightbulbs (they aren't switched off at night and attract all sorts of strange insects) and away from the engines, which usually emit noxious fumes.

If a long wait is involved, then Leticia (Colombia) has the best hotels and facilities. Weekly luxury 54-passenger boat, *Río Amazonas*, plies between Iquitos and Leticia, leaves Wed., operated by Amazon Camp, Putumayo 196, Iquitos, T 233931, US$400, US$250 without facilities, for 4 days. Canoes put out from Leticia and will take off passengers from passing boats at another mud bank called Puerto Ancorade, just opposite. There are also ferries from Benjamin Constant to Tabatinga and Leticia, US$0.50, 1½ hrs. The *Huallaga* is highly recommended for river journeys to Leticia or Pucallpa. It is easy to find a boat, but difficult to get it to move, though you can stay on board. Details on exit and entry formalities seem to change frequently, so when leaving Peru, check in Iquitos first (Immigration, Arica 477, office hours 0900-1300); latest indications are that exit stamps are given only at Puerto Alegría, not by the Peruvian Consulate in Leticia (0830-1430—the consul is elusive), while tourist cards for entry into Peru are given at Puerto Alegría, 2 hrs. upstream from Islandia, where the boat stops for police checks. Brazilian entry formalities are in Tabatinga, in town, 2 km. from the pier, or at the airport (taxis from riverfront to airport tend to overcharge). Boats to and across frontiers carry many smugglers and thieves.

THE INCA ROAD

We have had great pleasure since 1979 in incorporating an account by Christopher Portway, the explorer and author, of the Andean Inca road. His most interesting book Journey along the Spine of the Andes (Oxford Illustrated Press) was published in 1984. In view of space constraints, we have therefore shortened his account here.

Basically, there were two great roads in the Inca system. One was the royal road between Cuzco and Quito, progressively extended to take in northern Ecuador, southern Colombia, and southwards, Bolivia and northern Argentina. A mind-boggling 5,230 km. in length, its remains have been best preserved (more through remoteness than any preserving agency) in Peru. Much of the 4,050 km. of the coastal road between Tumbes and the River Maule in Chile has been built over by the Pan-American Highway.

The standard width of the royal road varied between 5 and 6 metres (as against the 8 metres of the less-obstructed coastal road). It was unpaved, except where there was unavoidable water or when climbing steep hillsides necessitating the use of stone steps.

A good section, bordered by stone, may be seen some 13 km. east of the village of Shelby, served by the railway from La Oroya to Cerro de Pasco. Its course is marked by the lonely ruins of Bonbón, an Inca community centre only recently identified, which in turn lies close to the modern dam holding back the Mantaro River as it flows out of the northern end of Lake Junín.

But perhaps the most astounding survival of Inca roads is the long stretch, displaying varied construction over differing terrain, between Yanahuanca and Wari (see page 979).

Yanahuanca is situated in the incredibly beautiful valley of the same name. It is rarely entered by foreigners and thus a visitor has to contend with a retinue of a hundred or more curious inhabitants in his passage through the village. Its amenities include a few bars, a simple restaurant and a community social centre, but no hotel.

Two km. up the Yanahuanca Valley a lesser valley cuts northwards between the towering crags. The road, its paving uneven and disturbed by countless horse and donkey convoys, leads up the smaller valley, its course sometimes shared by a stream, to the village of Huarautambo, a community of some 220 people, about 4 km. distant.

This village is surrounded by many pre-Inca remains and the schoolmaster, Sr. Valentín Inga Castro, will be only too happy to show visitors the many ruins of the area, as well as the cave-tomb full of deformed skulls only recently discovered by him, a crop of cave paintings and numerous underground chambers.

For more than 150 km. the *Camino Incaico* is not only in almost continuous existence from the Yanahuanca Valley but is actually shown on the map issued by the Instituto Geográfico Militar. From Huarautambo, in company with lesser tracks, it winds up the head of the Huarautambo valley and across rock-scattered grasslands, over escarpments, following valleys, then veering away to utilize more valleys hidden by saddles over which the road triumphs even if the weary 20th-century traveller wilts along the way. At a spot known locally as Incapoyo, superb views of the Cordillera Huayhuash, with peaks soaring to 6,000 metres and more, are to be seen.

While the road fades from sight or has become muddled with present day tracks the route is marked by the ruins of *tampus*—or Inca rest houses—and, occasionally, larger sites. *Tampus* were official and utilitarian. Some of them consisted of a single structure, others had a series of smaller rooms opening on a large corral where the llamas were stabled. Each was maintained by the local *ayllu* as part of its labour tax.

Between Yanahuanca and Wari pre-Inca *tampus* and other remains provide landmarks for the road. Thereafter traces of the road become fainter though short sections can be identified in the hills behind **San Luis, Piscobamba and Pomabamba**. Behind Pomabamba, far up upon the final crest of the mountains to the west, the road is revealed by a chain of old forts older than the highway itself, but it is left to such disintegrating edifices to mark the route to Cajamarca and northwards into Ecuador.

Townships and villages along the way include the following: *Tamboccocha* and *Gashapampa*: One single shop with little to offer enlivens these two remote villages. *Pilcocancha*: A few km. north of the township of Baños, notable only for its hot thermal pools lying a kilometre south. *La Unión* (see also page 989): A "double town" with its main residential section across the River Vizcarra in the sheer-sided valley of the same name. Several small hotels, simple but adequate at about US$1 per night but no hot water, a farce of a cinema and half a dozen restaurants. On the grass plateau above the town are the spectacular ruins of *Huánuco Viejo* (see page 989). *Pomachaca*: A small village with a couple of shops at a road and river junction. The roads lead to Wari (*Hotel Ideal*, F), San Marcos and Llamellín. *San Luis*: A village in the shadow of the Cordillera Blanca. A few small restaurants and an occasional bus service to Piscobamba, with a basic, but clean hotel with friendly owner, and another, both F, and a few shops and small restaurants.

The staff of the mayor's office are helpful and from behind the town views across the valley are superb. Occasional buses to *Pomabamba* (see page 884), a pleasant enough town. On both sides of the valley in which Pomabamba stands are pre-Inca ruins of considerable interest. *Sihuas*: A small township clinging to a hilltop. No hotel, but a couple of restaurants. *Huamachuco* (page 900). *Cajabamba* (see page 901), lively little town with a hotel or two and a number of restaurants (not to be confused with the Ecuadorean town of the same name). *Ichocán*: Pleasant village with an interesting church and a few small restaurants. The council do not object to overnight camping in the plaza with its fountain and trees. *San Marcos*: Lively little town with a hotel or two. *Cajamarca* (page 901).

(**Warning** The Andean Inca road in the north of Peru passes through extremely remote mountain territory. Travellers are advised, therefore, to take full precautions against starvation and exposure. There is, apparently, some danger of attack by cattle rustlers and part of the area has been affected by guerrilla activity).

INFORMATION FOR VISITORS

Documents No visa is necessary for citizens of Western European countries, South American countries (except Chile and Venezuela), Canada, the USA and Japan. Australians and New Zealanders must have visas. A Tourist Card (*Cédula C*, obligatory) is obtained free from the immigration authorities on arrival in Peru for visits up to 90 days (insist on getting the full 90 days, at some borders cards valid for 60, or even only 30 days have been given). It is in duplicate, the original given up on arrival and the copy on departure, and may be renewed (see below). A new tourist card must be obtained for each re-entry or when an extension is given. An International Certificate of Vaccination against smallpox is no longer required. Declaration of foreign currency no longer required. All foreigners should be able to produce on demand some recognizable means of identification, preferably a passport. You must present your passport when reserving tickets for internal, as well as, international travel. Officially, an exit ticket is required for entry into Peru to be allowed. At land frontiers, practices vary; an MCO may not be accepted as an onward ticket. One's best bet is a bus ticket Arequipa-Arica (Tepsa, valid for 6 months, sold as an onward ticket at the Ecuadorean border even though Tepsa have discontinued the route, and more expensive than Arequipa-Tacna, Tacna-Arica bus journeys) which may then be exchanged with persistence. Many travellers have reported that they have not been asked for a ticket at Aguas Verdes, Yunguyo or Desaguadero. If you do not have one on arrival at the border, you may be forced to pay US$15 minimum for an out-going bus ticket. Travellers arriving by air report no onward flight checks at Lima airport.

N.B. Tourist visas may be renewed for 60 days at the Ministerio del Interior, Paseo de la República at Av. 28 de Julio, Lima (also, we are told, in PIP offices in certain towns: check). On presentation of the visitor's passport, a valid return ticket to a destination outside Peru, a *solicitud* (written request for an extension) and on payment of US$20 or the equivalent in intis. If you wish to extend your entry permit after 90 days have already elapsed since your entry into Peru this is possible at the discretion of the authorities, but on payment of a fine of US$20. The maximum stay in such a case would be 150 days from the first entry. If you are in the Puno area when your visa expires, it is sometimes quicker and easier to cross the border to Bolivia for a day and return with a new visa, often for 90 days, which you would not get in Lima or Cuzco. To obtain a one-year student visa one must have: proof of adequate funds, affiliation to a Peruvian body, a letter of recommendation from your own and a Peruvian Consul, a letter of moral and economic guarantee from a Peruvian citizen and 4 photographs (frontal and profile). One must also have a health check certificate which takes 4 weeks to get and costs US$10. If your tourist card is stolen or lost, apply for a new one at Dirección General de Migración, Av. 28 de Julio 1118; very helpful.

Students are advised to take an international student's card in order to benefit from the student reductions available, especially in and around Cuzco (not as many student concessions are available as there used to be). To be any use in Peru, it must bear the owner's photograph. You can sometimes achieve benefits if "student" is on your tourist card as your occupation, but this can mean hours of haggling.

Export Ban No object of archaeological interest may be taken out of Peru.

Taxes There is a US$15 airport tax on international flight departures, payable in dollars (unless you have an Aeroflot ticket). There is a 21% tax on economy international flights originating in Peru. For non-Peruvians, there is a security tax of US$5 and an airport tax of US$2 on domestic flights (if you are working in Peru, carry a letter stating this and insist you are "residente" and pay local tax of US$0.20). Tax should not be charged on an MCO, but 9% often is.

Air Services from Europe   Direct flights from Frankfurt (Lufthansa), Paris (Air France), Amsterdam (KLM), and Madrid (Iberia). Cheap flights from London; one way is to go via Madrid with Iberia, or standby to Miami, then fly with Eastern/American, Ecuatoriana or AeroPerú to Lima, or Faucett to Iquitos and Lima. Setours, Jr. Unión 1011, Lima has cheap flights to Brussels fortnightly. Sobelair, the charter subsidiary of Sabena, has flights leaving Brussels Sun., 16 hrs., stopover of 1 hr. in Martinique, return Mon. Tickets available throughout West Germany, France, Belgium and Holland. Aeroflot fly to Peru from Moscow via Shannon and Havana, or via Luxembourg and Havana; the flight can be joined either in Moscow, or in Shannon or Luxembourg, but it is *vital* to check that these services are in operation when you want to travel. To avoid paying Peru's 21% tax on international air tickets, take your used outward ticket with you when buying return passage.

From USA and Canada   Miami is the main gateway to Peru with flights every day with Eastern/American and AeroPerú, Third Avenue, Miami (T 800-255-7378), Ecuatoriana 3 times a week, and Faucett. Other direct flights from New York (Eastern/American, Lan Chile), Los Angeles (Aerolíneas Argentinas, Varig) and Toronto (CP Air). Faucett has an office in Toronto. Ecuatoriana from Los Angeles via Quito is more expensive than other carriers, but you don't have to go via Miami (if taking AeroPéru or Faucett), you get 2 free stopovers in Quito, or, if you don't want to spend time in Quito, a free night in the *Hotel Quito*, lunch and a microbus tour of the city. Regular connections can be made from many other North American cities. AeroPerú offers a bargain, US$759 (US$999 1st class) for a round South America air pass, Miami-Miami, 45 days, plus discount flights inside Peru; can be arranged in USA, T 305-591 9420, or 800-327 7080.

From South America   Regular flights to all South American countries; in most cases, daily. Lloyd Aéreo Boliviano (LAB) is usually the cheapest airline for flights out of Lima but tickets bought in Peru are more expensive. LAB flies twice weekly between La Paz and Cuzco. Aerolíneas Argentinas and AeroPerú fly from Mexico. Beware of buying Viasa tickets in Peru, they often turn out to be forgeries. See above for AeroPerú's "Around South America" pass.

Trans-Pacific   Flights from Tokyo by Varig. From Australia and New Zealand to Tahiti by Air New Zealand, Qantas or UTA with a Lan-Chile connection to Lima via Santiago (stopover in Easter Island).

Trans-South Atlantic   From South Africa to Rio de Janeiro by South African Airlines or Varig, with immediate connections.

Duty-free Imports 400 cigarettes or 50 cigars or 500 grams of tobacco, 2 litres of alcoholic drinks, new articles for personal use or gifts up to value US$200.

Internal Air Services   link towns which are often far apart and can only be reached otherwise with difficulty. Virtually all the air traffic is in the hands of the Cía. de Aviación Faucett (who run bingo on board!) and AeroPerú. Tickets are not interchangeable between the two companies. See under Lima (page 874) for towns served, and above for taxes. Faucett offers cheap unlimited travel within Peru; the ticket costs £180 and is valid for 60 days. You must decide which places you want to go to in advance, but you don't have to go to all of them or fix the date in advance, and you must fly to Peru with Faucett and purchase the ticket outside South America. If you enter Peru with another carrier, a full airpass will in the mountains ask for the nearest mining or road construction camp. If you take your own car you are immediately a symbol of wealth and will be liable to have it broken into. Disadvantages of travelling in your own vehicle include the difficulties of getting insurance, theft, finding guarded parking lots, maintenance on appalling roads and nervous exhaustion, which may outweigh the advantages of mobility and independence.

Imported car spares available and cheaper than in neighbouring countries. Makes with well-established dealerships are easiest to obtain (e.g. Volvo, Peugeot, VW). VW Beetles, Toyota Coronas and Datsun Stanzas are assembled in Peru and therefore easier to get spares and service for. There is also a booming black market in motor parts involving both contraband and stolen parts. Must have international driving licence—especially with a number. If you don't have a number on your licence, improvise. (It has been reported that a UK driving licence is acceptable.)

The minimum age for renting a car is 25.

Note for Hitch-Hikers Hitch-hiking is difficult. Freight traffic has to stop at the police *garitas* outside each town and these are the best places to try (also, toll points, but these are further from towns). Drivers usually ask for money but don't always expect to get it. In mountain and jungle areas you usually have to pay drivers of lorries, vans and even private cars; ask the driver first how much he is going to charge, and then recheck with the locals (the Sierra Indians for whom it is normal method of travel). Private cars are very few and far between. Readers report that mining trucks are especially dirty to travel in, avoid if possible.

Taxis In most places taxi fares are fixed before the journey; therefore it is best to ask local advice on average charges before you bargain with taxi drivers. Taxis ordered at hotels are much more expensive than those hailed on the streets.

Railways There are passenger services on the following lines, which are often quicker and more comfortable than buses, though it is necessary to watch your belongings: Lima-La Oroya-Huancayo, La Oroya-Cerro de Pasco, Huancayo- Huancavelica, Arequipa-Juliaca-Puno, Puno-Juliaca-Cuzco, and Cuzco-Machu Picchu-Quillabamba. Details of services in the text. Good cheap meals are usually serviced on trains.

Walking Serious walkers are advised to get *Backpacking in Peru and Bolivia*, by Hilary Bradt which describes 3-5 day treks in the Cordilleras Blanca, Vilcabamba and Vilcanota (Cuzco region), and in the Cajamarca area. Also Jim Bartle's book: *Trails of the Cordilleras Blanca and Huayhuash of Perú*, Ed. Gráfica Pacific, Lima, 1980—out of print in 1990 (Jim Bartle has also published a series of excellent postcards of various peaks, sold in many bookshops in Lima). John Richter's *Yurak Yunka* can be obtained from the South American Explorers' Club or from *Lima 2000* bookshop, J. Bernal 271, Lima. Rob Rachowiecki's *Peru, a Travel Survival Guide*, has been recommended most warmly. For Charles Brod, *Apus and Incas*, see Cuzco, **Tourist Office** section.

When trekking, please do not drop litter; if you have the inclination, pick up that left by others.

Hotels The State Tourist Hotels (commonly known as *Hoteles de Turistas*) are run by Enturperú. They vary considerably but frequently offer the best accommodation in town in terms of cleanliness and reliable food. They provide safe garaging for cars at US$0.65 a night. Reservations can be made at Enturperú, Av. Javier Prado-Oeste 1358, San Isidro, P.O. Box 4475, Lima, T 287815, 282742, 274077, Telex: 20394.

Heating in rooms is often unsatisfactory. Good local maps can usually be obtained at the Tourist Hotels; in some of the smaller towns they function as tourist offices. All de luxe, 1st class and State Tourist Hotels charge a high 25% in taxes, which includes service charges; lower category hotels charge 20-23%. Most hotels have this surcharge included in their prices, but best check first. By law all places that offer accommodation now have a plaque outside bearing the letters H (Hotel), Hs (Hostal), HR (Hotel Residencial) or P (Pensión) according to type. A hotel has 51 rooms or more, a hostal 50 or fewer; the categories do not describe quality or facilities. Many hotels have safe parking for motor cycles. Check all bills most carefully. Bargaining is possible outside the peak July-August holiday season; all hotels seem to be crowded at the end of July, independence celebrations. It should be noted, even in the upper categories, that in general hotel standards are low. Also reception areas may be misleading; it is a good idea to see the room before booking. When booking a hotel from an airport, or station by phone, always talk to the hotel yourself; do not let anyone do it for you (except an accredited hotel booking service). You will be told the hotel of your choice is full and be directed to a more expensive one.

Note The Peruvian police seem to be sensitive about finding an unmarried Peruvian woman in a foreigner's hotel room after 1900 hours. They will charge her with prostitution, however innocent your intentions. (Non-Peruvian unmarried couples will not be bothered by the police.)

Camping Easy in Peru, especially along the coast. But following a number of attacks in the Andes on campers, it is not wise to camp in lonely places. Camping gas in little blue bottles is available in Lima, see under **Camping** in that section. Those with stoves designed for lead-free gasoline should use *ron de quemar*, available from hardware shops (*ferreterías*). White gas is called *bencina*, also available from hardware stores.

Food The high-class hotels and restaurants serve international food and, on demand, some native dishes, but the taverns (*chicherías*) and the local restaurants (*picanterías*) supply the highly seasoned native food at its best. It is generally found that the modest cafés are best value. Soups tend to be very good, and a meal in themselves. In the Lima area the most popular fish dishes are the *cebiche*—raw fish, seasoned with lemons, onions and red peppers; the *escabeche*—fish with onions, hot green pepper, red peppers, prawns (*langostinos*), cumin, hard eggs, olives, and sprinkled with cheese; and *chupe de camarones*, a shrimp stew made with varying and somewhat surprising ingredients. *Parihuela* is a popular bouillabaisse which includes *yuyo de mar*, a tangy seaweed. *Yacu-chupe*, or green soup, has a basis of potato, with cheese, garlic, coriander leaves, parsley, peppers, eggs, onions, and mint. *Causa* and *carapulca* are two good potato dishes; *causa* is made with yellow potatoes, lemons, pepper, hard-boiled eggs, olives, lettuce, sweet cooked corn, sweet cooked potato, fresh cheese, and served with onion sauce. Favourite meat dishes are *ollucos con charque* (a kind of potato with dried meat), *caucau*, made with tripe, potatoes, peppers, and parsley and served with rice; *anticuchos*, hearts of beef with garlic, peppers, cumin seeds and vinegar; *estofado de carne*, a stew which often contains wine; *carne en adobo*, a cut and seasoned steak; *fritos*, fried pork, usually eaten in the morning; *sancochado*, meat and all kinds of vegetables stewed together and seasoned with ground garlic; *lomo a la huancaína*, beef with egg and cheese sauce; *lomo saltado* is a beef stew with onions, vinegar, ginger, chilli, tomatoes and fried potatoes, served with rice; and *sopa a la criolla* containing thin noodles, beef heart, bits of egg and vegetables and pleasantly spiced. Any dish described as *arequipeño* can be expected to be hot and spicy. *Mondonguito* is a boiled small intestine. The best beef is imported from Argentina and is expensive. Duck is excellent. For snacks, Peruvian *empanadas* are good. *Palta rellena* is avocado filled with chicken salad.

Among the desserts and confections is *cocada al horno*—coconut, with yolk of egg, sesame seed, wine and butter; *picarones*—frittered cassava flour and eggs fried in fat and served with honey; *mazamorra morada*—purple maize, sweet potato starch, lemons, various dried fruits, sticks of ground cinnamon and cloves and perfumed pepper; *manjar blanco*—milk, sugar and eggs; *maná*—an almond paste with eggs, vanilla and milk; *alfajores*—shortbread biscuit with *manjar blanco*, pineapple, peanuts, etc.; *pastelillos*— yucas with sweet potato, sugar and anise fried in fat and powdered with sugar and served hot; and *zango de pasas*, made with maize, syrup, raisins and sugar. *Turrón*, the Lima nougat, is worth trying. *Tejas* are sugar candies wrapped in wax paper; the pecan-flavoured ones are tastiest. The various Peruvian fruits are of good quality: they include bananas, the citrus fruits, pineapples, dates, avocados (*paltas*), eggfruit (*lúcuma*), the custard apple (*chirimoya*) which can be as big as your head, quince, *papaya*, mango, guava, the passion-fruit (*maracuyá*) and the soursop (*guanábana*).

The tea hour starts about 1800 at the good hotels. If asked to a party ask the hostess what time you are *really* expected unless the time is specified on the invitation card as *hora inglesa*—English time; Peruvians tend to ask guests for dinner at 2000, but don't expect them till at least 2130.

A normal lunch or dinner costs about US$4.50, but can go up to about US$25 in a first-class restaurant, with drinks and wine included. Lunch is the main meal: dinner in restaurants is normally about 1900 onwards. There are plenty of cheap and good restaurants around the centre of Lima and most offer a "business lunch" called *menú fijo* for no more than US$2 for a 3-course meal. There are many Chinese restaurants (*chifas*) in Peru which serve good food at reasonable prices. For really economically-minded people the *Comedores Nacionales* in most cities of Peru offer a standard 3-course meal for only US$0.50-0.75. Meals at this price, or little more, can be found under name of *menú económico* at many restaurants throughout Peru.

Drinks The usual international drinks with several very good local ones: *pisco*, a brandy made in the Ica valley, from which pisco sour is made; *chilcano*, a longer refreshing drink also made with *guinda*, a local cherry brandy; and *algarrobina*, a sweet cocktail made with the syrup from the bark of the carob tree, egg whites, milk, pisco and cinnamon. Wine is acidic and not very good, the best of a poor lot are the Ica wines Tacama and Ocucaje; both come in red, white and rosé, sweet and dry varieties. Tacama blancs de blancs and brut champagne have been recommended, also Gran Tinto Reserva Especial. Viña Santo Tomás, from Chincha, is reasonable and cheap. Casapalca is not recommended. Beer is best in lager and porter types, especially the Cuzco and Arequipa brands (lager) and Trujillo Malta (porter). In Lima only Cristal and Pilsener (not related to true Pilsen) are readily available, others have to be sought out. *Chicha de jora* is a maize beer, usually homemade and not easy to come by, refreshing but strong, and *chicha morada* is a soft drink made with purple maize. Coffee is often brought to the table in a small jug accompanied by a mug of hot water to which you add the coffee. If you want coffee with milk, a mug of milk is brought. There are many different kinds of herb tea: the commonest are *manzanilla* and *hierbaluisa*.

Tips Hotel 10% in addition to the 10% on the bill. Restaurants: medium to luxury class 5% in addition to bill which includes tax and 10% service unless otherwise stated. Taxi drivers, none (in fact, bargain the price down, then pay extra for good service if you get it). Cloakroom attendants and hairdressers (very high class only), US$0.50-$1. Railway porters, US$0.15 per bag, according to distance carried. Airport porters, US$0.50, or US$1 for 8 bags or more. Note: anyone who as much as touches your bag will expect a tip. Usherettes, none. Car wash boys, US$0.25, car "watch" boys, US$0.10.

Security The following notes reflect the many comments we have received on the need to take special precautions when travelling in Peru. This should not hide the fact that the most Peruvians, particularly outside those areas affected by crime or terrorism, are hospitable and helpful.

Thieves are active in markets, streets, hotels, buses and trains, choosing especially tourists as their targets. The most common method of attack is bag-slashing. Take care everywhere, but especially when arriving in or leaving from a town at night by bus or train; in fact, it is better to travel by day whenever possible. For general hints on avoiding crime, please see the **Security** section on page 18. All the suggestions given there are valid for Peru. Avoid staying in hotels too near to bus companies, as drivers who stay overnight are sometimes in league with thieves; avoid restaurants near bus terminals if you have all your luggage with you, it is hard to keep an eye on all your gear when eating. On trains, one large bag is easier to watch, and lock to a rack, than lots of small ones. If alone, try to avoid walking around in the cities with a big backpack; take a taxi (look on it as an insurance policy). The police presence in Lima, Arequipa, Puno and Cuzco has been greatly stepped up. It is a good idea to inform your Embassy in Lima of your passport data (or leave a photocopy), so that if the passsport is stolen delays for replacement are minimized. In general, common sense is the best policy. Keep yourself fully informed, before going and while travelling: seek advice from others at all times (fellow travellers, your consulate, The South American Explorers Club, who issue a pamphlet entitled "How Not to Get Robbed in Peru", Foptur, etc.). Outside the July-August peak holiday period, there is less tension, less risk of crime, and more friendliness. A friendly attitude on your part, smiling even when you've thwarted a thief's attempt, can help you out of trouble. In addition, do not be discourteous to officials.

Although certain illegal drugs are readily available anyone carrying any is almost automatically assumed to be a drug trafficker. If arrested on any charge the wait for trial in prison can take a year and is particularly unpleasant. Unfortunately, we have received reports of drug-planting, or mere accusation of drug-trafficking by the PIP on foreigners in Lima, with US$500 demanded for release. If you are asked by the narcotics police to go to the toilets to have your bags searched, insist on taking a witness. **Drugs use or purchase is punishable by up to 15 years' imprisonment**.

Tricks employed to get foreigners into trouble over drugs include slipping a packet of cocaine into the money you are exchanging, being invited to a party or somewhere involving a taxi ride, or simply being asked on the street if you want to buy cocaine. In all cases, a plain clothes "policeman" will discover the planted cocaine, in your money, at your feet in the taxi, and will ask to see your passport and money. He will then return them, minus a large part of your cash. Do not get into a taxi, do not show your money, and try not to be intimidated.

Another Warning The activities of the guerrilla movements, Sendero Luminoso and Túpac Amaru (MRTA), are spreading. Avoid visiting places where they are reported as particularly active: they have no love for foreign tourists. Since Sendero Luminoso has been linked (supposedly) with the drugs trade, police and army searches have increased. Under state of siege legislation, be careful what you photograph. If possible carry an official letter stating your business. At times provinces are under martial law: a curfew (*toque de queda*) may be imposed; remember to make enquiries about this when you arrive in a new place. In late 1989/early 1990, the following Departments were under state of emergency: Ancash, Apurímac, Ayacucho, Huancavelica, Huánuco, Junín, Pasco, San Martín and Ucayalí, also the provinces of Lima, Yauyos and Huarochiri in the Department of Lima, the province of Callao, the province of Contamaná in Loreto. Do not enter the slums of any major city, nor of the river valley towns on the coast. As a general rule, do not travel alone and, outside the main centres, go as a group if possible. When travelling on buses in the mountains, there is the likelihood of the transport being stopped, either by guerrillas or by *comités* of villagers who will ask for "donations"; do not refuse to give. For up-to-date information, contact the Tourist Police in Lima (T 714579), the South American Explorers Club (address in Lima and Quito, Ecuador sections), or your Embassy or Consulate. The Country Officer for Peru, Office of Andean Affairs, Dept. of State, Washington D.C. 20520, T 202-632-3360, will inform US citizens on the advisability of travel.

Police Action If your belongings are stolen: (1) If the value is over US$20, go to PIP International Police (ask for the *Extranjeria* section if you encounter difficulties, the *comandante* or his second-in-command), if under US$20 go to the Guardia Civil. Alternatively, in Lima, one can go to the Tourist Police. (2) Make declaration of loss as soon as possible. (3) Buy *papel sellado* (stamped paper) from Banco de la Nación on which to make statement. A small inducement, say US$1, may help them to speed up the documentation process. See also under Cuzco, **page** 958. If you are robbed on a journey and want to obtain a *denuncia* for insurance purposes and for clearance from the authorities if you have a new passport after the original has been stolen, say you were robbed when the bus or train was moving. If it was standing at a bus stop or station at the time the offence was committed, you will be sent back to that particular place to make the *denuncia*, and that might be very inconvenient.

A *denuncia*—a statement of a theft signed by police—is valid in place of a student card if student card is taken, and is essential for insurance purposes and for clearance from the authorities if you have a new passport after the original has been stolen. If your American Express credit card is stolen apply immediately to American Express in your own country, or to Lima Tours in Lima or Cuzco. For other credit cards, there is now a combined office in Lima, T 461545 (day and night service).

Health Drinking water from the tap is generally not safe in the cities of Peru, but bottled water is available everywhere. Ask for drinks "sin hielo" (without ice) as the ice is likely to be made with ordinary tap water. Salads washed in tap water should be treated with caution on arrival in the country, but once accustomed, you are not likely to get "Inca Quickstep" from salads. Food at better hotels and restaurants is fine, even salads, but watch out for the typical dishes seasoned with highly spiced Peruvian peppers. In cases of diarrhoea, take "Colitina", an effective local remedy. Another recommended anti-diahorrea remedy is Donafan F, available without prescription. There are frequent outbreaks of typhoid in Lima and in many other parts of Peru. Outbreaks of virus hepatitis occur and can be protected against by taking immunoglobulins; be careful when eating in markets. Be careful about buying gamma globulin in Peru as most pharmacists do not keep it under refrigeration, rendering it valueless. Buy a disposable syringe for US$0.25 to obviate risk of hepatitis from the clinic or doctor's needle. In Lima, there is a Centro de Antirabia if you are unfortunate enough to be bitten by a rabid dog; in other cities, hospitals give anti-rabies injections. Because of a TB epidemic, avoid non-pasteurized dairy products.

Altitude is often a problem in the mountain cities. Also, when walking at high altitude, the body needs sugar, which can be carried conveniently in the form of a block of crystallized pure cane sugar, called *chancaca*, and easily found in markets. Tonopan has been recommended for altitude sickness and headaches. (See also **Health Information** at front of book.)

Best Time to Visit The coast is at its most agreeable from December to April inclusive, but this is the period when most rain falls in the Sierra. Business is more active later, but climate does not interfere much with business. During the cooler months, June to November, there is little or no rain but Lima's humidity is from 90 to 98%—and there is little sunshine from Paramonga S to Arica. During this period the temperature rarely falls below 13°C, or rises above 27°C. For the high Sierra heavier clothing should be taken—difference between day and night temperatures is great. The jungles beyond are tropical.

N.B. Between mid-July and mid-September, a great many Europeans go to Peru on holiday (also, many young Peruvians are on holiday in July and the first half of August), so it is better to avoid the country at this time: prices rise, transport is difficult, and the Peruvians tend to be less friendly.

Hours of Business *Shops*: Jan. to March, 0900-1230 and 1600-1900 (0930-1245, 1615-1900 in Lima). Rest of year: 0900-1230, 1530-1900. Some are closed on Sat.; many close later in the evening. *Banks*: Jan. to March, 0830-1130. Rest of year: 0830-1200 (some have introduced afternoon opening). Closed Sat. **N.B.** All banks close on June 30 and December 31 for balancing; if it falls on Sat. or Sun., banks may close one day before or after. *Offices*: Jan. to March, 0830-1130, and 1500-1830. Rest of year: 0830-1230 and 1500-1830. Many now work a through day, 0800-1500, and most close on Sat. *Government Offices*: Jan. to March, 0930-1130, Sat. 0900-1130. Rest of year: 0930-1100, 1500-1700; on Sat. 0930-1130.

British business travellers are strongly advised to get "Hints to Exporters: Peru", from Export Services Division, Department of Trade, Sanctuary Buildings, Great Smith St., London SW1P 3DB.

Public Holidays 1 January: New Year. March or April: Maundy Thursday (pm). Good Friday. 1 May: Labour Day. 29 June: SS. Peter and Paul. 28, 29 July: Independence (when all prices go up). 30 August: S. Rosa de Lima. 8 October: Battle of Angamos. 1 November: All Saints. 8 December: Immaculate Conception. 25 December: Christmas.

N.B. Everything closes on New Year's Eve, Christmas Eve, and other holidays designated "family holidays", especially July-August. At these times, expect prices to rise.

Time Zone 5 hours behind GMT, except January to April, when GMT -4 (exact date of clock change varies annually).

Currency On 1 January, 1986, the sol was replaced by the inti, worth 1,000 soles, but people still think in terms of the sol, or of "libras" (pounds) worth 10 soles (used for amounts under 1,000 soles only). The inti is divided into 100 céntimos. No coins are in use. Notes are of 10, 50, 100, 500, 1,000, 5,000, 10,000, 50,000 and 100,000 intis (10,000 and 50,000 sol notes are still in circulation). It is difficult to change currencies other than US dollars, and Deutsche marks, and other currencies carry higher commission fees. The Banco de la Nación at Lima airport, and at large towns near the frontier, will repurchase intis from departing travellers if you can produce official exchange slips; you will not be able to buy dollars at the frontier itself.

Warning We have been informed that a large number of forged notes are in circulation; check the numbers if possible, and hold notes up to the light to inspect the blank white space for silhouette portrait. We have also been told that there is a shortage of change in museums, post offices, railway stations and even shops, while taxi drivers are notorious in this regard—one is simply told "no change".

Foreign Exchange All banks change foreign currency at the official rate. They close Sat., Sun., holidays, and 30 June and 31 December for balancing the books, except that the Jorge Chávez Airport branch is open 24 hrs. every day of the year. Always count your money in the presence of the cashier, particularly the "pre-counted" bundles of notes. It is possible to have US$ or DM sent from your home country. Take the cheque to the Banco de la Nación and ask for a *liquidación por canje de moneda extranjera*. You will be charged 1% commission in US$ or intis. The main hotels and other banks are now allowed to exchange foreign currencies; however, hotels usually only provide this service for their guests, and many commercial banks charge 4% -5% commission. The services of the Banco de Crédito have been repeatedly recommended. US dollars are the most useful currency (take some small bills), but Deutsche marks can be negotiated in all large towns. *Casas de cambio* exchange travellers' cheques for cash dollars, usually at 5% commission, and are the safest places for changing dollars into intis. For changing dollars cash, the street changers give the best rates, but they also employ many ruses to give you a bad deal (check your intis before handing over your dollars, check their calculators, etc., and don't change money in crowded areas). The parallel market rate, now formally illegal but very much alive, is used by street money changers in the main centres, although 10% commission (2-3% in Lima) may be charged on travellers' cheques. Where street changers congregate is usually near an office where the exchange "wholesaler" operates; he will probably be offering better rates than on the street.

American Express state that they will sell travellers' cheques and give out emergency money, but only in Lima. Travel agents are allowed to accept foreign currencies in payment for their services, and to exchange small amounts. Outside Lima, Arequipa and Cuzco changing travellers' cheques can be a long, slow process and a photocopy of your passport may be required. Travellers have reported great difficulty in cashing travellers' cheques in the jungle area, even Iquitos, and other remote areas. Always sign travellers' cheques in blue or black ink or ballpen. There may be shortages of cash for changing travellers' cheques.

Credit Cards Visa—most common—Diners Club, and Mastercharge (Access) widely accepted, including at State Tourist Hotels; billed, of course, at the disadvantageous official rate, plus an 8% commission. Visa is accepted at Banco de Crédito, at better rates than for travellers' cheques. Some shops only accept cards issued in Peru or South America, and we are told that in Puno it is virtually impossible to use any type of credit card.

Cost of Living Living costs in the Provinces are from 10 to 20% below those of Lima. Peru is not too expensive for those who want comfort and reasonable food; eat the set meals when possible; they are served more quickly. Hotel prices compare very favourably with those in other Latin American countries.

Tourist Prices In 1989, in response to declining tourist numbers, taxes on tourism were increased so that foreigners had to pay far more than Peruvians for internal flights, museums and archaeological sites. This unpopular move led visitors to boycott some places, for instance Machu Picchu. Only foreigners working in Peru, and in possession of a Green Card/work permit were able to get reductions in hotels, etc., and (with some brazenness) on flights.

The **metric system** of weights and measures is compulsory.

Electric Current 220 volts A.C., 60 cycles throughout the country, except Arequipa (50 cycles).

Mail Sending parcels abroad must be done at Centro de Clasificación de Correos, Tomás Valle, block 600, Lima (take bus 128, direction San Germán). Staff in the post office help with all checking and then sew parcels into sacks for US$1. To avoid paying a tax of US$0.20 per kg. on parcels sent abroad, take your passport and onward ticket, plus a photocopy of each to the post office. Try not to have articles sent by post to Peru; pilfering is very serious. Strikes are also very common. Letters to the UK and European countries, cost US$0.65, to USA and Canada cost US$0.60. Letters of under 10 grammes within South America cost US$0.25 airmail. For US$0.50 extra letters can be sent "con certificado", which is recommended. Parcel post to USA, up to 1 kg. only, US$15; to Europe up to 2 kg.; US$32; to Australia and Canada, up to ½ kg; US$8.

Telephones Overseas calls cost on average US$3 per minute. Collect calls can now be made to North America and Europe (but not Switzerland or Denmark) at the Entel offices, off the Plaza San Martín in Lima. Deposit for international calls is more in Cuzco than in Lima. Local calls from private phones are free within city limits. Public telephone boxes need a token (*ficha*, 300 soles/30 céntimos called a *Rin*), often in short supply (there are street vendors who sell them, as well as news kiosks). 5,000 inti tokens are available for international calls, they last about 40 seconds each. Telephone directories found in most hotel rooms have a useful map of Lima and show itineraries of the buses. Telex to UK: US$15 for 3 minutes.

The Press Lima has 8 morning papers: *La Prensa, El Comercio, La República* (liberal-left) *La Crónica, Expreso, Ojo, El Diario, La Actualidad* . There is a weekly paper in English, the *Lima Times*, and a monthly economic and political report, the *Andean Report*. The main provincial cities have at least one newspaper each.

Sports Association football is the most popular. Basketball and other sports are also played on the coast, particularly around Lima and Callao. Golf clubs and racecourses are mentioned in the text. Riding is a favourite recreation in the Sierra, where horses can be hired at reasonable rates. Cricket is played at the Lima Cricket Club. Bullfights and cockfights are held in Lima. There is excellent deep-sea fishing off Ancón, N of Lima, and at the small port of Cabo Blanco, N of Talara (see text). In that part of the Andes easily reached from La Oroya, the lakes and streams have been stocked with trout, and fly fishing is quite good.

For details about the best rainbow trout fishing in Peru (near Juliaca and in Lakes Arapa and Titicaca) write to Sr. José Bernal Paredes, Casilla 874, Arequipa.

Swimming Between December and April the entire coast of Peru offers good bathing, but during the rest of the year only the northern beaches near Tumbes provide pleasantly warm water.There are many bathing resorts near Lima (do not take more than is absolutely necessary to the beach).

Language Spanish. Quechua, the language of the Inca empire, has been given some official status; it is spoken by millions of Sierra Indians who have little or no knowledge of Spanish. Another important Indian language is Aymará, used in the area around Lake Titicaca.

Tourist Information The Fondo de Promoción Turística (Foptur), at Av. Andrés Reyes 320, San Isidro, Lima, T 70 0781, has offices in the main cities of tourist interest: details in text. See also information under Lima, **page** 871. A new book of photographs of Peru, published by Aston Publications, was released in May 1990.

For new information on Peru we should like to thank Daniel Morgan (Wellington, NZ), Petra Schepens (South American Explorers Club, Lima), James Vreeland (Indiana Tours, Chiclayo), and the following residents and travellers Franck Abadie (Megève, France) and Marianne

Joelius (Stockholm), Dean A. Alper (Mill Valley, CA), Mike Altfillisch (USA), Martin Anderle, Susanne Riller and Tilo Timmermann (Fürth, W. Ger.), Stan Anderton (Preston, Lancs.), Eberhard Baer (Koeningsbrunn, W. Ger.), Sue Bennett (Kendal), Rop Bomer and Wilhelmien ter Haar (Mexico DF), J.N. Bowden and K.E. Badgery (Plymouth), Sara Braune (Stroud), Rachel Bridgeman (Harpenden), Lucy Broadbent and Rick Palmer (Palmerston North, NZ), Remo Bulgheroni (Killroergen, Switz.), David M. Butler (Belmont, Victoria), Susan Carroll (Bearwood, W. Midlands), Lucinda Coates (North Ryde, NSW), W.J. Coppock (Ukiah, CA), Rev John Corrie (Lima) Peter Crozier (Oslo), G.G.A. Cumming (Viña del Mar), Karen Dahl (Hamden, Conn.), Jan Van Dalfsen and Tineke Puister (Neths.), Dr. Tony Daniels (Cambridge), Heinz Ullrich-David (Ahnsen, W. Ger.), Christian Delbrouck (Freiburg, W. Ger.), Arturo Díaz Ruiz (Iquitos), Bernard van den Doof (de Lier, Neth.), Peter Driesch (Essen 1), Frank Dux (Detmold 18, W. Ger.), Kate Edwards (Freeport, Grand Bahama), Dag K. Ellingsen (Oslo 2), Dr Dietz Evers (Krumesse), Thomas Fedrizzi (Horgen, Switz.), Elisabeth Fischer and Thomas Winter (München 40), Anat and Arnon Fishbain (Tel-Aviv), Alexandra Fisher (London W8), Bruce Fitzwater (Portland, OR), Olivier and Paloma Foro (St-Moritz), Sharon Franklet (Lima 18), Paul Friedemann (Jorsten, W. Ger.), Andreas Gabel (Mainz), Ursula Gaedke (Konstanz, W. Ger.), Jens Gjerlev (Bodøn, Norway), Rudolf Graf (Genthod, Switz.), Andrew Grassie and Sara Gilbert (Lewes), D. Graves (Brooklyn, NY), Tamar Grossman (Montreal), Jon and Julia Gruffydd (Lima) A.M. De Boer-Van Hamel (Amstelveen), Mrs R.M. Hampson (Nassau), Astrid Hansen (Aars) and Jane Harfeld (Hornsyld, Dnmk.), Ellen Hansen and Morten Volden (Saupstad, Norway), Gina B. Hardin (Guayaquil), Jim Hardy (Waukesha, Wis.), Roy and Joan Harris (Nanaimo, BC), Wayne Harvey (South Australia), Kevin Healey (Melbourne, Vic.), Dr Paul Heaton (London NW6), Claudia Heilmann (Heidelberg, 11), Judith and Stephen Adler Hellman (Toronto), Paul Heller (Monrovia, CA), Olav Holger Helø (Copenhagen), Prof Maria-Sophia Jürgens de Hermoza (Consul of Federal Republic of Germany, Cuzco), David W. Heumann (Los Angeles, CA), Rosemary Hobin (San Francisco, CA), Ursula Hochuli (Switz.) and Vincent Choblet (Paris), Robin Holloway and Fiona Butler (Birmingham), Susan Holze and Astrid Brombosch (Heidelberg), Jorge Hopff (Rio de Janeiro), Edward Hutt (Stowmarket), Jeff Inglis (Seattle), Anne Jawer (Rydal, PA), Simon Jeffreys (Peterborough), Ursula Jenny (Bottmingen, Switz.), Allan Jensen and Vibeke Nageh (Munke-Bjergby, Dnmk.), Warren L. Johns (Auckland S, NZ), Martin Jung (Tübingen), Tobias Kämpf (Rupperswil, Switz.), Mrs E.A. Kelly (Symington, Ayrshire), Rosi Kerler (München 40), Marcel Kersten (Roosendaal, Neth.), Thomas Krauss and Petra Fadi (Glasgow 12), Philip Krippendorff and Matthias Bertsch (Marburg), Daniel Küng (Wohlen, Switz.), Loren Lacelle (Willits, CA), Antony and Elisabeth Lancaster (Lima 18), Toby Lanzer (Santiago de Chile), Kerstin Leibold (Münster), John M. Leonard, Moti Levin (K Byalek, Israel), Udo Lichtenthäler (Berlin 21), Helena van Maanen (Velp, Neths.), Mika Määttänen (Tampere, Fin.), Adeline Machler (Quito), Nelly Matthey (Lausanne), Cindy Miller (Vancouver, BC), Valerie and Bob Mitchell (Cottesloe, Western Australia), Eva and Günter Moser (München 40), Matthias Müller (Berlin 31), David, Christine, Philip and Catherine Mylan (Worksop), Stanley Nall (Viña del Mar), O. C Nathan (Remuera, Auckland, NZ), Stephen Newcomer (Centrevill, Iowa), Mette Nordaw and Claus Jørgensen (Lyngby, Dnmk.), Jonas Noreús (Varberg, Swe.), Dave Nutting (Melbourne), Ruth Owen (Lima 4), Lucy Paine and William Petrie (Watlington, Oxon.), Mag Reinhilde Pellinger (Enns, Aust.), Sandrine Pétremand and Gilles Maitre (Bevaix, Switz.), Ian Powell (Stafford) and Judy Proctor (London), Louis Prefontaine (St Malo, Manitoba), Robert Jan Prenger and André Kuipers (Amsterdam), Johan Reinhard (La Paz), Jörg Retzluff (Aurich, W. Ger.), Alan Riddell (Edinburgh), Marvin and Patricia Rosen (New York), Thomas Roztocil and Marie Gomez (Geneva), Richard and Yvonne Ruming (Bathurst, NSW), J.J. Schat (Zoetermeer, Neths.), Kathrin Schildknecht and Jürg Schmutz (Bern, Switz.), Ueli Schlatter (Hemmental, Switz.), Andrea Schneiber (Herborn, W. Ger.), Isabelle and Heinz Scholl-Kalt (Zürich), Daniel Schweimler and Claudia Ricca (London E7), Eleanor Sepora (New Zealand), Vivienne Shave (Truro), Irene Singer and Leonel Lurua (Buenos Aires), Alba Dawn Smith (Chicago, IL), Bette Smith and James Amidon (Winter Park, CO), Bob Snyder (Norwich, Ontario), John Spraos (London NW11), Dietrich Stahl (Bridgewater, Nova Scotia), Hans and Ina Stoffregen (Celle, W. Ger.), Douglas C. Stone (Trujillo), Fredi Suter (Goldau) and Claudia Räber (Oberkirch, Switz.), The Loving Team (London), Martin and Susanna Theander (Malmö), Dr Hans Uhlendorff (Worms/Rhein), Maarten van Vlerken (Amsterdam), Adrian Wainer (Dublin 16), Mike Warren (Sutton, Sy.), Roland Weitkamp (Braunschweig, W. Ger.), Michael R. White (Birmingham, B14), Urs Wigger (Menznau, Switz.), S. Wimder (Copenhagen), Tim Woodward (Tottenham, N15), F. Worthington (Leicester), Irene A. Zappia (Tucson, Arizona), Helmut Zettl (Ebergassing, Austria) and Ulrich Zimmermann (Oberursel, W. Ger.).

URUGUAY

INTRODUCTION

URUGUAY (area 186,926 square km.) is the smallest Hispanic country in South America, about the same size as England and Wales together, but its population is less than that of Wales alone. The country's official name is República Oriental del Uruguay. It has Brazil to the north, the River Uruguay between it and Argentina to the west, and the wide estuary of the Plate to the south. The Atlantic Ocean washes its shores on the east.

Apart from a narrow plain which fringes most of the coast (but not near Montevideo), and an alluvial flood plain stretching N from Colonia to Fray Bentos, the general character of the land is undulating, with little forest except on the banks of its rivers and streams. The long grass slopes rise gently to far-off hills, but none of these is higher than 600 metres. The Río Negro, which rises in Brazil, crosses Uruguay from NE to SW, where it empties, amid dense forest, into the Uruguay River.

History The Spanish explorer, Juan Díaz de Solís, sailed up the River Plate in 1516 and landed E of the site of Montevideo, near what is now Maldonado. His second landing was in the present Department of Colonia, where he was killed by the Charrúa Indians. There was no gold or silver in Uruguay, and it was only after about 1580 that the Spaniards showed any interest in it. Military expeditions against the Indians were unsuccessful, but Jesuit and Franciscan missionaries, landing in 1624, founded a settlement on Vizcaíno Island. It is said that cattle were first introduced during an unsuccessful expedition by Hernando Arias in 1607; they were successfully established between 1611 and 1620.

By 1680, the Portuguese in Brazil had pushed S to the Plate and founded Colonia as a rival to Buenos Aires, on the opposite shore. It was the Portuguese who planned, but the Spaniards who actually founded, the city of Montevideo in 1726. It changed hands several times and was actually taken by the British in 1807, but after their failure to hold Buenos Aires, they withdrew altogether. In 1808 Montevideo declared its independence from Buenos Aires. In 1811, the Brazilians attacked from the N, but the local patriot, José Gervasio Artigas, rose in arms against them. In the early stages he had some of the Argentine provinces for allies, but soon declared the independence of Uruguay from both Brazil and Argentina. Buenos Aires invaded again in 1812 and was able to enter Montevideo in June 1814. In January the following year the Orientales (Uruguayans) defeated the Argentines at Guayabos and regained Montevideo. The Portuguese then occupied all territory south of the Río Negro except Montevideo and Colonia. The struggle continued from 1814 to 1820, but Artigas had to flee to Paraguay when Brazil took Montevideo in 1820. In 1825 General Juan Lavalleja, at the head of 33 patriots (the Treinta y Tres Orientales), crossed the river and returned to Uruguay, with Argentine aid, to harass the invaders. After the defeat of the Brazilians at Ituzaingó on February 20, 1827, Britain intervened, both Argentina and Brazil relinquished their claims on the country, and independence was finally achieved in 1828.

The early history of the republic was wretchedly confused by civil war between two rival presidents, José Fructuoso Rivera with his Colorados and Manuel Oribe with his Blancos; these are still the two main parties today. Oribe, in this ten years' war, was helped by the Argentine dictator, Juan Manuel de Rosas, and Montevideo was besieged. Rosas fell from power in 1852, but the contest between Colorados and Blancos still went on. A Colorado, Gen. Venancio Flores, helped by Brazil, became president, and, in 1865, Uruguay was dragged into the war of the Triple Alliance against the Paraguayan dictator, López. Flores was assassinated in 1868 three days after his term as President ended. The country, wracked by civil war, dictatorship and intrigue, only emerged from its long political turmoil in 1903, when another Colorado, a great but controversial man, José Batlle y Ordóñez, was elected president.

During Batlle y Ordóñez' two terms as president, 1903-07 and 1911-15, Uruguay became within a short space of time the only "welfare state" in Latin America. The state has not only nationalized the public services but also controls many industries, including cement and chemicals. Its workers' charter provides free medical service, old age and service pensions and unemployment pay. Divorce has been legal for many years; illegitimate children have status and the right to inherit, and the investigation of paternity is obligatory. Education is free and compulsory, capital punishment abolished, and the church disestablished.

However, as the country's former prosperity has ebbed away over the past three decades, the welfare state has become increasingly fictitious. In 1973 the military promised to reduce the massive bureaucracy, spend more on the poor and development, and generally get the country moving again after the social and political turmoil of 1968-1973. In practice they expanded state spending by raising military and security programmes. Real wages fell to less than half their 1968 level. Less than ten per cent of the unemployed received social security payments. Montevideo began to sprout a few small shanty towns, once unheard of in this relatively affluent corner of the hemisphere. One of the most egalitarian countries in Latin America has increasingly come to resemble the rest of the continent, as only the very wealthy benefited from the military regime's attempted neo-liberal economic policies. Nevertheless, the country's middle class remains very large, if impoverished, and the return to democracy in 1985 raised hopes that the deterioration in the social structure would be halted, if not reversed. Almost ten per cent of the population emigrated for economic or political reasons during the 1960s and 1970s: the unemployed continue to leave, but the political and artistic exiles have returned en masse.

Allying himself with the Armed Forces in 1973, the elected President, Juan M. Bordaberry, decreed the closure of Parliament, and stayed on to rule as the military's figurehead until 1976. Scheduled elections were cancelled in that year, and a serious wave of political and trade union repression instituted. Unable to convince the population to vote for a new authoritarian constitution in 1980, the military became increasingly anxious to hand back power to conservative politicians. However, moderate politicians refused to accept the harsh conditions the military continued to try and impose. Finally, in August 1984 agreement was reached on the legalization of most of the banned leftist parties and elections

URUGUAY

117

km

0   80   160   240

N

ARGENTINA

BRAZIL

Uruguaiana

R. Cuareim

Bella Unión

Quaraí

Artigas

Isla Cabellas

Termas del Arapey

Concordia

Salto

Santana do Livramento

Rivera

Bagé

To Pelotas

Tacuarembó

To Pelotas and Porto Alegre

Tres Arboles

Piedra Sola

4

Colón

Paysandú

Algorta

R. Negro

Melo

Río Branco

To RÍO GRANDE

Paso de los Toros

Rincón del Bonete

Blanquillo

CUCHILLA GRANDE

Gualeguaychú

Mercedes

6

Durazno

Treinta Y Tres

Dolores

Trinidad

San Miguel

La Coronilla

Chuy

Nueva Palmira

Carmelo

Cardona

Florida

3

2

Tigre

Colonia

Juan Lacaze

Rosario

Valdense

Colonia Suiza

San José

Canelones

Minas

San Carlos

Rocha

La Paloma

BUENOS AIRES

RIVER PLATE

5

1

MONTEVIDEO

Atlántida

La Floresta

Pdo. Cps.

Piriápolis

Punta del Este

Maldonado

ATLANTIC OCEAN

1 Montevideo.
2 East from Montevideo.
3 Montevideo North-East to Brazil.
4 Montevideo North to Brazil.
5 West from Montevideo.
6 Up the River Uruguay.

1 Plaza de la Independencia
2 Plaza Cagancha/ Bus Terminal.
3 Parque Battle Y Ordóñez.

MONTEVIDEO

Artigas

Camino Carrasco

CARRASCO

Flores

8 de Octubre

Av. Italia

Docks

18 de Julio

Rivera

Av.

Bvia. España

1

3

Is. Inglesas

Playa Honda

Punta Gorda

Is. Brava

Playa Buceo

Playa Pocitos

Carrasco

RIVER

Playa Ramírez

Ramírez

Punta Brava

PLATE

were held in November. The euphoria was spoiled by the fact that the strongest opponent of the regime was not allowed to stand. The new moderate government of Julio María Sanguinetti (of the Colorado party) was inaugurated in March 1985 for a five year term of office. The process of national reconstruction and healing of political wounds began with a widespread political amnesty (endorsed by referendum in April 1989), but no new radical economic policies. The moderate conservative Partido Nacional (Blancos) won November 1989 presidential and congressional elections with only 38% of the vote, thereby failing to secure a working majority in either house. President Luis Alberto Lacalle took office on 1 March 1990 and secured the support of the Colorados in return for four cabinet posts. The Blancos hold 39 seats in the 99-seat House of Representatives, compared with 30 for the Colorados, 21 for the left wing Frente Amplio and 9 for Nuevo Espacio. Frente Amplio holds the powerful post of mayor of Montevideo.

Settlement There was little Spanish settlement in the early years and, for a long time, cattle were responsible for the social structure of Uruguay. Groups of nomadic *gauchos* trailed after the herds, killing them for food and selling their hides only. Organized commerce began with the arrival of cattle buyers from Buenos Aires who found it profitable to hire herdsmen to look after cattle in defined areas around their headquarters. By about 1800 most of the land had been parcelled out into large *estancias*. The only commercial farming was around Montevideo, where small *chacras* grew vegetables, wheat and maize for the near-by town.

It was only after independence in 1828 that immigration began on any scale. Montevideo was then a small town of 20,000 inhabitants. Between 1836 and 1926 about 648,000 immigrants arrived in Uruguay, mostly from Italy and Spain, some into the towns, some to grow crops and vegetables round Montevideo. The native Uruguayans never took to agriculture: they remained pastoralists, leaving commercial farming to the immigrants. More recent immigrants, however, Jewish, Armenian, Lebanese and others have chosen to enter the retail trades, textiles and leather production rather than farming.

The Uruguayan People The population was 3.08m by mid-1988; just under half live in Greater Montevideo. Only some 15% are rural, and the drift to the towns is 1.6% per year. The natural population increase is low for Latin America: 0.7% per annum. So is infant mortality, 37.6 per thousand; the death rate is 10.2 per thousand. Uruguayans are virtually all European, mostly of Spanish and Italian stock. A small percentage in parts of Montevideo and near the Brazilian border are of mixed African and European descent. Possibly 10% are *mestizos*. About 96% are literate. Gdp per capita is US$2,400.

The Economy Although accounting for only 11% of gdp (less than either manufacturing or commerce and catering), agriculture is the dominant sector of the economy, as a supplier and a consumer. It employs 17% of the workforce. 90% of the land area is suitable for farming, and only about 3% of that is unused. With a black soil, rich in potash, producing grasses superior even to those in Argentina, over three-quarters of the land is given over to livestock rearing, the rest for crop production.

Uruguay used to be second only to Argentina as a meat and meat-product exporter, but in the early 1980s, the beef-cattle sector suffered from low world prices and high interest rates, with the result that much of the herd was slaughtered. Slaughtering, domestic consumption and exports all declined in the 1983-85 period, but picked up thereafter, exports particularly in response to increased Brazilian demand in 1986. The number of sheep rose in the 1980s, despite increased demand for exports of live and slaughtered animals. This reflects the lower prices for meat than for wool, of which Uruguay accounts for about 3% of total world production. Livestock and its manufactures contribute the major proportion of exports: in 1988, raw wool and manufactures' share was 25%, beef 10%, and hides and skins 7%. The only cereal exported is rice, accounting for 6% of the total. Others grown are maize and wheat. Also important are oilseeds (sunflower and linseed) and citrus fruits, of which oranges and tangerines are the main crops. The fishing industry expanded in the 1970s and 1980s, but catches and exports fluctuated.

Manufacturing, which contributes 24% to gdp and employs 23% of the workforce, is concerned largely with agroindustrial activities. The most important of these are meat packing, drinks, tobacco, textiles, clothing and footwear. There are also some medium-technology industries such as oil refining, plastics, rubber products, electrical appliances and motor vehicle assembly. Import substitution behind tariff barriers encouraged growth until the 1960s, to be followed by stagnation until more export-oriented policies were introduced in the late 1970s. Various factors contributed to mixed results in the 1980s, not the least of which were economic problems in Argentina and Brazil. Construction accounts for 3% of gdp and 6% of employment. In the late 1970s, it benefited from Argentine investment, which was curtailed as the Uruguayan peso appreciated against its Argentine counterpart. The financial sector's fortunes also fluctuate according to the economic health of Argentina and Brazil. Uruguay has been called the Switzerland of Latin America, and is the repository of much of the region's flight capital.

Uruguay has no major mining industry, apart from the extraction of marble and various construction materials. It also has no known reserves of oil or natural gas. Its coal deposits are of poor quality and are not suitable for commercial mining. Almost 100% of electricity generation comes from hydroelectric plants, of which there are four. The combined installed capacity of their 14 turbines is 1,890 MW.

Like many Latin American debtors, Uruguay became unable to service its debts normally in the 1980s and had to reschedule its loans to commercial bank and government creditors in the context of an IMF stabilization programme. IMF targets were successfully met and when the agreement expired in 1987, it was replaced by enhanced surveillance. By the late 1980s Uruguay's external position had strengthened and net new borrowing from multilateral and commercial creditors took place on a voluntary basis, raising total external debt from US$4bn in 1985 to US$6.6bn. in 1989. Nevertheless, debt servicing absorbed over half of all exports of goods and services and the Government requested a debt reduction agreement from commercial banks, supported by another IMF programme and structural adjustment loans from other multilateral and bilateral lenders.

Government Uruguay is a republic with a bicameral legislature: a Senate with 31 seats and a Chamber of Representatives with 99 seats. The president, who is head of state and of the government, holds office for 5 years.

MONTEVIDEO (1)

Montevideo, the capital and the only large city in the country, was founded in 1726. Population, in and near: 1,760,000 (1990). The original site on a promontory between the River Plate and an inner bay, though the fortifications have been destroyed, still retains a certain colonial atmosphere. The city not only dominates the country's commerce and culture—almost 90% of all the imports and exports pass through it—but is also a summer resort and the point of departure for a string of seaside resorts along the coastline to the E.

A major landmark, the Palacio Salvo on Plaza Independencia, has recently undergone exterior renovation which removed its formerly splendid art-nouveau mouldings. It is not open to visitors. On the same plaza, the Victoria Palace hotel has a rooftop restaurant with fine views. Otherwise, the best place to get a view of the city is from the top of city hall (La Intendencia); external glass elevators take you up to a viewing platform, where there is a pastry shop, and an expensive restaurant. Entrance at the back of the building on Soriano, between Ejido and Santiago de Chile.

Set between the old town (Ciudad Vieja) and the new is the grandest of Montevideo's squares, Plaza Independencia with the impressive black marble mausoleum of Artigas in the middle. On most sides it is surrounded by colonnades, and there are three pavement cafés at the eastern end. The other end has been spoiled by rebuilding, particularly to the N and S beside Government House. In 1986 the government of President Sanguinetti moved the executive offices to the Palacio Libertad far from the centre, which the Armed Forces had put up to house the Ministry of Defence. The old government house, known as the Palacio Estévez, is now used for ceremonial purposes only. The long unfinished modern block to the West was originally intended to be the Palace of Justice, then presidential offices, but its future use is in doubt. Just off the plaza to the West is the splendid Solís Theatre, a Museum of Natural History alongside. In the old town, a short distance west of Plaza Independencia, is the oldest square in Montevideo: the Plaza Constitución, also known as the Plaza Matriz. Here on one side is the Cathedral (1790-1804), with the town hall (1804-1810) opposite. Still further west along Calle Rincón is the small Plaza Zabala, with a monument to Zabala, founder of the city. N of this Plaza are four buildings well worth seeing: the Banco de la República (Cerrito y Solís), the Aduana (Rambla 25 de Agosto), and the houses of Generals Rivera (Rincón y Misiones, 1300-1900) and Lavalleja (around the corner in 25 de Mayo, Tues., Wed. and Fri. 1100-1900). Together, the latter two buildings form the National History Museum.

The Avenida 18 de Julio, whose pavements are always thronged, begins at the Palacio Salvo. Along this avenue is the Plaza del Entrevero (with a statue of a group of *gauchos* engaged in battle), between Julio Herrera and Río Negro, a very pleasant place to sit; and the Plaza Cagancha (or Plaza Libertad), with a statue of Liberty and the main tourist office. The Municipal Palace (Intendencia), with the viewing platform, is on the South side of Av. 18 de Julio, just before it bends N, at the statue of the local equivalent of a cowboy (*El Gaucho*). In front of the Municipality is a plaza with a copy of Michelangelo's David in one corner. The road which forks S from the *Gaucho* is Constituyente, and leads to the fashionable beachside community of Pocitos. There are two museums inside the Municipal Palace, entered around the corner in Ejido: Museum of Art History, and Museum of Precolombian and Colonial Art (1700-2100 except Mondays). The latter is the more interesting. Beyond is the University, and nearby are the National Library, the French *lycée*, and the Ministry of Health. The avenue ends at an intersection with Bulevar General Artigas. Here is an obelisk commemorating the makers of the 1830 Constitution, by José Luis Zorrilla de San Martín (born 1891), and here, too, one may enter the Parque Batlle y Ordóñez (see below). The immense Legislative Palace, built of local marble, is reached from Av. 18 de Julio along Av. del Libertador Brig. Gen. Juan Lavalleja (normally known as Av. Libertador, formerly Av. Agraciada), 5 blocks E of Plaza Independencia (buses 150, 173, 175 from Calle Mercedes). (N.B. Calle Ibicuy is now called Hector Gutiérrez Ruiz.)

At the western end of the bay is the Cerro, or hill, 118 metres high (from which Montevideo gets its name), with an old fort on the top, now a military museum (0800-1800, entry US$0.20) with arms, flags and drums. The Cerro is surrounded by the oldest lighthouse in the country (1804). Bus from centre to Cerro: 125 "Cerro" from Mercedes, and others. In the port (which one can visit on Sat.—see Tourist Office), opposite the Port Administrative Building, the ship's bell of HMS *Ajax* has been set up to commemorate the scuttling of the *Graf Spee*. The anchor of the *Graf Spee* was set up at the entrance to the port area in 1964 to commemorate the 25th anniversary of the battle; the wreck itself lies about 3 km. offshore, but is no longer visible as it was dismantled some years ago. However, plates from its bulkheads have been used in the construction of the city stadium. One can still see the *Graf Spee*'s supply ship, listing but still afloat (used in the past as a prison hulk).

Of the many parks, El Prado (about 5 km. from Av. 18 de Julio, along Av. Libertador) is the oldest. Among fine lawns, trees and lakes is a rose garden planted with 850 varieties; also in the Prado is La Diligencia (the stage coach). The

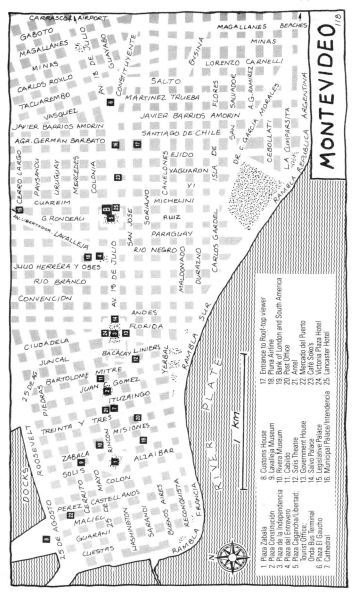

MONTEVIDEO

1. Plaza Zabala
2. Plaza Constitución
3. Plaza de la Independencia
4. Plaza del Entrevero
5. Plaza Cagancha/Libertad; Tourist Office; Onda Bus Terminal
6. Plaza El Gaucho
7. Cathedral

8. Customs House
9. Lavalleja Museum
10. Rivera Museum
11. Cabildo
12. Solís Theatre
13. Government House
14. Salvo Palace
15. Legislative Palace
16. Municipal Palace/Intendencia

17. Entrance to Roof-top viewer
18. Pluna Airline
19. Bank of London and South America
20. Post Office
21. Antel
22. Mercado del Puerto
23. Café Soko's
24. Victoria Plaza Hotel
25. Lancaster Hotel

RIVER PLATE

1 Km

two buildings of the Municipal Museums of Fine Art and History are in the grounds. During August, an annual farm show is held in the park. The largest and most popular park is Parque Rodó, on Rambla Presidente Wilson. Here are an open-air theatre, an amusement park, and a boating lake studded with islands. The National Museum of Fine Arts, with works by living artists, and a children's playground are at the eastern end. In Parque Batlle y Ordóñez (reached by a continuation eastwards of Av. 18 de Julio), are several statues: the most interesting group is the very well-known "La Carreta" monument, by José Belloni, showing three yoke of oxen drawing a waggon. In the grounds is the Estadio Centenario with a seating capacity of 70,000 and the main football pitch (Bus 177 from Av. 18 de Julio) but the 107 or 64 (a trolley-bus) are almost as convenient. There are a field for athletic sports and a bicycle race-track as well. The Zoological Gardens are a few blocks E of this park (open Wed.-Sun. until 2000); in the Gardens is a planetarium, one of the best in South America, displays Tues. 1730, Sat. and Sun. 1730 and 1830. Trolleybus 60 from Aduana (old city) passes the zoo gate. Entrance US$0.10. There is also a drive-in zoo in the Parque Lecoq, a few km. out of town on road to Colonia del Sacramento (entrance US$0.10 per car).

Festivals   Easter week is also Tourist Week (Fiesta Gaucha), with rodeo-type competitions held in the Parque El Prado (US$1.50 entry—bus 149 from Ejido in centre, or 183 from Pocitos) or Parque Roosevelt (horse-breaking and handicrafts), music (mostly folk). Large barbecues are held in the open air. Christmas Eve and New Year's Eve are celebrated with drummers and firecrackers in the streets. During carnival week and a few days after there are many live shows; especially recommended is the traditional *candombe* singing and dancing in the Barrio Sur in the centre (e.g. at *El Boliche* bar).

The Beaches (See inset map, page 1019) Nine sandy bathing beaches extend along almost the whole of the metropolitan water front, extending from Playa Ramírez in the W to Playa Carrasco at the eastern extension of the city. Along the whole waterfront runs the Rambla Naciones Unidas, named along its several stretches in honour of various nations. Bus 104 from Aduana, which goes along Av. 18 de Julio, gives a pleasant ride (further inland in winter) past Pocitos, Punta Gorda and all the beaches to Playa Miramar, beyond Carrasco. The express bus DI leaves from Plaza Matriz (Constitución) in front of the Cathedral and stops at special yellow bus stops; by using this service, which costs slightly more (US$0.40) about 30 minutes are saved on the journey time to Carrasco. The town beaches are reported still to be polluted, despite a major clean-up programme.

Among the main seaside residential areas are Pocitos, well supplied with hotels, restaurants and night-clubs (*boites*), with the reputation of being the "Copacabana" of Montevideo; and Carrasco, a delightful semi-rural place behind the beach of the same name at the end of the Rambla Sur, backed by a thick forest which has partly been turned into a national park. The international airport is nearby. E along the coast is a string of resorts, with much less polluted beaches, which are dealt with later in **East from Montevideo**.

Hotels   During the tourist season hotels should be booked in advance. At the beaches many hotels offer full board only during the season. After 1 April prices are greatly reduced and some hotel dining rooms shut down. For Carnival week, on the other hand, prices are raised by 20%. Many hotels increase prices at weekends, ask in advance.

Information on hotels from tourist office on Plaza Cagancha (Libertad), Cámara de la Industria Hotelera del Uruguay (CIHTU), Gutiérrez Ruiz 1217 (formerly Ibicuy), T 904287, and Centro de Hoteles y Restaurantes del Uruguay (Gutiérrez Ruiz 1213, T 900346, best for cheaper hotels). **Hint**: cheap hotel rooms in Uruguay are invariably gloomy. Bring your own 220V Edison-screw bulbs and hope they don't put too much strain on the wiring. When not included, breakfast usually costs US$1-$2. There is a 12% value-added tax on hotel bills.

Hostería del Lago, Arizona 9637, luxury, reported best in Montevideo area.

In the vicinity of the Onda bus terminal/Plaza Cagancha, and West towards Plaza Independencia are: **Internacional**, Colonia 823, A-L, rec. for business visits, however, no telex; **Victoria Plaza**, Plaza Independencia, A, a/c, excellent restaurant, friendly staff, faded old world charm which may be affected by development of large new extension, controlled by interests connected with Mr Moon's Unification Church; *Crillón*, Andes 1318, A, a/c, including breakfast, gloomy but clean; *London Palace*, Río Negro 1278, B, central, garage, parking. *Columbia Palace*, Rambla Rep. de Francia 473, T 960001, Fax 960192, B-A, first class accommodation with breakfast, restaurant, sauna.

Lancaster, C, a/c, incl. breakfast and bath, across plaza from bus terminal; *Oxford*, near Tourist Office, clean, good breakfast, C; *King's*, Andes 1491 casi Uruguay, N of Plaza Indpendencia, C with breakfast, rec.; *Alcalá*, Río Branco 1105, very clean and friendly, C (without bath); *Alvear*, Yí 1372, C, good service, friendly, rec. for business travellers.

Mediterráneo, Paraguay 1486, D with bath, family-run, clean, comfortable converted mansion; *Los Angeles*, Av. 18 de Julio 974, private bath, clean, old-style, friendly, rec., D (reductions for stays of over 3 days); *Aramaya*, Av. 18 de Julio 1103, E with bathroom, old, clean, comfortable; *Río de la Plata*, Av. 18 de Julio 937, E, clean, hot water; *Americana*, Av. 18 de Julio 1212, E with breakfast, rec.; *Balfer*, Cuareim 1328, one block off 18 de Julio, good, safe deposit, excellent breakfast. *Montevideo*, Yaguarón 1309, D, no breakfast but good rooms, rec., small garage.

Several on Uruguay: *Colonial*, 963, E; *Regencia*, 944, E; *Res Arapey*, 925, F.

Many on Soriano: *Hospedaje del Centro*, Soriano entre H Gutiérrez Ruiz y Paraguay, D with bath, clean, friendly, rec.; *Cervantes*, Soriano 868, plain but clean room with bath, C; *Nueva Pensión Ideal*, Soriano 1073, excellent washing facilities, friendly, no breakfast, E; *Royal*, Soriano, E, hot showers, clean, friendly; *Pensión del Este*, E, Guitiérrez Ruiz y Soriano, hot water, cold rooms, no clothes-washing allowed, nice cat, nosy dueña; *Libertad*, Gutiérrez Ruiz 1223, E, clean, quiet, laundry facilities and food available.

Cifre, E (10% discount on stays of over 2 weeks) Mercedes 1166, clean. *Claridge*, Mercedes 942, clean, friendly, E with bath, rec., undergoing renovation; *Casablanca*, San José 1039, friendly, E with bath; *Itá*, San José 1160, next to Onda terminal, E, clean and quiet; *Pensión Trinidad*, San José 1220, E, dark and not too clean, though friendly.

Several along Colonia, between Yí and Florida: *Ateneo*, Colonia 1147, clean, F with bath, friendly; *Windsor*, Michelini 1260, clean, pleasant, F with bath, rec.; *Hospedaje Diagonal 2*, Convención 1326 entre Av. 18 de Julio y San José, F, clean, friendly (not to be confused with *Diagonal 1*, Colonia 1168, which is red light).

Plenty of cheap hotels in and near the old city, e.g. *Lavalle*, Bartolomé Mitre 1314, T 962887, F, clean, basic; *Palacio*, Bartolomé Mitre 1364, T 963612, E, friendly, clean, safe, rec.; and *Matriz*, on Ituzaingó, E, clean and friendly, though run down. On Piedras are *Alojamiento Piedras*, No. 272, and *Pensión Universal*, No. 270, both E.

East of Plaza Cagancha: *Arosa*, Constituyente 1917, C, friendly, pleasant. *Parque*, Playa Ramírez, B inc. breakfast; *Ermitage*, Juan B Blanco 779-83, Playa Pocitos, B. At Carrasco: *Cottage*, B, friendly, no restaurant; *Casino Carrasco*, C with breakfast, good, "ancient splencour, reasonable service"; *Bristol*, B, built in 1926 in Louis XV style, must be seen, pleasant; *Oceania*, Mar Artico 1227, C, near airport (transport service), pleasant view, good restaurant and night club, highly rec. *Maracana*, Rambla Rep. de Chile 4667, Malvin Beach, E with bath single, clean, rec., take bus 60 from near Onda terminal.

Youth Hostel The headquarters of the Association are at Pablo de María 1583, 8th floor, T 404245, open 1300-1900 Mon.-Fri. Hostel (members only) is at Canelones 935, T 981324. US$1-2.30 p.p. according to season, probably the best bargain, friendly, clean, dormitory style, closed 1000-1700. Open all year.

Camping Parque Roosevelt, near Carrasco, about US$2 p.p., free, hot showers, safe, no electricity, 15 km. from centre, open all year, or superb camping in the wild can be had to the west of the Cerro on the flanks of the hill below the fort, amid pine trees. Also, Hugo A Morante has written to offer to rent a log cabin, 30 km out in the woods (T 989318/981107).

Restaurants The dinner hour is very late, from 2100 to 2400. (Less formal restaurants serve from 1930 onwards.) First-class restaurants at the centre are *El Aguila*, Buenos Aires 694, next to the Solís Theatre; *Morini*, Ciudadela 12-29, serves excellent steaks, simple but not cheap. *Bungalow Suizo*, Andes 1427, very good (about US$22 per head inc. wine), frequented by politicians and businessmen. *La Lutèce*, French, excellent, in Mercado del Puerto; *Panorámico*, 24th floor of Intendencia, pricey but worth it for the service and view. Don't miss eating at the Mercado del Puerto, opposite the Custom House, on Calle Piedras, between Maciel and Castellanas (take "Aduana" bus), grills cooked on huge charcoal grates (menus are limited to meat); colourful atmosphere and friendly; *Cabana Verónica* has been particularly rec. There are about a dozen grills open during market hrs. (though now the expanding numbers of grills and bars have largely replaced the market!); at night only *El Palenque* is open. Other good grill rooms (parrilladas) include *Las Tejas*, Av. Brasil, and *Nuevo García*, Calle Arocena, Carrasco. Also for lunch in the old city, *La Crêperie*, Bartolomé

Mitre, near Sarandí, in Mercado de Artesanatos, good unusual crêpes and salads, cheap.

In the central Plaza Cagancha/bus terminal district: *La Genovesa* (Spanish), San José 1242, excellent, reasonably priced; *Las Brasas*, San José 909, good typical food, moderate prices; *Viejo Sancho*, San José 1229, restaurant after 2000, excellent, popular, complimentary sherry or vermouth to early arrivals, tearoom by day; Italian restaurant at San José 1166, good; *El Fogón*, San José 1080. *El Gran César*, on Gutiérrez Ruiz, reasonable, rec. A good cheap place is restaurant on 6th floor of YMCA building, Colonia 1870, open for lunch and 1900-2200, US$2 (two courses) and plentiful with good views too; ask for the Asociación Cristiana de Jóvenes. *Cervecería La Pasiva* on Plaza Independencia, good, cheap; also *La Pasiva*, Ejido y 18 de Julio, rec. *Los Chivitos*, Río Branco y 18 de Julio, is a good cheap place to eat. *Gran Coco*, on Yí, offers a variety of good meat and vegetable dishes for about US$1.80; *Centro Residentes de Artigas*, San José 885, cheap, clean and friendly; *Antiquario*, Maldonado, atmospheric. In the Barrio Sur, *Bellini*, San Salvador y Minas, with piano music and singing.

Vegetarian: *Vegetariana*, Yí 1334, esq. Av. 18 de Julio, not very good, also San Juan 1056. *Kombi*, near Onda terminal, lunch Mon.-Fri., cheap, good.

Good cheap breakfasts at *Nuevo Metro*, San José 1200. A good place for lunch is the *Golf Club*, good food, excellent surroundings and grand view.

Many good restaurants on seafront in Pocitos, including *Doña Flor*, Blvd. España y Artigas, classy French restaurant, limited menu but superb, moves to Punta del Este in summer, US$25 p.p.; *Entrevero*, 21 de Setiembre, popular with Americans.

Tea Shops, known locally as *confiterías*. The most popular are along 18 de Julio, including *Latino, Facal, Manchester, Lusitano, Café del Rex, Lion D'Or, La Puerta del Sol*. Good ones are *Taberna Portofino*, Ituzaingó 1325, *Café Brazilero*, Ituzaingó 1477, founded 1877, closed Sun., and *Oro del Rhin* (0830-2100), Colonia y Convención (ex-Latorre), great cakes, rec. In Pocitos are *Cakes*, near Villa Beatriz (also in Carrasco), excellent; *Expresso Bar*, J.B. Blanco y Bulevard España, popular meeting place; *Virgilio's Café* at Punta Gorda on Rambla, good views, and many others. At Puerto Buceo Yacht Club, where tourists are allowed in.

Coctelerías Cocktails served with lots of side dishes: *Soko's*, 18 de Julio e Yí, also serves good food; *Bar Hispano*, Av. San José, excellent vermouths with 28 varieties of *hors d'oeuvres* and good food. *Payaso*, Galería Yaguarón, 18 de Julio; *Giorgio's*, Scocería and Rambla, Pocitos. Many others along the Rambla, with good sea views.

Heladerías Ice-cream parlours produce very good, unusual ice creams in the summer, and draw large crowds. Try *La Cigale*, on Scocería (Pocitos), on Ejido, or on Brandzen. *Las Delicias*, Carrasco, *Papitos*, at 18 de Julio 1054 or *Sorocabana*, Plaza Cayancha.

Shopping In general, Buenos Aires is better for shopping and business transactions. The main shopping area is Av. 18 de Julio, good for men's business suits. Suede and leather are not as cheap as in Buenos Aires, nor is quality as good; styling is more traditional; try *Casa Mario*, Piedras 641 (expensive); shops and workshops around Plaza Independencia may be a better bet. Amethysts and topazes are mined and polished in Uruguay and are good buys; see *Topaz International*, Victoria Plaza Hotel. For woollen wall hangings see *Manos del Uruguay*, which sells floor cushions, crafts, high quality woollen goods, etc. at Reconquista 616, and at San José 1111, and in the shopping centre in Carrasco near the Rambla. Other good craftwork (cheaper) in daily covered craft market on Plaza Cagancha, and Sat. a.m. craft fair in Villa Biarritz. The old city is said to be a good, cheap place to buy antiques. Antique shops on Plaza Independencia. On Sunday morning there is a large, crowded street market on Tristán Narvaja (good for silver and copper, and all sorts of collectibles) opposite Facultad de Derecho on 18 de Julio. Another flea market is held on Plaza Zabala, a couple of blocks behind the cathedral on Saturday mornings. On Sats. there is a market at Pocitos for fruit, leather and woollen handicrafts. Also in *Galería Diri*, 18 de Julio and Río Negro, which now has a branch in New York City. The Montevideo Shopping Center on the E edge of Pocitos (Herrera y Rivera) has wide range of shops including *Manos del Uruguay* as well as others selling leather goods (bus 141 or 142 from San José).

Cameras and Film Best place for developing films is *Photo Martin*, Av. Libertador and Uruguay; *Delucchi*, on Herrera y Obés, good for developing slides; *Foto Tecnifilm*, Av. 18 de Julio 1202, helpful, English spoken; camera repairs by *Fotocámara*, on Cuareim between Mercedes and Colonia. Film developing and equipment is quite expensive in Uruguay; better to bring film from abroad.

Bookshops English and American books: *Librería Barreiro y Ramos*, 25 de Mayo y J.C. Gómez; *Ibana*, International Book and News Agency, Convención (ex-Latorre) 1479, specializes in foreign publications. *Librería Ingleson*, Sarandí 580, specializes in language and children's books. Others include *Librería Mosca Hermanos*, Av. 18 de Julio 1578; *Feria del Libro*, Av. 18 de Julio 1308; *Paseo del Lector*, Av. 18 de Julio y Cuareim; *Librería Papacito*, Av. 18 de Julio 1415 and *Heritage Internacional*, Soriano 1610. There is a good one at Tristán Narvaja 1736. *Librería Oriente Occidente*, Cerrito 477 and *Librería El Aleph*, Bartolomé Mitre 1358, both sell used and rare books.

Taxis   US$0.30 for first 600 metres, and US$0.02 for each 140 metres afterwards; an additional 20% from midnight to 0600, charge for each hour of waiting, US$3.30. There is a small charge for each piece of luggage. Taxis can be hired, by agreement, by the hour within city limits.

City Transport   City and suburbs US$0.20 (at night it costs a third more). There are many buses to all parts from 18 de Julio; from other parts to the centre or old city, look for those marked "Aduana". For Pocitos from city centre take bus No. 121 from San José behind the Onda station.

Car Hire   without chauffeur, US$50 per 24 hrs., plus extra per kilometre if only hiring for the day; guarantee of US$100 required. Hire for 3-day weekend is US$130. The firms offering this are Hertz and National in Colonia, near Plaza Independencia, Avis at airport, American International Budget and Sudamcar, La Paz 1523, National Fill Service, Rambla Rep. del Perú 815, Esq. 813, self-drive hire is not recommended. With chauffeur, US$35 per 8-hr. day plus US$0.12 per kilometre, and payment for a chauffeur's lunch or supper. Rogelio Martinelli, Canelones 1450; Luis Moro e Hijos, Camino Ariel 4737; Empresa Salhon, Av. 8 de Octubre 4199; F. Miramonte, Magallanes 1446; ARI, 18 de Julio 2142; Hertz, Calle Colonia near Paza Independencia; National, nearby; Snappy, Andes 1363; and Avis.

Casinos   *Parque Hotel* at Playa Ramírez; *Hotel Carrasco* at Carrasco.

Discos   *People*, on Cuareim; *Eros*, on Boulevard Artigas. The best discotheques, called *boites*, are *Merek* and *Lancelot* in Carrasco (the former at lakeside, with swimming pool and chalet architecture, the latter a castle!); *Zum Zum* and *Privée* (Miguel Barreiro and Rambla) in Pocitos are good too. They admit couples only and have taped music, US$15 a couple, entrance included on 1st drinks. They are open until very late (2230-0500). Reservations are recommended on Sat. night. *Graffiti* is a cheap disco in Carrasco.

Night Clubs   The Bar and the Záfiro Room at the *Victoria Plaza* with Tropicana Show US$12 (incl. food), also *Lancaster Hotel*. The delights of the tango are available at *Tanguería del 40* at Hotel Columbia Palace or *La Cumparsita* in Calle Gardel (rec.). For music try *Cantores*, Gonzalo Ramírez 1417; there is a *peña* (folk-music show) at *El Templo del Sol*, Blvd. España 2109 (very varied, crowded and hot, similarly *St Elmo's* nearby), or *Pulpería* on Mercedes. Brazilian and Argentinian music at *Clave de Fu*, 26 de Marzo 1325, free entry, good atmosphere. In Pocitos, *Ratatouille*, Missini y J. Benito Blanco, Uruguayan, Brazilian and Argentine live music, US$4 incl. first drink; *House of Andrews*, live music, both best after 2300.

Sports   The beach is more popular than the water. Uruguay has three important yacht clubs, the Uruguayo, the Nautilus and the Punta del Este. Both the Montevideo Rowing Club and the Club Nacional de Regatas have club houses on the Bay. The German Rowing Club is on the Santa Lucía River. Fishing is becoming popular. Association football is played intensively. Rugby football is also played, and there is a yearly championship. There are two good 18-hole municipal links. There are several lawn tennis clubs, and two for polo. Horse races at Las Piedras (**see page** 1032). There is a national lottery. Massage is available at Suomi, Dr. José Scocería 2909.

Museums   Historical: Casa Lavalleja, Zabala 1464, open Tues., Wed. and Fri., 1100-1900, and Casa Rivera, Rincón 437, open daily 1300-1900. Natural History: Buenos Aires 652, 1400-1800 Tues.-Sat. (has a well-preserved, half-unwrapped mummy); closed during 1989 for alterations. Botanical: 19 de Abril 1179. Art: Museo Nacional de Bellas Artes, in Parque Rodó. Worth a visit for the park alone. Municipal: in large rooms upstairs at the Cabildo. The Intendencia (18 de Julio y Ejido) has occasional exhibitions. Zoological Museum, Rambla Chile 4215, on beach at Puerto Buceo. Gold Museum and Gaucho Museum in the sumptuous Banco de la República building, Av. 18 de Julio 996 (Mon.-Sat. 1300-1900). No entrance fees. The Sociedad de Amigos de Arqueología, Buenos Aires 652 (Casilla 6521) can provide professional advice. Museo Blanes, Millán 4015, has many Pedro Figari paintings, open 1400-1800, Tues.-Fri., free, rec. Automobile museum, Colonia e Yí, 6th floor, open 1700-2000, about 25 old models. Naval museum by the Buceo in Pocitos; air force museum near municipal stadium on Av. Larrañaga. Museum schedules are irregular: most are open Sun. and Tues. through Fri., but at times are open only in the afternoon, so make sure. Consult the newspaper *El Día* for current opening times of museums, exhibitions and libraries; also what's on generally (not always accurate).

Theatres Solís, housing the national theatre company and occasional visiting companies, worth seeing inside; cheap concerts on Mondays between March and November (US$0.30). El Galpón theatre company has now returned from exile. The Comedia Nacional plays at Sala Verdi, Soriano 914. Café Teatro "El Reloj"; Circular; Notariado; La Máscara, Río Negro 1180, Teatro del Anglo, San José 1426 (in the same complex free films are often shown, videos of ballet, opera, etc.). The national ballet company Ossodre is said to outperform the Buenos Aires company. Stella d'Italia; Círculo; Centro. All these are more or less professional. Occasionally, small amateur or semi-professional groups put on plays in cinemas or other places.

Cinema is very popular. Price is almost the same in all cinemas, at US$1.85-2 (some half-price on Thurs.). Classic films at Cinemateca. Films are released quite soon after the UK and USA, and often before they get to Buenos Aires. At least half Montevideo's cinemas show blue films—marked *sexo explícito*.

Music Concerts at Solís Theatre (see above). Pop concerts are held in Centenario stadium and Parque Rodó. Jazz at Alianza Francesa and Alianza Uruguay-Estados Unidos. For tango and other musical clubs etc. see above under **Night Clubs**. During the two weeks around Carnival there is a music and dance competition, in the Parque Rodó amphitheatre, in "Murga", a form of satirical revue, 4 hrs. every night, US$0.50 entry, starting at 2100.

Exchange Lloyds Bank, Calle Zabala 1500, and 11 city agencies; Citibank, Cerrito 455 (corner Misiones), no commission on own cheques; Banco Holandés Unido, 25 de Mayo 501; Banco Comercial, Cerrito 400 and Av. Libertador (up to US$1,000 available on Access or Visa, commission 3½%); and Banco Panamericano Uruguayo on Plaza Cajón. Only Banco de la República deals in US personal cheques for collection: 30 working days, high charge. American Express Bank, Rincón 473, T 960092, no commission on travellers' cheques to dollars (open 1300-1700 Mon.-Fri.—see Turisport under **Travel Agents**). There are exchange houses, especially along 18 de Julio, e.g. Gales at 1048, La Favorita at 1459 (both charge 3% commission on travellers' cheques), but do shop around for best rates—Exprinter on Plaza Independencia has been recommended. No restriction on foreign exchange transactions (i.e. an excellent place to stock up with US$ bills, though American Express and some banks refuse to do this for credit cards; most places charge 3% commission for such transactions). Airport bank open every day 0900-2200; so is Banco de la República exchange office on Plaza Cagancha. Note that rates for Brazilian currency are poor

Embassies and Consulates Argentine Consulate,Río Branco 1281, open 1400-1900, visa US$15, one day wait, English spoken. **Brazilian Consulate**, Blvd. Artigas 1257 (**Embassy** at No. 1328). **Paraguayan Consulate**, Blvd. Artigas 1191, open 0900-1200 summer, 1400-1730 winter. **Chilean Embassy**, Andes 1365, open 0900-1400, visa US$5, same day.
    US Embassy and Consulate, Rambla Wilson 1776, T 409051/409126. **Canadian Consulate**, Gómez 1348, T 958234. **British Embassy**, Marco Bruto 1073, T 723625/30/50, 723559/81/97. **Spanish Embassy**, Av. Brasil 2786. **Swedish Embassy**, Av. Brasil 3079, piso 6, Pocitos, T 780088. **Swiss Embassy**, Ing. Frederico Abadie 2934-40, T 704315. **West German Embassy**, La Cumparsita 1417-35, T 904958.

Chambers of Commerce and Cultural Institutions American Chamber of Commerce, Bartolomé Mitre 1337, esq. 108. T 959048/59. Uruguayan-American Library, Paraguay y Canelones, 1400-2000 Mon.-Fri., US publications and books. British Chamber of Commerce, Av. Libertador 1641, piso 2, of 201. T 900936. British Council (Instituto Cultural Anglo-Uruguayo), San José 1426, 3 piso. T 908468 (has good library with newspapers, sometimes shows free films). The British Hospital, Av. Italia 2420, T 409011. The English Club, Treinta y Tres 1309, T 995605. Alliance Française, Soriano 1176 (theatre, concerts, exhibitions in French and Spanish). Goethe Institut, Canelones 1524, T 405813/404432. The Apostleship of the Sea, Washington 274, T 952421.

Schools The British School at Carrasco and some 4 others, 1 French, 1 German, and the Crandon Institute, an American school for children up to 17. All have good scholastic ratings.

Churches The Roman Catholic Cathedral is known locally as the Iglesia San Juan. Anglican Church, Reconquista 522 (a national monument) T 908062 (English Service 1800 Sunday). Methodist services at Christ Church, Carrasco. Holy Trinity Episcopal (British), and the Emanuel Methodist Church (American), hold regular services in English. The German Evangelical Church holds services in German at Calle J M Blanco 2. There is a synagogue.

Post Office Misiones 1328 y Buenos Aires; 0800 (0730 in summer)-1845 Mon.-Fri., 0800-1245 Sat. and holidays (0730-1145 in summer). *Poste restante* at main post office will keep mail for 1 month, 2 if authorized in advance by administrator. Next to Pluna office at Plaza del Entrevero, and under Intendencia at corner of Av. 18 de Julio and Ejido. Closer to tourist area, there is one at Mercedes 929, at Convención.

Telecommunications All America Cables & Radio Inc., Plaza Independencia; Italcable SA, 25 de Mayo 400; Western Telegraph Co, Ltd, Cerrito 449; Telégrafo Nacional, Sarandí 478. Public telex booths (open 0700-2300) are available at Antel, Mercedes 884 or Rincón 501 and Treinta y Tres (open day and night also for international phone calls). Antel office at Sarandí 478 is open 24 hrs. a day for international phone calls.

Travel Agents *Muritelli*, Plaza del Entrevero, *J.P. Santos*, Colonia 951, and *Jetmar*, Plaza Independencia, all helpful. *Wagon-Lits* (Thomas Cook agents), Av. Gral. Rondeau 1392; Exprinter, Sarandí 700; *Turispanol Ltda*, Mercedes 942 (American Express for travel and mail services, good; sells Amex dollar travellers' cheques on Amex card and personal cheque at 1% commission); *Golden Tours*, Colonia 1221, T 90 7500, English spoken. *Viajes y Turismo*, Convención 1343 y 18 de Julio, 4th floor, T 916461, very helpful, English spoken. *Turinter*, Río Negro 1358, very helpful. *Sur Bus* does good US$10 day trip to Punta del Este, 0900-1800, with transfers from and to your hotel.

Tourist Commission Headquarters is at Av. Libertador 1409, fourth floor. Information Centre is on Plaza Cagancha; open every day, friendly though little English spoken, free maps, limited information. Also at Carrasco international airport.

Information Dial "214" for the central bureau of information (in front of Onda bus terminal) about communications, the weather, pharmacies on night duty and anything you want to know about streets in the city. Dial "6" for exact time. The *Guía del Ocios*, a weekly guide, gives information on entertainment, including addresses.

Maps An excellent map is produced by Ancap, the state oil company, US$1.50-2.

Airport The main airport is at Carrasco, 21 km. outside the city, modernized in 1990 with coffee shop and children's play area in departure lounge; left luggage about US$1 per day per item; if exchange facilities closed, buses will accept dollars for fares to town. To Montevideo 30 mins by taxi (US$13-15), or about 50 mins by bus No. 209 to Plaza del Entrevero (US$1.50), tell the driver where you want to get off. Onda and COT bus services to and from Punta del Este also call at the airport.

Rail All passenger services were withdrawn in January 1988.

Buses within Uruguay Good services to most towns; to Punta del Este, 2 hrs., US$ 3.50. Piriápolis US$2 (slow). La Paloma US$4 (slow). Maldonado US$3.25. To La Coronilla US$6.25 (5 hours). Colonia US$3.75, by Onda. During the summer holiday season buses are booked heavily; it is recommended to book in advance (also for Fri. and weekend travel all year round); Carmelo US$5; to Paysandú, US$8, 5½ or 7½ hours, according to route; to Salto, 4 a day, 7½ hrs., US$10. All services out of Montevideo to other parts of Uruguay leave Onda bus terminal on Plaza Cagancha; those to the east make a compulsory stop at Dante 1945/9; others at Terminal Goes, Av. General Flores y Domingo Aramburu. Onda runs services all over the country (the office is just off Av. 18 de Julio). The smaller competing services are just as fast and less expensive; differences in prices can sometimes be large. Services along Route 7 to Tala and San Jacinto are operated by Cita and leave from their office at Av. Libertador 1446. Arco office for buses to Colonia on Plaza Cagancha.

To Paraguay, Brazil, Chile twice a week (Wed. and Sat. 1500) by COIT and three times a week by Brújula bus (Tues., Fri. and Sun.) to Asunción, Paraguay (20 hours, US$30) alternatively take bus to Santa Fe, Argentina, via Paysandú bridge, for easy access to Asunción. As the journey involves crossing part of Argentina, British visitors will need a visa. There are very comfortable buses to Porto Alegre (US$21, 12 hrs.) and São Paulo (US$35 daily, 30 hours) at 2200 with Onda or TTL (Plaza Cagancha, opposite Onda), with drinks service on the *coche cama* and luxury service: often booked very early. A cheaper alternative route (which also avoids the risk of being stranded at the border by through-bus drivers) is to Chuy (US$7, 6 hrs.), then catch an onward bus to Porto Alegre (7½ hrs., US$5.50), either direct or via Pelotas. To Santiago (Empresa Gen. Artigas) via Buenos Aires and Mendoza, US$70, 28 hrs., departs Mon. 0800. Round trips to Argentina, Chile or Brazil by bus or plane, booked at travel agents are reported to be good value.

    N.B. One needs a passport when buying international tickets.

To Argentina: Ferries (Argentine immigration officer on ferries.) Direct to Buenos Aires, night service, alternate evenings at 2100 US$13 without sleeper or breakfast, US$20 sleeper, restaurant, bar, disco; also three daytime ferries, very convenient at each end. Cars about US$37. Services via Colonia: bus/ferry services by Buquebus (three crossings a day) and Ferry Líneas Argentinas (twice a day), 6-7½ hours, combined bus/ferry ticket US$15.40, ferry also takes cars (**see also under Colonia, page** 1033); bus/hydrofoil service by Aliscafos (Plaza Cagancha 1325, T 904608/905063), 5 sailings a day between 0200 and 1730 from Rinconada de Plaza Libertad, US$24, 4 hours, book in advance. It is cheaper to buy tickets for the whole journey than take a separate bus to Colonia and then buy ferry/hydrofoil tickets (break of journey in Colonia is allowed). Services via Carmelo and Tigre: bus/motor launch service by Deltanave from Plaza Cagancha, 8 hours, US$11, 0030 and 0800 daily; bus/ferry service by Buquebus, Río Negro 1400 (Plaza del Entrevero), 3-5 times daily depending on season (fewer on Sun.), efficient, 6-7½ hours, US$15-20. Bus service via Fray Bentos: joint service by Onda, CIT and COIT (offices at Sarandí 699) at 2200 and 2300 daily, US$11.80, 10 hours. Advanced booking is advisable on all services at busy periods.

EAST FROM MONTEVIDEO (2)

The beach season is from December to the end of February. This beautiful coastline, over 320 km. long, contains an endless succession of small bays, beaches and promontories set among hills and woods. There is a series of well equipped and modern camp sites all along the coast. Details are published in Friday's edition of *El Día* especially during the tourist season.

Two roads, both paved, go to Punta del Este. The northern branch (no tolls) via Pando and Soca, is Route 8; at Km. 75 Route 8 continues NE towards Minas (**see page** 1031); while Route 9 branches off to San Carlos (14½ km. N of Maldonado or 19 km. N of Punta del Este) through beautiful rolling country with views of the Laguna del Sauce and on to Chuy. The "Interbalnearia", runs largely along the coast, with short branches to some of the resorts, and is the one described in the text. There are toll posts (US$0.75) at Arroyo Pando and at Arroyo Solís Grande. There is an alternative road to the Interbalnearia route, running parallel between it and the coast—its use is recommended during heavy traffic periods due to the frequency of dangerous road junctions. Route 9, the road to Chuy, is now completely paved. A spur of the road turn S to La Paloma, and there are secondary roads to some of the resorts further along the coast.

Atlántida (*Rex*, C, is main hotel; *Munday*, C, is clean and friendly; many good *residenciales* charging E off season; some good restaurants—try the *Banzai*), 45 km. from Montevideo, is ringed by fir forest and has a good country club. A short distance beyond, in groves of eucalyptus and pine, is the small and intimate beach of Las Toscas, followed by Parque del Plata, on the Solís Chico river. An *asado* on the beach (with wine) costs about US$12. Shortly before Atlántida, in an old fortress set in pine woods, is *El Fortín de Santa Rosa* hotel and restaurant, 2 mins from a lovely sandy beach. Small zoo not far off.

At Km. 64.5 on the Interbalnearia is Sr. Garabedian's **campsite**. For bookings, telephone Sr. Garabedian at Montevideo 561230.

Crossing by a (toll) bridge we come to **La Floresta** (*Oriental*, highly rec.; *del Parque*), surrounded by woods. The chalets are pretty; the place reminds one of the villages of the Landes, near Biarritz. About 35 km. on, over a toll bridge, is **Solís** (*Solís Golf*; *El Chajá*), at the mouth of the River Solís. It has a very long beach, good fishing, delightful river and hill scenery. About 8 km. beyond Solís lies the small village of Las Flores, with a better beach than that at Solís. Accommodation is available at Edén Camping with room at US$3 p.p. or camping at km. 91 site.

Piriápolis, the next resort, 16 km. from Solís, 101 from Montevideo, may be reached either by turning south at the end of the Interbalnearia, and coming through Solís and then along the very beautiful R10, or by taking the original access road (R37) from Pan de Azúcar, which crosses the R93. It has a fine casino hotel and some 50 others, a good beach, a yacht harbour, a country club, a golf course, a motor-racing track and is particularly popular with Argentines. The town, set among hills, is laid out with an abundance of shade trees, and the district is rich in pine, eucalyptus and acacia woods. There are medicinal springs. Six km. to the N is Cerro Pan de Azúcar (Sugar Loaf), crowned by a tall cross with a circular stairway inside; there is only a path up to the cross. Just outside Piriápolis on the side road to Pan de Azúcar (town) by the entrance to the municipal park is a good zoo, containing among other things live specimens of all snakes and most animals native to Uruguay including endangered pampas deer. The bus from Piriápolis to Pan de Azúcar passes the gates. In the municipal park (La Cascada) is the Museo Castillo de Piriá, open 1300-1700, Fri., Sat., Sun. and holidays. The shortest route from Piriápolis to Punta de Este is by the Camino de las Bases which runs parallel to the R37 and joins the R93 some 4 km. east of the R37 junction.

Hotels Most close end-Feb. until mid-Dec. *Argentino*, B, with casino, medicinal springs, ice rink and dirty pool open to public for US$3.50, also sauna; *City*, D (closed in winter), with bath, ocean view, clean, friendly, rec.; *Rex*, next to Onda terminal, C, rec.; *Colón*, open off-season, C; *Centro*, E, rec.; *Colonial*, Rambla de los Ingleses, E with shower, breakfast, heating, clean, rec. *Luján*, C in season, E out of it, rec. The Centro de Hoteles y Anexos de Piriápolis runs a reservation office at Edificio Piriá on Rambla de los Argentinos. House and apartments for hire, Aloia—Colmegna Ltda, on Edif. Claramar on Rambla rec., English spoken.

Restaurants *Argentino*; *Don Quijote*, rec. for paella, cheap and good; *Parador Punta Fría*; *Puertito Don Anselmo* (shellfish, excellent, overlooking sea).

Youth Hostel Close to beach, behind *Hotel Argentino*, at Simón del Pino 1136, T 0432-2157, US$1.50 p.p. (open at least Nov.-March), mostly double bedrooms, hot showers, kitchen. Student cards accepted. There is also an international YMCA camp on the slope of Cerro del Toro, double rooms in bungalows, and tents.

Bus to Montevideo, US$2, 1½ hrs. Buses also to Rocha and Gen. José Artigas bridge (Argentina), US$17.

Tourist Information Asociación de Fomento y Turismo, Rambla de los Argentinos 1348.

Portezuelo has good beaches with the Laguna del Sauce and the fine Lussich woods behind. At **Punta Ballena** there is a wide crescent beach, calm water and very clean sand. The *Solana del Mar Hotel* (opens mid-December, payment in dollars cash is demanded unless you protest) modern, is on the beach, A with full board. The place is a residential resort but is still quiet. Casa Pueblo, the house of Uruguayan artist Carlos Páez Villaro, can be visited; it is built in a Spanish-Moroccan style on a cliff over the sea; there are paintings, collages and ceramics on display, and for sale; season: Nov. 1 to April 1. The Arboreto Lussich (only open 1030-1700 in winter) on the West slope of the Sierra de la Ballena (north of R10) contains a unique set of native and exotic trees. At the top of Punta Ballena there is a panoramic road with remarkable views of the coast. From Portezuelo it is possible to drive north towards the R9 by way of the R12 which then continues, unpaved, to Minas.

Maldonado, capital of Maldonado Department, 140 km. from Montevideo. This peaceful town, sacked by the British in 1806, is now a dormitory suburb of Punta del Este, but it has many colonial remains: the parish church, El Vigia watch tower, and fortifications on Gorriti Island in the semi-circular bay. Gorriti Island, densely wooded and with superb beaches, is an ideal spot for campers. See also the Mazzoni Museum (700 block of Ituzaingó, Tues.-Sat. 1200-1900, Sun. 1400-1900); San Fernando de Maldonado Museum (Sarandí y Rafael Pérez del Puerto, Tues.-Sat. 1300-2000); Museo de Arte Maldonado (José Dodera 648 y Treinta y Tres, private museum, interesting); and the windmill.

Hotels *Posta del Cangrejo*, Barra de Maldonado, L; *Maldonado*, quiet, clean, C; *Hospedaje Isla de Gorriti*, Calle Isla de Gorriti 884, D, rec.; *Celta*, Ituzaingó 839, a bit run down, friendly and helpful, D, Irish owner; *Dieciocho*, on Plaza, E with bath, rec.; *Le Petit Hotel*, Gral. Marco de los Reyes (1st floor), T 23044, shower, a/c, clean, E, rec.

Restaurants: *Matias Módena*, 3 de Febrero 642, good fish and meat, US$14 p.p.; *Santa Teresita*, José Ignacio, speciality seaweed omelette, good atmosphere, always crowded, good service, rec.; *La Posta del Crangrejo* has restaurant with a pleasant terrace, about US$16 p.p. Just after crossing the bridge to La Barra de Maldonado is the *Restaurant San Jorge*, speciality torta de mariscos; *Neuhausen*, pleasant, not too expensive; *Círculo Policial*, run by police, cheap place to eat.

Bus to Minas, Coom, 2 hrs., 5 a day, US$2.50. The railway track between Maldonado and

Punta del Este has been turned into a road.

Camping Two sites: one free, in Parque El Placer; the other charges.

San Carlos, on Route 8, 14½ km. N of Maldonado, is a charming town, half the size of Maldonado. Buses run from the plaza to Maldonado every 15 mins; it is a good point for connections to La Paloma, and Chuy on the Brazilian border. Excellent zoo, historical museum opposite *Hotel Reyes* (Olivera y Carlos Reyes, E, friendly, "immaculate"); other hotels: *Residencial Plaza*, Treinta y Tres, opposite plaza (E) and *El Amanecer*, Treinta y Tres 634. Free camping, with facilities, in lovely municipal park. 2 *cambios* which exchange travellers' cheques.

Punta del Este Seven km. on and 139 km. from Montevideo, facing the bay on one side and the open waters of the Atlantic on the other, lies the largest and best known of the resorts, Punta del Este, which is particularly popular among Argentines. Prices seem to have come down since the recession in Argentina. The narrow peninsula of Punta del Este has been entirely built over (a "concrete jungle"); it has excellent bathing beaches, the calm *playa mansa* on the bay side, the rough *playa brava* on the ocean side. There are an excellent yacht marina, yacht and fishing clubs, and many beautiful holiday houses. There is good fishing both at sea and in three near-by lakes and the river Maldonado (which the main road crosses at Manantiales by a unique inverted-W-shaped bridge). The rest of the area consists of sand dunes covered with pines. On Isla de Lobos, which is a government reserve within sight of the town, there is a huge sea-lion colony; excursions to it every morning at 0800, return at 1115, US$7 p.p.; ticket should be bought at the harbour the day before. Direct daily Boeing 737 flights from Buenos Aires to Punta del Este airport during the high season. On the land side, Punta del Este is flanked by large planted forests of eucalyptus, pine and mimosa. A large country club (the *Cantegril*) lets cottages and hotel apartments at a high price, or one may hire from an "Inmobiliaria". There are a golf course and two casinos. After the Easter vacation the place is all your own and on sunny days it is still warm enough to swim (even between 10 March and Easter it is quiet). Many of the best hotels and restaurants close after the end of the season in March.

Hotels Very many, but expensive: *Palace*, Gorlero y 11, L (A in March, closed in winter), breakfast only (but good restaurant, *El Aguila*, in the hotel), lovely courtyard, colonial style, well kept; *Amsterdam*, El Foque 759, L, ocean view; *San Rafael*, 1½ km. from centre on Atlantic side, B out of season (price doubles in season or with sea view), with breakfast, closed after Easter, luxurious; *Peninsula*, Gorlero 761, D-C off season, central, with bath, rec., open all year; *Tamaris* (in the woods), very modern but only showers; *Florinda*, Calle 27/24, A (C off season), T 40003, with bath, helpful, clean, central, friendly; *Playa Brava*, Calle 27 esq. 24, D off season, T 41618, similar good standard. *Charrúa*, near transport terminals. *Puerto*, Muergos 27, 4 blocks from Onda bus station, C, clean and friendly, English spoken; *Milano*, Calle 84, No. 880, C (E-D off season), family run, excellent, highly rec.; *Tourbillón*, Calles 9 and 12, basic, no hot water, E, in the off season. *L'Auberge*, near golf course, air-conditioned, "lo más refinado". Hotel rates are as much as halved in the winter months. In the high season, cheapest doubles cost about US$18; it is better to find a hotel in Maldonado and commute, or look for a hotel that is rebuilding, so that you can negotiate on prices. To stay at a hotel in the woods you will need a car; no public transport to beach or town.

Restaurants The most expensive restaurants are *La Floreal* (in the woods); *La Bourgogne*, Pedragosa Sierra, excellent, French-run, US$60 p.p.; and *La Lutèce*, Los Sauces casi Pedragosa Sierra, also French cuisine. *Bleu Blanc Rouge*, Calle 6 y 12, very good, US$25 p.p.; *Mariskonea*, one of the oldest establishments, US$25 p.p., good quality; *Doña Flor*, Deauville y Niza, French food, rec.; *Bungalow Suiza*, Av. Roosevelt y Parada 8, excellent, US$20 p.p.; *El Mastil* (behind port), charming atmosphere, open all year; *La Pomme*, Calle 11 esq. 12, Belgian-run, good food, US$15 p.p.; *El Ciclista*, Calle 20 801, one of the oldest restaurants, Italian food, US$10 p.p.; *El Viejo Marinero*, Las Palmeras, fish restaurant, very busy so go early, US$12 p.p.; *Forte di Makalle*, Calle 8-828 y 11, US$17.50, rec.; *Stromboli*, Gorlero y 11, excellent seafood, US$18 p.p., rec.; *Dackel*, Calle 20 y 28, very large, excellent seafood; *Andrés* on a terrace at the Edificio Vanguardia, US$13 p.p.; *da Carmela*, Gorlero 635 y Rambla Gen. Artigas, pizza and pasta, US$10 p.p., pleasant; *Blue Cheese*, overlooking yacht harbour, for steaks and unlimited salads; *Yacht Club Uruguayo* (not to be confused with the exclusive Yacht Club), Gral. Artigas y 8, simple, friendly, views over the port, US$9 p.p.; *El Metejón*, Gorlero y 17, US$20, good food but overpriced. On the main street, *La Fragata*, open 24 hours all year, a good meeting place; one block up the main street from bus station at Gorlero y 30 is *Country Cook*, US owned, good, cheap, wholesome. Many enticing ice-cream parlours such as *Confitería Gorlero* in Gorlero. A good disco is *New Faces*, Calle 20.

Crafts   *Manos del Uruguay* in front of the Casino Nogaró. Best sweaters from *San Carlos*.

Museum   Foundation museum of Contemporary Latin American Art, Barrio Beverly Hills, T 83477, open Dec. to end of Holy Week, Tues.-Sun. 1000-1400. Worth a visit but car needed to get there.

Tourist Information   Liga de Fomento, Parada 1, or Onda at Av. Gorlero and Calle 27, T 40023.

Exchange   Both Amex and Diner's Club have offices. Best rates of exchange from Banco de la República, which opens earlier and closes later than the other banks. Also *casas de cambio*.

Buses   New terminal on Av. Gorlero (served by local bus No. 7). To Montevideo, COT, Sur Bus or Onda (rec.) buses, US$3.50, less than 2 hrs., plenty of buses in the summer; to Piriápolis, US$1.50. To San Carlos (US$1.50) for connections to Porto Alegre (US$30), Rocha, La Paloma, Chuy. Direct to Chuy, 4 hrs., US$5. To Gen. José Artigas bridge (Argentina) US$20. Local bus fare about US$0.20.

Airport   El Jagüel (full customs facilities) as well as the airport on the southern shore of the Laguna del Sauce, Capitán Curbelo, which handles the Pluna and Aerolíneas Argentinas flights to Buenos Aires, US$66. Pluna to Porto Alegre and São Paulo. Airport tax US$2.50 and bus to town US$1.50. Exchange facilities, but no tax-free shopping yet.

Near Punta del Este, to the E, *Playa San Rafael*, where there is an 18-hole golf course, is growing rapidly. (*Casino San Rafael*, L high season (20/12-1/3), B low season, no credit cards, no a/c or balconies, much used for conferences, Telex 28035, T 042-82161; *San Marcos*, B, very pleasant; *Hotel Porto Beri*, new; *L'Auberge*, A). 30 km. from Punta del Este is the quiet fishing village of Faro José Ignacio, with lighthouse and the well-known restaurant Parador Santa Teresita, where seaweed omelette is a speciality. Further E are Punta del Diablo, with a beautiful beach, camping and a picturesque fishing village, and Cabo Colonia, which may be reached by horse-drawn carriage (look for signs on the road), or by bus from La Paloma and 1¾ hrs. walk.

Rocha   is 211 km. from Montevideo and 28 km. from the sea at La Paloma. Population: 20,000. Two casinos located at *Costas del Mar* and *Cabo Santa María* hotels. Groves of palms dotted about the fields give the area an unusual beauty.

Hotels   *Arrate; Trocadero*, C; *Roma; Municipal*, very good and cheap. *Hospedaje Plaza* on the plaza, budget, D/E (3 rooms only). Cheap food at *Las Vegas* on Ramírez.

Youth Hostel   at Barra de Valizas, open summer only.

Camping   Sites at Parque Andresito, Rocha, and Rancho Pucará, Barra de Valizas. There are also cabins for rent at US$6 (4 beds).

La Paloma   is a good port for yachts as it is protected by two islands. It has an oil refinery and a fishmeal plant which can smell bad but there is attractive scenery and good freshwater and sea fishing. Buses run to and from Rocha. Bike rental opposite the casino, US$2 a day; horses can be hired.

Hotels   *Bahía*, B, rec.; *Embeleco*, friendly, English spoken, B, rec.; *La Tuna* (T 0473-6083), C rec.; *Puertas del Sol*, C; *Parque*, clean, E. **Youth Hostel** at Parque Andresito, G, clean, friendly, good meals available, kitchen facilities, book at Montevideo office. Also thatched cabins in the woods for rent, US$13-21 a day with maid and kitchen, sleep 4-6, Dec.-Apr. only. **Restaurant** *Trattoria di Luigi*, highly rec., superb views.

10 km. north of La Paloma on the coastal road is *La Pedrera*, a beautiful village with sandy beaches and a campsite. (*Hotel La Pedrera*, D, swimming pool, tennis, comfortable rooms, rec.; *Hotel San Michel*,D; *Restaurant Costa Brava*, overlooking the sea.) From La Pedrera buses run north (on weekdays only) through pleasant fishing villages to Aguas Dulces and Castillos (from where buses are avialble to Chuy); accommodation in the villages is basic; visits to the islands of Castillos and Wolf can be arranged; look out for sea lions and penguins along the coast, for instance at Cabo Polonia.

North of Rocha, 306 km. from Montevideo lies the colonial fortress (converted into a museum) of Santa Teresa, begun by the Portuguese and finished by the Spaniards in the 1750s. (It was the other way round with the fortress of San Miguel—see below—neither smelt battle.) It is set in the Parque de Santa Teresa, with avenues of palms, a bird sanctuary, and fresh-water pools to bathe in. The fortress is very impressive; free admission. Open 0800-2000, closed Tuesdays. There are cottages to let for the summer season, beside the sea and excellent "wild" camping in the north of the park, so get off the bus at the Fortaleza steps, *not* at the main entrance. There is a small supermarket, a butcher's and a bar in the commercial area where campers are expected to register. Nine km. beyond and 15 km. S of Chuy is the bathing resort of **La Coronilla** with excellent ocean fishing for sharks, skate and black *corvina* from the rocks: there is an annual competition in January. Tour by taxi or Onda bus (US$9, daily) from La Coronilla to the Santa Teresa fortress and the strange and gloomy Laguna Negra, and the collection of native and exotic plants under glass. The beach stretches for many km., but there are too many waves for swimming.

Hotels *Gure-Exte*, B, on beach, small and very pleasant; *Parador La Coronilla*, C; *Costas del Mar*, C, on beach, rec., swimming pool; *Oceanía*, open all year, C (highly rec.), family runs restaurant close by; *Las Palmas*, D with shower (electric), clean, helpful, restaurant; both *Rivamar* and *Las Cholgas* claim to have heating.

Restaurants *La Ruta*, open all year, rec.

At **Chuy**, a run-down town, the frontier runs along the main street. Tourists may freely cross the border in either direction. *Hotel Chuy*, D, casino; *Hotel Plaza*, D; *International*, D (incl. own bath); *Hospedaje Vitoria*, 4 blocks E of *Hotel Chuy*, F, basic, clean, friendly, rec. *Restaurant Jesús*, ½ block from Onda, good, cheap, friendly. At present it is cheaper to eat in Brazil and pay for everything in cruzeiros. Money exchange at *Hotel Chuy* (open until 0300), and at 3 places opposite (open until 1830), giving slightly better rates. No exchange facilities on Sundays. Buy Brazilian currency here as the black market is difficult to find until São Paulo and is illegal. Banks won't change travellers cheques. There are many duty free shops in Chuy and tourists from Uruguay may buy limited amounts of manufactured goods on the Brazilian side without formalities (but see below).

The Uruguayan passport control is 2½ km. before the frontier on the road into Chuy. If travelling by bus, make sure the driver knows you want to stop at Uruguayan immigration. The Brazilian immigration is 2 km. from Chuy on the road to Pelotas. Buses from Chuy to Santa Vitoria or Pelotas stop at Brazilian customs; alternatively take a taxi. The office for the Pelotas bus is one block inside Brazil, near the *Hotel Quarain*. Make sure your passport is stamped or you may have difficulties leaving Brazil. Taking a car into Brazil is no trouble, especially if the car is not registered in Brazil or Uruguay.

Excursions from Chuy: on the Uruguyan side, overlooking the Laguna Merín, stands the fortress of **San Miguel**, set in a park in which many plants and animals are kept. (Bus from Chuy US$0.35, entry US$0.20, open Thurs.-Sun. only.) A casino nearby is open until 0400. From Chuy buses run every two hours to the Barra del Chuy; campsite, good bathing, many birds. The hotel nearby, the *Parador San Miguel*, is excellent. Onda runs daily excursion buses from La Coronilla to Barra del Chuy beach and from Chuy to San Miguel fort, US$9.

Transport Uruguayan taxis are allowed 25 km. beyond the frontier and vice versa. Buses: to Rio Grande (Rodoviaria) at 0700 and 1500, 4 hrs., with stop at immigration; to Porto Alegre, 7½ hrs., US$5; to Montevideo (Onda or Cita) US$9, also by Ruta del Sol US$7, 6 hrs., frequent stops; to Maldonado US$5; to La Paloma US$3, 3¾ hrs.

MONTEVIDEO NORTH-EAST TO BRAZIL (3)

The Pan-American Highway, 486 km. long, runs NE into the hills away from the coast. Route 8 is paved to about 30 km. beyond Minas, 120 km. from Montevideo; beyond it is all-weather.

Minas, with 34,000 inhabitants, is a picturesque small town set in the beautiful wooded hills, which supply granite and marble. Juan Lavalleja, the leader of the Thirty-Three who brought independence to the country, was born here (equestrian statue), and there is an equestrian statue to Artigas, said to be the largest such in the world, on the Cerro Artigas just out of town. The church's portico and towers, some caves in the neighbourhood, and the countryside around are worth seeing. The Parque Salus, on the slopes of Sierras de las Animas, is only 8 km. to the S and very attractive; take the town bus marked "Cervecería Salus" from plaza to the Salus brewery, then walk 2 km. to the mineral spring and bottling plant (*Parador Salus*, acceptable; reasonable set lunch.) The Cascada de Agua del Penitente waterfall, about 11 km. out of town, off the Minas-Aigue road, is interesting and you may see wild rheas (protected) nearby. It is difficult to get to the falls in the off-season. In March and April you can buy *butea* palm fruit, which is grape size, orange and tastes bitter-sweet. Good confectionery is made in Minas; the largest firm, opposite *Hotel Verdun*, shows tourists round its premises. Museum in the Casa de la Cultura.

Hotels *Verdun*, main plaza, clean, E; *Ramos*, 18 de Julio near bus station, basic, clean, E (discount for IYHA members); *Residencia Minas*, 25 de Mayo 502 on main plaza, clean, E.

Restaurants *San Francisco*, 25 de Mayo 586, is recommended as is *El Portal*, Aníbal del Campo 743, for parrillada. The best pastry shop is *Irisarri*, Calle Treinta y Tres 618, known for yemas (egg candy) and damasquitos (apricot sweets).

Exchange Lloyds Bank and national banks, open 1300-1700 Monday-Friday.

Youth Hostel Route 8, Km. 145, in small village of Villa Serrana, US$1.80 a night, 28 km. beyond Minas on road to Treinta y Tres; most attractive, but take plenty of food and drink as there is no shop. Direct bus from Montevideo or Minas, ask driver to set you down and walk 3 km. to Villa Serrana; essential to book through Montevideo office.

Air Service Daily flight by Tamu from Montevideo.

Bus To Montevideo, US$2.25, COT (4 a day) and many others, 2½ hrs. To Maldonado, Coom, US$2.50, 5 a day, 2 hrs.

The next centre of any importance, 286 km. from Montevideo, is **Treinta y Tres**, 15,000 people, picturesquely placed a little way from the Olimar River. Some 20 km. beyond, a dirt road, left, runs 19 km. among and over hills to a rocky region with small streams—the Quebrada de los Cuervos—now a beautiful and quite unspoilt national park. Free camping and swimming at Municipal Park at Río Olimar. Main plaza has all the main restaurants and grills.

Hotel *Central*, and pensions *Jorgito* or *Mota*.

Air Service Daily by Tamu from Montevideo.

The road goes on through **Melo** (111 km. from Treinta y Tres; *Hotel Internacional*, acceptable) to the border town of **Río Branco**, 88 km. from Melo, founded in 1914, on the Yaguarón River. The 1½ km.-long Mauá bridge across the river leads to the Brazilian town of Jaguarão

Hotel *Italiano*, D, with bath. **Youth Hostel** Av. Artigas 279

Restaurant *Oasis*, good, pollo a la brasa

This is where most international traffic used to cross the frontier; now the road via Chuy is better. Customs officials are at the international bridge, passport officials at the police station at Jaguarão. From Jaguarão buses run several times daily to Pelotas and Porto Alegre. There is usually a better rate of exchange at Melo than at the frontier.

MONTEVIDEO NORTH TO BRAZIL (4)

The 509 km. road from Montevideo to the border town of Rivera runs almost due north, at first over rolling hills through cattle country, vineyards, apple orchards, orange, lemon and olive groves. Further N, hilly cattle-range land is crossed.

Las Piedras, 24 km. from Montevideo, in vineyard country, has a Gothic Chapel of the Salesians. Race meetings (pari-mutuel betting) Thurs., Sat. and Sun.

Exchange Lloyds Bank, Calle General Artigas 652. Open 1300-1700, Mon.-Fri.

Canelones, 45 km. from the capital, is a typical small town of 10,000 people in a grain growing area. Further north is the pleasant country town of **Florida**, famous for a folklore festival on Independence Day each year. (*Hotel Español*, D; camp site; *Restaurant Negro el 8*, Italian food.)

Durazno, 182 km. from Montevideo on the Rio Yí, is a freindly provincial town with tree-lined avenues. There is a good view of the river from the western bridge. (*Hotel Central*, Manuel Cribe y Mons Arrospiede, D; **Youth Hostel**, Campus Municipal, T 2835 between 1300 and 1900.)

Paso de los Toros is close to the huge lake created by the Rincón del Bonete dam on the Río Negro (*Hotel Onda*, F, not very clean; beautiful camping by the river); next is Tacuarembó. There is a toll on Route 5, going north, 67.8 km. from Montevideo; the road is dual carriageway as far as Canelones. E of Paso de los Toros (1½ hrs. by Onda bus at 1700) is San Gregorio, cheap camping and bathing in Río Negro. Bus returns to Paso de los Toros 0245.

Rivera is a town of 55,400 people, on the Brazilian frontier. It is divided by a street from the Brazilian town of Santa Ana do Livramento, which has a good golf course, and a daily bus to Porto Alegre. Points of interest are the park (free camping facilities), the Plaza Internacional, and the dam of Cañapirú. There are an airport and a casino, and many duty-free shops.

Hotels *Casablanca*, Sarandí 484, T 3221, E, shower, breakfast, a/c, clean, pleasant. *Mabé* (near station); *Casino*; *Nuevo*.

Bus to Montevideo, US$10 or less, to Fray Bentos and Durazno, US$1.50; to Paysandú, by Onda 0400 and 1700, or take 1000 service to Tacuarembó and change.

WEST FROM MONTEVIDEO (5)

There is a toll on Route 1 (Montevideo-Colonia) at the Santa Lucía bridge (Km. 22.5). There are no tolls on Routes 2 to Fray Bentos and 3 to Paysandú and Salto.

Route 1, part of the Pan-American Highway, runs from Montevideo westwards for 177 km. to Colonia del Sacramento. There is a nice beach near the disused bull-ring, which is passed by regular buses. Much traffic from Argentina flows along this busy road; the surface has continued to deteriorate.

About 114 km. from Montevideo, a 5 km. branch leads N to **Colonia Suiza**, originally a Swiss settlement, with some 4,500 people. The Swiss national day is celebrated on 1 August with considerable zest. There are several hotels, the *Bungalow Suiza* restaurant and a Youth Hostel. Quite near is Nueva Helvecia, where the tourist can buy locally made Swiss musical boxes. At 120 km. along the main road, and just S, is **Colonia Valdense**, another colony, this time of Waldensians, who still cling to some of the old customs of the Piedmontese Alps. There is little for the budget traveller in either Nueva Helvecia or Colonia Valdense. Bus Montevideo-Colonia Valdense US$2.50; Colonia Valdense-Colonia Suiza US$0.50; Colonia Suiza-Colonia, US$1.20.

Hotels at Colonia Suiza *Nirvana*, A, restaurants, sports facilities, run down but good; *Hospedaje Comercio*, 18 de Julio 1209, E with bath and a/c; *Del Prado* (Youth Hostel), T 0522-4169.

Hotels at Colonia Valdense *Brisas del Plata*; *Parador los Ceibos*.

About 6½ km. further on, a paved main road branches off right to Rosario (5 km.), Mercedes

(164 km.), and Fray Bentos (34 km. further). **Rosario** is a typical agricultural town given over to dairying and grain production. Its port, Juan Lacaze, lies 22 km. SW. Population: 8,000.

Hotels *Ricardi* and *Riviera*, E, good.

Clubs Club Cyssa, a social, cultural and sporting club, with a stadium, football field and basketball ground. Two fishing clubs.

Colonia (del Sacramento), a charming small town (population 10,000) with an interesting historic section jutting into the River Plate, was founded by Portuguese settlers from Brazil in 1680. It contains rebuilt city walls and quite a number of colonial buildings and narrow streets in the older part of the town; all the more interesting because there are few such examples in this part of the continent. Worth seeing are the Parochial Church, the Municipal Museum in the old house of Almirante Brown (open Thurs. to Sun. 0800-1330), opposite it on the plaza (and with same hours) is the Museo Portugués; the Mansion of the Viceroy, the house of General Mitre, and the Farola (lighthouse). The plaza is particularly picturesque. The tourist office at Flores y Rivera offers good maps. Buenos Aires, to which there is a ferry service, is only 50 km. A "free zone" has been created here (no consumer goods). At Real San Carlos, just out of town (take the blue bus from the centre) are the racecourse (Hipódromo) and bull-ring (out of use). The best beach is Playa Ferrando, with campsite, 2 km. to the east. In the third week of January, festivities are held marking the founding of Colonia.

Hotels *Posada del Gobernador*, 18 de Julio 205, A, bed and breakfast, no dining room, charming, rec.; *El Mirador*, L, Av. Roosevelt, Km. 176½; *Royal*, General Flores 340, C, comfortable, good restaurant, pool, rec.; *Beltrán*, Gral. Flores 311, E, shared bath, clean; *Rincón del Río*, E, shower but no breakfast, clean, friendly; *Español*, Manuel Lobo 377, friendly, restaurant, rundown. Under same ownership: *Los Angeles*, small rooms, no restaurant, but clean and friendly, English spoken; *Leoncia*, Rivera 216, modern, good; *Esperanza* (Gral. Flores 237, clean, charming), all D. *Posada de la Ciudadela*, Washington Barbot 164, E, clean, pleasant, a/c, simple; *Italiano*, F without bath, friendly, clean, English spoken, good restaurant, rec. Several cheap *hospedajes* near the Plaza. *Hospedaje* at General Flores 311, E, no bath but clean, rec.

Restaurant *Esperanza* (at hotel) and *Yacht Club* (at harbour) are good; several good *parrilladas* along 18 de Julio. *Los Faroles*, rec., friendly; *La Casona* (coffee bar). *Canta Rana*, Comercio y Santa Rita, good and cheap, open weekends only off season, daily in Jan.-April.

Camping Site at Playa Ferrando.

Ferries Two ferries a day to Buenos Aires, four hours crossing, US$11 p.p., clean and comfortable (but more expensive than going by bus and ferry from Montevideo). Bus to ferry at Real San Carlos from town, US$0.50. The Argentine consulate is reported unfriendly to the British; best to use the one in Montevideo.

Hydrofoil Services to Buenos Aires, 7 a day, starting at 0430, last at 2000, US$17 (limited luggage allowance). It is substantially cheaper to buy ticket at the port than from a tourist agency. The company runs buses to their port in Colonia from Punta del Este, Piriápolis, Carrasco Hotel (Carrasco), and Montevideo (Plaza Libertad).

Air Service Lapa and Aero Uruguay both fly to Aeroparque, Buenos Aires 3 times a day, US$22. This is generally quicker than hydrofoil.

Bus to Montevideo, US$3.75 (2½ hrs.), Onda and COT, five a day each. US$1.50 to Carmelo, three times daily. To Salto, US$8, (8 hrs.), Chadre, at 0615 and 1430.

UP THE RIVER URUGUAY (6)

The road swings N and NW to reach the sleepy resort town of **Carmelo**, 74 km. from Colonia, on the shores of Las Vacas river. Population: 15,000. Across the bridge is a white restaurant on the left-hand side of the road: friendly, recommended. The port harbours several hundred yachts during the season. There is a free zone at the port. There are 2 companies with a launch service to Tigre, across the delta, a most interesting ride past innumerable islands (Cacciola, twice a day, 3 hrs., and Delta Nave twice daily, 3 times Sunday, 2½ hrs., US$3: Movilan SA, Constituyentes 263, T 418, office in Montevideo, Plaza Cagancha 1326, T 910755). You can pay at the Onda bus station in Montevideo for both bus and launch, US$11. Bus to Montevideo, 1210, 2240, US$5; to Fray Bentos, Salto, from main square 0710, 1540; bus to Colonia at 1700.

Hotels *Casino Carmelo; Comercio; La Unión*, Uruguay 368, E, very good value. *Centro*, next door, E. The bank will only exchange bills and not travellers' cheques.

Camping Site near the bridge (T 2058).

Some 30 km. up the river, by road, is **Nueva Palmira** (population 3,500). Worth visiting in the vicinity are the Pirámide of Solís (8 km. out of town), the Calera, the Camacho, and the Capilla de la Concepción and the Convento de la Reducción Jesuítica (1780—both in poor condition, 12 km. from town, and 3 km. off the road). A free zone at the port.

Some 20 km. away is the historic beach of La Agraciada, famous for the landing of the Thirty-Three patriots on 19 April, 1825, which led to Uruguayan independence. On the beach is a statue to General Juan Lavalleja, leader of the Treinta y Tres. A festival is held on each anniversary.

The road continues through the small river port of **Dolores** (population: 13,000), 32 km. up-river from the confluence of the Río San Salvador with the Río Uruguay, to

Mercedes, a livestock centre and resort best reached by road from the main Colonia-Montevideo highway (275 km.). It is set on the S bank of the Río Negro, 48 km. above its confluence with the Río Uruguay. This pleasant town of 34,000 inhabitants is a yachting and fishing centre during the season.

The charm of the town derives from its Spanish-colonial appearance, though it is not as old as the older parts of Colonia. There is a pleasant *costanera* (riverside drive).

Hotels *Brisas del Hum*, C; *Comercio; Petit Hotel*, D; *Himalaya*, D, with bath; *Martín*, D; *Universal*, D, rec. *Hospedaje Hotelcito*, Giménez 703, E. Cheap *hospedaje* (no name), Giménez 848, G; *Club de Remeros*, on riverside, G. Good food at *La Brasa*, Calle Castro y Careaga, and at *Círculo Policial*, Calle 25 de Mayo.

Camping Site at Mercedes, and beside Rivers Negro and Uruguay (US$0.45 p.p.).

Museums Palaeontology and Natural Sciences, a few kms. west of town; the Museum of Eusebio Giménez, with a gallery of paintings.

Tourist Office Artigas 215, T 2733.

Bus to Paysandú, 2½ hrs., US$4.

Excursions To the islands in the Río Negro—the largest has an inn. To the small town of **Santo Domingo** (Soriano), first town to be founded in Uruguay, to see a fine colonial church and an old house. Difficult to do this trip easily in one day.

The road continues westwards (34 km.) to

Fray Bentos, a port on the Uruguay River, 193 km. above Buenos Aires. An international bridge has been built across the Río Uruguay to Puerto Unzué (Argentina); toll US$2.10 per car, 3 buses a day to Gualeguaychú, Argentina, 0700, 1230, 1800. Main industry: meat packing and canning. Population: 14,000.

Hotels All on 25 de Mayo: *Colonial*, close to main Plaza and ETA bus office, hot water, E; *Gran Plaza* (satisfactory); *25 de Mayo*, E, clean, hot water. **Restaurant** *Club Armonía*.

River Boats Launch services four times a week to Gualeguaychú.

There is an ETA bus service to Rivera.

Paysandú, on the E bank of the Río Uruguay, 122 km. by good paved road from Fray Bentos (Route 2), and 480 by paved road via Trinidad from Montevideo (Route 3), has a population of about 80,000. Temperatures in summer can rise as high as 42°C. There is a golf club, and a rowing club which holds regattas. The cathedral is 19th century; the attached Salesian college has an interesting museum, opens 1700. The cemetery on the outskirts is worth a look. Also worth a visit is the Museo de la Tradición, with *gaucho* articles, at the Balneario Municipal beach, north of town. A historical museum has been opened at Florida 930. There is an international bridge to Colón, Argentina, (US$1.90 per car for crossing). It is about 8 km. to Colón. Airport with daily Tamu flights to Montevideo (US$12).

Hotels *Gran Hotel Paysandú*, D, 18 de Julio y 19 de Abril, T 3400, a/c, best; *Onda*, D, "super suites", good restaurant (one can reserve through Onda in Montevideo), rec.; *Pensión Popular*, E, with shower; *Concordia*, 18 de Julio, E, clean; *Rafaela*, 18 de Julio 1181, E, large rooms, modern and friendly, electric showers, no food but surrounded by cafés; *Lobato*, Leandro Gómez 1415, E, good. A good hotel, but not in the centre, is *Bulevar* at Bulevar Artigas and República Argentina. *Victoria*, 18 de Julio 979, F, highly rec., cheapest, very friendly.

Youth Hostel Liga Departamental de Fútbol, Gran Bretaña 872, T 4247, US$1 p.p., neither clean nor well-maintained. Cabins for 5 or more people.

Camping Free facilities available in a municipal park by the river.

Restaurant *Artemio*, Plaza de Constitución, 18 de Julio, "best food in town", but closed in winter. *Parrillada de Asturias*, good and cheap. *Don Diego's*, 19 de Abril, serves cheap *parrillada*, good value. *Pipan*, 2 blocks S of Cathedral, good and cheap.

Tourist Bureau Plaza de Constitución, 18 de Julio 1226.

Travel Agency Viñar Turismo, Artigas 1163, helpful.

Bus to Montevideo, 7½ hrs., US$8, by Onda, four buses daily. Other lines (Chadre, Agencia Central) are just as good. To Salto US$3. To Paso de los Toros 1430 (return 0430), US$4, or by Alonso bus to Guichón at 0600,1100, 1430 and change. For drivers, Route 3 via Mercedes is only 38 km. longer than the direct Route 2 via Trinidad, but in much better condition.

Excursions To the waterfalls of the River Quequay, a few km. to the N; the Termas del Guaviyú thermal springs 50 km. away (1½ hrs. by bus) with cheap camping, and to the Meseta de Artigas, 90 km. N of Paysandú, 13 km. off the highway to Salto. The Meseta, where General Artigas lived (statue), is 45 metres above the Uruguay river, which here narrows and forms whirlpools at the rapids of El Hervidero. A terrace commands a fine view, but the rapids are not visible from the Meseta. The statue, with the general's head topping a tall shaft, is very original. There are some pleasant, somewhat primitive, chalets available from Erwin Frey, 90 Estación Chapieny, Dept Paysandú. Early booking recommended. Bus to Km. 462 on Paysandú-Salto road.

Salto, 120 km. by paved road N of Paysandú, has a population of 80,000. It is a centre for cultivating and processing oranges and other citrus fruit. See the beautiful park of Solari; the Parque Harriague with an open air theatre and a well-kept zoo (closed Mon.., US$0.15—7 blocks from centre, feeding time 1400-1500); the fine-arts museum in the donated mansion, French style, of a rich *estanciero*, Uruguay 1067, opens at 1700, well worth a visit (the locals are justifiably proud of it); and the promenade along the River Uruguay. Across the river is Concordia, in Argentina, to which there are 5 ferries (US$1.10, 15 mins) on weekdays, 4 on Sat. but none on Sun.

Festival Shrove Tuesday carnival.

Hotels *Gran Hotel Salto*, Plaza Artigas, best, good restaurant, reasonably priced; *Los Cedros*, a/c, D, Uruguay 657 (T 3989); *Plaza*, Plaza Treinta y Tres, near bus station, simple, clean, good food, E. *Pensión 33*, Treinta y Tres 269, F, basic, central. *Concordia*, Uruguay 749, E, shower, a/c, central, clean, friendly; *Pensión Santa Catalina*, Brasil 1633 or *Pensión Las Tres Fronteras*, General Rivera 1155, cheaper, basic, E; *Artigas Plaza*, Plaza 18 de Julio next to Onda bus station, E with bath, hot water, very clean, log fire in winter, friendly (T4824), rec.; *Pensión Pocholo*, 18 de Julio opp. hospital, F, friendly but basic, others nearby at same price.

Youth Hostels Club de Remeros Salto (by the river) T 0732-3418, or Club de Leones, Uruguay 1626, if you can find a student to sign you in.

Camping Site at Salto.

Restaurants *Chef Restaurant*, Uruguay 639; *Sigo* at La Rueda, in the E, for parrillada, 10 blocks from the cathedral; *Club de Remeros de Salto*. *Club de Uruguay*, Uruguay, good breakfast and good value meals; *Club Bancario*, Brasil 765, lunch US$2, good.

Tourist Office Calle Uruguay 1052, free map.

Exchange Lloyds Bank, two agencies: Uruguay 585 and Blandengues y 8 de Octubre. Open 1300-1700, Mon.-Fri. (cashes cheques into dollars without commission). National banks. Cambio Pensotti has been recommended as helpful. The *cambio* at Uruguay 800 is open until 2000, Mon.-Sat.

Anglican Church Calle República de Argentina, close to Calle Uruguay.

Bus to Montevideo, US$10 (Onda); to Termas del Arapey, 2 hrs., daily, US$3.50. Paysandú US$3.65, four a day. To Rivera, US$8.50. To Colonia by Agencia Central, 0555, 8 hrs., US$8.

Air Service Daily to and from Montevideo via Paysandú, by Tamu, US$15 single. To Buenos Aires.

Excursions One excursion from Salto is by launch to the Salto Chico (uninteresting); another is to Salto Grande, where a ranch-style guest house for anglers is run by the Tourist Commission. Nearby is the resort *Hotel Horacio Quiroga*, B, sports facilities, staffed by nearby catering school. The most popular tourist site in the area is the large **Salto Grande** dam and hydroelectric plant 20 km. from Salto, built jointly by Argentina and Uruguay; a 2-hr. free tour can be arranged with the CTM (office on corner of *Hotel Gran Salto*). A road runs along the top of the dam. Medicinal springs at Fuente Salto, 6 km. N of the city. Bus No. 4 runs from Calle Artigas (US$0.15) to **Termas de Daymán**; beautifully laid out and eight swimming pools, with Youth Hostel on Route 3, Km. 490, T 0732-4361, restaurant, souvenir shop and campsite (entry to baths US$0.35, towel US$0.50, locker US$0.10).

The road to **Termas del Arapey** branches off the partially paved highway to Bella Unión, 61 km. N of Salto, and then runs 35 km. first E and then S Pampa birds, rheas and metre-long lizards much in evidence. Termas del Arapey is on the Arapey river S of Isla Cabellos (Baltazar Brum). The waters at these famous thermal baths contain bicarbonated salts, calcium and magnesium. There is a new hotel with pool (*Hotel Termas del Arapey*, A), a motel (very small bungalows with kitchens, no sheets provided), a nice swimming pool, a very simple *parador* (meals only) and a good Onda restaurant. Book ahead in Salto or Montevideo. Camping US$2 p.p.

The road (148 km.) runs N to the little town of **Bella Unión**, 5,000 people, (with free campsite, ask at Prefectura Naval, insect repellant needed), near the Brazilian frontier.

There is also a road from near Bella Unión E to **Artigas**, a frontier town in a cattle raising and agricultural area (excellent swimming upstream from the bridge). There is a bridge across the Río Cuaraim to the Brazilian town of Quaraí opposite. Population: 14,000.

Hotels *Concordia; Oriental, Pensión Uruguay* and *Hawaii*, basic but clean.

Camping US$0.25 p.p. a day, or at Agua Corriente—chance of camping at the yacht club on the river.

Youth Hostel Club Deportivo Artigas, Pte. Berreta and L.A. de Herrera, T 0642-3015.

Restaurants *Maricarmen*, Calle Lecueder 302, and *Municipal*, Lecueder y Berreta.

Bus service to Salto, 225 km. **Airport** at Bella Unión

INFORMATION FOR VISITORS

Documents A passport is necessary for entry except for nationals of other American countries, who can get in with national identity documents. Visas (about US$10) are not required by nationals of American and Western European countries, Israel and Japan. Tourist cards are valid for 3 months, extendable for a similar period. For extensions go to Migraciones office in Calle Misiones. A small fee is charged.

The Ministry of Tourism sells a "pasaporte turístico" at points of entry, about US$10, valid 30 days, which entitles the holder to discounts of 10%-20% for cash purchases of a wide range of goods and services from establishments listed (of limited value).

Airport Tax of US$4.50 on all air travellers leaving Uruguay for South American republics or Mexico (US$2.50 to Aeroparque, Buenos Aires); US$7 for all other countries, and a tax of 3% on all tickets issued and paid for in Uruguay.

Flights from Europe By air: direct flights by Pluna (Madrid), Iberia, KLM, and Lufthansa. Flying by other carriers, a change must be made at Rio or Buenos Aires.

From the USA Pan American World Airways (2 a week from New York), and Lan-Chile (from Montreal and/or New York), and (as far as Buenos Aires) by Canadian Pacific Airlines (from Toronto), Ecuatoriana and Avianca (both Los Angeles) and Aerolíneas Argentinas.

From Argentina Ferry services (Montevideo and Colonia to Buenos Aires), hydrofoil services (Colonia to Buenos Aires) and launch services (Carmelo to Tigre) are given in the text. Aerolíneas Argentinas and Pluna have several flights a day between Aeroparque in Buenos Aires and Carrasco Airport. Service intensified during holiday period (US$80 single). Also frequent flights to Punta del Este from Buenos Aires. Lapa and AeroUruguay fly between Colonia and Buenos Aires; US$22 single. From Colonia there is a fast bus service by Onda to Montevideo. Foreign airlines connect Carrasco with the Buenos Aires international airport at Ezeiza. Buses run across the Paysandú and Fray Bentos bridges. Direct bus between Buenos Aires and Montevideo by one of these routes takes about 10 hours. Ferries cross the Río Uruguay between Salto and Concordia.

  From Brazil Direct connection between Brazil and Uruguay by all the international airlines landing at Montevideo. Varig flies daily from Rio de Janeiro to Montevideo, via Buenos Aires. Cruzeiro do Sul has daily flights São Paulo, Porto Alegre and Montevideo. By road: the Pan-American Highway runs 2,880 km. from Rio de Janeiro to Montevideo and on to Colonia. It is poorly surfaced in parts. There are several bus services.

  From Chile Avianca and KLM (once), Pluna (twice) and Lan-Chile three times a week to Santiago. Lan-Chile flies between Santiago, Buenos Aires and Montevideo and between Montevideo and Lima. **NB** Tamu, the military airline, has flights to Santiago and Rio de Janeiro every other week; civilians are taken for US$15 but service is unreliable (ask at Pluna office in Montevideo or at Uruguayan consulates in Rio or Santiago).

  From Paraguay Once a week each by Pluna, and Líneas Aéreas Paraguayas (LAP). Twice-weekly buses Asunción-Montevideo.

Customs Duties are not usually charged on a reasonable quantity of goods (such as tobacco and spirits), brought in obviously for the traveller's own use: 200 cigarettes or 50 cigars or 3 small packets of tobacco are admitted duty-free; so is 1 bottle of alcoholic drink, 3 little bottles of perfume and gifts up to the value of US$5.

Local Air Services Internal flights are very cheap, e.g. US$15 to Salto, and to the Brazilian border at Rivera. Pluna will accept credit cards only at its office in Plaza del Entrevero, Montevideo. Tamu, the military airline, offers considerably reduced fares on many internal flights; tickets from Colonia 1021, Montevideo. Provincial airports are given in the text.

Roads There are 45,000 km. of roads, 80% of them paved or all-weather. The Comisión Nacional de Turismo will help to plan itineraries by car. Onda buses radiate into the interior from Montevideo, using comfortable American (they even use the Greyhound logo) long-distance coaches; other companies do not run the same extensive network, but are often cheaper and as fast. All hotels display Onda timetables. Hitch-hiking is fairly easy, along the coast, but difficult in the interior because the population is sparse; it is reportedly fairly safe for women to hitch alone. Gasoline prices are very high at US$3 a gallon for super. Route 5 as far as Canelones is now dual-carriageway.

Motoring Vehicles do not stop, nor is there a right of way, at uncontrolled intersections. Traffic is slow because there are so many ancient cars (1920s and 1930s models are called *cachilas* and skilled mechanics keep them on the road) outside Montevideo there is little traffic. Care is needed at night since vehicle lights do not always work. Insurance is not required by law. Uruguay is said to be much better than Argentina or Brazil to ship a car to.
Land-Rover garage in Montevideo at Cuareim 2082, near old railway station.

Railways All passenger services were withdrawn in January 1988.

Youth Hostels Asociación de Alberguistas del Uruguay, Calle Pablo de María 1583 (open 1300-1900), Montevideo (T 404245) operates hostels (IYHA members only) at Montevideo (Canelones 935), Artigas, Paysandú, Piriápolis, Salto, La Paloma, Colonia Suiza, Villa Serrana (near Minas), Barra de Valizas (near Rocha), Durazno and Rio Branco. A 10% rebate is available on Lapa plane tickets between Colonia and Buenos Aires—obtainable at the Onda terminal in Montevideo, and rebates have also been reported (10-20%) for bus fares and hotel prices.

Camping Several good sites in Montevideo and outside; see references in main text.

Food and Drink Beef is eaten at almost all meals; it is good and now always available. The majority of restaurants are *parrilladas* (grills) where the staple is beef. *Asado* (barbecued beef) is popular; the main cuts are *asado de tira* (ribs); *pulpa* (no bones), *lomo* (fillet steak) and entrecote. To get a lean piece of *asado*, ask for *asado flaco*. *Costilla* (chop) and *milanesa* (veal cutlet) are also popular; usually eaten with mixed salad or chips. *Chivitos* are Uruguayan steak burgers; *chivitos canadienses* are sandwiches filled with slices of meat, lettuce, tomato, egg, etc. (normally over US$2—very filling). Two other good local dishes are *puchero* (beef with vegetables, bacon, beans and sausages) and the local varieties of pizza, fast becoming a staple. Other specialities are barbecued pork, grilled chicken in wine, *cazuela* (or stew) usually with *mondongo* (tripe) or sea foods (e.g. squid, shark—*cazón*, mussels—*mejillones*). The sausages are very good and spicy (*chorizos, morcillas, salchichas*). *Morcilla dulce*, a sweet black sausage, made from blood, orange peel and walnuts, has been highly praised; so has the *morcilla salada*, which is savoury. For snacks, *media lunas mixtas* are a type of croissant filled with ham and cheese, either hot or cold; toasted sandwiches are readily available; *panchos* are hot dogs, *húngaros* are spicy sausage hot dogs. *Preparación* is a selection of crisps, nuts, vol-au-vent, etc. An excellent dessert is *chajá*, a type of sponge-cake ball with cream and jam inside—very sweet; others are *messini* (a cream sponge) and the common lemon pie. Pastries are very good indeed, and crystallized egg-yolks, known as *yemas*, are popular sweets. Ice cream is excellent everywhere.

The local wines are very varied: Santa Rosa Cabernet is a fair red and Santa Rosa Anticuario, also known as "The Old Museum", is good. Herbert Levi, a connoisseur from Buenos Aires, recommends Castel Pujol, Cabernet Sauvignon and Rosé. The beers are good. Imported drinks are freely available in Montevideo, e.g. whisky, US$2.50-3.00 and Chilean wines. *Mate* is a favourite drink between meal hours. The local spirits are *caña* and *grappa*; some find the locally-made whisky and gin acceptable. In the Mercado del Puerto, Montevideo, a *medio medio* is half still white wine, half sparkling white (a must! Elsewhere a *medio medio* is half *caña* and half whisky). *Espillinar* is a cross between whisky and rum. Try the *clérico*, a tasty mixture of wine, fruit juices and mate. Coffee is good: a *cortado* is a strong, white coffee, *café con leche* is milk with a little coffee. Milk is always available, either in bottles or plastic sacs. The dinner hour is late, usually from 2100 to 2400.

Tipping Normally all hotel and restaurant bills include a percentage service charge plus 20% value-added tax, but an additional small tip is expected. In other cases give 10% of the total bill. Porters at the airport expect about US$0.20 per piece of luggage; although there is an official rate of tips for porters at seaports, the actual charges are mostly higher. Taxi drivers are tipped 10% of the fare. Tips at cafés are about 10%. Cinema ushers get a small tip, as do cloakroom attendants and hairdressers (10%-15%).

Shopping Bargains See under Montevideo, page 1022.

Security Personal security offers few problems in Uruguay to travellers who are reasonably prudent.

Health Milk and fresh water can be drunk and fresh salads eaten fairly freely throughout the country. Medical services are not as good as they used to be. Under the Clínica Panamericana Plan, if you pay US$6 a month, a visit to a specialist costs US$0.60 plus free laboratory and emergency care. Many reports of hepatitis from injections and visits to the dentist. The British Hospital in Montevideo is recommended.

Climate Temperate, if somewhat damp and windy, and summer heat is tempered by Atlantic breezes, but there are occasional large variations. In winter (June-September), when the average temperature is 10° to 16°C, the temperature can fall now and then to well below freezing. It is generally humid and hardly ever snows. Summer (December-March), with an average temperature of 21° to 27°C, has irregular dry periods. There is always some wind and for the most part the nights are relatively cool. There are normally 120 sunny days in the year. The rainfall, with prolonged wet periods in July and August, averages about 1,200 mm at Montevideo and some 250 more in the N, but the amount of rain varies markedly from year to year.

Best times for visiting Most tourists visit during the summer (December-mid March), though hotels have to be booked in advance. Business visits can be paid throughout the year, but it is best to avoid the tourist months. In June, July, and August, orders are placed for the winter season 12 months ahead.

British business travellers are strongly advised to read "Hints to Exporters: Uruguay", obtainable from the Department of Trade, Sanctuary Buildings, 16-20 Great Smith Street, London SW1.

Hours of Business Most department stores generally are open 0900 to 1200, 1400 to 1900, but 0900 to 1230 on Sat. Business houses vary but most work from 0830 to 1200, 1430 to 1830 or 1900, according to whether they open on Sat. Banking hours are 1300 to 1700 in Montevideo; there are special summer hours (1 Dec.-15 March) in Montevideo (1330-1730), in the interior (0730-1130) and in Punta del Este (1600-2000); banks are closed on Sat. Government departments, mid-March to mid-November, 1300 to 1830 from Mon. to Fri.; rest of the year, 0700 to 1230, but not Sat.

Holidays 1, 6 Jan.; Carnival (see below); Easter week; 19 April; 1, 18 May; 19 June; 18 July; 25 August; 12 October; 2 November; 8, 25 December.

Carnival Week is officially the Monday and Tuesday immediately preceding Ash Wednesday, but a great many firms close for the whole of the week.
    Business comes to a standstill also during Holy Week, which coincides with La Semana Criolla (horse-breaking, stunt riding by cowboys, dances and song). Department stores close only from Good Friday. Banks close all week. Easter Monday is not a holiday.

Currency Bank notes issued are for 50, 100, 200, 500, 1,000, 5,000 and 10,000 new pesos, and coins for 10, 20 and 50 centésimos and 1, 2, 5 and 10 new pesos. Any amount of currency can be taken in or out.

Exchange Rates change frequently because of a floating exchange rate and inflation differentials against the US dollar; see the "Latest Exchange and Inflation Rates" table near end of book. Many banks and exchange houses (casas de cambio) will give you US$ cash for US$ travellers' cheques with no commission charged (some charge 1%). Obtaining US$ cash against a credit card is difficult; try the Banco Comercio Exterior and Caja Obrera. Dollars cash can be purchased when leaving the country. Exchanges from Brazilian and Argentine currency receive much worse rates than straightforward deals between dollars and pesos. Banks are closed on Saturday throughout the year; hours Monday-Friday 1300-1700.

Credit Cards Argencard is a member of the Mastercard organization, so one may use Access at outlets displaying their sign. Many shopkeepers are unaware of this but a phone call will confirm it. Also American Express, Diners Club and Visa. Most hotels outside Montevideo do not accept credit cards.

Cost of Living Several recent travellers have reported Uruguay as being very expensive, much more so than Argentina or Brazil. Prices vary considerable between summer and winter, Punta del Este being particularly expensive.

Weights and Measures Metric units alone are legal. Odd fact: the timber trade still uses inches for the cross section of lengths of timber.

Electric Power 220 volts 50 cycles AC.

Postal services are very unreliable; all items should be registered and sent by air mail to avoid delay (probably better to go direct to airport, avoiding chaos of the sorting office). Rates are low, e.g. US$0.25 for postcard, US$0.30 for a letter to Europe; US$2 for 1 kg surface-mail package, US$3.50 for 1 kg air-mail package (but best not to send parcels at all—if they do arrive they will probably have been opened).

Telecommunications Telex from most Antel centres, some 24 hrs.; cheaper than telegrams. Western Telegraph Co Ltd (British), ITT Comunicaciones Mundiales SA, and Italcable provide communication with all parts of the world through their cable stations at Montevideo.

The Government-owned Cerrito station supplies international radio-telegraph communication service. Press wireless service is provided by Press Wireless Uruguaya Ltda. Radio-telephone conversations with the United States and Europe, etc., are routed through Buenos Aires. The telephone service still has a poor reputation. Direct dialling abroad is possible. Collect calls only available to UK, USA, Spain, Italy and Canada (collect calls are the cheapest way of phoning USA and Canada). Cost: to USA about US$4 a minute; to Europe US$4.50; to New Zealand, US$5. Phone calls are cheaper by 20% between 2200 and 0700.

Media Of the 20 colour-TV stations, 4 transmit from Montevideo (channel 12 is the most popular). There are also 35 radio stations (8 private FM) in Montevideo and 65 in the rest of the country.

There are 6 Montevideo newspapers: *El País, El Día, La República* and *La Mañana*, and *El Diario* and *Mundo Color* which come out in the evening. *Búsqueda* is published weekly. The town of Paysandú has the *Telégrafo*. At noon the main Buenos Aires papers can be had in Montevideo.

Local Information Centres The Comisión Nacional de Turismo central office, at Plaza Cagancha, Montevideo, issues tourist literature. It has built a number of good guest houses at the various resorts and gives information about them at the Information Office. There is a good information kiosk at Montevideo's main bus station. The local papers publish "what's on" columns on Friday evenings and on Saturdays. Tourist section in Friday's *El Día*.

Maps Automóvil Club del Uruguay, Av. Libertador General Lavalleja (ex Agraciada) 1532, Montevideo, publishes road maps of the city and the country at large, and so do Esso and Ancap at about US$2 each. Official maps are issued by Instituto Geográfico Militar, Abreu y 8 de Octubre, open 0800-1230, T 816868.

We should like to thank Charlie Nurse for updating the Uruguay chapter and acknowledge the help given in revising the Uruguay section by Mrs P. Murphy (Montevideo) for some very useful material, Karl Alchorn (Oromocto, NB), Hans and Verónica Liechti-Avaneda (Santiago de Chile), Hans and Lena Bengtsson (Gothenburg, Swe.), Erik Bernesson (Båstad, Swe.), Fearon and Richard Blair (Kamloops BC, Canada), Jens Borchers (Herzberg/Harz, W. Ger.) and Michael Frantz (Sieber, W. Ger.), Alex Brand (Heidelberg 1), Binka Le Breton (Muriaé, Minas Gerais), Kirsten Bruun and Jesper Juel Rasmussen (Copenhagen), Daniel Buck and Anne Meadows (Washington DC), B Clark (Chelmsford), Dr Peter Dollinger (Liebefeld-Berne, Switz.), Jennifer Eberle (Westwood, NJ), John Edmunds (Harpenden, Herts.), Anthony Feeny (London EC1), D. Friend (Melbourne), Theodor A. Gevert (Barueri, SP, Brazil), Rod Glaubitz (Köln 91), Christian Gurney (Thornhill, Ont.), Simon Gustafson (Taby, Swe.), Dr Paul Heaton (London NW6), Frank Hermann (Nauheim), Ursula Jenny (Bottmingen, Switz.), Justin Koprowski (High Wycombe), Janet Krengel (Islington), Antony and Elisabeth Lancaster (Lima 18), Herbert S. Levi (Buenos Aires), Nelly Matthey (Lausanne), Kirk Mayer and Barbara Pearce (Macclesfield), Ralph-Peter Mechnik (Nürnberg 1), Barbara Meier and Thomas Ester (Essen 15, W. Ger.), Daniel Morgan (Wellington, NZ), Dimitri Moursellas (Manhattan Beach, CA), Richard Müller (Gümligen, Switz.), David, Christine, Philip and Catherine Mylan (Worksop), Steve Newman and Wendy Chilcott (Bahía Blanca), Jonas Noreús (Varberg, Swe.), Claus Nøgaard and Bitten Pedersen (Silkeborg, Dmk.), Lucy Paine and William Petrie (Watlington, Oxon.), Wulf Peters (Querenhurst, W. Ger.), John M. Raspey, Piero Scaruffi (Redwood City, CA), Kathrin Schildknecht and Jürg Schmutz (Bern, Switz.), Ueli Schlatter (Hemmental, Switz.), Jolanda Schneider (Malans, Switz.), Rolf Schneider (Effretikon, Switz.), Christian Stückle (Ingolstadt, W. Ger.), Thomas Thanner (München 40), Trevor Toone (Burnaby, BC, Canada), Karen Uemura (Hollister, CA), Ingrid Walter and Norbert Eisinger (Schnelldorf, W. Ger.), Regina Wetzer and Richard C. Brusca (San Diego, CA) and Urs Wigger (Menznau, Switz.).

VENEZUELA

INTRODUCTION

WHEN the Spaniards landed in Venezuela in 1498, in the course of Columbus' third voyage, they found a poor country sparsely populated by Indians who had created no distinctive culture. Four hundred years later it was still poor, almost exclusively agrarian, exporting little, importing less. The miracle year which changed all that was 1914, when oil was discovered near Maracaibo. Today, Venezuela is said to be the richest country in Latin America and is one of the largest producers and exporters of oil in the world. The oil revenues have been used to rebuild Caracas and Maracaibo and other cities, and to create the best network of roads on the continent. In view of recent new discoveries and the cutback of production, at the present rate of extraction oil reserves will last for at least 40 years. Vast investments have been poured into state industry and agrarian reform and into tackling the problems of education, housing and unemployment.

Venezuela has 2,800 km. of coastline on the Caribbean Sea, and 72 islands. To the east is Guyana, to the south Brazil, and to the west Colombia. Its area is 912,050 square km., and its population exceeds 18 million. It was given its name— "Little Venice"—by the Spanish navigators, who saw in the Indian pile dwellings on Lake Maracaibo a dim reminder of the buildings along Venetian waterways.

The country falls into four very different regions: the Venezuelan Highlands to the west and along the coast; the Maracaibo Lowlands around the fresh water lake of Maracaibo; the vast central plain of the Llanos of the Orinoco; and the Guayana Highlands, which take up over half the country.

The Venezuelan Highlands are an offshoot of the Andes. From the Colombian border they trend, at first, towards the NE to enfold the Maracaibo Lowlands. This section is known as the Sierra Nevada de Mérida. Beyond they broaden out into the Segovia Highlands N of Barquisimeto, and then turn E in parallel ridges along the coast to form the Central Highlands, dipping into the Caribbean Sea only to rise again into the North-Eastern Highlands of the peninsulas of Paria and

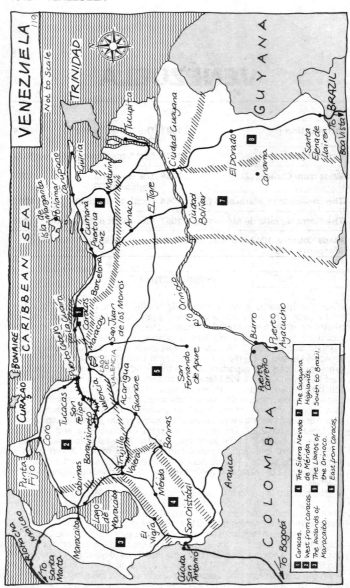

VENEZUELA

Not to Scale

CARIBBEAN SEA

TRINIDAD

GUYANA

COLOMBIA

BRAZIL

1 Caracas.
2 West from Caracas.
3 The lowlands of Maracaibo.
4 The Sierra Nevada de Mérida.
5 The Llanos of the Orinoco.
6 East from Caracas.
7 The Guayana Highlands.
8 South to Brazil.

Araya.

The general outline of each area will reveal that natural obstacles to farming, cattle breeding, and communications are formidable. It explains why the country was poverty-stricken for so long.

Climate is tropical, with little change between season and season. Temperature is a matter of altitude. Mean annual temperatures are given in the text. At Caracas it is 20°C, but during the dry season (December to April), there is a great difference between day and night temperatures, and during the whole year there is a burst of heat around mid-day. Rainfall in mm.: Caracas, 762; Maracaibo, 573; Barcelona, 660; Mérida, 1,295; Amazonas and parts of Barinas state 2,540.

History At the beginning of the 16th century, Venezuela was inhabited by various tribes of Caribs and Arawaks, who could make no effective resistance against the Spaniards. The first permanent Spanish settlement was at Cumaná, in 1520. Soon afterwards settlers reached Coro, at the foot of the Paraguaná Peninsula. Indian slaves were used to mine and pan for gold, but the results were disappointing and the settlers turned to agriculture, forming settlements at Barquisimeto in 1552, at Valencia in 1555, and at Caracas in 1567. It was not until after a century of consolidation in these areas that they began to occupy the rest of the country, intermarrying freely with the Indians and later introducing black slaves to work the sugar plantations. Centralized colonial control from Spain was as irksome here as in the rest of Latin America: three risings reflecting these discontents took place in 1749, 1775 and 1797, and there were two abortive attempts by Francisco Miranda to achieve independence in 1806 and 1811. After Miranda had been captured, the movement was led by Simón Bolívar, a *criollo* with a touch of Indian blood, born in Caracas in 1783. He met with mixed success until his capture of Angostura, now Ciudad Bolívar, in 1817. There he was joined by a contingent of experienced Peninsular veterans recruited in London. At their head, together with the horsemen of the *llanos* commanded by Gen. José Antonio Páez, he undertook a dramatic march over the Andes in 1819 to win the battle of Boyacá and capture Bogotá. Three months later, the revolutionary congress at Angostura—with most of Venezuela still in Spanish hands— declared the independence of Gran Colombia, a union of what is now Ecuador, Colombia, Venezuela, and Panama. Bolívar returned from Bogotá, and on June 24, 1821, the revolutionaries routed the Spanish forces at Carabobo. There was some desultory fighting for two more years, but the last of the Spanish forces surrendered at Puerto Cabello in 1823.

Before Bolívar's death in 1830 Páez declared Venezuela an independent republic. Other presidents of note were Guzmán Blanco, Juan Vicente Gómez (1909-1935), a brutal but efficient dictator, and Isaías Medina Angarita, who introduced the oil laws. There was much material progress under the 6-year dictatorship of Gen. Marcos Pérez Jiménez (1952-58), but his Gómez-like methods led to his overthrow in January 1958. A stable democracy has been created since, with regular presidential elections every five years. Sr. Carlos Andrés Pérez of the centre-left Democratic Action party took office in 1974, presiding over a period of rapid development following the first great oil-price rise, and was succeeded in 1979 by Sr. Luis Herrera Campins of the Christian Democratic party, Copei. Dr. Jaime Lusinchi of Democratic Action was elected president in 1983, to be followed by Carlos Andrés Pérez, who began his second term in 1989.

The People 53% are under 18. A large number are of mixed Spanish and Indian blood. There are some pure Indians, mostly in the Guayana Highlands and in the forests west of Lake Maracaibo. There are some pure-blooded Africans and a strong admixture of African blood along the coast, particularly at the ports. The arrival of 800,000 European immigrants since the war, mostly in the 1950s, has greatly modified the racial make-up in Venezuela. One in 6 of all Venezuelans is foreign born. Total population was 19,246,000 in 1989.

About 79% of the population is urban. Annual growth: 2.8%; urban growth: 3.3%. Birth-rate (1985) 33.0; mortality per 1,000 inhabitants: 5.6; expectation of life, 69 years.

Venezuela, despite its wealth, still faces serious social problems. About 12% are unemployed; about 10% are illiterate. Many rural dwellers have drifted to the cities; one result of this exodus is that Venezuelan farmers do not provide all the food the nation needs and imports of foodstuffs are necessary, even for items such as beans and rice.

The Economy Venezuela's economy has been dominated by petroleum, despite its contributing only 8% to gdp. Oil exports have inflated foreign exchange receipts and government fiscal revenues. Oil revenues have shaped the rest of the productive sector, even though employment creation has been minimal, and inter-industry links have been relatively underdeveloped. High earnings from oil have caused a tendency to overvalue the exchange rate, which has discouraged export-based production and hindered import substitution. Non-oil industry and agriculture are now being targeted for expansion as oil's role has diminished since the early 1980s.

Venezuela has vast natural resources, and is especially rich in energy, possessing 55.52 bn barrels of proved oil reserves. Apart from proved and exploitable reserves, there are another 1.2 trillion barrels in potential reserves of very heavy oil in the as yet unexploited Orinoco belt. There are 2.65 trillion cubic metres of natural gas reserves (plus 5 trillion probable), and 500 m tonnes of coal (9 bn estimated) in the provinces of Zulia and Táchira. There is believed to be a hydroelectricity potential (HEP) of 80,000 MW. The new hydroelectric generating capacity around Ciudad Guayana in the east is designed to act as the hub of economic growth. It includes the 10,300 MW **Guri dam project**, the second largest HEP station in the world after Haipú, and which in July 1986 provided just over half the country's generating capacity.

Venezuela is Opec's third largest oil producer, with a capacity of 2.6 m barrels a day. Oil production is concentrated in three major sedimentary basins: the Maracaibo, the eastern, and the Apure-Barinas basins. Petróleos de Venezuela (PDVSA), the state-owned oil company created out of the nationalization of oil companies in 1976, has been relatively successful in keeping its market share because of its forward-looking marketing strategy based on forming partnerships with refineries and marketing chains in Europe and the USA.

The mining sector has been probably the most buoyant part of the economy since 1984, and is likely to continue in this vein with important mining ventures in bauxite, iron ore, gold and coal. Venezuela could become the world's leading aluminium producer by the end of the century.

Only about 20% of the land surface is devoted to agriculture, and about three-quarters of this is pasture. Like mining, it is a small sector of the economy, accounting for 8% of gdp and employing 15% of the workforce. The main grain staples are maize and sorghum, while sugar and rice are also important. The main export crop is coffee, with other cash crops being cocoa and cotton.

Venezuela is Latin America's fourth largest debtor, and despite huge foreign reserves of over US$20 bn accumulated by the mid-1980s from oil wealth, the country became unable to service its external debt normally from 1982 because of a bunching of maturities. A US$21 bn debt rescheduling agreement was signed with commercial banks in 1986 but was almost immediately renegotiated, with longer repayment terms and lower interest rates, as falling oil prices that year caused unexpected foreign exchange constraints; oil revenues fell by 44% in 1986. The government avoided taking adjustment measures and chose instead to spend reserves until by end-1988 liquid foreign exchange reserves were exhausted. In 1989 the new administration turned to the IMF and World Bank for support for a comprehensive macroeconomic adjustment programme to rebuild reserves, encourage domestic savings and cut the public sector deficit. Previous policies were reversed with the freeing of interest rates and the exchange rate. The initial impact was a severe recession and gdp fell by 8.1% in 1989, accompanied by a burst of inflation and higher unemployment. Nevertheless, in 1990 the economy appeared to be on the road to recovery, strengthened by the reforms and a higher level of investment. A debt restructuring package was agreed in principle in March 1990 which allowed banks to choose from a menu of options including debt reduction, debt service reduction or new loans.

Government Venezuela is a federal republic of 20 states, a Federal District, and two territories. There are two legislative houses, a Senate with 47 seats and a Chamber of Deputies with 200 seats. The current Constitution is dated 23 January, 1961. Voting is now compulsory for all over 18.

Education Elementary schools are free, and education is compulsory from the age of 7 to the completion of the primary grade.

National Parks Venezuela has 35 national parks and 15 smaller national monuments, some of which are mentioned in the text. A full list is published by the Instituto Nacional de Parques (Inparques), Edificio CVB, Avenida Germania, Caracas. Each park has a regional director and its own guards (*guardaparques*). Permits (free) are required to stay in the parks, although this is not usually necessary for those visited frequently. For further information on the National Parks system, visit the Ministerio del Ambiente y de los Recursos Naturales Renovables (MARNR) at Parque del Este in Caracas. The book: *Guía de los Parques Nacionales y Monumentos Naturales de Venezuela*, is obtainable in Audubon headquarters, Las Mercedes shopping centre, Las Mercedes, Caracas.

CARACAS (1)

The capital, Caracas, and the cities of Valencia and Maracay are in the Central Highlands, the most important upland area in Venezuela. The mountains here rise abruptly from a lush green coast to heights of from two to three thousand metres. Caracas, lies in a small basin, a rift in the thickly forested mountains which runs some 24 km. east and west. This historic colonial town has been transformed into one of the most astonishing modern cities in Latin America.

Caracas, founded in 1567, now has a population of around 4 million. It lies at 960 metres, but the southern parts of the city are 120 metres lower. Temperatures are moderate (a maximum of 32°C in July and August, and an occasional minimum of 9°C in January and February) and it is always cool at night.

A comparatively low pass (1,040 metres) in the mountains gives Caracas access by road to its port, La Guaira, and its international and domestic airports nearby at Maiquetía. The distance by a magnificently engineered road is 28 km. or 30 mins. by car (toll US$0.10 when going up; going down is free). Much longer should be allowed, however, for anyone with a plane to catch, as there are often delays arising from heavy traffic.

The proportionate growth of Caracas since the war has been greater than that of any other Latin American capital. Colonial buildings have given way to modern multi-storeyed edifices, many of which are architecturally impressive. Excellent examples are the University City, the twin towers of the Parque Central (containing a Ministry of Transport exhibition, open Mon.-Fri. 0900-1530), the Centro Simón Bolívar, and the Círculo Militar.

Starting in Catia, an industrial area in the W where both roads from La Guaira enter, Avenida Sucre goes past the 23 de Enero workers' flats to join Av. Urdaneta between Palacio Miraflores and the Palacio Blanco, housing government offices. Later come the Post Office and Santa Capilla Church, looking like a wedding cake by a Parisian master pastrycook. Turn right here for Plaza Bolívar and the Capitol (the National Congress, do not take photographs in the vicinity or you may be arrested), or carry straight on down the Av. Urdaneta to San Bernardino (Colonial Museum). Here, we enter Av. Andrés Bello, which passes just below the cable railway station to join Av. Libertador to the Country Club and the E, or we can turn down the Av. La Salle to the eastern end of Los Caobos park, with the fine mahoganies which give it its popular name. From the Plaza Venezuela intersection at the eastern end of the park, the Avenida Abraham Lincoln leads E through

---

Caracas: Key to map

1. Plaza Bolívar; 2. Parque Carabobo; 3. Parque Los Caobos; 4. Plaza Candelaria; 5. Plaza O'Leary; 6. Plaza Miranda; 7. Plaza La Concordia; 8. Parque Central, Museo de Arte Contemporáneo, Museo de los Niños; Tourist Office; 9. Centro Simón Bolívar, CANTV; 10. Cathedral; 11. Capitolio Nacional; 12. San Francisco; 13. Santa Capilla; 14. Santa Teresa; 15. Casa y Museo de Bolívar; 16. Museo de Bellos Artes; 17. Museo de Ciencias Naturales; 18. National Library; 19. Jardín Botánico; 20. Post Office; 21. Consejo Municipal; 22. Banco Central; 23. Bus to Airport; 24. *Hotel Caracas Hilton*; 25. Road to Quinta Anauco and San Bernardino; 26. Road to Ciudad Universitaria; 27. Palacio Miraflores.

Sabana Grande and continues as the Avenida Francisco Miranda to the residential section of Altamira, with its fine plaza and obelisk (unfortunately a construction site for a new Metro station). Sabana Grande, a modern shopping, hotel and business centre, is now a pedestrian mall closed to vehicular traffic: a very popular place to take a stroll.

Alternatively, forking right out of Avenida Sucre and crossing the viaduct, we reach El Silencio, and thence pass through the Centro Simón Bolívar, with its twin skyscrapers and underground parking and shopping centre (with an interesting mosaic at the lowest level), and finally along the Avenida Bolívar past Nuevo Circo bullring towards University City, the Sports Stadium, the *Tamanaco Hotel* and La Casona, residence of the President. S of the Nuevo Circo is the Helicoide, planned as a commercial centre under the Pérez Jiménez regime but left uncompleted at his fall in 1958. From the viaduct, we can also take Av. Universidad past the National Library (former University), Capitol and San Francisco church. Two corners later, we glimpse, left, Bolívar's birthplace, before continuing to the Art Museum and on round Los Caobos park, or by the Av. Libertador, to the east.

Another west-east route is along the Avenida Boyacá from Avenida Baralt in the west to Petare in the east, connecting with the main road east to Barcelona (Route 9), which skirts the Cordillera de la Costa, including Avila mountain, and gives fine views along the length of the city. Towards the E end is a monument commemorating the battle of Boyacá, and a viaduct strides majestically over the recently remodelled park in Los Chorros suburb, to which access is signposted.

To the SW from El Silencio the Avenida San Martín leads towards the factories of Antímano. This area can also be reached direct from Catia by the Planicie tunnel. In the SW is also the older residential section of El Paraíso.

The shady Plaza Bolívar, with its fine equestrian statue of the Liberator and pleasant colonial cathedral, is still the official centre of the city, though no longer geographically so. In fact, several centres (Plaza Bolívar, Plaza Venezuela, Sabana Grande, Chacaíto, La Floresta, Boleíta) are strung along the valley with residential areas between.

Parks Jardín Botánico, near Plaza Venezuela, entrance by Ciudad Universitaria (free), is quite small, disorganized and noisy. Parque Los Caobos is being extended; it is peaceful and has a cafetería in the middle. By the entrance in Av. México is the cultural centre, Ateneo de Caracas, with a theatre, art gallery, concert rooms, bookshop and the imposing Teresa Carreño theatre complex. Parque Nacional del Este (renamed the Parque Rómulo Betancourt in 1989) has a zoo and is a peaceful place to relax, except at weekends, entrance US$0.10, closed on Mon. There is a boating lake and playground for children; many of the birds fly freely and there is an interesting collection of exotic flora. The Parque Caricuao is at the end of the Metro line, quite heavily wooded; it has the city's main zoo (the metro station is called Zoológico). Parque El Pinar also has a large zoo (Av. José Antonio Páez, El Pinar). The Parque Los Chorros at the foot of the mountain has impressive waterfalls, also recommended; El Calvario, west of Plaza O'Leary, is quiet and pleasant with a good view of Centro Simón Bolívar. A new park, Parque Vargas, is to replace the Nuevo Circo bus station. **See page** 1056 for El Avila National Park.

National Monuments

Panteón Nacional Open Tues.-Sun., 0900-1200 and 1500-1730. This was designed as the resting place of Bolívar, the Liberator, and Miranda, the Precursor of Independence. The remains of Bolívar lie there, but the tomb of Miranda, who died in a Spanish prison, has been left open to await the return of his body. There is a small military ceremony at 1515 daily.

Capitolio Nacional Open to visitors Tues.-Sun., 0900-1200 and 1500-1800. The Elliptical Salon has some impressive paintings by the Venezuelan artist Martín Tovar y Tovar and a bronze urn containing the 1811 Declaration of Independence. One of the paintings on the ceiling shows a British regiment fighting in the Battle of Carabobo, and the names of the officers appear on the wall; in acknowledgement of this assistance Bolívar granted the British armed forces the right to march through any city in Gran Colombia (Colombia, Ecuador, Panama and Venezuela) with bayonets fixed, drums beating and flags flying.

Museums

Museo de Bellas Artes, Plaza Morelos in Parque Los Caobos: open Tues.-Sun., 0900-1630. Pictures include an El Greco among works by mainly Venezuelan artists. Adjacent is the Galería de Arte Nacional, which also houses the Cinemateca Nacional.

Museo de Ciencias Naturales, also in Plaza Morelos in Parque Los Caobos; open 0900-1200, 1500-1730 except Mon.

Museo de Arte Colonial, Quinta Anauco, Av. Panteón, San Bernardino: open Tues.-Sat., 0900-1130, 1500-1700, Sun., 0900-1800. Guided tour in Spanish available. A delightful house built in 1720. Chamber concerts most Saturdays at 1800. The beautiful suburb of San Bernardino glories in tropical flowers and whole avenues of forest trees, smothered in blossom in season.

Casa Natal del Libertador   Open Tues.-Fri., 0900-1200 and 1430-1700, Sat., Sun., 1000-1300 and 1400-1700 (but closed for refurbishment in 1989). The present house is a reconstruction of the house where Bolívar was born. The first, of adobe, was destroyed by an earthquake. The second became a stable, and was later pulled down. The present building of stone was built by order of Gómez (whose birthday was the same as Bolívar's) in the early 1920s; it contains interesting pictures and furniture.

The Museo Bolivariano is alongside the Casa Natal and contains the Liberator's war relics.

House of Arturo Michelena, four blocks north of Miraflores palace, in the La Pastora section, is a typical 19th century home, now a museum. Open 0900-1200 and 1500-1700 (closed Mon. and Fri.).

Museo de Transporte, Parque Nacional del Este, includes a large collection of locomotives and old cars, as well as a fascinating series of scale models of Caracas a century ago. Open Sat., Sun., 0900-1800. Admission US$0.50 (closed in 1989).

In the Parque Central, between Av. Lecuna (E end) and the elevated section of Av. Bolívar there are four museums in a complex which includes 2 octagonal towers (56 floors each) and four large apartment buildings with shopping below.

Museo de Arte Contemporáneo, Parque Central, Cuadra Bolívar, near the *Caracas Hilton*, very good, European and Venezuelan painters represented. The museum is in two sections, the larger of which is downstairs and is easily missed. Open Tues.-Sun. 1000-1800.

Museo de los Niños, Parque Central, next to East Tower, is open to the public Wed.-Sun. and holidays, 0900-1200, 1400-1700, otherwise is for school visits; a highly sophisticated modern science museum, well worth a visit and extremely popular, US$0.75 (adults). Book a day or so in advance on school holidays or August. Also in the Parque Central complex, **Museo Audiovisual**, Tues.-Fri., 0900-1700, US$1, includes a library of Venezuelan television programmes, a practice TV studio, and **Museo del Teclado** (keyboard instruments).

Museo Histórico Militar, near Metro Gato Negro.

The Ministry of Foreign Relations contains pictures mostly of national heroes and historical events.

The Concejo Municipal (City Hall) on Plaza Bolívar contains three museums: a collection of the paintings of Emilio Boggio, a Venezuelan painter; the Raúl Santana Museum of the Creole Way of Life, a collection of miniature figures in costumes and poses characteristic of Venezuelan life, all handmade by Raúl Santana and extremely realistic; Francisco Pizarro's battle standard, presented by him to Sucre after the battle of Ayacucho and then given to Bolívar is shown here; and the Sala de Arqueología Gaspar Marcano, exhibiting ceramics, mostly discovered on the coast. All three open Tues.-Fri., 0930-1200, 1500-1800; Sat. and Sun., 0930-1800. Informative guides are available.

Those with a deeper interest in archaeology might like to contact the Junta Nacional Protectora y Conservadora del Patrimonio Histórico y Artístico de la Nación, Palacio de Miraflores, Av. Urdaneta.

Churches   The Cathedral should be seen for its beautiful façade, and pictures including alleged Rubens and Murillo. San Francisco should be seen for its colonial altars. Santa Teresa, between La Palma and Santa Teresa, just SE of the Centro Simón Bolívar, has good interior chapels.

N.B. Check museum schedules in *El Universal*, *El Nacional* or the *Daily Journal* (which also have details of events for children). Many museums and most religious buildings will refuse entry to anybody wearing shorts.

Modern Caracas

Visitors should see the Avenida de los Próceres with its twin monoliths and other monuments to the heroes of independence (it also has flowers and gardens); the magnificent Officers' Club on the same avenue, the Cuadra Bolívar near the *Caracas Hilton*; and the University City, an enormous and coherent complex of great buildings in which paintings, sculpture and stained glass are completely integrated with the architecture (which is now showing signs of wear).

N.B. In the centre of Caracas, each street corner has a name, and addresses are generally given as, for example, "Santa Capilla a Mijares", rather than the official "Calle Norte 2, No. 26". Maps can be bought at *Caracas Hilton*, and Lagovén service stations. Good street maps of Caracas can be bought in kiosks, or be found at the back of the yellow pages telephone directory.

Warning It is advisable not to arrive in Caracas at night and not to walk down narrow streets after dark. Police searches are common, especially in airports; if you have entered overland from Colombia, you can expect thorough investigation (once you've left the border, better to say you flew in).

Hotels Cheap *pensiones* are usually full of long-stay residents and have very few rooms available for travellers. Hotels tend to be particularly full at weekends and in July and August. In the centre all cheap hotels take only short stay customers on Fri. p.m. Better hotels often try to give you a suite instead of a double room. Hotels marked with an asterisk (*) are bookable through Fairmont International (see next page).

Recommended hotels not in the centre: The *Tamanaco** is the best hotel in Caracas, but it is difficult to get rooms as it is normally fully booked, changes travellers' cheques for guests only (poor rate), L+ (US$150d + 10% tax, rooms are priced in dollars). *Hotel Paseo de las Mercedes*, C, Las Mercedes is almost next door to the *Tamanaco*. *Nostrum*, Av. Orinoco con final Calle París, Las Mercedes (near *Paseo*), T 92-76-46, 92-66-46, a/c, hot water, clean, rec., E. The *Caracas Hilton**, L (US$115d + 10% tax, priced in dollars), is more central but noisy (traffic and air conditioning) and although the rooms are excellent and clean, the service has also been criticized; connected with the *Hilton* are the *Residencias Anauco Hilton**, Parque Central, an "apartotel", B, bad reports received about the travel agency at this hotel; another apartment hotel is the *CCT Venantur** in the Centro Ciudad Comercial Tamanaco, luxury, C; furnished flats also at *Crillón**, Av. Libertador, between Las Acacias and Los Jabillos, D, good value; *Ribot*, Av. Andres Eloy Blanco, La Mansión Fte. Viasa, La Candelaria (nr. *Hilton*), F, T 5713433/5713244. The *Ávila** is on Av. Jorge Washington in San Bernardino on the higher levels of the city (T 515128/515173, Telex: 21637 Avila), set in park-like gardens and very pleasant, A, good service, most of staff speak English and German, rooms vary, avoid top floor, pool, Metrobus nearby, good restaurant; *Aventura**, Av. Fco. Fajardo, San Bernardino, A, clean, modern, large rooms, pool, restaurant; *Waldorf*, Av. Industria, San Bernardino, Bellas Artes metro, T 571-4733, E, shower, restaurant, French, German and English spoken, good value, repeatedly rec.; *La Floresta**, Av. Avila, Sur Plaza Altamira, T 2844111, D, clean, friendly, helpful, but restaurant not very good. Also good, *Continental Altamira**, D, Av. San Juan Bosco (there is also *Altamira*, Av. J. F. Sosa, D). *Beethoven*, Av. Beethoven, Colinas de Bellomonte (½ block from Sears), D, with bath, TV, good, clean; *Centro Uslar*, 2a Av., Calles 1 y 2, Sector B, Urb. Montalbán, C, good but a long way from centre; *El Paseo*, Av. Los Ilustres, Urb. Los Chaguaramos, T 661-3438/3547/3315, D, good, clean. In the E of the city, *El Marqués*, Av. El Samán esq. Yaruari, El Marqués, medium-priced, comfortable, quiet, good restaurant.

Cheapest hotels can be found around the Nuevo Circo bus terminal, many of them on Av. Lecuna: e.g. *ABC*, F, with shower, very noisy (less so on higher floors, which are good value); *Center Park*, No. 20, T 5418619, F, helpful, safe; *Urupagua*, Limón and Rio Bravo, F, but this area is unpleasant and unsafe for women. Better to go several blocks WSW to a quieter area, e.g. *Príncipe*, Av. Sur 3, Gobernador a Pinto, G without bath; *Pensión San Marcos*, Hoyo a Santa Rosalía, T 5453723, G, noisy, basic; *Avenida*, Calle Sur 4 (nr. Capitolio), T 426440, E, hot water, a/c, safe, rec.; *La Neve*, Pilita a Glorieta No. 126—Sur 4, nr. Metro Capitolio, E, a/c or fan, bath, good, clean, safe, quiet, good restaurant, rec. For other cheap hotels look on Calle Sur 2.

In the downtown area: *Inter**, Ánimas a Calero on corner of Av. Urdaneta, E, very clean, shower and toilet with each room, friendly, English spoken, very popular so be sure to make a reservation, the queues for rooms begin before 0700 and the hotel is full by 0800, poor restaurant; *Ausonia*, Bolero a Pineda, D, with bath, hot-water, TV, central, clean; *Mara*, E, *Conde*, D, and *Veroes*, D, Av. Urdaneta, are in the centre, convenient for banks and business houses; also *Cervantes*, Av. Urdaneta, Norte 5, F, cheap but spartan, safe, very noisy. *Plaza Catedral**, Blvd. Plaza Bolívar, next to Cathedral, C, a/c, TV, phone, some English spoken, stays limited to 2 nights; *Caroni*, 2 blocks from Capitolio, near Cathedral, E, popular, good value, safe but a bit noisy; *Hospedaje Torreón*, San Agustín, Sur 11 Bolívar, E, clean, friendly, safe, rec.; *Grand Galaxie**, Truco a Caja de Agua, between Av. Baralt and Norte 4 on Salas Sta. Bárbara, T 83-90-11/83-90-44, D, deluxe, a/c, TV, phone, restaurant, central, comfortable; *Palais*, Norte 4 (Pilita a Glorieta), E, modern, clean, a/c, friendly, luggage stored, excellent restaurant; *Lider*, Baralt y Crespo, D, modern, a/c, friendly, rec; *Hispano—Venezolano*, Sur 4 (Reducto a Glorieta), T 422553, D, a/c, good value.

If you arrive in Caracas in doubt, ask a taxi driver to take you to Las Acacias in Sabana Grande, where you can choose a hotel from the very large number in that area. There are various grades all close together so you can walk from one to another until you find one suitable. However, many of the numerous small hotels on Av. Las Acacias do not cater for singles or for couples staying more than a few hours. If not using a taxi, take metro to Sabana Grande (for example). On Av. Las Acacias are *Bruno**, D, TV, air conditioning, fair, Peruvian restaurant with live entertainment, unremarkable; *Everest*, D; *Myriam*, E, few single rooms, off-street parking, clean but noisy; *Embassy*, E with bath, a/c, rec., expensive bar downstairs, *Restaurant Las Acacias* opp. is good value; *Tanausú**, E. On Av. Casanova are *Luna**, D, clean, friendly, rec. (with Calle El Colegio); *Capri-Casanova*, D, spartan but clean and friendly; *Broadway**, No. 4, convenient for Chacaíto metro station, D, private bathroom, TV, friendly, clean, a bit noisy, Italian specialities in restaurant. Others in Sabana Grande include *El Cóndor** (3a Av. Las Delicias), C, TV, air conditioning, businessmen on their own need to take suites because single rooms have no desks; *Plaza Palace*, Av. Los Mangos, Las Delicias, very good, friendly, good atmosphere, B; *Las Américas**, Los Cerritos, end of Casanova, D, classic 50's style, warm water, food passable but unexciting; *City** (Av. Bolivia, Los Caobos), E, all rooms have TV and private bath; *Ritz*, Av. Las Palmas y Av. Libertador, E, with bath, a/c, secure free parking; *Madrid*, F, Av. Chacaíto, small, hot water, showers in all rooms; *Capri*, F, Calle Las Flores, clean; *The King's Inn Hotel**, D, Calle Olimpo, near Av. Lincoln; *Tampa**, Av. Francisco Solano López, D; *Savoy**, Av. Francisco Solano López, Las Delicias, C, without food, good, efficient, clean, secure vehicle park. *Plaza Venezuela*, Av. La Salle, D, clean, friendly, noisy; *Critsal*, Plaza Venezuela, Av. Colegio, E, a/c, convenient, basic, comfortable, safe, good value, disco at weekends, good cheap Chilean food. Elena and Enrique Ganteaume (T 334276) rent out a colonial style villa and can arrange tours.

Hotel Reservations Fairmont International, Torre Capriles, Planta Baja, Plaza Venezuela, Caracas, T 782 8433, Telex 21232 SNRHO, Fax 782 4407, will book hotel rooms in Caracas and also in 102 hotels in the rest of the country. "Packages" organised by Fairmont International are reported to be much more expensive than hotel bookings. The airport tourist office is very helpful and will book hotel rooms. Finding a hotel, particularly in the middle-price range, is always difficult. If you book from abroad (e.g. Thomas Cook in England) make sure you receive confirmation before beginning your journey or you may turn up and find yourself without a room. **Economy tip**: most hotel rooms have a TV set for which you will be charged; if you don't want it, ask for it to be removed. For apartment rental, consult *El Universal* daily paper, small ads. columns.

Restaurants There is such a profusion of eating places in Caracas that we give the following general advice, with a mention of just a few places currently reported reliable, rather than attempt the impossible task of keeping up to date with all the changes. Guides to eating are published in the *VAAUW Guide to Caracas* and the magazine "Ve Venezuela". Also "Gourmet Dining out in Caracas", available at travel agencies and good hotels. Advertisements appear in the "Daily Journal" and the Yellow Pages of the telephone directory. Don't be shy about asking the price before you order in a bar as beer in one will cost three times as much as in another, and a modest portion of manchego cheese will cost more than a good steak. Food on display in a bar is free with your drink if they offer it as a *pasapalo*, but will be charged for if offered as a *ración*. You can save on the service charge by eating at the bar and not at a table. Coffee in a café is at government-controlled price if taken at the counter, but not if served at a table. Milk is subsidized and is cheaper than soft drinks. By decree, restaurants must put up a list of prices on or near the front door, and are prohibited from charging for place settings (cubiertos) or bread, butter, condiments etc. (guarnición).

For dining out, there is a selection of good restaurants around Avenida Urdaneta (*Bar Pas de Calais* for paella, *Mesón de Cervantes*—friendly multilingual manager, Nelson, *El Parador* and *Politena*), La Castellana (*La Estancia*), Plaza Altamira (*Mayfair Station*), Las Mercedes (*Piccolo Mundo*, *Hereford Grill*, *Farms Grill*, *Mr Ribs*, Av. Valle Arriba, barbecued ribs etc., very fashionable; *Era de Acuario*, vegetarian, open for dinner), El Rosal (*La Barba Roja*, Calle Venezuela, *El Jabaguero*, Calle Pichincha, both seafood) and Sabana Grande (see below). There are plenty of eating places around Plaza Bolívar. In the Parque Central (Edificio Anauco—basement) is *El Parque*, good food and service; *Tarzilandia*, 10th Transversal Altamira, San Juan Bosco, international food; *El Granjero del Este*, Rio de Janeiro, T 916619, traditional barbecues, excellent arepas. Very good Mexican/Peruvian dishes at *El Tizón*, CC Bello Campo, Sótano Local 80, T 316715/2613485. Excellent pastries and cheese from *Panadería y Pastelería Madona*, Av. Sur, near corner with Camejo (0800-2300). The *Sol y Sombra*, Sur 1 No. 110 at Velásquez, doubles as a betting shop on race days.

Although it is not practicable to cover the whole of Caracas, the following description of the Sabana Grande area will give an idea of what is available. Breakfast in your hotel is likely to be poor (poor bread or none, insipid coffee and orange juice which is half artificial). It is better and cheaper in a fuente de soda, and cheaper still in a pastelería or arepería. (One correspondent recommends *La Ermita* on Plaza Venezuela.) Tables in the open air on the boulevard, however, are expensive, e.g. US$0.40 for a batido which costs US$0.25 down a side street or US$0.20 at a green-grocer, yet it is exactly the same fruit drink. (The boulevard waiters overcharge. Check prices on the displayed list.) Mid-day is the most economical time to eat the main meal of the day and about the only opportunity to find fresh vegetables. Particularly good value is the "menú ejecutivo" or "cubierto", which is a three-course meal for US$1.50, e.g. at *Ventas de Madrid* on San Gerónimo, *O' Gran Sol* on Villa Flor between Casanova and Sabana Grande (excellent paella, reasonable prices) and *Rincón de Bucanero*, on Casanova (also has music in the evenings).

Good, economical meals in the evening at *Sorrentino* and *Jabillos* on Francisco Solano, *Coraveña* (next to *La Bússola*, one block east of Torre La Previsora), *La Soledad* (next block south on Casanova), *Tivoli* (El Colegio between Lincoln and Casanova, home made pasta) and *Tropical Room* (two blocks east on Casanova). For business and similar occasions: *La Bússola* (see above—try carpaccio), *Rugantino* in *Hotel Tampa* (speciality cartuccio), *El Chicote* behind La Previsora, and *Villa D'Este* in *Hotel Cóndor*. For variety: *Floridita* in La Previsora and *Esquina de Tejas* in *Hotel Kursaal* (both Cuban), *Le Coq d'Or*, Av. Los Mangos (French), *Hotel Bruno* (Peruvian), *Mario's* on Casanova (Brazilian—noisy), *Tasca, Tacos y Algo Más* on Casanova (Mexican), *Dragón Verde*, Ciné París, Av. Maturín (Chinese), *Le Chalet*, in *Hotel Crillón* (Swiss), good selection, highly rec., and *Buffet Vegetariano*, Av. Los Jardines. Other vegetarian restaurants are *El Acuarino*, Truco a Caja de Agua; *Super Bueno*, esq. Chorro a Dr Paúl, Edif. Plaza El Venezolano and in front of El Conde Hotel; *Chalet Naturista*, nr. Sabana Grande metro station; these four are not open for dinner. Roast lamb at *La Taberna*, Torre Capriles, Plaza Venezuela. Fast foods: there is a plethora of burger and pizza places, as well as the ubiquitous hot dog stalls of doubtful hygiene (when the police don't close them down).

Clubs There are 3 country clubs in Caracas, all of which have excellent restaurants. The Country Club in the eastern part has an 18-hole golf course. The Social Centre of the British Commonwealth Association, Quinta Alborada, Avenida 7 with Transversal 9, Altamira, Caracas, with bar and swimming pool; British and Commonwealth visitors only; entry fee according to length of stay; T 261-30-60. Membership of the better clubs is by the purchase of a share, which can run to thousands of dollars. An exception is the sports club run by the *Tamanaco Hotel*, open to non-guests and suitable for people staying a short time. The Military Club (Círculo de las Fuerzas Armadas) is well worth seeing and, if the visitors are soberly dressed, permission to view the premises is often granted. Flying Club, at La Carlota, near *Tamanaco Hotel*, mixed reports. Robert and Daisy Kunstaetter of Richmond Hill, Ontario (call sign VE300G) tell us the Radio Club Venezolano is a very welcoming, efficient organization of amateur radio operators which is eager to meet amateurs from around the world (address: P.O.Box 2285, Caracas 1010-A, T 781-4878, 781-8303—Av. Lima, Los Caobos; branches around the country).

Shopping For gems and fine jewellery, visit the *H. Stern* shops at the Hotels *Hilton* and *Tamanaco* and at the International Airport; try also *Labady*, Sabana Grande 98, beautifully-made gold jewellery, English spoken. *Pro-Venezuela Exposición y Venta de Arte Popular*, Gran Avenida at Calle Olimpo, between Plaza Venezuela and beginning of Av. Casanova (opp. Torre La Previsora), sells Venezuelan crafts, very crowded, no prices, bargain hard. Indian and Andean crafts can be found at the market in Las Mercedes. The CCCT shopping centre is worth a visit. Large-size shoes (up to 47) at Catedral Sur 4 y Mercaderes.

From Chacaíto, along Av. Abraham Lincoln, Sabana Grande, to Plaza Venezuela, is a pedestrian precinct, with good shops, handicrafts for sale, street traders and cafés.

Bookshops   English language ones include: *English Bookshop*, Concresa, Prados del Este; *Lectura*, Centro Comercial Chacaíto, and *Steele's Bookstore*, Calle Baruta, Sabana Grande. *Librería del Este*, Av. Francisco de Miranda 52, Edif. Galipán, *Librería Multilingua*, Concresa, and *Librería Unica*, Centro Capriles, ground floor local 13N, Plaza Venezuela, all have foreign language books. A French bookshop is *Librería La France*, Centro Comercial Chacaíto, Italian bookshop, *El Libro Italiano*, Pasaje La Concordia (between Sabana Grande pedestrian street and Av. Fco. Solano López), and for German books, *Librería Alemana* (Oscar Todtmann), Centro El Bosque, Avenida Libertador.

City Buses   Starting from the bus station at Nuevo Circo (due to be replaced in 1989— **see page 1054**), there are many buses, overcrowded in the rush hours, urban fare usually US$0.07 (the correct fare helps to speed things up). *Por puesto* minibuses running on regular routes charge between US$0.08 and US$0.15 depending on the distance travelled within the city; fares rise to US$1.40 for journeys outside. Many *por puesto* services start in Silencio.

Taxis are required by law to instal and use taxi-meters. The initial flag fee is US$0.25 plus US$0.10 for each km. and US$0.05 for each 30 seconds of the ride (hourly rate US$3). Taxi drivers are authorized to charge an extra 20% on night trips after 1800, on Sun. and all holidays, and US$0.45 for answering telephone calls. After 1800 drivers are selective about where they want to go. Beware of taxi drivers trying to renegotiate fixed rates because your destination is in "a difficult area". There are pirates, however, with possibly a taxi sign, but without yellow licence plates/registration-number plate, which are to be avoided. If you get in a taxi with no meter you must negotiate the price in advance.

The Metro, opened in 1983, operates 0600-2300. It is air-conditioned, clean, well-kept and more comfortable and quicker than any other form of city transport; no smoking, no large bags. There are 2 lines which interconnect at Capitolio and which are continually being extended. Tickets vary in price according to number of stations travelled. Ten-journey tickets, known as Multibono, are available (saves queuing): US$1.20 for up to 5 stations, US$1.40 for 6-8 stations, US$1.60 over 8 stations. Metrobuses (feeder buses) connect with the Metro system. Guide: *La Practiguía del Metro*, published by Practiguía Azul.

Driving   Self-drive cars (Hertz, National, Avis, Volkswagen, Budget) are available at the airport and in town. They are cheaper than guided excursions for less than full loads. Driver's licence from home country accepted. Major credit card or US$210 cash deposit required. The Government has fixed the rates and the cheapest available, in Nov. 1989, was US$9 per day plus US$0.10 per km. National Car Rental offers 10-15% discount with Amex cedit cards. Auto and personal insurance strongly recommended as you will be lucky to survive two or three days as a newcomer to Caracas traffic without a dent or a scrape. Carry spare battery water, fan belts, the obligatory breakdown triangle, a jack and spanners. Some cars have a security device to prevent the engine being started and this is recommended. Don't run out of fuel; you can incur a Bs.500 fine by so doing. Beware of potholes even in the best roads and avoid driving fast, particularly at night; a nationwide speed limit of 80 kph was imposed in 1982. The best road map can be bought from CVP petrol stations (US$1); it shows the distances between towns and is generally reliable. Many roads may be marked as dirt tracks but have been paved since the map was produced. The Guía Progreso map is very detailed but not very accurate, especially S of Orinoco.

Motorcycles may not be ridden in Caracas between 2300 and 0500. Pillion passengers are only permitted if of the opposite sex from the driver.

Garage   Yota-Box, 3a Transversal Mis Encantos, Quinta Morava, No. 1 15, Chacao, T 313772/331035, owner Gerardo Ayala, rec., especially for Toyota.

Night Clubs   Caracas is a lively city by night, and there are many and varied discotheques and night clubs. Caraqueños dine at home around 2000, and in restaurants from 2100 to 2300, so night clubs don't usually come to life until after 2300, and then go on to all hours of the morning. *Naiguatá* (*Hotel Tamanaco*), expensive; best show in town. *El Greco*, Av. Principal de Macaracuay (also restaurant in same building). *Hipocampo*, Plaza Chacaíto. *Mon Petit*, Plaza Altamira Sur (there are many small clubs, restaurants and bars on Plaza Altamira Sur). *México Típico*, on Av. Libertador. The "Noches Caraqueñas" show put on by the *Hilton* each Mon. evening makes a pleasant introduction to Caracas night-life. *Juan Sebastian Bar*, Av. Venezuela, El Rosal, is a jazz club (closed Sun.) and *Feelings*, Av. Tamanaco, El Rosal, is a popular *salsa* club. *Weekends*, San Juan Bosco, Altamira, is a hard rock café, no cover charge. *City Rock Café*, Chacaíto, looks like a shopping centre but is good for dancing. *Cervecería*

Nueva Esparta, Av. los Marquitos (Sabana Grande) is cheap, provides good music, but is another couples-only venue. Two gay clubs are *Ice Palace* at Altamira Sur (not exclusively gay, non members admitted for US$4) and *Zigzag* restaurant and piano bar, Av. Libertador, Ed. La Línea.

Discotheques *Water Point*, Centro Comercial, El Parque de Los Palos Grandes, and *Blow-up*, Plaza Altamira Sur, have been rec.; also *Teorema*, *La Jungla*, *Eva*, *The Flower*, and many others. Couples only seems to be the norm.

Sports and Recreations Golf, tennis, riding, fishing, horse-racing every Sat. and Sun. at La Rinconada (a truly magnificent grandstand), bull fights (in season; go to the *Bar-Restaurant Los Cuchilleros* on Av. Urdaneta next to Plaza Candelaria to meet bullfighters and *aficionados*; tickets sold there on bullfight Sunday mornings, ticket sales end 1400, bar closes 1530, bullfight starts 1600), baseball (October-January), football, swimming, etc. Horse-racing commences at 1300, admission price to grandstand US$1.10. Several buses go to La Rinconada. There are numerous cinemas (US$1-half price Mon.). Parque del Este (Av. Francisco Miranda) has a planetarium and a good jogging track. Wildlife Park (still under construction 1989) at Caricuao, west of the city, along the autopista Francisco Fajardo, T 431 9166. For flying try Halcón, Centro Comercial San Luis, T 987 1834. To hire fishing boats contact Ani Villanueva, T 740862. The recreational event of the year is the two days of Carnival.

Cultural Events There are frequent Sun. morning concerts in the Teatro Municipal, 1100, usually US$2.25. Concerts, ballet, theatre and film festivals at the Ateneo de Caracas, Paseo Colón, Plaza Morelos; and similar events, including foreign artists, at the Complejo Cultural Teresa Carreño, on Paseo Colón, just E of *Caracas Hilton* (an interesting building, too). For details of these and other events, see the newspapers, *El Universal*, *El Nacional* and *Daily Journal*, and the Sunday issue of *El Diario de Caracas*.

Exchange Citibank will exchange Citicorp cheques; Banco Unión for Visa transactions. For cash advances on Mastercard, go to Credimático for a voucher then to Banco Mercantil for the cash from a side office, up to US$250 a day. For Thomas Cook cheques try Banco Internacional or Banco Mercantil. For exchange go to Italcambio offices: esquina Veroes and Urdaneta, Av. Casanova (Sabana Grande), Av. L. Roche (Altamira Sur) Simón Bolívar Airport; La Moneda, Centro Financiero Latino, Urdaneta, Piso 8; Infesa, Av. Libertador, between Negrín and Jabillos; Confinanzas, Centro Comercial Paseo Las Mercedes, Local PA-CI, open 0800-1200, 1400-1700. Commission of US$0.04 charged per US$1 changed in travellers' cheques. American Express cheques, Banco Consolidado, Av. San Francisco, Edif. Torre California, piso 9, Urb. Colinas de La California, until 1100 only; AmEx rep is Turisol, Centro Comercial Tamanaco, level C-2, Chuao suburb, T 927922, also in *Hotel Tamanaco*.

Cultural Institutions British Council, Edificio Torre la Noria, 6th floor, Las Mercedes; English classes and modest library oriented towards English teaching, literature and fiction; Centro Venezolano-Americano, Av. Las Mercedes, good free library of books in English, and free concerts; also good for Spanish courses, US$195 for 2 months; Asociación Cultural Humboldt (Goethe Institut), Av. Juan Germán Roscio, San Bernardino, T 527634, library, lectures, films, concerts, Spanish courses.

Embassies and Consulates **Colombian Consulate**, Guaicaipuro, Sector Chacaíto, Urb. El Rosal, T 951-3631; open Mon.-Fri. 0800-1130 for visas, photo and US$10, can take anything from 2 hrs. to one day; **Brazilian Consulate**, Ed. Cen., Gerencial Mohedano, Av. Mohedano, T 261-4481; visas same day if requested at 0900, returned 1800; **Guyanese Embassy**, Quinta Roraima, Av. El Paseo, Prados del Este, T 771158, 9732781 (visa Mon., Wed., Fri., 0830-1200, same day if early, US$3, 2 application forms, 2 photos required); **Suriname Embassy**, 4a Avenida, between 7a and 8a Transversal, Urb. Altamira, T 324490; **Trinidadian Embassy**, Quinto Roraima, Av. El Paseo, Prados del Este (visa US$17, 2 photos, up to 1 week).

USA Embassy and Consulate, Av. Francisco Miranda, La Floresta, T 283 5035, nr. Metro Altamira; **Canadian Embassy**, Edificio Torre Europa, piso 7, Av. Francisco de Miranda, Chacao (T 33-9776); **Australian Embassy**, Luis Rocha y Av. 10, T 261-0658/4632, nr. Metro Altamira.

British Embassy and Consulate, Torre Las Mercedes, 3rd floor, Av. La Estancia, Chuao (T 7511022/1166/1966), Apartado 1246 for letters; **Danish Embassy**, Ed. EASO, 17th floor, Av. Francisco Miranda, nr. Chacaíto metro station, T 9514618/5606; **Finnish Embassy**, Torre C, piso 14, Centro Plaza, Av. Francisco de Miranda, T 284 5013; **French Embassy**, Ed. Las Frailes, La Guairita; **West German Embassy**, Edificio Panavén, piso 2, Av. San Juan Bosco, Altamira, T 2610181/310144; **Israeli Embassy**, Av. Francisco de Miranda, Centro Empresario Miranda, piso 4; **Spanish Embassy**, Ed. Banco Unión, Sabana Grande, piso 1; **Swedish Embassy**, Edificio Panavén, piso 5, Av. San Juan Bosco con Tercera Transversal, Altamira, T

2620176; **Swiss Embassy**, Torre Europa, piso 6, Av. Francisco de Miranda, Campo Alegre (T 334787/9510159).

Diex for visa renewal, Av. Baralt, El Silencia.

Non-Catholic Churches Anglican Church, Plaza Urape, San Román section of Las Mercedes (near *Tamanaco*; T 914727); The United Christian Church, interdenominational, Av. Arboleda, El Bosque.

Telecommunications are operated by the state company, CANTV, from El Silencio building in West Caracas, Centro Simón Bolívar, or Centro Plaza on Francisco Miranda in the east. Open 24 hrs., latter opens at 0700.

Post Office Central at Urdaneta y Norte 4, close to Plaza Bolívar. *Lista de correos* costs US$0.04, Mon.-Fri. only.

Hospitals Hospital de Clínicas, Av. Panteón y Av. Alameda, San Bernardino, T 5742011. Instituto Médico La Floresta, near US Embassy, T 2848111.

Dry Cleaning Tintorería Tulipán, Las Acacias Sur, next to *Hotel Colón*; nearby is a same-day launderette called De-Blan-Ro.

Tourist Office Information from floors 35-37, Torre Oeste, Parque Central (metro Bellas Artes is closest). T 507-8726/8814/8815. No maps but wonderful view. There is a smaller office at the airport, which has been highly praised and where English is spoken. **See page** 1102 for further recommended reading.

Travel Agents *BOT Tours*, Paseo Hilton, Nivel Lecuna, Parque Central (same building as Tourist Office), good. *Maso Internacional*, Plaza Altamira Sur, Av. San Juan Bosco, T 313577, reps. for Thomas Cook, generally good reports of tours. *Turven Tropical Travel*, Real Edificio Unión, local 13, Sabana Grande, PO Box 60622, Caracas 1050, T 9511032, varied tours. *Venezuelan Travel Advisers*, Venezuela, Edif. Policlínica Americana, Local D-PB, El Rosal, T 9514922. *Candes Turismo*, office in lobby of *Hilton*, T 571 0987; *Servicios Colectivos Especiales* in lobby of *Tamanaco*, T 283 6506, trips more varied and slightly cheaper. Also rec: *Paradise Expeditions*, Lacal 7, Ed. Unión 71, Chacaíto, T 9517741; *Airone*, Torre Lincoln, Sabana Grande con Las Acacias, T 781 2512; *Madrid Caracas*, Urdaneta 73, rec. for flights.

Airport Maiquetía, for national flights, Simón Bolívar for international flights, adjacent to each other (10 mins.' walk—taxi fare US$1.15), 28 km. from Caracas, near the port of La Guaira. The Tourist Office at the airport is very helpful; hotel bookings can be made there. *Casa de cambio* open 24 hrs. (Italcambio, good rates for cash, outside duty-free area). Check your change. Always allow plenty of time when going to the airport, whatever means of transport you are using: the route can be very congested and check-in procedures are very slow. Allow at least 2 hrs. checking-in time before your flight, especially if flying Viasa. Taxi fares from airport to Caracas cost on average US$6-8, depending on part of city but overcharging is rife. (Taxis are much cheaper to national terminal.) Fares are supposedly controlled: the taxi office in the airport issues you with a card with the official fare. Give this to the driver after you have checked the fare. After 2200 and at weekends a surcharge of 20% is included on the card. Drivers may only surcharge you for luggage (US$0.50 per large bag). If you think the taxi driver is overcharging you, make a complaint to Corpoturismo or tell him you will report him to the Departamento de Protección del Consumidor. The airport shuttle bus (blue and white) leaves from outside the airport for the city terminal (under the flyover at Bolívar and Av. Sur 17, 250 m. from Bellas Artes metro), regular service from 0600 to 0030, US$1.50. When checking in, keep 10 bolívar bills handy to pay departure tax levied at most large airports (see page 1096).

Long Distance Buses Although the Nuevo Circo bus station in the city centre was due to be closed, and replaced in 1989 by two new ones, at the E and W ends of the city (the latter near La Rinconada race track), it was still in use in Jan. 1990. Long-distance bus travel varies a lot in quality. However, buses from Caracas to Maracaibo, Mérida and San Cristóbal are usually in excellent condition; buses to Guayana are of poorer quality. Frequent service to Maracay, Valencia and Barquisimeto, but buses are often in bad shape; the Panamericana route is not recommended because it takes the old road on which there are many accidents. Aerobuses maintain regular services by air-conditioned coaches with reclining seats between Caracas and the main towns in eastern and western Venezuela, and also to Cúcuta, in Colombia. The fares of other good companies are a third less. The best lines are: to Maracaibo, Expresos los Llanos; to Guayana, Providencial. Buses stop frequently but there will not always be a toilet at the stop; always take your own toilet paper. Long distance *por puesto* services are twice as expensive as buses, less comfortable, but generally faster. On public holidays

CARACAS
ORIENTATION MAP
MAIN STREETS ONLY
NOT TO SCALE

1. Plaza Bolívar
2. Centro Simón Bolívar
3. Parque Central
4. Parque Los Caobos
5. Jardín Botánico
6. Plaza Venezuela
7. Parque Andrés Bello
8. Parque Arístides Rojas
9. Country Club
10. Ciudad Universitaria

11. Teleférico Station
12. Museo de Arte Colonial,
    Quinta Anauco
13. Hotel Ávila

INSET
14. Parque del Este
15. Francisco de Miranda
    Aerodrome
16. Hotel Tamanaco

buses are usually fully booked leaving Caracas and drivers often make long journeys without stopping. Sat. and Sun. morning are also bad for travel into/out of Caracas. Always take identification when booking a long-distance journey, the tickets only go on sale the day before travel (seats cannot be reserved). Half-price tickets are available for those with a student card but you may need to provide a photocopy. There is a left luggage store at the bus station. To avoid theft it is advisable not to sleep on the buses. Arrive early, buses may start before time.

Journey to Maracaibo, US$6.75, 10 hrs., *por puesto*, US$13; Maracay, US$0.90, 2 hrs., *por puesto*, US$1.80; Valencia, US$1.25, *por puesto*, US$2.50; Coro US$4.30 (overnight), *por puesto*, US$8.60; to Barquisimeto US$3. Overnight to Valera, US$5.10, 9 hrs. (Aerobuses). Buses to Mérida, Expresos Mérida, US$6, 12 hrs., *por puesto*, US$12; overnight to Mérida, via Panamericana or Los Llanos (12 hrs.) to San Cristóbal. Expresos Alianzas Caracas to Cúcuta, US$7.50, 8 hrs., daily at 1900. Get passport exit stamp at San Antonio; bus will stop there. Bus to San Antonio, US$6.75, *por puesto*, US$13.50. To Barinas, US$4.60, 8 hrs. To Puerto La Cruz, US$3.25, 6 hrs., *por puesto*, US$6.50; to Cumaná, US$3.80, 8 hrs., *por puesto*, US$7.60, to Margarita, US$10 including ferry; to Maturín, US$4.50, *por puesto*, US$9. To Ciudad Bolívar, US$6, 8 hrs. *por puesto*, US$12; Ciudad Guayana, US$6, *por puesto*, US$12; to Tucupita, US$6; Tumeremo, 1800, 14 hrs., US$6.75; El Dorado, US$7, 14½ hrs; San Fernando de Apure, US$3.75. Tepsa agents in Caracas: Rayco, Av. Olimpo, Edif. Anuncia, San Antonio, Sabana Grande, T 782-8276, reported to be very helpful and friendly.

Excursions The cable railway (*teleférico*) up Mount Avila from Av. Perimetral de Maripérez, giving a stupendous view of the city and the coast, was not operating in 1989 and in January 1990 was reported to be "awaiting repair". Check details beforehand (when in operation reservations are necessary 4 hrs. in advance; on Sundays queues are very long). The future of the *Humboldt Hotel* on the summit has still not been decided. It has been refurbished, but not reopened. Camping is possible with permission. At the summit there is a restaurant (closed in 1989), horseriding and an ice rink. Look out for 15 cm. moths with wood or leaf camouflage, trapped in corridor up to restaurant. A recommended trip, when the cable railway is operating, is to ride up and hike back down (note that it is cold at the summit, average temperature 13°C).

Good hiking: the three principal entrances to the **Avila National Park** are (a) 100 metres W of the restaurant *Tarzilandia* in Altamira (the easiest walk up); (b) the car park on the N side of Av. Boyacá above Urbanización Los Chorros (where there is a crude map)—8 hrs. to Pico Oriental, 2,650 metres; and (c) the entrance to Av. Boyacá from El Marqués (this route well signposted)—7 hrs. to Pico Naiguatá, 2,750 metres. A map of the paths (and entrance permit— US$2.85) is available from the Instituto Nacional de Parques, Edificio CVB, Av. Germania, Caracas, price US$1. A description of the park is included in *No Frills Guide to Venezuela*, published by Bradt Publications. Essential to carry your own drinking water and food, and to set out early. Serious danger of bush fires in the dry season January-April, so be careful with cigarettes, etc.

Another excursion is to the village of El Hatillo, ½ hr. from the city centre by car, where colonial style housing has been well preserved.

La Guaira is Venezuela's main port, only 20 mins. by road to Caracas, if the volume of traffic permits. Population: 20,775. Mean temperature: 29°C.

In the area are many seaside resorts and residential districts with a total population of about 70,000. There is a small museum (Museo Fundación John Boulton) in Calle Bolívar, open Tues.-Fri., 0930-1200 and 1500-1700, Sat.-Sun., 0900-1200. Old La Guaira is worth visiting and a short bus ride up the hill to the lighthouse gives a fine view of the port and its surroundings. A pleasant drive can be made along the Avenida Soublette eastwards to Macuto, Laguna Beach, Caraballeda and so on to **Los Caracas** (45 km.), a government holiday resort for workers. (All these places can be reached quite cheaply by bus.) Westward, on the way to Caracas, is the international airport. Taxi to airport, US$2.25.

The town of **Maiquetía** is not spoilt by proximity to the airport. *Hotel Salamanca*, Calle Real; *Hotel Senador*, Plaza Los Maestros, both F. The *Avila* is a good restaurant, near Los Maestros.

Macuto is a pleasant seaside resort with a fine, tree-lined promenade (the Paseo del Mar), a splendid yacht marina and a "pigeon housing estate". A good place to find some heat and sunshine in the rainy season and an ideal place to stay if "stopping-over" between flights to and from Caracas. A *por puesto* to Macuto from Caracas costs US$0.50 and takes less than 1 hr. The *por puesto* to the airport (domestic terminal) is US$0.60, or take Catia la Mar bus. The taxi fare from the airport is US$4 (plus US$0.50 for a large suitcase or rucksack). Anyone wanting to get on a *por puesto* back to Caracas at rush hour (weekend afternoons, etc.) is advised to walk to the *Macuto Sheraton*. Bus from Caracas is caught one street down from Universidad.

Hotels   On the coast, not too far from Maiquetía airport: *Macuto-Sheraton**, T 031-944-300, Fax 944-318, Apartado 65 La Guaira, L, luxury, at Caribe, 7 km. away; *Meliá Caribe**, A, luxury, also has hotel apartment block, good restaurant in main hotel, rec., Caraballeda; *Macuto**, Av. La Playa y Calle 3, Urb. Alamo, T 031-44561/2/3, 3-star, C with bath, a/c, hot water, 5 min. walk to beach, comfortable but poorly maintained, swimming pool. *Riviera*, Boulevard Caraballeda, D, clean, good food (French); *Hidalgo**, Av. La Playa, D, good; *Las Quince Letras**, D, Av. La Playa, rec, good restaurant; *Puerta del Sol*, E, bathless on weekdays, but friendly. *Alamo*, Av. La Playa, E (possible to bargain), with shower and fan, clean, good value, good restaurant on the shore, not cheap; *Santiago*, Av. La Playa, F p.p. with bath; *Diana*, D-F, Boulevard Caraballeda (T 031-44278), on the beach, bath, clean, a/c, helpful, noisy on ground floor especially, safe for motorcycles; *La Alemania*, Paseo del Mar, E, basic, old fashioned, pleasant; *Colonial*, on La Playa, E, good value, bath, a/c, smart, clean; *Isaibel*, corner of Isaibel and Calle 3, 2 mins. from sea, F, small, quiet, good; *Pensión Guanchez*, Calle Guzmania, F with fan, shower and toilet, breakfast US$1, no sign outside. (* = bookable through Fairmont International)

Restaurants   Recommended for paella is the *Solimar* in Urb. Caribe-Caraballeda. Also in Carabellada, along Av. Principal are *Neptuno*, good seafood, rec.; *El Bodegón del Lino*, Spanish-style; *El Portón del Timotes*, seafood, good service. Good cheap restaurant is *La Esquina*, near *Hotel Alamo*. *Mokambo* and *Apolo 17*, both on beach boulevard, good; many more on Paseo del Mar. *Panadería* Apdo. 8, on Alamo, good.

Beaches   Fishing (boats for hire at *Macuto-Sheraton* marina) just N of La Guaira (mostly marlin).

There are three beaches, with all facilities, along 27 km. of Caribbean seashore: one, Catia La Mar, W of La Guaira, and two—Macuto and Naiguatá—E of it. Catia La Mar is not recommended because it is industrial, very littered and the sea is heavily polluted, but it is very convenient for Maiquetía airport, taxi, US$2.10-2.35 depending on time of day. (*Hotel Bahía La Mar*, Av. La Playa, T 031-515940/515935, D with bath, very comfortable and clean, food good, swimming pool, *por puesto* minibus to Caracas 35 metres from door (US$0.30); handy for airport but under flight path; *Scorpio*, F, clean, modern but cockroaches; *Aeropuerto*, E, shower, a/c, OK). *Balneario Camuri Chico*, 3 good beaches, restaurant, showers, water fairly clean, rec. New beaches are being prepared. The beaches themselves are enclosed by breakwaters as the currents can be very strong. From Caracas, by car, it takes 30 mins. to the 1st, 45 mins. to the 2nd, and 1 hr. to the 3rd, provided there are not too many traffic jams. West of Catia La Mar are beaches at Puerto Carayaca (*Casa Francisco*, hotel and restaurant), Oricao (small, private beach), and Chichiriviche, no hotels or restaurants (not to be confused with the resort W of Puerto Cabello); hitch or take taxis to these beaches. Far better beaches are three or four hrs. by car from Caracas: Cata and Ocumare de la Costa (see page 1059), Chichiriviche (see page 1061) and several others in the Puerto Cabello area. These more distant beaches are recommended, but a day trip is tiring because of traffic jams, particularly when returning to Caracas.

The overnight trip to **Los Roques islands**, directly N of La Guaira, is well worth it. These islands are truly beautiful, with long stretches of white beaches and mile upon mile of coral reef. They constitute a national park, whose headquarters is in the largest island, Gran Roque. In all there are about 340 islands, islets, rocks and reefs. You can reach the islands by hitch hiking or a lift from the Aeroclub at La Carlota airport (often difficult). It is best to go in the morning or weekends; several planes leave then and often have spare places if you ask. Helicópteros del Caribe at Maiquetía sells flights for both one day and more than one day (return fare about US$175). Be prepared to wait at the airport. Also enquire in Barcelona for flights to the islands. You can take a small boat to other islands. Private accommodation is available for US$6-8 inc. meals. Beware of sunburn as there is no shade.

Other Excursions   Further afield, in **Yare**, a celebration is held on Corpus Christi day; the dance before the church of the enormously masked red devils, and of most of the villagers. It lasts the whole day. Yare is about 90 km. from Caracas; the road to it is through Petare and down the Río Guaira as far as Santa Teresa, and then up the Río Tuy. From Santa Teresa make a detour to the beautiful and little frequented **Guatopo National Park** on the road to Altagracia de Orituco, but you must return to Santa Teresa to continue your journey to Yare.

At the Parque Guatopo are various convenient places to picnic on the route through the forest. Take insect repellant. To stay the night in the park a permit must be obtained. There are a number of good nature trails in the park, for instance a 3-km. trail from Santa Crucita Recreation Area (well-signposted).

Another excursion is into the mountains to **Colonia Tovar** (1,890 metres), a village once so isolated that a few of its blond, blue-eyed people still speak the Black Forest German of their ancestors who settled there in 1843. Now it is very touristy. Strawberries, coffee, garlic, rhubarb and flowers are grown for the Caracas market. See the Scandinavian-style ceramics. Ask in Colonia Tovar for the *petroglifos*, rock paintings. The 1½-hr drive from Caracas is delightful. Along the road are small parks where picnic lunch can be taken (now in bad condition), but at weekends there are long traffic queues and you have to be early just to find a roadside spot to picnic and there are similar problems finding accommodation—no such difficulties in the week. Prices can be very inflated.

The road to Colonia Tovar passes through **El Junquito**, a small town with roadside stands selling fruit and barbecued meat (there are also pony stables). You see Caracas from one side of the road, the Caribbean from the other (*Parador Castilla* at Km. 43). 29 km. beyond El Junquito, a paved road with beautiful views winds down the mountain to the sea: it branches right to Oricao (see above), and Catia La Mar, or left to El Limón and Puerto Cruz (nice beach), from where one can go E, or W to Puerto Maya, a beautiful bay with nice swimming (there is another branch right to Puerto Cruz nearer Colonia Tovar). Another road, 34 km. (well-paved, but hair-raising), leads through glorious mountain scenery from Colonia Tovar to La Victoria on the Caracas-Valencia highway (4 buses a day).

Hotels in Colonia Tovar: *Bergland* (good, cheap breakfasts); *Selva Negra**, *Cabañas Baden; Edelweiss* (not rec.), *Freiburg, Kaiserstuhl*, all C; *Alta Baviera*. All serve German-style food in good restaurants. There is said to be a good spot for camping just below the town's cemetery, if you don't mind the company.

It is generally easy to get a lift if there are no buses. Taxi fare for the round trip from Caracas to Colonia Tovar (driver will wait) is about US$10. Bus from Av. Sur 9 y El Rosario, next to Nuevo Circo, to El Junquito (1 hr.), then change for Colonia Tovar (1 hr.). *Por puesto* from Plaza Catia or O'Leary (more frequently), Caracas, 1 hr., US$0.75. Alternatively, take a *por puesto* from Plaza Capuchino to El Junquito, then one from there to Colonia Tovar, US$0.70.

WEST FROM CARACAS (2)

A hundred km. W of Caracas is the great basin in which lies the Lake of Valencia and the towns of Maracay and Valencia. The basin, which is only 450 metres above sea-level, receives plenty of rain and is one of the most important agricultural areas in the country; sugar, cotton, maize, beans and rice are the main crops. In the other valleys and depressions in the Central Highlands are also grown manioc, bananas, cocoa and the superb local coffee.

The Pan-American Highway, which links Caracas by road with the other capitals of South America, follows closely the route of Gómez' Great Andean Highway as far as Lake Maracaibo, though many sections have been widened and straightened. At the start, there is the choice of a direct toll motorway to Valencia (with exit to Maracay), toll US$0.50, or the old road called, familiarly, "La Pan-americana" and known for its dangerous bends. (Hotels on "La Panamericana": *Colonial*, D, San Antonio de los Altos; *Cutlas*, D, Km. 10; *Panorama*, E, Km. 13; *Las Vegas*, D, Km. 14.) It leaves La Rinconada race course to its left, and climbs steadily but easily towards **Los Teques**, capital of Miranda state (pop.: 44,000, *Alemán*, E, Plaza Miranda, friendly, good food). This passes on its way the park of Las Colinas de Carrizal (collections of local fish and birds, and pleasant paths). Twenty-four km. beyond Los Teques on the way down into the fertile valleys of Aragua, we can either join the Caracas-Valencia tollway or take the older road through several attractive little towns such as La Victoria (see above). The Quinta de Bolívar is at San Mateo, between La Victoria and Maracay. A little nearer Maracay, a good road leads off to **San Juan de Los Morros (see page** 1075).

The Panamericana to Maracay should be taken at least once, for views and local colour, but winding up and down the mountains behind slow, smelly trucks is not much fun. The toll road also offers good views.

The new highway avoids city centres, so all that is seen of Maracay, Valencia and Barquisimeto are factories plus the huge concrete Barquisimeto Fourth Centenary Monument. Beyond Barquisimeto there are mountains like slag heaps, until we reach the green of the Andes.

Maracay, capital of Aragua State, has a population of 322,000, and is at an altitude of 495 metres. In its heyday it was the favourite city of General Gómez and some of his most fantastic whims are still there: the former *Hotel Jardín* (now a Government centre) with its beautiful zoo, park and fountain, built for his revels; the opera house opposite; his modest little house for personal use, and the bull ring, an exact replica of the one at Seville. The Gómez mausoleum, built in his honour, has a huge triumphal arch. Maracay is an attractive, peaceful city; it is the centre of an important agricultural area, and the school and experimental stations of the Ministry of Agriculture are worth visiting; it is also important industrially and militarily.

Hotels *Byblos**, D, Av. Las Delicias, high standard; *Maracay**, Las Delicias, B, swimming pool, gymnasium, night club; *San Luis*, Carabobo Sur 13, off the main shopping street, E, clean, showers, friendly; *Caroní*, Ayacucho Norte 197, Bolívar, E, a/c, comfortable, rec.; *Bolívar*, Av. Bolívar Este, E, adequate; *Wladimir*, F, Av. Bolívar Este 27, friendly, good restaurant at reasonable prices; *Italo*, E, Av. 6, Urb. La Soledad, service uninterested, ask for quiet side of building; *Pipo**, D, Av. Principal, El Castaño, swimming pool, discotheque, rec. restaurant (parrillas a speciality), in hills above the city; *Pensión Libertad*, Av. 99E y Calle Libertad (105 Sur), F with bath, clean, safe; (*-bookable through Fairmont International).

Restaurants *Tosca El Pescador*, Av. Sucre Norte 75, rec., especially for seafood; *Paella Valenciana*, rec.; *Napoli*, near Plaza Central, good selection, reasonably priced. There are many Chinese restaurants which are reliable.

Exchange Banco Consolidado (American Express), Av. Bolívar y Fuerzas Aéreas.

Tourist Office Ed. Fundaragua, La Soledad, friendly.

The FAV (Fuerza Aérea Venezolana) Museum in Maracay is open on Sun. from 0800 to 1800. About two dozen aircraft are displayed, including Second World War fighters and bombers, later jets and earlier aircraft from between the wars.

Excursions Lake Valencia; to Las Delicias, Gómez' crumbling country house, where he died, with its adjoining zoo. Take an Ocumare bus from the terminal. The huge 1,000-hectare **Henri Pittier National Park** (a birdwatcher's paradise) stretches from 24 km. N of Maracay to the Caribbean on both sides of the Andes; take a coat, it is cool in the cloud forest. There are no nature trails but many birds may be seen from the road, avoid weekends, best visibility in the morning. A road runs from Maracay over the 1,130-metre high Portachuelo pass, guarded by twin peaks, to three places by the sea: **Ocumare de la Costa**, 37 km. from Maracay; the naval base of Turiamo; and **Cata**, once the most beautiful beach in Venezuela, now overdeveloped, basic cabins for rent on beach, good fish restaurant, run by Pepe (Cuyagua beach, unspoilt, is 10 km. further on). The road was built by Gómez as an escape route if things grew too hot for him. Near the pass is Rancho Grande, the uncompleted palace Gómez was building when he died; it is in the shape of a question mark and is worth visiting. It is now the Rancho Grande Biological Station; permission to visit may be given to serious naturalists. A taxi can be hired at Maracay for a day's outing in the park for about US$15. The nearby town of **Victoria** has the oldest bullring in Venezuela and an interesting old hotel, *Hotel El Recreo*, D, originally a colonial house built in 1724 (also *Omni*, B). In the hills nearby is the *Hacienda San Mateo* formerly occupied by Simón Bolívar and now a museum. There is also a museum of sugar cane. Another excursion to the coast, also through the Henri Pittier National Park, goes over a more easterly pass (1,830 metres), on a paved but winding road (spectacular but not for timid drivers) to **Santa Clara de Choroni**, a beautiful colonial town (beautiful journey by bus from Maracay, US$1.10, 2½ hrs., 2 or 3 a day). *Hotel Club Cotoperix*, B p.p. for accommodation, T 573 5241, English spoken, full board and drinks in 3 colonial houses converted into guest houses, price also includes boat trips to otherwise inaccessible beaches, recommended; *Hospedaje La Montañita*, E. About 10 km. before Choroní are 2 waterfalls known as El Dique, where one can bathe; ask anyone for directions. There is also an electricity museum. Just beyond the town is the beach of Puerto Colombia

(*Hotel Alemania*, D; *Posada Bahía*, D, a/c, clean, excellent restaurant, Austrian owner; *Posada Alfonso*, E, clean; camping possible on the beach, dirty at weekends), from where launches (US$10) may be taken to the otherwise inaccessible colonial village of Chuao, famous in the past for its cocoa; the bay is very pleasant with a couple of bars.

Fifty km. to the west of Maracay the road reaches Valencia, through low hills thickly planted with citrus, coffee and sugar.

Valencia (population, about 495,000), the capital of Carabobo State, stands on the W bank of the Cabriales river, 5 km. before it empties into Lake Valencia (rather polluted). It is the third largest city in the republic, the centre of its most developed agricultural region, and the most industrialized. Annual mean temperature 24°C; altitude 490 metres; rainfall, 914 mm. a year. The atmosphere of the older and narrower streets is that of old Spain. The interesting 18th century Cathedral (open 0630-1130, 1500-1830 daily, 0630-1200, 1500-1900 Sun.) is on the central Plaza Bolívar. The statue of the Virgen del Socorro in the left transept is the most valued treasure; on the second Sunday in November it is paraded with a richly jewelled crown. See the Capitol, the Municipal Theatre, the old Carabobo University building and the handsome bullring, which holds the world record for takings at a single *corrida*. Also the Museo de Arte e Historia, Calle 98 and Av. 104 (open Tues.-Sat., 0800-1200 and 1400-1730), and the Aquarium de Valencia at the west end of Calle 107 beyond the *autopista*, featuring a dolphin show at 1630 (open Tues.-Sun., 0930-1800, admission US$0.25). There is a small zoo behind the aquarium. Like its Spanish namesake, Valencia is famous for its oranges. There is a nice country club. (**N.B.** Most of the interesting sights are closed on Sundays.)

Hotels *Intercontinental Valencia**, L-L+, Av. Juan Uslar, swimming pool, night club; *Residencias Ucaima**, Av. Boyacá, Centro Comercial La Viña, B; *Canaima*, Av. Lara con Branger, D, clean, TV, rec.; *Don Pelayo**, E, in town centre, Av. Díaz Moreno, rec., good restaurant; *Astor*, Calle Colombia, E, a/c, bath, clean, safe parking, good; *Central*, F, near main square, nice patio, quiet and clean, English spoken; *Bilboa*, F, Calle 100 (Colombia), 96-10, clean and quiet; *Metrópole*, F, central but dingy, Calle Comercial 103-47; *Palermo*, Calle Colombia, F, clean and friendly with laundry, other *residencias* on same street for the same price (*-bookable through Fairmont International).

Restaurants *Asociación de Ganaderos*; *Mar Chica*; *La Grillade*; *Venezuela*, rec.; *Fego*, Av. Bolívar 102-75, rec.

British Vice-Consul (Hon.): Corporación Mercantil Venezolana, Calle Silva No. 100-70, Edif. Comersa, T 50411/7.

Exchange Banco Consolidado (American Express), Av. Bolívar, Edif. Exterior; Turisol (also Amex); Italcambio, Av. Bolívar, Edif. Talia, Loc. 2.

Buses Bus terminus 3 km. from centre. To Caracas, US$1.25; to San Cristóbal, 10 hrs., US$5.85; Barquisimeto, US$1.85, 3 hrs; Maracay, 45 mins., US$0.25.

Excursions At the Safari Carabobo Reserva Animal, on the road from Valencia to Campo de Carabobo, you can see many wild animals, not all of them South American, in well-planned and quite spacious surroundings. Cars with roof racks are not permitted to enter. To the monument on the battlefield of Carabobo, laid out like a park with a *mirador* where Bolívar surveyed the battle, southwards on the road to San Carlos; the battle story is told in bronze: the British soldiers who helped Bolívar are particularly realistic. Buses to the battlefield leave from La Sanidad (Health Centre), US$0.25, 1 hr.

The Caracas-Valencia motorway continues down the mountains, reaching the sea near El Palito (refinery and pier). Here we turn right to Puerto Cabello. 18 km. from Valencia, the road passes Las Trincheras, a decaying spa with the second hottest springs in the world (98 °C); there are three baths (hot, hotter, very hot), a mud bath and a Turkish bath. Entrance US$1. Hotel* for patients only (D).

Puerto Cabello, 96 km. W of La Guaira, is the port for Valencia, 55 km. away by modern highway; it is in itself a large industrial centre. This, the second most important Venezuelan port, has an excellent harbour with a lighthouse, and a shipyard with dry dock. Average temperature, 28°C; population, 71,200. A standard-gauge 175-km. railway runs to Barquisimeto.

Hotels *Riviera*, with good restaurant. (Other good restaurants are *El Parque, Mar y Sol, Venezuela*, near the harbour and *San Antonio del Mar*.) Best hotels near are the *Cumboto*, D, Av. La Paz, Urb. Cumboto, swimming pool; *La Sultana*, F, Av. Juan José Flores; *El Ejecutivo*, F, good, friendly; *La Hacienda* (good German food).

Exchange Banco Italo de Venezuela.

About half an hour E of Puerto Cabello over a rough road is a beautiful horseshoe-shaped beach shaded by palms called La Bahía. It is well worth the drive, has a refreshment stand, changing rooms, toilet facilities and lifeguards, but take your own lunch. You can buy oysters from little boys who open them for you and douse them with lemon juice.

Puerto Cabello has another beach, Quizandal, with a coral reef, near the naval base. (Taxi fare, US$3.45 but you may find it hard to get one on the way back.) The nearby Country Club also has a beach with coral reefs within reach by boat. There are two Spanish forts at Puerto Cabello, one on the water (which can be reached by a small ferry boat), the other on a hill over the city (in a military zone and it is difficult to get permission to enter).

N.B. The beach to the W of Puerto Cabello is not so attractive; be careful of going beyond the bathing area as the beach is notorious for armed robbery.

Twenty-four km. W of Puerto Cabello, at the junction of the Pan-American Highway and the road to Tucacas, is **Morón**, where there is a state-owned petrochemical plant.

Quite near Morón is the lovely beach of **Palma Sola**, 16 km. long and deserted save at Easter time when Venezuelans camp out there in crowds. The water can be dangerous but the sands and palms are superb. There are hotels, many closed in the off season (*Balneario Canaima*, C, children's swimming pool; *Balneario Caribe*, D), restaurants and changing rooms. A road has been built from Morón to Coro via Tucacas, an hour from Puerto Cabello.

Tucacas (*Hotel Manaure-Tucacas*, E, Av. Silva, a/c, hot water, clean, restaurant; *Hotel Said*, at entrance, E, swimming pool, good; *La Palma*, F; *Centuca*, F; also rooms above the supermarket *La Suerte* on main street, E, but bargain, clean, good) is a small, dirty town of wooden shacks where bananas and other fruit are loaded for Curaçao and Aruba, but offshore is the **National Park of Morrocoy**, where there are hundreds of coral reefs, palm-studded islets, small cosy beaches and calm water for water-skiing, snorkelling, and skin-diving. The Park is reached on foot from Tucacas; camping allowed, no facilities, take food and drink, crowded at weekends (no alcohol for sale in the park). The largest, cleanest and most popular of the islands is Cayo Sombrero. Boats are for hire (US$10 to Cayo Sombrero, per boat, US$5.25 to nearer islands). Venezuelan skin-diving clubs come here for their contests. Scuba diving equipment can be hired from near the harbour for US$5 a day, but the diving is reported not very interesting. This is one of the two main fishing grounds of Venezuela; the other is off Puerto La Cruz.

A few km. beyond, towards Coro, is the favourite beach resort of **Chichiriviche**; the town is filthy but offshore are numerous lovely islands and coral reefs. *Hotel Mario**, B including 3 meals, swimming pool; *La Garza**, B (including 3 meals, but poor food and service) or D, pool; *Vaya*, C, small, new, clean, restaurant; *Náutico*, D with breakfast and dinner, friendly, recently refurbished, clean, good meals, fans but no a/c; *Capri*, near docks, E (bargain), shower and a/c, clean, pleasant Italian owned, good restaurant and supermarket; bakery opposite has rooms, F, fan. Restaurants (both near *Capri*), *Fregata*, rec.; *Falcón*, good, cheap, good coffee and juices. It is possible to hire a boat to any one of the islands; recommended for a weekend away from Caracas (note that prices posted onboard or on the jetty are per boat, not per person,, about US$5.25—take a snorkel). There is no direct bus, but frequent *por puestos* from Puerto Cabello, US$1, or from Valencia. You may camp on the islands, but there are no facilities or fresh water (good lunches on the beaches) and you may require a permit from Inparques (National Parks). Nearby is a vast nesting area for scarlet ibis, flamingoes and herons.

From Tucacas it is 177 km. to **Coro** (population 80,000), capital of the State of Falcón (*por puesto*, US$5), a charming town, with interesting colonial buildings (the town is a national monument), surrounded by sand dunes (*médanos*, themselves a **National Park**). Worth seeing are the Cathedral, the first in Venezuela, built 1531; San Francisco church; the cross of Cristobal Colón, 1527; San Clemente church and monastery; the Casa de Balcón, now the National Experimental University. There is an interesting xerophytic garden open to the public. Museo Diocesano, Calle Zamora 69 (open Tues. and Sun. 0900-1200, Wed.-Fri., 1600-1900, very interesting), Museo de Cerámica, Calle Zamora 98 (open Tues., 0900-1200, Wed.-Fri., 1600-1900, Sat. 1000-1300 and 1600-1900, Sun., 1000-1300). From Coro, there is a good but uninteresting road to Maracaibo and another paved road along the isthmus leading to the Paraguaná Peninsula, along whose beaches men fish, 15 to 20 a net. Near the village of La Vela along the Morón road the local handicraft is the production of rocking chairs of all sizes made from cactus wood. Airport (good restaurant on 1st floor, 10 mins. walk from centre) has a direct service to Curaçao (see below), Caracas and Las Piedras. Bus from Coro to Caracas US$4.30; to Maracaibo, US$2.10.

Hotels at Coro *Miranda**, B, Av. Josefa Camejo, opposite airport, swimming pool (very dirty, but non-residents can pay to use it); *Arenas*, opp. bus terminal, D, restaurant; *Caracas*, E, Calle Toledo 17, very good, charming, a/c; *Coro*, E, Av. Independencia, friendly, good value; *Venezia*, D, expensive food, but renovated and good; *Valencia*, E, with private shower; *Maracén*, E, with private shower; *Capri*, very basic but friendly. The *Bella Nápoli* is good, F, cheap, but run down; the *Pedregal* is cheaper, with bath, fan, friendly, patio; *Roma*, close to plaza, F, good.

Restaurant *Don Camilo*, by *Hotel Miranda* and airport, reasonable prices. *Cafetería El Indio*, Independencia, nr. statue, very good breakfast. *Cervecería Alhambra*, Calle Zamora.

Exchange Banco Consolidado, Calle Federación con Buchivacoa (for American Express). Exchange is not possible for Thomas Cook or Master Card.

There is a ferry service (Ferrys del Caribe) from La Vela de Coro and Punto Fijo (see below) to Aruba and Curaçao (several a week, but out of operation in 1989). The schedules are continually being changed, so apply to the company's offices. Buy tickets on morning of departure. The journey to both Aruba and Curaçao usually takes 4-6 hrs., but the bureaucracy can lengthen this period to 8-12 hrs. Fare to Curaçao US$25 (cabin extra). It is necessary to have ticket out of Curaçao before entering, even if you are Dutch. It is advisable to arrive at the terminal at least 4 hours in advance, because the immigration officers often leave their posts before the boat departs. The tourist office can provide more information. The office for the boat in Coro is at Av. Independencia, beside Supermercado Victoria; there are also offices in Caracas at Av. Urdaneta esq. Ibárrez, Edificio Riera. *Por puesto* between La Vela de Coro and Coro itself costs US$0.85 per seat, bus costs US$0.20; taxi from La Vela to the ferry dock (3 km.) is US$2.10; *por puesto* from Maracaibo to ferry terminal, US$7.50. If the ferry is not running, there are flights from Coro to Curaçao, 4 days a week, Aeropostal, US$40 one way, US$50 return (you must purchase a return ticket out of Curaçao).

The **Paraguaná Peninsula** is connected by pipelines with the oilfields of Lake Maracaibo. The Maravén (ex-Shell) and Lagovén (ex-Esso) groups have refineries, the former at Cardón, and the latter at Amuay. The airport, which has services to Maracaibo (30 min.), Coro, Maiquetía and Aruba (4 a week, US$45 single, Air Aruba, T 069-51605 or T Aeropostal 069-455534; Avensa, US$60) is known as **Las Piedras**, the town itself as **Punto Fijo** (Hotels: *Luigi*, E, Judibana, swimming pool; *Jardín**, D, Centro Comercial Judibana; *Caribe**, E, Calle Comercio 21-112; *Del Este*, F, Av. Táchira; also *Cardón**, D, *Safri*, Av. Colombia 78-15, clean, cheap, central; *Miami*, Calle Falcón No. 21-196). Taxi from Punto Fijo to Las Piedras, US$7. Eventually, all four places will merge into one large town. There is a seaport, Las Piedras-Paraguaná, between Amuay and Cardón, which also serves the town of Coro. The villages on the peninsula have interesting colonial churches, notably that of Santa Ana. There are many good beaches accessible by car, few visitors, good for camping but no facilities. Adicora is a nice little resort where you can rent a house by the week; good seafood restaurants.

The Segovia Highlands, lying N of Barquisimeto, suffer from droughts, and are only sparsely settled along the river valleys. From Morón the Pan-American Highway strikes up into the hills, reaching 550 metres at **San Felipe** (population 30,750), capital of Yaracuy State (Hotels: *Turístico Río Yurubí*, E; *Hostería Colonial**, E, Av. La Paz, pool; *El Fuerte**, E, Av. La Patria; *La Fuente*, E, Av. La Fuente).

If you do not want to go to Puerto Cabello and the coast, a newer section of the Highway from Valencia via Carabobo to just beyond San Felipe is 56 km. shorter.

Barquisimeto, capital of Lara State, has a population of 504,000. Altitude 565 metres, mean temperature 25°C. It stands on one of the alluvial fans so frequent in the Andes, and is Venezuela's fourth largest city, with the University of Lara. The Cathedral, an ultramodern structure of free-form concrete and glass, is very interesting. The Palacio Municipal at Carrera 17 with Calle 25 is an attractive modern building. Across the street is a large well-shaded plaza with a bronze equestrian statue of Bolívar. On Carrera 15 (Av. Francisco de Miranda) between Calles 41-43 there is a charming park, resplendent with lush vegetation, paths, fountains and another bronze statue of Bolívar. There is a road from Barquisimeto to Acarigua (**see page** 1074) on the alternative route from Caracas to Mérida.

Hotels The *Motel El Parador*, B, excellent, near El Obelisco, a great roundabout in the northern suburbs of the town in the middle of which stands a tower; *Hilton**, B, Carrera 5, Nueva Segovia; *Hostería El Obelisco**, D, Av. Panamericana, American motel-style, swimming pool, always full; *Gran Hotel Barquisimeto**, E, Av. Pedro León Torres, pool; *Curumato**, E, Av. 20, esq. Calle 34; *Del Centro*, F, Av. 20, between Calles 26-27, good value; *Hevelin*, E, Av. Vargas, between 20-21, with or without a/c; *La Casona*, F, Carrera 17 con Calle 27 near Plaza Bolívar (T 051-315311/317151), a/c, clean, hot water, excellent, parking, restaurant; *Principe**, E, Carrera 19, esq. Calle 23, swimming pool, good; *Yacambú*, E, Av. Vargas, between Carreras 19-20, swimming pool. *Avenida*, F, Av. Vargas, No. 21-124, 2nd floor, clean, economical. Many small cheap hotels near the bus terminal e.g. *Yaguara*, G, basic; *Rió*, F.

Restaurants *Mesón de la Campaña*, El Obelisco; *Guido's*, good, expensive; *Terminal Vargas*, food average, service good, expensive; railway station restaurant, excellent.

Exchange Banco Consolidado, Av. Vargas entre Calles 20 y 21, also Turisol (T 516743), both American Express.

Transport Railway to Puerto Cabello (Mon.-Fri. 0600 and 1600, Sat.-Sun. 0600, 1000, 1600, US$0.20), and an airport. (No bus from airport, only taxis. There is a single bus terminal on the edge of the city.) Bus to Mérida, only one a day, leaves at 0315, 8 hrs. via Agua Viva and El Vigía, US$4.20; to Acarigua, 1 hr., US$1; to Valera *por puesto*, 3½ hrs., US$2.75. To Coro some buses take 2 hours, some 7, check which is which. For renting cars (Volkswagen best), Av. Pedro León Torres y Calle 56, or agency in lobby of *Hotel Curumato*, Calle 34 with Av. 20, also at airport.

West of Barquisimeto, about half an hour's drive, is **El Tocuyo** with a good hotel in a delightful colonial setting, *La Posada Colonial*, D, with moderately priced restaurant. Between Barquisimeto and El Tocuyo is the main grape-growing area.

About 24 km. SW of Barquisimeto is the small town of **Quíbor** (*Hotel Duque*, F; outside the town is the *Posadas Turísticas de Sahare**, E). There is an interesting museum, Centro Antropológico de Quíbor, with exhibits of the Indians who used to live in the region. Stop in the plaza for a *chicha de maíz* or *arroz*, a refreshing traditional drink of the local Indians. Turn right a few km. before Quíbor to get to a tiny *rancho* in the village of El Tintoreto where "blankets" are made from local wool. These are in bright coloured stripes or plaids and serve well as colourful rugs, but not as what we call blankets. They are very good value. About 18 km. from Quíbor is the mountain village of Cubiro (two hotels) which stands at 1,600 metres, ideal for walking. Direct buses from Barquisimeto or change at Quíbor.

About 60 km. east of Barquisimeto is the little town of **Chivacoa**. Passing sugar-cane fields you reach the mountain of Sorte which is the holy region for the María-Lionza cult (similar to Voodoo) practised throughout Venezuela. Celebrations are held there mostly at weekends with 12 October (Día de la Raza) being the most important day. It is interesting to walk up the mountain when the pilgrims are camping beside the river and waterfalls, but do not go unless you are prepared to take it seriously, and use only the parking lot to park your car; other places are unsafe because of robbery.

Another pleasant excursion from Barquisimeto by bus or car is to **Río Claro**, about 28 km. inland, "where the Andes begin". You follow a lush river valley through the mountains. There are banana plantations in the area and many dirt trails you can follow on horseback or in a 4-wheel drive vehicle. From Río Claro a gravel road (dry season only) goes to Buena Vista and on to Quíbor; good views and pleasant villages.

Some 75 km. past Barquisimeto the Lara-Zulia motorway to Maracaibo forks off to the right (Caracas-Maracaibo 660 km.), through **Carora** (*Complejo Turístico Katuca*, D; *Motel* and *Restaurant Indio Mara*, F, reasonable; *Motel Posada Madrevieja*, F, both on Av. Francisco de Miranda; *Irpinia*, F, and *Parrilla Italia*, F, both on Av. 14 de Febrero).

THE LOWLANDS OF MARACAIBO (3)

The Lowlands of Maracaibo, lying in the encircling arms of the mountains, are more or less windless and extremely humid. Average annual temperature is higher than anywhere else in Latin America. Rainfall decreases steadily from the foothills of the Sierra Nevada to the coast. In these lowlands is the semi-salt Lake Maracaibo, of about 12,800 square km., 155 km. long and in places over 120 km. wide. It is joined to the sea by a waterway, 3 to 11 km. wide and 55 km. long, at the mouth of which is the bar of Maracaibo.

The area was once dependent on fishing and the transport of coffee across the lake from the Sierra. Since the discovery there of one of the world's greatest oilfields in 1914, there has been a great transformation, both in appearance (a forest of oil derricks covers the shore swamps and some of the lake), and in prosperity. The Lara-Zulia motorway reaches Maracaibo by the beautiful 8-km. long General Rafael Urdaneta bridge, which has the longest pre-stressed concrete span in the world.

Maracaibo, on the north-western shore of Lake Maracaibo, capital of the State of Zulia, is Venezuela's oil capital: 70% of the nation's output comes from the Lake area. Maracaibo, which is 55 mins. by jet from Caracas, is the country's second largest city. Population: 1.7 million. The airport is at La Chinita. The bus terminal is on the edge of the city.

The climate is damp and hot, but healthy. The hottest months are July, August and September, but there is usually a sea breeze from 1500 until morning. The mean temperature of 28°C and average humidity of 78% are most felt at sea level. The new part of the city round Bella Vista and towards the University is in vivid contrast with the old town near the docks; this, with narrow streets and colonial style adobe houses, is hardly changed from the last century (parts, especially around Santa Lucía church—blue and white, facing Parque Urdaneta, have been well-restored). A trip across the lake through the oil derricks is difficult to organize as the oilfields are a long way from Maracaibo. The zone begins at Cabimas (*Cabimas Internacional**, B, luxury, pool, discotheque) on the E shore of the lake and you can get a good view of the oil rigs from there (boat to Cabimas, US$1.75, *por puesto*, US$1.25, semi-legal trip in fishing boat among the derricks, US$3-5, ask behind the market) and from other towns further down, such as Lagunillas (*Hotel Lagunillas**, E, pool)—though don't take pictures without asking permission. A tourist taxi from *Hotel del Lago* to see the oil wells costs US$25.

From the port, you can take a ferry to Altagracia for US$0.65, the first at 0645, 25 mins. Return the same way or take a minibus (US$0.55), travelling through exotic scenery for almost an hour and crossing the General Urdaneta bridge.

Hotels It is difficult to obtain rooms without making reservations well in advance. *Hotel del Lago Intercontinental**, El Milagro, Av. 2, T 912167/911868, plastic atmosphere, pool open to non-residents; *Maracaibo Cumberland*, C, theft from hotel safe reported; *Gran Hotel Delicias**, D, Av. 15 esq. Calle 70, swimming pool, night club; *Motel Granada* (*Mogranca*), D, room service only, outside town on road to La Concepción; *Aparthotel Presidente**, D, Av. 11, 68-50, pool; *Maruma**, Circunvalación No.2, B, old and new sections, hot water, a/c, TV, reasonable restaurant; *Roma*, E, Calle 86, 3F-76, T 220868, a/c, popular with Italians, food is very good; *Kristof**, D, Av. 8 (Santa Rita), swimming pool, night club, poor exchange rates offered; *Londres*, Calle 94, Av. 6, F, with bath; *San José**, E, Av. 3Y (San Martín) 82-29, a/c, bath, good beds, friendly, Italian restaurant, rec.; several others nearby, e.g. *Caribe*, Av. 7, F, good value, a/c and shower; *Yacambú*, F, Av. Libertador, a/c, central, restaurant; *Aurora*, G, Calle 96, near waterfront, spacious, friendly. *Victoria*, Av. 6, Calle 99, in picturesque old part of town, F, rec.; *Novedades*, Calle 78 (antes Dr. Portillo) No. 9-43, Bella Vista, T 75766, E, a/c, shower, rec., safe, Italian owner Francesco Scherra; other hotels in Bella Vista include *Montevideo* (E), *Falcón* and *Mary* (both F), a US$0.50 taxi ride from bus terminal. *Santa Ana* is the cheapest, G, poor but friendly, opposite Occidente garage near main banking area on Av. 3, between Ciencias and Venezuela; nearby is *Pensión Familiar*, same price (beside *Restaurant La Friulana*).

Restaurants Most are closed on Sunday. *Chez Nicolás*, excellent food, highly rec.; *El Chicote* (seafood), Av. Bellavista (Av. 4), corner with Calle 70; *Rincón Boricua*, Av. 23, between Calles 66 and 67 (good meat); *El Pescadito* (Av. 2, 76-A-209), by lakeside, with agreeable breeze; *Mi Vaquita* (Av. 3H, Calle 76), steak house, very good; *La Carreta del Ché*, Av. 13A, No. 76-54; *Saint George*, Av. 12, No. 75-80, dear; *El Delfín*, Calle 75 and 3H, rec., especially for seafood; *Pizzería Napoletana*, Calle 77 near Av. 4, excellent, closed Tues.; *El Jardín*, Centro Comercial Costa Verde, Av. 4, good lunches; *Central Lunch*, Calle 98 (near the port), Chinese run, good helpings, cheap for Maracaibo, open when other places are shut; also in port district, *Café Comercio*, off Av. 4 and corner of Av. Libertador, good, "Bogart style". *ABC*, Av. Bella Vista near Calle 78, good Chinese, small, clean, open till 2100, closed Sun. *La Habana*, Av. Bella Vista (Av. 4) near Calle 76, good salads and milkshakes. *La Friulana*, Calle 95, Av. 3. for good cheap meal at less than US$2, repeatedly rec. For confectionery, *Café Samemrum*, Av. 5 de Julio between Avs. 10 and 11, and *Kabuki*, Av. 5 de Julio opp. Banco de Maracaibo, more fashionable. Health food store, *Larga Vida*, Av. 13A between Calles 75 and 76.

Taxis US$1 fixed fare.

Bookshops Librería Universal, Av. 5 de Julio y Av. 4, maps, stationery, Caracas newspapers; Librería Italiana, Av. 5 de Julio Ed Centro América, post cards and foreign publication (inc US).

Shopping Fin de Siglo department stores sell handicrafts, records, tapes, posters of local sights. The outdoor market, Las Pulgas, is enormous, take any bus S down Av. 4 (Bella Vista). Centro Comercial Costa Verde, Av. 4 (antes Bella Vista), good new shopping complex.

Exchange Banco Consolidado, Av. Bella Vista con Calle 67 (American Express, also Turisol Amex rep., T 70611); Citibank (Banco de Venezuela and local banks offer no exchange facilities). All banks shut at 1630 sharp, exchange in morning only. All Thomas Cook transactions have to be verified in Caracas. *Cambio* at bus terminal will change Colombian pesos into bolívares at a poor rate.

Colombian Consulate Av. 3Y (San Martín) 70-16 nr. Av. 4/Bella Vista (T 72232), 10 km. from centre, take bus or *por puesto* (Bellavista) out of town on Av. 4 to Calle 70; open Mon.-Fri., 0700-1100 prompt, 60-day visa in 5 hrs., no questions, no tickets required (better than Caracas).

Spanish Consulate Av. 15, No. 84-41, Delicias, T 526513.

British Vice-Consul Av. 9B con Calle 66A, No. 66-146, T 78642/82794.

Anglican Church Christ Church, Av. 8 (Santa Rita) a Calle 74.

Laundry Lavandería Laza, Calle 72 near Av. 3H, Bella Vista, rec.

Telecommunications Servicio de Telecomunicaciones de Venezuela, Calle 99, esq. Av. 3. CANTV, Calle 76 near Av. 3E, Bella Vista, open 0700-2330, inc. Sunday.

Post Office, Av. Libertador y Av. 3.

Doctors Dr. García, Hospital Coromoto, Av. 3C and Calle 72, T 912222, speaks English, as does Dr. Carlos Febres, a dentist, Av. 8, No. 84-129, Mon.-Fri. 0900-1200, 1500-1800, T

221504.

Air Services to Maiquetía Mérida, Valera, Barquisimeto, Las Piedras (for Amuay and Cardón), San Antonio (be early to guarantee seat) and other towns. Other airlines connect Maracaibo with Barranquilla (five flights a week), Curaçao, Trinidad, Miami, New York and Europe. (Pan Am Office, Centro Comercial Tamacuary, Av. 22 y Calle 72. T 529826/513199.) The airport is 14 km. S of the town. Taxis have a set fare of about US$3.50, there are no *por puestos*.

Buses Bus station is 15 mins. walk from centre, 1 km. S of the old town. There are several fast and comfortable buses daily to Valencia (US$4.65 by Expresos del Lago), San Cristóbal (US$4.50, 8 hrs., *por puesto*, US$9), Barquisimeto, 5½ hrs. including police stops and searches (US$2.95) and Caracas (US$6.75, 10 hrs.). Bus lines, other than Aerobuses de Venezuela, rec. are Occidente and Alianza, whose fares are cheaper. To Mérida, 5 hrs. (US$4.15), or take bus to El Vigía and change. To Maicao, Expreso Maicao bus, US$4.05, 3 hrs.; taxi US$20 per car (takes 5), 6 police checks en route.

On the W side of the lake, between the rivers Santa Ana and Catatumbo, a large area of swampland is crossed by the road to La Fría. The swamp is inhabited by the Motilones, who, until 1960, refused to have dealings either with white men or other Indians. The southern border of the Motilones' territory, the River Catatumbo, is famed for its almost nightly display of lightning for which there is, as yet, no accepted explanation and which caused it to be known in the old days as "The Lighthouse of Maracaibo". There are various missions you can visit: the easiest to reach is Los Angeles del Tocuco, 51 km. from Machiques, where they welcome visitors; it helps to take a present, such as dried milk. There is a priest at the mission who was attacked, and they now preserve in their museum the arrow head they took from his body. From here you can do a 5-day trek to Picci Cacao, through beautiful scenery to meet Yuspa Indians. Take them rice and blankets if you can carry them. Ask the padre for a guide and mules, take your own food and camping equipment. **Machiques** is on a fast road from San Cristóbal via La Fría to Maracaibo, and has the good *Motel Tukuko*, E.

The best sightseeing trip is north about 1 hr. to the Río Limón (it has another local name). Take a bus (US$0.40) to El Moján, riding with the Guajira Indians as they return to their homes on the peninsula. Another bus or taxi (US$1.75) can be taken to the river. Alternatively, take a Sinamaica bus from the new station, US$0.90 (*por puesto*, US$1.80, shorter delays from police searches make this worthwhile), then a colectivo to Puerto Cuervito, a small port on the Sinamaica lagoon, US$0.25. Hire a boat (bargaining rec. as the price is around US$30 for a boat holding 10 people; fix price, duration and route in advance to ensure full value), and go up the river for an hour to La Boquita (2,500 inhabitants) to see Indians living in houses made of woven reed mats built on stilts: the only place where they can be seen. Return by *por puesto* Sinamaica-El Moján (US$0.40), thence to Maracaibo (US$1.75). Excursions by boat to the Sinamaica lagoon from Maracaibo charge about US$10 for 1½ hrs., but if you think you are being overcharged, ask for *el libro de reclamaciones* which should give the maximum official price. By crossing the bridge over the river you come, in the north, to a paved road that leads to Riohacha, in Colombia, where border formalities are quick and easy, a recommended route, but the Colombian border town, Maicao, has a most unsavoury reputation; best not to stop there. If you enter Venezuela from Colombia at Maicao, you can expect very rigorous searches both at the border and on the way to Maracaibo (6 police checks in all). It is reported that a visa is essential despite what may be said by Venezuelan Consulates.

Along the way you see Guajira Indians, the men with bare legs, on horseback; the women with long, black, tent-shaped dresses and painted faces, wearing the sandals with big wool pom-poms which they make and sell for US$2, as against the US$7-10 in the tourist shops. The men do nothing: women do all the work, tending sheep and goats, selling slippers and raising very little on the dry, hot, scrubby Guajira Peninsula. If you don't do this trip, you can see these Indians in the Ziruma district of Maracaibo. There is an interesting Guajira market at Los Filuos, a mile beyond Paraguaipoa, where you can buy the local tent-dress (*manta*) for about US$5-10, depending on the quality, but much cheaper than in Maracaibo.

Those who wish to go on to the Sierra Nevada de Mérida or the State of Trujillo should return over the lake and turn sharp right through Cabimas, Lagunillas, Bachaquero and Mene Grande, all unattractive oil towns, to rejoin the Pan-American Highway at Agua Viva. For the Colombian frontier or San Cristóbal we follow the Pan-American Highway.

The Pan-American Highway from Agua Viva is a splendid asphalt speed track, but devoid of much scenic or historical attraction. It runs along the foot of the Andes through rolling country planted with sugar or bananas, or park-like cattle land. At Sabana de Mendoza, 24 km. S of

Agua Viva, is a possible stopover—*Hotel Panamérica* (good; air-conditioned). This road has plenty of restaurants, hotels and filling-stations, especially at Caja Seca and El Vigía, both rather new and raw looking towns. At **El Vigía** (*Hotel Gran Sasso*, E; *Hosteria El Vigía*, E; *La Suiza*, Av. 15, opposite bus terminal, F, rec.; restaurant, *Armarilla*, try armarilla asado), where the road from Mérida to Santa Bárbara (Zulia) crosses the Río Chama, there is a fine bridge over 1 km. long. Santa Bárbara (56 km. NW) is a milk, meat and plantain producing centre, with air and boat services to Maracaibo and an important annual cattle show.

From El Vigía, the road continues fairly flat until **La Fría**, with a large natural-gas fuelled power station, where it is joined by the road along the west side of Lake Maracaibo and begins to climb to San Cristóbal. La Fría has two hotels; the family-run *Hotel Turística*, F, on main square, basic but clean, is rec.

THE SIERRA NEVADA DE MERIDA (4)

The **Sierra Nevada de Mérida**, running from S of Maracaibo to the Colombian frontier, is the only range in Venezuela where snow lies permanently on the higher peaks. Near Mérida itself there are five such snowcaps of almost 5,000 metres. Several basins lying between the mountains are actively cultivated; the inhabitants are concentrated mainly in valleys and basins at between 800 and 1,300 metres above sea level. The three towns of Mérida, Valera and San Cristóbal are in this zone. There are two distinct rainy and dry seasons in the year. Two crops of the staple food, maize, can be harvested annually up to an elevation of about 2,000 metres.

Those who wish to visit the Sierra Nevada should turn left at Agua Viva to **Valera**, the most important town in the State of Trujillo, with a population of 117,000 and an airport with connections to Caracas and La Fría. The bus terminal is on the edge of the town. The Banco Consolidado, Av. Bolívar, changes Amex cheques. The US$7 trip by *por puesto* to Mérida across the Pico del Aguila pass (5½ hrs.) is well worth taking.

Hotels *Motel Valera**, Urb. La Plata, D, mixed reports; *Haack*, E, with private cold shower; *Victoria*, F, with bath, basic, noisy; *Pensión Lara*, Av. 13, Calle 8, G, clean, good, friendly. *Albergue Turístico*, F, Av. Independencia, good value; *Camino Real*, nearby, E; *Imperial*, E, Av. 4 esq. Calle 14. *Hidrotermal San Rafael*, 4 km. off road between Valera and Motatán, notable for its hot water springs and the thermal bath.

From Valera a visit can be made to the state capital, **Trujillo** (43,000 people), at 805 metres; a *por puesto* from Valera costs US$0.55. This politically important town is losing ground commercially to Valera. Trujillo runs up and down hill; at the top, across from the university, is a park (sadly rundown) with waterfalls and paths. The Centro de Historia de Trujillo is a restored colonial house, now a museum. Bolívar lived there and signed the "proclamation of war to the death" in the house. A monument to the Virgen de la Paz was built by the wife of President Herrera Campins in 1983; it stands on a mountain, at 1,608 metres, 2½ hr's walk from town; open 0900-1700, good views. (*Hotel Turística*, Av. Independencia 5-65, F with bath and hot water, highly rec.; *Hotel Roma*, F, good, clean, owner's daughter speaks English.)

From Trujillo there is a high, winding, spectacular paved road to **Boconó**, a town built on steep mountain sides. From there you can continue down to Guanare in the *llanos* via Biscucuy (where a very difficult road through Guárico leads to Barquisimeto).

Hotels *Hotel Vega del Río**, F, offers most services and food and is clean; *Colonial*, F, Av. Miranda; *Colina*, near the river at bottom of town, E, motel-style, clean, comfortable, restaurant; *Italia*, F, Calle Jáuregui.

Restaurants *Turística La Casa Vieja*, despite its name, good food, good value, lots of old photos of the area; *El Paisano*, popular restaurant with locals.

We are now in the Sierra Nevada de Mérida, the Western Andes of Venezuela.

The people are friendly, and very colourful in their red and navy blue ruanas. Forty km. beyond Trujillo on a good paved road we come to **Timotes** (hotels: *Las Truchas*, D, very nice, good food; *Posada Caribe*, F, good value; restaurant), a mountainous little place set high in the cold grain zone. Near Timotes are La Mesa de Esnujaque (*Hotel Tibisay**, E; *Miraflores*, F) and La Puerta (*Guadalupe**, D, a fine hotel; *Chiquinquirá*, E, Av. Bolívar 34; *Valeralta*, F, on road to Timotes; *Los Andes*, F, Av. Bolívar), both places hill resorts for Maracaibo and district. The road now climbs through increasingly wild, barren and rugged country and through the windy pass of *Pico del Aguila* (4,115 metres, best seen early in the morning, frequently in the clouds). This is the way Bolívar went when crossing the Andes to liberate Colombia, and on the peak is the statue of an eagle. In the pass is the very pleasant little *Restaurant Páramo Aguila* in chalet style. Behind it there is a small road leading up to the antenna and down towards the village of Piñango where there is trout fishing. Horses can be hired for treks to the Virgen del Carmen shrine and to the lake. The breath-taking scenery and the old village are worth the hardship of the 40 km. road; 4-wheel drive vehicles rec. if the road is wet.

The road then dips rapidly through **Apartaderos**, 12 km. away (*Hotel Parque Turístico*, E, clean, beautiful house, pricey restaurant; *Restaurant Mifiafi*, beautiful, with exquisite food, several rooms to let, gardener will give you seeds from his flowers); over the centuries the Indians have piled up stones from the rocky mountainside into walls and enclosures, hence the name. On Sunday they all stand and watch the tourists; the children sell flowers and fat puppies called *mucuchíes* (a variant of the Grand Pyrené) after a near-by town. Only 3 km. from Apartaderos is Laguna Mucubají, and a 1-hour walk takes you to Laguna Negra in the **Parque Nacional Sierra Nevada** for trout fishing; there is a campsite near the lake, restaurant and shop by the turn-off from the main road. A further 1½-hr. walk from Laguna Negra is the Laguna Los Patos (very beautiful if the weather is fine). Horses can be hired. Guides (not absolutely necessary) can be found at Laguna Mucubají or at the hotels in Santo Domingo (*Hotel Moruco**, D, food very good, bar expensive, reservations can be made through *Hotel Río Prado* in Mérida; *Santo Domingo*, E, hot water, clean, good restaurant but beware of overcharging; rooms for rent opp. *Restaurante Familia*, F). This quaint little hamlet lies a few km. away on the road which leads off to Barinas in the *llanos* and then on to Valencia. Between Santo Domingo and Laguna Mucubají is the *Hotel Los Frailes**, D, said to be one of the best in Venezuela, excellent food, international menus, expensive wines. Book well ahead through Avensa, but don't pay in advance as Avensa will not reimburse you in case of transport problems. *Mucubají* restaurant, at the highest point of the road that passes Laguna Mucubají, is very good for trout.

From Apartaderos the road to Mérida leads up to San Rafael de Mucuchíes, at 3,140 metres (Sra Crys, a French artist, will provide meals if you book in advance), from where you can walk up to a high valley where Indians tend cows and sheep (beware of the dogs that protect the houses), then down to **Mucuchíes** (*Hotel Los Andes*, F, old house above plaza, 4 rooms, clean hot water, shared bathrooms, excellent; *Hotel Faro*), where there is a trout farm. At Moconoque, to the NW there is a hot spring. An old colonial trail, El Camino Real, can be taken from Apartaderos to Mucuchíes (3-4 hrs.), sometimes joining the main road, sometimes passing through small villages; below San Rafael is an old flour mill still in operation. **Tabay**, 10 km. from Mérida, has a pleasant main square, look out for humming birds. Hotels: *Las Cumbres*, *El Castaño*; restaurant *Cancha de Bolas*. Gasoline here but not higher on Páramo circuit. There are two hot springs. From Plaza Bolívar in Tabay, a jeep can be taken to Aguas Calientes and the cloud forest at La Mucuy. We descend through striated zones of timber, grain, coffee and tropical products to reach level land at last and the city of Mérida. All through this part of the country you see a plant with curious felt-like leaves of pale grey-green, the *frailejón* (or great friar), which blooms with yellow flowers from September to December.

The patron saint of Mucuchíes is San Benito; his festival on 29 December is celebrated by participants wearing flower-decorated hats and firing blunderbusses continuously.

Mérida (173 km. from Valera and 674 km. from Caracas), founded 1558, is the capital of Mérida State. Its white towers are visible from far along the road, and it stands at 1,640 metres (mean temperature 19° C) on an alluvial terrace 15 km. long, 2½ km. wide, surrounded by cliffs and plantations and within sight of Pico Bolívar, the highest in Venezuela (5,007 metres), crowned with a bust of Bolívar. In January-February, the coldest months, and August-September, it rains almost every late afternoon. Mérida still retains some colonial buildings which contrast with the fine modern buildings, such as those of the University of the Andes (founded 1785), which has 37,000 students from all over South America and the Caribbean. The main square with rebuilt Cathedral is pleasant, but is no longer colonial. The *fiesta* is the week of 8 December; hotels will only let for the whole week. Mérida is also well known for its Feria del Sol, held on the week preceding Ash Wednesday. Population: 132,000, including students.

Mérida is known for its many parks (thirty three, some very small) and statues: the Parque de las Cinco Repúblicas (Calle 13, between Avs. 4 and 5), beside the barracks, has the first monument in the world to Bolívar (1842) and contains soil from each of the five countries he liberated (photography strictly prohibited). Bolívar is venerated in Venezuela and it is not permitted to cross a square containing his statue, if unsuitably dressed or carrying large bundles. The peaks known as the Five White Eagles (Bolívar, 5,007 m., Humboldt, 4,942 m., Bompland, 4,882 m., Toro, 4,755 m., León, 4,740 m.) can be clearly seen from here. There is a local legend that five Indian girls were transformed into mountains when they refused to submit to the Conquistadores. In the Plaza Beethoven, a different melody from Beethoven's works is chimed every hour (*por puestos* run along Av. 5, marked "Santa María" or "Chorro de Milla", US$0.10). The Parque Los Chorros de Milla has a zoo (some cages disgracefully small) in a hilly setting with a waterfall, closed Mon., it is some distance from the centre (minibus, US$0.35). On the way, there is a new chapel, built on the site where the Pope said mass in 1985. The Parque La Isla contains orchids, basketball and tennis courts, an amphitheatre and fountains; Jardín Acuario, besides the aquarium, is an exhibition centre, mainly devoted to the way of life and the crafts of the Andean peasants, admission US$0.10, open 0800-1200, 1400-2000 (*por puestos* leave from Av. 4 y Calle 25, US$0.10, passing airport). There is fishing and mountaineering in the neighbouring Sierra Nevada.

Hotels *Prado Río**, D, Cruz Verde 1, private bath, swimming pool, main building and individual cabins; *Belensate**, D, Urb. La Hacienda, La Punta; *Park Hotel**, Parque Glorias Patrias, C, but out of high season (i.e not Easter, August, Christmas or carnival) D, with discounts offered on car hire, noisy, but clean, good service, rec.; *Caribay**, Final Av. 2, noisy, D, good restaurant but poor service throughout; *Hostal Madrid*, F, Calle 23, Av. 7-8, basic, good value, good restaurant; *La Sierra*, E, Calle 23, No. 2-31, private bath, friendly, clean, good value, parking; *Luxemburgo*, E, Calle 24 (Rangel), between Avs. 6-7, private bath, excellent breakfast, friendly, rec.; *El Andinito*, Plaza Bolívar, clean and friendly, E, good restaurant; *Montecarlo*, Av. 7 with Calles 24 and 25, T 52-66-88, E, clean, safe, parking, hot water, good but restaurant poor (located between teleférico station and Plaza Bolívar); *Teleférico*, beside teleférico station, E, noisy, clean, hot water, good restaurant. *Chama*, E, Av. 4 con Calle 29, private bath, pleasant, friendly, rec., restaurant; *Posada La Merideña*, Av. 4 y Calle 16, clean, quiet, charming, E; *Plaza*, Av. 5 between C. 23 and 24, E with bath, good value, noisy (laundromat next door); *Santiago de los Caballeros*, E, Av. 3, between Calles 24-25, private bath; *Italia*, Calle 19 between Avs. 2 and 3, F, with bath, hot water (cheaper rooms available), clean, friendly; *Posada Luz Caraballo*, Plaza Mérida, F, small, clean, friendly, restaurant; *Encanto*, Av. Lora 25-30, entre Calles 25/26, F, friendly, take own lock, popular, cheapest; *Roje's*, Av. 2 y Calle 25, F with bath, clean, good value, English spoken; *Regent*, Av. 2, F, clean, safe, hot water, friendly; several hotels on Av. 2 between Calles 17 and 20. *Don Cándido*, Av. 2, F, good but noisy TV; *Mucubají*, Av. Universidad, E, clean and pleasant. It is difficult to get rooms during school holidays and the Feria del Sol. Recommended to book in advance.

Restaurants *Casa Vieja*, decorated as 19th-century Andean home, very good food, moderately priced, expect to pay about US$10 for two people; good food at *Chama Hotel; El "13"*, next to *Hostal Madrid*, good value; *Pekín*, Av. 3 y Calle 28, good set meal for US$3; *Hong Kong*, Av. 5 y Calle 25, good Chinese, reasonable prices; *Onde Jaime*, near Plaza Bolívar, Colombian food, very good; *La Paellera*, Av. 5, good food, reasonable prices; *Pabellón Criolla*, Calle 18 and Av. 8, good, cheap local food as well as hamburgers; *Pizzería Monte Carlo*, Av. 3, Calle 24, rec.; *Pizzería Club* is opposite, OK. Around the corner from *Roje's Hotel* are *Los Cibeles*, Spanish, good trout, and *La Puerta del Sol*, not so good.

Vegetarian restaurants: *Comida Vegetariana*, Calle 24, No. 8-205, opp. Parque Las Heroínas, lunch time only; *Fonda Vegetariana*, Calle 29/Av. 4, rec.; *Anfora de Acuario*, Av. 2, Calles 24 and 23, good set lunches; *Arco Iris*, Av. 4 and Calle 19, very nice; *Pizzería Vegetariano*, Av. 5 and Calle 26, good, cheap; *Gran Fraternidad*, Av. 4, Calle 26, *Macro-Mérida*, Av. 4, Calles 18 and 19. Cheap and filling restaurants are *Los Nevados*, Av. 2, No. 18-57 (rec.), *Comedor Popular*, Calle 23, No. 6. *Chipilino*, Av. 3 y Calle 19, popular with locals, open 24 hrs., rec. and *Restaurante Estudiantil Cuarta Avenida*, Av. 4 between C. 18 and 19. Good arepas at *Arepa Andina*, Av. 5, No. 21-46, and *La Arepera*, Plaza Bolívar. *El Lano*, Av. 3, Calles 28-9, excellent breakfast; *La Fresa*, Calle 26 near Av. 5, for desserts; *El Palacio*, Calle 23, good batidos; *Café Santa Rosa*, Av. 4 y Calle 23, good coffee; good tea shop on Av. 23 between Calle 25 and 26. The *Heladería La Coromoto*, Av. 3 y Calle 29, offers 292 flavours, 88 choices of ice cream each day, e.g., trout, cornflakes, garlic, spaghetti. Local specialities, trout, pastelitos (savoury); sweetmeats include dulces abrillantados, higo relleno, mantecado de maiz; also try the local drink, calentado.

Museums Colonial Art Museum, Av. 3 No. 18-48, three blocks from Plaza Bolívar (open Tues.-Fri., 0900-1200, 1500-1800, Sat. 1500-1800, and Sun., 1000-1200, 1500-1800). More interesting is the small Archaeology Museum on the main square. Museum of Modern Art, Plaza Beethoven. Instituto Municipal de Cultura, Av. 4, half block from Parque Bolívar, stages poetry readings, art shows etc.

Car Hire Several companies at the airport. For motorcycle hire try Buggy's Bikes, Av. Miranda, Quinta Sajomi 3-83, T 639145, US$12 per day.

Films One-day service, CA, Calle 23 between 5 y 6, T 527981.

Exchange No bank accepts travellers' cheques, except Banco Internacional and Banco Consolidado for American Express, at the end of Viaducto Calle 26, but only 1000 to 1200 at either bank, and Banco Mercantil for Thomas Cook; Banco Unido accepts Visa and Mastercard. Cheques accepted by the *Casa de Cambio* in Centro Comercial Las Tapias, Av. Andrés Bello and in airport arrivals, and by hotels. Turisol, Amex representative, T 631085. On Saturday, try the Latin Travel Agency by the *Park Hotel*.

Language Schools Several schools including Instituto Europa, rec. Try also Mailer Mattíc, Av. 7 between Calle 25 and 26, rec.

Colombian Consulate Calle 9, 2 blocks from C.C. Las Tapias, visas take 10 mins.

Post Office and Telephones CANTV, Calle 21 and Av. 14.

Laundry Lavandería La Vencedora, Av. 2 between Calles 24 and 25, same day service, US$0.75 a load; Lavandería Belén, Calle 21 between Av. 4 and 5.

Bullfights Mérida is a famous centre; the Feria del Sol in February is the peak time.

Tourist Offices Near the airport (good map, US$0.15) and near *Hotel Mucubají*. At Terminal Sur, helpful, map, hotel list, useful addresses and guide to events. At Oficina de Turismo Aeropuerto, Manuel, is very informative about excursions in the mountains, T 639330.

Travel Agencies Club de Turismo, Calle 24, No. 8-107 (opp. Teleférico), good advice on excursions, ask for Fanny. Occidente Turismo y Viajes, Av. 4 between Calles 18 and 19 for all flight bookings. Montaña offers climbing holidays (US$75-125 per day, including transport and equipment), mountain biking, trout fishing, and a 21-day tour of Venezuela, Ed. Las Américas P.B., Av. Las Américas, Mérida, T (074) 631740, Apartado Postal 645, Fax (5874) 631740; Sierra Tours, Park Hotel, T 630879, can book teleférico and has a range of excursions. It is cheaper to take a taxi for a day trip, Línea Tibisay, outside Park Hotel, T 637930, rec. Mountain Tours, Calle 24, No. 8-107, T 074-526402, offer a wide range of climbing tours and trips to the jungle. Nevada Tours at the airport offer interesting trips. They will take non-climbers up the Pico Bolívar, but owing to the altitude and weather conditions, this can be dangerous. Check all equipment carefully. Camilo Trujillo Medina, Parque Las Américas, Edificio M, T 637175, and Alan Highton, T 632958, both offer tours of Merida, speak English and have been recommended.

Air Services   Airport is on the main highway, *por puesto* into town US$0.10, taxi US$1.25. Aeropostal and Avensa. To Caracas 3 flights daily, 1 hr., also to San Antonio at 1730. In the rainy season, especially on afternoon flights, planes may be diverted to San Antonio (if they aren't, it's a hair-raising approach). Avensa pay for overnight accommodation or for *por puestos* to Mérida, 3-5 hrs. on winding roads where landslides are common. Sit on left side of plane from Caracas for views. A new airport is being built at El Vigía, 1 hr. from Mérida; much safer as it is on a plain.

Buses   The bus terminal is about 3 km. out of town on the W side of the valley, connected by frequent minibus service. To Caracas, US$6 (11-15 hrs.), *por puesto*, US$12; daily bus to Maracaibo, US$4.15, or *por puesto* service US$8.30, by Unión de Conductores, T 24364. Bus to San Cristóbal, 0600, US$3, 6 hrs; *por puesto* US$6. Buses to Barinas, US$1.75, 6 hrs. *Por puesto* to Apartaderos, US$1.75. Those hitchhiking east from Mérida should take a minibus to Tabay (US$0.25) and try from there. *Por puesto* to Valera, US$7 (6 hrs.), sit on the right side for best views.

The world's alleged highest and longest aerial cableway runs to **Pico Espejo** (4,765 metres) in four stages; it was built by the French in 1958. The trip up and down takes three hours and costs US$4, children US$2, discount for holders of any student card; it runs Tuesday to Sunday, except holidays, starting up at 0730, last trip up at 1200, last trip down at 1545 (only 2 rucksacks are allowed in each cabin, children are affected by the thin air, which makes them vomit). Check beforehand that the cable car is operating as it is periodically closed for maintenance. There is a quota of 200 people per hour and it is very popular at weekends and holiday periods. Book several days in advance from the ticket office on Calle 25 (T 074-525080). At busy periods queues start at 0600 and it may be worth booking at travel agencies or hotels (e.g. *Hotel Caribay*) which charge US$8. This is a "must", best done early in the morning (before 0830 ideally), before the clouds spoil the view, and from November to June. In summer the summit, with its statue to Our Lady of the Snows (patron saint of mountaineers), is clouded and covered with snow and there is no view. In the station in Mérida one can buy or or hire warm jackets, gloves, caps, and climbing equipment, although there is a café at the top which you don't have to leave if you feel the cold—temperatures can be as low as 0°C. August is the coldest month on the peaks. The glacier on Pico Bolívar can be seen clearly; so can Picos Humboldt and Bompland, forming the Corona, and to the E, on a clear day, the blue haze of the *llanos*. Electric storms in the mountains are not uncommon. There is a restaurant at La Montaña, 2,442 m.

If the peak is slightly clouded when you start, stop at the Loma Redonda station (4,045 metres) the last station but one. From this station there is a path to Los Nevados (2,711 metres), a pretty little place, plentiful accommodation G, guest house has food (5 or more hours' walking down, not recommended for the inexperienced, 7 hours up; be prepared for cold rain in the afternoon, start very early and rest before walking because of the sudden ascent in the cable car). Mules do the journey Tues.-Sun., US$3, 5 hrs. From Los Nevados you can continue to El Morro or take a jeep to Mérida (2½ hrs., very rough, US$2.50). It is possible to get a room to stay overnight (*Hospedaje Ariana*, G). Sr. Oviller Ruiz provides information on the history of the church and Indian cemetery. There is also an ice cave with dazzling crystal ice stalactites two hours' rough walk from the last station. Only those in good heart can make this high trip. At La Aguada station you can see the *frailejón* plant and throughout the area there is a great variety and quantity of flora. From La Aguada it is possible to trek on foot or by mule to the village of Los Aleros (see below), at 2,700 metres, 5 hours. From here you can continue to El Morro, 6 hours (beware of snakes on the path). A description of the Sierra Nevada is included in *No Frills Guide to Venezuela* published by Bradt Publications.

Note   Because this is a national park, you need a permit to leave the station area at the summit, or to walk this mountain range. It must be obtained from the Inparques (National Parks) ranger's office next to the *teleférico*, free; a mediocre topographical map is on sale. Permits are not given to single hikers: a minimum of 2 people is required. Camping gas may be bought in Mérida from a household shop near Plaza Bolívar. If camping, remember that the area is between 3,500 and 4,200 metres so acclimatization is necessary as is warm clothing for nighttime. Water purification is also recommended.

Mountain Guides   The Andean Club in Mérida organizes trips to the top and guides will provide all equipment; enquire at the *teleférico* station at the end of Calle 24, beyond Av. 8. Carlos Rodríguez C., can be contacted at the vegetarian restaurant of María Guerrero next to the *teleférico* (home address Av. Universidad, Edificio María Gracia, Piso 2, Apto. 5); he offers 1 to 7 day trips around Mérida, inc. in the price transportation, equipment and food.

Excursions 40 km. NW is the Centro de Investigaciones en Astronomía, responsible for the national observatory. Open daily 1030, 1400, 1530, 1900, 2200. There is a library, Mon.-Fri. 0900-1200, 1530-1730, T 791893, 791988. Visits to other resorts near Mérida: to Laguna de Mucubají, Laguna Negra or Pico del Aguila (**see page** 1068—*por puesto* to Pico de Aguila, US$2.50). Just outside Mérida is Los Aleros, a model of a 1930s Andean village; examples of traditional skills, fascinating collection of old cameras and photographs; a ride in an open-sided bus and other events; very touristy (however, no Coca Cola, only traditional refreshments), rec. as a "must" (*Hospedaje Florencia*, G, and other *pensiones*). *Antano* is a good nearby restaurant. **Jají**, 43 km. (good picnic spot en route overlooking Mérida), *por puesto* (US$1, sit on the left), famous for its colonial architecture, including a nice main square. Tourists can get advice from the Club Andino (P.O. Box 66) or Casa del Turista, La Compalla; T 3391. Recommended hotel and restaurant *Posada de Jají*, good food. Continuing for 62 km.—narrow, but mostly paved—beyond Jají, the Pan-American Highway is reached (several gas stations on the way). From La Azulita, between Jají and the Pan-American, one can visit La Cueva del Pirata. Through splendid scenery to Lagunilla, with pleasant lakeside restaurant; San Juan de Laqunillas, believed to be the first site of Mérida, has a striking church and is noted for its craftwork especially weaving. Fiestas from Christmas to Candlemas, 3 weeks in May (14 and 15 the highpoint) and in July. Thirty mins. beyond Lagunilla lies the little church of Estanques (seldom open except on Christmas Day) with a stupendous gold colonial altar. Near Estanques is the colonial village of Chiguará with mineral springs (*Posada Colonial Cantarranos*, F, friendly, try *El Merendero* for local delicacies), visited by exchange students; *por puesto* from Mérida, US$0.70. At El Pedregal there are botanical gardens and a good view over the town. Giant cacti in the area are said to be 300 years old.

After Mérida the road passes on through the Chama valley to Lagunilla. Ninety-six km. beyond Mérida comes **Tovar** (population 19,000; *Hostería Sabaneta*, E, private bath; *Pensión Ideal*, G, clean, basic, laundry facilities, friendly; *Hospedaje Tovar*, G; *Restaurant Kek Duna*, Hungarian owner speaks 6 languages and serves interesting food), a nice little town with pleasant excursions, whence we can rejoin the Pan-American via Zea or tackle the wild and beautiful old mountain road over La Negra to San Cristóbal. 15 km. from Tovar is Bailadores (*Hotel La Cascada*, C, modern— Wilfredo plays electric organ in the bar on Sat. night, and at Mass on Sun. in the beautiful church, entertaining on both occasions; *Hospedaje Villa*, F); beautiful walk to the waterfall with strawberries and cream half-way at La Capellería; *por puesto* to San Cristóbal US$3. Las Tapias, 2 km. away, has a hot spring. From Bailadores the road climbs up into the mountains. The *Hotel de Montaña*, C, private bath, T 077-82401/2, is rec., 7 km. before La Grita on the road from Mérida. Daily buses between Tovar and La Grita on the old road. **La Grita** is a pleasant town, still not entirely Americanized; Hotels: *La Casona*, F, Carrera 2A, No. 6-69, clean, friendly; *Capri*, F, Carrera 3, good value, bargain. Hard to find a reasonable restaurant.

San Cristóbal, capital of Táchira State, is on a plateau 55 km. from the Colombian border, at 830 metres. Average temperature 22°C, population 230,000. The city is on three levels, running N-S: a 112 km. wide level zone along the Torbes river, which flows S into the Orinoco basin, and two terraces, one of them 200 metres above the river, and 5°C cooler. This, and the La Concordia sector to the S, are the "select" suburbs. The city was founded in 1561, and the Spanish colonial appearance—the appearance only—is preserved. The Cathedral, finished in 1908, had its towers and façade rebuilt in colonial style for the 400th anniversary of the foundation. There is a good road over the mountains, with beautiful Andean views, to San Antonio.

Hotels *De Ferias El Tamá**, D, Av. 19 de Abril, overlooking the town, has an Olympic-size swimming pool; *Korinu*, D, Carrera 6 bis, rec., with restaurant; *Círculo Militar*, Av. 19 de Abril, E, all services including swimming pool and gymnasium; *Machirí*, E, Calle 7 No. 4-30, bath, hot water, clean, friendly, central, rec.; *Hamburgo*, Av. Libertador, F, clean; *Horizonte*, F, Av. 5, iced water provided; *Hospedaje El Almendro*, opp. old bus station, F, cheap and homely, near to *El Amparo* restaurant; *Motel Las Lomas**, E, Av. Libertador; *Ejecutivo*, F, old and basic but clean and central; *La Valencia*, F, run down, but clean and friendly; *Cariongi*, near bus terminal, F, basic but convenient; *Americano*, Calle 8, F, basic and good;

Tropicana, F, clean, spacious, just across the street behind the old bus terminal (billiard hall next door). There are several cheap hotels on Avenida 6A, just off the central plaza, in F category; *Residencia Hilton*, clean and friendly, is probably the most expensive; opposite is *Internacional*, F, cheaper and better; but neither are as grand as they sound.

Restaurants *Fung Wah*, on lower of 2 main thoroughfares, Chinese, expensive but good.

Exchange Banco Consolidado (American Express), 5a Av., Edif. Torre E.

Post Office Palacio Municipal, next to Cathedral.

Launderette in Cada shopping centre next to *Hotel El Tamá*, open 0800-1200, 1400-1800.

Airports for San Cristóbal: at San Antonio (1 hr.) and La Fría (90 mins.).

By Road To Maracaibo, 8 hrs., US$4.50, *por puesto*, US$9. To Mérida, US$6 by *por puesto* or bus, US$3. To Caracas, US$6.25-6.75, 12 hrs. by Llanos and Panamericana routes respectively; similarly to Valencia, US$5.50-5.85. To San Antonio, 2½ hrs. by bus, US$0.32, or *por puesto*, which continues to Cúcuta, US$1.25, stopping at Immigration in both countries, runs every 20 mins. By taxi to Cúcuta: US$9.25 to San Antonio, US$4.25 to wait at border, then US$5 to Cúcuta. San Cristóbal has a new bus terminal.

San Antonio, the frontier town (not a tourist attraction, although there is an attractive colonial cathedral, also some pleasant parks), is connected by international bridge with Cúcuta, Colombia, distant about 16 km. (bus US$0.65—in bolívares or pesos—to international bridge), whence you can continue by road or air to Bogotá. Be sure to get your Venezuelan exit stamp from the immigration office at the border bridge (building on left, upstairs, closed 1100-1300) or Colombian officials will send you back (unless you are only visiting Cúcuta). Once you are in Colombia go straight to the DAS office in Cúcuta to complete formalities there (**see page 647**). Entry charge, US$1.50. Entering Venezuela from Cúcuta, there is no point in buying a bus ticket to San Cristóbal before going through formalities. Go to DIEX on the other side of San Antonio, 3 blocks down from Carrera 9; entry stamp is only given after passport and visa have been photocopied at another office (US$0.20). If travelling on a Cúcuta-San Cristóbal bus, the driver should wait for you to go through formalities. 5 km. after San Antonio is a customs post; be prepared to be strip-searched. **N.B.** Venezuelan customs is often closed at weekends; it is therefore impossible to cross from Colombia at these times. Be prepared for long queues on the international bridge after 1500. Beware of all sorts of sharp practices at Cúcuta bus station (theft, contricks, selling tickets for buses that do not exist, e.g. Cúcuta-Caracas). Entering Venezuela in your own car presents no problems as long as you have obtained a visa in advance. You must visit Immigration in town, pay US$0.20 for a form on which to pay exit tax and have your passport photocopied. Once in Venezuela, you may find that local police are ignorant of documentation required for foreign cars. Thirteen km. N on the Venezuelan side lies the spa of Ureña, with natural hot springs (*Hotel Aguas Calientes**, C, private thermal bath, swimming pool).

Hotels At San Antonio: *Don Jorge*, F, a/c dining room expensive; *Táchira*, E, with bath, rec.; *Neveri*, E, Calle 3, No. 3-11, esq. Carrera 3, private bath, parking nearby, by border; *La Villa*, F, clean, fan; *Los Andes*, F, cheap; *San Antonio*, F, fan, clean, cheap meals; *Residencial Colonial*, Carrera 11, No. 251, F, clean, cheap restaurant, rec.; many hotels near town centre.

Exchange at the Banco de Venezuela on main square. *Casas de cambio* near the international bridge will not all change cheques and some will only change Colombian pesos, not even US dollars cash. The exchange rate for changing bolívares to pesos is better in San Antonio than in Cúcuta.

Colombian Consulate Carrera 6, No. 3-29, for visas, open until 0200.

Bus to Caracas US$6.75.

Airport has exchange facilities. Taxis run to DIEX (emigration) in town, and on to Cúcuta airport, US$5. *Por puesto* to airport, US$0.12. Internal flights, Avensa, to Maiquetía (US$30), Mérida, Barquisimeto, Coro, Maracaibo and Valencia; international to Aruba, Bonaire, Mexico, Miami, New York and Panama.

THE LLANOS OF THE ORINOCO (5)

This area of flat grasslands, 1,000 km. by 320 km., lies between the Andes and the Orinoco River and is reported to be one of the best places in the world to see birds. It is veined by numerous slow running rivers, forested along their banks. The vast flatland is only varied here and there by *mesas*, or slight upthrusts of the land. About 5 million of the country's 6.4 million cattle, many of the Zebu type from Brazil and India, are in the *llanos*, 30% of the country's area, but holding no more than 13% of the population. When the whole plain is periodically under water, the *llaneros* drive their cattle into the hills or through the flood from one *mesa* to another. When the plain is parched by the sun and the savanna grasses become uneatable they herd the cattle down to the damper region of the Apure and Orinoco. Finally they drive them into the valley of Valencia to be fattened for slaughter.

Parts of the area are coming under cultivation. The Guárico dam has created thousands of hectares of fertile land by controlling flood and drought. The *llanos* State of Portuguesa has now the largest cultivated area of any: rice and cotton are now produced.

Alternative route from Caracas to Mérida

There is a splendid road to the western *llanos* of Barinas, from Valencia through **San Carlos**, capital of Cojedes State (uninteresting, *Hotel Italo*, F, Av. Carabobo, a/c, private bath), **Acarigua**, a thriving agricultural centre (*Motel Payara**, D, on road to Guanare, pool, a/c; *Motel Rancho Grande*, E, on road to San Carlos; *Miraflores*, E, swimming pool) and **Guanare**, a national place of pilgrimage with an old parish church containing the much venerated relic of the Virgin of Coromoto, Patron of Venezuela. Population 32,500 (*Hotel Italia*, D, Carrera 5, No. 19-60, the most expensive; others, all E, include *Coromoto*, swimming pool; *Motel Portuguesa*, a/c, hot water, clean, good restaurant, pool).

After the first appearance of the Virgin, Chief Coromoto failed to be baptized, though he did hedge by getting other members of the tribe baptized. When the Virgin reappeared he made a grab at her and told her gruffly to be gone, but she vanished leaving in his hand a likeness of herself on the inner surface of a split stone now on display in the church. For years little attention was paid to the image, and it was only in 1946 that this Virgin was declared the Patron of Venezuela.

The road continues to **Barinas** (population 92,000), the capital of the cattle-raising and oil-rich State of Barinas. Fishing and game-watching excursions into the *llanos*. The rivers are full of *caribes* (*piranha*) and many kinds of fish good to eat. The local music at *Cantarama* bar near the bus terminal has been rec.; harp *cuatro*, singing, informal and very good.

Hotels *Motel El Cacique*, D, swimming pool; *Bristol**, Av. 23 de Enero, E; *Comercio**, F, Av. Marqués del Pumar, cooking facilities; *Plaza*, E, a/c, shower, good restaurant; *Motel La Media Avenida*, Av. 23 de Enero, E, cold showers, bar, restaurant, parking, clean, rec.; *Hostería Los Guasimitos*, F, a/c, clean, good restaurant, standard motel, on road to Guanare, swimming pool; *Suine*, quiet, F, with shower, no hot water, restaurant; *Lisboa*, opp. bus station, F, good, rec.

Restaurant Gladismar, Av. 7, good evening meals; *Heladería Metro*, Av. 7, good patisserie opposite the bus terminal.

Exchange Banco Consolidado (American Express), Av. Libertador con Calle Camejo.

Buses 4 a day for Mérida, US$1.75, magnificent ride through the mountains, 6 hrs. *Por puesto* costs US$3.50. Bus to Caracas, US$4.60, 8 hrs; to San Antonio, US$2.80. To Acarigua, US$1.60, 3 hrs; San Cristóbal, US$1, 4½ hrs. The bus terminal is on the edge of the town.

Airport with local services and to Caracas (2 a day US$24).

From Barinas there is a beautifully scenic road to Apartaderos, in the Sierra Nevada de Mérida (**see page** 1068).

Motorists travelling East from Mérida to Ciudad Bolívar can either go across the *llanos* or via San Carlos, El Sombrero, Valle de la Pascua and El Tigre, which route requires no ferry crossings and has more places with accommodation. In the *llanos*, near El Baúl (turn off main road E of San Carlos), is a safari-type lodge at Hato Piñero, including all meals, good room, and guide for bird- and animal-watching trips; address: Hato Piñero, Edif. General de Seguros, Piso 6, Ofic. 6B, Av. La Estancia, Chuao, Caracas 1060, T (2) 912011—contact Ani Villanueva.

Sixteen km. E of Maracay, a good road leads off to **San Juan de los Morros** where a cock-fighting tournament is held each year (Hotels: *Motel Santa Mónica*, E; *Gran Hotel Los Morros*, E, on Carretera Nacional towards Villa de Cura; *Excelsior*, E, Calle Marino; *Ana*, F). It has natural hot springs. Nearby are mountains with vertical cliffs, on which several climbing routes have been opened. The road divides later: S to the Guárico dam, the *llanos* and San Fernando de Apure, and E to Valle de la Pascua (*Hotel Venezuela*, E, Plaza Bolívar; *San Marcos*, E, Carretera Nacional towards El Socorro; *Gran Hotel Monte Carlo*, opp. bus station, F, a/c, shower) and El Tigre.

Going S, keep an eye open for egrets, which were almost exterminated early in the century for their feathers, once a valuable export. Crossing the bridge over the River Apure at Puerto Miranda we come to **San Fernando de Apure**, the capital of the western *llanos*. (Bus to Caracas, US$3.75.)

Hotels *Boulevard*, Av. Boulevard; *La Torraca*, Paseo Libertador; *La Fuente*, Av. Miranda; *Trinacria*, Av. Miranda; *El Río*, Av. Miranda; *Europa*, Paseo Libertador; all in E range with a/c, water spasmodic. *Hotel-Restaurant Apure*, good steaks, accommodation E; *Mister Pollo*, Av. Carabobo, good value chicken.

Exchange Banco Consolidado for American Express, Av. Miranda, Res. 19 de Abril.

Manfred W. Frischeisen recommends a detour from the Guárico dam: San Fernando road, turn left at Calabozo (*Motel Tiuna*, a/c and good restaurant) along a gravel road (being paved) to Paso del Caballo (81 km.). A little trail goes on to Cazorla (85 km.); on the swamps one can see egrets, parrots, alligators, monkeys (and hear howlers). Turn left in Cazorla to Guayabal, back on the main road, 21 km. from San Fernando (there is also a road to the right to Guayabal, very bad, only passable with 4-wheel-drive or a trail bike with effort).

From San Fernando you can drive W towards Barinas, the road is beautiful between Mantecal and Bruzual (2 buses a day San Fernando-Barinas). In the early morning, many animals and birds can be seen, and in the wet season alligators cross the road. At Bruzual, just S of Puente Nutrias over the Apure river, there are 3 primitive inns (e.g. *Los Llaneros*, F, you eat with the family). A fair, interesting road heads W after Mantecal at La Ye junction and goes over Guasdualito to San Cristóbal (take spare gasoline). Peter Straub recommends taking the bus from San Cristóbal to Guasdualito, then the mail plane to San Fernando, continuing to Ciudad Bolívar. Most travel agents do not know of this method: insist on seeing the timetables.

From San Fernando you can travel east to Ciudad Bolívar either by taking a boat (expensive and unreliable and not possible in the dry season) from opposite the airport to Caicara (see below), or by taking a bus to El Sombrero and catching the Ciudad Bolívar bus at 1700. South of San Fernando a paved road now continues to Puerto Ayacucho.

There is a route across the *llanos* to Ciudad Bolívar: from Chaguaramas on the road to Valle de la Pascua, turn S through Las Mercedes and flat cattle land to **Cabruta**, 179 km., daily bus to Caracas, US$3, there is no ferry to Puerto Ayacucho, but you can take a barge, US$10, 3-day trip, fix price with boat captain. Ask for Coronel Tefero about travelling on the river. There is a small hotel, infested with rats and cockroaches, but better accommodation in **Caicara**—ferry from Cabruta, about 1 hr., US$2 for car, passengers US$0.35. Hotels: *Tres Ríos*, E, a/c, parking, clean; *Central*, F; *Italia*, F; *Buenos Aires*, F; *Miami*, E; *Venezuela*, F; *Bella Guayana*, F. By bus from Caicara to Ciudad Bolívar, 5 hrs., US$4; to Puerto Ayacucho at 0600 and 1130, 6 hrs. US$3.50. There are two flights a week (Wed. and Sat.) to Puerto Ayacucho. Cargo boats take three days to Puerto Ayacucho but are unwilling to take passengers; better from Cabruta (see above).

Puerto Ayacucho is the capital of the Federal Territory of Amazonas, which has an area of 175,000 square kilometres and a population of only 15,000, a large proportion of whom live in Puerto Ayacucho. At the end of the dry season

(April), it is very hot and sticky. It is 800 km. up the Orinoco from Ciudad Bolívar, deep in the wild, but no direct boats do the five day journey up river. The opening of a new paved road north to San Fernando de Apure has led to a tourist boom during the last 3 years and the town is growing rapidly.

Hotels *Hotel Amazonas**, D, dilapidated, pool, expensive breakfast; *Hotel El Tobogán*, Orinoco, T (048) 21320, E, popular, fair, TV; *Italia*, F, with fan, very run down; *Residencia Internacional*, Av. Aguerrevere 18, T 21242, F, clean, safe, friendly, laundry; *Residencia Río Siapa*, Av. Orinoco, T 21138, E, modern, clean, friendly, hard to find; *Maguari*, F, friendly, will store luggage, rec., restaurant; *Gran Sarola*, opp. gas station, clean.

There is a good craft shop for souvenirs. The Friday market is worth a visit, but get there early (finishes at 0830); try Thursday.

Exchange Banco Unión, for Visa; Banco de Venezuela.

Transport Ferry across the Orinoco, US$0.50. Bus to Caicara, 0500, 0800, 1400 daily, 6 hrs; bus to Maracay and Caracas (11 hrs.) leaves from the "ferry town", 1630. Flights to Caracas, 2 a day via San Fernando de Apure, to Caicara and to Ciudad Bolívar.

Excursions Tobogán Tours, Av. Río Negro 44, Puerto Ayacucho (T (48)21700), owner Pepe Jaimes, arranges trips on the Orinoco, to Indian villages and to the Paraguena river through waterfalls, untouched jungle with fascinating wildlife, mixed reports. Turismo de la Selva also run a variety of tours, good reports. For tours of the Territorio Federal Amazonas, S of Puerto Ayacucho, a rec. guide is Yamal A. Nasser, Calle Crisanto Mato Coba 33, Barrio Virgen del Valle, Ciudad Bolívar, T 085-48969 (he may be contacted through the Tourist Office in Ciudad Bolívar). Pedro Lucchini, T (048) 21156, in *artesanía* shop to left of Tobogán Tours will advise and arranges some trips. Other rec. guides include Fernando Escobar, Av. Constitución, T 048-21946, very knowledgeable, speaks English; and Abid Seguias, T 048-24028, who organizes plane trips to villages. If planning to travel south from Puerto Ayacucho you need a permit from the Bureau of Indian Affairs (Orai) in Caracas, or possibly Puerto Ayacucho. Near Puerto Ayacucho is *Jungle Camp Calypso*, run by Calypso Tours, La Guaira (T 031-24683), US$150 p.p. for 2 days including food, cabin accommodation, highly rec., excursions in canoes. Also *Jungle Lodge Camturama* (T 048-22574), C, a/c, pool, buffet meals US$4-7, full day tours US$10, highly rec.
    For trips anywhere from Puerto Ayacucho check at the central service station. Other recommended trips include by *por puesto* to Samariapo and waterfalls at Tobogán de la Selva. From Samariapo boat to Isla de Ratón and Santa Rosa; also to Vichada and Santa Rita and thence bus to Villavicencio (Colombia).

Beyond Puerto Ayacucho are rapids, but smaller launches on the upper Orinoco can reach the Casiquiare and the Río Negro which flows into the Amazon. It is very difficult to find boats willing to take passengers. For information on travelling by boat to Manaus, ask for Alejandro. On the Río Negro, towards Brazil, is **San Carlos de Río Negro**. No hotel, so a hammock is essential. Flights to Puerto Ayacucho Wed. and Sat., US$25; military flights occasionally, if you pay for at least 7 passengers there will be an extra flight. It is possible to take a cargo boat from San Carlos up the Río Casiquiare and down the Orinoco (following Humboldt's route); it takes 8 days to Puerto Ayacucho. You can also rent a canoe to Santa Lucía on the Brazilian border on the Río Negro (US$20, 5 hrs. Santa Lucía-San Carlos); no hotel, food at the customs post.
    In 1955/56 two Americans successfully canoed to Argentina, continuing from the Amazon by way of the Tapajós, Paraguay and Paraná. The trip took about one year. The journey up the Amazon to the Casiquiare and Orinoco has also been successfully negotiated by a hovercraft with a British crew. It is impossible to go without a permit, available only for scientific expeditions. Permits are obtained from the Bureau of Indian Affairs (ORAI) in Caracas, or in Puerto Ayacucho itself. Buy your provisions here: nobody lives on the Casiquiare despite what the maps say. Do not travel alone. If you want to cross the border into Colombia at Puerto Ayacucho (ferry from the Guardia Nacional post on the northern edge of town), or further north at Puerto Carreño, you can expect difficulties with the local authorities. You will probably be asked for proof of how much money you have and where you are going; some travellers have had to obtain Colombian visas to enter the country when only a passport and ticket out of the country were strictly necessary. Some travellers have, however, reported no problems crossing for a few hours from Puerto Ayacucho, ferry departs 1100 and returns 1430, US$1 return. From Puerto Ayacucho there is a cargo boat to Puerto Páez, 4 hrs., for crossing to Colombia. Check with Guardia Nacional and insist on exit stamp (they are strangely reluctant). Ferry to Puerto Carreño US$0.75.

EAST FROM CARACAS (6)

The eastern part of the North-Eastern Highlands, with summits rising to 2,000 metres, has abundant rainfall in its tropical forest. The western part, which is comparatively dry, has most of the inhabitants and the two main cities, Cumaná and Barcelona.

Eastern Venezuela, with the Highlands in the NE, the great *llanos* of the Orinoco to the south, and south of the Orinoco again the range of Guayana Highlands, was until quite recently not of much account in the Venezuelan economy. Some coffee and cacao are grown on the eastern slopes of the north-eastern highlands in the tropical forest, but the western slopes are subject to drought. Cattle roam the *llanos*, and the Guayana Highlands produce gold and diamonds. The picture has now been changed, as about 30% of Venezuelan oil now comes from this area. South of the Orinoco vast iron ore deposits are mined.

It is now only five hours from Caracas to Barcelona by road through Caucagua, from which there is a 47-km. road NE to **Higuerote**, which has a number of beaches, currently the focus of large-scale tourist projects.

Higuerote can also be reached by a road, which is being paved, along the coastal mountain range from Los Caracas (92 km., **see page** 1056)—beautiful views, beaches everywhere, 4-wheel drive vehicles rec. (Higuerote hotels: *Campomar*, D; *Sol Mar*, D). One beach is at La Sabana (turn off after 37 km.); private rooms for rent, San Juan drum (*tambores*) festival at end-June. 4 km. beyond is Caruao, rebuilt in an old style—population is almost entirely black, friendly, good beach (one hotel, F ask for Josefa, who cooks delicious seafood, the sports club has a wild party each Sat. p.m.); follow the road for El Pozo del Cura, a waterfall and pool.

14 km. before Higuerote on the road from Caucagua is Tacarigua de Mamporal, where you can turn off to the **Laguna de Tacarigua National Park**. The road passes a Tunnel of Vegetation (almost 3 km. long), cocoa plantations, the towns of San José and Río Chico (*Hotel Italia*, E, a/c; excellent natural fruit icecream). In the fishing village of Tacarigua de la Laguna (rooms to rent), you can eat delicious *lebranche* fish; an unmotorized ferry crosses the lagoon, which has many water birds (including flamingoes, usually involving a day-long boat trip to see them), to the beach on the Caribbean.

41 km. from Barcelona is Píritu, which has an interesting Franciscan church, and the fishing village of Puerto Píritu (*Casacoima Puerto Píritu**, D).

Barcelona, population 112,000, mean temperature, 27°C, capital of Anzoátegui State, is on the W bank of the Neveri River, 5 km. from the ocean. You can see the ruins of the Casa Fuerte, grim relic of the War of Independence. Teatro Cajigal is a replica of the Teatro Municipal in Caracas. (Hotels: *Barcelona**, E, no restaurant; *Neveri*, D; restaurant *Castillo del Oriente*, unpretentious, not expensive.) Ships from La Guaira call at **Guanta**, 22 km. away, now connected with the 4-lane highway which goes through Puerto La Cruz and an airport with services to Caracas. Oficambio exchange facilities at the airport. Taxi Barcelona airport-Puerto La Cruz, US$5.

Barcelona has been surpassed commercially by **Puerto La Cruz**, 22 km. away by an asphalted highway skirting the pleasant residential and bathing resort of Lechería (*por puesto* US$0.20). Puerto La Cruz, once a fishing hamlet, is now a thriving town of 180,000 with two oil refineries, and famous for its watersports, fishing, diving, water skiing and surfing. Its seaport is also Guanta.

On the highway from Puerto La Cruz to Barcelona is the Polideportivo sports stadium seating 10,000 people: covered gymnasium, velodrome, tennis, volleyball, and basket-ball courts and two swimming pools. A new Institute of Technology, part of the Universidad del Oriente, is near the stadium.

Hotels at Puerto La Cruz tend to be fully booked with package tours. *Meliá**, B, on Paseo Colón, luxury hotel with all services and facilities; *Doral Beach**, D, swimming pool, beach, nearer Barcelona than Puerto La Cruz; *Europa*, Calle Sucre, esq. Plaza Bolívar, E, good, clean, safe, a/c; *Neptuno**, D, Paseo Colón, a/c, good restaurant; next door is *Margelino*, F with bath, a/c, safe, clean, very good; *San Remo*, D, Calle Simón Rodríguez 55, rec., near bus station; *Regis*, Paseo Colón 73, F, with fan in old part, E with a/c in new. *Tama*, Rómulo Gallegos, showers, a/c, helpful, courteous; *Colón*, Libertad, F with a/c, TV, 2 blocks from beach; *Equus*, Bolívar, E, shower, a/c, clean; *Monte Carlo*, E, good; *Mi Hotel*, Calle Libertad, D, a/c, showers, comfortable, clean, rec. *Sorrento**, E, Av. 5 de Julio, shower, comfortable; *Noray*, Av. Libertad, E with a/c, good, friendly; *Pensión Rancho Grande*, Paseo Colón, F with fan; *Residencial Turística Marina*, F, clean, friendly.

Restaurants *El Parador*, Paseo Colón, excellent food and service (Caesar Salad rec.). Also on or near Paseo Colón: *Da Luigi*, Italian, good; *El Chalet*, opposite, good European food; *Marisquería Guatarasco*; *Big Garden*, delicious sea food; *El Tejas*; *La Bella China*, best Chinese; plenty of others. *Nature*, vegetarian, Constitución 70, lunch and dinner. *Rincón Criollo*, Av. Libertad, popular with locals; *Guatacrazo* bar, all staff in fancy dress, fun, drinks and surprises, rec. Good bacon and eggs for breakfast at *Reale; Christophe's*, English-style pub, food, live music at weekends. *Swing* night club, 13 km. from Puerto La Cruz, US$3.30 one way by taxi, free entry, good music.

Shopping Vendors of paintings, jewellery, leather, etc. on Paseo Colón in evenings. Good hammocks may be bought, US$6-12. Perfectfoto SA, Carabobo, Fuente Torre Oriente, T 22821 for film processing; also Fotolisto, Paseo Colón, US$1.70 per film without mounts.

Laundry Lavandería Margarita, Bolívar 160.

Exchange Banco Consolidado (American Express), Av. 5 de Julio, Local No. 43; Turisol, Am Ex rep., T 662161/669910. Banco Royal Venezolano. Casa de Cambio: Oficambio Oriente, Calle Maneiro 17, Edif. Latina; also *cambio* in *Hotel Riviera*.

Post Office and Telecommunications Freitas y Bolívar, one block from Paseo Colón.

Travel Agency Viajes Ven-Mex, Av. Alberto Ravell 15, recommended. Venezuelan Travel Advisers, Municipal esq. Freitas, Edif. Montalero, T (081) 660113/669204.

Buses to Caracas, 6 hrs., US$3.25; to Ciudad Bolívar US$2.50, but often full since service starts at Cumaná.

Excursions To the islands of La Plata and La Chimana for swimming: take taxi to harbour, or *por puesto* to Pamatacualito then walk 10 mins. to harbour, then boat (to La Plata US$1, to La Chimana, US$13 return but pay on return trip, beautiful beaches). A tourist complex, El Morro, covering 20 sq. km. is being built at Salto La Sirena, 8 km. away in the Guanta valley.

The Coastal Zone Starting east from Puerto La Cruz, the road passes through the most beautiful coastal scenery in Venezuela, the **Mochima National Park**—a less crowded Côte d'Azur—to the seaport of Cumaná, 84 km. from Puerto La Cruz. On the way it passes Playa Blanca, by boat US$5 return from Puerto La Cruz, excellent snorkelling, take own equipment. The locals cook and sell fish.

Further along past Playa Arapito, where boats can be hired to the lovely, little La Piscina beach for good snorkelling, is the popular but dirtier beach of Playa Colorada with its red sands and palm trees (*por puesto* from Mercado Municipal in Puerto La Cruz or hitch). Here accommodation is available, camping is permitted for a small fee and there is a restaurant. Nearby are Playa Santa Cruz and Playa Vallecito (free camping, car US$0.80, bar with good food, plenty of palm trees for hammock-slinging).

Further east is **Santa Fe**, a good place to relax; Christoph Realini, who speaks German, English, Italian and Spanish, organises accommodation and boat trips (US$10), contact him at the *Restaurant Cochaima* or phone him on 004981-664330; gasoline is available; *por puesto* and bus to Cumaná and Puerto La Cruz. The village of Mochima, beyond Santa Fe, is 4 km. off the main road, hitching difficult; here Sra Cellita Día and Doña Luisa both let out rooms, F, eat at *Los Mochimeros*, good and friendly; boats to nearby beaches and around the islands, fares negotiable, about US$10 to one island US$20 trip round the islands (up to 6 people). **N.B.** At holiday times this coast is very busy.

Cumaná, population 155,000, capital of Sucre State, founded 1520, is the oldest Hispanic city in South America. It straddles both banks of the Manzanares,

1½ km. from Puerto Sucre. The castle of San Antonio has been fully restored, and there are good walks along the tree-lined Manzanares. San Luis beach, short local bus ride, recommended, but the water is somewhat dirty. Cumaná has an important sardine canning industry. Beware mosquitoes from the stagnant river. The port area is not safe at night. New airport 10 km. from centre (taxi fare US$2.50). Average temperature 27°C. Car ferry to Margarita Island. Famous for its carnival. A museum was built in 1974 to commemorate the 150th anniversary of the battle of Ayacucho; mainly portraits, relics and letters of Bolívar and Sucre. There is also a maritime museum (Museo del Mar) with good exhibits of tropical marine life, at the old airport, Av. Universidad with Av. Industrial, open Tues.-Sun. 0830-1130, 1430-1630, US$0.75.

Hotels *Cumanagoto**, C, Av. Universidad, poor food and service, excellent swimming pool and beach, travel agency for trips to Angel Falls, etc.; *Los Bordones*, B, Final Av. Universidad, 8 km. from the bus station, rec., beautifully situated on a good beach with excellent food and a swimming pool; *Villa Mar*, D, Av. Universidad, clean, comfortable, restaurant; these three are a long way from the centre of town. *Gran Hotel**, D, Av. Universidad, beach, mid-way between **Cumanagoto** and town centre; in same area, *Caribe*, on beach, E with bath and a/c, clean, basic, English spoken, no restaurant. *Minerva**, E, clean, modern, Av. Cristóbal Colón, US$1 taxi ride from centre; *Turismo Guaiqueri*, Av. Bermúdez 26 T (093) 24230/663444, E, comfortable, clean, a/c, bath, friendly, no restaurant; *El Río*, F, Av. Bermúdez, a/c, bath, phone, reasonable restaurant; *Residencias Trevi*, E, with bath and fan, on Av. Universidad, 2 km. from San Luis beach. *Regina*, Av. Arismendi, E with bath, a/c, restaurant, good value; *Mariño*, E, near centre on Av. Mariño with Junín, private bath, a/c, clean. Cheaper hotels can be found across the river from those above, around Plaza Ayacucho, especially on Calle Sucre: *Hospedaje La Gloria*, Sucre 31, opposite Sta. Inés church, F with fan and bath, basic, clean; on same street *Astoria*, F with bath, clean and friendly; *Italia*, F with fan, or a/c with bath, good (around the corner is *Madrid* bar, good cheap food, music); *Macuto*, *Cumaná*, *Colón*, all reasonably priced. Private accommodation at Bolívar 8, G, clean, fan.

Restaurants   Good food at *El Colmao* restaurant in the centre as well as *El Teide* (seafood); *Parrilla Ribera* on Av. Las Palomas; *Italia*, Sucre, cheap and good; *Jardín de Sport*, only outdoor café, good food, rec. *El Ilustre*, Av. Humbolt (opp. Plaza Sucre), for sandwiches, hamburgers, juices; *Pastelería Sucre*, Calle Mariño, breakfasts, cakes, coffee. *Helados Bariloche*, Plaza Ayacucho. All central restaurants close Sun. lunchtime.

Exchange   Banco Consolidado, Av. Bermúdez. Perimetral. Edif. Ajounián. Exchange at Oficambio, Calle Mariño, Edificio Funcal.

Panamanian Consulate   in a one-way street, next to Grupo Escolar José Silvero Córdova in Parcelamiento Miranda Sector D, T 663525; take a taxi.

Travel Agent   Happy Tour, Centro Comercial, La Banca, P.B., Local No. 6, T 24592; also at *Hotel Cumanagoto*, T 653111.

Bus   Bus terminal some distance from city centre, buses are often fully booked. *Por puesto* to Puerto La Cruz, US$1.50, bus US$0.75, 1¼ hrs. To Güiria (**see page 1085**), US$2.15, *por puesto* US$4.30 (5 hrs.), often stop in Carúpano. To Caracas, US$3.80 upwards depending on company (7 hrs.), frequent service; many daily to Ciudad Guayana and Ciudad Bolívar (7 hrs.)

Excursion   The Parque Nacional Cueva del Guáchero (**see page 1086**) can be visited from Cumaná by taking a daily bus at 0730 and 1200 hrs. to Caripe (US$2.15, 4 hrs.) or frequent *por puestos* (US$4.20, try bargaining, 2 hrs., OK for going there, almost impossible to get back in p.m.). 44 km. east of Cumaná is the beautiful beach of Cachamaure, on the Golfo de Cariaco, cabins US$18, barbeque equipment US$2. To the Araya Peninsula with its desert landscape and purple salt lakes, either by road, turning off the Cumaná-Carúpano road at Cariaco: the road on the peninsula soon becomes very rough; last chance to eat at Chacopata; or by ferry Cumaná-Araya (return ferries haphazard and difficult to get on as more cars than spaces). *Hotel Turístico* in Araya, E, with bar, restaurant, discotheque.

ISLA DE MARGARITA

Isla de Margarita and two close neighbours, Coche and Cubagua, form the state of Nueva Esparta.

Isla de Margarita is in fact one island whose two sections are tenuously linked by the 18 kilometre sandspit which separates the sea from the Restinga lagoon. At its largest, Margarita is about 32 kilometres from north to south and 67 kilometres from east to west. Most of its people live in the developed eastern part, which has some wooded areas and fertile valleys. The western part, the Peninsula de Macanao, is hotter and more barren, with scrub, sand dunes and marshes. Wild deer, goats and hares roam the interior, but four-wheel drive vehicles are needed to penetrate it. The entrance to the Peninsula de Macanao is a pair of hills known as Las Tetas de María Guevara, a national monument covering 1,670 hectares.

The climate is exceptionally good, but rain is scant. Water is piped from the mainland. The roads are good, and a bridge connects the two parts. Nueva Esparta's population is over 200,000, of whom about 20,000 live in the main city, Porlamar (which is not the capital, that is La Asunción).

The island has enjoyed a boom since 1983, largely as a result of the fall in the value of the bolívar and the consequent tendency of Venezuelans to spend their holidays at home. Margarita's status as a duty-free zone also helps. Venezuelan shoppers go in droves for clothing, electronic goods and other consumer items. Gold and gems are good value, but many things are not. There has been extensive building in Porlamar, with new shopping areas and Miami-style hotels going up. A number of beaches are also being developed. The island now has little to offer budget travellers, who would be better advised to stay on the mainland for the beaches and islands around Puerto La Cruz.

Local industries are fishing and fibre work, such as hammocks and straw hats. Weaving, pottery and sweets are being pushed as handicraft items for the tourists. An exhibition centre has been opened at El Cercado, near Santa Ana, on Calle Principal, near the church.

Despite the property boom and frenetic building on much of the coast and in Porlamar, much of the island has been given over to natural parks. Of these the most striking is the **Laguna La Restinga**. Launches provide lengthy runs around the mangrove swamps, but they create a lot of wash and noise. The mangroves are fascinating, with shellfish clinging to the roots. The launch will leave you on a shingle and shell beach (don't forget to arrange with your boatman to collect you), and you can rummage for shellfish in the shallows (protection against the sun essential). Flamingos live in the lagoon.

There are mangroves also in the **Laguna de las Marites** natural monument, west of Porlamar. Other parks are **Las Tetas de María Guevara, Cerro el Copey**, 7,130 hectares, and **Cerro Matasiete y Guayamurí**, 1,672 hectares (both reached from La Asunción).

By boat from Porlamar you can go to the Isla de los Pájaros, or Morro Blanco, for both bird-spotting and underwater fishing. In Boca del Río there is a Museum of the Sea.

Beaches   Apart from the shopping, what attracts the holidaymakers from Venezuela and abroad are the beaches: long white stretches of sand bordered by palms, but rather hot, with little shade (sunscreen essential—local wisdom is that you can burn even when sitting in the shade). Topless bathing is not seen, but the tanga (*hilo dental*—dental floss) is fairly common.

In Porlamar, the beach by the *Concorde* hotel is excellent: calm shallow water, pedalos for hire, windsurf classes; but that by the *Bella Vista* is crowded with foreign tourists and polluted. For a more Venezuelan atmosphere go northwest to **Pampatar**, which is set around a bay favoured by foreign yachtsmen as a summer anchorage. A scale model of Columbus' *Santa María* is used for taking tourists on trips. (*Residencial Don Juan*, E with bath and fan; apartments sleeping 6 are available, bargain over price; beach restaurant *Antonio's*,

CARIBBEAN SEA

Cabo Negro
Manzanillo
El Agua
Punta Cabo Blanco
Puerto Fermín
El Cardón
Paraguachí
Playa Guacuco
Laguna de Gasparía
Punta Ballena
Pampatar
El Morro
Pozo
Bella Vista
La Mar
Playa Manzanillo
Puerto La Cruz
La Galera
Pedro González
Santa Ana
Tacarigua
Guayamurí
Matasiete
LOS
Robles
Los Millanes
San Sebastián
LA ASUNCIÓN
Fuenfeduño
M.º Copey
El Valle del Espíritu Santo
San Juan
La Guardia
El Espinal
Punta de Tigre
Playa Ariba
Bahía de Juan Griego
La Guardia
Ensenada La Guardia
El Yaque
Laguna de las Marites
Laguna las Rejas
Punta Mosquito
ISLA DE COCHE
Güinima
San Pedro
Punta Mangle
Guamache
Punta de Mangle
Llano de María Guevara
Punta de Piedra
Ferry Terminal
Ruins of Nueva Cádiz
ISLA DE CUBAGUA
Laguna La Restinga
Launches
El Saco
San Francisco
Boca del Río
Manzanillo
Guayacancito
PENÍNSULA DE MACANAO
El Tunal
Robledal
Boca de Pozo (Macanao)
Punta Arenas
Relámpago
El Manglillo
Boca Chica

ISLA DE MARGARITA
NOT TO SCALE
124A

rec.; also *Trimar*, good value) Pampatar has the island's largest fort, San Carlos Borromeo, and the smaller La Caranta, where the cannon show signs of having been spiked. Visit also the church of Cristo del Buen Viaje, the Library/Museum and the customs house (now the offices of Fondene, the local development agency). The beach at Pampatar is not very good, but there are lots of fishing boats and fishermen mending their nets. A fishing boat can be hired for US$12 for 2½ hours, 4-6 passengers; shop around for best price, good fun and fishing. New hotels are being put up along this stretch.

A number of good beaches are being developed on the eastern side. These are divided into ocean and calm beaches, according to their location in relation to the open sea. The former tend to be rougher (good surfing and windsurfing) and colder. Water is uniformly clear and unpolluted. Not all the beaches have local services yet, such as restaurants, though these, *churuatas* (bars built like Indian huts), sunshades and deckchairs are becoming more widespread. (Hire charges are about US$1.30 per item.) It is still possible, even in high season, to find practically deserted beaches.

On the eastern coast is Playa Guacuco, reached from La Asunción by a road through the Guayamurí reserve: a lot of surf, fairly shallow, palm trees, restaurant and parking lot, liquor shop at La Sabana sells ice by the bucket, cheap, 1 km. before the beach; Parguito: long and open; Paraguachí: some *churuatas*; Playa del Agua: sea very rough for children, but fairly shallow, the fashionable part is at the southern end (interesting range of vendors on the beach—quail's eggs, caipirinha cocktails, coconuts, *cachapa* maize buns; *Restaurant El Paradiso*, rents out cabins, US$12, small but comfortable; *Kiosko El Agua*, helpful, English spoken; *Posada Shangri-Lá*, rec., and many other seafood restaurants open till 1900, most are pricey but *La Dorada* rec. as good value); the northern end is less touristy, has fewer facilities, and less shade. Manzanillo: water gets deep rather suddenly, fishing huts, fish sold on beach, new apartments under construction, Playa Escondida at the far end; Puerto Fermín/El Tirano (Lope de Aguirre, the infamous conquistador, landed here in 1561 on his flight from Peru), El Caserío handicrafts museum is nearby; Punta Cabo Blanco: attractive limestone outcrop; El Cardón: some development.

The coast road is interesting, with glimpses of the sea and beaches to one side, inland vistas on the other. There are a number of clifftop look-out points. The road improves radically beyond Manzanillo, winding from one beach to the next. Playa Puerto la Cruz adjoins Pedro González, another fashionable spot with a broad sweeping beach, running from a promontory (easy to climb) to scrub and brush that reach down almost to the water's edge (ask for Antonietta Luciani at *Restaurant Pedrogonzález*, she has an apartment to rent, US$40 per day, sleeps 6, well-equiped, rec. as is her restaurant). The next bay is accessible by scrambling over rocks (major building work under way). One advantage of Pedro González beach is that there is a large lagoon on the other side of the coast road, so it will be impossible to spoil the bay with speculative building. There are a lot of pelicans and sea urchins (harmless).

Further west is **Juan Griego** bay and town, famous for its sunsets (tours go to see them). The town is marred by a number of cheap clothing bazaars and the beach has little sand. (*Hotel La Galera*, rec.; several others; also cabins for 5 with cooking facilities US$20. *Restaurant Mi Isla* is rec., also the Lebanese restaurant on the beach.) Playas Caribe and Galera are less spoilt. Fortín La Galera is worth a visit for the view of Juan Griego and Galera bays; children will breathlessly recite the epic siege fought here during the wars of independence.

South of Juan Griego, the road goes inland to San Juan, then to Punta de Piedra (a pleasant stretch through cultivated land and farms at regular intervals). Near San Juan is Fuentedueño park which has special walks. A branch goes northwest to La Guardia at the eastern end of La Restinga. The dyke of broken seashells stretches to the Peninsula de Macanao: on its right a spotlessly clean beach, on its left the lagoon. At the far end is a cluster of fishermen's huts with landing stages from which the launches make trips into the labyrinth of canals in the lagoon (US$3.50).

The Peninsula de Macanao is quite underdeveloped, although it is hardly an untouched paradise. Construction companies are extracting large amounts of ballast for the building boom in Porlamar, while urban waste is simply being dumped in large quantities along the roadside. Some of the beaches, however, are highly regarded: Manzanilla, Guayaconcito, Boca de Pozo, Macanao, Punta Arenas and El Manglillo. Harbour at Chacachacare.

The capital, **La Asunción** (population 8,000), is a few kilometres inland from Porlamar. It has several colonial buildings, a cathedral, and the fort of Santa Rosa, with a famous bottle dungeon (open Monday 0800-1500, other days 0800-1800). There is a museum in the Casa Capitular, and a local market, good for handicrafts. Nearby are the Cerro Matasiete historical site and the Félix Gómez look-out in the Sierra Copuy.

Between La Asunción and Porlamar are the Parque Francisco Fajardo, beside the Universidad de Oriente, and El Valle del Espíritu Santo. Here is the church of the Virgen del Valle, a picturesque building with twin towers, painted white and pink. The Madonna is richly dressed (one dress has pearls, the other diamonds); the adjoining museum opens at 1400, it displays costumes and presents for the Virgin, including the "milagro de la pierna de perla", a leg-shaped pearl. A pilgrimage is held in early September. Proper dress is requested to enter the church.

Throughout the island, the churches are attractive: fairly small, with baroque towers and adornments and, in many cases, painted pink.

Most of the hotels are at **Porlamar**, 11 kilometres from the airport and about 28 kilometres from Punta de Piedra, where most of the ferries dock. It has a magnificent cathedral. At Igualdad y Díaz is the Museo de Arte Francisco Narváez. The main, and most expensive, shopping area is Avenida Santiago Mariño; better bargains and a wider range of shops are to be found on Gómez and Guevara. At night everything closes by 2300; women alone should avoid the centre after dark.

Ferries go to the Isla de Coche (11 kilometres by 6), which has over 5,000 inhabitants and one of the richest salt mines in the country. They also go, on hire only, to Isla de Cubagua, which is totally deserted, but you can visit the ruins of Nueva Cádiz (which have been excavated).

N.B. August and September are the vacation months when flights and hotels are fully booked.

Hotels at Porlamar *Hilton*, L (+10% tax), new, sailing dinghies for hire; other top class establishments, *Concorde*, Bahía de El Morro, and *Bella Vista**, Av. Santiago, B-A, swimming pool, beach; *For You**, Patiño y Av. Santiago Mariño, C, rec.; *Caribbean*, Vía El Morro, D, pool, beach; *Vista Mar*, D, Urb. Bella Vista, on the way to El Morro, beach; *Agila Inn*, Narváez, D-E, clean, swimming pool, restaurant, rec.; *Dos Primos*, Calle Mariño entre Zamora y San Nicolás, E, clean and modern, rec.; on the Boulevard, *Italia*, San Nicolás, D with bath, cold water, a/c, clean, safe, rec., but district is a bit rough; *Brasilia*, San Nicolás, F, quiet, clean, nice new rooms at back; *Cardón*, B, opposite old airport at Playa Cardón, peaceful, good rooms and restaurant, swimming pool, diving and snorkelling trips organized; *María Luisa**, Vía El Morro, E, beach; *Chez David*, E, a/c, on beach, modern; *Evdama*, Bella Vista y Campos, E, helpful, also holiday flats with parking; opposite is *Imperial*, D, clean, comfortable, safe, rec., but restaurant only average; *Tamá*, E (more with a/c, hot water, TV, etc.), very nice, Vía El Morro, beach; *Marítimo*, E, Calle Maneiro Este 6; *Porlamar*, Igualdad, E, clean, good restaurant; *Chez Toni*, San Nicolás 14-56, E, English spoken, cheap restaurant, rec; *Nueva Casa*, F with bathroom and fan, clean and friendly. *La Opera*, Igualdad y Fraternidad, E with bath (just off plaza); *Residencia Paraíso*, near main square, F, basic but clean, fan; *Residencia Don Francisco*, Igualdad, 2 blocks from plaza, F with bath, quiet, good; *Hotel España*, Marino 6-35, E, hot shower, very clean, friendly, rec; better value is *Rioja*, F with fan and bath, clean, safe. Many others round Plaza Bolívar. Cheaper places on Maneiro, e.g. *Res. Javi*, G, very basic, but friendly. *Cabañas Turísticas*, La Isleta, US\$35 for a cabin, sleeps 4, pool, restaurant. For longer stays, Enrique and Elena Ganteaume rent apartments in Porlamar, Juan Griego and La Asunción (Av. Principal 41, Urb. Santa Lucía, La Asunción, T 095-610467, friendly, English spoken).

Restaurants *El Peñero*, vía El Morro, service slow but good food; *Vecchia Marina*, Vía El Morro, good but more expensive; *Bahía* bar-restaurant, Av. Raúl Leoni y Vía El Morro, excellent value, live music; good breakfast at *Panadería*, Av. 4 de Mayo y Fermín; *Flamingo*, 4 de Mayo (in hotel), cheap, good, but small portions; *El Yate*, next to *Hotel For You* main entrance, highly rec. for food and service, steaks superb, US\$20-25 for 2, but wine can double the bill; *Café de París*, outside *Hotel For You*, croissants and enormous ice creams, a good meeting place; also *París Croissant* on Blvd. Santiago Mariño; *Los 3 Delfines*, Cedeño 26-9, seafood, rec.; *Guanaguanara*, pedestrian boulevard by sea, good food and service, reasonable prices. *La Isla*, Mariño y Cedeño, 8 fast food counters ranging from hamburgers to sausages from around the world. *La Cotorrera*, Av. Santiago Mariño, steaks; *Kiosco La Nena*, Av. Raúl Leoni, Italian and local dishes, highly rec. for food and value if not atmosphere, try pabellón margariteño (white fish, rice, black beans, fried plantains—add sugar and chilli sauce to taste). *Jardín de Italo*, Calle Campos, French, classy, little atmosphere; *Centro*

Vegetariano Mariuxu, Fermín 12-79, yellow and green house, no sign, lunch only, rec.

Entertainment   discotheque for singles (the only good one), *Village Club*, Av. Santiago Mariño.

Shopping   Besides all the duty-free shops, *Del Bellorín*, Cedeño, near Santiago Mariño, is good for handicrafts. Good selection of jewellery at *Sonia Gems*, on Cedeño; *Ivan Joyería* and *Inter Gold*, both on 4 de Mayo (latter is between *Ivan* and *Hotel Flamingo*); many other places on the main street are overpriced. When purchasing jewellery, bargain hard, don't pay by credit card (surcharges are imposed), get a detailed guarantee of the item and, if unsure, get another jeweller to check its validity.

Exchange   Banco Consolidado (American Express), Guevara y San Nicolás; banks generally slow with poor rates; best at Banco Construcción, Guevara or at *Hotel Contemporáneo* next to Banco Consolidado. *Casa de cambio* at Igualdad y Av. Santiago Mariño. Most shops accept credit cards.

Post Office   Calle Arismendi. **Phones**   CANTV, Bolívar, between Fajardo and Fraternidad.

Information   Tourist Office, Miranda, near cathedral, free city map. An English-language newspaper, *Mira*, is published on the island; the editor/publisher acts also as an inexpensive tour guide; Av. Santiago Mariño, Ed. Carcaleo Suites, Apartamento 2-A, Porlamar (T 095-613351). The best map is available from Corpoven.

Travel Agents   Turisol, Calle Hernández, friendly and helpful; Supertours, Calle Larez, Quinta Thaid, T 618781, Fax 617061, tours of the island and elsewhere; Zuluoga Tours, very helpful; Tourismo Guaiquerí, Santiago Mariño y Marcano, English spoken, mixed reports.

Car Hire   An economic proposition for any number above one and probably the best way of getting around the island, about US$27 a day, several competing offices at the airport, Avis also at *Hotel Bella Vista*, others also on Av. Santiago Mariño. Lizmar is the cheapest, US$23 per day unlimited mileage, insurance included (excess US$300), but cars are in poor condition. In all cases, check the brakes. Scooters can also be hired for about US$14 a day from Diversion Rentals, Calle Amador Hernández, Maruba Motor Rentals, La Marina (English spoken, good maps, highly rec.) or Auto Camping Margarita (boats and bicycles also for rent). Motor cycles may not be ridden between 2000 and 0500; although this (apparently) should not apply to tourists, police officers have been known to confiscate tourists' machines and impose heavy fines. **N.B.** Remember to keep an eye on the fuel gauge; there are service stations in towns, but air conditioning is heavy on fuel. Driving on Isla Margarita: the roads are generally good and most are paved. Sign posts are often poorly-positioned (behind bushes, round corners), which adds to the night time hazard of vehicles with badly-adjusted lights. It is best not to drive outside Porlamar after dark.

Public Transport   *Por Puestos* serve most of the island, leaving mainly from the corners of Plaza Bolívar in Porlamar. Fares: to Punta de Piedra, US$0.70; to La Asunción, US$0.20; to Pampatar, US$0.35; to La Restinga (from La Marina y Mariño), US$0.70, El Agua, US$0.35; Juan Griego, US$0.35.

Communications   There are 8-12 flights a day from Caracas, with Avensa and Aeropostal, 30-40 mins. flight; tickets are much cheaper if purchased in Venezuela in local currency (about US$21 one way). Daily flight from Cumaná at 0730, Aeropostal, and 2020, Avensa. Viasa, Av. 4 de Mayo, Edif. Banco Royal, Porlamar (T 32273, airport 691137); Avensa and Aeropostal are both on Calle Fajardo, Porlamar, opposite each other (Aeropostal hours 0800-1200, 1400-1800, T 617064, airport 691128; Avensa T 617111, airport 691021). (Airport: General Santiago Mariño, between Porlamar and Punta de Piedras; taxi US$6.)

Ferries (very busy at weekends) leave Puerto La Cruz for the island 4 times a day (4 hrs., cars, about US$6, passengers US$3.20 first class, breezy, or US$2.30 second, a/c) and from Cumaná at 0630 and 1530, return 1100 and 2000, 3 hrs., US$3 p.p.; the *Gran Cacique II* is a hydrofoil from Cumaná taking only 2 hrs., US$2.15 (0730 and 1600, return 1030 and 1730); the *Gran Cacique I* from Puerto La Cruz takes 2½ hrs., US$3.50 (2 times daily); check all ferry times in advance; book in high season, Calle Marcano, Porlamar, T 616780. Several bus companies in Caracas sell through tickets (US$10) from Caracas to Porlamar, arriving about midday. By car from Caracas, it takes about 4 hrs., but will be reduced to 2½ when the Sucre motorway is opened.

A ferry sails from Mercado Viejo to Chacopata on the mainland at 1000 and 1200, US$1.20, also takes cars. A ferry to Grenada, *The Eastward*, sails once a month. Go to the Puerto de Pescadores, El Guamache, near Punta de Piedra, and ask boat captains about taking a boat to the Leeward or Windward Islands; e.g. US$50 p.p. to Martinique (very difficult to find boats willing to take passengers).

The road from Cumaná goes on to the port of **Carúpano**, on the Paría Peninsula. The coastal route from Cumaná to Carúpano is beautiful, first passing the Gulf of Cariaco, then crossing to the shores of the Caribbean. Carúpano is famous throughout Venezuela for its pre-Lenten Carnival celebrations, and becomes a focus for tourists at that time. Population 80,000; airport.

Hotels *San Francisco*, F, Av. Juncal 87A (try the mussels); *Bologna*, F, a/c, owner speaks German, rec.; *El Yunque*, Av. Perimetral, E, dirty, beach, new restaurant with good seafood; *Lilma*, E, Av. Independencia 161, good restaurant; *Victoria**, D, Av. Perimetral, seen better days but good, swimming pool, restaurant.

Bus to Caracas, Responsable de Venezuela, US$4.80, 8 hrs; Cumaná, US$1.10; *por puesto* Cumaná US$2.20, Güiria US$2.20.

On the coastal drive W of Carúpano are Cereza, famed for its basket-making, and Guaca, where clams packed with peppers are sold. 10 km. E of Carúpano is the fishing village of El Morro de Puerto Santo, in itself not very interesting but in a beautiful setting.

The road continues East for 135 km. to **Güiria**. En route is Irapa, with hotel and restaurant (G with bath, clean). Güiria can also be reached from Maturín by bus, US$3.25, 6 hrs. (Also flights from Isla de Margarita or Tucupita each morning, best booked in advance.) Güiria is rather run down and very hot, dress is more casual than is common elsewhere. (*Hotel Gran Puerto*, E with bath and a/c, best restaurant in town; *Hotel Plaza*, F, basic; *Hotel Nayade*, F; *Hotel Fortuna*, restaurant rec. The Librería, on Bolívar opposite, is helpful with travel information, including boats to Trinidad. There are a couple of small places to eat on the main square: Heladería Güiria or Exprex, rec.) In one of the coves E of Güiria (exactly which one is not known) Spaniards of Columbus' crew made the first recorded European landing on the continent on 5 August, 1498, and took formal possession the following day.

A good excursion from Güiria is to **Macuro**, a village of 1,000 people on the tip of the Paria Peninsula. It is accessible only by boat, being surrounded on its landward sides by jungle. Boats leave Güiria daily at 1000 (US$2.10, take protection against sun and plastic sheeting in case of rough seas—ask for Don Pedro), returning 0530, taking 3 hrs., passing dense jungle which reaches down to the sea, and deserted, palm-fringed beaches. Macuro is friendly, with a good beach, a few understocked shops, one restaurant, no hotel but rooms to let (easy to camp or sling your hammock somewhere). Eduardo (who speaks English, French and German) has a bar at the end of the street and a museum of the history of the area; he is knowledgeable about boats to Trinidad for US$6.25 p.p.; trips to the Orinoco delta, and hiking on the peninsula. Boats may be hired to explore the coast and to go to Trinidad. If leaving for Trinidad, get your exit stamp in Usquire.

You can visit the Orinoco delta from Güiria; there are occasional motor boats trading between Güiria and **Pedernales** in the delta. The trip takes about 5 hrs., check for boats at the harbour or the *Hotel Fortuna* (not always open). Pedernales is a small village only a few km. from the south-western point of Trinidad. It is only accessible by boat from Güiria (ask for Andrecito, who lives on N side of small plaza nearest harbour entrance, or ask owner of *Hotel Plaza*—boats are very hard to find), or from Tucupita (much easier—page 1092), or boats from Trinidad costing about US$30-60, the more official, the more expensive. Sisiliano Bottini is a shipping agent. (Some cheap boats carry contraband and unless you avoid Trinidadian or Venezuelan immigration controls you will find this method both difficult and very risky: the Trinidadian authorities are reluctant to let even legal boats in for fear of drug smuggling.) Only one hotel, *Gran Arturo*, F, very basic, bar and restaurant, take your own hammock; the store on the riverbank also has rooms with cooking facilities, F. For a shower, ask Jesús, who runs a fish-freezing business. Only Indians live in the northern part of the village. Travel out of Pedernales is often difficult—to Tucupita by fishing boat, US$25, rec. as the boat stops in some of the Indian villages, where you can buy the best hammocks (*chinchorros*) and some beautiful carved animal figures made of balsa wood (see also page 1092).

From Puerto La Cruz a toll road goes inland, skirting Barcelona. At Km. 52 (where there is a restaurant) a road forks left to (near) Santa Bárbara (airport) and goes on to Jusepín, Quiriquire, and Caripito, all Lagovén oil camps.

In Santa Bárbara can be bought the native *chinchorros*, hammocks made by hand of woven *moriche* palm leaves, decorated with coloured yarn. They can also be found in Tucupita (see page 1091). They "give" when you lie on them and do not absorb moisture when used on the beach. Very good for camping.

Maturín, capital of Monagas State, an important commercial centre, is 16 km. beyond Jusepín. Population 152,000.

Hotels *El Cacique*, D, Av. Bolívar; *Pensión El Nacional* and *Latino*, both F, are rec. as simple and clean. *Friuli*, E, Carrera 9 with Calle 30; *Trinidad*, F, clean, English speaking, rec.; *Europa*, F, rec. as being as good as the *Trinidad* but with larger rooms; *Manolo*, Av. Bolívar, F, pleasant, restaurant with good food, bar; *Tamanaco*, F, is reasonable; *Mallorca*, F, Calle Mariño, reasonable with good food; *Comercio*, F with bath, not too clean, English spoken, central; *Asturias*, F, with cheap restaurant which serves excellent rice pudding. All hotel rooms have private bathroom and a/c.

Exchange Banco Consolidado (American Express), Av.Raúl Leoni, Edif. D'Amico.

Transport Air services to Caracas, and to Ciudad Bolívar (Aeropostal, 20 mins.). Buses leave three times a day for Caracas from the central bus terminal, 2030, 2200 and 2245 hrs. (US$4.20, 8 hrs.); buses for Ciudad Guayana (US$2.10) and El Dorado leave from the terminus near the airport. To Puerto La Cruz or Barcelona, take a *por puesto* to Cumaná and change, 2 hrs., US$3.50. Bus only to Ciudad Bolívar, US$2.75. Travelling between the airport and town: *por puesto* Nos. 1,5,6 (US$0.25), or bus from main road outside airport (US$0.10). Taxis from the Reponsable de Venezuela office will try to charge much more.

There are no exchange facilities in the airport except at the Aeropostal desk or the bar in the departure lounge, and they give a very bad rate.

Just beyond Jusepín an unpaved 32-km. road, left, joins the Maturín-Cumaná road (212 km.), all paved but twisty; beautiful tropical mountain scenery; accommodation at Cumanacoa, 56 km. before Cumaná, 2 hotels—E and F). At San Francisco on this road is a branch road running 22½ km. NE to **Caripe**, a small town set in a mountain valley. There is a huge *samán* tree in purple glory when the orchids which cover it bloom in May. There is also a paved road between Carúpano and Caripe via Santa Cruz and Santa María, 2 hrs.

Hotels *Samán**, Enrique Charner 29, D, excellent value and atmosphere, restaurant; *Caripe*, F, restaurant; *San Francisco*, E with bath, hot water, clean, rec., good restaurant; *Las Chaimas*, F, T 51141. New hotel *Venezia*, E, with excellent *Coba Longa* restaurant, owner speaks English. *Humboldt Cabañas*, between Teresén and Caripe, good, clean, sleep 4 for C, full cooking facilities, little hot water. *Lonchería Arabe*, rec.

12 km. from Caripe is the remarkable **Cueva del Guácharo** National Monument; open 0830-1700, entrance US$1, tour with guide, 2 hrs. Also a caving museum, US$0.15, with a good range of publications for sale and a cafeteria; *Hotel Guácgaro* nearby. A bus from Cumaná to Caripe—0730, returns 1300—takes 4 hrs. and costs US$2.15, or take the *por puesto*, 2 hrs., US$4.20, buses stop 3 km. from caves; if staying in Caripe, take a *por puesto* at 0800, see the caves and waterfall and catch the Cumaná bus which goes past the caves between 1200 and 1230. Taxis from Caripe US$1.50, hitching difficult. The cave was discovered by Humboldt, and has since been penetrated 10½ km. along a small, crystal-clear stream. First come the caves in which live about 30,000 *guácharos* (oil birds) with an in-built radar system for sightless flight. Their presence supports a variety of wildlife in the cave: blind mice, fish and crabs in the stream, yellow-green plants, crickets, ants, etc. For two hours at dusk (about 1900) the birds pour out of the cave's mouth, continously making the clicking sounds of their echo-location system, coming back at dawn with their crops full of the oily fruit of certain local palms. Through a very narrow entrance is the *Cueva del Silencio* (Cave of Silence), where you can hear a pin drop. About 2 km. in is the *Pozo del Viento* (Well of the Wind). No backpacks allowed in the caves (leave them at the ticket office); tape recorders are permitted, check if cameras, torches and flashlights are allowed. Guides are compulsory (included in entry price); to go further than 1½ km. into the caves, permits from Inparques in Caracas and special equipment are needed . The streams are now bridged, but there is still quite a lot of water around; wear old clothes, stout shoes and be prepared to take off your shoes and socks. In the wet season it is very slippery with mud and guano (bird droppings); tours into the cave may be shortened. Opposite the road is a path to Salto Paila, a 25-metre waterfall, about 30 minutes' walk, guides available (but not necessary); orange and other fruit trees along the way.

Continuing straight on from Km. 52, the road passes W of **Anaco** (*Motel Bowling Anaco*, E; *Motel Canaima*, E; *Internacional*, E). It has an airport, is an important centre for oil-well service contracting companies. Beyond Anaco a branch road leads to the oilfields of San Joaquín and San Roque.

The main road passes near Cantaura, a market town, and goes on to **El Tigre** (hotels include *Internacional Gran Hotel*, D, swimming pool, night club; *Milelvi*, F with bath, good, clean, parking in courtyard; and *Santa Cruz*, F; nearby Chilean restaurant serves excellent Chilean food and salads), and El Tigrito (*Hotel Rancho Grande*, D); two important trading centres within 20 km. of one another.

About 8 km. along the road is San Tomé (airport), the eastern headquarters of Menevén, the former Mene Grande oil company.

From El Tigre a good asphalt road leads off to Caracas; the one we are following leads, straight and flat, 120 km. over the *llanos* to the Angostura bridge over the Orinoco to Ciudad Bolívar, 282 km. from Puerto La Cruz.

THE GUAYANA HIGHLANDS (7)

These uplands, lying S of the Orinoco River, constitute half of Venezuela. They rise, in rounded forested hills and narrow valleys, to flat topped tablelands on the borders of Brazil. These lands with savannas interspersed with semi-deciduous forest are very sparsely populated. So far, communications have been the main difficulty, but a road has now been opened to Santa Elena de Uairen on the Brazilian frontier (**see page 1094**). This road can be followed to Manaus, and thence, by a suitable vehicle, to Brasília and southern Brazil. The area is Venezuela's largest gold and diamond source, but its immense reserves of iron ore, manganese and bauxite are of far greater economic importance.

Ciudad Bolívar, on the S bank of the Orinoco, is 400 km. from its delta and 640 km. by road from Caracas. Average temperature 29°C, but a cool and refreshing breeze usually springs up in the evening. It still has much colonial building but is changing rapidly. Population 115,000. It stands by the narrows of the Orinoco, with its Cathedral (completed 1840), on a small hill, and the Zanuro hill fort (1902), on another hill in the narrows, dominating the city.

The narrows, not more than 300 metres wide, gave the town its old name of Angostura. It was here that Bolívar came after defeat to reorganize his forces, and the British Legionnaires joined him; it was at Angostura that he was declared President of that Gran Colombia which he had yet to build, and which was to fragment before his death. At the Congress of Angostura, 15 February, 1819, the representatives of the present day Venezuela, Colombia and Ecuador met to proclaim Gran Colombia. The building, on Plaza Bolívar, houses a museum (Casa del Congreso de Angostura). Also on this historic square is the Cathedral, the Casa de Los Gobernadores de la Colonia, the Real Intendencia, and the Casa de la Cultura. When the town was still known as Angostura a physician invented the famous bitters there in 1824; the factory moved to Port of Spain in 1875.

There is a floating pontoon dock where ocean-going cargo boats can discharge, but the harbour is now naval. A walk along the river bank is rec. at dusk when the sun is setting. Launches take passengers across the river, but there are no other passenger boat services.

You can buy baskets and items made by the Indians. It is also the best place in Venezuela for anything made of gold. There are beautiful hand-made charms for charm bracelets and, most typical of all, the Venezuelan orchid, made by hand, of red, yellow and green gold. The gold orchid pin or earrings, or a gold nugget (known as *cochano*), are the best souvenirs of Venezuela. There are many jewellers on Pasaje Guayana, which runs off Paseo Orinoco. Gold shops also in Pasaje Gran Hotel Bolívar: for nuggets, Irma Lapeña has the most beautiful and the most expensive—bargain for a good price. A feature is the netting of *sapoara*, a delicious fish 30 to 35 cm. long which pours from the inlets when the river begins to swell in late June at the start of the rainy season and swims up stream to spawn. During its short season this is the favourite dish of the town.

Hotels *Orinoco*, on outskirts, overlooking river, A, pool, tourist agency; **Don Salo***, Av.

Bolívar, nr. Av. Táchira, D, seen better days, disappointing restaurant; difficult to find, though quite near the airport; *Laja Real**, opp. airport, D, swimming pool open to non-residents, excellent restaurant; *Canaima*, Av. Upata (far from centre), E, bath, a/c, clean, noisy; *La Cumbre*, Av. 5 de Julio, good view of town but rather run down, E, without food; *Gran Hotel Bolívar**, Paseo Orinoco, E, a/c, comfortable, good restaurant, café on balcony overlooking river; *Hotel del Sur*, Plaza las Banderas, T 206241, E, clean, a/c, rec.; *Mimo,* E, on the corner of Paseo Orinoco and Calle Amazonas, not rec. except for superb views of the river, suspension bridge and sunsets; *Sicilia*, Paseo Orinoco y Dalla Acosta, E, clean, friendly, modern, Italian and German spoken; *Caracas*, Paseo Orinoco, F, friendly, safe, balcony overlooking river; *Universal*, on edge of town, E, safe parking, rec; *Residencias Delicias*, Venezuela, F, clean, good value; *Italia*, Paseo Orinoco, E, a/c and bath, a few single rooms with fan, no bath, restaurant; *Unión*, Calle Urica, nr. *Italia*, F with a/c (cheaper with fan), clean, safe, good value, rec., good restaurant; *Pensión Panamericana*, Calle Rocía 6, F, shower, fan, safe, clean, laundry facilities, rec. *Pensión Boyacá*, Calle Babilonia, F, central, basic, friendly, a bit grubby, one shower for all, hourly rentals; *Brasilia*, D, ¾ km. from bus terminal; *Terminal y Adriana*, E, Av. Moreno de Mendoza, near bus terminal, friendly. It is often difficult to find rooms in hotels here. For the cheaper hotels, take a red bus from the airport to Paseo Orinoco; at the eastern end there are many to choose from.

Restaurants *Alfonso*, Av. Maracay; *Almanola*, Av. Cumaná; *La Cabaña*, Paseo Meneses; *Las Cibeles*, Paseo Orinoco; *La Cumbre*, Av. 5 de Julio; *La Paragua*, Av. La Mariquita; *Mirador*, prettily situated on the Orinoco, relaxed atmosphere, good at the expensive end of the menu; *La Playa*, Paseo Orinoco 84, fish; *Savoy*, Venezuela y Dalla Acosta, good value breakfast and lunch; good restaurant at Venezuela y Igualdad. Chinese restaurant on Av. Upata, opp. *Hotel Canaima*, good, open late. *Mi Casa*, Venezuela, open air, good value; *Bonbonería* Exquisito, near airport, pizzas, cakes, milkshakes and coffee. Cheap food at the market at the east end of Paseo Orinoco, need to bargain.

Museum The Museo Soto, Av. Germania, on the outskirts of the town has works by Venezuela's José Rafael Soto and other artists, open Tues.-Sun. 1000-1800, good. Museum at Casa del Correo del Orinoco, Paseo Orinoco y Carabobo, modern art and some exhibits of history of the city, and a fat precolumbian goddess, including the printing press of the newspaper which spread the cause of independence; Tues.-Sat. 0900-1200, 1500-1800, Sun. 0900-1200. Has free town map (poor) and booklet on Ciudad Bolívar. Museo Geológico y Minero at the School of Mines in the University of the East (UDO), Av. Principal, La Sabanita. Regional Museum of Guayana, housed in the former prison, 2 blocks from Cathedral on Paseo Orinoco. Many other museums in the city.

Taxis Under US$1 to virtually anywhere in town.

Exchange Banco Consolidado (American Express), Edif. Pinemar, Av. Andrés Bello, Centro Comercial Canaima; Banco Royal Venezolano (Calle Orinoco 38) and Banco Mercantil y Agrícola (Av. Jesús Soto) will change dollars cash. Banco Unión or Filanbanco handle Visa transactions. Travellers' cheques accepted by Banco Consolidado near airport.

Brazilian Consulate near Paseo Orinoco.

Post Offices Av. Táchira, 15 mins' walk from centre.

Tourist Offices On Dalla Acosta, provides free map of state and city, but otherwise little information. The small offices in the airport car park and the bus station in particular are very friendly and helpful. You will need a map: the town has a rather confusing layout.

Travel Agencies Venezolano Internacional de Turismo, Av. Andrés Bello and at the airport, rec. for tours to Canaima and Gran Sabana, English spoken; Agencia de Viajes Auyantepuy, Av. Bolívar, Ed. Roque, Centro No. 8, English and French spoken.

Airport Minibuses and buses marked Terminal to town centre. Taxi to Paseo Orinoco US$1.75.Served by Avensa, and Aeropostal which flies daily to Sta. Elena de Uairen for connections to Manaus and Brazil. (Reserve well in advance at the Aeropostal counter at the airport.) Also flights to Tucupita, and to Porlamar (Isla de Margarita—daily). Three flights daily to Caracas. Aerotuy to Santa Elena de Uairen and villages near the Brazilian border. Charter airline, Utaca, is rec.; ask for Jorge, and verify all prices.

Buses To get to the bus station take a bus marked Terminal going W along the Paseo Orinoco. Several daily to Caracas 8 hrs., US$6, and to the coast: to Puerto La Cruz, US$2.50, 4½ hrs.; to Cumaná, US$1.80; to Maracay US$2.50, 10 hrs. Tumeremo US$2.80; Tumeremo bus through to El Dorado US$3, 3 daily. To Santa Elena de Uairen direct with Línea Orinoco, Transportes Mundial or Expreso Rápidos de Güiria leave at 0500, 0800 and 1900, spectacular views of the Gran Sabana at sunset (book in advance), US$8, 14 hours. To Boa Vista with Transportes Mundial, Mon and Thurs at 2000, US$25, 20 hrs. To Ciudad Guayana hourly from 0700 by Expresos Guayanera, US$1, 1½ hrs., *por puesto*, US$2, 1½ hrs. Terminal at junction of Av. República and Av. Sucre. Bus to Caicara, 7½ hrs., including 2 ferry crossings.

For an excursion to see gold mining at Río Claro, take a bus to Guri and ask to be set down at the gate to Río Claro. Minibuses run to the mines, where the people are very friendly and will take visitors by boat to the workings. Return with workers going to Ciudad Bolívar.

73 km. E of Ciudad Bolívar is La Encrucijada (junction). To the left is the freeway to Ciudad Guayana (37 km.); straight on is the road to Upata via the Paso Carnachi (Caroní ferry); to the right is the road to Ciudad Piar (97 km.) and the iron ore mountain (Cerro Bolívar—cheaper to visit from Ciudad Bolívar than from Ciudad Guayana). Following this route through typical Guayana landscape you reach the village of La Paragua (107 km.) on a good, paved road. If you like adventure and untouched nature, take two ferries crossing the Río Paragua, towards El Paúl (4-wheel drive vehicles Dec.-May). There is usually transport available. From El Paúl you can get a ride towards the nearest river to Canaima, which you can cross on a *curiara* (passengers only), and from there hike about 15 km. to Canaima. Alternatively, from La Encrucijada, on the right hand road (in the direction of La Paragua) turn left after 8 km., past enormous black rocks, on to an almost hidden trail. After a further 2 km. is the Cueva del Elefante, where precolumbian relics were found and rock paintings can be seen. Following the track (10 km.) one comes to Playa Blanca on the Río Caroní, where miners dive for gold and diamonds. Mario Venarusso does boat trips.

Angel Falls, the highest fall in the world (979 metres) and **Canaima**, a nearby tourist lodge and hotel, 70 km. down-river, are best reached from Caracas or from Ciudad Bolívar. The lodge is on the edge of a tannin-stained lagoon with soft beige beaches; the Río Carrao tumbles over seven splendid falls into the lagoon below. The country is very beautiful. Lodging is in quite comfortable cabins; each is complete with shower and toilet; there are no hardships whatsoever. If travelling independently, one night's accommodation with 3 meals costs about US$25; the meals are basic, self-service, no choice. You could save yourself some money by taking food with you. Drinks are also expensive.

Avensa airline has inclusive charges for tours which leave twice daily from Maiquetía airport (first at 0710). The flights stop at Ciudad Bolívar, which can be the starting point for the trip. A Boeing 727 takes passengers from there to Canaima arriving in the morning, and will fly over the Angel Falls before landing, weather permitting. Trips to the falls may have to be booked weeks in advance in the holiday season. From Caracas the return flight, two nights' accommodation, six meals and a free boat trip around the lagoon costs about US$170 (June 1990); from Ciudad Bolívar the return flight with two nights' accommodation is about US$135 (US$100 for one night and 3 meals). All arrangements are made through Avensa, direct (best in Caracas) or through travel agencies. One-night trips are possible, as are longer stays (open flights can be booked from Ciudad Bolívar). Reductions are available for parties (note that these trips do not include a visit to Angel Falls, and that you may not even see the falls from the air in the rainy season). At Canaima itself there are expensive gift shops, but no alternative accommodation or restaurant.

Although the quickest and most convenient way to visit Canaima is on an Avensa excursion, it is also possible to travel independently and camp near Canaima: obtain a permit (free) from Inparques, Ed. CVB, Av. Germania, Caracas (without this Avensa will not sell you a ticket) and take it to the Avensa office in Ciudad Bolívar (not the one at the airport), return flight US$24, advisable to take food, though the Indian village near Canaima has a small store selling mainly canned foods; some families in the village also offer basic accommodation.

Many travel agencies, especially in Caracas, Isla Margarita and Ciudad Bolívar, book one-day excursions on Cessna planes (Aerobol, 5 seaters; Aerotuy, 9 seaters), from Caracas US$150, from Ciudad Bolívar US$130, includes guide, flight over falls, lunch at Canaima, boat tour of the lagoon, swimming. The cheapest way to fly over the falls is on scheduled flights from Ciudad Bolívar with

Aerotuy to Kavanayen or Icaburú, or to Santa Elena de Uairen, calling at either of these villages, about US$24 single, sit on right-hand side.

There are various excursions from Canaima, which are all worthwhile (and usually crowded): upriver to the **Angel Falls** costs up to US$150 (June 1990); 5 operators organize this trip at short notice, including Isidoro Sandoval of Excursiones Churun-Vena S.R.L. (rec., he has a video of a Japanese expedition which climbed the Falls in 1980), and "Jungle Rudy", the most expensive (he has his own hotel, US$80 with 3 meals, at Campamento Ucaima, just above the Hacha Falls, 2 hrs. walk from Canaima). All *curiaras* (dug-outs) must have 2 motors, by law, and carry first aid, life jackets, etc. Take wet weather gear, swimwear, mosquito net for hammock and insect repellant. Trips by boat to the Falls only go June-November, leaving usually in the afternoon, staying the first night at Isla Orquídea, continuing to the Falls next day. Depending on the river, the trip takes on average 3 days (best to go Mon.-Wed. as everything is fully booked at weekends). The flat-topped Auyan-Tepuy, from which spring the Angel Falls, was the setting for W. H. Hudson's *Green Mansions*. The sheer rock face of the Falls, named after Jimmy Angel, the US airman who discovered them in 1937, was climbed in 1971 by three Americans and an Englishman, David Nott, who recounted the ten-day adventure in his book *Angels Four* (Prentice-Hall).

You can also make walking expeditions into the jungle to Indian villages with a guide (e.g. Tomás), but bargain hard on the price. Recommended Indian guide is Matherson, ask for him at the camp. A highly recommended flight by Cessna 5-seater costs US$60 p.p., takes 45 mins. and does some circuits over and alongside the falls (better than organized flights is to go to the airstrip and ask around the pilots waiting there on business if they will fly over the Falls for the same price as a tour). Other excursions to Mayupa (US$45, half day), to Yuri Falls (US$30, half day); to Isla Orquídea (US$50, full day, good).

Auyan-Tepuy can also be reached by a 2-3-hr. hike from the village of **Kamarata**, reached only by air from Ciudad Bolívar (with Aeropostal or Utaca, 2½ hrs., book at least a week ahead in Ciudad Bolívar or Caracas, flights 4 times a week). In the dry season you can take a 3-4 day excursion to Kamarata from Canaima by boat. A friendly village with no hotels or restaurants, but rooms to let, about US$2 p.p.; camping also possible (mosquito nets necessary); take food, though locals may sell you dinner. Several good day-long hiking trips; guides to Auyan-Tepuy, waterfalls and the Cuevas de Kavac, US$10.

In Caracas contact *Hotel Tamanaco*, T 914555, or Caribex Tours, T 728271/2, for trips to Falls. Italcambio, T 820611, organizes camping trips up the River Paragua for parties of four at a cost of US$220 for three days, or US$325 four days. The travel agency at the *Caracas Hilton* has also been recommended; also Edgar Belstar, Caracas T 978 4245, 978 0813 or at home 978 1628, friendly. Tours can usually be booked on the spot, with no reservation problems.

N.B. Travellers' cheques can be cashed, but at a poor rate.

Warning Necklaces of poisonous red and black seeds (rosary peas) are on sale here.

In an area rich in natural resources 105 km. down-river from Ciudad Bolívar an entirely new metropolis, known as **Ciudad Guayana**, is still being built. It is forging into one the four separate centres of San Félix, Palúa, Puerto Ordaz and Matanzas. Its population is already approaching half of the planned million, on the south bank of the Orinoco and both sides of the Caroní river before it spills into the Orinoco. The mixing of the rivers' waters is like "pouring cream into coffee". East of the Caroní are the commercial port of **San Félix** (extensive work in progress near a riverside walk and park) and the Palúa iron-ore terminal of the railway from El Pao. Crossing the Caroní by the 470-metre concrete bridge we come to **Puerto Ordaz** (airport), the iron-ore loading port connected by rail with the famous Cerro Bolívar open-cast iron mine (see below). The iron-tinted waterfall, which looks like a beerfall, in the pretty Parque Cachamay is worth a visit. To the west are the government-owned Siderúrgica del Orinoco whose production is being raised to 4.8m tonnes of steel a year, and an aluminium plant, Venalum. About 3 km. away, across bare savanna, is an area reserved for smaller industries. The Casa Machupicchu, Calle Guasipati, sells a city map for US$0.70.

Just up the Caroní is the Macagua hydroelectric plant (with a second phase under construction); there are some truly beautiful cataracts called Salto Llovizna as you enter the grounds (known as Parque La Llovizna, reached by bus from San Félix most of the way, then hitch). Higher up the river is the massive Guri dam and hydroelectric undertaking, **see page 1044**. The trip to Guri takes 90 minutes by taxi; the plant is open daily 0900-1030, 1415-1515, for a conducted tour (4 daily, 1 hr.) phone Edelca, Puerto Ordaz 20-80-66 (Relaciones Institucionales del Guri); the area gets very full during holidays, Easter or carnival. You can also visit the rest of the complex including the hotel, D, a/c, comfortable; camping possible outside the entrance with permission. *Por puesto* from Ciudad Bolívar, Route 70, US$12.50

one way; for return, ask at Alcabala Río Claro (gatehouse) if they can get you a free lift.

Hotels *Intercontinental Guayana**, Parque Punta Vista, L-L+, all facilities, swimming pool, food and service poor; nearby is *Habana Cuba*, Av. Américas, E, cheapest in Puerto Ordaz, a/c, clean, unfriendly; *Dos Ríos*, México esq. Ecuador, D, shower, a/c, clean, swimming pool; *El Rasil*, C, Centro Cívico, with all comforts, swimming pool, overpriced, rooms good but food and service poor; tour agency organises trips to Orinoco delta, rec.; *Tepuy**, F, a/c, Carrera Upata, Edif. Arichuna; *La Guayana**, F, Av. Las Américas, clean, a/c, no hot water; *Residencias Puerto Ordaz*, Vía Caracas, E with bath; *Turismo*, F, basic, cheap; *Jardín*, F, Italian run, friendly, fan, will store luggage, not too safe. Many cheaper hotels in San Félix, the historical town, have been removed or closed down in the restoration works. Only *Aguila* (D) and *Yoli* (F, no hot water, otherwise OK) in San Félix have decent restaurants. It is difficult to find hotels because of the influx of workers, who live in them for lack of other housing.

Restaurants In Puerto Ordaz: *Hotel Guayana Restaurant*, under different management from hotel, good service but expensive; near *Hotel Guayana* are *Casa del Roti*, Calle Tumeremo, good, inexpensive, *Siria-Lebanon*, Calle Ciudad Piar, Arab food, *Archie's Soda Fountain*, Tumeremo below *Casa del Roti*, and beyond is a Chinese restaurant; the market at the intersection of Tumeremo and Guasipati has many cheap food stalls; two *areperías* on Vía Las Américas above *Hotel Guayana*, and reasonable restaurants at corners of Las Américas with Calle Upata and Calle El Palmar, further up the hill. More expensive on Las Américas is *Rincón Bavaria* (German); two steak restaurants on Calle La Urbana (one next to cinema is best); Italian restaurants: *Paolo's*, Calle Guasipati, fair, *Romanino's*, Calle Ciudad Piar, good, family place, and, opposite but cheaper and less good, *Mario's*; *The Key Club*, via Caracas (opp. Banco Royal), good seafood, expensive; good seafood also at *Porrua*, but further from centre.

Car Hire 18 different operators at the airport, Puma cars rec.; Hertz, Puerto Ordaz, rents 4-wheel drive vehicles, US$25 a day with unlimited mileage. A car is very useful in this area, especially for visiting the Cerro Bolívar mine and Guri dam.

Exchange Banco Consolidado (American Express), Calle Urbana, Edif. Don Andrés, Banco Royal Venezolano and Banco Provincial at Puerto Ordaz. Banco Mercantil. Very difficult to change travellers' cheques. Hotels give poor rates.

Brazilian Consulate Av. Las Américas, nr. CANTV, can issue visas but there is delay and a charge for authorisation.

Buses Bus station at San Félix (can be a dangerous place). Bus from Ciudad Guayana to Santa Elena de Uairen, US$6.50 with Líneas Orinoco, 0700 at least 12 hrs., via El Callao, Tumeremo (US$2.75, 5 hrs.), El Dorado and Km. 88; book a day in advance to Ciudad Bolívar US$0.50, 1½ hrs; *Por puesto* to Ciudad Bolívar US$2 (bus US$1); to Maturín US$4.20, 3 hrs., 0800 every day (bus US$2.10); to Caracas, US$6, 10½ hrs. To Barcelona and Puerto La Cruz, 8 a day; to Cumaná, 4 a day. Minibuses in town are fast, frequent and cheap; fare San Félix-Puerto Ordaz US$0.20-0.30; buses run until about 2100. Taxis San Félix—Puerto Ordaz US$1, Puerto Ordaz—airport US$1.50, airport—bus station US$2.20.

Air Transport Airport, with daily flights to Caracas, and twice weekly to Boa Vista (US$130), walk 600 metres to main road for buses to San Félix or Puerto Ordaz.

Excursions To Cerro Bolívar mine, take a *por puesto* (US$4.65) or hitchhike to Ciudad Piar, or go with guided tour organized by Ferrominera Orinoco at their headquarters building in Ciudad Guayana. Tours are free, and leave Ciudad Piar at 0900 and 1400. To visit industries in the area, ask at the Corporación Venezolana de Guayana, Departamento de Relaciones Públicas.

From San Félix or Puerto Ordaz go down the Orinoco to Los Castillos (either by *por puesto*, 1 hr., US$1.25, or by bus to Aceiles, US$0.30, ask to be let off where pick-up goes to Los Castillos 0700, 1130, 1530, returns 0830, 1300 and 1700, US$0.85; difficult to get there by boat). It is possible to camp on the beach. Candes Tours run an excursion from Puerto Ordaz but only if there are four people. There are two old forts here: one on a huge rock near the water, the other on top of a hill and both in good condition. A tiny village lies at their feet. It is said to have been here that Sir Walter Raleigh's son was killed in battle while searching for El Dorado. From Los Barrancos, on the N bank of the Orinoco, opposite San Félix, *curiaras* and other boats can be taken to the delta; settle prices before setting out, take hammock, mosquito net and repellant, and canned food (in the rainy season, take a raincoat).

A most interesting side trip along asphalted roads can be made to *Tucupita*, a river town in the Orinoco delta with an interesting cathedral. The climate is very humid and Tucupita often suffers from flooding and subsequent loss of electricity. The cafés on the edge of the plaza are rec. and are said to be "especially interesting at night, without electricity, with your feet virtually awash in the Orinoco." Travellers' cheques only accepted in the Banco Unión.

Hotels *Gran Hotel Amacuro*, Calle Bolívar 23, E, a/c, very good; *Delta*, F, Calle Pativilca 28, a/c, basic; *Victoria*, near Cathedral, F with a/c, cheaper with fan, reasonable; *Pequeño*, Calle La Paz, F, clean, safe, good value; and a few cheaper *hospedajes*. *Pequeña Venezia* campsite, 20 km. from Tucupita, good, with showers; will arrange river trips. Also 1 star hotel and restaurant beside river.

Restaurants: *Tucupita*, Calle Bolívar, good; *El Río*, rec.; *Refresquería La Cascada*, Monomo 25, English spoken; *Rincón Criollo*, cheap; *Latinaja*, large portions.

Transport Bus from San Félix at 0600 and 1400, *por puesto* 2 hrs., US$2.50. Flights are also available from Caracas, Ciudad Bolívar, Porlamar and Güiria with Aeropostal. Taxi from airport to village US$3. *Por puesto* from Maturín or Ciudad Guayana about US$5, 2-3 hrs. Tucupita-Caracas by bus, 10 hrs., 2000, US$6; for Puerto La Cruz at 1530, US$4, 6 hrs.

For a 3-4 day trip to see the delta, its fauna and the Indians, boats may be arranged by asking for help at the information office near Plaza Bolívar, or contact Juan Carrión (all the taxi drivers know him, but he is very expensive), but they are not easy to come by and are expensive except for large groups. The only recognized tours of the delta are run by Delta Tours, about which poor reports received, US$20 p.p. (it is possible to negotiate). Some boat owners visit hotels in the evenings looking for clients and may negotiate a price, about US$30 per day minimum. Delta trips can be arranged in Puerto Ordaz at Happy Tours, *Hotel Intercontinental*, T (086) 223257/227748, up-market but good. For shorter excursions by boat, ask at gas station (*bomba*) by the river. Excursions often only travel on the main river, not in the *caños* where wildlife can be seen. To avoid disappointment, check all details before committing yourself. Alternatively, take a *por puesto* from Plaza Bolívar to the village of La Horqueta (US$0.40), where it is easier to get a boat and where there are many Indians. Be warned, if the river level rises after a downpour, arrangements may be cancelled. Take enough food for yourselves, the guide and the Indians, and plenty of water. Hammocks and mosquito repellants are essential. If you go to a *ranchería* take gifts such as fresh fruit, needles, thread, knives and only give them individually. You can buy hammocks and local handicrafts; always ask permission to take photographs.

An interesting dead-end village is **Barrancas** (2 hotels) on the Orinoco, reached by road from Tucupita, 63 km. (*por puesto* to San Félix US$3.30) or from Maturín. From Barrancas you can take a boat to Curiapo (Indian village) and Amacuro (near Guyana border), check at the harbour. It is also possible to go to Georgetown from here; ask for boats to Amacuro and then on to Mabaruma (only for the adventurous) or check with the lady at the *librería* on the river at the bottom of the village, she is from Georgetown and travels there occasionally.

SOUTH TO BRAZIL (8)

Travelling South from Ciudad Guayana to the Brazilian border is becoming an increasingly popular excursion for Venezuelan tourists, as well as for overland travellers heading for Manaus and the Amazon. It is no longer an arduous trip; the road to the border at Santa Elena de Uairen is now paved for all but the last 32 km., with all bridges in place. Four-wheel drive is only necessary if one wanders off the main road, particularly in the rainy season. It is forbidden to travel beyond Km. 88 or off the main road without a spare 20 litres of gasoline (spare tanks are available there, but better and cheaper to get one earlier); all petrol pumps have fuel, but not all octane levels. It is also advisable to carry extra water and plenty of food. Camping is possible but a tent with good waterproofing is essential. There are police checks at the Río Cuyuní and at Km. 126, and a military check at San Ignacio de Yuruaní all driving permits, car registration papers, and identification must be shown.

South from Ciudad Guayana the road goes through Upata (Hotels: *Andrea**, E, credit cards accepted, restaurant, good; *Yocoima*, *Comercio*, *Adriático*, F, good and *La Palma*, which also has a restaurant), Guasipati (*Hotel La Reina*, D, a/c, good) and El Callao (Hotels: *Italia* and *Ritz*, both F, on Calle Ricaurte), which has a good carnival, and is a good place to buy gold nuggets (8 km. away are the underground goldmines of El Perú).

On another 40 km. is **Tumeremo** (Hotels: *Leocar*, 3 blocks from plaza, F, fair, with shower and toilet, fan, restaurant rec.; *Central*, near plaza, good (but may be "full", try again later), bakery and snackbar, clean, F; *Florida*, E, not too good; restaurant *El Esturión*, good, friendly, Calle El Dorado, Edificio Bolívar; *Restaurante Turístico* expensive but OK, does not serve yucca with everything). There is a chronic water shortage, check when it is available in your hotel. Tumeremo is recommended as the best place to buy provisions, there is Banco de la Unión (which does not change money), and gasoline (all grades) at a normal price (better than El Dorado). 5 km. from Tumeremo towards the Fuerte Tarabay is the beautiful artificial lake of San Pedro with an attractive campsite. From Tumeremo you can go to the Isla Anacoco, on the River Venamo which forms the border with Guyana. A paved road runs through the jungle to San Martín (one military and one police post en route), where you can arrange a visit to the island. Much English spoken in San Martín; in a house opposite the water tank are some stuffed animals. By bus to Santa Elena, US$5.20 (8-10 hrs., Líneas Orinoco, 1100, 2 blocks from plaza near *Leocar*); bus to Ciudad Bolívar, US$3.25, 6 a day, 6½ hrs or *por puesto* (via San Félix and Puerto Ordaz, 5 hrs, US$2.75); *por puesto* to San Félix (Ciudad Guayana), US$4.50; bus Tumeremo-Caracas, US$6.75.

285 km. from Ciudad Guayana and 108 km. from Tumeremo is **El Dorado**, where stands the regional prison made famous by Papillon's stay there (take a taxi, can't get in without a car, though even this does not guarantee entry, US$5 for an hour, arrange price with official, not driver). Exchange at El Dorado is possible with the gold buyer on the main street; cash only, poor rates. There is a gas station, open 0800-1900 daily. Bus from Caracas to El Dorado, Expresos del Oriente, at 1830 daily, US$7, 14½ hrs., return at 1400 (925 km.). The Orinoco bus line connects with Ciudad Bolívar (6 hrs.) and Santa Elena, as does Transmundial (better buses).

Hotels *Cervino*, next to bus stop, E, fan, clean; *El Dorado*, next to gas station, E, fair, no water in new annex; *Alfonso*, quite good, will make excursions to the mines; *San Agostino*, main plaza; *Hospedaje Portugal*, F, only six rooms, the Portuguese owner also runs the store next door. *Campamento Turístico*, run by Richard Sidney Coles (speaks English and German), F, with bath, basic.

6 km. south of El Dorado, is the Río Cuyuní: distances further south are measured from the bridge. At Km. 83, is Barquilla de Fresa, where tropical fish are bred (Henry Cleve speaks English and German). From Km. 85 (*Las Claritas*, small hotel, restaurant; big market for food and gold; safe parking at Las Hermanitas de los Pobres Convent) it's a ½-hr. drive (US$2 by jeep) to the nearest gold-digging village; other villages can only be reached by helicopter (US$15 one way). These villages are built out of oil cans and other rubbish, but are complete with hotels, restaurants, small shops, hairdressers, brothels, etc.

At Km. 88 (also called San Isidro), there is gasoline (rarely 92 octane), a number of eating places and hotels: *La Pilonera*, opp. Vargas store, F with fan, some rooms with bath, restaurant with good fruit drinks, very friendly; *El Parador del Via*, with restaurant, O.K. Everything is expensive. Gold is sold here; ask Francisco Vargas at the grocery store and restaurant. Bus Km. 88-Caracas, US$7.50. Frequent *por puestos* from El Dorado to Km. 88, 1 hr., US$2. The only reliable public transport out of Km. 88 is the bus from Ciudad Bolívar, which stops at Vargas store at 1400 daily, 6 hrs. to Santa Elena, US$3.25; the alternative is to get a ride with passing jeeps and trucks (very little passes after 1030). The 40 km. beyond Km. 88 up to the Gran Sabana are very steep. At Km. 100 is the huge, black Piedra de la Virgen; from here the steep climb begins up to La Escalera and the beginning of the beautiful **Gran Sabana National Park**. Characteristic of this area are the large abrupt *tepuyes* (flat-topped mountains or *mesas*) and the hundreds of waterfalls. To visit the national park, a permit must be obtained from Inparques.

At Km. 123 a short trail leads to the 40-metre Danto Falls. If you are paying for your ride, try to persuade the driver to make a short stop at the falls; they are close to the road (about

5 mins.' slippery walk) but not visible from it. 4 km. beyond the Monumento al Soldado Pionero (Km. 141) is a popular camping place at Luepa (on right going South, ask permission at the fort); 6 km. beyond is the military checkpoint at Ciudadela.

At Km. 148 is an unpaved road leading to **Kavanayén**, four-wheel drive needed except in dry season, off this road after 25 km. are the falls of Torón Merú (17 km.) and, further on, a left turn to the falls of Chinak-Merú, 100 metres high and very impressive (take the trail to the Río Aponguao and the Pemón Indian village of Iboribó, tip someone to ferry you across the river and walk 30 mins. to the falls; 30-min. boat trips to the falls cost US\$15; this trip is reported not to be possible by normal car, take great care near the falls. 18 km. before Kavanayén is a road to the *Hotel Chivaton*, E, good beds but icy water, no food, very isolated. Kavanayén is the site of a Franciscan mission, accommodation at the mission F, grocery store, airport (bargain with pilots to fly you over the Gran Sabana). Beyond Kavanayén a beautiful but risky trail leads along flat-topped mountains to the Karuari-Merú Falls.

For the remaining 200 km. to Santa Elena de Uairen few people or villages are seen. The Pemón Indian village of Kamoiran is at Km. 176 (restaurant, gasoline). The impressive falls at the Kama river should not be missed (Km. 211); there is also a small lake, possible to camp. At Km. 259 is the Río Yuruaní, from where it is a 15-minute hike to the Yuruaní waterfall—leave the main road 250 metres after the crossing, turn left; then comes the Pemón village of San Francisco de Yuruaní **(see page** 1095), then the checkpoint of San Ignacio de Yuruaní (excellent regional food). A trail at Km. 289 leads to the Quebrada de Jaspe where a river falls over red rocks.

Santa Elena de Uairen is a growing, pleasant, frontier town. The festival of Santa Elena, 9-19 August, features music, dance and handicrafts. The bank does not change money—instead try the shops in the centre, e.g. the gold shop S of main plaza, which changes travellers' cheques, the grocery store *El Gordito*, or the *Hotel Fronteras*. Generally the rates are poor (check with travellers going in opposite direction what rates should be); to obtain better rates you must wait until Ciudad Guayana, or Boa Vista if going to Brazil. If the service station is dry, ask for Sr. Lucca who sells gasoline out of barrels. Grocery store: *Tienda Mixta El Gordito*, opp. *Hotel MacKing*, English and French spoken. Passports and car documents must be stamped here if leaving or entering the country; the immigration office is on the north edge of the town on a hill opposite the Corpovén gas station (open 0700-1700 except Sun., and holidays). If shut, go to No. 26, uphill from gas station and ask for help. CANTV phone office for international calls, but not all day.

Hotels and Restaurants *Fronteras**, E with bath, clean, quiet, comfortable, rec., good restaurant; *Hospedaje Uairen*, F, good, clean, rec.; *Hospedaje Roraima*, noisy, mosquitoes, not rec.; *Hotel MacKing*, with private bathroom, and restaurant attached, service slow, F; *Turístico*, Yarimá, F, rec, good food; *Aurantepuy*, opp. Ciudad Bolívar bus stop, F with bath (cheaper rooms available), basic, clean; *Mini Hospedaje*, F, 2 blocks from *Fronteras*, clean, basic, friendly, some rooms with private shower; *Yarima*, F, good restaurant, sometimes sends free taxi to meet bus; *Hospedaje La Rica*, F, very clean, hot water, good value; *Tropical*, modern, clean. Opposite airport, rooms to let at Sergio's *granja*, friendly, cheap. 2 good restaurants on S side of town, *3 Vs* and a *Lonchería*, within a block of each other; *La Perla*, good grill; *Gran Sabana*, was good but has declined. Rooms are difficult to find during the fiesta (if stuck, ask for Charlie at the *Hotel Fronteras*, he may be able to find you somewhere else to stay).

For excursions into the Gran Sabana contact Willy or Carol at *Hospedaje Uairen*; take food, water, warm clothing and insect repellant. Alternatively, ask for Frank.

An office nr. *Hotel Uairen* dispenses malaria tablets during office hours, Mon.-Fri. Yellow fever inoculations are not available.

Mechanic Antonio Mejías, good, cheap, a miracle-worker.

Leaving by private car may involve a bit of a run-around, up to 2 hrs. **N.B.** U.S. citizens need a visa for Brazil; don't leave it until Santa Elena, it can take 2 weeks to get there. The new road to Brazil links Caracas with Manaus in three days if you drive hard, although it is only a dirt road with gravel on top. The Brazilian section has been described as "that rutted track which has no business being called a road." Be prepared.

Transport to and from Santa Elena All regular transport appears to call at the Immigration office when leaving Santa Elena. There is a daily bus to Boa Vista (Brazil) at about 0700 from *Hotel Fronteras*, 6 hrs., US$8 (cheaper in cruzeiros; money changers on buses). From Caracas it is best to go to Ciudad Bolívar and take either the Expreso Brazil-Venezuela bus direct to Boa Vista, or the Línea Orinoco bus straight through to Santa Elena, US$8, 13-14 hrs., returns from Santa Elena at 1600, take food. Alternatively take a daily bus to Tumeremo or El Dorado; Transmundial runs from Tumeremo to Santa Elena (US$5.20) and from El Dorado (US$4.65), returning from Santa Elena at 0830. From Tumeremo you can get a bus to San Félix (Ciudad Guayana), 4 hrs., or colectivo to Maturín, 2 hrs., but Líneas Orinoco go direct Santa Elena-Ciudad Guayana (US$6.50, 12-13 hrs.), or Expreso Maturín goes to Ciudad Guayana (US$6.50) and Maturín daily. Aeropostal has flights to Tumeremo and Ciudad Bolívar (US$24), 3 times a week, but the planes may be fully booked in advance in the high season (timetable uncertain, check on arrival); also Aerotuy to Ciudad Bolívar. On Wednesdays there is an interesting flight available to Tumeremo via Icabarú and the Indian villages of Uriman, Wonkin, and Kamarata. Book a week in advance.

116 km. W of Santa Elena is Icabarú, a diamond-producing centre (daily jeep from Santa Elena, US$5). 5 km. before Icabarú is *Villa Tranquila*, a well-appointed, more expensive camp. 58 km. from Santa Elena is a Guardia Nacional checkpoint at Parai-Tepuy, with a waterfall nearby. At Km. 68 is Shaiilili-ko camp, English, Italian and French spoken, rec. At *El Pauji* (Km. 85, US$3 by jeep from Santa Elena, 3 hrs.; ask in Santa Elena for possibility of a lift with families returning after buying supplies), ask for Luigi, an Italian at El Cajón mine (he speaks English). It is in a lovely area, with good walking and bird-watching. A good walk is to the small hill, 2 km. from El Pauji beyond the airfield; views from the crest into El Abismo, a huge valley.

In El Pauji, Danielle operates *El Caminante* tourist camp, just after the bridge, coming from Santa Elena, F p.p., helpful and friendly, camping, trips arranged, restaurant; in the village is the *hospedaje* of Rodrigo and Margarita, near the airstrip and small store, cabins F, no bath, clean, very knowledgeable and friendly place; just before the bridge is *El Merendero* restaurant. At *La Bodega* general store, Victoriano has information on guides for tourists. Jeep hire in El Pauji, US$50 per day. 15 km. from El Pauji, at Solís, Arquimedes and Philippe have a tourist camp; they organize tours. 25 km. from the town is the *Canta Rana* tourist camp with basic accommodation (owners, Alfonso and Barbara Borrero, speak German, English and Spanish); waterfall and lovely surroundings; they have a private plane that collects people from Puerto Ordaz (T 086-22-68-51 or 22-07-09, Sr. Haissan Al Atrache).

Mount Roraima An exciting trip is to walk to Mt. Roraima (2,810 metres), which it has been suggested was the **"Lost World"** made famous by Arthur Conan Doyle's novel (although conflicting evidence points to the Brazilian Serra Ricardo Franco near the Bolivian border west of Cuiabá as the site). Supplies for a week or more should be bought in Santa Elena or El Dorado. You can start walking from **San Francisco de Yuruani**, an Indian village (built of concrete and corrugated iron) on the main road 60 km. north of Santa Elena, and 10 km. north of the San Ignacio military check post (bus from Santa Elena, by jeep prices vary from US$2.25 to US$5.50). Meals are available, grocery store selling canned food and Coca Cola, but it is better to take all food from Ciudad Bolívar. The chief has a tent for hire, US$3.75/day. The National Guard require you to have a guide beyond Parai-Tepuy: hire one in San Francisco, about US$7 a day, Basilio is highly rec. though Carmelo is also good, or in Parai-Tepuy itself. Follow the virtually unused dirt road to Parai-Tepuy across open savanna with patches of jungle in the river valleys (jeep San Francisco-Parai-Tepuy US$12.50; to walk this stretch takes a day). Parai-Tepuy is the nearest village to the mountain. Short cuts can be taken—ask the friendly and interested local people. Beyond Parai-Tepuy it is easy to get lost on the many trails criss-crossing. Looking from the village, Roraima is the mountain on the right, the other massive outcrop on the left is Mata Hui (sometimes known as Mt. Kukenaan after the river which rises within it). The Kukenaan river quickly goes into flood; take a 50 m. rope if not going in a party and be prepared to get wet. It is about a 2-day walk to the jungle at the foot of Roraima and then it is possible to climb to the plateau along the "easy" gully which is the only route to the top.

This gully is the more central of two which run diagonally up the cliff face. The ascent takes 3-5 hrs. and it is possible to camp on the eerie plateau, but beware of lightning from the frequent electrical storms which the mountains attract.

There is plenty of water en route (too much in the rainy season, which makes some rivers impassable) but no accommodation. Full camping equipment is essential, and wear thick socks and boots to protect legs from snakes, also essential are warm clothing for the summit and effective insect repellant. The whole trip can take anywhere between five days and two weeks.

INFORMATION FOR VISITORS

Documents Entry is by passport and visa, or by passport and tourist card. Tourist cards (*tarjetas de ingreso*) are valid only for those entering by air and are issued by most airlines to visitors from 25 countries including the USA, Canada, Japan and all Western European countries except Spain and Portugal. They are valid for 60 days with, theoretically, 2 extensions of 30 days each permissible, at a cost of US$40 each. DIEX offices in many cities do not offer extensions—best to go to DIEX in Caracas, take passport, photograph and return ticket. If you enter the country overland, you will be required to obtain a visa from a Venezuelan consulate prior to arrival. Visas cost US$10, but free to Danes and US$3 to US citizens; you will need your passport, return ticket and letter of reference from your employer and bank. You must fill in an application form and the visa will take about three working days to come through, sometimes longer if authorization has to come from Venezuela. It appears that you cannot get a visa in advance in the USA or Canada, so to apply for an overland visa in Colombia or Brazil you need: passport, one photo and an onward ticket. A tourist card issued by Viasa in Bogotá is only valid for arriving in Caracas by air from Bogotá, not if you travel overland. To extend a visa for one month, in any city, costs US$26.50 (passport photo needed); it is best to leave the country (e.g. to Curaçao) and get a new one free. To change a tourist visa to a business visa, or to extend the latter, costs US$50. A business visa costs about US$25. Tourist visas are multiple entry. Transit passengers to another country can stay only 72 hrs.

N.B. Carry your passport with you all the time you are in Venezuela as the police are increasing spot checks and anyone found without identification is immediately detained (carrying a certified copy for greater safety is permissible). A press card as identification is reported to work wonders.

Information for business visitors is given in "Hints to Exporters: Venezuela", issued by the Export Services Division, Dept. of Trade, Sanctuary Buildings, 16-20 Great Smith Street, London SW1. Businessmen on short visits are strongly advised to enter the country as tourists, otherwise they will have to obtain a tax clearance certificate (*solvencia*) before they can leave.

Taxes All non-tourists leaving the country, except nationals of Denmark and transit passengers who stay for 7 days or less (who pay one bolívar), must pay US$15 at the airport or port of embarkation (payable in bolívares only). Minors under seven years of age do not pay the exit tax. There is also an airport tax of US$1.30 for those passengers on internal flights.

Travel by Air from UK and Europe British Airways and Viasa fly from London to Simón Bolívar, the international airport for Caracas; the former twice a week each way via either Port of Spain or St. Lucia. Viasa fly via a European city such as Paris or Lisbon. Viasa also serves Amsterdam, Frankfurt, Madrid, Milan, Porto, Rome, Santiago de Compostela and Zurich. The cheapest route from Europe is with Air Portugal from Lisbon to Caracas. There are also services from Europe by Air France, KLM, Iberia, Alitalia, Lufthansa, Swissair and Avianca. Iberia has a weekly service to Tenerife, Canary Islands, from where connections can be made to various North and West African countries.

From North America By air, passengers may reach Venezuela by Pan American, (Miami, New York, San Francisco), American Airlines (Washington, Miami), Viasa (Houston, Miami, New York), and Avensa (Miami, New York, also). Viasa and Air Canada fly to Toronto; there are also many charters at holiday times.

From Colombia There are direct flights by Viasa, British Airways, Alitalia and Avianca.

From Argentina, Brazil and Uruguay There are direct air services by Viasa, Aerolíneas Argentinas and Varig.

Others Lacsa flies from San José (Costa Rica), Panama and Barranquilla (Colombia) to Caracas. Aeropostal has services to Port of Spain (5 times a week from Caracas). BWIA flies the same route 4 times a week. **Difficulties have been reported in entering Trinidad** unless with a UK, US or Canadian passport. LIAT (4 times a week) and Aeropostal (twice) fly to Bridgetown, Barbados; Aeropostal also to Grenada, Martinique (also Air France, both to Pointe-á-Pitre, Guadeloupe, as well); Viasa 4 times a week to Havana (Viasa's outward flights London-Caracas connect with this service). There is direct air service from Chile (Viasa and LAN Chile both have 2 weekly flights; connections can also be made via Bogotá on Avianca), Peru (Aero Perú and Viasa—Viasa tickets purchased in Peru should be checked most carefully), Ecuador (Ecuatoriana and Viasa—to Quito and Guayaquil), Santo Domingo (Viasa, Aeropostal, Dominicana de Aviación), Puerto Rico (American, Aeropostal, Viasa), Curaçao (ALM, Dominicana; Aeropostal, cheaper), Aruba (Air Aruba, Avensa, Aeropostal and Viasa; Air Aruba flights cheaper from Las Piedras, **see page** 1062 than from Caracas).

International **road** connections are given in the text. **Shipping** routes are given in the Introduction and Hints, apart from those with Curaçao and Aruba, which can be found in the text under Coro.

Shipping a car from the USA From Miami: Venezuelan Line (agent Oceanic Steamship Co.—rec.) and Delta Line, US$500-650 for a VW minibus (in the other direction, Maracaibo-Miami, it costs US$300); no passengers. From New Orleans: Delta Line, VW minibus, US$1,400-1,700, passengers carried, but for US$1,200. Alternatively, agent Hansen and Tiedemann charges same price as Delta for vehicle, but you can accompany it for US$190 p.p. (5 days, including meals). Also recommended: Coordinadora del Caribe Transmodal C.A. (CCT) Calle Veracruz, Ed. Torreón, Piso 7, Las Mercedes, Caracas, T 92-71-33. Also Seaboard Marine, agent in Venezuela, Conavén, US$650 for a VW Kombi; their route is advertised as La Guaira-Miami, but actually goes to West Palm Beach, 80 miles North of Miami; almost impossible to travel with your vehicle. Vencaribe (shipping) agent is Taurel y cía, Edif. Taurel, Calle Cuji a Romualdo No. 69, Apto. de Correos 1592, Caracas; representative is Sonigar on 3rd floor, but Paul Paulheim on 1st floor is helpful. In port of La Guaira Taurel is on main street, just ask; Johnny Hilahl is the representative, but Wendy the receptionist and Bobby Momighan are also helpful, all speak English. Taurel's shipping department is called "vapores".

On arrival in Venezuela (La Guaira), you must go to the Tourism Department at Simón Bolívar airport where you must obtain a document identifying your car (take photocopies of driving licence, passport, car documents and bill of lading). With this you can get your car out of the port: a shipping agent is not necessary, though knowledge of Spanish is useful. Go then to Aduanas Marítimas at the port with your bill of lading, ownership documents and passport, and 5 hours to spare. They stop for lunch 1200-1300 and close at weekends.

Customs You may bring into Venezuela, free of duty, 25 cigars and 200 cigarettes, 2 litres of alcoholic drinks, 4 small bottles of perfume, and gifts at the inspector's discretion.

Air Services Most places of importance are served by Avensa (private) and/or Aeropostal (government-owned, both heavily overbooked always). Aeropostal also has international service (Viasa does not have domestic services). Both internal airlines offer special family discounts and 15% off for students. Beware of overbooking during holiday time, especially at Caracas airport; it is recommended that you check in two hours before departure, particularly at Easter. Internal night-time flights are scarce, and there is no late hour discount. If you travel with Viasa or any other airline for which Viasa is agent, it is possible to check in the day before flying out of Caracas by taking baggage, ticket and passport to their office at Centro Comercial Tamanaco, Nivel C.2, "Predespacho", between 1500 and 2100 (cost US$0.40); take bus from Chacaíto. To avoid overbooking the

Government now obliges airlines to post a passenger list, but it is important to obtain clear instructions from the travel agent regarding confirmation of your flight and checking-in time. Passengers leaving Caracas on international flights must reconfirm their reservations not less than 72 hours in advance; it is safer to do so in person than by telephone; 24 hours for national flights (if you fail to do this, you lose all rights to free accommodation, food, transport, etc. if your flight is cancelled). Beware of counterfeit tickets; buy only from agencies. If told by an agent that a flight is fully booked, try at the airport anyway. International passengers must check in two hours before departure or they may lose their seat to someone on a waiting list. Read carefully any notice you see posted with the relevant instructions. Handling charge for your luggage US$0.50. All flights are subject to delays or cancellation. Avensa operates an air-pass system, open only to non-residents and purchasable only outside Venezuela: unlimited travel for 21 days for US$139. Passengers are issued with an MCO (Miscellaneous Charges Order) in the country of purchase, this is exchanged in Caracas at Pasajes Avensa, Esq. El Conde. At the same time ask for a timetable of all Avensa flights. (In view of the cheapness of internal flights and the good bus services, the pass may not be worth buying).

Motoring   A tourist can bring in his/her car without paying duty, and the only documentation required is a visa for overland entry (this is necessary despite what Consulates may tell you). An entry permit for a car costs US$10 and requires one photograph (takes 24 hrs.); ask for a permit for 6 months, or unspecified time. **See also page** 1073. For vehicles with Venezuelan registration leaving Venezuela the following documents are required: an Automóvil passport book from the Touring y Automóvil Club de Venezuela, Apartado 68102, Centro Integral Santa Rosa, Locales 11 y 12, Calle A, Av. Principal, Santa Rosa de Lima, Caracas, T 914879; the original car papers; the registration document; a police *revisión* obtained from the Policía Técnica Judicial; and a temporary import/export licence for a vehicle obtainable from the Ministerio de Hacienda, Caracas, or from a customs agent in San Antonio de Táchira (border town) for about US$100. The export/import licence and the passport book must be signed and stamped by the Customs Administrator. If possible, check all details on bringing in/taking out a car in advance.

All visitors to Venezuela can drive if they are over 18 and have a valid driving licence from their own country. It is a good idea to hire a car (**see page** 1052); many of the best places are off the beaten track. If planning to hire a car for any length of time it is worth the trouble to obtain a *licencia temporal para conducir*; for this you require a medical certificate (eye examination, blood pressure, US$2, issued by an authorised medical centre, try Torre Phelps, Plaza Venezuela, Caracas), photocopy of your home driver's licence and two black-and-white passport photos which must be presented at the Ministerio de Transporte y Comunicaciones, Torre Este, Parque Central, Dep. Licencias, full details in Venamcham's *Executive Newcomer's Guide*. If you have an accident and someone is injured, you will be detained as a matter of routine, even if you are not at fault. Do not drive at night if you can help it. Carry insect spray if you do; if you stop and get out, the car will fill with biting insects.

In 1982 a nationwide speed limit of 80 k.p.h. was imposed. The roads in Venezuela are very good, all major routes are fully paved and even the dirt and gravel roads are reliable. Motoring restrictions in Caracas include a ban on parking in front of a bank; motorcycles may not be driven at night; pillion passengers may not be carried on motorcycles if of the same sex as the driver. You are more likely to be penalized for infringing these rules than for driving through a red light; they are designed to improve security for banks and pedestrians. In addition, motorcyclists are obliged to wear a crash helmet but it must not be of a type which obscures the face.

There are 5 grades of gasoline: "normal", 83 octane (Bs.2.55 a litre); 87 octane (Bs.2.62 a litre); 89 octane (Bs.2.65 a litre); 91 octane (Bs.2.68 a litre); and "alta", 95 octane (Bs.2.75 a litre). Diesel is hard to find, for example only one station in Caracas sells it; ask around. Service stations are open 0500-2100, Mon.-Sat., except those on highways which are open longer hours. Only those designated to handle emergencies are open on Sun. In the event of breakdown, Venezuelans are usually very helpful. There are many garages, even in rural areas; service charges are not high, but being able to speak Spanish will greatly assist in sorting out problems. Road maps are available for US$1 at most service stations, but the best map is the Guía Progreso, published by the insurance company Seguros Progreso SA, available at the company's offices and in major hotels. **Warning** There is an automatic US$20 fine for running out of fuel.

Road Transport There are excellent (but slow) bus services between the major cities, but the colectivo taxis and minibuses, known in Venezuela as *por puesto*, seem to monopolize transport to and from smaller towns and villages. Outside Caracas, town taxis are relatively expensive.

Railways The only passenger traffic of any importance is on the Barquisimeto to Puerto Cabello line. The 110-km. Yaritagua-Acarigua-Turén electric railway line was opened at the beginning of 1983 but was closed after the inaugural run because of damage to the track. It is intended mostly to transport agricultural products.

Hitch-Hiking (*Cola*) is not very easy but the Venezuelans are usually friendly and helpful if you know some Spanish. The best places to try are Guardia Nacional posts outside cities (may get free bus rides from them).

Hotel Reservations Fairmont International (**see page** 1050) will book hotel rooms both in Caracas and in other towns, where they have 102 hotels on their books, not all of which are mentioned in these pages. Hotels marked with an asterisk (*) are bookable through Fairmont. Officially controlled prices exist for one-star and two star hotels. In 1988 a 10% tourist tax was added to hotel prices, not for the benefit of hoteliers but for the construction and maintenance of tourist amenities.

Camping Equipment is available at sports-goods shops in Caracas. It is impossible, infact illegal, to refill portable gas cylinders. Camping in Venezuela is a popular recreation, for spending a weekend at the beach, on the islands, in the *llanos* and in the mountains. (People pitch their tents on Mount Avila overlooking Caracas.) Camping is not however used by travellers as a substitute for hotels on the main highways, and no special camp sites are yet provided for this purpose. If camping on the beach, for the sake of security, pitch your tent close to others, even though they play their radios loud. For information on hiking, climbing and relevant equipment, telephone Alexander on (02)573-00-56 (Spanish only).

Food Both in Caracas and to a lesser extent in Maracaibo there are excellent restaurants specializing in foreign regional cuisines. Venezuelan beef is comparable with Argentina's and, surprisingly, portions are larger. There is excellent local fish (we recommend *pargo* or red snapper), crayfish, small oysters and prawns, though sole, trout and large oysters are imported. Sometimes there is turtle, though it is a protected species. For those without a conservationist conscience, turtle may appear on menus in the Peninsula de Paraguaná as *ropa especial*. The *Tarzilandia* restaurant in Caracas also serves it. Of true Venezuelan food there is *sancocho* (a stew of vegetables, especially yuca, with meat, chicken or fish); *arepas*, a kind of white maize bread, very bland in flavour; toasted *arepas* served with a wide selection of relishes, fillings or the local somewhat salty white cheese are cheap, filling and nutritious; *cachapas*, a maize pancake (soft, not hard like Mexican *tortillas*) wrapped around white cheese; *pabellón*, made of shredded meat, beans, rice and fried plantains; and *empanadas*, maize-flour pies containing cheese, meat or fish. At Christmas only there are *hallacas*, maize pancakes stuffed with chicken, pork, olives, etc. boiled in a plantain leaf (but don't eat the leaf). The nearest thing to a boiled egg in most places is a *huevo tibio*. It comes without the shell because there are no eggcups. A *muchacho* (boy) on the menu is not a sign of cannibalism; it is a cut of beef. *Ganso* is also not goose but beef. *Solomo* and *lomito* are other cuts of beef. *Hervido* is chicken or beef with vegetables. *Caraotas* are beans; *cachitos* are *croissants* of bread. *Pasticho* is what the Venezuelans call Italian *lasagne*. The main fruits are bananas, oranges, grapefruit, mangoes, pineapple and pawpaws. Excellent strawberries are grown at Colonia Tovar, 90 minutes from Caracas. A delicious sweet is *huevos chimbos*—egg yolk boiled and bottled in sugar syrup. The Caracas *Daily Journal* (in English) lists many reliable restaurants in Caracas and Maracaibo. Venezuelans dine late.

Drink There is no good local wine though some foreign wines are bottled locally. Local wine is used only in cooking or in *sangría*. There are four good local beers: Polar (the most popular), Regional (with a strong flavour of hops), Cardenal and Nacional (a *lisa* is a glass of keg beer; for a bottle of beer ask for a *tercio*), mineral waters, gin and excellent rum. The citizens of Mérida sometimes drink a cocktail of beer and milk. The coffee is very good (*café con leche* has a lot of milk, *café marrón* much less); visitors should also try a *merengada*, a delicious drink made from fruit pulp, ice, milk and sugar; a *batido* is the same but with water, not milk. A *plus-café* is an after-dinner liqueur. Water is free in all restaurants even if no food is bought. Bottled water in *cervecerías* is often from the tap; no deception is intended, bottles are simply used as convenient jugs. Insist on seeing the bottle opened if you do not want a mouthful of chlorine with your whisky. *Chicha de arroz* is a sweet drink made of milk, rice starch, sugar and vanilla; fruit juices are very good. Gin and rum at about US$2 and coffee beans at US$1.50 per kilo are good buys.

Tipping Taxi drivers are tipped if the taxi has a meter (Caracas only, so far), but not if you have agreed the fare in advance. Usherettes are not tipped. Hotel porters, Bs.2; airport porters Bs.2 per piece of baggage. Restaurants, between 5 and 10% of bill.

Shopping Goods in shops bear a label "PVP" followed by the price. This is the maximum authorized price; you may be able to negotiate a discount but should never pay more than the PVP price.

Security In the cities, take the usual precautions to protect your valuables and belongings, but in addition, carry handbags, cameras etc. on the side away from the street as motor-cycle purse-snatchers are notorious, especially in Caracas. Hotel thefts are becoming more frequent.

Health Conditions are good. Water in all main towns is heavily chlorinated, so safe to drink, although most people drink bottled water. Medical attention is good. State health care is free and said to be good (the Clínica Metropolitana in Caracas has been recommended). Some rivers are infected with bilharzia and in some areas there are warning signs; check before bathing. Inoculation against typhoid and yellow fever, and protection against malaria, is recommended for the Orinoco and other swampy or forest regions. Malaria tablets may be obtained from Hospital Padre Machado (left-hand building as you face it), T 61-8211, no charge; or Ministerio de Sanidad y Asistencia Social (MSAS), Torre del Silencio (SW corner of Plaza Caracas), División de Malariología, free, English spoken; alternatively, bring malaria tablets with you. It is as well to carry some remedy in case of gastric upsets. Factor 15 sun-tan cream is widely available.

Clothing Tropical weight in normal city colours is best for business in Caracas, otherwise clothing is less formal, but smart jackets and ties are required in the most exclusive restaurants and clubs. In Maracaibo and the hot, humid coastal and low-lying areas, regular washable tropical clothing is used. For women: blouse and trousers (shorts quite acceptable on the coast); cotton dresses, with a wrap for cool evenings, and for air-conditioned restaurants and cinemas. Shoes are very good value.

Hours of Business Banks are open from 0830 to 1130 and 1400 to 1630. Mon. to Fri., but are no longer open on Sat. Government office hours vary, but 0800-1200 are usual morning hours. Government officials have fixed hours, usually 0900-1000 or 1500-1600, for receiving visitors. Business firms generally start work about 0800 and some continue until about 1800 with a midday break. Shops, 0900-1300, 1500-1900, Mon.-Sat. Generally speaking, the Venezuelan begins his day early, and by seven in the morning everything is in full swing. Most firms and offices close on Sat.

Holidays There are two sorts of holidays, those enjoyed by everybody and those taken by employees of banks and insurance companies. Holidays applying to all businesses include: 1 January, Carnival on the Monday and Tuesday before Ash Wednesday, Thursday-Saturday of Holy Week, 19 April, 1 May, 24 June, 5, 24July, 12 October, 25 December. Holidays for banks and insurance companies only include all the above and also: 19 March and the nearest Monday to 6 January, Ascension Day, 29 June, 15 August, 1 November and 8 December. There are also holidays applying to certain occupations such as Doctor's Day or Traffic Policeman's Day. On New Year's Eve, everything closes and does not open for a least a day; public transport runs, but booking offices are not open. Queues for tickets, and traffic jams, are long. Business travellers should not visit during Holy week or Carnival.
    Local: La Guaira: 10 March. Maracaibo 24: October, 18 November.

Official Time in Venezuela is 4 hrs. behind GMT, 1 hour ahead of EST.

Currency The unit of currency is the bolívar, which is divided into 100 céntimos. There are nickel alloy coins for 25 and 50 céntimos and 1, 2 and 5 bolívares, and notes for 5, 10, 20, 50, 100 and 500 bolívares. The 1,000-bolívares note no longer circulates, because of extensive counterfeiting. There is a shortage of small coinage: many shops round up prices unless you have small change and bars may refuse to serve you unless you produce the correct change. In 1989, the official and free rates of exchange were unified. Change travellers' cheques or US dollar notes in a *casa de cambio* for optimum rates; of the banks, Banco Unión and Banco de Venezuela change cheques and cash, but the latter usually only change money after 1500. The majority of banks do not cash travellers' cheques; in major towns, one or two banks may, but this varies from branch to branch. American Express cheques are widely accepted as is the Visa card (Banco Consolidado is affiliated with American Express, no commission, some branches cash personal cheques from abroad on an Amex card; Banco Unión handles Visa transactions and Banco Mercantil handle Mastercard). When changing dollars cash in banks, it is best to go in the morning. If changing money in hotels, do not take sterling or any other European currencies. It is impossible to change sterling in Ciudad Guayana or Ciudad Bolívar. Have money sent to you by telex and not by post, which can take weeks. Rates of exchange in hotels are generally poor.

Popular names for coins: Fuerte. Bs.5; Real, Bs.0.50; Medio, 0.25; Puya or Centavo, 0.05.

Weights and Measures are metric.

Voltage 110 volts, 60 cycles, throughout the country.

Postal Services The postal service is extremely slow, unreliable and expensive. Air mail letters to the USA or Europe can take from one to four weeks and registered mail is no quicker. Internal mail also travels slowly, especially if there is no P.O. Box number. If you want money sent to you from abroad, have it sent by telex. Avoid the mail boxes in pharmacies as some no longer have collections.

Telephone Service All international and long distance calls are operated by CANTV from El Silencio building in west Caracas, Centro Simón Bolívar or Centro Plaza on Fco. Miranda near US Embassy in east Caracas, open 24 hrs. Most major cities are now linked by direct dialling (*Discado Directo*), with a 3-figure prefix for each town in Venezuela. Otherwise CANTV offices deal with most long-distance and international calls in the cities outside Caracas. Collect calls have recently become possible, at least in Caracas, though staff in offices may not be sure of this. Calls out of Venezuela are more expensive than calls into it and are subject to long delays. Local calls are troublesome and the connection is often cut in the middle of your conversation; calls are best made from hotels or CANTV offices, rather than from booths. Local calls in Caracas cost US$0.06. Many public phones operate with phonecards (*tarjetas*), available for many different values, though many small shops impose a 25% handling charge and *tarjetas* may be out of stock. International calls are cheaper with a *tarjeta*.

Note Telephone, fax or telex are far preferable to cables. Ask your hotel for use of its telex or fax machine.

Press: Caracas: El *Universal*, *El Nacional* and *El Diario de Caracas*, *La Religión*, *Ultimas Noticias*. The *Daily Journal* (English), *El Mundo* and *2001* (evening), *Número* (weekly), *Resumen* (weekly), *Elite* (weekly), *Momento* (weekly), *Venezuela Gráfica* (weekly), *Páginas* (weekly), *Semana* (weekly), *Ve Venezuela*, tourist bi-monthly. Maracaibo: *Panorama*, *La*

Crítica. Puerto La Cruz: *El Tiempo*.

Radio Write to Radio Nacional, Caracas 101, Apartado 3979, for details about their plans for English-language broadcasts.

Tourist Information may be obtained from Corpoturismo, Apartado 50.200, Caracas, main office for information is floors 35-7, Torre Oeste, Parque Central. A useful publication is the *Guía Turística y Hoteles de Venezuela, Colombia y el Caribe*, published every July by Corpoturismo, which includes not only hotel details, but also road maps and tourist attractions. For businessmen setting up home in Caracas, the Venezuelan American Chamber of Commerce publication, *Executive Newcomer's Guide, Welcome to Venezuela*, is recommended, with useful chapters on housing, employment, schools, services, recreation facilities and legal matters. Also useful is the *Atlas Geográfico y Económico—Venezuela Visualizada* by Levi Marrero, Ed. Cultural Venezolana, 1977, which contains maps, tourist information and statistics of every state, available in all good bookshops. The *Guide to Venezuela* (1981), by Janice Bauman, Leni Young and others, in English (freely available in Caracas) is a mine of information and maps. Bradt Publications of 41 Nortoft Road, Chalfont St. Peter, Bucks, SL9 0LA, UK, publish *No Frills Guide to Venezuela*, by Hilary Dunsterville Branch and others, containing information on hikes and excursions and on Caracas.

We should like to thank Charlie Nurse for doing the updating, and the following travellers for help in revising the Venezuelan section: Franck Abadie (Megève, France) and Marianne Joelius (Stockholm), Lindsay Adam (Forest Row, W. Sussex), Tam Agosti-Gisler (Anchorage, Alaska), Arnold and Jannie (Maarssen, Neths.), Brian Bass (Clun/Craven Arms, Shropshire), David Burford (Templestowe, Victoria), Dorothea Bornholdt (Lutzhorn, W. Ger.), J.N. Bowden and K.E. Badgery (Plymouth), Jutta Brück (Nürnberg 60), Peter Caesar (Bogotá), Paul Stacey (London) and Ione Christiansen (Denmark), Bryan Crawford (Beauly, Inverness-shire), Joanne Cross and Frank Pinelli (Oak Park, IL), Ailsa J. Donnelly (Binghamton, NY), Barbara Evans and Hugh O'Donnell (London), Dr Dietz Evers (Krumesse), Thom Van Every (Edgbaston), Pauline Fearon (Hornchurch), Joachim Feld (Boeblingen, W. Ger.), Mo Fini (*Tumi*, Bath), Margaret Fleming (Karlsfeld, W. Ger.), Petra Franke (Gundelsheim, W. Ger.), Sharon Franklet (Lima 18), D. Friend (Melbourne), John N. Fugelso (Durham NC), Theodor A. Gevert (Barueri, SP, Brazil), Tony Gowers (Bristol), Rudy Graf (Geneva), Andrew Grassie and Sara Gilbert (Lewes), D. Graves (Brooklyn, NY), Jacqueline Greig (Cuckfield, E Sussex), Karl Gugler and Konstanze Mittendorfer (Vienna), Manuel G. Gutiérrez (Mountain Tours CA, Mérida), Jim Hardy (Waukesha, Wis.), Roy and Joan Harris (Nanaimo, BC), Martin and Susan Hockey (Oxford), Thomas Hodel (Kaufdorf, Switz.), Jacqueline L. Hodge (Creixell, Tarragona), Robin Holloway and Fiona Butler (Birmingham), David Jeffcock (Worthing), Allan Jensen and Vibeke Nageh (Munke-Bjergby, Dnmk.), Chris John (Poynton, Stockport) and Michelle Chaplow (Durham), Tobias Kämpf (Rupperswil, Switz.), Marcel Kersten (Roosendaal, Neths.), Rudi Lamparter (Gaechingen, W. Ger.), Binka Le Breton (Muriaé, Brazil), Melchior Lengsfeld (Basel), John Lewis (London NW2), Helena van Maanen (Velp, Neths.), Trevor J. Mason (Winchester), Kirk Mayer and Barbara Pearce (Macclesfield), Ralph-Peter Mechnik (Nürnberg 1), Gino Meir (Israel), Andreas Mietzsch (Braunschweig), Martha van Mil and Monica van Eysden ('s-Hertogenbosch, Neths.), Daniel Morgan (Wellington, NZ), Steve Morris (Saint John, NB, Canada), David, Christine, Philip and Catherine Mylan (Worksop), Stephen Newcomer (Centrevill, Iowa), Mette Nordaw and Claus Jørgensen (Lyngby, Dnmk.), Harrie Nouwens (Eindhoven, Neths.), Barry Oldham (Plymouth, Devon), Shawn and Jeff Olsen (St Paul, Minnesota), Carlo Ottavio (Potenza, Italy), Ruth Owen (Lima 4), Lucy Paine and William Petrie (Watlington, Oxon.), Jeff Perk (Carbondale, IL), W.V. Ralph (London SE12), Yves Rougeaux (Montreuil, France), Rick and Su Sareen (Thailand), Alex Scherer (Brugg, Switz.), Tina Scheftelowitz and Lasse Thielfoldt (Copenhagen), Ueli Schlatter (Hemmental, Switz.), Leon van der Schoor (Den Bosch, Neth.), Thorsten Schüller (Aschen, W. Ger.), Matthew Shugart (San Diego, CA), Ann Simon (Saffron Walden, Essex), Andrejs Skaburskis (Kingston, Canada), Dave Statham (London NW10), R.W. Le Sueur (Jersey), Joseph Swillen (Sint-Jaris-Winge, Belgium), Raquel Rotnes Thalenberg (Brazil) and Guiora Thalenberg (Israel), Martin and Susanna Theander (Malmö), Steve and Leslie Urban (Portsmouth, NH), Levy Venanzius (Disentis, Switz.), Mark D. Viner and Kim Hutchings (Bromley, Kent), Maarten van Vlerken (Amsterdam), Ingrid Walter and Norbert Eisinger (Schnelldorf, W. Ger.), Markus Weder (Binningen, Switz.), Roland Weitkamp (Braunschweig, W. Ger.), Huw Williams (Sutton Abinger), Johannes Witt and Andreas Diet (Regensbürg), Tim Woodward (Tottenham, N15) and S.L. Wyatt.

THE GUIANAS

LIKE the West Indians, the people of the three Guianas, Guyana (formerly British Guiana), Suriname (formerly Dutch Guiana) and French Guyane, are not regarded as belonging to Latin America. The explanation of these three non-Iberian countries on the South American continent goes back to the early days of the Spanish conquest of the New World. There was no gold or any other apparent source of wealth to attract the attention of the Spanish discoverers. This part of the coast, which Columbus had first sighted in 1498, seemed to them not only barren but scantily populated and seemingly uninhabitable. The English, the French and the Dutch, anxious to establish a foothold in this part of the world, were not so fastidious.

All three countries are geographically very similar: along the coast runs a belt of narrow, flat marshy land, at its widest in Suriname. This coastland carries almost all the crops and most of the population. Behind lies a belt of crystalline upland, heavily gouged and weathered. The bauxite, gold and diamonds are in this area. Behind this again is the massif of the Guiana Highlands. They reach a height of 3,000 feet (915 metres), in the Tumuc-Humac range, the divide between French Guyane and Suriname, and Brazil, and 9,219 feet (2,810 metres) at flat-topped Mount Roraima (**see page** 1095), where Guyana, Venezuela and Brazil all meet.

N.B. You need to have your own shoe-cleaning equipment; there seem to be no shoeshine boys in any of the Guianas.

Thanks and acknowledgements for help with the Guianas sections will be found at the end of the chapter on French Guyane.

GUYANA

GUYANA has an area of 83,000 square miles, nearly the size of Britain, but only about 0.5% (or 280,000 acres) is cultivated. The population numbers some 750,000, of whom about 91% are literate. There has been considerable emigration to the USA, Canada and Britain.

About 90% of the population lives on the narrow coastal plain, most of which is below sea level. A sea wall keeps out the Atlantic and the fertile clay soil is drained by a system of dykes. Sluice gates are opened to let out water at low tide; and separate irrigation channels are used to bring water back to the fields in dry weather. In several places fresh water is supplied by reservoirs, known as conservancies. Most of the western third of the coastal plain is undrained and uninhabited. Most people live either in Georgetown, the capital, or in villages which are strung along the main road running from Charity in the west to the Suriname border. Large wooden houses stand on stilts above the damp soil. The strange cultural mix—Dutch place names and drainage techniques, Hindu temples, mosques, coconut palms and calypso music—reflect the chequered history of the country. The rich agricultural land of this area is used for producing rice and sugar and for raising cattle. Coffee, fruit and vegetables are also grown.

Four major rivers cross the coastal plain—(from west to east) the Essequibo, the Demerara, the Berbice, and the Courantyne (which forms the frontier with Suriname). Only the Demerara is crossed by a bridge. Elsewhere ferries must be used. In the mouth of the Essequibo river are islands the size of Barbados. The lower reaches of these rivers are navigable; but waterfalls and rapids prevent them being used by large boats to reach the interior.

Inland from the coastal plain most of the country is covered by thick rain forest, although in the east there is a large area of grassland. Although some timber has been extracted, the main economic activity is mining: bauxite is extracted at Linden, Ituni and Kwakwani; gold and diamonds are sifted from the sand and gravel of the river beds by small teams of miners using mercury (at considerable environmental cost). Large areas of rain forest are still undisturbed, however, and even the more accessible areas have varied and spectacular wildlife, including brightly-plumaged birds. Towards the Venezuelan border the rain forest rises in a series of steep escarpments, with spectacular waterfalls, the highest and best-known of which are the Kaieteur Falls on the Potero river.

In the south west of the country is the Rupununi Savanna, an area of open grassland more easily reached from Brazil than from Georgetown.

The area west of the Essequibo river—about 70% of the national territory—is claimed by Venezuela. Another area in the south east, between the Koeroeni and New rivers, is claimed by Suriname.

The **climate**, although hot, is not unhealthy. Mean shade temperature throughout the year is 80°F; the mean maximum is about 87°F and the mean minimum 75°F. The heat is greatly tempered by cooling breezes from the sea and is most felt from August to October. There are two wet seasons, from the middle of April to the middle of August, and from the middle of November to the end of January. Rainfall averages 91 inches a year in Georgetown.

History The country was first partially settled between 1616 and 1621 by the Dutch West India Company, who erected a fort and depot at Fort Kyk-over-al (County of Essequibo). The first English attempt at settlement was made by Captain Leigh on the Oiapoque River (now French Guyane) in 1604, but it failed to establish a permanent settlement. Lord Willoughby, famous in the early history of Barbados, founded a settlement in 1663 at Suriname, which was captured by the Dutch in 1667 and ceded to them at the Peace of Breda in exchange for New York. The Dutch held the three colonies till 1796 when they were captured by a British fleet. The territory was restored to the Dutch in 1802, but in the following year was retaken by Great Britain, which finally gained it in 1814, when the three counties of Essequibo, Berbice and Demerara were merged to form British Guiana.

During the 17th century the Dutch and English settlers established posts up-river, in the hills, mostly as trading points with the Amerindian natives. Plantations were laid out and worked by slaves from Africa. Poor soil defeated this venture, and the settlers retreated with their slaves to the coastal area in mid-18th century: the old plantation sites can still be detected from the air. Coffee and cotton were the main crops up to the end of the 18th century, but sugar had become the dominant crop by 1820. In 1834 slavery was abolished. Many of the slaves scattered as small landholders, and the plantation owners had to look for another source of labour. It was found in indentured workers from India, a few Chinese, and some Portuguese labourers from the Azores and Madeira. About 240,000 had come from India alone by 1914. At the end of their indentures many settled in Guyana.

The end of the colonial period was politically turbulent, with rioting between the mainly East Indian People's Progressive Party (PPP), led by Dr. Cheddi Jagan, and the mainly African People's National Congress (PNC), under Mr. Forbes

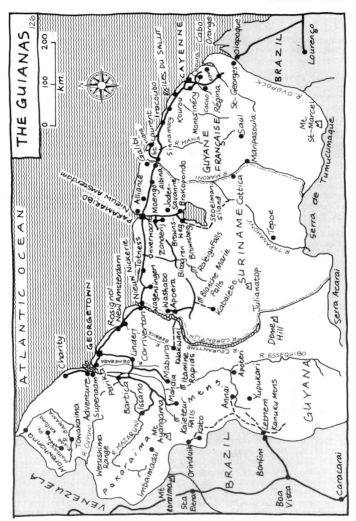

Burnham. The PNC, favoured over the PPP by the colonial authorities, formed a government in 1964 and has retained office since.

On 26 May 1966 Guyana gained independence, and on 23 February 1970 it became a cooperative republic within the Commonwealth, adopting a new constitution. Another new constitution was adopted in 1980; this declared Guyana to be in transition from capitalism to socialism. Many industries, including bauxite and sugar, were nationalised in the 1970s and close relations with the USSR and Eastern Europe were developed. Following the death of President Forbes Burnham in August 1985, Mr Desmond Hoyte became President. Since then, overseas investors have been invited back and relations with the United States have improved.

Elections to the National Assembly and to the Presidency have been held regularly since independence, but have been widely criticised as fraudulent. The main opposition parties are the PPP, still led by Dr. Jagan, and the Working People's Alliance, which attracts support from both East Indian and African communities. Elections due to be held in 1990.

The People Until the 1920s there was little natural increase in population, but the eradication of malaria and other diseases has since led to a rapid growth in population, particularly among the East Indians (Asian), who, according to most estimates comprise over 50% of the population. The results of the 1980 census have still not been published, possibly because of embarrassment over the high level of emigration, but more likely because of the extreme sensitivity of the racial balance between the East Indian and African (black) communities. Descendants of the original Amerindian inhabitants form a very small minority who have rapidly lost their isolation and moved to the urban areas.

The Economy Apart from instant, temporary prosperity brought about by the brief non-oil commodities boom in the mid-1970s, which raised gdp growth to 10.4% in 1975, Guyana's economy has been in almost permanent recession in the last two decades, despite considerable, unexploited potential in hydroelectric power, minerals and forestry. While Venezuela's long standing claim to the Essequibo region, within which most of these resources are situated, has discouraged investment, other factors are more to blame. Inefficient management in the dominant state sector covering vital sugar and bauxite industries, an investment climate discouraging both domestic and foreign savings, and an acute foreign exchange shortage, have resulted in poor performances from the key agricultural and mining sectors, and a largely moribund manufacturing sector.

Most agriculture is concentrated on the coastal plain, and many sugar plantations are below sea level, necessitating an extensive system of dams, dykes, canals and pumps to prevent inundation. Sugar is the main crop, and has vied with bauxite and alumina as the most important source of export earnings. Rice is the second most important crop, and a useful foreign exchange earner, though significant quantities of rice production are bartered or export proceeds are undeclared through trade with South American neighbours, especially Suriname and Brazil.

Guyana is the world's largest producer of calcined bauxite, the highest grade of the mineral, and currently has roughly half the world market, though competition from China is becoming stronger. Production is currently concentrated at Linden, on the Demarara river, and at Kwakwani in Berbice county. No alumina (refined bauxite) has been exported since 1982 because the Linden refinery still awaits investment for refurbishment.

In January 1987 the Government devalued the Guyana dollar. This and other adjustment measures proved beneficial both for the current account and for government finances but the economy remained depressed. Further devaluation was necessary in 1989 and again in 1990 as the Government struggled to come to terms with the IMF and other creditors to resume capital inflows. The IMF declared Guyana ineligible for further assistance in May 1985, because of payment arrears, although intermittent policy discussions continued as Guyana sought help from bilateral donors to enable it to pay its arrears to the Fund.

Guyana has suffered from serious economic problems for over 15 years; some estimates now put per capita income below that of Haiti. Wages are very low and many people depend on overseas remittances or "parallel market" activities to survive. There are frequent shortages of many basic items including some foodstuffs, gasoline and spare parts. The country's infrastructure is seriously run down. There are frequent electricity blackouts—sometimes lasting over 12 hours—and during these no water is available, except in larger hotels and businesses which have emergency generators and water pumps.

Government A Prime Minister and cabinet are responsible to the National Assembly, which has 65 members elected for a maximum term of 5 years. The President is Head of State. The country is divided into ten administrative regions.

Georgetown, the capital, and the chief town and port, is on the right bank of the River Demerara, at its mouth. Its population is roughly 200,000. The climate is tropical, with a mean temperature of 27°C, but the trade winds often provide welcome relief. The city is built on a grid plan, with wide tree-lined streets and drainage canals following the layout of the old sugar estates. Despite being located on the Atlantic coast, Georgetown is known as the "Garden City of the Caribbean". Parts of the city are very attractive, with white-painted wooden nineteenth century houses raised on stilts and a profusion of flowering trees. Lying, like most of the coastal area, below sea level, the city is protected from the ocean by a sea wall; in the evening this is crowded with strollers and at Easter it is a mass of colourful paper kites. Although part of the old city centre was destroyed by fire in 1945, there are some fine nineteenth century buildings, particularly on or near the Avenue of the Republic. The Gothic-style City Hall dates from 1887. St George's Anglican Cathedral, which dates from 1889, is 44 metres (143 feet) high and is reputed to be the tallest wooden building in the world. The Public Buildings, which house Parliament, are an imposing neo-classical structure built in 1839. Much of the city centre is dominated by the imposing tower above Stabroek market (1880). At the head of Brickdam, one of the main streets, is an aluminium arch commemorating independence. Nearby is a monument to the 1763 slave rebellion, surmounted by an impressive statue of Cuffy, its best-known leader. Near the Pegasus Hotel on High Street is the Umana Yana, a conical thatched structure built by a group of Wai Wai Amerindians using traditional techniques for the 1972 conference of the Non-Aligned Movement.

The National Museum, opposite the post office, houses an idiosyncratic collection of exhibits from Guayana and elsewhere, including a model of Georgetown before the 1945 fire. The Walter Roth Museum of Anthropology has a good collection of Amerindian artefacts.

The Botanical Gardens (entry free), covering 120 acres (50 hectares), are beautifully laid out, with Victorian bridges and pavilions, palms and lily-ponds. Near the south west corner is the residence of the President and there is also a large mausoleum containing the remains of the former president, Forbes Burnham, which is decorated with reliefs depicting scenes from his political career. Look out for the rare cannonball tree (Couroupita Guianensis), named after the appearance of its poisonous fruit. The zoo has a fine collection of local animals and the manatees in the ponds will eat grass from your hand. The police band gives a free concert on Thursdays, 1730-1830. There are also beautiful tropical plants in the Promenade Gardens on Middle Street and in the National Park on Carifesta Avenue.

The Georgetown Cricket Club at Bourda has one of the finest cricket grounds in the tropics. Near the south east corner of the Botanic Gardens is a well-equipped National Sports Centre. Nearby is the Cultural Centre, an impressive air-conditioned theatre with a large stage. Performances are also given at the Playhouse Theatre in Parade Street.

Warning Georgetown is a dangerous city at night, especially during blackouts and periods of reduced electricity. There are frequent "choke and rob" attacks. Don't walk the streets at night; taxis are cheap and easy to find. Most areas are fairly safe by day, provided the usual precautions are taken. Particular care is required around the Stabroek Market area and on Main Street. Avoid Albouystown (south of the centre) and Tiger Bay (along the Demerara River).

Hotels In the following large hotels foreigners have to pay in foreign currency (US, Canadian, East Caribbean, Barbadian or British): *Pegasus*, High St., L+, a/c, pool, restaurant, small rooms; *Park*, Main St., A (some rooms C), a/c, secure, beautiful Victorian ballroom (worth a visit); *Tower*, Main St., A, a/c, recently renovated, lively bar, restaurant, pool open to public, rec; *Woodbine*, New Market St., T 59430, a/c, rec; *Campala*, Camp St., T 52951, modern, a/c, near prison.

There are also many smaller, cheaper hotels which take payment in Guyanese dollars. Recommended are: *Demico*, near Stabroek Market, T 56372, D with a/c, E without; *Waterchris*, Water St., T 71980, E, a/c, good restaurant, friendly; *Rima Guest House*, 92 Middle St., T 57401, F, modernised, good value. Others include: *Belvedere*, Camp St., D, noisy; opposite is *Alpha Guest House*, E, 2nd floor with shower and mosquito net (no fan), 1st floor cheaper but usually short stay, bar downstairs; *Penthouse*, D; *La Chalet*, D; *Waggon Wheel*, E, noisy; *Le Grille*, 176 Middle St., T 57493, D, repeated reports of theft from rooms; *Chinese Dragon*, D, restaurant; *Palm Court*, D; *Roma*, Main St., D, used by short-stay clients; *Elizabeth Guest House*, Wellington St. Many small hotels and guest houses are full of long-stay residents, while some are rented by the hour. Try to book in advance. If in doubt, go to a larger hotel for first night and look around next day in daylight.

Restaurants Eating out is very cheap at present because of the favourable exchange rate. Best in town are *Del Casa* and *Caribbean Rose*, both on Middle St., US$10; also rec. are *Palm Court*, Main St., and the *Tower Hotel* restaurant, both US$4; and *Arawak Steak House*, in roof garden above *Demico Hotel*. Buffet breakfast at *Woodbine Hotel*, US$2.40; breakfast at *Waterchris* US$1. Good lunches for around US$2 at the *Rice Bowl* and *Country Pride*, both in Robb St., the *Coalpot* in New Town and *Hack's Hallai* (all of these close in the evening). Many Chinese restaurants, inc. *Kwang Chow*, Camp St., *Double Dragon*, Av. of the Republic; and *Diamond Food House*, 9 Camp St. For late night eating there are several Chinese restaurants on Sheriff St. inc. *Double Happiness*. For fast food, try *Red Rooster*, Regent St.; *Arapaima*, Main St.; *Idaho*, Brickdam; *Forest Hills*, Camp St.; *Calypso*, Regent St.

Night Life Georgetown is surprisingly lively at night, mainly with gold miners, traders and overseas Guyanese throwing US$ around. Liveliest disco is *Hollywood*, Camp St., though The *Library*, also on Camp St, *The Cave*, Regent St. and *The Dark*, in the *Park Hotel*, are also lively. *Palm Court Bar*, Main Street; *Mingles*, Crown St., is a good bar with live music and dancing (entrance US$0.40). Near the Kitty Market are *Jazzy Jacks*, Alexander St., and *We Place*, Lamaha St, but this area is unsafe unless you go with locals. Sheriff St., is some way from the centre but is "the street that never sleeps" full of late night Chinese restaurants and has some good bars inc. *Tennessee Lounge*, *Burns Beat*, *Halloween Bar* and *Shuttle Club*.

Shopping Normal shopping hours are 0900-1700 (Sat. 0900-1300). The main shopping area is Regent St. The two main department stores are *Guyana Stores* in Church St., and *Fogarty's*, but neither has a wide range of goods. Most Guyanese do their regular shopping at the four big markets—Stabroek, Bourda, La Penitence and Kitty. Craft items are a good buy; Amerindian basketwork, hammocks, wood carvings, pottery, and small figures made out of Balata, a rubbery substance tapped from trees in the interior. *Houseproud*, on Avenue of the Republic has a good selection of craftwork, but there are many other craft shops inc. *Creations*, near *Fogarty's*. Gold is also sold widely, often at good prices but make sure you know what you are buying. Imported goods are available for foreign currency at *Sijan Plaza*. Developing film takes time and is not always reliable—*Risans* on Main St. rec. as quick and efficient.

Bookshops Some interesting local books in *Houseproud*. Try also *GNTC* on Water St., *Argosy* and *Kharg* both on Regent St., *Dimension* on Cummings St., as well as *Guyana Stores* and *Fogarty's*.

Local Transport Car hire is virtually impossible. Minibuses run regularly to most parts of the city, mostly from Stabroek market or Avenue of the Republic, standard fare US$0.20. It is difficult to get a seat during rush hours. Taxis charge US$1.20 for short journeys, US$2.20 for longer runs, with higher rates at night and outside the city limits.

Exchange National Bank of Industry and Commerce; Guyana Bank of Trade and Industry; Bank of Baroda; Bank of Nova Scotia. Bank hours are 0800-1230 Mon.-Fri., plus 1500-1700 on Fri. Exchange houses (*cambios*) in shops may be open longer hours.

Embassies and Consulates There are a surprisingly large number of embassies, including: **British High Commission** (Main St.); **Canadian High Commission** (Young St.) and the Embassies of the **United States** (Main St, though moving to a new building near the sea wall), **Venezuela** (Thomas St.), **Brazil** (Church St.), **Cuba** (Main St.) and **Suriname** (Turkeyan).

Post Office Main one on Avenue of the Republic, slow service.

Churches Anglican: St. Georges Cathedral, Christ Church, Waterloo Street; St. Andrews (Presbyterian), Avenue of the Republic; Roman Catholic Cathedral, Brickdam.

Travel Agencies Try *Frandec Travel Service*, Main St., repeatedly rec.; *M's Tour Service*, 66 First Av., Subryanville, T 62860.

Bus Services There are regular services by minibuses and collective taxis to most coastal towns from the Stabroek Market. To Rosignol (for New Amsterdam, Springlands and Suriname), 1½ hrs, US$1.50; to Parika US$2; to Linden US$2.

Airport The international airport is at Timehri, 25 miles south of Georgetown. Minibus No. 42 to Georgetown US$0.40, taxi US$4-5. There is a small duty-free shop where local goods are reportedly slightly cheaper than in the capital and an exchange house, open at times of incoming flights. (For internal flights see **Information for Visitors**).

Linden (pop. 30,000), the second-largest town in Guyana, is a bauxite mining town 70 miles south of Georgetown on the Demerara river. A good (toll) road connects the two towns. On the west bank of the river, Linden is a company mining town with an executive area and golf course. Across the river (bridge or ferry) are the poorer suburbs of Wismar and Christianburg. The town is dominated by a disused alumina plant and scarred by old bauxite pits. Accommodation is scarce (*Mackenzie Hotel*, pleasantly situated on the river, T 04-2183, D; *Hotel Star Bonnett*, clean, good lunches).

From Linden rough roads suitable for four-wheel drive vehicles run south to the bauxite mining towns of Ituni and Kwakwani; south to the logging centre at Mabura Hill and on to Kurupukari; and west to Rockstone ferry on the Essequibo river. From Rockstone very bad roads run north to Bartica and south to Issano. It is planned to build a road from Kurupukari south to Annai, Lethem and Boa Vista by 1991, but it is not clear what standard the road will be or when it will be completed.

New Amsterdam (pop. 20,000) is 65 miles south-east of Georgetown on the east bank of the Berbice river, near its mouth. From Georgetown, take a minibus or collective taxi to Rosignol on the west bank of the Berbice, then cross the river by ferry (US$0.10; also takes vehicles). The town is run-down but picturesque.

Hotels *Penguin*, T 03-2012, a/c, D; *Church View Guest House*, D, inc. meals; *Hotel Embassy*, at Rose Hall.

Banks National Bank of Industry and Commerce; Guyana National Commercial Bank; Bank of Baroda.

From New Amsterdam, it is sometimes possible to get a lift on a bauxite barge up the Berbice river to the small mining town of Kwakwani.

The road continues east from New Amsterdam (minibus, US$1), to **Springlands** and Skeldon at the mouth of the Courantyne river. The two towns are officially known as **Corriverton** (Courantyne River Town).

Hotels In Springlands: *Ambassador*, near point for ferry to Nieuw Nickerie; *Swiss Hotel*, Pakistani run, rough but helpful. In Skeldon: *Mahogony*, D, fan, clean, friendly, rec.; *Parapak*, E, no fan, no mosquito net, poor value; *Arawak*, G, rough, avoid. Several good Chinese restaurants within a few blocks of Springlands town centre.

Exchange National Bank of Industry and Commerce; Guyana National Commercial Bank. *Cambio* (National Bank of Industry and Commerce) at Skeldon for arriving ferry passengers.

Transport To Georgetown by minibus to New Amsterdam, ferry to Rosignol and minibus from Rosignol, US$2.50.

Crossing to Suriname Before you leave Georgetown, check with the Suriname embassy whether you need a visa. From Springlands there is a daily ferry (not Sunday or national holidays of either country) to Nieuw Nickerie (foot passengers only). Queue at the booking office near the jetty from 0700, office opens 0800, booking fee US$0.25, all passports must be present when booking, tickets are sold later on the ferry, US$7 one way, payable in Suriname guilders only.

Immigration and customs formalities (very slow and thorough) take place from 0900, ferry sails from 1100 depending on tides and weather, crossing time normally 2 hours. (A new ferry, partly paid for by the EEC, was due to replace this service in 1990).

Travelling west from Georgetown, the road crosses the Demerara bridge (toll) and continues to **Parika**, a small town on the east bank of the Essequibo river. If you need accommodation, there are two small brothels where you can stay fairly safely. From here ferries cross the river to Adventure on the west bank at 1700 daily and 0830 Wed. and Fri., returning at 0300 daily and 1330 Wed. and Fri. (See *Three Singles to Adventure* by Gerald Durrell). There are also three ferries a day to Leguan Island (½ hr, US$0.25); accommodation available at the *Hotel President*.

From Parika there is also a ferry up the Essequibo river to Bartica on Tues. and Fri. at 0700, Sat. 1330, returning on Mon. and Thurs. at 0930, Sat. 0815, US$1 one way. The 36 mile journey takes 6 hours, stopping at Fort Island where you can buy sweetcorn and pastries; small boats come out from riverside settlements to load up with fruit. Local people generally prefer to take a speedboat, US$5 p.p., 2 hours.

Bartica, at the junction of the Essequibo and Mazaruni rivers, is the "take-off" town for the gold and diamond fields, Kaieteur Falls, and the interior generally. Here an Amazon-like mass of waters meets, but with an effect vastly more beautiful, for they are coloured the "glossy copper" of all Guyanese rivers and not the dull mud-brown of most of the Amazon. Swimming very good. There is a direct weekly ferry connection with Georgetown.

Hotels *Marin; **The Nest** on Fifth Avenue, E, unsafe, very noisy, meals to be had from disco after 1730, or "Robbie's". **Modern**, near ferry, good food. Book ahead if possible. Mrs Payne, near Hospital, basic, clean.

The Essequibo is navigable to large boats for some miles above Bartica. The Cuyuni flows into the Mazaruni 3 miles above Bartica, and above this confluence the Mazaruni is impeded for 120 miles by thousands of islands, rapids and waterfalls. To avoid this stretch of treacherous river a road has been built from Bartica to Issano, where boats can be taken up the more tranquil upper Mazaruni.

The **Kaieteur Falls**, on the Potaro River, rank with the Niagara, Victoria, and Iguazú Falls in majesty and beauty, but have the added attraction of being surrounded by unspoilt forest. The Falls, nearly five times the height of Niagara, with a sheer drop of 228 metres, are nearly 100 metres wide. They are unspoilt because of their isolation. M's Tour Service and Pisces, both in Georgetown, sometimes arrange tours depending on demand for about US$100 p.p. or you can charter a small plane in Georgetown.

The overland route to the falls takes 7-10 days. In Bartica ask around for trucks (which can be hired for around US$200) or for gold prospectors going to the Mahdia area. The journey to Kangaruma (government rest house, F, reservations can be made by radio from Georgetown) is 113 miles, via Garraway Stream with its fine suspension bridge over the Potaro, along a very poor jungle road which is often impassable especially during the rainy season and can take over 7 hours. From Kangaruma take a boat up the river (with portages around the Amatuk and Waratuk Falls) to Tukeit (government rest house, F, take your own food). The climb to the top of the Kaieteur Falls takes at least two hours but is worth it to watch the blue, white and brown water tumbling into a stupendous gorge. The rest house at the top of the Falls is closed. It is also possible to walk to the Falls from Mahdia—allow 4-6 days each way. Avoid April and October, which are the dry months when the flow of the falls is reduced, and June, which is the height of the wet season when the route is impassable.

The Kaieteur Falls lie within the **Kaieteur National Park**, where there is a variety of wildlife—tapirs, ocelots, monkeys, armadillos, anteaters, and jungle and river birds. The Pakaraima Mountains stretch from Kaieteur westwards to include the highest peak in Guyana, Mt. Roraima, the possible inspiration for Conan Doyle's *Lost World* (**see page** 1095). Roraima is very difficult to climb from the

Guyanese side.

There are several other spectacular waterfalls in the interior, including Imbaimadai and Oronduik, but none is very easy to reach.

Precautions Permits are required for travelling in many parts of the interior—obtainable from the Department of the Interior, Water Street, Georgetown. Detailed planning and a guide are essential. Take adequate supplies of food and drink, a sleeping bag, a sheet and blanket, a mosquito net, and kerosene for Tilley lamps.

The north-western coastal area is mainly accessible by boat only. From **Adventure** on the west bank of the Essequibo a road runs north through Anna Regina. Nearby is Lake Mainstay, a small resort, reached by taxi; it is also known as the hot and cold lake because it varies in temperature from one place to another. Then goes on to **Charity**, a pleasant little town with two small hotels and a lively market on Mondays.

Near the border with Venezuela is the small port of **Morawhanna** (Morajuana to the Venezuelans), which may be reached by an unreliable ferry from Georgetown. Mark Wilson reports that the journey is surprisingly rough and that "you will have to fight for hammock space and watch your possessions like a hawk". From Morawhanna boats sail up the river to Port Kaituma, 40 miles inland, from where a small passenger railway connects with the isolated settlement of Matthews Ridge (more easily reached by chartered aircraft from Georgetown). The site of the Jonestown mass-suicide is nearby.

The **Rupununi Savanna** in the south west is an extensive area of dry grassland with scattered trees, termite mounds and wooded hills. The freshwater creeks, lined with Ite palms, are good for swimming. The region is scattered with occasional Amerindian villages and a few large cattle ranches which date from the late nineteenth century: the descendants of some of the Scots settlers still live here. Between the 1920s and 1950s a rough cattle trail led to the coastal region, but this has since reverted to bush. Balata, a rubbery substance bled from trees, was once a source of income but it no longer has commercial value, having been replaced by synthetic substances; craft items are still made from it. Most of the airstrips used to transport balata are now closed. Links with Brazil are much closer than with the Guyanese coast; many people speak Portuguese and most trade, both legal and illegal, is with Brazil.

Avoid visiting the Rupununi in the wet season (May to August) as much of the Savanna is flooded and malaria mosquitoes widespread.

Lethem, a small but scattered town on the Brazilian frontier, is the service centre for the Rupununi and for trade with Brazil. There are a few stores, a small hospital, a police station and government offices which have radio telephone links with Georgetown. About 1½ miles south of town at St Ignatius there is a Jesuit mission dating from 1911.

A road link between Lethem and the Guyanese coast via Kurupakari and Linden is planned to open in 1991. Skyvan and regular charter planes link the town with Georgetown, about US$60 one way. Chartering an 8 seater plane from Georgetown to Lethem costs about US$800 round trip—pay extra for a detour over the Kaieteur Falls en route. Seats on private charter flights are often available for US$0.50 per pound bodyweight and luggage—travel light and don't eat breakfast.

Transport around the Rupununi is difficult; there are a few four-wheel drive vehicles, but ox-carts and bicycles are more common on the rough roads. From Lethem trucks can be hired for day-trips to the Moco-Moco Falls and the Kamu Falls and to the Kanuku Mountains. Trucks may also be hired to visit Aishalton, 70 miles south along a very bad road, 6 hour journey, US$260; and to Annai, 60 miles north east along a better road, 3 hour journey, US$110. An interesting trip is to the Amerindian village of Yukupari, where the Alan Knight Training Centre, a theological college training Amerindians for the Anglican priesthood, is always happy to see visitors and can, on occasion, provide accommodation for stranded travellers.

Truck-hire and tours can be arranged through Don and Shirley Melville, who run a bar near the air-strip in Lethem.

To visit Amerindian villages, a special permit must be obtained from the District Council in Revolution Square, Lethem.

An extraordinary account of an overland journey from Georgetown to the Rupununi and on to Boa Vista in the 1930s is to be found in *Ninety-Two Days* by Evelyn Waugh.

Hotels in the Rupununi In Lethem: Mr Arthur Bobb's *Takutu Hotel*, near airfield, C, full board, reports of theft; *Cacique Guesthouse*, F, full board also available, clean, highly rec.; try also the government rest house next to Guyana Stores, F, good meals, clean, efficient, rec. The *Manari Ranch Hotel*, 7 miles north of Lethem, D p.p. inc. meals, creek for swimming, rec. *Dadanawa Ranch*, 50 miles south of Lethem, takes guests and organises tours, as does Diane McTurk at *Karanambo Ranch*, 50 miles north-east of Lethem; they can both be contacted via Peter Seabra in the offices of the Rupununi Livestock Producers' Association, above Gapoor's shop, America Street, Georgetown.

Exchange Mr Jardin, the Portuguese shopkeeper, may exchange travellers' cheques (technically illegal), at a poor rate; Mr Mahoney gives better rates for cash. Changing money is much better on the Brazilian side of the frontier.

Crossing to Brazil Formalities are generally reported to be very lax on both sides of the border, but it is important to observe them as there are reports of people being refused entry to Guyana for not having the correct papers, including visa. In Lethem all procedures are dealt with at the police station; report there also with a visa if arriving from Brazil. The Takutu river, the frontier between the two countries, is about 1 mile north of Lethem (taxis available). There are small boats for foot passengers and a pontoon for vehicles. Just over the river is a shop and the Brazilian customs post. From here it is 1½ mile walk to the village of Bom Fim, from where a bus leaves for Boa Vista at 0800 (from Boa Vista to Bom Fim at 1600), 3½ hours, US$10. (Note that Brazilian time is one hour behind Guyanese time).

INFORMATION FOR VISITORS

Documents All visitors require passports and all, apart from nationals of Caribbean Community countries, require visas, obtainable from Embassies, High Commissions and Consulates in London, Washington, Port of Spain, Bridgetown, Caracas, Brasília, Paramaribo and elsewhere. Visas cost US$3 and two photos, an onward ticket and yellow fever certificate are required. Visitors arriving without visas are refused entry.

A permit from the Department of the Interior, Water St., Georgetown, is required for visiting the interior. This may take some time to obtain.

Taxes There is an airport tax of US$3, payable in Guyanese dollars, and a 10% tax on international airline tickets bought in the country.

International Air Services There are no direct flights to Guyana from either Europe or North America. BWIA flies to Guyana from Trinidad five times a week, LIAT flies from Barbados three times a week and Cubana from Cuba and Barbados fortnightly. There are also weekly flights from Caracas by Aeropostal and from Boa Vista and Manaus by Varig. Suriname Airways flies three times a week from Paramaribo, but these flights are difficult to book from outside the Guianas. Guyana Airways run no international or internal flights and operate mainly as a handling agency.

Flights are often booked weeks in advance, especially at Christmas when overseas Guyanese return to visit relatives. Flights are frequently overbooked, so it is essential to reconfirm your outward flight and difficult to change your travel plans at the last minute. Foreigners must pay for airline tickets in US$ or other specified currencies. Luggage should be securely locked as theft from checked-in baggage is common.

Customs Baggage examination is very thorough. Jewellery and foreign currency must be declared on arrival or else you will not be allowed to take them out of the country. Duties are high on goods imported in commercial quantities.

Internal Air Services There are no scheduled internal services. The Civil Aviation Department, Wright's Lane, Georgetown, operates a Skyvan service from Ogle airfield, east of Georgetown, to Lethem, US$60 one way. There are also several charter companies, including Mazerally, Air Service, Correia and Sankar. Surplus seats on privately chartered flights are sometimes available and are advertised in the press.

Road Transport Most coastal towns are linked by a good 185 mile road from Springlands in the east to Charity in the west; the Berbice and Essequibo rivers are crossed by ferries, the Demerara by a toll bridge near Georgetown. Apart from a good road connecting Georgetown and Bartica, most other roads in the interior are very poor. Car hire is virtually impossible. There are shortages of car spares. Gasoline costs US$1.20 a gallon but is subject to periodic shortages. Traffic drives on the left. Minibuses and collective taxis run between Georgetown and most towns in the coastal belt.

River Transport There are over 600 miles of navigable river, which provide an important means of communication. Ferries and river boats are referred to in the text, but for further details contact the Transport and Harbours Department, Water St., Georgetown. Note that there is no vehicle ferry across the Courantyne to Suriname.

Accommodation The largest hotels in Georgetown have their own emergency electricity generators and water pumps to deal with the frequent interruptions in supply. Other hotels usually provide a bucket of water in your room—fill this up when water is available. When booking an air-conditioned room, make sure it also has natural ventilation.

Food and Drink The blend of different national influences—Indian, African, Chinese, Creole, English, Portuguese, Amerindian, North American—gives a distinctive flavour to Guyanese cuisine. One well-known dish, traditional at Christmas, is pepper-pot, meat cooked in bitter cassava juice with peppers and herbs. Seafood is plentiful and varied, as is the wide variety of tropical fruits and vegetables. Staple foods are rice and long thin bora beans. The food shortages and import ban of the early 1980s have ended, but they did have the positive effect of encouraging experimentation with local ingredients, sometimes with interesting results. In the interior wild meat is often available—try wild cow, or else labba (a small rodent).

Rum is the most popular drink. There is a wide variety of brands, all cheap, including the best which are very good and cost less than US$2 a bottle. High wine is a strong local rum. There is also local brandy and whisky (Diamond Club), which are worth trying. The local beer, Banks, made partly from rice is acceptable and cheap. There is a wide variety of fruit juices.

Health There is a high risk of both types of malaria in the interior, especially in the wet season. Recommended prophylaxis is chloroquine 500 mg weekly plus paludrine 200 mg daily. If travelling to the interior for long periods carry drugs for treatment as these may not be available. Sleep under a mosquito net. Although there are plenty of mosquitoes on the coast, they are not malarial.

There is some risk of typhoid and water-borne diseases owing to low water pressure. Local people and many foreigners drink water with impunity, but purification tablets are a good idea. Tapwater is sometimes brown and contains sediment, but this is not a cause for concern. The Georgetown Hospital is run down, understaffed and lacking equipment, but there are a number of well-equipped private hospitals, including St Joseph's on Parade St., Kingston; Prasad's on Thomas St.; and the Davis Memorial Hospital on Lodge Backlands. Charges are US$2 to US$8 per day and medical consultations cost US$2 to US$4. If admitted to hospital you are expected to provide your own sheets and food (St.

Joseph's provides all these).

Travellers should examine shower pipes, bedding, shoes and clothing for snakes, especially in the interior.

Public Holidays 1 January, New Years' Day; 23 February, Republic Day and Mashramani festival; Good Friday, Easter Monday; Labour Day, 1 May; Caricom Day, first Monday in July; Freedom Day, first Monday in August; Christmas Day, 25 December, and Boxing Day, 26 December.

The following public holidays are for Hindu and Muslim festivals; they follow a lunar calender, and dates should be checked as required: Phagwah, usually March; Eid el Fitr, end of Ramadan; Eid el Azah; Youm un Nabi; Deepavali, usually November.

Note that the Republic Day celebrations last about a week: during this time hotels in Georgetown are very full.

Official Time 3 hrs behind GMT; one hour ahead of neighbouring regions of Brazil, Venezuela and Trinidad.

Currency The unit is the Guyanese dollar. There are notes for 1, 5, 10, 20 and 100 dollars, though devaluation and inflation mean that even the largest of these is worth very little. Coins for amounts under a dollar exist but are of little practical use.

The official exchange rate is G$45 = US$1, but licensed exchange houses (known as *cambios*) are allowed to buy and sell currency at their own rates. In June 1990 the cambio rate was around G$65 = US$1. At present *cambios* only buy US or Canadian dollars and pounds sterling. Most *cambios* accept drafts (subject to verification), travellers' cheques and telegraphic transfers, but not credit cards. Rates vary slightly between *cambios* and from day to day and some *cambios* offer better rates for changing over US$100. Note that to sell Guyanese dollars on leaving the country, you will need to produce your *cambio* receipt. The illegal black market on America St. ("Wall Street") in Georgetown still operates, but the rates offered are not significantly better than the *cambio* rate and there is a strong risk of being robbed or cheated.

Cost of Living The cambio rate means that, for foreigners, prices are very low at present. Even imported goods may be cheaper than elsewhere and locally produced goods such as fruit are very cheap. For Guyanese dependent on local salaries, the country is expensive and becoming more so with rising inflation.

Weights and Measures Although Guyana went metric in 1982, imperial measures are still widely used.

Voltage 100 v in Georgetown; 220 v in most other places, including some Georgetown suburbs.

Postal and Telephone Services Overseas postal and telephone charges are very low. There are no public telephones. Some businesses and hotels may allow you to use their phone for local calls if you are buying something—usual charge about US$0.05. Overseas calls can be made from the Guyana International Telecommunications Corporation office in the Bank of Guyana building (arrive early and be prepared for a long wait), or from the *Tower Hotel* (more expensive but more comfortable). Travel agencies may allow you to make overseas collect calls when buying tickets. International calls from private houses and from outside Georgetown are practically impossible.

Press *The Chronicle*, daily, government-run; *The Mirror*, weekly, opposition PPP-run; *The Stabroek News*, twice a week, independent; *The Catholic Standard*, weekly, well-respected and widely read. Street vendors charge more than the cover price—this is normal and helps them make a living.

Broadcasting There are two TV channels, mainly broadcasting programmes from US satellite television. GBC Radio is government-run and is often difficult to receive.

Things to Take Take a good supply of small gift items (e.g. imported cigarettes, batteries, good quality toiletries); these won't be asked for but will be well received. A good torch (for the electricity cuts) is essential.

SURINAME

SURINAME has a coast line on the Atlantic to the N; it is bounded on the W by Guyana and on the E by French Guyane; Brazil is to the S. Its area is 163,820 sq. km.

The principal rivers in the country are the Marowijne in the E, the Corantijn in the W, and the Suriname, Commewijne (with its tributary, the Cottica), Coppename, Saramacca and Nickerie. The country is divided into topographically quite diverse natural regions: lowland, savanna, and highland.

The northern part of the country consists of lowland, with a width in the E of 25 km., and in the W of about 80 km. The soil (clay) is covered with swamps with a layer of humus under them. Marks of the old sea-shores can be seen in the shell and sand ridges, overgrown with tall trees.

There follows a region, 5-6 km. wide, of a loamy and very white sandy soil, then a slightly undulating region, about 30 km. wide. It is mainly savanna, mostly covered with quartz sand, and overgrown with grass and shrubs.

South of this lies the interior highland, almost entirely overgrown with dense tropical forest and intersected by streams. At the southern boundary with Brazil there are again savannas. These, however, differ in soil and vegetation from the northern ones. A large area in the SW is in dispute between Guyana and Suriname. There is a less serious border dispute with Guyane in the SE.

Climate Tropical and moist, but not very hot, since the north-east trade wind makes itself felt during the whole year. In the coastal area the temperature varies on an average from 23° to 31°C, during the day; the annual mean is 27°C, and the monthly mean ranges from 26° to 28°C, only. The mean annual rainfall is about 2,340 mm. for Paramaribo and 1,930 mm for the western division. The seasons are: minor rainy season, November-February; minor dry season, February-April; main rainy season, April-August; main dry season, August-November. None of these seasons is, however, usually either very dry or very wet. The degree of cloudiness is fairly high and the average humidity is 82%. The climate of the interior is similar but with higher rainfall.

History Although Amsterdam merchants had been trading with the "wild coast" of Guiana as early as 1613 (the name Parmurbo-Paramaribo was already known) it was not until 1630 that 60 English settlers came to Suriname under Captain Marshall and planted tobacco. The real founder of the colony was Baron Willoughby of Parham, governor of Barbados, who sent an expedition to Suriname in 1651 under Anthony Rowse to find a suitable place for settlement. Willoughbyland became an agricultural colony with 500 little sugar plantations, 1,000 white inhabitants and 2,000 African slaves. Jews from Holland and Italy joined them, as well as Dutch Jews ejected from Brazil after 1654. On 27 February, 1667, Admiral Crynssen conquered the colony for the states of Zeeland and Willoughbyfort became the present Fort Zeelandia. By the Peace of Breda—31 July, 1667—it was agreed that Suriname should remain with the Netherlands, while Nieuw Amsterdam (New York) should be given to England. The colony was conquered by the British in 1799, and not until the Treaty of Paris in 1814 was it finally restored to the Netherlands. Slavery was forbidden in 1818 and formally abolished in 1863. Indentured labour from China and the East Indies took its place.

On 25 November, 1975, the country became an independent republic, which signed a treaty with the Netherlands for an economic aid programme worth US$1.5bn until 1985. A military coup on 25 February, 1980 overthrew the elected government. A state of emergency was declared, with censorship for press, radio and TV. The military leader, Col. Desi Bouterse, and his associates came under pressure from the Dutch and the USA as a result of dictatorial tendencies. After the execution of 15 opposition leaders on 8 December, 1982, the Netherlands broke off relations and suspended its aid programme, which was restored in 1988.

The ban on political parties was lifted in late 1985 and a new constitution was drafted. As a result of these movements towards redemocratization the Dutch Government announced the resumption of partial economic aid early in 1986, but later in that year, guerrilla rebels (the Jungle Commando), led by a former bodyguard of Col. Bouterse, Ronny Brunswijk, mounted a campaign to overthrow the government, disrupting both plans for political change, and the economy. Nevertheless, elections for the National Assembly were held in November 1987. A three-party coalition (the Front for Democracy and Development) gained a landslide victory over the military, winning 40 of the 51 seats. In January 1988, a former agriculture minister, Mr Ramsewak Shankar, was elected President by the Assembly for a 5-year term. Although a basis for peace was drawn up in mid-1989 (the Kourou Accord), tension had not diminished a year later, with a number of factions fighting to achieve various political ends. The relationships between the different groups, Government, army, Jungle Commando, bush blacks and Amerindians, were complex, with the added dimension of involvement by some groups in the cocaine trade undermining efforts to end the civil war.

Population The 1980 census showed that the population had declined to 352,041, because of heavy emigration to the Netherlands. By 1989 it was estimated to have grown to 362,000. The 1983 population consisted of East Indians (known locally as Hindustanis), 37%; Creoles (European-African and other descent), 31%; Indonesians, 14%; Chinese, 3%; Amerindians, 3%, and Bush Blacks (retribalized descendants of slaves who escaped in the 17th century, living on the upper Saramacca, Suriname and Marowijne rivers), 8.5%; Europeans and others, 3%. About 90% of the existing population live in or around Paramaribo or in the coastal towns; the remainder, mostly Carib and Arawak Indians and Bush Blacks, are widely scattered. Life expectancy 68 years; birth rate, 29.5 per 1,000; death rate, 6.1 per 1,000; infant mortality 27.6 per thousand; literacy, 80.2%.

The Asian people originally entered the country as contracted estate labourers, and settled in agriculture or commerce after completion of their term. They dominate the countryside, whereas Paramaribo is a predominantly Creole city. One of Suriname's main problems is the racial tension between Creoles and East Indians.

The official language is Dutch. The native dialect, called negro English (Sranan Tongo or Taki-Taki) originally the speech of the Creoles, is now a *lingua franca* understood by all groups, and standard English is widely spoken and understood. The Asians still speak their own languages among themselves.

The Economy Agriculture is restricted to some districts of the alluvial coastal zone, covering about 0.8m hectares and employing about 16.7% of the labour force. At least two-thirds of permanent crop and arable land is under irrigation. Farming accounts for 9.4% of gdp and 10% of exports. The main crops are rice (the staple), sugar cane and citrus fruits, all of which are exported to Europe, along with small quantities of coffee and bananas. Apart from rice, Suriname is a net importer of food; priority is being given to rice and livestock. Between 1981 and 1983, the sector registered annual declines in output, but after 1984, positive growth was restored with the rice and shrimp sectors receiving new incentives. Suriname has vast timber resources, but exports account for only 1.1% of the total and development has been hampered by a lack of investment. There is a small fishing industry, the chief catch being shrimps.

Manufacturing's contribution to gdp is 16.0%, employing 10.6% of the workforce. Import substitution, using both imported goods and local raw materials, is the main activity, with food processing accounting for 60% of the total.

Suriname is the world's sixth largest producer of bauxite, with reserves estimated at 1.9% of the world's total. The country has the capability to process the extracted ore into alumina and aluminium ingot. The bauxite/aluminium industry accounts for 80% of exports, while the mining sector as a whole contributes 6.6% of gdp and employs 4.0% of the workforce. Two companies control the industry, the Suriname Aluminium Company (Suralco), a subsidiary of Alcoa, and Billiton Maatschappij, part of Royal Dutch Shell. Their progressive merging of operations to improve competitiveness on world markets began to yield positive results in 1986 until the industry was severely disrupted by the civil war which started in that year.

Oil production from the Tambaredjo heavy oil deposit, operated by the state oil company, Staatsolie, is about 2,000 bpd. Exploratory wells in the Saramacca district have also yielded oil. Installed electricity generating capacity is 415 MW, of which 54% is thermal, 46% hydroelectric.

In 1988 growth began to recover, after 5 years of decline and a fall in gdp of 8.1% in 1987 alone, helped by resumption of activity in the bauxite industry, the attenuation of the domestic insurgency and the resumption of aid from the Dutch Government. The newly elected Government managed to stabilize the parallel exchange market and lowered political and economic uncertainties, but was under pressure from The Netherlands to devalue and reduce state involvement in the economy.

Government There is one legislative house, the National Assembly, which has 51 members. The President is both head of state and government. Suriname is divided into ten districts, of which the capital is one.

Warning: Those caught taking pictures of Fort Zeelandia, the People's Palace, police stations, military installations etc. face confiscation of their film, at least. Be careful also when taking pictures from ferries.

As a result of the civil war which began in 1986, the interior and east of the country were closed to travellers; only the Nieuw Nickerie-Paramaribo route was open. We retain our information on other places in the hope that the situation will improve (peace had not been restored by July 1990).

Paramaribo, the capital and chief port, lies on the Suriname river, 12 km. from the sea. It has a population of about 192,000, mainly Creoles. There are many attractive colonial buildings.

The People's Palace (the old Governor's Mansion) is on Eenheidsplein (formerly Onafhankelijkheidsplein, and before that, Oranjeplein) and many beautiful 18th and 19th century buildings in Dutch (neo-Normanic) style are in the same area. The recently restored Fort Zeelandia used to house the Suriname Museum, but the fort has been repossessed by the military (the whole area is fenced off); very few exhibits remain in the old museum in the residential suburb of Zorg-en-Hoop. Look for Mr. F. Lim-A-Po-straat if you wish to see what Paramaribo looked like only a comparatively short time ago. The nineteenth-century Roman Catholic Peter and Paul cathedral, said to be the largest wooden building in the Americas, is built entirely of wood and is well worth a visit. Much of the old town and its churches have been restored, and date only from the nineteenth century. Other things to see are the colourful market and the waterfront, Hindu temples in Koningstraat, the Caribbean's largest mosque at Keizerstraat and the Synagogue (1854) at Heerenstraat (under renovation and closed in 1989). A new harbour has been constructed about 1½ km. upstream. Two pleasant parks are the Palmentuin and the Cultuurtuin (with zoo, US$1.20, busy on Sun.)—but the latter is quite a distance from the town and there are no buses to it. National dress is normally only worn by the Asians on national holidays and at wedding parties, but some Javanese women still go about in sarong and klambi. A university was opened in 1968. There is one public swimming pool at Weidestraat, US$0.60 p.p. There is an exotic Asian flavour to the market and nearby streets. Cinemas show US, Indian and Chinese movies, with subtitles.

Hotels *Krasnapolsky*, (T 74050) A, swimming pool and shops, good breakfast, launderette on 1st floor, and bank (open until 1430); *Torarica*, A-L, swimming pool, casino, nightclub, tropical gardens, fully air conditioned, central, the largest breakfast US$2 (T 71500); *Ambassador*, A (T 77555), Sophie-Redmondstraat, friendly, clean, restaurant, under new management; *Riverclub*, at Leonsberg (8 km. from city), B, many very-short-stay customers, swimming pool; *Lashley*, B-D. All have a/c. Service charge at hotels is 10-15%.

For budget travellers, best is still the recently refurbished *YWCA Guesthouse* at Heerenstraat 11, D (at official exchange rate), cheaper weekly rates, clean, full of permanent residents, essential to book in advance (office open 0800-1400); if it's full try the *Graaf Van Zinzendorff-Herberg* at Gravenstraat 100, the same price as the YWCA. Advance booking advisable. Otherwise, try *Continental Inn*, E; *Fanna*, Princessestraat 31, C, clean, friendly; *Au Soleil Levant*, E. *La Vida* on the way in from the airport is "cheap but nice". *Blue Moon*, D, overpriced, fleas; *Balden*, Kwathweg 183, 2 km. from centre on the road to Nickerie is probably the cheapest available accommodation; its Chinese restaurant serves cheap meals. Beware: many cheap hotels not listed above are "hot pillow" establishments. The *Salvation Army* will give the hard up a bed for Sf4.50 a night (Saramaccastraat).

Restaurants There are some good restaurants, mainly Indonesian and Chinese dishes. Try a rijsttafel in an Indonesian restaurant, best is *Sarinah* (open-air dining), Verlengde Gemenelandsweg 187. A good restaurant is the *Bali*, Dr J. F. Nassy Laan 5; *Fa Tai*, Maagdenstraat 64, air conditioned; *Tai Toong*, Keizerstraat (good and interesting); for the best Chinese food, but not cheap, try *Iwan's*, Grote Hofstraat, or *Sheraton* (no relation), Heiligenweg. Many other Chinese restaurants: *Chi Wan* for its egg foo yung and won ton soup, Keizerstraat and Zwartenhovenbrugstraat 16. The *YWCA Cafeteria* is quite good. Meat and noodles from stalls in the market costs Sf3.00. Along the river there are cheap Javanese foodstalls, lit at night by candles. Try bami (spicy noodles) for Sf1 and petjil (vegetables) for Sf0.50. Especially rec. on Sundays when the area is busiest. In restaurants a dish to try is gadogado, an Indonesian vegetable and peanut concoction, available for about Sf5. Good places for lunch include *Orlando's* opposite the Post Office and *Hola's Terrace*, Domineestraat. For breakfast, try *Lie a Loi*, Heerenstraat, or *Klein Maar Fijn*, Watermolenstraat. The ice-cream parlour in Keizerstraat has been rec. as selling the best ice-cream in the Guianas. A nice place for a drink and dance is *Old Inn Cassiri Club* off the road to Afobakka.

Shopping Arts & Crafts, Neumanpad 13a. Amerindian goods, batik prints, carvings, basket work, drums are attractive. Cultuurwinkel, Anton de Kom Straat, bushnegro carvings, also available at Hotel Torarica. Carvings are better value at the workshops on Nieuwe Dominee Straat and the Neumanpad.

Bookshops The two main bookshops are Vaco and Kersten, both on Domineestraat, and both sell English-language books. Also Hoeksteen (Gravenstraat 17) and the kiosk in Krasnapolsky Hotel. Boekhandel Univers N.V., Gravenstraat 61, is recommended for nature, linguistic and scholarly books on Suriname. Second hand books, English and Dutch, are bought and sold in the market. Most bookshops sell a large map of Paramaribo, price US$7.

Local Transport Buses run regularly to most parts of the city; most services leave from Waterkant or Dr. Sophie Redmondstraat. There are also privately run "wild buses", also known as "numbered buses" which run on fixed routes around the city.

Taxis generally have no meters. The price should be agreed on beforehand to avoid trouble. A trip inside the city costs about US$3.

Self-Drive Cars City Taxi charges US$20 a day plus US$0.20 per km. after the first 100 km. Other rental agencies with similar prices: Purperhart, Kariem, Intercar. Kentax (T 72078) is open 24 hours a day. All driving licences accepted, but you need a stamp from the local police and a deposit of US$140-420. Gasoline costs US$0.50 a litre for "regular" and US$0.60 for "extra".

Bicycles Can be bought for about US$50 from A. Seymonson, Rijwielhersteller, Rust en Vredestraat. Recommended rides include to Nieuw Amsterdam, Marienburg, Alkmaar and back via Tamanredjo in the Javanese Commewijne district or from Rust en Werk to Spieringshoek to Reijnsdorp (3½ hours) and return to Leonsberg via ferry, whence it is a 30 minute ride to Paramaribo.

Exchange Algemene Bank Nederland (Kerkplein 1), Surinaamse Bank and Hakrin Bank, 0700-1400. Surinaamse branch in Hotel Krasnapolsky open 0700-1430; 0800-1200 Sat., Amex agents, charges Sf1.30 flat rate commission on each travellers cheque exchanged. Black market (illegal) around Waterkant market.

Church The Anglican Church is St. Bridget's, Hoogestraat 44 (Sunday 0900 service in English).

Golf Club Introduction from a member required.

Tourist Bureau On waterfront, Waterkant 8, T 71163/78421 (P.O.Box 656). Has useful handouts on lodgings in town and rural areas as well as restaurants. Free city map. English spoken, friendly and helpful; organizes tours (4 days at Sf275) and bus journeys.

Tourist Agencies *Stinasu*, the Foundation for Nature Preservation in Suriname, Jongbawstraat 14, offers reasonably priced accommodation and provide tour guides on the extensive nature reserves throughout the country. One can see "true wilderness and wildlife" with them. (*See page* 1120.) Mrs. W. J. Robles-Cornelissen, Rosenveltkade 34, T 74770, organizes excursions to the interior. *Does Travel Service*, Domineestraat. *Saramaccan Jungle Safaris* (John Ligeon), PO Box 676, Zwartenhovenbrugstraat 19, Paramaribo, has been recommended for visits by canoe to Saramaccan Bush Black villages and wildlife tours. *Suriname Safari Tours*.

Bus Services Most westbound buses leave from Waaldijkstraat, including services to Nickerie at 0500, 1100 and 1300 (or earlier if full), US$8 (plus US$5 for large bag), and to Totness at 1300, US$3. To Afobaka via Brokopondo, leaves from Saramaccastraat, at 0700, US$2. To Brownsberg at 0930, US$1.50. In 1989/90 there were no services eastwards to Albina via Moengo. For full details enquire at the tourist office.

Local Shipping The three ferries across the main rivers operate only in daytime (the Paramaribo-Meerzorg ferry until 2200). Two bridges have been built. The Suriname Navigation Co. (SMS) has a daily service, leaving 0700, on the Commewijne river (a nice four-hour trip; one can get off—see below—at *De Nieuwe Grond*, a plantation owned by an English couple, and stay overnight). The SMS has a daily service to Reynsdorp, leaving Paramaribo early in the morning. SMS also has infrequent services on other rivers (Wayombo and Cottica). The coastal service to Nieuw Nickerie has been discontinued, but there is a weekly (Mon.) 36-hour run there over inland waterways (**see page** 1121).

Airports The international airport is Zanderij, 45 km. S. of Paramaribo. Minibus or shared taxi to town costs US$12; ordinary taxi, US$50, regular minibus, marked PZB or POZ, which leaves from the service station 15 minutes' walk from the centre on the south highway, US$0.30, daytime only. De Paarl minibus rec. as cheaper (T 79600).
Money exchange facilities (now compulsory—**see page** 1124): Hakrin Bank between Customs and Immigration (closed Sundays). There is a new guest house near Zanderij airport.
Internal flights leave from Zorg-en-Hoop airfield in a suburb of Paramaribo; in 1988, local flights were restricted to two destinations: Nieuw Nickerie and Apoera.

Note It is advisable to check the weather conditions and probabilities of returning on schedule before you set out on a trip to the interior. Heavy rains can make it impossible for planes to land in some jungle areas; little or no provision is made for such delays and it can be a long and hungry wait for better conditions. Check also that entry to the area you wish to visit is permitted.

Excursions Powaka, about 90 minutes outside the capital, is a primitive village of thatched huts but with electric light and a small church. In the surrounding forest one can pick mangoes and other exotic fruit. By bus, take Route 4, 0800, US$2, or taxi or ferry to Nieuw Amsterdam, the capital of the predominantly Javanese district of Commewijne. There is an open-air museum inside the old fortress (open only in mornings except Fri. 1700-1900), which guarded the confluence of the Suriname and Commewijne rivers. There are some old plantation mansions left in the Commewijne district which are of interest; Mariënburg is the last sugar estate in operation in Suriname.
By private car to **Jodensavanne** (Jews' Savanna, established 1639), S of Paramaribo on the opposite bank of the Suriname river, where part of one of the oldest synagogues in the Western Hemisphere has been restored. It has a small museum. There are interesting Amerindian villages nearby. You need permission from the Forestry Department (LBB), in Jongbawstraat, to use the ferry to Jodensavanne. There is a new guesthouse, D (with six rooms), at Blakkawatra, nearby. Accommodation is available through Stinasu (see above) and camping is possible. Near Zanderij Airport there is a resort called Kola Kreek, with swimming area.
By bus or car to **Afobakka**, where there is a large hydro-electric dam on the

Suriname river. There is a government guesthouse, C (including 3 meals a day) in nearby **Brokopondo**. Victoria is an oil-palm plantation in the same area. The Brownsberg National Park is one hour by car from here.

The narrow-gauge railway, originally built for the Lawa goldfields, between Onverwacht (½ hour from Paramaribo by bus, Sf1, route PBO) and Brownsweg (87 km.) is no longer in operation. There is no hotel at Brownsweg, but transport (14 km. up hill) to **Brownsberg**, where there is accommodation, can be arranged, US$20 (T 75845, Ext 34). The return bus is supposed to leave at 1100. Guest house, C. A bus to Paramaribo leaves Brownsweg every morning (price doubles between low and high seasons—**see page** 1123).

Stinasu arranges trips to the Brownsberg Park (entry US$1) as well as the Raleigh Falls/Voltzberg Nature Reserve on the Coppename river (good swimming), the Wia-Wia reserve on the northeast coast where giant sea-turtles nest, and the Galibi reserve on the Marowijne river, another nesting place for turtles. There is accommodation of sorts in all these places. Soft drinks are generally available from Park offices. See below for more details on Nature Reserves.

Suriname Airways (SLM) has organized tours to **Stoelmanseiland** on the Lawa River (guest house with full board, C, including meals) in the interior, and to the Bush Black villages and rapids in that area. Price US$150 p.p. for 3 days (5 persons, minimum). SLM and other airlines (Gonini, GumAir) organize occasional charters to Tepoe, up the Tapanahony river in the S, where one can visit the Trio and Wayana Indians.

Nature Reserves N.B. In 1989 all reserves except Matapica were closed due to the civil war. *Raleighvallen/Voltzberg Nature Reserve* (57,000 hectares) is one of the more accessible rain-forest parks. In normal conditions, flights go from Paramaribo (40 mins.) to Foengoe Island in the Reserve. For a more scenic trip, you can take a three-or four-hour car ride from Paramaribo to Bitagron, a colourful Bush-Black village on the Coppename River (swimming good, but do not swim at Moedervallen because of electric fish), where the car can be left with the guard of the Government Geological Service. (The village was reported destroyed in 1987.) From there it is a four-hour boat trip up the Coppename to the reserve (round-trip). There is no electricity, refrigerator, beds or tents at Voltzberg Camp. However, climbing Voltzberg peak at the sunrise is unforgettable. The camp is 6 km. from the lodge. *Lolopasi Lodge*—with a secluded beach and view of the rapids—accommodates twelve. The *Foengoe Island Lodge* has accommodation for 64 people with complete kitchen facilities (drinks may be purchased from the manager, but you must bring linen and food), electricity, and shower. Group accommodation with kitchen privileges (twelve people, three rooms) available; or you may stay for less without kitchen privileges. Bedding is extra. Otherwise there are huts at Gonini, Koejaké, Tamanoea or Sonloir.

The *Coppename Estuary* is also a national park, protecting many bird colonies.

Only two or three hours by car from Paramaribo is the *Brownsberg Nature Park* (6,000 hectares). Alternative methods of transport from the city include a combination bus and van. In this tropical rain-forest park live giant toads, communal spiders, monkeys, jaguars, peccaries, agoutis, and a variety of birds. Rooms in the *Central Lodge*, or cottage or bungalow sleeping eight to ten people—with toilet, shower, and complete kitchen facilities (again, bring your own food). Hiking maps are available at the Park office, and a guidebook to the birds of Brownsberg can be purchased in the **Stinasu office** in Paramaribo. A useful contact is Lesley Hattun (English speaking) Stinasu, P.O.B. 436, Paramaribo. T 75845/71856, who is the organization tour organizer.

Two reserves are located on the northeast coast of Suriname. Known primarily as a major nesting site for sea turtles—five species including the huge leatherback turtle come ashore to lay their eggs—*Wia-Wia Nature Reserve* (36,000 hectares), also has nesting grounds for some magnificent birds. The nesting activity of sea turtles is best observed February-July. Since the beaches and consequently the turtles have shifted westwards out of the reserve, accommodation is now at Matapica beach, not in the reserve itself. (After a visit to the reserves please send any comments to Hilde Viane at Stinasu. Your support is needed to keep the reserve functioning.) There may also be mosquitoes and sandflies, depending on the season. A riverboat leaves Paramaribo daily at 0700 (buy ticket on board) and arrives in Alliance by way of the Commewijne River at 1100. You then transfer to a Stinasu motorboat for a one-hour ride to Matapica. The motorboat costs US$50 for 4 people, round trip. Suitable waterproof clothing should be worn. The beach hut accommodates 18 people in 4 rooms, and costs US$4 p.p. Take your own bedding/food. Cooking facilities provided. Book the hut and boat through Stinasu and keep your receipts or you will be refused entry. Early booking is essential as the closure of the other reserves has made Matapica very popular.

The *Galibi Nature Reserve*, where there are more turtle-nesting places, is near the mouth of the Marowijne River. There are Carib Indian villages. From Albina it is a 3-hour (incl. ½ hr. on the open sea) boat trip to Galibi where the beach hut holds 12 people; or one bed in group accommodation or to Eilanti, where the beach hut holds six people.

Nieuw Nickerie, on the S bank of the Nickerie River 5 km. from its mouth, opposite Guyana is the main town and port of the Nickerie district and is distinguished for its ricefields and for the number and voraciousness of its mosquitoes. The town has a population of more than 8,000, the district of 35,000, mostly East Indian. Paramaribo is 237 km. away by road. Buses leave hourly or when full, US$8 (plus US$5 for large bag) and take less time (5 hrs.) with the opening of the bridge than they did before. Sit on the left-hand side of the bus to get the best views of the bird-life in the swamps. SLM has two daily flights to the capital (US$25). The coastal ferry service has been discontinued, but once a week the SMS company makes an interesting water trip, using inland waterways, to Nieuw Nickerie taking 36 hours; it leaves Paramaribo on Mondays at 0800, departs Nieuw Nickerie 1200 Wednesday (times subject to 2 hrs variation due to tides) US$4, no cabins, only slatted seats, but there is hammock space; take food and drink; lots of mosquitoes.

Hotels *Blue Hawaii*, E, central, reported to overcharge foreigners; *Dorien*, C, bed and breakfast; *Amer Ali*, near ferry, clean, B; *De-Vesting*, similar quality, B; *Ashoko*, F; *Nickerie Logeergebouw*, B; *Sjiem Fat*, C, without meals; *Luxor*, E-F, among the cheapest; *Diamond*, D, clean, good value; *Oasis* (men only), F, basic. The *Ajai* (E) guest house is dirty and noisy, but has a balcony for "interesting conversations".

Restaurant *Tokyo*, rather basic. Good food at the Asanredjo foodstand (unmarked), ask to be directed, two blocks east of *Ajai*, on Oranjenassaustraat. Cheap filling meals can be obtained on the street for as little as US$1.50.

Banks Algemene Bank Nederland, Hakrin Bank, Post Office Savings Bank, People's Credit Bank, Surinaamse Bank. The bank at the immigration office is reported to close at 1500 Mon.-Fri., whether or not the ferry has arrived.

Ferry to Springlands, Guyana, US$7, one way, 2 hrs., no service Sun. or national holidays of either country, foot passengers only. Best to book 24 hrs. in advance, though it is possible to book on day of departure if space is available. Book for same day departures by handing in your passport at the Immigration Office, 200 metres below ferry point, opens 0700, be there 0630. Book in advance either at Immigration Office or at military police station, corner of Maynardstraat and Bataviastraat, Mon.-Fri. 0900-1200, Sat. 0900-1100. Lengthy customs inspection and passport return procedure begins at 0730. Currency declaration forms must also be handed in (see page 1124). Guyanese entry and currency forms available on ferry, US$0.50. For entry to Guyana a return ferry ticket (US$12) will suffice as an onward ticket: without one you can be sent back on the next ferry. The EEC has approved a grant of ECU 12m to finance the provision of a new ferry service to Guyana; a new terminal for the ferry is to be constructed 25 km. up river from Nieuw Nickerie; it had not been brought into service by April 1990.

Note Immigration officials have been known to insist on travellers changing US$50 for each day of stay: claim you are in transit and get your entry permit extended in Paramaribo.

Totness is the largest village in the Coronie district, along the coast between Paramaribo and Nieuw Nickerie. There is a good government guesthouse, E. The road (bad, liable to flooding) leads through an extensive forest of coconut palms. Bus to Paramaribo US$3 at 0600.

Wageningen is a modern little town, the centre of the Suriname rice-growing area. The road from Nickerie has recently been renewed. One of the largest fully mechanized rice farms in the world is found here. (*Hotel de Wereld*, C.) The Bigi-Pan area of mangroves is a bird-watchers' paradise; boats may be hired from local fishermen.

Vast reserves of bauxite have been discovered in the Bakhuis Mountains, in the northern part of Nickerie District. A road has been built from Zanderij to Apoera, but the laterite roads to the Bakhuis Mountains and on to the Kabalebo River, where a large hydro-electric station is planned are now overgrown and almost impassable. Gasoline available at Apoera only. **Apoera** is on the Corantijn and can also be reached by sea-going vessels. **Blanche Marie Falls**, 320 km. from Paramaribo on the Apoera road, is a popular destination. There is a guesthouse, *Dubois*, B, contact Eldoradolaan 22, Paramaribo T 76904/2. Camping is Sf30 tent/day. There is a good guesthouse at Apoera (C, with 3 meals, advance booking from Paramaribo advisable). **Washabo** near Apoera, which has an airstrip, is an Amerindian village. There is no public transport from Paramaribo to the Apoera-Bakhuis area, but many private cars and trucks go there and there are frequent charter flights to the Washabo airstrip. Irregular small boats go from Apoera to Nieuw Nickerie and to Springlands (Guyana). Try to rent a canoe to visit the Amerindian settlement of Orealla in Guyana or Kaboeri creek, 12 km. downstream, where giant river otters may possibly be seen in October or March.

N.B. As a result of civil war since 1986, the road between Paramaribo and Albina has been closed. A special permit is reportedly required to visit Albina, which has been severely damaged and depopulated, and the border was reported still closed in April 1990.

Moengo, 160 km. up the Cottica River from Paramaribo, is a bauxite mining and loading centre for the Suriname Aluminium Company (Suralco) a subsidiary of Alcoa. (*Government Guesthouse*, B, annex D.) Paranam, another loading centre for the Company, is on the left bank of the Suriname River. It can be reached by medium draught ships and by cars. Near Paranam is Smalkalden, where bauxite is loaded by the Billiton company on the road to Paramaribo.

Albina, the eastern frontier village, is 140 km. from Paramaribo, 29 km. from the mouth of the Marowijne River—the boundary with French Guyane. In normal times Albina is the centre for trips by powered dugouts to Amerindian and Bush Black villages on the Marowijne, Tapanahoni and Lawa rivers (about Sf50 plus). It takes 1½-2 days to get to the beautiful Stoelmanseiland (**see Excursions, page** 1120). There is a park along the Marowijne river (about 15 minutes walk from the town centre) called Het Park with free hammock places. Opposite Albina, in French Guyane, is St.-Laurent (**see page** 1128), with good restaurants and the old penal settlement to see.

INFORMATION FOR VISITORS

Documents Visitors must have a valid passport (issued by any government other than those of the communist countries or Hong Kong), a visa, or tourist card, and a through ticket to another country or a return ticket home from any of the Guianas. Visas cost US$14 and must be obtained in advance by citizens of all countries except Japan, Israel, The Gambia, South Korea, Denmark, Finland, Sweden, Switzerland, Netherlands Antilles, Brazil, Ecuador, Canada, Chile and Guyana (these require a tourist card, obtainable at the airport, US$14). There are consulates in Caracas, Brasília, Georgetown and Cayenne. Even with a visa you may on arrival be given only an eight day entry permit, but extensions may be obtained by reporting to the Immigration Office, van't Hogerhuystraat, Nieuwe Haven, Paramaribo, as soon as possible after arrival, with two passport-size photos (extension costs US$6). Any foreign currency must be declared on entry and exit; don't lose the double entry form.

Airport Tax There is an exit tax of US$17.

Air Services Zanderij airport is served by SLM (Suriname Airways), KLM, Air

France, ALM and Cruzeiro do Sul. SLM flies to Miami (twice weekly), Amsterdam (4 a week), Belém, Aruba, Curaçao and Port-au-Prince (Haiti), once a week each, Cayenne (3 times a week), and Georgetown (4 times a week). KLM flies from Amsterdam twice a week, once via Port of Spain; Air France flies from Cayenne once a week, and ALM from Curaçao once a week. Cruzeiro do Sul flies to Cayenne (US$85) and Belém on Mondays. Many people go to Cayenne to take advantage of cheap Air France tickets to Europe as well as increased seat availability. Internal services are maintained by SLM and two small air charter firms.

Travelling to Guyana and Guyane The ferry crossing to Guyana is covered in the text. There is no overland crossing to Guyane owing to the war in eastern Suriname, but note that GUM-Air flies to St.-Laurent du Maroni in western Guyane from the Zorg-en-Hoop airfield near Paramaribo.

Visa for Guyana Nearly everyone now needs a visa to enter Guyana. The application form costs US$0.50, visa US$9, from the Guyanese Embassy at 82 Gravenstraat, open Mon., Wed., Fri., 0800-1300. Same day service if you make an early application. Take three passport photos and onward ticket from Guyana.

Embassies USA (Dr. Sophie Redmondstraat 129, P.O. Box 1821, T 72900), Netherlands, Belgium, Brazil, Cuba, France, Mexico, Venezuela, South Korea, India, Indonesia, Guyana, India, Japan, China (People's Republic), USSR.

Consulates There are consuls-general, vice-consuls or consular agents for Canada, Denmark, Dominican Republic, Ecuador, Finland, W. Germany, Haiti, UK, Mexico, Norway, Spain, and Sweden—all in Paramaribo.

Customs Duty-free imports include (if declared) 400 cigarettes or 100 cigars or ½ kg. of tobacco, 2 litres of spirits and 4 litres of wine, 50 grams of perfume and 1 litre of toilet water, 8 rolls of still film and 60 metres of cinefilm, 100 metres of recording tape, and other goods up to a value of Sf40. Personal baggage is free of duty. Customs examination of baggage can be very thorough.

Communications There are 2,500 km of main roads, of which 850 km are paved. The main east-west road, 390 km in length, links Albina (inaccessible in 1990) with Nieuw Nickerie. Driving is on the left. Most settlements have an airstrip, but internal air services are limited. Internal bus services are poor.

Tourism Points of interest are: some colonial architecture, especially in and around Paramaribo; and the tropical flora and fauna in this very sparsely populated country. There are no beaches to speak of; the sea and the rivers in the coastal area are muddy, and mosquitoes can be a worry in places. Hotels and restaurants are outside the capital, and you usually have to bring your own hammock and mosquito net, and food. A tent is less useful in this climate. Hitchhiking is not common, but it is possible. The **high seasons**, when everything is more expensive, are 15 March-15 May, July-September and 15 December-15 January. Travelling is only cheap if you can change cash dollars on the black market, but taking your own hammock and food will reduce costs. Note that travel has been limited within Suriname since 1986, especially eastward to Albina and French Guyane.

Health No special precautions necessary except for a trip to the malarial interior; for free malaria prophylaxis contact the Public Health Department (BOG). Mosquito nets should be used at night over beds in rooms not air-conditioned or screened. Outside Paramaribo drinking water should still be boiled despite protestations. In some coastal districts there is a risk of bilharzia (schistosomiasis). Vaccinations: yellow fever and tetanus advisable, typhoid only for trips into the interior. Swim only in running water because of poisonous fish. There is good swimming on the Marowijne river and at Matapica beach and on the Coppename river. There are 5 hospitals in Paramaribo.

Clothing Except for official meetings, informal tropical clothing is worn, but not shorts. An umbrella or plastic raincoat is very useful.

Hours of Business Shops and Businesses: Mon.-Thurs 0730-1630, Fri. 0730-1300 and 1700-2000, Sat. 0730-1300. Government departments: Mon.-Fri. 0700-1500. Banks are open Mon.-Fri. 0730-1400. The airport bank is open at flight arrival and departure times.

Public Holidays 1 January, New Year; Holi Phagwa (1 day in March); Good Friday; Easter (2 days); 1 May (Labour Day); 1 July (National Unity); 25 November (Independence Day); Christmas (2 days). For Moslem holidays see note under Guyana (**page** 1114).

Time is 3 hrs. behind GMT.

Currency The unit of currency is the Suriname guilder (Sf) divided into 100 cents. There are notes for 1, 2½, 5, 10, 25, 100 and 1,000 guilders. Since end-1982 only notes showing the revolutionary symbol have been legal tender: do not accept the old ones. Coins are for 1 guilder and 1, 5, 10 and 25 cents (the 25-cent coin is usually known as a *kwartje*). Suriname's monetary system is quite independent of Holland's; the Suriname guilder is valued against the US dollar at US$1 = Sf1.78 (fixed), which has resulted in the country becoming expensive for the tourist. There has been a crackdown on the black market in cash US dollars (which rose as high as Sf12=US$ in 1989), which operates mainly from cheap hotel rooms and near the market in Paramaribo. Don't go looking for dealers; they will approach you.

Exchange Regulations are very strict. Everybody has to fill out a foreign currency declaration when entering and leaving. On departure, the imported foreign currency can be exported again provided a validated exchange permit is presented. Bank receipts must also be provided on departure to account for any currency transactions. Travellers' cheques can only be exchanged into guilders at banks. Only Sf100 in local currency and up to US$2,800 in foreign currency may be imported or exported without currency declaration. Expect to be searched thoroughly on entry.

Persons arriving at Zanderij airport and at Nieuw Nickerie are required to exchange US$280 per person at official rates if staying over 10 days. For shorter stays the requirement is to change US$30 per day. At other land borders (or if you say at the airport that you are in transit) the sum may be reduced to US$170 or US$17 per day for less than 10 days' stay (or ignored altogether); for children, half these rates. Exchange facilities are now situated at exit-entrance points.

The **metric** system is in general use.

Electricity Supply 127 volts AC, 60 cycles. Plug fittings are usually 2-pin round (European continental type). Lamp fittings are screw type.

Post, Telegraph, Telephone Telegrams can be sent from 0700 until 2200 and from Government Telegraph Service, Gravenstraat, in urgent cases.

There is a telephone and telegraph office on Vaillantplein. Book and pay in advance. Calls can be made to the US and UK via satellite. The office is open 0700-2000; calls booked before 2000 can be made up till midnight. Censorship is reported to be in operation on telephones and mail.

Newspaper in Dutch: *De Ware Tijd*.

Broadcasting There are several stations in Paramaribo and in the districts, broadcasting in Dutch, Hindi, Negro English and Javanese. There is also one state-controlled television station called Surinaamse Televisie Stichting (STVS), transmitting for 4 hours daily in colour on channel 8 (in Dutch).

Information about Suriname can be had from: the Suriname Embassy, Alex. Gogelweg 2, The Hague, Netherlands (T 070-65-08-44) or the Tourist Board, Waterkant 8, P.O.B. 656 (T 71163/78421; telex 292 Surair SN), Paramaribo, or Stinasu, Cornelis Jongbawstraat 14, P.O.B. 436 (T 75845). Also from embassies.

GUYANE

GUYANE, an Overseas Department of France, has its eastern frontier with Brazil formed partly by the River Oiapoque (Oyapoc in French) and its southern, also with Brazil, formed by the Tumuc-Humac mountains. The western frontier with Suriname is along the River Maroni-Itani. To the north is the Atlantic coastline of 320 km. The area is estimated at 89,941 square km., or one-sixth that of France. The land rises gradually from a coastal strip some 15-40 km. wide to the higher slopes and plains or savannas, about 80 km. inland. Forests cover some 8 million hectares of the hills and valleys of the interior, and timber production is increasing rapidly.

The territory is well watered, for over twenty rivers run to the Atlantic. Besides those named above, there are the Mana, Cayenne, Sinnamarie (with its tributary the Coureibo), Maroni, Oyack, and Approuage. Smaller rivers are the Inini, Ardoua, and Camopi.

The only mountain range of importance is the Tumuc-Humac. Among the higher peaks are Mounts Mitarka, Temorairem, Leblond, and Timotakem; this last in the extreme S on the Brazilian frontier. The mountains reach a height of 800 metres.

Climate is tropical with a very heavy rainfall. Average temperature at sea-level is 27°C, and fairly constant at that. Night and day temperatures vary more in the highlands. The rainy season is from November to July, with (sometimes) a short dry interruption in February and March. The great rains begin in May. The dry season is from July to mid-November.

History Awarded to France by the Peace of Breda in 1667, Guyane was twice attacked, first by the British in 1654 and later by the Dutch in 1676. In the same year the French retook possession and remained undisturbed until 1809. In that year a combined Anglo-Portuguese naval force captured the colony, which was handed over to the Portuguese (Brazilians). Though the land was restored to France by the Treaty of Paris in 1814, the Portuguese remained until 1817. Gold was discovered in 1853, and disputes arose about the frontiers of the colony with Suriname and Brazil. These were settled by arbitration in 1891, 1899, and 1915. By the law of 19 March, 1946, the Colony of Cayenne, or Guyane Française, became the Department of Guyane, with the same laws, regulations, and administration as a department in metropolitan France. The seat of the Prefect and of the principal courts is at Cayenne. The colony was used as a prison for French convicts with camps scattered throughout the country; Saint-Laurent was the port of entry. After serving prison terms convicts spent an equal number of years in exile and were usually unable to earn their return passage to France. Those interested should read *Papillon* by Henri Charrière. Majority opinion seems to be in favour of greater autonomy: about 5% of the population are thought to favour independence.

The People The total population is estimated 95,000, the work force 38,000. The basic population consists of Creoles, who, by the widest measure, account for 72% of the population; bush negroes, 6.4%; Amerindians, 4.2%; Asians, Europeans and others (including Brazilians), 17.1%. There are an estimated 15,000 migrant workers from Haiti and nearby countries. Their presence has contributed to a rise in the school age population from 13,215 in 1973 to 21,660 by 1987/88; the literacy rate is 82%.

Note The **Amerindian villages** in the Haut-Maroni and Haut-Oyapoc areas may only be visited if permission has been obtained from the Préfecture in Cayenne *before* departure to Guyane.

The Economy Guyane has renewable natural riches in its timber forests (about 80,000 sq km.) with 15 sawmills and mineral resources. Farming employs only 13% of the population and the country is very sparsely populated. An estimated 42 million tons of extractable bauxite have been located in the Kaw mountains to the SE of Cayenne by Alcoa and Pechiney. Some 40m tonnes of kaolin have been located at St.-Laurent du Maroni and gold is again being mined.

Guyane imports most of its foodstuffs and manufactured goods, of which about 50% come from France. The value of exports, mainly shrimps, rum, essence of rosewood, hardwoods and gold, is very low; France buys just over 20% and the USA about 50%.

At end-1982 the French Government announced plans to step up the Department's development in consultation with local parties: the so-called Green Plan (Plan Vert), backed by the Société Financière de Développement de la Guyane. Under the plan local production of basic foodstuffs, such as meat and eggs, was to be raised, and areas of timber plantations doubled to 22,000 hectares. In recent years new building has taken place and facilities for visitors have been much improved.

Government The head of state is the President of France; the local heads of government are a Commissioner of the Republic, for France, and the Presidents of the local General and Regional Councils. The General Council (19 seats) and the Regional Council (31 seats) are the two legislative houses. Guyane is divided into two *arrondissements*, Cayenne and St. Laurent du Maroni.

Cayenne, the capital and the chief port, is on the island of Cayenne at the mouth of the Cayenne River. It is 645 km. from Georgetown (Guyana) and 420 km. from Paramaribo (Suriname) by sea. Population 37,100. There is an interesting museum in Rue de Remire, near the Place de Palmistes, which includes paintings of convict life on the Iles du Salut (open Tues.-Sat. 0800-1300, Sun. 0900-1200, Mon. 1000-1300, Tues. and Fri. 1600-1830; free admission). Also worth a visit are Crique, the colourful but dangerous area around the Canal Laussant (built by Malouet in 1777); the Jesuit-built residence (circa 1890) of the Prefect (L'Hôtel-de-Ville) in the Place de Grenoble; the Place des Armandiers (also known as the Place Auguste-Horth) by the sea; Botanical Gardens; the Place des Palmistes, with assorted palms; a swimming pool; a municipal library and five cinemas. There are bathing beaches (water rather muddy) around the island, the best is Montjoly (no bus), but watch out for sharks.

Hotels *Novotel Cayenne*, on beach, A, restaurant, a/c, very good; *Hotel Cayenne Studios*, Rue Molé, A; *Amazonia*, Av. Gen. de Gaulle, A, good, friendly, a/c, luggage stored, central location, T 30-03-02; *Chez Mathilde*, Av. Gen. de Gaulle 42, D-C, hammock space, friendly, clean, noisy, not safe for left luggage, always full; *Neptima*, Rue F. Eboué 21 (15 rooms), B, best value, a/c, clean, friendly. *Ket-Tai*, corner of Avs. de la Liberté and Jubelin, C with shower and toilet, dirty, but a good view. *Madeleine*, B, a/c, breakfast, will book Raffinel bus to St.-Laurent, 1 km. out of town, friendly (good Surinamese snackbar nearby). Cheapest in town is *Foyer Paul VI*, Rue Yasim, T 30-04-16, E, cheap meals. About 9 km. from Cayenne is the *Beauregard*, A. Also *Hotel M*, a motel with air conditioned rooms and a small swimming pool; the owner hires out small cars, rec. for businessmen, 15F breakfast, T 35 4100, Telex 010 310. Mme. Izeros, T 31-06-55, lets out rooms, D, without breakfast. Most hotels do not add tax and service to their bill, but stick to prices posted outside or at the desk. Hotel rooms are expensive—at the end of 1989 none cost less than 140F a night double. Bed and breakfast accommodation is available for about US$20-30 a night—contact the tourist office for details. There is a great shortage of rooms, even in off-seasons: arrive early or book ahead. Amex cards often not accepted but Visa OK.

Restaurants and Bars Main hotels. *L'Auberge des Amandiers*, Place Auguste-Horth, excellent, good value; *Cap St. Jacques*, Rue Docteur E. Gippet, excellent Vietnamese food, reasonable. *Maxim'um*, Av. Estrée. *La Croix du Sud*, 80, Av. de Gaulle; *Le Snack Créole*, 17 Rue Eboué; *Club 106*, about 4 km. outside Cayenne; *Montjoly Bar; Palmiste*, 12 Av. de Gaulle, central and spacious; *Frégate*, Av. de Gaulle; *Le Traiteur de la Fôret*, Blvd. Jubelin, friendly, good; *Marveen Snack Bar*, Rue Ch. Colombe, near Canal de L'Est, food and staff pleasant, the patrons are very helpful regarding air travel and excursions (the elder of the two is a pilot for the Guyane Flying Club). *Ko Fei*, 18, Rue Lalouette, T 312888, good Chinese; *Apsara*, 95 Rue Colombe, Chinese, good value. Along the Canal Laussant there are Javanese snack bars; try bami (spicy noodles) or saté (barbecued meat in a spicy peanut sauce). Vans around Place des Palmistes in evenings sell cheap, filling sandwiches. *Bar Cayenne Palace*, 45 Av. de Gaulle, disco 80F with first drink. *Delifrance*, Av. de Gaulle, hot chocolate and croissants; *Epi D'or*, Av. Jubelin, good sweets and cakes, rec.

Bookshops Librairie AJC, 31 Boulevard Jubelin, has some stock in English. Also old maps and prints. Current map sold at Librairie Alain Pion, Av. de Gaulle and in most bookshops.

Car Hire 16 companies incuding both Hertz and Avis at airport. Full list available from ARDTLG (see **Tourist Office** below). An international driving licence is required.

Bank Banque Nacional de Paris-Guyane, 2 Place Schoelcher; no exchange facilities on Sat. Banque Française Commerciale, 2 Place des Palmistes; Crédit Populaire Guyanais, 93 Rue Lalouette. There are no exchange facilities at the airport; if in extreme need on Sat. you may be able to change money at Air France office in Place des Palmistes. Central drugstore may help when banks closed. Buy francs before arrival if possible.

Laundromat Corner of Rue F. Roosevelt and Rue Eboué, US$5 load all in.

Post Office 2 km. out from town (15F by taxi or 20 minutes on foot). Poste Restante letters are only kept for 2 weeks maximum. Post Office annex opp. Préfecture open a.m. (Place Grenoble).

Tourist Office Agence Régionale de Développement du Tourisme et des Loisirs de la Guyane (ARDTLG), 12 Rue Lalouette (T 30-09-00) and in botanical gardens. Free map and tourist guide (Guyane Poche). The SLM manager is reported to be very helpful with advice.

Travel Agent *Takari Tour*, Colline du Montabo, T 31-19-60 (BP 513). *Somarig*, Place L. Heder, is reported to be good for South American and European airline tickets. It also sells boat tickets to Ile Royale as well as meal tickets for the Auberge which are recommended. *JAL Voyages*, T 38-23-70 and *Guyane Excursions*, Centre Commercial Simarouba, T 32-05-41, both organise a varied programme of tours.

Bus Only westbound bus is run by Ruffinel & Cie, Av. Galmot, T 31-26-68 (Kourou 50F, St Laurent 120F) leaves 0515; will pick up at hotel if ticket bought day before. Otherwise transport is by shared taxis (collectifs), which leave from Av. de la Liberté, near the fish market early in the morning (Kourou 60F, St. Laurent 150F).

International Airport Cayenne-Rochambeau is 16 km. from Cayenne, 20 mins. by taxi. (See Air Routes to Guyane, page 1130.) Local air services: Air Guyane to all main centres. No public transport; only taxis (80F daytime, 100F night, but you can probably bargain or share). No exchange facilities. Cheaper taxi: Richard Lugret, T 31-29-89.

Excursions Trips by motor-canoe (*pirogue*) up-river into the jungle can be arranged. Six-and-a-half km. outside Cayenne is a restaurant with paintings of prison life by Huguet, an ex-convict, whose work can also be seen in the church at Iracoubo, between Kourou and St.-Laurent. Ten km. out, near the bridge to the mainland, is an American shrimp-packing plant.

Forty km. away is Ile Connétable, a small offshore island with large frigate-bird colonies; although a restricted area for tourists, some tour operators may take you.

Kourou, 56 km. W of Cayenne, where the main French space centre (Central Spatial Guyanais), used for the European Space Agency's Ariane programme, is located, is referred to by the Guyanais as "white city" because of the number of metropolitan French families living there; its population is about 6,450. It has two excellent hotels and a number of good restaurants, but the project and population have been substantially reduced. Tourist attractions include bathing, fishing, sporting and aero club, and a variety of organized excursions. The space centre occupies an area of about 4 km. deep along some 30 km. of coast, bisected by the Kourou river. It is open to the public on Tues., Weds., and Thurs. 0800-1130. Phone 33-49-19 to reserve a place on a tour (in French only) of the centre (max 40), often booked up days ahead; closed during Carnival. Kourou has its own port facilities, 4 km. out of town. There are no buses, but one can sometimes hitch a lift with the Space Centre bus to the cross roads 1 km. from the port. *Taxis collectifs* leave for Cayenne at 0600 and 1400 from Shell petrol station. Taxi from Cayenne or from airport, 300F.

Hotels *Relais de Guyane*, Les Roches (T 32-00-66), L; *Diamant*, A; *Auberge des Iles du Salut*, B; *Studio Sodecho*, Place Newton (T 32-06-11); *Des Roches*, A, pool, beach, good restaurants; *Centre D'Accueil*, de Gaulle, D, basic, clean, friendly.

Restaurants Many, esp. on de Gaulle inc. *Le Catouri, Cachiri, Auberge de Père Jean* (all Creole), *Vieux Montmartre* and *L'Aubrevoir* (French). Cheapest in town is *La Légion*, very good value. Snack Bars: *La Cage*, Av. Les Roches; *Felicio*, Allée des Tamanoirs. Night Clubs: *Bellevue* and *Club des Roches*, Av. Les Roches, *Le Vieux Montmartre*, de Gaulle.

Exchange Banque National de Paris Guyane, Place Newton; Banque Française Commerciale, Place Jeanne d'Arc; Crédit Populaire Guyanais, de Gaulle.

Travel Agency Guyane Excursions, T 32-05-41.

The **Iles du Salut** islands (many visitors at weekends), opposite Kourou, include the Ile Royale, the Ile Saint-Joseph, and the Ile du Diable. They were the scene of the notorious convict settlement built in 1852; the last prisoners left in 1953. The Ile du Diable ("Devil's Island"), a rocky palm-covered islet almost inaccessible from the sea, was where political prisoners, including Alfred Dreyfus, were held. There is a 60-bed hotel on Ile Royale, *Auberge Iles du Salut* (address Sothis, 97310 Kourou, T 32-11-00); former guard's bungalow, main meals (excellent) 150-250F, breakfast 30F (ex-mess hall for warders, with good food; bottled water sold). Camping is possible, but suitable sites are limited; take food and water (you can also sling a hammock in the open). You can see agoutis, turtles, humming birds and macaws, and there are many un-owned coconut palms. Paintings of prison life are on show in the tiny church. Boat from next to *Hotel des Roches*, Kourou 120F (130F weekends) return, leaves 0830, returns from island at 1600, 1 hr. each way. Tickets may be obtained from Somarig Voyager, Place Heder, Cayenne and from other tour agencies. Four daily crossings (40F return) by small boat from Ile Royale to Ile Saint-Joseph, which is wilder and more beautiful, with a small beach (this island had solitary-confinement cells and the warders' graveyard). Surfing and swimming are possible between Ile Royale and Ile du Diable. Boat owners are very reluctant to visit Devil's Island except around July-August when the sea is calmer.

Between Kourou and Iracoubo, on the road W to St.-Laurent, is **Sinnamary**, where Galibi Indians at a mission make artifical flowers from feathers, for sale to tourists (Hotels *Sinnarive*, B, and *Eldo Grill*, A, or contact M. Derain, T 34-53-09, who lets out rooms, D p.p.). Scarlet ibis can be seen in numbers on the Sinnamary estuary. A hydroelectric project is under construction on the Sinnamary River.

St.-Laurent du Maroni, population 5,000, formerly a penal transportation camp, is now a quiet colonial town 250 km. from Cayenne on the River Maroni, bordering Suriname. (Nearby is St.-Jean du Maroni, an Indian village.) There are three acceptable hotels and several restaurants. *Hotel Toucan*, B, unfriendly, poor value. *Hotel Bacadel*, above *Le Saramarca* restaurant, E, airy; the owner, Mme. Bacadel, is friendly. *Star Hotel*, A, a/c, friendly, rec. *Restaurants Vietnam* and *Le Point d'Intérrogation* have been rec. The old Camp de Transportation (the original penal centre but now full of squatters) can be wandered round at will (an absolute must if visiting the country), though if you want to see the cells you will have to apply to the local *gendarmerie*. The bank in St.-Laurent will not change Suriname guilders. Bus to Cayenne, 100F, 0500 daily; *taxis collectifs* to and from Cayenne, 140F a head, 3½-hr. trip.

The frontier with Suriname was still closed in March 1990 due to the civil war in that country. GUM airways fly from St-Laurent to Paramaribo, 303F one way, enquire at the *Star Hotel*.

40 km north of St.-Laurent du Maroni is **Mana**, a delightful town with rustic architecture near the coast (*Gîte d'Etape*, rooms OK, filthy kitchen, mosquitoes, disco next door; or contact Mme. Hidair, T 34-80-62, who has rooms, C). 16 km south of Mana following the river along a single track access road is Les Hattes (*Gîte Rureau*, B, clean) an Amerindian village (ask M. Daniel for permission to stay in the church); 4 km. further on is Les Hattes beach where leatherback-turtles lay their eggs at night; season April-August with its peak in June-July.

Between St.-Laurent and Mana is the house of Mathieu Witmandt, a Dutch biologist who welcomes visitors to his property in 300 acres of unspoilt tropical rain forest. For a reasonable price you may rent a hut or sling a hammock, buy meals (or bring your own food), and go on expeditions on foot or by boat. From St.- Laurent du Maroni, hitch to the police station 8 km. along the road to Cayenne; turn left here on to the Mana road for 7½ km., then turn left for 1 km. to the house.

Aouara, an Amerindian village with hammock places, is a few kilometres south of Les Hattes. It also has a beach where the leatherback turtles lay their eggs; they take about three hours over it. Take mosquito nets, hammock and insect repellant.

There are daily flights from Cayenne to **Maripasoula** (*Auberge Chez Dedè*) up the Maroni from St.-Laurent (2-4 day journey up river in *pirogue*). There may be freight canoes which take passengers (200F) or private boats (750F) which leave from St.-Laurent; 5-day tour with Takari Tour US$450 p.p. If going up the Maroni, take malaria prophylaxis.

Jef D. Boeke of Boston, Mass., has recommended a visit to **Saül**, a remote gold-mining settlement in the "central massif". The main attractions are for the nature-loving tourist—beautiful undisturbed tropical forests are accessible by a very well-maintained system of 90 km. of marked trails, including several circular routes. The place has running water, a radiotelephone, and electricity. A hostal (*Gîte d'Etape*) is run by Michel Modde (who also runs the tourist office), 70-100F per day with 3 meals, maps of local trails provided, own hammock and bedding useful but not essential. *Restaurant Chez Joseph*. Tourist Office: Syndicat d'Initiative 97314 Saül, Guyane Française. Air service Mon., Tues., Wed., Fri. with Air Guyane from Cayenne or via Maripasoula; try at airport even if flight said to be full. By *pirogue* from Mana up Mana River, 9-12 days, then one day's walk to Saül, or from St-Laurent via Maripasoula along Moroni and Inimi Rivers, 15 days and one day's walk to Saül, both routes expensive.

South-East of Cayenne is the small town of **Roura** (*Hotel La Pirogue*, B, clean, good views), which has an interesting church; an excursion may be made to the Fourgassier Falls several km. away. From Cayenne take a minibus to Stoupan, then catch the ferry across the River Comte (departs every hour 0730-1830). From Roura an unpaved road runs south-east towards the village of Kaw. At Km. 36 from Cayenne is the *Hotel Relais de Patawa* (T 31-93-95), C, or sling your hammock for 30F, cheaper rates for longer stays, highly rec. The owners, M and Mme Baloué, who are entomologists, will show you their collection, take you on guided tours of local sights and introduce you to their pet anaconda and boa constrictors. At Km. 80 is Cacao, where Hmong refugees from Laos are settled; they are farmers and produce fine traditional handicrafts. **Kaw**, at Km. 83, is on an island amid swamps which are home to much rare wildlife including caymans. The village is reached by dugout either from the Cayenne road or from Régina; basic accommodation available (Mme Musron, T 31-88-15), take insect repellant. South-West of Kaw on the River Approuague is Régina, linked with Cayenne by an unpaved road.

St.-Georges de l'Oyapoc is 15 min. down river from Oiapoque (Brazil) US$2 p.p. (canoe), *Hotel Damas*, *Hotel Modestina*, E, restaurant, also *Theofila*, lunch US$3, other restaurants and a night club. Several duty-free shops with French specialities. Immigration (*gendarmerie*) ½ km. from docks—French and Spanish spoken. There is nowhere to change dollars into francs; if entering the country here, you must change money before arriving in St.-Georges. There is a beautiful 19 metre waterfall one day up the Oyapoc River at Saut Maripa.

Air Guyane (office opposite Post Office) has daily flights to Régina and regular flights to and from St.-Georges (US$42, usually booked up a week in advance, but go to the airport if they say the flight is full). If the Air Guyane flights to St.-Georges are fully booked, it is probably cheaper not to wait for a standby (and pay Cayenne prices), but to find 2 or 4 others and take a Cessna from the Guyane Flying Club for US$90 (price includes baggage), 50 minute flight, recommended.

Camopi is an Indian village 2-3 days up the Oyapoc from St.-Georges (*pirogue*, 600F); to go beyond Saut-Maripa requires a special permit from the Préfecture in Cayenne, which takes 6 weeks and is usually granted only to scientists. Tours from Cayenne, 4,800F p.p. for 6 days.

INFORMATION FOR VISITORS

Documents   Passport not required by nationals of France and most French-speaking African countries carrying identity cards. No visa (45F) required for most nationalities (except for those of U.S.A., Guyana, the communist bloc and Asian—not Japan—and other African countries) for a stay of up to 3 months, but an exit ticket out of the country is essential (a ticket out of one of the other Guianas is not sufficient); a deposit is required otherwise. If one stays more than three months, income tax clearance is required before leaving the country. Inoculation against yellow-fever officially required only for those staying in Guyane longer than 2 weeks, but advisable for all. Travel to certain Amerindian villages is restricted (**see page 1126**).

Air Routes to Guyane   Air France flies 3 times a week direct to Guyane from Paris and 5 times a week from Pointe-à-Pitre (Guadeloupe) and Fort-de-France (Martinique). Cheapest flight from Europe is reported to be with Minerve (Paris T 45-22-08-50), once a week from Paris. Cruzeiro do Sul fly to Belém on Tues. and Fri. (return Mon. and Fri.) and to/from Paramaribo on Mon. Suriname Airways fly to Paramaribo 3 times a week; for Georgetown you have to change in Paramaribo. **NB** Do not accept verbal confirmation of flights from Air France in Cayenne: insist on a time/date stamped confirmation to avoid later misunderstandings.

Surface Transport to Guyane   The Compagnie Général Maritime runs a passenger service to France once a month via Martinique and a freight service every 3 months. There are no boat or bus connections with Suriname. To Brazil by motorized dugout from St. Georges to Oiapoque, no custom or immigration post but foreigners are still sometimes returned to Guyane if their papers are not in order. Make sure you get an exit stamp from Gendarmerie in St-Georges. This journey is possible in reverse.

Internal Transport   There are no railways, and about 1,000 km. of road (65% asphalted). The main road, narrow but now paved, runs for 130 km. from Pointe Macouris, on the roadstead of Cayenne, to Iracoubo. Another 117 km. takes it to Mana and St.-Laurent. One-to three-ton boats which can be hauled over the rapids are used by the gold-seekers, the forest workers, and the rosewood establishments. There is a twice-a-month shipping service which calls at nearly all the coastal towns of Guyane. Ferries are free. Internal air services by Air Guyane; bookings are made through Air France. These flights are always heavily booked, so be prepared to wait or write or telephone Air Guyane in Cayenne (T 317200). There are regular connections with Maripasoula, daily at 0930, 900F return; St-Georges, daily at 0745 and Mon. Tues., Thur., and Fri., at 1500, 560F return; Saül on Mon., Tues., Thur., and Fri., at 0930, 650F return; Régina, daily at 0745, 300F return. No services on Sun.

Road Transport   There is a lack of public transport; car hire can be a great convenience (there are 16 agencies in Cayenne). Gasoline/petrol costs 5F a litre.

Accommodation Details of hotels are given in the text. For information on *Gîtes* and *Chambres chez l'habitant* write to Agence Régionale de Développement du Tourisme et des Loisirs de la Guyane (ARDTLG), 12, rue Lalouette, 97338, Cayenne Cedex, T 30-09-00, Telex 910364 FG; also, for *Gîtes*, Association pour le Tourisme Vert en Guyane, 27, rue Justin Cataye, 97300 Cayenne, T 31-10-11.

Food Most is imported, except seafood; it is of very high quality but expensive.

Health Tropical diseases, dysentery, malaria, etc., occur, but the country is fairly healthy. Malaria prophylaxis recommended. In 1987 there were 5 hospitals with 861 beds and 237 physicians.

The best months to visit are between August and November, which are the usual months for trips to the jungle.

Public Holidays In addition to the feasts of the Church: 1 January, New Year's Day and 14 July, Fête Nationale. Moslem holidays are observed, but the dates vary because of the shorter Moslem year; see note under Guyana, **page** 1114 .

Time Zone 3 hours behind GMT.

Currency The currency is the French franc. Try to take francs with you as the exchange rate for dollars is low, many banks do not offer exchange facilities and most places demand cash. A better rate can be obtained by using Visa cards to withdraw cash from the Banque Nacional de Paris Guyane, Place Victor Schoelcher, Cayenne.

Weights and Measures The metric system is in use.

Telecommunications There is telephone communication throughout the territory. International telephone calls via STD to Europe and French Antilles. Foreign telegraph communication is via Paramaribo or Fort-de-France, from the TSF station at Cayenne.

Consulates British, 16 Av. Monnerville (B.P. 664, Cayenne 97300, T 31-10-34); Brazilian, 12 Rue L. Helder, at corner of Place des Palmistes, near Air France offices (closed Sats. T 30-04-67). Suriname, 38 rue Christophe Colombe (T 30-04-61).

General The language is French, with officials not usually speaking anything else. The religion is predominantly Roman Catholic.

Media *La Presse de la Guyane* is the daily paper (circ. 1,500). *France-Guyane-Antilles* is a weekly newspaper with a good information page for the tourist.

Tourist Information The French Government tourist offices generally have leaflets on Guyane; there is a special office in Paris, L'Office du Tourisme des Antilles et de la Guyane, 12 rue Auber, 75009 Paris, T 268-11-07. The Cayenne offices are at Jardin Botanique, BP 801, 97338 (Telex 910356, T 300900); 12, rue Lalouette, Cayenne (same phone number); Délégation Régionale, 10, rue L.-Heder, 97307 Cayenne, T 31-84-91; Syndicat d'initiative de Cayenne, Jardin Botanique, P.O. Box 702, 97338 Cayenne, T 31-29-19; St.-Laurent du Maroni, 16, rue du Colonel Chandon, T 34-10-86; Syndicat d'Initiative Rémire-Montjoly, Mairie de Rémire, 97305 Rémire, T 35-41-10.

We are most grateful to Charlie Nurse for updating the Guianas section, to Mark Wilson of The Crane, Barbados, for a complete revision of Guyana, to Aimée Azur, head of the Service des Relations Extérieures, Guyane, and to the following travellers: Daniel Morgan (Wellington, NZ), Stephen Newcomer (Centerville, Iowa), Erik Bernesson (Båstad, Swe.), Edith M. Coulton (Bedford), Graham Davis (Hove), Bill Forman (Fort Lauderdale, Florida), Thomas Hodel (Kaufdorf, Switzerland), Melchior Lengsfeld (Basel) and Peter.

FALKLAND ISLANDS
ISLAS MALVINAS

(In accordance with the practice suggested by the UN, we are calling the Islands by both their English and Spanish names.)

The Falkland Islands (Malvinas) comprise two groups: East Falkland (Isla Soledad) with its adjacent islands, about 2,600 square miles; and West Falkland (Gran Malvina), with its islands, about 2,100 square miles. Approximately 480 miles northeast of Cape Horn, the Islands lie between latitudes 51° and 53° S and between longitudes 57° and 62° W. Nearly all land combat during the 1982 war was confined to the northern half of East Falkland; its southern peninsula of Lafonia, and West Falkland were little affected. According to the 1986 census, two-thirds of the 1,916 residents are Falklands-born; another quarter were born in the United Kingdom. Slightly more than one-third live and work on sheep farms. During the past decade, land reform through sale and subdivision of traditional large stations has resulted in more broadly based local ownership of pastoral land.

Early History Records of early voyages are ambiguous, but Dutchman Sebald de Weert made the first universally acknowledged sighting in 1598. The Englishman Strong landed in 1690 and named the Falkland Sound for a British peer; this name was later applied to the entire group. The Islands acquired their French appellation, Iles Malouines, from 17th century seafarers from the channel port of St Malo. This in turn became the Spanish Islas Malvinas.

In 1764 France established a small colony of Acadians at Port Louis under Bougainville. Two years later France ceded the settlement to Spain, under which it became a military garrison and penal colony. At about the same time as France, Britain had built an outpost at Saunders Island, West Falkland, whose occupants Spain discovered and expelled in 1770. Restored in the following year after threat of war, the post was abandoned in 1774.

Deserted by Spain in 1811, during the South American wars of independence, the Islands lacked formal authority until 1820, when the United Provinces of the River Plate (later Argentina) raised their flag at Port Louis (Soledad). In 1831, an American warship destroyed a promising colonization project under the auspices of a German-born merchant from Buenos Aires, who had arrested and imprisoned American sealers operating in the area. After British warships expelled a token Argentine force in 1833, the Islands experienced nearly 150 years of stability until April 1982, when Argentina invaded and occupied. Britain's counter-invasion recaptured the Islands by June of that year.

Administration The Islands' Constitution provides for a Governor, appointed from London, an Executive Council composed of appointed and elected members, and an elected Legislative Council. **Education** A Junior and Senior School in Stanley cater to the needs of town children and rural children who board in the School Hostel. Instruction to GCSE Level is available locally (compulsory to the age of 15), but higher education requires overseas travel, usually to Britain. Rural children receive attention from settlement instructors or travelling teachers. Radio is used to keep in contact with the more isolated farms.

Climate Although the *Sunday Express* once referred to a mutton freezer in the Falklands as a "Colonial Development project near the South Pole" (8 March, 1953), the Islands are in the same latitude South as London is North. Mean monthly temperatures are lower than in London, but London experiences greater extremes. Normal temperature range is 20°F to 70°F, with an annual mean of 42°F. Though not always inclement, weather is very changeable. Persistent westerlies, blowing at an annual average of 14 knots, are the most trying aspect of the climate. Calm is more common in winter than summer. Stanley's annual rainfall of about 26 inches is slightly higher than London's. In the drier camp, outside Stanley, summer drought sometimes threatens local water supplies. Spring, autumn and winter clothing, as used in the United Kingdom, is suitable.

Stanley, the capital, is the major population centre on East Falkland. Its 1,232 residents live mostly in brightly-painted houses, many of which have corrugated iron roofs. Stanley Harbour, surrounded by rolling moorland, resembles parts of the Hebrides. The outer harbour of Port William is larger but less protected. East Cove, 30 miles southeast of the capital, is the principal port for the new military installations at Mount Pleasant.

Accommodation *Upland Goose Hotel*, Ross Road, T 21455, Fax 21520, £45 full board, £32 bed and breakfast, evening meal £12; *Emma's Guest House*, Ross Road, T 21056, Fax 21573, £27.50 full board; *Malvina House Hotel*, 3 Ross Road, T 21355, Fax 21357, £21.70-£32.65 bed and breakfast. Prices subject to change. Full meals at all three, with reservations recommended at *Upland Goose* and *Malvina*. *Fenton Guest House*, 7 Fitzroy Road, T 21282, £30 bed and breakfast; *Goodwins Guest House*, John Street, T 21252, £27 full board, £20 bed and breakfast. Pasties and ice cream at *Poole's* snack bar, John Street. Fish and chips and pizza at *Woodbine Cafe*, Fitzroy Road. *Monty's* bistro, on John Street, under new management and undergoing expansion, food OK but expensive.

On Sea Lion Island: *Sea Lion Lodge*, T 32004, £34.50 full board; at Port Howard, *Port Howard Lodge*, T 42187, £34.50 full board; on Pebble Island, *Pebble Island Lodge*, T 41097, £34.50 full board; *Chartres Lodge*, at Chartres, T 42250, £34 full board; and *Salvador Lodge*, Salvador, T 31150, £26.50 full board, £10 self-catering. Each lodge has a long wheelbase Land Rover for transport to the airstrip and points of interest nearby. The comfortable tourist lodges at Sea Lion Island, the most southerly inhabited island of the group (35 minutes flight fom Port Stanley), and Pebble Island (40 minutes flight) are good bases to view wildlife. Also on Pebble Island is a shanty that can be hired for £4 a night, room for up to 4. It is 12 miles from the rest of the population so is peaceful with plenty of wildlife (3 types of penguin within ½ hrs. walk). Bring food and bedding, all else provided. Scenic Port Howard's lodge on West Falkland, offers excellent trout fishing, a small but interesting war museum, and an opportunity to see the operations of a traditional large sheep station. The lodge at Salvador (Gibraltar Station), East Falkland, features fishing and wildlife and a beautiful northern coast.

Fred Clark's *Great Britain Hotel*, on the highway near Fitzroy, serves alcoholic beverages and snacks during normal licensing hours. Accommodation is limited on the islands but most farms help if they can.

Stanley has an excellent new civilian-military hospital, replacing the one damaged by fire early in 1984. Dental services are also available. Post Office, Philatelic Bureau, library and some other Government services are in Town Hall, Ross Road. Other Government offices are in the nearby Secretariat. Cable and Wireless operate overseas telephone, telegraph and telex services. The islands' telephone system has been completely replaced. There are some fairly well-stocked stores, open mainly Monday to Friday. The few pubs, such as the *Globe*, the *Rose*, and the *Victory* are popular meeting places during their strict drinking hours (Sundays only from 1200 to 1300, the "Glory Hour").

The new Museum at Britannia House, Ross Road West, merits a visit. Mr John Smith, Sparrow Hawk House, Allardyce Street, is knowledgeable on the Islands' maritime history. Government House, the Anglican Cathedral (most southerly in the world, built in 1890), and monuments commemorating the naval battle of 1914 and the 1982 liberation are also worth seeing. During the December holidays, the annual sports meeting at the race course attracts visitors from all over the Islands. The equally popular West Falkland sports, at the end of the shearing season in February or March, rotate among various settlements.

National Tourism Bureau Falkland Islands Tourism, Graham Bound, Managing Director, John Street, Port Stanley, T (010500) 22215, Telex 2433, Fax 27210, will provide all information on holidays on the islands. See below under communications for the Falklands Islands Government Office.

Rentals The Falkland Islands Company, Stanley, rents Fiat Strada 4 x 4 cars for about £125 per week, for road use only. Dave Eynon, South Atlantic Marine Services, P.O. Box 140, Stanley, T 21145, Telex 2413, hires out Land Rovers and his dinghy *Zodiac* with diving equipment, also arranges diving and fishing trips. Ian Bury on Davis Street rentsLand Rovers for £50 a day. Insurance is extra from the Falkland Islands Company. For boat hire for trips to Kidney Island and Narrows Island (50 ft. *Beaulie*) contact the owners, Jimmy and Owen Smith, T 31399.

Tourists For wildlife enthusiasts, especially birders, the Islands are an exceptional destination. Best months to visit are October to March. Make allowance for unpredictable weather. Outside Stanley, the only major road is that to the new airport at Mount Pleasant; elsewhere, tracks require Land Rovers or motorbikes. Remember to phone farms in the camp for permission to drive across private land. Off-road driving in the boggy terrain is a skill not easily learned by short-term visitors. Near Stanley and a few farm settlements there are still unexploded mines, but hazardous areas are clearly marked and fenced. Visitors should *never* enter these areas, and should report suspicious objects to the police or military authorities in Stanley. Ordnance Survey maps of the Islands are available from the Secretariat, £2 each for the 1:50,000 sheets; there is also a two-sheet, 1:250,000 map suitable for most purposes.

Travel outside the vicinity of Stanley is mainly by air. The Falkland Islands Government Air Service (FIGAS) operates three Islander aircraft to farm settlements and settled outer islands according to bookings, seat availability, and weather. To book a seat, visitors should telephone FIGAS no later than the morning of the day before travelling; flight schedules are announced that evening on local radio (airfares are about £1 per minute for non-islanders). Regular service operates 7 days a week, but it is also possible to arrange charter flights to wildlife sites on weekends (£400 per hour flying time, contact Mr Gerald Cheek, FIGAS, T 27219). Flights leave from Stanley Airport, three miles east of town on the Cape Pembroke peninsula; Stanley Bus Service carries passengers for £1.50.

Points of interest Sparrow Cove, Kidney Cove, and adjacent areas, only a short distance across Stanley Harbour by boat and out into Port William, are good areas to see penguins and other wildlife; dolphins often follow in the wake of your boat near The Narrows. Gypsy Cove, walking distance from Stanley, features a colony of burrowing Magellanic penguins and other shorebirds. Observe minefield fences which prevent close inspection of the penguins. At Cape Pembroke, around the old airport and lighthouse one can see ground-nesting birds such as dotterels, snipe, and Upland geese.

Kidney Island, a very small island densely covered with tussock grass, is a Nature Reserve. By arrangement in Stanley, it is possible for hardy and dedicated bird lovers to stay in the basic shanty. Rockhopper penguins, King cormorants and many other species nest here. Kidney Island is accessible by boat, 1½ hours from Stanley. Permission to visit must be obtained from the government Lands Officer. Trips—all day—are organized occasionally by Falklands Island Tourism.

Of particular interest are the hulls of old sailing ships at Stanley and Darwin. Examples at Stanley are the *Jhelum* (built in 1839 for the East India Company) near Government House, the *Charles Cooper* (the last US sailing packet to sail out of New York Harbour; in the Islands since 1866), and the iron-built *Lady Elizabeth* at the far end of the harbour (228 ft long, with three masts still standing). *Snow Squall*, one of the last American clipper ships, was removed by a team of marine archaeologists from Harvard University in 1987. At Darwin are the *Vicar of Bray* (last survivor of the California Gold Rush fleet), and another old iron ship, the *Garland*. Some of these hulls are still used for storage. There are interesting old French buildings and ruins at Port Louis.

Volunteer Point, north of Stanley, is a wildlife sanctuary. Permission to visit must be obtained from the owner, Mr Osmond Smith, at Johnson's Harbour; he charges £5 to visit—the fee goes towards the time used receiving the aircraft and looking after the penguins. By arrangement with Mr Smith it is possible to camp at the shepherd's house at Volunteer Point (you must take your own food and sleeping bag—don't drink the stream water, it is polluted by the penguins). Falklands Islands Tourism occasionally arrange tours; a 15-minute flight to Johnson's Harbour, then a 1½ hr. Land Rover trip across the camp. On other occasions, the farmer will drive you to the point if they are not busy; otherwise it is a 10 mile walk. Volunteer contains the only substantial nesting colony of King penguins in the Falklands. Gentoo penguins, Magellanic penguins, geese, ducks, and elephant seals are very tame and easily photographed. An exceptional wildlife hike is along the north coast of East Falkland, from Seal Bay to Volunteer Point. Ask permission of the manager of Port Louis as well, and allow three to four days.

The smaller islands off West Falkland, such as West Point, Carcass and New Island, are the most spectacular and attractive for wildlife and scenery. New Island, on the extreme west of the archipelago, is run as a nature reserve, but access is difficult. Enquiries should be addressed to Tony Chater, The Pink Shop, Stanley, or to Ian or Maria Strange. The Island has large colonies of rockhopper penguins, black-browed albatrosses, Gentoo and Magellanic penguins, King and Rock cormorants and many other birds, as well as a fur-seal colony. Carcass can be visited more easily and has two self-catering cottages. Saunders Island, besides a representative sample of wildlife, contains the ruins of the 18th-century British outpost at Port Egmont. At nearby Keppel Island are ruins of the South American Missionary Society, which used the site to catechize Indians from Tierra del Fuego during the latter half of the 19th century.

Economy Since the declaration of a 150-mile fisheries protection zone in 1986, the economy has been transformed. License fees from Asian and European fleets exploiting the Islands' squid, hake, and whiting have quadrupled Government revenue, to about £30 million a year. Much of this revenue is being used to fund overdue improvement in education and infrastructure, as well as social expenditures for increased pensions. A new telephone system has been installed and a new secondary school is planned. The housing stock has doubled since the 1982 war and there are many more vehicles in use. A new swimming pool is under construction in Stanley.

Most of the camp, as the countryside is known locally, is covered with grass and low heath. Almost all land outside Stanley is devoted to sheep grazing. There are some 600,000 sheep, all of whose wool is exported to the United Kingdom. Native tussock grass, the most valuable fodder, grows to seven feet or more and also shelters wildlife. It has disappeared from East and West Falkland because of grazing pressure, but still abounds on some smaller islands. There are only a few trees, introduced and carefully cultivated at settlements such as Hill Cove.

Entry requirements All travellers must have passports. Only Argentine visitors require advance visas, which are not readily granted. The new airport at Mount Pleasant, 30 miles from Stanley, is built to international specifications. Bob Stewart's Stanley Bus Service, St Mary's Walk, Stanley, T 20850, transports passengers and luggage to and from the capital for £10 single. Departing passengers should make reservations.

Communications The RAF presently operates two Tri-Star flights a week from Brize Norton, Oxfordshire, to the new airport at Mount Pleasant (Thursday and Monday, returning to UK Saturday and Wednesday). Standard fare is £1,900 return or £1,180 return on 28-day advance purchase; Falkland Islands residents receive a discount. Enquiries about passages can be addressed to Miss Victoria Poland, Falkland Islands Government London Office, Falkland House, 14 Broadway, Westminster, London SW1H 0BH, T 071-222 2542, Telex 8950476 FIGLON, Fax 2222375, for the Tourism Coordinator, T 071-222 5852. This office should be contacted for information on organized tours by UK companies, most of which specialize in birdwatching packages. Mountain Travel, 6420 Fairmount Avenue, El Cerrito, California 94530, T (415) 527-8100, includes the Falklands in its Antarctica programme, on the Norwegian vessel MV *Nordbrise*; full details from the above address.

It is hoped that scheduled airline service to the South American continent may begin soon. Aerovías DAP of Chile began charter flights between Punta Arenas and Port Stanley in April 1990; they have a fortnightly service. It is occasionally possible to obtain passage to Montevideo on European fishing boats, but this requires some patience and is undependable.

Scheduled service of the ferry *Indiana*, carrying passengers and freight between the Falklands and Montevideo, Uruguay and Punta Arenas, Chile, has recommenced. Passenger capacity is 12. For more details contact Stanley Services Ltd, City House, 190-196 City Road, London EC1V 2QH, T 071 252 5150; in the

Falklands T 22622, Fax 22623, Telex 2438. In Punta Arenas, go to Ultragas, Av. Independencia 865.

Cost of living is about the same as in Britain. Freight adds to the price of imported groceries. Since the construction of a hydroponic market garden near Stanley, fresh produce such as lettuce, tomatoes and aubergines are available year-round. Potatoes and other vegetables are grown in gardens and conservatories for household use, but are not readily purchased.

There is no value-added tax; only tobacco, wine, spirits and beer pay import duty. Small luxury goods on which freight is correspondingly low are sometimes cheaper than in the UK. Colour slide film, which can be scarce, should be brought from Britain.

Currency The local £ is on a par with sterling. Local notes and coins. UK notes and coins also legal tender. Currency from Ascension Island, where the RAF Tri-Star stops for refueling, is not accepted, nor are Falklands notes or coins legal in the United Kingdom. Foreign currency may be changed at Standard Chartered Bank, Ross Road, Stanley.

Mails Since the opening of Mount Pleasant, there is direct and dependable air mail service from the United Kingdom. Heavy parcels come by sea from the UK four or five times a year. Inter-island mail service is carried out by FIGAS and by the vessels *Monsunen* and *Forrest*.

SOUTH GEORGIA

South Georgia, in latitude 54½° S and longitude 36° to 38° W, has an area of about 1,450 square miles, and a small transient population of soldiers and British Antarctic Survey scientists. During the summer months, tourists may book a passage on the merchant supply vessel *Sir Bedivere* at Stanley for £400 return, but weather conditions sometimes prevent passengers from going ashore. Intending visitors must submit a request through the Government Secretary, Stanley. The Island was occupied by Argentina in April-May 1982.

South Georgia is a mass of high, snow-covered mountains and glaciers. Between 1951 and 1980 at King Edward Point, at sea level, snow fell an average of nearly 200 days per annum, but the coastal area is free from snow and partially covered by vegetation in summer. Wildlife consists of most of the same species found in the Falklands, but in much larger numbers. Reindeer, introduced by Norwegian whalers at the turn of the century, have flourished. Other points of interest are several abandoned whaling stations, the little white church, and many sailing-ship hulks.

We are deeply grateful to Graham Bound of Falkland Islands Tourism, Dr. Carlo Andreis (Monza, Milan), Wayne Bernhardson (Oakland, CA), B Clark (Chelmsford) and Hallam Murray (London SW11) for valuable new information.

CLIMATIC TABLES

The following tables have been very kindly furnished by Mr. R. K. Headland. Each weather station is given with its altitude in metres (m.). Temperatures (Centigrade) are given as averages for each month; the first line is the maximum and the second the minimum. The third line is the average number of wet days encountered in each month.

SOUTH AMERICA

	Jan.	Feb.	Mar.	Apr.	May	June	July	Aug.	Sept.	Oct.	Nov.	Dec.
Arica, Chile 29m.	26	26	25	23	21	19	19	18	19	21	22	24
	18	18	17	16	14	14	12	13	13	14	16	17
	0	0	0	0	0	0	0	0	0	0	0	0
Asunción, Par. 64m.	34	34	33	28	25	22	24	25	27	29	31	33
	22	22	21	18	14	13	14	14	16	17	19	21
	7	6	9	7	5	4	4	4	6	5	6	7
Bariloche, Arg. 825m.	21	21	18	14	10	7	6	8	10	11	16	18
	8	8	6	4	2	1	0	0	1	3	5	6
	2	3	5	7	11	13	11	11	8	6	4	4
Barranquilla, Col. 12m.	31	31	32	33	34	33	33	33	33	32	32	30
	22	22	23	24	25	25	25	25	25	24	24	23
	0	0	0	1	4	8	5	6	8	11	6	4
Belém, Braz. 24m.	31	30	30	31	31	32	32	32	32	32	32	32
	23	23	23	23	23	23	22	22	22	22	22	22
	24	26	25	22	24	15	14	15	13	10	11	14
Belo Horizonte 857m.	27	27	27	27	25	24	24	25	27	27	27	26
	18	18	17	16	12	10	10	12	14	16	17	18
	15	13	9	4	4	2	2	1	2	10	12	14
Bogotá 2560m.	21	21	21	20	20	19	19	19	20	20	20	21
	7	7	9	10	10	9	8	8	9	8	7	7
	9	7	10	18	16	10	16	10	13	18	16	13
Brasilia 912m.	27	28	28	28	27	26	26	28	30	29	27	27
	18	18	18	17	15	13	13	14	16	18	18	18
	19	16	15	9	3	1	0	2	4	11	15	20
Buenos Aires 25m.	30	29	26	22	18	15	15	16	18	21	25	29
	18	17	15	12	9	6	6	6	8	11	13	16
	5	5	6	6	4	4	5	6	5	7	7	7
Caracas 1035m.	26	26	28	28	28	27	26	27	28	27	27	26
	15	15	16	17	18	18	17	17	17	17	17	16
	4	3	2	4	8	13	13	11	11	11	8	6
Córdoba, Arg. 425m.	32	31	28	25	21	19	19	20	23	26	28	31
	17	16	14	11	7	4	4	5	8	11	13	16
	8	9	9	6	4	2	2	1	3	7	9	10
Cuzco 3310m.	20	21	21	22	21	21	21	21	22	22	23	22
	7	7	7	4	2	1	-1	1	4	6	6	7
	18	13	11	8	3	2	2	2	7	8	12	16
Guayaquil 6m.	31	31	32	31	31	29	28	29	30	29	30	31
	22	22	23	23	22	21	20	20	20	20	21	22
	12	13	15	10	4	1	0	0	0	1	0	2
La Paz, Bol. 3632m.	18	18	18	19	17	17	17	17	17	18	19	19
	6	6	6	5	3	2	1	2	3	5	6	6
	21	18	16	9	5	2	2	4	9	9	11	18
Lima 137m.	25	26	26	24	21	19	17	17	17	19	20	23
	19	20	19	18	16	15	14	13	13	14	16	17
	1	0	0	0	1	1	1	2	1	0	0	0
Manaus 48m.	30	30	30	30	31	31	32	33	33	33	32	31
	23	23	23	23	23	23	24	24	24	24	24	24
	20	18	21	20	18	12	12	5	7	4	12	16
Montevideo 22m.	28	28	26	22	18	15	14	15	17	20	23	26
	17	16	15	12	9	6	6	6	8	9	12	15
	6	5	5	6	6	5	6	7	6	6	6	7

SOUTH AMERICA (Cont.)

	Jan.	Feb.	Mar.	Apr.	May	June	July	Aug.	Sept.	Oct.	Nov.	Dec.
Porto Alegre, Braz.	31	30	29	25	22	20	20	21	22	24	27	29
10m.	20	20	19	16	13	11	10	11	13	15	17	18
	9	10	10	6	6	8	8	8	11	10	8	8
Punta Arenas,	15	14	13	9	6	4	3	4	7	10	12	14
Chile	7	7	6	4	2	1	1	1	2	3	4	6
28m.	6	5	7	9	6	8	6	5	5	5	5	8
Quito	21	21	20	21	21	21	21	22	22	21	21	21
2818m.	8	8	8	8	8	7	7	7	7	8	8	8
	9	11	11	15	10	9	3	3	8	13	13	7
Recife, Braz.	30	30	30	30	29	28	27	27	28	29	30	30
56m.	24	25	24	23	23	22	21	21	22	23	24	24
	7	8	10	11	17	16	17	14	7	3	4	4
Rio de Janeiro	30	30	29	27	26	25	25	25	26	26	28	28
30m.	23	23	23	21	20	18	18	18	19	20	20	22
	13	11	9	9	6	5	5	4	5	11	10	12
Salvador (Bahia)	29	29	29	28	27	26	26	26	27	28	28	29
8m.	23	23	24	23	22	21	21	21	21	22	23	23
	6	9	17	19	22	23	18	15	10	8	9	11
Santa Cruz, Bol.	30	31	30	28	25	23	24	28	28	29	30	31
437m.	21	21	20	19	16	15	15	16	19	20	20	21
	14	10	12	9	11	8	5	4	5	7	8	11
Santiago de Chile	29	29	27	23	18	14	15	17	19	22	26	28
520m.	12	11	9	7	5	3	3	4	6	7	9	11
	0	0	1	1	5	6	6	5	3	3	1	0
São Paulo	28	28	27	25	23	22	21	23	25	25	25	26
792m.	18	18	17	15	13	11	10	11	13	14	15	16
	15	13	12	6	3	4	4	3	5	12	11	14

Sources:—H.M.S.O. Meteorological Reports
K.L.M. Climatic Data Publication

TEMPERATURES CONVERSION TABLE

°C	°F	°C	°F	°C	°F	°C	°F
1	34	11	52	21	70	31	88
2	36	12	54	22	72	32	90
3	38	13	56	23	74	33	92
4	39	14	57	24	75	34	93
5	41	15	59	25	77	35	95
6	43	16	61	26	79	36	97
7	45	17	63	27	81	37	99
8	46	18	64	28	82	38	100
9	48	19	66	29	84	39	102
10	50	20	68	30	86	40	104

The formula for converting °C to °F is: °C x 9 ÷ 5 + 32 = °F.

STANDARD TIME ZONES

Argentina	3	Paraguay	4(3†)
Falkland Islands	4	Peru	5
Bolivia	4	Uruguay	3
Brazil	3*(2*1)	Venezuela	4
Chile	4(3†)	Guyana	3¾
Colombia	5	Suriname	3½
Ecuador	5	Guyane	3

* Standard time, except for Fernando de Noronha (2); Amazonia W of the Jari and Xingu rivers and E of the Tabatinga-Porto Acre line, and the States of Mato Grosso and Mato Grosso do Sul (4); and Amazonia W of the Tabatinga-Porto Acre line (5). † Summer time, October-March.

ECONOMIC INDICATORS

COUNTRY	US$ GNP per head (1988)†	% change pa (1980-88)†	Annual Inflation*	Exchange rate/US$	Parallel rate/US$
ARGENTINA	2,640	-1.6%	16,904	5,310	
BOLIVIA	570	-4.3%	16.1	3.15	3.15
BRAZIL	2,280	1.2%	6,585	61	87
CHILE	1,510	-0.1%	24.8	304	308
COLOMBIA	1,240	1.2%	28.4	501	502
ECUADOR	1,080	-1.1%	46.0	756	861
PARAGUAY	1,180	-2.1%	41.8	1,185	
PERU	1,287	-1.2%	1,903	33,721	63,500
URUGUAY	2,470	-1.4%	98.7	1,171	
VENEZUELA	3,170	-2.4%	37.4	48	

† Source: World Bank
* % change April 1990/April 1989
Exchange rates at 30 June 1990

WEIGHTS AND MEASURES

Metric

Weight:
1 kilogram (kg.) = 2,205 pounds
1 metric ton = 1.102 short tons
= 0.984 long ton

Length:
1 millimetre (mm.) = 0.03937 inch
1 metre = 3.281 feet
1 kilometre (km.) = 0.621 mile

Area:
1 hectare = 2.471 acres
1 square km. (km²) = 0.386 sq. mile

Capacity:
1 litre = 0.220 Imperial gallon
= 0.264 U.S. gallon

Volume:
1 cubic metre (m³) = 35.31 cubic feet
= 1.31 cubic yards

British and U.S.

1 pound (lb.) = 454 grams
1 short ton (2,000 lb.) = 0.907 metric ton
1 long ton (2,240 lb.) = 1.016 metric tons

1 inch = 25.417 millimetres
1 foot (ft.) = 0.305 metre
1 mile = 1.609 kilometres

1 acre = 0.405 hectare
1 square mile (sq. mile) = 2,590 km²

1 Imperial gallon = 4.546 litres
1 U.S. gallon = 3.785 litres
(5 Imperial gallons are approximately equal to 6 U.S. gallons)

1 cubic foot (cu. ft) = 0.028 m³
1 cubic yard (cu. yd.) = 0.765 m³

N.B. The *manzana*, used in Central America, is about 0.7 hectare (1.73 acres).

WILL YOU HELP US?

We do all we can to get our facts right in **The South American Handbook.** Each chapter is thoroughly revised each year, but the territory covered is vast, and our eyes cannot be everywhere. A new highway or airport is built; a hotel, a restaurant, a cabaret dies; another, a good one is born; a building we describe is pulled down, a street renamed. Names and addresses of good hotels and restaurants for "budget-minded" travellers are always very welcome. We would especially like to receive diagrams of walks, national parks and other interesting areas to use as source material for the Handbook and other forthcoming titles.

Your information may be far more up-to-date than ours. If your letter reaches us early enough in the year it will be used in the next edition, but write whenever you want to, for all your letters are used sooner or later.

Thank you very much indeed for you help.

Trade & Travel Publications Limited
6 Riverside Court
Riverside Road
Lower Bristol Road
Bath BA2 3DZ. England

INDEX TO PLACES

INDEX TO TOWN AND REGIONAL MAPS

let TUMI *carry that load!*

LATIN AMERICAN CRAFT CENTRES

We have Crafts, Music and Jewellery from the artizans of Mexico, Peru, Guatemala, El Savador, Ecuador, Chile, Nicaragua, Colombia & Bolivia.

Publishers and suppliers of Andean & Latin American Music, Postcards, Maps and Books.
Mail order service available from our Bath address.
Tumi shops at

8/9 NEW BOND STREET PLACE, BATH, AVON BA1 1BH, UK. (0225) 462367

2 LITTLE CLARENDON STREET, OXFORD, OX1 2HJ. UK. (0865) 512307

23/24 CHALK FARM ROAD, CAMDEN TOWN, LONDON NW1, UK. 071-485-4152.